INTERNATIONAL
WHO'S WHO IN POETRY
and
POETS' ENCYCLOPAEDIA

INTERNATIONAL WHO'S WHO IN POETRY
and POETS' ENCYCLOPAEDIA

Publisher:
Nicholas S. Law

Consultant Editors:
David Cummings
Dennis K McIntire

Senior Editor:
Jocelyn Timothy

Assistant Editors:
Barbara Cooper
Janine Lawrence

All communications to: International Who's Who in Poetry and Poets' Encyclopaedia
International Biographical Centre
Cambridge CB2 3QP, England

INTERNATIONAL
WHO'S WHO IN POETRY
and
POETS' ENCYCLOPAEDIA

EIGHTH EDITION
1997

Consultant Editors:
David Cummings
Dennis K McIntire

Routledge
Taylor & Francis Group

LONDON AND NEW YORK

This edition published 2014 by Routledge
2 Park Square, Milton Park, Abingdon, Oxon, OX14 4RN
711 Third Avenue, New York, NY 10017

Routledge is an imprint of the Taylor & Francis Group, an informa business

First Published	1957
Second Edition	1970
Third Edition	1972
Fourth Edition	1974
Fifth Edition	1977
Sixth Edition	1982
Seventh Edition	1993
Eighth Edition	1997

ISBN 978-0-948-87537-3 (hbk)

FOREWORD

With this eighth edition of the **International Who's Who in Poetry and Poets' Encyclopaedia**, a now well-established reference work celebrates its fortieth anniversary. We are honoured that the publisher, Nicholas Law, has charged us with serving as consultant editors for this major revision.

From the outset of our labours, we have pursued an exhaustive plan of revision. While the last edition served as a foundation upon which to build, for all practical purposes this edition constitutes an entirely new volume. Every biographee was sent a typescript of his or her entry for review, and every effort was made to make the needed amendments. We hereby offer our deepest thanks for all those who responded to our request for assistance. We express our regrets if any errors mar this edition, but we stand ready to make adjustments in the next edition.

In addition to the revision of existing entries, the consultant editors have been most anxious to expand the coverage afforded biographees missing from previous editions. Several hundred new entries now grace its pages, including not only all of the major poets of the day but many talented younger poets as well. In addition to poets from the UK, the Commonwealth, the USA, and Canada, every effort has been made to include poets whose work has become widely known via English translations.

While much attention was given to the biographical section of the volume, the appendices were also greatly expanded and thoroughly revised. They now stand as an accurate and up-to-date quick reference guide for future reference.

The Consultant Editors and the Publisher's staff, most ably headed by Senior Editor Jocelyn Timothy, are most pleased to send this fortieth anniversary edition of the **International Who's Who in Poetry and Poets' Encyclopaedia** out into the world. We have every confidence that it will find a welcome place on the reference shelf as an accurate, up-to-date, and comprehensive source of information.

David Cummings
Consultant Editor
UK, Commonwealth & Europe

Dennis K McIntire
Consultant Editor
Canada & USA

June 1997

June 1997

INTERNATIONAL BIOGRAPHICAL CENTRE
RANGE OF REFERENCE TITLES

From one of the widest ranges of contemporary biographical reference works published under any one imprint, some IBC titles date back to the 1930's. Each edition is compiled from information supplied by those listed, who include leading personalities of particular countries or professions. Information offered usually includes date and place of birth; family details; qualifications; career histories; awards and honours received; books published or other creative work; other relevant information including postal address. Naturally there is no charge or fee for inclusion.

New editions are freshly compiled and contain on average 80-90% new information. New titles are regularly added to the IBC reference library.

Titles include:

Dictionary of International Biography

Who's Who in Australasia and the Pacific Nations

Who's Who in Western Europe

Dictionary of Scandinavian Biography

International Who's Who in Art and Antiques

International Authors and Writers Who's Who

International Leaders in Achievement

International Who's Who in Community Service

International Who's Who in Education

International Who's Who in Engineering

International Who's Who in Medicine

International Who's Who in Music and Musicians' Directory - Volume One - Classical and Light Classical

International Who's Who in Music - Volume Two - Popular Music

Men of Achievement

The World Who's Who of Women

The World Who's Who of Women in Education

International Youth of Achievement

Foremost Women of the Twentieth Century

International Who's Who in Poetry and Poets' Encyclopaedia

Enquiries to:
International Biographical Centre
Cambridge CB2 3QP, England

CONTENTS

Page

FOREWORD BY THE CONSULTANT EDITORS   v

BIOGRAPHICAL SECTION   1 - 390

APPENDIX A:
   A Summary of Poetic Forms and Rhyme Schemes   391 - 392

APPENDIX B:
   Poets and Other Literary Figures of the Past   393 - 427

APPENDIX C:
   Poets Laureate of the United Kingdom   428

APPENDIX D:
   Poets Laureate of the United States of America   429

APPENDIX E:
   Poets Who Have Won the Nobel Prize for Literature   430

APPENDIX F:
   The Pulitzer Prize for American Poetry   431

APPENDIX G:
   King's/Queen's Gold Medal for Poetry   432

APPENDIX H:
   Oxford University Professors of Poetry   433 - 434

APPENDIX I:
   Poetry Prizes and Prizewinners   435 - 444

APPENDIX J:
   Organizations and Events of Interest to Poets   445 - 446

APPENDIX K:
   Poetry Book Publishers   447 - 455

APPENDIX L:
   Poetry Magazines   456 - 476

A

A'BEAR Howard. See: **BOALCH Donald Howard.**

AALFS Janet Elizabeth, b. 14 Aug 1956, Elmira, New York, USA. Writer; Martial Arts Instructor. Education: BA, 1979; MFA, Poetry, 1990; 3rd Degree Black Belt in Karate, 1986. Appointments: Poet and Writer since 13 years of age; Martial Arts & Self Defense Instructor, 1980-. Publications: Against The Odds, 1980; Where I Go the Grass Grows Lush, 1984; Of Angels and Survivors, 1992. Contributions to: Sinister Wisdom; Evergreen Chronicles; The Sarah Lawrence Review; Earth's Daughters; Onion; River Review; Encodings; Women Unlimited; Metis; California State Poetry Quarterly. Honours: Finalist, Cleveland State University Press Poetry Prize, 1995; Alumni Scholar Award, University of Massachusetts, 1978; 125 Alumni To Watch, University of Massachusetts, 1989. Memberships: Academy of American Poets; National Writers Union. Address: 29 Fort Street, Northampton, MA 01060, USA.

AANAN Taura Rai. See: **BLASOR-BERNHARDT Donna Jo.**

AARON Ada. See: **AHARONI Ada Andree.**

AAZIM Muzaffar, b. 29 Apr 1934, Kasmir, India. Poet; Writer; Administrator; Educator. m. 14 Oct 1956, 2 sons. Education: BSc, 1954; Various administrative courses. Appointments: Examiner in Kashmiri, Kashmir University up to PhD Level; Director Sericulture. Publications: Zolana, 1964; Man-I-Kaman, 1974. Contributions to: All India Radio; Doorshan, Indian National TV; Indian Poetry Review; AAJ KAL; NEB; Kashir Shairi. Honours: Best Book of the Year for Zolana, 1965; Best Book Award for Manikaman, 1975. Memberships: General Council of Sahitya Akademi, India; General Council, J & Kasmir Art, Culture & Languages; The Brontë Society, England; Advisory Committee, Kashmir University. Address: 11215 Oakleaf Drive #802, Silver Spring, MD 20901, USA.

ABBOTT Dickon John, b. 9 Jan 1962, Horsham, West Sussex, England. Social Services Officer. m. Hazel Dole, 25 July 1992. Education: BA, Honours, Modern History, Lincoln College, Oxford, 1984; Post-graduate Certificate in Education, Charlotte Mason College, Ambleside, 1986. Appointment: Parliamentary Candidate (Labour), Westmorland & Lonsdale, 1992. Contributions to: Poetry Review; Poetry Wales; New Prospects; Westwords; Orbis; Echo Room; Bogg; Pennine Platform; Envoi; Sol; Iota; Resurgence; Staple; Frogmore Papers; Westmorland Gazette. Honour: Prize Winner, anthology competition, Lancaster Literature Festival Poetry Competition. Membership: Poetry Society. Address: 17 Lamb Park, Rosside, Ulverston, Cumbria LA12 7NS, England.

ABBOTT Keith George, b. 2 Feb 1944, Tacoma, Washington, USA. Writer. m. Lani, 1 daughter. Appointment: Assistant Professor, Naropa Institute. Publications: Harum Scarum, 1984; Mordecai of Monterey, 1985; The First Thing Coming, 1987; Downstream From Trout Fishing in America, 1989; The Last Part, 1991; Skin And Bone, 1993. Address: Naropa Institute, Poetics, 2130 Arapahoe, Boulder, CO 80302, USA.

ABBS Peter Francis, b. 22 Feb 1942, Norfolk, England. Reader in Education. m. Barbara Beazeley, 29 June 1963, 1 son, 2 daughters. Education: BA, Hons, Literature and Philosophy, Bristol; PhD, Sussex. Appointments: Lecturer in Education, 1975, Senior Lecturer in Education, 1989, Reader in Education, 1991, University of Sussex. Publications: For Man and Islands, 1978; Songs of a New Taliesin, 1981; Icons of Time, 1991; Personae and Other Selected Poems, 1995; Angelic Imagination, 1996. Contributions to: Observer; Critical Quarterly; Use of English; Poetry Wales; Spectator; Country Life; Anglo-Welsh Review; Celtic Dawn; Human World; Outposts; Lapiz Lazuli; Y Seith; Acumen; Spokes; Agenda; Critical Survey; The Independent; Urthona; Forward Book of Poetry; Illuminations. Honours: Recommendation, Arvon International Poetry Competition, 1980, 1987; First Prize, Yeats Club Poetry Competition, 1990; Third Prize, Cardiff International Poetry Competition, 1991. Memberships: Poetry Society; Verbal Arts Association; Society of Authors. Address: 38 Prince Edwards Road, Lewes, Sussex BN7 1BE, England.

ABELL Carol Louise, b. 25 Sept 1940, Indiana, USA. Editor; Permanent Secretary, Federation of International Poetry Associations of UNESCO. m. Jeno Platthy, 25 Sep 1976. Education: National Institute of America, New York, 1965; PhD, University Asia, 1977; DLitt, University of New York, 1979. Appointments: Editor, New Muses, 1976-; Permanent Secretary of Federation of International Poetry Associations of UNESCO, 1976-; International Broadcasting, 1979-86. Publications: Morning Glory World, 1977; Five-Leaf Clover, 1983; Moonflowers, 1985; Mrs Orpheus, 1988; Fleurs de Lune, 1991; Timegraphs, 1993. Contributions to: New Muses; Jointure; Festschriften. Honours: Poet Laureateship, 1976; Diploma Aureum Honoris Causa, 1976; Hon DLitt, World Academy of Culture, 1984. Memberships: International PEN Club; International Poetry Society; Die Literarische Union. Address: PO Box 579, Santa Claus, IN 47579, USA.

ABLEY Mark, b. 13 May 1955, England. Poet; Journalist. m. Annie Beer, 15 Aug 1981, 2 daughters. Education: BA, Honours, English, University of Saskatchewan, 1975; BA, Honours, English, St John's College, Oxford, 1977; MA(Oxon), 1983. Appointments: Freelance Writer, 1978-87; Contributing Editor, Saturday Night, 1986-; Literary Editor, Montreal Gazette, 1989-91; Literary Columnist and Feature Writer, Montreal Gazette, 1991-. Publications: Blue Sand, Blue Moon, 1988; Glasburyon, 1994. Contributions to: Times Literary Supplement; Malahat Review; New Statesman; Encounter; The Listener; Montreal Gazette; London Review of Books; Quarto; Outposts; Dandelion; Grain; Matrix; Border Crossings; Fiddlehead; Poetry Review. Honours: Eric Gregory Award, 1981; Shortlisted, QSpell Award, 1989, 1995; Mark Harrison Prize, 1992. Memberships: Writers' Union of Canada; Federation of English-Language Writers of Quebec. Address: 38 Drayton Road, Pointe-Claire, Quebec H9S 4V2, Canada.

ABSE Dannie, b. 22 Sept 1923, Cardiff, Wales. Author. m. Joan Mercer, 4 Aug 1951, 1 son, 2 daughters. Education: MD, Westminster Hospital, London, 1950. Appointment: Manager, Central Medical Establishment Chest Clinic, 1954-82. Publications: Editor, The Hutchinson Book of Post-War British Poets, 1989; White Coat, Purple Coat, Collected Poems 1948-88, 1989, 1990; Remembrance of Crimes Past, 1990, 1992; On The Evening Road, 1994; Penguin Selected Poems, 1994. Contributions to: BBC; Leading publications in Britain and USA. Honours: Welsh Arts Council Literature Prize, 1971, 1987; Cholmondeley Award, 1985; DLitt, University of Wales; President of The Welsh Academy, 1995. Memberships: President, The British Poetry Society, 1979-92; Senior Fellow in Humanities, Princeton University, USA, 1973-74; Fellow, Royal Society of Literature, 1983; Fellow, 1990, President, 1995, The Welsh Academy. Address: c/o Anthony Sheilland Associates, 43 Doughty Street, London WC1N 2LF, England.

ACHEBE Chinua, b. 16 Nov 1930, Ogidi, Nigeria. Writer. m. Christie Okoli, 10 Sept 1961, 2 sons, 2 daughters. Education: University College, Ibadan, 1948-53; BA (London). Appointments: Nigerian Broadcasting Corporation, 1954-66; Senior Research Fellow, University of Nigeria, Nsukka, 1967-72; Professor of English, University of Massachusetts, 1972-75; Professor of English, University of Nigeria, 1975-83; Charles P Stevenson Professor, Bard College, 1990-. Publications: Novels: Things Fall Apart, 1958; No Longer at Ease, 1960; Arrow of God, 1964; A Man of the People, 1966; Anthills of the Savannah, 1987; Beware, Soul Brother, 1972, US edition as Christmas in Biafra, Italian edition as Attento; Soul Brother, 1995. Other Fiction: The Sacrificial Egg and Other Stories, 1962; Girls at War, short stories, 1972; Juvenile Fiction: Chike and the River, 1966; How the Leopard Got His Claws, with John Iroaganachi, 1972; The Flute, 1978; The Drum, 1978. Poetry: Beware, Soul-Brother and Other Poems, 1971; Christmas in Biafra and Other Poems, 1973. Essays: Morning Yet on Creation Day, 1975; The Trouble with Nigeria, 1983; Hopes and Impediments, 1988. Editor: Don't Let Him Die: An Anthology of Memorial Poems for Christopher Okigbo (with Dubem Okafor), 1978; Aka Weta: An Anthology of Igbo Poetry (with Obiora Udechukwu), 1982; African Short Stories (with C L Innes), 1984; The Heinemann Book of Contemporary African Short Stories (with C L Innes), 1992. Contributions to: New York Review of Books; Transition; Callaloo; Okike. Honours: Margaret Wrong Memorial Prize, 1959; Nigerian National Trophy, 1961; Jock Campbell/New Statesman Award, 1965; Commonwealth Poetry Prize, 1972; Neil Gunn International Fellow, Scottish Arts Council, 1975; Lotus Award for Afro-Asian Writers, 1975; Nigerian Merit Award, 1979; Order of the Federal Republic of Nigeria, 1979; Commonwealth Foundation Senior

Visiting Practitioner Award, 1984; Booker Prize Nomination, 1987; Commonwealth Poetry Prize, 1972; Several honorary doctorates. Memberships: Association of Nigerian Authors, President 1981-86; Commonwealth Arts Organization; Modern Language Association of America, Honorary Fellow; Writers and Scholars International, London; Writers and Scholars Educational Trust, London; Founder/President, Association of Nigerian Authors; Foreign Hon Member, American Academy of Arts and Letters; Fellow, Royal Society of Literature. Address: Bard College, Annandale on Hudson, NY 12504, USA.

ACHIM George, b. 30 May 1950, Pausesti-Otasau, Romania. Librarian. m. Achim Elena, 17 May 1980, 1 son, 1 daughter. Education: High School for Librarians; School of Drama. Appointments: Teacher; Educator; Administrator; Librarian; Copyright Inspector for Union of Composers. Publications: Killing Sitting on the Chair, 1992; End of the Road, 1994; Eminescu or the Tenths Laws of the Romanian Language, 1995; The Christening of the Bears, 1995; Thinks of the Olt, 1995. Contributions to: Beginning; Orizont; Review: Arges; Ramuri; Vatra; Tribuna; Contemporanul; Anthology: Pornire In Timp; Trepte; Arc Peste Timp; Vorbiri Si Convorbiri. Honours: Prizes of Reviews: Contemporanul and Agora Literara, 1984; Luceafarul, 1985; Vatra, 1986; Pr I Vacarescu, 1987; The Big Prize of City, 1988. Memberships: Literary Societies. Address: 1000 Rm Valcea, Str Daniil Ionescu, Bl 20, Sc A, Ap 11, Romania.

ACHYUTHAN NAMBUDIRI Akkitham, (Akkitham), b. 18 Mar 1926, Kumaranallur, India. Printer; Publisher; Writer; Editor. m. Sreedevi Antharjanam, June 1949, 2 sons, 4 daughters. Education: Undergraduate, Zamorins College, Kozhikode. Appointments: Printer and Publisher, Unninambndiri Magazine; Sub-Editor, Yogakshemam Weekly, Mangaladayam Magazine; Scriptwriter, Editor, All India Radio; Secretary and President, Ponani Kendra Kalasamithi; Vice President, Kerala Sahitya Akademi; President, Idasseri Smaraka Samithi; Taddpasya Vice President, Samskar Bharati, Agra; Senior Fellow, Central (Delhi) Government Department of Education, 1978-82. Publications: Poetry: Manoratham; Idinjupolinja Lokom; Balidar Shanam; Sparshamanikal. Essays: Hridayathilekku Nokki Ezhuthoo; 5 works of prose, 2 songs, 1 story, 1 play and 4 nursery poems. Contributions to: Mathrubhumi and other periodicals in Malayalam. Honours: Keralasahitya Akademi Award, 1972; Central Sahitya Akademi (Delhi) Award, 1973; Gold Medals, Writers' Co-Operative Society, 1973; Odakkuzhal Award, 1973; Ulloor Award, 1994; Kumaran Asan Award, Madras, 1994; Participated in the American Malayalee Conference, Fokana, Torento, 1994; Lalithaubika Antharjanam Award, 1996. Memberships: Numerous associations. Address: Devayanam, Kumaranallur, 679552 Palakkad, Kerala, India.

ACKERMAN Diane, b. 7 Oct 1948, Waukegan, Illinois, USA. Writer. Education: BA, English, Pennsylvania State University, 1970; MFA, Creative Writing, 1973; MA, English, 1976, PhD, 1978, Cornell University. Appointments: Writer-in-Residence, College of William and Mary, 1982, Ohio University, 1983, Washington University, 1983; Director, Writers Programme, Washington University, St Louis, 1984-86; Visiting Writer, Cooper Union, 1984, New York University, 1986, Columbia University, 1986-87, Cornell University, 1987. Publications: Poetry: The Planets: A Cosmic Pastoral, 1976; Wife of Light, 1978; Lady Faustus, 1984; Jaguar of Sweet Laughter, 1990. Prose: Twilight of the Tenderfoot, 1980; On Extended Wings, 1985, 1987; Reverse Thunder, 1989; A Natural History of The Senses, 1990; The Moon By Whalelight, 1990. Contributions to: Newyorker; Life; New York Times; Parade; National Geographic. Honours: Advisory Board, Planetary Society, 1980-; Board of Directors, Associated Writing Programme, 1982-85; Poetry Panel, New York Foundation for The Arts, 1985; Peter I B Lavan Award, Academy of American Poets, 1985; NEA, 1986; Poetry Judge for various awards and festivals; Panellist, various bodies. Literary Agent: Morton Janklow. Address: c/o Morton Janklow, 598 Madison Avenue, New York, NY 10022, USA.

ADAM Cornel. See: **LENGYEL Cornel Adam.**

ADAMO Ralph, b. 28 Apr 1948, New Orleans, Louisiana, USA. University Professor; Journalist. Education: BA, English, Loyola University of New Orleans; MFA, University of Arkansas. Appointments: English Department, University of New Orleans; Reporter for various newspapers; Scriptwriter for various television programmes. Publications: The Tiger Who Spoke French and Other Poems, 1972; Why We Have Friends, 1975; Sadness at The Private University, 1977; The End of the World, 1979; Hanoi Rose, 1989. Contributions to: American Scholar; Shenandoah; Poetry Northwest;

Barataria; Black Warrior Review; Poem; New Orleans Review; Motive; Epoch; Pacific Review; Voyages; Prism International Anthologies; Contemporary Poetry in America; The Made Thing; Maple Leaf Rag. Honour: Sal K Hall Memorial Poetry Prize, 1978-79. Membership: Writers Guild of America West Inc. Address: Department of English, University of New Orleans, Lakefront Campus, New Orleans, LA 70148, USA.

ADAMS Anna Theresa, (Theresa Butt, Anna Butt as painter), b. 9 Mar 1926, London, England. Writer; Artist. m. Norman Adams, 18 Jan 1947, 2 sons. Education: NDD Painting, Harrow School of Art, 1945; NDD, Sculpture, Hornsey College of Art, 1950. Appointments: Teaching at various schools; Designer, Chelsea Pottery, 1953-55; Part-time Art Teacher, Manchester, 1966-70; Art Teacher, Settle High School, 1971-74; Poetry Editor, Green Book, 1989-92. Publications: Journey Through Winter, 1969; Rainbow Plantation, 1971; Memorial Tree, 1972; A Reply to Intercepted Mail, 1979; Brother Fox, 1983; Trees in Sheep Country, 1986; Dear Vincent, 1986; Six Legs Good, 1987; Angels of Soho, 1988; Nobodies, 1990; Island Chapters, 1991; Life on Limestone, 1994. Contributions to: Poetry Review; P N Review; The Countryman; 10th Muse; Country Life; Yorkshire Life; Dalesman; Pennine Platform; Western Mail; Stand; Sunday Telegraph; Poetry Durham; Poetry Canada; Poetry Nottingham; Poetry Matters; Encounter; Spokes; Meridian; Acumen; Aquarius; Orbis; Spectator; North Yorkshire Journal. Honours: 1st Prize, Yorkshire Poets, 1974, 1976, 1977; 1st Prize, Arnold Vincent Bowen, 1976; Several Prizes, Lancaster Festival Poetry Competition; 1st Prize, Lincoln Open, 1984; 1st Prize, Rhyme International, 1986; 2nd Prize, Cardiff Festival Poetry Competition, 1987. Memberships: Poetry Society, London; Committee, Piccadilly Poets. Address: Butts Hill, Horton in Ribblesdale, Settle, North Yorkshire BD24 0HD, England.

ADAMS Barbara, (B B Adams), b. 23 Mar 1932, New York, New York, USA. Professor of American and English Literature. m. Elwood Adams, 6 June 1952, 2 sons, 2 daughters. Education: BS, 1962, MA, 1970, State University of New York at New Paltz; PhD, New York University, 1981. Appointment: Professor, Department of English, Pace University, 1984-. Publications: Double Solitaire, 1982; Hapax Legomena, 1990; The Enemy Self: Poetry and Criticism of Laura Riding, 1990. Contributions to: Nation; Psychoanalytic Review; Confrontation; Antigonish Review; Wooster Review; Negative Capability; Madison Review; European Judaism. Memberships: PEN, 1990; Poetry Society of America; Yeats Society, 1993-. Address: Department of English, Pace University, Pace Plaza, New York, NY 10038, USA.

ADAMS Mary Elizabeth Auman, b. 29 Nov 1940, North Carolina, USA. Teacher; Writer. m. Richard Chad Adams, 30 Mar 1962, 1 son, 3 daughters. Education: Diploma, Seagrove High School, North Carolina, 1959; BS, Pfeiffer College, Misenheimer, North Carolina, 1966. Appointments: Elementary School Teacher, Milford Elementary School, Marietta, Georgia, 1966-67, Kennesaw Elementary School, Georgia, 1967-68, Robbinsville Elementary School, North Carolina, 1975-88; Educational Department, North Carolina Zoological Park, Asheboro, North Carolina, 1989-; Adult Education Instructor, Randolph Community College, Asheboro, North Carolina, 1990-. Publication: A Collection of Poems by Mary Elizabeth Auman Adams, self published, 1987. Contributions to: Various anthologies. Honours: Golden Awards, World of Poetry, 1988, 1989, 1990; Poet of Merit, American Poetry Association, 1989; Outstanding Poetry Writers Award, National Arts Society, 1990; Caldwell W Nixon Jr Award, North Carolina Poetry Society, 1990. Memberships: North Carolina Poetry Society; Southern Poetry Association; National Arts Society; Sparrowgrass Poetry Forum; World of Poetry; Great Lakes Poetry Press; American Poetry Association. Address: 5911 US Highway 220 South, Asheboro, NC 27203, USA.

ADAMS Michael Louis, (Diano), b. 17 Apr 1948, Philadelphia, Pennsylvania, USA. Entrepreneur; Sales Marketing Professional; Writer. Education: BA, Mathematics, Cheyney University of Pennsylvania, 1972; Doctor of Literature, World University, 1981; Diplomas, International Poets Academy, Madras, India, 1987-88. Appointments: Substitute Teacher, Philadelphia Board of Education, 1972-81; Producer, Communicator, WPEB Community Radio, 1981-85; Mathematics Instructor, Rittenhouse Academy, Philadelphia, 1982-87; Sales Marketing Representative, Tiffany/American Lubricants Co, 1987-. Publication: Private Class Reunion/ a drop of river upstream, 1991. Contributions to: National and international anthologies; Poet International Monthly; Premier Poets; World Poetry; Poetry

Americas; Arulo; Vega Journal; Black Forum; Negro History Bulletin. Honours: 3rd Place, World Wide Poetry Competition, 1979; Writer of the Month, Modus Operandi, 1980; Best Original Material, WPEB Radio. 1983; Silver Poet Award, World of Poetry, 1986, 1990; Golden Poet Award, World of Poetry, 1987, 1988, 1989; Albert Einstein Medal, 1995. Memberships: World Academy of Arts and Culture - World Congress of Poets; International Poets Academy; World Poetry Society; World of Poetry. Address: 936 South 49th Street, Philadelphia, PA 19143, USA.

ADAMS Perseus, b. 11 Mar 1933, Cape Town, South Africa. Teacher (Retired). m. 1958. Education: BA, University of Cape Town, 1952; STC, 1961. Appointments: Clerk Psychologist; Journalist; Teacher. Publications: The Land at My Door, 1965; Grass for the Unicorn, 1975; Cries and Silences - Selected Poems, 1996. Contributions to: Standpunte; New Nation; Contrast. Honours: South Africa Poetry Prize for the Land at My Door, 1963; The Man Outside - E P Herald, South Africa, 1964; Festival of Rhodesia International Prize for Folio of 5 poems, 1970; 2nd Prize in John Keats Memorial Competition, England, 1972; 2nd Prize in Bridport Arts Festival Poetry Competition, 1984; Co-Winner in the Writing Section of the Bard of the Year Competition, 1993. Address: 21 Mapesbury Road, Cricklewood, London NW2 4HS, England.

ADAMS Richard (George), b. 9 May 1920, Newbury, Berkshire, England. Author. m. Barbara Elizabeth Acland, 26 Sept 1949, 2 daughters. Education: Bradfield College, Berkshire, 1933-38; Worcester College, Oxford, 1938-40, 1946-48, MA(Oxon), Modern History, 1948. Appointments: Army Service, 1940-46; Entered Civil Service in 1948, retired as Assistant Secretary, 1974. Publications: The Tyger Voyage (narrative poem), 1976; The Ship's Cat (narrative poem), 1977; The Legend of Te Tuna (narrative poem), 1986; Editor and Contributor to Occasional Poets Anthology, 1986. Memberships: Fellow, Royal Society of Literature; Fellow, Royal Society of Arts; John Clare Society. Address: Benwell's, 26 Church Street, Whitchurch, Hampshire RG28 7AR, England.

ADAMS Wilfried M G, b. 23 Nov 1947, Flanders, Belgium. 1 son. Education: Candidate Law, 1967, Licentiate, Germanic Philosophy, 1972, Catholic University of Louvain. Appointments: Biographer; Teacher; Translator; Literary Critic. Publications: Graafschap, 1970; Dagwaarts Eeen Woord, 1972; Geen Vogelkreet de Roos, 1975; Ontginning, 1976; Aanspraak, 1981; Lettre de Cachet, 1982; Uw Afwezigheid, 1986; Dicta Dura, 1988; Zayin, 1992; VII Sirventes, 1993. Contributions to: Several Flemish and Dutch literary periodicals. Honours: Prys Vlaamse Poeziedagen, 1971; Knokke-Heist, 1976; Provincie Antwerpen, 1988. Memberships: Vereiniging van Vloarnse Letterkundigen, 1973; Maatschappy der Nederlandse Letterkunde, 1974; Confraria de Recerques. Address: c/o Mr Dirk Adams, Bovenbosstraat 78A, B-3052 Haasrode, Belgium.

ADAMSON Donald, b. 15 June 1943, Dumfries, Scotland. Writer; Editor. Education: MA, English Literature, 1965, MLitt, Applied Linguistics, 1975, Edinburgh University. Appointments: EFL posts in France, Finland, Iran and Kuwait; Longman EFL Division, R & D Unit; Freelance EFL Writer and Editor; Editor, Markings, 1995-. Contributions to: Lines Review, Orbis, New Writing Scotland. Honours: Glasgow University/Radio Clyde Poetry Prize, 1985; 2nd Prize, Northwords Competition, 1995; Scottish Arts Council Writer's Bursary, 1995. Address: Highfields, Barrhill Road, Dalbeattie, Scotland.

ADAMSON Robert Harry, b. 17 May 1943, Sydney, New South Wales, Australia. Poet; Publisher. m. (1) Cheryl Adamson, 1973, (2) Juno Adamson, 19 Feb 1989, 1 son. Appointments: Editorial positions, New Poetry Magazine, Sydney, 1968-77; Editor and Director, Prism Books, Sydney, 1970-77; Founding Editor and Director (with Dorothy Hewett), Big Smoke Books, Sydney, 1979-. Publications: Canticles on the Skin, 1970; The Rumour, 1971; Swamp Riddles, 1973; Cross the Border, 1977; Selected Poems, 1977; The Law at Heart's Desire, 1982; The Clean Dark, 1989; Wards of the State, 1991. Contributions to: Various periodicals. Honours: Grace Levin Prize for Poetry, 1977; Kenneth Slessor Award, 1990; Turnbull-Fox Philips Poetry Prize, 1990; C J Dennis Prize for Poetry, 1990. Memberships: Australian Society of Authors; Poetry Society of Australia, president, 1970-80. Address: PO Box 59, Brooklyn, New South Wales 2083, Australia.

ADCOCK Elizabeth (Betty) S, b. 16 Sept 1938, Fort Worth, Texas, USA. Teacher. m. Donald Brandt Adcock, 22 June 1957, 1 daughter. Education: Hockaday Preparatory School, Dallas, Texas,

1954-56; Studied at Texas Technical University, 1956-57; North Carolina State University, 1965-67; Goddard College, Vermont, 1967-69. Appointments: Copywriter, Ralph Johnson Associates; Advertising, Copywriter and Creative Director, Percivall Advertising and Marketing; Visiting Lecturer in Creative Writing, Duke University, 1977; Writer-in-Residence, Kalamazoo College, Michigan, 1983; Kenan Writer-in-Residence, Meridith College, Raleigh, North Carolina, 1984-. Publications: Walking Out, 1975; Nettles, 1983; Beholdings, 1988. Contributions to: The Nation; Kenyon Review; Mississippi Review; TriQuarterly; Georgia Review; South Carolina Review; Southern Review; Poetry Northwest; Southern Poetry Review; Chicago Review; American Literary Review. Honours: New Writing Award, Great Lakes Colleges Association, 1975; Roanoke-Chowan Award, 1984; Fellowship in Poetry, National Endowment for The Arts, 1984; Individual Arts Grant, State of North Carolina, 1985; Zoe Kineaid Brockman Award, 1989; Invitation to read at Library of Congress, Washington DC, 1989. Memberships: Poetry Society of America; Academy of American Poets. Address: 817 Runnymede Road, Raleigh, NC 27607, USA.

ADCOCK Fleur, b. 1934, New Zealand. Poet. Publications: The Eye of the Hurricane, 1964; Tigers, 1967; High Tide in the Garden, 1971; The Scenic Route, 1974; The Inner Harbour, 1979; Below Loughrigg, 1979; Selected Poems, 1983; The Virgin and the Nightingale, 1983; The Incident Book, 1986; Time Zones, 1991; Editor: The Oxford Book of Contemporary New Zealand Poetry, 1982; The Faber Book of 20th Century Women's Poetry, 1987; Translator and Editor: Hugh Primas and the Archpoet, 1994. Honour: Order of the British Empire, 1996. Membership: Fellow, Royal Society of Literature. Address: 14 Lincoln Road, London N2 9DL, England.

ADHIKARI Santosh Kumar, b. 24 Nov 1923, West Bengal, India. Retired Principal of Banking Staff College; Writer. m. Mar 1948, 1 son, 2 daughters. Education: Graduated, Calcutta University, 1943; CAIIB, Diploma in Industrial Finance, The Indian Institute of Bankers, Bombay; Diploma in Management, Indian Institute of Management. Appointments: Vidyasagar Lecturer, University of Calcutta, 1979; Former Principal, Staff College, United Bank of India, Calcutta, retired 1983; Speaker, University of Chicago, Bengal Studies Conference, 1990. Publications: Books of Poetry: Ekla Chalo Re, 1948; Diganter Mogh, 1953; Anya Kono Khane; Blossoms in the Dust; Paari, 1986; Author: Santrasbad O Bhagat Singh, 1979; Vidyasagar and the New National Consciousness, Netaji Subhas Chandra. Contributions to: Kabi O'Kabita; Dhrupadi; Ekak, Prabasi; Udichi; Udbodhan. Honours: Prasad Puraskar for Poetry, 1986; Awarded the honorary title of Bharat Bhasa Bhusan, 1991; Former Editor, Spark. Memberships: Ex-Secretary, PEN, West Bengal Branch; Ex-Secretary, Vidyasagar Research Centre, Calcutta; National Committee, Akhil Bharat, Bhasa Sahity Sammelan, Bhopal; Asiatic Society, Calcutta. Address: 81 Raja Basanta Roy Road, Calcutta 700 029, India.

ADNAN Etel, b. 24 Feb 1925, Beirut, Lebanon. Poet; Writer; Painter; Tapestry Designer. Education: Sorbonne, University of Paris; University of California at Berkeley; Harvard University. Appointments: Teacher, Philosophy of Art and Humanities, Dominican College, San Rafael, California, 1958-72; Cultural Editor, Al-Safa Newspaper, Lebanon, 1972-79; Paintings exhibited around the world. Publications: Poetry: Moonshots, 1966; Five Senses for One Death, 1971; From A to Z, 1982; The Indian Never Had a Horse and Other Poems, 1985; The Arab Apocalypse, 1989; The Spring Flowers Own and the Manifestations of the Voyage, 1990. Novel: Sitt Marie-Rose, 1982. Other: Journey to Mount Tamalpais, 1986; Of Cities and Women, 1993; Paris, When It's Naked, 1993. Contributions to: Poems and short stories in many publications. Honour: France-Pays-Arabes Prize, 1978. Membership: Poetry Center, San Francisco. Address: 35 Marie Street, Sausalito, CA 94965, USA.

ADOFF Arnold, b. 16 July 1935, New York, New York, USA. Poet; Writer; Literary Agent. m. Virginia Hamilton, 19 Mar 1960, 2 children. Education: BA, City College of New York, 1956; Columbia University, 1956-58; New School for Social Research Poetry Workshops, New York City, 1965-67. Appointments: Teacher, New York City Public Schools, 1957-69; Literary Agent, Yellow Springs, Ohio, 1977-; Distinguished Visiting Professor, Queens College, 1986-87; Guest Lecturer in many US venues. Publications: Poetry: Black is Brown is Tan, 1973; Make a Circle Keep Us In: Poems for a Good Day, 1975; Big Sister Tells Me That I'm Black, 1976; Tornado!: Poems, 1977; Under the Early Morning Trees, 1978; Where Wild Willie, 1978; Eats: Poems, 1979; I Am the Running Girl, 1979; Friend

Dog, 1980; OUTside INside Poems, 1981; Today We Are Brother and Sister, 1981; Birds, 1982; All the Colors of the Race, 1982; The Cabbages are Chasing the Rabbits, 1985; Sports Pages, 1986; Flamboyan, 1988; Greens, 1988; Chocolate Dreams, 1989; Hard to Be Six, 1990; In for Winter, Out for Spring, 1991; Other: Malcolm X, biography, 1970; MA nDA LA, picture book, 1971. Editor: I am the Darker Brother: An Anthology of Modern Poems by Negro Americans, 1968; Black on Black: Commentaries by Negro Americans, 1970; Brothers and Sisters: Modern Stories by Black Americans, 1970; It Is the Poem Singing into Your Eyes: An Anthology of New Young Poets, 1971; The Poetry of Black America: An Anthology of the 20th Century, 1973; My Black Me: A Beginning Book of Black Poetry, 1974; Celebration: New Anthology of Black American Poetry, 1978. Contributions to: Articles and reviews in periodicals. Honours: Children's Book of the Year Citations, Child Study Association of America, 1968, 1969, 1986; American Library Association Notable Book Awards, 1968, 1970, 1971, 1972, 1979; Best Children's Book Citations, School Library Journal, 1971, 1973; Notable Children's Trade Book Citation, Children's Book Council-National Council for Social Studies, 1974; Jane Addams Peace Association Special Certificate, 1983; Children's Choice Citation, International Reading Association-Children's Book Council, 1985; National Council of Teachers of English Poetry Award, 1988. Address: Arnold Adoff Agency, PO Box 293, Yellow Springs, OH 45387, USA.

ADONH Overnak C Antoine, (Okama Okanza), b. 7 July 1954, Cotonou, Benin, West Africa. Librarian. Education: BTh, 1981; Degree in Literature, 1989, 1990. Contributions to: World of Poetry Anthologies, USA; Revue Noire, Afrique en Creations, France; Journals and magazines of various poetry associations. Honours: Certificate of Merit with Honorable Mention, World of Poetry, California, USA, 1989; Certificate of Merit with Honorable Mention, World of Poetry, Sacramento, California, 1990; Golden Poet Laureate Award, World of Poetry and American Academy and Institute of Arts and Letters, USA, 1990. Memberships: World of Poetry, Sacramento, California, USA; World Academy of Arts and Sciences, USA; World Academy of Arts and Culture, USA; World Poetry Intercontinental, India; Poets International Organisation, India; Honorary Member, American Academy and Institute of Arts and Letters, USA; Afrique en Creations, France; PEN International, Britain. Address: BP 03-1051 Cotonou, Republic of Benin, West Africa.

ADONIS. See: **ESBER Ali Ahmad Said.**

AFRA Kwesi. See: **THERSON-COFIE Larweh.**

AFTERMAN Susan, b. 11 May 1947, Melbourne, Australia. Poet; Architect. m. Allen Afterman, dec 1992, 4 sons. Education: BArch, Honours, Melbourne University, 1970. Publications: Rites, 1978; Rain, 1987, Hebrew edition as Ayallah, 1991. Contributions to: Various magazines in Australia and UK. Honour: Australian Arts Council Poetry Grant. Address: Kfar Clil, D N Ashrat, Israel.

AGEE Chris(topher Robert), b. 18 Jan 1956, San Francisco, California, USA. Educator. m. Nórín McKinney, 22 Aug 1990. Education: BA, Honours, cum laude, English and American Literature and Language, Harvard University, 1979; MA, English (Irish Writing), The Queen's University of Belfast, 1987. Appointments: Tutor, Faculty of Arts, Open University in Ireland; Education Adviser, University of East London. Publication: In the New Hampshire Woods, 1992; The Sierra de Zacatecas, 1995. Contributions to: Irish Times; Poetry Ireland Review; Editor, Special North American Issue, Poetry Ireland Review, 1994; Co-Editor, Contemporary Irish Poetry, Poetry, Chicago, 1995. Honour: Award of International Writers' Exchange with Russia, Irish Writers' Centre, 1992. Membership: Board of Directors, Poetry Ireland. Address: 102 North Parade, Belfast BT7 2GJ, Northern Ireland.

AGEE Jonis, b. 31 May 1943, Omaha, Nebraska, USA. Writer; Poet; Teacher. m. Paul McDonough, 1 daughter. Education: BA, University of Iowa, 1966; MA, 1969, PhD, 1976, State University of New York at Binghamton. Appointments: Teacher, College of St Catherine, St Paul, Minnesota, 1975-95; Literary Consultant, Walker Arts Center, Minneapolis, 1978-84; Adjunct Teacher, Macalester College, St Paul, Minnesota, 1980-88; Teacher and Editor, Literary Post Program for Senior Citizen Writers, 1986-89; Many poetry readings. Publications: Houses (poem), 1976; Mercury (poems), 1981; Two Poems, 1982; Border Crossings (editor), 1984; Stiller's Pond (editor), 1988, expanded edition, 1991; Bend This Heart, (stories),

1989; Pretend We've Never Met (stories), 1989; Sweet Eyes, (novel), 1991; Strange Angels (novel), 1993. Contributions to: Anthologies and periodicals. Honours: Minnesota State Arts Board Award, 1977; National Endowment for the Arts Fellowship, 1978; Loft-McKnight Awards, 1987, 1991. Memberships: Literary Guild; Society of American Poets. Address: c/o Ticknor and Fields, Houghton Mifflin Co, 215 Park Avenue South, NY 10003, USA.

AGGARWAL Bishan Swaroop (Ropari), b. 22 Oct 1937, Ropar, Punjab, India. Writer; Astrologer. m. 4 July 1961, 1 son, 2 daughters. Education: BA, 1956, BT, 1957, MA, 1965, Punjab University, India. Publication: Selected Poems, 1954. Contributions to: Silch Review; Canopy; Poesie Berhampur; Kavita India; Samvedna; Poeterit; Punjab Red Cross Journal; Haryana Scout Guide Patrika; 50 Other magazines of regional importance; In all, 1200 English and Hindi poems published in journals of national and regional importance. Honour: Awarded title of Rambha Shri, 1988. Address: Master Nand Lal Bhawan, Old Post Office Road, Ropar 140001, Punjab, India.

AGRAFIOTIS Demosthenes, b. 29 Dec 1946. Professor of Sociology. m. 1 daughter. Education: Diploma of Chemical Engineering, Technical University of Athens, 1969; MS Chemical Engineering, University of Wisconsin, 1970; Business Administration, Graduate Diploma, School of Economics and Commerce of Athens, 1972; Doctorat 3e Cycle en Sciences des Organisations, Gestion, Université de Paris IX, Dauphine, 1976; Doctorat d'Etat, Sciences des Organisations-Gestion, Universite Paris IX, Dauphine, 1978. Appointments: Engineering, Marketing, Teaching, R/D Management, Research, 1968, 1971-72, 1978-84; Elected Professor, 1984. Contribution to: The Elaboration of R/D Objectives and Programmes. Honours: Recipient of 7 scholarships. Memberships: New York Academy of Sciences; 20 Scientific Societies and Committees. Address: 96 Alexandras Avenue, 115 21 Athens, Greece.

AHARONI Ada Andree, (Ada Aaron), b. 30 July 1933, Egypt. Writer; Poet; Professor of Literature and Modern Poetry. m. Chaim Aharoni, 26 Mar 1951, 1 son, 1 daughter. Education: BA, English and Sociology, 1965, PhD, English Literature, 1975, Hebrew University, Jerusalem; MPhil, English Literature, University of London, 1967. Appointments: Lecturer, Department of English, Haifa University, 1967-77; Senior Lecturer, Department of General Studies, Technion, Haifa, Israel, 1977-93; President, International Friends of Literature Association, 1995-. Publications: Poems From Israel, 1972; Poems From Israel and Other Poems, 1974; From The Pyramids to Mount Carmel, 1979; Love Poems, 1980; Shin Shalom: Poems, 1984; Shin Shalom: New Poems, English/Hebrew edition, 1986; A Green Week, 1988; Metal et Violettes, 1989; Selected Poems From Israel and Around The World, 1992; Selected Poems: In My Carmel Woods, 1993; In The Curve of Your Palm, 1994; Peace Flower, 1995. Contributions to: Poetry Nippon; Jewish Chronicle; Voices; Arc; New Society; International Poetry Review; El Shark, Galilee, 1995; Poet, 1995. Honours: British Council Poetry Grant, 1972; Haifa and Bremen Poetry Award, 1975; The President of Israel's Literature Award: Keren Amos, 1977; Bank Discount Literary Award, 1979; Boston Forum Prize, 1981; Haifa Culture Poetry Prize, 1984; The Bemaaracha, Jerusalem Poetry Grant, 1987; Pennsylvania Poetry Award, 1989; Yunus Imri Poetry Award, 1992; Shin Shalom Peace Poetry Award, 1993; International Poetry Prize, 1994. Memberships: PEN; Editor of literary magazine, President, Galim Writers Association; Committee, Hebrew Writers Organization. Literary Agent: Rubin Mass, PO Box 990, Jerusalem 91009, Israel. Address: 57 Horev Street, Haifa 34343, Israel.

AHERN Thomas (Tom) Gregory, (Phillip Gregory), b. 2 Nov 1918, Westerly, Rhode Island, USA. Retired Public Relations Executive; Poet. m. Joyce Helen Schmidt, 11 Sept 1948, 2 sons, 3 daughters. Education: Brown University, 1942; Calvin Coolidge Law School, 6 months. Appointments: President, Ahern Textile Corporation, 1946-58; Public Relations, Raymond O'Connell Associates, 1966-67; Public Relations, Senior Vice President, Wallach Associates, 1968-79; Consultant to major corporation, 1979-1990. Publications: Book of memoirs; Novel in progress. Contributions to: Co-Host of TV literary programme, Talking About Books, 1991-94; Critiques include poetry, fiction and biography; Interviewed authors and recited poetry including his own. Membership: Academy of American Poets. Address: One Arraquat Road, Watch Hill, RI 02891, USA.

AHMED Shafi Uddin Abul Hasnat, b. 1 Jan 1937, Faridpur, Bangladesh. Marine Engineer. m. Ruhani Lily Khandkar, 25 Sept 1960,

2 sons. Education: RN, Dockyard College, Plymouth, 1952-56; Chartered Engineer, 1970; LLB, Hons, 1976; BA, Hons, Open University, 1992; European Engineer, 1994. Appointments: Engineer Officer, Associated Training Academies and Government Agencies, Merchant Navy, 1956-71; Marine Surveyor, Government of England, 1971-80; IMO Advisor to Bangladesh, 1980-82; Marine Survey Service, England, 1982-96. Publications: Free Translations From Rabindranath Tagore, 1982; Tagore's Eleven (ten poems and one song), 1985. Contributions to: Open University Poetry Society Anthology; Civil Service Poetry Anthology; International Society of Poets Anthology; Bengali Newsweekly Janomot, (UK). Honour: Peterloo Poet's Award, 1992. Memberships: Civil Service Society of Authors; Open University Poetry Society; National Poetry Society; South Asian Literature Society; Bengali Literary Society (UK). Address: 100 Western Avenue, East Acton, London W3 7TX, England.

AKHMADULINE Bella Akhatovna, b. 10 Apr 1937, Moscow, Russia. Poet. m. Boris Besserer, 1974. Education: Gorky Literary Institute, Moscow, 1960. Appointment: Secretary, Union of Soviet, later Russian Writers, 1986-. Publications: Fire Tree, 1958; String, 1962; Tale of the Rain, 1963; My Genealogy, 1963; Adventure in an Antique Store, 1967; Fever and Other Poems, 1968; Snowstorm, 1968; Music Lessons, 1969; Candle, 1977; Three Russian Poets, 1979; The Garden, 1987; Seashore, 1991. Honour: American Academy of Arts and Letters, 1977. Address: Chemiachovskoho Street 4, Apt 37, 125319 Moscow, Russia.

AKKITHAM. See: ACHYUTHAN NAMBUDIRI Akkitham.

AKMAKJIAN Alan Paul, b. 18 July 1948, Highland Park, Michigan, USA. University Teacher. Education: BA, MA, Eastern Michigan University, 1973-74; PhD, Wayne State University, 1979; MFA, California State University, San Francisco, 1991; PhD, St John's University and University of Texas. Publications: Treading Pages of Water, 1992; Let the Sun Go, 1992; California Picnic, 1992; Grounded Angels, 1993; Breaking the Silence, 1993; California Picnic and Other Poems, 1996.Contributions to: Ararat; Atom Mind; Blackbear Review; Black Buzzard Review; Context South; Green's Magazine; Mother Earth Journal; On The Bus; Poem; Small Pond; Wind; Wormwood Review. Honours: Texas Public Educational Grant, 1996; The University of Texas Fellowship, 1996; Jordan Fellowship in the Arts, 1995; St John's University Fellowship, 1994; Alex Manoogian Cultural Fund Award, 1992; Poets in the Schools Program, California. Memberships: Academy of American Poets; Directory of American Poets and Fiction Writers (AWP); MLA; PEN; Poetry Society of America; Writers Garret. Address: 2200 Waterview Parkway, Apt 2134, Richardson, TX 75080-2268, USA.

AL HAGAG Kanar. See: KACHEL Zeev.

ALANAH Patrica. See: COSENTINO Patricia Alanah.

ALBARELLA Joan, b. 22 Sept 1944, New York, New York, USA. Teacher of English. Education: BS, 1966, MSEd, 1971, State University of New York, Buffalo. Appointments: Actress, Director, Indigo Productions, 1973-85; Journalist, Photographer, Western New York Catholic, 1975-88; Associate Professor, State University of New York at Buffalo, Educational Opportunity Centre, 1986-. Publications: Mirror Me, 1973; Poems for the Asking, 1975; Women, Flowers, Fantasy, 1987; Spirit and Joy, 1993. Contributions to: Sunshine Magazine; Buffalo Courier Express; Western New York Catholic; North American Voice of Fatima. Honours: Poet of the Year, National Poetry Publications, New York, 1974, 1975, 1976. Memberships: Poets and Writers; Niagara Erie Writers; Founder, Co-ordinator, West Seneca Writers Club. Address: 923 Center Road, Buffalo, NY 14224, USA.

ALBERT Gwendolyn Hubka, b. 11 Jan 1967, Oakland, California, USA. Poet. Education: BA, Linguistics, University of California, 1989; Fulbright Scholar, Charles Univerity, Prague, 1989-90. Appointment: Editor, Je June: America Eats Its Young, 1993-. Publications: Dogs, 1991; Green, Green, 1992. Contributions to: Berkeley Poetry Review; Blind Date; Byzantium; Carbuncle; CUPS; Cyanosis; East Bay Guardian; Exquisite Corpse; GRIST online; House Organ; MacGuffin; Real Poetik; Sour Grapes. Honour: 1st Prize, Kingfisher Fiction Contest, 1991. Address: c/o Farnsworth, Box 85, 110 01 Prague 1, Czech Republic; PO Box 4565, Berkeley, CA 94705, USA.

ALCOSSER Sandra, b. 3 Feb 1944, Washington, District of Columbia, USA. Director of Creative Writing; Poet. m. 10 May 1978. Education: Lake Forest Academy; BA, Purdue University, 1966; MFA, University of Montana, 1982. Appointments: Director, Poets in The Park, Central Park, New York, 1975-77; Writer in Residence, Poet in The Schools, Solo Artist for National Endowment for The Arts, 1977-85; Assistant Professor, Louisiana State University, 1985-87; Director of Creative Writing, San Diego State University, 1988-92. Publications: Each Bone a Prayer, 1982; A Fish to Feed All Hunger, 1986. Contributions to: American Scholar; New Yorker; Paris Review; Poetry; Pushcart Prize VIII; North American Review; Yale Review; American Poetry Review. Honours: Guest Editor, Fiction and Poetry, Mademoiselle Magazine, 1966; Dylan Thomas Poetry Award, New School, 1976; National University Chapbook Award, 1980; Breadloaf Scholar, 1983; American Scholar Poetry Award, 1983; Associated Writing Programmes Award, Series Winner in Poetry, 1984; Fellowship, National Endowment for The Arts, 1985, 1991; Syndicated Fiction Project Winner, PEN, 1986; Breadloaf Fellow, 1986; Pushcart Prize for Poetry, 1988. Memberships: Poets and Writers; Associated Writing Programmes. Address: 5791 West Countyline, Florence, MT 59833, USA.

ALDERSON Bill (William), b. 14 Oct 1921, New Silksworth, Near Sunderland, England. Mechanical Engineer, Methods and Works Study. m. Doris Elisha Hart, 11 May 1946. Education: Further Education Courses in Management, English and other subjects, Sunderland Technical College. Publication: Poems From the Cliff Top, 1990. Contributions to: Short stories, Witney Gazette, 1962-64. Membership: Warwick Writers Club. Address: 25 Chandlers Walk, Whitnash, Leamington Spa, Warwickshire CV31 2LL, England.

ALDISS Brian Wilson, b. 18 Aug 1925, East Dereham, Norfolk, England. Writer; Critic. m. (1) 1 son, 1 daughter, (2) Margaret Manson, 11 Dec 1965, 1 son, 1 daughter. Education: Framlingham College, 1936-39. Appointments: Literary Editor, Oxford Mail, 1957-69; Fellow of the Royal Society of Literature. Publications: Pile, 1979; Farewell To A Child, 1982; Home Life With Cats, 1992; At The Caligula Hotel, 1995. Contributions to: Magazine of Fantasy and Science Fiction, USA; Priapus; Queen Magazine, 1960's; Times Literary Supplement; Times; PEN New Poetry; New Statesman; Keats-Shelley Review. Honour: Fellow, Royal Society of Literature, 1992. Memberships: Arts Council Literature Panel, 1978-80; Chairman, Society of Authors Committee of Management, 1977-78; President, British Science Fiction Association, 1960-64; Council, Science Fiction Foundation; Judge, Booker McConnell Prize, 1981; Founder Member, President, 1982-84, World Science Fiction; Permanent Special Guest, IAFA, 1985-. Literary Agents: Michael Shaw, UK; Robin Straus, USA. Address: Hambleden, 39 St Andrews Road, Old Headington, Oxford OX3 9DL, England.

ALEGRIA Claribel, b. 12 May 1924, Esteli, Nicaragua. Writer. m. Darwin J Flakoll, 29 Dec 1947, 1 son, 3 daughters. Education: BA, George Washington University, Washington, DC, USA. Publications: Anillo de Silencio, 1948; Suite, 1950; Vigilias, 1953; Acuario, 1955; Huesped de mi Tiempo, 1961; Via Unica, 1965; Aprendizenje, 1972; Pagare a Cobrar y Otros Poemas, 1973; Sobevivo, 1978; Suma y Sigue, 1981; Y este Poema Rio, 1989; Luisa en El Pais de la Realidad, 1989; Fugues, 1993; Works translated into 11 languages. Contributions to: Casa de las Americas; Repertorio Americano; Sur; Koeyu; Marcha; Brecha; Nuevo Amanecer Cultural; Paris Review; Soma; many others. Honour: Premio Casa de las Americas, Havana, Cuba, 1978. Literary Agent: Curbstone Press, USA. Address: Apartado Postal A-36, Managua, Nicaragua.

ALENIER Karren LaLonde, b. 7 May 1947, Cheverly, Maryland, USA. Poet; Writer; Special Assistant. m. Howard Scott Alenier, 22 June 1969, div 1979, 1 son. Education: BA, Honours, French, University of Maryland, College Park, 1969. Appointments: Computer Programmer, US Federal Power Commission, 1969-71; Computer Systems Analyst, US Department of Labour, 1972-77; Computer Specialist, US Department of Energy, 1977-82; Management Analyst, US Department of Justice, 1983-; Computer Specialist, US Department of Agriculture, 1991-. Publications: Editor, Whose Woods Are These, 1983; The Dancer's Muse, 1981; Wandering On The Outside, 1975, 1978. Contributions to: Negative Capability; Poet Lore. Honours: 1st Prize, Billee Murray Denny Award, Lincoln College, Illinois, 1981; Finalist, Eve of St Agnes Prize, Negative Capability; Fellow, Virginia Centre for The Creative Arts, 1989, 1990, 1991, 1992; Reading at the Library of Congress, Washington DC, 1995 and at Viola Café, Prague,

Czechoslovakia, 1995. Memberships: Founding President, Chairperson of the Board, Poetry Committee, Greater Washington, DC Area, 1986-90; President, Chairperson of the Board, 1986-; The Word Works; Poetry Society of America. Hobbies: Book Collecting; Cross Country Skiing; Photography; Gourmet Cooking; Travel; Dancing; Bicycling. Address: 4601 North Park Avenue 301, Chevy Chase, MD 20815, USA.

ALEXANDER Eric John, b. 26 Feb 1935, London, England. Technical Author. m. Frances Winifred Pelling, 31 July 1963, 1 son, 1 daughter. Education: PGCE, London, 1959; BSc, London Ext, 1955; BA, 1956, MA, 1960, Cantab. Appointments: Teaching, 1959-68; Technical Author, 1969-. Publications: Jonah at Large, 1986; Guide to the Realm of Mammon, 1986. Contributions to: Orbis; Poetry Nottingham; New Hope International; The Third Half; New Spokes; Foolscap; Krax Magazine; Bound Spiral; Odyssey; Tops. Memberships: Wycombe District Arts Association, secretary, 1986-93; Chiltern Writers Group, vice chairman, 1989-92, chairman, 1992-94; Chameleon Poets. Address: 8A Chestnut Avenue, High Wycombe, Buckinghamshire HP11 1DJ, England.

ALEXANDER Francis Wesley, b. 3 Nov 1949, Sandusky, Ohio, USA. Teacher. 1 son. Education: BS, Psychology, Wayne State University, 1973-77; Secondary Provisional Teaching Certificate, Mathematics, Eastern Michigan University, 1985-87. Appointments: Teacher, Adult Education, Detroit, Ypsilanti, Michigan, Toledo, Ohio, 1977-; Substitute Teacher, Ann Arbor, Michigan, Pittsburgh, 1981-87. Contributions to: Bare Bones; Red Pagoda; Mainichi Daily News, Japan; Dragonfly; Black Bear Review; Haiku Quarterly; Brussels Sprout; Modern Haiku; New Cicada, Japan; Beyond, Ko, Japan; Psychopoetica; Black Bough; Japanophile; Star Line; Scavenger's Newsletter; Haiku Headlines; Starsong; Contemporary Education; Black American Literature Forum; Piedmont Literary Review. Honours: Honourable Mention, Mainichi Daily News Annual Haiku Contest, 1989. Memberships: Haiku Society of America; Science Fiction Poetry Association. Address: 1816 Harrison Street, Sandusky, OH 44870, USA.

ALEXANDER Meena, b. 17 Feb 1951, Allahabad, India. Writer; Poet; Professor. m. David Lelyveld, 1 May 1979, 1 son, 1 daughter. Education: BA, Khartoum University, 1969; PhD, Nottingham University, 1973. Appointments: Lecturer, Miranda House, Delhi University 1974, Jawaharlal Nehru University 1975, Central Institute of English & Foreign Languages, Hyderabad 1975-77; Lecturer, 1977-79, Reader, 1979, University of Hyderabad; Assistant Professor, Fordham University, 1980-87, Hunter College, 1987-89; Associate Professor, Member, Graduate Faculty, City University of New York, 1989-92; Lecturer in Poetry, Columbia University, 1991-; Professor of English and Women's Studies, Hunter College and the Graduate Center, City University of New York, 1992-. Publications: The Bird's Bright Ring, poem, 1976; In The Middle Earth, play, 1977; Without Place, poem, 1977; I Root My Name, poems, 1977; The Poetic Self: Towards a Phenomenology of Romanticism, 1979; Stone Roots, poems, 1980; House of a Thousand Doors, poetry and prose, 1988; Women in Romanticism: Mary Wollstonecraft, Dorothy Wordsworth and Mary Shelley, 1989; The Storm: A Poem in Five Parts, 1989; Nampally Road, novel, 1991; Night-Scene: The Garden, poem, 1992; Fault Lines, memoir, 1993; River and Bridge, poems, 1995, expanded edition, 1996; The Shock of Arrival: Reflections on Postcolonial Experience, 1996; Manhattan Music, novel, 1997. Contributions to: Poetry and prose in various publications. Honours: Altrusa International Award, 1973; MacDowell Fellow, 1993; International Writer in Residence, Arts Council of England, 1995; Various grants. Address: 730 Fort Washington Avenue, No 2B, New York, NY 10040, USA.

ALI Agha Shahid, b. 4 Feb 1949, New Delhi, India. Professor of English and Creative Writing. Education: BA, University of Kashmir, 1968; MA, University of Delhi, 1970; MA, 1981, PhD, 1984, Pennsylvania State University; MFA, University of Arizona, 1985. Publications: Bone Sculpture, 1972; In Memory of Begum Akhtar and Other Poems, 1979; The Half-Inch Himalayas, 1987; A Walk Through the Yellow Pages, 1987; A Nostalgist's Map of America, 1991; Translation of Urdu poet, Faiz Ahmed Faiz: The Rebel's Silhouette, 1991. Contributions to: Antioch Review; Agni Review; Chelsea; Denver Quarterly; Grand Street; Helix; Ironwood; Kayak; Malahat Review; Massachusetts Review; Missouri Review; New England Review; Poetry; Paris Review; Virginia Quarterly Review; Yale Journal of Criticism. Honours: Government of India National Scholarship,

1968-70; Academy of American Poets Prize, 1983; Fellowship, Pennsylvania Council on The Arts, 1983; Tucson Poetry Festival Prize, 1985; Ingram-Merrill Fellowship, 1987; Alan Collins Fellow, Bread Loaf Writers Conference, 1987. Membership: Poetry Society of America. Address: Department of English, Hamilton College, Clinton, NY 13323, USA.

ALIESAN Jody, b. 22 Apr 1943, Kansas City, Missouri, USA. Poet. Education: BA, English and American Literature, Occidental College, 1965; MA, Brandeis University, 1966. Appointments: Board, The Poem in the World, 1995; Poetry Editor, Raven Chronicles, 1995. Publications: Thunder in the Sun, 1971; To Set Free, 1972; Soul Claiming, 1975; As If It Will Matter, 1978; Desire, 1985; Doing Least Harm, 1985; Grief Sweat, 1991; States of Grace, 1992. Contributions to: Wall Street Journal; Los Angeles Times; Portland Review; California Quarterly; Contemporary Quarterly; Negative Capability; Poetry Northwest; Quarry West; Studia Mystica; Calyx; Berkeley Poets Cooperative; Northwest Review; The Advocate; Yellow Silk. Honours include: Seattle Arts Commission Performance Grant, 1973; Seattle Arts Festival, Written Works Award, 1973, 1976, 1990, 1992; National Endowment for the Arts Fellowship, 1978; Pierce County Arts Commission, Six Washington Poets, 1978; Artist in Residence, Seattle Arts Commission, 1983; Thompson Visiting Poet, Babson College, 1988; Kings County Arts Commission, New Works, 1988, Work in Progress, 1979; Grants for Artists, Artists Trust, 1992; Seattle Arts Commission, Seattle Artists, 1994. Membership: Phi Beta Kappa. Address: 5043 22nd Avenue, Northeast, Seattle, WA 98105, USA.

ALKALAY Karen. See: **ALKALAY-GUT Karen Hillary.**

ALKALAY-GUT Karen Hillary (Karen Alkalay, Karen Gut, Hillary Keren), b. 29 Mar 1945, London, England. Lecturer. m. (1) 4 July 1967, (2) Exra Gut, 26 July 1980, 2 sons, 2 daughters. Education: BA, 1966, MA, 1967, PhD, 1975, University of Rochester, New York, USA. Appointments: Lecturer, State University of New York, Geneseo, 1967-70, University of the Negev in Beer Sheva, 1972-76, Tel Aviv University, 1977-. Publications: Making Love, 1980; Butter Sculptures (in Hebrew), 1983; Mechitza, 1986; Alone in the Dawn, biography, 1988; Ignorant Armies, 1991; Love and War, 1991; Love Soup, 1992; Harmonies/Disharmonies, 1994; Recipes, 1994. Contributions to: American Voice; Massachusetts Review; Forward; Webster Review; Jerusalem Post; Present Tense; Arc, Israel; Pilgrims, New Zealand; Voices; New Outlook; Rochester Jewish Ledger; International Quarterly; Amelia; Grasslands Review; Lilliput Review; Kerem; Sheila-na-gig. Honours: Tel Aviv Fund, 1980; Shvut Publication Award, Israel Writers' Association, 1983; Dulchin, Jewish Agency Award, 1984; 1st Prize, BBC World Service Poetry Award, 1990; Prairie Schooner Readers' Choice, 1992; Commendation, Arvon Poetry Competition, 1993. Memberships: Founder, 1982, Chair, 1982-84, 1991-, Secretary, 1987-89, Israel Association of Writers in English; PEN; Board, Federation of Writers in Israel; Poetry Society of America; Voices Israel; Chair, American Studies Association, Israel, 1991-95; Modern Language Association. Address: Department of English, Tel Aviv University, Ramat Aviv, Israel.

ALLBERY Debra, b. 3 Mar 1957, Lancaster, Ohio, USA. Instructor in Creative Writing. Education: Denison University, Granville, Ohio, 1975-77; BA, English, The College of Wooster, Ohio, 1979; MFA, University of Iowa, Iowa City, 1982; University of Virginia, 1991-93. Appointments: Writer in Residence, Phillips Exeter Academy, Exeter, New Hampshire, 1985-86, Brooks School, North Andover, Massachusetts, 1988, Dickinson College, Carlisle, Pennsylvania; Writer in Residence, 1989-90, Creative Writing Instructor, 1990-91, Interlochen Arts Academy. Publications: Poems in Anthology of Magazine Verse and Yearbook of American Poetry, 1986-88; Walking Distance, 1991; Pittsburgh Book of Contemporary American Poets, 1993. Contributions to: Poetry; Nation; Yale Review; Kenyon Review; Poetry Northwest; Ploughshares; Iowa Review; Western Humanities Review; Ironwood; Crazyhorse. Honours: George Bennett Memorial Fellowship, Phillips Exeter Academy, 1985-86; National Endowment for the Arts Fellowships, 1986-87, 1993-94; Discovery, Nation Poetry Prize, 1989; Resident Fellow, MacDowell and Yaddo, 1987, 1990; Fellowships, New Hampshire State Council on The Arts, 1987, 1990; Chubb Life America Fellowship, MacDowell Colony, 1990; Agnes Lynch Starrett Prize, University of Pittsburgh Press, 1990; Hawthornden Fellowship, for residency Hawthorne Castle, Scotland, 1991. Memberships: Academy of American Poets; Associated Writing Programmes. Address: 508 N Mulberry Stree, Clyde, OH 43410-1550, USA.

ALLEN Blair H, b. 2 July 1933, Los Angeles, California, USA. Writer; Artist; Poet. m. Juanita Aguilar Raya, 27 Jan 1968, 1 son, 1 daughter. Education: AA, San Diego City College, 1964; Studied at University of Washington, 1965-66; BA, Graphic Art, San Diego State University, 1970. Appointments: Book Reviewer, Los Angeles Times, 1977-78; Special Feature Editor, Cerulean Press and Kent Publications, 1982-. Publications: Televisial Po-ums for Bloodshot Eyeballs, 1973; Malice in Blunderland, 1974; N/Z, 1979; The Atlantis Trilogy, 1982; Dreamwish of the Magician, 1983; Right Through the Silver-Lined, 1984; Looking Glass, 1984; Trapped in a Cold-War Travelogue, 1991; May Burning into August, 1992; The Subway Poems, 1993; Editor, The Magical World of David Cole, 1984; Editor, Snow Summits in The Sun, poetry anthology, 1988; Editor, Bonfire on the Beach (poems by John Brander), 1993. Contributions to: Intermedia; Cage; Momentum; Bachy; Electrum; Margins; California State Poetry Journal; San Fernando Poetry Journal; News Letter Inago; First Inago Anthology; Assembling; Red Dancefloor; Pudding; Gypsy; Our Own Thing, anthology. Honours: First prize for Poetry Competition, Pacificus Foundation, Los Angeles, California, 1992; Various honours and awards. Memberships: Beyond Baroque Foundation; Medina Foundation; California State Poetry Society; Association for Applied Poetry. Address: 9651 Estacia Court, Cucamonga, CA 91730, USA.

ALLEN Bryan John, b. 27 Apr 1954, Tynemouth, England. Poet; Author; Journalist. Appointments: Regular Recitals on Radio 1 & 2, BBC World Service, Talk Radio UK, Great North Radio, BBC Newcastle, Wear FM, Metro FM, TFM, Radio Tyneside and on all BBC Regional Radio Networks; Appearances on Good Morning Show, BBC1; This Morning Show, ITV; Lifestyle, Cable; Wire TV, Cable; TTTV & BBC North; Organized the 24hr Poetry Charity Marathon Event, 1993; Resident Poet on GNR (Joe Poulters Show) and Radio Tyneside; Co-Presenter & Present, Wear in Focus Show, Wear FM. Publications: Feelings, 1990; Poetry Marathon Charity (anthology), 1993; Journeys, 1994. Contributions to: Newspapers: Mail on Sunday; Sunday Post; Sunday Mirror; Sunday Express; News of the World; People; Evening Chronicle; Journal; Northern Echo; Star Series; Northumberland Gazette; Magazines: North-East Times Magazine; First Time; Auteur; Link-Up; Northumbrian; Fanzines; Poets Gallery; Charity Magazines; Works included in anthologies throughout the country: First Time; North East 92-94; Poetry Marathon Charity 1993; Cassell's 94 (How can you write a poem when you're dying of AIDS); Bereavement/Comfort Poems used worldwide in Candlelit Services by many support groups and charities; Works used in Undying Heart Requiem, Manchester and London; Works used in greeting cards; Works shown in Poets Gallery; Works translated into French, Italian, German and Spanish. Memberships: The Royal Society of Literature; Writers Guild of England (UK); Poetry Society; European Association for the Promotion of Poetry; British Association of Journalists; Broadcasting Press Guild; Royal Television Society. Address: 16D Clayton Street West, Newcastle-upon-Tyne, NE1 5DZ, England.

ALLEN Judith, b. 5 Jan 1957, Nottingham, England. University Teacher. 1 daughter. Education: Masters in South African Literature, 1991; Honours Degree in English Literature, 1990; Batchelors Degree in English Literature and Social Anthropology, 1989. Appointments: Lecturer, English Department, University of Natal, Durban, South Africa, 1992-93; Adjunct Lecturer, English Department, State University of New York, Oneonta, New York, USA, 1993-. Contributions to: Parnassus Literary Journal, 1994. Address: 13.5 Franklin Street, Oneonta, NY 13820, USA.

ALLEN Paula Gunn, b. 1939, Cubero, New Mexico, USA. Writer; Poet; University Lecturer. Education: BA; MFA; PhD. Appointments: Lecturer, San Francisco State University, University of New Mexico, Fort Lewis College, University of California at Berkeley. Publications: The Blind Lion, 1974; Sipapu: A Cultural Perspective, 1975; Coyote's Daylight Trip, 1978; A Cannon Between My Knees, 1981; From The Center: A Folio of Native American Art and Poetry, editor, 1981; Shadow Country, 1982; Studies in American Indian Literature: Critical Essays and Course Designs, editor, 1983; The Woman Who Owned the Shadows, 1983; The Sacred Hoop: Recovering the Feminine in American Indian Traditions, essays, 1986, new edition, 1992; Skins and Bones, 1988; Spider Woman's Granddaughters: Traditional Tales and Contemporary Writing by Native American Women, editor, 1989; Grandmothers of the Light: A Medicine Woman's Sourcebook, 1991; Columbus and Beyond, 1992; Voice of the Turtle, 1994. Honours: American Book Award, 1990; Ford Foundation Grant; National Endowment for the Arts Award. Address:

c/o Diane Cleaver Inc, 55 Fifth Avenue, 15th Floor, New York, NY 10003, USA.

ALLOCATI Beatriz Olga, b. 2 Sept 1935, Buenos Aires, Argentina. Former Music Professor; Municipal Officer; Poet. m. Jorge C Zanardi, 2 Apr 1971. Education: Bachelor's Degree, 1955; Professor of Music, Conservatorio Nacional de Música, 1955; Cambridge Certificate of Proficiency in English (Literature), 1957. Appointments: Secretary, National Bank of Boston, Eli Lilly & Co, 1955-68; Secretary to the Mayor of Buenos Aires, 1983-86; Alternate Director-General of Municipal Libraries, 1986-89; Interinstitutional Coordination Director, Dirección General de Enseñanza Artística, 1989-. Publications: Poemas para una noche de lluvia (with poet Jorge Riveiro), 1972; A Sueno Partido, 1981; Los Infinitivos Infinitos de la Tia Bettona, in 5 Parfiles de Mujer, 1982; De Todos Modos, 1985; Interrupcion del Exilio, 1987; Por la Senal de Septiembre, 1988; Honrar al Hermano, 1993; Prose: Un Hombre de Derecho, Amadeo Allocati (biography of her father), 1992. Contributions to: Ronda Literaria magazine and provincial newspapers. Memberships: Sociedad Argentina de Escritores; Promotora del Libro Argentino; Asociación de Poetas Argentinos. Address: Carlos Calvo 1305, 5o 23, 1102 Buenos Aires, Argentina.

ALMON Bert, b. 29 July 1943, Port Arthur, Texas, USA. Professor of English. m. Olga Costopoulos, 23 Nov 1984, 1 son, 3 daughters. Education: BA, University of Texas, El Paso, 1965; MA, 1967, PhD, 1971, University of New Mexico. Appointments: Professor of English, University of Alberta, Edmonton, Canada, 1968-. Publications: The Return, 1968; Taking Possession, 1976; Poems for The Nuclear Family, 1979; Blue Sunrise, 1980; Deep North, 1984; Calling Texas, 1990; Earth Prime, 1994. Contributions to: Chicago Review; Orbis; Malahat Review; Kansas Quarterly; Iron; The North; Poetry Durham. Honours: Second Prize, Cardiff Poetry Festival Competition, 1991; Writers' Guild of Alberta Prize for Poetry, 1995. Memberships: Writer's Guild of Alberta; Poetry Society, London; Associated Writing Programs. Address: Department of English, University of Alberta, Edmonton, Alberta T6G 2E5, Canada.

ALONSO URIARTE Santiago, b. 13 July 1915, Spain. Writer; Lyricist. m. 7 July 1942. Education: Diploma, Academico Laureado, Diploma, Solemne de Academico e Merito como Poeta, Academia Internacional de Pontzen, Italy; Honorary Member, Academia Gazeta de Felgueiras, Portugal; Honorary Academician, Centro Cultural, Literario y Artistico Agustin Garcia Alonso, Spain. Publications: Volver a Vir, 1982, 1983; Encontraando Caminos, 1986; La Paz se Acerca, 1988; En Busca de Justicia, 1990; El Encanto de la Musica, 1990. Contributions to: Se Roqueta; Gemma; Clarin; Arboleda; Nirvana Populi; El Eria; Orchilla; Ruskal Herriko Poetak; Pegaleda; Setima Antologia de Poesia Contemporanea, 1990; Antologia Clarinde Poesia; Antologia Poetica Nigolaki; and others. Honours: El Paisaje Prize for Poetry, 1983; First Prize for Poetry, Curculo Cultural de Puerto de Pollensa, Balearic Islands, 1983; Acentor Prize for Poetry, 1987; Ayuda Poetry Prize, 1989. Memberships: Centro Cultural O Jornal de Felgueiras; Asociacion Mundial de Escritores; Sociedad General de Autores de Espana; World Academy of Arts and Culture, USA; Poetry Writers Association, USA; Accademia Internazionale de Pontzen, Italy. Address: Calle Mestral S/N, Apartado 86, Puerto Pollensa 07470, Mallorca, Spain.

ALONZO Eugene. See: HARR Lorraine Ellis.

ALPHONSO-KARKALA John B, b. 30 May 1923, South Kanara, Mysore State, India. Writer; Poet; Professor of Literature. m. Leena Anneli Hakalehto, 20 Dec 1964, 3 children. Education: BA, 1950, MA, 1953, Bombay University; University of London, 1954-55; PhD, Columbia University, 1964. Appointments: Visiting Lecturer, City College of the City University of New York, 1963; Assistant Professor, 1964-65, Associate Professor, 1965-68, Professor of Literature, 1969-. State University of New York at New Paltz; Visiting Professor, Columbia University, 1969-70. Publications: Indo-English Literature in the Nineteenth Century, 1970; Anthology of Indian Literature, editor, 1971; Bibliography of Indo-English Literature, 1800-1966, editor (with Leena Karkala), 1974; Comparative World Literature: Seven Essays, 1974; Passions of the Nightless Night, novel, 1974; Jawaharlal Nehru: A Literary Portrait, 1975; When Night Falls, poems, 1980; Vedic Vision, editor, 1980; Joys of Jayanagara, novel, 1981; Anthology of Indian Literature: Rishis, Buddha, Acharyas, Bhaktas, Mahatma, 1987; Indo-English Literature: Essays (with Leena A Karakala), 1994. Memberships: American Oriental Society; Association for Asian

Studies; International Congress of Comparative Literature; International Congress of Orientalists; Modern Language Association of America. Address: 20 Millrock Road, New Paltz, NY 12561, USA.

ALURISTA, b. 8 Aug 1947, Mexico City, Mexico. Professor of Spanish, Chicano, Mexican and Latin American Literature and Culture. 3 sons, 1 daughter. Education: BA, Psychology, San Diego State University, 1970; MA, Spanish Literature, 1979, PhD, Spanish Literature, 1982, University of California, San Diego. Appointments: Lecturer of Chicano Studies, University of Texas, Austin, 1974-76; Distinguished Visiting Lecturer of Chicano Literature and Creative Writing, University of Nebraska, Omaha, 1979; Lecturer of Spanish and Chicano Studies, San Diego State University, Calexio Campus, Calexio, California, 1976-83; Assistant Professor, Romance Languages Department, Colorado College, Colorado Springs, 1983-86; California State University, San Marcos, School of Education. Publications: Floricanto en aztlán, 1971; Nationchild plumaroja, 1972; Timespace huracán, 1976; Z Eros, 1995; Et tú, raza?. Poetry collections: Anque-Collected Works, 1976-1979, 1979; Spik in glyph?. 1981; Return (poems collected and new), 1982. Books for children: Coleccion Tula y Tonan, 9 volumes, 1973; Poems in numerous anthologies; Short stories, plays, essays and literary criticism; Audio and video tapes; Numerous edited works; Papers presented to scholarly meetings. Contributions to: Many journals, magazines and newspapers. Honours: A number of distinguished grants, fellowships and honours. Memberships: Association of Mexican American Educators; International Academy of Poets; Modern Language Association; National Association of Chicano Studies. Address: 4112 Calmoor Street, National City, CA 91950, USA.

ALVAREZ Alfred, b. 5 Aug 1929, London, England. Poet; Author. m. 7 April 1966, 2 sons, 1 daughter. Education: Oundle School; BA, 1952, MA, 1956. Corpus Christi College, Oxford. Appointments: Poetry Critic and Editor, Observer, 1956-66; Advisory Editor, Penguin Modern European Poets, 1964-76. Publications: The Shaping Spirit, 1958; The School of Donne, 1961; The New Poetry, 1962; Under Pressure, 1965; Beyond All the Fiddle, 1968; Penguin Modern Poets No 18, 1970; Apparition, 1971; The Savage God, 1971; Beckett, 1973; Hers, 1974; Autumn to Autumn and Selected Poems, 1978; Hunt, 1978; Life After Marriage, 1982; The Biggest Game in Town, 1983; Offshore, 1986; Feeding the Rat, 1988; Rain Forest, 1988; Day of Atonement, 1991; Faber Book of Modern European Poetry, 1992; Night, 1995. Contributions to: Many magazines and journals. Honour: Vachel Lindsay Prize for Poetry, 1961. Memberships: Alpine; Beefsteak; Climbers. Address: c/o Aitken & Stone, 29 Fernshaw Road, London SW10 0TG, England.

ALVES Euridice (Alice Verdi), b. 16 Aug 1946, Brazil. Administrador de Empresas. Education: Faculdade Administracao de Empresas. Publications: Retalhos; Libelo; Perolas; Ramalmete; Nas pegadas do Gigante; Reflexos; Silencios; Trajetoria; Aguia Solitária. Contributions to: Garatuja; Revista Nacional Da Legiao; Leia; Revista Nacional Da Anfip; International Poetry Yearbook. Memberships: International Writers and Artists Association; Academia de Letras. Address: Rua Fabio Jose Bezerra, 722 Apt 112, 03805-000 Sao Paulo, SP, Brazil.

AMALI Idris Odumu Onche, b. 6 June 1953, Benue State, Nigeria. Lecturer. m. Otumenyi Amali, 9 Sept 1978, 4 sons, 2 daughters. Education: St Andrews, Otukpo; Methodist School, 1966; University of Jos; Degrees: BA, Theatre & Drama; MA, PhD in English (Oral Literature). Appointments: National Assistant Secretary; Chairman, Borno State Association of Nigerian Authors; Poetry workshop, Vice-Chairman, Borno State, ANA; Member, Bilingual Committee of PEN; Senior Lecturer and Head of Department, Unimaid. Publications: A Week of Broken Pains and Other Poems; Waves Across Maiduguri and Other Poems; A Mountain of Desire. Contributions to: Kuka; Okike; Postgrats; Liwuram; Vultures in the Air, in Voices from Northern Nigeria: an Anthology; Africana Marburgensia; Frankfurter Afrikanische Blätter; Stepping Stone; Nigeria Magazine; Ufahamu; African Theatre Review; Chelsea; Fajar; Voices From the Fringe; ANA Review; Presence Africane; Opon Ifa. Memberships: Association of Nigerian Authors; Society of Nigerian Theatre Artists; African Literature Association; PEN International; Folklore Society of Nigeria; Borno Museum Association; Archaelogical Association of Nigeria; African Studies Association, Washington; Folklore Fellow, Oral Epics, Associate Member of Folklore Fellows, International Network of Folklorists. Address: Department of English, University of Maiduguri, PMB 1069, Maiduguri, Borno State, Nigeria.

AMBER Claude. See: BERNSTEIN Charles.

AMEEN Mark J, b. 18 Aug 1958, Lowell, Massachusetts, USA. Writer. Education: Bachelor's Degree, University of Massachusetts, 1980. Publications: A Circle of Sirens, 1985; The Buried Body, 1990. Honour: Poetry Fellowship, New York Foundation for the Arts, 1989-90. Address: 235 East 4th Street, New York, NY 10009, USA.

AMEERUDDIN Syed, b. 5 Dec 1942, Guntakal, India. Teacher; Professor. m. Sayeeda Be, 11 Apr 1968, 1 son. Education: BA, 1964; MA, 1966; MPhil, 1980. Appointment: Professor of English, New College, University of Madras. Publications: What the Himalaya Said; Doom to Come; A Lover and A Wanderer; Pe Tallic Love Times; Visioned Summits, poems; Indian Verse in English; Indian Voices; International Voices; International Poets. Contributions to: Number of leading Indian and international literary journals. Honours: DLitt, awarded at the 5th World Congress of Poets; Michael Madhusudan Award; Elected Honorary Professor; Australia Day Award; Certificate of Merit. Memberships: World Poetry Society; United Poets International; Editor, International Poets Academy; Indian Association for English Studies; Authors Guild of India. Address: 5 Mohamed Hussain Khan Lane, Royapettah, Madras 600014, India.

AMICHAI Yehuda, b. 1924, Wurzburg, Germany (Israeli citizen). Poet. m. Hana Sokolov. Education: Hebrew University, Jerusalem. Appointments: Visiting Poet, University of California at Berkeley, 1976, New York University, 1987. Publications: Poems translated into over 30 languages; Now and in Other Days, 1955; Two Hopes Away, 1958; In the Park, 1959; Now in the Turmoil, 1968; And Not in Order to Remember, 1971; Songs of Jerusalem and Myself, 1973; Behind All This Lies Happiness, 1974; Amen, 1978; On New Years Day, Next to a House Being Built, 1979; Time, 1979; Love Poems, 1981; Hour of Charity, 1982; Great Tranquility: Questions and Answers, 1983; From Many You Came, and to Men You Will Return, 1985; The Selected Poetry of Yehuda Amichai, 1986; Poems of Jerusalem, 1987; Even a Fist was Once an Open Palm with Fingers, 1991. Honour: Honorary Doctorate, Hebrew University, 1990. Address: 26 Malki Street, Yemin Moshe, Jerusalem, Israel.

AMIKA. See: DEVIDE Vladimir.

AMIRTHANAYAGAM Indran, b. 17 Nov 1960, Sri Lanka. Journalist; Poet. Education: BA, Haverford College. 1982; MA, Columbia University, 1985. Appointments: Editor, PB Securities; Guest Editor, The Portable Lower East Side; Contributing Editor, Night. Publication: The Elephants of Reckoning, 1993. Contributions to: Massachusetts Review; Literary Review; Portable Lower East Side; Bomb; Night; Hanging Loose; St Andrews Review; Pivot; Downtown; Dispatch. Honour: Pushcart Prize. Membership: Poetry Society of America. Address: 4810 Mercury Drive, Rockville, MD 20853, USA.

AMMONS A(rchie) R(andolph), b. 18 Feb 1926, Whiteville, North Carolina, USA. Poet; Professor of English. m. Phyllis Plumbo, 26 Nov 1949, 1 son. Education: BS, Wake Forest College, 1949; University of California at Berkeley, 1950-52. Appointments: Principal, Elementary School, Hatteras, North Carolina, 1949-50; Executive Vice-President, Friedrich and Dimmock Inc, Millville, New Jersey, 1952-62; Poetry Editor, Nation, New York City, 1963; Assistant Professor 1964-68, Associate Professor 1968-71, Professor of English 1971-73, Goldwin Smith Professor of English 1973-, Cornell University; Visiting Professor, Wake Forest University, 1974-75. Publications: Ommateum, with Doxology, 1955; Expressions of Sea Level, 1964; Corsons Inlet, 1965; Tape for the Turn of the Year, 1965; Northfield Poems, 1966; Selected Poems, 1968; Uplands, 1970; Briefings, 1971; Collected Poems, 1951-71, 1972; Sphere: The Form of a Motion, 1973; Diversifications, 1975; For Doyle Fosso, 1977; Highgate Road, 1977; The Snow Poems, 1977; The Selected Poems, 1951-1977, 1977, expanded edition, 1987; Breaking Out, 1978; Six-Piece Suite, 1981; Worldly Hopes, 1982; Lake Effect Country, 1982; Sumerian Vistas, 1987; The Really Short Poems of A R Ammons, 1991; Garbage, 1993. Contributions to: Periodicals. Honours: Guggenheim Fellowship, 1966; Levinson Prize, 1970; National Book Awards for Poetry, 1973, 1993; Bollingen Prize for Poetry, 1974-75; John D and Catharine T MacArthur Foundation Prize, 1981-86; National Book Critics Circle Award, 1982; North Carolina Award for Literature, 1986; Frost Silver Medal, Poetry Society of America, 1994. Address: Department of English, Cornell University, Ithaca, NY 14853, USA.

ANANIA Michael (Angelo), b. 1938, USA. Author; Poet. Appointments: Coordinator, Council of Literary Magazines; Bibliographer, Lockwood Library; Editor, 1963-64, Co-Editor, 1963-67, Audit; Instructor, State University of New York, 1964-65, Northwestern University, Illinois, 1965-68; Literary Editor, Swallow Press, 1968-; Assistant Professor, Department of English, University of Illinois, Chicago, 1970-. Publications: New Poetry Anthology; The Color of Dust; Set Sorts; Riversongs; The Red Menace; Constructions/Variations; The Sky at Ashland. Address: Department of English, University of Illinois, Chicago, IL 60680, USA.

ANDERSON Alex (Anthony), b. 17 June 1932, Liverpool, England. m. Elizabeth, 16 Sept 1963, 2 daughters. Education: Cert Ed, Liverpool University; Advanced Dip Ed, Lancaster University. Appointments: Apprentice Butcher; Army Service; Registered Yacht Master, Royal Engineers; Forester; Machine Operator, Printing Trade, 1959-64; Student Nurse; Registered Master Diver with Underwater Work Ltd, Devon; Teacher; Writer; Poet. Publications: Hobgoblins Also Dream, 1982; The Apple Tree, 1988; Landscape with Figures, 1989; The Caves of Mali, 1990; Tortoise in The Snow, 1990; Poets are the Priesthood of the World, 1995; Game Over, 1996; The Land of the Young, 1997. Memberships: Toadbirds; Liverpool Parliamentary Debating Society, Wrexham Member. Address: c/o Guild of St George, 17 Haddassah Grove, Liverpool L17 9XH, England.

ANDERSON Chester, b. 1932, USA. Author; Poet. Appointments: Editor, The Communication Company, 1967, Crawdaddy Magazine, 1968-69. Publications: Colloguy: A Liturgy for Dragons; The Pink Palace; Ten Years to Doomsday; The Butterfly Kid; Puppies; Fox and Hare. Address: PO Box 80, Rio Nido, CA 95471, USA.

ANDERSON Mark Ransom, b. 3 Sept 1951, Kansas, USA. Poet; Teacher. m. Susan Aileen Grimes, 29 July 1984, 1 son. Education: AB, Cornell University, 1973; MA, University of Minnesota, 1976; MFA, 1977, MA, 1979, PhD, 1983, Cornell University. Appointments: Visiting Assistant Professor, Emory University, 1984-85; Assistant Professor, Rhode Island College, 1985-91; Associate Professor, 1991-. Publications: The Broken Boat; Serious Joy. Contributions to: Poetry; Hudson Review; Poetry Northwest; Epoch; Kansas Quarterly; Cimarron Review; Green Mountains Review; Cumberland Poetry Review; Southern Poetry Review. Memberships: Associated Writing Programmes; Poetry Society of America; Modern Language Association; Academy of American Poets; National Council of Teachers of English. Address: 8 Lake View Drive, Greenville, RI 02828, USA.

ANDERSON Martin Lawrence, b. 31 Jan 1948, Essex, England. University Teacher. Div. Education: BA, Honours, University of Ulster, 1971; MPhil, University of Stirling, 1991. Appointments: Lecturer, Leeds Metropolitan University; Lecturer, University of Grenoble, France; Lecturer, University of Hong Kong; Professor at University of the Philippines, Diliman, Quezon City, 1997. Publications: The Kneeling Room, 1981; The Ash Circle, 1986, 1991; Heardlanes, 1989; Dried Flowers, 1990; Swamp Fever, 1991; The Stillness of Gardens, 1994. Contributions to: Sulfur; Longhouse Anthology; Tamarisk; O Ars; Paper Air; Waves; Prism; Antigonish Review; West Coast Review; Oasis; Palantir; Shearsman; Iron; Kudos; Ninth Decade. Address: English Centre, University of Hong Kong, Pokfulam Road, Hong Kong.

ANDRE (Kenneth) Michael, b. 31 Aug 1946, Halifax, Nova Scotia, Canada. Poet; Editor; Publisher; Critic. 1 son. Education: BA, McGill University; MA, University of Chicago; PhD, Columbia University. Appointments: Executive Director, Unmuzzled Ox Books and Magazine; Treasurer, Solto Baroque Opera Company. Publications: Get Serious; Studying the Ground for Holes; Letters Home; Jabbing the A is High Comedy; It As It; Tin Clothes. Contributions to: Little Magazine; Zymergy; Some; Telephone; Mudfish; Abraxas; Spectacular Diseases; Far Point; Canadian Forum. Memberships: Modern Language Association; CCLM; COSMEP; Small Press Center. Address: 105 Hudson Street, No 311, New York, NY 10013, USA.

ANDREWS Lyman Henry, b. 2 Apr 1938, Denver, Colorado, USA. Writer. Education: BA, Brandeis University, 1960. Appointments: Assistant Lecturer, University of Wales, Swansea, 1964-65; Lecturer, University of Leicester, 1965-88; Poetry Critic, Sunday Times, 1969-78; Visiting Professor, Indiana University, 1978-79. Publications: Ash Flowers; Fugitive Visions; The Death of Mayakovsky;

Kaleidoscope. Contributions to: Times; Sunday Times; Times Higher Educational Supplement; British Book News; San Francisco Examiner; Denver Post; Partisan Review; Encounter; El Corno Empurnado; Les Lettres Nouvelles; New Mexico Quarterly; Carolina Quarterly; Transatlantic Review; Anglo Welsh Review; Poetry Quarterly; Root and Branch. Honours: Fulbright Fellowship; James Phelan Travelling Fellowship; Woodrow Wilson National Fellowship. Address: c/o Marion Boyars Ltd, 24 Lacey Road, London SW1 1NL, England.

ANDRUP Claus Erik, b. 10 Aug 1949, Stockholm, Sweden. Public Relations Consultant; Boat Builder. m. (1) Arabella Patricia Lloyd, 28 July 1978, 1 son, 1 daughter, (2) Deborah Alice Sharp, 27 Apr 1989, 1 daughter. Education: Christian Brothers College, Sea Point, Cape Town, South Africa; Diploma in Communications, Advertising and Marketing, London Polytechnic, Metropolitan College. Appointments: Account Manager, Tibbenham Public Relations, Norwich, Norfolk; Director, Concord Group of Companies, London; President, Fair Harbour Mining Corporation, Vancouver, Canada; Director, The Randle Yacht Corporation, Port Coquitlam, British Columbia. Publications: New Nation, 1971, 1972; IZWI, 1971, 1972; Winter Collection, 1991; Poems, 1964-74 (self-published), 1974; New Contrast, 1992. Memberships: Poetry Society; Chelsea Arts Club. Address: 101-1340 Duchess Avenue, West Vancouver, British Columbia V7T 1H6, Canada.

ANGELIDOU Klairi, b. 19 Nov 1932, Ammochostos, Famagu Sta, Cyprus. Minister of Education and Culture. m. Nicos Angelides, 1 May 1955, 3 sons. Education: University of Athens, School of Philosophy. Appointments: Teacher to Gymnasium, 1956-61; Assistant Headmistress, 1962-80; Headmistress, 1980-91; Member of Parliament, 1991-93; Minister, 1993. Publications: Poiemata, 1967; Tou Xerizomou (Uprooting), 1975; Nostimon Imar, 1982; En Demo Anathountos, 1988, 2nd edition, 1989; Pentadaktylos, My Son, 1991, Bi-lingual Edition, 1994; The Silence of Statues, 1994. Contributions to: Efthini, Greece; Akti, Cyprus; Pnevmatiki Kypros, Cyprus; Aigiopelagitica, Greece; Kypriakos Logos, Cyprus. Honours: 1st Prize, Association of Greek Lyceum of Women, 1974; 1st Prize, National Association of Greek Authors, 1978, 1988. Memberships: National Association of Greek Authors of Cyprus and Greece; PEN; Greek Association of Translators. Address: Kimonos 11, Lefkosia, Nicosia, Cyprus.

ANGELO M. See: **ATRE Madhav V.**

ANGELOU Maya, b. 4 Apr 1928, St Louis, Missouri, USA. Writer; Poet; Professor. m. (1) Tosh Angelou, div, (2) Paul du Feu, 1973, div, 1 son. Education: Studied music; Modern dance training with Martha Graham, Pearl Primus and Ann Halprin; Studied drama with Frank Silvera and Gene Frankel. Appointments: Taught modern dance at Rome Opera and Hambina Theatre, Tel Aviv, 1955; Appeared in Off-Broadway plays; Assistant Administrator, School of Music and Drama, Institute of African Studies, University of Ghana, 1963-66; Writer-in-Residence, University of Kansas, 1970; Distinguished Visiting Professor, Wake Forest University, 1974, Wichita State University, 1974; California State University, Sacramento, 1974; 1st Reynolds Professor of American Studies, lifetime appointment, Wake Forest University, 1981-; Many appearances on television in various capacities. Publications: Poetry: Oh Pray My Wings are Gonna Fit Me Well, 1975; And Still I Rise, 1978; Shaker, Why Don't You Sing?, 1983; I Shall Not Be Moved, 1990; On the Pulse of Morning (for the inauguration of President Bill Clinton), 1993; The Complete Poems of Maya Angelou, 1994; Phenomenal Woman: Four Poems Celebrating Women, 1995. Fiction: Mrs Flowers: A Moment of Friendship, 1986; Short stories, stage, film and television plays. Non-Fiction: All God's Children Need Travelling Shoes, 1986. Contributions to: Many publications. Honours: North Carolina Award in Literature, 1987; Horatio Alger Award, 1992; Grammy Award for On the Pulse of Morning, 1994. Memberships: American Federation of Television and Radio Artists; Trustee, American Film Institute; Directors Guild; Equity; Advisory Board, Women's Prison Association. Address: c/o Dave La Camera, Lordly and Dame Inc, 51 Church Street, Boston, MA 02116, USA.

ANGHELAKI-ROOKE Katerina, b. 22 Feb 1939, Athens, Greece. Poet; Translator. Education: Universities of Nice, Athens, and Geneva, 1957-63. Appointments: Freelance Translator, 1962-; Visiting Professor, Harvard University, 1980; Visiting Fellow, Princeton University, 1987. Publications: Wolves and Clouds, 1963; Poems, 1963-69, 1971; The Body is the Victory and the Defeat of Dreams,

1975; The Scattered Papers of Penelope, 1977; The Triumph of Constant Loss, 1978; Counter Love, 1982; The Suitors, 1984; Beings and Things on Their Own, 1986; When the Body, 1988; Wind Epilogue, 1990; Empty Nature, 1993. Translator: Works by Shakespeare, Kazantzakis, Dylan Thomas and Beckett. Honour: Greek National Poetry Prize, 1985. Address: Synesiou Kyrenes 4, 114 71 Athens, Greece.

ANGLE Roger, b. 2 Aug 1938, Kansas, USA. Writer; Advertising Consultant. m. Fontelle Slater, 1960, 1 son. Education: BA, University of Wichita, Kansas, 1962; MFA, University of California, 1972. Appointments: Copy Editor, The Beacon, Wichita, 1964-67; Investigative Reporter, The Gazette and Daily, 1967-69; Coordinator, National Endowment for the Arts, 1973-76; Editor, Reporter, The Newport Ensign, California, 1979-85; Public Relations, Advertising Consultant, 1986-. Publications include: The Farm, 1962; Execution, 1963; The Day is Woman, 1966; The Young Girl, 1966; The Hunted Bird, 1975; My Tongue Has Been Everywhere, 1994. Short Fiction and Literary Prose includes: Moshohoni My Love, 1975; Violence Happens, 1976; Self Portrait at 38, 1976; Whims, 1979; Performance, 1980. Various other screenplays and plays. Honours: Several awards in fiction and journalism. Address: 2225 Pacific Avenue, Apt D, Costa Mesa, CA 92627, USA.

ANNAND James King, b. 2 Feb 1908, Edinburgh, Scotland. Teacher. m. Beatrice Lindosy, 1 Apr 1936, 4 daughters. Education: MA, University of Edinburgh, 1926-30. Appointments: Assistant Teacher; Headmaster, Whithorn. Publications: Two Voices; Twice for Joy; Poems and Translations; Songs from Carmina Burana; Thrice to Show Ye; Dod and Darier; A Wale and Rhymes. Contributions to: Glasgow Herald; Scotsman; Scots Magazine; Burns Chronicle; Lines Review; Voice of Scotland; Saltire Review; Akros; Press and Journal; Chapman; English World Wide. Honours: Burns Chronicle Poetry Prize; Scottish Arts Council Special Award. Membership: International PEN. Address: 173-314 Comely Bank Road, Edinburgh EH4 1DJ, Scotland.

ANNWN David. See: **JONES David James.**

ANSEN Alan, b. 23 Jan 1922, New York, New York, USA. Poet. Education: Woodmere Academy, 1929-38; Harvard College, 1938-42; New School for Social Research, 1946-47. Appointments: Secretary, 1948-53; Lecturer, 1969-86. Publications: The Old Religion; Tibor de Nagy; Various privately printed volumes; Contact Highs; Selected Poems; The Table of Talk of W H Auden; William Burroughs; The Vigilantes; Fragment of a Novel. Memberships: PEN America; Poetry Society of America. Address: 26 Timoleontos Philimonos, Marasleion, Athens 11521, Greece.

ANTHONY Frank, b. 6 June 1922, Minnesota, USA. Poet; Teacher; Writer. Education: St Johns University, 1946-47; BA, University of Minnesota, 1950; University of Iowa, 1951; MA, Dartmouth College, 1984; PhD, Florida State University, 1990. Appointments: Editor, Columnist, Beacon Publications; Producer, Vermont Public Radio; Media Consultant, Dartmouth College; Teacher, Cambridge Center, Community College Vermont, Florida State University. Publications: 24 Poems; Vermont Poems; Selected Poems; Collected Poems; That Special Voice; Poetry of the Unconscious; Beyond The Fruited Plain; Terminus. Contributions to: Celebrating T S Eliot; Frost in Spring; North of Wakulla; Edgar Allan Poe; Anthology of New England Writers; Dream International Quarterly; Jugglers World; Negative Capability; Northern New England Review; The Sucarnochee Review; Thirteen Poetry Magazine; Northwest Review; American String Teacher; Elk River Review; Life on The Line; Pleiades; A Vermont Scrapbook; Thoughts on High School and Beyond. Honours: Grant, Minnesota Council of The Arts; Citation, Dartmouth College. Memberships: Academy of American Poets; National Federation of State Poetry Societies; New England Poetry Club; New England Writers; Vermont Poets Association. Address: PO Box 483, 151 Main Street, Windsor, VT 05089, USA.

ANTHONY Geneva Jo, b. 10 Apr 1946, Minden, Louisiana, USA. Poet. Appointments: Vice President, 1987-90, Installation Officer, 1994, Recording Secretary, Mississippi Poetry Society, South Branch. Publications: Diamonds and Dewdrops; Special People; Poetry Premiere; Sweet Southern Dreams. Contributions to: Voices of the South; Yarn Spinner; XV; Poems of the Great South; Times and Seasons; Poems to Remember, II; Moments in Time; Secrets of Poetic Vision; Poems of Great America; Five South Mississippi Poets; Haiku

Happenings; To the Stars; Holiday Gems; The Heritage; The Spirit; Seven Stars Sentinel; Stories published in various magazines. Honours: Silver Poet Award, Golden Poet Award, 1992, Award of Merit, World of Poetry; 4 Blue Ribbon Awards, Southern Poetry Association; Several Presidents Awards, Runner-up, Poet of the Year, 1988, Poet of the Year, 1992, Mississippi Poetry Society, South Branch; Southern Literature and Southern Poets Officer, United Daughters of the Confederacy. Memberships: Mississippi Poetry Society; Southern Poetry Association. Address: 8417 Shady Rest Road, Vancleave, MS 39565, USA.

ANTHONY Steve, b. 20 Dec 1958, Perivale, Middlesex, England. Freelance Writer; Editor; Tutor. Education: BA, English and Philosophy, Hull University, 1983; MPhil, Modern Poetry in English, Stirling University, 1989; Cert Ed in Further Education, Thames Polytechnic, 1990. Publications: Take Any Train, Book of Gay Men's Poetry, 1990; The Gregory Anthology 1987-1990, 1990; The Crazy Jig, Lesbian and Gay Writing Scotland 2, 1992; Of Eros and Dust: Poems from the City (editor), 1992; Language of Water, Language of Fire, 1992; Risk Behaviour, 1993; Co-Editor, Jugular Defences: An AIDS Anthology, 1994. Contributions to: Author; Clanjamfrie; Encounter; Orbis; Sound Press for The Blind; Ambit; Poetry London Newsletter. Honours: Eric Gregory Award, Society of Authors, 1987; Winner, Bloodaxe Poetry Book Competition, 1987; Finalist, Scottish Open Poetry Competition, 1988; Finalist, Kent and Sussex Poetry Competition, 1988; Specially Commended, Lace Poetry Competition, 1990; Runner-up, Skoob/Index on Censorship Poetry Competition, 1992. Memberships: President, 1979-80, Secretary, 1988, Hull University Poetry Society; Poetry Society; Editorial Panel, Oscars Press; Advisory Board, Terrible Beauty Poetry Readings. Address: The Cottage, 40 Chiltern Close, Ickenham, Middlesex UB10 8JT, England.

ANTIN David, b. 1 Feb 1932, New York, New York, USA. Professor of Visual Arts; Poet. m. Eleanor Fineman, 1960, 1 son. Education: BA, City College, New York City, 1955; MA, Linguistics, New York University, 1966. Appointments: Chief Editor and Scientific Director, Research Information Service, 1958-60; Curator, Institute of Contemporary Art, Boston, 1967; Director, University Art Gallery, 1968-72, Assistant Professor, 1968-72, Professor of Visual Arts, 1972-, University of California, San Diego. Publications: Definitions, 1967; Autobiography, 1967; Code of Flag Behavior, 1968; Meditations, 1971; Talking, 1972; After the War, 1973; Talking at the Boundaries, 1976; Who's Listening Out There?, 1980; Tuning, 1984; Poèmes Parlés, 1984; Selected Poems 1963-1973, 1991; What It Means to be Avant Garde, 1993. Contributions to: Periodicals. Honours: Longview Award, 1960; University of California Creative Arts Award, 1972; Guggenheim Fellowship, 1976; National Endowment for the Humanities Fellowship, 1983; PEN Award for Poetry, 1984. Address: PO Box 1147, Del Mar, CA 92014, USA.

ANYIDOHO Kofi, b. 1947, Wheta, Ghana. Education: BA in English and Linguistics, University of Ghana. Appointments: Lecturer in English, University of Ghana. Publications: Elegy for the Revolution, 1978; Earthchild, 1985; Co-Editor, Our Soul's Harvest, 1978; Co-editor, The Fate of Vultures: New Poetry of Africa, 1989. Honours: BBC Arts and Africa Award. Address: Department of English, University of Ghana, PO Box 25, Legon, Near Accra, Ghana.

ANZRANNII Avikm Axim, (Vikram Mehta), b. 18 June 1947, Shimla, India. Lecturer in English. m. 5 May 1979, 1 son, 1 daughter. Education: BSc, Engineering, Delhi College of English, 1966; BA, Economics, SDB College, Shimla, 1968; MA, English, Regional Centre for P G Studies, Shimla, 1970. Appointment: Lecturer in English, Head of Department of Applied Science and Humanities, Government Polytechnic for Women, Kandaghat, India. Publications: General English for Polytechnic students, 1974; The Lover (for private circulation), 1976; Lillian O Ranni: A Love Song, 1987; Prem Geet (Hindi verses), 1990; 55 Love Songs of Anzrannii, 1995; other unpublished works. Contributions to: Poetcrit; Poet, Madras; Marande; Durst; Ranchi. Honours: DLitt, WAAC, USA, 1990; Diploma of Excellence in Poetry, International Poets Academy, Madras, 1990. Memberships: World Poetry Society, Madras; Writer's Forum, Ranchi; The Journal of the Poetry Society, India; World Congress of Poets, California, USA. Address: Chail View Palace, Kandaghat HP 173215, India.

AP-THOMAS Ifan, b. 27 July 1917, Manchester, England. Retired Radiologist. m. Beti Robinson Owen, 29 Mar 1958, 1 son, 1

daughter. Education: MB, University of Edinburgh, 1939. Publications: Journey to the Silverless Island; The Oakwoods of Love. Membership: Poetry Society. Address: 7 Bryn Estyn Road, Wrexham LL13 9ND, Wales.

APONICK Kathleen, b. 26 Sept 1941, Massachusetts, USA. Freelance Writer; Poet. m. Anthony A Aponick, 3 Jan 1970, 1 son. Education: BS, Framlingham State College, 1963; MA, Warren Wilson College, 1989. Appointments: Schoolteacher; Editor, Allyn and Bacon Inc, Boston; Freelance Writer. Publications: Merrimack: A Poetry Anthology; Near the River's Edge (poetry chapbook), 1995. Contributions to: Tar River Poetry; Worcester Review; Calliope; Seneca Review. Memberships: Poetry Society of America; New England Poetry Club. Address: 5 Skopelos Circle, Andover, MA 01810, USA.

APPLEMAN M(arjorie) H(aberkorn), b. Fort Wayne, Indiana, USA. Dramatist; Poet. m. Philip Appleman. Education: BA, Northwestern University; MA, Indiana University; Degré Supérieur, Sorbonne, University of Paris. Appointments: Professor of English and Playwriting, New York University, Columbia University; International Honors Program, Indiana University. Publications: Plays: Seduction Duet, 1982; The Commuter, 1985; Other: Over 25 plays given in full productions or staged readings, 1971-97; Poetry: Against Time, 1994; Opera libretto: Let's Not Talk About Lenny Anymore, 1989. Contributions to: Numerous anthologies and journals. Honours: Several playwriting awards. Memberships: Academy of American Poets; Authors League of America; Circle Repertory Company Playwrights Unit; Dramatists Guild; League of Professional Theatre; PEN American Center; Poets and Writers. Address: PO Box 39, Sagaponack, NY 11962, USA.

APPLEMAN Philip (Dean), b. 8 Feb 1926, Kendallville, Indiana, USA. Writer; Poet; Distinguished Professor of English Emeritus. m. Marjorie Ann Haberkorn, 19 Aug 1950. Education: BS, 1950, PhD, 1955, Northwestern University; AM, University of Michigan, 1951. Appointments: Fulbright Scholar, University of Lyon, 1951-52; Instructor to Professor, 1955-67, Professor, 1967-84, Distinguished Professor of English, 1984-86, Emeritus, 1986-, Indiana University; Director and Instructor, International School of America, 1960-61, 1962-63; Visiting Professor, State University of New College at Purchase, 1973, Columbia University, 1974; Visiting Scholar, New York University, University of Southern California at Los Angeles; John Steinbeck Visiting Writer, Long Island University of Southampton, 1992. Publications: Novels: In the Twelfth Year of the War, 1970; Shame the Devil, 1981; Apes and Angels, 1989. Poetry: Kites on a Windy Day, 1967; Summer Love and Surf, 1968; Open Doorways, 1976; Darwin's Ark, 1984; Darwin's Bestiary, 1986; Let There Be Light, 1991; New and Selected Poems, 1956-1996, 1996. Non-Fiction: The Silent Explosion, 1965. Editor: 1859: Entering an Age of Crisis, 1959; Darwin, 1970, 2nd edition, revised, 1979; The Origin of Species, 1975; An Essay on the Principle of Population, 1976. Contributions to: Numerous publications; The Paris Review. Honours: Ferguson Memorial Award, Friends of Literature Society, 1969; Christopher Morley Awards, Poetry Society of America, 1970, 1975; Castanola Award, Poetry Society of America, 1975; National Endowment for the Arts Fellowship, 1975; Pushcart Prize, 1985; Humanist Arts Award, American Humanist Association, 1994. Memberships: Academy of American Poets; American Association of University Professors; Authors Guild of America; Modern Language Association; National Council of Teachers of English; PEN American Center; Poetry Society of America; Poets and Writers. Address: PO Box 39, Sagaponack, NY 11962, USA.

APPLETON Joan Hazel, (Joan Downar), b. 12 Oct 1930, London, England. Teacher; Freelance Journalist. m. Albert Appleton, 10 Apr 1972. Education: Certificate in Education. Appointment: Teacher of Creative Writing, University of Nottingham Adult Education Centre. Publications: River People, 1976; The Empire of Light, 1984; From the First Word, 1985; The Old Noise of Truth, 1989. Contributions to: Sunday Times; Poetry Review; Encounter; New Statesman; Arts Council Anthologies. Honours: Runner-up: Stroud, 1976, Cheltenham, 1981, National Poetry Competition, 1985; First Prize Winner, Stroud, 1981. Memberships: National Poetry Society; Nottingham Poetry Society. Address: The Grange, Thrumpton, Nottinghamshire NG11 0AX, England.

ARCHIBALD Mary-Ann, b. 25 Oct 1963, Truro, Nova Scotia, Canada. Writer. Education: BA, Political Science, Acadia University,

Wolfville, Nova Scotia. Publication: Amethyst Review, 1995. Contributions to: Chronicle Herald; Outdoor Canada; Field & Stream; Farm Focus; The Farmer; Truro Magazine; Central Nova Business News; Dunhill. Memberships: Nova Scotia Writer's Federation; Periodical Writers of Canada. Address: PO Box 1122, Truro, Nova Scotia B2N 5H1, Canada.

ARDEN Hava. See: TICE Arden A.

ARGOW Sylvia, (Meletusa), b. New York, New York, USA. Author; Poet; Songwriter. Education: City University of New York; Bronx Community College; New York University. Appointments: Associate Editor, American Mosaic Poetry Magazine. Creative works: Composer of Songs; Author: Murmur in the Myrtle, Series 2 (quotella collection), 1980; The Transparent Wall, 1980; Hurrah for Johnny (children's short stories), 1989; The Jaded Mask (selected poems), 1987; The Journey, 1989; Book of Ten-a-Mins, 1990. Poetry: Charge and Pray; Mediocrity; Unbridled; Phenomenon; Primrose; Dominion; Sorceror. Creator of 7 new poetry forms: Argonelle; Quotella; Snare; Karina; Hermalee; Sherelle; Pondelle. Honours include: World Belletrist Award; Poetry's Hall of Fame, International Belles-Lettres Society, 1975; Poets Hall of Fame, Parnassus Literary Journal, 1981; Knight Grande Dame of Merit, Knights of Malta, 1986; Certificate of Award in Recognition as Poet, Vesta's Who's Who of North American Poets, 1st edition, Canada, 1991. Memberships: Woman's Press Club of New York; National League of State Poetry Societies; Composers, Authors and Artists of America; Poets and Writers; International Academy of Poets, UK; Life Member, World Institute of Achievement; American Society of Composers, Authors and Publishers; American Guild of Authors and Composers. Address: 2150 Wallace Avenue, No 4B, Bronx, NY 10462, USA.

ARGYLE Keith, b. 8 Feb 1951, Worksop, Nottinghamshire, England. Education: City and Guilds Catering, 1978. Appointments: Co-op Shop Assistant; Lyle Builder; Wall Tiler; Lorry Driver; Catering College; Catering Profession; Founder and Chair of White Tower Writers Association. Publications: The Good, The Fair & The Funny, 1994; A Week at Cleethorps, 1996. Memberships: Chair, Network of Writer and Doncaster Area; Founder and Chair, White Tower Writers Association. Address: 33 Wellgate, Conisborough, Doncaster, S. Yorks DN12 3HN, England.

ARIMA Takashi Nishida, b. 19 Dec 1931, Kyoto, Japan. Director. m. Yoshiko Oota, 15 Nov 1957, 1 son, 1 daughter. Education: Graduate, Doshisha University, 1954. Appointments: Manager, Kyoto Bank Branch, 1974-78; Vice Chairman, Takarabune Corporation, 1989-; President, Pegasus Leasing Company Ltd, 1987-; Teacher, Osaka College of Literature, 1968, Kyoto College of Art; Consultant Editor, Shi to shiso magazine. Publications: Songs: Someone Somewhere, 1968' Changing Course, 1969; Price Increase, 1970; Broadcasting Banned Songs, 1972; O Little Planet, 1985; Sounds of Asia, 1990; Owl's Lullaby, 1990; Poetry: Song of Little Odysseus; North, South, East and West; Journey to the Real; Memory of Twilight; The Memory of India; Stranger's Songs; Contemporary Japanese poetry; Mongolian Horses; Ilands; From the Labyrinth; The Beginning of the End; A Woman from the Sea; Metamorphosis; For children: New Children's Song, 1963; My Stamp My Promise; Haa Too Too, 1969; Kyoto Children, 1974; Rakuchu, Rakugai, Rakugai, 1975; Thanks. Honour: International Eminent Poet's Diploma, International Poets Academy, 1993. Memberships: Representative, Kyoto Contemporary Poetry Association; Japan Poets' Association; Japan Writers' Association; Japan PEN Club; World Academy of Art and Culture. Address: 1-29-103 Izumikawa-cho, Shimogamo, Sakyo-ku, Kyoto 606, Japan.

ARMANTROUT (Mary) Rae, b. 13 Apr 1947, Vallejo, California, USA. College Teacher. m. Charles Korkegian, 21 Aug 1971, 1 son. Education: AB, University of California, 1970; MA, California State University, San Francisco, 1975. Appointments: Teaching Assistant, 1972-74; Lecturer, 1978-82; Lecturer, University of California, 1982-. Publications: Necromance; Precedence; The Invention of Hunger! Extremities; Made To Seem. Contributions to: Partisan Review; Boundary 2; Sulfur; Conjunctions; Canary Islands Review; San Diego Union Newspaper; Best American Poetry of 1988. Honour: California Arts Council Fellowship. Address: 4774 East Mountain View Drive, San Diego, CA 92116, USA.

ARMITAGE Simon Robert, b. 26 May 1963, Huddersfield, West Yorkshire, England. Poet. m. Alison Tootell, 21 Sept 1991. Education:

Portsmouth Polytechnic, 1981-84; BA, Honours, Geography, 1984, MA, Manchester University, 1986-88. Appointments: Probation Officer, Greater Manchester Probation Service, 1988-93; Poetry Editor, Chatto And Windos, 1993-95. Publications: Zoom!, 1989; Xanadu, 1992; Kid, 1992; Book of Matches, 1993; The Dead Sea Poems, 1995. Contributions to: The Sunday Times; Times Literary Supplement; Guardian; Observer; Independent. Honours: Eric Gregory Award, 1988; Sunday Times Young Writer of The Year, 1993; Forward Poetry Prize, 1993; Lannan Award, 1994. Address: 3 Netherley, Marsden, Huddersfield HD7 6XN, England.

ARMSTRONG Blair Morton, b. 9 Sept 1925, Tulsa, Oklahoma, USA. Poet; Artist; Publisher; Explorer of Interrelationships Between the Arts. m. 20 Mar 1951, 1 son, 3 daughters. Education: 9 Years attendance and graduate of Spence School, New York; American Academy of Dramatic Art; Maryland Institute of Art, Baltimore. Appointments: Founder, Mnemosyne Press of Arizona; Lecturer on the Correlation of the Arts, American Museum, Bath, England; Developed the Mnemosyne Principle from her career of integrating the Arts, a very different approach to the administration of the Arts in public education, introduced in 1988 to 7 schools throughout Arizona; Founder, Flagstaff Festival of the Arts Poetry Competition; Six week exhibit, Sense of the Sea, expressed in 4 mediums: paintings, photography, poetry and shell design, Arizona State University, 1992-93. Publications: Memory of the Mogollon, collection of poems; Arizona Anthem, collection of poems. Contributions to: Saturday Evening Post. Honours: Letter of Appreciation from Her Majesty Queen Elizabeth II for An Anglophile's Cookery Book; Arizona Anthem was awarded Ambassador of Honour designation in Books-Across-the-Sea Programme, 1984. Memberships: Arizona Poetry Society; Founding Vice President, National Society of Arts and Letters, Phoenix Branch. Address: 6246 Joshua Tree Lane, Paradise Valley, AZ 85253, USA.

ARMSTRONG Naomi Young, (Gloria Young), b. 17 Oct 1918, Dermott, Arkansas, USA. Actress; Teacher. 1 child. Education: BSc, Speech Theatre, Northwestern University, Evanston, Illinois, 1961; AA, Wilson Junior College, 1957; DDiv, Universal Orthodox College, 1988. Appointments: Silk Dress Operator, ILGWU, 1947-55; IRS, 1956-59; Teacher, Chicago Board of Education, 1962-83; Actress, Screen Actors Guild and AFTRA, 1989-. Publications: A Child's Easter, 1971; Expression I, 1973; Expression III, 1976; Naomis Two-Line Sillies (A Guide for Living), 1985; Expression V, 1994. Contributions to: New Voices in American Poetry, 1972; Poet From Sea to Sea, 1986; United States Poets; Premier Poets. Honours: Doctor of Letters, 1980; LittD, 1981; Honorary Gold Diploma, 1976; PhD Ed, 1979; Awards, World Congress of Poets, 1973-1979, 1986, 1994; Numerous others. Memberships: IPA, Board of Governors, Chairman, Author Autographing Committee; LIFE; WAAC; UPLI, Honorary Member, Executive Board; Founder/Director, Chrysopoets Inc; World Poets Resource Centre; Poetry Society of London; Centre Studi e Scambi; Intercontinental Biog Association; World Poetry Society.

ARMSTRONG Terry Lee, (Terry Lee, Milo Rosebud), b. 23 Dec 1949, Elgin, Nebraska, USA. Carpenter. m. Chris Alvarez, 16 Nov 1991, 1 daughter. Education: Associate in Arts; San Antonio College; North Texas State University; University of Texas at San Antonio. Appointments: Editor and Publisher, Milo Rosebud, Lone Stars Magazine, Armstrong Publishing Company. Publications: Call It Love; When The Soul Speaks; Heart Thoughts and I Love Yous. Contributions to: National Library of Poetry; Omnific; Poetic Eloquence; My Legacy; Telstar; Moments in Time; Mobius; The Plowman. Honours: 1st Place, Grand Prize, North American Open Poetry Contest, 1990; Poet of the Year, Poetry Break Journal, 1991; Man of the Year, International Men of Achievement, 1992. Memberships: Library of Congress, Texas; National Endowment for the Arts Applicant, 1991, 1992, 1994. Address: 4219 Flint Hill, San Antonio, TX 78230, USA.

ARNOLD Bob, b. 5 Aug 1952, Adams, Massachusetts, USA. Stonemason; Builder. m. Susan Eileen Paules, 28 Aug 1974, 1 son. Education: Graduated, Brewster Academy, 1970. Appointment: Editor, Publisher, Longhouse Publishers and Booksellers, 1973-. Publications: Rope of Bells, 1974; Along the Way, 1979; Habitat, 1979; Thread, 1980; Self-employed, 1983; Back Road Caller, 1985; Gaze, 1985; Sky, 1986; Go West, 1987; Long Time Together, 1987; Cache, 1987; On Stone, 1988; Souvenir, 1989; Where Rivers Meet, 1990; By Heart, 1991; Our Guardian Angel, 1991; This Romance, 1992; Happy As You Are, 1993; Farm Hand, 1994; American Train Letters, 1995; Honeymoon, 1996. Contributions to: Country Journal; Harper's; Poetry

East; Coyotes Journal; Falk, West Germany; Edge, Japan; New Letters; Ploughshares; White Pine Journal; Aspect; Flute; Spoor; Heaven Bone; Tel-Let. Address: Jacksonville Stage, Brattleboro, VT 05301, USA.

ARRABAL Fernando, b. 11 Aug 1932, Melilla, Spain. Writer; Poet; Dramatist. m. Luce Moreau, 1958, 1 son, 1 daughter. Education: University of Madrid. Appointment: Co-Founder, Panique Movement. Publications: Novels: Baal Babylone, 1959; The Burial of Sardine, 1962; Fêtes et Rites de la Confusion, 1965; The Tower Struck by Lightning, 1983; The Compass Stone; The Red Madonna; La Fille de King Kong; L'Estravagante Croisade d'un castrat Amoureux; El Mono. Poetry: Le Pierre de La Folie, 1963; 100 Sonnets, 1966; Liberte Couleur De Femme; Arrabalesques, 1994; Humbles Paradis, 1986. Plays: Numerous published works. Honours: Ford Foundation Fellowship, 1959; Société des Auteurs Prize, 1966; Grand Prix du Théâtre, 1967; Grand Prix Humour Noir, 1968; Obie Award, Village Voice Newspaper, New York City, 1976; Premio Nadal, 1983; World's Theatre Prize, 1984; Prix du Theatre, Académie Francaise, 1993; Prix International Nabokov, 1994. Address: 22 Rue Jouffroy d'Abbans, Paris 75017, France.

ARROWSMITH Pat, b. 2 Mar 1930, England. Retired Assistant Editor, Amnesty International. Education: BA, History, Cambridge University, 1951; Social Science Certificate, Liverpool University, 1955; University of Ohio, USA, 1952-53. Appointments: Social Caseworker, late 1950's; Full-time peace movement worker, 1960's-70's; Staff Member, Amnesty International, 1972-94. Publications: Breakout, 1975; On The Brink, 1980; Thin Ice, 1982; Nine Lives, 1990. Contributions to: Many newspapers, magazines and journals including: Guardian; New Statesman; Tribune; Independent. Honours: 2nd Prize, Hornsey, London Competition, 1977; Highly Commended, Westminster, London Competition, 1978; Prize, Ver Poets Competition, 1993. Memberships: Ver Poets; London Poetry Society. Address: 132C Middle Lane, London N8 7JP, England.

ARROWSMITH William, b. 13 Apr 1924, Orange, New Jersey, USA. Translator; Educator; Critic. Div. 2 daughters. Education: AB, 1947, PhD, 1954, Princeton University; BA, 1951, MA, 1958, Oxford University. Appointments: Visiting Henry McCormick Professor of Dramatic Literature and Criticism, The Drama School, Yale University, 1976-77; Professor of Classics and Humanities, Johns Hopkins University, 1977-80; Visiting Presidential Professor, Georgetown University, 1981; Lecturer, The Folger Library, 1981; Visiting David B Kriser Professor of Humanities, New York University, 1982-84; Robert W Woodruff Professor of Classics and Comparative Literature, Emory University, 1982-86. Publications: General Editor, The Greek Tragedy in New Translations, 33 volumes, 1973-; Translation and introduction, The Alcestis of Euripides, 1974-89; The Poems as Palimpsest: A Dialogue on Eliot's Sweeney Erect, 1981; Eros in Terre Haute: T S Eliot's Lune de Miel, 1982; The Occasions by Eugenio Montale, translation with introduction and notes, 1987; Grave Prattle: Eliot's Le Directeur, Yale Review. Contributions to: Arion; Hudson Review; Chimera; The Nation; Harper's; New Yorker; Antaeus; Paris Review; American Poetry Review; Interim; Bostonia; Ploughshares. Honours: Landon Translation Prize, American Academy of Poets, 1986; Jerome J Shestack Poetry Prize for Translations, 1987; International Eugenio Montale Prize, Parma, Italy, 1990. Memberships: PEN; Poetry Society of America. Address: Department of Classical Studies, Boston University, 745 Commonwealth Avenue, Boston, MA 02215, USA.

ARROYO-GOMEZ Mario Vernon, b. 22 Apr 1948, Gibraltar. Teacher; Poet; Actor; Dancer. Education: Studied Drama, Dance, Speech and English, Leeds, 1967-1970; Studied Dance, Laban School of Dance, London, 1979-80. Appointments: Teacher, Head of Drama, Boy's Comprehensive School, Gibraltar, 4 years; Worked extensively with youth groups and adults and his productions as director and choreographer include: Job, A Masque for Dancing, Vaughan Williams; The Rite of Spring, Stravinsky; Jeux, L'Apres Midi d'un Faune, Debussy; Cantico Espiritual, Corelli, Verdi, Ives; Poetas Andaluces de Ahora; Jesus Christ Superstar, Lloyd Webber; Pioneered work in modern dance and in dance-drama in local community. Publication: Profiles...Perfiles, 1990. Honours: Number of awards from IBC and ABI including Fellow; Most Admired Man of the Decade; Nominated for: Man of the Year, World Intellectual, International Man of the Year, and Grand Ambassador of Achievement; Biographical Roll of Honour; Twentieth Century Award for Achievement; World Lifetime Achievement Award. Address: 16 George Jeger House, Glacis, Gibraltar.

ARTEAGA Alfred, b. 2 May 1950, Los Angeles, California, USA. University Professor. m. Paula Contreras, 27 Dec 1972, 3 daughters. Education: MFA, Creative Writing, Columbia University, 1974; PhD, Literature, University of California, Santa Cruz, 1987. Appointments: Assistant Professor of English, University of Houston, Texas, 1987-90, University of California, Berkeley, 1990-. Publication: Cantos, 1991. Contributions to: Blue Mesa Review; Berkeley Poetry Review; Baldus; Quarry West; Mango. Membership: PEN, USA; Centro de Escritores Chicanos. Address: Department of English, University of California, 322 Wheeler, Berkeley, CA 94720, USA.

ARTHUR Eagin. See: **REIFF Andrew Edwin.**

ASANTE Molefi Kete, b. 14 Aug 1942. Professor; Author. Education: Oklahoma Christian University, 1964; MA, Pepperdine University, 1965; PhD, University of California, Los Angeles, 1968. Appointments: Professor; University of California, Los Angeles, 1969-73, State University of New York, Buffalo, 1973-84, Temple University, 1984-. Publications: Break of Dawn, 1964; Epic in Search of African Kings, 1979. Contributions to: New Directions; Transitions. Honour: Christian Guild Writers Award, 1966. Memberships: Xanadu Poetry Club; Buffalo Writers Guild; Christian Guild Writers. Address: 707 Medary Avenue, Philadelphia, PA 19126, USA.

ASH John, b. 29 June 1948, Manchester, England. Writer; Poet; Teacher. Education: BA in English, University of Birmingham, 1969. Publications: The Golden Hordes: International Tourism and the Pleasure Periphery, with Louis Turner, 1975; Casino: A Poem in Three Parts, 1978; The Bed and Other Poems, 1981; The Goodbyes, 1982; The Branching Stairs, 1984; Disbelief, 1987; The Burnt Pages, 1991. Contributions to: Periodicals. Honours: Ingram Merrill Foundation Grant, 1985; Whiting Foundation Award, 1986. Address: c/o Carcanet Press Ltd, 208-212 Corn Exchange Buildings, Manchester M4 3BQ, England.

ASHANTI Baron James, b. 5 Sept 1950, New York, New York, USA. Poet; Writer; Editor; Critic; Lecturer. m. Brenda Cummings, 11 Sept 1979, 1 son, 1 daughter. Appointments: Literary Editor, Impressions Magazine, 1972-75; City and Third World Editor, Liberation News Service, 1974-79; Contributing Editor, The Paper, 1978; Lecturer; Director, Arts-in-Education Program, Frederick Douglass Creative Arts Center, New York City, 1988-. Publications: Nubiana, 1977; Nova, 1990. Contributions to: Many periodicals. Honours: Killen Prize for Poetry, St Peter's College, 1982; PEN Fellowships, 1985, 1987; Pulitzer Prize in Poetry Nomination, 1991. Address: 274 West 140th Street, Apt No 45, New York, NY 10030, USA.

ASHBERY John Lawrence, b. 28 July 1927, Rochester, New York, USA. Author; Critic. Education: BA, English Literature, Harvard College, Cambridge, 1949; MA, English Literature, Columbia University at New York, 1951; Graduate study in French Literature, New York University, 1957-58. Appointments: Art Critic, European Edition of New York Herald Tribune, Paris, 1960-65; Editor, Locus Solus, Lansen-Vercors, France, 1960-62, Art and Literature, Paris, 1963-66; Executive Editor, Art News, New York, 1965-72; Professor, English, Co-Director of MFA Programme in Creative Writing, CUNY, Brooklyn College, 1974-90; Distinguished Professor, CUNY, Brooklyn College, 1980-90; Art Critic, Newsweek, New York, 1980-85; Charles P Stevenson Jr Professor of Languages and Literature, Bard College, New York, 1990-. Publications: Selected Poems, 1967; Three Poems, 1972, 1977, 1989; Houseboat Days, 1976, 1977; Selected Poems, 1985, 1986, 1987; April Galleons, 1987, 1988, 1989, 1990; And The Stars Were Shining, 1993; Can You Hear, Bird, 1995; Also non-fiction, novels, plays and other publications. Honours: Fulbright Scholarship, 1955-56, Montpelier France and Rennes, 1956-57; Ingram Merrill Foundation Grant, 1962, 1972; Guggenheim Fellowship, 1967, 1973; Pulitzer Prize, 1976, Levinson Prize, 1977, Bollingen Prize in Poetry, Yale University Library, 1985, Ruth Lilley Poetry Prize, Poetry Magazine, The Modern Poetry Association and the American Council for The Arts, 1992, Antonio Feltinelli International Prize for Poetry, Accademia Nazionale dei Lincei, Rome, 1992, Chevalier de l'Ordre des Arts et des Lettres, Paris, 1993. Robert Frost Medal, Poetry Society of America, 1995. Address: c/o George Borchardt Inc, 136 East 57th Street, New York, NY 10022, USA.

ASHBY Jack (Sydney Edward), b. 11 Feb 1919, Mitcham, Surrey, England. Retired Managing Director. m. Ivy Wheatman, 12 Aug 1944, 2 sons. Education: Matriculation (university qualification), 1935.

Appointments: Production Manager, Philips Electrical, 1950-57; Director, 1957-71, Managing Director, 1971-89, Garage Company. Publications: Unscrambled Words No 1, 1992; No 2, 1992, No 3, 1992; Anthology of Unscrambled Words, 1992. Membership: Poetry Society. Address: c/o SEA Publishing Company, 39 Longhill Road, Ovingdean, Brighton, East Sussex BN2 7BF, England.

ASHLANDONIAN. See: **CHAMBERLAIN Kent Clair.**

ASHLEY J(ohn) R(andle), b. 18 Jan 1926, Northwich, Cheshire, England. Retired Personnel Manager. m. Freda Gittens, 13 Feb 1950, dec, 1 son. Appointments: Chemical Works Personnel Manager, Management Development, Senior Staff Job Evaluation Manager, ICI Mond Division until retirement. Contributions to: Northwich Guardian, mid 1940's; Willow Poetry, 1980's. Membership: Poetry Society. Address: Bodavon, Crows Nest Lane, Great Budworth, Northwich, Cheshire CW9 6HZ, England.

ASHOKAMITRAN Jagadisa Thyagarajan (Ashokamitran), b. 22 Sept 1931, Secunderabad, India. Editor; Writer. m. Rajeswari, 5 Sept 1963, 3 sons. Education: BSc, Mathematics, Physics and Chemistry. Appointments: Tutor, Popular Tutorials, Secunderabad, 1950-52; Public Relations Officer, Gemini Studios, Madras, 1952-66; Executive Editor, Kanaiyazhi (monthly), 1966-88; Editor, Munril literary journal, 1989-. Publications: Karainda Nizhalgal, 1969; Vaazhvilay Oru Murai, 1971; Innum Sila Naatkal, 1972; Thanneer, 1973; Kaalamum 5 Kuzhan Daigalum, 1974; 18th Parallel, 1977; Viduthalai, 1979; Unmai Vetkai, 1979; Akaya Thamarai, 1980; En Payanam, 1981; Vimochanam, 1982; Thanthaikkaka, 1983; Inru, 1984; Muraippen, 1984; Moonru Paarvaigal, 1984; Otran!, 1985; Sila Asiriyargal, Noolgal, 1987; Padaippu Kalai, 1987; Uttara Ramayanam, 1988; Mamasarovar, 1989; Oru Gramattu Adyayam, 1990; Appavin Snehidar, 1991; Water and 18th Parallel (in English), 1993. Contributions to: Illustrated Weekly of India; Indian Literature; Poet. Honours: Story of the Month Award, 5 times; Book of the Year Award, 1977, 1985; Story of the Year Award, 1985; Fiction of the Year Award, 1985, 1987, 1990; Santhome Award for Values, 1985; Honorary DLitt, World Academy of Art and Culture, 1990. Memberships: Founder Member, Ilakkia Sangram (literary forum); Founder Member, Creative Forum (writers and painters); Authors Guild of India, New Delhi, 1974-; PEN, India. Address: 23 Damodara Reddy Street, T Nagar, Madras 600017, India.

ASHRAF Allama Syed Waheed, b. 4 Feb 1933, Kichhauchha, India. Educator; Researcher. m. Ale Fatima Farzana, 28 Dec 1969, 3 sons, 1 daughter. Education: BA, 1960, MA, Persian, 1962, PhD, Persian, 1965, AMU Aligarh. Appointments: Lecturer in Persian, MS University Baroda, Gujrat, India, 1971-77; Reader in Persian, 1977-85, Professor of Persian, 1986-, Head of Department of Arabic, Persian and Urdu, 1986-, University of Madras, Tamil Nadu, India. Publications: Rubai, 1987; Rubai, part II, 1990. Contributions to: Danesh (quarterly journal); Gulbun (Urdu bimonthly); Sabarnama (Urdu quarterly); Nagd-o-Nazar (Urdu monthly); East-West Voices (international anthology). Memberships: Editorial Board, Annual of Oriental Research Institute, University of Madras; President, Anjuman-e-Danish Mandam-e-Urdu, University of Madras; Advisory Committee of State Encyclopaedia, Trivandrum, Kerala. Address: University of Madras, Tamil Nadu, South India.

ASHTON Keith William, b. 2 May 1951, Lincoln, England. Writer. Education: BA, Honours, Fine Art, Reading University, 1975. Appointments: Editor, Wordshare Magazine, 1989-91; Reviewer, Disability Arts Magazine, 1991-. Publication: Fair Moving, 1992. Contributions to: Prospice; Staple; Bete Noire; Orbis; The Green Book; Lincolnshire Life; The North; New Prospects; Sink Island Review; Poetry Review; Disability Arts Magazine. Membership: Poetry Society. Address: 3 Grainsby Close, Lincoln, England.

ASHWORTH Anne, b. 24 July 1931, Blackpool, England. Librarian. m. 3 Apr 1957, 1 son. Education: BA, Open University; ALA, Associate of the Library Association. Appointment: Librarian, Blackpool Sixth Form College, 1971-92. Publication: Mirrorwork, 1989. Contributions to: Poetry Review; Orbis; Rialto; Staple; Writing Women; Envoi; Iota; Pennine Platform; Other Poetry; Reform; and others. Honour: 1st Prize, Rhyme Revival, 1987. Membership: Poetry Society. Address: 2 Belle Vue Place, Blackpool, Lancashire FY3 9EG, England.

ASKOLD Markian Melnyczck, (Askold Melnyczck), b. 12 Dec 1954, Irvington, New Jersey, USA. Writer; Educator; Editor. Education: Antioch College, 1972-73; BA, Rutgers University, Newark, 1976; MA,

Boston University, 1978. Appointments: Editor, Agni Review, 1972-; Preceptor, Boston University, 1982-; Visiting Lecturer, Harvard University, 1990. Publications: Poems, 1975-1980; Under 35: The New Generation of American Poets, anthology, 1989. Contributions: Nation; Grand Street; Poetry; Antioch Review; Denver Quarterly; Pequod; Gettysburg Review; Partisan Review; Chelsea. Membership: Board of Directors, New England Poetry Club. Honours: Finalist Award, Massachusetts Arts Council, 1989, 1990. Address: c/o Agni, 236 Bay State Road, Boston University, Boston, MA 02138, USA.

ASNER Marie A, b. 28 Feb 1947, Minnesota, USA. Musician; Music Teacher; Journalist. m. 18 Aug 1968. Education: BS, Music, 1965; MS, Music, 1968; PhD, Music Education, 1982. Appointments: Music Teacher, Minnesota School Systems; Private Music Teacher and Journalist, Nebraska; Private Music Teacher, Journalist and Poet, Kansas, 1982-. Publications: Secret Place, 1991; Man of Miracles, 1992; An Inquiring Mind, 1993; Man of Miracles, Part II, 1994. Contributions to: Omaha World Herald; Shawnee Journal; Potpourri Literary Journal; Poets; Poets of Now; Encore; Metis; Collage; Chronicle; CSS Publications; Great Bend Poetry Anthology; Poets at Work; Sunflower Petals; Byline; Poets of the Vineyard; Sisyphus; Broken Streets; Prairie Woman; Texture; Writer's Companion; Passages North. Honours: Winner, CSS Publications National Poetry Contest, 1988; Winner, Jubilee Press National Chapbook Contest, 1989; 2nd Place Winner, Great Bend Poetry Contest, 1991; Honourable Mention, Poet Magazine Poetry Contest, 1992; 2nd Place Winner, Minnesota Poet Laureate Contest, 1994; Nominated for Kansas Governor's Art Award, 1995. Memberships: Poets and Writers; Working Press of America; Kansas State Poetry Society; Music Teachers National Association; American Federation of Musicians; American Guild of Organists. Address: 9000 West 82nd Place, Overland Park, KS 66204, USA.

ASTOR Susan Irene, b. 2 Apr 1946, New York, New York, USA. Poetry Teacher; Writer. Div. 2 daughters. Education: Brandeis University; BA, Adelphi University; Graduate work at C W Post (Long Island University) and Adelphi University. Appointments: Poet in various Long Island public schools, including Manhasset, Garden City and North Shore, 1980-. Publications: Silent Voices: Recent American Poems on Nature, 1978; Anthology of Magazine Poetry, 1979, 1980, 1981, 1983; Dame, 1980; Portfolio One, 1984; Three Grey Geese, 1985. Contributions to: Paris Review; Partisan Review; Confrontation; Poet Lore; Kansas Quarterly; California Quarterly. Honours: 1st Place, CW Post (Long Island University) Poetry Award, 1980, 1987; 1st Place, Schyllil County Council for the Arts Award, 1983; 1st Place, California Quarterly Poetry Contest, 1984; Award of Excellence, Composers and Songwriters International (with N K Brown), 1985. Membership: Poets and Writers. Address: 113 Princeton Street, Roslyn Heights, NY 11577, USA.

ATKINS John Alfred, b. 26 May 1916, Carshalton, Surrey, England. Teacher. m. Dorothy Joan Grey, 24 May 1940, 2 daughters. Education: BA, Honours, History, University of Bristol, 1938. Appointments: Head of English Department, Higher Teacher Training Institute, Omdurman, Sudan, 1966-68; Senior Lecturer, English Department, Benghazi University, Libya, 1968-70; Docent in English Literature, Lodz, Poland, 1970-76. Publications: Experience of England, 1941; Today's New Poets (group of poems), 1944; Co-Author, The Pleasure Ground (group of poems), 1947; Co-Author, Triad (group of poems), 1947. Contributions to: New Poetry, PEN; New Poetry, Arts Council; Penguin New Writing; Windmill; Poems of this War; Life and Letters Today; New Saxon Pamphlets; Mercury; Oasis; Australian International Quarterly; Outposts; Writing Today; Gangrel; Variegation; Voices; Million; HPJ (Hartforde Poets Journal); Numerous small magazines.' Membership: Chairman, Balkerne Writers, Colchester, 1986-89; Awarded Bursary, Tyrone Guthrie Centre (Eastern Arts Association), Ireland, 1991. Address: Braeside Cottage, Mill Lane, Birch, Colchester CO2 0NH, England.

ATKINS Russell, b. 25 Feb 1926, Cleveland, Ohio, USA. Composer; Poet. Education: Cleveland School (now Institute) of Art, 1943; Cleveland Institute of Music, 1945-46; Private music study in composition with J Harold Bron, 1950-54. Appointments: Editor, Free Lance Magazine, 1950-80; Publicity Office Manager, Sutphen Music School, 1957-60; Creative Writing Instructor, Karamu Theatre, 1972-86; Writer-in-Residence, Cuyahoga Community College, 1973; Instructor, Ohio Programme in Humanities, 1978. Publications: Phenomena, 1961; Objects, 1963; Heretofore, 1968; Podium Presentations, 1969; Here in The, 1976; Whichever, 1978; Beyond the

Reef, 1991. Contributions to: View; Beloit Poetry Journal; New York Times; Western Review; Botteghe Oscure; Writers Forum; Poetry Now; Coventry Reader; Cornfield Review; Stagebill. Honours: Monograph on music introduced at Darmstadt Festival, Germany, 1956; Karamu Theatre Tribute Award, 1971; Honorary Doctorate, Cleveland State University, 1976; Individual Artists Fellowship, Ohio Arts Council, 1978; Poem set to music, By Yearning and By Beautiful, and performed at Lincoln Centre for the Performing Arts, New York, 1986. Memberships: Writer-in-the-Schools Programme of Ohio Arts Council and National Endowment for the Arts, 1973-75; Invited, Breadloaf Writers Conference, 1956; Literary Advisory Panel, Ohio Arts Council, 1973-76; Cleveland State University Poetry Forum, 1967-; Consultant, Karamu Writers Conference, 1971 and to other conferences and workshops including East Cleveland Public Library, 1979; Trustee, Poets League of Greater Cleveland, University Circle Inc's Artist-in-Education Programme, 1988; Consultant, WVIZ Television, 1969-72. Address: 6005 Grand Avenue, Cleveland, OH 44104, USA.

ATKINS Timothy Clifford, b. 13 Aug 1962, London, England. Teacher. Education: BA, Honours, Religious Studies, King's College, London, 1985; MPhil, Poetics, University of Stirling, 1987; RSA Certificate, TEFL London, 1988. Appointments: TEFL Teacher, Barcelona, 1989-92, Rio de Janeiro, 1992-93; Creative Writing Teacher, San Francisco, 1993-94, University of London, 1994-. Publications: Some Poems, Scotland, 1987; Folklore (1-25), Paris, 1995. Contributions to: Harpers & Queen; City Limits, London; Psalm 151, Boulder, USA; Mirage, San Francisco; UCSF, San Francisco; EM, Barcelona. Address: 668B Fulham Road, London SW6 5RX, England.

ATKINSON Donald, b. 15 June 1931, Sheffield, Yorkshire, England. m. (1) 1953, (2) 1973, 1 son, 4 daughters. Education: BA, Honours, 1954, MA 1957, Cambridge; Chichester Theological College, 1954-56. Appointments: Teacher of English and for 11 years, Headmaster of secondary schools. Publications: St Boniface - A Life in Verse, 1955; A Sleep of Drowned Fathers, 1989; Graffiti for Hard Hearts, 1992; Othello in the Pyramid of Dreams, 1996. Contributions to: Guardian; Times Literary Supplement; Poetry Review; Stand; Ambit; Rialto; Lines Review; Writing Ulster; Anthologies: Forward; Blue-Nose; Klaonica; New Writing 5, British Council. Honours: Peterloo Poets Competition, 1988; Times Literary Supplement, Cheltenham Festival Competition, 1988; Leek Arts Festival Competition, 1989; Aldeburgh Poetry Festival Prize, 1990; Editor, Spokes Magazine, 1990-; 1st Prize, Sheffield Thursday Competition, 1994; Writer's Award, Arts Council of England, 1995. Address: Casa degli Scrittori, 40 Debden Road, Saffron Walden, Essex CB11 4AB, England.

ATKINSON Susan Jane, b. 9 Oct 1964, Blackburn, Lancashire, England. Artist; Film Technician. m. Rick Fester, 5 Oct 1991, 2 daughters. Education: BA, English Literature & Film Studies, Carleton University, Ottawa, Canada, 1986. Appointment: Freelance Film Technician, 1987-. Contributions to: Amber; Marsh & Maple; Carleton Arts Review; Greens Magazine; Reach Magazine; White Wall Review; Teak International; Focus. Address: 305 Indian Grove, Toronto, Ontario, M6P 2H6, Canada.

ATRE Madhav V, (M Angelo), b. 4 Aug 1938, Nasirabad, Pakistan. Teacher. m. Rekha Atre, 25 Feb 1968, 1 son, 1 daughter. Education: Visharad, Hindi equivalent to BA, 1958; BA, 1963; BA, Education, 1973; MA, English, 1979. Appointments: Clerk, 1956-64; Private Tutor, 1964-66; Teacher, English Medium Secondary School, 1967-80; Principal, English Medium Secondary School, 1981-, retiring Aug 1996. Publications: Not yet published: Erotic Eloquence, 1993; Anguished Embers, 1994; Love Bird and Other Selected Poems, 1995. Contributions to: Snows to the Seas (anthology from Amravati); World Poetry, 1995, 1996; Poetcrit; The Quest (bi-annuals from Ranchi & Maranda); Skylark India; Kavita India; Parichay Mein Parichay (quarterly from Bombay); Young Poets; Poet; Poets; Mirror; Magazines from Kerala, Madras, Bangalore, Bombay. Honours: Many letters of appreciation from readers and editors; Certificate of Merit, The Quest All-India Poetry Contest, 1993. Memberships: World Poetry Society, Madras; The Poetry Society, New Delhi. Address: 11-5 The Sewa Samiti Nagar, Sion Koliwada, Bombay 400 037, India.

ATWOOD Margaret (Eleanor), b. 18 Nov 1939, Ottawa, Canada. Poet; Author; Critic. Education: BA, Victoria College, University of Toronto, 1961; AM, Radcliffe College, Cambridge, Massachusetts, 1962; Attended Harvard University, 1962-63, 1965-67.

Appointments: Teacher, University of British Columbia, 1964-65; Sir George Williams University, Montreal, 1967-68; University of Alberta, 1969-70; York University, 1971-72; Writer-in-Residence, University of Toronto, 1972-73; University of Alabama, Tuscaloosa, 1985; Macquarie University, Australia, 1987; Holder, Berg Chair, New York University, 1986. Publications: Poetry: Double Persephone, 1961; The Circle Game, 1964; Kaleidoscopes Baroque, 1965; Talismans for Children, 1965; Speeches for Doctor Frankenstein, 1966; The Animals in That Country, 1968; The Journals of Susanna Moodie, 1970; Procedures for Underground, 1970; Oratorio for Sasquatch, Man and Two Androids, 1970; Power Politics, 1971; You Are Happy, 1974; Selected Poems, 1976; Marsh Hawk, 1977; Two-Headed Poems, 1978; True Stories, 1981; Notes Towards A Poem That Can Never Be Written, 1981; Snake Poems, 1983; Interlunar, 1984; Selected Poems II: Poems Selected and New, 1976-1986, 1986; Selected Poems 1966-1984, 1990; Margaret Atwood Poems 1965-75, 1992; Morning in The Burned House, 1995; Fiction: The Edible Woman, 1969; Surfacing, 1972; Lady Oracle, 1976; Dancing Girls, 1977; Life Before Man, 1979; Bodily Harm, 1981; Encounters With The Element Man, 1982; Murder in The Dark, 1983; Bluebeard's Egg, 1983; Unearthing Suite, 1983; The Handmaid's Tale, 1985; Cat's Eye, 1988; Wilderness Tips, 1991; Good Bones, 1992; The Robber Bride, 1993; Alias Grace, 1996. Non-Fiction: Survival: A Thematic Guide to Canadian Literature, 1972; Days of The Rebels 1815-1840, 1977; Second Words: Selected Critical Prose, 1982; Editor, The Oxford Book of Canadian Verse in English, 1982; Co-editor with Shannon Ravenel, The Best American Short Stories, 1989; Strange Things: Fictions of The Malevolent North in Canadian Literature, 1995. Contributions to: Books in Canada; Canadian Literature; Globe and Mail; Harvard Educational Review; The Nation; New York Times Book Review; Washington Post. Honours: Guggenheim Fellowship, 1981; Companion of the Order of Canada, 1981; Fellow, Royal Society of Canada; Foreign Honorary Member, American Academy of Arts and Sciences, 1988; Order of Ontario, 1990; Centennial Medal, Harvard University, 1990; Commemorative Medal, 125th Anniversary of Canadian Confederation, 1992; Honorary degrees. Memberships: Writers Union of Canada, President, 1981-82; PEN International, President, 1985-86. Address: c/o Oxford University Press, 70 Wynford Drive, Don Mills, Ontario M3C 1J9, Canada.

AUBERT Alvin (Bernard), b. 12 Mar 1930, Lutcher, Louisiana, USA. Professor of English Emeritus; Poet. m. (1) Olga Alexis, 1948 div, 1 daughter, (2) Bernadine Tenant, 1960, 2 daughters. Education: BA, Southern University, Baton Rouge, Louisiana, 1959; AM, University of Michigan, 1960; University of Illinois, Urbana-Champaign, 1963-64, 1966-67. Appointments: Instructor, 1960-62, Assistant Professor, 1962-65, Associate Professor of English, 1965-70, Southern University; Visiting Professor of English, University of Oregon, Eugene, 1970; Associate Professor, 1970-74, Professor of English, 1974-79, State University of New York, Fredonia; Founder-Editor, Obsidian Magazine, 1975-85; Professor of English, 1980-92, Professor Emeritus, 1992-, Wayne State University, Detroit. Publications: Against the Blues, 1972; Feeling Through, 1975; South Louisiana: New and Selected Poems, 1985; If Winter Come: Collected Poems, 1994; Harlem Wrestler, 1995. Honours: Bread Loaf Writers Conference Scholarship, 1968; National Endowment for the Arts Grants, 1973, 1981; Coordinating Council of Literary Magazines Grant, 1979; Annual Callaloo Award, 1989. Address: 18234 Parkside Avenue, Detroit, MI 48202, USA.

AUER Benedict, Father, b. 4 Nov 1939, Chicago, Illinois, USA. Father Benedict of St Martin's College and Abbey. Education: BSc, Humanities, Loyola University, Chicago, 1962; MA, History, Creighton University, 1964; MDiv, St Meinrad School of Theology, 1980; Doctor of Ministry in Christian Spirituality, San Francisco Theological Seminary, 1993. Appointments: Novitiate, 1976, Simple Profession, 1977, Lector, 1978, Acolyte, 1979, Solemn Vows, 1980, Deacon, 1980, Marmion Abbey, Aurora, Illinois; Priesthood, Annunciation Church, Aurora, Illnois, 1980; Various Pastoral assignments, Illinois, 1980-88; Director of Campus Ministry, St Martin's College, Washington, 1988-94; Assistant Professor of Education, Adjunct in Religious Studies, Speech and Geography, St Martin's College, Lacey, Washington, 1988-; Certification as Campus Minister, National Campus Ministry Association, 1993-. Publications: Touching Fingers with God, 1986; Priestless People, 1990; Godspeak: Thirteen Characters in Search of an Author, 1993. Contributions to: Pastoral Life; New Catholic Review; Priest; Human Development; New Renaissance; American Educator; Momentum; Per Se, Japan; Poetry published in 200 magazines including Lutheran Journal; Inquirer;

Croton Review; Blue Buildings; Wind; Daybreak, Canada; Gypsy, Germany; Kansas Quarterly; Bitterroot; Gryphon; Forum; Nexus; Windless Orchard; Short stories in various publications. Honours: Pi Gamma Mu, 1962; Phi Alpha Theta, 1964; Scholarship, Creighton University, 1963-64; 4 year scholarship, St Meinrad Seminary, 1977-80; Poem of the Year, Jubilee Press, Florida, 1987; Hon DH, London Institute for Applied Research, England, 1991; Citation and Award, Medallion of St Andrew, 1993. Address: Saint Martin's College/Abbey, Lacey, WA 98503, USA.

AUGUSTINE Jane, b. 6 Apr 1931, Berkeley, California, USA. Poet; Professor of Literature. m. (1) 1 daughter, (2) Michael D Heller, 5 Mar 1979, 3 sons. Education: AB, cum laude, Bryn Mawr College, 1952; MA, Washington University, St Louis, Missouri, 1965; PhD, City University of New York, 1988. Appointment: Associate Professor of English and Humanities, Pratt Institute, Brooklyn, New York. Publications: Lit By the Earth's Dark Blood, 1977; Journeys, 1985. Contributions to: MS; Aphra; Chrysalis; Pequod; Montemora, US; Staple Diet; Figs, UK. Honours: Fellowships in Poetry, New York State Council of the Arts, 1976, 1979; HD Fellowship in American Literature, Beinecke Library, Yale University, 1994-95. Memberships: Poetry Society of America; Modern Language Association; International Association for Philosophy and Literature. Address: PO Box 1289, Stuyvesant Station, New York, NY 10009, USA.

AUGUSTUS Reuben. See: HALEY Patricia.

AUM Leya, b. 27 Dec 1943, Albuquerque, New Mexico, USA. Teacher; Counselor. 1 daughter. Education: AB, English Literature, University of California, Berkeley, 1968; MA, Psychology, Sonoma State University, 1973; Feldenkrais Professional Training in Neuromuscular Relearning, 1977. Career: Psychotherapist and Feldenkrais Teacher in Private Practice; Instructor, Santa Rosa Junior College, 1977-. Contributions to: Poet's Pen, 1994; Sparrowgrass, Whispers, Peer Poetry Competition, 1996. Address: PO Box 5081, Santa Rosa, CA 95402, USA.

AURA Alejandro, b. Mar 1944, Mexico City, Mexico. Writer; Actor. m. Carmen Boullosa, 1981, 2 sons, 2 daughters. Publications: Poesia joven de Mexico, 1967; Alianza para vivir, 1969; Varios desnudes y dos docenas de naturalezas muertas, 1971; Volver a casa, 1974; Tambor interno, 1974; Hemisferio sur, 1982; La patria vieja, 1986; Cinco veces, 1988; Poeta en la manana, 1991. Contributions to: Revista Mester; Revista Volatin; Revista de la Universidad Nacional Autonoma de Mexico; Sabado; El Nacional; El Semanario de Novedades; La Journado Semanal; Los Universitarios; Revista Vuelta; and others. Honours: Grants form the Centro Mexicano de Escritores, 1964; Premio Nacional de Poesia, 1973. Address: Tiepolo 20, Mixcoac, DF 03710, Mexico.

AUSALA Margarita Bebrupe Palite, b. 13 July 1919, Smiltene, Latvia. Poet; Writer; International Journalist; Broadcaster. m. 8 Mar 1948, 1 son, 2 daughters. Education: Philology, History of Art, University of Riga, Latvia. Appointments: Assistant Editor, monthly magazine of Ministry of Education and Latvian newsapaper in London; Deputy Head of Information Department, Latvian Council in Great Britain; Press Office, Latvian Welfare Fund; Executive Member, Latvian Song Festivals in England and Europe; Press Secretary, Ramare Latvian Academicians; Honorary Editor, Latvia, Canada. Publications: Essays, 2 volumes, 1955; Patiesibasvins, poems, 1965; Agni un asmeni, poems, 1987. Contributions to: Laiks; Latrija; Tilts; Zintis; World Poetry, Korea, 1981-90; World Poet Anthology, 1980; Laurel Leaves, USA, 1968-90; Orbis, 1968-89; English PEN Magazine. Honours: Gold Badge of Distinction, Futtsian Academy, Taiwan, 1973; Poet Laureate, UPLI, Taiwan, 1973; Medal of Distinction, Florida, Chinese Poets Society, 1985; Poet Laureate of Fredom, UPLI, New York, 1987; Various honorary degrees; Gold Badge of Distinction, Daugavas Vanagi, 1980; Honorary Member, Cinque Port Poets, New Romney, England; 5 Medals for poems and lectures, United Poets Laureate International; Poet Laureate of Freedom, Academy of Leadership, New York. Memberships: Fellow, International PEN, English Centre; International Delegate, International PEN, Latvian Centre; Vice President, United Poets Laureate International; International Poetry Society; International Federation of Free Journalists, Great Britain; Newspaper Guild, USA; Grade Programmer, Radio Free Europe. Address: 243 Rockingham Road, Corby, Northamptonshire, England.

AUSSANT Paule Jeannine Louise, b. 27 Oct 1930, Saint-Vit, France. Retired Teacher. m. Aussant Bernard, 17 May 1956, 2 sons. Education: Baccalaureat, 1949; Teacher Training College, Paris; Studies in University of Sorbonne, Paris, 1952; Training courses in Pedagogy, Paris, 1970; School of Arts, ABC, Paris, 1960. Appointments: Courville Sur Eure, La Roche sur Yon, Papara-Tahiti, Polynésie Française, Collège Enseignement Secondaire, France. Publications: Hirako, 1972; Krizehmurmur, 1980; Poèmes d'amour, 1983; Rêve de l'aurore, 1986; Testament de l'étrange Planète, 1991; Marcher sur les étoiles, 1993; Visions du routard, 1993; Adieu au Pacifique, 1996. Contributions to: Froissart, Visages du XXe siècle; Flammes Vives; Poetic 7; Trilles; Regart; Cahiers de la Baule; Plumes au Vent; Sol'air; Le Moulin de la Poesie. Honours: Many prizes for poems in poetic recitals, shows in different towns including: La Baule, 1991, La Roche Syon 1967-83, Carnac, 1992. Membership: Société des Poètes Français, 1990-93. Address: 13 rue du Pont, 25920 Mouthier, Hauterpierre, France.

AUSTER Paul, b. 3 Feb 1947, Newark, New Jersey, USA. Writer; Poet. m. (1) Lydia Davis, 6 Oct 1974, div 1979, 1 son, (2) Siri Hustvedt, 16 June 1981, 1 daughter. Education: BA,1969, MA,1970, Columbia University. Appointment: Lecturer, Princeton University, 1986-90. Publications: Novels: City of Glass, 1985; Ghosts, 1986; The Locked Room, 1986; In The Country of Last Things, 1987; Moon Palace, 1989; The Music of Chance, 1990; Leviathan, 1992; Mr Vertigo, 1994. Poetry: Unearth, 1974; Wall Writing, 1976; Fragments from Cold, 1977; Facing the Music, 1980; Disappearances: Selected Poems, 1988. Non-Fiction: White Spaces, 1980; The Invention of Solitude, 1982; The Art of Hunger, 1982, augmented edition, 1992. Editor: The Random House of Twentieth Century French Poetry, 1982. Films: Smoke, 1995; Blue in the Face, 1995. Contributions to: Numerous periodicals. Honours: National Endowment for the Arts Fellowships, 1979, 1985; Chevalier, l'Order des Art et des Lettres, France; Priz Medicis Etranger, 1993. Membership: PEN. Address: c/o Carol Mann Agency, 55 Fifth Avenue, New York, NY 10003, USA.

AUSTIN Josephine, b. Richmond, Yorkshire, England. Education: Reading and Hastings. Publications: In Focus; Further into Focus; Spaces Between; Pisces Collection of Poems; Knee Deep in Short Buttercups; The Hurting Kind; Black Currant Stain; I Hear You Shouting Sister; There is Always an Old Tin Bath in the Meadow. Contributions to: Spring Anthology; Poetry Workshop; South Eastern Arts; Bog; Blick; BBC Second Selection; Thursday Magazine; Skylark; Impack; Poetry Review; Sussex Life; Folio; Outposts; Tops; Womans Hour. Honours: Dorothy Tutin Award for Services to Poetry; Hastings Mayoral Award for Services to Poetry, 1995; Adjudicator, Poetry Competition, 1981-; Festival Director, Hastings National Poetry Festival, 1968-. Membership: Sussex Society of Authors. Address: 4 Burdett Place, George Street, Hastings, East Sussex TN34 3ED, England.

AUTUMN. See: **KNELL William H.**

AVERY Raymond Kenneth, b. 10 Feb 1948, Dumfries, Scotland. m. Gloria, 27 Sept 1969, 2 daughters. Publications: Self Flagellation, 1993. Contributions to: Purple Patch; Disability Arts Magazine; Pot Pourri; Long Islander; Iota; Poetry Nottingham; Kray Desire; Poetry Manchester; Doors; Helicon; Exile; People to People; Dial 174; Dandelion; Banshee. Address: 19 Bell Close, Chelmsley Wood, Birmingham B36 0PZ, England.

AVGERINOS Cecily T Grazio, b. 16 Apr 1945, New York, New York, USA. Poet; Novelist. m. Robert T Avgerinos, 24 May 1969, 2 sons, 1 daughter. Education: BA, New York University. Appointments: Mayor's Commission; Church Ministries. Publications: My Tatterdamalion; Sunrises; Eternity; Summer Fantasy; My Prayer; Lunch in the Park; Circle of Gold; Lord, I Wonder; The Fig Tree; Fishing; Septecential; Loss; Bridge Across Tomorrow; To My Children; The Stringless Guitar; Pink Socks; My Dogwoods Loves Analogy; Merry Go Round; Strawsticks. Contributions to: Numerous anthologies. Honours: 4 Golden Poet Awards. Address: 173 Momar Drive, Ramsey, NJ 07446, USA.

AVISON Margaret (Kirkland), b. 23 Apr 1918, Galt, Ontario, Canada. Poet; Translator. Education: BA, English, University of Toronto, 1940. Appointments: Writer-in-Residence, University of Western Ontario, 1972-73; Staff, Mustard Seed Mission, Toronto, 1978-. Publications: History of Toronto, 1951; Winter Sun, 1960; The Research Compendium, 1964; The Dumbfoundling, 1966; Sunblue,

1978. Co-Translator: The Plough and The Pen: Writings from Hungary 1930-1956, 1963; Acta Sanctorum and Other Tales, 1970. Honours: Guggenheim Fellowship, 1956; Governor-General's Award, 1961. Address: c/o Mustard Seed Mission, Toronto, Ontario, Canada.

AWOONOR Kofi, b. 13 Mar 1935, Wheta, Ghana. 5 children. Education: BA, University of Ghana, 1960; MA, University of London, 1968; PhD in Comparative Literature, State University of New York at Stony Brook, 1973. Career: Reseach Fellow, Institute of American Studies, 1960-64; Director, Ghana Ministry of Information Film Corporation, 1964-67; Poet-in-Residence, 1968, Assistant Professor of English, 1968-72, Associate Professor, 1973-74, Chair of Department of Comparative Literature, 1974-75, State University of New York; Senior Lecturer, Professor of Literature and Dean of Arts Faculty, University of Cape Coast, 1977-82; Ghana Ambassador to: Brazil, 1984-88, Cuba, 1988-90, United Nations, 1990-. Publications: Rediscovery and Other Poems, 1964; Night of My Blood, 1971; Ride Me, Memory, 1973; The House by the Sea, 1978; Until the Morning After: Collected Poems 1963-1985, 1987; Latin American and Caribbean Notebook, 1992; Former Editor, Okyeame, Accra, Ghana; Co-Editor, Black Orpheus, Ibadan, Ghana; Associate Editor, World View, and Okike. Honours: Commonwealth Poetry Prize, 1989. Address: Ghana Mission to the United Nations, 19 East 47th Street, New York, NY 10017, USA.

AYLEN Leo William, b. Vryheid, Zululand, South Africa. Poet. m. Annette Battams. Education: Classical Scholar, New College, Oxford, England; MA, 1st Class in Honour Moderations (Classics); PhD in Drama, University of Bristol, England. Appointments: Numerous appearances as a Poet on TV and Radio in Britain, USA, South Africa; BBC Radio 3 programmes: An Unconquered God, 1988, 1989, Le Far West, 1989; Men and Women, 1991; Poetry in Action, 1993, 1994, 1995; Zulu Dream Time, 1994; Dancing Bach, 1995; Poetry for Children on BBC TV; Playschool, 1984, 1985, 1986, and Walrus, 1987; Subject of three nationwide American TV programmes, CBS; Poet at Large, 1974-75. Publications: Greek Tradedy in the Modern World, 1964; Discontinued Design, 1969; I, Odysseus, 1971; Sunflower, 1976, 4th imprint, 1985; Return to Zululand, 1980, 6th imprint, 1988; Red Alert: This is a God Warning, 1981; Jumping Shoes, 1983; Dancing the Impossible, Selected Poems, 1996; Feast of the Bones: New and Selected Poems, 1996; Poetry for Children: Rhymoceros, 1989; Children's Opera: The Apples of Youth, 1980. Contributions to: Anthologies; Written lyrics for musicals on the London stage, most notably Down the Arches; Translated poetry for broadcasting on radio and TV. Honours: Poet-in-Residence, Fairleigh Dickinson University, New Jersey, 1972-74; Cecil Day Lewis Fellow, 1979-80; Hooker Distinguished Visiting Professor, McMaster University, Ontario, Canada, 1982; Runner-up prizewinner, Arvon International Competition, 1992. Memberships: Poetry Society of Britain; Poetry Society of America; Writer's Guild of Great Britain; Writer's Guild of America; PEN. Address: 13 St Saviour's Road, London SW2 5HP, England.

AYYANARAPPAN Kavikkuil Pon, (Pasumpon), b. 5 May 1945, Arasur, India. Senior Section Supervisor; Director of Telecommunication Stores. m. Kamatchi, 6 Jun 1974, 1 son, 1 daughter. Education: BSc, 1974. Appointments: Divisional Secretary, NUTEECI III, FNPTO, O/o The DTS Madras - Staff Welfare; Secretary, O/o The DTS Madras - 6; Founder, Marumalarchi Mandram Arasoor, Chengai Anna Dt, Tamil Nadu, India. Publications: Nava Manigal, 1985; Malaithendral, 1985; Kavimurasu, 1990. Contributions to: Newspaper Dinamani, Malaysia; Magazines: Tamilppani; Kavithaiuravu; Tele News; Kuraliyam; Kavikkondal; Poet. Honours: 1st Prize Winner, for the Epic of Pannokku Panippori, Lion Ramesh and Lion Mahresh Literary Award, 1990; Recipient of VGP Literary Award for his Poetical Service, 1990. Memberships: World Congress of Poets, USA; All India Tamil Writers Association, Madras; Federation of World Tamils, Madras; Executive Member, Tamil Poetry Association, Madras; Assistant Secretary, World Tamil Poets Association, Madras; Founder Leader, World Literary Academy, Madras. Address: E 15 D Postal Telegraphs, Staff Quarters, Anna Nagar, Madras 600 040, India.

AZAD Shamim, b. 11 Nov 1954. Educator. m. Abul K Azad, 23 Apr 1972, 1 son, 1 daughter. Education: BA, Honours, 1972; MA 1973, 16th, 2nd class BA and MA. Publications: Bhalobashar Kabita, 1981; Sparsher Apekhaya, 1983; Hey Jubak, Tomar Bhabishyat, 1989. Contributions to: Overseas Correspondent, Bichitra (national weekly of Bangladesh). Memberships: National Education Advisory Board,

Primery, Bangladesh; Bangla Academy, Dhaka, Bangladesh; Bangla Shahittayar Parishad, London; Bishwa Shahitya Kendra, Dhaka, Bangladesh. Address: 188 Perth Road, Ilford, Essex IG2 6DZ, England.

AZOFEIFA Isaac Felipe, b. 11 Apr 1909, Santo Domingo de Heredia, Costa Rica. State Professor of Spanish. m. Clemencia Camacho Mora, 4 Jan 1936, 4 sons, 2 daughters. Education: Pedagogical Institute of Chile, 1933. Appointments: Director-General, Secondary Education, 1948-52; Professor of Literature, Psychology and Education, 1943-79, Director of School of General Studies, 1972-79, Professor Emeritus, 1980-, University of Costa Rica. Publications: Trunca Unidad, 1958; Vigilia en Pie de Muerte, 1961; Cancion, 1964; Estaciones, 1967; Dias y Territorios, 1969; Cima del Gozo, 1974; Cruce de Via, 1982; Ensayo Sobre la Palabra en seie discursos liricos, 1992. Contributions to: Repertorio Americano; Universidad, weeklies; Diario de Costa Rica; La Nación; Revista Nacional de Cultura, El Salvador; Revista Kanina de la Facultad de Letras de la Universidad de Costa Rica; Revista de Artes y Letras de la Universidad Nacional, Costa Rica; Revista Nacional de Cultura de la Universidad Nacional a Distancia, Costa Rica. Honours: Aquileo Echeverria National Prize for Poetry, 1964, 1969, 1974; Joaquin Garcia Monge Prize for Cultural Journalism, 1972; Magon National Prize for Culture, 1980; Doctor, hc, Universidad Estatal a Distancia, 1987; Premio Obra y Vida Omar Dengo Universidad Nacional, 1988. Memberships: Academia Costarricense de la Lengua; Corresponding Member, Real Academia Espanola, 1989 and Academia Chilena de la Lengua, 1985; Grupo Fuego de la Poesia de Santiago de Chile; Taller 66 de Santiago de Chile. Address: Apdo 444 - 2050 San Pedro de Montes de Oca, Costa Rica, Central America.

AZPITARTE ROUSSE Juan, (Juan Berekiz), b. 27 Apr 1959, Bilbao, Spain. Writer. Education: Graduated in Philosophy and Theology, University of Deurto, Bilbao. Appointments: President, Gerekiz Artistic Association; Founder Member, Graphologic Association in Basque Country. Publications: La Armonia y El Vitalismo, 1985; El Poeta y el Payaso, 1986; Poemas Raros, 1987; Mi Poesia Para Ti, 1988; Meditaciones en el asfalto, 1988; Sentimentios y Sonidos, 1988; A la Pintura, 1990. Contributions to: Gemma; Clarin; Mensajero; Redención; Bilbocio; Club CCC. Honours: Prize, Proyecto Hombre de Bizkaia, 1990; Patrocinado por la Asociación Artística Vizcaina. Memberships: Centro Cultural, Literario e Artistico de Gazeta de Felgueiras, Portugal; International Poetry, USA; Asociación Mundial de Escritores y Centro Cultural, Literario y Artistico Agustin Garcia Alonso-La Penorra 8, Vizcaya, Spain; Asociación Artistica Vizcaina, Spain. Address: Avda Zumalacarregui 119-9a C, 48007 Bilbao, Spain.

B

BABCOCK Wendell Keith, b. 21 Nov 1925, Genessee County, Michigan, USA. Baptist Pastor; Professor of Music and Religious Studies. m. Esther Marie Winger, 23 Aug 1951, 2 sons. Education: BA, Bob Jones University, 1967; MA, PhD, Columbia Pacific, San Rafael, California, 1984. Appointments: Professor, Biblical Studies; Instructor in Keyboard and Choral Techniques; Pastor and Choral Conductor at churches in Caledonia and Wyoming, Michigan; Teacher, Grand Rapids School of the Bible and Music; Chairman of English Department; General Bible Ministries; Publications Editor and Keyboard Musician, Grand Rapids campus station, WGNR; Keyboard Artist, various radio stations; Recording Artist, Staff Musician, Maranatha Bible Conference and Gull Lake Bible Conference, 1960-; Convention Organist, Gideons International from 1977; Currently: Professor of Music Pedagogy, Cornerstone College, Grand Rapids, Michigan; Pastor of White Hills Bible Church, Grand Rapids. Publications: Various articles in religious magazines, essays and a biblical commentary; Music works; Cantatas and sacred songs including: Everywhere You Go, It's Christmas, Easter Cantata, Echoes of Easter; The Church in Crisis, Acts commentary; Favourite Hymn Duets for Piano and Organ; Glimpses of Worship, volume of poetry, 1990; Great and Mighty Things: A History of Gull Lake, 1993. Honours include: Plaque for music composition and public production, 1970; Alumnus of the Year, Grand Rapids School, 1975; Golden Poets Award, 1988, 1989. Memberships: ABIRA; IBC; National Audubon Society; National Wildlife Association; Smithsonian; New York Academy of Science; World Literary Academy; International Society of Poets. Address: 3455 Williamson NE, Grand Rapids, MI 49505, USA.

BACHAR Gregory Paul, b. 3 Dec 1964, Cheektowaga, New York, USA. Musician. Education: BA, English/American Studies, University of California, Los Angeles, 1987; MFA, English/Creative Writing, University of Massachusetts, Amherst, 1993. Appointments: Editor, Rowhouse Press, Jack Mackerel Magazine, 1992-; Creative Writing Instructor, University of Massachusetts, Amherst, 1992-93; Writing Instructor, Seattle Central, 1994; Curator, Jack Mackerel Art Gallery, Seattle, 1996-. Publications: 47 Poems, 1994; The Cage Writings, 1995; Fragments, 1995; Steuben's 47, 1996; Green Clown on a Black Cross, 1996; Permeke's Constant, 1998. Contributions to: Conduit; Old Crow; Hawaii Review; Kansas Quarterly; Takahe; Colorado North Review; Portlandia Review of Books. Address: P O Box 23134, Seattle, Washington 98102-0434, USA.

BADMAN May Edith (May Ivimy), b. 10 Nov 1912, Greenwich, London, England. m. Raymond Frank Badman, 19 Oct 1968, 1 son, 1 daughter. Appointments: Founder, Organiser, Ver Poets, 1966-. Publications: Night is Another World, 1964; Midway This Path, 1966; Late Swings, 1980; Prayer Stocks, 1980; Parting the Leaves, 1984; Strawberries in the Salad, 1992; The Best Part of the Day, 1992. Contributions to: Time and Tide; BBC Radio 3, Poetry Now; Literary Review; Poetry Review; Tribune; Poetry Workshop; Meridian; Pembroke Magazine; Grand Piano; Iota; Outposts; Country Life; Countryside; Among others. Honours: Manifold Chapbook Competition, 1966; Greenwich Festival, 1981; Dorothy Tutin Award for Services to Poetry, 1983; National Poetry Competition, 1988; Howard Sergeant Memorial Award, 1990; Invitation to Buckingham Palace Royal Garden Party for services to the community, 1990. Memberships: Former Treasurer Poetry Society; Society of Women Writers and Journalists; St Albans Art Society, Associate. Address: Haycroft, 61 & 63 Chiswell Green Lane, St Albans, Hertfordshire AL2 3AL, England.

BADOSA Enrique, b. 16 Mar 1927, Barcelona, Spain. Writer. Education: Licentiate in Philosophy and Letters. Appointments: Literary Critic, El Noticiero Universal Newspaper, Barcelona; Literary Editor, Department of Spanish, Plaza and Janes Publishing House, Barcelona. Publications: Mas alla del viento, 1956; Tiempo de esperar, tiempo de esperanza, 1959; Baladas para la paz, 1963; Arte poetica, 1968; En roman paladino, 1970; Historias en Venecia, 1971; Poesia, 1956-1971, 1973; Dad este escrito a las llamas, 1976; Mapa de Grecia, 1979; Cuadernos de barlovento, 1986; Epigramas confidenciales, 1989. Contributions to: ABC; El Noticiero Universal; La Esatfeta Literaria; Papeles de Son Armadans; Insula; Poesia Espanola; Poesia de Espana; Caracola; Cuadernos Hispanoamericanos; Agora; Alamo; Barcarola; Fablas; Camp de l'Arpa; Hora de Poesi; Anfora Nova. Honours: Francisco de Quevedo Prize for Poetry, 1986; Poetry Prize of City of Barcelona, 1989; Fastenrath Prize, Real Academia Espanola de la Lengua, 1992. Memberships: Asociacion Colegial de Escritores; Asociacion Prometeo de Poesia; Academia Iberoamericana de Poesia. Address: Marc Aureli 14, 08006 Barcelona, Spain.

BAI Hua, b. 20 Nov 1930, He Nan, China. Writer. m. Wang Pei, 30 Dec 1956, 1 son. Education: Fine Arts Department, Hsin Yang College of Education. Appointments: Cultural Propaganda, People's Liberation Army, 1947-52; Club-in-Charge, Field Division, People's Liberation Army, 1952-55; Literary and Creative activities, General Office of Political Affairs of the Army, 1955-58; Skilled Worker, August 1st Film Factory, 1958-62; Editor, Shanghai Movies Production Company, 1962-64; Army Writer, 1964-85; Writer, Shanghai Writers' Association, 1985-. Publications: A Flock of Eagles, 1956; The Princess of Peacock, 1957. Contributions to: Numerous magazines and journals. Honour: National Best Poems Award, 1981. Memberships: Vice Chairman, Shanghai Writers' Association; Council of Chinese Writers' Association; Council of Chinese Film Artists Association; Beijing Pen centre; Chinese Opera Artists Association. Address: Room 706, No 4, Lane 83, Jiangning Road, Shanghai, China.

BAIGENT Beryl, b. 16 Dec 1937, Llay, Wrexham, North Wales. Teacher; Writer. m. Alan H Baigent, 19 Jan 1963, 3 daughters. Education: BA, Physical Education, MA, Literature, University of Western Ontario, London, Ontario. Appointments: Teacher, Oxford Co Board of Education; Freelance Journalist; Tutor; Secretary; Judge, Pat Lowther Award, 1992; Ontario Representative League of Canadian Poets, 1994-96. Publications: The Quiet Village, 1972; Pause, 1974; In Counter Point, 1976; Ancestral Dreams, 1981; The Sacred Beech, 1985; Mystic Animals, 1988; Absorbing the Dark, 1990; Undress Stress, (articles), 1991; Hiraeth: In Search of Celtic Origins, 1994; Triptych: Virgins Victims Votives, 1996; Published in anthologies: Northern Spirit, 1988, A Discord of Flags, 1992, The Magic Tree, 1995; Bite to Eat Place, 1995; Eramosa; Wayzgoose; Between Cultures On the Threshold: Writing Towards the Year 2000. Contributions to: Poetry Canada; Poetry Toronto; Momentum, UK; Porn Seed; Canadian Humanist; Poet; Poets Gallery; Public Works; Contemporary Verse II; Amaranth Review; Garm Lu; Tabula Rasa Ninnau; Wayzgoose Anthology; Y Drych; Poetry Australia; Pierian Spring; Alberta Poetry Yearbook; Implosion; Dog's Breath; Herspectives; Sage Woman; Hecate's Loom; Prairie Journal; Kairos. Honours: Ontario Weekly Newspaper Award, 1979; Fritch Memorial, Canadian Authors Association, 1982; Ontario Arts Council, 1983, 1985, 1987; Kent Writers Award, 1986; Black Mountain Award, 1986; Canada Council Touring Award, 1990, 1992, 1993, 1994; Forest City Poetry Award, 1991; International Affairs Touring Award, 1991; North Wales Arts Association Award, 1993, 1994; Muse Journal Award, 1994. Memberships: League of Canadian Poets; Canadian Poetry Association; World Poetry Society Intercontinental; Celtic Arts Association. Address: 137 Byron Avenue, Thamesford, Ontario N0M 2M0, Canada.

BAILEY Frank Edward (Frankie), b. 25 Sept 1948, Chicago, Illinois, USA. Laboratory Technician; X-Ray Technician; Singer. Education: Diplomas for Laboratory Technician and X-Ray Technician, Bryant College. Appointments: Singer, Poet and Composer, 1981-. Contributions to: Our Western World's Greatest Poems, 1983; Today's Greatest Poems, 1983; Our World's Best Loved Poems, 1984; Our World's Most Beloved Poems, 1984; Our Western World's Most Beautiful Poems, 1985; Our World's Most Cherished Poems, 1985; World Poetry Anthology, 1986; The Great American Poetry Anthology: Great Poems of Today, 1987; New American Poetry Anthology, 1988; Golden Treasury of Great Poems, 1988; World Treasury of Great Poems, 1989; Great Poems of the Western World, 1989; World of Poetry Anthology, 1990; World Treasury of Golden Poems, 1990; Our World's Favourite Gold and Silver Poems, 1991; Love is Priceless, Parnassus of World Poets, India, 1994; If the World Would Only See, National Library of Poetry, A Water's Edge, 1995. Honours: 6 Golden Poet Coveted Awards, 1985-90, 1 Silver Poet Coveted Award, 1986, World of Poetry; 21 Certificates of Honourable Mention, 1984-91; International Black Writers Conference, Honourable Mention for the poem The Ghetto Dreams 1985; Nomination as Poet of the Year, International Poet Merit and Honour Member, 1995. Memberships: World of Poetry; Society of American Poets; American Poetry Association. Address: 6045 South Prairie Avenue, Chicago, IL 60637, USA.

BAILEY Gordon, b. 22 Feb 1936, Stockport, Cheshire, England. Chief Executive of Charity. m. Corrine, 2 Aug 1958, 1 son, 3 daughters. Education: BA, Honours, Pastoral Theology. Publications: Plastic World, 1971; Mothballed Religion, 1972; Patchwork Quill, 1975; Can a Man Change?, 1979; 100 Contemporary Christian Poets, 1983; I Want to Tell You How I Feel, God, 1983; Stuff and Nonsense, 1989. Address: The Birches, 9 Wentworth Drive, Blackwell, Worcestershire B60 1BE, England.

BAILEY Kevin Neil Leroy, b. 16 Mar 1954, Wallingford-on-Thames, Berkshire, England. Psychologist; Editor. Div, 1 daughter. Education: Teacher's Certificate, Bulmershe College, University of Reading, 1976; BSc, Honours, Psychology, University of York, 1986; BA, Classics, Open University. Appointments: Fruit Picker; Pensions Clerk; Psychiatric Nurse; Labourer in brewery; Education Social Worker. Publications: Country Poems 1974-1979, 1979; Blue Ornaments, 1980; Anglo-Saxon Poems, 1980; Sappho, 1983; Poems and Translations, 1987; Founder of the Day Dream Press; Editor and Publisher, The Haiku Quarterly. Contributions to: Civil Service Anthologies, 1977-79; Poetry Nippon, Japan; Mainioki Daily News, Japan; Ko Magazine, Japan; New Cicada Haiku, Japan; Outposts; Envoi; Ore; Iota; Woodnotes; Frogpond, USA; Missors, USA; Hertfordshire Countryside; Essex Countryside; Berks and Bucks Countryside; Wiltshire Life; Haiku Quarterly. Memberships: Poetry Society of Japan; British Haiku Society. Address: 39 Exmouth Street, Kingshall, Swindon, Wiltshire SN1 3PU, England.

BAILEY Louise Slagle, b. 26 June 1930, Gainesville, Florida, USA. Educator. m. Grayson A Bailey Jr, 1961, div, 1 daughter. Education: BA, Honours, 1951, MA, 1953, University of Florida; Doctoral work, University of Tennessee, 1955-59. Appointments: Instructor, University of Tennessee, 1959-61; Instructor in English, 1961-63, Assistant Professor of English, 1961-87, Emeritus Professor, 1987-, Marshall University. Contributions to: Lucidity; Z Miscellaneous; The Poets of Now; American Poetry Annual; North American Poetry Review; Word & Image; Winter Fantasy; A Poetry Anthology; Images in Poetry; New Life Wings; The Illustrated Journal IV; The Independent Review; Rainbows & Roses; Verve; American Poetry Showcase; Wide Open Magazine; New York Poetry Society Anthology, (book 1); Best of Hill & Valley; Faith...Words; Innisfree Magazine; Poet's Review; Esc! Magazine; New Voices; Songs on The Wind; New Life Wings; A Poetic Garden of Verse; Annual Anthology of South Florida Poetry Institute. Memberships: Phi Beta Kappa; Phi Kappa Phi; West Virginia Writers; Guyandotte Poets Society; West Virginia Poetry Society. Address: 1204 9th Avenue, Huntington, WV 25701, USA.

BAIRD Dorothy Anne Scott, b. 5 Mar 1960, Edinburgh, Scotland. Teacher. m. John Philip Shinton, 6 Sept 1986, 1 son, 2 daughters. Appointments: English Language Teacher, Moscow; Resources Officer, Stourbridge; Teacher, F E and Rudolf Steiner School, Edinburgh. Publications: In the Gold of Flesh, 1990; With My Heart in My Mouth, (anthology), 1994. Contributions to: Acumen; Distaff; Grand Piano; Giant Steps; Spokes; Resurgence. Membership: National Poetry Society. Address: 117 Lanark Road West, Currie, Midlothian EH14 5N2, England.

BAKER David (Anthony), b. 27 Dec 1954, Bangor, Maine, USA. Associate Professor of English; Poet; Editor. m. Ann Townsend, 19 July 1987. Education: BSE, 1976, MA, 1977, Central Missouri State University; PhD, University of Utah, 1983. Appointments: Poetry Editor, 1980-81, Editor-in-Chief, 1981-83, Quarterly West; Visiting Assistant Professor, Kenyon College, 1983-84; Assistant Editor, 1983-89, Poetry Editor/Consulting Poetry Editor, 1989-94, Poetry Editor, 1994-, Kenyon Review; Assistant Professor of English, 1984-90, Associate Professor of English, 1990-, Denison University; Visiting Telluride Professor, Cornell University, 1985; Visiting Associate Professor, University of Michigan, 1996; Contributing Editor, The Pushcart Prize, 1992-; Many poetry readings. Publications: Poetry: Looking Ahead, 1975; Rivers in the Sea, 1977; Laws of the Land, 1981; Summer Sleep, 1984; Haunts, 1985; Sweet Home, Saturday Night, 1991; Echo for an Anniversary, 1992; After the Reunion, 1994; Holding Katherine, 1997. Editor: The Soil is Suited to the Seed: A Miscellany in Honor of Paul Bennett, 1986; Meter in English: A Critical Engagement, 1996. Contributions to: Anthologies and periodicals. Honours: Margaret Bridgman Scholar of Poetry, Bread Loaf, 1982; Outstanding Writer, Pushcart Press, 1982, 1984, 1985, 1986, 1990, 1991, 1994, 1995; James Wright Prize for Poetry, Mid-American Review, 1983; National Endowment for the Arts Fellowship, 1985-86; Bread Loaf Poetry Fellow, 1989; Pushcart Prize, 1992; Mary Carolyn Davies Award, Poetry Society of America, 1995;

Thomas B Fordham Endowed Chair in Creative Writing, Denison University, 1996. Memberships: Associated Writing Programs; Modern Languages Association; National Book Critics Circle; Poetry Society of America; Poets and Writers. Address: 135 Granview Road, Granville, OH 43023, USA.

BAKER June Frankland Marilyn, b. 27 May 1935, New York, New York, USA. Teacher. m. David A Baker, 6 July 1962, 2 daughters. Education: AB, State University of New York, Albany, 1957; MA, University of Pennsylvania, 1958. Appointments: Teacher, 1958-64; Writer, 1964-; Substitute Teacher, Journalism, Columbia Basin College, 1987. Publication: Co-Editor, Sand Tracks (anthology), 1976. Contributions to: Christian Science Monitor; Bellingham Review; Berkeley Poetry Review; Blue Unicorn; Commonweal; Crab Creek Review; Crosscurrents, A Quarterly; Gulf Stream Magazine; Kaleidoscope; Kansas Quarterly; Louisville Review; Southern Poetry Review; Three Rivers Poetry Journal; Writers Forum. Membership: Secretary, Vice President, Mid-Columbia Writers. Address: 614 Lynnwood Court, Richland, WA 99352, USA.

BAKER Lillian (Liliane L Baker, Miss Elbee), b. 12 Dec 1921, Yonkers, New York, USA. Writer; Poet; Editor. m. Roscoe Albert Baker, 1 son, 1 daughter. Education: El Camino College, 1952; University of California at Los Angeles, 1968. Appointments: Continuity Writer, WINS Radio, New York City, 1945-46; Columnist, Freelance Writer, Reviewer, Gardena Valley News, 1964-76; Founder, International Club for Collectors of Hatpins & Hatpin Holders, 1977; Editor, Points Newsletter, 1977-. Publications: A Book of Alms, 1964; Collector's Encyclopedia of Hatpins & Hatpin Holders, 1976; One Hundred Years of Collectable Jewelry 1850-1950, 1978, 6th edition, 1992; Art Nouveau & Art Deco Jewelry, 1980, 5th edition, 1990; The Concentration Camp Conspiracy: A Second Pearl Harbor, 1981; Hatpins & Hatpin Holders: An Illustrated Value Guide, 1983, 4th edition, 1991; Creative & Collectible Miniatures, 1984, revised edition 1991; War-Torn Woman, 1985; Fifty Years of Collectible Fashion Jewelry 1925-1975, 3rd edition, 1991; Dishonoring America: The Collective Guilt of American Japanese, 1988; American and Japanese Relocation in World War II: Fact, Fiction and Fallacy, 1989, revised edition 1991; The Japanning of America: Redress and Reparations Demands by Japanese-Americans, 1991; Twentieth Century Fashionable Plastic Jewelry, 1992; The Common Doom, 1992; The Coming of Dawn, poems, 1993. Contributions to: Anthologies. Honours: George Washington Honor Medal, Freedoms Foundation, 1991; Semi-finalist, North American Poetry Contest, 1993. Memberships: Americans for Historical Accuracy, Co-Founder 1972; Society of Jewelry Historians of the USA. Address: 15237 Chanera Avenue, Gardena, CA 90249, USA.

BAKER Winona Louise, b. 18 Mar 1924, Saskatchewan, British Columbia, Canada. Poet; Educator. m. Arthur Baker, 9 May 1945, 3 sons, 1 daughter. Education: Teaching degree. Publications: Clouds Empty Themselves, 1987; Not So Scarlet A Woman, 1987; Moss-hung Trees, 1992; Beyond The Lighthouse, 1992; Anthologies: An Invisible Accordion; Do Whales Jump at Night; The Haiku Hundred; Haiku International Anthology; Here Is A Poem; Inside Poetry; Milkweed; Musicanada; New Morningside Papers; Poetry Alive; Round the Pond; Short and Sweet; Sixty Singing Years; Themes For All Times; The Virago Book of Wicked Verse; Wind Five-folded; Witness to Wilderness; Womansong. Poetry Contributions to: Publications in North America, Europe, New Zealand and Japan. Honours: Shikishi, for Haiku in English, 1986; Expo Japan Book Award: Haiku, 1986; Foreign Minister's Prize, World Haiku Contest, 1989; Fundatia Nipponica Societatea Romana De Haiku Commemorative Medal 1994; Romanian Medal; Sonnet, Humour and Modern Haiku poetry prizes. Memberships: League of Canadian Poets; Federation of British Columbia Writers; Canadian, American, European and Japanese Haiku Associations. Address: 606 First Street, Nanaimo, British Columbia V9R 1Y9, Canada.

BALABAN John, b. 2 Dec 1943, Philadelphia, Pennsylvania, USA. Professor of English; Writer; Poet; Translator. m. 28 Nov 1970, 1 daughter. Education: BA, Penn State University, 1966; AM, Harvard University, 1967. Appointments: Instructor in Linguistics, University of Can Tho, South Vietnam, 1967-68; Instructor, 1970-73, Assistant Professor, 1973-76, Associate Professor, 1976-82, Professor, 1982-92, of English, Penn State University; Professor of English, Director of Creative Writing, University of Miami, 1992-. Publications: Vietnam Poems, 1970; Vietnamese Folk Poetry, editor and translator, 1974; After Our War, poems, 1974; Letters From Across the Sea, poems, 1978; Ca Dao Vietnam: A Bilingual Anthology of Vietnamese Folk Poetry, editor and translator, 1980; Blue Mountain, poems, 1982; Coming Down Again, novel, 1985, revised edition, 1989; The Hawk's Tale, children's fiction, 1988; Three Poems, 1989; Vietnam: The Land We Never Knew, 1989; Words for My Daughter, poems, 1991; Remembering Heaven's Face, memoir, 1991; Vietnam: A Literary Companion, editor (with Nguyen Qui Duc), 1996; New and Selected Poems and Translations, 1997. Contributions to: Anthologies, books, scholarly journals and periodicals. Honours: National Endowment for the Humanities Younger Humanist Fellow, 1971-72; Lamont Selection, Academy of American Poets, 1974; Fulbright-Hayes Senior Lectureship in Romania, 1976-77; Steaua Prize, Romanian Writers Union, 1978; Fulbright Distinguished Visiting Lectureship in Romania, 1979; National Endowment for the Arts Fellowship, 1978, 1985; Vaptsarov Medal, Union of Bulgarian Writers, 1980; National Poetry Series Book Selection, 1990; Pushcart Prize XV, 1990. Memberships: American Literary Translators Association, President, 1994-; National Endowment for the Arts Translation Panel, Chair, 1993-94. Address: Department of English, University of Miami, PO Box 248145, Coral Gables, FL 33124, USA.

BALACHANDRAN Kannaiya, (Crescent Virgo), b. 15 Sept 1951, Chidambaram, India. Reader in English. m. Ponni, 3 Sept 1989, 1 son. Education: BA, English, Annamalai University, 1971; MA, English, Annamalai University, 1974; MPhil, English, Annamalai University, 1984. Appointments: Tutor in English, Annamalai University, 1974-78; Lecturer in English 1979-89, Reader in English 1989-, Annamalai University. Publications: Annai Oru Agal Vilakku, 1975; Longing For You, 1986; For A Future & Heart's Chair, 1988, 1995; Oru Puthiya Kathai, 1995; Rusthiyin Veera Deerangal, 1995. Contributions to: Poetry; Byword; Bharat Protiva; The English Magazine; The Mahanadi Review; Scholar Critic; The Month; Hesperus Review; Journal of India Writing in English; Canopy; The Quest. Honours: Special Prize, All India Students One-Act Play Writing Competition, 1974; V.A.M.K. Dhavmaraja Gold Medal, 1974; Poetry Prize X World Congress of Poets; International Poet of Merit for 1995-96; Gold Coin in Kumudam-Readers' Guess Competition, 1996. Memberships: World Academy of Arts & Culture; International Society of Poets; American Studies Research Centre; Indian Association for American Studies. Address: Annamalai University, Annamalai Nagar 608002, India.

BALAZS Mary (Elizabeth Webber), b. 2 Aug 1939, Lakewood, Ohio, USA. Poet; College Professor in English. m. Gabriel George Balazs, 18 June 1960, 2 sons. Education: BA, 1960, MA, 1962, PhD, 1965, Pennsylvania State University. Appointments: Associate Professor of English, Virginia Military Institute, 1967-; Poets-in-Schools, National Endowment for The Arts, 1974-. Publications: Associate Editor, I That Am Ever Stranger, anthology, 1974; Editor, Puddingstone, volume of children's poetry, 1975. Poetry books: The Voice of Thy Brother's Blood, 1976, The Stones Refuse Their Peace, 1979, Out of Darkness, 1991; Co-Editor: Touching This Earth, anthology, 1977; Poems in anthologies: Peeling The Onion; Pierced By A Ray Of Sun; Best of Wind Anthology; Coming Together; The Tie That Binds. Contributions to: Kansas Quarterly; Poet & Critic; Roanoke Review; New Laurel Review; Inlet; West Coast Poetry Review; Green's Magazine; Cold Mountain Review; Matrix; Wind Literary Magazine; Literature and Belief; The Galley Sail Review; Poetry WLU, Canada. Honours: Best Poem of Issue, Patterns, 1971, Baby John, 1972; Irene Leache Literary Award, 1980, 1985; Piedmont Literary Contest, 1983; Kansas Quarterly, Kansas Arts Commission Award, 1987; Sam Ragan Poetry Prize, 1987; 1st Place, 1990, 1st Honourable Mention, 1994, 3rd Place, 1995, Jim Wayne Miller Poetry Contest; 1st and 2nd Place, Kate M Reis Poetry Contest, 1995. Memberships: Poetry Society of Virginia; Virginia Writers' Club; Virginia Association of Teachers of English. Address: Department of English & Fine Arts, The Virginia Military Institute, Lexington, VA 24450, USA.

BALCON Jill. See: **DAY-LEWIS Jill Angela Henriette.**

BALDERSTON Jean Merrill, b. 29 Aug 1936, Providence, Rhode Island, USA. Psychotherapist; Writer of Poetry. m. David Chase Balderston, 1 June 1957. Education: BA, University of Connecticut, 1957; MA, 1965, EdD, 1968, Teachers College, Columbia University. Appointments: Adjunctive University Faculty, Douglas College for Women, Rutgers University, Mountclair State College, New Jersey, Hunter and Queen's Colleges, City University of New York and Teachers College, Coloumbia University, 1965-70; Psychotherapist in

private practice, 1968-. Contributions to: New York Quarterly; Kayak; Poetry Now; Little Magazine; The Wormwood Review; Light: A Quarterly of Humorous, Occasional, Ephemeral and Light Verse; Various other literary magazines; Literary anthologies, including: Anthology of Magazine Verses and Yearbook of American Poetry. Memberships: American Psychological Association; Poetry Society of America; American Association for Marital and Family Therapy; Emily Dickinson International Society. Address: 1225 Park Avenue, New York, NY 10128, USA.

BALDWIN Michael, b. 1 May 1930, Gravesend, Kent, England. Author. Education: Open Scholar, 1949, Senior Scholar, 1953, St Edmund Hall, Oxford, 1950-55. Appointments: Assistant Master, St Clement Danes Grammar School, 1955-59; Lecturer, Senior Lecturer, Principal Lecturer, Head of English and Drama Department, Whitelands College, 1959-78. Publications: The Silent Mirror, 1951; Voyage From Spring, 1956; Death on a Live Wire, 1962; How Chas Egget Lost His Way in a Creation Myth, 1967; Hob, 1972; Snook, 1980; King Horn, 1983; Many novels and short stories, 1959-96. Contributions to: Listener; Encounter; New Statesman; Texas Review; BBC Wildlife Magazine; Outposts. Honours: Cholmondeley Award, 1984; Fellow, Royal Society of Literature, 1985. Memberships: Vice Chairman, Arvon Foundation, 1974-90; Chairman, Arvon Foundation at Lumb Bank, 1980-89; Crime Writer's Association. Address: 35 Gilbert Road, Bromley, Kent BR1 3QP, England.

BALK Christianne, b. 25 Aug 1952, Oswego, New York, USA. Teacher; Writer. m. 24 Aug 1985, 1 daughter. Education: BA, Biology, Grinnell College, 1974; MA, English, MFA, Creative Writing, University of Iowa. Publications: Bindweed, 1986; Desiring Flight, 1995. Contributions to: New Yorker; Harper's; Crazyhorse; Country Journal; Sonora Review; Pequod; Poetry Northwest; Missouri Review; Cutbank; Minnesota Monthly; Alaska Today; Iowa Journal of Literature Studies; Bellingham Review; Grinnell Magazine; Heartland; New Republic; Ploughshares. Honours: Walt Whitman Award, Academy of American Poets, 1985; Ingram Merrill Foundation Writing Grant, 1988; Verna Emery Award, Purdue University Press, 1995. Address: PO Box 15633, Seattle, WA 98115-0633, USA.

BALL Frank, b. 28 Sept 1935, Bloxwich, Staffordshire, England. Retired Fire Officer. m. 15 Mar 1958, 2 sons, 1 daughter. Appointments: Soldier, Grenadier Guards, 1953-57; Fire Officer until retirement, 1964-87. Publications: Fire & Thought, 1983; Verse on Fire, 1985; Fire Our Dreams, 1987; Cats in the Grass, 1989; These Parkinson Times, 1990; Half Penny Pride, 1991; Poets Ghost, 1992. Contributions to: Fire Service Magazines; Parkinsons Disease Society Newsletter. Honour: 1st Prize, Young Parkinsons Society, 1990. Memberships: Poetry Society; Betjeman Society. Address: Allandale, Walsall Road, Muckley Corner, Lichfield, Staffordshire WS14 0BP, England.

BALL Richard, b. 25 Dec 1919, Knighton, Powys, Wales. Poet; Literary Critic. 1 daughter, dec 1965. Education: Advanced French (Army), North Western Polytechnic College, Kentish Town, London, 1938-39; Monastery College, Ampleforth, 1942. Appointments: Invoice Clerk, Milling Office, 1936-38; Professional Soldier, 1st Battalion Grenadier Guards, 1938-46; War Service, Europe; Government Service, 1946-75, now retired; Contributing Editor, The Pembroke Magazine, North Carolina, USA, 17 years; Reviewer, The Plowman, Ontario, Canada, 8 years. Publications: Books: The Last Voyage of the Titanic, 1968; Avalon One, 1968; Avalon Two, 1969; Avalon Three, 1969; In Memory of Dylan Thomas, 1969; Chain, 1974; Silhouette of an Artist Walking, 1974; Mask of Aeschylus, 1981; Parable of the Man-Child, 1988; Anabase en Retard, 1991; Last Ten from the Gulag, 1992; Selected Poems 1933-1993, 1994. Contributions to: Many magazines, journals, newspapers and anthologies, including: Borderlines; Counterpoint; Global Tapestry Journal; Movement; New Age; OM Poetry and Prose; Orbis; Outposts; The Pembroke Magazine; Pennine Platform; Poetry and Audience; Poetry Nottingham; Poetry Now hardbacks; Pommegranate; Prospice; Radix; Strath, Rannock and Gilmore Poets; The Plowman; Tangent; Transatlanic Review (London, New York); Welcome Magazine; Weyfarers; Xenia; Zapizdat Poetry Anthologies. Honours: Numerous poetry competition awards including: 1st Prize, An Ode-Prometheus Re-Incarnated, Shelley Society of New York International, 1976; 1st Prize, Animals, Dodman Press Poemcard Competition, 1978; 1st Prize, Hill Farmer, 1978, 3rd Prize, Buzzard, 1979, Michael Johnson Memorial Awards International; 1st Prize, Staff of God, The Plowman Open, 1990; 1st Prize, Voltage, Crewe and Nantwich International,

1992; Several Diplomas for Excellence, Scottish National Opens, including UK Section, 1995. Memberships: University of Bristol Literary Society, 1966-72; Avon Poetry Group, Bristol, 1968-74; Life Member, Ver Poets Poetry Society, St Albans; Associate Member, Welsh Academy of Letters; Bristol Arts Centre, 1966-74. Address: Llwyn Huan, Llansantffraid, Ym Mechain, Powys SY22 6AA, North Wales.

BALLARD-HARVEY Margie, b. 12 July 1910, Grand Saline, Texas, USA. Poet. m. W F Harvey, 1933. Education: Graduated, Kaufman School, 1930. Contributions to: Ten Anthologies by Young Publications, 1960-76; World Treasury of Great Poems, 1993; Arcadia Poetry Anthology, 1994; National Library of Poetry: Best Poems, 1995; Windows of the Soul; Poetry Column in Southeast Star, 1948, 1949; Kaufman Herald. Honours: Golden Poet Awards, 1985-1989; Laurel Publisher Honorary Award; National Library of Poetry Editor's Choice Award, 1995. Memberships: The Poetry Society of Texas; Lifetime Membership, International Clover Association; World Literary Academy, Suburbia News, 1994. Address: 205 Water Street, Seagoville, TX 75159, USA.

BALLEM John Bishop, b. 2 Feb 1925, New Glasgow, Nova Scotia, Canada. Lawyer. m. Grace Louise Flavelle, 31 Aug 1951, 2 sons, 1 daughter. Education: BA, 1946, MA, 1948, LLB, 1949, Dalhousie University, Halifax, Nova Scotia; LLM, Harvard University Law School, Boston, Massachusetts, 1950. Appointment: Queen's Counsel, 1966. Contributions to: Writer's Block Magazine; Teak Roundup; International Prose & Poetry Quarterly; Western People; Mustico News. Honour: Honorary Doctor of Law Degree, University of Calgary, 1993. Memberships: Writer's Guild of Alberta; Writer's Union of Canada; Crime Writer's of Canada; Calgary Writers Association. Address: 1800, 350-7th Avenue SW, Calgary, Alberta T2P 3N9, Canada.

BALLOWE James, b. 28 Nov 1933, Carbondale, Illinois, USA. Professor of English. m. 24 Apr 1982, 1 son, 1 daughter. Education: BA, Millikin University, 1954; MA, 1956, PhD, 1963, University of Illinois. Appointments: Teacher, Junior High School, 1954-55; Assistant in Teaching, University of Illinois, 1955-61; Assistant Professor, Millikin University, 1961-63; Professor of English, Dean of Graduate School, Dean, College of Communications and Fine Arts, Department Chair, 1963-. Publications: The Coal Miners, 1979; Co-Editor, Anglo-Welsh Poetry: A Selection, 1989. Contributions to: Encounter, London; Salmagundi; Southern Review; Kansas Quarterly; Boundary 2. Honours: Illinois Arts Council Poetry Award, 1975, 1977; Creative Non-Fiction Award, 1992. Address: Bradley University, Peoria, IL 61625, USA.

BALON Brett John Steven, (John Peterson, Steve Johnson), b. 26 Apr 1953, Regina, Saskatchewan, Canada. Manager. Education: BA, Honours, Anthropology, Champion College, CDP, 1987, University of Regina; MLS, University of Western Ontario, 1978; CRM, Institute of Certified Records Managers, Prairie Village, Kansas, 1991; PhD, Information Science, Greenwich University, Hilo, Hawaii. Appointments: Senior Branch Supervisor, Southeast Regional Library, 1978-82; Records Management Supervisor, 1982-83; Record Systems Co-ordinator, 1983-88, 1989-90, 1991-, Systems Liaison Officer for Corporate Services, 1988-89, Acting Manager, Office Systems, 1990-91, City of Regina. Publications: Anthologies: 100% Cracked Wheat, 1983; Heading Out: The New Saskatchewan Poets, 1986. Contributions to: Carillon; Fort Sanity VII; Freelance; Grain; NeWest Review; New Quarterly; Perspectives; Queen's Quarterly; Western People. Memberships: Chairman, Western Writers Federation, 1983-84; President, Saskatchewan Writers Guild, 1983-84; Vice President, Sakatchewan Writers Guild, 1981-83; Solipsists Anonymous, 1991-; Rollers, 1990-91; The Writer's Group, 1984-85; Co-founder, 1980, President, 1980-82, Weyburn Writers Group; Chairman, Coreau Books, Board of Directors, 1987-88, 1992-93, Member, Board Directors, 1984-. Address: 2-4341 Rae Street, Regina, Saskatchewan S4S 3B2, Canada.

BAMDAD A. See: **SHAMLOU Ahmad.**

BAN Eva. See: **MARTINOVICH BAN Eva Maria.**

BANARASI Das, b. 16 Oct 1955, Akorhi, Mirzapur, India. Teacher. m. Vimala Devi, 10 Mar 1972, 1 son. Education: Sahityacharya (Equivalent to MA in Sanskrit), 1982; BTC, 1988; MA, Hindi Literature, 1993. Appointments: Assistant Teacher, Government Basic School, Mirzapur. Publications: Srivindhyavasinicharitamrit,

1989; Sriashtabhujakathamanjari, 1991; Paryavarankaumudi in Sanskrit, Hindi, English, 1993; Utsarg, 1995; Hymn to Lord (Hanuman), 1995; Gandhari; Silver Poems. Contributions to: Poet International, Anthologised in Poems 96, World Poetry, 1996, 1997. Honours: Sanskrit Literature Award, Uttar Pradesh Government Sanskrit Academy, 1995; Gram Ratna Award by Gram Panchayat Akorhi, Mirzapur, 1996. Memberships: Literary Secretary, Sanskar Bharati, Mirzapur, Address: s/o Srimolai, Village-Post Akorhi, District, Mirzapur 231307, UP, India.

BANDLER Rhoda Uttal, b. 6 June 1909. m. Nathan W Bandler, 6 Sept 1928, 2 sons. Education: BA, Hunter College, 1927; Postgraduate work at Columbia University. Contributions to: New York Times; Wall Street Journal; Oregonian; The Lyric; Second Air Division Journal; Writers Journal. Honours: Contest, New York Magazine, 1977; Distinguished Service Citation, National League of American Penwomen, 1988; Numerous small cash awards from the National League of American Penwomen and others. Memberships: Poetry Society of America; Secretary, National League of American Penwomen; Women Poets of New York; Craftsman Group. Address: 30 Lincoln Plaza, 17N, New York, NY 10023, USA.

BANDYOPADHYAY Prayag, (B Brayag), b. 19 Apr 1945, India. m. Mitali, 16 Apr 1984, 1 daughter. Education: MA; Honorary DLitt. Appointments: Lecturer, 1969-74; Senior Assistant Professor, 1974-. Publications: Prelude; Summer Thoughts; Shadows in a Subway; Selected Poems; The Highway Penguins; The Blue Threads; The Voice of a Terror; The Words Upside Down. Contributions to: Youth Times; Illustrated Weekly of India; Asian Modern Poetry, 1982, 1984, 1988; Li Poetry, Taiwan, 1989. Honours: 1st Prize, 5th World Congress of Poets, 1981; Mentioned as Poet Extraordinary in Tokyo. Membership: Chairman, Asian Poetry Centre. Address: 357/1/12/1, Prince Anwar Shah Road, Calcutta 68, India.

BANG Mary-Jo, b. 22 Oct 1946, Waynesville, Missouri, USA. Writing Teacher; Photographer. 2 sons. Education: BA, Sociology and English, 1972, summa cum laude, MA, 1975, Northwestern University, Evanston, Illinois; School of Art Institute of Chicago, 1984-86; BA, Distinction, Polytechnic of Central London, 1989. Appointments: Instructor, Department of English, 1991-, Instructor, Liberal Arts Department, 1992-, Columbia College, Chicago. Publications: Whatever You Desire, Editor, 1990; Anthologies: The Women Writer's Handbook, 1990; World of Mouth, Vol 2, 1990; Life on the Line, 1992. Contributions to: Mississippi Valley Review; Earth's Daughters; Kalliope; Poets On; Orbis; Oxford Poetry; Poetry Nottingham; Echoes; Outposts Poetry Quarterly; Envoi; Poetry Durham. Honours: 3rd Place, Jo-Anne Hirshfield Memorial Poetry Prize, 1990; 3rd Place, The Muse Inc 8th Annual Poetry Prize, 1990. Address: 4247 North Hermitage 1A, Chicago, IL 60613, USA.

BANKS David, b. 10 Oct 1943, Newcastle, England. University Lecturer. m. Christiane Ganchou, 7 July 1973, 2 daughters. Education: BA, 1975, MA, 1979, University of Cambridge; Licence, 1978, Maitrise, 1979, DEA, 1980, Doctorat, 1983, Université de Nantes, France. Appointments: Executive Officer, British Civil Service, 1969-72; Assistant Lecturer, University of Mosul, Iraq, 1975-76; Lecturer, ENSM, Nantes, 1977-81; Assistant, 1981-88, Maitre de Conferences, 1988-, Université de Bretagne Occidentale, Brest, France. Publications: Broken Ice, 1975; The Ones the Censor Didn't See, 1977; Death and Ever After, 1987; Vole File, 1995. Contributions to: Ludd's Mill; Ore; Krax; Eureka; Out of Sight; Little Word Machine; Bogg; Star West; Windless Orchard; Poetry North East; Grapeshot; Trends; Pacific Quarterly; Sepia; Iron; Oasis; Orbis. Address: 2 Rue des Saules, 29217 Plougonvelin, France.

BANTOCK Gavin, b. 4 July 1939, Worcestershire, England. Education: MA, New College Oxford, 1964. Career: Professor of English, Reitaku University, Japan, 1969-. Publications: Christ: A Poem in Twenty-Six Parts, 1965; Juggernaut, 1968; A New Thing Breathing, 1969; Anhaga, 1970; Gleeman, 1972; Eirenikon, 1972; Isles, 1974; Dragons, 1979. Honours include: Eric Gregory Award, 1969. Address: c/o Peter Jay, 69 King George Street, London SE10 8PX, England.

BARANCZAK Stanislaw, b. 13 Nov 1946, Poznan, Poland. Professor; Poet; Writer; Editor; Translator. m. 2 children. Education: MA 1969, PhD 1973, Adam Mickiewicz University, Poznan. Appointments: Assistant Professor, Institute of Polish Philology, Adam Mickiewicz University, 1969-77, 1980; Co-Founder and Member, KOR, human rights group, 1976-81; Unemployed and blacklisted for political reasons, 1977-80; Associate Professor of Slavic Languages and Literatures, 1981-84, Alfred Jurzykowski Professor of Polish Language and Literature, 1984-, Harvard University; Co-Editor, Zeszyty Literackie, 1982-; Associate Editor, 1986-87, Editor-in-Chief, 1987-90, The Polish Review. Publications: Poetry: Selected Poems: The Weight of the Body, 1989; 18 other books in Polish, 1968-96; Criticism and Essays: Breathing Under Water, and Other East European Essays, 1990; 14 other books in Polish, 1971-96; Other: 43 books translated from English into Polish, 1974-96. Contributions to: Many scholarly journals and periodicals. Honours: Alfred Jurzykowski Foundation Literary Award, 1980; Guggenheim Fellowship, 1989; Terrence Des Pres Poetry Prize, 1989; Chivalric Cross of the Order of Polonia Restituta, 1991; Special Diploma for Lifetime Achievement in Promoting Polish Culture Abroad, Polish Minister of Foreign Affairs, 1993; PEN and Book-of-the-Month Club Award for the Best Literary Translation (with Clare Cavanagh), 1996. Memberships: American Association for Advancement of Slavic Studies; American Association for Polish-Jewish Studies; PEN Polish Center; Polish Institute of Arts and Sciences in America; Polish Writers' Association; Union of Polish Writers Abroad; ZAIKS (Union of Polish Authors). Address: c/o Department of Slavic Languages and Literatures, Harvard University, 301 Boylston Hall, Cambridge, MA 02138, USA.

BARANOW Joan Marie, b. 10 Oct 1958, Cincinnati, Ohio, USA. Teacher. Education: BA, English, Hollins College, 1980; MA, English, State University of New York, 1983; PhD, English, Rutgers University, 1992. Appointments: Teaching Assistant, State University of New York, 1981-83, Rutgers University, 1984-89; Assistant Professor, Ashland University, 1989-92. Publication: Co-Editor, 80 On The 80's - A Decade's History of Verse, 1990. Contributions to: USI Worksheets; Sirens; Poetry Miscellany; Pegasus Review; Emily Dickinson: A First Book Affair; Little Magazine; Hollins Critic; Artemis; Window. Honours: Award, Academy of American Poets, 1983; Fellowship, Ohio Arts Council, 1992; Squaw Valley Community of Writers, 1990, 1991, 1992. Memberships: Poets and Writers; Associated Writing Programmes; Modern Language Association. Address: 73 Hillside Avenue, Mill Valley, CA 94941, USA.

BARBARESE Joseph Thomas, b. 18 May 1948, Pennsylvania, USA. Educator. m. Karen Henly, 7 June 1980, 2 sons, 1 daughter. Education: BA, Franklin and Marshall College, 1976; MA, Temple University, 1980. Appointments: Associate Fellow, Journal of Modern Literature, Temple University, 1989-94; Visiting Professor, Rutgers University, 1988-92; Chair, English Department, Friends Select School, Philadelphia, 1984-. Publications: Under the Blue Moon, 1985; New Science, 1989. Contributions to: Atlantic; Southern Review; Sewanee Review; North American Review; Kenyon Review. Honour: Penn State Arts Council Fellowship, 1989. Membership: National Council of Teachers of English. Address: 7128 Cresheim Road, Philadelphia, PA 19119, USA.

BARBATO John Allan, b. 4 Sept 1945, Chicago, Illinois, USA. Artist. m. Martha Turner, 11 Nov 1978, 2 sons, 2 daughters. Appointments: 36 years of writing and painting interspersed with various and sundry menial jobs. Publications: Commedia dell Arte, 1981; Music Once Made Like Love, 1985; Because I Dreamed of You Last Night, 1990; Face Up On Dash (audio cassette), 1990, Exuberance, Despair Vision, 1995. Contributions to: Deep Valley Review; Childbirth Alternative; Tule Review; Community Endeavour; Glyphs I, II, III; Wild Duck Review. Memberships: Poets Playhouse, Bd Dirs. Address: 20391, New Rome Road, Nevada City, CA 95959, USA.

BARBOUR Douglas (Fleming), b. 21 March 1940, Winnipeg, Manitoba, Canada. Professor of English; Poet; Writer. m. M Sharon Nicoll, 21 May 1966. Education: BA, Acadia University, 1962; MA, Dalhousie University, 1964; PhD, Queen's University, Kingston, Ontario, 1976. Appointments: Teacher, Alderwood Collegiate Institute, 1968-69; Assistant Professor, 1969-77, Associate Professor, 1977-82, Professor of English, 1982-, University of Alberta. Publications: Poetry: Land Fall, 1971; A Poem As Long As The Highway, 1971; White, 1972; Song Book, 1973; He And She And, 1974; Visions Of My Grandfather, 1977; Shore Lines, 1979; Vision/Sounding, 1980; The Pirates Of Pen's Chance (with Stephen Scobie), 1981; The Harbingers, 1984; Visible Visions: Selected Poems, 1984; Canadian Poetry Chronicle, 1985. Other: Worlds Out Of Words: The Science Fictions Novels Of Samuel R Delany, 1978; The Maple Laugh Forever: An Anthology Of Canadian Comic Poetry (editor with Stephen Scobie), 1981; Writing Right: New Poetry By Canadian Women (editor with Marni Stanley), 1982;

Tesseracts (editor with Phyllis Gollieb), 1987; B P Nichol And His Works, 1992; Daphne Marlatt And Her Works, 1992; John Newlove And His Works, 1992; Michael Ondaatje, 1993. Memberships: Association of Canadian University Teachers; Co-Chairman, League of Canadian Poets, 1972-74. Address: c/o Department of English, University of Alberta, Edmonton, Alberta T6G 2E5, Canada.

BARDIS Panos D(emetrios), b. 24 Sept 1924, Lefcohori, Arcadia, Greece. Professor of Sociology; Writer; Poet; Editor. m. Donna Jean Decker, 26 Dec 1964, 2 sons. Education: Panteios University, Athens, 1945-47; BA, Bethany College, West Virginia, 1950; MA, Notre Dame University, 1953; PhD, Purdue University, 1955. Appointments: Instructor to Associate Professor of Sociology, 1955-59, Acting Head, Sociology Department, 1958-59, Albion College, Michigan; Associate Professor 1959-62, Professor 1963-, of Sociology, University of Toledo; Editor, Social Science 1959-81, Co-Editor 1970-72, Book Review Editor 1995-, Revue Internationale de Sociologie; Editor, Book Review Editor, International Social Science Review, 1982-; Founder, Editor-in-Chief, International Journal on World Peace, 1983-. Publications: Non-Fiction: The Family in Changing Civilizations, 1967; Encyclopedia of Campus Unrest, 1971; History of the Family, 1975; The Future of the Greek Language in the United States, 1976; The Family in Asia (editor with Man Das), 1978; Sociology as a Science, 1980; History of Thanatology, 1981; Atlas of Human Reproductive Anatomy, 1983; Evolution of the Family in the West, 1983; Global Marriage and Family Customs, 1983; Dictionary of Quotations in Sociology, 1985; Marriage and Family: Continuity, Change and Adjustment, 1988; History of Sociology, 1988; South Africa and the Marxist Movement, 1989; Urania Smiles Now!: Universal Peace and Cosmic Harmony, 1993; Cronus in the Eternal City: Scientific, Social and Philosophical Aspects of Time in Ancient Rome, 1995. Fiction: Ivan and Artemis, novel, 1957. Poetry: Nine Oriental Muses, 1983; A Cosmic Whirl of Melodies, 1985; Ode to Orion: An Epic Poem in Twenty Rhapsodies, 1994; Ho Orionas: To Phengobolema Mias Chrysocentetes Astrothalassas, epic poem, 1996. Contributions to: Numerous publications. Honours: Many poetry awards and prizes. Memberships: American Association for the Advancement of Science; American Sociological Association; American Association of University Professors; Academy of American Poets; International Poets Academy; World Academy of Scholars; International Institute of Arts and Letters; Institut International de Sociologie. Address: 2533 Orkney Drive, Ottawa Hills, Toledo, OH 43606, USA.

BARDWELL (Constan Olive) Leland, b. 25 Feb 1928, India. Writer; Poet; Novelist; Playwright. m. Michael Bardwell, Apr 1947, 4 sons, 2 daughters. Education: Extra Mural, London University, 1949-50. Appointments: Groom; Secretary; Various jobs in London and Birmingham, 1944-46; Teacher, Kilquhanity House School, 1947-49; Various jobs as Teacher in Vocational Studies in Creative Writing. Publications: The Mad Cyclist, 1970; The Fly and The Bedbug, 1984; Dostoyevsky's Grave, 1991. Contributions to: Cyphers; Aquarius; Poetry Ireland; Arena; Irish Times; Translated into French, German, Hungarian and Hebrew. Honours: Awarded Arts Council Bursary, 1979-80; Elected Member, Adsdana, 1982-; Marten Toonder Award for Literature, 1992. Memberships: Chairman, Irish Writers Co-Op Publishing House, Dublin, 1978-82; Irish Writers' Union; Society of Irish Playwrights. Address: Cloonagh, Cloughboley, Ballinfull, Co Sligo, Ireland.

BARGEN Walter, b. 20 July 1948, Fort Bragg, North Carolina, USA. m. Mary Bobette Rose Bargen, 1 son, 1 daughter. Education: BA, cum laude, Philosophy, 1970, MEd, English Education, 1990, University of Missouri. Appointments: Specification Writer; Writer in Residence. Publications: Fields of Thenar, 1980; Yet Other Waters, 1990; Mysteries in The Public Domain, 1990; Rising Waters, 1994; The Vertical River, 1996. Contributions to: Denver Quarterly; Kansas Quarterly; New Letters; Puerto del Sol; New Mexico Humanities Review; Webster Review; Spoon River Quarterly; Farmers Market; Laurel Review; Phantasm; Abraxas; Missouri Review; South Dakota Review. Honours: National Endowment for the Arts Writing Fellowship, 1991; St Louis Poetry Centre Open Competition Prizes, 1991, 1992. Address: PO Box 19, Ashland, MO 65010, USA.

BARLOW Lolete Falck, b. 23 Aug 1932, Mobile, Alabama, USA. Writer. m. John Woodman Bryan Barlow, 13 May 1952, 1 son, 2 daughters. Education: Florida State University, 1950-51. Appointment: Poetry Editor, The Pen Woman Magazine, 1992-. Publication: Unheard Melodies, 1996. Contributions to: Midwest Poetry Review; Negative

Capability; Alexandrian Magazine; Insight, 1985; Anthology of Magazine Verse and Yearbook of American Poetry; Journal Newspapers; How to Write and Publish Poetry, Textbook; Washington Diocese; Chatterbox; Nativity Notes; Knight Kap; Days of Future's Past, Vol 2; Published in Poet's Domain, volumes 4-7. Honours: Della Crowder Miller Memorial Award, 1979; 3rd Place, Alexandria Branch, NLAPW, 1980; 1st Place, Midwest Poetry Gala, 1981; Free Verse, Alex Branch NLAPW, 1982; 2nd Place, Midwest Poetry Gala; 2nd Place, Alex Branch NLAPW Historical, 1983; 1st Place, Midwest Poetry Gala, 1987; Midwest Poetry Honoured Poet Award, 1988; 3rd Place, National Library of Poetry, 1990. Memberships: National League of American Pen Women, Alex Branch President, 1988-90. Secretary, 1982-88; Poetry Society of Virginia. Address: 8902 Bay Avenue, Box 754, North Beach, MD 20714, USA.

BARLOW Timothy Edward, b. 18 April 1952, Calais, Maine, USA. Educator. m. Beverly Marie Peakall, 21 June 1975. Education: BS, summa cum laude, University of Maine at Machias, 1974; MEd, University of Maine at Orono, 1990. Publications: The Golden Treasury of Great Poems, 1988l; New American Poetry Anthology, 1988; World Treasury of Great Poems, 1989; World Treasury of Golden Poems, 1990. Honours: Honourable Mention, New American Contest, World of Poetry, 1987; Golden Poet Award, World of Poetry. 1988, 1989; Honourable Mention, World of Poetry, 1988. Membership: Poetry Fellowship of Maine. Address: RFD No 3, Box 41, Ellsworth, ME 04605, USA.

BARNARD Keith, b. 26 Oct 1950, London, England. Composer; Poet; Teacher of Music and English. Education: AMus, Trinity College of Music, London, 1971; Diplomas, International Writers Association, 1989; International Poets Academy, Madras, India, 1990. Publications: Privately printed booklets; Outer World Poems, 1982; The Sacred Cup, 1982; The Legend of Bran, 1982; The Legend of Fonn, 1983; The Adventures of Fionn Mac Chumail, 1984; Heroes and Rituals, 1984; Dreams of Wisdom, 1986; Visions, 1988; Perspectives, 1989; Dream Soul, 1990; Kingdoms, 1991. Contributions to: East-West Voices; Rising Stars; Samvedana-Creative Bulletin; Poet International; Souvenir Tribute to Professor Saidhana; Canopy, Indian Literary Journal. Memberships: Performing Rights Association; Musicians' Union; New Age Music Association. Address: 13 Platts Lane, London NW3 7NP, England.

BARNES Bruce, b. 3 Mar 1948, Leytonstone, London, England. Legal Advice Worker. Education: LLB, University of London External, 1973; PGCE, University of Keele, 1975. Appointments: Advice Worker: London Borough of Waltham Forest, 1983-90; London Borough of Islington, 1990-92; Nucleus Legal Advice Centre, 1992-. Publication: Four Ways (anthology representing work of 4 poets), 1985. Contributions to: Kudos; Sandwiches; Poetry Wales; Foolscap; Bound Spiral; Doctor's Dilemma; Anthology: Affirming Flame, 1988. Honours: Runner up, Poetry Business Competition, 1988; Hornsey Library Campaign Competition, 1992. Memberships: Poetry Society; Institute of Contemporary Arts; Co-Ordinator, Islington Poetry Workshop; Blue Nose Poets Collective. Address: 19A Marriott Road, London N4 3QN, England.

BARNES Kate, b. 9 Apr 1932, Boston, Massachusetts, USA. Teacher; Writer. Div, 2 sons, 2 daughters. Education: BA, Scripps College, 1952. Appointments: English Literature Teacher, girls' boarding school; Ran riding school; Ghost writer. Publications: Co-author, The Big Golden Book of Horses (children's book); Talking in Your Sleep (small chapbook), 1987; Co-author: book of poetry, 1992. Contributions to: Harper's magazine; New Yorker; New York Herald Tribune; Beloit Poetry Journal; Village Voice. Honour: Included in New Yorker Book of Poems. Address: RR1, Box 1390, Union, ME 04862, USA.

BARNES Mary Jane, b. 23 Apr 1913, Kentucky, USA. Retired English Teacher; Author; Poet. m. (1) Howard A Beattie, 11 Nov 1930, dec, (2) Paul E Barnes, dec, 3 sons, (3) Alexander G Lawson, 1993. Education: AB, Morehead State University; MA, University of Arizona, Tempe; Diploma of Proficiency, Rome, Italy. Appointments: Chairman, Language Arts Department, Liberty Union High School, 13 years; Appeared on KYEL-TV, 1985, 1990; Co-Owner, Publisher and Editor, Emeritus Communications Inc, (3 newspapers), 1992-; Co-Organizer, Readers' Theater, Yuma, Arizona, 1992 and Yuma Live Poets Society, 1994. Publications include: Poems on US radio stations; Edited poetry column for newspaper; Conducted poetry readings; Poetry books: Delta Portraits, 1962, 1972; Rising Tides of Splendour, 1976; Shadows

on April's Hills, 1981; Songs From an Islander, 1982; Naomi and Ruth, 1984; Images, 1988; Another View of Paradise, 1990; Ring of Peace, 1990, 3rd edition in Mandarin, 1992, French, 1992, Spanish, 1993 and Hindu, 1995; Currently writing a book of Haiku on Canadian themes in the Basho style. Contributions to: World Poetry Anthology; Poet Magazine; Yuma Daily Sun and Valley Foothill News, 1991-; The Times, BC, Canada; United States Poets. Honours: Hon DLitt, World Academy of Arts and Culture, 1988; Golden Crown World Poetry Award, World Poetry Research Institute, Korea, 1990; Nominee, Nobel Prize, 1990; Woman of Year, National League of American Pen Women, California, 1993. Memberships include: Associate, Academy of American Poets, 1993-; Committee, Olympoetry Movement, 1994-; President, National League of American Pen Women, Berkeley Branch. Address: 4603 Balfour Road No 36, Brentwood, CA 94513, USA.

BARNES Richard Gordon, b. 5 Nov 1932, San Bernardino, California, USA. Poet; Rubboardist; Dole Professor of English; Director of Creative Writing. m. Patricia Casey, 30 July 1982, 5 sons, 4 daughters. Education: BA, magna cum laude, Pomona College, 1954; AM, Harvard, 1957; PhD, Claremont, 1960. Appointments: Acting Instructor, UC Riverside, 1958-59; Freelance living in Mexico, 1959-61; Pomona College, 1961-. Publications: The Complete Poems of R G Barnes, 1972; 31 Views of San Bernardino, 1975; Hungry Again The Next Day, 1978; Lyrical Ballads, 1979; A Lake on The Earth, 1982; All Sorts of Tremendous Things Can Happen, 1982; A Pentecostal, 1985; The Real Time Jazz Band Songbook, 1990; Few and Far Between, 1994. Contributions to: Antioch Review; Beloit Poetry Journal; Bachy; Buttons; Cage; Canard Anthology; Crosscurrents; Green House; Grove; Harvard Magazine; Horned Toad Gazette; Ironwood; Light Year; Little Creatures; Marilyn; Momentum; Ohio Review; Onthebus; Pacific; Pacific Review; Paris Review; Poetry; Poetry Claremont; Poetry Now; Poetry Project Newsletter; Practices of The Wind; Santa Monica Review; Spectrum; Telephone; World Order; Wormwood Review; Yearbook of Langland Studies; Zyzzyva. Memberships: Phi Beta Kappa; Association of Literary Scholars and Critics. Literary Agent: Writers' Representatives Inc. Address: Department of English, Pomona College, 140 West 6th Street, Claremont, CA 91711, USA.

BARNETT SCHARF Lauren Ileene, b. 9 May 1956, Chicago, Illinois, USA. Editor; Publisher. m. Craig Allen Scharf, 8 April 1979. Education: BA, State of Connecticut Board for State Academic Awards, 1980. Appointments: Editor, Publisher, Lone Star Publications, 1981-. Publications: Stand Up Poems, 1975; The Multi-Billion Dollar Blues, 1990. Contributions to: Numerous books and periodicals. Memberships: Association of Comedy Artists; Society of Professional and Ethical Publishers of Literature. Address: Lone Star Publications, PO Box 29000, No 103, San Antonio, TX 78229, USA.

BARNIE John Edward, b. 27 Mar 1941, Abergavenny, Gwent, Wales. Editor. m. Helle Michelsen, 28 Oct 1980, 1 son. Education: BA, Honours, 1963, MA, 1966, PhD, 1971, Birmingham University; Dip Ed, Nottingham University, 1964. Appointments: Lecturer, English Literature, Copenhagen University, 1969-82; Assistant, then Editor, Planet: The Welsh International, 1985-. Publications: Borderland, 1984; Lightning Country, 1987; Clay, 1989; The Confirmation, 1992; Y Felan a Finnau, 1992; The City, 1993; Heroes, 1996; No Hiding Place, 1996. Contributions to: American Poetry Review; Critical Quarterly; Poetry Wales; New Welsh Review; Anglo-Welsh Review; Kunapipi. Honour: Welsh Arts Council Prize for Literature, for The King of Ashes (a collection of essays), 1990. Memberships: Yr Academi Gymreig; Harry Martinson-Sällskapet; Committee Member, Welsh PEN. Address: Greenfields, Comins Coch, Aberystwyth, Dyfed, Wales.

BARNSTONE Willis, b. 13 Nov 1927, Lewiston, Maine, USA. Scholar; Poet; Novelist; Professor of Comparative Literature. 2 sons, 1 daughter. Education: BA, cum laude, French and Philosophy, Bowdoin College, 1948; MA, High Honours, English and Comparative Literature, Columbia University, 1956; PhD, Distinction, Comparative Literature, Yale University, 1960. Appointments: Assistant Professor of Romance Languages, 1959-62, Wesleyan University; Visiting Professor, various universities, 1967-73; Senior Fulbright Professor, English Literature, Instituto Superior del Profesorado, Profesorado de Lenguas Vivas, Buenos Aires, 1975-76; Senior Fulbright Professor, English and American Literature, Peking Foreign Studies University, 1984-85; Full Professor, Comparative Literature, Spanish and Portuguese, 1966-, Indiana University. Publications: From This White Island, 1959; A Sky of Days, 1967; A Day in The Country, 1971; China Poems, 1976; Stickball on 88th Street, 1978; Overheard, 1979; Ten

Gospels and a Nightingale, 1981; The Alphabet of Night, 1984; Five AM in Beijing, 1987; With Borges on an Ordinary Evening in Buenos Aires, 1992. Honours: Pulitzer Prize for Poetry, 1960, 1977; Cecil Hemley Memorial Award, 1968, Lucille Medwick Memorial Award, 1978, 1982, Gustav Davidson Memorial Award, 1980, 1988, Emily Dickinson Award, 1985, Poetry Society of America: Breakthrough Award, University of Missouri Press, 1976; Colorado Quarterly Annual Poetry Award, 1978; Best Poem of the Year Award, Chicago Review, 1980; W H Auden Award, New York State Arts Council, 1986; National Poetry Competition Award, Chester H Jones Foundation, 1988. Memberships: PEN; Poetry Society of America. Address: Department of Comparative Literature, Indiana University, Bloomington, IN 47405, USA.

BARON Emilio, b. 21 Mar 1954, Almeria, Spain. Professor. Education: BA, 1975, MA, 1976, PhD, 1982, University of Montreal. Appointments: Assistant Professor, University of Waterloo, Canada, 1982-83; Assistant Professor, Queen's University, Kingston, Canada, 1983-90; Universidad de Granada, Spain, 1990-93; Universidad de Almeria, 1993-. Publications: Cuenco de Soledad, 1974; La Soledad, La Lluvia, Los Caminos, 1977; De Este Lado, 1983; Poemas, 1974-1986, 1987; Llegan los Anos, 1993. Contributions to: Poesia Española; Papeles de Son Armadans; Fin de Siglo; Hora de Poesia; Anthos, in English, Canada; Criticism on Poetry (books): Manuel Machado: El Mal Poema, 1984; Agua oculta que ilora (Lorca), 1989; Luis Cenuda: Vida y Obra, 1990; Despues de Cernuda, 1991; Lirismo y Humor, 1992; T S Eliot en Espana, 1996; Poetry Criticism in: Revista Hispanica Moderna; Cuadernos Hispanoamericanos; Cuadernos Americanos; Latin-American Series; Insula; Los Cuadernos del Norte; Anales de Literatura Hispanoamericana; Cuadernos de Traduccion e Interpretacion. Honours: Access 1st, Premio Jorge Guillen, 1979. Membership: Asociacion de Escritores Espanoles. Address: Dept de Filologia Francesa e Inglesa, Universidad de Almeria, 04120 Almeria, Spain.

BARR Marylin Lytle, b. 11 Aug 1920. Poet; Writer. m. Orlando Sydney Barr, 6 Nov 1942, 1 son, 2 daughters. Education: BA, Beecher College, 1942; MA, Bank Street College of Education, 1967; Graduate courses, Syracuse University, Cambridge University, New York University, 1969-77. Appointments: Teacher, Glen Parkway School, New Haven, Connecticut; Teacher, The Chelsea School, New York Board of Education. Publications: Drawn from the Shadows, 1991; Concrete Considerations, 1993. Contributions to: Oxalis; Outloud; Piedmont Literary Review; Catskill Life; Tucumcari Literary Review; Pegasus Review; Poet's Gallery; Zephyr; Poetry Peddler; Confetti; Echoes; Apple Blossom Connection; Poet; S S Calliope; Implosion; Times Herald Almanac; Glens Falls Review; Mohawk Valley USA; Still Night Writings; Blue Light Review; Wide Open; Anthologies and various collections. Honours: Recognition in poetry contests with publication by The Hudson Valley Writers Association, 1988; The Stone Ridge Poetry Society, 1990. Memberships: Alchemy Club; Stone Ridge Poetry Society; Poetry Society of American Poets and Writers Inc; Massachusetts State Poetry Society; Greater Haverhill Poetry Society; North Shore Poets; Catskill Reading Society. Address: PO Box 75, Grahamsville, NY 12740, USA.

BARRETT Cathlene Gillespie, b. 14 Aug 1962, Utah, USA. Poet; Publisher; Editor. m. Kevin Barrett, 29 Aug 1981, 1 son, 1 daughter. Education: College. Appointment: Publisher, Editor, Midge Literary Magazine, 1991-. Contributions to: Anthologies and periodicals. Honours: Golden Poet Award; Honorable Mention, Poet of the Year, Utah State Poetry Society. Membership: Utah State Poetry Society. Address: 2330 Tierra Rose Drive, West Jordan, UT 84084, USA.

BARRIERE William J, (Vassillil Vidor), b. 15 Feb 1936, Canada. Writer; Poet. Education: Loyola College, Montreal; New York Institute of Finance, New York, USA. Publications: Work appears in various periodicals including Scimitar; Song; Vermont Life; American Poetry Journal. Honour: World of Poetry Honorable Mention, National Library of Poetry. Address: Drawer G, Angel Fire, NM 87710, USA.

BARROW Jedediah. See: **BENSON Gerard John.**

BARTLETT Elizabeth, b. 28 April 1924, Deal, Kent, England. Poet. Appointments: West Sussex Health Authority and West Sussex County Council, 1966-86. Appointments: Lecturer, Workers Education Association, Burgess Hill, 1960-63. Publications: A Lifetime of Dying, 1979; Strange Territory, 1983; The Czar is Dead, 1986; Look, No Face,

1991; Instead of a Mass, 1991; Two Women Dancing, 1994. Honours: Cheltenham Poetry Competition Prize, 1982; Arts Council Bursary, 1985; Cholmondeley Award, Society of Authors, 1996. Address: 17 St John's Avenue, Burgess Hill, West Sussex RH15 8HJ, England.

BARTLETT Elizabeth R, b. 20 July 1921, New York, New York, USA. Editor; Literary Director. m. 19 Apr 1943, 1 son. Education: BS, New York Teacher's College, 1941; Graduate Studies, Columbia University, 1941-42. Appointments: Instructor, Speech and Theatre, Southern Methodist University, Dallas, 1946-49; Director, Creative Writers Association, New School for Social Research, 1955; Assistant Professor of English, San Jose State University, 1960-61; Associate Professor, University of California at Santa Barbara, 1962-64; Poetry Editor, ETC, 1963-76; Professor of Creative Writing, San Jose State University, 1979, 1981; Poetry Editor, Crosscurrents, 1983-88; Editor/Director, International Anthology, Literary Olympians, 1992. Publications: Poems of Yes and No, 1952; Behold This Dreamer, 1959; Poetry Concerto, 1961; It Takes Practice Not To Die, 1964; Threads, 1968; Twelve-tone Poems, 1968; Selected Poems, 1970; The House of Sleep, 1975; In Search of Identity, 1977; Dialogue of Dust, 1977; Address in Time, 1979; A Zodiac of Poems, 1979; Memory is No Stranger, 1981; The Gemini Poems, 1984; Candles, 1987; Around the Clock, 1989. Contributions to: US: Harper's Bazaar; Saturday Review; New York Times; Literary Review; Virginia Quarterly; National Forum; Canada: Queen's Quarterly; Windsor Review; Dalhousie Review; Tamarack Review; Antigonish Review; Fiddlehead; Canadian Forum; England: London Times; Orbis; Outposts; Candelabrum; Prospice; Delhi-London Poetry Journal; Westwords. Honours: Writing Fellowships, 1959, 1960, 1961, 1970, 1977, 1979, 1985; Syndicated Fiction Awards, 1983, 1985. Memberships: PSA; PEN International; Author's Guild; International Women's Writing Guild. Address: 2875 Cowley Way No 1302, San Diego, CA 92110. USA.

BARTOLOME Efrain, b. 15 Dec 1950, Ocosingo, Chiapas. Mexico. Poet. m. Guadalupe Belmontes Stringel, July 1986, 1 son, 1 daughter. Appointment: Psychotherapist. Publications: Ojo de Jaguar, 1982; Ciudad Bajo el Relampago, 1983; Musica Solar, 1984; Cuadernos Contra el Angel, 1985; Ojo de Jaguar (augmented edition), 1990; Musica Lunar, 1991; Cantos Para La Joven Concubine, 1991. Contributions to: Vuelta; Proceso; Casa del Tiempo; Sabado; Siempre; Mexico en el Arte; Revista de la Universidad; La Palabra y el Hombre; Periodico de Poesia; La Jornado Semanal. Honours: Premio de Poesia Tuchtlan, 1980; Premio Ciudad de Mexico, 1982; Premio Nacional de Poesia Aguascalientes, 1984; Premio Nacional de Poesia Universidad de Queretaro, 1987. Address: Conkal No 266 (Esq Becal), Colonia Torres de Padierna, 14200 Mexico DF, Mexico.

BARTOSY Francisca Judith, (Judy Bartosy), b. 29 Oct 1929. Budapest, Hungary. Poet; Literary Translator; Reviewer. m. Francis Michael Bartosy, 14 June 1952, 2 sons, 1 daughter. Education: Educated in Budapest; Private tuition in English and German, Bavaria; Studied Creative Writing, Deakin University, 1985; Poetry course, 1986. Appointments: Kindergarten Teacher, 1958-86; Research Librarian at US Military Government, Munich; Typist and Interpreter, Commonwealth Public Service, Melbourne; Assistant Director, Fairyland (private kindergarten), Melbourne. Literary Appointment: Committee Member, Melbourne Poetry Society. Publications: Co-author, Island Roses, book of poetry, 1975; Pebbles, bilingual (Hungarian/English) book of poetry, 1990; From Silver Pines to Blue Gums', book of poetry, 1997. Contributions to: Skyspin (anthology), 1991; Acolades and Jellybeans, anthology, Society of Women Writers, 1992; Patchwork of Poetry, Australian anthology, Vol 3 and 4, 1992, 1994; Reviews in: Australian Multicultural Book Review - Vol 1 No 1, 1993, Vol 2 No 1, 1994, Vol 2 No 2, 1994, Vol 1, 1995; Poem in International Poets, 1993; 20 Poems and Translations, Women in Harmony: An Anthology, 1994; Poem in World Poetry, 1994; Translations of poems by Endre Ady, Hungarian into English, 1994, 1995; A Stitch in The Petal Of A Daisy, anthology, 1995. Honours: Commendation, Melbourne Poetry Society, Poetry Day, Australia, 1990; 1st Prize, Coolum J Interstate Writers Association Competition, 1991; 2 Certificates of Merit, Coolum Writers, 1991; Medallion of Achievement, Melbourne Poetry Society, Australia Day Council, 1991; Award for Best Poem, Society of Women Writers, Australia, Awards Day, 1991. Memberships: Committee Member, Melbourne Poetry Society; Fellowship of Australian Writers; Thursday Poets; Committee Member, Society of Women Writers, Australia, 1993; Australian Literary Translators' Association; Australian Association of Multicultural Writers; Victorian Writers' Centre. Address: 73 Church Road, Carrum, Victoria 3197, Australia.

BARUA Bhaben, b. 27 Nov 1941, Jhaji, Assam, India. m. Mamata Barua, 12 Dec 1970, 2 sons. Education: BA, Calcutta University, 1960; MA, Delhi University, 1963. Appointments: Staff, English Department, Punjabi University, Punjab, and Guwahati University, Assam. Publication: Sonali Jahaj (The Golden Ship), collected poems, 1977. Contributions to: In 3 volumes of collected poems in progress, first due in 1996. Honours: Assam Publication Board Award, 1978; Sahitya Akademie Award, 1979. Membership: Sole Indian Representative, International Writers' Conference in Yugoslavia, 1990. Address: Flat no 402, Swati Apartments, G S Road, Guwahati, India.

BASINGER William Daniel, b. 14 Feb 1952, Washington, District of Columbia, USA. Computer Specialist. m. Mary, 11 June 1988. Education: BA, University MD, 1974; MS, Georgetown University, 1977; MS, Johns Hopkins University, 1989. Appointments: Computer Programmer, Analsyst; Evaluation Technologies, Arlington, Virginia, 1977-78; Vitro Corp, Silver Spring, Maryland, 1978-84; 1987-88; Tracor Applied Sciences, Rockville, Maryland, 1984-88; Planning Research Corporation, McLean, Virginia, 1988-89; George Washington University/SCT, Washington DC, 1989-. Publications: Set Theory and the Monoid, 1977; An Analysis of the Interplay of Condition Parameters and Boolean Functions in Job Control Language, 1982; Discrete Data Modeling and Programming of Causes of Downtime, 1984; Logistic Resource Analysis of Causes of Downtime, 1986; Voice of the Earth: Poem, The Infinite Cosmos, 1995. Honours: Technical Achievement Award, Vitro Corp, 1984. Memberships: Association for Computing Machines; New York Acadamy of Science; American Geographys Union; Statue of Liberty and Ellis Island Foundation. Hobbies: Bible study; Violin; Viola; Poetry; Science Fiction; Bridge; Outdoor activities. Address: 11342 Cherry Hill Road T-203, Beltsville, MD 20705, USA.

BASLER Sabra Jane, b. 6 July 1950, Sacramento, California, USA. Div, 1 daughter. Education: BA, University of California, 1977; MA, California State University, Sacramento, 1984. Appointments: Director, Tooth of Time Books; Registrar, Rare Books and Poetry Collections, University of California, Davis. Publications: Men of Mind, 1990; AH!, 1990; Cycladic Code, 1991; Opening the Gate, 1992. Contributions to: Coyote's Journal; Quercus; Wind Chimes; Poet News; Sierra Journal; Nexus; Colt Drill; Valley Spirit. Memberships: Poets and Writers, New York; AWP; Council for Creative Projects. Address: 1920 Gold Southeast, Albuquerque, NM 87106, USA.

BASS Clara May Overy, (Clara May Overy), b. 11 May 1910, Grimsby, England. Authoress; Poetess; Former Singer; Musician; Artist. m. Donald Lesley Bass, 27 July 1937, 1 son. Education: Training in Music, Ballet and Voice Production. Appointments: Grimsby Amateur Operatics, 1920-45; Proprietor, Ladies' Hairdressing Salon, 1927-37; Singing Teacher, 1945-50; International Committee Member, Centro Studi e Scambi, Rome, Italy; Founder Fellow, International Poetry Society. Publications: Dreams of a Singer, 1963; Parnassus (anthology), 1967; Living Poetry, 1968; Major & Minor, 1975; Reflections, 1985. Contributions to: Collected Poems Anthology; Masters of Modern Poetry, Rome; Anthologies Centro di Cultura; SS Croce, Taranto, Italy; Religious Poetry, 1974, 1977, 1978, 1980, 1981; Ipso Facto; Quaderni di Poesia; Mosaic; Twist; City & Nachine Age Poetry; Orbis; Expression One; Village Review; Nature Poetry. Honours: Diploma di Premiazione Targa, Sheild, Holy Cross, 1977, 1978, 1979; Long Service, Silver Medal, Operatic Society; Diplomas, Piano, singing, 1st Prize Trophy, Premiazione Diploma, Targa Silver Medals. Memberships: Writers Guild of Great Britain; Poetry Society, London. Address: 68 Lestrange Street, Cleethorpes, South Humberside DN35 7HL, England.

BASS Ellen, b. 16 June 1947, Philadelphia, Pennsylvania, USA. Poet; Writer; Educator. 1 son, 1 daughter. Education: BA, Goucher College, 1968; MA, Boston University. Appointments: National Educator in child sexual abuse and healing; Co-founder, Survivors Healing Centre. Publications: No More Masks: An Anthology of Poems by 20th Century Women (Co-editor), 1973; I'm Not Your Laughing Daughter, 1973; Of Seperateness and Merging, 1977; For Earthly Survival, 1980; Our Stunning Harvest, 1985; Co-author, The Courage to Heal: A Guide for Women Survivors of Child Sexual Abuse (self-help book), 1988; Co-editor: I Never Told Anyone: Writings by Women Survivors of Child Sexual Abuse, 1983; Author, I like you to make jokes with me, but I don't want you to touch me (children's book), 1985; Free Your Mind: The Book for Gay, Lesbian and Bisexual Youth and Their Allies (Co-author), 1996. Contributions to: Atlantic Monthly;

Ms; Calyx; Conditions; Sinister Wisdom; Nimrod; Sojourner; Ploughshares. Honours: Elliston Poetry Award, University of Concinnati, 1980; Finalist, William Carlos Williams Award of Poetry Society of America, 1978. Membership National Writers Union. Literary Agent: Charlotte Raymond. Address: PO Box 5296, Santa Cruz, CA 95060, USA.

BASSANI Giorgio, b. 4 Apr 1916, Bologna, Italy. Novelist; Poet. m. Valeria Sinigallia, 1943. Education: University of Bologna. Appointment: President, Italia Nostra, 1966-. Publications: Poetry: Te lucis ante, 1947; Un'altra liberta, 1951; L'alba ai vetri: Poesie 1942-50, 1963; Epitaffio, 1974; In gran segreto, 1979; In rime e senza, 1982; Rolls Royce and Other Poems, 1982. Fiction: Gli ultima anni di Clelia Trotti, 1955; Cinque storie ferraresi, 1956; The Gold-Rimmed Spectacles, 1960; Una notte del '43, 1960; The Garden of the Finzi-Continis, 1965; The Heron, 1970; Behind the Door, 1972; Il romanza di Ferrara, 1974; The Smell of Hay, 1975; Di la dal cuore, 1984; Italian Stories, 1989. Honour: Bagutta Prize, 1983.

BASSO Eric, b. 29 June 1947, Baltimore, Maryland, USA. Novelist; Dramatist; Poet; Essayist; Artist; Photographer; Translator. Education: Catonsville Community College. 1965-67; BSc, Towson State University, 1970. Publications: The Beak Doctor: Short Fiction, Volume One, 1974-75, 1987; A History in Smallwood Cuts, 1990; Equus Caballus, 1991; The Golem Triptych, 1994; Bartholomew Fair, 1997. Contributions to: Chicago Review; Asylum; Central Park; Mr Cogito; Nocturne; Open; Oyez; Cold-drill; Vice Versa; Archer; Amputated Fingers. Address: 3623 Templar Road, Randallstown, MD 21133, USA.

BASU Krishnabasu, b. 17 Nov 1917, Chandernagore, West Bengal, India. College Teacher. m. Aparajito Basu, 22 July 1969, 1 daughter. Education: MA, 1973; PhD, 1986. Appointments: Lecturer; Senior Lecturer. Publications: Sabder Sarir, 1976; Jaler Saralve, 1982; Kardigane Kusum Prastab, 1986; Narsicus Fute Aache, Eka, 1988; Jal Batase Andhakare, 1990. Contributions to: Deshi; Ananda Bazar Patrika; Parichay; Jugantar; Aajkal; Bivab; Prama; Kritibas; Pratikhan; Maha Nagar; Amrita; Ananda Mela; Basumati. Honour: Pratishruti Puraskar, 1981. Address: B 16/8 Kalindi Housing Estate, Calcutta 700 089, India.

BATE John Leonard, b. 27 Dec 1919, London, England. Librarian. m. Margaret Mary Banks, 6 June 1945, 6 sons, 6 daughters. Education: Fellow of Library Association (FLA), 1953; MA, 1961, Dip Ed, 1962, St Andrews University. Appointment: Chief Librarian, Napier Polytechnic of Edinburgh, 1964-85. Publications: Damaged Beauty Needs a New Design, 1981; Florence Nightingale: a Dramatic Poem, 1983; Pictures of Edinburgh, 1984; Tablet-ed: a poem sheet, 1985; Title Deeds: a poem sheet, 1988; The Ballad of Gwen John, revised edition, 1992; Glimpses of a School Year, 1990; Meditations on Simple Themes, 1991; No Stones, No Scorpions, 1993. Contributions to: Tribune; Poetry Review; Orbis; Outposts; The Tablet; The Month. Honour: Member of the Order of the British Empire for Services to Education in Scotland, 1982. Membership: Secretary, School of Poets, Edinburgh, 1981-82. Address: 15 Bowness Avenue, Oxford OX3 0AJ, England.

BATEMAN David Robert, b. 26 Aug 1957, River Hill, Kent, England. Performance Poet; Writer; Tutor. Education: BSc, Honours, Social Studies, Teesside Polytechnic, 1979; Diploma in Psychology, 1981, Diploma in Landscape Interpretation, 1990, University of Liverpool. Appointments: Hospital Cleaner; Printer's Divvy; Co-writer and Performer with Magix Ox outdoor theatre company; Co-writer and Vocalist with poetry-and-music band Petra & The Probes; Ecologist for Landlife Urban Wildlife Unit; Coast Ranger, Sefton Ranger Service; Performance Poet; Stand-up Comedian; Lecturer, creative writing University of Liverpool. Publications: The Ideal God Competition, 1989; David Bateman's Golden Treasury of Dinosaurs, 1993; From Jellybeans To Reprobation, 1996; Curse of the Killer Hedge, 1996. Contributions to: Allusions; Bogg; Caprice; Echo Room; Iron; New Scientist; BBC Radio Merseyside; BBC Radio 1; Shout; Smoke; Numerous small magazines. Honour: 1st Prize, Edinburgh Performance Poetry Competition, 1990. Membership: Performer and Co-organiser with Evil Dead Poets Society. Address: Flat 7, 7 Gambier Terrace, Liverpool L1 7BG, England.

BATEMAN John Henry, b. 16 May 1918, London, England. Educator. m. 1950, 2 daughters. Education: MA, Sidney Sussex, Cambridge, 1946; Diploma of Education with Distinction, London

University, 1948. Appointments: Education Officer, 1948-54; Tutor; Schoolmaster, 1954-63; Lecturer, Senior Lecturer, Manchester Polytechnic, 1963-79. Publications: Verses, and Russia, 1970; Werther, and Wilhelm Begins, 1972; Poems for John Clare and Others, 19734; An Anthology of Student Poetry, Editor, 19174; An Anthology of School Poetry. Editor, 1975. Contributor to: Cambridge Review; Spectrum. Membership: Corresponding Member, Sidmouth Poetry Reading Circle, 1979. Address: 24 Manstone Mead, Sidmouth, Devon EX10 9RX, England.

BATES Scott, b. 13 June 1923, Evanston, Illinois, USA. m. 17 April 1948, 4 sons. Education: BA, Carleton College, 1947; PhD, University of Wisconsin, 1954. Appointments: French Professor, Sewanee, Tennessee, 1954-87; Film Professor, University of the South, 1970-. Publications: The ABC of Radical Ecology, 1982, 1990; Lupo's Fables, 1983; Merry Green Peace, 1991; Songs for the Queen of the Animals, 1992. Contributions to: New Yorker; Furioso; Sewanee Review; Partisan Review; New Republic; Southern Poetry Review; Tennessee Poetry Journal; Lyric; Quixote; Mountain Summer; Diliman Review; Delos. Honours: American Literary Anthology Prize, 1970. Address: Box 1263, 735 University Avenue, Sewanee, TN 37375, USA.

BATSTONE Stephanie, b. 22 Dec 1922, Croydon, Surrey, England. Medical Social Worker. Education: Oxford School Certificate Matric Exemption, 1939; Certificate Social Studies, Southampton University, 1956; Associate, Institute of Medical Social Workers, 1957. Appointments: WRNS, 1943-45; Secretarial, 1945-54; MSW, University College Hospital, Guys Hospital, St Helier Hospital, 1957-75; Retired, 1975. Publications: Poems of The Second World War, 1985; More Poems of The Second World War, 1989. Contributions to: The Tablet, Daily Mail D-Day Supplement. Membership: Associate, The Society of Authors. Address: 39 Beechwood Court, West Street Lane, Carshalton, Surrey SM5 2QA, England.

BAUER Steven (Albert), b. 10 Sept 1948, New Jersey, USA. Professor of English; Writer; Poet. m. Elizabeth Arthur, 19 June 1982. Education: BA, Trinity College, Hartford, Connecticut, 1970; MFA, University of Massachusetts, Amherst, 1975. Appointments: Instructor, 1979-81, Assistant Professor, 1981-82, Colby College, Waterville, Maine; Assistant Professor, 1982-86, Associate Professor, 1986-96, Professor, 1996-, of English, Director of Creative Writing, 1986-96, Internal Director of Creative Writing, 1996-, Miami University, Oxford, Ohio. Publications: Satyrday, novel, 1980; The River, novel, 1985; Steven Spielberg's Amazing Stories, 2 volumes, 1986; Daylight Savings, poems, 1989; The Strange and Wonderful Tale of Robert McDoodle (Who Wanted to be a Dog), children's verse collection, 1997. Contributions to: Essays, stories and poems in many periodicals. Honours: Strouse Award for Poetry, Prairie Schooner, 1982; Master Artist Fellowship Award, Indiana Arts Council, 1988; Peregrine Smith Poetry Prize, 1988. Address: 14100 Harmony Road, Bath, IN 47010, USA.

BAWER Bruce, b. 31 Oct 1956, New York, New York, USA. Poet; Critic. Education: BA, English, 1978, MA, English, 1982, PhD, English, 1983, State University of New York at Stony Brook. Appointment: Literary Editor, Arrival Magazine, 1986-87. Publication: Innocence, 1988. Contributions to: Poetry; Paris Review; New Criterion; Hudson Review; American Scholar; Poetry East; Poetry Northwest; Boulevard; Chelsea; Pequod; Agni; Crosscurrents; Verse; 2 Plus 2; Arizona Quarterly; Kansas Quarterly; Wall Street Journal. Honour: Residency, Djerassi Foundation, 1987. Memberships: Poetry Society of America; PEN; Board of Directors, National Book Critics Circle, 1989-. Address: 425 East 65th Street No 26, New York, NY 10021, USA.

BAYATI Abdal, b. 1926, Baghdad, Iraq. Poet. Education: Baghdad Teachers Training College. Appointment: Cultural Adviser, Ministry of Culture and Fine Arts, Baghdad. Publications: Angels and Devils, 1950; Broken Pitchers, 1954; Glory Be to Children and the Olive Branch, 1956; Poems in Exile, 1957; 15 Poems from Vienna, 1958; 20 Poems from Berlin, 1959; Words That Never Die, 1960; Fire and Words, 1964; The Book of Poverty and Revolution, 1965; That Which Comes and Does Not Come, 1966; Death in Life, 1968; Dead Dogs' Eyes, 1969; The Writing on Clay, 1970; Love Poems on the Seven Gates of the World, 1971; Collected Poems, 1971; Lilies and Death, 1972; The Moon of Shiraz, 1975; The Singer and the Moon, 1976; Eye of the Sun, 1978; Kingdom of the Spike, 1979; Love in the

Rain, 1985; Love, Death and Exile, 1990. Address: c/o Georgetown University Press, Intercultural Center, Room 111, Washington, DC 20057, USA.

BAYBARS Taner, b. 18 June 1936, Nicosia, Cyprus. Education: Turkish Lycee, Nicosia. Appointment: British Council, 1966-88. Publications: Corners of a Handkerchief, 1953; To Catch a Falling Man, 1963; Susila in the Autumn Woods, 1974; Narcissus in a Dry Pool, 1978; Pregnent Shadows, 1981; Co-translator, A Sad State of Freedom by Nazim Hikmet, 1990. Address: c/o MBA Literary Agents, 45 Fitzroy Street, London W1P 5HR, England.

BEAM Jeffrey Scott, b. 4 Apr 1953, Concord, North Carolina, USA. Poet; Library Technical Assistant. Education: Bachelor, Creative Arts in Poetry, University of North Carolina, Charlotte, 1975. Publications: The Golden Legend, 1981; Two Preludes for The Beautiful, 1981; Midwinters Fire, 1990; The Fountain, 1992; Visions of Dame Kind, The Jargon Society, 1995; Anthologies: Son of The Male Muse; Black Men/White Men; Sparks of Fire; Blake in a New Age; Yellow Silk-10th Anniversary Anthology. Contributions to: Carolina Quarterly; Yellow Silk; Dreamworks; Mouth of The Dragon; James While Review; Asheville Review; The Double Dealer Redux. Honour: Emerging Artist Grant, Orange and Durham Counties Art Councils. Memberships: Poets and Writers; North Carolina Writers Network. Address: Golgonooza at Frog Level, 3212 Arthur Minnis Road, Hillsborough, NC 27278, USA.

BEARDSLEY J(ohn) Douglas, b. 27 Apr 1941, Montreal, Quebec, Canada. Writer; Poet; Editor; Reviewer; Teacher. Education: BA, University of Victoria, British Columbia, 1976; MA, York University, Toronto, Ontario, 1978. Appointments: Chief Editor, Gregson Graham Ltd, 1980-82; Senior Instructor, Department of English, University of Victoria, 1981-; Writer, Editor, and Graphic Designer, Osborne, Beardsley and Associates, Victoria, 1982-85; Writer, Editor, and Proofreader, Beardsley and Associates, Victoria, 1985-. Publications: Going Down Into History, 1976; The Only Country in the World Called Canada, 1976; Six Saanich Poems, 1977; Play on the Water: The Paul Klee Poems, 1978; Premonitions and Gifts (with Theresa Kishkan), 1979; Poems (with Charles Lillard), 1979; Pacific Sands, 1980; Kissing the Body of My Lord: The Marie Poems, 1982; Country on Ice, 1987; A Dancing Star, 1988; Editor, The Rocket, The Flower, The Hammer, and Me (anthology of Canadian hockey fiction), 1988; Free to Talk, 1992; Inside Passage, 1993; Wrestling with Angels (Selected Poems, 1960-1995), 1996. Contributions to: Anthologies, newspapers, magazines and periodicals. Honours: Canada Council Arts Award, 1978; British Columbia Book Prize for Poetry Nomination, 1989. Address: 1074 Lodge Avenue, Victoria, British Columbia V8X 3A8, Canada.

BEASLEY Joan Helen Ostrom, b. 27 April 1941, Seattle, Washington, USA. Professor. m. Jon Steven Beasley, 16 July 1965. Education: BA, Latin, Seattle, Washington, 1962; MA, Classics, Seattle, 1963; MA, History, California State University at Long Beach, 1971; PhD, Higher Education, University of Denver, 1985. Appointments: Teaching Assistant, Latin Department, Bryn Mawr College, Bryn Mawr, Pennsylvania, 1963-64; Teacher of Latin, The Annie Wright Seminary, Tacoma, Washington, 1964-65; Teacher of Latin, The Katherine Branson School, Ross, California, 1965-67; Teacher of Latin, English and Yearbook, Redondo Union High School, Redondo Beach, California, 1968-70; Teacher of Latin and History, Bear Creek High School, Morrison Colorado, 1970-71; Substitute Teacher, Douglas County School District, Castle Rock, Colorado, 1982-83; Teacher of Latin, Natrona County High School, Casper, Wyoming, 1991-94; Adjunct Faculty, History, Western Civilization 101 and 102, Castle Rock Campus, Arapahoe Community College, Castle Rock, Colorado, 1994-. Publications: Poetry: Ostie, 1994; Resignation and Renewal, 1994; Teacher, 1994; Eurydice in Me, 1994; Morning Walk, 1994; Josh, 1994; Family Portraits, 1994; Juggernaut, 1994; April on Wolf Creek, 1994; Promethean Cycle, 1994; Shawn, 1994; Family Portraits, 1994; Lockstep, 1994; Together, 1994; The Wifely Poet's Dilemma, 1995; Ecstacy, 1995; Unison, 1995; Perspectives on December, 1996; Coming of Age at 50, 1996; On Living with Beau, 1996; Depression, 1996; Short Prose, Sagebrush Cache, 1996. Honours: Honorable Mention in Poetry Contest, 1994; Editor's Choice, Poetry Contest, 1994; Honorable Mention, 1994; Celebrating Excellence, The 1995 President's Awards, 1995; Fifth Place Winner, 1995; Achieving Excellence, the 1996 President's Awards. Address: 8902 Thunderbird Court, PO Box 4070, Parker, CO 80134, USA.

BEAUMONT Jeanne Marie, b. 15 June 1954, Darby, Pennsylvania, USA. Editor. Education: BA, English, magna cum laude, Eastern College, St Davids, Pennsylvania, 1973-78; MFA, Writing, Columbia University School of the Arts, 1988-89. Appointments: Resident Faculty, The Frost Place Annual Festival of Poetry, 1991-94; Editor, Co-Publisher, American Letters & Commentary, 1992-. Contributions to: Poetry; The Nation; Harpers; Antioch Review; Boulevard; New American Writing; Poetry East; Seneca Review; Southern Humanities Review; Gettysburg Review; 20 others. Honours: Winner, Benjamin T Burns Poetry Contest, 1989; Honorable Mentions, Billee Murray Denny Poetry Awards, 1992, 1993. Membership: Poets House, New York. Address: 120 West 70th Street, New York, NY 10023, USA.

BEAVER Bruce Victor, b. 14 Feb 1928, Australia. Writer. m. Brenda Bellam, 30 Sept 1963. Appointments: Contributing Editor, Poetry Australia. Publications: Under the Bridge, 1961; Seawall and Shoreline, 1964; Open at Random, 1967; Letters to Live Poets, 1969; Lauds and Plaints, 1972; Death's Directives, 1977; Selected Pub Angus and Robertson, 1978; As It Was, 1979; Headlands, 1986; Charmed Lives, 1988; New and Selected Pub, 1991. Contributions to: Sydney Morning Herald; Australian; Meanjin; Southerly; Scripsi; Voices; Bulletin. Honours: Poetry Society Awards, 1964, 1970; Grace Leven Award, 1971; Patrick White Award, 1982; FAW Christopher Brennan Award, 1983; NSW State Literary Awards Special Citation, 1990; AM Award, 1991. Memberships: Contributing Editor, Poetry Australia; Australian Society of Authors. Address: 15/14-16 Malvern Avenue, Manly, New South Wales 2095, Australia.

BECATOROS Stefanos, b. 23 Sept 1946, Athens, Greece. m. Mary, 30 Apr 1977, 1 son. Education: Chemistry, University of Athens; Librarianship, Technological Institute of Athens, 1982-85. Appointments: Librarian, Municipal Library of Athens, Folklore Part, 1975-. Publications: Terra Rossa, 1968; Knowing of One's Fatherland, 1972; Limited Space, 1975; Knowing of One's Fatherland-Collected Poems 1969-1981, 1985; Kithathineon Street, 1991; Wheel with Sky, 1994; Essays: The Spirit of Resistance, 1993; Texts on Culture, Politics. Contributions to: Dentro; Letters and Arts; Planodion; Porphiras; Graphi; Enteuctirion; Parateretes. Memberships: Union of Greek Librarians; Society of Greek Writers. Address: 69a Hippocrates Street, 10680 Athens, Greece.

BECKWITH Merle Ray, b. 16 July 1942, East Grand Rapids, Michigan, USA. Freelance Writer. m. 19 June 1982. Education: BA, Political Science, Western Michigan University, Kalamazoo, 1964; Graduate study in Anthropology and Education, University of California at Los Angeles, 1966-68. Appointments: Peace Corp Volunteer, Nigeria; Teacher, Grand Rapids, Michigan, Public Schools; Instructor, Western Michigan University; Teacher, Metro Adult Education, San Jose, California; Consumer Research, Gallup Polls; Clerk, Association for Retarded Citizens. Publications: Nature and Love, 1980; Nature, 1980; Meditations: a Collection of Contemplative Reflections, 1991. Contributions to: Piedmont Literary Review; Poetry Press; Ursus Press; New Worlds Unlimited Anthologies; Vesta Publications; World of Poetry Anthologies; American Poetry Anthologies; Trouvere's Laureate; Fine Arts Press; Earthwise Poetry Journal; Manna; Wyndham Hall Press Memorial Series; Jean's Journal; Yes Press; Broken Streets; Channels; New Hope International; Silver Wings; Being; A Pilgrim Press Publication; Abingdon Press Publication. Honours: Golden Poetry Award, World of Poetry, Sacramento, 1985, 1986, 1987. Memberships: California State Poetry Society; California Chapparal Poets, Ballard Chapter; Christian Writers League; ASCAP. Address: 3732 Monterey Pine No A109, Santa Barbara, CA 93105, USA.

BECTON Henry Jr, (H B Kamau), b. 21 Nov 1953, Chicago, Illinois, USA. Poet; Playwright; Publisher; Television and Radio; Producer. Education: Antioch College, 1971-74; Kennedy-King City College of Chicago, 1983-84. Appointments: Creative Writing Instructor, Cultural Arts Project, Baltimore, 1977-78, Hyde Park YMCA, Chicago, 1979; Artist-in-Residence, Chicago Council on Fine Arts, 1979-80; Co-ordinator, Writers' Seminar and Poetry Festival, DuSable Museum of African American History, Chicago, 1983; Producer and Host, Chicago Renaissance, Radio Station WHPK, University of Chicago, 1986-87; Host, Book Break, Chicago Access Corporation (cable tv), 1988-. Publication: Editor, Where Men Gather, anthology of 8 men's poetry and prose, 1982. Contributions to: Wooden Angels, anthology of poetry and prose, 1980; Nit and Wit Magazine; Black Book Bulletin; Chicago Literary Review; Chicory; Nurturing News;

Chicago Men's Gathering Newsletter; Chatham-Southeast Citizen Newspaper; Chicago Defender. Honours: Barbara Broome Literary Scholarship for Poetry, Chicago, 1978; Finalist, Walt Whitman Award, Academy of American Poets, 1980. Memberships: American Poetry Society; International Black Writers' Conference; The Perspectivist; Chairperson, The Triumverate. Address: 935 East 50th Street, Chicago, IL 60615, USA.

BEDOLACH Hanna, b. 15 Apr 1931, Israel. Dyslexic Children's Teacher. m. Mr Epshtein, 9 Sept 1949, 2 sons, 1 daughter. Education: Senior Teacher, 1967; BA, Literature, 1980. Appointments: Teacher; Teacher's Tutor in Linguistics Studies. Publications: My Flower-Bed River, 1983; Secure Space, 1986; The Cactus Scheme, 1989; Slow Motion, 1993; Imprisoned City, 1996. Contributions to: Literary columns in: Yediot Achranot; Maariv; Israeli newspapers and literary magazines including: Prose; Mahut; North. Honours: Creators and Researchers Association Prize, 1986-96; Encouragement Award, Literature Art Research Association, 1993; Amos Fund Award, 1996. Memberships: Hebrew Writers Association; Literature Fans Association; Music Association; Poets and Composers Association. Address: 3 Aharon Street, Givat-Shmuel 54019, Israel.

BEECHING Jack. Writer. Publications: Aspects of Love, 1950; Truth is a Naked Lady, 1957; The Polythene Maidenhead, 1970; Images Au Miroir/Mirror Images, 1979; Twenty Five Short Poems, 1982; The View From the Balloon, 1990. Address: c/o Tessa Sayle Agency, 11 Jubilee Place, London SW3 3TE, England.

BEER Ernest M V. See: BREMNER Stephen (Steve) George.

BEER Hilda Doreen, b. 29 Jan 1934, Thorverton, Nr Exeter, Devon, England. m. Wilfred Beer, 7 Sept 1957, 2 daughters. Appointments: Eastmond & Son Limited, Department Stores, Tiverton. Publications: Poems From A Devon Village, 1977, 2nd edition, 1985; Poems of The English Countryside, 1996. Contributions to: Express And Echo; Mid Devon Gazette; This England Magazine And Calenders; Local Focus; Spotlight South West TV; Graham Danton Radio Devon; Review Devon Life; The Golden Book of Poetry; Poetry of The World; Poetry Galaxy; Poetry Now; The South West; Under A Southern Sky; Anthologies; UK 2000 Magazine; Poetry Digest. Address: 10 Broadlands, Thorverton, Nr Exeter, Devon, England.

BEER Patricia, b. 4 Nov 1924, Exmouth, Devon, England. Writer; Poet. m. (2) John Damien Parsons, 1964. Education: BA, University of London; BLitt, St Hugh's College, Oxford. Appointments: Lecturer in English, University of Padua, 1946-48, Ministero Aeronautica, Rome, 1950-53; Senior Lecturer in English, Goldsmith's College, University of London, 1962-68. Publications: Loss of the Magyar and Other Poems, 1959; New Poems (edited with Ted Hughes and Vernon Scannell), 1962; The Survivors, 1963; Just Like the Resurrection, 1967; Mrs Beer's House (autobiography), 1968; The Estuary, 1971; An Introduction to the Metaphysical Poets, 1972; Spanish Balcony, 1973; Reader, I Married Him, 1974; Driving West, 1975; Moon's Ottery, 1978; Poems 1967-79, Selected Poems, 1979; The Lie of the Land, 1983; Wessex, 1985; Collected Poems, 1988. Contributions to: London Review of Books; Listener. Address: Tiphayes, Up Ottery, Near Honiton, Devon, England.

BEESON Diane Kay, b. 3 Sept 1949, Boulder, Colorado, USA. EFL/ESL Teacher; Translator. Education: BA, Lindenwood College, 1972; MA, Middlebury College, 1974; TOEFL Certificate, Fundacion Ponce de Leon, Madrid, Spain, 1981; Diploma, Translation, Institute of Linguists, England, 1987; PhD, Candidate, New York University. Appointments: Professor, Department of English, University of Cluny of Paris, Madrid, 1992-93; Staff Member, English for Banking, Law, Business, Economics and Secretarial Use, Linguacentre Academy, 1984-89; Director, English Classes, Grupo Anaya, 1983-92; Faculty Member, History and West European History, University of Delaware at University of Madrid, 1988-89; Maintenance, Writing conversational and advanced grammar, (ACHNA) Association Cultural Hispano y Norteamericano courses, 1988-92; Interpreter, Translator for companies, Madrid, 1984-94; Staff Member, British Institute for Young Learners, British Council, Madrid, 1994-97. Publications: 8 books (co-author); Translator, 4 books, 2 articles, texts, grammars, readers; Author of 7 articles, 1973-92. Contributions to: Gusto; New England Sampler; Pegasus Review; American Poetry Association; The Voice Within; San Fernando Poetry Journal; Zest, Canada; Broken Streets III; ARC Press; Latin Journal; Mechanics; Driftwood East; Perceptions II Anthology; Tiatis; Valhalla; Parnassus of World Poets, Madras, 1994.

Honours: Outstanding Woman of America, 1975; Joyce Kilmer Contest, Colorado, 1982; Sandcutters, Arizona, 1st Prize monthly, Honourable Mention Annual, 1983; 4th Honourable Mention, Caddo National Writer's Centre, 1987. Memberships: Modern Language Association; Association of Teachers of Spanish and Portuguese; National League of American Pen Women; American Association of University Women; Institute of Linguists; Teachers of English to Speakers of Other Languages, Spain. Address: 1615 South La Canada, Green Valley, AZ 85614, USA.

BEEVERS Mark (Busy), b. 29 Jan 1955, Carlton, North Yorkshire, England. Publications: A Cuckoo in the Coop, 1988; CHRYME, 1988; Ball and Chain, 1988; Black Sheep, 1988; Dark Angel, 1988; Death is My Lady, 1988; Heathen Heart, 1989; Savage Soul, 1989; Turning Over an Old Leaf, 1989; Blank, Broker & Best of Beevers?, 1989; Behind These Shades, 1989; Vicously Fair, 1989; A Lone Wolf's Whistle, 1989; Poetry Partisan, 1989; Driven by Daemons, 1990; Mirroring Madness, 1990; Pagan Pages, 1990; Bards, Bandits, Bohemians, 1990; Jester Years, 1990; Punch Lines, 1990; Unmasked, 1990; Lion of Love, 1991; A Double-Edged Sword, 1991; Both Barrels Blazing, 1991; Scallywag, 1991; De Sade Serenade, 1991; Bewitched, Bemused, Bedevilled & Beguiled, 1991; Hermit's Hot Pot, 1992; Pyrate Potshots, 1992; Gunning for Gurus, 1992; The Dead & The Divine, 1992; Pen Pages, 1992; Sorcery Sauce, 1993; Punch Daze, collection of plays, 1992; Founder, Saltburn Scene, literary magazine, 1992. Contributions to: Evening Gazette; Outlet; Purple Patch; Psychopoetica; Rapture; Top Copy; Peace & Freedom; Welcome; Super Trouper; Thurdays; Krax, White Rose; Exile; Third Half; ET; Tops; Something for Nothing; Cardengate News; Write Around (Cleveland anthology); Radio Cleveland; BBC2 Open Space (television). Honour: 1st Prize, Outlet Magazine Competition. Address: Glenside Cottage, Saltburn, Cleveland, England.

BEHERA Bhagaban, b. 3 Feb 1953, Pathuria, Nayagarh, Orissa, India. Broadcaster. m. Anjali, 3 Feb 1953. Education: MA, Political Science, Delhi University; PhD, J.N.U New Delhi. Appointments: Research Scholar, J.N.U, New Delhi; News Reader, Translator, Oriya Unit, All India Radio. Publications: Two books under print in English and one book in Oriya. Contributions to: Major provincial journals and newspapers. Honour: Invited to Recite at Delhi for The Ancient Tradition of Orissa, 1992. Memberships: Founder, Kalinga Poetry Society, 1996. Address: I-171 Garnali Monalla, Laxmi Nagar, Delhi 110092, India.

BEHLEN Charles (William), b. 29 Jan 1949, Slaton, Texas, USA. Poet. 1 daughter. Education: New Mexico Junior College, 1968-70. Publications: Perdition's Keepsake; Three Texas Poets; Dreaming at the Wheel; Uirsche's First Three Decades; The Voices Under the Floor. Contributions to: Bloomsbury Review; Cedar Rock; New Mexico Humanities Review; Poetry Now; Puerto del Sol; The Smith; Texas Observer. Honours: Pushcart Prize Nomination; Ruth Stephan Reader; Manuscripts Displayed and Placed in Time Capsule by San Antonio Museum of Art. Membership: Texas Association of Creative Writing, Texas Circuit. Address: 501 West Industrial Drive, Apartment 503-B, Sulphur Springs, TX 75482, USA.

BEISSEL Henry, b. 12 Apr 1929, Cologne, Germany. Poet; Dramatist; Writer; Translator; Editor; Teacher. m. (1) 2 daughters, (2) Arlette Francière, 3 April 1981, 1 daughter. Education: University of London, 1949; MA, University of Toronto, 1960. Appointments: Teacher, University of Edmonton, 1962-64, University of Trinidad, 1964-66, Concordia University, Montreal; Founder-Editor, Edge journal, 1963-69. Publications: Poetry: Witness The Heart, 1963; New Wings For Icarus, 1966; The World Is A Rainbow, 1968; Face On The Dark, 1970; The Salt I Taste, 1975; Cantos North, 1980; Season Of Blood, 1984; Poems New And Selected, 1987; Ammonite, 1987; Stones To Harvest, 1987; Dying I Was Born, 1992; Plays: Inook And The Sun, 1974; Goya, 1978; Under Coyote's Eye, 1980; The Noose, 1989; Improvisations For Mr X, 1989. Fiction: Winter Crossing; The Sniper. Other: Kanada: Romantik Und Wirklichkeit, 1981; Raging Like A Fire: A Celebration of Irving Layton, editor with Joy Bennett, 1993; Translations of poetry and plays. Contributions to: Various journals. Honours: Epstein Award, 1958; Davidson Award, 1959; Deustcher Akademischer Austauschdienst Fellowship, 1977; Walter-Bauer Literaturpreis, Germany, 1994. Memberships: International Academy of Poets; President, League of Canadian Poets, 1980-81; PEN; Playwrights Canada. Address: Box 339, Alexandria, Ontario K0C 1A0, Canada.

BEJERANO Maya, b. 23 Feb 1949, Haifa, Israel. Libarian; Teacher. m. Oct 1983, div 1988, 1 daughter. Education: BA, 1973, 1974, MA, 1978, Bar-Ilan University and Hebrew University, Jerusalem. Appointments: Librarian, Teacher, Main Public Library, Tel-Aviv. Publications: Ostrich, 1978; The Heat and the Cold, 1981; Data Processing, 1982; The Song of Birds, 1985; Selected Poems, 1987; Voice, 1987, Whale, 1990. Contributions to: Achjhav; Simon Kria; Jediot-Achronoth newspaper; Davar; Al-Hamishman; Haaretz; Mioznaim Hadarim. Honours: Prize of Levi Eschol, Rosh Hamemshola, 1986 for literature; Hary Harshon Prize for short story, 1976; Bernstein Prize for poetry book, Selected Poems, 1989. Membership: Agudat Aasofrim of Israel.

BELITT Ben, b. 2 May 1911, New York, New York, USA. Professor of Literature and Languages; Poet; Writer. Education: BA 1932, MA 1934, Postgraduate Studies 1934-36, University of Virginia. Appointments: Assistant Literary Editor, The Nation, 1936-37; Faculty Member to Professor of Literature and Languages, Bennington College, Vermont, 1938-. Publications: Poetry: Wilderness Stair, 1955; The Enemy Joy: New and Selected Poems, 1964; Nowhere But Light: Poems, 1964-69, 1970; The Double Witness: Poems, 1970-76; Possessions: New and Selected Poems, 1938-85, 1986; Graffiti, 1990. Other: School of the Soldier, 1949; Adam's Dream: A Preface to Translation, 1978; The Forged Feature: Toward a Poetics of Uncertainty, 1994; Editor and translator of several volumes. Contributions to: Books. Honours: Shelley Memorial Award in Poetry, 1936; Guggenheim Fellowship, 1947; Brandeis University Creative Arts Award, 1962; National Institute of Arts and Letters Award, 1965; National Endowment for the Arts Grant, 1967-68; Ben Belitt Lectureship Endowment, Bennington College, 1977; Russell Loines Award for Poetry, American Academy and Institute of Arts and Letters, 1981; Rockefeller Foundation Residency, Bellagio, Italy, 1984; Williams/Derwood Award for Poetry, 1986. Memberships: Authors Guild; Phi Beta Kappa; PEN; Vermont Academy of Arts and Sciences, Fellow. Address: PO Box 88, North Bennington, VT 05257, USA.

BELL Antoinette, b. 25 Jan 1938, Brentwood, Los Angeles, California, USA. Poet. m. Raymond J Bell, 24 Dec 1971, 1 son, 1 daughter. Education: Liberal Arts, University of California at Los Angeles, 5 years; Certified Youth Advisor; Department of Criminology, University of California at Berkeley. Appointments: Professional Model, 1959; Pacific Telephone Service Representative, 1961; Military Spouse, 1971-88; Poet, 1980-. Publication: The Edge of Vision, 1995. Contributions to: Approximately 100 poems, 2 Spanish language; US Poet; The Sounds of Poetry; California Federation of Chaparral Poets; In the West of Ireland; Fu Jen University; Poets of the Vineyard; World of Poetry; National Library of Poetry; Pipers Song. Honours: Certificate of Merit Shakespeare Sonnet US, 1996; Grand Prize, Pipers Collection, 1995; Eleanor Cox Award, CFCP, 1993; World of Poetry Eight Golden Poets Awards, 1985-92; Six Editor's Choice Awards, National Library of Poetry. Memberships: Ina Coolbirth Circle; The Academy of American Poets; California Federation of Chaparral Poets; Library of Congress Associates, USA; Poets of the Vineyard, CA; United States Poets. Address: 2884 Cypress Way, Fairfield, CA 94533, USA.

BELL Charles Greenleaf, b. 31 Oct 1916, Greenville, Mississippi, USA. Teacher; Writer. Education: BS, University of Virginia, 1936; BA, 1938, LittB, 1939, MA, 1966, University of Oxford, England. Appointment: Tutor Emeritus, St John's College, Santa Fe. Publications: Verse: Songs for a New America, 1953, revised, 1966; Delta Return, 1955, revised, 1969; Five Chambered Heart, 1985; Novels: The Married Land, 1962; The Half Gods, 1968 Other: Film, The Spirit of Rome, 1965; Symbolic History: Through Sight and Sound (40 slide tape/video dramas). Contributions to: Harper's magazine; New Yorker; Atlantic Monthly; Philosophic Essays in Philosophy of Science; Common Cause; Diogenes. Honours: Rhodes Scholarship; Ford Foundation Fellowship; Rockefeller Grant, 1948. Address: 1260 Canyon Road, Santa Fe, NM 87501, USA.

BELL Marvin Hartley, b. 3 Aug 1937, New York, New York, USA. College Professor. m. Dorothy Murphy, 2 sons. Education: BA, Alfred University, 1958; MA, Literature, University of Chicago, 1961; MFA, Literature, University of Iowa, 1963. Appointments: Visiting Lecturer, Goddard College, 1970; Columnist, Homage To The Runner, The American Poetry Review, 1975-78, 1990-92; Visiting Professor, University of Hawaii, 1981, University of Washington, 1982; Flannery O'Connor Professor of Letters, Faculty, Writers Workshop, 1965-, University of Iowa; Lila Wallace Reader's Digest Writing Fellow,

Woodrow Wilson Foundation, 1991-92, 1992-93. Publications: A Probable Volume of Dreams, 1969; The Escape Into You, 1971, 1974; Residue of Song, 1974; Stars Which See, Stars Which Do Not See, 1977, 1992; These Green-Going-To-Yellow, 1981; Co-author, Segues: A Correspondence in Poetry, 1983; Old Snow Just Melting: Essays and Interviews, 1983; Drawn By Stones, by Earth, by Things That Have Been in The Fire, 1984; New and Selected Poems, 1987; Iris of Creation, 1990; The Book of The Dead Man, 1994, A Marvin Bell Reader poems, journals, memoirs and essays, 1994; Everpresence: The Book of the Dead Man, Vol 2, forthcoming; Selected Poems, forthcoming. Contributions to: New Yorker; Nation; Poetry; American Poetry Review; Antioch Review; Antaeus; North American Review; Ploughshares; Crazyhorse; Verse; Zyzzyva; Anthologies: The Longman Anthology of Contemporary American Poetry, 1950-1980, 1983, Contemporary American Poetry, 1985, 1991, 1996, The Norton Introduction to Poetry, 1986, 1989, The Best American Poetry, 1990, The Vintage Book of Contemporary American Poetry, 1990. Honours include: Guggenheim Fellowship, 1977; National Endowment of the Arts Fellowships, 1978 and 1984; Flannery O'Connor Professorship for Letters, University of Iowa, 1986; Honorary Doctorate of Letters, Alfred University, 1986; Senior Fulbright Scholar to Yugoslavia, 1983 and Australia 1986; Award in Literature, American Academy of Arts and Letters, 1994. Address: Writers Workshop, University of Iowa, Iowa City, IA 52242, USA.

BELL Robin, b. 4 Jan 1945, Dundee, Scotland. Poet. 2 daughters. Education: MA, St Andrew's University, Scotland; MS, Columbia University, USA. Appointments: Publishing and University Teaching, New York, London and Edinburgh, 1968-82. Publications: The Invisible Mirror, 1965; Culdee, Culdee, 1966; Sawing Logs, 1980; Strathinver, 1984; Radio Poems, 1989; Editor: The Best of Scottish Poetry, 1989, Collected Poems of the Marquis of Montrose, 1990, Bittersweet Within My Heart, The Collected Poems of Mary, Queen of Scots. Contributions to: Many publications. Honours: Best Documentary, Television and Radio Industries of Scotland Award, 1984; Best British Radio Feature, Sony Award, 1985. Membership: Secretary, Poetry Association of Scotland, 1983-. Address: 38 Dovecot Road, Edinburgh EH12 7LE, Scotland.

BELL Sy(lvia) M(arie Dobbs), b. 16 Aug 1952, Harrodson County, Mississippi, USA. Freelance Writer; Photographer; Author. m. 24 Nov 1968, 2 sons. Education: Diploma Cumberland Academy. Appointment: Advisory Board Member, Southern Poetry Association. Publications: Memories, 1988; Thorns & Roses, 1990. Contributions to: Arkansas Gazette; Sun Herald; Mississippi Magazine; Poets of Now; Southern Poetry Association; WOP; APA; White Birches Magazine. Honours: 5 Golden Poetry Awards, 1987-91; Canterbury Productions, 4 Merit Awards; Blue Ribbon Award, Southern Poetry Association; WOP, 43 Awards; Writers Unlimited, 15 Awards. Memberships: Gulf Coast Writer's Association; Poets of Now; Bell's Letters; Southern Poetry Association; National Federation of State Poetry Societies Inc. Address: 1419 Georgia Place, Gulfport, MS 39507, USA.

BELLIVEAU Cynthia Judy, b. 17 Sept 1974, Brandon, Manitoba, Canada. Student. Appointments: Attending College, 1996; Cashier, 1993-96. Contributions to: National Poetry Association, And Time Stood Still (anthology), 1994; Daily Herald, 1994; Oatmeal and Poetry, 1995. Address: 1982 13th Street West. Prince Albert, Saskatchewan S6V 3K5, Canada.

BELLOTTI Antonio, b. 20 May 1959, Algeciras. Spain. Sculptor; Poet. m. Feb 1983, 1 son, 1 daughter. Education: BA, Honours, Essex, 1987; MA, Cambridge. Publication: The Established Order of Words and Things, 1991. Contributions to: Rialto; North; Oxford Poetry; Smiths Knoll; Odyssey; Spoils Anthology; Bradford Poetry; Staple. Membership: Poetry Society, London. Address: 101 High Street, Cherry Hinton, Cambridge CB1 4LU, England.

BELLUOMINI Ronald Joseph, b. 19 July 1946, Chicago, Illinois, USA. Teacher. m. Marilyn Naselli, 27 Sept 1969, 2 sons. Education: BS, Education, MA, Geography, Chicago State University. Appointment: Teacher, 1968-. Publication: The Thirteenth Labor, 1985. Contributions to: Menagerie, 1985; Rhino, 1986; Menagerie, 1989; FOC Review, 1990. Honour: Robert and Hazel Ferguson Memorial Award, Friends of Literature, 1986. Membership: Poetry Society of America. Address: 1721 Juliet Lane, Libertyville, IL 60048, USA.

BELOOF Robert Lawrence, b. 30 Dec 1923, Wichita, Kansas, USA. University Professor. m. Ruth M La Barre, 14 June 1946, div 1972, 4 sons. Education: BA, Friends University, 1946; MA, Middlebury College, 1948; MA, 1948, PhD, 1954, Northwestern University. Appointments: Assistant Professor, Associate Professor, Professor, University of California, Berkeley, 1948-89; Fulbright Professor of American Literature, Instituto Orientale, 1960-61; Chairman, Department of Rhetoric, 1964-69. Publications: The One-Eyed Gunner, 1956; Good Poems, 1973; The Children of Venus and Mars, 1974. Contributions to: Poetry, Chicago; Saturday Review of Literature; Humanist; Poetry Review; Recurrence; Variegation; University of Kansas City Review; Arena; Western Humanities Review; Poetry Quarterly; Shenandoah; Perspective; Dalhousie Review; Window; Contact; Listen; New Departures. Honours: Atlantic Monthly Scholarship, 1946; Elinor Frost Scholarship, 1947; Committee for Creative Arts, Fellowships, 1963. Address: 1613 Josephine Street, Berkeley, CA 94703, USA.

BELSKY Robert William, b. 14 Mar 1952, New York, New York, USA. Writer; Poet. Education: Nassau County School of PN, 1979; Portland Community College, 1982. Appointments: Nurse, Freelance Poet, Writer, 1979-84; Special Education Teacher, Part-time Poet and Writer, 1984-88; Writer, 1988-. Publications: An Autumn's Day, 1984; At the End of the Rainbow, 1984; A Step Into the Land of Thought, 1985. Contributions to: Silver Syllables, 1989; Rainbows and Roses, 1987; Poet's Memorable Songs, 1988; Impressions, 1986; A Time to be Free, 1989' The Poets Handbook, 1987; Seasons, 1987; Bluebells and Other Dreams, 1988; Glowing Embers, 1984; Heart Songs, 1987; Moments, Moods & Memories, 1987; New Poets, 1984; Chasing Rainbow, 1988; Lyrical Classics, 1987; American Anthology of Southern Poetry, 1989. Honours: Golden Poetry Award, 1988; Silver Poetry Award, 1989. Memberships: PEN; American Academy of Poets; Poetry Society of New Hampshire; New Hampshire Writer's Association. Address: 5 'C' Street, Hudson, NH 03051, USA.

BEN JELLOUN Tahar, b. 1 Dec 1944, Fez, Morocco. Writer; Poet; Dramatist. m. Aicha Ben Jelloun, 8 Aug 1986, 1 daughter. Education: University of Rabat, 1963-68; PhD, University of Paris, 1975. Publications: Fiction: Harrouda, 1973; La Réclusion solitaire, 1976, English translation as Solitaire, 1988; Moha le fou, Moha le sage, 1978; La Priere de l'absent, 1981; Muha al-ma'twah, Muha al-hakim, 1982; L'Ecrivain public, 1983; L'Enfant de sable, 1985, English translation as The Sand Child, 1987; La Nuit sacrée, 1987, English translation as The Sacred Night, 1989; Jour de silence a Tanger, 1990, English translation as Silent Day in Tangier, 1991; Les Yeux baissés, 1991. Poetry: Hommes sous linceul de silence, 1970; Cicatrices du soleil, 1972; Le Discours du chameau, 1974; La Memoire future: Anthologie de la nouvelle poesie du Maroc, 1976; Les Amandiers sont morts de leurs blessures, 1976; A l'insu du souvenir, 1980; Sahara, 1987; La Remontée des cendres, 1991. Plays: Chronique d'une solitude, 1976; Entretien avec Monsieur Said Hammadi, ouvrier algerien, 1982; La Fiancée de l'eau, 1984. Non-Fiction: La Plus Haute des solitudes: Misere sexuelle d'emigres nord-africains, 1977; Haut Atlas: L'Exil de pierres, 1982; Hospitalité francaise: Racisme et immigration maghrebine, 1984; Marseille, comme un matin d'insomnie, 1986; Giacometti, 1991. Honours: Prix Goncort, 1987; Chevalier de la Légion d'Honneur, 1988; Prix des Hemispheres, 1991. Address: 27 Rue Jacob 75, Paris 6, France.

BENDER Kathie Jane, (Kathie Kali), b. 3 Oct 1954, Dayton, Ohio, USA. Artist; Musician. m. James Leach, 3 Dec 1983. Appointments: Lead Singer: Smegmarines, 1984; Suicide Pact, 1986; Antiband, 1987-; Kali and the Thugs, 1996. Publication: Sex, Death and the Devil, 1993. Address: PO Box 69401, West Hollywood, CA 90069, USA.

BENDON Chris(topher Graham), b. 27 Mar 1950, Leeds, Yorkshire, England. Freelance Writer; Critic. m. Sue Moules, 30 Aug 1979, 1 daughter. Education: BA, English, St David's University College, Lampeter, 1980. Appointments: Clerk in various offices, 1966-76; Hellenic Cruise Staff, WF & RK Swan Ltd, 1971-76; Chairman, SDUC Rag Committee, 1977-78; President, SDUC Literary Society, 1979-80; Editor, Spectrum Magazine, 1983-88. Publications: Books: In Praise of Low Music, 1981, 1982; Software, 1984; Matter, 1986; Cork Memory, 1987; Ridings Writings - Scottish Gothic, 1990; Constructions, 1991; Perspective Lessons, Virtual Lines..., 1992; Jewry, 195; Crossover, 1996. Chapbooks: Testaments, 1983; Quanta, 1984; Aetat 23, 1985; The Posthumous Poem, 1988; A Dyfed Quartet, 1991. Contributions to: The Guardian; Poetry Review; Stand; London

Magazine; Bete Noir; Rialto; Anglo-Welsh Review; Acumen; Resurgence; Iron; Poetry Cumbria; Poetry Nottingham; New Welsh Review; Poetry Wales; Planet; Poetry Australia; Poetry Canada Review; California State Poetry Quarterly; Prospice; New England Review; Bread Loaf Quarterly; Stride; Owl; Lines Review; Chapman; Margin; Verse; Green Book; Anthologies: Orange Dove of Fiji; The Scottish Dog; Outposts 50th Anniversary; The Third Day; The Urgency of Identity. Honours: Hugh MacDiarmid Memorial Trophy, 1st Prize, Scottish Open Poetry Competition, 1988; £1000 Prize, Guardian/WWF Poetry Competition, 1989; £500 Award, The Royal Literary Fund, 1991. Memberships: The Welsh Academy; Welsh Union of Writers. Address: 14 Maesyderi, Lampeter, Dyfed, SA48 7EP, Wales.

BENEDICT Elinor, b. 4 June 1931, Chattanooga, USA. Writer; Editor. m. Samuel S Benedict, 3 Oct 1953, 2 sons, 1 daughter. Education: BA, Duke University, 1953; MA, Wright State University, 1977; MFA, Vermont College, 1983. Appointments: Staff Writer, Times Publications, Kettering, Ohio, 1969-76; Editor, Passages North, 1979-89; Part-time Instructor, Writers Workshop, Bay de Noc Community College, 1977-86; Freelance Writer and Poet, 1979-. Publications: Landfarer, 1978; A Bridge To China, 1983; The Green Heart, 1995; Chinavision, 1995; Editor, Passage North Anthology, 1990. Contributions to: Christian Science Monitor; Pennsylvania Review; Southern Humanities Review; Helicon Nine; Sing Heavenly Muse; Hayden's Ferry Review; Eclectic Literary Review. Honours: Michigan Council for the Arts Creative Artist Award, 1985; American Association of University Women Individual Grant Award, 1983; First Place, National Writers Union Poetry; Illinois Writers Inc Chapbook Award, 1993. Memberships: Poets & Writers; Poetry Society of America; The Academy of American Poets. Address: 8627 South Lakeside Drive, Rapid River, MI 49878, USA.

BENEDIKT Michael, b. 26 May 1935, New York, New York, USA. Writer; Poet; Critic; Editor. Education: BA, New York University, 1956; MA, Columbia University, 1961. Appointments: Professorships in Literature and Poetry, Bennington College, 1968-69, Sarah Lawrence College, 1969-73, Hampshire College, 1973-75, Vassar College, 1976-77, Boston University, 1977-79; Contributing Editor, American Poetry Review, 1973-; Poetry Editor, Paris Review, 1974-78. Publications: The Body, verse, 1968; Sky, verse, 1970; Mole Notes, prose poems, 1971; Night Cries, prose poems, 1976; The Badminton At Great Barrington Or Gustav Mahler And The Chattanooga Choo-Choo, poems, 1980; Anthologies: Modern French Theatre: The Avant-Garde, Dada And Surrealism (with George E Wellwarth), 1964, UK edition as Modern French Plays: An Anthology From Jarry To Ionesco, 1965; Post-War German Theatre (with George E Wellwarth), 1967; Modern Spanish Theatre (with George E Wellwarth), 1968; Theatre Experiment, 1968; The Poetry Of Surrealism, 1975; The Prose Poem: An International Anthology, 1976. Contributions to: Agni Review; Ambit; Art International; Art News; London Magazine; Massachusetts Review; New York Quarterly; Paris Review; Partisan Review; Poetry. Honours: Guggenheim Fellowship, 1968-69; Bess Hokin Prize, 1969; National Endowment for the Arts Prize, 1970; Benedikt: A Profile, critical monograph, Festschrift, 1978; National Endowment for the Arts Fellowship, 1979-80; Retrospective, Library of Congress, videotape, 1986. Memberships: PEN Club of America; Poetry Society of America. Address: 315 West 98th Street, No 6 A, New York, NY 10025, USA.

BENGTSON (John) Erik (Robert), b. 21 July 1938. Degerfors, Sweden. Teacher. m. Peggy Lundberg, 26 July 1963, 2 daughters. Education: MA, Uppsala University, 1964. Appointments: Teacher, Sundstagymnasiet, Karlstad. Publications: I somras, 1963; Orfeus tolv sanger, 1963; Som en a, 1964; Pep Talk, 1977; 10 novels. Honours: Various literary prizes. Address: Hantverkaregatan 12, 654 60 Karlstad, Sweden.

BENJAMIN David. See: SLAVITT David R(ytman).

BENNETT John M(ichael), b. 12 Oct 1942, Chicago, Illinois, USA. Poet; Librarian. m. C Mehrl Bennett, 3 children. Education: BA, cum laude, Spanish & English, 1964, MA, Spanish, 1966, Certificate of Competence in Latin American Studies, 1966, Washington University, St Louis; PhD, Spanish, University of California, Los Angeles, 1970; Certified Poetry Therapist, National Association for Poetry Therapy, 1985. Appointments: Editor, Lost and Found Times, 1974-; Latin American Bibliographic Assistant and Editor, Ohio State University, 1976-; Volunteer Poetry Therapist, Central Ohio Psychiatric Hospital, 1978-86; Publisher, Editor, Luna Bisonte Productions, 1974-.

Publications: White Screen, 1976; Nips Poems, 1980; Jerks, 1980; Blender, 1983; Antpath, 1984; No Boy, 1985; Co-author, Ax Tongue, cassette, 1986; Cascade, 1987; Stones in The Lake, 1987; Twitch, 1988; Swelling, 1988; Milk, 1990; Was Ah, 1991; Fenestration, 1991; Somation, 1992; Pod King, cassette, 1992; Blind On The Temple, 1993; Autophagia, cassette, 1993; Wave, 1993; Blanksmanship, 1994; Just Feet, 1994; Spinal Speech, 1995; Fish, Man, Control, Room, 1995. Contributions to: Poetry, word art, graphics, articles, reviews and translations to numerous publications; Readings and performances in many galleries, bookstores and universities in USA and Canada; Participant in numerous group shows worldwide; Curated exhibition, Tampon d'Artistes, Musée de la Poste, Paris, France, 1995. Honours: 10 Ohio Arts Council Awards, 1979-95. Address: 137 Leland Avenue, Columbus, OH 43214, USA.

BENNETT (Simone) Louise, b. 7 Sept 1919, Kingston, Jamaica. m. Eric Coverley. Education: Royal Academy of Dramatic Art, London. Career: Resident Artist, BBC (West Indies Section), 1945-46, 1950-53; Residencies in Coventry, Huddersfield and Amersham, England; Drama Specialist, Jamaica Social Welfare Commission, 1955-60; Lecturer, Drama and Jamaican Folklore, University of West Indies, Kingston, 1959-61; Lecturer, TV and Radio Commentator. Publications: Dialect Verses, 1940; Jamaican Dialect Verses, 1942; Jamaican Humour in Dialect, 1943; Miss Lulu Sez, 1948; Anancy Stories and Dialect Verse, 1950; Laugh with Louise, 1960; Jamaica Labrish, 1966; Anancy and Miss Lou, 1979; Selected Poems, 1982; Aunty Roachy Seh, 1993; Recordings: The Honorable Miss Lou, 1981; Miss Lou Live, 1983. Honours: Order of Jamaica; Member of the Order of the British Empire; Silver Musgrave Medal, Institute of Jamaica; Norman Manly Award of Excellence, University of West Indies. Address: Enfield House, Gordon Town, St Andrew, Jamaica.

BENNETT Michael Andrew, b. 8 Feb 1945, Southampton, Hampshire, England. English Teacher. Education: AIST, 1966; ONC Sciences, 1968; HND Chemistry, 1973; BEd Honours, English, 1984; LRPS, 1991. Appointments: Laboratory Technician; Social Worker/Playleader, Adventure Playgrounds; Research Technician; English Teacher. Publications: Then Came the Dove, 1980; Mornings and Other Trees, 1990; Feathers, 1992; Tracks, 1992. Contributions to: Acumen; Delhi London Poetry Quarterly; Envoi; Envoi Anthologies, 1988-90; First Time; NATE Newsletter; Orbis; Outposts; Articles in Schools Poetry Review; English in Education. Memberships: Poetry Society; Schools Poetry Association; NAEA; WIG; National Poetry Foundation. Address: 3 Wellington Avenue, Hounslow, Middlesex TW3 3SY, England.

BENNETT Paul (Lewis), b. 10 Jan 1921, Gnadenhutten, Ohio, USA. Professor of English (Retired); Poet; Writer; Gardener; Orchardist. m. Martha Jeanne Leonhart, 31 Dec 1942, 2 sons. Education: BA, Ohio University, 1942; AM, Harvard University, 1947. Appointments: Instructor, Samuel Adams School of Social Studies, Boston, 1945-46; Teaching Assistant, Harvard University, 1945-46; Instructor in English, University of Maine, Orono, 1946-47; Instructor to Professor of English ,1947-86, Poet-in-Residence, 1986-. Denison University; Gardener and Orchardist, 1948-; Consultant, Aerospace Laboratories, Owens-Corning Fiberglass Corp, 1964-67, Ohio Arts Council, 1978-81, Ohio Board of Regents, 1985-86. Publications: Poetry: A Strange Affinity, 1975; The Eye of Reason, 1976; Building a House, 1986; The Sun and What It Says Endlessly, 1995. Novels: Robbery on the Highway, 1961; The Living Things, 1975; Follow the River, 1987. Contributions to: Many periodicals. Honours: National Endowment for the Arts Fellowship, 1973-74; Phi Beta Kappa; Pi Delta Epsilon; Significant Achievement Award, Ohio University, 1992. Address: 1281 Burg Street, Granville, OH 43023, USA.

BENSLEY Connie, b. 28 July 1929, London, England. Writer. m. J A Bensley, 2 Aug 1952, 2 sons. Education: Diploma Social Sciences, London University, 1962. Publications: Progress Report, 1981; Moving In, 1984; Central Reservations, 1990; Choosing to be a Swan, 1994. Contributions to: Times Literary Supplement; Spectator; Observer; Poetry Review. Honours: Tate Gallery Poetry Competition 2nd Place, 1995; Times Literary Supplement Poetry Competition, 1st Place, 1986; Leek Poetry Competition, 2nd Place, 1988; Prizewinner, Arvon/Observer Poetry Competition, 1994. Memberships: Poetry Society; PEN; Poetry Editor, PEN Magazine, 1984-85. Address: 49 Westfields Avenue, Barnes, London SW13 0AT, England.

BENSON Gerard John, (Jedediah Barrow), b. 9 Apr 1931, London, England. Writer. m. (2) 1 son, 1 daughter, (3). Education:

Rendcomb College; Exeter University; Diplomas, Distinction, Drama and Education, Central School of Speech and Drama; Diplomas, Distinction, Drama and Education, London University; IPA First Class. Appointments: Senior Lecturer, Central School of Speech and Drama, London; Former Resident Tutor, Arvon Foundation and Taliesin Centre; Arts Council Poet-in-Residence at Dove Cottage for The Wordsworth Trust, 1994-. Publications: Name Game, 1971; Gorgon, 1983; Editor, This Poem Doesn't Rhyme, 1990, 1992; Editor, 100 Poems on The Underground, 1991; The Magnificent Callisto, 1993; Editor, Poems on The Underground, illustrated edition, 1992, 5th edition, 1995; Editor, Does W Trouble You?, 1994-95; Evidence of Elephants, 1995; In Wordsworth's Chair, 1995; Lone Poems on the Underground, 1996; Editor and Participating Poet, Poems on The Underground, audio-cassette, 1995. Contributions to: New Statesman; Times Literary Supplement; TES; Spectator; Anglo-Welsh Review; Aquarius; Strawberry Fare; New Humanist; Literary Review; The Page. Honours: Signal Award for Poetry, 1991; His book, In Wordsworth Chair, put on internet, Shareware, as a completely new poetry initiative, 1995; Evidence of Elephants, nominated for the Carnegie Medal, 1996. Memberships: Past Chairman, National Association of Writers in Education; Barrow Poets; Poems on the Underground; Writers' Guild; Poetry Society's Education Advisory Panel. Literary Agent: John McLaughlin of Campbell, Thomson, McLaughlin. Address: 46 Ashwell Road, Manningham, Bradford, West Yorkshire BD8 9DU, England.

BENSON Judi (Lamar Parish), b. 20 Dec 1947, Coronado, California, USA. Poet; Artist; Editor. m. Ken Smith, 6 July 1981, 1 son. Education: BA, Literature and Communications, University of North Florida; MA, Creative Writing, Antioch University, London. Appointments: Public Relations Director, Jacksonville Symphony Orchestra, 1975-78; Assistant Director and Creative Writing Tutor, Antioch University, London, 1980-87; Freelance Writer and Artist, 1987-; Editor, Foolscap Magazine, 1987-96; Writer-in-Schools, Huddersfield, World Poetry Festival, 1995. Publications: Making The Family Again, 1987; Somewhere Else, 1990; In The Pockets of Strangers, 1993; Co-Editor, Klaonica: Poems for Bosnia, 1993; Editor, What Poets Eat, food-related poems and recipes, 1994; Co-Editor, The Long Pale Corridor, 1996. Contributions to: Kalliope; Atlantic Review; Ambit; Orbis; Writing Women; The Rialto; Iron; Neon Clouds; Harry's Hand; Foolscap; Sunk Island Review; Bete Noire; Staple; Slow Dancer; Affirming Flame, anthology; Broadsheet Series; Arts Assembler; Time for Verse, BBC Radio 4 broadcast; Stanza; Poetry Please. Honours: 1st Prize, Jacksonville Arts Festival, 1976; Reader's Choice, Orbis Magazine, 1986; Honourable Mention, Staple Competition, 1989. Address: 78 Friars Road, East Ham, London E6 1LL, England.

BENSON Steve, b. 14 June 1949, Princeton, New Jersey, USA. Proofreader. Education: BA, Yale College, 1971; MFA, University of California at Irvine, 1973; MA, The Wright Institute. Publications: As Is, 1978; The Busses, 1980; Blindspots, 1980; Dominance, 1984; Briarcombe Paragraphs, 1984; Blue Book, 1989; Reverse Order, 1990. Contributions to: Oblek; Poetics Journal; Temblor; Avec; Tasted Screens and Parallels; New American Review; Writing; Raddle Moon. Honour: National Endowment for the Arts Poetry Fellowship, 1990. Address: 507 Cottekill Road, Stone Ridge, NY 12484, USA.

BENZING Rosemary Anne, b. 18 Sept 1945, South India. Teacher; Counsellor; Freelance Journalist. m. Richard Benzing, 5 Apr 1969, 1 son, 1 daughter. Education: BA, Honours, English and Philosophy, University College of North Wales, Bangor, 1968; Diploma in Education, 1969; Diploma in Counselling, 1990. Appointments: Teacher, Edward Shelley High School, Walsall, 1968-71; Babies, 1971-80, Supply Teacher, Shropshire LEA, 1980-; Counsellor, SRCC, 1988-. Contributions to: Hybrid; Foolscap; Folded Sheets; Smoke; Borderlines; Envoi; First Time; Purple Patch; Shropshire Magazine; Plowman; White Rose; Poetry Nottingham; Symphony; Psycho Poetica; Third Half; Krax; Bare Wires; Housewife Writers' Forum. Honour: Anglo Welsh Poetry Competition, 1986. Membership: Poetry Society. Address: Roden House, Shawbury, Shrewsbury, Shropshire, England.

BEOBIDE Isabel, b. 12 June 1942, Barcelona, Spain. Poet. 3 sons, 3 daughters. Appointments: President of European Arts Academy; Dutch National Committee and International Public Relations. Publications: Donner sa Main, 1974; Poetes Face à La Vie, 1976; Cuaderno Literario Azor, 1981; Poetes sans Frontieres, 1987; International Poetry Yearbook, 1992. Contributions to: Revues

Poetiques Cumbres; Alto Malon; El Molino de Viento; Periodicals: El Eria, Ayuda, Atalaya, Clarin; Newspapers: Diario de Las Palmas, Spain, Perigree, Netherlands, Volkskrant, Netherlands, La Religion, Venezuela. Honours: Honorary Diploma Mencion, Netherlands; Honorary Academic Award, Hispanic Cultural Centre, 1981; Special Recognition Diploma, Netherlands, 1984; 2nd Prize Diploma, Netherlands, 1984; Certificate of Participation, Puerto Rico, 1988; Silver Medal, AEA Paris, 1990; Gold Medal, AEA Paris, 1991; Gold Medal, International, AEA Luxembourg, 1991; Bronze Medal, HALAF, 1991; Silver Medal, International, AEA Belgium, 1992. Memberships: Agustin Garcia Alonco Centro Cultural Literario y Artistico, Spain; AEA; Poetry Writers Association. Address: Klieverink 814, 1104 KC Amsterdam, Netherlands.

BEREKIZ Juan. See: AZPITARTE ROUSSE Juan.

BERESFORD Anne. See: HAMBURGER Anne (Ellen).

BERG Hans (Cornelisten), b. 24 Dec 1938, Netherlands. Poet; Writer; Editor. Appointments: Lecturer, Art Academy, Arnhem; Writer-in-Residence, University of Texas; Editor, Raster, Grid, literary journals. Publications: Poetry: Gedichten, 3 volumes, 1969; White Shaman, 1973; Poetry of the Aztecs, 1972; Va-banque, 1977; Semblance of Reality, 1981; Texas Elegies, 1983; Songs of Anxiety and Despair, 1988. Novels: Zelfportret met witte muts, 1985; Het geheim van een oppewekt humeur, 1986. Other: The Defence of Poetry, essays, 1988; Prose Books; Books of Myths and Fables of Arctic Peoples; Numerous Poetry Translations. Contributions to: Periodicals. Honours: Van der Hoogt Prize, 1968; Prose Prize, City of Amsterdam, 1971. Memberships: PEN; Society of Dutch Literature. Address: c/o Meulenhoff Publishers, PO Box 100, 1000 AC Amsterdam, Netherlands.

BERG Stephen (Walter), b. 2 Aug 1934, Philadelphia, Pennsylvania, USA. Poet; Writer; Editor. m. Millie Lane, 1959, 2 daughters. Education: University of Pennsylvania; Boston University; BA, University of Iowa, 1959; Indiana University. Appointments: Teacher, Temple University, Philadelphia, Princeton University, Haverford College, Pennsylvania; Professor, Philadelphia College of Art; Poetry Editor, Saturday Evening Post, 1961-62; Founding Editor (with Stephen Parker and Rhoda Schwartz), American Poetry Review, 1972-. Publications: Poetry: Berg Goodman Mezey, 1957; Bearing Weapons, 1963; The Queen's Triangle: A Romance, 1970; The Daughters, 1971; Nothing in the Word: Versions of Aztec Poetry, 1972; Grief: Poems and Versions of Poems, 1975; With Akmatova at the Black Gates: Variations, 1981; In It, 1986; First Song, Bankei, 1653, 1989; Homage to the Afterlife, 1991; New and Selected Poems, 1992; Oblivion: Poems, 1995; Editor: Naked Poetry: Recent American Poetry in Open Forums (with Robert Mezey), 1969; Between People (with S J Marks), 1972; About Women (with S J Marks), 1973; The New Naked Poetry (with Robert Mezey), 1976; In Praise of What Persists, 1983; Singular Voices: American Poetry Today, 1985; Other: Sea Ice: Versions of Eskimo Songs, 1988. Contributions to: Periodicals. Honours: Rockefeller Centro Mexicano de Escritores Grant, 1959-61; National Translation Center Grant, 1969; Frank O'Hara Prize, Poetry magazine, 1970; Gugenheim Fellowship, 1974; National Endowment for the Arts Grant, 1976; Columbia University Translation Center Award, 1976. Address: 2005 Mount Vernon Street, Philadelphia, PA 19130, USA.

BERGAN Brooke, b. 6 Dec June 1945, Indianapolis, Indiana, USA. Writer; Editor. Education: BA, English, Marian College, Indianapolis, Indiana, 1967; MA, English, 1973; PhD, English, 1989, University of Illinois, Chicago. Literary Appointments: Technical Writer, 1973-76, Senior Editor, 1976-82, Managing Editor, 1982-86, Executive Editor, 1986-94, Associate Director of Publications, 1994-, University of Illinois, Chicago; Lecturer, Newberry Library, Chicago, 1989-; Literary Editor, Private Arts, 1992-. Publications: Windowpane, 1974; Distant Topologies, 1976; Storyville: A Hidden Mirror, 1994. Contributions to: The American PEN; Another Chicago Magazine; Private Arts; The Yale Lit. Honours: Illinois Arts Council Literary Award, 1975; Illinois Arts Council Writer-In-Residence, 1976-77, 1977-78; Fellowship, Illinois Arts Council, 1986; Runner-Up, George Bogin Memorial Award, Poetry Society of America, 1991. Address: 1150 North Lake Shore Drive 19F, Chicago, IL 60611, USA.

BERGÉ Carol, b. 4 Oct 1928, New York, New York, USA. Fiction Writer; Poet; Editor; Publisher; Antiques Dealer. m. Jack Henry Berge, June 1955, 1 son. Education: New York University; New School for

Social Research, New York City. Appointments: Editor 1970-84, Publisher 1991-. CENTER Magazine and Press; Distinguished Professor of Literature, Thomas Jefferson College, Allendale, Michigan, 1975-76; Instructor, Goddard College, 1976; Teacher, University of California Extension Program, Berkeley, 1976-77; Associate Professor, University of Southern Mississippi, 1977-78; Editor, Mississippi Review, 1977-78; Visiting Professor, University of New Mexico, 1978-79, 1987; Visiting Lecturer, Wright State University, Dayton, Ohio, 1979, State University of New York at Albany 1980-81; Proprietor, Blue Gate Gallery of Art and Antiques, 1988-; Editor-Publisher, Center Press, 1991-93. Publications: Fiction: The Unfolding, 1969; A Couple Called Moebius, 1972; Acts of Love: An American Novel, 1973; Timepieces, 1977; The Doppler Effect, 1979; Fierce Metronome, 1981; Secrets, Gossip and Slander, 1984; Zebras, or, Contour Lines, 1991. Poetry: The Vulnerable Island, 1964; Lumina, 1965; Poems Made of Skin, 1968; The Chambers, 1969; Circles, as in the Eye, 1969; An American Romance, 1969; From a Soft Angle: Poems About Women, 1972; The Unexpected, 1976; Rituals and Gargoyles, 1976; A Song, A Chant, 1978; Alba Genesis, 1979; Alba Nemesis, 1979. Other: LIGHT YEARS, The New York City Coffeehouse Poets of the 1960's, 1997. Reportage: The Vancouver Report, 1965. Contributions to: Literary periodicals, Anthologies, Art and Antiques magazines. Honours: New York State Council on the Arts CAPS Award, 1974; National Endowment for the Arts Fellowship, 1979-80. Memberships: Authors League; MacDowell Fellows Association; National Press Women; Poets & Writers. Address: 562 Onate Place, Santa Fe, NM 87501, USA.

BERGESEN Charles Racine, b. 21 Apr 1922, Stavanger, Norway. Shipowner. m. (1) Herdis Bryne, 1946, (2) Anne Marie Aanestad, 26 Sept 1964, 4 sons, 1 daughter. Education: Market Gardener, 1945. Appointments: Market Gardener on Firm, 1945-53; Partner Sigval Bergesen (Shipping), 1953-96; Swedish Consul 1955; Consul General for Sweden, 1982-84; French Consul, 1966-78. Publications: Oh Time, My Time (under pseudonym), 1986; Underway, 1990; Summer Flowers and Thistles, 1992; The Sensitive Plant, poems by P B Shelley, translated into Norwegian; Labyrinths, 1994; That I May Live (translated into English), 1996. Memberships: Chairman Stavanger Defense Association, 1955-60; Chairman, Stavanger Conservative Party, 1959-61; Member of board, Rogaland Conservative Party, 1960-64; Vice President Norwegian Defense Association, 1962-63; Chairman, Stavanger Shipowners Association, 1963-65, 1970-71, 1976-77; Member of Board, Norwegian Shipowners Association, 1972; Vice President, 1974-75, President, 1976-77; Chairman, Shipping Employers Association, 1976-77. Address: Ramsvik 50 D, 4015 Stavanger, Norway.

BERGHASH Rachel, b. 14 Nov 1935, Jerusalem, Israel. Teacher. m. Mark Berghash, 21 Jan 1962, 2 sons. Education: Rubin Academy of Music, Jerusalem, 1955-59; MSW, Yeshiva University, 1991. Appointments: Producer, A World Elsewhere, programme featuring poets and writers, WBAI-FM, New York, 1983-87. Contributions to: Images; Chicago Review; Pulp; Blue Unicorn; Bitterroot; Jewish Frontier; Waterways; Anima. Membership: Poets and Writers Inc. Address: 7 East 20th Street, New York, NY 10003, USA.

BERGMAN David, b. 13 Mar 1950, Fitchburg, Massachusetts, USA. English Professor. Education: BA, Kenyon College, 1972; MA, 1974, PhD, 1977, Johns Hopkins University. Appointment: English Professor, Towson State University, 1978-. Publications: Cracking the Code, 1985; Gaiety Transfigured, 1991. Contributions to: American Scholar; New Criterion; New Republic; Poetry; Paris Review; Raritan; Yale Review. Honours: Donor Award, American Society for Arts and Letters, 1982; Towson State Prize for Literature, 1985; George Elliston Poetry Prize, 1985. Memberships: MLA; Poetry Society of America. Address: 3024 North Calvert Street, Apt C5, Baltimore, MD 21218, USA.

BERGONZI Bernard, b. 13 April 1929, London, England. Author; Poet; Professor of English Emeritus. Education: Blitt, 1961, MA, 1962, Wadham College, Oxford. Appointments: Senior Lecturer 1966-71, Professor of English 1971-92, Professor Emeritus 1992-, University of Warwick, Coventry. Publications: The Early H G Wells, 1961; Heroes' Twilight, 1965, 2nd edition, 1980; Innovations: Essays on Art and Ideas, 1968; T S Eliot: Four Quartets: A Casebook, 1969; The Situation of the Novel, 1970, 2nd edition, 1979; T S Eliot, 1972, 2nd edition, 1978; The Turn of a Century, 1973; H G Wells: A Collection of Critical Essays, 1975; Gerard Manley Hopkins, 1977; Reading the Thirties, 1978; Years: Sixteen Poems, 1979; Poetry 1870-1914, 1980; The

Roman Persuasion (novel), 1981; The Myth of Modernism and Twentieth Century Literature, 1986; Exploding English, 1990; Wartime and Aftermath, 1993; David Lodge, 1995. Address: 19 St Mary's Crescent, Leamington Spa CV31 1JL, England.

BERKSON William Craig (Bill), b. 30 Aug 1939, New York, New York, USA. Poet; Critic; Editor; Teacher. m. Lynn O'Hare, 17 July 1975, 1 son, 1 daughter. Education: Brown University, 1957-59; Columbia University, 1959-60; New School for Social Research, New York City, 1959-61; New York University Institute of Fine Arts, 1960-61. Appointments: Instructor, New School for Social Research, 1964-69; Editor and Publisher, Big Sky Magazine and books, 1971-78; Adjunct Professor, Southampton College, Long Island University, 1980; Associate Professor, Graduate Seminars, California College of Arts and Crafts, 1983-84; Instructor, Marin Community College, 1983-84; Professor and Coordinator of Public Lectures Program, San Francisco Art Institute, 1984-; Poetry Editor, Video & the Arts, 1985-86; Contributing Editor, Zyzzyva, 1987-92; Corresponding Editor, Art in America, 1988-; Visiting Artist/Scholar, American Academy in Rome, 1991. Publications: Poetry: Saturday Night: Poems 1960-61, 1961; Shining Leaves, 1969; Two Serious Poems and One Other (with Larry Fagin), 1972; Recent Visitors, 1973; Hymns of St Bridget (with Frank O'Hara), 1975; Enigma Variations, 1975; Ants, 1975; 100 Women, 1975; The World of Leon (with Ron Padgett, Larry Fagin and Michael Brownstein), 1976; Blue is the Hero, 1976; Red Devil, 1983; Lush Life, 1983; Start Over, 1984. Criticism: Ronald Bladen: Early and Late, 1991. Editor: Frank O'Hara: In Memory of My Feelings, 1967; Best and Company, 1969; Alex Katz (with Irving Sandler), 1971; Homage to Frank O'Hara, with Joe LeSueur, 1978; Special De Kooning Issue, Art Journal, with Rackstraw Downes, 1989. Contributions to: Anthologies and periodicals. Honours: Poets Foundation Grant, 1968; Yaddo Fellowship, 1968; National Endowment for the Arts Fellowship, 1980; Briarcombe Fellowship, 1983; Artspace Award for New Writing in Art Criticism, 1990. Memberships: International Art Critics Association; PEN West. Address: 787B Castro Street, San Francisco, CA 94114, USA.

BERLANDT Herman Joseph, b. 7 May 1923, Chelm, Poland. Writer; Editor; Publisher; Administrator. m. 27 Sept 1967, 1 son, 2 daughters. Education: AA, University of California; Self Educated. Appointments: Programme Director, International Festivals Inc, New York City, 1965-67; Editor, Poets Commune Publications, 1969-71; Director of 16 Poetry-Film Festivals, 1975-91; Editor of Poetry, USA, 1985-90; Chairman of Board of Directors, National Poetry Association, 1987-; Received grant for workshop for senior citizens, A Stampede of Memories, Marin Arts Council, 1995-96; Publisher and Editor, Mother Earth International. Publications: I Spent One Lifetime Dancing, 1972; Poems from the Delphi EpiCentre, 1978; The Street Vendor (a scenario for the poetry-documentary), 1979; Yu-Me Love Songs, 1986; A Musical Offering, 1990; Soviet Poetry Since Glasnost (Editor of American Samizdat Edition), 1990; Uniting the World Through Poetry, international anthology, 1991; A Hippie Garden of Verses, 1992; In Praise of The Muses, 1994; Suicide Meditations, 1995; 50 Years Married To The Muse, Collected Poems, forthcoming; Publisher and Editor, Mother Earth International. Contributions to: Poetry; Poetry Flash; Three Penny Poets; The Folio. Honours: Ambassador for Poetry, Medallion, Artists Embassy Annual Award, 1990; Marin Arts Council Grant, 1995. Memberships: Founding Chairman, Chairman, 1987-93, National Poetry Association; PEN, Oakland; Artists Embassy International; Programme Director, Literary Section, Commonwealth Club. Address: c/o National Poetry Association, Fort Mason Centre, Building D, San Francisco, CA 94123, USA.

BERLIND Bruce, b. 17 July 1926, Brooklyn, New York, USA. Writer. m. (1) 2 sons, 3 daughters, (2) Jo Anne Pagano, 17 Jan 1985. Education: AB, Princeton University, 1947; MA, 1950, PhD, 1958, Johns Hopkins University. Appointments: Instructor to Professor, 1954-88, Charles A Dana Professor of English Emeritus, 1988-, Colgate University. Publications: Co-Editor, Bred in The Bone: An Anthology of Verse, 1945; Three Larks For a Loony, 1957; Ways of Happenings, 1959; Companion Pieces, 1971; Selected Poems of Agnes Nemes Nagy, translations, 1980; Birds and Other Relations: Selected Poetry of Dezso Tandori, translations, 1987; Co-Translator, Through the Smoke: Selected Poetry of Istvan Vas, 1989; Imre Oravecz's When You Became She, translations, 1994. Contributions to: Encounter; London Magazine; Stand; New Letters; Poetry; Transatlantic Review; TriQuarterly; Chicago Review; Paris Review; Grand Street; New England Review; Kenyon Review; Translation Review; Honest Ulsterman; Massachusetts Review; American Poetry

Review. Honours: Fulbright Award for Translation, 1984; Hungarian PEN Memorial Medal, 1986. Memberships: Poetry Society of America; PEN American Centre; American Literary Translators Association. Address: Box 237, Hamilton, NY 13346, USA.

BERMAN Cassia, b. 5 Apr 1949, New York, New York, USA. Writer; Teacher. Education: BA, Sarah Lawrence College, 1970; Certified Qi Healer, Qi Gong Therapist, Chinese Healing Arts Center, 1991, 1994. Appointments: New York City CETA Arts Project; Poet-in-Residence, many community organizations. Publication: Divine Mother Within Me, 1995. Contributions to: American Poetry Review; Divine Mosaic; Women's Images of The Sacred; Mothers of the Universe; Visions of the Goddess; Tantric Hymns of Enlightenment. Memberships: Member of the Board, SRV Retreat Center; Founding Member of the Board, Vedautic Light. Address: 11 1/2 Tannery Brook Road, Woodstock, NY 12498, USA.

BERNARD Chris, b. 26 Jan 1943, Lyon, France. Teacher. m. Gabrielle Farge, 2 Aug 1969, 2 sons. Education: Baccalaureat, University of Lyon, 1961. Appointments: President, Poesie Vivante, 1988; Director, Portique (publication), 1991. Publications: Soleil de Prieres; L'Amour en-vers; La Maison de N, 1991; Le Vol des Abeilles, 1986; Trois Perles d'Ame; Le Poete Sourire, 1988; Poemes d'Azur, 1992; Respirs, Grand Prix, 1994. Contributions to: Sciences et Avenir; L'Inconnu; Le Monde; L'Etrave; Albatros; L'Art et Poesie. Honours: Gold Medal, Internationale d'Arts et Lettres, 1992; Grand Poetry Prize, Festival de Nyons, 1988; Gold Medal de l'Education Sociale, 1989; Rene Boisleve Prize; Medaille d'Argent de la Poesies Contemporaraire Francaise; Charles Baudelaire Prize; Prix de Poesie Libre; Prix du Sonnet; Honorary Doctorate, Interamerican University of Humanistic Studies, 1989. Memberships: Academie International de Lutece; Societaire des Poetes Francais. Address: Le Theron, 84110 Puymeras, France.

BERNARD Oliver Owen, b. 6 Dec 1925, Chalfont St Peter, Buckinghamshire, England. Writer. 2 sons, 2 daughters. Education: BA, Goldsmiths College, 1953; ACSD, 1971. Appointments: Copywriter, Notley Advertising, 1958-64; English Teacher, Suffolk and Norfolk, 1964-74; Advisory Teacher of Drama, Norfolk Education Committee, 1974-81. Publications: Country Matters, 1960; Rimbaud collected poems, translating editor and introduction, 1961; Apollinaire selected poems, translator, 1965, new expanded edition, 1983; Moons and Tides, 1978; Poems, 1983; Five Peace Poems, 1985; The Finger Points at the Moon, translation, 1989; Salvador Espriu: Forms and Words, 1990; Getting Over It, autobiography, 1992; Quia Amore Langneo, translation, 1995. Contributions to: Poetry Chicago; Encounter; Botteghe Oscure; Times Literary Supplement; New Statesman; Spectator; Listener; Ambit; New Poetry; Only Poetry; North; Mabon; Child Education; Jerusalem Post. Honour: Poetry Society Gold Medal for Verse Speaking. Memberships: Poetry Society; William Morris Society. Literary Agent: Aitken & Stone, 29 Fernshaw Road, London SW10 0TG, England. Address: 1 East Church Street, Kenninghall, Norwich NR16 2EP, England.

BERNSTEIN Charles, (Claude Amber), b. 4 Apr 1950, New York, New York, USA. Professor of Poetry and Poetics; Poet; Writer; Editor. m. Susan Bee Laufer, 1977, 1 son, 1 daughter. Education: AB, Harvard College, 1972. Appointments: Freelance Writer in the medical field, 1976-89; Visiting Lecturer in Literature, University of California at San Diego, 1987; Visiting Professor of English, Queens College, City University of New York, 1988; Faculty and Series Coordinator, Wolfson Center for National Affairs, New School for Social Research, New York City, 1988; Visiting Butler Professor of English, State University of New York at Buffalo, 1989; Lecturer in Creative Writing, Princeton University, 1989, 1990; David Gray Professor of Poetry and Letters, State University of New York at Buffalo, 1990-. Publications: Poetry: Asylums, 1975; Parsing, 1976; Shade, 1978; Poetic Justice, 1979; Senses of Responsibility, 1979; Legend (with others), 1980; Controlling Interests, 1980; Disfrutes, 1981; The Occurence of Tune, 1981; Stigma, 1981; Islets/Irritations, 1983; Resistance, 1983; Veil, 1987; The Sophist, 1987; Four Poems, 1988; The Nude Formalism, 1989; The Absent Father in Dumbo, 1990; Fool's Gold (with Susan Bee), 1991; Rough Trades, 1991; Dark City, 1994; The Subject, 1995; Republics of Reality: Poems 1975-1995, 1996. Essays: Content's Dream: Essays 1975-1984, 1986; A Poetics, 1992. Editor: L=A=N=G=U=A=G=E (with Bruce Andrews), 4 volumes, 1978-81; The L=A=N=G=U=A=G=E Book (with Bruce Andrews), 1984; The Politics of Poetic Form: Poetry and Public Policy, 1990; Clone Listening: Poetry and the Performed Word, 1997. Contributions to: Numerous

anthologies, collections and periodicals. Honours: Phi Beta Kappa, 1972; William Lyon Mackenzie King Fellowship, 1980; Guggenheim Fellowship, 1985; University of Auckland Foundation Fellowship, 1986; New York Foundation for the Arts Fellowship, 1990, 1995; ASCAP Standard Award, 1993-95. Address: Poetics Program, Department of English, 438 Clemens Hall, State University of New York at Buffalo, Buffalo, NY 14260, USA.

BERROA Rei, b. 11 Mar 1949, Dominican Republic. Professor of Spanish Literature. Education: Diploma, Consejo Superior de Investigaciones Científicas, Madrid, 1977-78; MA, 1977, Middlebury College, Vermont and Madrid, Spain; MA, 1980, PhD, 1983, University of Pittsburgh, Pennsylvania. Appointments: Assistant Professor of Spanish and Latin American Literature, Humboldt State University, California, 1982-83; Blackburn College, Illinois, 1983-84; Associate Professor of Modern Spanish Literature, Stylistics and Literary Criticism, George Mason University, Virginia, 1984-. Publications: Retazos para un traje de tierra, 1979; En el reino de la ausencia, 1979; Los otros, 1983; Libro de los fragmentos, 1989; Book of Fragments, India, 1992. Contributions to: Compass; El Arco y la Lira; Isla Abierta; Cuadernos de Poetica; Cuadernos Americanos; Ahora!; Discurso Literario; Revista de Poeticas; Revista Mexicana de Cultura; Mundo; Problemas y Confrontaciones; Cuadernos Hispanoamericanos; Insula. Honours: Recorded a selection of his poetic works for the Library of Congress Poetry Archives, 1987; Readings at several councils, libraries and universities; Poet-in-Residence, Cincinnati Conference of Literature, and Oklahoma State University, 1985. Memberships: Vice-Editor for Creative Writing, Discurso Literario, 1988-; Editorial Board, Gradiva: Revista Literaria, 1987-; Editorial Board of Codice: Revista de Poeticas, 1987-; Poetry Society of America, 1991-; Latin American Writers Institute, New York, 1990-. Address: 3505 Spring Lake Terrace, Fairfax, VA 22030, USA.

BERRY Francis, b. 23 Mar 1915, Ipoh, Malaysia. Poet; Writer; Professor Emeritus. m. (1) Nancy Melloney Graham, 4 Sept 1947, 1 son, 1 daughter, (2) Eileen Marjorie Lear, 9 April 1970. Education: University College of South West, 1937-39, 1946-47; BA, University of London, 1947; MA, University of Exeter, 1949. Appointments: Professor of English Literature, University of Sheffield, 1967-70; Professor of English, Royal Holloway, University of London, 1970-80. Publications: Gospel of Fire, 1933; Snake in the Moon, 1936; The Iron Christ, 1938; Fall of a Tower, 1943; The Galloping Centaur, 1952; Murdock and Other Poems, 1955; Poets' Grammar, 1958; Morant Bay and Other Poems, 1961; Poetry and the Physical Voice, 1962; Ghosts of Greenland, 1966; The Shakespeare Inset, 1966; I Tell of Greenland, 1977; From the Red Fort, 1984; Collected Poems, 1994. Contributions to: Periodicals; BBC; Observer; Notes; Queries. Membership: Fellow, Royal Society of Literature. Address: 4 Eastgate Street, Winchester, Hampshire SO23 8EB, England.

BERRY Ila, b. 9 June 1922. Poet; Writer. Education: AA, Fullerton College, California; BA, John F Kennedy University, Orinda, California; MA, English and Creative Writing, San Francisco State University, 1985. Publications: Poetry: Come Walk With Me, 1979; Rearranging the Landscape, 1986; Rowing in Eden, 1987; Behold the Bright Demons, 1993. Contributions to: Periodicals. Honours: Jessamyn West Creative Award, 1969; Woman of Distinction, Fullerton College, 1969. Memberships: California Federation of Chaparral Poets, Robert Frost Chapter; California State Poetry Society; California Writers Club; Ina Coolbrith Circle, president, 1977-79; National League of American Pen Women. Address: 761 Sequoia Woods Place, Concord, CA 94518, USA.

BERRY Jake, b. 16 June 1959, Florence, Alabama, USA. Poet. Education: Graduate, Brooks High School, 1977; Northwest Alabama Junior College, University of North Alabama, International Bible College. Appointments: Editor, Outré (Literary Journal); Editor, Anomaly (An Audio and Print Literary Journal); Editor, The Experioddicist (A Print and Electronic Literary Journal). Publications: Species of Abandoned Light, 1995; Brambu Drezi, 1994; Phaseostrophes, 1995; Equations, 1991; The Tongue Bearer's Daughter, 1990; Unnon Theories, 1989; Psyclstomp, 1989; Hairbone Stew, 1988; Idiot Menagerie, 1987; The Pandemonium Spirit, 1986. Contributions to: Rolling Stone; Central Park; Poetry USA; Taproot Review; Heaven Bone; Juxta; Lost and Found Times; Antenynn; New Orleans Review; Score. Address: PO Box 2113, Florence, AL 35630, USA.

BERRY James, b. 1925, Fair Prospect, Jamaica. Poet; Writer; Editor. Publications: Bluefoot Traveller: An Anthology of West Indian Poets in Britain, editor, 1976; Fractured Circles, 1979; News for Babylon: The Chatto Book of West Indian-British Poetry, editor, 1984; Chain of Days, 1985; The Girls and Yanga Marshall, stories, 1987; A Thief in the Village and Other Stories, 1988; Don't Leave an Elephant to Go and Chase a Bird, 1990; When I Dance, poems, 1991; Ajeema and His Son, 1992. Honours: C Day-Lewis Fellowship; Poetry Society Prize, 1981; Boston Globe/Horn Book Award, 1993. Address: c/o Hamish Hamilton Ltd, 27 Wrights Lane, London W8 5TZ, England.

BERRY Wendell, b. 5 Aug 1934, Henry County, Kentucky, USA. Writer; Poet; Professor. m. Tanya Amyx Berry, 29 May 1957, 1 son, 1 daughter. Education: BA, 1956, MA, 1957, University of Kentucky. Appointments: Instructor, Georgetown College, 1957-58; E H Jones Lecturer in Creative Writing, 1959-60; Visiting Professor of Creative Writing, 1968-69; Stanford University; Assistant Professor, New York University, 1962-64; Faculty Member 1964-77, Professor, 1987-93, University of Kentucky; Elliston Poet, University of Cincinnati, 1974; Writer-in-Residence, Centre College, 1977; Bucknell University, 1987. Publications: Fiction: Nathan Coulter, 1960, revised edition, 1985; A Place on North, 1967, revised edition, 1985; The Memory of Old Jack, 1974; The Wild Birds, 1986; Remembering, 1988; The Discovery of Kentucky, 1991; Fidelity, 1992; A Consent, 1993; Watch With Me, 1994; A World Lost, 1996. Poetry: The Broken Ground, 1964; Openings, 1968; Findings, 1969; Farming: A Handbook, 1970; The Country of Marriage, 1973; Sayings and Doings, 1975; Clearing, 1977; A Part, 1980; The Wheel, 1982; Collected Poems, 1985; Sabbaths, 1987; Sayings and Doings and an Eastward Look, 1990; Entries, 1994; The Farm, 1995. Non-Fiction: The Long-Legged House, 1969; The Hidden Wound, 1970, revised edition 1989; The Unforeseen Wilderness, 1971, revised edition, 1991; A Continuous Harmony, 1972; The Unsettling of America, 1977; Recollected Essays 1965-1980, 1981; The Gift of Good Land, 1981; Standing by Words, 1983; Home Economics, 1987; What Are People For?, 1990; Harlan Hubbard: Life and Work, 1990; Standing for Earth, 1991; Sex, Economy, Freedom and Community, 1993; Another Turn of the Crank, 1995. Honours: Guggenheim Fellowship, 1962; Rockefeller Fellowship, 1965; National Institute of Arts and Letters Award, 1971; Jean Stein Award, American Academy of Arts and Letters, 1987; Lannan Foundation Award for Non-Fiction, 1989; T S Eliot Award, Ingersoll Foundation, 1994; Award for Excellence in Poetry, The Christian Century, 1994; Harry M Caudill Conservationist Award, Cumberland Chapter, Sierra Club, 1996. Address: Lanes Landing Farm, Port Royal, KY 40058, USA.

BERTOLINO James, b. 4 Oct 1942, Hurley, Wisconsin, USA. Poet; Writer; University Teacher. m. Lois Behling, 29 Nov 1966. Education: BS, University of Wisconsin, 1970; MFA, Cornell University, 1973. Appointments: Teacher, Washington State University, 1970-71, Cornell University, 1971-74, University of Cincinnati, 1974-84, Washington Community Colleges, 1984-91, Chapman University, 1989-96, Western Washington University, 1991-96. Publications: Poetry: Employed, 1972; Soft Rock, 1973; The Gestures, 1975; Making Space for Our Living, 1975; The Alleged Conception, 1976; New & Selected Poems, 1978; Precint Kali, 1982; First Credo, 1986; Snail River, 1995. Chapbooks: Drool, 1968; Day of Change, 1968; Stone Marrow, 1969; Becoming Human, 1970; Edging Through, 1972; Terminal Placebos, 1975; Are You Tough Enough for the Eighties?, 1979; Like a Planet, 1993. Contributions to: Poetry in 27 anthologies; prose in 3 anthologies; poetry, stories, essays and reviews in periodicals. Honours: Hart Crane Poetry Award, 1969; Discovery Award, 1972; National Endowment for the Arts Fellowship, 1974; Quarterly Review of Literature International Book Awards, 1986, 1995; Djerassi Foundation Residency, 1987; Bumbershoot Big Book Award, 1994. Address: 533 Section Avenue, Anacortes, WA 98221, USA.

BESWICK Zanna, b. 15 Oct 1952, London, England. Television Drama Editor; Lecturer in Dramatic Literature. m. Andrew Alexander Paterson, 3 June 1989. Education: 1st Class Honours, Drama, Bristol University, 1971-75. Appointments: Theatre Designer and Script Reader; BBC Script Editor in drama series, serials; Thames TV Editor of Young People's Drama Department; Producer, comedy series, The Faint Hearted Feminist, BBC; Thames TV Series Editor, The Bill; Lecturer in Drama, Wake Forest University, USA. Publication: And for the Footsteps, 1984. Contributions to: Camden Voices; Resurgence; Writing Women; 3 X 4; Neney; Second Shift; Female Eye. Anthologies: In the Gold of Flesh, 1990; Mirror Image, 1995; The Upper Hand, 1995; Earth Ascending, 1996. Membership: Poetry Society. Address: 18 Chisholm Road, Richmond, Surrey, England.

BETAKI Vassily, b. 29 Sept 1930, Rostov on Don, Russia. Poet; Translator of Poetry; Literary Critic; Architectural Historian. 2 daughters. Education: MA, Institute of Literature, Moscow. Appointments: Teacher, high school, 1950-55; Science Director, Pavlovsk Palace Museum, 1956-62; Critic, Radio Liberty, Munich-Paris, 1973-88. Publications: The Flame of Earth, 1965; Short Circuit of the Time, 1974; Europe-Island, 1981; The Fifth Horseman, 1985; In Kitej Town, 1991; Selected Poems, 1992; Poems 1990-1993, 1994. Contributions to: Zvezda Aurore; Grani; Continent; Strelez; Den Poezii; Neva, 1994; Zvesga, St Petersburg, 1995. Honours: Winner, translation Competition, Moscow's edition, Literature, for translating the major poems of E A Poe, 1971. Membership: Writers Union of USSR, 1966-72. Address: 4 rue Michel Vignaud, 92360 Mendon-la-Foret, France.

BETTENCOURT-PINTO Eduardo, b. 23 April 1954, Gabela, Angola. Accountant. m. Rosa Pinto, 17 Dec 1980, 2 sons. Education: Post Secondary Education in Commercial and Accounting, Labor Law, 1975. Appointments: Various occupations including: Journalism; Correspondent; Personnel Director; Computer Output Designer; Federal Employee in Canada. Publications: Deusa da Chuva, 1991; Emoção, 1978; Poemas, c/Jorge Arrimar, 1979; Razões, 1979; Mão Tardia, 1981; Emersos Vestigios, 1985. Contributions to: Correio dos Agores; Diario Insular; Gavea Brown Magazine; Prism International Suplemento Agoriano de Cultura. Honours: Contexto, Poetry Award, 1981; Portuguese Cultural Association, France, 1986. Membership: Portuguese Writers' Association. Address: 11528-198 St Pitt Meadows, BC V3Y 1N9, Canada.

BEVERIDGE Judith Helen, b. 3 Aug 1956, London, England. m. Surinder Singh Joson, 4 Aug 1990, 1 son. Education: BA, Communications, University of Technology, Sydney. Publications: The Domesticity of Giraffes, 1987; Accidental Grace, 2nd volume, forthcoming. Contributions to: Poetry Australia; Meanjin; Island Magazine; New Poetry; Southerly; Sydney Morning Herald; The Age; Penguin Book of Modern Australian Poetry; Oxford Book of Australian Poetry; Compass; P76; Phoenix Review. Honours: Dame Mary Gilmore Award, 1988; New South Wales State Literary Award for Poetry, 1988; Victorian Premier's Literary Award for Poetry, 1988; Shortlisted for South Australian Premiers Award, 1988, Commonwealth Poetry Prize for a First Book, 1989. Membership: Secretary, 1986-87, New South Wales Branch of Poets Union. Address: 12 Cobham Avenue, West Ryde, New South Wales 2114, Australia.

BEZNER Kevin, b. 21 Mar 1953, Bainbridge, Maryland, USA. English Professor. m. Lili Corbus, 16 Nov 1980, 1 son. Education: BA, American Studies, Roger Williams College, 1975; MA, American Studies, 1976, MA, English, 1989, University of Maryland; PhD, English, Ohio University, 1991. Appointments: Florida Community College, Jacksonville, 1986-88; Humanities, University of Montana, 1991-93; English, Idaho State University, 1994-95; Livingstone College, Salisbury, North Carolina, 1995-96. Publications: About Water, 1993; In the City of Troy, 1994; Co-Editor, The Wilderness of Vision: On the Poetry of John Haines, 1996. Contributions to: Big Scream; Calapooya Collage; Cincinnati Poetry Review; Elf; Eclectic Literary Forum; On the Bus; Snowy Egret; Turning Wheel. Memberships: PEN West; Associated Writing Programs; Western American Literature. Address: 4710 Walker Road, Charlotte, NC 28211, USA.

BHARATHI Madhura. See: **GANAPATHI Subramanyam.**

BHATIA H S, b. 15 Aug 1936, Lala Musa, Pakistan. Teacher. m. Sita Bhatia, 18 Nov 1962, 2 sons. Education: BA, Panjab University, Chandigarh, 1961; MA, English Literature, Meerut University, Meerut, 1970. Appointments: School Teacher, Jalandhar, 1955; Accounts Official, 1955-70; College Lecturer, degree classes, Panjab University, Chandigarh, 1970-94, retired as Senior Lecturer in English, Reader's Grade, 1994. Publications: Editor, Modern Trends in Indo-Anglian Poetry, 1982-83; Editor, Prevalent Aspects of Indian English Poetry, 1983-84; Burning Petals, collection of poems, 1983-84; The Necklace Wild, collection of poems, 1994; Social Reality in Indian English Poetry, 1994. Contributions to: Poetry Times; Poet; Homeros, Turkey; Skylark; Poetcrit; Eureka; Commonwealth Quarterly; Kavita India; Journal of Indian Writing in English; Youth Age; Canopy; Creative Forum; Bharat Protiva. Address: B 4-301 Nandi Colony, Chandigarh Road, Khanna, Punjab 141401, India.

BHATTACHARJYA Hiren, b. 28 July 1932, Jorhat, India. Writer. m. Parul, 6 Dec 1973, 1 son, 1 daughter. Education: BA, Guwahati University. Publications: Mor Desh Mor Premor Kabita, 1972; Bivinna Dinar Kabita, 1974; Kabita Road, 1976; Sugandhi Pakhila, 1981; Sashyor Pathar Manuh, 1991; Jonakimon O Annyanya, 1991. Contributions to: Assamese Daily; Periodicals. Honours: Raghunath Chowdhury Poetry Award, 1976; Bishnu Rava Award, 1985; Rajaji Literary Award, 1986; Soviet Land Nehru Award, 1988-89. Memberships: All India Progressive Writers Association; Progressive Writers and Artists Association. Address: Sheha Tirtha, RG Barua Road, Guwahati 781003, India.

BHATTACHARYA Indrajit, b. 22 Mar 1960, India. m. Chandana Bhattacharya, 20 Feb 1992. Education: BA, Honours, Economics, Calcutta, 1980; MA, English Literature, 1983, PhD, American Literature, 1991, Ravi Shankar University. Appointments: Assistant Contributing Editor, Ocarina, 1987. Publications: Song of the Morrow, 1988; Bubbles, 1991; Hattali, 1991. Contributions to: Poetry; Poetry Time; Ken; Literary Endeavour Eureka; Literary Horizon; Quest; Byword; Canopy; Ocarina; Madhya Valaya; Prasangawash; Skylark; Alakta; Homeros, Turkey. Memberships: American Studies Research Centre, Hyderabad; Comparative Literature Association of India; Indian Association for Canadian Studies; United Writers' Association; PEN All India Centre. Address: Department of English, SN Mor College, Tumsar Maharashtra 441912, India.

BHIMANN Boyi, b. 19 Sept 1911, Mamidi Kuduru, India. Retired Government Officer; Writer. Education: Double Graduation, 1935, 1940. Appointments: Journalist, 1936-55; Teacher, 1942-45; Director, Translations, Government of Andhra Pradesh, 1955-66; Member, legislative Council, Andhra Pradesh, 1978-84; Member Senate, Andhra and Osmania Universities, 1940-71; Member Syndicate, S K University, 1983. Publications: A Farm Boy, 1940; The Labour King, 1947; The Parliament of Lights, 1955; The Seventh Season, 1964; Raaga Vysaakhi, 1965; Fight for Social Justice, 1968; Raabhilu, 1971; The Huts are on Fire, 1973; The Photo, 1975; Janmantara Vyram, 1980; Ambedkara Suprabhatam, 1984; Salvation is My Birth Right, 1987; Idigo, Idee Bhagavadgita, 1990; Paatalalo Ambedkar, 1992; Drug Addicts, 1993; How Deep the Darkness and How Many the Lights, 1994; The Great Harijan and Girijan Personalities of Puranic Age, 1995. Contributions to: Numerous newspapers, magazines and journals. Honours: Awarded title Maha Kavi at Kakinada, 1968; Honorary Doctorate, Kalaa Prapoorna, Andhra University, 1971; Awards of Padma Shri, President of India, 1973; National Award, Central Saahitya Akademi for Poetry, 1975; Honorary DLitt, Kashi Vidyapeeth, Vaarnai, 1976; Rajalakshmi Literary Award, 1991; Telugu University Visishta Puraskaram, 1992; Honorary Doctorate, Nagarjuna University, 1993; Sahasra Poorna Chandra Darsanotsavan, 1994; B N Reddy Literary Award, 1995; Telugu Aatma Gourava Award, 1996. Memberships: Organised All India Telugu Writers Conferences as President of Navya Saahithi Samithi, 1959; Executive member, Fellow, State Sahitya Akademi, 1958-83; Governing Boards, Telugu Akademi and International Telugu Institute; Chairman, reception Committee, All India Dalit Writers Conference, 1985. Address: 1C 85, Irrum Manzil Colony, Hyderabad 500 082, Andhra Pradesh, India.

BIAN Zhilin, b. 8 Dec 1910, China. Research Fellow. m. Qing Lin, 1 Oct 1955, 1 daughter. Education: BA, Peking University, 1933. Appointments: Associate Professor, Southwestern Associated University, 1943-46; Professor, Nankai University, 1946-47; Professor, Beijing University, 1949-52; Research Fellow, Institute of Literature, Chinese Academy of Sciences, 1958-78; Research Fellow, Foreign Literature Institute, Chinese Academy of Social Sciences. Publications: Poems of a Decade 1930-39, 1942, 1989; Collected Poems 1930-58, 1982, 1984; Selected Poetry and Prose, 1990; Verse translation of Shakespeare's 4 major tragedies, 1956, 1988; A Chinese Selection of English Poetry with 12 modern French Poems, 1983. Contributions to: Various major Chinese periodicals and a few English magazines. Honour: Fellowship, British Council, 1947-48. Membership: Council, Chinese Writers Association. Address: Foreign Literature Institute, CASS, Beijing 100732, China.

BIANCHI Herman (Thomas Cashet), b. 14 Dec 1924, Rotterdam, Netherlands. Professor. 1 son. Education: LLD, Legal Studies, 1956. Appointments: Professor of Law, Free University, Amsterdam, 1960-89; Retired 1989. Publications: A Breviary of Torment, 1991. Memberships: Maatschappij der Nederlandse Letterkunde, Leiden. Address: Albrecht Dürerstraat 48, 1077 MB Amsterdam, Netherlands.

BIARUJIA Javant, b. 8 Aug 1955, Melbourne, Victoria, Australia. Education: Monash University, Clayton, Victoria, (no degree). Appointments: Editor, Nosukumo, 1982-96, Labassa Quarterly, 1995-, Australian-Indonesian Association News, Victoria, 1995-. Publications: Fallen Angels, 1980; Warrior Dolls, 1981; Thalassa Thalassa, 1983; Eye in the Anus, 1985; Autumn Silks, 1988; Gakai, 1989; Calqueneauz, 1989; This is a Table, 1989; Ra, 1991. Contributions to: Pink Ink; An Anthology of Australian Lesbian and Gay Writers; Australian Gay and Lesbian Writing, 1993; Outrider 90: A Year of Australian Literature; Patterns/Contexts/Time: A Symposium on Contemporary Poetry; Pictures From an Exhibition; Australian Writing Now; Love and Death; Edge City on Two Different Plans; Instructions for Honey Ants; Rialto; James White Review; Carrionflower Writ; Verandah; Pataphysics; Tyuonyi; Spit; Blue Jacket; Ping-Pong (journal of the Henry Miller library); The Illinois Review. Honours: 1st Place in HIV/AIDS Radio Plays, 1991; 1st Prize in the inaugural Irene Mitchell Award for short plays, 1996. Memberships: Society of Editors; Fellowship of Australian Writers; Imago; Co-Founder, Carringbush Writers, 1981. Address: GPO Box 994-H, Melbourne, Vic 3001, Australia.

BIASE Angela Maria Rocha de, (Monica de Oliveira Moulin), b. 12 Dec 1949, Muniz Freire-Espirito Santo, Brazil. Lawyer; Attorney. Education: Law School, University of São Paulo, 1968-72; Master degree,. FADUSP, 1973-75; Courses in legal area and international private law seminars. Appointments: Attorney, Municipality of São Paulo, 1977; Chief Attorney, 1981-87; Legal Counsel, Regional Administration Office, 1987-88; Director, Property Department, General Law Office, Municipality of São Paulo, 1989-90; Member of Legal Studies Centre, General Law Office, São Paulo, 1990-. Publications: Cantos do Encontrar, 1986; International Poetry Year Book, 1988; International Poetry, 1990, 1991, 1992; Cahiers Jaions, 1992. Contributions to: Pan Artes. Honours: Citation, contest Mulheres entre Linhas, State Culture Office, São Paulo, 1985; Golden Crown of World Poets Award, World Poetry Research Institute, Korea, 1992. Memberships: World Poetry Research Institute, Cheong Ju, Korea; Interdisciplinary Law Studies Institute, São Paulo. Address: Avenida Silvio Sciumbata No 595, Interlagos, São Paulo SP, CEP 04789-010, Brazil.

BICKERSTAFF Patsy Anne, b. 7 Jan 1940, Virginia, USA. Attorney. m. Wilson Lee Seay, 7 Jan 1988, 3 sons, 1 daughter. Education: BA, English, University of Richmond, 1963; JD, T C Williams School of Law, University of Richmond, 1978. Appointments: Attorney at Law, 1978-; Writing Reviewer, Henrico County Schools, 1990. Publications: City Rain, 1989. Contributions to: Caribbean Writer; Poetry Society of Virginia Anthologies; Faces of Freedom; South Coast Poetry Review; Ariel; Virginia Country; Modern Liturgy; Bellingham Review; Lyric; Showcase; Cumberland Poetry Review, 1995; Piedmont Literary Review, 1995; Edge City Review, 1995; Potomac Review, 1995. Honours: International Shakespearean Contest 1st Prize, 1985; Finalist, Capricorn Poetry Awards, 1992; Hackney Literary Awards, 1986; Virginia Highlands Festival Award, 1986; Poetry Society of Virginia Award, 1987, 1993; Black Hills Writers Group Prize, 1988; American Pen Women Award, 1988; New York Poetry Forum Award, 1988; Writer's Digest 5th place, 1994; Black Hills NLAPW, 1995; Arkansas NLAPW, 1995; Sparrowgrass Poetry Forum, 1995; Robert Penn Warren Award, 1st Place, 1995. Memberships: Regional Vice President, Poetry Society of Virginia; Virginia Writers Club. Address: PO Box 156, Weyers Cave, VA 24486, USA.

BIDGOOD Ruth, b. 20 July 1922, Seven Sisters, Glamorgan, Wales. Writer. m. David Edgar Bidgood, 31 Dec 1946, 2 sons, 1 daughter. Education: BA, 1943, MA, 1947, Oxford University. Appointments: Coder, WRNS; Sub Editor, Chambers Encyclopaedia. Publications: The Given Time, 1972; Not Without Homage, 1975; The Print of Miracle, 1978; Lighting Candles, 1982; Kindred, 1986; Selected Poems, 1992; The Fluent Moment, 1996. Contributions to: Country Life; Countryman; Poetry Wales; Planet; Anglo-Welsh Review; New Welsh Review; Aquarius; Poetry Nation Review; The Interpreter's House; New England Review; Bread Loaf Quarterly; Fine Frenzy; Malahat Review. Honours: Welsh Arts Council Award, 1975; Runner-up to Welsh Book of the Year, 1993. Membership: Academi Gymreig, English Speaking Section. Address: Tyhaeam, Abergwesyn, Llanwrtyd Wells, Powys, Wales.

BIELAWA Michael Joseph, b. 12 June 1960, Amsterdam, New York, USA. Library Director. 1 son. Education: AA, Housatonic Community College; BA, Southern Connecticut State College, 1982;

AA, Sacred Heart University, 1990; MLS, Southern Connecticut State University, 1993. Contributions to: Orphic Lute; Stratford Magazine; Trumbull Arts Festival; Bean Feast; Rycenda Symposiuml; Alura; Stratford Life, Section of Bridgeport Post; Polish-American Journal; BEI Compass; Vytis; Poetry for Peace. Honours: 1st Place, Stratford, Connecticut's 350th Anniversary Poetry Contest, 1989. Memberships: Connecticut Poetry Society; National Hawthorne Society. Address: 38 William Street, Ansonia, CT 906401, USA.

BIELBY John Nicholas Lyne, b. 4 June 1939, London, England. Lecturer. m. Sheila Marland, 22 Aug 1964, 1 son, 1 daughter. Education: BA, 1961; MA, 1983; Dip Primary Ed, 1972; Dip Psych and Sociology of Ed, 1973. Appointments: Lecturer, St John's College, Agra, India; Teacher, Bradley Junior School, Huddersfield; Lecturer, Senior Lecturer, Bradford and Ilkley Community College; Lecturer, Leeds University. Publications: Three Early Tudor Poets, 1976; An Invitation to Supper, 1978; Making Sense of Reading, 1994. Contributions to: Penine Platform; New Poetry; Orbis; Honest Ulsterman; Poetry & Audience; English; Poetry Reviewing, Times Educational Supplement. Honours: Awards from New Poetry, Lancaster (3 times) and Yorkshire Open; Rhyme International, 1989; Runner-up, Arvon, 1991. Memberships: Pennine Poets; Bradford and Baildon Poetry Society; Gowland Poets. Address: Frizingley Hall, Frizinghall Road, Bradford BD9 4LD, West Yorkshire, England.

BIELSKI Alison Joy Prosser, b. 24 Nov 1925, Newport, Gwent, Wales. Personal Secretary. m. (1) Dennis Ford Treverton Jones, dec 1948, (2) Anthony Edward Bielski, dec 1955, 1 son, 1 daughter. Education: Secretary to Press Officer, Bristol Aircraft; Secretary in Newport Engineering, family firm; Welfare Assistant, British Red Cross; Writer; Lecturer, Writers on Tour, Welsh Arts Council, 20 years. Publications: Across the Burning Sand, 1970; Eve, 1973; Shapes and Colours, 1974; The Lovetree, 1974; Mermaid Poems, 1974; Seth, 1980; Night Sequence, 1981; Eagles, 1983. Contributions to: Anglo-Welsh Review; New Welsh Review; Acumen; Poetry Wales; Planet; Workshop; New Poetry; Xenia; Prospice; Pembroke Magazine, USA; Borestone Mountain Poetry Awards; Social Care Education; The Works; Dragon's Hoard; Contemporary Women Poets; University of Salzburg Press. Honours: Premium Prize Poetry Society, 1964; 2nd Prize, Festival of Spoken Poetry, 1967; Anglo-Welsh Review Poetry Prize, 1970; 3rd Place, Alice Gregory Memorial Competition, 1979; Society of Women Writers and Journalists Christmas Prize, 1977; Orbis Poetry Prize, Poems for Peace, 1984; 2nd Prize, Julia Cairns Trophy, Society of Women Writers and Journalists, 1984, 1992. Memberships: Past Joint Honorary Secretary, Welsh Academy; Folklore Society; Traditional Cosmology Society; Committee, Gwent Poetry Society; Society of Women Writers and Journalists; Association of Little Presses. Address: 92 Clifton Road, Paugnton, Devon TQ3 3LD, England.

BIGGS Margaret Key, b. 26 Oct 1933, Needmore, Alabama, USA. Poet. m. 1 April 1956. Publications: Swampfire, 1980; Sister to the Sun, 1981; Magnolias and Such, 1982; Petals from the Womanflower, 1983; Plumage of the Sun, 1986. Contributions to: Earthwise Poetry Journal; Lively Arts Magazine; Ochlockonee Review; International University Poetry Quarterly; Thoreau Journal Quarterly; Limberlost Review; Jump River Review; Sackbut Review; The Poet; Modern Images; Poetry Magazine; Negative Capability; Poetry Monthly; San Francisco Poetry Journal; Midwest Poetry Review; Piedmont Literary Society; Old Hickory Review; Centre Stage; Pen Woman; Many others; Various anthologies. Honours: Numerous awards. Memberships: National Federation of State Poetry Societies; National League of American Pen Women; Life Member, Panhandle Writers Guild, Bay County; Alabama State Poetry Society; Alabama Writers' Conclave. Address: Box 2600, County Road 852, AL 36264, USA.

BIMGO. See: **MARGOLIS William J.**

BINNS John, b. 12 Nov 1947, Bradford, West Yorkshire, England. Publication: A Phoenix Rising, 1991. Contributions to: Rialto; Purple Patch; Third Half; Roads; Momentum; Peace and Freedom; Kissing the Sky; Barddoni; Songs; Dream Cell; Exile; Wire; Pennine Platform; Bare Wires; Poetry Nottingham; Wayfarers; Enigma; US magazines: Omnific; Minotaur; Nocturnal Lyric; Irreversible Man, anthology; Make Mine Canine, anthology. Honours: Runner-up, Mosaic Competition, 1990. Address: 14 Silver Royd Close, Wortley, Leeds LS12 4QZ, England.

BIRD Polly, b. 30 Sept 1950, London, England. Author. m. Dr J M Bird, 27 July 1974, 2 sons, 1 daughter. Education: BEd, Cantab, 1973; Certificate Field Archaeology, University of London, 1978. Appointment: Primary Teacher, Vice-Chair, School Governors. Publications: Included in: Reedham Reflections,1985; New Christian Poetry, 1990; A Long Journey, 1991; 1991 Envoi Summer Anthology; Environment Care-Caring Poetry Festival Anthology, 1991. Contributions to: Oregonian; Writers Review; The Lady; Envoi; Norfolk Fair; Bradford Poetry Quarterly; Nottingham Poetry. Honours: 1st Prize, C J Poetry Competition, 1987; 2nd Prize, Speakeasy Poetry Competition, 1991. Memberships: Poetry Society; Society of Authors. Address: 49 Oakhurst Grove, East Dulwich, London SE22 9AH, England.

BIRDI Saranjit (Sam), b. 8 Feb 1960, Punjab, India. Chartered Architect. Education: Diploma in Architecture, 1984; BA, Honours, Architecture, Bristol University, 1982. Publications: Shakti, 1983; Poems: Red, White and Blue; The Colour of Dirt; Me, You and the Clouds. Contributions to: Read poems and interview on BBC, 1983; Read poems on Bristol Radio, 1983. Memberships: Poetry Society; PEN. Address: 37 Cecil Road, Erdington, Birmingham B24 8AU, England.

BISHOP Patricia Julia Rose, b. London, England. Poet. m. 4 sons. Education: Cert Ed. Appointments: Civil Servant; Teacher; Smallholder. Publications: Double Exposure, 1988; All Wings & Bones (co-author Spacex), 1992; Aubergine is a Gravid Woman, 1993. Contributions to: New Welsh Review; Planet International; Envoi; Ostinato; Odyssey; Writing Women; Rialto; Radio 4; Radio Cornwall; Radio Stoke, Long Pale Corridor, Bloodaxe Anthology. Honour: Joint 2nd Place, National Poetry Competition, 1994; Arts Council/BBC North Award, Write Out Loud, 1996. Address: Newburn, Cockwells, Nr Penzance, Cornwall TR20 8DB, England.

BISHOP Robert Gregory, b. 23 Sept 1936, Clapham, London, England. Lecturer; Teacher; Translator. Education: BA, Arts, London, 1968; Certificate of Education, Leeds University, 1972. Appointments: National Service, RAF, 1954-55; Library Staff, London Evening News, 1959-62, Guardian Library, 1962-64; Teacher of English, Munich, 1968-69; Teacher of A' Level Students, Watford College of Further Education. 2 years; Translator, Lecturer and Teacher, Sprachen-und-Dolmetscher Institut and at various companies, Munich, 1972-. Publications: 165 poems published in Germany, England, Spain, USA, Australia; Anthology of his poems compiled by Artists for Nature; Included in Poetry Postcard Quarterly's 1996 Anthology of Winners, Haiku Championships; Heyue Anthology forthcoming. Contributions to: S Fest Magazine, SC, USA; Purple Patch; Frogmore Papers; The Good Society Review; Egonibs; Chronicles; Journal of Contemporary Anglo-Scandinavian Poetry; First Time; Weyfarers; Poetry Now; Germany: Munich Now Magazine; Schwabing Extra, Munich; Freyburger (language magazine), University of Freiburg. Honours: Special Commendation, Poetry Society, for a poem in its anthology, 1992; Special Commendation, English Explorer Magazine, 1992; Joint 4th Prize, The Kent and Sussex Society, 1995. Membership: Poetry Society of Great Britain. Address: Paschstr 56, 80637 Munich, Germany.

BISHOP Wendy, b. 13 Jan 1953, Japan. Professor of English; Teacher of Writing. m. Marvin E Pollard Jr, 1 son, 1 daughter. Education: BA, English, BA, Studio Art, 1975, MA, English, Creative Writing, 1976, MA, English, Teaching Writing, 1979, University of California, Davis; PhD, English, Rhetoric and Linguistics, Indiana University of Pennsylvania, 1988. Appointments: Chairperson, Communications, Humanities and Fine Arts, Navajo Community College, Tsaile, Arizona, 1984-85; Assistant Professor of English, University of Alaska, Fairbanks, 1985-89; Professor of English, Florida State University, 1989-. Publications: Released into Language: Options for Teaching Creative Writing, 1990; Something Old, Something New: College Writing Teachers and Classroom Change, 1990; Working Words: The Process of Creative Writing, 1992; The Subject Is Writing: Essays by Teachers and Students, 1993. Contributions to: American Poetry Review; Prairie Schooner; Western Humanities Review; Threepenny Review; Denver Quarterly; Chronicle of Higher Education. Honours: Joseph Henry Jackson Award, 1980; Several Fellowships; Many literary awards and readerships. Memberships: Modern Language Association; Poetry Society of America; Associated Writing Programmes; National Writing Centres Association; National Council of Teachers of English. Address: Department of English, Florida State University, Tallahassee, FL 32306, USA.

BISSETT Bill, b. 23 Nov 1939, Halifax, Nova Scotia, Canada. Education: University of British Columbia, 1963-65. Appointments: Writer-in-Residence, University of Western Ontario, 1985-86; Artist, with one-man shows throughout Canada. Publications: Lebanon Voices, 1967; Awake in the Red Desert, 1968; Medicine My Mouths on Fire, 1974; The Fifth Sun, 1975; An Alluyshun to Macbeth, 1976; Selected Poems, 1980; Animal Uproar, 1987; Inkorrekt Thots, 1992; Th Last Photo uv the Human Soul, 1993. Honours: Canada Council Grants. Address: PO Box 178, Station 8, London, Ontario N6A 5K2, Canada.

BISWAS Arabinda, b. 6 May 1925, Rangpur, India. Indian Administrative Service (Retired). m. Shyamala Biswas, 21 Nov 1951, 1 son. Education: MA, English, 1947; MA, Political Science, 1952; MEd, 1972; Educational Administration, University of California, 1967-68. Appointments: Lecturer, 1948; Principal, 1954; Deputy Director of Education, 1967; Indian Administrative Service, 1968; Director of Education, Delhi, 1974; Finance Secretary, Government of Goa, 1977; Secretary to the Lieutenant Governor, 1978-1983; Presently, Director, New Green Field Public School, New Delhi. Publications: Published 12 books, including Encyclopedic Dictionary of Education, 2 volumes, 1971; Comparative Education, 1976; Development of Education in India, 1986. Contributions to: Poet; International Monthly. Memberships: World Poetry Society, Madras. Address: 162 Kailash Hills, New Delhi 110065, India.

BIXBY Robert J, b. 9 Nov 1952, Michigan, USA. Editor. m. Kathleen Mae Beal, 1971, 1 son, 1 daughter. Education: BS, Central Michigan University, 1978; MSW, Western Michigan University, 1980; MFA. University of North Carolina, 1992. Appointments: Social Worker, 1980-87; Editor, General Media, 1987-96; Editor/Publisher, March Street Press; Editor/Publisher, Parting Gifts. Contributions to: Gypsy; Abbey; Aleron; Albany Review; Amelia; Blue Light Review; Celery; Chrysalis; Connecticut River Review; Green River Review; Greensboro Review; Impetus; Lucky Star; Magic Changes; Open 24 Hours; Passages North; Poetic Space; Prophetic Voices; Pulpsmith; Slipstream; South Coast Review; Cathartic; Thirteen Touchstone; Verse and Universe; Wooster Review; Xanadu. Address: 3413 Wilshire, Greensboro, NC 27408, USA.

BJELKHAGEN Teresa Grace, b. 28 June 1951, Poland. Linguist. Education: BA, English and Russian, 1974; MA, Applied Linguistics, 1977; Diploma in Applied, Descriptive and Theoretical Linguistics, Exeter University, England, 1982. Appointments: Freelance Translator and Language Editor in English, 1974-; Lecturer, English Communication, South Africa, 1985-86; Lecturer, Applied Linguistics, University of South Africa, 1987; Translator, Stockholm University, 1995-. Publications: Poems: Why Once Again, 1988; The Laughing Jacaranda, 1988; Fleurs de la Cote d'Azur, 1988; All That's You is Light, 1988; Engele, 1989; Encounters, 1989; Posh Array, 1989; Life's Perverse Cabooze, 1990; Lips of Scarlet, 1992; Squeezeling, 1992; Your Phantom of the Night, 1992; Chirping Like a Bird, 1993; I Look in Long Mirrors, 1994. Contributions to: Pasque Petals. Membership: South Dakota State Poetry Society, USA. Address: Hälsingegatan 8, 11323 Stockholm, Sweden.

BLACK Charles (Lund Jr), b. 22 Sept 1915, Austin, Texas, USA. Professor of Law. m. Barbara Ann Aronstein, 11 Apr 1954, 2 sons, 1 daughter. Education: BA, 1935, MA, 1938, University of Texas; LLB, Yale Law School, 1943; Honorary LLD, Boston University, 1975. Appointments: Professor of Law, Columbia University, New York, 1947-56; Luce Professor of Jurisprudence, Yale University Law School, 1956-75; Sterling Professor of Law, Yale University, 1975-86, now Emeritus; Adjunct Professor of Law, Columbia University, 1986-. Publications: Telescopes and Islands, 1963, 1975; Owls Bay in Babylon, 1980; The Walking Passenger, 1983. Contributions to: Antioch Review; Approach; Arizona Quarterly; Beloit Poetry Journal; Boston University Journal; Carleton Miscellany; Chicago Review; Colorado Quarterly; Fiddlehead, Canada; Laomedon Review, Canada; Little Magazine; New Orleans Review; New Orleans Poetry Journal; Perspective; Quest; New York Times; Sewanee Review; Southern Review; Southern Humanities Review; Southwest Review; University of Kansas City Review; Yale Literary Magazine; Whetstone; British: Delta; Pawn; Oasis; Ulfjotur, Iceland. Membership: Poetry Society of America. Address: c/o Columbia Law School, 435 West 116th Street, New York, NY 10027, USA.

BLACK David Macleod, b. 8 Nov 1941, Cape Town, South Africa. m. Jeanne Magagna, 28 Jan 1984. Publications: With Decorum,

1967; Penguin Modern Poets 11, 1968; The Educators, 1969; The Happy Crow, 1974; Gravitations, 1979; Collected Poems 1964-1987, 1991. Contributions to: Akros; Chapman; Lines Review; Scottish International. Honours: Scottish Arts Council Awards, 1967, 1968, 1992. Address: 30 Cholmley Gardens, London NW6 1AG, England.

BLACK Matt(hew), b. 26 Oct 1956, Oxford, England. Writer. 2 sons. Education: BA, 1st class, English Literature, University of Sheffield, 1988. Publications: Now We Are Twenty-Six, 1984; The Scent of Sweat, 1985; Soft Fruit Centre, 1987; In The Kitchen With The Candlestick, 1990; The Sofa or On Liberty, 1991; The Garden, 1993; Squeezing Lemons, 1994. Contributions to: Over 500 performances. Honours: 1st Prize, Avon Poetry Competition, 1984; Performance of Lost Magic Kingdoms poems, Sheffield Arts Department, 1988; Public Arts Commissions: Lynton PLC, Poem cast in bronze tablets for floor of Guildford Shopping Centre, Lynton PLC, 1989; Hubble Bubble, collaboration with Ralph Steadman for Cheltenham Festival of Literature, 1994; Oppenheim John-Downes Memorial Award, 1990. Membership: Poetry Society of Great Britain. Address: 51 Pearson Place, Sheffield S8 9DE, England.

BLACKBURN Michael Anthony, b. 8 Mar 1954, Newton Aycliffe, Co Durham, England. Freelance Writer; Publisher. m. Sylvia Dann, 14 July 1990, 1 stepson, 1 stepdaughter. Education: MA, English, Leeds University, 1977. Publications: The Constitutions of Things, 1984; Why Should Anyone Be Here and Singing?, 1987; Backwards into Bedlam, 1987; The Lean Man Shaving, 1988; The Prophecy of Christos, 1992. Contributions to: The North; Hubbub, USA; Stand; Tribune; Pen; Noorus; Estonia; Echo Room; Wide Skirt; Joe Soap's Canoe. Address: Sunk Island Publishing, PO Box 74, Lincoln LN1 1QG, England.

BLACKHALL Sheena Booth, b. 18 Aug 1947, Aberdeen, Scotland. Poet. Div, 2 sons, 2 daughters. Education: Gray's School of Art, Aberdeen, 1964-65; Diploma in Primary Education, College of Education, Aberdeen, 1965-68; BSc, Honours, Psychology, Open University, 1995. Appointments: Teaching in Glasgow, Fraserburgh, Aberdeen, Durham, 1968-72; Teaching at Beechwood Special School, Aberdeen, 1973-75; Freelance Illustrator, Short Story Writer and Poet, 1975-. Publications: The Cyard's Kist, 1984; The Spik o' the Lan, 1986; Hamedrauchtit, 1987; Nor'East Neuk, 1989; Fite-Doo/Black Crow, 1989; Nippick o' Nor'East Tales, 1989; A Toosht o' Whigmaleeries, 1991; Reets, 1991; A Hint o' Granite, 1992; Back o' Bennachie, 1993; Braeheid an Ither Doric Tales, 1993; Selected Poems, cassette, 1993; Druids, Drachts, Drochles, 1994; Kenspeckle Creel, 1995; Lament for The Raj, 1995; Selected Poems, Stagwyes, 1995; Plays broadcast on BBC TV: The Broken Hert and The Nicht Bus. Contributions to: Cencrastus; Chapman; Orbis; Lallans; Northern Lights Schools Anthology; Lines Review; Fresh Oceans; Stramullion; Irish Review; Sleeping with Monsters; Guid Gear/Sma Buike, Schools Collection; The Broken Fiddle; Mak It Now; Northwords; The Kist. Honours: Prizewinner, Scottish International Open Competition, 1989; Winner, Hugh MacDiarmid Silver Tassie for Best Poem in SLS Competition, 1990; Winner, Robert McClellan Tassie for Best Scots Short Story, 1988, 1990; Prizewinner, Sloane Competition in Scots, St Andrews University, 1993. Memberships: Scottish Poetry Library; Scots Language Society; Aberdeen Artists' Society; Aberdeen Gaelic Choir. Literary Agent: Charles King, Hammerfield Publishing. Address: 17 Montrose Drive, Garthdee, Aberdeen AB1 7DA, Scotland.

BLACKMAN Roy Alfred Arthur, (Arthur Peasmair), b. 15 May 1943, Burnham, England. Retired. m. Jillian Frances, 11 Dec 1965, 1 son, 1 daughter. Education: BSc Honours, Zoology with Geology, Bristol, 1964; PhD, Marine Zoology, Newcastle upon Tyne, 1971; BA, 1st Class Honours, Open University, 1990. Appointments: Senior Scientific Officer, Ministry of Agriculture, Fisheries and Food, 1971-92; Co-Editor, Smiths Knoll, 1991-. Contributions to: Stand; Staple; Rialto; Outposts; Other Poetry; Thames Poetry; Foolscap; Spokes; Slow Dancer; New Welsh Review; Grand Piano; Margin; Poetry Nottingham; Pennine Platform; Envoi; Frogmore Papers; Odyssey; Honest Ulsterman; Seam; Lines Review; North; Interpreter's House; Acumen; As Lords Expected, 1996; BBC Radio 4. Honour: Hawthornden Fellow, 1993. Address: 49 Church Road, Little Glemham, Woodbridge, Suffolk IP13 0BJ, England.

BLAINE Julien, b. 19 Sept 1942, Rognac, France. Editor. m. Catherinne Poitevin, 1 Dec 1962, 1 son, 2 daughters. Education: Faculte de Lettres, Aix en Provence. Appointments: Author; Editor; Actor; Lectures and performances worldwide, 1963-; Co-Ordinator,

Co-Organiser, Polyphonix, 1979-94; Co-Founder, Festival of Poetry, Cogolin, 1984; International Poetry Meetings, Tarascon, France, 1988-; Co-Creator, Centre International de Poésie, Marseille; Venezia Poesia, 1996. Publications: Calmar, Ed Spectres Familiers, 1992; Horizons Partiels, Ed Adriano Parise, 1996; Calmar, 1993; Carnet(s) de Piste, 1993; Pour tous Ceux Qui Flambent, 1994; Clostrophobie, 1994; Balimeke, 1995; Parodies et Brouillons, 1995; LA PHRA, 1995. Editor: Les Anthologies de l'An 2000, 1973, Les Anartistes, 1972-88. Recording, Creative Workshop, Radiophonique de France-Culture, Paris, 1986, 1992, 1994. Personal shows include: Ch'i ou Qi, Paris, 1992, Horizon, Paris, 1992, Vertigo Signi, 1992, Rétrospective des 4 Sortie de Quarantaine, Verone, 1995. Contributions to: Numerous Reviews, anthologies, exhibitions, meetings and festivals worldwide. Memberships: Co-Ordinator, Polyphonix; Editor, Docks International; Secretary, Festival of Tarascon. Address: Le Moulin de Ventabren, 13122 Ventabren, France.

BLAKE Michael (Mike) Bernard, b. 28 Mar 1956, Liverpool, England. Electrical and Electronics Technician/Engineer; Songwriter; Lyricist. Education: HND Electrical and Electronic Engineering, 1989; BTec ONC Electronics Engineering, 1987; City and Guilds Radio and Television Servicing, 1978. Appointments: Served in HM Royal Navy, 1973-77; Radio Operator 1st Class. Publication: Matters of Urgency, series 1, 1992. Contributions to: National Library of Poetry, USA; On the Threshold of a Dream, Vol III. Memberships: Poetry Society; Associate Member, IEE. Address: 10 Cromer Court, Liden, Swindon, Wiltshire SN3 6HQ, England.

BLAKE Olive. See: **SUPRANER Robyn.**

BLAKE Rachel, b. 28 Sept 1923, Dorking, Surrey, England. Educator; Lecturer. Education: BA, Honours, English, University of Durham, 1950; Slade School of Fine Art, University College London, 1953-55. Appointments: Lecturer in Further Education, ILEA, 1966-73; Lecturer in Literature, Camden Adult Institute, 1970-73; Lecturer in English Literature, University of Botswana, Lesotho and Swaziland, 1973-75; Special Needs Teacher, ILEA, 1976-83; Special Needs Teacher, Islington Individual Tuition centre, ILEA, 1984-87. Publications: Included in anthologies: Arts Council, New Poetry Nos 2, 1976, 4, 1978, 7, 1981, 8, 1982; Mandeville Home Truths, 1987; New Women Poets, 1990; Poet's England 10, 1991; Poet's England 12, 1992; Poet and Printer, 1994; Lifedrawings (pamphlet collection). Contributions to: Encounter; PEN International; New Blackfriars Teribune; Country Life; Acumen; PEN International Outposts; New Welsh Review; Aquarius; Rialto; Iron; BBC Radio 3 Poetry Now. Honours: 3rd Prize, Bloodaxe Books National Competition, 1987; Runner-up, Skoob/Index Poetry Competition, 1989; Runner-up Prizewinner, Skoob-Index Competition, 1992. Memberships: PEN; Poetry Society. Address: 4 Kettles Cottages, Trig Street, Beare Green, Surrey RH5 4QF, England.

BLANCHARD Enrique Daniel, b. 14 Dec 1944, Buenos Aires, Argentina. Writer; Professor. m. Elisa Ruiz-Toranzo, 3 July 1975. Education: Self-taught; Studied literature at University of Buenos Aires and University del Salvador, Buenos Aires, scriptwriting at University of La Plata, Buenos Aires, and Museology at Town Hall of Buenos Aires. Appointments: Editor-in-Chief, Nuevo Milenio, publishing house specialising in poetry; Professor, University of Buenos Aires; Director of literary workshops. Publications: El Fantasma Y Su Límite, 1982; Silveta De Polvo, 1982; El Disfraz Del Cuerpo, 1982; Función Del Ventrílocuo, 1984; Idolo De Niebla, 1984; Reo De Redes, 1986; El Locutor Físico, 1989; Retrato De Antifaz, 1990; Desnudo De Espectro, 1991; Viajero De Una Mano, 1994; Escenas En Las Estaciones Terminales, 1994; Physicus Loquutor I, 1995; Bootleg books: Gaucho Concreto, 1990; Guascalia O El Extasis Esquimal, 1990. Contributions to: Newspapers and literary magazines from Europe, USA and Latin America including: Lost and Found Times; Droomschaar; Norte; Calandrajas; Nicolau. Honour: Best Book of the Year for, Reo De Redes, Buenos Aires Lawyers Association, 1986. Address: Casilla de Correo 2847, 1000 Correo Central, Buenos Aires, Argentina.

BLAND Peter, b. 12 May 1934, Scarborough, North Yorkshire, England. Education: Victoria University, Wellington, New Zealand. Career: Co-Founder, Director, Downstage Theatre Company, Wellington, 1964-69; Actor and Writer in London. Publications: My Side of the Story, 1964; Domestic Interiors, 1964; Mr Maui, 1976; Primitives, 1979; Stone Tents, 1981; The Crusoe Factor, 1985; Selected Poems, 1987; Paper Boats, 1990. Honour: Cholmondeley

Award, 1977. Address: 2 Westrow, Westleigh Avenue, Putney, London SW15, England.

BLANDIANA Ana, (Otila Valeria Rusan), b. 25 Mar 1942, Timisoara, Romania. Poet; Writer; Librarian. m. Romulus Rusan. Education: Graduated, University of Cluj, 1967. Appointments: Columnist, Romania Literary Magazine, 1974-88; Librarian, Institute of Fine Arts, Bucharest, 1975-. Publications: First-Person Plural, 1964; The Wounded Heel, 1966; The Third Sacrament, 1969; To Be a Witness, 1970; 50 Poems, 1972; October, November, December, 1972; Poems, 1974; The Sleep Within the Sleep, 1977; Four Seasons, 1977; Poems, 1978; The Most Beautiful of All Possible Worlds, 1978; Events in My Garden, 1980; The Cricket's Eye, 1981; Poems, 1982; Projects for the Past, 1982; Corridor of Mirrors, 1984; Star of Prey, 1985; The Hour of Sand: Selected Poems, 1969-89, 1989. Honour: Herder Prize, Vienna, 1982. Address: c/o Cartea Romaneasca, str Nuferilor 41, 79721 Bucharest, Romania.

BLASER Robin (Francis), b. 18 May 1925, Denver, Colorado, USA. Professor of English; Poet. Education: MA, 1954, MLS, 1955, University of California at Berkeley. Appointment: Professor of English, Centre for the Arts, Simon Fraser University, Burnaby, British Columbia, Canada, 1972-86. Publications: The Moth Poem, 1964; Les Chimères, 1965; Cups, 1968; The Holy Forest Section, 1970; Image-Nations 1-12 and The Stadium of the Mirror, 1974; Image-nations 13-14, 1975; Syntax, 1983; The Faerie Queene and the Park, 1987; Pell Mell, 1988; The Holy Forest, 1993. Honours: Poetry Society Award, 1965; Canada Council Grant, 1989-90; Fund for Poetry Award, New York, 1995. Address: 1636 Trafalgar Street, Vancouver, British Columbia V6K 3R7, Canada.

BLASOR-BERNHARDT Donna Jo, (Taura Rai Aanan), b. Pittsburgh, Kansas, USA. Writer; Poet. m. Richard Wayne Bernhardt, 29 Oct 1964, dec, 1 son, 1 daughter. Education: WSI Rating, University of Alaska, Anchorage, 1962. Appointments: Treasurer, Tok Medical Clinic, 1982-83; Correspondence Secretary, Tok Chamber of Commerce, 1989-91; Board Member, Tok Chamber of Commerce, 1990-91; Field Editor, Birds & Blooms magazine. Publications: A Tent in Tok, Vol 1, 1980, 3rd edition, 1990; More..A Tent in Tok, Vol II, 1982, 6th edition, 1994; Friends..of the Tent in Tok, Vol III, 1988, 1990; Beyond..The Tent in Tok, Vol IV, 1990; Love..and the Tent in Tok, 1994; Tok..The Real Story, 1996. Contributions to: Numerous anthologies and newspapers. Memberships: Frigio Poets Society, Co-founder; National Writers Union; International Women's Writing Guild; International Platform Association; American Arts Association. Address: PO Box 110, Tok, AK 99780, USA.

BLITZER (Ilse) Hanna, b. 9 April 1915, Beuthen, Germany. Retired; Teacher of Private Lessons in English, French and German. m. S Blitzer, 31 July 1934, dec, 2 sons, 1 daughter. Education: Matriculation, Cambridge Proficiency in English Language, 1964. Publications: Staub und Sterne (Dust and Stars), 1982; Hánna Blitzer Lyrics, 1984; Noch ein Akkord (Another Accord), 1987; Od Akkord, Hebrew version, 1988; Ein Zeichen Setzen (To Set a Mark), 1991; Worte die Leben Sagen (Words That Say Life), 1994. Contributions to: Das Neue Israel; Die Stimme; Israel Nachrichten; Gauke's Jahrbuch; Impressum; Anthology Auf dem Weg; Mnemosyne; Nachrichten; Impressum; Feuerprobe; Kaleidoscope Israel; Alekto, Austria. Memberships: Writers Association of Israel; German Writing Authors; International Writers Association, Regensburg, Germany; Vice President, German Writers Association in Israel. Address: Kehilat-Sofia 14, 69018 Tel Aviv, Israel.

BLOCH Chana (Florence), b. 15 Mar 1940, New York, New York, USA. Professor of English; Poet; Translator; Critic; Essayist. m. Ariel Bloch, 26 Oct 1969, 2 sons. Education: BA, Cornell University, 1961; MA, 1963, MA, 1965, Brandeis University; PhD, University of California at Berkeley, 1975. Appointments: Instructor in English, Hebrew University, Jerusalem, 1964-67; Associate in Near Eastern Studies, University of California at Berkeley, 1967-69; Instructor, 1973-75, Assistant Professor, 1975-81, Associate Professor, 1981-87, Chairman, Department of English, 1986-89, Professor of English, 1987-, Director, Creative Writing Program, 1993-, Mills College, Oakland, California. Publications: Poetry: The Secrets of the Tribe, 1981; The Past Keeps Changing, 1992. Other: Spelling the Word: George Herbert and the Bible, 1985. Translator: Dahlia Ravikovitch: A Dress of Fire, 1978; Yehuda Amichai: The Selected Poetry, with Stephen Mitchell, 1986, revised edition, 1996; Dahlia Ravikovitch: The Window: New and Selected Poems (with Ariel Bloch), 1989; The Song of Songs: A New Translation, Introduction and Commentary (with Ariel Bloch), 1995. Contributions to: Poetry, translations, criticism, and essays in various anthologies and periodicals. Honours: Translation Award, Columbia University, 1978; National Endowment for the Humanities Fellowship, 1980; Book of the Year Award, Conference on Christianity and Literature, 1986; Writers Exchange Award, Poets and Writers, 1988; Yaddo Residencies, 1988, 1990, 1993, 1994, 1995, 1996; MacDowell Colony Residencies, 1988, 1992, 1993; Djerassi Foundation Residencies, 1989, 1991; National Endowment for the Arts Fellowship, 1989-90. Address: c/o Department of English, Mills College, Oakland, CA 94613, USA.

BLOMFIELD Richard Massie, b. 25 June 1913, Poole, Dorset, England. Public Relations; Advertising. m. 11 Jan 1943, 1 son, 1 daughter. Education: MA, Modern Languages, Oxford. Publications: Poole: Harbour, Heath and Islands, 1973; The Seal That Made Friends, 1974; Poole: Town and Harbour, 1989; Lyrics for musicals, co-writer. Contributions to: Orbis; Poetry Review; Acumen; Literary Review; Spectator. Address: 147 Banks Road, Sandbanks, Poole, Dorset, England.

BLOOM Harold, b. 11 July 1930, New York, New York, USA. Professor of Humanities; Writer. m. Jeanne Gould, 8 May 1958, 2 sons. Education: BA, Cornell University, 1951; PhD, Yale University, 1955. Appointments: Faculty, 1955-65, Professor of English, 1965-77, DeVane Professor of Humanities, 1974-77, Professor of Humanities, 1977-83, Sterling Professor of Humanities, 1983-, Yale University; Visiting Professor, Hebrew University, Jerusalem, 1959; Breadloaf Summer School, 1965-66, Cornell University, 1968-69; Visiting University Professor, New School for Social Research, New York City, 1982-84; Charles Eliot Norton Professor of Poetry, Harvard University, 1987-88; Berg Professor of English, New York University, 1988-. Publications: Shelley's Mythmaking, 1959; The Visionary Company, 1961; Blake's Apocalypse, 1963; Commentary to Blake, 1965; Yeats, 1970; The Ringers in the Tower, 1971; The Anxiety Influence, 1973; A Map of Misreading, 1975; Kabbalah and Criticism, 1975; Poetry and Repression, 1976; Figures of Capable Imagination, 1976; Wallace Stevens: The Poems of Our Climate, 1977; The Flight of Lucifer: A Gnostic Fantasy, 1979; Agon: Towards a Theory of Revisionism, 1981; The Breaking of the Vessels, 1981; The Strong Light of the Canonical, 1987; Freud: Transference and Authority, 1988; Poetics of Influence: New and Selected Criticism, 1988; Ruin the Sacred Truths, 1988; The Book of J, 1989; The American Religion, 1990; The Western Canon, 1994; Omens of Millenium: The Gnosis of Angels, Dreams and Resurrection, 1996. Contributions to: Scholarly books and journals. Honours: Fulbright Fellowship, 1955; Guggenheim Fellowship, 1962; Newton Arvin Award, 1967; Melville Caine Award, 1970; Zabel Prize, 1982; John D and Catharine T MacArthur Foundation Fellowship, 1985; Christian Gauss Prize, 1989. Membership: American Academy of Arts and Letters. Address: 179 Linden Street, New Haven, CT 06511, USA.

BLOOMFIELD Lawrence (Larry) E(dward), b. 5 Oct 1956, Wheeling, West Virginia, USA. m. (1) 1 son, 1 daughter, (2) Norma Jean Scott, 29 Nov 1980, 2 daughters. Education: Certificate in Graphic Arts, McKinley Vocational Technical Centre, 1974; Classes at West Virginia Career College, Belmont Technical College, Northern Community College, 1978-83. Publications: All My Own: Poems by Lawrence E Bloomfield; Over 70 poems published, including: Reflections in a Family Plot; Lamentations Over Carol; Deer Hunters Lament; The Jockey; Grandpap's Farm; Butterfly Dreamer; Words for my Mother; The Road; Octavian's Promise to Caesar; A Warrior's Plea. Contributions to: Poetic Page Magazine; Poet's Ink; Southern Poetry Association. Honours: Several awards in various poetry competitions; Columnist, Poet's Ink, 1991-93; Listed in several Who's Who in Poetry books. Memberships: Wheeling Area Chapter, West Virginia Poetry Society, Treasurer, 1991-95; West Virginia Poetry Society, Treasurer, 1995-96, State Treasurer, 1996-; Southern Poetry Association; Parnassus of World Poets. Address: Box 617-A Boggs Run Road, Benwood, WV 26031, USA.

BLOSSOM Laurel, b. 9 June 1943, Washington, District of Columbia, USA. Poet; Writer. Div, 1 daughter. Education: BA, Radcliffe College, 1966. Appointments: Director of Development, P & W, 1979-80. Publications: Any Minute, 1979; What's Wrong, 1987; The Papers Said, 1993. Contributions to: Poetry; Paris Review; Pequod; New York Quarterly; Confrontation; Carolina Quarterly; American Poetry Review; Columbia; Harper's. Honours: Scholar, Bread Loaf Writers Conference, 1976; Fellow, Squaw Valley Community of

Writers, 1977; Elliston Book Award Finalist, 1979; Yaddo Residency, 1979; Fellow, Ohio Arts Council, 1980-81; Nomination, Pushcart Prize, 1983, 1984, 1985, 1992; Finalist, National Poetry Series, 1985; Fellow, National Endowment for The Arts, 1987; Fellow, New York Foundation for The Arts, 1988; Associate, Atlantic Centre for The Arts, 1989. Memberships: Chair, Programme Committee, National Writer's Voice Project, 1990-95; Founder, The Writers Community, 1976. Address: 920 Park Avenue, No 2B, New York, NY 10028, USA.

BLUMENTHAL Michael Charles, b. 8 Mar 1949, Vineland, New Jersey, USA. Writer; Professor. 1 son. Education: BA, Philosophy, 1969; JD, Cornell Law School, 1974. Appointments: Bingham Distinguished Poet-in-Residence, University of Louisville, 1982; Briggs-Copeland Lecturer, Assistant Professor of Poetry, 1983-88, Associate Professor of English, Director of Creative Writing, 1988-93, Harvard University; Senior Fulbright Lecturer in American Literature, Eotvos Lorand University, 1992-95; Distinguished Visiting Writer-in-Residence, Boise State University, Idaho, 1996; Associate Professor of English, University of Haifa, Israel, 1996. Publications: Sympathetic Magic, 1980; Days We Would Rather Know, 1984; Laps, 1984; Against Romance, 1987; The Wages of Goodness, 1992; To Wed & To Woo: Poets on Marriage (editor), 1992; Weinstock Among the Dying, 1993. Contributions to: Poetry; The American Scholar; The Nation; Acni; Antaeus; Verse; The Lines Review; Prairie Schooner; New Criterion; Georgia Review. Honours: First Book Prize, Water Mark Poets of North America, 1980; Juniper Prize, University of Massachusetts, 1984; Lavan Younger Poets Prize, Academy of American Poets, 1986; Guggenheim Fellow, 1989; Harold U Ribelow Prize for Jewish Fiction, Hadassah magazine, 1994. Memberships: Poetry Society of America; Associated Writing Programs; Poets & Writers; PEN American Center. Address: c/o Dept of English, University of Haifa, Mt Carmel, Haifa 31905, Israel.

BLY Robert (Elwood), b. 23 Dec 1926, Madison, Minnesota, USA. Poet; Translator; Editor; Publisher. m. (1) Carolyn McLean, 1955, div 1979, (2) Ruth Counsell, 1980, 2 sons, 2 daughters. Education: St Olaf College, 1946-47; AB, Harvard University, 1950; MA, University of Iowa, 1956. Appointments: Publisher, Editor, 1958-; Various writing workshops. Publications: Poetry: The Lion's Tail and Eyes: Poems Written Out of Laziness and Silence, 1962; Silence in the Snowy Fields, 1962; A Love of Minute Particulars, 1985; What Have I Ever Lost By Dying?: Collected Prose Poems, 1993. Editor: The Sea and The Honeycomb, 1966; A Poetry Reading Against the Vietnam War, 1967; Translator: Over 35 books. Other: A Broadsheet Against the New York Times Book Review, 1961; Talking All Morning: Colleted Conversations and Interviews, 1980; The Eight Stages of Translation, 1983, 2nd edition, 1986; American Poetry: Wildness and Domesticity, 1990; Remembering James Wright, 1991; The Sibling Society, 1996. Honours: Fulbright Grant, 1956-57; Lowell Travelling Fellowship, 1964; Guggenheim Fellowships, 1964, 1972; American Academy of Arts and Letters Grant, 1965; Rockefeller Foundation Fellowship, 1967; National Book Award, 1968. Memberships: American Institute of Arts and Letters; Association of Literary Magazines of America, Executive Committee. Address: 1904 Girard Avenue South, Minneapolis, MN 54403, USA.

BOALCH Donald Howard, (Howard a'Bear), b. 25 Oct 1914, London, England. Librarian. m. Joyce Helen Coppock, 19 Feb 1948, 1 son, 1 daughter. Education: Corpus Christi College, Cambridge, 1933-36; MA, Cantab, 1940; MA, Oxon, 1962. Appointments: Assistant Keeper, Department of Oriental Antiquities, British Museum, 1947-48; Librarian, Archivist, Rothamsted Experimental Station, Harpenden, 1950-62; Sublibrarian in charge of scientific books, Bodleian Library, Oxford, 1962-75; Fellow, Corpus Christi College, Oxford, 1965-75. Publications: Caterwauls, 2nd edition, 1984; That Brave Vibration, 2nd edition, 1984; Each Way Free, 1985. Address: 4 Hill Top Road, Oxford, England.

BOBYSHEV Dmitry (Vasilievich), b. 11 Apr 1936, Russia. Writer of Russian Poetry and literary criticism; Teacher of Russian language and literature. Education: Diploma of Engineer, Leningrad Technological Institute, 1959. Appointments: Lecturer, Department of Slavic Languages and Literatures, University of Wisconsin at Milwaukee, 1982-85; Assistant Professor, Department of Slavic Languages and Literatures, University of Illinois, Urbana-Champaign, 1985-. Publications: Ziianiia, 1979; Zveri Sv Antoniia, 1989; Polnota Vsego, 1992; Russkie Tertsiny, 1992. Contributions to: USA periodicals: AGNI; TriQuarterly; Visions; Cumberland Poetry Review; Cream City Review; Clockwatch Review; Lucky Star; Poetry from the

Russian Underground; Russian Poetry; The Modern Period; Contemporary Russian Poetry; USSR Periodicals: Yunost; Den' poezil; Molodoi Leningrad; Zvezda; Znamia; Smena; Petropol; Leningradskii rabochii; Leningradskii universitet; Russian emigre periodicals: Kontinent; Grani; Russkaia Mysl: 22; Novyi Zhurnal; Perekriostki; Russki Al'manakh; Vstrechi; Vestnik RSKD; Streletz. Honour: Anna Akhmatova dedicated her poem Piataia rosa (The Fifth Rose) to him as a poet. Memberships: Modern Language Association; American Association of Teachers of East European Languages; Beast Fable Society; Writers Union, St Petersburg; Academy of American Poets. Literary Agent: Andrei Yurievich Ariev, Russia. Address: University of Illinois, Department of Slavic, 3092 FLB, 707 South Mathews Avenue. Urbana-Champaign, IL 61801, USA.

BOCCHORITANO A S. See: **SEGUI BENNASSAR Antoni.**

BOCK Layeh A, (Layeh Bock-Pallant), b. 11 Jan 1937, Montreal, Quebec, Canada. Writing Consultant. Div, 3 daughters. Education: BA, Swarthmore College; MA, University of New Mexico; PhD, Stanford University. Publication: Gestatten, 1967; Contributions to: Yellow Silk; Poetry Flash; Hasight-Ashberry Literary Journal; Beatitude; Probes; Various anthologies; Cafe Solo; Hyperem. Honour: Annual Poetry Prize, 1972. Membership: Poets and Writers Inc. Address: 642 Alcatraz No 106, Oakland, CA 94609, USA.

BOFFA Giovanni, b. 7 May 1922, Agno, Switzerland. Retired Professor. Education: PhD Literature, University of Florence, 1954. Appointments: Professor of Italian, Lugano Technicum, until 1985. Publications: Notturna, 1947; Mosaico disperso, 1951; Vigilia, 1956; Piccolo Rospo, 1958; Il vestito di legno, 1958; Pastelli fiorentini, 1958; Paesaggi, 1965; Signor Giacomo, 1966; Pastelli fiorentini, 1968; Sabbia del tempo, 1969; Al cielo del tuo sguardo, 19890. Contributions to: Several newspapers and reviews published in Italian; Founder, history and archaeology museum, Agno, Switzerland, 1955. Honours: Various important poetry and literary international awards. Memberships: Member of several literary and poetry societies worldwide; Member of several Knights Orders including Order of Malta.

BOGEN Don, b. 27 May 1949. Wisconsin, USA. Associate Professor of English. m. Cathryn Jeanne Long, 5 Sept 1976, 1 son, 1 daughter. Education: AB, 1971. MA, 1974, PhD, 1976, University of California at Berkeley. Appointments: Assistant Professor of English, 1976-82, Associate Professor of English, 1982-, University of Cincinnati. Publication: After the Splendid Display, 1986. Contributions to: New Republic; Nation; Paris Review; Poetry; Yale Review; Partisan Review; Kenyon Review; Ploughshares; Shenandoah; Stand; American Poetry Review. Honours: Edwin Markham Award, Eugene V Debs Foundation, 1976; Grand Prize, AWP Anniversary Awards. 1982; Individual Artists Fellowship, Ohio Arts Council, 1985; Ingram Merrill Foundation Grant, 1989; National Endowment for the Arts Fellowship, 1989; Camargo Foundation Fellowship, 1993. Memberships: National Book Critics Circle; Associated Writing Programmes. Address: 362 Terrace Avenue, Cincinnati, OH 45220, USA.

BOGLIUN Loredana, b. 18 Jan 1955, Pula-Pola, Croatia. Social Psychologist. m. Dino Bogliun, 2 Sept 1978, 1 son, 1 daughter. Education: Laurea in Psychology, 1978; Master in Psychology, 1986; PhD, Social Psychology, 1992. Appointments: University Professor, 1991-; Vice President of Istrian Region, Croatia, 1993-. Publications: Poesie, 1988; Vorbind Despre Noi, 1989; Mazere, 1993; Istarskite Zidišta, 1996; La Peicia, 1996; La Trasparenza, 1996. Contributions to: La Battana; Istra; Alfabeta; Il Territorio; Diverse Lingue; Balcanica; Republica; Issimo; Razgledi; Erasmus; Vilenica; Sodobnost; Corrispondenze; Approdi; Istria Nobilissima; Voci Nostre; Flowers of Peace. Honours: Istria Nobilissima, 1977, 1979, 1983, 1987, 1988, 1989, 1991, 1995; Trofeo Del Buonconsiglio Trento, 1987; Premio Drago Gervais Rijeka-Fiume, 1989. Address: Rudine 20, 52460 Buje-Buie, Istria, Croatia.

BOLAND Michael (John), b. 14 Nov 1950, Kingston, Surrey, England. Poet; Civil Servant. Appointment: Editor, The Arcadian (poetry magazine). Publications: The Midnight Circus; The Trout...Minus One, co-author, 1993. Contributions to: Envoi; Firing Squad; Purple Patch; Weyfarers; Various anthologies. Honour: Patricia Chown Sonnet Award. Memberships: Friends of Coleridge; Keats-Shelley Memorial Association; MIAP; PEN; Society of Civil Service Authors; Wordsworth Trust. Address: 11 Boxtree Lane, Harrow Weald, Middlesex HA3 6JU, England.

BOLD Alan, b. 20 Apr 1943, Edinburgh, Scotland. Writer. m. 29 June 1963, 1 daughter. Education: Edinburgh University, 1961-64. Appointments: Journalist. Times Educational Supplement, 1965-66; Reviewer, The Scotsman, 1970-88; Reviewer, Glasgow Herald, 1989-. Publications: Society Inebrious, 1965; To Find The New. 1967; The Voyage, 1968; A Perpetual Motion Machine, 1969; Penguin Modern Poets 15, 1969; The State of The Nation, 1969; The Auld Symie, 1971; He Will Be Greatly Missed, 1971; A Century of People, 1971; A Pint of Bitter, 1971; Scotland. Yes, 1978; This Fine Day, 1979; In This Corner, 1983; Summoned by Knox, 1985; Bright Lights Blaze Out, 1986. Contributions to: New York Times; Times Literary Supplement; London Review of Books; New Statesman; Glasgow Herald; Scotsman; 2 Plus 2; Poetry Review; Stand. Memberships: Scotish Poetry Library; Society of Authors; Society of Scottish Artists. Address: Balbirnie Burns East Cottage, Balbirnie Park, Markinch, Fife KY7 6NE, Scotland.

BOLEK Juliusz Erazm, b. 25 Nov 1963, Warsaw, Poland. Poet; Writer of Short Stories; Literary and Arts Critic; Journalist. Education: Faculty of Journalism and Political Sciences, University of Warsaw, 1985-91. Appointments: Editor-in-Chief, Enigma (magazine for young intellectuals), 1987-; Supervisor, Public Opinion Surveys Centre, 1988; Owner, I'm God Sent Enterprise (publishing house), 1990-91; Press Spokesman, Central Student Club of Warsaw Technical College, Stodota, 1991-93; Director, Studio-Kineo Arts Gallery, Warsaw, 1991-. Publications: Collections of Poems: Teksty. 1985; Nago, 1986; Miniatury, 1987; Prywatne Zagrozenie, 1989; Skroty Szalenstwa, 1991; Serge Btyskawicy, 1995. Contributions to: Radar; Razem; Walka Mlodych Przeglad Tygodniwy; Tygodnik Kulturalny; Kierunki; Zycie Literackie; Namietnosci; Cherwell, Oxford University Weekly; Miesiecznik Literacki; Nurt; Okolice; Miraz Premiera; Missland: Slowo Powszechne; Trybuna; Sztandar Mlodych; Ekran; Ekran; Dziennik Polski (The Polish Daily, London). Membership: The Polish Journalists Association; The Polish Writers' Association. Address: ul Chmielna 35 m 199, 00-117 Warsaw, Poland.

BOLTON Ken, b. 24 June 1949, Sydney, New South Wales, Australia. Poet; Art Critic. Education: BA, University of Sydney, 1974. Publications: Selected Poems, 1992; Two Poems - A Drawing of the Sky; The Ferrara Poems (co-author); Talking to You; Blazing Shoes; Sestina to the Centre of the Brain; Airborne Dogs (co-author); Notes for Poems; Blonde & French; Four Poems. Contributions to: Scripsi; Otis Rush; Salt; Meanjin; Ear in the Wheatfield; Overland. Honour: Michel Wesley Wright Award, Melbourne University, 1990. Address: PO Box 21, North Adelaide, South Australia 5006, Australia.

BOND Edward, b. 18 July 1934, London, England. Playwright; Director; Translator; Poet. Publications: Plays, 4 volumes, 1977-92; Theatre Poems and Songs, 1978; Collected Poems, 1978-85, 1985; Selected Letters, 4 volumes, 1994-95; Opera libretti for Hans Werner Henze: We Come to the River, 1976 and The English Cat, 1983; Translations. Honour: Honorary DLitt, Yale University, 1977. Membership: Theatre Writers Union. Address: c/o Margaret Ramsay Ltd, 14A Goodwin's Court, London WC2N 4LL, England.

BOND Harold, b. 2 Dec 1939, Boston, Massachusetts, USA. Poet; Teacher; Editor. Education: AB, English and Journalism, Northeastern University, 1962; MFA, Creative Writing, University of Iowa, 1967. Appointments: Instructor, Center for Adult Education, Cambridge, Massachusetts, 1968-; Copy Editor, Boston Globe, 1969-71; Editor, 1969-70, Editorial Board, 1971-, Ararat magazine; Vice President, Poets Who Teach, Massachusetts, 1978-79; Various teaching positions, adult education, poetry, Poet-in-Schools, Massachusetts; Founder, Director, Seminars in Poetry Writing, Belmont, Massachusetts, 1978-. Publications: Poetry: The Northern Wall, 1969; Dancing on Water, 1970; The Way It Happens to You, 1979; Other Worlds. Contributions to: Books and anthologies, including: Young American Poets, 1968; New Yorker Book of Poems, 1969; 11 Boston Poets, 1970; Getting Into Poetry, 1972; Armenian-North American Poets, 1974; I Sing The Song of Myself: Autobiographical Poems, 1978; Despite This Flesh: The Disabled in Stories and Poems, 1985; Light Year '87, 1986, Sutured Words: Contemporary Poetry About Medicine, 1987; The Villanelle: The Evolution of a Poetic Form, 1988; Introduction to Special Education: Teaching in an Age of Challenge, 1992; The Magical Pine Ring: Culture and the Imagination in Armenian-American Literature, 1992; Articulations: The Body in Poetry, 1994; Journals include: American Literary Review, Beloit Poetry Journal, Boston Globe, Harper's Magazine, Literary Review, New Republic, New Yorker, North

American Review, Saturday Review, Shenandoah, Yankee. Honours: Awards from: Armenian Allied Arts Association of America; Kansas City Star; Associated Writing Programmes; Authors League; PEN Fellowship, National Endowment for the Arts, 1976; Fellowship Finalist, Artists Foundation, MA, 1977. Address: 11 Chestnut Street, Melrose, MA 02176, USA.

BOND Katherine (Kay) L, b. 7 June 1949, Sardis, Mississippi, USA. Transcriptionist. m. John R Bond IV, 27 July 1969, 2 daughters. Contributions to: Treasured Poems of America Winter, 1996; Poetic Voices of America; Treasured Poems of America Summer, 1996; American Poetry Annual; Impressions; Echoes from the Silence; Ages and Stages; Freedom; Celebration of Life; Best Poems of 1996; Mists of Enchantment; Spirit of the Age; A Tapestry of Thoughts; At Water's Edge. Anthologies: Journey to our Dreams; Our Captured Moments; Promises to Keep; Inspirations; Meditations; Famous Poems of the Twentieth Century; Poet's Corner; Perspectives; Achieving Excellence. Honours: Award for International Poet of Merit, 1995; Editor's Choice Awards, National Library of Poetry; Two Honorable Mention Awards, 1995; President's Award for Literary Excellence, 1996; Four Achievement of Merit Awards through Creative Arts and Science Enterprises; Editor's Preference Award of Excellence. Memberships: International Society of Poets; National Authors Registry; International Society of Authors and Artists; Poet's Guild; The National Poet's Association. Address: 316 Notre Dame Avenue, Joliet, IL 60436-1254, USA.

BONTRIDDER Albert, b. 4 April 1921, Brussels, Belgium. Poet; Architect. m. Olga Dohnalova, 17 Sept 1953, 1 son, 1 daughter. Education: Diploma in Architecture, 1942. Publications: Hoog Water, 1951; Dood Hout, 1955; Bagatelle, 1962; Open Einde, 1967; Zelfverbranding, 1971; Gedichten, 1942-1972, 1973; Huizen Vieren Haat, 1979; Een oog te Veel, 1983; Groeten van Mijnheer en Mevrouw Ledepop, 1990; Poesie Flamade d'aujourd'hui, 1986, 1988. Contributions to: Tijd En Mens; Kentering; Architecture. Honours: Arkpreis Van het Vrije Woord, 1957; Prix de la Province du Brabant, 1960; Prix de la ville Heist-Duinbergen, 1969; Prix Dirk Martens, 1970; Prix Jan Campert. 1972; Prix SABAM for La Traduction, 1990. Memberships: PEN Club International, Belgium, President, 1975-80; Academie Royale des Sciences, des Lettres et des Beaux-Arts de Belgique; President, 1989, European Association for the Promotion of Poetry, Louvain, 1987. Address: Avenue Lequime 16a, B-1640 Rhode Saint Genese, Belgium.

BOOTH Philip, b. 8 Oct 1925, Hanover, New Hampshire, USA. Professor of English (Retired); Poet. m. Margaret Tillman, 1946, 3 daughters. Education: AB, Dartmouth College, 1948; MA, Columbia University, 1949. Appointments: Assistant Professor, Wellesley College, 1954-61; Associate Professor 1961-65, Professor of English and Poet-in-Residence 1965-85. Syracuse University. Publications: Letter from a Distant Land, 1957; The Islanders, 1961; North by East, 1966; Weathers and Edges, 1966; Margins: A Sequence of New and Selected Poems, 1970; Available Light, 1976; Before Sleep, 1980; Relations: Selected Poems, 1950-85, 1986; Selves, 1990; Pairs: New Poems, 1994; Trying to Say It: Outlooks and Insights on How Poems Happen, 1996. Honours: Guggenheim Fellowships, 1958, 1965; Theodore Roethke Prize, 1970; National Endowment for the Arts Fellowship, 1980; Academy of American Poets Fellowship, 1983; Rockefeller Fellowship, 1966; Maurice English Poetry Award, 1987. Address: PO Box 330, Castine, ME 04421, USA.

BOOTHROYD Christine, b. 31 Mar 1934, Batley, Yorkshire, England. Linguist. m. Don Brinkley, 10 Apr 1982, 1 stepson, 1 stepdaughter. Education: Leeds College of Commerce, 1951-52; UCW Teachers Certificate, University College of Wales, Aberystwyth, 1965-66; Diplomas in Italian, Perugia and Florence. Appointments: Secretarial Posts, Harrogate, Paris, Rome, Vienna, 1952-63; Teacher of French/Italian, Leeds, 1963-65; Lecturer in charge of Modern Languages, North Oxfordshire Technical College, 1966-77; Part-time Lecturer, French/Italian, Banbury and Harrogate. Publications: The Floating World, 1975; The Snow Island, 1982; The Lost Moon, 1992. Contributions to: Arts Council Anthology 3; Workshop New Poetry; Orbis; Glasgow Magazine; Writers in Concert; Doors; Krax; Moorlands Review; Dalesman; Yorkshire Journal. Membership: Harrogate Writers' Circle. Address: 35 St George's Road, Harrogate, North Yorkshire HG2 9BP, England.

BORDEN William (Vickers), b. 27 Jan 1938, Indianapolis, Indiana, USA; Chester Fritz Distinguished Professor of English; Writer;

Poet; Dramatist; Editor. m. Nancy Lee Johnson, 17 Dec 1960, 1 son, 2 daughters. Education: AB, Columbia University, 1960; MA, University of California at Berkeley, 1962. Appointments: Instructor 1962-64, Assistant Professor 1966-70, Associate Professor 1970-82, Professor of English 1982-, University of North Dakota; Fiction Editor, North Dakota Quarterly. Publications: Fiction: Superstoe, novel, 1967, 1996; Many short stories; Poetry: Slow Step and Dance, chapbook, 1991; Other: Numerous plays, including: The Last Prostitute, 1980; Tap Dancing Across the Universe, 1981; Loon Dance, 1982; The Only Woman Awake is the Woman Who Has Heard the Flute, 1983; Makin' It, 1984; The Consolation of Philosophy, 1986; Meet Again, 1992; Don't Dance Me Outside, 1993; Musical Drama: Sakakawea, 1987; Also Screenplays, radio plays, video scripts. Contributions to: Many anthologies and periodicals. Honours: North Dakota Centennial Drama Prize, 1989; ASCAP Awards, 1990, 1991, 1992; Burlington Northern Award, University of North Dakota, 1990; Minnesota Distinguished Artist Award, 1992; Minnesota State Arts Board Career Opportunity Grant, 1996. Memberships: American Society of Composers, Authors, and Publishers; Associated Writing Programs; Authors League of America; Dramatists Guild; PEN. Address: Route 6, Box 284, Bemidji, MN 56601, USA.

BORLAND Betty Jean, b. 17 Oct 1919, Oil City, Pennsylvania, USA. Retired Secretary. Education: High School, Dubois, Pennsylvania, 1937. Publications: Treasures From The Heart, 1988, vol II, 1991. Contributions to: World of Poetry; The National Library of Poetry; Parnassus of World Poets, 1994. Honours include: Award of Merit Certificate, 1988, 1990 (twice); Golden Poet Award, 1990. Membership: National League of American Pen Women. Address: 1311 Delaware Avenue South, No 445 SW, Washington, DC 20024, USA.

BORN Anne Rosemary, b. 9 July 1925, Cooden Beach, Sussex, England. History Writer; Poet; Translator. m. 1 June 1946, 3 sons, 1 daughter. Education: MA, Copenhagen University, 1952; MLitt, Oxford University, 1976. Appointments: Tutor, St Clare's Hall, Oxford; Tutor in Danish, Cambridge University; Tutor for Oxford Department of Education; Occasional Tutor for Exeter University, Tutor, Arvon Foundation and WEA; Tutor of Advanced Poetry Course, Exeter and Devon Arts Centre. Publications: Salcombe Shipyards, 1978, 1980; Airy Lines, 1978; Changing Views, 1979; Lighting Effects, 1987; Figures for Landscape, 1990; Poems of Landscape, 1990; Drake, 1993; Seeing Through, 1994; Slant as an Open Door, 1994. Contributions to: Encounter; Ambit; Rialto; Interactions; Outposts; Quartz; Green Book; Argo; Acumen; Bound Spiral; Orbis; Envoi; The Independent; Iron; Odyssey; Sean; Scratch; Smiths Knoll; Spokes; Tears in the Fence; Times Literary Supplement; Verse; Anthologies: Arvon Poetry Competition Anthology, 1987; Klaonica (Bosnia Poems), 1993; 4 Company of Poets Anthologies, 1990-93; Ripley Poetry Association Competition Anthology, 1993; South West Poetry Competitions Anthologies, 1992, 1993; Words International, 1989; What Poets Eat, 1994. Honours: 1st Prize, New Poetry Competition, 1980; 4th Newbury Competition, 1985; 2nd Other Poetry Competition, 1985; 2nd Rhyme Revival Competition, 1987; Special Commendation Arvon Competition, 1987; Commended SW Poetry Competition, 1991; Runner-up, Yorkshire Poetry Competition, 1991; Jersey Eisteddfod Competition, 1995. Memberships: Poetry Society; Society of Authors Translators Association, Committee Member, Chair, 1992-95; Company of Poets Group, Devon; Committee Member, Swedish-English Literary Translators Association. Address: Oversteps, Froude Road, Salcombe, Devon TQ8 8LH, England.

BOROWSKY Neal, b. 28 June 1966, Brooklyn, New York, USA. Graphic Designer; Sculptor. Education: BFA, School of Visual Arts, 1988. Appointments: Designer, Martha Vartas Productions. Contributions to: American Poetry Anthology. Membership: Poetry Society of America. Address: 106 Livingstone Avenue, Edison, NJ 00820, USA.

BORSON Roo, b. 20 Jan 1952, Berkeley, California, USA. Poet; Essayist. Education: University of California, Santa Barbara, 1969-71; BA, Goddard College, 1973; MFA, University of British Columbia, 1977. Appointments: Writer-in-Residence, University of Western Ontario, 1987-88, Concordia University, 1993. Publications: Landfall, 1977; In The Smoky Light of the Fields, 1980; Rain, 1980; A Sad Device, 1981; The Whole Night, Coming Home, 1984; Co-Author, The Transparence of November/Snow, 1985; Intent or The Weight of The World, 1989; Night Walk: Selected Poems, 1994; Water Memory, 1996. Contributions to: American Poetry Review; Saturday Night;

Poetry Australia; De Tweede Ronde; Literary Half-Yearly; Queens Quarterly. Honours: MacMillan Poetry Prize, 1977; CBC Prize for Poetry, 1982, 1989, for Personal Essay, 1991; Nominee, Governor General's Award, 1985, 1994. Memberships: PEN International; Writers' Union of Canada; League of Canadian Poets. Address: c/o Writers' Union of Canada, 24 Ryerson Avenue, Toronto, Ontario M5T 2P3, Canada.

BOSLEY John E, b. 26 Aug 1937, Stevenage, Hertfordshire, England. Writer; Counsellor. Div. 2 sons, 2 daughters. Education: BA, 1961, PGCE, 1962, Manchester; MSc, Bradford, 1982. Appointments: Teacher, London, Sudan, Leeds; Youth Worker, Bradford; Substance Counsellor, Leeds; Writer, Huddersfield. Contributions to: Bogg; X-Calibre; Envoi; Foolscap; Iota; Klik; North; Odyssey; Pennine Platform; Psychopoetica; Scratch; Sepia; The Wide Skirt; Local radio and buses (Yorkshire Rider). Honour: Huddersfield Poetry Competition 2nd, 1990. Membership: Poetry Society. Address: 9 Wheatroyd Lane, Huddersfield HD5 8XS, Yorkshire, England.

BOSLEY Keith Anthony, b. 16 Sept 1937, England. Poet; Translator. m. Satu Salo, 27 Aug 1982, 3 sons. Education: Universities of Reading, Paris and Caen, 1956-60; BA, Honours, French. Appointments: BBC Staff, 1961-93; Visiting Lecturer for BBC and British Council, Middle East, 1981. Publications: The Possibility of Angels, 1969; And I Dance, 1972; Dark Summer, 1976; Stations, 1979; A Chiltern Hundred, 1987; Translations of poetry include: The Song of Songs, 1976, Mallarmé: The Poems, 1977, Eino Leino: Whitsongs, 1978, The Elek Book of Oriental Verse, 1979, Jerzy Ficowski: A Reading of Ashes, 1981, From The Theorems of Master Jean de La Ceppède, 1983, The Kalevala, 1989, Luis de Camões: Epic and Lyric, 1990, The Kanteletar, 1992; The Great Bear, 1993; Odes by Aleksis Kivi, 1994; A Centenary Pessoa, 1995. Contributions to: Many newspapers, reviews, magazines, journals and periodicals. Honours: Finnish State Prize for Translators, 1978; 1st Prize in British Comparative Literature Association Translation Competition, 1979-80; 1st Prize, Goethe Society Translation Competition, 1982; Knight, First Class, Order of the White Rose of Finland, 1991. Membership: Corresponding Member, Finnish Literature Society, Helsinki. Address: 108 Upton Road, Upton-cum-Chalvey, Slough SL1 2AW, England.

BOSVELD Jennifer Miller, (Jennifer DeRhodes, Jennifer Groce, Jennifer Welch), b. 24 Jan 1945, Columbus, Ohio, USA. Poet; Writer; Publisher; Writing Centre Director; Teacher of Poetry; Career Counsellor; Consultant. m. (1) Raoul DeRhodes, 1963, 1 son, (2) Richard Groce, 1971, 1 son, (3)1981, (4) 1986. Education: Ohio State University, School of Social Work. Appointments: Executive Director, Friends of the Homeless Inc; Administrative Rules Liaison, Ohio Department of Mental Retardation and Developmental Disabilities; Executive Director, Disaster Research Centre, Ohio State University; Publisher, Pudding House Publications and Pudding Magazine: The International Journal of Applied Poetry; The Poetry Publishing Workshop and The Poetry Writing Workshop. Publications: Earthdays, 1976 Magic House, 1979; The Pulling, 1981; Free With the Purchase of a Spaghetti Fork, 1981; Topics for Getting in Touch: A Poetry Therapy Songbook, 1981, 39th printing, 1996; Criminal Hands, 1985; Jazz Kills the Paperboy, 1995; The Unitarian Universalist Poets: A Contemporary American Survey, Editor, 1996. Contributions to: Hiram Poetry Review; Negative Capability; Amelia; Christian Science Monitor; Smackwarm; Pteranadon; Chiron Review; Bottomfish; Cornfield Review; Wind; Pig Iron; Maryland Poetry Review; Coffeehouse Poems, An Anthology, 1996; Over 400 others. Honour: Ohio Arts Council Individual Artist Fellowship, 1995; Pioneer Award, National Association for Poetry Therapy, 1996. Memberships: Numerous past poetry memberships including Women's Poetry Workshop; Montage. Address: Pudding House, 60 North Main Street, Johnstown, OH 43031, USA.

BOSWORTH J(ames) A(lfred), b. 16 Feb 1936, Hastings, Sussex, England. m. Anne Elizabeth Moran, 19 Dec 1960, 5 sons. Education: BA, Open University, 1994. Appointments: Army Officer, NS and Reg Commissions, 1955-78; Self-employed Administrator of nursing home/hotel, 1978-85; Articulated Heavy Goods and Public Service Vehicle Operator, 1985-. Publications: Neknus and Other Poems, 1984; Clouds of Glory and Other Poems, 1985; Natural Memories, 1992; A Theory for Art, 1993; Prefaces, 1994. Contributions to: Numerous periodicals and competitions. Memberships: Poetry Society; British Society of Aesthetics; Open University Poets; Founder Member, New-Tradition Movement. Address: c/o The Midland Bank Plc, Old Town Hall, Bradford-On-Avon, Wiltshire BA15 1LS, England.

BOULLATA Issa J, b. 25 Feb 1929, Jerusalem, Palestine. Professor of Arabic Literature; Literary Critic and Scholar; Writer; Translator. m. Marita Seward, 12 Aug 1960, 3 sons, 1 daughter. Education: BA, 1st class honours, 1964, PhD, Arabic Literature, 1969, University of London. Appointments: Senior Teacher of Arabic Literature, De La Salle College, Jerusalem, 1949-52, Ahliyyah College, Ramallah, 1952-53, St George's School, Jerusalem, 1953-68; Professor of Arabic Literature and Language, Hartford Seminary, Connecticut, 1968-75, McGill University, Montreal, 1975-; Editorial Board, Al-Arabiyya, journal of American Association of Teachers of Arabic, 1995-97. Publications: Modern Arab Poets, 1950-1975, 1976; Critical Perpsectives on Modern Arabic Literature, 1980; Poems in: Modern Arabic Poetry, an Anthology, 1987, Trends and Issues in Contemporary Arab Thought, 1990; Translations from Arabic: The First Well: A Bethlehem Boyhood, by Jabra Ibrahim Jabra, 1995; The Game of Forgetting, by Mohamed Berrada, 1996. Contributions to: Journal of Arabic Literature; Edebiyat; Muslim World; Middle East Journal; Religion and Literature; Islamic Quarterly; Al-Arabiyya; Arab Studies Quarterly; Encyclopaedia of World Literature in the 20th Century; Jusoor; Book reviews in World Literature Today. Honours: Arberry Memorial Prize for Arabic Literature, Pembroke Arabic Research Group of Cambridge, England, 1972; Award for Arabic Literature in Translation, University of Arkansas Press, 1993. Memberships include: Middle East Studies Association of North America; Canadian Comparative Literature Association; International Association of Middle East Studies. Address: Institute of Islamic Studies, McGill University, 3485 McTavish Street, Montreal, Quebec H3A 1Y1, Canada.

BOULLOSA Carmen, b. 4 Sept 1954, Mexico City, Mexico. Writer. m. Alejandro Aura, 1981, 1 son, 1 daughter. Publications: El Hilo olvida; La Memoria Vacia; Ingobernable; Lealtad; Abierta; La Salvaja; Soledumbre. Contributions to: Revista Vuelta; Periodico de poesia; Revista de la UNAM; Los Universitario; El Paseante; Mandorla; TriQuarterly; Magazine Dominical de El Espectador; Sabado' El Semanario de Novedades. Honour: Premio Xavier Villaurrutia; Guggenheim Fellowship. Address: Tiepolo 20, Mixcoac DF 03710, Mexico.

BOUVARD Marguerite Anne, (Marguerite Guzman Bouvard), b. 10 Jan 1937, Trieste, Italy. Professor; Writer. m. Jacques Bouvard, 25 Nov 1959, 1 son, 1 daughter. Education: BA, Northwestern University, 1958; MA, Political Science, Radcliffe College, 1960; PhD, Political Science, Harvard University, 1965; MA, Creative Writing, Boston University, 1977. Appointment: Professor of Political Science and English, Regis College, 1966-. Publications: Journeys Over Water, 1980; Editor, Landscape and Exile, 1985; Voices From An Island, 1985; Of Light and Silence, 1990; With the Mothers of the Plaza de Mayo, 1993. Contributions to: Ploughshares; Partisan Review; Ohio Journal; Mid-West Quarterly; West Branch; Southern Humanities Review; Sojourner; Yarrow; Radcliffe Quarterly; Literary Review; Centennial Review; Caesura; San Jose Studies; Christian Science Monitor. Honours: All Nations Poetry Contest, 1975; Scholarship in Poetry, Bread Loaf Writers' Conference, 1976; Residencies at the MacDowell Colony, The Leighton Arts Colony Banff, Yaddo, The Virginia Centre for The Creative Arts, The Djerassi Foundation, Villa Montalvo, The Cottages at Hedgebrook, 1978-90; Quarterly Review of Literature Contest for book, 1985. Memberships: New England Poetry Club; PEN; Poetry Society of America. Address: 6 Brookfield Circle, Wellesley, MA 02181, USA.

BOWDEN Roland Heywood, b. 19 Dec 1916, Lincoln, England. Teacher of Art and English. m. Regine Rainer, 2 Jan 1946, 1 son, 1 daughter. Education: BArch, Liverpool School of Architecture, 1939. Appointments: Head, Art Department, Black Well School, Harrow, 1949-54; Head, Art Department, Manhood Community College, Selsey, 1954-80. Publications: Poems From Italy, 1970; Every Season is Another, 1986. Contributions to: A Celebration, South West Review; Poetry Matters; Words; Words International; Words Book, 1985-86. Honours: 1st Prize, Cheltenham Festival Poetry Competition, 1982; 1st Prize, Downland All Sussex Poetry Competition, 1983. Memberships: National Poetry Secretariat; Chichester Poetry Circle. Address: 2 Roughmere Cottage, Lavant, Chichester, West Sussex PO18 0BG, England.

BOWERING George Harry, b. 1 Dec 1936, Penticton, British Columbia, Canada. Professor of English. m. Angela Luoma, 14 Dec 1963, 1 daughter. Education: BA, 1960, MA, 1963, University of British Columbia. Appointments: Professor, Simon Fraser University; Writer-in-Residence, Sir George Williams University, Montreal.

1967-68. Publications: In The Flesh, 1974; The Catch, 1976; Another Mouth, 1979; Particular Accidents, 1981; West Window, 1982; Kerrisdale Elegies, 1984; Delayed Mercy, 1986; Sticks and Stones, 1989; Urban Snow, 1991; George Bowering: Selected Poems 1961-1992, 1993. Contributions to: Origin; Poetry, Chicago; Atlantic Monthly; London Magazine; Prism International; Nation; El Corno Emplumado. Honours: Governor-General's Award, 1969; Award for Poetry, Canadian Authors Association, 1994. Literary Agent: Denise Bukowski, Toronto, Canada. Address: 2499 West 37 Avenue, Vancouver, British Columbia V6M 1P4, Canada.

BOWERING Marilyn (Ruthe), b. 13 Apr 1949, Winnipeg, Ontario, Canada. Poet; Writer. m. Michael S Elcock, 3 Sept 1982, 1 daughter. Education: University of British Columbia, 1968-69; BA 1971, MA 1973, University of Victoria; University of New Brunswick, 1975-78. Appointments: Writer-in-Residence, Aegean School of Fine Arts, Paros, Greece, 1973-74; Visiting Lecturer 1978-82, Lecturer in Creative Writing 1982-86, 1989, Visiting Associate Professor of Creative Writing, 1993-96, University of Victoria, British Columbia; Faculty, 1992, Writer-in-Residence, 1993-94, Banff Centre, Alberta; Writer in Residence, Memorial University of Newfoundland, 1995. Publications: Poetry: The Liberation of Newfoundland, 1973; One Who Became Lost, 1976; The Killing Room, 1977; Third/Child Zian, 1978; The Book of Glass, 1978; Sleeping with Lambs, 1980; Giving Back Diamonds, 1982; The Sunday Before Winter, 1984; Anyone Can See I Love You, 1987; Grandfather was a Soldier, 1987; Calling All the World, 1989; Love As It Is, 1993. Novels: Autobiography, 1996; The Visitors Have All Returned, 1979; To All Appearances a Lady, 1990-. Editor: Many Voices: An Anthology of Contemporary Canadian Indian Poetry (with David A Day), 1977; Guide to a Labor Code of British Columbia, 1980. Contributions to: Anthologies and journals. Honours: Many Canada Council Awards for Poetry; Du Maurier Award for Poetry, 1978; National Magazine Award for Poetry, 1989; Long Poem Prize, Malahat Review, 1994. Memberships: League of Canadian Poets; Writers Union of Canada. Address: 3777 Jennifer Road, Victoria, British Columbia V8P 3X1, Canada.

BOWERS Edgar, b. 2 Mar 1924, Rome, Georgia, USA. Poet; Emeritus Professor of English. Education: Erskine College, 1941-42; Princeton University, 1943-44; BA, University of North Carolina, 1947; PhD, Stanford University, 1953. Appointments: Instructor in English, Duke University, 1952-55; Assistant Professor of English, Harpur College, State University of New York at Endicott, 1955-58; Assistant Professor, 1958-61, Associate Professor, 1961-67, Professor of English, 1967-91, Professor Emeritus, 1991-, University of California at Santa Barbara. Publications: The Form of Loss, 1956; The Astronomers, 1965; Living Together, 1973; Witnesses, 1981; Chaco Canyon, 1987; Thirteen Views of Santa Barbara, 1989; For Louis Pasteur, 1990; How We Came From Paris to Blois, 1991. Contributions to: Anthologies and periodicals. Honours: Fulbright Fellowship, 1950-51; Guggenheim Fellowships, 1959, 1969; University of California Creative Arts Award, 1963; Ingram Merrill Award, 1976; Brandeis University Creative Arts Award, 1978; Bollingen Prize, 1989; Harriet Monroe Prize, 1989; American Institute of Arts and Letters Award, 1991. Address: 1201 Greenwich Street, Apt 601, San Francisco, CA 94109, USA.

BOWERS Fleur(ette E), b. 8 Nov 1918, Jamaica, West Indies. Ex Government Officer. m. Donald Thomas Bowers, 31 July 1944, dec, 1 son, 1 daughter. Education: Associate Student in 20th Century Poetry, Open University, 1980. Publication: The Golden Thread, in aid of UNICEF Outposts, 1979; Breaking the Silence, 1993. Contributions to: Kites Anthology, 1977, Editor, Publisher to 1984, 1992; Highgate Poets, annually to 1995; Honorary Secretary and Treasurer, Envoi; Buzz Quarterly Magazine; Highgate Society; Regional Anthologies Poetry Now, 1993. Honours: Dorothy Tutin, 2nd Prize, Hastings, 1990; Local Library Support Group, 1st Prize, 1992. Memberships: Arts Council Poetry Library; Highgate Poets; Ver Poets. Address: 5 Springfield Avenue, Muswell Hill, London N10 3SU, England.

BOWLES Paul (Frederic), b. 30 Dec 1910, New York, New York, USA. Author; Poet; Composer. m. Jane Sydney Auer, Feb 1938 (dec 1973). Education: Studied music with Aaron Copland and Nadia Boulanger. Publications: Novels: The Sheltering Sky, 1949; Let It Come Down, 1952; The Spider's House, 1955; Up Above the World, 1966; Stories: A Little Stone, 1950; Collected Stories, 1979; A Delicate Episode, 1988; Unwelcome Words, 1989; Poetry: The Thicket of Spring, 1972; Next to Nothing, 1981; Other: Their Heads Are Green and Their Hands Are Blue, 1963; Without Stopping (autobiography),

1972; Points in Time, 1982; In Touch: The Letters of Paul Bowles, 1994; Paul Bowles: Music (essays, interviews, reviews), 1995. Honours: Guggenheim Fellowship, 1941; Rockefeller Grant, 1959. Address: c/o Ecco Press, 100 West Broad Street, Hopewell, NJ 08525, USA.

BOWMAN Roberta Pipes, b. 1 July 1915, USA. Writer; Painter. m. Elton Nuel Bowman, 24 Jan 1948, 2 sons. Education: Business College, 1941; Texas Christian University, 1942-48. Appointments: Secretary, Pure Oil Company, Texaco; Administrative Assistant, Federal Aviation Administration. Publications: Make Room for Joy, 1942; In This Our Times, 1977; Writing That Certain Poem, 1988; Poems for Christmas, 1990; Wind, Be Still, 1992; C & W Poems, 1995; Welcome to Today, 1995. Contributions to: Galaxy of Verse; Channels; Pentecostal Evangel; Pocket Inspirations; Numerous others including: Fort Worth Star Telegram; Fort Worth Press; World Poetry Society International; New York Herald Tribune; Rotarian; Capper's Weekly; Baptist Standard; Composers and Authors Magazine; Poetry Society of Texas Yearbook; National Federation of State Poetry Society Prize Poems. Honours: 11 Poetry Society of Texas Awards, 1956-1996; National Poetry Day, 1966, 1970, 1990, 1995; Chas Hanna Award, 1985, 1990; Composers, Authors and Artists Mason Sonnet Award, 1986, 1990, 1996; Welcome to Today, Winner, Lucidity Chapbook Contest, 1995. Memberships: Poetry Society of America; Poetry Society of Texas; Poets of Tarrant County; Composers, Authors, Artists of America; National Composers, Authors and Artists Association. Address: 3521 Eastridge Drive, Fort Worth, TX 76117, USA.

BOYD Megan E, b. 19 Aug 1956, New Mexico, USA. Poet. m. Scott Chaskey, 3 June 1982, 1 son, 1 daughter. Education: BA, Bennington College, 1980; MA, Lesley College, 1981; Writer's Year Abroad, Antioch International, London, England, 1977-78. Publications: Blue is the Color that Made the World, 1969; Heartwood, 1980; New Voices, Academy of American Poets Anthology, 1984; Gathering to Deep Water, 1988; Peace on Earth, book of prayers from around the world, 1992. Contributions to: Silo; The Hamprons; Boadside; Manhatten Poetry Review, Issue 10. Honours: Creative Writing Awards, junior and senior years, 1973-74, Sewickly Academy; Academy of American Poets, Poetry Prize, 1980; Hamptons International Poetry Prize, 1989. Address: PO Box 27, Sag Harbor, NY 11963, USA.

BRACKENBURY Alison, b. 20 May 1953, Gainsborough, Lincolnshire, England. Poet. Education: BA, English, St Hugh's College, Oxford, 1975. Publications: Journey to a Cornish Wedding, 1977; Two Poems, 1979; Dreams of Power and Other Poems, 1981; Breaking Ground and Other Poems, 1984; Christmas Roses and Other Poems, 1988; Seleected Poems, 1991; 1892, 1995. Honour: Eric Gregory Award, 1982. Address: c/o Carcanet Press, 208-212 Corn Exchange Buildings, Manchester M4 3BQ, England.

BRACKENBURY Rosalind, b. 14 May 1942, London, England. Writer. 1 son, 1 daughter. Education: MA, History, Cambridge University, 1963; PGCE with distinction, London University, 1964. Appointments: Leicester University Extra-Mural Department, 1975-82; Edinburgh University Extra-Mural Department, 1982-86; Writer-in-Residence, Dumfries and Galloway, 1989. Publications: Telling Each Other It Is Possible, 1986; Making for the Secret Places, 1989; Coming Home the Long Way Round the Mountain, 1993. Contributions to: Stand; Other Poetry; Writing Women; Chapman; Cencrastus; Poetry Now; Lines Review; Meanjin (Australia); Adelaide Review; Green Book; Resurgence; Anthologies: Sleeping With Monsters; Frankestein's Daughter; Small School Anthology. Memberships: Founder Member, Shore Poets, Eith, Scotland, 1991-; Key West Poets' Guild, Florida, USA, 1992. Address: 14 Enverleith Terrace, Edinburgh EH3 5NS, Scotland.

BRADBURY Ray (Douglas), b. 22 Aug 1920, Waukegan, Illinois, USA. Writer; Poet; Dramatist. m. Marguerite Susan McClure, 27 Sept 1947, 4 daughters. Education: Public Schools. Publications: Novels: The Martian Chronicles, 1950; Dandelion Wine, 1957; Something Wicked This Way Comes, 1962; Death is a Lonely Business, 1985; A Graveyard for Lunatics, 1990; Green Shadows, White Whale, 1992. Short Story Collections: Dark Carnival, 1947; The Illustrated Man, 1951; The Golden Apples of the Sun, 1953; Fahrenheit 451, 1953; The October Country, 1955; A Medicine for Melancholy, 1959; The Ghoul Keepers, 1961; The Small Assassin, 1962; The Machineries of Joy, 1964; The Vintage Bradbury, 1965; The Autumn People, 1965;

Tomorrow Midnight, 1966; Twice Twenty-Two, 1966; I Sing the Body Electric!, 1969; Bloch and Bradbury: Ten Masterpieces of Science Fiction (with Robert Bloch), 1969; Whispers From Beyond (with Robert Bloch), 1972; Harrap, 1975; Long After Midnight, 1976; To Sing Strange Songs, 1979; Dinosaur Tales, 1983; A Memory of Murder, 1984; The Toynbee Convector, 1988; Kaleidoscope, 1994. Poetry: Old Ahab's Friend, and Friend to Noah, Speaks His Piece: A Celebration, 1971; When Elephants Last in the Dooryard Bloomed: Celebrations for Almost Any Day in the Year, 1973; That Son of Richard III: A Birth Announcement, 1974; Where Robot Mice and Robot Men Run Round in Robot Towns, 1977; Twin Hieroglyphs That Swim the River Dust, 1978; The Bike Repairman, 1978; The Author Considers His Resources, 1979; The Aqueduct, 1979; The Attic Where the Meadow Greens, 1979; The Last Circus, 1980; The Ghosts of Forever, 1980; The Haunted Computer and the Android Pope, 1981; The Complete Poems of Ray Bradbury, 1982; The Love Affair, 1983; Forever and the Earth, 1984; Death Has Lost Its Charm for Me, 1987. Plays: The Meadow, 1960; Way in the Middle of the Air, 1962; The Anthem Sprinters and Other Antics, 1963; The World of Ray Bradbury, 1964; Leviathan 99, 1966; The Day it Rained Forever, 1966; The Pedestrian, 1966; Dandelion Wine, 1967; Christus Apollo, 1969; The Wonderful Ice-Cream Suit and Other Plays, 1972; Madrigals for the Space Age, 1972; Pillars of Fire and Other Plays for Today, Tomorrow and Beyond Tomorrow, 1975; That Ghost, That Bride of Time: Exerts from a Play-in-Progress, 1976; The Martian Chronicles, 1977; Farenheit 451, 1979; A Device Out of Time, 1986; Falling Upward, 1988. Non-Fiction: Teacher's Guide: Science Fiction, 1968; Zen and the Art of Writing, 1973; Mars and the Mind of Man, 1973; The Mummies of Guanajuato, 1978; Beyond 1984: Remembrance of Things Future, 1979; Los Angeles, 1984; Orange County, 1985; The Art of Playboy, 1985; Yestermorrow: Obvious Answers to Impossible Futures, 1991; Ray Bradbury on Stage: A Chrestomathy of His Plays, 1991; Journey to Far Metaphor: Further Essays on Creativity, Writing, Literature and the Arts, 1994; The First Book of Dichotomy, The Second Book of Symbiosis, 1995. Other: Television and film scripts. Honours: O Henry Prizes, 1947, 1948; National Institute of Arts and Letters Award, 1954; Writers Guild Award, 1974; Balrog Award for Best Poet, 1979; PEN Body of Work Award, 1985. Memberships: Science Fantasy Writers of America; Screen Writers Guild of America; Writers Guild of America. Address: 10265 Cheviot Drive, Los Angeles, CA 90064, USA.

BRADLEY George, b. 22 Jan 1953, Roslyn, New York, USA. Writer; Poet. m. Spencer Boyd, 8 Sept 1984. Education: BA, Yale Uniersity, 1975; University of Virginia, 1977-78. Publications: Terms to be Met, 1986; Of the Knowledge of Good and Evil, 1991. Other: Screenplays; Criticism. Contributions to: Periodicals. Honours: Academy of American Poets Prize, 1978; Yale Younger Poets Prize, 1985; Lavan Younger Poets Award, 1990. Address: 82 West Main Street, Chester, CT 06412, USA.

BRADLEY John M, b. 26 Sept 1950, Brooklyn, New York, USA. Teacher. m. Jana Brubaker, 1 son. Education: BA, University of Minnesota, 1973, 1977; MA, Colorado State University, 1981; MFA, Bowling Green State University, 1989. Publications: All For Blanca; Love-in-Idleness, 1989; The New Wine Dreaming in the Vat, 1993; Atomic Ghost. Contributions to: Caliban; Rolling Stone; Haydens Ferry Review; Poetry East; Exquisite Corpse; Sonora Review; Numerous others. Honours: National Endowment of the Arts Fellowship; Mary Roberts Rinehart Grant; Washington Prize. Memberships: Poets and Writers; Associated Writing Programs; Modern Language Association. Address: 504 Sycamore Road, DeKalb, IL 60115, USA.

BRADLEY Marjorie, b. 22 May 1916, Portsmouth, Hampshire, England. Retired Civil Servant. m. Reuben Stephen Bradley, 22 June 1938, 3 sons. Education: Municipal College, Portsmouth. Appointments: Junior Clerk, 1933-37; Tax Officer, 1937-38; Secretary, West Riding County Council, 1951-58; Clerical Officer, Department of Health and Social Security, 1958-73. Publication: Coffee Spoons. Contributions to: Envoi; Writer; London Calling; Purple Patch; Civil Service Author; Focus; Weyfarers; Success Magazine. Honours: Civil Service Authors, Herbert Spencer Competition; Open Poetry Competition; Envoi Magazine Open Competition; Salopian Poetry Competition; Success Magazine Competitions. Memberships: Society of Civil Service Authors; Patchway Writers Group; Wilfred Owen Association. Address: 88 Oak Close, Little Stoke, Bristol BS12 6RD, England.

BRADY Adrienne Sophia, b. 23 Aug 1936, Maymyo, Burma. Teacher. Widow, 1 son, 3 daughters. Education: BA Honours, English and History, London University, 1983; MA, Creative Writing, Lancaster University, 1985. Appointments: Head of English, Ursuline High School, Brentwood, 1985; Humanities Tutor, Singapore, 1987-89; English Language Instructor, Brunei, Borneo, 1990-92. Publications: Quintet: Staple First Editions, 1993; Summer Comes Barefoot Now, teaching anthology of poetry, General Editor, 1989. Contributions to: Spectator; Poetry Review; Schools Poetry Review; Anthologies: I Want to Be Me; Poetry 2. Honours: Late Aske Memorial Award, 1984; Basil Bunting Poetry Competition 3rd Prize, 1984; Surrey Poetry Competition 2nd Prize, 1985; Lancaster Literature Festival, 2 poems, 1986; Leek Arts Festival Runner-up, 1989; Greenwich Festival, 4th Prize, 1990; Staple Open Poetry Competition, 3 poems, 1991; Leek Arts Festival 1st Prize, 1992. Memberships: Schools Poetry Association, Committee, 1982-84; Poetry Society. Address: 34 Parklands, Billericay, Essex CM11 1AS, England.

BRADY Philip, b. 15 Aug 1955, New York, New York, USA. English Professor. Education: BA, Buckwell University, 1977; MA, University of Delaware, 1980; MA, San Francisco State University, 1984; PhD, State University of New York at Binghamton, 1990. Appointments: Professor of English, University of Lubumbashi, Zaire; Tutor, University College Cork, Ireland; Associate Professor of English, Youngstown University. Contributions to: Belfast Literary Supplement; Honest Ulsterman; Poetry Northwest; Massachusetts Review. Honours: Thayer Fellowship, 1990; Yaddo Residency, 1992; Ohio Arts Fellowship, 1993. Membership: Associated Writers Program. Address: English Department, Youngstown State University, Youngstown, PA 44555-3415, USA.

BRAMHARAJAN. See: RAJARAM A.

BRANDI John, b. 5 Nov 1943. Poet; Painter. Education: BFA, California State University at Northridge. Publications: A Question of Journey; Weeping the Cosmos; Shadow Play; Hymn for a Night Feast; In the Desert We Do Not Count the Days; That Back Road In; Diary from a Journey to the Middle of the World; That Crow That Visited Was Flying Backwards; Narrow Gauge to Riobamba; Desde Alla; Zulekah's Book; Heartbeat Geography: Poems 1966-1994, 1995. Contributions to: Atlantic; Denver Post; LA Free Press; Blue Mesa Review; Chelsea; IO; River Styx; Kyoto Journal. Honour: National Endowment for the Arts Fellowship for Poetry, 1980. Address: Holy Cow! Press, PO Box 3170, Mt Royal Station, Duluth, MN 55803, USA.

BRANDT Di(ana Ruth), b. 31 Jan 1952, Winkler, Manitoba, Canada. Writer. m. Les Brandt, 1971, Div 1990, 2 daughters. Education: BTh, Canadian Mennonite Bible College, 1972; BA Honours, University of Manitoba, 1974; MA, University of Toronto, 1975; PhD, University of Manitoba, 1993. Appointments: Instructor in English and Creative Writing, University of Winnipeg, 1987-95; Poetry Editor, Prairie Fire, 1988-92; Writer-in-Residence, University of Alberta, 1995-96. Publications: questions i asked my mother, 1987; Agnes in the sky, 1990; mother, not mother, 1992; Wild Mother Dancing: Maternal Narrative in Canadian Literature, 1993; Jerusalem, beloved, 1995. Contributions to: Prairie Fire; Border Crossings; Contemporary Verse 2; Prism International; New Quarterly; Arc; Tessera; Line; Dinosaur Review; Orbis; Moosehead Review; Others. Honours: Gerald Lampert Award for Best First Book of Poetry in Canada, 1987; Nominee, Governor General's Award for Poetry, 1987; Nominee, Dillon's Commonwealth Poetry Prize, 1988; Patrick Mary Plunkett Scholarship, University of Manitoba, 1989; McNally Robinson Award for Manitoba Book of the Year, 1990; Drummond Fellowship in Canadian Studies, University of Manitoba, 1991; Silver National Magazine Award, 1995; Nominee, McNally Robinson Award for Manitoba Book of the Year, 1993, 1995; Nominee, Govenor General's Award for Poetry, 1995. Memberships: League of Canadian Poets, Manitoba Representative, 1988-90, 2nd Vice-President, 1990-91; Writers' Union of Canada, 1988-, Prairies/North West Territories Representative, 1994-95, Floating Representative, 1995-96; Canadian PEN, 1991-, Manitoba Representative, 1992-94; Manitoba Writers' Guild, 1988-; Hiatus (feminist writing group), 1984-87; ACCUTE, 1993-. Address: 932 Jessie Avenue, Winnipeg, Manitoba R3M 1A9, Canada.

BRANDT Per Aage, b. 26 Apr 1944, Buenos Aires, Argentina. Professor in Semiotics and Hispanic Studies. m. Mette Brudevold, 1966, div 1983, 1 daughter. Education: MA, University of Copenhagen, 1971; Doctorate d'Etat, Semiolinguistics, Sorbonne, Paris, 1987. Appointments: Lectureship, Roskilde Universitetscentrum, Roskilde, Denmark, 1972-75; Lectureship, 1975-88, Professorship (docentur),

1988, University of Aarhus; Research Professorship, 1996-. Publications: Poesi I, II, 1969; Pamplona, 1971; Wie die Zeit vergeht, 1973; Dødshjælp, 1977; Beskyttelse, 1978; Indsigt i det nødvendige, 1979; Det skulle ikke være sådan, 1982; Ondskab, 1982; Livet i himlen, 1985; Fraværsmusik, 1986; Credo, 1988; Ostinato, 1989; Ingen kan vaagne, 1990; Rubato, 1991; Physis, 1992; Largo, 1994; Ups and downs, 1996; Numerous translations of Borges, Jabès, Roubaud, Bataille, Sade. Contributions to: Poesie; Action poétique; Zuk; Hvedekorn; Manuskripte Carpe, Carpe, Carpe, performance by Hotel Proforma, Kirsten Dehlholm, 1990. Honours: Prize for Pamplona, Danish Ministry of Culture, 1971; Largo, 1994; Emil Aarestrup Medal, 1993. Membership: Co-Founder (with Danish poet Poul Borum), regular Teacher, School of Writers, Copenhagen, 1987-. Address: Reventlowsgade 24, DK-1651 Copenhagen V, Denmark.

BRANTLEY Nancy Simpson, (Nancy Simpson), b. 16 Dec 1938, Miami, Florida, USA. Teacher; Writer. m. Ernest William Brantley, 1 Feb 1957, div 1977, 3 sons. Education: BS, Western Carolina University, 1978; MFA, Warren Wilson College, 1983. Appointments: Teacher, Clay County School, 1975-; Exceptional Children's Programme, Tri County Community College, 1988-. Publications: Across Water; Night Student. Contributions to: Georgia Review; Indiana Review; Southern Poetry Review; New Virginia Review; Florida Review; Atlanta Magazine; Seneca Review; Catalyst; Confrontation; Georgia Journal. Honour: North Carolina Artist Fellowship. Memberships: Clay County Arts Council; North Carolina Writers Network. Address: RT2, Box 232A, Hayesville, NC 28904, USA.

BRASFIELD James, b. 19 Jan 1952, Savannah, Georgia, USA. College Teacher. m. 7 Mar 1983, 1 son. Education: BA, English, Armstrong State College, 1975; MFA, Columbia University, 1979. Appointments: Editorial Assistant, Paris Review, 1981-82; Instructor, Western Carolina University, 1984-87; Lecturer, Pennsylvania State University, University Park, 1987-. Publication: Inheritance and Other Poems, chapbook, 1983. Contributions to: Antaeus; Berkeley Poetry Review; Black Warrior Review; Blue Buildings; Chicago Review; College English; Columbia; Iowa Review; Poetry East; Quarterly West; Seattle Review; New Virginia Review; Glas: New Russian Writing; Talisman; Other literary magazines. Honour: Fulbright Creative Arts Award to Ukraine, 1993-94. Memberships: Poetry Society of America; Associated Writing Program. Address: Department of English, 119 Burrowes Building, Pennsylvania State University, University Park, PA 16802, USA.

BRASS Perry M, b. 15 Sept 1947, Savannah, Georgia, USA. Writer. Education: BS, Art Education, New York University, 1974. Publications: Published 7 books, including: Sex-Charge, 1991. Contributions to: Christopher Street; Amethyst; The Everard Review; Anthologies: The Penguin Book of Homosexual Verse; The Columbia University Press Book of Gay Literature; The Male Muse; Angels of the Lyre; Under the Planet of the Male Muse; The Bad Boy Book of Erotic Poetry. Honours: The Jane Chambers International Gay Playwriting Contest, 1985. Membership: Secretary, The Publishing Triangle, New York, 1994-95. Address: 2501 Palisade Avenue, Apt A1, Bronx, NY 10463, USA.

BRATESCH Verona, b. 28 Mar 1922, Brasov, Romania. Writer; Poet. Div, 1 son, 1 daughter. Publications: Bleibende Spur, 1966; Klarheit, 1969; Octave, 1969; Wiege im All. 1971; Locul sub stele, 1975; Ausserhalb des Kreises, 1978; Efeuranken, anthology, 1980; O clipa de vint, translation, 1980; Stein neben Stein, 1982, as Sten efter Sten, 1985; Carmina, 1982; Gefahrdete Insel, 1983; Aufanderem Gestirn, 1984; Les yeux et les mains, 1984; Sur une autre étoile, 1985, as Sub uma outra estrela, 1987; Phönix, 1986; Laufvogel Mensch, 1987; Verlangen nach Menschen, 1990. Contributions to: 1700 poems in many journals and anthologies in various countries during 52 years. Honours: Brasov Prize, Romanian Writers' Union, 1978, 1982; Prize, Der Karlsruher Bote journal, 1978; Immortal Rose Medal, Witten, 1982; Dr Heinrich Mock Medal, Göttingen, 1984; Doctor of Literature (honoris causa), World Academy of Arts and Culture, 1984; 1st Prize for Poesia estera, Accademia Internazionale Iblea, Sicily, 1986; Medal, Certificate of Merit, 10th World Congress of Poetry and 1st World Congress of Culture, New York, 1987. Memberships: Romanian Writers' Union, 1967; International Lenau Society, 1969; International Union of Writers, Regensburg, 1976; Circle of Friends, Walchum, 1978; Literary Circle of Plesse, Göttingen, 1978; World Poetry Society. Address: Str Piatra Mare 117, R-2200 Brasov, Romania.

BRATHWAITE Edward, b. 11 May 1930, Bridgetown, Barbados. Education: Pembroke College, Cambridge; DPhil, University of Sussex, 1968. Appointment: Professor, University of the West Indies, Kingston, Jamaica, 1982-. Publications: The Arrivants: A New World Trilogy, 1973; Days and Nights, 1975; Other Exiles, 1975; Black + Blues, 1976; Mother Poem, 1977; Soweto, 1979; Sun Poem, 1982; Third World Poems, 1983; X-Self, 1987; Sappho Sakyi's Mediatations, 1989; Shar, 1990. Honour: Fulbright Fellowships, 1982-88. Address: Department of History, University of the West Indies, Mona, Kingston 7, Jamaica.

BRAUD Janice L, b. 22 Oct 1941, Corpus Christi, Texas, USA. Computer Analyst; Business Owner. m. Nolan J Braud, 23 Feb 1963, 3 daughters. Education: BA, Psychology, University of Houston, 1972; ASM, Business, Thomas A Edison College, New Jersey, 1984; BSBA, Business Data Processing, Thomas A Edison State College, New Jersey, 1987. Appointments: Elementary School Teacher and High School English Teacher, 1957-62; Teacher, 1963-65; Mental Health Field, 1966-73; Computer Programmer/Systems Analyst with Major Oil/Gas Companies, 1973-78; Owner/President, Cypress Systems Company Inc, 1978-. Publications: Through a Glass Darkly, 1994. Contributions to: Bellowing Ark; Catharsis; Color Wheel; Orphic Lute; Touchstone; Poetic Page; Feelings; Lucidity; Opus; Poet; Many Voices; Writer's Journal; Sophomore Jinx; Poetry Society of Texas Yearbooks. Honours: Poetry Society of Texas Annual Awards: 1st Place, 1991, Two 1st Place Awards, 1992, Nine 1st Place Awards, 1993, Six 1st Place Awards, 1994, Six 1st Place Awards, 1995. Poet of the Year, Poetic Page, 1994. Memberships: Poets Northwest (A Chapter of Poetry Society of Texas), President, 1996, Membership Chairman, 1992-93; Poetry Society of Texas; National Federation of State Poetry Societies; Poets At Work; Houston Chapter of Poetry Society of Texas. Address: 30103 Bashaw Drive, Spring, TX 77386, USA.

BRAUN Richard Emil, b. 22 Nov 1934, Detroit, Michigan, USA. Professor of Latin. 1 son. Education: AB, 1956, AM, Latin, 1957, University of Michigan; PhD, Classical Languages, University of Texas, 1969. Appointments: Lecturer, 1962-64, Assistant Professor, 1964-69, Associate Professor, 1969-76, Professor, 1976-, University of Alberta, Edmonton, Canada. Publications: Children Passing, 1962; Bad Land, 1971; The Foreclosure, 1972; Last Man In, 1990; Translations: Sophocles' Antigone, 1973; Euripides' Rhesos, 1978; Persius's Satires, 1984. Contributions to: Grosseteste Review; Modern Poetry Studies; Prism; Poetry Now; University of Georgia Review; Others. Honours: President's Medal, Western Ontario, 1965; Robert Frost Fellowship, 1968. Address: University of Alberta, Department of Classics, Edmonton, Alberta T6G 2E5, Canada.

BRAVERMAN Kate, b. 2 May 1949, Philadelphia, Pennsylvania, USA. Poet; Novelist; Short Story Writer. m. Alan Goldstein, 15 June 1991, 1 daughter. Education: BA, Anthropology, 1971; MA, English, 1986. Appointments: Professor of Creative Writing, California State University at Los Angeles. Publications: Milk Run, poems, 1977; Lithium for Medea, novel, 1979; Lullaby for Sinners, poems, 1980; Hurricane Warnings, poems, 1987; Palm Latitudes, novel, 1988; Postcard From August, poems, 1990; Squandering the Blue, stories, 1990. Contributions to: Many and varied magazines and journals. Memberships: PEN Los Angeles West; National Book Critics' Circle. Address: English Department, California State University at Los Angeles, 5151 State University Drive, Los Angeles, CA 90032, USA.

BRAWN M A. See: MINEO Melanie.

BRAXTON Joanne M(argaret), b. 25 May 1950, Washington, District of Columbia, USA. Poet; Critic; Professor. 1 daughter. Education: BA, Sarah Lawrence College, 1972; MA, 1974, PhD, 1984, Yale University. Appointments: Lecturer, University of Michigan, 1979; Assistant Professor, 1980-86, Associate Professor, 1986-89, Professor of English, 1989-, College of William and Mary. Publications: Sometimes I Think Of Maryland, poems, 1977; Black Women Writing Autobiography: A Tradition Within A Tradition, 1989; Wild Women In The Whirlwind: The Renaissance In Contemporary Afro-American Writing, editor with Andree N McLaughlin, 1990; The Collected Poems Of Paul Laurence Dunbar, editor, 1993. Contributions to: Books, anthologies, journals, and periodicals. Honours: Outstanding Faculty Award, State Council for Higher Education for Virginia, 1992; Fellowships and grants. Memberships: American Studies Association; College Language Association; Modern Language Association.

Address: c/o Department of English, St George Tucker Hall, College of William and Mary, Williamsburg, VA 23185, USA.

BRAY J(ohn) J(efferson), b. 16 Sept 1912, Adelaide, South Australia. Barrister; Chief Justice. Education: LLB, 1932, LLB Honours, 1933, LLD, 1937, University of Adelaide. Appointments: Admitted to South Australian Bar, 1933; QC, 1957; Chief Justice of South Australia, 1967-78; Chancellor, 1968-83, AC, 1979, University of Adelaide. Publications: Poems, 1962; Poems 1961-1971, 1972; Poems 1972-1979, 1979; The Bay of Salamis and Other Poems, 1986; Satura: Selected Poetry and Prose, 1988; Seventy Seven, 1990. Contributions to: Adelaide Review; Overland; Australian. Honour: South Australian Non-Fiction Award for Adelaide Festival of Arts, 1990. Memberships: Australian Society of Authors; Friendly Street Poets, Adelaide. Address: 39 Hurtle Square, Adelaide, South Australia 5000, Australia.

BRAYAG B. See: **BANDYOPADHYAY Prayag.**

BRAYBROOKE Neville, b. 30 May 1925, London, England. Writer. Publication: Four Poems for Christmas, 1986. Contributions to: Radio: BBC 3, BBC 4; Television: BBC TV, ITV; New Yorker; New Statesman; Sunday Times; Spectator; Tablet. Address: 10 Gardnor Road, Flask Walk, London NW3 1HA, England.

BRECKENRIDGE Jill, b. 23 Oct 1938, Idaho, USA. Writer; Writing Consultant. Div, 3 sons. Education: BA, University of Minnesota, 1972; MA, St Marys College, Winona, 1987; MFA, Goddard College, Vermont, 1980. Appointments: Teacher, workshops and seminars; Writing Consultant; Writer in the Schools; Teacher; Judge. Publications: How to be Lucky; Civil Blood; Three Women Poets; Poems in Milweed Chronicle; Moons and Lion Tailes; Steelhead; 25 Minnesota Poets. Honours: Loft McKnight Writers Award; Minnesota State Arts Board Grants; Bush Foundation Individual Artist Fellowship; Lake Superior Regional Writers Contest; Ragdale Writing Fellowship. Address: 42 South St Albans No 3, St Paul, MN 55105, USA.

BREDON John. See: **ENG Steve.**

BREEDEN David, b. 23 Mar 1958, Illinois, USA. English Professor. m. Joan Bishop-Breeden, 15 Oct 1983, 2 sons, 1 daughter. Education: BA, 1981; MFA, 1985; PhD, 1988. Appointment: Faculty, Schreiner College. Publications: Picnics, 1985; Hey, Schliemann, 1990; Double-Headed End Wrench, 1992; Building A Boat, 1995; The Guiltless Traveler, 1996. Contributions to: Poet Lore; Mid-American Review; Quarterly; North Atlantic Review; Literary Review; Paragraph. Memberships: PEN Center, USA West; Poets and Writers; Associated Writing Programmes. Address: Campus Box 4504, Schreiner College, 2100 Memorial Bouelvard, Kerrville, TX 78028, USA.

BREMNER Betty Avice, b. 12 Feb 1921, Christchurch, New Zealand. Freelance Journalist. m. William Laohlan Bremner, 26 Jan 1946, dec, 1 daughter. Education: Canterbury University, Christchurch; BA, Victoria University of Wellington, 1989. Publication: The Scarlet Runners, 1991-92. Contributions to: Sport; Kapiti Poems, III-VI; King's Cross Poets; Dominion. Memberships: President, Women Writer's Society Inc; PEN International; L'Alliance Francaise; Poetry Society. Address: 20 Dowse Drive, Maungaraki, Lower Hutt, New Zealand.

BREMNER Stephen (Steve) George, (Ernest M V Beer), b. 7 June 1956, London, England. Library Assistant. Contributions to: Spectator; New Statesman and Society; Poetry Review; London Drinker; Fellowship of Depressives Anonymous Newsletter. Honours: Mid Sussex Competitive Music Festival Literary Classes, Poetry 1st Place, 1991; Poetry Digest Fun 91 Humorous Poetry Competition, Grand Champion and 1st Prize England,1992. Address: 12 Block O, Peabody Estate, Abbey Orchard Street, London SW1P 2DW, England.

BRENER Rochelle (Diane), (Shelley Squire, Shelley Brener-Squire), b. 27 Feb 1945, Syracuse, New York, USA. Writer; Poet; Lecturer in Fine Arts; Personal Growth Consultant; Poetry Therapy Trainee; Photographer. m. Donald A Squire, 4 Oct 1965, div, 1 son, 1 daughter. Education: BA, English, Philosophy, Russell Sage College, New York, 1974; Diploma, Chicago School of Interior Design, 1968; MFA, Writing, Vermont College, Norwich University, Montpelier, 1989; Certified Practitioner, Neuro-Linguistic Programming (NLP), 1989; Pursuing Master's degree in Herbology, Emerson College. Appointments: Teacher; Art Teacher; Photojournalist; Contributing Editor, Poetry Forum, 1985-77; General Editor, Woman Locally Magazine, 1977-78; Freelance Photographer, 1981-; Medical Editor,

1982-83; Manuscript Critic, National Writers' Club, 1986-; Poetry Editor, The Albany Review, 1987-90; Teacher, Knowledge Network poetry workshops, 1988-89; Self-employed Personal Growth Consultant and NLP Practitioner, 1989-; Facilitator, poetry therapy support group sponsored by Capital District Psychiatric Center, 1990-; Lecturer, Fine Arts, Siena College, 1990-. Publications: Packrat, 1974; The Bottom Line, 1974. Contributions to: Albany Times-Union; Knickerbocker News weekly column; Kite; Between the Sheets; Poetry Forum; Albany Magazine; Albany Review; Crazyquilt Literary Quarterly; 3rd Annual Cal Anthology: It's On My Wall; Dan River Anthology; Men's Issues: An Anthology. Honours: Various for literary work; Several listings. Memberships: Academy of American Poets; Hudson Valley Writers' Guild; International Women Writers' Guild; Milton Society; National Association for Poetry Therapy; National Writers' Club; Poets and Writers Inc. Address: 69 Huntersfield Road, Delmar, NY 12054, USA.

BRENER-SQUIRE Shelley. See: **BRENER Rochelle (Diane).**

BRENNAN Matthew Cannon, b. 18 Jan 1955, Richmond Heights, Missouri, USA. Professor of English. m. (1) Laura L Fredendall, 13 Aug 1977, div 1987, 1 son, (2) Beverley Simms, 21 May 1997. Education: AB, Grinnell College, 1977; MA, 1980, PhD, 1984, University of Minnesota. Appointments: Visiting Assistant Professor of English, University of Minnesota, 1984-85; Assistant Professor of English, 1985-88, Associate Professor of English, 1988-92, Professor of English, 1992-, Indiana State University, Terre Haute. Publication: Seeing in the Dark, 1993; The Music of Exile, 1994. Contributions to: Poet Lore; Kansas Quarterly; Poetry Ireland Review; New Mexico Humanities Review; Louisville Review; Kentucky Poetry Review; Passages North; Tar River Poetry; Mississippi Valley Review; Anthology of Magazine Verse and Yearbook of American Poetry; Cape Rock; Webster Review; Context South; Toad Highway; Tampa Bay Review; Journal of Popular Culture; Sou'Wester; Wind. Honours: Indiana Arts Commission Master Fellowship in Poetry, 1997-95; Indiana State University Art, Endowment Grant, 1993; Honourable Mention, Academy of American Poets, 1979, 1980, 1984. Memberships: Poets and Writers' Inc; Writers' Center of Indianapolis. Address: Department of English, Indiana State University, Terre Haute, IN 47809, USA.

BREVET Jan, b. 4 May 1917, Lochen, Netherlands. Retired. Publications: Works included in many anthologies. Contributions to: National Library of Poetry Annual; North American Open Poetry Contest; Parnassus Literary Journal; Poet's Fantasy; Feelings; The Funny Side of Feelings; The Son of the Funny Side; Poetry Forum Literary Journal; Opus Literary Review; Lines 'n' Rhymes; Poet's Paradise. Honour: 1st Place Winner, Paris Anniversary Issue, 1992.

BREW Kwesi, b. 1928, Cape Coast, Ghana. Education: University of the Gold Coast. Appointments: Former Ambassador for Ghana to Britain, France, Germany and the USSR. Publications: The Shadows of Laughter, 1968; Pergamon Poets 2: Poetry from Africa, 1968; African Panorama, 1981. Honours include: British Council Prize. Address: c/o Greenfield Press Review, PO Box 80, Greenfield Center, New York, NY 12833, USA.

BREWSTER Elizabeth (Winifred), b. 26 Aug 1922, Chipman, New Brunswick, Canada. Professor Emeritus of English; Poet; Novelist. Education: BA, University of New Brunswick, 1946; MA, Radcliffe College, Cambridge, Massachusetts, 1947; BLS, University of Toronto, 1953; PhD, Indiana University, 1962. Appointments: Faculty, Department of English, University of Victoria, 1960-61; Reference Librarian, Mt Allison University, 1961-65; Visiting Assistant Professor of English, University of Alberta, 1970-71; Assistant Professor, 1972-75, Associate Professor, 1975-80, Professor, 1980-90, Professor Emeritus, 1990-, of English, University of Saskatchewan. Publications: East Coast, 1951; Lilooet, 1954; Roads, 1957; Passage of Summer: Selected Poems, 1969; Sunrise North, 1972; In Search of Eros, 1974; The Sisters, 1974; It's Easy to Fall on the Ice, 1977; Sometimes I Think of Moving, 1977; Digging In, 1982; Junction, 1982; The Way Home, 1982; A House Full of Women, 1983; Selected Poems of Elizabeth Brewster, 1944-84, 1985; Entertaining Angels, 1988; Spring Again, 1990; The Invention of Truth, 1991; Wheel of Change, 1993; Footnotes to the Book of Job, 1995. Honours: E J Pratt Award for Poetry, University of Toronto, 1953; President's Medal for Poetry, University of Western Ontario, 1980; Honorary LittD, University of New Brunswick, 1982; Canada Council Award, 1985. Memberships: League of Canadian Poets; Writers' Union of Canada.

Address: c/o Department of English, University of Saskatchewan, Saskatoon, Saskatchewan S7N 0W0, Canada.

BRICK Terence, b. 12 Sept 1942, London, England. m. Yvonne Boudier, 4 April 1964, 2 daughters. Contributions to: PEN and South East Arts anthologies; Creative Writing by John Fairfax, 1989; Spoils, 1991; Outposts; Envoi; Poetry Nottingham; Cobweb; Orbis; Iota; Pennine Platform; Response; Other Poetry; Pick; New Poetry (workshop); Flyover, Hammersmith and Fulham Poetry Festival; Prospice; Ore; South East Arts Review. Honour: Greenwich Festival Prizewinner, 1979. Address: 25 Abbey Close, Newbury, Berkshire, England.

BRIDGES Judith Fuller, b. 19 June 1955, Massachusetts, USA. Counsellor. Education: Graduate, Harvard Extension School; BA, Literature, York University, Toronto, Canada, 1983. Appointments: Counsellor, Case Manager, Advocates, 1987-90; Counsellor, Work Inc, 1990-. Contributions to: Persona, Warmth, Existere, 1981; Echo, Alberta Poetry Yearbook, 1982; Men in My Womb, anti-war anthology, 1984; Stories on the Door, 1990; Wail Magazine. Address: 108 Pearl Street, Cambridge, MA 02139, USA.

BRIDGES Lee Norris, b. 31 May 1927, Thomasville, Georgia, USA. Poet. m. Grietje Antjy Boontje, 4 May 1973, 1 son. Education: Detroit Institute of Arts, Music, 1952-54; City College of New York. Publications: The Rhythm Man, 1987; The Blue Bird Sings, 1989. Contributions to: Association for the Study of Afro-American Life and History; Presense Africain; Black Scholar; Third Half Literary Magazine; Tucumari Literary Review. Honours: Fine Points Area Youth Festival Award, Performance, Brooklyn, New York, 1979; Poetalk Quarterly Awards, Certificate for Excellence, 1991. Membership: Poets and Writers, New York. Address: Postbox 1346, 1000 BH Amsterdam, Netherlands.

BRIGHAM Faith Elizabeth Huckabone, (Fay Huckabone, Faith Mairee), b. 14 May 1953, Pittsburgh, Pennsylvania, USA. Fiscal Clerk. m. John Jefferson Brigham, 20 Dec 1980. Contributions to: Poet Magazine; Revelry; Wide Open Magazine; Cableweek; World of Poetry's Anthologies; Alley Cat Magazine; By-Line Magazine; Southern Poetry Review; American Poetry Annuals; Best Poems of 1995, Best Poems of 1995, Best Poems of 1996, National OLibrary of Poetry. Honours: Golden Poet Award and 7 Honourable Mention Awards, 1988, Golden Poet Award, 1988, 1989, 5 Honourable Mentions, 1989-91, Golden Poet Award and Honourable Mention, 1990, Who's Who in Poetry for Outstanding Achievement in Poetry, 1990, World of Poetry; Blue Ribbon Award, Southern Poetry Association; Creative Endeavors Honorable Mention Award. Memberships: Poet's Guild; Southern Poetry Association; International Society for the Advancement of Poetry. Address: 6725 Corto Road, Cocoa, FL 32927, USA.

BRIN Herb(ert Henry), b. 17 Feb 1915, Chicago, Illinois, USA. Poet; Journalist. 3 sons. Education: Member, Great Book Series, University of Chicago. Appointments: Feature Writer, Los Angeles Times; Publisher, Heritage Publications of California. Publications: Poetry: Wild Flowers, 1965; Justice, Justice, 1967; Conflicts, 1971; My Spanish Years and Other Poems, 1985. Memberships: American Poetry Society; Academy of American Poets. Address: 1101 East Loma Alta Drive, Calradena, CA 91001, USA.

BRINGHURST Robert, b. 16 Oct 1946, Los Angeles, California, USA. Poet. 1 daughter. Education: Physics, Linguistics, Massachusetts Institute of Technology, 1963-64, 1970-71; Philosophy, Oriental Languages, University of Utah, 1964-65; Arabic, Defense Language Institute, 1966-67; BA, Comparative Literature, Indiana University, 1973; MFA, University of British Columbia, 1975. Appointments: Visiting Lecturer, 1975-77, Lecturer, 1979-80, University of British Columbia; Poet-in-Residence, Banff School of Fine Arts, Alberta, 1983; Adjunct Lecturer, Simon Fraser University, Burnaby, 1983-84; Lecturer, Trent University, Peterborough, Ontario, 1984; Poet-in-Residence, Ojibway and Cree Cultural Centre Writers' Workshops, 1985; Writer-in-Residence, University of Winnipeg, 1986; Exchange Fellow, Writer-in-Residence, University of Edinburgh, Scotland, 1989-90. Publications: Poetry: Stonecutter's Horses, 1979; Tzuhalem's Mountain, 1982; The Beauty of the Weapons: Selected Poems 1972-82, 1982; Tending the Fire, 1985; The Blue Roofs of Japan, 1986; Pieces of Map, Pieces of Music, 1986; Conversations with Toad, 1987; The Calling: Selected Poems 1970-1995, 1995; Elements, 1995; New World Suite No 3, 1996; Prose: Visions:

Contemporary Art in Canada, 1983; Raven Steals the Light, 1984, 2nd edition, 1988; Ocean/Paper/Stone, 1984; The Black Canoe, 1991, 2nd edition 1992; The Elements of Typographic Style, 1992; A Story as Sharp as a Knife: An Introduction to Classical Haida Literature, 1996. Contributions to: Many anthologies including: Poets of Canada, 1978; Witness to Wilderness, 1984; New Canadian Poets, 1985; Words We Call Home, 1990; Coming to Light: Norton Introduction to Poetry, 1994; Contemporary Translations of the Native Literatures of North America, 1995; Norton Introduction to Literature, 1995; Poetry and Knowing, 1995. Honours: Guggenheim Fellowship in Poetry, 1988; Multiple Canada Council Awards. Address: Box 357, 1917 W 4th Avenue, Vancouver, British Columbia V6J 1M7, Canada.

BRINKLOW Win(nie Melvin), b. 1 Jan 1941, Fearn, Ross-shire, Scotland. m. 20 Sept 1957, 1 son, 1 daughter. Publications: She Thought It Was Naughty and Other Poems, 1990; Anthology: O' Mice & Men, 1992; Tartan Custard. Contributions to: Writers News; Poetry Digest. Honour: 1st Prize Dornoch Firth Bridge Poetry Competition, Sutherland, 1991. Address: Gneiss House, Invershin, By Lairg, Sutherland IV27 4ET, Scotland.

BRIONES MIGUEL Alicia, b. 5 Nov 1961, Barcelona, Spain. Teacher. Education: MA, Greek, 1985; Curs de Capacitacio del Catala a Secundaria, 1989. Appointments: Teacher, secondary school. Publications: Anuario del Rio Eria, no 5, 1983; Antologia Clarin de Poesia, 1983; Antologia Rosas Rojas, 1985; Las tres son de Editorial el Paisaje de Spain; International Poetry, 1986-90; World Poetry, 1990; Todo Desejo, 1990; VI Antologia de Poesia Contemporanea, 1989. Contributions to: Va i ve; Letraferit; Gemma; Clarin; Lea; Trebelde; Acentor; Promesas; Atalaya Cultural; El Eria; Manuscritos Poeticos; Gazeta de Felgueiras; Rocinante; Folha da Planta. Honours: Election to academies. Memberships: Asociacion Mundial de Escritores no 82; World Academy of Arts and Culture; Centre Cultural e Literario de Felgueiras, Portugal; Associacio de Joves Escritores en Liengua Catalana; Centro Cultural la Marcilla de Castrocalbon. Address: C/Bonavista no 107, Baixos, 08960 Sant Just Desvern, Barcelona, Spain.

BRISSETT Linda May, b. 16 Aug 19840, Kingston, Jamaica, West Indies. Registered Nurse; Certified Midwife. m. Louis Floyd Brissett, 19 Jun 1971, 1 son. Education: Diploma in Short Story Writing and Journalism; Registered General Nurse, 1960; Certified Midwife, 1962; Certificate in Nursing Unit Administration, 1971; Effective Supervision Certificate, 1975. Appointments: Registered Nurse, Jamaica; Staff Midwife, Bellshill Maternity Hospital, 1962-63; Registered Nurse, Maternity, Oshawa General Hospital, Ontario, 1963-64; Head Nurse, Neonatal Unit, Henderson General Hospital, Hamilton, Ontario, Canada, 1965-93; President, Briss Books Inc; Poet; Author. Publications: In Fields of Dream and Other Poems, 1991; Sunshine in the Shadows, 1993; Give Us This Day, 1995; Ingots (A Hamilton, Ontario Sesquicentenial Anthology with 5 other Poets), 1996; Carols of Christmases Past, 1996. Contributions to: New World Focus; The Spectator; The Bulletin; National Library of Poetry, USA; Quill Books, USA; Authors; Poemata. Honours: 2nd Prize, Quills, 1990; Certificate of Merit, National Library of Poetry, 1993. Memberships: Canadian Authors Association; Canadian Poetry Association, Hamilton Chapter. Address: 58 Skyview Drive, Hamilton, Ontario L9B 1X5, Canada.

BRITO Casimiro de, b. 14 Jan 1938, Algarve, Portugal. Writer; Bank Director. Education: Graduated in Commercial Studies. Appointments: Editor of literary magazines Cadernos do Meio-Dia, 1956-58, Cadernos de Poesia, 1971-72, Loreto 13, 1975-77. Publications: Poemas da Solidao Imperfeita, 1957; Carta a Pablo Picasso, 1958; Telegramas, 1959; Canto Adolescente, 1961; Poemas Orientais, Japanese translations, 1963; Jardins de Guerra, 1966; Mesa do Amor, 1970; Negaçao da Morte, 1974; Corpo Sitiado, 1976; Labyrinthus, 1981; Ode & Ceia - Collected Poems 1955-84, 1985; Ni Maître, Ni Serviteur, 1986; Onde se acumula o po, 1987; Arte de Respiraçao, 1988; Duas Aguas, Um Rio, 1989; Subitamente o Silencio, 1991; Opus Affettuso, 1993; Intensidades, 1995. Contributions to: Many publications in several countries. Honours: Ministry of Culture Prize; Writers' Association Prize; Versilia-Viareggio Prize. Membership: President, Past Vice-President, Portuguese PEN. Address: Rua Prof Prado Coelho, Lote 16, 6° frente, 1600 Lisbon, Portugal.

BROADHURST Valorie Anne. See: **WOERDEHOFF Valorie Anne Breyfogle.**

BROCK Edwin, b. 19 Oct 1927, Dulwich, London, England. Writer; Poet; Editor. Appointments: Advertising Writer, 1959-88; Poetry Editor, Ambit Magazine, London, 1960-. Publications: An Attempt at Exorcism, 1959; Night Duty on Eleven Beat, radio play, 1960; A Family Affair: Two Sonnet Sequences, 1960; The Little White God, novel, 1962, televised 1964; With Love from Judas, 1963; Penguin Modern Poets 8, co-author, 1966; Fred's Primer: A Little Girl's Guide to the World Around Her, 1969; A Cold Day at the Zoo, 1970; Invisibility is the Art of Survival: Selected Poems, 1973; Paroxisms, 1974; I Never Saw it Lit, 1974; The Blocked Heart, 1975; Song of Battery Hen: Selected Poems, 1959-65, 1977; Here, Now, Always, autobiography, 1977; The River and the Train, 1979; Five Ways to Kill a Man: New and Selected Poems, 1990. Address: The Granary, Lower Tharston, Norfolk NR15 2YN, England.

BROCK Randal(l), (C K Randall), b. 24 Nov 1943, Colfax, Washington, USA. Poet. Education: BA, History, BA, Education, Eastern Washington University, 1970; MFA, University of Oregon, 1973. Publications: Mouse Poems, 1971; Poems and Photographs, 1979; I Am Poems, 1982; Pockets of Origin, photographs, 1983; Shadows of Seclusion, 1983; The Goat Poems, 1984; Solid Blue, 1985; Stranger to the Stars, 1986; Cold Fire Poems, 1988; Variations, 1994; A Message from the other side, 1995; Images in Stone, 1995; Love and Other Secrets of the Sea, 1995; Anthologies: The Abraxas/Five Anthology, 1972; Encore Encore Anthology, 1976. Contributions to: Late Knocking; Look Quick; Random Weirdness; Cache Review; Nantucket Review; Syd's Journal; Tight; Encore; Measure; The White Elephant; Cross-Time Journal; Small Pond; Charas; Central Park; NRG; Taurus; Dan River Anthology; Deep Down Things Anthology; Prophetic Voices; Catalyst; Egorag; Hippo; Poetalk; Howling Mantra; Gone Soft; The Imperfect Pitch; Mutated Viruses; Salome; Amython; Piedmont Literary Review; The Fault; Gamut; Innisfree; Transmog; Shockbox; The Quest; First Time; Found Street; Indefinite Space; Headveins; Caprice; The Third Half; Lazer; Sivullinen. Honours: Lecture Artists Series 1974, Washington State University; Centrum Scholarship, Port Townsend, Washington, 1977. Memberships include: Poets and Writers; Modern Language Association; AWP; Piedmont Literary Society; PEN West, USA. Address: PO Box 1673, Spokane, WA 99210, USA.

BROCK Van(dall) K(line), b. 31 Oct 1932. Professor of Literature. 2 sons, 2 step-daughters. Education: BA, Emory University, 1954; MA, 1963, MFA, 1964, PhD, 1970, Univesity of Iowa. Appointments: Poetry Workshop, 1963-64, World Literature, Poetry Writing, 1968-70, University of Iowa; Assistant Professor, Humanities, Writing, Oglethorpe University, 1964-68; Assistant Professor, 1970-75, Associate Professor, 1975-78, Professor, 1978-87, Florida State University; Co-Director, Writing Programme, Florida State University Study Centre, London, England, 1976, Florence, Italy, 1984, 1987; Book/Publication Editor. Publications: Chapbooks: Final Belief, 1972; Weighing the Penalties, 1977; Spelunking, 1978; The Window, 1981; Long Poems: Ossabow Tabby, 1990; A Conversation with Martin Heidegger, 1990; Unpublished: Unspeakable Strangers: Descents into a Dark Self, Ascents into Light. Contributions to: Anthologies: The New York Book of Poems, 1969; New Voices in American Poetry, 1973, 1976; Young American Poets, Japanese translation, 1976; Contemporary Southern Poetry, 1978; Introduction to Poetry, Introduction to Literature, 1983, 1984, 1986; Strong Measures: Contemporary American Poetry in Traditional Forms, 1985; The Made Thing: Anthology of Contemporary Southern Poetry, 1987; Blood to Remember: American Poets on the Holocaust, 1989; Sweet Nothings: An Anthology of Rock'n'Roll in American Poetry, 1990; Articles of War: Poets of World War II, 1991; Many poetry periodicals. Honours: 6 Resident Fellowships; Borestone Mountain Poetry Awards; Best Poem, Pacific Books, Palo Alto, 1965, 1972; 1st Prize, Florida Poetry Contest, Florida Review, 1977; 1st Creative Writing Award, 1977, Individual Artist's Award, 1982-83, Fine Arts Council, Florida; 1st featured poet, Poets in the South, 1977; Rockefeller Fellowship, Centre for Study of Southern Culture, 1978-79. Memberships: Poetry Society of America; Associated Writing Programs. Address: Department of English, Florida State University, Tallahassee, FL 32306, USA.

BROCKWAY James Thomas, b. 21 Oct 1916, Birmingham, England. Writer; Translator. Education: London School of Economics; Leverhulme Post-Intermediate Scholarship, 1938; Wartime military service, 1940. Appointments: Self-employed. Publications: No Summer Song, 1949; Translations: The Prospect and the River, 1987; A World Beyond Myself, 1991; A Way of Getting Through, poems, 1995; Singers Behind Glass, Eight Modern Dutch Poets, translations,

1995; Dutch essays in book form. Contributions to: Poetry Review; London Magazine; Stand Magazine; Times Literary Supplement; Encounter; Listener. Honours: Belgian Government Translators Award, 1965; Dutch Martinus Nijhoff Prize, 1966. Memberships: Poetry Society; International PEN. Address: Riouwstraat 114, The Hague, The Netherlands.

BRODRIBB (Arthur) Gerald Norcott, b. 21 May 1915, St Leonards-on-Sea, Sussex, England. Schoolmaster; Writer; Archaeologist. m. Jessica Barr, 3 Apr 1954, 1 son. Education: University College, Oxford; MA, Oxon; Dip Ed, Oxon; Fellow, Society of Antiquaries; PhD, University of London. Appointments: Schoolmaster, St Peters School, Seaford, Christ's Hospital, Canford School; Headmaster, Hydneye House School, 1954-70; Co-Director of Roman Excavation at Beauport Park, East Sussex. Publications: 20, mostly on cricket or archaeology; The Bay and Other Poems, 1953. Contributions to: Cricketer; Hydneye Magazine. Memberships: Martlets, University College, Oxford; Twenty Club, Hastings; Eclectics Book Society, Ewhurst Green, East Sussex. Address: Stubbles, Ewhurst Green, East Sussex TN32 5TD, England.

BRODSKY Joseph Alexandrovich, b. 24 May 1940, Leningrad, Russia. Poet; Educator. 1 child. Education: 5 Honorary Doctorates. Appointments: Poet, 1955-; Milling Machine Operator; Hospital Morgue Worker; Metalworker; Labourer; Stoker; Translator; Poet-in-Residence, University of Michigan at Ann Arbor, 1972-73, 1974-79; Teacher, poetry and literature, Columbia University; New York University; Queens College; Smith College; Cambridge University; Andrew W Mellon Professor of Literature, Mount Holyoke College, South Hadley, Massachusetts, 1986-; Fellow, New York Institute of Humanities, New York University; Associate, Russian Institute, Columbia University. Publications: Work includes poems and essays in Russian and English; Selected Poems, 1973; A Part of Speech, 1980; Marbles, 1989; Essays: Less Than One, 1981. Contributions to: Numerous publications. Honours: Grantee, John D and Catherine T MacArthur Foundation, 1981; Nobel Prize for Literature, 1987; Poet Laureate for United States, 1991-92; National Book Critics Circle Award, for Less Than One. Address: Farrar Straus & Giroux, 19 Union Square West, New York, NY 10003, USA.

BRODSKY Louis Daniel, b. 17 Apr 1941, St Louis, Missouri, USA. Poet. m. 1 son, 1 daughter. Education: BA magna cum laude, Yale, 1963; MA, English Literature, Washington University, 1967; MA, Creative Writing, San Francisco State University, 1968. Appointments: Executive Officer, Biltwell Co, St Louis, 1968-87; Creative Writing Instructor, Mineral Area Junior College, Flat River, Missouri, 1980-90; Curator, Brodsky Faulkner Collection, Southeast Missouri State University, Cape Girardeau, 1984-. Publications: Poetry: Five Facets of Myself, 1967, 1995; The Easy Philosopher, 1967, 1995; A Hard Coming of It and Other Poems, 1967, 1995; The Foul Rag-and-Bone Shop, 1967, 1969, 1995; Points in Time, 1971, 1995; Taking the Back Road Home, 1972; Trip to Tipton and Other Compulsions, 1972; The Talking Machine and Other Poems, 1973; Cold, Companionable Streams, 1974; Tiffany Shade, 1974; Trilogy: A Birth Cycle, 1974; Monday's Child, 1975; The Kingdom of Gewgaw, 1976; Point of Americas II, 1976; Preparing for Incarnations, 1976; La Preciosa, 1977; Stranded in the Land of Transients, 1978; The Uncelebrated Ceremony of Pants Factory Fatso, 1978; Birds in Passage, 1980; Résumé of a Scrapegoat, 1980; A Mississippi Trilogy: Vol 1, Mississippi Vistas, 1983, 1990, Vol 2, Mistress Mississippi, 1992, Vol 3, Disappearing in Mississippi Latitudes, 1994; You Can't Go Back, Exactly, 1988; The Thorough Earth, 1989; Four and Twenty Blackbirds Soaring, 1989; Falling from Heaven: Holocaust Poems of a Jew and a Gentile (co-author), 1991; Forever, for Now: Poems for a Later Love, 1991; A Gleam in the Eye: Poems for a First Baby, 1992; Gestapo Crows: Holocaust Poems, 1992; The Capital Café: Poems of Redneck, USA, 1993; Paper-Whites for Lady Jane: Second-Love Poems, 1995. Contributions to: Harper's; Southern Review; Amelia; Texas Quarterly; Kansas Quarterly; American Scholar; Anthology of Magazine Verse; National Forum; New Welsh Review; Ariel; Orbis; Literary Review. Address: 10411 Clayton Road, Suites 201-203, St Louis, MO 63131, USA.

BROGAARD-PEDERSEN Berit Oskar, b. 28 Aug 1970, Copenhagen, Denmark. PhD Researcher. Education: MSc, Biochemistry, 1989-94; BA, Danish Literature and Theatre, 1994-96. Publications: Danskere til Salg, 1991; Livet I lysthuset, 1992; Solnedgangens Orange Born, 1994; Manden der fandt ud af livets gåde; Marcos. Contributions to: Pseudo-Pop Magazine, 1995; Kritik,

1995. Memberships: The Danisk Writers Union. Address: Attika Strandlejen 429, DK 2930 Klampenborg, Gyldendal, Denmark; Klareboderne 3, 1001 Copenhagen, Denmark.

BROHL Ted, b. 18 Feb 1924, Pittsburgh, Pennsylvania, USA. Retired. m. Ellie Johnes, 27 June 1948, 1 son, 2 daughters. Publications: Ted Brohl's Gargoyles and Other Muses, 1990; In a Fine Frenzy Rolling, 1992; A Simple Grace, 1994; I Don't Talk Down to Kids, 1996. Contributions to: NPA Market-Letter, The National Poets Association; Oatmeal & Poetry; The Poet's Corner; Diamond Memories; Poetic Page; Washington Township News Report; New Jersey Legionnaire; Midnight Zoo; Cochran's Corner; Police Times Newspaper. Honours: 1st Honorary Poet Laureate in Gloucester County, New Jersey, 1991; Poet Laureate, Washington Township, New Jersey, 1991; Poet of Merit, American Poetry Association, 1990; Author's Award, New Jersey Writers Conference, 1993. Memberships: Patron Member, Poetry Society of America; Charter Member, The International Society of Poets; Walt Whitman Cultural Arts Center; The Writer's Center. Address: 812 Saratoga Terrace, Turnersville, New Jersey 08012, USA.

BROLL Brandon William, b. 18 Aug 1960, Johannesburg, South Africa. Poet; Writer; Scientist; Senior Writer at Science Photo Library, London. Education: Graduated with Distinction in Natural Science, University of Cape Town, 1980; BSc, Honours, 1981; Read for a Doctorate in Zoology, 1985. Appointments: Editor, Civil Rights League, South Africa, 1988-89; Helped launch a conference on a South African Bill of Rights, 1989. Publication: Not Merely White-South African poems 1986-88. Contributions to: Numerous publications in Britain, USA, South Africa and India; Anthologies: Twenty Five Years of English South African Poetry, 1989; Camden Voices Anthology, 1991; Vertical Images Anthology, 1991; Kites Anthology, 1992; Sojourners: New Writing by Africans in Britain, 1994; Parnassus of World Poets, 1994. Honours: Invited to perform at Poetry Festivals in Edinburgh, Hastings and London. Memberships: Poetry Society, London; Poetry Library, London. Address: 50A North View Road, Hornsey, London N8 7LL, England.

BROMIGE David (Mansfield), b. 22 Oct 1933, London, England (Canadian citizen, 1961). Poet; Writer; Professor of English. m. 1 son, 1 daughter. Education: BA, University of British Columbia, 1962; MA, 1964, ABD, 1969, University of California at Berkeley. Appointments: Poetry Editor, Northwest Review, 1962-64; Instructor, University of California at Berkeley, 1965-69; Professor of English, Sonoma State University, California, 1979-93. Publications: The Gathering, 1965; Please, Like Me, 1968; The Ends of the Earth, 1968; The Quivering Roadway, 1969; Threads, 1970; Ten Years in the Making, 1973; Three Stories, 1973; Birds of the West, 1974; Out of My Hands, 1974; Spells and Blessings, 1974; Tight Cornors and What's Around Them, 1974; Credences of Winter, 1976; Living in Advance, 1976; My Poetry, 1980; P-E-A-C-E, 1981; In the Uneven Steps of Hung Chow, 1982; It's the Same Only Different, 1984; The Melancholy Owed Categories, 1984; You See, 1985; Red Hats, 1986; Desire, 1988; Men, Women, and Vehicles, 1990; Tiny Courts in a World Without Scales, 1991; They Ate, 1992; The Harbormaster of Hong Kong, 1993; A Cast of Tens, 1994; From the First Century, 1995. Contributions to: Anthologies and periodicals. Honours: Poet Laureate, University of California (all campuses), 1965; Discovery Award, 1969; Poetry Fellowship, 1980; National Endowment for the Arts; Canada Council Grant in Poetry, 1976-77; Pushcart Prize in Poetry, 1980; Western States Art Federation Prize in Poetry, 1988; Gertrude Stein Award in Innovative Writing, 1994. Address: 461 High Street, Sebastopol, CA 95472, USA.

BRONSON Wolf. See: **RABORG Frederick Ashton, Jr.**

BROOKS Gwendolyn, b. 7 June 1917, Topeka, Kansas, USA. Poet; Writer. m. Henry L Blakely, 17 Sept 1939, 1 son, 1 daughter. Education: Graduated, Wilson Junior College, Chicago, 1936. Appointments: Teacher, Northeastern Illinois State College, Chicago; Columbia College, Chicago; Elmhurst College, Illinois; Rennebohm Professor of English, University of Wisconsin, Madison; Distinguished Professor of the Arts, City College of the City University of New York, 1971; Consultant in Poetry, Library of Congress, Washington DC, 1985-86; Jefferson Lecturer, 1994. Publications: Poetry: A Street in Bronzeville, 1945; Annie Allen, 1949; Bronzeville Boys and Girls, 1956; The Bean Eaters, 1960; Selected Poems, 1963; We Real Cool, 1966; The Wall, 1967; In the Mecca, 1968; Riot, 1969; Family Pictures, 1970; Black Steel: Joe Frazier and Muhammad Ali, 1971; Aloneness, 1971; Aurora, 1972; Beckonings, 1975; To Disembark, 1981; Black Love,

1982; Mayor Harold Washington, and Chicago, The I Will City, 1983; The Near-Johannesburg Boy and Other Poems, 1986; Blacks, 1987; Winnie, 1988; Gottschalk and the Grande Tarantelle, 1988; Children Coming Home, 1991; Other includes: Report from Part Two, 1995. Contributions to: Various publications. Honours: American Academy of Arts and Letters Grant, 1946; Guggenheim Fellowship, 1946-47; Pulitzer Prize in Poetry, 1950; Thormod Monsen Award, 1964; Ferguson Memorial Award, 1964; Poet Laureate of Illinois, 1968; Anisfield-Wolf Award, 1968; Black Academy Award, 1971; Shelley Memorial Award, 1976; Frost Medal, Poetry Society of America, 1988; National Endowment for the Arts Lifetime Achievement Award, 1989; Aiken-Taylor Award, 1992; National Book Foundation Medal, 1994. Memberships: National Women's Hall of Fame; Society of Midland Authors. Address: 5530 South Shore Drive, Apt 2A, Chicago, IL 60637, USA.

BROOKS Katherine Elizabeth Howes, b. 14 Oct 1922, Framingham, Massachusetts, USA. Homemaker. m. Wendell C Brooks, 1 Aug 1943, 2 daughters. Education: BA, Colby College, Waterville, Maine, 1944. Publications: The Nine Lives of Frank and Natalie, 1995; Off Limits, 1995; Unsung Creatures from A to Z, 1996. Contributions to: Poets' Review; Apropos; Omnific; Feelings; Cliff Island Seagull; Anterior Bitewing; Poets' Pouch; Ellery Queen; Housewife's Humor; Poetpourri. Honours: Numerous 1st places, 1985-96; Joan Brown Award for Humorous Poetry, Poetpourri, 1989; Poet of the Year, Poets' Review, 1992, 1994. Address: 25 Fessenden Street, Portland, Maine 04103, USA.

BROSMAN Catharine Savage, b. 7 June 1934, Denver, Colorado, USA. Professor. m. Paul W Brosman Jr, 21 Aug 1970, 1 daughter. Education: BA, 1955; MA, 1957; PhD, 1960. Appointments: Instructor, Rice University, 1960-62; Assistant Professor of French, Sweet Briar College, 1962-63; Assistant Professor of French, University of Florida, 1963-66; Associate Professor of French, Mary Baldwin College, 1966-68; Associate Professor of French, 1968-72, Professor of French, 1972-92, Kathryn B Gore Professor of French, 1992-, Tulane University, New Orleans, Louisiana; De Velling and Willis Visiting Professor, University of Sheffield, 1996. Publications: Watering; Abiding Winter, 1983; Journeying from Canyon de Chelly, 1990; The Shimmering Maya and Other Essays, 1994; Passages, 1996. Contributions to: Southern Review; Sewanee Review; Southwest Review; Georgia Review; Southern Humanities Review; Critical Quarterly; Interim; American Scholar. Honours: 3rd Place Award, Best Poems of 1973. Address: Department of French and Italian, Tulane University, New Orleans, LA 70118, USA.

BROSSARD Nicole, b. 27 Nov 1943, Montreal, Quebec, Canada. Poet; Author. Education: Licence ès Lettres, 1968, Scolarité de Maîtrise en lettres, 1972, Université de Montréal; Bacc Spéecialisé en Pédagogie, Université du Québec a Montréal, 1971. Publications: Poetry: Mécanique Jongleuse, 1973, English translation as Daydream Mechanics, 1980; Le Centre blanc, 1978; Amantes, 1980, English translation as Lovers, 1986; Double Impressions, 1984; Mauve, 1984; Character/Jeu de Lettres, 1986; Sous la langue/Under Tongue, bilingual edition, 1987; La Nuite verte duparc labyrinthe, trilingual edition, 1992. Fiction: Un Livre, 1970, English translation as A Book, 1976; Sold-Out, 1973; English translation as Turn of a Pang, 1976; French Kiss, 1974, English translation, 1986; L'amer, 1977; English translation as These Our Mothers, or, the Disintegrating Chapter, 1983; Les Sens apparent, 1980, English translation as Surfaces of Sense, 1989; Picture Theory, 1982, English translation, 1991; La Désert mauve, 1987, English translation as Mauve Desert, 1990; Baroque d'aube, 1995, English translation as Baroque at Dawn, 1996. Contributions to: Numerous anthologies. Honours: Governor-General Prizes, 1974, 1984; Chapbook Award, Therafields Foundation, 1986; Grand Prix de Poésie, Fondation Les Forges, 1989; Honorary Doctorate, University of Western Ontario, 1991; Prix Athanase-David, 1991. Membership: L'Acadèmie des Lettres du Québec, 1993-. Address: 34 Avenue Robert, Outrement, Quebec H3S 2P2, Canada.

BROSTROM Kerri Rochelle, b. 22 July 1961, Minneapolis, Minnesota, USA. Publicist. m. Peter Masters, 29 Mar 1996, 1 son, 2 daughters. Education: Attended St Cloud State University, University of Minnesota; Majored in Marketing and minored in Political Science. Appointments: Staff, GTE, 3 years; Staff, Northwest Airlines, 3 years; Currently, Publicist, Movement Records. Contributions to: Nassau Review; Aura; Potpourri; Oregon East; Oyez Review; Byline; Black River Review; Touchstone; OLD Red Kimono; Poetpourri; The Pointed Circle; Negative Capability; Rag Mag; Sidewalks; Artword Quarterly;

Explorations; Mind in Motion; Fox Cry; Wisconsin Review; Greenfuse; Cafe Review; Cape Rock; Sonoma; Mandala; Nightsun; Djinni; Rockford Review; Ellipses; Prairie Winds; Maryland Poetry Review. Address: 2512 East 125th Street, Burnsville, MN 55337, USA.

BROUGHTON James, b. 10 Nov 1913, USA. Poet; Filmmaker. m. Suzanne Hart. 6 Dec 1962, 1 son, 1 daughter. Education: BA, Stanford University, 1936. Appointments: Associate Professor, San Francisco State University; Special Instructor, San Francisco Art Institute. Publications: Making LIght of it; The Androgyne Journal; Special Deliveries; Hooplas; 75 Lifelines; A to Z; Ecstasies; Graffiti for the Johns of Heaven; Hymns to Hermes; A Long Undressing; High Kukas; Tidings; True & False Unicorn; Musical Chairs; The Playground; Making Light of It, 1992; Coming Unbuttoned, 1993. Contributions to: Credences; Exquisite Corpse; Saturday Review; New Yorker; Beatitude; Vortex; City Lights Review; Zyzzva; Several anthologies. Honours: Distinguished Service Award; Lifetime Achievement Award. Membership: Poetry Society of America. Address: PO Box 1330, Port Townsend, WA 98368, USA.

BROUMAS Olga, b. 6 May 1949, Hermoupolis, Greece. Poet. m. Stephen Edward Bangs, 1973, div 1979. Education: BA, University of Pennsylvania, 1970; MFA, University of Oregon, Eugene, 1973. Appointments: Instructor, University of Oregon, 1972-76; Visiting Associate Professor, University of Idaho, 1978; Poet-in-Residence, Goddard College, Plainfield, Vermont, 1979-81, Women Writers Center, Cazenovia, New York, 1981-82; Founder-Associate Faculty, Freehand Women Writers and Photographers Community, Provincetown, Massachusetts, 1982-87; Visiting Associate Professor, Boston University, 1988-90; Fanny Hurst Poet-in-Residence, Brandeis University, 1990. Publications: Restlessness, 1967; Caritas, 1976; Beginning with O, 1977; Soie Sauvage, 1980; Pastoral Jazz, 1983; Black Holes, Black Stockings, 1985; Perpetua, 1989; Sappho's Gymnasium, 1994. Honours: Yale Younger Poets Award, 1977; National Endowment for the Arts Grant, 1978; Guggenheim Fellowship, 1981-82. Address: 162 Mill Pond Drive, Brewster, MA 02631, USA.

BROWN Barbara Marie, b. 6 Dec 1934, London, England. Secretary; Typist. m. Philip Brown, 30 Mar 1954, dec, 1 son, 1 daughter. Publication: First Time, 1992. Contributions to: Brighton Festival, 1992; National Poetry Society; Ouse Valley Poetry; Hastings Festival, 1992. Membership: Poetry Society. Address: 22 London Prospect, Oakwood Drive, Central Hill, Upper Norwood, London SE19, England.

BROWN (Mary) Charline Hayes, b. 13 Dec 1919, USA. Business Manager; Accountant. m. Joseph Cecil Brown Jr, 30 Sept 1945, 1 son, 2 daughters, 1 dec. Education: BS, Louisiana State University, 1941. Appointments: Accountant-Secretary, H R Hayes Library Co, Monroe, 1941-45; Personnel Clerk, Veterans Administration, Marietta, 1945-46; Insurance Examiner, Veterans Administration, 1946; Secretary-Treasurer, Lumberman's Supply Co Inc, Monroe, 1953-85; Estate Administrator, 1977-78, 1983-86; Manager, Hayes Co, Monroe, 1978-90. Publications: Brief Lightning, 1979. Contributions to: Oregonian; Hearthstone; Conquest; Christian Home; Furrow; Writer; Grit; American Haiku; Swordsman Review; American Bard; Archer; Westminster Magazine; Sonnet Sequences; Green World; Step Ladder; Poet's Reed; Kansas City Poetry Magazine; Charleston Evening Post; Scimitar and Song; The Lyric; Lyric Louisiana; Lincoln Young Anthologies; Avalon Anthologies; American Poetry Anthologies. Memberships: National League of American Penwomen; Louisiana State Poetry Society; Mississippi State Poetry Society. Address: 5200 Bon Air Drive, Monroe, LA 71203, USA.

BROWN Fred, b. 18 Sept 1948, Birmingham, England. Teacher. m. Kate, 16 June 1979. Education: BEd. Appointments: Teacher, Somerdale High School; Oakleigh Special School; Beechlawn Special School; Jaffe Centre; Home Tuition, Jaffe Centre. Contributions to: Orbis; Belfast Review; Fiction Magazine; Pennine Ink; Poetry Audience; Nutshell; Iota. Honour: 3rd Point North, 1988. Address: 320 Castlereach Road, Belfast BT5 6FG, Northerm Ireland.

BROWN James Willie, Jr. See: **KOMUNYAKAA Yusef.**

BROWN John Gracen, b. 8 Oct 1936, Martinsburg, West Virginia, USA. Writer. Education: BS, 1961, MS, 1962, Southern Illinois University. Appointments: Camp Counsellor (Leader) for Children;

Teacher; Guidance Director; Restoration Worker. Publications: Variation in Verse, 1975; A Sojourn of the Spirit, 1981; Passages in the Wind, 1985; Eight Dramas, 1991; The Search, 1994. Honours: Music based on poems from 2 of his books won 1st Prize, International Double Bass Convention, 1984; Poetry used extensively by over 150 composers around the world. Memberships: American Society of Composers, Authors and Publishers. Address: 430 Virginia Avenue, Martinsburg, WV 25401, USA.

BROWN Rita Mae, b. 28 Nov 1944, Hanover, Pennsylvania, USA. Author; Poet. Education: Broward Junior College, 1965; BA, New York University, 1968; Cinematography Certificate, New York School of Visual Arts, 1968; PhD, Institute for Policy Studies, Washington, DC, 1973. Publications: The Hand That Cradles The Rock, poems, 1971; Rubyfruit, novel, 1973; Songs To A Handsome Woman, poems, 1973; In Her Day, novel, 1976; A Plain Brown Rapper, essays, 1976; Six Of One, novel, 1978; Southern Discomfort, novel, 1982; Sudden Death, novel, 1983; High Hearts, novel, 1986; The Poems Of Rita Mae Brown, 1987; Starting From Scratch: A Different Kind of Writer's Manual, 1988; Bingo, novel, 1988; Wish You Were Here, mystery, 1990; Rest In Pieces, 1992; Venus Envy, 1993; Dolley: A Novel of Dolley Madison In Love And War, 1994; Other: screenplays. Contributions to: Various magazines. Address: c/o Wendy Weil Agency, 747 Third Avenue, 4th Floor, New York, NY 10017, USA.

BROWN Rosellen, b. 12 May 1939, Philadelphia, Pennsylvania, USA. Writer; Poet; Associate Professor. m. Marvin Hoffman, 16 March 1963, 2 daughters. Education: BA, Barnard College, 1960; MA, Brandeis University, 1962. Appointments: Instructor, Tougaloo College, Mississippi, 1965-67; Staff, Bread Loaf Writer's Conference, Middlebury, Vermont, 1974, 1991, 1992; Instructor, Goddard College, Plainfield, Vermont, 1976; Visiting Professor of Creative Writing, Boston University, 1977-78; Associate Professor in Creative Writing, University of Houston, 1982-85, 1989-. Publications: Some Deaths In The Delta And Other Poems, 1970; The Whole World Catalog: Creative Writing Ideas For Elementary And Secondary Schools (with others), 1972; Street Games: A Neighbourhood, stories, 1974; The Autobiography Of My Mother, novel, 1976; Cora Fry, poems, 1977; Banquet: Five Short Stories, 1978; Tender Mercies, novel, 1978; Civil Wars: A Novel, 1984; A Rosellen Brown Reader: Selected Poetry And Prose, 1992; Before And After, novel, 1992. Contributions to: Books, anthologies and periodicals. Honours: Woodrow Wilson Fellow, 1960; Howard Foundation Grant, 1971-72; National Endowment for the Humanities Grants, 1973-74, 1981-82; Radcliffe Institute Fellow, 1973-75; Great Lakes Colleges New Writers Award, 1976; Guggenheim Fellowship, 1976-77; American Academy and Institute of Arts and Letters Award, 1988; Ingram-Merrill Grant, 1989-90. Address: c/o Creative Writing Program, University of Houston, Houston, TX 77204, USA.

BROWN Stewart, b. 14 Mar 1951, Lymington, Hampshire, England. University Lecturer in African and Caribbean Literature; Writer; Poet; Editor. m. Priscilla Margaret Brant, 1976, 1 son, 1 daughter. Education: BA, Falmouth School of Art, 1978; MA, University of Sussex, 1979; PhD, University of Wales, 1987. Appointments: Lecturer in English, Bayero University, Kano, Nigeria, 1980-83; Lecturer in African and Caribbean Literature, University of Birmingham, 1988-. Publications: Mekin Foolishness, poems, 1981; Caribbean Poetry Now, 1984, new edition, 1992; Zinder, poems, 1986; Lugard's Bridge, poems, 1989; Voiceprint: An Anthology of Oral and Related Poetry from the Caribbean, editor with Mervyn Morris and Gordon Rohler, 1989; Writers from Africa: A Reader's Guide, 1989; New Wave: The Contemporary Caribbean Short Story, 1990; The Art of Derek Walcott: A Collection of Critical Essays, 1991; Caribbean Stories Now, 1991; The Pressures of the Text; orality, texts and the Telling of Tales, 1995; The Art of Kamau Brathwaite: A Collection of Critical Essays, 1992; The Heinemann Book of Caribbean Poetry, with Ian McDonald, 1992; Caribbean New Voices I, 1996. Contributions to: Anthologies and periodicals. Honours: Eric Gregory Award, 1976; Southwest Arts Literature Award, 1978; Honorary Fellow, Centre for Caribbean Studies, University of Warwick, 1978. Memberships: Welsh Academy; Welsh Union of Writers. Address: Centre of West African Studies, University of Birmingham, Edgbaston, Birmingham B15 2TT, England.

BROWN William Imray, b. 11 May 1929, Aberdeen, Scotland. Teacher; Lecturer; Poet. m. Roma Learmonth Robertson, 22 Dec 1951, 3 sons. Education: University of Aberdeen, 1946-50; MA, Aberdeen College of Education, 1962. Appointments: Teacher, Glasgow Schools, 1952-53; Teacher, Dufftown, Banffshire, 1953-57;

Principal Teacher, Benwick High School, 1957-62; Senior Lecturer, Aberdeen College of Education, 1962-78. Publications: Pools Cycle; Langstene Nou and Syne. Contributions to: Acumen; Iota; Orbis; Apostrophe; Iron; Ore; Celtic Dawn; Isthmus; Outposts; Chapman; Lallans; Pennine Platform; Spokes; Envoi; Lines Review; Poetry Nottingham; Programore Papers; New Hope International Poetry Digest; Staple; Gairm; New Prospects. Honours: Nottingham Poetry Society; Open University Poets; Poetry Digest General Competition; Scottish International Competition; Yeats Club. Address: The Coach House, Huntly Place, Aboyne, Aberdeenshire AB34 5HD, Scotland.

BROWNE Michael Dennis, b. 28 May 1940, Walton-on-Thames, England (US citizen, 1978). Professor; Writer; Poet. m. Lisa Furlong McLean, 18 July 1981, 1 son, 2 daughters. Education: BA, Hull University, 1962; Oxford University, 1962-63; Ministry of Education Teacher's Certificate, 1963; MA, University of Iowa, 1967. Appointments: Visiting Lecturer, University of Iowa, 1967-68; Instructor, 1967, 1968, Visiting Adjunct Assistant Professor, 1968, Columbia University; Faculty, Bennington College, Vermont, 1969-71; Visiting Assistant Professor, 1971-72, Assistant Professor, 1972-75, Associate Professor, 1975-83, Professor, 1983-, University of Minnesota. Publications: The Wife of Winter, 1970; Sun Exercises, 1976; The Sun Fetcher, 1978; Smoke From the Fires, 1985; You Won't Remeber This, 1992; Selected Poems 1965-1995, 1997. Contributions to: Numerous anthologies and journals; Other: Texts for various musical compositions. Honours: Fulbright Scholarship, 1965-67; Borestone Poetry Prize, 1974; National Endowment for the Arts Fellowships, 1977, 1978; Bush Fellowship, 1981; Loft-McKnight Writers' Award, 1986; Minnesota Book Award for Poetry, 1993. Memberships; The Loft: Poetry Society of America. Address: 2111 East 22nd Street, Minneapolis, MN 55404, USA.

BROWNING Stella, b. 22 June 1917, New Romney, Kent, England. Retired; Literary Consultant; Poet; Author; Editor; Lecturer. m. (1) J J Duffey, div, (2) Kenneth Martin, dec, 2 sons. Education: Higher Schools Certificate, hons, English, Psychology, London University; MA, French, English; Diploma, Music, Convent, Loire Valley, 1939. Appointments: Part-time English Teacher, World War II; Lecturer, English, Oban High School; Journalist, Poetry Promotions; Broadcaster, USA, Scotland, England; Reader, BBC Medway, 5 years; Magazine Editor; Executive Editor, World Poetry Society Anthologies, 1990, 1991, 1993, 1995, 1996; Soka Gakkai, Tokyo, 1994, 1995, 1996; Carta Internacional De Posia, Argentina, 1995, 1996; Request Readership, Edinburgh Festival, Guest Editor, Poetry Now, England, Guest Editor, Literary Advisor, Literary Review, India, Adjudicator, National Anthologies, 1995; Editor-in-Chief, Posie India, 1996; Co-Coordinator, Milton Trust/United Poets Laureate Congress, 1997. Publications: Hoodie the Crow, Pilgrimage and other Poems, 1972; Butter-in-the-Buttercups, 1972-77; Notail at Wesley, 1980; On Wings of Sound, autobiography, 1980; Wings of the Wind, 1986; To Hold a Wildbird in the Hand, 1991-92; Brigg Flatts Re-Visited: Tribute to Basil Bunting, 1995; Childhood; Shaft of Light, 1992, translated into 5 languages, 1994-96; Tapes of spiritual readings and spiritual verse extracts. Contributions to: Kent Life; Now; Outposts; New Hope International; Colorado Review; Kentish Express; Oban Times; Glasgow Herald; Times Literary Supplement; Laurel Leaves; Poets for Africa; Rainbows of Peace; World Poetry Anthologies; Positively Poetry; others. Honours include: 2 Gold, 1 Silver Medals; Silver Cross, Citation, Elna M Smith Foundation, Arkansas, 1985; Laurel Leaves Crown, Florida, 1985; Bronze Medal, W P Society; Honorary Doctorate, Marquis Giuseppe Scicluna International University, 1985; London Literary Review Award for Shaft of Light, 1992; Romney Bookshop display of works, 1994; Nominee, Australian Dove of Peace, 1995-96. Memberships: Founder, Editor, Cinque Ports Poets, 1970-95; Silver Jubilee, 1995; Vice-President, United Poets Laureate, 1985; PEN International; Honorary Member, Ayrshire Writers and Artists; Maltese Cross. Address: 2 Highfield, Sussex Road, New Romney, Kent TN28 8DS, England.

BROWNJOHN Alan (Charles), b. 28 July 1931, Catford, London, England. Poet; Writer; Critic. Education: BA, 1953, MA, 1961, Merton College, Oxford, England. Appointments: Lecturer, Battersea College of Education, 1965-79; Tutor, Polytechnic of North London, 1981-83; Poetry Critic, New Statesman, 1968-76, Encounter, 1978-82, Sunday Times, 1990-; Chairman, Poetry Society, 1982-88. Publications: Poetry: Travellers Alone, 1954; The Railings, 1961; The Lions' Mouths, 1967; Sandgrains on a Tray, 1969; Penguin Modern Poets 14, 1969; First I Say This: A Selection of Poems for Reading Aloud, 1969; Brownjohn's Beasts, 1970; Warrior's Career, 1972; A

Song of Good Life, 1975; The Old Flea-Pit, 1987; The Observation Car, 1990; In the Cruel Arcade, 1994; Fiction: To Clear the River, 1964; The Way You Tell Them, 1990; Other: Philip Larkin, 1975; Meet and Write, 1985-87; The Gregory Anthology, 1990. Honours: Cholmondeley Award, 1979; Author's Club (London) Award, Best First Novel, 1990. Memberships: Arts Council of Great Britain Literature Panel, 1968-72; Poetry Society, London; Writer's Guild of Great Britain; Society of Authors. Address: 2 Belsize Park, London NW3, England.

BROWNSTEIN Michael H, b. 17 July 1953, Evanston, Illinois, USA. Teacher. m. Deborah Wymbs, 10 Oct 1988, 2 sons, 2 daughters. Education: BA, Elementary Education, Northern Illinois University, 1974; MA, Curriculum and Development, National College of Education, 1988. Appointments: Writer, Publisher, Editor, Paper Bag Press, 1988-; Editor, Wymbs Broadside, 1989-91; Contributing Editor, Letter X, 1992-95; Educational Columnist, South Street Journal, 1994-. Publications: The Shouting Gallery, 1988; Poems From the Body Bags, 1989; Reflections, 1991; The Principal of Things, 1994; Recessions & Other Poems, 1996. Contributions to: Chicago Reader; Chicago Sun Times; Learning Magazine; Bogg; Phonex Press; Ariel Words; Tomorrow Magazine; Several others. Honours: Chapbook First Prize, 1989; Triton College of International Poetry First Place, 1991, 1992, 1993, 1994, 1996. Address: PO Box 268805, Chicago, IL 60626-8805, USA.

BRUCE George, b. 10 Mar 1909, Fraserburgh, Aberdeenshire, Scotland. Poet; Writer; Broadcaster; Lecturer. m. Elizabeth Duncan, 25 July 1935, 1 son, 1 daughter. Education: MA, Aberdeen University, 1932. Appointments: English Master, Dundee High School, 1934-46; Producer, BBC, Aberdeen, 1946-56, Edinburgh, 1956-70; First Fellow in Creative Writing, Glasgow University, 1971-73; Lecturer in Scotland and abroad. Publications: Sea Talk, 1944; Landscapes and Figures, 1967; Collected Poems, 1940-70, 1970; Perspectives: Selected Poems, 1970-86, 1986; The Land Out There, 1991; Other: Anne Redpath: A Monograph of the Scottish Painter, 1975; Some Practical Good: The Cockburn Association, 1875-1975, 1975; Festival in the North, 1947-75, 1975. Contributions to: Anthologies, books, and periodicals. Honours: Scottish Arts Council Awards, 1967, 1971; Honorary DLitt, College of Wooster, Ohio, 1977; Officer of the Order of the British Empire, 1984. Memberships: Saltire Society; Scottish Poetry Library; Poetry Society. Address: 25 Warriston Crescent, Edinburgh EH3 5LB, Scotland.

BRUCE Lennart, b. 21 Feb 1919, Stockholm, Sweden. Writer. m. Sonja Bruce, 22 July 1960, 1 son, 1 daughter. Education: College and University, 1928-40. Appointment: International Financier, 1945-64. Publications: English: Making the Rounds, 1967; Observations, 1968; Moments of Doubt, 1969; Mullioned Windows, 1970; The Robot Failure, 1971; Exposure, 1972, 2nd edition, 1972; Subpoemas, 1974; Letter of Credit, 1973; The Broker, 1984; Swedish: En Sannsaga, 1982; Utan Synbar Anledning, 1988; Forskningringen, 1990; En Nasares Gang, 1993; Kafferepet, 1995; Translations: Agenda, 1976; The Second Light, 1986; Speak to Me, 1989; The Ways of a Carpetbagger, 1993; Instructions for Undressing the Human Race, with Matthew Zion, 1968. Honours: Royal Swedish Academy of Letters, 1978, 1988. Memberships: Swedish Writers Association; PEN American Centre; Poetry Society of America. Address: 31 Los Cerros Place, Walnut Creek, CA 94598, USA.

BRUCHAC Joseph, b. 16 Oct 1942, Saratoga Springs, New York, USA. Author; Poet; Storyteller; Publisher; Editor. m. Carol Worthen, 12 June 1964, 2 sons. Education: AB, Cornell University, 1965; MA, Syracuse University, 1966; Graduate Studies, State University of New York at Albany, 1971-73; PhD, Union Institute, Ohio, 1975. Appointments: Co-Founder, Director, Greenfield Review Press, 1969-; Editor, Greenfield Review Literary Magazine, 1971-90; Visiting Scholar and Writer-in-Residence at various institutions; Member, Dawnland Singers, 1993-. Publications: Fiction and Poetry: Indian Mountain and Other Poems, 1971; Turkey Brother and Other Iroquois Folk Tales, 1976; The Dreams of Jesse Brown, novel, 1977; Stone Giants and Flying Heads: More Iroquois Folk Tales, 1978; The Wind Eagle and Other Abenaki Stories, 1984; Iroquois Stories, 1985; Walking With My Sons and Other Poems, 1986; Near the Mountains: New and Selected Poems, 1987; Keepers of the Earth, stories, 1988; The Faithful Hunter: Abenaki Stories, 1988; Long Memory and Other Poems, 1989; Return of the Sun: Native American Tales from the Northeast Woodlands, 1989; Hoop Snakes, Hide-Behinds and Side-Hill Winders: Tall Tales from the Adirondacks, 1991; Keepers of the

Animals, with Michael Caduto, stories, 1991; Thirteen Moons on Turtle's Back, with Jonathan London, poems and stories, 1992; Dawn Land, novel, 1993; The First Strawberries, 1993; Flying with the Eagle, Racing the Great Bear, stories, 1993; The Girl Who Married the Moon, with Gayle Ross, stories, 1994; A Boy Called Slow, 1995; The Boy Who Lived with the Bears, stories, 1995; Dog People, stories, 1995; Long River, novel, 1995; The Story of the Milky Way, with Gayle Ross, 1995; Beneath Earth and Sky, 1996; Children of the Long House, novel, 1996; Four Ancestors: Stories, Songs and Poems from Native North America, 1996; Other: Survival This Way: Interviews with Native American Poets, 1987; The Native American Sweat Lodge: History and Legends, 1993; Roots of Survival: Native American Storytelling and the Sacred, 1993; Editor: Words from the House of the Dead: An Anthology of Prison Writings from Soledad, with William Witherup, 1971; The Last Stop: Writings from Comstock Prison, 1974; Aftermath: An Anthology of Poems in English from Africa, Asia and the Caribbean, 1977; The Next World: Poems by Thirty-Two Third-World Americans, 1978; Songs from This Earth on Turtle's Back: Contemporary American Indian Poetry, 1983; The Light from Another Country: Poetry from American Prisons, 1984; Breaking Silence: An Anthology of Asian American Poetry, 1984; North Country: An Anthology of Contemporary Writing from the Adirondacks and the Upper Hudson Valley, with others, 1985; New Voices from the Longhouse: An Anthology of Contemporary Iroquois Writing, 1985; Returning the Gift: Poetry and Prose from the First North American Native Writers Festival, 1994; Smoke Rising: The Native North American Literary Companion, with others, 1995. Contributions to: Many anthologies, books, and periodicals. Honours: National Endowment for the Arts Fellowship, 1974; Rockefeller Foundation Humanities Fellowship, 1982-83; American Book Award, 1985; Notable Children's Book in the Language Arts Award, 1993; American Library Association Notable Book Award, 1996; Knickerbocker Award for Juvenile Literature, New York Library Association, 1996. Memberships: National Association for the Preservation and Perpetuation of Storytelling; PEN; Poetry Society of America. Address: PO Box 308, Greenfield Center, NY 12833, USA.

BRUTUS Dennis, b. 28 Nov 1924, Salisbury, Rhodesia. Education: BA, Witwatersrand University, Johannesburg, 1947. Appointments: Professor at universities in Pittsburgh, Austin, Dartmouth and Boston; Active on behalf of organizations countering racism in sport. Publications: Sirens, Knuckles, Boots, 1963; Letters to Martha and Other Poems from a South African Prison, 1968; Poems from Algiers, 1970; Thoughts Abroad, 1970; A Simple Lust: Selected Poems, 1973; China Poems, 1975; Strains, 1982; Stubborn Hope, 1978; Salutes and Censures, 1984; Airs and Tributes, 1988; Still the Sirens, 1993. Address: 3812 Bates Street, Pittsburgh, PA 15213, USA.

BRUUN Mette Tine, b. 5 Apr 1956, Copenhagen, Denmark. Writer. m. L Bohm, 16 June 1984, 1 son, 3 daughters. Education: Nurse, 1980. Publications: De Betydningsfulde Kvinder, 1992; Natmasker, 1995. Membership: Dansk Forfatter Forening. Address: Skipper Clements Alle 5 1, 2300 Copenhagen S, Denmark.

BRYAN Sharon, b. 10 Feb 1943, Salt Lake City, Utah, USA. Poet; Writer. Education: BA, Philosophy, University of Utah, 1965; MA, Anthropology, Cornell University, 1969; MFA, Poetry, University of Iowa, 1977. Appointments: Adjunct Faculty, University of Washington, 1987-93; Associate Professor, Memphis State University, 1987-93; Visiting Professor, Dartmouth College, University of Houston, 1993-. Publications: Salt Air, 1983; Objects of Affection, 1987; Flying Blind, 1996. Contributions to: Atlantic; Georgia Review; Ploughshares; Poetry Northwest; Nation; Southern Review; Quarterly West; Seattle Review; Tar River Poetry. Honours: Academy of American Poets Prize, 1977; Discovery, The Nation, 1977; Arvon Foundation Prize, 1985; Governor's Award, Washington, 1985; NEA, 1987; Tennessee Arts Fellowship, 1991. Memberships: Poetry Society of America; Academy of American Poets; Poets and Writers; AWP. Address: 1254 West 1000 North, Salt Lake City, UT 84116, USA.

BU Ba Yan, b. 28 Mar 1941, Molidawa, Inner Mongolia, China. Teacher; Editor; Writer. m. Yu Minghua, 12 Mar 1973, 1 daughter. Education: Middle School, Beijing Central National University, 1960. Appointments: Teacher of Chinese, Middle School, Harbin, 1960-73; Editor, Poems and Novels, Periodical, 1973-84; Head, Editorial Department, Poetry Forest Magazine, Associate Editor-in-Chief, Harbin Literature and Art Magazine Agency, 1984-89; Professional Writer; Associate Chairman, Harbin Writers Association, 1990-. Publications: Fresh Milk and Flowers, 1980; Unbosom My Love, 1983;

The Flying Colour, 1987. Contributions to: Poetry Periodical; People's Daily; Literature and Art Newspaper; PLA Literature & Art; National Literature; October; European Times; Vast Ocean Poetry Magazine. Honours: Several awards. Memberships: Chinese Writers Association; Council Member, Chinese Mongolia Literature Association; Founder, Council Member, World Association of Chinese Poets; Standing Council, Chinese Minority Nationality Writers Association; Associate Chairman, Heilongjiang Writers Association Branch in Poetry; Council Member, Heilongjiang Poetry Association; World Congress of Poets, San Francisco. Address: 17 5-303 Hezhou Street, Daoli, Harbin, China.

BUCHAN Tom, b. 19 June 1931, Glasgow, Scotland. Education: MA, University of Glasgow, 1953. Appointments: Lecturer in Scotland, including Senior Lecturer in English and Drama, Clydebank Technical College, Glasgow, 1967-70; Director, theatre ensembles. Publications include: Ikons, 1958; Dolphins at Cochin, 1969; Exorcism, 1972; Poems 1969-72, 1972; Forwards, 1978. Honours include: Scottish Arts Council Awards. Address: Scoraig, Dundonnell, Wester Ross IV23 2RE, Scotland.

BUCHAN Vivian Eileen Eaton, b. 19 May 1911, Eagle Grove, Iowa, USA. Freelance Writer. m. Warren Joseph Buchan, 4 Sept 1933. Education: BA, English, Coe College, 1933; MA, English, University of Illinois, 1958. Appointments: Teacher in Rhetoric Programme, University of Illinois, 1957-58; University of Iowa, 1959-67. Publications: English Compositions, manual, 1960; Sun Signs, 1979; Make Presentations with Confidence, 1991, translated into Portugese, 1995. Contributions to: Approx 900 articles, essays, columns, poems in over 80 national and international publications. Honours: 2nd Place, Lyrical Iowa, 1964; Merlit Award, Coe College, for distinguished contributions to education as an editor, educator and writer, 1983; 4th Place, 1989, Grand Prize Award, 1991, 2nd Place, 1989, 2 Grand Prizes, 1991, World of Poetry; 2nd Place, Iowa Poetry Association, 1981; Iowa Poetry Association 3rd Place, 1987; Other awards in state and national poetry contests; 1st Place, General Adult Category, Iowa Poetry Association, 1995; 1st Place, The Lifted Hood, Iowa Poetry Association, 1996. Address: Walden Place No 225, 2423 Walden Road, Iowa City, IA 52246, USA.

BUCK Heather, b. 6 Apr 1926, Kent, England. Writer. m. Hadley J Buck, 23 May 1952, 1 son, 1 daughter. Publications: The Opposite Direction, 1971; At the Window, 1982; The Sign of the Water Bearer, 1987; Psyche Unbound, 1995; TS Eliot's, Four Quartets, 1996. Contributions to: Acumen; Agenda; Critical Quarterly; Encounter; English; Poetry Review; Rialto: Pen New Poems 1976-77; New Poetry 7; Interactions; Understanding & Response; The Independent; The Month; Anthologies: Sixty Women Poets; Completing the Picture. Memberships: Poetry Society; English Association. Address: 14 High Street, Lavenham, Suffolk CO10 9PT, England.

BUCKHOLTS Claudia, b. 29 Dec 1944, Ardmore, Oklahoma, USA. Poet. m. Thomas Glannon, 19 Sept 1987. Education: Matthew Vassar Scholar, Vassar College; BA, History, University of Michigan, 1967. Appointments: Editorial Assistant, Houghton Mifflin Company, 1968, 1969; Director, Cambridge Poets Workshop, 1973-83; Editor, Gargoyle poetry magazine, 1975-82; Harvard University Press, Foreign Rights, 1979-. Publications: Bitterwater, 1975; Travelling Through the Body, 1979; The Book of Q, prose and poetry, 1993. Contributions to: Alaska Quarterly Review; Connecticut Poetry Review; Kansas Quarterly; Midwest Quarterly; Minnesota Review; Paintbrush; Prairie Schooner; Sojourner; Soundings East; Hiram Poetry Review; Indiana Review; Dark Horses; Gargoyle; Shadowgraphs; Night House Anthology; 48 Younger American Poets; Provincetown Poets; Polis; Zeugma; Noise; Sri Chinmoy Awards Anthologies. Honours: Hopwood Awards, 1965, 1967; Grolier Poetry Prize, 1976; Snr Chinmoy Poetry Awards, 1977, 1978; Editor's Choice, Best Poems of 1980 (Dark Horse; Massachusetts Artists' Foundation Fellowship, 1981; National Endowment for the Arts Fellowship, 1988. Membership: Academy of American Poets. Address: 15 Clarendon Avenue, Somerville, MA 02144, USA.

BUCKLEY William K, b. 14 Nov 1946, San Diego, California, USA. Teacher. m. Mary Patricia, 25 Nov 1969, 1 son. Education: MA, San Diego State University; PhD, Miami University, Oxford, Ohio. Appointment: Associate Professor, Indiana University. Publications: Meditations on the Grid; Images Entitled to their Recoil from Utopia. Contributions to: Cafe Review; Lynx Eye; Left Curve; Coe Review; Peace Magazine; Rain Dog Review. Membership: American Academy of Poets. Address: English Department, Indiana University, 3400 Broadway, IN 46408, USA.

BUCKNER Sally (Beaver), b. 3 Nov 1931, Statesville, North Carolina, USA. College Teacher. m. Robert Lynn Buckner, 21 Aug 1954, 2 sons, 1 daughter. Education, AB, English, 1953; MA, English, 1970; PhD, English Education, 1980. Appointments: Public School Teacher, Gastonia, North Carolina, 1954-55; Kindergarten Teacher, Goldsboro, 1962-65; Journalist, Raleigh Times, 1966-68; Teaching Assistant, North Carolina State University, 1968-70; English Faculty, Peace College, 1970-; Co-Director, Capital Area Writing Project, 1983-. Publication: Strawberry Harvest, 1986. Contributions to: Christian Century; Woman's Day; Southern Poetry Review; Pembroke Review; Crab Creek Review; Embers; Sunrust; Uwharrie Review; Crucible. Honours: Crucible 1st Award, 1976; San Ragan Prize, 1986, 1989; Nostalgia 2nd Prize, 1989; Chester Jones Special Merit, 1989. Memberships: Chair, North Carolina Writers Conference; Conference Director, North Carolina Poetry Society; Planning Committee, North Carolina Women Writers Conference. Address: 3231 Birnamwood Road, Raleigh, NC 27607, USA.

BUDBILL David, b. 13 June 1940, Cleveland, Ohio, USA. Writer; Poet. Education: BA Honours, Philosophy, minor Art History, Muskingum College, New Concord, Ohio, 1962; Philosophy, Columbia University, 1961; MDiv, Theology, Literature, Union Theological Seminary, New York, 1967. Appointments: Poet-in-Residence: Niagara Erie Writers, Buffalo, New York, 1984; Jamestown Community College, Jamestown, New York, 1986, 1987. Publications: Barking Dog, 1968; The Chain Saw Dance, 1977; Pulp Cutters' Nativity, 1981; From Down to the Village, 1981; Why I Came to Judevine, 1987; Judevine: The Complete Poems, 1991; Editor, Danvis Tales, Selected Stories by Rowland Robinson, 1995; Plays include Little Acts of Kindness, 1995. Contributions to: Best American Poetry, 1989; An Ear to the Ground: An Anthology of Contemporary American Poetry, 1989; Working Classics: Poems on Industrial Life, 1990; The Rag and Bone Shop of the Heart, 1992; New American Plays, 1992; Best Men's Stage Monologues, 1992; Broadsides: Litany for Today, 1981; Poem Called Pome, 1982; Periodicals: Harper's; Slow Dancer; Sun; Beloit Poetry Journal; Quest 79; Review; Country Journal; Quest 79; Poetry Now; Vermont Life; New Farm; Longhouse; Organic Gardening; Greensboro Review; Ohio Review; North by Northeast; Seeds of Change; Great Circumpolar Bear Cult; West Branch; Green Mountains Review. Honours: Williamstown Repertory Theatre Playwright's Fellowship, 1965; Publication Grant, American Studies Institute, 1967; Poetry Fellowship, Vermont Council on the Arts, 1973, 1977, 1979; Kirkus Reviews Best Books, for Christmas Tree Farm, 1974; Snowshoe Trek to Otter River, 1976; Nominee, Dorothy Canfield Fisher Best Young Adult Fiction Award, 1976, 1980; Guggenheim Award in Poetry, 1982-83; Playwriting Fellowship, National Endowment for the Arts, 1991; San Francisco Bay Area Critics' Circle Award, 1991. Memberships: PEN; Dramatists' Guild. Literary Agent: Susan Schulman, 454 West 44th St, New York, NY 10036, USA. Address: RR 1, Box 2080, Wolcott, VT 05680, USA.

BUDDANNA. See: **HINGAMIRE Buddappa.**

BUDDEE Paul (Edgar), b. 12 Mar 1913, Western Australia. Retired School Principal; Author; Poet. m. Elizabeth Vere Bremner, 1944, 1 son, 1 daughter. Education: Claremont Teachers College. Appointment: School principal, 1935-72. Publications: 30 children's and adult works published in Australia, UK, Europe, 1944-84, including: Stand to and Other War Poems, 1943; The Oscar and Olga Trilogy, 1943-47; The Unwilling Adventurers, 1967; The Mystery of Moma Island, 1969; The Air Patrol Series, 1972; The Ann Rankin Series, 1972; The Escape of the Fenians, 1972; The Peter Devlin Series, 1972; The Escape of John O'Reilly, 1973; The Call of the Sky, 1978; The Fate of the Artful Dodger, 1984; Poems of the Second World War, 1986. Contributions to: Many periodicals. Honours: Australia Citizen of the Year, 1979; Australia Commonwealth Literary Board Grants, 1977, 1978, 1984; OAM, 1989. Memberships: Australian Society of Authors; Fellowship of Writers; PEN International. Address: 2 Butson Road, Leeming, WA 6149, Australia.

BUI Khoi Tien, (Huy-Luc), b. 23 Dec 1937, Binh-dinh, Vietnam. College Counsellor; Poet Laureate. m. Yen Kim Nguyen, 7 Dec 1962, 3 children. Education: BS, Law; MS, Business Management; National Planner Training, Taiwan, 1963, Philippines, 1965, Japan, 1970, Thailand, 1971. Appointments include: Counsellor at Houston Community College, 1976-; Chairman, Indochinese Culture and

Refugee Information Centre, Houston Community College, 1981-; Founder, Moderator, radio programme The Voice of Free Vietnam, 1980-; Oriental Culture Adviser, Rice University and University of Houston, 1980-; Oriental Culture Lecturer, University of Texas, University of Houston, 1982-. Publications: 7 poetry books. Contributions to: Vietnamese and English magazines. Honours: Many medals and decorations, Govenment of the Republic of Vietnam, 1965-75; National Literature Prize, 1966; Houston's Poet Laureate Award, 1984; Golden Poet Award, 1985; Ambassador to Vietnamese and American Culture Award, 1986; Education Award, 1986. Memberships: Executive Member, PEN Vietnamese Centre, 1960-75; PEN American Centre, 1982-; Galaxy Verse; American Poetry Society. Address: PO Box 720236, Houston, TX 77272, USA.

BULBURIAN Y Stephan, b. 11 Mar 1950, Fresno, California, USA. Farmer; Poet. m. Christine B Barile, 19 July 1980, 2 sons. Education: Fresno City College; California State University; Fresno College; Fresno Pacific College. Appointments: Grape Farmer, San Joaquin Valley, California. Publications: Vintage, anthology, Poets of the Vineyard, 1995; Ararat, quarterly literary journal, 1955; The Armenian Weekly, 1995. Contributions to: Armenian Weekly; Asbarez; Hye Sharzhoom; Norttayastan. Honour: Art Award Winner in Poetry, Armenian General Benevolent Union, 1990. Memberships: New England Poetry Club; Poets of the Vineyard; The Fresno Poets Association. Address: 113 Carter Way, Fowler, CA 93625, USA.

BULLEY Anne. See: **MAIER Anne Winifred.**

BULLOCK Kenneth Jr, b. 17 Aug 1950, New Orleans, Louisiana, USA. Writer. 2 daughters. Education: Associate of Arts, Jones County Junior College. Appointments: Served in US Marine Rifle Company (7th Marines), Vietnam, 1970. Contributions to: Fuel; Alternative Press; Night Roses; Prutea Poetry; Context South; Mobius; The Journal Poetry Forum; Poetry Motel; Riverrun; Lost Creek Letters; Nexus; Dream International Quarterly; Press of the Third Mind; Plowman Press (Chapbook); Wayne Literary Review; Poet Magazine; Pokeday Sticks; Minature; Sanscrity; Oyez Review; White Wall; Muddy River Poetry Review; Aileron. Honours: Honorable Mention in Poetry Forum Book Competition; Chosen to be published in White Wall 20th Edition (Competition). Memberships: The Academy of American Poets. Address: 1113 Parker Drive, Laurel, MS 39440, USA.

BULLOCK Michael, b. 19 Apr 1918, London, England. Professor Emeritus; Poet; Dramatist; Writer; Translator. Education: Homsey College of Art. Appointments: Commonwealth Fellow 1968, Professor of Creative Writing 1969-83, Professor Emeritus 1983-, University of British Columbia, Vancouver, Canada; McGuffey Visiting Professor of English, Ohio University, Athens, Ohio, 1969; New Asia Ming Yu Visiting Scholar, 1989, Writer-in-Residence, 1996, New Asia College, Chinese University of Hong Kong; Adviser, New Poetry Society of China, 1995-. Publications: Poetry: Transmutations, 1938; Sunday is a Day of Incest, 1961; World Without Beginning Amen, 1963, 2nd edition, 1973; Two Voices of My Mouth/Zwei Stimmen in meinem mund, bilingual edition, 1967; A Savage Darkness, 1969; Black Wings White Dead, 1978; Lines in the Dark Wood, 1981; Quadriga for Judy, 1982; Prisoner of the Rain, poems in prose, 1983; Brambled Heart, 1985; Dark Water, 1987; Poems on Green Paper, 1988; The Secret Garden, 1990; Avatars of the Moon, 1990; Labyrinths, 1992; The Walled Garden, 1992; The Sorcerer with Deadly Nightshade Eyes, 1993; The Inflowing River, 1993; Moons and Mirrors, 1994; Dark Roses, 1994; Stone and Shadow, 1996; Fiction: Sixteen Stories as They Happened, 1969; Green Beginning Black Ending, 1971; Randolph Cranstone and the Persuing River, 1975; Randolph Cranstone and the Glass Thimble, 1977; The Man with Flowers through His Hands, 1985; The Double Ego, 1985; Randolph Cranstone and the Veil of Maya, 1986; The Story of Noire, 1987; Randolph Cranstone Takes the Inward Path, 1988; The Burning Chapel, 1991; The Invulnerable Ovoid Aura, Stories and Poems, 1995; Voices of the River, 1995; Other: Selected Works, edited by Peter Loeffler and Jack Stewart, 1996. Contributions to: Many anthologies. Honours: Schlegel-Tieck German Translation Prize, 1966; British New Fiction Society Book of the Month, 1977; Canada Council French Translation Award, 1979; San Francisco Review of Books Best Book List, 1982; San Jose Mercury News Best Book, 1984; Okanagan Short Fiction Award, 1986. Address: 103-3626 West 28th Avenue, Vancouver, British Columbia V6S 1S4, Canada.

BULMAN Aaron E, (Aharon Eliyahu), b. 12 Jan 1948, Lawrence, Massachusetts, USA. Corporate Manager. m. Rachelle L

Schwartzman, 29 Aug 1971, 2 sons, 2 daughters. Education: BA, Yeshiva University, 1969; BA, City College of the City University of New York, 1970; Rabbi Isaac Elchonow Theological Seminary, 1969-71. Appointments: Teacher, 5-8 Grade, Yeshiva Torch Vamonah, Bronx, 1969-70; Teacher, Assistant Principal, Cosp City J Centre, Bronx, 1970-74; Manager of Planning Area, Equitable Insurance Company, New York, 1974-. Contributions to Ten Jewish American Poets; Christian Science Monitor; Voices International; Home Planet News; Images; Jewish Currents; Paris Review; Partisan Review; Small Pond. Membership: Poets and Writers. Address: 15 Magaw Place, Apt 1-B, New York, NY 10033, USA.

BULMER April Helen, b. 4 May 1963, Toronto, Ontario, Canada. Writer. Education: BA, York University, 1986; MA, Concordia University, 1990. Appointments: Administrative Assistant, TV Ontario, Toronto, 1985-88; Researcher/Reporter, Maclean's Magazine, Toronto, 1990-92. Publication: A Salve for Every Sore, 1991. Contributions to: The Malahat Review; Event; Contemporary Verse 2; Zymergy; Orbis; Globe and Mail; Cross-Canada Writers Magazine. Membership: League of Canadian Poets.

BUNCH Richard Alan, b. 1 June 1945, Honolulu, Hawaii, USA. Educator; Writer. m. Rita Anne Glazar, 11 Aug 1990, 1 son, 1 daughter. Education: AA, Napa Valley College, 1965; BA, Stanford University, 1967; MA, University of Arizona, 1969; MDiv, Vanderbilt University, 1970; DD, Vanderbilt University, 1971; Graduate studies in Philosophy, Vanderbilt University, 1972-75; Graduate Studies in Asian Religions, Temple University, 1975-76; JD, University of Memphis, 1980; Teaching Credential, Sonoma State University, 1988. Appointments: Attorney, Horne and Peppel, PC, Memphis, Tennessee, 1981-83; Associate News Editor, Napa Valley Times, 1985-86; Adjunct Humanities Faculty, Napa Valley College, 1985-. Publications: Summer Hawk, 1991; Wading the Russian River, 1993; Santa Rosa Plums, 1996; A Foggy Morning, 1996. Contributions to: Slant; Sonoma Mandala; Mandrake Poetry Magazine; Hawaii Review; Poetry Nottingham; Brownstone Review; Takahe; Nebo; The Plaza; West Wind Review; Sivullinen; Xavier Review; Prairie Winds. Honours: Pushcart Prize Nomination, 1988; Grand Prize, Ina Coolbrith National Poetry Day Contest, 1989; Jessamyn West Prize, 1990. Memberships: Academy of American Poets; Russian River Writers' Guild; Ina Coolbrith Poetry Circle. Address: 248 Sandpiper Drive, Davis, CA 95616, USA.

BUNTON Hope, b. 11 Jan 1921, Willingham, Cambridgeshire, England. Teacher. m. John Bunton, 15 July 1961, div. Education: University of London, 1939-42; International Language School, London, 1971. Appointments: Our Lady's Convent, Brigg; Edmund Campion Comprehensive School; 6th Form College, Preston. Publication: Until All Is Silence. Contributions to: Envoi; Writer's Voice; Lancashire Life; Cambridgeshire Life; Lincolnshire Writers; Liverpool Echo; Viewpoint; Breakthru; Bedsitter; Lantern Light; Journal of Indian Writing in English; Anthology of Peace Poems for Lancashire Literature Festival; Haiku magazine; Radio Merseyside; Radio Lancashire; Poetry Now; New Hope International; Parnassus of World Poets; Darius Anthology; Inclusion in: Railway Anthology, Marigolds Now Grow on Railway Platforms, 1996. Honours: 2nd Prize, Religious Section, Chorley Arts Poetry Competition; 3rd Prize, Topical Section. Membership: Preston Writers Circle. Address: 10 Clifton Street, Preston, Lancashire PR1 8EE, England.

BURACK Alexandra, b. 13 Jan 1960, Boston, Massachusetts, USA. Poet; Editor. Education: BA, cum laude, Sociology, Manhattanville College, Purchase, New York, 1982. Appointments: Founding Member, Brick Walk Poets Collective, West Hartford, 1995-; Founder, Executive Director, The Boris Burack Memorial Poetry Reading Series, Middletown, 1996-. Contributions to: The Bound Spiral, 1995; Araby, 1997; Invert, 1991; The Boston Collection of Women's Poetry, Vol I, 1984. Honours: Commendation, 1994 UK Poets-of-the-Year Competition; Honorable Mention, Connecticut Poetry Society, 1987; Co-Winner, Brush Hill Press Poetry Competition, 1984. Memberships: Poetry Society of America, 1995; Associate Member, Academy of American Poets, 1996; Connecticut Poetry Society, 1987-88. Address: 62 Arkay Drive, Higganum, CT 06441, USA.

BURCH Claire, b. 19 Feb 1925, New York, New York, USA. Writer; Poet; Filmmaker. m. Bradley Burch, 14 Apr 1944, dec, 1 son, dec, 2 daughters. Education: BA, Washington Square College, 1947. Publications: Poetry: Winter Bargains; Notes of a Survivor; Shredded

Millions; Homeless In The Eighties, 1989; Homeless In The Nineties, 1994; Novels: Goodbye My Coney Island Baby; You Be The Mother Follies, 1994; Non-Fiction: The Small Book of Laurie; Stranger In The Family, 1972; Solid Gold Illusion, 1991. Contributions to: Various periodicals. Honours: Carnegie Awards, 1978, 1979; City of Berkeley, 1989-93; California Arts Council Grants, 1991, 1992, 1993, 1994; Seva Foundation, 1996 Memberships: Poetry Society of America; Writers' Guild. Address: c/o Regent Press, 6020A Adeline, Oakland, CA 94608, USA.

BURDICK Carol, b. 8 Aug 1928, Salem, West Virginia, USA. Educator; Writer. m. Robert Hudson, 19 June 1949, div 1970, 2 sons, 1 daughter. Education: BA, Milton College, 1949; MS, State University of New York at Geneseo, 1963. Appointments: Teaching, Alfred University, 1974; Co-Director, Ossabaw Island Project, 1979-82. Publications: Destination Unknown, 1968; Stop Calling Me Mr Darling, 1989; Woman Alone: A Farmhouse Journal, 1990. Contributions to: Maine Times; Maine Edition; Alfred Review; Poet Lore; Down East; Maine Sunday Paper; English Journal; Lyrics for songs by Klaus Roy, Tom Benjamin. Honours: 1st Prize, Alfred Review, 1989; Distinguished Teaching Award, 1996. Memberships: Poetry Society of America; MacDowell Colony Fellow. Address: Pondhouse, Alfred Station, NY 14803, USA.

BURFORD Edward (Ted), b. 11 Feb 1926, Leeds, Yorkshire, England. Writer; Poet. Appointments: Radio Technician; Electrician; Air Traffic Engineer; Joint Editor, Limestone Publications, 1973-82. Publications: Cranefly Incident, 1975; Imaginary Absences, 1983; Sycamore Broadsheet No 30, 1985; Quintet, 1993. Contributions to: London Magazine; Ambit; Rialto; New Poetry Anthologies, Arts Council, Vols 1, 2, 3, 6, 8; BBC 3, Radio London; Of Eros and Dust, poetry anthology, 1992; Observer; Spectator. Honours: 1st Prize, Camden Poetry, 1969; Yorkshire Arts Award, 1985; Prizewinner, National Poetry Competition, 1988; 1st Prize, Bridport Short Story Competition, 1989. Membership: Poetry Society, 1969-. Address: 15 Woodfield Road, Ealing, London W5 1SL, England.

BURKE Colleen Zeita, b. 3 Feb 1943, Sydney, Australia. Poet; Author. m. Declan Affley, 11 Dec 1967, dec, 1985, 1 son, 1 daughter. Education: BA, Sydney University, 1974. Appointments: Shorthand Typist, GIO, 1959-67; Research Assistant and Community Worker, Royal Prince Alfred Hospital, 1974-87; Tutor, Adult & Community Education, 1985-. Publications: Go Down Singing, 1974; Hags Rags & Scriptures, 1977; The Incurable Romantic, 1979; She Moves Mountains, 1984; Doherty's Corner - Biography of Australian Poet Marie E J Pitt, 1985; the edge of it, 1992; Wildlife in Newtown, 1994. Contributions to: Westerly; Sydney Morning Herald; Hecate; Overland; Blast; Southerly; Poetry Australia; Hobo; New South Wales School Magazine; The Salmon (Ireland). Honours: Shortlisted, New South Wales State Literary Awards, 1993; Three Literature Board of the Australian Council Grants. Memberships: Poets Union; Australian Society of Authors; New South Wales Writers Centre. Address: 126 Lennox Street, Newtown, NSW 2042, Australia.

BURNETT Alfred David, b. 15 Aug 1937, Edinburgh, Scotland. University Librarian. Education: MA (Hons), English Language and Literature, University of Edinburgh, 1959; ALA, University of Strathclyde, 1964. Appointments: Library Assistant, Glasgow University Library, 1959-64; Assistant Librarian, Durham University Library, England, 1964-90. Publications: Mandala, 1967; Diversities, 1968; A Ballad Upon a Wedding, 1969; Columbaria, 1971; Shimabara, 1972; Fescennines, 1974; Thirty Snow Poems, 1973; Hero and Leander, 1975; The True Vine, 1975; He and She, 1976; The Heart's Undesign, 1977; Figures and Spaces, 1978; Jackdaw, 1980; Thais, 1981; Romans, 1983; Vines, 1984; Autolycus, 1987; Kantharos, 1989; Lesbos, 1990; Mirror and Pool, translations from Chinese (with John Cayley), 1992; Nine Poets, 1993; The Island, 1994, 2nd edition, 1996; Twelve Poems, 1994; Something of Myself, 1994; Six Poems, 1995; Transfusions, 1995; Editor, anthologies. Contributions to: Poetry Durham; Numerous professional and critical periodical contributions and monographs. Honours: Essay Prize, 1956, Patterson Bursary in Anglo-Saxon, 1958, University of Edinburgh; Kelso Memorial Prize, University of Strathclyde, 1964; Essay Prize, Library Association, 1966; Sevensma Prize, International Federation of Library Associations, 1971; Hawthornden Fellowship, 1988, 1992; Panizzi Medal, British Library, 1991; Fellow, British Centre for Literary Translation, Norwich, 1994. Memberships: Poetry Book Society; Bibliographical Society; Private Libraries Association. Address: 33 Hastings Avenue, Merry Oaks, Durham DH1 3QG, England.

BURNS Jim, b. 19 Feb 1936, Preston, Lancashire, England. Tutor; Local Government Employee. 2 sons. Education: BA, Bolton Institute of Technology, 1980. Appointments: Editor, Move, 1964-68; Editor, Palantir, 1976-83; Jazz Editor, Beat Scene, 1990-. Publications: The Store of Things; A Single Flower; Leben in Preston; The Goldfish Speaks From Beyond the Grave; Fred Engeles Bei Woolworth; Notes from a Greasy Spoon; Internal Memorandum; Out of the Past; Confessions of an Old Believer, 1996. Contributions to: Guardian; Tribune; New Statesman; New Society; London Magazine; Ambit; Poetry Review; Critical Survey; Beat Scene; Kerouac Connection; Prose. Address: 11 Gatley Green, Gatley, Cheadle, Cheshire SK8 4NF, England.

BURNSHAW Stanley, b. 20 June 1906, New York, New York, USA. Publisher; Poet; Writer. m. Lydia Powsner, 2 Sept 1942, dec, 1 daughter. Education: BA, University of Pittsburgh, 1925; University of Poitiers, France, 1927; University of Paris, 1927; MA, Cornell University, 1933. Appointments: President and Editor-in-Chief, Dryden Press, 1937-58; Program Director, Graduate Institute of Book Publishing, New York University, 1958-62; Vice-President, Holt, Rinehart and Winston, publishers, 1958-66; Regents Visiting Lecturer, University of California, 1980; Visiting Distinguished Professor, Miami University, 1989. Publications: Poems, 1927; The Great Dark Love, 1932; Andre Spire and His Poetry, 1933; The Iron Land, 1936; The Bridge, 1945; The Revolt of the Cats in Paradise, 1945; Early and Late Testament, 1952; Caged in an Animal's Mind, 1963; The Hero of Silence, 1965; In the Terrified Radiance, 1972; Mirages: Travel Notes in the Promised Land, 1977; Robert Frost Himself, 1986; A Stanley Burnshaw Reader, 1990; The Seamless Web, 1991. Contributions to: Many periodicals. Honours: National Institute of Arts and Letters Award, 1971; Honorary Doctorate of Humane Letters, Hebrew Union College, 1983; Honorary Doctorate of Letters, City University of New York, 1996. Address: 250 West 89th Street, No PH2G, New York, NY 10024, USA.

BURNSIDE John, b. 19 Mar 1955, Fife, Scotland. Knowledge Engineer. Publications: The Hoop, 1988; Common Knowledge, 1991; Feast Days, 1992; The Myth of the Twin, 1994; Swimming in the Flood, 1995. Contributions to: Sunday Times; Observer; Encounter; Poetry Review; PN Review; Poetry Durham; Poetry Wales; Verse; Times Literary Supplement; New Yorker. Honours: Scottish Arts Council Book Award, 1988, 1991; Geoffrey Faber Memorial Prize, 1994. Address: c/o Jonathan Cape, 20 Vauxhall Bridge Road, London SW1V 2SA, England.

BURROWAY Janet (Gay), b. 21 Sept 1936, Tucson, Arizona, USA. Professor; Writer; Poet. m. (1) Walter Eysselinck, 1961, div 1973, 2 sons, (2) William Dean Humphries, 1978, div 1981, (3) Peter Ruppert, 1993, 1 stepdaughter. Education: University of Arizona, 1954-55; AB, Barnard College, 1958; BA 1960, MA 1965, Cambridge University, England; Yale School of Drama, 1960-61. Appointments: Instructor, Harpur College, Binghampton, New York, 1961-62; Lecturer, University of Sussex, 1965-70; Associate Professor 1972-77, Professor 1977-, MacKenzie Professor of English, 1989-95, Robert O Lawson Distinguished Professor, 1995-, Florida State University; Fiction Reviewer, Philadelphia Enquirer, 1986-90; Reviewer, New York Times Book Review, 1991-; Essay-Columnist, New Letters: A Magazine of Writing and Art, 1994-. Publications: Fiction: Descend Again, 1960; The Dancer from the Dance, 1965; Eyes, 1966; The Buzzards, 1969; The Truck on the Track, children's book, 1970; The Giant Jam Sandwich, children's book, 1972; Raw Silk, 1977; Opening Nights, 1985; Cutting Stone, 1992; Poetry: But to the Season, 1961; Material Goods, 1980; Other: Writing Fiction: A Guide to Narrative Craft, 1982, 4th edition, 1995. Contributions to: Numerous journals and periodicals. Honours: National Endowment for the Arts Fellowship, 1976; Yaddo Residency Fellowships, 1985, 1987; Lila Wallace-Reader's Digest Fellow, 1993-94; Carolyn Benton Cockefaire Distinguished Writer-in-Residence, University of Missouri, 1995; Woodrow Wilson Visiting Fellow, Furman University, Greenville, South Carolina, 1995. Memberships: Associated Writing Programs, Vice President, 1988-89; Authors Guild. Address: 240 De Soto Street, Tallahassee, FL 32303, USA.

BURROWS Edwin Gladding, b. 23 July 1917, Dallas, Texas, USA. m. Beth Elpern, 7 Dec 1972, 3 sons. Education: BA, Yale University, 1938; MA, University of Michigan, 1940. Appointments: Manager of University Michigan Radio Stations, 1945-70; Director, Centre for Audio Research, University of Wisconsin, 1970-73; Retired. Publications: The Arctic Tern; Man Fishing; The Crossings; Kiva; On

the Road to Baileys; Properties; The House of August; Handsigns for Rain. Contributions to: American Poetry Review; Atlantic Monthly; Ascent; Gettysburg Review; Hawaii Review; Massachusetts Review; Michigan Quarterly Review; Paris Review; Poetry; Poetry Northwest; Seattle Review; Virginia Quarterly Review; Wilderness Magazine. Honours: John Masefield Award; Major Hopwood Award; Ohio State Award; 1st Poetry Prize Ascent; Nominated for National Book Award. Address: 20319 92nd Avenue West, Edmonds, WA 98020, USA.

BURROWS Michael James, b. 4 Mar 1962, Cheltenham, Gloucester, England. Poet. Education: Diploma in Higher Education in English and Theology, Leeds University, 1990. Apppointments: 'A' Level English Tutor, 1985; Editor, University College Literary Magazine, 1986-88; Editor, Hospital Literary Magazine, 1991-92; Creative Writing Tutor, 1992-93; Editor and (occasional) Creative Writing Tutor, Poetry Magazine, 1993-. Publications: Flexham's Shadow, 1996. Contributions to: Smoke; Poetry and Audience; T O P S; First Time; A Hairshirt of Words; Snapshot Poems; Under the Asylum Tree; The Ripon Gazette; Big Plug; Still Waters; Cliff Hanger; Merseyside Poets CD. Address: Flat 2, 52A County Road, Walton, Liverpool L4 3QL, England.

BURTON Gabrielle, b. 21 Feb 1939, Lansing, Michigan, USA. Writer; Poet. m. Roger V Burton, 18 Aug 1962, 5 daughters. Education: BA, Marygrove College, Michigan, 1960. Appointments: Teacher, Fiction in the Schools, Writers in Education Project, New York, 1985; Fellow, American Film Institute, Los Angeles, 1995-97; Various poetry readings and workshops. Publications: I'm Running Away From Home But I'm Not Allowed to Cross the Street (non-fiction), 1972; Heartbreak Hotel (novel), 1986. Contributions to: Articles, essays, poems, and reviews in numerous publications. Honours: MacDowell Colony Fellow, 1982, 1987, 1989; Yaddo Fellow, 1983; Maxwell Perkins Prize, 1986; Great Lakes Colleges Association Award, 1987; Bernard De Voto Fellow in Non-Fiction, Breadloaf Writer's Conference, 1994; Mary Pickford Foundation Award for 1st Year Screenwriter, 1996. Address: 4600 Los Felix Boulevard, No 106, Los Angeles, CA 90027, USA.

BURTON Michael Hedley, b. 20 July 1955, New Zealand. Speech Artist; Teacher; Reciter. Education: BA, Waikato University, 1977; Diploma in Drama, Auckland University, 1977; Diploma in Speech, Goetheanum, Basel, Switzerland, 1987. Appointments: Teacher, Christchurch, New Zealand, 1983-86; Speech Teacher, Remedial, Napier, 1988-90; Speech Teacher, Botton School of Eurythmy, 1990-91; Actor and Speech Teacher, English Eurythmy Theatre, 1991-93; Actor and Translator, Portal Productions, 1993-95. Publications: In the Light of a Child; 1989; In Celebration of Being Human, 1990; Songs of a Washing Machine and Other Loony Poems, 1992; The Very Old Donkey, 1995. Contributions to: New Zealand School Journal. Address: 2 Lower Street, Ruscombe, Stroud, Gloucestershire GL6 6BU, England.

BUSACCA Helle Fathma, b. 21 Dec 1915, San Piero-Patti, Sicily, Italy. Teacher; Poet; Writer; Painter. Education: PhD, Classic Letters, Universita Statale di Milano, 1938; Abilitatione (State competition) all Insegnamento, 1939. Appointments: Teacher of Italian, Latin, Greek, Arts History at Varese and Pavia, 1940-45, Milan, 1945-54, 1960-71, Napoles, 1954-55, Siena, 1955-60 and Florence, 1971-. Publications: Books of poetry: Memory Game, 1949, Rhythms, 1965, The Quanta of Suicide, 1972, The Quanta of Karma, 1976, Nothing Poetry From Babele, 1980, The Book of Whirl, 1990, The Book of Chinese Shadows, 1991, Love's Labour's Lost, 1994; Summer Wind, novel, 1987; Tales Of A Lost World, short stories, 1991. Contributions to: La Fiera Letteraria; Hellas, Florence; Letteratura, Florence; Le Proporzioni Poetiche, Milan; Civiltà Delle Macchine, Rome; L'Albero, Lecce; Poetry, Madras; Salvo Imprevisti, Florence; Lunario Nuovo, Catania; Nord Europa, Luxembourg; International Poets, Madras; Rising Stars, Bangalore; Parnassus of World Poets, Madras. Honours: Premio Prizes: Pesaro, 1950, Pisa and Palermo, 1967, Gabicce Mare, 1973, Senigallia, 1979, Bologna, 1980, Albericao Sala, 1993, Tirinnanzi, Legnano, 1988, Marsa Siklah, Sicily, 1989, Ack-Pegon, 1990, Libero de Libero, Fondi, Latina, 1990, L'Incontro, 1991; 2nd Premio, Citta di Pompei per la Poesia, 1986; Premio Brianza e Betocchi, 1990, Bologna, 1990; Premio Lodi, Citta di Ada Negri, 1990; Premio, Cisternino per la Poesia, 1991; Premio Sabaushia, 1995. Memberships: Poetry, Madras; Tommaso Campanella (Literature); Honorary Member, Academy in Rome; ASLA; ASA. Address: Via delle Panche 103, 50141 Florence, Italy.

BUSBY SMITH C. See: **SMITH John Charles**.

BUSH Duncan, b. 6 Apr 1946, Cardiff, Wales. Poet; Writer; Teacher. m. Annette Jane Weaver, 4 June 1981, 2 sons. Education: BA, 1st Class Honours, in English and European Literature, Warwick University, 1978; Exchange Scholarship, Duke University, USA, 1976-77; DPhil, Research in English Literature, Wadham College, Oxford, 1978-81. European Editor, The Kansas Quarterly & Arkansas review; Writing Tutor with various institutions. Publications: Aquarium, 1983; Salt, 1985; Black Faces, Red Mouth, 1986; The Genre of Silence, 1987; Glass Shot, 1991; Masks, 1994; Editor: On Censorship, 1985. Contributions to: BBC and Periodicals. Honours: Eric Gregory Award for Poetry, 1978; Barbara Campion Memorial Award for Poetry, 1982; Welsh Arts Council Prizes for Poetry, Arts Council of Wales, Book of the Year, 1995, for Masks. Memberships: Welsh Academy; Welsh Union of Writers, Vice Chairman, 1982-86. Address: Godre Waun Oleu, Brecon Road, Ynyswen, Penycae, Powys SA9 1YY, Wales.

BUSHE Paddy, b. 18 Aug 1948, Dublin, Ireland. Writer. m. Fiona Ni Chinnsealaigh, 26 Dec 1970, 1 son, 1 daughter. Education: BA, University College Dublin, 1969. Appointments: Teacher: Dublin, 1970-71, Australia, 1971-73, County Kerry, 1973-91; Writer, 1991-. Publications: Poems with Amergin, 1989; Teanga, 1990; Counsellor, 1991. Contributions to: Cyphers; Poetry Ireland Review; Great Book of Ireland; Arvon International Anthology; Irish University Review; Labour Party Congress Journal; Steeple Salmon; others. Honours: Specially Commended, Arvon Competition, 1987; Runner-up, Patrick Kavanagh Award, 1988; Poetry Prize, Listowel Writers' Week, 1990. Memberships: Poetry Ireland; Irish Writers' Union; The Poetry Society, London. Address: Cliff Road, Waterville, County Kerry, Ireland.

BUTCHER Barbara, b. 21 Dec 1937, Stanmore, Middlesex, England. Hypnotherapist. 1 son, 1 daughter. Education: Pitmans College; National College Food Tech; Buckinghamshire School of Music; Thames Valley University. Appointments: Milk Analyst; Microbiologist; Secretary Personal Assistant; Music Teacher; Hypnotherapist; Psychotherapist; Reflexologist. Publication: Talking Trees. Contributions to: Weyfarers; Rio; Cheshire Poetry Magazine; Buckinghamshire Examiner; Buckighamshire Free Press; Autistic States in Adults; Maidenhead Advertiser. Honours: Chesham Poetry Competition; Wycombe Arts; Nottingham Lace; Ripley Poetry Competition; Age Concern; Manchester Poetry. Memberships: Chesham Poetry Society; Poetry, Arvon Foundation; Orbis. Address: 35 Lowfield Way, Hazelmere, Bucks HP15 7RR, England.

BUTLER Allen Todd, (Cool Al), b. 6 May 1961, Portsmouth, Virginia, USA. Advertising Representative. Education: BS, Mass Communication, Norfolk State University, 1985. Appointment: Vice President, Creative Writers Club. Contributions to: World Book of Poetry; Sagacity Magazine; National Library of Poetry; Jeff Roberts Publishing Company; Quill Books, 1987-88; Midwest Poetry Review; Oatmeal Studios Greetings Cards; American Poetry; Caldora Music Publishing; Creative Record; Essence Magazine; Poetry Centre. Honours: Distinguished Achievements Awards, 1983-84; Honourable Mention Award, 1989; Golden Poet Awards, 1989-91; Who's Who in Poetry for Outstanding Achievement in Poetry, 1990. Memberships: DJ Music Services, 1983-84; National Writers Club; American Songwriters Organization, 1993-94; Top Records Songwriters Association, 1995. Address: 1273 West 27th Street, Norfolk, VA 23508, USA.

BUTLER (Frederick) Guy, b. 21 Jan 1918, Cradock, Cape Province, South Africa. Retired Professor of English Literature. m. 7 Dec 1940, 2 sons, 2 daughters. Education: BA, 1938, MA, 1939, Rhodes University College; BA, 1947, MA, 1951, Brasenose College, Oxford. Appointments: Schoolmaster, St John's College, Johannesburg, 1940; War Service, Middle East, Italy and UK, 1940-45; Lecturer, University of Witwatersrand, Johannesburg, 1948-50; Senior Lecturer, 1951, Professor of English 1952-86, Rhodes University, Grahamstown. Publications: Stranger to Europe 1939-49, 1952, with additional poems, 1960; South of the Zambesi: Poems from South Africa, London and New York, 1966; On First Seeing Florence, 1968; Selected Poems, 1975, with additional poems, 1989; Songs and Ballads, 1978; Pilgrimage to Dias Cross, 1987; Out of the African Ark, Animal Poems (editor with David Butler), 1988; The Magic Tree: South African Stories in Verse (editor with Jeff Opland), 1989; Guy Butler: Essays and Lectures (edited by Stephen Watson), 1994; Editor: A Book of South African Verse, 1959; When Boys Were Men, 1969; The 1820 Settlers, 1974. Contributions to: Vandag; The Malahat Review; Standpunte; UNISA English Studies; Cape Argus; Ishmael; Contrast; Sesame; New Coin; PN Review; New South African Writing; New World Writing. Honours include: South African Broadcasting Corporation, 1st and 2nd Prizes for Poetry, 1949, 1953; DLitt hc, University of Natal, 1970; Central News Agency Award, 1976; Literary Award, Cape Tercentenary Foundation, 1981; DLitt hc, University of Witwatersrand, 1984; DLitt et Phil hc, University of South Africa, 1989; Lady Usher Prize for Literature, 1992; DLitt hc, Rhodes University, 1994; Freedom of the City of Grahamstown, 1994. Memberships: Honorary Life Member, English Academy of South Africa; Shakespeare Society of South Africa, National President 1985. Hobbies: Nature conservation; Restoring old buildings. Address: High Corner, 122 High St, Grahamstown, Cape Province 0461, South Africa.

BUTLER Michael David, b. 18 Sept 1931, London, England. Poet. m. Veronica Helen Freudenberg, 15 May 1971, 1 son, 2 daughters. Education: MA, English Literature, Jesus College, Oxford, 1953. Appointments: Member of Order of Friars Minor Capuchin, 1955-69; Ordained Priest, 1963; Worker Priest, Layman, 1966-73; Part-time Teacher of English Literature, The City Lit, London, 1973-76; Part-time Teacher of English as a Foreign Language, then Adult Literacy, Holloway AEI, 1974-79. Publication: Street and Sky, 1980. Contributions to: Orbis; Iron; Stride; Voices; South; Doors. Membership: Poetry Society. Address: 29 Cattistock Road, Maiden Newton, Dorchester, Dorset DT2 0AG, England.

BUTLER Michael Gregory, b. 1 Nov 1935, Nottingham, England. Professor. m. Jean Mary Griffith, 31 Dec 1961, 1 son, 1 daughter. Education: BA, 1957, MA, 1960, Cambridge University; DipEd, Oxford University, 1958; FIL, 1967; PhD (CNAA), 1974. Appointments: Assistant Master, Kings School, Worcester, 1958-61; Assistant Master, Reuchlin Gymnasium, Pforzheim, Germany, 1961-62; Head of German, Ipswich School, Ipswich, England, 1962-70; Lecturer in German, 1970-80, Senior Lecturer, 1980-86, Head, Department of German Studies, 1984, Professor of Modern German Literature, 1986-, Head, School of Modern Languages, 1988-93, University of Birmingham. Publications: Nails and other Poems, 1967; Samphire (co-editor), 3 volumes, 1968-83; The Novels of Max Frisch, 1975; Englische Lyrik der Gegenwart (edited with Ilsabe Arnold Dielewicz), 1981; The Plays of Max Frisch, 1985; Frisch: 'Andorra', 1985, revised edition 1994; Rejection and Emancipation - Writing in German-speaking Switzerland 1945-1991 (edited with M Pender), 1991; The Narrative Fiction of Heinrich Böll, 1994. Contributions to: Migrant; Mica (California); Samphire; Poetry Review; BBC; Sceptre Press; Vagabond (Munich); Universities Poetry; others. Honours: Taras Schevchenko Memorial Prize, 1961. Address: 45 Westfields, Catshill, Bromsgrove B61 9HJ, England.

BUTLIN Ron, b. 17 Nov 1939, Edinburgh, Scotland. Education: MA, University of Edinburgh, 1975. Appointments: Writer-in-Residence at various Scottish institutions, including University of Edinburgh, 1982, 1985, Midlothian Region, 1989-90; Writing Fellow, Stirling University, 1993. Publications: Sretto, 1976; Creatures Tamed by Cruelty, 1979; Ragtime in Unfamiliar Bars, 1985; Opera libretti, Markheim and Dark Country, 1990, 1992. Honours: Scottish Arts Council Bursaries. Address: Gordon and Sheil Ltd, 43 Doughty Street, London WC1N 2LF, England.

BUTOR Michel (Marie François), b. 14 Sept 1926, Mons-en-Barcoeul, Nord, France. Author; Poet; Professor. m. Marie-Josephe Mas, 22 Aug 1958, 4 daughters. Education: License en philosophie, 1946; Diplome d'études superieures de philosophie, 1947, Sorbonne, University of Paris. Appointments: Associate Professor, University of Vincennes, 1969, University of Nice, 1970-73; Professor of Modern French Language and Literature, University of Geneva, 1975-91; Visiting Professorships in the US. Publications: Passage de Milan, 1954; L'Emploi du temps, 1956, English translation as Passing Time, 1960; La Modification, 1957, English translation as Change of Heart, 1959; La Génie du Lieu, 4 volumes, 1958, 1971, 1978, 1988; Degrés, 1960, English translation as Degrees, 1961; Répertoire, 5 volumes, 1960, 1964, 1968, 1974, 1982; Une histoire extraordinaire: Essai sur un reve de Baudelaire, 1961, English translation as Histoire extraordinaire: Essay on a Dream of Baudelaire's, 1969; Mobile: Etude pour un representation des Etats-Unis, 1962, English translation as Mobile: Study for a Representation of the United States, 1963; Description de San Marco, 1963, English translation as Description of San Marco, 1983; Illustrations, 4 volumes, 1964, 1969, 1973, 1976; 6,810,00 litres d'eau par seconde: Etude stereophonic, 1965, English translation as Niagara, 1969; Essai sur "Les Essais", 1968; La Rose des vents: 32 rhumbs pour Charles Fourier, 1970; Matiè de reves, 5 volumes, 1975, 1976, 1977, 1981, 1985; Improvisations sur Rimbaud, 1989; Improvisations sur Michel Butor, 1994; Numerous other volumes of fiction, poetry and essays. Honours: Chevalier de l'Ordre National du Mérite; Chevalier des Arts et des Lettres; Several literary prizes. Address: a l'Ecart, Lucinges, 74380 Bonne, France.

BUTT Theresa. See: **ADAMS Anna Theresa.**

BUTTACI Salvatore (Amico) M, b. 12 June 1941, New York, New York, USA. English Teacher; Document Examiner; Entrepreneur. Education: BA, Communication Arts, Seton Hall University, 1965; Total Certification in Psychology of Handwriting, Felician College, 1989; Graduate Handwriting Analyst (GHA), highest level handwriting analyst. Appointments: English Teacher, 1966-68, 1971-80; Vice-Principal, 1968-70; Principal, 1970-71; Marketing Executive, 1980-91; Document Examiner, 1989-; Teacher, 1992-; Former Editor, New Worlds Unlimited, showcase for new and established poets. Publications: Stops and Pauses on the Scrapbook Express, 1974; Grandpa: Memory Poems, 1976; Bread and Tears and 35 other poems, 1986. Contributions to: Christian Science Monitor; The Aquarian Weekly; The Writer; New Jersey Poetry Monthly; Impact: A Quarterly of Contemporary Poetry; Archer; Miscellany: A Davidson Review; Gravida; Anemone; Wind; Eleven; Thirteen; El Viento; Rufus; Bardic Echoes; Ocarina (India); Weid: Sensibility Review; Reach Out; Footwork; Circus Maximus; Karmic Runes; Parnassus; Tempo; Quill; Pudding; Lunch; Cyclo Flame; Gallery Series; Bachaet; Stonehinge; Modus Operandi; Metrosphere; Passaic Review; Convidado (Portuguese); Spirit: A Magazine of Poetry; Third Eye; Philadelphia Poets; Nitty Gritty; Odessa Poetry Review; Many others. Memberships: Poets and Writers Inc; New Jersey Poetry Society; American Society of Composers, Authors and Publishers; Songwriters' Guild; National Writers' Club. Address: PO Box 887, Saddle Brook, NJ 07663, USA.

BUTTRESS Derrick, b. 2 Jan 1932, England. Teacher. m. 17 May 1952, 2 daughters. Education: Fircroft College, 1973; University of York, 1974-77. Appointments: Factory Worker; Student; English Teacher. Publications: It Is You We Are Trying To Love; Connie; Hoppy. Contributions to: Ambit; Phoenix; Prospice; Slow Dancer; Bogg; Ion; Yorkshire Review; Anglo Welsh Review; Oasis; Global Tapestry; Zenos; The Stage. Address: 76 Brinkhill Crescent, Clifton, Nottingham NG11 8FF, England.

BUYS Anna (Anneke), b. 11 Nov 1945, Leiden, Netherlands. m. Klaas Schouten, 1 July 1965, 2 sons. Appointments: Post Office Clerk; Old People's Help. Publications: Growth - in millimetres, 1984; Lines of Fracture, 1985. Contributions to: Gist; Lifte; Iambe; 't Kofschip; Frase; Tower Poetry, Canada; Glory, India; Poets for Africa, USA; Rhythm-and-Rhyme, New Zealand; Chikyu, Japan; Chinese Daily; Li Poetry; Blue Stars Poetry, Taiwan; In her translation: Bulgaria Esperantisto; Esperanto en Skotlando. Honours: Poezie prijs Izegem, Belgium, 1984; Prijs van de Bibliotheek, Rotterdam, 1986. Membership: Vrienden van het schrijven, Almelo. Address: Dintel 20, 7333 Apeldoorn, Netherlands.

BYARD Olivia Elizabeth, b. 23 Apr 1946, Newport, Gwent, Wales. Writer; Creative Writing Tutor. m. Aug 1980, 2 sons. Education: BA, Honours, Queen's University, Kingston, Canada. Publication: Collection Peterloo Poets, 1997. Membership: The Poetry Society. Address: Oxford, England.

BYRD Robert (Bobby) James, b. 15 Apr 1942, Memphis, Tennessee, USA. Poet; Publisher. m. Lee Merrill Byrd, 2 Dec 1967, 2 sons, 1 daughter. Education: BA, University of Arizona, Tucson, 1965; MA, University of Washington, Seattle, 1967. Appointment: Co-Publisher, Cinco Puntos Press, 1985-. Publications: Places Is and Memphis Poems, 1971; Here, 1975; Pomegranates, 1984; Get Some Fuses for the House, 1987; On the Transmigration of Souls in El Paso, 1993. Contributions to: Blue Mesa Review; Puerto del Sol; Exquisite Corpse; Io; Cayote's Journal; Rolling Stock; Rio Grande Review; From a Window; Longhouse; Bombay Gin; New Dog II; Aethlon: A Journal of Sports Literature; Talking from the Heart; Dead Tree; Starving Artist Times; Truck; The Spirit That Wants Me. Honours: National Endowment for the Arts Fellowship, 1990; D H Lawrence Fellowship, 1990; Memberships: PEN West; Rio Grande Writers' Association, President, 1984. Address: State University of New York at Albany, 1400 Washington, English Department, Albany, NY 12222, USA.

C

CABRAL DEL HOYO Roberto, b. 7 Aug 1913, Mexico. Poet. m. Alicia Bowling, 1944, 3 sons, 2 daughters. Education: Bachillerato, Instituto de Ciencias, Zacatecas. Appointments: Various positions, cultural programmes, radio and TV stations; Editorial positions, Fondo de Cultura Economica and Reader's Digest of Mexico. Publications: De tu amor y de tu olvido y otros poemas, 1948; Por merecer la gracia, 1950; Contra el oscuro viento, 1959; Tres de sus palabras, 1962; Palabra (Antologia), 1964; Potra de nacar, 1966; De mis raices en la tierra, 1968; Rastro en la arena (Antologia), 1970; Poetic Works, 1940-80, 1980; Estas cosas que escribo, 1988; Camino caminado, 1991; Codicilos, 1992. Contributions to: Various national newspapers and magazines, including Excelsior, El Universal, El Nacional, Novedades, Universitarios. Honours: Various prizes, national literary competitions. Membership: PEN Mexico. Address: Cerrada do Calyecac 19-4, Campestre, San Angel, Mexico DF 01040, Mexico.

CABRAL KURTZ Olga Marie (Olga Cabral), b. 14 Sept 1909, Trinidad, British West Indies. Poet; Writer. m. Aaron Samuel Kurtz, dec, 27 June 1951. Education: Several art courses, New School for Social Research, New York, 1961-62. Appointments: Co-Owner, Little Art Centre, Brooklyn, New York, 1950-56; Owner and Manager, French-American Art Gallery, Long Beach, New York, 1958-66. Publications: Cities and Deserts, 1959; The Evaporated Man, 1968; Tape Found in a Bottle, 1971; Occupied Country, 1976; The Darkness in My Pockets, 1976; In the Empire of Ice, 1980; The Green Dream, 1990; Voice/Over: Selected Poems, 1993. Contributions to: 36 anthologies in the US and Europe, including: We Believe in Humanity; A Geography of Poets; We Become New; Poems by Contemporary American Women; For Neruda, For Chile; From the Belly of the Shark; Imaginative Literature; Also 40 literary journals. Honours: Emily Dickinson Award of the Poetry Society of America, 1971; Lucille Medwick Memorial Award of the Poetry Society of America, 1976. Memberships: Poetry Society of America; Authors Guild; Authors League of America. Literary Agent: Frances Goldin, Frances Goldin Literary Agency. Address: 463 West Street, Apt H-523, New York, NY 10014, USA.

CABRINETY Patricia Ann Butler, b. 4 Sept 1932, Earlville, New York, USA. Writer; Illustrator; Inventor; Teacher; Company President. m. Lawrence P Cabrinety, 20 Aug 1955, 1 son, 2 daughters. Education: BS, Education and Music; AS, Paralegal. Publications: Charis Series; Songs. Paulette Fry and Mi Cazone. Contributions to: World of Poetry; Editor's Desk; Vantage Press; All Seasons of Poetry; Poetry Centre; American Press; WPBS Poetry. Honours: Five Times Winner, Golden Poet Award; Six Time Winner, Vantage Press International Award; Poet of the Month Award; Numerous Honorable Mentions with Award of Publication; 2 Awards, Parnassus of Parnassus of World Poets, India. Memberships: American Management Association; American Professional and Executive Women; National Writers Association of University Women; National Writers Association; Florida Freelance Writers; Worcester Country Poetry Association; Worcester County Music Association; Minneapolis Music Teachers Forum; Edina Chamber of Commerce; National Female Executives; Computer History Institute for the Preservation of Software; National Notary Association; National Association of Legal Assistants. Address: 925 Pearl Hill Road, Fitchburg, MA 01420, USA.

CADAVAL Rudy De. See: **CAMPEDELLI Giancarlo.**

CADET Maurice, b. Jacmel, Haiti. Professor of Literature (retired); Poet. div, 2 sons, 3 daughters. Education: Diplomas in Letters and Modern Languages, Haiti and France; BS in Law, Haiti. Appointment: Professor of Literature, College of Alma, 1967-95. Publications: Turbulences, 1989; Chalè Piman, 1990; Haute Dissidence, 1991; Itinéraires d'un enchantement, 1992; Réjouissances, 1994; l'illusoire éternité de l'été, 1996. Contributions to: Magazines. Memberships: Association professionnelle des écrivains de la Sagamie; National Authors Union of Quebec. Address: 630 Robert Jean, Apt 2, Alma, Quebec G8B 7H1, Canada.

CAHIT Neriman, b. 21 May 1937, Kirni, Cyprus. Journalist. m. Ahmet Gursel, 6 Sept 1959, div 1980, 1 son, 1 daughter. Education: Diploma, 1957, Teachers Training Centre. Appointments: Primary School Teacher, 1957-90; Journalist, 1957-. Publications: Distress

That is Knotted, 1988; KTOS Struggle History (The history of the Turkish Cypriot Teachers' Trade Union), 2 volumes, 1988-91; Our Children and Sexuality, 1990; Subject Woman, 1990; Ayseferi (A Journey to the Moon): Poems 1995-. Contributions to: Nacak; Soz; Halkin Sesi; Bozkurt; Kibris Postasi; Ortam; Besparmak; 502; Poet; World Poetry; newspapers and magazines. Honours: Nine prizes in the field of Journalism and Literature. Memberships: Cyprus Turkish Artist and Writers Union; World Academy of Arts and Culture; Teacher's Trade Union; Women Research Centre, Founder; Journalists' Association; Greenpeace; Conflict Resolution Studies, Cyprus. Address: 14 Ogretmenler Cad, Ogretmen Evleri, Ortakoty Lefkosa, Mersin 10, Turkey.

CAIMBEUL Maoilios MacAonghais, b. 23 Mar 1944, Isle of Skye, Scotland. Writer. m. Margaret Hutchison, 2 Dec 1971, 1 son. Education: BA, Edinburgh University; Teaching Diploma, Jordanhill College, Glasgow, 1978. Appointments: Various jobs before university; Gaelic Teacher, Tobermory High School, 1978-84; Gaelic Development Officer, Highlands and Islands Development Board, 1984-87; Writer, 1987-. Publications: Eileanan, 1980; Bailtean, 1987; A Caradh an Rathaid, 1988; An Aghaidh na Siorraidheachd, anthology with 7 other Gaelic poets, 1991. Contributions to: Gairm; Lines Review; Chapman; Cencrastus; Orbis; Poetry Ireland Review; Comhar; Gairfish; Baragab; Weekend Scotsman; West Highland Free Press; Anthologies: Air Ghleus 2, 1989; Twenty of the Best, 1990; The Patched Fool, 1991; Somhairle, Dain is Deilbh, 1991. Honours: Award, Gaelic Books Council Poetry Competition, 1978-79; Poetry/Fiction Prize, Gaelic Books Council, 1982-83. Membership: Scottish PEN. Address: 12 Na Dunanan, Stamhain, An t-Eilean Sgitheanach IV51 9HZ, Scotland.

CAINE Shulamith Wechter, b. USA. Professor; Poet. Education: BA, MA, University of Pennsylvania. Appointment: Drexel University, Philadelphia. Publication: World and Local News. Contributions to: American Poetry Review; American Scholar; Chronical of Higher Education; Denver Quarterly; Greensboro Review; Images of Israel; Midland Review; Negative Capability; Philadelphia Poets; Southern Poetry Review; South Street Star; Tucumari Literary Review; Voices Israel; Womens Studies Quarterly; Feminist Press. Honour: Winner, Gerald Cable Prize for Love Fugue; Pennsylvania Council on the Arts Fellowship. Membership: Poetry Committee. Address: 122 Grasmere Road, Bala, Cynwyd, PA 19004, USA.

CAIRD Janet Hinshaw, b. 24 Apr 1913, Livingstonia, Malawi. Teacher of English. m. James Bowman Caird, 19 July 1938, 2 daughters. Education: MA Hons, English Literature, University of Edinburgh, 1935; University of Grenoble and Sorbonne, 1935-36; St George's College, Edinburgh, 1935-36. Appointments: Teaching in Department of English: Park School for Girls, Glasgow, 1937-38; Royal High School, Edinburgh, 1940-41; Dollar Academy, 1942-43. Publications: Some Walk a Narrow Path, 1977; Distant Urn, 1983; John Donne You Were Wrong, 1988. Contributions to: Glasgow Herald; Lines Review; Chapman. Memberships: Poetry Society, London; Scottish Poetry Library; Association of Scottish Literary Studies; Society of Antiquaries of Scotland. Address: 1 Drummond Crescent, Inverness IV2 4QW, Scotland.

CALAIS Jean. See: **RODEFER Stephen.**

CALDER Angus, b. 5 Feb 1942, Sutton, Surrey, England. Educator. Education: MA, English, King's College, Cambridge; DPhil, Social Studies, University of Sussex, 1968. Appointments: Lecturer in Literature, University of Nairobi, Kenya, 1968-71; Staff Tutor, Reader in Literature, Open University in Scotland, 1979-94; Visiting Professor in English, University of Zimbabwe, 1992. Contributions to: New Statesman; Chapman; Cencrastus; Others. Honour: Eric Gregory Award, 1968. Memberships: Convenor, Scottish Poetry Library, 1982-88; Panel of Scottish Board of the Year Award Judges, 1983-; Saltire Society. Address: 15 Spittal Street, Edinburgh EH3 9DY, Scotland.

CALDER Robert Russell, b. 22 Apr 1950, Burbank, Scotland. Writer; Editor; Critic. Education: Glasgow University, 1967-71; Edinburgh University, 1972-74; MA, Philosophy, History, 1973. Appointments: Co-Editor, 1973-76, Associate Editor, 1988-, Chapman; Editor, Lanes Review, 1976-77. Publications: Il Re Giovane, 1972; Serapion, 1993; Featured in: European Poetry in Scotland, 1989; The New Makers, 1991. Contributions to: PN Review; NER; Edinburgh

Review; Poetry Ireland; Chapman; Others. Address: 23 Glenlee Street, Burnbank, Hamilton, Lanarkshire ML3 9JB, Scotland.

CALDWELL Robert Francis, b. 7 Mar 1931, Greenwich, Connecticut, USA. Retired US Government Civil Servant. Education: DPsy, 1961; MsD, 1965; DD Diploma of Naturopathy (ND) Great Britain, 1967; PhD, 1968; Knight of Justice, 1989. Appointments: Sergeant, US Army, 1952-57; City Carrier, 1967-74; Former Chaplain, American Legion, Pulaski, New York; Past Worthy Chaplain, Fraternal Order of Eagles, Stamford, Connecticut; Ordained Minister. Publication: A Poet's Reflections, 1993. Contributions to: Florida Gardener; Azalea Review: Golden Lifestyles; Sparrowgrass; Contemporary Poets of America; National Library of Poetry; Poets at Work; Poetry in Motion; Florida State Poets Association; Famous Poets Society. Honours: Outstanding Poets of 1994; Poet's PEN; Award of Merit, Illiad Press; President's Award for Literary Excellence, NAR; Award of Merit, NAR; Honourable Mention, Longfellow Awards; Accomplishment of Merit Certificate of Poetic Achievement, Amherst Society; Poet Laureate of Lake County Senior Citizens Center, Leesburg, Florida; Famous Poet for 1995; President, Vice President, National Association of Retired Federal Employees. Memberships: Poets and Writers Inc, New York City; National Authors Registry; Life Member, International Society of Poets Inc; South Florida Poetry Institute. Address: Griffwood Mobile Home Park, Picciola Road 03896-132, Fruitland Park, FL 34731, USA.

CALIBAN. See: **KNELL William H.**

CALLAGHAN Barry, b. 5 July 1937, Toronto, Ontario, Canada. Education: MA, University of Toronto, 1963. Appointments: Professor, Toronto University, 1965-. Publications include: The Hogg Poem and Drawings, 1978; As Close as We Came, 1982; Stone Blind Love, 1988; Exile's Exiles, 1992; Editor, Lords of Winter and of Love: A Book of Canadian Love Poems in English and French, 1983. Honours include: Prix Italia, 1977; National Magazine Awards. Address: 69 Sullivan Street, Toronto, Ontario M5T 1C2, Canada.

CALLAWAY Kathy J, b. 19 Feb 1943, Springfield, Massachusetts, USA. Writer; Assistant Professor. 1 son. Education: BA, 1978, MFA, 1979, University of Montana, Missouri, USA. Appointments: Several intensive writing workshops nationwide, sponsored by the National Endowment for The Arts and State Arts Boards, 1982-92; Writer-in-Residence, Assistant Professor of English, Mankato State University, Minnesota, 1982-84; Assistant Professor of English, Moorhead State University, Minnesota, 1987-88; Visiting Assistant Professor of English, University of Alaska/Fairbanks, Nome, Alaska, 1989-90, 1993; Soros Foundation Fellow to Tartu, Estonia, 1993-94; United Nations Volunteer, Graduate Teacher-Training, North East Agricultural University, Harbin, China, 1995. Publications: Heart of the Garfish, Pitt Poetry Series, 1982; The Bloodroot Flower, novel, 1982. Contributions to: Antaeus; Iowa Review; Ploughshares; The Nation; Crazyhorse; Parnassas; The Pushcart Prize: V Anthology. Honours: PEN New Writer, 1980; Loring Williams Prize for Poetry, 1980; The Pushcart Prize, 1982; Agnes Lynch Starrett Award for Poetry, 1982; National Endowment For The Arts Fellowships, 1984, 1990. Membership: Poets and Writers. Address: 2727 1/2 Fourth Avenue East, Hibbing, MN 55746-0006, USA.

CALVET Marta Gloria (Koala), b. 28 Oct 1941, Buenos Aires, Argentina. Educator; Communicator; Writer. div, 1 son, 1 daughter. Education: BA Psychology, University of Alaska; MA, Humanities, Arizona State University; PhD candidate, Berkeley, California, 1971. Appointments: Professor of World Literature and Psychology, Montevideo, Uruguay, 1970s; Director, Language Arts Institute, Argentina, 1980-90; Professor of French and Spanish, Southern University, New Orleans, 1991-. Publications: Fata Morgana, 1989; Pirate's Laughter; Sueno de Nomade. Contributions to: Pagina 12; Exquisite Corpse; Pinched Nerves; Les Amis; New Orleans Opera Association. Honours: Fondo Nacional de Las Artes, 1989; Southern University at New Orleans Poetry Award, 1991. Memberships: Associcion Argentina de Escritores; New Orleans Poetry Forum; Modern Language Association. Address: 1225 Chartres, Apt 8, New Orleans, LA 70116, USA.

CAMERON Esther Beatrice, b. 10 Sept 1941, New York, New York, USA. Translator; Lawyer. Education: BA, University of Wisconsin, 1964; MA, 1966, PhD, 1973, University of California at Berkeley; University of Wisconsin Law School, 1993. Appointment: Associate Professor of German, State University of New York at

Buffalo, 1969-71. Publications: A Gradual Light, in Hebrew Translation, 1983; Various collections distributed privately, including: Here and There, 1992. Contributions to: Poetry Northwest; Primavera; Gryphon; Jewish Spectator; Ma'Ariv; 'Al Ha-Mishmar; B'Or Hatorah; Seven Gates; Lyris; Orbis; Wisconsin Poets' Calendar; Arc. Honours: Peter Schwiefert Poetry Prize, 1985; Orbis Rhyme International Contest, First Prize in Formal Poetry Category, 1990. Memberships: Israel Association of Writers in English; Voices Group, Jerusalem. Address: 4414 Rolla Lane, Madison, WI 53711, USA.

CAMERON Lori Michelle, b. 18 Mar 1965, Valdosta, Georgia, USA. English Professor; Editor. m. Brian S Cameron, 30 July 1994. Education: MA, English, 1992; BA, Writing, 1988; AA, Religion, 1986. Appointments: English Instructor, Chaffey College, 1992-94; English Professor, DeVry Institute of Technology, 1995-; Editor, Penwood Review, 1996-. Contributions to: Spring Harvest; Thalia: Studies in Literary Humor; At Water's Edge; Best Poems of 1996. Honours: 3rd Place, National Library of Poetry Annual Contest, 1995; Editor's Choice Award, National Library of Poetry, 1995, 1996. Memberships: International Society of Poets, 1994-96; International English Honor Society, Sigma Tau Delta, 1991-92. Address: 3910 Howard Avenue, Los Alamitos, CA 90720, USA.

CAMNER Howard, b. 14 Jan 1957, Miami, Florida, USA. English Teacher; Writer. Education: BA, English, Florida International University, 1982. Appointments: English Teacher; Screen Writer; Producer and Host of cable TV talk show; New York Performance Poet. Publications: Notes From The Eye of a Hurricane, 1979; Transitions, 1980; Scattered Shadows, 1980; Road Note Elegy, 1980; A Work in Progress, 1981; Poetry From Hell to Breakfast, 1981; Midnight at The Laundromat and Other Poems, 1983; Hard Times On Easy Street, 1987; Madman In The Alley, 1989; Stray Dog Wail, 1991; Banned In Babylon, 1993; Jammed Zipper, 1994; Bed of Nails, 1995. Contributions to: Howling Mantra; New York Magazine; Poet's Voice; Without Halos; Poetry Journal; The Diversifier; Amanda Blue; Eleventh MUSE; Louder Than Bombs; Cuthbert's Treasury; Gathering Stars; Poetpourri; Palmetto Review; Perceptions; Florida in Poetry; Poems That Thump In The Dark; Tributary; Security Blanket; Poetry: An American Heritage; After The Meeting on Elbe; American Poets 1990's. Honours: Works included in 100 prominent literary collections worldwide; Nominated for Poet Laureate of Florida, 1980; Inducted into The Last Poets, Honorary Member, 1980; Fine Arts Press Poetry Award, 1988; Golden Poet Award, 1988; Silver Poet Award, 1989; Inducted into the Homer Honour Society of International Poets, 1992. Memberships: Poets and Writers Inc; Academy of American Poets; Poetry Society of America; South Florida Poetry Institute; Writers' Exchange; National Writers Association. Address: 10440 S W 76th Street, Miami, FL 33173, USA.

CAMPBELL Alistair Te Ariki, b. 25 June 1925, Rarotonga, New Zealand. Writer. m. (1) Fleur Adcock, 1952, (2) Meg Andersen, 1958, 3 sons, 2 daughters. Education: BA, Victoria University of Wellington, 1953; Diploma of Teaching, Wellington Teachers' College, 1954. Appointments: Teacher, Newtown Primary School, Wellington; Editor, New Zealand Department of Education; Senior Editor, New Zealand Council for Educational Research; Writer's Fellow, Victoria University of Wellington, 1992. Publications: Verse: Mine Eyes Dazzle, 1950; Sanctuary of Spirits, 1963; Wild Honey, 1964; Blue Rain, 1967; Kapiti: Selected Poems, 1972; Dreams, Yellow Lions, 1975; The Dark Lord of Savaiki, 1980; Collected Poems, 1981; Soul Traps, 1985; Stone Rain: The Polynesian Strain, 1992; Death and the Tagua, 1995; Pocket Collected Poems, 1995; Novels: The Frigate Bird, 1989; Sidewinder, 1991; Tia, 1993. Autobiography: Island to Island, 1984. Drama: The Suicide, 1965; When the Bough Breaks, 1970. Contributions to: Landfall; New Zealand Listener; Poetry New Zealand; New Zealand Poetry Yearbook; Comment; Poetry Australia. Honours: Gold Medal for TV documentary Island of Spirits, La Spezia International Film Festival, 1974; New Zealand Book Award for Poetry, 1982. Membership: Treasurer, President, President of Honour, PEN International, New Zealand Centre. Address: 4B Rawhiti Road, Pukerua Bay, Wellington, New Zealand.

CAMPBELL Donald, b. 25 Feb 1940, Caithness, Scotland. m. Jean Fairgrieve, 1966, 1 son. Appointments: Writer-in-Residence at various Scottish institutions, including Edinburgh Education Department, 1974-77; Writer-in-Residence, Royal Lyceum Theatre, 1981-82. Publications: Poems, 1971; Rhymes 'n Reasons, 1972; Murals: Poems in Scots, 1975; Blether: A Collection of Poems, 1979; A Brighter Sunshine, 1983; Anm Audience for McGonagall, 1987;

Selected Poems 1970-90, 1990; Plays for stage, radio and television. Address: 85 Spottiswoode Street, Edinburgh EH9 1BZ, Scotland.

CAMPBELL George, b. 26 Dec 1916, Panama (Jamaican citizen). m. Odilia Crane, 1948, 4 daughters. Education: St George's College, Kingston. Appointment: Programme Director for Jewish Centres in New York. Publications: First Poems, 1945, revised edition, 1981; Earth Testament, 1983. Address: c/o Garland Publishing, 136 Madison Avenue, New York, NY 10016, USA.

CAMPBELL Rona Mary, b. 7 Oct 1945, Chichester, England. Poet; Singer. m. (1) 1967, div 1970, 2 sons, 1 daughter, (2) Roderick Campbell, 1972, div, 1992. Education: Finals in Singing, Theory and General Musicianship, Cardiff College of Music and Drama, 1963-68; Studied Drama, Spanish, Italian, some German. Appointments: Principal Soprano, Metropolitana Opera de Caracas, Venezuela; Director, The Third Room, Performance, Poetry Venue, Everyman Bistro, Everyman Theatre, 1988-91; Singing Teacher, Natural Health Centre, Liverpool, 1992; Director, Founder, Central Academy of Singing, Liverpool, 1994; Founder, Director, Voice Link, Liverpool, 1994. Publications: Poetry: David of the Mines, narrative poem in Sotheby's Anthology, 1982; The Hedge, first collection, 1988; Broadcasts: BBC Radio Ulster, TV Ulster's programme Spectrum; BBC Radio Merseyside, Radio Wales, The Today Programme; BBC's Kaleidoscope. Contributions to: Anthologies: Of Caterpillars, Cats and Cattle, 1987; Niffs and Whiffs, 1991; Minibeasts, 1992; 2 tours of Ireland. Honours: Runner-up (from 44,000 entrants), Sotheby's International Poetry Competition, 1982. Memberships: Poetry Society; Aldeburgh Poetry; Friend of The Arvon Foundation; Association of Teachers of Singing; Voicecare Network UK. Address: 19 Elmsley Road, Mossley Hill, Liverpool L18 8AY, Merseyside, England.

CAMPEDELLI Giancarlo, (Rudy de Cadaval), b. 1 Jan 1933, Verona, Italy. Writer. m. Grazia Corsini, 31 Mar, 1 son, 1 daughter. Education: Pro Dea University, Albany, New York, 1993; World Academy of Arts and Culture, Sacramento, California, 1995; St Petersburg University, Russia, 1995. Appointments: Director, Grolier International Inc, 1972-83; Vice President, Kronos Europea SPA and IBI Inc, New York. Publications: Cocktail di Poesie, 1959; 23 Poemas Contemporaines, 1968; Schiavo 1933, 1979; Et Apres, 1983; L'Albero del silenzio, 1988; Colloquio con la pietra, 1988; Viaggio Nello Specchio Della Vita, 1994. Contributions to: Discorso Diretto, Treviso; Inter Muses, Paris; Sequence, Paris; La Lampada, Brasil; La Battana, Lubiana; Poetry, Chicago, USA; Durak, New York, USA; Literaria, Buenos Aires; MPT, London, England; La Prora, Rome. Honours: National Poetry Prize, 10 times, 1959-1990; International Poetry Prize, 4 times, 1959-1994; Lupa Capitalina Prize, City Hall, Roma, 1979; Knight, Grand Officer of the Order of Merit of Italian Republic, 1989; Knight Commander of the Sovereign Order of St John of Jerusalem, 1990; 3 Honorary Doctorates, New York and St Petersburg, 1993 and 1995; Knight of the Sovereign Military Teutonic Order of Levante, 1994. Memberships: Centro Cultural Literario Artisico de Portugal; International Writers and Artist Association, Bluffon; Accademia Degli Abruzzi, Chieti; World Academy of Arts and Culture, California, USA; World Literary Academy, Cambridge, England; Internationale Burckhardt Akademie, Basle. Address: Via Mascagni 5, 37024 Arbizzano di Negrar, Verona, Italy.

CAMPION D(aniel Ray), b. 23 Aug 1949, Oak Park, Illinois, USA. Editor. Education: AB, University of Chicago, 1970; MA, University of Illinois at Chicago, 1975; PhD, University of Iowa, 1989. Appointments: Production Editor, Encyclopaedia Britannica, 1971-74; Editor of Children's Books, Follett Publishing Co, 1977-78; Teaching and Research Assistant, 1978-84, Visiting Assistant Professor of English, 1991-, University of Iowa; Test Specialist, 1984-86, Senior Test Specialist, 1986-94, Senior Test Editor, 1994-, The American College Testing Programme. Publications: Calypso, 1981; Walt Whitman: The Measure of His Song (edited with Ed Folsom and Jim Perlman), 1981; Peter de Vries and Surrealism, 1995. Contributions to: Anthologies: Banyan Anthology 2, 1982; Light Year 1985, 1986; Anthology of Magazine Verse and Yearbook of American Poetry, 1985 edition, 1986-88 edition; Lives in Translation: An Anthology of Contemporary Franco-American Writings, 1991; Other: Ascent; The Atlanta Review; Caliban; Great Lakes Review; Iron; Invisible City; Journal of Popular Culture; Light; Little Magazine; Laurel Review; Mississippi Valley Review; Nantucket Review; Negative Capability; North Dakota Quarterly; Poet Lore; Poetry; Rolling Stone; The Spirit That Moves Us; Telephone; Timbuktu. Honours: University of Chicago Festival of the Arts Award, 1967; All-Nations Poetry Contest Award,

1975; Literary Award, Illinois Arts Council, 1979. Memberships: Modern Language Association; Midwest Modern Language Association; National Council of Teachers of English; Society for the Study of Midwestern Literature. Address: 1700 East Rochester Avenue, Iowa City, IA 52245, USA.

CANALES Jacque, b. 18 July 1932, Uncastillo, Zaragoza, Spain. Writer; Poet. m. Manuel Galdeano, 29 Mar 1962, 2 sons, 2 daughters. Appointments: English Teacher; Journalist; Philosophy Studies. Publications: Un Viento en el Espejo, 1985; Entre la Transparencia y la Musica, 1985; Ese Perfume de la Puerta Sellada, 1985; En la Piel de la Palabra, 1986; La Noche y sus Sandalias, 1986; Un Largo Pez de Plata, 1987; Nietzsche Tambien Se Rie. 1987; Colon, Presencia entre Dos Olas, 1987; Safo, 1987; Tiempo de Sed, 1988; De Vita et Moribus, 1989; Urgentes Amapolas, 1991; Unpublished: Resonancias de Americo Desnuda; Alba Detenida; El Niño de los Ojos de Agua; Consideraciones de Colon; Part-published: Isla de Agua Dulce; Several essays. Contributions to: Several Spanish and international anthologies; Mairena Review of Poetry; La Tarde; Burgos daily; ABC daily, Madrid; Huelva daily; Madinat Al-Zhara Review, Cordoba; El Mirador; Zaragoza Review; Antipodes Review; World Poetry, 1991; El Urogallo Review; Mairena Review. Honours: 42 important Spanish and international prizes for books including: Gold Medals for Poetry; Gold Pen for Poetry; Lady of Olympoetry; Silver Key of Poetry; Lady of Spanishness; Lady of Elche. Memberships: Spanish Writers' and Artists' Association; National Union of Spanish Writers; Worthy Member ad honorem, Cultural Literary and Artistic Centre of Felgueiras, Portugal; General Secretary, Latin-American Academy of Poetry; Co-Founder, Nemesis Literary Social Group; World Academy of Arts and Culture, California. Address: c/o Fernando Gabriel, 18-80-E, 28017 Madrid, Spain.

CANAN Janine, b. 2 Nov 1942, Los Angeles, California, USA. Poet. Education: BA, Stanford University 1963; University of California, 1963-66; New York University, 1972-76. Appointments: Private Psychiatrist, Berkeley, California, 1979-. Publications: Of Your Seed; The Hunger; Daughter; Who Buried the Breast of Dreams; Shapes of Self; Her Magnificent Body; She Rises Like the Sun; Invocation of the Goddess. Contributions to: Colorado North Review; Caprice; California Quarterly; Tree Kalliope; New Directions; Conditions; Synapse; Exquisite Corpse; Earth's Daughters; Thesmophoria; Manhattan Poetry Review; No Apologies; We Moon. Honour: Swan Koppelman Award, Membership: Poetry Society of America. Address: 466 Cascade Drive, Fairlax, CA 94930, USA.

CANDEIAS Marcolino, b. 28 Aug 1952, Cinco Riberas, Terceira, Azores, Portugal. Executive Secretary. m. Valdeci Purim, 22 Sept 1990, 1 son, 1 daughter. Education: Bachelor in Romanic Philology, University of Coimbra, Portugal, 1978; Grade of Licenciate in Modern Languages and Literatures, Portuguese and French Branch, University of Coimbra, Portugal. Appointments: Assistant Professor, Linguistics, University of Azores, Portugal, 1979-80; Assistant Professor, Linguistics, University of Coimbra, Portugal, 1980-86; Lecturer, Portuguese and Brazilian Culture and Portuguese Language, University of Montreal, Quebec, Canada, 1986-90; Executive Secretary, General Direction and Board of Directors, Caisse d'économie des Portugais de Montréal, Montreal, Canada. Publications: Por ter escrito Amor, 1971; Na distância deste tempo, 1984. Contributions to: Antologia de Poesia Açoriana do Séc, 1975; Antologia de Poesia Açoriana; Sempre disse tais coisas esperançado na vulcanologia; The Sea Within; Pai sua bênçao; Os Nove Rumores do Mar; Cadernos de Literatura; Vértice; New Canadian Review; Correio dos Açores; Diário Insular; A Uniao. Memberships: Instituto Açoriano de Cultura. Address: 4132 Hillcrest, Pierrefonds, Quebec H9J 1W3, Canada.

CANNELLA Vincent, b. 19 May 1927, Tampa, Florida, USA. Poet; Illustrator. Education: Museum of Modern Art School; Janice Franklyn School of Art; Art Student League of New York. Contributions to: American Poetry Association; Poetry Anthology; Editor's Choice; Days of Future Past; Quill Books Chasing Rainbows; Dan River Anthology; American Anthology of Midwestern Poetry; Voices of the South; Tabula Rasa Magazine; Lucidity Quarterly; First Time Publications: Poetry Forum; Kola; Riverun Fall; Wide Open Magazine; Se La Vie Writer's Journal, Aug 1995. Honours: 1st Prize, Amardilio State Fair; Honourable Mention, Bronte Street; American Poetry Association Poetry Contest. Address: 953 East 211th Street, Bronx, NY 10469, USA.

CANNON Frank. See: **MAYHAR Ardath.**

CANNON Janet, b. 8 Oct 1945, USA. Poet; Teacher. 1 daughter. Education: BA, University of Iowa, 1970; MA (clearance), 1972. Appointments: Writing Workshops, Taos Schools, 1979; Martin Luther King High School, 1985; New York City Public Library, 1987-88; Contributing Editor; Radio Host; Founder, Editor, Crow Call; Collective Poetry Editor; Plexus; Arts Reviewer; KXRT Radio; Editor, Scholastic Books, 1994, McClanahan & Co, 1994-95, American Bureau of Shipping, 1995. Publications: The Last Night in New York; Percipience. Contributions to: Literary journals, pamphlets and periodicals. Honours: Honorable Mention, Rio Grande Writers' Association Poetry Contest; Kimo Theatre Writing Contest; Honourable Mention, Minimuse Poetry Contest; American Society of Composers, Authors and Publishers Award. Memberships: Poetry Society of America; American Society of Composers, Authors and Publishers; Directory of American Poets and Fiction Writers. Address: 12832 125th Lane NE, #D4, Kirkland, WA 98034, USA.

CANTALUPO Charles, b. 17 October 1951, Orange, New Jersey, USA. Professor of English; Poet; Writer. m. (1) Catherine Musello, 21 August 1976, dec 1983, 1 son, dec 1979, (2) Barbara Dorosh, 29 October 1988, 3 daughters, 1 son. Education: University of Kent, Canterbury, 1972; BA, Washington University, St Louis, 1973; MA, 1978, PhD, 1980, Rutgers University. Appointments: Teaching Assistant, 1973-76, Instructor, 1977-79, Rutgers University; Instructor, 1980-81, Assistant Professor, 1981-89, Associate Professor, 1989-96, Professor of English, 1996-, Penn State University, Schuylkill Haven. Publications: The Art of Hope, poems, 1983. A Literary Leviathan: Thomas Hobbes's Masterpiece Of Language, 1991; Editor, The World Of Ngugi Wa Thiong'o, 1995; Poetry, Mysticism And Feminism: from th' nave to the chops, 1995; Editor, Ngugi Wa Thiong'o: Text And Contexts, 1995; Anima/I Wo/man And Other Spirits, 1996. Contributions to: Books, anthologies, scholarly journals and periodicals. Honour: American Academy of Poets Prize, 1976. Address: c/o Department of English, Penn State University, 200 University Drive, Schuylkill Haven, PA 17972, USA.

CAPE Judith. See: **PAGE P(atricia) K(athleen).**

CARDILLO Joe, b. 1 Aug 1951, Norwich, New York, USA. Poet; Recording Artist; Associate Professor. Education: MA, State University of New York at Albany, 1978; BA, Siena College, 1973. Appointment: Assistant Professor, Hudson Valley Community College, 1978-. Publications: No Surrender; The Rock 'N' Roll Journals; Artifact; No Denials; Turning Toward Morning; Legacy of Desire; Forever September. Contributions to: Rolling Stone; Iron; North County Anthology; Lactuca; Crab Creek Review; Duega Chapbook Award; National Book Award Nominee; Featured on Legendary John Peel Show; Narrative Poetry Award; 2 FM Hit poetry singles; 9 DJ Listed Poetry CDs. Membership: Poets and Writers, New York. Address: MRV 207, Hudson Valley Community College, Troy, NY 12180, USA.

CAREW Jan Rynveld, b. 24 Sept 1925, Agricola, Guyana. Writer; Educator. m. Joy Gleason Carew, 28 Sept 1975, 1 son, 2 daughters. Education: Howard University, 1945-46; Western Reserve University, 1946-48; Charles University, Prague, 1949-51; La Sorbonne, Paris, 1951-52. Appointments: Professor, Princeton University, 1969-72; Lecturer, Rutgers University, 1969-72; Professor, North Western University, 1973-87, now Emeritus Professor; Visiting Clarence J Robinson Professor, George Mason University, 1989-91; Visiting Professor of International Studies, Illinois Wesleyan University. Publications: Sea Drums In My Blood; Street of Eternity. Contributions to: Penguin Book of Caribbean Verse; Black American Literature Forum; Pacific Quarterly; Journal of African Civilization; Caribbean Quarterly; New Writing in the Caribbean. Address: African American Studies Department, North Western University, 2003 Sheridan Road, Evanston, IL 60208, USA.

CAREW Rivers Verain, b. 17 Oct 1935, Guildford, Surrey, England. Journalist. m. (1) Susan Babington Hill, 7 Dec 1968, div, 1 son, 3 daughters, (2) Siobhán Nie Charthaigh, 9 Apr 1992. Education: BA, Trinity College, Dublin, 1956; MA, 1960. Appointments: Assistant Editor, Ireland of the Welcomes, 1963-67; Joint Editor, Dublin Magazine, 1964-69; Sub Editor, 1967-77, Deputy Chief Sub Editor, 1977-82, Chief Sub Editor, 1982-87, RTE; Chief Sub Editor, BBC World Service, 1987-. Publication: Figures Out of Mist. Contributions to: Irish Times; A Review of English Literature; Dublin Magazine. Address: 148 Catharine Street, Cambridge CB1 3AR, England.

CARIAGE Paul Marie Joseph, b. 3 Feb 1922, Algiers, Algeria. Retired French Internal Ministry. m. Vassallo Suzanne Marie, 30 July 1949, 1 son, 1 daughter. Education: Des Beaux Arts. Appointments: Artist Painter. Publications: Reveries; A Coeur Oovert; D'Esperance et D'Amour; Arc En Ciel; Libre Champ; Comme un Chant D'Oiseau; Ombre et Lumiere; Gerbe; Pele Mele. Contributions to: Several Reviews and Anthologies. Honours: Hundred Prizes. Memberships: Societé des Poets Francais; International Writers Artists Association; World Academy of Arts and Culture; World Poetry Research Institute; World Poetry Society. Address: 34 Chemin de Malpeigne, 84000 Avignon, France.

CARLILE Henry David, b. 6 May 1934, San Francisco, California, USA. Professor. 1 daughter. Education: AA, Grays Harbor College, 1960; BA, University of Washington, 1962; MA, 1967. Appointments: Instructor, 1967-69; Assistant Professor, 1969, 1972; Associate Professor, 1972-79; Professor, 1980-. Publications: The Rough Hewn Table; Running Lights; Rain, 1993. Contributions to: American Poetry Review; Concerning Poetry; Missouri Review; New Yorker; Parnassus; Portland Review; Shenandoah. Honours: Discovery Grant and Poetry Fellowship, National Endowment for the Arts; Devins Award; Ingram Merrill Poetry Fellowship; 2 Pushcart Prizes; Crazy Horse Poetry Award. Address: 7349 South East 30th Avenue, Portland, OR 97202, USA.

CARLIN Vuyelwa Susan, b. 13 Sept 1949, South Africa. Poet. m. Brian Wigston, 8 Mar 1969, 1 son, 1 daughter. Education: English Honours degree, Upper Second, Bristol University, 1972. Appointments: Secretary, 1974-76; Artists Model, 1984-91; House Mother, Bedstone College, 1992-. Publications: Midas' Daughter, 1991; How We Dream Of The Dead, 1995; Included in anthologies: Images for Africa, 1988; Poetry Wales 25 Years, 1990; New Christian Poetry, 1990; Seren Poets 2, 1990; New Women Poets, 1990; Sing Freedom!, 1991. Contributions to: Poetry Review; Stand; London Review of Books; London Magazine; New Welsh Review; Poetry Wales; Poetry Durham; Orbis; Chapman; Lines Review; Poetry, USA; Gettysburg Review, USA. Honours: 3rd Prize, Cardiff International Poetry Competition, 1988; Prize, National Poetry Competition, 1988. Memberships: The Poetry Society; Out of Bounds Poetry Group; Anglo-Welsh Poetry Society. Address: c/o Seren Books, 1st Floor, 2 Wyndham Street, Bridgend, Mid Glamorgan CF31 1EF, Wales.

CARMEN Marilyn Elain, b. 23 Nov 1941. Writer. 2 sons, 2 daughters. Education: MA, English Creative Writing, Iowa State University, 1987. Appointment: Professor, Community College of Philadelphia, 1991-. Publication: Born of the Wind, 1997. Contributions to: Paterson Literary Review, 1997. Honour: Fellowship, Pennsylvania State Council on the Arts, 1990. Address: Community College of Philadelphia, 17th and Springgarden Streets, Philadelphia, PA, USA.

CARMI T. See: **CHARNY Carmi.**

CARMICHAEL Jack B(lake), b. 31 Jan 1938, Ravenswood, West Virginia, USA. Writer; Poet; Editor. m. Julie Ann Carmichael, 2 Oct 1981, 4 daughters. Education: BA, Ohio Wesleyan University, 1959; PhD, Michigan State University, 1964; Postdoctoral Studies, University of Oregon, 1966-67. Appointment: Editor and Publisher, Dynamic Press, 1990-. Publications: Novels: A New Slain Knight, 1991; Black Knight, 1991; Tales of the Cousin, 1992; Memoirs of the Great Georgeous, 1992; The Humpty Boys in Michigan, 1995. Contributions to: Poems in various anthologies and journals. Honour: Outstanding Achievement Award, American Poetry Association, 1990. Membership: Academy of American Poets. Address: c/o Dynamic Press, 519 South Rogers Street, Mason, MI 48854, USA.

CARPATHIOS Neil Emmanuel, b. 4 Mar 1961, Columbus, Ohio, USA. English Teacher; Adjunct Professor. m. Danielle Marie Cacioppo, 28 Dec 1989. Education: Ohio State University, BA, 1983; University of Iowa, MFA, 1986; University of Akron, 1988. Appointments: Writer-in-Residence, Iowa Schools; Writing Instructional Aide, Akron City Schools; Substitute Teacher, Cuyahoga Falls Schools; College Instructor, University of Akron; English Teacher, Archbishop Hoban High School; Jackson High School, 1991-. Publications: Its Own Kind of Beauty, 1989; I the Father, 1993. Contributions to: Kansas Quarterly; Sun; South Coast Poetry Journal; Stone Country; Plain Song; Albany Review; Ohio Journal; Poetry Magazine. Honours: Pushcart Prize; Ohio Arts Council Community of Poets Award; Ohio Arts Council, Poetry in the Park. Address: 7954 Daytona North West, Masillon, OH 44646, USA.

CARPENTER Carol Maureen, b. 9 Nov 1943, Highland Park, Michigan, USA. Writer; Instructional Designer. m. Mack L Carpenter, 5 Apr 1963, 1 son, 1 daughter. Education: BS, 1966, MEd, 1972, EdD, 1984, Wayne State University. Appointments: English Teacher, Detroit Public School, 1966-71; English Instructor, Oakland Community College. 1971-73; Program Co-Ordinator, Instructor, Detroit Institute of Technology, 1974-80; Curriculum Developer, Oakland University, 1980-81; Creative Manager, Planning, Sandy Corp, 1982-85; Principal, Vice President, Board of Directors, The High Performance Group Inc, 1985-. Contributions to: Wisconsin Review; Indiana Review; Bellingham Review; Writer's Forum; Cape Rock. Honours: Tompkins Award, Graduate Division, 1979, 1980; 1st Place, Poetry, Writers Digest Annual Competition, 1992. Address: 10005 Berwick, Livonia, MI 48150, USA.

CARPENTER John Randell, b. 14 April 1936, Cambridge, Massachusetts, USA. Writer; Translator; Editor; Teacher. m. Bogdana Maria-Magdalena Chetkowska, 15 April 1963, 1 son, 1 daughter. Education: BA, Harvard College, 1958; Sorbonne, Paris, 1962-66. Appointments: Translator, Editor, Freelance, 1966-74; Poet-in-Residence, Teacher, 1975-76, 1977-80; Fellow, National Endowment for the Arts, 1976-77, 1980-81; Lecturer, 1980; Assistant Professor, Lecturer, 1983-88. Publications: Gathering Water; Egret; Pebble, Cedar, Star; Translation of poetry. Contributions to: New York Times; Quarterly Review of Literature; Southwest Review; Minnesota Review; Epoch; Perspective; Mister Cogito; Penny Dreadful; Cafe Solo; Slant; Embers; Poet Lore; The Humanist. Honours: Writter Bynner Poetry Award; Islands and Continents Translation Award; Award, Andrew Mellon Foundation. Memberships: American Language Teachers Association; PEN; Poets and Writers. Address: 1606 Granger Avenue, Ann Arbor, MI 48104, USA.

CARPENTER Lucas, b. 23 Apr 1947, Elberton, Georgia, USA. Professor of English; Writer; Poet; Editor. m. Judith Leidner, 2 Sept 1972, 1 daughter. Education: BS, College of Charleston, 1968; MA, University of North Carolina at Chapel Hill, 1973; PhD, State University of New York at Stony Brook, 1982. Appointments: Instructor, State University of New York at Stony Brook, 1973-78; Instructor, 1978-80, Associate Professor of English, 1980-85, Suffolk Community College; Editorial Consultant, Prentice-Hall Inc, 1981-; Associate Professor of English, Oxford College of Emory University, 1985-94; Professor of English, 1994-. Publications: A Year for the Spider,poems, 1972; The Selected Poems of John Gould Fletcher (editor with E Leighton Rudolph), 1988; The Selected Essays of John Gould Fletcher (editor), 1989; John Gould Fletcher and Southern Modernism, 1990; The Selected Correspondence of John Gould Fletcher (editor with E Leighton Rudolph), 1996. Contributions to: Anthologies, scholarly journals, and periodicals. Honours: Resident Fellow in Poetry and Fiction Writing, Hambidge Center for the Creative Arts, 1991; Oxford College Professor of the Year Awards, 1994, 1996. Memberships: National Council of Teachers of English; Poetry Atlanta; Poetry Society of America; Southeast Modern Language Association. Address: c/o Department of English, Oxford College of Emory University, Oxford, GA 30267, USA.

CARPENTER William, b. 31 Oct 1940. Writer; Teacher. 2 sons. Education: BA, Dartmouth College, 1962; PhD, University of Minnesota, 1969. Appointments: Assistant Professor, University of Chicago, Illinois, 1967-72; Faculty Member, College of the Atlantic, 1972-. Publications: The Hours of Morning; Rain; Speaking Fire At Stones; A Keeper of Sheep. Contributions to: American Poetry Review; Poetry; New England Review. Honours: Associated Writing Programs Award; National Endowment for the Arts Fellowship; Samuel Frency Morse Prize. Literary Agent: Alison Bond. Address: Box 1297, Stockton Springs, ME 04981, USA.

CARR Rosemary Sally, b. 5 Feb 1948, Runcorn, Cheshire, England. English Teacher. m. Michael Carr, 15 Aug 1970, 1 son, 1 daughter. Education: BA Hons, English and American Literature, University of Kent, 1969; Dip Ed, University of Bath, 1970. Appointment: English Teacher, 1970-74, 1982-84. Contributions to: Poetry Review; London Magazine; Agenda; Honest Ulsterman; New Welsh Review; Poetry Durham; The Rialto; Stand. Memberships: Poetry Society; Friends of Arvon. Address: Glebe House, Grittleton, Chippenham, Wilts SN14 6AP, England.

CARRIER Warren (Pendleton), b. 3 July 1918, Cheviot, Ohio, USA. University Chancellor (retired); Writer; Poet. m. (1) Marjorie J Regan, 3 Apr 1947, dec, 1 son, (2) Judy L Hall, 14 June 1973, 1 son.

Education: Wabash College, 1938-40; AB, Miami University, Oxford, Ohio, 1942; MA, Harvard University, 1948; PhD, Occidental College, 1962. Appointments: Founder-Editor, Quarterly Review of Literature, 1943-44; Associate Editor, Western Review, 1949-51; Assistant Professor, University of Iowa, 1949-52; Associate Professor, Bard College, 1953-57; Faculty, Bennington College, 1955-58; Visiting Professor, Sweet Briar College, 1958-60; Professor, Deep Springs College, California, 1960-62; Portland State University, Oregon, 1962-64; Professor, Chairman, Department of English, University of Montana, 1964-68; Associate Dean, Professor of English and Comparative Literature, Chairman, Department of Comparative Literature, Livingston College, Rutgers University, 1968-69; Dean, College of Arts and Letters, San Diego State University, 1969-72; Vice-President, Academic Affairs, University of Bridgeport, Connecticut, 1972-75; Chancellor, University of Wisconsin, Platteville, 1975-82. Publications include: Reading Modern Poetry, co-editor, 1955, 2nd edition, 1968; Bay Of The Damned, 1957; Toward Montebello, 1966; Leave Your Sugar For The Cold Morning, 1977; Guide To World Literature, editor, 1980; Literature From The World, co-editor, 1981; The Diver, 1986; Death Of A Chancellor, 1986; An Honorable Spy, 1992; Murder At The Strawberry Festival, 1993. Contributions to: Periodicals. Honours: Phi Beta Kappa, 1942; Award for Poetry, National Foundation for the Arts, 1971; Collady Prize for Poetry, 1986. Address: 69 Colony Park Circle, Galveston, TX 77551, USA.

CARROLL Paul (Donnelly Michael), b. 15 July 1927, Chicago, Illinois, USA. Professor of English; Poet; Writer. m. Maryrose Carroll, June 1979, 1 son. Education: MA, University of Chicago, 1952. Appointments: Poetry Editor, Chicago Review, 1957-59; Editor, Big Table Magazine, 1959-61, Big Table Books, Follett Publishing Company, 1966-71; Visiting Poet and Professor, University of Iowa, 1966-67; Professor of English, University of Illinois, 1968-. Publications: Edward Dahlberg Reader, editor, 1966; The Young American Poets, 1968; The Luke Poets, 1971; New And Selected Poems, 1978; The Garden Of Earthly Delights, 1986; Poems, 1950-1990, 1990. Contributions to: Various periodicals. Address: 1682 North Ada Street, Chicago, IL 60622, USA.

CARRUTH Hayden, b. 3 Aug 1921, Waterbury, Connecticut, USA. Poet; Writer; Professor. m. (1) Sara Anderson, 14 Mar 1943, 1 daughter, (2) Eleanor Ray, 29 Nov 1952, (3) Rosie Marie Dorn, 28 Oct 1961, 1 son, (4) Joe-Anne McLaughlin, 29 Dec 1989. Education: AB, University of North Carolina,1943; MA, University of Chicago, 1948. Appointments: Editor-in-Chief, Poetry Magazine, 1949-50; Associate Editor, University of Chicago Press, 1950-51; Project Administrator, Intercultural Publications Inc, New York City, 1952-53; Poet-in-Residence, Johnson State College, Vermont, 1972-74; Adjunct Professor, University of Vermont, 1975-78; Poetry Editor, Harper's Magazine, 1977-83; Professor, Syracuse University, 1979-85; Professor, Bucknell University, 1985-86; Professor, 1986-91, Professor Emeritus, 1991-, Syracuse University. Publications: Poetry: The Crow and the Heart, 1946-59, 1959; In Memorium: G V C, 1960; Journey to a Known Place, 1961; The Norfolk Poems: 1 June to 1 September 1961, 1962; North Winter, 1964; Nothing for Tigers: Poems, 1959-64, 1965; Contra Mortem, 1967; For You, 1970; The Clay Hill Anthology, 1970; From Snow and Rock, From Chaos: Poems, 1965-72, 1973; Dark World, 1974; The Bloomingdale Papers, 1975; Loneliness: An Outburst of Hexasyllables, 1976; Aura, 1977; Brothers, I Love You All, 1978; Almanach du Printemps Vivarois, 1979; The Mythology of Dark and Lights, 1982; The Sleeping Beauty, 1983, revised edition, 1990; If You Call This Cry a Song, 1983; Asphalt Georgics, 1985; Lighter Than Air Craft, 1985; The Oldest Killed Lake in North America, 1995; Mother, 1985; The Selected Poetry of Hayden Carruth, 1986; Sonnets, 1989; Tell Me Again How the White Heron Rises and Flies Across the Nacreous River at Twilight Toward the Distant Islands, 1989; Collected Shorter Poems, 1946-91, 1992; Collected Longer Poems, 1994. Other: Appendix A, novel, 1963; After The Stranger: Imaginary Dialogues with Camus, 1964; Working Papers: Selected Essays and Reviews, 1984; Sitting In: Selected Writings on Jazz, Blues and related topics, 1986; Editor: A New Directions Reader (with James Laughlin), 1964; The Voice That is Great Within Us: American Poetry of the Twentieth Century, 1970; The Bird/Poem Book: Poems on the Wild Birds of North America, 1970. Contributions to: Various periodicals. Honours: Bess Hokin Prize, 1954; Vachel Lindsay Prize, 1956; Levinson Prize, 1958; Harriet Monroe Poetry Prize, 1960; Bollingen Foundation Fellowship, 1962; Helen Bullis Award, 1962; Carl Sandburg Award, 1963; Emily Clark Balch Prize, 1964; Eunice Tietjens Memorial Prize, 1964; Guggenheim Fellowships, 1965, 1979; Morton Dauwen Zabel Prize,

1967; National Endowment for the Humanities Fellowship, 1967; Governor's Medal, Vermont, 1974; Shelley Memorial Award, 1978; Lenore Marshall Poetry Prize, 1978; Whiting Writers Award, 1986; National Endowment for the Arts Senior Fellowship, 1988; Ruth Lilly Poetry Prize, 1990; National Book Critics Circle Award in Poetry, 1993. Address: RR1, Box 128, Munnsville, NY 13409, USA.

CARSON Ciaran, b. 9 Oct 1948, Belfast, Ireland. Arts Administrator. m. Deidre Shannon, 16 Oct 1982, 2 sons, 1 daughter. Education: BA, Queens University, Belfast. Appointments: Traditional Arts Officer, Arts Council of Northern Ireland, 1975-. Publications: The New Estate; The Irish For No; Belfast Confetti. Contributions to: Times Literary Supplement; New Yorker; Irish Review; Honest Ulsterman; London Review of Books. Honours: Gregory Award; Alice Hunt Bartlett Award; Irish Times/Her Lingus Award. Address: Arts Council of Northern Ireland, 181A Stranmillis Road, Belfast BT9 5DU, Ireland.

CARSON Timotheu H, b. 8 June 1933, Little Rock, Arkansas, USA. Instructor. m. Lillian B Carson, 21 Dec 1957, 1 son. Education: BA, Theology, English, French, German, Butler University, Indianapolis, Indiana; MA, English, French, German, Indianapolis University, Indiana Universitites, Purdue, Sorbonne. Appointments: Indianapolis Public Schools, 1961-72; English, French, German, Russian & Spanish Teacher in High School, St Louis Christian College, 1972-73; Taught Messianic Prophets, Spanish for Missionaries, Evangelism in Multi-Ethnic Society, Jennings School System, Jennings, Missouri, 1972-76. Publications: Selected Poetry of T H Carson, 1994; Trnlflint, 1993; Echoes of Dark Heartbeats, 1994; Warbook of the Lamb, 1994; Shepherd's Calendar of the Royal Bard, 1994. Contributions to: Argus of St Louis, Missouri; Butler University Manuscript; Iliad Press; American Poetry Society; Amherst Society; Sparrowgrass; National Library of Poetry; International Society. Honours: Editor's Choice Award, 1994; Presidential Award, 1994, 1995, 1996; National Poetry Registry Citation; Honorable Mention, Sparrowgrass Publishers; Letters of Acknowledgements from Her Majesty Elizabeth II, 1994-95 and President Clinton. Memberships: National Poetry Registry: Sterling Heights, Michigan; National Authors Registry; Symulto Publishers of Chicago. Address: 2020 West Farwell, Box 502, Chicago, IL 60645, USA.

CARTER Cassandra June, b. 10 June 1945, Doncaster, England. Scriptwriter; Editor. m. Colin Vancad, 31 July 1975, dec. Education: BA, University of Queensland, Australia, 1967; MA, Bryn Manor College, 1969; Fulbright Scholar, 1967-69. Contributions to: Maker; Kindred Spirits Quarterly; Moonstone; Age; Australian. Honour: University of Queensland Poetry Prize. Membership: Australian Writers Guild. Address: 12 Diamond Street, East Preston, Victoria 3072, Australia.

CARTER Martin (Wylde), b. 7 June 1927, Georgetown, British Guiana. Politician; Poet; Senior Research Fellow. Education: Queens College, Georgetown. Appointments: Chief Information Officer, Booker Group of Companies, 1959-66; United Nations Representative, 1966-67, Minister of Information, 1967-71, Republic of Guyana; Lecturer, Essex University, England, 1975-76; Writer-in-Residence, 1977-81, Senior Research Fellow, 1981-, University of Guyana. Publications: Poetry: The Hill Of Fire Glows, 1951; To A Dead Slave, 1951; The Kind Eagle, 1952; The Hidden Man, 1952; Returning, 1953; Poems Of Resistance From British Guiana, 1954; Poems Of Succession, 1977; Poems Of Affinity, 1978-80, 1980; Selected Poems, 1989; Other: New World: Guyana Independence Issue, editor, 1966; Man And Making - Victim And Vehicle, 1971; Creation: Works Of Art, 1977. Contributions to: Various anthologies and periodicals. Address: c/o New Beacon Books, 76 Stroud Green Road, London N4 3EN, England.

CARTER Mavis, b. 9 Mar 1939, London, England. Teacher. m. Edwin Carter, 3 sons, 3 daughters, 2 foster daughters. Education: Digby Stuart Training College, 1957-59. Publication: Seasonal Change. Contributions to: Distaff; Fatchance; Froghore Papers; Orbis; Outposts; Poetry Nottingham; Smiths Knoll; Thursdays; Westwords; Hepworth, A Celebration, anthology; Chayns, a Cornish Anthology. Memberships: Arvon Centres Limited; Taliesin Trust. Address: West Barn, Tarlton, Cirencester, Gloucestershire GL7 6PA, England.

CASE Angelo, b. 16 Dec 1936, Locarno, Switzerland. Elementary School Teacher. m. Elena Uehlinger Pianista, 20 Oct 1962. Education: Teaching Certificate 1955, Teacher Training College, Locarno. Publications: Books of Poetry: Il Silos, 1960; I Compagni Del

Cribbio, 1965; Le Precarie Certezze, 1976; Die Rote Piazza, 1976; Al Dunque, 1986. Contributions to: Rivista Cenobio; Rivista La Scuola; Rivista Svizzera Italians; Almanacco Valmaggese; Daily: Eco Di Locarno; Giornale Del Popolo; Weekly: Azione; Cooperazione; Radio Della Svizzera Italiana (Monte Ceneri). Honours: Premio Schiller due volte, 1966, 1976. Address: Via San Quirico 11, 6648 Minusio (Ticino), CH, Switzerland.

CASEY Michael, b. 1947, Lowell, Massachusetts, USA. Civil Servant; Poet; Editor. m. Kathleen Davey, 26 July 1975. Education: BS, Lowell Technological Institute, 1968; MA, State University of New York at Buffalo, 1973. Appointments: Editorial Advisor, Alice James Press, Cambridge, Massachusetts, 1972-; Civil Servant, 1974. Publications: Obscenities, 1972; On Scales, 1972; My Youngest That Tall, 1972; My Brother-in-Law and Me, 1974; The Company Pool, 1976. Contributions to: New York Times; Nation; Quarterly; Rolling Stone; Araet. Honour: Younger Poet Award, Yale University, 1972. Address: c/o Ashod Press, PO Box 1147, Madison Square Station, New York, NY 10159, USA.

CASHET Thomas. See: **BIANCHI Herman.**

CASTRO Jan Garden, b. 8 June 1945, St Louis, Missouri, USA. Author; Arts Consultant. Education: BA English, University of Wisconsin, 1967; Publishing Certificate, Radcliffe College, 1967; MAT, Washington University, St Louis, 1974; MA, 1994. Appointments: Life Certificate Teacher, Secondary English, Speech, Drama & Social Studies, Missouri; Teacher, Writer, St Louis, 1970-; Director, Big River Association, St Louis, 1975-85; Lecturer, Lindenwood College, 1980-; Co-Founder, Director, Duff's Poetry Series, St Louis, 1975-81; Founder, Director, River Styx PM Series, St Louis, 1981-83; Arts Consultant, Harris-Stowe State College, 1986-87. Publications: Contributing Author: San Francisco Review Books, 1982-85; American Book Review, 1990-; Missouri Review, 1991; Newsletters, 1993; Tampa Review, 1994-; The National American Poetry Review. Author: Mandala of the Five Senses, 1975; The Art and Life of Georgia O'Keeffe, 1985. Editor: River Styx Magazine, 1975-86; Co-editor: Margaret Atwood: Vision and Forms, 1988; TV host and Co-producer, The Writers Circle, Double Helix, St Louis, 1987-89. Honours: Member, University City Arts and Letters Commission, Missouri, 1983-84; Recipient, Arts and Letters Award, St Louis Magazine, 1985; Editor's Award and Editor during GE Younger Writer's Award to River Styx Magazine; Coordinating Council for Literary Magazines, 1986; Arts Award Mandrake Society Charity Ball, 1988; Leadership Award, YWCA St Louis, 1988; NEH Fellow, UCLA, 1988; Johns Hopkins University, 1990; Fellow, Camargo Foundation Fall, 1996; Member, MLA, Margaret Atwood Society (Founder). Address: Home: 7420 Cornell Avenue, Saint Louis, MO 63130-2914, USA; Office: Lindenwood College, Saint Charles, MO 63301, USA.

CASTRO Michael, b. 28 July 1945, New York, New York, USA. Educator. m. Adelia Parker, 2 sons, 1 daughter. Education: BA cum laude, English, State University of New York at Buffalo, 1967; MA, American Literature, 1971, PhD, English, 1981, Washington University at St Louis. Appointments: Senior and Founding Editor, River Styx Magazine, 1975-; Assistant Professor, 1980-86, Associate Professor, 1987-92, Professor of Humanities, 1992-, Lindenwood College, St Charles, Missouri; Director, River Styx at Duffs Poetry Series, 1986-; Host, Poetry Beat Radio Programme, 1989-. Publications: The Kokopilau Cycle, 1975; Ghost Hiways and Other Homes, 1976; Cracks, 1977, US edition, 1991. Contributions to: Edge; World's Edge, Japan; Sagarin Review; Tampa Review; Mississippi Valley Review; Printed Matter, Japan; Not a Single Answer; Literati Internazionale; Visions; Shadows Project; River Styx; Noctiluca. Honour: 1st Prize for Poetry, Visions Magazine/Art Barn of Washington DC, 1987. Address: LCIE, Lindenwood College, 209 North Kingshighway, St Charles, MO 63301, USA.

CASTRO SOTOMAYOR Maria Cristina, b. 4 Aug 1931, Rancagua, Chile. Teacher in English. Education: Bachiller Letras Universidad de Chile, 1951; Professor Normalista Urbana, 1962. Appointments: Secretary and Accountant, PROTINFA, 1952-55; Elementary School Teacher, 1958-66; Teacher in English Nght High School, 1958-71; Agriculture School, 1966-79; Industrial School, 1961-68; High School for Boys, 1958-80; Own Private Academy for Adults, 1980-92; Only English. Publications: Regreso a la Esperanza, 1952; Poemas, 1989; En Familia, 1992; Epistolario, 1993. Contributions to: Her works had been published in newspapers, magazines, journals, in Chile, Guatemala, Argentina, Uruguay, Spain,

Germany, India. Honours: Children's International Year, 1979; Honour Member, Ruben Dario Institute, Stgo, 1990; Electrotype Plate Chilean Teacher's School, 1990, 1996; Diploma Major, 1994; Distinction, Ines Oliveira de Núnez, 1994, 1995, 1996. Memberships: Co-founder ARIEL, 1952-73; Director of publications of Retired Teachers from 1988; Member of ALIRE V Region, Cultural Corporation of the Major in San Felipe. Address: Casilla 308, San Felipe, Aconcagua, Chile.

CATES Edward William, b. 11 Mar 1952, New Hampshire, USA. Social Worker. Education: BA, Boston University, 1974. Appointments: Coordinator, Boston Poetry Film Festival, 1973-77; Coordinator, First Night Poetry Event, 1979. Publications: Geopolitics; Remember Your Dreams; The Gypsy's Bible: Selected Poems of John Tuwim, translated from Polish. Contributions to: Small Moon; Door no 3; Noctiluca; Miscellaneous; Boston Literary Review; Modularist Review; Moody Street Review; Words; Imagine. Honour: Massachusetts Artist Foundation Fellowship. Membership: New England Poetry Club. Address: 72 Moreland Street, 1st Floor, Somerville, MA 02145, USA.

CAULFIELD Lotti Lota Carlotta, b. 16 Jan 1953, Havana, Cuba. Editor; Publisher. 1 son. Education: MA, University of Havana, 1979; MA, San Francisco State University, 1986; PhD, Tulane University, 1991. Appointments: Editor, Publisher, El Gato Tuerto, 1984-; Lecturer, San Francisco State University, California, 1984-86; Lecturer, Tulane University, New Orleans, Louisiana, 1988-. Publications: Fanaim; Oscuridad Divine; Sometimes I Call Myself Childhood; El Tiempo Es Una Mujer Que Espera; 34th Street and Other Poems; Angel Dust. Contributions to: Visions; Haight Ashbury Literary Journal; Poetry San Francisco; Lyra; Mairena; Termino Magazine; La Papirola; Codice; El Faro; Le Nuez; Linden Lane Magazine. Honours: Honourable Mention, Mairena International Poetry Competition; Ultimo Novecento International Prize; Honourable Mention, La Torre do Calafuria; Cintas Fellowship. Memberships: Internazionale Accademia di Lettura, Pisa; Libera Accademia Galileo Galilei; Modern Language Association; PEN; American Association of Teachers of Spanish and Portuguese. Address: Box 5028, Tulane University Station, New Orleans, LA 70118, USA.

CAUNT Lorna Margaret, b. 30 Nov 1927. Teacher; Secretary; Laboratory Technician; Housewife. m. Tony Caunt, 27 Feb 1954, 2 sons, 1 daughter. Education: BSc (London) Zoology, 1949. Publications: Keeping Company, 1989; No Sense of Grandeur, 1991; No One About, 1993. Contributions to: Outposts; Envoi; Weyfarers; Iota; Staple; Pause; First Time; Doors; Poetry Nottingham; Poet's England; The Countryman; Spokes; Vision On (Ver); Ver Poets' Voices; Arcadian; Psychopoetica; Success Magazine. Honours: 2nd prize, Arts Council/David bookshops, 1985, 1987, 1988; Ver Poets Internal Competitions, 1988 twice, 1990,1991, 1992 twice; Various mentions. Memberships: Ver Poets; Welwyn Garden City Literary Society; Ware Poetry Reading Group. Address: 1 Templewood, Welwyn Garden City, Hertfordshire AL8 7HT, England.

CAUSLEY Charles, b. 24 Aug 1917, Launceston, Cornwall, England. Appointment: Teacher in Cornwall, 1947-76. Publications include: Survivor's Leave, 1953; Union Street, 1957; Penguin Modern Poets 3, 1962; Underneath Underneath The Water, 1968; Six Women, 1974; Collected Poems 1951-75, 1975; Secret Destinations, 1984; 21 Poems, 1986; A Field of Vision, 1988; Secret Destinations, 1989; The Young Man of Cury, 1991; Bring in the Holly, 1992; Collected Poems, 1992; Collected Poems for Children, 1996; Penguin Modern Poets 6, 1996; Collected Poems 1951-9, 1997. Honours: Queen's Gold Medal for Poetry, 1967; Commander of the Order of the British Empire, 1986; Ingersoll/TS Eliot Award, USA, 1990. Address: 2 Cyprus Well, Launceston, Cornwall PL15 8BT, England.

CAWS Ian, b. 19 Mar 1945, Bramshott, England. Local Government Officer. m. Hilary Walsh, 20 June 1970, 3 sons, 2 daughters. Education: Churcher's College, Petersfield, 1957-64; Certificate in Social Work, 1970, Certificate for Social Workers with the Deaf, 1973, North Western Polytechnic. Appointments: Social Worker, 1970-74; Senior Social Worker, 1975-86; County Team Leader, 1986-91; Arts Development Officer, 1991-. Publications: Looking for Bonfires, 1975; Bruised Madonna, 1979; Boy With a Kite, 1981; The Ragman Totts, 1990; Chamomile, 1994; The Feast of Fools, 1994. Contributions to: Critical Quarterly; Dalhousie Review; Encounter; Honest Ulsterman; Listener; Literary Review; London Magazine; Malahat Review; Month; New Edinburgh Review; New Statesman; Observer; Poetry Australia; Poetry Review; Scotsman; Spectator; Stand; Tablet; Times Literary Supplement; Tribune; Wascana Review.

Honours: Eric Gregory Award, 1973; Southern Arts Literature Bursary, 1977; Sussex Poet of the Year, 1985; National Poetry Competition, Prizewinner, 1987, 2nd Prize, 1988; Cheltenham Festival Poetry Competition, 3rd Prize, 1987; Poetry Book Society Recommendation, The Ragman Totts, 1990. Membership: Poetry Society. Address: 9 Tennyson Avenue, Rustington, West Sussex BN16 2PB, England.

CAYLEY John Howland, b. Ottawa, Ontario, Canada. Publisher; Bookseller. 1 son, 2 daughters. Education: American School in London, 1969-72; Bedales School, Hampshire, 1972-74; BA (Hons) Oriental Studies (Chinese) 1978, Durham University. Appointments: Research Associate, University of Newcastle Upon Tyne, 1984-86; Curator, British Library, Oriental Collections, Chinese Section, 1986-88; Han-Shang Tang Ltd (Specialist Booksellers) & Bamboo Publishing Ltd, 1988-; Publisher, Editor, Founder, The Wellsweep Press, specialising in translation from Chinese Literature, especially poetry, 1988-. Publications: Statements of the New Chinese Poetry of Duoduo, co-translator, 1989, revised and enlarged as: Looking Out From Death: From the Cultural Revolution to Tiananmen Square, 1989; Wine-Flying: A Chinese Quatrain, translator and adaptor, 1989; Gu Cheng, Selected Poems: An Authorized Translation, co-translator, 1990; Mirror and Pool: Translation from the Chinese, co-translator, 1991; Under It All, poetry, 1993; An Essay on the Golden Lion, poetry, 1995; Ink Bamboo, poems, 1996; Various Electronic Publications. Contributions to: Agenda; Patched Fool; Haiku Quarterly; Poetry Durham; Numbers; Outposts Poetry Quarterly; New Statesman; Renditions, Hong Kong; PEN International; Eonta; Times Literary Supplement; Paideuma; Independent; Sunk Island Review; The Guardian; Visible Language. Address: Wellsweep Press, 1 Grove End House, 150 Highgate Road, London NW5 1PD, England.

CECIL Richard, b. 14 Mar 1944, Baltimore, Maryland, USA. Poet. m. Maura Stanton, 10 Apr 1971. Education: BA, University of Maryland, 1966; MA, University of Iowa, 1972; MFA, Indiana University, 1985. Appointments: Visiting Assistant Professor, Lockham University, 1986-87; Visiting Assistant Professor, 1987-88, Assistant Professor, 1989-, Indiana University, Bloomington; Assistant Professor, Rhodes College, 1988-89. Publications: Einstein's Brain, 1986; Alcatraz, 1992. Contributions to: Poetry; American Poetry Review; Southern Review; Crazy Horse; Virginia Quarterly Review; Chelsea; Louisville Review; Georgia Review; Ohio Review; New England Review; Antioch Review; Sycamore Review; Carolina Quarterly. Honour: Verna Emory Prize. Membership: Associated Writing Programs. Address: Department of English, Indiana University, Bloomington, IN 47405, USA.

CÉCILE. See: SMITH Cecile Musson.

CEDERING Siv, b. 5 Feb 1939, Sweden. Poet; Novelist; Children's Book Writer; Illustrator; Artist. m. David Swickard, 11 Sept 1983, 1 son, 2 daughters. Appointments: Visiting Writer, University of Pittsburgh, 1987; Visiting Writer, Interlochen Arts Academy, 1983; Visiting Writer, University of Massachusetts, 1973. Publications: Oxen; The Blue Horse; Cup of Cold Water; Mother Is; Letters From the Island. Contributions to: Harpers; Ms; Science; New Republic; New York Times; Paris Review; Partisan Review; Georgia Review; Fiction International; Shenandoah; Confrontation. Honours: New York Foundation Fellowship; Best Book of the Year Award; Rhysling Award. Memberships: Poetry Society of America; CCLM; American PEN; Swedish Writers Union. Address: Box 800, Amagansett, NY 11930, USA.

CELA Camilo José, b. 11 May 1916, Iria Flavia, La Coruna, Spain. Writer; Poet. m. (1) Maria del Rosario Conde Picavea, 12 Mar 1944, 1 son, (2) Marina Castano, 1991. Education: University of Madrid, 1933-36, 1939-43. Publications: Fiction: La Familia de Pascual Duarte, 1942, English translation as Pascual Duarte's Family, 1946; Pabellon de reposo, 1943, English translation as Rest Home, 1961; Nuevas andanzas y desventuras de Lazarillo de Tormes, 1944; Caminos inciertos: La colmena, 1951, English translation as The Hive, 1953; Santa Balbina 37: Gas en cada piso, 1952; Timoteo, el incomprendido, 1952; Mrs Caldwell habla con su hijo, English translation as Mrs Caldwell Speaks to Her Son, 1968; Café de artistas, 1955; Historias de Venezuela: La catira, 1955; Tobogan de hambrientos, 1962; Visperas, festividad y octava de San Camilo del ano 1936 en Madrid, 1969; Oficio de tinieblas 5, o, Novela de tesis escrita para ser cantada por un coro de enfermos, 1973; Mazurca para dos muertos, 1983; Cristo versus Arizona, 1988; Also many volumes of stories. Poetry: Pisando la dudosa luz del dia, 1945; Reloj de

Sangre, 1989. Non-Fiction: Diccionario Secreto, 2 volumes, 1968, 1971; Enciclopedia del Erotismo, 1976-77; Memorias, entendimientos y voluntades, memoirs, 1993. Other: Volumes of essays and travel books. Honours: Premio de la critica, 1955; Spanish National Prize for Literature, 1984; Nobel Prize for Literature, 1989; Planeta Prize, 1994. Membership: Real Academia Espanola, 1957. Address: c/o Agencia Literaria Carmen Balcells, Diagonal 580, 08021 Barcelona, Spain.

CERVANTES James V, b. 2 Apr 1941, Houston, Texas, USA. Professor of English. 3 daughters. Education: BA, English, Writing, University of Washington, 1972; MFA, Poetry, University of Iowa, 1974. Appointments: Instructor in Humanities, Community College of Vermont, 1974-77; Lecturer in Creative Writing, Arizona State University, 1978-81; Instructor in English, Northern Arizona University, 1985-88; Assistant Professor of Learning Skills and English, California State University at Sacramento, 1988-92; Professor of English, Mesa Community College, Mesa, Arizona, 1992-. Publications: The Fires in Oil Drums, 1980; The Year is Approaching Snow, 1981; The Headlong Future, 1990. Contributions to: Southwest; Pacific Review; Hayden's Ferry Review; Telescope; Northwest Review; Nebraska Review; Seattle Review; Cincinnati Poetry Review; Michigan Quarterly Review; Western Humanities Review; Christian Science Monitor; Tumblewords: Writers Reading the West; Blue Mesa Review; Lucid Stone; Gruene Street; Thin Air; Others. Honours: Poetry Fellowship, Arizona Commission on the Arts, 1981; The Capricorn Award, 1987. Memberships: Modern Language Association; CCCC; American Studies Association; Associated Writing Programs; The Writer's Voice. Address: 511 N MacDonald, Mesa, AZ 85201, USA.

CHAARITHRA. See: VIJAY BHANU A K.

CHABEREK Edward John (Makyo), b. Torrington, Connecticut, USA. Writer. m. Guna Kupcs, 29 Mar 1976. Education: BA cum laude, Philosophy, University of Connecticut, 1974. Appointments: Reporter: Hartford Courant; Waterbury Republican; Litchfield Enquirer; Litchfield County Times. Contributions to: Acumen; Poetry Nottingham; Bitterroot; Galley Sail; Plainsongs; Cornfield Review; Asylum. Address: 329 East Front Street, No C-3, Missoula, MT 59802, USA.

CHAFFIN Randall. See: CHAFFIN-KASH Lillie D.

CHAFFIN-KASH Lillie D, (Lila Day, Randall Chaffin), b. 1 Feb 1925, Varney, Kentucky, USA. Teacher; Librarian. 1 son. Education: BA, 1952; MA, 1971; LHD, 1972. Appointments: Teacher, 1947-67; Librarian, 1968-78. Publications: Lines and Paints; First Notes; Eighth Day 13th Moon; Appalachian History; Bear Weather. Contributions to: New York Times; Christian Science Monitor; Courier Journal; Who Speaks for Appalachia. Honours: Child Study Association Award; Alice Lloyd Award. Memberships: Poetry Society of America; Kentucky State Poetry Society; Florida State Poetry Association/Childrens Book Writers; American PEN Women. Address: 4270 8th Street Road, Huntington, WV 25701, USA.

CHALLIS Chris, b. 11 Feb 1952, Essex, England. Writer; Lecturer. Education: BA (Hons), Class II, 1973, MA (Distinction), 1974, PhD, 1979, Leicester University. Appointments: Editor, Luciad, Leicester University; Judge, numerous poetry competitions; Editor, Jewry Wall Irregulars magazine. Publications: Highfields Landscape, 1979; William of Cloudslee, 1980; The Wild Thing Went From Side To Side, 1984; Editor, Common Ground anthologies, 1984, A Sense of Place, 1986, Word Scan, 1990, others; Jack Kerouac, Charles Bukowski and Me, 1984, 2nd edition, 1987; Four Stout Shoes, 1988; A Little Earth for Charity, 1992; 20 braodsheets in Phoenix Broadsheet Series; The Leicester Poems, 1992; Together in Eternity, 1993-94; Meaning Light, excerpted and full version. Contributions to: Omens; Luciad; Southwest Review; Poetry LUFBRA; Palantir; Ludd's Mill; Folio International; Global Tapestry; Iota; Poetry Nottingham; Leicester CND News; Leicester Haymarket Theatre Programmes; Zenos; Literary Review; Wire; The Face; Daily Telegraph; Foreword; BSH magazine's Taleteller Series; Anthologies including: Poet's England, 1993; Write Here, 1993; Valleys of Thought, 1994. Honours: Work published in anthologies, USA, Belgium, Denmark, Germany; Winner, Lancaster Literature Festival, 1985; Judge, Miniwords Competition, 1995; Numerous bursaries, awards and writer's residencies. Membership: East Midlands Arts Association Literature Panel, 1979-84. Address: 65 High Street, Ingatestone, Essex CM4 0AT, England.

CHAMBERLAIN Kent Clair, (Ashlandonian), b. 22 Jan 1943, Abilene, Kansas, USA. Poet; Short Fiction Writer. Education: Short

Fiction Course Writers Digest; Junior Accounting Graduate, One College of Business. Publications: Ship Bound for Where; Slant Lined; Rarely Published; Winter's Bird. Contributions to: Lithian Ashlandonian; Poets Corner; Silk Screen; Beau Coca. Honours: Various. Memberships: President, United Amateur Press Association, 1980-81. Address: 625 Holly Street, Ashland, OR 97520, USA.

CHAMBERLAIN Velma. See: RICHESON C(ena) G(older).

CHAMBERS Alan, b. 6 Sept 1929, Manchester, England. Educator. Education: BA (Admin), MEd, Dip Ed, Manchester University. Appointments: Primary School Teacher, Manchester; Lecturer in Education, Furzedown College; Head of Education, Battersea College, later amalgamated into South Bank Polytechnic. Publications: A Gregarious Creature?, 1988; Hooves and Horns and Music, unpublished, poems for children; Your Voice on My Ear. Contributions to: Outposts; Brentford Poets; Cobweb. Memberships: Poetry Society, London; Wooden Lambs; Founder, Poets at Questors and Mattock Press. Address: Flat L, Mattock Lane, Ealing, London W5 5BG, England.

CHAMBIAL D C, b. 29 Sept 1950, Bajrol, India. Teacher. m. Kanta, 5 Mar 1975, 2 sons. Education: BSc, 1970; BEd, 1971; MA, 1975; MPhil, 1976; PhD, 1994. Appointments: School Teacher, 1971-87; School Lecturer, 1987-89; College Lecturer, 1989-. Publications: Broken Images, 1983; Cargoes of Bleeding Hearts, 1984; Poetry of Himachal, 1985; Perceptions, 1986; S A Cobweb of Words, 1990. Contributions to: Tribune; Indian Express; Poet; Poetry; Poetry Time; Indian Literature; JIWE; Quest; Bharat Protiva; Commonwealth Quarterly; Byword; Poeterit. Honours: Trans-Word Poetry Expo Medal, 1987; 7th Poetry Day Australia Medal, 1988; Poetry Day Australia, 1991-92; Intern Writer of Excellence Certificate, 1992; Michael Madhusudan Academy Award, 1995. Memberships: Poetry Society of America; Poetry Society of India; PMLA; Rachna. Address: Chambial Niwas, Maranda 176 102, India.

CHAMIEL Haim Itzchak (Hai Chamiel Ben Efraim), b. 18 Jan 1917, Poland. Educator; Poet; Publisher; Editor; Author; Writer. m. Hava, 12 Sept 1944, 2 sons, 1 daughter. Education: MA, Hebrew University 1950; PhD, 1953; Bar Ilan University, 1956, 1980. Appointments: Hebrew Teacher, Yavne School, Poland, 1936-37; Headmaster, Hebrew School; Youth Leader, 1939-44; Publisher, Jersusalem, 1945-50; Director General, Jewish Agency, 1950-80; Lecturer, Bar Han University, 1956-58; Senior Lecturer, 1968. Publications: Avivim; Meofek; Moked; Neroth; Benofei; Strains of Homage and Delight; Unto the Heart of My Heaven; As Long As I Have Being; But a Glimmer of Light. Contributions to: Beith Mikra; Sinai; Hebeitimes. Honours: Klausner Prize; Tel Aviv Municipality Prize; Hebrew University Prize; Shapira Prize. Memberships: ACUM; World Hebrew Universities; Ramath Shapira Education Centre; International Academy of Poets. Address: 7 Fichman Street, Jerusalem 92 584, Israel.

CHAMPAGNE Lenora Louise, b. 13 Dec 1951, Louisiana, USA. Theatre Artist. m. Robert C Lyons, 17 Aug 1991, 1 daughter. Education: BA, English, Louisiana State University, 1972; MA, Drama, 1975, PhD, Performance Studies, 1980, New York University. Appointments: Faculty, Gallatin School of Individualized Study, New York University, 1981-; Visiting Artist, Trinity College, 1985-89; Faculty, State University of New York, Purchase, 1990-95. Publication: Editor and Contributor, Out From Under: Texts by Women Performance Artists, 1990. Contributions to: Heresies; Benzene; Between C & D; Poetry Project Newsletter; Blatant Artifice; Iowa Review. Honour: Native Voice Visions Prize, Louisiana State University, Baton Rouge, 1993. Memberships: New Dramatists, 1993-; Dramatists Guild. Address: 3 Horatio Street, New York, NY 10014, USA.

CHAN Stephen, b. 11 May 1949, Auckland, New Zealand. Dean and Professor in International Relations and Ethics; Writer; Poet. Education: BA, 1972, MA, 1975, University of Auckland; MA, Kings College, London, 1977; PhD, University of Kent, Canterbury, 1992. Appointments: International Civil Servant, Commonwealth Secretariat, 1977-83; Lecturer in International Relations, University of Zambia, 1983-85; Visiting Lecturer in International Relations, Victoria University of Wellington, 1986; Faculty, University of Kent, 1987-96; Visiting Professor, Graduate Institute of International Studies, Geneva, 1991, University of Tampere, 1994-95; Visiting Lecturer, University of Natal, 1992; Professor in International Relations and Ethics, Head of

International Studies, Dean of Humanities, Nottingham Trent University, 1996-. Publications: Scholarly: The Commonwealth Observer Group in Zimbabwe: A Personal Memoir, 1985; Issues in International Relations: A View from Africa, 1987; The Commonwealth in World Politics: A Study of International Action, 1965-85, 1988; Exporting Apartheid: Foreign Policies in Southern Africa, 1978-1988, 1990; Social Development in Africa Today: Some Radical Proposals, 1991; Kaunda and Southern Africa: Image and Reality in Foreign Policy, 1991; Twelve Years of Commonwealth Diplomatic History: Commonwealth Summit Meetings, 1979-1991, 1992; Mediation in Southern Africa (editor with Vivienne Jabri), 1993; Renegade States: The Foreign Policies of Revolutionary States (editor with Andrew Williams), 1994; Towards a Multicultural Roshomon Paradigm in International Relations, 1996; Portuguese Foreign Policy in Southern Africa (with Moises Venancio), 1996; Snarling at Each Other: Students and Masters in International Relations (editor with Jarrod Wiener), 1996; Poetry: Postcards from Paradise (with Rupert Glover and Merlene Young), 1971; A Charlatan's Mosaic: New Zealand Universities Literary Yearbook (editor), 1972; Arden's Summer, 1975; Songs of the Maori King, 1986; Crimson Rain, 1991. Honours: Visiting Fellowships; Honorary LittD, WAAC, Istanbul; Honorary Professor, University of Zambia, 1993-95. Address: c/o Faculty of Humanitites, Nottingham Trent University, Nottingham NG11 8NS, England.

CHANCE Jane, (Jane Chance Nitzsche), b. 26 Oct 1945, Missouri, USA. Professor. m. (1) Dennis Carl Nitzsche, June 1966, div, 1967, 1 daughter, (2) Paolo Passaro, 30 April 1981, 2 sons. Education: BA, Purdue University, 1967; AM, 1968, PhD, 1971, University of Illinois. Appointments: Lecturer, 1971-72, Assistant Professor, 1972-73, University of Saskatchewan, Canada; Assistant Professor, 1973-77, Associate Professor, 1977-80, Professor, 1980-, Rice University, Houston, Texas; Honorary Research Fellow, University College, London, England, 1978; Member, Institute for Advanced Study, Princeton, USA, 1988-89; Rockefeller Foundation Resident, Bellagio, Italy, 1988; Visiting Research Fellow, Institute for Advanced Studies in the Humanities, University of Edinburgh, Scotland, 1994; Eccles Fellow, University of Utah Humanities Center, 1994-95. Publications: The Genius Figure in Antiquity and the Middle Ages, 1975; Tolkien's Art: A Mythology for England, 1979; Woman as Hero in Old English Literature, 1985; Christine de Pizan's Letter of Othea to Hector, 1990; The Lord of the Rings: The Mythology of Power, 1992; Studies in Medievalism: The Inklings; The Lord of the Rings; The Mythology of Power; Medieval Mythography: From Roman Africa to the School of Chartres, 1994; The Mythographic Chaucer: The Fabulation of Sexual Poetics, 1995; Gender and Text in the Late Middle Ages, 1996. Contributions to: Ariel; Antigonish Review; Dalhousie Review; Icarus; Kansas Quarterly; The Lyric; Literary Review; Nimrod; New America; Primavera; Quartet; Poetry; Southern Humanities Review; Wascana Review; University Blue. Honours: National Endowment for the Humanities, Guggenheim and many others. Memberships: PEN; Authors' Guild; Elected Member-at-large, Texas Faculty Association, 1995-97. Address: 2306 Wroxton Road, Houston, TX 77005-1538, USA.

CHANDLER Rose Wiley, b. 3 Oct 1921, Kentucky, USA. Teacher; Antique Collector and Dealer; Poet. m. Claude Chandler, 31 May 1942, dec, 2 daughters. Education: Eastern State Teachers College, 1939-40; Music Course, 1959; University of Kentucky, 1962; Writers Digest Writing School, 1989. Appointments: Secretary, Kentucky State Poetry Society, 1969; Secretary and President, SPS, 1970; President, Contest Chairman, 1971; Founder, Johnson County Poetry Society, 1978. Publications: A Gypsy's Delight, 1971; Moonlight Mystique, 1988; Traveling Through Atlanta at Night in the Rain, National Library of Poetry to Publishing in Best Poems, 1996. Contributions to: Numerous. Honours: Golden Poet Award; Prize KSPS Contest; Prize, Ocala Chapter of the National League of American Pen Women, 1995. Published in newspapers, poetry columns, many anthologies. Memberships: International Society of Poetry; The National Library of Poetry. Address: 10962 South West 79th Terrace, Ocala, FL 34476, USA.

CHANDRA SEKHAR K, (Srivatsa), b. 3 Dec 1925, Mysore City, India. Linguist. Education: BSc, 1951, LittD, 1980, University of Arizona, USA. Appointments: Language Teacher, School of International Training, Vermont, USA, 1965; Orientation Teacher, Callison College, Stockton, California, USA (Bangalore, India). Publications: Anthologised in World Poetry in 6 editions, published in Madras, India; Books. Contributions to: Deccan Herald; Bangalore; India; Indian Express; Bangalore; India; Saptagiri; Thirupati Hills;

Andhra, India. Honours: Participaton in World Poetry, Madras, India, 1990; Presentation of English Poetry, widely acclaimed and honoured. Memberships: Vice president, Poetry International Organisation, Banglore, for 25 years. Address: 637, 11th Main Road, HAL 2nd Stage, Indiranagar, Banglaore 560008, India.

CHANDRASEKARAN S, b. 8 Aug 1953, Salem, India. Teacher. m. Maheswari, 27 Apr 1978, 1 son, 1 daughter. Education: BA, English, 1980; BEd, English, 1983; MA, English, 1987. Appointments: Teacher, 1974-95; Warden in Government College Boys Hostel, 1995-. Contributions to: Poet; World Poetry; Metverse Muse; Poems-96; Kamakoti Vani. Honours: 2nd Prize, Poetics Competition, Sri Sankaracharya Swamigal of Kanchi Kamakoti Mutt, 1991. Memberships: Metverse Muse and Tradverse and Friends; Poet. Address: Iswaramurthi Palayam, Via Mangalapuram, Salem District 636202, Tamilnadu, India.

CHAPMAN David Charles, (Charles Davies), b. 15 Apr 1944, Williamsport, Pennsylvania, USA. Maintenance Mechanic. m. Carol Jane Livermore, 23 May 1964, 2 daughters. Education: Lincoln University, 1964-70; Penn College, 1979-81. Appointments: Lead Person, Second Shift Supervisor, 1964-73; Mechanic, 1973-79; Head of Security, 1982-84; Stockroom Attendent, 1984-89; Tester, 1989-91. Publication: Lavander Moments. Contributions to: Grit Publishing Company; American Anthology of Contemporary Poetry. Honour: Golden Poet Award. Address: 1217 Race Street, Williamsport, PA 17701, USA.

CHAPMAN Janice Noreen, b. 25 Dec 1941, Woodward, Oklahoma, USA. m. (1) Donald Plain, div 1968, 1 son, 2 daughters, (2) Donald Cleve Johns, Nov 1968, div, 2 sons, 1 dec, 1 daughter, (3) Leon Sylvan Chapman Jr, 4 Dec 1985, 3 stepsons, 3 stepdaughters. Appointments: Switchboard Operator, Columbus Medical Center Hospital; Taxi Driver; Cashier, Wal Mart 1311 Store, Columbus, Georgia. Contributions to: Various anthologies and other publications including: National Poetry Anthology, 1985; Odessa Poetry Review; Voices in Poetry, 1985; Poems of the Century, 1985; American Poetry Association Anthology, vol 1, 1985, Vol 2, 1986; Lines 'n' Rhymes; The Space Between, 1994; Joys of the Journey, 1995; Impressions, 1995; Echoes from the Silence, 1995; Inspirations, 1995; Best New Poems, 1995; Endless Harmony, 1996; Best Poems of 1996; The Poet's Corner, 1996; Watch for the Ice on the Bridge, 1996; Sound of Poetry, 1996. Honours: Editor's Choice Award, National Library of Poetry, 1995; Nominee, Poet of the Year, International Society of Poets, 1995; Accomplishment of Merit Award, Creative Arts and Sciences, 1995; Nominee, One of Poets of the Year, National Library of Poetry, 1996. Memberships: Distinguished Member, International Society of Poets. Address: 1900 Wellborn Drive, Columbus, GA 31907, USA.

CHAPPELL Fred (Davis), b. 28 May 1936, Canton, North Carolina, USA. University Teacher; Poet; Writer. m. Susan Nicholls, 2 Aug 1959, 1 son. Education: BA, 1961, MA, 1964, Duke University. Appointment: Teacher, University of North Carolina, Greensboro, 1964-. Publications: Poetry: The World Between The Eyes, 1971; River, 1975; The Man Twice Married To Fire, 1977; Bloodfire, 1978; Awakening To Music, 1979; Wind Mountain, 1979; Earthsleep, 1980; Driftlake: A Lieder Cycle, 1981; Midquest, 1981; Castle Tzingal, 1984; Source, 1985; First And Last Words, 1989; C: 100 Poems, 1993; Spring Garden: New And Selected Poems, 1995; Novels: It Is Time, Lord, 1963; The Inkling, 1965; Dagon, 1968; The Gaudy Place, 1972; I Am One Of You Forever, 1985; Brighten The Corner Where You Are, 1989; Farewell, I'm Bound To Leave You, 1996; Short Fiction: Moments Of Light, 1980; More Shapes Than One, 1991; Collection: The Fred Chappell Reader, 1987; Other: Plow Naked: Selected Writings On Poetry, 1993. Honours: Rockefeller Grant, 1967-68; National Institute of Arts and Letters Award, 1968; Prix de Meilleur des Livres Etrangers, Académie Française, 1972; Sir Walter Raleigh Prize, 1972; Roanoke-Chowan Poetry Prizes, 1972, 1975, 1979, 1980, 1985, 1989, 1996; North Carolina Award in Literature, 1980; Bollingen Prize in Poetry, 1985; World Fantasy Awards, 1992, 1994; T S Eliot Prize, Ingersoll Foundation, 1993; Aiken Taylor Award in Poetry, 1996. Literary Agent: Weyr Literary Agency, Brooklyn, New York, USA. Address: 305 Kensington Road, Greensboro, NC 27403, USA.

CHARLES Nicholas J. See: KUSKIN Karla.

CHARLES Tony, b. 4 Apr 1947, Birmingham, England. Writer. 1 son, 1 daughter. Education: Cert Ed (Drama), Bretton Hall, 1969; BA, Open University, 1984. Appointments: Itinerant labourer; Teacher;

Writer-in-Residence, Bishops Castle, 1991; Yeovil, 1992, Barrow-in-Furness, 1993. Publications: The Wonderful Rubbish Tip, 1976; The Bear and Ragged Staff, 1984; Wake, 1992. Contributions to: Acumen; Agenda; Bull; Candelabrum; Cobweb; Country Life; Ecologist; Envoi; Folio International; Foolscap; Interactions; Iron; Issue One; Odyssey; Outposts; Poetry Express; Prospice; Sepia; Spokes; Thursdays; Westwards; Wide Skirt; Others. Memberships: Poetry Society; Friends of Arvon. Address: 33 Lillebonne Close, Wellington, Somerset TA21 9EX, England.

CHARNEY Lena London, b. 26 Jan 1919, Symiatycze, Poland. Administrator; Educator; Poet. m. Roy L Charney, 10 Nov 1955, 1 son. Education: BA, cum laude, Hunter College, New York, 1941; MA, Clark University, Worcester, Massachusetts, 1942; PhD Candidate, Columbia University, New York, 1947-53. Appointments: Millinery Designer, Co-Owner, Sanjour (Millinery) Studio, New York, 1937, 1939-41, and of Lenblac (Millinery), New York, 1938; Co-Owner, Co-Manager, Golden Dawn, bungalow colony, Mohegan Lake, New York, 1939-46; Assistant Editor, Insurance Weekly, 1945-46; Co-manager, 1950-59, Owner/Manager, 1959-, London's Studio Apartments; Teacher, Principal, St Basil's Academy, Garrison, NY, 1968-73; Substitute Teacher, Lakeland, Mahopac, Peekskill, Yorktown and Hendrik Hudson School Districts, 1974-82; Poet, 1984-. Contributions to: Anthologies: We Speak for Peace; Out of Season; The Best of Breakthrough Magazine's First Five Years; Forthcoming: The Color of Gold; Rage Before Pardon, forthcoming; Reviews, magazines, journals and other publications include: Pleiades; Poet's Sanctuary; Black Buzzard Review; Wind; Plastic Tower; Gypsy; Elf; Bitterroot; Nostalgia; Hydra; Neon Journal; Israel Horizons; Art Times; Second Glance; The Lucid Stone; The Westchester Writer; Poems that Thump in the Dark. Honours: Finalist, Verve Poetry Competition, 1990; Finalist, Verve Poetry Competition, 1990; Honorable Mention, Nostalgia Poetry Contest, 1991; Finalist, 22nd Annual Poetry Competition, Greenburgh, 1993. Memberships: AXA; OBK; Peregrine Poets; Hudson Valley Writers Center; National Writers Union. Address: PO Box 145, Mohegan Lake, NY 10547, USA.

CHARNY Carmi, (T Carmi), b. 31 Dec 1925, New York, New York, USA (Israeli citizen). Poet; Editor; Teacher. m. Lilach Peled, 3 sons. Education: BA, Yeshiva University, 1946; Graduate Studies, Columbia University, 1946, Sorbonne, Paris, 1946-47, Hebrew University, 1947, 1949-51. Appointments: Co-Editor, Massa, bi-weekly, Tel Aviv, 951-54; Editor, Orot, quarterly, Jerusalem, 1955; Editor, Sifriat Hapoalim Publishers, Tel Aviv, 1957-62, Am Oved Publishers, Tel Aviv, 1963-70; Zisking Visiting Professor of Humanities, Brandeis University, 1969-70; Adjunct Associate Professor, University of Tel Aviv, 1971-73; Editor-in-Chief, Ariel, quarterly, Jerusalem, 1971-74; Visiting Fellow, Oxford Centre for Postgraduate Hebrew Studies, 1974-76; Visiting Professor, Hebrew Union College, Jerusalem, 1978-; Visiting Professor, Stanford University, 1979, Yale University, 1986, New York University, 1986, University of Texas at Austin, 1987. Publications: Poetry: As T Carmi: Mum Vahalom, 1951; Eyn Prahim Shehorim, 1953; Sheleg Birushalayim, 1955; Hayam Ha'aharon, 1958; Nehash Hanehoshet, 1961, English translation as The Brass Serpent, 1964; Ha'unicorn Mistakel Bamar'ah, 1967; Tevi'ah, 1967; Davar Aher/Selected Poems, 1951-69, 1970; Somebody Likes You, 1971; Hitnatslut Hamehaber, 1974; T Carmi and Dan Pagis: Selected Poems (with Dan Pagis), 1976; El Erets Aheret, 1977; Leyad Even Hato'im, 1981; English translation as At the Stone of Losses, 1983; Hatsi Ta'avati, 1984; Ahat Hi Li, 1985; Shirim Min Ha'azuva, 1989; Emet Yehova, 1993; Editor: As T Carmi: The Modern Hebrew Poem Itself (with Stanley Burnshaw and Exra Spicehandler), 1965; The Penguin Book of Hebrew Verse, 1981; Other: Translations of plays into Hebrew. Contributions to: Periodicals. Honours: Brenner Prize for Literature, 1972; Prime Minister's Awards for Creative Writing, 1973, 1994; Jewish Memorial Foundation Grants, 1975, 1990; Kovner Award for Poetry, Jewish Book Council, 1978; Guggenheim Fellowship, 1987-88; Tel Aviv Foundation for Literature and Art Grant, 1988; Bialik Prize, 1990; Honorary Doctor of Humane Letters, Hebrew Union College, Jewish Institute of Religion, 1993. Memberships: Academy for the Hebrew Language Writers Association of Israel. Address: Hebrew Union College, Jewish Institute of Religion, 13 King David Street, Jerusalem 94101, Israel.

CHATERGIE Annand. See: SCHOENFELD Ilan.

CHATTARJI Chandak, b. 17 Aug 1935. Teacher. m. Rina Banerjee. 8 Dec 1961, 1 son, 1 daughter. Education: BA, Viswa Bharati University, 1955; MA, Calcutta University, 1957; Associate of the College Preceptors, London, 1970. Appointments: English Teacher, La Martiniere College, Lucknow; English Teacher, La Martiniere College, Lucknow; English Teacher, Housemaker, Sainik School, Rewa; Senior English Master, Housemaker, Tashi Namgyal Academy; Senior English Master, Housemaker, St Pauls School, Darjeeling; Principal, Dr Virendra Swarup Public School, Kanpur; Principal, Air Force School, Kanpur. Publications: Another Dorian Gray. Contributions to: Telegraph; Poetry India; Poet. Membership: World Poetry Society. Address: Air Force School, 402 Air Force Station, Chakeri, Kanpur 208008, Udra Pradesh, India.

CHATTERJEE Debjani, b. 21 Nov 1952, Delhi, India. Poet; Writer; Editor. m. Brian D'Arcy, 20 July 1983. Education: BA, American University in Cairo, 1972; MA, University of Kent, Canterbury, 1973; PhD, University of Lancaster, 1977; PGCE Sheffield City Polytechnic, 1981. Appointments: Lecturer, Didsbury College of Education, Manchester, 1975-76; Export Sales and Sector Manager, Marketing British Steel Corporation, 1977-80; Secondary School Teacher, Sheffield, 1981-84; Racial Equality Director, Sheffield, 1984-94, Oxfordshire, 1994; Distance Learning Project Co-ordinator, Sheffield, 1995-. Publications: Peaces; Poems for Peace; Whistling Still: Bloody Lyres; I Was That Woman; Barbed Lines; The Sun Rises in the North; Northern Poetry Vol II. Contributions to: Guardian; Poetry Review, Poetry London Newsletter, Poetry Nottingham; Outposts Poetry Quarterly; Poetry Matters; Artrage; Iron; Giant Steps; Nahan; Indian Literature; Journal of Indian Writing in English; Delhi London Poetry Quarterly; Illustrated Weekly of India; Journal of the Poetry Society of India; Wasafiri. Honours: Shankars International Childrens Competition Poetry Prize; Lancaster Literature Festival Poems Competition Winner; Peterloo Poets Open Poetry Competition Afro-Caribbean/Asian Prize; Southport Writer's Circle Poetry Competition; Artrage Annual Literature Award. Memberships: Life Member of Poetry Society, India, UK; National Association of Writers in Education; Yorkshire Arts Literature Policy Group, 1991; Password Books Limited, 1991, 1994; Arts Council of England Literature Panel, 1996. Address: 11 Donnington Road, Sheffield S2 2RF, England.

CHAUDHARY Ajit Kumar Shankar, (Ajit Kumar), b. 9 June 1933, Lucknow, Udra Pradesh, India. Educator. m. Snehmayi Chaudhary, 20 May 1959, 1 son. Education: MA, Allahabad University, India, 1952. Appointments: Lecturer in Hindi, D A V College, Kanpur, 1953-56; Hindi Translator, Ministry of External Affairs, New Delhi, 1956-62; Lecturer then Reader in Hindi, Kirorimal College, Delhi University, 1962-. Publications include: Akele Kanth Ki Pukar, 1958; Ankit Hone Do, 1962; Ye Phool Nahin, 1970; Gharonda, 1987; Hirni Ke Liye, 1993. Contributions to: Pratik; Nayi Kavita; Kalpana; Dharmayug; Saptahik Hindustan; Poorvagraha; Hansa; Scores of other journals. Honours: Honoured to recite poems in literary symposiums organised by All India Radio, Indian Television Centres and Private Bodies; Recipient of Prizes for criticism and travelogues. Memberships: Hindi Advisory Board, National Book Trust, New Delhi; Advisory Board, Sahitya Kala Parishad, Delhi Administration, Delhi; Numerous selection committees for central and state awards. Address: Kirorimal College, Delhi University, Delhi 110007, India.

CHEATWOOD Kiarri Teule-HeKima, b. Virginia, USA. Poet; Writer. m. Imani Znia, Jan 1973, 2 sons, 1 daughter. Education: BA, Elmhurst College, 1968-71; Predoctoral Fellow, University of Michigan, 1972-73. Appointments: Certified Teacher of Moo Duk Kwan Tae Kwon Do; Teacher, Writing, University of Illinois, Chicago; Guest Lecturer, Mass-Communications, Center for Inner City Studies, Northeastern Illinois University; Teacher, Creative Writing and Afrikan World History, Richmond Community High School for the Gifted; Architect; Author. Publications: Valley of the Anointers, 1979; Psalms of Redemption, 1983; Elegies for Patrice, 1984; Bloodstorm: Five Books of Poems and Docu-Poems, 1986; The Race, 1991; Seeds of Consistency, Fruits of Life, 1990; The Butcher's Grand Ball, 1993; To Save The Blood of Black Babies, 1995. Contributions to: Black World; The Chicago Sun Times; Transition/Ch'indaba; Contemporary Literary Criticism; Nimrod; Nommo; Nkombo; First World; The New York Amsterdam News; The Richmond News Leader; The Black Scholar. Honours: Nominated for HMH First Amendment Award for Investigative Journalism and for his literary column in The Richmond News Leader, 1988. Address: c/o Native Sun Publishers, PO Box 13394, Richmond, VA 23225, USA.

CHEN Jianhua, (Ji Hua, You Chen), b. 16 July 1947, Shanghai, China. Poet; Scholar of Chinese Literature and Culture. m. Wei Xing Wang, 26 Apr 1981, 1 son. Education: Fudan University, 1982; PhD, 1988. Appointments: Teacher, College of Liberal Arts, Shanghai

University, 1982-85; Lecturer, Fudan University, 1988-90; Academic Consultant, Chinese Great Dictionary Publishing House, 1988-90; Visiting Scholar, University of California, USA, 1988-. Publications: Poetry and Death; The Literature of Jiangsu and Zhejiang in the Ming Dynasty; Hua Jian Ji. Contributions to: Chung Wai Literary Monthly; Ideology Letters; Dong Xiang; Fudan Journal; Academic Monthly; Numerous others. Honours: Academic Award, Fudan University; Zhao Jingshen Chinese Classics Award. Memberships: Classical Drama Association of China; American Association for Asian Studies; International Center for Asian Studies, Hong Kong. Address: 220 Miller Court, Santa Cruz, CA 95060, USA.

CHEN Share Tan, b. 21 Nov 1934, China. Poet; Political Commentator; Author; Journalist. m. 9 Jan 1961, 4 sons, 1 daughter. Education: Graduate, Shaanxi Normal University, 1962. Appointments: Literary Teacher in China, 1953-63; Cadre in a County in China, 1963-79; Artistic Editor in China, 1979-80; Poet, Author and Political Commentator in USA, 1980-. Publications: China, 1985; Missing, 1989; You Are the Wind, 1989; Shui Tiao Keh Tou, classical poem, 1990. Contributions to: Chinese News; China Spring; Central Daily News; Square. Memberships: World Academy of Arts and Culture Inc, Governing Board of the World Congress of Poets; World Brotherhood and Peace Through Poetry; Association of Modern Chinese Literature and Arts of North America. Address: 1831 33rd Avenue, San Francisco, CA 94122, USA.

CHEN You. See: **CHEN Jianhua.**

CHENG Chou Yu. See: **CHENG Wen Tao.**

CHENG Wen Tao, (Cheng Chou Yu, Chou Yu Cheng), b. 4 Dec 1933, Jinan, Shangdong Province, China. Teacher. m. 11 Nov 1962, 1 son, 2 daughters. Education: Taiwan National Chung Hsing University, BA, 1955-58; University of Iowa, 1969-70; MFA, 1971-72; PhD, 1972-73. Appointments: Literary Editor, 1958-59; Lecturer, 1965-66; Executive Director, 1967-68; Artist-in-Residence, 1968-70; Instructor/Lecturer, 1969-74; Senior Lecturer, 1974-; Visiting Professor, 1984-88. Publications: Above the Space of Dream; The Prayers Robe and Pot; Long Song; The Odalisquest Outside the Window; Selected Poems of Cheng Cho'ou Yu; Cheng Ch'ou Yu Shih Ji; Yen Ren Hsing; All the Possibilities of Snow; Shi Hua Sha Na. Contributions to: China Times; United Daily News; United Literary Monthly; Central Daily News. Honours: Fulbright-Hays Grant; Keynote Lecturer. Memberships: Modern Poetry Society; World Chinese Writers Association. Address: 434 Temple Street, 3963 Yale Station, New Haven, CT 06520, USA.

CHERRY Kelly, b. Baton Rouge, Louisiana, USA. Professor in the Humanities; Writer; Poet. m. Jonathan B Silver, 23 Dec 1966, div 1969. Education: Du Pont Fellow, University of Virginia, 1961-63; MFA, University of North Carolina, 1967. Appointments: Faculty, 1977-82, Professor, 1982-83, Romnes Professor of English, 1983-88, Evjue-Bascom Professor in the Humanities, 1993-, University of Wisconsin, Madison; Writer-in-Residence, Southwest State University, Marshall, Minnesota, 1974, 1975; Visiting Professor and Distinguished Writer-in-Residence, Western Washington University, 1981; Faculty, MFA Program, Vermont College, 1982, 1983; Distinguished Visiting Professor, Rhodes College, Tennessee, 1985. Publications: Fiction includes: Sick And Full Of Burning, 1974; Conversion, 1979; Augusta Played, 1979; In The Wink Of An Eye, 1983; The Lost Traveller's Dream, 1984; My Life And Dr Joyce Brothers, 1990; Poetry: Lovers And Agnostics, 1975, revised edition, 1995; Relativity: A Point Of View, 1977; Songs For A Soviet Composer, 1980; Natural Theology, 1988; Benjamin John, 1993; God's Loud Hand, 1993; Time Out Of Mind, 1994; Death And Transfiguration, 1997; Other: The Exiled Heart: A Meditative Autobiography, 1991; Writing The World, essays and criticism, 1995. Contributions to: Anthologies and periodicals. Honours: Canaras Award, 1974; Bread Loaf Fellow, 1975; Yaddo Fellow, 1979, 1989; National Endowment for the Arts Fellowship, 1979; Romnes Fellowship, 1983; Wisconsin Arts Board Fellowships, 1984, 1989, 1994; Hanes Prize for Poetry, Fellowship of Southern Writers, 1989; Wisconsin Notable Author, 1991; Hawthornden Fellowship, Scotland, 1994; E B Coker Visiting Writer, Converse, 1996. Membership: Board of Directors, Associated Writing Programs, 1990-93. Address: c/o Department of English, University of Wisconsin at Madison, Madison, WI 53706, USA.

CHESSA Charles E, b. 16 Feb 1955, Warren, Maine, USA. Maintenance Worker; Poet; Writer. Education: Graduated with Honors and Scholarship, Penquis Valley High School, Maine, 1974. Appointment: US Army Veteran. Publications: Chapbooks: Ink River, 1994; Poetry 9-4-8-4, 1996. Contributions to: Writers World, 1995; The Long Islander, Walts Corner, 1993; GRIT, 1994; Just Write, 1995; Cat's Magazine, 1995; Westbury Anthology, 1995; The Pointed Circle, 1995. Honours: Runner Up, Scottish International Open Poetry Competition, Scotland, 1995; President's Award for Literary Excellence, 1994. Memberships: The Maine Poets Society; The Poets Study Club. Address: P O Box 520, #6, McIntosh TP, Bar Harbor, Maine 04609, USA.

CHESTERFIELD Reginald Alan, b. 8 Nov 1925, Exeter, Devon, England. Medical Practitioner; Dairy Farmer. m. Patricia Mary, 14 July 1951, 2 sons. Education: Royal College of Physicians, 1949; Royal College of Surgeons, 1950. Publications: Requiem for Innocence; A Lovely Slice of Bread; It Gets Late Early Now, 1995. Contributions to: Oribs; Pause; Staple; BBC; TSW; Countryman; Farmers Weekly. Membership: Company of Poets. Literary Agent: Jonathon Clifford, National Poetry Foundation, 27 Mill Road, Fareham, Hants PO16 0TH, England. Address: South Hayne, Bishops Nympton, South Molton, Devon EX36 3QR, England.

CHEUNG Judy Hardin, b. 3 Feb 1945, USA. Teacher. m. Benjamin Szeshing Cheung, 16 Aug 1990, 2 sons. Education: BA, Sonoma State University, 1966; MA, University of San Francisco, 1981. Appointments: Teacher, Special Education, Sonoma Developmental Center, 1972-. Publications: Welcome to the Inside; Caltions; Flying on the Wings of a Dragon; Phoenix and the Dragon. Contributions to: Numerous. Honours: Silver Pegasus Award; Poets of the Vineyard Award. Memberships: California Federation of Chaparral Poets; Ina Coolbirth Circle; Poets of the Vineyard. Address: 704 Bringham Avenue, Santa Rosa, CA 95404, USA.

CHEWNING Rose Ardeth, b. 13 July 1940, Virginia, Minnesota, USA. Homemaker; Singer; Songwriter. 2 daughters. Publications: Poems. Contributions to: American Anthology of Mid Western Poetry; Great Poems of the Western World. Honour: Golden Poet Award. Address: 5561 Raintree Drive, 5D, Mountain Iron, MN 55768, USA.

CHEYNEY-COKER Syl, b. 28 June 1945, Freetown, Sierra Leone. Education: Universities of Oregon, 1967-70, California, 1970, and Wisconsin, 1971-72. Appointments: Visiting Professor of English, University of the Philippines, Quezon City, 1975-77; Senior Lecturer, University of Maiduguri, Nigeria, 1979-. Publications: Concerto for an Exile, 1973; The Graveyard Also Has Teeth, 1974; The Blood in the Desert's Eyes: Poems, 1990. Address: Department of English, University of Maiduguri, PMB 1069, Maiduguri, Nigeria.

CHIANG Robert, b. 5 July 1963, New York, New York, USA. Physician. Education: BA, Augustana College, Rock Island, 1985; MD, Rush Medical College, Chicago, 1990. Contributions to: SAGA; American Anthology of Mid Western Poetry; American Anthology of Southern Poetry. Memberships: American Academy of Ophthalmology; American Society of Cataract and Refractive Surgery. Address: 10406 Owensmouth Avenue, Chatsworth, CA 91311, USA.

CHIBEAU Edmond, b. 20 Oct 1947, New York, New York, USA. Video Producer. m. Amy Reusch, 20 June 1987. Education: BA, Long Island University, 1973; University of California at Santa Barbara, 1973; MA, University of Pennsylvania, 1992; PhD, Northwestern University, 1996. Appointments: Assistant Professor, Pace University; Video Producer, Time Warner Manhattan; Video Curator, Childrens Museum of Manhattan. Contributions to: Nation; Santa Barbara News Press; California Quarterly; Ear; Glants Play Well; Red Weather; Shuttle; Flute; Assembling; Gallery Works; Pan Arts; The Fly. Honours: Ace Award; New York State Foundation for the Arts; CEEBA. Memberships: Authors League of America; Poets and Writers. Address: 7522 North East Lake Terrace, Chicago, IL 60626, USA.

CHICHETTO James William, b. Boston, Massachusetts, USA. Assistant Professor. m. 5 June 1941. Education: Stonehill College, 1964; Holy Cross College, 1968; Wesleyan University, 1978. Appointments: Assistant Editor, Gargoyle Magazine, 1976-80; Editor, Connecticut Poetry Review, 1986; Artist, Illustrator, Connecticut Poetry Review and East and West Literary Quarterly. Publications: Poems; Dialogue: Emily Dickinson and Christopher Cauldwell; Stones, A Litany; Gilgamesh and Other Poems; Victims; Homage To Father Edward Sorin. Contributions to: America; Boston Globe; Boston Phoenix; Christian Century; Colorado Review; Connecticut Poetry

Review; Footwork; Gargoyle Magazine; Other Side; Manhattan Review; Others. Honours: Sri Chinmoy Poetry Award; National Endowment for the Arts Grants. Memberships: National Writers' Union; Connecticut Poetry Forum; New England Artists Inc; Priest, Congregation of Holy Cross. Address: Stonehill College, North Easton, MA 02357, USA.

CHIDANANDA K. See: **GOWDA Chidananda Kolambe.**

CHILDERS Joanne, b. 5 Sept 1926, Ohio, USA. Retired Editor. m. 20 Aug 1951, 3 sons. Education: BA 1948, University of Cincinnati; MA 1952, University of Florida. Appointments: Welfare Worker; Social Worker; Editor. Publications: The Long Distance, 1989; Moving Mother Out, 1992. Contributions to: Sewannee Review; Massachusetts Review; College English; Commonwealth; Carolina Quarterly; Forum; Kentucky Poetry Review; Cumberland Poetry Review; and others. Honour: Individual Artist Grant, Florida State of the Arts, 1988. Address: 3504 North West 7th Place, Gainesville, FL 32607, USA.

CHILTON Joan Shaw, b. 27 May 1917, York, England. Retired. Education: Midland Agricultural College, 1935-37; Leicester University, 1937-39; Diploma in Christian Studies, Southampton University, 1992-95. Appointments: Trainee Industrial Welfare Worker; Local Ambulance Service; Opened Second Hand China, Glass Shop; Work with the Blind. Publication: Various Poems. Contributions to: Selsey Chronicle; Selsey Parish Magazine; Anthology, 1992. Honour: Certificate for 30 years work with the blind in West Sussex (voluntary). Memberships: National Poetry Society; Poetry Now Society; Selsey Poetry Society. Address: 1 Selsey Court, Hillfield Road, Selsey, Chichester, West Sussex PO20 0LD, England.

CHIN Ch'ang. See: **YEH Victor Wei Hsin.**

CHISHOLM Alison (Fiona Williams), b. 25 July 1952, Liverpool, England. Teacher of Speech and Drama and Creative Writing. m. Malcolm Chisholm, 10 July 1971, 2 daughters. Education: ATCL, 1969; FLCM, 1971; LLAM, 1973. Appointments: Teacher, Oxford Academy of Speech and Drama, Middlesbrough; Principal, Richmond Academy of Speech, Southport; Poetry and Creative Writing Tutor, Southport Arts Centre. Publications: Alone No More (co-author), 1977; Flying Free, 1985; The Need for Unicorns, 1987; Single Return, 1988; Paper Birds, 1990; The Craft of Writing Poetry, textbook, 1992; A Practical Poetry Course, 1994; How to Write 5-Minute Features, 1996. Contributions to: Envoi; Outposts; Doors; Orbis; Smoke; Staple; Others; Various anthologies; BBC Radio Merseyside and Network Northwest; Articles on poetry in numerous writers' magazines. Honours: Prizes in Mary Wilkins Memorial Competition (twice), Success Open, Grey Friars, Rhyme International, Lace, KQBX, Chester, Banstead, Lake Aske, Envoi, Julia Cairns, Ouse Valley, Sefton, New Prospects and Yorkshire Competitions, and US competitions in various categories of World Order of Narrative and Formalist Poets and NFSPS, Ohio Poetry Day Competitions, 1985-. Memberships: Society of Women Writers and Journalists; Poetry Society; The Verse Writers' Guild of Ohio; The Fellowship of Christian Writers; The London Writers' Circle; Southport Writers' Circle, Past Chairman. Address: 53 Richmond Road, Birkdale, Southport, Merseyside PR8 4SB, England.

CHISM-PEACE Yvonne, b. 23 Jan 1945, Philadelphia, Pennsylvania, USA. Poet; Essayist; Filmmaker. Education: BA, Rosemont College, 1966; MA, New York University, 1968; MA, Bank Street College of Education, 1996. Appointments: Poetry Editor, MS Magazine, 1973-86; Adjunct Professor of English, City University of New York, 1977-86; Writer-in-Residence, Poets in the Schools, 1979-86; Writer-in-Residence, Bronx Council on the Arts, 1982-84; Independent Filmmaker, 1983-; Adjunct Professor of English, Rosemont College, 1996-. Publications: IWILLA/Soil, 1985; IWILLA/Scourge, 1986. Contributions to: MS Magazine; Daily Fare; The Third Woman; We Become New; Callaloo; Pushcart Press; Catholic Girls; Bless Me Father. Honours: National Endowment for the Arts (twice); Mary Roberts Rinehart Fellowship; Creative Artists in Public Service; Brio Award. Memberships: Poetry Society of America; Poets and Writers; Bronx Council on the Arts; Schomburg Center; American Association of University Women. Address: Greene Street Artists Corporation, 5225 Greene Street 16, Philadelphia, PA 19144, USA.

CHIU Pai. See: **HO Chiung Jung.**

CHOATE Alec Herbert, b. 5 April 1915, High Barnet, Hertfordshire, England. Writer. m. 26 Feb 1943, 1 son, 2 daughters. Appointments: Soldier, 2nd World War; AIF Service in Egypt, Palestine, Syria, Borneo; Surveyor, 1945-75. Publications: Gifts Upon the Water, 1978; A Marking of Fire, 1986; Schoolgirls at Borobudur, 1990; Mind in Need of a Desert, 1995. Contributions to: Fremantle Arts Review; Habitat Australia; Patterns; Quadrant; Salt; Southerly; Westerly. Honours: Tom Collins Poetry Prize; Western Australia Week Literary Award; Patricia Hackett Prize. Memberships: Fellowship of Australian Writers (WA Section Inc); International PEN; Perth PEN Centre. Address: 11A Joseph Street, West Leederville, Western Australian 6007, Australia.

CHONG RUIZ Eustorgio Antonio, b. 21 Feb 1934, Los Santos, Panamá. Education: BS, University of Panamá, 1958. Appointments: Director, Felix E Oller High School, 1958-62; Assistant Professor, University of Panamá, 1965-68; High School Teacher, 1962-92. Publications: Canción del Hombre en la Ventana; Yaya; Y Entonces tu; Del mar y la Selva; A la Luz del Fogón; Detrás de la Noche; Otra vez, Pueblo; Techumbres, Guijarros y Pueblo; Después del Manglar; Diario de una noche de camino. Contributions to: Revista Boreal; Revista Amancer; Revista Pliego de Murmurios; Revista Puerto Norte Sur; Revista Galaxia 71; Periódico El Sol de Azuero. Honour: Poetry Award. Memberships: Sociedad Bolivariana de Panamá; Academia Panaména de la Historia; Asociación de Professors de la Republica de Panamá; Sociedad Amigos Museo Afro Antillano. Address: Apartado 6507, Panamá 5, Panamá.

CHORLTON David, b. 15 Feb 1948, Spittal-an-der-Drau, Austria. Artist; Writer. m. Roberta Elliott, 21 June 1976. Appointments: Graphic Designer: Pifco, Manchester, England, 1968-71, Steinbock, Vienna, Austria, 1971-72, Persil GmbH, Vienna, 1972-75. Publications: Without Shoes, 1987; The Village Painters, 1990; Measuring Time, 1990; Forget the Country You Came From, 1992; Outposts, 1994; The Insomniacs, 1994. Contributions to: Abraxas; Blue Mesa Review; Blue Unicorn; Contact II; Chaminade Literary Review; The Devil's Millhopper; Green's Magazine; Hawaii Pacific Review; Hawaii Review; International Poetry Review; Mississippi Mud; New Mexico Humanities Review; Pembroke Magazine; Poem; Poet Lore; Nexus; Santa Clara Review; Slipstream; Webster Review. Memberships: Board Member, Arizona State Poetry Society, 1982-83; Board Member, Rio Grande Writers' Association, 1984-85. Address: 118 West Palm Lane, Phoenix, AZ 85003, USA.

CHOROSINSKI Eugene Conrad, b. 1 Jan 1930, Sienno, Poland. Author; Poet. Education: University Studies, 4 years. Publications: Through the Years, 1995. Contributions to: Several anthologies. Honours: 4 Editors Choice Awards, 1994-95; Numerous others. Membership: International Society of Poets. Address: 131 Madrona Drive, Eustis, FL 32726, USA.

CHOU Po-Nai, b. 14 Aug 1933, Wu Hwa County, Guangzhou Province, China. Editor; Writer. m. 21 May 1960, 1 son, 4 daughters. Education: Communication Electronics School of Chinese Air Force, 1955; Taiwan University, 1958, 1959. Appointments: Secretary, Literary Editor, Central Daily News, 1977-80; Council Secretary, Cultural Planning & Development, Executive Yuan, 1981-90; Chairman, Chief Editor, World Tribune, 1990-. Publications: A Deserted Town; Cool Autumn Again; If Only Because of Loneliness; On Realism; Trends of Literary Thoughts of 20th Century; A Study on Modern Fiction. Contributions to: Central Daily News; United Daily News; World Tribune. Honours: Literary Medal & Golden Statue Award, 1970; Poetry Education Prize, Ministry of Education, China, 1994. Membership: Vice Chairman, Poetry Association of China, 1995-. Address: 3F3 No 5, Lane 68, Sanmin Road, Taipei, Taiwan, China.

CHOU Yu Cheng. See: **CHENG Wen Tao.**

CHOUDHURI Pradip, b. 5 Feb 1943, Bengal, India. Teacher. m. Gouri Choudhuri, 29 May 1967, 1 son. Education: MA in English; PG Diploma, Teaching of English; Diploma in French. Appointments: Teacher, English Language and English Poetry Editing Numerous Poetry Journals. Publications: My Rapid Activities; Skin Disease; Poetry, Religion; 64 Ghosts Ferry; A Few Concepts to be Abandoned in Poetry; The Black Hole. Contributions to: Second Aeon; Cosmos; Robot; Swakal; Alpha Beat Soup; The Blue Jacket; Décharge; Rimbaud Revue; An Amzer; La Toison d'Or; Press-Stances; Art et Poésie de Touraine; L'écriture; Noréal; Inédit, Bouillabaisse; Tamanoir;

Lieux d'Asile, Lieux d'Exil. Memberships: Le Club Kerouac; Nimporte quelle Route. Address: 2nd Floor Apt 6, 73 Regent Estate, Calcutta, 700 092 India.

CHOWDHRY Maya, b. 2 Feb 1964, Edinburgh, Scotland. Writer; Poet; Poetry Performer; Filmmaker; Photographer. Education: MA, Scriptwriting for film and television, Northern School of Film and Television, Leeds Metropolitan University, 1994; Short courses, Arvon Foundation. Appointments: Administrator, Edinburgh Fringe Film Festival, 1986; Producer, Director, Sheffield Film Cooperative, 1987-91; Tutor, Manchester Writing Festival, 1993, 1994; Resident Dramatist, Red Ladder Theatre Company, 1994; Currently writing poetry, screenplays and plays. Publication: Putting in the Pickle Where the Jam Should Be, 1989. Contributions to: Feminist Arts News, 1990, 1991, 1992; Talking Poetry, Radio 5, 1991; Anthologies: Language of Water, Language of Fire; The Popular Front of Contemporary Poetry; Risk Behaviour; Crazy Jig, 1992; Daskat, 1993; Engelsk Meddelelser, 1993; Kiss, 1994; As Girls Could Boast, 1994. Honour: Cardiff International Poetry Competition, 1992. Memberships: Asian Women Writers' Collective; Poetry Society. Address: 14 Sturton Road, Sheffield S4 7DF, England.

CHOYCE Lesley, b. 21 Mar 1951, Riverside, New Jersey, USA (Canadian citizen). Professor; Writer; Poet; Editor. m. Terry Paul, 19 Aug 1974, 2 daughters. Education: BA, Rutgers University, 1972; MA, Montclair State College, 1974; MA, City University of New York, 1983. Appointments: Editor, Pottersfield Press, 1979-; Professor, Dalhousie University, 1986-. Publications: Adult Fiction: Eastern Sure, 1981; Billy Botzweiler's Last Dance, 1984; Downwind, 1984; Conventional Emotions, 1985; The Dream Auditor, 1986; Coming Up for Air, 1988; The Second Season of Jonas McPherson, 1989; Magnificent Obsessions, 1991; Ecstacy Conspiracy, 1992; Margin of Error, 1992; The Republic of Nothing, 1994; The Trap Door to Heaven, 1996; Young Adult Fiction: Skateboard Shakedown, 1989; Hungry Lizards, 1990; Wavewatch, 1990; Some Kind of Hero, 1991; Wrong Time, Wrong Place, 1991; Clearcut Danger, 1992; Full Tilt, 1993; Good Idea Gone Bad, 1993; Dark End of Dream Street, 1994; Big Burn, 1995; Falling Through the Cracks, 1996; Poetry: Re-Inventing the Wheel, 1980; Fast Living, 1982; The End of Ice, 1985; The Top of the Heart, 1986; The Man Who Borrowed the Bay of Fundy, 1988; The Coastline of Forgetting, 1995; Non-Fiction: An Avalanche of Ocean, 1987; December Six: The Halifax Solution, 1988; Transcendental Anarchy (autobiography), 1993; Nova Scotia: Shaped by the Sea, 1996; Editor: Chezzetcook, 1977; The Pottersfield Portfolio, 7 volumes, 1979-85; Visions from the Edge (with John Bell), 1981; The Cape Breton Collection, 1984; Ark of Ice: Canadian Futurefiction, 1992. Honours: Event magazine's Creative Nonfiction Competition Winner, 1990; Dartmouth Book Awards, 1990, 1995; Ann Connor Brimer Award for Children's Literature, 1994; Authors Award, Foundation for the Advancement of Canadian Letters, 1995. Address: RR 2, Lawrencetown Beach, Porters Lake, Nova Scotia B0J 2S0, Canada.

CHRANOVA Albena Vladimirova, b. 12 May 1962, Plovdiv, Bulgaria. Div, 1 daughter. Education: English Language School, 1980; Plovdiv University, 1985. Appointments: Assistant, Plovdiv University, 1986; Senior Assistant, 1990; Publications: Till Beyond; A Woman in the Shadow; The Two Bulgarian Literatures. Contributions to: Rodna Retch; Trakija; Prilep; Litavra; Struma; Zornica; Literaturen Front; Puls; Studentska Tribuna; ABV. Honours: First Poetry Prize, Plovdiv University; First Poetry Prize, National Students Literature Fest; Second Poetry Prize, Young Writers Competition; Silver Medal for Poetry; Debut Book of Poetry. Memberships: National Young Writers Club; Writers Society, Plovdiv; Department of New Bulgarian Studies. Address: Tzar Assen Str 33, 4000 Plovdiv, Bulgaria.

CHRISCADEN. See: **HINDS Sallie A.**

CHRISTENSEN Inger, b. 16 Jan 1935, Vejle, Denmark. Writer. Publications: Light; Grass; It; Letter in April; Alphabet; Poem of Death; Butterfly Valley. Contributions to: Change; New Directions; Akzente; Die Hören; Letres Internationals; L'Autre. Honours: Kritikerprisen; Boghandlernes Gyldne Laurbær; Aarestrup Medaljen; Tåge Brandts Rejselegat; Kjeld Abell Prisen; Morten Nielsens Mindelegat; Soren Gyldendal Prisen; Fredslegatet. Membership: The Danish Academy. Address: Dag Hammarskjölds Allé 5, 4 tv, DK 2100 Copenhagen O, Denmark.

CHRISTENSEN Paul, b. 18 Mar 1943, Pennsylvania, USA. Professor. m. Catherine Anne Tensing, 20 Aug 1969, 2 sons, 2

daughters. Education: William and Mary College, 1967; University of Cincinnati, 1970; University of Pennsylvania, 1975. Appointments: Instructor, 1974-75, Assistant Professor, 1975-79, Associate Professor, 1979-83, Professor, 1983-, Texas A&M University. Publications: In Seven Poets; Old and Lost Rivers; Sign of the Whelming; Weights and Measures; Where Three Roads Meet, 1995; The Two of Us (with Leslie Ullman), 1995. Contrtibutions to: Washington Post; LA Times; American Statesman; Sulfur; Parnassus; Southwest Review; Temblor; Madison Review; Quarter After Eight. Honours: Writer's Grant, National Endowment for the Arts. Membership: Texas Circuit, Modern Language Association. Literary Agent: Gloria Stein. Address: Department of English, Texas A&M University, College Station, TX 77843, USA.

CHRISTIAN Dudley Noel, b. 15 Nov 1944, Port of Spain, Trinidad, West Indies. Engineer; Inventor. m. Grace Sujkowski, 18 Sept 1967, 2 sons, 1 daughter. Education: Taxidermy Certificate, 1964; Electrical Certificate, 1964; Plastics Certificate, 1964; World Trade and Business Management, 1966; Certificate of Import-Export Achievement, 1976; Certificate of Appreciation, Cable TV, 1978; 4th Class Engineering, 1980; 2nd Class Engineering, 1987; Marine Computer Certificate, 1995. Appointments: Oiler, 1972-81; Junior Engineer, 1981-86; 3rd Engineer, 1986-87; 2nd Engineer, 1987-88; Chief Engineer, 1988-; Creator, host, director, co-producer, TV programme for new unknown poets, 1975-82. Publications: Poets Pen, 1971; The Seelaats, 1988; Judge Me Not Without a Trial, 1975; Only Children of the Universe Are We, 1973; Legends, Lives and Loves along the Inside Passage, 1976; Sonnets of Life-Love-Racism and Hate, 1973; Inside a Heart, 1974; Lifes-Illusive-Zenith, 1981; That We Too Free May Live, 1980; Loves Reflections, 1983; Short Stories for Guidance of Children, 1992. Contributions to: Van Sun; Province; Times (Local); Chilliwack Review; Mission Record; Caymanian Paper. Honours: Royal Patronage Status Title, 1995; Various Certificates and Acknowledgements; Inclusions: Harlo's Anthology of Poets and Writers, 1975; World of Poetry, 1977; Toronto Poetry Association, 1981. Memberships: Burnaby Arts Club; Vancouver Poetry Association; Fraser Valley Poets Potpourri and Pause for Poetry. Address: 8573 McEwen Terrace, Mission, BC V2V 6R2, Canada.

CHRISTOPHER Nicholas, b. 28 Feb 1951, New York, New York, USA. Poet; Writer. m. Constance Barbara Davidson, 20 Nov 1980. Education: AB, Harvard College, 1973. Appointments: Adjunct Professor of English, New York University; Adjunct Associate Professor of Writing, Columbia University. Publications: On Tour With Rita, poems, 1982; A Short History Of The Island Of Butterflies, poems, 1986; The Soloist, novel, 1986; Desperate Characters, poems, 1988; Under 35: The New Generation Of American Poets, editor, 1989; In The Year Of The Comet, poems, 1992; 5 Degrees And Other Poems, 1995; Walk On The Wild Side: Urban American Poetry Since 1975, editor, 1994; Veronica, novel, 1996; Somewhere in the Night: Film Noir and the American City, 1997. Contributions to: Anthologies and periodicals. Honours: New York Foundation for the Arts Fellowship, 1986; National Endowment for the Arts Fellowship, 1987; Peter I B Lavan Award, Academy of American Poets, 1991; Guggenheim Fellowship, 1993; Melville Cane Award, 1994. Address: c/o Janklow and Nesbit Associates, 598 Madison Avenue, New York, NY 10022, USA.

CHRISTY David, b. 28 Jan 1952, Philadelphia, Pennsylvania, USA. Editor; Publisher; Writer. 1 son, 1 daughter. Appointments: Editor, Publisher, Alpha Beat Soup, 1986-; Co-Editor, Moody Street Irregulars. Publication: Loose Stones. Contributions to: Bouillabaisse; Global Tapestry Journal; Moody Street Irregulars; Blue Jacket; Kerouac Connection; Tempus; Window Panes; Cokefish; Impetus; Canadian Poetry Review; PPHOO. Address: Alpha Beat Press, 31 Waterloo Street, New Hope, PA 18938, USA.

CHRYSTOS Christina, (Singingarrow-Smith), b. 7 Nov 1946, San Francisco, California, USA. Poet; Performer. Education: Self-educated. Appointments: 48 readings, 1977-90, 21 in 1991, 15 in 1992, including: Mazer Collection, Lesbian Archives, Los Angeles; Women of All Red Nations, Conference on Genocide, Chicago; Returning the Gift, 1st Native Writers' Conference, Oklahoma; Rainbow Voices, San Francisco; Vancouver International Writers' Festival, British Columbia; People Like Us, Chicago. Publications: Not Vanishing, 1988; Dream On, 1991. Contributions to: Anthologies: This Bridge Called My Back; A Gathering of Spirit; Inversions; Dancing On the Rim of the World; Living the Spirit; Naming the Waves; Gay and Lesbian Poetry of Our Times; Periodicals: Taos Review; Sunbury;

Sinister Wisdom; Conditions; Fireweed; Maenad. Honours: Barbara Demming Memorial Award, 1988; Poetry Grant, National Endowment for the Arts, 1990; Freedom of Expression Award, Human Rights Fund, 1991; Lannan Foundation, Poetry, 1991. Memberships: Poets and Writers; Northwest Native Writers; Returning the Gift. Address: 9551 South Beach No A, Bainbridge Island, WA 98110, USA.

CHULA Margaret, b. 10 Oct 1947, Vermont, USA. Writer; Small Press Owner. Education: MA, 1961-65, AS cum laude, 1965-67, Bay Path College; Northeastern University, 1967-69. Appointments: Institute for The Future, Menlo Park, CA, 1974-77; University Teacher, Kyoto Seika College, Kyoto, Japan, 1982-92, Doshisha Women's College, Kyoto, Japan, 1983-92; Owner, Katsura Press, 1992-. Publications: Grinding My Ink, 1993; This Moment, 1995. Contributions to: Poet Lore; Kyoto Journal; Modern Haiku; Kansai Time Out, Kobe, Japan; Ezra Pound Anthology; 1988 Anthology of Contemporary Poetry. Honours: 2nd Prize, Japan Airlines National Haiku Contest, 1987; 1st Prize, Third International English Tanka Contest, 1993; Haiku Society of America's National Book Award, 1994; 1st Prize, Kansai Time Out 7th Annual Writing Contest, 1994. Memberships: PEN West; Haiku Society of America; Poetry Society of Japan; The Japan Tanku Poets' Club; Northwest Association of Book Publishers. Address: 206 South West Carey Lane, Portland, OR 97219, USA.

CHURCH Avery Grenfell, b. 21 Feb 1937, North Wilkesboro, North Carolina, USA. Educator; Scientist; Poet. m. Dora Ann Creed, 1991. Education: University of North Carolina; BA, Baylor University, 1962; MA, University of Colorado, 1965. Appointments: US Navy, 1955-57; Programme Chairman, Anthropology Club, 1962-63, Teaching Assistant, 1965, University of Colorado; Assistant Professor, Memphis State University, Tennessee, 1965-66, 1969-72; Lecturer, University of South Alabama, 1972-83; Vice-Chairman of Anthropology, 1975-76, Vice-President, 1976-77, Executive Committee, 1975-77, Alabama Academy of Science; Editorial Advisory Board, American Biographical Institute, 1980-83. Publications: Rainbows of the Mind; Patterns of Thought; Waves of Life, 1995. Contributions to: American Bard; Anthology on World Brotherhood and Peace; Dan River Anthology; Dakota: Plains and Fancy; Jeans Journal; Parnassus Literary Journal; San Fernando Poetry Journal; Yearbook of Modern Poetry; Numerous others. Honours: Cultural Doctorate (honorary), World University, 1981; Doctor of Humanities (honorary), London Institute for Applied Research, 1993; Book Award; Poets' Hall of Fame; Poet Laureate of the Month; Poet of the Year Award; Lloyd Frank Merrell Award; Certificates of Merit. Memberships: Poetry Society of America; Academy of American Poets; Presidents' Club Silver Circle, University of Colorado at Boulder, 1994-95. Address: 2749 Park Oak Drive, Clemmons, NC 27012, USA.

CHURCH David Randall, b. 20 Jan 1947, Providence, Rhode Island, USA. Taxi Driver. Div, 5 sons, 1 daughter. Education: Christian Brothers Academy, Providence, Rhode Island, 1961-65; Self taught through own studies in English, Psychology and Philosophy. Appointments: Poetry Editor and Contributor to 247 Arts Magazine, Providence, Rhode Island; Promoter of monthly Jam Sessions, mixing poetry and song at performing art establishments in and around Providence, Rhode Island. Publications: Cool Earth, 1977; Blue Balls, 1995. Contributions to: Newport Review; Poets Press; Cer-Ber-Us; Spoken Word Anthology of Providence Poets, 1993; Alpha Beat Press; Cokefish; Bouillabaise; Sunspot Press. Address: 30 Forest Street, Providence, RI 02906, USA.

CHUTE Robert Maurice, b. 13 Feb 1926, Naples, Maine, USA. Professor Emeritus. m. Virginia Hinds, 24 June 1946, 1 son, 1 daughter. Education: BA, University of Maine, 1950; ScD, The John Hopkins University, 1953. Appointments: Instructor, Assistant Professor, Middlebury College; Assistant Professor, San Fernando Valley State College; Associate Professor, Lincoln University; Professor, Bates College; Professor Emeritus, Bates College, 1993-. Publications: Quiet Thunder; Uncle George; Voices Great and Small; Thirteen Moons; Samuel Sewall Sails for Home; When Grand Mother Decides to Die; The Crooked Place. Contributions to: Kansas Quarterly; Beloit Poetry Review; Bitterroot; South Florida Poetry Review; North Dalcota Review; Cape Rock; Fiddlehead; Greenfield Review; Literary Review. Honours: Phi Beta Kappa; Sigma Xi, 1950; Maine Humanities Chapbook Award. Memberships: American Poetry Society; Fellow, American Association for the Advancement of Science. Literary Agent: Nancy Heyward. Address: 85 Echo Cove Lane, Poland, ME 04274, USA.

CIMINO Lorenzo, b. 26 May 1938, Bari, Italy. Psychologist. m. Tiziana Peduzzi, 28 June 1975. Education: Highest Diploma for Piano, Conservatory of Music, Bari, 1957; PhD, University of Bari, 1965. Appointments include: Psychologist, Public Administration, 1971-; Pianist. Publications: G Gentile and K Marx, unpublished thesis, 1966; Musical reviews in magazines, 1979-91; 3 Books of Lyrics, 1989, 1991, 1996; Scientific articles in reviews; Papers presented at national and international conferences; Lyrics in anthologies. Honours: Numerous academic honours; Numerous prizes for poetry and journalism. Memberships: Italian Society for Scientific Psychology (SIPS); Italian Psychological Society for the Artistic and Literary Creation (SIPCAL); Società Italiana Psicologia Scientifica; Associazione Italiana Scienze Psicologiche; Centro Studi G Bateson; Società Italiana Educazione Musicale; Istituto Comasco per la Storia del Movimento di Liberazione; Unione Legion d'Oro; Accademia AILAS, Bologna. Address: Via Nosee 4, I-22020 Schignano (CO), Italy.

CINGOLANI Charles L, b. 18 Jan 1933, Butler, Pennsylvania, USA. Teacher. m. Roswitha Volkmann, 12 July 1969, 1 son, 1 daughter. Education: BA, Stonehill College, 1955; MA, Duquesne University, 1966; PhD, University of Basel, 1972. Appointment: Point Park College, Pittsburgh, Pennsylvania. Publication: In the Wheat. Contributions to: Poetry Quarterly; New Hope International Quartos Magazine; Lundian; New Europe; Purple Patch; Foolscap. Address: Waldshuterstrasse 6, 79862 Hoechenschwand, Germany.

CIRINO Leonard John, b. 11 Sept 1943. Teacher; Writer; Editor; Painter; Musician. Education: BA, Sonoma State University, 1977. Appointments: Instructor, Mendocino Branch, College of the Redwoods, California, 1980-88. Publications: The Source of Precious Life; For You/On Stones; A Small Boot of Changes; Her Poems; A Collage; Rattlenate Logic; Personae Ca 50 Minute Tape; Ballard of the Mad Boy and His Shadow; Poems After the Spaniards of 27, 1992; Sweeney Everyman, 1992; Poems From Some Latins, 1992; Rocking Over Dawn: Selected Poems, 1988-1991; Waiting For The Sun To Fill With Courage, prose, poems, 1994; Henry's Will: A Tribute To John Berryman, 1995; The Widow Poems, 1996. Contributions to: Amelia; Anderson Valley Advertiser; Blue Unicorn; The Cape Rock; Plains Poetry Journal; Paper Radio; Paragraph; Canada Poetry Review; Fiddlehead; West Branch; New Settle Interview; Arts and Entertainment; Sisters Today; Epiphany; Exquisite Corpse. Address: PO Box 591, Albion, CA 95410, USA.

CIVASAQUI José, (Sosuku Shibasaki), b. 2 Jan 1916, Saitama Ken, Japan. Lecturer; Translator; Poet. m. Setsuko Hirose, 18 Sept 1940, 2 sons, 1 daughter. Education: Yokohama Central Army Education Program School; World University, Tucson, USA. Appointments: Civilian Employee, US Army, Yokohama, 1946-48; Lt Staff, Toshiba EMI Ltd, 1955-76; Lecturer, Japan Translation Academy, 1978-84; Lecturer, Sunshine Business College, 1985-94. Publications: In His Bosom; In Thy Grace; Beyond Seeing; Living Water; Invitation To The World of Haiku; Doshin Shien; Green Pastures, book of poems, 1993. Contributions to: Japan Times; Come Come Club; New Age; Mainichi; Poetry Nippon; Laurel Leaves Quarterly; Anthology of World Poetry. Honours: Excellence in Poetry; Plaque of Distinction; Honourable Poet Laureate; Recognition of Outstanding Christian Poetry, and as Poet Humanities; Premio Speciale; Decretum Christian Men of Letters; Premio Internazionale, San Valentino d'Oro, Italia, 1989; 3rd Class Medal for Peace, Albert Einstein Int Academy Foundation, USA, 1990; Medallion, Poetry Day Australia and Melbourne Poetry Society Competition, 1991-92; Michael Madhusudan Academy Award, Calcutta, India, 1992; Congress Medallion for Distinguished Participation, IBC and ABI, 1993; Fourth Order of Merit, Japan, 1993; Man of Year, IBA, 1994; Silver Medallion Dove in Peace, Poetry Day Australia, 1995. Memberships: United Poets Laureate International; Poetry Society of Japan; Japan Song Translators Society; Japan League of Poets; Japan Guild of Authors and Composers; PEN; Poetry Society; International Shakespeare Association. Address: Honcho 2-12-11, Ikebukuro, Toshima-ku, Tokyo 170, Japan.

CLAIRE William, b. 4 Oct 1935, Northampton, Massachusetts, USA. Consultant. m. Sedgley Mellon Schmidt, div, 1 son. Education: BA, Columbia College, Columbia University, 1958; MLS, Georgetown University, 1979. Appointments: Director, Washington Office, American Paper Institute; Ex Director, World Federalists, USA; Director, Washington Office, State University of New York; President, Senior Partner, Washington Resources; Founding Editor, Publisher, Voyages: A National and International Literary Magazine, 1967-73. Publications:

Poems from a Southern France Notebook; Strange Coherence of Our Dreams; Publishing in West: Alan Swallow, 1976; Mark Van Doren: Selected Essays: 1924-1972, 1981. Contributions to: New York Times; American Scholar; The Nation; Chelsea; Carleton Miscellany; New York Quarterly; West Coast Review. Honours: National Endowment for the Arts; Yaddo Fellowship; Rockefeller Foundation. Memberships: PEN America; Cosmos Club; National Press Club. Literary Agent: Gloria Sterm Agency, New York City, New York, USA. Address: 4705 Butterworth Place NW, Washington, DC 20016, USA.

CLARK Anne, b. 14 May 1960, Croydon, Surrey, England. Wordsmith; Musician. Appointments: Editor, Paul Wellers, Riot Stories, 1980-82; Co-Editor, Faber & Faber's Hard Lines. Publications: The Sitting Room; Changing Places; Joined Up Writing; Pressure Points; Hopeless Cases; RSVP; Unstill Life. Contributions to: Numerous. Honours: Runner Up, Poem for a Nuclear Romance. Address: c/o 56-60 Islington Part Street, London N1 1PX, England.

CLARK Douglas George Duncan, b. 3 Oct 1942, Darlington, England. Retired. Education: Bsc, Hons, Mathematics, Glasgow University, 1966. Appointments: Actuarial Student, Scottish Widows Fund, Edinburgh, 1966-69; Research Investigator, British Steel, Teesside, 1971-73; Computer Officer, Bath University Computing Services, Bath, 1973-93. Publications: The Horseman Trilogy in 4 books: Troubador, 1985; Horsemen, 1988; Coatham, 1989; Disbanded, 1991; Dysholm, 1993; Selected Poems, 1995. Contributions to: Lines Review; Cencrastus; Avon Literary Intelligencer; Outposts; Acumen; Sand Rivers Journal; Rialto; Completing the Picture: Exiles, Outsiders and Independents; Poet's Voice; Mount Holyoke News; Isibango; Agnieszka's Dowry. Membership: Bath Writers' Workshop, 1982-. Address: 69 Hillcrest Drive, Bath, Avon BA2 1HD, England.

CLARK Gary Osgood, b. 14 Nov 1945, Norfolk, Massachusetts, USA. Library Assistant. m. Dawn McClain, 24 Mar 1979, div 1991, 1 son. Education: BA, English, California State University, San Jose, California, 1975. Appointments: Publishing, 1979-; Poetry readings in Sacremento area: Hosted a poetry series, Davis Art Center, 1985-87. Publications: Letting the Eye to Wonder, 1990; 7 Degrees of Something, 1991. Contributions to: Sonoma Mandala; Manhattan Poetry Review; Vincent Brothers Review; Phase & Cycle; Wormwood Review; Next Phase; Pirate Writings; South Coast Poetry Journal. Memberships: Science Fiction Poetry Association. Address: PO Box 72364, Davis. CA 95617, USA.

CLARK John Pepper, b. 6 Apr 1935, Kiagbodo, Nigeria. Education: University of Ibadan, 1955-64. Appointments: Professor of African Literature, University of Lagos, 1966-85. Publications: Poems, 1962; A Reed in the Tide: A Selection of Poems, 1965; Casualties: Poems 1966-68, 1970; Urhobo Poetry, 1980; A Decade of Tongues: Selected Poems 1958-1968, 1981; State of the Union, 1985; Mandela and Other Poems, 1988; Also plays for stage and radio. Address: c/o Andrew Best, Curtis Brown, Haymarket House, 28-29 Haymarket, London SW1Y 4SP, England.

CLARK Marjorie Russell McMillan, (Lisa Russell McMillan), b. 23 Mar 1925, Edinburgh, Scotland. Plant Pathologist, Retired. Education: BSc (Hons), Edinburgh, 1947; PhD, 1949. Appointments: Plant Pathologist, West of Scotland Agricultural College, 1949-85. Publication: Organisms. Contributions to: Little Word Machine; Edinburgh Festival Fringe; Broadcasts; BBC Tape, Inspired By Nature, 1995. Honours: Scottish Open Poetry Competition; Poet of the Year, Runner Up. Membership: Association of Applied Biologists. Address: Woodlands, Gattonside, Melrose, Roxburghshire, Scotland.

CLARK Thomas Willard, b. 1 Mar 1941, Oak Park, Illinois, USA. Poet. m. Angelica Heinegg, 22 Mar 1968, 1 daughter. Education: BA, University of Michigan, 1963; MA, Cambridge University, England, 1965; Instructor in American Poetry, University of Essex, 1966-67. Appointments: Poetry Editor, The Paris Review, 1963-74; Core Faculty in Poetics, New College of California, 1987-. Publications: Stones, 1969; Air, 1970; When Things Get Tough on Easy Street, 1978; Paradise Resisted, 1984; Disorded Ideas, 1987; Easter Sunday, 1987; Fractured Karma, 1990; Sleepwalker's Fate, 1992; Junkets ona Sad Planets Scenes from the Life of John Keats, 1993; Like Real People, 1995. Contributions to: New Statesman; Kulchua; The Listener; TLS; Encounter; Poetry, Chgo; The Nation. Honoiurs: Hopwood Award, 1963; Bess Hokin Prize for Poetry, 1966; George Dillon Memorial Prize for Poetry, 1968; Poets Foundation Award, 1978; Rockefeller Fellow, 1968; Guggenheim Fellow, 1970; NEA Grants, 1985; Jerome

Shestack Award for Poetry, 1992. Address: 1740 Marin Avenue, Berkeley, CA 94707, USA.

CLARKE Gillian, b. 8 June 1937, Cardiff, Glamorgan, Wales. Poet; Editor; Tutor, Creative Writing. Education: BA, University College, Cardiff, 1958. Appointments: Lecturer, Gwent College of Art and Design, Newport, 1975-82; Editor, Anglo-Welsh Review, 1976-84; Freelance Writer, 1985-; Chair, Welsh Academy, 1988-93; Chair. Taliesin Trust, 1989-94; President, Ty Nwydd, 1993-; Editor, Life President of the Welsh creative writers' house, Ty Newydd in Gwynedd; Tutor of Creative Writing for all ages. Publications: Poetry: Snow on the Mountain, 1971; The Sundial, 1978; Letter from a Far Country, 1982; Selected Poems, 1985; Letting in the Rumour, 1989; The King of Britain's Daughter, 1993; Editor: The Anglo Welsh Review, 1976-84, Poetry Book Society Anthology, 1987-1988, 1987; I Can Move the Sea, 1996; The Whispering Room, 1996; Drama: The Time of the Wolf, 1996; Translations: One Moonlit Night (T. Llew Jones); Poems by Menna Elfyn, 1996; Forthcoming Publications: Collected Poems, 1997; One Bright Morning by Kate Roberts (translation); The Poet's Boast; Other works: Talking in the Dark, 1975; Letter From a Far Country, 1979; The King of Britain's Daughter, 1993. Address: Blaen Cwrt, Talgarreg, Llandysul, Dyfed, Wales.

CLEARY Brendan, b. 6 June1958, County Antrim, Ireland. Part Time Lecturer; Performance Poet; Stand Up Comic. Education: BA, 1980; MA, 1985. Appointments: Co-Editor, Stand Magazine, 1981-82; Founder, Editor, Ecto Room Machine, 1985. Publications: Tears in the Burger Store; Expecting Cameras; Late Night Bouts; The Parties Upstairs; Newcastle Is Benidorm; Crack; White Bread and ITV; The Irish Card. Contributions to: New Younger Irish Poets; Blackstaff; 12 Bar Blues; New Statesman; New England Review; Stand; Sunk Island Review; Tribune; The North; The Wipe Skirt; Salmon; The Echo Room. Honour: Basil Bunting Award. Membership: Morden Tower Readings. Address: c/o 45 Bewick Court, Princes Square, Newcastle upon Tyne, Tyne & Wear NE1 8EG, England.

CLEVERLY Henry David, b. 20 Nov 1962. Poet. Publication: Walking Willacome Well. Contributions to: Agog; Amonite; Arcadian Celtic Dawn; Hybrid; Lines Review; Nutshell; Orbis; Rialto; Third Half; Vigil; Wyrd; Ambit; Envoi. Address: 2 Pantile Cottages, Kettlestone Road, Little Snoring, Norfolk NR21 0JE, England.

CLIFTON (Thelma) Lucille, b. 27 June 1956, Depew, New York, USA. Professor of Literature and Creative Writing; Poet. m. Fred J Clifton, 1958, dec 1984, 2 sons, 4 daughters. Education: Howard University, Washington, DC, 1953-55; Fredonia State Teachers College, New York, 1955. Appointments: Poet-in-Residence, Coppin State College, Baltimore, 1972-76; Poet Laureate of Maryland, 1976-85; Visiting Writer, George Washington University. Washington, DC, 1982-83; Professor of Literature and Creative Writing, University of California, Santa Cruz, 1985-; Distinguished Visiting Professor, St Mary's College, Maryland, 1989-91. Publications: Poetry: Good Times, 1969; Good News About The Earth, 1972; An Ordinary Woman, 1974; Two-Headed Woman, 1980; Good Woman: Poems and a Memoir, 1969-1980, 1987; Next, 1987; Ten Oxherding Pictures, 1989; Quilting: Poems, 1987-1990, 1991; The Book of Light, 1993; Other: Generations, 1976; Children's books: 14 books, 1970-81. Honours: YM-YWHA Poetry Center Discovery Award, 1969; National Endowment for the Arts Grants, 1970, 1972; Juniper Prize, 1980; Coretta Scott King Award, 1984. Address: c/o Curtis Brown, 10 Astor Place, New York, NY 10003, USA.

CLINE Charles William, b. 1 Mar 1937, Waleska, Georgia, USA. Professor. m. Sandra Lee Williamson, 11 June 1966, 1 son. Education: AA, Reinhardt College, 1957; University of Cincinnati, 1957-58; BA, 1960, MA, 1963, Vanderbilt University. Appointments: Assistant Professor, Shorter College, 1963-64; Instructor, West Georgia College, 1964-68; Manuscript Procurement Editor, 1968; Associate Professor, 1969-95, Professor, 1975-, Kellogg Community College. Publications: Forty Salutes to Michigan Poets (editor); Crossing the Ohio; Questions for the Snow; Ultima Thule; Wholeness of Dreams (co-author). Contributions to: Poet; Voices International; New Laurel Review; Great Lakes Review; Green River Review; Wind Literary Journal; SouWester; Orbis; Ocarina; IBC Magazine; World Institute of Achievement Newsletter; Bardic Echoes; Modus Operandi; North American Mentor Magazine; Invictus; New Europe; New Muses. Honours: LittD, World University, 1981; Gold Medal; International Academy of Poets Award; World Institute of Achievement; Commemorative Silver Medal; Life Patron, International Biographical

Association; World Fellowship Award; Medallion for Distinguished Participation, 20th International Congress on Arts and Communications, 1993. Memberships include: World Poetry Society; Tagore Institute of Creative Writing; Academy of American Poets; Poetry Society of America; Wordsworth-Coleridge Association; Association of Literary Scholars and Critics; Modern Language Association. Address: 9866 South Westnedge Avenue, Portage, MI 49002, USA.

CLINTON (Lloyd) Dewitt, b. 29 Aug 1946, Topeka, Kansas, USA. Professor. m. 14 July 1973. 1 stepdaughter. Education: BA, Southwestern College, 1968; MA, Wichita State University, 1972; MFA, 1975, PhD, 1981, Bowling Green State University. Appointments: Lecturer, 1981-85; Assistant Professor, 1985-88; Associate Professor, 1988-95; Professor, University of Wisconsin at Whitewater, 1995-. Publications: Conquistador, Dog Texts; The Rand McNally Poems; Coyot, Dog Texts; Das Illustrite Mississippithal Revisited; Night Jungle Bird Life; Active Death: Unholy Rhymes. Contributions to: Journal of Reform Judaism; Kenyon Review; Great River Review; Wisconsin Review; Birmingham Poetry Review; Apalachee Quarterly; Eleven Wisconsin Poets; Heartland II: Poets of the Midwest; Southern California Quarterly; Abiko Quarterly; Cross Currents: Religion and Intellectual Life; Louisiana Literature; Southern California Quarterly; Abiko Quarterly; Cross Currents: Religion and Intellectual Life; Louisiana Literature. Honours: New Work Award (Wisconsin Arts Board); System Teaching Fellow, University of Wisconsin; Individual Artist Grant (WAB); Creative Artist Grant (Michigan Council for the Arts); MacDowell Colony Fellow; Ann Stanford Poetry Prize, University of Southern California, 1994; Summer Enhancement Grant, University of Wisconsin at Whitewater, 1994; Ann Stanford Poetry Prize, University of Southern California, 1994; Summer Enhancement Grant, University of Wisconsin at Whitewater, 1994. Memberships: Associated Writing Programs; Wisconsin Fell of Poets. Address: 3567 North Murray Avenue, Shorewood, WI 53211, USA.

CLITHEROE Frederic, b. 25 Sept 1941, Bury, Lancashire, England. Librarian. m. Catherine Eyre, 1 July 1971, 1 son, 1 daughter. Education: BA, Honours, English, University of Exeter, 1966-69; ALA, 1970. Appointments: University of Sussex, 1970-71; Assistant Librarian, University of Keele, 1971-90; Freelance Writerr, 1990-. Publications: Ellipsis, 1961; Poems, 1968; Meerbrook, 1979; Forsbrook, 1981; Countess Torsy, 1989; Harecastle Mint, 1993. Contributions to: University Poetry, 1968; Sceptre; Daedalus; Jordan Review; National Poetry Anthology, 1983; Outposts, 1978; Exeter Review, 1991. Honours: Dunn-Wilson Prize, 1966; Award from Beanica Foundation, 1981. Memberships: Secretary, University Literary Society, 1968-69. Address: Greenfields, Agger Hill, Finney Green, Newcastle, Staffordshire ST5 6AA, England.

CLOUDSLEY Timothy, b. 18 Sept 1948, Cambridge, England. University Lecturer. m. Rhona Cleugh, 18 July 1987, 2 sons. Education: BA (Hons) Cantab, 1971; Postgraduate Research, Durham University, 1972-74. Appointments: Lecturer, Sociology, Newcastle University, 1972-74; Napier University, Edinburgh, 1974-76; Heriot-Watt University, Edinburgh, 1976-77; Glasgow Caledonian University, 1977-. Publications: Poems to Light (Through Love and Blood), 1980; Mair Licht (Anthology), 1988; Coincidence (Anthology), 1995. Contributions to: Northlight Poetry Review; Understanding Magazine; Interactions; Romantic Heir; The People's Poetry; The Cadmium Blue Literary Journal; Journal des Poetes. Memberships: Open Circle (Arts and Literature Organisation), Glasgow, Literary Secretary, 1990-96. Address: 31 Hamilton Drive, Glasgow G12 8DN, Scotland.

CLOVIS Donna Lucille, b. 22 Aug 1957, East Orange, New Jersey, USA. Educator; Writer. 2 sons, 1 daughter. Education: BA, Trenton State College, 1978. Appointments: New Brunswick Board of Education, Teacher, 1981-86; North Brunswick, Teacher, 1986-89; Voorhees, Teacher, 1989-. Publications: Metamorphosis: Survival Through These Hard Times; Struggles for Freedom, 1994. Contributions to: Instructor Magazine; True Love Magazine; Black Masks Magazine. Honours: New Jersey Institute of Technology Writers Award for Poetry; ESL Success Award; Blue Ribbon Award. Memberships: Poets & Writers Guild; Southern Jersey Poetry Association; New Jersey Poetry Society; National Council of Teachers of English. Address: PO Box 0741, Princeton Junction, NJ 08550, USA.

CLUYSENAAR Alice Andree (Anne), b. 15 Mar 1936, Brussels, Belgium. Educator; Poet. m. Walter Freeman Jackson, 30 Oct 1976. Education: BA, Trinity College, Dublin, 1957; University of Edinburgh, 1963. Appointments: Teacher, Manchester University, England, 1957-58; Trinity College, Dublin, Ireland, 1961-62; Kings College, Aberdeen, Scotland, 1963-65; University of Lancaster, England, 1965-71; Huddersfield Polytechnic, 1982; University of Birmingham, 1973-76; Sheffield City Polytechnic, 1976-87. Publications: Fan of Shadows; Nodes; An Introduction to Literary Stylistics; Selected Poems of James Burns Singer; Double Helix. Contributions to: New Poets of Ireland; English Poetry, 1960-; Faber Poetry Introduction; Virago Anthology of Women's Love Poetry; Poems and Criticism. Address: Little Wentwood Farm, Llantrisant, Usk, Gwent NP5 1ND, South Wales.

COATES Ruth Allison, b. 18 May 1915, Mount Carmel, Illinois, USA. Writer. m. Robert E Coates, 24 Dec 1939, 2 sons, 2 daughters. Education: Graduated from Mount Carmel High School, 1933; Graduated from Bethel Women's College, Hopkinsville, Kentucky, 1936, AA degree; Indiana University, Bloomington, Indiana, AB, English, 1938. Appointments: Published Freelance Writer,1936-; Commercial Artist, Department Stores, Indianapolis, Indiana and San Antonio, Texas, 1939-42. Publications: Waiting for the Westbound, 1992; Great American Naturalists, 1974. Contributions to: Byline; Rand-McNally Anthology; Indiana Writes; National Library of Poetry; Humpty-Dumpty's Magazine. Honour: James Land Jones Memorial Prize, 1993. Membership: Poetry Society of America. Address: 8140 Township Line Road, Apartment 5306, Indianapolis, IN 46260, USA.

COBB David Jeffery, (Kobu), b. 12 Mar 1926, Harrow, England. Educational Adviser; Writer. m. Pannee Siripongpreeda, 10 July 1979, 2 sons, 3 daughters. Education: BA, 1954; PGCE, 1955. Appointments: German Teacher, 1955-58; Assistant, Unesco Institute for Education, Hamburg, 1958-62; British Council, English Teacher, Bangkok, Dhonburi, 1962-68; Assistant Professor, Asian Institute of Technology, 1968-72; In-house adviser/writer for educational publishers, 1972-84; Freelance, 1985-. Publication: A Leap in the Light, 1991; Mounting Shadows, 1992; Chips Off the Old Great Wall, 1994; The Shield-Raven of Wittenham, 1995; Jumping from Kiyomizu, 1996. Contributions to: Rialto; Iron; Modern Haiku; Frogpond; Ko; Haiku Canada; Quartos; Haiku Quarterly; Mainichi Daily News; Woodnotes; Blithe Spirit; Albatross; Nineties Poetry; Contemporanul. Honour: 1st Prize, Cardiff International Haiku Competition, 1990. Memberships: British Haiku Society, Secretary; Haiku Society of America; Royal Bangkok Sports Club; Life Guards Association. Address: Sinodun, Shalford, Braintree, Essex CM7 5HN, England.

COBB Esther Jane, b. 23 May 1928, Sonyea, New York, USA. Nurse (retired). m. George Cobb, 12 Dec 1959, dec. Education: Graduated High School, 1945; Nurses Training, 1949; 30 college credits. Publication: Book in progress. Contributions to: National Library of Poetry. Address: 4513 Red School Road, Dansville, NY 14437, USA.

COBBING Bob, b. 1920, England. Poet. Publications: Selected Poems: Bill Jubobe, 1976; Bob Jubile, 1990; Collected Poems: Cygnet Ring, 1977; ABC/Wan Do Tree, 1978; A Peal in Air, 1978; The Kollekted Kris Kringle, 1979; Bob Cobbing's Girlie Poems, 1983; Sockless in Sandals, 1985; Vowels and Consequences, 1985; Astound and Risible, 1987; Lame, Limping, Mangled, Marred and Mutilated, 1986; Processual, 1987; Entitled: Entitled, 1987; Improvisation is a Dirty Word, 1989; Voice Prints, 1993; Poems by RWC for RWC, 1995. Address: 89A Petherton Road, London N5 2QT, England.

COCCO-ANGIOY Marisa, b. 18 Dec 1938, Benevento, Italy. Professor. Education: University of Spain. Appointments: Writer. Publications: Tristezas y Recuerdos; Encuentros; Acquasola; Confesiones De Hoy; Reflexiones; Tramonta Il Sole, 1990; I Morti Di Palermo, 1993; El Amor, 1994. Contributions to: L'Unione Sarda; Bacherontius, S Marsherita Ligure; Voce, Della Sardegna. Honours: Renato Serra; Versilia; C Capodieci; Premio, San Valentino, 1990. Memberships: UESA; AEPE. Address: Via Pisacane, 17-16129 Genova, Italy.

CODRESCU Andrei, b. 20 Dec 1946, Sibiu, Romania (US citizen, 1981). Professor of English; Author; Poet; Editor; Radio and Television Commentator. m. Alice Henderson, 12 Sept 1969, 2 sons. Education: BA, University of Bucharest, 1965. Appointments: Professor of English, Louisiana State University, 1966-; Commentator,

All Things Considered, National Public Radio; Editor, Exquisite Corpse, literary journal. Publications: Novels: The Repentance of Lorraine, 1994; The Blood Countess, 1995. Poetry: Comrade Past and Mister Present, 1991; Belligerence, 1993; Alien Candor: Selected Poems, 1970-1995, 1996. Essays: Raised by Puppets Only to Be Killed by Research, 1987; Craving for Swan, 1988; The Disappearance of the Outside: A Manifesto for Escape, 1990; The Hole in the Flag: A Romanian Exile's Story of Return and Revolution, 1991; Road Scholar: Coast to Coast Late in the Century, 1993; The Muse is Always Half-Dressed in New Orleans, 1995; Zombification: Essays from NPR, 1995; The Dog With the Chip in His Neck: Essays from NPR & Elsewhere, 1996. Editor: American Poetry Since 1970; Up Late, 1988; The Stiffest of the Corpse: An Exquisite Corpse Reader, 1983-1990, 1990; American Poets Say Goodbye to the 20th Century, 1996. Film: Road Scholar, Public Broadcasting Service, 1994. Honours: George Foster Peabody Award, 1995; Freedom of Speech Award, American Civil Liberties Union, 1995; Literature Prize, Romanian Cultural Foundation, 1996. Address: 1114 Peniston, New Orleans, LA 70115, USA.

COEN Christiana, b. 18 Dec 1943, Shanghai, China. Teacher. m. Dr Massimo A Tosini, 28 Dec 1992. Education: Degree in Literature and Philosophy, Genova University. Appointments: Founder, art gallery specializing in visual poetry, Spazio Tre, Parma, 1968; Participant in many public multi-media performances and festivals, 1975-, including: Diversi in Versi, Parma, 1984; Salento Poesia, Lecce, 1988; Pescart, Milano, 1990; Umanitaria, Milano, 1991-92; Teatro Lirico di Milano, Milano, 1993; Festival di Poesia Sonora, Pescara, 1994; Contemporanea Mente Poesia, Milano, 1995-96; Enrico Baj's Patafisica Exhibition, Milano, 1994; Founder, various artists (poets, musicians, filmmakers) working together, Casacoen, 1994. Publications: Qualcosa Che Ritorna, 1966; Storia di Ingrid La Viaggiatrice, 1995. Contributions to: L'Incantiere, poetry review. Honours: Finalist, Lerici-Pea Award, 1966; Finalist, National Lorenzo Montano Award, 1996. Membership: Baobab (Sound Poets Association). Address: Via Casale 7, 20144 Milano, Italy.

COFFEY Brian, b. 8 June 1905, Kingstown, County Dublin. Mathematics Teacher; Lecturer in Philosophy. m. 8 Oct 1938, 4 sons, 5 daughters. Education: Baccalareat in Classics both parts, 1923, 1924, Paris; BSc Chemistry 1st Hon 1928; MSc Chemistry 1929; MA Mathematics 2nd Hon 1929; PhD 1946, Paris. Appointments: Assistant Professor in Philosophy, St Louis University, Missouri, 1947-52; Head of Mathematics, St Benedicts, Ealing, London, 1955-68; Various tuition posts. Publications: Poems, co-author, 1929; Three Poems, 1933; Third Person, 1938; Various poems; essays in Irish University Review, 1951-60; Also in Niagara Press, USA; Selected Poems, 1971; Chanterelles, 1985; Poems 1925-1990; Death of Hector, 1979. Contributions to: Articles, reviews in The Criterion, London, 1939-84; Occasional articles in Irish & English journals; Translations from French and Spanish at various times. Honour: Irish Arts Council Prize. Address: 48 Alma Road, Portswood, Southampton SO2 1BP, England.

COFFEY Marilyn June, b. 22 July 1937, Alma, Nebraska, USA. Writer; Teacher; Performer; Publisher. m. 15 April 1961, 1 son. Education: BA, University of Nebraska, 1959; MFA, Brooklyn College, 1981. Appointment: Currently Associate Professor, Department of English, Fort Hays State University, Kansas. Publications: A Cretan Cycle; Eostre. Contributions to: Manhattan Poetry Review; 13th Moon; Woodstock Times; Sunbury; Aphra; Snake Roots; New American Review. Honours: 1976 Pushcart Prize; Named Master Alumnus. Memberships: Poets and Writers; Poetry Society of America. Address: 305 West 15 Street, Hays, KS 67601, USA.

COGSWELL Fred(erick William), b. 8 Nov 1917, East Centreville, New Brunswick, Canada. Professor Emeritus; Author; Poet; Editor; Translator. m. (1) Margaret Hynes, 3 July 1944, dec 1985, 2 daughters, (2) Gail Fox, 8 Nov 1985. Education: BA, 1949, MA, 1950, University of New Brunswick; PhD, University of Edinburgh, 1952. Appointments: Assistant Professor, 1952-57, Associate Professor, 1957-61, Professor, 1961-83, Professor Emeritus, 1983-, University of New Brunswick; Editor, Fiddlehead Magazine, 1952-66, Humanities Association Bulletin, 1967-72. Publications: The Stunted Strong, 1955; The Haloed Tree, 1956; Testament of Cresseid, 1957; Descent From Eden, 1959; Lost Dimensions, 1960; A Canadian Anthology, 1960; Five New Brunswick Poets, 1962; The Arts In New Brunswick, 1966; Star People, 1968; Immortal Plowman, 1969; In Praise Of Chastity, 1970; One Hundred Poems Of Modern Quebec, 1971; The Chains Of Liliput, 1971; The House Without A Door, 1973; Against Perspective,

1979; A Long Apprenticeship: Collected Poems, 1980; Pearls, 1983; The Edge To Life, 1987; The Best Notes Merge, 1988: Unfinished Dreams: Contemporary Poetry Of Acadie, 1990; In My Own Growing, 1993; As I See It, 1994. Honours: Various medals and awards; Order of Canada. Memberships: League of Canadian Poets; PEN; Writers Federation of New Brunswick. Address: Camp A6, Site 6, RR 4, Fredericton, New Brunswick E3B 4X5, Canada.

COHEN Helen Degen, b. 19 Nov 1934. Writer. m. Arnold L Cohen, 4 Mar 1956, div, 2 sons, 1 daughter. Education: BS, University of San Antonio; MA, University of Illinois, 1977. Appointments: School Teacher, 1958-60; Instructor, Roosevelt University, 1979-84; Artist in Education, Illinois Arts Council, 1983-90. Contributions to: Partisan Review; Spoon River Quarterly; The House in Via Gambito; Concert at Chapins House; Another Chicago Magazine; Outerbridge. Honours: National Endowment for the Arts; Literary Award, Illinois Arts Council; 1st Prize, Stand Magazine; 1st Prize, Korone; Special Award, Indiana University Writer's Conference. Memberships: Poetry Forum; Poetry Society of America; Illinois Writers Inc. Address: 1166 Osterman, Deerfield, IL 60015, USA.

COHEN Leonard, b. 21 Sept 1934, Montreal, Quebec, Canada. Singer; Composer; Poet. Education: McGill University; Columbia University. Appointments: Singer and Composer, with concerts throughout North America and Europe. Publications: Let Us Compare Mythologies, 1956; The Spice Box of Earth, 1961; Flowers for Hitler, 1964; Parasites of Heaven, 1966; Selected Poems, 1956-1968, 1968; Leonard Cohen's Song Book, 1969; The Energy of Slaves, 1972; Two Views, 1980; Book of Mercy, 1984. Honours include: Quebec Literary Award, 1964. Address: c/o Stranger Music Inc, 146 West 75th Street, 2A, New York, NY 10023, USA.

COHEN Selma (Phoebe), b. 13 Mar 1925, New York, New York, USA. Secretarial. m. Philip Cohen, 3 July 1947, dec, 3 sons 1 dec, 1 daughter. Education: Girls Commercial High School, 1942. Appointment: Secretary in Department of Computer Science at San Francisco State University, 1984-92. Publications: Poems, Prose, Drawings From the Hand, Mind and Heart, 1990; This Tree and More Poems, Prose and Beginnings Endings, 1990; She's My Woman, a woman's point of view of a man's point of view, and other poems, 1990; Emotion - Mostly Poems, 1990; Looking Into a Mirror, Prose Poems, 1991; Touch Me, and other poems, 1993. Address: 1501 Lincoln Way, No 201, San Francisco, CA 94132, USA.

COHN Jim, b. 17 Apr 1953, Illinois, USA. Poet; Scholar. Education: BA, University of Colorado; Jack Kerouac Fellowship, Naropa Institute; MSEd, University of Rochester and The National Technical Institute for the Deaf. Publications: Green Sky; Mangrove; Divine April; Prairie Falcon. Contributions to: Rolling Stone; Brief; Heaven Bone; Napalm Health Spa; Nada Anthology; The Temple of Baseball; Nice to See You: Talking with Tranquility; Sign Language Studies; Akwesasne Notes. Honours: Walt Whitman Award. Memberships: Poets and Writers; Writers and Books. Address: Birdsfoot Farm, Star Route, Box 138, Canton, NY 17617, USA.

COLBY Beulah M Wadsworth, b. 10 May 1941, Maine, USA. Housewife; Town Clerk; Columnist. 1 son, 4 daughters. Contributions to: Republican Journal; Golden Treasury of Great Poems. Honours: National Honor Society, Golden Poet Award; Silver Poet Award. Address: HCR 80, Box 4, Liberty, ME 04949, USA.

COLDWELL John Walter, b. 10 Apr 1950, London, England. Teacher. m. Rosemary John, 19 Apr 1982, 2 sons. Appointments: Bank Clerk, 1967-74; Teacher, Temple Boys School, 1974-86; Head of English, 1986-89; Publicity Officer, St Georges High School, 1989-. Publications: Hoo Sir, Me Sir; More Lasting Than A Fish Supper; Well, Well; Daleks On Ramsey Street; Beast in the Bedroom; The Bees Knees; The Slack Jawed Camel; Thunder Clap; Bees Sneeze. Contributions to: Issue One; Brandos Hat; The North; Working Titles; The Third Half; The Rialto; Ioata; Foolscap; Poetry Now; Terrible Work Purple Patch. Membership: Salford Poems, Swop Scheme. Address: 11 Park Road, Ramsgate, Kent CT11 7QN, England.

COLE Eugene Roger (Peter E Locre), b. 14 Nov 1930, Cleveland, Ohio, USA. Freelance Writer; Editor; Researcher. Education: BA, 1954; MDiv, 1958; AB, 1960; MA, 1970. Appointments: Ordained Roman Catholic Priest, 1958; Newman Moderator, Central Washington University, 1958-59; English Instructor, Department Chairman, Schools of Northwest, 1959-69; Business Manager,

Experiment Press, 1959-60; Freelance Writer, Editor, Researcher, 1969-; Poetry Critic, National Writers' Club, 1969-72; Founder, Director, Godspeople Inc, 1985-. Publications: Which End; Spring as Ballet; Have You; Woman, You: Falling Up; Act and Potency; Ding An Sich; Uneasy Camber. Contributions to: Saturday Review; Northwest Review; International Poetry Review; Cape Rock Journal; Laurel Review; Discourse; Numerous others. Honours: Poetry Broadcast Award; Danae International Poetry Award; Distinguished Service to Poetry Award. Memberships: Authors' Guild; National Writers' Club; Friends of the Lilly Society. Address: PO Box 91277, Cleveland, OH 44101, USA.

COLE Henri, b. 9 May 1956, Japan. Poet; Teacher; Editor. Education: BA, College of William and Mary, 1978; MA, University of Wisconsin, 1980; MFA, Columbia University, 1982. Appointments: Executive Director, Academy of American Poets, 1982-88; Visiting Lecturer, Yale College, 1989; Associate Professor, Columbia University, New York, 1989; Visiting Writer, University of Maryland, 1990; Briggs-Copeland Lecturer in Poetry, Harvard University, Cambridge, Massachusetts, 1993-. Publications: The Zoo Wheel of Knowledge; The Marble Queen. Contributions to: Antaeus; Atlantic Monthly; Boulevard; Gettysburg Review; Grand Street; The Hudson Review; Nation; New Yorker; Ontario Review; Paris Review; Poetry; Southern Review; Yale Review. Honours: Pushcart Prize; Fellowship, Ingram Merrill Foundation; Amy Lowell Poetry Travelling Scholarship; Fellowship, New York Foundation for the Arts; The National Endowment for the Arts. Memberships: Academy of American Poets; PEN; Poetry Society of America. Address: 410 East 88th Street 3B, New York, NY 10128, USA.

COLE William (Rossa), b. 20 Nov 1919, Staten Island, New York, USA. Author; Poet; Reviewer. m. (1) Peggy Bennett, May 1947 div, 2 daughters, (2) Galen Williams, 10 July 1967, 2 sons. Appointments: Publicity Director, 1946-58, Publicity Director and Editor, 1958-61, Simon and Schuster Inc, New York City; Columnist, Saturday Review, 1974-79; Book Reviewer, Endless Vacation, 1990-. Publications: A Cat Hater's Handbook, or, The Ailurophobe's Delight (with Tomi Ungerer), 1963; Uncoupled Couplets: A Game of Rhymes, 1966; Editor: 8 poetry anthologies and 10 other anthologies; 7 anthologies for children; 35 cartoon anthologies. Contributions to: Various periodicals. Honour: American Library Association Notable Books, 1958, 1964, 1965. Memberships: Authors Guild; American PEN; International PEN; Poets and Writers; Poetry Society of America. Address: 201 West 54th Street, New York, NY 10019, USA.

COLE-EARNEY Beverly. See: EARNEY Beverly (Verna).

COLEMAN Mary Ann, b. 3 Jan 1928, USA. Writer. m. Oliver McCarter Coleman, 4 Mar 1955. Education: Indiana University, 1945-49; BSEd Auburn University, 1950. Appointments: Teacher, Pompano Beach, Florida, 1951-52; Welfare Worker, Atlanta, 1952-53; Teacher, East Point, 1953-55; Teacher of Poetry Workshops, 1970-. Publications: Disappearances; Secret Passageway; Recognizing the Angel; The Dreams of Hummingbirds: Poems from Nature. Honours: Poetry Society of America Consuelo Ford Memorial Award; Anhinga Press Cynthia Cahn Memorial Award; Hororable Mention, International Sri Chinmoy Contest. Memberships: Poetry Society of America; National League of American Penwomen; Poetry Atlanta; Society of Childrens Book Writers; Georgia State Poetry Society. Address: 205 Sherwood Drive, Athens, GA 30606, USA.

COLES Donald Langdon, b. 12 April 1928, Woodstock, Ontario, Canada. Professor; Poet. m. 28 December 1958, 1 son, 1 daughter. Education: BA, Victoria College; MA, University of Toronto; MA (Cantab), 1954. Appointments: Fiction Editor, The Canadian Forum, 1975-76; Director, Creative Writing Programme, York University, 1979-85; Poetry Editor, May Studio, Banff Centre for the Fine Arts, 1984-93. Publications: Sometimes All Over, 1975; Anniversaries, 1979; The Prinzhom Collection, 1982; Landslides, 1986; K In Love, 1987; Little Bird, 1991; Forests Of The Medieval World, 1993; My Death as the Wren Library, 1993; Someone Has Stayed In Stockholm: Selected and New Poems, 1994. Contributions to: Various periodicals. Honours: CBC Literary Competition, 1980; Gold Medal for Poetry, National Magazine Awards, 1986; Governor-General's Award for Poetry, 1993. Membership: PEN International. Address: 122 Glenview Avenue, Toronto, Ontario M4R 1P8, Canada.

COLES Robert, b. 10 Dec 1929, Boston, Massachusetts, USA. Writer; Teacher; Physician. m. Jane Hallowell, 3 sons. Education: AB,

Harvard College, 1950; Columbia University, MD, 1954. Appointments: Psychiatric Resident, Massachusetts General Hospital, 1955-56; Research Psychiatrist, Harvard University Health Service, 1963-; Professor, Harvard University, 1977-; Visiting Professor, Dartmouth College, 1988-. Publications: A Festering Sweetness; Rumors of Separate Worlds. Contributions to: American Poetry Review; Poetry; Massachusetts Review. Address: University Health Services, 75 Mt Auburn Street, Cambridge, MA 02138, USA.

COLLIER Michael Robert, b. 25 May 1953, Arizona, USA. Professor. m. Katherine A Branch, 2 May 1981, 2 sons. Education: BA, Connecticut College, 1976; MFA, University of Arizona, 1979. Appointments: Lecturer, George Mason University, 1982; Lecturer, Trinity College, 1982-83; Director of Poetry Programmes, Folger Shakespeare Library, 1983-84; Lecturer, 1984, Assistant Professor, Associate Professor, 1984-96, Professor, 1996-, University of Maryland; Lecturer, Johns Hopkins University, 1985-88; Visiting Lecturer, Yale University, 1990-92; Writing Staff, Warren Wilson College, 1991-. Publications: The Clasp and Other Poems; The Folded Heart; The Wesleyan Tradition: Four Decades of American Poetry, 1993; The Neighbor, 1995. Contributions to: New Yorker; Atlantic; Nation; New Republic; Poetry; American Poetry Review; Antaeus; Antioch Review; Southern Review; Denver Quarterly; Partisan Review. Honours: Fellowship, National Endowment for the Arts; Thomas Watson Fellowship; Alice Faye di Castagnola Prize; Pushcart Prize; Discovery Award, The Nation; Fellowship, Fine Arts Center, Provincetown; Guggenheim Fellowship; Directorship, Bread Loaf Writers' Conference. Memberships: Poetry Society of America; Academy of American Poets. Address: Department of English, University of Maryland at College Park, College Park, MD 20742, USA.

COLLINS Martha, b. 25 Nov 1940, Omaha, Nebraska, USA. Writer; Teacher. m. Theodore M Space, 6 Apr 1991. Education: AB, Stanford University, 1962; MA, University of Iowa, 1965; PhD, 1971. Appointments: Assistant Professor, Northeast Missouri University, 1965-66; Professor, University of Massachusetts, Boston, 1966-. Publications: The Catastrophe of Rainbows; The Arrangement of Space; A History of Small Life on a Windy Planet, 1993. Contributions to: Pushcart Prize Anthology; American Poetry Review; Field; Poetry; Kenyon Review; Partisan Review; Southern Review; Virginia Quarterly Review; New England Review; Agni; Ploughshares. Honours: Gordon Barber Memorial Award; Fellowship, National Endowment for the Arts; Alice Fay Di Castagnola Award; Peregrine Poetry Prize; Ingram Merrill Fellowship; Pushcart Prize; Mary Carolyn Davies Award; Bunting Fellowship. Memberships: Poetry Society of America; Associated Writing Programs; New England Poetry Club. Address: 66 Martin Street 3, Cambridge, MA 02138, USA.

COLOMBO John Robert, b. 24 Mar 1936, Kitchener, Ontario, Canada. Author; Editor. m. Ruth, 3 children. Appointments: Advisor, Canada Council, Ontario Arts Council, North York Arts Council; Writer in Residence, Mohawk College, Hamilton, 1979-80. Publications: Over 110 books, including: Selected Poems, Selected Translations, Off Earth, Luna Park, Some Hungarian Poems, Songs of the Indians, Poems of the Inuit, Mysterious Canada, The Mystery of the Shaking Tent, Walt Whitman's Canada, Voices of Rama. Honours: Harbourfront Literary Award, 1985; Order of Cyril and Methodius; Esteemed Knight of Mark Twain. Address: 42 Dell Park Avenue, Toronto, Ontario M6B 2T6, Canada.

COLON ALVARADO Roberto, b. 11 May 1929. Professor. Education: University of Puerto Rico, 1957; Stanford University, California, 1962-64. Appointments: US Army, 1950-54; Professor, University of Puerto Rico, 1961-62. Publications: Fronda Verde; El Jibaro Magazine; Yerbajos; Resolana. Contributions to: Magazines in Puerto Rico and the US; Alma Latina; Bohemia; Periodico El Mundo; El Vocero; Don Quixote. Honours: Novelist Manuel Zeno Gandia Prize; Roberto Colon Alvarado Poetry Contest; Resolution. Memberships: Puerto Rican Authors' Society; International Writers and Artists; World Academy of Arts and Culture. Address: Las Palmas Bldg 5 Apt 32, Coamo, PR 00769, USA.

COMBS Maxine, b. 14 June 1937, Dallas, Texas, USA. Teacher; Writer. m. 1 son, 1 daughter. Education: BA, Mills College, 1958; MA, Wayne State University, 1961; PhD, University of Oregon, 1967. Appointments: Instructor, Idaho State University, 1963-65; Lecturer, Lane Community College, 1966-69; Lecturer, American University, 1970-74; Instructor, 1972-77, 1981-88, Assistant Professor, 1990-, University of the District of Columbia, 1972-77, 1981-88; Assistant

Professor, George Mason University, 1979-80; Instructor, Howard University, 1988, 1990. Publications: Swimming Out of the Collective Unconscious; The Foam of Perilous Seas. Contributions to: South Florida Poetry Review; Backbone; Ariel; Up Against the Wall; Poets' Domain; Echoes; Literary Review; Finding The Name; Round Table; Iris. Honours: Honourable Mention, National League of American Pen Women; Finalist, Signpost Press Chapbook Contest; Semi-finalist, The Nation Chapbook Contest; Winner, Larry Neal Award in Fiction. Memberships: The Writers' Center; Academy of American Poets. Address: 2216 King Place NW, Washington, DC 20007, USA.

COMFORT Alex(ander), b. 10 Feb 1920, London, England. Physician; Adjunct Professor; Writer; Poet. m. (1) Ruth M. Harris, 1943, div 1973, 1 son, (2) Jane T Henderson, 1973, dec 1991. Education: BA, 1943, MB, BCh, 1944, MA, 1945, Cambridge University; MRCS, LRCP, London Hospital, 1944; DCH 1946, PhD, 1949, DSc, 1963, University of London. Appointments include: Honorary Research Associate, Department of Zoology, 1951-73, and Director of Research, Gerontology, 1966-73, University College, London; Clinical Lecturer, Department of Psychiatry, Stanford University, 1974-83; Professor, Department of Pathology, University of California School of Medicine, Irvine, 1976-78; Consultant Psychiatrist, Brentwood Veterans Administration Hospital, Los Angeles, 1978-81; Adjunct Professor, Neuropsychiatric Institute, University of California, Los Angeles, 1980-; Consultant, Ventura County Hospital, California, 1981-91. Publications: Non-fiction includes: The New Joy Of Sex, 1991; Writings Against Power And Death, 1993; Fiction includes: Imperial Patient: The Memoirs of Nero's Doctor, 1987; The Philosophers, 1989; Poetry includes: France And Other Poems, 1942; The Song Of Lazarus, 1945; The Signal To Engage, 1946; And All But He Departed, 1951; Haste To The Wedding, 1962; Poems For Jane, 1979; Mikrokosmos, 1994. Honours: Ciba Foundation Prize for Research in Gerontology, 1958; 2nd Prize, Borestone Poetry Award, 1962; Karger Memorial Prize, 1969. Memberships: American Association of Sex Educators, Counselors and Therapists; American Medical Association; American Psychiatric Association; British Society for Research on Aging; Gerontological Society; Peace Pledge Union; Royal Society of Medicine. Address: 2 Fitzwarren House, Hornsey Lane, London N6 5LX, England.

COMPTON Suzette Childeroy, b. 27 Oct 1925, India. Writer. m. (1) Eric Burn, div, (2) Alfred Busiel, dec, 1 daughter, (3) Angus Mackintosh, div, (4) Roddy Wilson, div. Education: Private Tuition; St Helen's, Northwood. Publications: Debrett's Book of Antiques; Christmas Cards for The Collector. Contributions to: Parnassou Book of World Poets, 1995; Anchor Poets of the Southeast, England; Kettleshill Press Anthology; Blue Dragon Press Anthology; Over 70 poems, illustrated with paintings by Michael Garady; Phoenix Poets; Lings Greetings Cards, Paintings and Poetry Series. Honours: Dame of the Order of St Michael of The Wing. Memberships: London Writers Circle; Phoenix Poets. Address: 9 The Hoo, Church Street, Old Willingdon, Eastbourne, East Sussex BN20 9HR, England.

CONGDON Kirby, b. 13 Nov 1924, West Chester, Pennsylvania, USA. Retired Writer. Education: BA, Columbia College, 1951. Publications: Hourglass, Nine Poems, 1947; Iron Ark, A Bestiary, 1962; Juggernaut, 1966; A Key West Rebus, 1969; Dream-Work, 1970; Black Sun, 1973; Chain Drive, 1976; Animals, 1978; Fantoccini, 1981; Here We Are, 1989. Contributions to: New York Times; Contact II; Colorado Quarterly; Confrontations. Address: 715 Baker's Lane, Key West, FL 33040, USA.

CONLEE Heather M, b. 14 Jul 1966, Rochester, New York, USA. Mother; Student; Writer. 1 son, 1 daughter. Education: Currently studying for AAS. Publications: Through the Hourglass; Sounds of Poetry. Contributions to: National Library of Poetry. Honours: Accomplishment of Merit, 1995. Address: 15 North Front Street, #6R, Hudson, NY 12534, USA.

CONN Jeanne Emily Louise, b. 18 Dec 1931, Ilford, Essex, England. Letter Writer. m. Victor William Amos Conn, 5 Apr 1956. Education: University of Leicester. Appointments: Editor, Connections, Literary Quarterly. Contributions to: Kerouac Connection; Atlantean; Sol; Global Tapestry; Alpha Beat Soup; Connections; Matrix. Memberships: Goldsmiths Literary Society; Luciad Leicester University Literary Magazine. Address: 165 Domonic Drive, New Eltham, London SE9 3LE, England.

CONN Stewart, b. 5 Nov 1936, Glasgow, Scotland. Poet. Appointments: Radio Producer, BBC, Glasgow, 1962-77; Literary Adviser, Edinburgh Royal Lyceum Theatre, 1972-75; Head of Radio Drama, BBC, Edinburgh, 1977-92. Publications: Thunder In The Air, poems, 1967; The Chinese Tower, poems, 1967; Stoats In The Sunlight: Poems (in the US as Ambush And Other Poems), 1968; The Burning, 1971; In Transit: An Ear To The Ground, poems, 1972; PEN New Poems, 1973-74 (editor), 1974; Thistlewood, 1975; The Aquarium, The Man In The Green Muffler, I Didn't Always Live Here, 1976; Under The Ice, poems, 1978; Play Donkey, 1980; In The Kibble Palace: New And Selected Poems, 1987; The Luncheon Of The Boating Party, poems, 1992; In The Blood, poems, 1995; At The Aviary, 1995. Contributions to: Anthologies, journals and radio programmes. Honours: E C Gregory Award, 1964; Scottish Arts Council Awards and Poetry Prize, 1968, 1978, 1992; Fellow, Royal Scottish Academy of Music and Drama; Society of Authors Travel Bursary, 1996. Membership: Knight of Mark Twain. Address: 1 Fettes Row, Edinburgh EH3 6SF, Scotland.

CONNERS Logan T. See: MASON (H)enry (C)onner.

CONNOR Margaret Lamorna, b. 10 Sept 1929, Bedford, England. Teacher. Education: Ripon College of Education, 1952-54. Appointments: Ramsgate, 1954; Birmingham, 1959; Senior Mistress: Bradford, 1963, 1975-80; Leeds, 1969. Publications: Introducing Fabric Collage, 1969, 1970; Pilgrimage, poems, 1995; B H Latrobe, Architect, history pamphlet, 1995. Contributions to: Verse for the Eighties; New Christian Poetry; Liturgy of Life; Aireloom; Pennine Platform; Weyfarers; Aireings; 4 Poetry Now Anthologies; Northeast '93; Yorkshire Anthology, 1994; Samaritan Poets; Simply Read; Springboard; Christian; Reform; Catholic Pictorial; Church of Ireland Gazette; Life and Work; New Fire; Moravian Messenger; Moravian, USA; Leeds Grapevine; City Vision; Parnassus of World Poets; Yorkshire Journal; Yorkshire Evening Post; Home Gardening, Northern Ireland; Moravian History, IOTA, articles; Psychopoetica; Poetry Today. Honours: Exhibitions of Collage, including Commonwealth Institute, London, 1970; Colleges in educational and private collections; 3rd Prize, Society of Teachers of Speech and Drama, 1985; Runner-up, Yorkshire Television Poetry Competition, 1985; Joint Recipient, 1st Prize, Poetry, Swarthmore Creative Writing Competition, 1995. Memberships: Swarthmore Writers Workshop; Ilkley and Aireings Literary Festivals. Membership: Northern Society of Costume and Textiles. Address: 13 Fulneck, Pudsey, West Yorkshire LS28 8NT, England.

CONNOR Tony, b. 16 Mar 1930, Manchester, England. m. Frances Foad, 1961. Appointments: Professor of English, Wesleyan University, Connecticut, 1971-. Publications include: With Love Somehow, 1962; Lodgers, 1965; 12 Secret Poems, 1965; Kon in Springtime, 1968; In the Happy Valley, 1971; The Memoirs of Uncle Harry, 1974; Twelve Villanelles, 1977; New and Selected Poems, 1982; Spirits of the Place, 1987; Metamorphic Adventures, 1996. Address: 44 Brainerd Avenue, Middletown, CT 06457, USA.

CONNORS Bruton. See: ROHEN Edward.

CONQUEST (George) Robert (Acworth), (Ted Pauker, Victor Gray), b. 15 July 1917, Malvern, Worcestershire, England. Writer. m. (1) Joan Watkins, 2 sons, (4) Elizabeth Neece, 1 Dec 1979. Education: University of Grenoble, 1935-36; Magdalen College, Oxford, 1936-39; MA (Oxon), 1972; DLitt, 1975. Appointments: Visiting Poet, University of Buffalo, USA, 1959-60; Literary Editor, The Spectator, 1962-63. Publications: Poems; A World of Difference; Power and Policy in the USSR; Between Mars and Venus; The Egyptologists; The Great Terror; Arias From A Love Opera; The Nation Killers; Lenin; Kolyma; Forays; The Abomination of Moab; We and They; Inside Stalin's Secret Police; The Harvest of Sorrow; New and Collected Poems; Stalin and the Kirov Murder; Tyrants and Typewriters; Stalin, Breaker of Nations. Contributions to: London Magazine; Times Literary Supplement; Analog Science Fiction; Soviet Studies; Neva, St Petersburg; Novy Mir, Moscow; Poetry; Chicago; New Republic; Spectator. Memberships: British Academy; Royal Society of Literature; Travellers' Club; British Interplanetary Society; Society for the Promotion of Roman Studies; American Association for the Advancement of Slavic Studies. Address: 52 Peter Coutts Circle, Stanford, CA 94305, USA.

CONRADI-BLEIBTREU Ellen (Ellen Schmidt-Bleibtreu), b. 11 June 1929, Heidelberg, Germany. Author. m. Dr Bruno Schmidt-Bleibtreu, 5 June 1956, 1 son, 1 daughter. Education: English,

Spanish, Philosophy, University of Mainz. Appointments: Delegate and 10 years as Regional Consultant for Europe International Council of Women Committee, Arts, Letters and Music, Paris. Publications: Jahre m FJ, 1950; Kraniche, 1970; Fragmente, 1973; Unter dem Windsegel, 1978; Zeitzeichen, 1983; Klimawechsel, 1989. Contributions to: Westermanns Hefte; Canadian Newspaper, Vancouver; Dt Tagespost; Ev Sonntagsblatt; Bonner Rundschau; General Auzeiger. Honours: Urban Prize, 1976; Honorary Prize, Literary Union, 1977; World Culture Prize, Accademia Italia, 1984; Professor, hc, Istitute Europe di Cultura, 1989. Memberships: Gedok, 1967; Professional Advisor of Literature, 5 years; Die Kogge European Authors Union, 1973; Humboldt-Gesellschaft, 1993. Address: Pregelstrasse 5, 53127 Bonn, Germany.

CONRAN Anthony, b. 7 April 1931, Kharghpur, India. Poet; Writer. Education: BA, 1953, MA, 1956, University of Wales. Appointments: Research Assistant, 1957-66, Tutor in English, 1966-, University of Wales. Publications: Formal Poems, 1960; Icons, Asymptotes, A String o Blethers, Sequence of the Blu Flower, The Mountain, For The Marriage Of Gerald And Linda, 1963; Stalae And Other Poems, 1965; Guernica, 1966; The Penguin Book Of Welsh Verse, 1967; Claim, Claim, A Book Of Poems, 1969; Life Fund, On To The Fields Of Praise: Essays On The English Poets Of Wales, 1979; The Cost Of Strangeness, 1982; Welsh Verse, 1987. Address: 1 Frondirion, Glanrafon, Bangor, Caernarvonshire, Wales.

CONSTABLE Geoffrey David, b. 7 Aug 1958, Prestwood, Buckinghamshire, England. New Age Christian Mystic Poet and Musician. Education: BA (Hons), English. 1989, Information Technology course, 1992, St David's University College of Wales. Publications: The Island of Storms, 1981; Leavings, 1985; The Prophetic Tapes. 1995. Contributions to: Poetry Review; Ostinato; Poetry Now; Poetry Business; CND Cymru. Honours: 3rd Prize, CND National Poems for Peace Competition, 1983; 3rd Prize, Poetry Society National Competition, 1990; Runner-up Prize, 1st Cardiff International Poetry Competition; Runner-up Prize, Poetry Business 1990 Competition. Memberships: Poetry Society; Welsh Union of Writers; Early English Texts Society; Founder Member, Leader, New Age Christian Movement; President, former George Formby Appreciation Society; Former Member, Lampeter Writers Workshop. Address: 6 Twitchell Road, Gt Missenden, Bucks HP16 0BQ, England.

CONSTANTINE David (John), b. 4 Mar 1944, Salford, Lancashire, England. Fellow in German; Poet; Writer; Translator. m. Helen Frances Best, 9 July 1966, 1 son, 1 daughter. Education: BA, 1966. PhD, 1971, Wadham College, Oxford. Appointments: Lecturer to Senior Lecturer in German, University of Durham, 1969-81; Fellow in German, Queen's College, Oxford, 1981-. Publications: Poetry: A Brightness to Cast Shadows, 1980; Watching for Dolphins, 1983; Mappi Mundi, 1984; Madder, 1987; Selected Poems, 1991; Caspar Hauser, 1994; Sleeper, 1995; Fiction: Davies, 1985; Back at the Spike, 1994; Non-fiction: The Significance of Locality in the Poetry of Friedrich Hölderlin, 1979; Early Greek Travellers and the Hellenic Ideal, 1984; Hölderlin, 1988; Friedrich Hölderlin, 1992; Translator: Hölderlin: Selected Poems, 1990, enlarged edition, 1996; Henri Michaux: Spaced, Displaced (with Helen Constantine), 1992; Philippe Jaccottet: Under Clouded Skies/Beauregard (with Mark Treharne), 1994; Goethe: Elective Affinities, 1994; Kleist: Stories and Plays, 1997; Editor: German Short Stories 2, 1972. Honours: Alice Hunt Bartlett Prize, 1984; Runciman Prize, 1985; Southern Arts Literature Prize, 1987. Membership: Poetry Society. Address: 1 Hilltop Road, Oxford OX4 1PB, England.

CONTOGENIS Constantine, b. 21 June 1947, New York, New York, USA. Teacher. Education: BA, City College of the City University of New York, 1973. Publication: Brief Songs of the Kisang. Contributions to: Ironwood; Poetry New York; Triquarterly; Grand Street; Chicago Review; Nimrod; Beloit Poetry Journal; Pulpsmith; New England Review; Bread Loaf Quarterly; Poetry East; Pequod. Honours: Poetry Grants, Edward Albee Foundation, Ragdale Foundation, Hélène Wurlitzer, Korean Arts and Culture Foundation. Membership: Poetry Society of America. Address: 65 Sullivan Street, New York, NY 10012, USA.

COOK Geoffrey Arthur, b. 9 Apr 1946, Cleveland, Ohio, USA. Scholar; Artist; Writer. Education: Kenyon College, 1964-67; BA, University of California, 1982; MA, 1987; PhD. Appointments: Contributing Editor, Margins, 1975-78; Contributing Editor, La Mamelle Art Contemporary, 1977-81; California Poets in the Schools, 1981-83;

Berkeley Ecumenical Chaplaincy for the Homeless. Publications: Tolle Lege; A Basket of Chestnuts: From the Miscellanea of Venantius Fortunatus; Love and Hate; Azrael. Contributions to: Nation; West Coast Poetry Review; Invisible City; Isthmus; Took; West Consciousness Review; Berkeley Review of Books; Minotaur; Poetry USA; The Hartford Courant; Androgyny; Free Lance; Zahir; India Currents; Global Tapestry Journal; Buddhist Third Class Junkmail Oracle; Orbis; Kings Review; Fiction International: Forum on Political Correctness. Memberships include: PEN; The American Literary Translators' Association; Association of Asian Studies; American Oriental Society; Indo-British Historical Society. Address: PO Box 4233, Berkeley, CA 94704, USA.

COOK Robert Leslie, b. 2 May 1921, Edinburgh, Scotland. Officer, Royal Navy; Secretary. m. Janet Ritchie, 28 Oct 1942, 2 daughters. Education: Edinburgh University, 1952-57. Publications: Hebrides Overture and Other Poems; Within the Tavern Caught; Sometimes a Word; Time With a Drooping Hand; The Daylight Lingers; World Elsewhere; Voices From Ithaca. Contributions to: Antioch Review; Candelabrum; Countryman; Linq; Negative Capability; New English Weekly; Nimrod; Orbis; Outposts; Poetry Review; Prairie Schooner; Several anthologies. Honour: Grierson Verse Prize. Memberships: Scottish Association for the Speaking of Verse; Edinburgh University Poetry Society. Address: 4 Whitecraigs, Kinnesswood, Kinross KY13 7JN, Scotland.

COOKE William, b. 27 Dec 1942, Stoke-on-Trent, Staffordshire, England. Lecturer. Education: BA, 1964; MA, 1966; PhD, 1969. Appointments: Teacher, Thistley Hough Grammar School; Tutor, Sixth Form College, City of Stoke-on-Trent; Lecturer, Stoke-on-Trent College. Publications: Builder; Small Ads; Edward Thomas: A Critical Biography, 1970. Contributions to: Critical Quarterly; Anglo Welsh Review; Poetry Wales; Outposts; English; New Poetry 1, 2 and 4; BBC Radio 3. Honour: Writer's Bursary. Membership: West Midland Arts, Literature Advisory Panel. Address: 17 Stuart Avenue, Trentham, Stoke-on-Trent ST4 8BG, England.

COOKSON William George, b. 8 May 1939, London, England. Editor; Publisher. m. Margaret Elizabeth Craddock, 20 July 1985, 1 daughter. Education: New College, Oxford, 1960-63. Appointments: Editor, Agenda Magazine, 1959-. Publications: Ezra Pound - Selected Prose 1909-1965 (editor), 1973; Dream Traces, a sequence, 1975; A Guide to the Cantos of Ezra Pound, 1985; Spell, 1986; Vestiges, 1987. Address: 5 Cranbourne Court, Albert Bridge Road, London SW11 4PE, England.

COOL AL. See: BUTLER Allen Todd.

COOLEY Peter John, b. 19 Nov 1940, Detroit, Michigan, USA. Professor. m. Jacqueline Marks, 12 June 1965, 1 son, 2 daughters. Education: AB, Shimer College, 1962; MA, University of Chicago, 1969; PhD, University of Iowa, 1970. Appointments: Assistant Professor, Associate Professor, University of Wisconsin, 1970-75; Associate Professor, Professor, Tulane University, New Orleans, Louisiana, 1975-. Publications: The Company of Strangers; The Room Where Summer Ends; Night Seasons; The Van Gogh Notebook; The Astonished Hours. Contributions to: New Yorker; Atlantic; Poetry; Harper's; Nation; New Republic. Honours: Pushcart Prize; Robert Frost Fellowship; Breadloaf Writers' Conference. Memberships: PEN; Poets and Writers; Poetry Society of America. Address: Tulane University, New Orleans, LA 70118, USA.

COOLIDGE Clark, b. 26 Feb 1939, Providence, Rhode Island, USA. Poet. m. Susan Hopkins, 1 daughter. Education: Brown University, 1956-58. Publications: Flag Flutter and US Electric, 1966; (Poems), 1967; Ing, 1969; Space, 1970; The So, 1971; Moroccan Variations, 1971; Suite V, 1973; The Maintains, 1974; Polaroid, 1975; Quartz Hearts, 1978; Own Face, 1978; Smithsonian Depositions, and Subjects to a Film, 1980; American Ones, 1981; A Geology, 1981; Research, 1982; Mine: The One That Enters the Stories, 1982; Solution Passage: Poems, 1978-1981, 1986; The Crystal Text, 1986; Mesh, 1988; At Egypt, 1988; Sound as Thought: Poems, 1982-1984, 1990; The Book of During, 1991; Odes of Roba, 1991; Baffling Means, 1991; On the Slates, 1992; Lowell Connector: Lines and Shots from Kerouac's Town, 1993; Own Face, 1994; Registers: (People in All), 1994; The ROVA Improvisations, 1994. Honours: National Endowment for the Arts Grant, 1966; New York Poets Foundation Award, 1968. Address: c/o The Figures, 5 Castle Hill, Great Barrington, MA 01230, USA.

COONEY Anthony Paul, b. 3 July 1932, Liverpool, England. Schoolmaster. m. 12 Apr 1958, 2 daughters. Education: Gregg Commercial College, Liverpool, 1948-50; Ethel Wormald College of Education, 1968-70; Open University. Appointments: Messenger Boy, 1946-48; Leading Aircraftman, Royal Air Force, 1950-52; Shipping Clerk, 1952-67; Assistant Master, 1971-91. Publications: Liverpool Newsletter; The Old Police Station Poetry Magazine; Georgian Sequence; The Wheel of Fire; Germinal; Inflections; Mersey Poems; Personations; Land of My Dreams. Contributions to: Various small press magazines. Address: Rose Cottage, 17 Hadassah Grove, Lark Lane, Liverpool L17 8XH, England.

COONS Susan Anderson, b. 21 June 1937, Minnesota, USA. Insurance Employee Benefit Specialist. Div, 1 son, 1 daughter. Education: BA, College of Wooster, Ohio; Sonons State University. Appointments: Teacher; Freelance Writer; Insurance Agent; Publisher. Publications: Harnassing Motion; Party in the Fields; Wine Song; What Did Slena Do. Contributions to: Poet; Blue Unicorn; Rooftops. Honours: Ina Coolbrith Golden Award; Poets of Vineyard World of Poetry. Membership: California Writers Club. Address: PO 2808, Rohnert Park, CA 94927, USA.

COOPER Jane (Marvel), b. 9 Oct 1924, Atlantic City, New Jersey, USA. Professor. Education: BA, University of Wisconsin, 1946; MA, University of Iowa, 1954. Appointments: Sarah Lawrence College, 1950-87; Visiting Professor, Graduate Writing Division, Columbia University School of the Arts, 1979, 1987-88, 1990; Visiting Professor, University of Iowa, 1980-81. Publications: The Weather of Six Mornings, 1969; Maps and Windows, 1974; Scaffolding: New and Selected Poems, 1984, 2nd edition, 1993; Green Notebook, Winter Road, 1994. Contributions to: American Poetry Review; American Voice; Iowa Review; Kenyon Review; New Yorker; Paris Review; Ploughshares. Honours include: Lamont Award, 1968; Shelley Award, 1978; Maurice English Award, 1985; Award in Literature, American Academy of Arts and Letters, 1995; New York State Poet, 1995-97. Memberships: PEN; Poets House, Poets' Advisory Board; Phi Beta Kappa. Address: 545 West 111th Street, Apt 8K, New York, NY 10025, USA.

COOPER John Charles, (Charles Greene), b. 3 Apr 1933, Charleston, South Carolina, USA. Professor of Philosophy and Religion; Lutheran Pastor. 4 sons, 2 daughters. Education: AB, University of South Carolina, 1955; MA, 1964, PhD, 1966, University of Chicago; MDiv, Lutheran Seminary, Columbia; STM, Lutheran Seminary, Chicago. Appointments: Professor of Philosophy and Religion: Newberry College; Eastern Kentucky University; Winebrenner Theological Seminary; Susquehanna University; Asbury College, 1993; University of Kentucky, 1994; Pastor: Faith Lutheran Church, Tampa; All Saints Lutheran Church, Nicholasville, Kentucky. Publications: The Unexamined Life, 1975; Vickie's Lake, Kentucky, 1989; Four Quartets, 1991 Cast a Single Shadow, 1995. Contributions to: Christianity Today; Christian Century; Time of Singing; Carolina Review; Wind; Merton Seasonal; Scripset. Honours: Euphrosynean Award, University of South Carolina, 1956; Phi Beta Kappa, 1956; 2nd Prize, Time of Singing, 1992; Phi Sigma Tau, University of Kentucky, 1995. Address: Writers Retreat, 2441 Bohon Road, Harrodsburg, KY 40330, USA.

COOPER Marti(ne Linda), b. 29 Nov 1955, Sheffield, England. 1 son. Education: BA, Leeds University, 1977. Appointments: Assistant Manager, Print Shop, 1977-85. Publications: Contemporary Yorkshire Poetry; Poems for Peace; Poetry Now Political. Contributions to: Staple; Weyfarers; Counterpoint; Aireings; Pennine Platform; New Hope International. Address: 10 Sheepwalk Lane, Castleford, West Yorkshire WF10 3HP, England.

COOPER Thomas (Edward), b. 12 July 1932, Ashton under Lyne, Lancashire, England. Social Worker (retired). Education: BA, Social Work, North Lancashire Polytechnic, 1967-70. Appointments: Royal Navy, 1947-55; ICI, Cheshire, 1955-1966; Social Work, Greater Manchester MBC, 1970-92; Freelance Writer, 1992-. Publications: Tameside Tales, 1992; Cheshire Odes, 1993; Fenland Fables, 1995. Contributions to: Newspapers and periodicals. Honours: Honourable mentions in many competitions in local and national newspapers and periodicals. Address: 3 Regal Lane, Soham, Cambridgeshire, CB7 5BA, England.

COOPER FRATRIK Julie, b. 8 Dec 1941, Philadelphia, Pennsylvania, USA. Poet. 4 daughters. Education: BA, 1980; MFA,

1983; MA. Publication: Where Our Voices Lie. Contributions to: Louisville Review; Texas Review; Tondril. Honour: Bucks County, Pennsylvania Poet. Memberships: Academy of American Poets; Poetry Society of America; Pennsylvania Arts Commission; Poets and Writers. Address: 6144 Upper Mountain Road, New Hope, PA 18938, USA.

COOVER Robert (Lowell), b. 4 Feb 1932, Charles City, Iowa, USA. Writer; Dramatist; Poet; University Teacher. m. Maria del Pilar Sans-Mallagre, 3 June 1959, 1 son, 2 daughters. Education: Southern Illinois University; BA, Indiana University, 1953; MA, University of Chicago, 1965. Appointments: Teacher, Bard College, 1966-67, University of Iowa, 1967-69, Princeton University, 1972-73, Brown University, 1980-; Various guest lectureships and professorships. Publications: The Origin Of The Brunists, 1966; The Universal Baseball Association, J Henry Waugh, Prop., 1968; Pricksongs And Descants, short fictions, 1969; A Theological Position, plays, 1972; The Public Burning, 1977; A Political Fable (The Cat In The Hat For President), 1980; Spanking The Maid, 1982; Gerald's Party, 1986; A Night At The Movies, 1987; Whatever Happened To Gloomy Gus Of The Chicago Bears?, 1987; Pinocchio In Venice, 1991; John's Wife, 1996; Briar Rose, 1997. Contributions to: Plays, poems, fiction, translations, essays, and criticism in various publications. Honours: William Faulkner Award for Best First Novel, 1966; Rockefeller Foundation Grant, 1969; Guggenheim Fellowships, 1971, 1974; Obie Awards, 1972-73; American Academy of Arts and Letters Award, 1976; National Endowment for the Arts Grant, 1985; Rhode Island Governor's Arts Award, 1988; Deutscher Akademischer Austauschdienst Fellowship, Berlin, 1990. Memberships: American Academy and Institute of Arts and Letters; PEN International. Address: c/o Department of English, Brown University, Providence, RI 02912, USA.

COPE Robert Knox (Jack Cope), b. 3 June 1913, Mooi River, Natal, South Africa. Writer; Poet; Editor. m. Lesley de Villiers, 4 June 1942, 2 sons. Appointment: Co-Founder and Editor, Contrast, South African literary magazine, 1960-80. Publications: Lyrics And Diatribes, 1948; Selected Poems Of Igrid Jonker, co-translator, 1968, revised edition, 1988; The Rain Maker, 1971; The Student Of Zend, 1972; My Son Max, 1977; Editor: Penguin Book Of South African Verse; Other: Stage, radio, and television adaptations. Contributions to: School textbooks and magazines. Honours: British Council Award, 1960; Carnegie Fellowship, 1966; CNA Prize, Argus Prize, and Gold Medalist for Literature, Veld Trust Prize, 1971; Honorary DLitt, Rhodes. Address: 21 Bearton Road, Hitchin, Hertfordshire, SG5 1UB, England.

COPE Wendy Mary, b. 21 July 1945, Erith, Kent, England. Writer. Education: BA, History, St Hilda's College, Oxford, 1966; Diploma in Education, 1967. Appointments: Primary School Teacher, London Borough of Newham, 1967-69, Inner London Education Authority, 1969-86. Publications: Making Cocoa for Kingsley Amis, 1986; Twiddling Your Thumbs, 1988; The River Girl, 1990; Serious Concerns, 1992. Contributions include: London Review of Books; Poetry Review; Daily Telegraph; Independent; Guardian; Sunday Times; Observer. Honours: Cholmondeley Award for Poetry, 1987; Fellow, Royal Society of Literature, 1993; Michael Braude Award for Light Verse, American Academy of Arts and Letters, 1995. Membership: Management Committee, 1992-95, Society of Authors. Address: c/o Faber and Faber, 3 Queen Square, London WC1N 3A4, England.

CORBETT-FIACCO Christopher, b. 2 Apr 1961, Albany, New York, USA. Writer. Appointment: Publisher, Editor, Sisyphus, 1990-. Publication: Pieces of Eight, anthology, 1992. Contributions to: American Poetry Annual, Amherst Society; Archer; Chiron Review; Fennel Stalk; Frugal Chariot; Hemispheres; Kana; Pegasus; Plowman; Renovated Lighthouse; Vandeloecht's Fiction Magazine. Address: 8 Asticou Road, Boston, MA 02130, USA.

CORBLUTH Elsa, b. 2 Aug 1928, Beckenham, Kent, England. Writer; Photographer. m. David Boadella, div 1987, 1 son, 1 daughter, dec 1980. Education: As mature student: BA, Combined Creative Arts, 1st Class Honours, Alsager College, 1982; MA, Creative Writing, Lancaster University, 1984. Publications: St Patrick's Night, poems on daughter's death in charity hostel fire while working there; Various booklets; Wilds, travelling exhibition of poems illustrated by her photographs, accompanied by poetry readings. Contributions to: Poetry Review; Outposts; The Rialto; Times Literary Supplement; Others; Anthologies: Green Book; Arts Council of Great Britain (several); PEN; Others. Honours: 1st Prize, South-West Arts (Bridport) Competition, 1979-1981; Joint 1st, Cheltenham Festival Competition, 1981; 1st, Sheffield Competition, 1981; 1st, ORBIS Rhyme Revival, 1986, 1993, 1995; Runner-up, Arvon and National Competition; Poems broadcast on Radio 3; BBC Radio 4 programme on St Patrick;s Night poems and daughter Eilidh's poems, 18 Mar 1995; Others. Address: Hawthorn Cottage, Rodden, Near Weymouth, Dorset DT3 4JE, England.

CORDANI Albert, b. 15 July 1947, Torrington, Connecticut, USA. Mason Labourer. m. 3 Feb 1979, 1 son, 1 daughter. Appointments: Labourer, Maintenance, Truck Driver, Cook, Automobile Products Sales. Publications: Treasured Poems of America; Awaken to a Dream; Festival of Voices; American Poetry Anthology; Windows on the World; Treasured from the Heart; Expressions; Word of Poems. Honours: Silver Poetry Award; Best Poet of the 90s. Address: 113 Funston Avenue, Torrington, CT 06790, USA.

CORDELLI Franco, b. 20 Feb 1943, Rome, Italy. Theatre Critic; Writer; Translator; Poetry Critic; Author. Education: Modern American Literature, University of Urbino, 1971. Appointments: Theatre Critic, 1968-89; Theatre Critic, Europeo, 1986; Vice-Director, Nuovi Argomenti, 1990-. Publications: Fuoco Celeste; Il Pubblico della Poesia; Il Poeta Postumo; Pro Prieta Perduta. Contributions to: Nuovi Argomenti; Poesia; Russian and Swedish anthologies. Honours: Teatrale Award; Sila Opera Prima; Sila; Brutium; Villa; Fondi. Memberships: Jury of Mondello Literary Prize; Colosseo Theatre; Teatro delle Arti; International Poetry Festival of Rome. Address: Via Francesco Mengotti 39, 00191 Rome, Italy.

CORDER Louise Pugh, b. 24 Apr 1936, Asheboro, North Carolina, USA. Media Coordinator. m. Leo D Corder, 16 Aug 1958, 3 sons. Education: BA, High Point College, 1958; MEd, University of North Carolina at Greensboro, 1972. Appointments: High School Teacher, 1958-59; Teacher, Grays Chapel High School, 1959-62; School Media Coordinator, 1976-93. Publications: Several poems in My Search; Poems in Ta Ke Time; Today's Greatest Poems; Candles of Hope, Poems to Cherish; Bridge of Faith; Here to the Land. Contributions to: Ideals; Muse; New Earth; Herald Holiness; Christian Advocate; Grit. Honours: Award Winner, Burlington Writers Club Annual Contest; North Carolina Poetry Society Winner; Winner, Christian Writers Fellowship International Contest. Memberships: North Carolina Poetry Society; National Endowment for the Arts; North Carolina Library Association; Alpha Delta Kappa Educational Fraternity; Randolph Asheoro Media Association. Address: 2713 Bruce Pugh Road, Franklinville, NC 27248, USA.

COREY Stephen Dale, b. 30 Aug 1948, Buffalo, New York, USA. Poet; Literary Editor; Essayist; English Professor. m. Mary Elizabeth Gibson, 28 Jan 1970, 4 daughters. Education: BA English 1971; MA English 1974; PhD English 1979. Appointments: Instructor of English, University of Florida 1979-80; Assistant Professor of English, University of South Carolina 1980-83; Assistant Editor 1983-86, Associate Editor 1986-, The Georgia Review. Publications: Synchronized Swimming, 1985, reissued, 1993; The Last Magician, 1981, reissued 1987; All These Lands You Call One Country, 1992; Poetry Chapbooks: Fighting Death, 1983; Gentle Iron Lace, 1984; Attacking the Pieta, 1988. Contributions to: Poetry; American Poetry Review; Kenyon Review; New Republic; Kansas Quarterly; Georgia Review; Poets & Writers; Antioch Review; Yellow Silk; Laurel Review. Honours: Writing Fellowships from the state arts councils of Florida 1978-79, South Carolina 1981-82 and Georgia 1985-86, 1988-89; Water Mark Poets First Book Award, 1981, for The Last Magician; Swallow's Tale Press Poetry Award, 1984, for Synchronized Swimming. Address: 357 Parkway Drive, Athens, GA 30606, USA.

CORMAN Cid (Sidney), b. 29 June 1924, Boston, Massachusetts, USA. Poet; Writer; Editor. m. Shizumi Konishi, 1965. Education: AB, Tufts University, 1945; Graduate Studies, University of Michigan, 1946-47, University of North Carolina, 1947, Sorbonne, University of Paris, 1954-55. Appointments: Poetry Broadcaster, WMEX, Boston, 1949-51; Editor, Origin Magazine and Origin Press, Kyoto, Japan, 1951-71. Publications: Poetry: Sabluna, 1945; Thanksgiving Eclogue, 1954; The Responses, 1956; Stances And Distances, 1957; A Table In Provence, 1958; The Descent From Daimonji, 1959; For Sure, 1959; For Instance, 1959; For Good, 1961; In Good Time, 1964; In No Time, 1964; All In All, 1965; For Granted, 1966; At Bottom, 1966; Words For Each Other, 1967; And Without End, 1968; No Less, 1968; No More, 1969; Nigh, 1969; Livingdying,

1970; Of The Breath Of, 1970; For Keeps, 1970; For Now, 1971; Out And Out, 1972; A Language Without Words, 1973; So Far, 1973; Breathing, 1973; 0/1, 1974; Once And For All, 1976; Auspices, 1978; Aegis: Selected Poems, 1970-1980, 1983; And The Word, 1987; Other: The Gist Of Origin: An Anthology, editor, 1973; At Their Word: Essays On The Arts Of Language, 2 volumes, 1977-78; Where We Are Now: Essays And Postcription, 1991. Honours: Fulbright Fellowship, 1954; Lenore Marshall Memorial Poetry Award, 1974; National Endowment For The Arts Award, 1974. Address: c/o Black Sparrow Press, PO Box 3993, Santa Barbara, CA 93130, USA.

CORN Alfred, b. 14 Aug 1943, Bainbridge, Georgia, USA. Poet; Writer; Critic; Translator. m. Ann Jones, 1967, div 1971. Education: BA, Emory University, 1965; MA, Columbia University, 1967. Appointments: Poet-in-Residence, George Mason University, 1980, Blaffer Foundation, New Harmony, Indiana, 1989, James Thurber House, 1990; Humanities Lecturer, New School for Social Research, New York City, 1988; Ellison chair in Poetry, University of Cincinnati, 1989; Bell Distinguished Visiting Professor, University of Tulsa, 1992; Hurst Residency in Poetry, Washington University, St Louis, 1994; Numerous college and university seminars and workshops; Many poetry readings. Publications: Poetry: All Roads at Once, 1976; A Call in the Midst of the Crowd, 1978; The Various Light, 1980; Tongues on Trees, 1980; The New Life, 1983; Notes from a Child of Paradise, 1984; An Xmas Murder, 1987; The West Door, 1988; Autobiographies, 1992; Present, 1997; Novel: Part of His Story, 1997; Criticism: The Metamorphoses of Metaphor, 1987; Editor, Incarnation: Contemporary Writers on the New Testament, 1990; The Pith Helmet, 1992; A Manual of Prosody, 1997. Contributions to: Books, anthologies, scholarly journals and periodicals. Honours: Woodrow Wilson Fellow, 1965-66; Fulbright Fellow, Paris, 1967-68; Ingram Merrill Fellowship, 1974, 1981; National Endowment for the Arts Fellowships for Poetry, 1980, 1991; Gustav Davidson Prize, Poetry Society of America, 1983; American Academy and Institute of Arts and Letters Award, 1983; New York Foundation for the Arts Fellowships, 1986, 1995; Guggenheim Fellowship, 1986-87; Academy of American Poets Prize, 1987; Yaddo Corporation Fellowship in Poetry, 1989; Djerassi Foundation Fellowship in Poetry, 1990; Rockefeller Foundation Fellowship in Poetry, Bellagio, Italy, 1992; MacDowell Colony Fellowships in Poetry, 1994, 1996. Memberships: National Book Critics Circle; PEN; Poetry Society of America. Address: 350 West 14th Street, Apt 6A, New York, NY 10014, USA.

CORNEL Adam. See: LENGYEL Cornel Adam.

CORNISH Sam(uel James), b. 22 Dec 1935, Baltimore, Maryland, USA. Poet; Writer; Teacher. m. Jean Faxon, 1967. Education: Goddard College, Vermont; Northwestern University. Appointments: Teacher of Creative Writing, Highland Park Free School, Roxbury, Massachusetts; Instructor in Afro-American Studies, Emerson College, Boston. Publications: Poetry: In This Corner: Sam Cornish and Verses, 1961; People Beneath the Window, 1962; Angles, 1965; Winters, 1968; Short Beers, 1969; Generations, 1971; Streets, 1973; Sometimes: Ten Poems, 1973; Sam's World, 1978; Songs of Jubilee: New and Selected Poems, 1969-1983, 1986; Folks Like Me, 1993; Other: Your Hand in Mine, 1970; My Daddy's People Were Very Black, 1976; 1935: A Memoir, 1990; Editor: Chicory: Young Voices from the Black Ghetto (with Lucian W Dixon), 1969; The Living Underground: An Anthology of Contemporary American Poetry (with Hugh Fox), 1969. Honour: National Endowment for the Arts Grants, 1967, 1969. Address: c/o Department of English, Emerson College, 100 Beacon Street, Boston, MA 02116, USA.

CORR John Franz, b. 29 May 1937, New York, New York, USA. Reader to Blind. m. Ruth Immerwahr, Sept 1972, 1 son. Education: BA, English, Whitman College, Walla Walla, Washington, 1959; Teaching Certificate, Western Washington State College, Bellingham, Washington, USA, 1965. Appointments: Carpenter 20 years; Research Technician; Teacher, Hilo High School, 1 year; Work Evaluator, 4 years; Reader to Blind, 12 years; Mental Health Consumer Intern, 9 months. Publications: Woodfrogs in Chaos - Anthology, 7 pages, 1996. Contributions to: Seattle Post Intelligencer. Memberships: 19th Draft, Auburn's Literary Arts Society. Address: 304 15th St SE #7, Auburn, AW 98002-6660, USA.

CORSERI Gary Steven, b. 31 Mar 1946, New York, New York, USA. Writer. m. May 1982. Education: BA, University of Florida, 1967; MAT, Harvard University, 1969; PhD, Florida State University, 1988. Publications: Random Desert, 1989. Contributions to: Poetry

Northwest; Poetry Lore; Florida Review; Buffalo Spree Magazine; Southern Humanities Review; International Poetry Review; Harvard Advocate; Florida Quarterly; West Branch; Atlantic Gazette; Premiere; Pyramid; University of Tampa Poetry Review; Woodrider; Your Place; Your Grace. Honours: 1st Prize, Stephen Vincent Benet Narrative Poem Contest, 1972; 1st Prize, Florida Poetry Contest, 1975; Co-winner, Georgia Poetry Circuit, 1989; Tennessee Williams Scholarship, 1990. Membership: Poetry Society of America. Address: c/o Pat Kenning, 2732 Williams, Denver, CO 80205, USA.

CORSO Gregory, b. 26 Mar 1930, New York, New York, USA. Poet; Dramatist; Writer. m. (1) Sally November, 7 May 1963, div, 1 daughter, (2) Belle Carpenter, 1968, 1 son, 1 daughter. Publications: Poetry: The Vestal Lady of Brattle, and Other Poems, 1955; Bomb, 1958; Gasoline, 1958, new edition, 1992; A Pulp Magazine for the Dead Generation: Poems (with Henk Marsman), 1959; The Happy Birthday of Death, 1960; Long Liv Man, 1962; Selected Poems, 1962; There is Yet Time to Run Back Through Life and Expiate All That's Been Sadly Done, 1965; The Geometric Poem: A Long Experimental Poem, Composite of Many Lines and Angles Selective, 1966; 10 Times a Poem: Collected at Random From 2 Suitcases Filled With Poems: The Gathering of 5 Years, 1967; Elegiac Feelings: American, 1970; Herald of the Autochthonc Spirit, 1981; Wings, Words, Windows, 1982; Mindfield: New and Selected Poems, 1989; Many others. Novel: American Express, 1961. Plays: This Hung-up Age, 1955; Way Out: A Poem in Discord, 1974; Collected Plays, 1980; Non-Fiction: Some of My Beginnings and What I Feel Right New, 1982. Contributions to: Penguin Modern Poets 5, 1963; A Controversy of Poets, 1965; Several periodicals. Honours: Jean Stein Award for Poetry, American Academy & Institute of Arts & Letters, 1986; Longview Award; Poetry Foundation Award. Address: c/o Roger Richards Rare Books, 26 Horatio Street No 24, New York, NY 10014, USA.

CORTI Doris Joyce, b. 29 Dec 1928, Plaistow, London, England. Poet; Freelance Writer; Housewife. m. Arthur George Stump, 6 Aug 1949. Education: RSA English Literature, Grove-Russell Central School, 1942; GCE A Level, English Literature and Language, Havering College of Further Education. Appointments: Secretary to Manager Export Company; Secretary to Bank Manager. Publications: Poetry Booklets: The Space Between, 1982 (illustrated by Michael Stump), New Moves, 1987, Rituals and Reminders, 1991 (illustrated by Michael Stump); Poems included in two sociology books: Let's Call the Whole Thing Off, 1989, Through the Fear Barrier, 1992. Book: Writing Poetry, published by D Thomas & Luchar, Oct 1994; Poetry Booklet, The Moon is a Letter C, 1995. Contributions to: Poetry to: Acumen; Envoi; Poetry Voice; Feature contributions to: Writers News; Report; Social Work Today; Writing Magazine; Contributions to anthologies: One in a Million; The Unsaid Goodnight; Envoi Summer Anthologies. Honours: Third Prize, Stamford Literature Festival, 1990; Second Prize, Brentwood Poetry Group, 1980; 1st Prize, poetry, 1994, 2nd Prize, poetry, 1995, The Centenary Competition of The Society of Women Writers and Journalists. Memberships: Poetry Advisor to Society of Women Writers and Journalists; Included in Poetry Society's Poets in Schools scheme; Included in Eastern Arts Literary Scheme for Schools (WORDS); Speaker for National Association of Women's Clubs. Address: 52 Poors Lane, Hadleigh, Essex SS7 2LN, England.

COSENTINO Patricia Alanah, (Patricia Alanah), b. 6 June 1925. Antique Dealer. m. David A Cosentino, 28 June 1990, 2 sons. Education: MEd, Regis College, 1984. Appointments: Director, Learning Laboratory, Newton College, 1967-70; Assistant Director, MAT, Harvard School of Education, 1970-72; Teacher, Wellesley, Massachusetts, 1972-90. Publications: Cat in the Mirror, 1970; The Spring Anthology Magazine; Author-Poet: Haiku Highlights; Cardinal Poetry Review; Premiere Phylon; Fireflower. Contributions to: Southern Poetry Review; Quoin; Melange; Translator, Prota. Honours: 1st Honours, Kentucky State Poetry Society; Mary F Lindsley Award, New York Poetry Forum. Memberships: Past Treasurer, New England Poetry Club; American Society of Poets, New York City; American Academy of Poetry; Poetry Society of America. Address: 33 Leo drive, Gardner, MA 01440, USA.

COSMOS Eddie. See: THERSON-COFIE Larweh.

COSTELLO Rita D, b. 22 June 1973, New York, USA. Poet; Student; College English Instructor. Education: BFA, Bowling Green State University (in Creative Writing and English), 1995; Currently an MFA student in poetry at Wichita State University. Appointments: Technical Editor for the Anathema Review, 1994-95; Graduate

Teaching Assistant at Wichita State University, 1996-. Publication: Rapeseed, chapbook from Doll Drag Press, 1996. Contributions to: Seattle Review; The Slate; Coal City Review; Midland Review; Plainsong; Anathema Review; Half Tones to Jubilee; The Panhandler; Radiance; Onionhead. Address: 4064 Cessna Drive, Wichita, Kansas 67210, USA.

COSTLEY William Kirkwood Jr (Bill), b. 21 May 1942, Salem, Massachusetts, USA. Writer; Journalist; Poet; Playwright. m. 6 June 1964, 1 son, 1 daughter. Education: AB, English, Boston College of Arts and Sciences, 1963; MFA coursework, Boston University, 1967-. Appointments: With many newspapers, later computer manufacturers including: Digital Equipment Corporation; Data General Corporation; International Data Group's Installed Technology International; Harte-Hanks Community Newspapers, Costley's Wellesley (Middlesex News); Wellesley Symphony (The Townsman). Publications: Knosh I Cir, selected poems 1964-75, 1975; R(A)G(A)S, 2 travel poems, 1978; A(Y)S(H)A, 16 poems on birth of twin grandsons, 1988; Terrazzo, 18 poems (partially in Italian), 1992; Siliconia, poems written in Santa Clara of Carmel-by-the-Sea on 1st trip to California, 1995. Contributions to: Ploughshares Vol 1, No 1; Arts in Society; The Smith; Small Pond; Nostoc; Scrievens; Last Glasgow Magazine; Occasionally to: Edinburgh Review; ER Encyclopaedia, 1987-. Honour: Honourable Mention, 1985 Anthology, Poetry Society, UK. Memberships: Scottish Poetry Library Association, Edinburgh; Robinson Jeffers Association, Santa Clara University; Tor House Foundation, Carmel-by-the-Sea; Boston Media Action Committee; National Writers Union, (Boston Local 1981), Steering Committee 1982-83, Member 1992-. Literary Agent: Marshall Brooks, Arts End Books, PO Box 1962, Waban, MAS 02168, USA. Address: One Sunset Road, Wellesley, MA 02181-4615, USA.

COTTON John, b. 7 Mar 1925, London, England. Education: BA, University of London, 1956. Appointment: Headmaster, Highfield Comprehensive, Hemel Hempstead, 1963-85. Publications include: Fourteen Poems, 1967; Outside the Garden of Eden and Other Poems, 1969; Roman Wall, 1973; Photographs, 1973; Powers, 1977; A Letter for a Wedding, 1980; Somme Man, 1980; The Totleigh Riddles, 1981; Day Book Continued, 1982; Oh Those Happy Feet, 1986; The Poetry File, 1988; Here's Looking at You Kid: New and Selected Poems, 1990. Address: 37 Lombardy Drive, Berkhamsted, Hertfordshire HP4 2LQ, England.

COUPER John Mill, b. 7 Sept 1914, Dundee, Scotland. University Lecturer in English Literature. m. Katharine Boyd, 17 July 1940, 2 sons, 1 daughter. Education: MA, 1936, PhD, 1948, Aberdeen University. Appointments: Lecturer, University of Queensland, Australia, 1951-54; Headmaster, Knox Grammar School, 1954-55; Lecturer, University of New South Wales, 1958-67; Senior Lecturer, Associate Professor, Macquarie University, 1968-78. Publications: East of Living, 1967; The Book of Bligh, 1969; In From the Sea, 1974; The Lee Shore, 1979; Canterbury Folk, 1984. Contributions to: Sydney Morning Herald; Australian; The Bulletin; Meanjin; Southerly; Melbourne Age. Honour: Moomba Prize for The Book of Bligh, 1970. Address: 9 Dudley Street, Asquith, New South Wales 2077, Australia.

COURT Wesli. See: TURCO Lewis Putnam.

COUTO Nancy Vieira, b. 11 June 1942, New Bedford, Massachusetts, USA. Poet. m. Joseph A Martin, 13 Aug 1988. Education: BS, Education, Bridgewater State College, 1964; MFA, English, Cornell University, 1980. Appointments: Subsidiary Rights Manager, Cornell University Press, 1982-94; Lecturer, Department of English, Cornell University, 1994; Consultant and Editor, Leatherstocking Literary Services, 1994-. Publications: The Face in the Water, 1990. Contributions to: Gettysburg Review; Epoch; American Poetry Review; Hudson Review; Iowa Review; Milkweed Chronicle; Poetry Northwest; Priarie Schooner. Honours: Gettysburg Review Award, 1994; Agnes Lynch Starrett Prize, 1989; National Endowment for the Arts Fellowship, 1987; New York State CAPS Fellowship, 1982-83. Memberships: Associated Writing Programs. Address: 508 Turner Place, Ithaca, NY 14850, USA.

COUZYN Jeni, b. South Africa. Psychotherapist. 1 daughter. Education: BA, Hons, University of Natal. Publications: Flying, 1970; Monkey's Wedding, 1972; Christmas in Africa, 1975; House of Changes, 1978; Life by Drowning, 1983, 1985; In the Skin House, 1993; Children's books: Bad Day; Tom-Cat-Lion; Various works published in Canada and South Africa; Editor: Bloodaxe Book of

Contemporary Women Poets, 1985; Singing Down the Bones, 1989. Memberships: Society of Authors; Guild of Psychotherapists. Address: c/o Anne Dewe, Andrew Mann Ltd, 1 Old Compton Street, London W1, England.

COWEN Athol Ernest, b. 18 Jan 1942, Wales. Writer. Publications: Word Pictures (Brain Soup), 1989; Huh!, 1991. Memberships: Publishers Association; Writers Guild of Great Britain; The Poetry Society; Guild of International Songwriters and Composers; Musicians Union. Address: 40 Gibson Street, Wrexham, Wales.

COWLAN Paul Francis, b. 7 June 1950, Farnborough, Kent, England. Songwriter; Performer; Peripatetic Tutor-Lecturer. Education: BEd Hons, 1974. Contributions to: Psychopoetica; Orbis; Envoi; Poetry Digest. Honours: 2nd Place, Poetry Digest Bard of the Year, 1994; Winner, Envoi Poetry Competition No 111, 1995. Address: 4 Court Hall, Kenton, Devon EX6 8NA, England.

COWLIN Dorothy. See: WHALLEY Dorothy.

COY David Lavar, b. 24 Apr 1951, Powell, Wyoming, USA. Professor of English and Creative Writing, Poetry. m. 19 Nov 1975, 1 son, 1 daughter. Education: BA, English Literature, University of Wyoming, 1975; MFA, Creative Writing, University of Arkansas, Fayetteville, 1983. Appointments: Graduate Assistant, University of Arkansas, 1979-83; Instructor, 1983-87, Assistant Professor, 1987-88, Southwest Missouri State University; Professor, Director of Writing School, Arizona Western College, 1988-. Publications: Rural News, 1991. Contributions to: Antioch Review; Aracne; Colorado North Review; Intro; Jumping Pond; Plainsong; Poetry NOW; Slant; Sow's Ear; Spoon River Quarterly; Widener Review. Honour: Academy of American Poets Prize, University of Arizona, 1982. Membership: Associated Writing Programs. Address: 2465 West 3rd St, Yuma, AZ 85364, USA.

CRAIG Shawna Anne Hudson, b. 1 July 1955, Vancouver, Washington, USA. Researcher. m. Patrick Naughtin, 31 Jan 1992, 2 daughters. Education: AAS, Anthropology, 1980; BA cum laude, Anthropology, 1982; MA, Anthropology, 1984. Appointments: Mother; Teaching Assistant; Research Assistant; Migrant Head Start Teacher; Circulation Manager; Researcher; Student Nurse. Contributions to: Journals: CLASS; Opossum Holler Tarot Newsletter; Writer's Voice; Dactylus; Writers Exchange Newsletter; Lucidity; Books: Chasing Rainbows; Poets' Memorable Songs; RSUP Press Anthology Poets, 1987; On the Threshold of a Dream, in American Poetry Anthology; Orchids and Daffodils, A Lyrical Bouquet, Rainbows and Rhapsodies, in Poetry of the 80s; Awaken to a Dream, in Poetic Voices of America, 1987; A Time To Be Free, in The World's Best Poems of 1987; The Best Poems of 1988. Honours: Honourable Mention, March Quarterly Poetry Competition, Writers Exchange, 1988; Poet of the Year, 1988; Honourable Mention, Chapbook Competition, 1990. Membership: International Society for the Advancement of Poetry. Address: 303 White Oak Drive, Austin, TX 78753, USA.

CRAIG Timothy, (Janet Turpin, Theresa Mullholland), b. 22 July 1940, USA. Librarian; Garden Designer. m. Sarah Brewster Coy, 20 Aug, 1994, 1 son. Education: BA, University of Maryland, 1962; MA, New York University, 1963; PhD, 1972; DLitt, Trinity College, Cambridge, 1974. Appointments: Assistant Professor, City University of New York; Assistant Keeper, British Museum; Editorial Assistant, Wellesley Index; Curator, Mansell Collection. Publications: Heart Slums; Everything in Its Path; Knots and Fans; Advice to the Rain; One If By Land. Contributions to: Xanadu; Plains Poetry Review; Pale Fire Review; Romantist; Thirteen; Lyric; Prairie Light. Memberships: Modern Language Association; Hidden Chiefs. Address: PO Box 784, Salem, NY 12865, USA.

CRAM David, b. 5 Apr 1945, Sutton-on-Sea, Lincolnshire, England. Lecturer in General Linguistics. Education: BA 1967, Oxford University; PhD 1973, Cornell University. Appointments: Aberdeen University 1974-88; Jesus College, Oxford, 1988-. Contributions to: Aberdeen Evening Express; Acta Victoriana; Ambit; Honest Ulsterman; Light Year; Literary Review; London Magazine; Spectator. Address: Jesus College, Oxford OX1 3DW, England.

CRAMER Steven, b. 24 July 1953, Orange, New Jersey, USA. Lecturer; Regular Book Reviewer. m. Hilary Rao, 20 Sept 1987. Education: University of Iowa, 1976-78; Antioch College, 1972-76; BA, 1978. Appointments: Poetry Editor, David R Godine, Publisher;

Instructor, Massachusetts Institute of Technology; Staff Editor, Atlantic Monthly; Lecturer, Boston University; Lecturer, Tufts University; Visiting Instructor, Massachusetts Institute of Technology. Publications: The Eye That Desires to Look Upward; The World Book. Contributions to: Antioch Review; Atlantic; Iowa Review; Nation; New England Review; New Republic; North American Review; Ohio Review; Paris Review; Partisan Review; Ploughshares; Poetry. Honours: Stanley Young Fellowship; National Endowment for the Arts Fellowship. Memberships: Associated Writing Programs; Poetry Society of America. Address: English Department, Tufts University, Medford, MA 02155, USA.

CRASE Douglas, b. 5 July 1944, Battle Creek, Michigan, USA. Poet. Education: AB, Princeton University, 1966. Appointments: Fellow, New York Institute for the Humanities, 1983-86. Publications: The Revisionist, 1981. Contributions to: New Yorker; Poetry; American Poetry Review; Partisan Review; Paris Review; Nation; Oxford Poetry; Spazio Umano. Honours: Witter Bynner Prize, American Academy and Institute of Arts and Letters, 1983; Guggenheim Fellowship, 1984; Whiting Writers Award, 1985; John D and Catherine T MacArthur Fellowship, 1987-92. Address: 470 West 24th Street, Apt 6D, New York, NY 10011, USA.

CRATE Joan, (Louise Imida), b. 15 June 1953, Yellowknife, Northwest Territories, Canada. English Instructor at University Level. 3 sons, 1 daughter. Education: Certificate of Communications Media; BA Hons; MA. Appointments: Instructor, University of Calgary, 1988; Instructor for Fiction Course, Correspondence, Lakeland College, Cold Lake, Alberta 1988-; Instructor, Red Deer College, Red Deer, Alberta 1991-; Writer in Residence, Calgary Public Library 1992. Publications: Pale as Real Ladies, poetry book, 1989; Breathing Water, novel, 1989; Anthologies: Native Writers and Canadian Writing, 1990; Literature in English: Writers and Styles From Anglo-Saxon Times to the Present, 1992. Contributions to: Grain; Dandelion; Fiddlehead; Orbis; Quarry; Canadian Literature; Ariel; Sanscrit; Arc; Canadian Author and Bookman; Canadian Forum; Newest Review; Calgary Herald, newspaper; CBC Radio. Honours: Third Place in Kalamalka New Writers Poetry Competition, 1987; Bliss Carmen Award for Poetry, 1988. Memberships: Alberta Writers Guild 1986-, past member at large 1987-88; Served with Calgary Creative Reading Series 1986-92, President 1989-91; The Dandelion Society; Co-Editor, poetry 1989-90, Dandelion. Address: 71 Marion Crescent, Red Deer, Alberta, T4R 1N1, Canada.

CRAWFORD John William, b. 9 Feb 1936, Ashdown, Arkansas, USA. College Professor. m. Kathryn Bizzell, 17 June 1962, 1 son, 1 daughter. Education: AA, Texarkana College, 1956; BA, BSE, Ouachita Baptist University, 1959; MSE, Drake University, 1962; EdD, Oklahoma University, 1968. Appointments: Instructor, English, Clinton College, 1962-66; Instructor, English, Oklahoma University, 1966-67; Associate Proffessor, English, 1967-73, Director of Freshman English, 1970-76, Chairman, Department of English, 1976-86, Professor, English, 1973-, Henderson State University. Publications: Making The Connection, 1989; Just Off Highway 71, 1992; I Have Become Familiar With The Rain, 1995. Contributions to: Rendezvous; Theology Today; ELF; Inlet; Lucidity; Voices International; Rivers Edge; Black Buzzard Review; Another Small Magazine; Potpourri; Independent Review; Soundings; Zephyr. Honours: 1st in Childrens Poetry, Deep South Writers Conference, 1975; Sybil Nash Abrams Awards, Arkansas Poets Roundtable Poetry Day, 1982, 1995; Byron Reece Narrative Award, Georgia Poetry Society, 1985; Merit Award for Service, Arkansas Poets Roundtable Poetry Day, 1988. Memberships: Arkansas Poets Roundtable; Arkansas Writers Conference; Arkansas Philological Association; Mississippi Philological Association; Philological Association of Louisiana; South Central Modern Language Association. Address: Box 7813, Henderson University, AR 71999-0001, USA.

CRAWFORD Robert, b. 23 Feb 1959, Bellshill, Scotland. University Professor. m. Alice Wales, 2 Sept 1988. Education: MA, 1981; DPhil, 1985. Appointments: Elizabeth Wordsworth Junior Research Fellow, Oxford, 1984-87; British Academy Postdoctoral Fellow, Glasgow University, 1987-89; Lecturer, University of St Andrews, 1989-; Professor of English, Modern South Literature, University of St Andrews, 1995-. Publications: Sterts & Stobies; Severe Burns; New Chatto poets 2; A Scottish Assembly; Sharawaggi; Talkies; The Savage and the City in the Work of T S Eliot, 1987; Devolving English Literature, 1992; Identifying Poets: Self and Territory in Twentieth Century Poetry, 1993; Masculinity, poems, 1996.

Contributions to: Gairfish; Akros; Chapman; Lines Review; London Magazine; London Review of Books; New Writing Scotland; New Yorker; Oxford; Poetry Review; Times Literary Supplement; Verse. Honours: Gregory Award; Runner Up, National Poetry Competition; Poetry Book Society Recommendations; Selected for Arts Council of Great Britain's New Generation Poets, 1994. Memberships: Society of Authors. Literary Agent: David Godwin, Henrietta House, 17-18 Henrietta Street, Covent Garden, London WC2E 8QX. Address: School of English, University of St Andrews, Fife, KY16 9AL, Scotland.

CREELEY Robert White, b. 21 May 1926, Arlington, Massachusetts, USA. Writer; Professor. m. (1) Ann McKinnon, 1946, div 1955, 2 sons, 1 daughter, (2) Bobbie Louise Hall, 1957, div 1976, 4 daughters, (3) Penelope Highton, 1977, 1 son, 1 daughter. Education: BA, Black Mountain College, 1954; MA, University of New Mexico, 1960. Appointments: Lecturer, Black Mountain College, 1954-55; University of British Columbia, 1962-63; Professor, 1967-78; David Grey Professor, 1978-89; State University of New York at Buffalo; Advisory Editor, American Book Review, 1983-; New York Quarterly, 1984-; Samuel P Capen Professor of Poetry and The Humanities, 1989. Publications: Poetry; For Love; Words; Pieces: A Day Book; Selected Poems; Memory Gardens; Prose: The Island; The Gold Diggers; Mabel: A story; The Collected Prose; Criticism; Was That a Real Poem; Collected Essays; The Essential Burns. Honours include: Guggenheim Fellow; Sheeley Memorial Award; National Endowment for the Arts; Frost Medal; Distinguished Fulbright Award; State University of New York Distinguished Professor. Memberships: American Academy and Institute of Arts and Letters; PEN. Address: 64 Amherst Street, Buffalo, NY 14207, USA.

CREMONA John, b. 6 Jan 1918, Gozo, Malta. Jurist. m. Marchioness Beatrice Barbaro of St George, 20 Sept 1949, 1 son, 2 daughters. Education: BA 1939, LLD cum laude 1942, Malta University; DLitt 1939, Rome University; BA 1st Class Hons 1946, PhD in Laws 1951, London University; Dr Jur, Trieste University. Appointments: Lecturer, Professor, University of Malta; Attorney-General, member Executive Council of Government and Consultative Council of Government; Vice President, Contitutional Court of Malta; Chief Justice of Malta; President of the Council of the University of Malta; Judge then Vice President, of the European Court of Human Rights, Strasbourg; member then Chairman, United Nations Committee on the Elimination of Racial Discrimination (CERD), New York and Geneva; Member of Editorial Board, various international human rights reviews. Publications: Eliotropi, 1937; Songbook of the South, 1940; Limestone 84, with others, 1978; Malta Malta, 1992. Contributions to: Italy: Poeti d'Oggi; Quaderni di Poesia; Il Piccolo dilla Sera; Il Giornale di Politica e di Letteratura; Belgium: La Revue Nationale; Greece: Olimpo; Japan: Poetry Nippon; UK: Outposts; Orbis; English; Anglo-Welsh Review; Scottish International; Envoi; Tribune; Workshop; New Poetry; USA, The Smith. Honours: Mostra Nazionale di Poesia Contemporanea, Italy, 1937, 1938; Hon Fellow LSE; Hon Fellow, Real Academia de Jurisprudencia y Legislacion, Spain; Fellow, Royal Historical Society, England; Chevalier de la Legion d'Honneur, France; Knight Grand Cross of the Order of Merit, Italy; Knight of the Sovereign Military Order of Malta, of the Venerable Order of St John of Jerusalem and of the Order of St Gregory the Great; Knight Grand Cross of the Constantinian Order; Companion of the Order of Merit, Malta. Memberships: Vice President, International Poetry Society, UK; Vice President, Malta Poetry Society. Address: Villa Barbaro, Main Street, Attard, Malta.

CRIPPS Dame Joy Beaudette, (H E Nobless), b. 13 June 1923, Melbourne, Victoria, Australia. Publisher; Poet; Photographer. m. Charles John Cripps, 2 Dec 1944, 2 sons. Appointments: Founder, Melbourne Poetry Society, 1982; Founder, Publisher, Festivals, Poetry Day Australia, 1982-93; Founder, Dove in Peace Award, 1993; Photographic illustrations for books, Exhibitions, 1983-86. Publications: Magpie Bridge, poems on Chinese Mythology, 1981; Getting Published, 1983; Tatters of Hessian, 1985; India Where Life Revolves around the Well, 1989; Poetry of Journey (with Xiao Luo China), 1990; Doves of Peace, collection, 1990; Poetry, Joy Beaudette Cripps, 1990; Tanabata, with calligraphy, China, Japan, Korrea & Thai translations, 1992; Poems for Thailand, dedicated to Queen Sirikit 60th Anniversary, 1992. Contributions to: Many poems, some articles to: Australia Women's Day Magazine; Women Writers of Australia; AEA newsletters; Kadimah, Melbourne Chronicle; Yukei Teiki Haiku, USA, Canada; Struga International Poetry Review, Yugoslavia; IBC Magazine, Cambridge; Australian Mordialloc News; The Age; Mainichi News, Tokyo; Canta Internaqcional de Poesia, Argentina; Poetcrit

Maranda, India; World Poetry, Korea. Anthologies: Poetry Day Australia, 1985, Books 1 and 2, 1988; Beneath the Southern Cross, 1988; Editor: Actinia, collection of 12 Australian poets, 1983; Celebration, international and Australian Anthology, 1984. Honours: LittD, Marquis Scicluna International University, 1986; LittD, Poet Laureate, World Academy of Arts and Culture, 1986; Gold Medallion, Red Shawl of Honour, Madras Congress, 1986; President's Medal, Australia Bicentennial, 1988; Taipei Medal, 1989; Gold Crown Kaya, Korea, 1991; Premio, La Gloire, 1982; Princess of Poetry, 1985; International High Committee Leonardo Da Vinci Accadamia, Rome, 1987; Professeur Attache de Recherche, (AUPAC), Paris, Bruxelles, 1993; others. Memberships: Founder, Past President, Melbourne Poetry Society; PEN Melbourne, International Committee, Member 1985; Oceania Regent Poet Intercontinental, India; Vice President, World Poetry Research Institute, Korea, 1993. Address: 3 Mill Street, Aspendale, Victoria 3195, Australia.

CRONIN Anthony, b. 23 Dec 1928, Enniscorthy, County Wexford, Ireland. Education: BA, University College, Dublin, 1948. Appointments: Columnist, The Irish Times, Dublin, 1973-86; Artistic Adviser to the Irish Prime Minister. Publications include: Poems, 1957; Collected Poems 1950-73, 1973; 41 Sonnet-Poems 82, 1982; New and Selected Poems, 1982; Letters to an Englishman, 1985; The End of the Modern World, 1989; Relationships, 1994. Honour: Marten Toonder Award, 1983. Address: 9 Rainsford Avenue, Dublin 8, Ireland.

CROOKER Barbara Poti, b. 21 Nov 1945, Cold Spring, New York, USA. Writer. m. Richard McMaster Crooker, 26 July 1975, 1 son, 3 daughters. Education: BA, Douglass College, Rutgers University, 1967; MS Education, Elmira College, 1975. Appointments: Instructor, English, Corning Community College, 1974-76; Instructor, English, County College of Morris, 1978-79; Assistant Professor, English, Northampton County Area Community College, 1980-82; Instructor, Women's Center, Cedar Crest College, 1982-85; Artist in Education (poet in the schools), 1989-; Instructor, Lehish County Community College, 1993. Publications: Writing Home, 1983; Starting from Zero, 1987; Looking for the Comet Halley, 1987; The Last Children, 1989; Obbligato, 1992; Moving Poems. Contributions to: Yankee; Family Circle; Organic Gardening; Country Journal; Anthology of Magazine Verse and Yearbook of American Poetry; America;Christian Science Monitor; Passages North; Hiram Poetry Review; Negative Capability; West Branch; Yarrow; Poets On; Madison Review; South Dakota Review; Passages North Anthology; This Sporting Life; Psychological Perspectives; McCall's; Pharos; Zone 3; Plains Poetry Journal; Bereavement; Potato Eyes; Highlights for Children; Denver Quarterly; Four Quarters; Pennsylvania Review.Honours: Nominee, Pushcast Prize, 1978, 1989; Fellowship in Literature, Pennsylvania Council on the Arts, 1985, 1989, 1993; Winner, Passages North and National Endowment for the Arts Emerging Writers Competition, 1987; The Phillips Award, Stone Country, 1988; Finalist, Felix Pollak Prize in Poetry, 1988; Finalist, The Brittingham Prize, 1988; Emerald Muse Award, 1989; Fellow, Virginia Center for the Creative Arts, 1990, 1992, 1994, 1995. Membership: Poetry Society of America. Address: 7928 Woodsbluff Run, Fogelsville, PA 18051, USA.

CROSHAW Michael, b. 12 Mar 1943, Warwick, England. m. Theresa Belt, 6 June 1970, div 1976, 2 sons. Appointments: British Telecom, 1973-91; Associate Editor, Orbis Magazine, 1980-87. Publications: Alum Rock, 1992; Mercia Poets, 1980 Collection. Contributions to: Acumen; Babel; Bogg; Bradford Poetry Quarterly; Bull; Chapman; Core; Envoi; Envoi Book of Quotes on Poetry; Jennings; Manhattan Poetry Review; Moorlands Review; New Hope International; Orbis; Ore; Other Poetry; Outposts Poetry Quarterly; Pennine Platform; Poetry Australia; Poetry Nottingham; Poet's Voice; Psychopoetica; Stride; Weyfarers. Memberships: George Eliot Fellowship, Secretary, 1960-62; Mercia Poets 1975-81. Address: Queen's Road, Nuneaton, Warwickshire CV11 5ND, England.

CROSS Beryl Mary, b. 5 Oct 1929, London, England. Journalist; Poet. Education: Exemption from Matriculation, University of London, 1945; GCE, Advanced Level, English Economic History, Economics, University of London, 1953; Diploma in Economics and Political Science, University of Oxford, 1955. Literary Appointments include: Editor of, Bank Officer; Research and Publicity Officer, National Union of Bank Employees; Publications Editor, National Association for Mental Health; Editor of, Rural District Review; Editor of, District Councils Review, journal of the Association of District Councils. Publications: Works included in, Anthology of Phoenix Poets 1972-1994, 1994; Finishing Touches, Mother and Sons, Sussex

Drought, included in Writing Poetry, by Doris Corti, 1994. Contributions to: Acumen; Outposts; Envoi; Poetry Nottingham; Weyfarers; Iota; Symphony; Seam; The Poet's Voice. Honours: Certificate of Distinction, for Finishing Touches, WB Yeats Club International Competition; Seal of Achievement Certificate for Concerto, WB Yeats Club International Competition. Memberships: Vice Chairman, Society Women Writers and Journalists; Committee, Phoenix Poets. Address: 32 Silver Crescent, Gunnersbury, London W4 5SE, England.

CROSSLEY-HOLLAND Kevin (John William), b. 7 Feb 1941, Mursley, Buckinghamshire, England. Professor; Poet; Writer; Editor; Translator. m. (1) Caroline Fendall Thompson, 1963, 2 sons, (2) Ruth Marris, 1972, (3) Gillian Paula Cook, 1982, 2 daughters. Education: MA, St Edmund Hall, Oxford. Appointments: Editor, Macmillan & Co, 1962-69; Lecturer in English, Tufts-in-London Program, 1967-78, University of Regensburg, 1978-80; Gregory Fellow in Poetry, University of Leeds, 1969-71; Talks Producer, BBC, 1972; Editorial Director, Victor Gollancz, 1972-77; Arts Council Fellow in Writing, Winchester School of Arts, 1983, 1984; Visiting Professor of English and Fulbright Scholar-in-Residence, St Olaf College, Minnesota, 1987-90; Professor and Endowed Chair in Humanities and Fine Arts, University of St Thomas, St Paul, Minnesota, 1991-95; Director, Minnesota Composers Forum, 1993-. Publications: Poetry: The Rain-Giver, 1972; The Dream-House, 1976; Time's Oriel, 1983; Waterslain, 1986; The Painting-Room, 1988; New And Selected Poems, 1991; The Language of Yes, 1996; Forthcoming: Poems from East Anglia, 1997; For children includes: Storm, 1985; British Folk Tales, 1987; Tales From Europe, 1991; Taliesin (with Gwyn Thomas), 1992; The Labours of Herakles, 1993; Norse Myths, 1993; The Green Children, 1994; The Dark Horseman, 1995; Non-fiction includes: The Stones Remain (with Andrew Rafferty), 1989; Editor, includes: Peter Grimes by George Crabbe, 1990; Translations from Old English includes: Beowulf (with Bruce Mitchell), 1968; The Wildman (with Nicola LeFanu), 1995; Opera: The Green Children (with Nicola LeFanu), 1990; The Wildman (with Nicola LeFanu), 1990. Contributions to: Numerous journals and magazines. Honours: Arts Council Award, Best Book for Young Children, 1966; Poetry Book Society Choice, 1976, and Recommendation, 1986; Carnegie Medal, 1985. Address: c/o Rogers, Coleridge and White, 20 Powis Mews, London, W11 1JN, England.

CROUCH Lynitta, (LaNita Crouch Moses), b. Colloaway, New York, USA. Administrative Secretary. Education: Communications Management Public Relations degree, Memphis State University; Writers Workshops; Creative Writing Workshop, Kentucky State University. Appointments: Self-employed, Personnel Counsellor; Administrative Assistant. Publication: Almost Touch. Contributions to: Literary journals; Anthologies; A Different Drummer; Galaxy of Verse; Old Hickory Review; The Tennesseans Anthology; Affinities; Florida Poets; Pegasus; Tennessee Voices Yearbook; Light; Insight Review. Honours: Elected Poet Laureate, 1987; Armstrong State College Chapbook Award; Several Kenneth Beaudoin and William Young Elliot Gemstone Awards; Numerous awards in contests. Memberships: Poetry Society of Tennessee; Kentucky State Poetry Society; International Women's Writing Guild; Memphis Music Association. Address: PO Box 111102, Memphis, TN 38111, USA.

CROW Mary, b. 14 July 1933, Mansfield, Ohio, USA. Poet. Div, 2 sons. Education: BA 1955, College of Wooster; MA, 1963, Indiana University; Study at The Writers' Workshop, University of Iowa. Appointments: Faculty Member, 1964-, Professor of English, Colorado State University, Ft Collins. Publications, Poetry: Going Home, 1979; The Business of Literature, 1980; Borders, 1989; I have Tasted the Apple, 1996. Contributions to: American Poetry Review; Ploughshares; Prairie Schooner; Literary Review; Beloit Poetry Review; New Letters; Massachusetts Review; Quilt; Three Rivers Poetry Journal; and others. Honours: Poetry Fellowship, National Endowment for the Arts, 1984; Fulbright Creative Writing Award to Yugoslavia, 1988; Colorado Book Award, 1992. Membership: Poetry Society of America; PEN; AWP. Address: English Department, Colorado State University, Fort Collins, CO 80523, USA.

CROWDEN James Pascoe, b. 27 Jan 1954, Plymouth, Devon, England. Shepherd; Woodman; Anthropologist. m. Olivia Joan Sanders. 6 July 1985. 1 daughter. Education: BSc Hons, Civil Engineering. Appointment: 2nd Lieutenant, Royal Engineers. Publication: Blood, Earth and Medicine, 1991; In Time of Flood, 1996. Contributions to: Whitehorse Star; Yukon; Country Living. Address:

Forge House, Fore Street, Winsham, Chard, Somerset TA20 4DY, England.

CROWE Thomas Rain, b. 23 Aug 1949, Chicago, Illinois, USA. Poet; Publisher. Education: BA, Anthropology and English, Furman University, Greenville, South Carolina, 1972. Appointments: Editor, Beatitude Magazine and Books, San Francisco; Founder/Director, San Francisco Poetry Festival, 1976; Founding Editor, Katuah Journal, North Carolina; Founder and Publisher, New Native Press and Fern Hill Records, 1979; International Editor, The Asheville Poetry Review, 1994; Feature Writer and Reviewer, The Arts Journal and other arts/review journals; Translator; Essayist; Poet; Author. Publications: Learning to Dance, 1986, Poems for Che Guevara's Dream, 1991; The Personified Street; New Native; Water From The Moon, 1994; Why I Am A Monster, 1992; Deep Language, 1993. Contributions to: The Arts Journal; Arts Papers; Art Vu; Southern Exposure; Nexus; Oxygen; Beatitude; Cold Mountain Review; Black Mountain Review; Point; WNC Greenline; Cuirt Journal, Ireland; Northwords, Scotland; Iron, England; Western Telegraph, Wales; Southern Pines Pilot; The Wofford Journal. Honours: North Carolina Poetry Society Award Winning Poems, 1981; Award of Merit, Phoenix Design Group, 1982; 1st Place for Collaboration with Melody Schaper (Spoken-Word and Dance Performance Piece), American College Dance Festival, 1994; International Merit Award, Atlanta Review, 1996. Address: PO Box 661, Cullowhee, NC 28723, USA.

CROZIER Andrew, b. 1943, England. Education: MA, Cambridge University; PhD, University of Essex, Wivenhoe. Appointment: Reader in English, University of Sussex. Publications include: Loved Litter of Time Spent, 1967; Walking on Grass, 1969; Neglected Information, 1973; Printed Circuit, 1974; Pleats, 1975; Residing, 1976; High Zero, 1978; Were There, 1978; All Where Each Is, 1985; Anthology: A Various Art, 1987. Address: Arts Building, University of Sussex, Brighton, Sussex BN1 9QN, England.

CROZIER Lorna, b. 24 May 1948, Swift Current, Saskatchewan, Canada. Associate Professor; Poet. Education: BA, University of Saskatchewan, 1969; MA, University of Alberta, 1980. Appointments: Creative Writing Teacher, Saskatchewan Summer School of the Arts, Fort San, 1977-81; Writer-in-Residence, Cypress Hills Community College, Swift Current, 1980-81, Regina Public Library, Saskatchewan, 1984-85, University of Toronto, 1989-90; Broadcaster and Writer, CBC Radio, 1986; Guest Instructor, Banff School of Fine Arts, Alberta, 1986, 1987; Special Lecturer, University of Saskatchewan, 1986-91; Associate Professor, University of Victoria, British Columbia 1991-. Publications: Inside is the Sky, 1976; Crow's Black Joy, 1978; No Longer Two People (with Patrick Lane), 1979; Animals of Fall, 1979; Humans and Other Beasts, 1980; The Weather, 1983; The Garden Going On Without Us, 1985; Angels of Flesh, Angels of Silence, 1988; Inventing the Hawk, 1992; Everything Arrives at the Light, 1995; Editor: A Sudden Radiance: Saskatchewan Poetry (with Gary Hyland), 1987; Breathing Fire: The New Generation of Canadian Poets (with Patrick Lane), 1995. Honours: CBC Prize, 1987; Governor General's Award for Poetry, 1992; Canadian Author's Award for Poetry, 1992; Pat Lowther Award, League of Canadian Poets, 1992. Membership: Saskatchewan Writers' Guild. Address: c/o McClelland and Stewart Inc, 481 University Avenue, Suite 900, Toronto, Ontario M5G 2E9, Canada.

CRUCEFIX Martyn, b. 11 Feb 1956, Trowbridge, Wiltshire, England. Teacher; Lecturer. m. Louise Tulip, 24 July 1992. Education: BA English 1st Class 1979, Lancaster University; DPhil English 1985, Worcester College, Oxford University. Publications: The Gregory Poems Anthology, 1985; Beneath Tremendous Rain, 1990; At The Mountjoy Hotel, 1993; On Whistler Mountain, 1994; A Madder Ghost, forthcoming. Contributions to: Anthologies: Voices in the Gallery, 1986; Touchstones, 1987; Contemporary Christian Poetry, 1990; Beneath the Wide Wide Heaven, 1992; Journals: Ambit; Acumen; Critical Quarterly; Literary Review; London Review of Books; Outposts; Oxford Poetry Poetry Review; Poetry Wales; Rialto; Times Literary Supplement. Honours: E C Gregory Award, 1984; Hawthornden Fellowship, 1991; Competitions: Prizewinner in Lancaster Festival Competition, 1985; Kent Festival Competition, 1988; World Wildlife Fund Competition, 1989; National poetry Competition, 1989, 1990; Poetry Business Competition, 1991; Second Place in Arvon/Observer Competition, 1991; Joint Winner, Sheffield Thursday Poetry Competition, 1993. Memberships: Poetry Society, member General Council. Memberships: Poetry Society, member General Council; Blue Nose Poetry, Founder member of this London based reading & workshop organisation. Address: 10 Topsfield Rd, London N8 8SN, England.

CSORBA Gyozo, b. 21 Nov 1916, Pecs, Hungary. Librarian. m. 12 Nov 1944, 3 daughters. Education: Doctor Rei Publicae 1939, University. Appointment: Immobility, poems, 1938. Publications: Seasons of the Soul: Selected Poems, 1970; Collected Poems, 1978; Back to Ithake: Selected Poems, 1986; Look Death Boldly in the Face, poems, 1991; Faust II, translation, 1953, Janus Pannonius, Selected Poems of Latin; Other translations. Contributions to: Kortars; The Present Generation; Jelenkor; Modern Times. Honours: Baumgarten Prize, 1947; Jozsef Attila Prize, 1957, 1972; Kossuth Prize, 1985. Memberships: Magyar Irok Szovetsege; Society of Hungarian Writers; Committee of Confederacy; Accademy Széchenyi of Writers and Artists, 1992. Address: Damjanich u 17, H-7624 Pecs, Hungary.

CUBA Ivan, b. 1920, Nottinghamshire, England. Author; Poet; Academic. Education: Poetry with Kenneth Turtill, Art with Ida G Eise, University of Auckland. Appointments: Army Service, World War II; Artist, exponent of nude in oil painting and war sketches; Psychiatric writer on Art; Honorary Representative, Centre Studi E Scambi, Italy; Honorary Representative, Temple of Arts Museum, USA. Publications: Battlefield; Madness in Art; Gold Medal Poems, Poems by Ivan Cuba, 1990. Honours: Poet Laureate, Gold Medal, Rome, 1979; DLitt, World Academy of Arts and Culture, 1988; International Poets Academy, India; Recipient, Greek Gold Medal for defending Khalkis Swing Bridge, Greece, 1941. Memberships: Elected Life Fellow, Academy Leonardo da Vinci, Rome; Elected to Academies, USA, India, Switzerland, Australasia; Editor, Pacific Islands International Poets Academy, India. Address: PO Box 5199, Auckland, New Zealand.

CULLA Daniel De, b. 28 Jan 1945, Valleldao, Spain. CS. m. Rita de Diego, 22 Apr 1977, 1 daughter. Education: DD; BA; Master of Dada; MA. Appointments: Priest of Pagan Church; Magician of Isthar; Knight of Malta; Poet Laureate, World Poetry (India, Korea, Japan, California, Brussels). Publications include: God' Eye Eye Eye; The Papamoscas of Kremlin; D de Descencanto; De Este Vino Nos Hemos Cuidado Nosotros; Blues de Perro Curto; Colom' Letter to Liberty; El Sí de Mi Niña. Contributions include: Suck; Smuck; Eidos; Poesía Hispánica; Hora de Poesía; La Pata de Palo; La Campana; La Lletra A; Al Margen; Red Mole; República de las Lettras. Honours: Laureated by: World Poetry; World Press Photo; Poet; Les Fils de Mr Hyde; Le Temps Deborde; War Resisters League; Asociación Colegial de Escritores; Planet Drum; ABC (Cruz Negra A); Poet; Polémica; Coevolution. Memberships: International Society for Individual Liberty; World Poetry; Nuclear Resister; Norla, Norway; Green Peace; Alaska Wildlife Alliance; Friends of the Wolf; War Resisters League; Asociación Colegial de Escritores; Poetas del Mundo Uníos. Address: Poetas del Mundo Uníos, PO Box 2 117, 09080 Burgos, Spain.

CUMBERLEGE Marcus (Crossley), b. 23 Dec 1938, Antibes, France. Poet; Translator. m. (1) Ava Nicole Paranjoti, 11 Dec 1965, div 1972, (2) Maria Lefever, 9 Nov 1973, 1 daughter. Education: BA, St John's College, Oxford, 1961. Appointments: Lecturer, Universities of Hilversum and Lugano, 1978-83. Publications: Oases, 1968; Poems For Quena And Tabla, 1970; Running Towards A New Life, 1973; Bruges, Bruges (with Owen Davis), 1975; Firelines, 1977; The Poetry Millionaire, 1977; La Nuit Noire, 1977; Twintig Vriendelijke Vragen (with Horst de Blaere), 1977; Northern Lights, 1981; Life Is A Flower, 1981; Vlaamse Fables, 1982; Sweet Poor Hobo, 1984; Things I Cannot Change, 1993. Honour: Eric Gregory Award, 1967. Address: Eekhoutstraat 42, 8000 Bruges, Belgium.

CUNLIFFE Ruth E, b. Lancaster, Ohio, USA. Author; Poet. 1 daughter. Education: Journalism and Literature, Ohio State University. Career: 1st published poem, age 10; Teacher, Poetry, Lake Placid High School, Florida, 1984-; Lectures on Art of Reading Poetry, Poetry the Best Therapy, other topics; Teaches poetry class, elderly day care centres; Editor, own publication, Just for Fun. Publications: 4 poetry books including: Sweet Nectar, 1988. Contributions to: Over 2500 poems and over 100 short stories to various publications including: Omnific; Poet's Voice; Ajax Poetry Letter; Poets Corner weekly newsletter, local newspaper. Honours: Over 50 awards and trophies including: Golden Poet Award, World of Poetry, 4 times. Memberships: President, Past Vice-President, Florida State Poets Association Inc; Founder, President, Lake Placid Heritage Poets; Verse Writers Guild of Ohio; Poets at Work, Pennsylvania; National League of American Penwomen; National Federation of State Poetry Societies; Affiliate: Academy of American Poets; World Wide Poetry Circle; Poets of Now. Address: 2105 Rainbow Avenue, Sebring, FL 33870, USA.

CUNNING Alfred. See: **HOLLIDAY David John Gregory.**

CUNNINGHAM Michael, b. 25 Apr 1950, Liverpool, England. Accountant; Legal Cashier. Education: BA Hons Class II, History of Art, Manchester University, 1971; Certificate in Education, Manchester Polytechnic, 1972. Appointments: Art Teacher, Chatham Grammar School, 1972; Trainee Accountant, Louis Nicholas & Co, Liverpool, 1977; Audit Clerk, King Nagley Bakerman & Co, Liverpool, 1982; Accountant, Office Manager, David Matthews & Co, Solicitors, Liverpool, 1991. Contributions to: Magazines: Echo Room; Iota; Smoke; Verse; Poetry Nottingham; North; Wide Skirt; Slow Dancer; Tops; Sepia; Krax; Orbis; Outposts; Radio: BBC North West, Write Now. Memberships: Evil Dead Poets Society; Dead Good Poets Society; Performance Sessions in Liverpool; Former member, M & MX Performance Duo; Poetry Society. Address: 162 Booker Avenue, Liverpool L18 9TB, England.

CURNOW Thomas Allen Monro, b. 17 June 1911, Timaru, New Zealand. Poet; Dramatist; Critic. m. (1) Elizabeth Jaumaud LeCren, 1936, 2 sons, 1 daughter, (2) Jenifer Mary Tole, 1965. Education: BA, University of New Zealand, Canterbury, Auckland, 1931-34; College of St John the Evangelist, Auckland, 1931-33; LittD, University of Auckland, 1966. Appointments: Reporter, Sub-Editor, The Press, Christchurch, 1935-48; News Chronicle, London, England, 1949; Senior Lecturer, Associate Professor of English, University of Auckland, 1951-76. Publications: Valley of Decision, 1933; Three Poems, 1935; Enemies: Poems 1934-36, 1937; Not in Narrow Seas, 1939; Island and Time, 1941; Sailing or Drowning, 1943; Jack Without Magic, 1946; At Dead Low Water and Sonnets, 1949; Poems 1949-57, 1957; A Small Room with Large Windows: Selected Poems 1962; Trees, Effigies, Moving Objects: A Sequence of 18 Poems, 1972; An Abominable Temper and Other Poems, 1973; Collected Poems 1933-73, 1974; An Incorrigible Music, a Sequence, 1979; Selected Poems, 1982; You Will Know When You Get There, 1982; The Loop in Lone Kauri Road, Poems, 1983-85, 1986; Continum, New and Later Poems, 1971-88, 1988; Selected Poems 1940-89, 1990; Penguin Modern Poets, with Donald Davie and Samuel Menashe, 1996. Editor: A Book of New Zealand Verse, 1945, 1951; The Penguin Book of New Zealand Verse, 1960; Look Back Harder, critical writings, 1935-84, 1987; Four Plays: The Axe, The Overseas Expert, The Duke's Miracle, Resident of Nowhere, 1972. Contributions to: Encounter; Islands; Landfall; Partisan Review; Penguin New Writing; Poetry, Chicago; Poetry London; PN Review; The Age Monthly, Melbourne; The Bulletin; Sport; Times Literary Supplement; London Magazine; London Review of Books; Verse. Honours: New Zealand Book Award for Poetry, 1963, 1975, 1979, 1983, 1987; Katherine Mansfield Memorial Fellowship, 1983; Commander of the Order of the British Empire, 1986; Dillons Commonwealth Poetry Prize, 1989; Queen's Gold Medal for Poetry, 1989; Order of New Zealand, 1990; Cholmondeley Award, 1992. Literary Agent: Curtis Brown. Address: 62 Tohunga Crescent, Parnell, Auckland 1, New Zealand.

CURRY Duncan Charles, b. 5 Oct 1957, Southall, Middlesex, England. Teacher. Education: BA Hons, 1979; PGCE, 1984; MA, 1993. Publications: Contemporary Yorkshire Poetry, 1984; Oranges, 1986; Against the Grain, 1989; The Darts and the Commentary, 1996. Contributions to: Orbis; Iron; Rialto; Harry's Hand; The Wide Skirt; North; Outposts; Poetry and Audience; Poetry Nottingham; Bradford Poetry Quarterly; English in Education, NATE periodical. Honours: Prizewinner in the Louth Writer's Circle Poetry Competition, 1985; 2nd Prize in Stamford Poetry Festival Competition, 1990. Memberships: Tutor for the Poetry Business, Westgate, Huddersfield; Competition for above 1987-. Address: 79 School Street, Moldgreen, Huddersfield HD5 8AX, England.

CURRY Elizabeth R, b. 31 Jan 1934, Evanston, Illinois, USA. University Professor of English and Women's Studies. m. Stephen J Curry, 10 June 1958, 1 son. Education: BA, Northwestern University, 1956; PhD, University of Wisconsin-Madison, 1963. Appointment: Currently University Professor, English, Slippery Rock University, Slippery Rock, Pennsylvania. Publications: Earth Against Heaven: A Tiananmen Square Anthology, 1990; 27 chapbooks, 1985-91; Clinical Pain Log Book; Thinking About Your Creative Writing, 1995. Contributions to: Oxford Magazine; Taproot; Colorado North Review; Socrates Is Dead; Western Ohio Journal; Alfred Review; Outlook; Limberlost Review; Focus; Boston Women's Art Collective; Poetry Motel; Ginger Hill; Pennsylvania English; Lucidity; Odessa Review; Ego Flights; Up Against the Wall; Mother...; Poetry Forum; New Poets' Review; The Green Hills Literary Lantern, Lynx Eye; Others. Honours: Phi Beta Kappa, 1956; 1st Prize, Southern California Poets PEN Contest, 1987; 2nd Prize, Macomb College, 1987; 2nd Prize, K-Bar of

California, 1987; Finalist, Negative Capability Eve of St Agnes Contest, 1989; Finalist, Central Pennsylvania Council of Arts Competition, 1989. Address: c/o English Department, 314 SWC, Slippery Rock University, Slippery Rock, PA 16057, USA.

CURRY Mary Earle Lowry, b. 13 May 1917, Seneca, South Carolina, USA. Homemaker; Poet; Church Worker. m. Rev Peden Gene Curry, 25 Dec 1941, 1 son, 1 daughter, dec. Education: Furman University, 1945; Special courses. Publications: Looking Up!, 1949; Looking Within, 1961, reprint, 1980; Church in The Heart of The City, hymn, 1973. Contributions to: Yearbook of Modern Poetry; Poets of America; Poetic Voice of America; We, The People; Poetry Digest; Poetry Anthology of Verse; International Anthology on World Brotherhood and Peace; The State; The Greenville News; Inman Times; Fountain Inn Times; Fort Mill Times; Laurens Advertiser; Ware Shaols Life; Wesleyan Advocate, Georgia; South Carolina Advocate; Living in South Carolina; Personal poetry broadcasts, Virginia; Parnassus of World Poets. Honours: World Award for Culture, Statue of Victory, Centro Studi e Richerche delle Nazioni, Italy, 1985. Memberships: Aux Rotary, Charleston, 1972-74; Centro Studi Scambi Internazionale, Rome; United Methodist Church Women's Organizations, and Church Ministers Wives Clubs; Community clubs. Address: 345 Curry Drive, Seneca, SC 29678, USA.

CURTIS David, b. 21 Feb 1946, Providence, Rhode Island, USA. Teacher. m. Elaine B Davis, 6 Jan 1990, 3 sons. Education: AB, Rhode Island College, 1968; PhD, Brown University, 1977. Appointments: Assistant Professor, English, Wilkes College, 1977-78; Associate Professor, English, Sacred Heart University, 1981-. Publication: Update from Pahrump, 1992. Contributions to: Dalhousie Review; Poem; Four Quarters; Coe Review; Karamu; Midwest Poetry Review; Plains Poetry Journal; Shorelines; Candelabrum; Literature and Film Quarterly. Honours: Honourable Mention, Quarterly Poetry Review, 1987; 3rd Prize, North American Open Poetry Competition, 1990. Membership: Poetry Society of America. Address: 126 Ardmore Road, Milford, CT 06460, USA.

CURTIS Linda Lee (Herren), b. 18 Apr 1950, Stafford, Kansas, USA. Poet; Writer. m. Ronald Benson Curtis, 8 June 1979. Education: AA, Barton County Community College, Great Bend, Kansas, 1978. Appointments: Editor, Publisher, Winter Wheat Newsletter, 1985-; President, Founder, Poems Against Pushers, 1990-. Publications: Books: Midnight Echoes, 1976; Sonnets and Sunbonnets, 1976; The Cheater's Almanac, 1976; Smoke Rings, 1977; More Than My Share, 1979; Intermissio, 1982; Ghetto Rain, 1990; When I Wear Red, 1990; Head Shots, book of poetry, 1993. Contributions to: Over 1000 poems to: Portable Wall; Complete Woman; Sagacity; Innisfree; Bronte Street; Poetic Justics; Free Focus; Hob Nob; Parnassus Literary Journal; First Inago Anthology of Poetry; Mallife; Soundboard; Open Window; Phoenix Gazette; Arizona Republic; Poems published in: Life Scribes; Poets' Voice; An Eliza Bleecker Anthology; John Thumbull Anthology; In the West of Ireland; Perceptions; Java; Singles Profile; The Grapevine; Poetree and others. Honours: Soundboard Poet of the Year Award, 1984; Arizona Women's Partnership Songwriting Award, 1985; The Poets' Voice Best Poem of the Issue Award, 1994. Membership: Poets and Writers, New York. Address: 1919 W Adams, Phoenix, AZ 85009, USA.

CURTIS Nancy Jo, b. 22 Sept 1943, Indiana, USA. Storekeeper. m. (1) Thomas N Farace, 2 Nov 1958, (2) Herman L Schulenberg, 12 Dec 1973, 2 sons, 2 daughters. Contributions to: Calvary Lutheran Church Newsletter; Trades Newspaper; Bedford Newspaper; Great American Poetry Anthology; American Anthology of Southern Poetry; New American Poetry Anthology; Pathways. Honours: Vintage Golden Poet, World of Poetry, 1987; Golden Poet, 1988; Silver Poet, 1989, 1990. Memberships: Lutheran Library Association; World of Poetry. Address: 202 Washington Boulevard, Lake Placid, FL 33852, USA.

CURTIS Tony, b. 26 Dec 1946, Carmarthen, Wales. Education: BA, University College of Swansea, 1968. Appointment: Senior Lecturer in English, Polytechnic of Wales, Pontypridd, 1979-. Publications include: Peveril Castle, 1971; Walk Down a Welsh Wind, 1972; Album, 1974; The Deerslayers, 1978; Carnival, 1978; Preparations: Poems 1974-79, 1980; Letting Go, 1983; Selected Poems 1970-85, 1986; Poems Selected and New, 1986; The Last Candles, 1989; Co-editor, Love From Wales, 1991; Taken for Pearls, 1993. Honours include: Eric Gregory Award, 1972. Address: Pentwyn, 55 Colcot Street, Barry, South Glamorgan CF6 8BQ, Wales.

CUTHBERT Valerie, b. 30 Oct 1923, London, England. Writer; Journalist; Poet; Secretarial Teacher (retired). m. 27 Nov 1965. Education: PENU and privately tutored in Tanzania; Pitman Teaching Certificates; PCT; PCTT; FIPS; FSCT; MFTCom. Appointments: Service in First Aid Nursing Yeomanry (WTS East Africa), 1941-44; Secretary to 1965; Secretarial College Teacher, 1965-70; Secretarial College Owner and Manager, Mombasa, 1970-78; Full-time Writer, 1978-. Publications: The Great Siege of Fort Jesus, 1970, 1988, reprinted, 1990, 1992; Yusuf Bin Hasan, 1972, 4th Impression, 1992; Jomo Kenyatta - The Burning Spear, 1982; Dust and the Shadow, 1988; To be published: Thoughts on Writing; Muted Music, poetry collection; Wind Song, poetry collection; A Guide to Study, textbook; Wings of the Wind. Contributions to: Poem, Anthology of American Poetry, 1987; Articles, short stories and poems to: Presence; First Time; Swarm; Writers' Rostrum; London Calling; Nation; Coast Week; Youth; Viva; Standard; Lady (UK and Kenya); Catholic Herald; Personal Secretary; Professional Lady; Parents; Weekly article on writing/education to Trend, East African Standard Education; Mombasa Notebook to Daily Nation Wednesday Magazine Supplement; Jacaranda Designs Anthology. Honours: 2nd Prize for Short Story, Viva Magazine, 1980's; Dust and the Shadow shortlisted, Commonwealth Writers Competition, African Section; 2nd Prize, Short Story Competition, Writers Association of Kenya, 1993; Placing, International Society of Poets (UK) Competition, 1996. Memberships: Writers Association of Kenya; Formerly: Poetry Society, UK; Poetry Association of Kenya. Literary Agent: Mrs Terry Temple, The International Press Agency (Pty) Ltd, PO Box 67, Howard Place, South Africa. Address: PO Box 82727, Mombasa, Kenya, East Africa.

CZAJKOWSKI Jerzy Stanisław, b. 13 Jan 1931, Oścísłowo, Mazowsze, Poland. Poet; Essayist; Novelist. Education: Faculty of History and Sociology, 1961-68; MA, Cultural Sociology, 1968. Appointments: Camera Reporter, 1953-55; Editorial Secretary, Współzeność fortnightly literary review, 1956-59; Senior Editor, Artistic and Film Publishing House, 1961-67; Senior Editor, State Scientific Publishing House, 1968-71; Editorial Secretary, Literatura na Swiecie literary monthly, 1971-73; Senior Editor, Polish Contemporary Poetry Series, Home Publishing Agency KAW, 1974-80; Senior Editor, Publishing House Kiw, 1980-89; Literary Consultant. Publications include: Smoky Landscapes, 1958; Disant Tree, 1978; Passions and Patiences, 1978; Laughter of Pompea, 1987; Anateme of Wernyhora, poem, 1990; The Forest is Silent, 1995; Contributions to: anthologies: Vertige de bien vivre; Les eclats du legende; Poesie de Opinogóra. Contributions to: Various anthologies, literary journals, throughout the world, including poetry in Polish, French, Russian, Ukranian. Honours: Writer's Award, Współczesność fortnightly literary review, 1958; Editor's Award for monograph on S Jaracz, Theatre and Actor, 1964; Editor's Award for monograph on Europe, 1978. Memberships: ZPL; ZAIKS; PTWK; Współczesność Group of Poets and Painters, 1957-60. Address: ul Świetojerska 4-10 m 57, 00-236 Warsaw, Poland.

CZCIBOR-PIOTROWSKI Andrzej. See: PIOTROWSKI Andrzej Stanislaw.

CZERNIAWSKI Adam, b. 20 Dec 1934, Warsaw, Poland. Writer; Translator. m. Ann Christine Daker, 27 July 1957, 1 son, 1 daughter. Education: BA, English, London, 1955; BA, Philosophy, London, 1967; MA, Philosophy, Sussex, 1968; BPhil, Philosophy, Oxford, 1970. Appointments: Broadcaster; Insurance Official; Philosophy Lecturer; Administrator, Hawthornden Castle; Translator-in-Residence, University of East Anglia, Norwich; Assistant Director, British Centre for Literary Translation, University of East Anglia. Publications: Hunting the Unicorn; Interior Topography; A Dream, a Citadel, a Grove; A View of Delft; Golden Age; Selected Poems; Autumn; Collected Poems; Scenes from a Disturbed Childhood, 1991; The Mature Laurel, Essays on Modern Polish Poetry (editor), 1991; The Muses and the Owl of Minerva, 1994. Contributions to: Kultura; Literatura; Odra; Metafora; Naglos; Kresy; Poetry Review; Modern Poetry in Translation; The Rialto; Bête Noire; Cahiers de l'Est; Cogito; Akcente; Comparative Criticism; Literatur und Kritik; Kerala Kavita; Der Prokurist; La Main de Singe; Romania Literara. Honours: Woursell Foundation; Koscielski Foundation; Rockefeller Foundation Fellowship, 1993. Address: 24 Calabria Road, London N5 1AJ, England.

D

D'AGUIAR Fred, b. 2 Feb 1960, London, England. Editor; Poet; Novelist. Education: BA Hons, University of Kent, 1985. Appointments: Writer in Residence, London Borough of Lewisham, 1986-87; Birmingham Polytechnic, 1988-89; Visiting Writer, Amherst College, 1992-94; Assistant Professor of English, Bates College, 1994-95; Tchr, University of Miami, Florida, 1995-. Publications: Mama Dot, 1985, 1989; Airy Hall, 1989; British Subjects, 1993; Co-Editor: The New British Poetry, 1988; Novels: The Longest Memory, 1994 (Eight translations and a Channel 4 film); Dear Future, 1996; Play: A Jamaican Airman Forsees His Death, 1995; Television: Sweet Thames (poem/documentary for BBC), 1992; Rain (poem/documentary for BBC), 1994; Radio: 1492 (a long poem commissioned by BBC Radio broadcast), 1992. Honours: T S Eliot Prize for Poetry, University of Kent, 1984; The Malcolm X Prize, 1986; The Guyana Prize, 1989; BBC Race in the Media Award, 1992; Most Innovative Film Award, British Film Institute, 1993; David Higham Award; Whitbread Best First Novel Award. Address: c/o Curtis Brown, Haymarket House, 28-29 Haymarket, London SW1Y 4SP, England.

D'ALFONSO Antonio, b. 6 Aug 1953, Montreal, Quebec, Canada. Writer; Editor. m. Julia Mary Gualtieri, 8 Sept 1990. Education: BA, Communication Arts, Loyola College, Montreal, 1975; MSc, Communications in Semiology of Film, Université de Montréal, 1979. Appointments: Teacher, 1974-79; Editor-in-Chief, Guernica Editions, Montreal, 1979-. Publications: La Chanson du Shaman Sedna, 1973; Queror, 1979; Black Tongue, 1983; The Other Shore, 1986; L'Autre Rivage, 1987; L'Amour panique, 1987; Avril ou l'anti-passion, 1990; Panick Love, 1992; Lettre a Julia, 1992. Contributions to: Le Devoir; The Gazette; La Presse. Membership: Union des écrivains, Quebec. Address: Guernica Editions, PO Box 633, Stn NDG, Montreal, Quebec H4A 3R1, Canada.

D'AMBRA Adrian Lewis, b. 15 Dec 1957, Melbourne, Victoria, Australia. Secondary English Teacher; Freelance Travel Journalist. m. Maria Consiglia Zammit, 21 Apr 1991. Education: BA 1984, Dip Ed 1985, University of Melbourne. Appointments: Process Worker; Pre-School Childcare Worker; Tram Conductor; Author; Publisher; Teacher, Victorian Ministry of Education; Teacher, ISTEK VAKFI, Istanbul. Publications: The Flowers of Impotence, 1983; Cavafy's Room, chapbook, 1987. Contributions to: Journals and magazines. Memberships: Poetry Society, London; Fellowship of Australian Writers, Victoria Branch. Address: 37 Venice Street, Mornington, Victoria 3931, Australia.

D'AMBROSIO Vinni Marie, b. 5 Apr 1928, New York, New York, USA. College Professor. 1 daughter. Education: BA, Smith College; PhD, New York University. Appointments: Lecturer to Full Professor, English, Brooklyn College, City University of New York; Coordinator for Poetry Readings, Brooklyn Arts Council, to 1984. Publications: Life of Touching Mouths, 1972; Eliot Possessed: T S Eliot and FitzGerald's Rubaiyat, 1989. Contributions to: New York Times; Light; Pivot; Confrontation; Others. Honours: 1st Prize, American Academy of Poets, 1969; Christopher Morley Award, Poetry Society of America, 1971; Pat Davis Award, Pen and Brush, 1984, 1987. Memberships: President, T S Eliot Society; Board of Directors, Pen and Brush Inc; Poetry Society of America; Modern Language Association; Director at Large, American Association of University Women; Medieval Club of New York; American Literature Association; PEN American Center. Address: Brooklyn College, City University of New York, NY 11210, USA.

DABYDEEN Cyril, b. 15 Oct 1945, Guyana. Poet; Writer. m. 6 June 1989, 1 daughter. Education: BA (Hons), Lakehead University, Thunder Bay, Ontario, 1973; MA, 1974, MPA, Queen's University, Ottawa. Publications: Poetry: Distances, 1977; Goatsong, 1977; This Planet Earth, 1980; Still Close to the Island, 1980; Islands Lovlier Than a Vision, 1988; The Wizard Swami, 1989; Dark Swirl, 1989; Jogging in Havana, 1992; Stoning the Wind, 1994; Discussing Columbus, 1996; Fiction: Sometimes Hard, novel, 1994; Berbice Crossing, stories, 1996; Black Jesus and Other Stories, 1997; Editor: A Shapely Fire: Changing the Literary Landscape, 1987; Another Way to Dance: Asian-Canadian Poetry, 1990; Another Way To Dance: Contemporary Voices of Asian Poetry in America and Canada, 2nd edition. Contributions to: Canadian Forum; Canadian Fiction Magazine; Fiddlehead; Dalhousie Review;

Antigonish Review; Canadian Author and Bookman; Toronto South Asian Review; Journal of South Asian Literature; Wascana Review; Literary Review; Globe and Mail; Caribbean Quarterly. Honours: Sandbach Parker Gold Medal; A J Seymour Lyric Poetry Prize; Poet Laureate of Ottawa; Okanagan Fiction Award. Memberships: Canadian Association of Commonwealth Language and Literature Studies. Address: 106 Blackburn, Ottawa, Ontario K1N BA7, Canada.

DABYDEEN David, b. 9 Dec 1955, Guyana. Poet; Writer; Senior Lecturer. Education: BA, Cambridge University, 1978; PhD, London University, 1982. Appointments: Junior Research Fellow, Oxford University, 1983-87; Senior Lecturer, Warwick University, 1987-. Publications: Slave Song, 1984; Coolie Odyssey, 1988; Disappearance, 1993; Turner, 1994. Contributions to: Various periodicals. Honours: Commonwealth Poetry Prize, 1984; Guyana Literature Prize, 1992. Memberships: Literature Panel, Arts Council of Great Britain, 1985-89; Fellow, Royal Society of the Arts. Address: c/o Warwick University, Coventry, CV4 7AL, England.

DACEY Philip, b. 9 May 1939, St Louis, Missouri, USA. Poet; Teacher. m. Florence Chard, 1963, div 1986, 2 sons, 1 daughter. Education: BA, St Louis University, 1961; MA, Stanford University, 1967; MFA, University of Iowa, 1970. Appointments: Instructor in English, University of Missouri, St Louis, 1967-68; Faculty, Department of English, Southwest State University, Marshall, Minnesota, 1970-; Distinguished Writer-in-Residence, Wichita State University, 1985. Publications: Poetry: The Beast With Two Backs, 1969; Fist, Sweet Giraffe, The Lion, Snake, and Owl, 1970; Four Nudes, 1971; How I Escaped from the Labyrinth and Other Poems, 1977; The Boy Under the Bed, 1979; The Condom Poems, 1979; Gerard Manley Hopkins Meets Walt Whitman in Heaven and Other Poems, 1982; Fives, 1984; The Man with Red Suspenders, 1986; The Condom Poems II, 1989; Night Shift at the Crucifix Factory, 1991; Editor: I Love You All Day: It Is That Simple (with Gerald M Knoll), 1970; Strong Measures: Contemporary American Poetry in Traditional Forms (with David Jaus), 1986. Honours: Woodrow Wilson Fellowship, 1961; New York YM-YWHA Discovery Award, 1974; National Endowment for the Arts Fellowships, 1975, 1980; Minnesota State Arts Board Fellowships, 1975, 1983; Bush Foundation Fellowship, 1977; Loft-McKnight Fellowship, 1984; Fulbright Lecturer, 1988. Address: Route 1, Box 89, Lynd, MN 56157, USA.

DAELMAN Jos (Walter Zone), b. 1 Aug 1937, Zwijndrecht, Belgium. Librarian. m. Yolanda Stroobant, 24 Nov 1959, 1 daughter. Education: Graduate in Library Science, 1970; Graduate in Scientific and Technical Documentation, 1972. Appointments: Branch Librarian, 1958; Teacher, Library School, Antwerp, 1973; Head, Reference Department, 1982, currently, Head, Psycho-Pedagogical Department, Central Public Library, Antwerp. Publications: Land tussen Zee en Aarde, 1974; De Stilte toewaarts, 1979; De Landschapstuin, 1980; Buiten de Roedel, 1983; Het Verlangzamen, 1986; Een Haas in Winterkoren, 1989; Letters from Sark and Other Places, 1992; Huiswaarts, 1994; Herdersuur, 1996; With painter Cel Overberghe: Vacuum, 1972; De zwarte Wandelaar, 1982. Contributions to: Nieuw Vlaams Tijdschrift; Deus Ex Machina. Honour: Gieriek; Award for Poetry, Province of Antwerp, 1984. Membership: Vereniging voor Vlaamse Letterkundigen; PEN. Address: Oostvaart 42, 9180 Moerbeke-Waas, Belgium.

DALAL Suresh, b. 11 Oct 1932, Bombay, Thane, India. University Professor; Head of Department of Gujarati. m. Sushila, 11 May 1960, 2 daughters. Education: MA, Gujarati 1955, PhD, Gujarati 1969, University of Bombay. Appointments: Lecturer, K C College 1956-64; Lecturer, H R College 1960-64; Professor and Head, Department of Gujarati, K J Somaiya College 1964-73; Professor and Head, Department of Gujarati, SNDT Women's University, 1973-; Director, Department of P G Studies & Research, SNDT Women's University over 8 times; Editor, Kavita magazine last 25 years. Publications: 22 books of poems and 14 books of children's verses 1966-92. Contributions to: Janmabhoomi; Pravasi; Most of prestigious magazines of Gujarati literature. Honours: Prizes of Gujarat Government and Ranjitram Gold Medal for Creative Writing, 1983. Address: 133 Hassa Mahal, Dalamal Park, Cuffe Parade, Bombay 400 005, India.

DALE Peter John, b. 21 Aug 1938, Addlestone, Surrey, England. Poet; Writer; Translator. m. Pauline Strouvelle, 29 June 1963, 1 son, 1 daughter. Education: BA (Hons), English, St Peter's College, Oxford, 1963. Appointments: Teacher, Howden County Secondary

School, East Yorkshire, 1963-64, Glastonbury County Secondary School, Sutton, Surrey, 1964-72, Hinchley Wood County Secondary School, Esher, Surrey, 1972-93; Co-Editor, Agenda, 1972-96. Publications: Poetry: Walk From the House, 1962; The Storms, 1968; Mortal Fire, 1976; One Another, sonnet sequence, 1978; Too Much of Water, 1983; A Set of Darts: Epigrams (with W S Milne and Robert Richardson), 1990; Earth Light: New Poems, 1991; Translator: Selected Poems of François Villon, 1978, 4th edition, 1994; The Divine Comedy, terza rima version, 1996. Contributions to: Various journals and periodicals. Honour: Arts Council Bursary, 1970. Membership: Society of Authors. Address: 10 Selwood Road, Sutton, Surrey SM3 9JU, England.

DALIBARD Jill E Dawson, b. 24 July 1936, Long Melford, Suffolk, England. Social Worker. Education: BA, 1958, Bristol, England; MSW 1969, McGill University, Canada; MA, 1988, Concordia, Canada. Appointments: Lecturer in English, Concordia University, Canada; Social Worker, Royal Victoria Hospital, Montreal, Canada; Director of Hospital Services, Ville Marie Social Service Centre, Montreal, Canada. Publication: Deed of Gift, 1995. Contributions to: Waves; Canadian Forum; Antigonish Review; Wascana Review; Poetry Canada Review; League of Canadian Poets Annual Anthology. Memberships: British Poetry Society; National Association for Poetry Therapy, USA. Address: 3550 Ridgewood Avenue, Apt 34, Montreal, Quebec H3V 1C2, Canada.

DALVEN Rae, b. 25 Apr 1904, Preveza, Greece. English Teacher. m. Jack Negrin, 1928, div 1938. Education: BA, Hunter College, USA, 1925; MA, New York University, 1928; MFA, Yale Drama School, 1941; PhD, New York University. Appointments: Assistant Professor, Drama, Fisk University, Nashville, Tennessee, 1954; English Instructor, Fairleigh Dickinson University, 1958-61; Adjunct Professor, Race College, 1961-68; Professor of English, Chairman, English Department, Ladycliff College, Highlands Falls, New York, 1962-73. Publications: 90 verse translations from Greek by Joseph Eliyia, 1945; Modern Greek Poetry, selections from 60 poets, 1949, 2nd edition, 1971; The Complete Poems of Cavafy, 1961, 2nd edition, 1972; Fourth Dimension: selected poems of Yannis Ritsos, 1977. Contributions to: Poetry; Literary Review; Colorado Review; Partisan Review; Confrontation; Others. Honours: Fellow, MacDowell Colony,1965, 1966-67, 1968, 1977, 1989; Glatstein Poetry Award, Poetry Magazine, 1972; Hall of Fame Award, Hunter College Alumni Association, 1973; Gold Key Award, Columbia Scholastic Press Endowment for the Arts, to translate Greek women poets, 1984; Outstanding Educator of America Scroll, Ladycliff College, 1993. Memberships: Poetry Society of America; PEN; Dramatists Guild; Authors Guild. Address: Ladycliff College, Highland Falls, NY 10928, USA.

DALY Padraig John, b. 25 June 1943, Dungarvan, County Waterford, Ireland. Priest of the Order of St Augustine. Education: BA, 1967, H Dip Ed, 1973, University College, Dublin; BD, 1969, Gregorian, Rome. Appointments: Prior, St John's Priory, Dublin 1981-85; Prior, St Augustine's, Ballyboden 1985-89; Parish Priest, Ballyboden 1989-. Publications: Nowhere But in Praise, 1978; This Day's Importance, 1981; Dall' Orlo Marino Del Mondo, 1981; A Celibate Affair, 1984; Poems, Selected and New, 1988; Out of Silence, 1993. Contributions to: Books, magazines and journals in Ireland. Memberships: Poetry Ireland; Irish Writers Union. Address: St Augustine's, Ballyboden, Dublin 16, Ireland.

DANA Robert (Patrick), b. 2 June 1929, Allston, Massachusetts, USA. Professor of English; Poet. m. (1) Mary Kowalke, 2 June 1951 (div 1973), 3 children, (2) Margaret Sellen, 14 Sept 1974. Education: AB, Drake University, 1951; MA, University of Iowa, 1954. Appointments: Assistant Professor to Professor of English, Cornell College, Mount Vernon, Iowa, 1953-94; Editor, Hillside Press, Mount Vernon, Iowa, 1957-67; Editor, 1964-68, Contributing Editor, 1991-, North American Review; Contributing Editor, American Poetry Review, 1973-88, New Letters, 1980-83. Publications: My Glass Brother and Other Poems, 1957; The Dark Flags of Waking, 1964; Journeys from the Skin: A Poem in Two Parts, 1966; Some Versions of Silence: Poems, 1967; The Power of the Visible, 1971; In a Fugitive Season, 1980; What the Stones Know, 1984; Blood Harvest, 1986; Against the Grain: Interviews with Maverick American Publishers, 1986; Starting Out for the Difficult World, 1987; What I Think I Know: New and Selected Poems, 1990; Wildebeest, 1993; Yes, Everything, 1994. Contributions to: Various periodicals. Honours: Rainer Maria Rilke Prize, 1984; National Endowment for the Arts Fellowships, 1985, 1993;

Delmore Schwartz Memorial Poetry Award, 1989; Carl Sandburg Medal for Poetry, 1994. Memberships: Academy of American Poets; Associated Writing Programs; PEN; Poetry Society of America. Address: 1466 Westview Drive, Coralville, IA 52241, USA.

DANIEL Geoffrey Peter, (Peter Thorne), b. 5 Mar 1955, Bedford, England. Teacher. m. Iseabal Flora MacDonald, 12 July 1980, 1 son, 1 daughter. Education: Kings Canterbury, 1968-72; Durham University, 1977-78; Hamilton College of Education, 1980. Appointments: Head of Drama, Kamuzu Academy, Malawi; Glenalmond College, Perthshire; Head of English, Reeds School, Surrey; Head of Sixth Form, Reed's School, 1995. Contributions to: Books, magazines and journals. Honour: International Haiku. Memberships: British Haiku Society; Fellowship of Christian Writers; Fellow, Society of Antiquaries, Scotland. Address: Reeds School, Cobham, Surrey KT11 2ES, England.

DANIELS Margaret, b. 16 June 1921, Colorado, USA. Artist-Painter. m. 9 May 1941, 2 sons, 1 daughter. Education: BFA, Drake University, 1965; MA, Iowa State University, 1977. Appointments: Art Teacher, 1965-75; Currently self-employed Artist; Conducts workshops. Publications: Poems in: Lyrical Iowa, 1987, 1988, 1989; American Anthology of Contemporary Poetry, 1989; CSS Publications, 1990; Great Poems of the Western World, 1990. Honours: Merit Award, Walt Whitman Guild, 1988; Golden Poet Award, World of Poetry, 1989; Poetry Award, Iowa National League of American Pen Women, President, Des Moines Branch; Iowa Poetry Association; Walt Whitman Guild. Address: Rt 4, Squaw Valley, Ames, IA 50010, USA.

DANIELS Peter John, b. 20 July 1954, Cambridge, England. Librarian; Indexer. Education: BA, Hons, English, Reading University, 1978; Postgraduate Diploma in Librarianship, Birmingham Polytechnic, 1981. Appointment: Assistant Librarian, Religious Society of Friends. Publications: Breakfast in Bed, 1987; Take Any Train: A Book of Gay Men's Poetry (editor), 1990; Peacock Luggage (co-author), 1992. Contributions to: James White Review, Minneapolis, Guest Editor 1992, and British Representative; various British Magazines. Honours: Runner-up, National Poetry Competition, 1990; Winner, Poetry Business Pamphlet Competition, 1991. Memberships: Oscars (gay poetry group), treasurer, 1986-; Attender at various London workshop groups including Thurlow Road. Address: c/o Oscars Press, B M Oscars, London WC1N 3XX, England.

DANTE Jack, b. 15 Feb 1945, Johnson City, New York, USA. Freelance Writer and Lecturer; Editor. Education: BA, State University of New York at Binghampton, 1968. Appointments: Managing Editor, Science Fiction Writers of America Bulletin, 1970-75; Instructor, Writing, Science Fiction, Broome Community College, Binghampton, New York, 1972, 1990, 1991; Assistant Professor, Cornell University, Ithaca, New York, 1973; Member, Board of Directors, National Home Life Assurance Company, New York City; Principal Partner, Aultman Robertson and Associates advertising and public relations firm. Publications: Faster Than Light: An Anthology of Stories about Interstellar Travel (editor with George Zenrowski), 1976; Starhiker, novel, 1977; Christs and Other Poems, 1978; Timetipping, short stories, 1980; Junction, 1981; The Man Who Melted, 1984; In the Field of Fire (edited with Jeanne Dann), 1987; Slow Dancing Through Time (with Gardner Dozois, Michael Swanwick, Susan Casper, Jack L Haldeman II), short stories; Echoes of Thunder (with Jack C Haldeman II), short novel, 1991; Editor: Wandering Stars: An Anthology of Jewish Fantasy and Science Fiction, 1974; Immortal, 1977; Editor with Gardner Dozois: Future Power, 1976; Aliens!, 1980; Unicorns!, 1984; Magicals!, 1984; Bestiary!, 1985; Mermaids!, 1985; Sorcerers!, 1986; Demons!, 1988; Dogtails!; Seaserpents!, 1989; Dinosaurs!, 1990. Address: 825 Front Street, Binghampton, NY 13905, USA.

DANTE Robert, b. 12 Feb 1953, Lytham St Annes, Lancashire, England. Writer; Correspondent. Education: BA, University of Houston, 1992. Appointments: Writer; Editor; Theatre Critic; Poet; Publisher, Boudoir Noir Magazine. Publication: Silent Command, 1993. Contributions to: Stone Drum; Aileron; Cincinnati Poetry Review; En Passant; Phosphene; Harvest. Memberships: International Association of Theatre Critics; Canadian Magazine Publishers Association; Canadian Editors Association. Address: PO Box 5, Stn F, Toronto, Ontario M4Y 2L4, Canada.

DAO Bei. See: **ZHAO Zhenkai.**

DARDEN Kathryn E, (Mary Edwards), b. 19 Dec 1958, Nashville, Tennessee, USA. Publisher. Education: MA, David Lipscomb University, 1976. Appointments: Teacher, Nashville Christian School, 1990-95; President, Darden and Associates, 1982-; Publisher, 1988-. Publications: Publisher: Christian Activites Nashville; Creative ReSOURCE Director; Anthology of Christian Poetry; American Poetry Anthology; Best Poems of the 90's; Distinguished Poets of America; Outstanding Poets of 1994; Poetic Voices of America, 1995; After the Storm, Best Poems of 1995; Christian Poet's Pen; Poetry in Motion; Christian Poet #59. Honours: Numerous awards; Honorable Mention, Who's Who in International Poetry; International Woman of the Year, 1995, 1996; Editor's Choice Awards. Address: PO Box 210182, Nashville, TN 37221-0182, USA.

DARDEN-SMITH Patricia, b. 21 Dec 1955, Savannah, Georgia, USA. Para Professional. m. DeWitt Smith, 5 Oct 1981, 1 son. Appointments: Teacher's Assistant; Nurse's Assistant; Girl Scout Leader; Substitute Teacher Certificate. Publications: In a Different Light, 1991; Language of the Soul, 1991; Poetic Voices of America, 1992; Impressions, 1995; Freedom, 1995; Endless Harmony, 1995; Perspectives, 1995; Best New Poems, 1995; The Rainbow's End, 1996; Mirrors of the Mind, 1996; Our Captured Moments, 1996; Treasured Poems of America, 1996; Crossings, 1996; Skyline, 1996; Sweetheart, 1997. Contributions to: Starburst; Journal of the International Society of Authors & Artists Verses; Journal of Cader Publishing. Honours: Certificate of Accomplishment of Merit, 1995; Honorable Mention Certificate; Honorable Mention Certificate; President's Award, 1996; Famous Poet of 1996, Famous Poets' Society, Hollywood, California, 1996. Memberships: International Society of Authors and Artists; Creative Arts and Sciences; National Poets Association; The Georgia State Poetry Society. Address: POB 1637, Vidalia, GA 30475, USA.

DARRAGH Simon Timothy, b. 12 June 1944, Walmer, Kent, England. Plumber; Translator. Education: BA (Hons), Philosophy, University College London, 1971. Publication: Poem in The Literary Review Anthology of Real Poetry, 1990. Contributions to: Poems to: Literary Review, Orbis and The Rialto (England); Orphic Lute, Amelia, S P S M and H (USA). Honour: 2nd Prize, Literary Review Poetry Competition, 1988. Address: Alonnisos, Sporades, Greece.

DARUWALLA K(eki) N(asserwanji), b. 24 Jan 1937, Lahore, India. Bureaucrat. m. Khorshed Keki Daruwalla, 10 May 1965. Education: MA English, Punjab University. Appointment: Visiting Fellow, Queen Elizabeth House, Oxford, 1980-81. Publications: Under Orion, 1970; Apparation in April, 1971; Crossing of Rivers, 1976; Winter Poems, 1980; Keeper of the Dead, 1982; Landscapes, 1987; Anthology: Two Decades of Indian Poetry 1960-80 (editor). Fiction: Sword and Abyss, 1979; Poetry Book for Children: Mr Mugger and Mr Stripes. Contributions to: Anthologies, journals and periodicals. Honours: Sahitya Akademi, National Academy of Letters, Award, 1984; Commonwealth Poetry Award, Asia Region, 1987. Membership: Advisory Board for English, Sahitya Akademi, 1983-87. Address: c/o Oxford University Press, YMCA Library Building, First Floor, Jai Singh Rd, Post Box 43, New Delhi-110 001, India.

DAS Jagannath Prasad, b. 26 Apr 1935, Orissa, India. Writer; Researcher. m. Mitra, 7 May 1960, 1 daughter. Education: MA; PhD. Publications: First Person, 1976; Love Is a Season, 1978; Timescapes, 1980; Silences, 1989; 8 collections of poems in Oriya language. Contributions to: Illustrated Weekly of India; Indian Literature; Poetry Society Journal. Honour: Sahitya Akademi Award, 1991. Membership: President, Poetry Society of India. Address: 305-SFS, Hauz Khas, New Delhi 110016, India.

DAS Kamala, b. 31 Mar 1934, Malabar, South India. Appointments: Poetry Editor, Director of Book Point, Bombay; Political Activist (Independent). Publications: Summer in Calcutta: Fifty Poems, 1965; The Descendants, 1967; The Old Playhouse and Other Poems, 1973; Tonight This Savage Rite, 1979; Collected Poems, 1984. Honour: PEN Prize, 1964. Address: Sthanuvilas Bungalow, Sashamangalam, Trivandrum 10, Kerala, India.

DAS Sisir Kumar, b. 7 Nov 1936, Calcutta, India. Educator. m. 11 Aug 1960, 2 sons, 1 daughter. Education: MA, 1957, Calcutta; PhD, 1963, Calcutta and London. Appointments: Lecturer in Bengali, SOAS, University of London, 1960-63; Reader in Bengali, 1963-80, Tagore Professor, 1980-, University of Delhi. Publications: In Bengali Language: Jama Lagna, 1956; Hayto Daroja Ache, 1986; Abalupta

Chaturtha Charan, 1986; Baj Pakhir Sange, 1992. Memberships: President, Comparative Indian Literature Association, Delhi, 1977-87; Vice President, Comparative Literature Association of India, 1989-. Address: Department of Modern Indian Language, University of Delhi, Delhi 110007, India.

DASGUPTA Buddhadeb, b. 11 Feb 1944, Anara, India. Film Director. m. 27 June 1975, 2 daughters. Education: MA, Economics, University of Calcutta. Appointment: Professor, Economics, Calcutta, 1969-76. Publications: Govir Aerialey, 1962; Coffin Kimba Suitcase, 1971; Himjug, 1978; Chatakahini, 1982; Roboter Gan, 1986; Srestha Kobita, 1990. Contributions to: Krittibash; Shotobhisha; Alinda; Desh; Ananda Bazar Patrika. Address: 32-1F Gariahat Road South, Flat 3A, Calcutta 700031, India.

DASGUPTA Manjush, (Sumitra Gupta), b. 12 Sept 1942, India. Government Servant; Regional Planner. m. S Dasgupta, 8 Mar 1967, 1 son. Education: MA, Economics, Calcutta University; Diploma in National Economic Planning, School of Planning and Statistics, Warsaw, Poland. Appointments: Survey Analyst; Urban Economist; Regional Planner. Publications: Pratham Diner Surya, 1962; Annya Banabhumi, 1966; Siuarga Theke Telephone, 1983; Bholobasa Jhakhan Prabase, 1986; Ghar I Akasher Galpa, 1989; Aguner Dana, 1991. Contributions to: Annanda Bazar; Desh; Bartaman; Aajkaal; Dainik Basumati; Monorama; Chaturanga; Telegraphy; Alinda; Kalpratima; Bharat Bichitra; Jugantar; Anandamela; Sandesh. Address: Flat 302, Block 46, Behala Govt QRS, Calcutta 700 060, India.

DASH Braja Kishore, b. 25 Sept 1958, Kaladia, Namouza, Cutlack, India. Teacher; Poet; Writer. Education: ISC, BA, with distinction; BEd, First Class; MA, First Class. Appointments: Teacher, Government High School, Machkund, Koraput, India. Publications: Love; My Livelong Here Peace of Dove; Truth; My Life Is Your Eternal Game; I Am Potentially Divine; Meditation; Oriya Poem Collection, forthcoming. Contributions to: Poetry 96; Poet; Poetry Time; Poetcrit; Poetry; Heaven; Triveni; Kavita India; Vedic Light; Skylark; Genadaishi. Honours: World Congress of Poetry; Bharat Chakra Memorial Award, Sambalpur University; Gem of Oriental Knowledge, Kalikrishna, Jeypore, Koraput; Certificate, Bhakta Charan Charitable Trust; Gem of Oriental Knowledge, Kali Krishna. Address: Government High School, Machkund, Koraput, Orissa 764 040, India.

DASH Brusaketu, (Kuna), b. 1 Feb 1962, Buguda, India. Headmaster. m. 9 Mar 1991. Education: HSC, BSE, Orissa, 1978; Intermediate Arts, 1980, BA, 1982, MEd, 1983, MEd, 1984, MA, English, 1987, Berhampur University. Appointments: Editor, Premika literary monthly; Reporter, Sambad, Sun Times; Headmaster, Budhagiri Bidyapitha, B D Pur. Publications: Pasu Pakshyenka Kahani (story for children), 1989; Nadi Naree Namaskar (short story), 1990; Rutu O'Rati (poetry collection), 1991. Contributions to: Periodicals and magazines. Honours: Jadumani Sahitya Sansad, Udayapur, 1988; Palli Shree Poetry Awards, 1990. Memberships: Yuba Lekhaka Samilana; General Secretary, Chinta O'Chetana, Orissa; General Secretary, Ossta, Buguda Zone; Darnik Asha Sahitya Ashara; Secretary, Sakala Sahitya Sansad. Address: Buguda 761118, Gianjam, Orissa 761118, India.

DASSANOWSKY Robert von, b. 28 Jan 1960, New York, New York, USA. Writer; Poet; Dramatist; Editor; University Professor. Education: American Academy of Dramatic Arts, Pasadena, California, 1977-78; American Film Institute Conservatory Program, Los Angeles, 1979-81; BA, 1985, MA, 1988, PhD, 1992, University of California at Los Angeles. Appointments: Editor, New German Review, 1986-91; Founding Editor, Rohwedder: International Magazine of Literature and Art, 1986-91; Teaching Fellow, Department of Germanic Languages, 1989-92, Visiting Assistant Professor of German, 1992-93, University of California at Los Angeles; Writer/Researcher, The Disney Channel, 1990-92; Corresponding Editor, Rampike, 1991-; German Language Editor, Osiris, 1991-; Associate Editor, Center, 1992-; Managing Editor, Writers' Forum, 1993-96; Assistant Professor of German, Head, German Studies, Development Director of Film Studies, University of Colorado At Colorado Springs, 1993-; Founding President, PEN Colorado, 1993-. Publications: Phantom Empires: The Novels of Alexander Lernet-Holenia and the Question of Postimperial Austrian Identity, 1996; Hans Raimund: Verses of a Marriage (translator), 1996; Telegrams from the Metropole: Selected Poetry 1980-1995, 1997; Alexander Lernet-Holenia: Mars in Aries (translator), 1997; Other: Several plays and television scripts. Contributions to: Many periodicals and anthologies. Honours: Julie Harris/Beverly Hills Theatre Guild Playwriting Award, 1984; Accademico Honoris Causa, Accademia Culturale d'Europa, Italy, 1989; University of Colorado President's Fund for the Humanities Grant, 1996. Memberships: Authors League; Dramatists Guild; Paneuropa Union, Austria; Modern Language Association; PEN; Poets and Writers; Society for Cinema Studies; Screen Actors Guild. Address: c/o Department of Languages and Cultures, University of Colorado at Colorado Springs, Colorado Springs, CO 80933, USA.

DATTA Bidhan, b. Mar 1948, Akherpur, India. Poet; Writer; Lyricist Service. m. June 1975, 1 daughter. Publications: Rakta-Tyies; Nirvasito Sahytiek and Sambo Bad; Parliament Theke Janapath; Sadamanuser Deshe; Donrao PathikBar; Madhusudan Smriti; Yobaraj; Ayatou Raja. Contributions to: Jugantor; Harold; World Poetry; Canopy; New Global Verse; Anthology of contemporary Universal Most Important Poet. Creative works: Has written over 1000 songs. Honours: World Poet Award, 1986; Bangladesh Tribuj Parisad, 1994; President, Jibananda Prize; Secretary, Michael Madhusudan Academy; Secretary, Vivekananda Award; Secretary, Sayendranath Dutta Award. Address: 284 MNK Road (N), (BJF) PO Alambazar, Calcutta 700035, India.

DAUNT Jon, b. 1 Mar 1951, Columbus, Ohio, USA. Poet. m. 16 Dec 1979, 2 sons. Education: BA, Stanford University, 1973; MA, University of California, 1983. Contributions to: California Quarterly; Cincinnati Poetry Review; Connecticut Poetry Review; Denver Quarterly; Descant; Louisiana Literature; Malahat Review; Mississippi Review; Nimrod; Prairie Schooner; Shenandoah; South Carolina Review; South Dakota Review. Honours: Academy of American Poets Award, 1984; Alice Sherry Memorial Prize, Poetry Society of Virginia, 1985; Wildwood Poetry Prize, 1985-86; Black Bear Poetry Awards, 1985-86, 1988-89; Fulbright-Hays Grant, 1987-88. Memberships: Poetry Society of America; Philological Association of the Pacific Coast. Address: 609 D Street, Davis, CA 95616, USA.

DAVENPORT Christine Elaine, b. 9 May 1980, Greenwood, South Carolina, USA. Student. Education: Honors Program, Emerald High School, Greenwood, South Carolina. Contributions to: Nature Medley Vol IV; Kids Playyard. Honours: Poetic Achievement highlighted in local newspaper, Index Journal, 1996. Address: 401 Lorenzo Road, Greenwood, South Carolina 29646, USA.

DAVEY Frank(land), b. 19 Apr 1940, Vancouver, British Columbia, Canada. Professor of Canadian Literature; Writer; Poet; Editor. m. (1) Helen Simmons, 1962, div 1969, (2) Linda McCartney, 1969, 1 son, 1 daughter. Education: BA, 1961, MA, 1963, University of British Columbia, Vancouver; PhD, University of Southern California, Los Angeles, 1968. Appointments: Founding Editor, Tish magazine, Vancouver, 1961-63; Open Letter, Toronto, 1965-; Writer-in-Residence, Sir George Williams University, Montreal, 1969-70; Assistant Professor, 1970-72, Associate Professor, 1972-79, Professor of English, 1980-90, Chair, Department of English, 1985-90, York University, Toronto; General Editor, Quebec Translations Series, 1973-90, New Canadian Criticism Series, 1977-; Visiting Professor, Shastri Indo-Canadian Institute, Karnatak University, India, 1982; Director, Swift Current Literary Database amd Magazine Project, 1984-90; Carl F Klinck Professor of Canadian Literature, University of Western Ontario, London, 1990-. Publications: Poetry includes: Four Myths for Sam Perry, 1970; Weeds, 1970; Griffon, 1972; King of Swords, 1972; L'An Trentiesme: Selected Poems 1961-1970, 1972; Arcana, 1973; The Clallam, or, Old Glory in Juan de Fuca, 1973; War Poems, 1979; The Arches: Selected Poems, 1980; Capitalistic Affection, 1982; Edward and Patricia, 1984; The Louis Riel Organ and Piano Company, 1985; The Abbotsford Guide to India, 1986; Postcard Translations, 1988; Popular Narratives, 1991; Reading Kim Right, 1993; Canadian Literary Power, 1994; Cultural Mischief, 1996; Others include: Karla's Web: A Cultural Examination of the Mahaffy-French Murders, 1994. Contributions to: Books and journals. Honours: Macmillan Prize, 1962; Department of Defence Arts Research Grants, 1965, 1966, 1968; Canada Council Fellowships, 1966, 1974; Humanities Research Council of Canada Grants, 1974, 1981; Canadian Federation for the Humanities Grants, 1979, 1992; Social Sciences and Humanities Research Council Fellowship, 1981; Membership: President, Association of Canadian College and University Teachers of English, 1994-96. Address: c/o University of Western Ontario, London, Ontario N6A 5B8, Canada.

DAVEY William, b. 20 Mar 1913, New York, New York, USA. Poet; Writer. m. (7) Susan Steenrod, 19 Nov 1965. Education: Princeton University; University of California at Berkeley; New York University; Sorbonne, Paris. Appointments: 1st poem, age 7; Commando, 1st Special Service Force, Canadian-American Elite Unit, World War II; High-goal polo player, amateur astronomer and chess player; Contributing and Foreign Language Editor, The Long Story, 1991-96. Publications: Dawn Breaks the Heart (novel), 1932; Arms, Angels, Epitaphs, poetry; The Angry Dust, novel, 1995; The Trail of Pythagoras (poetry), 1996; Splendor from Darkness (novel), in progress. Contributions to: Anthologies, periodicals and magazines. Honour: Nominated four times for Literary Prizes. Memberships: Poetry Society of America; Poetry Society of Virginia. Address: Lions Watch Farm, PO Box 129, Keene, VA 22946, USA.

DAVIDE Adele, b. 12 Dec 1937, Manchester, England. Jungian Analyst; Astrologer. m. 1959, div 1971, 2 daughters. Education: National Diploma of Art, Painting Special, 1962; MAJA (Member of the Association of Jungian Analysts), 1985; MIAJA (Member of the International Association of Jungian Analysts), 1985. Appointments: Lecturer in Drawing, Chelsea College of Art, 1962-63; Lecturer in Drawing and Painting, Plymouth College of Art, 1964-65; Lecturer in Creative Writing and Literature, Enfield College of Higher Education, 1974-83; Private Practice as Analyst and Lecturer in Psychology, 1985-; Supervisor and Lecturer at the Centre for Psychology, 1990-; Training Analyst, 1993-. Publication: Becoming, 1980. Contributions to: Anthologies, newspapers and journals. Honours: Prize Caernarvon Festival, 1978; First Prize, Cheltenham Open Competitive Festival, 1993. Address: 49 Llanvanor Road, Child's Hill, London NW2 2AR, England.

DAVIDSON Michael, b. 18 Dec 1944, Oakland, California, USA. Professor of Literature; Poet; Writer. m. (1) Carol Wikarska, 1970, div 1974, (2) Lois Chamberlain, 1988, 2 children. Education: BA, San Francisco State University, 1967; PhD, State University of New York, Buffalo, 1971; Post-Doctoral Fellow, University of California, Berkeley, 1974-75. Appointments: Visiting Lecturer, San Diego State University, 1973-76; Curator, Archive for New Poetry, 1975-85, Professor of Literature, 1977-, University of California, San Diego. Publications: Poetry: Exchanges, 1972; Two Views of Pears, 1973; The Mutabilities, and the Foul Papers, 1976; Summer Letters, 1976; Grillwork, 1980; Discovering Motion, 1980; The Prose of Fact, 1981; The Landing of Rochambeau, 1985; Analogy of the Ion, 1988; Post Hoc, 1990; Other: The San Francisco Renaissance: Poetics and Community at Mid-Century, 1989. Contributions to: Periodicals. Honour: National Endowment for the Arts Grant, 1976. Address: c/o Department of Literature, University of California at San Diego, La Jolla, CA 92093, USA.

DAVIDSON Phebe Elizabeth, b. 25 Mar 1944, Summit, New Jersey, USA. Professor of English. m. Stephen Davidson, 29 May 1968, 2 sons. Education: BA, English, Trenton State College, 1967; MA, English Rutgers, 1987; PhD, English, Rutgers, 1991. Appointments: Teacher, High School English, 1967-76; Writing Instructor, Rutgers, 1990-91; Assistant Professor of English, 1991-96, Associate Professor of English, 1996-, University of South Carolina. Publications: Milk and Brittle Bone, 1991; Two Seasons, 1993; The Silence and Other Poems, 1995; The Artists' Colony, 1996. Contributions to: The Kenyon Review; Calliope; The Literary Review; Confluence; Elephants & Other Gods; Poetry East; South East Poetry Journal; Southern Poetry Review. Honours: Amelia Award, 1988; Lester Cash Short Poem Award, 1991; H R Roberts Foundation Award, 1992; Joanna Burgoyne Prize, 1993; Porter Fleming, 1994, 1995. Memberships: Associated Writing Programs; South Carolina Poetry Society; South Carolina Writer's Workshop. Address: Department of English, University of South Carolina - Aiken, SC 29801, USA.

DAVIES Charles. See: **CHAPMAN David Charles**.

DAVIES Josie Ennis, b. 8 Dec 1928, Coventry, Warwickshire, England. School Teacher; College Lecturer. m. Harold Henry Davies, 26 Dec 1967. Education: Teaching Diploma, 1952, 1964. Appointments: Tax Officer, Inland Revenue, 1946-50; School Teacher, 1952-62; Lecturer, Coventry Technical College, 1962-72. Publications: Waiting for Hollyhocks; Shadows on the Lawn; The Tuning Tree; Marmalade and Mayhem; Miscellany; Understanding Stone, 1994; A Press of Nails, 1996. Contributions to: Folio International; Pennine Platform; Iota; Periaktos; Poetry Nottingham; Spokes; Success; The

Countryman; Weyfarers; The Writers Voice; The Lady; Vigil; Haiku Quarterly; Period Piece and Paperback; Envoi; Poetry Digest. Membership: National Poetry Foundation. Address: 349 Holyhead Road, Coventry, Warwickshire CV5 8LD, England.

DAVIES Piers (Anthony David), b. 15 June 1941, Sydney, New South Wales, Australia. Barrister; Solicitor; Screenwriter; Poet. m. Margaret Elaine Haswell, 24 Aug 1973, 1 daughter. Education: LLB, University of Auckland, 1964; Diploma in English and Comparative Law, City of London College, 1967. Appointments: Barrister and Solicitor, Jordan Smith & Davies, Auckland, New Zealand (qualified, 1965); Chairperson, Short Film Fund, New Zealand Film Commission, 1987-91. Publications: East and Other Gong Songs, 1967; The Life and Flight of Rev Buck Shotte (with Peter Weir), screenplay, 1969; Day Trip from Mount Meru, 1969; Homesdale (with Peter Weir), screenplay, 1971; The Cars That Ate Paris (with Peter Weir), screenplay, 1973; Diaspora, 1974; Bourgeois Homage to Dada, 1974; Editor, Central Almanac, 1974; Skin Deep, screenplay, 1978; R V Huckleberry Finn, video documentary, 1979; Olaf's Coast, documentary, 1982; Jetsam, 1984; The Lamb of God, screenplay, 1985; A Fair Hearing, screenplay, 1995. Contributions to: Shipping Law Section, Encyclopedia of New Zealand Formsand Precedents, 1994. Contributions to: Anthologies and periodicals. Address: 16 Crocus Place, Remuera, Auckland 5, New Zealand.

DAVIS Dick, b. 18 Apr 1945, Portsmsouth, Hampshire, England. Education: BA, King's College, Cambridge, 1966; PhD in Persian, University of Manchester, 1988. Appointment: Professor of Persian, Ohio State University, USA, 1988-. Publications include: In the Distance, 1975; Seeing the World, 1980; Visitations, 1983; The Covenant, 1984; What the Mind Wants, 1984; Lares, 1986; Devices and Desires: New and Selected Poems 1967-87, 1989; Editions and translations of poetry. Address: Department of Judaic Languages, Ohio State University, 190 North Oval Mall, Columbus, OH 43210, USA.

DAVIS Eunice Christine, b. 5 July 1914, Brooklyn, Mississippi, USA. Retired Teacher. m. George Vernon Barnes, 17 July 1949. Education: BS, University of South Mississippi, 1935. Appointments: Teacher of English in Southern Mississippi Schools, 1939-49; High School and Junior High Teacher, Williamsburg High School, Collins, 1935-37, Puckett High School, 1937--39, Brayton High School, 1939-41, Rynnelstown High School, Perry County, 1941-43, Hattiesburo, Mississippi Junior High School, 1943-49. Publications: To The Stars, 1992; Moments in Time; Autumn Leaves, 1994; Back Porch; Dreams Wander, 1994; Haiku Happenings, 1995. Contributions to: Voices International; Mississippi Poetry Society Journals & Special Publications as Lyric Mississippi; South Mississippi Poets; Many others. Honours include: Poet of the Year, 1988; Most Published Poet, 1991. Memberships: Mississippi Poetry Society; Writers Unlimited; Waiku of America; Southern Poetry Association; South Branch of Mississippi Poetry Society. Address: 712 Irving Street, Pascagoula, MS 39567, USA.

DAVIS Jack (Leonard), b. 11 Mar 1917, Perth, Western Australia. Poet; Dramatist; Writer. m. Madelon Jantine Wilkens, 12 Dec 1987, 1 daughter. Appointment: Writer-in-Residence, Murdoch University, 1982. Publications: The First Born and Other Poems, 1968; Jagardoo Poems from Aboriginal Australia, 1978; The Dreamers, play, 1983; Kullark, play, 1983; John Pat and Other Poems, 1988; Burungin (Smell the Wind), play, 1989; Plays from Black Australia, 1989. Contributions to: Identity. Honours: Human Rights Award, 1987; BHP Award, 1988; Australian Artists Creative Fellowship, 1989; Honorary doctorates. Memberships: Chairman, Aboriginal Writers Oral Literature and Dramatists Association; Australian Writers Guild; Life Member, PEN International. Address: 3 Little Howard Street, Fremantle, Western Australia, Australia.

DAVIS John Clarence Jr, b. Knoxville, Tennessee, USA. Professional Doctoral Minister; Writer; Broadcaster; Poet. m. Alma Coleen Beets, 4 June 1962, 1 son. Education: Baccalaureate degree, Business Education and Adminsitration, Metropolitan University, Los Angeles; Master's Degree, magna cum laude, Bible Interpretation; DMin, Theological Seminary; Certifed Teacher, Humanities, Broadcasting, State of Tennessee; Graduate Emeritus, Dr Billy Graham School of Evangelism. Appointments: Educator; Feature Writer; Clergyman Evangelist; Founder, The Chaplain's Hour, broadcast programmes for US Army; Founder, Doctor Davis Media Ministries. Publications: The Poet's Guide to Getting Published; Reach Out America; Anthologies: A Poem in Simple Prayer for Our American

Hostages, in World of Poetry, 1987; Treasured Poems of America, 1990; World of Poetry; American Poetry Anthology. Contributions to: Award-winning articles in newspapers and journals. Honours: Creative Journalism Award, Great Commonwealth of Kentucky Award of Merit Certificate, World of Poetry, 1987; 2 Silver Poet Awards, 2 Golden Poet Awards, World of Poetry; Emeritus PhD, Alumni Society; Metropolitan-Cosmopolitan University, Los Angeles; Honorary Collegiatus DLitt for Outstanding Broadcasting and Writing. Address: Doctor Davis Ministries, Study and Studios, 1728 Fair Drive Northeast, Knoxville, TN 37928, USA.

DAVIS Melody D, b. 19 Sept 1959, Harrisburg, Pennsylvania, USA. Writer; Photographer. m. Shahan Islam, 29 Jan 1983. Education: BA, Columbia University, 1981; MA, State University of New York at Stony Brook, 1989. Appointments: President, Founder, Poetlink, 1989-93; Adjunct Professor, State University of New York at Stony Brook, 1989, 1993; Montclair State College, 1990. Publications: The Center of Distance; The Male Nude in Contemporary Photography. Contributions to: Anthologies, journals and periodicals. Honours: Alice Moser Claudel Poetry Contest, 1st Place; Amy Loveman Prize for Poetry; Lenore Marshall Prize for Poetry; National Endowment for the Arts Fellowship in Poetry, 1995; Finalist, National Poetry Series, 1995, for Private Cosmologies. Memberships: Poetlink; Poets and Writers; New Orleans Poetry Forum. Address: 24 Childsworth Ave, Bernardsville, NJ 07924, USA.

DAVIS Owen, b. 27 Jan 1939, Kuala Lumpur, Malaysia. Poet. m. 30 Jan 1986, 2 sons, 1 daughter. Appointment: Editor, South West Review, 1979-81. Publications: Ace of Fools, 1980; The Reflective Arrangement, Galloping Dog, 1982; One Plus One (with Jeremy Hilton), 1986; Two Stones, One Bird (with Paul Mathews), 1989. Poetry-music cassette: Traveller, 1985; Into Another World, 1989. Contributions to: Magazines and anthologies. Honour: South West Arts Writer's Bursary, 1975. Address: 15 Argyle Road, Swanage, Dorset BH19 1HZ, England.

DAVIS Selwyn Sylvester, (Niwles Sivad), b. 18 Sept 1945, Trinidad and Tobago. Town Planner; Environment Consultant; Martial Arts Instructor; Researcher; Playwright-Poet; Actor. m. Violet Nidali Nyasoka Sakala, 3 Jan 1992, 1 son, 1 daughter. Education: BA (Hons), Geography, 1969, Postgraduate Diploma, City Planning, 1977, Univerity of Manitoba; Advanced Reading Dynamics Certificate, Evelyn Wood Institute, Halifax, Winnipeg, 1976; Postgraduate Diploma, Financial Management, Conductor Ltd, Toronto, 1980. Appointments: Consultant, Dunbar Patterson Rose Landscape Architects, Winnipeg, Canada, 1980; Chief Town Planner, Lusaka City Council, Zambia; Environment Research Consultant, UN Centre for Regional Development, Nagoya, Japan; Director, International Tae Kwon Do Federation, Vienna. Publications: Manitoba 1874-1974 Centennial Poetry Contest Anthology, 1974; I Want to Meet You There, anthology, 1976; Selected Slips, (Teachers Guidebook), 1980; My Africa Rebirth (Teacher's Guidebook), 1991; Zambia National Association of Writers Poetry Contest Anthology (editor). Contributions to: Contemporary Verse 2; Writers News Manitoba Journal; British Columbia Society of Landscape Architects Newsletter; Caribe; Yearbook Poetry Contest Anthology, Canadian Authors Association; Newsletters: Save the Children; Zambia Institute of Planners; British Columbia Society of Landscape Architects. Honours: Honourable Mention, Poetry Contests: Manitoba Centennial, 1974; Canadian Authors Association, 1980; Producer, Host Poetry Talks, Cable TV, 1970s; Commissioned poetry readings: Manitoba Poetry Conference, 1976; Southern Africa Development Coordinating Conference, 1990; Poetry Adjudicator, National Theatre Arts Association Annual Festival, Zambia, 1988-; Best 1-Act Play, Lusaka Theatre Club, 1988; Books chosen for School Grades, Zambia Ministry of Education, 1992. Memberships: Poetry Committee, Zambia National Association of Writers, chair; Poetry Society, National Poetry Centre, London; Canadian Authors Association; Lusaka Press Club; Lusaka Theatre Club; Morvant EC Ex-Pupils Literary and Cultural Association, chair; Pegasus Literary and Cultural Association, Port of Spain. Address: PO Box 835, 36 Adelaide Street, Toronto, Ontario M5C 2K1, Canada.

DAVIS William Virgil, b. 26 May 1940, Canton, Ohio, USA. Professor of English. m. Carol Demske, 17 July 1971, 1 son. Education: AB, 1962, MA, 1965, PhD, 1967, Ohio University; MDiv, Pittsburgh Theological Seminary, 1965. Appointments: Assistant Professor, English: Ohio University, 1967-68; Central Connecticut State University, 1968-72; University of Illinois, Chicago, 1972-77; Associate Professor, English, 1977-78; Professor, English,

Writer-in-Residence, 1979-, Baylor University, Waco, Texas; Visiting Professor, University of Vienna, Austria, 1979-80, 1989-90; Writer-in-Residence, University of Montana, 1983; Visiting Scholar/Guest Professor, University of Wales, Swansea, 1983; University of Copenhagen, Denmark, 1984. Publications: One Way to Reconstruct the Scene, 1980; The Dark Hours, 1984; Understanding Robert Bly, 1988; Winter Light, 1990; Critical Essays on Robert Bly, 1992; Miraculous Simplicity: Essays on R S Thomas, 1993; Living Away; Robert Bly: The Poet and His Critics, 1994; The Bones Poems, forthcoming. Contributions to: Critical articles and poems in magazines and journals. Honours: Yale Series of Younger Poets Award, 1979; John Atherton Fellow in Poetry, Bread Loaf Writers Conference, 1980; Chapbook Prize, Calliope Press, 1984. Memberships: Academy of American Poets; PEN; Tau Kappa Alpha; International Association of University Professor of English; Modern Language Association; Phi Kappa Phi; Poetry Society of America; Poets and Writers; Texas Institute of Letters; Texas Association of Creative Writing Teachers. Address: 2633 Lake Oaks Road, Waco, TX 76710, USA.

DAVISON Peter (Hubert), b. 27 June 1928, New York, New York, USA. Poet; Writer; Editor. m. (1) Jane Truslow, 7 Mar 1959, dec 1981, 1 son, 1 daughter, (2) Joan Edelman Goody, 11 Aug 1984. Education: AB, Harvard College, 1949; Fulbright Scholar, St John's College, Cambridge University, 1949-50. Appointments: Page, US Senate, 1944; Assistant Editor, Harcourt Brace and Co, 1950-51, 1953-55; Assistant to Director, Harvard University Press, 1955-56; Associate Editor, 1956-59, Executive Editor, 1959-64, Director, 1964-79, Senior Editor, 1979-85, Atlantic Monthly Press; Poetry Editor, The Atlantic, 1972-; Editor, Peter Davison imprint, Houghton Mifflin Company, 1985-. Publications: The Breaking of the Day, 1964; The City and the Island, 1966; Pretending to Be Asleep, 1970; Walking the Boundaries, 1974; A Voice in the Mountain, 1977; Barn Fever, 1981; Praying Wrong: New and Selected Poems, 1959-84, 1984; The Great Ledge, New Poems, 1989; Prose: Half Remembered: A Personal History, 1973, revised edition, 1991; One of the Dangerous Trades: Essays on The Work and Workings of Poetry, 1991; The Fading Smile: Poets in Boston 1955-1960, 1994; Poetry: The Poems of Peter Davison, 1957-95, 1995. Contributions to: Atlantic Monthly; New York Times Book Review; Washington Post Book World; New England Monthly; Encounter; Poetry, Chicago; New Yorker; Harper's; New Criterion; Hudson Review; Sewanee Review; Southern Review. Honours: Winner, Yale Series of Younger Poets, 1963; Award, National Institute American Academy of Arts and Letters, 1972; James Michener Prize, 1981, 1985; New England Booksellers Award for Literary Excellence, 1995. Address: 70 River Street, No 2, Boston, MA 02108, USA.

DAVITT Michael, b. 20 Apr 1950, Cork, Ireland. TV Producer; Director. m. Maire Nic Fhinn, 26 July 1975, 1 son, 2 daughters. Education: University College, Cork; BA, Celtic Studies, 1971; TTG Diploma, 1st Hons 1983. Appointments: Teacher of Irish; Linguistic Researcher; Manager of Slogadh Youth Festival; TV Presenter; Editor of Innti Poetry Journal; Theatre Manager; TV Producer/Director. Publications: In the Irish (Gaelic) Language: Gleann Ar Ghleann, 1982; Bligeard Sraide, 1983; Rogha Danta/Selected Poems, Bilingual; Galar Gan Naire, cassette, 1990; An Tost A Scagadh, 1993. Anthologies: Original Irish & English Translations: The Bright Wave, 1986; The Flowering Tree, 1990; Penguin Book of Contemporary Irish Poetry, 1990; Field Day Anthology, 1991; Compiler of Sruth Na Maoile (Gaelic Poetry from Scotland and Ireland), 1993. Contributions to: Innti; Comhar; Poetry Ireland Review; Eire-Ireland; Translation; Die Horen; Graph; Antioch Review, USA. Honours: Arts Council (Ireland) Writing Bursaries 1980, 1990; Oireachtas Award, 1981; Butler Award for Literature, Irish-American Cultural Institute, 1994. Memberships: Irish Writers' Union; National Union of Journalists. Address: 32 Albany Road, Ranelagh, Dublin 6, Ireland.

DAWE (Donald) Bruce, b. 15 Feb 1930, Geelong, Victoria, Australia. Associate Professor; Poet; Writer. m. Gloria Desley Blain, 27 Jan 1964, 2 sons, 2 daughters. Education: BA, 1969, MLitt, 1973, MA, 1975, PhD, 1980, University of Queensland. Appointments: Lecturer, 1971-78, Senior Lecturer, 1978-83, DDIAE; Writer-in-Residence, University of Queensland, 1984; Senior Lecturer, 1985-90, Associate Professor, 1990-93, School of Arts, Darling Heights, Toowoomba. Publications: No Fixed Address, 1962; A Need of Similar Name, 1964; Beyond the Subdivision, 1968; An Eye for a Tooth, 1969; Heat-Wave, 1970; Condolences of the Season: Selected Poems, 1971; Just a Dugong at Twilight, 1974; Sometimes Gladness: Collected Poems, 1978, 4th edition, revised, 1993; Over Here Harv!

and Other Stories, 1983; Towards Sunrise, 1986; This Side of Silence, 1990; Bruce Dawe: Essays and Opinions, 1990; Mortal Instruments: Poems, 1990-1995, 1995. Contributions to: Various periodicals. Honours: Myer Poetry Prizes, 1966, 1969; Ampol Arts Award for Creative Literature, 1967; Dame Mary Gilmore Medal, Australian Literary Society, 1973; Braille Book of the Year, 1978; Grace Leven Prize for Poetry, 1978; Patrick White Literary Award, 1980; Christopher Brennan Award, 1984; Order of Australia, 1992; Distinguished Alumni Award, UNE, 1996. Memberships: Honorary Life Member, Australian Association for Teaching English; Centre for Australian Studies in Literature; Honorary Life Member, Victorian Association for Teaching of English. Address: 30 Cumming Street, Toowoomba, Queensland 4350, Australia.

DAWE Gerald Chartres, b. 22 Apr 1952, Belfast, Northern Ireland. Writer. m. Dorothea Meluin, 28 Oct 1979, 1 son, 1 daughter. Education: BA Hons, University of Ulster; MA, University College, Galway. Appointments: Tutor in English, Assistant Lecturer, University College, Galway, Republic of Ireland, 1978-87; Assistant Lecturer, Trinity College, Dublin, 1989-. Publications: Sheltering Places, 1978; The Lundy Letter, 1985; Sunday School, 1991; Heart of Hearts, 1995. Editor: The Younger Irish Poets, 1982; The New Younger Irish Poets, 1991; Krino: The paperback review of the arts, 1986-. Critical prose: Across a Roaring Hill: The Protestant Imagination in Modern Ireland (with Edna Longley), 1985; How's the Poetry Going? Literary Politics and Ireland Today, 1991; The Poet's Place (with John Wilson Foster), 1991; A Real Life Elsewhere, 1993; False Faces: Poetry, Politics & Place, 1994; Against Piety: Essays in Irish Poetry, 1995. Contributions to: Irish Times; Fortnight; Linen Hall Review; Honest Ulsterman; Poetry Review, UK. Honours: Major State Award, 1974-77; Arts Council Bursary for Poetry, 1980; Macaulay Fellowship in Literature, 1984; Hawthornden International Writers Fellowship, 1988. Memberships: Irish Writers Union; Poetry Ireland; International Association for the Study of Anglo-Irish Literature. Address: 21 Mulgrave Street, Dun Laohaire, Co Dublin, Republic of Ireland.

DAWSON Jean, b. 14 Oct 1946, West Midlands, England. Teacher (retired); Voluntary Worker for Worcestershire Nature Conservation Trust. m. Anthony Rowland Dawson, 29 Aug 1970. Education: Honours degreee in Zoology, University of Nottingham; Postgraduate Certificate of Education, Leeds. Appointments: Assistant Teacher at various schools in Kent, Gloucestershire and Worcestershire. Contributions to: Outposts PQ; Orbis; Envoi; Iron; Rialto; Green Book; Honest Ulsterman; Poetry Nottingham; Other Poetry; Westwords. Honour: 3rd Prize in Orbis Rhyme International Poetry Competition, 1989. Membership: Poetry Society. Address: Ciderpress, Cotheridge Lane, Eckington, Pershore, Worcestershire WR10 3BA, England.

DAY Kevin K Markwick, (Felix Jaffa, A J Spar), b. 27 May 1959, Hampshire, England. Writer. m. Kim Elizabeth Markwick Day, 17 Oct 1986, 1 son, 2 daughters. Education: 2nd BDS, Bristol University, 1980-85; BA, 1988. Appointments: Deputy Editor, Mens World, 1990-91; Managing Editor, Phoenix Roman, 1991-92; Writer-in-Residence, Good Directions Ltd, 1992-. Publications: From Soft Hues to Half Light; The Amorist. Contributions to: Guardian; Xenos; Rattlers Tale; Staple; Envoi; Writer's Monthly; Expressions. Honour: Best Poem by Her Dad This Year, Aj's Hug Award. Memberships: Poetry Society; Founder of the Campaign for Real Poetry. Address: Writer in Residence, Good Directions Ltd, 15 Talisman Business Centre, Duncan Road, Park Gate, Hampshire S03 7BX, England.

DAY Lila. See: **CHAFFIN-KASH Lillie D.**

DAY-LEWIS Jill Angela Henriette, (Jill Balcon), b. 3 Jan 1925, London, England. Actress; Broadcaster; Editor. m. C Day-Lewis, 27 Apr 1951, 1 son, 1 daughter. Education: Gold Medallist, Central School of Speech and Drama; Hon Degree 1992, Open University. Publications: Editor: A Lasting Joy, 1973; Posthumous Poems of C Day-Lewis, 1979; The Pity of War, 1985; Complete Poems of C Day-Lewis, 1992; Alec, An 80th Birthday Present for Alec Guinness (co-editor, with Christopher Sinclair-Stevenson), 1994. Memberships: Honorary Fellow, Royal Society of Literature; President, Society of Teachers of Speech and Drama; Vice President, Thomas Hardy Society; Vice President, Poetry Society; Vice President, Wilfred Owen Association. Address: Vine Cottage, Steep, Petersfield, Hampshire GU32 2DP, England.

DAYTON Irene Catherine, b. 6 Aug 1922, Lake Ariel, Pennsylvania, USA. Poet; Novelist. m. Benjamin B Dayton, 16 Oct 1943, 2 sons. Education: Associate Degree, Robert Wesleyan College, 1942. Appointments: Poetry Consultant, 1971-73, Poet-in-Residence, 1972-73, New York State Arts Council, Rochester, New York; Instructor, Modern Poetry Writing, Adult Education, Blue Ridge Community College, Flat Rock, North Carolina, 1978-85. Publications: The Sixth Sense Quivers, 1970; The Panther's Eye, 1974; Seven Times the Wind, 1977; In Oxbow of Time's River, 1978; Forthcoming: The Blackbird's Wing; The Falcon's Flight; Tale of the Vercors (novel); House of Zorayan (novel); The Israel Poems. Contributions to: Anthologies and magazines. Honours: Finalist, Yale Series of Younger Poets, 1958; 1st Prize Awards, Rochester Festival of Religious Art, 1959. 1960; Guiness Award, Cheltenham Festival of Literature, 1963; Distinguished Submission Award, Shenandoah Valley Academy of Literature, 1979. Memberships: Honorary Life Member, Past President, Rochester New York Poetry Society; Life Member, Poetry Society of America; Life Member, North Carolina Poetry Society; Founder Fellow, International Academy of Poets, Marquis Library Society, New York City. Address: 209 South Hillandale Drive, East Flat Rock, NC 28726, USA.

DE ANDA Graciela, b. 1 Nov 1969, French Camp, California, USA. Poet. Education: BA, Political Science, University of Texas, Pan American, Edinburgh, 1992. Publications: Windows of the Soul, 1990; 1990 American Anthology of Southern Poets, 1990; Selected Works of Our World's Best Poets, 1991; American Poetry Annual, 1991; Awaken to a Dream, 1991. Address: 308 East Peter, Edinburg, TX 78539, USA.

DE CAMP L(yon) Sprague, b. 27 Nov 1907, New York, New York, USA. Writer; Poet. m. Catherine Adelaide Crook, 12 Aug 1939, 2 sons. Education: BS, Aeronautical Engineering, California Institute of Technology, 1930; MS, Engineering and Economics, Stevens Institute of Technology, 1933. Publications: Over 130 books, including science fiction, fantasy, historical novels, history, biography, textbooks, and juvenile among others. Contributions to: Numerous stories, articles and poems in anthologies, periodicals and other publications. Honours: International Fantasy Award, 1953; Grandmaster Fantasy Award, 1976; Nebula Award, Science Fiction Writers of America, 1978; World Fantasy Conference Award, 1984. Memberships: Authors Guild; History of Science Society; Science Fiction and Fantasy Writers of America; Society for the History of Technology. Address: 3453 Hearst Castle Way, Plano, TX 75025, USA.

DE CONVINCK Herman, b. 21 Feb 1944, Belgium. Editor. m. Kristien Hemmerechts, 14 Mar 1992. Education: University of Louvain. Appointments: Journalist; Editor. Publications: Onbegonnen Werk; De Hectaren Van het Geheugen; Enkelvoud; Over de Troost Van Pessimisme; Over Marieke van De Bakker; De Flaplekstlezer; Schoolslag, poetry; Essays on poetry: Intimiteit onder de melkweg; De vliegende keeper. Contributions to: Most Dutch Literary Magazines. Honours: Prize of the Flemish Provinces; Jan Compert Prize. Membership: PEN. Address: Cogels-Osylei 65, 2600 Antwerp, Belgium.

DE CORMIER-SHEKEYIAN Regina, b. New York, New York, USA. Writer; Poet. m. Haig Shekerjian, 2 sons. Publications: Flutes of Bone, Bones of Clay, 1991; Hoofbeats on the Door, 1993. Anthologies: Voices for Peace, 1990; Many Voices, 1986; Changes, 1987; No Hay Fronteras (bilingual), 1990; Looking for Home: Women Writing About Exile, 1990; Only Morning in Her Shoes, 1990; Helicon Nine Reader, 1991; Translations for The Writings of Christine de Pizan, 1994. Contributions to: Anthologies, journals and magazines. Honours: Pablo Neruda Award, 1984; Rubén Darío Poetry Award, 1988; J W Andrews Narrative Poetry Award, 1990. Memberships: Authors Guild Inc; Poetry Society of America; Academy of American Poets. Address: 4 Sparkling Ridge, New Paltz, NY 12561, USA.

DE FRANCE Stephen David, (Steve De France), b. 29 Dec 1939, Denver, Colorado, USA. College Professor; Writer. Education: BA, English; BA, Theatre Arts; MEd; MA, English Literature; Postgraduate Work, University of Southern California. Appointments: Actor, motion pictures and television; Businessman; Currently Tenured Professor, Literature, Writing, Los Angeles Trade Technical College, California. Publications: Voices at the Way Station, 1968; Another Night in the Dog Breath Cafe, 1974; Angel's Flight: L A Poems, 1980; Lost in Hollywood, 1989; To The Eye It Seems Not To Move, 1991; Poems of Ordinary Anger, 1993. Contributions to: Trellis; Hornspoon;

Community of Friends; Jesture Magazine; Cardinal Poetry Quarterly; Orbis; Apostrophe; California State Poetry Quarterly, 1992. Honours: Honoured as only living poet with subtle sense of rhythm, Deaf Triangle Players Society, Pecos, Texas. Address: 2125 East Ocean Boulevard, Suite 3B, Long Beach, CA 90803, USA.

DE KOK Ingrid Jean, b. 4 June 1951, South Africa. Educator. 1 son. Education: BA, English, Political Science, Witwatersrand University; BA (Hons), English, University of Cape Town; MA, English, Queen's University, Canada. Appointments: Junior Lecturer, English Department, University of Cape Town; Research Assistant, Department of Film Studies, Queen's University, Kingston, Canada; Planning Coordinator, Khanya College, SACHED Trust, South Africa; Director, Extra-Mural Studies, Department of Adult Education, University of Cape Town, 1988-. Publications: Familiar Ground, 1988; Represented in anthologies and collections: The Paperbook of South African English Poetry, 1986; I Quabane Labantu: Poetry in the Emergency, 1989; Breaking the Silence: A Century of South African Women's Poetry, 1990. Contributions to: American Poetry Review, USA; Descant; Event; Brick; Canada; South Africa: South African Review of Books; New Coin; Staffrider; Sesame; Contrast; New Contrast; Upstream; Congress of South African Writers publications; Triquarterly, USA. Membership: Congress of South African Writers. Address: Department of Adult Education, University of Cape Town, Rondebosch 2200, South Africa.

DE LINT Charles (Henri Diederick Hoefsmit), b. 22 Dec 1951, Bussum, Netherlands (Canadian citizen, 1961). Editor; Poet. m. Mary Ann Harris, 15 Sept 1980. Appointments: Owner-Editor, Triskell Press; Writer-in-Residence, Ottawa and Gloucester Public Libraries, 1995. Publications: Drink Down the Moon: A Novel of Urban Faerie, 1990; Death Leaves an Echo, 1991; Dreamimg Place, 1992; From A Whisper to a Scream, 1992; Dreams Underfoot: The Newford Collection, 1993; Memory and Dream, 1994. Contributions to: Anthologies and periodicals. Honours: Various awards. Memberships: Horror Writers of America, vice-president, 1992-93; Science Fiction Writers of America; Small Press Writers and Artists Organization. Address: PO Box 9480, Ottawa, Ontario K1G 3V2, Canada.

DE PAZZI Ellen Eugenia Bosley, (e e de pazzi), b. 7 April 1915, Elcador, Iowa, USA. Poet; Writer; Artist. m. Passino de Pazzi (Marchese), 17 Aug 1940, 2 sons. Education: Design Studies, Indiana University, 1934-37; Art Student, Ateliar Caterina Baratelli, Rio de Janeiro, 1949-52; Degree, Fine Arts, Suffolk Community College, 1987. Appointments: Children's Art Workshop Sponsor, Hampton Center Gallery Inc, New York, 1975-91; Special Education Art Class, Parent-Teacher Association Project for Children, 1985-86; Boces Art Enrichment Programme, 1985-87; Artist-in-Residence, Kids Crafts, Painting, West Hampton Library Classes; TV Master Artist Series, producer, host; Frequent Guest Poetry Readings, radio stations, college campuses and bookstores. Contributions to: Taproot Annual Anthology, 1978, 1984, 1989, 1990, 1991; Ellen de Pazzi Visits Old Italy with Poetry, as guest on: Ideas and Images, CableVision CH 27 programme, 1991; Sound Wave Bi-Annual Poetry and Essay Magazine; Westhampton Chronicle; East End Arts Poetry Corner; Thank You Gorbachev, 1991. Honours: Poetry Prize for Floodtide, 1983, Contadino, 1986, Sound Waves Magazine. Memberships: Tap Root for Older Poets and Writers, 1979-91; Westhampton Writers Festival, 1985-91; Sound Waves SSC Poetry Club, Editorial Staff, 1985-90; Westhampton Library Poetry Group. Address: The Studio, 44 Bayfield Lane, Westhampton Beach, NY 11978, USA.

DE REGNIERS Beatrice Schenk (Tamara Kitt), b. 16 Aug 1914, Lafayette, Indiana, USA. Writer. m. Francis de Regniers, May 1953. Education: PhB, University of Chicago, 1935; Sorbonne, Paris, 1935-36; Summer School University of Toulouse, France; Med, Winnetka Graduate Teachers College. Appointments: Copywriter, Scott Foresman & Co, Illinois, 1943-44; Welfare Officer, UNRRA, Egypt, 1944-46; Copywriter, American Book Co, 1948-49; Director of Educational Materials, American Heart Association, 1949-61; Editor, Lucky Book Club, 1961-81. Publications: The Giant Story; A Little House of Your Own; What Can You Do With a Shoe; A Child's Book of Dreams; Something Special; Cats Cats Cats Cats Cats; Who Likes the Sun; Circus; Red Riding Hood Retold in Verse; It Does Not Say Meow; A Bunch of Poems and Verses; This Big Cat and Other Cats I've Known; So Many Cats; Jack and the Beanstalk, retold in verse; The Snow Party; The Shadow Book; The Abraham Lincoln Joke Book; David and Goliath; Jack The Giant Book; The Boy, the Rat and the Butterfly; The Enchanted Forest; Laura's Story; Picture Book Theatre;

Waiting for Mama; The Giant Killer, retold in verse; The Secret Act; The Boy Who Fooled the Giant; The Boy, The Cat and the Magic Fiddle; Sam and the Impossible Thing. Memberships: Authors Guild; PEN; Dramatists Guild; Society of Childrens Book Writers. Address: 180 West 58th Street, New York, NY 10019, USA.

DE SOUZA Eunice b. 1 Aug 1940, Poona, India. Education: BA, University of Bombay, 1960. Appointments: Lecturer in English, St Xavier's College, Bombay, 1969-. Publications: Fix, 1979; Women in Dutch Painting, 1988; Ways of Belonging: Selected Poems, 1990. Address: St Xavier's College, Bombay 4000 001, India.

DEADY John Joseph, b. 11 Dec 1936, Lancashire, England. School Teacher. Contributions to: Aireings; Poetry Now; North West. Address: 20 Chorley Road, Standish, Wigan, Lancashire WN6 0AA, England.

DEAHL James Edward, b. 5 Dec 1945, Pittsburgh, Pennsylvania, USA. Author; Editor; Teacher. m. Gilda L Mekler, 23 May 1982, 3 daughters. Appointments: Editor, publisher, Poemata; Managing partner, Mekler & Deahl, publishers. Publications: In The Lost Horn's Call, 1982; No Cold Ash, 1984; Blue Ridge, 1985; Geschriebene Bilder, 1990; Opening The Stone Heart, 1992; Heartland, 1993; Even This Land Was Born Of Light, 1993; Under The Watchful Eye, 1995; Tasting The Winter Grapes, 1995. Honour: Mainichi Award, 1985. Memberships: International PEN; League of Canadian Poets; Haiku Canada; Poetry Society, UK; Academy of American Poets, USA. Address: 237 Prospect Street South, Hamilton, Ontario LM8 2Z6, Canada.

DEAL Susan Strayer, b. 21 Feb 1948, Lincoln, Nebraska, USA. Poet. Education: BA, Kearney State College, 1973; MA, University of Lincoln, 1980. Appointments: Teacher; Adjunct Professor. Publications: No Moving Parts, 1980; The Dark is a Door, 1984; Sometimes So Easy, 1991. Contributions to: Bay Windows; Northwest Review; Sows Ear; Prairie Schooner; Black Warrior Review; Mid America Review; En Passant; Abraxas; Blue Unicorn; Potato Eye; Oxford Magazine; Oxlis; Anemone; Sandhills Press. Honours: Pushcart Prize, 1974; Triton Poetry Contest, 1978; Mississippi Poetry Contest, 1984; Writers Choice, 1984; Poetry on the Buses, 1984. Address: 3825 Woods Boulevard, Lincoln, NE 68502, USA.

DEAN Melfyn, b. 31 Oct 1943, Caerphilly, Wales. m. Inga Dean, 4 Nov 1995. Education: St Loyes College, Exeter; Catering Diploma, 1968; Telephonist Diploma, 1969. Appointments: CS's Shop Manager; Shop Assistant, Exeter Pram Toy Shop; Fruit Manager, Tesco Limited; Deputy Manager, J Menzies; Chef, Queens Hotel, Cardiff; Chef, Lord Nelson, Haverford West; Chef/Head Barman, Lewis Arms Hotel, Stornoway; Caretaker, Arfon Baha'i Centre, Bangor, North Wales. Publications: Poems and Things, 1995; White Tower Relics and Jewels, 1996; White Tower; 5 Personal Anthologies. Contributions to: BBC North; Mind; Breakthrough; Helicon; White Tower Writers; Forward Press Group; 21 Poems for Various Books; Cherry Bite Publications. Memberships: Wentworth Writers, Barnsley; Bridlington Writers; White Tower Writers Association, Conisborough. Address: Enshala, 28 Maidwell Way, Laceby Acres, Grimsby DN34 5UP, England.

DEAN-RICHARDS Wayne, b. 3 Sept 1961, England. Lecturer. m. Julia, 12 Apr 1996, 2 sons, 1 daughters. Education: BA (Hons), Creative Arts, Nottingham, 1983; PGCE, University of Wolverhampton, 1994; MA, English Language, University of Central England, 1996. Appointments: Factory worker; Professional Boxer; Actor; Freelance Writer; Painter/Decorator; Caretaker; School Teacher; Lecturer in English. Publications: Poems By Two Fat Men, 1986; Tea and Biscuits for Two, 1996. Contributions to: New Yorker; Colorado Review; Understanding; People To People; Heartthrob; Chronicles of Disorder; Vigil; Scratch; Helix; Art Review. Address: 191 Pound Road, Oldbury, Warley, West Midland B68 8NF, England.

DEANE Seamus, b. 9 Feb 1940, Northern Ireland. University Teacher. m. 19 Aug 1963, 3 sons, 1 daughter. Education: BA, Queens University, Belfast, 1961; MA, 1963; PhD, Cambridge University, 1966. Appointments: Visiting Fulbright and Woodrow Wilson Lecturer, Reed College, USA, 1966-67; Visiting Professor, University of Notre Dame, 1977; Carleton College, 1987-88; University of Washington, 1987; Professor, University College, Dublin, 1980-. Publications: Gradual Wars; Rumours; History Lessons; Selected Poems. Contributions to: Grand Street; Listener; Irish University Review; Cambridge Review;

Times Literary Supplement. Honours: AE Award for Literature; American - Ireland Fund Literary Award. Memberships: Royal Irish Academy; Field Day Company; Aosdana. Address: English Department, University College, Dublin, Ireland.

DEAR Catherine Elizabeth (Eliza), b. 13 Apr 1935, Stroud, Gloucestershire, England. Social Worker; Freelance Counselling. m. 25 July 1957, div 1977, 2 sons, 1 daughter. Education: Dip Soc Studies, Trinity College, Dublin, 1956; Dip A S S CQSW, University College, Dublin, 1976. Appointments: Child Care Officer, Royal Borough Chelsea and Kensington, 1969; Psyciatric Social Worker, Mater Child and Family Center, 1973; Freelance Work with groups and individuals, Creative and Counselling 1980; Writer, 1989-. Contributions to: Cyphers; Salmon; Poetry Ireland; Kilkenny Anthology. Honours: Diploma, Scottish International Open Poetry Competition, 1991; Limerick 3rd Prize in Poetry, 1991; Literary Festival, Commendation in Poetry, 1991. Memberships: Irish Writers Union; The Poetry Society. Address: Legan, Thomastown, County Kilkenny, Ireland.

DECKER Donna, b. 15 Aug 1956, Staten Island, New York, USA. Assistant Professor of English. Education: BA, hons, English, College of Staten Island, 1981; MA, English, City College of New York, 1984; PhD, English (Creative Writing), Florida State University, 1990. Appointments: Adjunct Instructor, Pace University, New York and College of Staten Island, New York, 1985-86; Teaching Assistant, English, Florida State University, 1986-90; Assistant Professor, English, University of Wisconsin, Stevens Point, 1990-. Publications: Three Thirds (with N Rasheed and C Acuna-Gomez), 1984; North of Wakulla (editor with Mary Jane Ryals), 1990. Contributions to: IKON; Apalachee Quarterly; Genre; Sundog. Honour: Outstanding Creative Writing Award to Graduate Student, Florida State University, 1987. Memberships: Poets and Writers; M & D Harbor Series; Associated Writing Programs. Address: 317 6th Avenue, Stevens Point, WI 54481, USA.

DEEMER Bill, b. 4 Mar 1945, Norfolk, Virginia, USA. Poet. m. Toby Joy Murray. Publications: Poems, 1964; Diana, 1966; The King's Bounty, 1968; A Few for Lew, 1972; A Few for Lew and Other Poems, 1974; All Wet, 1975; This is Just to Say, 1981; Subjects, 1984. Contributions to: Coyote's Journal; Longhouse. Honour: National Endowment for the Arts Award, 1968. Address: 92400 River Road, Junction City, OR 97448, USA.

DEEN Cheryl Ann, b. 24 Jan 1943, Pomona, California, USA. Floral Designer (retired). m. Jack Deen, 14 May 1966, 2 sons, 2 daughters. Education: University of San Francisco, 2 years. Appointments: Bookkeeper, Continental Life Insurance Company, San Francisco, California, 2 years; Inventory Control Clerk, Arabol Chemical Company, San Francisco, 2 years; Owner, Floral Designer, Bouquet Florist, Redlands, California, 25 years. Publications: Moments More to Go, 1990; The Fountain, 1990; Something for Everyone, 1991; Urania, 1991; Represented in publications: American Poetry Association Volume X, No 2; Amherst Society, 1991; Fine Arts Press, 1991. Contributions to: Poetry Society of America; Wide Open Magazine; Midwest Poetry Review; Sparrowgrass Poetry Forum; Poetry Unlimited; Poetry Press; Poetry Center; Creative Arts and Sciences Enterprises; Zander Press. Honours: Silver Poet Award, 1989; Golden Poet Award, 1990; World of Poetry; Bronze Quill Award, International Society of the Advancement of Poetry, 1990; Best New Poet Distinction Award, 1990; 7 Honourable Mentions, World of Poetry; 1st Place Award, Poetry Forum; Honourable Mention, International Society for the Advancement of Poetry; 3rd Place Award, Watermark Press. Memberships: International Society for the Advancement of Poetry; Mile High Poetry Society; National Library of Poetry. Address: 4040 East Piedmont 375, Highland, CA 92346, USA.

DEFORD Sara Whitcraft, b. 9 Nov 1916, Youngstown, Ohio, USA. Professor. Education: BA, 1936; MA, 1938; PhD, 1942. Appointment: College English Teacher, 1942-81. Publications: Return to Eden; Lectures on Modern American Poetry; City of Love; The Pearl; Lectures on Paradise Lost; Short Loves Poems of John Donne; Forms of Verse with Clarinda Lott; Japanese Scroll Painting; The Circle; Lily of the Valley. Contributions to: Professional journals and magazines. Honours: Sigma Theta Chi Alumnae Poetry Prize; Albert Stanburrough Cook Prize; Eugene Saxton Memorial Fellowship; Fulbright Professorship. Membership: Poetry Society of America. Address: 1961 South Josephine, No 302, Denver, CO 80210, USA.

DELEANU Daniel, b. 12 Sept 1972, Sibiu, Romania. Teacher. Education: BA, English and Romanian, University of Sibiu, 1995; MA, English, University of Sibiu, 1996. Appointment: Teacher of English, Romanian and World Literature, Christian High School, of Sibiu, 1995-. Publications: Efigiile Himerei, 1992; Taci, 1993; The Sunset at Sundown, 1993; Self-Portraits and Other Visionary Indiscretions, 1995. Contributions to: Luceafarul; Euphorion; Tribuna; Saeculum; North Words; Psychopoetica; 100 Words; Back to Godhead; Anthologies: A Break in the Clouds, 1993; The Sound of Poetry, 1993. Honours: International Poet of Merit, 1995; Nominated as Poet of the Year, International Society of Poets, 1995. Address: Str George Cosbuc 30, Sibiu 2400, Jud Sibiu, Romania.

DELFANO M M. See: **FLAMMONDE Paris.**

DEMETILLO Ricaredo, b. 2 June 1920, Dumangas, Iloilo, Philippines. Education: University of Iowa, Iowa City, USA. Appointment: Professor, University of Philippines, Quezon City, until 1986. Publications: No Certain Weather, 1956; La Via: A Special Journey, 1958; Daedalus and Other Poems, 1961; Barter in Panay, 1961; Masks and Signature, 1968; The City and the Thread of Light and Other Poems, 1974; Lazarus, Troubadour, 1974; Sun, Silhouettes and Shadow, 1975; First and Last Fruits, 1989. Address: 38 Bulacan Street, West Avenue, Quezon City, Philippines.

DEMING Alison Hawthorne, b. 13 July 1946. Writer. 1 daughter. Education: MFA, Vermont College, 1983; Stegner Fellow, Stanford University, 1987-88. Appointments: Director, University of Arizona Poetry Center, 1990-. Publications: Science and Other Poems, 1994; Temporary Homelands, 1994. Contributions to: Georgia Review; Denver Quarterly; Sierra; Orion; Wilderness; Alaska Quarterly; Third Coast. Honours: Pablo Neruda Prize, 1983; National Endowment for the Arts Fellowship, 1990, 1995; Gertrude Claytor Award, Poetry Society of America, 1991; Walt Whitman Award, Academy of American Poets, 1993. Memberships: Academy of American Poets; Poetry Society of America; Association for the Study of Literature and The Environment. Address: University of Arizona Poetry Center, 1216 North Cherry Avenue, Tucson, AZ 85719, USA.

DENIORD Richard (Chard) Newnham, b. 17 Dec 1952, New Haven, Connecticut, USA. Teacher. m. 20 June 1971, 1 son, 1 daughter. Education: BA, 1975; MDiv, Yale University, 1978; MFA, University of Iowa, 1985. Appointments: Psychotherapist, Connecticut Mental Health Centerm 1 978-82; Teacher, The Gunnery, 1985-89; Teacher, The Putney School, 1989-. Comparative Religions, 1989-. Publication: Asleep in the Fire. Contributions to: Iowa Review; Ploughshares; Denver Review; North American Review; Bad Henry Review; Agni; Quarterly West; Mississippi Review; Poetry East; Graham House Review; Antioch Review. Honour: Emily Dickinson Award. Membership: Poetry Society of America. Address: RR4, Box 929, Putney, VT 05346, USA.

DENNISTON Edward Connor, b. 13 Nov 1956, Longford, Ireland. Teacher of English, Drama and Media Studies. m. Gillian Doonan, 26 July 1980, 2 daughters. Education: BA, H Dip Ed, Trinity College, Dublin. Appointments: Assistant Head Teacher, 1980; Head of English, 1983. Contributions to: Fortnight; Belfast; Poetry Ireland; Honest Ulsterman; Riverine; Salmon Magazine; Belfast Review. Memberships: Poetry Society; Poetry Ireland; Poetry Wales. Address: 11 Alder Grove, Mt Pleasant, Waterford, Ireland.

DEPAOR Louis, b. 27 June 1961, Cork, Ireland. Writer. m. Shirley Bourke, 1 son, 4 daughters. Education: University College, Cork, 1978-81; PhD, 1986. Appointments: Assistant Lecturer, University College Cork, 1984-85; Thomond College, 1985-87; Moved to Australia, 1987; Community Radio, Melbourne; Visiting Professor, University of Sydney. Publications: Próca Solais is Luatha; 30 Dán; Aimsir Bhreicneach/Freckled Weather; Gobán Cré is Cloch/Sentances of Earth and Stone. Contributions to: Innti; Comhar; Stet; Australian Short Stories; Modern Writing; Meanjin; Melbourne Age; Melbourne Times; Chapman. Honours: Duais Sheáin Uí Ríordáin, 1988, 1992; Writers Project Grant, 1990, 1991; Australia Council Fellowship, 1995; Shortlisted Victorian Premiers Award, 1994. Membership: Flann O'Brien Society. Address: 117 Shaftsbury Street, Coburg 3058, Australia.

DER-HOVANESSIAN Diana, b. USA. Poet. m. James Dalley, sep, 2 daughters. Education: AB, Boston University College of Liberal Arts; Graduate Work, Harvard University; Courses at Radcliffe Seminars. Appointments: Editor, Young America; Teacher-Lecturer various universities; Writer in residence teaching poetry and creative writing, Newton and Quincy Schools, Massachusetts, 12 years. Publications: Anthology of Armenian Poetry (translator), 1978; How to Choose Your Past, 1979; The Arc, 1981; Sacred Wrath, 1982; Land of Fire, poems of Egh Charents, 1985; About Time, 1986; Come Sit Beside Me and Listen to Kouchag, 1986; Songs of Bread, Songs of Salt, 1990; Coming to Terms, 1992; Across Bucharest After Rain: selected poems of Maria Banus (translation), 1996. Contributions to: American Scholar; Agni Review; Christian Science Monitor; American Poetry Review; Nation; New Republic; Paris Review; Partisan Review; Sands; Ararat; New York Times; New York Herald Tribune; Yankee; American Poetry Review; Translation; Delos; and others. Honours: New England Poetry Club Gretchen Warren Award, 1976; PEN/Translation Centre Grant, 1977; Poetry Society of America Mary Carolyn Davies Award, 1978; Phoenix Barcelona Peace Prize for Poem, 1985; Armand Erpf Award for Excellence in Literary Translation from Columbia University, 1986; Anahid Literary Award, Columbia University Armenian Centre, 1991; Golden Pen Award from Boston Writers Union, 1992, 1993-94; Fulbright Fellowship; National Endowment of the Arts Fellowship, 1993-94; Selected Poems of Diana Der-Hovanessian, 1994, nominated for Pulitzer Prize. Memberships: Poetry Society of America, Board Member; New England Poetry Club, President, 1979-; PEN; American Literary Translators Association; Columbia University Translation Centre, Board of Governors; Editorial Board, Agni Review, Ararat and Delos, Compost. Address: 2 Farrar Street, Cambridge, MA 02138, USA.

DERHODES Jennifer. See: **BOSVELD Jennifer Miller.**

DERRICOTTE Toi, b. 11 Apr 1941, Hamtramck, Michigan, USA. Poet; Teacher. m. C Bruce Derricotte, 30 Dec 1967, 1 son. Education: BA, 1965; MA, 1984. Appointments: Educational Consultant, Columbia University, 1979-82; Poet-in-the-School, 1974-88, Master Teacher, 1984-88, New Jersey State Council on the Arts, 1974-88; Poetry Teacher, Writers Voice Series, Manhattan West Side Y, 1985-86; Poet-in-the School, Maryland State Arts Council, 1987-88; Poet, Workshop Leader, The Frost Place, Franconia, New Hampshire, 1988; Associate Professor, English Literature, Old Dominion University, 1988-90; Commonwealth Professor, English Department, George Mason University, 1990-91; Associate Professor, English Department, University of Pittsburgh, 1991-. Publications: The Empress of the Death House, 1978; Natural Birth, 1983; Captivity, 1989. Contributions to: Over 150 poems to periodicals and anthologies. Honours: Poetry Fellow, New Jersey State Council on the Arts, 1983; Lucille Medwick Memorial Award, Poetry Society of America, 1985; Creative Writing Grant, National Endowment for the Arts, 1985, 1990; Maryland State Arts Council Grant, 1987; Pushcart Prize, 1989; Nominee, Poets Prize, Paragon, 1990; Poetry Committee Book Award, Folger Library, 1990. Memberships: Advisory Panel, Writers-in-Residence Program, New Jersey State Council on the Arts; Advisory Board: Geraldine R Dodge Foundation Poetry Festival, 1986; Mount Vernon College Curriculum Development; Center for Visual History Voices and Visions series, New York; Editorial Board: Issues; Poet Lore; Advisory Editorial Board, Caribbean Writer; Modern Language Association; Academy of American Poets; Poetry Society of America; PEN; Associated Writing Programs. Address: 7958 Inverness Ridge Road, Potomac, MD 20854, USA.

DERRY Paul ('X'), b. 28 Sept 1930, Council Bluffs, Iowa, USA. Chief Editor. m. Donalee Jacobs, 8 Aug 1953, 1 son, 1 daughter. Education: Sociology major, 1955-57, Journalism, 1958-61, BA, hons, Journalism, 1961, University of Nebraska, Omaha. Appointments: Investigator, Hooper-Holmes Bureau, Omaha, Nebraska, 1955-57; Investigator, Retail Credit Co, Omaha, 1957-60; Reporter, Photographer, Omaha Sun Newspapers, 1960-61; Editor, Aerojet-General Corporation, Sacramento, California, 1961-66; Joined, 1966, currently Chief Editor, Technical Publications Department, Lockheed Missiles and Space Company Inc, Sunnyvale, California. Publication: Love Me-and I'll pay you back, chapbook, 1988. Contributions to: Poems in The Ledge; quick brown fox; The Poetry Peddler; Poetry Forum; HEATHENzine; Writer's Voice; Experiment in Words; Aurora Poetry Letter and Terse Tales; MOBIUS; The Advocate; tight. Honour: Outstanding Journalism Student, University of Nebraska at Omaha, 1961. Memberships: Academy of American Poets; Poetry Society of America; Friends of PEN. Address: 185 Union Avenue, No 3, Campbell, CA 95008, USA.

DESCHOEMAEKER Frans, b. 8 Sept 1954, Belgium. Official, Flemish Ministry of Education. Education: Institute for Psychical and Social Training, Kortrijk, 1973-74. Publications: Down the River; Autumns Halls of Mirrors; The Chuckle of the Country Squire; Elements of Archaeology. Contributions to: De Periscoop; Diogenes; The Critical Lexicon of Dutch Literature After 1945; Dietsche Warande & Belfort; Kreatief; De Vlaamse Gids; Elseviers Magazine. Honours: Poetry Prize, Flemish Club Brussels; Poetry Prize of West Flanders; Maurice Gilliams Prize of the Royal Academy of Dutch Linguistics and Literature, 1995. Memberships: Diogenes; Nieuwe Stemmen; Filter. Address: Vontstraat 61, 9700 Oudenaarde, Belgium.

DESHPANDE Renukadas Yeshwant, b. 17 Apr 1931, Maharashtra, India. Teaching. m. Suniti, 9 June 1962, 1 son. Education: MSc, Physics, 1955. Appointments: Research Scientist, Tata Institute of Fundamental Research, Bombay; Bhabha Atomic Research Centre, Bombay; Lawrence Radiation Laboratory Berkeley, USA; Currently, Sri Aurobindo International Centre of Education, Pondicherry; Associate Editor, Motherindra, Pondicherry. Publications: Poetry: The Rhododendron Valley, 1988; All is Dream-Blaze, 1992; Under the Raintree, 1994; Prose: Nirodbaran: Poet and Sadhak; Amal-Kiran: Poet and Critic; The Ancient Tale of Savitri; Satyawan Must Die; Vyasa's Savitri, in press. Contributions to: Mother India; Sri Aurobindo Circle; Sri Aurobindo Action; POET; Bridge-in-Making. Address: Sri Aurobindo International Centre of Education, Pondicherry 605002, India.

DESMOND. See: **FLAMMONDE Paris.**

DEUTSCH-BENAROYA Shelley, b. 3 May 1953, New York, New York, USA. Editor; Freelance Writer. m. Haym Benaroya, 1 Oct 1983, 1 son, 1 daughter. Education: BA, magna cum laude, English Education, Judaic Studies, State Univerity of New York, Albany and Hebrew University, Jerusalem, 1975; MS cum laude, Broadcast Management, Newhouse School of Communications, Syracuse University, 1976. Appointments: Writer, NBC News, New York City; Editor, CES Publishing Company, New York City; Associate Director, Media Tours, The Rowland Company, New York City; Director, Broadcast Media, Policano Inc, New York City; Adjunct Professor, English Department, Kean College, Union, New Jersey. Honours: Honourable Mention, Queens Poetry Competition, Queens Council on the Arts, 1979; Poetry Fellowship, New Jersey Council on the Arts, 1990-91. Memberships: Poetry Society of America; Academy of American Poets. Address: 23 Peach Orchard Drive, East Brunswick, NJ 08816, USA.

DEVAPOOJITHAYA Arikkady Srisha, b. 11 Dec 1944, Kasaragod, India. Teacher; Professor. m. B V Usharani, 26 Apr 1969, 1 son, 1 daughter. Education: MA, English Language, 1966; MA, Kannada, 1971; MA, Sanskrit, 1973; MA, Hindi, 1975. Appointments: Professor, Government College, 1966; Head of Department, 1988; Attending poets' conferences for many years as a Kannada poet in Indian States of Kerala and Karnataka; Regular Broadcast of Poems, All India Radio. Publications: Kasaragodina Kavithegalu; Idu Varthamana; Thappenu; Kavi Goshthi, 1994; Banjaru Bhoomi, 1996. Contributions to: Udayavani; Thushara; Mallige; Novabharatha; Tainudi; Hosa Digantha; Articles in The English Journal, Suguna Digest. Honour: Muddana Kavya Rajya Prashasthi. Memberships: Navya Sahithya Sangha; Executive Committee, Kasaragodu Jilla Lekhakara Sangha; Kasaragod; The Kerala Government College Teachers' Association, 1966-. Address: Head of Department of English, Government College, Kasaragod, PO Vidyanagar Pin 671123, Kerala, India.

DEVARAJ Ramasamy, b. 4 Dec 1941, Sankaralingapuram, Tinneveli District, India. Collegiate and Higher Secondary Physics Teacher. m. Rukmani, 16 Sept 1973, dec, 1 son, 2 daughters. Education: MSc, Physics, 1969, MPhil, Physics, 1977, BL, 1982, Madras, MEd, 1984, Annamalai University. Appointments: Formerly Assistant Professor, Physics, Madras Christian College, Tambaram, Madras; Currently Subject Teacher, Physics, Government Model Higher Secondary School, Government College of Education, Saidapet, Madras. Publications: Songs of Good Hope, 1995. Books of poetry in English: Lamps of Lightning, 1990; Poems of Ramasamy Devaraj, 1991; One Hundred Love-Poems, 1991. Books of poetry in Tamil: Sayi Avataram, 1985; Odukkappattore Ulagatthup Parani, 1990; Ramasamy Devarasan Kavithaigal, 1991; Oru Nooru Kaadhal Kavithaigal, 1991. The People of the Hoaxama Islands, a collection of Surrealistic Plays and Poems in English, 1993. Translations:

Upanishads (from Vedas), 1974; Bhagavad-Gita, 1974. Contributions: Periodicals and magazines. Honour: Honorary DLitt, World University, Tucson, Arizona, USA, 1984. Memberships: Founder-President, World Parnassians Guild International, Madras, India; Editor in Chief, Parnassus of World Poets, An International Poetry Annual in English. Address: K-13, Todhunter Nagar, Saidpet, Madras 600015, India.

DEVEREAUX Emily. See: **LEWIS-SMITH Anne Elizabeth.**

DEVIDE Vladimir, (Amika), b. 3 May 1925, Zagreb, Croatia. Mathematician. m. Yasuyo Hondo, 26 Dec 1981, 1 son. Education: Diploma of Civil Engineering, 1951; DSc, Mathematics, 1956. Appointments: Member, Croatian (formerly Yugoslav) Academy of Sciences and Arts, 1973; Full Professor of Mathematics, University of Zagreb, retired, 1990. Publications: Japanska haiku poezija, 1970, 1976, 1977, 1985; Iz japanske knjizevnosti, 1985; Japan - poezija i zbilja, 1987; Bijeli cvijet, 1988, 1994; Varijante, 1989; Zen, 1992, 1993; Antidnevnik prisjecanja, 1995. Contributions to: Mainichi Daily News; Japan Times, Ko, Nihon Bunka, Haiku International (Japan); Modern Haiku, Studia Mystica, Point Judith Light (USA); Republika, Forum, 15 Dana, Haiku (Croatia). Honours: Order Zuihosho (Sacred Treasure) of the Japanese Government; Encouragement Prize at the Japanese International Haiku ITOEN Contest 1991, 1993, 1994; Prize Rugjer Boskovic of Republic of Croatia. Memberships: Union of Croatian Writers; Croatian PEN Club; Croatian (formerly Yugoslav) Academy of Sciences and Arts; Haiku International Association, Japan. Address: Vinogradska 10, 10000 Zagreb, Croatia.

DEVILLE Edward Samuel, b. 31 Aug 1950, Hertford, England. m. Deborah Marie Booty, 18 Apr 1992. Publication: A Bone to Pick With the Sea, 1970. Contributions to: Telegraph Magazine; Outposts; Poetry Review. Honour: Cheltenham Festival, 1981. Membership: Poetry Society. Address: 74 Fordwich Rise, Hertford SG14 2DE, England.

DEWDNEY Christopher, b. 9 May 1951, London, Ontario, Canada. Poet; Writer. m. (1) Suzanne Dennison, 1971 div 1975, 1 daughter, (2) Lise Downe, 1977, 1 son. Education: South and Westminster Collegiate Institutes, London, Ontario; H B Beal Art Annex, London, Ontario. Appointments: Associate Fellow, Winters College, York University, Toronto, 1984; Éminence Verte, Society for the Preservation of Wild Culture, Toronto, 1987; Poetry Editor, Coach House Publishing, Toronto, 1988. Publications: Poetry: Golders Green, 1972; A Paleozoic Geology of London, Ontario, 1973; Fovea Centralis, 1975; Spring Trances in the Control Emerald Night, 1978; Alter Sublime, 1980; The Cenozoic Asylum, 1983; Predators of the Adoration: Selected Poems 1972-1982, 1983; Permugenesis, 1987; The Radiant Inventory, 1988; Demon Pond, 1994; Other: The Immaculate Perception, 1986; Recent Artifacts From the Institute of Applied Fiction, 1990; Concordant Proviso Ascendant: A Natural History of Southwestern Ontario, Book III, 1991; The Secular Grail, 1993. Contributions to: Periodicals. Honours: Design Canada Award, 1974; Canada Council Grants, 1974, 1976, 1981, 1985; CBC Prize, 1986. Address: c/o McClelland and Stewart Inc, 481 University Avenue, Suite 900, Toronto, Ontario M5G 2E9, Canada.

DEWHIRST Ian, b. 17 Oct 1936, Keighley, West Yorkshire, England. Librarian. Education: BA, hons, English, University of Manchester, 1958; Associate, Library Association, 1967. Appointment: Keighley Reference Librarian, 1967-91. Publications: The Handloom Weaver and Other Poems, 1965; Scar Top and Other Poems, 1968. Contributions to: Dalesman; Transactions of the Yorkshire Dialect Society; Yorkshire Ridings Magazine; Pennine Platform; Yorkshire Journal. Memberships: Brontë Society; Yorkshire Dialect Society; Past Honorary General Secretary; Edward Thomas Fellowship. Address: 14 Raglan Avenue, Fell Lane, Keighley, West Yorkshire BD22 6BJ, England.

DEY Richard Addison, (Richard Morris Dey), b. 28 Nov 1945, USA. Writer. 2 sons. Education: Harvard College, BA, 1973. Appointments: Freelance Journalist; Commercial Fisherman; Yacht Captain. Publications: The Beguia Poems, 1988; In the Way of Adventure, 1989. Contributions to: Poetry; New Republic; Harvard Advocate; Harvard Magazine; Sail; Country Journal; Indian Express; Lokmat Times; Nagpur; Florescence; Haryana. Memberships: Poets and Writers; New England Poetry Society; CLIC, Nagpur. Address: 178 Gardner Street, Hingham, MA 02043, USA.

DEY Tapati, b. 13 Sept 1957, Gwahati, Assam, India. Government Servant. Education: MA, English Literature, 1980. Appointment: Personal Assistant (Secretary) to Director, Telecom Microwave Project, Nagpur. Contributions to: Hitavada, Nagpur; Tribune, New Delhi and Chandigarh; Telegraph, Calcutta; All India Radio, Nagpur; Telecom Journals, New Delhi and Bombay. Honours: 2nd Prize in Poetry (English), All India Posts and Telegraphs Literary Competition, 1983; Selected amongst Accomplished Writers of the Year, All India Radio Annual Journal, 1983-84; Consolation Prizes for Fiction, Hitavada newspaper-magazine, 1986, 1987, 1988; Best Writer and Best Article Award, 1990. Address: Munmun, 32 Yogendra Nagar, Nagpur 440013, Maharashtra, India.

DHOOMKETU Kaviraj. See: **DWIVEDI Suresh Chandra.**

DI CICCO Pier Giorgio, b. 5 July 1949, Arezzo, Italy. Roman Catholic Priest; Poet. Education: BA, 1972, BEd, 1973, Master of Divinity, 1990, University of Toronto; Bachelor of Sacred Theology, St Paul's University, 1990. Appointments: Founder, Poetry Editor, Poetry Toronto Newsletter, 1976-77; Associate Editor, Books in Canada, 1976-79; Co-Editor, 1976-79, Poetry Editor, 1980-82, Waves; Ordained Roman Catholic Priest and Associate Pastor, Anne's Church, Brampton, Ontario, 1993-. Publications: We Are the Light Turning, 1975; The Sad Facts, 1977; The Circular Dark, 1977; Dancing in the House of Cards, 1977; A Burning Patience, 1978; Roman Candles: An Anthology of 17 Italo-Canadian Poets (Editor), 1978; Dolce-Amaro, 1979; The Tough Romance, 1979; A Straw Hat for Everything, 1981; Flying Deeper Into the Century, 1982; Dark to Light: Reasons for Humanness: Poems 1976-1979, 1983; Women We Never See Again, 1984; Twenty Poems, 1984; Post-Sixties Nocturne, 1985; Virgin Science: Hunting Holistic Paradigms, 1986. Honours: Canada Council Awards, 1974, 1976, 1980; Carleton University Italo-Canadian Literature Award, 1979. Address: PO Box 344, King City, Ontario L0G 1K0, Canada.

DI PASQUALE Emanuel, b. 25 Jan 1943, Sicily, Italy. English Professor. m. (1) div, 1 son, 1 daughter, (2) Mary, 1 daughter. Education: BA, English, Adelphi University, USA, 1965; MA, English, New York State University, 1966. Appointments: Elizabeth City State University, North Carolina, USA; Middlesex County College, Edison, New Jersey. Publication: Genesis, 1989. Contributions to: New York Times; Nation; Sewanee Review; Cricket; Christian Science Monitor; New York Quarterly. Address: English Department, Middlesex County College, Edison, NJ 08818, USA.

DI PRIMA Diane, b. 6 Aug 1934, New York, New York, USA. Poet; Writer; Dramatist; Artist. m. (1) Alan S Marlowe, 1962 div 1969, (2) Grant Fisher, 1972, div 1975, 2 sons, 3 daughters. Education: Swarthmore College, 1951-53. Appointments: Co-Founder, New York Poets Theater, 1961-65; Co-Editor (with LeRoi Jones), 1961-63, Editor, 1963-69, Floating Bear magazine; Publisher, Poets Press, 1964-69, Eidolon Editions, 1974-; Faculty, Naropa Institute, 1974-; Faculty, New College of California, San Francisco, 1980-87; Co-Founder, San Francisco Institute of Magical and Healing Arts, 1983-91; Senior Lecturer, California College of Arts and Crafts, Oakland, 1990-92; Visiting Faculty, San Francisco Art Institute, 1992; Adjunct Faculty, California Institute of Integral Studies, 1994-95. Publications: Poetry includes: This Kind of Bird Flies Backward, 1958; The New Handbook of Heaven, 1963; Poets Vaudeville, 1964; Kerhonkson Journal 1966, 1971; The Book of Hours, 1970; Prayer to the Mothers, 1971; So Fine, 1971; XV Dedications, 1971; Revolutionary Letters, 1971; The Calculus of Variation, 1972; Loba, Part I, 1973; Freddie Poems, 1974; Brass Furnace Going Out: Song, After an Abortion, 1975; Selected Poems 1956-1975, 1975, revised edition, 1977; Loba as Eve, 1975; Loba, Part 2, 1976; Loba, Parts 1-8, 1978; Wyoming Series, 1988; The Mysteries of Vision, 1988; Pieces of a Song: Selected Poems, 1990; Seminary Poems, 1991; The Mask is the Path of the Star, 1993; Death Poems for All Seasons, forthcoming. Fiction includes: Memoirs of a Beatnik, 1969; Not Quite Buffalo Stew, forthcoming. Other includes: Notes on the Summer Solstice, 1969; Recollections of My Life as a Woman (autobiography), forthcoming; The Mysteries of Vision: Book of Essays on HD, forthcoming; One Too Like Thee (criticism), forthcoming. Contributions to: Various publications. Honours: National Endowment for the Arts Grants, 1966, 1973; Coordinating Council of Little Magazines Grants, 1967, 1970; Lapis Foundation Awards, 1978, 1979; Institute for Aesthetic Development Award, 1986; Lifetime Service Award, National Poetry Association, 1993. Address: 584 Castro Street, Suite 346, San Francisco, CA 94114, USA.

DIACHUK Naomi Joy, (Naomi Lange), b. 4 Mar 1948, Lancaster, Lancashire,England. Mother; Community Volunteer. m. (1) 2 sons, 1 daughter, (2) James Diachuk, 9 Feb 1992. Publications: Itineraries, 1990; 3 poems in Watch Her Colours Fly. Contributions to: Possibilities, Baptist Women's magazine. Address: 63 Rodney Street, Howick, Auckland, New Zealand.

DIAMOND Sandy, b. 20 Jan 1939, Iowa, USA. Media Specialist. Div. Education: BS, Education; MS, Media, Certification, Reading. Appointments: Teacher, Media Specialist, Wellcome Memorial Lake Crystal Middle School, Minnesota School District; Media Specialist, Mankato Public Library, Minnesota. Publications: Ever, Never, and Sometimes, 1978; Poetic Treasures, 1980; Honey Creek Anthology, 1980; Mirrors of the Wistful Dreamer, 1980; Yearbook of Modern Poetry, 1981; Turning Wheel, 1982; Eternal Echoes, 1982; American Poetry Anthology, 1986; American Anthology of Midwestern Poetry, 1988. Contributions to: Vega, 1978, 1979; Grit: Choral Music (2 with Carolyn Bayerkohler), 1981; Mankato High School 20th Reunion Booklet, 1986. Honours: Certificate of Creative Talent, 1979; Flame's 1st Place, 1979; 1 of Mankato State University Alumni honoured as published author, 1983; Golden Poet Award, 1989, 1990. Memberships: Friends of the Library; Former Member, Southern Minnesota Poets Society. Address: 309 North Broad Street, Mankato, MN 56001, USA.

DIANO. See: **ADAMS Michael Louis.**

DICKENSON George Therese, b. 23 Oct 1951, California, USA. Writer. Education: BA, 1976. Appointments: Proofreader, Copy Editor, 1977; Director, Founder, Incisions Arts, 1978-88; Senior Editor, New York Magazine, 1982-88; Editor, Freelance, 1988-; Writer, Freelance, 1990-. Publications: Transducing Segue; Striations. Contributions to: Big Allis; Assassin; Baltimore Sun; Black Rose; Body Politic; Blues 10; Gay Community News; The News and the Weather; The World; Artzone; Ahnoi; Pegasus; Contact 11; Dream Helmut. Honours: American Academy of Poets Award; Wellesley Entrant to Glassioch Poetry Contest; Massachusetts Arts and Humanities Foundation. Membership: Poets and Writers. Address: 65 Second Avenue, No 2H, New York, NY 10003, USA.

DICKEY R(obert) P(reston), b. 24 Sept 1942, Flat River, Missouri, USA. University Professor of English (retired). Education: BA, 1967; MA, 1969; PhD, 1975. Appointments: Instructor in English, University of Missouri, 1964-69; Assistant Professor of English, University of Southern Colorado, 1969-74; Instructor in English, Pima College,1974-80. Publications: Running Lucky, 1969; Acting Immortal, 1970; Concise Dictionary of Lead River, Missouri, 1972; The Basic Stuff of Poetry, 1972; Life-Cycle of Seventy Songs, 1984; The Poetica Erotica of R P Dickey, 1989; The Little Book on Racism and Politics, 1990; Ode on Liberty, 1996. Contributions to: Poetry; New Yorker; Atlantic; Harper's; Sewanee Review; Poetry Northwest; Hudson Review; Western Review; New York Times; American Poetry Review; Salmagundi; Poetry Bag; Black Bear Review; Poet (India); Revue Moderne (France); Chicago Review; Big Table; Southern Review. Address: PO Box 87, Ranchos de Taos, NM 87557, USA.

DICKEY William, b. 15 Dec 1928, Bellingham, Washington, USA. Educator. Education: BA, Reed College, 1951; MA, Harvard University, 1955; MFA, Writers Workshop, University of Iowa, 1956; Advanced study, Jesus College, Oxford University, 1959-60. Appointments: Cornell University, 1956-59; Denison University, 1960-62; Joined, 1962, Former Chair, Professor, English, Creative Writing, San Francisco State University, California; Visiting Professor, English, University of Hawaii, 1978. Publications: Interpreter's House, 1954; Of the Festivity, 1959, reprint, 1971; Rivers of the Pacific Northwest, 1969; More Under Saturn, 1972; The Rainbow Grovery, 1978; The Sacrifice Consenting, 1981; Six Philosophical Songs, 1983; Joy, 1986; Metamorphoses, 1991; Night Journey, 1992. Contributions to: Atlantic; Harper's; New Yorker; Poetry; New England Review-Bread Loaf Quarterly; Yale Review; Massachusetts Review; Carolina Quarterly; Kenyon Review; Many others. Honours: Yale Series of Younger Poets, 1959; Juniper Prize, 1978; Creative Writing Letters, 1980; Bay Area Book Reviewers' Poetry Award, 1987. Memberships: PEN American Center; Modern Language Association; California Association of Teachers of English. Address: 1476 Willard Street, San Francisco, CA 94117, USA.

DIGOT Jean, b. 19 June 1912, France. Poet. m. Simone Ayme, 23 Aug 1946. Education: Bachelier, Latin, Sciences, Philosophy,

University of Toulouse; Certificate, Advanced Studies in Psychology (Aesthetics), Faculty of Paris-Sorbonne. Publications: 10 collections of poetry, 1946-90; Espace des sources, poems. Contributions to: Revue Sud, Marseille (special number Jean Digot), 1985; Le Journal des Poetes, Brussels, 1990. Honours: Grand Prix for Poetry, Mont Saint-Michel, 1975. Memberships: Societe des Gens de Lettres de France; President, Association des Ecrivains du Rouergue; President, Jury, Prix de poesie Antonin Artaud. Address: 7 rue de Saunhac, 12000 Rodez, France.

DILLARD R(ichard) H(enry) W(ilde), b. 11 Oct 1937, Roanoke, Virginia, USA. Professor of English; Writer; Poet; Editor. m. (1) Annie Doak, 1965, div 1972, (2) Cathy Hankla, 1979. Education: BA, Roanoke College, Salem, Virginia, 1958; MA, 1959, PhD, 1965, University of Virginia. Appointments: Instructor, Roanoke College, 1961, University of Virginia, 1961-64; Assistant Professor, 1964-68, Associate Professor, 1968-74, Professor of English, 1974-, Hollins College, Virginia; Contributing Editor, Hollins Critic, 1966-77; Editor-in-Chief, Children's Literature, 1992-. Publications: Fiction: The Book of Changes, 1974; The First Man on the Sun, 1983; Omniphobia, 1995; Poetry: The Day I Stopped Dreaming About Barbara Steele and Other Poems, 1966; News of the Nile, 1971; After Borges, 1972; The Greeting: New and Selected Poems, 1981; Just Here, Just Now, 1994; Non-fiction: Horror Films, 1976; Understanding George Garrett, 1988; Editor: The Experience of America: A Book of Readings (with Louis D Rubin Jr), 1969; The Sounder Few: Essays from "The Hollins Critic" (with George Garrett and John Rees Moore), 1971. Contributions to: Periodicals. Honours: Academy of American Poets Prize, 1961; Ford Foundation Grant, 1972; O B Hardison, Jr Poetry Award, Folger Shakespeare Library, Washington, DC, 1994. Address: Box 9671, Hollins College, VA 24020, USA.

DILLON Enoch (LaRoy), b. 18 Oct 1925, Hillsboro, Oregon, USA. Poet; Former President's Budget Specialist. m. Jean Marie Lang, 3 Feb 1951, 2 sons, 4 daughters. Education: BS, Economics, Pacific University, 1948; MA, Economics, Catholic University of America, 1952. Appointments: 2nd Lieutenant, 1945-46, 1st Lieutenant, 1951-52, US Army; Public Administration Specialist, 1948-51, 1952-55; Budget Specialist, Executive Office of the President of the US, 1955-71; Executive Assistant, Budgets, National Science Foundation, 1971-80; Retired to write, 1981-. Publications: The Bicentennial Blues, 1988; Love, from the ends of the earth, 1990. Contributions to: Poet Lore; Visions; Poultry; Gryphon; San Fernando Poetry Journal; Odyssey; Federal Poet; Country Cottage Poetry Journal; Light, Deus Ex Machina, Heaven Bone. Memberships: Writers Center, Bethesda, Maryland; Federal Poets, Washington, DC. Address: 6310 Hollins Drive, Bethesda, MD 20817, USA.

DILSAVER Paul, b. 8 Dec 1949, Colorado, USA. English Instructor. Education: BA, Philosophy, University of Southern Colorado, 1972; MA, English, Colorado State University, 1973; MFA, Creative Writing, Bowling Green State University, Ohio, 1979. Appointments: Instructor, English, Casper College, Wyoming; Instructor, English, University of Western Illinois; Assistant Professor, English, Carroll College, Montana; Lecturer, English, University of Southern Colorado. Publications: Malignant Blues, 1976; A Brutal Blacksmith, An Anvil of Bruised Tissue, 1979; Encounters with the Antichrist, 1982; Character Scatology, 1984. Contributions to: New York Quarterly; Denver Post; DeKalb Literary Arts Journal; Writers' Forum; Pulpsmith; Wind; Bogg; RE: Artes Liberales; Post; Cathartic; Dog River Review; Z Miscellaneous; Colorado North Review; Colorado State Review; Ascent; Sou'wester; Gumbo; Snakeroot; Spoon River Quarterly; Penny Dreadful; Phantasm. Address: PO Box 1621, Pueblo, CO 81002, USA.

DIMIT Emma, b. 24 Nov 1922, Johnstown, Pennsylvania, USA. Credit Union Manager (retired). m. Robert Morgan Dimit, 15 June 1946, 3 sons, 1 daughter. Education: BS, Home Economics, Indiana University of Pennsylvania, 1944; Further study: Ohio State University, 1962-63; South Dakota State University, 1976-79. Appointments: Teacher, West Deer Township and Johnstown, Pennsylvania; Substitute Teacher, Columbus, Ohio, and Volga, South Dakota; Manager, Federal Credit Union, South Dakota State University. Publications: In Black and White, 1989. Contributions to: Prize Poems of National Federation of State Poetry Societies; Pteranodon Magazine; Country Poet; Oakwood; Pasque Petals; Voices of South Dakota I, II, III; People Hold Balloons Softly; South Dakota Sentinel; Brookings County History Book. Honours: Numerous, South Dakota State Poetry Society, 1977-92; 1st Prize, Pteranodon Magazine, 1980;

National; Federation of State Poetry Societies Prizes, 1981, 1986; Centennial Poet and Poet of the Year, South Dakota State, 1989; League of Minnesota Poets, 1989. Memberships: South Dakota State Poetry Society Inc, Treasurer, School Contest Judge, Critiqueing Round Robin Organiser and Coordinator, Board Member; National Federation of State Poetry Societies, Delegate, National and State Contest Judge; Secretary, Bardic Round Table; Arizona State Poetry Society; Tri City Poetry Society of Arizona. Address: 330 Marian Avenue, Brookings, SD 57006, USA.

DINO Isiodoro D, Rev Fr (Sacerdux), b. 4 Apr 1910, Bacon, Sorsogon, Philippines. Catholic Priest; College Professor; Former Military Chaplain. Education: Secondary, Philosophy, Theology, Holy Rosary Diocesan Seminary, Naga City, 1927-37; PhD, Education, McKinley-Roosevelt College, Chicago, USA, 1947; LittB (Journalism), BSE, MA (English), PhD (Philosophy), University of Santo Tomas, Manila, 1948-52. Appointments: Parish Chaplain, School Director, 1937-43; Chaplain, military positions, 1943-54; Parish Pastor, School Director, 1954-60; Vice-Rector, Principal, Rector, Our Lady of Penafrancia Seminary, Sorsogon, 1960-77; President, Dean of Graduate School, Annunciation College, Sorsogon, 1961-; Member, Diocesan Finance Council, Sorsogon, 1987-. Publications: My Lyre, 1940; Seashells on the Shore, 1973; String of Pearls, 1980; A Sheaf of Golden Grain. Contributions to: Survey of Philippine Literature; Seminarium; La Defenza; Bikols of the Philippines; Bicol Voices, poem and essay collection; Anthologies include: Spring Anthology, UK, 1973; Friends, Foreign Poetry, Korea, 1979; World Anthology, USA, 1980; Anthology of World Brotherhood and Peace, Manila, 1981; Asian Modern Poetry, 1982; Metaphor Beyond Time, 1990; Laurel Leaves. Honours: Poet Laureate: in English, Holy Rosary Seminary, 1933, in Bicol, Bicol Vernacular Guild, 1936; 1st Prize, World Contest, Bicol Translation of Jose Rizal's Ultimo Adios, Award of Honour, Distinguished Filipino Catholic Poet, United Poets Laureate International, 1967; Honorary Fernando Ma Guerrero Family Award, Literature, 1975, Talaang Pangdangal, 1976, University of Santo Tomas Alumni Association; Golden Wreath, Honorary Catholic Poet Laureate, World Congress of Poets, 1990. Memberships: Committee Chair, World Congresses of Poets; United Poets Laureate International Formerly; Fellow, International Poetry Society; Greater National Society of Published Poets; Stella Woodall Poetry Society International. Address: Annunciation College, 479 Magsaysay Avenue, 4700 Sorsogon, Philippines.

DINSMORE Danika, b. 17 Feb 1968, Glendale, California, USA. Teacher; Writer. m. David Johnson, 12 June 1993. Education: BA, English, 1990; MFA, Writing and Poetics, 1993; Certificate, Screenwriting, 1996. Appointments: English Teacher, 1991; Spring Quarter (for advanced writing class), 1992, full year, 1994-95; Admission Assistant, University Preparatory Academy, Seattle, Washington; Executive Director, North West Spoken World Laboratory. Publication: Traffic, 1996; Editor-in-Chief, Morning Glory 1988-90; Co-Editor, Bombay Gin, 1991-92, Hyena, 1992-94. Contributions to: 13th Moon; Chain; Dark Ages Clasp The Daisy Root; New Censorship; Thousand Oaks City News; Bombay Gin; Morning Glory; Woodfrogs in Chaos (anthology). Honours: Helicon Award, Editing of Morning Glory, 1990; IPIPP Creative Community Organizing Award, 1996. Membership: Core Member, 19th Draft Literary Series of Auburn, Washington. Address: 28915 North East 34th Court, Redmond, WA 98053, USA.

DIOMEDE Matthew, b. 8 June 1940, Yonkers, New York, USA. Educator. m. Barbara Diomede, 29 June 1968. Education: BA, Fordham College; MS, Fordham University; MA, Long Island University; PhD, St Louis University, 1992. Appointments: Teacher, Connecticut, New York, 1962-79; Lecturer, Coordinator, University of Missouri, St Louis, 1979-82; Lecturer, Assistant Professor, English, Parks College, St Louis University, 1982-92; English Instructor, St Louis Community College, Forest Park, 1992-95; English Instructor, University of South Florida, Tampa and University of Tampa, 1995-. Publications: Anthologies: Poetry of Our Time; A Yearbook of Modern Poetry, 1971; Black Cat Bone; Outstanding Contemporary Poetry, 1971; International Who's Who in Poetry Anthology, 1972; National Poetry Anthology, 1972, 1973; Book: Pietro Di Donato, 1995. Contributions to: Journals and magazines. Honours: Bronze Medal of Honour, Centre Studi e Scambi Internazionali, 1972; Graduate Poetry Award, Long Island University, 1975; Award Finalist, Virginia Commonwealth University Contemporary Poetry Series, 1975; Long Island University Alumni Poetry Award, 1978; Special Merit, IVA Mary Williams Inspirational Poetry Competition, 1990; Poetry Scholarship,

Rope Walk Writers Retreat, 1990; Certificate of Merit, J Mark Press; Poetry Prize, State of Maine Writers Conference. Memberships: Modern Language Association; National Council of Teachers of English; Poets and Writers; Association of Literary Scholars and Critics. Address: 815 Bourbon Red Drive, Des Peres, MO 63131, USA.

DISCH Thomas M(ichael), (Leonie Hargrave, Dobbin Thorpe), b. 2 Feb 1940, Des Moines, Iowa, USA. Writer; Poet; Dramatist; Librettist; Lecturer. Education: Cooper Union, New York; New York University. Appointments: Lecturer at colleges and universities; Artist-in-Residence, College of William and Mary, 1996. Publications: Novels: The Genocides, 1965; Mankind Under the Leash, 1966; The House That Fear Built (with John Sladek), 1966; Echo Round His Bones, 1967; Black Alice (with John Sladek), 1968; Camp Concentration, 1968; The Prisoner, 1969; 334, 1974; Clara Reeve, 1975; On Wings of Song, 1979; Triplicity, 1980; Neighbouring Lives (with Charles Naylor), 1981; The Businessman: A Tale of Terror, 1984; Amnesia, 1985; The M.D.: A Horror Story, 1991; The Priest: A Gothic Romance, 1995; Poetry: The Right Way to Figure Plumbing, 1972; ABCDEFG HIJKLM NOPQRST UVWXYZ, 1981; Orders of the Retina, 1982; Burn This, 1982; Here I Am, There You Are, Where Were We, 1984; Yes, Let's: New and Selected Poetry, 1989; Dark Verses and Light, 1991; The Dark Old House, 1995; Criticism: The Castle of Indolence, 1995; Other: Short story collections; plays; opera libretti; juvenile books. Contributions to: Many anthologies and periodicals. Honours: O Henry Prizes, 1975, 1979; John W Campbell Memorial Award, 1980; British Science Fiction Award, 1981. Memberships: National Book Critics Circle; PEN; Writers Guild. Address: Box 226, Barryville, NY 12719, USA.

DITZ Cordula Alexandra, b. 9 Mar 1972, Hamburg, Germany. Artist. Education: Abitur, Hamburg, 1991; Studies, 1994-. Appointments: Exhibitions in Hamburg, 1992-, Taber, Tschechien, 1995, Helsinki, Finland, 1996, Wien, Austria, 1996; Band Projects, 1992-. Publications: Die Differenz Aus Sontag & Montag, 1994; Tot & Mordschlag, 1996. Membership: FACT, EV, Hamburg. Address: c/o Bobs Bar, Marktstrobe 41, 20357 Hamburg, Germany.

DIVOK Mario J, b. 22 Sept 1944, Benus, Czechoslovakia. Real Estate Broker; Investments Executive; Poet; Dramatist. m. Eva Pytlova, 6 Oct 1990, 1 daughter. Education: MA, Pedagogic Institute, Martin, Czechoslovakia, 1967; MPA, California State University, Long Beach, 1977. Publications: The Relations, 1975; The Voice, 1975; The Wind of Changes, 1978; Equinox, 1978; The Collection, 1978; I Walk the Earth, 1980; The Blind Man, 1980; Looking for the Road to the Earth, 1983; The Birthday, 1984; Stranger in the Land, 1989; Selected Works, 1992. Contributions to: Various periodicals. Honours: Schlossar Award, Hall Publishers, Switzerland, 1980; American Poetry Association Award, 1988; World of Poetry Award, 1990. Memberships: American Association of Poets; American Playwrights Association. Address: 5 Misty Meadow Drive, Irvine, CA 92715, USA.

DIXON Peter, b. 6 Apr 1937, London, England. Lecturer in Primary Education. m. Marion Blades, 8 Aug 1964, 1 son, 1 daughter. Education: Qualified as a Teacher in 1960. Appointments: Teacher, primary and secondary schools, 1960-70; Lecturer in Art and Education, Saffron Walden, 1970-75; Senior Lecturer in Art and Education, King Alfred College, Winchester, 1975-. Publications: Grow Your Own Poems, 1988, 2nd reprint 1992; I Heard a Spider Sobbing, 1989; Big Billy, 1990. Contributions to: Times Newspapers; Learning magazine, USA; Parents magazine, UK. Membership: National Poetry Society, London. Address: 30 Cheriton Road, Winchester, Hampshire SO22 5AX, England.

DJURDJEVICH Miloš, b. 2 Aug 1961, Rab, Island Rab, Croatia. Literature Critic and Poet. Education: Studied Law, Philosophy and Comparative Literature, University of Zagreb; BA, Philosophy and Comparative Literature, 1991; MA, Literature, 1997. Appointments: Literature Critic for Radio 101, Radio Zagreb; Literary Critic and Translator for Croatian Radio; Poetry Editor for cultural magazine, Vijenac. Publications: Landscapes Or Circling for Words, 1989; In the Mirror, 1994; Harvest, 1997. Contributions to: Quorum, Republika-Croatia; Literatura, Dialogi-Slovenia; Orpheus-Hungary; Euphorion, Romania; Central Europe Now-Slovakia. Memberships: Croatian Centre of International PEN; Croatian Association of Writers. Address: 1 Ferenščica 27, 10000 Zagreb, Croatia.

DOANE Myrtle Caroline, b. 19 May 1914, Lynn, Massachusetts, USA. Schoolteacher; Freelance Writer of Prose and Poetry. m. Alfred M Doane, 6 Nov 1959, 1 stepson, 2 daughters (1 adopted). Education: Bachelor of General Studies, University of New Hampshire, Durham Campus, 1975. Appointments: Bookkeeper; Payroll Clerk; School Teacher. Publications: Lyrical Echoes of Freedom, 1961; Sounds of Maine, 1970; Think Ecology with Haiku, 1972; Sounds of Arkansas, 1978; Sounds of Heaven, 1978; Sounds of Liberty, 1979; Sounds of New Hampshire, 1980; Treasures of Laughter, 1983; Sounds of Bethlehem, 1988; My Father's World, 1990; Included: Famous Maine Writers Collection for Women, Westbrook College; Folger's Library Special Collection, University of Maine. Contributions to: Anthologies, magazines and newspapers. Honours: Poetry on Trees Award, Inspirational and Humorous Poetry, State of Maine Writers Conference, 1960-90; George Washington Medal, Poetry, Freedoms Foundation, Valley Forge, Pennsylvania, 1961, 1972; Arkansas Poetry Day Contest, 1988. Memberships: Poetry Fellowship of Maine, Project Chair; Poetry Society of Massachusetts; Round Table of Arkansas Poets; Maine Writers Conference, Chairman, Founder of Gospel Awards; Maine Radio, TV and Press Women; Freedoms Foundation, Valley Forge; American Arts Association; Co-Founder, Bethlehem Poetry Council; Co-Founder, Bethlehem as New Hampshire Poetry Capital; Founder, Chairperson, New England Poetry Conference. Address: PO Box 567, Bethlehem, NH 03574, USA.

DOBYNS Stephen, b. 19 Feb 1941, Orange, New Jersey, USA. Professor of Creative Writing; Poet; Writer. m. 2 children. Education: Shimer College, Mount Carroll, Illinois, 1959-60; BA, Wayne State University, 1964; MFA, University of Iowa, 1967. Appointments: Instructor, State University of New York College, Brockport, 1968-69; Reporter, Detroit News, 1969-71; Visiting Writer, University of New Hampshire, 1973-75, University of Iowa, 1977-78, Boston University, 1978-79, 1980-81, Syracuse University, 1986; Faculty, Goddard College, Plainfield, Vermont, 1978-80, Warren Wilson College, Swannanoa, North Carolina, 1982-87; Professor of Creative Writing, Syracuse University, New York, 1987-. Publications: Poetry: Concurring Beasts, 1972; Griffon, 1976; Heat Death, 1980; The Balthus Poems, 1982; Black Dog, Red Dog, 1984; Cemetery Nights, 1987; Body Traffic, 1991; Velocities: New and Selected Poems, 1966-1992, 1994; Fiction: A Man of Little Evils, 1973; Saratoga Longshot, 1976; Saratoga Swimmer, 1981; Dancer with One Leg, 1983; Saratoga Headhunter, 1985; Cold Dog Soup, 1985; Saratoga Snapper, 1986; A Boat Off the Coast, 1987; The Two Deaths of Señora Puccini, 1988; Saratoga Bestiary, 1988; The House of Alexandrine, 1989; Saratoga Hexameter, 1990; After Shocks/Near Escapes, 1991; Saratoga Haunting, 1993; The Wrestler's Cruel Study, 1993; Saratoga Backtalk, 1994; Saratoga Fleshpot, 1995; Saratoga Trifecta, 1995. Honours: Lamont Poetry Selection Award, 1971; MacDowell Colony Fellowships, 1972, 1976; Yaddo Fellowships, 1972, 1973. 1977, 1981, 1982; National Endowment for the Arts Grants, 1974, 1981; Guggenheim Fellowship, 1983; National Poetry Series Prize, 1984. Address: 208 Brattle Road, Syracuse, NY 13203, USA.

DOCHERTY Brian, b. 19 Aug 1953, Glasgow, Scotland. Lecturer in English and American Literature. m. Rosemary Docherty, 4 Aug 1984. Education: BA, Humanities, Middlesex Polytechnic; MA, American Poetry, University of Essex; PGCE, London University Institute of Education. Appointment: Part-time Tutor in Literature, Birkbeck College of Extra-Mural Studies. Publications: Ventrilquism, 1991; The Andy Warhol Happy Hour, 1992. Contributions to: ABSA Annual Report, 1990; Smith's Knoll; Echo Room; Foolscap; Ambit; Cobweb. Membership: Poetry Society. Address: Special Sorts Press, 10A Dickenson Road, London N8 9ET, England.

DOCHERTY John. See: **SILLS-DOCHERTY Jonathan John.**

DOLIS John, b. 25 Apr 1945, St Louis, Missouri, USA. Professor. Education: BA, English, St Louis University, 1967; MA, English, 1969, PhD, English, 1978, Loyola University of Chicago. Appointments: TV Script Writer, CBS & WTTW, Chicago, Illinois, 1966, 1971; Instructor, English, University of Kansas, 1981-85; Assistant Professor, 1985-92, Associate Professor, 1992-95, English, Pennsylvania State University, Scranton; Visiting Professor of American Culture and Literature, Bilkent University, Ankara, Turkey, 1995-96. Editorial Work includes: Editorial Board, Illinois English Bulletin, poetry issues, 1970, 1971; Editor, Information Systems Newsletter, Loyola University of Chicago Computer Journal, 1972; Editorial Board, Nathaniel Hawthorne Review, 1993-. Publications: BI( )nk Space, 1993; Ghost of ( ) Chance: (A) Quantum Epic, 1996; Many articles in various publications; Poems published in various magazines and anthologies: Best in Poetry, Echoes of the Unlocked Odyssey,

Journal of Contemporary Poets, Midwest Poetry Review, Notable American Poets, Overtures, Poetry of Our Time, New Orleans Review; Several book reviews and speaker at numerous conferences. Honours: National Endowment for the Humanities Fellowship, 1979, 1988; Fulbright Fellowship, 1980, 1989; CIES Scholarship, East European Language Institute, University of Pittsburgh, 1989; Award for Excellence in Scholarly Activities, Pharmakon Research International, Penn State University, 1991. Memberships: American Literature Association; International Association for The Fantastic in the Arts; Modern Language Association; World Phenomenology Institute. Address: Department of English, Pennsylvania State University, Dunmore, PA 18512, USA.

DOLLARHIDE Louis Edgar, b. 23 Apr 1918, America, Oklahoma, USA. University Professor of English. m. Betty Jane Zachry, 15 Aug 1949, 3 sons, 2 daughters. Education: BA, Mississippi College, 1942; MA, Harvard University, 1947; PhD, University of North Carolina, Chapel Hill, 1954. Appointments: President, Southern Literary Festival; Literary Columnist, Jackson (Mississippi) Daily News-Clarion Ledger, 1956-76; Editor, Founder, Mississippi Poetry Journal. Contributions to: Texas Quarterly; Lyric; Images; Old Hickory Review. Membership: President, Lifetime Member, Mississippi Poetry Society. Address: 1407 Fillmore Avenue, Oxford, MS 38655, USA.

DONALDSON Leigh, b. USA. Journalist. Education: BA, hons, Journalism, Mass Communications, University of Michigan, 1977; Georgetown Law School, Washington, DC, 1977-78; Graduate study, English, Comparative Literature, Columbia University, 1980. Appointments: Assistant Teacher, Cheremoya School, Los Angeles, California, 1982-83; Publications Coordinator, Boston Life Underwriters Association, Boston, Massachusetts, 1984; Editorial Assistant, Unitarian Universalist Service Committee, Boston, 1985; Permissions Editor, Houghton Mifflin Publishing Co, Boston, 1987-89; Correspondent, Rockingham County Newspapers, Portsmouth, New Hampshire; Publisher, North East Arts Literary Journal; Poetry readings. Publications: Poetry collections: Departures; Why We Sat and Waited; Boston Days; Jazz Poems; I Want to Write, illustrated children's books. Contributions to: Crisis; AIM Quarterly; Obsidian II Literary Journal; Poetry South; Tucumari Literary Review; Skylark Magazine; Catalyst Magazine; Minnesota Ink; Colorlines Magazine; Shooting Star Review; Poetry Corner; Manhattan Poetry Review; City River of Voices Anthology, 1992; San Fernando Poetry Journal; International Poetry Review; Cafe Review, 1992; Atelier, 1993; Jambalaya Magazine, 1995. Honours: Overall Winner, Fields of Earth Poetry Competition, 1991; National Press Foundation Award, 1992; Abraham Woursell Prize; Writer's Digest Achievement Award (poetry), 1993. Memberships: Seacoast Arts and Cultural Alliance; New Hampshire Writers and Publishers Project; New England Poetry Club; Seacoast Writers Association; Dramatists Guild; Maine's Writer's Association. Address: NorthEastARTS, PO Box 94, Kittery, Maine 03904, USA.

DONG Jiping, b. 13 Aug 1962, Chongqing, China. Teacher. Education: Sichuan Tourism School, 1979-81. Publications: Octavio Paz: Selected Poems; Maple Leaves in Four Seasons. Contributions to: Orbis; Salmon; Scripsi; Westerly; Indigo; Prism International; Footwork; Paterson Literary Review; Contemporary Poetry; Poetry Press Monthly; Modern Chinese Poetry. Honours: International Canadian Studies Award; International Writing Program and International Visitor Program, USA, 1993. Memberships: Haiku Society of America; World Poetry Society; Chinese Prose Poetry Society; Association for International Canadian Studies; Centre for Studies in Australian Literature. Address: 6 Yizijie St, Central District, Chongqing 630012, China.

DONOVAN D(eborah) A(nn Delmore), b. 14 Jan 1953, Lowell, Massachusetts, USA. Writer; Poet; Homemaker. m. Shawn Paul Donovan, 20 Oct 1972, 2 sons, 1 daughter. Education: Graduated with honours, High School, 1970; Associates degree, Lifelong Learning, University of New Hampshire, 1990. Appointments: Secretary, Board of Directors, Art Alive!, Lowell, 1982-83; Poetry Editor, 25% Rag, New England literary magazine; Also Proofreader, Seamstress, Retail Clerk and Secretary. Contributions to: Deros, 1982; Up Against the Wall, Mother, 1982; Earthshine, 1982; Art Alive! Newsletter, 1983; 25% Rag, 1990. Honour: 1st Prize, New England Poetry Group, 1989. Address: 28 Church Street, Lebanon, NH 03766, USA.

DOOLEY Maura, b. 18 May 1957, Cornwall, England. Arts Administration. Education: University of York, 1975-78; University of

Bristol, 1980-81. Appointments: Centre Director, Arvon Foundation, 1982-87; Literature Officer, Royal Festival Hall, 1987-. Publications: Ivy Leaves and Arrows; Turbulence; Explaining Magnetism. Contributions to: Poetry Review; Observer; Critical Quarterly; North; Southern Review; Independent. Honours: Major Eric Gregory Award; Poetry Book Society Recommendation. Memberships: Arvon Foundation; Poetry Books Society; Southern Arts Literature Panel; London Arts Board. Address: c/o Bloodaxe Books, PO Box 1SN, Newcastle Upon Tyne NE99 1SN, England.

DOORTY John, b. 7 Feb 1959, County Clare, Ireland. Teacher. Education: BA, National University of Ireland, 1980; Higher Diploma in Education, National University of Ireland, 1981; Postgraduate Diploma in Computing, University of Limerick, 1989. Appointments: Teacher of Creative Writing and Complementary Studies at Co Act College of Art, Commerce and Technology, Limerick, 1983-90; Coordinator of Ennistymon 84 Visual Arts Project, 1984; Teacher of English Language in Valencia, Spain, 1990-96. Contributions to: Bellingham Review; Flaming Arrows; Dal of Cais; Departures; North-Clare Writers Workshop Collection. Memberships: Founder of Departures Literary Journal, Editor of Departures 1987-95; Founder of New Series Literary Journal, 1996; Editor of New Series; Writers Union. Address: Carrowkeal, Kilshanny, Co Clare, Ireland.

DORCAS. See: WILDHAGEN Dorothy Mabel.

DORESKI William, b. 10 Jan 1946, Stafford, Connecticut, USA. Professor. m. 17 June 1981. Education: BA, 1975, MA, 1977, Goddard College; PhD, 1983, Boston University. Appointments: Instructor, Emerson College; Professor: Goddard College; Keene State College. Publications: The Testament of Israel Potter, 1976; Half of the Map, 1980; Ghost Train, 1991; The Years of Our Friendship: Robert Lowell and Allen Tate, 1990; The Modern Voice in American Poetry, 1995. Contributions to: Antioch Review; Massachusetts Review; Kansas Quarterly; Colorado Review; Cimarron Review; Agni Review; Mudfish; Epoch; Salmagundi; Literary Review; Innisfree; America; Mississippi Quarterly; Beloit Poetry Journal; Small Pond; Wormwood Review. Memberships: Modern Language Association; Academy of American Poets; Associated Writing Programmes. Address: Department of English, Keene State College, Keene, NH 03431, USA.

DORET Michel R, b. 5 Jan 1938, Haiti. Writer; Architect. m. Liselotte Bencze, 30 Nov 1970. Education: BA, 1970, Pace College of New York; MA, 1972, New University. Appointments: Worked with various consulting firms in New York City, 1969; Doret Product Design and Development 1969-; Architect in private practice and Writer, 1982-. Publications: Isolement, 1979; Cinq Dialogues, 1980; Esquisses, 1980; Topologie, 1981; Antipalinodie, 1981; Poésie 83, 1984; Les Mamelles de Lutèce, 1991; L'Univers de Marie, 1991; Lyrisme du Moi, 1992; Les Versets de L'Alliance, 1992; Caryatides, 1992; Amphore, 1992; Situation Poésie 93, 1993; La Vie et L'Oeuvre, 1994; The History of the Architecture of Ayiti: Vol I, The Republic of Haiti; Vol 2, The Dominican Republic, 1995; several research studies on francophone poetry, especially Swiss and Haitian. Contributions to: Les Poésiades 1990-92; Séquences no 37; Portique no 9; Encyclopédie Poétique (La Montagne, Le Temps); La Grande Anthologie Encyclopédique (Dieu; Les Poètes et L Amérique; Les Poètes et l'Art); Ex Tempore; Feuillets Artistiques et Littérires; Florilège; Anthologie Cristal 92; Les Saisons du Poème; Arbol de Fuego; Pléiade; Carta Internacional de Poesia; and others. Honours: Prix de Poésie de la Qualité de la Vie Société des Poètes et Artistes de France: Diploma d'Excellence au Palmarès Général des Prix et Concours, 1991; Médaille de Bronze de la Haute Académie littéraire et artistique de France HALAF 1991; Brevet de Mérite, 1994; Médaille d'Argent Internationale de la Poésie, 1994; Médaille d'Argent de L'Encouragement Au Bien, 1995; Numerous Diplômes d'Honneur, Mentions d'Honneur. Memberships: Société des Gens de lettres de France; Association Royale des Ecrivains Wallons; International Comparative Literature Association; Société des Poètes et Artistes de France; Cercle International de la Pensée et des Arts Francais; Les Poètes de l'Amitié; Poésie Vivante en Pays Voconce; Société Francaise de Littérature Générale et Comparée; Asociación Mundial de Escritores. Address: 1364, rue de Gex Maconnex 01210 Ornex, France.

DORN Ed(ward Merton), b. 2 Apr 1929, Villa Grove, Illinois, USA. Poet; Writer; Translator; Anthropologist; Ethnologist; Professor. m. Jennifer Dunbar, 1969. Education: University of Illinois at Urbana-Champaign, 1949-50; BA, Black Mountain College, 1954.

Appointments: Lecturer, Idaho State University, Pocatello, 1961-65; Co-Editor, Wild Dog, Pocatello, 1964-65; Fulbright Lecturer, 1965-67, Visiting Professor of English 1967-68, 1974-75, University of Essex, Colchester, England; Visiting Professor, University of Kansas, Lawrence, 1968-69; Regent's Lecturer, University of California at Riverside, 1973-74; Writer-in-Residence, University of California at San Diego, La Jolla, 1976; Professor, University of Colorado at Boulder, 1977-. Publications: Poetry: The Newly Fallen, 1961; Hands Up!, 1964; From Gloucester Out, 1964; Idaho Out, 1965; Geography, 1965; The North Atlantic Turbine, 1967; Gunslinger I, 1968, and I, 1969; The Midwest It That Space Between the Buffalo Statler and the Lawrence Eldridge, 1969; The Cosmology of Finding Your Spot, 1969; Twenty-four Love Songs, 1969; Songs: Set Two, A Short Count, 1970; Spectrum Breakdown: A Microbook, 1971; By the Sound, 1971; The Cycle, 1971; A Poem Called Alexander Hamilton, 1971; The Hamadryas Baboon at the Lincoln Park Zoo, 1972; Gunslinger, Book III: The Winterbook, Prologue to the Great Book IV Kornerstone, 1972; Recollections of Gran Apacheria, 1974; Manchester Square (with Jennifer Dunbar), 1975; Collected Poems: 1956-1974, 1975; Hello, La Jolla, 1978; Selected Poems, 1978; Abhorrences, 1989. Fiction: Some Business Recently Transacted in the White World, short stories, 1971. Non-Fiction: What I See in the Maximum Poems, 1960; Prose 1, (with Michael Rumaker and Warren Tallman), 1964; The Rites of Passage: A Brief History, 1965; The Shoshoneans: The People of the Basin-Plateau, 1966; Way West: Essays and Verse Accounts 1963-1993, 1993. Translations: Our World: Guerilla Poems From Latin America (with Gordon Brotherston), 1968; Tree Between Two Walls (with Gordon Brotherston), 1969; Selected Poems of Cesar Vallejo, 1976. Honours: D H Lawrence Fellow, 1969. Address: 1035 Mapleton, Boulder, CO 80302, USA.

DORRIS Michael (Anthony), b. 30 Jan 1945, Dayton, Washington, USA. Anthropologist; Adjunct Professor; Author; Poet. m. Louise Erdrich, 10 Oct 1981, 6 children. Education: Graduate, Georgetown University, 1967; MPhil, Yale University, 1971. Appointments: Assistant Professor of Anthropology, Johnston College, California, 1970, Franconia College, New Hampshire, 1971-72; Professor, 1972-89, Adjunct Full Professor, 1989-, Dartmouth College; Faculty, Mount St Vincent University, Halifax, Nova Scotia, 1975; Visiting Senior Lecturer, Auckland University, 1980. Publications: Native Americans; Five Hundred Years After, 1977; A Guide to Research on North American Indians (with Arlene Hirschfelder and Mary Lou Byler), 1983; A Yellow Raft in Blue Water (novel), 1987; The Broken Cord, 1989; Route Two and Back (with Louise Erdrich), 1991; The Crown of Columbus (novel with Louise Erdrich), 1991; Morning Girl, 1992; Rooms in the House of Stone, 1993; Working Men (stories), 1993; Paper Trail: Essays, 1994; Guests, 1994; Sees Behind Trees, 1996; Cloud Chamber (novel), 1996; The Window, 1997; Matter of Conscience, 1998. Contributions to: Numerous books, journals, and newspapers. Honours: Guggenheim Fellowship, 1978; Rockefeller Foundation Research Fellowship, 1985; Indian Achievement Award, 1985; PEN Syndicated Fiction Award, 1988; National Endowment for the Arts Fellowship, 1989; Christopher Awards, 1990, 1992; Notable Book of the Year Citations, American Library Association, 1990, 1994; Heartland Prize, 1990; National Book Critics Circle Award, 1990; Sarah Josepha Hale Literary Award, 1991; Scott O'Dell Award, 1992. Memberships: American Anthropological Association; American Association for the Advancement of Science; Authors Guild; Modern Language Association; National Congress of American Indians; National Indian Education Association; PEN; Writer's Guild. Address: c/o Charles Rembar, Rembar and Curtis, 19 West 44th Street, No 711, New York, NY 10036, USA.

DORSEY John Victor, b. 27 Nov 1976, Honolulu, Hawaii, USA. Poet; Editor. Education: Diploma, Student, Westmoreland County Community College, Fall 1995-. Appointments: Editor, Traditionalist Poetry Review, 1994-95; Editor, Heaven Train, 1996-. Publications: When It's Over and Other Poems, 1995; B Poems and Other short miscellaneous; Thoughts of Anguish, forthcoming. Contributions to: MOON Magazine; Poet's Fantasy; Stretchmarks; Report to Hell; Twisted Nipples; Lines 'N' Rhymes; The Laureate Letter. Honours: Editor's Choice Award Winner, National Library of Poetry, 1994; International Poet of Merit Award; Poet of the Year Nominee, 1995; International Society of Poets. Address: Rd 1, Box 858, Greensburg, PA 15601, USA.

DOSAL Carmen, b. 10 Oct 1928, Santander, Spain. Professional Painter; Art Journalist; Poet. Education: Diploma, Museo Arte Moderno, Barcelona. Publications: Paloma Rosa del amor, collection

of poems 1973-82; Mareas, 1983; Viajero del Viento, 1991; Bosquejos desde mi Bahia; Represented in Brias Poetica Moderna anthology; Essays on art. Contributions to: El Diario Montanes. Honours: Diploma of Honour, Palme d'Or des Beaux Arts, Monte Carlo; Academician of Merit with Silver Palm, Accademia Internazionale di Pontzen, Italy, 1992; Hon DLitt, World Academy of Arts and Culture, California; Honorary Member, Centro Cultural de O Jornal de Felgueiras, Portugal. Memberships: Artistic and Literary Circle, California; Centro Cultural Agustin Garcia Alonso, Aranguren; Centro Cultural O Jornal de Felgueiras; World Academy of Arts and Culture; Accademia Internazionale di Pontzen; Asociacion de Poesiam, Madrid; Instituto Literario y Cultural Hispanico. Address: Ruiz Zorrilla 17-A 1-A, Santander, Spain.

DOSTAL Cyril, b. 30 Apr 1930, Cleveland, Ohio, USA. Writer; Editor specialising in scientific and technical subjects. Div 1982, 2 sons, 1 daughter. Education: BA, English Literature, 1956, summa cum laude, Hons in English, MA, English Literature 1958, Miami University, Oxford, Ohio. Appointments: Teacher, Miami University, Ohio University, University of Akron, various times; Writer for a variety of Industrial Firms; Full Time Freelance Writer. Publications: Poetry: Emergency Exit, 1975; A Great Day for Butterflies (working title: I Like Doing Carpentry Because it Makes Me Feel Like Jesus), in preparation; Collections and Anthologies: Voices in Concert, 1974; Poetry: Cleveland, 1971. Contributions to: Over 150 poems in anthologies, collections, journals and magazines. Memberships: Trustee, Poet's League of Greater Cleveland, 1974-, Founding President 1974-76, President 1989-; Staff Poetry Consultant, Indiana University Writers' Conference 1970-76. Address: 3283 Dellwood Road, Cleveland Heights, OH 44118, USA.

DOTY Mark, b. 10 Aug 1953, Maryville, Tennessee, USA. Writer; Poet; Professor. Education: BA, Drake University, 1978; MFA, Goddard College, 1980. Appointments: Faculty, MFA Writing Program, Vermont College, 1981-94, Writing and Literature, Goddard College, 1985-90; Guest Faculty, Sarah Lawrence College, 1990-94, 1996; Fannie Hurst Visiting Professor, Brandeis University, 1994; Visiting Faculty, University of Iowa, 1995, 1996, Columbia University, 1996; Professor, Creative Writing Program, University of Utah, 1997-. Publications: Turtle, Swan, 1987; Bethlehem in Broad Daylight, 1991; My Alexandria, 1993; Atlantis, 1995; Heaven's Coast (memoir), 1996. Contributions to: Many anthologies and journals. Honours: Theodore Roethke Prize, 1986; National Endowment for the Arts Fellowships in Poetry, 1987, 1995; Pushcart Prizes, 1987, 1989; Los Angeles Times Book Prize, 1993; Ingram Merrill Foundation Award, 1994; National Book Critics Circle Award, 1994; Guggenheim Fellowship, 1994; Whiting Writers Award, 1994; Rockefeller Foundation Fellowship, Bellagio, Italy, 1995; New York Times Notable Book of the Year, 1995, 1996; American Library Association Notable Book of the Year, 1995; T S Eliot Prize, 1996; Bingham Poetry Prize, 1996; Ambassador Book Award, 1996; Lambda Literary Award, 1996. Address: c/o Creative Writing Program, University of Utah, Salt Lake City, UT 84112, USA.

DOUGLAS George William, b. 9 May 1952, Corbridge, Northumberland, England. Local Government Officer. Publications: Poetry, Now Heart of England Regional Anthology, 1995. Contributions to: Poetic Voices of America, 1995, 1996; Poetry International, Anthology of Contemporary Poetry, 1972; Poetry Now; South East Poetry Anthology, 1992. Honours: Honorary Membership: World Parnassians Guild International, 1995; First ever entry into a major competition, via Poetic Voices of America, Poem received Honorable Mention Entry Status, 1995. Membership: Friends of the Dymock Poets, Herefordshire, England. Address: 14 Barnes Road, Farncombe, Godalming, Surrey GU7 3RG, England.

DOVE Rita (Frances), b. 28 Aug 1952, Akron, Ohio, USA. Poet; Writer; Professor. m. Fred Viebahn, 23 Mar 1979, 1 daughter. Education: BA, summa cum laude, Miami University, Oxford, Ohio, 1973; Postgraduate studies, University of Tubingen, 1974-75; MFA, University of Iowa, 1977. Appointments: Assistant Professor 1981-84, Associate Professor 1984-87, Professor of English 1987-89, Arizona State University, Tempe; Writer-in-Residence, Tuskegee Institute, 1982; Associate Editor, Callaloo, 1986-; Advisor and Contributing Editor, Gettysburg Review, 1987-, TriQuarterly, 1988-, Georgia Review, 1994; Professor of English 1989-93, Commonwealth Professor 1993-, University of Virginia; Poet Laureate of the USA, 1993-95. Publications: Poetry: Ten Poems, 1977; The Only Dark Spot in the Sky, 1980; The Yellow House on the Corner, 1980; Mandolin, 1982; Museum, 1983; Thomas and Beulah, 1986; The Other Side of the House, 1988; Grace Notes, 1989; Selected Poems, 1993; Lady Freedom Among Us, 1994; Mother Love, 1995. Other: Fifth Sunday (short stories), 1985; Through the Ivory Gate (novel), 1992; The Darker Face of the Earth (verse play), 1994; The Poet's World (essays), 1995. Contributions to: Magazines and journals. Honours: Fulbright Fellow, 1974-75; National Endowment for the Arts Grants, 1978, 1989; Portia Pittman Fellow, Tuskegee Institute, 1982; Guggenheim Fellowship, 1983-84; Peter I.B. Lavan Younger Poets Award, Academy of American Poets, 1986; Pulitzer Prize in Poetry, 1987; General Electric Foundation Award for Younger Writers, 1987; Rockefeller Foundation Residency, Bellagio, Italy, 1988; Ohio Governor's Award, 1988; Mellon Fellow, National Humanities Center, 1988-89; Fellow, Center for Advanced Studies, University of Virginia, 1989-92; NAACP Great American Artist Award, 1993; Renaissance Forum Award, Folger Shakespeare Library, 1994; Many Honorary Doctorates. Memberships: Literature Panel 1984-86, Chair, Poetry Grants 1985, National Endowment for the Arts; Editorial Board, National Forum 1984-, Iris 1989-; Commissioner, Schomburg Center for the Preservation of Black Culture, New York Public Library, 1987; Renaissance Forum, Folger Shakespeare Library, 1993-; Council of Scholars, Library of Congress, 1994-; Pen Club; ASCAP; American Philosophical Society; Academy of American Poets; Associate Writing Programs; Phi Beta Kappa, Senator, 1994-; Phi Kappa Phi; Poetry Society of America; Poets and Writers. Address: Department of English, 219 Bryan Hall, University of Virginia, Charlottesville, VA 22903, USA.

DOWDEN George Kaviraj (Duncan Jr), b. 15 Sept 1932, USA. Poet; Writer. m. Annie Dowden, 22 Sept 1982. Education: BA, Bucknell University, 1957; MA, New York University, 1960. Appointments: Graduate Assistant, New York University, 1959; English Teacher, Brooklyn College, 1960-63, 1966-67. Publications: Flight from America, 1965; Renew Jerusalem, 1969; Earth Incantations-Body Chants, 1976; A Message to Isis, 1977; From the Stone through You, and White Faces, 1978; The Moving I, 1987; Great Love Desiderata, 1988; Flowers of Consciousness, 1991; The Deepening, 1994. Contributions to: Anthologies and magazines. Address: Top Flat, 82 Marine Parade, Brighton, East Sussex BN2 1AJ, England.

DOWLING Basil Cairns, b. 29 Apr 1910, Southbridge, Canterbury, New Zealand. English Master. m. Margaret Wilson, 11 June 1938, 1 son, 2 daughters. Education: St Andrew's College, Christchurch, New Zealand; MA, Canterbury University College, Christchurch, 1933; Library Diploma, Wellington, 1946. Appointments: Reference Librarian, 1947-49, Deputy Librarian, 1950-51, Otago University; Assistant Master, Downside School, Surrey, England, 1952-54; Assistant Master, 1954-75, Head, English Department, 1965-75, Raine's Foundation School, London. Publications: A Day's Journey, 1941; Signs and Wonders, 1944; Canterbury and Other Poems, 1949; Hatherley: Recollective Lyrics, 1968; A Little Gallery of Characters, 1971; Bedlam: A Mid-Century Satire, 1972; The Unreturning Native, 1973; The Stream, a Reverie of Boyhood, 1979; Windfalls, 1983. Contributions to: John O'London's Weekly; New Poems (PEN), 1954; Painter and Sculptor; Landfall, New Zealand; Times Literary Supplement; Time and Tide; Countryman; New Zealand Listener. Honour: Jessie Mackay Memorial Award, 1961. Membership: International PEN. Address: 12 Mill Road, Rye, East Sussex TN31 7NN, England.

DOWNAR Joan Hazel. See: APPLETON Joan Hazel.

DOYLE Charles Desmond, (Mike Doyle), b. 18 Oct 1928. Professor Emeritus of English. Education: Dip Teach, 1956, BA, 1957, MA, 1959, University of New Zealand; PhD, Auckland University, 1968. Appointments: Professor of English, University of Victoria, British Columbia, Canada, 1976-93. Publications: A Splinter of Glass, 1956; The Night Shift (with others), 1957; Distances, 1963; Messages for Herod, 1965; A Sense of Place, 1965; Quorum-Noah, 1970; Abandoned Sofa, 1971; Earth Meditations, 1971; Earthshot, 1972; Preparing for the Ark, 1973; Planes, 1975; Stonedancer, 1976; A Month Away from Home, 1980; A Steady Hand, 1982; The Urge to Raise Hats, 1989; Separate Fidelities, 1991; Intimate Absences: Selected Poems 1954-1992, 1993. Contributions to: Canadian Literature; Canadian Forum; Malahat Review; Poetry, Chicago; San Francisco Review; Meanjin, Australia; Quadrant, Australia; Landfall, New Zealand; Akzente, Germany; Nation, USA; Tuatara; Ellipse; Others. Honours: Creative Arts Fellowships, UNESCO, 1958-59. Memberships: Writers Union of Canada; New Canterbury Literary Society. Address: 641 Oliver Street, Victoria, British Columbia V85 4WZ, Canada.

DR G. See: GLYNN Martin Roy.

DRAKE Albert Dee, b. 26 Mar 1935, Portland, Oregon, USA. Professor Emeritus. m. 28 Dec 1960, div 1985, 1 son, 2 daughters. Education: Portland State College, 1956-59; BA, English, 1962, MFA, English, 1966, University of Oregon. Appointments: Research Assistant, 1965, Teaching Assistant, 1965-66, English Department, University of Oregon; Assistant Professor, English, 1966-70, Associate Professor, English, 1970-79, Professor, English, 1979-91, Michigan State University, East Lansing; Professor Emeritus, English, Michigan State University, 1995. Publications: Michigan Signatures (editor), 1969; 3 Northwest Poets, 1970; Poems, 1972; Assuming the Position, 1972; Riding Bike, 1972; By Breathing In and Out, 1974; Cheap Thrills, 1975; Returning to Oregon, 1975; Roadsalt, 1976; Reaching for the Sun, 1979; Garage, 1980; Homesick, 1988. Editor: Happiness Holding Tank, 1969-92, 1968-; Hot Rodder, 1993. Contributions to: Poetry Northwest; Poetry Now; Northwest Review; Shenandoah; South Dakota Review; Arts in Society; Wormwood Review; West Coast Poetry Review; Windsor Review; Midwest Quarterly; Assembling; TransPacific; December. Honours: Poetry Prize, St Andrews Review, 1974; National Endowment for the Arts, 1975, 1984; Michigan Council for the Arts, 1981. Address: 9727 South East Reedway, Portland, OR 97266, USA.

DRAKE Bobbie Alice, b. 20 Jan 1945, Jasper, Texas, USA. Reviewer; Co-Ordinator, Poet Of The Month for People Plus. m. Nelson Arden Drake, 20 Jan 1964, 2 son, 1 daughter. Education: AA, 1986; BA, Literature, 1995, currently pursuing MA in Literature, University of Houston, Clear Lake. Publication: A Skein of Varigated Thread, 1995. Contributions to: Poetry Society of Texas Book of The Year; Baylor House of Poetry; Bayousphere; Chrysalis; Gulf Breeze; Houston Poetry Festival, 1991; Lagniappe; Patchwork; Premier Poets; Vineyard Poetry Quarterly; The Wounded Heart; Voice for Conversion!; When The Wind Stops; Writer's Lifeline. Honours: Critics Choice Award; Juried Poet, Houston Poetry Festival, 1991; World Congress of Poets Certificate, 1992; Lady Olympoetry, 1992; San Jacinto College Writer of the Year, 1993; Honorary Doctorate of Literature, London Institute for Applied Research, 1993; Honorary Doctor of Letters and Lifetime Fellowship, Australian Institute for Co-Ordinated Research, 1994; United Poets Laureate International, Laureate, Woman of Letters, 1995; Many local and state awards; All American Scholar, 1992; Shield of Valor, 1992; ABI Medal of Honour, 1993. Memberships: Poetry Society of Texas; Vice President, San Jacinto Chapter; Poets Northwest; PST; Director, United Poets Laureate International; University of Houston Clear Lake Literature Club; National Council of Teachers of English; Maison International des Intellectuals Academy, MIDI, France; Sigma Tau Delta; Phi Theta Kappa. Address: 1609 Blackburn, Pasadena, TX 77502, USA.

DREYER Inge b. 12 June 1933, Berlin, Germany. Writer. Publications: Achtung Stolperstelle, 1982; Schule mit Dachschaden, 1985; Toenende Stille, 1985; Die Streuner von Pangkor, 1987. Contributions to: Several contributions to German and International Anthologies and Literature Magazines: Silhouette, Gauckes Jahrbuch, World Poetry. Honours: World Poets Award Golden Crown, 1990; Honorary Doctor of Literature, London, 1992; Honorary Professor of Literature, Paris, 1992; International Cultural Diploma of Honour, 1995. Memberships: VS; GEDOK; NGL; World Academy of Arts and Culture; World Poetry Society. Address: Winkler Strasse 4A, 14193 Berlin, Grunewald, Germany.

DRINKARD Dianna (Phoebe) Phyllis Marcia Salicoff, (Diannamight Press), b. 2 Apr 1947, Detroit, Michigan, USA. Poet; Painter; Mystic; Reiki Soul Therapist. m. David Roy Drinkard, 20 Mar 1976. Education: Diploma, Southfield High School, 1965; BA, University of Michigan, 1969; MA, University of Michigan, 1970; Summer Studies, Shakespeare/English Literature, Farleigh-Dickensen University, Banbury, England, 1971; Diploma/Master of Herbology/Fellowship/Master of Botanical Medicine, The Emerson College of Herbology and Botanical Pharmacopeia, Montreal, Canada, 1981; Minister License, The Universal Life Church, Modesta, California, 1990; Certificate, Reiki Master, The Reiki Center, Southfield, Michigan, 1990; Certificate, Soul Therapist, The Universal Life Church, Modesta, California, 1992. Appointments: Tutor, Professional Assistant, Learning Laboratory Consultant, Paraprofessional Library and Administrative Testing Assistant, Oakland Community College, 1970-75; Playwright/Children's Programmer, Southfield Public Library, Southfield, Michigan, 1978; Recreation Editor, Senior News, City of Southfield Department of

Parks and Recreation, Southfield, Michigan, 1978-79; Reiki Master/Healer and Soul Therapist, 1990-. Publications: Rainbow Dances, 1991; Reiki Healing, 1992; Reiki Healer, 1993; Reiki Master Healer, 1994; Reiki Master Teacher, 1995; In Soul Elations, 1996. Contributions to: The Sound of Poetry; The Best Poets of 1996; The Best Poets of the 90's; Voices of America; The Heartland Quarterly; Up Against the Wall-Mother; The World of Poetry. Honours: Golden Poet, World of Poetry, 1991; Editor's Choice, National Library of Poetry, 1993, 1996. Address: 10131 Sakura Drive #C, St Louis, Missouri 63128-1370, USA.

DRISCOLL Mary Harris, b. 6 June 1928, Worcester, Massachusetts, USA. Corporate Treasurer. m. Joseph F Driscoll, 21 June 1952, 3 sons, 6 daughters. Education: AB, magna cum laude, Phi Beta Kappa 1949, Smith College; MA, Romance Languages and Literature, 1952, Wellesley College, Harvard. Appointments: Treasurer, Harris Oil Corporation; Green Gold Tree Corporation. Publications: In Formal Gardens, 1980; Brief Lightning, 1981. Contributions to: Journals and periodicals. Address: 206 West Main Street, Milbury, MA 01527, USA.

DROOGENBROODT Germain, b. 11 Sept 1944, Belgium. Translator; Poet; Editor. m. Liliane Leroy, 8 June 1968, 1 son, 1 daughter. Education: Languages, 1967. Appointments: President, TTI Belgium, 1969-88; President, Chief Editor, Point, 1984-. Publications: Appearances; Forty at the Wall; Do You Know the Country; Poems; Waves, What Shall I Do; When The Dark Blue Night Smashes Down; Poetry translated and published: The Balm of Dawn; China, China; When they Torture Me; The Paces of the Night in the Grass; 7 x Japan; The Shadow's Cool Corners and Sides; Thirty-Three Flemish Poets; Because your Dreams are Fake; Entrusted to Time; Conversation with the Sound of Silence; No Pasaran! No Pasaran? Contributions to: Spectator; Argus; Revolver; Point; Marina D'Art; Trenc D'Alba; Aiguadolc; Kruispunt; Vlaanderen. Honours: Literature Award; Poetry Award; Honorary Degree of Doctor of Literature; Hawthornden International Retreat for Writers Fellowship. Address: Ithaca, Camino Monte Molar 69, E03590 Altea, Alicante, Spain.

DROR Shlomo. See: **SCHOENFELD Ilan.**

DROZDIK Ladislav, b. 3 Mar 1930, Nova Bana, Czechoslovakia. Associate Professor. m. Jarmila Sikova, 21 Sept 1953, 2 sons, 1 daughter. Education: BA, 1953; Dr, 1967; Habilitation thesis, 1979. Appointments: Assistant Professor, 1953-79; Associate Professor, 1979-92; Professor, 1992-. Publications: High Shade Celebration; The Close Orbit; Tormenting Passion of the Sun; Selections from the Love Poetry of Nizar Qabbani; Homeless Poems. Honour: National Jan Holly Prize. Memberships: Slovak Oriental Society; Linguistic Society of America. Address: Zahrebska 6, 81105 Bratislava, Czech Republic.

DRUMMOND LaVena May, b. 23 June 1931, USA. Teacher; Executive Secretary; Homemaker; Self-Employed Rancher. m. Jack W Drummond, 15 July 1948, 1 son, 1 daughter. Education: Fort Scott Junior College. Appointments: Teacher, Blueprint Control; Executive Secretary, Cessna Aircraft Wichita; Owner, Operator, J & L Ranch, Severy. Publications: Pegasus Aloft; Music; Whom to Love; Vacation; Counsellor Arabia. Honours: Golden Poet Award; Silver Poet Award. Membership: World of Poetry. Address: RR1, Box 142, Severy, KS 67137, USA.

DRURY Finvola Margaret, b. 7 Aug 1926, Cleveland, Ohio, USA. Poet; Teacher. m. George Drury, 28 Aug 1948, 1 son, 1 daughter. Education: BA, State University of New York, 1976; MA, 1984. Appointments: Lecturer, Toledo Museum of Art, 1946-48; Visiting Professor, Rochester Institute of Technology, 1990. Publications: Casualties of War; Elegy for Joric Ross; Burning the Snow. Contributions to: Poetry Magazine; AD; Social Text; 60's Without Apology; Conservatory of American Letters Anthology; New Rivers Irish American Anthology. Memberships: Miles Modern Poetry Committee; Writers and Books Literary Center; Conductor of Writing Workshops. Address: RR1 Box 96A, Brooksville, Maine 04617, USA.

DU Yunxie, (Wu Jin, Wu Dahan), b. 17 Mar 1918, Sitiawan, Malaysia. Editor; Teacher; Magazine Editor.m. Li Lijun, 22 April 1982, 2 sons, 4 daughters, 2 stepsons. Education: Trinity College, 1934-37; Xiamen University, 1938-39; BA, Southwest Associated University, 1945. Appointments: Interpreter, American Volunteers Group; News Editor, Ta Kung Pao, Chongqing; Teacher, Nanyang Girls High School and Chinese High School, Singapore; Translator,

Editor, Hong Kong, Ta Kung Pao; Translator, News Editor, Xinhua News Agency; Teacher, Director, Foreign Languages Department, Shanxi Teachers College. Publications: Forty Poems; Nine Leaves Anthology; Late Paddies; Sitiawan, You Are My First Beloved; Selected 100 Poems of Du Yunxie, 1995. Contributions to: Ta Kung Pao; Wen Ju Magazine; Chinese New Poetry; Renaissance; Poetry Magazine; Chinese Poets; People's Daily. Memberships: Chinese Writers Association; PEN; Dongqing Literature Society; Council member, China Poetry Institute. Address: Flat 8-6, Bldg 17, 3 Yangfangdian Road, Beijing 100038, China.

DU PLESSIS Nancy Ellen, b. 20 Aug 1954, Hartford, Connecticut, USA. Writer-Performer; Teacher (specialist in ordinary English, acting, diction, poetry). Education: State University of New York, College at Purchase, 1972-74; BA, Urban Design Studies, Journalism, New York University, Washington Square College, 1975-77; Institut des Etudes Théâtrales, 1987-89; Department of Theatre, l'Université de Paris VIII, 1989-92; Diploma, Etudes Superieures Universitaires, 1992; TOEFL Certificate, WICE, Paris, 1992. Appointments: Freelance Editor and Writer, New York City, 1977-85; EFC Teacher, Paris, Performer, Lecturer, Theatre in English, Université de Paris VIII, 1986-93; Freelance Writer, Performer, Acting, EFL Teacher, based in Munich, Germany, 1994-. Publications: Bud, 1981; Notes From The Moroccan Journals, and, Art New York, bilingual edition of 2 long texts, 1995. Contributions to: Women and Performance Journals; La Tribune Internationale des Langues Vivantes; River Styx; Home Planet News; The Tie That Binds, anthology. Honours: Development Grant, Center for Peace Through Culture, New York City; Travel Grant for Poetry Performance, Richardson Foundation, Washington. Memberships: Poets and Writers, New York; Société des Auteurs et Compositeurs Dramatiques, Paris. Address: Kyreinstr 11, D-81371 Munich, Germany.

DUBERSTEIN Helen Laura, b. 3 June 1926, New York, New York, USA. Poet. m. 10 Apr 1949, 2 daughters. Appointments: Writer, 1986; Teacher, New York University, 1987; Guest Lecturer, Manhattan Community College, 1987; Poetry Judge, Pen American Center Prison Writing, 1988; Book: Pursuit of the Goddess; Arrived Safely; Changes; The Voyage Out; Succubus/Incubus; The Human Dimension. Publications: Confrontation; For Now; Jewish Dialogue; The Shameless Old Lady, 1994; Shadow Self & Other Tales, 1994; Anthologies: Looking Forward (The Cord and the Track); The Radical Theatre Journal. Contributions to: New Republic; United Teacher; Majority Report; Village Voice; Poets Fortnightly; WIV; Second Growth. Honours: Tenth Annual Editors Book Award; Interlochen Awards for Best Play; Iowa School of Short Fiction Award; National Foundation for the Arts Grant. Memberships: PEN; Dramatists Guild; Poetry Society of America; League of Professional Theatre Women. Address: 463 West Street No 904 D, New York, NY 10014, USA.

DUBIE Norman (Evans Jr), b. 10 Apr 1945, Barre, Vermont, USA. Professor of English; Poet; Writer. Education: BA, Goddard College, 1969; MFA, University of Iowa, 1971. Appointments: Teaching Assistant, Goddard College, 1967-69; Teaching Assistant, 1969-70, Writing Fellow, 1970-71, Distinguished Lecturer and Member of the Graduate Faculty, 1971-74, University of Iowa; Poetry Editor, Iowa Review, 1971-72, Now Magazine, 1973-74; Assistant Professor, Ohio University, 1974-75; Lecturer, 1975-76, Director, Creative Writing, 1976-77, Associate Professor, 1978-81, Professor of English, 1982-, Arizona State University. Publications: The Horsehair Sofa, 1969; Alehouse Sonnets, 1971; Indian Summer, 1973; The Prayers of the North American Martyrs, 1975; Popham of the New Song, 1975; In the Dead of Night, 1975; The Illustrations, 1977; A Thousand Little Things, 1977; Odalisque in White, 1978; The City of the Olesha Fruit, 1979; Comes Winter, the Sea Hunting, 1979; The Everlastings, 1980; The Window in the Field, 1982; Selected and New Poems, 1983, new edition, 1996; The Springhouse, 1986; Groom Falconer, 1989; Radio Sky, 1991; The Clouds of Magellan, 1991; The Choirs of June and January, 1993. Contributions to: Anthologies and periodicals. Honours: Bess Hokin Prize, 1976; Guggenheim Fellowship, 1977-78; Pushcart Prize, 1978-79; National Endowment for the Arts Grant, 1986; Ingram Merrill Grant, 1987. Address: c/o Department of English, Arizona State University, Tempe, AZ 85281, USA.

DUBOIS Frédéric, (Julien Dunilac), b. 24 Sept 1923, Neuchatel, Switzerland. Diplomat. m. Lydia Induni, 14 Apr 1947, 1 son, 2 daughters. Education: Formation Classique a Neuchatel, Switzerland, sciences sociales á Paris. Appointments: Secrétaire puis Conseiller d'Ambassade á Paris (affaires culturelles); Directeur de l'Office Fédéral de la Culture, Berne, Switzerland 1980-85. Publications: La Vue Courte, 1952; La Past du Feu, 1954; Corps et Biens, 1957; Les Mauvaises Tetes, 1958; Passager clandestin, 1962; Futur mémorable, 1970; L'Un, 1974; La Passion alon Belle, 1985; Plein ciel, 1985; Mythologiques, 1987; Précaire Victoire, 1991. Contributions to: George Sand sous la loupe, 1978; Francois Mitterrand sous la loupe, 1981; Le Conseil fédéral sous la loupe, 1991; Numerous dramatic pieces for radio. Memberships: Société Ecrivains neuchatelois et jurassiens; Société Suisse des Ecrivains; Société Suisse des Auteurs. Address: Rue des Parcs 5, CH 2000 Neuchatel, Switzerland.

DUBOIS Jean, b. 4 Jan 1926, Denver, Colorado, USA. Writer. m. Edward N Dubois, 21 Aug 1947, 1 sons, 2 daughters. Education: BA, University of Wyoming, 1947; MA, The Pennsylvania State University, 1963. Publications: Silent Stones, Empty Passageways, 1992; The Same Sweet Yellow, 1994. Contributions to: Poets On; Thema; Modern Haiku; Brussels Sprout; Wall Street Journal; Mayfly. Memberships: Haiku Society of America, Co-Editor, Members Anthology, 1995. Address: P O Box 1430, Golden, CO 80402, USA.

DUBOIS Rochelle Holt. See: HOLT Rochelle Lynn.

DUCHARME Mark Edward, b. 27 Oct 1960, Detroit, Michigan, USA. Shift Manager. m. Lori S Cushman, 31 Dec 1989, 1 daughter. Education: BA, Communication, University of Michigan, 1982; MFA, Writing and Poetics, Naropa Institute, 1992. Appointments: Adjunct Faculty, Department of Writing and Poetics, 1993, Adjunct Faculty, Department of Continuing Education, 1995-96, Naropa Institute. Publications: Life Could Be a Dream, 1990; Emphasis, 1993; i, a series, 1995; 4 sections from Infringement, 1996; Contracting Scale, 1996. Contributions to: Talisman; Lingo; New American Writing; First Intensity; ACM; Washington Review; Situation; Big Allis; Torque; B City; Ribot; Mirage # 4 Period(ical); Juxta; The Impercipient; Texture; Lost and Found Times. Honour: Selected for Gertrude Stein Awards in Innovative American Poetry: 1994-1995, Sun and Moon Press. Address: 2965 13th Street, Boulder, CO 80304, USA.

DUCKER Carolyn, b. 15 Oct 1968, Cirencester, GloucestershireEngland. Florist; Translator. Education: St Annes College, Oxford, 1987-92. Contributions to: Envoi; Frogmore Papers; Hybrid; Journal of Refugee Studies; Memes; Cascando; Angel Exhaust. Address: 7 Northmoor Place, Northmoor Road, Oxford OX2 6XB, England.

DUEMER Joseph, b. 31 May 1951, San Diego, California, USA. Professor. m. Carole A Mathey, 31 Dec 1987. Education: BA, University of Washington, 1978; MFA, University of Iowa, 1980. Appointments: Lecturer, Western Washington University, 1981-83; San Diego State University, 1983-87; Assistant Professor, Clarkson University, 1987-. Publications: Fools Paradise; The Light of Common Day; Customs; Static, poetry, 1995 Dog Music, poetry anthology, 1996. Contributions to: New England Review; Tar River Poetry; Manoa; Poetry Northwest; Wallace Stevens Journal; Seattle Review; Boulevard; Tendril; Kansas Quarterly; Carolina Quarterly; American Poetry Review; Pacific Review. Honours: National Endowment for the Arts Fellowship; Associated Writing Programs Anniversary Award; Bread Loaf Fellow; Yaddo Residency; Blue Mountain Center Fellow. Memberships: Modern Language Association; National Council of Teachers of English; Poets and Writers; Society for Literature and Science. Literary Agent: Sydelle Kramer, The Franes Golding Literary Agency. Address: Center for Liberal Studies, Box 5750, Clarkson University, Potsdam, NY 13699, USA.

DUERRSON Werner, b. 12 Sept 1932, Schwenningen/Neckar, Germany. Writer. Education: Music Studies, Trossingen, 1953; German and French Literature Studies, Túbingen, Munich, 1957; PhD, 1962. Publications: Poetry, prose, essays, dramas and translations including: Dreizehn Gedichte, 1965; Schattengeschlecht, 1966; Flugballade, 1966; Drei Dichtungen, 1970; Mitgegangen mitgehangen, 1975; Werner Dürrson liest Lyrik und Prosa, 1978; Schubart-Feier Eine Deutsche Moritat, 1980; Schubart, drama, 1980; Stehend bewegt (drama), 1980; Zeit-Gedichte, 1981; Stehend bewegt (poem), 1982; Der Luftkünstler (prose), 1983; Das Kattenhorner Schweigen (poems), 1984; Feierabend (poems), 1985; Blochaden (poems), 1986; Wie ich lese? (essay), 1986; Kosmose (poem), 1987; Denkmal fürs Wasser (poems), 1987; Ausleben (poems of 12 years), 1988; Abbreviaturen, aphorisms, 1989; Katzen-Suite (poems), 1989; Werke in vier Bänden (poetry and prose), 1992; Ausgewählte Gedichte (poems), 1995; The

Kattenhorn Silence (translated by Michael Hamburger), 1995; Several works in co-operation with painters (Klaus Staeck, Erich Heckel, HAP Grieshaber, Jonny Friedlaender) and musicians (Klaus Fessmann and others); Translations of authors including Guillaume d'Aquitaine, Marguerite de Navarre, Mallarmé, Rimbaud, Yvan Goll, Rene Char and Henri Michaux. Contributions to: Anthologies and broadcasting. Honours: Lyric Poem Prize, S W German press, 1953; German Award for short stories, 1973, 1983; Literary Prize of Stuttgart, 1978; Literary Prize Schubart, 1980; Literary Prize of Ueberlingen, 1985. Memberships: PEN; Association of German Writers; Association Internationaleides Critiques littéraires, Paris. Address: Schloss Neufra, D-88499 Riedlingen/DO, Germany.

DUFFETT Michael Frank, b. 23 Feb 1943. Writer-in-Residence. m. Debra Faye Jones, 31 July 1982, 2 sons, 4 daughters. Education: BA, 1964, MA, 1968, Sidney Sussex College, Cambridge. Appointments: English Teacher: Saudi Arabia; British Council, Edinburgh; Associate Professor, Kawamura Gakuen University, Tokyo; Assistant Professor, Chaminade University, Honolulu; Visiting Professor, Pepperdine University, Malibu, California; Contract Artist in Poetry, William James Association, California. Publications: Evolution: A Japanese Journal, 1976; The Land of Nifty Noonah, 1987; Mountain, A Metaphysical Verse Melodrama, 1988; A Baker's Dozen, 1987; Forever Avenue, 1987; Elements 1943-2013, 1991. Contributions to: Japan Times; New Zealand Listener; Printed Matter; Cow in the Road; Michi; Journal; Poetry Round Up. Honours: Tokyo Engish Literature Society, 1975; Multi-Residency Artist, Sierra Conservation Center, 1989. Memberships: Tokyo English Literature Society; Board, Cow in the Road Literary Journal; Poetry Society of America. Address: PO Box 917, Valley Springs, CA 95252, USA.

DUFFIELD Jeremy, b. 25 June 1946, Alfreton, Derbyshire, England. Chartered Textile Technologist. m. Andrea Bramley, 7 Sept 1968, 1 daughter. Education: Derby and District College of Art and Technology, 1963-69; Associateship of Textile Institute (ATI). Appointments: Laboratory Assistant and Dyer, Derby, 1963-68; Hosiery and Fabric Dyer, Nottingham, 1968-82; Dyehouse Manager, Leicester, 1982-. Publication: Danced By The Light of The Moon, 1993. Contributions to: Poetry Nottingham; Poetry Digest; Envoi; Iota; She; Countryman; Nottingham Topic; Poetry Society Newsletter. Honours: 1st Prize, Open Section, CISWO Mining Poems Competition, 1988; 1st Prize, Swanage Arts Festival Poetry group, 1991; 1st prize, Queenie Lee Poetry Competition, 1993. Memberships: Nottingham Poetry Society, Chairman, Treasurer; Poetry Society, London; Nottingham Writers' Club, Publicity Secretary; Robert Louis Stevenson Club, Edinburgh; Herrick Society, Leicestershire. Address: 71 Saxton Avenue, Heanor, Derbyshire DE75 7PZ, England.

DUFFY Carol Ann, b. 23 Dec 1955, Glasgow, Scotland. Poet. Education: BA, Hons, Philosophy, University of Liverpool, 1977. Publications: Standing Female Nude, 1985; Selling Manhattan, 1987; The Other Country, 1990. Honours: C Day Lewis Fellowships, 1982-84; Eric Gregory Award, 1983; Scottish Arts Council Book Award of Merit, 1985, 1987; Somerset Maugham Award, 1988; Dylan Thomas Award, 1990. Address: 4 Camp View, London SW19 4UL, England.

DUFFY Maureen Patricia, b. 21 Oct 1933, Worthing, Sussex, England. Author. Education: BA, Kings College, 1956. Publications: That's How It Was; The Microcosm; Wounds; Love Child; The Venus Touch; The Erotic World of Gaery; I Want to Go to Moscow; Capital; Housespy; Evesong; Memorials of the Quick and the Dead; Visual Art; Londoners; Change; A Thousand Capriscious Chances. Contributions to: New Statesman. Memberships: Writers Action Group; Writers Guild of Great Britain. Address: 18 Fabian Road, London SW6 7TZ, England.

DUGAN Alan, b. 12 Feb 1923, Brooklyn, New York, USA. Poet. m. Judith Shahn. Education: Queens College; Olivet College; BA, Mexico City College. Appointments: Teacher, Sarah Lawrence College, 1967-71, Fine Arts Work Center, Provincetown, Massachusetts, 1971-. Publications: General Prothalamion in Populous Times, 1961; Poems, 1961; Poems 2, 1963; Poems 3, 1967; Collected Poems, 1969; Poems 4, 1974; Sequence,1976; Collected Poems, 1961-1983, 1983; Poems 6, 1989. Contributions to: Several magazines. Honours: Yale Series of Younger Poets Award, 1961; National Book Award, 1961; Pulitzer Prizes in Poetry, 1962, 1967; Rome Fellowship, American Academy of Arts and Letters, 1962-63; Guggenheim Fellowship, 1963-64; Rockefeller Foundation Fellowship, 1966-67; Levinson Poetry Prize, 1967. Address: Box 97, Truro, MA 02666, USA.

DUHIG Robert Ian, b. 9 Feb 1954, London, England. Homelessness Worker; Poet. m. Jane Vincent, 1 son. Education: BA, Leeds University; Postgraduate Certificate in Education, Leeds University. Publication: The Bradford Count, 1991. Contributions to: Irish Review; Times Literary Supplement; New Statesman; Society; Honest Ulsterman; Arion; Bottlenose Review. Honours: 1st Prize, British National Poetry Competition, 1987; Bradford Count shortlisted for Whitbread Poetry Prize, 1991. Address: c/o Bloodaxe Books, PO Box 1SN, Newcastle-upon-Tyne NE99 1SN, England.

DULING Paul, b. 14 Nov 1916, Spokane, Washington, USA. Writer; Poet; Journalist: Public Relations. m. Helen Julia Pendexter, 5 Jan 1946, 2 daughters. Education: BA, University of Washington, 1939. Appointments: Copywriter, Prudential Insurance Company, 1941-51; Director, Sales Promotion, Advertising, Public Relations, Postal Life Insurance Company, 1951-59; Americans United for Separation of Church and State, 1959-67; Alumni Relations, Pratt Institute, 1967; Retired, 1971. Publications: Lunch Hour Girls/Lunch Hour Man, 1979; Love Until the Sun Goes Down, 1984; Whispering Without Walls, 1990. Contributions to: Saturday Evening Post; Poet Lore; Euterpe; Connecticut River Review; Wings Press; Greens; Embers; Bean Feast; Connecticut Artists; San Fernando Poetry Journal; Small Pond; Fair Press; Reader, Walt Whitman International Poetry Center, 1978-79; Poet of the Month, New York Poetry Forum, 1985. Memberships: Connecticut Poetry Society; State Chairman, World Poetry Day. Address: 49 Taquoshe Place, Fairfield, CT 06430, USA.

DUNCAN Andrew Charles Maitland, b. 26 Nov 1956, Leeds, Yorkshire, England. Engineer. Publications: Cut Memories and False Commands, 1991; Sound Surface, 1992; Alien Skies, 1992. Contributions to: Ochre; Eduofinality; Grosseteste Review; Memes; First Offence. Address: Flat 6 Avon Court, Holden Road, London N12 8HR, England.

DUNCAN Stephen Thomas, b. 19 Mar 1952, London, England. Writer; Artist. m. Marilyn Rogers, 1981, 2 sons, 1 daughter. Education: BA, 1st class Hons, Fine Art, 1974, Wimbledon School of Art; Postgraduate Certificate, Royal Academy of Art, 1977; Postgraduate studies, Accademia Di Belle Arti, Rome, 1979. Appointments: Part-time Lecturer in Fine Art and Cultural Studies Departments, number of colleges and polytechnics. Publications: Arts Council Anthologies: New Poetry 5, 1979; New Poetry 6, 1980; New Poetry 7, 1981; PEN Anthology, New Poetry 11, Quartet, 1988; Peterloo Preview 1, 1988. Contributions to: Times Literary Supplement; Critical Review; Poetry Review; Poetry Matters; The Observer Arvon Poetry Collection, Guardian, 1994; and others. Honours: 1st Prize Winner 1981, 2nd Prize Winner 1987, Wandsworth London Writers Competition; 1st Prize Winner, Greenwich Festival Poetry Competition, 1985; 2nd Prize Winner, Times Literary Supplement/Cheltenham Festival Poetry Competition, 1986; 2nd Prize Winner, Bridport Literary Competition, 1989; 2nd Prize Winner, Jewish Quarterly National Poetry Competition, 1994; Arts Council Writers Award, 1994; 4th Prize Winner, Cardiff International Poetry Competition, 1995. Membership: Poetry Society, UK. Address: 56 Mervan Road, London SW2 1DU, England.

DUNETZ Lora. Occupational Therapist. Education: BA, MA, 1943, Columbia University; Certificate of Occupational Therapy, New York University, 1945; Diplôme, Ecole de Hautes Etudes Françaises, 1962. Appointments: Occupational Therapist: University Hospital, Baltimore County, 1947-53; Public Schools in Baltimore, 1954-75; US Army during Korean Conflict, 1st Lieutenant, Women's Medical Specialist Corps. Publication: To Guard Your Sleep and Other Poems, 1988. Contributions to: Ararat; Mediphors; Hellas; Passager; New York Times; Georgia Review; Literary Review; Lyric; Poet Lore; Imagi; Icarus; Without Halos; Brussels Sprout; Anthology of American Magazine Verse. Honours: Lyric Memorial Award, 1982. Memberships: Poetry Society of America; New Jersey Poetry Society. Address: Box 113, Whiting, NJ 08759, USA.

DUNETZ Mildred, b. New York, New York, USA. Social Worker. Education: BA, Brooklyn College; MSC, Western Reserve University, Cleveland, Ohio, 1946. Appointments: Family Society of Philadelphia, 1946-48; Sheltering Arms Children's Service, 1948-64; Family Counselling of New Haven, Connecticut, 1964-76, Contributions to: Lyric; Classical Outlook; St Joseph's Magazine. Honours: The Panola Prize, 1977; The Margaret Haley Carpenter Prize, 1987; Writer's Digest Poetry Competition, Top 100. Address: 20B Homestead Drive, Whiting, NJ 08759, USA.

DUNILAC Julien. See: DUBOIS Frédéric.

DUNKERLEY Hugh David, b. 30 July 1963, Surrey, England. College Lecturer. m. Alison MacLeod, 6 Apr 1991. Education: BA, Christchurch College, 1982-85; University of Bristol, 1986-87; BA, University of Lancaster, 1987-88. Appointments: Lecturer, West Sussex Institute of Higher Education. Contributions to: Orbis; Westmords; Giant Steps; Stand; Experience of Poetry. Honours: Lancaster Literary Festival Poetry Competition Prizewinner; Eric Gregory Award. Address: 68 Oving Road, Chichester, West Sussex PO19 4EW, England.

DUNN Douglas Eaglesham, b. 23 Oct 1942, Inchinnan, Scotland. University Professor. m. Lesley Lane Bathgate, 10 Aug 1985, 1 son, 1 daughter. Education: BA, Hull, 1969; FRSL, 1981; Hon LLD, Dundee, 1987; Hon Fellow, Humberside College, 1987; Hon DLitt, Hull, 1995. Appointments: Freelance Writer, 1971-91; Professor of English, University of St Andrews, 1991-; Director, St Andrews Scottish Studies Institute. Publications: Terry Street, 1969; The Happier Life, 1972; Love or Nothing, 1974; Barbarians, 1979; St Kilda's Parliament, 1981; Europa's Lover, 1982; Elegies, 1985; Selected Poems, 1986; Northlight, 1988; New and Selected Poems, USA, 1989; Andromache, 1990; Head of School of English, 1994-. Books edited: Scotland, An Anthology, 1991; Faber Book of 20th Century Scottish Poetry, 1992; Dante's Drum-kit, 1993 (poems); Oxford Book of Scottish Short Stories (editor), 1995. Contributions to: Times Literary Supplement; New Statesman; New Yorker; Glasgow Herald; Scotland on Sunday; Listener; Poetry Review; and others. Honours: Somerset Maugham Award, 1972; Geoffrey Faber Memorial Prize, 1975; Hawthornden Prize, 1982; Whitbread Poetry Award, 1985; Whitbread Book of the Year Award for 1985, 1986; Cholmondeley Award, 1989; Hon D Litt, Hull, 1995. Memberships: Literature Panel, Arts Council of Great Britain 1981-83; Literature Committee, Scottish Arts Council 1991-; Scottish Arts Council, 1992-94. Literary Agent: Peters, Fraser & Dunlop. Address: School of English, University of St Andrews, St Andrews, Fife KY16 9AL, Scotland.

DUNN Stephen, b. 24 June 1939, New York, New York, USA. Poet; Writer. m. Lois Kelly, 1964, 2 daughters. Education: BA, History, Hofstra University, 1962; New School for Social Research, New York City, 1964-66; MA, Creative Writing, Syracuse University, 1970. Appointments: Assistant Professor, Southwest Minnesota State College, Marshall, 1970-73; Visiting Poet, Syracuse University, 1973-74, University of Washington, Seattle, 1980; Associate Professor to Professor, 1974-90, Stockton State College, New Jersey; Adjunct Professor of Poetry, Columbia University, 1983-87. Publications: Poetry: Five Impersonations, 1971; Looking for Holes in the Ceiling, 1974; Full of Lust and Good Usage, 1976; A Circus of Needs, 1978; Work and Love, 1981; Not Dancing, 1984; Local Time, 1986; Between Angels, 1989; Landscape at the End of the Century, 1991; New and Selected Poems, 1974-1994, 1994; Loosestrife, 1996; Forthcoming Publications: Double Standards, 1998; Other: Walking Light: Essays and Memoirs, 1993. Contributions to: Periodicals. Honours: Academy of American Poets Prize, 1970; National Endowment for the Arts Fellowships, 1973, 1982, 1989; Bread Loaf Writers Conference Robert Frost Fellowship, 1975; Theodore Roethke Prize, 1977; New Jersey Arts Council Fellowships, 1979, 1983; Helen Bullis Prize, 1982; Guggenheim Fellowship, 1984; Levinson Prize, 1988; Oscar Blumenthal Prize, 1991; James Wright Prize, 1993; Academy Award, American Academy of Arts and Letters, 1995. Address: 445 Chestnut Neck Road, Port Republic, NJ 08241, USA.

DUNNETT Alan David Michael, b. 7 July 1953, London, England. Playwright; Theatre Director. Education: English Degree, Trinity College, Oxford University, 1971-74. Appointments: Creative Writing Tutor, Aspley Library, Nottingham, 1989-90; Writer-in-Residence, Ashwell Prison, 1991-92. Publications: In the Savage Gap, 1989; Hurt Under Your Arm, 1991. Contributions to: New Poetry 6; Rialto; Prospice; Smoke; Pennine Platform; Orbis; Grand Piano; Staple; Stepping Out; Zenos; Weyfarers; Poetry Nottingham; Iota; Frogmore Papers; Skoob Occult Review; Envoi; Methuen Book of Theatre Verse. Honour: East Midlands Arts Literature Bursary, 1989. Membership; Poetry Society Register of Poets. Address: 3 Tintern Street, London SW4 7QQ, England.

DUNNETT Denzil Inglis, b. 21 Oct 1917, Sirsa, India. HM Diplomatic Service. m. Ruth Rawcliffe, 20 Mar 1946, 2 sons, 1 daughter. Education: Edinburgh Academy, 1922-35; MA Lit Hum, Corpus Christi College, Oxford, 1939. Appointments: War Service,

Royal Artillery, 1939-46; Editorial Staff, The Scotsman, 1946-47; Diplomatic posts include: Bulgaria, Paris, Buenos Aires, Congo, Madrid, Mexico, Senegal, 1946-77. Publication: Bird Poems, 1989. Contributions to: The Scottish Review; Scottish Bookman; Satire Review; Anthology of the Anarhyme. Membership: Secretary, Chairman, English Society, Oxford, 1936-38. Address: 11 Victoria Grove, London W8 5RW, England.

DUQUETTE Georges J, b. 18 Feb 1947, Thunder Bay, Ontario, Canada. Professor of Education. Education: BA, Philosophy and English, 1970; BEd, English Methods, 1971; MEd, Educational Psychology, 1981; PhD, Second Foreign Language in Education, 1986. Appointments: High School Teacher, English, 1971-81; Assistant Professor, Saint Mary's University, Halifax, 1986-88; Associate Professor, Laurentian University, Sudbury, 1988-. Address: School of Education, Laurentian University, Sudbury, Ontario P3E 2C6, Canada.

DURCAN Paul, b. 16 Oct 1944, Dublin, Ireland. Writer; Poet. m. Nessa O'Neill, 8 May 1969, 2 daughters. Education: BA Hons, Archaeology and Mediaeval History, University College, Cork, Ireland. Appointment: Writer-in-Residence, Trinity College, Dublin, 1990. Publications: Selected Poems, 1982; The Berlin Wall Café, 1985; Going Home to Russia, 1987; Daddy, Daddy, 1990; Crazy About Women, 1991; A Snail In My Prime, 1993; Give Me Your Hand, 1994. Honours: Patrick Kavanagh Award, 1974; Poetry Society Choice, 1985; Poetry Award, Irish-American Cultural Institute, 1989; Whitbread Poetry Award, 1990. Membership: Aosdana. Address: 14 Cambridge Avenue, Ringsend, Dublin 4, Ireland.

DUTRO Pauline Joan Tedrick, b. 10 July 1925, Winterset, Ohio, USA. Poet; Songwriter; Short Story Writer. m. 19 Apr 1948, Ralph R Dutro, 1 son, 2 daughters. Education: Business Course, Cambridge, Ohio, 1944; Diploma, Children's Books, 1996. Appointments: Inspector, Shell Plant BF Goodyear, 1942, Greyhound Lines, 1944, B & O Billing, 1945; Dress Shop Manager, 1946; Ohio Bell Telephone, 1948. Publications: Life's Truly Greatest Treasure, poem (Golden Award); Cast Your Bread Upon the Waters, poem. Contributions to: Local newspapers. Honours: Golden Award, World of Poetry, 1987; Honourable Mentions, 1987, 1988; Honorable Mention Award, 1988; Golden Silver Awards, 1990; Certificate, Nightingale-Conant of Management Excellence, 1990. Address: 1490 Lectric Ln, Zanesville, OH 43701, USA.

DUTTON Geoffrey (Piers Henry), b. 2 Aug 1922, Anlaby, South Australia. Education: University of Adelaide; Magdalen College, Oxford. Appointment: Editorial Director, Sun Books Pty, 1965-80. Publications: Night Flight and Sunrise, 1944; Antipodes in Shoes, 1958; Flowers and Fury, 1962; On My Island: Poems for Children, 1967; Poems Soft and Loud, 1967; Findings and Keepings: Selected Poems 1940-70, 1970; New Poems to 1972, 1972; A Body of Words, 1977; Selective Affinities, 1985; The Innovators, 1989; Flying Low, 1992; New and Selected Poems, 1993. Honours include: Officer, Order of Australia, 1976. Address: c/o Curtis Brown Ltd, PO Box 19, Paddington, New South Wales 2021, Australia.

DUTTON G(eoffrey John) F(raser), (G F Dutton), b. 30 Dec 1924, Chester, England. Medical Science. m. Elizabeth Caird, 22 Sept 1957, 2 sons, 1 daughter. Education: BSc Honours, 1949, PhD, 1954, Edinburgh; DSc, Dundee, 1968. Appointments: Research Fellow, Medical Research Council; Emeritus Professor of Biochemistry. Publications: Camp One, 1978; Squaring the Waves, 1986; The Concrete Garden, 1991. Contributions to: Lines Review; New Writing Scotland; Akros; Chapman. Honours: Hon DPhil, Kuopio, 1978; Hon D de l'Univ, Nancy, 1979. Scottish Arts Council Awards, 1979, 1988; Poetry Book Society Recommendation, 1991. Address: Druimchardain, Bridge of Cally, Blairgowrie PH10 7JX, Scotland.

DWIVEDI Suresh Chandra, (Kaviraj Dhoomketu), b. 29 Mar 1950, Ballia, Uttar Pradesh, India. Professor of English. m. Prabha Dwivedi, 14 June 1975, 1 son , 2 daughters. Education: BA, 1967; MA, English, 1969; PhD, 1976; DLitt, 1988. Appointments: IUGC Fellow, Kashi Vidyapith Varanasi, 1969-72; Lecturer in English, Allahabad Degree College, 1972-84; Lecturer in English, Shri Aurobindo College, Delhi University, 1975; Reader in English, 1984-96, Professor of English, 1996-, Allahabad University, India. Publications include: Ek Aur Sabera, 1978; Haira Pipar Kabahun Na Dole, 1988; Poems included in World Poetry Anthology, 1989, 1990, 1991, 1992, 1993, 1994, 1995. Contributions to: Aaz; Rashtrabhasha Sandesh; Poetry Time; Pratibna India; Youth Age; Madhya Dhara; Shashwati; Naee

Azadi; Kavita India; Commonwealth Quarterly; Also poetry in other anthologies and in numerous books. Honours: Rahul Sankrityayan Award, Uttar Prasdesh Hindi Sansthan, 1986; George Abrahim Grierson Award, Akhil Bharatiya Bhojpuri Bhasha Parishad, 1988; Honorary DLitt, World Academy of Arts & Letters, USA, 1988; Janapadiya Samman, 1989; Rastra Kavi, 1995; Vani Ratna Award, 1996. Memberships: Life Member, American Studies Research Centre, Hyderabad; Life Member, Indian Association for English and American Studies; Literary Criterion; Associate Editor, Kavita India and Points of View; Secretary, Bharatiya Sahitya Sansthan; President, World Bhojpuri Association; Founder, Samagra Dharma. Address: Poet's Corner 125-3, Ome Gayatri Nagar, PO Teliarganj, Allahabad 211004, India.

DWYER Deirdre Diana (Dee), b. 18 Jun 1958, Liverpool, Nova Scotia, Canada. Poet; Teacher. m. Hans von Hammerstein, 12 Oct 1992. Education: MA, English and Creative Writing; BA, Philosophy, Studio Writing I & II, Banff Centre for the Arts. Appointments: Tutor, 1993, 1995; Instructor of English, Nova Scotia College of Art and Design, 1995. Contributions to: Event; Canadian Literature; Poetry Canada Review. Honours: Honorable Mention in Fiddle/Grain Head's Dress Code Contest, 1996; Honorable Mention Short Grain Contest, 1993; Various Scholarships and Grants. Memberships: The Writer's Federation of Nova Scotia; The League of Canadian Poets. Address: 2375 June Street, Halifax NS B3K 4K3, Canada.

DYBEK Stuart, b. 10 Apr 1942, Chicago, Illinois, USA. Poet; Writer; Professor of English. m. Caren Bassett, 1966, 1 son, 1 daughter. Education: BS, 1964, MA, 1967, Loyola University; MFA, University of Iowa, 1973. Appointments: Teaching Assistant, 1970-72, Teaching and Writing Fellow, 1972-73, University of Iowa; Professor of English, Western Michigan University, 1973-; Guest Writer and Teacher, Michigan Council for the Arts' Writer in the Schools Program, 1973-92; Faculty, Warren Wilson MFA Program in Creative Writing, 1985-89; Visiting Professor of Creative Writing, Princeton University, 1990, University of California, Irvine, 1995; Numerous readings, lectures and workshops. Publications: Brass Knuckles, poems, 1979; Childhood and Other Neighbourhoods, stories, 1980; The Coast of Chicago, stories, 1990; The Story of Mist, short fiction and prose poems, 1994. Contributions to: Many anthologies and magazines. Honours: Award in Fiction, Society of Midwest Authors, 1981; Cliffdwellers Award for Fiction, Friends of American Literature, 1981; Special Citation, PEN/Hemingway Prize Committee, 1981; Michigan Council for the Arts Grants, 1981, 1992; Guggenheim Fellowship, 1982; National Endowment for the Arts Fellowships, 1982, 1994; Pushcart Prize, 1985; 1st Prize, O Henry Award, 1985; Nelson Algren Prize, 1985; Whiting Writers Award, 1985; Michigan Arts Award, Arts Foundation of Michigan, 1986; American Academy of Arts and Letters Award for Fiction, 1994; PEN/Malamud Award, 1995; Rockefeller Foundation Residency, Bellagio, Italy, 1996. Address: 310 Monroe, Kalamazoo, MI 49006, USA.

DYER Bernadette Elaine, b. 19 Apr 1946, Kingston, Jamaica, West Indies. Library Assistant. m. Terry Dyer, 15 May 1971, 2 sons, 1 daughter. Education: Art College Diploma, 1968. Appointments: Display Artist; Library Worker. Publications: Bite to Eat Place, 1995; An Invisible Accordian, 1995. Contributions to: Jones Ave; Alpha Beat Soup; Word Up; Poemata; Paper Plates; Artery; Next Exit; Egorag. Honours: Winner of The League of Canadian Black Artists Competition, 1995. Membership: The Canadian Poetry Association. Address: PO Box 22571, St George Postal Station, Toronto, Ontario M5S 1U0, Canada.

DYER Geraldine (Geri) A, b. 4 Nov 1921, Brooklyn, New York, USA. Artist; Poet. m. Ralph Dyer, 26 Oct 1956. Education: Brooklyn College and Brooklyn Museum Art School; New York Phoenix School of Design; Voice Culture, Madame Julia Gille. Appointments: Analyst; Executrix; Chairwoman, Artist Run Gallery; Fine and Graphic Artist; Exhibited in solo and group art shows; Poet. Contributions to: Brooklyn Historical Society; Brooklyn Heights Library; First Presbyterian Church; Cadman Towers Newsletter; Grace Church Anthology; Poems in: Edge of Twilight, 1994, Echoes of Yesterday, 1994, Parnassus of World Poets, 1994, 1995, Best Poems, National Library of Poetry, 1995, Tomorrow Who Knows, 1995. Honours: International Competition Award, Watercolour Certificate of Excellence, 1988; Outstanding Accomplishment, Alma E Wright Memorial Poetry Contest, 1989, 1990; 1st Prize for sonnet, Brooklyn Poetry Circle Memorial Contest, 1994; Several Editor's Choice Awards, 1994, 1995. Memberships: Former Vice President, Steering Committee, 1994-95, Brooklyn Poetry

Circle; Poetry Society of America; MOMA. Address: 101B Clark Street 9D, Brooklyn Heights, NY 11201, USA.

DYKEMAN Therese (Marie) B(oos), b. 11 Apr 1936, Iowa, USA. m. King John Dykeman, 7 Feb 1959, 1 son, 2 daughters. Education: BS, Creighton University, 1958; MA, Loyola University; PhD, Union Institute, Ohio, 1980. Appointments: Adjunct Professor, Loop City College, Chicago, 1965-67, Housatonic Community College, 1970-80, University of Bridgeport, 1980-90, Fairfield University, Connecticut, 1990-. Publications: Eleven Voices, 1990; American Women Philosophers 1650-1930; Six Exemplary Thinkers, 1993; Thinking of Women: Twelfth to the Twentieth Century. Contributions to: Western Voice, 1987-89. Honour: Honourable Mention, Connecticut Poetry Society, 1988. Memberships: Connecticut Poetry Society; Centre for Independent Study, President, 1989-91; Rhetoric Society of America; Modern Language Association; President, Danforth Associates of New England, 1992-93. Address: 47 Woods End Road, Fairfield, CT 06430, USA.

E

EARLEY Thomas (Tom) Powell, b. 13 Sept 1911, South Wales. m. 13 Apr 1939, 2 daughters. Education: Trinity College, Carmathen. Appointments: Senior English Master; Headmaster, Preparatory School. Publications: Welshman in Bloomsbury, 1968; The Sad Mountain, 1970; Rebel's Progress, 1979; All These Trees, 1992. Contributions to: New Statesman; Tribune; Poetry Wales; Anglo-Welsh Review; Planet; Welsh Nation; London Welshman; Western Mail; Second Aeon; Country Quest; Breakthrough; Poet; Outposts; Anthologies: Lilting House; Oxford Book of Welsh Verse; Voices of Today; London Lines; Anglo-Welsh Poetry. Honours: Poems discussed on BBC and read on several radio channels; Film of life work shown on television, 1970. Memberships: Elected Member, Welsh Academy of Writers; Welsh Union of Writers; Tutor, City Literary Institute; Poetry Society. Address: 21 Bloomsbury Square, London WC1A 2NS, England.

EARNEY Beverly (Verna), (Beverly Cole-Earney), b. 15 Aug 1951, Auckland, New Zealand. m. Michael David Frederick Earney, 9 Aug 1980, 2 sons, 1 daughter. Education: Diploma in German, Auckland Goethe Society, 1967; Hamilton Teachers' College, New Zealand; University of Waikato, New Zealand. Appointments: Policewoman, New Zealand Police Department; Freelance Artist; Assistant Curator, National Museum of Victoria; Operation Theatre Receptionist Clerk, Royal Victorian Eye and Ear Hospital, Melbourne. Publication: Beneath The Southern Cross, 1988. Contributions to: Earwig; Parnassus of World Poets, 1994, 1995; V Anthology of Olympoetry, 1995-96; World Poetry Anthology, 1996. Honours: Commendation, Poetry Day Competition, 1987; Melbourne Poetry Society Haiku Selections, 1989; Poetry Day Manuscripts Certificate, 1991. Membership: Melbourne Poetry Society. Address: 17 Vandeven Court, Ferntree Gully 3156, Victoria, Australia.

EASTON Earnest Lee, b. 1 May 1943, Indiana, USA. Education: AA, Loop College, Chicago, 1958; BA, University of Illinois, 1970; MPA, Syracuse University, 1971; MA, 1975; PhD, Cornell University, 1978. Contributions to: Wrapped Up In Nature, 1983. Honours: Honour Student, Loop College, 1967, University of Illinois, 1970; Fellowship, Syracuse University, 1970; Scholarship, University of Salzburg, 1969. Memberships: Hollywood Chaparral Poetry Society; California State Poetry Society; Naval Reserve Association; American Legion Guild of Authers and Composers; Concerts for Humanity. Address: 605 South Normandie Street, Los Angeles, CA 90005, USA.

EATON Charles Edward, b. 25 June 1916, Winston-Salem, North Carolina, USA. Poet; Writer. m. Isabel Patterson, 1950. Education: Duke University, 1932-33; BA, University of North Carolina, Chapel Hill, 1936; Princeton University, 1936-37; MA, English, Harvard University, 1940. Appointments: Instructor in Creative Writing, University of Missouri, 1940-42; Vice Consul, American Embassy, Rio de Janeiro, 1942-46; Professor of Creative Writing, University of North Carolina, 1946-52. Publications: Poetry: The Bright Plain, 1942; The Shadow of the Swimmer, 1951; The Greenhouse in the Garden, 1956; Countermoves, 1963; On the Edge of the Knife, 1970; The Man in the Green Chair, 1977; Colophon of the Rover, 1980; The Thing King, 1983; The Work of the Wrench, 1985; New and Selected Poems 1942-1987, 1987; A Guest on Mild Evenings, 1991; The Country of the Blue, 1994; The Fox and I, 1996; Novel: A Lady of Pleasure, 1993; Short stories: Write Me from Rio, 1959; The Girl from Ipanema, 1972; The Case of the Missing Photographs, 1978; New and Selected Stories 1959-1989, 1989. Contributions to: Periodicals. Honours: Bread Loaf Writers Conference Robert Frost Fellowship, 1941; Ridgely Torrence Memorial Award, 1951; Gertrude Boatwright Harris Award, 1955; Arizona Quarterly Awards, 1956, 1975, 1977, 1979, 1982; Roanoke-Chowan Awards, 1970, 1987, 1991; Oscar Arnold Young Award, 1971; O Henry Award, 1972; Alice Faye di Castagnola Award, 1974; Arvon Foundation Award, 1980; Hollins Critic Award, 1984; Brockman Awards, 1984, 1986; Kansas Quarterly Awards, 1987; North Carolina Literature Award, 1988; Fortner Award, 1993. Membership: American Academy of Poets. Address: 808 Greenwood Road, Chapel Hill, NC 27514, USA.

ECHERUO Michael, b. 14 Mar 1937, Umunomo, Nigeria. Education: PhD, Cornell University, Ithaca, USA, 1965. Appointments: Vice Chancellor, Imo State University, Owerri, 1981-. Publications

include: Mortality, 1968; Distanced: New Poems, 1975; Poets, Prophets and Professors, 1977; Editor, The Tempest by Shakespeare, 1980. Honour: All-Africa Competition for Poetry, 1963. Address: Vice Chancellor's Office, Imo State University, Owerri, Nigeria.

ECKLES Arden. See: **TICE Arden A.**

EDELMANN Carolyn Foote, b. 28 Nov 1937, Toledo, Ohio, USA. Author. m. Werner J Edelmann MD, 2 Sept 1961, div 1983, 2 daughters. Education: BS, St Mary of the Woods College, SMW, Indiana; 1st Member of community accepted for Princeton University Creative Writing Program: Advanced Poetry with Theodore Weiss, Galway Kinnell, and Stanley Plumly. Appointments: Began writing poetry, 1974; Gives regular readings in Princeton, New Hope, and Philadelphia areas; Appearances on public and commercial radio and television (poetry); Recent public radio appearance on WDVR FM, Sergeantsville; Recent readings: Encore Books, Princeton; Beaver Pond Poetry Forum, New Hope, Pennsylvania. Publication: Gatherings, 1987, with first public reading aboard QEII; Between The Dark and The Daylight, 1996 Articles in: Boston Magazine; Fellowship in Prayer; Packet Publications; Cape Cod Compass; Changes Magazine; Thirteen Magazine; Dream International Quarterly; Delaware Journal for Literature and Science; Kelsey Review. Contributions to: Journal of New Jersey Poets; US 1 Worksheets; Snake Nation Press; Up Against the Wall Mother; Psychological Perspectives; Maryland Review; Footwork; Voices International; In the Mail; New Jersey Poetry Monthly; Princeton University Alumni Weekly; Princeton Library Poems. Honours: Winner, New Jersey Poetry Monthly Prize, 1970's; William Carlos Williams Prize, Paterson Library, 1970's; Viola Hays Parsons Award, 1970's; Delaware Valley Poets Prize, 1990's; IE Magazine Contest Winner for Between The Dark and The Daylight, 1996. Memberships: National League of American Penwomen; Academy of American Poets; Poets and Writers; International Women's Writing Guild; National Writers' Union. Address: 203 Salem Court #10, Princeton, NJ 08540, USA.

EDLOSI Mario. See: **LEIH Grace Janet.**

EDMOND Lauris Dorothy, b. 2 Apr 1924, Dannevirke, New Zealand. University Tutor. m. Trevor Charles Edmond, 16 May 1945, 1 son, 5 daughters. Education: Certificate, Wellington Teachers' College, 1943; Speech Therapy Diploma, Christchurch Teachers' College, 1944; BA Hons, Waikato University, 1968; MA 1st Class Hons, Victoria University, 1972. Appointments: High School Teacher, French, English, 1967-73; Editor, Post Primary Teachers' Journal, 1973-81; Tutor, Massey University, 1980-; Visiting Performer, Festivals: Cambridge Poetry, 1985; Perth Arts, 1987; National Word, Canberra, 1987; Adelaide, 1988; World Poetry, Harbourfront, Toronto, 1989; Wellington Festival of the Arts, 1990; International Writers', Vancouver, 1993; Melbourne Writers', 1995. Publications include: In Middle Air, 1975; The Pear Tree and Other Poems, 1977; Wellington Letter: A Sequence of Poems, 1980; Seven, 1980; Salt From the North, 1980; Catching It, 1983; Selected Poems, 1984; Seasons and Creatures, 1986; Summer Near the Arctic Circle, 1988; New and Selected Poems, 1991; Scenes from a Small City, 1994; Selected Poems 1975-1994, 1994; In Position, 1996. Contributions to: Magazines and journals, New Zealand, Australia, UK; Anthologies. Honours: Best First Book Award, 1975; Lilian Ida Smith Award for Poetry, New Zealand PEN, 1987; Katherine Mansfield Memorial Fellowship, 1981; Commonwealth Poetry Prize, 1985; Writer's Residency, Deakin University, Melbourne, 1985; Order of the British Empire, 1986; Honorary DLitt, Massey University, 1988. Memberships: PEN New Zealand Centre; Wellington Poetry Society; Stout Research Centre Board, 1986-90; Founding Member, Peppercorn Press, 1990-. Address: 22 Grass Street, Oriental Bay, Wellington, New Zealand.

EDMOND Murray (Donald), b. 1949, New Zealand. Appointments: Director, Actor and Writer with the Town and Country Players, Wellington. Publications: Entering the Eye, 1973; Patchwork, 1978; End Wall, 1981; Letters and Paragraphs, 1987; From the Word Go, 1992; The Switch, 1994; Names Manes, 1996; Co-Editor, The New Poets of the 80's: Initiatives in New Zealand Poetry, 1987. Address: c/o University of Auckland, Private Bag 92019, Auckland, New Zealand.

EDSON Russell, b. 9 Apr 1935, USA. Poet; Writer. m. Frances Edson. Education: Art Students League, New York City; New School for Social Research, New York City; Columbia University; Black Mountain College, North Carolina. Publications: Poetry: Appearances: Fables and Drawings, 1961; A Stone is Nobody's: Fables and

Drawings, 1961; The Boundary, 1964; The Very Thing That Happens: Fables and Drawings, 1964; The Brain Kitchen: Writings and Woodcuts, 1965; What a Man Can See, 1969; The Childhood of an Equestrian, 1973; The Clam Theatre, 1973; A Roof with Some Clouds Behind It, 1975; The Intuitive Journey and Other Works, 1976; The Reason Why the Closet-Man is Never Sad, 1977; Edson's Mentality, 1977; The Traffic, 1978; The Wounded Breakfast: Ten Poems, 1978; With Sincerest Regrets, 1981; Wuck Wuck Wuck!, 1984; The Wounded Breakfast, 1985; Tick Tock, 1992; The Tunnel: Selected Poems, 1994; Fiction: Gulping's Recital, 1984; The Song of Percival Peacock, 1992. Honours: Guggenheim Fellowship, 1974; National Endowment for the Arts Grants, 1976, and Fellowship, 1982; Whiting Foundation Award, 1989. Address: 149 Weed Avenue, Stamford, CT 06902, USA.

EDWARDES Peter Ivan. Retired. Appointments: Bank Clerk; Officer, Merchant Navy; Teacher; War Service; RN Reserve and Royal Indian Naval VoLunteer Reserve; Journalist; Teacher. Contributions to: Anthologies: New Poets; 20th Century Poetry; Poetry Today; Golden Eagle Treasury; Editors Choice; Kaleidoscope of Verse; Poetry International; A Treasury of Modern Poets; Spring Poets; Autumn Anthology; Contemporary Poets; Modern Poets; Journals: Hants Telegraph; Best of Modern Verse; Havant News Extra; New Horizons; Weald Monthly; Muse; Havant and District Writers Circle Magazine; Broadcast various poetry and some set tomusic. Honours: Highly Commended, Poetry Competitions, analytical services, autumn, 1967, Spring, 1968; Summer, 1968; Member of the Order of the British Empire; 5 Medals for war service. Memberships: Founder, Havant and District Writers Circle, 1958; President, Fellow, International Academy of Poets. Address: 51 Kingston Crescent, North End, Portsmouth, Hampshire, England.

EDWARDS Mansell, b. 13 May 1921, Camborne, Cornwall, England. Civil Engineer. m. Betty Eloise Saunders, 7 July 1945, 1 son, 1 daughter. Education: Camborne School of Mines, 1936-40; HND, Willesden College of Technology, 1952. Appointments: Civil Engineer, 1958-. Contributions to: Uxbridge and West Drayton Gazette. Honours: Letter from HM the Queen, 1991; Letter of Thanks, Marylebone Cricket Club for poem in tribute to Sir George Allen, 1989. Memberships: Chartered Institute of Building; Electrical Power Engineers Association; Literary Review; Poetry Society; Marylebone Cricket Club. Address: Plymbryn, 131 Belmount Road, Uxbridge, Middlesex UB8 1QZ, England.

EDWARDS Mary. See: DARDEN Kathryn R.

EDWARDS Rebecca Jane, b. 4 April 1969, Batlow, New South Wales, Australia. Writer; Artist. 1 daughter. Education: BA with double major in Japanese Language and Culture, University of Queensland, 1992. Appointment: Writer-in-Residence, James Cook University, Townsville, Queensland, 1996. Publications: Eating the Experience, 1994; Contributor to, Eat the Ocean, 1996. Contributions to: Imago; Quadrant; Island Magazine; Northern Prospective; Northern Territories Literary Awards Anthology, 1995; Two Centuries of Australian Poetry, 2nd edition, 1995. Honours: Red Earth Award, Northern Territoires Section, 1989; Ford Memorial Medal, University of Queensland, 1991, 1992; Fifth Regional Illustrated Poetry Competition, 1995. Memberships: Queensland Writers' Centre; New South Wales Poets' Union; Fellowship, Australian Writers Queensland Artworkers' Alliance. Address: PO Box 1055, Spring Hill, Brisbane, Queensland 4004, Australia.

EDWIN Robert. See: VIERECK Peter.

EFRAIM Hai Chamiel Ben. See: CHAMIEL Haim Itzchak.

EGLINTON Edna Mary, b. 26 Oct 1924, London, England. Poet. m. George Arthur Eglinton, 12 Jan 1946, 1 son, 1 daughter. Publications: Pisgah, 1977; Holiday Viewing, 1982; Listen to Us (1 of 6 poets), 1983; Hands Together (with David Santer), 1994; Included in anthologies: New Poetry 9, 1983; A Mirror to Our Day, 1983; Affirming Flame, 1989; Company of Poets, 1, 2 and Journeys, 1989-1991; Included in books for children: Violet Poetry Book, 1986; Unicorn and Lions, 1987; Language in Colour, 1989; Big World Little World, 1992; One in a Million, 1992. Contributions to: Christian; Cobweb; Counterpoint; Distaff; Envoi; Foolscap; Franciscan; Frogmore; Hampshire Poets; Honest Ulsterman; Iota; Meridian; Odyssey; Orbis; Otter; Outposts; Palantir; Psychopoetica; Poems from Portsmouth; Poetry Nottingham; Poetry Wales; Phoenix; Schools Poetry Review;

South Coast Poetry Journal, California; Staple; 10th Muse; TOPS; Ver; Weyfarers; Woman Journalist. Honours: South Wales Miners' Eisteddfod, for English Poem, 1982; Humberside Children's Book Group Poetry Competition, 1991; Runner-up in minor competitions. Memberships: Company of Poets; Friends of the Arvon Foundation, Honorary Secretary, 1979-92; Society of Women Writers and Journalists. Address: 9 North Street, North Tawton, Devon EX20 2DE, England.

EIBEL Deborah, b. 25 June 1940, Montreal, Quebec, Canada. Poet. Education: BA, McGill University, 1960; AM, Radcliffe College, 1962; MA, Johns Hopkins University, 1971. Publications: Kayak Sickness, 1972; Streets Too Narrow for Parades, 1985; Making Fun of Travellers, 1991. Contributions to: Malahat Review; Canadian Woman Studies; Prairie Schooner; Anthologies: Celebrating Canadian Women; And Other Travels; Soundings. Honours: Arthur Davison Ficke Sonnet Award, Poetry Society of America, 1965; Arts Bursary, Canada Council, 1967; Residency, Leighton Artists' Colony, 1988. Memberships: Poetry Society of America; League of Canadian Poets. Address: 6657 Wilderton Avenue, Montreal, Quebec H3S 2L8 Canada.

EINARSSON Kristinn, b. 15 July 1948, Reykjavík, Iceland. Hydrologist. m. Margret Hallsdottir, 20 July 1984, 1 son, 2 daughters. Education: BSc, University of Copenhagen, 1977. Appointments: Hydrologist, Hydro Power Division, National Energy Authority, Reykjavik, 1978; General Secretary, Icelandic Hydrological Committee, 1986-. Publications: Imatra, 1970; A Bandi Rimbanda, 1973. Contributions to: Samvinnan; TMM. Memberships: Writers Union of Iceland, former member, Admission Committee. Address: Laugalaekur 3, IS 105 Reykjavik, Iceland.

EINBOND Bernard Lionel, b. 19 May 1939, New York, New York, USA. College Professor. m. Linda Saxe, 20 Feb 1977, 1 son, 1 daughter. Education: AB, 1958, AM, 1960, PhD, 1966, Columbia University. Appointments: Professor of English, Lehman College, 1968-; Adjunct Professor of English, Columbia University, New York City, 1989-90. Publication: The Coming Indoors and Other Poems, 1979; The Tree As It Is, 1994. Contributions to: Bogg; Modern Haiku; Sunbury; Frogpond. Honours: Keats Poetry Prize, 1975; Grand Prize Winner, Japan Air Lines Haiku Competition, 1988; Mirrors International Tanka Award, 1990. Membership: Haiku Society of America, President 1975. Address: PO Box 307, Fort George Station, New York, NY 10040, USA.

EL-SHAHAWY Ahmed Ibrahim, b. 12 Nov 1960, Domyetta, Egypt. Editor. Education: Graduate, Journalism, Assyot University. Appointments: Editor, Alahram Daily, 1986; Assistant Managing Director, Nisf-el-Dunya Weekly, 1990. Publications: Two Prayers for Love, 1988; Al Ahadith, 1991; The Book of Love, 1992; States of the Lover, 1995; The Hadilhs II, 1994. Contributions to: Al-Akhbar; Rose Al Yussuf; Al-Hayat; Sahab El Kheir; Al Arab; Al She'r; Al Kahera; Poet Lore; Odjak. Honours: 1st prize, Poetry Contest, Ministry of Culture, Egypt, 1983; Fellowship Certificate in Literary Writing, University of Iowa, USA, 1991; Certificate of Fellows of Literature, Aiwa University, 1991; Special Diploma in Culture and Science, Ionic Centre, Greece, 1994; UNESCO Literary Award, 1995. Memberships: Writers and Artists Society; Egyptian Writers Union; International Writing Programme; Press Syndicate. Address: Al-Ahram Newspaper, Al-Galaa Street, Cairo, Egypt.

ELBEE Miss. See: BAKER Lillian.

ELFICK Hilary Margaret, b. 25 April 1940, Warwickshire, England. Writer. m. Richard Elfick FCA, 15 Mar 1968, 1 son, 2 daughters. Education: Hons BA, English Language and History, Diploma in Education, University of Keele, 1962. Appointments: BBC Studio Manager (Radio), 1962; BBC Producer, Radio 4, 1964-68; Taught at Danes Hill Prep School, rising to Head of English and Sixth Form Tutor, 1988-92; Freelance for Settlement and Vietnamese Refugees and the Hospice Movement, 1993-; International Coordinator, Voices for Hospices. Publications: Folk and Vision, 1971; The Horse Might Sing, 1990; Unexpected Spring, 1992; Going Places, 1994. Contributions to: The Sydney Morning Herald; The Tablet; Envoi Magazine (poetry); Reviews for Orbis, Times Literary Supplement, Times Educational Supplement. Honour: Highly Commended Envoi International Poetry Competition, 1996. Memberships: Surrey Poets, Weyfarers; Joint Head, Young Writers Group South. Address: 74 Middle Street, Brockham, Betchworth, Surrey RH3 7HW, England.

ELIYAHU Aharon. See: **BULMAN Aaron E.**

ELKAYAM (Rachel) Shelley, b. 18 Nov 1955, Haifa, Israel. Literary Editor; Counsellor in Education and Organisation. Education: BA, Jewish History, Counselling, School of Education, Haifa University, 1976-80; MA, Counselling, School of Education, Hebrew University, Jerusalem, 1987. Appointments: Co-founder, East for Peace: Spokesperson, World Conference on Religion and Peace (WRCP), 1983, International Coordinator, Youth, 1984, Youth Against Racism, 1985; Chair, WRCP Israel, 1987-95; Chief Editor, Tarmil, Israel Defence Forces (IDF) Literature Publishing House 1991; Editor, MC, literary programmes, Gale Zahal (IDF Radio); Editor, Publication, Hebrew Writers' Association, Jerusalem, 1992-95; Speaker, Women's Federation for World Peace, 2nd Convention, Seoul, 1995; Speaker, Organiser, Situation of the Poetess in Israel meeting, Knesset Committee on Status of Women, 1995. Publications: English: Simple Days, 1983; Hebrew, Dutch: Selected Poems, 1984; Hebrew: The Essence of Oneself, 1981; The Lemon-Bud's Light, 1983; Song of the Architect, 1987; When the Mouse and the Snake First Met, 1987; Editor: Women's Poetry inside Jerusalem, audio cassette, 1995. Contributions to: Shdeemot, The Kibbutz Movement, 1979-80; Piyoot Dafshar Shevu'ee, 1982-84; Dante (The Hell) Anthology of Translation, 1984; Sheret V-Am, 1985; BBC; Kol-Israel (IBA Radio); On Translating Dante, Poetry International; After Jews and Arabs, Remaking Levantine Culture (Ammiel Alcalay), 1993; Modern Literatures of the Non-Western World, 1995; Literary Review, 1994. Honours: Keren Adler Young Poet Prize, Haifa University, 1980; Speech at Opening Assembly, XXII International Writers' Conference, 1985; Nominated to represent Sephardic Jewry, World Conference on Religion and Peace, International Council, 1986; Nominated Literary Editor, IDF Publication for Soldiers. Memberships: Executive Board, Hebrew Writers' Associations, Israel, Jerusalem; Editorial Council, New Options, USA; Poetry International; One World Poetry; Organiser, Rainbow Poetry Festival; Board, Council for Advancement of Women, Jerusalem; Founder, Editor, Poetess Platform; MC, Founder, 1st Poetesses' Festival, Jerusalem. Address: PO Box 9552, Malkha, Manachat, Jerusalem 96901, Israel.

ELKIN Roger James, b. 14 Mar 1943, Congleton, Cheshire, England. Curriculum Director in Continuing Education. m. Eileen Baddley, 22 Aug 1965, 1 son, 1 daughter. Education: BA Hons, History, 1965; PGCE, 1966; MA, Keele University, 1982. Appointment: Curriculum Director in Continuing Education, Leek College of Further Education, Leek, Staffordshire. Publications: Pricking Out, 1988; Points of Reference, 1996. Contributions to: Poetry Canada; Outposts; Orbis; Staple; Tees Valley Writer; Green Book; Prospice; Weyfarers; Acumen; Envoi; Poetry Nottingham; Resurgence; Psychopoetica; Tribune; Poetry Wales; Purple Patch; Reviews in: Stand (Wilfred Owen); Outposts (Ted Hughes, Frances Horowitz); Chapter in the Challenge of Ted Hughes, Edit Keith Sagar. Honours: Lake Aske Memorial Award, 1982, 1987; Douglas Gibson Memorial Award, 1986; Sylvia Plath Award, 1986; Howard Sergeant Memorial Award for Services to Poetry, 1987; Poet of the Year, 1991; Writers' Rostrum. Memberships: Co-Editor, Prospice issues 17-25, 1985-88; Editor, Envoi from issue 101, 1992; Founder, Organiser, Leek Arts Festival International Poetry Competition, 1983-92. Address: 44 Rudyard Road, Biddulph Moor, Stoke-on-Trent, Staffordshire ST8 7JN, England.

ELLIOT Alistair, b. 13 Oct 1932, Liverpool, England. Poet; Verse Translator; Former Librarian. m. 1956, 2 sons. Education: MA, Litterae Humaniores, Christ Church, Oxford. Appointments: Actor, 1957-59; Librarian: Kensington Public Library, London, 1959-61; Keele University, 1961-65; Pahlavi University, Iran, 1965-67; Newcastle University, 1967-82; His version of Medea performed at Almeida Theatre, Islington, London and in New York, with actress Diana Rigg winning awards (including Tony Award, 1994). Publications: Contentions, 1977; Kisses, 1978; Talking Back, 1982; On the Appian Way, 1984; My Country, 1989; Turning the Stones, 1993; Translations: Verlaine: Femmes Hombres, 1979; Heine: The Lazarus Poems, 1979; French Love Poems, 1991; Italian Landscape Poems, 1993; Euripides: Medea, 1993; Editor: Virgil and Dryden: The Georgics, 1981. Contributions to: Observer; Times Literary Supplement; Listener; London Magazine; London Review of Books; Poetry Review; Stand; New Statesman; Spectator; Paris Review; North Dakota Review; Arion; PN Review; Poetry London; Poetry Now; Critical Inquiry; Encounter; Thames Poetry; Many more. Honours: Grant, Arts Council of Great Britain, 1979; Ingram Merrill Award, 1983, 1989; Prudence Farmer Award, 1983, 1991; Djerassi Foundation Fellowship, 1984. Address: 27 Hawthorn Road, Newcastle-upon-Tyne NE3 4DE, England.

ELLIOT Bruce. See: **FIELD Edward.**

ELLIS Mayne, (Y S Lem), b. 20 Mar 1954, Vancouver, British Columbia, Canada. Education: University studies. Appointments: Secretary; PA; Retail Clerk; Freelance Editor; Gas Station Attendant; Church Caretaker. Publications: For PHE appeared in Listen! Songs and Poems of Canada, 1972; Scientists Find Universe Awash in Tiny Diamonds, appeared in Cries of the Spirit, 1991. Contributions to: Orbis; Condisitons; Rites; Phoenix; Earthi's Daughters; Exit 13. Honours: Prize for Ice is Uncertain, Phoenix, Winter, 1986; Prize for Glacier, Writer's Poetry Contest. Address: c/o 115 Wells Way, London SE5 7SZ, England.

ELLIS Royston, (Richard Tresillian), b. 10 Feb 1941, England. Author; Travel Writer; Editor. 1 son. Publications: Jiving to Gyp, 1959; Rave, 1960; The Mattress Flowers, 1961; The Rainbow Walking Stick, 1962; The Cherry Boy, 1967; Burn Up, 1965. Contributions to: Penguin Book of Homosexual Verse; Various magazines; TV and live performances reading poetry to music. Honour: Dominica National Day Poetry prize, 1966. Address: Royal Cottage, Bentota, Sri Lanka.

ELLSON Peter Kenneth, b. 22 July 1937, Surrey, England. Poet; Painter; Publisher. m. (1) Barbara Norman, 1966, dec 1972, (2) Anke Kornmuller, 1978, div 1993. Publications: Poems, 1978; Halde, 1983. Contributions to: Tuba Magazine; New Leaf. Memberships: Poetry Book Fair Organiser, Edinburgh Fringe Festival, 1980-82. Address: Route des Vans, La Republique, 30160 Bordezac-Gard, France.

ELMAN Richard, b. 23 Apr 1934, Brooklyn, New York, USA. Professor. m. Alice Goode Elman, 12 Apr 1978. Education: BA, Syracuse University, 1955; MA, Stanford University, 1957. Appointments: Notre Dame University, 1990; Numerous other professorships, University of Michigan, University of Pennsylvania, Columbia University and State University of New York at Stony Brook. Publications: The Man Who Ate New York, 1973; Homage to Fats Navarro, 1976; In Chantales, 1980; Cathedral-Tree-Train, 1993. Contributions to: New Yorker; St Marks Poetry Newsletter; Witness; Commonwealth; Nation. Honour: Prix Schmnatte, Halifax, 1980. Membership: PEN. Address: PO Box 216, Stony Brook, NY 11790, USA.

ELMQUIST Evangeline, b. Hoffmann, Minnesota, USA. Writer. Education: Bible Study Course; Writers Correspondence Course. Appointments: Writer; President of a Writer's Club, 1968. Publications: A Treasure of Memories Dearest to My Heart, 1983; Beautiful Horizons, 1983; Poems of a Singing Heart, 1971. Contributions to: Writers Journal; National Library of Poetry; Poetry Forum; Express Magazine; Iliad Press; Arcadia Poetry Press; Fine Arts Press; World of Poetry; Author/Poet Magazine; American Poetry Anthology; Writers Journal; Camarederie Magazine; Poets Guild; Dover Beach Poetry Press; Poetry International; Sparrow Grass Poetry Forum; Creative Arts. Honours: Editor's Choice Award for Outstanding Achievement in Poetry, National Library of Poetry, 1994, 1995; Sound of Poetry Award for Cassette Tape of poems, The Singing Heart, 1994 and Memories Live Forever, 1995; Poet of the Year, Writers Journal, 1994; Editor's Special Award for Writing, Writers Journal, 1985; Laureate Award for Writing in Writers Journal, 1990; Named Poet of the Year, Poets on Parade, 1976. Memberships: Poetry Publishers Association; International Society of Poets. Address: Rt 1, Box 82, Hoffman, MN 56339, USA.

ELMQUIST May Violetta, b. Hoffman, Minnesota, USA. Writer. Education: Bible Study Course; Correspondence Courses and Studies. Appointment: Writer. Publications: A Bouquet of Verse from the Garden of My Heart, 1968; May's Memory Album, 1971; Seasons of My Heart, 1982; Through Gardens of Splendour, 1983. Contributions to: Harbor Lights; Bluenose Rambler; Express Magazine; Hob Nob; UAP Press; Quill Books; The Christian Way; Nutmugger; Vesto Publications; Golden Dreams Anthology. Honours: Award for Best Poem in Bluenose Rambler, 1971; Poet of the Month; Honorable Mention for Poem in Clover Collection of Verse, 1969; Quill Book Awards; Atlas Award; Accomplishment of Merit Award; Creative Art Science, 1992; Poetry Read on TV Channel America, 1995. Memberships: Minnesota Society of Poetry; League of Minnesota Poets. Address: Rt # 1, Box 82, Hoffman, MN 56339, USA.

ELMSLIE Kenward Gray, b. 27 Apr 1929, New York, New York, USA. Poet; Librettist. Education: BA, Harvard University, 1950.

Publications: The Champ, 1968, new edition, 1994; Album, 1969; Circus Nerves, 1971; Motor Disturbance, 1971; The Orchid Stories, 1972; Tropicalism, 1976; The Alphabet Work, 1977; Communications Equipment, 1979; Moving Right Along, 1980; Bimbo Dirt, 1981; 26 Bars, 1986; Sung Sex, 1989; Pay Dirt (with Joe Brainard), 1992; Champ Dust, 1994; Bare Bones, 1995; Opera libretti: Lizzie Borden, 1966; Miss Julie, 1966; The Sweet Bye and Bye, 1973; The Seagull, 1974; Washington Square, 1976; Three Sisters, 1986; Play: City Junket, 1987; Muiscal Play: Postcards on Parade, 1993; Reference work: Kenward Elmslie: A Bibliogaphical Profile (by William C Bamberger), 1993. Contributions to: Paris Review; Art and Literature; New American Writing; Oxford Review; Partisan Review; Sun and Moon; Folder; Big Sky; Locus Solus; Adventures in Poetry; Conjunctions; Oblek; Mississippi Review; Sun; United Artists; Barney; Mother; Brooklyn Review; Brilliant Corners; Oink!; Penguin Modern Poets 24; Best American Poetry, 1988; The Beat Scene; A Century in Two Decades. Honour: Frank O'Hara Poetry Award, 1971. Membership: American Society of Composers, Authors and Publishers. Address: Poets Corner, Calais, VT 05648, USA.

ELSBERG John William, b. 4 Aug 1945, New York, New York, USA. Publications Manager. m. Constance Waeber, 17 June 1967, 1 son. Education: BA, Columbia College, 1967; MA, University of Cambridge, England, 1973. Appointments: Editor in Chief, US Army Centre of Military History; Adjunct Professor, University of Maryland; Lecturer, Northern Virginia Community College; Editor, Bogg Magazine, 1980-. Publications: Cornwall and Other Poems, 1972; Poems by Lyn Lifshin and John Elsberg, 1979; The Price of Reindeer, 1979, 1983; Walking as a Controlled Fall, 1980; Home-style Cooking on Third Avenue, 1982; Limey and the Yank, 1982, 1981; Torn Nylon Comes with the Night, 1987; 10 or Less, 1989; The Affair, 1991; Father Poems, 1993; Offsets, 1994; The Randomness of E, 1995. Contributions to: Poetry Now; Gargoyle; Tribune; Orbis; Cambridge Review; Maryland Poetry Review; Amelia; Real Poetry; New Hope International; Outposts; Impulse; New Laurel Review; Hanging Loose; Lost and Found Times; Printed Matter; Wind; Tight; Atom Mind; Ruby; Membrane; Blue Unicorn. Memberships: Fellow, Virginia Centre for the Creative Arts; Writers' Centre, Bethesda, Maryland; Poets and Writers; Poetry Committee, Folger Shakespeare Library; Poetry Society of America. Address: 422 North Cleveland Street, Arlington, VA 22201, USA.

ELTON William R, b. 15 Aug 1921, New York, New York, USA. Professor. m. Mary Elizabeth Bowen, 1970, div 1974. Education: Studied at Columbia University and University of London; PhD, Ohio State University, 1956. Appointments: Professor, University of California, Riverside, 1955-69; Professor of English Literature, Graduate School, City University of New York, 1969-. Publications: Wittgenstein's Trousers: Poems, 1991; Circus in Nirvana: Poems, forthcoming. Contributions to include: Partisan Review; Poetry New York; Denver Quarterly; Christian Science Monitor; Medicinal Purposes; Experiment. Memberships: Honorary Member, Shelley Society. Address: c/o PhD Program in English, Graduate School, City University of New York, 33 West 42 Street, New York, NY 10036, USA.

ELWES Clare, b. 8 Oct 1966, London, England. Writer. Education: International Baccalaureate, 1984; BA, Honours, Visual and Performing Arts, 1988. Appointments: Film and television work; Designer and Performer, theatre festivals. Honours: Hopkins Society of Ireland Certificate of Merit, 1991; International Summer School. Membership: Poetry Society. Address: 24 Cheyne Row, London SW3 5HL, England.

EMANUEL James Andrew, b. 15 June 1921, Nebraska, USA. University Professor. m. Mattie Etha Johnson, div 1974, 1 son, dec. Education: BA summa cum laude, Howard University, Washington DC, 1950; MA, Northwestern University, Evanston, Illinois, 1953; PhD, Columbia University, New York, 1962. Appointments: Lecturer through to Professor of English, City College of the City University of New York, 1957-84; Fulbright Professor, Universities of Grenoble, 1968-69, Warsaw, 1975-76; Visiting Professor, University of Toulouse, 1971-73, 1979-81. Publications: The Treehouse and Other Poems, 1968; Panther Man, 1970; Black Man Abroad: The Toulouse Poems, 1978; A Chisel in the Dark, 1980; A Poet's Mind, 1983; The Broken Bowl, 1983; Deadly James and Other Poems, 1987; The Quagmire Effect, 1988; Whole Grain: Collected Poems, 1958-89, 1991; De la Rage au Coeur, 1992; Blues in Black and White, 1992, with Godelieve Simons. Contributions to: Kenyon Review; New York Times; Phylon; Negro Digest/Black World; Freedomways; Afro American History Bulletin;

African American Review; Freelance; Interculture; Midwest Quarterly; Ararat; Negative Capability; La Vague á l'Ame; Inédit; Les Elytres du Hanneton; Jubilarni Sarajevski Dani Poezije; Change; La Traductière; Obaje; Il Tarocco; Rovesnik; Article, Entre bruit et silence: le poète trans Jean Migrenne, 1996 issue Sources in Namur, Belgium. Honours: Flame Magazine Citation of Merit, 1958; Black American Literature Forum Special Distinction Award, 1978; Special Tutor, J Emanuel Poems at University of Toulouse, 1979-80. Memberships: Association Festival Franco-Anglais de Poésie in Paris; Assocation Grenier Jane Tony in Brussels. Address: Boite Postale 339, 75006 Paris Cedex 06, France.

EMBERSON Ian McDonald, b. 29 July 1936, Hove, Sussex, England. Retired Librarian. Publications: Doodles in the Margins of My Life, 1981; Swallows Return, 1986; Pirouette of Earth, novel in verse, 1995. Contributions to: Pennine Platform; Envoi; Orbis; New Hope International; Bradford Poetry Quarterly; Dalesman; Countryman. Honour: William Alwyn International Poetry Society Award, 1981. Memberships: Pennine Poets; Brontë Society; Gaskell Society. Address: Eastroyd, 1 Highcroft Road, Todmorden, Lancashire OL14 5LZ, England.

EMMOTT Stewart Earl, b. 6 Oct 1950, Manchester, England. Freelance Author and Archivist. 1 son. Education: Part 1 English Literature, Drama, Hull University Teachers' Training College, 1971-73. Appointments: Founder, Archive of Modern Poetry, Fylde Coast. Publications: Forgotten Woodland, unpublished, 1968-69; Poetical Offerings, 1970; Plaintive Poems, 1973; The Frailest Flowers, 1975; Burnt Leaves, 1976; Little Verses, 1978; Fading Innocence, 1980; A College Romance, a 3 act play, 1981; The Northern Romantic, 1981; Particles of Rain, new poems, 1985; Patterns of Life, new poems, 1986; Catching the Rain, 1987; Burning the Sad Dreams, Collection of Poems 1989 to 1993, unpublished; Hidden Worlds, 1990; The Dark Harvest, 1991; Short Story: Ghosts of the Past; Poem: The Ghost of a Girl; Unpublished: The Children of the Previous Owner. Contributions to: The Parnassus of World Poets' Anthology, 1994; Viking Gifts, 1996; Poems; Dalesman; Cumbria Life; Lancashire Life; Record; Preston Arts News; The Gothic Society Magazine. Memberships: Life Member, Cumbrian Trust for Nature Conservation. Address: 15 Bolton Avenue, Carleton, Poulton le Fylde, Lancashire FY6 7TW, England.

EMRICK Ernestine Hoff, b. 25 Oct 1918, Chicago, Illinois, USA. Teacher; Pastor's Wife. m. Leland B Emrick, 31 May 1941, 1 son. Education: BS Music, 1940. Appointments: Public school music and art supervisor; Library technician, Educational Media Department. Publications: Look to the Light, 1954; His Kingdom in My Kitchen, 1955. Contributions to: Prize Poems of the National Federation of State Poetry Societies, 1978, 1980, 1981, 1985, 1987, 1992; Bretheren Life and Thought; Gospel Messenger; Time of Singing; Christian Century; Cat Fancy; CQ; Anthologies: This is Chaparral; His Pen in Her Hand; Crossroads; Brief Encounters; Poetry Fullerton. Honours: California Federation of Chaparral Poets: Golden Pegasus Award, 1988, Archie Rosenhouse Memorial Award, 1988, Theme Poem, 1976; National Federation of State Poetry Societies Awards, 1975-94; Beth Martin Haas Memorial Award, California Federation of Chaparral Poets, 1995. Memberships: California Federation of Chaparral Poets; California State Poetry Society; Associate Editor, CQ, CSPS publications, annual CSPS contest Chairman. Address: 2780 Hillcrest Drive, La Verne, CA 91750, USA.

ENCARNACION Pisonero, b. 7 June 1951, Valladolid, Spain. Publications: El Jardin de las Hesperides; Si se Cubre de musgo la Memoria; Adamas. Contributions to: Rey Legarto; Alaluz; Religion y Cultura; Empresa de Mudanzas. Memberships: Pertenezco a la Asociacion de Escritores y Artistas Espanoles. Address: Lope de Haro 74D, 28039 Madrid, Spain.

ENEKWE Onuora Osmond, b. 12 Nov 1942, Afa, Nigeria. Researcher; Lecturer. m. Josephine Chioma Adinde, 9 Apr 1974, 1 son, 6 daughters. Education: BA Hons, English, University of Nigeria, 1971; MFA, Creative Writing, 1974, MPhil Theatre, 1977, PhD Theatre, 1982, Columbia University. Appointments: Senior Lecturer, 1980-84, Associate Professor 1984, Coordinator, Department of Dramatic Arts 1986-89, Associate Dean, Faculty of Arts, 1989-91, University of Nigeria. Publications: Broken Pots, 1977; Marching to Kilimanjaro, 1991. Contributions to: Mundus Artium: Selection of African Writers and Artists, 1977; Aftermath (anthology), 1977; Rhythms of Creation, 1978; Jungle Muse, 1987; Anthill Annual, 1989; Literary Review, 1991; English for Senior Secondary Schools; Daily Times; Weekend

Concord. Honour: Commonwealth Poetry Prize Nomination, 1978. Memberships: New York State Poets in the Schools Inc, 1974-82; Assistant Editor, 1978-87, Editor 1987-, Okike: An African Journal of New Writing. Address: Department of Dramatic Arts, University of Nigeria, Nsukka, Nigeria.

ENG Steve, (John Bredon), b. 31 Oct 1940, San Diego, California, USA. Author; Literary Journalist. m. Anne Jeanne Kangas, 15 May 1969, 2 sons, 2 daughters. Education: BA, English Literature, George Washington University, Washington, DC, USA, 1963; MS Education (Counseling), Portland State University, Portland, Oregon, USA, 1973. Publications: Edited Collections: Bob Lind, Elusive Butterfly and Other Lyrics, 1971; Mary Elizabeth Counselman, The Face of Fear and Other Poems, 1984; Lucile Coleman, Hunter of Time: Gnomic Verses, 1984; John Gawsworth, Torreros, 1990; Editor with Marge Simon: Poets of the Fantastic: An Anthology of Horror, Fantasy and Science Fiction, 1992; Forthcoming collection: Yellow Rider and Other Lyrics, 1997. Contributions to: The Twilight Zone; Eldritch Tales; The Romantist; Night Songs; Cumberland Poetry Review; The Arkham Collector; The Lyric; Amazing; Fantasy Tales (UK); Argonaut; Whispers; Star Line; Fantasy Commentator. Honours: Focus Poet, Rachael, 1971; 1st Poetry Prize, The Rufus, 1973; American Poets Fellowship Society Certificate of Merit, 1973; Co-winner, Rhysling Awd for Short Poem, Science Fiction Poetry Association, 1979; 2nd Prize, Narrative Ballad, Chapparal Poets, 1980; Best Writer: Poetry, Small Press Writers and Artists Organization, 1979, 1983. Memberships: Small Press Writers and Artists Organization, Poetry Consultant, 1980-90; Chmn, poetry panel, 1987; Member, Broadcast Music Inc (BMI), Blue Meadow Music, for original songs including five songs recorded by Lonnie Lynne La Cour, written by Steve Eng, 1972-. Address: Po Box 111864, Nashville, TN 37222, USA.

ENGELHARDT Robert Michael, b. 19 Sept 1964, Albany, New York, USA. Writer; Poet. Education: College of Saint Rose, 1984. Publications: Release..., 1992; Sacred Days, 1994; Hearse, 1995. Contributions to: Atlier; Mobius; The Charles Bukowski Newsletter #10; Delirium; Pumpkinhead; Chronicles of Disorder; Happy Kitty; Mertz! Times Union; Source; Metroland; Volume. Membership: Hudson Valley Writers Guild.

ENGELS Deen. See: **FERMIN Bert.**

ENGELS John (David), b. 19 Jan 1931, South Bend, Indiana, USA. Professor of English; Poet; Writer. m. Gail Jochimsen, 1957, 4 sons, 2 daughters. Education: AB, University of Notre Dame, 1952; University College, Dublin, 1955; MFA, University of Iowa, 1957. Appointments: Instructor, Norbert College, West de Pere, Wisconsin, 1957-62; Assistant Professor, 1962-70, Professor of English, 1970-, St Michael's College, Winooski Park, Vermont; Visiting Lecturer, University of Vermont, 1974, 1975, 1976; Slaughter Lecturer, Sweet Briar College, 1976; Writer-in-Residence, Randolph Macon Woman's College, 1992. Publications: Poetry; The Homer Mitchell Place, 1968; Signals from the Safety Coffin, 1975; Blood Mountain, 1977; Vivaldi in Early Fall, 1981; The Seasons in Vermont, 1982; Weather-Fear: New and Selected Poems 1958-1982, 1983; Cardinals in the Ice Age, 1987; Walking to Cootehill: New and Selected Poems 1958-1992, 1993; Big Water, 1995; Other: Writing Techniques (with Norbert Engels), 1962; Experience and Imagination (with Norbert Engels), 1965; The Merrill Guide to William Carlos Williams (Editor), 1969; The Merrill Checklist of William Carlos Williams (Editor), 1969; The Merrill Studies in Paterson (Editor), 1971. Honours: Bread Loaf Writers Conference Scholarship, 1960, and Robert Frost Fellowship, 1976; Guggenheim Fellowship, 1979. Address: c/o Department of English, St Michael's College, Winooski Park, VT 05404, USA.

ENGLAND Gerald, b. 21 Dec 1946, Ackworth, England. Insurance Agent; Poet; Editor. m. Christine Ann Smedley, 22 June 1974, 2 sons. Education: Strathclyde University, 1964-66; Leeds College of Technology, 1967-68; HNC Chemistry, Sheffield Polytechnic, 1969-71; Open University, 1973-74. Appointments: Technician, Sheffield University, 1969-74; Agent, Britannic Assurance, 1974-; Editor, Headland, 1969-79, New Hope International, 1980-; Secretary, Yorkshire Poets Association, 1971-73. Publications: Poetic Sequence for Five Voices, 1966; Mousings, 1970; The Wine, The Women and the Song, 1972; For Her Volume One, 1972; Meetings at the Moors Edge, 1976; The Rainbow, 1980; Daddycation, 1982; Futures, (with Christine England), 1986; Stealing Kisses, 1992. Contributions to: Bogg; Brussel Sprout; Candelabrum; Crooked Roads; Envoi; Folio; Green's Magazine; Haiku Quarterly; Hybrid; Inkshed;

International Journal on World Peace; Krax; Legend; Lo Straniero; Moorlands Review; New Wave; Owen Wister Review; Pennine Ink; Periaktos; Pididdle; Prophetic Voices; Radio Void; Verve; Vincent Bros Review; Waterways; Wormwood Review; Z Miscellaneous; Numerous others worldwide. Memberships: Yorkshire Dialect Society, Council Member; Pennine Poets; Association of Little Presses; Tameside Arts Association; International Writers and Authors Association. Address: 20 Werneth Avenue, Gee Cross, Hyde, Cheshire SK14 5NL, England.

ENGLER Robert Klein, b. 20 May 1948, Chicago, Illinois, USA. Tutor; Writer. Education: Divinity Degree, University of Chicago, 1976. Appointment: Chairman, Social Sciences Department, Richard J Daley College, Chicago. Publication: Sonnets by Degree, 1986. Contributions to: Christopher Street; James Wright Review; Tribe. Honour: Illinois Arts Council Award for Poetry, 1989. Address: Richard J Daley College, 7500 South Polaski, Chicago, IL 60652, USA.

ENGLISH June Vincent, b. 16 June 1936, Dover, Kent, England. Writer. m. (1) Alan E John, 9 May 1959, 1 son. m. (2) John Brian English, 7 July 1979, 1 son. Education: BA, English and History, University of Kent, 1989; MA, Humanities, Christchurch, England, 1992. Appointments: Writer; Teacher, Creative Writing at Local Schools. Contributions to: Acumen; Psychopoetica; Poetry Digest; Peace & Freedom; Dam; Hen House; Other Small Press Magazines. Memberships: The Poetry Society. Address: Four Winds, Pommeus Lane, Ripple, Nr Deal, Kent CT14 8HZ, England.

ENRIGHT D(ennis) J(oseph), b. 11 Mar 1920, Leamington, Warwickshire, England. Education: MA, Downing College, Cambridge, 1946. Appointments: Professor of English in the Far East, 1947-70; Director, Chatto & Windus Publishers, 1974-82. Publications: The Laughing Hyena and Other Poems, 1953; Bread Rather Than Blossoms, 1956; Some Men are Brothers, 1960; Selected Poems, 1969; Daughters of Earth, 1972; The Terrible Shears: Scenes From a Twenties Childhood, 1974; Sad Ires and Others, 1975; Paradise Illustrated, 1978; A Faust Book, 1979; Collected Poems, 1987; Selected Poems, 1990; Under the Circumstances, 1991; Old Men and Comets, 1993. Honours include: Queen's Gold Medal for Poetry, 1981; OBE, 1991. Address: 35A Viewfield Road, London SW18 5TD, England.

ENSLIN Theodore (Vernon), b. 25 Mar 1925, Chester, Pennsylvania, USA. Poet; Writer. m. (1) Mildred Marie Stout, 1945, div 1961, 1 son, 1 daughter, (2) Alison Jane Jose, 1969, 1 son. Education: Public and Private; Studied composition with Nadia Boulanger. Appointment: Columnist, The Cape Codder, Orleans, Massachusetts, 1949-56. Publications: Poetry: The Work Proposed, 1958; New Sharon's Prospect, 1962; The Place Where I Am Standing, 1964; To Come To Have Become, 1966; The Diabelli Variations and Other Poems, 1967; Poems 1967, 1967; The Poems, 1970; Forms, 5 volumes, 1970-74; The Median Flow: Poems 1943-1973, 1974; Ranger, Ranger 2, 2 volumes, 1979, 1980; Music for Several Occasions, 1985; Case Book, 1987; Love and Science, 1990; A Sonare, 1994; Fiction: 2 + 12, short stories, 1979; Play: Barometric Pressure 29-83 and Steady, 1965; Other: Mahler, 1975; The July Book, 1976. Honours: Nieman Award for Journalism, 1955; National Endowment for the Arts Grant, 1976. Address: RFD Box 289, Kansas Road, Milbridge, MA 04658, USA.

EPSTEIN George, b. 28 Aug 1919, New York, New York, USA. Salesman; Semi-retired Poet. m. Mae Gold, 30 Aug 1942, 1 son, 1 daughter. Appointments: Salesman, Seiko Watches; Poet. Publication: Ramblin' Round the North Country, 1986. Contributions to: Theodore Roosevelt Association Journal; American Jewish Historical Association; Mary Hitchcock Hospital Clarion; Courier; Boston Globe; Union Leader; Mountaineer. Honour: Honourable Mention, Mountaineer. Membership: Founder, Co-Director, Poetry Council of Bethlehem. Address: Main Street, PO Box 122, Bethlehem 03574, USA.

ERDRICH (Karen) Louise, b. 7 June 1954, Little Falls, Minnesota, USA. Writer; Poet. m. Michael Anthony Dorris, 10 Oct 1981, 7 children. Education: BA, Dartmouth College, 1976; MA, Johns Hopkins University, 1979. Appointments: Visiting Poet and Teacher, North Dakota State Arts Council, 1977-78; Writing Instructor, Johns Hopkins University, 1978-79; Communications Director, Editor of Circle of the Boston Indian Council, 1979-80. Publications: Fiction: Love Medicine, 1984, augmented edition, 1993; The Beet Queen, 1986; Tracks, 1988; The Crown of Columbus (with Michael Anthony

Dorris), 1991; The Bingo Palace, 1994. Poetry: Jacklight, 1984; Baptism of Desire, 1989. Other: Imagination, textbook, 1980. Contributions to: Anthologies; American Indian Quarterly; Atlantic; Frontiers; Kenyon Review; Ms; New England Review; New York Times Book Review; New Yorker; North American Review; Redbook; Others. Honours: MacDowell Colony Fellowship, 1980; Yaddo Colony Fellowship, 1981; Dartmouth College Visiting Fellow, 1981; National Magazine Fiction Awards, 1983, 1987; National Book Critics Circle Award for Best Work of Fiction, 1984; Virginia McCormick Scully Prize for Best Book of the Year, 1984; Best First Fiction Award, American Academy and Institute of Arts and Letters, 1985; Guggenheim Fellowship, 1985-86; First Prize, O Henry Awards, 1987. Address: c/o Rambar & Curtis, 19W 45th Street, New York, NY 10036, USA.

ERICKSON Rollie, b. 17 Jan 1953, Madison, Wisconsin, USA. Artist. m. Cass Erickson, 4 July 1992. Education: BFA, State University of New York at Purchase, 1981. Appointment: Artist (painter). Contributions to: Wordimage; Asheville Poetry Review. Address: POB 867, Weaverville, NC 28787, USA.

ERLENDSSON Eyvindur, b. 14 Feb 1937, Grindavik, Iceland. Theatre and Film Director; Writer; Poet; Designer; Painter; Actor; Teacher. m. Sjofn Halldorsdottir, 26 May 1958, 3 sons, 2 daughters. Education: Master of Cabinet Making, 1958; Diploma, Acting School of National Theatre, Reykjavík, 1960; Reykjavík Art School, 1958-59; BA, State Institute of Theatrical Art, Moscow, 1967. Publications: Ode for a Grandfather, poem in living pictures, 1981; A memorandum of a picture on a wall and the Holy Ghost in the kitchen drawer, Icelandic Radio, 1978.. Contributions to: Timarit Mals og Menninger; Lesbok Morgunblaosins; Pjoviljinn; Albyoublaoio-Helgarposturinn; Utvorour; Baendablaoio; RUV-TV; RUV-Radio; translations of Plays for the National theatre, Icelandic Theatre School and others. Memberships: Writers Union of Iceland; Icelandic Filmakers Association; Actors Union of Iceland; Theatre Directors Association of Iceland. Address: Hatun, Offusi, 801 Selfoss, Iceland.

ERLENDSSON Sverrir Pall, b. 15 July 1948, Iceland. Teacher. Education: BA, Icelandic Grammar and Litterature, History, University of Iceland, 1974. Appointments: Teacher, Middle School of Neskaupstadur, 1969-70; Akureyri Junior College, 1974; Social Activities Counsellor, 1976; Part-time jobs, Reporter, Programme Producer. Publications: You and Home, 1988; Litlar Sogur, short stories, 1992. Membership: Writers Union of Iceland. Address: Asvegi 29, IS 600 Akureyri, Iceland.

ESBER Ali Ahmad Said, (Adonis), b. 1930, Oassabin, Syria. Associate Professor; Poet. Education: BA, Damascus University, Syria, 1951-54; PhD, University of St Joseph, Beirut, 1970-73. Appointments: Professor, Arabic Literature, Lebanese University, 1971-85; PhD Advisor, University of St Joseph, Beirut, 1971-85; Visiting Professor, Arabic Literature, Université de la Sorbonne Nouvelle, France, 1980-81; Invited Lecturer, Arab Poetics, College de France, Paris, 1983; Invited Lecturer, Modernity in Arab Culture, Georgetown University, 1985; Associate Professor, Arab Poetry, Geneva University, 1989-95. Publications: Poetry in French: Chants de Mihyar le Damascene, 1983; Tombeau pour New York suivi de Prologue a l'histoire des rois des ta'ifa et de Ceci est mon nom, 1986; Le Temps les Villes, 1990; Célébrations, 1991; Chronique des branches, 1991; Mémoire du vent, anthology, 1991; Soleils Seconds, 1994; Singuliers, 1995. In English: An Introduction to Arab Poetics, 1990; The Pages of Day and Night, 1994. Numerous Poetry in Arabic Published. Honours: Prix des Amis du Livre, Beirut, 1968; Syria-Lebanon Award, International Poetry Forum, Pittsburgh, 1971; National Prize of Poetry, Beirut, 1974; Officer des Arts et des Lettres, Ministry of Culture, Paris, 1983; Exhibit at the Maison de la Poésie, Paris, 1984; Poet-in-Residence, Georgetown University, 1985; Guest of Honour, Pen Club Week, New York, 1986; Grand Prix des Biennales Internationales de la Poésie de Liege, Brussels, 1986; Prix Jean Malnieu-étranger, Marseille, 1991; Feronia-Cita di Fiano, Rome, 1993; Nazim Hikmat Prize, Istanbul, 1994; Prix, Méditerranée-Etranger, Paris, 1995; Prize of Lebanese Culture Forum, France, 1995. Memberships: Haut Conseil de Réflexion du College International de Philosophie, Paris, 1983; Académie Stéphane Mallarmé, Paris, 1983. Address: 1 Square Henri Regnault, 92400 Courbevoie, France.

ESCANDELL Noemi, b. 27 Sept 1936, Havana, Cuba. Professor of Spanish language and Literature. m. Peter Knapp, 1 June 1957, div 1972, 2 sons, 2 daughters. Education: BA, Queens College, City University of New York, 1968; MA, 1971, PhD, 1976, Harvard

University. Appointments: Assistant Professor, Bard College, New York, 1976-83; Language Programme Director, Nuevo Instituto de Centroamerica, Esteli, Nicaragua, 1987-88; Spanish Professor, Westfield State College, 1983-93; Director, Afterschool Programme, Ross School, Washington DC, 1995-96. Publications: Palabras/Words, Slusa (Spanish Literature in the USA), 1986; Cuadros, 1982; Ciclos, Editorial Gahe, Madrid, 1982; Poems in No Hay Fronteras, 1990. Contributions to: The Caribbean Writer; El Gato Tuerto; Stone Country; Plaza; Verbena; Revista de Literatura; Peregrine; Letras femeninas; Third Woman; Horizontes, 2000; Horizontes; El Comercio; CPU Review. Honours: Poet-in-Residence, Millay Colony for the Arts, Austerlitz, New York, 1983, 1991; Special Mention, Certamen Poetico Federico Garcia Lorca Poetry Contest, 1995; First Prize in Poetry, XXXII Certamen Literario International Odon Betanzos Palacio, 1996. Membership: Academia Iberoamericana de Poesia, Washington DC Chapter. Address: 1525 Q Street Northwest No 11, Washington DC 20009, USA.

ESH Eshed. See: **SCHOENFELD Ilan.**

ESHLEMAN Clayton, b. 1 June 1935, Indianapolis, Indiana, USA. Professor of English; Poet; Writer; Translator. m. (1) Barbara Novak, 1961, div 1967, 1 son, (2) Caryl Reiter, 1969. Education: BA, Philosophy, 1958, MA, Creative Writing, 1961, Indiana University. Appointments include: Dreyfuss Poet-in-Residence and Lecturer, California Institute of Technology, Pasadena, 1979-84; Visiting Lecturer in Creative Writing, University of California, San Diego, Riverside, Los Angeles and Santa Barbara, 1979-86; Reviewer, Los Angeles Times Book Review, 1979-86; Founder Editor, Sulfur magazine, 1981-; Professor of English, Eastern Michigan University, 1986-. Publications: Poetry includes: Yellow River Record, 1969; A Pitchblende, 1969; The Wand, 1971; Bearings, 1971; Altars, 1971; The Sandjo Bridge, 1972; Coils, 1973; Human Wedding, 1973; The Last Judgement: For Caryl Her Thirty-First Birthday, The End of Her Pain, 1973; Aux Morts, 1974; Realignment, 1974; Portrait of Francis Bacon, 1975; The Cull Wall: Poems and Essays, 1975; Cogollo, 1976; The Woman Who Saw Through Paradise, 1976; Grotesca, 1977; On Mules Sent from Chavin: A Journal and Poems, 1965-66, 1977; Core Meander, 1977; The Name Encanyoned River, 1977; The Gospel of Celine Arnauld, 1978; What She Means, 1978; A Note on Apprenticeship, 1979; The Lich Gate, 1980; Nights We Put the Rock Together, 1980; Our Lady of the Three-Pronged Devil, 1981; Hades in Manganese, 1981; Foetus Graffiti, 1981; Fracture, 1983; Visions of the Fathers of Lascaux, 1983; The Name Encanyoned River: Selected Poems 1960-1985, 1986; Hotel Cro-Magnon, 1989; Other includes: Novices: A Study of Poetic Apprenticeship, 1989; Translations: 19 books, 1962-90. Honours: National Endowment for the Arts Grant, 1969, and Fellowships, 1979, 1981; Guggenheim Fellowship, 1978; National Book Award for Translation, 1979; National Endowment for the Humanities Grant, 1980, and Fellowship, 1981; Michigan Arts Council Grant, 1988. Address: 210 Washtenaw Avenue, Ypsilanti, MI 48197, USA.

ESKUBI Juanita Nicolasa, b. 27 Aug 1956, Farnborough, Hampshire, England. Freelance Technical Translator. Education: Diploma in Spanish, Institute of Linguistics, 1979; Aptitud de Inglis, Escuela Oficial de Idiomas, Bilbao, 1980. Appointments: Translator, Wellcome Foundation, Woking, 1979; Freelance Technical Translator, Private Teacher of English as a Foreign Language, Bilbao, Spain, 1979-92. Contributions to: Plowman; Exile. Honours: 3rd prize, Cranleigh Poetry Competition, 1972; Poetry Course, Arvon Foundation, 1971. Memberships: Institute of Linguistics; Poetry Society. Address: Plaza San Pio X-2-80, 48014 Bilbao, Vizcaya, Spain.

ESPOSITO Nancy, b. 1 Jan 1942, Dallas, Texas, USA. Poet ; Professor. Education: BA, English, MA, English, New York University; PhD, Comparative Literature, ongoing. Appointments: Adjunct Assistant Professor, Creative Writing and Poetry, Bentley College, 1986-, Lecturer, Creative Writing and Poetry, Tufts University, 1986-93; Translator, Managua, Nicaragua, 1985-86; Copy Editor, Ginn Press, Prentice-Hall, 1989-. Publications: Book: Changing Hands, 1984; Anthologies: Ixok-Amar-Go (translation), 1987; Two Decades of New Poets, 1984; The Handbook of Executive Communication, 1986; Foreign Affairs Bibliography, 1954-64, 1964; Quarterly Review of Literature Anthology of Poets, 1993. Contributions to: South Dakota Review; Nation; Carolina Quarterly; Blue Buildings; North American Review; Mississippi Review; Threepenny Review; Poet and Critic; Black Warrior Review; Harvard Business Review; Seattle Review;

American Poetry Review; Imagine; Sojourner; Antioch Review; Denver Quarterly; Prairie Schooner; Seattle Review; Delos. Honours: Discovery, Nation Award, 1979; Pushcart Prize Finalist, 1980-81; Massachusetts Arts Lottery Grant, 1984; Colladay Award, 1984; Poetry Society of America Gordon Barber Memorial Award, 1987; Fulbright to Egypt, 1988; Publishing Award, Bentley College, 1988. Memberships: Poetry Society of America; Academy of American Poets; Poets and Writers Inc; Associated Writing Programs; Oxfam America. Address: 11 Chauncy Street, Cambridge, MA 02138, USA.

ESTRELLA. See: GRESS Esther Johanne.

ETTER Dave (David Pearson), b. 18 Mar 1928, Huntington Park, California, USA. Poet; Editor. m. Margaret A Cochran, 8 Aug 1959, 1 son, 1 daughter. Education: BA History, University of Iowa, 1953. Appointments: Promotion Department, Indiana University, 1959-60; Rand McNally Publishing Co, 1960-61; Assistant Editor, Encyclopaedia Britannica, Chicago, 1964-73; Editor, Northern Illinois University Press, 1974-80; Freelance Writer, Poet and Editor, 1981-. Publications: Open to the Wind, 1978; Riding the Rock Island Through Kansas, 1979; Cornfields, 1980; West of Chicago, 1981; Boondocks, 1982; Alliance, Illinois, 1983; Home State, 1985; Live at the Silver Dollar, 1986; Selected Poems, 1987; Midlanders, 1988; Electric Avenue, 1988; Carnival, 1990; Sunflower County, 1994. Contributions to: Poetry; Nation; Chicago Review; Kansas Quarterly; Prairie Schooner; Poetry Northwest; TriQuarterly; Massachusetts Review; North American Review; Ohio Review; New Letters; Shenandoah; Beloit Poetry Journal; El Corno Emplumado; San Francisco Review; New Mexico Quarterly; Mark Twain Journal; Slow Dancer (England), among others. Honours: Society of Midland Authors Poetry Prize, 1967; Friends of Literature Poetry Prize, 1967; Illinois Sesquicentennial Poetry Prize, 1968; Theodore Roethke Poetry Prize, 1971; Carl Sandburg Poetry Prize, 1982; Bread Loaf Writers' Conference Fellowship in Poetry, 1967. Address: 414 Gates Street, PO Box 413, Elburn, IL 60119, USA.

ETTY Robert, b. 6 Nov 1949, Waltham, Lincolnshire, England. Schoolteacher. m. Anne Levison, 3 Apr 1975, 1 son, 1 daughter. Education: BA. Publications: Hovendens Violets, 1989; New Pastorals, 1992; Marking Places, 1994. Contributions to: Poetry Review; Orbis; Spectator; Outposts; Rialto; Staple; Envoi; Iron; The Independent. Honours: Lake Aske Award, Nottingham Poetry Society, 1990; 1st Prize, Wykeham Poetry Competition, 1991; 1st Prize, Kent and Sussex Open Poetry Competition, 1992; Other Competition Prizes, 1989-96. Address: Evenlode, Church Lane, Keddington, Louth, Lincolnshire LN11 7HG, England.

EVANS Donald, (Onwy), b. 12 June 1940, Cardiganshire, Wales. Welsh Master. m. Pat Thomas, 29 Dec 1972, 1 son. Education: Honours Degree, Welsh, 1962, Diploma, Education, 1963, University College of Wales, Aberystwyth. Appointments: Welsh Master, Ardwyn Grammar School, Aberystwyth, 1963-73; Welsh Master, Penglais Comprehensive School, Aberystwyth, 1973-84; Welsh Specialist, Cardigan Junior School, 1984-91. Publications: Egin, 1976; Haidd, 1977; Grawn, 1979; Cread Crist, 1986; O'r Bannau Duon, 1987; Iasau, 1988; Seren Poets 2 (with others), 1990; Wrth Reddf, 1994. Contributions to: Welsh Poetry Society Magazine; Poetry Wales; Modern Poetry in Translation; Welsh. Honours: The National Eisteddfod Crown & Chair, 1977, 1980; Welsh Arts Council Poetry Prize, 1977, 1983, 1989; The Welsh Academy Poetry Award, 1989. Memberships: The Welsh Poetry Society; The Welsh Academy. Address: Y Plas, Talgarreg, Llandysul, County of Ceredigion SA44 4XA, Wales.

EVANS Mari, b. 16 July 1923, Toledo, Ohio, USA. Poet; Writer. Div, 2 sons. Education: University of Toledo. Appointments: Writer, Producer, and Director, The Black Experience television programme, Indianapolis, 1968-73; Writer-in-Residence and Instructor in Black Literature, Indiana University-Purdue University at Indianapolis, 1969-70; Assistant Professor of Black Literature and Writer-in-Residence, Indiana University, 1970-78, Purdue University, 1978-80; Writer-in-Residence and Visiting Assistant Professor, Northwestern University, 1972-73; Visiting Professor, Washington University, 1980, Cornell University, 1981-84, University of Miami, Coral Gables, 1989; Associate Professor, State University of New York, Albany, 1985-86; Writer-in-Residence, Spelman College, Atlanta, 1989-90. Publications: Poetry: Where Is All the Music?, 1968; I Am a Black Woman, 1970; Whisper, 1979; Nightstar, 1981; A Dark and Splendid Mass, 1992; Other: Rap Stories, 1973; J D, 1973; I Look at

Me, 1974; Singing Black, 1976; Jim Flying High, 1979; Black Women Writers 1950-1980: A Critical Evaluation (Editor), 1984. Honours: John Hay Whitney Fellowship, 1965; Woodrow Wilson Foundation Grant, 1968; Black Academy of Arts and Letters Award, 1971; MacDowell Fellowship, 1975; Copeland Fellowship, 1980; National Endowment for the Arts Award, 1981; Yaddo Fellowship, 1984. Address: PO Box 483, Indianapolis, IN 46206, USA.

EVANS Martina Mary Lelia, b. 11 Aug 1961, Cork, Ireland. Radiographer. m. Declan Evans, 5 Oct 1985, 1 daughter. Education: BA, Open University, 1991. Contributions to: Poetry Ireland Review; Celtic Dawn; Scratch; Rialto; Iota; Hybrid; Brandos Hat; Third Half; Symphony; Cobweb; New Hope International Fat Chance; Bound Spiral; New Irish Writing; New Virago Poets. Honours: Frances Martin College Prize; Hennessy Award Nomination, 1992. Address: 47B Landseer Road, Upper Holloway, London N19 4JU, England.

EVERETT Graham, b. 23 Dec 1947, USA. Professor; Writer; Publisher. m. Elyse Arnow, 27 Dec 1981, 1 son. Education: MA, English, 1987; PhD, English, 1994, State University of New York at Stony Brook. Appointments: Interim Director of Poetry Centre at State University of New York at Stony Brook; Publisher/Editor, Street Magazine and Press. Publications: Casting Bones From a Turtle Shell, 1975; The Trees, 1978; Strange Coast, 1979; Sunlit Sidewalk, 1985; Minus Green, 1992; Minus Green Plus, 1995. Contributions to: Confrontation; Contact II; Long Pond Review; West Hills Review; Mojo Navigator; Intrepid; Grubstreet; Bluefish; San Fernando Review; Scree; Fire Island Tide; Bird Effort; Wetlands; Voyeur; Redstart; Long Island Quarterly; Live Poets, Caprice and Others. Memberships: President, Backstreet Editions Inc; Editor, Blackhole School of Poethnics; Trustee, 1990, Walt Whitman Birthplace Association; Modern Language Association; NCTE; AWP. Address: PO Box 772, Sound Beach, NY 11789, USA.

EVERS Jason Harvey, (Jason Hurcot, Herbert Neal), b. 8 July 1963, Westminster, London, England. Horticulturalist. Education: Welsh College of Horticulture, 1983-86; BTec HND, Business Studies and Horticultural Marketing, Merrist Wood Agricultural College, 1989; RCA Certificate in Effective Speaking; Polytechnic Certificate in Drama, Geography and History. Appointments: Buyer, The Chelsea Gardener, London, 1986-88; Self-employed, 1989-. Publications: The Peacock Magazine, 1977, 1980. Contributions to: Private Eye; The Big Issue; Charlottes Magazine. Memberships: Associate, Institute of Horticulture; Poetry Society; Founder-Member, Independent Covent Garden Venture for New Commissioned Operas, 1989; Keats Society; Funded and Initiated, 1st prizes given for Poetry and Prose submitted to magazine, Peacock Prize for Poetry and Prose. Address: 12 Cleaver Street, Kennington, London SW11 4DP, England.

EWING Gillian, b. Scotland. 3 sons. Education: MA, Glasgow. Contributions to: TES; Iota; Literary review; Spectator; Orbis; North; New prospects; Nutshell. Address: 10 The Mount, Malton, North Yorkshire YO17 0ND, England.

EZEKIEL Nissim, b. 16 Dec 1924, Bombay, India. Retired Professor. m. Daisy Jacob, 23 Nov 1952. Education: BA, 1945, MA, 1947, English Literature. Appointments: Editorial Assistant, Illustrated Weekly of India, 1952-54; Manager, Shilpi Advertising, 1954-61; Professor, Head of English Department and Vice Principal, Mithibai College of Arts, 1962-73; Professor, Department of English, Bombay University, 1973-85. Publications: A Time to Change, 1952; Sixty Poems; The Third; The Unfinished Man; The Exact Name; Hymns in Darkness; Latter-Day Psalms; Collected Poems 1952-88, 1989. Contributions to: Times of India; Illustrated Weekly; Quest; Kavita India; Debonair; Indian Literature; Journal of Indian Writing in English. Honours: Best Book of the Year, National Academy of Letters, 1983; Padma Shri Award for Contribution to Indian Literature in English, 1987. Memberships: PEN All India Centre; Honorary Secretary and Editor, Indian PEN; Bombay English Association, Managing Committee. Address: 18 Kala Niketan, 6th Floor, 47c, Bhulabhai Desai Road, Bombay 400026, India.

F

FABILLI Mary, b. 16 Feb 1914, USA. Poet; Artist. Education: AB, University of California at Berkeley, 1941. Appointments: Associate Curator of History, Oakland Museum, California, 1949-77. Publications: The Old Ones, 1966; Aurora Bligh and Early Poems, 1968; The Animal Kingdom, 1975; Poems, 1976-81, 1981; Winter Poems, 1983; Simple Pleasures, 1987; Shingles and Other Poems, 1990. Contributions to: New Directions; Experimental Review; Talisman; Bristol Banner Books, 1995; Journal, 1995. Address: 2445 Ashby Avenue, Berkeley, CA 94705, USA.

FACOS James, b. 28 July 1924, Lawrence, Massachusetts, USA. Professor. m. Cleo Chigos, 1 Dec 1956, 1 son, 2 daughters. Education: AB, Bates College, 1949; MA, Florida State University, 1958; DHL, Norwich Univerity, 1989. Appointments: Professor, Vermont College of Norwich University, 1958-89. Publications: Mornings Come Singing, 1981; The Piper O The May, 1962. Contributions to: Poetry; Saturday Evening Post; Lyric; Christian Science Monitor. Honours: Walter Peach Award, 1962; Corinne Davis Award, 1970. Address: 333 Elm Street, Montpelier, VT 05602, USA.

FAERBER Meir Marcell, (Meir Re'ubeni), b. 29 Apr 1908, Ostrava, Austria-Hungary. Journalist. m. Sara Ilana Tutelman, 2 sons. Education: Deutsches Staatsgymnasium, Ostrava; Deutsche Staats-Handelsakademie, Brno. Appointments: Chairman, Israel-Austria Association of Israel, 1956-63, Tel Aviv Branch, 1963-1993; Editor, German monthly, Die Stimme, Tel Aviv, 1975-. Publications: Mein Tel Aviv, 1940; Ringende Seelen, 1974; Worte, 1980; Der Wandernde Bote, 1981; Brennende Eifersucht, 1983; Dreimal drei Glieder einer Kette, 1985; Ernstes und Heiteres, 1986; Israel in Tanka-Versen, 1987; Aus unbekannten Motiven, 1991; Von Abraham bis Salomo, 1991; Editor of two anthologies: Stimmen aus Israel, 1979, and Auf dem Weg, 1989. Contributions to: Various newspapers and periodicals. Honours: Das Goldene Ehrenzeichen, Republik Oesterreich, 1971; Jakob Landau Preis, Bnai Brith-Lodge, Theodor Herzl, Tel Aviv, 1980; Medal, Studiosis Humanitatis, Literarischen Union, Germany, 1981; Verdienstkreuz 1 Klasse Bundesrepublik Deutschland, 1983. Memberships: Chairman, Association of German Writing Authors in Israel, 1975-; Board, Organisation of Authors Association of Israel, and Organisation of the German Writing Authors, Berlin; PEN Centre Israel; National Federation of Israeli Journalists; International Federation of Journalists, Brussels; International Authors Circle, Plesse; Regensburger Schriftsteller-Gruppe International, Germany. Address: POB 1356, Tel Aviv 61013, Israel.

FAGUNDO Ana Maria, b. 13 Mar 1938, Spain. Professor of Spanish Contemporary Literature. Education: BA, MA, PhD, English, University of Redlands, California; MA, PhD, University of Washington, Seattle. Appointments: Assistant Professor, Associate Professor, Full Professor, University of California, Riverside, 1967-92; Visiting Professor, Stanford University, 1984; Director of Education Abroad, Universidad Central, Barcelona, Spain, 1976-78. Publications: Brotes, 1965; Isla Adentro, 1969; Diario de una muerte, 1970; Configurado tiempo, 1974; Invencion de la luz, 1978; Desde Chanatel, el canto, 1982; Como quien no dice voz alguna al viento, 1984; Retornos sobre la siempre ausencia, 1989; Obra Poetica, 1990; Isla en si, 1992. Contributions to: Poesia Espanola; Vanguardia; Papeles de Son Armadans; Cuadernos Americanos; Arbol de Fuego; Arequipa; Cosmos; Seneca Review; Poesia de Venezuela; Caracole; Bahia; Ganigo; Azor; Alamo; Hora de Poesia. Honours: Carabela de Oro, Barcelona, 1977; Finalist Angaro, 1980. Memberships: Sociedad General de Autores de Espana. Address: Spanish Department, University of California, Riverside, CA 92507, USA.

FAHEY Diane Mary, b. 2 Jan 1945, Melbourne, Victoria, Australia. Writer. Education: BA, 1966, Dip Ed (Secondary), 1972, MA (First Class), University of Melbourne, 1975. Appointments: Teacher, Humanities, Box Hill Technical College, 1973; English Tutor, Deakin University, Burwood Campus, 1976-79; Lecturer, Literary Studies, University of SA, Salisbury Campus, 1986. Publications: Voices from the Honeycomb, 1986; Metamorphoses, 1988; Turning the Hourglass, 1990; Mayflies in Amber, 1993; The Body in Time, 1995. Contributions to: The Age; The Canberra Times; Island; Meanjin; Overland; Scripsi; Southerly; Southern Review; Voices; Westerly, Australia; Ambit;

Modern Painters; The Poetry Review; Resurgence; The New Welsh Review; Planet; Poetry Wales; Ariel; Kunapipi; Poetry Ireland. Honours include: Mattara Poetry Prize, 1985; John Shaw Neilson Prize, 1989; The Wesley Michel Poetry Prize, 1987; 3 Writers Fellowships from the Literature Board of Australia. Memberships: Victoria Writers Centre; S A Writers Centre; New South Wales Writers Centre; Fellowship of Australian Writers. Address: 12 Noble Street, Barwon Heads, Victoria 3227, Australia.

FAINLIGHT Ruth, b. 2 May 1931, New York, New York, USA. Writer. m. Alan Sillitoe, 19 Nov 1959, 1 son, 1 daughter. Education: College of Arts and Crafts, England. Appointments: Poet-in-Residence, Vanderbilt University, Nashville, Tennessee, 1985, 1990. Publications: Cages, 1966; To See the Matter Clearly, 1968; The Region's Violence, 1973; Another Full Moon, 1976; Sibyls and Others, 1980; Fifteen to Infinity, 1983; Climates, 1983; Selected Poems, 1987; The Knot, 1990; This Time of the Yaer, 1994; Selected Poems, revised 2nd edition, 1995. Contributions to: English; Hudson Review; Lettre Internationale; London Magazine; London Review of Books; New Yorker; Poetry Review; Poetry; Threepenny Review; Times Literary Supplement; Yale Review. Honour: Cholmondeley Award for Poetry, 1994. Memberships: PEN; Writers in Prison Committee. Address: 14 Ladbroke Terrace, London W11 3PG, England.

FAIRBRASS Graham John, b. 14 Jan 1953, Meopham, Kent, England. Traveller; Writer; Painter. Education: BA, Arts, Open University, 1991; Coleg Harlech, 1995-96; Diploma, University of Wales, 1996. Appointments: Accounts Clerk, 1969-70; Editorial Assistant, 1971-74; Stock Clerk, 1974-77; General Stores Clerk, 1977-88; Traveller, Writer, Painter, 1988-90; Student, 1991-. Publication: Conquistadors Shuffle Moon, 1989. Contributions to: Poetry Now, 1994; Anthology South East; Parnassus of World Poets, 1994, 1995, 1997; Poetry Club Anthology, Vol I, 1995. Address: 6 Hornfield Cottages, Harvel, Gravesend, Kent DA13 0BU, England.

FAIRFAX John, b. 9 Nov 1930, London, England. Poet. 2 sons. Appointments: Co-Founder, and Member of Council of Management, Arvon Foundation; Director, Phoenix Press; Director, Arts Workshop, Newbury, Poetry Editor Resurgence. Publications: This I Say, 1966; The 5th Horseman of the Apocalypse, 1969; Adrift to the Staf Brow of Taliesin, 1974; Bone Harvest Done, 1980; Wild Children, 1984; 100 Poem, 1992. Contributions to: Times Literary Supplement; Temenos; Malahat Review; Europe; Psychopoetica; Prospice; Acumen; Anglo-Welsh Review; Resurgence; Pearl. Memberships: Poets in Schools Scheme, Poetry Society; Writers in Education Scheme. Address: The Thatched Cottage, Eling, Hermitage, Newbury, Berks RG16 9XR, England.

FALCK Colin, b. 14 July 1934, London, England. Writer; University Professor. 1 daughter. Education: BA, Oxon, 1957, 1959; PhD, London, 1988. Appointments: Lecturer, Sociology, London School of Economics, 1961-62, Literature, Chelsea College, 1964-84; Adjunct Professor in English Literature, Syracuse University, London Centre, 1985-89; Associate Professor, York College, Pennsylvania, 1989-; Associate Editor, The Review, Oxford and London, 1962-72; Poetry Editor, The New Review, London, 1974-78. Publications: The Garden in the Evening, 1964; Promises, 1969; Backwards into the Smoke, 1973; In this Dark Light, 1978; Poems Since 1900: An Anthology (co-editor), 1975; Robinson Jeffers: Selected Poems (editor), 1987; Myth, Truth and Literature: Towards a Time Post-Modernism, 1989; Edna St Vincent Millay: Selected Poems (editor), 1991; Memorabilia, 1992; Myth, Truth and Literature: Towards a True Post Modernism, 2nd edition, 1994. Contributions to: Agenda; Boston Review; Encounter; Iron; London Magazine; London Review of Books; New Leaf; New Review; New Statesman; Outposts Poetry Quarterly; PN Review; Partisan Review; Poetry Book Society Supplement; Poetry Durham; Poetry Nation; Times Literary Supplement. Address: c/o 20 Thurlow Road, London NW3 5PP, England.

FALLON Peter, b. 26 Feb 1951, Osnabruck, Germany. Education: BA, Trinity College, Dublin, 1975. Appointments: Fiction Editor, O'Brien Press, Dublin, 1980-. Publications: Among the Walls, 1971; Co-incidence of Flesh, 1972; The First Affair, 1974; Finding the Dead, 1978; The Speaking Stones, 1978; Winter Work, 1983; The News and Weather, 1987; Editor of volumes of Irish poetry. Address: Gallery Press, Loughcrew, Oldcastle, County Meath, Ireland.

FAMA Maria, b. 3 Mar 1951, Philadelphia, Pennsylvania, USA. Writer; Educator; Researcher. Education: BA, 1971, MA, 1973, Temple University. Appointments: Teacher, 1972-79; Research Writer, Temple University School of Dentistry, 1979-87; Bibliographic Assistant, Charles L Blockson, Afro-American Collection, 1987-89; Public Services Coordinator, Temple University, 1990-. Publications: Current, 1988; Poetry Videos, Fig Tree in the Yard, and Sneakers, 1989; Identification, 1991; Italian Notebook, 1995. Contributions to: Pearl; Piedmont Literary Review; South Street Star; Cardinal Review; Sons of Italy Times; La Bella Figura; City Paper of Philadelphia; Labyrinth; Hyacinths and Biscuits; Giornale di Matera; In the Public Eye; Heat; Modern Haiku; Poetry; Poet; Philadelphia Poets; La Bella Figura; A Choice, 1993; Via: Voices in Italian Americana; Laurel Leaves; North Star Poets; Joy and Tears; Seven Arts Magazine; Labyrinth, American Writing; Footwork - The Paterson Literary Review; Italian American and Italian Canadian Poets: An Anthology. Honours: Philadelphia Writers Conference Poetry Award, 1976, 1977, 1990; Read work on radio as part of Philadelphia Writers Series, 1990. Memberships: American Poetry Center; Penn Laurel Poets, Recording Secretary; Philadelphia Writers Organization and Writers Conference. Address: 1322 Sigel Street, Philadelphia, PA 19148, USA.

FANG Jing, b. 26 Apr 1914, Wanxian, Sichuan, China. University Professor. m. Miss He Pinjia, 2 Oct 1938, 2 sons, 2 daughters. Education: Graduate, China Public College, Shanghai, 1931; BA, High Honours, National Peking University, 1939. Appointments: Associate Professor, National Guizhou University, Guiyang, Guizhou, 1944-47; Professor, National Teachers College for Women, Chongqing and National Chongqing University, 1947-50; Professor, Dean, Vice President, Southwest China Teachers University, 1950-88. Publications: Rainy Vision, 1942; Voice, 1943; Victims, 1948; Songs of a Minstrel, 1948; Grain Gleanings, 1981; Flower Seeds, 1989; The Shadow of Flying Bird, 1990. Contributions to: New Poetry; Poetry; Stars Poetry Monthly; Shi Bi-Monthly (poetry, Hong Kong); Galaxy; Literary Quarterly; Ocean (literary, Hong Kong). Honour: Awarded Sichuan Guo Moruo Honorary Prize for Literature, Poetry, 1988. Memberships: Chinese Writers' Association; Honorary Chairman, Sichuan Writers' Association; Chairman, Chongqing Poetry Society; Editor-in-Chief, Galaxy Poetry (magazine). Address: Southwest China Teachers University, Beibei, Chongqing, Sichuan 630715, China.

FANNING Micheal, (O Fionnain), b. 3 Mar 1954. Writer; Medical Doctor. Publications: The Love Letters of Daniel O'Connell, 1983; Tombolo, 1994; Deithe an t Solais, 1994. Contributions to: Ulsterman; Envoi; Acumen; Comhar. Address: The Wood, Dingle, County Kerry, Ireland.

FANTHORPE U(rsula) A(skham), b. 22 July 1929, Kent, England. Writer. Education: St Anne's College, Oxford, 1950-53. Appointments: Writer-in-Residence, St Martin's College, Lancaster, 1983-85; Northern Arts Literary Fellow, University of Durham and Newcastle, 1987-88. Publications: Side Effects, 1978; Standing To, 1982; Voices Off, 1984; Selected Poems, 1986; A Watching Brief, 1987; Neck Verse, 1992; Safe as Houses, 1995. Contributions to: Various publications. Honours: Travelling Scholarship from the Society of Authors, 1983; Hawthornden Scholarship, 1987; Cholmondeley Award, Arts Council Bursary, 1995; Hon DLitt, University of the West of England, 1995. Memberships: Fellow, Royal Society of Literature; PEN. Address: Culverhay House, Wotton under Edge, Gloucestershire GL12 7LS, England.

FARAGHER E(ric) S(teven), b. 23 Apr 1957, Liverpool, England. Librarian. Education: Diploma of Higher Education, 1988; BA Hons Combined Studies (Humanities) English, Philosophy, Writing, 1989; Postgraduate Diploma in Information and Library Studies, 1990-91. Appointments: Shelf Attendant, Liverpool City Libraries, 1974-85; Librarian, Sefton School of Health Studies, 1992-93; Senior Library Assistant, City of Liverpool Community College. Publications: Anthologies: 1992 Poets, 1992; Peppermint Dream, 1992; Poetry Now North West, 1992, 1992; Altogether Now, 1993. Contributions to: Write Now, BBC Radio Cumbria; The Toadbird (TOPS); Krax; Staple; New Hope International; Poetry Nottingham; White Rose; Third Half; Sepia; Iota; Outposts; Orbis; Boundary; Writers' Own Magazine; Folio; Weyfarers; Linq (Australia); Poet (USA); ...And of Tomorrow? Psychopoetica. Memberships: Liverpool Writers' Club, Committee Member, 1975-80, Chairman 1981-82; Library Association. Address: 31 Tudor Street, Liverpool L6 6AG, England.

FARHI Musa Moris, b. 5 July 1935, Ankara, Turkey. Novelist. m. Nina Ruth Gould, 2 July 1978, 1 stepdaughter. Education: BA, Humanities, Istanbul American College, 1954; Diploma, Royal Academy of Dramatic Art, London, 1956. Publication: Voices Within The Art: The Modern Jewish Poets, 1980. Contributions to: Menard Press; Men Cards; European Judaism; Modern Poetry In Translation; Frank; Jewish Quarterly; Steaua (Romania); Confrontation (USA); North Atlantic Review (USA). Memberships: Society of Authors; Writers Guild; PEN. Address: 11 North Square, London NW11 7AB, England.

FARLEY Jennifer, b. Nottinghamshire, England. Journalist; Fiction Writer; Creative Writing Tutor. Education: St Mary and St Anne, Abbots Bromley. Appointments: Runs courses and workshops in poetry and creative writing and workshops for poetry readings. Contributions to: New Welsh Review; Writing Women; Oxford Poetry; Poetry Durham; Slow Dancer; and others. Honours: 1st Prize, Kent and Sussex Open Poetry Competition, 1989; Runner-Up, South West Arts Poetry Competition, 1991; Shortlisted, Bridport, 1990. Membership: Poetry Society. Address: Hetton Cottage, 40 Cudnall Street, Charlton Kings, Cheltenham, Gloucestershire GL53 8HG, England.

FARLEY Joseph Michael, b. 28 Dec 1961, Philadelphia, Pennsylvania, USA. Speechwriter; Publicist; Writer; Researcher; Investigator. m. Juan Xu, 25 Aug 1988. Education: BA, English, St Joseph's University, Philadelphia, 1983; MA, English and Creative Writing, Temple University, 1988. Appointments: Library Assistant, 1983-85; Social Worker, Philadelphia Department of Human Services, 1985-86; Public Relations Specialist, Philadelphia Commission on Human Relations, 1987-92; Human Relations Representative II, Investigator, 1993-. Publications: Editor: Axe Factory I, 1986, III, 1990, V, 1996. Chapbooks: January, 1985; Beat Ballad Blues, 1995; Souvenir or Evolution, 1996. Contributions to: The Next Parish Over: Collection of Irish American Writing; Painted Bride Quarterly; Pearl Magazine; Bogg Magazine; Wayfarers; Iota. Address: 2653 Sperry Street, Philadelphia, PA 19152, USA.

FARMER Rod, b. 9 June 1947, Carthage, Missouri, USA. Professor of Education and History. m. Margaret Eastman Farmer, 8 Aug 1986. Education: BS, Social Science, 1968, MA, History, 1972, Central Missouri State University; PhD, Social Science Education, University of Missouri at Columbia, 1978; Postgraduate Study in History, University of Maine, 1984-85. Appointments: Professor of Education and History, University of Maine at Farmington, 1978-; US Army 1969-70. Publication: Universal Essence, 1986. Contributions to: Amaranth Review; Black Fly Review; Bitterroot; Black Buzzard Review; Cafe Review; Dog River Review; ELF; Ellipsis; The Galley Sail Review; Phase and Cycle; Poetry Pedler; Psychopoetica; Sandscript; San Fernando Poetry Journal; Skylark; Riverrun; Coe Review; Hollins Critic; Potato Eyes; Pegasus; Connecticut River Review; Manna; Infinity Limited; Canal Lines; Parnassus Literary Review; Prophetic Voices; Chaminade Literary Review; Philomel; Fathoms; Mind in Motion; Mobius; Delirium, and others. Over 600 poems published in journals. Membership: Maine Writers and Publishers Alliance. Address: Franklin Hall, 104 Main Street, University of Maine at Farmington, Farmington, ME 04938, USA.

FARNSWORTH Robert Lambton, b. 8 Apr 1954, Boston, Massachusetts, USA. College Professor. m. Georgia N Nigro, 28 Aug 1977, 2 sons. Education: AB English, Brown University, 1976; MFA, Columbia University, 1979. Appointments: Visiting Assistant Professor: Ithaca College, Colby College and Bates College. Publications: Three or Four Hills and a Cloud, 1982; Honest Water, 1989. Contributions to: American Poetry Review; Poetry; Missouri Review; Carolina Quarterly; New England Review; Poetry Northwest; Ironwood; Ploughshares; Michigan Quarterly Review; Antioch Review. Honour: National Endowment for the Arts Fellowship in Poetry, 1989-90. Address: 19 Ware Street, Lewiston, ME 04240, USA.

FARRELL Michael John, b. 7 July 1964, Ashton under Lyne, Lancashire, England. Poet; Artist. Education: BA, English Literature, Sunderland University, 1984; Studying Life, Foundation in Fine Art, Bilston, Wolverhampton, 1992. Appointments: Hotel Porter, The Mount Hotel, Wolverhampton; Librarian, Winter Hill, Wolverhampton; Insurance Clerk, Wolverhampton; Fine Artist at Bilston, Wolverhampton. Publications: Ghosts on Glass, 1983; Christmas Box, 1991; Editor, The Memo Bowl, a new literary magazine, 1992. Contributions to: Ambit 119; Iron 62; several dozen small presses.

Honour: A Reading in Chester, 1983-84. Memberships: Poetry Society; Dances With Wolves Fan Club. Address: 45 Heantun Rise, Francis Street, Wolverhampton WV1 4RE, England.

FARUQI Moeen, b. 2 Feb 1958, Karachi, Pakistan. Educator; Art Critic; Artist. 2 sons. Education: BSc, Physics, California State University, 1981; MEd, University of Wales College of Cardiff, Wales, 1992. Appointments: School Administrator, Modern Education Society, 1983-; Art Critic for Pakistan Press International, 1986-. Publications: UK: Orbis; Verse; Iron; Rialto. Memberships: International Association of Art Critics; Commonwealth Council of Educational Administration. Address: 95 Jamshed Road, Karachi 74800, Pakistan.

FASEL Ida, b. 9 May 1909, Portland, Maine, USA. University Professor; Poet. m. Oskar A Fasel, 24 Dec 1946. Education: BA, 1931, MA, 1945, Boston University; PhD, University of Denver, 1963. Appointments: University of Connecticut, New London; Midwestern University, Wichita Falls, Texas; Colorado Woman's College, Denver, University of Colorado, Denver, 1962-77; Professor Emeritus of English, 1977. Publications: On the Meanings of Cleave, 1979; Thanking the Flowers, 1981; West of Whitcaps, 1982; All of Us Dancers, 1984; Amphora Full of Light, 1985; Available Light, 1988; Basics, 1988; Where is the Center of the World?, 1991. Contributions to: Renaissance and Baroque Lyrics; Study and Writing of Poetry; Anthology of Magazine Verse; Yearbook of American Poetry; Clap Hands and Sing; Cape Rock; Nimrod; Poet Lore; Creeping Bent; Blue Unicorn; others. Honours: Faculty Fellowship, University of Colorado, 1967; Collegium of Distinguished Alumni, Boston University, 1979; 1st Prize, Boston University Poetry Competition, 1986, 1990; Colorado Poet Honor, Denver Public Library Friends, 1991. Memberships: Poetry Society of America; Milton Society of America; Friends of Milton's Cottage; Conference on Christianity and Literature; Denver Women's Press Club; Colorado Author's League. Address: 165 Ivy Street, Denver, CO 80220, USA.

FATCHEN Max(well Edgar), b. 3 Aug 1920, Adelaide, South Australia. Journalist; Author. m. Jean Wohlers, 15 May 1942, 2 sons, 1 daughter. Appointments: Reporter and Special Writer, Adelaide News, 1946-55; Special Writer, 1955-84, Literary Editor, 1972-82, Adelaide Advertiser. Publications: Children's poetry: Songs for My Dog, 1982; Wry Rhymes for Troublesome Times, 1983, 1985; A Paddock of Poems, 1987; A Pocketful of Rhymes, 1989; A Country Christmas, 1990; The Country Mail is Coming, 1990; Tea for Three (with Colin Thiele), 1994; Peculiar Rhymes and Lunatic Lines, 1995. Contributions to: Poetry included in over 90 anthologies as well as in the Denver Post, Adelaide Advertiser, New South Wales Children's Magazine and on BBC and ABC; Something About the Author, autobiographical essay, 1995. Honours: Book of the Year Award, Children's Book Council; Member of the Order of Australia for Services to Journalism and Literature. Memberships: Australian Society of Authors; Fellowship of Australian Writers; South Australian Writers Centre; Australian Journalists' Association. Address: PO Box 6, Smithfield, South Australia 5114, Australia.

FAUGSTAD Åse Marie Lilleskare, b. 3 Apr 1941, Dale i Bruvik, Norway. Poet; Translator; Teacher. m. Bjorn Oistein Faugstad, 23 Feb 1963, 3 daughters. Education: Cand Philol, Bergen University, Norway, 1984. Appointments: High School Teacher for 15 years; Teacher in Junior College for 3 years. Publications: Ved mitt altar, poems, 1966; Stilt pa min tanke, poems, 1968; Stjernene, poems, 1974; I dette huset, poems, 1977; Den gylne kokongen, poems, 1988; Tidevatnet kjem inn, poems, 1989; Straumar, 20th Century Poetry in English, anthology of poems in the poet's translation, with the poet's introduction of each poet, 1992. Contributions to: Gula Tidend, Bergen; Ergo, Oslo; Passport and Adam, England; Caracoa, Philippines. Memberships: Norwegian Authors' Association; Literary Council of NAA; Norwegian Language Council; Norwegian Translators' Association. Address: Holhovdvegen 4, 5280 Dalekvam, Norway.

FAUST Naomi F(lowe), b. 1940, Salisbury, North Carolina, USA. Educator; Author; Poet. m. Roy M Faust. Education: AB, Bennett College, Greensboro, North Carolina; MA, University of Michigan; PhD, New York University, 1963. Appointments: Instructor of English, Bennett College and Southern University; Professor of English, Morgan State College, Baltimore; Teacher of English, Greensboro Public School and New York City Public Schools; Professor of English Education, Queens College of the City University of New York. Publications: Speaking in Verse, 1974; All Beautiful Things, 1983; And I Travel By Rhythms And Words, 1990. Contributions to: Adam of Ife;

Black Women in Praise of Black Men; Afro-American Newspapers; Biennial Anthology of Premier Poets; Bitter Root; Cyclo Flame; Dear Dark Faces: Portraits of a People; Essence Magazine; Gusto; International Poets; A Milestone Sampler; New York Amsterdam News; New York Voice; Poems By Blacks, (anthology); Poet Magazine; South and West; World Poetry. Honours: Cooper Hill Writers Conference Prize and Certificate of Merit, 1970; Certificate of Merit for poem in anthology, Poems By Blacks, 1970; Cyclo Flame Magazine Prize, 1970; International Eminent Poet, International Poets Academy, 1988; Contributions Prize, The Creative Record, 1989. Memberships: World Poetry Society Intercontinental; New York Poetry Forum; National Women's Book Association; National Council of Teachers of English; American Association of University Professors. Address: 112-01 175th Street, Jamaica, New York 11433, USA.

FAUX Elizabeth Christine (Liz), b. 14 Apr 1953, Taplow, Buckinghamshire, England. Special Needs Teacher. m. 2 sons. Education: BA Hons, Humanities, majoring in English Literature and Linguistics, Hatfield Polytechnic, 1982; Certificate in Education, Herts College of Higher Education; Currently studying for MA in Creative Writing at Glam University; Advanced Diploma in Special Needs Education, 1995. Appointment: Lecturer in Special Needs, Oaklands College, St Albans. Publication: First collection, Between the Islands, 1994. Contributions to: Poetry Post; Vision On; Acumen; New Spokes; Poetry Durham; World Parnassus of Poetry, 1994; Poetry included in Anthology for Women Writers, forthcoming. Honours: 1st Prize, 1990, 2nd Prize, 1991, VER Poets Open Competition; 1 Highly Commended, 2 Commended, Ripley Open Poetry Competition, 1992; 1st Prize in Specialist Category, Barnet Open Competiton, 1994; Joint Winner of the Blue Nose Poetry Competition, 1996. Memberships: Ver Poets, workshop group run by May Badman based in St Albans; Poetry Society, 1987-; Publicity Officer, Toddington Poetry Society, 1991-92. Address: 15 Holcroft Road, Harpenden, Hertfordshire AL5 5BG, England.

FEDERICI Tersilla, b. 15 June 1956, Mantoua, Italy. Education: Faculty of Medicine and Surgery, University of Parma, five years. Contributions to: Poetry published in various anthologies and reviews. Honours: International Competition of Poetry Prize, Mantoua, 1981, 1984, 1985, 1986; Honourable Mention, 1982; International Prize Christmas, Rome, 1983; City of Mantoua Poetry Prize, 1983; S Bettinelli International Prize, 1983; Honour Diploma, F Garcia Lorca, Rome, 1986; Golden Plate, City of Sabbioneta International Poetry Prize, 1990; Finalist, Poesie in Cornice '94, Melegnano, 1994; M Yourcenar Prize Anthology, CDE Melegnano, 1995; Lions Club Viadana-Ogliopo Prize, 1996. Address: 46010 Commessaggio Inf, Mantoua, Italy.

FEDERMAN Raymond, b. 15 May 1928, Paris, France. Novelist; Poet; Translator; Professor. m. Erica Hubscher, 14 Sept 1960, 1 daughter. Education: BA cum laude, Columbia University, 1957; MA, 1958, PhD, 1963, University of California at Los Angeles. Appointments: Assistant Professor, University of California, 1960-64; Associate Professor of French and Comparative Literature, 1964-68, Professor of Comparative Literature, 1964-68, Professor of English and Comparative Literature, 1973-90, Distinguished Professor, 1990-, State University of New York at Buffalo. Publications: Temporary Landscapes, 1965; Among the Beasts, 1967; Me Too, 1975; Duel, 1989; Autobiographic Poems, 1991. Contributions to: Paris Review; Westcoast Review, Review of Australian Poetry; Caliban; Mississippi Review; Buffalo News; Niagara Magazine; Big Table; Evergreen Review; Zone; Esprit. Honours: Guggenheim Fellowship, 1966-67; Frances Steloff Prize, 1971; Panache Experimental Prize, 1972; American Book Award, 1986. Memberships: American PEN Centre; The Fiction Collective, Director, 1989-94, Board, 1988-. Address: 46 Four Seasons West, Eggertsville, NY 14226, USA.

FEINSTEIN Elaine Barbara, b. 24 Oct 1930, England. 3 sons. Education: Newnham College, University of Cambridge, 1949-52. Publications: In a Green Eye, 1966; The Magic Apple Tree, 1971; At the Edge, 1972; The Celebrants and Other Poems, 1973; Some Unease and Angels: Selected Poems, 1977; The Feast of Eurydice, 1980; Badlands, 1987; City Music, 1990; Selectecd Poems, 1994; Poems in Translation: The Selected Poems of Marine Tsvetayeva, 1971, 1987; Three Russian Poets: Margarite Aliger, Yunna Morits Bella Akhmaduline, 1976. Contributions to: Times; Sunday Times; Times Literary Supplement; New York Review of Books. Honours: Cholmondeley Award, 1990; Honorary DLett, Leicester University, 1990; Fellow, Royal Society of Literature, 1980. Membership:

Executive Committee, International PEN. Address: c/o Gill Coleridge, Rogers Coleridge & White, 20 Powis Mews, London W11, England.

FELDMAN Irving (Mordecai), b. 22 Sept 1928, Brooklyn, New York, USA. Professor of English; Poet. m. Carmen Alvarez del Olmo, 1955, 1 son. Education: BS, City College, New York City, 1950; MA, Columbia University, 1953. Appointments: Teacher, University of Puerto Rico, Rio Piedras, 1954-56, University of Lyons, France, 1957-58, Kenyon College, Gambier, Ohio, 1958-64; Professor of English, State University of New York, Buffalo, 1964-. Publications: Poetry: Work and Days and Other Poems, 1961; The Pripet Marshes and Other Poems, 1965; Magic Papers and Other Poems, 1970; Lost Originals, 1972; Leaping Clear, 1976; New and Selected Poems, 1979; Teach Me, Dear Sister, and Other Poems, 1983; All of Us Here and Other Poems, 1986; Other: The Life and Letters, 1994. Honours: Kovner Award, Jewish Book Council of America, 1962; Ingram Merrill Foundation Grant, 1963; American Academy of Arts and Letters Grant, 1973; Guggenheim Fellowship, 1973; Creative Artists Public Service Grant, 1980; Academy of American Poets Fellowship, 1986; John D and Catharine T MacArthur Foundation Fellowship, 1992. Address: c/o Department of English, State University of New York at Buffalo, Buffalo, NY 14260, USA.

FENECH Raymond Mario Paul, b. 6 Jan 1958, St Julians, Malta. Copywriter. m. Angela Fenech, 12 Dec 1987. Education: CACC Diploma, Journalism and Professional Writing, England, 1979; LEA Diploma, Journalism, London Educational Association, England, 1982; The Writing School Diploma, Creative Writing, England, 1996. Appointments: Reporter, Independence Print, 1978-79; Journalist, The Times of Malta, 1980-85; Sales Manager, Inernational Skypak Couriers Limited, 1986-88; Executive, CSB Limited, 1988-90; Director, Promarketing International Limited, 1990-92; Copywriter, Crown Advertising Limited, 1992-. Publications: Within The Edges of Immortality, 1992; Expressions, 1992. Contributions to: The Times of Malta; Il-Mument; Tune In Magazine; Rustic Rub; Poetry Now; Cadium Blue; Poetry Network; Poet's Pen; Dream Inter. Quaterly; Writers Viewpoint; Canadian Writers Journal. Honours: Poet of the Year Award of Merit, National Authors Registry and Cader Publishing, USA, 1993; Best Poem of the Month Award, Verses Magazine, USA, 1993; 2nd Prize, Poetry Network Newsletters Poetry Competition, 1993; Presidents Award, Literary Excellence, National Authors Registry, USA, 1994, 1995, 1996; High Commendation Award, Tears In The Fence International Poetry Competition, 1996. Memberships: Freelance Press Services; Registerd Author, National Authors Registry; Society of American Poets; Salopian Poetry Society; Bay Area Coalition Poets; Malta Delegate for the European Association for the Promotion of Poetry, Brussels, Belgium; Poetry Book Society; Capricorn International Authors Guild; Poetry Society; Sharkti Laureate; Canadian Poetry Association. Address: No 2 Carmen Flats, C. von Brockdorff Street, MSDO2, Malta.

FENTON James, b. 25 Apr 1949, Lincoln, England. Education: BA, Magdalen College, Oxford, 1970. Appointments: Literary journalist with various newspapers including: Guardian, Times, Sunday Times and Independent; Columnist, Arts Poetica, London Sunday Independent, 1990-. Publications include: Our Eastern Furniture, 1968; Put Thou Thy Tears into My Bottle, 1969; Terminal Moraine, 1972; A Vacant Possession, 1978; Dead Soldiers, 1981; A German Requiem, 1981; The Memory of War, 1982; Children in Exile, 1983; Partingtime Hall, 1987. Honours include: Cholmondeley Award, 1986. Address: 1 Bartlemans Road, Oxford OX4 1XU, England.

FERENCZ Gyozo, b. 4 Apr 1954, Budapest, Hungary. University Lecturer. m. Katalin Gadoros, 28 Oct 1977, 2 sons, 1 daughter. Education: MA, Hungarian and English Language and Literature, Eötvös Lorand University, Budapest, 1978; PhD, 1982. Appointments: Literary Editor, Europa Publishing House, 1983-85, 1986-; Lecturer, Eotvos Lorand University, 1985-86. Publications: If There Were no Traces at All, 1981; Danger of Collapse, 1989; John Donne: Negative Love, translation, 1987; An Anthology of American Poetry, editor, 1990. Contributions to: New Moon; Thing; 2000; Moving World. Honours: Robert Graves Prize for Poetry, 1987; Tibor Dery Award, 1990; Forintos Prize for Poetry Translation, 1990. Memberships: Hungarian PEN Club, 1988; Association of Hungarian Writers, 1988; Editor of New Moon, bi-yearly literary anthology, 1989-91; Hungarian Correspondent of International Poetry Magazine, 1988. Address: Ajtosi Düer sor 19-21, Budapest 1146, Hungary.

FERGAR Feyyaz (Feyyaz Kayacan), b. 20 Dec 1919, Istanbul, Turkey. Broadcaster. m. (1) 1942, dec, (2) 1958, dec 1993, 3 sons, 3 daughters. Education: Diploma, Ecole Libre de Sciences Politiques, Paris, 1939; B Comm, Durham University, 1946. Appointments: Announcer and Translator, 1942-44, Programme Assistant, 1947-74, Head of Section, 1974-79, Turkish Section, BBC External Services, retired. Publications: Les Gammes Insolites, 1936; Gestes a la Mer, 1943; A Talent for Shrouds, 1991. Contributions to: Zenos; Acumen; New Canadian Review; Core; Haiku Quarterly; Sell. Membership: International PEN Club. Address: 27 Ravensbourne Road, Bromley, Kent BR1 1HN, England.

FERGUSON Joseph, b. USA. Writer; Editor; Reviewer. Appointments: Former Editor and Reviewer, Hudson Valley Magazine; Ran the Fiction Writing Workshop for the Greater Poughkeepsie Library District; Media Representative, Maryknoll Media Relations Office; Reviews for Times-Herald Record, 1988-; Reviewer for numerous publications. Publications: Fiction, Humour includes: May, Sunshine and No Ice, in Off Belay, 1979; After the Crux, in Swift Kick, 1987; Beware, Joe Tennis, in Climbing, 1995; Poetry in various publications and anthologies include: View from the Graveyard Shift; Grave Dreams; The Altar, 1991; Autumn Road Kill, 1991; Duecy and Detour, 1991; Night Image, 1992; End of Daylight in a Mirror, 1993; Autumn Poem, 1993; Lefty, 1993; Bronx Break Dance, 1994; Two Sisters Who Own a Store, 1994; He Looked Good, 1996; Monotone Morning, 1995; The Steamy Roadside World, 1995; Swept Back, 1995; Reflections on the Way to Work, forthcoming; Nonfiction: Against the Tide: The Life of Skip Storch, Marathon Swimmer, in progress. Contributions to: Numerous articles and columns for various local, national and international publications on many topics as reporter, freelancer, editor and staff writer. Honours: Honourable Mention, American Poetry Association Contest, 1989; Finalist, American Book Series, San Diego Poets Press, 1990; Honourable Mention, World of Poetry Contest, 1990; World of Poetry Golden Poet, 1990; Distinguished Poets of America, 1993; Semi-Finalist, North American Open Poetry Contest, 1993. Address: 26 Bank Street, Cold Spring, NY 10516, USA.

FERGUSON William (Rotch), b. 14 Feb 1943, Fall River, Massachusetts, USA. Associate Professor of Spanish; Writer; Poet. m. Nancy King, 26 Nov 1983. Education: BA, 1965, MA, 1970, PhD, 1975, Harvard University. Appointments: Instructor, 1971-75, Assistant Professor, 1975-77, Boston University; Visiting Professor, 1977-79, Associate Professor of Spanish, 1983-, Adjunct Professor of English, 1989-, Chairman, Foreign Languages, 1990-, Clark University, Worcester, Massachusetts; Visiting Lecturer in Spanish Renaissance Literature, University of Pennsylvania, 1986-87; Associate Editor, Hispanic Review, 1986-87. Publications: Dream Reader (poems), 1973; Light of Paradise (poems), 1973; La versificación imitativa en Fernando de Herrera, 1981; Freedom and Other Fictions (stories), 1984. Contributions to: Scholarly journals, anthologies, periodicals, and magazines. Memberships: American Association of University Professors; International Institute in Spain; Modern Language Association; Phi Beta Kappa; Sigma Delta Pi. Address: 1 Tahanto Road, Worcester, MA 01602, USA.

FERLINGHETTI Lawrence (Monsanto), b. 24 Mar 1920, Yonkers, New York, USA. Poet; Writer; Dramatist; Publisher; Editor; Painter. m. Selden Kirby-Smith, Apr 1951, div, 1 son, 1 daughter. Education: AB, University of North Carolina, 1941; MA, Columbia University, 1948; Doctorat with honours, University of Paris, Sorbonne, 1951. Appointments: Co-owner, City Lights Pocket Bookshop, later City Lights Books, San Francisco, 1953-; Founder Editor, City Lights Books, Publishing, San Francisco, 1955-; Many poetry readings; Participation in many national and interational literary conferences. Publications include: Poetry: Pictures of the Gone World, 1955; A Coney Island of the Mind, 1958; Berlin, 1961; Starting from San Francisco, 1961, revised edition, 1967; Where is Vietnam?, 1965; An Eye on the World: Selected Poems, 1967; After the Cries of the Birds, 1967; The Secret Meaning of Things, 1969; Tyrannus Nix?, 1969; Back Roads to Far Places, 1971; Open Eye, Open Heart, 1973; Who Are We Now?, 1976; Landscapes of Living and Dying, 1979; A Trip to Italy and France, 1980; Endless Life: Selected Poems, 1984; Over All the Obscene Boundaries: European Poems and Transitions, 1985; Inside the Trojan Horse, 1987; When I Look at Pictures, 1990; These Are My Rivers: New and Selected Poems, 1955-1993, 1993. Novels: Her, 1960; Love in the Days of Rage, 1988. Other Writings: The Mexican Night: Travel Journal, 1970; Northwest Ecolog, 1978; Plays: Unfair Arguments with Existence: Seven Plays for a New Theatre, 1963.

Contributions to: Numerous books and periodicals. Creative Works: Painting exhibitions include: retrospective one-man shows: Butler Museum of American Art; University of Maryland Art Gallery; University of California, Santa Cruz, Art Gallery; Palazzo delle Esposizioni, Rome, 1996. Honours: National Book Award Nomination, 1970; Notable Book of 1979 Citation, Library Journal, 1980; Silver Medal for Poetry, Commonwealth Club of California, 1986; Poetry Prize, City of Rome, 1993. Address: c/o City Light Books, 261 Columbus Avenue, San Francisco, CA 94133, USA.

FERMIN Bert, (Deen Engels), b. 7 Dec 1926, Indonesia. Retired Teacher. m. Cili van Neer, 1 Mar 1958, 1 son, 4 daughters. Education: Diploma Teachers Training, Heerlen, 1957; Diploma Teachers Training Special Education, Tilburg, 1961. Appointments: Schools for Retarded Children, 1958-64; Gipsy Childrens School, 1964-66; School for Children with Difficulties in Learning and Education, Maastricht, 1966-68; School for Children with Difficulties in Hearing and Speech, Hoensbroek, 1968-90. Retired. Publications: Poems by Ulrich Bouchard and Deen Engels, 1980; Don't Blow, 1981; Kicking Occiput, 1983; Together in the Holes, 1986; Menu for Surviving, 1987; The Tricks of the Death, 1988; The Snares of Existence, 1989; Abiding in the Fridge, 1991; The Flowers Shark, 1992; Whitehaven, 1994. Contributions to: Appel; Gist; Concept; Vlam; WeL; In zekere zin; Horizon; Karree; Vlaanderen; Nieuw Vlaams Tijdschrift-Gierik; International Poetry. Honours: Poetry Prize, Sint-Truiden, 1979; Secundo Precio en la Categoria Prosa y Poesia, Consulado de Costa Rica, The Hague, 1990. Membership: Vereniging van Limburgse Auteurs. Address: Mauritslaan 1, 6371 ED Landograaf, Netherlands.

FERNANDEZ Antonio J Ruiz, b. 1 Mar 1929, Fonelas, Guadix, Granada. Poet. m. Vida María Sàez Carcelén, 1 son, 3 daughters. Education: High School Graduate. Appointments: Joined Military Academy Los Pachecos, Guadix; Engineer's Corp, Group of Mobilization and Practices of Railroad, 4 years; Various positions, Spanish National Railway Network; Engineers' Chief (civil) and Sublieutenant in ECH(FFCC) Engineers' Corp (military), 1981. Publications: Love and Its Passions, book of poetry (Fourth Summons Acentor Prize, International Poetry Competition Help); Cultural Train of Stories; Life and Love are Better in Granada; Everything is Possible in Granada; Collection of Poems - The Dragon; also several short stories. Contributions to: Anthologies and literary reviews including: Spanish and Latin American Present Authors, 6th and 7th volumes; Bugle of Poetry, 8th and 10th volumes; Great Promises; Poetical Antenna; We; Encyclopaedia of Writers of Spanish Language; Poetical Breezes; Gemma; Cultural World; Andrade; Alba; Caliope; Trianera; Eira. Honours include: Nomination, International Writers and Artists Association; 1st Prize for The Man and the Nature, 9th Literary Tender Agustin García Alonso; Meritorious Member of Honour, Cultural, Literary and Artistic Centre Gazette of Felgueira, Portugal, 1989; International Writers Certificate, Colorado University, USA; Diploma of Honour, Directory of International Literature and University; Nominated Favourite Son, home town District Council, 1990; Founder Member of Merit and Orden Pegasus, World Association of Cultural World Congresses. Memberships: International Writers and Artists Association; Marcilla, cultural group, 1983-; Honorable Member, Cultural, Literary and Artistic Centre AEG; Cultural Association, 1985-; Club of Friends, 1985-. Address: Magnolia 1-2-2, 18015, Granada.

FERNANDEZ Querubin D, Jr (Efren Banez Nuqui, Quefer), b. 30 Jan 1936, Manila, The Philippines. m. Victoria S Talens, 20 July 1964, 2 sons, 2 daughters. Education: BA, English, 1969, BSc, Education, 1970, Angeles University Foundation, The Philippines. Appointments: Managing Editor, Columnist, The Voice; Municipal Secretary, then Assistant Municipal Assessor, Mabalacat, Pampanga. Publications: Anthology on World Brotherhood and Peace, 1979; Bulun Dutung, 1982; Kapampangan Writing, A Compilation and Critique, 1984; Yamut Dikut, 1991. Contributions to: Ing Mayap a Balita Magazine; Central Luzon Newsweekly; Voice. Honours: Crown Poet Laureate by Agtaka, 1973; Alternate Poet Laureate of Emerme, 1975; 1st Place, Don Gonzalo Puyat Memorial Awards for Pampango Literature, 1980; 1st Prize Winner, Contest in Commemoration of the 418th Foundation Day of Pampanga, 1990. Memberships: Secretary, Aguman Talasulat Kapampangan, 1978-82; Vice President, Aguman Poeta at Taladalit Ning Amanung Siswan, 1990-94. Address: Mabalacat, Pampanga 2010, The Philippines.

FERNANDEZ DE LA PUENTE Amando Jesus (Amando Fernandez), b. 16 Mar 1949, Havana, Cuba. College Instructor. Education: BA, 1983, MSc, Modern Language Education, 1984, MA,

Hispanic Studies, 1988, Florida International University. Publications: Herir at Tiempo, 1986; Perfil de la Materia, 1986; Azar en Sombra, 1987; Pentagrama, 1987; El Ruisenor y la Espada, 1988; Materia y Forma, 1990; Los Siete Circulos, 1991. Honours: 1st Prizes for Poetry include: Jose Maria Heredia, 1986, 1987; Mairena, 1986; Agustin Acosta, 1987; Jaen de Poesia, 1987; Odon Betanzos, 1987; Luis de Gongora, 1987; Antonio Gonzalez de Lama, 1988; Ciudad de Badajoz, 1989. Address: 4803 North West 7th Street, Apt 302, Miami, FL 33126, USA.

FERRARA Ranieri Walter, b. 17 June 1954, Naples, Italy. Philosopher. Publications: Ritrattazioni, 1988; La correzione, 1990; La sostituzione, 1993. Contributions to: Quinta Generazione; Visionario; Offerta Speciale; Anterem; Mito; Ballyhoo-Letterature; Annales; Gemma; Pliego de Murmurios; Escamotage; Presencias; Anthologies: International Poetry, 1990; World Poetry, 1992; La Poésie des Palmipedes, 1992. Membership: World Academy of Arts and Culture, USA. Address: Via Saverio Altamura 22, 80128 Naples, Italy.

FERRARI Mauro, b. 16 Feb 1959, Novi Ligure, Italy. English Teacher. m. Arezzi Marina, 3 Oct 1987. Education: Scientific High School; Degree summa cum laude, Foreign Languages, University of Genoa, 1983. Appointments: English Teacher, High School, 1985-; English Literature Teacher, Third-Age University, Genoa, 1988-90, Novi Ligure, 1990-91; Director, publishing company, Edizioni Joker, Novi Ligure; Director, literary magazine, La Clessidra; Editor, Joker. Publications: Forme, 1989; Almanacco del Poeta, 3 poems, 1990; I Ventidue, 4 poems, 1990; Al Fondo delle Cose, 1995. Contributions to: Il Lettore di Provincia; Margo; Zeta; Altri Termini; Clandestino; Testuale; L'Altra Europa (mostly essays on British poetry); Margo and Clandestino (mostly poems); Galleria; La Clessidra. Memberships: Editorial Staff, Margo, Milan, 1991-; Poetry Society; Editorial Staff, L'Altra Europa, Cosenza. Address: Via Baiardi 12, 15067 Novi Ligure (AL), Italy.

FERREL Carl Gene, b. 29 July 1950, Iowa, USA. Manager; Septic Repair Specialist. Education: Art Degree, Colorado Mountain College, 1971-72; Real Estate Certificate, Blackhawk College, Illinois, 1981. Appointments: Self Employed Business and Personal Consultant, 1977-78; Record Company President, 1978-79; Manager, Septic Repair Specialist, 1982-91. Publications: Poems in anthologies: These Too Shall Be Heard, Vols I and II, 1989; Golden Voices Past and Present, 1989; American Poetry Anthology, 1989, 1990; 1990 Anthology of Southern Poetry, 1990; Whispers in the Wind, 1990; Down Peaceful Paths, 1990; Moment of Memory. Contributions to: Rock Island Argus Dispatch. Honours: Golden Poet, 1990; Honourable Mentions, 1990, 1991. Memberships: Florida State Poets Association; National Federation of State Poetry Societies. Address: 2630 78th Avenue, Milan, IL 61264, USA.

FERRETT Mabel (Mrs Wuzzle, MF), b. 30 Apr 1917, Leeds, Yorkshire, England. Educator. m. Harold Ferrett, 7 Aug 1947, 1 son. Education: Teacher's Certificate, Ripon Training College. Appointments: Teacher in Leeds; Part-time work for Kirklees Museums Service; Freelance Journalist. Publications: The Lynx-Eyed Strangers, 1956; The Tall Tower, 1970; Years of the Right Hand, 1975; A Question of Menhirs, 1984; Humber Bridge, Selected Poems, 1955-85, 1986; Scathed Earth, poems, 1986; Poetry tape, Poems by Ian Emberson and Mabel Ferrett, 1983. Contributions to: BBC Radio 4; Radio Leeds Educational Services; Pennine Radio; Yorkshire Post; Outposts; John O'London's Weekly; Orbis; Woman Journalist; Pennine Platform; New Hope International; Yorkshire Ridings Magazine; John Bull; Pennine Poets Anthology 1966-1986; Pennine 25, 1991; and others; Editor, Pennine Platform, 1973-76; Editor, Ipso Facto, poetry anthology, 1975; Editor, Orbis, 1978-80. Honours: 2nd Prize, Kirklees Festival, 1975; Special Prize, Phoenix Anag-rhyme Competition, 1975; 1st Prize, Julian Cairns Award, Society of Women Writers and Journalists, 1976; Yorkshire Arts Association Bursaries, 1979, 1983; Poetry Adjudication, Wharfedale Festival Poetry Competitions, 1984, 1985, 1988, 1992. Memberships: Pennine Poets; Life President, Spen Valley Historical Society. Address: 2 Vernon Road, Heckmondwike, West Yorkshire WF16 9LU, England.

FIELD Edward, (Bruce Elliot), b. 7 June 1924, Brooklyn, New York, USA. Writer. Education: New York University (no degree). Publications: Stand Up, Friend, with Me, 1963; Variety Photoplays, 1967; A Full Heart, 1977; A Geography of Poets, editor, 1979; Village, (with Neil Derrick as Bruce Elliot); New and Selected Poems, 1987; Counting Myself Lucky, 1992; Editor, A New Geography of Poets,

1992; The Office, with Neil Derrick (as Bruce Elliot); Eskimo Songs and Stories, 1973. Contributions to: New Yorker; New York Review of Books; Partisan Review; Evergreen Review; Listener. Honours: Lamont Award, 1963; Guggenheim Fellowship, 1963; Shelley Memorial Award, 1978; Fellow, American Academy of Rome, 1980. Membership: Authors Guild. Address: 463 West Street, No A323, New York, NY 10014, USA.

FIELD Simon, b. 21 Nov 1955, Cookham, Berkshire, England. Nurse. Education: BA, Philosophy, Leicester University, 1979. Contributions to: Rialto; Orbis; Staple; New Hope International; Mildred; Southern Review; Bogg; Poetry New Zealand; Takalie; and others. Membership: Auckland Poetry Workshop, New Zealand. Address: 55 Finch Street, Morningside, Auckland, New Zealand.

FIELDER Mildred, b. 14 Jan 1913, South Dakota, USA. Author. m. Ronald G Fielder, 17 Sept 1932, 2 sons. Education: Huron College, 1931-32; University of Colorado, 1937. Appointments: Various posts in national offices for National League of American Pen Women; Book Review Editor, The Pen Woman Magazine. Publications: Wandering Foot in the West, 1955; The Edzards Family and Related Lines, 1965; The Treasure of Homestake Gold, 1970; Potato Creek Johnny, 1973; Wild Bill Hickok, Gun Man, 1974; Deadwood Dick and the Dime Novels, 1974; Poker Alice, 1978; Preacher Smith of Deadwood, 1981; Wild Fruits, An Illustrated Field Guide and Cookbook, 1983; Invitation to Fans, 1988; Love is Forever, 1992; Story Poems, 1993. Contributions to: Anthology of American Poetry, 1962; Rhyme Time for the Very Young, 1964; Yearbook of Modern Poetry, 1971; Outstanding Contemporary Poetry, 1972; Denver Post; Grit; Pacific Spectator; and others. Honours: Prize Winner: Pennsylvania Poetry Contest; Jesse Stuart Contest; Palo Alto Sonnet Contest; New York Poetry Forum; Tracy Souers Memorial Religious Poetry Contest; California Federation of Chaparral Poets; World of Poetry; South Dakota State Fair. Memberships: Life, Society of American Historians; Regional Vice President, South Dakota Poetry Society; Life. South Dakota Historical Society; National Federation of Press Women; National League of American Pen Women; Western Writers of America; New York Poetry Forum; California Federation of Chaparral Poets. Address: 5202 North Fort Yuma Trail, Tucson, AZ 85715, USA.

FIELDING Amber. See: **MONEYSMITH Carol Louise Giesbrecht.**

FIELDS Nancy Carlene Sexton, b. 20 Jan 1952, Wise County, Virginia, USA. Poet; Novelist; Songwriter. m. Vester Fields Jr, 3 Feb 1967, 2 sons. Education: Graduated, Public Schools, Wise County, Virginia. Appointments: Writer of poetry, gospel, rock and country songs; Author of romantic novels; Artist. Contributions to: Great Poems of the Western World; Golden Treasures; Poems That Will Live Forever. Honours: World of Poetry Hall of Fame; Honourable Mention, 1988, 1989, 1990; Awards of Merit, 1988-1990; Golden Poet Awards, 1988-1992; Silver Poet Awards, 1990-1992. Memberships: International Platform Association; Homer Honor Society of International Poets; Editors and Poets in the United States and Canada, 1989-90. Address: Rt 1, Box 621, T Branch, Norton, VA 24273, USA.

FIGUEROA John (Joseph Maria), b. 4 Aug 1920, Kingston, Jamaica. Professor (retired); Writer; Poet. m. Dorothy Grace Murray Alexander, 3 Aug 1944, 4 sons, 3 daughters. Education: AB, College of the Holy Cross, 1942; Teachers Diploma, 1947, MA, 1950, University of London; Graduate Studies, Indiana University, 1964. Appointments: Lecturer, University of London, 1948-53; Senior Lecturer, 1953-57, Professor of Education, 1957-73, Dean of the Faculty of Education, 1966-69, University College of the West Indies, Kingston; Professor of English and Consultant to the President, University of Puerto Rico, 1971-73; Professor of Humanities, El Centro Caribeno de Estudios Postgraduados, Puerto Rico, 1973-76; Professor of Education, University of Jos, Nigeria, 1976-80; Visiting Professor of Humanities, Bradford College, Yorkshire, England, 1980; Fellow, Centre of Caribbean Studies, Warwick University, 1988.Publications: Blue Mountain Peak, poems and prose, 1944; Love Leaps Here, poems, 1962; Editor, Caribbean Voices: An Anthology of West Indian Poetry, 2 volumes, 1966, 1970; Society, Schools and Progress in the West Indies, 1971; Ignoring Hurts: Poems, 1976; Editor, Dreams and Realities: Six One-Act Comedies, 1978; Co-Editor, Caribbean Writers, 1979; Editor, An Anthology of African and Caribbean Writing in English, 1982; Editor: Third World Studies: Caribbean Sampler, 1983; The Chase: The Collected Poems of John Figueroa, 1991.

Contributions to: Journals and periodicals. Honours: British Council Fellowship, 1946-47; Carnegie Fellowship, 1960; Guggenheim Fellowship, 1964; Lilly Foundation Grant, 1973; Institute of Jamaica Medal, 1993; Medal, Bourg-en-Bresse, France. Address: 77 Station Road, Woburn Sands, Buckinghamshire, MK17 8SH, England.

FINALE Frank, b. 10 Mar 1942, Brooklyn, New York, USA. Educator. m. Barbara Long, 20 Oct 1973, 3 sons. Education: BS, Education, Ohio State University, 1964; MA, Human Development, Fairleigh Dickinson University, 1976. Appointments: Founding Member, and Editor-in-Chief, Without Halos, 1985-95; Poetry Editor, the new renaissance, 1996-. Publications: Anthologies in: Life on the Line, 1992; A Loving Voice, Vol 2, 1993; Dear Winter, 1984; Anthology of Magazine Verse and Yearbook of American Poetry, 1985, 1986-88; Blood to Remember, 1991; Movieworks, 1990; Co-Editor, Anthology of Jersey Shore Poems and Photographs, forthcoming 1996; Under a Gull's Wing. Contributions to: Christian Science Monitor; Georgia Review; New York Quarterly; Kansas Quarterly; the new renaissance; Negative Capability; Poet Lore; Poetry Now; Blue Unicorn; Brooklyn Review; Long Pond Review; Journal of New Jersey Poets; Footwork; Pig Iron; Long Story; Descant; Piedmont Literary Review; ELF; LIPS; XANADU. Honour: Literacy Award from International Reading Association and The Ocean County Reading Council, 1993. Membership: Founding Member, Ocean County Poets Collective, 1983. Address: 19 Quail Run Drive, Bayville, NJ 08721, USA.

FINCH Annie Ridley Crane, b. 31 Oct 1956, New Rochelle, New York, USA. Poet; Editor; Teacher; Critic. m. Glen Brand, 6 Dec 1985, 1 son. Education: BA, Yale University, 1979; MA, Creative Writing, University of Houston, 1986; PhD, English, Stanford University, 1990. Appointments: Editor, Poems: A Journal of Poetry Reviews and Essays; Editor and Poetry Editor, Sequoia; Graduate Fellow, Stanford Humanities Centre; Assistant Professor, Prosody and Creative Writing, University of Northern Iowa. Publications: The Encyclopaedia of Scotland, 1982; The Ghost of Meter: Culture and Prosody in American Free Verse, 1993. Contributions to: Hellas; Salmon; Formalist; (How)ever; Outposts; South Dakota Review; Plains Poetry Journal; Kansas Quarterly; Weber Studies; MacGuffin. Honours: Editors Award, The MacGuffin, 1990; Nicholas Roerich Fellowship, 1993. Memberships: Poetry Society of America; Academy of American Poets; Emily Pickinson International Society (charter member). Address: English Department, University of Northern Iowa, Cedar Falls, IA 50614, USA.

FINCH Peter, b. 6 Mar 1947, Cardiff, Wales. Poet; Writer. 2 sons, 1 daughter. Education: Glamorgan Polytechnic. Appointment: Editor, Second Aeon, 1966-75. Publications: Wanted, 1967; Pieces of the Universe, 1968; How to Learn Welsh, 1977; Between 35 and 42, short stories, 1982; Some Music and a Little War, 1984; How to Publish Your Poetry, 1985; Reds in the Bed, 1986; Selected Poems, 1987; How to Publish Yourself, 1988; Make 1990; Poems for Ghosts, 1991; Useful, 1997; Antibodies, 1997. Contributions to: Various magazines and journals. Memberships: Welsh Academy; Welsh Union of Writers. Address: 19 Southminster Road, Roath, Cardiff CF2 5AT, Wales.

FINCH Roger, b. 17 Apr 1937, Pittsburgh, Pennsylvania, USA. Professor of English and Linguistics. Education: BA, Music Theory, George Washington University, 1968; PhD, Near Eastern Language and Literature, Harvard University, 1977. Appointments: Lecturer, Sophia University, Tokyo, 1978-; Professor, Surugadai University, Saitama, 1990-. Publications: What Is Written in the Wind; According to Lilies, Carcanet, 1993. Contributions to: PN Review; London Magazine; Beloit; Michigan Quarterly; Horam Poetry Review; Poet Lore; Wormwood; Literary Review; Prairie Schooner; Cimarron Review; Clockwatch Review; San Jose Studies; Waascana Review; Antigonish Review; Windsor Review. Honour: 1st Prize, Bridport Arts Centre, 1988. Address: O-Aza Kitagawa 176-6 Hanno-shi, Saitama, Japan.

FINCKE Gary W, b. 7 July 1945, Pittsburgh, Pennsylvania, USA. University Professor. m. Elizabeth Locker, 17 Aug 1968, 2 sons, 1 daughter. Education: BA, Thiel College, 1967; MA, Miami University, 1969; PhD, Kent State University, 1974. Appointments: English Instructor, Penn State University, 1969-75; Chair, English Department, LeRoy Central School, 1975-80; Associate Professor, English, Susquehanna University, 1980-. Publications: The Double Negatives of the Living, 1992; Plant Voices, 1991; Handing the Self Back, 1990; The Days of Uncertain Health, 1988; The Coat in the Heart, 1985;

Breath, 1984; For Keepsies, 1993; Inventing Angels, 1994. Contributions to: Paris Review; Poetry; Yankee; Quarterly Poetry Northwest; Georgia Review; Prairie Schooner; Beloit Poetry Journal; Gettysburg Review; Pequod; Cimarron Review; Southwest Review; New England Review and Breadloaf Quarterly; Laurel Review; Green Mountains Review; Boulevard; Harper's. Honours: Pennsylvania Arts Council Fellowships, 1982, 1985, 1987, 1991, 1995. Memberships: Poets and Writers; Associated Writing Programs; Poetry Society of America. Address: 3 Melody Lane, Selinsgrove, PA 17870, USA.

FINKEL Donald, b. 21 Oct 1929, New York, New York, USA. Poet; University Teacher (retired). m. Constance Urdang, 1956, 1 son, 2 daughters. Education: BS, 1952, MA, 1953, Columbia University. Appointments: Teacher, University of Iowa, 1957-58; Bard College, 1958-60; Faculty, 1960-92, Poet-in-Residence, 1965-92, Poet-in-Residence Emeritus, 1992-, Washington University, St Louis; Visiting Lecturer, Bennington College, 1966-67; Princeton University, 1985. Publications: The Clothing's New Emperor and Other Poems, 1959; Simeon, 1964; A Joyful Noise, 1966; Answer Back, 1968; The Garbage Wars, 1970; Adequate Earth, 1972; A Note in Heaven's Eye, 1975; Going Under, and Endurance: An Arctic Idyll: Two Poems, 1978; What Manner of Beast, 1981; The Detachable Man, 1984; Selected Shorter Poems, 1987; The Wake of the Electron, 1987; Beyond Despair, 1994. Honours: Helen Bullis Prize, 1964; Guggenheim Fellowship, 1967; National Endowment for the Arts Grants, 1969, 1973; Ingram-Merrill Foundation Grant, 1972; Theodore Roethke Memorial Prize, 1974; Morton Dauwen Zabel Award, American Academy of Arts and Letters, 1980. Membership: Phi Beta Kappa. Address: 2051 Park Avenue, Apt D, St Louis, MO 63104, USA.

FIORENTINO Carmine, b. 11 Sept 1932, Brooklyn, New York, USA. Education: LLB, Blackstone School of Law, Chicago, 1954; LLB, John Marshall Law School, Georgia, 1957. Appointment: Presently engaged in Private Law Practice. Publications: Non Fiction; Poetry; Composer, words and music of popular songs and hymns. Contributions to: Evening Star; National Observer. Honours: Private Tutor and Monitor, Georgia State Board of Bar Examiners; Atlanta Lawyer Reference Panel, 1953-63; Commendation, Director of US Department of Housing and Urban Development, Elmira New York Disaster Field Office; Statue of Victory, World Culture Prize, 1985. Memberships: American, Federal, Atlanta and Decatur-Dekalb Bar Associations; American Judicature Society; Old War Horse Lawyers Club; Association of Trial Lawyers. Address: 4717 Roswell Road North East, Suite R-4, Atlanta, GA 30342, USA.

FIRER Susan, b. 14 Oct 1948, Milwaukee, Wisconsin, USA. Writer; Educator. 1 son, 2 daughters. Education: BA, 1973, MA, 1982, University of Wisconsin, Milwaukee. Appointments: Lecturer in English; Adjunct Assistant Professor, University of Wisconsin at Milwaukee, 1988-. Publications: My Life With the Tsar and Other Poems, 1979; The Underground Communion Rail, 1992; The Lives of the Saints and Everything, 1993. Contributions to: Chicago Tribune; Christian Science Monitor; Best American Poetry, 1992; Iowa Review; Boundaries of Twilight: Czecho-Slovak Writing from the New World, 1991; Hummers, Knucklers and Slow Curves: Contemporary Baseball Poems, 1991; Mixed Voices: Contemporary Poems About Music, 1991. Honours: Academy of American Poets Prize, University of Wisconsin, 1977; Wisconsin Arts Board Fellowship, 1979; The Best American Poetry, 1992; Cleveland State University Poetry Centre Prize, 1992. Address: 1514 East Kensington Boulevard, Milwaukee, WI 53211, USA.

FIRTH A Lee, b. 22 May 1962, Pontefract, Yorkshire, England. Director of Local Charity. Publications: Co-Author, Undue Vibrations, 1989; Snapshots, Vol 1, 1991, Vol 2, 1992; Poems 1988-92, 1992. Contributions to: Envoi Summer 1991 Anthology; Poetry Now; North West Anthology, 1992; Guardians of the State Anthology, 1992; Numerous poetry magazines; Frequent performer at Northern Literature and Arts Festivals. Address: 109 High Street, Thurnscoe, Rotherham, Yorkshire S63 0QZ, England.

FISCHER Maria. See: **SAUER Annmarie.**

FISHER Allen, b. 1 Nov 1944, Norbury, London, England. Educator; Painter. Education: Goldsmiths' College, University of London, 1983-86; Masters degree, Essex University. Appointments: Head of Academic Affairs, Herefordshire College of Art & Design; Publisher with various book firms; Painter. Publications include: Long Shout to Kernewek, 1975; Paxton's Beacon, 1976; Gripping the Rail,

1976; Doing, 1977; London Blight, 1977; Apocalyptic Sonnets, 1978; Unpolished Mirrors, 1981; Bending Windows, 1982; Defamiliarising, 1983; African Boog, 1983; Brixton Fractals, 1985; Buzzards and Bees, 1987; Camel Walk, 1988; Stepping Out, 1989; Convalescence, 1992; Co-author, Future Exiles, 1992; Breadboard, 1994; Dispossession & Cure, 1995; Civic Crime, 1995. Address: 14 Hopton Road, Hereford HR1 1BE, England.

FISHER Leona. See: **KERR Kathryn Ann.**

FISHER Roy, b. 11 June 1930, Birmingham, England. Writer; Musician. Education: BA, 1951, MA, 1970, Birmingham University. Publications: City, 1961; The Ship's Orchestra, 1967; Matrix, 1971; The Cut Pages, 1971, 1986; The Thing About Joe Sullivan, 1978; A Furnace, 1986; Birmingham River, 1994; The Dow Low Drop, 1996. Contributions to: Numerous journals and magazines. Honours: Andrew Kelus Prize, 1979; Cholmondeley Award, 1981. Memberships: Society of Authors; Musicians Union. Address: Four Ways, Earl Sterndale, Buxton, Derbyshire SK17 0EP, England.

FISHMAN Charles Munro, b. 10 July 1942, Oceanside, New York, USA. m. Ellen M Haselkorn, 25 June 1967, 2 daughters. Education: BA, 1964, MA, 1965, Hofstra University; DA, State University of New York at Albany, 1982. Appointments: Distinguished Service Professor of English and Humanities and Director, Visiting Writers Program, State University of New York at Farmingdale. Publications: The Firewalkers, 1996; Nineteenth-Century Rain, 1994; As the Sun Goes Down in Fire, 1992; Zoom, 1990; The Death Mazurka, 1987, 1989; Warm-Blooded Animales, 1977; Aurora, 1974; Editor, Blood to Remember: American Poets on the Holocaust, 1991; Co-Translator, Katzenleben (Catlives), 1991. Contributions to: American Writing; Epoch; Southern Poetry Review; New York Times; European Judaism; Prism International; New York Quarterly; New England Review; Poetry Now; Poetry East; Georgia Review; Anthology of Magazine Verse and Yearbook of American Poetry; Midstream. Honours: New York Foundation for the Arts Fellowship in Poetry, 1995; Winner Firman Houghton Poetry Award, New England Poetry Club, 1995; Gertrude B Claytor Memorial Award, 1987; Poet in the Community Award, 1979, 1982; Writer's Market Poetry Competition First Prize, 1972; Pinkie Gordon Lane Nature Poetry Award, 1979. Memberships: Associated Writing Programs; American PEN; Poetry Society of America; Poets and Writers; Long Island Poetry Collective (Co-Founder). Address: Visiting Writers Program, Knapp Hall, State University of New York at Farmingdale, NY 11735, USA.

FITTS Gus. See: **RABORG Frederick Ashton, Jr.**

FITZGERALD Judith, b. 11 Nov 1952, Toronto, Ontario, Canada. Poet; Critic. Education: MA, English Literature, York University, 1977. Publications: Beneath the Skin of Paradise: The Piaf Poems, 1984; My Orange Gorange, 1985, children's poetry, illustrated by Maureen Paxton; Given Names: New and Selected Poems, 1972-85, 1985, poetry, edited by Frank Davey; Whale Waddleby, 1986, children's poetry, illustrated by Maureen Paxton; SP/ELLES: Poetry by Canadian Women: Poesie de femmes canadiennes, edited with an introduction, 1986; Diary of Desire, 1987, poetry; First Person Plural, 1987, anthology; Raptuous Chronicles, 1991, prose poem; Ultimate Midnight, 1992, poetry and prose poem; Daybook for a Habit of Blues, 1993, Prose-poem novella; River, poems, 1995. Contributions to: Poems in anthologies, broadcasts and periodicals. Honours: Canada Council Project Grant, 1988; Canada Council Arts Grant A, 1988; Toronto Arts Council Research and Development Award, 1990; Canada Council Project Grant, 1990, 1991; Canada Council Arts Grant A, 1990; Short-listed for The Governor-General's Award for poetry, Raptuous Chronicles, 1992. Address: 1805-2285 Lakeshore West, Mimico, Ontario M8V 3X9, Canada.

FITZGERALD Mary Joan, b. 2 Oct 1928, Chicago, Illinois, USA. Musician; Teacher; Educator. Education: BA, Music Education, Alverno College, Milwaukee, Wisconsin, 1967; MPS, Institute of Pastoral Studies, Loyola University, Chicago, 1987; Master's Equivalent in Church Music, DePaul University, Chicago. Appointments: Piano Teacher, Music Education Teacher, Church Musician, 1949-88; Organist, St Henry Catholic Church, Chicago, 1981-88; Secretary, 1988-. Contributions to: 1987 American Anthology of Midwestern Poetry; Writer of 137 poetic English Sequences for Sacred Liturgy, unpublished. Address: 8937 North Lamon Avenue, Skokie, IL 60077, USA.

FITZGERALD-CLARKE Michael, b. 11 Mar 1959, Doncaster, Yorkshire, England. Poet. m. Kim, 17 Mar 1995. Education: Bachelor of Economics, Monash University, Australia. 1980. Appointments: Various positions in the Australian Public Service. Publications: Paralytic Mountain; S-h-h-hideIplonk, both forthcoming. Contributions to: Poems published in Australia, USA and England. Address: 9 Holder Street, Turner, ACT 2612, Australia.

FITZMAURICE Gabriel John, b. 7 Dec 1952, Moyvane, County Kerry, Ireland. Primary Teacher. m. Brenda Downey, 17 Aug 1981, 1 son, 1 daughter. Education: Leaving Certificate, Honours, St Michael's College, Listowel, County Kerry. 1965-70; Diploma in Primary Teaching, Mary Immaculate College, Limerick, 1970-72. Appointments: Assistant Teacher, Avoca National School, County Wicklow, 1972-74; Teacher, Christ The King National School, Limerick City, 1974-75, Moyvane National School, 1975-. Publications include: Poetry in English: Rainsong, 1984, Road to the Horizon, 1987, Dancing Through, 1990, The Father's Part, 1992, The Space Between: New and Selected Poems 1984-92, 1993, The Village Sings, 1996; Poetry in Irish: Nocht, 1989, Ag Síobshiul Chun An Rince, 1995; Children's poetry in English: The Moving Stair, 1989, enlarged edition, 1993, But Dad!, 1995; Children's poetry in Irish: Nach Iontach Mar Atá, 1994; Translation, The Purge, by Mícheál Ó Airtnéide, 1989, Poems I Wish I'd Written, selected translations from the Irish, 1996; Editor: The Flowering Tree, 1991, Between the Hills and Sea: Songs and Ballads of Kerry, 1991, Irish Poetry Now: Other Voices, 1993, Kerry Through Its Writers, 1993. Contributions to: Spectator; Tablet; Sunday Tribune, Dublin; Irish Times, Dublin; Poetry Ireland Review; Poetry Review, Belgium; Fiddlehead, Canada; Etudes Irlandaises, France. Honours: Represented Ireland at Europees Poeziefestival, Leuven, Belgium, 1987, 1991; Award Winner, Gerard Manley Hopkins Centenary Poetry Competition, 1989. Memberships: Former Chairman and Literary Advisor, Writers' Week, Listowel, County Kerry; Patron, Kerry International Summer School of Living Irish Authors, Tralee, Co Kerry. Address: Applegarth, Moyvane, County Kerry, Ireland.

FITZSIMMONS Thomas, b. 21 Oct 1926. Professor of English. m. 2 sons. Education: BA English Literature, Stanford University, 1951; MA English and Comparative Literature, Columbia University, New York, 1952. Appointments: Consulting Editor, Office of the Secretary of Defence, 1952-; Writer and Editor, New Republic Magazine, Washington, DC, 1952-55; Research Team Chairman, 1955-56, Director of Research for Publication 1956-68, Director and Editor 1958-59, HRAF, Yale University; Assistant Professor 1966-88, Emeritus 1989-, Oakland University, Rochester, Michigan. Publications: Water Ground Stone, 1993; Muscle and Machine Dream, 1986; Rocking Mirror Daybreak, Linked Poems with Ooka Makoto, 1982; With the Water, 1972; Translations: The New Poetry of Japan (co-editor), 1993; A Play of Mirrors: Eight Major Poets of Modern Japan, 1987 (co-editor); A String Around Autumn: Selected Poems of Ooka Makoto, 1952-80, 1982; Japanese Poetry Now, 1972; Ghazals of Ghalib, 1971; Dream Machine, 1996. Contributions to: Antioch Review; Art Presse; Astra; Beloit Poetry Journal; Black Mountain Review; Chelsea Review; Crosscurrants; Evergreen Review; Floating Bear; Goliards; Kenyon Review; Tri Quarterly; Wormwood. Honours: Numerous including: National Endowment for the Arts Fellowships, 1967, 1982, 1989-90 and Grants, 1984, 1986; Fulbright Lectureships, 1962-64, 1967-68; Fulbright Research Fellowship, 1988-89. Address: KatyDid Books, 1 Balsa Road, Sante Fe, NM 87505, USA.

FLAMMONDE Paris, (M M Delfano, Adolf Nemm, Desmond), b. 1932, Richmond, Virginia, USA. Poet; Author; Journalist; Critic; Columnist; Broadcaster; Director; Painter; Composer. m. Marcia Damian Sadagursky, 8 Feb 1963. Education: University of Chicago; Chicago Art Institute; New York University; New School for Social Research. Appointments: Broadcast Panelist; Producer; Director; Lecturer. Publications: Books: The Kennedy Conspiracy, 1969; The Age of Flying Saucers, 1971; The Mystic Healers, 1974; UFO Exist! 1976; The Living Prophets, 1972; Poetry Books: Phantasmagoria, 1958; The Grey Man, 1965. Contributions to: Saturday Review; Harper's; National Review; East; Georgia Review; Cavalier; Epos; Bluestone; Cape Rock; Bardic Echoes; The Lyric: Vespers; Unusual; Peace and Poets International; Bowery News; Pegasus; Emily Dickenson Studies; Odessa; Candelabrum (England); The Westerly (Australia). Honours: First Prize, Peace and Poets International; Third Prize, International Shakespeare Sonnet Competition; First, Greenwich Village Laureate Prize. Memberships: Author's Guild; Author's League; Poetry Society of American; Co-Founder, The Creative Workshop, New York City, and the Prometheans; Founder, The Merlin Society of

Poetry and other Arts. Address: Tarot Box 6199 RR 6, Stroudsburg, PA 18360, USA.

FLETCHER Harvey Dupree, b. 28 Feb 1936, Spartanburg, South Carolina, USA. Retired US Marine. Education: University of South Carolina, 1977-79. Appointments: US Marine Corps, 1952-71; Veteran of Korea, 1953; Veteran of Vietnam, 1964, 1967-68, 1970-71; TV shows, 1987-89; Lecturer, University of South Carolina, 1989. Publications: Visions of NAM, 1987, Vol II, 1987, Vol III, 1988, Vol IV, 1991. Address: 4189 Sheppard Crossing Way, Stone Mountain, GA 30083, USA.

FLORSHEIM Stewart, b. 14 Nov 1952, New York, New York, USA. Company Director. m. Judy Rosloff, 24 May 1987, 2 daughters. Education: BA, Journalism and Philosophy, Syracuse University, 1974; MA, English, San Francisco State University, 1978. Appointments: Assistant Editor, Excerpta Medica, 1974-76; Manager, German Books, Cody's Book Store, Berkeley, California, 1976-78; Director, Technical Communications, ASK, 1978-94; Group Manager, Documentation, Intuit, 1994-96; Documentation Manager, Advent Software, 1996-. Publications: Ghosts of the Holocaust, 1989; Unsettling America, 1994. Contributions to: Berkeley Poets Cooperative; Dremples; Round Table; Dimension; Blue Unicorn; Syracuse Poems; Yoga Journal; Double Take. Honour: Honourable Mention, Whiffen Prize, Syracuse University, 1974. Membership: Berkeley Poets Cooperative, 1976-80. Address: 170 Sandringham Road, Piedmont, CA 94611, USA.

FLORY Sheldon, b. 28 June 1927, USA. Retired Episcopal (Anglican) Priest. 3 sons. Education: AB French, Middlebury College, Vermont, 1950; MA English Comparative Literature, Columbia University, New York City, 1952; MDiv, General Theology Seminary, New York, 1958. Appointments: Fellow and Tutor, General Theological Seminary 1958-60; Rector, St Margaret's Church, Belfast, Maine 1960-63; Rector, Trinity Church, Geneva, New York, 1963-69; Chaplain, Brown University, Providence, Rhode Island, 1969-74; Chaplain and Dean of Faculty, Darrow School, New Lebanon, New York, 1974-90; Part-time Priest-in-Charge, St Peter's Church, Bloomfield, New York, 1991-. Publications: A Winter's Journey, 1979; Open Winter, 1994. Contributions to: New Yorker; Poetry; Epoch; Iowa; Seneca and Northern Reviews; Lamp in the Spine; Williwaw; Separate Doors; London Sunday Observer; Anglican Theological Review. Honours: Borestone Mountain Anthology, 1955; Williwaw Annual Competition, Hon Mention, 1988; Arvon International Poetry Competition, First Prize, 1989; Judge, Arvon Competition, 1991. Memberships: PEN 1980-85; Poets and Writers 1974-. Address: 6981 R 21, Naples, NY 14512, USA.

FLYNN Sharon Washburn, b. 14 Jan 1949, Winchester, Massachusetts, USA. Billing Clerk. m. Bill Flynn, 10 Dec 1977, 2 sons, 2 daughters. Education: Diploma, Technical High School, 1967; Basic and Advanced Courses, Institute of Children's Literature, 1988-90; External Studies, Creative Writing/Poetry, University of Wisconsin, 1990-91. Appointments: Directory Assistance Operator; Receptionist/Clerical; Lumber Clerk (Accounts Payable); Claims Assistant; Claims Examiner/Processor; Billing Clerk (Accounts Payable/Accounts Receivable). Publications: Lions, Lizards and Lady Bugs, 1989; Bears, Bunnies and Bees, 1990; A Voyage to Remember, 1996; Best Poems of 1995; Numerous Anthologies, 1988-96. Contributions to: Poet Magazine; Poet's Review; Midwest Poetry Review; Lucidity; Parnassus Literary Journal; Sharing and Caring; Hayden's Poetry Review; The Inspirational Poet. Honours: Honorable Mention, Writer's Digest Writing Competition, 1992; Commendable Award, New England Writers/Vermont Poets Free Verse, 1992; 1st Place, Best of Book for Vol 6 of Sharing and Caring, Hayden's Poetry Review, November Issue. Memberships: New England Writers/Vermont Poets Association; American Academy of Poets. Address: 106 Lang Street, Springfield, MA 01104-2138, USA.

FOERSTER Richard Alfons, b. 29 Oct 1949, New York, New York, USA. Writer; Editor. m. Valerie Elizabeth Malinowski, 28 Oct 1972, div 1985. Education: BA English, Fordham University, 1971; MA English, Univerity of Virginia, 1972; Teacher Certificate, Manhattanville College, 1975. Appointments: Assistant Editor, Clarence L Barnhart Inc, 1973-75; Editor, Prentice Hall Inc, 1976-78; Associate Editor, Chelsea Magazine, 1978-94; Editor, Chelsea Magazine, 1994-; Reviewer, Maine in Print, 1989-91. Publications: Transfigured Nights, 1990; Sudden Harbor, 1992; Patterns of Descent, 1993. Contributions to: Poetry; Nation; New Criterion; Shenandoah; Boulevard; Southwest Review; Epoch; Kenyon Review; Southern Review. Honours:

Discovery/The Nation Award, 1985; Bess Hokin Prize, 1992; Hawthornden Fellow, 1993; National Endowment for the Arts Creative Writing Fellowship in Poetry, 1995. Memberships: Poetry Society of America; Maine Writers and Publishers Alliance; Academy of American Poets; Society for the Arts, Religion and Contemporary Culture. Address: PO Box 1040, York Beach, ME 03910, USA.

FOGDEN Barry, b. 28 June 1948, Sussex, England. m. Celia Marjorie Avard, 16 Sept 1980. Education: BSc Psychology, University of Surrey, 1980; BA Humanities, The Open University, 1981; MA Philosophy, University of Sussex, 1981. Appointments: Legal Draftsman, 1968-77; Tutor in Creative Writing, Salisbury Tech College, 1983-86; Tutor for University of Sussex; Freelance Writer and Editor, 1986-. Publications: Displaced Person, 1989; De Fordrevne, 1990; Swede, 1993; In the Darkroom, An Exploding Still, 1994; Utan Identitet, 1994; A Chalk Stream in Sussex, 1995; The Black Heralds, 1995. Contributions to: South; Acumen; Downlander; Wessex Poets 1 and 2; Vision On; Orbis; Envoi; Staple; Psychopoetica; Iron; Foolscap; Iota; Skoob Review; Index on Censorship; Verse; Hippo; Parting Gifts; Ambit; ELF; Poet's Market; New York Echoes. Honours: Sussex Poet of the Year, 1987; Skoob/Index of Censorship International Competition Winner, 1989; Leek Arts Festival Competition, 1990; Surrey Open Competition, 1990. Membership: Poetry Society. Address: 27 Bradbourne Park Road, Sevenoaks, Kent TN13 3LJ, England.

FOLEY John Wayne Harold (Jack), b. 9 Aug 1940, Neptune, New Jersey, USA. Writer; Performer; Editor. m. Adelle Foley, 21 Dec 1961, 1 son. Education: BA Cornell University, 1963; MA, University of California at Berkeley, 1965. Appointments: Executive Producer in Charge of Poetry, Berkeley Radio Station, KPFA: Editor in Chief, Poetry USA; 1990-96; Reviewer, Contributing Editor Poetry Flash. Publications: Letters/Lights - Words for Adelle, 1987; Gershwin, 1991; Adrift, 1993; Exiles, 1996. Contributions to: Malthus; Galley Sail Review; Barque; Mallife; Poly: New Speculative Writing; Blind Date; Brief; Poetry Flash; Poetry USA: Modom; Fiction Review; Exquisite Corpse; NRG; Took. Honours: Yang Poetry Prize, 1971; New York State Regents Scholarship, 1958-63; Western Union Scholarship, 1958-63; Cornell University Work Scholarship, 1962; Woodrow Willson Fellowship, 1963-65; Adrift nominated for Bay Area Book Reviewers Association Award, 1993. Memberships: PEN Oakland, Programme Director; Poets and Writers; Modern Language Association. Address: 2569 Maxwell Avenue, Oakland, CA 94601, USA.

FONTIER Jaak, b. 27 July 1927, Bruges, Belgium. Author; Art Critic; Retired Teacher. m. Christiane Bruyooghe, 26 Dec 1953, 1 son, 2 daughters. Education: Teacher of Germanic Languages, Training College, Ghent, 1946-48. Publications: Zen maan en sterren, essay, 1975; In de zon van zen, essay, 1977; Friedrich Hölderlin, Wat blijft stichten de dichters, German-Dutch Anthology, translation of 48 poems, 1981; Keramiek in Vlaanderen, essay, 1986; Monographs: Luc Peire, 1984, Swimberghe, 1989, Gaston De Mey, 1990 and Vic Gentils, 1992. Contributions to: Nieuw Vlaams Tijdschrift; De Vlaamse Gids; Het 5de Wiel; Yang; Ons Erfdeel; Kreatief. Honour: Award for Essay, Province West Flanders, 1969. Memberships: Vereniging Westvlaamse Schrijvers; Vereniging Vlaamse Letterkundigen; Association Internationale des Critiques d'Art. Address: Sint-Ewoudsstraat 34, B-8200 Bruges, Belgium.

FOOTE Arthur Dawson, b. 19 Mar 1931, Toxteth, Liverpool, England. Former Assistant Minister, Warden of Voluntary Service Centre, Library Assistant. Education: MA, Balliol College, Oxford, 1949-53; Diploma in Theology, Manchester College, Oxford, 1953-56. Appointments: Assistant Minister, Hammond Hill Church, Chatham, Kent; Warden, International Voluntary Service Centre, London; Library Assistant, British National Book Centre, London. Publications: Angla Antologio, 1952; Esperanto Anthology, original and translated verse in Esperanto, 1958; The House Not Right in the Head, original poems in English, 1986; The Sunken Well, 1988; Behind the Lines, contributor, 1990. Contributions to: AMF; Gairfish; Gallimaufry; Inquirer; Life and Work; Northlight; Orbis; Scrievins; and others. Address: Flat 1/A, 12 Peddie Street, Dundee DD1 5LS, Scotland.

FOQUÉ Richard K V, Professor, b. 21 Nov 1943, Willebroek, Belgium. Professor; Architect. 2 sons, 1 daughter. Education: Engineer-Architect, University Leuven, 1967; Postgraduate Diploma, Hochschüle für Gestaltung, Ulm, Brd, 1968; MSc, Design Technology, University of Manchester, Institute of Science and Technology, 1969. Publications: Alleen Kringen, Bladen voor Poëzie, 1967; De Dieren

Komen, Bladen voor Poëzie, 1969; Poetical Functions, The Use of Poetry, Manchester Poetry Society, 1969; De Mekanische Priester, integration in 5 movements, premiere in town theatre of Louvain, 1971 and various performances in 1971-72; Drie Millivolt van Oneindig, poems, Yang Poetry Series, Ghent, 1972. Contributions to: Poems in various literary magazines including Heibel, Yang, Grafiek and Gedichten, Revolver; Co-founder and inspirator of the international poetry event, Dichters in het Elzenveld, Antwerp, 1988, 1989, 1993, 1994 and 1995. Memberships: Flemish Literary Society; Fellow, World Literary Academy; International Academy of Poets. Address: Hortside, Bruinstraat 14, B-2275 Lille, Belgium.

FORAKER Nelda Sue Branch, b. 23 Nov 1951, Louisiana, USA. Poet; Songwriter. m. Tommy Joe Foraker, 16 Mar 1968, 1 son, 2 daughters. Education: Honours Graduate, Delta School of Business and Technology, Louisiana, 1985. Publications: Poems in the 1987 American Poetry Anthology; The Anthology of Southern Poetry, 1987; Love's Greatest Treasures; Today's Poets Speak from the Heart, 1988. Contributions to: Southwest Daily News; Moss Bluff/Westlake News; Beauregard News; Louisiana Gospel Hayride Magazine. Honours: Poet of Merit, American Poetry Society, 1988, 1989; Best New Poet of 1988, and 1989; Poet of the Month, Southwest Louisiana Poetry Guild, 1988; Honourable Mention, World of Poetry, 1991. Memberships: Southwest Louisiana Poetry Guild; American Poetry Association; Louisiana Gospel Hayride; Christian Songwriters Association. Address: Rt 13, Box 30, No 38, Lake Charles, LA 70611, USA.

FORBES John, b. 1 Sept 1950, Melbourne, Victoria, Australia. Poet; Writer. Education: BA, University of Sydney, 1973. Appointment: Editor, Surfer's Paradise, 1974-83. Publications: Tropical Skiing, 1976; On the Beach, 1977; Drugs, 1980; Stalin's Holidays, 1981; The Stunned Mullet and Other Poems, 1988; New and Selected Poems, 1992. Contributions to: Newspapers and magazines. Honours: New Poetry Prize, 1973; Southerly Prize, 1976; Grace Leverson Prize, 1993. Membership: Australian Society of Authors. Address: 54 Morris Street, Summerhill, New South Wales, Australia.

FORCHE Carolyn (Louise), b. 28 Apr 1950, Detroit, Michigan, USA. Poet; Writer; Associate Professor. m. Henry E Mattison, 27 Dec 1984, 1 son. Education: BA, Michigan State University, 1972; MFA, Bowling Green State University, 1975. Appointments: Visiting Lecturer in Poetry, Michigan State University, Justin Morrill College, East Lansing, 1974; Visiting Lecturer, 1975, Assistant Professor, 1976-78, San Diego State University; Journalist and Human Rights Activist, El Salvador, 1978-80; Visiting Lecturer, 1979, Visiting Associate Professor, 1982-83, University of Virginia; Assistant Professor, 1980, Associate Professor, 1981, University of Arkansas at Fayetteville; Visiting Writer, New York University, 1983, 1985, Vassar College, 1984; Adjunct Associate Professor, Columbia University, 1984-85; Visiting Associate Professor, University of Minnesota, 1985; Writer-in-Residence, State University of New York at Albany, 1985; Associate Professor, George Mason University, 1994-. Publications: Poetry: Gathering the Tribes, 1976; The Country Between Us, 1981; The Angel of History, 1994. Non-Fiction: Women in the Labor Movement, 1835-1925: An Annotated Bibliography (with Martha Jane Soltow), 1972; Women and War in El Salvador (editor), 1980; El Salvador: The Work of Thirty Photographers (with others), 1983. Other: Claribel Alegria: Flowers from the Volcano (translator), 1982; Against Forgetting: Twentieth-Century Poetry of Witness (editor), 1993. Contributions to: Anthologies and periodicals. Honours: Devine Memorial Fellowship in Poetry, 1975; Yale Series of Younger Poets Award, 1975; Tennessee Williams Fellowship in Poetry, Bread Loaf Writers Conference, 1976; National Endowment for Arts Fellowships, 1977, 1984; Guggenheim Fellowship, 1978; Emily Clark Balch Prize, Virginia Quarterly Review, 1979; Alice Fay di Castagnola Award, Poetry Society of America, 1981; Lamont Poetry Selection Award, Academy of American Poets, 1981; Los Angeles Times Book Award for Poetry, 1994. Memberships: Academy of American Poets; Amnesty International; Associated Writing Programs, president, 1994-; PEN American center; Poetry Society of America; Theta Sigma Phi. Address: c/o Department of English, George Mason University, 4400 University Drive, Fairfax, VA 22030, USA.

FORD Charles Henri, b. 10 Feb 1913, Brookhaven, Mississippi, USA. Poet. Publications: A Pamphlet of Sonnets, 1936; The Garden of Disorder, poetry, 1938; ABC's, poetry, 1940; The Overturned Lake, poetry, 1941; Poems for Painters, 1945; The Half-Thoughts, The Distances of Pain, 1947; Sleep in a Nest of Flames, poetry, 1949; Spare Parts, 1966; Silver Flower Coo, paste-up poems, 1968; Flag of

Ecstasy, selected poems, 1972; Om Krishna I, 1979, 11, 1981, III, 1982; Haiku and Imprints, 1984; Handshakes from Heaven, 1985, II, 1986; Emblems of Arachne, 1986; Out of the Labyrinth, 1991; Water From a Bucket, 1997; Editor: Blues 10, A Special Issue of Un Muzzled Ox Magazine; I Will Be What I Am; Exhibitions: From Dali to Mapplethorpe, Portrait Photographs, Akehurst Gallery, London, 1993; The Young and Evil, novel, 1993. Address: 1 West 72nd Street, New York, NY 10023, USA.

FORD R(obert) A(rthur) D(ouglass), b. 8 Jan 1915, Ottawa, Ontario, Canada. Retired Diplomat. m. Maria Thereza Gomes, 27 June 1946, dec. Education: BA Hons English and History, University of Western Ontario, 1938; MA, History, Cornell University, 1939. Appointment: Canadian Diplomatic Service, 1940-64. Publications: A Window on the North 1956; The Solitary City, 1969; Holes in Space, 1979; Needle in the Eye, 1983; Russian Poetry, 1984 (translation); Doors Words and Silence, 1985; Dostoyevsky and Other Poems, 1988; Coming from Afar: Selected Poems, 1990. Contributions to: Encounter; Maclean's; Queen's Quarterly; Canadian Forum; University of Toronto Quarterly; First Statement; Northern Review; Tamarack Review; Prism International; Malahat Review; Maryland Quarterly. Honours: Hon DLit, 1965; Hon LLD, 1988; Companion of the Order of Canada, 1971; Award of Merit, UWO, 1989; Governor General's Poetry Prize, 1958. Membership: League of Canadian Poets. Address: La Poivriere, 63310 Randan, France.

FORD-CHOYKE Phyllis May, b. 25 Oct 1921, Buffalo, New York, USA. Editor; Poet. m. Arthur Davis Choyke Jr, 18 Aug 1945, 2 sons. Education: BS, summa cum laude, Northwestern University, 1942. Appointments: Reporter, City News, Chicago, 1942-43; Metropolitan Section, Chicago Tribune, 1943-44; Feature Writer, Office of War Information, New York City, 1944-45; Corporate Section, Artcrest Products Co Inc, Chicago, 1958-88; Vice President, 1964-88, President, 1988-90, The Partford Corporation, Chicago; Founder, Director, Harper Square Press Division, 1966-. Publications: Apertures to Anywhere, 1979; Editor: Gallery Series One, Poets, 1967; Gallery Series Two, Poets-Poems of the Real World, 1968; Gallery Series Three, Poets: Levitations and Observations, 1970; Gallery Series Four, Poets, I Am Talking About Revolution, 1973; Gallery Series Five, Poets, To An Aging Nation, 1977. Honour: Bonbright Scholar, 1942. Memberships: Daughters of the American Revolution; Board of Directors, 1987-93, Treasurer, 1988-93, Society of Midland Authors, Board of Directors, 1988-96, Treasurer, 1987-93, President, 1994-95; Mystery Writers of America; Chicago Press Veterans Association; Arts Club, Chicago; John Evans Club of Northwestern University; Phi Beta Kappa. Address: 29 East Division Street, Chicago, IL 60610, USA.

FORELLE Helen. See: **LEIH Grace Janet.**

FOREST Jody, b. 11 Jan 1949, Summerland, California, USA. Fisherman. Education: Santa Barbara City College, 1969-72; Medieval Metaphysics, Miskatonic University, 1972-76. Appointments: 2 Years Paratrooper in Vietnam; Fisherman. Publications: Strange Days in Spookville; Outsiders, 1971; The Bank of America of New Orleans, 1976. Contributions to: Santa Barbara News & Review; Tales of Lovecraftian Horror; Cemetery Dance; Rouge et Noir; Surrealist Toiler; Firesignal; Scavenger's; Santa Barbara Independent. Honours: Salvador Dali Fan Club Poet of Year, 1971; Busby Berkley Memorial Award, 1972; Killer Frog Award, 1986; Jim Morrison Award for Poetry, 1977. Memberships: Clark Ashton Smith Fan Club, 1972-; Sci-Fi Poetry Society, 1976-; Vietnam Veteran's Against War, 1969-. Address: PO Box 666, Summerland, CA 93067, USA.

FORSHAW Cliff, b. 20 July 1953, Liverpool, England. Freelance Writer. Div. Education: Liverpool Art College, 1971-72; BA, Honours, English and European Literature, Warwick University, 1972-75. Publications: Spectra, 1977; Bombed Out, 1979; Himalnan Fish, 1991; Esau's Children, 1991. Contributions to: London Poetry Quarterly; Envoi; Heaven Bone; Not Otherwise; Orbis; Outposts; Poetry Wales; Prospice; Quartz; Rialto; Resurgence; Poetry Nottingham. Honours: Prizes: Impress New Writing Competition, 1986; Orbis Rhyme Revival, 1987; Lancaster Literature Festival, 1987, 1990; Runner Up, Bridport Poetry Competition, 1986, 1988; Supplementary Prize, 1991; Rhyme International, 1989, 1990; Greenwich Festival, 1990. Membership: Writers' Guild. Address: 341 Victoria Park Road, London E9 5DX, England.

FORSYTH Sheila Constance, b. 5 Sept 1938, Irvington, New Jersey, USA. Clerk Cashier. Education: Graduated, Irvington High School. Appointments: Sales Clerk, F W Woolworth & Co; Clerk Cashier, Kerr Electrical Service; Bookkeeper, Cashier, Underwood Mortgage Co. Publications: Poem in anthology, Graces, 1994. Contributions to: Irvington Herald/Vailsburg Leader; Cape Cod Life; Writer; Independent Review; Christian Creative Arts; Ariel, Vols VIII, IX and X; Amherst Society; National Library of Poetry; Red Clay, native American poetry, 1993; Grandmother Earth Creations, To Love a Whale, Anthology, 1995. Honours: Honourable Mention, Writers' Digest Magazine Contest, 1979, 1983, 1985; 2nd Prize, Hawaii Education Association, 1980; Blue Ribbons, Contra Costa County Fair, 3 categories of poetry, 1980; 1st Place in Haiku, Arizona State Poetry Society, 1980; 1st Prize, Louisiana State Poetry Society, 1982; 3rd Place, World of Poetry International Contest, 1984; Silver Poet Award, World of Poetry, 1986; Honourable Mention, World Order of Narrative Poets, 1985, 1987; Winner, Salute to the Arts Contest, 1989, 1990, 1991; 1st Prize, Indiana State Contest, 1993; University of Baltimore Passager Contest Winner, 1995. Membership: Suburban Poets Guild. Address: 1207 Clinton Avenue, Irvington, NJ 07111, USA.

FORT Gary W, b. 23 July 1956, St Louis, Missouri, USA. m. 1 daughter. Education: BA, Communications, University of Missouri, 1990. Appointments: Teacher; Advertisement Writer. Publication: In the Writers Mind, 1991. Contributions to: Essence Magazine; World of Poetry; Poet's Forum; Quill Press; Poetry Magiz; Warner Press; and others. Honours: Five Golden Poet Awards, World of Poetry, 1985-89; Certificate of Achievement, Hollywood Song Jubilee, 1987; Music City Song Festival Award, 1989. Memberships: Society and Academy of American Poets; Midwest Writer's Association; Writer's World International; International Society of Poets; Songwriters and Lyricist Club; America's Songwriter Club; Poets Page Literary Club; Staff Writer, Apple Blossom Connection. Address: 4735 Lewis Place, St Louis, MO 63113, USA.

FORTH John, b. 15 June 1950, Bethnal Green, London, England. Teacher of English. m. 30 July 1977, 2 daughters. Education: BEd Honours, 1975, MEd 1980, West London Institute of Higher Education. Appointments: Head of English, Feltham School; Head of English, Kingswood School; East Midlands Arts New Voices Tour, 1994. Publication: Malcontents, 1994. Contributions to: London Magazine; Poetry Durham; Verse; Owl; Outposts; A Sense of Place, East Midlands Arts; Spoils, Poetry Business Anthology; New Prospects; North; Risk Behaviour, Poetry Business Anthology; Envoi. Honour: East Midlands Arts Development Award for Work on 2nd Collection. Membership: Poetry Society. Address: 32 High Street, Gretton, Northamptonshire, England.

FOSS Phillip, b. 20 Oct 1950, Portland, Oregon, USA. Writer. m. Joyce Begay, 1 son, 1 daughter. Education: BA, English, 1973; MEA, Writing, 1977. Appointments: Director, Creative Writing Programme, Institute of American Indian Arts, 1979-89; Publishing Director, Recursos de Santa Fe, 1989-92; Director, Pedernal Inc, 1991-. Publications: Roaring Fork Passage, 1977; Grace; The Snakes and the Dogs, 1978; Yana, 1978; House of Eagles, 1979; Somata, 1982; The Composition of Glass, 1988; The Excesses, the Caprices, 1990; Courtesan of Seizure, 1992. Contributions to: Conjunctions; Sulfur; Tyuonyi; Shearsman; Esquire and others. Honour: National Endowment for the Arts Fellowship in Poetry, 1987. Address: PO Box 23266, Santa Fe, NM 87502, USA.

FOSTER Edward (Halsey), b. 17 Dec 1942, Northampton, Massachusetts, USA. Poet; Publisher; Editor; Teacher. Div. 1 son, 1 daughter. Education: AB, Columbia College, 1965; MA, Columbia University, 1966; PhD, Columbia University, 1970. Appointments: Assistant Professor, Associate Professor, Professor, Stevens Institute of Technology, 1985-; Visiting Professor, Ankara University, Turkey, 1978-79; Visiting Professor, University of Istanbul, Turkey, 1985-86; Visiting Professor, Drew University Graduate Faculty, 1990, 1992, 1994, 1996; Poetry Editor, MultiCultural Review, 1991-95; Editor, Talisman: A Journal of Contemporary Poetry and Poetics, 1988-; President, Talisman House Publishers, 1993-. Publications: The Space Between Her Bed and Clock, 1993; The Understanding, 1994; All Acts Are Simple Acts, 1995. Contributions to: Five Fingers Review; Bombay Gin; American Letters and Commentary; MultiCultural Review; New Jersey History; Rendezvous; Hudson Valley Review; Ararat: A Quarterly Small Press, Western American Literature; Journal of The West; The Greenfield Review; Sagetrieb; American Book Review; Double Eye; Exact Change; First Intent; Poetry New York; Poetry USA. Membership: Modern Language Association. Address: PO Box 3157, Jersey City, NJ 07303-3157, USA.

FOSTER John Louis, (Derek Stuart), b. 12 Oct 1941, Carlisle, Cumbria, England. Teacher. m. Christine Eileen Paul, 2 Apr 1966, 2 sons. Education: Denstone College, 1954-60; BA, Brasenose College, Oxford, 1963, Dip Ed 1965, MA (Oxon). Appointments: Vice-Principal, Lord William's School, Thame, 1977-88. Publications: Four O'Clock Friday, 1991; Standing on the Sidelines, 1995. Editor of numerous poetry anthologies including: Once I Ate a Jellyfish, 1989; Spaceways, 1986; School's Out, 1988; Let's Celebrate, 1989; Never Say Boo to a Ghost! 1990; Jackdaws Poetry Books, 1990; Knockout Book of Poems, 1988; Dragon Poems, 1991; Twinkle Twinkle Chocolate Bar, 1991; More Jackdaws Poetry Books, 1991; Another First Poetry Book, 1987; Another Secondary Poetry Book, 1988; Another Third Poetry Book, 1988; Another Fourth Poetry Book, 1989; Another Fifth Poetry Book, 1989; Dinosaurs Poems, 1993; Poetry Paintbox Series, 1994; Monster Poems, 1995. Contributions to: Talking Poetry (BBC Radio); Poetry Corner (BBC radio); Words and Pictures (BBC TV). Membership: Poetry Society. Address: 18 Galley Field, Abingdon, Oxon OX14 3RT, England.

FOSTER Leslie Donley, b. 19 Oct 1930, Chicago, Illinois, USA. Professor of English. 1 daughter. Education: AB Liberal Arts, 1954, AM English, 1960, University of Chicago; PhD, University of Notre Dame, 1973. Appointments: Instructor, Valparaiso University, Indiana, 1959-62, 1963-64; Instructor, 1967-72, Assistant Professor 1972-75, Associate Professor 1975-82, Professor 1982-; Visiting Professor of English, Njala University College, University of Sierra Leone, 1982-84. Contributions to: Georgia Review; Anglican Theological Review; Ariel; Interim; Rolling Coulter; Northeast; Ellipsis; Peninsula Poets; among others. Address: Box 357, Marquette, MI 49855, USA.

FOSTER Linda Nemec, b. 29 May 1950, Ohio, USA. Poet; Writer; Teacher. m. Anthony J Foster, 26 Oct 1974, 1 son, 1 daughter. Education: BA, Aquinas College, Michigan, 1972; MFA, Goddard College, Vermont, 1979. Appointments: Teacher of Creative Writing and Poetry, Michigan Council for the Arts, 1980-93; Instructor of English Composition, Ferris State University, 1983-84; Guest Lecturer and Speaker, various schools, colleges and conferences; Director of Literature Programming, Urban Institute for Contemporary Arts, Grand Rapids, Michigan, 1989-95. Publications: A History of the Body, 1987; A Modern Fairy Tale: The Baba Yaga Poems, 1992; Trying to Balance the Heart, 1993; Living in the Fire Nest, 1996. Contributions to: Manhattan Poetry Review; Mid-American Review; Poetry Now; Onthebus; Oxford Magazine; Sierra Madre Review; Georgia Review; Permafrost; Bellingham Review; Contemporary Michigan Poetry; Indiana Review; Literatura; Quarterly West; Artful Dodge; Puerto del Sol; Virago Book of Birth Poetry; Witness; International Poetry Review. Honours: Creative Artist Grants in Poetry, Michigan Council for the Arts, 1984, 1990, 1996; Grand Prize, American Poetry Association, 1986; Honourable Mention, Writers' Digest, 1987; Prizewinner, McGuffin Poetry Contest, 1987; Passages North National Poetry Competition, 1988; Poetry/Visual Art Selection, Sage College, New York, 1994, 1995. Memberships: Executive Committee, Poetry Resource Center of Michigan; Academy of American Poets; Detroit Women Writers; Urban Institute for Contemporary Arts. Address: 2024 Wilshire Drive South East, Grand Rapids, MI 49506, USA.

FOSTIERIS Antonis, b. 16 May 1953, Athens, Greece; Editor; Director of Literary Magazine. m. 1991. Education: Degree in Law, Athens University; MPhil in History of Law, University of Paris. Appointments: Editor, Director of Magazine, The New Poetry 1974-76; Co-Director, Annual anthology of poetry, (Poetry 1975-Poetry 1981) 1975-81; Co-Editor and Director, most established Greek literary magazine, He Lexi (The Word) 1981-. Publications: The Long Journey, 1971; Interiors-or-The Twenty, 1973; Poetry Within Poetry, 1977; Dark Eros, 1977, 3rd edition 1985, Translated, California, USA, 1984; The Devil Sang in Tune, 1981, 2nd edition 1985, Translated, California, USA, 1984; The Shall and the Must of Death, 1987, 2nd edition 1990. Contributions to: All established Greek literary magazines and also to many foreign periodicals and anthologies, England, France, Germany, Italy, Romania, USA. Membership: Greek Writers' Association. Address: Dionyssiou Aiginitou 46, 115 28 Athens, Greece.

FOULON Roger, b. 3 Aug 1923. Poet. m. Marcelle Cordier, 5 Apr 1947, 1 son. Education: Institut Superieur de Pedagogie, Hainaut. Publications: L'exil terrestre; D'entre les songes; Naissances; Prieres pour un vivant; Eve et le songe; Pur enfant de moi-meme; Le pain de tous les jours; La joie humaine; La route vers la mer; Aulne; Visages du monde; Chants d'un captif; Poemes choises; Chemins d'un vivant; Bestiaire; Silex; L'envers du decor; Rites pour conjurer la mort;

Laudes pour elle et le monde; Le denombrement des choses; Petit reliquaire pour les oiseaux; Variations sur l'amour; Petite suite pour Eglantine; Neuvaine sous la pluie; Croquis matinaux; Jardins; Le dit de la presse; Nocturnes; Poems pour l'enfant qui vient; Poesie des signes; Icariennes; Clartes; Saisons; Passages; Bruxelles millenaire; Paroles pour une naissance; Pour saluer le jour; Tout est parole; Ex-libris; Variations sur une parole de Tagore; Le temps des sorbes; Itineraires; Quotidiennes; Images d'une petite ville; Elements; Paroles pour la pluie; Joie du temps; Les charmes de la terre; Poemes pour un amour qui ne s'eteint; Antiphonaire pour la pluie; Jeux d'aube; Chateau-poesie; Poemes sur des dessins d'Armand Simon; Senteurs sauvages; Ombres chinoises; Iberiques, 1990; Norvegiennes, 1990; Croix, 1991; Prodiges, 1991; Printemps, 1992; Resurgence, 1993; Julia, 1993; Volières, 1993; Lègendes, 1993; Contigues, 1995. Honours: Prix Max Rose; Prix Auguste Marin; Prix Unimuse; Prix Interfrance; Prix Charles Plisnier; Prix Malpertuis. Memberships: President, Association des Escrivaius belges de langue francaise; Artistes de Thudinie; Founding Director, Le Spantole Literary Review, 1956. Address: 12 rue du Fosteau, B-6530 Thuin, Belgium.

FOURIE Jeanette Beatrice, b. 22 Mar 1949, Springs, South Africa. Freelance Translator. Education: JMB Matric, Vereeniging, South Africa, 1966; BA, University of South Africa, 1981; Yoga Teacher's Diploma, Amsterdam, 1989. Appointments: Head of Accounting, Head of Computer Operations, The Perm, Johannesburg, 1970-81; Credit Department, NED Bank Ltd, Johannesburg, 1981-82; Administrative Assistant to Credit Manager, Continental Bank, Amsterdam, 1983-85; Regional Assistant, Head Office, ING Bank Amsterdam, 1985-90; Freelane Translator, 1990-. Publications: The Haunted Heart, 1992; Poetry included in the anthology: A Question of Balance, 1992; Poetry featured on tape, The Sound of Poetry; Poetry included in the calendar of National Library of Poetry, USA, 1993; Poetry included in Best Poems of 1996, National Library of Poetry, USA. Membership: Netherlands Society of Translators. Address: Ymertstraat 8, 1611 BD Bovenkarspel, Netherlands.

FOWLER Alastair David Shaw, b. 17 Aug 1930, Glasgow, Scotland. University Professor. m. Jenny Catherine Simpson, 23 Dec 1950, 1 son, 1 daughter. Education: Queen's Park School, Glasgow; University of Glasgow; MA, University of Edinburgh, 1952; MA, Pembroke College, Oxford, 1955; DPhil (Oxon) 1957; DLitt (Oxon) 1972. Appointments: Junior Research Fellow, Queen's College, Oxford, 1955-59; Instructor, Indiana University, 1957; Lecturer, University College Swansea, 1959; Fellow and Tutor in English Literature, Brasenose College, Oxford, 1962-71; Regius Professor of Rhetoric and English Literature, University of Edinburgh, 1972-84; Visiting Professor, Columbia University, 1964; University of Virginia, 1969, 1979, 1985-90, Professor of English, University of Virginia, 1990-; Member, Institute for Advanced Study, Princeton, 1966, 1980; Visiting Fellow: Council of the Humanities, Princeton University, 1974, Humanities Research Centre, Canberra, 1980, All Souls College, Oxford, 1984; Member, Scottish Arts Council, 1976-77; Advisory Editor, New Literary History, 1972-; General Editor, Longman Annotated Anthologies of English Verse, 1977-80; Member, Editorial Board: English Literary Renaissance, 1978-, Word and Image, 1984-, The Seventeenth Century, 1987-, Connotations 1990, Translation and Literature, 1990, English Review, 1990. Publications: Seventeen, 1971; Catacomb Suburb, 1976; From the Domain of Arnheim, 1982. Contributions to: Scotsman; Times Literary Supplement; Lines; Ambit; Akros. Membership: Scottish Poety Library Association. Address: Department of English, University of Virginia, Bryan Hall, Charlottesville, VA 22903, USA.

FOX Connie. See: FOX Hugh Bernard.

FOX Hugh Bernard, (Connie Fox), b. 12 Feb 1932, Chicago, Illinois, USA. University Professor. m. Maria Bernadette Costa, 14 Apr 1988, 2 sons, 4 daughters. Education: BA, 1955, MA, English, 1956, Loyola University, Chicago; PhD, American Literature, University of Illinois, 1958. Appointments: Professor of American Literature, University of Illinois, 1958-68; Department of American Thought and Language, Michigan State University, 1968-. Publications: The Industrial Ablution, 1971; Handbook Against Gorgons, 1971; Ecological Suicide Bus, 1971; Survival Handbook, 1972; People, 1973; Huaca, 1975; Yo Yo Poems, 1977; Almazora 42, 1982; The Dream of the Black Topaze Chamber, 1983; Oma, 1985; 10107, 1986; Babicka, 1986; Nachthymnen, 1986; Skull-Worship, 1991; Our Lady of Laussel, 1991; A Month in the Country, 1991; The Sacred Cave, 1992; Shaman, 1993; Once, poems, 1996; The Last Summer, 1995. Contributions to:

New York Quarterly; Wormwood Review; Poetry Motel; No Exit; Slipstream; Postcards Con Carne; MacGuffin; Nutshell; Alternative Fiction and Poetry, among others. Memberships: Founter COSMEP, International Organization of Independent Publishers, Board 1968-78, Chairman 1978. Address: ATL/EBH Michigan State University, East Lansing, MI 48824, USA.

FRANCE Linda, b. 21 May 1958, Newcastle-upon-Tyne, England. Poet; Tutor in Adult Education. 2 sons. Education: BA, Hons, English/History, University of Leeds, 1979. Publications: Acts of Love, 1990; Red, 1992; Acknowledged Land, 1993; Sixty Women Poets (editor), 1993; The Gentleness of the Very Tall, 1994. Contributions to: Anthologies: New Women Poets, 1990; Wordworks, 1992; Magazines: North; Rialto; Iron; Stand; London Magazine; Poetry Durham; Writing Women; Wide Skirt and others. Honours: Basil Bunting Award, 1988, 1990; Northern Arts Writers' Award, 1989, 1995; Tyrone Guthrie Award, 1990; Author's Foundation Award, 1993; Arts Foundation Poetry Fellowship, 1993. Address: c/o Bloodaxe Books, PO Box 1SN, Newcastle-upon-Tyne NE99 1SN, England.

FRANK John Frederick, b. 7 Sept 1917, Milwaukee, Wisconsin, USA. Poet. m. L Page Gooch, 8 Mar 1944, 1 daughter. Education: BS, Northwestern University, Illinois, 1939; MA, Johns Hopkins University, 1953; ABD, University of Pennsylvania, 1961. Appointments: Assistant Instructor, Pennsylvania State University, 1953; Instructor, University of North Carolina, 1958-60; Lecturer in Writing, Southern Illinois University, 1960-63; Assistant Professor, Kutztown State University, 1963-65; Lecturer in English, City University of New York, 1965-66. Publications: America Sings, National Poetry Association, 1951; The Golden Year, Poetry Society of America Anthology, 1960; Americana Anthology, volume I, 1976; Love Lyrics Anthology, 1985; Johnny Appleseed, 1989. Contributions to: Poetry; Voices; New Quarterly of Poetry; Pennsylvania Literary Magazine; New York Poetry Forum; Poet. Honours: Writers Conference Award, 1941; S V Benet Award, Pasadena Playhouse, 1945; Award, World Literature, University of Rome, 1969; Concorso Internazionale di Poesia, Italy, 1983; Fellow, International Poets Academy Award, 1987. Memberships: World Poetry Society; New York Poetry Forum; Modern Language Association; American Association of University Professors. Address: Fishel Creek Road, RD No 3, Seven Valleys, PA 17360, USA.

FRANKLIN Walt, b. 19 June 1950, Schwabach, Germany. Poet; Editor of Great Elm Press; Natural History Writer. m. Leighanne Parkins, 4 Sept 1982, 1 son, 1 daughter. Education: BS Psychology, 1973, Elementary Education Teaching Certificate 1975, Alfred University; Self-taught in ecology, homesteading, bioregionalism. Appointments: Counselor, Grafton School, 1976-80; Advisor, Human Services, ARC, Alfred, New York 1981-90; Publisher and Editor, Great Elm Press, Greenwood, New York, 1984-92. Publications: Talking to the Owls, 1984; Topographies, 1984; The Glass Also Rises, 1985; Little Water Company, 1986; Ekos. a Journal Poem, 1986; The Ice Harvest, 1988; Instrument, 1988; Rootwork and Other Poems, 1988; The Wild Trout, 1989, 1991; Uplands Haunted by the Sea, 1992; The Flutes of Power, 1995; Letters from Susquehannock, 1995. Contributions to: About 350 publications including: Anthology of Magazine Verse & Yearbook of American Poetry; Organic Gardening; Poem; Earth Prayers; Cutting Edge Quarterly; North Atlantic Review; Bird Watchers' Digest; Blue Unicorn; Signal; Transnational Perspectives. Honours: Numerous small press awards including Abacus and Rose, 1988. Memberships: Poets Theatre, Hornell, New York; Appalachian Writers Association; Poets and Writers. Address: 1205 Co Rt 60, Rexville, NY 14877, USA.

FRASER Douglas Jamieson, b. 12 Jan 1910, Edinburgh, Scotland. m. Eva Nisbet Greenshields, 30 Mar 1940, 2 sons, 1 daughter. Publications: Landscape of Delight, 1967; Rhymes O'Auld Reekie, 1973; Where the Dark Branches Part, 1977; Treasure for Eyes to Hold, 1981. Contributions to: Lines Review; Scots Magazine; Lallans; Burns Chronicle. Honour: Queen's Silver Jubilee Medal, 1977. Memberships: Scottish PEN; Poetry Association of Scotland; Edinburgh Poetry Club. Address: 2 Keith Terrace, Edinburgh EH4 3NJ, Scotland.

FRASER Kathleen, b. 22 Mar 1937, Tulsa, Oklahoma, USA. Professor; Poet. m. Jack Marshall, 1961, div 1970, 1 son. Education: BA, Occidental College, Los Angeles, 1959; Columbia University, 1960-61; New School for Social Research, New York City, 1960-61; Doctoral Equivalency in Creative Writing, San Francisco State University, 1976-77. Appointments: Visiting Professor, University of

Iowa, 1969-71; Writer-in-Residence, Reed College, Portland, Oregon, 1971-72; Director, Poetry Center, 1972-75, Associate Professor, 1975-78, Professor, 1978-, San Francisco State University. Publications: Poetry: Change of Address and Other Poems, 1966; In Defiance of the Rains, 1969; Little Notes to You from Lucas Street, 1972; What I Want, 1974; Magritte Series, 1978; New Shoes, 1978; Each Next, 1980; Something (Even Human Voices) in the Foreground, A Lake, 1984; Notes Preceding Trust, 1987; Boundary, 1988; Giotto, Arena, 1991; When New Time Folds Up, 1993; Il Cuore: The Heart, New and Selected Poems 1970-95, 1997; Editor: Feminist Poetics: A Consideration of the Female Construction of Language, 1984. Honours: YM-YWHA Discovery Award, 1964; National Endowment for the Arts Grant, 1969, and Fellowship, 1978; Guggenheim Fellowship in Poetry, 1981. Address: 1936 Leavenworth Street, San Francisco, CA 94133, USA.

FRAZEUR Gisele Barling, b. 16 Jan 1961, Rochester, New York, USA. Actress. Education: BA, State University of New York, Fredonia. Appointments: Producer Playwright of All Souls' Night; Actor; Published Poet; Freelance Journalist. Contributions to: Sierra Madre News; Wretch Magazine; Lucidity Poetry Journal; Poetpourri Poetry Journal; Sparrowgrass Poetry Forum. Honour: Editors Choice Award, National Library of Poetry. Address: 418 North Lima, Sierra Madre, CA 91024, USA.

FRAZEUR Joyce Jaeckle, b. 17 Jan 1931, Lewisburg, Pensylvania, USA. Poet; Short Story Writer; Novelist. m. Theodore C Frazeur Jr, 24 July 1954, 1 son, 2 daughters. Education: BA, William Smith College, 1952. Publications: A Slip of Greenness, 1989; By Lunar Light, novel, 1995; The Bovine Affliction, chapbooks, 1991; Flower Soup, chapbooks, 1993; Chirruping, chapbooks, 1994; Cycles, chapbooks, 1996. Contributions to: Pegasus; Peace and Freedom; For Poets Only; Emerald Reflections; Independent Review; Poetry Forum; Free Focus; Thirteen Poetry Magazine; Buffalo News; Poetpourri; Se La Vie Writers' Journal; Buffalo Spree; Buffalo Journal; Wide Open Magazine; Pandora; Odessa Poetry Review; Poet; Liberated Voice. Address: 390 Juniper Drive, Sedona, AZ 86336, USA.

FREEMAN William T, b. 26 May 1948, Waterbury, Connecticut, USA. Contributions to: Parnassus Literary Journal; Obsidian; Anthology of Magazine Verse; Yearbook of American Poetry. Honour: Connecticut Commission on the Arts Grant, 1981. Address: 205 Orange Street, Waterbury, CT 06704, USA.

FREET Paul Irvin, b. 16 Sept 1943, Concord, Pennsylvania, USA. Retail Manager. Education: Graduated, Fannett Metal High School; Courses in Writing, Famous Writers School, Westport; Poetry Courses, Shippensburg University. Appointments: Shoe Factory, 1962-73; Thrift Drug Co, 1973-; Tarot Card Reader, 1982-. Publications: Reflections on a Clear Stream, 1993. Contributions to: Midwest Poetry Review; Apprise; Poetic Page; Patriot; Apropos; Rhyme Time. Honour: 2 top awards at Midwest Poetry Review, 1994; 2 first place awards, Poetic Page, 1995, 1996. Membership: Academy of American Poets. Address: 728 Brookens Road, Fayetteville, PA 17222, USA.

FREIBERG Stanley Kenneth, b. 26 Aug 1923, Wisconsin, USA. Teacher; Writer. m. Marjorie Ellen Speckhard, 29 June 1947, 1 son, 1 daughter. Education: BA, 1948, MA, 1949, PhD, 1957, University of Wisconsin. Appointments: Chairman, English Department, Cottey Cottage, Nevada, Missouri, 1954-58; Chairman, Board of Foreign Language Studies, University of Baghdad, 1964-65. Publications: The Baskets of Baghdad: Poems of the Middle East, 1968; Plumes of the Serpent: Poems of Mexico, 1973; The Caplin-Crowded Seas: Poems of Newfoundland, 1975; The Hidden City: A Poem of Peru, 1988. Contributions to: Redlands Review; Christian Century; Dalhousie Review; Queen's Quarterly; Ariel; Parnassus of World Poets, 1994. Honour: Canada Council Award, 1978. Address: 1523 York Place, Victoria, British Columbia V8R 5X1, Canada.

FREIRE DA SILVA Marinalva, b. 13 Sept 1948, Joao Pessoa, Paraiba, Brazil. Professor of Philology of Romance Languages; Researcher of Lusohispanic Language and Literature. Education: Licentiate Litt (Portuguese); Licentiate, Pedagogy-specialised, Portuguese and Spanish Language, Brazilian, Portuguese and Spanish Literature; MLitt, Educational Administration; Doctor of Romance Philology. Appointments: Professor, Universidad Federal de Paraiba, 1978-; Honorary Assistant Professor, Department of Romance Philology, Universidad Complutense de Madrid, 1988-89,

1989-90; Escritoria; Conferencista. Publications: Various essays on the Brazilian poet, Augusto dos Anjos, and on novelist, Graciliano Ramos; Di Tames do Coracao, 1989; Poetry in anthologies. Contributions to: Various Brazilian periodicals. Honours: Poet Laureate, International Poetry Competition, Academica Internacional de Lettres, Cultura e Fraternidade, 1987; International Writers and Artist Association Fraternity, USA, 1989. Memberships: Associacao Portuguese de Linguistica, Lisbon; Asociacion Cultural Brazil; Academia Paraibana de Poesia, Brazil; Uniao Brasileira de Escritores, Brazil; International Writers and Artists Association, USA; Academia Paraibana de Literatura; Uniao Paraibana de Escritores Joao Pessoa. Address: Rua Jose Vieira 675 Tambauzinho, 58043 Joao Pessoa, Paraiba, Brazil.

FREISINGER Randall Roy, b. 6 Feb 1942, Kansas City, Missouri, USA. College Teacher. 2 sons. Education: BJ, Journalism 1962, MA, English Literature, 1964, PhD, English Literature, 1975, University of Missouri. Appointments: Instructor, Jefferson College 1964-68; Resident Lecturer, University of Maryland Overseas Programme 1968-69, 1975-76; Assistant Professor, Columbia College 1976-77; Assistant and Associate Professor, Michigan Technological University, 1977-; Associate Editor, Laurel Review, 1989-. Publications: Running Patterns, 1985; Hand Shadows, 1988. Contributions to: Aspen Leaves; Chariton Review; Mississippi Valley Review; Passages North; Cottonwood; Kansas Quarterly; Tendril; Stone County; Milkweed Chronicle; Mickle Street Review; Interim; New Letters; Laurel Review; Nebraska Review; Poet and Critic; South Coast Poetry Journal; Hiram Poetry Review; Great River Review; Northern Review; Caesura; Anthology of American Verse and Yearbook of American Poetry, 1984, 1985; Passages North Anthology, 1990. Honours: Selected for the Bread Loaf Writers' Conference, Middlebury, Vermont, 1982, 1983; Flume Press National Chapbook Prize, 1985; Pushcart Prize nominations in 1985, 1988. Memberships: Associated Writing Programmes; National Council of Teachers of English. Address: 200 Prospect Street, Houghton, MI 49931. USA.

FRENCH Wendy Rowena, (Rowena Morgan-Jones), b. 4 Sept 1945, Neath, Wales. Teacher. m. Dr William Marshall, 3 Jan 1992, 2 sons, 2 stepdaughters. Education: Certificate of Education, 1967; BA, Open University, 1983; Certificate in Counselling and Psychotherapy, 1989. Appointments: Teacher in various schools; Headteacher, St Paul's, Hampstead, 6 years; Senior Teacher, Children's Department, Maudsley Hospital School, London; Currently, Headteacher, Bethlem Hospital School, Kensington, London. Contributions to: Envoi; Rialto; Poetry Nottingham; Iota; Weyfarers; White Rose; Aeropagns; Poems in anthology, Angels of the Heart; Envoi Anthology; Spokes, Smoke and Pennine Platform; Poems in: What Poets Eat, 1994; The Long Pale Corridor, 1995. Honour: 3rd Prize for, Sibelius is Dead, Envoi Competition, 1990. Memberships: Committee, Ripley Poetry Society; Poetry Society, London; Founder Member, Words and Music, Dulwich Poetry Group. Address: 4 Myton Road, West Dulwich, London SE21 8EB, England.

FRESTA Maria Catina, b. 24 Aug 1952, Tully, Queensland, Australia. Teacher. 1 son, 1 daughter. Education: BEd, 1975. Appointments: Research Officer, Water Management, Norfolk Island; Teacher, Shalom College, Bundaberg, Australia. Publications: An Australian Mix, 1992; Mix Don't Blend, 1993. Contributions to: Linq; Quadrant; Rebout; Imago; Ulitarra; Hecate; Idiom 25; North of Capricorn; Social Alternatives; The Guide; Range Writers; Heartland; Northern Perspective; From all Walks of Life; Courier Mail; Canberra Times. Honours: Eaglehawk Dahlia Award, 1993; Mt Isa Mines Short Story, 1993; 2 Literary Grants from Queensland Government, 1992, 1994; Numerous 2nd and 3rd Prizes and Highly Commended Awards around Australia and Overseas. Memberships: Australian Society of Authors; Queensland Writers Centre; Regional Poets Society; Victorian Writers Society. Address: 2/90 Boundary Street, Bundaberg, Queensland 4670, Australia.

FREUND Philip (Herbert), b. 5 Feb 1909, Vancouver, British Columbia, Canada. Emeritus Professor; Novelist; Playwright; Literary Critic; Historian. Education: BA cum laude, 1929, MA, 1931, Cornell University. Appointments: Lecturer, City College of New York; Lecturer, Hunter College; Guest Lecturer, Cornell University, University of British Columbia (summers); Professor, Fordham University, New York City. Publications: Prince Hamlet, 1953; Private Speech, 1955, 1956; The Bacchae, 1970, 1973. Contributions to: Opinion Magazine. Membership: Sigma Delta Chi. Address: 1025 Fifth Avenue, New York, NY 10028, USA.

FRIAR Will. See: **MARGOLIS William J.**

FRICKER Richard Gorman, b. 13 May 1926, Hackney, London, England. Doctor of Medicine; Anaesthetist; Dental Surgeon. m. Catherine Margaret Evans, 8 June 1955, 3 sons. Education: LRCP & SI; LDS RCS I; MSc, University of Surrey; DA, University of London. Appointments: Queen Mary Hospital for Children, Carshalton; Hackney Hospital; St Nicholas Hospital, Plumstead; Ashford Hospital, Kent. Publications: A Dunce in Poverty, 1974; Clatterface to Mute, 1986. Contributions to: Apollo, 1990. Memberships: Concert Director, Wagner Society of London, 1964-71; Founder Chairman, Music Club of London, 1968. Address: Burrell Cottage, 73 Wickham Road, Beckenham, Kent, England.

FRIED Philip Henry, b. 8 Jan 1945, Georgia, USA. Editor. m. Lynn Saville, 5 Oct 1985. Education: BA English, Antioch College, 1966; MFA Poetry, University of Iowa Writers Workshop, 1968; PhD, English State University of New York, 1978. Appointments: Editor: Mitchell and Titus, CPAs, 1979-84, Holt, Rinehart and Winston, 1984-86, Prentice Hall, 1986-; Founder and Editor, Manhattan Review; Founder, National Poetry Initiative, 1994. Publications: Mutual Trespasses, 1988; Editor, Acquainted with the Night, 1997. Contributions to: Beloit Poetry Journal; Chicago Review; Partisan Review; Paris Review; Poetry Northwest; Cream City Review; Maryland Poetry Review; Orim; Poet and Critic; Sequoia; Raccoon; Southern Poetry Review; Poet Lore; Magazine of Speculative Poetry, among others. Honours: Grant, Council of Literary Magazines and Presses, 1984. Memberships: Council of Literary Magazines and Presses; Poets House; National Writers Union; Poets and Writers; Poetry Society of America; PEN. Address: The Manhattan Review, 440 Riverside Drive, No 45, New York, NY 10027, USA.

FRIEDMAN Debbie (Dina), b. 13 June 1957, Takoma Park, Maryland, USA. Writer. m. Shef Horowitz, 9 Oct 1983, 1 son, 1 daughter. Education: BA, English, Cornell University, 1978; MSW, University of Connecticut, 1985. Appointments: Workshop Leader, private workshops and through Amherst Writers and Artists; Instructor, Holyoke Community College and University of Massachusetts; Co-Director, Accurate Writing and More. Contributions include: Pacific Poetry and Fiction Review; Calyx; Peregrine; Slant; Jewish Currents; Permafrost; Black Bean Review; Pig Iron; Rhino; Hurricane Alice. Address: PO Box 1164, Northampton, MA 01061, USA.

FRIEDMAN Norman, b. 10 Apr 1925, Boston, Massachusetts, USA. Poet; Critic; Teacher; Psychotherapist. m. Zelda Nathanson, 7 June 1945, 1 son, 1 daughter. Education: AB, 1948, AM, 1949, PhD, 1952, Harvard University; MSW, Adelphi University School of Social Work, 1978. Appointments: Teaching Assistant, 1949-50, Teaching Fellow, Harvard University, 1950-52; Instructor, Associate Professor, University of Connecticut, 1952-63; Associate-Full Professor, Queens College, and City University of New York Graduate Center, 1963-88. Publications: The Magic Badge: Poems, 1953-84, 1984; The Intrusions of Love: Poems 1992. Contributions to: Beloit Poetry Journal; New Mexico Quarterly; New Voices 2; New Orleans Poetry Journal; Georgia Review; Northwest Review; Antioch Review; Choice; Nation; Texas Quarterly; Centennial Review. Honours: Northwest Review Annual Poetry Prize, 1963; Borestone Mountain Poetry Awards, 1964, 1967; Fourth, All Nations Poetry Contest, 1977; North American Mentor Magazine Annual Poetry Award Certificate of Merit, 1982. Memberships: Modern Language Association; Poetry Society of America; Academy of American Poets and Writers; National Writers Union. Address: 33-54 164th Street, Flushing, NY 11358-1442, USA.

FRIEDMAN S(amuel) L, b. 12 Feb 1908. Retired Business Executive. m. 14 Feb 1935, 1 son, 1 daughter. Education: High School Graduate. Publications: The Glass Shore, 1982; Some Light Through the Blindfold, 1990; Baudelaire, documentary, 1991, full length play. Contributions to: Poet and Critic; Borestone Mountain Poetry Anthology; Southern Poetry Review. Honours: First Prize, Poet and Critic; 1st and 5th Honourable Mention, California State Poetry Contest, 1995. Address: 732 North June Street, Los Angeles, CA 90038, USA.

FRIEDRICH Paul William, b. 22 Oct 1927, Massachusetts, USA. Anthropologist; Linguist; Poet. 2 sons, 4 daughters. Education: BA, 1950, MA, 1951, Harvard University; PhD, Yale, 1957. Appointments: Instructor, Harvard University, 1957-58; Deccan College, Linguistic Scholar, 1959-59; Assistant Professor: University of Pennsylvania, 1959-62, University of Chicago, 1962-; Currently Professor of

Anthropology, Linguistics and Social Thought. Publications: Bastard Moons, 1979; Sonata, 1987. Contributions to: Spoon River Quarterly; Blue Unicorn; Beloit Poetry Journal; Kansas Quarterly; Great River Review; Mississippi Valley Review; Literary Review; Matatis Mutandis Intergalatic Poetry Messenger. Memberships: American Academy of Poets; American Academy of Arts and Sciences. Address: University of Chicago, 1126 East 59th Street, Chicago, IL 60637, USA.

FRIMAN Alice Ruth, b. 20 Oct 1933, New York, New York, USA. Professor. m. (1) Elmer Friman, 3 July 1955, (2) Marshall Bruce Gentry, 24 Sept 1989, 2 sons, 1 daughter. Education: BA, Brooklyn College, 1954; Indiana University, 1964-66; MA, English, Butler University, 1971. Appointments: Professor of English, University of Indianapolis, 1990-; Writer in Residence, Curtin University, Perth, Australia, 1989; Visiting Professor of Creative Writing, Indiana State University, 1982; Lecturer in English, Indiana and Purdue Universities, 1971-74. Publications: Insomniac Heart, 1990; Reporting from Corinth, 1984; Loaves and Fishes: Women Poets of Indiana (ed), 1983; Song to my Sister, 1979; A Question of Innocence, 1978; Driving for Jimmy Wonderland, 1992. Contributions to: Beloit Poetry Journal; Poetry; Prairie Schooner; Puerto del Sol; Shenandoah; Southern Poetry Review; London Magazine; Manoa; Poetry Review; Rialto. Honours: Consuelo Ford Award, 1988; Erika Mumford Prize, 1990; Midwest Poetry Award, 1990; Cecil Hemley Memorial Award, 1990; First Prize, Start with Art Literary Competition, 1992; Lucille Medwick Memorial Award, 1993; First Prize, Abiko Quarterly International Poetry Contest, 1993; Award for Excellence in Poetry, Hopewell Review, 1995. Memberships: Poetry Society of America; Poets and Writers; Writers' Centre of Indianapolis; Society for the Study of Midwestern Literature. Address: 6312 Central Avenue, Indianapolis, IN 46220, USA.

FRITZ Leah Hurwit, b. 31 May 1931, New York, New York, USA. Poet. m. Howard William Fritz, 25 Dec 1955, 2 daughters. Publications: UK - From Cookie to Witch is an Old Story (poems), 1987; Somewhere en Route: Poems 1987-92, 1992; Books of Prose: USA - Thinking Like a Woman (essays), 1975; Dreamers and Dealers: An Intimate Appraisal of the Women's Movement, 1977, paperback 1980. Contributions to: USA: Sojourner; Sisterhood is Powerful, anthology; MS Magazine; UK: Poetry Review; Pen International; Acumen; Orbis; Foolscap; PN Review; Swansea Review; Italy; Decoder; UK anthology, Rhythm of Our Days, 1991; UK anthology, Touching the Sun: Poems in Memory of Adam Johnson, editor Leah Fritz, 1995.Memberships: Poetry Society; English Centre of PEN. Address: 47 Regent's Park Road, London NW1 7SY, England.

FRITZ Walter Helmut, b. 26 Aug 1929, Karlsruhe, Germany. Writer. Education: Studied Literature and Philosophy, University of Heidelberg, 1949-54. Publications: Veröffentlichung von Gedichtbüchern seit 1956, new edition as Gesammelte Gedichte, 1979; Wunschtraum Alptraum, 1981; Werkzeuge der Freiheit, 1983; Immer einfacher, immer schwieriger, 1987; Die Schlüssel sind vertauscht, 1992; Gesammelte Gedichte 1979-94, 1994. Contributions to: Akzente; Neue Deutsche Literatur; Neue Rundschau; Merku. Honours: Literaturpreis der Stadt Karlsruhe, 1960; Preis der Bayerischen Akademie der Schönen, Künste, 1962; Villa Massimo-Stipendium, 1963; Preis des Kulturkreises im Bundesverband der deutschen Industrie, 1973; Stuttgarter Literaturpreis, 1986; Georg-Trakl-Preis, 1992. Memberships: Akademie der Wissenschaften u der Literatur, Mainz; Deutsche Akademie der Schönen Kunste, Munich; Deutsche Akademie für Spache und Dichtung, Darmstadt; PEN. Address: Kolbergerstrasse 2a, 7500 Karlsruhe 1, Germany.

FROEHLICH Joey, (W J Stephens), b. 13 Nov 1954, Honolulu, Hawaii, USA. US Government Printer; Clerk. Education: BA, English and Political Science, Brescia College. Publications: The Fuel of Tender Years, poetry collection, 1996. Contributions to: Amazing SF; Masques 3, poetry featured with Ray Bradbury's; Swords Against Darkness; Midnight Graffiti 3, poem side-barred with a Stephen King story; Scavenger's Newsletter; Space and Time; Haunts; Weirdbook; Poets of The Fantastic; Psychos; Argonaut; The Romantist; Beyond The Fields We Know; Dark Fantasy; Eldritch Tales; Night Songs, Supernatural Poetry, Diversifier, Spwao Showcase, Spwao Newsletter, Evermist, Prelude to Fantasy, Science Fiction Poetry Association's Newsletter, Deathrealm, Dreams & Nightmares, Dead of Night Magazine, Dragonfields, Amanita Brandy, Eerie Country, Owlfight, The Miskatonic, Palace Coribie, Clowns and Cages, Ian II, Last Tango in The Twilight Zone; Editor, publisher: Whispered Legends, Violent

Legends. Honours: Nominated for the Spwao, Kelly and Balrog Awards in Poetry. Address: PO Box 155, Frankfort, KY 40602, USA.

FROST Erica. See: SUPRANER Robyn.

FRUCHTMANN Benno, b. 5 Sep 1913, Meuselwitz, Germany. Writer; Poet; Playwright. m. Mirjam David, 2 Nov 1951, 2 sons. Appointments: Commercial Artist, Ministry of Agriculture. Publications: Maskerade; Anthologies in German language and translation into Hebrew; 16 Radio plays, short stories and ballads, metric prose. Contributions to: Neue Rundschau; Neue Deutsche Hefte; Europaische Indeen; Dimensions; Neue Zurcher Zeitung; Translations in Hebrew newspapers and periodicals. Honours: Stipend Atelierhaus, Worpswede, Germany, 1986; Participant, International Colloquium of Jewish Authors, Osnabruck, 1991. Memberships: Israel Writers Association; Association of German Writers. Address: 10 Liesin Street, 62977 Tel Aviv, Israel.

FRY Christopher, b. 18 Dec 1907, Bristol, England. Playwright. m. Phyllis Marjorie Hart, 1936, 1 son. Education: Bedford Modern School. Appointments: Actor, Citizen House, Bath, 1927; Primary School Teacher, 1928-31; Director, Tunbridge Wells Repertory Players, 1932-35; Director, Oxford Repertory Players, 1940, 1944-46; Arts Theatre, London, 1945. Publications: The Boy With The Cart, 1939; The Firstborn, 1946; A Phoenix Too Frequent, 1946; The Lady's Not For Burning, 1949; Thor With Angels, 1949; Venus Observed, 1950; A Sleep of Prisoners, 1952; The Dark is Light Enough, 1954; Curtmantle, 1962; A Yard of Sun, 1970; The Brontës of Haworth, TV play, 1973; Can You Find Me, 1978; Translation: Ring Round The Moon, 1950; The Lark, 1954; Tiger at the Gates, 1955; Duel of Angels, 1958; Judith, 1962; Peer Gynt, 1970; Cyrano de Bergerac, 1975; The Best of Enemies, TV play, 1976; Sister Dora, TV play, 1977, introduction and text, Charlie Hammond's Sketchbook, 1980, Selected plays, 1985; One Thing More, or Caedmon Construed, 1986; Genius, Talent and Failure, 1991; Looking for a Language, 1992. Honours: Fellow, Royal Society of Literature, 1950; Hon Diploma in Arts, Manchester, 1962; Queen's Gold Medal for Poetry, 1962; R S L Heinemann Award, 1962; DLitt, Lambeth, 1988; Hon Fellow, Manchester Metropolitan University, 1988; Hon DLitt, Sussex University, 1994; Hon DLitt, De Montfort University, 1994. Address: The Toft, East Dean, Near Chichester, Sussex, England.

FRYM Gloria, b. 28 Feb 1947, New York, New York, USA. Writer. m. Jeffrey J Carter, 1 daughter. Education: BA, 1968, MA, 1973, University of New Mexico. Appointments: Core Faculty, Poetics Programme, New College of California; Instructor, Creative Writing, San Francisco State University. Publications: Impossible Affection, 1979; Back to Forth, 1982; By Ear, 1990; How I Learned, 1992. Honour: San Francisco State University Poetry Center Book Award, 1983. Address: 2119 Eunice Street, Berkeley, CA 94709, USA.

FULLER Bruce Thomas, b. 10 Jan 1954, Harvey, Illinois, USA. Education: BSc, Computer Sciences, Sonoma State University, 1985. Publications: The Fifty Cent Poet, 1979; Speculation of the Spirit, Supposition of the Soul, 1980; The Opinions Expressed by the Poet are not Necessarily Those of the Reader, 1981. Contributions to: Toyon '82; The Literature Annual of Humboldt State University Contact, 1983. Address: 829 Queen Anne Street, Woodstock, IL 60098, USA.

FULLER Jean Violet Overton, b. 7 Mar 1915, Iver Heath, Buckinghamshire, England. Author. Education: Royal Academy of Dramatic Art, 1931-32; BA Honours, English, University of London, 1944; University College of London, 1948-50. Appointment: Founding Director, Fuller D'Arch Smith Ltd (rare books), 1969-. Publications: Venus Protected, 1964; Carthage and the Midnight Sun, 1966; African Violets, 1968; Darun and Pitar, 1970; Tintagel, 1970; Conversations with a Captor, 1973; The Great Adventure of the Much Travelled Little Oak Tree, 1984; The Mystical Tale of Two Hens, 1986; Bambina the Thanksgiving Picture, 1988; The Nightingale, 1989; The Passing of Bambina and the Coming of Chalcedony, 1990; Chalcedony's Kittens, 1991; Leo and America, 1992; Cats and Burglars, 1993; The Bombed Years, 1995; Tinta's Toe, 1995. Contributions to: Poetry Review; Manifold; Expression I; Wave. Honours: Manifold Poems of the Decade Competition, 1970; Manifold Chapbook Prize, 1978. Membership: Society of Authors. Address: Fuller D'Arch Smith Ltd, 37b New Cavendish Street, London, England.

FULLER John Leopold, b. 1 Jan 1937. College Tutor. Education: New College, Oxford. Appointments: Visiting Lecturer,

University of Buffalo, 1962-63; Assistant Lecturer, English, University of Manchester, 1963-65; Fellow, Tutor in English, Magdalen College, Oxford, 1966-; Fellow, Royal Society of Literature. Publications: Fairground Music, 1961; The Tree That Walked, 1967; Cannibals and Missionaries, 1972; Epistles to Several Persons, 1973; Penguin Modern Poets, 22, 1974; Squeaking Crust, 1974; The Mountain in The Sea, 1975; Lies and Secrets, 1979; The Illusionists, 1980; Selected Poems, 1953-1982, 1982; The Beautiful Inventions, 1983; Partingtime Hall, 1989; The Grey Among The Green, 1988; The Mechanical Body and Other Poems, 1991; Stones and Fires, 1996. Contributions to: New Statesman; Times Literary Supplement; Listener; Encounter; London Magazine; New Yorker; New Review; Quarto; Thames Poetry; Spectator. Honours: Newdigate Prize, 1960; Richard Hillary Award, 1962; E C Gregory Award, 1965. Address: Magdalen College, Oxford, England.

FULTON Alice, b. 25 Jan 1952, Troy, New York, USA. Professor of English; Poet. m. Hank De Leo, 1980. Education: BA, Empire State College, Albany, New York, 1978; MFA, Cornell University, 1982. Appointments: Assistant Professor, 1983-86, William Wilhartz Professor, 1986-89, Associate Professor, 1989-92, Professor of English, 1992-, University of Michigan; Visiting Professor of Creative Writing, Vermont College, 1987, University of California, Los Angeles, 1991. Publications: Anchors of Light, 1979; Dance Script with Electric Ballerina, 1983; Palladium, 1986; Powers of Congress, 1990; Sensual Math, 1995. Honours: MacDowell Colony Fellowships, 1978, 1979; Millay Colony Fellowship, 1980; Emily Dickinson Award, 1980; Academy of American Poets Prize, 1982; Consuelo Ford Award, 1984; Rainer Maria Rilke Award, 1984; Michigan Council for the Arts Grants, 1986, 1991; Guggenheim Fellowship, 1986-87; Yaddo Colony Fellowship, 1987; Bess Hokin Prize, 1989; Ingram-Merrill Foundation Award, 1990; John D and Catharine T MacArthur Foundation Fellowship, 1991-96; Elizabeth Matchett Stover Award, 1994. Address: 2370 Le Forge Road, RR 2, Ypsilanti, MI 48198, USA.

FULTON Robin, b. 6 May 1937, Isle of Aran, Scotland. Education: PhD, Edinburgh University, 1972. Appointment: Senior Lecturer in English, Stavanger, Norway. Publications: A Matter of Definition, 1963; Instances, 1967; The Space Between the Stones, 1971; Tree-Lines, 1974; Between Flight: Eighteen Poems, 1976; Following a Mirror, 1980; Selected Poems 1963-78, 1980; Fields of Focus, 1982; Coming Down to Earth and Spring is Soon, 1990; Editions and translations of Scandinavian poetry. Address: Postboks 467, N-4001 Stavanger, Norway.

FUNKHOUSER Erica, b. 17 Sept 1949, Cambridge, Massachusetts, USA. m. Thaddeus Beal, 1 Sept 1973, 1 son, 1 daughter. Education: BA, English, Vassar College, 1971; MA, English, Stanford University, 1973. Appointments: Lecturer in English, Lesley College, Massachusetts; Dramaturg, Revels Inc, Cambridge, Massachusetts. Publications: Natural Affinities, 1983; Sure Shot, 1992. Contributions to: Poetry; New Yorker; Ploughshares; Paris Review; Anthologies: Working Classics; Poems on Industrial Life, 1990; Contemporary New England Poetry, 1987. Honours: Sylvia Plath Poetry Contest Winner, 1979; Fellowship, The Artists Foundation, Massachusetts Council on The Arts and Humanities, 1982; Consuelo Ford Award, Poetry Society of America, 1989. Membership: Poetry Society of America. Address: 179 Southern Avenue, Essex, MA 01929, USA.

FURNIVAL Christine Mary Twiston, b. London, England. Writer; Homeopath. m. Robert Graham Furnival, 6 June 1957, 3 daughters. Education: BA, Honours, English, University of Cambridge, 1953; Diploma in Homoepathy, 1990. Appointments: Advertising Copy Writer; Teacher, ILEA; Copywright Researcher, British Council; Teacher in Adult Education of Creative Writing and of Adult Literacy. Publications: A Bare-Fisted Catch, 1968; The Animals to Orpheus, 1975; Prince of Sapphires, 1977; Towards Praising, 1978. Contributions to: New Statesman; Poetry Wales; Anglo-Welsh Review; Aquarius; Meridian; Workshop; Poetry of The Seventies, anthology; PEN, anthology, 1971; Has also broadcast on BBC 2 and Radio Wales. Memberships: Writers' Guild of Great Britain; Theatre Writers' Union; Poetry Society; PEN; Playwrights' Co-Operative. Address: 33 West Street, Stratford upon Avon, Warwickshire CV37 6DN, England.

G

GABRIEL Stella, b. 2 June 1921. Senior Lecturer; Student Counsellor. Div. Education: BA Honours, Manchester University, 1969. Appointments: Editor, then Assistant Personnel Manager and Staff Trainer, House Magazine, Liverpool, 1953-64; Teacher, English and Russian, 1970-73; Teacher-Trainer and Lecturer in English, 1973-80; Senior Lecturer, Student Counsellor, 1980-86. Contributions to: Poetry Now; Brando's Hat; Mainly performing poet at evenings of entertainment for charity. Membership: Committee, Manchester Poet. Address: 1 Brayton Avenue, Didsbury, Manchester M20 0LP, England.

GAGE Maura R, (Maura Liebman), b. 27 Apr 1963, Pittsburgh, Pennsylvania, USA. Instructor of English. m. Dennis Gage, 19 Aug 1990, div 1993. Education: BA, English, California University of Pennsylvania, 1984; MA, English, Colorado State University, 1987; Currently pursuing PhD in English, University of South Florida. Appointments: English Instructor, Pasco-Hernando Community College, 1988-89; Teaching Assistant, English, 1989-, Student Support Services Programme, 1995-, University of South Florida; Instructor of English and Creative Writing, Hillsborough Community College, Tampa, Florida, 1993-. Publications: Jackets, booklet, 1991; Spun From the Gold in David's Hair, chapbook, 1994; Sweet Man of Morning, broadside, 1994; Wanderin', postcard, 1994. Contributions include: Scrape; Valley Spirit; Ripples; Bogg; Tandava; Time to Pause; Poets Corner; Krax; Alura; Image; Bitterroot; Chicago Sheet; Hobo Stew Review; Parnassus Literary Journal; Truly Fine Review; Green's Magazine; Treasured Poems of America; Candelabrum; Art; Higginson Journal; Proof Rock; The Cathartic; Poetic Justice; Reflections; Impetus; Nycticorax; Nostoc; Poetalk. Honours: Honourable Mention, 4th Place, California Federation of Chaparral Poets, Robert Frost Chapter, 1987; 2nd Prize, Many Voices, Many Lands, 1988; Winner, Florida Suncoast Writers' Conference Poetry Contest, 1990; Honourable Mention, Academy of American Poets, 1990; Winner, Estelle J Zbar, Poetry Award, 1991; 1st Prize, Sparrowgrass Poetry Forum, 1992; Editor's Choice Award for His Compeer, National Library of Poetry, 1994. Membership: Vice President, 1983-84, Sigma Tau Delta. Address: 212 Heritage Lane, K-204, Temple Terrace, FL 33617, USA.

GALANES Miguel. See: JIMENZ DE LOS GALANES Y DE LA FLOR Miguel.

GALATI Jacqueline A, b. 2 May 1965, Chicago, Illinois, USA. Executive Secretary. Education: Degree: Poetry, Short Story/Novel Writing. Appointment: Executive Secretary. Publication: Contributions to: Midwest Anthology of Poetry, 1988; Iliad Press, National Library of Poetry, Sparrowgrass, Creative Arts & Sciences, The Poetry Guild, Poets Guild, The Amherst Society. Honours: Golden Poet Award, 1988, 1991; Honorarium, World of Poetry, 1990; President's Award, 1993, 1994, 1995, 1996. Address: 2800 Broadway Street, Blue Island, IL 60406, USA.

GALL Sally Moore, b. 28 July 1941, New York, New York, USA. Librettist. m. William Einar Gall, 8 Dec 1967. Education: BA, cum laude, Harvard University, 1963; MA, 1971, PhD, 1976, New York University. Appointments: Poetry Editor, Free Inquiry, 1981-84; Founding Editor, Eidos, The International Prosody Bulletin, 1984-88. Publications: Co-Author, The Modern Poetic Sequence: The Genius of Modern Poetry, 1983, paperback, 1986; Editor, Ramon Guthrie's Maximum Security Ward and Other Poems, 1984; Versification Editor, Poetry in English: An Anthology, 1987; Author: Ramon Guthrie's Maximum Security Ward. Contributions to: Reference books, professional journals and literary magazines; Also music collaborator as librettist for opera and musical theatre. Honours: Penfield Fellow, New York University, 1973-74; Academy of American Poets Award, 1975, Key Pin and Scroll Award, 1976, New York University; Co-Winner, Explicator Literary Foundation Award, 1984. Memberships: Dramatists Guild; Lyrica; Modern Language Association; Opera America; National Opera Association; Opera for Youth Board; International Alliance of Women in Music; Poets and Writers. Address: 5820 Folsom Drive, La Jolla, CA 92037, USA.

GALLAGHER Katherine, b. 7 Sept 1935, Maldon, Australia. Writer; Teacher. m. 8 April 1978, 1 son. Education: BA, 1962, Diploma of Education, 1963, Melbourne University. Appointments: Teacher of English as a Second Language, Paris, 1971-78; Secondary Teaching, part-time, London Borough of Haringey, 1982-; Creative Writing Teacher, London, Australia, 1984-; Poetry Society, Open College of The Arts, Barnet College, 1990. Publications: The Eye's Circle, 1975, 1979; Tributaries of the Love-Song, 1978; Passengers to the City, 1985; Fish-Rings on Water, 1989; Finding The Prince, 1993; Translation of Jean Jacques Celly's Poems, The Sleepwalker with Eyes of Clay, 1994; Anthologies include: Ain't I a Woman, 1987; Virago Book of Love-Poetry, 1990; In The Gold of Flesh, 1990; Poetry of War, BBC, 1990; Sing Freedom, 1991; Longman Book Project, 1994; Chatto Book of Ghosts, 1994; In Australia: Penguin Book of Australian Women's Poetry, 1986; Kiwi and Emu, 1989; New Oxford Book of Australian Verse, 1991; Oxford Book of Australian Love Poetry, 1994; Changing Places, 1994, among others. Contributions: Acumen; Honest Ulsterman; Outposts; Poetry Review; Time Out; Poetry Ireland; Age; Bulletin; Canberra Times; Meanjin; New Poetry; Poetry Australia; Quadrant; Kunapipi; Antipodes; Waves; Struga International Poetry Review. Honours: Fellowship, Australian Literature Board, 1978; Warana Poetry Prize, Brisbane, 1981; Runner-up, She Magazine Poetry Competition, UK, 1985; Book shortlisted for Australian National Poetry Award, 1986. Membership: Co-Editor, Poetry London Newsletter. Address: 49 Myddleton Road, Wood Green, London N22 4LZ, England.

GALLAGHER Tess, b. 21 July 1943, Port Angeles, Washington, USA. Poet; Writer. m. Raymond Carver, 17 June 1988. Education: MFA, University of Iowa, Writers Workshop, 1974. Appointments: Teaching Fellow, University of Iowa, 1974-75; Assistant Professor, St Lawrence University, 1974-75, Kirkland College, 1975-76; Visiting Lecturer, University of Montana, 1976-77; Assistant Professor, University of Arizona, 1979-80; Professor, Syracuse University, 1980-89; Writing Poems, 1990-. Publications: Stepping Outside, 1974; Instructions to The Double, 1976; Under Stars, 1978; Willingly, 1984; A Concert of Tenses, essays, 1986; Amplitude: New and Selected, 1987; Moon-Bridge Crossing, 1992; Portable Kisses, 1992; The Lover of Horses, stories, 1992; Portable Kisses Expanded, 1994; My Black Horse, 1995. Contributions to: Zyzziva; New Yorker; Atlantic Monthly; Ploughshares; Caliban; Vogue; Parnassus; Michigan Quarterly; American Poetry Review; Cimmaron Review. Honours: 2 National Endowment for the Arts Grants; Guggenheim Fellowship, 1978-79; Lyndhurst Prize, 1993. Memberships: American Poetry Society; PEN. Address: Skyhouse, Port Angeles, WA 98362, USA.

GALLAS John Edward, b. 11 Jan 1950, Wellington, New Zealand. Teacher in Student Support Service, Leicestershire. Education: Nelson College, New Zealand, 1961-67; BA, Honours, English, Otago University, Dunedin, New Zealand, 1968-71; MPhil, English Literature, 1100-1400, Merton College, Oxford, 1972-74; PGCE, North Staffs Polytechnic, 1980-81. Appointments: Assistant Lecturer in English, Otago University; Assistant Chef, York; English Teacher, Bursa, Turkey; Archivist, Liverpool; English Teacher, Market Harborough; English Teacher, Diyarbakir, Turkey; Teacher in Leicestershire, Student Support Service. Publications: Practical Anarchy, 1989; Flying Carpets Over Filbert Street, 1993; Third Collection, untitled, due 1997. Contributions to: PN Review; Landfall; Thames Poetry; Staple; Outposts; Stand; Rialto. Honours: Rutland Poetry Prize, 1984; Runner-up, National Poetry Prize, 1985; East Midlands Arts Bursary, 1986; Charnwood Poetry Prize, 1987; New Voices Midlands Reading Tour, 1990; Surrey Poetry Centre Prize, 1992. Address: 40 London Road, Coalville, Leicestershire LE67 2JA, England.

GALLETTI de MASTRANGELO Irma, b. 11 Dec 1928, Argentina. m. Hugo Mastrangelo, 1 July 1950, 1 son, 1 daughter. Education: Teaching Qualifications at First and Adult Level; CIE, Assessor, Centre of Educational Investigations. Appointments: Teacher, Buenos Aires; Participant, Scholastic Commission of Municipal Government. Publications: Anthologies include: Antologia Poetica, 4, 1981; Poesia '82, 1982; Cuento y Poesia, 1982; El Amor en la Poesia Argentina, 1983; Neuvos Autores Nacionales, 1983; La Mujer en la Poesia Hispanoamericana, 1983; Diccionario de Poetas Argentinos, 1984; El Soneto Hispanoamericano, 1984; Poesia Argentina Contemporanea, 1986; America Poetica, 1988; Poetas Hispanoamericanas Contemporaneas, 1989; Patria Plural, 1990; Suma de Armor, 1991; America Poetica, 1992. Contributions to: Semper Fidelis; Illustrated Poem; Democracia. Honours: Special Mention, Poesia Argentina Contemporanea; General Administration of Schools and Culture Invitation, National Library of the Argentine Republic. Memberships: Argentine Society of Writers. Address:

Zelarrayan 317 p10 Dpto 6, 8000 Bahia Blanca, Buenos Aires, Argentina.

GALVIN Brendan, b. 20 Oct 1938, Everett, Massachusetts, USA. Professor of English; Poet. m. Ellen Baer, 1968, 1 son, 1 daughter. Education: BS, Boston College, 1960; MA, Northeastern University, 1964; MFA, 1967, PhD, 1970, University of Massachusetts. Appointments: Instructor, Northeastern University, 1964-65; Assistant Professor, Slippery Rock State College, 1968-69; Assistant Professor, 1969-74, Associate Professor, 1974-80, Professor of English, 1980-, Central Connecticut State University; Visiting Professor, Connecticut College, 1975-76; Editor (with George Garrett), Poultry: A Magazine of Voice, 1981-; Coal Royalty Chairholder in Creative Writing, University of Alabama, 1993. Publications: The Narrow Land, 1971; The Salt Farm, 1972; No Time For Good Reasons, 1974; The Minutes No One Owns, 1977; Atlantic Flyway, 1980; Winter Oysters, 1983; A Birder's Dozen, 1984; Seals in the Inner Harbor, 1985; Wampanoag Traveler, 1989; Raising Irish Walls, 1989; Great Blue: New and Selected Poems, 1990; Early Returns, 1992; Saints in Their Ox-Hide Boat, 1992; Islands, 1993. Honours: National Endowment for the Arts Fellowships, 1974, 1988; Connecticut Commission on the Arts Fellowships, 1981, 1984; Guggenheim Fellowship, 1988; Sotheby Prize, Arvon International Foundation, 1988; Levinson Prize, Poetry magazine, 1989; O B Hardison Jr Poetry Prize, Folger Shakespeare Library, 1991; Charity Randall Citation, International Poetry Forum, 1994. Address: PO Box 54, Durham, CT 06422, USA.

GALVIN Patrick, b. 1927, Cork, Ireland. m. Diana Ferrier, 2 sons. Appointments: Writer-in-Residence, Editor and Film Critic, Northern Ireland and England; Ballad Singer, England and USA, 1955-60; Resident Dramatist, Lyric Theatre, Belfast, 1974-77. Publications: Heart of Grace, 1957; Christ in London, 1960; By Nature Diffident, 1971; Lon Chaney, 1971; The Woodburners, 1973; Man on the Porch, 1980; Collected Poems and Letters, 1985; Let the Seahorse Take Me and Other Poems, 1986. Address: c/o Brian and O'Keefe, 78 Coleraine Road, Blackheath, London SE3, England.

GAMSON Leland Pablo, b. 30 Dec 1950, Minneapolis, Minnesota, USA. Social Worker. m. Bonnie Lou Campbell, 24 Aug 1985. Education: MSW Catholic University, 1981; MEd, American University, 1974; BA, Religion, Hiram College, 1973. Appointments: Editor, As Is, 1975-79; Economics Assistant, US Department of Labor, 1977-79; Veterans Administration Social Worker, 1981-; Editor, Bacon and Eggs News, 1982-; USAR Officer, 1983-. Publication: Sinia and Olympus, 1977. Contributions to: Friends Journal; Gargoyle; American Magazine; As Is; Higgison Journal of Poetry; Federal Poet; James Whitcomb Riley Celebration Anthology; Bacon and Eggs; Edgar Allan Poe Celebration Anthology; Quaker Life; Parnassus of World Poets. Honours: Gold Quill, 1969; Grant County Poetry Contest, 1992. Memberships: Federal Poets; President, Creative Writers, Grant County, Indiana, 1993-; American Scientific Affiliation. Address: 607 West Spencer, Marion, IN 46952, USA.

GANAPATHI Subramanyam, (Madhura Bharathi), b. 25 Mar 1953, Tirunelveli, India. Banker. m. G Meenakshi, 20 Oct 1983, 1 s. Education: BS, 1974; Postgraduate Diploma in Journalism, 1978. Appointments: Employed with Syndicate Bank, a leading public sector bank, 1978-. Contributions to: The Hindustan Times; Debonair; Indian Literature; Poetry India, 1989; Anthology Poetry India, 1990; Anthology, Femina. Honours: Consolation Prize in first ever National Level Poetry Contest jointly sponsored by the Poetry Society, Delhi and the British Council Division in India, 1988. Memberships: Founder President of Bharathi Iyakkam, a socio-literary mission. Address: 56 Satsangam Street, Madipakkam, Chennai 600 091, India.

GANDER Forrest, b. 21 Jan 1956, Barstow, California, USA. Professor of English. Education: BS, Geology, College of William and Mary; MA, English, San Francisco State University. Appointments: Professor, Providence College, Rhode Island, 1984-; Co-Editor, Last Roads Publishers. Publications: Rush to The Lake, 1988; Eggplants and Lotus Root, 1991; Lynchburg, 1993; Deeds of Utmost Kindness, 1994; Editor, Mouth to Mouth: Poetry by 12 Contemporary Mexican Women, 1993. Contributions to: Conjunctions; Sulfur; Southern Review; New Directions Anthology; Partisan Review. Honour: National Endowment for the Arts Fellowship in Poetry, 1988. Membership: Associated Writing Programs. Address: 351 Nayatt Road, Barrington, RI 02806, USA.

GANDHI Madan Gopal Kalra Yayati (Yayati Madan G Gandhi), b. 31 Aug 1940, Lahore, India. Poet; Painter; Teacher. m. Sushma Gandhi Devayani, 14 Apr 1976. Education: Matriculation, High School, Punjab University, 1956; MA, English, 1964, MA, First class, (Gold Medallist), Political Science, 1966, PhD, Political Science, 1974, Punjab University. Appointments: Professor and Director, Centre for Third World Studies and Political Science, Director, Directorate Education, M D University, Rohtak; Visiting Fellow, St John's College, Cambridge, 1989-90. Publications: Ashes and Embers, 1982; Kundalini, 1982; Haikus and Quatrains, 1983; Petals of Flame, 1985; Luteous Serpent, 1986; Meandering Maze, 1987; Freak Stair, 1988; Ring of Silence, 1989; Enchanting Flute, 1990; Shunyata in Trance, 1991; The Imperilled Earth, 1993; Cam Musings, 1994; Divine Dancer, 1994. Contributions to: Poet, Madras; World Poetry Anthology, Madras, 1990, 1991; Reviews published in: The Poet, Madras, Sky Lark, Aligarh, Literary Half Yearly, Mysore, Tribune (Chandigarh). Honours: Tagore Centenary Medal for Poetry, 1961; Varamihir and Aryabhatt Awards for Astrology, 1992, 1993. Memberships: President, Poetry Society of India, Delhi; World Poetry Society, Madras; Director, Chairman, Vikas Bharti, Delhi; Convener, Kala Bharti, Delhi. Address: 3239 Sector 21 D, Chandigarh, India.

GANNELLO Alfreda Mavis, b. 17 Nov 1926, London, England. Freelance Writer; Author; Poet; Columnist. m. Charles Carmelo Gannello, 2 Jan 1954. Education: High School through College, Post Graduate. Appointments: Medical Assistant; Information and Referral Aide; Medical Insurance Assessor. Publication: Meet Carmelo, 1988. Contributions to: Black Creek Review; Potpourri International; New York Poetry Society; Writer's Dream; Quill Books; American Poetry Association; Suwannee Poetry; New York Poetry Anthology; Villager; National Library of Poetry; Poets Corner; Poetry International; Amherst Poetry Society; Sparrowgrass Poetry Forum; Poetry Unlimited; World of Poetry; Break Out; Literary Pathways; Famous Poets Anthology; Arcadia Poetry Anthology; Iliad Press; Views to Muse; Yes Press; Poets Guild. Honours: Numerous Awards, Honourable Mentions and Certificates of Merit, 1987-91; Browning Poetry Awards, 1994. Memberships: International Society for the Advancement of Poetry; National Audubon Society. Address: PO Box 2272, Oak Park, Illinois 60302-2272, USA.

GARCIA ALONSO Agustin, b. 14 Jan 1947, Castrocalbon, Spain. Author; Poet. m. Marid de las Candelas Ranz Hormazabal, 18 Aug 1973, 2 sons, 1 daughter. Education: Certificado de Bachiller; Gazeta de Felgueiras Poetural; Academician Lauredo, Accademia Internazionale Pontzen, Naples; World Academy of Arts and Culture, California; Academy Letras e Ciencias, Sao Lourenco, Brazil. Appointments: Photographer; Editor; President, cultural associations. Publications: Numerous. Contributions: Various Spanish publications. Honours: El Paisaje de Poesia, 1987, El Paisaje de Novela, 1975, 1977; El Paisaje de Sonetos, 1984. Memberships include: World Academy of Arts and Culture. Address: La Penorra No 8, 2, 48850 Aranguren, Vizcaya, Spain.

GARCIA FERNANDEZ Eugenio, b. 5 Mar 1951, Sueros de Cepeda, Leon, Spain. University Professor of Literature. Education: Licentiate in Philosophy and Letters, specialising in Hispanic Literature, Universidad Complutense de Madrid. Appointments: Professor of Literature for University Matriculation, INB Jorge Guillen. Publications: Juegos de la Memoria, 1989; Clima Interior, 1989; Sombras de un Verano, 1991. Contributions to: Poetry Critic for daily newspaper, El Mundo, Madrid; Critical articles in several magazines and journals. Address: Plaza de Cristo Rey no 1, 28040 Madrid, Spain.

GARCIA TERRES Jamie, b. 15 May 1924, Mexico. Poet; Writer; Publisher. m. Celia Chavez Rivera, 4 Feb 1960, 2 sons, 1 daughter. Education: University National Automona de Mexico, 1942-46; University of Paris, 1950. Appointment: General Subdirector, National Institute of Fine Arts, 1948-49; Editor, Mexico en el Arte, 1948-53; Chief of Press Department, 1951-53; General Director, Universidad Nacional Autonoma de Mexico, 1953-65; Editor, 1953-65; Ambassador to Greece, 1965-68; General Director, 1968-71; Editor, 1971-89; Editor, 1989-. Publications: El Hermano Menor; Correonoctumo; Las Provincias del Aire; La Fuente Oscura; Los Reinos Combatientes; 100 Imagenes del Mar; Carne de Dios; Breve Antologia de Girorgos Seferis; Todo lo mas por decir; Honores a Francisco de Terrzas; Parte de Vida; Las Manchas del Sol; Baile de Mascaras. Contributions to: Mexico en el Arte; El Espectador; Evergreen Review; Mito; Alarce; Pauta; Marcha; Plural; Eco; Vuelta; Syntaxis. Honour: Premio Magda

Donato. Address: Paseo de la Reforma num 1310, Lomas de Chapultepec, Mexico 11000 DF, Mexico.

GARCIA-SIMMS Michael. See: **SIMMS Michael Arlin.**

GARDNER Nancy Bruff, (Nancy Bruff, Nancy Gardner), b. 15 Nov 1909, Fairfield County, Connecticut, USA. m. (1) 1 son, 1 daughter, (2) Esmond Gardner, 20 July 1963. Education: Private School in New York, Connecticut and University of Sorbonne, Paris. Publications: My Talon in Your Heart, 1946; Walk Lightly on the Planet, 1985. Contributions to: Various newspapers; Collection of writings in Boston University Library. Memberships: Poetry Society of America; Authors League; Authors Guild; Dramatists Guild, New York; Poets and Writers. Address: 200 East 66th Street, Apt D803, New York, NY 10021, USA.

GARDNER Stephen Leroy, b. 8 Apr 1948, South Carolina, USA. Professor of English. m. Mignon P W Derrick. Education: MA, English, 1970, MA, Honours, English, 1972, University of South Carolina; PhD, English and Creative Writing, Oklahoma State University. Appointments: Teaching Fellow, 1970-72, Co-Ordinator, 1975-81, Assistant, Associate, Professor of English, 1972-84, Professor of English and Chair, Division of Arts and Letters, 1984-86, Dean, College of Humanities and Social Sciences, 1986-93, University of South Carolina at Aiken; Editor, The Devil's Millhopper Press, 1986-. Contributions: Southern Review; Language of Poems; Sandlapper; Mississippi Review; Yearbook of Modern Poetry, 1976; Southern Poetry Review; Tinderbox; Stone Country; Hollins Critic; American Poets; Anthology of Magazine Verse and Yearbook of American Poetry; Black Willow; Texas Review; Kansas Quarterly; New Delta Review; Chariton Review. Honours: Honourable Mention, Hollins Critic Poetry Contest, 1972; Best Poem, Borestone Mountain Poetry Awards, 1976; First Prize, Oklahoma State University Academy of American Poets Competition, 1978; University of South Carolina Grants, 1982, 1983; South Carolina Arts Commission Readers Circuit, 1988; Selected for SC Arts Commission Approved Artists List, 1989-; Eyster Prize for Poetry, 1994. Memberships: Board of Directors, 1992-96, Aiken Center for The Arts; Treasurer, Board of Governors, 1993-96, Chairman, 1996-, SC Academy of Authors; Associated Writing Programmes; Hemingway Society; Walt Whitman Association; Council of Colleges of Arts and Sciences. Address: PO Box 40, Ballentine, SC 29002, USA.

GARDONS S S. See: **SNODGRASS W D.**

GARFITT Roger, b. 12 Apr 1944, Melksham, Wiltshire, England. Poet; Prose Writer. Education: BA, Honours, Merton College, Oxford, 1968. Appointments: Arts Council Creative Writing Fellow, University College of North Wales, Bangor, 1975-77; Arts Council Poet in Residence, Sunderland Polytechnic, 1978-80; Editor, Poetry Review, 1977-82; Welsh Arts Council Poet in Residence in Ebbw Vale, 1984; Poet in Residence, Pilgrim College, Boston, 1986-87; Blyth Valley Disabled Forum, 1992. Publications: Caught On Blue, 1970; West of Elm, 1974; The Broken Road, 1982; Rowlstone Haiku, with Frances Horovitz, 1982; Given Ground, 1989; Border Songs, 1996. Contributions to: Times Literary Supplement; New Statesman; Encounter; London Magazine; Stand; Poetry Wales; La Traductiere, Paris; Granta; London Review of Books; PN Review; Poetry Review. Honours: Guinness International Poetry Prize, 1973; Gregory Award, 1974. Memberships: Poetry Society; Welsh Academy; National Association of Writers in Education. Literary Agent: Jane Turnbull. Address: c/o Jane Turnbull, 13 Wendell Road, London W12 9RS, England.

GARLICK Raymond, b. 21 Sept 1926, London, England. Education: BA, University College of North Wales, Bangor, 1948. Appointments: Lecturer, Trinity College, Carmarthen, 1967-86. Publications include: Poems from the Mountain House, 1950; Requiem for a Poet, 1954; Poets from Pembrokeshire, 1954; The Welsh-Speaking Sea, 1954; Landscapes and Figures: Selected Poems 1949-63; A Sense of Europe: Collected Poems 1965-68, 1968; A Sense of Time: Poems and Antipodeans 1969-72, 1972; Incense: Poems 1972-75, 1976; Collected Poems 1946-86, 1987. Address: 30 Glannant House, College Road, Carmarthen SA31 3EF, Wales.

GARNER Van Dee, b. 25 Jan 1933, Sherwood, Tennessee, USA. Disabled Veteran. m. Helen Lively, 18 Nov 1967. Appointments: World of Poetry, International Society of Poets, Washington, DC. Publications: Deep Within, 1987; Special Edition of the Poems of Van

Garner, 1989; The Collected Works of Van Garner, 1990. Contributions to: Jean's Journal, Veteran's Voices Magazine. Honours: International Poet of Merit, 1995; Delaware Heritage Bill of Rights Award, 1991. Address: 3725 Jarren Drive, Chattanooga, TN 37415-3526, USA.

GARRETT Evvy, b. 28 Jan 1946, Kansas City, Missouri, USA. Poet; Writer. 1 son, 1 daughter. Contributions include: New York Quarterly; Poetic Space; Anemone; Riverrun; Pearl; Chicago Street; Rapping Paper; San Diego Lesbian Press; Journal; AKA; Poetic Space First Anthology; The Shadows Project; Cappers; Copper Hill Quarterly; Rant; We Accept Donations; Writer's Info; Psychopoetica; Alura; December Rose. Address: 4350 West Point Loma Boulevard, San Diego, CA 92107, USA.

GARRETT George (Palmer, Jr), b. 11 June 1929, Orlando, Florida, USA. Professor of English; Writer; Poet; Editor. m. Susan Parrish Jackson, 1952, 2 sons, 1 daughter. Education: BA, 1952, MA, 1956, PhD, 1985, Princeton University. Appointments: US Poetry Editor, Transatlantic Review, 1958-71; Visiting Lecturer, Rice University, 1961-62; Associate Professor, 1962-67, Hoyns Professor of English, 1984-, University of Virginia; Writer-in-Residence, Princeton University, 1964-65, Bennington College, Vermont, 1979, University of Michigan, 1979-80, 1983-84; Co-Editor, Hollins Critic, 1965-71, Worksheet, 1972-, Poultry: A Magazine of Voice, 1981-; Professor of English, Hollins College, Virginia, 1967-71; Professor of English and Writer-in-Residence, University of South Carolina, 1971-73; Senior Fellow, Council of the Humanities, Princeton University, 1974-78; Adjunct Professor, Columbia University, 1977-78. Publications: Poetry: The Reverend Ghost, 1957; The Sleeping Gypsy and Other Poems, 1958; Abraham's Knife and Other Poems, 1961; For a Bitter Season: New and Selected Poems, 1967; Welcome to the Medicine Show: Postcards, Flashcards, Snapshots, 1978; Luck's Shining Child: A Miscellany of Poems and Verses, 1981; The Collected Poems of George Garrett, 1984; Novels include: The Old Army Game, 1994; Short stories include: An Evening Performance: New and Selected Short Stories, 1985; Other includes: My Silk Purse and Yours, 1993; Editor: 18 books, 1963-93. Honours: Sewanee Review Fellowship, 1958; American Academy in Rome Fellowship, 1958; Ford Foundation Grant, 1960; National Endowment for the Arts Grant, 1967; Contempora Award, 1971; Guggenheim Fellowship, 1974; American Academy of Arts and Letters Award, 1985; Cultural Laureate of Virginia, 1986; T S Eliot Award, 1989. Membership: Vice Chancellor, 1987-93, Chancellor, 1993-, Fellowship of Southern Letters. Address: 1845 Wayside Place, Charlottesville, VA 22903, USA.

GARRIGAN Sean. See: **BENNETT John Frederic.**

GARSTON Maureen Beatrice Courtnay, (Maureen Weldon), b. 4 Oct 1940, Leicester, England. Ballet Dancer; Ballet Teacher; Poet. 1 daughter. Education: Diploma, Royal Academy of Dancing, 1973; Chester College, Cheshire, 1980's. Appointments: Dancer with Irish Theatre Ballet Company, 1960's; TV work, RTE, Ireland, 1965; Small ballet school, Weldon School of Dancing, 1973-78; Own poetry performances, 1991-92; Readings in London at Torriano Meeting House and Vertical Images, 1993, Chester Festival, 1993, 1994, Telford's Chester on National Poetry Day, 1994, and in Liverpool. Publications: Poems From The Back Room, pamphlet, 1991; No Pawns in This Play, pamphlet; Leap, book, 1992. Contributions include: About 500 poems published; New Hope International; Purple Patch; Weyfarers; Irreversible Man; TOPS; Coal City Review; Quest, India; Third Half; Poetry Now; Green's Magazine; Poetalk; Psychopoetica; Grasslands Review; Quickenings; News Letter Inago, USA; Voices Israel; Parnassus of World Poets, India; Paris Atlantic; Deadlock. Membership: Society of Women Writers and Journalists, 1994-. Address: 16 Glastonbury Avenue, Off St James Avenue, Upton by Chester, Cheshire CH2 1NG, England.

GASCOYNE David Emery, b. 10 Oct 1916, Harrow, Middlesex, England. Poet. m. Judy Tyler Lewis, 19 May 1975, 2 stepsons, 2 stepdaughters. Education: Salisbury Cathedral Choir School; Regent Street Polytechnic Secondary School, London. Publications: Roman Balcony, 1932; Man's Life in This Meat, 1936; Hölderlin's Madness, 1938; Poems, 1937-1942, 1943; A Vagrant and Other Poems, 1950; Night Thoughts, 1956, 1958, 1995; Collected Poems, 1954, 1988; Collected Verse Translations, 1970; Selected Poems, 1995; Collected Verse Translations, 1965-88, 1996. Contributions to: New Verse; Contemporary Poetry and Prose; New English Weekly; Listener; Delta; Poetry London; Cahiers du Sud; Partisan Review; New Statesman; Nation; Horizon; Adam International Review; Times Literary

Supplement; Botteghe Oscure; Poetry Review; Temenos; Agenda. Honours: Premio Biella Poesia Europea, 1982; Literature Award, Fellow, Royal Society of Literature; Chevalier des Arts et Lettres, French Government, 1995. Memberships: Cultural Committee, World Organization for Poets; Committee, Biennales Internationales de Poesie, Belgium. Address: 48 Oxford Street, Northwood, Cowes, Isle of Wight PO31 9PT, England.

GASTON Elaine (Ailsa Craig), b. 9 Feb 1960, Newry, County Down, Northern Ireland. Arts Administrator. Education: BA Honours, French and Spanish, St Anne's College, Oxford University, 1983; International Therapy Examination Council Diploma in Anatomy and Physiology, 1992; Diploma in Reflexology, Almitra School of Reflexology, 1992. Appointments: Actress with various fringe companies in UK, 1983-86; Director, Pegasus Youth Theatre, Oxford, 1986-90; Development Officer, Old Museum Arts Centre, 1990-92. Publications: Working on first anthology; Poetry Matter No 8, Peterloo Poets Anthology, 1990. Contributions to: Honest Ulsterman; Poetry Ireland; FAN, London. Honours: Second Prize, Ouse Valley Poetry Competition, 1989; Second Prize, Manchester Open Poetry Competition, 1990; Highly Commended, Peterloo Poetry Competition, 1990. Memberships: Founder-Member, Fine Lines, Irish Women Writers Network, London, 1987-90; Founder-Member, Word of Mouth, Poetry Group, Belfast, 1991. Address: c/o Old Museum Arts Centre, 7 College Square North, Belfast BT1 6AR, Northern Ireland.

GATENBY Greg, b. 5 May 1950, Toronto, Ontario, Canada. Poet; Editor; Literary Impressario. Education: BA, English Literature, York University, 1972. Appointments: Editor, McClelland and Stewart, Toronto, 1973-75; Artistic Director, Harbourfront Reading Series, 1975-; Artistic Director, Humber College School of Creative Writing, 1992-93. Publications: Rondeaus for Erica, 1976; Adrienne's Blessing, 1976; The Brown Stealer, 1977; The Salmon Country, 1978; Growing Still, 1981; Anthologies: 52 Pickup, 1977; Whales Sound, 1977; Whales: A Celebration, 1983; The Definitive Notes, 1991; The Wild is Always There, 1993; The Very Richness of That Past, 1995. Honours: City of Toronto Arts Award in Literature, 1989; Honorary Lifetime Member, League of Canadian Poets, 1991. Memberships: Writers' Union of Canada; PEN, Canadian Centre; Friends of Fisher Rare Book Library. Address: c/o Harbourfront Reading Series, 410 Queen's Quay West, Toronto, Ontario M5V 2Z3, Canada.

GEDDES Gary, b. 9 June 1940, Vancouver, British Columbia, Canada. Writer; Teacher; Editor. m. Jan Geddes, 2 May 1972, 3 daughter. Education: BA, University of British Columbia, 1962; DipEd, Reading University, England, 1964; MA, 1966, PhD, 1975, English, University of Toronto. Appointments: Lecturer, 1971-74; Writer-in-Residence, University of Alberta, 1976-77; Professor of English, Concordia, 1978-. Publications: Poems, 1971; Rivers Inlet, 1972; Snakeroot, 1973; Letter of the Master of Horse, 1973; War and Other Measures, 1976; The Acid Test, 1980; The Terracotta Army, 1984; Changes of State, 1986; Hong Kong, 1987; Selected Writings of Gary Geddes, 1988; No Easy Exit, 1989; Light of Burning Towers, 1990; Girl by The Water, 1994; The Perfect Cold Warrior, 1995; Active Trading: Selected Poems, 1970-95, 1996; The Perfect Cold Warrior, 1995. Honours: E J Pratt Medal and Prize, 1969; National Poetry Prize, 1980; America's Best Book, Commonwealth Poetry Competition, 1985; National Magazine Gold Award, 1987; Writers Choice Award, 1988; Lampman Poetry Prize, 1990; Gabriela Mistral Prize, 1995. Memberships: League of Canadian Poets; Writers' Union of Canada; Playwrights Union; PEN International. Address: RR1 Dunvegan, Ontario K0C 1J0, Canada.

GEIER Joan Austin, b. 6 Mar 1934, New York, New York, USA. Writer. m. Walter Geier, 15 Sept 1956, 2 son, 1 daughter. Education: BS, Humanities, Hunter College. Publications: Garbage Can Cat, 1976; Mother of Tribes, 1987; A Formal Feeling Comes, 1994. Contributions to: Good Housekeeping; Christian Science Monitor; New York Newsday; Catholic Digest; Poetry Society of America Quarterly; SPSM&H; A Formal Feeling Comes; The Lyric; Poetpourri; Negative Capability; Hiram Poetry Review. Honours: Poetry Awards, World Order of Narrative Poets, 1980, 1987, 1990, 1992; Gustav Davidson Award, Poetry Society of America, 1982; John Masefield Award, World Order of Narrative Poets, 1983; Amelia Special Award for Haiku, 1985. Memberships: Critic, President, Brooklyn Poetry Circle; Poetry Society of America. Address: 556 H 102 Main Street, Roosevelt Island, NY 10044, USA.

GELDMAN Mordechai, b. 16 Apr 1946, Germany. Clinical Psychologist. Education: MA, Clinical Psychology. Appointments: Psychotherapist; Literary Critic. Publications: Sea Time Land Time, 1970; Bird, 1975; Window, 1980; 66-83, a collection of old and new poems, 1983; Milano, 1988; Eye, 1993; Dark Mirror, 1995. Contributions to: Ha'aretz, lediot Acharonot; Siman; Kri'a; Achshav; Eton 77; Hadarim. Honours: Homsky Prize for Poetry, Hebrew Writers Association, 1983; Prime Minister's Prize, 1995. Membership: Hebrew Writers Association; Society of Hebrew Writers. Address: 73 Shlomtzion Hamalka Street, Tel Aviv 62266, Israel.

GELLIS Willard, b. 9 June 1936, New York, New York, USA. Poet; Writer. m. Shirley Routten, 23 Aug 1981, 1 daughter. Education: AB, Hofstra University, 1958; MA, University of Maryland, 1961; PhD, New York University, 1970. Appointments: Assistant Professor of English, Lockhaven College, Pennsylvania; Associate Professor of English, Purdue University, Indiana; Associate Professor of English, New York Institute of Technology; Visiting Professor, English Literature, State University of New York, Farmingdale, 1989. Publications: Moon inna Bood House, 1984; Ballad of Making Nightmares Pay, 1987; Sin and Hoodoo Memory, 1987; Satan's Suckhole, 1987; Old Sparky, 1987; The Bigfoot Songbook, 1989; St Joe Road, 1989; Bamboo and Cotton, 1991; Go Slow Swift of Heart, 1991; Popped, 1992; Bronco Junky, 1994. Contributions to: Analecta; Hanging Loose; Goodly Co; New American and Canadian Poetry; Mountain Ways; North America Book; Long Shot; Best of The Penny Dreadful Review. Memberships: Poets and Writers; Westhampton Cultural Consortium; Alliance for Community Media. Address: 57 Seafield Lane, Bay Shore, NY 11706, USA.

GELPI Albert, 19 July 1931, New Orleans, Louisiana, USA. Coe Professor of American Literature; Writer. Education: AB, Loyola University, 1951; MA, Tulane University, 1956; PhD, Harvard University, 1962. Appointments: Assistant Professor, Harvard University, 1962-68; Associate Professor, 1968-74, Professor, 1974-78, Coe Professor of American Literature, 1978-, Stanford University. Publications: Emily Dickinson: The Mind of the Poet, 1965; The Poet in America, 1950 to the Present, 1973; Co-Editor, Adrienne Rich's Poetry, 1975; The Tenth Muse: The Psyche of the American Poet, 1975; Editor, Wallace Stevens: The Poetics of Modernism, 1986; A Coherent Splendor: The American Poetic Renaissance 1910-1950, 1987; Co-Editor, Adrienne Rich's Poetry and Poetry, 1993; Denise Levertov: Selected Criticism, 1993; The Blood of the Poet: Selected Poetry of William Everson, 1993. Address: Department of English, Stanford University, Stanford, CA 94305, USA.

GENTRY Mary E, b. 19 Oct 1933, California, USA. m. Harlan C Gentry, 21 Feb 1964, 1 son, 3 daughters. Education: Effective Speech and Human Relations, Simmons Institute, 1959. Appointments: Various. Publications: Hearts on Fire: A Treasury of Poems on Love, 1983; These Too Shall Be Heard, 1991; Down Peaceful Paths, 1991; Listen With Your Heart, 1992; The National Library of Poetry's, The Sound of Poetry, 1992; The Best Poems of the 90's, 1992. Contributions to: American Poetry Anthology, 1982, 1990; Great American Anthology, 1988; American Anthology of Contemporary Poetry, 1988. Honours: Awards of Merit, 1987, 1988, Golden Poet, 1987, 1988, Silver Poet, 1990, World of Poetry. Address: 7045 Molokai Drive, Paradise, CA 95969, USA.

GENZELIS Bronislovas, b. 16 Feb 1934, Republic of Lithuania. Lecturer. m. 17 Oct 1959. Education: Moscow University, 1959; Insitute of Lithuanian History, 1965; Doctor of History of Philosophy, Moscow, 1974; Docent of Vilnius University, 1969; Professor of Vilnius University, 1976. Appointments: Siouliai Pedogogical Insitute, Vilnius University, 1959-92; Member of Supreme Council of the USSR, 1989-90; Member of the Parliament of Lithuania, 1990-96; Chairman of the Committee of Education, Science and Culture of the Parliament of Lithuania, from February, 1997-; Professor of Vytautos Magnus University. Publications: Enlightenment Ideas in Lithuania, 1972; Essay About Thinkers, 1986; An Outline of the Renaissance Philosophy, 1988; The Interaction of Cultures, 1989; Stories About Lithuanian Thinkers, 1994; Philosophy of Ancient, 1997. Contributions to: Journals: Revue Bultique; Problemos; Kulturos Gazai (Domains of Culture); Pergole; Mokslos Irgyvenimes; Philosophy - Sociology; Weekly magazine: Literature i Menos; Atoimimos. Address: Smelio 3-10, Vilnius 2055, Lithuania.

GEORGALAS Robert Nicholas, b. 11 Nov 1951, New York, New York, USA. Professor of English. m. Joanne Pepe, 5 Sept 1981.

Education: AA, Bronx Community College, 1970; BA, Herbert H Lehman College, 1972; MA, City College of New York, 1974. Appointments: Adjunct Lecturer, Herbert Lehman College, 1974-77; Adjunct Professor of English, Marymount Manhattan College, 1979-88; Professor of English, College of DuPage. Contributions to: Great Lakes Poetry Newsletter; Gotta Write; Prairie Light Review; Anthologies: American Anthology of Midwestern Poetry, 1989; Poetry Cafe, 1990; Contemporary Poets of America and Britain, 1992; Distinguished Poets of America, 1993; Daughter of Joy, in Tears of Fire, 1993; Yankees 2, in Sport Literate, 1995. Honours: Second Prize, Chicagoland Poetry Contest, 1989; Third Prize, Autumn Harvest Poetry Festival, 1989; Editor's Choice Award, National Library of Poetry, 1993, 1994. Memberships: Modern Language Association; National Council of Teachers of English. Address: 360 East Randolph, Apt 1407, Chicago, IL 60601, USA.

GEORGE Etty (Elsa), b. 5 July 1937, Cochin. Educator. m. Abraham George, 15 July 1979. Education: MA, English Literature, 1960; DLitt, 1980. Appointments: Lecturer, 1962-80, Professor, 1981-92; Head of Department, 1984-92; Vice Principal, 1988-92; Member of Board of Studies, MG University, Kerala, India, 1989-91. Publications: Pope Poet, 1980; Gusto, Driftwood, poetry journals, 1982-85; World Poetry, 1986-92; Spring Showers, 1989; Whispering Heart, 1987. Honour: International Eminent Poet Award and Honours Fellow, International Academy of Poets. Memberships: World of Poetry Society Intercontinental; Christian Society of Poets, USA; Society of Poets, Australia. Address: BCM College, Kottayam, Kerala, India.

GEORGE Victor André Gilles Joseph, b. 27 Oct 1937, Bois-et-Borsu, Belgium. Teacher. m. 22 July 1967, dec 1982. Education: Graduate, French, History, Geography and Dutch, Secondary Schools. Appointments: Teaching career. Publications: Adju K'pagnon, 1963; Gris Pwin, 1965; In Paradisum, 1978; Recineyes, 1979; Totes les Ameurs de Monde, 1983; Tchonson d'a ci qu'a Passe l'Baye. Contributions to: Les Cahiers Wallons; La Vie Wallonne; Dialectes de Wallonie. Honours: Prix des Critiques Wallons, 1963; Prix Biennal de la Ville de Liege, 1965; Prix Dunbuy, Huy, 1966; Prix Michaux, Namur, 1978; Prix du Ministere de la Communate Francaise, 1982. Memberships: Societe de Langue et de Litterature Wallones, Liege; Vice President, Relis Namurwes, Namur. Address: Tier Laurent 6, B-4560 Bois-et-Borsu, Belgium.

GERALD John Bart, b. 25 Sept 1940, New York, New York, USA. Author; Publisher. m. Julie Maas, 3 Oct 1970. Education: AB, Harvard College, 1962. Publications: Translation, Poèmes 34 Poems, René Tavernier, 1984; Translation, The Difficulty of Ethics in the Evolution of Human Thought (Albert Schweitzer), 1985; Plainsongs, 1985; Country Poems, 1991; Stories: Internal Exile, 1992; New Englanders, 1992. Contributions to: Potato Eyes; Akwesasne Notes. Membership: PEN American Center; PEN Canada; Associate, PEN Club Français. Address: 206 St Patrick Street, Ottawa, Ontario K1N 5K3, Canada.

GERARD David, b. 19 Oct 1923, Glasgow, Scotland. Librarian. Education: BA (London), 1955; BA (Dunelm), 1985; Fellow, Library Association; Churchill Fellow, 1967. Appointments: Deputy City Librarian, Exeter, 1955-57; Deputy City Librarian, Nottingham, 1957-64; City Librarian, Nottingham, 1964-68; Senior Lecturer, College of Librarianship, Wales, 1968-82. Publications: Personalia, 1983; Revenants, 1985; Piano Piano, 1988; This Year, Next Year, 1991; Aller Retour, 1993. Address: 9 Crofter's Green, Wilmslow, Cheshire SK9 6AY, England.

GERAS Adele Daphne, b. 15 Mar 1944, Jerusalem, Israel. Children's Author. m. Norman Geras, 7 Aug 1967, 2 daughters. Education: BA Honours, Modern Languages, St Hilda's College, Oxford, 1966. Publications: Up on the Roof, pamphlet shared with Pauline Stainer, 1987; Sampler, pamphlet printed privately in limited edition, 1991; Poetry included in New Women Poets, 1991; Voices From the Dolls' House, 1994. Contributions to: Literary Review; Ambit; Other Poetry; Rialto; Writing Women; North; Spokes; Numbers. Honours: Up on the Roof won the first Smith-Doorstop Pamphlet Competition; Prizewinner, Northern Poetry One and Northern Poetry Two, both published by Littlewood; Included in many commended anthologies; Jewish Quarterly Poetry Prize, 1993. Memberships: Poetry Society; Society of Authors; National Association of Writers in Education: VER Poets. Address: 10 Danesmoor Road, Manchester M20 3JS, England.

GEREIGHTY Andrea (Ann) S(aunders), b. 20 July 1938, New Orleans, Louisiana, USA. Owner of Public Opinion Polls Bureau Business. m. Dennis Anthony Gereighty Jr, 9 May 1959, dec, 1 son, 2 daughters. Education: BA, English Education, University of New Orleans, 1974; Summer programme on English-Speaking Union Scholarship, Exeter College, England, summer 1972; BA, English Education, 1974, MA, English, 1978, University of New Orleans. Appointments: Head Start and Special Education Teacher, High School and University Instructor in New Orleans and Berlin, Germany; Door-to-Door Opinion Pollster; Currently, Owner and Manager, public opinion polls business, New Orleans Field Services Associates. Publications: Illusions and Other Realities, 1974; Season of the Crane; Restless for Cool Weather. Contributions to: San Francisco Quarterly; Beggars' Bowl; National Poetry Review; Tulane University Literary Journal; Dalliance; New Laurel Review; Ellipsis; University of New Orleans Literary Journal; Negative Capability, Literary Journal. Honours: First Place, Deep South Literary Award for Poetry, 1973; Honourable Mention, Poetry Award, Deep South Writers, 1983; First Place, National League of American Pen Women, 1984; First Runner-Up, Gibbons Award for Poetry, 1984; 2nd Palce Nuyorican Poetry Competition, New York City, 1994. Memberships: Co-Ordinator, 1990-, Editor and Publisher, President, Lend Us An Ear, monthly publication, New Orleans Poetry Forum; CODA Poets and Writers; Deep South Literary Society. Address: 257 Bonnabel Boulevard, Metairie, LA 70005-3738, USA.

GEROLD Charles, (Charles Perdu, Carlos Perdido), b. 21 Feb 1927, Chicago, Illinois, USA. m. Adriana Youssif, 15 June 1967, 3 sons, 1 daughter. Education: BA, 1949; MA, 1953; PhD, 1983. Appointments: Editor; US Government Official; Aerospace Systems Analyst; Hospital Administration. Contributions to: American Poetry Anthology, 1990. Honour: Alden Award for Drama, Dramatists Alliance, San Francisco. Address: 17 Woodford Drive, Moraga, CA 94556, USA.

GERSHON Karen, b. 29 Aug 1923, Germany. Writer. m. Val Tripp, 2 sons, 2 daughters. Publications: The Relentless Year, 1960; Selected Poems, 1966; Legacies and Encounters, 1972; My Daughters, My Sisters, 1975; Coming Back From Babylon, 1979; Collected Poems, 1990. Contributions to: Times Literary Supplement; Listener; Transatlantic Review; Review of English Literature; Twentieth Century; Critical Quarterly; Jewish Quarterly; Outposts; Tribune; New York Times; Jerusalem Post; Jewish Chronicle; Pacific Quarterly. Honours: Arts Council, 1967; Jewish Chronicle Book of The Year Prize, 1967; Haim Greenberg Pioneer Women's Award, 1968. Address: The Coach House, Coach House Lane, St Austell, Cornwall PL25 5AD, England.

GERSTLER Amy, b. 24 Oct 1956, San Diego, California, USA. Poet; Writer. Education: BA, Pitzer College. Publications: Poetry: Yonder, 1981; Christy's Alpine Inn, 1982; White Marriage/Recovery, 1984; Early Heavens, 1984; The True Bride, 1986; Bitter Angel, 1990; Nerve Storm, 1993. Fiction: Martine's Mouth, 1985; Primitive Man, 1987. Other: Past Lives (with Alexis Smith), 1989. Contributions to: Magazines. Honour: National Book Critics Circle Award, 1991. Address: c/o Viking Penguin, 375 Hudson Street, New York, NY 10014, USA.

GERVAIS C(harles) H(enry), b. 20 Oct 1946, Windsor, Ontario, Canada. Poet; Writer; Editor. m. Donna Wright, 1968, 2 sons, 1 daughter. Education: BA, University of Guelph, 1971; MA, University of Windsor, 1972. Appointments: Staff, Toronto Globe and Mail, 1966; Canadian Press, Toronto, 1967; Reporter, Daily Commercial News, Toronto, 1967, Chatham Daily News, 1972-73; Teacher of Creative Writing, St Clair College, Windsor, 1969-71; Publisher, Black Moss Press, Windsor, 1969-; Editor, Sunday Standard, Windsor, 1972; General News Reporter, 1973-74, 1976-81, Bureau Chief, 1974-76, Religion Editor, 1979-80, Book Editor, 1980-, Entertainment Writer, 1990-, Windsor Star. Publications: Poetry: Sister Saint Anne, 1968; Something, 1969; Other Marriage Vows, 1969; A Sympathy Orchestra, 1970; Bittersweet, 1972; Poems for American Daughters, 1976; The Believable Body, 1979; Up Country Lines, 1979; Silence Comes with Lake Voices, 1980; Into a Blue Morning: Selected Poems, 1982; Public Fantasy: The Maggie T Poems, 1983; Letters from the Equator, 1986; Autobiographies, 1989; Playing God: New Poems, 1994; Other: The Rumrunners: A Prohibition Scrapbook, 1980; Voices Like Thunder, 1984; The Border Police: One Hundred and Twenty Five Years of Policing in Windsor, 1992; Seeds in the Wilderness: Profiles of World Religious Leaders, 1994; From America Sent: Letters to Henry Miller, 1995; Editor: The Writing Life: Historical and Critical Views of the Tish

Movement, 1976; Children's books: How Bruises Lost His Secret, 1975; Doctor Troyer and the Secret in the Moonstone, 1976; If I Had a Birthday Everyday, 1983. Honours: Western Ontario Newspaper Awards, 1983, 1984, 1987. Address: 1939 Alsace Avenue, Windsor, Ontario N8W 1M5, Canada.

GERY John Roy Octavius, b. 2 Jun 1953, Reading, Pennsylvania, USA. Professor of English. Education: AB, Honours, Princeton University, 1975; MA, English, University of Chicago, 1976; MA, Creative Writing, Stanford University, 1978. Appointments: Lecturer, Stanford University and San Jose State University, 1977-79; Instructor, 1979-84, Assistant Professor, 1984-88, Associate Professor, 1988-95, Professor of English, 1995-, University of New Orleans; Visiting Professor, University of Iowa, 1991-92. Publications: Charlemagne: A Song of Gestures, 1983; The Burning of New Orleans, 1988; Three Poems, 1989; The Enemies of Leisure, 1995; Nuclear Annihilation and Contemporary American Poetry, 1996. Contributions to: Chicago Review; Crosscurrents; Nebo; Kenyon Review; Iowa Review; Paris Review. Honours: Deep South Writers Poetry Award, 1987; Charles William Duke Long Poem Award, 1987; Wesleyan Writers Conference Poetry Fellowship, 1989; W B Yeats Chair in Poetry, Italy, 1990; National Endowment for The Arts Creative Writing Fellowship, 1992-93. Memberships: Academy of American Poets; Associated Writing Programmes; Poets and Writers; Modern Poetry Association; Consultant, Louisiana State Poetry Society; Editorial Board, New Orleans Poetry Journal Press. Address: Department of English, University of New Orleans, New Orleans, LA 70148, USA.

GESTSSON Magnus, (Magnus Gezzon), b. 7 April 1956, Reykjavik, Iceland. Writer. m. Thorgerdur Sigurdardottir, 2 daughters. Education: History and Art History, University of Iceland. Appointments: Library Assistant, 1977-83; Poetry Critic at Pjodviljinn, 1989-91. Publications: Vasabok, 1979; Samlyndi badvordurinn (astarljod), 1983; Laug ad blaum straumi, 1986; Ljod, 1988; Syngjandi Solkerfi, 1995; Co-Author, Fyrrvera (Hrafn Hardarson og Thorhallur Thorhallsson), 1982; Tröllasögur, 1991; Translations from Danish, Likami borgarinnar; Translator of other authors. Contributions to: Timarit Mals og menningar; Teningur; Sky; Lesbok Morgunblaosins; Icelandic State Radio; Interviews and articles in various magazines and newspapers. Membership: Writers' Union of Iceland, 1987-. Address: Kötlufelli 7, 111-Reykjavik, Iceland.

GEVIRTZ Susan, b. 27 Oct 1955, Los Angeles, California, USA. Writer; Professor. m. David Delp, 15 Aug 1992. Education: BA, The Evergreen State College, 1977; MA, St John's Graduate Institute, 1980; PhD, University of California, Santa Cruz, 1990. Appointments: Assistant Professor, Hutchins School of Liberal Studies, Sonoma State University, 1989-; Instructor, California College of Arts and Crafts, 1989-91; Instructor, University of San Francisco, 1988-89. Publications: Prothesis: Caesarea, 1994; Taken Place, 1993; Linen minus, 1992; Domino: Point of Entry, 1992; Narrative's Journey: The Fiction and Film Writing of Dorothy Richardson, 1996. Contributions to: AVEC; The Art of Practice, anthology; Moving Borders: Three Decades of Innovative W Chain: Writing by Women, anthology; Poetics of Criticism; Writing from the New Coast; Raddle Moon. Memberships: Syntax Project for the Arts Advisory Board; Small Press Traffic; Small Press Distribution. Address: 1939 Jones Street, San Francisco, CA 94133, USA.

GEZZON Magnus. See: GESTSSON Magnus.

GHANDI Bipin Ramanlal, b. 7 Feb 1949, Amreli, India. Agrochemical Engineer. m. Veena, 26 Nov 1973, 1 son, 1 daughter. Education: BEC, Mechanical Engineering, 1971. Publication: Udbhav, collection of English poems, 1986. Contributions to: Poet; Premier Poets; Skylark; Mudrankan; Eureka. Honour: International Eminent Poet Award, 1988. Memberships: Fellow, International Poets Academy, Madras, India; Life, Mudra Amreli, Gujarat, India. Address: Mangal Mandir, Manekpara, Amreli, Gujarat 364601, India.

GHIGNA Charles Vincent, b. 25 Aug 1946, Long Island, New York, USA. Poet; Children's Author. m. Debra Ghigna, 2 Aug 1975, 1 son, 1 daughter. Education: BA, English; MEd, English and Education. Appointments: Former Poetry Editor, English Journal for the National Council of Teachers of English and Poet in Residence, Alabama School of Fine Arts; Currently: Correspondent for Writer's Digest Magazine; Nationally Syndicated Writer, humourous newspaper feature, Snickers; Speaker at schools, colleges, book fairs and conferences. Publications: Returning to Earth, 1989; Good Dog/Bad

Dog, 1992; Good Cat/Bad Cat, 1992; Tickle Day: Poems from Father Goose, 1994; Riddle Rhymes, 1995; Speaking in Tongues: New and Selected Poems 1974-1995. Contributions to: Harper's; Playboy; McCall's; New York Quarterly; Writer's Digest; Artist's Magazine; Writer; Rolling Stone; Saturday Evening Post; Ladies Home Journal; Good Housekeeping; Guideposts; Wall Street Journal; Village Voice; Christian Science Monitor; Highlights for Children; Ranger Rick; Child Life; Humpty Dumpty; Jack and Jill; Children's Digest; Children's Playmate; Turtle; Lollipops. Honours: Pulitzer Prize Nomination for, Returning to Earth; Grant, Alabama Poet in Schools Programme, 1974. Address: 204 West Linwood Drive, Homewood, AL 35209, USA.

GHOSE Zulfikar, b. 1935, Sial Kot, Pakistan. Author; Poet; Professor. Appointments: Cricket Correspondent, Observer, London, 1960-65; Teacher, London, 1963-69. Publications: Co-author, Statement Against Corpes, 1964; The Loss of India, verse, 1964; Confessions of a Native-Alien, 1965; The Contradictions, novel, 1966; The Murder of Aziz Khan, novel, 1967; Jets from Orange, verse, 1967; The Incredible Brazilian Book 1, novel, 1972; The Violent West, verse, 1972; Co-author, Penguin Modern Poets 25, 1974; Crump's Terms, novel, 1975; The Beautiful Empire, novel, 1975; Hamlet, Prufrock and Language, 1978; A Different World, novel, 1978; Hulme's Investigations into the Bogart Script, novel, 1981; A New History of Torments, novel, 1982; The Fiction of Reality, criticism, 1983; Don Bueno, novel, 1983; A Memory of Asia, poetry, 1984; Figures of Enchantment, novel, 1986; Selected Poems, 1991; The Art of Creating Fiction, criticism, 1991; The Triple Mirror of the Self, novel, 1992; Shakespeare's Mortal Knowledge, criticism, 1993. Address: Department of English, University of Texas at Austin, Austin, TX 78712, USA.

GHOSH Pratima, b. 25 Dec 1943, Calcutta, India. Information and Broadcasting Officer. Education: MA, Economics, University of Calcutta, 1964; Diploma in Public Administration, IIPA, New Delhi. Appointment: Currently, Officer of Information and Broadcasting Ministry, Government of India. Publications: Ghuranta Manche, 1974; Akhan Mohana Chere, 1978. Contributions to: Desk Magazine, Kabi o Kabita Magazine, among others. Honour: Participant, All-India Poet's Convention, Calcutta, India. Address: Kutir Math South West House 21, PO Chandannagar PIN 712136, Hooghly, West Bengal, India.

GIANNINI David, b. 19 Mar 1948, USA. Poet. Publications: Opens, 1970; Stories, poems, 1974; Fourfield, 1976; Close Packet, 1978; Three, 1978; Stem, 1982; Antonio and Clara, 1992; Keys, 1992. Contributions to: Sonora Review; Longhouse; Shadowplay; Tel-Let; Talisman; Room; George Mason Review; Shearsman, Malaysia; MJP, Canada. Honours: Massachusetts Artists Foundation Fellowship Award, 1990; University of Florida Award, 1991; Osa and Lee Mays Award for Poetry, 1970; Numerous other grants and awards. Address: PO Box 630, Otis, MA 01253, USA.

GIBBONS (William) Reginald Jr, b. 7 Jan 1947, Houston, Texas, USA. Poet; Writer; Editor; Professor. m. Cornelia Maude Spelman, 18 Aug 1983, 1 stepson, 1 stepdaughter. Education: AB, Princeton University, 1969; MA, 1971, PhD, 1974, Stanford University. Appointments: Instructor in Spanish, Livingston College, Rutgers University; Lecturer, Princeton and Columbia Universities; Lecturer then Professor, Northwestern University; Editor, TriQuarterly Magazine. Publications: Roofs, Voices, Roads, 1979; The Ruined Motel, 1981; Saints, 1986; Maybe It Was So, 1991; Other works include translation, fiction and literary criticism. Contributions to: American Poetry Review; Nation; Southwest Review; Yale Review; Partisan Review; New Republic; Atlantic; Hudson Review; Southern Review. Honours: Guggenheim Fellowship for Poetry; National Endowment for The Arts and Illinois Arts Council Fellowships; Short Story Award, Texas Institute of Letters; Denver Quarterly Translation Award; Anisfield-Wolf Book Award, 1995; Jesse Jones Award, Texas Institute of Letters, 1995. Memberships: PEN American Centre; Poetry Society of America; Texas Institute of Letters. Address: Department of English, Northwestern University, University Hall 215, Evanston, IL 60208, USA.

GIBSON Edwin W, b. 18 June 1910, Lubbock, Texas, USA. Machine Manufacturing. m. Frances Ernst, 30 May 1987. Education: BA, Berea College, Berea, Kentucky, 1934; Warner College, Eastland, Texas. Appointment: Wrote Poetry of Gonnets for College Classmates. Publications include: Music Lovers' Cook Book, with Frances Gibson. Western Novels; Screen Plays; Poetry; Contributions to: Eastland; Texas Daily News; The Citizen Paper, Berea, Kentucky; Citizen.

Memberships: Writers Group West California; Writers Workshop, Texas. Address: 809 W Travis Street, Fredericksburg, TX 78624, USA.

GIBSON Grace Evelyn Loving, b. 29 Oct 1919, Drakes Branch, Virginia, USA. Educator. m. Alton Brooks Gibson, 16 Dec 1944, 3 sons. Education: BA, University of North Carolina, Greensboro, 1940; MA, English, Duke University, Durham, 1943. Appointments: Instructor in English, St Andrews College, 1963-65; Assistant, then Associate Professor, Communicative Arts Department, Pembroke State University, 1966-86; Adjunct Professor, English Literature, St Andrews College, 1986-. Publications: Home in Time, 1977; Drakes Branch, 1982; Wind Burial, co-translation, 1990; Editor, The Pocket John Charles McNeill, 1990; Editor, By Reason of Strength, by Gerald W Johnson, reprint 1994; Frayed Edges, poems, 1995. Contributions to: Pembroke Magazine; St Andrews Review; Crucible; Arts Journal; Cape Rock International Poetry Review; Pilot. Honours: Fartner Writer and Community Award, 1989; Sam Ragan Award, The Crucible, 1992. Memberships: Second Vice President, North Carolina Poetry Society; Nominating Committee, North Carolina Writers' Network, 1994-96. Address: 709 McLean Street, Laurinburg, NC 28352, USA.

GIBSON Keiko Matsui, b. 4 Sept 1953, Kyoto, Japan. University Professor. m. Morgan Gibson, 14 Sep 1978, 1 son. Education: BA, English, Kwansei Gakvin University, Japan, 1976; MA, Comparative Literature, University of Illinois, 1983; PhD, Indiana University, 1992-. Appointments: Instructor, Japanese, Northwestern Michigan College, 1980; Associate Instructor, Comparative Literature, Indiana University, 1984-85; Instructor, 1991-92, Assistant Professor, 1992-93, Comparative Literature, Pennsylvania State University; Associate Professor, British-American Studies, Kanda University of International Studies, Chiba, Japan, 1993-. Publications: Stir up the Precipitable World, 1983; Kokoro: Heart-Mind, 1981; Tremble of Morning, 1979. Contributions to: Other Side River; Anthology of Magazine Verse and Yearbook of American Poetry; For Rexroth; Passages North; Vajradhattu Sun; Sackbut Review; Nexus; New Letters; Crosscurrents; Kyoto Review; Ao; Kansai Time Out; Blue Jacket; Jandararin; Edge. Honour: Kenneth Rexroth Special Award for Poetry, Kyoto, Japan. Memberships: Japan, American and International Comparative Literature Associations. Address: Department of English, Kanda Gai University of International Studies, 1-4-1 Wakaba, Mihama-ku, Chiba-Shi, Chiba-Ken 261, Japan.

GIBSON Margaret, b. 4 June 1948, Toronto, Ontario, Canada. Poet; Writer. m. S Silboord, sep, 1 son. Education: High School, Toronto. Publications: Lunes: Poems, 1973; On the Cutting Edge, 1976; The Butterfly Ward, 1977; Considering the Condition, 1978; Signs: Poems, 1979; Long Walks in the Afternoon, 1982; Memories of the Future: The Daybooks of Tina Modotti, 1986; Out in the Open, 1989; The Vigil: A Poem in 4 Voices, 1993. Honours: Literary Award, City of Toronto, 1976; Melville Cane Award, 1988. Address: c/o Louisiana State University Press, PO Box 25053, Baton Rouge, LA 70894, USA.

GIBSON Margaret Leigh Ferguson, b. 17 Feb 1944, Philadelphia, Pennsylvania, USA. Poet. m. David McKain, 27 Dec 1975, 1 stepson, 1 stepdaughter. Education: BA, Hollins College, 1966; MA, University of Virginia, 1967. Appointments: Assistant Professor, George Mason University, 1970-75; Writer in Residence, Phillips Academy, Andover; Visiting Professor, MFA Programme, Virginia Commonwealth University, 1991, University of Massachusetts, 1992-93. Publications: Signs, 1979; Long Walks In The Afternoon, 1982; Memories of The Future, 1986; Out in The Open, 1989; The Vigil, 1993. Contributions to: Georgia Review; Southern Review; New England Review; Parnassus; Michigan Quarterly Review; Poetry; Shenandoah. Honours: Lamont Selection, Academy of American Poets, 1982; Melville Cane Award, Poetry Society of America, 1986-87. Memberships: Phi Beta Kappa; Woodrow Wilson Fellow, Poetry Society of America. Address: 19 School Street, Bradford, PA 16701, USA.

GIBSON Morgan, b. 6 June 1929, Cleveland, Ohio, USA. m. Keiko Matsui Gibson, 14 Sept 1978. Education: BA, English Literature, Oberlin College, 1947-50; MA, English and American Literature and Creative Writing, 1952, PhD, 1959, University of Iowa. Appointments: Assistant then Associate Professor of English, University of Wisconsin, Milwaukee, 1961-72; Chair, Graduate Faculty, Goddard College, Vermont, 1972-75, Osaka University, Japan, 1975-79; Visiting Professorships, Michigan State University, 1979, University of Illinois, 1982, Knox College, 1989-91; Professorships, Chukyo University,

1987-89, Japan Women's University, Tokyo, 1993-; Lecturer, Penn State University, 1991-93. Publications include: Stones Glow Like Lovers' Eyes, 1970; Crystal Sunlake, 1971; Dark Summer, 1977; Wakeup, 1978; Speaking of Light, 1979; Kokoro: Heart Mind, 1980; The Great Brook Book, 1981; Among Buddhas in Japan, 1988; Revolutionary Rexroth: Poet of East-West Wisdom, 1986; Tantric Poetry of Kukai (Kobo Daishi) Japan's Buddhist Saint, 1987; Winter Pilgrim, 1993; Poetry Editor, Arts in Society, 1965-72; Contributing Editor, Printed Matter, Tokyo, 1989-91, Electric Rexroth, 1992, Kyoto Journal, 1994-95; Poetry Editor, Japan Environment Monitor, 1993-95. Contributions: Buddhism and the Emerging World Civilization; Practices of the Wind Anthology; Brewing Anthology; Crosscurrents; For Rexroth; Edge; Outposts; Vermont Anthology. Honours: Fiction First Award, Munity, 1960; Uhrig Award for Excellent Teaching, 1965, Research and Writing Grants, University of Wisconsin, 1965-69. Memberships: PEN American Centre; Poetry Society of America; Buddhist Peace Fellowship; Japan Anglo-American Poetry Society. Address: 202 Flat Fukuju 5, 1-2 Hongo-cho, Naka-ku, Yokohama-shi, Kanagawa-ken 231, Japan.

GIFFORD Terry, b. 28 June 1946, Cambridge, England. Senior Lecturer in English. 1 son, 1 daughter. Education: BEd, Lancaster, 1973; MA, Sheffield, 1978; PhD, Lancaster, 1992. Publications: The Stone Spiral, 1987, 2nd edition, 1988; Ten Letters to John Muir, 1990; Outcrops, 1991; The Rope, 1996; Contributions to: Poetry Wales; North; Alpine Journal; Pennine Platform; Cencrastus; Climbing Art, USA; High; Critical Quarterly. Honours: Lancaster Literature Festival Anthology, 1982, 1983, 1985; 1st Prize, South Yorkshire Literary Competition, 1983; South Yorkshire Mike Hayward Award, 1986. Memberships: Founder, Co-Coordinator, Sheffield Writers' Sticky Bun Club; Director, International Festival of Mountaineering Literature. Address: 56 Conduit Road, Sheffield S10 1EW, England.

GIL Lourdes, b. 14 Dec 1951, Havana, Cuba. Writer; Editor. m. Ariel Rodriguez, 20 Nov 1983, 1 son. Education: Certificate, University of Madrid, Spain, 1973; BA, Fordham University, 1974; ABD, MA, 1978, New York University. Appointments: Editor, Romanica Journal, New York University, 1975-82; Translator, Hearst Publishers, New York, 1977-83; President, Giralt Publishers Co, New York, 1984-; Editor, Lyra Quarterly, New Jersey, 1987-. Publications: Pneumas, 1977; Manuscrito Nina Avsente, 1980; Vencido Fuego Especie, 1983; Blanca Aldaba Preludes, 1989. Contributions to: Linden Lane Magazine; Romanica Journal; EN/ACE Review; Inti; Kantil Review; Spectrum; Latino Stuff Review; Gato Tuerto; Michigan Literary Quarterly; Poesia Venezuela; Hudson Literary Quarterly. Honours: Cintas Fellowship, United Nations, 1979, 1991; Alenco-Barcelona, Venezuela, 1982; Outstanding Young Women of America, 1985; Bensalem Association of Women Writers, 1985. Memberships: Co-Ordinator, Literary Programme, Ollantay Centre for The Arts; Americas Society; Poetry Society of America; Latin American Writers Institute; Friends of PEN; Association of Hispanic Arts; Pan-American Literary Circle; President, Lyra Society for The Arts. Address: Lyra Society for The Arts Inc, PO Box 3188, Guttenberg, NJ 07093, USA.

GILBERT Virginia, b. 19 Dec 1946, Elgin, Illinois, USA. Education: BA, English, Iowa Wesleyan College, 1965-69; MFA, Creative Writing, Poetry, University of Iowa, 1969-71; PhD, Creative Writing, Poetry and English, University of Nebraska, 1991. Appointments: Instructor, Peace Corps Volunteer, South Korea, 1971-73; English as a Second Language, Department of Defense Subcontracts in Iran with Datex and Telemedia Inc, 1976-79; ESL Instructor, 1979, College of Lake County, Illinois, 1979; Teaching Assistant, University of Nebraska, 1984-87; Assistant Professor, 1980-92, Associate Professor, 1992-, English, Alabama A & M University. Publications: To Keep at Bay The Hounds, 1985; The Earth Above, 1993; That Other Brightness, 1996. Contributions to: Beloit Poetry Journal; Seneca Review; Prairie Schooner; Poetry Now; Sumac; North American Review; Southern Poetry Review; New York Quarterly; MSS. Honours: Harlan Award, Iowa Wesleyan College, 1966-69; National Endowment for The Arts Fellowship, 1976-77; Nebraska Poets' Association's Chapbook Series, 1984; Second Place, Hackney Awards, 1990; Title III, Federally Funder Faculty Development Grant, Alabama A & M University, 1990-91; 1st Place, Sakura Festival 2nd Annual Haiku Contest, 1992. Memberships: Modern Language Association; Associated Writing Programmes; Poets and Writers; Poetry Society of America; Peace Corps Volunteer Assn; Peace Corps Volunteer Readers and Writers Association. Address: Alabama A & M University, Department of English, Box 453, Normal, AL 35762, USA.

GILCHRIST Ellen, b. 20 Feb 1935, Vicksburg, Mississippi, USA. Author; Poet. Education: BA, Millsaps College, Jackson, Mississippi, 1967; Postgraduate Studies, University of Arkansas, 1976. Publications: The Land Surveyor's Daughter (poems), 1979; The Land of Dreamy Dreams (stories), 1981; The Annunciation (novel), 1983; Victory Over Japan: A Book of Stories, 1984; Drunk With Love (stories), 1986; Riding Out the Tropial Depression (poems), 1986; Falling Through Space: The Journals of Ellen Gilchrist, 1987; The Anna Papers (novel), 1988; Light Can Be Both Wave and Particle: A Book of Stories, 1989; I Cannot Get You Close Enough (3 novellas), 1990; Net of Jewels (novel), 1992; Anabasis: A Journey to the Interior, 1994; Starcarbon: A Meditation on Love, 1994; The Age of Miracles (stories), 1995; Rhoda: A Life in Stories, 1995. Contributions to: Many journals and periodicals. Honours: National Endowment for the Arts Grant in Fiction, 1979; Pushcart Prizes, 1979-80, 1983; Louisiana Library Association Honor Book, 1981; Mississippi Academy of Arts and Sciences Awards, 1982, 1985; Saxifrage Award, 1983; American Book Award for Fiction, 1984; J William Fulbright Award for Literature, University of Arkansas, 1985; Mississippi Institute of Arts and Letters Literature Award, 1985. Memberships: Authors Guild; Authors League of America. Address: 834 Eastwood Drive, Fayetteville, AR 72701, USA.

GILDERSLEVE. See: WACHENJE Vivienne.

GILL David Lawrence William, b. 3 July 1934, Chislehurst, Kent, England. Teacher; Lecturer. m. Irene Henry, 5 July 1958, 2 sons, 1 daughter. Education: BA, Honours, German, University College, London, 1955; Certificate in Education, Birmingham University, 1958; BA, Honours, English, London External, 1970. Appointments: Assistant Teacher, Bedales, Nyakasura, Uganda, Magdalen College School, Oxford, Lecturer, 1971-79; Senior Lecturer, Newland Park College of Education, became incorporated into Bucks College of Higher Education, 1979-87. Publications: Men Without Evenings, 1966; The Pagoda and Other Poems, 1969; In The Eye of The Storm, 1975; The Upkeep of The Castle, 1978; Karel Klimsa, translated from Ondra Lysohorsky, 1984; One Potato, Two Potato, with Dorothy Clancy, 1985; Legends, Please, 1986; The White Raven, 1989; The New Hesperides, 1991. Contributions to: Observer; London Magazine; Encounter; Tribune; Listener; Critical Quarterly; Verse; Anglo-Welsh Review; Chapman;Countryman; Country Life; The Use of English; Orbis; Pennine Platform; Iota; Weyfarers; Transition, Uganda; Staple. Address: 38 Yarnells Hill, Botley, Oxford OX2 9BE, England.

GILLAN Maria Mazziotti, b. 12 Mar 1940, Paterson, New Jersey, USA. Poet; Poetry Centre Director. m. Dennis Gillan, 30 June 1964, 1 son, 1 daughter. Education: BA, English, Seton Hall University, 1961; MA, English, New York University, 1963; Postgraduate, Drew University, 1977-80. Appointments: Director, Poetry Centre, Passaic County Community College, 1980-; Geraldine R Dodge Foundation Poetry Teacher, 1986-; Numerous readings/workshops. Publications include: Winter Light, 1985; Lice D'Inverno, 1989; Cries of The Spirit, 1990; Taking Back My Name, 1991; Where I Come From: Selected and New Poems, 1995; Anthologies: International Women Poets Anthology, 1990; Literature Across Cultures: A Reader in Writing, 1994; I Feel a Little Jumpy Around You, 1995; Editor, Footwork: The Paterson Literary Review, 1980-; Co-Editor, Unsettling America: Contemporary Ethnic American Poetry, 1994. Contributions to: Professional journals. Honours include: Fellow in Poetry, New Jersey State Council on The Arts, 1981, 1985; Sri Chinmoy Award, 1981, 1982, 1983; Editor's Choice Award, 1985; American Literary Translators Award, 1987; Recipient, National Poetry Competition Commendation, Chester H Jones Foundation, 1990; Semifinalist, PEN Syndicated Fiction Competition, 1994. Memberships include: Pen, America; Poets and Writers; Poetry Society of America. Address: 40 Post Avenue, Hawthorne, NJ 07506, USA.

GILLIARD Emile, b. 12 April 1928, Malonne, Namur, Belgium. Librarian (Pens). m. Jeanine Schmitz, 27 Nov 1957, 1 son. Education: Diploma, Baccalaureate, Greco-Latin, 1948; Certificate of Philosophy, 1951; Certificate of Librarian, 1959. Appointments: Teacher, College du Sacré-Coeur, Profondeville, 1954-57; Secretary, 1957-59, Librarian and Director of Library, 1960-93, Les Comtes de Hainaut, Mons, Hainaut, Belgium. Publications: Chîmagrawes, 1955; Pâtêrs Po Tote One Sôte Di Djins, 1959; Vias d'Mârs, 1961; Rukes di Têre, 1966; Li Dêrene Saison, 1976; Silicose Valley, 1989; Paurt èt R'Vindje, 1990; A lpe, 1992; Vicadje, 1992; Li Navia dèl Pîrète, 1992; Come dès Gayes Su On Baston, 1995. Contributions to: Les Cahiers Wallons, Namur; Vers L'Avenir, Namur; Micromania, Châtelet. Honours: J Durbuy Prize,

1952; Ville de Liège Prize, 1959; Prize of Government, 1970; G Michaux Prize, Ville de Namur, 1980. Memberships: President, 1995-, Société de Langue et de Littérature Wallones, Liège, 1976-; Rèlis Namurwès, Namur, 1953-. Address: 321 Rue Saint Laurent, B-4000 Liège, Belgium.

GILLIES Valerie, b. 4 June 1948, Alberta, Canada. Freelance Writer. m. William Gillies, 24 June 1972, 1 son, 2 daughter. Education: MA, Honours, 1970; MLitt, Edinburgh, 1974. Appointments: Writer, Boroughmuir High School, Edinburgh Academy; Commissioned Poet, Borders Festival, 1989; Writer in Residence, Duncan of Jordanstone College of Art, Dundee, 1988-90; Writer in Residence, University of Edinburgh, 1995-96. Publications: Trio: New Poets From Edinburgh, 1971; Poetry 3, 1975; Each Bright Eye, 1976; Bed of Stone, 1984; Tweed Journey, 1989; Twelve More Scottish Poets, 1988; Leopardi: A Scottish Quair, 1987; The Chanter's Tune, 1990; The Jordanstone Folio, 1990; The Ringing Rock, 1995. Contributions to: Lines Review; Chapman; Rubicon; L'Arco; Orgini; Il Segnale; Poetry Ireland Review; Green Book. Honours: Eric Gregory Award; Two Scottish Arts Council Book Awards. Memberships: PEN Scotland; Scottish Poetry Library Association. Address: 67 Braid Avenue, Edinburgh EH10 6ED, Scotland.

GILLILAN Pamela, b. London, England. Civil Servant; Meteorologist; Interior Decorator. m. David James Gillilan, 12 Mar 1948, 1 son, 2 daughters. Appointments: Poet-in-Residence, Avon County Library Service, 1986; Tutor, Arvon Foundation, various times; Faculty Member, Summer Conference, Poets' House, Portmuck, Northern Ireland, 1991-96. Publications: That Winter, 1986; The Turnspit Dog, 1993; All-Steel Traveller, New and Selected, 1994. Contributions to: Poetry Review; Stand; Iron; Outposts; Orbis; Listener; Giant Steps; Southwest Review; Smoke; Anglo-Welsh Review; Honest Ulsterman; Oxford Poetry; and others. Honours: Hawthornden Castle Fellowship; Winner, Cheltenham Poetry Prize, 1979; Prizes in National Poetry Competition. Memberships: Natioanl Association of Writers in Education; West Country Writers' Association. Address: 25 Caledonia Place, Clifton, Bristol BS8 4DL, England.

GILLILAND Brian Keith, (Martin Musick), b. 1 May 1959, Wichita, Kansas, USA. Custodian. Education: GED, State of Arkansas, 1978. Appointment: Poetry Editor, The Pioneer Express, North Arkansas Community College Student Paper, 1978. Publications: Sex with a Barren Landscape, 1987. Contributions to: Implosion Press; Quickenings; Midwest Poetry Review; Green Gale Publishing; Poetry Plus; The Mountain Echo; Cosmic Trend; M Talacico & Daughter Publications; Sparrowarass Poetry Forum Inc; Moose Bound Press; Aztec; Peak. Honours: Honourable Mention, Music City Song Festival, 1985; Golden Poet Award, 1988; Honourable Mention, World of Poetry, 1988; Honourable Mention, Music World Song Contest, 1986; 7th Place, Cash in the Star Contest, 1994. Memberships: Top Records Songwriters Association. Address: 1661 Vassier Avenue, St Louis, Missouri 63133, USA.

GILLON Adam, b. 17 July 1921, Poland. Professor of English. m. Isabella Zamojre, 1946, 1 son, 1 daughter. Education: MA, Hebrew University of Jerusalem, 1949; PhD, English and Comparative Literature, Columbia University, New York, 1954. Appointments: Professor of English, Acadia University, Nova Scotia, Canada, 1957-62; Emeritus Professor, State University of New York, 1962-81; Professor of English, University of Haifa, Israel, 1979-84. Publications: Selected Poems and Translations, 1962; Editor, Translator, Introduction to Modern Polish Poetry, 1964, 1967; In A Manner of Haiku: Seven Aspects of Man, 1967, 1970; Editor, Translator, The Dancing Socrates and Other Poems by Julian Tuwim, 1968; Poems of The Ghetto: A Testament of Lost Men, Editor, Translator, 1973; Daily New and Old, 1971; Strange Mutations, 1973; Summer Morn, Winter Weather, 1975; The Withered Leaf: A Medley of Haiku and Senryu, 1982; Joseph Conrad, 1982; Joseph Conrad: Comparative Essays, 1994. Contributions to: Fiddlehead; James Joyce Quarterly; Haiku Magazine; Polish Review; Jerusalem Post; Chicago Jewish Forum. Honours: Alfred Jurzykowski Foundation Award, 1967; Joseph Fels Foundation Award, 1970; National Endowment for the Humanities, 1985; Gold Award, Worldfest International Festival, 1993. Memberships: Modern Language Association; Haiku Society of America; Joseph Conrad Society of America; Polish Institute of Arts and Sciences. Address: 490 Rt 299 West, New Paltz, NY 12561, USA.

GIOIA (Michael) Dana, b. 24 Dec 1950, Los Angeles, California, USA. Writer. m. Mary Hiecke, 23 Feb 1980, 3 sons, 1 dec. Education:

BA, English, Stanford University, 1973; MA, Comparative Literature, Harvard, 1975; MBA, Graduate School of Business, Stanford, 1977. Appointments: Business Executive, General Foods Corporation, 1977-92; Full-time Writer, 1992-. Publications: Editor, The Ceremony and Other Stories, 1984; Poems From Italy, anthology, 1985; Daily Horoscope, 1986; Translator, Mottetti: Poems of Love, 1990; The Gods of Winter, 1991; Can Poetry Matter?, 1992; An Introduction to Poetry, 1994. Contributions to: New Yorker; Hudson Review; Nation; Paris Review; New York Times Book Review; Atlantic Monthly; Washington Post Book World. Honours: Best of the New Generation Award, Esquire, 1984; Frederick Bock Prize for Poetry, 1985. Memberships: Board, Poetry Society of America, and Wesleyan University Writers Conference; Contribution Editor, The Hudson Review. Address: 7190 Faught Rd, Santa Rosa, CA 95403, USA.

GIOVANNI Nikki, (Yolande Cornelia Giovanni), b. 7 June 1943, Knoxville, Tennessee, USA. Poet; Writer; Professor of Creative Writing. 1 son. Education: BA, Fisk University, 1967; School of Social Work, University of Pennsylvania, 1967; Columbia University, 1968. Appointments: Assistant Professor, Queens College, City University of New York, 1968; Associate Professor, Livingston College, Rutgers University, 1968-72; Founder-Publisher, Niktom Publishers, 1970-74; Visiting Professor, Ohio State University, 1984; Professor of Creative Writing, Mount St Joseph on the Ohio, 1985-. Publications: Poetry: Black Judgement, 1968; Black Feeling, Black Talk, 1968; Re: Creation, 1970; Poem of Angela Yvonne Davis, 1970; My House, 1972; The Women and the Men, 1975; Cotton Candy on a Rainy Day, 1978; Those Who Ride the Night Winds, 1983; Children's poetry: Spin a Soft Black Song, 1971, revised edition, 1985; Ego Tripping and Other Poems for Young Readers, 1973; Vacation Time, 1980; Knoxville, Tennessee, 1994; Non-fiction: Gemini: An Extended Autobiographical Statement on my First Twenty-Five Years of Being a Black Poet, 1971; A Dialogue: James Baldwin and Nikki Giovanni, 1973; A Poetic Equation: Conversations between Nikki Giovanni and Margaret Walker, 1974; Sacred Cows... and Other Edibles, 1988; Conversations with Nikki Giovanni, 1992; Racism 101, 1994; Editor: Night Comes Softly: An Anthology of Black Female Voices, 1970; Appalachian Elders: A Warm Hearth Sampler (with Cathee Dennison), 1991; Grandmothers: Poems, Reminiscences, and Short Stories About the Keepers of Our Traditions, 1994. Honours: Ford Foundation Grant, 1968; National Endowment for the Arts Grant, 1969; Honorary doctorates. Address: c/o William Morrow Inc, 105 Madison Avenue, New York, NY 10016, USA.

GITIN David, b. 19 Dec 1941, Buffalo, New York, USA. University of New York, Buffalo; MA, English, San Francisco State University; 2 Years further coursework in English, University of Wisconsin-Madison. Appointments: Teacher at various universities and colleges, including present work for Chapman University, Monterey Peninsula College and Hartnell College. Publications: Guitar Against the Wall, 1972; City Air, 1974; Ideal Space Relations, 1976; Legwork, 1977; This Once: New and Selected Poems, 1965-1978, 1979; Vacuum Tapestries: Poems From Haight Ashbury Notebooks, 1967-69, 1981; Fire Dance, 1989. Contributions to: Over 200 periodicals including: Ant's Forefoot; Audit; Bombay Gin; Epoch; Floating Island; Greenfield Review; Hills; Ironwood; Invisible City; American and Canadian Poetry; New York Times; Paideuma; Poetry Nippon;Western; Humanities Review. Honours: Arx Foundation Award, 1970; Doris Green Award, 1975. Address: PO Box 505, Monterey, CA 93942, USA.

GIULIANI Marilyn Kay, b. 16 Mar 1948, Missoula, Montana, USA. Teacher. Education: BA, Education; MEd, University of Montana. Appointments: Teacher, 2nd and 3rd Grades, 25 years. Publication: In The Shadow of Your Wings. Contributions to: Silver Wings; Poetic Eloquence; National Library of Poetry; Cappers Magazine; Montana Poet Magazine; The Apostolic Crusade. Membership: Society of American Poets. Address: 301 West Lawrence #Apt 303, PO Box 493, Helena, MT 59601, USA.

GIUSTI Mariangela, b. 26 Aug 1951, Empoli, Italy. Teacher; Journalist. m. 8 Dec 1973, 1 son, 2 daughter. Education: Science Degree, Philosophy, 1975, Masters Degree, 1977, University of Florence. Appointments: Teacher of Italian Literature, Secondary Upper School, 1980-88; Teacher, Department of Science Education, University of Florence, 1989-. Publications: Fare on Non Fare, 1975; Ripartire la Successione, 1977; Il Tempo non E'Uno, 1982; Il Cavaliere, 1983; Poeti Della Toscana, 1985; Poesie di Dogana, 1988. Contributions to: Lettera; Silarus; Collettivo; Erba D'Arno; Poesia

Nuova; Ann Magazine. Honours include: Honourable Mention, Academy of Science, Torino, 1980; Second Prize, Letterasio Trinita, 1981; Premio Estate Locridea, 1986; Premil il Portone Pisa, 1988; Premio Naz E Montale, Roma, 1988. Membership: International Centre Eugenio Monale, Roma. Address: Viale Giotto 12, 50053 Empoli, Firenze, Italy.

GIVANS Raymond John, b. 20 July 1951, Portadown, County Armagh, Northern Ireland. Secondary School Teacher. m. Eileen Watt, 2 Aug 1978, 2 sons. Education: BEd, Queen's University, Belfast, 1974; MEd, University of Bath, Avon, England, 1977. Contributions to: Poetry Ireland; Studies: An Irish Quarterly; Irish Press; Cyphers; Connacht Tribune; Salmon; Threshold; Orbis; Acumen; Pamphlet Collection: No Surrender, Castlecaulfield, 1993; Other Poetry; Poetry Nottingham; Poetry Post; Germination, Canada. Memberships: Poetry Ireland, Dublin; Postal, Vers Poets, St Albans, England. Address: 26 Kingsland Park, Dundonald, Belfast BT5 7FB, Northern Ireland.

GIVENS Violet Banks Robinson, b. 1 Jan 1924, Kentucky, USA. m. (1) Samuel Fleming Robinson, 11 Aug 1943, (2) Montgomery Douglas Givens, 2 Feb 1954, 2 daughters. Education: Diploma, Booth School of Business, 1942; BA, Heidelberg University, 1961. Appointments: Various posts including Co-Editor of Stylus Literary Magazine, and Shaw AFB Page Sumter Daily. Publication: Singings of the Damned, 1970. Contributions to: North American Mentor Magazine; Stylus; Rainbow Quarterly; Educational Forum; Kauri; Pegasus; Jean's Journal; Wind; Ave Maria; Podium; Salisbury Cathedral Poet; Avant Garde; Bitch; Journal of Women's Ministries. Honours: St Contes Annual Contest, 1968; American Society of Pen Women, Colorado Branch, 1968; Kentucky State Poetry Society Contest, 1968; Kentucky Writers Guild, 1969; National State Poetry Societies Contest, 1990. Memberships: Life, Kentucky State Poetry Society; Texas State Poetry Society; Verse Writers Guild of Ohio. Address: 604 Wild Briar Cove, Buttercup Creek, Cedar Park, TX 78613, USA.

GJUZEL Bogomil, b. 9 Feb 1939, Cacak, Yugoslavia. Poet. m. (1) Alexandra Judith Rainsford, 24 Dec 1966, div 1987, 1 daughter, (2) 1 son. Education: BA, English, University of Skopje, 1963; University of Edinburgh, 1965. Appointments: Journalist, 1962; TV Skopje Director, 1963-66; Dramaturgist, Dramski Theatre, Skopje, 1966-70, 1985-; Programme Director, Struga Poetry Evenings, 1971-73; Member, International Writing Programme, Iowa City, 1972-73; Bibliographer, 1976-85. Publications: Mead, 1962, 1971; Alchemical Rose, 1963; Libation Bearers, 1965; Odysseus in Hell, selection, 1969; The Well in Time, 1972; The Wheel of the Year, 1977; Reality is All, 1980; A State of Siege, 1981; The Empty Space, 1982; Darkness and Milk, 1986; Naked Life, 1994; Destroying the Wall, 1989; Selected Poems, 1991. Honours: Brothers Miladinov Award for Best Book of the Year in Macedonian, 1965, 1972; Aleksa Šantić Yugoslav Award, 1985-88. Memberships: Secretary, 1967-69, Macedonian PEN; Secretary, Relations Abroad, Macedonian Writers Union, 1970-72. Address: Ivan Cankar 113a, Vlae, 91000 Skopje, Macedonia, Yugoslavia.

GLANG Gabriele, b. 18 July 1959, Arlington, Virginia, USA. Editor; Graphic Designer. m. Rudi Ebert, 21 May 1992, 2 sons. Education: Certificate, Publications Specialist Program, George Washington University, Washington, DC, 1982; BA, English Writing, George Mason University, Fairfax, Virginia, 1979. Appointments: Features Editor/Arts Writer, George Mason University, 1977-79; Editorial Assistant, National Jogging Association, Washington, DC, 1979-80; Editorial Assistant, American Chemical Society, Books Department, Washington, DC, 1980-81; Copy Editor, American Chemical Society, Journals Department, Washington, DC, 1981-82; Freelance Editor/Designer, Dublin, Ireland, 1982-83; Managing Editor, American Politics Magazine, Washington, DC, 1983; Editor, National Telephone Cooperative Association, Washington, DC, 1984; Editor, District of Columbia Budget Office, Washington, DC, 1984-85; Director of Publications, American Association of Dental Schools, Washington, DC, 1985-90; Freelancer, Washington, DC, 1984-90; Freelance DTP Business, Geislingen, Germany, 1990-. Publications: Books: Stark Naked on a Cold Irish Morning, 1990; Free State: A Harvest of Maryland Poets, 1989; Roundelay, 1981. Contributions to include: T Stroheker's "Come" leporello; Kent County News; Amherst Society's American Poetry Annual; The Hollins Critic; Quarry Magazine; California Quarterly; Visions; Lip Service; Phoebe; Poet Lore; Unicorn; Crop Dust; Bogg; Dalhousie Review. Honours: Fellowship, Virginia Center for Creative Arts, 1988; Dr Antonio J Waring Jr, Memorial Prize,

1978; John Ciardi Memorial Prize for Poetry, National Society of Arts and Letters, 1987; Negative Capability Eve of St Agnes' Poetry Prize, 1987. Address: Schwarzwiesenstr 48, D 73312 Geislingen, Germany.

GLANVILLE Ade, b. 7 May 1966, Winchester, Hampshire, England. Actor. Appointments: Gardener, 1982-83; Stock Controller, 1983-86; Sales Assistant, 1986-87; Manager, 1987-88; Civil Servant. Contributions to: Peace and Freedom, 1996; First Time. Address: 1 Whitmoor Cottage, Whitmoor Common, Worplesdon, Guildford, Surrey GU3 3RP, England.

GLASER Elton Albert II, b. 13 Jan 1945, New Orleans, Louisiana, USA. Professor of English. m. Helen Christensen, 14 Aug 1968, 1 son, 1 daughter. Education: BA, English, 1967, MA, English, 1969, University of New Orleans; MFA, Creative Writing, University of California, Irvine, 1972. Appointments: Instructor of English, Western Michigan University, 1968-70; Instructor, Professor of English, University of Akron, 1972-; Director, University of Akron Press, 1993-; Editor, Akron Poetry Series. Publications: Relics, 1984; Tropical Depressions, 1988; Color Photographs of the Ruins, 1992. Contributions to: Poetry; Georgia Review; Iowa Review; Poetry Northwest; North Dakota Quarterly; Southern Poetry Review; Parnassus; Poem in The Best American Poetry, 1995. Honours: Theodore Roethke Award, Poetry Northwest, 1979; Hart Crane Memorial Poetry Award, Icon, 1981; Fellowships, Ohio Arts Council, 1983, 1987, 1995, National Endowment for the Arts, 1983, 1990; Iowa Poetry Prize, 1987; Poetry Prize, Louisiana Literature, 1989; Nancy Dasher Award, College English Association of Ohio, 1990; Randall Jarrell Poetry Prize, North Carolina Writers' Network, 1990. Address: Department of English, University of Akron, Akron, OH 44325, USA.

GLASER Michael Schmidt, b. 20 Mar 1943, Chicago, Illinois, USA. Professor of English. m. 8 May 1976, 3 sons, 2 daughters. Education: BA, Denison University, 1965; MA, 1967, PhD, 1971, Kent State University. Appointments: Assistant, Associate, Full Professor, Director of Festival and Poets and Poetry, Co-Ordinator of Oxford Programme, St Mary's College of Maryland; Executive Board, Poetry Committee of Greater Washington, DC Area. Publications: Marmalade, 1976; On Being a Father, 1987; The Cooke Book: A Seasoning of Poets, 1987; A Lover's Eye, 1991. Contributions to: Hartford Courant; Christian Century; Christian Science Monitor; Green's Magazine; Eleven; Poets On; Poet Lore; Colorado North Review; Samsadat; Poem; Sh'ma; New Letters; America; Roanoke Review. Honours: Chester H Jones National Poetry Prize Competition, 1983; Publications Prize, 1987; Columbia Merit Award for Service to Poetry, 1995. Memberships: Writers Centre, Bethesda; Poets and Writers; Ebenezer Cooke Poetry Society. Address: PO Box 1, St Mary's City, MD 20686, USA.

GLASGOW Eric, b. 10 June 1924, Leeds, Yorkshire, England. University Teacher. Education: MA, St Johns College, Cambridge, 1948; PhD, Victoria University of Manchester, 1951. Appointments: Teacher, 1954-70; Tutor: History, Open University, 1974-78; History and English, London University External Students, 1984-. Contributions to: Year's Poetry; Contemporary Review. Address: Flat 37 Clairville, 21 Lulworth Road, Birkdale, Southport, Merseyside PR8 2FA, England.

GLASSCOTT Alison Julia, b. 25 May 1973, Reading, Berkshire, England. Creative Writing Tutor; Poet. 1 son, dec 1993, 1 daughter. Education: St Joseph's, Reading, 1983-91. Appointment: Creative Writing Tutor, Chiltern Edge Adult Education Centre, Oxfordshire, 1991-92. Publication: The Fragile Continent, 1991. Contributions to: Rialto; Bare Bones; Weyfarers; Haiku Quarterly; Editions of Word for Word; Shell Young Poet of The Year Collection, 1990. Honours: Joint Second Prize, Shell Young Poet of the Year Award, 1990; Joint First Prize, Charterhouse International Poetry Competition, 1991. Memberships: Steering Committee, Berkshire Literature Festival, 1990-92; Co-Leader, Thin Raft Poetics, 1990-92; National Poetry Society. Address: Omey Island, Claddaghduff, Co Galway, Ireland.

GLEE Glenna, b. 1 Feb 1918, Anderson, Indiana, USA. Labourer. m. Robert Paul Williamson, 24 Dec 1939, 2 sons. Education: High School, 1935; General, International Graphoanalysis Society, 1970; Master, International Graphoanalysis Society, 1972. Appointments: Poet Laureate, Indiana State Federation of Poetry Clubs, 1980-81; Resolution of Indiana General Assembly, 101st Session, 1980. Publications: Kerosene Lamp, 1978; Mindwind, 1983; A Bard's Eye View of Graphoanalysis, 1981; After All, Introduction by

Lee Pennington, 1990. Contributions to: Grit Poet; World Poetry Society; North American Mentor; National Federation of State Poetry Societies, Prize Poems, 1984. Honour: Poet Laureate, Indiana State Federation of Poetry Clubs, 1980-81. Memberships: Anderson Poetry Corner; Indiana State Federation of Poetry Clubs; Kentucky State Poetry Society; Poets Study Club of Terre Haute, Indiana. Address: 808 East 32nd Street, Anderson, IN 46016, USA.

GLEN Duncan Munro, b. 11 Jan 1933, Cambuslang, Lanarkshire, Scotland. Professor. m. Margaret Eadie, 4 Jan 1957, 1 son, 1 daughter. Education: Rutherglen Academy and Edinburgh College of Art. Appointments: Book Designer in London, 1958-62; Editor, Robert Gibson, Educational Publishers, Glasgow, 1962-65; Sole Owner, Akros Publications, 1965-; Lecturer, Senior Lecturer, Principal Lecturer, South Lancashire University, 1965-78; Professor and Head of Department of Visual Communication, Nottingham Trent University, 1978-87. Publications: In Appearances, 1971; Mr and Mrs J L Stoddart at Home, 1975; Buits and Wellies, 1976; Of Philosophers and Tinks, 1977; Ten Sangs of Love, 1977; Ten Bird Sangs, 1978; Poet at Work, 1979; Realities Poems, 1980; On Midsummer Evenin Merriest of Nichts? 1981; The State of Scotland, 1983; The Stones of Time, 1984; The Turn of the Earth, 1985; Tales to be Told, 1987; A Poem and Etchings, 1990; Selected Poems, 1965-90, 1991; The Poetry of the Scots, 1991; Beyond Exile: Poems, 1991; A Journey into Scotland: Poems, 1991; Hugh MacDiarmid: Out of Langholm and into the World, 1992; Echoes: Frae Classical and Italian Poetry, 1992; Contributions to: Glasgow Herald; Guardian; Independent; Akros; Lines Review; Chapman. Honours: Special Award from Scottish Arts Council for Services to Literature, 1992; Howard Sergeant Poetry Award, 1993. Address: 33 Lady Nairn Avenue, Kirkcaldy KY1 2AW, Scotland.

GLOVER Jon Martin, b. 13 May 1943, Sheffield, Yorkshire, England. Professor; Head of Division of Humanities. m. Elaine Alice Shaver, 3 Oct 1965, 2 daughter. Education: BA, Honours, English and Philosophy, 1965, MPhil, Philosophy, 1969, University of Leeds. Appointments: Professor and Head of Division of Humanities, Bolton Institute of Higher Education, Bolton Institute. Publications: The Grass's Time, 1970; The Wall and The Candle, 1982; Our Photographs, 1986; Co-Editor, The Penguin Book of First World War Prose, 1989; To The Niagara Frontier, poems, 1994. Contributions to: Stand; PN Review; Acumen; Poet's Voice; Notes and Queries. Address: 3 Lightburne Avenue, Bolton, Lancashire, England.

GLÜCK Louise (Elisabeth), b. 22 April 1943, New York, New York, USA. Poet; Writer; Professor. m. (1) Charles Hertz, div, 1 son, (2) John Dranow, 1977, div 1996. Education: Sarah Lawrence College, 1962; Columbia University, 1963-66, 1967-68. Appointments: Faculty and Board Member of MFA Writing Program, 1976-80, Ellison Professor of Poetry, 1978, University of Cincinnati; Faculty and Board Member of MFA Writing Program, Warren Wilson College, Swannanoa, North Carolina, 1980-84; Holloway Lecturer, University of California, Berkeley, 1982; Scott Professor of Poetry, 1983, Senior Lecturer in English, part-time, 1984-, Williams College, Williamstown, Massachusetts; Regents Professor of Poetry, University of California, Los Angeles, 1985-88; Visiting Professor, 1995, Harvard University; Hurst Professor, Brandeis University, 1996. Publications: Poetry: Firstborn, 1968; The House on Marshland, 1975; The Garden, 1976; Descending Figure, 1980; The Triumph of Achilles, 1985; Ararat, 1990; The Wild Iris, 1992; The First Four Book of Poems, 1995; Other: Proofs and Theories: Essays on Poetry, 1994; Meadowlands, 1996. Contributions to: Many anthologies and periodicals. Honours: Academy of American Poets Prize, 1967; Fellowship, National Endowment for the Arts, 1969-70, 1979-80, 1988-89; Guggenheim Fellowships, 1975-76, 1987-88; American Academy and Institute of Arts and Letters Award, 1981; Melville Crane Award, Poetry Society of America, 1985; Sara Teasdale Memorial Prize, Wellesley College, 1986; Phi Beta Kappa Poet, Harvard, 1990; Co-Recipient, Bobbitt National Prize, 1992; Pulitzer Prize in Poetry, 1993; Poet Laureate of Vermont, 1994; PEN/Martha Albrand Award, 1995. Memberships: Fellow, American Academy of Arts and Sciences; PEN; Phi Beta Kappa; American Academy and Institute of Arts and Letters. Address: Creamery Road, Plainfield, VT 05667, USA.

GLYNN Martin Roy, (Dr G), b. 26 July 1957, Nottingham, England. Writer. 2 daughters. Education: Certificate of Education; British Equity Card; Member, Institution of Production Engineers. Appointment: Literature Development Office, Nottingham, 1989-90. Publications: Poetic Vibrations, 1981; Fuel, 1982; True Reflections, 1983; Subtle Racist Top 10, 1984; De Rachet a Talk, 1985; So You

Say, 1989; Angola, 1990; Rage/Warzone, 1991. Contributions to: You'll Love This Stuff, 1986; Dub Poetry, 1986; Too Little Toffee, 1989; Poem Street, 1990. Memberships: Board, East Midlands ALTS; Equity Actors Union; Director, Shomali ALTS Development Agency. Address: 195 Rock Street, Pitsmoor, Sheffield, Yorkshire S3 9JF, England.

GODBERT Geoffrey Harold, b. 11 June 1937, Manchester, England. Government Information Officer. 1 son, 1 daughter. Education: Royal Manchester College of Music, Performance. Publications: Ides of March, 1975; The Lover Will Dance Incredibly, 1981; Co-Author, Still Lifes, 1983; Journey to the Edge of Light, 1985; The Brooklyn Bridge, 1985; The Theatre of Decision, 1985; Co-Author, For Now, 1991; Are You Interested in Tattooing, 1996; I Was Not, Was Not, Mad Today, 1996. Contributions to: Acumen; Envoi; Gnosis; many other small magazines; Poetry in anthologies: Angels of Fire; Transformations; Completing the Picture, 1995; Co-Editor: 100 Poems by 100 Poets; 99 Poems in Translation, 1994. Address: 5 Berners Mansions, 34-36 Berners Street, London W1P 3DA, England.

GODEL Vahé, b. 16 Aug 1931. Professor. 2 sons. Education: Licencié es Lettres, University of Geneva. Publications: Signes Particuliers, 1969; Cendres Brûlantes, 1970; L'Oeil Étant la Fenêtre de L'Ame, 1972; Poussières, 1977; Du Même Désert à la Même Nuit, 1978; Obscures Besognes, 1979; Qui Parle? Que Voyez-vous?, 1982; Faits et Gestes, 1983; L'Heure d'Or, 1985; Les Frontières Naturelles, 1986; Quelque Chose Quelqu'un, 1987; Exclu Inclus, 1988; La Chute des Feuilles, 1989; Vous, 1990; Ov, 1992; Le Goût de la Lecture, 1992; De Plus Belle, 1993; Arthur Autre, 1994; Le Congrès d'Automne, 1995; P.S., 1995; Le Charme des Vestiges, 1996. Contributions to: Journal de Genève; Revue de Belles-Lettres; Cahiers Du Sud; Europe; Cahiers de la Différence; Poésie 90; Cahiers du Centre International d'Etude Poétiques; Le Journal des Poètes. Memberships: Centre International d'Etudes Poétiques; Groupe d'Olten; World Academy of Arts and Culture; Société Civile des Auteurs Multimedia. Address: 25 Avenue des Cavaliers, 1224 Chêne Bougeries, Geneva, Switzerland.

GOEDICKE Patricia, b. 21 June 1931, Boston, Massachusetts, USA. Poet. m. Leonard Wallace Robinson, 3 June 1971. Education: BA, Middlebury College, 1953; MA, Ohio University, 1965. Appointments: Lecturer, Ohio University, 1963-68, Hunter College, 1969-71; Associate Professor, University of Guanajuato, Mexico, 1972-79; Visiting Writer, Kalamazoo College, 1977; Guest Poet, Sarah Lawrence College, 1980-81; Visiting Poet, 1981-83; Associate Professor, 1988-90, Professor, 1991-, University of Montana. Publications: Between Oceans, 1968; For the Four Corners, 1976; The Trail That Turns on Itself, 1978; The Dog That Was Barking Yesterday, 1980; Crossing the Same River, 1980; The King of Childhood, 1984; The Wind of Our Going, 1985; Listen Love, 1986; The Tongues We Speak: New and Selected Poems, 1989; Paul Bunyan's Bearskin, 1992; Invisible Horses, book of poems, 1996. Contributions include: New Yorker; Harper's; Poetry Magazine; American Poetry Review; Ploughshares; New York Times; New Letters; Paris Review; Beloit Poetry Review. Honours: Honourable Award, Memphis State Review, 1988; Honourable Mention, Arvon International Poetry Competition, 1987; Research Grant, 1989, Distinguished Scholar, 1991, University of Montana. Memberships: McDowell Colony Fellow; Poetry Society of America; Academy of American Poets; Associated Writing Programmes. Address: 310 McLeod Avenue, Missoula, MT 59801, USA.

GOLDBARTH Albert, b. 31 Jan 1948, Chicago, Illinois, USA. Poet; Writer; Assistant Professor of Creative Writing. Education: BA, University of Illinois, 1969; MFA, University of Iowa, 1971; University of Utah, 1973-74. Appointments: Instructor, Elgin Community College, Illinois, 1971-72, Central YMCA Community College, Chicago, 1971-73, University of Utah, 1973-74; Assistant Professor, Cornell University, 1974-76; Visiting Professor, Syracuse University, 1976; Assistant Professor of Creative Writing, University of Texas, Austin, 1977-. Publications: Poetry: Under Cover, 1973; Coprolites, 1973; Opticks: A Poem in Seven Sections, 1974; Jan 31, 1974; Keeping, 1975; A Year of Happy, 1976; Comings Back: A Sequence of Poems, 1976; Curve: Overlapping Narratives, 1977; Different Flashes, 1979; Eurekas, 1980; Ink Blood Semen, 1980; The Smugglers Handbook, 1980; Faith, 1981; Who Gathered and Whispered Behind Me, 1981; Goldbarth's Book of Occult Phenomena, 1982; Original Light: New and Selected Poems, 1973-1983, 1983; Albert's Horoscope Almanac, 1986; Arts and Sciences, 1986; Popular Culture, 1989; Delft: An Essay Poem, 1990; Heaven and Earth: A Cosmology, 1991; Across the Layers: Poems Old and New, 1993; The Gods, 1993; Fiction: Marriage

and Other Science Fiction, 1994; Essays: A Sympathy of Souls, 1990; Great Topics of the World: Essays, 1994; Editor: Every Pleasure: The "Seneca Review" Long Poem Anthology, 1979. Honours: Theodore Roethke Prize, 1972; Ark River Review Prizes, 1973, 1975; National Endowment for the Arts Grants, 1974, 1979; Gugenheim Fellowship, 1983. Address: c/o Department of English, University of Texas at Austin, Austin, TX 78712, USA.

GOLDENSOHN Barry Nathan, b. 26 Apr 1937, New York, New York, USA. m. Lorraine Goldensohn, 5 Aug 1956, 1 son, 1 daughter. Education: BA, Philosophy, Oberlin College, 1957; MA, English Literature, University of Wisconsin, 1959. Appointments: Teacher, Goddard College, 1965-77; Dean, School of Humanities and Arts, 1977-81, Professor of Literature and Writing, 1980-82, Hampshire College; Professor of English, Skidmore College, 1982-. Publications: Gulliver's Travels, 1961; Saint Venus Eve, 1972; Uncarving The Block, 1978; The Marrano, 1988; Dance Music, 1992. Contributions to: Poetry; Agenda; Salmagundi; Yale Review; Massachusetts Review; Southern Review; New Republic. Honours: MacDowell Fellowships; Vermont Council for The Arts Poetry Award, 1977; 6 Faculty Research Grants, Skidmore; Residency Fellowships at MacDowell, Millay and Djerassi Foundations; Poetry Award, New York Foundation for The Arts, 1985. Address: 11 Seward Street, Saratoga Springs, NY 12866, USA.

GOLDIE Joyce Marion (Ortolan), b. 11 Feb 1930, London, England. Housewife and Mother. m. Derek George Goldie, 8 Aug 1953, 3 daughters. Publications: Treasuries of Inspiration, 1986; First Time Magazine, 1987, 1988; Salt and Icing, 1989; York and District Writers Anthology, 1990, and 5 other anthologies, 1993-96; London Calling, 1990; Grieving with Grace, 1991. Contributions to: Candis, 1991; Channel 4 TV, 1991, 1993; Writer's Forum, 1994. Honours: Runner-Up, York and District Poetry Competition, 1990; First Prize, Kym Whybrow Memorial Competition; Certificate of Merit, London Calling. Address: Ivy Cottage, Portloe, Truro, Cornwall TR2 5RG, England.

GOLDLEAF Steven, b. 18 June 1953, Brooklyn, New York, USA. Professor; Writer. m. Carolyn Yalkat, 23 Aug 1981, 2 daughters. Education: AB, Columbia University, 1976; MA, Johns Hopkins University, 1980; PhD, University of Denver, 1985. Appointments: Assistant Professor, Le Moyne College; Lecturer, State University of New York, Albany; Assistant Professor, Pace University. Contributions to: Denver Quarterly; Spitball; Northeast Journal. Honours: American Academy of Poets Award, 1984; Gerald Warmer Bruce Prize for Poetry, 1979; Spitball Honorable Mention, 1985. Address: 1096 Regent Street, Niskayana, NY 12309, USA.

GOLDSCHMIDT Allan David, b. 7 July 1944, USA. Payroll Clerk. Education: Academic Diploma, George Washington High School, 1959; Dean's List, Bronx Community College, 1963; AAS, 1965; BA, Social Work, Empire State College, State University of New York, 1985. Appointments: Gimbels Department Store, New York, 1967-86; Advertising Executive, Payroll Clerk, Faculty Payroll, New York University, 1993-. Publications: Of Sun And Wind, 1994; Wood Winds, 1996, original illustrations included in both. Contributions include: Medicinal Purposes; New Press; Literary Quarterly; Literary Review; Feelings; Kamban Poetry Edge; Tom Weiss' Up Front Muse International Review; Salonika. Honours: Second Place, French Poetry Recital Contest, Bronx Community College, 1964; Talent Contest Winner, Poetry-Flute, New York University, 1994; Honorable Mention, Tom Catterson's Stop Short Poetry Contest, 1996. Memberships: Staff Art Editor, Assistant Editor, Medicinal Purposes; Assistant Poetry Editor, New Press; Poet at recitals and improvisation flutist, Bronx Poets and Writers Alliance, 1984-90; Poetry Co-Ordinator, Stepping Out, monthly magazine; Editorial Assistant, Recording Secretary, Empire State College Paper. Address: 33-06 34th Avenue 2A, LIC, NY 11106, USA.

GOLDSTEIN Laurence Alan, b. 5 Jan 1943. Professor of English. m. Nancy Jo Copeland, 28 Apr 1968, 2 sons. Education: BA, University of California, Los Angeles, 1965; PhD, Brown University, 1970. Appointments: Assistant Professor, 1970-77, Associate Professor, 1978-85, Professor of English, 1985-, University of Michigan; Editor, Michigan Quarterly Review, 1978-. Publications: Altamira, 1978; The Three Gardens, 1987; The American Poet at The Movies: A Critical History, 1994; Anthology: The Faber Book of Movie Verse, 1994; Cold Reading, book of poems, 1995. Contributions to: Poetry; Southern Review; Iowa Review; Salmagundi; Ontario Review;

Indiana Review; Ploughshares; New York Quarterly; Best American Poetry, 1995. Address: c/o Department of English, University of Michigan, Ann Arbor, MI 48109, USA.

GOLDSTEIN-JACKSON Kevin Grierson, b. 2 Nov 1946, Windsor, Berkshire, England. Writer. m. Mei Leng Ng, 6 Sept 1975, 2 daughters. Education: BA, Reading University; MPhil, Southampton University; FRSA. Appointments: Programme Organizer, Southern TV, 1970-73; Assistant Producer, HK-TVB, Hong Kong, 1973; Freelance Writer, TV Producer, 1974-75; Head of Film, Dhofar Region TV Service, Sultanate of Oman, 1975-76; Assistant to Head of Drama, Anglia TV, 1977-81; Founder, TSW, Television South West and Chief Executive and Programme Controller, 1981-85; Freelance Writer, 1985-. Contributions to: Hampshire Poets; Sandwiches; Bogg; Contemporary Poets; Doors; Envoi; Haiku Quarterly; Iota; Krax; Ellery Queen's Mystery Magazine; Kangaroo; Tidepool; New England Review. Memberships: Writers' Guild; Society of Authors; Poetry Society. Address: c/o Alcazar, 18 Martello Road, Branksome Park, Poole, Dorset BH13 7DH, England.

GOLDSTONE Tim John, b. 2 June 1958, Hertford, England. Screen Writer. Education: BA, English and History, St David's University College, Lampeter, Wales. Appointments: Kitchen Assistant; Fruit-Picker; Mill Hand; Labourer; Farmworker, and others. Publications: Material broadcast on television and radio; Currently preparing collections of short stories and poems. Contributions to: Spectrum, Dyfed; Momentum, Clwyd; TOPS, Toxteth, Liverpool; New Welsh Review; Cambrensis; Cardiff Poet; Stand (forthcoming). Honours: Winner, Radio Times Comedy Awards, for a 30 minute radio play, 1991; Scholarship to Hay-on-Wye Festival of Literature Short Story Masterclass, Welsh Arts Council, 1992; Runner-Up, Bridport Prize, 1994. Address: Clifton House, Penllyn, Cilgerran, Cardigan, Dyfed SA43 2RZ, Wales.

GOLDSWORTHY Peter, b. 12 Oct 1951, Minlaton, South Australia, Australia. Education: B Surg, University of South Australia, 1974. Publications: Readings from Ecclesiastes, 1982; This Goes With This, 1988; This Goes With That, 1991; Co-Editor, Number Three Friendly Street: Poetry Reader, 1988. Honours: South Australia Poetry Award, 1988. Address: 8 Rose Street, Prospect, South Australia 5082, Australia.

GOMBOS Susan, b. 11 Dec 1952, Brooklyn, New York, USA. Family Therapist. m. 6 Aug 1972, 1 son, 1 daughter. Education: Masters in Social Work, 1975; Advanced Certificate, Family Therapy, 1989. Appointments: Clinical Private Practice; New York City Board of Education; Jewish Board of Family and Children's Services. Contributions to: Visions International; Feelings; Reflections; Womens' News, Westchester County. Honour: First Place, Town of Greenburgh Poetry Contest, 1992. Memberships: Hudson Valley Writers Center; Poetry Society of America. Address: 22 Treetop Lane, Dobbs Ferry, NY 10522, USA.

GOMEZ Jewelle Lydia, b. 11 Sept 1948, Boston, Massachusetts, USA. Writer. Education: BA, Northeastern University, Boston, 1971; MS, Columbia Graduate School of Journalism, 1973. Appointments: Associate, New York State Council on the Arts, 1984-91; Director of Literature, New York State Council on the Arts, 1991-93; Adjunct Professor, New College of California, 1994; Adjunct Professor, Menlo College, California, 1994; Writer in Residence, California Arts Council, 1995-96. Publications: The Gilda Stories, 1991; Forty-Three Septembers, 1993; Oral Tradition, 1995. Contributions to: Women on Women; Gay & Lesbian Poetry in Our Time; Occidental; The Key To Everything; Conditions; Mosaique. Memberships: PEN; American Center of Poets & Writers. Address: c/o Frances Goldin Literary Agency, 57 E 11th Street, New York, NY 10003, USA.

GÓMEZ Mercedes Estíbaliz, b. 24 Sept 1932, Santurce, Vizcaya, Spain. Housewife. m. Mario Angel Marrodán, 1 son, 1 daughter. Education: Colegio Santa Ana de Portugalete; Artistic Studies, private academy. Publications: Poetry: Estrofas De Una Mujer; El Alma Iluminada; El Limbo Dorado; El Parnaso Intimo; Los Dones del Azar. Contributons to: Numerous poetry journals into Spain and abroad; Included in various anthologies; Translations into Italian and Austrian dialect. Honours: Poetry Prizes; Abanto y Zierbana; Amigos de Galicia (de Sestao); Poesía Mínima (de Baracalo). Memberships: Asociación Artística Vizcaina; A Garibaldi, Portugal; Asociación Colegial De Escritore De Espana; AGA. Address: Cristobal

Mello 7-20, Izqda Apartado Postal 16, 48920 Portugalete, Vizcaya, Spain.

GONZALEZ Anson (John), b. 21 Aug 1936, Trinidad & Tobago, West Indies. Educationist. m. Sylvia Figuero, 6 Aug 1961, 2 daughters. Education: Teachers Diploma, 1959; BA, 1971; MPhil, 1982. Appointments: Primary School Teacher, 1953-71; Teachers College Lecturer, 1971-72; Educational Publisher, 1972-86; School Supervisor, 1986-89; University Lecturer, 1988; Sixth Form School Principal, 1991-96. Publications: Score (with V D Duestel), 1972; Love Song of Boysie, 1974; Collected Poems 1969-1979, 1979; Postcard & Haiku, 1984; Moksha: Poems of Light & Sound, 1988; Merry-Go-Round & Other Poems, 1992. Contributions to: The New Voices; Bian; Now; Guardian; Express; Caribbean Poetry Now; West Indian Poetry; Growing Water; Lion Book of Christian Poetry; Education Journal. Honours: Fellow, International Poetry Society; Life Fellow, World Literary Academy; Writers Union of Trinidad & Tobago; Certificate of Merit, University of Miami Carribbean Writers Institue, 1996; Writer of the Year, 1988; Wutt Award for Services to Poetry Day, 1990. Memberships: Writers Union of Trinidad & Tobago, Founding Member & President, 1988-90; John Clifford Sealey Foundation, 1994; Founder-Editor, The New Voices and the New Voices Newsletter. Address: PO Box 3254, Diego Martin, Trinidad & Tobago, West Indies.

GONZALEZ-MARINA Jacqueline (Joaquina), b. 19 Feb 1935, Madrid, Spain. University Lecturer. m. (2) Desmond Savage, 22 Dec 1982, (1) 2 sons, 1 daughter. Education: BA, Modern Philology, Barcelona University, 1959; MA, Modern Philology, Barcelona University, 1962; Royal Academician, Royal Academy of St Telmo, Malaga, Spain, 1975. Appointments: Lecturer, Barcelona University, 1960-68; St Godrics College, London, 1970-91; Research for books on Education and Poetry (a total of 12 published), American College in London; Lecturer in Modern Languages, 1994-. Publications include: Dieciocho Segundos, 1953; Tijeras Sin Filo, 1955; Antologia de Temas, 1961; Short Stories, 1972; Brian Patten, 1975; A Survival Course, 1975; Once Poemas, 1977; Poesia Andaluza, 1977; Adrian Henri, 1980; Historias y Conversaciones, 1995. Contributions to: Wheels Magazine; The Islander; Verde Blanco; Hydra; El Postillon; Caracola; Sur; Tribune; Mundo Español; Insula; Life Images (Anthology) Living Verse (Anthology); Interactions (Anthology); Link Magazine. Honours: Honorary Title of Royal Academician for the RA in Malaga, Spain; Lecturer in the Liberal Arts Department at the American College in London. Memberships: Royal Academy in London; Poetry Society in London; Honorary Member of the Athenaeum in Alicante and of the Poetry Society in the Isle of Wight; Editor, Dandelion Magazine (Poetry and The Arts), 1979-. Address: "Casa Alba", 24 Frosty Hollow, East Hunsbury, Northants NN4 0SY, England.

GOODALE David John, b. 5 Mar 1972, Hartford, Connecticut, USA. Student. Education: BA, Cum Laude, English, Western Connecticut State University, 1994. Appointments: Community Service Volunteer, Broadstairs, England; Tour Guide, New England Carousel Museum, Bristol, Connecticut, USA; Teacher, English as a Foreign Language, Boston Area. Contributions to: National Library of Poetry; Psychopoetica, 1994. Address: 1741 Main Street, Newington, CT 06111, USA.

GOODALL David Arthur, b. 3 May 1945, England. Retired Teacher. m. Vivien Ann, 15 Feb 1975, 3 daughters. Education: BA, 1966; Diploma in Education, 1967; Fellow, College of Preceptors, 1976; ACP Diploma, 1983. Appointments: Teacher of History and English, Rhyddings School, Oswaldtwistle, Lancs, 1967-77; Head of History, Willingdon School, East Sussex, 1977-92. Contributions to: Education Today; Odyssey; New Hope International; Staple; Outposts; Envoi; Acumen; Frogmore Papers; Pennine Platform; Symphony; Third Half; Moonstone; First Time; Poetry Nottingham; Exile; Iota; Nutshell; Cobweb; Aeirings; Purple Patch; White Rose; Poetry Digest; Hybrid; Peace and Freedom; Eastern Rainbow; Pause; Firing Squad; Work broadcast on BBC Radio and TV; Work included in Poetry Now anthologies and in Siren Books in 1994; An Idea of Bosnia, 1996. Honour: Third Place, Poetry Digest Competition; Runner-Up, 22nd Place, 1994, Poetry Digest Bard of the Year Competition; Finalist, Woodman's Press Competition, 1993. Address: 64 Hawkswood Drive, Hailsham, East Sussex BN27 1UR, England.

GOODISON Lorna, b. 1 Aug 1947, Kingston, Jamaica. Education: Studies in Kingston and New York. Appointments: Writer-in-Residence, University of the West Indies, Kingston, 1973;

Employed in advertising and as Freelance Writer, 1977-. Publications include: Poems, 1974; Tamarind Season, 1980; I Am Becoming My Mother, 1986; Heartease, 1988; Lorna Goodison, 1989; To Us All Flowers Are Roses, 1990. Honour: Commonwealth Poetry Prize, 1986. Address: 8 Marley Close, Kingston 6, Jamaica.

GOODWYN Frank, b. 28 June 1911, Alice, Texas, USA. Writer; Professor Emeritus. m. 3 June 1938, 2 sons. Education: BA, 1939, MA, 1940, Texas College of Arts and Industries; PhD, University of Texas, 1946. Appointments: School Teacher, 1933-39; Teaching Assistant, Texas A & M University, Kingsville, 1939-40; Instructor in English, University of Texas, 1944-46; Assistant Professor of Spanish: Colorado University, 1946, Northwestern University, Illinois, 1946-50; Professor of Spanish and Folklore, University of Maryland, 1950-81. Publication: Poems About the West, 1975. Contributions to: Over 103 poems in popular magazines. Memberships: President, Federal Poets, Washington, DC, 1988-; Ellicott Street Poets, 1989-. Address: 9709 Lorain Avenue, Silver Springs, MD 20901, USA.

GOON Fatt Chee, b. 8 Jan 1924, China. m. Phuah Guay Kee, 12 Jan 1955, 1 son, 1 daughter. Education: Teacher's Training, Penang Free School, Malaya, 1949; BA Honours, London University. Appointments: Teacher, 1946-64; Curriculum and Textbook Officer, Statistician, Ministry of Education, Malaysia, 1965-69; Principal: Clifford Secondary School, Kuala Kangsar, 1969-71, Cochrane Road School, Kuala Lumpur, 1971-74, Penang Free School, 1974-79. Publications: Tatarakyat Memengah Baru 4, 1977; Modern Civics for Secondary Schools, book 4, 1978; The Role of the Principal in Malaysia, 1980. Contributions to: Poet; World Poetry; Eminent Poets; Dawn of a New Era; Dance on the Horizon; Parnassus of World Poets; Best Poems of 1996. Honours: Fulbright Scholarship, 1966-67; Title of PKT conferred by Governor of Penang; Cultural Doctorate in Literature, World University, Arizona, 1987; International Poetry Competition, 1989; International Order of Merit, International Biographical Centre, Cambridge, 1993. Memberships: World Poetry Society Intercontinental; International Editorial Board, World Poetry; International Advisory Board, World University, Benson, USA, 1994-; Board of Trustees, World University Roundtable, Benson, USA, 1995-. Address: 85 Jalan Durian, Taman Cheras, 56100 Kuala Lumpur, Malaysia.

GOONERATNE Malini Yasmine, b. 22 Dec 1935, Colombo, Sri Lanka. Writer; Poet; Editor; Professor. m. Brendon Gooneratne, 31 Dec 1962, 1 son, 1 daughter. Education: BA, 1st Class Honours, Ceylon, 1959; PhD, English Literature, Cambridge University, 1962; DLitt, English and Commonwealth Literature, Macquarie University, Australia, 1981. Appointments: Editor, New Ceylon Writing, 1971-; Director, Post-Colonial Literature and Language Research Centre, 1988-93, Personal Chair in English Literature, Macquarie University, 1991; Visiting Professor of English, University of Michigan, USA, Edith Cowan University, Western Australia, 1991; External Advisor, Department of English, University of the South Pacific, 1993. Publications: English Literature in Ceylon 1815-1878: The Development of an Anglo-Ceylonese Literature, 1968; Jane Austen, 1970; Word Bird, Motif, 53 Poems, 1971; The Lizard's Cry and Other Poems, 1972; Alexander Pope, 1976; Poems from India, Sri Lanka, Malaysia and Singapore (editor), 1979; Stories from Sri Lanka (editor), 1979; Diverse Inheritance: A Personal Perspective on Commonwealth Literature, 1980; 6000 Foot Death Dive (poems), 1981; Silence, Exile and Cunning: The Fiction of Ruth Prawer Jhabvala, 1983; Relative Merits, 1986; Celebrations and Departures (poems), 1991; A Change of Skies (novel), 1991; The Pleasures of Conquest (novel), 1995. Contributions to: Various publications. Honours: Order of Australia, 1990; Eleanor Dark Writers Fellowship, 1991; Marjorie Barnard Literary Award for Fiction, 1991; Several research and travel grants. Memberships: Australian Society of Authors; Fédération Internationales des Langues et Littératures Modernes, vice-president, 1990-96; International Association of University Professors of English; Patron, Jane Austen Society of Australia; New South Wales Writers Centre; South Asian Studies Association of Australia; South Pacific Branch of the Association for Commonwealth Literature and Language Studies. Address: c/o School of English, Linguistics and Media, Macquarie University, North Ryde, New South Wales 2109, Australia.

GOORHIGIAN Martin, b. 1 July 1932, New York, New York, USA. Teacher. m. Louise Zarifian, 23 June 1963, 1 son, 1 daughter. Education: BA, University of Connecticut, 1954; MS, University of Bridgeport, 1966. Publications: Ani, 1989; Between Ice Floes, 1990; The Road Narrows, 1991. Contributions to: Meriden Record Journal;

High Tide; Sound and Waves of West Haven; Laurels; Hob Nob; Prophetic Voices; Parnassus; Night Roses; Wide Open; Plowman; Tucumcari. Honour: Fourth Prize for Poetry, Sparrowgrass Poetry Forum, 1991. Memberships: Chairman, Letters Committee, Milford Fine Arts, 1986-88. Address: 12 Cardinal Drive, Milford, CT 06460, USA.

GORDON Coco, b. 16 Sept 1938, Italy. Artist; Poet; Publisher. 1 son, 2 daughters. Publications: Raw Hands and Bagging, 1978; Water Mark Papers, 1979; Co-author, Loose Pages, 1983; Co-author, Opaque Glass, 1985; Things in Loops and Knots I Pick From The Ground Become a Small Italian Opera, 1987; Acquaterra, MetaEcology and Culture, 1995; New Observations May, 1995; SuperSky Woman: La Caduta (V-idea), 1995. Contributions to: Bachy; Images; Xanadu; Confrontation; Swift Kick; Four Zoas Nighthouse Anthology; Saturday's Women Anthology; American Classic Anthology; Lotta Poetica; Ear Magazine; High Performance; Howling Mantra; Infolio; Assembling; Heresies; Pig Iron Press Anthology No 18; Environmental, Essence and Issue, 1992; Reviews: San Francisco Review of Books, Northeast Rising Sun, Small Pond Magazines, Small Press Magazine, Vernissage (Vienna). Honours: Residency: Banff Centre, 1991, Djerassi Foundation, 1996; Grant, Harvestworks, 1993. Address: 138 Duane Street, New York, NY 10013, USA.

GORDON Gerald Timothy, b. 19 Apr 1943, Pennsylvania, USA. University Professor; Writer. m. Kathleen O'Neill, 25 May 1969, 4 daughters. Education: BA, La Salle University; MA, Duquesne University; MFA, New Mexico State University; PhD, Kent State University. Appointments: Professor, University of Maine, University of Cincinnati, Kirkwood Community College, Black Hills State University. Publications: Night Company; Blacks and Blues. Contributions to: Agni; Beacon Review; American Literary Review; English Journal; Great River Review; Kansas Quarterly; Loon; Mixed Voices; Contemporary Poems About Music, anthology; Rio Grande Writers' Quarterly; Out of Season, anthology; Riverrun; Sonora Review; California State Poetry Quarterly; The Best New Voices in Poetry and Prose Anthology. Honours: Robert A Wichert Poetry Prize, New Mexico State University, 1987; Awarded Associate Artist Residency, Atlantic Centre for The Arts, 1992; Awarded 6 month Artist Residency for Poetry, Helene Wurlizter Foundation of New Mexico, 1994; Night Company nominated for the Naational Endowment for the Arts Western States Book Awards and was semi-finalist for the Bluestem Award. Memberships: Poets and Writers; Maine Society of Poets; Lambda Iota Tau; Associated Writing Programmes; Ohio Writers' Society. Address: 931 West Jackson Boulevard No 5, Spearfish, SD 57783, USA.

GORDON M. See: **LAVIN S R.**

GOREC-ROSINSKI Jan, b. 6 Jan 1920, Króglik, Poland. Writer; Essayist; Journalist. m. Maria Barbara Dobrzalska-Górec, 15 Aug 1938, 3 sons. Education: Master of Law, Nicolai Copernici University, Torun, 1952. Appointments: Journalist, Polish Radio, 1957-58; Editor: Fakty, 1989-, Metafora (literary magazine), 1989-. Publications: Jamark arlekinów, 1963; Ucieczka z Wiezy Babel, 1964; Bluznierstwo garncarza, 1965; Zaprzesze horyzonty, 1968; Molitwa za dobrinu, 1968; Czas odnajdywania, 1970; Zywa galaz, 1971; W kamieniu, 1973; Poezje wybrane, 1976; Ulica Sokratesa, 1978; Eroica, 1980; Sen Syzyfa, 1982; Wzejscie slonc, 1985; Departures, 1985; Czyje bedzie królestwo, 1987; Kredowy Bóg, 1987; Cztowiek Podzielony, 1988; Czarnopis, poezje wybrane, 1989; Siedem wieczerników, 1990; Krzyczec beda kamienie, 1991; Czarna perla, 1992; Sloneczny splot, 1993; Demony, 1994; Przechodzien róz, 1995. Contributions to: Yucie Literackie; Nowa Kultura; Tworczosc; Poezja; Kultura; Fakty; Polityka; Odra; Kamena; Litery; Nurt; Tak i Nie; Poglady; New Europe; and others. Honours: Council Award, Bydgoszcz People's Province, 1968; Workers Publishing Cooperative Award, 1979; Klemens Janicki Award, 1986; International Poetic November Award, 1987; Professor T Kotarbinski Prize, 1989. Membership: President of Bydgoszcz City Branch, Union of Polish Writers in Warsaw. Address: ul Siddlecka 79a, 85-412 Bydgoszcz, Poland.

GORRELL Dena Ruth, b. 8 June 1932, Loyal, Oklahoma, USA. Writer; Poet. m. John S Gorrell, 14 Nov 1953, 1 son, 1 daughter. Education: Associate in Commerce, Oklahoma State University, 1952; Diploma, Institute of Children's Literature, CT, 1989. Publications: Truths, Tenderness and Trifles, 1986; Sunshine and Shadow, 1989. Contributions to: Edmond Sun; Living Streams; Poets at Work; Muse; Wide Open Magazine; Odessa Poetry Review; Independent Review.

Honours: Grand Prize, 1989, 2nd Prize, 1989, International Society for The Advancement of Poetry; 1st Prize, Creative Endeavors Spring Contest, 1990, Cimarron Valley Writers, 1990, Poets at Work, 1990, Tulsa Tuesday Writers, 1990; 2nd Prize, Poetry Press, 1990. Memberships: Poetry Society of Oklahoma; Academy of American Poets; International Society for the Advancement of Poetry; National Federation of State Poetry Societies; National League of American Pen Women Inc. Address: 14024 Gateway Drive, Edmond, OK 73013, USA.

GORZELSKI Roman, b. 12 April 1934, Luck, Poland. Writer; Journalist. Education: College, Lodz, 1954; University of Warsaw, 1962. Appointments: Teacher, 1962-70; Journalist and Writer, 1970-. Publications: Three Blueses, 1964; Metamorphosis, 1973; The Town and the Poem, 1975; Pronunciation of Words, 1977; Return to the Point, 1981; The Bitter Man, 1982; Stadium Full of Sun, 1980; The Pichna River, 1986; Silver Thoughts, 1986; The Warta River, 1988; Cathing of Heads, 1990; The Grain of Anxiety, 1991; Thoughts in Section, 1995. Contributions to: Poezja; Przekroj; Zycie Literackie; Miesiecznik Literack; Szpilki; Tygodnik Kulturalny. Honours: Nike Warszawska Award, 1969; Awards of Merit: Lodz Town, 1986, Polish Culture Award, 1977. Memberships: Union of Polish Writers; Polish Society of Authors; Association of Authors and Composers. Address: ul Chodkiewicza 6, 94-028 Lodz, Poland.

GOTO Takahiko, (Naoya Shibasawa), b. 8 Dec 1940, Japan. Teacher. m. Yasuko, 18 Nov 1966, 1 daughter. Education: BA, Education, University of Gifu, 1963. Appointment: High School Teacher, 1963-. Publications: The Summer I Found, 1965; The Jumper Over the Butterfly, 1985; A Crawfish in the Rain, 1993. Contributions to: Mainichi; Shi to Shisoh. Honour: International Poets Academy Award, 1995. Membership: International Writers and Artists Association, USA. Address: 1512-50 Masaki, Gifu City 502, Japan.

GOTTLIEB Andrew Carl, b. 13 Aug 1969, Ottawa, Ontario, Canada. Student. Education: BA Psychology, University of Rochester, Rochester, New York, USA, 1993. Appointments: Assistant Director of Public Relations, National Association of Life Underwriters, 1994-96; Attending Iowa State University for Master's Degree, 1996-. Contributions to: Mobius; Ihcut. Honour: 3rd Place William Gaines Writing Competition. Address: 311 E Glendale Avenue Apt 1, Alexandria, VA 22301, USA.

GOUDGE John Barnaby, b. 9 July 1921, India. Personnel Manager. m. 20 Sept 1952, 2 daughters. Education: MA Honours, Modern History, Trinity College, Oxford, 1946-48; Barrister at Law, Inner Temple, 1955-57. Appointments: Served in Burma and India, 1941-46; British Petroleum, 1949-51, 1960-78; Colonial Development Corp, 1952-60. Publications: Selected Poems of Baudelaire, translations, 1979; October Sun, 1985. Contributions to: Outposts; Times Literary Supplement; Orbis; Envoi; Green Book; Celtic Dawn; Foolscap; Bound Spiral; South East Arts Review; Poetry World. Honours: Verse Translation First Prizes, Yeats Club, 1987; Skoob Books, Index on Censorship Poetry Competition, 1988; First Prize for a Rhymed Poem, Envoi, 1991. Address: Capers, Dormansland, Lingfield, Surrey RH7 6NP, England.

GOULD Alan David, b. 22 Mar 1949, London, England. Writer; Novelist; Poet; Essayist. m. Anne Langridge, 17 Jan 1984, 2 sons. Education: BA, honours, 1971; DipEd, 1974. Appointments: Full Time Writer, 1975-; Occasional Teacher; Creative Fellow, Australian National University, 1978; Writer-in-Residence, Geelong College, 1978, 1980, 1982, 1985; Writer-in-Residence, Australian Defence Forces Academy, 1986; Writer-in-Residence, Lincoln Humberside Arts Centre, 1988. Publications: Icelandic Solitaries, 1978; Astral Sea, 1981; The Pausing of The Hours, 1984; The Twofold Place, 1986; Years Found in Likeness, 1988; Former Light, selected poems, 1992; Momentum, 1992; Mermaid, 1996. Contributions to: Most Australian outlets. Honours: New South Wales Premiers Prize for Poetry, 1981; Prizes for Fiction, 1985, 1992. Address: 6 Mulga Street, O'Connor, ACT 2602, Australia.

GOUMAS Yannis, b. 20 Oct 1935, Athens, Greece. Shipping Executive. Education: Hove College, 1946-49; Seaford College, 1949-53; University of Southampton School of Navigation, 1953-54. Appointments: Apprentice, 1954-58; Officer on Greek Ships, 1958-60; Rethymnis and Kulukundis Ltd, London, 1960-64; Vice President, J G Goumas Shipping Co SA, Piraeus, 1974-. Publications: Take One, 1967; Sorry, Wrong Number, 1973; Athens Blues, 1974; Signing On,

1977; Thorns in Each Other's Flesh, 1977; Athenians Go to Work, 1978; Past the Tollgate, 1983; The Silence of Others, 1990. Contributions to: Poetry Review; London Magazine; Mundus Artium; Malahat Review; Prism International; Tribune; Shenandoah; Iron; Prospice; Contemporary Literature in Translation: Waves; Samphire; Sycamore Review; Oasis; Verse; Second Aeon; Xenia; Eureka; Kudos; Poesie Vivante; Roots; and others. Membership: Poetry Society. Address: J G Goumas Shipping Co SA, 1-3 Filellinon Street, GR 185-36 Piraeus, Greece.

GOUSSELAND Pascale Christine, b. 20 Dec 1949, France. Psychotherapist. m. John Copen, 28 Oct 1989. Education: Baccalaureat, Philosophy, France, 1968; MA, Science of Information, Law, Assas, Paris, 1973; MA, English, Sorbonne, Paris, 1974; Continuing studies at CG Jung Foundation and Mid Manhattan Institute for Psychoanalysis, 1994-. Appointments: Fashion, Import and Export, Takano Inc, Tokyo, 1975-80; Securities Executive, EF Hutton, New York, 1980-85; Importer of Gousseland Cognac, writer and poet, and supporter and advisor to several contemporary artists, 1985-95; Vice President, Service Express Inc, 1988-94; Poet, performing poet and writer, 1991-95; Psychotherapist and Certified Master Hypnotherapist, 1991-. Publications: Screenplay writer of: GO, 1989, One Hour Photo, 1990-91, and Uranium 235, 1992; Poems include: This Heart Which Beats Too Fast, 1995; Poems Message On A Painting, 1995; Wintertime Savings, 1995; Different Suicide, 1995; Cosmic Feedback, 1995; Visions 1, 1995; I Became Something, 1995; A Week At A Glance, 1995; Many poetry readings, 1991-95; Assistant Editor and French Language Editor, The New Press Literary Magazine, 1993; Poems on TV: Inner Joy, Flying Fish, and New Press, 1994. Honour: Gradiva Award for Best Poetry, National Association for the Advancement of Psychoanalysis, 1995. Memberships: National League of American PEN Women; CG Jung Foundation for Analytical Psychology; Associate Member, American Boards of Accreditation and Certification; American Society for Psychical Research; International Association of Counselors and Therapists. Hobbies include: Animal and Human Rights; Art; Nature; Travel. Address: 135 East 71 St, New York, NY 10021, USA.

GOVINDA RAO K V, (Jyothikumari), b. 4 Oct 1927, Andhra Pradesh, India. Editor. m. 7 Mar 1952, 2 sons. Education: BA; LLB; Doctor in Homoeopathy. Appointment: Editor of, Wisdom, an international monthly digest. Publications: Merise Merikallu, short stories, 1946; Mahatma Gandhi, lyrics, 1948; Durapu Kondalu, short stories, 1950; Rationingu Kathalu, short stories, 1950; Bala Geethalu, poems for children, 1958; Murali, novel, 1959; Manushulu Manasulu, novel, 1960; Antha Abaddam, humorous play, 1961. Contributions to: Wisdom; Ideas Exchange; Poet. Membership: Authors Guild of India, Madras. Address: c/o Wisdom, 9 Desika Road, Mylapore, Madras 600 004, India.

GOWDA Chidananda Kolambe, (K Chidananda), b. 15 June 1942, India. m. Tarini Chidananda, 17 May 1973, 1 daughter. Education: BEng, 1964; MEng, 1969; PhD, Computer Science and Engineering, 1979. Appointments: Lecturer, 1964-69, Assistant Professor, 1969-79, Electrical Engineering; Professor of Computer Science and Engineering, S J College of Engineering, Mysore, 1979-. Publications: Engineering geethegalu, 1980; Engineering Lyrics, 1981; Vignana Vachanagalu, 1984; Putanigala Vignana Padyagalu, 1985; Pattedari Padyagalu, 1989. Contributions to: Chikyu Anthology, 1984; Indo Australian Flowers, 1984; Decades of Poetry, 1985; Pearl Edition, 1985. Honour: State Literature Award, Best Children's Book of Poems, 1985. Address: Professor of Computer Science and Engineering, S J College of Engineering, Mysore 570 006, Kernataka State, India.

GOWLAND Mary Lee (Mary Lee), b. 6 May 1949, Los Angeles, California, USA. Publications: Tender Bough, 1969; Hand in Hand, 1971; The Guest, 1973; Snow Summits in the Sun, 1989; Remembering August, 1994. Contributions to: Poetry LA; Sierra Star; Mountain Times; Blue Window; Onthebus; Women in Photography; Brentwood Bla Bla; Poetry Motel; Fat Tuesday; B-City; Impetus; Random Weirdness. Memberships: Poetry on the Sand, 1985-87; Mountain Arts Council; California Poets in the Schools (C-Pitts); Presenting Arts to Children in Elementary School (P.A.C.E.S.). Address: 49386 Cavin Lane, Coarsegold, CA 93614, USA.

GOYER BUSHNO Lila Joan, b. 9 Aug 1931, Pomona, Missouri, USA. Nurse. m. John J Bushno, 1954, 3 sons, 4 daughters. Education: AA, 1980, AS, 1989, Black Hawk College. Contributions to: Many anthologies in newspapers and magazines. Honours: Many poetry awards and honours including: Six Yearly Golden Poets Awards, 1985-90; Editor's Choice, 1988; Poet of Merit, 1988; Poet of the Year, International Society of Poets; Honorary Member, World Parnassian Guild International; Editor's Choice Award, National Library of Poetry. Memberships: Academy of American Poets; International Society of Poets. Address: 714 East 5th Street, Kewanee, IL 61443, USA.

GRABILL James Roscoe, b. 29 Nov 1949, Ohio, USA. Teacher; Poet; Essayist; Editor. Education: National Presbyterian Scholar, The College of Wooster, 1967-70; BFA, Bowling Green State University, 1974; MA, Graduate Fellow, 1984, MFA, Graduate Fellow, 1988, Colorado State University. Appointments: Producer, Radio Transmissions, 1979-80; Editor, Leaping Mountain Press, 1985-89; Poetry Co-Ordinator, Power Plant Arts Centre, 1986-88; Director, Oregon Writers' Workshop, 1990-91; Currently, Educator. Publications: One River, 1974; Clouds Blowing Away, 1976; To Other Beings, 1981; In The Coiled Light, 1985; The Poem Rising Out of the Earth and Standing Up in Someone, 1994; Through the Green Fire, 1994. Contributions: East West Journal; Sun; A Magazine of Ideas; Kayak; Granite; Momentum; Caliban; Another Chicago Magazine; Mid-American Review; Greenfield Review; Mississippi Mud; High Plains Literary Review; Poetry Northwest; New Letters; Minnesota Review; NRG; Madison Review; Intro; Bloomsbury Review; Colorado Review; Germination; Northern Light; Inroads; Editor's Choice II; Wooster Review; Seizure; Writers' Forum; Plainsong; Willamette Week; Quartet; New Orleans Review. Address: 9835 South West 53rd Avenue, Portland, OR 97219, USA.

GRABOWSKA-STEFFEN Alicja Wanda, (Alicja Wanda Patey-Grabowska), b. 24 July 1939, Warsaw, Poland. Poet; Teacher; Editor. m. Jan Steffen, 9 Dec 1978, 1 son. Education: MA, Polish Philology, Warsaw University. Publications: From the Circle, 1968; Adam Ewa, 1975; A Tree From The Inside, 1979; A Lullaby, 1981; You and I, 1982; A Wound of the Earth, 1983; Here Am I Women, 1984; Zoo, 1988; Przed Snem, 1990. Contributions to: Poetry Canada Review; Neue Züricher Zeitung; Lichtungen; Jalons; Anthologies: Polnische Liebesgedichte; The Scream in The Morning, 1994; In The Name of Love, 1995, in Poems by Polish Women Poets; Children's books: Christmas Eve, 1992; Dwarfs, Elves, Gnomes, Trolls, 1993. Honours: 1st Prize for Theatrical Play, 1985; Silver Wreath, Accademia Internazionale di Pontzen, Naples, 1989. Memberships: Society of Authors; Accademia Internazionale di Pontzen, Naples; Societe Europenne de Culture. Literary Agent: Authors Agency, ul Grzybowska 32, PO Box 133, 00-950 Warsaw, Poland. Address: Orlowicza 6m 30, 00-414 Warsaw, Poland.

GRACE Eugene Vernon, b. 12 Dec 1927, Jackson, Tennessee, USA. Physician. Div, 1 son, 3 daughters. Education: BS, MD, University of Michigan, Ann Arbor; Ophthalmology Speciality, University of North Carolina. Appointments: Private Practice in Ophthalmology; Foreign Expert, American Poetry and Literature, Guangzhou Teachers College, China, 1988-89. Publications: The Most Beautiful Love Poetry in the English Language, Sonnets from the Portuguese, 1984; Mash, Central America, 1985; Poetry of a Bible Reader, 1985; Vision of Job, 1985; Life's Too Short and the Weeks are Too Long, 1986; Wildness, 1986; From These Stones, 1986; Cave, 1988; American Sonnets, The First Century, 1989; The China Chronicle, 1990. Contributions to: Poetry Under the Stars, 1978; England and Roanoke, A Collection of Poems, 1548-1987; Durham Morning Herald; People's Daily, Beijing; Inkling; Writer's Journal; Parnassus; Z Miscellaneous; Corradi. Memberships: North Carolina Poetry Society; President, North Carolina Writers Conference, 1976; Founder, Friday Noon Poets, 1978. Address: 911 Broad Street, Durham, NC 27705, USA.

GRADEL Charles T, b. 4 Dec 1972, Oregon, Ohio, USA. Student. Education: Graduate, Clay High School, 1991; Currently studying for Bachelor's Degree, University of Toledo. Appointments: Freelance Poet, 1992-. Contributions to: The National Library of Poetry's New Anthology, Shadows and Lights; The Best Poems of the '90's. Honours: Received Editor's Choice Award for Poem published in Shadows and Light, 1996. Address: 619 B Roxbury Court, Oregon, OH 43616, USA.

GRAHAM Henry, b. 1 Dec 1930, Liverpool, England. Lecturer. Education: Liverpool College of Art, 1950-52. Appointment: Poetry Editor, literary magazine, Ambit, London, 1969-90. Publications: Good Luck to You Kafka/You'll Never Need It Boss, 1969; Soup City Zoo, 1969; Passport to Earth, 1971; Poker in Paradise Lost, 1977; Europe

After Rain, 1981; Bomb, 1985; The Very Fragrant Death of Paul Gauguin, 1987; Jardin Gobe Avions, 1991. Contributions to: Ambit; Transatlantic Review; Prism International; Evergreen Review; Edinburgh Review; Agenda; Numerous anthologies worldwide including: The New Makars, 1992. Honours: Arts Council Literature Awards, 1967, 1971, 1975; National Poetry Competition, 1992. Address: Flat 5, 23 Marmion Road, Liverpool L17 8TT, England.

GRAHAM Jorie, b. 9 May 1951, New York, New York, USA. Poet; Teacher. m. James Galvin. Education: BFA, New York University, 1973; MFA, University of Iowa, 1978. Appointments: Poetry Editor, Crazy Horse, 1978-81; Assistant Professor, Murray State University, Kentucky, 1978-79, Humboldt State University, Arcata, California, 1979-81; Instructor, Columbia University, 1981-83; Staff, University of Iowa, 1983-. Publications: Hybrids of Plants and of Ghosts, 1980; Erosion, 1983; The End of Beauty, 1987; Editor with David Lehman, The Best American Poetry, 1990; Region of Unlikeness, 1991; Materialism, 1993; The Dream of the Unified Field, 1995. Honours: American Academy of Poets Award, 1977; Young Poets Prize, Poetry Northwest, 1980; Pushcart Prizes, 1980, 1982; Ingram Merrill Foundation Grant, 1981; Great Lakes Colleges Association Award, 1981; American Poetry Review Prize, 1982; Bunting Fellow, Radcliffe Institute, 1982; Guggenheim Fellowship, 1983-84; MacArthur Foundation Fellowship, 1990; Pulitzer Prize in Poetry, 1996. Address: c/o Department of Creative Writing, University of Iowa, Iowa City, IA 52242, USA.

GRAHN Judy (Judith Rae), b. 28 July 1940, Chicago, Illinois, USA. Poet; Writer. Education: BA, San Francisco State University; Medical Laboratory Technician, Washington DC. Appointments: Speaker; Freelance Teacher; Publisher; Medical Laboratory Technician in 1960's; Lectured or read poetry at most major American universities and taught classes at Stanford and New College of California. Publications: The Common Women Poems, 1969; Edward the Dyke and Other Poems, 1971; A Woman is Talking to Death, 1974; She Who, 1977; The Work of a Common Woman, 1978; The Queen of Wands, 1982; The Queen of Swords, 1987; Cassettes: March to The Mother Sea, 1990; A Woman is Talking to Death, 1990; Her work is included in many anthologies. Honours: Poem of the Year, American Poetry Review, 1979; NEA, 1980; American Book Award, 1983; Editor's Choice, 1984. Membership: Founder, Women's Press Collective, 1970. Address: Beacon Press, 25 Beacon Street, Boston, MA 01208, USA.

GRANT James Russell, b. 14 Dec 1924, Bellshill, Scotland. Physician. m. (1) Olga Zarb, 23 Mar 1955, div, 1 son, (2) Susan Tierney, 22 April 1994. Education: Institute of Psychiatry, University of London, 1954-55; Medal in English, Hamilton Academy, 1941; MB CHb, University of Glasgow, 1951. Appointments: Various medical posts. Publications: Hyphens, 1959; Poems, 1959; The Excitement of Being Sam, 1977; Myths of My Age, 1985; Hattonrig Rod, 1986; Histories and Idylls of the 20th Century, forthcoming. Contributions to: Glasgow University Magazine; Botteghe Oscure; Saltire Review; Prism International; Fiddlehead; Chapman; Ambit; BBC; CBC; Agenda; Edinburgh Review; Anthologies: Christian Poetry, 1988; Oxford Book of Travel Verse, 1985; Book of Machars, 1991. Honour: 3rd Prize, Scottish Open Poetry Competition, 1976; 3rd Prize, UK National Poetry Competition. Memberships: National Poetry Society; British Medical Association. Address: 255 Creighton Avenue, London N2 9BP, England.

GRAU B H. See: BERGESEN Charles Racine.

GRAVES Michael David, b. 21 Mar 1951, New York, New York, USA. College Instructor. m. BA English, Hunter College, 1978; MA English, Temple University, 1984. Appointments: Instructor, English Department, The Pennsylvania State University, University Park State College, 1986-88; Adjunct Instructor, Borough of Manhattan Community College, English as Second Language, 1988-92; Adjunct Instructor of English, various colleges in the City University of New York, 1988-90; Touro College, Division of New Americans, 1992-95. Publications: Outside St Jude's, 1990. Contributions to: The Journal of Irish Literature; James Joyce Quarterly; The Classical Outlook; European Judaism; The Hollins Critic; Aeraiocht Press; The Poetry Newsletter; Wind; Green's Magazine; Writer's Forum. Membership: Poetry Society of America. Address: 462 83 Street, Brooklyn, NY 11209, USA.

GRAVES Roy Neil, b. 2 Feb 1939, Tennessee, USA. College Teacher. m. Sue Lain Hunt, 5 June 1965, div 1982, 1 son, 2 daughter. Education: BA, Honours, English, Princeton University, 1961; MA, ABD, Duke University, 1964; DA, University of Mississippi, 1977. Appointments: Graduate Instructor, Duke University, 1964-65; Lecturer, University of Virginia, Roanoke, 1965, 1967; Assistant Professor of English, University of Virginia, Lynchburg, 1965-67; Assistant, Associate Professor of English, Co-Ordinator, Humanities and Social Sciences, Central Virginia Community College, Lynchburg, 1967-69; Assistant, Associate, Professor of English, University of Tennessee, Martin, 1969-; Instructor, Tennessee Governor's School for Humanities, summers 1985-. Publications: Medina and Other Poems, 1976; Somewhere on the Interstate, 1987. Contributions to: Christian Science Monitor; Miscellany: A Davidson Review; New York Magazine; Appalachian Journal; Goddard Journal; Mississippi Review; Hampden-Sydney Review; Small Farm; Vanderbilt Poetry Review; Celebration: A Bicentennial Anthology; Lyric; Old Hickory Review; Windmills; Bean Switch; Contemporary American Poetry; Specilia 6; Publications of the Arkansas Philological Association; Mountain Review; Homeworks: A Book of Tennessee Writers; Panhandler; New Ground; Journal of the Jackson Purchase Historical Society; Educational Catalyst. Honours: Bain-Swiggett Prize for Poetry, 1960; The Manners Prize, 1961; 1st Place for Poetry, The Miscellany, A Davidson Review, 1976; Winner, 2nd Mid-South Chapbook Competition, Ion Books, Memphis, 1987. Address: Route 2, Box 473, Martin, TN 38237, USA.

GRAY Robert, b. 23 Feb 1945, Australia. Appointment: Writer-in-Residence, Tokyo, 1985-. Publications: Introspect, Retrospect, 1970; Creekwater Journal, 1974; Grass Script, 1978; The Skylight, 1983; Selected Poems 1963-83, 1985, revised edition, 1990; Piano, 1988; Co-Editor, The Younger Australian Poets, 1983. Honours: New South Wales Premier's Award, 1986.

GRAY Victor. See: CONQUEST (George) Robert (Acworth).

GRECZYNKA. See: SIDERIDOU Niki-Stella.

GREEN Catherine Anne Mary Durkin, b. 3 Mar 1970, Liverpool, England. Actress. Education: St Edwards College, Liverpool; BA Honours, English Literature, Hertford College, Oxford; Central School of Speech and Drama. Honour: Poetry Society's Gold Medal, 1991. Memberships: Poetry Society; English Speaking Union. Address: 10 Golborne Road, Winwick, Near Warrington, Cheshire WA2 8SZ, England.

GREEN Fay, b. 30 Jan 1954, Kent, England. Solicitor; Poet; Breeder of Rare Sheep. Education: Law Society Examinations, Honours, 1978. Appointments: Solicitor; Secretary, Kent Rare Breeds Survival Trust Group; Committee, Federation of Kent Writers, 1994-. Publications: Pure Green, 1990; Colours, 1991; No Telegrams, 1992; Fragile Ground, 1994; Poems-in-Law, 1995. Contributions to: Kent and Sussex Poetry Society Folio Competition Winners Anthologies; Law Society's Gazette; Angels of the Heart Anthology, 1992; Heart and Soul Anthology (Poetry Now), 1996; Kentish Poems (Aegis Press), 1996. Honours: Kent and Sussex Poetry Society, Commendation, 1992, 1994. Memberships: Kent and Sussex Poetry Society; L'Etrave Revue des Arts et des Lettres. Address: Charity Farmhouse, Pilgrims Way, Hollingbourne, Kent ME17 1RB, England.

GREEN Frederick Pratt, b. 2 Sept 1903. Retired Methodist Minister. m. Marjorie Mildred Dowsett, 6 Aug 1931. Education: Didsbury Training College (Methodist), 1925-28. Publications: This Unlikely Earth, 1952; The Skating Parson, 1963; The Old Couple, 1976; The Last Lap, 1991. Contributions to: Poetry Review; English; New Yorker; Time and Tide; Listener; Outposts; New Poetry; Yorkshire Post; Countryman; Norfolk Fair; Hibbert Journal; Anthologies in Oxford Book of Twentieth Century English Verse. Honour: LHD, Emory University, Atlanta, for Contributions to Hymnody, 1982. Membership: PEN International. Address: Cromwell House, Cecil Road, Norwich NR1 2QL, England.

GREENBERG Alvin David, b. 10 May 1932, Cincinnati, Ohio, USA. Writer; Educator. 2 sons, 1 daughter. Education: BA, 1954, MA, 1960, University of Cincinnati; PhD, University of Washington, 1964. Appointments: University of Kentucky, 1963-65; Macalester College, 1965-. Publications: The Metaphysical Giraffe, 1968; The House of the Would-Be Gardener, 1972; Dark Lands, 1973; Metaform, 1975; In Direction, 1978; And Yet, 1981; Heavy Wings, 1988; Why We Live

With Animals, 1990. Contributions to: American Poetry Review; Gettysburg Review; Georgia Review; Chelsea; Nimrod; Cincinnati Poetry Review. Honours: Short Fiction Award, Associated Writing Programmes, 1982; Pablo Neruda Prize in Poetry, 1988. Memberships: Associated Writing Programmes; Poets and Writers; Modern Language Association. Address: 1113 Lincoln Avenue, St Paul, MN 55105, USA.

GREENBERG Barbara (Levenson), b. 27 Aug 1932, Boston, Massachusetts, USA. Poet; Fiction Writer. 2 sons. Education: BA, Wellesley College, 1953; MA, Simmons College, 1973. Appointments: Teaching of Creative Writing at various colleges including Goddard, Warren Wilson, New York University and Massachusetts Institute of Technology. Publications: Spoils of August, poems, 1974; Fire Drills, stories, 1982; The Never-Not Sonnets, 1989. Address: 770 Boylston Street, No 6-1, Boston, MA 02199, USA.

GREENE Jeffrey, b. 22 May 1952, Norwalk, Connecticut, USA. Professor of English. Education: BA, Goddard College, 1975; MFA, University of Iowa, 1977; PhD, University of Houston, 1986. Appointments: Assistant Professor, Associate Professor of English, University of New Haven. Publications: To The Left of The Worshipper, 1991; Glimpses of the Invisible World in New Haven, 1995. Contributions to: New Yorker; Nation; American Scholar; Iowa Review; Antioch Review; Sewanee Review; Ploughshares; Missouri Review; Prairie Schooner; Indiana Review; Seneca Review; Ohio Review; Denver Quarterly. Honours: Discovery, The Nation Award; Mary Roberts Rinehart Grant; Brazos Prize in Poetry; 2nd Prize, National Poetry Competition; Connecticut Commission on The Arts Grant. Memberships: Associated Writing Programmes; Poetry Society of America. Address: 254 Bradley Street, New Haven, CT 06510-1103, USA.

GREENE Jonathan Edward, b. 19 Apr 1943, New York, New York, USA. Writer; Publisher; Book Designer. 1 son, 2 daughters. Education: BA, Bard College, 1965. Appointments: Design and Production Manager, University Press of Kentucky, 1966-75; Director, Gnomon Press, 1965. Publications: The Reckoning, 1966; Instance, 1968; The Lapidary, 1969; A 17th Century Garner, 1969; Scaling the Walls, 1974; Glossary of the Everyday, 1974; Peripatetics, 1978; Once a Kingdom Again, 1979; Quiet Goods, 1980; Idylls, 1983, revised and enlarged edition, 1990; Small Change for The Long Haul, 1984; Trickster Tales, 1985; Les Chambres des Poetes, 1990; The Man Came to Haul Stone, 1995. Contributions to: Quarterly Review of Literature; Monks Pond; New Directions Annual; Origin; Poetry; American Literary Anthology; Tree; Active Anthology; Truck; Text; The Small Farm; Montemora; New World Journal; Sulphur. Honours: National Endowment for the Arts Fellowship, 1969, 1978; Southern Federation of States Arts Agencies Fellowship, 1977. Address: PO Box 475, Frankfort, KY 40602, USA.

GREENHALGH Christopher David, b. 17 Mar 1963, Bury, Lancashire, England. Education: BA Honours, English, University of Hull, 1981-84; PGCE, English, University of East Anglia, 1986-87; PhD, University of Hull, 1993. Appointments: English Teacher, International School, Athens, 1987-90. Contributions to: Many poems published in Bete Noire magazine, 1984-; Poem broadcast on BBC Radio 4, Time for Verse programme, 1991. Honours: 1st Prize, Thetford Open Poetry Competition, 1987; Gregory Award Winner, 1992. Membership: Poetry Society, 1990-. Address: 17 Kew Gardens, Penwortham, Preston, Lancashire PR1 0DR, England.

GREENING John David, b. 20 Mar 1954, London, England. Teacher of English. m. Jane Woodland, 29 Apr 1978, 2 daughters. Education: BA, Honours, English, University College of Swansea, 1975; University of Mannheim, Germany, 1975-76; MA, Drama, University of Exeter, 1977. Appointments: Clerk to Hans Keller, BBC Radio 3; EFL Teacher in Aswan, Upper Egypt and then to Vietnamese Boat People in North-east Scotland; Currently Teacher of English, Kimbolton School, Huntingdon. Publications: Westerners, 1982; Winter Journeys, 1984; Boat People, 1988; The Tutankhamun Variations, 1991. Contributions to: Observer; Spectator; Encounter; World and I; Stand; Poetry Review; Bananas; Rialto; Poetry Wales; Outposts; Poetry Durham; Oxford Poetry; Cumberland Poetry Review; PBS Anthology; Gregory Anthology. Honours: First prize, Alexandria International Poetry Prize, 1981; Twice a top winner, Arvon/Sotheby's International Poetry Competition, 1987, 1989; Scottish Arts Council Writer's Bursary, 1982. Membership: Poetry Society. Address: 27

Hatchet Lane, Stonely, Huntingdon, Cambridgeshire PE18 0EG, England.

GREENWALD Roger Gordon, b. Neptune, New Jersey, USA. University Teacher. Education: BA, City College of New York, 1966; MA, 1969, PhD, 1978, University of Toronto. Appointments: Tutor, Senior Tutor, Innis College, 1969-; Director, Innis College Writing Centre, 1994-, University of Toronto. Publications: Joint Author, A Mustard Sandwich, limited edition chapbook, 1980; Connecting Flight, 1993; Translator, Editor, Introduction by him, The Silence Afterwards: Selected Poems of Rolf Jacobsen, 1985; Co-Translator, Introduction by him, Stone Fences by Paal-Helge Haugen, 1986; Co-Translator, Ten Poems by Pia Tafdrup, 1989; Translator, Introduction by him, The Time in Malmö on the Earth by Jacques Werup, 1989; Translator, A Story About Mr Silberstein, novel by Erland Josephson, 1995. Contributions to: Alcatraz; Exile; Northward Journal; Panjandrum; Pequod; Poetry East; Promethean; Rubicon; Scandinavian Review; The Spirit That Moves Us; Stand; Artes International; Translation; World; Editor, WRIT Magazine, 1970-95. Honours: Winner for Poetry, Norma Epstein National Competition, Canada, 1977; Translation Centre Award, Columbia University, 1983; Richard Wilbur Translation Prize, 1985; F R Scott Translation Prize, 1986; American-Scandinavian Foundation Translation Prize, 1990; CBC Radio "Saturday Night" Literary Award, 1994; Inger Sjöberg Translation Prize, 1995. Memberships: Translation Committee, PEN American Centre; American Literary Translators Association; Association for the Advancement of Scandinavian Studies in Canada; Associated Writing Programs. Address: Innis College, University of Toronto, 2 Sussex Avenue, Toronto, Ontario M5S 1J5, Canada.

GREENWAY-WHITE Melanie Robin, b. 30 May 1956, Carlisle, Pennsylvania, USA. Artist. m. Randy Dee White, 17 Dec 1979, 2 sons, 3 daughters. Education: Carlisle Senior High School, Pennsylvania, 1974; Associate Degree, Ricks College, Rexburg, Idaho, 1976; BSc, Brigham Young University, Provo, Utah, 1978. Publication: Afterthoughts, 1996. Contributions to: Ensign; Northwest Herald. Membership: Northwest Area Arts Council. Address: 3810 Tecoma Drive, Crystal Lake, IL 60012, USA.

GREGOR Arthur, b. 18 Nov 1923, Vienna, Austria. Writer; Teacher; Editor. Education: BS, New Jersey Institute of Technology, 1945. Appointments: Senior Editor, Macmillan Company, 1962-70; Professor of English, 1974-88, Poet in Residence, 1988, Hofstra University. Publications: Octavian Shooting Targets, 1954; Declensions of a Refrain, 1957; Basic Movements, 1966; Figure in The Door, 1968; A Bed By The Sea, 1970; Selected Poems, 1971; The Past Now, 1975; Embodiment and Other Poems, 1982; Secret Citizen, 1989; The River Serpent, 1995. Contributions to: New Yorker; Nation; New Republic; New York Times; New York Herald Tribune; Saturday Review; Esquire; Harper's; Commentary; Commonweal; Poetry; Sewanee Review; Kenyon Review; Hudson Review; Botteghe Oscura; New World Writing; Quarterly Review of Literature; Southern Review; Minnesota Review; Michigan Quarterly. Honours: First Appearance Prize, Poetry, Chicago, 1948; The Palmer Award, Poetry Society of America, 1962. Memberships: Poetry Society of America; PEN; Authors' Guild. Address: 250 West 94th Street, New York, NY 10025, USA.

GREGORY R G, b. 6 Jan 1928, Southampton, Hampshire, England. Language Worker; Arts Writer. Education: BA English, London, 1952; Diploma in Drama, Inst of Education, Newcastle, England, 1972. Appointments: Teacher, English/Drama, Hampshire, Uganda, Shropshire, 1952-72; Founder, Word and Action (Dorset), Language Arts Organisation, 1972-. Publication: Glimpses of Dorset, 1996. Contributions to: Outposts; New Poetry; Ambit. Address: 77 Wimborne Road, Colehill, Wimborne, Dorset BH21 2RP, England.

GREGORY Joan. See: POULSON Joan.

GREGORY Phillip. See: AHERN Thomas (Tom) Gregory.

GRENIER Arpine Konyalian, b. 29 June 1943, Beirut, Lebanon. Poet. 1 son. Education: BSc, 1965; MSc, 1967; MFA, 1997. Appointments: Research in Veterinary Medicine, University of California, Davis, 1967-70; Medical Research, Huntington Medical Research Institute, 1973-90; Financial Research Analyst, Southern California Edison Company, 1980-93. Publications: St Gregory;s Daughter, 1991; Whores From Samarkand, 1993. Contributions to: Ararat; Sulfur; Chiron Review; Columbia Review; California Quarterly;

Asbarez. Memberships: Academy of American Poets. Address: 990 South Marengo Avenue, Pasadena, CA 91106, USA.

GRENNAN Eamon, b. 13 Nov 1941, Dublin, Ireland. Professor; Poet. 1 son, 2 daughters. Education: BA, 1963, MA, 1964, University College, Dublin; PhD, Harvard University, 1973. Appointments: Lecturer in English, University College, Dublin, 1966-67; Assistant Professor, Herbert Lehman College, City University of New York, 1971-74; Assistant Professor, 1974-83, Associate Professor, 1983-89, Professor, 1989-, Vassar College. Publications: Wildly for Days, 1983; What Light There Is, 1987; Twelve Poems, 1988; What Light There Is and Other Poems, 1989; As If It Matters, 1991; So It Goes, 1995; Selected Poems of Giacomo Leopardi (translator), 1995. Contributions to: Anthologies and periodicals. Honours: National Endowment for the Humanities Grant, 1986; National Endowment for the Arts Grant, 1991; Guggenheim Fellowship, 1995. Address: c/o Department of English, Vassar College, Poughkeepsie, NY 12604-0352, USA.

GRESS Esther Johanne, (Estrella), b. 20 Aug 1921, Copenhagen, Denmark. Publisher; Editor; Poet. Education: Degrees in Commerce. Appointments: Book Publishing, 8 years; Editor of Encyclopedias and various other publications; Newspaper Berlingske Tidende, 1950-; Radio, Film and Theatre Columnist and Picture Editor; Congress Organizer and Lecturer, Publishing House Estrella, Humlebaek. Publications: Skal, 1974; Liv, 1977; Ville vejen i vejen, 1979; Det sker maske, 1982, 1985; Det gik, 1983; Raise, English poems, 1984; Raise, English and Indian translations, 1989; Raise, translation into Chinese, 1992; En ny begyndelse, 1993; Let Us, in 27 languages, 1995; Hvad du gør mod andre, theme-book about Survival, 1997; Grow with English Poems, 1989-1991; Poems set to music in English, Danish, Italian. Contributions to: Numerous anthologies, papers and magazines in USA, England, Italy, Switzerland, Austria, Korea, India, Japan, Portugal, Egypt, Australia, Thailand, Greece, Taiwan, Israel, Brazil and Denmark. Honours: Awards from USA, India, England, Taiwan and in Italy, Naples, Rome, Mantova, Como, Milan; Danish Academy Consul for Accademia d'Europa, Naples, 1982; Guest of Honor New York Poetry Forum, 1983; Doctor of Literature (Hon), 1984; Grand Dame, Knights of Malta, 1984; Dr Amado Yuzon's Medal for Exemplary Services for World Brotherhood and Peace, Rome, 1988; Grand Prix, Mediterranee d'Europe Trofeo Italia, 1989; Appointed President for the World Congress of Poets, 1997; Woman of the Year, USA, 1990; Women's Inner Circle Achievement, 1992. Memberships: Academy of Arts and Culture; Regional Co-Ordinator for Europe, World Congress of Poets; Co-Founder and International Regent, International Poets Academy, India; Numerous poetry and authors associations in Denmark, Sweden, USA, Italy and Malta. Address: Ny Strandvej 27, 3050 Humlebaek, Denmark.

GRESSER Sy (Seymour Gerald), b. 9 May 1926, Baltimore, Maryland, USA. Stone Sculptor; Writer. 3 sons, 1 daughter. Education: BS, 1949, MA, 1972, Zoological Sciences, English and American Literature, University of Maryland; Institute of Contemporary Arts, Washington, DC, 1949-50. Appointments: Publications Consultant for various firms, 1960-; Teacher, 1965-70; Private Students, present. Publications: Stone Elegies, 1955; Coming of the Atom, 1957; Poems From Mexico, 1964; Voyages, 1969; A Garland for Stephen, 1971; A Departure for Sons, 1973; Fragments and Others, 1982; Hagar and Her Elders, 1989. Contributions to: Poetry Quarterly; Stand; Antioch Review; Western Humanities Review; Johns Hopkins Review; Atavist Magazine; New York Times Book Review. Address: 1015 Ruatan Street, Silver Spring, MD 20903, USA.

GREY Eilonwy. See: LLOYD-JONES Jenafer.

GREY John Anthony, b. 14 Aug 1949, Brisbane, Australia. Data Processing. m. Gale Grey, 12 Jan 1980. Publications: First, 1989; Devil in the River, 1990; Chainsaw Massacre Suite and Other Poems of Psychotic Bliss, 1991; Dance to the Window, 1993. Contributions to: Paintbrush; Osiris; Sequoia; Greensboro Review; Wisconsin Poetry Review; Spoon River Quarterly; Miocoro Review; Green Mountains Review; Bugg; Seams; Cape Rock; Birmingham Poetry Review; Roanoke Poetry Review; Seattle Review; Louisville Review; many others; Over 3000 poems in print since 1986. Honours: Poet of the Year Award, Small Press Writers of America Organization, 1990, 1991. Memberships: Small Press Writers of America Organization; Science Fiction Poetry Association. Address: 72 Fruit Hill Avenue, Providence, RI 02909, USA.

GRIEDER Ted, b. 25 Feb 1926. Curator, New York University, now Retired. Education: BA, University of Southern California, 1948; MA, 1950, PhD, 1958, Stanford University; MLS, University of California at Berkeley, 1962. Appointments: Chief Bibliographer at University of California at Santa Barbara, 1962-63, University of California at Davis, 1963-66, New York University, 1966-70; Associate Curator, Full Curator, Rare Books, New York University, 1970-82. Publications: Corpus, 1967; I Shall Come to You, 1973; The High Country, 1985; Williamsburg Ramble, 1988; The Broken Country, 1990; Coastlands, 1993. Contributions to: Nexus. Honours: American Phil Society, 1966-68; ALS, 1977-79; Honorary Poet Laureate, Flagler County, Florida, 1989-. Memberships: Modern Language Association; Life Member, Poetry Society of America; Grolier Club. Address: 276 Ocean Palm, Flagler Beach, FL 32136, USA.

GRIFFIN Ted (Edward Francis), b. 1962, Pinner, Middlesex, England. Journalist. m. Education: BA, Honours, Open University, 1987. Appointments: Poetry Reviewer, Topical Books, 1990-93; Editor, The Betjemanian Journal of The Betjeman Society, 1991-94; Occasional Reviewer for Orbis, Envoi and Outposts Poetry Quarterly. Contributions to: Outposts Poetry Quarterly; Acumen; Poetry Nottingham; Spokes; Openings; Folio International; BBC Radio. Memberships: Chairman, 1985-88, Open University Poets; Francis Brett Young Society. Address: Manor Farm House, Steeple Claydon, Buckinghamshire MK18 2QF, England.

GRIFFITHS (Brian Bransom) Bill, b. 20 Aug 1948, London, England. Self-Employed Writer; Small Press Publisher; Researcher. Education: BA, Honours, Medieval and Modern History, University College, London, 1969; MA, 1983, PhD, 1987, Old English, King's College, London. Appointments: Printshop Manager, National Poetry Centre, Poetry Society, 1974-76; Artist in Residence, Westfield College, London, 1984-85; Small Press Publisher, Amra Imprint. Publications: War With Windsor, 1974; Tract Against The Giants, 1984; Editor, Alfred's Metres of Boethius, 1991; Co-Author, Paladin's (Re)Active Anthology, No 1, 1992; Star Fish Jail, poetry, 1993. Contributions to: Poetry Review; Talus; Figs; Fragmente. Honours: Joint Winner, Alice Hunt Bartlett Award, Poetry Society, 1974; Caedmon Prize for Old English Verse, Pa Engliscan Gesitas, 1988. Memberships: Honorary Chairman, Association of Little Presses, 1989-92. Address: 21 Alfred Street, Seaham Harbour, Co Durham SR7 7LH, England.

GRIFO Lionello. See: **VAGGE Ornello.**

GRINKER Morton, b. 19 May 1928, Paterson, New Jersey, USA. Writer. m. Lynn Grinker, 28 June 1963. Education: BA, English, University of Idaho, 1952. Publications: To the Straying Aramaean, 1972; The Gran Phenician Rover, books one through to six, due 1996. Contributions to: Shig's Review; S-B Gazette; Perspectives; Or; Dust; Manhattan Review; Work; Tampa Poetry Review; Amphora; Buffalo Stamps; Hyperion; Illuminations Reader; Poems Read in the Spirit of Peace and Gladness; San Francisco Bark. Address: 1367 Noe Street, San Francisco, CA 94131, USA.

GROCE Jennifer. See: **BOSVELD Jennifer Miller.**

GROCH Erik, b. 25 Apr 1957, Kosice, Czechoslovakia. Editor. m. Monika Torok, 2 sons. Appointments: Railway Worker; Night Watchman; Journalist for Kulturny Zivot (Cultural Life), literary weekly; Editor, publishing house, Timotej, Kosice. Publications: Sukromne hodiny smutku (Private Lessons in Sadness), 1989; Baba Jaga: Zalospevy (Baba Yaga: Elegies), 1991; Bratsestra (Brothersister), 1992. Contributions to: Kulturny Zivot; Slovenske Pohlady; Romboid; Dotyky; Ticha Voda; Fragment K; Inostrannaya Literatura, Russia; Prairie Schooner, USA. Honour: Ivan Krasko Prize for Best Debut of the Year, 1989. Membership: Obec Spisovatelov Slovenska, PEN Club. Address: Tomasikova 19, 04001 Kosice, Slovakia.

GROLLMES Eugene E, b. 9 Nov 1931, Kansas, Missouri, USA. University Administrator. Education: AB, MA, 1961, St Louis University; PhD, Boston College, 1969. Appointments: High School Teacher; University Professor; Assistant Dean of Arts and Sciences, St Louis University, 1974-. Publication: At The Vietnam Veterans Memorial, Washington DC: Between The Lines, 1988. Contributions to: Alura; Bitterroot; Blue Unicorn; Daring Poetry Quarterly; Deros; Earthwise; Encore; Great River Review; MacGuffin; Manhattan Poetry Review; Manna; Midwest Poetry Review; New Voices; Orphic Lute; Peninsula Poets; Piedmont Literary Review; Sands; Spoon River

Quarterly; The Villager. Membership: Academy of American Poets. Address: 3601 Lindell Boulevard Street, St Louis, MO 63108, USA.

GROSMAN Ernesto Luis, b. 2 Mar 1956, Buenos Aires, Argentina. Professor. Education: Poetic Fellowship, English Department, State University of New York at Buffalo, 1993; MA, Humanities, 1994, Doctoral Candidate in Latin American Literature, New York University. Appointment: Senior Lecturer, Department of Spanish and Portuguese, Yale University, 1994-. Publications: Xul, anthology of Argentine poetry, 1996; Charles Olson, anthology in Spanish, 1996. Contributions to: American Poetry Review; Rift; Xul; Exact Change; Mandorla. Address: 19 Off Twin Lake Road, North Branford, CT 06471, USA.

GROSS Dan S. See: **SNODGRASS W D.**

GROSS Natan, b. 16 Nov 1919, Cracow, Poland. Film Director; Journalist; Poet; Translator. Education: Law and Art Studies; Polish Film Institute. Appointment: Polish Film Institute, 1945-46. Publications: Wybor Wapólczesnej Poezji Hebrajskiej (Selection of New Hebrew Poetry), 1947; Piesni o Jzraelu (Song of Israel), 1948; Co nam zostalo z tych lat (What is Left of It All), 1971; Co-Editor, Ha'shoa beshira haivrit (Holocaust in Hebrew Poetry), anthology, 1974; Wiersze Buntu i Zaglady (Songs of Holocaust and Rebellion), 1975; Okruszyny mlodosci (Crumbs of Youth), 1976; Co-Author, Yeladim be'getto (Children in the Ghetto), 1978; Palukstart monogr, 1982; Co-Editor, Mehawa Le'Korczak (Homage to Korczak), anthology, 1986; Mi Ata Adon Grymek? (Who Are You Mr Grymek?), 1986; Editor, To byla Szkola Hebrajska w Krakowie (This was the Hebrew School in Cracow), 1989; Toldot ha'kolnoa ha'jeheudi be Polin (History of the Jewish Film in Poland), 1989; Co-Author, Haseret Ha'ivri (History of Israel Film), 1991. Contributions to: Various publications. Honours: Ben-Dor Prize, Davar Newspaper, 1960; Jugendpreis, Film Festival Berlin for feature, The Cellar, 1964; Numerous Israeli and International Film Festival Awards; Leon Lustig Prize for, Who are You Mr Grymek?, 1986; Israeli Union Performing Artists Award, 1989; Lifetime Acheievement Award Film Academy, 1991; Echo Krakowa Newspaper Prize for, Kim pan jest, panie Grymek, 1991. Memberships: Film Critics Section, Association Israeli Journalists; Film and TV Directors Guild, Israel. Address: 14 Herzog Street, Entr 3, Givataim 53586, Israel.

GROSS Philip John, b. 27 Feb 1952, Delabole. Freelance Writer; Creative Writing Tutor. m. Helen Gamsa, 1 son, 1 daughter. Education: BA, Honours, University of Sussex, 1973; Postgraduate Diploma in Librarianship, Polytechnic of North London, 1977. Appointments: Numerous residencies and teaching posts, most recently at Bath College of Higher Education. Publications: Familiars, 1983; The Ice Factory, 1984; Cat's Whiskers, 1987; The Air Mines of Mistila, 1988; Manifold Manor, for young people, 1989; The Song of Gail and Fludd, novel, 1991; The Son of the Duke of Nowhere, 1991; The All-Nite Café, 1993; I.D., poetry, 1994; The Wind Gate, novel, 1995. Contributions to: Numerous magazines and journals. Honours: Eric Gregory Award, 1981; Poetry Book Society Choice for, Air Mines of Mistila, 1988; Arts Council Bursary for Writing for Young People, 1990; Signal Award for Children's Poetry, 1994. Literary Agent: Lesley Hadcroft, Laurence Pollinger Ltd, 18 Maddox Street, London W1R 0EU, England. Address: 87 Berkeley Road, Bristol BS7 8HO, England.

GROVES Gene Tierney, b. 14 Aug 1951, Prestatyn, North Wales. Teacher. m. Richard Geoffrey Groves, 2 sons. Education: Rhyl High School, 1963-70; Certificate of Education, Elizabeth Gaskell College of Education, Manchester, 1974. Appointments: Various clerical and administrative jobs; Currently, Supply Teacher for Northumberland. Contributions to: New Welsh Review; Iron; Staple; Foolscap; Poetry Nottingham; Tees Valley Writer; Tidelines Anthology. Address: 3 Turners Way, Morpeth, Northumberland NE61 2YE, England.

GROVES Paul Raymond, b. 28 July 1947, Gloucester, England. Teacher. m. Annette Rushton Kelsall, 1 June 1972, 2 daughters. Education: Monmouth School, 1958-65; Teaching Certificate, Caerleon College of Education, 1969. Appointments: Assistant Master in various state schools; Evening Class Lecturer in Creative Writing; Visiting Poet in Schools, Poetry Society. Publications: Poetry Introduction 3, 1975; Green Horse, 1978; Academe, 1988; The Bright Field, 1991; Ménage à Trois, 1995. Contributions to: Critical Quarterly; Literary Review; London Magazine; New Statesman Society; Outposts Poetry Quarterly; Poetry Review; Poetry Wales; Dalhousie Review; Oxford

Poetry; Stand; Spectator; Times Literary Supplement; Wascana Review. Honours: Eric Gregory Award, 1976; First Prizes: The Times Literary Supplement/Cheltenham Festival, 1986, Green Book, 1986, Yeats Club, 1987, Surrey Poetry Group, 1987, 1988, 1991, Charterhouse International, 1989, 1990, Rainforest Trust, 1991; Orbis International, 1992; Bournemouth Festival, 1994. Membership: Poetry Society. Address: 44 Birch Park, Coleford, Gloucestershire GL16 7RU, England.

GRUBER Loren Charles, b. 17 Sept 1941, Carroll, Iowa, USA. Medievalist; Scholar; Writer. m. Meredith A Crellin, 22 Jan 1983, 1 son, 1 daughter. Education: BA, Simpson College, Iowa, 1963; MA, Western Reserve University, Ohio, 1964; PhD, University of Denver, Colorado, 1972. Appointments: Instructor to Associate Professor of English, Simpson College, Iowa; Chief Executive Consultant, Stanley, Barber, Southard, Brown and Associates, San Diego, California; Account Executive, Manager and News Director, Radio Stations; Assistant Professor of English, Northwest Missouri State University, Maryville, 1989-. Publications: Motion, Perception and Oppaet in Beowulf, 1974; The Agnostic Anglo-Saxon Gnomes: Maxims I and II, Germania and the Boundaries of Northern Wisdom, 1976; The Rites of Passage: Havamal, Stanzas 1-5, 1977; Co-Bibliographer, Middle English Research in Progress, Neuphilologische Mitteilungen, 1978-80; Editor, In Geardagum series, 1973-80. Contributions to: American Haiku; Lyrical Iowa; North American Mentor; Midstream; Sequel. Memberships: Life, Medieval Academy of America; Life, Society for the Advancement of Scandinavian Studies; Modern Language Association of America; Society for New Language Studies; Iowa Poetry Association; Indianola, Iowa Fine Arts Commission. Address: 310 West Clark, Clarinda, IA 51632, USA.

GRUMBACK Doris (Isaac), b. 12 July 1918, New York, New York, USA. Author; Critic; Former Professor of English. m. Leonard Grumbach, 15 Oct 1941, div 1972, 4 daughters. Education: AB, Washington Square College, 1939; MA, Cornell University, 1940. Appointments: Associate Editor, Architectural Forum, 1942-43; Teacher of English, Albany Academy for Girls, New York, 1952-55; Instructor, 1955-58, Assistant Professor, 1958-60, Associate Professor, 1960-69, Professor of English, 1969-73, College of Saint Rose, Albany; Visiting University Fellow, Empire State College, 1972-73; Literary Editor, New Republic, 1973-75; Adjunct Professor of English, University of Maryland, 1974-75; Professor of American Literature, American University, Washington, DC, 1975-85; Columnist and reviewer for various publications, radio, and television. Publications: The Spoil of the Flowers, 1962; The Short Throat, The Tender Mouth, 1964; The Company She Kept (biography of Mary McCarthy), 1967; Chamber Music, 1979; The Missing Person, 1981; The Ladies, 1984; The Magician's Girl, 1987; Coming Into the End Zone, 1992; Extra Innings: A Memoir, 1993; Fifty Days of Solitude, 1994; The Book of Knowledge: A Novel, 1995. Contributions to: Books and periodicals. Memberships: PEN; Phi Beta Kappa. Address: c/o Maxine Groffsky, 2 Fifth Avenue, New York, NY 10011, USA.

GRUMMAN Robert Jeremy, b. 2 Feb 1941, Norwalk, Connecticut, USA. Poet; Critic. Education: BA, English, California State University, Northridge, 1982. Publications: Of Manywhere-at-Once, 1990, 2nd edition, 1991; Spring Poem, 1990; Mathemaku 1-5, 1992; An April Poem, 1989; Mathemaku 6-12, 1994; Of Poem, 1995; Poems, 1996. Contributions to: Score; Kaldron; New Orleans Review; Poetry USA; Generator; Sub Bild, Germany; Freie Zeit Art, Austria; Offerta Speciale, Italy; Central Park; Sticks. Address: 1708 Hayworth Road, Port Charlotte, FL 33952-4529, USA.

GUBERMAN Jayseth, b. 4 April 1960, Bridgeport, Connecticut, USA. Freelance Writer. Education: BA, History, Sacred Heart University, Fairfield, Connecticut, 1981; Arabic and Islamic Studies, Yale University Graduate School, 1983-84; MA, Near East Studies, New York University, 1985. Appointments: Assistant Professor, Adjunct, Political Science, Sacred Heart University, Fairfield, Connecticut, 1987; Currently, Freelance Writer. Contributions to: Jewish Spectator; Jewish Currents; Judaism; Orim; A Jewish Journal at Yale; Israel Horizons; Response; Reconstructionist; New Zealand Jewish Chronicle; Black Buzzard Review; Prophetic Voices; Plowman Anthologies; Voices Israel; European Judaism; Martydom and Resistance. Memberships: Writers and Artists for Peace in the Middle East; International Society for Yad Va-Shem; Poets and Writers; Corresponding Member, New Zealand Association for the Study of Jewish Civilization; APS; SIP; JHPS; Phi Alpha Theta. Address: 294 South Quaker Lane, West Hartford, CT 06119, USA.

GUENTHER Charles John, b. 29 April 1920, St Louis, Missouri, USA. Writer; Teacher. m. Esther Laura (Klund) Guenther, 11 April 1942, 1 son, 2 daughters. Education: AA, Harris Teachers College, St Louis, 1940; BA 1973, MA 1974, Webster University; PhD Fellow, St Louis University, 1976-79; LHD, Southern Illinois University, 1979. Appointments: US Army Engineers; US Air Force Aero Chart and Information Service; Adjunct Professor or Instructor, various colleges and universities in USA. Publications: Modern Italian Poets, 1961; Phrase-Paraphrase, 1970; Paul Valéry in English, 1970; Voices in the Dark, 1974; Jules Laforgue Selected Poems, 1984; The Hippopotamus: Selected Translations 1945-85, 1986; High Sundowns, Translation J R Jimenez Poems, 1974; The Pluralism of Poetry, 1973; Moving the Seasons: Selected Poems, 1994. Contributions to: Poetry; American Poetry Review; Quarterly Review of Literature; Kenyon Review; Partisan Review; Nation; Reporter, Edge; Accent; Perspective; Minnesota Review; Priarie Schooner; Formalist; Critic; Literary Review; Audience; New Directions; American Women Poets, anthology, editor. Honours: James Joyce Award, Poetry Society of America, 1974; The Missouri Library Association Literary Award, 1974; Witter Bynner Poetry Translation Grant, Poetry Society of America, 1979; The Missouri Writers Guild Poetry Award, 1983, 1986, 1993; The Walter Williams Award for Major Work, 1987, 1995; Decorated Commander, Order of Merit of the Italian Republic, 1973; Awarded Doctor of Humane Letters, Southern Illinois University, 1979. Memberships: Academy of American Poets; Poetry Society of America, Midwest Vice-President, 1976-90; Past President, Missouri Writers Guild, St Louis Writers Guild and St Louis Poetry Center; American Literary Translators Association; Special Libraries Association. Address: 9877 Allendale Drive, St Louis, MO 63123, USA.

GUEST Barbara, b. 6 Sept 1920, Wilmington, North Carolina, USA. Writer; Poet; Novelist; Biographer. m. (1) Stephen, Lord Haden-Guest, 1948, div, (2) Trumbull Higgins, 1955, dec, 1 son, 1 daughter. Education: BA, University of California, Berkeley, 1943. Appointment: Associate, Art News, 1953-68. Publications: The Location of Things, 1960; Poems, 1963; The Blue Stairs, 1968; Moscow Mansions, 1973; Quilts, 1974; The Countess from Minneapolis, 1976; Seeking Air, novel, 1978; The Turler Losses, 1980; Biography, 1980; Herself Defined: H.D. The Poet and Her World, biography, 1984; Musicality, 1989; Fair Realism, 1989; The Altos, with artist, Richard Tuttle, 1991; Defensive Rapture, 1993; Selected Poems, 1995; Stripped Tales, with artist, Anne Dunn, 1995. Contributions to: Conjunctions; O-blek; New American Writing; American Poetry Review; Pembroke; Hambone; Art in America; Art News; Paris Review; Blue Mesa Review; Denver Quarterly; Iowa Review; New American Letters; Arshile; Chelsea Review. Honours: Longview Award, 1960; Laurence Lipton Award for Literature, University of Southern California, 1989; Poetry Award for, Defensive Rapture, San Francisco State University, 1995. Memberships: Poetry Society of America; PEN. Address: 49 West 16th Street, New York, NY 10011, USA.

GUEST (Henry) Harry (Bayly), b. 6 Oct 1932, Penarth, Glamorganshire, Wales. Retired. m. Lynn Dunbar, 28 Dec 1963, 1 son, 1 daughter. Education: BA, Trinity Hall, Cambridge; DES, Sorbonne, Paris. Appointments: Assistant Master, Felsted, 1955-61; Head of Modern Languages, Lancing, 1961-66; Lecturer, Yokohama National University, 1966-72; Head of Modern Languages, Exeter School, 1972-91; Japanese Teacher, Exeter University, 1979-95; Hawthornden Fellow, 1993; Honorary Research Fellow, Exeter University, 1994-. Publications: Arrangements, 1968; The Cutting-Room, 1970; A House Against The Night, 1976; Lost and Found, 1983; Coming to Terms, 1994. Contributions to: Ambit; Poetry Review; Atlantic Review; Pacific Quarterly; PN Review; English; Critical Quarterly; Poetry Australia; Comparative Criticism. Membership: General Council, Poetry Society, 1972-76. Address: 1 Alexandra Terrace, Exeter, Devon EX4 6SY, England.

GUETHE M Baugher, b. 21 Feb 1951, Lafayette, Indiana, USA. Medical Technologist. m. Richard, 18 May 1984, 1 son, 1 daughter. Education: Completed Lafayette Home Hospital Medical Technologist Program, 1970; Received Certification, 1971; Obtained Upgraded Certification by HEW, 1981. Appointments: Supervisor, RIA Laboratory, University of Lafayette, Department of Pediatrics; Supervisor, Pediatric Endoscopy Satellite Laboratory. Contributions to: Dream International Quarterly; Feelings; Capper's Poetry Explosion Newsletter; The Plowman; Tight; Penny Dreadful Review; Ralph's Review; One Earth, Scotland; En Plein Air, Switzerland; Sivullinen, Finland; First Time, England. Memberships: The Academy of

American Poets. Address: 1905 East Oak Street, New Albany, IN 47150-1727, USA.

GUGLIELMI Joseph Julien, b. 30 Dec 1929, Marseille, France. Primary School Teacher. m. Therese Bonnelalbay, dec, 2 sons, 1 daughter. Education: Baccalaureat Philosophie-Lettres, 1950; Propedentique lettres classiques, 1952; Primary School Teacher's Certificate, 1960. Publications: La Preparation des Titres, 1980; Aube, 1984; Fins de vers, 1986; Le Mouvement de la mort, 1988; Joe's Bunker, 1991; Principe de paysage, 1991. Contributions to: Action Poetique; Les Cahiers du Sud; Manteia; Change; Critique; La Quinzaine Litteraire; Ragile; Le Bulletin critique du Livre Francais; "A"; L'in Plano; Llanfair; Zuc; Nioque; Java; Oblek; Scripsi; Grosseteste; Acts; Moving Letters; Digraphe; Les Lettres Francaises; Docks; Translation; OARS; Notus; Skoria; Ironwood; and others. Honours: Sabbatical years granted by Le Centre National des Lettres, 1980, 1988. Address: 6 allee du Parc, 94200 Ivry sur Seine, France.

GUGLIELMO Dolores, b. 29 Aug 1928, Corona, Long Island, New York, USA. Poet. Education: BA, English, Queen's College, 1983; Currently pursuing Masters Degree in English, St John's University, Jamaica, New York. Appointments: Accounts Clerk, Mathieson Alkali Co, 1946-51; Secretary, Receptionist, Pan American Airways, 1951-55; Secretary to Vice President, Advertising, Pepsi Cola Co, 1955-67. Publications: Comet Racer, 1994; Black Picasso, 1994; He Was Mike, 1994; Ballad of Uriah Cabe, 1994; Heatwave, 1995; In a Japanese Tea Room, 1995; Shapes, 1995; House on Half Moon Street, 1995; Gas Station Cat, 1995; Ritual, 1995; The Forest, 1995; Truckline Cafe, 1995. Contributions to: The Ascent; Paper Salad; Poetic Page; Opus; Black Buzzard; Voices International; The Plowman; Rant; The Villager; Simply Words; Sivllinneki, collection, Finland, 1995-96; Summer Stream, collection, 1995-96; Oakham House, collection, 1995-96; Poetry in Motion; US Poets, collection, 1995-96; Lone Stars. Honours: Winner, International Poetry Contest, Seven Magazine, 1967; Poetry Recital on David Frost Show, 1970; English Honours Award, Queen's College, 1983; Writers Club Award for Excellence in Poetry, Queenborough Community College, 1992; Finalist, Guggenheim Fellowship, 1996, and Boxcar Poetry Competition, 1996. Memberships: World Poetry Society, Madras, India and Napa, CA, USA. Address: 43-44 Kissena Boulevard, Flushing, NY 11355, USA.

GUHA Ananya Sankar, b. 18 Feb 1957, Shillong, India. Academic Administrator. m. Punam Guha, 9 Mar 1995. Education: MA, English Literature, 1980, PhD, Fiction novels of William Golding, 1992, North Eastern University, Shillong. Appointments: Lecturer, Senior Lecturer, Department of English, St Edmund's College, Shillong, 1981-92; Assistant Regional Director and now Regional Director in Charge in Indira Gandhi, National Open University, Shillong, 1992-. Publications: What Else Is Alive, 1988; In This My Land, 1989. Contributions to: Poiesis, Bombay; Poetry Chronicle, Bombay; The Telegraph, Calcutta; New Welsh Review, Wales; Winterspin, New Zealand; Green's magazine, Canada; Brown Critique, Bombay. Honours: 1st Prize, All India Poetry Festival in Bombay (Youth of India Festival), 1979. Memberships: Assistant General Secretary of the Shillong Poetry Society, Writer's Forum, Ranchi; National Institute of Research in Indian English Literature, Gulbanga, India; Co-editor, Lyric (Shillong). Address: 'Mitali', Latumkhrah, Shillong 793003, Meghalaya, India.

GUIDA George, b. 17 Nov 1967, Brooklyn, New York, USA. College Instructor. Education: BA, Columbia College, 1989; MA, 1994, MPhil, 1995, City University of New York. Appointments: Instructor, City College, 1989-91; Instructor, Hunter College, 1991-95; Instructor, Barnard College, 1995-. Publications: In Low Italian, 1995; Stiletto Tongues, 1995. Contributions to: Voices in Italian American; Footwork: Patterson Literary Review; Poetry New York; Dream International Quarterly; Upstart; Columbia Guide to New York. Membership: Italian American Writers Association. Address: 120 West 44th Street, #1404, New York, NY 10036, USA.

GUINANE Alison Maria, b. 22 May 1948, Manchester, England. Retired Teacher. 1 daughter. Education: Hollies FCJ Convent, 1959-66; BA Honours, English, University of York, 1969; PGCE (Primary), University of Manchester, 1977; MA with Distinction, Creative Writing, University of Lancaster, 1993. Appointments: Teacher of English in charge of Integrated Humanities, Lower Secondary School, 1977-82; Teacher of English, in charge of Information Technology and Audio-Visual Resources, Sixth Form

College, 1982-94, retired. Publication: Through the Railings, 1991. Contributions to: Numerous poems published in small magazines and in anthologies; Orbis; Lancaster Lifefest, 1990, 1991, 1994; Staple. Membership: National Poetry Foundation, 1988-92. Address: Quince Cottage, 26 Upcast Lane, Wilmslow, Cheshire SK9 6EH, England.

GUJRAL Shiela, (Shiela), b. 24 Jan 1924, Lahore, India. Educationalist; Social Worker; Writer. m. I K Gujral, 26 May 1945, 2 sons. Education: MA, Economics, 1943; Diploma in Journalism, 1945; Diploma, Montessori Training, 1946. Appointments: Teacher in the 1950s; Later, Social Work and Writing; Editor, Seema Raksha (Hindi), 1963-64. Publications: Jagi Janata (Hindi), 1963; Ghungat Ke Pat (Hindi), 1974; Sagar Tat Par (Hindi), 1980; Two Black Cinders (English), 1985; Anunad (Hindi), 1986; Amar Vel (Punjabi), 1986; Niara Hindustan (Punjabi), 1989; Nishwas (Hindi), 1989; Signature of Silence (English), 1991; Mahak, short stories in Punjabi, 1992; Tapovan Mae Bawandei, short stories in Hindi, 1992; Throttled Dove, English poetry, 1995; Jab Mai Na Rahu, Hindi poetry, 1995; Sangli, Punjabi Poetry, 1995. Contributions to: Indian English Poetry Journals and Literary Journals in Hindi and Punjabi; Translations of poems published in Urdu, Arabic, Russian, Uzbek and Latvian. Honours: DLitt, World Academy of Art and Culture, 1992; Golden Poet Awards, 1989, 1990; Nirala Award, Hindi Poetry, 1989. Memberships: Chairman, various Child Welfare Organisations, 1960-76; President, Country Women's Club, 1972-76; President, Delhi Parent-Teacher Association, 1972-76; President, Lekhika Sangh, Women Writers Association, 1981-86; PEN; Authors Guild; Indian Poetry Society. Address: G-13 Maharani Bagh, New Delhi 110065, India.

GULDAGER Katrine Marie, b. 29 Dec 1966, Maglegaard, Copenhagen, Denmark. Writer. Education: Candidate Phil in Danish Literature, 1994. Publications: Days Are Changing Hands, 1994; Crash, 1995; Blank, 1996. Honours: Prize for Days Are Changing Hands, 1994; Travel Grant to Southern Africa, 1994; 3 Year Working Grant, 1995; The Humour Prize, 1996; Henri Nathansens Memory Grant, 1996. Memberships: The Danish Writers Union. Address: c/o Gyldendal, Klareboderne 3, 1001 Copenhagen N, Denmark.

GUNDERSON Joanna, b. 14 May 1932, New York, New York, USA. Writer; Publisher. m. Warren Gunderson, 2 May 1970, 1 son, 1 daughter. Education: BS, Columbia University, 1954. Appointments: Writer, 1955-; Publisher, Red Dust, 1963-. Publications: Indrani and I; Sights; Three Novellas. Creative works: Plays: Kaleidoscope, full-length play, 1969; Adult Education, short play, 1985; She, full-length play; Voice from the Field; Color, full-length play; Crystal, full-length play; One-Act Plays: Plants; Motion; Voices of This Century; Hieroglyphics of the Night; Bells. Contributions to: Rampike; Midland Review; Northeast Journal; How(ever); Frank. Address: 1148 Fifth Avenue No 12B, New York, NY 10128, USA.

GUNDERSON Keith Robert, b. 29 Aug 1935, New Ulm, Minnesota, USA. Professor of Philosophy; Writer. m. (1) 3 sons, (2) Sandra Riekki, 28 July 1979. Education: BA, Philosophy, Macalester College, St Paul, Minnesota, 1957; BA, Philosophy, Worcester College, Oxford University, 1959; PhD, Philosophy, Princeton University, 1963. Appointments: Instructor of Philosophy, Princeton University, 1962-64; Assistant Professor, University of California at Los Angeles, 1964-67; Associate Professor, 1967-70, Professor, 1971-, of Philosophy, University of Minnesota. Publications: A Continual Interest in The Sun and Sea, 1971; 3142 Lyndale Avenue So, Apt 24, 20 selections of prose poems, 1974; To See a Thing, 1975; A Continual Interest in The Sun and Sea and Inland, Missing the Sea, 1976. Contributions to: Western Humanities Review; Prairie Schooner; Massachusetts Review; American Poetry Review; North Stone Review; Milkweed; Chronicle; South and West; Burning Water; Trace; New Mexico Quarterly; Epoch; Black Flag; Chelsea; others; Various poems set to music by composers, Sydney Hodkinson, Eastman School of Music, and Eric Stokes, University of Minnesota. Honours: National Endowment for The Arts Grant for Poetry, 1974; Minnesota State Arts Board Grant, 1979. Memberships: Los Angeles Incognoscent, 1964-; Managing Editor, Minnesota Writers Publishing House, 1979-83. Address: 1212 Lakeview Avenue South, Minneapolis, MN 55416, USA.

GUNESEKERA Romesh, b. 26 Feb 1954, Sri Lanka. Appointments: Tutor, Arvon Foundation Writing Course, 1991; Judge, Peterloo Open Poetry Competition, 1991. Publication: Special Issue Poetry Durham, No 11, Winter 1985. Contributions to: Ambit; Artrage; Guardian; London Magazine; London Review of Books; Other Poetry;

Pen; Poetry Durham; Poetry Matters; Poetry Now. Honours: Commendation, Poetry Society National Poetry Competition, 1988; Commendation, Peterloo Open Poetry Competition, 1988; 1st Prize, Peterloo Open Poetry Competition, Afro-Caribbean/Asian Section, 1988; Joint 1st Prize, Stanzas 85, London, 1985; Best First Work Award, Yorkshire Post, 1994. Address: c/o Granta Books, 2-3 Hanover Yard, Noel Road, Islington, London N1 8BE, England.

GUNN Thom(son William), b. 29 Aug 1929, Gravesend, England. Teacher. Education: BA, 1953, MA, 1958, Cambridge University. Appointments: Lecturer, 1958-61, Assistant Professor, 1961-64, Associate Professor, 1964-66, University of California at Berkeley; Freelance, 1967-73; Visiting Lecturer, 1973-89, Senior Lecturer, 1989-, University of California at Berkeley. Publications: Fighting Terms, 1954; The Sense of Movement, 1957; My Sad Captains, 1961; Positives, with Ander Gunn, 1966; Touch, 1967; Moly, 1971; Jack Straw's Castle, 1976; Selected Poems, 1979; The Passages of Joy, 1982; The Occasions of Poetry, prose, 1982; The Man with Night Sweats, 1992; Collected Poems, 1993; Shelf Life, prose, 1993. Contributions to: Times Literary Supplement; Threepenny Review; PN Review. Honours: Levinson Prize for Poetry, 1955; W H Smith Prize, 1979; Sara Teasdale Prize, 1988; Robert Kirsch Award, Los Angeles Times, 1988; Shelley Memorial Award, 1990; Lila Wallace Reader's Digest Grant, 1991-93; 1st Prize, Forward Poetry Prize, 1992; Bay Area Book Reviewers' Award for Poetry, 1993; PEN USA West Prize for Poetry, 1993; Fellow of American Academy of Arts and Sciences, 1993; MacArthur Fellow, 1993; Lenore Marshall Poetry Prize, 1993. Address: 1216 Cole Street, San Francisco, CA 94117, USA.

GUNNARSDOTTIR (Asta) Berglind, b. 5 Dec 1953, Reykjavík, Iceland. Writer; Teacher of Spanish. 3 daughters. Education: Commercial College of Iceland; BA, Spanish and Linguistics, University of Iceland, including one year at Universidad de Complutense, Madrid, Spain. Appointments: Various part-time jobs; Freelance Writer and Teacher, programmes for radio and translating; Editorial work, two publications of Yearbook of Icelandic Poetry. Publications: Ljod Fyrir Lifi, 1983; Ljodsott, 1986; Ljosbrot i Skuggann, 1990; Flugfiskur, 1992; Allsherjargodinn, 1992; Bragd Af Eilifd, 1995. Contributions to: Timarit Mals og Menningar; Lesbok Morgunbladsins; Andvari; Sky; Bjartur og Fru Emilia; Arbok, 1988. Membership: Rithöfundasamband Islands (Writer's Union of Iceland). Address: Holtsgata 37, 101 Reykjavík, Iceland.

GUNTON DEAL Kathleen, b. 12 Oct 1946, Santa Monica, California, USA. Writer; Teacher. m. 2 sons, 1 daughter. Education: AA, Orange Coast College, 1978; BA, California State University, Long Beach, 1982. Contributions to: America; Lyric; Christian Science Monitor; California State Poetry Quarterly; The Rectangle; Abbey; Vintage 45. Honours: Professor Foote Writing Award, California State University, Long Beach, 1982; Sigma Tau Delta Writer's Key, 1985; UFCW Writing Award, 1986; Honourable Mention, Writer's Digest, 1988, 1989, 1990; Robert Frost Gold Award, San Mateo, 1989; Edna St Vincent Millay, San Mateo, 1990. Memberships: Sigma Tau Delta; California State Poetry Society. Address: 1209 South Mohawk Drive, Santa Ana, CA 92704, USA.

GUPTA Sumitra. See: **DASGUPTA Manjush.**

GURKIN Mary Kathryn Bright, b. 23 Nov 1934, Whiteville, North Carolina, USA. Poet. m. Worth Wicker Gurkin, 9 July 1955, 3 sons. Education: Valedictorian, Class Poet, Whiteville, North Carolina, 1953; Meredith College, 1953-55. Appointments: Founding President, 1972-73, Executive Director, 1975-76, Sampson County Arts Council. Publications: Rorschach, 1977; Terra Amata, 1980; Stainless Steel Soprano, 1990. Contributions to: Pembroke Magazine; St Andrews Review; Southern Poetry Review; International Poetry Review; Texas Review; Crucible. Honours: St Andrews Poetry Award, 1977; Zoe Kincaid Brockman Book Award, 1980; Nomination for Pulitzer Prize for, Stainless Steel Soprano, 1990. Memberships: Corresponding Secretary, 1974, North Carolina Poetry Society; North Carolina Writers; Dead Poets Society, Edenton, North Carolina. Address: 1009 West Queen Street, Edenton, NC 27932, USA.

GUT Karen. See: **ALKALAY-GUT Karen Hillary.**

GUTIERREZ VEGA Hugo, b. 11 Feb 1934, Mexico. Diplomat; Lecturer. m. 21 Nov 1960, 3 daughters. Education: Degrees in Law, Mexico, Italian Literature, Rome, and English Literature, London.

Appointments: Dean, University of Queretaro, Mexico; Director of Cultural Extension, National University of Mexico; Diplomat in Rome, Italy, Moscow, London, Madrid, Washington and Rio de Janeiro; Ambassador of Mexico in Greece, Lebanon, Cyprus, Romania and Moldova; Lecturer, National University, Mexico. Publications: Buscado Amor, 1965; Des de Inglaterra, 1969; Cantos de Plasencia; Resistencia de Particulares, 1976; Cuando el Placer Termine, 1976; Meridiano 8-0, 1980; Antologia, 1980; Cantos de Tomelloso, 1982; Las Peregrinaciones del Deseo, Poesia Revnida, 1965-86; Audar En Brasil, 1985; Los Soles Griegos, 1986; Cantos del Despotado de Morea, 1991; His poems are translated into English, French, Italian, Portuguese, Russian, Romanian and Greek. Contributions to: Cuadernos Hispano Americanos; Siglo XX; Estafeta; Times Literary Supplement; Vuelta; Nexos. Honours: National Prize for Poetry, Mexico, 1976; Order of Alfonso X Elsabio, Isabel la Catolica, and Commendatore. Memberships: Director, Revista de la Universidad de Mexico; PEN Club of Mexico. Address: Mexican Embassy, Diamandidou 73, Paleo Psychico, Athens 15452, Greece.

GUTTERIDGE Donald George, b. 30 Sept 1937, Sarnia, Ontario, Canada. Professor Emeritus. m. Margaret Anne Barnett, 30 June 1961, 1 son, 1 daughter. Education: BA, Honours, English, University of Western Ontario, London, Canada. Appointments: Teacher, 1960-67; Professor of English Methods, now Professor Emeritus, 1968-; Director, The Althouse Press, 1990-. Publications: Riel: A Poem for Voices, 1968; The Village Within, 1970; Death at Quebec, 1971; Saying Grace: An Elegy, 1972; Coppermine: The Quest for North, 1973; Tecumseh, 1975; Borderlands, 1976; A True History of Lambton County, 1977; God's Geography, 1982; The Exiled Heart, 1986; Love in the Wintertime, 1990. Contributions to: Queens Quarterly; Fiddlehead; Contemporary Verse II; Poetry Canada Review. Honour: President's Medal, University of Western Ontario, 1972. Memberships: League of Canadian Poets, 1970-81; Writers Union of Canada, 1988-. Address: 114 Victoria Street, London, Ontario N6A 2B5, Canada.

GUTTMAN Naomi, b. 10 July 1960, Montreal, Quebec, Canada. Teacher. m. Jonathan Mead, 6 July 1986. Education: BFA, Concordia University, 1985; MFA, Warren Wilson College, 1988; MA, English, Loyola Marymount University, Los Angeles, 1992. Publication: Reasons for Winter, 1991. Contributions to: Malahat Review; Matrix. Honours: Bliss Carman Award for Poetry, Banff School of Fine Arts, 1989; QSpell Award for Poetry, 1992. Address: 356 North Spaulding Avenue, Los Angeles, CA 90036, USA.

GUY Scott, b. 26 Nov 1958, Chicago, Illinois, USA. Television and Film Writer. Education: BS, magna cum laude, Northwestern University, 1979; MFA, University of California at Los Angeles, 1981. Appointments: Artistic Director, Passage Theatre; Head Writer, NBC's Our Place, Flying Whales and Peacock Tales; Collaborations with Milcho Leviev, Ed Zelnis, Ken Nevfeld and John Vorhaus. Publications: Verse: The Loot of Loma, 1979; Hugh Selwyn Mauberley (after Pound), 1980; Edward II, 1980; Our Place, 1986; Flying Whales and Peacock Tales, 1987; A Christmas Warning, 1989; The Pooblies, 1991; The Green House, 1991; Kensington Gardens, 1992; Der Curmudgeon Lieder, 1992; The Coming of Madness, 1993; Outcasts of the Dark Boneyard, 1993. Contributions to: Passage Theatre; Children's Classical Theatre; Urban Gateways; Encino Playhouse; Performing Tree; Los Angeles Jazz Choir; NBC; C and K Productions; Xanadu Theatre. Honours: Illinois Arts Council Individual Artist Grant, 1981; Rosenbaum Foundation Musical Comedy Grant, 1986; Multiple Emmy Award nominations for lyrics and scripts for NBC, 1986, 1987; Commission from Los Angeles Jazz Choir to write libretto of, The Green House, a jazz cantata in 7 movements; California Arts Council Screenwriting Fellowship, 1992; Los Angeles Cultural Affairs Department Fellowship, 1992; Finalist, Eugene O'Neill Musical Theatre Conference, 1993. Address: 6650 Hayvenhurst, No 229, Van Nuys, CA 91406, USA.

GYŐRI Ladislao Pablo, b. 13 July 1963, Buenos Aires, Argentina. Engineer. Education: Graduated as Electronic Engineer, National Technological University of Buenos Aires, 1989. Appointment: Assistant to sculptor Kosice, responsible for technical advice, maintenance, project and construction of water circulation, lighting, electronics and movement systems, 1990-95. Publication: Estiajes, Creator of Virtual Poetry, 1994. Contributions to: Dimensao; Intimacy; Teraz Mowie; P.O.Box; Piel de Leopardo; Visible Language; Luz en Arte & Literatura. Memberships: Argentinian Society of Writers; Co-Founder, Argentinian Tevat Group for the Research and Diffusion

of Poetry and Arts and New Technology. Address: Avenue Federico
Lacroze 3814 2do 10 (1427), Buenos Aires, Argentina.

H

HA Kil-Nam, b. 4 Mar 1934, Nakano, Japan. Managing Director of University Library. m. Ham chun-ja, 28 Nov 1968, 3 sons. Education: Graduate, Kyungbuk National University, Korea, 1958; Graduate, Graduate School of Education, Kyungnam University, 1986. Appointments: Chief Editor, Kyungnam University Press, 1980-; Director, Chungang Library, Kyungnam University, 1989-. Publications: Essays: The Legacy That I'd Like to Possess, 1982; Friendship Like the Sunset, 1983; In the Name of Longing, 1989; Poetry: The Wind Blowing in the Deep Sea, Indangsu, 1986. Contributions to: Literary Books, Newspapers, Professional Poetry Books, Professional Essay Books, Literary Poetry Books. Honours: Prize of Masan City's Culture, 1990; Literary Prize of Poetry and Consciousness, 1990. Memberships: Korea Literary Society; Korean Poets Association; Korean Modern Poets Association; Korean New Poetry Studies Association; International Poets Association; Korean Essayists Association. Address: 503 Weol Young Apartment, 2-11 Weolpo-dong, Hapo-gu, Masan 631-410, South Korea.

HACKER Marilyn, b. 27 Nov 1942, New York, New York, USA. Poet; Writer; Critic; Editor; Teacher. 1 daughter. Education: BA, Romance Languages, New York University, 1964. Appointments: Editor, Quark: A Quarterly of Speculative Fiction, 1969-71, The Kenyon Review, 1990-94; Jenny McKean Moore Chair in Writing, George Washington University, 1976-77; Member, Editorial Collective, 1977-80, Editor-in-Chief, 1979, The Little Magazine; Teacher, School of General Studies, Columbia University, 1979-81; Visiting Artist, Fine Arts Work Center, Provincetown, Massachusetts, 1981; Visiting Professor, University of Idaho, 1982; Editor-in-Chief, Thirteenth Moon: A Feminist Literary Magazine, 1982-86; Writer-in-Residence, State University of New York, Albany, 1988, Columbia University, 1988; George Elliston Poet-in-Residence, University of Cincinnati, 1988; Distinguished Writer-in-Residence, American University, Washington DC, 1989; Visiting Professor of Creative Writing, State University of New York, Binghamton, 1990, University of Utah, 1995, Barnard College, 1995, Princeton University, 1997; Fannie Hurst Poet-in-Residence, Brandeis University, 1996. Publications: Presentation Piece, 1974; Separations, 1976; Taking Notice, 1980; Assumptions, 1985; Love, Death and the Changing of the Seasons, 1986; The Hang-Glider's Daughter: New and Selected Poems, 1990; Selected Poems: 1965-1990, 1994; Winter Numbers, 1994; Edge (translator of poems by Claire Malroux), 1996. Contributions to: Numerous anthologies and other publications. Honours: National Endowments for the Arts Grants, 1973-74, 1985-86, 1995; National Book Award in Poetry, 1975; Guggenheim Fellowship, 1980-81; Ingram-Merrill Foundation Grant, 1984-85; Robert F Winner Awards, 1987, 1989, John Masefield Memorial Award, 1994, Poetry Society of America; Lambda Literary Awards, 1991, 1995; Lenore Marshall Award, Academy of American Poets, 1995; Poets' Prize, 1995. Address: 230 West 105th Street, New York, NY 10025, USA.

HACKNEY Frances Marie Veda, b. 14 July 1917, Sydney, New South Wales, Australia. Botanist; General and Human Biologist. m. Walter Frederick Frohlich, 19 Mar 1949, 3 sons, 3 daughters. Education: BSc, 1st Class Honours, 1938, MSc, 1940, DSc, 1949, Sydney University; Postgraduate Studies in Zoology, Human Histology. Appointments: Linnaean Macleay Fellow, Research; Council for Scientific and Industrial Research and Botany Department, Sydney University, 1940-49; Various positions, Sydney University, University of New South Wales, Macquarie University, 1964-81. Publications: Bread and Butter Moon, 1956; Australian Science, Essays, 1964; For All I Have Loved, Poetry, 1994. Contributions to: Sydney Morning Herald; Northern Herald; SMH Supplement; Bulletin Press; Catholic Weekly; Annals Australia; Beneath the Southern Cross I and II, anthology; World Poetry, Annual Anthology, 1990-1997; International Poetry Magazine, 1990-; Art Voice, 1994; Compass, 1994. Honours: Australian Women's Weekly Poetry Prize, 1965; Australia Day Council's Medal for Achievement, 1987; Australia Day Council's Bicentennial Gold Medal, 1988; New South Wales Senior Citizens Gold Medal, 1989; Australia Day Council's Medal for Achievement, Jan, Aug, 1991; Binalong Banjo Paterson Poetry prize, 1991; Twice 1st Prize Winner, Melbourne Poetry Society, 1987, 1991; Writing Fellow, Fellowship of Australian Writers, 1993; Citizenship's Award, for Services to Music and the Arts, 1996. Memberships: Archivist, Fellowship of Australian Writers; Fellow Member, International Poets

HADAS Rachel, b. 8 Nov 1948, New York, New York, USA. Professor of English; Poet; Writer. m. (1) Stavros Kondilis, 7 Nov 1970 div 1978, (2) George Edwards, 22 July 1978, 1 son. Education: BA, Classics, Radcliffe College, 1969; MA, Poetry, Johns Hopkins University, 1977; PhD, Comparative Literature, Princeton University, 1982. Appointments: Assistant Professor, 1982-87, Associate Professor, 1987-92, Professor of English, 1992-, Rutgers University; Adjunct Professor, Columbia University, 1992-93; Visiting Professor, Princeton University, 1995. Publications: Starting From Troy, 1975; Slow Transparency, 1983; A Son From Sleep, 1987; Pass It On, 1989; Living in Time, 1990; Unending Dialogue, 1991; Mirrors of Astonishment, 1992; Other Worlds Than This, 1994; The Empty Bed, 1995; The Double Legacy, 1995. Contributions to: Periodicals. Honours: Ingram-Merrill Foundation Fellowship, 1976-77; Guggenheim Fellowship, 1988-89; American Academy and Institute of Arts and Letters Award, 1990. Memberships: Fellow, American Academy of Arts and Sciences; Modern Greek Studies Association; Modern Language Association; PEN; Poetry Society of America. Address: 838 West End Avenue 3A, New York, NY 10025, USA.

HAECKER Hans Joachim, b. 25 Mar 1910, Königsberg, Germany. Retired Assistant Master of Secondary School; Writer; Poet; Dramatist. m. Irmtraut Krause, 14 Aug 1938, dec 1976, 2 sons, 2 daughters. Education: Abitur, 1929; University Examination in Philosophy, English and German, 1934; Teachers Examination, 1936. Appointments: Assistant Master, various secondary schools, 1941-72. Publications: Hiob, drama, 1937; Die Insel Leben, poems, 1942; Teppich der Geschichte, poems, 1947; Der Tod des Odysseus, drama, 1947; Dreht euch nuicht um, drama, 1961; Gedenktag, drama, 1962; Der Brieftrager Kommt, drama, 1962; Nicht im Hause-Nicht auf der Strausse, drama, 1978; Lauztloser Alarm, poems, 1977; Werke Michel Angelos, poems, 1975; Der Traum vom Traume des Lazrus, essay, 1978; Registriert im XX Jahrhundert, poems, 1980; Existentielismus der Distanz, essay, 1984; Gedichte, 1985; Rauchzeichen, stories, 1990; Haikuge dichte, 1993. Contributions to: Die Horen; Rheinischer Merkur; Frankfurter Allgemeine Zeitung; Die Welt; Universität; Österreichische Furche; Podium, Vienna. Honours: Gerhart Hauptmann Prize, 1961; Niedersächsuches Künstlerstipendum, 1979; Plesse Literatur Prize, 1986; Kogge, Ring of Honour, 1989. Memberships: European Writers Association; International Press Association; German Writers Association. Address: Krasseltweg 34, D-3000 Hanover, Germany.

HAGEN Edna (Sue), b. 9 April 1957, Sandpoint, Idaho, USA. Preparatory Cook; Poet; Songwriter. m. Curtis Hagen, 3 August 1992. Education: Studied at Kalispell College, 2 years. Appointments: Poet, working from home on poetry and songs; Founder of Poetry for the Gifted and Talented Program, School District 5, Kalispell, Montana, 1982; Involved with the Poets Convention for nine years and was invited to attend a poetry convention in Washington DC, 1995. Publications: Satin and Lace by Edna Hagen, 1989; Selected Poetry by Edna Hagen, 1995; April's Song, 1996. Honours include: Golden Poetry Award, Library of Poets, 1991; Editor's Choice Award, Inter Lake newspaper, 1994; Blue Ribbon Winner for poem, Southern Poetry Association, 1994; Honourable Mention, Poet of the Year Competition, 1994; Magic Key Award, for songs and production, 1994; Won song writing award for, Pieces Of The Heart, 1994; Special Recording Award, Edlee Music, 1995; Winner, Top Writer Award, Song Writers Association, 1995; Certificate of Excellence for poem, And Time Stood Still, National Poetry Association, 1995; Included in World of Poetry for Springtime in Montana; Special Certificate, New Voices, JMV Publishing, 1996; Certificate of Publication, Impressions, 1996; Poem, Underneath Montana Skies in the National Authors Registry; Winner, Happiness Award for, Poetry is Happiness Booklet; Golden Poetry Award for poem, My Father's Home. Memberships: National Poetry Association, 1982-; Kalispell Poetry Association. Address: 526 4th Street West, Kalispell, MT 59901, USA.

HAIG Margaret Jane Darrah, b. 7 Dec 1919, Gambusnethan, Strathclyde, Scotland. Co-Director of London School of English. m. James Peacock Haig, 15 Dec 1964, 1 son. Education: ASCT, 1956; FSCT, 1964; AIST, 1965; WHO, 1967. Appointments: Head, Department of Cardiological Technicians; Reader of English, University of Parma, Italy; Co-Director, London School of English, Parma. Publications: Fragmentary Thoughts of Time Place and Space,

1990; Beyond the Frontiers, 1991; Along the Banks of Time, 1992. Contributions to: James Joyce Quarterly Journal, USA; Plowman International Journal of Poetry, Canada; Eavesdropper Journal of Poetry, London. Honours: 1990 Xth International Award for Literature; Colombini Cenelli Award; Finishing with Poem Montalcino written in English and Italian. Memberships: National Poetry Society, London; Plowman Journal of Poetry and Literature, Canada; Poetry Society, Palma; Eavesdropper Society, London. Address: Via Bruno Longht 11, 43100 Parma, Italy.

HAINES Brian William, b. 24 Jan 1918, Devonport, Devon, England. Writer; Researcher. Appointments: Solicitor and Barrister, Supreme Court, Victoria, Australia, 1967. Publications: Four Winds, 1948; A Book of Epigrams, 1950; Lark in the Morning, 1952; Block Towers, 1960; Other publications include technical writing, short stories and novels. Contributions to: Poetry and reviews: Daily Herald; News Chronicle. Membership: Life Member, Poetry Society, London. Address: 9a Sharpleshall Street, London NW1 8YN, England.

HAINES John (Meade), b. 29 June 1924, Norfolk, Virginia, USA. Poet; Writer; Teacher. m. (1) Jo Ella Hussey, 10 Oct 1960, (2) Jane McWhorter, 23 Nov 1970, div 1974, (3) Leslie Sennett, Oct 1978, div, 4 children. Education: National Art School, Washington DC, 1946-47; American University, 1948-49; Hans Hoffmann School of Fine Art, New York City, 1950-52; University of Washington, 1974. Appointments: Poet-in-Residence, University of Alaska, 1972-73; Visiting Professor in English, University of Washington, 1974; Visiting Lecturer in English, University of Montana, 1974; Writer-in-Residence, Sheldon Jackson College 1982-83, Uncross Foundation 1987, Montalvo Center for the Arts 1988, Djerassi Foundation 1988; Visiting Lecturer, University of California at Santa Cruz, 1986; Visiting Writer, The Loft Mentor Series, 1987; Visiting Professor, Ohio University, 1989-90; Visiting Writer, George Washington University, 1991-92; Chair in Creative Arts, Austin Peay State University, Clarksville, Tennessee, 1993; Visiting Lecturer, Annual Wordsworth Conference, Grasmere, UK, 1996. Publications: Poetry: Winter News, 1966, revised edition 1983; Suite for the Pied Piper, 1968; The Legend of Paper Plates, 1970; The Mirror, 1970; The Stone Harp, 1971; Twenty Poems, 1971, 3rd edition, 1982; Leaves and Ashes, 1975; In Five Years, 1976; Cicada, 1977; In a Dusty Light, 1977; The Sun on Your Shoulder, 1977; News from the Glacier: Selected Poems 1960-1980, 1982; New Poems: 1980-1988, 1990; Rain Country, 1990; The Owl in the Mask of a Dreamer, 1993; Fables and Distances, New and Selected Essays, 1996; A Guide to the Four-Chambered Heart, 1996. Contributions to: Various periodicals and anthologies. Honours include: Elliston Fellow in Poetry, University of Cincinnati, 1992; Lenore Marshall Nation Award, 1991; Literary Award, American Academy of Arts & Letters, 1995. Memberships include: Academy of American Poets; PEN American Center; Poetry Society of America; Sierra Club. Address: PO Box 103431, Anchorage, AK 99510, USA.

HAINES John Francis, b. 30 Nov 1947, Chelmsford, Essex, England. Local Government Officer. m. Margaret Rosemary Davies, 19 Mar 1977. Education: Hull High School for Commerce, 1959-66; Padgate College of Education, 1966-69; ONC in Public Administration, Millbank College of Commerce, 1972. Appointments: General Assistant; Payments Assistant. Publications: Other Places, Other Times, 1981; Spacewain, 1989; After the Android Wars, 1992. Contributions to: Dark Horizons; Fantasy Commentator; First Time; Folio; Idomo; Iota; Macabre; New Hope International; Not To Be Named; Overspace; Purple Patch; Sandor; The Scanner; Simply Thrilled Honey; Spokes; Star Line; Stride; Third Half; Yellow Dwarf; A Child's Garden of Olaf; A Northern Chorus; Ammonite; Boggers All; Eldritch Science; Foolscap; Heliocentric Net; Lines of Light; Ore; Pablo Lennis; Pleiade; Premonitions; Mentor; Rampant Guinea Pig; Zone; Positively Poetry; What Poets Eat; Mexicon 6 - The Party; Terrible Work; Xenophilia. Memberships: Science Fiction Poetry Association; British Fantasy Society; Founder Member, The Eight Hand Gang, an association of British Science Fiction Poets. Address: 5 Cross Farm, Station Road, Padgate, Warrington WA2 0QG, England.

HAKAK Balfour Medad, b. 26 Apr 1948, Iraq. Education: Hebrew Literature and Bible Studies, The Hebrew University, Jerusalem, 1970-77; BA, MA degrees with distinction. Appointments: Young Journalist, Ma'ariv Lanoar, 1963-66; Teaching in High School, 1974-87; Curriculum Planning, Israeli Curriculum Centre, Ministry of Educatin, 1977-; Editing a Teachers' Journal, 1986-. Publications: 4 poetry books, 1970, 1972, 1978, 1987. Honours: Won 2 literary prizes. Memberships: Hebrew Writers Association, 1982-; Founder,

Assocation of Zionist Writers; Jerusalem Sepharadi Board; Association for the Jewish-Iraqi Heritage. Address: PO Box 1508, Mevaseret Zion 90805, Israel.

HAKAK Herzl, b. 1948, Iraq. m. 3 sons, 1 daughter. Education: Hebrew University, Jerusalem, 1970-77. Appointment: Young Journalists, Ma'ariv Lanoar, 1963-66. Publications: 4 poetry books, 1970, 1972, 1978, 1987. Honours: 2 literary prizes. Memberships: Hebrew Writers Association, 1982-, Chairman Criticism Committee; Zionist Writers; Jerusalem Sepharadi Board; Association for the Jewish Iraqi Heritage. Address: PO Box 1506, Mevaseret, Zion 90805, Israel.

HAKIM Sy (Seymour), b. 23 Jan 1933, New York, New York, USA. Artist; Poet. m. Odetta Roverso, 18 Aug 1970. Education: AB, Eastern New Mexico University, 1954; MA, New York University, 1960; Postgraduate work at various universities including: University of California, Pennsylvania, Massachusetts, Brigham Young University, and Clemson. Appointments: Teacher of Art, Tucumcari, New Mexico, 1957; English Guidance, New York City, 1958-60; Teacher of Art, English and Photography, Department of Defense Schools in Germany, Italy and England, 1960-93; Chairperson, Language Arts Department, Vicenza School, 1980-93. Publications: Manhattan Goodbye, 1970; Undermoon, 1970; In The Museum of The Mind, 1971; Wine Theorem, 1972; Substituting Memories, 1975; Iris Elegy, 1979; Balancing Act, 1981; Eleanor Goodbye, 1988. Contributions to: Consultant Editor, Poet Gallery Press, 1970-83; Editor, Overseas Teacher, 1977; Works in various magazines and journals including California State Quarterly, American Writing, Dan River Anthology, It's On My Wall, and Older Eyes. Memberships: Association of Writers and Poets; National Photo Instructors Association, 1980-88; Italo-Brittanica Association. Address: 3726 Manayunk Avenue, Philadelphia, PA 19128, USA.

HALEY Patricia, (Rosie Lee, Reuben Augustus), b. 17 Jan 1951, Waxachie, Texas, USA. Therapist; Teacher; Writer. Education: BA, Texas Woman's University, 1973; MEd, University of North Texas, 1994; Licensed Professional Counselor. Appointments: Staff Therapist, Columbia Medical Center, Lancaster, Texas; Teacher, Business English, St Philips College, San Antonio, Texas; School Councelor, Ferris Elementary School, Ferris, Texas; Teacher, Supervisor, Life Skills Centre, Ennis Junior High School, Texas; Founder, Editor, Publisher, Poetic Perspective Inc, 1988-. Publications: Family Tributes, 1989; Therapeutic Poetry, 1990; Heroes: A Poetic Perspective, 1991. Contributions to: American Poetry Anthology; Images; Silver Wings; Diamonds and Rust; Poetry Press; Poetry Unlimited. Honours: Honourable Mention, Galaxy's James Spencer Contest 1989; Poet of Merit, American Poetry Association and Certificate of Poetic Achievement, 1989; Honourable Mention, Poetry Arts Project, 1990. Memberships: National Association of Poetry Therapy; Poetry Society of America; Poetry Society of Texas; Galaxy of Verse Foundation; American Counceling Association; Texas Counseling Association. Address: 110 Onieda Street, Waxahachie, TX 75165, USA.

HALIM Huri. See: **OFFEN Yehuda.**

HALL Bernadette Mary, b. 6 Dec 1945, Alexandra, South Island, New Zealand. Secondary School Teacher. m. John Hall, 13 Jan 1968, 2 sons, 1 daughter. Education: MA, Honours, Otago University, 1968. Appointments: Assistant Teacher, Villa Maria College; Tutor in Creative Writing, University of Canterbury. Publications: Heartwood, 1989; Of Elephants, etc. 1990; The Persistent Leviator, 1994. Contributions to: Soho Square; Landfall; Sport; Poetry NZ; Contemporary New Zealand Poetry; Vital Writing; Carcanet; Takahe magazine, Editor (poetry). Honours: Writer-in-Residence, University of Canterbury, Christchurch, 1991; Robert Burns Fellowship, Otago University, Dunedin, 1996. Membership: New Zealand Society of Authors (PEN Inc). Address: 19 Bryndwr Road, Fendalton, Christchurch 5, New Zealand.

HALL David, (David Iveson), b. 30 Dec 1946. Teacher. m. Valerie E Walters, 19 May 1984, 1 daughter. Education: BA, Honours, English, London University. Publications: A Bit of England, illustrated by John Cornelius, 1990; Birds of Passage, 1991. Contributions to: Ore; Orbis; Scratch; North; Odyssey; Foolscap. Address: 54 Poll Hill Road, Heswall, Wirral, Merseyside L60 7SW, England.

HALL Donald (Andrew, Jr), b. 20 Sept 1928, New Haven, Connecticut, USA. Poet; Writer; Professor of English (retired). m. (1)

Korby Thompson, 1952, div 1969, 1 son, 1 daughter, (2) Jane Kenyon, 1972, dec 1995. Education: BA, Harvard University, 1951; BLitt, Oxford University, 1953; Stanford University, 1953-54. Appointments: Poetry Editor, Paris Review, 1953-62; Junior Fellow, Society of Fellows, Harvard University, 1954-57; Assistant Professor, 1957-61, Associate Professor, 1961-66, Professor of English, 1966-75, University of Michigan. Publications include: Poetry: The Alligator Bride: Poems New and Selected, 1969; The Yellow Room: Love Poems, 1971; A Blue Tit Tilts at the Edge of the Sea: Selected Poems 1964-74, 1975; The Town of Hill, 1975; Kicking the Leaves, 1978; The Toy Bone, 1979; The Twelve Seasons, 1983; Brief Lives, 1983; Great Day at the Cows' House, 1984; The Happy Man, 1986; The One Day: A Poem in Three Parts, 1988; Old and New Poems, 1990; The One Day and Poems, 1947-1990, 1991; The Museum of Clear Ideas, 1993; Short stories: The Ideal Bakery, 1987; Other: Principal Products of Portugal, 1995; Editor: The Essential E A Robinson, 1993. Honours: Edna St Vincent Millay Memorial Prize, 1956; Longview Foundation Award, 1960; Guggenheim Fellowships, 1963, 1972; Sarah Josepha Hale Award, 1983; Poet Laureate of New Hampshire, 1984-89; Lenore Marshall Award, 1987; National Book Critics Circle Award, 1989; Los Angeles Times Book Award, 1989; Robert Frost Silver Medal, Poetry Society of America, 1991; Lifetime Achievement Award, New Hampshire Writers and Publishers Project, 1992; New England Book Award for Non-Fiction, 1993; Ruth Lilly Prize for Poetry, 1994; Honorary Doctorates. Address: Eagle Pond Farm, Danbury, NH 03230, USA.

HALL Fiona Jane, b. 15 July 1955, Swinton, South Yorkshire, England. Teacher. 2 daughters. Education: BA, Honours, St Hugh's College, Oxford, 1976. Postgraduate Certificate in Education, Oxford Polytechnic, 1977. Appointments: Teacher, Thornhill School, Gaborone, Botswana, 1977; Teacher, Naledi Aduction Centre, Gaborone, 1978-79; Part-time/Supply Teacher, Northumberland County Council, 1986-. Publications: New Women Poets, 1990; Other anthologies: What Big Eyes You've Got, 1988; New Writing from the North, 1988; Tidelines, 1988; New Christian Poetry, 1990; I Wouldn't Thank You for a Valentine, 1992. Contributions to: Rialto; Staple; Writing Women; Outposts; Reform; Tyne and Wear Metro Poetry Poster. Honours: Bloodaxe/Evening Chronicle Edward Boyle Prize for Most Promising New Poet, 1988, Runner-up, 1990, 1991; Northern Arts Bursary, 1989; Northern Arts Tyrone Guthrie Award, 1990; 1st Prize, Durham Litfest Competition, 1992. Membership: Poetry Society. Address: The School House, Whittingham, Alnwick, Northumberland NE66 4UP, England.

HALL Floriana Frances, b. 2 Oct 1927, Pittsburgh, Pennsylvania, USA. m. Robert E Hall, 31 Dec 1948, 2 sons, 3 daughters. Education: Akron University. Appointments: Writer, High School Newspaper, 1944-45; Writing Autobiography, Childrens Book. Publications: Tomorrows Dream; Choices; Parallels; The Harmony of The Daffodils; The Boomerang Effect; Maturity; Love Never Dies, 1995. Contributions to: Poets Corner; PEN; Sparrow Grass Poetry Forum; Akron Beacon Journal Review. Honours: Editors Choice Award, National Library of Poetry, 1995, 1996. Membership: Distinguished Member, National Library of Poetry. Address: 1232 Clifton Avenue, Akron, OH 44310, USA.

HALL Jane Anna, b. 4 April 1959, New London, Connecticut, USA. Writer; Poet; Model. Education: Professional Model, Barbizon School, 1976. Appointments: Model, Barbizon Agency, 1977; Career Planning, Wesleyan University, 1985-86; Freelance Poet and Writer, 1986-. Publications: Cedar and Lace, 1986; Satin and Pinstripe, 1987; Fireworks and Diamonds, 1988; Stars and Daffodils, 1989; Sunrises and Stonewalls, 1990; Mountains and Meadows, 1991; Moonlight and Water Lilies, 1992; Founder-Editor, Poetry in Your Mailbox Newsletter, 1989-; Sunset and Beaches, 1993; Under Par Recipes, 1994; New and Selected Poems 1986-1994, 1994; Poems for Children 1986-1994, 1995. Contributions to: Bell Buoy; Expressions I and II; Pictorial Gazette; Connecticut River Review; Connecticut Chapter Romance Writers of America Newsletter; Contributing Editor, Matchbook Magazine, 1993; One Woman Shows, Westbrook Public Library Westbrook, Connecticut, 1989-96. Honours: 2nd Prize for Post Dawn Enchantment, Connecticut Poetry Society Contest, 1983; 2nd Prize for poem Polar Bear Frolic in Connecticut Poetry Society Contest, 1986; Various Certificates. Memberships: Romance Writers of America, 1989-; Romance Writers of America, Connecticut Chapter, 1989-. Address: PO Box 629, Westbrook, CT 06498, USA.

HALL J(ohn) C(live), b. 12 Sept 1920, London, England. Education: Oriel College, Oxford. Appointment: Staff Member, Encounter Magazine, 1955-91. Publications: Selected Poems, 1943; The Summer Dance and Other Poems, 1951; The Burning Hare, 1966; A House of Voices, 1973; Selected and New Poems 1939-1984, 1985; Editor of poems by Edwin Muir, Keith Douglas and others. Address: 9 Warwick Road, Mount Sion, Tunbridge Wells, Kent TN1 1YL, England.

HALL Rodney, b. 18 Nov 1935, Solihull, Warwickshire, England. Education: BA, University of Queensland at Brisbane, 1971. Appointment: Poetry Editor, The Australian newspaper, 1967-78. Publications: Penniless Till Doomsday, 1962; Eyewitness, 1967; The Autobiography of a Gorgon, 1968; The Law of Karma: A Progression of Poems, 1968; Heaven, In A Way, 1970; A Soapbox Omnibus, 1973; Selected Poems, 1975; Black Bagatelles, 1978; The Most Beautiful World: Fictions and Sermons, 1981; Journey Through Australia, 1989. Address: c/o Penguin Books, PO Box 257, Ringwood, Victoria 3134, Australia.

HALLMUNDSSON Hallberg, b. 29 Oct 1930, Iceland. Editor; Translator. m. May Newman, 29 July 1960. Education: BA, University of Iceland, 1954; University of Barcelona, 1955-56; New York University, 1961. Appointments: Columnist, Frjals Thjod, Iceland, 1954-60; Assistant, Associate, Senior Editor, Encyclopedia International, New York, 1961-76; Senior Editor, Americana Annual, 1976-78, Funk & Wagnalls New Encyclopedia, 1979-82; Production Copy Editor, Business Week, 1984-. Publications: Haustmal, 1968; Neikvaeda, 1977; Song of the Stone, translation, 1977; Spjaldvisur, 1985; Threatubok, 1990; Spjaldvisur II, 1991; Svartir Riddarar, translation, 1992; Skyggnur, 1993; 100 Kvaedi, translation, 1994; Vandraedur, 1995. Contributions to: Lesbok Morgunbladsins; Samvinnan; Timarit Mals Og Menningar; Andvari; Icelandic Canadian; Iceland Review; American-Scandinavian Review; World Literature Today; Visions International; Georgia Review; Andblaer; Grand Street. Honours: 1st Prize, Short Story Contest, Reykjavik, 1953; First Prize, Translation of Norwegian Poetry, Minneapolis, 1966; Grant, Translation Center, New York, 1975, Government of Iceland, 1976-79; Iceland Writers Fund, 1985, American-Scandinavian Society, New York, 1991, and Translation Fund, Iceland, 1994; Selected Scandinavian of the Month, American-Scandinavian Bulletin, 1981. Memberships: Writers Union of Iceland; American Literary Translators Association. Address: 30 Fifth Avenue, New York, NY 10011, USA.

HALPERN Daniel, b. 11 Sept 1945, Syracuse, New York, USA. Associate Professor; Poet; Editor. m. Jeanne Catherine Carter, 1982. Education: San Francisco State College, 1963-64; BA, California State University, Northridge, 1969; MFA, Columbia University, 1972. Appointments: Editor, Antaeus magazine, 1969-; Instructor, New School for Social Research, New York City, 1971-76; Editor-in-Chief, Ecco Press, 1971-; Visiting Professor, Princeton University, 1975-76, 1987-88; Associate Professor, 1976-, Chairman, School of the Arts, 1978-, Columbia University; Founder-Director, National Poetry Series, 1978-. Publications: Poetry: Traveling on Credit, 1972; The Keeper of Height, 1974; The Lady Knife-Thrower, 1975; Treble Poets 2 (with Gerda Mayer and Florence Elon), 1975; Street Fire, 1975; Life Among Others, 1978; Seasonal Rights, 1982; Tango, 1987; Foreign Neon, 1991; Selected Poems, 1994; Non-fiction: The Good Food: Soups, Stews and Pasta (with Julie Strand), 1985; Halpern's Guide to the Essential Restaurants of Italy, 1990; Editor, includes: The Autobiographical Eye, 1993; Too Far From Home: The Selected Writings of Paul Bowles, 1993; Dante's Inferno: Translations by Twenty Contemporary Poets, 1993; Not For Bread Alone: Writers on Food, Wine, and the Art of Eating, 1993; Nine Visionary Poets and the Quest for Enlightenment, 1994; On Music (with Jeanne Wilmot Carter), 1994; Who's Writing This?: Notations on the Authorial I, with Self Portraits, 1994. Honours: Rehder Award, Southern Poetry Review, 1971; YM-YWHA Discovery Award, 1971; Bread Loaf Writers Conference Robert Frost Fellowship, 1974; National Endowment for the Arts Fellowships, 1974, 1975, 1987; Creative Arts Public Service Grant, 1978; Guggenheim Fellowship, 1988-89. Address: c/o Ecco Press Ltd, 100 West Broad Street, Hopewell, NJ 08525, USA.

HALSE Frank Adams Jr, b. 3 May 1927, Troy, New York, USA. Clergyman. m. Joyce Holcomb, 7 June 1952, 2 daughters. Education: AB, Psychology and Religion, 1955; STM, Psychology and Religion, 1958; MA, Family Studies, 1974. Appointments: Pastor; Campus Minister; Director of Education, Psychiatric Centre; Director, Outreach, Child and Family Service Agency; retired. Publications: Poems of the Spirit, 1962; Sidewalks of Fog, 1981; View from the Catacombs, 1988;

A Portable Ark, 1989. Contributions to: Frying Pan; Lake Effect; Daily Change. Membership: Poetry Society of America. Address: 506 3rd Street, Brandon, FL 33511, USA.

HALSEY Alan, b. 22 Sept 1949, Croydon, Surrey, England. Bookseller. Education: BA, Honours, London. Publications: Yearspace, 1979; Another Loop in Our Days, 1980; Present State, 1981; Perspectives on The Reach, 1981; The Book of Coming Forth in Official Secrecy, 1981; Auto Dada Cafe, 1987; A Book of Changes, 1988; Five Years Out, 1989; Reasonable Distance, 1992; The Text of Shelley's Death, 1995. Contributions to: Critical Quarterly; Conjunctions; North Dakota Quarterly; Writing; Ninth Decade; Poetica; South West Review; Poetry Wales; Poesie Europe; O Ars; Figs; Interstate; Prospice; Reality Studios; Fragmente; Screens and Tasted Parallels; Avec; Purge; Grille; Acumen; Shearsman; Oasis; New American Writing. Address: West House, Broad Street, Hay on Wye, Via Hereford HR3 5DB, England.

HALTER Aloma, b. 25 Nov 1954, London, England. Poet; Editor. Education: BA, Honours, Newnham College, Cambridge, 1978. Appointments: Various positions in Jerusalem, 1980-85; English Correspondent to Minister of Science and Technology; Literary Critic, Jerusalem Post; Bureau Manager, Baltimore Sun, Jerusalem; Assistant to Director; Jerusalem Film Archive; Assistant Editor, Ariel, Israel Review of Arts and Letters, 1985-; Literary Critic, Jerusalem Post, 1983-. Publication: The Mosaic Press. Contributions to: Ambit; Tel Aviv Review; Jewish Chronicle; Jerusalem Quarterly; Jerusalem International Poetry Festival; European Judaism. Address: c/o Ariel, 214 Jaffa Street, Jerusalem 91130, Israel.

HAMBERGER Robert, b. 30 June 1957, London, England. Social Worker, 3 children. Education: BA, Honours, Sussex University, 1978; MA, Leicester University, 1988. Appointment: Writing Consultant for Corby Community Arts, 1985-. Publications: No Green Leaves, 1979; The Tunes of Risky Weather, 1985; Journey to a Birth, 1987. Contributions to: Ambit; Envoi; Green Book; Iron; Orbis; Outposts; Poetry Wales; Rialto; Spectator; Staple; Tribune; Verse; New Statesman; The Observer; Anthologies: Hard Lines 2; Seven Years On; Affirming Flame. Honours: East Midlands Arts Writers' Bursary, 1985; Prizewinner, National Poetry Competition, 1991; Hawthornden Fellowship, 1995. Membership: John Claren Society. Address: Ivy House, Main Street, East Farndon, Nr Market Harborough, Leicestershire LE16 9SH, England.

HAMBURGER Anne (Ellen), (Anne Beresford), b. 10 Sept 1928, Redhill, Surrey, England. Poet; Writer; Actress; Teacher. m. Michael Hamburger, 28 July 1951, 1 son, 2 daughters. Education: Central School of Dramatic Art, London, 1944-46. Appointments: Actress, various repertory companies, 1946-48, BBC Radio, 1960-78; Teacher; General Council, Poetry Society, 1976-78; Committee Member, 1989, Advisor on Agenda, Editorial Board, 1993-, Aldeburgh Poetry Festival. Publications: Poetry: Walking Without Moving, 1967; The Lair, 1968; The Courtship, 1972; Footsteps on Snow, 1972; The Curving Shore, 1975; Songs a Thracian Taught Me, 1980; The Songs of Almut, 1980; The Sele of the Morning, 1988; Landscape With Figures, 1994. Other: Struck by Apollo, radio play (with Michael Hamburger), 1965; The Villa, radio short story, 1968; Alexandros Poems of Vera Lungu, translator, 1974; Duet for Three Voices, dramatised poems for Anglia TV, 1982; Snapshots from an Album 1884-1895, 1992. Contributions to: Periodicals. Address: Marsh Acres, Middleton, Saxmundham, Suffolk 1P17 3NH, England.

HAMBURGER Michael Peter Leopold, b. 22 Mar 1924, Berlin, Germany. Writer. m. Anne Ellen File, 1951, 1 son, 2 daughters. Education: Christ Church, Oxford, 1955; MA (Oxon). Appointments: Lecturer, Reader, German, University of Reading, 1955-65; Bollingen Foundation Fellow, 1959-61, 1965-66; Florence Purington Lecturer, Mount Holyoke College, Massachusetts, USA, 1966-67; Visiting Professor, State University of New York, Buffalo, 1969, Stony Brook, 1971; Visiting Fellow, Center for Humanities, Wesleyan University, Connecticut, 1970; Regent's Lecturer, University of California, San Diego, 1983; Visiting Professor: University of South Caroline, 1973, Boston University, 1975-77; Part-time Professor, University of Essex, 1978. Publications: Poetry: Flowering Cactus, 1950; Poems 1950-51, 1952; The Dual Site, 1958; Weather and Season, 1963; Feeding the Chickadees, 1968; Penguin Modern Poets (with A Brownjohn and C Tomlinson), 1969; Travelling I-V, 1969, VI, 1975; Ownerless Earth, 1973; Real Estate, 1977; Moralities, 1977; Variations, 1981; Collected Poems, 1984; Trees, 1988; Selected Poems, 1988; Roots in the Air,

1991; Collected Poems 1941-1994, 1995; Translations including poems by F Hölderlin, H M Enzensberger, N Sachs, G Grass, Paul Celan, Peter Huchel, Franco Fortini, Goethe, Günter Eich; East German Poetry (editor), 1972; Prose and criticism including: The Truth of Poetry, 1970, 1982. Contributions to: The Take-Over, short story in Best Stories, 1995; Numerous others. Honours: Order of the British Empire, 1992; Fellow, Royal Society of Literature, 1972-86; Honorary DLitt, University of East Anglia, 1988; Honorary PhD, Technical University, Berlin, 1995; Translation prizes including: Medal, Institute of Linguists, 1977; Wilhelm-Heinse Prize, 1978; Schlegel-Tieck Prize, London, 1978, 1981; Goethe Medal, 1986; Austrian State Prize, 1988; European Translation Prize, 1990. Memberships: Corresponding Member, Deutsche Akademie für Sprache und Dichtung, Darmstadt, 1973. Address: c/o John Johnson Ltd, Clerkenwell House, 45-47 Clerkenwell Green, London EC1R 0HT, England.

HAMBY James Allan, b. 16 May 1943, Oakland, California, USA. University Administrator; Freelance Writer. m. Laura A Roche, 30 July 1988, 3 daughters. Education: BS, 1965, MA, 1970, Southern Oregon State College. Appointments: Assistant, Southern Oregon State College, 1965-66; Director, Oregon Museum of Natural History, 1966-67; Faculty, Medford (Oregon) High School System, 1967-70; Instructor, Utah State University, 1970-71; Administrator, Humboldt State University, 1971-. Publication: Collection: Lake Ice Splitting. Contributions to: Forum; The Old Red Kimono; Driftwood East Quarterly; Transactions of the Pacific Circle; Poem; Lowlands Review; Pandora; Song; Waters; Western Poetry; Toyon; New Mexico Magazine; Idaho Heritage; Bitterroot Review; South Dakota Review; Hartford Courant; Quartet; University of Portland Review; Pacifica; Descant; Cardinal Poetry Quarterly; Above Ground Review; New Laurel Review; Western Review; Oyez!; Energy West; Bardic Echoes; Humboldt Journal of Social Relations; The Mainstreeter; El Viento. Honours: Poetry Award, Utah Fine Arts Institute, 1971; Various Editor's Choice Citations. Memberships: Academy of American Poets; Poets and Writers Inc. Address: PO Box 1124, Arcata, CA 95521, USA.

HAMILTON (Robert) Ian, b. 24 Mar 1938, King's Lynn, Norfolk, England. Education: BA, Keble College, Oxford, 1962. Appointments: Poetry Editor and Reviewer for London newspapers, 1962-. Publications: Pretending Not to Sleep, 1964; The Visit, 1970; Anniversary and Vigil, 1971; Returning, 1976; Fifty Poems, 1988; A Poetry Chronicle: Essays and Reviews, 1973; Editions of poetry, Honours include: English-Speaking Union Award, 1984. Address: 54 Queen's Road, London SW19, England.

HAMILTON-ALLAN Nigel, b. 27 July 1960, Scotland. Writer. Education: Currently Studying for Psychology Degree. Appointments: Scientist; Music Presenter; Office Manager and Chief Disc-Jockey, company contracted to independent UK radio station; Organiser, Promoter and Presenter within Music Industry; Entrepreneur; Poet; Author; Lyricist; Composer. Publications: Kaleidoscope, 1995; Poetic Forces, 1995; Poets Parade, 1995; Seasons of the Garden, 1995; Poems From The Stables, 1995; To Mum and Dad with Love, 1995; Life After Life, 1995; The Heart of It, 1995; Walk Through Paradise, 1995; The Sound of Poetry, 1995; Glasgow and Strathclyde Unabridged, 1996. Contributions to: End of Millennium; Psychopoetica; Changes; Writers Viewpoint; Peace & Freedom. Honours: 3rd Place, The Northampton Poets, 1995; Runner-up, British Small Press Guild, 1995; Highly Commended, In-House Poetry Competition, 1995; Semi-Finalist, National Library of Poetry, 1995; Entry in Best Poems of the 90's. Address: 52 Trainard Avenue (1/2), Glasgow G32 7RD, Scotland.

HAMMICK Georgina, b. 24 May 1939, Hampshire, England. Writer; Poet. m. 24 Oct 1961, 1 son, 2 daughters. Education: Academie Julian, Paris, 1956-57; Salisbury Art School, 1957-59. Publications: A Poetry Quintet (poems), 1976; People for Lunch, 1987; Spoilt (short stories), 1992; The Virago Book of Love and Loss (Editor), 1992. Contributions to: Journals and periodicals. Membership: Writers Guild. Address: Bridgewalk House, Brixton, Deverill, Warminster, Wiltshire BA12 7EJ, England.

HAMMOND Clifford, b. 16 Sept 1915, Epping, Essex, England. Retired Life Assurance Official. Education: Fellow, Chartered Insurance Institute, 1954. Publications: Reflections, 1977; Further Reflections, 1987; Envoi Book of Quotes on Poetry, 1991, Selected by Clifford Hammond and edited by Anne Lewis-Smith; One Hundred Aphorisms, 1992. Contributions to: Envoi; Orbis; Southern Evening

Echo. Address: 38 Hocombe Drive, Chandlers Ford, Hampshire SO5 1QE, England.

HAMMOND Karla Marie, b. 26 Apr 1949, Middletown, Connecticut, USA. Consultant. Education: BA, English, Goucher College, 1971; MA, English, Trinity College, 1973. Appointments: Executive Staff Administration, Connecticut Student Loan; Consultant, Aetna Life and Casualty; Manager, Planning and Communications, ADVO; Managing Partner, KMH Communications; Vice President Executive Search, People Management. Contributions to: Over 185 publications in USA, Canada, England, Sweden, Italy, Japan, Australia and Greece. Honour: Nominated for Pushcart Prize. Address: 12 West Drive, East Hampton, CT 06424, USA.

HAMMOND Mary Stewart, b. Richmond, Virginia, USA. Poet. m. Arthur Yorke Allen, 22 May 1971. Education: BA with Honours in Poetry, Goucher College. Appointments: Poet-in-Residence, Writer's Community, 1992; Teacher, Advaced Poetry, Writers's Voice, 1992-. Publication: Out of Canaan, W W Norton, 1991. Contributions to: New Yorker; Atlantic Monthly; New Criterion; Yale Review; American Voice; Gettysburg Review; New England Review and Bread Loaf Quarterly; Paris Review; American Review; Boulevard; Field. Honours: First Prize, 1985, Finalist, 1986, 1990, Narrative Poem Contest, New England Review and Bread Loaf Quarterly; 1992 Winner, Best First Collection of Poetry Award, Great Lakes Colleges' Association. Memberships: Academy of American Poets; Poetry Society of America. Address: 1095 Park Avenue, Apartment 4A, New York, NY 10128, USA.

HAMMOND Peter, b. 13 July 1942. Mining Supervisor. m. Diane Ivy, 12 Aug 1989. Education: Modules Diploma of Higher Education, 1985. Appointments: Environmental and Mining Supervisor; Public Speaker on Poetry and Literature Black Country in Colleges and Universities, Schools and Art Societies nationwide. Publications: Two in Staffordshire with Graham Metcalf, 1979; Love Poems, 1982. Contributions to: New Age Poetry; Outposts; Charter Poetry; Chase Post; Swansea Festival, 1982. Honour: School Poetry Prize, 1956. Memberships: Rugeley Literary Society; Co-Founder, Cannock Poetry Group; Poetry Society Readings. Address: 14 Ascot Drive, Cannock, Staffordshire WS11 1PD, England.

HAMPDEN Holly. See: **ROEDER Jill Mary.**

HAMRI Thorsteinn Fra. See: **JONSSON Thorsteinn.**

HAN Jen-Tsun, (Lomen), b. 20 Nov 1928, Wenchang, Kwangtung, China. Poet. m. 14 Apr 1955. Education: Flight School of Chinese Air Force; Studied Aircraft Accident Investigation School of FAA, USA. Appointments: Chief Editor, Blue Star Poetry; Director, The World Association of Chinese Poets, 1989; Director, Poetry Workshop, The Chinese Literature and Art Association, 1990; Judge, Poetry Competitions. Publications: Poetry: Aurora, 1958; Undercurrent of Ninth Day, 1963; The Tower of Death, 1969; The Invisible Chair, 1973; Lomen's Select Poetry Anthology, 1975; The Wilderness, 1980; The Trace of the Sun and Moon, 1981; Lomen's Poetry Anthology, 1984; The Whole World Stops Breathing at the Start Point of Race, 1988; The Forever Way, 1989; Criticisms: The Tragic Mind of Modern Man and Modern Poet, 1964; The Interview of Poetic Mind, 1969; The Man Forever On Trial, 1973; The Resonance of Time and Space, 1981; Seeing the World by Poetry Eye, 1989. Honours: Blue Star Prize, Chinese Poetry Association, 1958; Fort McKinley cited as Great Poet, United Poets Laureate International and won Gold Medal from President Ferdinand E Marcos, Philippines; Nominated with wife as Distinguished Literary Couple, 1st World Congress of Poets in Philippines and awarded Gold Medal, 1969; Honorary Doctor of Literature, World Academy of Arts and Culture, 1986; Citation for Poetry Education, Ministry of Education, China, 1988; Major Poetry Prize, China Time Newspaper, 1988; Encyclopaedia Americana, Chinese Edition, 1992. Address: 4th Floor, No 8 Taishun Street, Taipei, Taiwan, China.

HAN Yeping. See: **SHAO Yan Xiang.**

HANDLIN James P, b. 14 Nov 1943, Boston, Massachusetts, USA. School Head Teacher. m. Diane Rubin, 14 Nov 1981, 1 son, 2 daughters. Education: BA, Iona College, 1965; MS, Bank Street College of Education, 1985; EdD, Columbia University, 1988. Appointments: Head of Upper School, Pingry School, Martinsville; Head of School, Brooklyn Friends' School, Brooklyn, New York.

Publications: Where the Picture Book Ends, 1979; The Distance in a Door, 1980; The Haiku Anthology, 1986; Blue Stones and Salt Hay: An Anthology of New Jersey Writers, 1990; Editor's Choice III, 1992. Contributions to: Poetry; Prairie Schooner; Lips; Patterson Review; Footwork. Honours: Dylan Thomas Award, New School for Social Research, 1979; Gusto Press Discovery Award, 1979; Gusto Press Haiku Award, 1980; Grant, 1985, Award, 1988, New Jersey State Council of the Arts; 1st Prize, Passaic County College Poetry Award, 1986. Membership: American Directory of Poets and Fiction Writers. Address: 969 Cedarbrook Road, Plainfield, NJ 07060, USA.

HANF James Alphonso, (James Wildwood), b. 3 Feb 1923, Chehalis, Washington, USA. Naval Architect Technician; Poet. m. 16 Aug 1947, 1 daughter. Education: Graduate, Centralia Junior College, Washington, 1943. Appointments: Poetry Editor, Coffee Break Magazine, 1977-82; Lecturer, new Americana version of Haiku (originator), 1977; Lecturer, Haiku and Siamese poetry to professional and civic groups. Contributions to: Numerous literary journals, anthologies and popular magazines. Honours: Poet Laureate, Outstanding Poet of the Year, Inky Trails, 1978; Award, Dragonfly; Diploma di merito, Universita delle Arti, Italy; Distinguished Service Award, American Biographical Institute, 1981; Honorary DLitt, World University, 1981; Nomination, Poet Laureate, Washington State, 1981; Grand Prize, World Poetry Society Convention, 1985-86; Golden Poet Award, World of Poetry, California, 1985-88; Silver Poet Award, 1989; Grand Prize Winner, Las Vegas World Poetry Convention, 1990. Memberships: Honorary Member, Stella Woodall Poetry Society; World Poets Resource Centre; California Federation of Chaparral Poets; Ina Coolbrith Circle; Literarische Union; New York Poetry Forum; Illinois State Poetry Society; World and National Poetry Day Committees; Western World Haiku Society; International Poetry Society, India. Address: PO Box 374, Bremerton, WA 98337, USA.

HANFORD Mary. See: **HANFORD BRUCE Mary.**

HANFORD BRUCE Mary, (Mary Hanford, June Minim), b. 18 June 1940, Washington, District of Columbia, USA. Associate Professor of English. m. Guy Steven Bruce, 23 Mar 1991, 2 sons. Education: BA, University of Texas, Arlington, 1965; MA, Southern Methodist University, 1968; PhD, Arizona State University, 1986. Appointments: Instructor in English, Arizona State University, Tempe, 1981-85; Associate Professor of English, Monmouth College, Illinois, 1985-; Senior Scholar in American Literature, Fulbright Professor of American Literature, Ecole Normale Supérieure, Yaounde, Cameroon, Africa, 1988-90. Publications: Swamproot featuring Mary Hanford's African Poetry, 1989; Holding to the Light, 1991. Contributions to: Poetry View; New Earth Review; Mockingbird; Poetry Scope; Cedar Rock; Louisville Review; KMCR Anthology; Bisbee Times; Prickly Pear; Slipstream; Brush Fire; New Kauri; Signalfire; Visions; Oasis; Bisbee Observer; The Carillon; Spoon River Quarterly; Embassy Echo; Huskyn News; Spectrum; Poems Across Our Land; Jane's Stories; World Parnassus of Poets; The Lucid Stone. Honours: Prize, Arizona Poetry Society, 1983; Nomination for Guggenheim Fellowship, 1984; Runner-up, Jonquil Trevor Sonnet Contest, 1984; Runner-up, Flume Press National Chapbook Contest, 1990. Memberships: The Academy of American Poets; American Association of University Professors; Warren County Writers' Bloc; Free Fall, Monmouth College; Illinos Writers Association. Address: 511 E Boston, Monmouth, IL 61462, USA.

HANSEN Jefferson, b. 8 Feb 1965, Sturgeon Bay, Wisconsin, USA. Poet; Teacher. m. Elizabeth Burns, 19 Oct 1991, 2 daughters. Education: BA, Beloit College, 1987; MA, State University of New York, Buffalo, 1992. Appointments: Teacher of English, Albany Academy, New York, 1993-95; Blake School, Minneapolis, Minnesota, 1995-. Publications: Gods to the Elbows, 1991; Red Streams of George Through Pages, 1993; The Dramatic Monologues of Joe Blow Only Artsy, 1994; A Particular Pluralist Poem, 1996. Contributions to: Sulfur; O-blek; Avec; Washington Review; B-City; Abacus; Writers from the New Coast, anthology. Address: 2510 Highway 100 South #333, St Louis Park, MN 55416, USA.

HANSEN Margaret Standish, b. 24 June 1917, Big Spring, Wisconsin, USA. m. 15 Oct 1939, 2 sons. Education: 1st grade Teaching Certificate, Juneau County Teachers College, 1937. Publications: Gingerbread and Calico, 1984; Silver Raindrops, 1987; Patterns, 1989. Contributions to: Sunshine; Grit; Idaho Statesman; Artisan; Spokane Chronicle; CAAA National Magazine; Senior Times; Senior Outlook. Honours: 3rd Place, Byline Magazine, 1985; 1st Place,

National Chapter, CAAA, 1986; 1st Place, Spokane Chapter, CAAA, 1987; 2nd Place, Washington State Federation of Women's Clubs, 1989. Memberships: Poetry Scribes, Spokane; Composers, Authors and Artists of America, Spokane. Address: 1105 North Rudolf Road, Spokane, WA 99206, USA.

HANSEN Merle Charles, b. 28 Mar 1923, Chicago, Illinois, USA. Writer; Editor; Nurse. m. Betty Tayeko Ogawa, 10 Jan 1949, 1 son, 3 daughters. Education: AB, Philosophy, Elmhurst College, 1946; Languages, English, Philosophy, Graduate School, California State University, Long Beach. Appointments: Assistant Editor, 1947-50; Editor, Writer, 1950s; Assistant Advertising Manager; Teachnical Writer; Nurse; Retired. Publications: Over 100 books of poetry. Contributions to: Anthologies. Honours: Golden Poet's Award, 1988-92; 14 Honourable Mentions, 1988, 1992; 1st Runner-up Award, 1989; Editor's Choice Award, 1990; Poetic Achievement Award, 1990, 1991. Memberships: California State Poetry Society; International Society of Poets. Address: PO Box 14735, Long Beach, CA 90803, USA.

HARALDSDOTTIR Ingjiborg, b. 21 Oct 1942, Reykjavík, Iceland. Writer; Translator; Poet. 1 son, 1 daughter. Education: Diploma, Feature Film Director; MA, All Union State Institute of Cinematography, Moscow, USSR, 1969. Appointments: Assistant Director of Theatre, Havana, Cuba, 1970-75; Film Critic, Reykjavík, 1976-85; Journalist, Reykjavík, 1978-81. Publications: Thangad vil eg fljuga; Ordspor daganna, 1983; Nu eru adrir timar, 1989; Ljód, collected poems, 1991; Höfud konunnar, 1995. Contributions to: Timarit Mals og Menningar; Skirnir. Honours: Nu eru adrir timar nominated for Icelandic Literature Award, 1990, for Nordic Literature Prize, 1993. Membership: Writers' Union of Iceland, Chairman 1994-. Address: Drápuhlid 13, 105 Reykjavík, Iceland.

HARBOUR Josephine, (Singleton Harbour), b. 22 Jan 1923, Goody Hills, Cumberland, England. Women's Auxiliary Air Force; Motherhood; Shop Assistant. m. Stanley Harbour, 8 Feb 1946, 2 sons, 1 daughter. Publications: Everyday Poems, 1982; Second Everyday Poems, 1983; My World, 1986; Verse from the Bible, 1986; In Search of a Dream, 1986; Treasured Thoughts, 1987; Of Changing Scienes, 1988; Bob's Story, 1989; Peals in Words, 1991. Contributions to: Christian Herald; The Lady; Writers Rostrum; Woman's Own, magazine; Third Half; Folio; Ploughman, Canada; White Rose. Honours: 1st prize, local competition, 1985; Runner-up, White Rose Competition, 1991. Address: 65 Moorgate Road, Dereham, Norfolk NR19 1NU, England.

HARBUS Maynam. See: **SUBRAHMANYAM K V V.**

HARDARSON Hrafn Andres, b. 9 Apr 1948, Kopavogur, Iceland. Librarian. m. Anna S Einarsdottir, Oct 1969, 1 son, 1 daughter. Education: Chartered Librarian (UK), 1972; Fellow, Library Association (UK), 1994. Appointments: Assistant Librarian, 1968-72, Branch Librarian, 1973-76, City Library Reykjavík; Chief Librarian, Kopavogur Town Library, 1976-. Publications: Fyrrvera, 1982; Thrileikur Ad Ordum, 1990; Tonmyndaljod, 1992; Tone-Picture-Poems, 1993; Hafid Brennur (translation of Vizma Belsevica), 1994; Hler, 1995; Mylsna, 1995. Contributions include: Morgunbladid-Lesbok; Andblaer; TMM; Lystraeninginn. Honour: 2nd Prize, Eyjafjardarsveit, 1995. Membership: Writers Union of Iceland. Address: Medalbr 2, 200 Kopavogur, Iceland.

HARDY Alan William, b. 10 Mar 1951, Luton, Bedfordshire, England. Director and Teacher, Language School. m. Shelby Mory, 24 Aug 1985, 1 daughter. Education: BA, English and Italian Literature, 1973, MA, Comparative Literature, 1976, Warwick University; Dip TEFL, Christ Church College, Kent University, 1983. Appointments: English Teacher, Sir Joseph Williamson's Mathematical School, Rochester, Kent; English Language Teacher, Whitehill Estate School of English, Flamstead, Hertfordshire. Contributions to: Envoi; Iota; New Hope International; Nutshell; Kangaroo; TOPS; Foolscap; Sepia; Hybrid; Purple Patch. Honours: 2nd Prize, Hastings National Poetry Competition, 1994. Address: Whitehill Estate School of English, Flamstead, St Albans, Hertfordshire AL3 8DN, England.

HARDY Dorothy C, b. Town Creek, Alabama, USA. Education Administrator; Freelance Writer and Poet; Business Owner. 1 daughter. Education: BS, English, 1956; MEd, Counselling 1960; EdD, Counselor, Educator, 1976. Appointments: Director, Student Development Services, Southeast Missouri State University;

Commissioner, DBA, Ohio Department of Mental Health; President, Cincinnati Life Adjustment Institute; Employment Recruitment Specialist, Kansas State University; Director, Handicapped Student Programmes, Director, Special Student Services, Assistant Dean of Student Groups, University of Cincinnati. Publication: Promises: Bright and Broken, 1989. Contributions to: Essence Magazine; Midwest Poetry Review; Summerfield Journal; Kwibidt Publisher; American Press; Hometown Press; Wide Open Magazine; Independent Review; Odessa Poetry Review; Quill Books; American Poetry Association; Sewannee Poetry; New York Poetry Foundation. Honours: Golden Poet Award, World of Poetry, 1986, 1987; Certificate of Achievement for short fiction, Writers Digest, 1986; Creative Enterprises Certificate of Merit for Poetry, 1987 and World's Best Poets of 1987; 2nd place, Pensters Award, 1987; Winner, Chapbook Poetry Contest, Slough Press, 1988. Address: 901 N Pine Street, Florence, AL 35630, USA.

HARGRAVE Leonie. See: **DISCH Thomas M.**

HARJO Joy, b. 9 May 1951, Tulsa, Oklahoma, USA. Poet; Professor; Musician. 1 son, 1 daughter. Education: Institute of American Indian Arts, 1968; BA, University of New Mexico, 1976; MFA, University of Iowa, 1978. Appointments: Assistant Professor, University of Colorado, Boulder, 1985-88; Associate Professor, University of Arizona, 1988-91; Professor, University of New Mexico, Albuquerque, 1991-. Publications: The Last Song, chapbook, 1975; What Moon Drove Me To This?, 1980; She Had Some Horses, 1984; Secrets from the Center of the World, 1989; In Mad Love and War, 1990; The Woman Who Fell from the Sky, 1994; The Spiral of Memory, 1996. Contributions to: Ploughshares; River Styx; Contact II; Bloomsbury Review; Sonora Review; Grant Street Review; American Voice; Journal of Ethnic Studies. Honours: Writing Fellowship, National Endowment for the Arts, 1978-92; Fellowship, Arizona Commission on the Arts, 1989; Pushcart Prize XV Edition; American Indian Distinguished Achievement in the Arts Award, 1990; William Carlos Williams Award, Poetry Society of America; Josephine Miles Poetry Award, Oakland PEN, 1991; Oklahoma Book Arts Award, 1995; Lifetime Achievement Award, Native Writers' Circle of the Americas, 1995. Memberships: International PEN; Executive Board, US PEN. Literary Agent: Charlotte Sheedy, 65 Bleeker Street, 12th Floor, New York, NY 10012, USA. Address: PO Box 4999, Albuquerque, NM 87196, USA.

HARLESS Margaret Michael, (Tamarack), b. 8 Dec 1930, Pennsylvania, USA. Teacher. m. Marion Harless, 20 Dec 1968. Education: BS, Elementary Education, Frostburg College, 1952; MS, Elementary Education, Western Maryland College, 1968. Appointments: Teacher, Maryland Public Schools; Librarian, County System; Plant Nursery Worker. Publications: Taming the Savage River, prose and poetry, 1968, 1988. Contributions to: Journal of the Alleghenies; Oakland Republican, Maryland; Glades Star. Membership: West Virginia Poetry Society. Address: 13800 Frederick Road, West Friendship, MD 21794, USA.

HARLOW Michael, b. 1937, New Zealand. Appointment: Lecturer in English, Christ Church Teachers College. Publications: The Book of Quiet, 1974; Edges, 1974; The Identikit, 1978; Text Identities, 1978; Nothing But Switzerland and Lemonade, 1980; Today is the Piano's Birthday, 1981; Vlaminck's Tie, 1985; Take a Risk, Trust Your Language, Make a Poem, 1985. Address: c/o Auckland University Press, University of Auckland, Private Bag, Auckland, New Zealand.

HARPER Albert William John, b. 25 July 1917, Fullarton, Ontario, Canada. Retired Teacher. Education: BA, Psychology and Philosophy, University of Western Ontario, 1949; MA, Philosophy, University of Toronto, 1952; PhD, Philosophy, Mellen University, Lewiston, New York, 1996. Appointments: Secondary School Teaching, 1955-72. Publications: Adventures in Ideas, 1985; Poems of Reflection, 1995. Contributions to: Poemata, Canadian Poetry Association; Reach Magazine, Hawaii. Memberships: Canadian Poetry Association. Address: 59 Victor Street, London, Ontario N6C 1B9, Canada.

HARPER Michael S(teven), b. 18 Mar 1938, New York, New York, USA. Professor of English; Poet. m. 3 children. Education: BA 1961, MA 1963, California State University, Los Angeles; MA, University of Iowa Writers Workshop, 1963; ad eundem, Brown University, 1972. Appointments: Visiting Professor, Lewis and Clark College, 1968-69, Reed College, 1968-69, Harvard University, 1974-77, Yale University, 1976; Professor of English, Brown

University, 1970-; Benedict Distinguished Professor, Carleton College, 1979; Elliston Poet and Distinguished Professor, University of Cincinnati, 1979; National Endowment for the Humanities Professor, Colgate University, 1985; Distinguished Minority Professor, University of Delaware, 1988, Macalester College, 1989; 1st Poet Laureate of the State of Rhode Island, 1988-93; Phi Beta Kappa Visiting Scholar, 1991; Berg Distinguished Visiting Professor, New York University, 1992. Publications: Dear John, Dear Coltrane, 1970; History is Your Own Heartbeat, 1971; History As Apple Tree, 1972; Song: I Want a Witness, 1972; Debridement, 1973; Nightmare Begins Responsibility, 1975; Images of Kin, 1977; Chant of Saints (Co-Editor), 1979; Healing Song for the Inner Ear, 1985; Songlines: Mosaics, 1991; Every Shut Eye Aint Asleep, 1994; Honorable Amendments, 1995; Collected Poems, 1996. Honours: Black Academy of Arts and Letters Award, 1972; National Institute of Arts and Letters Grants, 1975, 1976, 1985; Guggenheim Fellowship, 1976; Melville Cane Award, Poetry Society of America, 1978; Governor's Poetry Award, Rhode Island Council of the Arts, 1987; Robert Hayden Memorial Poetry Award, United Negro College Fund, 1990; Literary Lion, New York Public Library, 1992; Honorary doctorates. Membership: American Academy of Arts and Sciences. Address: c/o Department of English, Brown University, Providence, RI 02912, USA.

HARR Lorraine Ellis, (Tombo, Dolores Mundi, Eugene Alonzo), b. Sullivan, Illinois, USA. Writer; Poet; Housewife; Mother. m. 18 Aug 1958, 2 sons. Education: Many college courses; Self-educated; Workshops. Publications: Editor, Dragonfly haiku quarterly, all editions, 1972-84; Cats, Crows, Frogs and Scarecrows, 1971; Tombo: 226 Dragonfly Haiku, 1975; The Red Barn, Americana Haiku, 1975; Snowflakes in the Wind: Winter Haiku, Selected Senryu of Leh, 1976; Haiku and Commentary, Anthology of Western World Haiku Society: Haiku Award Winners, 1974-81; A Flight of Herons: Seascapes in Haiku, 1977; China Sojourn: Haibun, 1981; Ripe Papaya and Orange Slices: Poems of Mexico, translated by Maria Hacketti, 1986; 70 Sevens: Pathways of the Dragonfly, Haiku Sequences. 1986; Collected articles from Dragonfly, 1991. Contributions to: Oregon Journal; Northwest Magazine; Oregonian; Denver Post; American Haiku; Press; Versecraft; Human Voice Quarterly; Beloit Journal; Poetry Dial; Poetry Pendulum; Hoosier Challenge; Janus-SCTH; Windless Orchard; Shorelines; Blue Print; Tweed; Lunatic Fringe; Haiku West; Orphic Lute; Modern Haiku; Haiku Highlights; Ascent; Ranger; East-West Journal; Instructor; Journal of Aesthetic Education; Green World; Swordsman Review; Westward; Haiku Magazine; Archer; Messages from Matsuyama (Yagi). Honours: Japan Air Lines Contest, 1964; Black Ship Festival, 1967; Haiku Awards, Mainichi Daily Newspapers, 1982-87, 1989-92; New Tea Contest, 1992-93; Numerous others. Memberships: Founder, Western World Haiku Society, 1972; Oregon State Poetry Association; International Ikebana; Editor, High School Annual, The Ranger, senior year. Address: 4102 North East 130th Place, Portland, OR 97230, USA.

HARRIS Edna Beulah Mae Warren, (End), b. 28 Feb 1950, Milford, Deleware, USA. Writer. m. A Harris, 7 Feb 1970, 2 sons, 1 daughter. Education: BS, Education, 1982; MA, Educational Psychology, 1982, ANU; Delaware Technical Community College in Nursing; Certificate in Human Service Work I and II. Appointments: Poultry Worker; Poet; Songwriter; Writer; Instructor, Delaware Technical College. Publication: Talking About All Kinds of Things. Contributions to: American Poetry Association; National Library of Poetry; Watermark Press; World of Poetry. Honours: Golden Poet Award, 1985-89; Silver Poet Award, 1990; Editor's Choice Award, 1985-89; Certificates of Merit, 1984-86; Who's Who in Poetry Honour for Outstanding Achievement in Poetry, 1990; Royal Award, 1995; Certificate of Attendance, 1995. Memberships: American Poetry Association; Amherst Society; National Library of Poetry; Watermark Press; Honorary Member, World Parnassians' Guild International, 1995. Address: Box 272, Route 1, Lincoln, DE 19960, USA.

HARRIS Marie, b. 7 Nov 1943, New York, New York, USA. Writer. m. Charter Weeks, 4 Nov 1977, 3 sons. Education: BA, Goddard College, 1971. Appointments: Freelance Writer; Partner, Isinglass Studio. Publications: Raw Honey, 1975; Interstate, 1980; Weasel in the Turkey Pen, 1993. Contributions to: Poet Lore; Sojourner; Bluefish; Hanging Loose; Longhouse. Honours: Fellowship, National Endowment for the Arts, 1976; Fellowship, New Hampshire Council on the Arts, 1981. Memberships: National Writers Union; Poetry Society of America. Address: PO Box 203, Barrington, NH 03825, USA.

HARRIS Robert F(ranklin), b. 14 Jan 1949, Mayfield, Kentucky, USA. Preacher. m. Sandra, 6 June 1971, 1 son, 1 daughter. Education: BA, Central Bible College, 1980; Graduate Work University of Louisville, 1983-84; Graduate Programme in English, Murray State University. Appointments: Ordained Minister, Assemblies of God, 1986; Kentucky State Chaplain, Military Order of the Purple Heart, 1989-90; Vice-Commander, Four Rivers Chapter, Military Order of the Purple Heart, 1990; Teacher, English, History, Charles Shedd Research Academy, Mayfield, Kentucky. Publications: Do You Know, 1989; Alpha, 1990; The Scout, 1990; One Act Plays: Seasoned with Love, 1992; IndoChina, 1994; Woodbridge Monuments, 1995; Truly Pure Diary, 1995; Our Feathered Friends, 1995. Contributions to: Fulton Leader; New Life Church Bulletins; Stanley Hanks Poetry Chapbook Contest, St Louis Poetry Centre Inc; Kentucky Arts Council, Al Smith Fellowship Programme, 1992; National Library of Poetry, 1993; Parnassus of World Poets, 1994; Best Poems of 1996; Best Poems of 1995; Outstanding Poets of 1994; National Library of Poetry; Kaleidoscpe, 1994; Notations, 1995. Honours: Awards of Merit, 1987, 1988, 1988, 1990, 1990. Memberships include: National Arts Society; Kentucky State Poetry Society; Mayfield Graves County Art Guild; International Society of Poets; National Council of Teachers of English; National Federation of State Poetry Societies. Address: Route 2, Box 728-3, Mayfield, KY 42066, USA.

HARRIS (Theodore) Wilson, b. 24 Mar 1921, New Amsterdam, British Guiana. Education: Graduated, Queen's College, Georgetown, 1939. Appointments: Writer and Lecturer throughout the Commonwealth and at the University of New York, Buffalo, USA. Publications: Fetish, 1951; The Well and the Land, 1952; Eternity to Season, 1954, revised, 1979; The Radical Imagination (essays), 1992; The Resurrection at Sorrow Hill, 1993. Honours include: DLitt, University of West Indies, 1984, University of Kent, Canterbury, 1988. Address: c/o Faber and Faber Ltd, 3 Queen Square, London WC1N 3AU, England.

HARRISON James (Thomas), (Jim Harrison), b. 11 Dec 1937, Grayling, Michigan, USA. Author; Poet. m. Linda May King, 10 Oct 1959, 2 daughters. Education: BA, 1960, MA, 1964, Michigan State University. Appointment: Instructor, State University of New York, Stony Brook, 1965-66. Publications: Fiction: Wolf: A False Memoir, 1971; A Good Day to Die, 1973; Farmer, 1976; Legends of the Fall, 1979; Warlock, 1981; Sundog, 1984; Dalva, 1988; The Woman Lit by Fireflies, 1990; Sunset Limited, 1990; Julip, 1994; Poetry: Plain Song, 1965; Locations, 1968; Walking, 1969; Outlyer and Ghazals, 1971; Letters to Yesinin, 1973; Returning to Earth, 1977; New and Selected Poems, 1961-1981, 1982; The Theory and Practice of Rivers, 1986; Country Stores, 1993; Screenplays: Cold Feet (with Tom McGuane), 1989; Revenge (with Jeffrey Fishkin), 1990; Wolf (with Wesley Strick), 1994; Non-fiction: Just Before Dark, 1991. Honours: National Endowment for the Arts Grant, 1967-69; Guggenheim Fellowship, 1968-69. Address: PO Box 135, Lake Leelanau, MI 49653, USA.

HARRISON James. See: **LIGHTFOOT David James.**

HARRISON Jeffrey Woods, b. 10 Oct 1957, Cincinnati, Ohio, USA. Poet; University Teacher. m. Julie Wells, 28 Nov 1981. Education: BA cum laude, Columbia University, 1980; MFA, English, University of Iowa, 1984; Stegner Fellowship in Creative Writing, Stanford University, 1985-86. Appointments: English Teacher, Berlitz Schools, Japan, 1980-81; Researcher and Writer for book World Artists, H W Wilson Publishing Company, 1981-82; Teaching Assistant, University of Iowa, 1983-84; Museum Assistant, Researcher, The Phillips Collection, 1985-87; Instructor, Johns Hopkins University, 1989; Lecturer, George Washington University, Washington DC, 1990-92; Roger E Murray Chair in Creative Writing at Phillips Academy, Andover, Massachusetts, 1997. Publication: The Singing Underneath, 1988; Sign of Arrival, 1996. Contributions to: New Yorker; Poetry; New Republic; Hudson Review; Yale Review; Antioch Review; Paris Review; Partisan Review; Kenyon Review; Sewanee Review; Nation; Boulevard; Crazyhorse; Harvard Magazine; Margin; Missouri Review; Ontario Review; Quarterly; Southwest Review; Verse; New Criterion; Southern Review; Anthology of Magazine and Verse; Yearbook of American Poetry; Arvon Foundation International Poetry Competition, 1985 Anthology; New Voices; The Uncommon Touch. Honours: Prize, Academy of American Poets, 1983; McAfee Discovery Prize, Missouri Review, 1986; Ingram Merrill Foundation Fellowship, 1988; Amy Lowell Fellowship, 1988-89; Peter I B Lavan Younger Poets Award, Academy of American Poets, 1989; Fellowship, National Endowment for the Arts, 1992. Memberships: Academy of

American Poets; Poetry Society of America. Address: 4040 Mt Carmel Road, Cincinnati, OH 45244, USA.

HARRISON Pamela Alice, b. 16 Aug 1946, USA. Poet; Teacher. m. Dennis M McCullough, 12 June 1971, 1 daughter. Education: BA, English Literature, Smith College, 1968; Special student, Philosophy, University of Western Ontario, 1973-75; MFA, Writing Poetry, Vermont College, 1983. Appointments: Instructor, English Literature, Writing, University System of New Hampshire, 1987-94; Teacher, 9-10th Grade English Language and Literature, Beaver School, Boston, Massachusetts; Instructor, Dartmouth College, Creative Writing, 1995. Publication: Noah's Daughter, chapbook, 1988. Contributions to: Poetry; Poetry Now; Poetry Miscellany; Cimarron Review; Laurel Review; New England Review; Seneca Review; Fiction International; Green Mountain Review; Great River Review; Connecticut River Review; Passages North; Calliope; Caribbean Writer; South Florida Poetry Festival; College Handbook of Creative Writing; Contemporary Review; Gulf Stream; Yankee Magazine; Visions International. Honours: Merit Scholar, MFA Programme in Writing, Vermont College; Winner, Leona Jones Smith Memorial Award, NFSP Societies, 1984; Finalist, Brittingham Prize, University of Wisconsin Press, 1987, 1988, 1990; Winner, Panhandler Chapbook Competition, 1988; Winner, Merit Scholarship to Wesleyan Writers' Conference, 1989; Finalist, Walt Whitman, Academy of American Poets, 1990; Nominee, Pushcart Prize, 1990, 1993, 1994, 1995. Memberships: Poetry Society of America; Academy of American Poets; Associated Writing Programs. Address: PO Box 1106, Norwich, VT 05055, USA.

HARRISON Tony, b. 30 Apr 1937, Leeds, Yorkshire, England. Poet; Translator. m. Publications: Earthworks, 1964; Aitkin Mata (play with J Simmons), 1965; Newcastle is Peru, 1969; The Loiners, 1970; Voortrekker, 1972; The Misanthrope (translation of Molière's play), 1973; Poems of Palladas of Alexandria (Editor and Translator), 1973; Phaedra Britannica (translation of Racine's Phèdre), 1975; Bow Down (music theatre), 1977; The Passion (play), 1977; The Bartered Bride (libretto), 1978; From the "School of Eloquence" and Other Poems, 1978; Continuous, 1981; A Kumquat for John Keats, 1981; The Oresteia (translation), 1981; US Martial, 1981; Selected Poems, 1984, revised edition, 1987; Dramatic Verse, 1973-1985, 1985; The Fire-Gap, 1985; The Mysteries, 1985; V, 1985; Theatre Works, 1973-1985, 1986; Loving Memory, 1987; The Blasphemers' Banquet, 1989; The Trackers of Oxryhynchus, 1990; V and Other Poems, 1990; A Cold Coming: Gulf War Poems, 1991; The Common Chorus, 1992; The Gaze of the Gorgon, 1992; Square Rounds, 1992; Black Daisies for the Bride, 1993; Poetry or Bust, 1993; A Maybe Day in Kazakhstan, 1994; The Shadow of Hiroshima, 1995; Permanently Bard, 1995; The Kaisers of Carnuntum , 1995; The Labours of Herakles, 1995; The Prince's Play, 1996; Plays 3, 1996. Honours: Cholmondley Award for Poetry, 1969; Geoffrey Faber Memorial Prize, 1972; European Poetry Translation Prize, 1983; Whitbread Award for Poetry, 1992; Prix d'Italia, 1994; W H Heinemann Award, 1996. Memberships: President, Classical Association, 1987-88; Fellow, Royal Society of Literature. Address: c/o 2 Crescent Grove, Clapham Common, London SW4 7AH, England.

HARRISS Malcolm Stuart, b. 27 Nov 1967, Sandwich, Kent, England. m. Sylvia Pienkowski, 24 April, 1996. Education: BA (Hons), English and Media Studies, University of Southampton, 1985-88; MA, University of East Anglia, 1988-89. Appointments: Management Trainee, Boots the Chemist Ltd, Norwich, 1989-91; Technical Writer, Thorburn Kirkpatrick, Harlesden, Norfolk, 1991-92; Assistant Editor, Willesedeane Press, Cambridge, 1992-94; Freelance Writer, 1994-. Publications: The Rockpool and Other Poems, 1992; Blood and Rainbows, 1994; Little Bagatelle (with Jamie Sanders and Ann Marie Watkins), 1995; Stargazy Pie, 1996; Bullets, forthcoming. Contributions to: Newspapers, literary magazines and journals; many writers' workshops. Address: 26 Seymour Street, Cambridge, CB1 3DQ, England.

HARROLD William Eugene, b. 24 June 1936, Winston-Salem, North Carolina, USA. Professor of English, Writer. Education: BA, Wake Forest University, 1959; MA, 1961, PhD, 1967, University of North Carolina, Chapel Hill. Appointments: Teaching Assistant, University of North Carolina, Chapel Hill, 1962-65; Instructor, Assistant Professor, Associate Professor, Professor, University of Wisconsin, Milwaukee, 1965-96. Publications: Beyond the Dream, 1972; Trails Filled with Lighted Notions, 1988; The Variance and the Unity; Boat with a Daffodil Sail, 1994. Anthologies: Sutured Words; Gathering Place of the Waters; A Garland for John Berryman; Ardentic Verba.

Contributions to: Literary journals and periodicals. Honours: Oscar Arnold Young Award, 1973; Trinton All Nations Prize, 1977; Ann Stanford Prize, 1988. Memberships: Modern Language Association; Browning Institute; Tennyson Society; Midwest Modern Language Association; Wisconsin Fellowship of Poets. Address: Box 413, Department of English, University of Wisconsin, Milwaukee, WI 53201, USA.

HARROW Ian, b. 27 Jan 1945, Bamburgh, Northumberland, England. Lecturer in Art History. m. Anne Slater, 1 son, 1 daughter. Education: BA Hons, Fine Art, Leeds University, 1967. Appointments: Lecturer, Art History, 1972-75, Senior Lecturer, 1975-83, Head, School of Art, 1983-, University of Central Lancashire (formerly Lancashire Polytechnic), Preston, Lancashire. Publications: Pen New Poems 1977-78; Adam's Dream, 1980; Hume's Study, 1986. Contributions to: Stand Magazine; London Magazine; Literary Review; Poetry Wales; English; Rialto; Grand Piano; Poetry and Audience; Magyar Pen; Hungarian Quarterly. Membership: Poetry Society, London. Address: 3 Woodbine Terrace, Headingley, Leeds LS6 4AF, England.

HARRY J S, b. 1939, Adelaide, South Australia, Australia. Appointments: Writer-in-Residence, Australian National University, Canberra, 1989-. Publications: The Deer Under the Skin, 1970; Hold, for a Little While, and Turn Gently, 1979; A Dandelion for Van Gogh, 1985. Honours include: PEN International Prize, 1987. Address: PO Box 184, Randwick, New South Wales 2031, Australia.

HARSENT David, b. 9 Dec 1942, Devon, England. Poet; Writer. m. (1) div, 2 sons, 1 daughter, (2) 1 daughter. Appointments: Fiction Critic, Times Literary Supplement, London, 1965-73; Poetry Critic, Spectator, London, 1970-73. Publications: Poetry: Tonight's Lover, 1968; A Violent Country, 1969; Ashridge, 1970; After Dark, 1973; Truce, 1973; Dreams of the Dead, 1977; Mister Punch, 1984; Playback, 1997; Selected Poems, 1989; News From the Front, 1993; The Sorrow of Sarajevo (English versions of poems by Goran Simic); Novel: From an Inland Sea, 1985; Libretto: Gawain (for Harrison Birtwistle's opera), 1991; Editor: New Poetry 7, 1981; Poetry Book Society Supplement, 1983; Savremena Britanska Poezija, 1988. Honours: Eric Gregory Award, 1967; Cheltenham Festival Prize, 1968; Arts Council Bursaries, 1969, 1984; Geoffrey Faber Memorial Prize, 1978; Society of Authors Travel Fellowship, 1989. Address: c/o 10 Iron Bridge House, Bridge Approach, London NW1 8BD, England.

HART Kevin, b. 5 July 1954, London, England. Education: Canberra, Stanford and Melbourne Universities; PhD, 1987. Appointments: Lecturer, Deakin University, Victoria, 1987-90; Senior Lecturer, Deakin University, 1990; Associate Professor, Monash University, 1991-95; Professor, Monash University 1995-. Publications include: Nebuchadnezzar, 1976; The Departure, 1978; The Lines of the Hand: Poems 1976-79, 1981; Your Shadow, 1984; Peniel, 1990; The Buried Harbour, 1990; New and Selected Poems, 1995; Dark Angel, 1996. Honours: Victorian and New South Wales Premiers' Awards, 1985. Address: 247 Richardson Street, North Carlton, Victoria 3054, Australia.

HARTNETT Michael, b. 18 Sept 1941, County Limerick, Ireland. Education: University and Trinity Colleges, Dublin. Appointment: Teacher, National College of Physical Education. Publications include: Anatomy of a Cliché, 1968; Selected Poems, 1971; A Farewell to English and Other Poems, 1975; Poems in English, 1977; Prisoners, 1978; Collected Poems Volumes 1 and 2, 1985-87; A Necklace of Wrens: Poems in English and Irish, 1987; House of Moon; Poetry in Gaelic. Honours include: Irish Arts Council Award, 1975. Address: Gallery Press, Loughcrew, Oldcastle, County Meath, Ireland.

HARTSHORN Willard Lansing (Bud), b. 28 Sept 1922, Waterbury, Vermont, USA. Retired. m. Mary Eugenie (Jean) Ruda, 30 Jan 1942, 3 sons, 2 daughters. Education: University of Connecticut, 1957; US Civil Service Rating, 1966; Qualification, Live Literature Programme of New England Foundation for the Arts, 1984. Appointments: Teacher, Creative Writing, Abbot Terrace Health Care Center, Waterbury; Volunteer Teacher, Creative Writing Course; Volunteer Teacher, Senior Citizen Groups. Publications: Poems by Willard L Hartshorn, 1973; As I See It, audio tape, 75 poems, 1988; What Spilled When the Door of Life Was Left Ajar, 1991; On Borrowed Time. Contributions to: Waterbury Republican; New Haven Register; Cheshire Herald; Red Shield Magazine; Stars and Stripes; Leaves of Laurel; War Cry; Our Western World's Greates Poems; Today's Greates Poems; Our World's Best Loved Poems. Honours: 1st Prize,

Waterbury Republican, 1934; 1st Prize, Artists and Writers of Connecticut, 1972; 1st Prize, Connecticut Poetry Society, 1984; 4th Prize, Golden Poet Award, World of Poetry, 1988; 5th Prize, Silver Poet Award, 1989, Over-all Standing Award, Silver Poet Award, 1990, World of Poetry. Memberships: Artists and Writers of Connecticut, Treasurer, 1966-; Connecticut Poetry Society; National Federation of State Poetry Societies Inc; National Academy of Repertory Poetry. Address: 1256 Summit Road, Cheshire, CT 06410, USA.

HARVEY Anne Berenice, b. 27 Apr 1933, London, England. Actress; Broadcaster; Writer; Editor. m. Alan Harvey, 13 Apr 1957, 1 son, 1 daughter. Education: Guildhall School of Music and Drama, 1950-53; AGSM, Performer's; LGSM, Teacher's, Performer's. Appointments: Assistant Stage Manager, Leatherhead Theatre; Director, Guildhall Theatre, Perranporth, Cornwall, 1954-57; Drama Teacher, 1962-84; Freelance Writer, Actress, Drama Examiner, Adjudicator; Lecturer, Director, Pegasus Programmes; Series Editor, Poetry Originals, Viking Penguin. Publications: Editor: Poets in Hand: A Puffin Quintet, 1985; Of Caterpillars, Cats and Cattle, 1987; In Time of War, 1987; Something I Remember: Poems of Eleanor Farjeon, 1987; A Picnic of Poetry, 1988; Six of the Best, 1989; The Language of Love, 1989, 1991; Headlines from the Jungle with Virginia McKenna, 1990; Faces in a Crowd, 1990; Occasions; Shades of Green, 1991; Elected Friends, Poems to and about Edward Thomas, 1991; He Said, She Said, They Said, 1993; Methuen Audition Book for Young Actors, 1993; Criminal Records, 1994; Methuen Book of Duologues, 1995; Starlight, Starbright, 1995. Contributions to: Guardian; Independent; Times Literary Supplement; Times Educational Supplement; Tablet; Speech and Drama. Honours: Grant, The Arts Council's Compton Poetry Fund for Promoting Poetry to a Wider Audience, 1984, 1986; Signal Poetry Award, 1992. Memberships: British Federation of Festivals for Music, Speech and Dance, Central Board Member; Edward Thomas Fellowship; Children's Books History Society; John Masefield Society; Charlotte Mary Yonge Fellowship; Friends of the Dymock Poets. Address: 37 St Stephens Road, Ealing, London W13 8HJ, England.

HARVEY Francis, b. 13 April 1925, Enniskillen, Ireland. Bank Official. m. Marie A Gormley, 22 June 1955, 5 daughters. Education: University College, Dublin. Publications: In the Light on the Stones, 1978; The Rainmakers, 1988. Contributions to: Irish Times; Guardian; Cyphers; Dublin Magazine; Hibernia; Honest Ulsterman; Irish Independent; Irish press; New Poetry; Orbis; Poetry Ireland Review; Donegal Democrat (The Rat Pit); Orange Dove of Fiji; New Poems 1977-78; The Long Embrace, 20th Century Irish Love Poems. Honours: Irish Times-Yeats International Summer School Poetry Prize, 1977; Worldwide Fund for Nature Hutchinson-Guardian Prize, 1989 Peterloo Poets Prize, 1990. Memberships: Poetry Ireland; Poetry Society, London; Society of Irish Playwrights; Irish Writer's Union. Address: Trienna, Upper Main Street, Donegal Town, County Donegal, Ireland.

HARVEY Marshall L, (Thomas Norman), b. 23 Aug 1950, New Mexico, USA. Teacher; Technical Writer. m. Virginia, 28 Dec 1972, 1 daughter. Education: BA, cum laude, Williams College, 1972; MA, Indiana University, 1974; PhD, University of Chicago, 1979. Appointments: Instructor, English, Columbia College; Technical Writer, Digital Engineering Corp; Writer, Boston Technology. Publications: Painted Light, 1994; Iambic Pentameter from Shakespeare to Browning, 1996. Contributions to: Berkeley Poetry Review; Hawaii Review; NRG; Impetus; Boston Poet; Next Exit. Honour: Bay Area Poetry Coalition. Membership: Poetry Society of New Hampshire, 1983-. Address: 59 Boulder Drive, Londonderry, NH 03053, USA.

HARVEY Pamela Ann, b. 15 Oct 1934, Bush Hill Park, Edmonton, London, England. Writer. Education: RSA Diploma. Appointments: Secretarial Work, London; Library Work, Southgate Library. Publications: Poetry, 1994; Quiet Lines, 1996. Contributions to: The People's Poetry; Romantic Heir; Cadmium Blue Literary Journal; Pendragon; Keltria, USA; Celtic Connections; Silver Wheel; Sharkti Laureate; Time Haiku; Azami, Japan. Memberships: Enfield Writers Group; New Renaissance Poets Society.

HARWOOD Edmund Donald, b. 9 Jan 1924, Cannes, France. Royal Navy Officer; Translator. m. Penelope Ann St Clair Morford, 2 Apr 1949, 1 son, 1 daughter. Education: Naval Translator in German, 1949, Norwegian, 1969. Appointments: Naval Officer, retiring as Commander, 1942-72; Freelance Translator, 5 languages, 1972-. Publications: A Clutch of Words, 1980; A Flight of Words, 1985.

Contributions to: Acumen; Argo; Country Life; Countryman; Envoi; Field; Iron; Orbis; Outposts; Pennine Platform; Poetry Nottingham; Rialto; Spokes; Stand; Staple; Weyfarers; Doors; Global Tapestry; Iota; Sepia; South. Honours: Rhyme Revival, 1983; Stanza, 1984; Chester, Staple, 1986; Surrey Competition, 1988; Queenie Lee Competition, 1989; Vert Poets Open, 1990; Ouse Valley Poetry Competition, 1992; Christchurch Poetry Competition, 1992. Address: Wadswell, Haythorne Common, Horton, Wimborne, Dorset BH21 7JG, England.

HARWOOD Lee, b. 6 June 1939, Leicester, England. Writer. Div, 2 sons, 1 daughter. Education: BA (Hons), English, Queen Mary College, University of London, 1961. Publications: Title Illegible, 1965; The Man With Blue Eyes, 1966; The White Room, 1968; Landscapes, 1969; The Sinking Colony, 1971; HMS Little Fox, 1976; Boston Brighton, 1977; All The Wrong Notes, 1981; Monster Masks, 1985; Dream Quilt, 30 assorted stories, 1985; Rope Boy to the Rescue, 1988; Crossing the Frozen River: Selected Poems, 1988; In the Mists: Mountain Poems, 1993; As translator: Tristan Tzara - Selected Poems, 1975; Tristan Tzara: Chanson Dada, 1987; Co-editor with Peter Bailey: The Empty Hill. Memories and Praises of Paul Evans, 1945-1991, 1992. Contributions to: Ambit; London Magazine; Montemora; Paris Review; Partisan Review; Poetry Review, London; Transatlantic Review. Honours: Annual Award, Poetry Foundation, New York, 1966; Alice Hunt Bartlett Prize, Poetry Society, London, 1976. Memberships: National Poetry Secretariat, Chairman 1974-76; The Poetry Society, London, Chairman 1976-77. Address: 2 Ivy Place, off Waterloo Street, Hove, Sussex BN3 1AP, England.

HASAN Rabiul, b. Dhaka, Bangladesh (American citizen). Student. Education: BA, Hons, Political Science, MA, Political Science, University of Dhaka, Bangladesh; MSEd, Social Science, MSEd, English, Alcorn State University, USA. Appointments: Adjunct Instructor of English, Delgado Community College, New Orleans, Louisiana; Adjunct Instructor of English, Alcorn State University, Lionman, Mississippi; Adjunct Instructor of Political Science and History, Alcorn State University; Public Relations Officer, Alcorn State University. Publication: Protima Esai Bolay, Jai (Protime Comes to Say Goodbye), 1992. Contributions to: Colonnades; Poet Lore; Transom; Modern Images; Bloomsbury Review; Wind; Images; Writers' Forum; Permafrost; Widener Review; Plainsongs. Honour: Certificate of Achievement, Potpourri International Publishers. Memberships: Mississippi Philological Association; Academy of American Poets. Address: 2609 MacGregor Downs Road, Apt #17 Greenville, NC 27834, USA.

HASHMI (Aurangzeb) Alamgir, b. 15 Nov 1951, Lahore, Pakistan. Professor of English and Comparative Literature; Editor; Broadcaster. Education: MA, 1972; MA, 1977; DLitt, 1984. Appointments: Academic posts, various universities, 1971-. Publications: Poetry: The Oath and Amen, 1976; An Old Chair, 1979; America Is a Punjab Word, 1979; My Second in Kentucky, 1981; This Time in Lahore, 1983; Neither This Time/Nor That Place, 1984; Inland and Other Poems, 1988; The Poems of Alamgir Hashmi, 1992; Sun and Moon and Other Poems, 1992; Also: Pakistani Literature, 1978; Commonwealth Literature, 1983; Ezra Pound, 1983; The Worlds of Muslim Imagination, 1986; The Commonwealth, Comparative Literature and the World, 1988; Pakistani Short Stories in English, 1996. Contributions to: Edinburgh Review; Boston Literary Review; Washington Review; Poetry Australia; The Poetry Review; Landfall; Helix; Pacific Quarterly; New Letters; Modern Poetry Studies; Chicago Review; Span; Pen International; Sapriphage; Journal of South Asian Literature; Screever; New Mexico Humanities Review; Bridge; Terra Poetica; Poetry Nottingham; Asiaweek; Aspect; The New Quarterly; Origins; Centerpoint; West Branch; Cincinnati Poetry Review; Omens; Telescope; Wascana Review; Ariel; Portland Review; Word Loom; Canto; Greenfield Review; Westerly; Confrontation; Cape Rock; Lamar Review; Seneca Review; Capilano Review; Connecticut Quarterly; DeKalb Literary Arts Journal; Green River Review; Contemporary Review; Chelsea; Postmodern Culture; Paris Voices; Toronto Review; Kunapipi; The Literary Review; Others. Honours: First Prize, All Pakistan Creative Writing Contest, 1972; The Patras Bokhari Award (National Literature Prize), The Pakistan Academy of Letters, 1985; Rockefeller Fellow, 1994; The Roberto Celli Memorial Award, 1994. Memberships: Several literature associations, Pakistan, England, USA. Address: c/o Indus Books, PO Box 2905, Islamabad GPO, Pakistan.

HASS Robert (Louis), b. 1 Mar 1941, San Francisco, California, USA. Poet; Writer; Translator; Editor; Professor. m. Earlene Joan Leif,

1 Sept 1962, div 1986, 2 sons, 1 daughter. Education: BA, St Mary's College of California, 1963; MA, 1965, PhD, 1971, Stanford University. Appointments: Assistant Professor, State University of New York, Buffalo, 1967-71; Professor of English, St Mary's College of California, 1971-89, and University of California at Berkeley, 1989-; Visiting Lecturer, University of Virginia, 1974, Goddard College, 1976, Columbia University, 1982, and University of California at Berkeley, 1983; Poet-in-Residence, The Frost Place, Franconia, New Hampshire, 1978; Poet Laureate of USA, 1995-97. Publications: Poetry: Field Guide, 1973; Winter Morning in Charlottesville, 1977; Praise, 1979; Human Wishes, 1989; Sun Under Wood, 1996; Other: Twentieth Century Pleasures: Prose on Poetry, 1984; Into the Garden - A Wedding Anthology: Poetry and Prose on Love and Marriage, 1993; Translator: Czeslaw Milosz's Unattainable Earth (with Czeslaw Milosz), 1986; Editor: Rock and Hawk: A Selection of Shorter Poems by Robinson Jeffers, 1987; The Pushcart Prize XII (with Bill Henderson and Jorie Graham), 1987; Tomaz Salamun: Selected Poems (with Charles Simic), 1988; Selected Poems of Tomas Tranströmer, 1954-1986 (with others), 1989; The Essential Haiku: Versions of Basho, Buson and Issa, 1994. Contributions to: Anthologies and other publications. Honours: Woodrow Wilson Fellowship, 1963-64; Danforth Fellowship, 1963-67; Yale Series of Younger Poets Award, Yale University Press, 1972; US-Great Britain Bicentennial Exchange Fellow in the Arts, 1976-77; William Carlos Williams Award, 1979; National Book Critics Circle Award, 1984; Award of Merit, American Academy of Arts and Letters, 1984; MacArthur Foundation Grant, 1984. Address: PO Box 807, Inverness, CA 94937, USA.

HASTINGS Jennifer Sue, b. 31 Oct 1965, Cincinnati, Ohio, USA. Library Clerical Worker. Education: BA, International Business, Muskingum College, Ohio, 1987; Diploma, Institute of Children's Literature, 1991. Appointments: Secretary, Human Resources Division, Huntington Bank Inc; Clerk, Kenton County, Kentucky; Public Library. Contributions to: American Poetry Anthology, 1989; Publisher's Choice: Selected Poems of the New Era, 1989; Best New Poets of 1989; Great Poems of the Western World Vol II, 1990; Poetic Voices of America, 1990; American Anthology of Southern Poetry, 1990. Honours: 3rd place, National French Creative Writing Contest, Poetry, 1981; Poet of Merit, American Poetry Association, 1989, 1990; Golden Poet, World of Poetry, 1989, 1990; Inclusion in World of Poetry's Who's Who in Poetry, 1990. Memberships: Poetry Society of America; Academy of American Poets; American Poetry Association; World of Poetry; Muskingum College Literary Magazine Association, Secretary, Assistant Editor; Night Writers; Phi Sigma Iota; International Foreign Language Honorary Society. Chapter President, Chapter Secretary. Address: 1518 Diamond Court, No 12, Fort Wright, KY 41011, USA.

HATHAWAY Michael, b. 20 Sept 1961, El Paso, Texas, USA. Appointment: Typesetter, Great Bend Daily Tribune, Kansas. Publications: Shadows of Myself, 1980; Inconspicuous, 1988; Excerpt, 1989; Come Winter and Other Poems, 1989; God Poems, 1991. Contributions to: Fire!; Calliopes Corner; Waterways; Manna; Golden Isis; RFD; Up Against the Wall, Mother; Raw Bone; Nothing Sinister; ArtiMag; Psychopoetica; Forum for Universal Spokesmen; Clock Radio; New Sins; Daring Poetry Quarterly; Thirteen; River Rat Review; Silver Wings; Parnassus Literary Journal; Gypsy; Impetus; Anemone; Pididdle; Cats Eye; Off My Fare; Poets Perspective; Proof Rock; Heigh-Ashbury Literary Journal; Cat Fancy; Pearl; Ransom; Poet; Abbey. Honour: 1st Place, Jubilee Press Contest, 1987. Address: 1514 Stone, Great Bend, KS 67530, USA.

HAUGEN Paal-Helge, b. 26 Apr 1945, Valle, Norway. Poet; Writer; Dramatist. Education: Medicine, film and theatre, Norway and the USA. Appointments: Chairman, Norwegian State Film Production Board, 1980-85; Chairman, Board of Literary Advisors, Association of Norwegian Authors, 1984-88; International Pegasus Prize Committee, 1988. Publications: 28 books including: Anne (novel), 1968; A (libretto for monodrama by Iannis Xenakis), 1993; Poesi: Collected Poems, 1965-95, 1995; Other: Plays for stage, radio, and television; Opera libretti. Contributions to: Professional journals translated into 20 languages. Address: Skrefjellv 5, 4645 Nodeland, Norway.

HAUGOVA Mila, (Mila Srnková), b. 14 June 1942, Budapest, Hungary. Magazine Editor. m. (1) Edgar Haug, 16 Sept 1967, divorced, 1 daughter, (2) Ladislav Kvasz, 1993. Education: Engineer in Agronomy degree, Nitra, 1965. Appointments: Teacher, Technical High School; Teacher, Grammar School; Editor, Romboid literature and critical theory magazine; Close relationship to painter Peter Ondreicka, illustrator of her 2 poetry books, 1984-90. Publications: Rusty Earth,

1980; Variable Surface, 1981; Possible Tenderness, 1984; Clean Days, 1990; Prime Love, 1991; Nostalgia, 1992; Lady with Unicorn, 1995. Contributions to: Romboid; Slovenske Pohlady (Slovak View); Literary Weekly; Cultural Life; New Writing; Several programmes on Slovak Radio and TV. Honours: Prize for book Rusty Earth, Literary Foundation, 1981; Prize for poetry book Prime Love, Slovensky Spisovatel Publishing House, 1992. Memberships: Club of Independent Writers; PEN Slovak Centre, Secretary 1992-. Address: Nejedlého 27, 84102 Bratislava, Slovakia.

HAWKINS Hunt, b. 23 Dec 1943, Washington, District of Columbia, USA. Professor of English. m. Elaine Smith, 4 Sept 1976, 1 son, 1 daughter. Education: BA, Williams College, 1965; MA, 1969, PhD, 1976, Stanford University. Appointments: Instructor, Texas Southern University, 1968-70; Assistant Professor, University of Minnesota, 1977-78; Assistant Professor, 1978-83, Associate Professor, 1983-94, Professor of English, 1994-, Florida State University, Tallahassee. Publication: The Domestic Life, 1994. Contributions to: Poetry; Southern Review; Georgia Review; Tri-Quarterly; Carleton Miscellany; Poetry Northwest; Beloit Poetry Journal; Harvard Magazine; Minnesota Review; Kayak; Wormwood Review; Kansas Quarterly; Yankee Magazine; Bellingham Review; Florida Review; Southern Poetry Review; Apalachee Quarterly. Honours: Prize, Academy of American Poets, 1963, 1965, 1973; Agnes Lynch Starrett Poetry Prize, 1992; Florida Individual Artist Fellowship, 1993-94. Memberships: Modern Language Association; South Atlantic Modern Language Association; Joseph Conrad Society; Mark Twain Circle. Address: English Department, Florida State University, Tallahassee, FL 32306, USA.

HAWTHORNE Susan, b. 30 Nov 1951, Wagga Wagga, New South Wales, Australia. Publisher; Writer; Academic. Education: Diploma in Primary Teaching, Melbourne Teachers College, 1973; BA, Honours, Philosophy, La Trobe University, 1976; MA, prelim, Classics, University of Melbourne, 1981. Appointments: Music, Theatre and Writing Co-Ordinator, Women 150 Festival, 1984; Tutor, Koori Teacher Education Program, Deakin University, 1986; Editor and Commissioning Editor, Penguin Books, Australia, 1987-91; Publisher, Spinifex Press, 1991-; Lecturer, Department of Communication and Language Studies, Victoria University of Technology, 1995-. Publication: The Language in My Tongue, Four New Poets, 1993. Contributions to: Australia: Meanjin; Overland; Fine Line; Age; Australian Women's Book Review; Canada: Tessera; UK: Slow Dancer; USA: Sinister Wisdom. Honours: Shortlisted for Mattara Poetry prize, 1991; Shortlisted for ABC Radio National Poetry Award, 1994. Memberships: PEN International; Australian Society of Authors; Fellowship of Australian Writers; Victorian Writers Centre. Address: PO Box 212, North Melbourne, Victoria 3051, Australia.

HAXTON Brooks, b. 1 Dec 1950, Greenville, Mississippi, USA. Teacher; Poet. m. 5 June 1983, 1 son. Education: BA, Beloit College, Wisconsin; MA, Syracuse University. Appointments: Resident Poet, Warren Wilson College, 1990-; Resident Poet, Syracuse University, Syracuse, New York, 1993-. Publications: The Lay of Eleanor and Irene, 1985; Dominion, 1986; Traveling Company, 1989; Dead Reckoning, 1989. Contributions to: American Poetry Review; Atlantic; Beloit Poetry Journal; Kenyon Review; Missouri Review; Southern Review; Tri-Quarterly Review. Honours: Fellowships from: Syracuse University, 1979-81; Council for the Arts, Washington, DC, 1984; Ingram Merrill Foundation, 1985; National Endowment for the Arts, 1987; New York Foundation for the Arts, 1988. Membership: Poetry Society of America. Address: 21 Bloomingdale Road, White Plains, NY 10605, USA.

HAYES Ann Louise, b. 13 May 1924, Los Angeles, California, USA. Professor of English. Education: AB summa cum laude, English, 1948, MA, English, 1950, Stanford University. Appointments: Acting Instructor, Stanford University, 1950; Teaching Associate, Indiana University, 1953-55; Instructor, Coe College, 1955-57; Instructor, 1957-60, Assistant Professor, 1960-65, Carnegie Institute of Technology; Associate Professor, 1965-74, Professor, 1974-, Carnegie Mellon University, Pittsburgh, Pennsylvania. Publications: For Sally Barnes, 1963; Amo Ergo Sum, Amo Ergo Est, 1969; The Dancer's Step, 1973; The Living and the Dead, 1975; Witness How All Occasions..., 1977; Progress, Dancing, 1986; Circle of the Earth, 1990; Letters at Christmas and Other Poems, 1995. Contributions to: New Mexico Quarterly Review; City Lights; American Scholar; Southern Review; Virginia Quarterly Review; Carnegie Review; Three Rivers Poetry Journal; Oakland Review; Cloud Chamber; Fountain; Focus;

Poema Convidada; New England Journal of Medicine; Hudson Review; Confrontation; Maryland Review; The Epigrammatist; La Fontana. Honours: Irene Hardy Poetry Award, Stanford University, 1943; Clarence Urmy Poetry Prize, Stanford University, 1943, 1947, 1950; Ina Coolbrith Award, University of California, Stanford University and Mills College, 1943; Honourable Mention, James D Phelan Award in Poetry, 1947; Borestone Mountain Poetry Award, 1968; Best Poems of 1969. Address: Department of English, Baker Hall 259, Carnegie Mellon University, Pittsburgh, PA 15213, USA.

HAYNA Lois Ruth Beebe, b. 28 Jan 1913, Idaho, USA. Teacher. m. Joseph Hayna, 17 June 1959, 1 son, 2 daughters. Education: University of Wisconsin, Madison. Publications: Book of Charms, Co-author, 1983; Never Trust a Crow, 1990; Northern Gothic, 1992. Contributions to: Plains Poetry Journal; South Coast Poetry Journal; Bulletin of the Poetry Society of America; Chowder Review; Croton Review. Honours: Literary Fellowship Award, Colorado, 1984; Nominated for Governor's Award, 1990; Nominated, Pushcart Poetry Prize, 1991; Awarded Residence at Ragdale Writers Colony and Helene Wurlitzer Foundation, Taos, New Mexico. Memberships: Poetry Society of America; Academy of American Poets; Poetry West, Board Member, Secretary; National Federation of State Poetry Societies. Address: 403 Locust Drive, Colorado Springs, CO 30907, USA.

HAYWOOD April, (Sheila Smith), b. 10 Apr 1948, Georgia, USA. Writer. 1 daughter. Appointments: Bank Clerk; Photographer of Fine Art; Foster Mother; Youth and Community Worker; Claims Negotiator; Technical Sales Representative; Zone Manager, Avon Cosmetics. Contributions to: Vole; Stubble; Poetry of the 70's; First Time; Frogmore Papers; Poetry Now. Memberships: Poetry Society; Poets Anonymous. Address: 193 Green Lane, Norbury, London SW16 3LZ, England.

HAZARA Singh, b. 30 Nov 1922, Sheikhpura District, India. Retired University Teacher. m. Phool Kaur, 13 Mar 1949, 2 sons, 2 daughters. Education: BA, Punjab University, Lahore, 1945; MA, 1950, LLB, 1955, Punjab University, Chandigarh. Appointments: Lecturer, English, Khalsa College, Amritsar, 1950-53; Assistant Professor, English, Government Agricultural College, Ludhiana, 1954-66; Associate Professor of English, 1966-84, Head, Department of Languages and Journalism, 1977-82, Punjab Agricultural University, Ludhiana; Secretary to Vice-Chancellor, Guru Nanak Dev University, Amritsar, 1985-88. Publications: Aspirations, 1980; Yearnings, 1987. Contributions to: Advance, Chandigarth; Samvedana, Mangalore; Poet, Madras; Poetcrit, Maranda; Poets International, Banglore; Quest, Ranchi; Canopy, Bareilly; Metverse Muse, Visakhapatnam; Brainwave, Madras. Anthologies: Indian Verse by Young Poets, 1980; New Voices in Indian Poetry, in English, 1981; Rising Columns: Some Indian Poets in English, 1982; East-West Winds: An International Anthology of Poetry, 1982; Modern Trends in Indo-Anglian Poetry, 1982; Prevalent Aspects of Indian English Poetry, 1983; Indo-Australian Flowers, 1984; Prism: An Anthology of English Verse, 1984; New Talents in Indo-English Poetry, 1985; Moods: An Anthology of Futuristic English Verse, 1985; East-West Voices, 1988; World Poetry, 1991, 1992, 1994, 1995, 1996; Rising Stars, 1991; New Global Voices, 1994; Golden Thoughts, 1995; Poetry 200 AD, 1996. Memberships: Indian Society of Authors; World Poetry International; Punjabi Sahitya Academy, Ludhiana. Address: 3-C Udham Singh Nagar, Ludhiana 141001, India.

HAZO Samuel (John), b. 19 July 1928, Pittsburgh, Pennsylvania, USA. Professor of English; Writer; Poet. Education: BA, University of Notre Dame, 1948; MA, Duquesne University, 1955; PhD, University of Pittsburgh, 1957. Appointments: Faculty, 1955-65, Dean, College of Arts and Sciences, 1961-66, Professor of English, 1965-, Duquesne University; Director, International Poetry Forum, 1966-. Publications: Discovery and Other Poems, 1959; The Quiet Wars, 1962; Hart Crane: An Introduction and Interpretation, 1963, new edition as Smithereened Apart: A Critique of Hart Crane, 1978; The Christian Intellectual Studies in the Relation of Catholicism to the Human Sciences (Editor), 1963; A Selection of Contemporary Religious Poetry (Editor), 1963; Listen with the Eye, 1964; My Sons in God: Selected and New Poems 1965; Blood Rights, 1968; The Blood of Adonis (with Ali Ahmed Said), 1971; Twelve Poems (with George Nama), 1972; Seascript: A Mediterranean Logbook, 1972; Once for the Last Bandit: New and Previous Poems, 1972; Quartered, 1974; Inscripts, 1975; The Very Fall of the Sun, 1978; To Paris, 1981; The Wanton Summer Air, 1982; Thank a Bored Angel, 1983; The Feast of Icarus, 1984; The

Color of Reluctance, 1986; The Pittsburgh That Starts Within You, 1986; Silence Spoken Here, 1988; Stills, 1989; The Rest is Prose, 1989; Lebanon, 1990; Picks, 1990; The Past Won't Stay Behind You, 1993; The Pages of Day and Night, 1995; The Holy Surprise of Right Now, 1996; Latching the Fist, 1996. Address: 785 Somerville Drive, Pittsburgh, PA 15243, USA.

HEANEY Seamus (Justin), b. 13 Apr 1939, County Londonderry, Northern Ireland. Poet; Writer; Professor. m. Marie Devlin, 1965, 2 sons, 1 daughter. Education: St Columb's College, Derry; BA 1st Class, Queen's University, Belfast, 1961. Appointments: Teacher, St Thomas's Secondary School, Belfast, 1962-63; Lecturer, St Joseph's College of Education, Belfast, 1963-66, Queen's University, Belfast, 1966-72, Carysfort College, 1975-81; Senior Visiting Lecturer 1982-85, Boylston Professor of Rhetoric & Oratory 1985-, Harvard University; Professor of Poetry, Oxford University, 1989-94. Publications: Eleven Poems, 1965; Death of a Naturalist, 1966; Door Into the Dark, 1969; Wintering Out, 1972; North, 1975; Field Work, 1979; Selected Poems, 1965-1975, 1980; Sweeney Astray, 1984, revised edition as Sweeney's Flight, 1992; Station Island, 1984; The Haw Lantern, 1987; New Selected Poems 1966-1987, 1990; Seeing Things, 1991, The Spirit Level, 1996. Prose: Preoccupations: Selected Prose 1968-1978, 1980; The Government of the Tongue, 1988; The Place of Writing, 1989; The Redress of Poetry, 1995. Editor: The May Anthology of Oxford and Cambridge Poetry, with Ted Hughes, 1993; The Rattle Bag, 1982. Other: The Cure at Troy, version of Sophocles's Philoctetes, 1990; Laments, translated from the polish of Jan Kochanowski, with Stanislaw Baranczak, 1995. Honours: Somerset Maugham Award, 1967; Cholmondeley Award, 1968; W H Smith Award, 1975; Duff Cooper Prize, 1975; Whitbread Award, 1987; Nobel Prize for Literature, 1995. Memberships: Irish Academy of Letters. Address: c/o Faber & Faber, 3 Queen Square, London WC1N 3RU, England.

HEARLE Kevin James, b. 17 Mar 1958, Santa Ana, California, USA. Poet; Professor. m. Elizabeth Libby Henderson, 26 Nov 1983. Education: AB, English with Distinction, Stanford University, 1980; MFA English, University of Iowa, 1983; MA, Literature, 1990; PhD, Literature, 1991, University of Santa Cruz. Appointments: Lecturer, Department of English, California State University, Los Angeles; Lecturer, Department of English, San Jose State University; Lecturer in American Literature; Univerity of California at Santa Cruz; Research Assistant, National Endowment for the Humanities Summer Institutes on Literary Translation; Poetry Co-Editor, Quarry West; Lecturer, Department of English, Coe College; Instructor, General Education Program, University of Iowa; Outreach Instructor, Iowa Center for the Arts. Publication: Each Thing We Know is Changed Because We Know It and Other Poems, 1994. Contributions to: Georgia Review; Yale Review; University of Windsor Review (Canada) Quarterly West; New Orleans Review; Sonora Review; Petroglyph; Poetry Flash. Honours: Poems nominated for Pushcart Prize, 1993; Finalist; National Poetry Series, 1992; Finalist, Yales Series of Younger Poets, 1992; Finalist, Discovery, The Nation Poetry Contest, 1984. Memberships: PEN Center USA West; The Literary Network; American Literary Translator's Assocation; Western Literature Association; Modern Language Association; Robinson Jeffers Association; Friends of Steinbeck. Address: 320 N Palm Drive #304, Beverly Hills, CA 90210, USA.

HEARNE Vicki, b. 13 Feb 1946, Austin, Texas, USA. Assistant Professor of English; Writer; Poet. m. (1) div, 1 daughter, (2) Robert Tragesser, 1980. Education: BA, University of California, Riverside. Appointments: Lecturer in English, University of California, Riverside, 1981-84; Assistant Professor of English, Yale University, 1984-. Publications: Nervous Horses (poems), 1980; In the Absence of Horses (poems), 1983; Adam's Task: Calling Animals by Name, 1986; The White German Shepherd (novel), 1988; Bandit: Dossier of a Dangerous Dog, 1991; Animal Happiness, 1993; The Parts of Light (poems), 1994. Honours: Peter Lavan Younger Poets Award, Academy of American Poets, 1984; American Academy and Institute of Arts and Letters Award, 1992. Memberships: American Working Dog Association; PEN; Endangered Breeds Association. Address: c/o Yale Institution for Social and Policy Studies, Yale University, New Haven, CT 16520, USA.

HEATH Desmond Butterworth, b. 27 Feb 1927, London, England. Musician (Violinist). m. Sylvia Noel Putterill, 21 June 1952, 1 son, 2 daughters. Education: ARCM, Royal College of Music, 1942-47. Appointments: BBC Symphony Orchestra, 1948-57;

Philharmonia, 1961-70; Freelance Player, English Baroque Soloists, London Classical Players, Academy of Ancient Music and others; Violin Teacher, Eton and Westminster (peripatetic). Publications: After This Sky, 1968; Chiaroscuro, 1985; Country Night and Other Poems, 1990; Roden Noel - A Wide Angle, compiled and presented, 1996. Contributions to: New Hope International Writing; Poetry Wales; Iota; Breakthru; Poetry Nottingham; Envoi. Honours: Highly Commended, Lake Aske Competition, Poetry Nottingham, 1983; 1st Prize, Queenie Lee Memorial Competition, Poetry Nottingham, 1986; Merit Award, Queenie Lee Poetry Competition, Poetry Nottingham, 1991; 3rd Prize, Phras 94 Open Poetry Competition. Address: 60 Esmond Road, Bedford Park, London W4 1JF, England.

HEATH-STUBBS John (Francis Alexander), b. 9 July 1918, London, England. Poet. Education: Worcester College for the Blind; Queen's College, Oxford. Appointments: English Tutor, 1944-45; Editorial Assistant, Hutchinsons, 1945-46; Gregory Fellow, Poetry, University of Leeds, 1952-55; Visiting Professor of English, University of Alexandria, 1955-58, University of Michigan, 1960-61; Lecturer in English Literature, College of St Mark and St John, Chelsea, 1963-73. Publications: Poetry: Wounded Thammuz; Beauty and the Beast; The Divided Ways; The Swarming of the Bees; A Charm Against the Toothache; The Triumph of the Muse; The Blue Fly in His Head; Selected Poems; Satires and Epigrams; Artorius; A Parliament of Birds; The Watchman's Flute; Birds Reconvened; Buzz Buzz; Naming of the Best; The Immolation of Adelphi; Cats Parnassus; Time Pieces; Partridge in a Pear Tree; Ninefold of Charms; Collected Poems; The Game of Love and Death, 1991; David Gray: In the Shadows, 1991; The Parson's Cat, 1992; Sweet Apple Earth, 1993; Chimeras, 1994; Hindsights, autobiography, 1993; Translations: Hafir of Shiraz (co-translator); The Rubiyat of Omar Khayyam; Leopardi: Selected Prose and Poetry; The Poems of Anyte; Editor, Selected poems of Jonathan Swift, Tennyson, Alexander Pope and others; Drama and criticism. Honours: Queen's Gold Medal for Poetry, 1973; Order of the British Empire. Address: 22 Artesian Road, London W2 5AR, England.

HEATHERLEY A Celeste. See: **MORGAN Ariel Celeste Heatherley**.

HECHT Anthony (Evan), b. 16 Jan 1923, New York, New York, USA. Poet; Professor. m. (1) Patricia Harris, 27 Feb 1954, div 1961, 2 sons, (2) Helen D'Alessandro, 12 June 1971, 1 son. Education: BA, Bard College, 1944; MA, Columbia University, 1950. Appointments: Teacher, Kenyon College 1947-48, State University of Iowa 1948-49, New York University 1949-56, Smith College 1956-59; Associate Professor of English, Bard College, 1961-67; Faculty 1967-68, John D Deane Professor of Rhetoric and Poetry 1968-85, University of Rochester; Hurst Professor, Washington University, St Louis, 1971; Visiting Professor, Harvard University 1973, Yale University 1977; Faculty, Salzburg Seminar in American Studies, 1977; Professor, Georgetown University, 1985-93; Consultant in Poetry, Library of Congress, Washington, DC, 1982-84; Andrew Mellon Lecturer in Fine Arts, National Gallery of Art, Washington, DC, 1992. Publications: A Summoning of Stones, 1954; The Seven Deadly Sins, 1958; A Bestiary, 1960; The Hard Hours, 1968; Millions of Strange Shadows, 1977; The Venetian Vespers, 1977; Obbligati: Essays in criticsm, 1986; The Transparent Man, 1990; Collected Earlier Poems, 1990; The Hidden Law: The Poetry of W H Auden, 1993; On the Laws of the Poetic Art, 1995; The Presumption of Death, 1995; Flight Among the Tombs, 1996. Co-Author and Co-Editor: Jiggery-Pokery: A Compendium of Double Dactyls (with John Hollander), 1967. Editor: The Essential Herbert, 1987. Translator: Seven Against Thebes (with Helen Bacon), 1973. Contributions to: Many anthologies; Hudson Review; New York Review of Books; Quarterly Review of Literature; Transatlantic Review; Voices. Honours: Priz de Rome Fellowshp, 1950; Guggenheim Fellowships, 1954, 1959; Hudson Review Fellowship, 1958; Ford Foundation Fellowships, 1960, 1968; Brandeis University Creative Arts Award, 1965; Pulitzer Prize in Poetry, 1968; Academy of American Poets Fellowship, 1969; Bollingen Prize, 1983; Eugenio Montale Award. 1983; Harriet Monroe Award, 1987; Ruth Lilly Award, 1988; Aiken Taylor Award of The Sewanee Review, 1988; National Endowment for the Arts Grant, 1989. Memberships: Academy of American Poets, honorary chancellor 1971-95; American Academy of Arts & Sciences; American Academy of Arts & Letters; Phi Beta Kappa. Address: 4256 Nebraska Avenue North West, Washington, DC 20016, USA.

HEFFERNAN Michael, b. 20 Dec 1942, Detroit, Michigan, USA. Professor. m. (1) Kathleen Spigarelli, 9 Aug 1975, div 1994, 3 sons, (2)

Anna Monardo, Sept 1995. Education: AB, University of Detroit, 1964; MA, 1967, PhD, 1970, University of Massachusetts. Appointments: Instructor, Oakland University, Michigan, 1967-69; Professor, Pittsburg State University, Kansas, 1969-86; Professor, University of Arkansas, Fayetteville, 1986-. Publications: The Cry of Oliver Hardy, 1979; To the Wreakers of Havoc, 1984; The Man at Home, 1988; Love's Answer, 1994; The Back Road to Arcadia, 1994. Contributions to: American Poetry Review; Georgia Review; Gettysburg Review; Iowa Review; Shenandoah; Quarterly; TriQuarterly. Honours: Bread Loaf Scholarship, 1977; Fellowships, National Endowment for the Arts, 1978, 1987, 1993. Membership: Poetry Society of America, 1975-. Address: c/o University of Arkansas, Fayetteville, Arkansas, USA.

HEFFERNAN Thomas (Patrick) Carroll, b. 19 Aug 1939, Hyannis, Massachusetts, USA. Lecturer in English, Philosophy and Humanities. m. Nancy Eller, 14 July 1972, diss 1977. Education: AB, Boston College, 1961; MA, English Literature, University of Manchester, England, 1963; Università per Stranieri, Perugia, Italy, summer 1965; PhD, English Literature, Sophia University, Tokyo, Japan, 1991. Appointments: Poet in Schools, North Carolina Department of Public Instruction, Raleigh, 1973-77; Visiting Artist, Poetry: North Carolina Department of Community Colleges, 1977-81, South Carolina Arts Commission, 1981-82; Lecturer in English, Philosophy and Humanities, University of Maryland Asian Division. Publications: Mobiles, 1974; A Poem Is A Smile You Can Hear (editor), 1976; A Narrative of Jeremy Bentham, 1978; The Liam Poems, 1981; City Renewing Itself, 1983. Contributions to: Ploughshares; Midwest Quarterly; Southern Poetry Review; St Andrews Review; Yankee; Mainichi; Poetry Nippon; Several other publications. Honours: National Endowment for the Arts Literary Fellowship in Poetry and Fiction, Southern Arts Foundation, 1977; Gordon Barber Memorial Award, Poetry Society of American, 1977; Mainichi Awards, Tokyo, 1985, 1987, 1988; Haiku Award, JAL Mainichi Culture Seminar, 1986; Itoen International Haiku Award, Tokyo, 1991. Memberships: Poetry Society of America; Haiku Society of America; Modern Language Association; Association of Writers and Poets. Address: University of Maryland, Asian Division, PSC 80, Box 14591, APO AP 96367, USA.

HEGI Ursula (Johanna), b. 23 May 1946, Büderich, Germany. Professor of English; Writer; Poet; Critic. 2 sons. Education: BA, 1978, MA, 1979, University of New Hampshire. Appointments: Instructor, University of New Hampshire, 1980-84; Book Critic, Los Angeles Times, New York Times, Washington Post, 1982-; Assistant Professor, 1984-89, Associate Professor, 1989-95, Professor of English, 1995-, Eastern Washington University; Visiting Writer, various universities. Publications: Fiction: Intrusions, 1981; Unearned Pleasures and Other Stories, 1988; Floating in My Mother's Palm, 1990; Stones from the River, 1994; Salt Dancers, 1995; Non-fiction: Tearing the Silence: On Being German in America, 1997. Contributions to: Anthologies, newspapers, journals, and magazines. Honours: Indiana Fiction Award, 1988; National Endowment for the Arts Fellowship, 1990; New York Times Best Books Selections, 1990, 1994; Pacific Northwest Booksellers Association Award, 1991; Governor's Writers Awards, 1991, 1994. Memberships: Associated Writing Programs; Board of Directors, National Book Critics Circle, 1992-94. Address: c/o Department of English, Eastern Washington University, Cheney, WA 99004, USA.

HEINRICH Peggy, b. 20 Feb 1929, USA. Writer. m. Martin R Heinrich, 4 Apr 1952, dec 1976, 2 daughters. Education: BA, Hunter College, New York City, 1949. Appointment: Editor, Connecticut River Review, 1985-87. Publications: Haiga Haiku (with artist Barbara Gray), 1982; A Patch of Grass, 1984; Sharing the Woods, 1992; Forty-four Freckles, 1995. Contributions to: Connecticut Artist; Blue Unicorn; Footwork; Calliope; Poet Lore; Frogpond; Connecticut River Review; The New Renaissance; Mainichi (Tokyo) Daily News; Embers; San Fernando Poetry Journal; DeKalb Literary Arts Journal; Z Misc; Passager; Iconoclast; Basho Festival Anthology; Women and Death Anthology. Honours: Sri Chinmoy Award, Committee for Spiritual Poetry, 1980; 2nd Prize, North Carolina Haiku Society, 1984; Medal for Literary Achievement, State of Connecticut, 1985; Connecticut Writers' League, 1985; Blue Unicorn, 1985; Poetry Contest, Hartford, Connecticut, 1986; National League of American Pen Women, 1986; Haiku Contest, Japan Air Lines, 1988; Poetry Society of Virginia, 1989; 3rd Prize, Henderson Award, Haiku Society of America, 1994; 1st Prize, Hawaii Education Association International Haiku Contest. Memberships: Poetry Society of America; Academy of American Poets; Poets and Writers; Dramatists' Guild; Haiku Society of America.

Past Treasurer; Connecticut Poetry Society. Address: 30 Burr Farm Road, Westport, CT 06880, USA.

HEINZ Evelyn M, b. 24 Oct 1939, Streator, Illinois, USA. Part-time Writer and Poet. m. John C Heinz, 7 June 1958, 3 sons, 4 daughters. Education: Institute of Childrens Literature, Redding Ridge, Connecticut. Publication: Reflections, 1989; Nature's Beckoning, 1995. Contributions to: Sunshine Magazine; Ideals and Mature Living; Lutheran Digest, Voice of Fatima; Poetry Anthology, Great Lakes Poetry Press; Poetry Anthology, American Poetry Association; Poetry Anthology, World of Poetry Press; Poetry Anthology, Sparrowgrass Poetry Forum; Poetry Anthology, Poetry Press, Texas; Poetry Anthology, Florida State Poets Association Inc. Honours: Numerous Honourable Mentions and Golden Poet Awards, 1985-90. Membership: International Society of Poets, Washington DC. Address: 3707 West Bradley Court, McHenry, IL 60050, USA.

HELER Ziv. See: **SCHOENFELD Ilan.**

HELLER Janet Ruth, b. 8 July 1949, Milwaukee, Wisconsin, USA. College Professor. m. Michael A Krischer, 13 June 1982. Education: Oberlin College, 1967-70; BA honours, 1971, MA, 1973, English Literature, University of Wisconsin, Madison; University of Chicago, 1973-75; PhD, English Literature, 1987. Appointments: Coordinator, Writing Tutor Programme, University of Chicago, 1976-81; Instructor, Northern Illinois University, 1982-88; Assistant Professor, Arts and Sciences, Nazareth College, 1989-90; Assistant Professor, English Language and Literature, Grand Valley State University, 1990-. Publication: Coleridge, Lamb, Hazlitt, and the Reader of Drama, 1990. Contributions to: Anima; Modern Maturity; Women: A Journal of Liberation; Organic Gardening; Capper's Weekly; Kentucky Poetry Review; Lilith; Reconstructionist; Writer; Response; Light Year '85; New Poets' Anthology; Poets' Voices 1984; San Fernando Poetry Journal; Mothers Today; Earth's Daughters; Primavera; Cottonwood Review; Spoon River Quarterly; Celebrate the Midwest!; Women's Glib: A Collection of Women's Humor; Our Mothers' Daughters; Hysteria; Pegasus Review; Shofar; Artful Dodge; Filtered Images: Women Remembering Their Grandmothers; Women's Spirituality, Women's Lives; Modern Poems on the Bible; Criticism: Women's Studies; 20th-Century Literature; Language and Style; 19th-Century Prose; Poetics; Concerning Poetry; Women and Language; Theatre Journal. Honours: Dean's List, Oberlin College, 1967-70; Finalist, poem in amateur poetry contest anthology Winds of the World, Poetry Press, 1977; Winner, Friends of Poetry Contest, Kalamazoo, 1989; Commissioned poem, Friends of Poetry, 1990-91. Memberships: Modern and Midwest Language Associations; Byron Society; Michigan College English Association; National and Michigan Councils of Teachers of English; Society for the Study of Midwestern Literature; Council of Writing Program Administrators. Address: Department of English, Grand Valley State University, Allendale, MI 49401, USA.

HELLER Michael, b. 11 May 1937, New York, New York, USA. Writer; Teacher. m. Jane Augustine Heller, 5 Mar 1979, 1 son. Education: BS, 1959; MA, English, 1986. Appointment: Academic Coordinator, American Language Institute, New York University. Pubications: Two Poems, 1970; Accidental Center, 1972; Figures of Speaking, 1977; Knowledge, 1980; Marginlia In A Desperate Hand, 1985; In The Builded Place, 1990; Carl Rakosi: Man and Poet (editor), 1993. Contributions to: Paris Review; Ohio Review; American Poetry Review; Nation; New Letters; Conjunctions; Pequod; Frank; Boundary 2; Manoa; Tel Aviv Review; Margins; Harper's; New York Poetry. Honours: New York Poetry Prize, 1964; New York State Fellowship in the Arts, 1976; Poet-Scholar Award, National Endowment for the Humanities; Di Castagiola Prize, Poetry Society of America, 1980; Seminar Award, National Endowment for the Humanities, 1986; Fellowship, New York Foundation on the Arts, 1998. Memberships: Poetry Society of America; PEN; Poets and Writers; American Academy of Poets; Poets in Public Service; Modern Language Association; Associated Writing Programs; Poets' House. Address: Box 1289, New York, NY 10009, USA.

HELLERSTEIN Kathryn A, b. 27 July 1952, Cleveland, Ohio, USA. Assistant Professor of Yiddish Literature and Language; Translator of Yiddish Poetry; Poet. 1 son, 1 daughter. Education: BA (Hons) magna cum laude, English, Brandeis University, 1974; MA, Creative Writing, English, 1976, PhD, English and American Literature, 1981, Stanford University. Appointments: Assistant Professor of English, Wellesley College, 1982-86; Visiting Assistant Professor of English, Haverford College, 1988-90; Adjunct Assistant Professor of Yiddish, University of Pennsylvania, 1991-93; Visiting Assistant Professor of Judaic Studies, University of Washington, 1992; Lecturer in Yiddish, University of Pennsylvania, 1993-. Publications: Yiddish Poems of Moyshe-Leyl Halpern (translator), 1982; American Yiddish Poetry: A Bilingual Anthology (contributor, translator), 1986; Selected Poems of Kadya Molodowsky (translation). Contributions to: Poetry; Kenyon Review; New York Review of Books; Partisan Review; Bridges; Midstream. Honours: Edith Mirrielees Fellowship in Creative Writing, Poetry, Stanford University, 1974-75; National Endowment for the Arts Literature Program Fellowship for Translators Grant, 1986-87; Honourable Mention for Group of Poems, Anna Davidson Rosenberg Poetry Award, 1987; Marie Syrkin Fellowship, 1991. Memberships: Modern Language Association, Chair of Executive Committee, Yiddish Discussion Group, 1989-90; Association of Jewish Studies; Yivo Institute for Jewish Research. Address: 7205 Lincoln Drive, Philadelphia, PA 19119, USA.

HELLYER Jill, b. 17 Apr 1925, North Sydney, New South Wales, Australia. Writer. Div, 2 sons, 1 daughter. Appointment: Foundation Executive Secretary, Australian Society of Authors. Publications: The Exile, 1969; Song of the Humpback Whales, 1981. Contributions to: Sydney Morning Herald; Australian; Age; Meanjin; Southerly; Overland; Westerly. Honours: Grenfell Henry Lawson Award, 1963; Poetry Magazine Award, 1965. Membership: Australian Society of Authors. Address: 25 Berowra Road, Mount Colah, New South Wales 2079, Australia.

HELMES Leslie Scott, b. 27 Oct 1945, Fort Snelling, Minnesota, USA. Architect; Graphic Designer; Photographer. m. Julie Holbrook Williams, 15 Sept 1967, div 1974. Education: BArch, University of Minnesota, Minneapolis, 1968. Appointments: Draftsperson, Freerks Sperl Flynn; Programme Co-ordinator, Minnesota Historical Society; Director, Physical Planning and Design, Park Nicollett Medical Centre, Minneapolis; Vice President, Skaaden-Helmes Architects Inc. Publications: Autistext, 1987; Our Bodies, Our Icons, 1991; Red Letters, 1991; Xpos, 1991; Postcards from the Back of the Eye, 1991; Archaeology Structures, 1992; Mental Activities, 1992. Contributions to: Paris Review; Clown War; Kaldron; Scope; O; White Walls; Interstate; Tam-Tam; Shishi News; Aticus Review; Lost and Found; NRG; Mosumumo; Anterum; Eleven; Oars; Lake Street Review; Pigiron. Honour: 1st Prize, Concrete Poetry Contest, Gamut Magazine, 1982. Memberships: Ampersand Club of Minnesota; Minnesota Center for Book Arts. Address: 862 Tuscarora, St Paul, MN 55102, USA.

HELWIG David (Gordon), b. 5 Apr 1938, Toronto, Ontario, Canada. Poet; Writer; Editor. m. Nancy Keeling, 1959, 2 daughters. Education: Graduated, Stamford Collegiate Institute, 1956; BA, University of Toronto, 1960; MA, University of Liverpool, 1962. Appointments: Faculty, Department of English, Queen's University, Kingston, Ontario, 1962-80; Co-Editor, Quarry magazine. Publications: Poetry: Figurines in a Landscape, 1967; The Sign of the Gunman, 1969; The Best Name of Silence, 1972; Atlantic Crossings, 1974; A Book of the Hours, 1979; The Rain Falls Like Rain, 1982; Catchpenny Poems, 1983; The Hundred Old Names, 1988; The Beloved, 1992; Fiction: The Day Before Tomorrow, 1971; The Glass Knight, 1976; Jennifer, 1979; The King's Evil, 1981; It Is Always Summer, 1982; A Sound Like Laughter, 1983; The Only Son, 1984; The Bishop, 1986; A Postcard from Rome, 1988; Old Wars, 1989; Of Desire, 1990; Blueberry Cliffs, 1993; Just Say the Words, 1994; Editor: Fourteen Stories High: Best Canadian Stories of 71 (with Tom Marshall), 1971-75; New Canadian Stories (with Joan Harcourt), 4 volumes, 1972-75; Words from Inside, 1972; The Human Elements: Critical Essays, 2 volumes, 1978, 1981; Love and Money: The Politics of Culture, 1980, 1983-86; Best Canadian Stories (with Sandra Martin), 4 volumes, 1983-86; Coming Attractions 1983-86 (with Sandra Martin), 4 volumes, 1983-86; Coming Attractions 1987 and 1988 (with Maggie Helwig), 2 volumes, 1987, 1988; Best Canadian Stories (with Maggie Helwig), 4 volumes, 1987-89, 1991. Honour: CBC Literary Prize, 1983. Address: 106 Montreal Street, Kingston, Ontario K7K 3E8, Canada.

HENDERSON Hamish, b. 11 Nov 1919, Blairgowrie, Perthshire, Scotland. Education: MA, Downing College, Cambridge. Appointment: Lecturer and Fellow, School of Scottish Studies, University of Edinburgh, 1951-. Publications include: Elegies for the Dead in Cyrenaica, 1948; Freedom Come-All-Ye, 1967; Alias MacAlias, 1990; Editor, Ballads of World War II Collected by Seumas Mór Maceanruig, 1947. Honours include: Somerset Maugham Award, 1949. Address:

School of Scottish Studies, University of Edinburgh, 27 George Square, Edinburgh EH8 9LD, Scotland.

HENDRIKS A(rthur) L(emiere), b. 17 Apr 1922, Kingston, Jamaica. Education: Studied in Jamaica and England. Appointment: Freelance Writer, 1971-. Publications: On This Mountain and Other Poems, 1965; These Green Islands and Other Poems, 1971; Muet, 1971; Madonna of the Unknown Nation, 1974; The Islanders and Other Poems, 1983; The Naked Ghost and Other Poems, 1984; To Speak Simply: Selected Poems 1961-86, 1988; Co-Editor, The Independence Anthology of Jamaican Literature, 1962. Address: 7 Park Hill, Toddington, Bedfordshire LU5 6AW, England.

HENDRY Diana (Lois), b. 2 Oct 1941, Meols, Wirral, Cheshire, England. Teacher; Poet; Writer. m. George Hendry, 9 Oct 1965, div 1981, 1 son, 1 daughter. Education: BA, Honours, 1984, MLitt, 1986, University of Bristol. Appointments: Assistant to Literature Editor, Sunday Times, London, 1958-60; Reporter and Feature Writer, Western Mail, Cardiff, 1960-65; Freelance Journalist, 1965-80; Part-Time English Teacher, Clifton College, 1984-87; Part-Time Lecturer, Bristol Polytechnic, 1987; WEA, Modern Poets Course, 1987-; Tutor, Open University, 1991-92; Part-Time Tutor, University of Bristol, 1993-. Publications: Midnight Pirate, 1984; Fiona Finds Her Tongue, 1985; Hetty's First Fling, 1985; The Not Anywhere House, 1989; The Rainbow Watchers, 1989; The Carey Street Cat, 1989; Christmas on Exeter Street, 1989; Sam Sticks and Delilah, 1990; A Camel Called April, 1990; Double Vision, 1990; Harvey Angell, 1991; Kid Kibble, 1992; The Thing-in-a-Box, 1992; Wonderful Robert and Sweetie-Pie Nell, 1992; Back Soon, 1993. Making Blue, 1995; Strange Going's-On, 1995. Contributions to: Anthologies and periodicals. Honours: Stroud Festival International Poetry Competition, 1976; 3rd Prize, 1991, 2nd Prize, 1993, Peterloo Poetry Competition; Whitbread Award for Children's Novel, 1991; 1st Prize, Housman Poetry Society Competition, 1996. Address: 52 York Road, Montpelier, Bristol, BS6 5QF, England.

HENDRY Joy McLaggan, b. 3 Feb 1953, Perth, Scotland. Writer; Editor; Teacher; Broadcaster. m. Ian Montgomery, 25 July 1986. Education: Honours in Mental Philosophy, University of Edinburgh; DipEd, University of Edinburgh and Moray House College of Education. Appointments: Editor, Chapman, 1972-; Teacher of English, 1977-84; Freelance Writer and Broadcaster, 1984-; Radio Critic, The Scotsman, 1987-. Publications: Chapman editions, 1972-; Scots: The Way Forward, 1981; Poems and Pictures of Wendy Wood, 1985; The Land for the People, 1985; Critical Essays on Sorley MacLean, 1986; Gang Doun Wi' a Sang, play on life and works of poet William Soutar, 1995; Critical Essays on Norman MacCaig, 1991; The Waa' at the Warld's End, radio play broadcast Radio 3, Oct 1993. Contributions to: Scotsman; Herald; Guardian; Northwords; Chapman; Temenos; Cencrastus; Lallans; Poetry Ireland; Radio Scotland; Others. Memberships: Scottish PEN; National Union of Journalists; Advisory Council for the Arts in Scotland. Address: 4 Broughton Place, Edinburgh EH1 3RX, Scotland.

HENN Mary Ann, b. 17 June 1930, Frazee, Minnesota, USA. Teacher. Education: BA in Elementary Education, Spanish and English, 1964. Appointments: Worked in college library, cafeteria, college development and secretarial offices. Publications: Chapbooks: Just Beyond Sight, 1984; Jigsaw Solver, 1986; Light Through Stained Glass, 1986; Nu Plus, 1990; Nu-N-Human, 1993. Contributions to: Parnassus' Poetry Peddlar; Poetry Review; Silver Wings; Felicity; Omnific; Puck and Pluck; Waterways; Inside Joke; Ajax; Channels; CAL Anthologies; Coal City Review; Poet Band Co; Wide Open; Christian Century; Helter Skelter; New Hope International; My Legacy; Bogg; Orphic Lute; Apropos; Wide Open; Reflect; Just Between Us; Amateur Writers Journal; Hob Nob; Se La Vie; Chiron; Ludicity; Manna; Creative Hodge Podge; Bitterroot; Pet gazxette; Quickenings; Gotta Writer; Bits Scapes; Bell's Letters. Address: 104 Chapel Lane, St Joseph, MN 56374, USA.

HENRI Adrian (Maurice), b. 10 Apr 1932, Birkenhead, Merseyside, England. Poet; Painter; Playwright; Singer; Songwriter. m. Joyce Wilson, 28 Oct 1959, div June 1974, dec Aug 1987. Education: Department of Fine Arts, King College, Newcastle, 1951-55; BA (Hons), Fine Arts, Dunelm, 1955. Appointments: Scenic Artist; Schoolteacher: Manchester College of Art, 1961-64; Liverpool College of Art, 1964-67; Writer-in-Residence, Tattenhall Centre, Cheshire, 1980-82; Writer-in-Residence, Department of Education, University of Liverpool, 1989; Visiting Lecturer, John Moores, Liverpool University,

1995. Publications: Tonight at Noon, 1968; City, 1969; Autobiography, poems, 1971; The Best of Henri, 1975; City Hedges, 1977; From the Loveless Motel, 1980; Penny Arcade, 1983; All Now O O P, collected in Adrian Henri Collected Poems, 1986; Wish You Were Here, 1990; Not Fade Away, poems, 1994; Poems for Children: The Phantom Lollipop Lady, 1986; Rhinestone Rhino, 1989; Box and Other Poems, 1990; Dinner with the Spratts, 1993; Co-author: The Mersey Sound, 1967, 1974, 1983, new volume, 1983. Honour: Honorary DLitt, CNAA on behalf of Liverpool Polytechnic, 1990. Memberships: Liverpool Academy of Art, President 1972-81; Merseyside Arts Association, President 1978-80. Literary Agent: Rogers, Coleridge and White, 20 Powis Mews, London W11 1JN, England. Address: 21 Mount Street, Liverpool L1 9HD, England.

HENSON Stuart, b. 18 May 1954, Little Paxton, Cambridgeshire, England. Writer; Teacher. m. Katherine Lunn, 6 Apr 1977, 2 sons. Education: BEd, Cert Ed, Nottingham College of Education, 1972-76; Lock Haven State College, Pennsylvania, USA, 1973. Appointments: Head of Drama, Kimbolton School; Tutor, Northamptonshire Local Education Authority courses; Visiting Writer, Littlehey Prison. Publications: The Impossible Jigsaw, 1985; Ember Music, 1993. Contributions to: Argo; Critical Survey; English; Encounter; The Fiction Magazine; Green Book; Literary Review; New Statesman; New Welsh Review; Outposts; Other Poetry; Poetry Review; Poetry Durham; Poetry Wales; Quarto; Rialto; Spectator; New Poetry 4; PEN New Petry II; The Poetry Book Society Anthology, 1988-90. Honours: Eric Gregory Award, 1979; 1st Prize, Open University Open Poetry Competition, 1990; 2nd Prize, Peterloo Open Poetry Competition, 1992. Membership: Poetry Society. Address: Brickyard Cottage, Covington Lane, Catworth, Huntingdon, Cambridgeshire PE18 0SD, England.

HENTHORNE Marjorie L (Emerson), b. 16 May 1921, Osawatomie, Kansas, USA. Designer, Patentee, Washington, DC; Captain, US Navy. m. Huston Burns McClure, 28 June 1947, 1 daughter. Education: William and Mary Professional Institute; Business Certificate, Junior College, Kansas City; King-Smith School of Dramatic Dance; Kansas City Art Institute Fashions Certificate. Appointments: Art Department, Kansas City Star; Aide to Correspondent, Washington, DC; Aide to US Senator William F Knowland, California; Owner, Oakland Tribune, California; Times Herald, Washington, DC; Harzfelds, Ladies Fashions, Kansas City, Missouri; Chief, Land Lease Control Office, French Government, Washington, DC. Publications: New Voices in American Poetry, 1980, 1981, 1982, 1984, 1986; Patriot Poems; Greeting Cards; Echos of Freedom, war poems, 1991-1993, Historical Libraries; Pioneers and Modern Folk. Contributions to: Northeast News, Kansas City, Times Herald News, 1947, Washington DC - Parnassus World Poets. Memberships: Poetry Corner, Norfolk, Virginia, 1948-49; Parnassus World Guild; International Platform Association; International Relations Council; Kansas City Clubs and Associations. Address: 133 North Lawn, Kansas City, MO 64123, USA.

HERMAN Grace Gales, b. 12 May 1926, Lawrence, New York, USA. Physician; Poet. m. Roland B Herman, 22 July 1945, div 1981, 2 daughters. Education: Diploma, High School Music and Art, 1942; BA Hons, Cornell University, 1945; MD, College of Physicians and Surgeons, Columbia, 1949. Appointments: Intern, 1949-50, Cancer Research, 1962-65, Mount Sinai Hospital, New York City; Pathology Resident, White Plains (New York) Hospital, 1950-51; Cancer Research, Gynaecology, College of Physicians and Surgeons, Columbia, 1957-62; Examining MD, Employee Health, Metropolitan Life Insurance Company, 1969-88; Active in poetry, 1957-. Publication: Set Against Darkness, 1992. Contributions to: Minnesota Review; Colorado Quarterly; Poetry Review of the Poetry Society of America; Pembroke Magazine; Purchase Poetry Review; Literature and Medicine; Jewish Frontier; Embers; Yet Another Small Magazine; Slow Motion Magazine; Poetpourri; Pharos; New York Herald Tribune; Poetalk; Also medical articles. Honours: 2nd Prize, Director's Prize, Chautauqua Institute Poetry Center, 1990; Finalist, Poetpourri, 1991 and 1992 National Awards Editions. Memberships: Phi Beta Kappa; Phi Kappa Phi; Alpha Omega Alpha (honorary medical); Poetry Society of America. Chairperson of Peer Workshop 1982-92. Address: 370 First Avenue 9C, New York, NY 10010, USA.

HERMAN-SEKULICH Maya (Marija), (Maja Herman), b. 17 Feb 1949, Belgrade, Yugoslavia. Essayist; Poet; Translator. m. Milosh Sekulich. Education: MA, Belgrade University, 1977; PhD, Princeton University, 1986. Appointments: Fulbright Visiting Lecturer, Rutgers

University, USA, 1982-84; Lecturer, Princeton University, 1986, 1987-88. Publications: Micromegas Modern Yugoslav Poetry (guest editor), 1985; Camerography, poems, 1990; Catography, poems, 1992; Sketches for Portraits, essays, 1992; Translations, introductions in 10 books and 3 anthologies. Contributions to: Paris Review; Printed Matter; Antaeus; Confrontation; Night; Knjizevne Novine, Irene, Belgrade. Honours: Fellowship, Princeton University, 1980-85; American Association of University Women, 1981-82; Fulbright Fellowship, 1982-84. Memberships: American PEN Center, New York; Serbian PEN Centre, Belgrade; Poetry Society of America; Serbian Writers' Association; Modern Language Association. Address: 7 West 16th Street, Apt 3, New York, NY 10011, USA.

HERREN. See: **CURTIS Linda Lee.**

HERREWEGHEN Hubert F A van, b. 16 Feb 1920, Pamel, Belgium. Television Executive. m. Maria B Botte, 18 July 1946, 2 sons, 3 daughters. Appointment: Currently Head of Drama Department, BRTN (Flemish TV). Publications: Het Jaar der Gedachtenis, 1943; Liedjes van de Liefde en van de Dood, 1949; Gedichten, 1953; Gedichten II, 1958; Gedichten III, 1961; Gedichten IV, 1968; Gedichten V, 1977; Verzamelde Gedichten, 1977, 1986; Kort Dag, 1988; Twee Fazanten, 1988; Korf en Trog, 1993; Karakol, 1995. Contributions to: Editor, literary review Dietsche Warande en Belfort, 1947-. Honours: Staatsprijs voor Poezie, 1962; Prijs de Standaard, 1985; Prize, SABAM. Memberships: Koninklijke Academie voor Nederlandse Taal en Letterkunde, Gent, Belgium; Maatschappij der Nederlandse Letterkunde, Leiden, Netherlands. Address: Grilstraat 4, 1080 Brussels, Belgium.

HERSVEINN Gunnar. See: **SIGURSTINSSON Gunnar Hersveinn.**

HERTZ Dalia, b. 19 May 1942, Israel. Lecturer. Education: Studied Philosophy at Oxford, England, 1964-68; BA, Philosophy, 1974, MA with distinction, Philosophy, 1978, Tel-Aviv University. Appointments: Editor and Presenter, Literary Programmes, Israel's Radio; Teacher of Philosophy, Tel-Aviv University; Visiting Lecturer, Hebrew Literature Department, Tel-Aviv University; Creative Writing Director, Hebrew University; Member, Repertory Committee; Habima Theatre; Member, Drama Department, Israel's TV. Publications: Quartet, 1962; The Tel-Aviv Poets (co-editor), 1990; Ir-Shirim, City of Poems, 1990. Contributions to: Poetlore, USA; Argo, England; Riel, Israel; Siman-Kriea, Israel; Achshav, Israel; Ha-aretz Literary Supplement, Tel-Aviv; Yadiot-hahroniot's Literary Supplement, Israel; Davar Literary Supplement, Israel. Honours: Creative Writing Grant, America-Israel Cultural Foundation, 1986; Creative Writing Grant, Tel-Aviv Foundation for Literature and the Arts, 1988; Participated at International Poetry Festival, Rotterdam, Netherlands, 1990; Israeli Publishers' Prize for Ir-Shirim, City of Poems, 1991. Memberships: Union of Hebrew Writers, Israel; PEN; ACUM, Union of Writers and Composers in Israel. Address: The Union of Hebrew Writers, Beit Ha-Sofez, Kaplan 6, Tel-Aviv, Israel.

HESTER Alan William Walter, b. 3 Nov 1957, Reading, Berkshire, England. Civil Servant. m. Eunice Hester, 11 July 1987, 1 son, 1 daughter. Education: BA Honours, English Literature, University College, Cardiff, 1979. Appointments: Editor, Gair Rhydd, Cardiff Student Union Newspaper, 1977-78; Department of Employment; Youth Training Manager, Manpower Services Commission; Education Manager, Training Enterprise Council. Contributions to: Rialto; Orbis; Acumen; Iron; Spokes; Grand Piano; Wide Skirt; Echo Room; Envoi; Weyfarers; Inkshed; South Coast Poetry Journal, California; Hybrid; Anthologies: Poems for Peace; Grovoi Summer Anthology, 1988, 1989, 1990, 1991. Honour: 2nd Prize, Ver Poets Open Poetry Competition, 1985. Address: 67 Skilton Road, Tilehurst, Reading, Berkshire RG3 6SA, England.

HEWETT Dorothy, b. 21 May 1923, Perth, Western Australia. Education: Perth College, University of Western Australia. Appointments: Writer-in-Residence at various Australian universities. Publications: What About the People, 1962; Windmill Country, 1968; The Hidden Journey, 1969; Late Night Bulletin, 1970; Rapunzel in Suburbia, 1975; Greenhouse, 1979; Alice in Wormland, 1987; Selected Poems, 1990; Wild Card, autobiography, 1990. Honours include: Member, Order of Australia, 1986. Address: 195 Bourke Street, Darlinghurst, New South Wales 2011, Australia.

HEWITT Bernard (Robert), b. 11 Feb 1927, Greenwich, New South Wales, Australia. Consultant, Environmental Engineering. m. Betty Lorna Mills, 2 Jan 1956, div 1975, 3 daughters. Education: BA, Queensland, 1961; MPhil, Hull, 1977; Eur Ing, 1990. Appointments: University and Government positions in Australia, 1950-64; University and Government positions, 1965-90. Publications: Over 1300; Artifacts of a Generation, short stories; Falling Leaves and Visions, short stories; The Ends of Expediency, poetry; Images: Jungle and Sea; Jungle Green Sky Blue and Sea Quest; Yet Four Seasons Go Round; Scratches on the Surface. Contributions to: Mainichi Daily News; Sentinel Record, Arkansas; Legerete, Alabama; Parnassus; Prophetic Voices; Mirrors; Lucidity; New Cicada; Bitterroot; Poetry Forum; Poesie, India; Amateur Writers Journal; Mirrors; Hob-Nob; Quickenings; Snake River Reflections; Z, New York; Thirteen; Unknowns; New Renaissance; Grab-a-Nickel; Northeast Arts; Others. Honours: Over 100 literary prizes, 1984-93. Address: PO Box 6215, Cairns, Queensland 4870, Australia.

HEYEN William (Helmuth), b. 1 Nov 1940, Brooklyn, New York, USA. Professor of English; Poet; Writer. m. Hannelore Greiner, 7 July 1962, 1 son, 1 daughter. Education: BS, Education, State University of New York College, Brockport, 1961; MA, English, 1963, PhD, English, 1967, Ohio University. Appointments: Instructor, State University of New York College, Cortland, 1963-65; Assistant Professor to Professor of English and Poet-in-Residence, State University of New York, Brockport, 1967-; Teacher, University of Hannover, Germany, 1971-72; Visiting Creative Writer, University of Wisconsin, Milwaukee, 1980; Visiting Writer, Hofstra University, 1981, 1983, Southampton College, 1984, 1985; Visiting Professor of English, University of Hawaii, 1985. Publications include: Lord Dragonfly: Five Sequences, 1981; Erika: Poems of the Holocaust, 1984; The Generation of 2000: Contemporary American Poets (Editor), 1984; Vic Holyfield and the Class of 1957: A Romance, 1986; The Chestnut Rain: A Poem, 1986; Brockport, New York: Beginning with "And", 1988; Falling From Heaven (Co-Author), 1991; Pterodactyl Rose: Poems of Ecology, 1991; Ribbons: The Gulf War, 1991; The Host: Selected Poems 1965-1990, 1994; With Me Far Away: A Memoir, 1994, Crazy Horse in Stillness, 1996. Contributions to: Many books, chapbooks, journals and magazines. Honours: Borestone Mountain Poetry Prize, 1965; National Endowment for the Arts Fellowships, 1973-1974, 1984-85; American Library Association Notable American Book, 1974; Ontario Review Poetry Prize, 1977; Guggenheim Fellowship, 1977-78; Eunice Tietjens Memorial Award, 1978; Witter Bynner Prize for Poetry, 1982; New York Foundation for the Arts Poetry Fellowship, 1984-85; Lillian Fairchild Award, 1996. Address: c/o Department of English, State University of New York College at Brockport, Brockport, NY 14420, USA.

HIBSHMAN Kevin M, b. 29 Aug 1964, Philadelphia, Pennsylvania, USA. Musician; Clothing firm worker. Publications: Producer, monthly underground poetry magazine, Disturbing Dreams and Dried Blood, 1990-; Retribution, 1990. Contributions to: Small underground magazines in Pennsylvania, California and New Jersey; Music Reviews, Splatter Effect Magazine; Numerous anthologies; Golden in Hearts and Wings Newsletter. Honours: Silver Poet Award, World of Poetry, 1986, 1989; Golden Poet Award, World of Poetry, 1990; Honourable Mention for Retribution, World of Poetry's Free Contest, 1990; Honourable Mention for After Reading Rimbaud, World of Poetry's Great Free Contest, 1990. Membership: World of Poetry. Address: 103 North Cedar Street, Lititz, PA 17543, USA.

HIEMSTRA Marvin R, b. 27 July 1939, Iowa, USA. Poet; Scholar; Drollist. Education: BA (Hons), Creative Writing and Literature, State University of Iowa, 1962; MA, English Literature and Folklore, Indiana University, Bloomington, 1966. Publications: MRH, 1960; I'd Rather Be a Phoenix!, 1976; Sun Cat, 1986; Jasmine, Opera Libretto about Tahiti, 1987; Golden Gate Treasure, 1987; Cats in Charge, 1989; Dream Tees, Poems from Dreams, 1991; San Francisco Cats, 1991; 26 Compliments, 1991; Redwood Burl, 1992; Seasons, 1993; Star Molen, 1994; Snow on Golden Bamboo, 1995. Contributions to: North American Review; Abstract; Knickerbocker; Microbibliophile. Honours: Browning Society Award, 1975; American Poetry Society, 1982; Villa Montalvo Poetry Competition, 1985; Villa Montalvo Solo Reading Performance, 1986; Lilly Library, Poetry in Performance, 1986; Glendale Public Library, Poetry Cats, 1990; Miniature Book Society, Distinguished Book Award for Golden Gate Treasure, 1990; Dream Tees- Pulitzer Prize in Poetry Nomination, 1991; In Deepest USA, performance with music by Doni Harvey for CD, 1996. Memberships: The Poetry Society of America; The Dramatists Guild; The Authors League of America; Miniature Book

Society Inc; The Academy of American Poets. Address: c/o Juniper Von Phitzer Press, 166 Bonview Street, San Francisco, CA 94110-5147, USA.

HIGGINBOTHAM Patricia, b. 19 Oct 1941, Pittsburgh, Pennsylvania, USA. Teacher. m. S Roy Higginbotham, 8 May 1963, 1 son, 1 daughter. Education: BA, English, University of Florida, 1963; MA, English Education, University of South Florida, 1988. Appointments: Insurance Sales and Claims, The Co-operators Group and Insurance Company of British Columbia, 1978-84; Teacher, Hillsborough County Schools, Tampa, Florida, 1984-95; Presently assigned to Robinson High School, Tampa, Florida. Contributions to: Co-Editor, Florida English Journal, 1990-93; Lyric; Poet Magazine; Journalist, USA; Tower Poetry, Canada; Orbis; Inkshed, UK; Poetry also published in many other small press journals; More than 150 poems published in 32 journals. Membership: Academy of American Poets. Address: 3211 Swann Avenue, Apt 310, Tampa, FL 33609, USA.

HIGGINS Richard (Dick) Carter, b. 15 Mar 1938, Cambridge, England. Composer; Performer; Music Publisher; Writer; Poet. m. (1) 1960, div 1970, (2) 1984, 2 daughters. Education: BS, Columbia University, 1960; MA, New York University, 1977. Appointments: Co-Founder, Fluxus, 1961; Founder-Director, Something Else Press, 1964-73, Unpublished Editions, 1972-78, Printed Editions, 1978-85; Teacher, California Institute of the Arts, 1970-71; Research Associate in Visual Arts, State University of New York, Purchase, 1983-89; Professor in Art, Williams College, 1987. Publications: Over 40 books, from poetry to criticism, 1960-96. Contributions to: Numerous anthologies, group books, magazines, and museum catalogues. Honours: Bill C Davis Drama Award, 1986-87; Pollock-Krasner Foundation Grant, 1993; Various other grants. Address: PO Box 27, Barrytown, NY 1507, USA.

HIGHWATER Jamake, Writer; Poet; Lecturer. Appointments: Senior Editor, Fodor Travel Guides, 1970-75; Classical Music Editor, Soho Weekly News, 1975-79; Graduate Lecturer, School of Continuing Education, New York University, 1979-83; Assistant Adjunct Professor, Graduate School of Architecture, Columbia University, 1983-84; Contributing Arts Critic, Christian Science Monitor, 1988-92; Contributing Editor to several periodicals. Publications include: Indian America: A Cultural and Travel Guide, 1975; Song From The Earth: American Indian Painting, 1976; Ritual of the Wind: North American Indian Ceremonies, Music and Dances, 1977; Anpao: An American Indian Odyssey, 1977; Journey to the Sky, 1978; Many Smokes, Many Moons, 1978; Dance: Rituals of Experience, 1978; Masterpieces of American Indian Painting, 2 volumes, 1978, 1980; The Sun, He Dies, 1980; The Sweet Grass Lives On: Fifty Contemporary North American Indian Artists, 1980; Rama, 1994; The Language of Vision, 1995; The Mythology of Transgression, 1996; Songs for the Seasons, poems, 1995. Other: Writer, Host & Narrator, PBS TV series, Native Land, 1986. Honours: Newbery Honor Award, 1978; Best Book for Young Adults Awards, American Library Association, 1978, 1986; Virginia McCormick Scully Literary Award, 1982; National Educational Film Festival Best Film of the Year Award, 1986; Ace Award, Discovery Channel, 1991; Best Book for Young Adults Award, New York Public Library, 1994. Memberships include: American Federation of Television & Radio Artists; Authors Guild; Authors League; Indian Art Foundation, founder member 1980-87; Native American Rights Fund, national advisory board member 1980-87; PEN. Address: Native Lands Foundation, 1201 Larrabee Street, Suite 202, Los Angeles, CA 90069, USA.

HIGSON Philip, b. 21 Feb 1933, Newcastle-under-Lyme, Staffordshire, England. Poet; Translator and Editor (Poetry); Historian; Art Historian; sometime Senior Lecturer in History (Renaissance Course Leader). Education: BA (Hons), Liverpool University, 1956; MA, 1959, PhD, 1971; PGCE, Keele University, 1972. Appointments: Lecturer and Senior Lecturer, Chester College of Higher Education, 1972-89; Visiting Lecturer, 1990. Publications include: Poems of Protest and Pilgrimage, 1966; To Make Love's Harbour..., 1966; The Riposte and Other Poems, 1971; A Warning to Europe: The Testimony of Limouse, 1992; Limouse Nudes Inspired by Baudelaire, 1994; Childhood in Wartime Keele: Poems of Reminiscence, 1995; Sonnets to My Goddess, in this life and the next, 1995. Translations: Baudelaire: The Flowers of Evil and all other authenticated poems, 1974; Maurice Rollinat's Les Névroses: Selected English Versions, 1986; The Complete Poems of Baudelaire with Selected Illustrations by Limouse, 1992. Contributions to: Critical Quarterly; Making Love:

Picador Book of Erotic Verse, 1978; Poets England; Piranha, Madeley College; Collegian, Chester College; Chester Poets Anthologies; Excalibur, Chester; Cheshire Vista; International Rhyme Revival Anthology; Candelabrum Poetry Magazine, Cambridgeshire; Eclectic Muse, Vancouver; L'Amateur d'Art, Paris; Bulletin de la Société Les Amis de Maurice Rollinat, Argenton-sur-Creuse. Honours: Brian O'Connor Trophy, Cheshire, 1981-1983; First Prize, Eclectic Muse, Vancouver, 1990. Memberships: President, Baudelaire Society of France, 1992-; FRSA; FSA; Society of Authors; Chester Poets, President and Anthology Editor, 1974-92; Chester College of Higher Education Poetry Society, President and Anthology Editor, 1988-89. Address: 1 Westlands Avenue, Newcastle-under-Lyme, Staffordshire ST5 2PU, England.

HILBERS Betty M (Gaylor), b. Muncie, Indiana, USA. Domestic Engineer. m. Vernon W Hilbers, 10 June 1951, 1 son, 1 daughter. Appointments: Bookkeeper; Domestic Engineer; Musician; Typist. Publications: American Poetry Anthology, 1987, 1988; Love's Greatest Treasures, 1988; Editor's Choice, 1989; A Rendezvous, 1989; Moods and Inspirations Western Style, 1990; Record: Under the Master's Care, released on Gospel album, Hallelujah, 1993. Contributions to: Verde Independent; Bugle Call; Journal. Honours: Poet of Merit Trophy, American Poetry Association Convention; 1989; Rendition of The Library hung in Campe Verde Public Library, 1990. Membership: Arizona State Poetry Society. Address: HC 62, Box 114, Campe Verde, AZ 86322, USA.

HILBERT Ernie, b. 4 Apr 1970, Philadelphia, Pennsylvania, USA. Graduate Student. Education: BA, Summa Cum Laude, English, Rutgers University; MSt, Research Methods in English, Oxford University, England; Currently pursuing PhD in English Literature at Oxford University. Appointments: Published Poetry, Fiction, Reviews in Magazines throughout UK and USA; Chief Editor, Oxford Quarterly Review. Publications: Lust the Experiment, 1994. Contributions to: Long Shot; Painted Bride Quarterly; Mind Matters Review; Axiom. Address: St Catherines College, Oxford OX1 3UJ, England.

HILL Brian Merrikin, b. 6 Jan 1917, Newcastle-upon-Tyne, Tyne and Wear, England. Schoolmaster. m. Irene Salkeld, 8 Aug 1955, 1 son, 1 daughter. Education: St Catherine's Society, University of Oxford, 1935-39; BA (Oxon) Hons, School of English, 1939; MA, 1942. Appointments: Assistant, Glenhow Preparatory School, Saltburn; Senior French Master, Abbotsholme School, Derbyshire, 1942-48; Senior English Master, 1948-68, Headmaster, 1968-73, Wennington School, Wetherby; Head of English, Knottingley High School, 1973-78; Editor, Pennine Platform, 1977-. Publications: Eighteen Poems, 1947; Two Poems of Pilgrimage, 1977; Wakeful in the Sleep of Time, 1984; Local History, 1985; The Unifying Prism, selected translations from Saint-Pol-Roux, 1986; The European Letters, 1987; Dolphins and Outlaws, 1993; With Planetary Eyes, translations of Pierre Emmanuel and Saint-Pol-Roux, 1993. Contributions to: Lire Pierre Emmanuel, article, 1994; New English Weekly; Adelphi; Outposts; Orbis; Meridian; Tribune; The Poet's Voice; Stand Modern Poetry in Translation; Acumen; Temenos; Sheaf; Poetry Nottingham; Anthologies: Poems of the Mid Century; A Mingling of Streams, 1989; Yorkshire Poetry, 1984. Honours: Winner, Yorkshire Open Poetry Competition, 1977; Bursaries, Yorkshire Arts, 1978, 1979; Runner-up, 1983, 1988, Winner (only poet to have won twice), 1987, 1989, Scottish International Open Poetry Competition; Only poet to win Hugh MacDiarmid Trophy twice, Memberships: Pennine Poets; Past Chairman, Wetherby Arts Society; Former Member: Wetherby Arts Festival Committee; Literature Panel, Yorkshire Arts. Address: Ingmanthorpe Hall Farm Cottage, Wetherby, West Yorkshire LS22 5EQ, England.

HILL David Anthony, b. 22 Aug 1952, Walsall, West Midlands, England. English Teaching Adviser. Education: CEd, BEd, St Paul's College, Cheltenham, 1970-74; DipEd, English Language Teaching (Exeter), College of St Mark and St John, Plymouth, 1980; MPhil, Applied Linguistics, Exeter University, 1987. Appointments: Primary Teacher: Aston, Oxfordshire, 1974-75; Swindon, Wiltshire, 1975-77; Teacher, English as a Foreign Language, Riva, Italy, 1977-79; British Council Lektor: Prizren, 1980-82, Nis, 1982-86, Yugoslavia; Director of Studies, 1986-87; English Teaching Adviser, 1987-, British Council, Milan, Italy. Publications: The Eagles and the Sun, 1986; The Judas Tree, 1993. Contributions to: Poetry Review; Relations, translations from Serbo-Croat; Knjizene Novine, in translation; Knjizevna Rec, in translation; Mediaeval and Renaissance Serbian Poetry (language editor, translator); The Pre-Raphaelitism of Ezra Pound, 1995. Honours: Competition Winner, Poetry Review. Memberships: William

Morris Society; Poetry Society; Poetry Book Society; International Association of Teachers of English as a Foreign Language; Teaching English to Speakers of Other Languages. Address: Piazzale G de Agostini 3, 20146 Milan, Italy.

HILL Geoffrey (William), b. 18 June 1932, Bromsgrove, Worcestershire, England. Professor of Literature and Religion; Poet; Writer. m. (1) Nancy Whittaker, 1956, div 1983, 3 sons, 1 daughter, (2) Alice Goodman, 1987, 1 daughter. Education: BA, 1953, MA, 1959, Keble College, Oxford. Appointments: Staff, 1954-76, Professor of English Literature, 1976-80, University of Leeds; Churchill Fellow, University of Bristol, 1980; University Lecturer in English and Fellow, Emmanuel College, Cambridge, 1981-88; Clark Lecturer, Trinity College, Cambridge, 1986; University Professor and Professor of Literature and Religion, Boston University, 1988-. Publications: Poetry: Poems, 1952; For the Unfallen: Poems 1952-1958, 1959; Preghiere, 1964; King Log, 1968; Mercian Hymns, 1971; Somewhere is Such a Kingdom: Poems 1952-72, 1975; Tenebrae, 1978; The Mystery of the Charity of Charles Péguy, 1983; New and Collected Poems 1952-1992, 1994; Canaan, 1996; Criticism: The Lords of Limit, 1984; The Enemy's Country, 1991; Other: Brand (adaption of Henrik Ibsen's play), 1978. Honours: Gregory Award, 1961; Hawthornden Prize, 1969; Alice Hunt Bartlett Award, 1971; Geoffrey Faber Memorial Prize, 1971; Whitbread Award, 1971; Duff Cooper Memorial Prize, 1979; Honorary Fellow, Keble College, Oxford, 1981, Emmanuel College, Cambridge, 1990; Loines Award, American Academy and Institute of Arts and Letters, 1983; Ingram-Merrill Foundation Award, 1988; Honorary DLitt, University of Leeds, 1988. Membership: Fellow, Royal Society of Literature; Elected Fellow of the American Academy of Arts and Sciences, 1996. Address: The University Professors, Boston University, 745 Commonwealth Avenue, Boston, MA 02215, USA.

HILL Harriet. See: TURNER Stella.

HILL Selima, b. 13 Oct 1945, London, England. m. Roderic Hill, 1968, 2 sons, 1 daughter. Education: New Hall College, Cambridge. Publications: Saying Hello to the Station, 1984; My Darling Camel, 1988; The Accumulation of Small Acts of Kindness, 1989. Honour: Cholmondeley Prize, 1986. Address: c/o Chatto and Windus, 20 Vauxhall Bridge Road, London SW1V 2SA, England.

HILLIS Rick, b. 3 Feb 1956, Nipawin, Saskatchewan, Canada. Writer; Poet; Teacher. m. Patricia Appelgren, 29 Aug 1988, 1 son, 1 daughter. Education: University of Victoria, 1977-78; BEd, University of Saskatchewan, 1979; Graduate Studies, Concordia University, 1983; MFA, University of Iowa, 1984; Stanford University, 1988-90. Appointments: Stegner Fellow, Stanford University, 1988-90; Lecturer, California State University, Hayward, 1990; Jones Lecturer, Stanford University, 1990-92; Chesterfield Film Writer's Fellowship, 1991-92; Visiting Assistant Professor of English, Reed College, 1994-96. Publications: The Blue Machines of Night (poems), 1988; Coming Attractions (Co-Author), 1988; Canadian Brash (Co-Author), 1990; Limbo Stories, 1990. Contributions to: Anthologies and periodicals. Honour: Drue Heinz Literature Prize, 1990. Address: c/o Department of English, Lewis & Clark College, Portland, OR 97202, USA.

HILLRINGHOUSE Mark, b. 5 Nov 1905, Guthrie, Kentucky, USA. Poet; Professor. m. Ariane Arendshorst, 7 Dec 1927, 1 son, 1 daughter. Education: BA summa cum laude, Vanderbilt University; MA, University of California at Berkeley, 1927; Yale, 1927-28; Rhodes Scholar, BLitt, 1930. Appointments: Poetry Consultant, Library of Congress, Washington, DC, 1944-45. Publications: At Heaven's Gate: Selected Poems 1923-1943; All The King's Men, Blackberry Winter, The Circus in the Attic; World Enough and Time; Segregation; Brother to Dragons; Band of Angels; The Inner Conflict in the South; Promises: Poems 1954-1956; Selected Essays, The Cave; All The King's Men, play; You, Emperors, and Others; Poems 1957-1960; The Legacy of the Civil War; Wilderness; Floods; Who Speaks for the Negro?; Selected Poems: New and Old, 1923-1966; Incarnations: Poems 1966-68; Audubon: A Vision; Homage to Theodore Dreiser; Meet Me in the Garden; Or Else-Poem, Poems 1968-1974; Democracy and Poetry; Selected Poems 1975. Contributions to: Poetry; Co-founder, Southern Review; Partisan Review; Conjunctions; New Yorker; Raritan; Paris Review; Parnassus; Pequod; Iowa Review; Antioch; Verse; Atlantic Monthly; Oblek; Antaeus; The World; Little Magazine; American Poetry Review; Hudson Review; Northwest Review; New York Times; Georgia Review; Temblor. Honours: Pulitzer Prize, 1946, 1957, 1979; Shelley Memorial Award, 1957; Edna St Vincent Millay Prize, Poetry Society of America; National Book Award; Bolligen Prize,

1967; National Medal, Literature, 1970; Van Wyck Brooks Award, book-length poem, 1970; 3rd Annual Jefferson Lecture in Humanities, 1974; Emerson-Thoreau Award, American Academy of Arts and Sciences; Copernicus Award, Academy of American Poets; Harriet Monro Prize, 1977; Wilma and Roswell Messing Jr Award, 1977; Connecticut Arts Council Award; Presidential Medal of Freedom; Commonwealth Award, Literature; Hubbell Memorial Award; MacArthur Grant. Memberships: American Philosophical Society; American Academy of Arts and Letters; American Academy of Arts and Sciences. Address: 170 College Boulevard, PCCC, Paterson, NJ 07505, USA.

HIND Steven, b. 24 Feb 1943, Emporia, Kansas, USA. Teacher of Writing and Literature. m. Annabeth Dall, 10 July 1965, 1 son, 1 daughter. Education: BSE, Kansas State Teachers College, 1965; MSE, Emporia State University, 1968; MA English, University of Kansas, 1970. Appointments: English Teacher, Topeka High School, 1965-69; Teacher of Writing and Literature, Hutchinson Community College, 1970-. Publications: Familiar Ground, 1980, 1984; That Trick of Silence, 1990. Contributions to: Farmer's Market; As Far As I Can See, anthology; The Book of Contemporary Myth; Ellipsis; Midwest Quarterly; Kansas Quarterly; Cottonwood Magazine; American Land Forum; Art River Review; Borderlands; Others. Honours: Scholarship Winner, Colorado Writers Conference, Boulder, 1977, and Kansas Quarterly Award Winner, 1977; He is the subject of a television course programme on Kansas literature broadcast and taught regularly by Washburn University. Address: 503 Monterey Place, Hutchinson, KS 67502, USA.

HINDS Sallie A, (Chriscaden), b. 8 June 1930, Saginaw, Michigan, USA. Retired Sims Township Treasurer. m. James F Hinds, 25 Aug 1951, 2 daughters. Education: MacMurray College for Women, 1948-49; Michigan State University; Bay Arenac Skill Centre. Appointments: Research Secretary, 1949-51; Insurance Secretary, 1951-52; TV Traffic Manager, Women's Director and Model, 1953-59; Sims Township Treasurer, 1980-92; Retired; East Tawas Planning-Zoning Commission, 1993-. Publications: Bits and Pieces of Nature's Seasons, 1986; Simple Words...Quiet Thoughts, 1994. Contributions to: Anthologies: American Poetry, 1982; Hearts on Fire, 1983; Treasury of Poems, 1983; Today's Greatest Poems, 1989; New American Poetry Anthology, 1989; World Treasury of Golden Poems, 1990; Poems That Will Live Forever, 1991; A Time to be Free, 1988; Whispers in the Wind, 1989; Down Peaceful Paths, 1990; Navigator; Mature Living; Country Magazine; Amateur Writers Journal; Callis Tales; Arenac County Independent; All My Tomorrows, 1992; Echoes from the Silence, 1995; Treasured Poems of America, 1995. Honours: Silver Poet Award, World of Poetry, 1986; Golden Poet Award, 1987-92; 2nd Place, 1986; 5th Place, 1987; 4th Place, 1990, 1991; Numerous Honourable Mentions, 1986-; 1st Place Blue Ribbon, Arenac County Fair, 1990; Editors Choice Award, National Library of Poetry, 1995. Memberships: World of Poetry; Four Seasons Poetry Club; Lifetime Member, International Library of Poetry; East Tawas Ladies Literary Club, Treasurer; National Library of Poetry; Northeast Michigan Arts Council. Address: 1216 East Lincoln, East Tawas, MI 48730, USA.

HINE (William) Daryl, b. 24 Feb 1936, Burnaby, British Columbia, Canada. Poet; Writer; Translator. Education: McGill University, 1954-58; MA, 1965, PhD, 1967, University of Chicago. Appointments: Assistant Professor of English, University of Chicago, 1967-69; Editor, Poetry magazine, Chicago, 1968-78. Publications: Poetry: Five Poems 1954, 1955; The Carnal and the Crane, 1957; The Devil's Picture Book, 1960; Heroics, 1961; The Wooden Horse, 1965; Minutes, 1968; Resident Alien, 1975; In and Out: A Confessional Poem, 1975; Daylight Saving, 1978; Selected Poems, 1980; Academic Festival Overtures, 1985; Arrondissements, 1988; Postscripts, 1992; Novel: The Prince of Darkness and Co 1961; Other: Polish Subtitles: Impressions from a Journey, 1962; The "Poetry" Anthology 1912-1977 (Editor with Joseph Parisi), 1978; Translator: The Homeric Hymns and the Battle of the Frogs and the Mice, 1972; Theocritus: Idylls and Epigrams, 1982; Ovid's Heroines: A Verse Translation of the Heroides, 1991. Honours: Canada Foundation-Rockefeller Fellowship, 1958; Canada Council Grants, 1959, 1979; Ingram-Merrill Foundation Grants, 1962, 1963, 1983; Guggenheim Fellowship, 1980; American Academy of Arts and Letters Award, 1982; John D and Catharine T MacArthur Foundation Fellowship, 1986. Address: 2740 Ridge Avenue, Evanston, IL 60201, USA.

HINGAMIRE Buddappa, (Buddanna), b. 4 Sept 1933, Arag, India. Teacher; Reader. m. Kashakka, 1965, 1 son, 2 daughters. Education: BA, 1958, MA Russian, 1958, Karnatak University; MA, 1962, PhD, 1967, University of Poona. Appointments: Teacher, high schools, college and university; Lecturer, Reader, Institute of Kannada Studies, Karnatak University. Publications: Hullu Gejje, 1962; Shabda Rakta Mamsa, 1968; Bapu Belaku, Editor, 1969; Hosa Janangada Kavitegale, 1970; Haddugala Headu, 1977; I Nadiya Madilalli, 1978; Pushkin Kavitegalu, 1980; Taras Shevencko Kavitegalu; Byelorussian Kavitegalu, 1985; Avetik Issakyan Kavit, 1986. Contributions to: Prabuddha Karnatak; Prajavani; Udayavani; Samyukta Karnatak; Prapancha; Sankramana; Karnatak Bharati; Kannadiga; Tai-Nudi Karmaveer. Honours: Golden Jubilee Award, Mysore University, 1978; Sahitya Akedemi Award, 1978; Soviet Land Nehru Award, 1980. Memberships: Kannada Board, Central Sahitya Akademi; Literary Society; Secretary, Sahitya Mantap, Kattimani Literary Forum. Address: Attikolla Road, No 3, Malmaddi, Dharwad 58007, India.

HINO Seiji, b. 8 Dec 1927, Tokyo, Japan. High School Teacher. m. Yamagata-Shi, 31 Oct 1959, 1 son, 1 daughter. Education: MA, Western Philosophy, Tohoku University, 1956. Appointments: Teacher, Nihon Daigaku Yamagata High School, 1958-; Yamagata Johoku Girls High School; Lecturer, Yamagata Medical Treatment College, 1995. Publications: Nikogori (Frozen Dishes), 1984; Letters to Young Friends, 1989. Contributions to: Shinto no Tomo, monthly; Poet, monthly, India; Parnassus, India. Honours: Michael Madhusudan Academy Award, 1994. Memberships: Research for Modern Poetry; World Poetry Research Institute, President, Kimyoung Sam, Korea; Poet; World Academy of Arts and Culture; Governing Board of World Congress of Poets; FIBA; IWA; International Poets Academy, Madras, India. Address: 1-4-33 Kiyozumi-cho, Yamagata-shi, 990 Japan.

HIRSCH Edward (Mark), b. 20 Jan 1950, Chicago, Illinois, USA. Professor of English; Poet; Writer. m. Janet Landay, 29 May 1977, 1 son. Education: BA, Grinnell College, 1972; PhD, University of Pennsylvania, 1979. Appointments: Assistant Professor, 1979-82, Associate Professor of English, 1982-85, Wayne State University; Associate Professor, 1985-88, Professor of English, 1988-, University of Houston. Publications: For the Sleepwalkers, 1981; Wild Gratitude, 1986; The Night Parade, 1989; Earthly Measures, 1994; Editor: Transforming Vision: Writers on Art, 1994. Contributions to: Periodicals. Honours: Awards, 1975-77; Peter I B Lavan Younger Poets Award, 1983, Academy of American Poets; Ingram-Merrill Foundation Award, 1978-79; American Council of Learned Societies Fellow, 1981; National Endowment for the Arts Fellowship, 1982; Delmore Schwartz Memorial Poetry Award, New York University, 1985; Guggenheim Fellowship, 1985-86; National Book Critics Circle Award, 1987; Rome Prize, American Academy and Institute of Arts and Letters, 1988; William Riley Parker Prize, Modern Language Association, 1992. Memberships: Authors Guild; Authors League of America; Modern Language Association; PEN; Phi Beta Kappa; Poetry Society of America. Address: c/o Department of English, University of Houston, Houston, TX 77204, USA.

HIRSCHFIELD Theodore H, b. 25 May 1941, Nordenburg, East Prussia, Germany. Assistant Professor of English. m. Margaret Allen, 26 Jan 1963, 1 daughter. Education: BA, English, Ottawa University, Kansas, 1963; MA, Creative Writing, Hollins College, Virginia, 1964; 23 hours towards PhD in English, Southern Illinois University at Carbondale, 1964-65, 1977-79; 60 hours toward PhD in English, Vanderbilt University, 1970-73. Appointments: Instructor of English, 1965-74, Assistant Professor of English, 1974-, Southeast Missouri State University at Cape Girardeau. Publications: After Durer - Knight, Death and the Devil, 1964; Numerous poems including: The Cape Rock, 1965; A Poem for My Wife, 1966; Human Weather, volume of verse, 1992; German Requiem, volume of verse and audio cassette, 1993; Orbiting God, volume of verse, 1993. Contributions to: Cape Rock; Today; Hollins Critic; Cargoes; Ariel; LIT; Ottawa University Campus Literary Supplement; Tauy Talk. Honours: Induction into Lambda Iota Tau, 1959; Grand Prize, Ottawa University Campus Literary Supplement, 1960, 1961, 1962; 3rd Prize, National Student Poets' Association, San Francisco, California, 1962. Memberships: Modern Language Association, 1965-; Lambda Iota Tau, International College Chapter, 1959-63. Address: 1557 Lexington, Cape Girardeau, MO 63701, USA.

HIRSCHMAN Jack, b. 13 Dec 1933, New York, New York, USA. Poet; Translator. m. Ruth Epstein, 1954, 1 son, 1 daughter. Education: BA, City College of New York, 1955; AM, 1957, PhD, 1961, Indiana

University. Publications: Poetry: Fragments, 1952; Correspondence of Americans, 1960; Two, 1963; Interchange, 1964; Kline Sky, 1965; Yod, 1966; London Seen Directly, 1967l; Wasn't It Like This is in Woodcut, 1967; William Blake, 1967; A Word in Your Season (with Asa Benveniste), 1967; Ltd. Interchangeable in Eternity: Poems of Jackruthdavidcelia Hirschman, 1967; Jerusalem, 1968; Aleph, Benoni and Zaddik, 1968; Jerusalem Ltd, 1968; Shekinah, 1969; Broadside Golem, 1969; Black Alephs: Poems 1960-1968, 1969; NHR, 1970; Scintilla, 1970; Soledeth, 1971; DT, 1971; The Burning of Los Angeles, 1971; HNYC, 1971; Les Vidanges, 1972; The R of the Ari's Raziel, 1972; Adamnan, 1972; K'wai Sing: The Origin of the Dragon, 1973; Cantillations, 1973; Aur Sea, 1974; Djackson, 1974; Cockroach Street, 1975; The Cool Boyetz Cycle, 1975; Kashtaniyah Segodnyah, 1976; Lyripol, 1976; The Arcanes of Le Compte de St Germain, 1977; The Proletarian Arcane, 1978; The Jonestown Arcane, 1979; The Cagliostro Arcane, 1981; The David Arcane, 1982; Class Questions, 1982; Kallatumba, 1984; The Necessary Is, 1984; The Bottom Line, 1988; Sunsong, 1988; The Tirana Arcane, 1991; The Satin Arcane, 1991; Endless Threshold, 1992; The Back of a Spoon, 1992; The Heartbeat Arcane, 1993; The Xibalba Arcane, 1994; Editor: Artaud Anthology, 1965; Would You Wear My Eyes: A Tribute to Bob Kaufman, 1989; Translator: Over 25 volumes, 1970-95. Address: PO Box 26517, San Francisco, CA 94126, USA.

HIRSHFIELD Jane, b. 24 Feb 1953, New York, New York, USA. Poet. Education: AB magna cum laude, Princeton University, 1973. Appointments: Instructor, University of San Francisco Masters in Writing Program; Poet-Teacher, California Poets in the Schools; Faculty, Port Townsend Writers' Conference; Napa Poetry Conference; Foothills Writers' Conference; Visiting Associate Professor, Creative Writing, University of California at Berkeley, 1995; Adjunct Professor, University of Minnesota, 1995. Publications: Alaya, Quarterly Review of Literature Poetry Series, 1982; Of Gravity and Angels, 1988; The Ink Dark Moon: Poems by Komachi and Shikibu, Women of the Ancient Court of Japan, 1990; The October Palace, 1994; Women in Praise of the Sacred: 43 Centuries of Spiritual Writing by Women, 1994. Contributions to: New Yorker; Atlantic; Nation; American Poetry Review; Paris Review; Christian Science Monitor; Georgia Review; Antioch Review; Ontario Review; Yellow Silk; Ironwood; Denver Quarterly; Missouri Review; The Yale Review; Parabola; Tricycle; Sierra; Anthologies. Honours: Yaddo Fellow, 1983, 1985, 1987, 1989; Guggenheim Fellow, 1985; Joseph Henry Jackson Award, 1986; Columbia University Translation Center Award, 1987; Artist-in-Residence, Djerassi Foundation, 1987-1990; Poetry Society of America Awards, 1987, 1988; Pushcart Prize, 1988; Dewar's Young Artist Recognition Award, 1990; Poetry Center Book Award, 1994; Commonwealth Club of California Poetry Medal, 1994; Bay Area Book Reviewers' Award in Poetry, 1994; Rockefeller Fellow, Bellagio Study Center, 1995. Memberships: PEN; Poetry Society of America; Associated Writing Porgrams; Board, Marin Poetry Center; Board, Marin Arts Council; Author's Guild. Address: c/o Michael Katz, Literary Agent, 367 Moline Avenue, Mill Valley, CA 94941, USA.

HISEY James Huffman II, b. 29 Apr 1943, Detroit, Michigan, USA. Business Executive. m. Martha Louise Cadwell, 21 Mar 1970, 1 son. Education: BA, University of Miami, Florida, 1973; Graduate work to MBA, 1985. Appointments: Consultant, Hull & Company, Greenwich, Connecticut; President, JCM Industries, Fairfield, Connecticut; Director of Marketing, MicroAge, Fairfield; Trader, Great Lakes Carbon Corporation, New York. Publication: Songs for a Season With Love, 1988. Membership: Connecticut Poetry Society. Address: 384 Ronald Drive, Fairfield, CT 06930, USA.

HLAVSA Virginia Victoria (James), b. 28 Mar 1933, Doylestown, Pennsylvania, USA. Writer. m. Richard Auton Hlavsa, 22 Dec 1951, 1 son. Education: BA, 1967, MA, 1971, Queen's College, New York; PhD, State University of New York at Stony Brook, 1978. Appointments: Assistant Adjunct Professor of English, Queen's College, Flushing, New York, 1968-88; Private Tutor in Reading and Writing, 1979-; Guest Editor, special issue of Women's Studies, 1992. Publications: Squinnied for a Sign, 1992; Festilifes, 1992; Waking October Leaves: Reammations by a Small Town Girl, 1993. Contributions to: Dalhousie Review; Fox Cry; Manhattan Review; New York Times; Psychopoetica; Religious Humanism; SPSM&H. Membership: The International Women's Writing Guild.

HO Chiung Jung, (Pai Chiu), b. 8 June 1937, Taichung, Taiwan. Advertising and Interior Decoration Designer. m. 1 April 1962, 1 son, 3 daughters. Education: Graduate, Taichung Junior College of

Commerce, 1956. Appointments: President, Li Pai Advertising Co Ltd; President, Jin Jan Interior and Exterior Decoration Co Ltd; Managing Director, Interior Design Association, China; Director, Art Design Association, China; First and Second Chief Director of Interior Decoration Design Horizontal Union, Taichung; Prime Consultant, Interior Decoration Design Union Association of Taichung and Taiwan; Prime Consultant, Interior Decorating Design National Union Association, China; Chief Editor, Li Poetry Society, 4 times; Executive Editor, Asian Modern Poetry; Editor, Epoch Poetry Society. Publications: Death of The Moth, 1959; Rose of The Wind, 1965; The Sky Symbol, 1969; Pai Chiu Anthology, 1971; Criticism on Modern Poetry, 1972; Chansons, 1972; Poetry Square, 1984; The Wind Blowing, You Feel A Tree's Existence, 1989; Cherish, 1990; Images From Observation and Measurement, 1991. Contributions to: Li Poetry; Blue Stars Poetry; Modernist School; Epoch Poetry; Free China Review; China Times and Union Days. Honours: The First National Literary Award for Poetry, 1955; Judge of modern poetry for many poetry societies, magazines, reviews and newspapers; The Fourth Taiwan Kong-How Award for Poetry, 1994. Address: 198-1, Sec 4, Tian Jin Road, Taichung, Taiwan.

HOBSBAUM Hannah, (Hannah Kelly), b. 27 July 1937, Poona, India. Secretary. m. Philip Hobsbaum, 1957, div 1966. Education: Studied Violin, Trinity College of Music; Read English at Birkbeck College, University of London, 1966-71. Appointments: Secretary and Research Assistant to Philip Hobsbaum; Secretary to Mr C M Lind Holmes; Currently Secretary to Mr A K Misra; Founder Member, group producing A Group Anthology, Oxford University Press; Belfast Poetry Group; Poets' Workshop, London; Chairman, Camden Poetry Group; Member, Birkbeck Poetry Workshop. Publications: Prelude, 1974; A Game of Cards, 1981; The Butterfly, 1985; The Promised Land, 1991; Co-editor, Camden Group anthologies: New Furrows; The Voice and Its Moment; The Seventh Wave; Looking Out Looking In; The Silver Snake, 9th Anthology (edited with Roy Batt), 1994. Contributions to: Outposts; Minerva; The Owl; Ver Poets; Orpington Arts Festival. Honours: Citation of Meritorious Achievement for Services to Literature, 1994. Address: 64 Lilyville Road, London SW6 5DW, England.

HOBSBAUM Philip Dennis, b. 29 June 1932, London, England. Writer; Professor of English Literature. m. Rosemary Phillips, 20 July 1976. Education: BA, 1955, MA, 1961, Downing College, Cambridge; Royal Academy of Music, 1955-56; LRAM, 1956; PhD, University of Sheffield, 1968. Appointments: Lecturer in English, Queen's University, Belfast, Northern Ireland, 1962-66; Lecturer, 1966-72, Senior Lecturer, 1972-79, Reader, 1979-85, Professor of English Literature, 1985-, University of Glasgow, Scotland; Judge, Whitbread Book of the Year Competition, 1994. Publications: The Place's Fault, 1964; In Retreat, 1966; Coming Out Fighting, 1969; A Theory of Communication, 1970; Women and Animals, 1972; Tradition and Experiment in English Poetry, 1979; A Reader's Guide to D H Lawrence, 1981; Essentials of Literary Criticism, 1983; A Reader's Guide to Robert Lowell, 1988; Metre, Rhythm and Verse Form, 1995; Anthologies. Contributions to: Times Literary Supplement; Spectator; Encounter; Poetry Review; Beloit Poetry Journal; Kansas Quarterly; New York Times; Outposts; Ambit; Glasgow University Magazine; Scotsman; Northern Review; Texas Quarterly; Phoenix; Medical News; Developmental Psychology and Child Health; Times Higher Education Supplement; Keats-Shelley Review; Review of Contemporary Fiction. Honours: DLitt, University of Glasgow, 1994. Membership: Association for Scottish Literary Studies. Address: c/o Department of English Literature, University of Glasgow, Glasgow G12 8QQ, Scotland.

HOCHERMAN Ehud, b. 26 June 1962, Israel. Bookseller. m. Sharon Estrik, 7 Jan 1991, 1 daughter. Publication: Gimgum, 1989. Contributions to: Newspapers: Al Hamishar; Ma'ariv; Davar; Literary magazines: Moznaim; Shofra. Address: Shenkin 63, Givataim 53305, Israel.

HOFF Kay, b. 15 Aug 1924, Neustadt, Holstein, Germany. Freelance Writer. m. Marianne Schilling, 12 Jan 1951, 3 sons, 1 daughter. Education: DPhil, University of Kiel, 1949. Appointments: Librarian, 1950-52; Freelance Journalist, 1952-58; Editor, Neues Rheinland, 1958-67; Publisher, Guido Hildebrandt Verlag, 1965-72; Director, German Cultural Centre, Tel Aviv, Israel, 1969-73; Freelance Writer, 1973-. Publications: In Babel zuhaus, 1958; Zeitzeichen, 1962; Skeptische Psalmen, 1965; Netzwerk, 1969; Zwischen-zeilen, 1970; Bestandsaufnahme, 1977; Gegen den Stundenschlag, 1982; Zur Zeit, 1987; Zeitgewinn, Gesammelte Gedichte, 1953-1989, 1989; Fruehe

Gedichte 1951-52, 1994. Contributions to: Frankfurter Allgemeine Zeitung; Suddeutsche Zeitung; Die Welt; Frankfurter Hefte; Neue Deutsche Hefte; Neue Rundschau. Honours: Poetry Prize, Young Authors Competition, Schleswig-Holstein, 1952; 2nd Prize, Radio Play Competition, South German Radio, 1957; North Rhein-Westphalian Award of Achievement, 1960; Ernst Reuter Prize, 1965; Georg Mackensen Prize, 1968; Guest of Honour, Villa Massimo, Rome, 1994. Membership: PEN Zentrum Bundesrepublik Deutschland. Address: Stresemannstrasse 30, D-23564 Lübeck, Germany.

HOFFMAN Barbara A, b. 19 Dec 1941, Rochester, New York, USA. College Professor. Education: AB, D'Youville College, 1963; MA, Catholic University of America, 1965; ABD, Duquesne University, 1969. Appointment: Professor of English, Marywood College, 1969-. Publication: Cliffs of Fall, 1979. Contributions to: Studin Mystreu; Endless Mountain Review; Best Sellers; Scanlou's Poetry Journal. Memberships: Mulberry Poets and Writers Association; Lambda Iota Tau. Address: 1749 Jefferson Avenue, Dunmore, PA 18509, USA.

HOFFMAN Daniel (Gerard), b. 3 Apr 1923, New York, New York, USA. Professor of English Emeritus; Poet; Writer. m. Elizabeth McFarland, 1948, 2 children. Education: AB, 1947, PhD, 1956, Columbia University. Appointments: Fellow, School of Letters, Indiana University, 1959; Elliston Lecturer, University of Cincinnati, 1964; Lecturer, International School of Yeats Studies, Sligo, Ireland, 1965; Professor of English, 1966-83, Poet-in-Residence, 1978-, Felix E Schelling Professor of English, 1983-93, Professor Emeritus, 1993-, University of Pennsylvania; Consultant in Poetry, 1973-74, Honorary Consultant in American Letters, 1974-77, Library of Congress, Washington, DC; Poet-in-Residence, Cathedral of St John the Divine, New York City, 1988-; Visiting Professor of English, King's College, London, 1991-92. Publications: Poetry: An Armada of Thirty Whales, 1954; A Little Geste and Other Poems, 1960; The City of Satisfactions, 1963; Striking the Stones, 1968; Broken Laws, 1970; Corgi Modern Poets in Focus 4 (with others), 1971; The Center of Attention, 1974; Able Was I Ere I Saw Elba: Selected Poems 1954-1974, 1977; Brotherly Love, 1981; Hang-Gliding from Helicon: New and Selected Poems 1948-1988, 1988; Middens of the Tribe, 1995; Others include: The Poetry of Stephen Crane, 1957; Poe Poe Poe Poe Poe Poe Poe, 1972; Ezra Pound and William Carlos Williams: The University of Pennsylvania Conference Papers, 1983. Honours: Yale Series of Younger Poets Award, 1954; Ansley Prize, 1957; American Council of Learned Societies Fellowships, 1961-62, 1966-67; Columbia University Medal for Excellence, 1964; American Academy of Arts and Letters Grant, 1967; Ingram Merrill Foundation Grant, 1971; National Endowment for the Humanities Fellowship, 1975-76; Hungarian PEN Medal, 1980; Guggenheim Fellowship, 1983; Hazlett Memorial Award, 1984; Paterson Poetry Prize, 1989. Membership: Chancellor, Academy of American Poets, 1972-. Address: c/o Department of English, University of Pennsylvania, Philadelphia, PA 19104-6273, USA.

HOFFMANN Roald, b. 18 July 1937, Zloczow, Poland. Chemist; Poet. m. Eva Borjesson, 30 Apr 1960, 1 son, 1 daughter. Education: BA, Columbia University, 1958; PhD, Harvard University, 1962. Appointments: Junior Fellow, Society of Fellows, Harvard University, 1962-65; Associate Professor to John A Newman Professor of Physical Science, Cornell University, 1965-. Publications: The Metamict State, 1987; Gaps and Verges, 1990. Contributions to: Paris Review; Literaturnaya Gazeta; Prairie Schooner; New England Review; Bread Loaf Quarterly; Lyrikvännen; TriQuarterly. Honour: Pergamon Press Fellowship in Literature, Djerassi Foundation, 1988. Address: Department of Chemistry, Cornell University, Ithaca, NY 14853, USA.

HOFMANN Michael, b. 25 Aug 1957, Freiburg, Germany. Education: BA, Magdalene College, Cambridge, 1979. Appointments: Freelance Writer, 1983-. Publications: Nights in the Iron Hotel, 1983; Acrimony, 1986; K S in Lakeland: New and Selected Poems, 1990; Corona, Corona, 1993. Honours: Cholmondeley Award, 1984; Geoffrey Faber Memorial Prize, 1988. Address: c/o Faber and Faber, 3 Queen Square, London WC1N 3AU, England.

HOGGARD James (Martin), b. 21 June 1941, Wichita Falls, Texas, USA. Teacher. m. Lynn Taylor, 23 May 1976, 1 son, 1 daughter. Education: BA, Southern Methodist University, 1963; MA, University of Kansas, 1965. Appointment: Reporter, Wichita Falls Record News, 1965-66; Instructor, Assistant Professor, Associate Professor, Professor of English, Midwestern State University, Wichita Falls, 1966-. Publications: Eyesigns, 1977; The Shaper Poems, 1983;

Two Gulls, One Hawk, 1983; Breaking an Indelicate Statue, 1986; The Art of Dying, translation, 1988; Love Breaks, translation, 1991; Chronicle of My Worst Years, translation, 1994. Contributions to: Southwest Review; The Texas Observer; Manoa; Mundus Artium; Ohio Review; Mississippi Review; Vanderbilt Review; New Mexico Humanities Review; Cedar Rock; Colorado Review; Kansas Quarterly; New Letters; Latin American Literary Review; Concho River Review; Sou'wester; Southern Poetry Review; The Smith; South Florida Poetry Journal; TriQuarterly; University of Tampa Review; Others. Honours: Award, The Hart Crane and Alice Crane Williams Memorial Fund, 1970. Memberships: President, The Texas Institute of Letters; Past President, Texas Association of Creative Writing Teachers; American Literary Translators' Association. Address: English Department, Midwestern State University, Wichita Falls, TX 76308, USA.

HOGUE Cynthia Anne, b. 26 Aug 1951, Moline, Illinois, USA. Professor of English. m. Jon Jaukur Ingimundarson, 17 July 1983. Education: BA, 1973; Master of Arts and Humanities, 1975; PhD, English, 1990. Publications: Touchwood, 1978; Where The Parallels Cross, 1983; The Woman in Red, 1989. Contributions to: American Poetry Review; American Poetry; Central Park; Cut Bank; Fiction International; Field; Hayden's Ferry; How(ever); Ironwood; Negative Capability; Passages North; Ploughshares; Quarterly West; Sequoia; University Publishing; Willow Springs; Women's Quarterly Review. Honours: Fulbright-Hayes Fellowship, 1979-80; Judith Siegel Pearson Award in Poetry, 1987; Fellowship, National Endowment for the Arts, 1990. Memberships: Modern Language Association; Associated Writing Programs; National Council of Teachers of English; Freedom Writers' Association (associated with Amnesty International); Poets and Writers, USA. Address: Department of English, University of New Orleans, Lakefront, LA 70148, USA.

HOKE Leon Edward. Minister; Writer. Education: Graduated with Honour, Lincoln High School, 1966; Attended Community College of the United States Air Force, graduate of the 3628th St.Sq.; LMTC, Applied Aerospace Science Technical School, 1967; Other Diplomas. Appointments: Orderly, North Carolina Orthopaedic Hospital, 1967; Non Commissioned Officer, United States Air Forces, Europe, 1967-73; Subsidiary Corporation of United Airlines, 1974-75; Security Agent, Arlex Associates, 1977-79; Minister, 16th Street Church, 1978-79; Apartments Manager, Hoke Company, 1979-83. Publications include: "Heart Beats" from the Throne, 1982. Contributions to: Reviews of published work have appeared in: Weekly Book Newsletter, Nigerian Publishers Association News; Numerous journals and anthologies. Honours include: Nominated, Queen's Gold Medal for Poetry, 1983; Finalist, McDonalds Food Corporation Literary Awards, 1989. Memberships: Deputy Governor, ABIRA; World Poetry Society; North Carolina Writers Network; International Academy of Poets. Address: 311 South Rhyne Street, Dallas, NC 28034, USA.

HOLBROOK David Kenneth, b. 9 Jan 1923, Norwich, Norfolk, England. Emeritus Fellow, Downing College; Author. m. France Margaret (Margot) Davies-Jones, 23 April 1949, 2 sons, 2 daughters. Education: Downing College, University of Cambridge, 1941-42, 1945-47; BA (Hons), English, 1946; MA, 1951. Appointments: Lieutenant, Armoured Corps, 1952-45; Tutor, Bassingbourn Village College, 1954-61; Fellow, King's College, Cambridge, 1961-65; College Lecturer, Jesus College, Cambridge, 1966-67; Writer-in-Residence, Dartington Hall, 1971-73; Fellow, Director of English Studies, Downing College, Cambridge, 1981-88; Leverhulme Emeritus Research Fellow, 1988-90. Publications: Imaginings, 1961; Against the Cruel Frost, 1963; Old World, New World, 1969; Object Relations, 1969; Chance of a Lifetime, 1977; Moments in Italy, 1976; Selected Poems, 1980; Carpe Diem, to be published. Contributions to: Listener; Outposts; London Magazine; Transatlantic Review; PEN; Critical Quarterly; Twentieth Century; Encounter; New Statesman; Harper's Bazaar; Blackwood's; Poetry Workshop; Use of English; Bananas; New Poetry 6 and 9; Acquarius; Spectrum; Words; Observer; Scotsman; New York Times; Prospice; English; Acumen; Stonechat; Geste; Human World; Stand; Cuirimo; Polymus; Samphire; Tiltyard; Tagus; Athos; Times Literary Supplement. Honours: Poetry Book Society Choice, 1961, 1969; 3 Arts Council Writer's Bursaries, 1968, 1970, 1976; Prize, International Who's Who Competition, 1973; Prize, Keats Poetry Competition, 1975. Membership: Society of Authors. Address: Denmore Lodge, Brunswick Gardens, Cambridge CB5 8DQ, England.

HOLDEN Kim Michelle, b. 29 Jan 1970, Edmonton, Alberta, Canada. Special Needs Child Care Worker. Education: Licenced

Nurses Aid Graduate with Distinction, 1992. Appointments: Pre-school Teachers Assistant working with Special Needs Children; Writer. Publications: Whispers in the Wind, 1991; Dawn Peaceful Paths, 1992; Apex One, 1992; I'm Only Shaken not Stirred, 1995. Contributions to: Quill Book Anthology; Daily Courier; Kelowna BC; Plowmen Quarterly Publication. Honours: Caprice Poetry Award, 1994. Address: #2-2355 Marshall Road, Kelowna, BC V1Z 1E9, Canada.

HOLDT David M, b. 12 May 1941, Cleveland, Ohio, USA. Teacher; Writer. m. Sandra B Wood-Holdt, 26 June 1976, 1 son, 1 daughter. Education: BA, 1963, CAS, 1993, Wesleyan University, Middletown, Connecticut; MA, Duke University, Durham, North Carolina, 1967. Appointments: Teacher, Hotchkiss School, 1963-65; Germantown Friends School, 1967-70; Westledge School, 1970-77; Director of Writing Programme, Teacher, Principal, 1992-; Writer-in-Residence, Watkinson School, Hartford, Connecticut, 1978-. Publications: Sun Through Trees, 1972; Rivers Edge, 1985; Waterscapes, 1987. Contributions to: Northwoods Journal; Chelsea; Maine Life; Cambric Poetry I, II, III; Just Pulp; Spectrum; Pastiche; Poet; Firelands Review; Spitball; Connecticut River Review; Stone Country; Poets On; Embers; Clearwater Navigator; Amelia; Connecticut Writer; Blueline; Lake Effect; River of Dreams. Honour: 2nd Prize, Connecticut Writers League, 1987. Memberships: Poets and Writers; Teachers and Writers Collaborative. Address: 3 Orchard Hill Road, Canton, CT 06019, USA.

HOLENDER Barbara D, b. 15 Mar 1927, Buffalo, New York, USA. Poet. m. H William Holender, 8 May 1949, dec, 1 son, 1 daughter. Education: Cornell University, 1944-46; BA, University of Buffalo, 1948. Appointments: Instructor, English: University at Buffalo, 1973-76; New York State Poets in the Schools, 1976. Publications: Shivah Poems: Poems of Mourning, 1986; Ladies of Genesis, 1991; Is This the Way to Athens?, 1996. Contributions to: New York Times; Christian Science Monitor; Literary Review; Prairie Schooner; Helicon Nine; Anthologies: New York Times Book of Verse, 1970; Sarah's Daughters Sing, 1990; 80 on the 80's, 1990; Helicon Nine Reader, 1990; Scarecrow Poetry, 1994; Lifecycles, 1994. Honours: Hans S Bodenheimer Award for Poetry, 1984; Western New York Writers in Residence Award, 1988. Memberships: Poetry Society of America; Poets and Writers. Address: 263 Brantwood Road, Snyder, NY 14226, USA.

HOLLAND Walter R, b. 11 Nov 1953, New York, New York, USA. Physical Therapist. Education: HS Diploma, 1972; BA, Dance and Literature, Bard College, New York, 1976; MS, Physical Therapy, Columbia University, New York, 1985; MA, Creative Writing (Poetry), City College, City Univ of New York, 1991; PhD English Literature (pending), ABD Level III Student, Graduate Center, City University of New York, 1996. Publications: A Journal of the Plague Years: Poems 1979-1992, 1992. Contributions to: Anthologies: Jugular Defences: An AIDS Anthology, 1994; Poetry for Life: Seventy Six Poets Respond to AIDS; Magazines: James White Review; Christopher Street; Found Object; Bay Windows; Art and Understanding; RFD; Men's Style Magazine. Memberships: Publishing Triangle, New York City; Center for Lesbian and Gay Studies. Address: 46 West 83rd Street, Apt 4H, New York, NY 10024, USA.

HOLLANDER Jean, b. Vienna, Austria. Poet; Teacher; m. Robert B Hollander, 1 son, 1 daughter. Education: MA, Columbia University. Appointments: Teacher of Literature and Writing, Columbia University, Brooklyn College, Trenton State College; Poetry Writing, Hunterdon Adult Education; Lecturer, Princeton University; Director, Writers Conferences, Trenton State College. Publications: Crushed into Honey, 1986; I Am My Own Woman, translation, 1995; Moondog, 1996. Contributions to: Sewanee Review; American Scholar; Literary review; Poet Lore; New England Review; Numerous others. Honours: Finally the Manager, Best Poems of 1973, Borestone Mountain Poetry Awards, 1974; 1st Prize for single poem, Billie Murray Denny Poetry Contest; Poetry Fellowships, New Jersey State Council on the Arts, 1980, 1984, 1993; Eileen W Barnes Award, for Crushed into Honey, 1986. Membership: Poetry Society of America. Address: 592 Province Line Road, Hopewell, NJ 08525, USA.

HOLLANDER John, b. 28 Oct 1929, New York, New York, USA. Professor of English; Poet; Critic; Editor. m. (1) Anne Loesser, 15 June 1953, div, 2 daughters, (2) Natalie Charkow, 17 Dec 1982. Education: AB, 1950, MA, 1952, Columbia University; PhD, Indiana University, 1959. Appointments include: Instructor to Professor of English, 1959-86, A Bartlett Giamatti Professor of English, 1986-95, Sterling

Professor of English, 1995-, Yale University; Christian Gauss Seminarian, Princeton University, 1962; Visiting Professor, 1964, Patten Lecturer, 1986, Fellow, Institute for Advanced Study, 1986, Indiana University; Faculty, Salzburg Seminar in American Studies, 1965; Professor of English, Hunter College and the Graduate Center, City University of New York, 1966-77; Overseas Fellow, Churchill College, Cambridge, 1967-68; Elliston Professor of Poetry, University of Cincinnati, 1969; Resident Guest Writer, City of Jerusalem, 1980; Phi Beta Kappa Lecturer, 1981-82; Glasgow Lecturer, Washington and Lee University, 1984. Publications: Poetry includes: Types of Shape, 1968, expanded edition, 1991; The Night Mirror, 1971; Town and Country Matters, 1972; Selected Poems, 1972; Tales Told of the Fathers, 1975; Reflections on Espionage, 1976; Spectral Emanations: New and Selected Poems, 1978; Blue Wine, 1979; Flowers of Thirteen, 1983; In Time and Place, 1986; Harp Lake, 1988; Selected Poetry, 1993; Tesserae, 1993; Criticism includes: The Work of Poetry, 1997; As Editor, includes: Garden Poems, 1996; Other: The Death of Moses (libretto for Alexander Goehr's opera), 1992. Honours include: National Institute of Arts and Letters Award, 1963; National Endowment for the Humanities Senior Fellowship, 1973-74; Levinson Prize, 1974; Washington Monthly Prize, 1976; Guggenheim Fellowship, 1979-80; Mina P Shaughnessy Award, Modern Language Association, 1982; Bollingen Prize, 1983; Shenandoah Prize, 1985; John D and Catharine T MacArthur Foundation Fellowship, 1990-95. Memberships: Academy of American Poets; American Academy of Arts and Letters; Fellow, American Academy of Arts and Sciences. Address: c/o Department of English, Yale University, PO Box 208302, New Haven, CT 06520, USA.

HOLLIDAY David John Gregory, (William Speaker, Alfred Cunning), b. 20 Aug 1931, Isleworth, Middlesex, England. Poetry Magazine Editor. m. Ruth Brick, 29 Feb 1960, 1 son, 1 daughter. Education: Member, Association of Accounting Technicians, 1980-87. Appointments: Joint Editor, Deuce, 1956-61; Member, Editorial Board, Envoi, 1957-60; Editor, Scrip, 1961-73; Editor, iota, 1988-. Publications: Pictures from an Exhibition (with Patrick Snelling), 1959; Compositions of Place, 1961; Jerusalem, 1982; The Abbot Speaks, 1995. Contributions to: Breakthru; Chetwynd Post; Cornhill; Envoi; Here Now; Ipse; Limbo; Littack; Manifold; New Christian; Orbis; Outposts; Symphony; Poetry Nottingham; Two Tone; Others. Honour: Founder Fellow, International Poetry Society, 1976. Memberships: Past Chairman, Nottingham Poetry Society; Past Chairman, Wensley Poetry Group. Address: 67 Hady Crescent, Chesterfield, Derbyshire S41 0EB, England.

HOLLINS Amy, b. Birkenhead, Merseyside, England. Poet; Novelist. m. THB Hollins, 2 sons, 2 daughters. Education: BA Hons, Modern Languages, Diploma in Education, Liverpool University. Appointments: Assistant Editor, Workshop New Poetry; Former Tutor on Critical Service Panel, The Poetry Society. Publications: Axe and Tree, 1973; Many People, Many Voices (co-editor), 1978; The Quality, 1985; Centrepiece, 1994. Contributions to: Observer; Spectator; Use of English; Ally, USA; Poet, India; Others; Anthologies: 2 from Hutchinson; 1, English Speaking Board; 1, Yorkshire Arts Association; BBC publication and radio broadcasts. Memberships: Society of Authors; Yorkshire and Humberside Arts; Authors Lending and Copyright Society; The Royal Society of Literature; The National Poetry Society; The International Society of Poets; Women Writers' Network. Address: 2 Lidgett Park Avenue, Leeds, West Yorkshire LS8 1DP, England.

HOLLOWAY (Percival) Geoffrey, b. 23 May 1918, Birmingham, England. Field Officer in Mental Welfare. m. (1) 2 daughters, (2) Patricia Pogson, 27 Aug 1977. Education: Certificate in Social Science. Appointments: Assistant, Shropshire County Library, 5 years; Agent, Prisoners' Aid Society, 2 years; Mental Welfare Officer, Local Authority Mental Health Department, 33 years; Retired, 1983. Publications: To Have Eyes, 1972; Rhine Jump, 1974; All I Can Say, 1978; The Crones of Aphrodite, 1985; Salt, Roses, Vinegar, 1986; Percepts without Deference, 1987; My Ghost in Your Eye, 1988; The Strangest Thing, 1991; Mongoose On My Shoulder, 1992; The Leaping Pool, 1993; A Sheaf of Flowers, 1994. Contributions to: Times Literary Supplement; Listener; London Magazine; Encounter; John O'Londons; Yorkshire Post; Stand; Outposts; Orbis; Poetry Wales; Aquarius; Bête Noire; Acumen; The Green Book; Iron; Lines Review; New Welsh Review; Pennine Platform; Poetry Durham; Rialto; Staple; Envoi; Samphire; Tribune; Poetry Review; Ambit; Literary Review; Country Life; Grand Piano; Prospice; Anglo Welsh Review; Sheaf. Honours: Rhine Jump, Poetry Book Choice. Memberships: Secretary, Brewery

Poets, Brewery Arts Centre, Highgate, Kendal; Keswick Poetry Group. Address: 4 Gowan Crescent, Staveley, nr Kendal, Cumbria LA8 9NF, England.

HOLLOWAY Glenna Preston, b. 7 Feb 1928. Artist; Specialist in Enamelling, Silversmithing and Lapidary. m. Robert Wesley Holloway, 20 Feb 1948. Education: Ward Belmont College. Publications: Anthologies: Diamond Anthology, Poetry Society of America, 1971; National Federation of State Poetry Societies Prize Poems, 1977-95; The Reach of Song, 1984, 5th edition, 1995; Soundings, 1985; The Poet's Job: To Go Too Far, 1985; Shorelines, 1987, 1988; Sound and Light, 1987; Red Mountain Rendezvous, 1995; Rhysling, 1995. Contributions to: Good Housekeeping; Saturday Evening Post; Christian Century; National Forum; Hollins Critic; Iowa Woman; South Coast Poetry Journal; Elf; Cape Rock; Poet; Silver Web; Western Humanities Review; Georgia Review; McCall's; America; Christian Science Monitor; Poet Lore; Orbis; Crazy Quilt Quarterly; Blue Unicorn; Japanophile; Poet India; Icon; Kansas City Star; Formalist; Louisiana Literature; Verve; Paterson Poetry Review; Spectrum; New World; Touchstone; Columbia Pacific University; Crucible; Connecticut River Review; Many others. Honours: Daniel Whitehead Hicky Award, 1984; Best of Best, Chicago Poets and Patrons, 1984, 1986-1989, 1991; Best of Best, National League of American Pen Women, 1985, 1990; Grand Prize, National Federation of State Poetry Societies, 1986; Hart Crane Memorial Award, Kent State University, Ohio, 1988; Ragdale Foundation Fellow, 1989; World Order of Narrative and Formalist Poets, 1991-95; Chicago Poets and Patrons, 1991-95; National League of American Pen Women, Chicago Branch and Biennial, 1993; Edward D Vickers Award, Georgia, 1994; Winchell Award, Connecticut, 1995; Poets of the Palm Beaches, 1995; Arkansas Writers' Conference, 1995; CPU Review, 1995; Numerous others. Memberships: National League of American Pen Women; National Federation of State Poetry Societies; Illinois State Poetry Society, President 1991-93; Chicago Poets' Club; Poetry Society of Florida. Address: 913 E Bailey Rd, Naperville, IL 60565, USA.

HOLLOWAY John, b. 1 Aug 1920, Croydon, Surrey, England. Professor of Modern English (retired); Writer; Poet. m. (1) Audrey Gooding, 1946, 1 son, 1 daughter, (2) Joan Black, 1978. Education: 1st Class Modern Greats, New College, Oxford, 1941; DPhil, Oxon, 1947. Appointments: Temporary Lecturer in Philosophy, New College, Oxford, 1945; Fellow, All Souls College, Oxford, 1946-60; Lecturer in English, University of Aberdeen, 1949-54, University of Cambridge, 1954-66; Fellow, 1955-82, Life Fellow, 1982-, Queens' College, Cambridge; Reader, 1966-72, Professor of Modern English, 1972-82, University of Cambridge; Various visiting lectureships and professorships. Publications: Language and Intelligence, 1951; The Victorian Sage, 1953; Poems of the Mid-Century (Editor), 1957; The Charted Mirror (essays), 1960; Selections from Shelley (Editor), 1960; Shakespeare's Tragedies, 1961; The Colours of Clarity (essays), 1964; The Lion Hunt, 1964; Widening Horizons in English Verse, 1966; A London Childhood, 1966; Blake: The Lyric Poetry, 1968; The Establishment of English, 1972; Later English Broadside Ballads (Editor with J Black), 2 volumes, 1975, 1979; The Proud Knowledge, 1977; Narrative and Structure, 1979; The Slumber of Apollo, 1983; The Oxford Book of Local Verses (Editor), 1987; Poetry: The Minute, 1956; The Fugue, 1960; The Landfallers, 1962; Wood and Windfall, 1965; New Poems, 1970; Planet of Winds, 1977; Civitatula: Cambridge, The Little City, 1994. Contributions to: Professional journals. Honours: Honorary doctorates. Membership: Fellow, Royal Society of Literature, 1956. Address: c/o Queens' College, Cambridge CB3 9ET, England.

HOLLOWAY Patricia, (Patricia Pogson), b. 8 Mar 1944, Rosyth, Scotland. Yoga Teacher. m. (1) 1 son, 1 daughter, (2) Geoffrey Holloway, 27 Aug 1977. Education: National Diploma in Design, 1964; Teaching Certificate, 1971; Diploma, British Wheel of Yoga, 1987. Appointments: Draughtswoman Restorer, Ashmolean Museum, Oxford, 1964-66; Part-time Yoga Teacher; Poetry Tutor, Schools and Writing Centres, Libraries. Publications: Before the Road Show, 1983; Snakeskin, Belladonna, 1986; Rattling the Handle, 1991; A Crackle from the Larder, 1991; The Tides in the Basin, 1994. Contributions to: Tribune; Yorkshire Post; Newcastle Chronicle; Ambit; Literary Review; Country Life; Orbis; Palantir; Outposts; Writing Women; Staple; Rialto; Aquarius; Sheaf; Prospice; Anglo Welsh Review; Bananas; Bête Noire; Lancashire Life; Grand Piano; Poetry Review Supplement; Green Book; Poetry Durham; Iron; Odyssey; Scratch; Smiths Knoll; Spokes; London Magazine; Other Poetry; Anthologies: Purple and Green; No Holds Barred; Ladder to the Next Floor; Adam's Dream; Between Comets; New Lake Poets; Children's anthologies. Honours: 1st Prize,

York Open Competition, 1985; 3rd Prize, Manchester Open, 1989; 2nd Prize, National Poetry Competition, 1989; 1st Prize, BBC Kaleidoscope Competition, 1990. Memberships: Brewery Poets, Brewery Arts Centre, Kendal; Keswick Poetry Group. Address: 4 Gowan Crescent, Staveley, nr Kendal, Cumbria LA8 9NF, England.

HOLMES Clyde, b. 20 Oct 1940, Barnet, London, England. Landscape Painter; Poet. m. Gudrun Jakob, 19 Oct 1871, 1 son, 2 daughters. Education: Hornsey School of Art, St Martin's School of Art, London, 1960-65, BA, 1965. Publications: Cwm Hesgin, 1977; Standing Stone, 1978; In Season, 1988; Westering, 1992. Contributions to: Anglo-Welsh Review; Aquarius; Country Life; Countryman; Gallery; Honest Ulsterman; London Magazine; New Poetry; Ninth Decade; Outposts; Poetry Review; Poetry Wales; Samphire; Counterpoint; Poetry Nottingham; Vision On; Anthologies: Here in North Wales; Speak to the Hills; Sports Anthology; Anthology of Twentieth Century British and Irish Mountain Poetry; Poems read on HTV Cymru Wild Wales education programmes, BBC Radio Cymru. Honours: New Poetry Prize, 1976; Finalist, Arnold Vincent Bowen Prize, 1976; Certificate of Distinction, 1977; Finalist, Stroud Festival; Michael John Memorial Prize, 1977, 1979; Diploma Winner, Scottish Open Poetry Competition, 1977, 1978, 1979; Special Commendation, Welsh Arts Council New Poets Competition, 1978; Edmund Blunden Prize, 1979. Membership: International Poetry Society. Address: Cwm Hesgin, Capel Celyn, Frongoch, Y Bala, Gwynedd LL23 7NU, North Wales.

HOLMES John. See: **SOUSTER Raymond Holmes.**

HOLMES John, b. 7 June 1955, Arusha, Tanzania. English Teacher; Language Consultant. m. Boel Marie Larsson, 30 July 1983, 1 son. Education: BA, Honours, Manchester University, 1977; Postgraduate Certificate of Education, Sheffield University, 1978; MA, Teaching English as a Foreign Language. Appointments: Lecturer, English, King Saud University, Riyadh, Saudi Arabia, 1978; English Teacher, Studieframiandet, Malmö, Sweden, 19780-87; Head, English Department, Skurups Folkhogskola, 1987-92; Director, Professional English Language Consultants, Malmö, 1989-92. Publications: At This Time, illustrated by Jake Attree, 1984; The Purblind Men, illustrated by Jake Attree, 1991; 5 radio plays for Sveriges Utbildningsradio AB, 1985-92. Membership: Poetry Society, London. Address: Ostra Forstadsgatan 14, 21131 Malmö, Sweden.

HOLMES Raymond. See: **SOUSTER Raymond Holmes.**

HOLMES Richard (Gordon Heath), b. 5 Nov 1945, London, England. Writer; Poet. Education: BA, Churchill College, Cambridge. Appointments: Reviewer and Historical Features Writer, The Times, London, 1967-92; Ernest Jones Memorial Lecturer, British Institute of Psycho-Analysis, 1990; John Keats Memorial Lecturer, Royal College of Surgeons, 1995; Houzinga Lecturer, University of Leiden, Netherlands, 1997. Publications: Thomas Chatterton: The Case Re-Opened, 1970; One for Sorrows (poems), 1970; Shelley: The Pursuit, 1974; Shelley on Love (Editor), 1980; Coleridge, 1982; Nerval: The Chimeras (with Peter Jay), 1985; Footsteps: Adventures of a Romantic Biographer, 1985; Mary Wollstonecraft and William Godwin (Editor), 1987; Kipling: Something Myself (Editor with Robert Hampson), 1987; Coleridge: Early Visions, 1989; Dr Johnson and Mr Savage, 1993; Coleridge: Selected Poems (Editor), 1996. Honours: Somerset Maugham Award, 1977; Whitbread Book of the Year Prize, 1989; Officer of the Order of the British Empire, 1992; James Tait Black Memorial Prize, 1994. Membership: Fellow, Royal Society of Literature. Address: c/o Harper Collins, 77 Fulham Palace Road, London W6 8JB, England.

HOLMES Stewart Quentin, b. 25 Dec 1929, London, England. Actor; Journalist. Education: Royal Society of Arts Credits, English-Typewriting, Pitman's Shorthand, 1950; Mandarin Chinese, Hong Kong University, 1971-72. Appointments: BBC Correspondent, Tehran, Iran, 1971; Features Editor, Hong Kong Standard, 1971-72; London Correspondent, International Press Bureau and Union Jack newspaper, 1981. Publications: Odes and Ends, 1985; Once Upon A Rhyme, 1987. Contributions to: Outpost; British MENSA Magazine; Union Jack newspaper. Honour: Golden Poet, World of Poetry, California, 1990. Memberships: London Poetry Society; Stanza Poets; British MENSA; British Actors Equity; Chartered Institute of Journalists; Foreign Press Association, London. Address: 146 Clarence Gate Gardens, Baker Street, London NW1 6AN, England.

HOLT Rochelle Lynn, (Rochelle Holt Dubois), b. 17 Mar 1946, Chicago, Illinois, USA. Writer; Teacher. Education: BA with honours, English, University of Illinois, Chicago, 1967; MFA, English, University of Iowa Writers' Workshop, Iowa City, 1970; PhD, English, Psychology, Columbia Pacific University, 1980. Appointments: Consulting Editor, Merging Media Publications, Westfield, New Jersey, 1978-92; Adjunct: Union College, Westfield, 1983-; Kean College of New Jersey, 1988-; Writer in Residence, English Teacher, Elizabeth High School, Elizabeth, New Jersey, 1988-; Fiction Instructor, Writer's Digest School, 1989-. Publications: Two Plus One, poetic play, 1984; Extended Family, 1986; Uno-Duo, 1988; Bushels of Broken Glass, poetic novella, 1989; Chords, 1990; Anove-Underground Anthology (editor), 1990; Author's Choice, 1991; Warm Storm, 1991; Panes, Fiction As Therapy, 1993; The Rivers Shadow, 1993; Jokers are Wild: 39 Plays to Ruffle Your Lover, 1994. Contributions to: Over 2000 poems and over 300 stories to magazines and periodicals, 1970-. Honours: Writer-in-Residence, National Endowment for the Arts, 1976, 1977; Poet in Schools, Virginia, late 1970s; Several grants including: Grant for Book Discussion, New Jersey Humanities Council, Westfield, 1985; Reading Grant, Dodge Foundation, 1980s; Literature Award, Willow Bee Publishing House, Wyoming, 1986. Memberships: International Women Writers' Guild; Associated Writing Programs; Poetry Society of America; American Academy of Poets; Feminist Writers' Guild; Women for Freedom of the Press. Address: c/o Olga G Holt, 5111 North 42nd Avenue, Phoenix, AZ 85019, USA.

HOLTON John Clark, b. 14 Apr 1959, Washington, District of Columbia, USA. Editor. Education: Atlantic College, 1975-77; American University, 1980-82. Appointments: Editor, Acclaim, 1977, Creative Expressions, 1983, Swinging Light, Voyager 83, 1996. Publication: Cry of the Invisible, 1991. Contributions to: Tropos; The Pearl; Influence; Expressions. Address: 2633 Guilford Avenue, Baltimore, MD 21218, USA.

HONIG Edwin, b. 3 Sept 1919, New York, New York, USA. Poet; Educator. m. (1) Charlotte Gilchrist, 1 Apr 1940, dec 1963, (2) Margot Dennes, 15 Dec 1963, div 1978, 2 sons. Education: BA, 1939, MA, 1947, University of Wisconsin, Madison; MA (ad eundem), Brown University, 1948. Appointments: Instructor, English: Purdue University, West Lafayette, Indiana, 1942-43; University of New Mexico, 1947-48; Claremont College, California, 1948; Instructor, 1949-52, Briggs Copeland Assistant Professor, 1952-57, Harvard University; Professor, English, 1957-82, Emeritus Professor, 1982-, Brown University, Providence, Rhode Island. Publications: García Lorca, 1944, 1963; Poems: The Moral Circus, 1955; The Gazabos: 41 poems, 1960; Survivals, 1964; Spring Journal, 1968; Four Springs, 1972; At Sixes, 1974; Shake a Spear with Me, John Berryman, 1974, edited as Affinities of Orpheus, 1976; Selected Poems 1955-1976, 1979; Cow Lines, 1982; Interrupted Praise, 1983; Gifts of Light, 1983; Calderón - Six Plays, translation, 1993; The Imminence of Love, Poems 1962-1992, 1993. Contributions to: New York Times; Kenyon Review; Nation; Poetry Magazine; New Republic; New Directions Annual; Sewanee Review; New Yorker; Michigan Quarterly Review; Poetry Review; Agni; Norton Anthology of Modern Poetry, 1988; Others. Honours: Poetry Prize, Saturday Review of Literature, 1957; Golden Rose, New England Poetry Society, 1961; Phi Beta Kappa, Brown University, 1961, 1982; Amy Lowell Travelling Poetry Fellowship, 1968; Rhode Island Governor's Award, Excellence in the Arts, 1970; Decorated by President of Portugal for translation of Fernande Pessoa, 1976; Translation Award, Poetry Society of America, 1984; Decorated by King of Spain for translation of Calderón, 1996; Other fellowships. Memberships: Past Board Member, Poetry Society of America; Dante Society of America. Address: 99 Post Road, Unit F-5, Warwick, RI 02888-1666, USA.

HOOKER Jeremy, b. 23 Mar 1941, Warsash, Hampshire, England. Education: BA, University of Southampton, 1963. Appointments: Lecturer in English, Bath College of Higher Education, 1988-. Publications include: The Elements, 1972; Soliloquies of a Chalk Giant, 1974; Solent Shore: New Poems, 1978; Landscape of the Daylight Moon, 1978; Englishman's Road, 1980; Their Silence a Language, 1993. A View from the Source: Selected Poems, 1982; Itchen Water, 1982; Master of the Leaping Figures, 1987; In Praise of Windmills, 1990. Honours include: Eric Gregory Award, 1969. Address: Old School House, 7 Sunnyside, Frome, Somerset, England.

HOOVER Paul, b. 30 Apr 1946, Harrisonburg, Virginia, USA. Writer; Poet; Teacher. m. Maxine Chernoff, 5 Oct 1974, 2 sons, 1 daughter. Education: BA cum laude, Manchester College, 1968; MA,

University of Illinois, 1973. Appointments: Poet-in-Residence, Columbia College, Chicago, 1974-; Editor, New American Writing, journal. Publications: Idea, 1987; The Novel, 1990; Postmodern American Poetry (Editor), 1993. Contributions to: Periodicals. Honours: National Endowment for the Arts Fellowship in Poetry, 1980; General Electric Foundation Award for Younger Writers, 1984; Carl Sandburg Award for Poetry, 1987. Memberships: Associated Writing Programs; Modern Language Association. Address: 2920 West Pratt, Chicago, IL 60645, USA.

HOPE Akua Lezli, b. 7 June 1957, New York, New York, USA. Writer; Poet. Education: BA, Williams College, 1975; MSJ, 1977, MBA, 1978, Columbia University. Appointments: Public Relations Associate, AT&T Network Systems, 1979-85; Marketing Communications Supervisor, Corning Incorporated, 1985-; Editor, New Heat, 1989-. Publications: Lovecycles, 1977; Shard, 1989; Sister Fire, 1994; Embouchure, poems on jazz and other musics, 1995; Contributions to: Obsidian II; Ikon; Hambone; Contact II; Black American Literature Forum; Erotique Noire, An Anthology of Erotic Writing by Black Writers, 1992; Confirmation, An Anthology of Afrikan American Women Writers; Extended Outlooks, An Anthology of American Women Writers. Honours: US-Africa Fellowship, Ragdale Foundation, 1993; Sterling Brown Award, 1975; Finalist, Walt Whitman Prize, 1983; Poetry Fellowship, New York Foundation for the Arts, 1987-88; Finalist, MacDonalds Literary Achievement Award Competition, 1989; Creative Writing Fellowship, National Endowment for the Arts, 1990; Finalist, Barnard New Women Poets Series, 1990. Memberships: Poetry Society of America; Science Fiction Poetry Association; Teachers and Writers; Poets and Writers; Founding Member, New Renaissance Writers' Guild. Address: PO Box 33, Corning, NY 14830, USA.

HOPMAN Ellen Evert, b. 31 July 1952, Salzburg, Austria. Author; Herbalist; Lay Homeopath. Education: MEd, Mental Health Counseling, University of Massachusetts, 1990. Appointments: Author; Health Educator; Teacher and Practitioner of Herbalism, 1983-. Publications: Tree Medicine, Tree Magic, 1992; A Druid's Herbal For the Sacred Earth Year, 1994; People of the Earth - The New Pagans Speak Out, co-author, 1995. Videos: Gifts from the Healing Earth, Vol I. Audio Tapes: The Herbal and Magical Powers of Trees; The Druid Path - Herbs and Festivals; Celtic Goddesses and Gods. Address: P O Box 219, Amherst, MA 01004, USA.

HOROVITZ Michael, b. 4 Apr 1935, Frankfurt, Germany. Education: BA, Brasnose College, Oxford. Appointments: Editor and Publisher, New Departures magazine, 1959-. Publications: Strangers, 1965; Bank Holiday: A New Testament for the Love Generation, 1967; The Wolverhampton Wanderer: An Epic of Britannia, 1971; Love Poems: Nineteen Poems of Love, Lust, and Spirit, 1971; Growing Up: Selected Poems and Pictures 1951-79, 1979; Midsummer Morning Jog Log, 1986; Bop Paintings, Collages, Drawings and Picture Poems, 1989; Co-editor, Grandchildren of Albion, 1992; Wordsounds & Sightlines: New & Selected Poems, 1994; The Pow Anthology, 1996. Address: PO Box 9819, London W11 299.

HORVATH Elemer G, b. 15 April 1933, Hungary. Printer. m. 29 May 1968. Education: University of Budapest, 1953-56; University of Florence, Italy, 1957-61. Publications: A mindennapok arca, 1962; Egy feher neger naplojabol, 1976; A homokora nyaka, 1980; Maya tukor, 1982; A szelrozsa gyokerei, selected poems, 1990; Scaliger Rosa (poems), 1995. Contributions to: Almost all major Hungarian language literary magazines abroad; Literary magazines, Hungary, 1978-. Honour: Robert Graves Award, 1992; Book of the Year Award, 1995. Memberships: International PEN Club; Poetry Society of America; Hungarian Writers Association. Address: 209 Bullet Hole Road, Mahopac, NY 10541, USA.

HOTHERSALL Patricia Ann, b. 23 June 1942, Burnley, Lancashire, England. Teacher. m. Colin Hothersall, 28 Dec 1963, 2 sons. Education: Cert Ed; MA; PhD. Appointment: Department Head, rural school. Publications: Booklets: And on the 8th Day, 1978; Gemini, co-author; Images & Illusions, 1986; Occasional Reflections, with son Robert, 1990. Contributions to: Poets Voice; Periaktos; Weyfarers; Success; Counterpoint; Outrigger; TOPS; Others. Honours: Minor competitions in small magazines; Prize in The Writer. Address: Middlen, 23 Churchill Road, Thetford, Norfolk IP24 2JW, England.

HOUGHTON Timothy Dane, b. 1 Mar 1955, Dayton, Ohio, USA. Professor of English and Creative Writing. m. Cynthia Moore, 18 Aug 1990. Education; BA, English, Psychology, Sociology, University of

Pennsylvania; MA, English, Creative Writing, San Francisco State University, 1979; PhD, English, Creative Writing, University of Denver, 1984. Appointments: Professor: University of Nebraska; Currently University of Houston, Texas. Publications: High Bridges, 1989; Below Two Skies, 1993. Contributions to: Greensboro Review; College English; Poet Lore; Denver Quarterly; Stand Magazine; Carolina Quarterly; Brooklyn Review; Arizona Quarterly. Honours: Residencies, Artist Colonies: Yaddo, 1990; Virginia Center for the Creative Arts, 1990, 1991, 1992; Helene Wurlitzer Foundation, 1993. Membership: Creative Writing Programs. Address: Creative Writing Program, English Department, University of Houston, Houston, TX 77204, USA.

HOUNTONDJI Victor Mahouton, b. 22 Sept 1953, Sakete, Benin, West Africa. University Lecturer in French. 1 son. Education: Licences, Lettres, Anglais, Maitrise Lettres, 1975; Diplome, Etudes Superieures, 1977; Diplome, Etudes Approfondies, 1981. Appointments: Teacher, College St Thomas d'Aquin, Akrakra, Cotonou, 1971-72; Lyceums and colleges, Gabon, 1974-78; Lecturer, University of Calabar, Nigeria, 1979-80. Publications: Couleur de reves, poetry and prose, 1977; Paroles de poete, collection of articles, texts, interviews, poetry, prose; Le cahier d'un retour au pays natal, d'aime cesdaire; Evenement litteraire et facteur de revolution. Contributions to: Anthologies: 30 ans de poesie contemporaire, 1988; Poetes de nôtre temps, 1988; World Poetry, 1988; East-West Voices, 1988. Honours: Honorary DLitt, World Academy of Arts and Culture; Governing Board of World Congresses of Poets, 1985; Fellow, International Eminent Poet, International Poets Academy, 1990. Memberships: Société des Poètes Français; Association des Ecrivains de Langue Française; World Academy of Arts and Culture; Governing Board, World Congresses of Poets. Address: PO Box 1268, Cotonou, Benin, West Africa.

HOUSTON Libby. See: JEWELL Elizabeth Maynard.

HOWARD David Andrew, b. 20 Aug 1959, Christchurch, New Zealand. Writer; Poet; Editor. 1 son. Education: Diploma in Cabaret, Christchurch Academy, 1989. Appointments: Partner, Impress Editorial independent agency specialising in poetry assessment; Full-time Writer, 1984-88, 1989-; Member, The Curtainless Window Theatre Company, 1988; Partner, Takahe Publishing Collective, 1989-; Poetry Editor, Takahe literary quarterly, 1989-. Publications: In the First Place: Poems 1980-1990, 1991; Holding Company, 1995; Complete with Instructions, video, 1995. Contributions to: Chelsea; Descant; Landfall; New Zealand Listener; Poet Lore; Poetry Australia; Poetry New Zealand; Printout; Visions International; Anthologies: The Bird Catcher's Song, Australia, 1992; Catching the Light, New Zealand, 1992. Honours: 1st Prize, Gordon and Gotch Poetry Award, 1984; 1st Prize, New Zealand Poetry Society International Competition, 1987. Memberships: National Council, PEN New Zealand; Chair, Canterbury-Westland Branch, PEN New Zealand; New Zealand Book Council; Takahe Publishing Collective; Book Arts Society of New Zealand; Canterbury Poets' Collective; New Zealand Literature Association. Address: PO Box 13-335, Christchurch 1, New Zealand.

HOWARD Noni H E, b. 26 Dec 1949, Montreal, Quebec, Canada. Publisher; Educator; Writer; Poet. Education: BA, English, Religion, Bishop's University, Lennoxville, Quebec; MA, English, University of Alberta, 1972; PhD, Creative Writing, University of British Columbia, 1974. Appointments: Consulting Editor, The Phoenix, 171-80; Staff Writer: Vancouver City Magazine, and Gay Tide, 1972-74; Staff Teacher, Vancouver Free University, 1972-74; Features on poetry, women, Public TV, Vancouver, 1973-74; Staff Teacher, Orpheus Alternative University, San Francisco, USA, 1974-80; Editor-in-Chief, Publisher, New World Press, Daly City, California, 1974-; Produced films for Poetry Festivals, San Francisco: Annual Women's, 1977, 1979, Gay Pride Week, 1977-78; Bloodjet Literary Magazine, 1978-85; Haight-Ashbury Literary Journal, 1979-85; Consulting Editor: Catlin Press, Vancouver, 1978-85; Women Talking-Women Listening, 1979-80; Poetry readings, Canada, England, Mexico, USA. Publications: I Think of You, I Thought of You; I Will Think of You, 1967; A Transparent Quiet Sea, 1971; Politics of Separation, 1974; Almost Like Dancing; Anthology of 1st Annual Women's Poetry Festival of San Francisco, 1977; The Politics of Love: Selected Poems 1970-1996, 1996. Contributions to: Many publications including: Bristol Banner Books, 1991-95; In the West of Ireland, 1994, 1995; National Library of Poetry, 1994, 1995; Parnassus of World Poets, 1994, 1995; The Mitre, 1994, 1995; Olympoetry, 1994, 1995. Honours: First Prize, many Honourable Mentions, Alberta Poetry Contests, 1965-71; Kind Editor Award, Poetry Organization of Women,

California, 1980; Grants. Memberships: League of Canadian Poets; Poets and Writers; Poetry Organization of Women, California; Association of American Publishers; Women's Choice; Feminist Literary Guild; Poets and Writers; Honorary Member, World Parnassians' Guild International; Bay Area Poets' Coalition; Olympoetry Movement Committee. Address: 744 Stoneyford Drive, Daly City, CA 94015-3642, USA.

HOWARD Richard (Joseph), b. 13 Oct 1929, Cleveland, Ohio, USA. Poet; Critic; Editor; Translator. Education: BA, 1951, MA, 1952, Columbia University; Postgraduate Studies, Sorbonne, University of Paris, 1952-53. Appointments: Lexicographer, World Publishing company, 1954-58; Poetry Editor, New American Review, New Republic, Paris Review, Shenandoah; Rhodes Professor of Comparative Literature, University of Cincinnati. Publications: Poetry: Quantities, 1962; The Damages, 1967; Untitled Subjects, 1969; Findings, 1971; Two-Part Inventions, 1974; Fellow Feelings, 1976; Misgivings, 1979; Lining Up, 1984; Quantities/Damages, 1984; No Traveller, 1989; Like Most Revelations: New Poems, 1994; Criticism: Alone With America, 1969; Passengers Must Not Ride on Fenders, 1974; Editor: Preferences: Fifty-One American Poets Choose Poems From Their Own Work and From the Past, 1974; The War in Algeria, 1975; Translator: Over 65 books. Contributions to: Magazines and journals. Honours: Guggenheim Fellowship, 1966-67; Harriet Monroe Memorial Prize, 1969; Pulitzer Prize in Poetry, 1970; Levinson Prize, 1973; Cleveland Arts Prize, 1974; American Academy and Institute of Arts and Letters Medal for Poetry, 1980; American Book Award for Translation, 1984; PEN American Center Medal for Translation, 1986; France-American Foundation Award for Translation, 1987; National Endowment for the Arts Fellowship, 1987. Address: c/o Alfred A Knopf Inc, 201 East 50th Street, New York, NY 10022, USA.

HOWARD Roger, b. 19 June 1938, Warwick, England. Playwright; Lecturer in Literature. m. Anne Zemaitis, 13 Aug 1960, 1 son. Education includes: MA Litt (Drama), 1976. Appointments: Lecturer: Tientsin University, China, 1966-68; Peking University, 1972-74; Writer in Residence, University of York, England, 1976-78; Lecturer, Director of MA Drama, 1979-93, Senior Lecturer, 1993-, Essex University. Publication: Senile Poems, 1988. Contributions to: Argo; New Poetry; Only Poetry; Palantir; Poetry and Audience; Rock Drill; Stand; Straight Lines; Times Literary Supplement; Urbane Gorilla; Y; Anthologies: New Poetry 2 and 5; The Poets' Gift. Address: Department of Literature, University of Essex, Wivenhoe Park, Colchester, Essesx CO4 3SQ, England.

HOWARD Sherwin Ward, b. 19 Feb 1936, Safford, Arizona, USA. College Administrator. m. Annette Mina Shoup, 30 June 1960, 3 sons, 1 daughter. Education: BS, Mathematics, 1960, MA, Theatre, Music, 1963, Utah State University; MFA, Playwriting, Yale University; PhD, Higher Education Administration, University of Wisconsin, 1980. Appointments: Assistant to Provost, Ohio University, 1966-69; Assistant to President, Lawrence University, 1969-80; Dean, Arts and Humanities, Weber State University, 1980-. Publication: Sometime Voices, 1988. Contributions to: Dialogue; Redneck Review; Weber Studies; Ensign Magazine. Honours: Dialogue Prize for Best Poetry of the Year, 1987; Utah Poet of the Year, 1988. Memberships: Utah Poetry Society; Ben Lomond Poets. Address: 5150 Shawnee, Ogden, UT 84403, USA.

HOWE Fanny, b. 15 Oct 1940, Buffalo, New York, USA. Fiction Writer; Poet. 1 son, 2 daughters. Education: Stanford University, 1958-61. Appointments: Lecturer in Writing: Tufts University, 1968-71; Columbia University, 1974-77; Massachusetts Institute of Technology, 1978-87; Professor of Literature, University of California at San Diego, 1987-. Publications: Eggs, 1968; The Amerinlas Coastline Poem, 1975; Alsace-Lorraine, 1978; Robeson Street, 1984; The Vineyard, 1989; The Lives of the Spirit, 1989; The Quietest, 1992; The End, 1992; Saving History, 1993. Contributions to: Ploughshares; Sulfur; Conjunctions; Temblor; The New Yorker; O'blek; Grand Street; Others. Honours: National Endowment for the Arts, 1991. Memberships: Fiction Collective; Bunting Institute. Address: Literature Department 0410, University of California at San Diego, La Jolla, CA 92093, USA.

HOWE Susan, b. 1937, USA. Poet. Education: BFA, Painting, Museum of Fine Arts, Boston, 1961. Appointments: Butler Fellow in English, 1988, Professor of English, 1989, State University of New York, Buffalo; Visiting Scholar and Professor of English, Temple University, Philadelphia, 1990, 1991; Visiting Poet and Leo Block Professor, University of Denver, 1993-94; Visiting Brittingham Scholar,

University of Wisconsin, Madison, 1994; Visiting Poet, University of Arizona, 1994. Publications: Poetry: Hinge Picture, 1974; The Western Borders, 1976; Secret History of the Dividing Line, 1978; Cabbage Gardens, 1979; The Liberties, 1980; Pythagorean Silence, 1982; Defenestration of Prague, 1983; Articulation of Sound Forms in Time, 1987; A Bibliography of the King's Book, or, Eikon Basilike, 1989; The Europe of Trusts: Selected Poems, 1990; Singularities, 1990; The Nonconformist's Memorial, 1993; Frame Structures: Early Poems 1974-79, New Directions, 1996. Other: My Emily Dickinson, 1985; Incloser, 1990; The Birth-mark: Unsettling the Wilderness in American Literary History, 1993. Honours: Before Columbus Foundation Awards, 1980, 1986; New York State Council of the Arts Residency, 1986; Pushcart Prize, 1987; New York City Fund for Poetry Grant, 1988; Guggenheim Fellowship, 1996-97. Address: 115 New Quarry Road, Guilford, CT 06437, USA.

HOWELL Anthony, b. 20 Apr 1945, London, England. Education: Royal Ballet School, London. Appointment: Editor, Softly, Loudly Books, London. Publications: Sergei de Diaghileff (1929), 1968; Inside the Castle, 1969; Femina Deserta, 1971; Oslo: A Tantric Ode, 1975; The Mekon, 1976; Notions of a Mirror: Poems Previously Uncollected 1964-82, 1983; Winter's Not Gone, 1984; Why I May Never See the Walls of China, 1986; Howell's Law, 1990; Near Cavalry: Selected Poems of Nick Lafitte, 1992; Editor, Erotic Lyrics, 1970. Address: 21 Augusta Street, Adamstown, Cardiff CF2 1EN, Wales.

HOWELL Elmo, b. 5 Aug 1918, Tremont, Mississippi, USA. Retired English Teacher. Education: BA, University of Mississippi, 1940; MA, 1948, PhD, 1955, University of Florida. Appointments: Jackson State College, Jacksonville, Alabama, 1955-57; Memphis State University, 1957-83. Publications: Winter Verses, 1989; The Apricot Tree, and Other Poems, 1993; I Know a Planted Field, 1995. Membership: Mississippi Poetry Society. Address: 3733 Douglass Avenue, Memphis, TN 38111, USA.

HOWES Barbara, b. 1 May 1914, New York, New York, USA. Poet. m. William Jay Smith, 1 Oct 1947, 2 sons. Education: BA, Bennington College, 1937. Appointment: Editor, Chimera literary quarterly, 1943-47. Publications: The Undersea Farmer, 1948; In the Cold Country, 1954; Light and Dark, 1959; Looking Up at Leaves, 1966; The Blue Garden, 1972; A Private Signal: Poems New and Selected, 1977; Moving, 1983; Collected Poems: 1945-1990, 1995. Contributions to: American Scholar; Atlantic; Botteghe Oscure, Rome; Encounter, England; Isis, Oxford; Mandrake, Oxford; New Yorker; New York Times; Partisan Review; Poetry; Sewanee Review; Southern Review; Stand, England; Virginia Quarterly Review; Yale Review; Antaeus; Berkshire Review; Carleton Miscellany; Chimera; Conjunctions; Harper's Bazaar; Harvard Magazine; Inquiry; Saturday Review; Voices; Others. Honours: Guggenheim Fellowship, 1955; Brandeis University Creative Arts Poetry Grant, 1958; Award in Literature, National Institute in Arts and Letters, 1971; Golden Rose Award, New England Poetry Club, 1973; Christopher Award, 1974; Bennington Award for Outstanding Contributions to Poetry, 1980; Finalist, National Book Award, twice. Address: RR1, Box 175, North Pownal, VT 05260, USA.

HOWITZ Bettina, b. 23 Aug 1943, Copenhagen, Denmark. Writer; Painter. 2 sons, 1 daughter. Education: High School Diploma, 1961; Sorbonne Diploma, 1976; Diploma in French Language, Copenhagen School of Economic and Business Administration, 1983. Appointments: Painting Exhibitions, 1983-; Staff, The Danish Film Institute, 1985-90; Production Manager for film about Gypsies in Spain, 1991-92. Publications: Moments of Truth, New York, 1991; Anna's Song, New York, 1993; Støv (Dust), stories, 1994. Membership: The Danish Writer's Union. Address: Lille Strandstraede 18 St, 1254 Copenhagen K, Denmark.

HOYLAND Michael David, b. 1 Apr 1925, Nagpur, India. Retired Art Lecturer. m. Marette Nicol Fraser, 21 July 1948, 2 sons, 2 daughters. Education: Board of Education Drawing Exam, 1943; NDD, 1947; ATD, 1948. Publications: Art for Children, 1970; Variations, 1975; A Love Affair with War, 1981; The Bright Way In, 1984. Contributions to: Over 150 poems in journals and a collection; Also short stories; Reviewer, Ore. Address: Foxfoot House, South Luffenham, Nr Oakham, Rutland, Leicestershire LE15 8NP, England.

HUA Ji. See: CHEN Jianhua.

HUANG Min-Chi. See: **YEH Victor Wei Hsin.**

HUBBARD Thomas Frederick, b. 6 Nov 1950, Kirkcaldy, Scotland. Writer; Lecturer. m. 3 Apr 1982, 2 sons, 1 daughter. Education: MA 1st Class Hons, 1973, PhD, 1982, Aberdeen University; Diploma in Librarianship, with distinction, Strathclyde, 1978. Appointments: Senior Library Assistant, Edinburgh University Library, 1980-82; Librarian, Scottish Poetry Library, 1984-92; Lecturer, University of Grenoble, France, 1993; Visiting Assistant Professor, University of Connecticut, 1993-94, University of North Carolina at Asheville, 1996-98; Various teaching engagements, Edinburgh and Glasgow Universities and Glasgow School of Art; Appearance on In Verse series, Scottish Television. Publications: Four Fife Poets (co-author), 1988; The New Makers (editor); Seeking Mr Hyde; Numerous anthologies including: Behind the Lines, 1989; European Poetry in Scotland, 1991. Contributions to: Cencrastus; Chapman; Cyphers; Gairfish; Lines Review; Poetry Ireland; Poetry Wales; Scottish Slavonic Review; Tratti. Honour: Awarded Writer's Bursary, Scottish Arts Council, 1992. Membership: International PEN Scottish Centre. Address: 4 Asquith Street, Kirkcaldy, Fife KY1 1PW, Scotland.

HUCK Janet, b. 2 May 1960, Bournemouth, Dorset, England. Poet. m. David Huck, June 1983. Publication: First Poetry Collection, 1996. Contributions to: Winter Anthology, 1991; Poetry New South West Anthology, 1992. Honours: Highly Commended, Ouse Valley Poetry Competition, 1989. Membership: Poetry Society. Address: Ivy Cottage, Waterditch, Nr Christchurch, Dorset BH23 8JX, England.

HUCKABONE Fay. See: **BRIGHAM Faith Elizabeth Huckabone.**

HUDSON Louise Deborah, b. 2 Dec 1958, London, England. Writer. 2 sons. Education: Certificate in Recreational Arts for the Community. Appointments: Acting Education Officer, Publicity Secretary, Poetry Society; Arts Coordinator, Halton Borough Council; Centre Director, Arvon Foundation in Devon. Publications: Four Ways, 1985; Some People, 1989; Intimate Relations, 1993. Contributions to: Rialto; Slow Dancer; Orbis; Iron; Smoke; Foolscap; Wide Skirt. Membership: Founder Member, Company of Poets. Address: Elm Court, East Street, Sheepwash, Beaworthy, Devon EX21 5NL, England.

HUDSON Thomas Cyril, b. 25 Aug 1910, Cowes, Isle of Wight, England. Chief Engineering Estimator and Planning Engineer. Publication: Kairos (Selected Poems 1), 1960. Contributions to: The Boy's Own Paper; Humour Variety; Southern Evening Echo; Hampshire Poets; Isle of Wight Poets, Nos 1, 2, 3; Country Life; Island Images, anthology; A Whisper in the Rain, anthology; The Big Sleep, anthology; Nature: Paradise, anthology; Poets of the South, anthology; Poetic Inspirations, anthology; New Poetry 2; PEN Anthology; Isle of Wight County Press; Islandlife; Flickerings; Snap; Parnassus of World Poets; Skin Deep; Royal Poets; Millenium Blues. Honours: 1st Prize, 1971, 1972, W G and S F Tillyard Cup, 1974, Isle of Wight Writers Circle; Margery Hume Cup, Isle of Wight Festival, 1972-73, 1979, 1982, 1984-90, 1992, 1994, 1995; 1st Prize, Isle of Wight Arts Council, 1983. Address: Wyvern, 250 Newport Road, Cowes, Isle of Wight, England.

HUFANA Alejandrino, b. 22 Oct 1926, San Fernando, La Union, The Philippines. Education: Quezon City, California and Columbia Universities. Appointments: Professor of English, University of Philippines, 1979-. Publications include: 13 Kalisud, 1955; Sickle Season: Poems of a First Decade 1948-58, 1959; Poro Point: An Anthology of Lives: Poems 1955-60, 1961; The Wife of Lot and Other New Poems, 1971; Sing Heil: An Epic of the Third Reich, 1975; Imelda Marcos: A Tonal Epic, 1975; Obligations: Cheers of Conscience, 1975; Shining On, 1985. Address: 22 Casanova Street, B Culiat, Tanding Sora Avenue, Quezon City, The Philippines.

HUFFSTICKLER Albert, (Albert Huff), b. 17 Dec 1927. Education: BA, English, Southwest Texas State University, San Marcos, Texas, 1961. Appointment: Library Assistant, retired from the University of Texas. Publications: Night Diner, 1986; Walking Wounded, 1989; Working on My Death Chant, 1991; City of the Rain, 1993. Contributions to: Nimrod; Abraxas; Poetry East; New Mexico Humanities Review; Pig Iron; Iron; Journal of Anthroposophy; Poetry Motel. Honours: Austin Book Award, 1989; Senate Resolution, State of Texas honouring his contribution to Texas Poetry, 1989. Address: 312 East 43rd Street 103, Austin, TX 78751, USA.

HUGHES Annie. See: **SNUGGS Olive.**

HUGHES Glyn, b. Middlewich, Cheshire, England. Author. 1 son. Education: Regional College of Art, Manchester, 1952-56; Qualified Art Teacher, 1959. Appointments: Teaching, Lancashire and Yorkshire; Southern Arts Writer-in-Residence, Farnborough, Hampshire, 1982-84; Arts Council Writer-in-Residence, D H Lawrence Centenary Festival, Eastwood, Nottinghamshire, 1985; Readings of poetry and extracts from novels, venues including: Ohio Poetry Circuit, 1970; Greece, Czechoslovakia, 1988. Publications: Neighbours, 1970; Rest The Poor Struggler, 1972; Best of Neighbours (Selected Poems); 1979; Samuel Laycock, Selected Poems (editor), 1981; Novels: Where I Used To Play On The Green, 1982, paperback, 1984; The Hawthorn Goddess, 1984, 1992, paperback, 1985; The Rape Of The Rose, 1987, 1992, paperback, 1989; The Antique Collector, 1990, paperback, 1991; Roth, 1992, paperback, 1993; Bronte, 1996; Verse plays for BBC Radio: The Yorkshire Women, 1978; Dreamers, 1979; The Stranger, 1979. Honours: Poetry Book Society Recommendation and Poetry Prize, Welsh Arts Council, for Neighbours, 1970; Arts Council Fellow, Bishop Grossetese College, Lincoln, 1979-81; Guardian Fiction Prize and David Higham Prize, for Where I Used To Play On The Green, 1982. Literary Agent: Mic Cheetham, Mic Cheetham Agency, 139 Buckingham Palace Road, London SW1W 9SA, England. Address: 1 Millbank Road, Millbank, Sowerby Bridge, West Yorkshire HX6 3DY, England.

HUGHES Gwyneth, b. 10 May 1929, Berkeley, California, USA. Teacher of English as a Foreign Language. m. Henri Lasry, 13 Oct 1951, 2 sons, 1 daughter. Education: BA, University of California, Berkeley, 1949. Contributions to: Orbis; Outposts; Envoi; Staple; Pennine Platform; Iota; Writing Women; Wayfarers; Poetry Nottingham; Fatchance; Smiths Knoll; Cardiff Poet; Sphinx; Writer; Poet Lore; Cyclotron; New Athenean. Memberships: Theatre Writers' Union; New Playwrights' Trust; Women Writers' Network; Magdalena Project; Welsh Union of Writers; Poetry Society; Dramatists' Guild, USA; Poetry Society of America. Address: c/o Lasry, 106 Boulevard Diderot, 75012 Paris, France.

HUGHES Sophie, b. 24 Sept 1927, Houlton, Maine, USA. Art Teacher; Artist; Poet. Education: BA, English Literature, Barnard College, Columbia University, 1949; MA, Fine Arts, Columbia Teachers' College, 1951; 32 postgraduate credits, various New York colleges. Appointments: Assistant to Librarian, Columbia College Library, New York City, 1952-55; Art Teacher, Goddard Neighborhood Center, New York City, 1954-58; Painting Teacher, Adult Classes, YMCA, New York City, 1958; Art Teacher, Lexington School for the Deaf, New York City, 1958-83. Contributions to: Anthology of Magdalena Verse-Yearbook of American Poetry, 1986-88; Art-Life; Candelabrum Chelsea; Confrontation; Cotton Boll-Atlanta Review; Exquisite Corpse; Hollins Critic; Interim; New York Quarterly; Poem; Princeton Spectrum; Sing Heavenly Muse!; Tea Leaves; Many others. Memberships: Academy of American Poets; Poetry Society of America; Poets and Writers Inc; Poets House, New York City. Address: 29 West 12th Street, Apt 2H, New York, NY 10011, USA.

HUGHES Ted, (Edward James Hughes), b. 17 Aug 1930, Mytholmroyd, West Yorkshire, England. Poet; Dramatist; Author; Poet Laureate of England. m. (1) Sylvia Plath, 1956, dec 1963, 1 son, 1 daughter, (2) Carol Orchard, 1970. Education: BA, 1954, MA, 1959, Pembroke College, Cambridge. Appointments: Founding Editor (with Daniel Weissbort), Modern Poetry in Translation magazine, London, 1964-71; Poet Laureate of England, 1984-. Publications include: Poetry: A Solstice, 1978; Orts, 1978; Moortown Elegies, 1978; Adam and the Sacred Nine, 1979; Remains of Elmet: A Pennine Sequence, 1979, 3rd edition, revised, as Elmet: Poems, 1994; Four Tales Told by an Idiot, 1979; Moortown, 1979, revised edition as Moortown Diary, 1989; Sky-Furnace, 1981; A Primer of Birds, 1981; Selected Poems 1957-1981, 1982; River, 1983; Flowers and Insects: Some Birds and a Pair of Spiders, 1986; Tales of the Early Word, 1988; Wolfwatching, 1989; Capriccio, 1990; The Unicorn, 1992; Rain-Charm for the Duchy and Other Laureate Poems, 1993; Earth Dances, 1994; New Selected Poems 1957-1994, 1995; Poetry for children: 13 books, 1961-91; Plays: Eat Crow, 1971; Plays for children: several; Stories: Difficulties of a Bridegroom, 1996; Other: Winter Pollen: Occasional Prose, 1995; Editor: Sylvia Plath's Selected Poems, 1985. Honours: First Publication Award, New York Poetry Center, 1957; 1st Prize, Guinness Poetry Awards, 1958; Guggenheim Fellowship, 1959-60; Somerset Maugham Award, 1960; Hawthornden Prize, 1961; City of Florence International Poetry Prize, 1969; Premio Internazionale Taormina,

1973; Queen's Gold Medal for Poetry, 1974; Officer of the Order of the British Empire, 1977; Signal Poetry Awards, 1979, 1983, 1985; Heinemann Award, Royal Society of Literature, 1980; Poet Laureate of England, 1984-; Guardian Children's Fiction Award, 1985; Maschler Award, 1985; Honorary Fellow, Pembroke College, Cambridge, 1986. Address: c/o Faber and Faber, 3 Queen Square, London, WC1N 3AU, England.

HUGHEY David Vaughn, b. 19 Jan 1944, Henderson, Nevada, USA. College Professor. Education: BA, Sociology, Kent State University, 1967; PhD, Anthropology, University of Pittsburgh, 1977; BS, Business, International College of the Cayman Islands, 1987. Appointments: Instructor, Faculty Advisor, Duquesne Magazine, Duquesne University, 1978; Visiting Assistant Professor, University of Santa Clara, 1979-80; Associate Professor, 1981-87, Professor, 1992-, International College of the Cayman Islands, Grand Cayman; Assistant Professor, National-Louis University, Atlanta, Georgia, 1991-92. Contributions to: Driftwood East; CSP World News, Canada; Quintessence; New Earth Review; Bardic Echoes; Feelings; Adventures in Poetry Magazines; Bitterroot; Green Fuse; Hyperion; Journal of Contemporary Poets; McLean County Poetry Review; Orphic Lute; Parnassus Literary Review; Piedmont Literary Review; SPAFASWAP. Honours: Honourable Mention, Young America Sings, 1962; Honourable Mention, for Rhymed Verse and for Pattern of Choice, Inky Trails Poem of the Year, 1975; Honorary Editor, New Earth Review, 1978. Memberships: Poets and Writers Inc; Georgia State Poetry Society Inc. Address: International College of the Cayman Islands, Newlands, Grand Cayman, Cayman Islands.

HULL Coral Eileen, b. 12 Dec 1965, Sydney, New South Wales,Australia. Poet. Education: Bachelor, Creative Arts, University of Wollongong, New South Wales, Australia, 1987; MA, Deakin University, Victoria, Australia, 1994. Appointments: Visual Artist; Animal Rights Activist; Photographer; Education Officer, Animal Liberation, Victoria, Australia. Publications: In The Dog Box of Summer, 1995; William's Mongrels', 1996. Contributions to: Hecate; Island; Voices; Poetrix; Scratch; Fine Line; Poetry on Paper; Northern Perspective; Top Dog Journal; Women and Survival; Numerous others. Honours: Second Prize and Commended, Eaglehawk Dahila Arts Festival Literary Competition, 1985; The Philip Larkin Poetry Prize, Wollongong University, 1987; Winner, 1993 H M Butterfly - F Earle Hooper Award, The English Association Sydney Branch, University of Sydney; Highly Commended, The Red Earth Poetry (Open) Category, Northern Territory Literary Awards, Darwin, 1995. Address: PO Box 1630, Collingwood, Victoria 3066, Australia.

HULSE Michael, b. 12 June 1955, Stoke-on-Trent, Staffordshire, England. Education: MA in German, University of St Andrews, 1977. Appointment: Lecturer, University of Cologne, 1985-. Publications: Monochrome Blood, 1980; Dole Queue, 1981; Knowing and Forgetting, 1981; Propaganda, 1985; Eating Strawberries in the Necropolis. 1991; Translations of German poetry. Honours: Poetry Society Prize, 1978. Address: c/o Collins Harvill, 8 Grafton Street, London W1X 3LA, England.

HUMPHREY Paul, b. 14 Jan 1915, New York, New York, USA. Commercial Writer. m. Eleanor Nicholson, 22 Feb 1941, 2 sons, 1 daughter. Education: Graduate, DeVeaux Military Academy, 1936; Graduate, University of Rochester, 1940; MA, 1947-48. Appointments: Military Supplies Procuror, 1941-45; Teacher, Vice Principal, high school, 1946-47; Promotional Material Writer, F E Compton Co, 1948-61; Commercial Writer, 1962-. Publications: Verse: 1934; Burnt Toast, 1977; Suburban Briefs, 1986; Ballad Bar, 1991; The Lighter Touch, 1992. Contributions to: Rochester, New York Democrat & Chronicle; Boston Globe; New York Times; Cosmopolitan; Good Housekeeping; Ladies Home Journal; Modern Maturity; Pleasure Publications; Rotarian; True Love; Bitterroot; Midwest Review; Orbis; Plains Poetry Journal; Alura; Triad; Krax; St Martins Bedford Introduction to Literature; Lightyear Poets Market; Saturday Evening Post; Numerous others; Prose Books: How To Books; Co-author, Maud Humphrey Biography; 50 Features, Travel Brochures, 31 countries. Honours: Humour 1st Prize, Writers Digest, 1988; Various minor awards. Memberships: Rochester Poets, President, 1955-68; Authors League, New York City; Poets and Writers. Address: 2329 South Union Street, Spencerport, NY 14559, USA.

HUMPHRIES Martin Charles, b. 5 April 1955, Bristol, England. Museum Director. Education: AGSM, Guildhall School of Music and Drama, 1976; BEd, London University, 1977. Appointments:

Administrator, Oval House Arts Education Centre; Manager, Ronald Grant Archive; Director, The Cinema Museum; Editor, GMP Poetry Series, 1985-90. Publications: Mirrors, 1980; Searching for a Destination, 1982; Salt and Honey (co-author), 1989; Editor: Not Love Alone: A Modern Gay Anthology, 1985; So Long Desired: Poems by James Kirkup and John McRae, 1986; Dreams and Speculations: Poems by Paul Binding and John Horder, 1986; Three New York Poets, 1988; Tongues United: 5 Black Gay Poets, 1988; Twenty Something: Poems by Dinyar Godrej, Tim Neave, Pat O'Brien; The Sexuality of Men (co-editor), 1985; Heterosexuality (co-editor), 1987; Essays in: Men, Sex and Relationships, 1992; Between Men and Feminism, 1992. Contributions to: Impact; Oscar-cards; Performing Oscars; Gaypride Anthologies, 1986, 1987; Square Peg; RFD; Christopher Street; Eros in Boystown. Address: 7 Meru Close, London NW5 4AQ, England.

HUNT Laird Burnau, b. 3 Sept 1968, Singapore. Writer. Education: BA, Indiana University, 1990; French Literature, History, The Naropa Institute, Boulder; MFA, Writing and Politics, 1996; Paris, Lasorbonne Licence Lettres Modernes, 1996. Appointment: Literary Secretary to Bobbie Louise Hawkins, Boulder, 1993-94. Publications: Canon, 1993; Pieces, 1994; Snow Country, 1995; T.E.L., 1996. Contributions to: Printed Matter; Bombay Gin; Quarterly; World; Talisman; Trembling Ladders. Honours: T. Edith Drane Award for Outstanding Student in History, Indiana University, 1990; The Marianne Moore Scholarship for Poetry and Editing, 1994. Membership: Founder Publisher, Psalm 151, Literary Bi-annual. Address: 3 Rue Ruhmkorff, 75017 Paris, France.

HUNT Sam, b. 4 July 1946, New Zealand. Publications: Between Islands, 1964; Selected Poems 1965-69, 1970; Postcard of a Cabbage Tree, 1971; Letter to Jerusalem, 1971; Beware the Man, 1972; Birth on Bottle Creek, 1972; Time to Ride, 1975; Drunkard's Garden, 1978; Sailor's Morning: 100 Selected Poems 1966-79, 1979; Collected Poems 1963-80, 1980; Running Scared, 1982; Selected Poems, 1987. Honour: Queen's Service Medal. Address: c/o Laremata Post Office, Wellington, New Zealand.

HURCOT Jason. See: EVERS Jason Harvey.

HURFORD Christopher R, b. 10 Oct 1965, Bristol, England. Solicitor's Representative. Education: BA, Honours, English, St John's College, Cambridge, 1988; MA, Creative Writing, Lancaster University, 1989. Appointments: TV Researcher; Lecturer in English, Catholic University, Lublin, Poland; Harper-Wood Scholar for Poetry, 1991-92; Overseas Aid Worker. Publications: Love/Hate, co-author, 1991; Heroes, 1993; Tiger Book of Popular Verse, 1994; Erotic Verse, Editor, 1995. Contributions to: Verse; Rialto; Orbis; Contra-Flow; The North; BIS; Times Literary Supplement; Brulion. Honours: Master's Prize, Cambridge, 1988; North National Poetry Competition runner-up; Harper-Wood Scholar, 1991-92. Address: 1 Font Lane, West Coker, Yeovil, Somerset BA22 9BP, England.

HURLEY Maureen V, b. 24 Nov 1952, San Francisco, California, USA. Writer; Poet; Journalist; Photojournalist. Education: AA, Art, College of Marin, 1973; BA, Art, 1975, BA, Expressive Arts, 1981, MA, Creative Writing (Poetry), in progress, Sonoma State University, California. Appointments: Freelance Photojournalist, 1970-; Poet-Teacher, 1979-; Artist-in-Residence, various organisations and institutions, California, Montana, Mexico, Bahamas, Ukraine, Netherlands, 1980-; Appeared: many national, international festivals, radio, TV; Guest Lecturer, Presenter, professional organisations, universities, schools; Numerous readings. Publications include: Co-author: Falling to Sea Level, 1986; Dream Vessels, 1993; We Are Not Swans, 1993; Editor: The Poem is the Person's Life, 1985; Someone Inside Me, 1986; The Power of the Reckless Sleeper, 1987; Still Writing on Rocks, 1988; A Night Full of Doves, 1989; The Gift of Dreams, 1990; Poem for a Russian Child, 1991; This Body is to Ask, 1993; Co-editor, translator: Several issues of Mother Earth Journal, 1990-; Soviet Poetry Since Glasnost with Oleg Atbashian); Eastern European Poetry; African Poetry; Latin American Poetry; Others. Contributions to: Nebraska Review; Louisville Review; Caribbean Writer; Chaminade Literary Review; Negative Capability; Kalliope; Others; Anthologies: Looking for Home: Women Writing about Exile, 1990; House on Via Gombito, 1990; Atomic Ghost: Poets Respond to the Nuclear Age, 1995; The Hermit Kingdom: Korean War Conflict, 1995; Others. Honours: 9 Artist in Residency Awards, California and Montana Arts Councils, 1983-; San Francisco Arts Commission Achievement Award, 1986; 2 Writers Fellowships, Sonoma County

Community Foundation/National Endowment for the Arts, 1990, 1992; Nominee, Pushcart Prize, 1993; Winner, Anna Davidson Rosenberg Poetry Award on the Jewish Experience, 1994; Negative Capability, 1994; Richard Eberhart Poetry Prize, Florida State University; Chester H Jones National Poetry Prize, 1992; Many others. Memberships: Poets and Writers; National Poetry Association; California Confederation of the Arts; Board Member, Executive Director, Russian River Writers' Guild; Board Member, Area Coordinator, California Poets in the Schools. Address: 7491 Mirable Rd # 5, Forestville, CA 95436, USA.

HURST Frances. See: **MAYHAR Ardath.**

HUSAIN Masud, (Masud), b. 28 Jan 1919, Kaimganj, India. Teacher; Researcher. m. Najma Begum, 3 Feb 1948, 1 son, 4 daughters. Education: MA, Urdu, 1941, PhD, Urdu, 1945, Professor Emeritus, 1984, Aligarh Muslim University; Doctorat d'Université, Paris University, 1953. Appointments: Lecturer, Urdu, 1943-53, Reader, 1953-61, Professor of Linguistics, 1968-73, Aligarh Muslim University; Professor of Urdu, Osmania University, 1961-68; Vice Chancellor, Jamia Millia Islamia, New Delhi, 1973-78. Publications: Roop Bengal aur Dosre Geet, collection of lyrics in Hindi, 1948, 1954; Do Neem, collection of poems in Urdu, 1956, 1984. Contributions to: Hamari Zaban weekly; Monthly titles: Adab-e-Latif; Shahrah; Ajkal; Jamia. Honours: U P Urdu Akademi Award for Do Neem; Niaz Fateopuri Award, Pakistan; Member, Sahitya Akademi Award, New Delhi, 1984. Memberships: Life Member, Anjuman Taraqqi-e-Urdu, New Delhi; Vice Chairman, Urdu Taraqqi Bureau, New Delhi; Sahitya Akademi, New Delhi; Honorary Vice Chancellor, Jamia Urdu, Aligarh, 1973-. Address: Javed Manzil, Dodpur, Aligarh 202002, India.

HUSSEY Charlotte Anne, b. 20 Dec 1945, Portland, Maine, USA. Educator. m. Spiro Arriotis, 21 Apr 1991, 1 daughter. Education: BA, Wheaton College, Norton, Massachusetts, 1968; MA, Concordia University, Montreal, 1979; MFA, Warren Wilson College, Swannanod, North Carolina, 1991. Appointments: Coordinator, Teacher, Centre for Continuing Education and Creative Writing Programmes, McGill University, Montreal; Professor, Creative Writing Programme, Concordia University; Literary Critic, Montreal Gazette. Publication: Rue Sainte Famille, 1990. Contributions to: Moose Head Review; Warren Wilson Review; Antigonish Review; Rubicon; Matrix; Event; Poetry Canada Review; Stone Country; Garden Varieties: An Anthology of the Top Fifty Poems from the National Poetry Contest; Passions and Poisons; New Canadian Prose, Poetry and Plays, 1987; Relations; Family Portraits. Honours: Poetry Finalist, Quebec Society for the Promotion of English Language and Literature, 1991; Canada Council Sponsorship for Poetry Readings, 1991-. Memberships: League of Canadian Poets; Maine Writers and Publishers' Alliance; Women and Words/Les Femmes et les Mots, Writing Workshop; Montreal's Tuesday Night Group. Address: 3421 Rue Ste Famille No 3, Montreal, Quebec H2X 2K6, Canada.

HUTCHINSON (William Patrick Henry) Pearse, b. 16 Feb 1927, Glasgow, Scotland. Appointments: Former Translator and Drama Critic. Publications: Tongue Without Hands, 1963; Imperfect Confession, 1968; Expansions, 1969; Watching the Morning Grow, 1973; The Frost Is All Over, 1975; Selected Poems, 1982; Translator of Poems by Josef Carner and Friend Songs: Medieval Love-Songs from Galaico Portuguese, 1962, 1970. Address: c/o Gallery Press, Loughcrew, Oldcastle, County Meath, Ireland.

HUTTERLI Kurt, b. 18 Aug 1944, Bern, Switzerland. Writer. m. Marianne Buchler, 7 July 1966, 1 son, 1 daughter. Education: Secondary School Teacher Diploma, University of Bern, 1966. Publications: Aber, 1972; Kurzwaren, 1975; Ein Hausmann, 1980; Finnlandisiert, 1982; Stachelflieder, 1991; Katzensprung, 1994. Contributions to: Der Bund; Stuttgarter Zeitung; Drehpunkt; Einspruch. Honours: Poetry Prize, City of Bern, 1971; Book Prize for Aber, City of Bern, 1972. Memberships: PEN, Switzerland; Autoren Gruppe Olten; Berner Schriftsteller-Verein. Address: RR2 S53/C10, Oliver, British Columbia V0H 1T0, Canada.

HUY-LUC. See: **Bui Khoi Tien.**

HYLAND Paul Robert, b. 15 Sept 1947, Poole, Dorset, England. Author; Travel Writer; Poet; Broadcaster. m. Maggie Ware, 8 Dec 1990. Education: BSc (Hons), Bristol University, 1968. Publications: Riddles for Jack, 1978; Domingus, 1978; Poems of Z, 1982; The Stubborn Forest, 1984; Getting into Poetry, 1992, 2nd edition, 1996;

Indian Balm, 1994; Kicking Sawdust, 1995; Backwards Out of the Big World, 1996. Contributions to: Encounter; New Statesman; Other Poetry; PN Review; Poetry Review; Stand; Times Literary Supplement; Poetry Now; BBC Radio 3; Others. Honours: Eric Gregory Award, 1976; Alice Hunt Bartlett Award, 1985. Memberships: The Poetry Society; Society of Authors. Literary Agent: David Higham Associates Ltd. Address: 2 May's Leary, Filleigh, Barnstaple, Devon EX32 0TJ, England.

I

IBSEN Arni. See: **THORGEIRSSON Arni Ibsen.**

IDDINGS Kathleen, b. 25 June 1945, West Milton, Ohio, USA. Publisher; Editor; Writer. Div, 1 son, 3 daughters. Education: BS, Education, Miami University, Oxford, Ohio, 1968; Further study: University of California at San Diego, Napa College, Mira Costa College, others. Appointments: Elementary Teacher, 1960-73; Editor, Publisher: San Diego Poets Press, 1981-; La Jolla Poets Press, 1985-; Substitute Teacher, Mira-Costa College, 1985-86; Consultant in Talented and Gifted, San Diego City Schools, California, 1988-. Publications: Over 250 poems to: The Way of Things, 1984; Invincible Summer, 1985; Promised to Keep, 1987; Selected and New, 1980-90, 1991. Contributions to: McGraw Hill's college textbook Literature; Swenson's American Sports Poems; Pater's Yearbook of American Poetry; Fried's Gridback; Poets On; Cross Currents; Dragonfly; Ohioana Quarterly; California Quarterly; Writer's Digest; Los Angeles Times; Others. Honours: National Endowment for the Arts-Combo Fellowship, 1986; Writer's Grant, PEN America, 1989; Djerass, Artists Colony Residency, 1990; Napa Poetry Conference Scholarship. Memberships: PEN America; Academy of American Poets; World Poetry Society; Board of Directors, Independent Scholars, San Diego; Association of Women Poets. Address: PO Box 8638, La Jolla, CA 92038, USA.

IGLESIAS SERNA Amalia, b. 8 Jan 1962, Menaza, Palencia, Spain. Writer; Journalist. Education: Licentiate in Philosophy and Letters, University of Deusto, Bilbao. Publications: Un lugar para el fuego, 1985; Memorial de Amauta, 1988; Mar en sombra, 1989; Represented in anthologies: Las diosas blancas, 1986; Poetas de los 80, 1989; Literature Magazine, 1989; Poesia en Bilbao, 1991; Conversaciones y poemas, 1991. Contributions to: Insula; El Urogayo; La gaceta del Norte; La luna; El Correo Espanol; El pueblo Vasco; ABC; Diario 16; Zurgai; Pergola; Others. Honours: Adonais Prize, 1984; Alonso de Ercilla del Gobierno Vasco Prize, 1987. Address: c/o Constanilla de Santiago 2 - 4o Izd, 28013 Madrid, Spain.

IGNATOW David, b. 7 Feb 1914, Brooklyn, New York, USA. Poet; Teacher. m. Rose Graubart. Education: Academic Degree, New Utrecht High School, Brooklyn, New York, 1932. Appointments: President Emeritus, Poetry Society of America; Professor Emeritus, City University of New York, 1984; Visiting Professor, New York University, 1985; Senior Lecturer, Columbia University. Publications: Poems, 1948; The Gentle Weight Lifter, 1955; Say Pardon, 1962; Rescue the Dead, 1962; Figures of the Human, 1964; Figures of the Human, 1964; Rescue the Dead, 1968; Earth Hard; Poems 1934-69, 1970; Thread the Dark, 1970; Selected Poems, 1975; Facing the Tree, 1975; New and Collected Poems 1970-85, 1986; I Have A Name, 1996; The End Game and Other Stories, 1996; Chaptbooks: The Animal in the Bush, 1978; Sunlight: A Sequence for My Daughter, 1979; Conversations, 1980; Whisper to the Earth, 1981; Prose: The Notebooks of David Ignatow, 1973; Open Between Us, 1980; New and Collected Poems, 1970-85; The One in the Many: A Poet's Memoirs, 1988; Contributor to numerous journals and magazines. Honours include: National Institute of Arts and Letters, 1964; Guggenheim Fellowship, 1965, 1973; Shelley Memorial Prize, 1965; Rockefeller Foundation Fellowship, 1968; Wallace Stevens Fellowship, 1977; Bollingen Prize, 1977; Robert Frost Medal, 1994; The John Steinbeck Award, 1993. Memberships: PEN; Poetry Society of America. Address: PO Box 1458, East Hampton, NY 11937, USA.

IKEDA Kazuyosi, b. 15 July 1928, Fukuoka, Japan. Poet; Professor of Theoretical Physics. m. Mieko Ikeda, 20 Nov 1956, 1 son, 1 daughter. Education: Graduated, 1951, Postgraduate course, 1951-56, DSc, 1957, Department of Physics, Faculty of Science, Kyushu University. Appointments: Assistant, 1956, Associate Professor, 1960, Department of Physics, Faculty of Science, Kyushu University; Associate Professor, Department of Applied Physics, 1965, Professor, Theoretical Physics, Department of Applied Physics, 1968, Professor, Theoretical and Mathematical Physics, Department of Mathematical Sciences, 1989-, Professor Emeritus, 1992-, Faculty of Engineering, Osaka University; Professor,1992, President, 1995-, International Earth Environment University, Japan. Publications: Serialized Poems of Fixed Form in Seven and Five Syllable Metre, 1979-, subjects including Migratory Birds, 1989, Fierce Animals,

Marine Animals, Fierce Birds, Fishing Implements, 1990, Mountains, 1991; Essays on Poetry; Bansyoo Hyakusi (A Hundred Poems on All Creation), collection of poems, 1986; A Physicist's Modern Poems, 1989-91; The World of God, Creation and Poetry, 1991; Poems included in Olympic Anthologies, The First 100, Barcelona-92, The Relay of Opinions, Olympoetry-94; Intercultural Communication in Poetry, 1993; Poems on the Hearts of Creation, collection of English poems, 1993; Translations of Shakespeare's Sonnets into Japanese Poems of Fixed Form, 1994; International Intercourse among Poets, 1995; Mountains (World Poets Series Ferdinandea), 1995; North, South, East and West (World Poets Library of Olympoetry), 1996; Contributions to: Chishiki Magazine; Osaka University Newspaper; Mainichi Shimbun Newspaper; World Poetry; Modern Poetry; Shintenchi Magazine; International Poets Journal; Quest Journal. Honours: International Cultural Diploma of Honor, 1989; Grand Ambassador of Achievement, 1989; International Order of Merit, 1990; Chevalier Grand Cross, 1991; Golden Academy Award for Lifetime Achievement, 1991; International Honors Cup, 1992; Silver Shield of Valour, 1992; The 20th Century Award for Achievement, 1993; Award of International Eminent Poet, 1993; Prize Catania e il suo Vulcano, 1994; Prize Catania Duomo, 1995; Hon DLitt, 1995; IBC Director General's Honours List, 1996; World Who's Who Hall of Fame, 1996. Memberships: United Writers Association; World Literary Academy; International Poets Academy; World Congress of Poets; World Academy of Arts and Culture; World Institute of Achievement; Honorary Founder, Olympoetry Movement; Academician of Honour, Accademia Ferdinandea di Scienze, Lettere ed Arti; Charter Member, Order of International Fellowship; Honorary Director, World Parnassians Guild International; Senator, Maison Internationale des Intellectuels. Address: Nisi 7-7-11 Aomadani, Minoo-si, Osaka 562, Japan.

ILLO Maria, b. 6 July 1949, New York, New York, USA. Writer. Education: PhD, Philosophy, Columbia University, 1979. Publications: Mirrors for the Unnamed Flower, 1976; Songs of Flight and Song of the Lute, 1980; The Way of the Soul, 1990. Contributions to: Indian and Foreign Review, India; Korea Times; Ammonite Publications, England; USA: Odessa Poetry Review; Golden Isle; Willow Bee Publishing; Delong Publishers; Tapestry Magazine; Vision Magazine; Networker Magazine; Southern Rose Review; Mighty Natural Magazine. Honours: 1st Award, National Federation of State Poetry, 1979; 1st Prize, California State Poetry Society, 1979; Poet of the Month, New York Poetry Forum, 1980; Invited, Fourth World Congress of Poets; Grand International Prize, IFTO, 1986; 3 Delong Prizes, 1987-89; 1st Prize, Tokyo Literary Society, 1988; 2nd Place, National Writers Club, 1989; 1st Prize, Southern Rose Review, 1990; 1st Prize, Daly City Poetry Contest, 1990; 1st Prize, Poetic Page, 1992; 1st Prize, PN Magazine, 1992. Address: 1000 Jackson Keller, No 3101, San Antonio, TX 78213, USA.

IMIDA Louise. See: **CRATE Joan.**

INDERMILL Marilyn, (Marcus Ivan Windorquill), b. 8 Aug 1948, Colorado, USA. Stage Wardrobe Technician; Poet. Education: Alliance Française, Paris, 1969-70; BA, English Literature, University of Colorado, 1971. Appointments: Swimming Instructor, Boulder Parks and Recreation, 1966-70; University of Colorado Mountain Recreation and Lifeguard; Editorial Assistant, MacMillan Publishing Co Inc; Night Manager, Copley Plaza Hotel, Boston, Massachusetts; Wardrobe Technician, International Alliance of Theatrical Stage Employees. Publications: Tales of Ancient Trees, 1979; The Asboo Bampin Forest and Other Places I Have Know, 1985; A Photographic Essay, 1986; Quill on the Wind, 1986; Land of the Quick Draw Howdy, 1987; Asboo Bampin Forest Books For a Better Future: The Magical World, 1990. Contributions to: Riding A Dark Train, to Stone Soup Poetry, 1972; Twilight of Dream Reflected in Pools of May, 1972; Daffodils Laugh, 1986, to The Federal Poet; A Howdy Poem, Precious Posterity, 1984; A Corn Shower, A Season to Be Jolly, Christmas is A Time to Wish, to American Poetry Anthology, 1987; You First, Love is Not An Act, Comfortably Immortal, to Hearts on Fire: A Treasury of Poems on Love, 1989; Throbbing Jungle Drums, to Love's Greatest Treasures: Today's Poets Speak from the Heart, 1989, and to World Treasury of Great Poems Vol II, 1989; How Do I Love You, to Sparrowgrass Poetry Forum Inc, 1991; Make Our Talk Have Earnest Reality, to World's Favorite Gold and Silver Poems, 1991. Honours: 1st Place, Italian Prize, 1986; 5th Place, Love Category, American Poetry Association Poetry Contest, 1986; Golden Poet Awards, World of Poetry, 1989, 1990. Memberships: Federal Poets of Washington DC; Writer's Haven

Writers of San Diego, California. Address: 335 Madison Avenue No 235, San Diego, CA 92116, USA.

INDU. See: **SRINIVASAN Indira.**

INEZ Colette, b. 23 June 1931, Brussels, Belgium. Poet; Teacher. m. Saul Stadtmauer, 26 July 1964. Education: BA, English Literature, Hunter College, USA, 1961. Appointments: Faculty, The New School, New York City, 1973-83; Poetry Instructor, Kalamazoo College, 1975, 1976, 1978, 1985, 1989; State University of New York, Stony Brook, 1975; Visiting Professor, Hunter College, 1978; Poetry Instructor, Finkelstein Library, 1981, 1982, 1987; Instructor, Writing Programme, Columbia University, 1983-; Poetry Instructor: West Side YMCA, 1984-87; Cooper Union, 1988; Visiting Professor, Ohio University, 1990; Poet-in-Residence, Bucknell University, 1992. Publications: The Woman Who Loved Worms, 1972; Alive and Talking Names, 1977; Eight Minutes from the Sun, 1983; Family Life, 1988; Getting Underway: New and Selected Poetry, 1993; Naming the Moons, 1993; For Reasons of Music, 1994. Contributions to: Nation; Partisan Review; Hudson Review; Poetry; New Republic; Yale Review; Ohio Review; Beloit Poetry Journal; Harvard Magazine; Antioch Review; Chicago Review; Poetry Northwest; Ms Magazine; Texas Quarterly Review; American Voice; Prairie Schooner; Poetry; American Poetry Review; Michigan Quarterly Review; Humanist; Virginia Quarterly Review; Poetry Australia; Yankee; Helicon Nine; Antaes; Many others including anthologies. Honours: Reedy Memorial Award, 1973, Kreymborg Award, 1976, Poetry Society of America; National 1st Book Award, Great Lakes Colleges Association, 1973; Fellowships: National Endowment for the Arts, 1974, 1988; New York State CAPS, 1975; Yaddo, 1980, 1986, 1988, 1989, 1990; Rockefeller, 1980; Ragdale, 1982, 1984; Virginia Colony for the Creative Arts, 1983, 1986, 1987, 1988; Guggenheim, 1985-86; Pushcart Prize, 1986-87; Leighton Art Center, Banff, Canada, 1986; Blue Mountain Center, 1988-93; Djerassi Foundation, 1989; Norma Millay honoree, Millay Colony, 1991; New York State Foundation for the Arts, 1994. Memberships: Poetry Society of America, Governing Board, 1979-80; PEN American Center; Committee Member, The Poet's Prize. Address: 5 West 86th Street, New York, NY 10024, USA.

INFANTE Victor David, b. 5 Feb 1972, Pittsburgh, Pennsylvania, USA. Art Heretic. Education: BA International Politics Science and English Literature, New England College at Arundel, West Sussex, 1993; Class Valedictorian. Appointments: Producer, The Near Infamous; Poetry on Thursdays, Jara Gardens, Huntington Beach, California; Producer of the Tearing the Curtain and Words Xing the Line Series. Publications: Stale Cigarettes and Guinness, 1996; The Price of Getting What You Want, 1996. Contributions to: Poetry Flash; Blue Satellite; Freedom Isn't Free, 1951; Critical Reviews in Next Magazine & Impetuous Magazine. Honour: North Hills Press Poetry Contest, 1995. Address: 33891 Malaga Drive, Dana Point, CA 92691, USA.

INGALLS Jeremy, b. 2 Apr 1911, Gloucester, Massachusetts, USA. Poet; Translator; Professor (retired). Education: AB, 1932, AM, 1933, Tufts University; Student, 1938, 1939, Research Fellow, Classical Chinese, 1945-46, University of Chicago. Appointments: Assistant Professor, Western College, Oxford, Ohio, 1941-43; Resident Poet, 1947, Assistant Professor, 1948-50, Associate Professor, 1953-55, Professor of English and Asian Studies, 1955-60, Rockford College, Illinois; Visiting Lecturer at numerous colleges and universities. Publications: A Book of Legends (stories), 1941; The Metaphysical Sword (poems), 1941; Tahl (narrative poem), 1945; The Galilean Way, 1953; The Woman from the Island (poems), 1958; These Islands Also (poems), 1959; This Stubborn Quantum: Sixty Poems, 1983; Summer Liturgy (verse play), 1985; The Epic Tradition and Related Essays, 1988; Contributions to: Various publications. Honours: Yale Series of Younger Poets Prize, 1941; Guggenheim Fellowship, 1943-44; American Academy of Arts and Letters Grant, 1944-45; Shelley Memorial Award for Poetry, 1950; Lola Ridge Memorial Award for Poetry, 1951, 1952; Ford Foundation Faculty Fellow, 1952-53; Fulbright Lecturer, Kobe, Japan, 1957-58; Rockefeller Foundation Lecturer, Kyoto, Japan, 1960; Honorary Epic Poet Laureate, United Poets Laureate International, 1965; Honorary doctorates. Memberships: Dante Society; Modern Language Association; Phi Beta Kappa; Poetry Society of America. Address: 6269 East Rosewood, Tucson, AZ 85711, USA.

INSINGEL Mark, b. 3 May 1935, Antwerp, Belgium. Author. Education: Koninklijk Vlaams Muziekconservatorium Antwerp, Drama Studies, 1954-57; Sorbonne, Paris, French Literature 1957-59. Publications: Drijf-hout, 1963; Een Kooi Van Licht, 1966; Perpetuum Mobile, 1969; Modellen, 1970; Posters, 1974; Dat Wil Zeggen, 1975; Gezwel Van Wortels, 1978; Het Is Zo Niet Zo Is Het, 1978; Een Meisje Nam de Tram, 1983; Jij Noemt Stom Wat Taal Is, 1986; In Elkanders Armen, 1990; De Een En de Ander, 1991; De Druiven Die Te Hoog Hangen, 1993. Contributions to: Main literary magazines in the Netherlands and Belgium; Several books in English translation including: A Lapse of Time, 1970; When a Lady Shakes Hands With a Gentleman, 1975; My Territory, 1980; That Is to Say, 1985. Honours: Tweejaarlijkse Prijs van De Vlaamse Gids, 1970; Arthur Merghelynckprijs van de Koninklijke Academie voor Nederlandse Letterkunde, 1974; Visser-Neerlandiaprijs, 1974; Dirk Martensprijs, 1978. Memberships: Treasurer, PEN Centre, Belgian-Dutch speaking; Maatschappij voor Nederlandse Letterkunde te Leiden. Address: Rucaplein 205, B-2610 Antwerp, Belgium

IOANNIDES Klitos, b. 7 July 1944, Moutoullas, Cyprus. Researcher. m. Mary Contoyianni, 12 Feb 1984, 1 son. Education: Paedagogical Academy of Cyprus, 1962-64; MA, Religious Sciences, Sorbonne, Paris, 1967-71; PhD, Philosophy, University of Paris, Sorbonne, 1971-73. Appointments: Researcher, Maraslion Paedagogical Institute, 1974-76; Researcher, Cyprus Research Centre, 1977-. Publications: 6th Generation, 1967; Aspidouchi Kourites, 1971; Penthima, 1971; Thargelies, 1975; One Jot, 1977; Poems 1967-1987, 1988. Contributions to: Sous le Pavé la Plage, Paris; Elfthiui, Athens; Kypriaka Chronica; Nea Epochi; Kyklos Larnaca; Achti; Pneumatiki Kypros; Philia, Germany; PEN International, London. Memberships: Vice President, Secretary, PR, Cyprus PEN; Vice President, Philosophical Society of Cyprus; Committee, Union of Cypriot Writers; Union of Greek Writers, Athens. Address: 10 Hellados St Flat 401, Acropolis, 2003 Nicosia, Cyprus.

IOANNOU Susan, b. 4 Oct 1944, Toronto, Ontario, Canada. Writer; Editor. m. Lazaros Ioannou, 28 Aug 1967, 1 son, 1 daughter. Education: BA Honours, English Language and Literature, 1966, MA, English Literature, 1967, University of Toronto. Appointments: Managing Editor, Coiffure de Canada, 1979-80; Poetry Editor, Arts Scarborough Newsletter, 1980-85; Associate Editor, Cross-Canada Writers' Magazine, 1980-89; Managing Editor, Columbine Editions, 1981-85; Poetry Instructor, Toronto Board of Education, 1982-94; Director, Wordwrights Canada, 1985-; Poetry Instructor, School of Continuing Studies, University of Toronto, 1989-90. Publications: Spare Words, 1984; Motherpoems, 1985; The Crafted Poem, 1985; Familiar Faces, Private Griefs, 1986; Writing Reader-friendly Poems, 1989; Clarity Between Clouds: Poems of Midlife, 1991; Where the Light Waits, 1996. Contributions to: Antigonish Review; Ariel; Canadian Author; Contemporary Verse 2; Dandelion; Daybreak; Malahat Review; Canadian Literature; Matrix; Canadian Woman Studies; New Quarterly; Northward Journal; Pierian Spring; Poetry Canada; Prairie Fire; Prism International; Toronto Life; West Coast Review; Writer's Digest; Descant; Poetry Toronto; Poet's Gallery; Quarry; Scrivener; Squatchberry Journal; The Globe and Mail; Wascana Review; Waves; Whetstone; Grain; Various anthologies including: Canlit Food Book; Kitchen Talk; Other Channels; Relations; And Other Travels; Celebrating Canadian Women; Here is a Poem; Nova Scotia Poetry Awards Anthology; Songs From the North; Womansong; Vintage 94. Honours: Norma Epstein Award, Poetry, University of Toronto, 1965; Book Cellar Mother's Day Poetry Award, 1982; Winner, Arts Scarborough City Poetry Contest, 1987; Media Club of Canada Memorial Award, 1990; Okanagan Short Fiction Award, 1997. Memberships: Arts and Letters Club of Toronto; Canadian Poetry Association; Editors Association of Canada; The League of Canadian Poets. Address: PO Box 456, Station O, Toronto, Ontario M4A 2P1, Canada.

IRANI Rustom Bailty, b. 1 Aug 1962, London, England. Poet; Television Journalist. Education: Selwyn College, Cambridge, 1981-84; MA, Theology and Religious Studies, Cambridge University; Postgraduate Diploma in Journalism, City University, London, 1984-85. Contributions to: Grass Roots (anthology of new poets); Magazines including: Outposts; Speaking in Tongues. Address: 1 Queensborough Terrace, Queensway, London W2, England.

IRELAND Allen Lee, b. 10 Oct 1969, Quakertown, Pennsylvania, USA. Education: BA, English, 1990; Teacher Certification, 1992, MA, English, University of North Carolina, Greensboro. Appointments: Editor, college literary magazine, 1987-88; Graduate Assistant in Black Studies, 1990-91. Contributions to: Lyric; Breakthrough!; Candelabrum;

Parnassus Literary Journal; Eclectic Muse; Tucumcari Literary Review. Honours: 2nd Honourable Mention, Archibald Rutledge Contest, Poetry Council of North Carolina, 1989; Runner-up, 2nd Annual Poetry Contest, Eclectic Muse, 1992. Address: 2005 Spring Garden Street, Greensboro, NC 27403, USA.

IRELAND Kevin Mark, b. 18 July 1933, Auckland, New Zealand. Poet; Writer. m. Caroline Dalwood, 2 sons. Publications: Poetry: Face to Face, 1963; Educating the Body, 1967; A Letter From Amsterdam, 1972; Orchids, Hummingbirds and Other Poems, 1974; A Grammar of Dreams, 1975; Literary Cartoons, 1978; The Dangers of Art: Poems 1975-80, 1980; Practice Night in the Drill Hall, 1984; The Year of the Comet, 1986; Selected Poems (Oxford Poets Series), 1987; Tiberius at the Beehive, 1990; Skinning a Fish, 1994. Honours: New Zealand National Book Award for Poetry, 1979; Order of the British Empire for services to Literature, 1992. Membership: former President, PEN, New Zealand. Address: 8 Domain Street, Devonport, Auckland 1309, New Zealand.

IRENE C D, b. India. Medical Doctor. m. J Anthikad, 2 sons, 1 daughter. Appointments: Medical Doctor; Pathologist, Government of India. Publication: Flight to Freedom, 1993; Slaves of Society, short stories, 1993; Anthologies: Whispers of Love, 1992; Pearls and Pebbles, 1994. Contributions to: Poems, short stories, novellettes in national and international books and periodicals. Honours: Recipient of many prizes for her poems. Address: 836 10th Cross, 23rd Main, J P Nagar, II Phase, Bangalore 560 078, India.

IRION Mary Jean, b. 6 Nov 1922, Newport, Kentucky, USA. Freelance Writer; Director of Writer's Center. m. Paul Irion, 29 Aug 1944, 1 son, 1 daughter. Education: BA, Millersville State College, 1966. Appointments: English Teacher, Lancaster Country Day School, Pennsylvania, 1968-73; Visiting Lecturer, Theology, Literature, Lancaster Theological Seminary, Lancaster, 1985-; Founder, Director, The Writers Center, Chautauqua, New York, 1988-. Publications: Holding On. Contributions to: Poetry; Prairie Schooner; Yankee; New England Review; Western Humanities Review; Southern Humanities Review; The Christian Century; Southwest Review; Poet Lore; Poet and Critic; Ladies' Home Journal; The Literary Review; Others. Honours: 1st Place, Unicorn Award, 1976, 3rd Prize, Wisconsin Award, 1985, National Federation of State Poetry Societies; Prize, Chautauqua Poetry Workshop, 1976, 1977, 1978; Honourable Mention, Lucille Medwick Award, 1983; Honourable Mention, Wildwood Poetry Festival, 1988; Ruth Lake Memorial Award, Poetry Society of America, 1993. Memberships: Fellow, Society for the Arts and Religion in Contemporary Culture; Poets and Writers; Academy of American Poets; Poetry Society of America. Address: 149 Kready Avenue, Millersville, PA 17551, USA.

IRVING Jean Mary, b. 20 June 1926, Elsternwick, Victoria, Australia. Home Manager; Volunteer Worker. m. Norris Ramon Irving, 5 June 1954, 1 son, 1 daughter. Education: Zercho's Business College, 1939; Mature Student, english Certificate, Leongatha High School, 1983. Contributions to: Sentinel Times; Gippsland Regional Adult Literacy Council publication; Moomba Poetry Reading; Network; Melbourne Poetry Society; Life Writing. Honours: Commendation Award, Melbourne Poetry Society, Poetry day Australia, 1991-92; 1st Decade, 1991. Membership: Country Member, Melbourne Poetry Society. Address: 15 Koonwarra Road, Leongatha, Victoria 3953, Australia.

IRWIN P K. See: **PAGE P(atricia) K(athleen).**

ISSAIA Nana, b. 1 Oct 1934, Athens, Greece. Poet; Essayist; Prose Writer; Translator; Painter; Broadcaster. Education: Secretarial Course, Denson Secretarial College, London; 1st Pitman Diploma, 1953; Studied Painting, Free Workshop of Fine Arts, 1958-62. Appointments: Private Secretary to Prime Minister Karamanlis, 1958-63; Broadcasting, 4th National Programme, ERA 4, 1989. Publications: Poems, 1969; Six Poets, collective edition, 1971; Persona, 1972; One Glance, 1974; Nights and Days of No Importance, 1977; Alice in Wonderland, long poem, 1977; Form, 1980; The Tactics of Passion, prose and poetry, 1982; Realization of Forgetting, 1982; Translations include: The Poetry of Sylvia Plath, 1974. Contributions to: Kathimerini newspaper; Most good Greek magazines including: Doma; Tram; Planodion; Lexi; Thendro; New Estia; 2 major Greek anthologies; Modern Poetry in Translation, London; USA: Chicago Review; Manroot; Grove; International Portland Review; Charioteer; Pacific Moana Quarterly, New Zealand; Canada: Descand; Dandelion;

Grand; Nui Blanche, Quebec; Mozgo Vilag, Budapest; Orizont, Romania; Cuadernos de Poesia Nueva, Madrid; Skylark, India; Zenos, England; Philia, Germnay; Other foreign magazines; Anthologies: A Book of Women Poets from Antiquity to Now, USA; Contemporary Greek Poetry (Kimon Friar); Nuovi Poetic Greci, Lilan; Gerkai i my Sovremennaya Grecheskaya poeziya, Moscow; Raduga. Honours: 2nd State Prize for Poetry for collection Form, 1981. Memberships: World Congress of Poets, Governing Board, World Academy of Arts and Culture. Address: Iridanou 3, GR 115 28 Athens, Greece.

ISTENDAEL Geert van, b. 29 Mar 1947, Ukkel, Belgium. Journalist. 1 son, 1 daughter. Education: Bachelor, Philosophy, 1967; Licence, Sociology, 1969. Appointments: Fellow, National Scientific Research Fund, Belgium, 1969-76; Journalist, Belgian TV, Dutch Language, 1978-83. Publications: De iguanodons van Bernissart. Een Belgisch gedicht, 1983; Plattegronden, 1987. Contributions to: Newspapers: De Morgen, Brussels; De Volkskrant, Amsterdam; Periodicals; Maatstaf, Amsterdam; Septentrion; Rekkem; NWT, Antwerp; De Brakke Hond Antwerp; De Vlaamse Gids, Brussels. Memberships: PEN Club, Belgium; Goethe Gesellschaft, Weimar; Associacao Pessoana dos Amigos de Martinho da Arcada, Lisbon. Address: Kruisdagenlaan 58, 1200 Brussels, Belgium.

ITTYCHERIA Verghese, (Rajani), b. 11 Jan 1941, Munnar, India. Consultative Faculty Member; Editor. m. Leela Iype, 8 July 1968, 1 son, 1 daughter. Education: BSc, Chemistry, Physics; MA, English Language and Literature; Cultural Doctorate, World University, USA. Appointments: Consultative Faculty Member, World University, Artizona; Senator, Envoy to United Arab Emirates, International Parliament for Safety and Peace; Scientist, Indian Space Research Organisation; Editor, Poetry, Gulf Weekly. Publications: Count Down to Lift-Off, 1988; God's Peace Defeats Man's War. Cotributions to: Gulf Weekly; Poet International. Memberships: President, Malayalee Samajam Ranji Jabalpur; Founder Member, Aruvankadu Christian Association. Address: PO Box 336, Dubai, United Arab Emirates.

IVANOVA Mirela Tsvetkova, b. 11 May 1962, Sofia, Bulgaria. Writer; Editor. Education: German Language School, 1981; Plovdiv St Paissii Hilendarski University, 1985. Appointments: Editor, Literaturen front, weekly; Editor, Detsa, Izkoustvo, Knigi, bimonthly. Publications: Stone Wings, 1985; Whispers, 1990; Lonely Game, 1990; Memory for Details, 1992. Contributions to: Literaturen Vestnik; Plamak; Septemvri; Savremennik; Poetry Review; Litfass; Sunk Island Review; Scratch; Textura. Honour: Winner, Poetry Award, Union of Bulgarian Writers, 1992. Membership: Union of Bulgarian Writers. Address: Mladost II, bl 221-A, ap 19, Sofia 1799, Bulgaria.

IVENS Michael William, (Yorick), b. 15 Mar 1924. Director; Writer. m. (1) Rosalie Turnbull, (2) Katherine Laurence, 5 sons, 1 daughter. Appointments: Editor, Twentieth Century; Director, STD Telephone and Cable; Director, Aims of Industry; Director, Foundation for Business Responsibilities; Yorick Column, Time and Tide; Free Nation. Publications: Another Sky, 1963; Last Waltz, 1964; Private and Public, 1968; Born Early, 1975; No Woman is An Island, 1983; New Divine Comedy, 1990; Poetry Review; Outposts; Oxford Book of Twentieth Century Verse; New Poetry of the Commonwealth; After A War; Poetry and Business Life. Honour: Commander of the Order of the British Empire, 1983. Address: 2 Mulgrave Road, London NW10 1BT, England.

IVESON David. See: **HALL David.**

J

JACK Sheila Beryl, b. 26 Sept 1918, Liverpool, England. Teacher. m. Robert Lawrence Jack, 31 Jan 1942, dec, 1 son, 1 daughter. Education: Derby Diocesan Training College for Teachers; Teaching English as a Second Language, Wolverhampton Teachers College. Appointments: Full-time Supply Teacher, Salop Education Committee, 1953-63; Civil Servant, COD Donnington, 1963-65; Teacher, English as Second Language, Woden Road, Wolverhampton, 1965-74; English Teacher, Deansfield High School, Wolverhampton, 1974-75; Full-time Supply Teacher, Priority Area Schools, Wolverhampton Education Committee, 1975-78. Publications: 32 Poems, 1962; Another 32 Poems, 1973; Footsteps from our Past, script, 1977; To Save a Castle, 1989. Contributions to: Shrewsbury Chronicle; Monday World; Anglo-Welsh Borderlines; Scottish Home and Country. Honours: Fellow, World Literary Academy; Honorary Vice-President, 1978; Poet of the Month, 1981, Centro Studi e Scambi Internazionale; 1st Prize, Haiku/Haiga Competition - Gateway Japanese Festival, 1991. Memberships: Former Attingham Writers Club; Anglo-Welsh Poetry Society; Poetry Society; Centro Studi e Scambi Internazionale; Monday Club; National Union of Teachers. Address: Longacre, Wrockwardine, Nr Telford, Shropshire, England.

JACKOWSKA Nicolette (Susan), (Nicki Jackowska), b. 6 Aug 1942, Brighton, East Sussex, England. Poet; Novelist; Writer; Teacher. m. Andrzej Jackowski, 1 May 1970, div, 1 daughter. Education: ANEA Acting Diploma, 1965; BA, 1977, MA, 1978, University of Sussex. Appointments: Founder-Tutor, Brighton Writing School; Writer-in-Residence at various venues; Readings; Radio and television appearances. Publications: The House That Manda Built, 1981; Doctor Marbles and Marianne, 1982; Earthwalks, 1982; Letters to Superman, 1984; Gates to the City, 1985; The Road to Orc, 1985; The Islanders, 1987; News from the Brighton Front, 1993; Write for Life, 1997; Forthcoming Publication: Lighting a Slow Fuse - Selected Poems. Contributions to: Various publications. Honours: Winner, Stroud Festival Poetry Competition, 1972; Continental Bursary, South East Arts, 1978; C Day-Lewis Fellowship, 1982; Writer's Fellowship, 1984-85, Writer's Bursary, 1994, Arts Council. Membership: Poetry Society. Address: 98 Ewart Street, Brighton, Sussex BN2 2UQ, England.

JACKSON Alan, b. 6 Sept 1938, Liverpool, England. Education: Edinburgh University. Appointments: Founder and Director, Kevin Press, Edinburgh, 1965. Publications: Under Water Wedding, 1961; Sixpenny Poems, 1962; Well Ye Ken Noo, 1963; All Fall Down, 1965; The Worstest Beast, 1967; The Grim Wayfarer, 1969; Idiots are Freelance, 1973; Heart of the Sun, 1986; Salutations: Collected Poems 1960-89, 1990. Address: c/o Polygon, 22 George Square, Edinburgh EH8 9LF, Scotland.

JACKSON Andrew John, b. 27 Oct 1962, Winchester, Hampshire, England. Temporary Clerk. Education: BA, Honours, History/English, College of Ripon and York St John, 1985-89. Appointments: Civil Service, 1982; Archaeological Assistant, Southampton and Winchester, 1984-85, 1990-91 and 1992-94; Administrative Assistant, Benefits Agency Winchester, currently on temporary contract as Students Grant Assistant, Hampshire County Council. Contributions to: Poetry Now Anthology: Love Lines, 1995; Poetry Now Anthology: Book of Traditional Verse, 1995; Poetry Now: Indelible Ink, anthology, 1995; Poetry Now magazine; Rivet magazine. Address: 100 Priors Dean Road, Harestock, Winchester, Hampshire SO22 6LA, England.

JACKSON Michael (Derek), b. 1940, Nelson, New Zealand. Education: MA, University of Auckland; PhD, Cambridge University. Appointment: Senior Lecturer in Anthropology, Massey University, 1973-. Publications: Latitudes of Exile: Poems 1965-75, 1976; Wall, 19890; Going on, 1985; Rainshadow, 1987; Duty Free: Selected Poems 1965-1988, 1989. Honours sinclude: Commonwealth Poetry prize, 1976. Address: Department of Social Anthropology, Massey University, Palamerston North, New Zealand.

JACKSON Rueben M, b. 1 Oct 1956, Augusta, Georgia, USA. Archivist. m. Jacquelyn Carrie Kathleen Hunter, 24 Sept 1983. Education: BA English Literature 1978, Goddard College, Plainfield, Vermont; MLS Library and Information Science, 1984, University of the District of Columbia. Appointments: Library Technician, Smithsonian Institution Libraries, 1983-85; Assistant Librarian, Museum of African Art, 1985-87; Children's Librarian, District of Columbia Public Library, 1987-89; Archivist, Smithsonian Institutions Duke Ellington Collection, 1989-. Publication: Fingering the Keys, 1991. Contributions to: Indiana Review; Plum Review; Black American Literature Forum; Christian Science Monitor; Visions; Washington Review; Folio; Catalyst; Washington Post; Processed World; Painted Bride Quarterly; Chelsea; Washington City Paper; Lip Service; Tryst; NJSO Journal; Library Journal; Washington Post. Honours: Runner Up, Grolier Poetry Prize, Cambridge, Massachusetts, 1986; Honourable Mention, Visions Magazine Poetry Competition, 1989; Runner Up, Larry Neal Award, Washington DC, 1992. Address: 519 Powhatan Place, North West, Washington, DC 20011, USA.

JACKSON William David, b. 15 July 1947, Liverpool, England. English Language Course Designer and Teacher. m. Christa Antonie Range, 3 June 1972, 1 son, 1 daughter. Education: BA (Hons), English Language and Literature, St Catherine's College, Oxford, 1968. Contributions to: Agenda; Babel; Iroh; London Magazine; Modern Poetry in Translation; Orbis; Outposts; Poetry Nottingham; Pennine Platform; Stand; Rialto and others. Memberships: Poetry Society, London; British Haiku Society. Address: Clemensstrasse 66, 80796 Munich, Germany.

JACOB Thekkalthyparampil Samuel, b. 2 Oct 1941, Keezhuvaipur, Kerala, India. Teacher. m. Thankamma Jacob, 21 Nov 1971, 1 son, 1 daughter. Education: BA, 1968; MA, 1970. Appointments: Clerk, Mandle District Collector's Office, MP India, 1962; Postal Clerk, Indian Postal Department, 1963-70; Member, Executive Body, Kerala Cultural Association, Indore, 1968-70; High School Teacher, Uganda, 1972; Headmaster, Pro-High School Ungma, Nagaland, India, 1973-75; Lecturer, M T College, Wokha, Nagaland, 1976-; Guest Editor, Gruha Deepam magazine, Deepam Book Club, Vennikulam, Kerala, India, 1994; Editorial Board Member, Hon Director, International Socio Literary Foundation, Karnataka State, India, 1996-. Publications: Celestial Melody, 1991; Memorable Moments, 1995; Ikeda First: Rest Nowhere Review of Poet Ikeda: An Assessment of His Unique Poetry, 1994; Represented in anthologies: Samvedana; Poet; Rising Stars: A World of Anthology of Poetry; East West Voices; World Poetry, 1990, 1992. Contributions to: Poems included in World Poetry, 1990-1992, 1994-96; Mosaic by Writers Forum, Ranchi, 1994 & 1995. Honours: Complimented by distinguished persons such as Dr Krishna Srinivas, Madras, Dr Rosemary C Wilkinson, USA, Dr Narendrapal Singh, New Delhi; PhD, International University California, USA, 1993; Merit Certificate, Writers Forum, Ranchi, 1994. Memberships: Chetana Literary Group, Mangalore; United Writers Association, Madras; World Poetry Society, Madras; Writers Club of India. Address: PB No 16, Wokha 797 111, Nagaland, India.

JACOBIK Jane Gray, b. 21 May 1944, Newport News, Virginia, USA. Poet. m. Bruce N Gregory, 4 Jan 1983, 1 son, 1 daughter. Education: BA, Goddard College, Plainfield, Vermont, 1976; MA, British and American Literature, 1985, PhD, British and American Literature, 1990, Brandeis University. Appointments: Assistant Professor, English, Eastern Illinois University, Charleston, 1989-91; Associate Professor, Eastern Connecticut State University, Willimantic, 1991-. Publications: Jane's Song, 1976; Paradise Poems, 1978; Sandpainting, 1980. Contributions to: Ploughshares, Georgia Review; Prairie Schooner, Ontario Review; South Dakota Review; Cream City Review; Nebraska Review; Hollin's Critic; American Literary Review; Hiram Poetry Review; Alaska Quarterly Review; North American Review; Poetry East; Minnesota Review; Tar River Review; Bellingham Review; Kansas Quarterly Review. Memberships: Poetry Society of America; New England Poetry Club; Worcester Country Poetry Association. Address: 86 Fox Hill Road, Pomfret Center, CT 06259, USA.

JACOBS Alan John Lawrence, b. 9 Sept 1929, London, England. Retired Art Dealer. Publication: The Petal Fishers, 1994; Element Book of Mystical Verse, editor. Contributions to: Reflections; Self Enquiry; Mountain Path. Membership: Keats-Shelley Memorial Association. Address: 53 Broadfield, Broadhurst Gardens, London NW6 3BN, England.

JACOBS Clara Halstead, b. Jackson County, Illinois, USA. m. 10 Nov 1928. Appointment: Bookkeeper; Own business; Columnist; home town and area newspapers, 7 years. Publications: Golden Nuggets, Vol I, 1990, Vol II, 1991, Vol III, 1992; Devotionals, 1992, Vol IV, 1993. Contributions to: New American Poetry Anthology; In a Different Light; In a View from the Edge; A Question of Balance; Wind in the Night Sky; Whispers in the Wind; A Break in the Clouds; Home Town and area newspapers. Honours: Golden Poet Award, 1988-1990; Listed in Our World's Most Treasured Poems, 1991; Distinguished Poets of America; Golden Poet Award, 1991 and 1992; Numerous Awards of Merit. Membership: International Society of Poets. Address: Box 202, Elkville, IL 62932, USA.

JACOBS Ruth Harriet, b. 15 Nov 1924, Boston, Massachusetts, USA. Sociologist; Gerontologist; Writer. m. Neal Jacobs, 18 July 1948, div, 1 son, 1 daughter. Education: BS, 1964, Boston University, PhD, 1969, Brandeis University. Appointments: Professor, Boston University, 1969-82; Professor, 1982-89, Department Chair, 1982-87, Clark University; Senior Lecturer, Regis College, 1988-; Researcher, Wellesley College Center for Research on Women, 1979-; Teaches poetry writing to senior citizens, several communities and Elderhostels. Publications: Button, Button Who Has the Button, 1987; Out of Their Mouths, 1988; Be an Outrageous Older Woman A R A SP, 1991, revised edition 1993; Editor, We Speak for Peace, anthology, 1993; Women Who Have Touched My Life, 1996; 3 Prose books. Contributions to: Hickory Review; Hemetra; Poets; Friendly Woman; Broomstick; Wellesley Townsman; Hot Flash; Many anthologies including: If I Had a Hammer; When I am An Old Woman I Will Wear Purple; I Would Pick More Daisies; Above Underground Poets. Honours: Poetry Writing Fellowships: Edna St Vincent Millay; Ossabaw; Adlen Dow Creativity Center; Wurlitzer Foundation; Ragdale; Virginia Center for the Creative Arts; Alfred University Summer Place; Grants Massachusetts Arts Lottery Foundation, 1987; Massachusetts Foundation for the Humanities and Public Policy, 1988; Weston Arts Lottery Council, 1989. Memberships: Massachusetts Poetry Association; International Women Writers Guild. Address: 75 High Ledge Avenue, Wellesley, MA 02181, USA.

JACQUIER Nancy-Kelly, b. 15 Mar 1925, Le Locle Canton de Neuchâtel, Switzerland. Commercial Office Employee; Writer. m. 21 Oct 1950, 1 son, 3 daughters. Education: Primary, secondary and commercial school at Le Locle; Literary Studies: self-taught, then pre-college, also some courses in Latin and Greek. Publications: Sanitra, l'enfant de la colline, novel, 1971, new edition, 1990; Feuillets au vent, short stories, 1973; Entre ciel et terre, poems, 1975; Le vent de la revolte, novel, 1976; Sanitra et la Boule de cristal, 1990; Fables de ma caboche, poetry, 1990; Sous le regard de Venus, poems, 1990; Hymns al/amour, poems, 1990; Prelude a l'amour, poems, 1990. Contributions to: Poems, short stories, tales, in regional journals. Honours: Participated under pseudonym in International Francophone Contests 1971, 1973, 1974; Participant, Mai Litteraire, 1978; Concours QSL, 1979. Membership: Society of Swiss Writers, Zürich. Address: Tivoli 39, CH 2610 St-Imier, Switzerland.

JAEGER Sharon Ann, b. 15 Jan 1945, Douglas, Arizona, USA. Editor; Poet; Publisher; Translator. Education: BA summa cum laude, University of Dayton, 1966; MA, English, Boston College, 1971; Doctoral study, Communications, Rensselaer Polytechnic Institute, 1978-79; DA, English, State University of New York, Albany, 1982; MA, Comparative Literature, Literary Theory, University of Pennsylvania, 1990; PhD, Comparative Literature and Literary Theory, University of Pennsylvania, 1995. Appointments: Co-Editor, Sachem Press, 1980-82, Editor, Intertext, 1982-; Fulbright Lecturer, Universidade Nova da Lisboa, Universidade de Aveiro, 1983-84; Visiting Assistant Professor, Haverford College, 1987-88; Visiting Lecturer, University of Pennsylvania, 1988, 1990-95. Publications: Keeping the Lowest of Profiles, 1982; Filaments of Affinity, 1989; The Chain of Dead Desire, 1990; Why the Planets Do Not Speak, 1996; Co-translator, Rilke, Duino Elegies, 1991. Contributions to: Intro 13; Poet and Critic; Penn Review; Calyx; Plains Poetry Journal; Cimarron Review; Midwest Quarterly; Phoebe; Spoon River Quarterly; Western Poetry Quarterly; New Mexico Humanities Review; Ocra; Stone County; Mustang Review; Gold Dust 3; Harpoon; Cross-Connect; Contents Under Pressure; Graham House Review (translation). Honours: Best of Issue, Western Poetry Quarterly, 1978; 1st Place, Graduate Division, McKinney Literary Competition, 1979; 1st Place, Ezra Pound Competition, Literary Translation, 1988, 1990, 1991, 1993, 1995; 1st Place, William Carlos Williams Awards, Poetry, University of Pennsylvania 1992, honorable mention, 1988, 1991, 1994, 1995.

Memberships: PEN West; Academy of American Poets; American Comparative Literature Association; Rhetoric Society of America; Former Co-ordinator, Jawbone Reading Series. Address: Intertext, 2633 East 17th Avenue, Anchorage, AK 99508, USA.

JAFFA Felix. See: **DAY Kevin K Markwick.**

JAGGI Satya Dev, b. 15 Jan 1937, Punjab, Pindigheb, India. University Teacher. m. 3 Mar 1974. Education: BA Hons, English 1958; MA, Philosophy, 1960; MA, English, 1963; PhD, English, 1977. Appointments: Lecturer; Reader; Senior Lecturer; Acting Head. Publications: No More Words, 1966; Homewards and Other Poems, 1966; The Earthrise, 1969; The Moon Voyagers, 1970; One Looks Earthward Again, 1970; Our Awkward Earth, 1970; Readiness is All, 1970; Obscure Goodbyes, 1970; A City Within a City, 1983; Far in Maiduguri, 1983; A Passage to London, 1983; Coleridge's and Yeats' Theory of Poetry, 1966; End of Hunger, 1968; The Point of Light, 1968; Lead No One By the Nose (a play), 1983; Our Concern with Poetry, 1983; The Poet's Plenty, 1983; The Poet's Proposition, 1984; I A Richards on Poetic Truth, 1985; The Language of Poetry, 1990. Contributions to: Illustrated Weekly of India; Imprint; Opinion Quarterly; Quest; Literary Half-Yearly; Indian Writing in English; Nigeria Illustrated; Nigeria Standard; Times International; Punch; Daily Times; National Concord; Guardian. Honour: 3rd Prize in BBC Poetry Competition, 1990. Memberships: Chairman, Falcon Poetry Society, Delhi; Chairman, Indian Writers in English, Delhi. Address: 8258, B-XI, Vasant Kunj, New Delhi 110070, India.

JAINS Jessica. See: **RICHESON C(ena) G(older).**

JAMES Anthony Stephen, b. 27 Oct 1956, Penllergaer, South Wales. Writer; Poet. m. Penny Windsor, 24 May 1987, div 1994, 1 daughter. Education: BA, University College of Swansea, 1991. Publications: Poetry: All That the City Has to Offer; Introducing Kivi; Novel: A House with Blunt Knives; The Serpent in April (as Antonia James). Contributions to: Numerous publications. Honour: Eileen Illtyd David Award, 1983. Membership: Literature for More Than One Year Group. Address: 16B Buckingham Road, Bonymaen, Swansea SA1 7AL, Wales.

JAMES Clive (Vivian Leopold), b. 7 Oct 1939, Kogarah, New South Wales, Australia. Writer; Poet; Broadcaster; Journalist. Education: BA, Sydney University, 1960; MA, Pembroke College, Cambridge, 1967. Appointments: Assistant Editor, Morning Herald, Sydney, 1961; Television Critic 1972-82, Feature Writer 1972-, Observer, London; Various television series and documentaries. Publications: Poetry: Peregrine Prykke's Pilgrimage Through the London Literary World, 1974, revised edition, 1976; The Fate of Felicity Fark in the Land of the Media, 1975; Britannia Bright's Bewilderment in the Wilderness of Westminster, 1976; Fan-Mail, 1977; Charles Charming's Challenges on the Pathway to the Throne, 1981; Poem of the Year, 1983; Other Passports: Poems 1958-1985, 1986. Fiction: Brilliant Creatures, 1983; The Remake, 1987; Brrm! Brrm!, 1991. Non-Fiction: The Metropolitan Critic, 1974; Visions Before Midnight, 1977; At the Pillars of Hercules, 1979; Unreliable Memoirs, 1980; The Crystal Bucket, 1981; From the Land of Shadows, 1982; Glued to the Box, 1983; Flying Visits, 1984; Falling Towards England (Unreliable Memoirs Continued), 1985; Snakecharmers in Texas, 1988; May Week Was in June: Unreliable Memoirs III, 1990; Fame in the 20th Century, 1993. Contributions to: Commentary; Encounter; Listener; London Review of Books; Nation; New Review; New Statesman; New York Review of Books; New Yorker; Times Literary Supplement; Others. Address: c/o Observer, 8 St Andrew's Hill, London EC4V 5JA, England.

JAMES Maurice Alan, b. 22 Feb 1944, Aldershot, Hampshire, England. Editor; Publisher; Poet. m. Heather Baker, 1 July 1967, 2 daughters. Education: Suffolk College. Appointments: Editor, Joint Publisher, Isthmus Poetry Society Journal; Owner, Publisher, Editor, PFC (Poetry for Charity) Publications; Secretary, Founder, North Bedfordshire Poets (now Ouse Valley Poets), 1985-; Founder, Secretary, Administrator, Ouse Valley Poetry Competition Anthology (editor), 1986-91; A Space Where I Can Often Hide, 1988; Piper of Dreams by Lorraine van de Broucke (publisher), 1991. Address: Ouse Valley Poetry PFC Publications, 25 Totnes Close, Devon Park, Bedford, Bedfordshire MK40 3AX, England.

JAMIE Kathleen, b. 13 May 1962, Johnston, Renfrewshire, Scotland. Education: MA, Philosophy, University of Edinburgh.

Appointment: Writer-in-Residence, Dundee University, 1990-93. Publications include: Black Spiders, 1982; A Flame in Your Heart, 1986; The Way We Live, 1987; The Golden Peak, 1992; The Autonomous Region, 1993. Honours include: Eric Gregory Award, 1980; Scottish Arts Council Awards. Address: David Fletcher Associates, 58 John Street, Penicuik, Midlothian, Scotland.

JANAVICIUS Aldona Irena (Aldona Vesciunaite), b. 12 Jan 1923, Lithuania. Teacher; Painter; Writer. m. Vytautas Janavicius, 31 Oct 1947, 5 daughters. Education: Ecole des Arts et Metiers, Diploma, 1948; Certificate, department of Adult Education, University of Sydney. Publications: Poems in Lithuanian language: Zodziai Kaip Salos, 1976; Aidincios Upes, 1985. Contributions to: AM&M Publications, Chicago. Honours: Words Like Islands, and Echoing Rivers, nominated foir Vincas Kreve Literary Prize, Canada. Memberships: Worls Lithuanian Writers Association, New York. Address: 77 Barcom Avenue, Rushcutters Bay, New South Wales 2011, Australia.

JANES Adrian Clive, b. 8 May 1958, Kingston, Surrey, England. Librarian. Education: BA (Hons), English, St David's University College, Lampeter, 1982; Postgraduate Diploma in Library and Information Studies, Ealing College of Higher Education, 1987. Appointments: Lyricist, Drummer, with The Outsiders, 1976-79; Community Service Volunteer, Gravesham, 1982-83; Library Assistant, Kingston Polytechnic, 1985-86; Library Assistant/Assistant Librarian, Roehampton Institute, 1988; Assistant Librarian, L B Havering, 1989-95; Senior Assistant Librarian, L B Havering, 1995-. Publications: Failing Light, 1985; Attempted Communication, 1988. Contributions to: Orbis; Resurgence; Rouska; Spectrum; Digger's Magazine; Memes; Purple Patch. Honour: Associate of Library Association, 1992. Memberships: Blake Society; Library Association, 1985-. Address: c/o 39 Rushett Close, Long Ditton, Surrey KT7 0UT, England.

JANKIEWICZ Leo. See: **YANKEVICH Leo.**

JANOWITZ Phyllis, b. 3 Sept 1940, New York, New York, USA. Associate Professor of English; Poet. div, 1 son, 1 daughter. Education: MFA, University of Massachusetts, Amherst, 1970. Appointments: Writer-in-Residence, Indiana Central University, 1979; Visiting Lecturer, Princeton University, New Jersey, 1980; Visiting Assistant Professor, English, 1980-82, Poet-in-Residence, 1982-83, Assistant Professor, English, 1983-86, Associate Professor, 1986-92, Professor, 1992-, Cornell University, Ithaca, New York. Publications: Rites of Strangers, 1978; Visiting Rites, 1982; Temporary Dwellings, 1988. Contributions to: New Yorker; Boston Review; Atlantic; New Republic; Spazio Umano; Paris Review; Prairie Schooner; Ohio Review; Nation; Radcliffe Quarterly; Harvard Magazine; Shenandoah; Michigan Quarterly Review; Southwest Review; William and Mary Review; Vital Signs; Wisconsin Review; Esquire; Ploughshares; Writing Poems; Lightyear. Honours: Fellow, Bunting Institute, Radcliff College, 1971-73; National Endowment for the Arts, 1974, 1988-89; Stroud International Poetry Award, 1978, 1983; Aldred Hodder Fellow, Princeton, 1979-80; Emily Dickinson Award, 1978, 1983, Consuelo Ford Award, 1980, 1982, Lucille Medwick Award, 1981, Poetry Society of America, 1978, 1983; 1st Selection, Associated Writing Programs Poetry Series, 1978; National Book Critics Circle Nominee, 1983; AWP Anniversary Award, 1984. Memberships: Poetry Society of America; PEN International; Poets and Writers; Community Artists Program, New York State; Associated Writing Programs Inc; MacDowell Colony Fellows, Director, Cornell Creative Writing Committee. Address: One Lodge Way, Ithaca, NY 14850, USA.

JANSEN Garfield, Reverend Swami, (Mariananda), b. 15 Aug 1967, Coimbatore, India. Monk; Professional Model; Actor; Counsellor; Writer. Education: BA, Psychology, 1989; Courses in Counselling, Theology, Psychology, and Philosophy, 1989-90; PhD, (Mariology), 1997; DLitt, (Literature). Appointments: Ordained, Catholic Sanyasi, 1990; Principal in Toch School, Amala School, Good News School, 1990-92; Work as Model, Writer, Counsellor, and Lecturer, 1992-. Publications: Assumption of Our Lady Mary, 1994; Mary: Mother and Queen, 1995; Hail Mary: Full of Grace, 1996. Contributions to: Agnelo's Call; Malabar Herald; Coastal Observer; New Leader; Virgin of Poor; Messenger of Cross; Indian Currents; Journal of Spirituality; Proclaim; Voice of Delhi. Honours include: Title of Knight Immaculate; Doctorate. Memberships include: President, Indian Chapter, Stop the Killing; Executive Council Advisor. Social Literary International Foundation; The World Winged Award. Address: 1275 Trichy Road, Near Sreepathy Theatre, Coimbatore 641018, Tamil Nadu, India.

JARMAN Mark Foster, b. 5 June 1952, USA. Poet. m. Amy Kane, 28 Dec 1974, 2 daughters. Education: MFA, Poetry, University of Iowa; BA, English Literature, University of California, Santa Cruz. Appointments: Teaching-Writing Fellow, University of Iowa, 1974-76; Instructor, Indiana State University, Evansville, 1976-78; Visiting Lecturer, University of California, Irvine, 1979-80; Assistant Professor, Murray State University, Kentucky, 1980-83; Assistant Professor, 1983-86, Associate Professor, 1986-92, Professor, 1992-, Vanderbilt University, Nashville, Tennessee. Publications: North Sea, 1978, 2nd Edition, 1989; The Rote Walker, 1981; Far and Away, 1985; The Black Riviera, 1990; Iris, 1992. Contributions to: Hudson Review; PN Review; Poetry; New Yorker; Partisan Review; Sewanee Review; Antaeus; Ploughshares. Honours: Joseph Henry Jackson Award, 1974; Prize, Academy of American Poets, 1975; Grants, National Endowment for the Arts, 1977, 1983, 1992; Robert Frost Fellowship, Bread Loaf Writers' Conference, 1985; Guggenheim Fellowship in Poetry, 1991. Memberships: Associated Writing Programs; Modern Language Association; Poetry Society of America; Poets Prize Committee. Address: Department of English, Vanderbilt University, Nashville, TN 37235, USA.

JAYANATHAN T K, b. 20 Apr 1933, Trichur, Kerala, India. Banker. m. M Arya, 7 Feb 1956, 1 son, 2 daughters. Education: BA Statistics, 1957; CAIIB, 1966. Appointments: Clerk; Officer; Accountant; Sub-Manager; Currently Manager, Indian Overseas Bank, Regional Office, Kochi. Publications: Represented in anthologies: Contemporary Indian English Poetry, 1988; The Trapped Word, 1988; Contemporary Indian English Love Poetry, 1990; World Poetry, 1990; Cholkettu, 1990; Book of own Malayalam poems; Kudamattom (Malayalam anthology), 1992; 4 English anthologies. Contributions to: Indian Literature, New Delhi; Poet, Madras; Kavita India; Pratibha India; Poetry, Berhampur; Poetry Time, Berhampur; Quest, Ranchi; Mathrubhoomi Weekly; Kumkumum Weekly. Membership: Fellow, International Poets Academy. Address: Kadalayil, Kadalasseri, PO Vallachira - 680 562, Trichur District, Kerala, India.

JELENKOVIC Sasa, b. 8 Aug 1964, Zajecar, Yugoslavia. Writer. Education: Studies of Comparative Literature, University of Belgrade, finished 1990. Appointments: Editor-in-Chief of magazine Znak (Sign), 1988-90; Poetry editor of magazine Knjizevna rec (Literary Word), 1992-94; Poetry editor of magazine Rec (Word), 1994-. Publications: Neprijatna geometrija (Unpleasant Geometry), 1992; Ono sto ostaje (What Remains Behind), 1993; Heruvimske tajne (Cherub's Secrets), 1994. Contributions to: Knjizevna rec; Rec; Poezija (poetry); Letopis matice srpske. Honours: Matic's Scarf Award, 1992; Milan Rakic Award (the Serbian Writers Association Award), 1993. Membership: Serbian Writers Association. Address: Sasa Jelenkovic, Cara Dusana 7/26, 11000 Beograd, Yugoslavia.

JENNERMANN Donald L, b. 20 Dec 1939, Ladysmith, Wisconsin, USA. Professor. m. Gretchen Bauer, 7 Oct 1976, 2 sons, 2 daughters. Education: BA, MA, University of Wisconsin; PhD, Indiana University. Appointment: Professor, Indiana State University, 1964-. Publications: Born of a Cretan Spring, 1981; Bearing North, 1996. Contributions to: Esparavel, (Cali, Colombia); Indiana Writes; Stone Drum; South Dakota Review; Wisconsin Review; Hellas. Membership: Indianapolis Writer's Center. Address: University Honors Program, Indiana State University, Terre Haute, IN 47809, USA.

JENNINGS Elizabeth (Joan), b. 18 July 1926, Boston, Lincolnshire, England. Education: MA, St Anne's College, Oxford. Appointments: Freelance Writer, 1961-. Publications include: A Way of Looking, 1955; A Sense of the World, 1958; Recoveries, 1964; The Mind Has Mountains, 1966; The Animals' Arrival, 1966; Collected Poems, 1967; Relationships, 1972; Growing Points: New Poems, 1975; Moments of Grace, 1979; Celebrations and Elegies, 1982; In Shakespeare's Company, 1985; Collected Poems, 1953-85, 1986; Tributes, 1989; Let's Have Some Poetry, 1960; Poetry Today 1957-60; Christianity Today, 1965; Editions of poetry. Honours include: W H Smith Award, 1987. Address: 11 Winchester Road, Oxford OX2 6NA, England.

JENSEN Laura Linnea, b. 16 Nov 1948, Tacoma, Washington, USA. Poet; Occasional Teacher. Education: BA, University of Washington, 1972; MFA, University of Iowa, 1974. Appointments: Manuscript Judge, National Endowment for the Arts, 1977; Panel Member, National Endowment for the Arts, Washington DC, 1981; Prize Judge, Poetry Society of America, 1982, 1985; Hopwood Awards, University of Michigan, 1986; Visiting Poet, Oklahoma State

University, 1978. Publications: Chapbooks and Pamphlets: After I Have Voted, 1972; The Story Makes Them Whole, 1979; Tapwater, 1978; A Sky Empty of Orion, 1985 (awarded from Book Builders West); Anxiety and Ashes, 1976; Bad Boats, 1977; Memory, 1982; Shelter, 1985. Contributions to: American Poetry Review; Antaeus; Field; Iowa Review; Ironwood; New Yorker; Northwest Review; Poetry Northwest; Pushcart Prize No 3, No 10, No 14. Honours: Honours Award, 1978; Fellowship Grant, 1986-87; Washington State Arts Commission; Fellowship, National Endowment for the Arts, 1980-81; Grant, Ingram-Merrill Foundation, 1983; Theodore Roethke Award, poetry, Poetry Northwest, 1986; Guggenheim Fellowship, 1989-90; Lila Wallace-Reader's Digest Fund Award, 1993. Memberships: Poets and Writers; Associated Writing Programmes; Academy of American Poets, 1970's. Address: 302 North Yakima No C3, Tacoma, WA 98403, USA.

JEONG Ki Seok, (Wha-pyung), b. 25 Sept 1923, Kure, Jeon-Nam, Korea. Retired Teacher. m. Lee wha-yeoh, 1 son, 4 daughters. Education: BA, Seoul National University, 1949. Appointments: Principal of High School; Chairman of Chong-ho Literature; Establishment and Administration of Peace Literary Award; Establishment of A Poetry Park. Publications: Poetry: Drum of Peace; Praise of Life; Skater on Thin Ice; Drum of the Sun; Buy My Dream; I Want Vomit Heaven; Tracing Things; A Wild Goose; Illusional Date; P! P! Q; A Sea gull of Hiroshima; Man! Rise the Moon; Novel: Light, Sound and Wind!. Honours: The Order of National Service Merit, 1975; The Crown World Poets Award: Prize Winner; Korean Great Poets Award, Prize Winner. Address: 783-3 Sindori, Yongbang Myon, Kure, Jeon Nam, South Korea.

JESSENER Stephen, (Stephen Weild) b. 28 Dec 1966, Wanstead, London, England. Special Needs Teacher. Education: English Degree, North London Polytechnic, 1989; PGCE, Brentwood College, 1991. Appointments: Teacher, Handsworth Primary School, 1991-93; Special Needs Teacher, Chapel Primary School, 1994-. Contributions to: Bad Poetry Quarterly, (Staff poet), 1994-95; Editor, Zimmerframepileup, 1995-96. Address: 54 Hillcrest Road, Walthamstow, London E17 4AP, England.

JEWELL Elizabeth Maynard, (Libby Houston), b. 9 Dec 1941, North London, England. Poet. m. Mal Dean, 21 May 1966, dec, 1 son, 1 daughter. Education: BA Hons, English Language and Literature 1963, MA, 1987, Lady Margaret Hall, Oxford; Certificate in Science Biology, 1986, University of Bristol. Appointments: Founder Member, Holloway Neighbourhood Group, 1976-79; Conservation Planning Assistant, Avon Wildlife Trust, 1987-88; Research Assistant, Botany Department, University of Bristol, 1989-; Legal Co-Worker, Berry's Legal Services Cooperative, 1992-. Publications: A Stained Glass Raree Show, 1967; Plain Clothes, 1971; At the Mercy, 1981; Necessity, 1988; A Little Treachery, with Artist Julia Farrer, 1990; All Change, poems for children, 1993. Contributions to: New Statesman; New Departures; Transatlantic Review; Smoke; Foolscap; Slow Dancer; Orbit (NSW); New Worlds; Bananas; Poor Old Tired Horse; Anthologies include: High on the Walls, 1990; The Puffin Book of 20th Century Children's Verse, 1991; The Oxford Book of Story Poems, 1990; Mother Gave a Shout, 1990; Angels of Fire, 1986; Contributor of programmes of original poetry for children to BBC Schools radio (R4/R5) Series: Pictures in Your Mind, Stories and Rhymes, Contact, and Verse Universe, 1973-91. Memberships: Poetry Society 1970-72; Founder Member, Practising Poets, Bristol, 1983-87; Avon Poetry Festival Committee Member, 1988-91. Address: c/o 120 Grosvenor Road (Berry's), St Pauls, Bristol BS2 8YA, England.

JEWELL Terri L, b. 4 Oct 1954, Louisville, Kentucky, USA. Freelance Writer and Book Reviewer; Poet. Education: BS, Montclair State College, Upper Montclair, New Jersey, 1979. Appointments: Poetry Editor, Shooting Star Review, Pittsburgh, Pennsylvania, 1992; Creative Writers Grant Review Panel Member, Arts Foundation of Michigan, 1994-; Poet-in-Residence, Oak Park Public Library, Michigan, 1994. Publications: The Black Woman's Gumbo Ya-Ya: Quotations by Black Women, 1993; Succulent Heretic, 1994. Contributions to: African American Review; American Voice; International Poetry Review; Midland Review; Negative Capability; When I Grow Old I Shall Wear Purple, 1986; Kentucky Poetry Review; Bloomsbury Review; Black Scholar; Small Press Review; Poetry Flash; Chicago Magazine. Honours: Pushcart Prize Nominations, 1989; Residency, Wolf Pen Women Writers Colony, Prospect, Kentucky, 1990; Individual Creative Artist Grant, Arts Foundation of Michigan, 1993-94; Prism Award for Literature and Activism, Lansing,

1994. Memberships: Michigan Creative Writers-in-the-Schools Program; Teachers and Writer's Collaborative, New York. Address: PO Box 23154, Lansing, MI 48909, USA.

JI Hun. See: WOO Kwok Yin.

JIANG Feng, b. 30 July 1929, Shanghai, China. Reporter; Editor; Translator; Professor. m. Shutong Wei, 1 Oct 1964, 1 son, 1 daughter. Education: BA, Foreign Languages and Literature, Tsinghua University, 1950; BA, Chinese Language and Literature, Peking University, 1961. Appointments: Reporter and Editor of a newspaper of the PLA; Editor-in-Chief of literary magazines, Red Building, Grass; Translator and Professor, Institute of Modern History, Chinese Academy of Social Sciences. Publications: Along The Great Wall, 1980; Love Song, 1991; Translation: Selected Poems of Percy Shelley, 1980-89, 1991-92; Selected Poems of Emily Dickinson, 1986, 1988, 1992; An Anthology of American Modern Poetry, 1986; Selected Poems of Macedonia, 1988; Poems of P B Shelley, English/Chinese edition, 1993; Complete Lyrical Poems of P B Shelley, 1995. Contributions to: Poetry; People's Daily; Literature of PLA; Red Building; Grass; Chinese Poets; World Literature; Treatises on P B Shelley, E Dickinson, W Whitman; Poetry translation, Resemblance Implies Fidelity. Honours: Diploma for Distinguished Contribution to the Development of Social Sciences, State Council of China; Rainbow Prize for Life-time Achievement in Translation, Chinese Writers' Association. Memberships: Deputy Secretary-General, Smedley-Strong-Snow Society of China; Chinese Writers' Association; China PEN; Chinese Translators' Association; Honorary Advisor, IBC. Address: 707 Building 2, Changyungong, Beijing 100044, China.

JIMENEZ DE LOS GALANES Y DE LA FLOR Miguel, (Miguel Galanes), b. 5 Jan 1951, Daimiel, Cuidad Real, Spain. Teacher of Literature and Spanish Language. m. Esperanza Diaz Martin, 26 Nov 1973, 1 son, 1 daughter. Education: BA, Spanish Literature. Appointments: Critic for the journals El Sol and El Mundo. Publications: Inconexiones, 1979; Urgencias sin nombre, 1981; Opera ingenua para Isabel Maria, 1983; Condicion de una musica inestable, 1984; La Demencia consciente, 1987; Los restos de la juerga, 1991. Contributions to: Spanish and overseas critical reviews in literary supplements of El Mundo and El Sol; Nueva Estafeta, Transito, Arrecifa, Alaluz, Cuadernos Hispanoamericanos, Mairena. Membership: Creador del movimiento poetico El Sensismo. Address: c/o Pedro Rico, no 31 10 E, 28029 Madrid, Spain.

JODLOWSKI Marek, b. 5 May 1941, Kielce, Poland. Journalist; Theatre Critic; Theatrologist. m. Teresa Slowikowska, 13 Feb 1961, 1 daughter. Education: Wroclaw University, 1964. Appointments: Vice-Chief, Opole Monthly Magazine, 1975-81, 1985-91. Publications: Osad, 1973; Dowood osobisty, 1978; Psia fuga, 1990. Contributions to: Odra; Opole; Zycie Literakie; Poezja; Agora; Kontrasty Ordrzanskie; Nurt; Poglady; Literatura. Honours: Award for Best Debut of Year, Polish Poetry Festival, Lodz, 1974; Voivode of Opole Provice Award, 1986. Address: ul Grota-Roweckiego 9a-4, 45-256 Opole, Poland.

JOHN Jesus Christopher I. See: MOREN Rodney.

JOHN Mathew Pattacheril, b. 29 Sept 1911. Editor. m. Lena, 1 son, 1 daughter. Education: Madras University. Appointments: Teacher; Secretary, YMCA; Bank Assistant; Industrialist; Currently Editor, New Times Observer. Publications: Inner Space Voyages, 1973; Earth's Flowers, 1984; City Down Below, 1985. Contributions to: New Times Observer. Honours: Cultural Doctorate in Literature, World University, Arizona, 1980; Certificate of Merit, World Congress of Poets, Florida, 1985; Laureate Man of Letters, 1986; Poet Laureat of Pondicherry, 1988; United Poets Laureate International, California; Honorary Life Member, Cinque Ports Poets, England, 1988. Address: Consecration, 16 Rue de la Compagnie, Pondicherry 605001, India.

JOHN Roland, b. 14 Mar 1940, England. Freelance Writer. Education: Private. Publications: Report from the Desert, 1974; Boundaries, 1976; The Child Bride's Diary (from the Chinese), 1980; Believing Words are Real, 1985; To Weigh Alternatives, 1992; A Reader's Guide to the Cantos of Ezra Pound, 1995. Contributions to: Editor, Outposts Poetry Quarterly, 1986-; Agenda; Acumen; Envoi; Prospice; Poetry Review; South Coast Poetry Journal, USA; Printed Matter, Japan; Litteratura, Zagreb; Word and Image, Amsterdam; Outposts; Scripsi, Australia; Others. Address: 22 Whitewell Road, Frome, Somerset BA11 4EL, England.

JOHNSON Adam, b. 10 Apr 1965, Stalybridge, Cheshire, England. Poet. Appointments: Clerical Officer, City and Guilds of London Institute, 1985-86; Editor, Debrett's Peerage, 1989-91. Publication: Poems, 1992. Contributions to: Acumen; European Gay Review; Interim; Outposts; PEN International; P N Review; Prospice; Rialto. Address: 38 Redcliffe Gardens, London SW10 9HA, England.

JOHNSON Darren, b. 31 Jan 1970, Rome, New York, USA. Journalist. m. Eileen Murphy, 18 Oct 1995. Education: BA, English and Pre-Law, Southampton College, New York, 1992; Graduate work, State University of New York, Stony Brook. Appointment: Editor, Publisher, Rocket Literary Quarterly, New York, literary magazine of poetry and fiction. Publications: Novel: I Do Not Prefer to Have Sex; Chapbooks: Kayla, 1994; Clits in My Mouth Make Me Happy, 1995; Jazz Poems. Contributions to: Rocket Literary Quarterly; Plastic Tower; Alpha Beat Press; Impetus; Tight. Address: PO Box 672, Water Mill, NY 11976, USA.

JOHNSON (Edward) Stowers, b. England. Appointments: Principal, Dagenham Literary Institute, 1936-39; Headmaster, Aveley School, 1939-68; Editor, Anglo-Soviet Journal, 1966-68; Art Curator, National Liberal Club, London, 1974-79. Publications: Branches Green and Branches Black, 1944; London Saga, 1946; The Mundane Tree, 1947; Mountains and No Mules, Sonnets They Say, 1949; Before and After Puck, 1953; When Fountains Fall, 1961; Gay Bulgaria, 1964; Yugoslav Summer, 1967; Collector's Luck, 1968; Turkish Panorama, The Two Faces of Russia, 1969; Agents Extraordinary, 1975; Headmastering Man, 1986; Hearthstones in the Hills, 1987; Collector's World, 1989.

JOHNSON Halvard, b. 10 Sept 1936, Newburgh, New York, USA. Teacher; Writer. m. Lynda Schor, 10 Sept 1990, 2 stepsons, 1 stepdaughter. Education: BA, Ohio Wesleyan University, 1958; MA, University of Chicago, 1960. Appointments: Lecturer, Wright Junior College, Chicago; Instructor, University of Texas at El Paso; Assistant Professor, University of Puerto Rico; Lecturer, University of Maryland; Visiting Part-time Lecturer, Rutgers University, Newark; Instructor, American Language Institute, New York University. Publications: Transparencies and Projections, 1969; The Dance of the Red Swan, 1971; Eclipse, 1974; Winter Journey, 1979. Contributions to: West Coast Review; Latitudes; El Corno Emplumado; Monk's Pond; Sou'Wester; Gosis; Stony Brook; Cafe Solo; Sumac; For Review; Dacotah Territory; Poetry Now; Eureka; Puerto Del Sol; Ironwood; Arx; Images; Maryland Poetry Review; Pearl; Mudfish; Gulf Stream; Saint Andrews Review. Honours: National Endowment for the Arts Grant, Poetry, 1990; Baltimore City Arts Grants, poetry, 1991, 1992. Memberships: Poets and Writers; PEN; Associated Writing Programmes; The Writer's Centre, Bethesda, Maryland. Address: 118 S Collington Avenue, Baltimore, MD 21231, USA.

JOHNSON J Chester, b. 28 Sept 1944, Chattanooga, Tennessee, USA. Financial Services Executive; Poet. m. (1) 1 son, 1 daughter, (2) Freda Stern, 7 May 1989. Education: Harvard College, 1962-65; BSE, University of Arkansas, 1968. Appointments: Senior Analyst, Moody's Investors Service; Head, Public Finance Research and Advisory Group, Morgan Guaranty Trust; Deputy Assistant Secretary, US Treasury department; Chairman, Government Finance Associates Inc. Publications: Oh America! and January 1967, 1975; Family Ties, Intervecine Interregnum, 1981; For Conduct and Innocents, 1982; Shorts: On Reaching Forty, 1985; It's a Long Way Home and An American Sequence, 1985; Shorts: For Fun, Not for Instruction, 1985; Exile/Martin, 1986; The Professional Curiosity of a Martyr, 1987; Freda's Appetite, 1991; Lazarus, Come Forth and Plain Bob (Unbeh Aved), 1993. Contributions to: New York Times; Chicago Tribune; Choice; Voices International; Poetry Parade; Trace; Epos; South and West; Michigan and Wisconsin Reviews; Literary Times; Taproot; Broken Streets. Honour: Appointed with W H Auden as the two poets for the retranslation of the Psalms in the Book of Common Prayer, Episcopal CHurch, 1990s. Memberships: Poetry Society of America; American Academy of Poets; Poets and Writers. Address: 315 East 86th Street, Apt 16GE, New York, NY 10028, USA.

JOHNSON Jenny (Jennifer Hilary), b. 2 Nov 1945, Bristol, England. Poet; Adjudicator. m. Noel David Harrower, 28 Apr 1990, 1 son. Appointments: Various positions including Shop Assistant, Librarian, Civil Servant, Insurance Clerk, National Health Employee; Gives poetry readings, own and other poetry; Runs workshops. Publications: Going Home, 1980; Becoming and Other Poems, 1983; Poems 1983-86 (with Frances Lovell), 1987; Towards Dawn, 1991;

The Chromoscope, 1991; The Wisdom Tree: Poems, 1975-93. Contributions to: Stand Magazine; Resurgence; Green Book; Orbis; Acumen; Ore; Pennine Platform; Staple; A Mingling of Streams, Salzburg University Anthology. Honours: 1st Prize, 1978, 1979, 2nd Prize 1982, 3rd Prize, 1983, South West Arts Literature Award. Memberships: The Poetry Society, London. Address: Culross, 11 The Crescent, Woodthorpe, Nottingham NG5 4FX, England.

JOHNSON Linton Kwesi, b. 1952, Chapletown, Jamaica. Education: BA, Goldsmiths' College, London, England, 1973. Appointments: Arts Editor, Race Today magazine and Writer-in-Residence, London Borough of Lambeth. Publications: Voices of the Living and the Dead, 1974; Dread, Beat and Blood, 1975; Inglan is a Bitch, 1980; Recordings include: Making History, 1984; In Concert with the Dub Band, 1985. Honours include: C Day Lewis Fellowship. Address: c/o Island Records Ltd, 22 St Peters Square, London W6 9NW, England.

JOHNSON Nick (Nicholas H), b. 2 Dec 1944, Hartford, Connecticut, USA. Freelance Medical Advertising Editor; Adjunct Professor of English. Education: BA, English Literature, University of Connecticut, Storrs, 1967; ABD, English Literature, The Catholic University of America, Washington, DC, 1971; MFA, Creative Writing, Brooklyn College, New York, 1980. Appointments: Visiting Lecturer, Graduate Assistant, Creative Writing Instructor, Catholic University of America, Washington, DC, 1968-74; Graduate Assistant, Brooklyn College, Brooklyn, New York, 1979-80; Adjunct Professor, Autobiographical Writing, College of New Rochelle, New York, 1988. Contributions to: Men of Our Time; Journal; Movieworks; American Poetry Review; Shenandoah; Epoch; Brooklyn Literary Review; Aileron; Ledge; Mudfish; Berkeley Poets Cooperative; Quartet; Bitteroot; Hawaii Review. Honours: MacDowell Colony Residency, 1980; Finalist, New Poets Series, Wesleyan University Press, 1987, 1988; Finalist, Wisconsin Institute of Creative Writing, 1987. Memberships: The Writers Community, New York City; Poetry Society of America; Past President, English Graduate Organization, Brooklyn College. Address: 141 Huntington Street, Brooklyn, NY 11231, USA.

JOHNSON Peter Martin, b. 22 Feb 1951, Buffalo, New York, USA. Professor. m. Genevieve Allaire, 1 son. Education: PhD, University of New Hampshire. Appointment: Professor of English, Providence College, Rhode Island, 1985-. Publications: Editor, The Prose Poem: An International Journal, 4 volumes. Contributions to: Over 60 poems in 40 different journals including: Verse, Epoch, Iowa Review and Field. Membership: Academy of American Poets. Address: English Department, Providence College, Providence, RI 02918, USA.

JOHNSON Steve. See: **BALON Brett John Steven.**

JOHNSTON Allan James, b. 25 Oct 1949, San Diego, California, USA. Instructor; Editor. m. Guillemette Claude Johnston, 28 Nov 1980. Education: BA, English, California State University, Northridge, 1973; MA, Creative Writing, 1980; PhD, English, 1988, University of California, Davis. Appointments: Lecturer, University of California, Davis; Editor, Great Books Foundation, Chicago, Illinois; Lecturer and Instructor, Northeastern Illinois University, Chicago; Loyola University, Chicago; Lecturer, Oakton Community College. Publication: Tasks of Survival, selected poems, 1970-90, 1996. Contributions to: Americas Review; Androgyne; Asylum; Black Mountain II Review; California Quarterly; Dickinson Review; Green Fuse; Orbis; Riverrun; South Florida Poetry Review; Weber Studies; Z Miscellaneous; Stick; MacGuffin; Psychopoetica; Pig Iron; Pacific International; Lazy Bones Review; Strong Coffee; Wisdom; CQ; Black Bear Review; Black River Review; 20th Century Literature. Honours: 1st Prize, 2nd Prize, Fairfax Folio, 1980; Honourable Mention, C T Wright Poetry Contest, 1980, 1981; Honourable Mention, Flying Colors Anthology, 1980; September Achievement in Poetry, Z Miscellaneous, 1987; 2nd Prize, Riverrun Poetry Contest, 1989; Finalist, Roberts Writing Awards, 1991. Memberships: Modern Language Association. Address: 1105 Asbury, Evanston, IL 60202, USA.

JOINES Mary Elizabeth, b. 30 July 1911, Madison, Kansas, USA. Freelance Writer. m. Glenn V Joines, 7 June 1934, 1 son, 2 daughters. Education: BS, Cum Laude, Home Economics, Kansas State University, 1933; 20 Graduate Hours at University of Kansas and University of Missouri; Conversational French through French Embassy, Kuwait City, Kuwait; Adult short course in Advanced Poetry, Front Range College, Westminster, Colorado. Appointments: Teacher,

High School Home Economics and General Science, Erie, Kansas, 1934-35; Teacher, Pololei English Language School, Honolulu, Territory of Hawaii, 1953-55; Teacher, Elementary School, Topeka, Kansas and Shawnee Mission, Kansas, 1957-66; Tutor in Kansas and in Kuwait. Publications: Of Home and Other Hazards, 1986; Manuscript of Serious Verse Echoes in the Wind, forthcoming. Contributions to: Kansas City Star; Denver Post; Senior Edition; Pen Woman; Good Housekeeping; Saturday Evening Post; House of White Birches; Pegasus (Kentucky State Poetry Society's Winners); Swordsman Review; Poem in Anthology, Springfest, Mile High Poetry Society; Poem in Anthology, Tomorrow Never Knows, National Library of Poetry, 1995. Honours: 251 Cash Prizes (90 of which were 1st Place, 83 were 2nd Place), 1949-; Plaque, In Appreciation of Service, Kansas Authors Club, 1981. Memberships: Ionian Literary Society; Midwest Federation of Chaparral Poets; Kansas Authors Club, 1949-85; National League of American Pen Women, 1964-; Marshall Annual Open Contest; Poetry Society of Colorado, 1979-; Kentucky State Poetry Society, 1986-. Address: 8905 Oakwood Street, Westminster, CO 80030, USA.

JONAS Ann, b. 15 July 1919, Joplin, Missouri, USA. Poet. m. Walter H Jonas, 30 Mar 1944, 1 daughter. Education: Student, 1936-39, Graduate, 1939, Goodman Theatre, Chicago. Appointments: Commentator, Actress, Writer, Producer, WHAS, Radio, Louisville, Kentucky, 1942-47; Radio and TV Interview Host, Actress, Writer, WAVE Radio, Louisville, 1947-54; Began poetry publication, 1960. Publications: Anthologised in: Dark Unsleeping Land, 1960; Deep Summer, 1963; Kentucky Contemporary Poetry, No 1, 1964, No 2, 1967; Kentucky Harvest, 1968; The Diamond Anthology, 1971; Ipso Facto, England, 1975; Peopled Parables, 1975; Sampler-Contemporary Poets of the New South, 1977; Friendship Bridge-Anthology of World Poetry, 1979; The Kentucky Book, 1979; A Merton Concelebration, 1981; Lawrence of Nottingham, 1985. Contributions to: Journals: Poetry Review; Southern Review; Quest; Prism International, Canada; Colorado Quarterly; Carolina Quarterly; Southern Humanities Review; Orbis, England; Monk's Pond; Bitteroot; Midwest Quarterly; Midwestern University Quarterly; Latitudes; Adena; A Review of General Semantics; Kentucky Poetry Review; Approaches; Skylark, India; American Voice; Haiku Journals: American Haiku; Haiku, Canada; Haiku West; Modern Haiku; Janus-SCTH. Honours: Yaddo Fellowship, 1968; Finalist, Annual Award, 1970, Cecil Hemley Memorial Award, 1972, Poetry Society of America; Henry Rago Memorial Award, New York Poetry Forum, 1972; 1 of 5 finalists, Eleanor B North Award, International Poetry Society, 1975; Co-Winner, Edwin Markham Poetry Prize, Eugene V Debs Foundation, 1977; 1st Prize, Poetry, Yaddo National Writers Center, 1982. Memberships: Poetry Society of America; Fellow, International Poetry Society; Honorary Vice-President, Centro Studi e Scambi Internazionali; Poetry Fellowship, Virginia Center for the Creative Arts, 1993. Address: 2425 Ashwood Drive, Louisville, KY 40205, USA.

JONAS Edward Joseph, b. 30 Sept 1966, Wharton, Texas, USA. Former USAF; Student; Writer. m. Leira Laken-Lee Jonas, 1 daughter. Education: USAF Crew Chief Fire Protection, Hazardous Materials Technician, Emergecy Medical Technician; Course Certified Telecommunications Operator; Course Certified Emergency Medical Dispatcher; Fire Science Degree. Appointments: Stationed in Lubbock, TX; Desert Storm/Sand, Arabia; Korea; Alaska; San Antonio, TX and Italy. Publications: Words on the Rising Wind; Fire from Within; Poetic Voices of America, 1984; Rememberances; American Poetry Annual, 1994; After the Storm; And Time Stood Still; Best Poems of 1995; Poetuc Voices of America, 1986; Dusting off Dreams; River of Dreams; Golden Treasures; Walk Through Paradise; Journey to our Dreams. Honours: Distinguished Member Nomination, International Society of Poets, 1994-95; Invitation to the Academy of American Poets; Semi-Finalist, 1994; North American Open Poetry Contest; Invitation to International Society of Authors and Artists; Presidents Award Recipiant, 1995; Editors' Preference Award of Excellence; Editors Choice Award, 1994; Editors Choice Award, 1995; Accomplishment of Merit Certificate, 1994. Address: 3321 Turnabout Loop, Cibolo, TX 778108, USA.

JONES Brian, b. 1938, London, England. Appointment: Teacher of English at secondary level. Publications: Poems, 1966; A Family Album, 1968; Interior, 1969; The Mantis Hand and Other Poems, 1970; For Mad Mary, 1974; The Spitfire on the Northern Line, 1975; The Island Normal, 1980; The Children of Separation, 1985. Honours include: Eric Gregory Award, 1968. Address: c/o Carcanet Press, 208-212 Corn Exchange Buildings, Manchester M4 3BQ, England.

JONES David James, (David Annwn), b. 9 May 1953, Cheshire, England. Poet; Lecturer; Critic. Education: BA, Aberystwyth; PhD; PGCE, Bath University. Appointments: Postgraduate Tutor, University College of Wales, Aberystwyth; Head of A Level, Wakefield District College; Degree Coordinator, Wakefield District College. Publications: Shadings; Foster the Ghost; King Saturn's Book; The Other; Definitive; Primavera Violin; The Spirit That Kiss; Hear the Voice of the Bard; Poetry in the British Isles; Inner Celtia; Flare Head Lives in Leeds; Dantean Designs. Contributions to: Poetry Wales; Anglo Welsh Review; Iron; Bête Noire; AMF; Madog Staple Poets; Affirming Flame; Community Projects Anthology; Yorkshire Contemporary; The Third Day; Planet; Welsh Book News. Honours: Inter Collegiate Eisteddfod Prize; Bunford Prize; Warrington Writers Anthology, judge; Cardiff Literary Festival, judge, 1994; Blake Society, 1994. Memberships: The Welsh Academy; NAWE; New Note Poetics. Address: 3 Westfield Park, Wakefield, West Yorkshire WF1 3RP, England.

JONES Emory Davis, b. 30 Mar 1944, Starkville, Mississippi, USA. Instructor of English. m. Glenda Lynn Broughton, 14 Aug 1966, 2 daughters. Education: BAE, 1965, MA, 1966, PhD, 1981, University of Mississippi. Appointment: Instructor of English, Northeast Mississippi Community College, Booneville. Publications: Magic Medicine Show and Other Poems, 1987; Lodestone and Other Poems, 1989; Represented in: Mississippi Writers: Reflections of Childhood and Youth, Volume III: Poetry 1988. Contributions to: Voices International, 1981, 1985, 1987, 1990; White Rock Review, 1983; Muscadine, 1983, 1984; Negative Capability, 1983; Cotton Boll-Atlanta Review, 1986; Number One, 1988, 1989. Honours: Bela Egydi Award, 1983, 1984. Memberships: Founder, former President, current President, Historian, Mississippi Community College Creative Writing Association; Past President, North Branch, Mississippi Poetry Society Inc. Address: 608 North Pearl Street, Iuka, MS 38852, USA.

JONES Evan (Lloyd), b. 20 Nov 1931, Melbourne, Victoria, Australia. Education: MA, 1957, 1959, Melbourne and Stanford Universities. Appointment: Senior Lecturer in English, Melbourne University, 1965-89. Publications include: Inside the Whale, 1960; Understandings, 1967; Recognitions, 1978; Left at the Post, 1984; Co-editor, The Poems of Kenneth Mackenzie, 1972. Address: Department of English, University of Melbourne, Parkville, Victoria 3052, Australia.

JONES Frederick Malcolm Anthony, b. 14 Feb 1955, Middlesex, England. University Lecturer. m. Christina Jones, 2 sons. Education: BA, Classics, Newcastle-upon-Tyne, 1977; MA, Medieval Studies, Leeds, 1979; PhD, thesis on Satires of Juvenal, St Andrews, 1987. Appointments: Assistant Lecturer, Department of Classics, University of Cape Town, South Africa, 1982-86; Teacher, Department of Classics, Cobham Hall, Kent, England, 1987-89; Lecturer, Department of Classics and Ancient History, University of Liverpool, 1989-. Publication: Congreve's Balsamic Elixir, 1995. Contributions to: Northern Poetry Two, 1991; Peterloo Preview 3, 1993; Orbis; Poetry and Audience; Verse; Poetry Nottingham; Scratch; Weyfarers; Pennine Platform; Contrast, Capetown; Upstream, Capetown. Honours: 1 of 10 joint winners, Northern Poetry Competition, 1991; Felicia Hemans Prize for Lyrical Poetry, 1991. Memberships: Society for the Promotion of Roman Studies; Cambridge Philological Society. Address: Department of Classics and Ancient History, University of Liverpool, Liverpool L69 3BX, England.

JONES (Morgan) Glyn, b. 28 Feb 1905, Merthyr Tydfil, Glamorgan, Wales. Teacher of English (retired); Poet; Writer; Translator. m. Phyllis Doreen Jones, 19 Aug 1935. Education: St Paul's College, Cheltenham. Appointment: Teacher of English, South Wales Schools. Publications: Poetry: Poems, 1939; The Dream of Jake Hopkins, 1954; Selected Poems, 1975; Selected Poems, Fragments and Fictions, 1988; Fiction: The Blue Bed, 1937; The Water Music, 1944; The Valley, The City, The Village, 1956; The Learning Lark, 1960; The Island of Apples, 1965; Selected Short Stories, 1971; Welsh Heirs, 1977; Other: Books of criticism; Translations. Contributions to: Journals and periodicals. Honours: Honorary DLitt, University of Wales, 1974; Honorary Fellow, Trinity College, Carmarthen, Wales, 1993. Membership: Fellow, Welsh Academy. Address: 158 Manor Way, Whitchurch, Cardiff CF4 1RN, Wales.

JONES Huw Griffith, b. 5 Feb 1955, England. Teacher of Religious Education and Welsh. m. Janice Dixon, 28 July 1978, 2 daughters. Education: BD 1977, United Theological College, University

College of Wales, Aberystwyth; PGCE, University College of Wales, 1978. Appointment: Reviews Editor, Anglo-Welsh Review 1985-88. Publications: A Small Field, 1985; Included in anthology: The Bright Field, 1991; Lleuad y Bore, 1994. Contributions to: Poetry Wales; Taliesin. Honour: 2nd Prize, Welsh Arts Council's New Poets Competition, 1983. Membership: The Welsh Academy. Address: 5 Ffordd Coed Mawr, Bangor, Gwynedd LL57 4TB, Wales.

JONES Jill Patricia, b. 13 Oct 1951, Sydney, New South Wales, Australia. Poet; Reviewer. Education: BA (Hons), Sydney University; Graduate Diploma, Communications, New South Wales Institute of Technology; MA, University of New South Wales. Appointments: Editorial Assistant; Book Editor; Publications Officer; Newsletter Editor; Publicity and Information Officer; Policy Analyst; Senior Policy Analyst; Executive Policy Coordinator. Publications: The Mask and the Jagged Star, 1992; Flagging Down Time, 1993; A Parachute of Blue: First Choice of Australian Poetry, (co-editor). Contributions to: Australia; Age Monthly Review; Australian; Bulletin; Island; Meanjin; Overland; Poetry Australia; Southerly; Sydney Morning Herald; Westerly; UK; Oasis; Slow Dancer; Echo Room; USA: Antipodes; Visions; Canada: Prism International; Antigonish Review; New Zealand: Takahe. Honours: Writer' Project Grant, Australia Council, 1992; Highly Commended, FAW Anne Elder Award, 1992; Mary Gilmore Award, 1993; Category B Writers' Fellowship, 1995. Memberships: Australian Society of Authors; Poets Union of New South Wales; Fellowship of Australian Writers; Writers Centre New South Wales. Address: PO Box 155, Rozelle, NSW 2039, Australia.

JONES (Everett) LeRoi, (adopted the name Amiri Baraka), 7 Oct 1934, Newark, New Jersey, USA. Professor of Africana Studies; Poet; Dramatist; Writer. m. (1) Hettie Roberta Cohen, 1958, div 1965, 2 daughters, (2) Sylvia Robinson, 1967, 6 children and 2 stepdaughters. Education: Rutgers University, 1951-52; BA, English, Howard University, 1954. Appointments: Founder, Director, Black Arts Repertory Theatre, Harlem, New York, 1964-66; Spirit House, Newark, 1966-; Visiting Professor, San Francisco State College, 1966-67; Yale University, 1977-78, George Washington University, 1978-79; Chair, Congress of Afrikan People, 1972-75; Assistant Professor, 1980-82, Associate Professor, 1983-84, Professor of Africana Studies, 1985-, State University of New York, Stony Brook. Publications: Poetry includes: The Disguise, 1961; The Dead Lecturer, 1964; Black Art, 1966; A Poem for Black Hearts, 1967; Black Magic: Collected Poetry 1961-1967, 1970; It's Nation Time, 1970; In Our Terribleness: Some Elements and Meaning in Black Style (with Billy Abernathy), 1970; Spirit Reach, 1972; African Revolution, 1973; Hard Facts, 1976; Selected Poetry, 1979; AM/Trak, 1979; Spring Song, 1979; Reggae or Not!, 1982; Thoughts for You!, 1984; The LeRoi Jones/Amiri Baraka Reader, 1993; Plays include: General Hag's Skeezag, 1992; Fiction includes: Tales (short stories), 1967; Other includes: Conversations with Amiri Baraka, 1994; As Editor, includes: Confirmation: An Anthology of African American Women (with Amina Baraka), 1983. Honours: Obie Award, 1964; Guggenheim Fellowship, 1965; Yoruba Academy Fellowship, 1965; Dakar Festival Prize, 1966; Grant, 1966, Award, 1981, National Endowment for the Arts; DHL, Malcolm X College, Chicago, 1972; Rockefeller Foundation Grant, 1981; American Book Award, Before Columbus Foundation, 1984. Membership: Black Academy of Arts and Letters. Address: c/o Department of Africana Studies, State University of New York at Stony Brook, Stony Brook, NY 11794, USA.

JONES M(argaret) A(lice) B(artlett), b. 23 Oct 1906. Retired Educator. Education: BA, 1927; BA, Honours, 1928; BSc, Honours, 1944; Barrister-at-law, Middle Temple, 1952. Appointments: Head Teacher, schools, Essex, Gloucester City, Bristol, 1929-42; Administrative Officer, Gloucestershire County Council, 1942-56; Seconded for Gwilym Gibbon Fellowship, Nuffield College, Oxford, 1953-54; Principal, St Katharine's College of Education, Liverpool, 1956-65. Publications: Lake Vrynwy, 1972; Chinese Acrobats, 1975; Imagination All Compact, 1982; The Way We Live Now, 1982; A Field Full of Folk, 1986; A Poem is Made, 1991. Contributions to: Anthologies including: On Being Alone, 1970; Poems, 1974; News Item in Verse, 1977; Voices of Today, 1980; Alderney, 1980; Thirty, 1982; Poets England No 4, 1981, No 5, 1984, No 6, 1984, No 10, 1990; Magazines: Poetry Wales; Anglo-Welsh Review; Outposts; Orbis; Country Life; Ver Poets; Reynard; Envoi; Doors. Honours: 1st Prize, South Wales Eisteddford, 1986, 1992, 1994; 1st Prize, Ministerley Eisteddfod, 1991, 1995; Highly Commended Entries in World Order of Narrative and Formalist Poets (USA), 1993, 1994; BBC Midland Poets; Dial-a-Poem, South Wales Arts. Memberships: Ver Poets; Guildford

Poets. Address: 8 Mayfield Park, Shrewsbury, Shropshire SY2 6PD, England.

JONES (Glyn) Martin, b. 3 June 1937, Surbiton, Surrey, England. Lecturer. m. 1 Apr 1966, 1 son, 1 daughter. Education: BA, History, 1962, Postgraduate Certificate in Education, 1963, London University. Appointment: Co-editor, Weyfarers. Publication: The Pink Shiny Raincoat, 1992. Contributions to: Outposts; New Poetry; Poetry South-East; Samphire; Weyfarers; Envoi; Poetry Nottingham. Honour: Commended, Surrey Poetry Centre Competition, 1991. Membership: Surrey Poetry Centre, Guildford. Address: 1 Mountside, Guildford, Surrey GU2 5JD, England.

JONES Mike, b. 7 May 1951, Cheshire, England. Post Office Employee. Publication: Scars and Glory, 1980. Contributions to: Countryman; Outposts; Orbis; New Poetry; Envoi; Candelabrum; Artful reporter; Ipsel; Weyfarers; Chester Poets Vols 6-12; Meridian; Allusions. Memberships: Founder, Mid Cheshire Writers Group; Committee Member, Crewe and District Writers Group; Chester Poets. Address: Glyndwr Cottage, Birch Heath, Tarporley, Cheshire CW6 9UR, England.

JONES Paul McDonald, b. 5 Feb 1950, Hickory, North Carolina, USA. Poet; Research Computing Development Manager. m. Sally Greene. Education: BS Computer Science, North Carolina State University, 1972; MFA in Poetry, Warren Wilson College, 1992. Publication: What the Welsh and Chinese Have in Common, 1990. Contributions to: Thinker Review; Southern Humanities Review; Ohio Review; Georgia Review; Carolina Quarterly; American Literary Review; St Andrews Review; Ironwood; Pembroke Magazine; Crescent Review; Plainsong; Loblolly; Lyricist; Poet Lore; Hampden-Sydney Review; Crucible; Cold Moutain Review; Brix; Turning Dances. Honours: North Carolina Quarterly Poetry Prize, 1979; North Carolina Arts Council Fellowship, 1981; Emergent Poets Reading Series, 1987; North Carolina Writers and Readers Competition, 1988; Theodore Christian Hoefner Award, 1987; North Carolina Writers' Network Chapbook Award, 1990; Guy Owen-Tom Walters Poetry Prize, 2nd Place, 1992. Memberships: North Carolina Writers' Network, Vice President 1984-87; Art Centre of Carrboro, Poetry Director 1978-90; American Academy of Poets; Poets and Writers; North Carolina Writers' Conference. Address: 5526 Hideaway Drive, Chapel Hill, NC 27516, USA.

JONES Rodney, b. 11 Feb 1950, Hartselle, Alabama, USA. Poet; Writer. m. (1) Virginia Kremza, 1972, div 1979, (2) Gloria Nixon de Zepeda, 21 June 1981, 2 children. Education: BA, University of Alabama, 1971; MFA, University of North Carolina, Greensboro, 1973. Publications: Going Ahead, Looking Back, 1977; The Story They Told Us of Light, 1980; The Unborn, 1985; Transparent Gestures, 1989; Apocalyptic Narrative and Other Poems, 1993. Contributions to: Periodicals. Honours: Lavan Younger Poets Award, Academy of American Poets, 1986; Younger Writers Award, General Electric Foundation, 1986; Jean Stein Prize, American Academy and Institute of Arts and Letters, 1989; National Book Critics Circle Award, 1989. Memberships: Associated Writing Programs; Modern Language Association. Address: c/o Houghton Mifflin Co, 222 Berkeley Street, Boston, MA 02116, USA.

JONES Seaborn Gustavus, b. 10 Oct 1942, Macon, Georgia, USA. Natural History Interpretor. m. Loyce Kirkland, 10 Oct 1989, 1 daughter. Education: Mercer University, 1961-63. Appointment: Natural History Interpreter, Museum of Arts and Sciences, Macon, Georgia. Publications: Drowning from the Inside Out, 1982; X-Ray Movies. Contributions to: New York Quarterly; Bogg; Xanadu; 80 on the 80s Anthology; Snake Nation Review; City Scriptum; Coldspring Journal. Honours: Artist Initiated Award, Georgia Arts Council, 1988; Author of the Year Award in Poetry, Georgia Council of Authors and Journalists. Address: PO 469, Lizella, GA 31052, USA.

JONES Thomas (Tom) Claburn Jr, b. 4 May 1941, Chicago, Illinois, USA. Attorney-at-Law; Poet; Translator; Teacher. m. Karin K Krueger, 29 Nov 1980, 2 sons, 3 daughters. Education: BA cum laude, Harvard University, 1965; JD cum laude, Columbia University School of Law, 1968; MFA, George Mason University, 1992. Appointments: Attorney, Amnesty International, USA, 1972-79; District Attorney, Greenlake County, Wisconsin, 1983-84; Visiting Professor of Poetry, Visua Bharati University, West Bengal, India 1990; Private Practice, Passim, Navajo-Hopi Legal Services, 1992-. Publications: Songbook of Absences, Translations of poems by Miguel Hernandez, 1972, reprinted 1980; No Prisoners, 1976; Footbridge to India, 1990; Madmen and Bassoons, 1992. Contributions to: Greenfield Review; International Poetry Review; Kansas Quarterly; Nation; New Republic; Poet Lore; Southern Poetry Review; Wind Literary Journal; Wisconsin Review; Wisconsin Trails; Yale Review. Honour: Appointed Visiting Professor of Poetry, Visva Bharati University, West Bengal, India, 1992. Memberships: Academy of American Poets; Associated Writing Programmes; Poetry Society of America; Modern Language Association. Address: c/o Navajo-Hopi Legal Services, PO Box 2990, 117 Main Street, Tuba City, AZ 86045, USA.

JONES Volcano. See: **MITCHELL Adrian.**

JONG Erica (Mann), b. 26 Mar 1942, New York, New York, USA. Author; Poet. m. (1) Michael Werthman, 1963, div 1965, (2) Allan Jong, 1966, div 1975, (3) Jonathan Fast, 1977, div 1983, 1 daughter, (4) Kenneth David Burrows, 5 Aug 1989. Education: BA, Barnard College, 1963; MA, Columbia University, 1965. Appointments: Lecturer in English, City College of the City University of New York, 1964-66, 1969-70, University of Maryland Overseas Division, 1967-69; Faculty, Bread Loaf Writers Conference, Middlebury, Vermont, 1982, Salzburg Seminar, Austria, 1993. Publications: Fear of Flying, 173; How to Save Your Own Life, 1977; Fanny, Being the True History of the Adventures of Fanny Hackabout-Jones, 1980; Parachutes and Kisses, 1984; Serenissima: A Novel of Venice, 1987; Any Woman's Blues, 1990; Fear of Fifty: A Midlife Memoir, 1994; Poetry: Fruits and Vegetables, 1971; Half-Lives, 1973; Here Comes and Other Poems, 1975; Loveroot, 1975; The Poetry of Erica Jong, 1976; At the Edge of the Body, 1979; Ordinary Miracles: New Poems, 1983; Becoming Light: Poems, New and Selected, 1991; Other: Four Visions of America (with others), 1977; Witches, 1981; Megan's Book of Divorce: A Kid's Book for Adults, 1984; Erica Jong on Henry Miller: The Devil at Large, 1994. Contributions to: Various publications. Honours: Academy of American Poets Award, 1963; Bess Hokin Prize, 1971; New York State Council on the Arts Grant, 1971; Alice Faye di Castagnola Award, 1972; National Endowment for the Arts Grant, 1973. Memberships: Authors Guild; Phi Beta Kappa; Poetry Society of America; Poets and Writers; Writers Guild of America. Address: 425 Park Avenue, New York, NY 10022, USA.

JONSSON Thorsteinn, (Thorsteinn Fra Hamri), b. 15 Mar 1938, Hamar, West Iceland. Writer. Publications: I Svortum Kufli, 1958; Tannfe Handa Nyjum Heimi, 1960; Lifandi Manna Land, 1962; Langnaetti a Kaldadal, 1964; Jorvik, 1967; Vedra Hjalmur, 1972; Fidrid ur Saeng Daladrottningar, 1977; Spjotalog a Spegil, 1982; Ny Ljod, 1985; Urdargaldur, 1987; Vatns Gotur og Blods, 1989; Safarinn Sofandi, 1992. Contributions to: Various Icelandic and Scandinavian newspapers and magazines. Honours: Award from the Writers Fund of the State Radio, 1962; Award from the Ari Josefsson Memorial Fund, 1968; The Cultural Award of the newspaper Dagbladid in Reykjavik, 1981; Childrens Book Literary Award, given by the city of Reykjavik, for a translated book, 1981; Thorbergur Thordarson's Literary Prize, 1991; Four times participant in the annual Nordic Council Prize Competition; The Icelandic Literary Prize, 1992. Memberships: Writers' Association of Iceland; PEN. Address: Smaragata 2, 101 Reykjavík, Iceland.

JOPE Norman Francis, b. 28 May 1960, Plymouth, Devon, England. Administrator. Education: BA Hons Philosophy 1982, University of Wales. Appointments: Administrator with various public sector bodies including the Civil Service, the West Midlands Regional Health Authority, the University of Plymouth and the British Computer Society, 1983-. Publications: Spoil, 1989; Tors, 1990; In the Absence of a Summit, 1992; Zones of Impulse, 1994; Francis, 1995; Time Over, 1995; Air, 1995; Forthcoming: For the Wedding Guest: Terra Fabulosa; Editor, MEMES, 1989-94; Over 40 magazines of quality in UK, US and Europe; also featured in depth in three anthologies: Stonechat, 1992; Stumbling Dance, 1994; A Curious Architecture, 1996. Membership: Plymouth Poetry Exchange. Address: c/o 38 Molesworth Road, Plympton, Plymouth, Devon PL7 4NT, England.

JORDAN Andrew, b. 17 July 1959, Norfolk, England. Editor; Poet. Appointments: Editor, Publisher, 10th Muse Magazine. Publications: Living in the Shadow of the Weather, 1984; Ancestral Deaths, 1985; St Catherine's Buried Chapel, 1987; Decoded Chronicles, 1987; The Invisible Children, 1991; The Mute Bride, forthcoming 1996. Contributions to: Acumen; Orbis; Arts Bursary, 1989. Address: 33 Hartington Road, Southampton S014 0EW, England.

JORDAN June, b. 9 July 1936, New York, New York, USA. Professor; Poet; Writer. m. Michael Meyer, 5 Apr 1955, div 1966, 1 son. Education: Barnard College, 1953-55, 1956-57; University of Chicago, 1955-56. Appointments: Faculty, City College, City University of New York, 1967-69, Sarah Lawrence College, 1969-70, 1973-74; Professor of English, State University of New York at Stony Brook, 1978-89; Visiting Poet-in-Residence, MacAlester College, 1980; Chancellor's Distinguished Lecturer, 1986, Professor of Afro-American Studies and Women's Studies, 1989-93, Professor of African American Studies, 1994-, University of California, Berkeley; Playwright-in-Residence, 1987-88, Poet-in-Residence, 1988, New Dramatists, New York City; Visiting Professor, University of Wisconsin, Madison, 1988; Poet-in-Residence, Walt Whitman Birthplace Association, 1988. Publications include: Living Room: New Poems 1980-1984, 1985; On Call: New Political Essays, 1981-85; Lyrical Campaigns: Selected Poems, 1989; Moving Towards Home: Selected Political Essays, 1989; Naming Our Destiny: New and Selected Poems, 1989; Technical Difficulties: New Political Essays, 1992; The Haruko/Love Poetry of June Jordan, 1993; Other: I Was Looking at the Ceiling and Then I Saw the Sky (Libretto and lyrics for this Opera, music composed by John Adams), 1995. Contributions to: Magazines and professional journals. Honours: Rockefeller Foundation Grant, 1969; Prix de Rome, 1970; CAPS Grant in Poetry, 1978; Yaddo Fellow, 1979, 1980; National Endowment for the Arts Fellowship, 1982; Achievement Award for International Reporting, National Association of Black Journalists, 1984; New York Foundation for the Arts Fellowship, 1985; MADRE Award for Leadership, 1989; Freedom to Write Award, PEN West, 1991; Lila Wallace-Reader's Digest Writers Award, 1995. Memberships: American Writers Congress; PEN American Center; Poets and Writers. Address: c/o University of California at Berkeley, Berkeley, CA 94720, USA.

JORIS Pierre, b. 14 July 1946, Strasbourg, France. Poet; Translator; Teacher. Companion, Nicole Peyrafitte, 2 sons. Education: BA, Bard College, 1969; MA, Essex University, 1975; PhD, State University of New York at Binghamton, 1990. Appointments: Freelance Writer and Translator, 1969-; Editor, Sixpack Magazine, 1972-77; Teacher, University of Constantine, Algeria, 1976-79; Visiting Writer, University of Iowa, 1987, University of California 1990-92; Associate Professor, State University of New York, Albany, 1992-. Publications: Breccia (Selected Poems 1972-1986), 1987; Janus, 1988; The Irritation Ditch, 1991; Turbulence, 1991; Winnetou Old, 1994. Contributions to: Numerous professional journals, magazines, reviews and newspapers. Honours: CCLM Grant to Sixpack Magazine, 1975; Fel's Literary Award, (via CCLM) to the Editors of Sixpack, 1975; Centre National des Lettres, France, Translators Grant, 1993; Fonds Cultural National (Ministry of Culture, Luxembourg) Writers Grant, 1987; Faculty Research Award Program Grant, State University of New York at Albany, 1993; PEN Center USA West Award for Translation (with Jerome Rothenberg), 1994. 1996 Pen West (Oakland) Award, (with Jerome Rothenberg) 1995. Memberships: Founding Member, Luxembourg Writers Union, 1986-; PEN American Center. Address: 6 Madison Place, Albany, NY 12202, USA.

JOSEPH Jenny, b. 7 May 1932, Birmingham, England. Writer; Lecturer. m. C A Coles, Apr 1961, dec, 1 son, 2 daughters. Education: BA (Oxon), Hons, English. Publications: The Unlooked-for Season, 1960; Rose in the Afternoon, 1974; The Thinking Heart, 1978; Beyond Descartes, 1983; Persephone, fiction told in prose and poetry, 1986; The Inland Sea, 1989; Beached Boats, prose with Robert Mitchell's photographs, 1991; Ghosts and Other Company, 1995; Selected Poems, 1992. Honours: Gregory Award, 1960; Cholmondeley Prize, 1975; James Tait Black Prize for Persephone, 1986; The Society of Authors' Travelling Scholarship for 1995. Literary Agent: John Johnson Ltd, London. Address: 17 Windmill Road, Minchinhampton, Glos GL6 9DX, England.

JOSEPH Lawrence, b. 10 Mar 1948, Detroit, Michigan, USA. Professor of Law. m. 10 Apr 1976. Education: BA, 1970, JD, 1975, University of Michigan; BA, 1972, MA, 1976, Cambridge University. Appointment: Professor of Law, St John's University, School of Law, 1987-. Publications: Shouting at No One, 1983; Curriculum Vitae, 1988; Before Our Eyes, 1993. Contributions to: Paris Review; Nation; Village Voice; Partisan Review; Poetry; Boulevard; Kenyon Review. Honours: Hopwood Award for Poetry, 1970; Starrett Poetry Prize, 1982; National Endowment for the Arts Poetry Award, 1984. Memberships: PEN American Centre, Events Committee; Poetry Society of America, Board of Governors; Poets House, Advisory

Council; National Writers Voice, Advisory Committee. Address: 355 S End Ave Apartment 33N, New York, NY 10280-1060, USA.

JOSHY George Joseph, b. 30 May 1967, Meloor, India. Artist. Education: BSc; Internationally reputed Painter, Sculptor and Musician. Appointment: Poet, 1990-; Exhibitions of his paintings, sculptures and pencil sketches; Member, United Nations Youth Organisation, 1991-. Contributions include: Samvedhana, 1993, 1996; Autmnan, Poet, 1994; World Poetry, 1995; New Global Voice, 1995; Prophetic Voices, 1996; Poetcrit. Honours: Honorary Poesie, India, for distinguished contribution in the promotion of poetry and peace in the world; DLitt, Arts, World Academy of Arts and Culture, China. Memberships: World Poetry Society; Poetry Society India; Honorary Director, Socio-Literary Foundation. Address: Shee's International Art Centre, Meloor, PO 680311 CKDY-TCR, Kerala, India.

JOURDAN Pat, b. 19 Oct 1939, Liverpool, England. Artist. Div, 2 sons. Education: NDD Painting, Liverpool College of Art, 1961. Publications: The Common Thread, writings by working class women, 1989; Strictly Private, anthology chosen by Roger McGough, 1981, 1982; The Bedsit Girl, 1968. Contributions to: Over to You, anthology, 1975; Workshop; Aquarius; Rialto; SOL; Oyster; Straight Lines; Pentameters; Outposts; Many public readings in London and Norwich, 1968-. Honours: California US America, anthology, best poems of 1968; Borestone Mountain Poetry Awards, 1969; Norwich Writers Circle 2nd Prize, 1982. Membership: Norwich Poetry Group. Address: 5 Onley Street, Unthank Road, Norwich, Norfolk NR2 2EA. England.

JOYCE Veronica Dolores, b. 4 Feb 1939, New York, New York, USA. Teacher. Education: BS, 1963, MA, 1965, Fordham University; PhD, New York University, 1978. Appointments: English Teacher, Department Chairman, Holy Rosary Academy, Union City, New Jersey, 1965-68; English Teacher, Leonia Middle and Nigh Schools, Leonia, New Jersey, 1968-84; English Teacher, Bloomingdale Senior High, Florida, 1988-. Contributions to: California Quarterly; South Florida Poetry Review; Feelings; Florida English Jouranl (FEJ); Anthologies from Florida Suncoast Writers Conference, 1993-95. Honours: Poet in Attendance: Breadloaf Writers Conference, Middlebury, Vermont, 1989, Teachers as Writers, Workshop with Dr S Dunning; Honourable Mention, California Quarterly Poetry Competition, 1990. Memberships: Poetry Society of America; South Florida Poetry Society; Florida Council of Teachers of English (FCTE); Kappa Delt Pi; National Council of Teachers of English. Address: PO Box 5634, Sun City Center, FL 33571, USA.

JOYETTE Anthony, b. 21 Feb 1949, St Vincent, West Indies. Painter; Illustrator. m. 24 Sept 1977, 2 daughters. Education: Bishop's College, Kingstown, St Vincent, 1969; Diplome d'Etudes Collegiales, Marie Victorian College, Quebec, 1991. Publications: Germination of Feeling, 1980; Vincentian Poets 1950-1980, 1990. Contributions to: Kola, Quebec; Bim, Barbados; Vince World, St Vincent; Matrix, Quebec. Honours: World of Poetry Award, 1989. Memberships: Quebec Black Writers Guild; Canadian Poetry Association; World of Poetry. Address: PO Box 1381, St Laurent, Quebec H4L 4X3, Canada.

JOZEFACKA Maria Emilia, b. 2 Mar 1942, Opole, Poland. Writer. Education: MA, Catholic University of Lublin, 1964; DLitt, Lodz University, 1971. Appointment: Assistant, Catholic University of Lublin, 1965-69. Publications: The Edge, 1969; The Holocaust, 1970; The Epicentre, 1971; Advent, 1982; A Bedrock, 1983; The Borderland (Japanese translation), 1985; The Encounter Earth, 1988; A View from the Cross, 1992. Contributions to: Polish Radio and TV; Polish reviews and magazines: Tworczosc; Poezja; Wspolczesnosc; Kierunki; Kamena. Honours: Regional Prizes, 1968, 1972, 1983; National Prize for Best Poetry Book of the Young Generation, 1971; Award, Polish Ministry of Culture and Art, 1984. Memberships: Polish Writers Association; IBBY. Address: al Tumidajskiego nr 2B m 42, 20-247 Lublin, Poland.

JUANITA Judy, b. 19 July 1946, Berkeley, California, USA. College Instructor. 1 son. Education: BA, Psychology 1969, MFA, Creative Writing 1993, San Francisco State University. Appointments: San Francisco State University, 1969-71, 1992-93; Poet-in-the-Schools, New Jersey State Arts Council, 1982-88; Montclair (New Jersey) State College, 1983-84; Lecturer, Writing & Literature, Laney College, Oakland, 1993-; Holy Names College, and 1996. Publications: Heaven's Hold, 1993; Knocked Up, 1994-95. Contributions to: 13th Moon; Painted Bride Quarterly; Croton Review; Lips; Passaic Review; Aquarian Weekly Rock Magazine; Bergen

Poets; Rare Form; Rooms. Honours: New Jersey State Council on the Arts Fellowship for Poetry, 1982, 1986. Address: 6645 Eastlawn Street, Oakland, CA 94621, USA.

JULIUS Richard Todd, b. 30 Aug 1959, Buffalo, New York, USA. Publications Coordinator; Technical Editor. Education: BA, triple major, English, Comparative Literature, Arts and Ideas, Residential College, 1984, MFA, English-Creative Writing, Rackham Graduate School, 1988, University of Michigan; English Instructor Credential, California Community Colleges. Appointments: Publisher, Empty Mirror Press, 1985-90; Adjunct Lecturer, Composition-Creative Writing, University of Michigan, Ann Arbor, 1988-89; Instructor, City College of San Francisco, California, 1989-90; Publications Coordinator, Center for Project Management, San Ramon, California, 1989-. Contributions to: Slipstream, San Fernando Poetry Journal; Red Cedar Review; Cutting Edge Quarterly; Ripples Poetry and Fiction Magazine. Memberships: Academy of American Poets; Poetry Society of America; Newsletter Editor, Board Member, Berkeley Chapter, Society for Technical Communication. Address: PO Box 1558, Danville, CA 94526, USA.

JUNEMANN Edna Julia, b. 10 Jan 1914, New York, New York, USA. Education: BA, Hunter College, 1932-36. Appointments: Secretary, Austrian State Tourist Department, 1936, General Chemical Co, 1936-45, Union Theological Seminary, 1946-49, Maier Naval Architects, 1948-51; Office Manager, private doctor's office, Neurological and Psychiatric, 1951-69; Secretary: Cooper Union College, 1969-71, Flushing Hospital, 1971-73, American Scholarship Association, 1973-76. Contributions to: Poet, 1982-91; Grit, newspaper; American Poetry Anthology; National Library of Poetry Anthologies; Antologia Poetica. Honours: New York Poetry Forum Contest, 1982; Honorable Mention at international poetry contest, Academia Internationale di poesia, Italy, 1983; 2nd Place for Poetry, Senior Talent Shows, New York City, 1994, 1995. Memberships: New York Poetry Forum; Browning Society; Dickens Fellowship; Mark Twain Association. Address: Sanford Gardens, 144-41 Sanford Avenue No 5E, Flushing, NY 11355, USA.

JUNKINS Donald (Arthur), b. 19 Dec 1931, Saugus, Massachusetts, USA. Poet; Writer; Professor. m. Kaimei Zheng, 18 Dec 1993. Education: BA, University of Massachusetts, 1953; STB, 1956, STM, 1957, AM, 1959, PhD, 1963, Boston University. Appointments: Instructor 1961-62, Assistant Professor of English 1962-63, Emerson College, Boston; Assistant Professor of English, Chico State College, California, 1963-66; Assistant Professor 1966-69, Associate Professor 1969-74, Director, Master of Fine Arts Program in English 1970-78, 1989-90, and Professor of Engish 1974-95, Professor Emeritus, 1995-, University of Massachusetts, Amherst. Publications: Poetry: The Sunfish and the Partridge, 1965; The Graves of Scotland Parish, 1969; Walden, One Hundred Years After Thoreau, 1969; And Sandpipers She Said, 1970; Editor, The Contemporary World of Poets, 1976; The Uncle Harry Poems and Other Maine Reminiscences, 1977; Crossing by Ferry: Poems New and Selected, 1978; The Agamenticus Poems, 1984; Playing For Keeps: Poems 1978-1988, 1989; Journey to the Corrida, 1997; Euripides' Andromache, translator, 1997. Contributions to: Anthologies, including Classic Short Fiction 1972, Themes in American Literature 1972, The Longman Anthology of American Poetry, 1992; The New Yorker Book of Poems 1974; American Literature; Antioch Review; Atlantic; Critique; Early American Literature; Harper's; New Yorker; Northwest Review; Poetry; Sewanee Review; Studies in Short Fiction; Various others. Honours: Breadloaf Writers Conference Poetry Scholarship, 1959; Jennie Tane Award for Poetry, 1968; John Masefield Memorial Award, 1973; National Endowment for the Arts Fellowship, 1974, 1979. Address: 63 Hawks Road, Deerfield, MA 01342, USA.

JUNLAKAN Lesley Diane, b. 24 May 1955, Manchester, England. University English Teacher. m. Wilat Junlakan, 10 Mar 1988. Education: BA, Honours, 1976, MA, 1977, University of Manchester. Appointments: Tutor, College of Adult Education, Manchester, 1981-85; Lecturer, Thammasat University, Bangkok, Thailand, 1985-88; Srinakarinwirod University, Thailand, 1988-89; NIFS, Kanoya, Kagoshima, Japan, 1989-. Publications: Japanese Fan, Western Fingers, 1990; Plum Blossom and Persimmons. Contributions to: Azami; Haiku in English; Shi Miyaku; Katahira. Memberships: Azami, Osaka; National Poetry Foundation, England; Poetry Society, England. Address: Kimotsuki Cottage, Otemachi 12-15, Kanoya-shi, Kagoshima-ken 893, Japan.

JUSSAWALLA Adil, b. 8 Apr 1940, Bombay, India. Education: MA, University College, Oxford, 1964. Appointments: Lecturer in London and Bombay; Literary Editor, Bombay; Editor, Debonair, Bombay, 1989-. Publications include: Land's End, 1962; Missing Person, 1976. Address: Palm Springs, Flat R2, Cuffe Parade, Bombay 400 005, India.

JUSTICE Donald (Rodney), b. 12 Aug 1925, Miami, Florida, USA. Professor (retired); Poet; Writer. m. Jean Catherine Ross, 22 Aug 1947, 1 son. Education: BA, University of Miami, 1945; MA, University of North Carolina, 1947; Postgraduate Studies, Stanford University, 1948-49; PhD, University of Iowa, 1954. Appointments: Instructor, University of Miami, 1947-51; Assistant Professor, Hamline University, 1956-57; Lecturer, 1957-60, Assistant Professor, 1960-63, Associate Professor, 1963-66, Professor, 1971-82, University of Iowa; Professor, Syracuse University, 1966-70, University of Florida, Gainesville, 1982-92. Publications: Poetry: The Summer Anniversaries, 1960; Night Light, 1967; Departures, 1973; Selected Poems, 1979; The Sunset Maker, 1987; A Donald Justice Reader, 1992; New and Selected Poems, 1995; Other: The Collected Poems of Weldon Kees (Editor), 1962; Platonic Scripts (essays), 1984. Contributions to: Journals and magazines. Honours: Rockefeller Foundation Fellowship, 1954; Lamont Award, 1959; Ford Foundation Fellowship, 1964; National Endowment for the Arts Grants, 1967, 1973, 1980, 1989; Guggenheim Fellowship, 1976; Pulitzer Prize in Poetry, 1980; Academy of American Poets Fellowship, 1988; Co-Winner, Bollingen Prize, 1991. Memberships: American Academy and Institute of Arts and Letters. Address: 338 Rocky Shore Drive, Iowa City, IA 52246, USA.

JYOTHIKUMARI. See: **GOVINDA RAO K V.**

K

KABADI Dwarakanath H, b. 17 Feb 1936, Bangalore City, India. Auditor; Advocate, retired. m. Smt Chandrakantha D Kabadi, 24 May 1962, 3 sons. Education: BCom, 1958; BL, 1963; 2 Honorary DLitt; Honorary PhD. Appointment: Auditor and Advocate (retired). Publications: Symphony of Skeletons, poems, 1985; Ruptured Senses, long poem, 1985; Geetha Gangothri, lyrical poems, 1987; Minchina Butti, 3 line Kannada Flickers, 1988; Tender Wings, children's poems, 1988; Melting Moments, love poems, 1990; Swapna Sopana, Kannada poems, 1993; Naguva Mallige, Kannada rural folklore-songs, 1994; Kabadi's Glimmericks, nonsense poetry, 1994; A Tear on a Pancake, poems, 1995. Contributions to: Poet; Nouvelle Europe; Poetry Nippon; New Muses, USA; Laureal Leaves; Unilit; Deccan Herald; Rajasthan Journal of Indian Writing in English; JIWE; International Poetry Letter, Argentina; Li-Poetry Magazine, China; Indian Literature, Sahitya Akademi; Poetry Time; LittCrit; Canopy; Poetcrit; World Tribune; PIO Journal; Ocarina; Samvedana; Prophetic Voices. Honours: Chosen as Chancellor of the Congress and presented with Bronze Plaque, World Congress of Poets, Baltimore, USA, 1976; Diploma of Merit, Universite Delle Arte of Italy, 1982; Medallion of Honour for Tender Wings book, Melbourne Poetry Society; International Eminent Poet, International Poetry Academy, Madras; Michael Madhusudan International Poetry Award for 3 Line Flicker book. Memberships: Founder President, Poets International Organisation, Bangalore and Garden of World Poets, Madras; Life Fellow, World Poetry Society, USA; Executive Board, Federation of International Poetry Association, USA. Address: No 80, 5th Cross, 1st Main, BDA Hig Layout, RMV 2nd Stage, Bangalore 560 094, India.

KACHEL Zeev, (Wolf Kachel, Z Kachol Koch, Kanar al Hagag), b. 6 Apr 1912, Brest Litovsk, Russia. Electromechanical Engineer; Safety Engineer; Poet; Writer; Painter. m. Judith Yolanta Joseph, 12 May 1952, 1 son, 1 daughter. Education: Diploma, Electromechanical Engineer, Institut Technique de Normandie, France, 1934. Appointments: Secretary-General, Union of Jewish Societies of France, Paris, 1939-42; Secretary, Nationals of Brest-Litovsk Society, Israel; Director, Safety Department, Safety Engineer-in-Chief, Electrical Co, Israel, 1947-77. Publications: In Yiddish: The Drum, 1938; Ethiopia, 1938; In Hebrew: Hanuchai od Le'ehow, 1961; Eize Yom Hayom. Contributions to: Poet; Hebrew Journals: Bohagshama; Betichut; Barechev; Davar; Ha'areth; Yiddish: Theatre Welt. Honours: 2nd Prize, Nweie Presse, Paris, 1939. Memberships: Israeli Union of Editors of Periodicals; Association of Composers and Authors Israel; World Poetry Society. Address: 13 Yocheved Street 13, Haifa 34674, Israel.

KACHMAR Jessie, b. 28 Mar 1913, Portland, Oregon, USA. English Teacher. m. John F Kachmar, 23 Dec 1946, 1 daughter. Education: BA, 1935, MA work, 1935-37, University of Washington; Advanced study, Crane College, Chicago; Writing courses, University of Minnesota, St Paul and Minneapolis; Poetry Seminar, Loyola University, 1960. Publications: Snow Quiet, 1976; Apertures to Anywhere, 1979; Variations, 1992; Represented in 4 anthologies. Contributionsto: Gallery Series; Choice; Caprice; Chicago Dial a Poem, 1980s. Honours: Women Writers Honorary, University of Minnesota, 1953; Winner, 1980, Runner-up, 1981, All Nations Poetry Contest, Triton College, Illinois. Membership: Poetry Seminar, Executive Board, several years. Address: 13739 15th Avenue North East No B-1, Seattle, WA 98125, USA.

KADMON Jean Ball Kosloff, b. 1 Aug 1922, Denver, Colorado, USA. Poet; Novelist; Sculptor; Painter. m. 18 Aug 1945, 2 sons. Education: BA, University of Alberta, 1943; Graduate studies in Anthropology, University of Chicago, 1944-46. Appointments: Clerk-Typist, USED, Canol Project, Northwest Territories, Canada, 1943; Anthropologist, International Centre for Community Development, Haifa, Israel, 1964-65; Sociologist, Jewish Agency, Israel, 1966-68. Publications: Moshav Segev, 1972; Peering Out, 1996; Clais and Clock, 1988. Contributions to: Voices, Israel, Vols 1-24; Seven Gates, Israel, Vols 1-8; Arc 9 & 10, Literary Journal Israel, 1994, 1995; Jerusalem Post; AI Hamishmar. Honour: New Zealand International Writers Workshop 2nd Prize, 1981. Membership: Israel Association of Writers in English. Address: 12 Zerubabel Street, Jerusalem 93504, Israel.

KAHN Sy M, b. 15 Sept 1924, New York, New York, USA. Professor Emeritus; Freelance Writer; Theatre Director. Div, 1 son. Education: BA with honours, University of Pennsylvania, 1948; MA, University of Connecticut, 1951; PhD, University of Wisconsin, 1957. Appointments: Assistant Professor, English, Beloit College, 1955-60; Assistant Professor, English, Humanities, University of Southern Florida, 1960-63; Professor, English, Humanities, Raymond College, 1963-68; Professor, Drama, English, 1968-86, Chairman, Drama Department, 1970-81, Professor Emeritus, 1986-, University of the Pacific; Fulbright Professorship, American Literature: University of Salonika, Greece, 1958-59; University of Warsaw, Poland, 1966-67; University of Vienna, Austria, 1970-71; University of Porto, Portugal, 1985-86. Publications: Our Separate Darkness, 1963, 1965, 1968; Triptych, 1964; The Fight Is With Phantoms, 1966; A Later Sun, 1966; Another Time, 1968; Facing Mirrors, 1981; Devour the Fire: Selected Poems of Harry Crosby (editor), 1984; Between Tedium and Terror: A Soldier's World War II Diary, 1993. Contributions to: Beloit Poetry Journal; Mid-West Quarterly; Bitterroot; Epos; College English; Southern Poetry Today; San Fernando Poetry Journal; Far Point; Many Others; Various Anthologies. Honours: Gardner Writing Awards, University of Wisconsin, 1954, 1955; Crosby Writing Fellowship, 1962, 1963; Borestone Poetry Award, 1964; Promethean Lamp Prize, 1966; Grand Prize in Poetry, University of the Pacific, 1985. Membership: Modern Language Association. Address: Ravenshill House, 1212 Holcomb Street, Port Townsend, WA 98368, USA.

KALI Kathie. See: **BENDER Kathie Jane.**

KAMANDA Kama, b. 11 Nov 1952, Luebo, Zaire. Poet; Writer; Novelist; Lecturer. Education: State Diploma in Literary Humanities, 1968; Degree in Journalism, Journalism School, Kinshasa, Zaire, 1969; Degree in Political Sciences, University of Kinshasa, 1973; Law Degree, University of Liège, 1981, University of Strasbourg, 1988. Appointments: Journalist; Technical Assistant Infeurope; Lecturer at various universities, schools and cultural centres; Literary Critic for various newspapers. Publications: Les Contes des Veillées Africaines, 1967, 1985; Chants de Brumes, 1986; Les Résignations, 1986; Eclipse d'Etoiles, 1987; Les Contes du Griot, 2 volumes, 1988, 1991; La Somme du Néant, 1989; L'Exil des Songes, 1992; Les Myriades des Temps Vécus, 1992; Lointaines sont les Rives du Destin; Les Vents de l'Epreuve, 1993; L'Etreinte des Mots, 1995. Honours: Works referenced in noted works including: Kama Kamanda au Pays du Conte, 1993; Various awards of the French Academy including Prix Paul Verlaine, 1987, the Louise Labé Award for Poetical Merit, 1990, and Théophile Gautier Award, 1993; Literature Award of the Black African Association of French-Speaking Writers, 1991; Special Poetry Award, Academy Institute of Paris, 1992; Special Prize of French-Speaking Countries of the General Council of Agen; Silver Jasmin for Poetical Originality. Memberships: International PEN Club; Association of African Writers; Association of French Language Authors; Association of French Poets; Société des Gens de Lettres en France. Address: 21 rue d'Armagh, B-6780 Messancy, Belgium.

KAMAU H B. See: **BECTON Henry Jr.**

KAMERER Jocelyne Maria, b. 6 Sept 1950, Pont-A-Muussons, France. Secretary. Education: Upsala College, East Orange, New Jersey, 1 year. Appointments: Holiday Inn, Richmond, Virginia, 1970-77; Secretary, Hilton, Reno, 1978-82; Administration Assistant, Regional Transportation Agency, Reno, 1983-93. Publications: Reflections, 1990; Life Within. Contributions to: Plowman; Tel Star; Dusty Dog; Moments In Time; Poets of Now; Others. Honours: Golden Quill Award, 1990; Silver Quill Award, 1991; First Place, Plowman 91, Certificate of Special Honour, 1992; Third Place, Khepera, 1994; 4 Blue Ribbon Awards, Southern Poetry Association, 1991-; Award of Poetic Excellence, 1990. Memberships: Southern Poetry Association; National Poetry Association; The Society for the Advancement of Poetry; The Plowman. Address: 2816 Airport Road #122, Colorado Springs, CO 80910, USA.

KANE Julie, b. 20 July 1952, Boston, Massachusetts, USA. Writer. Education: BA with distinction, English, Cornell University, 1974; MA, Creative Writing, Boston University, 1975; Fellow in English, PhD Program, Louisiana State University, 1991-. Appointments: Writer-in-Residence, Phillips Exeter Academy, New Hampshire, 1975-76; Grantwriter, Federal Antipoverty Program, 1976-78; Technical Writer, Editor, Commercial Nuclear Power Industry, 1978-91. Publications: Two Into One, 1982; Body and Soul, 1987; The Bartender Poems, 1991. Contributions to: Boston Phoenix;

Chiaroscuro; Epoch; Eleventh Muse; Feminist Studies; Gabija; London Magazine; Louisiana Literature; Mademoiselle; Negative Capability; Nemunas; New Laurel Review; Nimrod; Only Poetry; Piedmont Literary Review; Pontchartrain Review; Remington Review; Sidewinder; The Stone; Thema; Tucumcari; Taos Review; Tulane Literary Magazine; Various anthologies. Honours: 1st Prize, College Poetry Competition, Mademoiselle Magazine, 1973; Scholarship, Boston University Graduate Writing Program, 1974-75; George Bennett Fellowship in Writing, Phillips Exeter Academy, 1975-76; Napa Poetry Competition Participant Reader Award, 1983; Honourable Mention, Boston University Graduate Poetry Contest, 1990; National Merit Award, Poetry Atlanta Prize, 1990; Louisiana State University Academy of American Poets Prize, 1993. Memberships: Poets and Writers; New Orleans Poetry Forum; Associate Member, New Orleans Gulf South Booksellers Association. Address: 7111 Walmsley Avenue, New Orleans, LA 70125, USA.

KANE Paul, b. 23 Mar 1950, Cobleskill, New York, USA. Associate Professor of English. m. Tina Kane, 21 June 1980. Education: BA, 1973, MA, 1987, MPhil, 1988, PhD, 1990, Yale University; MA, University of Melbourne, Australia, 1985. Appointments: Poet-in-Residence, Briarcliff College; Proprietor, Warwick Bookstore; Carpenter, Merritt Construction; Admissions Director, Wooster School; Visiting Lecturer, Yale University; Associate Professor, Vassar College. Publication: The Farther Shore, 1989. Contributions to: New Republic; Paris Review; Grand Street; Sewanee Review; Shenandoah; Scripsi; American Review; Meanjin. Honours: Fulbright Postgraduate Grant, 1984; Schweitzer Prize Preceptorship in Poetics, New York University, 1985. Memberships: Common Wealth of Letters, Yale University; PEN America; Poetry Society of America; American Association of Australian Literary Studies; Elizabethan Club, Yale University. Address: 8 Big Island, Warwick, NY 10990, USA.

KANG Shin II, b. 1 Apr 1943, Samye, Jeonbuk, Korea. Teacher. m. Sun Deok Jeon, 15 Feb 1971, 2 sons, 1 daughter. Education: BA, Jeonbuk National University, 1967; MEd, Educational Graduate School, Jeonbuk National University, 1985. Appointments: Secretary-General, Korea World Poetry Research Institute, 1993; Editor-in-Chief, World Poetry Korea, 1993; President, Jeonbuk Catholic Literary Fellowship Association, 1994; Acting President, Iksan Literary Men's Association. Publications: Getting Off the Last Stop of the Four Seasons, 1991; In the Place Where Colours of Solitude and Love Remain, 1995. Contributions to: Literary Magazine of Korea; Moonyesajo; Moonhak Kong-gan; Jeonbuk Literature; Iksan Literature; Anthology of World Poetry; World Poetry India; World Poetry Korea. Honours: New Poet Prize, Moonyesajo monthly, 1990; Kaya Gold Crown World Poets Award, Korea World Poetry Research Institute, 1996.Memberships: Korea Free Poets Association; Korea Space Poets Association. Address: 957-1 Samye-Ri, Samye-Eub, Wanju-Kun, Jeonbuk 565-800, Korea.

KANTARIS Sylvia, b. 9 Jan 1936, Grindleford, Derbyshire, England. Poet; Writer; Teacher. m. Emmanuel Kantaris, 11 Jan 1958, 1 son, 1 daughter. Education: Diplome d'Études Civilisation Française, Sorbonne, University of Paris, 1955; BA Honours, 1957, CertEd, 1958, Bristol University; MA, 1967, PhD, 1972, University of Queensland, Australia. Appointments: Tutor, University of Queensland, Australia, 1963-66, Open University, England, 1974-84; Extra-Mural Lecturer, Exeter University, 1974-. Publications: Time and Motion, 1975; Stocking Up, 1981; The Tenth Muse, 1983; News From the Front (with D M Thomas), 1983; The Sea at the Door, 1985; The Air Mines of Mistila (with Philip Gross), 1988; Dirty Washing: New and Selected Poems, 1989; Lad's Love, 1993. Contributions to: Many anthologies, newspapers, and magazines. Honours: National Poetry Competition Award, 1982; Honorary Doctor of Letters, Exeter University, 1989; Major Arts Council Literature Award, 1991; Society of Authors Award, 1992. Memberships: Poetry Society of Great Britain; Literature Panel, 1983-87, Literary Consultant, 1990-, South West Arts. Address: 14 Osborne Parc, Helston, Cornwall TR13 8PB, England.

KANTOR Peter, b. 5 Nov 1949, Budapest, Hungary. Poet. Education: MA, English and Russian Literature, 1973, MA, Hungarian Literature, 1980, Budapest ELTE University. Appointment: Literary Editor, Kortars magazine, 1984-86. Publications: Kavics, 1976; Halmadar, 1981; Sebbel Lobbal, 1982; Gradicsok, 1985; Hogy no az eg, 1988; Naplo, 1987-1989, 1991; Font lomb, lent avar, 1994; Mentafü (selected poems), 1994. Contributions to: Various publications. Honours: George Soros Fellowship, 1988-89; Wessely Laszlo Award, 1990; Dery Tibor Award, 1991; Fulbright Fellowship, 1991-92; Fust

Milan Award, 1992; Jozsef Attila Award, 1994. Memberships: Hungarian Writers Union; International PEN Club. Address: Stollar Bela u 3/a, Budapest 1055, Hungary.

KAPLAN Susan Robin, b. 13 Dec 1958, Philadelphia, Pennsylvania, USA. Assistant Professor of English Literature. Education: BA, Religion, Temple University, 1980; MA, English, University of Southern Mississippi, 1982; PhD, English, Creative Writing, University of Houston, 1987. Appointments: Instructor, University of Southern Mississippi; Assistant Editor, Mississippi Review; Assistant Professor, Virginia Military Institute, Lexington. Contributions to: Poetry; New Orleans Review; Boulevard. Honours: Academy of American Poets, 1986; Ruth Lake Memorial Award, Poetry Society of America, 1989. Memberships: Associated Writing Programs; Poetry Society of America. Address: Department of English, Virginia Military Institute, Lexington, VA 24450, USA.

KAPODISTRIAS Panagiotis, b. 16 Nov 1961, Zakynthos, Greece. Priest of Hellenic Orthodox Church; Professor of Theology (Orthodoxy). m. Fotini Papantoni, 5 Sept 1982, 2 sons, 1 daughter. Education: Orthodox Congregational Theology, University of Athens. Appointments: Ordained and Served in Zakynthos Cathedral; Parish Priest of Banato Church, Zakynthos, 1987-; Book-Keeper, Monastery of Strofades and Saint Dionysios 1983-; Assistant Secretary in offices of Zakynthos Bishopric and Press Section 1983-; Regular radio and television broadcasts on a variety of subjects 1989-; Professor, School of Music, Zakynthos, 1992-. Publications: As if Painting on Glass, 1987; Translucent Waters, 1992; When the Cave-owner Appears, 1995. Contributions to: Nea Estia; Periplous; Sinaxi; Kinonia; To Dentro; Eptanissiaka Filla; Mikri Hydria; Tetramina. Honour: Poetry Prize of Haiku, from the Embassy of Japan, Athens, 1993 Address: Banato (Village), GR 291 00 Zakynthos, Greece.

KAPSALIS John, b. 27 Jan 1927, Mytelene, Greece. Doctor of Food Science. m. Athena, 2 Sept 1956, 2 daughters. Education: BS, 1954; MS, 1955; PhD, 1959. Appointments: Postdoctoral, Ohio University, 1959; Chemist, Armed Forces Food and Container Institute, Chicago, 1960-63; Head, Biochemistry Branch, US Army Natick Laboratories, 1963-87. Publications: The Odds, 1972; Twentyeth and Other Centuries, 1974; The Saga of Chrysodontis Pappas, 1994. Contributions to: Dark Horse; Bitterroot; Northeast Journal; Nebraska Review; Joycean Lively Arts Guild Review Indigo. Honours: Massachusetts Artists Foundation Poetry Award, 1985. Memberships: Listed Directory of American Poets and Fiction Writers; Academy of American Poets. Address: 5776 Deauville Lake Cir #308, Naples, FL 33962, USA.

KARARACH Auma, b. 20 May 1965, Gulu, Uganda. Development Economist. Education: BA, Makerere University, 1989; MA, 1991, PhD, Leeds University, England. Appointments: Programme Coordinator (Sandwich), 1986-89. Publications: A Feast of Poison, 1986; The Pains of Our Heart, 1988. Contributions to: Lobo Mews; Dowing Magazine; Radio Uganda Writers Club Programme. Honours: Acoli Young Poets Award, 1987. Memberships: Poetry Society, London; Acoli Writing Club; Royal Economic Society. Address: Flat 5, 20 Kelso Road, Leeds LS2 9PR, England.

KARASEK Krzysztof, b. 19 Feb 1937, Warsaw, Poland. Editor; Literary Critic. 1 daughter. Education: Academy of Physical Education, Warsaw; Philosophy, University of Warsaw. Appointments: Co-Founder, Editor, Nowy Wyraz Literary Monthly, 1972-76; Editor, Poetry Section, Polish Radio, 1976-82; Editor, Essays, Literature Monthly, 1983-92; Editor, Poetry, Przedswit Publishing House, 1992-; Vice Director and Deputy in Chief, II Program, Polish Radio. Publications: Godzine Jastrzebl, 1970; Drozd I inne wiersze, 1972; Poszje, 1974, 1975; Prywatna historia ludzkosci, 1978, 1986; Trzyposmaty, 1982; Wietsze I poematy, 1982; Sceny z Grottgera I nne Wiersze, 1984; Foezje wybrane, 1986; Swierszoze, 1987; Lekoja biolog I Inne Wiersze, 1990; Poeta nie spoznia sie ne poema, 1991; Poezje, 1994; Gzsrwone Jabluszko, 1994; Poezja I jej sobowtor, Book of Essays on Poetry, 1986; Autopsychografia, Essays, 1993; Gottfried Benn: Selected Poema, translation from German, 1982. Contributions to: Main Polish Monthlies: Tworozosc; Literatura; Res Publics; Odra; Wiez; Foreign Magazines and Periodicals. Honours: Czerwona Roza Prize, 1969; Prize, Best Poetry Book of Year, Literature, 1990. Memberships: Polish PEN; Society of Polish Writers. Address: Walbrzyska 15-402, 02-739 Warsaw, Poland.

KARAVIA Lia Headzopoulou, b. 27 June 1932, Athens, Greece. Writer; Poet; Dramatist. m. Vassillis Caravias, 20 Sept 1953, 2 sons. Education: Diploma in English Literature, Pierce College, Athens, 1953; Diploma in French Literature, Institute of France, Athens, 1954; Diploma, Acting School, Athens, 1962; Classical Literature, University of Athens, 1972; Doctorat Nouveau Regime, Comparative Literature, Paris, 1991. Appointments: Actress; Teacher of Acting and the History of the Theatre, Public Schools, 1984-94. Publications: 10 novels; 10 poetry collections; Stage and radio plays; Television scripts. Contributions to: Anthologies, journals, and magazines. Honours: Menelaos Loudemis Prize, 1980; Michaela Averof Prize, 1981; Prizes for three plays for the Young, 1986, 1987, 1988; National Prize for Best Play for the Young, 1989; National Playwrights Prizes, 1990, 1991; President for Greece of European Institute for Theatre Research. Memberships: Actors League of Greece; International Theatre Centre; Maison International de Poeses, Liège; Society of Greek Writers; Union of Greek Playwrights. Address: 51 Aghiou Polycarpou Street, Nea Smyrni 17124, Athens, Greece.

KARIM Fawzi, b. 1 July 1945, Baghdad, Iraq. Poet; Writer. m. 31 Dec 1980, 2 sons. Education: BA, Arabic Literature, College of Arts, Baghdad, Iraq, 1967. Appointments: Taught Arabic, 1968; Freelance Writer, Lebanon, 1969-72; London as exile and freelance writer, 1979-. Publications: Where Things Begin, 1968; I Raise My Hand in Protest, 1973; Madness of Stone, 1977; Stumbling of a Bird, 1985; We Do Not Inherit the Earth, 1988; Schemes of Adam, 1991; Pestilential Continents, long poem, 1992; Exile to Awareness, essays; Edmon Sabri, study; City of Copper, short stories; Collected Poems, 1968-92, 1993. Contributions to: Shi'r; Al-adab; Al-Karmel; Mawaqif; Al-Kalima; Al Lahda Alshiria; Al Ightirab Al-adabi; Poetry Review; Editor-in-Chief/Owner/Publisher, Quarterly Magazine, Al-Lahda Al-Shiriya, London. Memberships: Union of Iraqi Writers; English Poetry Society. Address: PO Box 2137, London W13 0TY, England.

KAROL Pamala Marie, (La Loca), b. 29 Mar 1950, Hollywood, California, USA. Legal Secretary. Education: University of California, Berkeley, 1967-71; 1st Teaching Certificate in French, Sorbonne, University of Paris, 1973; BA, Communication Arts, Columbia College, 1974; Graduate Studies, Film, Loyola Marymount University; Poetry Workshop with Ron Koertge, Pasadena City College, 1985-. Appointment: Co-Instructor, Poetry Workshop, University of California, Los Angeles Extension Writers Program, 1990. Publications: The Mayan, 1988; Adventures on the Isle of Adolescence, 1989. Contributions to: Threepenny Review; Steaua; Kozmik Blues; Gridlock; Los Angeles Times; Poetry Australia; Jacaranda Review; City Lights Review; Pretext; Endless Party; Inscape; Sierra Madre Review. Honours: Fellowship for Graduate Studies in Film, Academy of Motion Picture Arts and Sciences, 1974, 1976; College Prize, Academy of American Poets, 1986; Official US Representative, Winter Olympic Writers Festival, Calgary, Canada, 1988; Artists Fellowship in Literature, California Arts Council, 1988-89; National Endowment for the Arts Fellowship in Literature, 1994. Memberships: PEN Center USA West; Poetry Society of America; Academy of American Poets; National Writers Union. Literary Agent: Carol Lees Management. Address: 1608 No Cahuenga Blvd # 562, Hollywood, California 90028-6202, USA.

KARUNAKARAN M Frederick, b. 12 Dec 1948, Palayamkottai, Tirunelvelli District, Madras, India. Professor of English. m. 8 May 1974, 1 son, 1 daughter. Education: BA, English, 1969, MA, English, 1971, MPhil, English, 1978, PhD, English, 1990, University of Madras. Appointments: Professor of English, Government Arts Colleges, Government of Tamil Nadu Collegiate Educational Service, 1971-; Presented papers on Modern Poetry, various seminars, India, Egypt, 1989, 1990. Publications: Books for College Students, 1987; Composition Notes for Degree Classes, 1987. Contributions to: Newspapers: Hindu; Indian Express; Journal of English Language Teaching; Poetry; Focus on English; College magazines. Honours: Invited to XIth Conference; World Congress of Poets; Honoured, 39th All India English Teachers Conference. Memberships: World Congress of Poets, USA; All India English Teachers Association; English Language Teachers Association; Focus on English. Address: Department of English, Government Arts College, Tiruttani, Tamil Nadu 631209, India

KASPER Stanley Frank, b. 11 May 1920, Erie, Pennsylvania, USA. Freelance Writer and Poet. m. Rita Marina Komiskey, 25 Mar 1944, 1 son, 2 daughters. Education: BA, 1972, MA, 1974, Goddard College, Vermont. Appointments: Served US Army, 1940-60; Office

Manager, American Electronics Lab, 1960-69; Office Manager, American Electronics Labs, 1960-69; Media Manager, Merck Sharp and Dohmne, West Point, Pennsylvania, 1969-84. Publications: Poems of Life, 1985; Slices of Life, 1988; Images of Life, 1990. Contributions to: Norristown Times Herald; Byline; Creative Enterprises; Poet's Review; Poetry Press; Fine Arts Press; Poetic Page; New York Poetry Foundation; Piper Calling; Lucidity; Cambridge Collection; Apropos; Suwanne Poetry. Honours: Best Valentine's Poem, Poet's Review, 1991; Award of Appreciation, Award of Merit, Creative Enterprises; 1st Place, Drama Professional, 1st Place, Serious Poetry, Methacton Intercom. Memberships: Pennsylvania Poetry Society; Philadelphia Writers Conference, Scholarship Chairman; St David's Christian Writers Conference, Assistant Treasurer. Address: 2803 Curtis Lane, Lansdale, PA 19446, USA.

KASPER Wayne Lee, b. 17 Oct 1956, Columbia, Missouri, USA. Poetry Editor; Naturalist. 1 son, 2 daughters. Education: BA, English, 1989, MA, English, 1991, Central Missouri State University; Cherokee Language, Northeastern State University, Tahlequah, Oklahoma, 1988. Appointment: Poetry Editor, Gray. Contributions to: Amherst Society, 1989, 1990; Trellis; Protea; Green Fuse; Poetry Explosion Newsletter; Pen; Minotaur; Old Hickory Review; Potpourri; Word and Image; Tin Wreath; Feelings; Reflections; Plowman; Onionhead; Portable Wall; Long Islander; My Legacy; Tandava; IaZer; World of Poetry. Address: 18212 Westwood Drive, Sterling, CO 80751, USA.

KATZ Steve, b. 14 May 1935, New York, New York, USA. Novelist; Short Story Writer; Poet; Screenwriter; Professor. m. Patricia Bell, 10 June 1956, div, 3 sons. Education: BA, Cornell University, 1956; MA, University of Oregon, 1959. Appointments: English Language Institute, Lecce, Italy, 1960; Overseas Faculty, University of Maryland, Lecce, Italy, 1961-62; Assistant Professor of English, Cornell University, 1962-67; Lecturer in Fiction, University of Iowa, 1969-70; Writer-in-Residence 1970-71, Co-Director, Projects in Innovative Fiction 1971-73, Brooklyn College, City University of New York; Adjunct Assistant Professor, Queens College, City University of New York, 1973-75; Associate Professor of English, University of Notre Dame, 1976-78; Associate Professor of English 1978-82, Professor of English 1982-, University of Colorado at Boulder. Publications: Novels: The Lestriad, 1962; The Exaggerations of Peter Prince, 1968; Posh, 1971; Saw, 1972; Moving Parts, 1977; Wier and Pouce, 1984; Florry of Washington Heights, 1987; Swanny's Ways, 1995. Short Stories: Creamy and Delicious: Eat My Words (in Other Words), 1970; Stolen Stories, 1985; 43 Fictions, 1991. Poetry: The Weight of Antony, 1964; Cheyenne River Wild Track, 1973; Journalism, 1990. Screenplay: Grassland, 1974. Honours: PEN Grant, 1972; Creative Artists Public Service Grant, 1976; National Educational Association Grants, 1976, 1982; GCAH Book of the Year, 1991; America Award in Fiction, for Swanny's Ways, 1995. Memberships: Authors League of America; PEN International; Writers Guild. Address: 669 Washington Street, No 602, Denver, CO 80203, USA.

KATZ Vincent, b. 4 June 1960, New York, New York, USA. Poet; Musician. m. Vivien Bittencourt, 16 Nov 1987. Education: BA, Music, Classics, University of Chicago, 1982; BA, MA, Classics, Oxford University, England, 1985. Appointments: Owner/Curator, She's Leaving Home, gallery-performance club, Boston, Massachusetts, 1986-87; Associate Editor, The Print Collectors Newsletter, New York City, 1988-90. Publications: Rooms, 1978; A Tremor in the Morning (with linocuts by Alex Katz), 1986; Cabal of Zealots, 1988; New York Hello! (with photographs by Rudy Burckhardt), 1990; Charm, translations from Latin of Roman poet Propertius, 1995. Contributions to: Bomb; Cover; World; New American Writing; Exquisite Corpse; Mudfish; Ghandabba; Broadway; Oink!; Mag City; Fred; Tranfer; Ars Electronica; New Censorship; Poetry Project Newsletter. Honours: Billings Fiske Poetry Prize, University of Chicago, 1982; Selected by Kenneth Koch to read at PEN Young Writers Series, 1988. Memberships: Poets and Writers; Founder, President, Pocket Poetics, University of Chicago, 1978-82. Address: 211 West 19 Street, #5, New York, NY 10011, USA.

KAUFMAN Azriel, b. 1 May 1929, Poland. Poet; Teacher; Artist. m. Mazal Kaufman, Apr 1984, 1 son, 3 daughters. Education: Studied Art with Abshalom Okashi, Akko; BA, Sociology, History, Hebrew University, Jerusalem, 1962; MA, Hebrew Literature, Tel-Aviv University, 1978; Additional Studies, Faculty of Arts, Hebrew University. Appointments: Teaching, elementary schools, Akko and Haifa, Israel, 1951-66; Director, Institute of Youth Leaders and Institute of Teachers Development, Haifa, 1967-69; Teacher, Literature, Youth Leaders Seminar, Tel Aviv Municipality and Manager, Art courses, 1969-70; Director, Tel-Aviv and Central Branch, Art and Culture Department, Ministry of Education, 1971-; Annual Exhibition, Artists House, Tel-Aviv, 1975; Other exhibitions: Zavti Gallery, Tel-Aviv, 1979; Art Pavilion, Yarkon Park, Tel-Aviv, 1980; Exhibition Hall, Kfar Saba, 1981; Mishkan Le Omanut, Ein Harod, 1982. Publications: Journey to the False Truth (with Zvi Raphaeli), 3 Volumes, 1968; Sonata of a Wandering Bird, 1983; A Bit of This, 1985; You Can Move Now, 1989. Contributions to: Poems and criticism to: Daily Israeli newspapers, Al Ha Mishmar, Ha'Aretz, Davan; Evening newspapers, YeDiot Aharonot, Maariv; Art and literary magazines; Achshav, Moznayim, Appirion, Iton 77 magazine. Honour: Prime Minister's Prize for Poetry in Homage of Levy Eshkol, 1989-90. Memberships: Hebrew Writers Society, Central Committee Member 1987-89; Israeli Artists and Sculptors Society. Address: 3 HaBaron Hirsch, Ramat-Aviv, Tel-Aviv, 64962 Israel.

KAUFMAN Merilee Dale, b. 24 June 1943, New York, New York, USA. Publicist; Public Relations Executive. Appointment: Currently Executive Vice President. Publications: Anthologised in Sarah's Daughter's Sing. Contributions to: New York Times; Confrontation; Long Pond Review; Centerfold; Albany Review; Jewish Ledger; Minnesota Ink. Honours: 2nd Prize, C W Post's 23rd Annual Poetry Competition, 1989; 1st Prize, Annual Centerfold Competition, Rockville Center Guild for the Arts, 1989; Honourable Mention, 1st Annual Open Competition, Fresh Meadows Poets, 1989. Membership: Poetry Society of America. Address: 3256 Elliott Bouelvard, Oceanside, NY 11572, USA.

KAUFMAN Shirley, b. 5 June 1923, Seattle, Washington, USA. Poet; Translator. m. (1), 3 daughters, (2), Hillel Daleski, 19 June 1974. Education: BA, University of California at Los Angeles, 1944; MA, California State University, San Francisco, 1967. Appointments: Visiting Lecturer, Department of English, University of Massachusetts, Amherst, 1974; Visiting Professor, Department of English, University of Washington, Seattle, 1977; Poet-in-Residence, Oberlin College, Oberlin, Ohio, 1979, 1989; Visiting Professor, Department of English, Hebrew University, Jerusalem, Israel, 1983-84. Publications: The Floor Keeps Turning, 1970; Gold Country, 1973; From One Life to Another, 1979; Looking at Henry Moore's Elephant Skull Etchings in Jerusalem During the War, 1977, 2nd Edition, 1979, Hebrew Translation (Dan Pagis), 1980; Claims, 1984; Rivers of Salt, 1993; Roots in the Air: New and Selected Poems, 1996; Translations include: My Little Sister, from Hebrew of Abba Kovner, 1971, revised, 1986; The Light of Lost Suns: Selected Poems of Amir Gilboa, 1979; But What, Selected Poems of Judith Herzberg, from Dutch (with Judith Hersberg), 1988; Others. Contributions to: American Poetry Review; Atlantic; Field; Harper's; Iowa Review; Nation; New Republic; New Yorker; Poetry; Western Humanities Review. Honours: 1st Prize, Academy of American Poets, San Francisco State University, 1964; Discovery Award, Poetry Center, YM-YWHA, New York, 1967; US Award, International Poetry Forum, Pittsburgh, 1969; Fellowship, National Endowment For the Arts, 1979; Cecil Hemley Memorial Award, 1985; Alice Fay Di Castagnola Award, 1989, Shelley Memorial Award, 1991, Poetry Society of America. Memberships: Poetry Society of America; PEN, Israel. Address: 7 Rashba Street, 92264 Jerusalem, Israel.

KAUL Madan Lel, b. 11 Aug 1923, Srmagar, Kashmir, India. College Teacher. m. Srat Gange Kaul, 9 May 1955, 2 sons, 1 daughter. Education: MA, English and Political Science; Bachelor of Teaching, 1950. Appointments: Teacher, 1948-49; Headmaster, High School, Fazilka; Government School Lecturer, 1950-58; College Professor, 1960-81. Publications: The Home Coming, 1992-93; The Pilgrimage, 1994-95. Contributions to: The Tribune; Indian Express; Poetcrit. Address: Taraniwas Depot, Bazar, Dharamasala, Humaschal Pradesh, India.

KAVANAGH P(atrick) J(oseph), b. 6 Jan 1931, England. Writer. m. (1) Sally Philipps, 1956, dec, (2) Catherine Ward, 1965, 2 sons. Education: Douai School; Lycèe Jaccard, Lausanne; MA, Merton College, Oxford. Appointments: British Council, 1957-59; Actor, 1959-70; Member, Kingham Committee of Enquiry into English Language, 1986-88. Publications: One and One, 1960; On the Way to the Depot, 1967; About Time, 1970; Edward Thomas in Heaven, 1974; Life Before Death, 1979; Selected Poems, 1982; Presences (new and selected poems), 1987; An Enchantment, 1991; Collected Poems, 1992; Voices in Ireland, 1994; Autobiography: The Perfect Stranger, 1966; Editor: Collected Poems of Ivor Gurney, 1982; Co-Editor, Oxford Book of Short Poems, 1985; The Bodley Head G K Chesterton, 1985;

Selected Poems of Ivor Gurney, 1990; A Book of Consolations, 1992. Contributions to: Columnist, The Spectator, 1983-. Honours: Richard Hillary Prize, for The Perfect Stranger, 1966; FRSL, 1986; Cholmondeley Poetry Prize for Collected Poems, 1993. Address: c/o A D Peters, The Chambers, Chelsea Harbour, London SW10 0XF, England.

KAVOUNAS Alice Juno, b. 7 July 1945, New York, New York, USA. Writer. m. Frederick Taylor, 20 May 1988, 1 stepson, 2 stepdaughters. Education: BA, English Literature, Vassar College, Poughkeepsie, New York, 1966. Appointments: Writer: Poetry, Short Stories and TV; Advertising Copywriter, New York City and London. Publications: 1st collection of poems, The Invited, 1995. Contributions to: Bananas; New Poetry 7, 9; Wordlife; Times Literary Supplement; London Magazine; Poetry Book Society Winter Supplement; London Review of Books; New England Review-Bread Loaf Quarterly; Poetry Now, BBC Radio 3. Memberships: Poetry Society, London; Society of Authors. Literary Agent: Jane Turnball, 13 Wendell Road, London W14. Address: Vallier, Trevalsoe, St Keverne, Cornwall TR12 6NU, England.

KAWAR Jamal, b. 1930, Nazareth, Israel. Education: BA, Haifa University; MA, Hebrew University, Jerusalem; PhD, Syntatic Analysis of the Glorious Quran, Tel-Aviv University. Appointments: Joined Democratic Arab Party, elected Member of the Executive Committee, and heading the Cultural Department; Teacher, Arabic Faculty in Haifa. Publications: 12 Collections of poetry; Editor, Elmawakib, monthly magazine in Arabic. Contributions to: Many articles on Arabic topics. Membership: Chairman, Palestinian Writers and Poets Association, Israel, 1988-. Address: International PEN - Israel, The Writers House, 6 Kaplan Street, Tel-Aviv, Israel.

KAWINSKI Wojciech, b. 22 May 1939, Poland. Poet. m. Helena Lorenz, 17 Apr 1964, 1 son, 1 daughter. Education: MA, 1964. Appointment: Sub-Director, Pismo Literacko-Artystyczne, 1985-89. Publications: Odleglosci Posluszne, 1964; Narysowane We Wnetrzu, 1965; Ziarno Rzeki, 1967; Pole Widzenia, 1970; Spiew Bezimienny, 1978; Pod Okiem Slonca, 1980; Listy Do Ciebie, 1982; Milosc Nienawistna, 1985; Ciemna strona jasnosci, 1989; Wieczorne sniegi, 1989; Czysty zmierzch, 1990; Pamiec zywa, 1990; Zwierciadlo sekund, 1991; Srebro lisei, 1993; Zelazna rosa, 1995. Contributions to: Numerous journals and magazines including: Echo Krakowa; Wiez; Metafora. Honours: Prize, City of Cracow, 1985; Red Rose Prize for Poetry, Gdansk, 1985; Prize KI Janicki, Bydgoszcz, 1995. Membership: Polish Writers Association. Address: ul Stachiewicza 22a, 31-303 Krakow, Poland.

KAY Jackie, b. 9 Nov 1961, Edinburgh, Scotland. Writer; Arts Administrator. 1 son. Education: BA Honours, English. Appointments: Writer-in-Residence, Hammersmith, London, 1988-90; Literature Touring Coordinator, Arts Council, 1990-92. Publications: The Adoption Papers, 1991; Two's Company, 1992. Contributions to: Poetry Review; Spare Rib; Conditions; Poetry Wales; Chapman; Rialto; Poetry matters; London Poetry Newsletter; City Limits. Honours: Eric Gregory Society of Authors Award, 1991; Book Award, Scottish Arts Council. Memberships: Poetry Society; Writers Guild. Address: 62 Kirkton Road, London N15 5EY, England.

KAZANTZIS Judith, b. 14 Aug 1940, Oxford, England. Poet; Fiction Writer. 1 son, 1 daughter. Education: Honours Degree, Modern History, Oxford, 1961. Publications: Poetry Collections: Minefield, 1977; The Wicked Queen, 1980; Touch Papers (co-author), 1982; Let's Pretend, 1984; Flame Tree, 1988; A Poem for Guatemala, pamphlet, 1988; The Rabbit Magician Plate, 1992; Selected Poems 1977-92, 1995. Contributions to: Stand; London Magazine; New Statesman; Poetry Review; Ambit; Verse; Honest Ulsterman; Bete Noire; Key West Reader; Faber Book of Blue Verse; Virago Book of Love Poetry. Memberships: Poetry Society; Labour Party. Literary Agent: A P Watt. Address: 9 Avondale Park Gardens, London W11 4PR, England.

KEARNS Lionel John, b. 16 Feb 1937. Writer; Consultant in Interactive Media. m. 31 Dec 1981, 4 sons, 1 daughter. Publications: Songs of Circumstances, 1963; Pointing, 1967; By the Light of the Silvery McLune: Media Parables, Poems, Signs, Gestures, and Other Assaults on the Interface, 1968; Practising Up to Be Human, 1978; Ignoring the Bomb, 1982; Convergences, 1985. Address: 1616 Charles Street, Vancouver, BC V5L 2T3, Canada.

KEARNS MORALES Rick, b. 3 Feb 1958, Harrisburgh, Pennsylvania, USA. Writer; Teacher. m. Ziza Almeido, 15 Oct 1989. Education: BA, Spanish, Millersville University of Pennsylvania, 1984; MS, Journalism, Columbia University School of Journalism, 1986. Appointments: Freelance Writer, Musician, 1988-; Instructor, Creative Writing, Pennsylvania School of Art & Design, 1992-95; Political Reporter, El Hispano Newspaper, 1994-; Instructor, Poetry of Protest of Latin America, Rutgers University, New Jersey, 1995-. Publications: Street of Knives, 1993; ALOUD - Voices from the Nuyorican Poets Cafe, anthology, 1995; In Defense of Mumia, anthology, 1996. Contributions to: Chicago Review; Massachusetts Review; Drum Voices; On the Bus. Memberships: Coordinator, Paper Sword Writers Organization, 1988-94; Board Member, Harrisburg Artists Factory, 1995-. Address: 3022 North Fifth Street, Harrisburg, PA 17110, USA.

KEELEY Edmund, b. 5 Feb 1928, Syria. Writer; Professor of English and Creative Writing. m. 18 Mar 1951. Education: BA, Princeton, 1949; DPhil, Oxford University, 1952. Appointments: Fulbright Teacher, American Farm School, Thessaloniki, Greece, 1949-50; Instructor, Brown University, 1952-53; Fulbright Lecturer, English and American Literature, University of Thessaloniki, 1953-54; Instructor, Assistant Professor, Associate Professor, Professor, Programme Director, Princeton University, 1954-; Several visiting appointments. Publications: The Libation, 1958; The Gold-Hatted Lover, 1961; Vassilis Vassilikos: The Plant, The Well, The Angel (with Mary Keeley), 1964; The Imposter, 1970; C P Cavafy: Passions and Ancient Days (with George Savidis), 1971; Modern Greek Writers (edited with Peter Bien), 1972; Voyage to a Dark Island, 1972; Odysseus Elytis: The Axion Esti (with George Savidis), 1974; Cavafy's Alexandria, 1976, revised 1996; Odysseus Elytis: Selected Poems (edited with Philip Sherrard), 1981; Yannis Ritsos: Return and Other Poems 1967-72, 1983; Modern Greek Poetry: Voice and Myth, 1983; Yannis Ritsos: Exile and Return: Selected Poems 1967-74, 1985; The Dark Crystal: Poems by Cavafy, Sikelianos, Seferis, Elytis, Gatsos, 1981; A Wilderness Called Peace, 1985; The Salonika Bay Murder, 1989; The Essential Cavafy, 1995. Honours: Rome Prize, American Academy of Arts and Letters, 1959; Selection Pushcart Prize IX, 1984-85; 1st European Prize, Poetry Translation, 1987; Honorary Doctorate, Athens University, 1994. Memberships: Poetry Society of America; PEN American Center; American Literary Translators Association. Address: 140 Littlebrook Road, Princeton, NJ 08540, USA.

KEEN Suzanne Parker, b. 10 Apr 1963, Bethlehem, Pennsylvania, USA. Assistant Professor of English. m. Francis MacDonnell, 7 Jun 1992. Education: AB, English, Studio Art, 1984, AM, Creative Writing, 1986, Brown University; PhD, English and American Literature, Harvard University, 1990. Appointments: Assistant Professor of English, Yale University, New Haven, Connecticut, 1990-95; Assistant Professor of English, Washington and Lee University, Lexington, Virginia, 1995-. Contributions to: Agni; Anthology of New England Writers; Anthology: On The Verge - Emerging Poets and Artists, 1994; Chelsea; Clerestory; English Journal; Graham House Review; Notus: New Writing; Ohio Review. Honours: Prize, Pawtucket Arts Council, 1985; Kim Ann Arstark Poetry Prize, Brown University, 1985; Academy of American Poets Prize, Harvard University, 1987; 2nd Prize, New England Poetry Competition, 1991. Memberships: MLA; Society for the Study of Narrative Literature. Address: Department of English, Washington and Lee University, Lexington, VA 24450, USA.

KEENEY Patricia, b. 21 June 1943, England. Editor; Critic; Teacher of Creative Writing. Education: BA, McGill University; MA, Sir George Williams University; Doctoral Work, University of Sussex. Appointments: Poetry Editor and Features Writer, Cross Canada Writers' Quarterly and the Canadian Forum; Columnist, Canadian Poetry Review. Publications: Swimming Alone, 1988; New Moon, Old Mattress, 1990; The New Pagans, 1991; The Book of Joan, 1994; Selected Poems, 1996; The Incredible Shrinking Wife, novel, 1995; Anthologies: Landscape, 1977; Other Channels, 1984; The Oberon Poetry Collection, 1992; Borderlines, 1995; The Incredible Shrinking Wife, 1995; Engenderings: Selected Works, 1996. Contributions to: Canadian Literature; Canadian Literature; Canadian Forum; Maclean's Magazine. Membership: International Editorial Board of Unesco's World Encyclopedia of Contemporary Theatre; League of Canadian Poets, Chair International Committee. Address: 42 Manor Road East, Toronto, Ontario M4S 1P8, Canada.

KELL Richard Alexander, b. 1 Nov 1927, Youghal, County Cork, Ireland. Teacher. m. Muriel Adelaide Nairn, 31 Dec 1953, 2 sons, 2 daughters. Education: BA, 1952, Higher Diploma in Education, 1953, University of Dublin. Appointments: Teacher and Librarian, 1953-59; Lecturer in English, Isleworth Polytechnic, England, 1960-70; Senior Lecturer in English, Newcastle-upon-Tyne Polytechnic, 1970-83; Joint Editor, Other Poetry, 1994. Publications: Control Tower, 1962; Differences, 1969; The Broken Circle, 1981; In Praise of Warmth, 1987; Rock and Water, 1993. Contributions to: PN Review; Encounter; Spectator; Listener; Stand; Irish Press; Irish Times. Address: 18 Rectory Grove, Gosforth, Newcastle-upon-Tyne NE3 1AL, England.

KELLBERG Joyce Eileen, b. 24 Oct 1947, Spokane, Washington, USA. Cashier. Appointments: Bookkeeper-Teller, Orofino Office, Idaho First National Bank, Orofino, Idaho, USA, 1967-77; Teller, Coeur d'Alene Office, The Idaho First National Bank, Coeur d'Alene, Idaho, USA, 1977-78; Teller, Equitable Savings and Loan Assurance Ltd, Coeur d'Alene, Idaho, 1979; Cashier, Pay 'N' Save Drug Stores Inc, Spokane, Washington, Parkade Plaza Stores 1979-88, Franklin Park Plaza Store 1988-89, Riverpark Square Store 1989-94; Cashier, Payless Drug Store Inc, Spokane, Washington, 1994-. Publications: Perspectives, 1995; Shadows and Light, 1996; Treasured Poems of America, 1996; Endless Harmony, 1996; Our Captured Moments, 1996; Recollections of Yesterday, 1996; The Best Poems of the 90's, 1996; Meditations, 1996. Honours: Editors Choice Award, 1996; Accomplishment of Merit, 1996. Memberships: International Society of Poets, 1996; The National Authors Registry, 1997. Address: POB 9001, Spokane, WA 99209, USA.

KELLER David Michael, b. 26 May 1941, Berkeley, California, USA. Poet. Education: AB, Harvard College, 1964; Iowa State College, 1962; AM, PhD, University of Wisconsin, 1964-73. Appointments include: Director of Admissions, Frost Place Festival of Poetry, 1980-; Consultant, Geraldine R Dodge Foundation, 1986-91. Publications: Starting-Points (with Donald Sheehan), 1066; Circling the Site (Annex 21), 1982; A New Room, 1987; Land That Wasn't Ours, 1989. Contributions to: Poetry; Poetry Northwest; Ohio Review; Ironwood; Prairie Schooner; Missouri Review; High Plains Literary Review; Pequod; Ploughshares; Poetry East; Poetry Miscellany. Honours: Grants for Poetry, 1979, 1982, 1992, Artistic Merit Grant, 1985, New Jersey State Council on the Arts; Best Poem in The Indiana Review, 1985; Colladay Award, QRL, 1989. Memberships: Board of Governors, Poetry Society of America, 1989-92; Board of Advisors, Poet's House, Northern Ireland; Staff Poet, Eldridge Park Artists/Clark Kent Troupe; Macedonians. Address: 151 Hughes Avenue, Lawrenceville, NJ 08648, USA.

KELLER Johanna, b. 26 Apr 1955, Ahoskie, North Carolina, USA. Writer; Librettist. Education: MMus Honours, University of Colorado, 1977; MA, Creative Writing/Poetry, Antioch University, 1996. Appointments: Workshop teacher, The Writers Voice, New York, Northern Westchester Center, Mount Kisco, Putnam Valley Schools and Newport Writers Conference. Publications: Moose, chapbook, 1995; Libretto, adaptation of Mark Twain's The War Prayer (with David Sampson), world premiere at Princeton University, 1995. Contributions to: Dark Horse (Scotland); Voices (Israel); US journals: Southwest Review; Chelsea; Plum Review; Pivot; Nimrod; Negative Capability; Connecticut Review; Reviewer for Antioch Review. Honours: Grand Prize, Green River Writers National Contest, 1994; Grand Prize, Community Writers Association National Contest, 1995; Finalist, Randall Jarrell Poetry Prize, Ireland, 1996; Artist Fellowship, New York Foundation for the Arts, 1997; Ludwig Vogelstein Foundation Grant, 1997; Annual Editor's Award, Florida Review, 1997; Residency Fellowship, Ragdale Foundation, 1997. Address: c/o Howard Morhaim Literary Agency, 841 Broadway #604, New York, NY 10003, USA.

KELLEY Alita, b. 19 Nov 1932, Bradford, West Yorkshire, England. Teacher; Translator. m. (1) Carlos de Luchi Lomellini, 17 Sept 1951, (2) Alec E Kelley, 29 May 1970, 2 daughters. Education: BA, 1981; MA, 1986; PhD, 1992, University of Arizona. Appointments: Teacher of English, British Council, Lima, Peru, 1962-68; Teacher of Italian, US Embassy, Lima, Peru, 1967-68; Commercial Translator and Office Manager, Wiesman and Co, Tucson, Arizona, USA, 1969-92; Assistant Professor of Spanish and French, Pennsylvania State University, Delaware Co Campus, Media, Pennslyvania, USA, 1992-. Publications: Shared Images, 1981; Dreams of Samarkand, 1982; Ineffable Joys, 1983; Antimacassars, 1984; Target Practice, 1994; Spanish Versions of Poems by Jane Radcliffe; Lima Rooftops: Chants in Two Immigrant Languages, 1978. Contributions to: Aireings; Ambit;

Outposts; Haravec (Lima, Peru); Tribune (London); Writing Women; Poetry Nottingham; Global Tapestry; Pennine Platform. Memberships: American Literary Translation Association; Latin American Indian Literature Association. Address: 1086 King Road, MP-215, Malvern, PA 19355-1975, USA.

KELLY Connie, b. 21 Jan 1970, Oregon City, Oregon, USA. Cook. 2 sons. Education: Certificate of Culinary Arts, School of Applied Technology, 1996. Appointments: McDonalds, 1989-92; The Steak Escape, 1993-94; Idaho State University School of Applied Technology, 1996-. Publications: The Amherst Society, 1995; American Poetry Annual, 1995; JMW Publishing - Impressions and Rhyme & Reason; Iliad - Voices and Crossings and Meditations, 1995; National lbrary of Poetry, At Watersedge - Sparkies in the Sand, The Sound of Poetry Tape, 1995. Honours: Honorable Mention, Iliad Press, 1995; Certificate of Merit, Lyric Writing, Chapel Recording, 1996; Certificate of Publication, JMW Publishing, 1996. Address: 4317 Opal Avenue #6, Pocatello, ID 83204, USA.

KELLY Hannah. See: **HOBSBAUM Hannah.**

KELLY Jeanne Lin Smith, b. 4 Feb 1945, Corinth, Mississippi, USA. Teacher. m. 13 Aug 1966, 2 sons. Education: BA, 1966, MEd, 1981, Mississippi College; Additional coursework, University of Southern Mississippi, Auburn University, University of Mississippi. Appointments: Teacher, English, Forrest County Agricultural High School, 1966-69; Reference Librarian, Hattiesburg Public Library, 1969-70; Teacher, English, French, Greenville Christian School, 1971-72; Teacher, English, Goodwater High School, Alabama, 1976-78; Teacher, English and reading, Alexander City Junior High School, Alabama, 1978-79; Teacher, English, Chairman, English Department, Honours Programme Coordinator, Madison-Ridgeland Academy, Madison, Mississippi, 1979-95; English Instructor, Holmes Community College, Ridgeland, MS, 1995-. Publication: Scrapbook, Chapbook, 1995. Contributions to: Southern Poetry Review; Decision; Home Life; Living with Teenagers; Mississippi Poetry Journal. Honours: Recognition, Spring Contests, Mississippi Poetry Society, 1986-96. Membership: Central Branch President, Past Newsletter Editor, Past State 2nd Vice President, State President, Mississippi Poetry Society, 1995-96. Address: 315 Church Street, Madison, MS 39110, USA.

KELLY Leonard, (Levi Tafari), b. 24 June 1960, Liverpool, England. Self-Employed Writer and Performer; Former Chef. Education: CGIL 705, 706-1, 706-2, 707-2, RIPHH, NWRAC PCPC, Certificate in Spoken English, Colquitt St Technical College, Liverpool. Publications: Duboetry, 1987, 1988; Liverpool Experience, 1989; Rhyme Don't Pay, 1994. Honours: Blackpenmanship Award, 1982; Won Nomination for Liverpool Echo and Daily Post Awards, 1992-93, 1993-94. Memberships: Poetry Secretaire; Musicians Union. Address: 16 Dombey Street, Liverpool, Merseyside L8 5TL, England.

KELLY M T(erry). Novelist; Playwright; Poet. m. 2 sons. Education: BA English, Glendon College, 1970; BEd, University of Toronto, 1976. Appointments: Columnist, 1979-81, Reviewer, 1979-91, Globe and Mail; Contributing Interviewer, Imprint literary show, TV Ontario. Publications: I Do Remember the Fall, novel, 1978; Country You Can't Walk In, 1979; The More Loving One, novella and stories, 1980; The Ruined Season, novel, 1982; Country You Can't Walk In and Other Poems, 1984; A Dream Like Mine, novel, 1987; Breath Dances Between Them and Other Stories, 1991; Out of the Whirlwind, 1995. Contributions to: Toronto Life; Globe and Mail; Canadian Forum; Poetry, Chicago; Scotsman, Edinburgh; Weekend; Queen's Quarterly; Books in Canada; Saturday Night; Others; Anthologies: Canadian Literary Landmarks; Whales, A Celebration; Whale Sound; Un Dozen: 13 Canadian Poets; Prism International; Semna de Bellas Artes, Mexico; Others. Honours: Arts Grant 'A' Canada Council, 1996; Finalist, Best 1st Novel of the Year for I Do Remember the Fall, Books in Canada, 1978; Unbodied Souls nominated Best Short Story, National Magazine Awards, 1983; Toronto Arts Council Award for Poetry, 1986; Governor General's Award for Literature, Fiction, for A Dream Like Mine, 1987; 3 short term awards and Arts Grant B, Canada Council. Address: 60 Kendal Ave, Toronto, Ontario M5R 1L9, Canada.

KELLY Robert, b. 24 Sept 1935, Brooklyn, New York, USA. Professor of Literature; Poet; Writer. Education: AB, City College, New York City, 1955; Columbia University, 1955-58. Appointments: Editor, Chelsea Review, 1957-60, Matter magazine and Matter publishing,

1964-, Los 1, 1977; Lecturer, Wagner College, 1960-61; Founding Editor (with George Economou), Trobar magazine, 1960-64, Trobar Books, 1962-65; Instructor, 1961-64, Assistant Professor, 1964-69, Associate Professor, 1969-74, Professor of English, 1974-86, Director, Writing Programme, 1980-93, Asher B Edelman Professor of Literature, 1986-, Bard College; Assistant Professor, State University of New York, Buffalo, 1964; Visiting Lecturer, Tufts University, 1966-67; Poet-in-Residence, California Institute of Technology, Pasadena, 1971-72, University of Kansas, 1975, Dickinson College, 1976. Publications include: Poetry: Kali Yuga, 1971; Flesh: Dream: Book, 1971; Ralegh, 1972; The Pastorals, 1972; Reading Her Notes, 1972l; The Tears of Edmund Burke, 1973; Whaler Frigate Clippership, 1973; The Bill of Particulars, 1973; The Belt, 1974; The Loom, 1975; Sixteen Odes, 1976; The Lady of, 1977; The Convections, 1978; The Book of Persephone, 1978, revised edition, 1983; The Cruise of the Pnyx, 1979; Kill the Messenger Who Brings the Bad News, 1979; Sentence, 1980; The Alchemist to Mercury, 1981; Spiritual Exercises, 1981; Mulberry Women, 1982; Under Words, 1983; Thor's Thrush, 1984; Not This Island Music, 1987; The Flowers of Unceasing Coincidence, 1988; Oahu, 1988; A Strange Market, 1992; Mont Blanc, 1994; Fiction: Queen of Terrors: Fictions, 1994; Other: A Line of Sight, 1974. Honours: Los Angeles Times Book Prize, 1980; American Academy of Arts and Letters Award, 1986. Address: c/o Department of English, Bard College, Annandale-on-Hudson, NY 12504, USA.

KELLY Tom, b. 22 May 1947, Jarrow, Tyne and Wear, England. College Lecturer. m. Carol Kelly, 20 Dec 1969, dec, 1 daughter. Education: BA, Honours. Appointment: Lecturer, Further Education College. Publications: The Gibbetting of William Jobling, 1972; Still With Me, 1986; John Donne in Jarrow, 1993; Their Lives, 1993; Riddle of Pain, 1995. Contributions to: Stand; Iron; Orbis; Rialto; Staple; Hybrid; Samphire; Working Titles; Purple Patch; Oasis; Sepia; First Time; Exile; Intoprint; Tees Valley Writer; Krax; Harry's Hand; Foolscap; Eavesdroppper; Here Now; Tourism; Reid Review; Iota; Pennine Platform; Poetry Nottingham; Westwords; Third Half; Overspill. Address: 69 Wood Terrace, Jarrow, Tyne and Wear NE32 5LU, England.

KEMP Harry Vincent, b. 11 Dec 1911, Singapore. Poet; Mathematician. m. Alix Eiermann, 9 July 1941, 1 son, 1 daughter. Education: Clare College, Cambridge, 1931-34. Publications: The Left Heresy (with Laura Riding and Robert Graves), 1939; Ten Messengers (with Witold Kawalec), 1977; Verses for Heidi (illustrated by Harry Gordon), 1978; Collected Poems, 1985; Poems for Erato, 1980; Poems for Mnemosyne, 1993. Address: 6 Western Villas, Western Road, Crediton, Devon EX17 3NA, England.

KEMP Jan, b. 12 Mar 1949, Hamilton, New Zealand. University Teacher of English. Education: BA, 1970, MA, Hons 1974, University of Auckland; Diploma of Teaching 1972, Auckland Teachers' College; RSA Certificate (TEFL) 1984, The British Council, Hong Kong. Appointments: University of Papua New Guinea 1980-82; University of Hong Kong 1982-85; University of Singapore, 1985-. Publications: Against the Softness of Woman, 1976; Diamonds and Gravel, 1979; Ice-Breaker Poems, 1980; The Other Hemisphere, 1991. Contributions to: Landfall; Islands; New Zealand Listener; New Zealand Herald; Radio New Zealand; Westerly, Australia; Pivot, USA. Honours: Four Poets Tour, New Zealand, 1979; QEII Arts Council Poetry Representative at South Pacific Festival of Arts, Papua New Guinea, 1980; PEN/Stout Centre Fellowship, Victoria University of Wellington, New Zealand, 1991. Memberships: PEN International, New Zealand Centre; PEN International, Writers in Exile Centre, USA. Address: ELPU, National University of Singapore, 10 Kent Ridge Crescent, 0511 Singapore.

KENDALL Tina, b. 6 Jan 1958, Bradford, West Yorkshire, England. Freelance Writer, 2 sons, 1 daughter. Education: BA Hons. Modern Languages: BA, English; MA, French; MA, English; MA, Scriptwriting for Film and TV. Appointments: Editor, Spare Rib Magazine; University Teacher; Equal Opportunities Officer; Writer-in-Residence. Contributions to: Beautiful Barbarian; Naming the Wares; Feminist Arts News; Peterloo Poets; Hambone 10; Language of Water, Language of Fire; Onlywomen Press; Virago. Honours: Highly Commended: Peterloo Poetry Competition; Turning Point. Address: c/o Sheba Feminist Press, 10a Bradbury St, London N16 8JN, England.

KENNEDY Joseph Charles, (X J Kennedy), b. 21 Aug 1929, Dover, New Jersey, USA. Poet; Writer. m. Dorothy Mintzlaff, 31 Jan

1962, 4 sons, 1 daughter. Education: BSc, Seton Hall University, 1950; MA, Columbia University, 1951; University of Paris, 1956. Appointments: Teaching Fellow, 1956-60, Instructor, 1960-62, University of Michigan; Poetry Editor, The Paris Review, 1961-64; Lecturer, Women's College of the University of North Carolina, 1962-63; Assistant Professor to Professor, Tufts University, 1963-79. Publications: Nude Descending a Staircase, 1961; An Introduction to Poetry (with Dana Gioia), 1968, 8th edition, 1994; The Bedford Reader, 1982, 6th edition (with Dorothy Kennedy and Jane Aarron), 1997; Cross Ties, 1985; Dark Horses, 1992; 13 children's books. Contributions to: Newspapers and journals. Honours: Lamont Award, 1961; Los Angeles Times Book Award, 1985. Memberships: Authors Guild; John Barton Wolgamot Society; Modern Language Association; PEN. Address: Fern Way, Bedford, MA 01730, USA.

KENNEDY Margaret Mary Downing, b. 13 July 1933, Stourbridge, Worcestershire, England. m. James Kennedy, 2 Nov 1963, 3 daughters. Education: Secretarial College, 1950-51. Appointments: Various positions, Civil Service and Clerical Work. Contributions to: John L Londons Weekly; BBC Poetry Programmes; Orbis. Membership: John Clare Society. Address: 22 Bridlington Road, Ferryvale, Nigel, Transvaal, South Africa.

KENNELLY Brendan, b. 17 Apr 1936, Ballylongford, County Kerry, Ireland. Education: MA, Trinity College, Dublin, 1964. Appointment: Professor of Modern Literature, Trinity College, Dublin, 1973-. Publications: Let Fall No Burning Leaf, 1963; My Dark Feathers, 1964; Collection One: Getting Up Early, 1966; Selected Poems, 1971; Bread, 1971; Love-Cry, 1972; The Voices: A Sequence of Poems, 1973; New and Selected Poems, 1976; The Visitor, 1978; In Spite of the Wise, 1979; The Boats are Home, 1980; The House that Jack Didn't Build, 1982; Cromwell, 1983; Moloney Up and At It, 1984; A Time for Voices: Selected Poems 1960-90; Editor, The Penguin Book of Irish Verse, 1970, revised, 1981. Address: 19 St Alban's Park, Sandymount, Dublin 4, Ireland.

KENNET Lady Elizabeth Ann, b. 14 April 1923, London, England. Writer. m. Wayland Hilton Young (now Lord Kennet), 24 Jan 1948, 1 son, 5 daughters. Education: MA, Oxford. Publications: Time is as Time Does, poetry, 1958; Other subjects include: Architecture, Arms Control, Maritime and International Affairs. Contributions to include: Sunday Times; Botteghe Oscure, 1954, 1958; Springtime, anthology, 1953; Best Articles and Stories, Indiana, 1959; Parnassus of World Poets, 1994, 1995. Honour: European Federation Tourist Press's overalll prize, Libro Per Il Turismo, 1990. Literary Agent: Ingrid T Schick International, Widenmayerstrasse 24/25, Munich D-80538, Germany. Address: 100 Bayswater Road, London W2 3HJ, England.

KENNEY Richard Laurence, b. 10 Aug 1948, USA. Poet; Teacher. m. Mary F Hedberg, 4 July 1982, 2 sons. Education: BA, Dartmouth College, 1970. Appointment: Assistant Professor to Associate Professor to Professor, University of Washington, 1987-. Publications: The Evolution of the Flightless Bird, 1983; Orrery, 1984; The Invention of the Zero, 1993. Contributions to: New Yorker; Poetry; New England Review; Yale Review. Honours: Yale Series of Younger Poets Prize, 1982; J S Guggenheim Fellowship, 1984; Rome Prize in Literature, 1986; MacArthur Fellowship, 1987-92; Lannan Literary Award, 1994. Address: c/o Department of English Box 354330, University of Washington, Seattle, WA 98195, USA.

KENNY Adele, b. 28 Nov 1948, Perth Amboy, New Jersey, USA. Poet; Writer; Editor; Consultant. Education: BA, English, Newark State College, 1970; MS, Education, College of New Rochelle, 1982. Appointments: Artist-in-Residence, Middlesex County Arts Council, 1979-80; Poetry Editor, New Jersey ArtForm, 1981-83; Associate Editor, Muse-Pie Press, 1988-. Publications: An Archeology of Ruins, 1982; Illegal Entries, 1984; The Roses Open 1984; Between Hail Marys, 1986; Migrating Geese, 1987; The Crystal Keepers Handbook, 1988; Counseling Gifted, Creative and Talented Youth Through the Arts, 1989; Castles and Dragons, 1990; Questi Momenti, 1990; Starship Earth, 1990; We Become By Being, 1994; Staffordshire Spaniels, 1997. Contributions to: Periodicals. Honours: Writer's Digest Award, 1981; New Jersey State Council on the Arts Fellowships, 1982, 1987; Merit Book Awards, 1983, 1987, 1990; Roselip Award, 1988; Haiku Quarterly Award, 1989. Memberships: President, Haiku Society of America, 1987-88, 1990; Poetry Society of America; Allen Ginsberg Poetry Award, 1993. Address: 207 Coriell Avenue, Fanwood, NJ 07023, USA.

KENT (Alice) Jean (Cranley), b. 30 Aug 1951, Chinchilla, Queensland, Australia. Psychologist. m. Martin Kent, 8 Jan 1974. Education: BA, University of Queensland, 1971. Appointments: Guidance Assistant, Department of Guidance and Special Education, Brisbane, Queensland, 1971-72; Assistant to Careers Counsellor, Canberra College of Advanced Education, 1975; TAFE Counsellor, Department of Technical and Further Education, New South Wales, 1977-79, 1983-89; also Lift Driver, Bookshop Assistant, Invalid's Home Help, Member of a Craft Co-Operative (handpainting clothes) and Writer for an encyclopaedia. Publications: Verandahs, 1990; Practising Breathing, 1991. Contributions to: Australia: Sydney Morning Herald; Australian; Bulletin; Canberra Times; Age; Adelaide Review; Imago; Island; Outrider; Meanjin; Phoenix Review; Poetry Australia; Salt; Southerly; Westerly; Overland: USA: Antipodes; Anthologies; Mother I'm Rooted; Penguin Book of Australian Women Poets; The Mattara Prize Anthologies for 1982, 1987, 1991; The ABC/ABA Australian Bicentennial Anthology; The Tin Wash Dish; First Rights; A Decade of Island Magazine; Nimrod; Canada: Poetry Canada. Honours: For Books: Anne Elder Award, 1990; Mary Gilmore Award, 1991; Short-listed for New State Wales State Literary Awards, 1991; For Poems: John Shaw Neilson Prize, 1980, 1991; Patricia Hackett Prize, 1981, 1990; Anne Danckwerts Memorial Prize, 1986; National Library Award (joint winner), 1988; Henry Kendall Award, 1988, 1989. Memberships: Australian Society of Authors. Address: 2 Kilaben Road, Kilaben Bay, New South Wales 2283, Australia.

KERCEL Stephanie Ann (Dorcas Tabitha), b. 7 Sept 1949, Germany. Private Duty Nurses Aide. Education: Radford College, 1967-69. Contributions to: Logos; Christadelphian Tidings; Caribbean Pioneer. Membership: Federal Poets. Address: 7843 Audubon Avenue, Alexandria, VA 22306, USA.

KEREN Hillary. See: ALKALAY-GUT Karen Hillary.

KERN Canyon. See: RABORG Frederick Ashton, Jr.

KERNSTEIN Kimberly, b. 2 May 1966, Terre Haute, Indiana, USA. m. Robert Kernstein, 17 Nov 1984, 1 son. Publications: Fortune; I Like the Way He Looks at Me; The Other Side of Life; The Vigil; The Nameless. Honour: 4th Place, World Poetry Contest. Address: PO Box 157, New Goshen, IN 47863, USA.

KERR Kathryn Ann, (Leona Fisher, Willi Red Bear), b. 15 Aug 1946, St Louis, Missouri, USA. Writer; Editor. m. Thomas A Palmer, 7 July 1990, 1 daughter. Education: BA, Southern Illinois University, 1971; MS, Eastern Illinois University, 1984. Appointments: Teacher, Librarian, Botanist, Editor. Publications: First Frost; Equinox; Coneflower. Contributions to: Another Chicago Magazine; Ascent; Great River Review; Spoon River Quarterly, Spring House Ponchatrain Review; Thema. Honours: Pushcart Foundation Writers Choice; Illinois Wesleyan Univerity Poetry Prize; Illinois Arts Council Fellowship; Illinois Arts Council Poetry Award; Eastern Illinois University Poetry Award. Memberships: Red Herning Poets; Illinois Writers. Address: RT4, Box 693, Marion, IL 62959, USA.

KERR-SMILEY Justin Robert, b. 25 Apr 1965. Journalist. Education: BA Honours, University of Newcastle-upon-Tyne, 1987; Postgraduate Diploma, TV and Radio Journalism, London College of Printing, 1990; Bursary, BBC South and East. Appointments: Reporter, ABC Radio 2BL, Sydney, New South Wales, Australia, 1990-91; Reporter, Associated Press, London, England, 1991-. Publication: Love, Loss and Other Seasons. Contributions to: Hourglass; Frogspawn; Courier; Santiago, Chile: Sociedad de Poesia; Palabras y Letras; Lengua. Membership: Poetry Society. Address: 2A Newby Street, London SW8 3BG, England.

KERRIGAN Thomas Sherman, b. 15 Mar 1939, Los Angeles, California, USA. Lawyer. m. Victoria Elizabeth Thompson, 31 Jan 1980, 2 sons, 4 daughters. Education: Loyola University, 1964; University of California at Berkeley, 1957-61. Appointments: Editor, Hierophant Press, 1969-73; Deputy Attorney General, 1965-69; Associate, law firm of McLaughlin and Irvin, 1970-74; Partner, 1974-; Drama Critic, 1993-. Publications: Only Morning in her Shoes; Celebration; New Writing II; Branches Among the Stars, 1990. Contributions to: Aspect; California State Poetry Quarterly; Hawaii Review; Kansas Quarterly; Northstone Review; Southern Review; Wisconsin Review; Illuminations; Outposts Poetry Quarterly. Memberships: California Bar Association; American Bar Association; Yeats Society; Augustan Society; Board Directors, Irish-American Bar

Association; Board Directors, Ensemble Studio Theatre, Los Angeles. Address: 13122 Weddington Street, Sherman Oaks, CA 91401, USA.

KESRI. See: **SRINIVAS Krishna.**

KESSLER Jascha (Frederick), b. 27 Nov 1929, New York, New York, USA. Professor; Poet; Writer; Dramatist. m. 17 July 1950, 2 sons, 1 daughter. Education: BA, University of Heights College of New York University, 1950; MA, 1951, PhD, 1955, University of Michigan. Appointments: Faculty, University of Michigan, 1951-54, New York University, 1954-55, Hunter College, 1955-56, Hamilton College, 1957-61; Professor, University of California at Los Angeles, 1961-. Publications: Poetry: Whatever Love Declares, 1969; After the Armies Have Passed, 1970 In Memory of the Future 1976; Fiction: An Egyptian Bondage, 1967; Death Comes for the Behaviorist 1983; Classical Illusions: 28 Stories, 1985; Transmigrations: 18 Mythologems, 1985; Siren Songs and Classical Illusions (50 stories), 1992; Other: Plays; The Cave (opera libretto); Translations: The Magician's Garden: 24 Stories by Geza Csáth, 1980; Rose of Mother-of-Pearl, 1983; Bride of Acacias: The Poetry of Forugh Farrokhzad, 1983; Under Gemini: The Selected Poetry of Miklós Radnóti, 1985; Medusa: The Selected Poetry of Nicolai Kantchev, 1986; The Face of Creation: 23 Contemporary Hungarian Poets, 1988; Catullan Games, 1989. Honours: National Endowment for the Arts Fellowship, 1974; Rockefeller Foundation Fellowship, 1979; Hungarian PEN Cub Memorial Medal, 1979; George Soros Foundation Prize, 1989; California Arts Council Fellowship, 1993-94. Memberships: American Literary Translators Association; American Society of Composers, Authors, and Publishers; Poetry Society of America. Address: c/o Department of English, University of California at Los Angeles, Los Angeles, CA 90095, USA.

KHAIR Tabish, b. 21 Mar 1966, Ranchi, India. Journalist; Teacher. Education: BA, Honours, 1988; Diploma in Journalism, 1988; MA, 1992. Appointments: Part-time Teacher, Nazareth Academy, 1986; District Correspondent, 1986-87; Staff Correspondent, 1990-92, Times of India; Co-Editor, Cultural Academy, Gaya, 1987-89. Publications: My World, 1991; A Reporter's Diary, 1993; The Book of Heroes, 1995; An Angel in Pyjamas, novel, 1996. Contributions to: PEN, Indian edition; Mirror, Bombay; Debonair, Bombay; Times of India; Telegraph, Calcutta; Hindustan Times; Poetry Chronicle, Bombay; Economic Times; London Magazine; PN Review; Iron; Planet; Source, UK; Malvis, Madrid; Greens Magazine, USA; Poetry Feur und Eis; Aristos, USA; Journal of Poetry Society of India; PN Review; Orbis; Iron; Poetry Nottingham; Planet. Honours: British Council's All India Prize, 1996. Memberships: Poetry Society of India. Address: Roarsvej 14 St tv, 2000 Frederiksberg, Denmark.

KHALIL Muhammad. See: **LANGE Eugene Samuel.**

KHALVATI Mimi, b. 28 Apr 1944, Tehran, Iran. Writer; Theatre Director. 1 son, 1 daughter. Education: University of Neuchatel, Switzerland, 1960-62; Drama Centre, London, 1967-70; SOAS, University of London, 1991. Appointments: Director, Theatre Workshop, Tehran; Director, Theatre in Exile. Publications: Persian Miniature-A Belfast Kiss, 1990; In White Ink, 1991; Mirrorwork, 1995. Contributions to: Poetry Review; PN Review; Writing Women; Acumen; North; Writing Ulster; Poetry Durham; Poetry Matters; Rialto; Artrage; Envoi; New Spokes; Orbis; Anvil New Poets, 1990; New Women Poets, 1990; Camden New Voices, 1990. Honours: Joint Winner, Poetry Business Pamphlet Competition, 1989; Joint Winner, Afro Caribbean-Asian Prize, Peterloo Poets, 1990; Writers Award, Arts Council of England, 1994. Address: 130C Evering Road, London N16 7BD, England.

KHERDIAN David, b. 17 Dec 1931, Racine, Wisconsin, USA. Author; Poet. m. (1) Kato Rozeboom, 1968, div 1970, (2) Nonny Hogorgian, 17 Mar 1971. Education: BS, University of Wisconsin, 1965. Appointments: Literary Consultant, Northwestern University, 1965; Founder-Editor, Giligia Press, 1966-72; Rare Book Consultant, 1968-69; Lecturer, 1969-70, Fresno State College; Poet-in-the-Schools, State of New Hampshire, 1971; Editor, Ararat magazine, 1971-72; Director, Two Rivers Press, 1978-86; Founder-Editor, The Press at Butternut Creek, 1987-88. Publications include: A Song for Uncle Harry, 1989; The Cat's Midsummer Jamboree, 1990; The Dividing River/The Meeting Shore, 1990; On a Spaceship with Beelzebub: By a Grandson of Gurdjieff, 1990; The Great Fishing Contest, 1991; Friends: A Memoir, 1993; Junas's Journey, 1993; Asking the River, 1993; By Myself, 1993; My Racine,

1994; Lullaby for Emily, 1995; Editor: Visions of America by the Poets of Our Time, 1973; Settling America: The Ethnic Expression of 14 Contemporary Poets, 1974; Poems Here and Now, 1976; Traveling America with Today's Poets, 1976; The Dog Writes on the Window with His Nose and Other Poems, 1977; If Dragon Flies Made Honey, 1977; I Sing the Song of Myself, 1978; Beat Voices: An Anthology of Beat Poetry, 1995; Co-Editor: Down at the Santa Fe Depot: 20 Fresno Poets, 1970; Other: Various translations. Honours: Jane Addams Peace Award, 1980; Banta Award, 1980; Boston Globe/Horn Book Award, 1980; Lewis Carroll Shelf Award, 1980; Newbery Honor Book Award, 1980; Friends of American Writers Award, 1982. Membership: PEN. Address: Box 150, Spencertown, NY 12165, USA.

KHETAN Gulab, b. 3 Nov 1946, Kathmandu, Nepal. Compere; Editor; Journalist; Lyricist; Scriptwriter; Translator. m. Vimala Khetan, 1 d. Education: BCom, 1964. Appointments include: Chief News Editor, News Reader, Radio Nepal, 3 years; Announcer, Narrator, Programme Compere, including number international programmess; Chief Editor: Anmol Gyan Sangalo general knowledge monthly, Vishleshan weekly, Kathmandu; Deputy Editor, Aarth-Jagat fortnightly, Birganj Chamber of Commerce and Industry; Guest Editor, Kalpana literary magazine. Publications include: How to Analyse, booklet, 1960; Andhyaro Aakash Ko, Nepali poems, Aalok-Antaha Karan Ko, short stories, Jeevan Saar - Safalta Ka Khudkilaharu, essays, articles, Suryodaya, revolutionary poem, Samata-Padavali, Hindi couplets, 1990; Parichaya - Manav Ka Manav Se, Hindi articles, Manavata Ma Lakschya, Hindi articles on relig, spiritualism, philosophy, Introduction of Man to Man, in English, 1992-93; Chief Editor, SASCE Souvenir, 1988. Honours: Number 1sts including: 1st and only literary person to receive title of Sutra kavya ke janmadata from late Mahadevi Verma; 1st Nepali poet to attend The World Urdu Mushaira; 1st Nepali poet and writer with 3 books released at 1 function, 1990; Numerous titles including: Saraswat-samman, highest literary award and title, cultural and literary organisation, Benaras Hindu University, Varanasi, 1990; Life Member, PEN All India Centre; Songs recorded for Bangladeshi and Pakistani films; International Excellence Gold Awd, International Friendship; Nepal's Best News Reader Award, Lions Club, Adarshnagar; Number of other honours and awards. Memberships include: Executive Member, Nepalganj Chamber of Commerce and Industry; Treasurer, Nepal Red Cross Society, Banke Dist; Treasurer, Nepal Family Planning Association, Banke Dist; Director, Bheri Vyapar Company Ltd; Treasurer, Federation Nepalese Chamber of Commerce and Industry; Rotary International, Kathmandu; 3 Lions Clubs. Address: Gyaneshwar, Post Box 2975, Kathmandu, Nepal.

KIGHTLY Ross, b. 29 Sept 1945, Melbourne, Victoria, Australia. Teacher. m. Carol Ann Stoker, 20 Dec 1986, 3 sons, 2 daughters. Education: BA, Honours, 1966, Diploma in Education, 1967, Monash University. Contributions to: Scratch; Oennine Ink; Inshed; Pennine Platform; Weyfarers; Acumen; Iota; Poetry Nottingham; Orbis. Honours: 3rd Prize, Orbis-Rhyme International Poetry Competition, 1991; 3rd Prize, Southport Writers Circle Poetry Competition, 1992. Address: 1 Heathy Avenue, Holmfield, Halifax, West Yorkshire HX2 9UP, England.

KIKEL Rudy John, b. 23 Feb 1942, Brooklyn, New York, USA. Editor; Writer. Education: BA, St John's University, Jamaica, New York, 1963; MA, Pennsylvania State University, 1965; PhD, Harvard University, 1975. Appointments: Teacher, English, Suffolk University, Boston, Massachusetts, to 1975; Freelance Journalist; Currently Art, Lifestyle and Poetry Editor, Bay Windows weekly newspaper, Boston. Publications: Shaping Possibilities, 1980; Lasting Relations, 1984; Long Division, 1992; Gents, Bad Boys and Barbarians: New Gay Poetry, 1995. Contributions to: Kenyon Review; Massachusetts Review; Shenandoah; American Review; Ploughshares; Mouth of the Dragon; Tribe: An American Gay Journal. Honour: The Grolier Prize, 1977. Address: 62 Chandler Street No 1, Boston, MA 02116, USA.

KILLDEER John. See: **MAYHAR Ardath.**

KILLEEN Kevin, b. 31 Oct 1966, London, England. Writer; English Teacher. Education: Philosophy, Liverpool University, 1984-87. Appointments: Advice Worker, Toxteth Citizens Advice Bureau, Liverpool, 1987-90; Teacher, Jamu Music and Drama Academy, Brno, Czechoslovakia, 1990-92; Poetry, Writing, Radio Prague, 1992. Publication: Evictions from the Nursery, 1989. Contributions to: Prague Post; Lidova Npveny, translations into Czech; Ambit; Poetry Now. Memberships: Organiser, Prague Radio Poetsl

Everyman Poetry Society. Liverpool; Former Organiser, Pilgrim Poets, Liverpool. Address: 116 Empire Avenue, London N18 1AG, England.

KILLICK (Edward) John, b. 18 July 1936, Southport, Merseyside, England. Teacher in Further, Adult and Prison Education. m. Carole Lesley Forrow, 5 Oct 1963, 1 son, 2 daughters. Education: Teacher's Certificate, Garnett College, 1965; BA, General Arts, Open University, 1979. Appointments: Vice-Principal for Adult Education, 1976-79; Deputy Education Officer, HMP Canterbury, 1979-80; Education Officer, HMDC Buckley Hall, Rochdale, 1980-83; Education Officer, HMP Drake Hall, Stafford, 1983-90; Editor, Littlewood Press, 1982-90; Editor, Littlewood Arc Press, 1990-92; Writer in Residence, HMP New Hall, Wakefield, 1990-92; Writer in Residence, Westminster Health Care, 1992-96. Publications: Continuous Creation, 1979; A Pennine Chain, 1983; Things Being Various, 1987; Singular Persons, 1988; The Times of Our Lives, 1994; Between the Lines Between the Bars, 1994; Would You Please Give Me Back My Personality, 1994; Openings - Dementia Poems, 1996; Wind-Horse, 1996. Contributions to: Times Literary Supplement; Scotsman; Lines Review; Poetry Review; PN Review; London Magazine; Green Book; North. Memberships: Former Adviser to Yorkshire Arts Association; Past Chairperson and Secretary, National Association of Writers in Education; Past Manager of Poetry Book Society; Past Member of Home Office's Arts in Prison Advisory Group. Address: 5 Slater Bank, Hebden Bridge, West Yorkshire HX7 7DY, England.

KIM Chol, b. 8 Aug 1941, Busan, Korea. Management Innovator. m. Kang Myong Ja, 29 Jan 1978, 1 son, 1 daughter. Education: Seoul National University, 1960. Appointment: Manager, 1991-. Contributions to: Columnist, Daewoo Motor Company. Honours: New Spring Literature Contest Prize; Korean Literature Translation Prize. Memberships: Korean Literary Persons Association; Korean Modern Poets Association; Poetic Coterie. Address: c/o Kang Moon-Shoo 205-52, 29 Tong 3 Ban, Mun-Hyun 3 dong, Nam-ku, Busan 608 0043, Korea.

KIM Unsong (William Soo), b. 1 Sept 1924, Seoul, Korea. Retired Professor. m. Sue, 17 Jan 1947, 4 sons. Education: BS, Seoul University, 1949; MS, University of Wisconsin, 1956; PhD, 1958; Hon DLitt, World Academy, Arts and Culture, 1991. Appointments: Assistant Professor, Michigan State University, 1958-59; Fellow, NASA Ames Research Centre, 1962-66; Fellow, Max Planck Institute, Germany, 1966-69; Professor, Yonsei University, Seoul, 1970-83. Publications: 100 Korean Poems; Classical Korean Poems; Search of Life; Hyangga; Poems by Mao Tsetung; Lao Tzu's Tao Teaching Lyrical; Anthology of Korean Poets in China selected and translated by Kim Unsong, 1993; Poems of Modern Sijo. Contributions to: Chosen Times; Korean American Journal; New Korea; American Poetry Anthology; New York Poetry Foundation Anthology; Poetry USA. Honour: 1st Prize, World Poetry Society. Memberships: World Poetry Society; International Poets Academy; World Congress of Poets; California Federation of Chaparral Poets; Korean Literary of America. Address: 120 Lassen Drive, San Bruno, CA 94066, USA.

KIM Yang Shik (Cho-ee), b. 4 Jan 1931, Seoul, Korea. Poet; Essayist; Translator. m. Ho Sok Chai, 15 Nov 1954, 1 son, 1 daughter. Education: BA, Ewha Women's University, 1954; Ma, Dong Kuk University, 1977. Publications: Legend of Jongup Fusa; Birds Sunrise; The Village of Magpies, Essays: Encounter with the World Poets; Modern Indian Literature; Crescent Moon. Contributions to: Newspapers and journals. Honours: 1st prize, Current Literature; Modern Korean Poetry Prize. Memberships: Modern Poetry Association; Korean Writers Association; Korean Women Writers Association; International Pen club; Tagore Society of Korea. Address: 3-1 Dongsan Villa, 1492-13 Sochdong, Seoul 137 070, Korea.

KIM Young-Sam, b. 1922, Korea. m. Jeng Chan Su, 1 son, 4 daughters. Appointments: Professor, Korean National University, 1953-86; National Policy Consulting Committee, President, Chief, Free Korea Press, 1985-. Publications: Modern Art; Life of Kim So Woll; Life of Kim Marie; Blue Island; Planet of Resistance; Dao dong Riverside; Love Song of Aran; Story of the Bear Women; Sonnet; 100 Volumes, 1988; Little Love Song of Shulam; The Encyclopedia of Korean Poetry. Honours: Award of May Literature; Award of Korean LIterature; MM Award; No San Literature Award of Korea; Award of Excellent Writer, 1987; World Poets Award, 1987-88; World Poets Conference, 1988, 1990. Memberships: PEN; National Poets Committee; President, World Poetry Research Institute, World Poets Club. Address: 1408 1 Dong Lucky A, Yulrang Dong, Cheongju 360, Korea.

KIND Anne, b. 16 May 1922, Berlin, Germany. Nurse; Administrator; Fundraiser. m. Robert William Kind, 26 July 1943, 1 son, 1 daughter. Education: Northern Polytechnic, Holloway, London, 1938-39; Kettering General Hospital, 1941-43. Appointments: Nursery Nurse; Student Nurse; Secretary then Branch Organiser, Family Planning Association; Administrator, LOROS, Leicester Organisation for Setting up a Hospice. Publications: Come and See This Folks, Biography of Jack Otter, 1994; Self-published: View in a Rear Mirror; Selective Memories. Contributions to: Stand; Weyfarer; Staple; E Midlands Arts; Dalesman; Scarlet Women; Mementum; Poet's England. Honours: Officer of the Order of the British Empire, 1990; Long Eaton Festival 3rd Prize, 1982; Staple Competition Runner-up, 1986; Cooperative Poetry Festival, 1989. Membership: Poetry Society; Leicester Poetry Society. Address: 8 Ridge Way, Oadby, Leicester LE2 5TN, England.

KING Charles, b. 29 Oct 1919, Edinburgh, Scotland. School Teacher. m. Vera Gall Thomson, 5 Apr 1956, 1 son, 2 daughters. Education: MA, Honours, Edinburgh University; Diploma in Education, 1951. Publications: Twelve Modern Scottish Poets, Editor, 1971; Twelve More Modern Scottish Poets, Co-editor, 1986; A Toosht o'Whigmalleries, Publisher, editor, 1991. Contributions to: Reviews on Scottish poetry to: Teaching English; The Use of English; Akros; Lines Review. Memberships: past Secretary, Scottish Branch, English Association; Former Council Member, Association of Scottish Literary Studies; Councillor, Grampian Regional Council, Aberdeen, 1986-94. Address: Hammerfield Publishing, 36 Hammerfield Avenue, Aberdeen AB10 7FJ, Scotland.

KING (Elizabeth) Ann (Ivy), b. 27 July 1959, Bruce, Mississippi, USA. Public Librarian; Freelance Children's Writer. m. Michael A King, 3 Sept 1981, 1 son. Education: University of Mississippi, 1981. Appointments: Director, Blackmur Memorial Library; Branch Head Librarian, Jesse Yancy Memorial Library. Publications: Heartsong: A Treasury of Verse. Contributions to: Mississippi Poetry Society Journal; NFSPS Journal. Honours: Mississippi State Poetry Contest; Epitaph Category NFSPS Contest. Memberships: Mississippi Poetry Society; National Federation of State Poetry Societies; National Association for the Preservation and Perpetuation of Storytelling. Address: PO Box 80, Bruce, MS 38915, USA.

KING Joy Rainey, b. 5 Aug 1939, Memphis, Tennessee, USA. Retired. m. Guy R King, 24 Dec 1956, 1 son, 1 daughter. Appointments: 4 years in banking; 10 years as medical secretary; 1 year as book keeper. Publications to: From the Gazebo, 1995. Contributions to: Best Poems of 1995, Best Poems of 1996, National Library of Poetry; World's Largest Poem for Peace; Upsouth magazine; Parnassus of World Poets, India; Sparrow International, Croatia; Amber, Nova Scotia; Amber, Nova Scotia; Planetaria Multilingual Anthology, Italy; Sounds of Poetry, the stereo album issued by the National Library of Poetry. Also in numerous anthologies in USA. Honours: Editor's Choice Award, National Library of Poetry, 1993, 1994, 1995, 1996; Also recorded in Sounds of Poetry from the National Library of Poetry. Memberships: The Poet's Guild; Southern Illinois Writer's Guild; Internatonal Society of Poets; The International Poetry Hall of Fame Museum on the Internet. Address: 3029 Willow Branch, Herrin, IL 62948, USA.

KING Robert, b. 6 Dec 1937, Denver, Colorado, USA. University Professor. Div, 1 son, 2 daughters. Education: BA, 1959, PhD, 1965, University of Iowa; MA, Colorado State University, 1961. Appointments: Assistant Professor, Alaska Writers Workshop, University of Alaska, 1965-68; Associate Professor, New School for Studies in Education, 1968-72; Professor, Department of english, 1972-, University of North Dakota. Publications: Standing Around Outside, 1979; A Circle of Land, 1990. Contributions to: Ascent; Kansas Quarterly; Painted Bride Quarterly; North Dakota Quarterly; Green Mountain Review; Anthologies: As Far As I Can See: Contemporary Writing of the Middle Plains, 1989; Beyond Borders: An Anthology of New Writing from Manitoba, Minnesota, Saskatchewan, and the Dakotas, 1992. Memberships: College Chairman, University of North Dakota, Academy of American Poets Poetry Prize; Co-Coordinator, Annual University of North Dakota Writers Conference. Address: Department of English, Box 7029, University Station, University of North Dakota, Grand Forks, ND 58202, USA.

KINLOCH David, b. 21 Nov 1959, Glasgow, Scotland. University Lecturer. Education: MA, Glasgow University, 1982; DPhil, Balliol College, Oxford, 1986. Appointments: Junior Research Fellow, St

Anne's College, Oxford, 1985-87; Research Fellow, University of Wales, 1987-89; Lecturer, University of Salford, 1989-90; Lecturer, 1990, Senior Lecturer, 1994, University of Strathclyde; Editor, Southfields Magazine. Publications: Co-Author, Other Tongues, 1990; Dustie-Fute, 1992; Paris-Forfar, Poems, 1994. Contributions to: London Magazine; New Writing Scotland; Cencrastus; Edinburgh Review; Jacarandah Review; Gairfish; Lines Review; Verse. Honour: Prize Winner in Poems Made Manifest Competition, 1992. Membership: Founder/Co-Editor, Verse Poetry Magazine. Address: Department of Modern Languages, University of Strathclyde, Glasgow, Scotland.

KINNELL Galway, b. 1 Feb 1927, Providence, Rhode Island, USA. Writer. 1 son, 1 daughter. Education: Princeton University. Publications: What a Kingdom it Was, 1960; Flower Herding on Mount Monadnock, 1963; Body Rags, 1966; Black Light (novel), 1966; The Book of Nightmares, 1971; The Avenue Bearing the Initial of Christ into the New World, 1974; Mortal Acts, Mortal Words, 1980; Selected Poems, 1982; How the Alligator Missed Breakfast, 1982; The Past, 1985; When One Has Lived a Long Time Alone, 1990; Imperfect Thirst, 1994; Translations: The Poems of François Villon, 1965; On the Motion and Immobility of Douve, 1968; The Lackawanna Elegy, 1970; Interviews: Walking Down the Stairs, 1977. Honours: Award, National Institute of Arts and Letters, 1962; Cecil Hemley Poetry Prize, 1969; Medal of Merit, 1975; Pulitzer Prize, 1983; National Book Award, 1983; MacArthur Fellowship, 1984; Vermont State Poet, 1989-93. Memberships: PEN; Poetry Society of America; National Institute of Arts and Letters; Poets House. Address: RFD, Sheffield, VY 05866, USA.

KINSELLA John, b. Perth, Western Australia. Poet. Education: University of Western Australia. Appointments: Full Time Writer; Editor, Literary Journal, Salt; Publisher, Editor, Folio (Salt). Publications include: Night Parrots, 1989; Eschatologies, 1991; Full Fathom Five, 1993; Syzygy, 1993; The Silo: A Pastoral Symphony, 1995; Erratum/Frame(d), 1995; The Undertow: New and Selected Poems, 1996. Contributions to: Newspapers and literary journals in Australia, USA, England, New Zealand, Canada and India. Honours: Creative Development Grants, Western Australian Department of The Arts, 1992, 1993; Category A and B Fellowships, The Literature Board of The Australia Council, 1993, 1995; Young Australian Creative Fellowship, for Outstanding Artistic Contribution to the Nation, 1996; Special Conference Allocation from The Literature Board of The Australia Council to perform at The Cambridge Conference of Contemporary Poetry, 1995; Shortlisted, Western Australia Premier's Award, 1990, 1992; Shortlisted, 1992 New South Wales Premier's Award; Winner, 1993 Washington Premier's Award; Winner, 1993 Harri-Jones Memorial Award; 1996 John Bray Award for Poetry. Address: PO Box 202, Applecross, Western Australia 6153, Australia.

KINSELLA Thomas, b. 4 May 1928, Dublin, Ireland. Poet; Teachers. m. Eleanor Walsh, 27 Dec 1955, 1 son, 2 daughters. Publications: Another September, 1958; Downstream, 1962; Nightwalker, 1969; Fifteen Dead, 1979; One and Other Poems, 1979; Peppercanister Poems, 1969-79; Blood and Family, 1988; Translations: The Tain, 1969; Poems of the Dispossessed, 1981; Editor, New Oxford Book of Irish Verse (with all new translations from the Irish), 1986. Contributions to: Numerous journals and magazines. Honours: Guiness Poetry Award, 1958; Choice of Poetry Book Society, 1958, 1962; Denis Devlin Memorial Award, 1966, 1969; Guggenheim Fellowships, 1968-69, 1971-72. Memberships: Irish Academy of Letters, Council 1979; Patron, Dublin Arts Festival; Director, Cuala Press. Address: 47 Percy Lane, Dublin 4, Ireland.

KINZIE Mary, b. 30 Sept 1944, Montgomery, Alabama, USA. Poet; Editor; Critic; Teacher. 1 daughter. Education: BA, Northwestern University, 1967; Free University of Berlin, 1967-68; The Johns Hopkins University, MA, 1972, PhD 1990. Appointments: Executive Editor, Tri Quarterly Magazine, 1975-78; Instructor, Northwestern University, 1975-78; Lecturer 1978-85; Director, English Major in Writing, 1979-; Associate Professor, 1985-90; Professor, 1990-. Publications: The Threshold of the Year; Masked Women; Summers of Vietnam and Other Poems; Autumn Eros, poetry; The Cure of Poetry in an Age of Prose, criticism; Ghost Ship, 1996. Contributions to: Salmagundi Magazine; Modern Philology; Festschrift; Many others. Honours: Illinois Arts Council Awards, 1977, 1978, 1980, 1982, 1984, 1988, 1990, 1993; Devins Award, 1982; The Elizabeth Matchett Stover Memorial Award in Poetry, 1987. Memberships: PEN; Poetry Society of America; Society of Midland Authors. Address: English Department,

University Hall 102, Northwestern University, Evanston, IL 60208, USA.

KIRK Pauline Marguerite, b. 14 Apr 1942, Birmingham, England. Writer. m. Peter Kirk, 4 Apr 1964, 1 son, 1 daughter. Education: Nottingham University, 1960-63; Sheffield University, 1963-64; Monash University, 1966-70. Appointments: Teacher, Methodist Ladies College, 1965-66; Teaching Fellow, Monash University, 1965-69; Tutor, 1970-87; Tutor Counsellor, Assistant Senior Counsellor, 1971-72; Voluntary Resource Co-ordinator, 1988-95; Full-time Writer, 1995-. Publications include: Poetry: Scorpion Days, 1982; Red Marl and Brick, 1985; Rights of Way, 1990; Travelling Solo, 1995; Return to Dreamtime, 1996. Novels: Waters of Time, 1988; The Keepers, 1996; Anthologies: Purple and Green: Poems by 33 Women Poets, 1985; Yesterday's Yorkshire, 1991; Cleopatra, 1994. Contributions to include: Early Risers; Poetry Nottingham; Poetry Monash; Mobius; She. Honours: Individual Writers Bursary; Yorkshire and Humberside Arts New Beginnings Award, 1994; Readings at wide range of venues. Memberships: Society of Authors; Editorial Board, Aireings; Pennine Poets; Fighting Cock Press. Address: 20 Lee Lane East, Horsforth, Leeds LS18 5RE, England.

KIRKUP James Falconer, b. 23 Apr 1925, South Shields, Tyne and Wear, England. Poet; Novelist; Translator. Education: BA, Kings College, University of Durham. Appointments: Gregory Fellowship, University of Leeds, 1950-52; Visiting Poet, Senior Lecturer, Bath Academy of Art, 1952-56; Travelling Lecturer, Swedish Ministry of Education, 1956-57; Professor, University of Salamanca, 1957-58; Kyoto University of Foreign Studies, Kyoto, Japan, 1974-89; British Centre for Literary Translation, University of East Anglia, Norwich, 1995. Publications include: The Drowned Sailor; The Cosmic Shape; The Submerged Village; The Creation; A Correct Compassion; A Spring Journey; The Descent into the Cave; The Prodigal Son; Refusal to Conform; Selected Poems of Takagi Kyozo; Paper Windows; White Shadows, Black Shadows; The Body Servant; A Bewick Bestiary; No More Hiroshimas; Zen Contemplations; The Guitar Player of Zuiganji; The Sense of the Visit, 1985; Throwback: Poems Towards an Autobiography, 1992; Look At It This Way! - Poems for Young People, 1993; Formulas for Chaos, 1994; Strange Attractors, 1995; A Certain State of Mind, 1995; No More Hiroshimas, 1995; Burning Giraffes, 1996; The Patient Obiturist, 1996; Figures in a Setting, 1996. Contributions to include: Times Literary Supplement; New Yorker; Poetry Review; Times; Guardian; Rialto; Orbis; Outposts; Atlas Anthology; Black Letter; Canadian Poetry Review; Prism International; Modern Poetry in Translation; London Magazine; New Statesman; Spectator; Translation; Gay Sunshine; Independent; Haiku Quarterly; Blithe Spirit; Ko Haiku Magazine; Nineties Poetry; Encounter; Lines. Honours: Japan PEN Prize for Poetry; Keats Prize for Poetry; Mabel Batchelder Award; Scott Moncrieff Prize for Translation, 1993. Memberships: Royal Society of Literature; British Haiku Society. Address: BM Box 2780, British Monomarks, London WC1N 3XX, England.

KIRSTEN-MARTIN Diane, b. 29 Mar 1950, Bronx, New York, USA. Poet; Writer. m. 2 Oct 1976, 1 son. Education: BA, University of Rochester, 1972; MA, San Francisco State University, 1986. Contributions to: Hayden's Ferry Review; Yellow Silk; Zyzzyua; On The Bus; Bellingham Review; Gomimomo; Torncat; Blue Mesa Review; Santa Clara Review. Honour: 2nd Prize, National Writers Union Competition, 1992. Address: 68 Ashton Avenue, San Francisco, CA 94112, USA.

KITONGA Ellen Mae (Syomwangangi), b. 19 Jan 1943, Merrill, Wisconsin, USA. Editor. m. Justus Muthangya Kitonga, 21 Dec 1968, 1 son, 1 daughter. Education: BA, English, 1965, MA, English Literature, 1966, English Literature and Linguistics, 1969, University of Wisconsin; KPA, Editorial Production Course, 1972; BPA, Editorial Management Course, 1980. Appointments: Lecturer, Department of Literature, University of Nairobi; Graduate Teacher, Kenya Institute of Education; English Editor, Longman Kenya Ltd; ELT Editor, Oxford University Press, East and Central Africa; Editor, Press Officer, UNCHS, Habitat. Publication: Co-editor with Jonathan Kariara, Introduction to East African Poetry, 1976, and later revised edition. Honours: Shortlisted for Jomo Kenyatta Prize in Literature, Judge's Choice, 1977. Memberships: Kenya Language Association; Secretary, Treasurer, Executive Committee Member, Co-Editor, Lugha; Kenyan Editor, Journal of the Language Association of Eastern Africa; Writer's Association of Kenya. Address: PO Box 67553, Nairobi, Kenya.

KITSON Helen Dawn, b. 6 June 1965. Leicester, England. Clerk-Typist. Contributions to: London Magazine; North; Wide Skirt; Rialto; Scratch; Staple. Membership: Poetry Society. Address: 11 St Clements Court, Tybridge Street, St Johns, Worcester WR2 5NW, England.

KIZER Carolyn Ashley, b. 10 Dec 1925, Spokane, Washington, USA. Poet; Professor. Education: BA, Sarah Lawrence College, 1945; Postgraduate studies, Columbia University, 1946-47; Studied poetry with Theodore Roethke, University of Washington, 1953-54. Appointments: Founder-Editor, Poetry North West, 1959-65; Specialist in Literature, US Department of State, Pakistan, 1964-65; 1st Director, Literature Programs, National Endowment for the Arts, 1966-60; Poet-in-Residence, University of North Carolina, Chapel Hill, 1970-74; Hurst Professor of Literature, Washington University, St Louis, 1971; Lecturer, Barnard College, 1972; Acting Director, Graduate Writing Program, Columbia University, 1972; Poet-in-Residence, Ohio University, 1974; Visiting Poet, Iowa Writer's Workshop, 1975; Professor, University of Maryland, 1976-77; Poet-in-Residence, Distinguished Visiting Lecturer, Centre College, Kentucky, 1979; Distinguished Visiting Poet, East Washington University, 1980; Ellison Professor of Poetry, University of Cincinnati, 1981; Senior Fellow, Humanities Council, Princeton University, 1986. Publications: The Ungrateful Garden, 1961; Knock Upon Silence, 1965; Midnight Was My Cry, 1971; Mermaids in the Basement: Poems for Women, 1984; Yin: New Poems, 1984; Carrying Over, 1988; Proses, 1993; Editor, The Essential John Clare, 1993. Contributions to: Poems and Articles in various American and British Journals. Honours: Governor's Awards, State of Washington, 1965, 1985; Pulitzer Prize in Poetry, 1985; American Institute of Arts and Letters, 1985; San Francisco Arts Commission Award in Literature, 1986. Memberships: American Civil Liberties Union; American Poets; Amnesty International; PEN. Address: 19772 8th Street East, Sonoma, CA 95476, USA.

KLAPPERT Peter, b. 14 Nov 1942, Rockville Center, New York, USA. Poet; Teacher. Education: BA, Cornell University, 1964; MA, University of Iowa, 1967; MFA, 1968. Appointments: Teaching Assistant, University of Iowa, 1965-68; Instructor, Rollins College, 1968-71; Briggs Copeland Lecturer, Harvard University, 1971-74; Visiting Professor, New College, 1972; Writer-in-Residence, 1976-77, Assistant Professor, 1977-78, College of William and Mary, 1976-77; Assistant Professor, 1978-80, Director of Writing Program, 1979-81, 1985-88, Associate Professor, 1981-91, Professor, 1991, Program in Poetry, 1996-, George Mason University. Publications: Lugging Vegetables to Nantucket; Circular Stairs, Distress in the Mirrors; Non Sequitur O Connor; The Idiot Princess of the Last Dynasty: 52-Pick Up; Internal Foreigner. Contributions to: Atlantic; Harpers; New Yorker; APR; Antaeus; Ploughshares; Saturday Review; Gettysburg Review; Parnassus; AWP Chronicle. Honours: Yale Series of Younger Poets Competition; National Endowment for the Arts Fellow; Ingram Merrill Foundation; Lucille Medwick Award. Memberships: Poetry Society of America; PEN; Associated Writing Programs; Academy of American Poets. Address: MS 3E4 - Department of English, George Mason University, Fairfax, VA 22030, USA.

KLEEFELD Carolyn Mary, b. 1935, Catford, London, England. Poet; Author; Painter. Education: Art and Psychology, University of California at Los Angeles. Publications: Climates of the Mind, 1979; Satan Sleeps with the Holy; Word Paintings, 1982; Lovers in Evolution, 1983; Songs of Ecstasy, 1990; Included in Mavericks of the Mind; Interviews for the New Millennium; Painting Exhibitions in various California locales.Contributions to: Poetry included in: Erotic by Nature; The Erotic Impulse. Memberships: Co-Founder, The New Forum, Monterey, California; Supporter of Amnesty International; Concerned Scientists and Ecologically Progressive Organizations. Address: P O Box 370, Big Sur, CA 93920, USA.

KLEIN Adelina, b. Romania. Poet. Education: Graduate, Faculty of Public Relations, Buber Institute; Graduate, Communications and Spokesperson Faculty, Institute for Communications, Hebrew University, Jerusalem, Israel. Appointment: Editor, Madregot poetry journal. Publications: Expressions, 1980; Passing, 1983; Boxes, 1987; Almond Clouds, 1994. Contributions to: World Poetry; Quest and Poems; International Poets; New Global Voice; Bat-kol; A Sharq. Honours: Special Award for editing journal Galim 7; Special Award for Literature and Poetry Advancement; Tip of the Pen Special Distinction Award. Memberships: Jerusalem Branch, National and International Association of Poetry. Address: PO Box 9516, Jerusalem 91094, Israel.

KLEINSCHMIDT Edward Joseph, b. 29 Oct 1951. Professor. Education: BA, St Marys College, 1974; MA, Hollins College, 1976. Appointments: Associate Professor, Santa Clara University. Publications: To Remain; First Languages: Magnetism. Contributions to: New Yorker; Best American Poetry; American Poetry Review; New England Review; Gettysburg Review; Poetry. Honours: Juniper Prize, Bay Area Book Reviewers Award; Gesù Award, 1990. Memberships: Poetry Society of America; PEN; Associated Writing Program. Address: English Department, Santa Clara University, Santa Clara, CA 95053, USA.

KNELL William H, (Sparrow, Caliban, Autumn, Von Wernich), b. 5 Mar 1927, New York, New York, USA. English Professor. m. 27 Aug 1977, 1 son. Education: BA, Highlands University, 1952; MA, Adelphi University, 1965. Appointments: Editor, Writer, New York Mirror, 1953-60; Las Vegas City Schools, 1960-65; Writer, Santa Fe New Mexican, 1960-65; Writer, Santa Fe New Mexican, 1960-62; Professor, New Mexico Highlands University, 1965-91; Professor Emeritus, 1992. Contributions to: Santa Fe New Mexican; International Poetry Review; Modern American Lyrics; Twigs; Manifold; Green World; Seydell Quarterly; Bouquets of Poems; Private Anthology; Poet; Mile High Poetry Society; New York Mirror. Memberships: World Poetry Society; Rio Grande Writers Association; Squares. Address: 862 Sperry Drive, Las Vegas, NM 87701, USA.

KNIGHT Arthur Winfield, b. 29 Dec 1937, San Francisco, California, USA. Writer. m. Kit Duell, 25 Aug 1976, 1 daughter. Education: BA, English, 1960, MA, Creative Writing, 1962, San Francisco State University. Appointments: College Professor, California University of Pennsylvania, 1966-93; Film Critic, Anderson Valley Advertiser, 1992-; College Professor, part-time, University of San Francisco, 1995. Publications: Co-author, with wife, A Marriage of Poets, 1984; Wanted, 1988; Tell Me An Erotic Story, 1993; Basically Tender, 1991; Outlaws, Lawmen and Bad Women, 1993; The Secret Life of Jesse James, 1996. Contributions to: New York Quarterly; College English; Cape Rock; Zone 3; Poet Lore; Cottonwood; Massachusetts Review; Atom Mind; Bakunin; Poetry Motel; Redneck Review. Honour: 1st Place Winner, Third Annual Joycean Lively Arts Guild Review Contest, 1982. Membership: Western Writers of America. Address: PO Box 2580, Petaluma, CA 94953, USA.

KNIGHT Kit, b. 21 Sept 1952, North Kingston, Rhode Island, USA. Writer. m. Arthur Winfield Knight, 25 Aug 1976, 1 daughter. Education: BA, Communications, California University, Pennsylvania, 1975. Appointments: Co-Editor, Unspeakable Visions of The Individual, 1976-88; Poet, Columnist, The Russian River News, Guerneville, California, 1988-92; Writer to date. Publications: Co-author with husband, A Marriage of Poets, 1984; Women of Wanted Man, book of poems, 1994. Contributions to: Waterways; Russian River News; Pittsburgh Quarterly; Blue Jacket, Japan; Green's Magazine, Canada; Slipstream; Billy The Kid Outlaw Gang. Honour: Perry Award for Best Achievement in Poetry, for book of poems, Women of Wanted Men, James-Younger Gang, Liberty, Missouri. Address: PO Box 2580, Petaluma, CA 94953, USA.

KNIGHT Stephen Edward, b. 10 June 1960, Swansea, Wales. Freelance Theatre Director. Education: BA, Honours, Jesus College, Oxford, 1981; Bristol Old Vic Theatre School, 1985-86. Appointment: Writer-in-Residence, West Glamorgan, 1984-85. Publications: Flowering Limbs, 1993; Included in anthologies: Poetry Introduction 6, 1985; The Gregory Anthology 1987-90, 1990; The Bright Field; Contemporary Poetry From Wales, 1991. Contributions to: Encounter; Guardian; Honest Ulsterman; London Magazine; London Review of Books; New Statesman; Observer; Oxford Poetry; Poetry Durham; Poetry Review; Poetry Wales; Verse; Times Literary Supplement; Western Mail. Honours: National Poetry Competition Prizewinner, 1984, 1987, 1st prize, 1992; Eric Gregory Award, 1987; Cardiff Poetry Competition, 2nd prize, 1989.

KNOX Ann B, b. 31 Jan 1926, Buffalo, New York, USA. Writer; Editor; Teacher. 3 sons, 2 daughters. Education: BA, Vassar College, 1946; MA, Catholic University of America, 1970; MFA, Warren Wilson College, 1981. Appointment: Editor-in-Chief, Antietam Review, 1984-. Publications: Stone Crop; Signatures. Contributions to: Poetry; Negativem Capability; New York Quarterly; Berkeley Review; Nimrod Poets; Soundings East; Blueline; Poet Love; Maryland Poetry Review. Honours: Washington Writers Publishing House Winner; Pennsylvania Council on the Arts Grant; Virginia Center for Creative Arts Fellowship. Memberships: Poets and Writers; Academy of American poets; Writers

Center; Associated Writing Program; International Womens Writing Guild; Poetry Society of America. Address: Box 65, Hancock, MD 21750, USA.

KOBU. See: **COBB David Jeffrey.**

KOCH Kenneth (Jay), b. 27 Feb 1925, Cincinnati, Ohio, USA. Poet; Professor of English; Dramatist; Writer. m. (1) Mary J Elwood, 1955, 1 daughter, (2) Karen Steinbrink, 1994. Education: AB, Harvard University, 1948; MA, 1953, PhD, 1959, Columbia University. Appointments: Lecturer, Rutgers University, 1953-54, 1955-56, 1957-58, Brooklyn College, 1957-59; Director, Poetry Workshop, New School for Social Research, New York City, 1958-66; Lecturer, 1959-61, Assistant Professor, 1962-66, Associate Professor, 1966-71, Professor of English, 1971-, Columbia University; Associated with Locus Solus magazine, Larsen-Vercours, France, 1960-62. Publications include: Poetry: Thank You and Other Poems, 1962; Poems from 1952 and 1953, 1968; When the Sun Tries to Go On, 1969; Sleeping with Women, 1969; The Pleasures of Peace and Other Poems, 1969; Penguin Modern Poets 24 (with Kenward Elmslie and James Schuyler), 1973; The Art of Love, 1975; The Duplications, 1977; The Burning Mystery of Anna in 1951, 1979; From the Air, 1979; Days and Nights, 1982; Selected Poems 1950-1982, 1985; On The Edge, 1986; Seasons on Earth, 1987; One Train, 1994; On the Great Atlantic Rainway: Selected Poems 1950-1988, 1994; Plays: One Thousand Avant-Garde Plays, 1988; Fiction: Hotel Lambosa, 1993; Editor: Talking to the Sun: An Illustrated Anthology of Poems for Young People (with Kate Farrell), 1985. Honours: Fulbright Fellowships, 1950, 1978; Guggenheim Fellowship, 1961; National Endowment for the Arts Grant, 1966; Ingram-Merrill Foundation Fellowship, 1969; Harbison Award for Teaching, 1970; Frank O'Hara Prize, 1973; National Institute of Arts and Letters Award, 1976; Award of Merit for Poetry, American Academy of Arts and Letters Award, 1976; Award of Merit for Poetry, American Academy of Arts and Letters, 1986; Bollingen Prize for Poetry, 1995; Rebekah Johnson Bobbitt National Prize for Poetry, 1996. Address: 25 Claremont Avenue, Apt 2-B, New York, NY 10027, USA.

KOCH Z Kachol. See: **KACHEL Zeev.**

KOESTENBAUM Phyllis, b. 16 Sept 1930, Brooklyn, New York, USA. Poet. m. (1) Peter Koestenbaum, 29 June 1952, div 1986, (2) Aaron Goldman, 16 July 1989, 3 sons, 1 daughter. Education: BA, Radcliffe College, 1952; MA, San Francisco State University, 1979. Appointments: Instructor, West Valley Community College; Lecturer, Santa Clara University; Lecturer, San Francisco State University; Affiliated Scholar, Institute for Research on Women and Gender, Stanford University, 1984-. Publications: 14 Criminal Sonnets, 1984; That Nakedness, 1982; Hunger Food, 1980; Oh I can't she says, 1980; Crazy Face, 1980. Contributions to: Threepenny Review; New England Review; Ironwood; Tendril; Five Fingers Review; Northwest Review; Anthology of Magazine Verse and Yearbook of American Poetry; Epoch; Brooklyn Review; Poet Lore; American Letters and Commentary; Arvon Foundation Poetry Competition 1980 Anthology: Woman Poet the West; Nimrod; Anthologies: The Best American Poetry, 1992, 1993; A Formal Feeling Comes: Poems in Form by Contemporary Women. Honours: Creative Writing Fellowship, National Endowment for the Arts; Honorable Mention, Annual Book Award, San Francisco State University Poetry Center; 1st Prize, Academy of American Poets Contest. Memberships: National Writers Union; Authors Guild. Address: 982 East La Mesa Terrace, Sunnyvale, CA 94086, USA.

KOESTENBAUM Wayne, b. 20 Sept 1958, San Jose, California, USA. Teacher; Poet. Education: BA, Harvard University, 1980; MA, Johns Hopkins University, 1981; PhD, Princeton University, 1988. Appointment: Faculty, Yale University, 1988-. Publications: Double Talk, 1990; Ode to Anna Moffo and Other Poems, 1990; The Queen's Throat, 1993; Rhapsodies of a Repeat Offender, 1994. Address: c/o Department of English, Yale University, New Haven, CT 06520, USA.

KOFALK Harriet, b. 12 Oct 1937, USA. Peace/Nature Poet. 1 son, 1 daughter. Education: BA, University of New Mexico, 1959. Appointments: Administration Assistant, American Optometric Association, 1965-67; Kimbro Associates, 1970-72; Executive Assistant, Santa Fe Opera, 1973-77; Research Administration, RAND Corporation, 1979-81; Freelance Writer. Publications: Wisdom of the 80's; Tamotzu in Haiku; Tamotzu Angels in the Garden, 1994; Speaking of Mother Eart, 1994; Haiku; Earth Prayers; Rainbows; Light;

Home; Pax Gaia; No Woman Tenderfoot - Florence Merriam Bailey, Pioneer Naturalist; The Peaceful Cook - More Than a Cookbook; Solar Cooking - Primer/Cookbook, 1995; Afternoon in a Japanese Garden. Contributions to: Christian Science Monitor; Newsweek; Sunstone Review; Mainichi Daily News; Hai; Ko. Honours: International Haiku Contest Runner Up; JAL Haiku Contest Runner Up; Honorable Mention, Kansas Poetry Contest. Memberships: Haiku Society of America; Northwest Writers; Oregon State Poetry Association. Address: Peace Place, 175 East 31, Eugene, OR 97405, USA.

KOGAWA Joy (Nozomi), b. 6 June 1935, Vancouver, British Columbia, Canada. Writer; Poet. m. David Kogawa, 2 May 1957, div 1968, 1 son, 1 daughter. Education: University of Alberta, 1954; Anglican Women's Training College, 1956; University of Saskatchewan, 1968. Appointment: Writer-in-Residence, University of Ottawa, 1978. Publications: Poetry: The Splintered Moon, 1967; A Choice of Dreams, 1974; Jericho Road, 1977; Woman in the Woods, 1985. Fiction: Obasan, 1981; Naomi's Road, 1986; Itsuka, 1992; The Rain Ascends, 1995. Contributions to: Canadian Forum; Chicago Review; Prism International; Quarry; Queen's Quarterly; West Coast Review; Others. Honours: First Novel Award, Books in Canada, 1982; Book of the Year Award, Canadian Authors Association, 1982; American Book Award, Before Columbus Foundation, 1982; Best Paperback Award, Periodical Distributors, 1982; Notable Book Citation, American Library Association, 1982; Order of Canada; Doctor of Laws, Honoris Causa, 1991, 1993; Doctor of Letters, Honoris Causa, 1992. Memberships: Canadian Civil Liberties Association, Director; Canadian Tribute to Human Rights, Patron; League of Canadian Poets; PEN International; Writers Union of Canada. Address: c/o Writers Union of Canada, 24 Ryerson, Toronto, Ontario M5T 2P3, Canada.

KOLLER James, b. 30 May 1936, Oak Park, Illinois, USA. 2 sons, 4 daughters. Education: BA, North Central College, 1958. Appointment: Editor, Coyote Books, Coyotes Journal, 1964-. Publications: Roses Love Sunshine; Great Things Are Happening; Poems for the Blue Sky; I Went to See My True Love; Some Cows; Two Hands; The Natural Order; This is What He Said. Honour: National Endowment for the Arts Fellowship. Address: P O Box 629, Brunswick, ME 04011, USA.

KOLUMBAN Nicholas, b. 17 June 1937, Budapest, Hungary. High School English Teacher. m. 11 June 1967, 1 daughter. Education: BA, 1962, MA, 1966, Pennsylvania State University. Appointments: College Instructor, Virginia Polytechnic Institute and State University, Blacksburg, 1965-70; High School German Teacher, Bridgewater, New Jersey, 1971-84; High School English Teacher, Paterson, New Jersey, 1985-. Publications: In Memory of My Third Decade, 1981; Reception at the Mongolian Embassy, 1987; The Porcelain Balloon, 1992; Surgery on My Soul, 1996. Contributions to: Another Chicago Magazine; Artful Dodge; Chariton Review; Hawaii Review; Hitel, Hungary; Michigan Quarterly Review; Mudfish; New Letters; Poetry East; Poetry Review. Honour: Poetry Prize, New Jersey State Arts Council, 1984-85. Address: 150 West Summit Street, Somerville, NJ 08876, USA.

KOMUNYAKAA Yusef, (James Willie Brown, Jr), b. 29 Apr 1947, Bogalusa, Louisiana, USA. Professor of Creative Writing; Poet. m. Mandy Sayer, 1985. Education: BA, University of Colorado, 1975; MA, Colorado State University, 1979; MFA, University of California, Irvine, 1980. Appointments: Visiting Professor, 1985, Associate Professor of Afro-American Studies, 1987-96, Indiana University; Professor of Creative Writing, Princeton University, 1997-; Many poetry readings. Publications: Dedications And Other Darkhorses, 1977; Lost In The Bonewheel Factory, 1979; Copacetic, 1984; I Apologize For The Eyes In My Head, 1986; Dien Cai Dau, 1988; The Jazz Poetry Anthology, Editor with Sascha Feinstein, 1991; Magic City, 1992; Neon Vernacular: New And Selected Poems, 1993. Contributions to: Anthologies and periodicals. Honours: Pulitzer Prize in Poetry, 1994; Kingsley Tufts Poetry Award, 1994. Address: c/o Department of English, Princeton University, Princeton, NJ 08544, USA.

KOONTS J Calvin, b. 19 Sept 1924, Lexington, North Carolina, USA. Retired College Professor; Administrator. m. Cortlandt Louise Morper, 6 Sept 1953, 1 son, 1 daughter. Education: AB, Catawba College, 1945; MA, Vanderbilt University, 1949; PhD, 1958; Postdoctoral Study, Harvard University, 1960; Independent Research, University of California at Los Angeles, 1977. Appointments: Boyden High School, Salisbury, North Carolina, 1945-48; Peabody College of Vanderbilt University, 1951-52; Erskine College, 1949-90; Professor

Emeritus, Erskine, 1990-. Publications: Since Promontory; Straws in the Wind; Under the Umbrella; Green Leaves in January; A Slice of the Sun; Inklings; A Stone's Throw; Lines, Opus 8. Contributions to: Catawba Totem; Erskine Review; Abbeville Press and Banner; Lexington Dispatch; Peabody Reflector; Village Observer; Clearing House. Honours: Jesse H Jones Scholarship; Peabody Harvard Scholarship; Unicorn Poetry Prize; Elizabeth Boatwright Coker Award; Twice Nominated Poet Laureate of South Carolina. Memberships: SCATE; Phi Delta Kappa; South Carolina State Board of Education; Poetry Society of South Carolina; Sigma Pi Alpha; Pi Gamma Mu. Address: P O Box 163, Due West, SC 29639, USA.

KOONTZ Thomas Wayne (Tom), b. 9 July 1939, Fort Wayne, Indiana, USA. Poet. m. Haven Skye Jarvis, 10 June 1987, 5 daughters. Education: BA, Miami University, 1961; MA, 1965, PhD, 1970, Indiana University. Appointments: Instructor, George Washington University, 1965-67; Professor, Ball State University, 1967-. Publications: To Begin With, 1983; Charms, 1983. Contributions to: Spoon River Quarterly; Asylum; Cicada; Frog Pond; Black Fly Review; Blue Unicorn; Forum; Indiannual; Windless Orchard. Membership: Associate Writing Program. Address: 2700 South Whitney Road, Selma, IN 47383, USA.

KOOSER Ted (Theodore Kooser), b. 25 Apr 1939, Ames, Iowa, USA. Poet; Teacher; Company Vice-President. m. (1) Diana Tresslar, 1962, div 1969, 1 son, (2) Kathleen Rutledge, 1977. Education: BS, Iowa State University, 1962; MA, University of Nebraska, 1968. Appointments: Underwriter, Bankers Life Nebraska, 1965-73; Part-Time Instructor in Creative Writing, University of Nebraska, 1970-; Senior Underwriter, 1973-84, Vice-President, 1984-, Lincoln Benefit Life. Publications: Poetry: Official Entry Blank, 1969; Grass Country, 1971; Twenty Poems, 1973; A Local Habitation, and a Name, 1974; Shooting a Farmhouse: So This is Nebraska, 1975; Not Coming to be Barked At, 1976; Hatcher, 1978; Old Marriage and New, 1978; Cottonwood County (with William Kloeflkorn), 1979; Sure Signs: New and Selected Poems, 1980; One World at a Time, 1985; The Blizzard Voices, 1986; Weather Central, 1994; Editor: The Windflower Home Almanac of Poetry, 1980; As Far As I Can See: Contemporary Writers of the Middle Plains, 1989. Honours: Prairie Schooner Prizes, 1975, 1978; National Endowment for the Arts Fellowships, 1976, 1984; Poetry Award, Society of Midland Authors, 1980; Stanley Kunitz Prize, 1984; Governor's Art Award, Nebraska, 1988; Richard Hugo Prize, 1994. Address: Route 1, Box 10, Garland, NE 68360, USA.

KOPPANY Zsolt, b. 20 Aug 1955, Budapest, Hugary. Editor. m. Aranka Hegyesi, 15 Aug 1981. Education: Qualification: Locksmith. Appointments: Mechanic; Shop Assistant; 24 months active service in the Hungarian People's Army; Office Attendent; Buyer; Storeman. Publications: Poems and other books: Poetic Play, poems, 1988; Words and Passions, essays, 1991; Everday Passion, short story, 1992; War of Book, novel, 1994; The Empire of Thoughts, essays, 1994; Ode of Alfernon-Lead Telephone, poems and drama, 1994; Acquarelle, poems, 1996; Anno Donini, selected poems, 1996; The Redeemer in Shade, essays and interviews, 1997. Contributions: Magyar Nemzet; Nepszava; Uz Magyarorszag; Hitel; Stadium; Viligia; Tiszataj; Magyar Naplo; Elet Es Irodalom; Eletunk; Jel; Emberhalasz. Honour: Josef Lengyel Grant, 1985. Membership: Hungarian Writers Association. Address: Fadrusz Utca Z IV/j, 1114 Hungary.

KOPS Bernard, b. 28 Nov 1926, London, England. Playwright; Poet. m. Erica Gordon, 1956, 4 children. Appointments: Lecturer in Drama, Spiro Institute, 1985-86; Surrey Education Authority, Ealing Education Authority, ILEA, Arts Educational School/The Acting Company, 1989-90; City Literary Institue, 1990-93. Publications: Poems, 1955; Poems and Songs, 1958; Anemone for Antigone, 1959; Erica, I Want to Read You Something, 1967; For the Record, 1971; Barricades in West Hampstead, 1988; also 9 novels; Neither Your Honey Nor Your Sting, offbeat History of the Jews, 1985; Autobiography, The World is a Wedding, 1963-75; 18 Plays; 21 Plays for Radio; 11 Plays, drama/documentary for television; Serial, The Survivor for television, 1991-92; Manuscript Collections: University of Texas at Austin, USA; Indiana University at Bloomington, Indiana, USA. Honours: Arts Council Award for Playing Sinatra, a play commissioned by the Croydon Warehouse Theatre; Arts Council Bursary, 1957, 1979, 1985; C Day Lewis Fellowship, 1981-83; Dreams of Anne Frank, Winner of London Fringe Awards, 1993; Sailing with Homer, Winner of Writer's Guild of Great Britain Award, 1995. Address: Flat 1, 35 Canfield Gardens, London NW6, England.

KORIYAMA Naoshi, b. 3 Nov 1926, Kikai Island, Japan. Professor. m. Ruriko Maeda, 13 Sept 1954, 2 sons, 1 daughter. Education: Kagoshima Normal College, 1941-47; Okinawa Foreign Language School, 1948-49; University of New Mexico, 1950-51; State University of New York at Albany, 1951-54. Appointments: Instructor, Assistant Professor, Obirin Junior College, 1956-61; Faculty Member, 1961-, Professor, 1967-, Tokyo University. Publications: Coral Reefs; Plum Tree in Japan; Songs from Sagamihara; By the Lakeshore and Other Poems; Time and Space; Posie Di Naoshi Koriyama; Another Bridge Over The Pacific; Eternal Grandeur and Other Poems. Contributions to: Poetry Nippon. Honour: 7th International Poetry Prize. Memberships: Poetry Society of Japan; G M Hopkins Society of Japan. Address: 2-15-9 Yaei, Sagamihara-shi, Kanagawa-ken 229, Japan.

KORNFELD Robert Jonathan, b. 3 Mar 1919, Newtonville, Massachusetts, USA. Playwright. m. 23 Aug 1945, 1 son. Education: BA, Harvard University, 1941. Appointments: Writer of Radio Dramas; Editor; Reporter; San Francisco Examiner; Freelance Writer; Photographer; Playwright; Poet; Travel Writer; Co-Chair, Literary Committee, National Arts Club. Publications: Cahiers d'Art det D'Amitie Paris; A Dream Within A Dream. Contributions to: Botteghe Oscure; La Prensa; Music for Saint Nicholas, performed in Alice Tully Hall, Lincoln Centre, 1992. Honours: 1st Prize, National Contest, Passage in Purgatory. Memberships: Authors League; Dramatists Guild; National Arts Club: Bronx Society of Science and Letters; PEN: American Centre; The Drama League. Address: The Withers Cottage, 5286 Sycamore Avenue, Riverdale, NY 10471, USA.

KOSOFF Flora M, b. 13 Oct 1926, Portland, Oregon, USA. Registered Nurse; Writer. 1 daughter. Education: St Josephs Hospital, Northern Idaho College of Education, Lewiston. Appointments: Harborview Hospital, Seattle; St Josephs Hospital. Publications: Little Boris and the Metterics; Further Adventures of Big Mike and Little Boris; Sounding in Silence; All The Young Nightingales; Come Light My Lamp; The Nursing Years, 1944-1983, journal in verse. Contributions to: Oregon Coast Magazine; Allevspark Wind; Midwest Poetry Review. Honours: Poetic Page Chapbook Contest, 1990, 1992. Memberships: Pipes Calling Poets; Poetic Page. Address: 215 Waldo Street, Spruce Haven Mobile Home Park, Crescent City, CA 95531, USA.

KOSTELANETZ Richard (Cory), b. 14 May 1940, New York, New York, USA. Writer; Poet; Critic; Artist; Composer. Education: AB, (Honours), Brown University, 1962; Graduate Studies, King's College, London, 1964-65; MA, Columbia University, 1966; Study in music and theatre, Morley College, London, and New School for Social Research, New York. Appointments: Co-Founder-President, Assembling Press, New York, 1970-82; Literary Director, Future Press, New York 1976-; Co-Editor-Publisher, Precisely: A Critical Magazine, 1977-84; Sole Proprietor, RK Editions, New York, 1978-. Co-ordinator-Interviewer, American Writing Today: Voice of America Forum Series, 1979-81; Contributing Editor to various journals; Guest Lecturer and Reader at many colleges and universities; Numerous exhibitions as an artist.Publications: Poetry: Visual Language, 1970; I Articulations/Short Fictions, 1974; Portraits from Memory, 1975; Numbers: Poems and Stories, 1976; Rain Rains Rain, 1976; Illuminations, 1977; Numbers Two, 1977; Richard Kostelanetz, 1980; Turfs/Arenas/Fields/Pitches, 1980; Arenas/Fields/Pitches/Turfs, 1982; Fields/Pitches/Turfs/Arenas, 1990; Solos, Duets, Trios, and Choruses, 1991; Repartitions-IV, 1992; Wordworks: Poems Selected and New, 1993; Partitions, 1993; Repartitions, 1994. Fiction: In the Beginning, novel, 1971; Constructs Vols I-VI, 1975-91; One Night Stood, novel, 1977; Tabula Rasa: A Constructivist Novel, 1978; Exhaustive Intervals, novel, 1979; Fifty Untitled Constructivist Fictions, 1991; Many others. Non-Fiction: Recyclings: A Literary Autobiography, 2 volumes, 1974, 1984; The End of Intelligent Writing: Literary Politics in America, 1974; Metamorphosis in the Arts, 1980; The Old Poetries and the New, 1981; The Grants-Fix: Publicly Funded Literary Granting in America, 1987; The Old Fictions and the New, 1987; On Innovative Music(ians)s, 1989; Unfinished Business: An Intellectual Non-History, 1990; The New Poetries and Some Old, 1991; Published Encomia, 1967-91, 1991; On Innovative Art(ist)s, 1992; The Dictionary of the Avant-Gardes, 1994; On Innovative Performance(s), 1994; The Fillmore East: 25 Years After: Recollections of Rock Theatre, 1995; An ABC of Contemporary Reading, 1995; Crimes of Culture, 1995; John Cage (Ex)plain(ed), 1996; One Million Words of Booknotes, 1958-1993, 1996; Many others. Editor: American Writing Today, 2 volumes, 1981, revised edition, 1991; The Avant-Garde Tradition in Literature, 1982; Gertrude Stein Advanced: An Anthology of Criticism, 1990; Writing About John Cage,

1993; Nicolas Slonimsky: The First 100 Years, 1994; A Portble Baker's Biographical Dictionary of Musicians, 1994; Classic Essays on 20th Century Music, 1996; Writing on Glass, 1996; A Frank Zappa Companion, 1996; A B B King Companion, 1996; Another E E Cummings, 1997; Many others. Other: Films; Videotapes; Radio Scripts; Recordings. Contributions to: Many anthologies; Numerous poems, articles, essays, reviews, in journals and other publications. Honours: Woodrow Wilson Fellowship, 1962-63; Fulbright Fellowship, 1964-65; Pulitzer Fellowship, 1965-66; Guggenheim Fellowship, 1967; One of Best books, American Institute of Graphic Arts, 1976; Several National Endowment for the Arts Grants; Pushcart Prize, 1977; Deutscher Akademischer Austauschdienst Stipend, Berlin, 1981-83; American Society of Composers, Authors, and Publishers Awards, 1983-91; Many others.Memberships: American PEN; American Society of Composers, Authors, and Publishers; Artists Equity; International Association of Art Critics; National Writers Union; Phi Beta Kappa; Others. Address: PO Box 444, Prince Street Station, New York, NY 10012, USA.

KOT Wieslaw, b. 14 Nov 1955, Zakliczyn, Poland. Teacher. 1 daughter. Education: MA, Philosophical and Historical Department, Jagiellonian University, Cracow, 1982. Appointments: Cracow, Rzeszow, 1982; Cracow, 1984; Cracow, Przemysl, 1985; Tarnow, 1986; Cracow, Sanok, 1988; Krosno, Cracow, 1989; Melbourne, Australia, 1990; Cracow, 1991. Publications: Rozmowy, 1980; Owoc winy, 1984; Nie nasz swiat, 1984; Szedl Czarodziej, anthology, 1986; Klucz do windy, 1989; Drugie niebo, 1989. Contributions to: Profile; Nowiny; Wiesci; Poezja. Membership: Zwiazek Literatow Polskich. Address: ul Krupnicza 22 2LP, Cracow 31-123, Poland.

KOTIKALAPUDI Venkata Suryanarayana Murti, (K V S Murti), b. 31 May 1929, Parlakhemundi, Orissa, India. Professor of English, Retired. Education: MA, English Language and Literature, 1963, PhD, English, 1972, Andhra University, Visakhapatnam; Intensive course in Linguistics and Phonetics, Central Institute of English and Foreign Languages, Hyderabad, 1969. Lecturer in English, until 1980, Assistant Professor of English, 1980-85, Professor of English, 1986-87, MMA Law College, Madras; Many international seminars and lectures, and poetry recitals. Publications: Books of criticism: Waves of Illumination, 1978; Sword and Sickle: Critical Study of Mulk Raj Anand's Novels, 1983; Kohinoor in the Crowns Critical Studies in Indian English Literature, 1987; Old Myth and New Myth: Letters from MRA to KVS, 1993; Books of Poetry in Telugu: Ihamlo Param, 1979; Liilaahela, 1981; Pranavamtho Pranayam, 1994; Books of poetry in English: Allegory of Eternity, 1975; Triple-Light, 1975; Sparks of the Absolute, 1976; Spectrum, 1976; Symphony of Discords, 1977; Araku, 1982; Comic and Absolute, 1995; Convex-Image and Concave-Mirror, 1995; Glimpses and Grandeur, in press. Contributions to: Several poems, book reviews, and research papers on English and Telugu Linguistics and Literature, in national and international publications. Honours include: Hon DLit, Free University of Asia, 1976, World University, Tucson, USA, 1977; Several Merit Certificates and Honours for Distinguished Achievement; Fellow, International Academy of Poets, UK, 1976. Memberships include: World University Round Table; Indian PEN; Authors Guild of India. Address: 43-21-9A Venkataraju Nahar, Visakhapatnam 530 016, AP, India.

KOUL Chaman Lal (Shakhtinternational), b. 27 July 1938, Kashmir, India. Senior Lecturer. m. Sarlabhan Ritajee, 26 May 1967, 1 son, 1 daughter. Education: MA, Hindi; MA, English; Nishnat, (MED); Dip Jour (IOJ); PGD, Jour (MSPI); Outstanding in CC in Acting and Diploma in Direction (IFTA, Delhi). Appointments: Teacher; Senior Teacher; Senior Master; Lecturer; Senior Lecturer; Head of Department of Hindi. Publications: Love Is God; Sher-i-Kashmir; International Shakmyi-Indra Gandhi; International Cricketers. Contributions to: Poet; Poets International; World Poetry, 1994, 1995. Honours: Second Prize in Self-Composing Poetry, Hindi Institute, Agra; Mark of Honour for Outstanding in Acting and Direction; Semi-Finalist in World Poetry Competition for a poem on Bhagawaan Gopinath. Memberships: World Poetry Society; Life Member, The Poetry Sociaety of India; Life Member, Bombay English Association; Life Member, The Indian PEN. Address: Interestellar, Shakhtinternational, c/o PM, PO Gangiyal, Jammu 180010, India.

KOULENTIANOS Denis, b. 7 June 1935, Piraeus, Greece. m. Toula Conomos, 10 Sept 1960, 2 sons. Education: College St Paul, Piraeus, 1954; Postgraduate Center of Public Relations, Athens, 1967; Brantridge Forest School, UK, 1966; University of Kansas, USA; Certificate in Philosophy, 1962. Appointments: Freelance Journalist

and Author, 1955-. Publications: Lyric Agonies, 1956; Thus Jesus Spoke, 1959; Bowings, 1962; The Bridge, 1965; Essence, 1979; In the Zodiak of Twins, 1981; Violets & Stilettos, 1989; DK: An Anthology, 1972; Aphorisms, 1976; Kytherian Yearnings, 1987; Pictures, 1992; My Debt to Poetry, 1994; Greek Smiles, 1996. Contributions to: Voice Universal; Il Messagero del Sud; The Inquirer; Metafisica; International Poet; Nea Estia; Laurel Leaves; Morias; Ei; Free Spirit; Spiritual Kithira; Literal Review. Honours: World Academy of Arts & Culture: Dr of Literature HC, 1988; International Poets Academy, Fellow Member-Intern Eminent Poet, 1991; Accademia del Fiorino, Accademico d'Onore, 1992; Academie de Lutece, Medaille d' Or, 1995. Memberships: United Poets Laureate Intern, Honorary Vice President; Panhellenic Union of Writers; Society of Kytherian Studies; Accademia Ferdinandea. Address: 28a Xenophon Street, 181 20 Korydallos, Greece.

KOUTSOUVELI Kassiani-Annita, b. Athens, Greece. Actress; Singer. Div, 1 daughter. Education: Dramatic School of Athens, Conservatory Actors Studies of New York; Music - voice teaching with Ismini Ippoleton in Athens and Susdy Radvani in New York. Appointments: Mermaid Club, Houston, USA, 1973; Asteria Glyphada, 1975; Village Gate, New York, 1975; Leading lady in American movie, The Song and The Silence, acclaimed in New York Times. Publications: Cosmos, 1972; Fossils, 1987; I Have The Eight, 1992; Bread and Some Hope, 1995. Contributions to: Philological to Vradini of Tziphiliak Estia; Eksotmissi newspaper Ipizofiki Estia European Art Centre; Ipirotikos Logos Prooodos. Memberships: National Society Greek Writers; Panhellenic Society of writers (PSW); European Society of Scientist, Artists, Writers. Address: Vdou 19, Glyphada 16675, Athens, Greece.

KOWIT Steve, b. 30 June 1938, New York, New York, USA. Poet; Teacher. m. Mary Petrangelo. Education: BA, Brooklyn College, 1965; MA, San Francisco State College, 1967; MFA, Warren Wilson College, 1991. Appointments: Instructor, San Diego State University, 1975-89; Visiting Professor, University of California, San Diego, 1978-79; Professor, US International University, 1979-80; Instructor, Southwestern College, 1989-. Publications: Cutting Our Losses, 1984; Lurid Confessions, 1985; Heart in Utter Confusion, 1986; Passionate Journey, 1988; Pranks, 1990. Contributions to: New York Quarterly; Exquisite Corpse; Poets Column, New York Times Book Review; Poet's Corner, Los Angeles Times Book Review; Beloit Poetry Journal; Anthologies: Up Late! American Poetry since 1970; A New Geography of Poets, 1992; Yellow Silk Anthology, 1990; The Maverick Poets; The Stand Up Poets; Poets for Life; Others. Honour: Fellowship in Poetry, National Endowment for the Arts, 1985. Address: PO Box 184, Potrero, CA 91963, USA.

KOZAK Jamie, b. 19 June 1947, Germany. Psychoanalyst. Appointments: Didactic member, psychoanalysis School Group Cero, Madrid. Publications: Para alguien en algun lugar; Psiconanalsis del Psiconanalisis; Transferencia y Sentido en Psicoanalisis; Psicpsis Infantiles; La Mirada de los Lobos; Artificios. Contributions to: International Poetry; World Poetry; Apocalipsis Cero. Memberships: International Writers Association; Poesia mas Poesia. Address: c/Real 114 2o, DS-28500 Arganda del Rey, Madrid, Spain.

KOZER José, b. 28 Mar 1940, Havana, Cuba. College Professor; Poet. m. Guadalupe, 15 Dec 1974, 2 daughters. Education: BA, New York University, 1965; MA, Queens College; PhD equivalent, 1983. Appointments: Profesor, Romance Languages, Queen's College, New York, 1965-. Publications: Padres Y Otras Profesiones, 1972; De Chepen A La Habana, co-author, 1973; Este Judio De Numeros Y Letras, 1975; Y Asi Tomaron Posesion En Las Ciudades, 1978, 1979; Jarron De Las Abreviaturas, 1980; La Rueca De Los Semblantes, 1980; Antologia Breve, 1981; Bajo Este Cien, 1983; La Garza Sin Sombras, 1985; El Carillon De Los Muertos, 1987; Carece De Causa, 1988; De Donde Oscilan Los Seres En Sus Proporciones, 1990; Chapbooks: Poemas De Guadaloupe, and editions, 1974; Nueve Laminas Y Otros Poemas, 1984; Diptico De La Restitucion, 1986; Somero Animal De La Especie, 1988; Verdehalago, 1990; Projimos, 1991. Contributions to: Over 200 literary journals, poetry magazines, newspapers, USA; Canada; Spain; Latin America. Honours: CINTAS Foundation Award, USA, 1973; Julio Tovar Poetry Prize, Spain, 1974; City University of New York/PSC Foundation Award, USA, 1991. Address: Queen's College, Romance Languages Department, Flushing, NY 11367, USA.

KRAMER Aaron, b. 13 Dec 1921, Brooklyn, New York, USA. Professor of English Emeritus; Author; Poet; Translator. m. Katherine Kolodny, 10 Mar 1942, 2 daughters. Education: BA, 1941, MA, 1951, Brooklyn College; PhD, New York University, 1966. Appointments: Instructor, 1961-63, Assistant Professor, 1963-66, Adelphi University; Lecturer, Queens College, Flushing, New York, 1966-68; Associate Professor, 1966-70, Professor of English, 1970-91, Professor Emeritus, 1991-, Dowling College, Oakdale, New York. Publications: The Glass Mountain, 1946; Poetry and Prose of Heine, 1948; Denmark Vesey, 1952; The Tinderbox, 1954; Serenade, 1957; Tune of the Calliope, 1958; Moses, 1962; Rumshinsky's Hat, 1964; Rilke: Visions of Christ, 1967; The Prophetic Tradition in American Poetry, 1968; Poetry Therapy (Co-Author), 1969; Melville's Poetry, 1972; On the Way to Palermo, 1973; Poetry the Healer (Co-Author), 1973; The Emperor of Atlantis, 1975; O Golden Land, 1976; Death Takes a Holiday, 1979; Carousel Parkway, 1980; The Burning Bush, 1983; In the Suburbs, 1986; A Century of Yiddish Poetry, 1989 Indigo, 1991; Life Guidance Through Literature (Co-Author), 1991; Dora Teitelboim: Selected Poems (Editor and Translator), 1995. Contributions to: Professional journals. Honours include: Hart Crane Memorial Award, 1969; Eugene O'Neill Theatre Center Prize, 1983; National Endowment for the Humanities Grant, 1993; Festschrift published in his honour, 1995. Memberships: American Society of Composers, Authors and Publishers; Association for Poetry Therapy; Edna St Vincent Millay Society; E E Cummings Society; International Academy of Poets; PEN; Executive Board, Walt Whitman Birthplace Association, 1969-85. Address: 96 Van Bomel Boulevard, Oakdale, NY 11769, USA.

KRAMER Lotte Karoline, b. 22 Oct 1923, Mainz, Rhine, Germany. Poet. m. Frederic Kramer, 20 Feb 1943, 1 son. Education: Art, History of Art, 1950-60's. Appointments: Laundry-hand; Lady's Companion; Dress Shop Assistant; Voluntary Worker, Peterborough Museum. Publications: Scrolls, 1979; Ice Break, 1980; Family Arrivals, 1981; A Lifelong House, 1983; The Shoemaker's Wife, 1987; The Desecration of Trees, 1994; Earthquake and Other Poems, 1994. Contributions: New York Times; Christian Science Monitor; Ariel, Canada; Poetry Canada Review; Cyphers, Eire; New Statesman; Spectator; Observer; Mainzer Geschichtsblatter, Germany; Jewish Chronicle; Jewish Quarterly; Agenda; Acumen; Outposts; Country Life; Countryman; Literary Review; Encounter; Chapman; Stand; PEN New Poetry; PEN International; Month; Green Book; Poetry Durham; New Humanist; Argo; Contemporary Review; Spokes; Rialto; Writing Women; Other Poetry; Ore; Quartz; Ambit; Anthologies include: Contemporary Women Poets, 1975; Poetry in the 70's, 1976; New Poetry, 1976, 1977, 1979, 1980, 1988; Writers of East Anglia, 1977; The Poetry of Chess, 1981; Chaos of the Night, 1984; In Time of War, 1987; A Picnic of Poetry, 1988; In The Gold of The Flesh, 1990; Holocaust Poetry, 1995; The Dybbuk of Delight, 1995; Completing the Picture, 1995. Honour: 2nd Prize, York International Poetry Competition, 1972. Memberships: Poetry Society; English PEN. Address: 4 Apsley Way, Longthorpe, Peterborough, Cambridgeshire PE3 9NE, England.

KRANZ Gisbert, (Kris Tanzberg), b. 9 Feb 1921, Essen, Germany. Writer. m. Brigitte Scholwer, 14 Aug 1951. Education: DPhil, University of Bonn, 1950; Staatsexamen, German and English, 1951, Theology, 1954. Appointments: Docent, Padagogische Hochschule, Paderborn, 1964; President, Inklings Gesellschaft, 1983. Publications: Englische Sonette; Epiphanien; Gedichte auf Bilder; Dome im gedicht; Freie Künste; Bilder und Personen; Martin und Prado; Niederwald und andere Gedichter. Contributions to: Babel; Besinnung; Braunschweiger Zeitung; Christ in der Gegenwart; Bas Boot; Die Waage; Echo der Zeit; FAZ; Hochland; Lyrica Germanica; Mindener Tageblatt; Packs; Westfalische Nechrichten; Inklings; Deutsche Tagespost; Many anthologies. Memberships: Inklings Gesellschaft für Literatur und Asthetik; Ovid Gesellschaft; dante Gesellschaft; C S Lewis Society. Address: Erster Rote Haag Weg 31, D-52076 Aachen, Germany.

KRATT Mary, b. 7 June 1936, Beckley, West Virginia, USA. Writer. m. Emil F Kratt, 29 Aug 1959, 1 son, 2 daughters. Education: BA, Agnes Scott College, 1958; MA, University of North Carolina at Charlotte, 1992. Publications: 11 published books of History, Biography and Poetry, 1980-; Poetry: Spirit Going Barefoot, 1982; The Only Thing I Fear is a Cow and a Drunken Man, 1991; On the Steep Side, 1993. Contributions to: Christian Science Monitor; Charlotte Observer; Christian Century; Shenandoah; Southern Poetry Review; Nimrod; Poem; New Mexico Humanities Review; Many other literary magazines. Honours: Lyricist Prize, 1982; Oscar Arnold Young Award

for best original poetry book by North Carolinian, 1983; Portfolio, Poetry Centre Southeast, 1984, 1985; Sidney Lanier Award, North Carolina Poetry Society, 1985; North Carolina Readers and Writers Series, North Carolina Writers Network, 1986; St Andrews Writer and Community Award, 1994; Distinguished Alumnae Writer Award, Agnes Scott College, 1994; MacDowell Colony Artist Residency Award North Carolina Arts Council, 1996. Memberships: Poets and Writers; Board Member, North Carolina Writers Network; Chairman/Vice-President/Secretary, North Carolina Writers Conference, 1989-92; Board Member, North Carolina Writers Workshop; Associate Editor, Southern Poetry Review. Address: 7001 Sardis Road, Charlotte, NC 28270, USA.

KRAUSE Nina, b. 11 Aug 1932, Delta, Ohio, USA. m. William Krause, 5 Mar 1955, 1 son, 1 daughter. Education: BA, Bowling Green State University, Ohio, 1954. Appointments: Various Writing and Editorial Work. Contributions to: Kentucky Poetry Review; Connecticut River Review; Dream Shop; Kentucky Book; Modern Lyrics Anthology; Contemporary Kentucky Poetry; Louisville Courier Journal Magazine. Memberships: Poetry Society of America; Academy of American Poets. Address: 1704 East Hunter Avenue, Bloomington, IN 47401, USA.

KRAUSS Beatrice Joy, b. 26 Dec 1943, Portland, Oregon, USA.. Principal Investigator. m. Herbert H Krauss, 28 Aug 1965, 2 sons. Education: PhD, City University of New York; MA, University of Kansas; BMus, Northwestern University, Illinois. Appointments: Director of Research, Community School District, Brooklyn, 1978-79; Assistant, Associate Professor, College of New Rochelle, 1979-90; Senior Research Associate, Memorial Sloan Kettering Cancer Centre, 1990-93;Principal Investigator, National Development and Research Institute Inc, 1993-; Principal Investigator, National Develoment and Research Institutes, 1995-. Contributions to: Blue Unicorn; River Run; Small Pond Magazine. Memberships: Poetry Society of America; Hudson Valley Writer's Center. Address: 6 Downing Court, Irvington, NY 10533, USA.

KREITER-FORONDA Carolyn, b 20 Dec 1946, Farmville, Virginia, USA. Teacher. m. Patricio Gomez-Foronda, 28 Mar 1991. Education: MEd, 1973; MA, 1979; DAE, 1983; PhD, 1995. Appointments: Teacher of English and Creative Writing, Fairfax County Public Schools, Virginia, USA, 1969-. Publications: Gathering Light, 1993; Contrary Visions, 1988. Contributions to: Antioch Review; Prairie Schooner; American Poets on the Holocaust; Mid-American Review; Bolivian Times; Anthology of Magazine Verse and Yearbook of American Poetry. Honours: Cultural Laureate Award of Virginia, 1991; Arts on the Road Poetry Winner, 1989; First Place Poetry Award, Poetry Society of Virginia, 1993; Arts-in-Education Grants (3 times), Virginia Commission, 1986, 1987, 1988. Memberships: The Poetry Committee of the Greater Washington DC Area; Editorial Board, SCOP Publications; Associated Writing Programs. Address: 5966 Annaberg Place, Burke, VA 22015, USA.

KREITMAN Norman, b. 5 July 1927, London, England. Physician. m. 26 Mar 1957, 1 son, 1 daughter. Education: MBBS, London; MD, London. Publications: Touching Rock, 1987; Against Leviathan, 1989. Contributions to: Acumen; Lines Review; Chapman; New Writing Scotland; Others. Membership: Chairman, Poetry Association of Scotland. Address: 24 Lauder Road, Edinburgh EH9 2JF, Scotland.

KREMERS Carolyn Sue, b. 2 Nov 1951, Denver, Colorado, USA. Writer; University Instructor. Education: BA, English, Humanities with Honours, Stanford University, 1973; BA, Flute Performance, summa cum laude, Metropolitan State College, Denver, Colorado, 1981; MFA, Creative Writing, University of Alaska, Fairbanks, 1991. Appointment: Lecturer, Department of English, University of Alaska, Fairbanks, 1993-. Publications: Essay in The Wilderness Of Vision: On The Poetry of John Haines, forthcoming; Musical setting of, Sestina Kyrie, for soprano, 3 percussionists and 3-person speaking chorus, by composer Lynette Westendorf. Contributions to: Alaska Quarterly Review; Life on the Line: Selections on Words and Healing, anthology; Permafrost; Poetry Alaska Women: Top of the World; The Prose Poem: An International Journal; Runner's World; Year of Alaskan Poets Calendar, 1992. Honour: Individual Artist Fellowship, monetary award, Alaska State Council on The Arts, 1992. Memberships: Associated Writing Programs; Modern Language Association of America; Wordcraft Circle of Native Writers and Storytellers. Address: PO Box 87231, Fairbanks, Alaska 99708, USA.

KRESH David, b. 13 Mar 1940, New York, New York, USA. Librarian. m. Diane Elizabeth Nester, 16 May 1986, 3 sons, 1 daughter. Education: BA, Swarthmore College, 1962; MSLS, Drexel University, 1966. Appointments: Reference Librarian, Library of Congress, 1967-. Publications: Bloody Joy; Sketches After Petes Beer. Contributions to: Poetry; Chicago Review; Salmagundi; Mississippi Review; Ironwood; Slow Dancer; High Plains Literary Review. Address: 601 North Carolina Avenue SE, Washington, DC 20003, USA.

KROLL Jeri, b. 7 Oct 1946, New York, New York, USA. Writer; Community Artsworker; Lecturer. m. Jeff Chilton, 1 son. Education: BA, Summa Laude, Smith College, USA, 1967; MA, English, University of Warwick, Coventry, England, 1968; PhD, English, Columbia University, USA, 1974. Appointments: Instructor, University of Maine, Presque Isle, 1974-75; Assistant Professor, Dickinson College, 1975-77; Tutor, Flinders University, Australia, 1978-81; Part-time, Adelaide University, 1981-83; Senior Lecturer in English, Flinders University; Publications: Death as Mr Right, 1982; Indian Movies, 1984; The Electrolux Man and Other Stories, 1987; Monster Love, 1990; House Arrest, 1993; Children's Picture Books: You Be the Witch; Sunny Faces; Swamp Soup (poems); Beaches; What Goes with Toes? Contributions to: Poetry Australia; Southerly; Canberra Times; Overland; Bulletin; Southern Review; Quadrant. Honours: Ethel Olin Corbin Poetry Prize, Smith College, 1966; Elizabeth Babcock Poetry Prize, Smith College, 1967; 3rd Prize, Grand Prize Competition, National Federation of State Poetry Societies, USA, 1977; Prize, Pennsylvania State Poetry Society Competition, 1978; 1st Prize, Esso Literary Competition, 1980; 1st Prize, Artlook National Poetry Contest, 1981; 2nd Prize, Anne Elder Award, for Death as Mr Right, 1982; Highly Commended, ABC Bicentennial Literary Awards, 1988. Memberships: Board of Management, South Australian Writers' Centre. Address: 29 Methuen Street, Fitzroy, Adelaide, South Australia 5082, Australia.

KRONENBERG Susan, b. 19 July 1948, New York, New York, USA. Poet; Writer; Performance Artist. Education: CA, Queens College, City University of New York, 1969. Appointments: Creative Writing and Poetry Teacher, New York State Council on The Arts, 1980-83; Teacher, CETA, 1979-80; National Writers Club, Poetry Panel, 1990. Publications: Always I Was Getting Ready To Go; Incantations Of The Grinning Dream Woman. Contributions to: Numerous include: The Manhattan Poetry Review; Poetry Now; The Helen Review; Home Planet News; Out There; Cactus Poets; Skyviews; The Writers Journal. Honours: Bumbershoot Arts Festival Poetry Prize; Capitol Hill Arts Commission Poetry Performance Grant; King County Arts Commission Poetry Prize; Writing Fellowships. Memberships: Poetry Society of America; Poets & Writers. Address: 920 North Stanley Avenue, No 208, West Hollywood, CA 90046, USA.

KRONENFELD Judy, b. 17 July 1943, New York, New York, USA. College Teacher. m. David Brian Kronenfeld, 21 June 1964, 1 son, 1 daughter. Education: BA summa cum laude, Smith College, Northampton, Massachusetts, 1964; PhD, English, specialisation in Renaissance Literature, Stanford University, California, 1971. Appointments: Lecturer, English and Comparative Literature, 1972-73, 1978-79, University of California at Irving; Visiting Associate Professor, 1987-; Assistant Professor, English, Purdue University, 1976-77; Visiting Assistant Professor, English, 1980-81, 1988-89, Lecturer, Creative Writing Programme, 1984-, University of California at Riverside. Publication: Shadow Of Wings, 1991. Contributions to: Plainsong; Passages North; Images; Lake Effect; Crosscurrents; MSS; California State Poetry Society Quarterly; Santa Barbara Independent; Electrum; Pinchpenny; Crescent Review; Hiram Poetry Review; Blue Unicorn; Shirim; Blow; Wind; Negative Capability; Third Eye; Abraxas. Memberships: Modern Language Association; Phi Beta Kappa. Address: 3314 Celeste Drive, Riverside, CA 92507, USA.

KU Yeonsik, (Songlang), b. 6 July 1925, Kyongnam, Korea. Poet; Professor. m. Im Oknam, 15 July 1952, 2 sons, 1 daughter. Education: PhD, Dong A University. Appointments: Professor, Dong A University, 1958-90; Dean Of Night School, 1979; Professor Emeritus, 1990; Professor, Kokusai University, 1989-. Publications: City Of Black Coral; Sensation; Fogs; Kyushu Diary. Contributions to: Modern Literature; Literature Monthly; Poetry; World Literature; Poetry and Consciousness; PEN Literature. Literary World; Current of Literary Ideas; World Poetry; Bamboo Shoot; Anthology of Contemporary Poets; Hangook Libo; Pusan Libo; Kukje Libo. Honours: Pusan Award; Sangwha Award. Memberships: International PEN; Modern Korean Poets Association; Korean Poetics Association; Korean Literary Critics

Association; Korean Literary Association; Korean Pusan Literary Association; Korean Writers Association. Address: Department of Korean Language and Literature, College of Humanities, Dong A University, 840 Hadagong Sashagu, Pusan, 604 714 South Korea.

KUAN Yun-Loong (Kuan Kuan), b. 9 Aug 1929. Soldier; Actor; Writer; Poet. m. Chong-Chong Wein, 1 son, 1 daughter. Education: Commerical High School; Army School; Self Study. Appointments: Colonel, army; Producer, television programmes; Editor, publishing company. Publications: Poetry Collection: The Isolated Faces; The Selected Poetry of Kuan Kuan; 4 essay collections. Contributions to: United Daily News; China Times; Literature Quarterly; Contemporary Literature; Torch Poetry Magazine. Honours: Poetry awards of contemporary literature and art associations in Hong Kong; China Contemporary Poetry Awards. Membership: Torch Poetry Society. Address: Feng Huang Lou No 504, Garden New City, Hsin Tien Taipei, Taiwan, China.

KUEPPER Philip Watson, b. 14 Aug 1948, Burlington, Iowa, USA. Poet. Education: BA, St Francis College, 1982. Contributions to: In RFD includes: Dimple The Dragon, fiction, 1985; I Know Not Cease, 1985; Making the Bed, 1994; In World of Poetry includes: Breaths of Restless Turn, 1987; The Stream of Consciousness, 1987; The Inheritance Factor, 1987; The Fisher of Words, 1987; My Heart in April Aches, 1988; The Fire in The Water, 1988; Morning Break, 1989; To Arrest the Dusk, 1989; Apartments Apart, 1990; Thanksgiving Day, 1990; A Primate Computing Geometry, 1990; The Message in the Fire, 1991; Irish Saraband, 1991; Flag in Snow, 1991; Invisible Walls, 1991; Of What I Am Made, 1991; Reading The Text, 1992; In American Poetry Annual includes: Extending The Symphony, 1990; After Seeing A Likeness of Andrew at the Hardware Store, 1994; The Infinite Isle, 1995. Others: A Coloring Fire, Poetry, 1975; Georgetown, The Washingtonian, 1975; Finding Sanctuary, play, Stamford Sight Site and Insight, 1989; The Echo in the Hour, 1991. Memberships: Amherst Society; Poets and Writers. Address: 233 Bouton Street West, Stamford, CT 06907, USA.

KUHNER Herbert, b. 29 Mar 1935, Vienna, Austria. Writer; Translator. Education: BA, Columbia University. Publications: Broadsides and Pratealls; Will The Stars Fall, 1995; Love of Austria, 1995. Contributions to: Dimension; European Judaism; Malahat Review; Confrontation; Poetry Australia; Skylark; Negative Capability; PEN International; Die Ziehharmonika. Honours: Golden Pen for Translation; Honorary Professorship, Austrian Ministry of Art and Science. Memberships: PEN; Poetry Society of America. Address: Gentzgasse 14/4, A-1180 Vienna, Austria.

KUIPER Koenraad, b. 22 Feb 1944, Hanover, Germany. Associate Professor in Linguistics. m. Alison Clare Wylde, 11 May 1968, 3 daughters. Education: MA Hons, Victoria University of Wellington, 1967; PhD, Simon Fraser University, 1972. Appointments: Master, Riccarton High School; Master, Burnside High School; Lecturer and Senior Lecturer, University of Canterbury. Publications: Signs of Life, 1981; Mikrokosmos, 1990. Contributions to: Comment; Island; Landfall; West Coast Review; Works; Tuatura; Untold; Takahe; Plainwraps; Poetry New Zealand. Honours: Runner Up, PEN Best First Book Award, 1991; Runner Up, New Zealand Poetry Society Annual Competition, 1991; Award Winner, Whitireia Poetry Competition, 1990, 1991, 1992. Address: 16 Tui Street, Christchurch 4, New Zealand.

KUMAR Ajit. See: **CHAUDHARY Ajit Kumar Shankar.**

KUMAR Shiv K(umar), b. 16 Aug 1921, Lahore, Punjab, India. Education: PhD, Fitzwilliam College, Cambridge, 1956. Appointment: Professor of English, Osmania University, 1959-86. Publications include: Articulate Silences, 1970; Cobwebs in the Sun, 1974; Subterfuges, 1976; Woodpeckers, 1979; Trapfalls in the Sky, 1986; Editor, British Romantic Poets: Recent Revelations, 1966; Editor, Indian Verse in English, 1970 (1971). Honours include: Fellow, Royal Society of Literature, 1978. Address: 2-F/Kakatiya Nagar, PO Jamia Osmania, Hyderabad 500 007, India.

KUMIN Maxine, b. 6 June 1925, Philadelphia, Pennsylvania, USA. Poet; Writer; Teacher. m. Victor M Kumin, 29 June 1946, 1 son, 2 daughters. Education: AB, 1946, MA, 1948, Radcliffe College. Appointments: Staff, Bread Loaf Writers Conference, 1969-71, 1973, 1975, 1977; Lecturer, Newton College of the Sacred Heart, Massachusetts, 1971; Visiting Lecturer, Professor, and Writer, University of Massachusetts, Amherst, 1972, Columbia University,

1975, Brandeis University, 1975, Washington University, St Louis, 1977, Princeton University, 1977, 1979, 1982, Randolph-Macon Women's College, Lynchburg, Virginia, 1978, Bucknell University, 1983, Atlantic Center for the Arts, New Smyrna Beach, Florida, 1984, University of Miami, 1995; Staff, Sewanee Writers Conference, 1993, 1994. Publications: Poetry: Halfway, 1961; The Privilege, 1965; The Nightmare Factory, 1970; Up Country: Poems of New England, New and Selected, 1972; House, Bridge, Fountain, Gate, 1975; The Retrieval System, 1978; Our Ground Time Here Will be Brief, 1982; Closing the Ring, 1984; The Long Approach, 1985; Nurture, 1989; Looking for Luck, 1992; Fiction includes: Why Can't We Live Together Like Civilized Human Beings?, 1982; Other includes: Women, Animals, and Vegetables: Essays and Stories, 1994; Various children's books. Contributions to: Numerous magazines and journals. Honours include: Pulitzer Prize in Poetry, 1973; American Academy of Arts and Letters Award, 1980; Academy of American Poets Fellowship, 1985; Levinson Award, 1987; Poet Laureate, State of New Hampshire, 1989; Sarah Joseph Hale Award, 1992; Poets' Prize, 1994; Various honorary doctorates. Memberships: PEN; Poetry Society of America; Writers Union. Address: Joppa Road, Warner, NH 03278, USA.

KUMMINGS Donald D, b. 28 July 1940, Lafayette, Indiana, USA. Professor of English; Chair, Department of English and Humanities. m. 21 Mar 1987, 2 sons. Education: BA, Purdue University, 1962; MA, Purdue University, 1964; PhD, English and American Studies, Indiana University, 1971. Appointments: Associate Instructor, Indiana University, 1966-70; Assistant Professor of English, 1970-75, Associate Professor of English, 1975-85, Professor of English, 1985-, University of Wisconsin-Parkside. Publication: The Open Road Trip: Poems, 1989. Contributions to: Bitterroot; Centering; Elizabeth; Goodly Co; Kansas Quarterly; Poetry Now; Quartet; Root River Poets; Spoon River Quarterly; Still Night Writings; Stoney Lonesome; West Hills Review; Wormwood Review; Anthologies: Mandala, 1970; LIT, 1986; Dolphins Arc, 1989. Honours: Frederick L Hovde Award for Poetry, Purdue University, 1964; Academy of American Poets Prize, Indiana University, 1969; Small Press Review Award, 1989; Posner Poetry Prize of the Council for Wisconsin Writers, 1990. Memberships: Walt Whitman Association, Camden, New Jersey; Walt Whitman Birthplace Association, Long Island, New York; Wisconsin Fellowship of Poets; Council of Wisconsin Writers; Sigma Tau Delta International English Honour Society. Address: 4101 5th Place, Kenosha, WI 53144, USA.

KUNA. See: **DASH Brusaketu.**

KUNERT Gunter, b. 6 Mar 1929, Berlin, Germany. Author. m. Marianne Todten, 1 Apr 1952. Education: Dr H C Allegheny College, Meadville, 1988. Publications: Fremd Daheim. Honours: Heinrich Mann Prize; J R Becher Prize; Heinrich Heine Prize; Hölderlin Prize; E R Curtius Prize. Memberships: Akademie Der Künste; Freie Akademie der Kunste; Akademie für Sprache und Dichtkunst; PEN. Address: Schulweg 7, D-2216 Kaisborstel, Germany.

KUNIHIRO Kei (Yoshihide), b. 11 Dec 1961, Harajuku, Tokyo, Japan. Poet; Writer; Actor; Singer. 1 daughter. Education: Graduated from Law School, Hosei University, 1985. Appointments: Novelist, Dancing on the Frying Pan in 1986, The Terrorist of the Holy Night in 1990, 1986-90; Actor, movie Down Town Heroes, 1988; Poet, Poet & Killer Chronicles, 1995. Publications: Poet & Killer 1st Edition, 1993; Poet & Killer 2nd Edition, 1994; Poetic Assassin, 1995; Poet & Killer Chronicles, 1995. Contributions to: Alpha Beat Press; Dharma Beat; Brouhaha; Kombat; Brunswick Publishing Corporation. Membership: Founder, Straight Edge Poetry System & Hard Core Reading Machine. Address: 3-33-19 Sakuragaoka Setagaya-ku, Tokyo 156, Japan.

KUNITZ Stanley J(asspon), b. 29 July 1905, Worcester, USA. Poet; Editor; Essayist; Educator. m. (1) Helen Pearce, 1930, div 1937, (2) Eleanor Evans, 21 Nov 1939, div 1958, 1 daughter, (3) Elise Asher, 21 June 1958. Education: AB (summa cum laude) 1926, MA 1927, Harvard University. Appointments: Editor, Wilson Library Bulletin, 1928-43; Professor of English, Potsdam State Teachers College, New York, 1949-50; Lecturer, New School for Social Research, New York City, 1950-57; Adjunct Professor in Writing, Graduate School for the Arts, 1967-85, Columbia University; Honorary Consultant in American Letters, Washington DC, 1976-83; Numerous poetry readings and lectures. Publications include: Poetry: Intellectual Things, 1930; Passport to the War: A Selection of Poems, 1944; Selected Poems 1928-1958, 1958; Passing Through: The Later Poems, 1995. Non-Fiction: Robert Lowell: Poet of Terribilita, 1974; A Kind of Order, A Kind of Folly: Essays and Conversations, 1975; Interviews and

Encounters, 1993. Editor: Living Authors: A Book of Biographies, 1931; The Junior Book of Authors: An Introduction to the Lives of Writers and Illustrators for Young Readers (with Howard Haycraft), 1934, 2nd edition, revised, 1951. Translator: Poems of Anna Akhmatova (with Max Hayward), 1973; Andrei Voznesensky: Story Under Full Sail, 1974. Contributions to: Many anthologies, books and periodicals. Honours include: Garrison Medal for Poetry, Harvard University, 1926; Levinson Prize for Poetry, 1956; Brandeis Creative Arts Award, 1964; National Medal of Arts, 1993; National Book Award for Poetry, 1995. Memberships include: Academy of American Poets, Chancellor, 1970-; Phi Beta Kappa; Poets House, New York, Founding President 1985-90. Address: 37 West 12th Street, NY 10011, USA.

KUNZ Carol Ann, b. 22 Mar 1940, Zanesville, Ohio, USA. Nurse. m. Robert J Kunz, 11 Mar 1976, 3 sons, 2 daughters. Education: Bachelors Degree of Arts in English/Journalism, Tarleton State University, 1995; Stephensville, Texas, 1979; Weatherford College of Nursing, Weatherford, Texas. Appointments: Nurse; Writer; Poet; Teacher. Publications: Anthologies: Great Poems of Our Times, 1993; Dark Side of the Moon, 1994; Outstanding Poets of 1994; Treasured Poem of America, 1994; Sharing Special Memories, 1995; Great Poems of the 90s, 1990. Contributions to: International Society of Poets Anthologies; Stephenville Empire Tribune; Oatmeal & Poetry; Editor: The Special PEN; Dublin Citizen; Lutheran Church Newsletter. Honours: Accomplishment of Merit for Ode to Midsummer Nights Dream, 1994; International Society of Poetry Cash Prize, 1995; Certificate of Excellence for Pitch N Peach, 1994; Honorable Mention for Silent, 1994. Memberships: International Society of Poets; The Wordrunners Writing Group; Dublin Shamrock Writers. Address: Route 5, Box 258, Dublin, TX 76446, USA.

KUPPNER Frank, b. 1951, Glasgow, Scotland. Publications include: A Bad Day for the Sung Dynasty, 1984; The Intelligent Observation of Naked Women, 1987; Ridiculous, Absurd, Disgusting, 1989. Address: c/o Carcanet Press Ltd, 208-212 Corn Exchange Buildings, Manchester M4 3BQ, England.

KURIATA Czesław, b. 29 Apr 1938, Marcelowka, Poland. 1 son, 1 daughter. Education: MA, A Mickiewicz University, 1960. Appointment: Manager, Literary Unit of Local Broadcastingg Station, Koszalin, 1965-83. Publications: The Sky Levelled With The Earth; The Girl Under Flowers; Gallop To The Great Forest; Prince Erics Return; Stone Fruit Wine; Boguslaw X; Selection Of Poems; The Simplest Confessions. Contributions to: All literary Polish magazines, journals, periodicals, newspapers. Honours: Best Poetic Debut Award; Monthly Pobrzeze Prize; 2 Radio Drama Prizes; 2 Artistic Work Prizes; Many prizes in literary competitions. Membership: Zaiks. Address: P O Box 79, ul Emilii Plater 2c/33, 75-348 Koszalin 9, Poland.

KURZ Elsie Bowman, b. 8 Aug 1919, Philadelphia, Pennsylvania, USA. m. Egon, 2 Apr 1939, 2 sons, 1 daughter. Publication: Poems for People. Contributions to: Bitterroot; Lyric; Z Miscellaneous; Byline; No Name Newsletter; Pinchpenny; M Muse. Honours: Lyric Roberts Memorial Award; Heersh Dadid Badonneh Award. Memberships: National Federation State Poetry Societies; Florida State Poets Association; Poets of the Palm Beaches; South Florida Poetry Institute. Address: Isle of Capri B50, Kings Point, Delray Beach, FL 33484, USA.

KUSHNER Aleksandr Semyonovich, b. 14 Sept 1936, Leningrad, Russia. Writer. m. Elena Vsevoldodovna Nevzglyadova, 1981, 1 daughter. Education: Leningrad Pedogogical Institute. Appointment: Lecturer, 1959-69. Publications: First Impressions; Night Watch; Omens; Letter; Direct Speech; Voice; Canvas' The Tavricjesky Garden; Daydreams; Poems; The Hedgrow; Nightly Melody; Appollo in the Snow. Contributions to: Novii mir; Znamya; Neva Yunost; Zvezda; Voprosi Literature; Literaturnaya Gazeta. Memberships: Russian Union of Writers; PEN. Address: Kaluzhsky Pereulor 9, Apt 48, St Petersburg 193015, Russia.

KUSHWAHA Tejnarayan, b. 24 Apr 1933, Singhandi, India. Retired HM. 3 sons, 1 daughter. Education: BA, 1958, MA (Hindi), 1960, MA (Sanskrit), PhD, 1971, Diploma in Education, 1971, Bhagalpuruni University; Sahityalankar (Deo 1963), Aurvedacharya, 1971. Appointments: Assistant Teacher at multi-purpose higher secondary school, Eshipur, 1960-94; HM to H/S Fullidumar, Banka, 1994-95; Honorary Kulsachiv (Vikram Shila, Hindi Vidyapith, Bhagalpur, 1969-. Publications: OMA (Doot Kavya/PrabandhKavya in Hindi), 1963; Savarna (an allegorie Angika Epic on Vedic Solar

Family), 1984; Geet Chirayeenke (Bhojpuri lyrics), 1992; Devata - Vedic Mythological Lyric Drama, 1993. Contributions to; Navbharat Times; Aaj; Aryavarta; Anga Madhuri; Saptahik Hindustan Jyotsna; Sanmarg; Ajtal; Adivasi; Dumka Darpan; Himshikar Dakshin Bharat; Bihar Bhumi; Bihar Jiwan; Prdeep Navrastra; Vishumitra. Honours: Ram Prasadsingh Sahitya Puraskar (Maghi Academy), 1984; Anup Puraskar (Sahitya Kunj), 1988; Griyarsan Puraskar (Bihar Sarkar), 1990; Bhavpritananad Balinaraya Puraskar all on Savarna; Supathga Samman. Memberships: Vikramshila Hindi Vidyapith Kulsachiva; Akhil Bhartiya Angika Sahitya Kala Manch, national president; Arhilbhartiya Bhasha Sahitya Sammelin Branch Bihar Vice President. Address: At-Gandhi Nagar Po Eshipur Dl-Bhagalpur (Bihar) Pin 813206, India.

KUSKIN Karla (Seidman), (Nicholas J Charles), b. 17 July 1932, New York, New York, USA. Writer and Illustrator of Children's Fiction and Verse. m. (1) Charles M Kuskin, 4 Dec 1955, div Aug 1987, 1 son, 1 daughter, (2) William L Bell, 24 July 1989. Education: Antioch College, 1950-53; BFA, Yale University, 1955. Appointments: Illustrator for several publishers; Conductor of poetry and writing workshops. Publications: Roar and More, 1956, revised edition, 1990; James and the Rain, 1957, new edition, 1995; In the Middle of the Trees, 1958; The Animals and the Ark, 1958; Just Like Everyone Else, 1959; Which Horse is William?, 1959, new edition, 1992; Square as a House, 1960; The Bear Who Saw the Spring, 1961; All Sizes of Noises, 1962; Alexander Soames: His Poems, 1962; How Do You Get From Here To There?, 1962; ABCDEFGHIJKLMNOPQRSTUVWXYZ, 1963; The Rose on My Cake, 1964; Sand and Snow, 1965; Jane Ann June Spoon and Her Very Adventurous Search for the Moon, 1966; The Walk the Mouse Girls Took, 1967; Watson, The Smartest Dog in the USA, 1968; In the Flaky Frosty Morning, 1969; Any Me I Want to Be: Poems, 1972; What Did You Bring Me?, 1973; Near the Window Tree: Poems and Notes, 1975; A Boy Had a Mother Who Bought Him a Hat, 1976; A Space Story, 1978; Herbert Hated Being Small, 1979; Dogs and Dragons, Trees and Dreams: A Collection of Poems, 1980; Night Again, 1981; The Philharmonic Gets Dressed, 1982; Something Sleeping in the Hall, 1985; The Dallas Titans Get Ready for Bed, 1986; Jerusalem, Shining Still, 1987; Soap Soup, 1992; A Great Miracle Happened Here: A Chanukah Story, 1993; Patchwork Island, 1994; The City Dog, 1994; City Noise, 1994; James and the Rain, 1995; Paul, 1994. Contributions to: Parent's Choice; House and Garden; New York Magazine; New York Times; Parents; Saturday Review; Village Voice; Wilson Library Bulletin. Honours: Book Show Awards, American Institute of Graphic Arts, 1955-60; Children's Book Award, International Reading Association, 1976; Children's Book Council Showcase Selections, 1976-77; National Council of Teachers of English Poetry Award, 1979; Children's Science Book Award, New York Academy of Sciences, 1980; American Library Association Awards, 1980, 1982, 1993; Best Book of 1987, School Library Journal; Others. Address: 96 Joralemon Street, Brooklyn, NY 11201, USA.

L

LA FORTUNE Knolly Stephen, b. 2 Jan 1920, Trinidad, West Indies. Teacher; Writer; Lecturer. m. Catherine Searle, 28 Aug 1971, 1 son, 1 daughter. Education: Trinidad Teachers College, 1943-45; ACP, College of Preceptors, London, 1954; ATC, Goldsmiths College, London University, 1954-56; FRGS, Royal Geographical Society, 1976; BA, Open University, 1977; PhD, International University, 1985. Appointments: Education Officer, Trinidad, 1959-60; Junior Librarian, St Pauls Sec, London, 1968-70; Teacher, 1959-80. Publications: Moments of Inspiration Poetry; Several poems. Contributions to: RAAbits English, Carnival Rhapsody, 1995; Trinidad & Tobago Guardian; Catholic News; Poet of Spain Gazette; London Regional Examination Board; Goldsmiths College Jubilee Magazine; World of Poetry Magazine West Indian Chronicle; Birm; West Indian Digest; Caribbean Times. Honours: Trinidad Teacher of the Year, 1952; Literary Diploma of Merit; International Academy of Poets Award; Statue of Victor Award; Man of Year Award; Best Poem Award. Memberships: Caribbean Teachers Association; Academy of Poets; Caribbean Art Society. Address: 68 Arthurdon Road, Brockley, London SE4 1JO, England.

LA GATTUTA Margo, b. 18 Sept 1942, Detroit, Michigan, USA. Poet; Teacher. m. Stephen La Gattuta, 14 Nov 1964, div June 1988, 3 sons. Education: BA, English honours, Oakland University, Rochester, Michigan, 1980; MFA, Writing, Vermont College, 1984. Appointments: Seminar Leader, Cranbrook PM, 1984-; Writing Consultant, schools, 1986-; English Instructor, Oakland Community College, Michigan, 1987-; Radio Host, weekly talk show, 1990-. Publications: Diversion Road, 1983; Noedgelines, 1986; The Dream Givers, 1990; Inventing The Invisible, audio tape, 1990; Video, 1992. Contributions to: Bridge; Passages North; Calliope; Cincinnati Poetry Review; Negative Capability; Moving Out; Sun; Earth's Daughters; Labyris; 5 AM; McGuffin; Green River Review; Little Magazine; Woamn Poet; Mobius; Odyssey; New Laurel Review; Metro Times; Detroit News; Rochester Clarion; Anthology of Outstanding Michigan Poets; Anthology for Magazine Verse and Yearbook of American Poetry; Waves; Reviews; Book Reader, California; Detroit News. Honours: Ohio Poetry Day Award, 1991; Gwendolyn Book Award, Poetry, Michigan State University, 1991; Florida State Poetry Award, National Federation of State Poetry Societies, Illinois Chapter; International Women's Writers Guild; Detroit Women Writers; Cranbrook Writers Guild. Address: 2134 West Gunn Road, Rochester, MI 48306, USA.

LA LOCA. See: KAROL Pamala Marie.

LAABS Joochen-Henning, b. 3 July 1937, Dresden, Germany. Traffic Engineer. 3 daughters. Education: Technical University, 1956-61. Appointments: Scientist, Institute for Public Transportation; Head of Department; Freelance Writer. Publications: Eine Strassenbahn für Nofretete; Himmel Straflicher Leichtsinn. Contributions to: Neue Deutsche Literatur; Neue Literatur; Micromegas; Literature Mesicnik; Plamik; Union. Honour: Martin Anderson Nexo Prize. Memberships: PEN; VS. Address: Husstrasse 126, 12489 Berlin, Germany.

LABOMBARD Joan, b. 2 July 1920, San Francisco, California, USA. Poet. m. Emerson H LaBombard, 17 July 1943, 1 daughter. Education: BA, University of California at Los Angeles, 1943. Publications: Calendar, 1985; The Counting of Grains, 1990; The Winter Watch of the Leaves, 1993. Contributions to: The Atlantic; Chicago Tribune; Colorado Review; Poetry; Poetry Northwest; The Nation; Prairie Schooner; Virginia Quarterly Review; several anthologies. Honours: Borestone Mountain Poetry Awards Annual Volumes, 1st Prize, 1958, 1969; PSA, Reedy Award, 1971; Lucile Medwick Award, 1974; Consuela Ford, 1977; Wagner Award, 1977; American Book Award for The Counting of Grains, 1989. Memberships: Academy of American Poets; Poetry Society of America; Associated Writing Programs; PEN Center USA West. Address: 814 Teakwood Road, Los Angeles, CA 90049, USA.

LACZKOWSKI Zdzislaw, (Tadeusz Seweryn), b. 27 Oct 1927, Zawiercie, Katowice, Poland. Novelist; Journalist; Poet. Education: Law Faculty, Jagiellonian University, 1948-49; Actor School, 1948-49; Catholic University of Lublin. Appointments: Art Editor, Slowo Powszechne, 1952-92; Slowo-Dziennik Katolicki, 1992-95. Publications: Poems and Poetical Prose: Gad; The Poem of John Paul; Collection of Selected Poems; Two Novels and Episode of Memoires; Short Plays; Author of 18 Books (Poetry and Poetical Prose) and two thousand critical publications. Honours: Wlodzimierz Pietrzak Literary Award (twice); Kierunki Magazine Award; International Giorgio La Pira Award. Memberships: European Culture Association; Union of Polish Writers, 1960-90; Dramaturgists and Stage Composers Association. Address: Falecka 5/7 m 65, 02-547 Warsaw, Poland.

LADY IN BLACK. See: SOLON Loretta Joseph.

LAIBI Shaker, b. 21 Mar 1955, Iraq. Writer; Painter. Education: Master's Degree, Baghdad, 1977; Diploma, Ecole Superieur d'Art Visuel, Geneva, 1982. Publications: Fingers of Stone, in Arabic, 1976; One of Three Texts, in Arabic, 1982; Calling for Help (Istigatat), 1984; Eloquence, Arabic-French, 1988; Text of Texts, in Arabic, 1993; These are the Guards, My Sublime, in Arabic, 1993; Mythaphisyque, in Arabic, 1995; Menga, la pastorale, 1996; L'inconographie de Sacré, 1996. Contributions to: Archipel, revue Belge; Nord-Sud, revue Suisse; Mawaqif; Al-Karmel; Al-Naqid; Al-Badil; Al-Adab; Others. Membership: Societe Suisse des Ecrivaines et Ecrivains. Address: 77 bd Carl-Vogt, 1205 Geneva, Switzerland.

LAIR Helen Humphrey, b. 3 Jan 1918, Indiana, USA. Poet; Artist; Art Teacher. m. Marvin Lair, 2 July 1966, 1 son, 2 daughters. Education: Anderson College; Herron School of Art; Wisconsin University; Gloucester School of Art. Publication: Earth Pilgrim and Lair of the Four Winds. Contributions to: Best Loved Contemporary Poems; Adventures in Poetry; Hibiscus Press; National Society of Art and Literature; Premier Poets; Poets of India; Poetry Review; The Criterion, 1994-95. Honours: Clover International Award; Bicentennial Poetry Award; Farnell Award; Miller Award; Golden Poet Award; Campbell Historical Award; National Federation of Poets Award; Hibiscus Press Award. Memberships: New York Poetry Forum; Raintree Writers; California Chaparrel Poets; World Congress Poets; Academy American Poets; International Platform Association; Indiana Federation of Poets; National Federation of Poets; Men and Women in Communication; Poets Achievement and World Congress of Poets. Address: 741 Kenwood Avenue, Fort Wayne, IN 46805, USA.

LAITER Saloman, b. 16 July 1937, Mexico City, Mexico. Poet; Film Director; Painter. 4 sons. Education: School of Architecture; MGM Studio, England. Publications: David; Women Of Lot; The Dungeons Of Hell; Memories Of An Architect; The Perpetual Exile; Area Of Silences; Mester De Juglaria. Contributions to: Uno Mas Uno; Siempre; Revista De Bellas Artes; Excelsior. Memberships: Society of Mexican Authors; Directors Guild. Address: Montanas Rocallasas Pte 210, Lomas de Chapultepec, Mexico 11000, DF Mexico.

LALLY Margaret, b. Cleveland, Ohio, USA. Associate Professor of English. m. Thomas R Lally, 21 Oct 1961, div 1976, 2 sons. Education: BA English, 1972, MA English, 1974, PhD, English Literature, 1982, Case Western Reserve University. Appointments: Graduate Assistant and Lecturer, Case Western Reserve University, 1975-83; Lecturer in English, University of Akron, Ohio, 1982-87; Professor, Citadel, Military College of South Carolina, USA, 1987-. Publication: Juliana's Room, 1988. Contributions to: Kenyon Review; Ohio Review; Literary Review; Hudson Review. Honours: Individual Artist's Award, Ohio Arts Council, 1984; Nomination, Los Angeles Times Book Prize, 1989. Membership: Poet's Prize Committee, D H Lawrence Society of North America. Address: Department of English, The Citadel, 171 Moultrie Street, Charleston, SC 29409, USA.

LAM Cecil Justin, b. 16 Dec 1957, Hong Kong. Poet; Painter; Performer. 1 son. Education: University Degrees; Honorary PhD Degree in Poetry and Philosophy. Appointments: Poet, Musician, Composer, Painter, Exhibiter, Performer, Sculptor, Calligrapher, Martial Artist, Herbalist, Naturopathic Medicine Exponent. Publications: The Poetry of God, 1995; Holy Blood: The Seven Seals, God and Man; Angel's Wings; Universe; Utoila; God and Angel; In His Image; The Poet in Disguise. Contributions to: Plowman magazines; Bet Magazines; Best Poems of Today; Toronto Sun newspaper; Toronto Star newspaper; Red Horse; The Orange X; The Purple X. Honours: Editor's Choice, Distinguished America's Poets; First Prize in Literature & Poetry, The Canadian Boys and Girls Agency; First Prize in Long Poem, Canadian Association for Civil Justice and Equality. Memberships: Canadian Poetry Association; Canadian League of

Poets; Associate Member, United Nation of Canadian Associates. Address: PO Box 22127, Thorncliffe PO Station, Toronto, M4H 1N9, Canada.

LAMANTIA Philip, b. 23 Oct 1927, San Francisco, California, USA. Poet. Education: University of California at Berkeley, 1947-49. Publications: Erotic Poems, 1946; Narcotica: I Demand Extinction of Laws Prohibiting Narcotic Drugs, 1959; Ekstasis, 1959; Destroyed Works, 1962; Touch of the Marvelous, 1966; Selected Poems, 1943-1966, 1967; Penguin Modern Poets 13 (with Charles Bukowski and Harold Norse), 1969; The Blood of the Air, 1970; Becoming Visible, 1981; Meadowland West, 1986. Address: c/o City Lights Books, 261 Columbus Avenue, San Francisco, CA 94133, USA.

LAMB Elizabeth Searle, b. 22 Jan 1917, Topeka, Kansas, USA. Freelance Writer; Poet; Editor. m. F Bruce Lamb, 11 Dec 1941, 1 daughter. Education: BA, University of Kansas, 1939; BMus, 1940. Appointments: Harpist, Harp Teacher, Kansas City Music Conservatory, 1940-41; Personnel Clerk, Walsh Driscoll Construction Co, Trinidad, British West Indies, 1942-43; Temporary Clerk, US Consulate, Belem, 1943; Published Freelance Writer, Poet, 1939-; Editor, Frogpond, 1984-91, 1994. Publications: Lines for My Mother, Dying; Casting into a Cloud; 39 Blossoms; Picasso's Bust of Sylvette; In this Blaze of Sun; Inside Me, Outside Me; Today and Every Day. Contributions to: Haiku Anthology, 1974, 1986; Erotic Haiku, 1983; Haiku Handbook, 1985, 1989; Haiku: Canadian Anthology, 1985; Anthology of International Haiku Poets, 1992; Haiku Moment, 1993; Short and Sweet, Vol I, 1994; A Haiku Path: Haiku Society of America 1968-88, 1994; New Mexico Poetry Renaissance, 1994; Saludos!, 1995. American Haiku; Haiku World: An International Poetry Almanac; Modern Haiku; Frogpond; Brussels Sprout; Fish Drum; Outch; Mainichi Daily News; New York Times; New York Herald Tribune; Blue Unicorn; Studia Mystica; Shanghai Art and Letters; English Coaching; Shi Kan Poetry; Lookout; Purpose; Unity; Ant Farm. Honours: 1st Prize, Penumbral Poetry Competition; Special Prize, World Haiku Contest; 1st Prize, Mainichi Daily News Contest; Wind Chimes Press Publication Prize; J Franklyn Dew Award; Ko Poetry Association Award; Haiku Society of America Biennial Book Award; Henderson Memorial Haiku Award; High/Coo Press Publication Award; Ruben Dario Memorial Award; First Annual Honorary Curatorship, American Haiku Archive, California State Library. Memberships: Haiku Society of America; Poetry Society of America; Haiku International Association; Association for International Renku. Address: 970 Acequia Madre Street, Santa Fe, NM 87501, USA.

LAMBOVSKI Boyko Panov, b. 13 Mar 1960, Sofia, Bulgaria. Literary Consultant. m. Liudmila Kirilova Koteva, 13 May 1992. Education: Lycée de Langue Française, Sofia, 1974-79; M Gorky, Literary Institute, Moscow, 1982-87. Appointments: Referrent, Union of Bulgarian Writers, 1987-89; Editor, auditoria students literary issue, 1989-90. Publications: Messenger, 1986; Scarlet Decadence, 1991; Evarda, 1992. Contributions to: Literaturen Vestnik; Plamak; Letopisi; Other Bulgarian publications; Akzente, Berlin; Latinsky Kvartal, Moscow; Child Of Europe, anthology, London; Kmen, Prague; Others. Honours: Vladimir Bashev National Prize, Poetical Book Debut, 1987; Annual Prize, Achievements in the Sphere of Art, Svoboden Narod paper, 1992. Memberships: Union of Bulgarian Writers; Co-founder, Friday 13th, avant garde literary movement for synthesis of arts. Address: Shipchenski Prokhod 7-11, Bl 228-A, Ap 65, Sofia 1111, Bulgaria.

LANCASTER William John, b. 18 Apr 1946. Writer; Teacher. m. Barbara Milligan, 2 sons. Education: BA, 1967, MA, 1970, University of Sheffield. Appointments: Lecturer in Creative Writing, University of Huddersfield and Open College of the Arts. Publications: Effects of War, 1986; Spilt Shift (with Geoff Hattersley), 1990. Contributions to: Poetry Review; London Magazine; Times Literary Supplement; Ambit; Iron; Encounter; Rialto; Wide Skirt; Echo Room; Pennine Platform; Slow Dancer; Orbis; Scratch; Verse; Aquarius; North; English In Education. Honours: 2nd Prize, National Poetry Competition, 1979; Writers Award, Yorkshire Arts, 1983. Membership: Committee Member, National Association of Writers in Education. Address: 32 Thornhill Road, Edgerton, Huddersfield, Yorkshire HD3 3DD, England.

LANCE Betty Rita Gomez, b. 28 Aug 1923, Costa Rica. Professor Emeritus; Writer. 2 sons. Education: Teaching Diploma, Universidad Nacional, Costa Rica, 1941; BA, Central Missouri State University, Warrensburg, 1944; MA, University of Missouri, Columbia, 1947; PhD, Washington University, St Louis, 1959. Appointment:

Professor Emeritus of Romance Languages and Literatures, Kalamazoo College. Publications: La Actitud Picaresca en la Novela Espanola del Siglo XX, 1969; Vivencias, 1981; Bebiendo Luna, 1983; Vendimia del Tiempo, 1984; Hoy Hacen Corro las Ardillas, short story, 1985; Alas en el Alba, 1987; Siete Cuerdas, 1996. Contributions to: Americas; Letras Femeninas; Caprice; and others. Memberships: Poets and Writers of America, USA; Asociacion De Escritores De Costa Rica; Asociacion Prometeo De Poesia, Madrid; Academia IberoAmericana De Poesia, Madrid. Address: 1562 Spruce Drive, Kalamazoo, MI 49008, USA.

LANDERT Walter, b. 3 Jan 1929, Zürich, Switzerland. Merchant. m. Elsy Weber, 15 Apr 1954, 3 sons, 1 daughter. Education: Swiss Mercantile School, London, 1950; Student Trainee, Westminster Bank, London, 1951. Appointments: Bank Employee; Sales Manager; Manager, Administration Department; Independent Merchant; Writer. Publications: Manager auf Zeit; Selbstbefragung Poems; Entwurf Schweiz; Koitzsch Novel; Traum einer Besseren Welt; Unkraut im Helvetischen Kulturgartchen; Meine Frau baut einen Bahnhof; S Huus us pilatusholz; Klemms Memorabilien; Umwerfende Zeiten; Treffpunkt: Fondue Bourguigonne, novel, 1992. Contributions to: Various newspapers and anthologies. Honours: Artemis Jubilee Prize; Poetry prize. Membership: Swiss Authors Group, Olten. Address: Lendikonerstrasse 54, CH-8484 Weisslingen ZH, Switzerland.

LANE M(illicent Elizabeth) Travis, b. 23 Sept 1934, USA. Poet. m. Lauriat Lane, 26 Aug 1957, 1 son, 1 daughter. Education: BA, Vassar College, 1956; MA, 1957,PhD, 1967, Cornell University. Publications: An Inch or So of Garden; Poems; Homecomings; Divinations and Shorter Poems; Reckonings; Solid Things; Temporary Shelter; Night Physics. Contributions to: Canadian Literature; Dalhousie Review; Fiddlehead; Exile; Event; Germination; Antigonish Review; New Quarterly; Canadian Forum; Canadian Literature; Room of Ones Own; Moosehead Review; Queens Quarterly; Cormorant; Waves; Scrivener; Other Voices; Pottersfield; Portfolio; Tidepool; Quarry; Poetry; Canada Review; Malahat; Southern Review; Wascana Review. Honours: Pat Lowther Prize; Fiddlehead; Writers Federation of New Brunswick, 1994. Memberships: League of Canadian Poets; Writers Federation of New Brunswick; Canadian Poetry Association. Address: 807 Windsor Street, Fredericton, New Brunswick E3B 4G7, Canada.

LANG-DILLENBURGER Elmy (Elmy Lang), b. 13 Aug 1921, Pirmasens, Germany. Writer; Painter; Interpreter. m. Franz Dillenburger, 9 Sept 1947, div 1974, 1 son. Appointment: Foreign Correspondent. Publications: Mitternachtsspritzer; Pingpong Pinguin; Das Wort; Blick ins Paradies; Limericks; Stufen zum Selbst Lebenszeichen; Verdammt geliebtes Leben - Vie maudite bien aimée. Contributions to: Philadelphia Gazette; Literat; Rheinpfalz; Mindener Tageblatt; Silhouette; Neue Westfalische; Westfalenblatt and others. Honours: Gran Premio d'Europe; La Musa Dell'Arte; Landgrafenmedaille der Stadt Pirmasens. Memberships: European Authors Association Die Kobge; German Writers Union; International Writers Union, Regensburg. Address: Strobelallee 62, D-66953 Pirmasens, Germany.

LANGE Eugene Samuel, (Muhammad Khalil), b. 7 July 1955, Liverpool, England. Teacher; Performance Artist; Freelance Performance Poet. 1 daughter. Education: Youth and Community Work, North East Wales, 1979-81; Millbrook College, 1988. Publications: Numerous Poems, Title and Introduction, Collection of Poetry by Levi Tafari, Ryme Don't Pay. Contributions to: Rasta Magazine; Window; Numerous anthologies; Under Currents; Smoke; Black Lynx; Black Arts. Honour: Black Penmanship Award. Address: Flat 321 Belvedere Road, Liverpool L8 3TF, England.

LANGE Naomi. See: **DIACHUK Naomi Joy.**

LANGLAND Joseph Thomas, b. 16 Feb 1917, Spring Grove, Minnesota, USA. Writer; Teacher. m. Judith Gail Wood, 26 June 1943, 2 sons, 1 daughter. Education: AA, Santa Ana College, 1936; BA, University of Iowa, 1940; MA, 1941; Graduate Study, 1946-48; Harvard and Columbia Universities, 1953-54. Appointments: Instructor, University of Iowa, 1946-48; Instructor, Dana College, 1941-42; Assistant and Associate Professor, University of Wyoming, 1948-49; Associate and Full Professor, University of Massachusetts, 1959-80; Professor Emeritus, 1980-. Publications: A Dream of Love, 1986; Twelve Poems, 1991; Selected Poems, 1992. Contributions to: New York Times Books; New Yorker; Atlantic; Paris Review; London

Magazine; Listen; Poetry Review; Nation; Harpers/Bazaar; Sewanee; Hudson; Virginia Quarterly; Massachusetts. Honours: Ford Faculty Fellowship; Amy Lowell Poetry Fellowship; New England Living Legend; Chancellors Prize. Memberships: Several. Address: 16 Morgan Circle, Amherst, MA 01002, USA.

LANGTON Daniel Joseph, b. 6 Sept 1927, New Jersey, USA. College Professor. m. 1 Feb 1949, 1 son. Education: St Pauls and Hayes; San Francisco State College; University of California. Appointments: High School Teacher, 1963-67; College Teacher, 1967-. Publications: Querencia; The Hogarth Selhush Letters; The Inheritance; Life Forms. Contributions to many periodicals. Honours: London Prize; Browning Award; Devins Award. Memberships: Poetry Society of America; American Academy of Poets. Address: Box 170012, San Francisco, CA 94117, USA.

LANNERS Paul, b. 25 June 1948, Luxembourg. Adult Educator. Education: Licence of Classical Philology, Catholic University of Louvain, Belgium, 1973; Licence of Catholic Theology, University of Strasbourg, France, 1988. Publications: Point de Convergence, Poèmes de 1967 à 1980, 1983. Contributions to: Littérature luxembourgeoise de langue française, Sherbrooke, 1980, collective works; Magazines and Journals: Les Nouvelles Pages de la SELF; Nos Cahiers; Présence francophone; Letzebuerger Almanach; and others; Poems translated into Dutch and Russian. Memberships: Former member of Board of Directors, Société des Ecrivains Luxembourgeois de Langue Française (SELF). Address: 28 Rue Charles-Arendt, L-1134 Luxembourg.

LANTAY Patricia, b. 6 Mar 1946, New York, New York, USA. Office Administrator. 2 daughters. Education: BA, Marymount College, 1982. Appointments: Editor of St Bartholomew's Review, 1972; Historian to the New York Poetry Forum, 1974. Contributions to: St Bartholomew's Review, 1972, 1973, 1976; West Virginia Poetry Society Anthology, 1994; Elk River review, 1996. Honours: Anna Phillips Bolling Memorial for Poetry, Greenwich Academy; Sylvia Plath Award, World Narrative of Poets, 1980; Graduation Medal of Honor, Marymount College, 1982; Eva Ban Award, New York Poetry Forum, 1983; Annette Feldman Award, New York Poetry Forum, 1983; West Virginia Poetry Society Annual Contest, 1994; Massachusetts State Poetry Society Award, 1994; California State Poetry Society August Contest, 1994; Miller Award, Green Rivers Writers, 1994; Jessee Poet July Award, 1995. Memberships: Academy of American Poets; New York Poetry Forum; National Federation of State Poetry Societies. Address: 333 East 43rd Street, New York, NY 10017, USA.

LAPERLE P(atricia) J(oan Karr), b. 4 Jan 1943, Springfield, Massachusetts, USA. Author. m. Donald A Laperle, 10 Oct 1981, 1 son, 4 stepsons, 2 stepdaughters. Education: Barrington College, 1960-62. Appointments: Assistant, Inventory Control, Dennison Manufacturing Co; Head of Inventory Control, Clearpoint Inc; Welfare Secretary, Salvation Army. Publications: Under His Wings; Land of Living Waters. Contributions to: World of Poetry Press; Odessa Poetry Review; Sparrow Grass Poetry; National Arts Society; Poetry; Caring Connection - John Milton Society for the Blind Publications. Honours: Golden Poet Award; Silver Poet Award; Robert Frost Poetry Festival; Apa Poet of Merit Award; Christian Writers Fellowship International Koala Book Award. Memberships: Poetry Society of America; National Arts Society; Massachusetts State Poetry Society; National Federation of State Poetry Societies; Christian Writers Fellowship International. Address: 2 Downey Street, Hopkinton, MA 01748, USA.

LAPIERRE Matthew Scott, b. 9 Oct 1968, Augusta, Maine, USA. Poet. Education: BA, Colby College, 1990; MFA, University Massachusetts, Amherst, 1993. Contributions to: Atom Mind; Chiron Review; Midwest Quarterly; Daedalus Anthology of Kinky Verse; Cokefish; Poetry Motel; Sheila-Na-Gig. Honours: 3rd Place, Chiron Review Poetry Contest, 1995; Winner, Rocket Press Poetry Contest, 1995; Nominated for 1996 Pushcart Prize. Address: PO Box 7615, Portland, ME 04112, USA.

LAPIERRE Pierre, b. 16 Jan 1932, Elisabethville, Zaire. Senior Lecturer. Div, 1 son, 5 daughters. Education: BSc, University of Cape Town, 1954; BA (Hons), Drama, French, 1979, PhD, 1993, UKC. Appointments: Freelance Poet, Playwright. Publications: Poster Poems; Celebration of Summer; State of the Kingdom; Ducks. Honours: Radio Medway 2nd Prize; Herbert Read Gallery. Membership: Poetry Society of Great Britain. Address: 160 Old Dover Road, Canterbury, Kent CT1 3EX, England.

LAPOLT Eda Marie, b. 11 Mar 1956, Monticello, New York, USA. Secretary. Education: Graduate, Monticello High School, 1974; AAS Degree, Secretarial Science with Word Processing, Orange County Community College, 1983. Appointments: Telephone Operator, New York Telephone Company for 10 years; Legal Secretary for 2 years; Administrative Secretary for 5 years. Contributions to: National Library of Poetry; Poetry in Motion; Poet's Corner; True Romance Magazine. Honours: 5 Editor's Choice Awards, National Library of Poetry. Memberships: The National Poet's Association; The International Society of Poets. Address: 7 Nelshore Drive, Monticello, NY 12701, USA.

LARGE Timothy Stoker, b. 11 Sept 1972, Iowa City, Iowa, USA. Education: BA, Honours, English, Balliol College, Oxford, 1992. Appointments: Editor, Corroboree; Guitarist; Songwriter. Publications: Wonderland and Other Poems, 1991; Wonderland and Thy Hand, 1992. Contributions to: Hybrid; Purple Patch; Poems; Others. Honours: 1st Prize, Under-19 Section, Charterhouse International Poetry Competition, 1991. Memberships: Poetry Society; President, Society of Lunatics, Lovers and Poets. Address: 78 Windsor Road, Cambridge CB4 3JN, England.

LARSEN Marianne, b. 27 Jan 1951, Kalundborg, Denmark. Poet. Publications: Several volumes of poems, 1971-; Free Compositions, 1991. Contributions to: Many Danish and foreign magazines. Honours: Adam Oehelagers Prize, 1980; Emil Aarestrup Prize, 1982; Beatrice Prize, 1989; Martin Andersen Nexo Prize, 1990; Egmont Fond Prize, 1991. Membership: Danish Ministry of Cultural Affairs Committee for Rewarding Poets and Writers with State Aid. Address: Worsaesvej 20, 2 tv, 1972 Frederiksbourg C, Denmark.

LARSON Edna (Doris) Miner, b. 6 Mar 1928, Cedar Rapids, Iowa, USA. Freelance Writer. m. Ted A Larson, 13 Aug 1974. Education: Coe College, 1949-53. Appointments: Administrative Director, Quad City Physicians Exchange; Treasurer, Waterloo Cedar Rapids Branch of National League of American Pen Women; President, Midwest Federation of Chaparral Poets. Contributions to: Cappers; C R Gazetts; Over 409 News & Views; Nostalgia; Bereavement; Zipper Room; Hospice Happenings; Calvin Comments. Honour: Iowa Lyrical. Memberships: National League of American Pen Women; Midwest Federation of Chaparral Poets; Iowa Poetry Association. Address: 1611 2nd Avenue Southeast, Cedar Rapids, IA 52403, USA.

LARSON Rosamond Winterton, b. 10 Dec 1932, Los Angeles, California, USA. m. Robert Patten Larson, 16 May 1977, 3 sons, 4 daughters. Education: St Joseph Hospital School of Nursing, 1950-52; Palomar Junior College, 1965-66. Publications: New American Poetry Anthology; The Golden Treasury of Great Poems; World Treasury of Great Poems; American Anthology of Contemporary Poetry; American Anthology of Midwestern Poetry; Poetic Voices of America. Contributions to: Glamour; Heuristagon; Dear Mr Gorbachev. Memberships: Academy of American Poets; Breast Cancer Action of San Francisco, USA; Amnesty International, USA. Address: PO Box 11912, Zephyr Cove, NV 89448, USA.

LASKEY Michael, b. 15 Aug 1944, Lichfield, Staffordshire, England. Poet; Educator. m. Kay Osler, 23 Apr 1974, 3 sons. Education: Open Exhibitioner, English, St John's College, Cambridge, 1962-65; BA, English, 1965. Appointments: Teacher, English for Foreigners, Berlitz School, Santander, Spain; Member, English Department, Colegio Gazelueta, Las Arenas, Vizcaya; Lecturer I, English and Liberal Studies, North Nottinghamshire College Of Further Education, Worksop, England. Teacher of English, Scale III, Richard Hale School, Hertford; Arvon Tutor; W H Smith Poet in Schools; Poetry Correspondent, BBC, Radio Suffolk; Freelance Writing Groups Coordinator, Arts and Libraries Department, Suffolk County Council, 1992; Co-Editor, Smiths Knoll Poetry Magazine. Publications: Cloves of Garlic, 1989; Represented in Peterloo Preview 2, 1990; Thinking of Happiness, 1991. Contributions to: Times Literary Supplement; London Review of Books; Spectator; Poetry Durham; Poetry Review; Rialto; Stand; London Magazine; Others. Honours: Joint Winner, Cloves of Garlic, Poetry Business Pamphlet Competition, 1988; Thinking of Happiness, Poetry Book Society Recommendation, 1991. Memberships: Founding Coordinator, Aldeburgh Poetry Festival; Honorary Secretary, Trustee, Aldeborough Poetry Trust; Founding Member, East Suffolk Poetry Workshop. Address: Goldings, Goldings Lane, Leiston, Suffolk IP16 4EB, England.

LASSELL Michael John, b. 15 July 1947, New York, New York, USA. Writer; Editor; Journalist. Education: AB, Colgate University, 1969; MFA, School of Drama, Yale University, 1976. Appointments: Articles Director, Metropolitan Home; Executive Editor, SI Magazine; Managing Editor, Interview; Managing Editor, LA Style. Publications: Poems for Lost and Un-Lost Boys, 1985; Decade Dance, 1990; The Hard Way, 1995; The Name of Love, 1995; Eros in Boystown, 1996; Anthologies: Gay and Lesbian Poetry in Our Time, 1988; Poets for Life, 1989; High Risk, 1990; Queer City, 1991. Contributions to: Los Angeles Times Magazine; Dance Magazine; Poetry New York; City Lights Review; Poetry LA; Zyzzyva; Central Park; Hanging Loose; Kansas Quarterly; Out; Advocate; Frontiers. Honours: Lambda Literary Award, 1991 for Decade Dance; Finalist, Gregory Kolovakos Award for Writing About AIDS; Nominated, American Library Association Award. Memberships: PEN American Centre; Poets and Writers; National Lesbian and Gay Journalists Association; The Publishing Triangle; American Society of Magazine Editors. Address: 114 Horatio Street, No 512, New York, NY 10014, USA.

LATHBURY Roger, (Roger Lewis) b. 9 Sept 1945, New York, New York, USA. University Professor. m. Begona, 6 Aug 1986. Education: Indiana University, 1968. Appointment: Associate Professor, George Mason University. Publication: The Carbon Gang. Address: Orchises Press, PO Box 20602, Alexandria, VA 22320, USA.

LATTIG Sharon, b. Dover, New Jersey, USA. Adjunct Lecturer; PhD Candidate. Education: BFA, New York University, 1985; MA, City College, 1995; PhD Candidate, The Graduate School and University Center, The City University of New York. Appointments: Adjunct Lecturer, English, The College of Staten Island, 1995-; Archivist, The Segue Poetry Archive, 1995-. Contributions to: Columbia Poetry Review; Whatever; Promethean. Honour: Alice M Sellers Prize, Academy of American Poets, 1995. Membership: Modern Language Association. Address: 230 Riverside Drive, Apartment 18-C, New York, NY 10025, USA.

LAUTURE Denizé, b. 11 May 1946, Haiti. Writer; Teacher. m. 2 sons. Education: BA, City College, New York, 1977; MA, 1981. Appointment: Assistant Professor, St Thomas Aquinas College. Publications: Boula Pou Yon Metamòfoz Zèklè; When the Denizen Weeps, 1989; 2 Childrens Books: Father and Son, 1993, Running the Road to ABC, 1996. Contributions to: Black American Literary Forum; African Commentary; Presence Africaine; Bitterroots; Innisfree; Poetry 13; Haiti Culture; Hatch and Billops Collections; Callaloo; Compost; Litoral: Poesia Norteamerican Contemporanea. Honours: Best Book of Poetry; Board of Trustees Award for Excellence, St Thomas Aquinas College, 1994. Memberships: The Poetry Society of America; Poets and Writers; American Association of Teachers of French. Address: St Thomas Aquinas College, Route 340, Sparkill, NY 10976, USA.

LAVERY Erin Margaret, b. 3 Mar 1979, Los Angeles, California, USA. Student. Education: Summer Writing and Literature Program, Oxford University. Publications: Works included in: Distinguished Poets of America, 1993; A Break in the Clouds, 1993; American Poetry Annual, 1994; Tears of Fire, 1995. Contributions to: World's Largest Peace Poem. Honours: Editor's Choice Award, twice, 1993, 1995; Accomplishment of Merit Certificate, Creative Arts and Sciences, 1994. Membership: International Society of Poets. Address: Los Angeles, California, USA.

LAVIN S R, (M Gordon), b. 2 Apr 1945, Springfield, Massachusetts, USA. Writer; Teacher. 2 sons, 4 daughters. Education: AIC, BA, 1967; MA, Literature, Trinity College, 1970. Appointments: Editor, The Four Zoas Press, 1972-80; Professor of English, Castleton State College, 1987-; Professor of English, CCV, 1988-. Publications: To A City Girl I Have Forgotten, 1968; The Stonecutters At War With The Cliff Dwellers, 1970; Cambodian Spring, 1973; Let Myself Shine, 1979; The Knew Me When, 1990. Contributions to: Stand Magazine; Hiram Poetry Review; Malcontent Cold Drill; Chelsea; Black Box; Broadway Boogie; Four Zoas Journal Of Poetry and Letters; Fag Rag Little Caesar; Lynx; Springfield Journal; Plowman Anthology. Honours: National Endowment for the Arts, 1973-76, 1980; Permanent Archive at University of Buffalo, 1989-. Membership: Poets and Writers. Address: 417 East Street, Middletown Springs, VT 05757, USA.

LAVOIE Steven Paul, b. 9 Oct 1953, Minnesota, USA. News Librarian. Education: AB, Humanaties, 1975, Master of Library and Information Studies, 1985, University of California at Berkeley.

Appointments: Reference Assistant, Cedar Rapids (Iowa) Public Library, 1982-84; Columnist, Editorial Writer, Oakland Tribune, 1991-; Librarian, Marin Independent Journal, 1986-89; Librarian, Oakland Tribune, California, 1989-. Publications: Snoring Practice, 1982; On the Way, 1982; Erosion Surface, 1984; Birth of a Brain (with Dave Morice), 1984; Plastic Rulers, 1984; Nine Further Plastics, 1985; Lipsynch, 1986; Original Panorama, 1995. Contributions to: Los Angeles, 1956; Komotion International; Life of Crime; East Bay Guardian; Signs of Life; Exquisite Corpse; Potrero Hill Literary Supplement; Punk; Instead of a Magazine; Blue Suede Shoes; End; Famous. Honours: Winner, Sonoma State University Poetry Festival, 1971; Doris Green Award, 1982; Mark Twain Prize, 1984. Memberships: Co-Founder, Black Bart Poetry Society; Pacific Center for the Book Arts; Society for American Baseball Research; Board of Directors, University of California, School of Library & Information Studies Alumni Association. Address: 4085B Lincoln Avenue, Oakland, CA 94602, USA.

LAWRENCE Christina. See: **LOOTS Barbara Kunz.**

LAWSON David Douglas Alexander, b. 20 June 1965, London, England. Writer. Education: Trinity College, Glenalmond, Scotland, 1979-83; Trinity College, Cambridge, 1984-87; Trinity College, Oxford, 1987-90. Contributions to: Haiku Hundred. Honour: Powell Prize. Memberships: Cambridge/Oxford; School of Poets, Edinburgh. Address: Pittarrow, Perth Road, Abernethy, Tayside PH2 9LW, Scotland.

LAWSON Sarah Anne, b. 4 Nov 1943, Indianapolis, Indiana, USA. Writer; Translator. Education: BA, Indiana University, 1965; MA, University of Pennsylvania, 1966; PhD, University of Glasgow, 1971. Publications: Dutch Interiors, 1985; Outside the Chain of Hands, with 3 others, 1994; Down Where the Willow is Washing Her Hair, 1995. Contributions to: Poetry Introduction 6, 1985; TLS, London Review of Books; New Statesman; Orbis; Quarto; English; Critical Quarterly; Quaker Monthly; The Pen; The Honest Ulsterman; The Rialto. Honour: C Day Lewis Fellowship, 1979-80. Memberships: English PEN, Fellow, Executive Committee; Poetry Society; Royal Society of Literature. Address: 186 Albyn Road, London SE8 4JQ, England.

LAXDAL Eggert, b. 5 April 1925, Iceland. Painter. 1 son, 4 daughters. Education: Photoengraver; Painter. Publications: 3 books of poetry; 4 other books; 3 books for children; 1 novel. Contributions to: Icelandic reviews. Membership: Writers Association, Iceland. Address: Frumskogum 14, Hverager i, Iceland.

LAXMAN Bhatia (Komal Laxman), b. 26 Mar 1936, Pakistan. Journalist. m. Godi Jagtiani, 30 Oct 1963, 1 son, 2 daughters. Education: Delhi University; PU School of Journalism. Appointments: Sub editor, Times of India; Chief Sub Editor. Publications: Nau Sabha; Jeea Jharoko; Folk Tales of Pakistan; Three Operas. Contributions to: Koonj; Rachna; Lotus; Anthologies of Poetry; Many magazines and journals. Honours: Soviet Land Nehru Award; Sahitja Akademi Award; Ministry of Education Award. Memberships: Authors Guild; Sahitja Akademi; Forum of Financial Writers. Address: B-26 Press Enclave, Saket, New Delhi 110017, India.

LAZARUS Henry. See: **SLAVITT David R(ytman).**

LE FAY Malefica Grendelwolf Pendragon. See: **SCARPA Michael L.**

LE HEGARAT Irene, b. 25 Dec 1923, Halden, Norway. Poet; Clerk; Secretary. Education: Gothenburg University, 1964-66; Foreningen Nordens Institute, 1966-69. Publications: Stenspiror/Stone Spires; In The World; Under Vintergatan; Tunnlarna. Contributions to: Poesie Europé; Ord Och Bild; Var Lösen; Profil; Kurpil; Orbis; Lyrikvännen; Anthology: Parnassus of World Poets, India, 1994-95; Journal of Contemporary Anglo-Scandinavian Poetry, England, 1994; International Board Honorary Directors, Parnassus of World Poets, 1995. Memberships: Poetry Society; Swedish Writers Foundation, Stockholm, Sweden. Address: Marklandsgatan 53, 4tr, 414 77 Gothenburg, Sweden.

LEALE B C, b. 1 Sept 1930, Ashford, Middlesex, England. Publications: Leviathan and Other Poems, 1984; The Colours of Ancient Dreams, 1984. Contributions to: Ambit; Encounter; Fiction Magazine; Kayak; Listener; Literary Review; London Review of Books; Montana Gothic; Observer; Pacific Quarterly; Poetry Review; A Review of English Literature; Second Aeon; Spectator; Stand; Times

Literary Supplement; Tribune; Anthologies: Best of the Poetry Year 6; Double Vision; A Group Anthology; New Poems 1963 & 1977-78; New Poetry 1, 2, 4, 6, 7 & 9; New Writing & Writers 16 & 18; PEN New Poetry 1; The Poetry Book Society Anthology 1986-87; Voices in the Gallery. Address: Flat E10, Peabody Estate, Wild Street, London WC2B 4AH, England.

LEALMAN Brenda, b. 12 June 1939, West Yorkshire, England. Religious Educator. Education: BA, University of Birmingham; University of London. Appointments: Religious Education Teacher, Staffordshire, 1963-69; Head of Department, Collegiate School, Leicester, 1970-79; National Religious Education Adviser, Christian Education Movement, 1979-92; Fellow, Westhill College, Birmingham, 1990-92; Warden, Westhill College, 1992-; School Inspector, 1994-. Publications: The Image of Life; Knowing and Unknowing; The Mystery of Creation. Contributions to: Envoi Summer Anthology; Studia Mystica. Honour: First Prize, Resurgence Writing Competition. Membership: Poetry Society. Address: Flat 5, 158 London Road, Leicester LE2 1ND, England.

LEBIODA Dariusz Thomas, (Michael Podhorodecki, Marek Rosenbaum), b. 23 April 1958, Bydgoszcz, Poland. University Teacher. m. Danuta Futyma, 25 June 1983, 1 son. Education: MA, Higher Pedagogical School, 1984; PhD, University of Gdansk, 1994. Appointment: Teacher, Higher Pedagogical School, 1985-. Publications: Sucides from Under the Charles River, 1980; The Newest Testament, 1983; A Moment Before the End of the World, 1988; Cry, My Generation, 1990; Mysteries of the Life of Karol Wojtyla, 1991; Mickiewicz Imagination and Element, 1996; The Land of Swallow, 1995. Contributions to: Art; Misiecznik Literacki; Literature Life; Culture; Poetry. Honours: Andrzej Bursa Prize; Red Rose Prize; Ianicius Prize; Stanislav Wyspianski Prize; Best Poetical Book in Poland Prize. Memberships: Adam Mickiewicz Literary Society; Henryk Sienkiewicz Literary Society; Polish Writers Union. Address: ul Osiedlowa 18/16, 85-794 Bydgoszcz, Poland.

LECKNER Carole H, b. 13 Jan 1946, Montreal, Quebec, Canada. Author; Poet; Consultant. Education: MA, English in Creative Writing, Concordia University, Montreal, 1979. Appointments: Writer-Researcher, 7 on 6, CBC-TV, 1966-67; Freelance Writer, Journalist, Montreal Gazette Weekend Magazine, 1967; Producer, Director, Literary Reading Series, Centaur Theatre, 1974; Publisher, Editor, Rufanthology, Protestant School Board of Greater Montreal, 1974-80; Editor, Viewpoints magazine, Canadian Jewish Congress, 1980-81; Poet-in-the-Schools Programme, League of Canadian Poets, 1984-; Educator, writing and creativity seminars, Paradigm Communications, 1984-; Personal Creativity and Writing, School of Continuing Studies, University of Toronto, 1986-; Writer-in-Residence, Simon Fraser University, 1987; Personal Consultant in Writing and Creativity, Reader and Performer of Poetry, Canada, USA, 1972-; Conference Presenter, Writing, Creativity, 1978-; Reader, Soloist, poems of The Hour Has Come, 1989. Publications: Daisies On a Whales Back, 1972; Seasons In Transition, 1980; Cityheart, 1988; The New Whaler, The Seeds Of Time; In anthologies: The Hour Has Come, choral symphony (poet-librettist) performed worldwide, 1988; Score, 1987; This Time Forever, feature film, 1977. Contributions to: Magazines: POET-Descant Poetry Canada; CVII; Montreal Poems; New Directions; Cyan Line; Sundance Dream Journal; Anthol; Cross Country; Anthologies: Cross Cut; There Is A Voice; Tributaries; Sampler. Honours: Awards for contribution to Jewish Letters, 1978; Grants, Canada, 1987-93. Memberships: League of Canadian Poets; PEN; Writers' Guild, Canada; Alliance, Canadian Cinema, Television and Radio Artists; Society, Composers, Authors, Music Publishers, Canada. Address: Paradigm Communications, 111 Raglan Avenue, Suite 603, Toronto, Ontario M6C 2K9, Canada.

LEE Amy Freeman, b 3 Oct 1914. Appointments: Lifetime Chairman, Young Pegasus Poetry Contest, San Antonio Public Library, 1984-. Publications: Remember Pearl Harbor, 1943; Ipso Facto, 1976; Inkwell Echoes, 1985; Parnassus of World Poetry, 1994. Contributions to: American Poetry Magazine, 1941. Honours: Certificate of Merit, International Who's Who in Poetry, 1969; Honorary Member, San Antonio Poets Association, 1985; Art and Letters Award, Friends of the San Antonio Public Library, 1985; Award for 50 Years of Service, Young Pegasus Poetry Contest, San Antonio Public Library, 1991. Memberships include: Poetry Society of America, 1940-; Poetry Society of Texas, 1991-; Texas Watercolor Society; Southwestern Watercolor Society; National Watercolor Society; International Art Critics Association; Advisory Council, College of Fine Arts, University of Texas; San Antonio Lighthouse for the Blind; National Trustee, The Humane Society of the United States; Texas Committee for the Humanities; Board Trustees, Institute for the Humanities at Salada, Texas; Texas Art Education Association; International Women's Forum, New York. Address: 127 Canterbury Hill, San Antonio, TX 78209, USA.

LEE Ann, b. 9 Aug 1923, Idaho, USA. Librarian. m. Thomas S Lee, 25 Feb 1946, 1 son, 1 daughter, dec. Education: BA, Scripps College, 1944; MA, University of Chicago, 1951; MA, University of California, 1966. Appointments: Psychological Counsellor, 1948; Information Service, 1951-52; Editor, 1952-54; Librarian, 1966-72. Publication: Mornings. Contributions to: Epoch; First the Blade; Spring Harvest; Creative Writing; Michigan Quarterly Review; Encore; Christian Century; Small Pond; Mongoose; Poet Lore; Writer; Poetry Today; Stone Country; Herald Press Publications. Memberships: Academy of American Poets; Valley Poets; California State Poetry Society; Chaparral Poets. Address: 520 West Colorado Avenue 13, Glendora, CA 91740, USA.

LEE Byung Suk, b. 30 May 1938, Korea. Buddhist Priest. Education: Korea Air and Correspondence University; Dong University. Appointments: Received Commandments of Buddhism; Resident Priest, Yon Kook Sa Temple. Publications: Korea Buddhist Priests Poems, Vols I-IV; A Stone of the World Beyond; A Dream Lane to the Moon. Contributions to: Modern Literature; Poetic Literature; Modern Poetic Science; Monthly Literature; South Poems; Friends; Album of International Poets; World Poetry; Laurel Leaves Asiatic Poems Collections. Memberships: Korean Literature Association; Korean Buddhist Monk Poets Association; Pusan Korea Affairs of UPLI; Tagore Institute of Creative Writing International. Address: Chun Ryong Sa Temple, 130 Cho Jang Dong, Pusan 602 040, Korea.

LEE Dennis Beynon, b. 31 Aug 1939, Toronto, Ontario, Canada. Writer. m. Susan Ruth Perly, 12 Oct 1985, 1 son, 2 daughters. Education: BA, University of Toronto, 1962; MA, 1965. Appointments: Lecturer, University of Toronto, 1963-67; Editor/Director, House of Anansi Press, 1967-72; Poetry Editor, McClelland and Stewart, 1981-84. Publications: Kingdom of Absence; Civil Elegies and Other Poems; The Gods; The Difficulty of Living on Other Planets; Riffs; Nightwatch: New and Selected Poems; Wiggle to the Laundromat; Alligator Pie; Nicholas Knock; Garbage Delight; Jelly Belly; Lizzy's Lion; The Ice Cream Store. Contributions to: Most major Canadian Periodicals. Honours: Governor General's Award for Poetry; CACL Medal; IODE Award; Ruth Schwartz Award; Vicky Metcalf Award; Order of Canada, 1994. Memberships: Writers Union of Canada; PEN; CAPAC/SOCAN. Literary Agent: Westwood Creative Artists. Address: c/o WCA, 10 St Marys Street 510, Toronto, Ontario M4Y 1P9, Canada.

LEE Hamilton, b. 10 Oct 1921, China. University Professor. m. Jean C Zhang, 24 Aug 1945, 1 son, 3 daughters. Education: BA, Beijing Normal University, 1948; MA, University of Minnesota, 1958; EdD, Wayne State University, Michigan, 1964. Appointments: English Teacher, Taiwan, 1948-56; Research Associate, Wayne State University, 1958-64; Visiting Professor, Summer School, Seton Hall University, summer 1964; Assistant Professor, Moorhead State University, Minnesota, 1964-65; Associate Professor, University of Wisconsin, La Crose, Wisconsin, 1965-66; Professor, East Stroudsburg University, 1966-; Visiting Scholar, Harvard University, summer 1965-1966; Visiting Fellow, Princeton University, 1976-78; Professor Emeritus, East Stroudsburg University, Pennsylvania. Publications: Chapbooks: Revelation and Reflection, 1989 and 1991. Contributions to: Byline; Poetry Norwest; Poets at Work; Portals; Numerous anthologies. Honours: Numerous awards from various poetry contests over about 20 years including: Editor's Choice, National Library of Poetry, 1994. Memberships: Poetry Society of America; The Academy of American Poets; Advisory Council, International Society of Poets. Address: 961 Long Woods Drive, Stroudsburg, PA 18360, USA.

LEE James Alan, b. 4 Oct 1958, Windber, Pennsylvania, USA. Freelance Writer. Education: Attended University of Pittsburgh at Johnstown, 1976-78. Appointments: Contributing or Assistant Editor at following magazines: Scavengers NL, 1988-; Pillow Talk, 1989; Dark Side, 1990. Contributions to: Aliens & Lovers Anthology (Unique Graphics), 1983; Magazines: Xenophilia; Tapestry; Z Miscellaneous; The Body Electric; The Tome; Beyond SF & F; Dark Side; Aberrations; Xizquil. Memberships: Southern Alleghenics Writers Guild, past president and currently secretary/treasurer; Pennwriters. Address: 801-26th Street, Windber, PA 15963-1952, USA.

LEE Kuei-Shien, b. 19 June 1937, Taipei, Taiwan. Patent Agent; Chemical Engineer; Corporation President. m. Huei-uei Wang, 1965, 1 son, 1 daughter. Education: Chemical Engineering, Taipei Institute of Technology, 1958; German Literature, European Language Center of Educational Ministry, 1964; PhD, Chemical Engineering (Honoris Causa), Marquis Giuseppe Scicluna International University Foundation, 1985. Appointments: Director, Li Poetry Society; Publisher, Inventors Journals; Examiner, Wu yong-fu Critique Prize; President, Taiwan PEN; Secretary General of the 1995 Asian Poets Conference. Publications: Essays include: Journey to Europe, 1971; Profile of the Souls, 1972; Essays on German Literature, 1973; On International Patent Practices, 1975; Critical Essays on Chinese Translation of English Poetry, 1976; Critical Essays: On Taiwanese Poems, 1987; Poetical Reaction, 1992; Poetical Witness, 1994; Poetry includes: Pagoda and Other Poems, 1963; The Loquat, 1964; Poems on Nankang, 1966; Naked Roses, 1976; Collected poems, 1985; Formation of Crystal, 1986; Transfusion, 1986; Eternal Territory, 1990; Praying, 1993; Image in the Evening, 1993; Anthologies include: Anthology of German Poems, 1970; Anthology of Black Orpheus, 1974; Year Book of Taiwanese Poems, 1987; Selected Poems of Li Poetry Society, 1992. Translations include: The Trial by Franz Kafka, 1969; Cat and Mouse by Gunter Grass, 1970; Duineser Elegien by R M Rilke, 1969; Die Sonnete an Orpheus by R M Rilke, 1969; Das Buch der Bilder, by R M Rilke, 1977; Selected Poems by Giosue Carducci, 1981; Selected Poems by Salvatore Quasimodo, 1981; Prussian Night by Alexander Solzhenitsyn, 1995. Honours include: Albert Einstein International Academy Foundation Alfred Nobel Medal for Peace, 1991; The Poetic Creation Award of Li Poetry Society, 1994. Memberships include: Founder Fellow, International Academy of Poets; Rilke-Gesellschaft; President, Taiwan PEN, 1995. Address: Room 705, Asia Enterprise Center, No 142 Minchuan East Road, Sec 3, Taipei, Taiwan, China.

LEE Lance Wilds, b. 25 Aug 1942, New York, New York, USA. Writer; Lecturer. M. Jeanne Barbara Lee, 30 Aug 1962, 2 daughters. Education: Boston University, 1960-62; BA, Brandeis University, 1962-64; MFA, Yale University, 1964-67. Appointments: University of Bridgeport; Southern Connecticut State College; University of Southern California; University of California at Los Angeles; California State University, Northridge. Publications: Wrestling With The Angel; Times Up; Fox Hound and Huntress; The Understructure Of Screenwriting. Contributionsto: Poetry LA; Poetry Northwest; Crosscurrents; Negative Capability; Agenda; Stand; Outposts; Hiram Poetry Review; Iron; Orsis; Midwest Poetry Review; Acumen; Poem; Cape Rock; Antioch Review; Nimrod. Honours: Wells Scholarship; National Endowment for the Arts, Creative Writing Fellowship. Memberships: American Academy of Poets; Poetry Society of America. Address: 1127 Galloway Street, Pacific Palisades, CA 90272, USA.

LEE Paul, (Poong Ho Lee), b. 23 Feb 1950, Yesan, Choongnam, Korea (US citizen, 1986-). Educator; Poet; Writer; Literary Translator; Critic, Publisher and General Editor; Caltrans Electrical Engineer; Publisher and editor of Modern Poetry. m. Lisa Park, 28 May 1994, 1 daughter. Education: BS, Electrical Engineering, Inha University, 1975; Inha University Graduate School of Engineering, Electrical Engineering, 1978-80; University of California at Los Angeles, 1981; Petroleum Engineering, University of Southern California, 1981; Fullerton College, 1983-84; Writers' Program, Poetry, University of California at Los Angeles, 1989; BA, English, California State University, Los Angeles, 1982-95. Appointments: Corporal of Signal Corps, ROK Army, 1971-74; Electrical Engineering Lecturer, Osan Technical College, 1979, Dongyang Technical College, 1980; Electrical Engineer, California Department of Transportation, 1981-; Principal, Korean School of Southern California, Peninsula, 1986-88; President, Eastwind Press, 1991-; Publisher and General Editor, Modern Poetry, 1996-. Publications: Desert Moon, 1989; Opening a New Horizon, 1989; Korea's Freedom Poetry, 1989; Literature/LA, 1990; Overseas Land, 1990; Autumn River, translation, 1990; Hanbit Tower and a Song of Asterism, translation, 1993; The Power of a Flower, 1993; Looking at Hanbit Tower, 1996; Modern Poetry, 1996. Contributions to: Korean American Christian Literature, 1987-; Korea Times Los Angeles, 1987-; The Echo, 1987, 1989; Modern Praxis, Japan, 1988-; Korean American Literature, 1989-; Monthly Literature, 1989-; Sijo Literature, 1989-; Poet India, 1989-; American Poetry Anthology, 1989; American Poetry Annual, 1989; Heartland Anthology of Poetry, 1989; National Poetry Anthology, 1989; Treasured Poems

of America, 1989; National Library of Poetry, 1989; Jangbaiksan, China, 1989; Southwest Manuscripts, 1989, 1991; Poetry Monthly, 1992-; University Times of California State University, Los Angeles, 1990; Statement, California State University, Los Angeles, 1991; Hoseo Literature, 1991-; Anthology of Contemporary Universal Most Important Poets, 1992; Taejon Literature, 1992-; Siwon Poet, Japan, 1993; New Intellectual Poetry International, 1993; Asian Poets II, 1993; Parnassus of World Poets, India, 1994, 1995; Jalons, France, 1995; Modern Literature, 1995-. Honours: Korean American Christian Literature Award in Poetry (Korean), 1986; The Echo Literary Prize in Poetry (English), 1987, 1989; Mona O'Connor Memorial Poetry Prize, 1989, 1991; Editor's Choice Award, North American Open Poetry Contest, 1989. Memberships: Poetry Society of America; Academy of American Poets; Modern Poetry Association; IBC; Modern Poets Association; Korean American Writers' Association; Korean Literary Writers' Association; Taejon Literary Writers' Association; Sijo Society of America. Literary Agent: Modern Poetry. Address: Modern Poetry/Eastwind Press, PO Box 348, Los Angeles, CA 90053-0348, USA.

LEE Rosie. See: **HALEY Patricia.**

LEE Terry. See: **ARMSTRONG Terry Lee.**

LEE William David, b. 13 Aug 1944, Matador, Texas, USA. University Administrator. m. Jan M Lee, 13 Aug 1971, 1 son, 1 daughter. Education: BA, Colorado State University, 1967; MA, Idaho State University, 1970; PhD, University of Utah, 1973. Appointment: Head, Department of Languange and Literature, 1971-. Publications: Porcine Legacy; Driving and Drinking; Shadow Weaver; Porcine Conticles; Day's Work; My Town, 1995. Contributions to: Kenyan Review; Haydens Feny Review; Poetry East; River Styx; Nebraska Tenitory; Willow Springs Magazine; Tailwind; Weber Studies; Ellipsis. Honours: Prize/Governors Award; Book Length Poetry Award; National Endowment for the Arts Creative Writing Fellowship; Western States Book Award, 1995; Mountain and Plains States Booksellers Award, 1996; Professor of the Year, 1995; Distinguished Service Award, 1995. Memberships: Utah Arts Council; Springville Arts Council; Zion Arts Panel. Address: Department of Language and Literature, Southern Utah University, Cedar City, UT 84720, USA.

LEGAGNEUR Serge, b. 10 Jan 1937, Jeremie, Haiti. Professor; Writer; Poet. Appointments: Professor of French Literature; Reader and Re-writer. Publications: Textes Interdits; Textes en croix; Le Crabe; Inalterable Glyphes. Contributions to: Lettres et Ecritures; Passe Partout; Estuaire; Nouvelle Optique; Possibles; Mot pout Mot; Nouvelliste; Haiti Litteraire; Le Matin. Memberships: Haiti Litteraire; Quebec Writers Union. Address 3320 Boulevard Gouin E, Apt 401, Montreal, Quebec H1H 5P3, Canada.

LEGGETT Andrew Alfred George, b. 25 Apr 1962, Brisbane, Queensland, Australia. Psychiatrist; Writer. 1 son, 1 daughter. Education: MBBS (Queensland); FRANZCP. Appointments: Consultant Psychiatrist in private practice in Brisbane, special interest in psychotherapy; Writer of poetry, occasional reviews, papers on ethical issues in psychiatry; Guest Editor and Brisbane contact person for Hobo Poetry Magazine. Publication: Old Time Religion, accepted for publication in Penguin Australian Poetry Series, not yet published. Contributions include: Australia includes: Australian; Bulletin; Canberra Times; Imago; Overland; Westerly; Quadrant; Linq; Northern Prospective; Ultarra; United Kingdom includes: Iron; USA includes: Antipodes; New Zealand: Spin; about 150 poems in about 50 different journals in four countries. Honour: Member of Queensland State of Origin performance poetry team, 1993-95. Memberships: Secretary, 1994, Readings Co-Ordinator, 1994, Queensland Poets Association; Queensland Writers Centre; Fellowship of Australian Writers; United Kingdom Poetry Society. Address: PO Box 5389, West BND, Queensland 4101, Australia.

LEHMAN David Cary, b. 11 June 1948, New York, New York, USA. Writer. m. Stefanie Green, 2 Dec 1978, 1 son. Education: BA, Magna Cum Laude, Columbia University, 1970; BA, MA, Cambridge University, 1972; PhD, English, Columbia University, 1978. Appointments: Assistant Professor of English, Hamilton College, 1976-80; Fellow, Society for Humanities, Cornell University, 1980-81; Freelance Writer, 1982-; Book Critic and Writer, Newsweek, 1982-89; Series Editor, The Best American Poetry, 1988-; Editorial Adviser in Poetry, W W Norton and Co, 1990-93; Series Editor, Poets on Poetry, 1994-. Publications: An Alternative to Speech, 1986; The Perfect

Murder: A Study in Detection, 1989; Operation Memory, 1990; The Line Forms Here, essays, 1992; Signs of the Times: Deconstruction and the Fall of Paul de Man, 1992; The Big Question, critical essays, 1995; Valentine Place, Book of Poems, 1996. Contributions to: New Yorker; New York Review of Books; New Republic; Nation; Paris Review; Times Literary Supplement; Partisan Review; Boulevard; Harvard Magazine; Yale Review; New York Times Book Review; New York Times Magazine; New York Observer; Washington Post; Boston Globe; Newsday; Los Angeles Times; Chicago Tribune; American Heritage. Honours: American Academy and Institute of Arts and Letters; Award in Literature; Guggenheim Fellowship in Poetry; National Endowment for the Arts Grant; Ingram Merrill Foundation Grants; Bernard F Conners Poetry Prize; Pushcart Prize; Consuelo Ford Award; Writers Award from The Lila Wallace-Readers Digest Fund, 1991-94. Membership: National Book Critics Circle. Address: 105 Valentine Place, Ithaca, NY 14850, USA.

LEHMANN Geoffrey (John), b. 20 June 1940, Sydney, New South Wales, Australia. Education: BA, University of Sydney, 1960. Appointment: Lecturer in Law, University of New South Wales. Publications: The Ilex Tree, 1965; A Voyage of Lions and Other Poems, 1968; Conversation with a Rider, 1972; From an Australian Country Sequence, 1973; Selected Poems, 1976; Ross' Poems, 1978; Nero's Poems: Translations of the Public and Private of the Emperor Nero, 1981; The Younger Australian Poets (co-editor), 1983. Address: 8 Highfield Road, Londfield, New South Wales 2070, Australia.

LEIH Grace Janet, (Helen Forelle, Mario Edlosi), b. 27 Jan 1936. Publisher. m. John Maxwell Jeffords, 2 Dec 1955, 1 son, 2 daughters. Education: New York State College for Teachers; Augustana College, Sioux Falls; Memphis State University. Appointments: Key Punch Operator; Data Entry Clerk; Programmer Analyst; Consultant; Secretary; Publisher; Writer; Poet; Owner of Tesseract Publications. Publications: Pearls Among The Swine; Mortimer Troll; Publication Indexing; A Writers Guide to Inventory; The Pasque Petals Index; The Teatotalers. Contributions to: Pasque Petals; Broomstick; Voices of South Dakota; Lincoln Logs; Mill Hunk Herald; Homestones; Lyrical Treasures; South Dakota Magazine; Bird Verse Portfolio; Poet Magazine; Grasp the Rainbow. Honours: Denver Pen Women; Best In Show, 1980-84; Honorable mentions, National Federation of State Poetry Societies; The Academy of American Poets; National Association of Desktop Publishers. Address: RR No 1 Box 27, Fairview, SD 57027, USA.

LEITHAUSER Brad, b. 27 Feb 1953, Detroit, Michigan, USA. Poet; Writer. m. Mary Jo Salter, 1980, 1 daughter. Education: BA, 1975, JD, 1980, Harvard University. Appointments: Research Fellow, Kyoto Comparative Law Center, 1980-83; Visiting Writer, Amherst College, 1984-85; Lecturer, Mount Holyoke College, 1987-88. Publications: Poetry: Hundreds of Fireflies, 1982; A Seaside Mountain: Eight Poems from Japan, 1985; Cats of the Temple, 1986; Between Leaps: Poems 1972-1985, 1987; The Mail from Anywhere: Poems, 1990; Fiction: The Line of Ladies, 1975; Equal Distance, 1985; Hence, 1989; Seaward, 1993; Non-fiction: Penchants and Places: Essay and Criticism, 1995; Editor: The Norton Book of Ghost Stories, 1994. Honours: Harvard University-Academy of American Poets Prizes, 1973, 1975; Harvard University McKim Garrison Prizes, 1974, 1975; Amy Lowell Traveling Scholarship, 1981-82; Guggenheim Fellowship, 1982-83; Lavan Younger Poets Award, 1983; John D and Catharine T MacArthur Foundation Fellowship, 1983-87. Address: c/o Alfred A Knopf Inc, 201 East 50th Street, New York, NY 10022, USA.

LEM Y S. See: **ELLIS Mayne.**

LEMASTER J(immie) R, b. 29 Mar 1934, Pike County, Ohio, USA. Professor. m. Wanda May Ohnesorge, 21 May 1966, 1 son, 2 daughters. Education: BA, Defiance College, 1959; MA, Bowling Green State University, 1962; PhD, 1970; Litt D, Defiance College, 1988. Appointments: Professor, Defiance College, 1962-77; Professor, Baylor University, 1977-; Professor, Beijing Second Institute of Foreign Languages, 1980-81, 1985-86. Publications: Poets of the Midwest; The Heart is a Gypsy; Children of Adam; Weeds and Wildflowers; First Person, Second; Purple Bamboo; Journey to Beijing. Contributions to: Negative Capability; Images; Xavier Review; Texas Review; Descant; International University Poetry Quarterly; Old Hickory Review; Kentucky Poetry Review; Mid South Writer; Phi Kappa Phi Journal. Honours: South and West Publishers Award; Ohio Poet of the Year. Memberships: Texas Association of Creative Writing Teachers; Modern Language Association; South Central Modern Language Association; Mark Twain Circle of America. Address: 201 Harrington Avenue, Waco, TX 76706, USA.

LENGYEL Cornel Adam, (Cornel Adam), b. 1 Jan 1915, Fairfield, Connecticut, USA. Historian. m. Teresa Murphy Delaney, 10 July 1933, 3 sons, 1 daughter. Education: Litt D, Taiwan. Appointments: Editor, 1938-41; Music Critic, 1937-41; Shipwright, 1942-44; Manager, The Forty-Niner Theatre, 1946-50; Editor, 1952-54; Founder, Executive, Editor, Dragons Teeth Press, 1969-; Visiting Professor, Lecturer, California State University, Sacramento, 1962-63; Writer in Residence, 1968-69; Guest Lecturer, Hamline University, 1968-69; Massachusetts, Institute of Technology, 1969. Publications: Thirty Pieces; The Shadow Trap; The Master Plan; Will of Stratford; The Declaration of Independence; Four Dozen Songs; Late News from Adams Acres; Doctor Franklin; The Courage to Grow Old, 1988; From These Hills, 1990; Blood to Remember, 1991; Anthology of Contemporary Poets, 1992; World Poetry, 1993; We Speak for Peace, 1993. Contributions to: Britannica Library of Great American Writing; Menorah Treasury; Interpretation for Our Time. Honours: Albert M Bender Award; Maritime Poetry Award; Maxwell Anderson Award; Castagnola Award; National Endowment for the Arts Award. Memberships: MLA; AAUP; PEN; Poetry Society. Address: El Dorado National Forest, 7700 Wentworth Springs Road, Georgetown, CA 95634, USA.

LENHART Gary A, b. 15 Oct 1947, Newark, Ohio, USA. Writer. m. Louise E Hamlin, 1 daughter. Education: BA, Siena College, 1969; MA, University of Wisconsin, 1973. Publications: Light Heart; One at a Time; Bulb in Socket; Anthologies: Aloud; Out of This World; Up Late. Contributions to: Hanging Loose Magazine; United Artists Magazine; Exquisite Corpse; Broadway 2; New American Writing; Gandhabba; Joe Soaps Canoe; The World. Membership: Poetry Project, New York City. Address: 166 Beaver Meadow Road, Norwich, VT 05055, USA.

LENIER Sue, b. 9 Oct 1957, Birmingham, England. Playwright; Poet; Solicitor. Education: MA, Clare College, Cambridge University, 1977-80; University of California, 1981-82; Drama Studio, London, 1982-83. Appointments: Teacher, Newstead Wood Girls School, 1985-86; Articled Clerk, Assistant Solicitor, 1989-91. Publications: Swansongs; Rain Following. Contributions to: Lines Review; Staple; New Prospects; Washington Post; New York Times. Honours: Harkness Fellowship; London Writers Competition Winner. Memberships: Playwrights Cooperative; New Playwrights Trust. Address: 24 Hunter Close, East Boldon, Tyne and Wear NE36 OTB, England.

LEON BASCUR Maria Del Carmen, b. 14 Aug 1944, Cabildo, Chile,. Newsreader. m. 20 Aug 1973, 1 son, 2 daughters. Publications: Antologia Vivencias, 1984; Antologia Vivencias II, 1986; Antologia Pupila Femenina, 1989; Editor, Director, SAFO; Revista Literaria Femenina; Editor, Antologia La Rosa Blindada. Contributions to: El Hombre y el Paisaje de Atacama, 1985; Por Norte, La Esperanza, 1987; Tres Muieres en la Poesia Copiapina, 1990; Poetas del Nuevo Mundo, 1991; 500 Poets Latinoamericanos, 1992. Honours: 1st Place in Poetry, Copiapo 3a Region, 1984, 1985; 1st Place Poetry, Chimbarongo 6a Region, 1988; International Contest, Women's Love Poetry, 1988; Escilda Greve National Competition, Santiago, 1990; Ruben Dario Medal for Intellectual Merit, 1992; Gabriela Mistral Medal. Memberships: Sociedad de Escritores de Chile; Public Relations Officer, Sociedad Escritores de Atacama 3rd Region; Public Relations Officer, Sociedad Escritores de Rancagua, 6th Region; Director, Editor, SAFO Women's Literary Magazine. Address: Avenida Santa Rosa 8171, Depto 207, Santiago, Chile.

LEONARD Tom, b. 22 Aug 1944, Glasgow, Scotland. Writer. m. Sonya Maria O'Brian, 24 Dec 1971, 2 sons. Education: MA, Glasgow University, 1976. Appointment: Writer in Residence, 1987-90. Publications: Six Glasgow Poems; A Priest Came On At Merkland Street; Bunnit Husslin; Three Glasgow Writers; My Name is Tom; If Only Bunty Was Here; Ghostle Men; Intimate Voices; Selected Work; Satires And Profanities. Contributions to: Radical Renfrew; Poetry From the French Revolution to the First World War. Honour: Joint Winner Saltire Society Scottish Book of the Year Award. Address: 56 Eldon Street, Glasgow G3 6NJ, Scotland.

LEONG Choy Yin, (Simon Leong), b. 5 Dec 1938, Kuala Lumpur, Malaysia. Retired Standard Chartered Banker. m. Teoh Kim Lean, 3 Feb 1966, 2 sons. Education: University of Cambridge, 1963;

Degree of Merit in Poetry; ICS Diploma, Freelance Journalism and English, 1989, 1992. Publications: American Poetry Anthology; As I See the World Today, 1994; Best Poems 1995; Best Poems 1996; Best of the 90's; Path Less Traveled; Heartland; Global Co-operation for a Better World. Contributions to: Malay Mail; Sunday Star; Malaysian Post; Standard Chartered News; Movie News,Singapore. Honours: Editor's Choice Awd, National Library of Poetry, 1993-96; Editor's Preference Awd of Excellence, National Library of Poetry and Artists, NY, USA, 1993-96. Memberships: Poetry Society; Charter Lifetime Member; International Society of Poets; National Library. Address: 56 Jin 35/26 Tmn Sri Tampal, Rampal Court J Blk, Setapak 53300 Kuala Lumpur, Malaysia.

LEONHARDT Joyce LaVon, b. 17 Dec 1927, Aurora, Nebraska, USA. Instructor. Education: BS, Union College, Lincoln, 1952. Appointments: High School Teacher, 1952-76; Junior College Instructor, 1981-90. Contributions to: Several books published by World of Poetry. Honours: Honourable Mention Certificates; Golden Poet; Silver Poet. Membership: World of Poetry. Address: 1824 Atwood Street, Longmont, CO 80501, USA.

LEOTTA Guido, b. 2 May 1957, Faenza, Italy. Publisher; Writer. Education: Diploma (Accountancy). Appointments: President of Tratti/Mobydick, Cultural Cooperative and Publishing House, 1987; Author and Coordinator, Tratti Folk Festival, 1989-95. Publications: Sacsaphone, first collection of novels, 1981; Anatre, short stories, 1989; Strategie di Viaggio Nel Non Amore, poetry, 1992; IL Bambino Ulisse, children's stories, 1995. Contributions to: Subway, Music & Literature Review, 1989-90; Tratti, Literature Magazine, 1987-95; Punto A Capo, Monthly Magazine, 1987-91. Honours: Premio Leonforte, Children's Stories, 1991; Comortas Filiochta, Dun Laoghaire, Ireland, Poetry Prize, 1994. Address: Via Bubani 4, I 48018 Faenza (RA), Italy.

LERNER Arthur, b. 10 Jan 1915, Chicago, Illinois, USA. Teacher; Psychologist. m. Matilda Fisher. Education: Roosevelt University, 1942; Northwestern University, 1946; University of Southern California, 1953, 1968. Appointments: Professor, Los Angeles City College, 1957-83; Lecturer, University of California, Los Angeles, 1970-74; Director, Poetry Therapy, Woodview Calabasas Hospital, 1971-86. Publications: Rhymed and Unrhymed; Follow Up Starting Points; Words for all Seasons. Contributions to: Literary Review; Writers Notes and Quotes; Canadian Poetry; Image; Orbis; Wallace Stevens Journal; Cats Eye; Phylon; Journal of Poetry Therapy; Spring; Journal of E E Cummings Society; California Quarterly; Poet; Poet and Critic; Moment; American Bard; Oak Leaves; International Poetry Review; Scimitar and Song; Sierra; Voices; American Poets Best; Poetry Editor, The Arts in Psychotherapy. Honour: Literary Achievement Book Award. Memberships: Poetry Society of America; Authors Guild; PEN. Address: 520 South Burnside Avenue No 11C, Los Angeles, CA 90036, USA.

LERNER Laurence David, b. 12 Dec 1925, Cape Town, South Africa. Poet; Professor. m. Natalie Winch, 15 June 1948, 4 sons. Education: MA, University of Cape Town, 1945; BA, Pembroke College, 1949. Appointments: Lecturer, University College of Gold Coast, 1949-53; Lecturer, Queens University, 1953-62; Lecturer, Reader, Professor, University of Sussex, 1962-84; Professor, Vanderbilt University, 1985-. Publications: Domestic Interior, 1959; The Direction of Memory, 1964; Selves, 1969; ARTHUR; The Man I Killed, 1980; Chapter and Verse: Bible Poems, 1984; Rembrandt's Mirror, 1987; Two Volumes of Computer Poems: ARTHUR: The Life and Opinions of a Digital Computer, 1974 and ARTHUR & MARTHA: The Loves of the Computer, 1982; Selected Poems, 1984; Critical Books: Love and Marriage, 1979; The Frontiers of Literature, 1987; Novel: My Grandfather's Grandfather, 1985. Contributions to: Sunday Times; New Statesman; Spectator; Times Literary Supplement; Poetry Review; Encounter; London Magazine; London Review of Books; Sewanee Review; BBC. Honours: Prudence Farmer Prize; Recommended by Poetry Book Society. Membership: Royal Society of Literature. Address: Abinger, 1B Gundreda Road, Lewes, East Sussex BN7 1PT, England.

LETKO Ken, b. 8 May 1953, Ashland, Wisconsin, USA. Educator. Education: BS, University of Wisconsin at Stevens Point, 1975; MFA, Bowling Green State University, 1983; MA, Bowling Green State University, 1988. Appointments: Lecturer, Bowling Green State University; Foreign Expert, Xian Foreign Languages University, China; Instructor in Writing and Literature, College of the Redwoods.

Publications: Chapbooks: Wisconversation, 1979; Shelter for Those Who Need It, 1985; All This Tangling, 1995. Contributions to: Greenfield Review; Cottonwood; Permafrost; Gambit. Memberships: Associated Writing Programs; Academy of American Poets. Address: College of the Redwoods, 883 West Washington Boulevard, Crescent City, CA 95531, USA.

LETRIA José Jorge, b. 8 June 1951, Cascais, Portugal. Writer; Journalist. m. Isabel Letria, 9 July 1973, 3 sons. Education: Law and History, University of Lisbon. Appointments: Journalist and Editor of the main daily and weekly newspapers in Portugal. 1970-94; Correspondent for Spanish newspapers; Teacher of Journalism and Mass Communication; Director of The National Radio, 1974-75; Playwright; Songwriter with 9 LP's; TV Author; Elected City Councillor for Culture in Cascais, 1994; The most awarded Portuguese Poet. Publications: Author of 30 children's books; Poetry books include: Capela Dos Ocios - Odes Mediterrânicas, 1993; Actas Da Desordem Do Dia, 1993; La Tentation Du Bonheur, 1993; O Fantasma Da Obra, 1994; Os Achados Da Noite, 1994; Lisboa, Capital Do Coracao, 1994; A Dúvida Melódica, 1994; O Dom Intranquilo, 1995. Contributions to: Portugal: Colóquio/Letras, Vértice, Hifen, Jornal de Letras, Nova Renascenca, Autores, Cadernos do Tâmega; Spain: Espacio Escrito, Boca Bilingue, Barcarola, Palim Psesto, Delibros; Germany: Lusorama; Mexico: Plural. Honours: ECA de Queiroz, City of Lisbon, 1989; Cidade de Ourense, Spain, 1989, 1994; Plural, Mexico, 1990; Internationale des Arts et des Lettres, Paris, 1991; Over 20 national awards including: Gulbenkian Prize, 1992; International UNESCO Prize, France, 1993. Memberships: Board Member, The Portuguese Author's Society; Portuguese Writers Association; The World Literary Academy; Correspondent, Le Collège de L'Europe; PEN Club; International Association of Critics. Address: Avenue General Humberto Delgado, No 5-7-B, 2745 Queluz, Portugal.

LEVENSON Christopher, b. 13 Feb 1934, England (Canadian citizen, 1973). Education: BA, Downing College, Cambridge, 1957. Appointment: Department of English, Carleton University, Ottawa, 1968-. Publications: New Poets, with others, 1959; Cairns, 1969; Stills, 1969; Into the Open, 1977; The Journey Back and Other Poems, 1978; No-Man's Land, 1980; Arriving at Night, 1986; The Return, 1986; Half Truths, 1990. Honours include: Eric Gregory Award, 1960. Address: Department of English, Carleton University, Ottawa, Ontario K1S 5B6, Canada.

LEVERTOV Denise, b. 24 October 1923, Ilford, Essex, England. Professor; Writer. m. Mitchell Goodman, 1947, div. 1 son. Appointments: Teacher, YM-YMCA Poetry Center, New York, 1964; Teacher, City College of New York, 1965; Teacher, Drew University, 1965; Teacher, Vassar College, 1966-67; Teacher, University of California at Berkeley, 1969; Visiting Professor: Massachusetts Institute of Technology, 1969-70; University of Cincinnati, 1973; Artist-in-Residence, Kirkland College, 1970-71; Elliston Lecturer, University of Cincinnati, 1973; Professor, Tufts University, 1973-79; Fannie Hurst Professor, Brandeis University, 1981-83; Professor, Stanford University, 1981-94; A L White Professor-at-Large, Cornell University, 1993-. Publications: Verse: The Sorrow Dance, 1968; Footprints, 1972; Life in the Forest, 1978; Candles in Babylon, 1982; Poems 1960-1967, 1983; Poems 1968-1972, 1987; Breathing the Water, 1987; A Door in the Hive, 1989; Evening Train, 1992; Sands of the Well, 1996; In the Night (short story), 1968; The Poet in the World (essays), 1973; Light up the Cave (essays), 1981; New and Selected Essays, 1992. Honours include: Longview Award, 1961; Guggenheim Fellowship, 1962; American Academy of Arts and Letters Award, 1966; Numerous Honorary Doctorates; Shelley Memorial Award, 1984; Robert Frost Medal, 1990; National Endowment for the Arts Senior Fellowship, 1991; Lannan Award, 1992; Fellowship, Academy of American Poets, 1995. Memberships: American Academy of Arts and Letters; Corresponding Member, Academie Mallarme. Address: c/o New Directions Publishers, 80 Eighth Avenue, New York, NY 10011, USA.

LEVETT John Anthony, b. 30 Oct 1950, London, England. Librarian. m. Wendy Dawn Peters, 1 July 1972, 1 son, 1 daughter. Education: ALA (Associate of the Library Association), 1974. Appointments: Professional Librarian, Greenwich and the City of London; Stock Editor, Bexley Libraries, London; Service Manager, Bromley Libraries. Publications: Changing Sides, 1983; Skedaddle, 1987; Their Perfect Lives, 1994. Contributions to: Encounter; Guardian; London Magazine; London Review of Books; Literary Review; New Statesman; Orbis; Poetry Review; Times Literary Supplement; BBC

Radio; Spectator. Honours: New Statesman Prudence Farmer Award, 1982; Joint Winner, National Poetry Competition, Poetry Society of Great Britain, 1991; Shortlisted for Whitbread Poetry Award, 1994; Also prizes in a number of International Poetry Competitions including Cheltenham, Stroud and York. Address: 94 Edison Road, Welling, Kent DA16 3NG, England.

LEVI Peter, (Chad Tigar), b. 16 May 1931, Ruislip, Middlesex, England. Poet; Writer; Translator; Professor. m. Deirdre Connolly, 1977, 1 stepson. Education: Beaumont College, 1946-48; Pass Degree. Campion Hall, Oxford, 1958; British School of Archaeology, Athens, 1965-68. Appointments: Member, Society of Jesus, 1948-77; Roman Catholic Priest, 1964-77; Tutor, Lecturer, Classics, Campion Hall, Oxford, 1965-77; Fellow 1977-91, Emeritus Fellow 1993-, St Catherine's College, Oxford; Lecturer, Classics, Christ Church, Oxford, 1979-82; Professor, Poetry, Oxford University, 1984-89. Publications: Poetry: Earthly Paradise, 1958; The Gravel Ponds, 1958; Beaumont 1861-1961, 1961; Orpheus Head, 1962; Water, Rock and Sand, 1962; The Shearwaters, 1965; Fresh Water, Sea Water, 1966; Pancakes for the Queen of Babylon: Ten Poems for Nikos Gatsos, 1968; Ruined Abbeys, 1968; Life is a Platform, 1971; Death is a Pulpit, 1971; Penguin Modern Poets 22 (with John Fuller and Adrian Mitchell), 1973; Collected Poems, 1955-1975, 1976; Five Ages, 1977; Private Ground, 1981; The Echoing Green: Three Elegies, 1983; Shakespeare's Birthday, 1985; Shadow and Bone: Poems 1981-1988, 1989; Goodbye to the Art of Poetry, 1989; The Marches (with Alan Powers), 1989; Rags of Time, 1994. Fiction: The Head in the Soup, novel, 1979; Grave Witness, mystery, 1985; Knit One, Drop One, mystery, 1986; To the Goat, novella, 1988; Shade Those Laurels (with Cyril Connolly), mystery, 1990. Non-Fiction: The Light Garden of the Angel King: Journeys in Afghanistan, 1972; The Noise Made by Poems, 1977; The Hill of Kronos, 1980; The Flutes of Autumn, 1983; The Lamentation of the Dead, 1984; A History of Greek Literature, 1985; The Frontiers of Paradise: A Study of Monks and Monasteries, 1987; The Life and Times of William Shakespeare, 1988; The Art of Poetry, 1990; Boris Pasternak, 1990; Life of Lord Tennyson, 1993; Edward Lear, 1994. Editor: Richard Selig: Poems, 1963; The English Bible 1534-1859, 1974; Pope, 1974; Atlas of the Greek World, 1980; The Penguin Book of English Christian Verse, 1984; New Verses by Shakespeare, 1988. Translator: Yevgeny Yevtushenko: Selected Poems (with Robin Milner-Gulland), 1962; Pausanias: Guide to Greece, 2 Volumes, 1971, revised edition 1984; The Psalms, 1977; George Pavlopoulos: The Cellar, 1977; Alexandros Papadiamantis: The Murderess, 1982; Marco the Prince: Serbo-Croat Heroic Songs (with Anne Pennington), 1983; The Holy Gospel of John, 1985; Revelation, 1992. Memberships: Corresponding Member, Society of Greek Writers, 1983; Kingman Committee on English, 1987-88; President, Virgil Society, 1993-95. Address: Prospect Cottage, The Green, Frampton on Severn, Glos GL2 7DY, England

LEVI Steven C, (Warren Sitka), b. 9 Dec 1948, Chicago, Illinois, USA. Freelance Writer. Education: BA, History, Unviersity of California at Davis, 1970; Teaching Credential, 1972; MA, History, San Jose State College, 1973. Publications: Alaskan Phantasmagoria, 1978; The Last Raven, 1979; The Phantom Bowhead, 1979; We Alaskans, 1980; Fish-Fed Maize, 1981; Our National Tapestry, 1986; A Destiny Going Sour, 1991. Contributions to: Poet; Writer's Digest; Harpoon, Co-editor; Frogpond; Permafrost; Vega; Crop Dust; Gryphon; Phoebe; Abraxas; The Album of International Poets, India; A Hard Row to Hoe; Tales of the Old West; Cube; Edge; Cokefish; Poet; Fireweed; Poetry Peddler; Haight-Ashbury Literary Journal; Amelia; Coffeehouse Poets; Quarterly; Finding the Boundaries; Mid American Review; Ghosts of the Holocaust. Address: 8512 East 4th, Anchorage, AK 99504, USA.

LEVINE Philip, b. 10 Jan 1928, Detroit, Michigan, USA. Poet; Writer; Professor. m. Frances Artley, 12 July 1954, 3 sons. Education: BA, 1950, AM, 1955, Wayne University; MFA, University of Iowa, 1957; Studies with John Berryman, 1954. Appointments: Instructor, University of Iowa, 1955-57; Instructor 1958-69, Professor of English 1969-92, California State University at Fresno; Elliston Professor of Poetry, University of Cincinnati, 1976; Poet-in-Residence, National University of Australia, Canberra, 1978; Visiting Professor of Poetry, Columbia University, 1978, 1981, 1984, New York University 1984, 1991, and Brown University, 1985; Chairman, Literature Panel, National Endowment for the Arts, 1985; Various poetry readings. Publications include: Poetry: On the Edge, 1961, 2nd edition, 1963; Silent in America: Vivas for Those Who Failed, 1965; Red Dust, 1971; They Feed They Lion, 1972; 1993, 1974; One for the Rose, 1981; Sweet Will, 1985; What Work Is, 1991; The Simple Truth: Poems,

1994. Non-Fiction: Don't Ask, interviews, 1979; The Bread of Time: Toward an Autobiography, 1994. Editor: Character & Crisis: A Contemporary Reader (with Henri Coulette), 1966; The Essential Keats, 1987. Contributions to: Many anthologies. Honours include: Joseph Henry Jackson Award, San Francisco Foundation, 1961; Frank O'Hara Prizes, 1973, 1974; Levinson Prize, 1974; Harriet Monroe Memorial Prize for Poetry, University of Chicago, 1976; National Book Critics Circle Award, 1979; Golden Rose Award, New England Poetry Society, 1985; Ruth Lilly Prize, 1987; National Book Award for Poetry, 1979, 1991; Pulitzer Prize in Poetry, 1995. Address: 4549 North Van Ness Boulevard, Fresno, CA 93704, USA.

LEWIN Peter Carrigue, b. 28 May 1946, Lancaster, Lancashire, England. Restauranteur. m. Carolyn Ann Gee, 3 June 1967, 2 daughters. Education: Teacher's Certificate. Appointments: Chef and Owner, The Olde Ship Inn, Pilling; Bennet's French Bistro, Lytham St Annes. Contributions to: Pennine Platform 25th Anniversary Edition, 1991; Iota Magazine, 1991; Lancashire Life; Radio Lancashire; Radio Mersey; GMR; Radio Cumbria. Membership: Northern Association of Writers in Education. Address: Flat 2, Heeley Road, Lytham St Annes, Lancashire FY8 2JY, England.

LEWIS D(esmond) F(rancis), b. 18 Jan 1948, Colchester, Essex, England. Former Insurance Broker. m. Denise Jean Woolgar, 23 May 1970, 1 son, 1 daughter. Education: BA Hons English, Lancaster University, 1969. Appointment: Company Pensions Negotiator, 1970-92. Contributions to: Over 450 prose poems and stories published in UK and USA, including literary journals: Stand; Iron; Panurge. Many DFL specials and interviews; Also horror stories. Address: 7 Lloyd Avenue, Coulsdon, Surrey CR5 2QS, England.

LEWIS Roger. See: LATHBURY Roger.

LEWIS William Edward (Bill), b. 1 Aug 1953, Maidstone, Kent, England. Poet; Storyteller; Mythographer. m Ann Frances Morris, 17 Oct 1981. Appointments: Writer-in-Residence, Brighton Festival, 1985; Editor, Pardigm Shift, 1992; Co-editor, The Book of North Kent Writers, 1996; Teacher, a course in Myth Magic and Spirituality, adult education, The Kent County Council. Publications: Poems, 1975-83; 1983; Night Clinic, 1984; Communion, 1986; Rage Without Anger, 1987; Skyclad Christ, 1992; Coyote Cosmos, short stories, 1994; Translation Women, 1996; Anthologies: Rivers of Life, 1980; Contemporary Christian Poetry, 1988; Worship the King, 1992. Contributions to: Social Work Today; Chile Fights; Pinch of Salt; Iron; Bogg; Sepia; Global Tapestry Journal; Stride; Prospiece; Christian; Chatham Standard; Brighton Echo; Wormwood Review, USA; Prophetic Voices, USA; Mother Earth Healing Society Newsletter, Canada. Membership: Founder Member, The Medway Poets. Address: 66 Glencoe Road, Chatham, Kent ME4 5QE, England.

LEWIS-SMITH Anne Elizabeth, (A McCormick, Quilla Slade, Emily Devereaux), b. 14 Apr 1925, Poet; Writer; Editor; Publisher. m. Peter Lewis-Smith, 17 May 1944, 1 son, 2 daughters. Appointments: 1st WRNS Magazine Editor, 1943; Feature Writer, Various Magazines; Editor, Aerostat, 1973-78; Editor, WWNT Bulletin; Editor, BAFM Newsletter; Assistant Editor, ENVOI, 1967-78; Editor, ENVOI Poets Publications, 1984-94; British Association of Friends of Museums Yearbook, 1985-91; Editor, ENVOI, 1983-91; Publisher, ENVOI Poets Publications. Publications: Seventh Bridge; The Beginning; Flesh and Flowers; Dandelion Flavour; Dinas Head; Places and Passions; In the Dawn; Circling Sound, 1996. Contributions to: Over 40 different magazines. Honours: Tissandier Diploma for Services to Aviation; Debbie Warley Award; Honorable Life Member Balloon Federation of America; Dorothy Tutin Award for Services to Poetry. Membership: Fellow, PEN. Address: Pen Ffordd, Newport, Pembrokeshire SA42 0QT, Wales.

LI Mingxia, (Zhang Er), b. 15 Sept 1960, Beijing, China. Scientist. m. L Schwartz, 7 Feb 1995. Education: Degree in Medicine, 1982; PhD, 1992. Appointment: Senior Research Scientist, American Home Product Co. Contributions to: China Press, New York; First Line, New York; Epoch Poetry Quarterly, Taiwan; Talisman, New Jersey; Five Fingers Review; Trafika; Journal of Chinese Religion. Memberships: First Line Poetry Circle; Overseas Correspondent, Journal of Contemporary Foreign Literature. Address: 120 Cabrini Boulevard, Apt 137, New York, NY 10033, USA.

LI Quing, b. 1 July 1933, China. President; Chief Editor. m. Ka Sang, 1 July 1956, 2 sons, 1 daughter. Education: Jinan University.

Appointments: Founder of Hong Kong, Literary World Association, 1987-; Delegate of International Conference on Hong Kong Literature, 1988; Speaker of 2nd International Conference on the Commonwealth of Chinese Literature, 1988; Speaker of 2nd International Conference on the Commonwealth of Chinese Literature, 1988. Publications: The Story of the Red Flower; The Songs of Jadeite Band; On the Equator; Come Over the Wave; Deep Loving Everywhere; Li Qings World; Of Hills and Water; Lyric Poems in Taiwan. Contributions to: Poetry; Literature of People; Literary World; Literature of Hong Kong; Blue Stars Poetry Quarterly. Honours: The Honorary Degree of Doctor of Literature (Litt D); World Academy of Arts and Culture; International Man Laureate Awardees with Laureate Honors (Wreath of Golden Laurel Leaves Crown); Memberships: The Hong Kong Writers Club; The Hong Kong Writers Association; Overseas Friendship Association of World Academy of Arts and Culture; World Congress of Poets;. Address: 109 Gloucester Road, RM 1303 Tung Wai Comm Bldg, Wan Chai, Hong Kong.

LI Ying, b. 8 Dec 1926. Editor; Publisher; Poet; Poetry Researcher. m. 22 Oct 1948, 1 son, 1 daughter. Education: BA Chinese Literature, minor Western Literature, Peking University, 1949. Appointments: Reporter, Xin Hua News Agency; Section Chief of Editing Department, Vice Editor-In-Chief; Head, Publishing House of Literature and Art, People's Liberation Army; Culture Minister, General Politics Department, People's Liberation Army; Currently: Vice Executive President, China Federation of Literary and Art Circles; Member of Presidium, Chinese Writers Association. Publications: Poetry: Green Seedlings in the Stone City, 1944; The Gun 1948; Poems On The Battlefield, 1951; Festival On The Battlefield, 1952; Red Lanterns On Tian An Men, 1954; Flowers Of Friendship, 1955; The Morning, 1957; Records Of The Present Times, 1959; Field Of Blossoms, 1963; To The Fiery Years, 1964; Date Village, 1972; People Who Have Stood Up, 1976; Poems Written On The March, 1976; Early Spring, 1979; On The Burning Battlefield, 1980; Proud Of Being A Tree, 1980; Watching Star, 1984; Travels In America, 1985; Blessing Youth, 1987; Love Peas, 1988; West Plateau Dreams, 1991; Sleeping Mountain and Waking River, 1992; The Paper Crane, 1993; Theoretical: Reflections On Poetry, 1991. Contributions to: Major newspapers and journals. Honours: Several. Memberships: Many. Address: 30 Building, No 21, Andeli Beijie, Beijing 10011, China.

LI Zhi, (Peng Xiang), b. 27 Apr 1962, Beijing, China. Journalist; Editor. Education: Peking University attached Primary and Middle School, 1969-80; Chinese Social University, 1982-86; Advanced Summer Courses, Peking University, 1985. Appointments: Administrator, Foreign Affairs, Peking University, 1986; Translator, Management, China International Airline, 1986-89. Publications: Rainbow's End; In the Fire; Destination. Contributions to: Poet International; Talk of the World; Japanese Daily; Voices of Israel; World Poetry; New Hope International (UK); New Global Voice (India). Honours: Honoured Guest Chinese Editor, Poet International; Director, International Board of Paramparaa Viswambhara; Prize Winner, World New Ancient Poetry Contest, 1994. Memberships: World Academy of Arts and Culture; World Poetry Society; DHP Society, Taiwan, 1994; Contemporary Poetry Society, Hong Kong, 1995. Address: 168 Lang Run Yuan, Peking University, Beijing 100871, China.

LIARDET Tim, b. 26 Sept 1949, London, England. Freelance Writer. m. Alison Liardet, 23 Jan 1983, 1 son. Education: BA, History, University of York; Two years' PhD research in History of The First World War. Appointments: Self Employed Cabinet Maker, 1974-88; Assistant Manager, White Collar Agency, 1988-90; Manager, Training and Marketing, North Shropshire College, 1990-95. Publications: Clay Hill, 1988; Fellini Beach, 1994. Contributions to: The Forward Book of Poetry; Poetry Book Society Anthology; Independent; Agenda; New Statesman, Outposts Poetry Quarterly; Poetry Review; Oxford Poetry; Thumbscrew, Poetry Durham; Poetry Ireland Review; Malahat Review; Chattahoochee Review; Dalhousie Review; Poetry Wales; Wascana Review; Kansas Quarterly; Redoubt; Envoi; Cimarron Review; Staple; Orbis; Planet, New Welsh Review; Poetry Nottingham. Address: Derwen Deg, 59 Oakhurst Road, Oswestry, Shropshire SY11 1BL, England.

LIDDY James Daniel Reeves, b. 1 July 1934. Writer; Professor. Education: MA, National University of Ireland; Barrister at Law, Dublin. Appointments: Irish Bar Visiting Poet; Professor, University of Wisconsin at Milwaukee. Publications: In a Blue Smoke; Blue Mountain; Baudelaire's Bar Flowers; A White Thought in a White Shade; The Slovak Bowling Alley; Art is not for Grown Ups; Collected Poems, 1994. Contributions to: New York Times; Irish Times; New England Review; Cypress; Irish Literary Supplement; University Review; Poetry Ireland; South Western Reviews; A Memoir of Katherine Kavanagh, London Magazine. Memberships: Aosdama, Ireland; American Committee for Irish Studies; Modern Language Association. Address: Department of English & Comparative Literature, University of Wisconson Milwaukee, PO Box 43, Milwaukee, WI 53201, USA.

LIDDY John Mario, b. 11 Apr 1954, Ireland. Teacher; Librarian. m. Pilar Gutierrez De Los Rios, 10 Dec 1990, 2 sons. Appointments: Curators Assistant, Hunt Museum; Co-Editor, Stony Thursday Book; Teacher; Librarian. Publications: Boundaries; The Angling Cot; Song of the Empty Cage. Contributions to: Bellingham Review; Cook Examiner; Limerick Journal; Paris/Atlantic; Poetry Island; Radio Telfis Eireann; Cyphers; Krino; Irish Press; Irish Poetry Now: Other Voices; Agenda; La Carava. Memberships: Poetry Ireland; Irish Writers Union; Irish Hispanic Society. Address: Duque De Sesto 23, 1-18, 28009 Madrid, Spain.

LIE Arvid Torgeir, b. 18 Aug 1938, Skafsaa, Norway. Author. m. Liv Greaker, 3 sons. Education: University of Oslo, 1959-62. Appointments: Member, Literary Council, Norwegian Author Union. Publications: Under The Birds Wing Cross; Snow Winter; From a Half of a Lifetime; Write and Think; Sun and Second; Seven Turns Up; A Strange House; In a Bergsto Year. Contributions to: Several Norwegian and foreign periodicals, poetry anthologies. Address: Bringsaas, 3840 Seljord, Norway.

LIEBERMAN Laurence, b. 16 Feb 1935, Detroit, Michigan, USA. Poet; Professor; Poetry Editor. m. Bernice Braun, 17 June 1956, 1 son, 2 daughters. Education: BA, University of Michigan, 1956; MA, 1958. Appointments: College of the Virgin Islands, 1964-68; University of Illinois, Professor, 1968; Poetry Editor, 1971. Publications: Unblinding; The Achievement of James Dickey; The Osprey Suicides; Unassigned Frequencies; American Poetry In Review; God's Measurements; Eros At The World Kite Pageant; Mural Of Wakeful Sleep; Creole Mephistoles; New And Selected Poems (Book), 1993; The St Kitts Monkey Feuds (Poetry), 1995; Beyond the Muse of Memory: Essays on Contemporary American Poets, 1995; Dark Songs: Slave House and Synagogue, 1996. Contributions to: New Yorker; Atlantic; Harpers; Nation; New Republic; Paris Review; Partisan Review; Hudson Review; Kenyon Review; Poetry; Boulevard; Saturday Review; Pequod: Tar River Poetry; Chariton Review. Honours: Jerome S Shestack Prize From American Poetry Review; Best American Poetry, 1991. Address: 208 English Building, 608 Wright Street, University of Illinois, Urbana, IL 61801, USA.

LIEBLER Michael Lynn, b. 24 Aug 1953, Detroit, Michigan, USA. Professor. m. Pamela Morrill, 5 Nov 1976. Education: BA. 1976; MA, 1980. Appointment: Professor of English, Wayne State University, Detroit, 1980-. Publications: Martyr of Pog; Knit Me a Pair of Your Shoes; Broken Man In A Perfect Mirror; Measuring Darkness; Whispers by the Lawn; Breaking the Voodoo; Stripping the Adult Century Bare. Contributions to: River Styx Literary Review; Cottonwood Literary Review; Licking River Literary; Cranbrook Literary Review; Rolling Stock Magazine; Relix Magazine; Oyez Literary Review. Memberships: Poetry Resource Centre. Address: 31725 Courtland, St Clair Shores, MI 48082, USA.

LIEBMAN Maura. See: **GAGE Maura R.**

LIFSHIN Lyn (Diane), b. 12 July 1944, Burlington, Vermont, USA. Poet; Teacher. Education: BA, Syracuse University, 1960; MA, University of Vermont, 1963. Appointments: Instructor, State University of New York, Cobleskill, 1968, 1970; Writing Consultant, New York State Mental Health Department, Albany, 1969; and Empire State College of the State University of New York at Saratoga Springs, 1973; Poet-in-Residence, Mansfield State College, Pennsylvania, 1974, University of Rochester, New York, 1986, and Antioch Writers' Conference, Ohio, 1987. Publications: Poetry: Over 75 collections including: Upstate Madonna: Poems, 1970-1974, 1975; Shaker House Poems, 1976; Some Madonna Poems, 1976; Leaning South, 1977; Madonna Who Shifts for Herself, 1983; Kiss the Skin Off, 1985; Camping Madonna at Indian Lake, 1986; Many Madonnas, 1988; The Doctor Poems, 1990; Apple Blossoms, 1993; Blue Tattoo, 1995; The Mad Girl Drives in a Daze, 1995. Editor: Tanged Wires: A Collection of Mother and Daughter Poems, 1978; Ariadne's Thread: A Collection of Contemporary Women's Journals, 1982; Unsealed Lips, 1988.

Contributions to: Many books and numerous other publications, including journals. Honours: Hart Crane Award; Bread Loaf Scholarship; Yaddo Fellowships, 1970, 1971, 1975, 1979, 1980; MacDowell Fellowship, 1973; Millay Colony Fellowships, 1975, 1979; Jack Kerouac Award, 1984; Centennial Review Poetry Prize, 1985; Madeline Sadin Award, New York Quarterly, 1986; Footwork Award, 1987; Estersceffler Award, 1987. Address: 2142 Appletree Lane, Niskayuna, NY 12309, USA.

LIGHTFOOT David James, (James Harrison), b. 7 Apr 1941, Wrexham, Wales. Former School Teacher. m. Valerie Elizabeth Lightfoot, 23 Oct 1965, 1 son, 1 daughter. Education: BA, Wales, 1962; MA, Wales, 1964; PhD, Leicester, 1980. Appointments: Head of Classics, St Margarets, Liverpool; Head of Classics, Boston Grammar School; Education Officer, Government of Kenya; Head of English, Monks Dyke School; Deputy Head, St Peter and Paul School, Lincoln. Publications: Down Private Lanes; Last Round. Contributions to: Acumen; Orbis; Outposts; Rialto; Prospice; Oxford Poetry; Pennine Platform; Proof; Bradford Poetry Quarterly; New Welsh Review; Iota; Inkshed; Staple. Honours: Muscular Dystrophy Competition; Rosemary Arthur Award; Frogmore; Orbis Rhyme Revival Runner Up, 1993. Membership: Society of Authors. Address: 1 Horncastle Road, Louth, Lincolnshire LN11 9LB, England.

LIKHI (Sukhdershan), b. 19 Apr 1932, Ludhiana, India. Indian Police Service. m. Veena Bahl, 27 Feb 1965, 1 son, 1 daughter. Education: BA Honours, English, 1952; MA, English, 1954; Police and Administration courses. Appointments: Lecturer in English, 1954-57; DSP, 1963; SP, 1971; Area Organiser SSB, Government of India, 1971-77; SP CID, 1978-81; SP, 1981-84; SSP, 1984-85; Commandant, 1985-90; Police Officer, 1990-91. Contributions to: Book reviews and poems: Daily Tribune; Poetry Society of India Journal; Poet; Asian Age; Poem, Going Middle East for Gold, in Poetry India New Voices, 1990. Membership: Poetry Society of India; President, Association for Social Organisation, 1993-. Address: H No 1787 Phase III B2, Sas Nagar, Mohari, Punjab, India.

LIMA Robert, b. 7 Nov 1935, Havana, Cuba. Professor. m. Sally A Murphy, 27 June 1964, 2 sons, 2 daughters. Education: BA, Villanova University, 1957; MA, 1961; PhD, New York University, 1968. Appointments: Lecturer, Hunter College, 1962-65; Assistant Professor, 1965-69, Associate Professor, 1969-73, Professor, 1973-, Penn State University; Fulbright Visiting Professor; Fulbright Poet in Residence in Peru. Publications: Seventh Street; Poems of Exile and Alienation; Fathoms; Corporal Works; The Olde Ground; Mayaland. Contributions to: Statements; Cimarron Review; Journal of General Education; Studia Mystica; Boundary 2; Literary Review; Anthology of Magazine Verse; Dreamworks; Prairie Schooner; Caribbean Writer; Kosmos; In the West of Ireland; Visions. Honours: Cintas Foundation Fellow; Fellow, Institute for the Arts and Humanistic Studies; Academia Norteamericana de la Lengua Espanola. Memberships: Poetry Society of America; PEN; Poets and Writers. Address: Institute for the Arts and Humanistic Studies, Penn State University, Ihlseng Cottage, University Park, PA 16802, USA.

LINDEMAN Jack, b. 31 Dec 1924. Poet; Professor. Education: BA, West Chester State College, University of Pennsylvania, 1949; University of Mississippi, 1949-50; American University Villanova University, 1971. Appointments: Instructor, African Center, Lincoln University, 1963-64; Temple University, 1964-65; Kutztown State University, 1969-85; Professor, Emeritus, 1985-. Publications: 21 Poems; Anthologies: Poets of Today; Where is Vietnam?; The Writing on the Wall; From Paragraph to Essay; In the West of Ireland; In The West of Ireland II, 1995; Parnassus of World Poets, 1994. Contributions to: Beloit Poetry Journal; Commonweal; California Quarterly; Harpers Bazaar; Literary Review; Massachusetts Review; Christian Science Monitor; New York Times; Modern Age; High Plains Review; Images; New World Writing; Nation; Prairie Schooner; Poetry; Southwest Review; Southern Poetry Review; Kansas Quarterly; Hollins Critic; Crazy Quilt; California State Poetry Quarterly; Bellowing Ark; San Fernando Poetry Journal; Home Planet News; California Quarterly; Slant; Oregon East; Synaesthetic; Blue Unicorn; Eureka Literary Magazine; Poet's Page; Apocalypse; Mew Authors Journal. Honour: Best Poems of 1966. Membership: American Friends of the Vatican Library. Address: 133 South Franklin Street, Fleetwood, PA 19522, USA.

LINDEN Eddie Sean, b. 5 May 1935, Northern Ireland. Writer; Poet; Editor. Education: Holy Family, Mossend; St Patrick's, New Stephenson; Catholic Workers College of Oxford. Appointments: Founder, Editor, Literary Magazine, Aquarius. Publications: City of Razors, poems; Contributions to: Penguin Book of Homosexual Verse; Best of Scottish Poetry; Poetry Society Anthology; Childrens Poems; Poetry Review; Tribune; Times; Tablet; Irish Times; Belfast Review; Belfast Fortnight and Agenda. Honour: Biography, Who is Eddie Linden, by Sebastian Barker, also play of the same title, Red Lion Theatre, Islington, London. Memberships: Poetry Society; Howard Sergant Memorial Award Committee. Address: Flat 10 Room A, 116 Sutherland Avenue, London W9, England.

LINDNER Carl Martin, b. 31 Aug 1940, New York, New York, USA. Professor of English, 1 son, 1 daughter. Education: BA, 1962, MA, 1965, City University of New York; PhD, University of Wisconsin at Madison, 1970. Appointments: Assistant Professor of English, 1969-74, Associate Professor of English, 1974-87, University of Wisconsin at Parkside; Professor of English, University of Wisconsin at Parkside, 1987-. Publications: Vampire, 1977; The Only Game, 1981; Shooting Baskets in a Dark Gymnasium, 1984. Contributions to: Poetry; Slant; Greensboro Review; Southern Poetry Review; Mid-American Review; Kansas Quarterly; South Carolina Review; Southwest Review; Literary Review; Beloit Poetry Journal; Poets On; Southern Humanities Review; Negative Capability; Cottonwood. Honour: Wisconsin Arts Board Creative Writing Fellowship, 1981. Address: c/o University of Wisconsin at Parkside, Box 2000, Kenosha, WI 53141, USA.

LINDOP Grevel Charles Garrett, b. 6 Oct 1948, Liverpool, England. Lecturer. m. Amanda Therese Marian, 4 July 1981, 1 son, 2 daughters. Education: BA, Wadham College, Oxford, 1969; MA, BLitt, Wolfson College, 1974. Appointments: Lecturer, University of Manchester, 1971-84; Senior Lecturer, 1984-93; Reader, 1993-. Publications: Against The Sea; Fools Paradise; Tourists; Moons Palette; A Prismatic Toy. Contributions to: Times Literary Supplement; Critical Quarterly; PN Review; Poetry Durham; Numbers. Address: Department of English, University of Manchester, Manchester, M13 9PL, England.

LINDSAY Graham Boyd, b. 16 Sept 1952, Wellington, New Zealand. Writer. Education: BA; Diploma in Teaching. Publications: Thousand-Eyed Eel, 1976; Public, 1980; Big Boy, 1986; Return to Earth, 1991; Editor, Morepork 1-3, 1979-80; The Subject, 1994. Contributions to: New Quarterly Cave; Islands; Spleen; Climate; Pilgrims; Parallax; Landfall; Splash; Untold; OUSA Review; Canta Critic; Frame; Metro; Takahe; Listener; Edge; Span; Poetry New Zealand; Plainwraps; Sport; Literary Half-Yearly; Origin; Quote Unquote; New Zealand Books; Printout. Membership: New Zealand Society of Authors. Address: 100 Main South Road, Christchurch 4, New Zealand.

LINDSAY (John) Maurice, b. 21 July 1918, Scotland. Writer; Former TV Executive. m. 3 Aug 1946, 1 son, 3 daughters. Education: Glasgow Academy, 1928-36; Scottish National Academy of Music, 1936-39. Appointments: Drama Critic, 1946-47; Music Critic, 1946-60; Programme Controller, Border Television, 1959-62; Production Controller, 1962-64; Features Executive, 1964-67; Director, Scottish Civic Trust, 1967-83; President, Association for Scottish Literary Studies, 1982-83; Honorary Secretary General, Europa Nostra, 1983-91. Publications: Robert Burns: The Man, His Work; The Legend; The Burns Encyclopaedia; History of Scottish Literature; The Castles of Scotland; Collected Poems 1940-90; On the Face of It, Collected Poems, Vol 2; News of the World: Last Poems; Francis George Scott and the Scottish Renaissance; The Scottish Dog (with Joyce Lindsay); The Chambers Guide to Good Scottish Gardens (with Joyce Lindsay). Contributions to: Glasgow Herald; Scotsman; New Scottish Writing; Stand; Lines Review. Honours: Territorial Decoration; Atlantic Rockerfeller Award; Commander of the Order of the British Empire; D Litt, University of Glasgow; Honorary Fellow, Royal Incorporation of Architects in Scotland. Address: 7 Milton Hall, Milton, Dumbarton G82 2TS, Scotland.

LINEBARGER James Morris (Jim), b. 6 July 1934, Abilene, Texas, USA. Professor. m. Lillian Tillery, 1958, div, 2 sons. Education: AB, Columbia University, 1952; MA, 1957; PhD, Emory University, 1963. Appointments: Instructor, Assistant Professor, Georgia Tech, 1957-62; Assistant Professor, 1963-65; Associate Professor, 1965-70; Full Professor, 1970-; Poet In Residence, University of North Texas, 1989-. Publications: The Worcester Poems, 1991; Anecdotal Evidence, 1993. Contributions to: Southwest Review; Laurel Review;

Descant; Cross Timbers Review; Southern Humanities Review; Pebble; Midwestern University Quarterly; Arts and Letters; Vanderbilt Review. Memberships: Poetry Society of America. Address: English Department, University of North Texas, Denton, TX 76203, USA.

LIST Anneliese, (Alice Pervin), b. 6 Jan 1922, Heroldsberg, Germany. Author. m. Huldreich List, 28 Feb 1947, dec. Education: Qualified Dancer, Opera-House (Nuremberg) Ballet School, 1926-38, Munich, 1939. Appointments: Dancer, Municipal Theatre Guben, 2 years; Dance Soubrette, Municipal Theatre of Landsberg-Warthe, 1 year; Operetten-Soubrette, Municipal Theatre of Elbing, 1944-45; Clerk, US European Exchange System, 1954; Secretary, Refugee and Migration Section, American Consulate General, United States Embassy Escapee Program, 1955-60; Clerk in Charge, Foreigners Office, Nuremberg, 1960-82; Author. Publications include: The Tree, 1973; What I'll Never Be Able To Forget In All My Life, 1975; My Long Way From The War Until Today, 1975; Not Before Today I Understood Why My Mother Left Me, 1975; How I Earned My First Money, 1977; The Little Witch, 1977; The Luck Behind The Mountains, booklet with 4 stories, 1978; A Fairy Tale, 1986; Ten Promises, 1987; First Love, 1987; Prayer in The Sunshine, 1989; Jubilate, 1991; The Rainbow, 1992; Her Most Beautiful Christmas, 1992; The Heroine, 1993; Am Waldsee, 1995; Forgotten, 1995; The Revenge is Mine, Says Our Lord, 1995. Contributions to: Stories, poems and articles published in Main-Echo, Frau Aktuell, 7 Tage, Welt am Sonnabend, True Stories, Goldenes Blatt and Zenit; Schoenbuch-Verlag. Honours include: 2nd Prize in an international contest for best story, True Stories Magazine, 1975; Gold Medal and Certificate for Honourable Service, City of Nuremberg, 1982; Fellow, World Literary Academy, 1986; International Cultural Diploma of Honour for Outstanding Contribution to Literature, 1988; Cultural Doctorate of Literature, World University Roundtable, 1988. Membership: World Literary Academy, England. Address: Ritter-von-Schuh Platz 15, 90459 Nurenberg, Germany.

LISTOPAD Frantisek. See: **SYNEK Jiri (George).**

LITHERLAND Sheila Jacqueline, b. 18 Sept 1936, Birmingham, England. Poet; Creative Writer; Literature Tutor. Div, 1 son, 1 daughter. Education: Regent Street Polytechnic, 1955; Ruskin College, Oxford, 1986; BA, University College, London, 1989. Publications: The Long Interval; Fourpack; Half Light; Modern Poets of Northern England; New Women Poets; The Poetry of Perestroika; Flowers of Fever. Contributions to: Iron Magazine; Writing Women Magazine; Oxford Magazine; Green Book. Honour: Annaghmakerrig Residence, 1994. Memberships: Colpitts Poetry; Modern Tower Committee; The Poetry Society. Address: 6 Waddington Street, Durham City DH1 4BG, England.

LITT Iris, b. 18 Mar 1928, New York, New York, USA. Freelance Writer; Poet. m. Gilbert Burris, 11 July 1948, 2 sons. Education: BA, Ohio State University, 1948; Exchange Student, Universidad de Las Americas, Mexico City, 1947. Appointments: New York Market Editor, Columnist, The Writer, 1949-54; Copywriter, The Gumbinner Agency, 1954-59; Copywriter, Ellington and Co, 1960-62; Copywriter, Norman, Craig and Kummel, 1960-62; Benton and Bowles, 1962-64; Clinton E Frank Advertising, 1964-71; ACR Advertising, 1971-84. Publications: Book of Poetry: Word Love, 1994, reprinted 1996. Contributions to: Poetry; Onthebus; Poetry Now; Central Park; Earth's Daughters; Ledge; Woodstock Poetry Review; DeKalb Literary Arts Journal; Blue Unicorn; Poet Lore; West End; Stone Country; Lactuca; Cape Rock Journal; Pearl; Bitterroot; Green Fuse; Scholastic; Compact; Poetry Chap Book; Atlantic Monthly. Honours: College Poetry, Atlantic Monthly Award; 2nd Prize, League of American Pen Women; French Bread Award, Pacific Coast Journal. Memberships: Poetry Society of America. Address: 252 West 11th Street, New York, NY 10014, USA.

LITTLE Geraldine Clinton, b. 23 Sept 1925, Northern Ireland. College Professor. m. Robert Knox Little, 26 Sept 1953, 2 sons. Education: BA, Goddard College, Vermont, 1971; MA, Trenton State College, 1976. Appointments: Adjunct Professor, Burlington County College, 1978-; Professor, Rutgers University, 1980; Trenton State College, 1986-87. Publications: Star Mapped; Heloise A Abelard; A Well Tuned Harp; Women: In the Mask and Beyond; Seasons in Space; Beyond the Boxwood Comb; Ministries; More Light, Larger Vision; Out of Darkness. Contributions to: Poetry Northwest; Yankee; Christian Science Monitor; Literary Review; California Review; Confrontation; Prairie Schooner; Nimrod; Hudson Review; St Andrews Review; Northwest Review; Poetry Now; Poetry Miscellany; Poet and Critic; Stone Country; Poet Lore; Raccoon. Honours: Gordon Barber

Award; Alfred Kreymborg Award; Cecil Hemley Award; Dustav Davidson Award; Pablo Neruda Award; Chas Angoff Award; The Charles Bosworth Jones Award; PEN Short Fiction Award; 4 Grants. Memberships: Poetry Society of America; Haiku Society of America; PEN International; New Jersey Poetry Society; New England Poetry Club. Address: 519 Jacksonville Road, Mt Holly, NJ 08060, USA.

LIU Ban-jiu. See: **LU Yuan.**

LIU Wen Yu, b. 5 Mar 1930, Liao Yuan, Jilin Province, China. Poet; Dramatist; Editor. m. Lian Jie Bao, 16 Aug 1952, 2 sons, 1 daughter. Education: Liao Bei College, 1948; DLit, World Academy of Arts and Culture, USA. Appointments: Editor, Liao Xi Literature and Art, 1949; Liao Ning Literature and Art; Poetry Section Leader, Youth of Literature, 1957; Poet, Dramatist, 1960; Chief Editor, Mang Zhong, Shi Chao, 1984; Chairman, Literary and Art Works Union of Shenyang, 1987; Vice Chairman, Literature and Art Works Union of Liaoning, Writers Union of Liaoning, 1989. Publications: Willow Flute; Paeans of Native Soil; Give You a Song; Green Feelings; White Love Flower; Selected Poems of Liu Wen Yu; Mine Beaconfire; Underground Fury; Sweet Heart. Contributions to: Poem; Shi Xhao; Chu Nu Di; Ya Lu Jiang; Dong Bei Wen Xue; Mang Zhong; Liao Ning Daily; Shen Yang Daily; People's Literature. Honour: Poetry of Liaoning Province Prize. Memberships: Writers Union; Dramatists Union; Musicians' Union; Folk Artists Union; Vice Chairman, Research Association of Prose Poem; Universal Chinese Poems Union; World Academy of Arts and Culture, USA. Address: 40 Sec 3 San jing Street, Heping, Shenyang 110003, China.

LIU Zhan-Qiu, b. 20 Nov 1935, Anhui, China. Editor. Education: Foreign Language Institute, 1955. Appointment: Editor-in-Chief, 1986-89. Publications: On the Early Spring Writing Paper; Warm Love; Lyrics and Thoughts; The Far Away Guitar; Titleless Lyric; Man, Love, Scene; Pure and Impure Lyric Poems; Seas Romance; The Melody of Lyric Poems; The Secret of Poetry. Honour: China New Poetry Award. Memberships: China Writers Association; Chinese Prose Poem Society; World Academy of Arts and Culture; International Poetry Association. Address: 15A Hufang Road, Beijing, China.

LIVINGSTONE Douglas (James), b. 5 Jan 1932, Kuala Lumpur, Malaysia. Marine Microbiologist. Education: PhD. Appointments: Officer in Charge, Pathological Diagnostic Laboratory, Kabwe General Hospital, North Rhodesia, 1959-63; Senior Marine Bacteriologist, Durban, 1964-. Publications: The Skull in the Mud; Sjambok and Other Poems from Africa; Poems: Eyes Closed Against the Sun; A Rosary of Bone; The Anvil's Undertone; Selected Poems: A Littoral Zone. Contributions to: London Magazine; New Contrat. Honours: Guinness Poetry Prize; Cholmondeley Award; CNA Literary Prize; Thomas Pringle Poetry Prize. Address: PO Box 17001, Congella 4013, South Africa.

LIYONG Taban, b. 1939, Kajo Kaji, Sudan. Education: BA, Howard University, Washington, 1966. Appointments: Lecturer in Nairobi, Tanzania and New Guinea. Publications include: Eating Chiefs: Lwo Culture from Lolwe to Malkal, 1970; Frantz Fanon's Uneven Ribs: With Poems More and More, 1971; Another Nigger Dead, 1972; Ballads of Underdevelopment: Poems and Thoughts, 1974; To Still a Passion, 1977. Address: Literature Unit, College of Education, University of Juba, PO Box 82, Juba, Sudan.

LLOYD-JONES Jenafer, (Eilonwy Grey, Greya Locke), b. 16 June 1971, Joplin, Missouri, USA. Opera Singer. Education: BM, Conservatory of Music, Cincinnati. Publication: The Babblings of an Insane Mind. Contributions to: Spectrum; Seven Hills Review. Membership: Poetry Society of America. Address: 1122 White Pine Court, Cincinnati, OH 45255, USA.

LOBO PRABHU Louella, b. 27 Dec 1942, Mangalore, India. Publisher; Editor; Columnist; Broadcaster. m. J M Lobo Prabhu, 12 May 1964, 1 daughter. Education: BA Honours, Literature, 1st Class, Bombay University, 1963. Appointments: Publisher, Editor, Insight, 1964-; "A" Grade Artist, National Radio and Television; Academie Council, Senate, Mangalore University, 1986-; Partner, Lobo Prabhu Enterprises; Director, Elite Cultural Centre. Publications: Literary Adviser, Indian Book Chronicle, Jaipur; A Musical Credo, 1987; The Grammar of Politics in Verse, 1988; My Temple of the Arts, 1991; My India is One India, 1992; The Heart of Eve, 1993; The Ascent of Mount Carmel, 1994; Tiaha, 1995-96. Contributions to: Times of India; Statesman; Herald; Indian Currents; Coastal Observer; Chetana;

Indian Book Chronicle; Kavita India; Poet; National Radio. Honours: Fellow, United Writers Association of India; Fellow, Indo-African Society, New Delhi; 1st ever winner, Sandesha Media Award for Arts, 1991; Life Associate, IWA; 1st ever winner, New Leader Award, 1994; Michael Madhusudan Dutt Award, 1995; IFSMH Award, 1995-96; Metverse Muse Premier Membership, 1996; Bethany Award for Guest Editing, 1996. Memberships: Adviser, Chetana Literary Group; Indian Book Chronicle; Editorial Board, Mangalore University Newsletter, Coastal Observer; All India Women Editors' Association. Address: Chateau De Lou, Light House Hill Road, Mangalore 575 001, Karnataka, India.

LOCHHEAD Douglas Grant, b. 25 Mar 1922, Guelph, Ontario, Canada. Writer; President of Board; m. 17 Sept 1949, 2 daughters. Education: BA, McGill University; MA, Toronto University; BLS, McGill University. Appointments: Librarian, Professor, Victoria College, 1951-52; Cornell University, 1952-53; University Librarian, Dalhousie University, 1953-60; Director of Libraries, York University, Toronto, 1960-63; Librarian, Fellow, Massey College, University of Toronto, 1963-75; Director, Mount Allison University, 1975-87. Publications: The Heart is Fire; Battle Sequence; A & E; Poet Talking; The Panic Field; A & B & C; Tiger in the Skull; Millwood Road Poems; Upper Cape Poems; Prayers in a Field; Dykelands; The Full Furnace; Homage to Henry Alline; High Mersh Road. Contributions to: Most Canadian Literary Journals. Honours: Golden Dog Award; Fellow, Royal Society of Canada; Tremaine Medal in Bibliography; Professor Emeritus. Memberships: Life Member, League of Canadian Poets, 1995-; Bibliographical Society of Canada. Address: PO Box 1108, Sackville, New Brunswick E0A 3C0, Canada.

LOCHHEAD Liz, b. 26 Dec 1947, Motherwell, Scotland. Poet; Playwright; Screenwriter; Teacher. Education: Diploma, Glasgow School of Art, 1970. Appointments: Art Teacher, Glasgow and Bristol Schools; Lecturer, University of Glasgow. Publications: Poetry: Memo for Spring, 1972; The Grimm Sisters, 1981; Dreaming Frankenstein and Collected Poems, 1984; True Confessions and New Clichés, 1985. Screenplay: Now and Then, 1972. Plays: Blood and Ice, 1982; Silver Service, 1984; Dracula and Mary Queen of Scots Got Her Head Chopped Off, 1989. Honours: BBC Scotland Prize, 1971; Scottish Arts Council Award, 1972. Address: 11 Kersland Street, Glasgow G12 8BW, Scotland.

LOCKE Greya. See: LLOYD-JONES Jenafer.

LOCKETT Reginald Franklin, (Tahid), b. 5 Nov 1947, Berkeley, California, USA. Instructor of English. m. Faye West, 18 Jan 1983, 1 daughter. Education: BA, English Literature, 1971, MA, English Literature, 1972, San Francisco State University. Appointments: Instructor of English, Peralta Community College District, 1973-76; Lecturer in Creative Writing, San Francisco State University, 1976-78; City College of San Francsico, 1982-90; Instructor of English, San Jose City College, 1990-. Publications: Good Times & No Bread, 1978; Where The Birds Sing Bass, 1995. Contributions to: Negro Digest; Iowa Review; Konceptualizations; Journal of Black Poetry; Visions Across the Americas; Thresholds; Black Dialogue; Soul Book; Black Fire; Quilt; Genetic Dancers. Honours: The PEN Oakland; Josephine Miles Literary Award for Where the Birds Sing Bass, 1996. Memberships: Board member, National Poetry Association; Former vice-president and founding member, PEN, Oakland. Address: 211 Hanover Avenue #6, Oakland, California 94606, USA.

LOCKLIN Gerald (Ivan), b. 17 Feb 1941, Rochester, New York, USA. Poet; Writer; Professor. m. (1) Mary Alice Keefe, 3 children, (2) Maureen McNicholas, 2 children, (3) Barbara Curry, 2 children. Education: BA, St John Fisher College, 1961; MA, 1963, PhD, 1964, University of Arizona. Appointments: Instructor, California State College at Los Angeles, 1964-65; Associate Professor, then Professor of English, California State University at Long Beach, 1965-. Publications: Poetry: The Toad Poems, 1970; Poop, and Other Poems, 1973; Tarzan and Shane Meet the Toad (with Ronald Koertge and Charles Stetler), 1975; The Criminal Mentality, 1976; Toad's Sabbatical, 1978; The Last of Toad, 1980; By Land, Sea, and Air, 1982; The Ensenada Poems (with Ray Zepeda), 1984; Gringo and Other Poems, 1987; The Death of Jean-Paul Sartré and Other Poems, 1988; Lost and Found, 1989; The Firebird Poems, 1992; The Old Mongoose and Other Poems, 1993; Toad Turns Fifty: Selected Poems by Gerald Locklin, 1993. Fiction: Locked In, short stories, 1973; The Chase, novel, 1976; The Four-Day Work Week and Other Stories, 1977; The Cure, novel, 1979; A Weekend in Canada, short stories,

1979; The Case of the Missing Blue Volkswagen, novella, 1984; The Gold Rush and Other Stories, 1989. Contributions to: Many periodicals. Membership: Phi Beta Kappa. Address: Department of English, California State University, Long Beach, CA 90840, USA.

LOCRE Peter E. See: COLE Eugene Roger.

LOFTON Ramona, (Sapphire), b. 4 Aug 1950, Fort Ord, California, USA. Literacy Educator; Poet; Writer. Education: BFA cum laude, City University of New York, 1983; MFA, Brooklyn College, 1995. Appointment: Writer, Writing Project of Teachers College, Columbia University, 1992-93. Publications: Books: American Dreams, 1994; Push, 1996. Contributions to: Outweek; Amaranth Review; Queer City; City Lights Review; The Washington Post; New York Post; New York Newsday; The Phoenix Review; The New York Times Magazine; Wild Thing (poem) excerpted in Dinitia Smith's The Poet Kings and the Populist Uprising, 1995; Anthologies: High Risk, 1994; Life Notes, 1994; Critical Condition: Women on the Edge of Violence, 1993; Aloud: Voices from the Nuyorican Poets Cafe, 1994; Women on Women, 1990. Honours: Amaranth Review, prize for poem, Rabbit Man, 1991; Harvest Works/Audio Arts, Artist-in-Residence Award, 1991. Literary Agent: Charlotte Sheedy, 65 Bleeker, 12th Floor, New York, NO 10012, USA. Address: PO Box 975, Manhattanville Station, New York, NY 10027, USA.

LOGAN William, b. 16 Nov 1950, Boston, Massachusetts, USA. Professor. m. Debora Greger. Education: BA, Yale University, 1972; University of Iowa, 1975. Appointments: Assistant Professor, 1983-87, Associate Professor, 1987-91, Professor, 1991- University of Florida at Gainesville. Publications: Sad Faced Men; Difficulty; Sullen Weedy Lakes. Contributions to: The New Yorker; Poetry; Harpers; The Nation; Sewanee Review; Critical Quarterly; Paris Review; Partisan Review. Honours: National Book Critics Circle Citation for Excellence; Peter I B Lavan Younger Poets Award. Address: 19 Mawson Road, Cambridge CB1 2DZ, England.

LOGGHE Joan Slesinger, b. 23 Aug 1947, Pittsburgh, Pennsylvania, USA. Poet; Editor; Writing Teacher. m. Michael Logghe, 2 Aug 1971, 1 son, 2 daughters. Education: BA Magna Cum Laude as Class Poet, Tufts University, 1969. Appointments: New Mexico Artist-In-Residence, Open Hands Arts With Elders; Poetry Editor; Mothering Magazine; Host for open reading series At Santa Fe Centre for Contemporary Arts. Publications: Poems From The Russian Room, 1989; A Lunch Date With Beauty, 1990; What Makes a Woman Beautiful, 1993. Contributions to: Writers Digest; Puerto Del Sol; Taos Review; Mothering Magazine; Anthologies from Faber & Faber, Harper Collins. Honours: National Academy of Poets College Award, 1966; National Endowment for the Arts Fellowship, 1992. Membership: PEN. Address: Rt 3 Box 180 A, Espanola, NM 87532, USA.

LOGUE Christopher (John), b. 23 Nov 1926, Portsmouth, Hampshire, England. Poet; Writer; Dramatist. m. Rosemary Hill, 1985. Education: Prior Park College, Bath. Publications: Poetry: Wand and Quadrant, 1953; Devil, Maggot and Son, 1954; The Weakdream Sonnets, 1955; The Man Who Told His Love: 20 Poems Based on P Neruda's "Los Cantos d'Amores", 1958, 2nd edition, 1959; Songs, 1960; Songs from "The Lily-White Boys", 1960; The Establishment Songs, 1966; The Girls, 1969; New Numbers, 1970; Abecedary, 1977; Ode to the Dodo, 1981; War Music: An Account of Books 16 to 19 of Homer's Iliad, 1981; Fluff, 1984; Kings: An Account of Books 1 and 2 of Homer's Iliad, 1991, revised edition, 1992; The Husbands: An Account of Books 3 and 4 of Homer's Iliad, 1994; Selected Poems, (edited by Christopher Reid), 1996. Plays: The Lily-White Boys (with Harry Cookson), 1959; The Trial of Cob and Leach, 1959; Antigone, 1961; War Music, 1978; Kings, 1993; Screenplay: Savage Messiah, 1972; Other: Lust, by Count Palmiro Vicarion, 1955; The Arrival of the Poet in the City: A Treatment for a Film, 1964; True Stories, 1966; The Bumper Book of True Stories, 1980; Editor: Count Palmiro Vicarion's Book of Limericks, 1959; The Children's Book of Comic Verse, 1979; London in Verse, 1982; Sweet and Sour: An Anthology of Comic Verse, 1983; The Children's Book of Children's Rhymes, 1986. Address: 41 Camberwell Grove, London, SE5 8JA, England.

LOMAS Herbert, b. 7 Feb 1924, Yorkshire, England. Poet; Critic. m. Mary Marshall Phelps, 27 June 1968, 1 son, 1 daughter. Education: BA, University of Liverpool, 1946-49; MA, 1952. Appointments: Army, Kings Liverpool Regiment, 1943-44; Officer, Royal Garhwal Rifles, 1944-46; Teacher, Spetsai, Greece, 1950-51; Lecturer, Senior Lecturer Finland, 1952-65; Senior Lecturer, Borough Road College, 1966-72;

Principal Lecturer, 1972-82; Poet; Critic; Freelance Writer; Translator. Publications: Chimpanzees are Blameless Creatures, 1969; Who Needs Money?, 1972; Private and Confidential, 1974; Public Footpath, 1981; Fire in the Garden, 1984; Letters in the Dark, 1986; Trouble, 1992; Selected Poems, 1995; Translations: Contemporary Finnish Poetry, 1991; Wings of Hope and Daring, 1992; Black and Red, 1993; Narcissus in Winter, 1994; The Year of the Hare, 1994. Contributions to: Adelphi; London Magazine; Encounter; Hudson Review; Ambit; London Lines; Spectator. Honours: Poetry Prize, Guinness Poetry Competition; Runner Up, Arvon Foundation Poetry Competition; Cholmondely Award; Poetry Book Society Biennial Translation Award; Knight First Class Order of the White Rose, Finland, 1991. Membership: Society of Authors. Address: North Gable, 30 Crag Path, Aldeburgh, Suffolk IP15 5BS, England.

LOMAX Marion, b. 20 Oct 1953, Newcastle upon Tyne, Tyne and Wear,England. Professor of Literature. m. Michael Lomax, 29 Aug 1974. Education: BA, Librarianship, 1974; BA, English and American Studies, 1979; DPhil, University of York, 1983. Appointments: Part-time Lecturer, King Alfreds College, 1983-86; University of Reading, 1983-87; Open University, 1983-88; Lecturer, St Mary's College, 1987-88; Creative Writing Fellow, University of Reading, 1987-88; Senior Lecturer, St Mary's University College, 1988-95; Professor of Literature, St Mary's University College, Strawberry Hill, 1995-. Publications: The Peepshow Girl; Time Present and Time Past, editor; Libretto to Opera: Beyond Men and Dreams, 1991; Raiding the Borders, 1996. Contributions to: Times Literary Supplement; Poetry Review; Literary Review; London Magazine; Writing Women; Poetry Durham; Forms of Poetry; Taking Reality by Surprise; Poetry with a Sharper Edge; Poetry Wales; Aquarius; Anthologies: Poetry with an Edge; Sixty Women Poets. Honour: E C Gregory Award, Cheltenham Festival Poetry Competition; Hawthornden Fellowship, 1993. Membership: Poetry Society; National Association for Writers in Education. Address: Bloodaxe Books, PO Box 1SN, Newcastle upon Tyne, Tyne and Wear NE99 1SN, England.

LOMBARDO Gian, b. 24 Sept 1953, Hartford, Connecticut, USA. m. Margaret Soussloff, 28 Apr 1991. Education: BA, Trinity College, 1980; MA, Boston University, 1981. Publications: Between Islands, 1984; Standing Room, 1989; Before Arguable Answers. Contributions to: Lift; Prose Poem International; Agni; Denver Quarterly; Talisman; Iowa Review. Membership: Writing Programs. Address: 781 East Guinea Road, Williamsburg, MA 01096, USA.

LOMEN. See: HAN Jen-Tsun.

LONG D(onald) S(tuart), b. 5 Jan 1950. Writer; Editor. m. Michele, 1 Aug 1981, 3 sons. Education: BA, MA Hons, University of Canterbury; Teaching Diploma, Christchurch College of Education; Maori, Samoan, Victoria University. Appointments: Editor, Edge, 1971-77; Pacific Editor, Learning Media, 1986-; Editor, (with Witi Ihimaera) Into the World of Light, and Te Ao Marama. Publications: Borrow Pit, 1971; Poems from the Fifth Season, 1977; The Winter Fisherman. Contributions to: Landfall; Poetry Australia; Manoa; Cutbank; Kayak; Chelsea; Laughing Bear; Wayside Review; Makar; Cafe Solo; Prism International. Memberships: New Zealand Society of Authors/PEN New Zealand Centre, Executive Committee; New Zealand Book Council's Writers in Schools Scheme. Address: 22 Marine Drive, Day's Bay, Eastbourne, New Zealand.

LONG Robert Hill, b. 23 Nov 1952, Raleigh, North Carolina, USA. Poet; Teacher. m. Sandra Morgen, 22 Mar, 1980, 1 son, 1 daughter. Education: BA, Honors Studies, Davidson College, 1975; MFA, Program for Writers, Warren Wilson College. Appointments: Visiting Lecturer, Clark University, 1988-91; Senior Instructor, Program in Creative Writing, University of Oregon, 1991-. Publications: The Power to Die, 1987; The Work of The Bow, 1996. Contributions to: Poetry; Hudson Review; Kenyon Review; New England Review; Massachusetts Review; Stand. Honours: Fellow, North Carolina Arts Council, 1986; Fellow, National Endowment for The Arts, 1988; Best American Poetry, 1995; Cleveland State University Poetry Center Prize, 1995. Address: Program in Creative Writing, University of Oregon, Eugene, OR 97403, USA.

LONGCHAMPS Renaud, b. 5 Nov 1952, St Ephrem, Quebec, Canada. Writer. m. Charlotte Poulin, 29 July 1973, 1 son, 2 daughters. Education: Diplom d'Etudes Collegiales; Francois Xavier Garneau College. Publications: Paroles d'ici; L'homme Imminent; Anticorps; Charpente Charnelle; Sur l'Aire du Lire; Ditatique; Main Armee; Terres Rares; Comme d'hasard Ovrable; L'Etat de Matiere; Le Desir de la Production; Miguasha; Anomalies; Le Detail de l'Apocalypse; Legendes; L'Echelle Des Etres; Babelle l'Apres le Deluge; Liescarfe; Americane. Contributions to: Les Herbes Rouges; La Nouvelle Barre du Jour; Hobo Quebec; Estuaire; Cross Country; Levres Urbaines; Urgenies; Possibles; International Litte Realite; Dalhousie French Studies; Jungle; Identites; Poetic Journal. Membership: Union des Ecrivains Quebecois. Address: 24 Boulevard Chartier, Saint Ephrem, Comte de Beauce, Quebec GOM 1R0, Canada.

LONGLEY Michael, b. 27 July 1939, Belfast, Northern Ireland. Poet; Arts Administrator. m. Edna Broderick, 1964, 1 son, 2 daughters. Education: BA, Trinity College, Dublin, 1963. Appointments: Assistant Master, Avoca School, Blackrock, 1962-63; Belfast High School and Erith Secondary School, 1963-64, and Royal Belfast Academical Institution, 1964-69; Director for Literature and the Traditional Arts, Arts Council of Northern Ireland, Belfast, 1970-. Publications: Poetry: Ten Poems, 1965; Room to Rhyme (with Seamus Heaney and David Hammond), 1968; Secret Marriages: Nine Short Poems, 1968; Three Regional Voices (with Barry Tebb and Iain Crichton Smith), 1968; No Continuing City: Poems 1963-1968, 1969; Lares, 1972; An Exploded View: Poems 1968-1972, 1973; Fishing in the Sky, 1975; Man Lying on a Wall, 1976; The Echo Gate: Poems 1975-1978, 1979; Selected Poems, 1963-1980, 1980; Patchwork, 1981; Poems 1963-1983, 1985; Gorse Fires, 1991. Editor: Causeway: The Arts in Ulster, 1971; Under the Moon, Over the Stars: Young People's Writing from Ulster, 1971; Selected Poems by Louis MacNeice, 1988. Contributions to: Periodicals. Honours: Eric Gregory Award, Society of Authors, 1965; Commonwealth Poetry Prize, 1985. Address: 32 Osborne Gardens, Malone, Belfast 9, Northern Ireland.

LONSFORD Florence Hutchinson, b. 7 Jan 1914, Lebanon, Indiana, USA. Artist; Designer; Writer; Art Teacher. m. Graydon Lee Lonsford, 18 Dec 1938. Education: MA, Hunter College; BS Science, Purdue University, 1936; Postgraduate, National Academy of Fine Arts, 1956-58; MA, Hunter College, 1963; Postgraduate, John Herron Art Institute, 1963. Appointments: Teacher of Fine Arts, New York Public Schools, 1960-80; Owner, Operator, Greeting Card Design Business, 1966-69; Illustrator, Freelance Artist, Designer. Publications: Poetry of Florence Lonsford; Bristol Banner Books; George Herbert; Samuel Coleridge; Samuel Johnson; T S Eliot; D H Lawrence; Edgar Allan Poe; Emily Dickinson. Contributions to: New York Times; Womens Day; Womens Home; Companion; Christian Science Monitor; The Islander; Episcopal New Yorker; Poetry Motel; Spotlight. Creative works: Group shows in National and International Exhibits including: New York, Ohio, West Virginia, Kentucky, France, Monaco. Honours include: Summer Festivals in Deauville, Cannes, France; National Art League, New York; International 22-Nations Show, Monaco; 1st Prize, Print Making, Indiana State Fair, 1995; Merit Award, Water Color Society of Indiana, 1995. Memberships include: National Society Independant Scholars; Metropolitan Portrait Society; National Art League; Poetry Society of America; Indiana Artists. Address: 311 East 72nd Street, New York, NY 10021, USA.

LOONEY George, b. 22 Mar 1959, Cincinnati, Ohio, USA. University Instructor in Literature and Writing. m. Mairi Meredith, 25 Aug 1984. Education: BFA in Art Education, University of Cincinnati, 1981; MFA in Creative Writing, Bowling Green State University, 1984. Appointments: Part-time Instructor, Loyola University of Chicago; Part-time Instructor, Roosevelt University and Columbia College, Chicago; Intern Instructor, Bowling Green State University; Resident Part-time Instructor, Bowling Green State University; Adjunct Instructor on the Graduate Faculty of Creative Writing and English, Bowling Green State University; Instructor in Creative Writing, Bowling Green State University. Publications: Animals Housed in the Pleasure of Flesh (collection of poems), 1995. Contributions to: Anthology of Magazine Verse and Yearbook of American Poetry; Black Warrior Review; Editor's Choice III; Gettysburg Review; High Plains Literary Review; Kenyon Review; Literary Review; Poetry East; Prairie Schooner; Puerto Del Sol; Southern Poetry Review; Tar River Poetry; Texas Review; Indiana Review; Mississippi Review; Poet Lore; Apalachee Quarterly; Cimarron Review; Cincinnati Poetry Review; Cottonwood; Oxford Magazine; Sulphur River Literary Review; Mississippi Valley Review; Panhandler; Permafrost; Riverwind; Southern Review; Denver Quarterly; Haydens Ferry Review. Honours: Charles Angoff Award, Literary Review, 1990; Ohio Arts Council Individual Artists Fellowship, 1991-92; National Endowment for the Arts Creative Writers Fellowship, 1992; Bluestem Award, 1995. Address: 325 Wallace, Bowling Green, OH 43402, USA.

LOOTS Barbara Kuntz, (Christina Lawrence), b. 30 Sept 1946, Kansas City, Missouri, USA. Writer. m. Larry Rolfe Loots, 20 July 1969. Education: BA, Winthrop College, 1967; MLA, Baker University, 1993. Appointments: Writing Stylist; Writer; Editorial Manager; Editor. Publications: The Brides Mirror Speaks; Sibyl and Sphinx, 1988; Snow Toward Evening, 1990; The Anthology of Magazine Verse and Year Book of American Poetry; The Random House Anthology of Poetry for Children; The Helicon Nine Reader. Contributions to: Christian Century; Cricket Magazine; Helicon Nine; Lyric; New Letters; Plains Poetry Journal. Honours: World Order of Narrative Poets; Hanks Competition, 2nd Award. Memberships: Poetry Society of America; Poets and Writers; Piedmont Literary Society. Address: 7943 Charlotte, Kansas City, MO 64131, USA.

LOPEZ ANGLADA Luis, b. 13 Sept 1919, Ceuta, Spain. m. Maria Guerra Vozmediano, 26 Nov 1946, 3 sons, 7 daughters. Education: Academoia Infanteria Zaragoza; University of Valladolid. Publications: Albor; Escribi Tu Nomnbre; Poemas Americanos y Otros Poemas, 1966; Arte de Amar, 1968; Los Amantes, 1972. Contributions to: Halcon; La Estafeta Literaria. Honours: National prize for Literature, 1961; National Prize, 1983; Quevado Prizes, Madrid City Council; Prize, City of Barcelona; Peace Prize, Dominican Republic, 1955; Premio Mairena, Puerto Rico, 1988; Silver Medal, Gold Shield, City of Ceuta; Commander, Order Isabel la Catolica; Numerous literary awards and prizes. Memberships: Academia Hispano-Americana de Cadiz de Bellas Artes; Purisima Concepcion de Valladolid San Telmo de Malaga; Academia Juglares San Juan de la Cruz; Association of International Art Critics. Address: Call de Aviacion Espanola num 5, 28003 Madrid, Spain.

LOVEDAY John, b. 1926, England. Appointment: Former Headmaster at primary school in Buckinghamshire. Publications: Particularities, 1977; Bones and Angels, with Shirley Toulson, 1978; The Agricultural Engineer, 1982; From the Old Foundrty, 1983; Particular Insights, 1986. Address: c/o Headland, 38 York Avenue, West Kirby, Wirral, Merseyside L48 3JF, England.

LOVELOCK Yann Rufus, b. 11 Feb 1939, Birmingham, England. Coordinator, Buddhist Prison Chaplaincy Organization. m. Ann Riddell, 28 Sept 1961. Education: BA, Oxford, 1963. Appointments: Secretary, Oxford Poetry Society, 1961-62; Literary Editor, Isis, 1961-62; Reviews Editors, Iron, 1974-82; Assistant Editor, Little Word Machine, 1975-79; Vice Chairman, Freundkreis Poesie Europe, 1977-; Associate Editor, Oasis, 1990-. Publications: Short Circuit; City and Beyond; Strangers in Amber; The Grid; Building Jerusalem; A Scattering Folder; Blue Cubes for a Catarrh; The Haiku Pavement; Landscape with Voices, 1995. Contributions to: Stand; P N Review; Observer; Ambit; Poetry Review; Agenda; Poetry Wales; Honest Ulsterman; Gairfish, Scotland; Krino, Ireland; Pearl, Denmark; Poesie Europe, Germany; Osiris, USA; New Cicada, Japan. Honours: Sheffield University Poetry Prize; Silver Medal, Haute Academie d'Art et de Littérature. Memberships: Corresponding Member, La Société de Langue et de Littérature Wallonnes. Address: 80 Doris Road, Birmingham, West Midlands B11 4NF, England.

LOW Denise Lea, b. 9 May 1949. College Teacher; Poet; Reviewer. m. 7 Dec 1994, 2 sons. Education: BA, University of Kansas, 1971; MA, 1974; MFA, Wichita State University, 1984. Appointments: Lecturer, Kansas State University, 1975-77; Lecturer, University of Kansas, 1977-84; Professor, Haskell Indian Nations University, 1984-. Publications: Spring Geese and Other Poems, 1984; Starwater, 1988; Vanishing Point, 1991; Tulip Elegies: An Alchemy of Writing, 1993. Contributions to: Helicon Nine; Kansas Quarterly; Monitor Anthology of Magazine Verse; Midwest Quarterly; Stiletto; Great Lakes Review; Mid America Review; Petroglyph; Tellas. Honours: Kansas Arts Commission Literary Award; Roberts Foundation Award. Memberships: Associated Writers Program; Modern Language Association; Poets and Writers. Address: 1916 Stratford Road, Lawrence, KS 66044, USA.

LOWBURY Edward (Joseph Lister), b. 6 Dec 1913, London, England. Physician; Poet; Writer on Medical, Scientific and Literary Subjects. m. Alison Young, 12 June 1954, 3 daughters. Education: BA 1936, BM and BCh 1939, University College, Oxford; MA, London Hospital Medical College, 1940; DM, Oxford University, 1957; Fellow, Royal College of Pathologists. Appointments: Bacteriologist, Medical Research Council Burns Research Unit, Birmingham Accident Hospital, 1949-79; Founder-Honorary Director, Hospital Infection Research Laboratory, Birmingham, 1964-79. Publications: Poetry:

Over 20 collections, including: Time For Sale, 1961; Daylight Astronomy, 1968; Poetry and Paradox: Poems and an Essay, 1976; The Night Watchman, 1974; Selected Poems, 1978; Selected and New Poems, 1990; Collected Poems, 1993; Mystic Bridge, 1996. Non-Fiction: Thomas Campion: Poet, Composer, Physician (with Alison Young and Timothy Salter), 1970; Drug Resistance in Antimicrobial Therapy (with G A Ayliffe), 1974; Hallmarks of Poetry: Reflections on a Theme, 1994. Editor: Control of Hospital Infection: A Practical Handbook (with others), 1975, 2nd edition, 1981, 3rd Edition, 1992; The Poetical Works of Andrew Young (with Alison Young), 1985. Contributions to: Numerous medical, scientific and literary publications, including reference works and journals. Honours: Newdigate Prize, 1934; Honorary Research Fellow, Birmingham University; John Keats Memorial Lecturer Award, 1973; Everett Evans Memorial Lecturer Award, 1977; DSc, Aston University, 1977; A B Wallace Memorial Lecturer and Medal, 1978; Honorary Professor of Medical Microbiology, Aston University, 1979; LLD, Birmingham University, 1980; Officer of the Order of the British Empire; Hon Fellow, Royal College of Surgeons; Fellow, Royal Society of Literature; Honorary Fellow, Royal College of Physicians; Fellow, Royal College of Pathologists. Memberships: British Medical Association; Society for Applied Bacteriology; Society for General Microbiology; Foundation President, Hospital Infection Society; Others. Address: 79 Vernon Road, Birmingham, West Midlands B16 9SQ, England.

LOWERY Martyn John, b. 8 July 1961, Rochdale, Lancashire, England. College Lecturer. Education: BA Hons English, 1982; MA, English, 1984; PhD, English, Exeter, 1990. Appointments: Lecturer in English, Salford University, 1989; Administrative Assistant, Department of Social Security, 1990; Lecturer in English, Worthing Sixth Form College, 1991. Publications: Our Love Now, anthologized in Strictly Private, 1980; The Dignity of Labour, 1984. Contributions to: Northern Line; Wayfarers; Pennine Platform; Bogg; Diversion; Krax; Sepia; New Hope International; North; Arcadian; Iota; Pennine Ink; Doors; Second Rapture; Psychopoetica; Ore; Frogmore Papers; First Time; Third Half; What Of Tomorrow; Songs; Momentum; Oxford Poetry; Cutting Room; Connections; Hybrid; Wire; White Rose; Paladin; Foolscap; Freelance Writing and Photography; Smith's Knoll; Lines; Spokes; Bound Spiral; Bradford Poetry; Westwords; Nutshell; Odyssey; Inkshed; New Welsh Review. Address: Hollies, 16 Wordsworth Road, Worthing, West Sussex BN11 3NH, England.

LOWITZ Leza, b. 12 Feb 1962, San Francisco, California, USA. Writer; Editor; Translator. m. Oketani Shogo, Feb 1995. Education: BA, English Literature, University of California at Berkeley, 1984; MA, English, Creative Writing, San Francisco State University, 1988. Appointments: Lecturer, San Francisco State University, 1989; Lecturer, Rikkyo Universty of Tokyo, 1991-92; Lecturer, Tokyo University, 1992-94. Publications: Old Ways to Fold/New Paper, 1996; Editor and co-translator of two volumes of Japanese Contemporary Women's Poetry entitled a Long Rainy Season, 1994; Other Side River Winds, 1995. Contributions to: Poetry translations: Harper's; Zyzzyua; Yellow Silk; Poetry; Prairie Schooner; Five Fingers Review; Poetry Flash; Poetry: USA; Kyoto Journal; Shearsman; Global City. Honours: U C Berkeley and Young Poetry Award, 1984; Browning Society Poetry Award, 1986, 1987; PEN Syndicate Fiction Award, 1989; Printed Matter Poetry Award, 1993; NEH Award, 1994; Benjamin Franklin Award, 1995; Austrian Arts Ministry Grant, 1995. Memberships: San Francisco Women Writers Workshop; Academy of American Poets; PEN; PEN Freedom to Write Committee.

LOYDELL Rupert Michael, b. 7 July 1960, London, England. Writer; Publisher; Artist. m. Susan Patrica Callaghan, 3 Sept 1983. Education: BA (Hons), Creative Arts, 1982-85. Appointments: Founder, Managing Editor, Stride Publications, 1979-; Editor, Event South West, 1988-89; Jazz Editor, Art Editor, Event South West, 1987-92; Design Editor, Third Way Magazine, 1989-93; Exeter Arts Development Officer, 1994-96. Publications: Fill These Days, 1990; Pitched At Silence, 1991; Between Dark Dreams, 1992; Timbers Across The Sun, 1993; The Giving of Flowers, 1994; Stone Angels: Prose 1979-1993, 1995; Trajectories, 1995; Fool's Paradise, 1995. Editor: How The Net is Gripped, 1992; Ladder To The Next Floor, 1993; The Stumbling Dance, 1994; A Curious Architecture, 1995. Contributions to: An Idea of Bosnia; Acumen; Bees Sneeze; Poems for Winter; Stand Up Poetry; Hepworth; Third Way; Strait; Orbis; Ostinato; Oasis; Tenth Muse; Outposts; South Coast Poetry Journal; Cornerstone; Scratch; Terrible Work; Chiron Review; EST. Address: c/o Stride Publications, 11 Sylvan Road, Exeter, Devon EX4 6EW, England.

LU Yuan, (Liu Ban-jiu), b. 8 Nov 1922, Huangpi, Hubei, China. Editor; Translator; Freelance Writer. m. Lou Hui, 12 Dec 1944, 2 sons, 2 daughters. Education: BA, Foreign Literature Department, National Fu Tan University, Chungking, 1944. Appointments: Ex-Deputy Editor-in-Chief, in charge of foreign literature publication, People's Literature Publishing House, Beijing; Co-Copy Editor, SHIKAN, poetry magazine, Chinese Writers Association. Publications: Poems: Innocent Talk, 1942; Starting-point, 1947; Collection, 1948; Songs of Man, 1983; A Sequel to Songs of Man, 1983; Another Song, 1985; Onions with Honey, 1986; Nach den Wirren: Deutschland-Gedichte (translated by Friedheim Denninghaus), 1988; Espoir (translated by Dominique Hoizey), 1988; Let's Go To The Sea, 1990; Sketchbook by a Doppelganger, prose poetry, 1992; Translations: Rilke (selected), 1993; Faust (2 parts), 1994; Anthology translations: My Neighbours' Flutes, 1986; Gehen Sie in Sich, 1987; Fingerlogik (Bestandteile einer chinesischen Zeichensprache), poems, (translated by Horst Keimig), 1995; Schopenhauers Essays (selected), 1995. Contributions to: Domestic and foreign journals. Honours: National Poetry Prize for Another Song, Chinese Writers Association, 1986. Memberships: PEN Club, China Centre; Goethe-Gesellschaft in Weimar EV; International Association for Germanic Studies; Council Member, Chinese Writers Association; Chinese Translators Association; National Foreign Literature Institute. Address: c/o Peoples' Literature Publishing House, 166 Chao Nei Street, Beijing 100705, China.

LUBWA P'CHONG Cliff, b. 20 Aug 1946, Gulu, Uganda. Educator. m. (1) 1 daughter, (2) Pat Hope Keshubi, 30 June 1992. Education: Diploma in Education, 1968; BA, 1976; MA, 1987; MEd, 1991. Appointments: Deputy Headmaster; Inspector of Schools; Head of Literature and Languages. Publication: Words of My Groaning, 1976. Contributions to: Pulsations, 1968; Poems from East Africa, 1971; Summer Fires, 1984; Many People, Many Voices; A Man with Lobelia Flute; Longman Book of Poetry, Book 1; Dhanal; Nanga; Heart-Throb. Honours: Runner-up, BBC Arts and Africa Poetry Award, 1982; Fellow in Creative Writing, University of Iowa, USA, 1987. Address: Institute of Teacher Education, PO Box 1, Kyambogo, Kampala, Uganda.

LUCAS Dennis Michael, b. 23 September 1968, Catskill, New York, USA. Musician; Writer. Education: High School Regent's Diploma, Hunter Tannersville Central, 1986; BA, English, Brooklyn College, 1991. Appointments: Musician; Writer. Publications: Haiku For Harry, 1989; Thirteen Ways Of Looking At A Crow, 1992; Poetic License, 1996. Contributions include: Amelia; Zone 3; Woodstock Times; Night Roses; Mountain Eagle; Black River Review; Art Times. Address: PO Box 263, Hunter, NY 12442, USA.

LUCAS John, b. 26 June 1937, Exeter, Devon, England. Professor of English. m. 30 Sept 1961, 1 son, 1 daughter. Education: 1st Class Honours, Philosophy and English Literature, 1959, PhD 1965, University of Reading. Appointments: Assistant Lecturer, Reading University, 1961-64; Lecturer, Senior Lecturer, Reader, Nottingham University, 1964-77; Visiting Professor, University of Maryland and Indiana, USA, 1967-68; Professor of English, Loughborough University, England, 1977-; Lord Byron Visiting Professor, University of Athens, Greece, 1984-85. Publications: About Nottingham, 1971; A Brief Bestiary, 1972; Egils Saga: Versions of the Poems, 1975, paperback, 1985; The Days of the Week, 1983; Studying Grosz on the Bus, 1989; Flying to Romania, 1992. Contributions to: New Statesman; Sunday Times; Tribune; New York Times; BBC Radios 3, 4; Poetry Review; Poetry Durham; Critical Survey; Arts Council Anthologies 2, 9; Best Poems of 1991 (Hutchinson); Two Plus Two; Diavaso, Greece; Voyages International, USA. Honours: Poetry Prize for Best 1st Full Volume of Poetry, Aldeburgh Festival, 1990. Memberships: Fellow, Royal Society of Arts; Chairman, Poetry Book Society, 1988-92; John Clare Society; William Morris Society; Publisher, Shoestring Press, 1994-. Address: 19 Devonshire Avenue, Beeston, Nottingham NG9 1BS, England.

LUCIE-SMITH (John) Edward (McKenzie), b. 27 Feb 1933, Kingston, Jamaica. Education: BA, Merton College, Oxford, 1954. Appointments: Freelance Journalist and Writer; Consultant and Curator, Art Exhibitions in Britain and USA. Publications: A Tropical Childhood and Other Poems, 1961; Confessions and Histories, 1964; Fir-Tree Song, 1965; Three Experiments, 1965; Gallipoli - Fifty Years After, 1966; Cloud Sun Fountain Statue, 1966; Towards Silence, 1968; Snow Poems, 1969; Lovers, 1970; A Girl Surveyed, 1971; Two Poems of Night, 1972; The Rabbit, 1973; The Well-Wishers, 1974; Seven Colours, 1974; Inscriptions/Inscripciones, 1975; Beasts with Bad

Morals, 1984; Two anthologies of poetry: Penguin Book of Elizabethan Verse and British Poetry Since 1945. Address: c/o Rogers Coleridge and White Ltd, 20 Powis Mews, London W11 1JN, England.

LUMSDEN Robert James, b. 7 Aug 1914, London, England. Teacher. m. 8 June 1940, 1 son. Education: BA, Queen Mary College, 1949. Appointments: Teacher, 28 years. Publications: Master Plan for Self Development, Achievement and Achievement, 1959; Cat on My Lap; The Beachcomber and the Swan; 23 Steps to Success and Achievement, 1972; Letter to Tennyson and Other Poems, 1992; A Deal of Wonder, 1995 Contributions to: New Welsh Review; Outposts Quarterly; Staple New Writing; Other Poetry; Envoi; Orbis; Pennine Platform. Honours: Endocrine National 2nd Prize; Isle of Wight 1st Prize. Memberships: Farringford Tennyson Society; Enfield Writers Workshop; Isle of Wight Poetry Society. Address: Spindrift. Heathfield Road, Freshwater, Isle of Wight PO40 9SH, England.

LUPPINO Vincent, b. 10 July 1937, New Britain, Connecticut, USA. Customer Service Representative. Education: BS, CCSC, 1959; MA, Trinity College, 1970. Contributions to: Tunxis Poetry Review; World of Poetry Anthologies; Poetry Press Anthology. Honours: State of Connecticut Medal for Literary Achievement; Gold Poet Award; Silver Poet Award. Membership: Connecticut Poetry Society. Address: 43 Lawlor Street, New Britain, CA 06051, USA.

LUTHER Susan Militzer, b. 28 May 1946, Lincoln, Nebraska, USA. Literary Scholar; Editor; Teacher; Poet. m. Robert N Luther, 18 July 1971. Education: BA, Louisiana State University, 1969; MA, University of Alabama, 1976; PhD, Vanderbilt University, 1986. Appointments: Assistant Editor, Poem, 1985-; Faculty Member, Department of English, University of Alabama, 1986-. Contributions to: Malahat Review; Negative Capability; Kansas Quarterly; Slow Dance; Kalliope Waterways; MacGuffin; Poem; Wordsworth Circle; Slant; Cumberland Poetry Review; Piedmont Lterary Review; Hellas Frontiers; California State Poetry Quarterly; Sonoma Mardala. Honours: Fellowship Vermont Studio Center; Finalist, Half Tones Jubilee Poetry Contest; Finalist, Anhinga Prize. Memberships: Modern Language Association; NCTE; Alabama State Poetry Society; Poetry Society of America; Literary Association Board Member; Arts Council Assembly Representative. Address: c/o Department of English, University of Alabama at Huntsville, Huntsville, AL 35899, USA.

LUX Thomas, b. 10 Dec 1946, Northampton, Massachusetts, USA. Poet; Teacher. m. Jean Kilbourne, 1983, 1 daughter. Education: BA, Emerson College, Boston, 1970; University of Iowa, 1971. Appointments: Managing Editor, Iowa Review, 1971-72, Ploughshares, 1973; Poet-in-Residence, Emerson College, 1972-75; Faculty, Sarah Lawrence College, 1975-, Warren Wilson College, 1980-, Columbia University, 1980-. Publications: The Land Sighted, 1970; Memory's Handgrenade, 1972; The Glassblower's Breath, 1976; Sunday, 1979; Like a Wide Anvil from the Moon the Light, 1980; Massachusetts, 1981; Tarantulas on the Lifebuoy, 1983; Half Promised Land, 1986; Sunday: Poems, 1989; The Drowned River, 1990; A Boat in the Forest, 1992; Pecked to Death by Swans, 1993; Split Horiznn, 1994; The Sanity of Earth and Grass (Editor with Jane Cooper and Sylvia Winner), 1994. Honours: Bread Loaf Scholarship, 1970; MacDowell Colony Fellowships, 1973, 1974, 1976, 1978, 1980, 1982; National Endowment for the Arts Grants, 1976, 1981, 1988; Guggenheim Fellowship, 1988; Kingsley Tufts Poetry Award, 1995. Address: 67 Temple Street; West Newton, MA 02164, USA.

LUZA Rad(omir Jr), b. 12 July 1963, Vienna, Austria. Actor; Writer; Comedian. Education: Diploma, Jesuit High School, 1981; BA, English, Tulane University, 1985. Appointments: Staff Writer, Tulane Hullabaloo, 1981; Co-Editor, Arts and Entertainment Section, Tulane Hullabaloo, 1983; Correspondent, Times, Picayune, 1984; Staff Writer, Goodwill Games in Atlanta, Georgia, 1985; President, Young Democrats of Bucks County, Pennsylvania, 1995. Publications: Harahan Journal, 1991; This N' That: Handwritings from a Wounded Heart, 1993; Porch Light Blues, 1995. Contributions to: Poet's Attic; Poet Magazine; Anterior Poetry Review; Mile High Poetry Society; Reflections; East and West Literary Quarterly; New Laurel Review; Papyrus; Dialogue. Honour: Certificate for Artistic Merit, The Mayor of Harahan, Los Angeles. Memberships: Poets and Writers, fiction and poetry; Poetry Society of America; The Academy of American Poets. Address: 18 Golf Club Drive, Langhorne, PA 19047-2163, USA.

LYKIARD Alexis Constantine, b. 2 Jan 1940, Athens, Greece. Writer. m. Erica Bowden, 20 Sept 1985, div, 1 son. Education: King's

College, Cambridge, 1959-62; MA 1966. Appointments: Writer in Residence, in several locations; Presenter, BBC Radio 4's Time for Verse, 1985-. Publications: 15 Poetry Collections; Robe of Skin; Milesian Fables; Cat Kin; Out of Exile; Safe Levels; Living Jazz; Beautiful is Enough; Omnibus Occasions, 1996. Contributions to: Adam; Ambit; Aquarius; English; Tribune; Ostinato; Poetry Wales; Outposts; Jazz Monthly; Transatlantic Review; Rialto; Iron; Lines Review; Poetry Ireland; Honest Ulsterman; Spokes; The Sun; Chapman; Haiku Quarterly; South West Review; Westwords; Acumen; Stride. Honours: ACGB Awards; TSW Video Poetry Competition Winner. Memberships: Literature Panel, ACGB; SWA; Writers Guild of Great Britain; ACE Prisons' Advisory Group, 1993-. Address: 77 Latimer Road, Exeter, Devon EX4 7JP, England.

LYMAN Harlan, b. 3 Dec 1975, Petersburg, Virginia, USA. Publications: Miles to Go Before I Sleep, 1996. Contributions to: Slug Fest; LTA; Mojo Risin; Small Press Review; Silent But Deadly; Blindman's Rainbow. Address: Route 3, Box 221, Cumberland, VA 23040, USA.

LYNCH Annette Peters, b. 23 Oct 1922, Marion, Indiana, USA. College Teacher. m. Thomas Millard Lynch, 24 Aug 1949, 2 sons, 2 daughters. Education: BA, Indiana University, 1944; MA, 1945; PhD, Occidental College, Los Angeles, 1960. Appointments: Instructor, Indiana University, 1945-49; Glendale College, 1949-50; Occidental College, 1950-55; Mount San Antonio College, 1955-93, retired. Publications: Ways Around The Heart. Contributions to: Alderbaran; Athena Incognito; California State Poetry Quarterly; Calapoyya College; Christian Science Monitor; Facet; Galley Sail Review; Inside English; Maryland Poetry Review; Toyon; Underpass; Wisconsin Review; Blue Unicorn; Cloverdale Review; Forum; Gaia; New Los Angeles Poets; Onthebus; Psychopoetica; Tempo; Voices. Honours: Anthology of Magazine Verse, 1986-88; 2nd Prize, Annual California Quarterly National Contest, 1992; Outstanding Faculty Emeritus, Mount San Antonio College, 1993. Memberships: Academy of American Poets; Poetry Society of America; California State Poetry Society. Address: 833 Garfield Avenue, South Pasandena, CA 91030, USA.

LYON Martin, b. 10 Feb 1954, Romford, Essex, England. Librarian. Education: BA, 1976. Appointments: Principal Library Assistant, University of London. Contributions to: Acumen; Agenda; Orbis; Outposts Poetry Quarterly; Pen International; Spokes. Honour: Lake Aske Memorial Award. Address: 63 Malford Court, The Drive, South Woodford, London E18 2HS, England.

LYON Richard Woodward (Rick), b. 24 Oct 1953, Puerto Rico. Launch Operator. Education: MFA, Columbia University; BA, Boston University. Appointments: Assistant Editor, Parnassus: Poetry in Review,. New York, 1980-82; Cataloguer, Clipper Ship Book Shop, 1983; Shipping/Receiving, H L Hayden Co, 1984; Launch Operator, Essex Island Marina, 1986-. Publication: Bell 8, 1994. Contributions to: Agni Review; American Poetry Review; Ironwood; Kansas Quarterly; Massachusetts Review; Nation and Partisan Review; The Missouri Review, 1995. Honours: Residency at Yaddo; Fellowship, Connecticut Commission on the Arts; Discovery/The Nation Award of 92nd Street YM-YWHA Winner; Writer-in-Residence, The Camargo Foundation, Cassis, France, 1995. Address: 29 Pratt Street, Essex, CT 06426, USA.

LYSENKO Myron, b. 15 Dec 1952, Heyfield, Victoria, Australia. Poet. 1 daughter. Education: Completed HSC, 1971. Appointments: Co-Editor of literary magazine, Going Down Swinging, 1979-94; Poet-in-Schools, 1989-; Organizer, La Mama Poetica, 1991, 1992; Assistant Director, 1992, 1993, Co-Director, 1994, Montsalvat National Poets Festival; Poet-in-Residence, Melbourne 200, 1993. Publications: Coughing with Confidence, 1988; Live Sentences, 1991; Nothing Personal, forthcoming. Contributions to: Going Down Swinging; Overland; Meanjin; Mattoid; Scarp; Southerly; Poetry Australia; Age; Australian; Wormwood Review (USA); Roads (England); Alpha Beat Soup (Canada); Suito Ved (Ukraine). Honours: 3rd Prize, Australian Sports Poet, 1995; 2nd Prize, Australian Olympic Sports Poet, 1996. Memberships: Poets Union; Victorian Writers Centre; Tasmanian Poetry Festival. Address: 21 Luscombe Street, East Brunswick, Victoria 3057, Australia.

M

MA Fei. See: **MARR William Wei-Yi.**

MA Mao Yang, (Peiji Ma), b. 1964, China. Contemporary Poet. Education: Philosophy. Appointments: Coal Miner; Editor, Economy Literature, Literature Review Monthly, Literature Review Paper; Chief Editor, Hebei Coal Poem, The New Century Poem Monthly; College Teacher. Publications: Poetry Anthologies: There Is No Way for Love; It Is, In Fact, A Pity (won Gold-Cow Literature Award, 1993, 1995); Multiplex Thougthts Anthology. Contributions to: Over 600 poems and poetry reviews in: China Coal Paper; Worker Daily; Contemporary Miner; Beijing Evening Paper; The Spirit of Poem; The South Poem; Xinhua Poem; Seed Monthly; Star Poem. Memberships: Beijing Writers' Association; Shanghai Writers' Association; China Writers' Association; China City Poem Research Association. Address: Beijing Youth College, Beijing 100015, China.

MACDONALD Alastair A, b. 24 Oct 1920, Scotland. Professor Emeritus. Education: MA, First Class Honours, Aberdeen University, 1948; BLitt, Christ Church, Oxford University, 1953; Senior Studentship, 1953-55, PhD, 1956, Manchester University. Appointments: Temporary Senior English Master, King William's College, Isle of Man, 1953; Professor, English, Memorial University, Newfoundland, Canda, 1955-87. Publications: Between Something and Something, 1970; Shape Enduring Mind, 1974; A Different Lens, 1981; Towards The Mystery, 1985; A Figure on the Move, 1991; Landscapes of Time, New, Uncollected, and Selected Poems, 1994. Contributions to: Aberdeen University Review; Antigonish Review; Atlantic Advocate; Cnadian Author and Bookman; Canadian Forum; Canadian Poetry; Dalhousie Review; Daybreak; English; Quarry; Green's Magazine; Lines Review; Fiddlehead; Midwest Quarterly; Newfoundland Quarterly; New York Times; Queen's Quarterly; Outposts; Scottish Field; Scottish Literary Journal; Twentieth Century; Umwelt; Anthologies include: Poets of Canada; East of Canada; New Voices In American Poetry; 31 Newfoundland Poets; Modern Newfoundland Verse; A Treasury Of Newfoundland Prose And Verse; 60 Atlantic Writers; No Other Place: Poetry from Aberdeen University Review, 1913-1995, 1995. Honours: Best Poem: Canadian Author And Bookman, 1972; New Voices In American Poetry, 1973; Newfoundland Government Arts and Letters Competition, Poetry Division: 1st, 1976; Hon Mention, 1978; 2nd, 1982. Memberships: Writers' Alliance of Newfoundland and Labrador; League of Canadian Poets; Scottish Poetry Library Association. Address: Department of English, Arts and Administration Building, Memorial University, St John's, Newfoundland, 4C1 5S7, Canada.

MACDONALD Cynthia, b. 2 Feb 1928, New York, New York, USA. Poet; Lecturer. m. E C Macdonald, 1954, div 1975, 1 son, 1 daughter. Education: BA, Bennington College, Vermont, 1950; Graduate Studies, Mannes College of Music, New York City, 1951-52; MA, Sarah Lawrence College, 1970. Appointments: Assistant Professor, 1970-74, Associate Professor, Acting Dean of Studies, 1974-75, Sarah Lawrence College; Professor, Johns Hopkins University, 1975-79; Consultant, 1977-78, Co-Director, Writing Program, 1979-, University of Houston; Guest Lecturer at various universities, colleges and seminars among others. Publications: Amputations, 1972; Transplants, 1976; Pruning the Annuals, 1976; (W)holes, 1980; Alternate Means of Transport, 1985; Living Wills: New and Selected Poems, 1991. Contributions to: Anthologies and other publications. Honours: MacDowell Colony Grant, 1970; National Endowment for the Arts Grants, 1973, 1979; Yaddo Foundation Grants, 1974, 1976, 1979; CAPS Grant, 1976; American Academy and Institute of Arts and Letters Award, 1977; Rockefeller Foundation Fellow, 1978. Memberships: American Society of Composers, Authors, and Publishers; Associated Writing Programs. Address: c/o Alfred A Knopf Inc, 201 East 50th Street, New York, NY 10022, USA.

MACHAN Katharyn Howd, b. 12 Sept 1952, Woodbury, Connecticut, USA. College Professor; Belly Dancer. m. Eric Machan Howd, 20 June 1991, 1 son, 1 daughter. Education: BA, College of Saint Rose, 1974; MA, University of Iowa, 1975; PhD, Northwestern University, 1984. Appointments: Teacher of Writing, Literature, Speech and Performance, Tompkins Cortland Community College, Ithaca College, Cornell University, Northwestern University. Publications: Sixteen collections, including, Belly Words, 1994. Contributions to:

Yankee; Seneca Review; Poets On; South Coast Poetry Journal; Zone 3; Kalliope. Honours: Two Awards, Poetry Society of America, 1981, 1983; Several grants for poetry in the past decade. Memberships: Board Director, Feminist Women's Writing Workshops. Address: PO Box 456, Ithaca, NY 14851-0456, USA.

MACINNES Mairi Clare, b. 5 Jan 1925, Norton on Tees, England. Writer. m. John McCormick, 4 Feb 1954, 2 sons, 1 daughter. Education: BA, MA, University of Oxford. Appointments: Various. Publications: Splinters; Herring; Oatmeal; Milk and Salt; The House on the Ridge Road; Elsewhere and Back. Contributions to: New Yorker; Spectator; Ploughshares; Massachusetts Review; Literary Review; Nation; Tri Quarterly Review; Prairie Schooner; Quarterly Review of Literature; Canto; Stand; Ontario Review; New Statesman; PN Review; Noble Savage; Lines; New Republic; Columbia. Honours: Witter Bynner Fellowship; New Jersey Council of the Arts Grant; National Endowment in the Arts Fellowship; Ingram Merrill Fellowship; Yorkshire Poetry Competition. Membership: Poetry Society. Address: Hovingham Lodge, Hovingham, York YO6 4NA, England.

MACKEY Mary, b. 21 Jan 1945, Indiana, USA. Poet; Novelist; Professor. Education: AB, Harvard College, 1966; PhD, Unversity of Michigan, 1970. Appointments: Poet, 1959-; Novelist, 1972-; Professor, Writer in Residence, California State University at Sacramento, 1972-. Publications: Split Ends; One Night Stand; Skin Deep; The Dear Dance of Eros. Contributions to: Yellow Silk; Harvard Advocate; MS Magazine; Poetry USA; Country Women; Wemoon; Switched-on Gutenberg (an on-line poetry magazine). Memberships: PEN, Chair, West Coast Branch, 1988-92; Bay Area Book Reviewers Association; Writers Guild; Authors Guild. Address: Department of English, California State University at Sacramento, 6000 J Street, Sacramento, CA 95819, USA.

MACKIE Peter George, b. 6 Jan 1957, Perth, Scotland. Industrial Worker. Education: Higher English, RSA in Typewriting, 1973; SCCAPE, Office Studies, 1973; Higher National Diploma, Data Processing, 1987. Appointments: Kitchen Porter, Hotel Wolf, Oberammergau, Germany, 1989-90; Kitchen Porter, Hotel Turmwirt, Oberammergau, 1990; Factory Worker, Jan Leenders BV, Tegelen, Netherlands, 1991; Temporary Industrial Worker, Adia Keser Uitsendburo, Venlo, 1991; Werknet Uitzenburo, Venlo Netherlands, 1991-92. Publications: All the Words under the Sun, 1973; The Madhouse of Love, 1992. Contributions to: Peace and Freedom; Silver Wolf; Little People; Workshop New Poetry No 35, 1977; Krax Magazine; Vigil; Bark; Bar Fax; Melodic Scribble; Padiham. Memberships: Association of Little Presses; Small Press Group of Great Britain; Small Press Center, New York; Associate Member of Society of Young Publishers. Address: Tetrahedron Books, 30 Birch Crescent, Blairgowrie, Perthshire PH10 6TS, Scotland.

MACKLIN Elizabeth, b. 28 Oct 1952, Poughkeepsie, New York, USA. Copy Editor. Education: BA Spanish, State University of New York at Potsdam, 1973; Graduate School of Arts and Sciences, New York University, 1975-78. Appointment: Poetry Editor, Wigwag Magazine, 1989-91. A Woman Kneeling in the Big City, 1992. Contributions to: The New Yorker; The Nation; The New Republic; Paris Review; The Threepenny Review; The New York Times. Honours: Guggenheim Fellowship in Poetry, 1994; Ingram Merrill Foundation Award in Poetry, 1990. Memberships: PEN American Center Executive Board; Poetry Society of America; Academy of American Poets. Address: 207 West 14th Street (5F), New York, NY 10011, USA.

MACKMIN Michael, b. 20 Apr 1941, London, England. Psychotherapist; Poet; Editor. Div, 2 daughters. Education: BA, 1963; MA, 1965. Publications: The Play of Rainbow; Connemara Shore; Co-editor, The Rialto. Contributions to: Various Magazines. Address: c/o The Rialto, 32 Grosvenor Road, Norwich NR2 2PZ, England.

MACLEAN Alasdair, b. 16 Mar 1926, Glasgow, Scotland. Publications: From the Wilderness, 1973; Waking the Dead, 1976; Night Falls on Ardnamurchan: The Twilight of a Crofting Family, 1984. Honours include: Cholmondeley Award, 1974. Address: c/o Victor Gollancz Ltd, 14 Henrietta Street, London WC2E 8QJ, England.

MACLENNAN Ian Alexander, b. 22 Aug 1924, London, England. Professor. m. Vivien Margery, 26 Apr 1974. Education: MSc, University of London, 1958; MA, University of Oxford, 1964. Appointments: Assistant Professor, Mathematics, University of Kings

College, 1947-53; Associate Professor, Philosophy, Dalhousie University, 1956-79. Publications: Winter Apples, 1987; In Celebration, 1991; Images, 1991. Contributions to: Dalhousie Review; Kansas Quarterly; Psychopoetica; Möbius; Whetstone Poetry; Poetry WLU; Canadian Author and Bookman; The Eclectic Muse; Colorado North Review. Honours: 2nd Prize, North American Poetry Competition, National Library of Poetry, USA, 1994. Address: Apt 310, Fort Massey Apts, 1263 Queen Street, Halifax, NS B3J 3L4, Canada.

MACLEOD Iris Jean, b. 18 May 1927, Calgary, Alberta, Canada. Musician; Poet. Div, 2 sons. Education: BA, English, Philosophy, Great Distinction, San Jose State University, 1961; Graduate studies in English, 1962; BA, Music, California State University, Hayward, 1982; 1 Year Business Course, Mt Royal College, Calgary, Alberta, Canada. Appointments: Teletypist, Canadian Pacific Railway, Calgary, 1945-46, Banff Springs Hotel, Lethbridge, Calgary, 1947; Secretary, University of Alberta Extension Department, 1947-48; Postal Clerk, Banff Springs Hotel, 1948; Secretary: Standard Iron Dominion Bridge, Edmonton, 1948-50, Zip Grip Sales, 1950 and 1952, National Groceries, Peterboro, 1951; A C Wickman, Toronto, 1951; Building Centre, Toronto, 1955; Secretary, Ampex Corporation, 1957-58; Secretary, Precision Instrument, San Carlos, 1958-59; Assorted Kelly girl and other short-time secretarial posts, including Stanford University, 1959-60; Secretary-Editor, Ampex Corporation Research Department, 1966-72; Piano Accompanist Student Assistant, College of San Mateo, 1979-80; Part-time art permit sales of poetry and music in fairs, and oil painting sale and street entertainment at Renaissance Fairs, 1972-76, 1976-78, pass-the-hat basis, Northern California. Publications: Channel 12 TV production of miniature music-drama, Selections from Alexander, 1975; Limited edition distribution of Seven Sonnets From Notes of a Winter Voyageur, 1989; Chord or Nonchord, music and poetry, 1977; A Masque for All-Souls Eve, miniature music-drama based on music and poetry of Iris MacLeod and poetry of Edith Sitwell, 1982. Contributions to: Poet, India; Two Steps In, Menlo Park; WPA; Palo Alto; American Poet; Peninsula Poets; Toyon Poets; International Poet; Featured Poet in International Poetry Special Edition, 1995. Honours: Koerner Foundation Scholarship for poetry from University of British Columbia, Canada, 1956; 2nd Prize, 1974, 1st prize and a 3rd Prize, 1975, and several Honorable Mentions, San Jose Friends of the Library Contests; San Mateo County Fair Walt Whitman Award Annual Poetry Competition, 1985; International Order of Merit in Music, 1991; International Honors Cup for Poetry and Music, ABI, 1992; Honorary DLitt, 1993. Memberships: World Poetry Society, 1978-; FIBA, 1988-; Dame des Lofsensischen Ursinius-Orden, 1993. Address: 1332 Paloma Avenue, Belmont, CA 94002, USA.

MACLEOD N(orma) J(ean), (Normajean Macleod, Cass Peru), b. 27 Feb 1929, Indiana, USA. Retired Data Systems Coordinator; Editor. m. John C Macleod, 13 Sept 1947, 1 son. Education: Motel Management School, Santa Barbara, 1973. Appointments: Motel Manager, 1972-74; Apartment Manager, 1972-74; Freelance Writer, Lecturer, Data Systems Coordinator, Indiana University, 1975-95; Editor, Publisher, 1988-93. Publications: Poetica Erotica; Womanclature; The Queen Bee Syndrome. Contributions to: Monterey Peninsula Herald; Bloomington Herald Times; Womankind; New America; Secret Songs; Voices for Peace; Several anthologies. Honours: Monterey Peninsula Herald Prize; National Federation of State Poetry Societies Annual Contest; Indiana State Federation of Poets Contest; Honorary Degrees; Guardian Award; Laureate Woman of Letters. Memberships: International Womens Writing Guild; Indiana State Federation of Poetry Clubs; National Federation of State Poetry Societies; United Poets Lauriate International. Address: 7123 N St Rd, 37, #2, Bloomington, IN 47404, USA.

MACNAB Arden. See: TICE Arden A.

MACNAB Roy Martin, b. 17 Sept 1923, Durban, South Africa. Diplomat; Foundation Officer. m. Rachel Mary Heron Maxwell, 6 Dec 1947, 1 son, 1 daughter. Education: MA, Jesus College, Oxford, 1946-47; DLitt, University of South Africa. Appointments: Cultural Attaché, South African High Commission, London, 1955-59; Counsellor, South African Embassy, Paris, 1959-67; London Director, South African Foundation, 1968-83. Publications: Testament of a South African; The Man of Grass; Winged Quagga; Oxford Poetry; South African Poetry. Contributions to: Oxford Book of South African Verse; Penguin Book of South African Verse; New Poems; Spectator; Poetry Review; Poetry Commonwealth; Journal des Poètes; Outposts. Membership: Royal Society of Arts. Address: 20 Sur le Cap Négre, 83980 Cavaliere, France.

MACNAUGHTAN Maureen, b. 31 Aug 1945, Glasgow, Scotland. Ceramic Artist. m. Gordon, 4 June 1966, 1 son, 2 daughters. Education: Open University, 1985-87; University of Aberdeen, 1992. Appointments: President of Moray and Nairn Writers Workshop, 1984-89; Secretary, Aberdeen Writers, 1989-91; Secretary, Postgraduate and Mature Students Society, 1990-92. Publications: Scotia Rampant; Scottish Primary School Anthology; US Poets for African Anthology; Scottish Poetry Macgregors Gathering; New Writing Scotland; Fresh Oceans; Gallimaufry; Original Prints; Galliard Anthology; Scratchings Anthology. Contributions to: Aynd; Iron; Poetry Nottingham; Interstate USA; Bradford Poetry Quarterly; ARC; Sepia; New Coin; Weyfarers; Firth Write; Spokes Ore; Sovereign Gold USA; Success Poetry; Toll Gate Journal; Ammonite; Gaudie; Period Piece and Paperback; White Rose; Voices Israel; Chapman; Poetry Review; Poetry Wales. Honours: Bursary from Scottish Arts; Dorothy Dunbar Trophy; Bobby Aiken Memorial Prize; Diplomas of Excellence. Memberships: Scottish Poetry Library; Poetry Society; World Development Association. Address: 122 Oldany Road, Glenrothes, Fife KY7 6RF, Scotland.

MACNEACAIL Aonghas, b. 7 June 1942, Isle of Skye, Scotland. Writer. m. Gerda Stevenson, 21 June 1980, 1 son. Education: Glasgow University. Appointments: Writers Fellowships, Gaelic College, Isle of Skye, 1977-79; Gaelic Association, 1979-81; Ross Cromarty Distict Council, 1988-90. Publications: Imaginary Wounds; Seeking Wise Salmon; The Great Snowbattle; The Avoiding; Rock Water. Contributions to: Numerous. Honours: Grampion Television Poetry Award; Gaelic Books Council Award; Scottish Association for the Speaking of Verse Diamond Jubilee Award; National Mod Literary Prize. Memberships: Poetry Society; Scottish Poetry Library. Address: 1 Roseneath Terrace, Edinburgh, EH9 1JJ, Scotland.

MACSWEENEY Barry, b. 17 July 1948, Newcastle-upon-Tyne, Tyne and Wesr England. m. Elaine Randell, 1972. Appointments: Former Journalist and Editor. Publications: Poems 1965-68, 1969; Lost is the Day, 1970; Our Mutual Scarlet Boulevard, 1971; Fools Gold, 1972; Dance Steps, 1972; Pelt Feather Leg, 1975; Black Torch, 1978; Odes, 1978; Ranter, 1985. Honours include: Arts Council Grant, 1971. Address: 55 Haydon Place, Denton Burn, Newcastle-upon-Tyne, Tyne and Wear, England.

MACTHOMAIS Ruaraidh. See: THOMSON Derick Smith.

MACVEAN Jean Elizabeth, m. 10 Oct 1952, 1 son, 1 daughter. Education: College d'Hulst, Versailles, Sorbonne, Paris. Publications: Ideas of Love; Eros Reflected; The Dolorous Death of King Arthur; The Adjacent Kingdom; The True and Holy Story of the Sangrail, 1995. Contributions to: Encounter; Agenda; Temenos; Tablet; Mandeville Press; Meridien; Aquarius; Poetry London; Apple; Yale Literary Magazine; Contemporary Literature Criticism; Big Little Poems; PEN, Poetry of the Seventies; Homage to Imagism; Luna; Envoi Book of Quotes on Poetry; Parnassus of World Poets, 1994; Outposts; Radio Programme, The Price of an Eye, Life and Work of the Poet Thomas Blackburn; Radio Play, Flight of the Swan. Memberships: Poetry Society; Fellow, PEN International. Address: 21 Peel Street, London W8 7PA, England.

MADU Ladi, b 28 June 1960, Lagos, Nigeria. Writer; Journalist; m. Ida Heidemans Madu, 6 Apr 1987, 1 son. Education: Diploma, D'Etudes Françaises, 1983; London School of Journalism, 1991. Contributions to: Poetry Nottingham; Orbis; Folio International; Prophetic Voices; Parallel; Barddowi; Songs. Address: 32 Witte Van Haemstedestraat, 3021 SZ Rotterdam, Netherlands.

MAGEE Wes(ley Leonard Johnston), b. 20 July 1939, Greenock, Scotland. Author. m. Janet Elizabeth Magee, 10 Aug 1969, 1 son, 1 daughter. Education: Goldsmiths College, University of London, 1964-67; University of Bristol, 1969-71. Appointments: Teacher, Primary School, 1967-76; Deputy Headteacher, 1976-78; Headteacher, 1978-90. Publications: Flesh, or Money; 40 Books for Children. Contributions to: Encounter; Poetry Review; Scotsman; New Statesman. Honours: Poetry Book Society Recommendation; New Poets Award; Cole Scholarship, USA. Address: Santone House, Low Street, Sancton, York YO4 3QZ, England.

MAGER Don(ald Northrop), b. 24 Aug 1942, New Mexico, USA. University Professor. m. (1) Barbara Feidman, div, (2) William A McDowell, 2 sons. Education: BA, Drake University, 1964; MA, Syracuse University, 1966; PhD, Wayne State University, 1985.

Appointments: Instructor, Syracuse University; Director, CALL; Executive Director, Michigan Organization for Human Rights; Professor, Johnson C Smith University. Publications: To Track the Wounded One, 1988; Glosses, 1992; Queering The Renaissance, 1994. Contributions to: Christopher Street; Mid America Review; Slant; Black Warrior Review; Lyracist; New Orleans Review; Kenyon Review; Mouth of the Dragon; Pebbles; Greenfield Review; Slant (1994); Cape Rock (1995); Sun Dog (1995). Honours: Hallmark Prize; Tompkins Award; Lyracist First Prize; Approach Magazine Award; Blumenthal Award, 1994. Memberships: Modern Language Association. Address: Department of English, Johnson C Smith University, Charlotte, NC 28216, USA.

MAGNUSDOTTIR Thorunn Magnea, b. 10 Nov 1945, Reykjavík, Iceland. Poetess; Actress; Play Director. 2 sons. Education: Private Acting School, 1959-62; Icelandic College of Arts and Crafts, Reykjavík, 1959-60; National Theatre School, Reykjavík, 1962-64; Jacques Lecocq Ecole de Mime et Theatre, Paris, 1964-66. Appointments: Acting, over 60 plays, National Theatre, 1966-; Assistant Director, Director, 27 plays, National Theatre and other Icelandic Theatres; Appeared, Films, TV and Radio Plays. Publications: Morgunregn, 1962; Islanske dikt, 1975; Laerebok i islandsk, 1976; Ljo asafn, 1980; Dikt av islanske kvinner, 1985; Ljo spor, 1988; Translations include works of Alphonse Daudet, Ray Bradbury, Gertrude Stein. Contributions to: Newspapers: Morgunbla i; Timin; Magazines: Vera; 19 June. Memberships: President, Alliance Francaise, Iceland; Writers Union, Iceland; Actors Union, Iceland. Address: Laufasveg 6, Reykjavík, Iceland.

MAGNUSSON Sigurdur A, b. 31 Mar 1928, Iceland. Writer. Div, 2 sons, 3 daughters. Education: University of Iceland, 1948-50; University of Copenhagen, 1950-51; University of Athens, 1951-52; University of Stockholm, 1952-53; New School for Social Research, New York, 1953-55. Appointments: Radio Commentator, United Nations, 1953-56; Teacher, 1954-56; Journalist, 1956-67; Editor-in-Chief, 1967-74; Principal of Correspondence School, 1974-77. Publications: Scribbled in Sand; Death of Balder; This is Your Life; 6 Novels; 4 Travel Books. Contributions to: New World Writing; To Avrio; Quest; Writers Workshop; Iceland Review; Islandske dikt fra vart hundrear; American Scandinavian Review; A Soviet Anthology of 5 Icelandic Poets. Honours: Golden Cross of the Greek Order of Phoenix; Cultural Councils Prize for Best Play; Cultural Prize for Best Novel; European Jean Monnet Prize for Literature, 1995. Memberships: Chairman, Writers Union of Iceland; Chairman, Nordic Writers Council; Chairman, Society of Icelandic Drama Critics; Chairman, Greek Icelandic Cultural Society; Chairman, Amnesty International, Icelandic Section, 1988-95. Address: Baronsstig 49, IS-101 Reykjavík, Iceland.

MAHAPATRA Jayanta, b. 22 Oct 1928, Cuttack, India. Retired Reader. m. Jyotsna Das, 16 Jan 1951, 1 son. Education: University of Cambridge, 1941; BSc, Utkal University, 1946; MSc, Patna University, 1949. Appointments: Lecturer, Reader, 1950-86; Poetry Editor, The Telegraph (Calcutta), 1994-. Publications: Close the Sky; A Fathers Hours; A Rain of Rites; Waiting; The False Start; Relationship; Life Signs; Dispossessed Nests; Burden of Waves and Fruit; Selected Poems; Temple; A Whiteness of Bone; Bali (poetry in Oriya), 1993; I Can, But Why Should I Go (translation), 1994; Kahibi Gotie Katha (Riya), 1995. Contributions to: Helix; Quadrant; Ariel; Malahat Review; Queens Quarterly; Boundary; Chicago Review; Kenyon Review; Sewanee Review; Nimrod; Western Humanities Review; River Styx; New Quest; Hudson Review (New York); Triquarterly (Evanston, Illinois). Honours: International Poetry Contest; Jacob Glatstein Memorial Award; Sahitya Akademi Award; Japan Foundation Visitors Award; Rockefeller Foundation Award; El Consejo Nacional Para La Cultura y Las Artes, Mexico, 1994; Poemas (selected poems in Spanish), 1994. Memberships: National Academy of Letters; Telegraph (Calcutta), Editor of Poetry. Address: Tinkonia Bagicha, Cuttack 753001, Orissa, India.

MAHAPATRA Laxmi Narayan, b. 20 Apr 1942, Phasi, India. Advocate. m. Binodina Mahapatra, 15 May 1964, 2 sons, 1 daughter. Education: LLB, 1962; MA, 1963. Publications: Rita and Other Poems; Lone Boatman; Bhuma; Dead River; Night without Moon; The Shadowed Sun. Contributions to: Illustrated Weekly of India; India Literature; International Poetry; World Poetry; Selected Writings; Prophetic Voices. Honours: Nehru Award; Michael Madlusndem Award; International Literature Award. Membership: International

Writers Association. Address: Gliri Road, Benhampuz 760005, Orissa, India.

MAHASHWETA Chaturvedi, b. 2 Feb 1950, Etawah, Uttar Pradesh, India. Reader. m. Dr Uma Kamt Chaturvedi, 11 Dec 1970, 2 sons, 1 daughter. Education: MA, English, 1966; MA, Sanskrit, 1969; Sangeet Prabhaker - Sitar, 1975, Tabla, 1976, Vocal, 1979; MA, Hindi, Sahityacharya, 1978; PhD ,1983; LL.B , 1993; DLitt, 1991. Appointment: Lecturer, RPPG College, Meerganj, Bareilly, 1984-. Publications include: Editor of various publications; Throbbing Lyre, Roaming Aroma (English poems), 1994; English poetry collections: Eternal Pilgrim, Immortal Wings, Stone God, Waves of Joy, 1997. Contributions to: Poetry Time; Bridge in Making; Poet-Crit; Heaven; Yuva Bharti; Kavita India; The Quest; Brain-Wave; Canopy; World Poetry; Prophetic Voices; Assam Express. Honours include: Certificate for Poetry, Melbourne Poetry, Australia, 1988; Sahitya Bharti, 1994; Gold Medal in Poetry, 1995; Michael Madhusudan Award, 1995; Subhadra Kumari Chauhan Padak, 1995. Memberships: International Poets Academy; Authors Guild of India; Hindi Sahitya Sammelan; Nagari Pracharinidt; Sabha; Varansi; Editor, international bi-lingual (Hindi-English) magazine, Mandakini; Secretary, Mandakini Sanstha, UP. Address: Professors Colony, Shyam Ganj, Bareilly 243 005, UP, India.

MAHER Mary Geraldine Kennedy, b. 29 Oct 1937, Yorkshire, England. m. Kenneth Maher, 6 Apr 1978, 1 daughter. Education: Diploma, Paget Gorman Sign System, 1974; Postgraduate Diploma, Special Education, 1978. Appointments: Teacher, Mainstream; Teacher, Special Schools; Head of Department, Special Needs; Deputy Head, Hospital School; Tutor, NNEB Education and Tutor, Further Education. Publications: Snowfruit; Stonechat; Dusting Round the Jelly; Taboo. Contributions to: Poetry Review; Poetry Durham; Rialto; Smoke; Scratch; Orbis; Odyssey. Honour: South West Arts Literary Award. Memberships: Poetry Society; Company of Poets. Address: Pippins, Hillhead, Chittlehampton, Umberleigh, North Devon EX37 9RG, England.

MAHON Derek, b. 23 Nov 1941, Belfast, Northern Ireland. Education: BA, Trinity College, Dublin, 1965. Appointments: Drama Critic, Editor, Poetry Editor, 1981-, New Statesman. Publications include: Twelve Poems, 1965; Night-Crossing, 1968; Lives, 1972; The Man Who Built His City in Snow, 1972; The Snow Party, 1975; Light Music, 1977; The Sea in Winter, 1979; Poems 1962-1978, 1979; Courtyards in Delft, 1981; The Hunt by Night, 1982; A Kensington Notebook, 1984; Antarctica, 1986; Editor, Modern Irish Poetry, 1972; Editor, The Penguin Book of Contemporary Irish Poetry, 1990. Address: Rogers Coleridge and White Ltd, 20 Powis Mews, London W11 1JN, England.

MAHORSKY Jody, b. 3 Nov 1952, Pennsylvania, USA. Teacher. 1 son, 2 daughters. Education: BS, Special Education of Mentally Retarded and Elementary Education, 1974; Early Childhood Education, 1975; Therapeutic Masseuse and Foot Reflexologist, 1993. Appointments: Special Education Teacher; Poet and Fiction Writer; Massage and Reflexologist Therapist; Shaman. Contributions to: Poet Talk; Cottage Cheese; Prophetic Voices; Golden Isis; Potpurri International; Impressions; Spirit of the Muse; Creative Spirit; First Time; Night Roses; Bold Print; Poetry Peddler; Wise Women. Memberships: Poets and Writers; Association of Bodyworkers & Massage Professionals; Pennsylvania Association of Massage & Bodywork Professionals. Address: 134 Mauch Chunk Street, Nazareth, PA 18064, USA.

MAIDEN Jennifer Margaret, b. 7 Apr 1949, Penrith, New South Wales, Australia. Author. m. David Toohey, 14 July 1984, 1 daughter. Education: BA, MacQuarie University, 1974. Appointments: 14 books published including 12 of poetry; Writer-in-Residence, Australian National University, University of Western Sydney, Springwood High School and New South Wales Torture and Trauma Rehabilitation Unit; Selected Poems set for New South Wales Higher School Certificate. Publications: Tactics, 1974; The Problem of Evil, 1975; The Occupying Forces, 1975; Mortal Details, 1975; Birthstones, 1981; The Trust, 1988; Elected Poems, 1990; Bastille Day, 1990; Acoustic Shadow, 1993. Contributions to: All major Australian Literary Magazines and Newspapers for 3 decades. Honours: English Association Prize; Harri Jones Memorial Prize; Grenfell Henry Lawson Award, 1979; New Souith Wales Premier's Prize, 1991; Victorian Premier's Prize, 1991; Several Fellowships from Australia Council. Membership: Australian Society of Authors. Address: PO Box 4, Penrith, NSW 2751, Australia.

MAIER Anne Winifred, (Anne Bulley), b. 15 April 1922, Grayshott, England. Retired Potter; History Researcher. m. 31 Mar 1947, 2 sons, 2 daughters. Education: St Anne's College, Oxford, England, 1946. Appointments: Served War Office and Women's Royal Naval Service, 2nd World War. Publications: Selected Poems, 1980; Free Mariner, 1992. Contributions to: Fleet Poetry Broadsheet, 1944-45; Anthologies: Hands Across the Sea, 1980; Chaos of the Night; Women's Poetry and Verse of 2nd World War, 1984; BBC Woman's Hour 50th Anniversary Poetry Collection, 1996. Membership: Elected Brother, Art Workers Guild, 1973. Address: Middle Ridge, Wambrook, Chard, Somerset TA20 3ES, England.

MAIETTA Diane Marie, b. 24 Apr 1957, Pittsburgh, Pennsylvania, USA. Writer. Div, 1 daughter. Education: BA, Point Park College, Pittsburgh; Indiana University. Appointments: Assistant Public Relations Manager; Retail Sales. Contributions to: Watermark Press; National Library of Poetry; Amherst Society; World of Poetry. Honours: Editor's Choice Award, National Library of Poetry; Honorable Mentions; Golden Poet Award. Membership: International Society of Poets. Address: PO Box 265, Apollo, PA 15613, USA.

MAIREE Faith. See: **BRIGHAM Faith Elizabeth Huckabone.**

MAJA-PEARCE Adewale, b. 3 June 1953, London, England. Researcher; Consultant; Writer. Education: BA, University College of Swansea, University of Wales, 1975; MA, School of Oriental and African Studies, London, 1986. Appointments: Researcher, Index on Censorship, London, 1986-; Consultant, Heinemann International, Oxford, 1986-94. Publications: Christopher Okigbo, Collected Poems (editor), 1986; The Heinemann Book of African Poetry in English, 1990. Contributions to: Various periodicals. Memberships: PEN; Society of Authors. Literary Agent: David Grossman Literary Agency, 168 Limpsfield Road, Sanderstead, Surrey CR2 9EF, England. Address: 33 St George's Road, Hastings, East Sussex TN34 3NH, England.

MAJOR Clarence, b. 31 Dec 1936, Atlanta, Georgia, USA. Poet;Writer; Artist; Professor. m. (1) Joyce Sparrow, 1958, div 1964, (2) Pamela Ritter. Education: New York City, 1972; BS, State University of New York, Albany, 1965; PhD, Union Graduate School, Cincinnati, 1978. Appointments: Columnist, 1973-76, Contributing Editor, 1976-86, American Poetry Review; Assistant Professor, Howard University, 1974-76, University of Washington, 1976-77; Visiting Assistant Professor, University of Maryland, College Park, 1976, State University of New York, Buffalo, 1976; Associate Professor, 1977-81, Professor, 1981-89, University of Colorado, Boulder; Editor, 1977-78, Associate Editor, 1978-, American Book Review; Professor, 1989-, Director, Creative Writing, 1991-, University of California, Davis. Publications include: Poetry: Swallow the Lake, 1970; Symptoms and Madness, 1971; Private Line, 1971; The Cotton Club: New Poems, 1972; The Syncopated Cakewalk, 1974; Inside Diameter: The France Poems, 1985; Surfaces and Masks, 1988; Some Observations of a Stranger in the Latter Part of the Century, 1989; Parking Lots, 1992; Fiction includes: Stories: Fun and Games, 1990; Novels: All-Night Visitors, 1969; NO, 1973; Emergency Exit, 1979; Such was the Season, 1987; Painted Turtle: Woman With Guitar, 1988; Dirty Bird Blues; Others include: Juba to Jive: A Dictionary of African-American Slang, 1994; Editor: The Garden Thrives: Twentieth Century African-American Poetry, 1995. Honours: Fulbright-Hays Exchange Award, 1981-83; Western States Book Award, 1986; Pushcart Prize, 1989. Address: c/o Department of English, University of California at Davis, Davis, CA 95616, USA.

MAJUMDER Pronab Kumar, b. 3 Jan 1941, Khulna, Bangladesh. Civil Service. m. 23 Jan 1973, 1 son. Education: First Class Graduate, Calcutta University, India. Appointments: Sub-Divisional Magistrate; Additional District Magistrate; Deputy Secretary to the Government of West Bengal; Joint Secretary to the Government of West Bengal, India. Publications: Collection of Poems in Bengali, 1973-93; Collection of Poems in English, 1993, 1995. Contributions to: Amrita Bazar Patrika; Telegraph; Asian Age; Poet; Quest; Canopy; Byword; Kavita India. Memberships: Poetry Society of India; Writers Forum, Ranchi, India. Address: P233, Block B, Lake Town, Calcutta 700089, India.

MAKEPEACE Eleanor Maria, b. 8 Nov 1946, Bishop Auckland, County Durham, England. Artist. Education: Cert Ed, Oxford, 1969; BEd, University of Newcastle-upon-Tyne, 1976. Appointments: Teaching, Art, Geography, English as a Foreign Language, Remedial,

all levels from Nursery to Adult, for 4 local Education Authorities and 1 private school; Supply Teaching and Home Tuition. Publications: Our Unofficial Tourist Guide, 1972; A Little Lower than the Angels, 1978; Uprooting, 1981; Echoes, 1979; Images, 1980; Tynes, 1986; Contradictions, 1990; Directions. Contributions to: Conjunction, USA; Lettera, Italy; Here Now; New Hope International; Meridian; Writing Women; Genera; Strong Words; Poetry North East; Not Poetry; BBC Local Radio. Address: Strada di Mociano 5, 53010 Taverne d'Arbia, Siena, Italy.

MAKOTO Ryu. See: **STROUD Drew McCord.**

MALASCHAK Dolores M, b. 19 Mar 1923, Illmo, Missouri, USA. Retired Educator; Freelance Writer. m. Anthony Malaschak, dec, 17 May 1941, 3 sons, 2 daughters. Education: BA, Secondary Education, Southern Illinois University, Edwardsville, 1972. Appointments: Practical Nurse, 1956-64; Educator, Creative Writing, Belleville College; Full-time Educator, Illinois High School and Wirth Junior High, 1971-84; Sub-Teacher, Gilman City, Missouri, 1984-89; Freelance Writer, 1984-. Publications: Run in the Morning, 1968; The Prodigal, 1987; Rainbow in My Hand, 1984; Garden Years, 1990; Greenwood Days, 1990; Harvest Time, 1990; Midnight in The Study, 1992. Contributions to: Imprints Quarterly; Poetry Australia; The Poet (India); Bitterroot; Alura Quarterly - Anthology; Cyclo Flame; Bell's Letters. Memberships: Past Co-Editor, Poetry Magazine, Lincoln Log; Co-Founder and Past President, National League of American Pen Women, Metro East Branch. Address: RR1, Box 96A, Gilman City, MO 64642, USA.

MALIK Kershav, b. 5 Nov 1934, Srinagar, India. Literary and Art Journalism. m. 7 Aug 1969. Education: BA, 1949; Italian and French Government Cultural Scholarships, 1950-55. Appointments: Literary Editor, Thought; Indian Literature; Art Critic, Times of India. Publications: Lake Surface and Other Poems; Rippled Shadow; Storm Warning; 26 Poems; Negatives; Between Nobodies and Stars; Shapes in Peeling Plaster; The Cut Off Point; Ten Poems; Islands of Mind. Contributions to: Temenos; Adam International Review; Literary Review; Bitterroot; Dalhousie Review; Eye; Opinion; Poetry Time; Poetry Canada; New Letters; Botteghe Oscure; Ascent; Hindustan Times; Illustrated Weekly; Damascus Road Poetry Quarterly; Poesie. Honour: Padma Shri National Award. Membership: Poetry Society. Address: 5/90P Connaught Circus, New Delhi 110 001, India.

MALLINSON John David, b. 14 Apr 1939, Oldham, Lancashire, England. Former School Master. m. Catharine Tillman Williams, 11 July 1970, 1 son, 2 daughters. Education: St Cassians College, 1952-55; London School of Economics, 1957-60; Institute of Linguists. Appointments: Oulu River Power Company, Finland; Inter Community School, Zurich; Stonyhurst Preparatory School; St Peters High School, Bury. Publications: Spirit of Place; By North West; Composition of a European City (Salzburg), 1996. Contributions to: Cenrastus; Contemporary Review; English; Envoi; Outposts; Orbis; Ore; Pause; Poetry Nottingham; Psychopoetica; Prospice; Stand; BBC Radio; New Welsh Review; Good Society Review; Poet's England-18, Lancashire; Journal of Contemporary Anglo-Scandinavian Poetry. Honour: North West Arts Publication Grant, 1989. Address: 8 Norwich Avenue, Oldham, Lancashire OL9 0BA, England.

MALOUF (George Joseph) David, b. 20 Mar 1934, Brisbane, Queensland, Australia. Poet; Novelist. Education: BA, University of Queensland, 1954. Appointments: Assistant Lecturer in English, University of Queensland, 1955-57; Supply Teacher, London, 1959-61; Teacher of Latin and English, Holland Park Comprehensive, 1962; Teacher, St Anselm's Grammar School, 1962-68; Senior Tutor and Lecturer in English, University of Sydney, 1968-77. Publications: Poetry: Bicycle and Other Poems, 1970; Neighbours in a Thicket: Poems, 1974; Poems, 1975-1976, 1976; Wild Lemons, 1980; First Things Last, 1981; Selected Poems, 1981; Selected Poems, 1959-1989, 1994. Fiction: Johnno, novel, 1975; An Imaginary Life, novel, 1978; Child's Play, novella, 1981; The Bread of Time to Come, novella, 1981, republished as Fly Away Peter, 1982; Eustace, short story, 1982; The Prowler, short story, 1982; Harland's Half Acre, novel, 1984; antipodes, short stories, 1985; The Great World, novel, 1990; Remembering Babylon, novel, 1993. Play: Blood Relations, 1988. Opera Libretti: Voss, 1986; Mer de Glace; Baa Baa Black Sheep, 1993. Memoir: Twelve Edmondstone Street, 1985. Editor: We Took Their Orders and Are Dead: An Anti-War Anthology, 1971; Gesture of a Hand, anthology, 1975. Contributions to: Four Poets: David Malouf, Don Maynard, Judith Green, Rodney Hall, 1962; Australian; New York

Review of Books; Poetry Australia; Southerly; Sydney Morning Herald. Honours: Grace Leven Prize for Poetry, 1974; Gold Medal, Australian Literature Society, 1975, 1982; Australian Council Fellowship, 1978; New South wales Premier's Fiction Award, 1979; Victorian Premier's Award for Fiction, 1985; New South Wales Premier's Drama Award, 1987; Commonwealth Writer's Prize, 1991; Miles Franklin Award, 1991; Prize Femina Etranger, 1991; Inaugural International IMPAC Dublin Literary Award, 1996. Address: 53 Myrtle Street, Chippendale, New South Wales 2008, Australia.

MALTMAN Kim Rendal, b. 23 Aug 1950, Canada. Physicist. Education: BSc, Chemistry and Mathematics, University of Calgary; MSc 1973; PhD, University of Toronto, 1983. Publications: The Country of the Mapmakers; For Nobody Else Should They Ask; The Sicknesses of Hats; Branch Lines; Softened Violence; The Transparence of November Snow; Technologies/Installations. Contributions to: Malahat Review; Canadian Literature; Canadian Forum; Dandelion; Canadian Dimension; University of Windsor Review; Quarry; Matrix; Fiddlehead; Poetry Australia; Orbus. Honour: 1st Prize, IBC Poetry Competition. Memberships: Writers Union of Canada; PEN. Address: Department of Mathematics and Statistics, York University, 4700 Keele Street, North York, Ontario M3J 1P3, Canada.

MANDEL Charlotte, b. 1 Apr 1925, Brooklyn, New York, USA. Poet; Editor. m. Irwin D Mandel, 1 Apr 1944, 1 son, 2 daughters. Education: BA, Brooklyn College, 1944; MA, Montclair State College, 1977. Publications: The Marriages of Jacob; Keeping Him Alive; The Life of Mary; Doll; A Disc of Clear Water. Contributions to: Iowa Review; Seneca Review; Raccoon; Nimrod; River Styx; West Branch. Honours: Fellowships; Open Voices Writers Voice Winner; Woman of Achievement Award; Geraldine E Dodge Foundation Fellow; Kavinoky Award. Address: c/o Saturday Press, PO Box 884, Upper Montclair, NJ 07043, USA.

MANGANO John Giovanni, (Giovanni Mangani), b. 9 Aug 1953, New Jersey, USA. Artist; Writer. Education: Glassboro State College, 1979-80. Publications: Recollections; Le Poesis di Giovanni Mangano. Contributions to: Mindy Inquire; Bob Monte Express; World of Dark Shadows; Hoofprints. Membership: Atlantic County Historical Society. Address: PO Box 255, Hammonton, NJ 08037, USA.

MANHEIM Werner, b. 17 Feb 1915, Lissa, Poland. University Professor; Pianist; Teacher. m. Eliane Housiaux, 18 Aug 1951. Education: BEd, Berlin University; Chicago Musical School of Roosevelt University. Appointments: Assistant Professor, 1947-54, Research Assistant, Kinsey Institute, 1955-58, Assistant and Associate Professor, 1958-80, Professor, 1980-82, Indiana University. Publications: Klänge der Nacht; Wanderwege; Im Abendrot Versunken; Wenn das Morgenrot Aufblüht; Noch Fliessen Die Tränen; Landschaft in Moll; Im Atem der Nacht; Geheimnisvoll das Licht; A Spark of Music; Herbstmusik; Timeless is a Silver Sparkle; Ein Halm im Wind; Im tiefsten Ich bist Du allein; In Der Dämmerung; Grün hebt die Erde; Monographs: Albert Conradi; Martin Buber. Contributions to: Prosa und Poesie; Unio; Silhouette. Honours: Dr Fine Arts; Dr Litt hc; Studiosis Humanitatis Medal; Certificate of Merit; Adolf Bartels Memorial Honor; Dr Heinrich Mock Medal; Golden Poet Award, 1989, 1990, 1991; United Poets Laureate; International Poets Academy. Memberships: Liason World Poetry Society; German Haiku Society; Plesse Society; Phi Mu Alpha Sinfoniam Fraternity. Address: 2906 Hazelwood Avenue, Fort Wayne, IN 46805, USA.

MANHIRE Bill, b. 27 Dec 1946, Invercargill, New Zealand. Education: BA, University of Otago at Dunedin, 1967; MPhil, University College London, 1973. Appointment: Lecturer, Victoria University, Wellington, 1973-. Publications : Malady, 1970; The Elaboration, 1972; Song Cycle, 1975; How to Take Your Clothes Off at the Picnic, 1977; Dawn/Water, 1980; Good Looks, 1982; Locating the Beloved and Other Stories, 1983; Zoetropes: Poems 1972-82, 1984; The Old Man's Example, 1990; Milky Way Bar, 1991. Honours include: New Zealand Book Award, 1985. Address: Department of English, Victoria University of Wellington, PO Box 600, Wellington 1, New Zealand.

MANI Philip, b. 14 Sept 1946, Kottayam, India. Industrial Engineer; Management Analyst. Education: BS, 1966; MS, 1972; MA, 1978; MS, 1988. Appointments: Manpower Planning Officer, 1975-80; Industrial Engineering Consultant, 1980-82; Industrial Engineer, 1982-88; Management Analysis Officer, 1989-, Publication: Federal

Poets Poetry Book. Membership: Federal Poets. Address: 12204 Red Church Court, Potomac, MD 20854, USA.

MANICOM David Alton, b. 19 July 1960, Ingersoll, Ontario, Canada. Diplomat. m. Teresa Marquis, 13 Aug 1983, 2 sons, 1 daughter. Education: BA, St Michael's College, University of Toronto, 1983; MA, 1985, PhD, 1989, McGill University. Appointments: Lecturer, McGill University, Montreal, 1988-89; 2nd Secretary, Vice-Consul, Canadian Embassy, Moscow, Russia, 1991-93; 1st Secreary, Canadian High Commission, Islamabad, Pakistan. Publications: Sense of Season, 1989; Theology of Swallows, 1991. Contributions to: Saturday Night; Malahat Review; Descant, Canada; Shenandoah, USA. Membership: Leauge of Canadian Poets. Address: PO Box 500, (Mosco) Station A, Ottawa, Ontario K1N 8T7, Canada.

MANN Christopher Michael, (Zithulele), b. 6 April 1948, Port Elizabeth, South Africa. Director, Operations, Grahamstown Foundation; Director, Valley Trust; Administrator, Vuleka Trust. m. Julia Georgina, 10 Dec 1981, 1 son, 1 daughter. Education: BA, 1970; MA, Oxon, 1973; MA, London, 1974. Appointments: School Teacher; Lecturer; Development Administrator. Publications: First Poems; A New Book of South African Verse in English; New Shades; Kites; Mann Alive (video of aural poems with book of the texts and interview with the author), 1992; South Africans, a Series of Portrait Poems, 1995; Plays: The Sand Labyrinth, 1980; Mahoon's Testimony, 1995. Contributions to: All Major South African Publications. Honours: Newdigate Prize; Olive Schreiner Award; South African Performing Arts Council Playwright Award; DLitt (honoris causa), University of Durban-Westville, 1993. Address: 19 Frances Street, Grahamstown 6140, South Africa.

MANSELL Chris, b. 1 Mar 1953, Sydney, New South Wales, Australia. Poet; Writer. m. Steven G Sturgess, Dec 1986, 1 son, 1 daughter. Education: BEc, Sydney University. Appointments: Lecturer, University of Wollongong, 1987-89, University of Western Sydney, 1989-91; Residencies, Curtis University 1985, University of Southern Queensland 1990, K S Prichard Centre 1992, Bundanon, 1996. Publications: Delta, 1978; Head, Heart and Stone, 1982; Redshift/Blueshift, 1988; Shining Like a Jinx, 1992; Day Easy Sunlight Fine, 1995; Lies, The River & Other Poems for Schodinger's Cat, 1996. Contributions to: Age; Antigonish Review; Ariel; Arc; Australian; Hecate; Imago; Kunapipi; Meanjin; Overland; Prism International; Southerly; Dandelion; New Quarterly and many others. Honours: Amelia Chapbook Award, 1987; Queensland Premiers Prize for Poetry, 1993. Memberships: Poets Union; Australian Society of Authors; Women in Publishing. Address: PO Box 94, Berry, NSW 2535, Australia.

MANWARING Randle (Gilbert), b. 3 May 1912, London, England. Managing Director. m. Betty Violet Rout, 9 Aug 1941, 3 sons, 1 daughter. Education: London University, 1929; MA, Keele University, 1982. Appointments: Wing Commander, Royal Air Force, 1946; Pensions Representative, 1954-56; Managing Director, 1960-77; Director, 1964-; President, Society of Pension Consultants, 1968-70. Publications: Several. Contributions to: Poetry Review; Field; Scrip; Envoi; Expression; This England; Oxford Magazine; Poetry Nottingham; Muse; Poetry Today; Cricket Quarterly; Circle in the Square; Orbis; New Poems. Memberships: Society of Authors; Society of Sussex Authors; Poetry Society; Downland Poets. Address: Marbles Barn, Newick, Nr Lewes, East Sussex BN8 4LG, England.

MARCUS Mordecai, b. 18 Jan 1925, Elizabeth, New Jersey, USA. University Professor of Literature and Writing. m. Erin J Gasper, 3 June 1955, 1 son, 1 daughter. Education: BA, Brooklyn College, 1949; MA, New York University, 1950; PhD, University of Kansas, 1958. Appointments: Teaching Assistant, Rutgers University, 1951-52; Assistant Instructor, Instructor, University of Kansas, 1952-58; Instructor, Assistant Professor, Purdue University, 1958-65; Associate Professor, Professor, University of Nebraska-Lincoln, 1965-. Publications: Five Minutes to Noon, 1971; Return from the Desert, 1977; Conversation Basketball, 1980; Talismans, 1981; Restorations, 1984; Critical Book: The Poems of Robert Frost, 1991; Poems: Pursuing the Lost, 1993. Contributions to: Shenandoah; South Dakota Review; Kansas Quarterly; Poet Lore; Poet and Critic; Southern Poetry Review; San Jose Studies; Christian Century; Prairie Schooner; Blue Unicorn; North American Review. Honours: Represented in 4 Alan F Pater Anthologies of Magazine Verse and in Best Poems of 1971. Memberships: Robert Frost Society. Address: Department of English, University of Nebraska-Lincoln, Lincoln, NE 68588, USA.

MARGOLIS William J, (Will Friar, Bimgo), b. 13 Aug 1927, USA. Poet. Education: BA, Roosevelt University, 1950. Appointments: Re-Writer, Editor, Wall Street Journal; Editor Publisher, Mendicant; Editor Publisher, Miscellaneous Man; Co-Editor, Co-Founder, Beatitude; Editor Publisher, Mendicant Editions. Publications: The Anteroom of Hell, 1957; The Little Love of our Yearning, 1960, 1962; The Eucalyptus Poems, 1974; Rustle and Break, 1987; The Summer Cycles, 1988; A Book of Touch, 1988. Contributions to: Beliot Poetry Journal; Ark; Beatitude; Coastlines; Colorado Review; Concept; Croupier; Galley Sail Review; Illuminations; Karamu; Kauru; Kayros; Los Angeles Free Press; Los Angeles Image; Mainstream; Odyssey; Manhattan Review; Mendicant; Mile High Underground; Miscellaneous Man; Morning Star; Naked Ear; Los Angeles Oracle; Outcry; Pendulum; Poetry; San Francisco Review; Semina; Snowy Egret; Smith; Sparrow; Stooge; Sunset Palms Hotel; Trace; Whetstone; Venice Poetry Co; Venice West Review; Black Ace, Grist, Grist on Line, Egg. Address: 1507 Cabrillo Avenue, Venice, CA 90291-3709, USA.

MARIANANDA. See: **JANSEN Garfield, Reverend Swami.**

MARIANI Paul L(ouis), b. 29 Feb 1940, New York, New York, USA. Professor. m. Eileen Spinosa, 24 Aug 1963, 3 sons. Education: BA, Manhattan College, 1962; MA, Colgate University, 1964; PhD, City University of New York, 1968. Appointment: Distinguished University Professor, University of Massachusetts. Publications: Timing Devices; Crossing Cocytus; Prime Mover; Salvage Operations; The Great Wheel, 1996. Contributions to: Hudson Review; Tri Quarterly Review; Denver Quarterly; New Criterion; Prairie Schooner; Gettysburg Review; Kenyon Review; New England Review; Nation; America. Honours: National Endowment for the Arts; National Endowment for the Humanities; Guggenheim Fellowship. Memberships: Modern Language Association; Poetry Society of America. Address: 63 Main Street, Montague, MA 01351, USA.

MARIE Charles P, (Mussy Sainte-Agathe), b. 23 Jan 1939, Nancy, France. Professor. Education: Licence ès lettres, 1963, Diplôme d'Etudes Supérieures, 1967, Nancy; MA, Exeter, England, 1971; PhD, Hull, England, 1979; CAPES, France, 1989. Appointments: University and School Posts, Ivory Coast, England, Nigeria, South Africa, France; Professor of French, Ahmadu Bello University, Nigeria, 1977; Assistant Master, Lycée Anna de Noailles, Evitan, 1991-; Chercheur-associé, Universités d'Angers et de Dijon. Publications: Petit vide poches, 1973; La Réalité humaine chez Jean Giraudoux, 1975; Virginia Water, 1976; La Mésangette, 1980; Poèmes au Nadir, 1981; Jean Giraudoux aux sources du sens, 1982; Luc Vuagnat dans le Voile d'Isis, 1984; Le Sens sous les mots, 1984; Genève et son Luth, 30 analyses de poètes, 1987; Torches de Lune, 1988; Florilège genevois-Poètes de l'Arbalète 1966-91, 1991; Féminalines au bois, 1992; Mademoiselle d'Ermelo, 1994; De Bergson à Bachelard Essai de poétique essentialiste, 1995. Contributions to: Annales des Arts et Lettres du Périgord; Art et Poésie; Fer de Lance; Courrier des Marches et d'Outre-Mer; Genève Lettres; Le Cerf-Volant; Yorkshire Review; Séquences; Interactions; La Nouvelle Proue; La Pensée Francaise; Rencontres Artistiques et Littéraires; Terre Lorraine; L'Etrave; La Toison d'Or; Les saisons du poème; Le Cerf-volant; Florilège; L'aéro-Page; Others; Criticism to many; Anthologies: Lorraine tes poètes; Poèmes et contes pour enfants; Anthologie de la Société des Poètes Français (1902-1982); 25 Ans de Poésie contemporaine; Poètes de notre temps; Anthologie de Notre Temps; Art et Poésie III-Reflets poétiques de l'éthnie française; World Poetry; L'Encyclopédie poétique, Vols XIII, XXXVI. Honours: Prizes and diplomas, poetry, 1976-96; Chevalier des Lettres et des Arts, Ordre de la Poèmeraie d'Olt, 1980; Prix Elie Faure, ALAP, 1981; Silver Medal, Academy Internationale, Lausanne, 1982; Prix, Franco-Suisse Michel-Ange, 1985; National Corresponding Associate, Académie de Stanislas, Nancy, 1986; Bronze Medals, Academie de Lutèce, 1988; City of Bordeaux, 1989; Renaissance internationale des Arts et Lettres, 1992; Correspondent, Academy Florimontane, Annecy, 1989; Prize, Criticism, Swiss SPAF, 1990; Prize, Criticism, SPAF International, 1991; Prix Wilfrid Lucas, 1992; Prix Marcel Beguey, 1995; Grand Prix du Vimeux, 1995. Memberships: Past Vice-President, Past Editor, Sociète des Ecrivains genevois; Société des Ecrivains d'Alsace Lorraine; Sociète des Poètes Francais; Société des Poètes et Artistes de France, Delegate-General; Societé Suisse des Ecrivains; Swiss PEN Club; Sociètaire des Gens de Lettres, Paris; Institute of Linguists; Society for French Studies, Oxford. Address: 78 Chemin de la Montagne, 1224 Geneva, Switzerland.

MARITIME George, b. 19 Feb 1942, Yonkers, New York, USA. Poet. Education: Syracuse University Schubert Fellowship in Writing to graduate school, Sarah Lawrence College, 1960's. Appointment: Director, Folk Music Hall of Fame. Publications: Columbus, 1991; The Cricket's Song, The Story of John Keats, 1992; The Ballad of Christopher Marley, 1994. Contributions to: New Press; Herald Statesman. Honour: Award, Composers, Artists and Authors of America. Memberships: Marlowe Society of America; New York Shelley Society; Melville Society; Marlowe Lives Association; Columbus' Countdown, 1992. Address: 44 Cherwing Road, Bryn Mawr Knolls, Yonkers, NY 10701, USA.

MARKHAM E(dward) A(rchibald), b. 1 Oct 1939, Montserrat, West Indies. Education: Universities of Wales, East Anglia and London. Appointments: Director, Creative Writing Fellow and Magazine Editor; Senior Lecturer at Sheffield Hallam University, 1991-. Publications: Cross-fire, 1972; Mad and Other Poems, 1973; Master Class, 1977; The Lamp, 1978; Love Poems, 1978; Games and Penalties, 1980; Love, Politics and Food, 1982; Family Matters, 1984; Human Rites: Selected Poems 1970-1982, 1984; Lambchops in Papua New Guinea, 1986; Living in Disguise, 1986; Towards the End of a Century, 1989; Caribbean Poetry from the West Indies and Britain, 1989; Letter from Ulster & The Hugo Poems, 1993; Misapprehensions, 1995; As editor: Hinterland: The Bloodaxe Book of Caribbean Poetry, 1989. Address: c/o Bloodaxe Books, PO Box 1SN, Newcastle-upon-Tyne NE99 1SN, England.

MARKHAM Jehane, b. 12 Feb 1949, Sussex, England. Poet; Playwright. 3 sons. Education: Central School of Art, 1969-71. Publication: The Captain's Death; Ten Poems, 1993; Virago New Poets, 1993. Plays for Radio include: More Cherry Cake, 1980; Thanksgiving, 1984; The Bell Tar; Frost in May. Play for TV: Nina, 1978. Contributions to: Women's Press; Longmans Study; Sunday Times; BBC 2 Epilogue; Bananas Literary Magazine; Camden Voices; Independent; Observer; Acorn; Ambit. Memberships: Poetry Book Society; Highgate Literary and Scientific Society. Address: 56 Lady Somerset Road, London NW5, England.

MARKUS Giovanna, b. 25 Sept 1927, Iglesias, Cagliari, Sardinia, Italy. Educator. m. 16 Dec 1954, 2 sons. Education: Laurea, Political Science. Appointments: Teacher, Law. Publications: Pressappoco, 1981; Il volo nello specchio, 1984; Fontanamare, 1992. Contributions to: Il Corriere di Roma; Silarus; L'Abruzzo Letterario; Misura. Honours: Winner, Bonnano Pisano Prize, Pisa, 1979; Citta di Venezia Prize, 1980; Casandrino Prize, Rome, 1981; Villa Alessandra Prize, 1984; 2nd Place, Citta della Spezia Prize, La Spezia, 1984. Memberships: Accademia Tiberina, Rome; Accademia Culturale d'Europa, Bassano Romano. Address: Via Gallia 52, 00183 Rome, Italy.

MARLATT Daphne, b. 11 July 1942, Melbourne, Victoria, Australia. Education: BA, University of British Columbia, 1964. Appointments: Writer-in-Residence, Manitoba and Alberta Universities. Publications: Frames of a Story, 1968; Poems, 1970; Vancouver Poems, 1972; Our Lives, 1975; Solstice: Lunade, 1980; Here and There, 1981; How Hug a Stone, 1983; Touch to My Tongue, 1984; Double Negative, 1988; Salvage, 1991. Honours include: Canada Council grants. Address: c/o Gynergy Books, 85 Water Street, PO Box 132, Charlottestown, Prince Edward Island C1A 7X2, Canada.

MARLOWE Ann Margaret, b. 29 Dec 1939, Garreti, Indiana, USA. Professor. Education: BA, St Francis College; MA, University of Dayton; PhD, University of New Mexico. Appointments: Teaching Assistant, University of Dayton; Teaching Assistant, University of New Mexico; Instructor, Tri-State University; Professor of English, Missouri Southern State College. Contributions to: Avalon; Alvernian; World of Poetry. Honours: Golden Poet Award; Honourable Mention, World of Poetry Contest. Memberships: Poetry Society of America; Rocky Mountain Modern Language Association; Modern Language Association; Missouri State Teachers Association. Address: 1811 Delaware, MO 64804, USA.

MARR William Wei-Yi, (Fei Ma), b. 3 Sept 1936, China. Energy and Environmental Engineer. m. Jane Jy Chyun Liu, 22 Sept 1962, 2 sons. Education: Taipei Institute of Technology, 1957; MS, Marquette University, 1963; PhD, University of Wisconsin, 1969. Appointments: Assistant Mechanical Engineer, 1959-61; Senior Engineering Analyst, 1963-67; Research Engineer, 1969-96; Editorial Advisor, New World Poetry (Los Angeles); Editorial Advisor, The Literati Bimonthly (San

Francisco). Publications: In the Windy City; Selected Poems; White Horse; Poems of Fei Ma; The Thumping Hoofbeats; Road; Selected Short Poems; Fly! Spirit; Selected Poems, China, 1993; Autumn Window, 1995. Contributions to: Li Poetry Bimonthly; Ren Min Wen Xue; Epoch Poetry; United News; China Times; First Line Poetry Magazine; New World Poetry Magazine; Wan Xiang Poetry Magazine. Honours: New Poetry Award. Memberships: Li Poetry Society; First Line Poetry Society; Chinese Artists Association of North America; President, Illinois State Poetry Society, 1993-95; Vice President, New Poetry, Beijing, 1994-; Poets Club of Chicago. Address: 737 Ridgeview Street, Downers Grove, IL 60516, USA.

MARRERO Melanie. See: MINEO Melanie.

MARRIOTT David Sylvester, b. 22 Oct 1963, Nottingham, England. Lecturer. Education: BA, Sussex University, 1983-86. Appointment: Lecturer in English. Publications: Mortgages; Light; Circles; Woodcutter; Airs and Ligatures; Lative. Contributions to: Verse; Avec; Folded Sheets; First Offense; Pearl; La Pagina; Archeus; Poetical Histoires; Scarlet. Address: 227 Mayall Road, London SE24 0PS, England.

MARRODÁN Mario Angel, b. 7 June 1932, Portugalete, Vizcaya, Spain. Lawyer; Writer; Poet; Editor. m. Mercedes Gómez Estíbaliz, 31 May 1961, 2 sons. Education: Bachillerato Superior; Licentiate in Law; Philosophy and Letters; Health. Publications: Over 250 books of poetry, aphorisms, essays, anthology contributions and art criticism, including: La Escultura Vasca; Panorama de la Acuarela Vasca; Diccionario de Pintores Vascos; Maestros de la Pintura Vasca; Ansia en Vida; Cronista del Presente; Aprendizaje en la Miseria; Homenaje al Dolor; Onagro: Luz de la Imagen; Soloquios Lunáticos; Dossier de un Cincuentón; Pálpitos del Pecho; Translated into French, Portuguese, English, Italian, Lithuanian, Austrian dialect, Catalan and Basque. Contributions to: About 2000 journals and magazines; Founder, Editor: Pleamar; Boletín Lírico de la Juventud Española; Alrededor de la Mesa; Others. Honours: City of Bilbao; Basterra; Abanto and Zierbana; Nirvana Populi; International Award for Love Poems; 2nd Prize, Amantes de Teruel; La Catorcena; Las Planas; Best Book in Catalan. Memberships: Asociacion Española de Críticos de Arte; International Association of Art Critics; Asociación Española de Críticos Literarios; Sociedad de Estudios Vascos; Asociación Vasca Bolivariana; Real Sociedad Bascongada de los Amigos del Pais; Academia Libre de Artes y Letras, San Antón; Asociación Colegial de Escritores de Espana. Address: Cristobal Mello 7, 2o izqda, Apartado Postal 16, 48920 Portugalete, Vizcaya, Spain.

MARSH Katherine C, b. 23 Apr 1956, Salem, Oregon, USA. Freelance Writer. Education: Chemeketa College, 1976, 1986; Linn-Benton College, 1977, 1985-86; Associate of Arts, University of Oregon, 1977-78; Writers Digest School, 1995. Appointments: Reporter, Correspondent, 1976-90; Freelance Writer. Publications: Co-Author of Several Books. Contributions to: Midwest Poetry Review; Poetic Expressions; The Lucid Stone; Toast; Alpha Beat Press; Poetalk; California State Quarterly. Honours: Nashville Newsletter Poetry Award, 1979, 1981; Newcomer's Award, Society of American Poets, 1994. Memberships: Poets & Writers; A Directory of American Poets & Fiction Writers 1997-1998; Poets Guild. Address: P O Box 613, Salem, OR 97308, USA.

MARSHALL Ron(ald E), b. 12 Aug 1947, North Dakota, USA. Media Marketing Consultant. m. (1) 12 Aug 1970, div, (2) 5 Aug 1991, 2 daughters. Education: University of North Dakota, 1969; MA, Lesley College, Cambridge, 1987. Appointments: Newspaper Reporter; Journalism Teacher; Advisor; Media Advisor; Commerical Aerial Photographer; Real Estate Broker; Television Reporter; Publisher; Executive Director. Publications: American Poetry Anthology; Todays Greatest Poems; Lyrical Treasures, Classic and Modern; Lyrical Treasures, An International Poetry Anthology. Contributions to: Full House Poets; Pastiche; Published Poet Newsletter; Phantasmagoria; New Voices; Leisuretime Magazine; Wildcat. Honour: Poetry Broadcast. Address: 4821 Chaparral Road, Colorado Springs, CO 80917, USA.

MARSHBURN Sandra, b. 6 Jan 1945, Benton Harbor, Michigan, USA. Associate Professor of English. m. Robert Marshburn, 10 Sept 1966, 1 daughter. Education: BA, English, 1969; MA, English, 1972, University of Maryland. Appointments: Part-time Instructor, Morris Harvey College, 1974-76; Associate Professor, West Virginia State College, 1976-. Publications: Controlled Flight, 1990; Undertow, 1992.

Contributions to: Yankee; Ohio Journal; Writer's Digest; Tar River Poetry; Greensboro Review; Cincinnati Poetry Review; Midwest Quarterly; MacGuffin; West Branch; Devil's Millhopper; Kentucky Poetry Review; Three Rivers Poetry Journal. Address: 201 Viking Road, Charleston, WV 25302, USA.

MARTIN Angus, b. 6 Feb 1952, Argyll, Scotland. Postman. m. Judith Honeyman, 28 Mar 1986, 3 daughters. Publication: The Larch Plantation. Contributions to: Weekend Scotsman; Lines Review; Chapman; Poetry Wales; PEN New Poetry; New Writing Scotland; An Canan; Northwords. Honour: Scottish Arts Council Spring Award. Address: 13 Saddell Street, Campbeltown, Argyll PA28 6DN, Scotland.

MARTIN Graham Dunstan, b. 21 Oct 1932, Leeds, Yorkshire, England. Senior Lecturer. m. (1) Ryllis Eleanor Daniel, 21 Aug 1954, 2 sons, 1 daughter, (2) Anne Moone Crombie, 14 June 1969, 2 sons. Education: Oriel College, Oxford, 1950-54; Manchester University, 1955. Appointments: Assistant Teacher, Various Secondary Schools, 1956-65; Assistant Lecturer, 1965-67, Lecturer, 1967-82, Senior Lecturer, 1982-, Edinburgh University. Publications: Remco Campert; Love and Protest; Le Cimetiere Marin; Anthology of Contemporary French Poetry; Sonnets; Selected Poems. Contributions to: Lines; London Magazine; Modern Poetry in Translation; Prospice; 2 Plus 2; New Edinburgh Review; Lost Voices of World War One. Address: French Department, Edinburgh University, 60 George Square, Edinburgh EH8 9JU, Scotland.

MARTIN FUMERO Graciliano, b. 18 Aug 1961, Venezuela. Education: Campos Academy, Valencia, Spain. Appointments: Under Secretary, Culture of the Canary Nationalist Party; Teacher, Nuestra Señora de la Paz School. Publications: Sentimientos; Numerous Anthologies: Directory of International Writers and Artists; World Poetry; Primer Indice de Poetas de Lengua Española. Contributions to: Various periodicals. Honours: Primer Premio de Poesia La Voz de Taco; XI Concurso Molino de Viento La Bella Quiteria; Premio International de Poesia La Valderia; Certamen de Poesia Mujer 90; V Premio de Poesia. Memberships: International Writers and Artists Association; 20th Century Association of America. Address: Apartado de Correos 152, 38108 Taco, Santa Cruz de Tenerife, Canary Islands.

MARTING Janet, b. 3 Apr 1951, Burlington, Vermont, USA. Associate Professor. m. 25 May 1986. Education: BA, University of Vermont, 1973; MA, Colorado State University, 1975; PhD, Michigan State University, 1982. Appointments: Instructor, Texas Technical University, 1975-78; Assistant Professor, Ohio State University, 1982-84; Director of Composition, 1984-89, Associate Professor, 1989-, University of Akron. Publications: The Heart's Geographer, 1979; Making a Living: A Real World Reader, 1993; The Voice of Reflection: A Writer's Reader, 1995; Commitment, Voice and Clarity: An Argument Rhetoric and Reader, 1996. Contributions to: Descant; New Orleans Review; Centennial Review; Ohio Journal; Red Cedar Review; Chariton Review; Sam Houston Literary Review; Aspen Leaves; Pawn Review; Rocky Mountain Arts Journal; Nebula; Travois; An Anthology of Texas Poetry; Texas Anthology; Texas Stories and Poems. Honours: Named Outstanding Writer, Colorado State University Poetry Contest, 1979; Honourable Mention, Community of Poets Award, Ohio. Membership: National Council of Writing Program Administration. Address: 373 Greenwood Avenue, Akron, OH 44320, USA.

MARTINOVICH BAN Eva Maria, (Eva Ban), b. 16 Mar 1934, Brazil. Journalist; Writer; Poet. m. Danilo Martinovich, 13 Jan 1964, 1 stepson. Education: Masters Degree, Cruz Alta Rio Grande Do Sul; University of Curtiba; University of Porto Alegre. Appointments: Foreign Correspondent, New York, 1967-79, 1987; Columnist, Ultima Hora. Publications: Oriental Poems; Poemas Orientais; Death and I; Center of the World; Green Boy; 3 Books of Short Stories; 9 Books of Poetry. Contributions to: Many periodicals. Honours: 18 Gold Medals; 2 Silver Medals. Memberships: International Academy of Letters; Union of Writers of the State of Rio de Janeiro; Brazilian Press Association; Poetry Society of America; International Pen Club. Address: Avenida Copacabana 959/503, 22060 Rio de Janeiro, Rio de Janeiro, Brazil.

MARX Anne, b. 8 Mar 1913, Bleicherode, Germany. Poet; Author; Lecturer; Editor. m. Frederick E Marx, 12 Feb 1937, 2 sons. Education: Medical Schools; Literary Studies at Colleges and Writers Conferences. Publications: Ein Buechlein; The Second Voice; By Way of People; Forty Love Poems for Forty Years; Holocaust; Wunden und

Narben; The World's Love Poetry; Love in Late Season; Hear of Israel, 1975; Face Lifts For All Seasons, 1980; A Further Semester, 1985; Love in Late Season, 1993. Contributions to: New York Times; New York Herald Tribune; Christian Science Monitor; Good Housekeeping Magazine; Ladies Home Journal; Gryphon; Lyric; Muse; South Florida Poetry Review; Midwest Poetry Review; Ann Arbor Review; Chicago Tribune Magazine; Manifold; Encore; Brotherhood Magazine. Honours: Cecil Hemley Memorial Prize; Greenwood Prize; Biennial Prizes of National League of American Pen Women; National Federation of Poetry Society Prizes; Chapbook Publication Awards; Anne Marx Collection of Papers in New York Public Library Archives. Memberships: Poetry Society of America; National League of American Penwomen. Address: 315 The Colony, Hartsdale, NY 10530, USA.

MASINI Donna, b. 13 Dec 1954, Brooklyn, New York, USA. Poet. m. Judd Tully, 28 June 1986. Education: BA Honours, English, Classics, Hunter College, 1985; MA, English, Creative Writing, New York University, 1988. Appointments: Instructor, English, Creative Writing, New York University, 1988; Instructor, Poetry Workshop, Writer's Voice, Hunter College, New York; Instructor, English, Creative Writing, Hunter College, 1995-. Publications: That Kind of Danger, poems, 1994; About Yvonne, forthcoming. Contributions to: Paris Review; Georgia Review; Boulevard; Parnassus; Pequod; High Plains Literary Review; Conditions; Thirteenth Noon; Early Ripening; American Women's Poetry, anthology. Honours: Phi Beta Kappa, 1985; College Prize, Academy of American Poets, 1985, 1986; New York Foundation for the Arts, 1986; Yaddo Fellow, 1989-91; National Endowment for the Arts, 1991; Felix Pollak Poetry Prize, University of Wisconsin, Madison, 1991. Memberships: Poets and Writers; Poets House; AWP. Address: PO Box 5, Prince Station, New York, NY 10012, USA.

MASON David (James), b. 11 Dec 1954, Bellingham, Washington, USA. Poet; Professor. m. Anne Lennox, 16 Oct 1988, 1 stepdaughter. Education: BA, Colorado College, 1978; MA, 1986, PhD, 1989, University of Rochester. Appointments: Assistant Professor, 1989-93, Associate Professor, 1993-, Moorhead State University. Publications: Blackened Peaches, 1989; Small Elegies, 1991; The Buried Houses, 1991; The Country I Remember, 1996. Contributions to: Spectator; Hudson Review; Sewanee Review; American Scholar; Poetry; Grand Street; Harvard Review. Honours: Nicholas Roerich Poetry Prize, 1991; Alice Fay Di Castaguola Award, Poetry Society of America, 1993. Address: 1333 5th Avenue South, Moorhead, MN 56560, USA.

MASON H(enry) C(onner), (Logan T Conners), b. 13 Mar 1952, Portsmouth, Ohio, USA. Poet; Lecturer; Musician; Tutor. 2 sons. Education: Shawnee State University, Portsmouth. Appointments: Editor, Shawnee State University Silhouette. Contributions to: Shawnee Silhouette; National Library of Poetry; Suwanee Poetry Review; Bad Haircut Quarterly; Villager; Plowman Anthology. Honours: 1st Prize, National Competition, American Scholastic Press Association; Phoenix Writers. Address: c/o Shawnee Silhouette, 940 Second Street, Portsmouth, OH 45662, USA.

MASON John Frederick, b. 28 Apr 1952, London, England. Teacher. Education: Marlborough College, 1964-68; St Catharine's College, 1970-73; MA, 1973. Appointments: Assistant Master, Christs Hospital, 1973-77; Lady Hawkins School, Kington, 1980-93; Arhus University, 1993-. Publication: From the Black Square. Contributions to: Resurgence; New Welsh Review; Other Poetry; New Democrat. Membership: Poetry Society. Address: Paradisuejen 78, 8600 Siliceborg, Denmark.

MASON Myriam (Adelaide), (Myriam Mason Mosonyi), b. 5 June 1928, Suffolk, England. Concert Singer; Opera Singer; Piano Tutor; Opera Producer; Workshop Director. m. Pierre Mosonyi, 1 daughter. Education: Conservatoire Internationale de Musique, 1952-55; Mannes College of Music, New York, 1959-61. Appointments: Singing Teacher, Huddersfield College of Music, 1969-70; Inner London Education Authority, 1974-89; Part-Time Lecturer, Enfield College, 1976-91. Publications: Short Story; Pebbles and Seagulls; Script; Handel Visits St George's, 1750; Opera Libretto; Beggar's Scrabble. Contributions to: Numerous. Memberships: Poetry Society; Marx Memorial Library; Worker's Music Association; Friend, Shakespeare's Globe. Address: 6A Fairbourne Road, London N17 6TP, England.

MASON Stanley Allen, b. 16 Apr 1917, Blairmore, Alberta, Canada. Editor; Translator. m. Cloris Ielmini, 29 July 1944, 1 daughter. Education: Oriel College, Oxford, 1935-38. Appointments: Teacher, Translator, 1939-43; Technical Translator, 1943-63; Literary Editor, Graphis Magazine, 1963-83; Editor, Elements, 1969-75. Publications: A Necklace of Words; A Reef of Hours; Send Out the Dove; The Alps; The Everlasting Snow; Collected Poems; A German Treasury, anthology, 1993-95. Contributions to: Adelphi; Poetry Review; Envoi; Orbis; Outposts; Pennine Platform; Doors; Odyssey; Canadian Forum; Dalhousie Review. Honours: Borestone Mountain Poetry Award; Living Playwright Award. Address: Im Zelgli 5, 8307 Effretikon, Switzerland.

MASSEY Alan Randolph Charles, b. 6 June 1932, Berkshire, England. Librarian. m. Gillian Elizabeth Petty, 30 Sept 1974. Publications: Trajectories in the Air; The Fire Garden. Contributions to: Agenda; Poetry Review; Workshop; Expression. Membership: Poetry Society. Address: 41 Albany Road, Windsor, Berkshire SL4 1HL, England.

MASSIMILLA Stephen T, b. 31 May 1964, New York, New York, USA. Professor; Poet. BA, Magna Cum Laude, 1986, Phi Beta Kappa, Williams College; With Writing Fellowship, MFA, Columbia University, 1985. Appointments: Editor, Art in America magazine; Writing Instructor, Columbia University, 1984, 1985; Art Instructor, School of Visual Arts, 1985, 1986; Professor of Writing, Barnard College, 1985-; Associate Director, Arthur Danziger Gallery, 1992-. Publication: Figure in the Tower, 1996. Contributions to: Tampa Review; Ariel; Descant; Re: Arts and Letters; Poetry; Cafe Eighties; Onionhead; Distillery; Atom Mind; Wind; Avra; Chants; Black Buzzard; Zuzus Petals Quarterly Online; National Poetry Library Anthology: Daydream on the Land. Honours: Kaufman Prize, 1986; Semi-Finalist, National Poetry Library Open Competition, 1996; Academy of American Poets Prizes, 1986, 1996. Membership: Poetry Society of America. Address: 55 10th Avenue, Sea Cliff, NY 11579, USA.

MAST Edward, b. 18 Aug 1954, Los Angeles, California, USA. Playwright. Education: Bachelor, Liberal Studies, California College at Sonoma, 1976; MFA, Theatre and Playwriting, University of California at Los Angeles, 1978. Publication: Suzy and her Husbands, 1996. Contributions to: Earthwise; Amaranth Review; Cicada; Point Judith Light; Talking Raven. Honour: Second Place, Still Waters Press Poetry Competition, 1995. Address: 520 3rd Avenue West, #B, Seattle, WA 98119, USA.

MASUD. See: HUSAIN Masud.

MATCHETT William H(enry), b. 5 Mar 1923, Chicago, Illinois, USA. Professor Emeritus. Appointments: Teaching Fellow, Harvard University, Cambridge, Massachusetts, 1953-54; Instructor, 1954-56; Assistant Professor, 1956-60, Associate Professor, 1960-66, Professor, English, 1966-82, Professor Emeritus, 1983-, University of Washington, Seattle; Editor, Modern Language Quarterly, 1963-82. Publications: Water Ouzel and Other Poems, 1955; Poetry: From Statement to Meaning (with J Beaty); The Phoenix and the Turtle; Shakespeare's Poems and Chester's Loues Martyr, 1965; The Life and Death of King John, by William Shakespeare (editor), 1966; Fireweed and Other Poems, 1980. Honours: Furioso Poetry Award, 1952; Washington State Governor's Award, 1982. Memberships: Editorial Board, Poetry Northwest, Seattle, 1961. Address: 1017 Minor Avenue No 702, Seattle, WA 98104, USA.

MATHENY Danny Lee, b. 6 Aug 1952, San Antonio, Texas, USA. Truck Driver. 1 daughter. Appointments: Truck Driver, 15 years; Smelter Worker, PHELPS Dodge Mining Co. Publications: A Family Affair; Modern Day Poems by A Family of Modern Day Poets; A Literary First by a Family of South Dakota Poets. Contributions to: A Tapestry of Thoughts; Where Dawn Lingers; Best Poems of the 90s. Honour: South Dakota State Poetry Contest, aged 7, 1960. Memberships: International Society of Poets; Induction Ceremony, 1996. Address: 101 Nth Bayard St, Box 2663, Silver City, NM 88062, USA.

MATHIS-EDDY Darlene Fern, b. 19 Mar 1937, Indiana, USA. Professor. m. Spencer Livingston Eddy, 23 May 1964, dec 1971. Education: BA, Summa cum Laude, Goshen College, 1959; MA, Rutgers University, 1961; PhD, 1966. Appointments: Instructor, Douglas College, 1962-64; Instructor, Rutgers University, 1964; Lecturer, 1965; Assistant Professor, 1967-70, Associate Professor, 1971-75, Professor, 1975-, Ball State University; Poet in Residence,

1989-93; Editor, The Hedgerow Press, 1995. Publications: Leaf Threads; Weathering. Contributions to: Amelia; Barnwood; Blue Unicorn; Bitterroot; Cottonwood; Dog River Review; Forum; Green River Review; Pebble; Snowy Egret; BSU Forum; The Anne Miniver Broadside Series, 1982; The Trumpet Vine Broadside Series, 1995. Honours: Poet in Residence; Woodrow Wilson National Fellow; Rutgers University Graduate Honors Fellow; Counsulting Editor, Blue Unicorn, 1995-. Memberships: American League of PEN Women; Midwest Writers Workshop. Address: Department of English, RB248, Ball State University, Muncie, IN 47306, USA.

MATSON Clive, b. 13 Mar 1941, Los Angeles, California, USA. Poet; Teacher. Education: University of Chicago, 1958-59; Columbia University, 1989. Appointments: Adjunct/faculty, Creative Writing, Pacific Oaks College, 1984-88; University of California Extension, 1985-; J F Kennedy University, Orinda, California, 1993-. Publictions: Hourglass; Equal in Desire; On the Inside; Heroin; Space Age; Mainline to the Heart. Contributions to: Nimrod; Exquisite Corpse; East Bay Express; Grist; Yodeler; Gallery Works; Association for Humanistic Psychology; Hanging Loose; Visions International. Honour: Columbia University Graduate Writing Fellowship. Membership: Poets & Writers. Address: 472 44th Street, Oakland, CA 94609, USA.

MATSON Suzanne Marie, b. 12 Nov 1959, Portland, Oregon, USA. Writer; Professor. m. Joseph Donnellan, 15 June 1991, 1 son. Education: BA, Portland State University, Oregon, 1981; MA, 1983, PhD, 1987, University of Washington. Appointments: Assistant Professor of English, 1988-94, Associate Professor of English, 1994-, Boston College. Publications: Sea Level, 1990; Durable Goods, 1993; The Hunger Moon, forthcoming. Contributions to: American Poetry Review; Poetry; Harvard Review; Shenandoah; Indiana Review; Poetry Northwest; Seattle Review; Southern Poetry Review. Honours: Young Poet's Prize, Poetry Northwest, 1983; Academy of American Poets Prize at the University of Washington, 1986. Memberships: PSA; AWP. Address: English Department, Boston College, Chestnut Hill, MA 02167, USA.

MATTHEWS Liv. See: **SNUGGS Olive.**

MATTHEWS William, b. 11 Nov 1942, Cincinnati, Ohio, USA. Poet; Teacher. m. (1) 2 sons, (2) Patrica Smith, 12 Dec 1989. Education: BA, Yale University; MA, University of North Carolina. Appointments: Teacher: Wells College, Cornell University, Emerson College, Sarah Lawrence College, University of Colorado, University of Iowa, University of Washington, University of Houston, Brooklyn College, Columbia University, City College, University of Michigan. Publications: Ruining the New Road; Sleek for the Long Flight; Sticks and Stones; Rising and Falling; A World Rich in Anniversaries; Flood; A Happy Childhood; Foreseeable Futures; Blues If You Want Curiosities; Selected Poems and Translations, 1969-1991; Time and Money, 1995; The Mortal City: 100 Epigrams of Martial, 1995. Contributions to: New Yorker; Poetry; Atlantic Monthly; Georgia Review; Ohio Review; Antaeus. Honours: Several Fellowships; Oscar Blumenthal Award; Governors Award for Literature; Eunice Tietjens Memorial Prize; National Book Critics Circle Award for Poetry, 1995. Memberships: PEN; Authors Guild; Associated Writing Programs; Poetry Society of America. Address 523 West 121 Street, New York City, NY 10027, USA.

MATTHIAS John (Edward), b. 5 Sept 1941, Columbus, Ohio, USA. Professor of English; Poet; Editor. m. Diana Adams, 1967, 2 children. Education: BA, Ohio State University, 1963; MA, Stanford University, 1966; Fulbright Fellow, University of London, 1966-67. Appointments: Assistant Professor, 1967-73, Associate Professor, 1973-80, Professor of English, 1980-, University of Notre Dame; Visiting Professor, Clare Hall, Cambridge, 1976-77; Skidmore College, Saratoga Springs, New York, 1978, University of Chicago, 1980. Publications: Poetry: Other Poems, 1971; Bucyrus, 1971; Herman's Poems, 1973; Turns, 1975; Double Derivation, Association and Cliché: From the Great Tournament Roll of Westminster, 1975; Two Poems, 1976; Crossing, 1979; Rostropovich at Aldeburgh, 1979; Bathory and Lermontov, 1980; Northern Summer: New and Selected Poems 1963-1983, 1984; Tva Dikter, 1989; A Gathering of Ways, 1991; Swimming at Midnight: Selected Shorter Poems, 1995; Beltane at Aphelion: Collected Longer Poems, 1995; Other: Reading Old Friends: Reviews, Essays, and Poems on Poetics, 1992; Editor: 23 Modern British Poets, 1971; Five American Poets, 1979; Introducing David Jones, 1980; Contemporary Swedish Poetry (with Göran Printz-Påhlson), 1980; David Jones: Man and Poet, 1989; Selected

Works of David Jones, 1993. Honours: Columbia University Translation Center Award, 1979; Ingram-Merrill Foundation Grant, 1984; Society of Midland Authors Prize, 1984; Slobadan Jovanovic Award, 1989. Address: c/o Department of English, University of Notre Dame, Notre Dame, IN 46556, USA.

MAWER Charles E, b. 1 Feb 1969, Haslemere, Surrey, England. Advertising. Education: Lady Margaret Hall, Oxford University. Publications: Down the Backs of Sofas; Learning Gumboot; Poetry Now South; Young Words. Contributions to: Poetry Nottingham; Envoi; Iota; Iron; People's Poet; First Time; Old Police Station; Surrey Advertiser; Oxford Literary Magazine. Honours: Major Award Winner, Young Writer of the Year; Pick of the Fringe. Memberships: Oxford Poetry Society; London Blue Nose Poets; Poetry Society. Address: Fernside Cottage, Brook Road, Wormley, Nr Godalming, Surrey GU8 5UA, England.

MAXTON Hugh. See: **McCORMACK William John.**

MAXWELL Glyn Meurig, b. 7 Nov 1962, Welwyn Garden City, Hertfordshire, England. Poet. Education: Worcester College, Oxford, 1982-85; Boston University, 1987-88. Appointments: Editorial Assistant, W H Allen Plc, 1989; Freelance Poet, Reviewer, Editor, 1989-. Publications: Tale of the Mayor's Son; Out of the Rain; Gynss The Magnificent and Other Verse Plays. Contributions to: Times Literary Supplement; Sunday Times; LRB; Spectator; Poetry Review; Verse; PEN International; PN Review; Atlantic; Akzente; Orbis. Honours: Eric Gregory Award; Poetry Book Society Choices; 3rd National Poetry Competition; Arvon International Poetry Competitions; John Llewellyn Rhys Memorial Prize; Sunday Times Young Writers Award. Memberships: Poetry Society; PEN. Address: c/o Bloodaxe Books, PO Box 1SN, Newcastle-upon-Tyne NE99 1SN, England.

MAY Brian James, b. 7 Jan 1945. Retired Teacher. m. 29 July 1967, 1 son, 2 daughters. Education: BA, 1957; MA, 1971; PGCE, 1973; MA, Education, 1991. Appointments: Assistant Warden, Adult Education, Dartington, 1968-70; Head of Drama, Arthur Terry School, Birmingham, 1970-81; Open University Tutor, 1973-; Head of English, Swanshurst School, Birmingham, 1981-83; Head of Arts Faculty, Chamberlain College, 1983-88; Vice Principal, Josiah Mason College, 1988-93. Contributions to: Orbis; Illuminations; Christ's College Magazine; Times Educational Supplement; Poetry Now. Membership: Fellow, College of Preceptors. Address: 3 Holte Drive, Sutton Coldfield, Birmingham B75 6PR, England.

MAYER Gerda (Kamilla), b. 9 June 1927, Czechoslovakia. m. 3 Sept 1949. Education: BA, Bedford College, University of London, 1963. Appointments: Landwork; Office Work. Publications: Gerda Mayer's Library Folder; Treble Poets 2; The Knockabout Show; Monkey on the Analyst's Couch; The Candy Floss Tree; March Postman; A Heartache of Grass; Time Watching, 1995. Contributions to: Penguin Book of Light Verse; Oxford Book of Travel Verse; With a Poet's Eye; Voices in the Gallery; The Faber Book of Blue Verse; Orange Dove of Fiji; Hutchinsons Book of Post War British Poets; Peace and War; Toughie Toffee; Making for the Open; What on Earth; The Oxford Book of Story Poems. Memberships: Society of Authors; Poetry Society. Address: 12 Margaret Avenue, Chingford, London E4 7NP, England.

MAYER-KOENIG Wolfgang, b. Vienna, Austria. University Professor. Education: Humanistisches Gymnasium, Matura, 1968; Studies: Language, Poetry, History of Arts, Law, University of Vienna, Saarbrücken, Los Angeles, California; DLitt and Dr Fine Arts; Fndr of Literary Situation Austrias University Cultural Center, 1969; Guest Lecturer, University in France, 1975-85. Appointments: Unanimously elected head of division, Austrias Student Union (Corporartion of Pulic Law), 1971-78; Personal Secretary of Austria's Chancellor Dr Kreisky, and Member of Cabinet; University Professor, 1986-; Editor of the International Poetry Magazine LOG, sponsored by UNESCO, 1983-. Publications: Visible Pavilions, 1968; Stichmarken, 1969; Morgue, 1974; Poetry and Drawing, 1976; in the Arms of Our Warden, 1980; Responsibilty of Writing, 1985; Temporary Denial, 1985; Chagrin non dechiffré, 1986; Colloquil nella stanza, 1986; The Corsellet of the Myghty, 1987; A Complicated Angel, 1988; A Hatalom Bonyolult Angyala, 1989; Coloquios nel Cuarto, 1990; Verzögerung des Vertrauens, 1995; Verkannte Tiefe, 1996; Grammatik der Modernen Poesie, 1996. Honours: Theodor Koerner Prize for Poetry, 1974; Cross of Honour for Science and Arts for Poetry, 1974; Chevalier des Arts et des Lettres of the French Republic for Poetry, 1987; Premio Prometeo doro per la Poesia Regione Lazio, 1983. Memberships: Austrias Poets and Writers Association; Accademia Tiberina, Rome Academy Cosentina, Cosenca. Burckhardt Acc St Gallen, Switzerland. Address: Haubenbiglstrabe 1 a, 1190 Vienna, Austria.

MAYFAIR Bertha. See: **RABORG Frederick Ashton, Jr.**

MAYHAR Ardath, (Frank Cannon, John Killdeer, Frances Hurst), b. 20 Feb 1930, USA. Fiction Writer. m. Joe E Mayhar, 8 June 1958, 4 sons. Education: Self-educated. Appointments: Farmer; Bookstore Owner; Postal Clerk; Newspaper Proofreader; Author; Poet. Publications: The Absolutely Perfect Horse; Blood Kin; Bloody Texas Trail; Carrots and Miggle; Exile on Vlahil; Far Horizons; Feud At Sweetwater Creek; Golden Dream: A Fuzzy Odyssey; High Mountain Winter; How The Gods Wove in Kyrannon; Hunters of the Plains; The Island in the Lake; Khi to Freedom; Lords of the Triple Moons; Makra Choria; Medicine Walk; Monkey Station; Passage West; People of the Mesa; A Place of Silver Silence; Runes of the Lyre; The Saga of Grittel Sundotha; Seekers of Shar-Nuhn; Slewfoot Sally and the Flying Mule; Soul-Singer of Tyrnos; BattleTech; The Sword and the Dagger; Texas Gunsmoke; Towers of the Earth; Trail of the Seahawks; The Untamed; The Wall; Warlock's Gift; Wild Country; Wilderness Rendezvous; The World Ends in Hickory Hollow; Through a Stone Wall. Contributions to: Texas Quarterly; Cardinal Poetry Quarterly; Poetry Today; Poetry Dial; Quoin; The Lyric Encore. Honours: Poetry Book Award; Sonnet Award; Publication Award, Book of Poetry; Margaret Haley Carpenter Prize; Jean Miliken Award. Memberships: Science Fiction Writers of America; Western Writers of America. Literary Agent: Jimmy Vines, 409 East 6th Street #4, New York, NY 10009, USA. Address: PO Box 180, Chireno, TX 75937, USA.

MAYNE Seymour, b. 18 May 1944, Montreal, Quebec, Canada. Poet; Editor; Translator. Education: BA, McGill University, 1965; MA, 1966; PhD, University of British Columbia, 1972. Appointments: Managing Editor, Very Stone House, 1966-69; Editor, Ingluvin Publications, 1970-73; Editor, Mosaic Press, 1974-83. Publications: Mouth, 1970; Name, 1975; Diasporas, 1977; The Impossible Promised Land, 1981; Vanguard of Dreams, 1984; Children of Abel, 1986; Simple Ceremony, 1990; Essential Words, 1985; Killing Time, 1992; Locust of Silence, 1993; The Song of Moses, 1995. Honours: Chester Macnaghten First Prize; J I Segal Prize; York Poetry Workshop Award; American Literary Translators Association Poetry Translation Award, 1990; Jewish Book Committee Prize, 1994. Memberships: PEN; AM Klein Research & Publication Committee. Address: Department of English, University of Ottawa, Ottawa, Ontario K1N 6N5, Canada.

MAZZARO Jerome, b. 25 Nov 1934, Detroit, Michigan, USA. College Professor. Education: AB, Wayne State University, 1954; MA, University of Iowa, 1956; PhD, Wayne State University, 1963. Appointments: University of Detroit, 1958-61; State University of New York, 1962-; Visiting Professor, San Diego State University, 1978; Bennington College, 1979-80. Publications: Changing the Windows; The Caves of Love; Rubbings. Contributions to: Accent; Bennington Review; Choice; Georgia Review; Hudson Review; Humanist; Literary Review; Modern Poetry Studies; Massachusetts Review; Nation; New Letters; Ohio Review; Ontario Review; Poetry; Salmagundi; Shenandoah; New Republic; Southwest Review; Yale Review. Honour: Guggenheim Fellowship. Membership: Dante Society of America. Address: 147 Capen Boulevard, Buffalo, NY 14226, USA.

MCALPINE Katherine, b. 31 Oct 1948, Plainfield, New Jersey, USA. Freelance Writer. 1 son. Education: Privately educated; Studied Voice with Leon Kurzer, Vienna Opera. Appointments: Singer and Voice Teacher; Freelance Writer. Publications: Anthologies: Glibquips, 1994; The Best Contemporary Women's Humor, 1994. Literature: The Human Experience, 1995. Contributions to: Nation; Formalist; Sparrow; Epigrammatist; Chronicles; Hellas; Lyric; Light; Cumberland Poetry Review; Plains Poetry Journal. Honours: Eva Le Fevre Award, 1988; Fluvanna Award, 1989; Galbraith Award, 1990; The Nation/Discovery Award, 1992; Judith's Room Award for Emerging Women Poets, 1992. Address: 11 Mitchell Street, Eastport, ME 04631, USA.

MCALPINE Rachel Phyllis, b. 24 Feb 1940, Fairlie, New Zealand. Writer. m. Grant McAlpine, 19 Dec 1959, div, 2 sons, 2 daughters. Education: BA, University of Canterbury, 1960; BA (Hons), Victoria University of Wellington, 1977; DipEd, Massey University, 1973. Appointments: Secondary School Teacher, 1960, 1972-77; Consular Clerk, 1961-63; Writer, 1984-. Publications: Lament for

Ariadne, 1975; Stay at the Dinner Party, 1977; Fancy Dress, 1978; House Poems, 1980; Recording Angel, 1983; Thirteen Waves, 1986; Selected Poems, 1988; Kiwi in Kyoto, 1993. Contributions to: Landfall; Islands; The New Zealand Listener; Southerly; Sydney Morning Herald; Meanjin; Kyoto Journal. Honours: New Zealand-Australia Writers Exchange, 1982; Writer-in-Residence, University of Canterbury, 1986; New Zealand Scholarship in Letters, 1990; Visiting Scholar, Doshisha Women's College of Liberal Arts, Kyoto, Japan, 1993-94. Memberships: PEN, New Zealand; New Zealand Writers Guild. Address: c/o Glenys Bean, Literary Agent, PO Box 42098, Auckland 2, New Zealand.

MCAULEY James J(ohn), b. 8 Jan 1936, Dublin, Ireland. Education: BA, University College, Dublin, 1962; MFA, University of Arkansas, 1971. Appointments: Professor of English, Eastern Washington State University, 1978-; Director, Eastern Washington University Press, 1993-. Publications include: Observations, 1960; A New Address, 1965; Draft Balance Sheet: Poems 1963-1969; After the Blizzard, 1975; The Exile's Recurring Nightmare, 1975; Praise! (Libretto), 1980; Recital: Poems 1975-1980, 1982; The Exile's Book of Hours, 1982; Coming and Going: New and Selected Poems, 1989; Editor, Dolmen Press, Dublin, 1978-85. Address: Creative Writing Program, MS#1, Spokame Center, Eastern Washington State University, 1st G Watt, Spokane, WA 99201, USA.

MCCALLISTER Weslynn, b. 18 May 1949, Evansville, Indiana, USA. Business Woman. m. R A Holway, dec, 2 sons, 1 daughter. Education: Liberal Arts; Fine Arts; Real Estate. Appointments: Real Estate Associate; Manager of Family Business; Poet and Aspiring Novelist. Publications: The Looking Glass of Yesterday, 1993; Reflections, 1995. Contributions to: Moments in Time; Writer's World; Poetic Eloquence; Feelings Poetry Magazine; Poetic Knight; Apropos; Catharsis; Poets in Motion; Poet and Pen Quarterly; Pipers Song; Gotto Write Lit Magazine; NPA Market Letter. Honours: 2nd Place, Poetry Contest, 1990; Award, Poet and Pen Quarterly, 1990; Chapbook Contest by Caro Lynn Publications, 1995. Memberships: Romance Writers of America, South West Florida Chapter. Address: 7350 S Tamiami, TR #229, Sarasota, FL 34231, USA.

MCCALLUM-PETERS Yvonne Veronica, b. 21 May 1944, Guyana. Teacher. m. Dereck George McCallum, 7 Nov 1964, 3 sons, 1 daughter. Education: Teachers College, 1971; BA, University of Guyana, 1979; University of Guyana, 1983; Brooklyn College, 1986-89; Teachers College, Columbia University, 1990. Appointments: Graduate Mistress, Queens College, Georgetown; Editor, St Marks Day School Newsletter; Director of Education; Principal, John Hus Moravian Church School; Adjunct Lecturer. Publications: American Poetry Anthology; World Anthology of Great Poetry. Contributions to: American Anthology of Poetry; World of Poetry. Honours: Golden Poet Award; Certificate of Merit; Silver Poet Award. Memberships: New York Consortium of Adult Basic Education Teachers; United Federation of Teachers; American Association of Higher Education. Address: 568 Powell Street, Brooklyn, NY 11212, USA.

MCCARRON Daniel Peter, b. 14 Dec 1933, Canada. Journalist; Publisher. m. (1) Jessie Drysdale, 2 sons, 3 daughters. (2) Diane Arssenault, 31 Dec 1993. Education: Arts, Journalism, St Mary's University, Halifax, Canada, 1957. Appointments: City Editor, Halifax Chronicle-Herald, 1957; Editor, The Globe & Mail, 1962; Editor, CBC, Toronto, 1964; Editor, own paper, The Strait News, 1972; Editor, various papers until 1996; Editor, Publisher, Ordinary Times. Contributions to: Atlantic Monthly; Maclean's Magazine; Several others. Honours: Named among Journalists of World Contest, International Society of Poets, 1995. Address: 2-15 Falconwood Road, Charlottetown, Prince Edward Island C1A 6B6, Canada.

MCCARTHY Joanne, b. 18 Mar 1935, Missoula, Montana, USA. College Faculty Member. divorced, 4 sons, 2 daughters. Education: BA, English (Creative Writing), University of Montana, 1955; MA, English (Literature), University of Puget Sound, 1969. Appointments: Teaching Fellow, English, University of Puget Sound, Washington, 1965-68; Faculty, Tacoma Community College, Washington, 1969-96; Fulbright Exchange Fellow, English, Berufsaufbauschule, Nürnberg, Federal Republic of Germany, 1984-85. Publication: Shadowlight, 1989. Contributions to: Green Fuse; Poets' Gallery, Canada; Writers Forum; Bellingham Review; Calyx; Earth's Daughters; Exhibition; Mediphors; Poets On; Thema; West Wind Review; Anthologies, If I Had My Life to Live Over (I Would Pick More Daisies), 1992; Each in Her Own Way, 1993, I Am Becoming the Woman I've Wanted, 1994;

Fingerlings, 1995. Honours: Winner, Writer's Omnibus Poetry Competition, 1980; Shadowlight Selected for New American Writing International Tour; Winner, Metro Arts Poetry Bus Project, Seattle; Brodie Herndon Memorial Poetry Society of Virginia, 1994. Address: 1322 North Cascade, Tacoma, WA 98406, USA.

MCCASLIN Susan Elizabeth, b. 3 June 1947, Indianapolis, Indiana, USA. College Instructor. m. Mark Haddock, 9 Aug 1979, 1 daughter. Education: BA, magna cum laude, Phi Beta Kappa, University of Washington, 1969; MA, Simon Fraser University, 1973; PhD, University of British Columbia, 1984. Appointments: Teaching Assistant, English Department, Simon Fraser University, 1969-71; Sessional Lecturer, English Department, University of Victoria, 1973-74; Instructor, English Department, Trinity Western College, 1974-77; Sessional Lecturer, 1977-79, 1984-85, Teaching Assistant, 1980-82, English Department, University of British Columbia; Assistant Professor, English Department, Trent University, Peterborough, Ontario, summer 1984; Instructor in English, Douglas College, New Westminster, BC, 1984-. Publications: Conversing with Paradise, 1986; Locutions, 1995. Contributions to: West Coast Review; Littack; Crux; Bellowing Ark; White Wall Review; Scrivener; Christianity and Literature; Carleton Arts Review; Kore; Anima; Journal of Human Experience; Journal of Feminist Studies in Religion; Canadian Woman Studies; Literature and Belief; Contemporary Verse 2; Ariel; New Quarterly; Grain. Honours: Honourable Mention, William Stafford Award, 1986; 2nd Place for Poem, Cecilia Lamont Literary Contest, 1994; 1st Place, Annual Poetry Contest, Burnaby Writers' Society, 1995. Memberships: Burnaby Writers' Society; Federation of British Columbia Writers; Canadian Authors' Association; League of Canadian Poets; Writers' Union of Canada; Canadian Children's Literature Organization. Address: 21 Brackenridge Place, Port Moody, British Columbia V3H 4G4, Canada.

MCCLANE Kenneth Anderson, b. 19 Feb 1951, New York, New York, USA. Professor. m. Rochelle Evette Woods, 22 Oct 1983. Education: BA, 1973, MA, 1974, MFA, 1976, Cornell University. Appointments: Instructor, Colby College, 1974-75; Assistant Supervisor, University of New York, 1978-79; Luce Visiting Professor, Williams College, 1984; Wayne State University, 1987; University of Michigan, 1989; Cornell University, 1989-; Washington University, 1991. Publications: Walls: Essays, 1985-90; Take Five: Collected Poems, 1988. Contributions to: Beloit Poetry Journal; Epoch; Northwest Review; Black American Literature Forum; Callaloo; Greenfield Review; Nimrod; Freedomways; Obsidian; Wind; Black Scholar; Crisis; Texas Review; Four Quarters; Wisconsin Review; Cape Rock; Cincinnati Poetry Review; West Hills Review; Abraxis; Counseling and Values; Hampton Sydney Poetry Review; Vineyard Gazette; Thoreau Journal Quarterly. Honours: George Harmon Coxe Award; Corson Morrison Poetry Prize; Clark Distinguished Teaching Award. Memberships: Poets and Writers; Poetry Society of America. Address: Department of English, Cornell University, Ithaca, NY 14853, USA.

MCCLOSKEY Phil(omena Mary), (Yvonne Somerville), b. 11 May 1940. Secretary; Housewife. m. Patrick Daniel McCloskey, 5 Sept 1959, 2 sons, 2 daughters. Education: Drake Business School, 1959. Appointments: Bank Clerk; Secretary; Administrative Assistant. Contributions to: Pause; Ratpit; No Asylum; Force 10; Poetry Ireland's Sense of Place Broadsheet; Steeple. Honours: John Player Trophy; 2nd Prize, McGill Poetry Competition; Donegal Poet of the Year; Highly Commended Certificate, Gerard M Hopkins Poetry Competition. Memberships: Killybegs Writers Workshop; Killybegs Literary Society; National Poetry Foundation. Address: Fintra, Killybegs, County Donegal, Ireland.

MCCLURE Michael (Thomas), b. 20 Oct 1932, Marysville, Kansas, USA. Professor; Poet; Dramatist; Writer. m. Joanna Kinnison, 1954, 1 daughter. Education: University of Wichita, 1951-53; University of Arizona, 1953-54; BA, San Francisco State College, 1955. Education: Assistant Professor, 1962-77, Associate Professor, 1977-78, Professor, 1978-, California College of Arts and Crafts, Oakland; Playwright-in-Residence, American Conservatory Theatre, San Francisco, 1975; Associate Fellow, Pierson College, Yale University, 1982. Publications: Poetry: Passage, 1956; For Artaud, 1959; Hymns to St Geryon and Other Poems, 1959; The New Book: A Book of Torture, 1961; Dark Brown, 1961; Ghost Tantras, 1964; 13 Mad Sonnets, 1964; Hail Thee Who Play, 1968, revised edition, 1974; The Sermons of Jean Harlow and the Curses of Billy the Kid, 1969; Star, 1971; The Book of Joanna, 1973; Rare Angel (writ with raven's

blood), 1974; September Blackberries, 1974; Jaguar Skies, 1975; Antechamber and Other Poems, 1978; The Book of Benjamin, 1982; Fragments of Perseus, 1983; Selected Poems, 1986; Rebel Lions, 1991; Simple Eyes and Other Poems, 1994; Plays include: Gargoyle Cartoons (11 plays), 1971; The Mammals, 1972; The Grabbing of the Fairy, 1973; Gorf, 1976; General Georgeous, 1975; Goethe: Ein Fragment, 1978; The Velvet Edge, 1982; The Beard and VKTMS: Two Plays, 1985; Novels: The Mad Club, 1970; The Adept, 1971; Other includes: Lighting the Corners: On Art, Nature, and the Visionary: Essays and Interviews, 1993. Honours: National Endowment for the Arts Grants, 1967, 1974; Guggenheim Fellowship, 1971; Magic Theatre Alfred Jarry Award, 1974; Rockefeller Foundation Fellowship, 1975; Obie Award, 1978. Address: 264 Downey Street, San Francisco, CA 94117, USA.

MCCONNELL Will. See: **SNODGRASS W D.**

MCCORKLE James Donald Bruland, b. 6 Feb 1954, St Petersburg, Florida, USA. College Professor. m. Cynthia Jane Williams, 16 July 1989. Education: BA, Hobart College, 1976; MA, 1977, MFA, 1981, PhD, 1984, University of Iowa. Appointments: Teaching Assistant, 1979-84; Visiting Assistant Professor, 1986-87; Assistant Professor, Hobart College, 1987-92; Visiting Assistant Professor, Keuka College, 1995. Publications: The Still Performance; Conversant Essays. Contributions to: ACM; Antioch Review; Boulevard; Chronicle of Higher Education; Columbia; Denver Quarterly; Little Magazine; Louisville Review; Manhattan Poetry Review; Manoa, New Delta Review; Maryland Review; Minnesota Review; Missouri Review; New Selta Review; Plum Review; Poet and Critic; Quarry West; Seneca Review; Southwest Review; Kenyon Review; Pequood; Verse; Green Mountains Review; Prairie Schooner. Honour: Ingram Merrill Foundation Fellowship. Memberships: Poetry Society of America; Associated Writing Program; Modern Language Association; Elizabeth Bishop Society. Address: 145 Hillcrest Avenue, Geneva, NY 14456, USA.

MCCORMACK William John, (Hugh Maxton), b. 15 Sept 1947, Dublin, Ireland. Writer; University Teacher. m. Sheelagh Grayson, 9 Jan 1971, 1 son. Education: BA, MA, Trinity College, 1967-71; DPhil, New University of Ulster, 1971-74. Appointments: Lecturer, Professor, New University of Ulster, University of Leeds, University of Budapest, Georgetown University, University of Antwerp. Publications: Stones; The Noise of the Fields; Jubilee for Renegades; At the Protestant Museum; The Engraved Passion; Swift-Mail, 1992. Honours: Poetry Book Society Choice; Hungarian Ministry of Culture Prize for Translation. Membership: Aosdana. Address: 3 Rosemount Terrace, Arbour Hill, Dublin 7, Ireland.

MCCORMICK A. See: **LEWIS-SMITH Anne Elizabeth.**

MCCORMICK Mary Joneve, b. Tiffin, Ohio, USA. Writer; Teacher. Education: BA, English, University of California; MA, Creative Writing, San Francisco College; MSed, Fordham University. Appointments: Writer; Teacher. Publication: Small Bird Bones, 1993; Publisher, Soul to Soul, Internet poetry journal. Contributions to: Art Times; Standard; Sisyphus; The New Press; Golden Isis; Smoke Signals; Nomad's Choir. Honour: Represented the University of California as Poet. Membership: Poets & Writers. Address: 427 West 51st Street, New York, NY 10019, USA.

MCCROSSAN Eamon, b. 12 Dec 1963, Belfast, Northern Ireland. Civil Servant; Freelance Journalist. Education: A Level Evening Education. Publications: After Rain; Snow Queen; Evacuated to Coalisland. Contributions to: Orbis; Northern Women; Ulster Tatler; Cyphers; Universe; Belfast Review; Poetry Ireland. Address: 24 La Salle Drive, Belfast BT12 6DB, Northern Ireland.

MCCULLOUGH Ken(neth), b. 18 July 1943, Staten Island, New York, USA. Poet; Writer; Teacher. Education: BA, University of Delaware, 1966; MFA, University of Iowa, 1968. Appointments: Teacher, Montana State University, 1970-75, University of Iowa, 1983-95, Kirkwood Community College, Cedar Rapids, 1987, St Mary's University, Winona, Minnesota, 1996; Writer-in-Residence, South Carolina ETV Network, 1975-78; Participant, Artist-in-the-Schools Program, Iowa Arts Council, 1981-96. Publications: Poetry: The Easy Wreckage, 1971; Migrations, 1972; Creosote, 1976; Elegy for Old Anna, 1985; Travelling Light, 1987; Sycamore Oriole, 1991; Walking Backwards, 1996. Contributions to: Numerous publications. Honours: Academy of American Poets Award,

1966; 2nd Place, Ark River Awards, 1972; Helene Wurlitzer Foundation of New Mexico Residencies, 1973, 1994; National Endowment for the Arts Fellowship, 1974; 2nd Prize, Sri Chinmoy Poetry Awards, 1980; Writers' Voice Capricorn Book Award, 1985; 2nd Prize, Pablo Neruda Award, Nimrod magazine, 1990; 3rd Prize, Kudzu Poetry Contest, 1990; Ucross Foundation Residency, Wyoming, 1991; Witter Bynner Foundation for Poetry Grant, 1993; Iowa Arts Council Grants, 1994, 1996. Memberships: Associated Writing Programs; Association of American University Professors; National Association of College Academic Advisers; Renaissance Artists and Writers Association and Renaissance International; Rocky Mountain Modern Language Association; Science Fiction Writers of America. Address: 372 Center Street, Winona, MN 55987, USA.

MCDONALD Paul John, b. 1 May 1961, Walsall, West Midlands, England. Poet; Lecturer; Reviewer. Education: Arts, Open University, 1983-86; 1st Class Hons degree, English, Birmingham Polytechnic, 1989; PhD Candidate, Central England University, 1990-94. Appointments: Former Saddlemaker, Walsall; Lecturer, Central England University, 1990-; Book Reviewer, The Birmingham Post; Editor, Publisher, Read This Poetry Broadsheet; Lecturer in American Literature, University of Wolverhampton, 1994-. Publications: Circles, 1992; First Communion, 1993; A Funny Old Game, 1994. Contributions to: Approx 50 magazines, England, USA, India, including: Arcadian; Foolscap; Frogmore Papers; Hybrid; Iota; Krax; New Hope International; Nutshell; People to People; Psychopoetica; Purple Patch; Odyssy; Old Police Station (YOPS); Third Half; White Rose; Wyro; Coal City Review; Prophetic Voices; Pluck and Pluck; Staple; Interactions; California Quarterly. Honour: PhD, 1994. Address: 70 Walstead Road, Delves, Walsall, West Midlands WS5 4LX, England.

MCDONOUGH William J, b. 5 May 1971, Pell City, Alabama, USA. Masonry. Education: Southern Union State College, Wadley, Alabama, USA, at present. Appointment: Brick Mason. Publications: Voyage to Remember, 1996; Best Poems of 90s; Iliad Press 96 Crossings; Sparrowgrass Poetry Forum 96; Treasured Poems of America; The Child Within, 1996. Contributions to: National Poets Association, 1996; NPA Marketletter. Honours: National Library of Poetry, Editor's Choice Award, 1996; Iliad Press, Honorable Mention 96; National Library of Poetry, Selected for Sound of Poetry, Cassette. Memberships: International Society of Poets; National Author's Registry. Address: PO Box 1267, Ashland, AL 36251, USA.

MCEWEN Christian, b. 21 April 1956, London, England. Writer; Teacher. Education: BA, English Literature, Social Anthropology, University of Cambridge, 1979; MA, English Literature, Creative Writing, University of California at Berkeley, USA, 1982. Appointments: Reader, Virago, British Feminist Press, 1983-86; Adult Literacy Counsellor, 1986-88; Writer, Teachers and Writers Collaborative, 1988-; Lecturer, Parsons and Eugene Lang, The New School, New York City, 1992-. Publications: Naming the Waves; Contemporary Lesbian Poetry (editor, contributor), 1988; Represented in: Poems for Peace, 1986; Love Poems by Women, 1990; The Poetry of Sex, 1992; The Crazy Jig, 1992. Contributions to: Sinister Wisdom; Transfer; Edinburgh Review of Books; Litmus; Sojourner; Others. Honours: Fulbright Scholarship, 1979; Lambda Literary Award, 1989; Grant, Fund for Poetry, 1991; Residencies: Yaddo (2); Millay; Virginia Center for the Creative Arts; Hambidge; Cottages at Hedgebrook and Cummington. Memberships: National Writers Union. Address: 28 Clesson Brook Road RR1, Charlemont, MA 01339, USA.

MCFADDEN Roy, b. 14 Nov 1921, Belfast, Northern Ireland. Publications: Swords and Ploughshares; Flowers for a Lady; The Hearts Townland; Elegy for the Dead of the Princess Victoria; The Garryowen; Verifications; A Watching Brief; The Selected Roy McFadden; Letters to the Hinterland; After Seymour's Funeral; Collected Poems 1943-95. Address: 13 Shrewsbury Gardens, Belfast BT9, Northern Ireland.

MCFADDEN Tom, b. 20 Sept 1945, Lancaster, Pennsylvania, USA. m. Loretta Yasson, 15 July 1967, 3 daughters. Education: BA, Pennsylvania State University, 1967. Contributions to: Writing; Dream International Quarterly; White Rose; Writers Own Magazine; Peace and Freedom; Limerick Tribune; Killarney Advertiser; Momentum; Writers Rostrum; Tidepool; Electric Muse; Breakthrough; Underpass; Midwest Poetry Review; Poets Review; Voices; Poet; For Poets Only; Nocturnal Lyric; Innisfree; Oak; My Legacy; Snake River Relections; Austin Chronicle; Poetry Pedler; Star Song; Poetic Page; Rhymes in

Lines; Poets at Work; Bells Letters; Word and Image. Address: 11704 Running Fox Trail, Austin, TX 78759, USA.

MCFARLAND Ron(ald Earl), b. 22 Sept 1942, Bellaire, Ohio, USA. Teacher. m. Elsie Roseland Watson, 29 Jan 1966, 1 son, 2 daughters. Education: AA, Brevard Junior College, 1962; BA, 1963, MA, 1965, Florida State University; PhD, University of Illinois, 1970. Appointments: Instructor, Department of English, Sam Houston State College, 1965-67; Assistant Professor to Professor, English, 1970-, Director, Creative Writing, 1992-95, University of Idaho, Moscow; Idaho State Writer-in-Residence, 1984-85; Exchange Professor, Ohio University, 1985-86. Publications: Idaho's Poetry: A Centennial Anthology; The Haunting Familiarity to Things; Composting at Forty; The Villanelle: The Evolution of a Poetic Form; Deep Down Things: Poems of the Inland Pacific Northwest, anthology; James Welch; Norman MacLean; David Wagoner; Tess Gallagher; American Controversy, composition textbook. Contributions to: Weber Studies; Lullwater Review; South Coast Poetry Journal; Birmingham Poetry Review; American Literary Review; Yarrow; West Wind Review; Palouse Journal; South Florida Poetry Review; Talking River Review; Spitball; Hampden-Sydney Poetry Review; Hiram Poetry Review. Honours: Idaho's 1st State Writer-in-Residence, 1984; Burlington Northern Faculty Achievement Award, 1990; Alumni Award for Faculty Excellence, 1991. Memberships: Presenter, Scholar, Let's Talk About It and Poets on Tape, reading-discussion series, Idaho State Library; Western Literature Association; Academy of American Poets. Address: 857 East 8th Street, Moscow, ID 83843, USA.

MCFERREN Martha Dean, b. 25 Apr 1947, Henderson, Texas, USA. Librarian. m. Dennis Scott Wall, 21 May 1977. Education: BS, North Texas State University, 1969; MLS, 1971; MFA, Warren Wilson College, 1988. Appointments: Librarian, San Jacinto Community College, Texas, 1971-75; Librarian, Jefferson Parish Libraries, Louisiana, 1976-81; Librarian, New Orleans Public Schools, 1984-85; Instructor, Dillard University, New Orleans, Louisiana, 1991. Publications: Delusions of a Popular Mind; Get Me Out of Here; Contours for Ritual; Women in Cars. Contributions to: New Laurel Review; Half Tones to Jubilee; Literary Review; Missouri Review; Willow Springs; College English; Greenfield Review; Kansas Quarterly; Chowder Review. Honours: Marianne Moore Poetry Prize; Creative Writing Fellowship, National Endowment for the Arts; Yaddo Fellowship; Deep South Poetry Prize; Louisiana Artist Fellowship; Finalist, AWP Anniversary Awards. Memberships: Poetry Society of America; Poets and Writers; New Orleans Poetry Forum. Address: 2679 Verbena Street, New Orleans, LA 70122, USA.

MCGILL Nicole Grace, b. 16 Oct 1978, St Louis Park, USA. Nursing Assistant. Education: Graduate, 1996. Appointments: McDonalds, 1994-95; Dental Assistant, 1995-96; Nursing Assistant, 1996-. Publication: Poetry, 1994, 1995. Contributions to: Star Tribune; Anoka Shopper. Honour: Editor's Choice Award, 1994. Membership: National Library of Poetry. Address: 3440 Placer Avenue, Anoka, MN 55303, USA.

MCGONIGAL James, b. 20 May 1947, Scotland. Head of Department of Language and Literature. m. Mary Alexander, 1 Aug 1971, 3 son, 3 daughters. Education: MA, University of Glasgow, 1970; MPhil, 1973; PhD, 1978; Jordanhill College, 1988. Appointments: Teacher of Secondary English, Head of Learning Support Unit, 1971-84; Lecturer, 1984-91; Head of English Education, 1991-92; Head of Language and Literature, 1992-. Publications: Unidentified Flying Poems; Several Anthologies. Contributions to: Aquarius; Akros; Edinburgh Review; Gairfish; New Blackfriars; Temenos; Words; A Sort of Hot Scotland, anthology, co-editor, 1994; Last Things First, 1995; Sons of Ezra: British Poets and Ezra Pound, 1995; Full Strength/Angels, 1996. Memberships: Association for Scottish Literary Studies; Poetry Society. Address: Department of Language and Literature, St Andrews College, Duntocher Road, Bearsden, Glasgow G61 4QA, Scotland.

MCGOUGH Roger, b. 9 Nov 1937, Liverpool, England. Poet. Education: St Marys College, Liverpool; Hull University. Appointments: Fellow of Poetry, Loughborough University, 1973-75; Writer-in-Residence, Western Australia College of Advanced Education, 1987; Honorary Professor, Thames Valley University. Publications: Watchwords; After the Merry Making; Gig; Sporting Relations; In the Glassroom; Holiday on Death Row; Summer with Monika; Waving at Trains; Melting into the Foreground; Blazing Fruit; You at the Back; Defying Gravity; Lucky; 12 books of poetry for children. Honours: Signal Award, Best Book of Poetry for Children; BAFTA Award; Royal Television Society Award. Memberships: General Council of the Poetry Society; Trustee and former Chairman, Chelsea Arts Club. Address: c/o Peters, Fraser & Dunlop, 5th Floor, The Chambers, Chelsea Harbour, Lots Road, London SW10 0XF, England.

MCGRATH Niall, b. Antrim, North Ireland. Education: MA, Edinburgh University; BA, Open University. Publications: Heart of a Heartless World, novel, 1995; First Sight, poetry selection, 1996. Contributions in: New Statesman and Society; Agenda; Acumen; Honest Ulsterman; Poetry Ireland Review; Asylum; Envoi; New Poetry Quarterly; Parnassus (USA); Wascana Review (Canada). Honour: Shortlisted, 1995 Tears in The Fence, Poetry Pamphlet Competition, England.

MCGRORY Edward, b. 6 Nov 1921, Stevenston, Ayrshire, Scotland. Retired Sales Consultant. m. Mary McDonald, 20 Nov 1948, 1 son, 1 daughter. Education: BA, Open University, 1985. Publications: Selected Poems, 1984; Plain and Coloured, 1985; Pied Beauty, 1986; Orchids and Daisies, 1987; Light Reflection - Mirror Images (introduction by Iris Murdoch), 1988; Chosen Poems by Celebrities; Eddie McGrory's Poems, 1988; Masks and Faces (introduction by Duncan Glen), 1989; Illuminations, 1990; Candles and Lasers: Lyrics for Musical Settings, 1992. Memberships: Various literary societies. Address: 41 Sythrum Crescent, Glenrothes, Fife KY7 5DG, Scotland.

MCGUCKIAN Medbh, b. 12 Aug 1950, Belfast, Northern Ireland. Poet; Teacher. m. John McGuckian, 1977, 3 sons, 1 daughter. Education: BA, 1972, MA, 1974, Queen's University, Belfast. Appointments: Teacher, Dominican Convent, Fortwilliam Park, Belfast, 1974; Instructor, St Patrick's College, Knock, Belfast, 1975-; Writer-in-Residence, Queen's University, Belfast, 1986-88. Publications: Poetry: Single Ladies: Sixteen Poems, 1980; Portrait of Joanna, 1980; Trio Poetry (with Damien Gorman and Douglas Marshall), 1981; The Flower Master, 1982; The Greenhouse, 1983; Venus and the Rain, 1984, revised edition, 1994; On Ballycastle Beach, 1988; Two Women, Two Shores, 1989; Marconi's Cottage, 1991; The Flower Master and Other Poems, 1993; Captain Lavender, 1994; Editor: The Big Striped Golfing Umbrella: Poems by Young People from Northern Ireland, 1985. Honours: National Poetry Competition Prize, 1979; Eric Gregory Award, 1980; Rooney Prize, 1982; Ireland Arts Council Award, 1982; Alice Hunt Bartlett Award, 1983; Cheltenham Literature Festival Poetry Competition Prize, 1989. Address: c/o Gallery Press, Oldcastle, County Meath, Ireland.

MCKEE Lois Hester Grace, b. 15 June 1938, Belfast, Northern Ireland. Administrative Officer. m. 14 July 1961, 3 sons, 1 daughter. Contributions to: Belfast Telegraph; Scottish Poetry Society; Orbis. Honour: Prize Winner, Scottish Poetry Society. Memberships: Orbis; Civil Service Author. Address: 49 Downpatrick Road, Clough BT30 8NL, Northern Ireland.

MCKENZIE Lillian Crawford, b. 15 June 1905, Dothan, Alabama, USA. Education: BA, Wesleyan College, Macon, Georgia, USA; Art Diploma, Huntingdon College, Montgomery, Alabama. Publications: Book of Poems, Dear Family; Author, Archives of History Book, Diary of a Young Southern Girl; Numerous poems published in various magazines and anthologies. Honours: Award for Volunteer Work at the Soldiers Service Centre during World War II; State PEN Women Prize, 1977; Listed as one of Miami's Most Distinguished Women, 1986. Memberships: Magna Charta Dames; English Speaking Union; Miami Vizayans; Debutante Committee for Society of Southern Families, Miami; Officer of Dade County Medical Auxiliary; Women's Guild of University of Miami. Address: 1101 Wyndegate Drive, Orange Park, FL 32073, USA.

MCKERNAN Llewellyn McKinnie, b. 7 Dec 1941, Hampton, Arkansas, USA. Poet; Children's Book Writer. m. John Joseph McKernan, 3 Sept 1967, 1 daughter. Education: BA, English, summa cum laude, Hendrix College, 1963; MA, English, University of Arkansas, 1966; MA, Creative Writing, Brown University, 1976. Appointments: English Instructor, Georgia Southern College, 1966-67; Adjunct Professor of English, Marshall University, 1980-86; Full-time Professor of English, St Mary's College, Fall Semester, 1989; Adjunct Professor of English, Marshall University, Fall Semester, 1991. Publications: Short and Simple Annals, 1979, 2nd edition, 1983; More Songs of Gladness, 1987; Bird Alphabet, 1988; Many Waters, 1993; This is The Day and This Is The Night, 1994. Contributions to:

Antietam Review; Kalliope; Kenyon Review; Southern Poetry Review; Poet and Critic; Amelia; Appalachian Journal; Appalachian Heritage; Agni Review; Nimrod. Honours: Best Poet in National Writing Project, AAUW, 1978; 3rd Prize, Chester H Jones National Poetry Competition, 1982; WVA Humanities Artist Grant, 1983; Poets and Writers Poetry Reading Grant, 1984; 2nd Prize, National Founders Award Contest, NFSPS, 1994. Memberships: Poetry Society of West Virginia; West Virginia Writers Association; Society of Children's Book Writers and Illustrators; International Women's Writing Guild. Address: Route 10, Box 4639B, Barboursville, WV 25504, USA.

MCKINLEY Hugh, b. 18 Feb 1924, Oxford, England. m. Deborah Waterfield, 15 Sept 1979. Appointments: Literary Editor, Athens Daily Post, 1966-77; European Editor, Poet, India, 1967-89; Editorial Panel, Bitterroot, USA, 1980-91. Publications: Poetry; Starmusic; Transformation of Faust; Poet in Transit; Exulting for the Light; Skylarking. Contributions to: London Magazine; Orbis; Weyfares; Pennine Platform; Candelabrum Magazine; Poetry Wales; Poets Voice; Hibernia; Kilkenny Magazine; Dublin Magazine; Malahat Review; Bitterroot; Smith Poetry International; Laurel Leaves; Poet India; Skylark; Poet's England; 15 Suffolk. Honours: DLitt, University of Asia, Karachi, 1972; International Academy of Leadership and President Marcos Medal, 1967. Memberships: Suffolk Poetry Society; Bahai World Faith. Address: Roseholme, Curlew Green, Kelsale, Suffolk, England.

MCLEMORE Monita Prine, b. 7 June 1927, Avera, Mississippi, USA. Teacher and Professional Harpist. m. Harry Kimbrell McLemore, 9 Mar 1952, 1 son, 1 daughter. Education: BMus, 1949, MMus, 1951, University of Southern Mississippi. Appointments: Teacher, Private Piano Lessons, 44 years; Professor of Music, University of Arkansas, 9 years; Teacher in Public and Private Schools, 5 years; Perkinston Junior College Professor of Music, 2 years; Gulf Coast Community College Professor of Music, 3 years; Teacher of Harp, 3 years. Publications: Poems by Monita, 1985; More Poems, 1987; Still More Poems, 1989; Ripples From The Edge, 1992; A Tapestry of Nature, 1994; Haiku Happenings, 1995. Fingerprints in Rhyme, 1996. Contributions to: Modern Haiku; Back Porch; Haiku Headlines; Frogpond; Moments in Time; Southern Poetry Society; Magnolia Muse; Mississippi Poetry Society; The Sentinal; The Sanddollar. Honours: Poet of the Year, South Chapter of Mississippi Poetry Society, 1994; Several awards from poetry competitions. Memberships: Poetry Society, State & South Chapter; National Federation of State Poetry Societies; Writers Unlimited. Address: 110 Winchester Drive, Ocean Springs, MS 39564, USA.

MCLOUGHLAND Beverly, b. 13 May 1946, Newark, New Jersey, USA. Writer. m. Keith F McLoughland, dec 4 April 1967. Education: BA, Early Childhood Education, Kean College, Union, New Jersey, 1973; Seton Hall University, Newark, New Jersey, 1963-65; Graduated, St Vincent Academy, 1963. Appointments: Second Grade Teacher, 1966-70; Professional Writer, 1976-. Publications: A Hippo's a Heap and Other Animal Poems, 1993; Anthologies which include author's poems: More Surprises, 1987; Side by Side, 1988; Good Books, Good Times, 1990; Dog Poems, 1990; Happy Birthday, 1991; A Cup of Starshine, 1991; Pterodactyls and Pizza, 1992; Ring Out, Wild Bells, 1992; Flit, Flutter, Fly, 1992; Through Our Eyes, 1992; The Walker Bear, A Children's Treasury, 1993; Early Years, Poems & Rhymes, 1993; Sorry for the Slug, 1993; Poetry from A to Z, 1994; Weather, 1994; Hand in Hand, An American History Through Poetry, 1994; April Bubbles Chocolate, An ABC of Poetry, 1994; The New Oxford Tresury of Children's Poems, 1995; Many poems have also appeared in numerous elementary school textbooks. Contributions to: Cricket; Highlights; Cobblestone; Ranger Rick; Your Big Backyard; Dolphin Log; Humpty Dumpty's; Children's Playmate; Jack and Jill; Weekly Reader; School Magazine (Australia); Instructor; Language Arts; Reading Teacher; Joy of Reading; Science and Children; Christian Science Monitor. Membership: Society of Children's Book Writers and Illustrators. Address: c/o Boyds Mills Press, 815 Church Street, Honesdale, PA 18431, USA.

MCMILLAN Lisa Russell. See: **CLARK Marjorie Russell McMillan.**

MCNAIR Wesley, b. 19 June 1941, Newport, New Hampshire, USA. Professor. m. Diane Reed McNair, 24 Dec 1962, 3 sons, 1 daughter. Education: BA, Keene State College, 1963; MA, Middlebury College, 1968. Appointments: Senior Fulbright Professor, Catholic University of Chile, 1977-78; Visiting Associate Professor, Dartmouth

College, 1984; Associate Professor, Colby Sawyer College, 1968-87; Professor, University of Maine, 1987-. Publications: My Brother Running; Twelve Journeys in Maine; The Town of No; The Faces of Americans in 1853; The Quotable Moose: A Contemporary Maine Reader. Contributions to: Atlantic; Poetry; Iowa Review; New England Review; New Criterion; Sewanee Review; Prairie Schooner; Harvard Magazine; Southern Review; Yankee. Honours: New England Emmy Award; Residency, Bellagio Center of The Rockefeller Foundation; National Endowment for the Arts Fellowship Grants; Robert Frost Fellowship; Guggenheim Fellowship; Pushcart Prize; Eunice Tietjens Memorial Prize; Theodore Roethke Prize; Devins Award, National Endowment for the Arts, Poet-in-Residence, 1977; 1st Prize in Poetry, Yankee Magazine, 1994. Address: 1 Chicken Street, Mercer, ME 04957, USA.

MCNALLY Marcy Ada, b. 29 Dec 1951, Tucson, Arizona, USA. Writer; Artist. Education: University of Arizona, Tucson. Appointments: Advertising, Public Relations, BBDO, Botsford Ketchum and San Francisco Chronicle/Examiner. Publications include: The Aftermath; The Arrow; The Autumn of Winter Becoming; Chekhov Reverie; Dangling Conversation; Dark Horse and Spring of Renaissance Ashes; Desert Broom; The Divine Fire; Dreams and Dust; The Empress; For an Aging Friend; Glass Ceiling; Gossamer Thread; Foever Young; High Desert Dawn; Homeless; Letter to Charlie; Love's Betrayal; Love's Solace; Monica Like Moonflowers; Sensuality; Solitude Gently Chiding. Honours: 1st Place 1996 Poetry Award; 2nd Place, Mountain Muse Editor's Choice Award, 1996; 3rd Place 1995 North American Open Poetry Competition, Editor's Choice Award, 1995; Honorable Mention, Anderie Press Award, 1995; Editor's Choice Award, The Poetry Guild, 1996. Memberships: Arizona State Poetry Society; National Federation of Poetry Societies; International Society of Poets; Natinal Authors Registry; National Writers Union. Address: 5326 East 6th Street, Tucson, AZ 85711, USA.

MCNAMARA Robert James, b. 28 Mar 1950, New York, New York, USA. Teacher. 1 daughter. Education: BA, Amherst College, 1971; MA, Colorado State University, 1975; PhD, University of Washington, 1985. Appointments: Lecturer, University of Washington, 1985-. Publication: Second Messengers, 1990. Contributions to: Agni Review; Antioch Review; Field; The Gettysburg Review; Massachusetts Review; North West Review; Ohio Review; Poetry Northwest. Honours: National Endowement for the Arts; Creative Writing Fellowship; Kansas Quarterly Arts Commission Prize. Memberships: Academy of American Poets; Artist Trust; Associated Writing Programs. Address: Department of English, University of Washington, Seattle, WA 98105, USA.

MCNEIL Florence Anne, b. 8 May 1940, Vancouver, British Columbia, Canada. Writer. m. David McNeil, 3 Jan 1973. Education: BA, 1961, MA, 1965, University of British Columbia. Appointments: Instructor, Western Washington University, 1965-68; Professor University of Calgary, 1968-73; Professor, 1973-76, Visiting Lecturer, 1989-90, University of British Columbia. Publications: Miss P and Me; All Kinds of Magic; Catriona's Island; Breathing Each Other's Air; A Silent Green Sky; Walhachin; The Rim of the Park; Emily; Ghost Towns; A Balancing Act; The Overlanders; Barkerville; Swimming Out of History: Poems. Contributions to: Prism International; Canadian Forum; Cross Canada; Writers Quarterly; Quarry; Event. Honours: MacMillan Prize for Poetry; National Magazine Award for Poetry; Harpers Crest Selection; British Columbia Book Award Silver Medal. Memberships: Writers Union of Canada; League of Canadian Poets; Canadian Society for Childrens Authors, Illustrators and Performers; British Columbia Writers Federation. Address: 20 Georgia Wynd, Delta, British Columbia V4M 1AS, Canada.

MCNEILL Christine, b. 4 Apr 1953, Vienna, Austria. Language Tutor. Education: EFL Teaching Certificate, 1976; German Teaching Certificate, 1976; ESL Teaching Certificate, 1977. Appointment: Language Tutor. Publications: Selection of Works in New Women Poets; Kissing the Night, 1993. Contributions to: Observer; New Statesman and Society; New Welsh Review; Chapman; Quadrant (Australia); Cyphers (Ireland); Ambit; Stand; London Magazine; Poetry Durham; PN Review; Critical Quarterly; Jewish Quarterly; Poetry Wales; Oxford Poetry; Outposts; Verse; Honest Ulsterman; Writing Women; Rialto; North; Iron. Honour: Joint Winner of Second Richard Ellmann Award, 1993. Membership: National Poetry Society. Address: The Cabin, Church Street, Cromer, Norfolk NR27 9ES, England.

MCQUEEN (Pris)Cilla (Muriel), b. 22 Jan 1949, Birmingham, England. Poet; Teacher. m. Ralph Hotere, 1974, div 1986, 1 daughter. Education: MA (Hons), 1st class, Otago University, Dunedin, New Zealand, 1970. Publications: Homing In, 1982; Anti Gravity, 1984; Wild Sweets, 1986; Benzina, 1988; Berlin Diary, 1990. Contributions to: New Zealand: Landfall; Islands; Climate; Parallax; Moreport; Rambling Jack; Untold; Printout; Australia: Compass; Island, Tasmania; Canada: Poetry Canada Review; Ariel; England: Poetry New; Resurgence. Honours: New Zealand Book Award for Poetry, 1983, 1989, 1991; Robert Burns Fellowship, Otago University, 1985, 1986; Fulbright Visiting Writers Fellowship, 1985; Australia-New Zealand Exchange Writers Fellowship, 1987; Scholarship, Goethe Institute, Berlin, 1988. Memberships: PEN, Past National Council Member; Writer Member, Australasian Performing Rights Association. Address: 33 Skibo Street, Kew, Dunedin, New Zealand.

MEDD Stephen David, b. 9 July 1951, Hull, Humberside, England. Teacher. m. 12 Aug 1972, 2 daughters. Education BEd, 1972. Appointments: Head of English; Head of Mathematics; Key Stage 3 Co-ordinator; Head of Year 8. Contributions to: Outposts; Orbis. Membership: Poetry Society. Address: 10 Cragside View, Rothbury, Morpeth, Northumberland NE65 7YU, England.

MEDINA José Ramón, b. 20 July 1921, San Francisco de Macaira, Venezuela. Writer; Lawyer; Journalist. 1 son, 1 daughter. Education: PhD, Political and Social Sciences, Universidad Central de Venezuela, 1950; Graduate courses: Criminal Law, Italy; Criminology, Paris, France. Appointments: Secretary, Universidad Central de Venezuela, 1963-68; Senator, 1963-68; Judge, Vice-President of Judicial Council, Magistrate, Prosecutor-General of the Republic, 1974-79; Venezuelan Ambassador to Greece, 1984; Comptroller General, elected by Congress, 1985, re-elected, 1989. Publications: Edad de la esperanza, 1943-44; Les collines et le vent, 1959; Memorias y elegias, 1960; Poesia plural, 1969; Testigo de verano, 1969; Rumor sobre diciembre, 1979; Ser verdadero, 1982; Certezas y presagios, 1984. Honours: Prize, Academia de Letras Castellanos, Instituto Nacional de Chile, 1944; Culture Prize, Universidad Central de Venezuela, 1949; Municipal Prize for Poetry, Caracas, 1949; Boscan Prize, Instituto Cultura Hispanica, Barcelona, Spain, 1952; International Prize for Latin, Siena, Italy, 1957; National Prize for Literature (Poetry), Venezuela, 1959-60; International Bolivariano Prize, Caracas, 1963. Memberships: Academia Venezolana de la Lengua, Past Director; Academia de Letras Ruben Dario, Argentina; Corresponding Member, Real Academia; Legal Advisor, Asociacion de Periodista Venezolanos. Address: Fundacion Biblioteca Ayacucho, Apartado Postal 14.413 y 2.122, Caracas, Venezuela.

MEEK Jay, b. 23 Aug 1937, Grand Rapids, Michigan, USA. Professor. m. Martha George, 29 Aug 1966, 1 daughter. Education: University of Michigan, 1959; Syracuse University, 1965. Appointments: Wake Forest University, 1977-80; Sarah Lawrence College, 1980-82; Massachusetts Institute of Technology, 1982-83; Memphis State University, 1984; University of North Dakota, 1985-. Publications: The Week the Dirigible Came, 1976; Drawing on the Walls, 1980; Earthly Purposes, 1984; Stations, 1989; Windows, 1993. Contributions to: Field; Georgia Reiew; Iowa Review; Kansas Quarterly; Massachusetts Review; New York Quarterly; Ohio Review; Poetry; Poetry North-West; Salamagundi; Three Rivers Poetry Journal; Virginia Quarterly Review; Yale Review. Honours: National Endowment for the Arts, 1973; Guggenheim Fellowship, 1986; Bush Artist Fellowship, 1989. Address: English Department, Box 7209, University Station, University of North Dakota, Grand Forks, ND 58202, USA.

MEGAW (Robert) Neill Ellison, 7 Oct 1920, Ottawa, Ontario, Canada. English Professor. m. Ann Barber, 20 Dec 1947, 1 son, 2 daughters. Education: MA, 1946, PhD, 1950, University of Chicago. Appointments: Instructor to Professor, Williams College, 1950-69; Professor (English), University of Texas, 1969-85. Contributions to: US: Lyric; Plains Poetry Journal; Writer's Digest; Modern Haiku; Frogpond; Sequoia; Jewish Currents; Spectator; Hellas; Nimrod; South Coast Poetry Journal; Negative Capability; Cumberland Poetry Review; London: Outposts; Frome; Poetry Nippon; Nagoya; Mainichi Daily News, Tokyo. Honours: Commendation, National Poetry Competition Winners, 1989 (Chester H Jones Foundation); 1st Grand Prix, Pegasus (Kentucky State Poetry Society), 1989. Memberships: American Poetry Society; National Federation of State Poetry Societies; Poetry Society of Texas. Address: 2805 Bowman Avenue, Austin, TX 78703, USA.

MEHTA Usha Praveen, b. 17 Apr 1968, Kelam Bakkam, Tamil Nadu, India. Adult Education Promoter; Sportswoman; Writer; Poetess; Translator. m. Praveen Mehta, 10 Dec 1990, 1 daughter. Education: MA, University of Madras. Appointments: Poetess in India; Poems broadcasted on All India Radio; Honorary Editor, Kalptas, Hindi weekly, Beawar, Rajasthan; Convenor: National Awareness Campaign; Bharat Mat Todo Campaign; Hind Men Hindi Ka Nam Va Kam Campaign; Jat Pant Todo Campaign; Industrial Development Syllabus for Women Entrepreneurs; Training Course in Taxation for Women Entrepreneurs; Vanaspati Vigyan Men Hinsa-Virodh Campaign. Honour: Usha Praveen Mehta's Contribution to the Modern Hindi Poem. Address: c/o Warsha Enterprises, Main Road, PO Wani 445304, Yavatmal District, Maharastra, India.

MEHTA Vikram. See: **ANZRANNII Avikam Axim.**

MEIER Herbert, b. 29 Aug 1928, Solothurn, Switzerland. Writer; Playwright; Translator. m. Yvonne Haas, 23 Sept 1954, 2 sons, 1 daughter. Appointments: Chefdramaturg, Schauspielhaus, Zürich, 1977-82: Writer-in-Residence, University of Southern California at Los Angeles, 1986. Publications: Gedichte und Märchen; Siebengestirn; Dem Unbekannten Gott; Elf Strassengesange; Sequenzen; Gli Spaziali; Vier Gedichte; Drei Gedichte. Contributions to: Literatur und Kunst. Memberships: Schweiz Schriftstellerverband; PEN. Address: Appenzeller Strasse 73, CH 8049 Zürich, Switzerland.

MEINKE Peter, b. 29 Dec 1932, Brooklyn, New York, USA. Writer; Professor. m. Jeanne Clark, 14 Dec 1957, 2 sons, 2 daughters. Education: AB, Hamilton College, New York, 1955; MA, University of Michigan, 1961; PhD, University of Minnesota, 1965. Appointments: English Teacher, Mt Lakes High School, New Jersey, 1958-60; Assistant Professor of English, Hamline University, St Paul, Minnesota, 1961-66; Professor of Literature and Director of the Writing Workshop, Eckerd College, St Petersburg, 1966-93; Visiting Distinguished Writer, University of Hawaii, 1993; Writer-in-Residence, Austin State University, 1995; Distinguished Visiting Writer, University of North Carolina, Greensboro, 1996. Publications: Lines from Neuchâtel, 1974; The Night Train and the Golden Bird, 1977; The Rat Poems, 1978; Trying to Surprise God, 1981; Underneath the Lantern, 1986; The Piano Tuner, 1986; Night Watch on the Chesapeake, 1987; Far From Home, 1988; Liquid Paper: New and Selected Poems, 1991; Scars, 1996; Campocorto, 1996. Contributions to: New Republic; New Yorker; Grand Street; Poetry (Chicago); Spectator (London); Virginia Quarterly Review; The Georgia Review; Yankee; Amicus; Michigan Review; and others. Honours: Olivet Sonnet Competition, First Prize, 1966; National Endowment for the Arts Creative Writing Fellowship, 1974; Gustav Davidson Memorial Award (Poetry Society of America), 1976; Writers Digest First Place Award, 1976; Lucille Medwick Memorial Award (Poetry Society of America), 1984; Flannery O'Connor Award, 1986; National Endowment for the Arts Creative Writing Fellowship, 1989; Robert A Staub Distinguished Teacher Award, 1990; Emily Dickinson Award (Poetry Society of America), 1992; Paumano Poetry Award, 1993; Master Artist's Fellowship, Fine Arts Work Center, Provincetown, 1995. Memberships: Poetry Society of America; PEN; National Book Critics Circle; Academy of American Poets. Address: 147 Wildwood Lane South East, St Petersburg, FL 33705-3222, USA.

MELETUSA. See: **ARGOW Sylvia.**

MELITAS Roula. See: **POLLARD Roula.**

MELLON Hilary Anne, b. 7 Nov 1949, Norwich, Norfolk, England. Creative Writing Tutor. m. David Buck, 1 daughter. Education: Currently Studying for Open University Degree. Appointments: Laboratory Assistant, 1965-69; Assistant Scientific Officer, 1969-88; Freelance Writer, 1988-90; Tutor, 1989. Publications: Spaces in Between; Fire Raiser; Disturbing the Night. Contributions to: Encounter; Outposts; Prospice; Rialto; Orbis; Bête Noir; Sol; Acumen; Literary Review; Smiths Knoll; Giant Steps; Grand Piano; Ostinato; Spokes; Contra Flow; Ore; Propositions; Next Exit; Cobweb; Odyssey; Haiku Quarterly; Weyfarers; Pennine Platform; Poetry Nottingham. Honours: FAIM Poetry Competition Winner. Memberships: Open University Poets; The Poetry Society. Address: 45 Carshalton Road, Norwich, Norfolk NR1 3BB, England.

MELLOR Robin Frederick, b. 16 Nov 1944, South Wales. Poet; Children's Writer. m. Frances Anne Mellor, 13 June 1988, 2 sons, 1 stepson, 1 stepdaughter. Education: BEd, London University, 1975.

Appointments: Teacher, 1967-80; Head Teacher, 1980-91. Publications: Much anthologised in works for children; Tree Roots and Evening Ice; Wild Monkey and Other Poems for Children; Don't Pull Up Your Trouser Legs Before You See the Sea. Contributions to: Infant Education; Junior Education; Poetry Wales. Memberships: Poetry Society; Society of Authors. Address: 51 Bush Road, Cuxton, Rochester, Kent ME2 1LS, England.

MELNYCZCK Askold. See: **ASKOLD Markian Melnyczck.**

MELTZER David, b. 17 Feb 1937, Rochester, New York, USA. Poet; Writer; Teacher; Editor; Musician. m. Christina Meyer, 1958, 1 son, 3 daughters. Education: Los Angeles City College, 1955-56; University of California at Los Angeles, 1956-57. Appointments: Editor, Maya, 1966-71, Tree magazine and Tree Books, 1970-; Faculty, Graduate Poetics Program, 1980-, Chair, Undergraduate Writing and Literature Program, Humanities, 1988-, New College of California, San Francisco. Publications: Poetry: Poems (with Donald Schenker), 1957; Ragas, 1959; The Clown, 1960; Station, 1964; The Blackest Rose, 1964; Oyez!, 1965; The Process, 1965; In Hope I Offer a Fire Wheel, 1965; The Dark Continent, 1967; Nature Poem, 1967; Santamaya (with Jack Shoemaker), 1968; Round the Poem Box: Rustic and Domestic Home Movies for Stan and Jane Brakhage, 1969; Yesod, 1969; From Eden Book, 1969; Abulafia Song, 1969; Greenspeech, 1970; Luna, 1970; Letters and Numbers, 1970; Bronx Lil/Head of Lillin S A C, 1970; 32 Beams of Light, 1970; Knots, 1971; Bark: A Polemic, 1973; Hero/Lil, 1973; Tens: Selected Poems 1961-1971, 1973; The Eyes, The Blood, 1973; French Broom, 1973; Blue Rags, 1974; Harps, 1975; Six, 1976; Bolero, 1976; The Art, The Veil, 1981; The Name: Selected Poetry 1973-1983, 1984; Arrows: Selected Poetry 1957-1992, 1994; Novels include: Out, 1994; Other includes: Two-Way Mirror: A Poetry Note-Book, 1977; As Editor, includes: Reading Jazz; The White Invention of Jazz, 1993; Writing Jazz, 1997. Honours: Council of Literary Magazine Grants, 1972, 1981; National Endowment for the Arts Grants, 1974, 1975; Tombstone Award for Poetry, James Ryan Morris Memorial Foundation, 1992. Address: Box 9005, Berkeley, CA 94709, USA.

MEMMOTT David Robert, b. 10 Dec 1948, Grand Rapids, Michigan, USA. Office Specialist; Publisher; Computer Typesetter; Desktop Publisher. m. Susan A Hoyt, 14 Sept 1974, 1 daughter. Education: BA, English, Eastern Oregon State College, La Grande, 1977; Workshops and Symposia in Letterpress Printing, Book Design, Editing, Proofreading, Communication Skills. Appointments: Editor, Oregon East, Eastern Oregon State College, 1976; Board of Directors, Blue Mountain Designers and Craftsmen, 1978-83; Board of Directors, Grande Ronde Resource Council, 1982-83; Director, This Land Is Your Land, 3-week Public Education Program on land use planning; Grant Guidelines Committee, Eastern Oregon Regional Arts Council; Editor, Publisher, Ice River: A Journal of Speculative Writing, 1986-90. Publication: House on Fire, 1992. Contributions to: Fourth Annual Year's Best Fantasy and Horror; Nebula 27; Alpha Gallery; Co-Lingua; Oregon East; In the West of Ireland; Rampike, Canada; Works, England; Magazine of Speculative Poetry; Quarterly West; Callapooya Collage; Live Poets; Poets of the Fantastic; Portland Review; Willow Springs; Crab Creek Review; North Colorado Review; North Coast Poetry Review; Gypsy; Intro 8, 9; Dreams and Nightmares; Urbanus; Ellipsis. Honours: Award, Atlantic College Poetry Contest, 1976; Selected for Travelling Poetry Gallery, Oregon Arts Commission, 1980; 2nd Place, Oregon State Poetry Association Poetry Day Competition, 1986; Fishtrap Fellow, Writers Conference, 1990; Rhysling Award for Best Science Fiction, Fantasy or Science Long Poem of the Year, 1991. Memberships: Science Fiction Poetry Association; Small Press Writers and Artists Organization. Address: 1003 Y Ave, La Grande, OR 97850, USA.

MENASHE Samuel, b. 16 Sept 1925, New York, New York, USA. Poet. Education: BA, Queen's College, Flushing, New York, 1947; Doctoral d'Université, Sorbonne, Paris, 1950. Appointments: Bard College, Annandale-on-Hudson; CW Post College, Greenvale, New York. Publications: The Many Named Beloved, 1961; No Jerusalem But This, 1971; Fringe of Fire, 1973; To Open, 1973; Collected Poems; Penguin Modern Poets, Vol 7, 1996. Contributions to: Times Literary Supplement; Poetry Nation Review; Temendos; New York Review of Books; New Yorker; Yale Review; Antioch Review; Poetry Durham; and others. Honour: The Longview Foundation Award, 1957. Address: 75 Thompson Street, Apt 15, New York, NY 10012, USA.

MENEBROKER Ann Reynolds (Ann R Bauman), b. 30 Mar 1936, Washington, District of Columbia, USA. Art Gallery Assistant. m. (1) Jerrol P Bauman, 25 Oct 1952, (2) Wayne L Menebroker, 23 May 1964, 1 son, 2 daughters. Appointments: Variety of working positions. Publications: It Isn't Everything; Slices; Three Drums for the Lady; If You are Creative I Will Vanish; The Habit of Wishing; Love, Drunks, Error and Myth; Going Nowhere; The Blue Fish; Dark Pleasure; Biting Through the Spine; On the Edge; Mailbox Boogie; Routines That Will Kill You; If I Had My Life To Live Over I Would Pick More Daisies, anthology, 1992; Dream Catcher, 1992; I Am Becoming the Woman I Wanted, anthology, 1994. Contributions to: San Francisco Chronicle; Kansas Quarterly; Carlton Miscellany. Membership: Sacramento Poetry Center. Address: 2738 4th Avenue, Sacramento, CA 95818, USA.

MENTZER G(eorge Speraw) (George Schiller Mentzer), b. 10 Feb 1923, Annville, Pennsylvania, USA. Retail Food Salesman. m. Catherine Jane Shay, 10 Dec 1943, 2 sons, 1 daughter. Education: Diploma, International School, 1950; Diploma, Air University, 1958; ThB, International Seminary, 1990. Appointments: Store Salesman; Union Steward; Night Foreman. Contributions to: Lebanon Daily News; Poets Digest; National Arts Today; Poems of Great America. Honours: Golden Poet Award, 1985; Silver Poet Award, 1989; Honourable Mention, 1990. Memberships: American Poetry Association; Great Lakes Poetry Association; National Arts Society; World of Poetry Association. Address: 616 Renova Avenue, Lebanon, PA 17042, USA.

MENZIES Rosemary Laura, b. 8 Mar 1939, Auckland, New Zealand. Teacher; Writer. m. Robert Gordon Menzies, 8 May 1967, 2 daughters. Education: Diploma of Physical Education, Otago University, 1958; Diploma of Teaching, New Zealand, 1964; Diploma of English Language Teaching, Auckland University, 1989. Appointments: Specialist Teacher, Physical Education, Dance, Science, Takapuna Grammar School, 1959-60; Lecturer in Physical Education, Dance, Health, Ardmore Teachers' College, 1960-62; Teacher, London, England and Edinburgh, Scotland, 1963-64; Teacher, Birkdale Intermediate School, 1965-69; Home Tutor for Refugee Family, 1983-; Contributor, Coordinator, Weekly Live Poetry Scene, Auckland, 1983-; Tutor, English Language, Auckland Language Schools and Carrington Polytechnic, 1994-; Joined International Peace Journey to Sarajevo and Mostar, 1995-96; Voluntary work in Croatia and Bosnia; Active Member of Peace Movement in New Zealand. Publications: I Asked The Moon, 1981; Whitewave and Undertow, 1986; To Where The Bare Earth Waits, 1988; Poems For Bosnia, 2 editions, English and Bilingual, 1995; The Globe Tapes: 2 books and 2 cassettes of 42 New Zealand poets reading their own work (producer, co-editor), 1985. Contributions to: Outrigger; Echoes; Printout; Poetry New Zealand; Kiwi; Emu; Many Poetry Readings. Honours: Public Speaking Cup, Auckland City Council, 1985. Memberships: PEN New Zealand; Writers-in-Schools. Address: 21 Wernham Place, Birkenhead, Auckland 10, New Zealand.

MENZIES Trixie (Te Arama) Thelma, b. 16 Aug 1936, Wellington, New Zealand. m. (1) William Stewart, 31 Jan 1958, (2) Barry Charles Menzies, 14 May 1979, 1 son, 2 daughters. Education: BA, Auckland University College. 1957; MA (Hons), Auckland University, 1979. Appointments: Assistant, Otahuhu College, Auckland; Tutor, University of Auckland. Publications: Uenuku, 1986; Papakainga, 1988; Rerenga, 1992. Contributions to: Landfall; Journal of New Zealand Literature; Printout Magazine, Auckland; Poetry New Zealand; Sunday Star-Times. Anthologised in The Penguin Book of Contemporary New Zealand Poetry, 1989; The Te Ao Marama Series of Maori Writing (Reed), nos 2 1993, and 4 1994; Between The Lines (Longman Paul 1994); Dangerous Landscapes (Longman Paul 1994). Honours: Co-Winner, PEN Award for Best First Book, Poetry, 1987, Uenuku; Finalist in New Zealand Book Awards, 1993, Poetry for Rerenga. Memberships: Nga Puna Waihanga (New Zealand Maori Writers and Artists Society); New Zealand Society of Authors; Waiata Koa (Maori Women Writers and Artists Collective); Te Ha (Maori Writers Group). Address: PO Box 87-082 Meadowbank, Auckland, New Zealand.

MEO Franca, b. 16 Dec 1939, Treviso, Italy. Writer. m. Piero Giacomini, 21 July 1961, 2 sons, 1 daughter. Education: Graduated, Foreign Languages and Literature. Appointment: Teacher of Art, Mogadiscio, Italy. Publications: Penso a un'ora più tenue, 1960; Ariête trevisane, 1961; Ci troviamo umili, 1966; Sapere d'essere vivi, 1972; Il sole negli occhi (illustrated by Gisella and Carmen Meo), 1978; Doni d'amore, 1979, 2nd edition, 1990; Questa vita questo amore (illustrated

by Nino Baldessari), 1982; Amore e disamore (illustrated by Enrico Muscetra), 1986; Come abbiamo potuto dimenticare il paradiso? (Spanish translation by Edda Piaggio), 1989; Storie di oggetti e di donne, 1990; Anthologies: Fermarsi un po'/Einen Augenblick innehalten (translated by Rolf Mäder), 1984; Poemas, 1987; Un coeur palpitant dans l'espace (translated by Jeanne Heaulmé), 1991; A Heart Beating in Space (translated by Alison Butcher), 1997; Has also published literary criticism and translations. Address: Via Gian Maria Mazzucchelli 2, 25080 Ciliverghe (BS), Italy.

MEREDITH Jennifer Margaret (Jenni), (Tonos), b. 8 Oct 1949, Middlesex, England. Freelance Journalist; Cartoonist; Arts Administrator; Animator. m. Tony Meredith, 10 Apr 1970, 1 son. Education: Diploma Course in Fine Art, Hammersmith-Chelsea Art College. Appointments: Founder, Snowball Press, 1991; Editorial Assistant Disability Arts Magazine, 1992-93; Director, SnowTracks Productions, 1995-. Publications: Snow Ewes Crowing Over Spilt Snails, 1991. Anthologies include: 4 Poems in The Bees Sneeze Anthology, 1992; Mustn't Grumble, 1994; Under the Asylum Tree, 1995; Flying Lambourghinis and Marshmallow Fish, Ed, 1991. Creative works: Wrote and Directed video of animated concrete poetry, Through The Pane, for the Arts Council of England, 1995. Contributions to: Disability Arts Magazine; Iron; Bare Bones; BBC Radio Three; Celebration Radio. Memberships: Poetry Society; Federation of Worker Writers and Community Publishers; Founder, Write to Belong, National Postal Forum of Disabled Writers, 1992. Address: 4 Argyll Street, Ryde, Isle of Wight PO33 3BZ, England.

MEREDITH Joseph Edward, b. 6 Jan 1948, Philadelphia, Pennsylvania, USA. Teacher. m. Jeanne M Koenig, 5 Aug 1972, 1 son, 1 daughter. Education: BA, La Salle University, 1970; MA, University of Florida, 1974. Appointments: Lecturer, English, 1974-90; Director, Writing Center, 1979-90; Poet-in-Residence, La Salle University, Philadelphia, Pennsylvania, 1988-90; President, Meredith Associates, Corporate Writing Consultants, 1990-; Adjunct Professor, Camden County College, Blackwood, New Jersey, 1991-. Publication: Hunter's Moon, 1993. Contributions to: American Scholar; Threepenny Review; Southwest Review; Four Quarters, Philadelphia; Kansas Quarterly; Florida Quarterly; Painted Bride Quarterly, Philadelphia. Honours: Mary Elinor Smith Prize, 1984; Hart Crane Award, 1986; Corcoran Prize, 1990, 1991, 1992. Address: 4625 Oakland Street, Philadelphia, PA 19124, USA.

MEREDITH William (Morris), b. 9 Jan 1919, New York, New York, USA. Poet; Professor. Education: AB, Princeton University, 1940. Appointments: Instructor in English and Woodrow Wilson Fellow in Writing, Princeton University, 1946-50; Associate Professor in English, University of Hawaii, 1950-51; Associate Professor 1955-65, Professor in English 1965-83, Connecticut College, New London; Instructor, Breadloaf School of English, Middlebury College, Vermont, 1958-62; Consultant in Poetry, Library of Congress, Washington DC, 1978-80. Publications include: Poetry: Love Letter from an Impossible Land, 1944; Ships and Other Figures, 1948; The Open Sea and Other Poems, 1958; The Wreck of the Thresher and Other Poems, 1964; Winter Verse, 1964; Year End Accounts, 1965; Two Pages From A Colorado Journal, 1967; Earth Walk: New and Selected Poems, 1970; Hazard, the Painter, 1975; The Cheer, 1980; Partial Accounts: New and Selected Poems, 1987; Poems Are Hard to Read, 1991. Editor: Shelley: Poems, 1962; University & College Poetry Prizes 1960-1966, 1966; Eighteenth-Century Minor Poets (with Mackie L Jarrell), 1968; Poets of Bulgaria (with others), 1985. Translator: Guillaume Apollinaire: Alcools: Poems 1898-1913, 1964. Honours include: Yale Series of Younger Poets Award, 1943; Van Wyck Brooks Award, 1971; International Vaptsarov Prize for Literature, Bulgaria, 1979; Los Angeles Times Prize, 1987; Pulitzer Prize in Poetry, 1988. Memberships: Academy of American Poets, chancellor; National Institute of Arts & Letters. Address: 6300 Bradley Avenue, Bethesda, MD 20817, USA.

MERRICK Beverly Georgianne Childers, b. 20 Nov 1944, Troy, Kansas, USA. Professor; Poet; Writer; Journalist. m. John Douglas Childers, 10 July 1963, 1 son, 2 daughters. Education: Double BA, 1980, Masters in Journalism, 1982, Marshall University, Huntington; Masters in Creative Writing 1986, Ohio University, Athens; Women's Studies Certificate, 1984; Doctor of Philosophy in Mass Communications, Tau Kappa Alpha, 1989. Appointments: Graduate Assistant, Dean of Student Life Office, Marshall University, 1980; Reporter, Ashland Daily Independent, 1981; Instructor and Associate Teacher, Ohio Unversity, 1981-84; Reporter, Rio Rancho Observer,

1986; Team Teacher, Albuquerque Public Schools, 1987-89; Assistant Professor in Communication, East Carolina University, North Carolina, 1990; Adjunct Faculty, Embry Riddle University, Kortland Air Force Base, Albuquerque, 1991-. Publications: Navigating the Platte, 1986; Grasshoppers on the Platte, 1989; Killing Day, 1990; Outracing the Train, 1990; Hanh Viet Nguyen, The Boat Baby, 1990; Cool Travelor News, 1991; 2 Poems in Riverrun, 1991; I Walk in Cornrow Rhythm, 1991; Why I Am Wanting to Solve Every Echo, anthology, 1991; Storm on the Inland Sea, 19B91. Contributions to: Periodicals. Honours: Jesse Stuart Writing Award, 1979; Winner of Past Presidents Award, National Federation of State Poetry Societies, 1987. Membership: President, New Mexico State Poetry Society 1987-89. Address: c/o 3716 Simms North East, Albuquerque, NM 87102, USA.

MERRILL Christopher (Lyall), b. 24 Feb 1957, Northampton, Massachusetts, USA. Poet; Writer; Editor; Teacher. m. Lisa Ellen Gowdy, 4 June 1983, 1 daughter. Education: BA, Middlebury College, Vermont, 1979; MA, University of Washington, 1982. Appointments: Director, Sata Fe Writer's Conference, 1987-90; Founder-Director, Taos Conference on Writing and the Natural World, 1987-92, Santa Fe Literary Center, 1988-92; General Editor, Peregrine Smith Poetry Series, 1987-; Adjunct Professor, Santa Fe Community College, 1988-90; Contributing Editor, Tyuonyi, 1989-, The Paris Review, 1991-; Adjunct Faculty, Lewis and Clark College, 1993-95; Poetry Editor, Orion Magazine, 1993-; Faculty, Open Society Institute/University of Sarajevo, 1995; William H Jenks Chair in Contemporary Letters, College of the Holy Cross, 1995-. Publications: Workbook (poems), 1988; Fevers & Tides (poems), 1989; The Forgotten Language: Contemporary Poets and Nature (editor), 1991; From The Faraway Nearby: Geoargia O'Keefe as Icon (with Ellen Bradbury), 1992; The Grass of Another Country: A Journey Through the World of Soccer, 1993; Watch Fire (poems), 1994; The Old Bridge: The Third Balkan War and the Age of the Refugee, 1995; What Will Suffice: Contemporary American Poets on the Art of Poetry (editor with Christopher Buckley), 1995; Only The Nails Remain: A Balkan Triptych, 1998; The Cauldron: Fifty American Poets (editor with Catherine Bowman), 1998. Contributions to: Books, journals, and periodicals. Honours: John Ciardi Fellow in Poetry, Bread Loaf Writers' Conference, 1989; Pushcart Prize in Poetry, 1990; Ingram Merrill Foundation Award in Poetry, 1191; Peter I B Lavan Younger Poets Award, Academy of American Poets, 1993. Membership: Academy of American Poets. Address: 12 Woodstock Road, Pomfret, CT 06258, USA.

MERRY Rosemary Elisabeth, b. 22 Feb 1925, Soham, Cambridgeshire, England. Retired Social Worker. m. Ian W Merry, 22 Nov 1947, 1 daughter. Education: Nottingham University then University College; Diploma, Social Studies, 1944. Appointments: WRNS, 1944-47; Editorial Assistant, 1947-50; Administration: Institute of Management and Institute of Personnel Management, 1950-56; Hospital Social Worker, 1968-78; Senior Social Worker, Diocese of Winchester, 1978-83. Publication: A Crack in a Wall, (Envoi Poets Publications), 1993. Contributions to: Writing Magazine; New Statesman; Envoi; Weyfarers; Doors Poetry Now; Several anthologies. Honours include: Open Poetry Competitions, 1990; Wilfred Owen Association Poetry Competition, 1992. Memberships: Society of Women Writers & Journalists, 1991-93; Suffolk Poetry Society; Suffolk Book League. Address: Farmgate Cottage, Wicks Lane, Earl Stoneham, Suffolk IP45 5HL, England.

MERWIN W(illiam) S(tanley), b. 30 Sept 1927, New York, New York, USA. Poet; Dramatist; Writer; Translator. m. Diana Whalley, 1954. Education: AB, Princeton University, 1947. Appointments: Playwright-in-Residence, Poet's Theatre, Cambridge, Massachusetts, 1956-57; Poetry Editor, The Nation, 1962; Associate, Théâtre de la Cité,Lyons, 1964-65. Publications: Poetry: A Mask for Janus, 1952; The Dancing Bears, 1954; Green with Beasts, 1956; The Drunk in the Furnace, 1960; The Moving Target, 1963; The Lice, 1967; Three Poems, 1968; Animae, 1969; The Carrier of Ladders, 1970; Signs, 1971; Writings to an Unfinished Accompaniment, 1973; The First Four Books of Poems, 1975; Three Poems, 1975; The Compass Flower, 1977; Feathers from the Hill, 1978; Finding the Islands, 1982; Opening the Hand, 1983; The Rain in the Trees, 1988; Selected Poems, 1988; Travels, 1993; Plays: Darkling Child (with Dido Milroy), 1956; Favor Island, 1957; The Gilded West, 1961; Adaptations of 5 other plays; Other includes: The Lost Upland, 1993; Editor: West Wind: Supplement of American Poetry, 1961; The Essential Wyatt, 1989; Translator: 19 books, 1959-89. Honours: Yale Series of Younger Poets Award, 1952; Bess Hokin Prize, 1962; Ford Foundation Grant, 1964;

Harriet Monroe Memorial Prize, 1967; PEN Translation Prize, 1969; Rockefeller Foundation Grant, 1969; Pulitzer Prize in Poetry, 1971; Academy of American Poets Fellowship, 1973; Shelley Memorial Award, 1974; National Endowment for the Arts Grant, 1978; Bollingen Prize, 1979; Aiken Taylor Award, 1990; Maurice English Award, 1990; Dorothea Tanning Prize, 1994; Lenore Marshall Award, 1994. Memberships: Academy of American Poets; American Academy of Arts and Letters. Address: c/o Georges Borchardt Inc, 136 East 57th Street, New York, NY 10022, USA.

MESSERLI Douglas John, b. 30 May 1947, Waterloo, Iowa, USA. Publisher; Poet; Fiction Writer. Education: BA, University of Wisconsin; MAS, 1974, PhD, 1979, University of Maryland. Appointments: Publisher, Sun and Moon Press, Los Angeles, California, 1976-; Assistant Professor of Literature, Temple University, 1979-85; Director, Contemporary Arts Educational Project Inc, 1982-. Publications: Djuna Barnes: A Bibliography, 1976; Dinner on the Lawn, 1979; Some Distance, 1982; River to River: A Poetic Manifesto, 1984; Maxims from My Mother's Milk-Hymns to Him: A Dialogue, 1988; Silence All Round Marked: An Historical Play in Hysteria Writ, 1992; Along Without: A Fiction in Film for Poetry, 1993; An Apple a Day, 1993; The Walls Come True: An Opera for Spoken Voices, 1993; Editor: Contemporary American Fiction, 1983; Language, Poetries, 1987. Contributions to: Roof; Mississippi Review; Paris Review; Boundary 2; Art Quarterly; Los Angeles Times. Membership: Modern Language Association. Address: Sun and Moon Press, 6026 Wilshire Boulevard, Los Angeles, CA 90036, USA.

MESTAS Jean Paul, b. 15 Nov 1925, Paris, France. Engineer; Poet; Critic; Essayist; Lecturer; Translator; Consultant. m. Christiane Schoubrenner, 23 Dec 1977, 2 sons, 1 daughter. Education: BA, 1947, LLB,1947, Institute of Political Studies, Paris. Appointment: Engineer, 1947-85. Publications: Traduire La Mémoire, 1975; Pays Nuptial, 1977; Mémoire D'Exil, 1978; Cette Idée Qui Ne Vivra Pas, 1979; Des Mouettes aux Portes du Silence, 1980; Au Fond des Choses, 1981; En Ce Royaume D'Ombre et D'Eau, 1982; Entre Deux Temps, 1983; En Ecoutant Vieillir Les Lampes, 1983; Ismène, 1984; Anamesa de Dyokapoye, 1984; Entre Les Colonnes Du Vent, 1984; Chambourg a Deux Voix, 1985; Dans La Longue Automne du Coeur, 1985; Poemas, 1985; Avec L'Eau de Ce Fleuve, 1986; L'Ancre et le Cyclone, 1987; Pluies de Juillet, 1988; La Terre Est Pleine de Haillons, 1988; Entre Les Violons du Silence, 1988; Tulipa Malva, 1988; Le Ciel Bougeait A Peine, 1989; Chant Pour Chris, 1989; La Lumière Arriva Des Mains, 1990; Among the Silent Violins, 1990; Cantico Para Chris, 1990; A Luz Chegara Das Maos, 1990; Roses de Sable, 1990; Rosas de Areia, 1991; Aliénor, 1992. Contributions to: Journal Des Poètes; Letras; Front Littéraire; L'Union; El Tiempo; Ariane; Bull Britique Du Livre Frs; Création; Figaro Magazine; La Montagne; Nelles Littéraires; Ouest-France; Voix du Nord; Dialog. Honours: Excellence in Poetry, International Poetry, New York, 1982; Premio de la Cultura, Palermo, 1991; Priz Marcel Beguey, Bergerac, 1992. Memberships: Fellow, International Academy, Madras, India; Board of Research Advisors, International Wrtiers and Artists, New York; Vice President, International Poetry, Cheong-Ju, Korea. Address: B401, 43 Quai Magellan, 44000-Nantes, France.

MEYER Lynn. See: SLAVITT David R(ytman).

MEYER Margaret (Maggi) H, b. 1 Feb 1916, Fargo, North Dakota, USA. Interior Decorator; Secretary; Technical Assistant. m. William C Meyer, 27 May 1938, div 1947, 1 son. Education: University of California at Los Angeles. Appointments: Legal Secretary; Interior Decorator; Technical Assistant, ICC; Editor, Bay Area Poets Coalition's POETALK, 1979-90. Publications: Mix With Love, 1977; Body and Soul, 1978; More, 1979; And More, 1980; It Came With Me, 1981; Sign of No Time, 1982; How Is It, 1983; Changing, 1984; Maggi, 3 Faces of Poetry, 1988; In Thrall, 1992; Et Cetera, 1995. Contributions to: 16 anthologies; Ally; Nail Down My Corner; Poets at Work; Minotaur; Milvia Street; California State Poetry Quarterly; Napa Review; 5 Alameda Poets anthologies; 5 Coolbrith anthologies; Poet; Metaphor Beyond Time, anthology. Honours: Many. Memberships: Bay Area Poets Coalition; Ina Coolbrith, Renegades and Alameda Poets. Address: 1527 Virginia Street, Berkeley, CA 94703, USA.

MEZEY Robert, b. 28 Feb 1935, Philadelphia, Pennsylvania, USA. Poet-in-Residence; Professor of English. m. Olivia Simpson, 14 July 1963, 1 son, 2 daughters. Education: Kenyon College, 1951-53; BA, University of Iowa, 1959; Graduate Study, University of Iowa and Stanford University, 1960-62. Appointments: Instructor or Lecturer,

Fresno State, Memphis State; Assistant Professor, Western Reserve University Professor, Franklin and Marshall College; Assistant Professor, Fresno StateUniversity; Associate Professor, University of Utah; Full Professor, Pomona College, 1976-. Publications: The Lovemaker, 1961; White Blossoms, 1965; A Book of Dying, 1970; The Door Standing Open: New and Selected Poems, 1970; Couplets, 1976; Small Song, 1978; Selected Translations, 1982; Evening Wind, 1987; Edited: Naked Poetry, 1968; New Naked Poetry, 1975; Poems from the Hebrew, 1969; Translated Tungsten by Cesar Vallejo, 1988. Contributions to: Poetry; New Yorker; Partisan Review; Kenyon Review; Raritan; Harper's; Paris Review; Hudson Review; Botteghe Oscura; Los Angeles Times; Antaeus. Honours include: Robert Frost Prize, 1952; Stegner Writing Fellowship, 1960; Lamont Selection of The Lovemaker, 1960; Ingram Merrill Fellowship, 1973; Guggenheim Fellowship, 1977; Poetry Award from National Institute and Academy of Arts and Letters, 1982; National Endowment for the Arts Fellowship, 1986; Ingram Merrill Fellowship, 1989. Address: Pomona College, Claremount, CA 91711, USA.

MICHAEL Christine, (Angela O'Brien), b. 3 Mar 1944, Nottingham, England. Performer; Writer; Publisher. 1 son, 1 daughter. Education: Bishop Grosseteste College, 1963-66; Open University, 1974-81; University College Cork, 1983-86. Appointments: Former Head of Religious Studies, Margaret Guen Bott School; Head of Religious Studies, Glaisdale Comprehensive School; Organiser, Community Expansions Literature; Known as Nottingham's Singing Poet. Publications: I Called the People Love; The Box Under the Bed; Who Made the Rainbow?; Somewhere There's Heaven; That's For Cats. Contributions to: Poetry Now; Cyphers; Envoi; Orbis; Poetry Digest; First Time; Outposts; Iota; Writers Review; Oxford Poetry; Third Half; Little Bears; Pen to Paper. Some songs, poems and stories translated and published in Germany. Honours: Mary Wilkins Competition; Years Club Poetry Competition; Muscular Dystrophy Competition; Charnwood Competition; Lake Aske Memorial Award. Memberships: International Songwriters Guild; International Songwriters Association; Performing Rights Society. Address: 54 Kingswood Road, West Bridgford, Nottingham NG2 7HS, England.

MICHALSKA-TUSZ Danuta (Dana), b. 3 Aug 1933, Lublin, Poland. Artist. m. Felix Tuszynski, 3 Aug 1989, 2 sons. Education: MD, Academy of Fine Arts, Warsaw, Poland; Postgraduate Diploma of Advertising, Warsaw, Poland; High School of Art, Warsaw, Poland. Appointments: Artists Agency Cplia, Poland, 1952-55; Self Employed, China and Glass Painting, Warsaw, Poland, 1955-66; Advertising Consultant, Polish Airlines, 1966-71; Advertising Consultant, FSO Car Industries, 1971-75; Fashion Designer, Warsaw, Poland, 1975-81; Self Employed Artist: Portrait, Oil, Tempera in Folk Style, Gouache, Unique and Very Original Style; 15 Solo Exhibitions in Poland, Europe and Australia; Over 60 Group Exhibitions. Publications: Max Germaine - Women Artists of Australia; Dictionary of Polish Artists, Warsaw, 1972; Alice in Wonderland 125 Catalogue; Publicity in Artists Newsletters and Press. Contributions to: Public and Private Collections: Miami, Florida, USA; Azoty, Pulawy, Poland; Polish National Gallery; Carrol Foundation, Melbourne; Mornington Peninsula Art Centre, Victoria, Australia; Sweden; Israel; Hungary; Libya; Russia; Switzerland; France; Iraq; Belgium. Honours: Artists Grant, Ministry of Culture, France, 1966; Artists Grant, Ministry of Culture, Poland, 1966; Honourary Award, Victoria Artists Society, S M Melbourne for Contribution and Services to the Arts; High Commended, Spring Exhibition, Victoria Artists Society, Melbourne, 1994; High Commended, Winter Exhibition, Victoria Artists Society, Melbourne, 1992; First Place, Contemporary Art Society, Victoria, 1989. Memberships: Polish Artists Society; Victoria Artists Society; Contemporary Artists Society; Five Plus Group, Melbourne, Australia. Address: 1/438 Hawthorn Road, South Caulfield, 3162 Victoria, Australia.

MICU Liliana Maria, (Liliana Ursu), b. 11 July 1949, Sibiu, Romania. Radio Producer; Poet. m. Dan Micu, 14 Oct 1979, 1 son. Education: BA, Faculty of English, University of Bucharest, 1972. Appointment: Producer, Weekly Cultural Programme, Book Reviewing, Interviews, Poetry Translations, 1st Channel, Romanian National Radio. Publications: Viata deasupra orasului, 1977; Ordinea Clipelor, 1978; Piata aurarioir, 1980; Zona de Protectie, 1983; Corali, 1986; Port Angeles, 1992; Wingless Victory: Poems from America, 1993. Contributions to: Luceafarul; Romania Literara; Transilvania; Steaua; Euphorion; Atheneum; Cronica; Viata Romaneasca; Convorbiri Literare; Secolul XX; Mihai Eminescu; Glasul Natiunii; Viata Noua; Contemporanul; Poetry Wales; Honest Ulsterman; The Applegarth

Review; Oxford Poetry; European Poetry Review II; Tribune; American Poetry Review; New Yorker; Ohio Review; Gettysburg Review; Hudson Literary Magazine. Honours: Prize for Poetry, Luceofarul Literary Magazine, 1976; Prize for Poetry, Romanian Writers Association, 1980. Memberships: European Association for the Promotion of Poetry; Romanian Writers Union; Romanian Journalists Association; Secretary, European Poetry Centre and Cultural Dialogue East West Constant, Noica, Sibiu. Address: Str Dr Victor Babes nr 20, Sector 5, Bucharest 35, Romania.

MIDDLETON Christopher, b. 10 June 1926, Truro, Cornwall, England. Professor of German Literature. 1 sons, 2 daughters. Education: University of Oxford, Merton College, 1948-52; DPhil, Oxford, 1954. Appointments: English Lektor at Zürich University, 1952-55; Lecturer at University of London King's College, 1955-65; Professor, University of Texas, Austin, 1966-. Publications: Selected Writings, 1989; The Balcony Tree, 1992; Andalusian Poems, 1993; Intimate Chronicles, 1996. Contributions to: PN Review; The New Yorker; Paris Review; The Threepenny Review; London Review of Books; Columbia Journal; Shearsman; Antaeus; O-Blek. Honours: Sir Geoffrey Faber Memorial Prize, 1964; Guggenheim Fellowship, 1974-75; National Endowment for the Arts Fellowship, 1980; Schlegel-Tieck Prize, 1987; Max Geilinger-Stiftung Prize, Zürich, 1988. Membership: Akademie der Künste Berlin. Address: Germanic Languages, EP Schoch 3, 102, University of Texas, Austin, TX 78712, USA.

MIHAILOVIC Vasa, b. 12 Aug 1926, Prokuplje, Yugoslavia. Professor. m. Branka, 28 Dec 1957, 2 sons. Education: BA, 1956; MA, 1957; PhD, 1966. Appointments: Professor, Slavic Languages and Literatures, University of North Carolina, Chapel Hill, North Carolina, USA, 1961-95. Publications: Stari i Novi Vilajet, 1977; Bdenja, 1980; Krugovi Na Vodi, 1982; Litija Malih Praznika, 1990; Na Brisanom Prostoru, 1994; Bozic u Starom Kraju, 1994. Honours: Serbian Pen Center, 1988; Zlatni Prsten, 1994. Memberships: Society of Serbian Writers and Artists Abroad; Association of Writers of Serbia. Address: 821 Emory Drive, Chapel Hill, NC 27514, USA.

MIKHAILUSENKO Igor Georgiyevich, b. 20 Apr 1932, Moscow, Russia. Poet; Translator; Journalist. Education: Graduated, Moscow Foreign Languages Institute after Maurice Thorez, 1958; Diploma, Higher Education, as a Translator from Russian into English. Appointments: International Soviet Travel Agency Intourist, Translator into Russian from English texts and Interpreter for tourists, 1959, 1960, 1964-68; Interpreter and Translator in English and Russian, Proofreader and Editor for Style in Russian, News Press Agency, 1964; Inspector of Translators' Department, Soviet State Copyright Agency, 1974; Freelance Journalist for Russian Press for many years. Publications: Poems for Peace, 1988; Poesia Para A Paz, 1985; Tres Poems de Mikhailusenko, 1987; Serie Galaxia, 1987; Poemas do Futuro, 1987; Five Poems Seen by the English Queen, 1995. Contributions to: Various publications including: Dostoinstvo newspaper, 1995-96. Honours: Badge of Honour, Moscow Peace Committee, 1982; Recognised by United Poets Laureate International, 1987; Award, Editors of Fine Arts Press, USA. Memberships: Laurel Leaves, Official Organ of United Poets Laureate International, 1984; Board of Directors, International Writers and Artists Association, Moorhead State University; Board of Directors, International Writers and Artists Association, Bluffton College, Ohio, USA. Address: Bolshaya Gruzinskaya Street, House 63 Apt 87, Moscow 123056, Russia.

MILES John Arthur, b. 24 Aug 1942, Erith, Kent, England. Writer. m. Kay Lesley Foster, 18 Feb 1972, 1 son, 2 daughters. Education: High School Matriculation, Urrbrae Agricultural College, South Australia, 1960. Appointments: Adelaide Festival Writer's Week, 1992; Poetry Editor, Australian Writer, 1994; Varuna Fellow, 1996. Publications: Anthology, 1987; Going Down Swinging, 1991; Homecoming, 1993; He Dances, 1994; Harvest, Five Seasons, 1995; Honor: A Vanuatu Suite and Envoi, 1996. Contributions to: Australia: Quadrant, Hecate, LiNQ, Courier-Mail, Advertiser, Studio, Webber's, Australian Poetry, Stet, Mattoid, Muse, Kangaroo, Scarp, Tamba, GDS, New England Review, Northern Perspective, Redoubt, Hopi, Grassroots, Social Alternatives, Small Times, Penola Pennant, Cobbitt's, Santos News, Eyre Peninsula Tribune, Writing, Wasteland, Heartland, Leader, Famous Reporter, The Ray, Australian Writer, Phoenix Review, Naracoorte Herald; North America: Antipodes, Impetus, Prairie Schooner, Green Fuse, Cicada, Atlanta Review; Voices International, Vintage Northwest, Parnassus, American

Buddhist Visions-International; Germany: Goethe Institute Literary Quarterly, Mosaic; South Africa: Natal Witness, New Contrast; England: Stand Magazine, Iota, Envoi, Poetry Nottingham, Orbis, Poetry, Periaktos, Inkshed, New Hope International; Japan: Mainichi Shimbun, Printed Matter, Kyoto Journal, Obiko; International: New Scientist; Radio in Australia. Honours: Studio Bicentenary Poetry Prize, 1988; Studio 10th Anniversary Poetry Prize, 1990; Mainichi Shimbun Haiku Awards, 1992; Penola Festival Max Harris Literary Awards Lyric Poetry, 1993; Shire of Eltham Alan Marshall Short Story Awards, 1994; National Library Illustrated Poetry Exhibition, 1994; Penola Festival Max Harris Literary Awards Fiction, 1994; Mainichi Shimbun Haiku Awards, 1994; National Library Illustrated Poetry Exhibition, 1995; Penola Festival Max Harris Literary Awards Open Poetry, 1995. Address: 17 Nunyah Drive, Banksia Park, South Australia 5091, Australia.

MILES Simon James, b. 18 Oct 1956, Birmingham, England. Poet; Writer. Appointments: Tutor in Creative Writing, Rampton Social Hospital and Mansfield Writers Workshop; Readings and Workshops Nationwide. Publications: 1st Collection - Reasons Why, 1990; Editor: The Archangel, annual collection of poetry to accompany the William Blake Congregations; Anthologies by the Mansfield Writers Workshop. Contributions to: Orbis; Pennine Platform; Staple; Stride; Celtic Dawn; Mosaic; Quartz; Poesis, Romania. Honours: Artist in Industry, Lace Manufacturers, Nottingham, 1986; Delivered paper, On Miracle Ground, International Conference for Lawrence Durrell, State College, Pennsylvania, 1986; Winner, Yeats Club Grand Prize, 1988. Memberships: Initiator, William Blake Congregations. Address: 134A Hartley Road, Radford, Nottingham NG7 3AJ, England.

MILLAR Gabriel Bradford, b. 30 Nov 1944, Writier; Rhythmical Masseuse. m. Graham Kennish, 18 July 1969, 2 daughters. Education: BA, Barnard College, Columbia Univesity; University of Edinburgh. Appointments: Part-time Teacher, Rudolf Steiner School; Writing Workshops. Publications: Mid Day; The Bloom on the Stone; The Brook Runs; Thresholds, 1995. Contributions to: New York Times; Lines Review; Scottish International; BBC TV Festival Now. Address: Severn Prospect, 13 Belmont Roud, Stroud, Glos GL5 1HH, England.

MILLER Aine, b. 15 Jan 1938, Ireland. Working Poet; Teacher; Workshop Co-Ordinator. m. Alexander Miller, 18 Apr 1960, 1 son, 3 daughters. Education: BA, University College Cork, 1958; Middlesex Board of Education, 1960. Appointments: Junior Demonstrator, University College Cork, 1958-59; Form Mistress, St Thomas School, 1959-61; Part Time Remedial Teacher, 1969-73; Part Time Teacher, Teacher of Creative Writing, 1990-; Writer-in-Residence D.A.T.E Centre, 1992-. Publications: Six for Gold; The Cloverdale Anthology of Irish Poetry; Goldfish in a Baby Bath, 1994; Jumping off Shadows, 1995. Contributions to: Poetry Ireland Review; Orbis; Rialto; West Coast; Salmon; Riverine; Womens Work; Poets Aloud; Interim; Visions; American Association Prize Winners Anthology; Limerick Broadsheet; Sense of Place Broadsheet; Odyssey; First Time. Honours: Gerard M Hopkins Prize; South Tipperary Literature Festival Poetry Prize; Cootehill Poetry Prize; Book Shop Poetry Prize; Syllables Poetry Competition Winner, Patrick Kavanagh Award, 1992; Allingham Trophy, 1992; Moore Medallion, 1994; Kilkenny Prize, 1994; Boyle Festival Prize, 1994; Birr Heritage Prize, 1994. Memberships: English Literature Society; Poetry Ireland; Wednesday Group. Address: 35 Finsbury Park, Upper Churchtown Road, Dublin 14, Ireland.

MILLER David, b. 2 Oct 1950, Melbourne, Australia. Librarian. Education: BA, History of Ideas, 1981; PhD, English Literature, 1986. Publications: The Caryatids, 1975; Primavera, 1979; Losing to Compassion, 1985; Messages, 1989; The Break, 1991; Pictures of Mercy: Selected Poems, 1991; Stromata, 1995; Elegy, 1996. Contributions to: Agenda; First Intensity; Notus; Acts; Stride; Reality Studios; Tel-let; Morning Star Folios; Intimacy; The Poet's Voice; Odyssey; Pearl. Address: 7 Waynflete House, Union Street, London SE1 0LE, England.

MILLER E(ugene) Ethelbert, b. 20 Nov 1950, New York, New York, USA. Director. m. Denise King, 25 Sept 1982, 1 son, 1 daughter. Education: BA, Howard University. Appointments: Director, African Resource Center, 1974-; Vice President, Associated Writing Programs; Vice President, PEN Faulkner Foundation; Associate Editor, African American Review; Board, Washington Independent Writers. Publications: First Light, 1994; In Search of Color Everywhere, 1994. Contributions to: Callaloo; Black American Literature Forum; Thinker

Review; Konch; New Essence; National Public Radio; Manoa; Sojourners. Honours: Mayors Arts Award; Public Humanities Award; Outstanding Author Award, Howard University, 1995. Memberships: Board Member, Washington Independent Writers; National Writers Union; PEN American Center; Washington Review; Middle Atlantic Writers Association Review. Address: PO Box 441, Howard University, Washington, DC 20059, USA.

MILLER Edmund, b. 18 July 1943, Queens, New York, USA. College Teacher. Education: BA, C W Post Campus, Long Island University, 1965; MA, Ohio State University, 1969; PhD, State University of New York at Stony Brook, 1975. Appointments: Assistant 1981-86, Deputy Chairman 1983-, Associate Professor 1986-90, Professor 1990-, English Department, C W Post Campus, Long Island University, New York. Publications: Fucking Animals: A Book of Poems, 1973; The Nadine Poems, 1973; Winter, 1975; A Rider of Currents, 1986; The Screwdriver's Apprentice, 1996; Scholarly books inc: George Herbert's Kinships. Contributions to: Long Island Quarterly; Numerous others. Memberships: Modern Language Association; Friends of Bemerton, Newsletter Cross-Bias Editor; Milton Society of America; Lewis Carroll Society of North America; Conference on Christianity and Literature, Past Regional President; Fellow, Augustan Society, Past Journal Editor. Address: English Department, C W Post Campus, Long Island, Brookville, NY 11548, USA.

MILLER Jim Wayne, b. 21 Oct 1936, Leicester, North Carolina, USA. Professor. m. Mary Ellen Yates, 17 Aug 1958, 2 sons, 1 daughter. Education: AB, English, Berea College, Kentucky, 1958; PhD, German and American Literature, Vanderbilt University, Nashville, 1965. Appointments: Instructor, German and English, Fort Knox Dependent Schools, 1958-60; National Defense Education Act Fellow, Vanderbilt University, 1960-63; Assistant Professor 1963-66, Associate Professor 1966-70, Professor 1970-, Western Kentucky State University. Publications: Copperhead Cane, 1964; The More Things Change The More They Stay The Same, 1971; Dialogue with a Dead Man, 1974; The Figure of Fulfillment, translation, 1975; The Mountains Have Come Closer, 1980; Vein of Words, 1984; Nostalgia for 70, 1986; Brier, His First Book, 1988; Newfound, (novel), 1989; His First, Best Country (novel), 1993; Copperhead Cane/Der Schlangenstock (Bilingual edition of 1964 poems), 1995; Co-editor with Robert J Higgs and Ambrose Manning of Appalachia Inside Out, 2 volumes, 1995. Contributions to: Louisville, Ky Courier Journal; Writer; Georgia Review; Appalachian Journal; Appalachian Heritage; Southern Poetry Review; Mississippi Review; Mountain Life and Work. Honours: Alice Lloyd Memorial Award for Appalachian Poetry, 1967; Thomas Wolfe Literary Award, 1980; Appalachian Writers Association Award, 1984; Jim Wayne Miller Festival, Sixth Annual Literary Festival, Emory and Henry College, Emory, 1988; Zoe Kinkaid Brockman Memorial Award for Poetry, North Carolina Poetry Society, 1989; Appalachian Writers Association Award for Outstanding Contributions to Appalachian Literature, 1990. Memberships: Kentucky State Poetry Society, 1967-; Appalachian Writers Association. Address: 1512 Eastland Drive, Bowling Green, KY 42104, USA.

MILLER Leslie Adrienne, b. 22 Oct 1956, Ohio, USA. Assistant Professor of English. Education: BA, English, Stephens College, 1978; MA, English, University of Missouri; MFA, Poetry Writing, University of Iowa, 1982; PhD, Literature, Creative Writing, University of Houston. Appointments: Director, Creative Writing Programme, Stephens College, Columbia, Missouri; Currently Assistant Professor, English, University of St Thomas, St Paul, Minnesota. Publications: Hanging on the Sunburned Arm of Some Homeboy, 1982; No River, 1987; Staying Up for Love, 1990; Ungodliness, 1993. Contributions to: American Voice; New England Review; Ploughshares; Kenyon Review; New Letters; Carnegie-Mellon Magazine; Pennsylvania Review; Missouri Review; American Poetry Review; Southern California Anthology; Quarterly West; Nebraska Review; Helicon Nine; Antioch Review; Southern Poetry Review; Ohio Journal; Kansas Quarterly; Prairie Schooner; Northwest Review; Georgia Review; North American Review. Honours: President's Award, Ohio Journal, 1985; Stella Erdhardt Fellowship, 1987; Stanley Hanks Chapbook Award, 1987; Writers at Work Poetry Fellowship, 1989; Stanley Young Poetry Fellowship, Bread Loaf, 1989; Billee Murray Denny Award, 1989; Poetry Fellowship, National Endowment for the Arts, 1989; Strousse Award, Prairie Schooner Magazine, 1991; Loft-McKnight Award, 1993; Minnesota State Arts Board Artist's Fellowship. Memberships: Associated Writing Programs; Modern Language Association; Poetry Society of America; Poets and Writers. Address: Department of

English, University of St Thomas, 2115 Summit Ave, St Paul, MN 55105, USA.

MILLER Marge, b. 17 Feb 1948, New York, New York, USA. Human Resources Supervisor. m. Donald Miller, 22 May 1966, 2 sons. Education: Human Resources Management, St Joseph's College, Patchogue, New York. Appointment: Production Manager, Book Mark, Literary Review. Publication: Fandango, 1987. Contributions to: American Poetry Anthology, 1988; Zephyr; Island Women; Prism; Colorado Old Times; Golden Gate Review. Honours: Runner-up, American Poetry Association Poetry Contest, 1988; 1st Prize, Sister Andrea Brown Memorial Award, 1991. Memberships: Vice President, Backstreet Editions; Founding Member, Great South Bay Poetry Cooperative. Address: 16 Clusterpine Street, Medford, NY 11763, USA.

MILLER Mona Rosa, b. 10 Mar 1909, London, England. Secretarial; Freelance Writer and Poet. m. Henry Miller, 7 Jan 1928, 1 son, 1 daughter. Education: 3 Diplomas, Royal Academy of Music; 4 Diplomas with Honours, Drawing, Royal of Arts. Appointments: Civil Servant during World War II; Company Secretary and Personnel Officer, 9 years; Accountancy, 5 years; Personal Secretary to Director until retirement. Publications: She Walks in Beauty, 1973; A Dialogue in Barnes, co-editors and authors, 1974; Loving, 1974; Fragment of a Dream, 1983; A Passage of Time, anthology, International Society of Poets, 1996; 3 children's books; Short stories and articles in various magazines. Contributions to: Book Weekly Examiner, 1972-74; Tell Tale; Richmond Poets; Voices; Israel; The Eastern Sun is Rising, India; Christian Herald; Parnassus, USA; International Society; Quintessence, USA; Amber, Canada; BBC Radio; Over 300 poems in various journals in UK, USA, Canada, Israel, India and Ireland. Honours: Diploma, Companion of Western Europe, 1981; Diploma of Merit, Università delle Arti, Italy, 1982; Editor's Choice Award, For Outstanding Achievement in Poetry, 1996. Memberships: Chairman, London Writers Circle Poetry Group; Fellow, International Poetry Society; Conductor, Sean Dornan Manuscript Society Circulators. Address: 30 Carmichael Court, Barnes, London SW13 0HA, England.

MILLER Scott Reamy, b. 19 July 1965, Port Arthur, Texas, USA. Teacher. Education: BA, Sociology, Baylor University, 1987; Secondary Teaching Certification, Trevecca Nazarene College, 1992. Appointments: Mathematics & English Supervisor, Madison Nazarene Christian Academy, 1993-94; Mathematics and Spanish Teacher, Apollo Middle School, 1994-95; Mathematics & Writing Tutor, 1993-96. Contributions to: Poets Pouch; Penny-A-Ciner; Poets Fantasy; Oatmeal & Poetry; Anthology of Christian Poetry. Honour: Drury's Best of 1996 Collection. Membership: Editor, Christian Poets Pen.

MILLER Stephen M, b. 18 Aug 1939, Appleton, Wisconsin, USA. Publisher. 2 sons. Education: University of Iowa, Iowa City; Graduate study at Writers Workshop, 1964. Publications: The Last Camp in America, 1982; Backwaters, 1983. Contributions to: Rolling Stone; Madrona; Abraxas; Marilyn; Midatlantic Review. Honour: Literary Arts Fellowship, Wisconsin Arts Board, 1987. Address: 17 North Franklin Avenue, Madison, WI 53705, USA.

MILLIGAN Spike (Terence Alan), b. 1918, India. Writer; Playwright; Screenwriter; Poet; Satirist; Radio and TV Personality. Appointments: Radio and TV appearances include: The Goon Show, BBC Radio; Show Called Fred, ITV; World of Beachcomber, Q1-Q5, BBC2 TV; Curry and Chips, BBC; Oh in Colour, BBC, A Milligan for All Seasons. Publications: Silly Verse for Kids, 1959; A Dustbin of Milligan, 1961; Puckoon, 1963; The Little Pot Boiler, 1963; A Book of Bits, 1965; The Bedside Milligan, 1968; Milliganimals, 1968; The Bald Twit Lion, 1970; Milligan's Ark, 1971; Adolf Hitler: My Part in His Downfall, 1971; Small Dreams of a Scorpion, 1972; Rommel? Gunner Who?, 1973; Badjelly the Witch, 1973; Spike Milligan's Transports of Delight, 1974; Dip the Puppy, 1974; The Great McGonagal Scrapbook, 1975; The Milligan Book of Records, Games, Cartoons and Commercials (with Jack Hobbs), 1975; Monty: His Part in My Victory, 1976; Mussolini: His Part in My Downfall, 1978; A Book of Goblins, 1978; Open Heart University, 1979; Indefinite Articles and Slunthorpe, 1981; The 101 Best and Only Limericks of Spike Milligan, 1982; Sir Nobonk and the Terrible Dragon, 1982; The Melting Pot, 1983; There's a Lot About, 1983; Further Transports of Delight, 1985; Floored Masterpieces and Worse Verse, 1985; Where Have All the Bullets Gone, 1985; Goodbye Soldier, 1986; The Mirror Running, 1987; Startling Verse for All The Family, 1987; The Looney, 1987; William McGonall Meets George Gershwin, 1988; It Ends With Majic..., 1990;

Peace Work, 1991; Condensed Animals, 1991; Dear Robert, Dear Spike, 1991; Depression and How to Survive It, 1993; Hidden Words, 1993; The Bible According To Spike Milligan, 1993; Lady Chatteley's Lover According to Spike Milligan, 1994; Wuthering Heights According to Spike Milligan, 1994; Spike Milligan: A Celebration, 1995; John Thomas and Lady Jane According to Spike Milligan, 1995. Address: Spike Milligan Productions, 9 Orme Court, London W2, England.

MILLIS Christopher, b. 27 May 1954, Hartford, Connecticut, USA. Writer; Teacher. m. Nina Davis, 30 July 1977, 1 son. Education: BA, Wesleyan University, 1976; MA, 1982, PhD, 1988, New York University. Appointments: Instructor, New York University, 1981-85; Assistant Professor, Writing, Hobart College, 1986-89; Assistant Professor of Writing, Boston University, 1990-. Publications: The Diary of the Delphic Oracle, 1990; The Dark of the Sun, 1994; Impossible Mirrors, 1995; Productions: The Shining House, 1980; Poems for the End of the World, 1982; The Magnetic Properties of Moonlight, 1984. Contributions to: Harvard Review; Quarterly; New Letters; Kansas Quarterly; Seneca Review; Hanging Loose; Croton Review; Central Park; and others. Honours: New York State Council on the Arts Award, 1984; First Prize, International Poems for Peace Competition, Barcelona, 1985; Fulbright Grant, 1986; Award, Massachusetts Arts Council, 1989; National Poetry Competition Award, Jones Foundation, 1990. Memberships: Poetry Society of America; Modern Language Association. Address: 290 Massachusetts Avenue, Cambridge, MA 02139, USA.

MILLS Ralph Joseph Jr, b. 16 Dec 1931, Chicago, Illinois, USA. Professor of English. m. 25 Nov 1959, 1 son, 2 daughters. Education: BA, Lake Forest College, 1954; MA, 1956, PhD, 1963, Northwestern University. Appointments: Instructor, English, University of Chicago, 1959-61; Assistant Professor, Committee on Social Thought, University of Chicago, 1961-65; Associate Professor 1965-68, Professor 1968-, English, University of Illinois at Chicago. Publications: Door to the Sun, 1974; A Man to His Shadow, 1975; Night Road/Poems, 1978; Living With Distance, 1979; With No Answer, 1980; March Light, 1983; For a Day, 1985; Each Branch, Poems 1976-1985, 1986; A While, 1989; A Window in Air, 9 Poems, 1993. Contributions to: American Poetry Review; Chicago Review; Ascent; Crazy Horse; Tar River Poetry; Choice; Poem;Descant; Kayak; Poetry New; Ironwood; Centennial Review; Mississippi Valley Review; Dacotah Territory; Northeast; New Letters; Beloit Poetry Journal; Midwest Quarterly; New England Review; Long House; New Mexico Humanities Review; Spoon River Quarterly; and others. Honours: Illinois Arts Council Awards for Poetry, 1979, 1983, 1984; Society of Midland Authors Poetry Prize, 1979; Carl Sandburg Prize for Poetry, 1983-84. Address: 1451 North Astor Street, Chicago, IL 60610, USA.

MILO ROSEBUD. See. ARMSTRONG Terry Lee.

MILOSZ Czeslaw, b. 30 June 1911, Szetejnie, Lithuania. (US citizen, 1970). Poet; Novelist; Critic; Essayist; Translator; Professor. Education: M Juris, University of Wilno, 1934. Appointments: Programmer, Polish National Radio, Warsaw, 1934-39; Diplomatic Service, Polish Ministry of Foreign Affairs, 1945-50; Visiting Lecturer 1960-61, Professor of Slavic Languages and Literatures 1961-78, Professor Emeritus 1978-, University of California at Berkeley. Publications in English Translation: Poetry: Three Winters, 1936; Selected Poems, 1973, revised edition, 1981; Selected Poems, 1976; The Bells in Winter, 1978; The Separate Notebooks, 1984; Unattainable Earth, 1986; Collected Poems, 1990; Provinces: Poems 1987-1991, 1991; Facing the River: New Poems, 1995. Novels: The Seizure of Power, 1955; The Issa Valley, 1981. Non-Fiction: The Captive Mind, essays, 1953; Native Realm: A Search for Self-Definition, essays, 1968; The History of Polish Literature, 1969, revised edition, 1983; Emperor of the Earth: Modes of Eccentric Vision, 1977; Nobel Lecture, 1981; Visions from San Francisco Bay, 1982; The Witness of Poetry, lectures, 1983; The Land of Ulro, 1984; Beginning With My Streets: Essays and Recollections, 1992. Editor & Translator: Postwar Polish Poetry: An Anthology, 1965, revised edition, 1983. Honours include: National Medal of Arts, 1990; Several honorary doctorates. Memberships include: American Institute of Arts & Letters; American Association for the Advancement of Slavic Studies; Polish Institute of Letters & Sciences in America. Address: c/o Department of Slavic Languages & Literatures, University of California at Berkeley, Berkeley, CA 94720, USA.

MINARIK John Paul, b. 6 Nov 1947, McKeesport, Pennsylvania, USA. Poet; Engineer. m. Susan Kay Minarik, 15 Oct 1988, 1 son.

Education: BS, Mechanical Engineering, Carnegie Mellon University, 1970; BA, Magna Cum Laude, English and Psychology, University of Pittsburgh, 1978. Appointments: Teaching Consultant, University of Pittsburgh; Chief Engineer, New Directions; Professional Poet, Pennsylvania Council of the Arts; Instructor, Community College of Allegheny County; Project Engineer/Consultant, Economy Industrial Corporation; Engineer, United States Steel Corporation. Publications: A Book, 1974; Patterns in the Dusk, 1978; Past the Unknown, Remembered Gate, 1980; Editor, Kicking Their Heels With Freedom, 1982; Advisory Editor, The Light From Another Country, 1984. Contributions to: Poems in over 100 newspapers across the USA; American Ethnic; Backspace; Confrontation; Gravida; Greenfield Review; Happiness Holding Tank; Interstate; Journal of Popular Culture; Mill Hunk Herald; New Orleans Review; Nitty-Gritty; Old Main; Poetry Society of America Bulletin; Small Pond; Carnegie-Mellon Magazine; Prison Writing Review; Painted Bride Quarterly; Caprice; Hyacinths and Biscuits; Joint Conference; Sunday Clothes; Poems read over Voice of America, Monitoradio, WQED-FM, WYEP & Reading Three Rivers Arts Festival & American Wind Symphony. Honours: Honourable Mention, PEN Writing Award, 1976-77; Nominated by Publisher for The Pushcart Prize, 1984; First, Poetry and Prose Contest, 1986; Fourth, Poetry and Prose Contest, 1989. Memberships: Editor and Founder, Academy of Prison Arts; Advisory Editor, Greenfield Review Press. Address: PO Box 99901, Pittsburgh, PA 15233, USA.

MINEO Melanie, (M A Brawn, Melanie Marrero), b. 11 July 1954, Dexter, Maine, USA. Poet; Professor; Counselor. m. Thomas Mineo, 3 July 1990, 1 son. Education: Attended California Institute of the Arts, MFA Theatre Programme, 1985-86; BA magna cum laude, Liberal Arts (Philosophy, Theatre, English), 1988; ESL Certification, 1990; Mediator Certification, 1991; PhD in progress. Appointment: Counselor. Contributions to: 1988 Anthology of Midwestern Poetry; Golden Isis; The Long Islander; Brook Spring; Sing Heavenly Muse!; World of Poetry Anthology. Honour: 4th Place, World of Poetry Contest, 1990. Memberships: American Association of University Women; Children International. Address: 58 Shinnecock Avenue, East Quogue, NY 11942, USA.

MING Chiu Yee. See: **YAU Emily (Yee Ming).**

MING Emily Yau Yee. See: **YAU Emily (Yee Ming).**

MINHINNICK Robert Christopher, b. 12 Aug 1952, 1 daughter. Education; BA, University College of Wales; PGCE. Publications: A Thread in the Maze; Native Ground; Life Sentences; The Dinosaur Park; The Looters. Contributions to: Planet; Poetry Wales; Western Mail; Pivot; Literary Review; Poetry Book Society Supplement; PEN Anthology. Honours: Literature Prize; Eric Gregory Award; John Morgan Award. Membership: Welsh Academy. Address: 11 Park Avenue, Porthcawl, Mid Glamorgan, South Wales.

MINIM June. See: **HANFORD BRUCE Mary.**

MINISH Geoffrey Roy Greer, b. 10 Mar 1929, Toronto, Ontario, Canada. Journalist. m. Pauline Marion Addison, 15 June 1987. Education: Jarvis Collegiate, 1941-46; MA, Trinity College, Dublin, 1957. Appointments: Police Reporter, Windsor Star, Ontario, 1954-55; Sub-Editor, Reuters, London, 1960-64; Police Reporter, The Daily Colonist, Victoria British Columbia, 1965; Sub-Editor, Visnews, London, 1966-67; Sub-Editor, Occasional Reporter, Agence France-Presse, Paris, 1967-87; Freelance Contributions: Irish Times, Jazz Journal International, Melody Maker, Sight and Sound, Take One (Paris Correspondent). Publications: 1960's anthologies: Poems for Peace; Poetry From the Left. Contributions to: New Stateman; Orbis; Poetry Now; Guardians of the State; Bare Bones; Breakthru'; Eavesdropper; Omens; Panurge; Peace News; Smiths Knoll; Verse, Britain; Antigonish Review; Fiddlehead; Plowman, Canada; Paris Metro, France; Holy Door; Icarus, Ireland; Creel; Village Voice, USA; 1993 Poets Diary for all Seasons. Honour: Co-Winner, Paris Metro Competition, 1977. Memberships: National Union of Journalists, Life Member; Poetry Society. Address: 133 Rue St Dominique, 75007 Paris, France.

MINTER Sheryl Ann, b. 2 Oct 1960, Huntington, Long Island, New York, USA. Poet. Div, 1 son. Education: One year, Law College. Appointment: Teachers Aide, Smithtown Central School District. Publications: Poetic Windows, 1993; Visions of Poetry, 1994; Images of Poetry, 1995; Poetic Views, 1995. Contributions to: Third Half;

Illinois Architectural and Historical Review; Horse People Magazine; Poetic Page; Poetic Eloquence; Poetry in Motion; Oatmeal and Poetry; Night Roses; Simply Words; Anderie; Christian Poets Pen; Pence and Freedom; Messenger; Newsday. Honours: Honorable Mention, National Authors Registry, 1994; Fourth Place, Poetic Page, Metaphors, 1995; Honorable Mention, Poetic Page Chapbook Competition, 1995; Honorable Mention, Christian Poets Pen, 1996. Memberships: Founding Member, Smithtown Poetry Society; Babylon Citizens Council on the Arts; Associate Member, National Poets Association. Address: 9 Fourth Street, Nesconset, NY 11767, USA.

MINTY Judith, b. 5 Aug 1937, Detroit, Michigan, USA. Writer. m. Egar Minty, 19 June 1957, 1 son, 2 daughters. Education: BS, Ithaca College, New York; MA, Western Michigan University. Appointments: Visiting Poet, Interlochen Centre for the Arts, Syracuse University; University of California, Santa Cruz; Professor, English, Humbolt State University, 1981-94. Publications: Lake Songs and Other Fears, 1974; Yellow Dog Journal, 1979; Letters to My Daughter, 1980; In the Presence of Mothers, 1981; Counting the Losses, 1986; Dancing the Fault, 1991; The Mad Painter Poems, 1996. Contributions to: Poetry; Poetry Northwest; Atlantic; New Yorker; Iowa Review; Missouri Review; Barat Review; Five Fingers Review; Small Towner; Ocooch Mountain News; Redstart; Hawaii Review; Great Lakes Review; Black Warrior Review; Green River Review; Seneca Review; Sou'wester; New York Quarterly. Honours: United States Award, International Poetry Forum, 1973; John Atherton Fellowship to Bread Loaf, 1974; Eunice Tietjens Award, Poetry Magazine, 1974; 2 Michigan Council for the Arts Creative Artists Grants, 1981, 1983; 2 PEN Syndicated Fiction Awards, 1985, 1986; PEN, Mead Foundation California Award, 1986; Villa Montalvo Award for Excellence in Poetry, 1989; Chrales Hackley Distinguished Lectureship, 1996; Honorary Doctrate in Humanities, Michigan Technological University, 1997. Memberships: PEN; Poets and Writers; Associated Writing Programmes; Poetry Society of America. Address: 7113 South Scenic Drive, New Era, MI 49446, USA.

MIRZA Baldev, b. 6 Mar 1932, Malerkotla, Punjab, India. Teacher; Publisher. Education: MA, English Literature, AMU Aligarh; BEd, AMU Aligarh; BA, Indian Classical Music, Paryag Samiti Allahabad. Appointments: Running a Nursery School, 1966-; Skylark India Poetry Magazine, 1970-. Publications: Shall I Speak Out; Words On Fire; Buddha My Love; Across the Falling Snow; When the Stars Ache; My Nursery Rhymes, 1973, 6th edition, 1996. Contributions to: Numerous worldwide. Memberships: Authors Guild of India; International Writers Association. Address: Kothi Zamirabad, Raghubirpuri, Aligarh UP, India.

MITCHELL Adrian, (Apeman Mudgeon, Volcano Jones, Gerald Stimpson), b. 24 Oct 1932, London, England. Performing Poet; Playwright; Novelist; Lyricist; Childrens Author. 2 sons, 3 daughters. Education: Oxford University, 1953-55. Appointments: Granada Fellow, University of Lancaster, 1968-70; Fellow, Wesleyan University, 1972; Resident Writer, Sherman Theatre, 1974-75; Visiting Writer, 1978-80; Resident Writer, Unicorn Theatre for Children, 1982-83; Fellow in Drama, Nanyang University, Singapore, 1995; Dylan Thomas Fellow, UK Festival of Literature, Swansea, 1995. Publications: Poems; Out Loud; Ride the Nightmare; The Apeman Cometh; For Beauty Douglas; On the Beach at Cambridge; Notringmas Day; Love Songs of World War Three; All My Own Stuff; Adrian Mitchell's Greatest Hits; Blue Coffee. Contributions to: Pieces of Peace. Honours: Gregory Award; PEN Translation Prize; Tokyo Festival TV Film Award. Memberships: Royal Society of Literature; Writers Guild; Society of Authors. Address: Peters, Fraser and Dunlop, 5th Floor, The Chambers, Chelsea Harbour, Lots Road, London SW10 0XF, England.

MITCHELL Elizabeth Manuel (Elma), b. 19 Nov 1919, Scotland. Librarian. Education: Somerville College, Oxford, 1938-41; BA (Oxon), 1941; MA (Oxon); Diploma, Librianship, University of London. Appointments: Librarian, 1941-47; Research Librarian; Now retired. Publications: The Poor Man in the Flesh; The Human Cage; Furnished Rooms; People Etcetera; Neighbours. Contributions to: BBC Poetry Please; Best of Scottish Poetry; Making for the Open; Several anthologies. Honours: Poetry Book Prize; Cheltenham Festival Poetry Competition. Memberships: Poetry Society; Dillington Poets; Poetry Book Society. Address: Tanlake Cottage, Buckland St Mary Chard, Somerset TA20 3QF, England.

MITCHELL Felicia, b. 22 Feb 1956, Sumter, South Carolina, USA. College Teacher; Poet. m. Barry A Love, 17 Mar 1989, 1 son. Education: Diploma, Booker T Washington High School, Columbia, 1973; BA, 1977, MA, 1980, University of South Carolina; PhD, Curriculum and Instruction, University of Texas, Austin, 1987. Appointments: Teaching Assistant, Multicultural Education, University of Texas, Austin, 1985-87; Instructor of Poetry Workshops, Texas Union Informal Classes, 1986-87; Assistant Professor of English, Director of the Writing Center, Co-Ordinator of the Writing Program, 1987-93; Associate Profesor of English, Director of the Writing Center and Writing Program, Co-Ordinator of Writing Across the Curriculum, 1993-; Numerous conference presentations; Poetry readings and workshops. Publications include: Books: Words and Quilts: A Selection of Quilt Poems, 1996; Case Hysterics, 1996; Poetry included in various books: We Speak for Peace. An Anthology, 1992; Our Mothers, Our Selves, Writers and Poets Celebrating Motherhood, 1996; Details Omitted from the Text, forthcoming; Other: Editorial Columnist, The Athens Observer, Georgia, 1981-83; Film Reviews: The Athens Observer and New Arts Review, 1981-83; The Best 50 Bundt Cakes, due 1997. Contributions to: Articles in various books and journals; Poetry in numerous journals including: Waterways, Poetry in the Mainstream; Cafe Review; Sow's Ear Poetry Review; Cape Rock. Honours include: Master's Thesis submitted to the Dickens Museum, 1982; Phi Kappa Phi; Various Grants; Bread Loaf Writers' Conference Scholarship, 1988; Fellowship, Virginia Center for the Creative Arts, 1995. Memberships include: Student Intern Advisory Council, 1989-; Chair, Academic Standards Committee, 1995-; Faculty Advisory Committee, 1996-. Address: 29511 Smyth Chapel Road, Meadowview, VA 24361-4203, USA.

MITCHELL Terry (Terrance LaMarr), b. 14 Dec 1970, Cleveland, Ohio, USA. Freelance Artist. Education: Shaw High School; Diploma, Kansas City Art Institute; Cleveland Institute of Art, 1 year; Various workshops and courses. Appointments: Designer of five T-shirts for Euclid Media Graphics, 1996; Sold various paintings; Currently part-time in Nursing Department, Mount Sinai Medical Center. Contributions to: The Fragrance of a Prophet, Given Free, and Native Dove, in Lamp Post Magazine, due 1997. Address: 24101 Lakeshore Boulevard, Apt 806A, Euclid, OH 44123, USA.

MITCHELL V(ernice) V(irginia), b. 11 Mar 1921, Scott, Mississippi, USA. Nurse. m. Willis Mitchell, 17 Aug 1940, 4 sons, 2 daughters. Education: Princeton Continuation School, 1954-55; Chicago Board of Education: LPN Certificate. Appointments: LPN, Cook County Hospital, 1951-59; LPN, University of Illinois, 1959-67; LPN (Intensive Care), Grant Hospital of Chicago, 1967-78; LPN (Orthopaedics), Northwestern Memorial Hospital, 1979-84; LPN (Private Duty), Aetna Nurses Registry, Chicago, 1984-91. Publications: Lyrics to music: I Thank You Lord, 1979; You Are in the Middle of My Life, 1983; Day and Night Dreams, 1988; Success Through Spiritual Truths, book, 1989. Contributions to: American Poetry Anthology; World of Poetry Press. Honours: Golden Poet Awards, 1985-88; Hall of Fame for Senior Citizens, Chicago. Address: 6726 South Emerald Avenue, Chicago, IL 60621, USA.

MNOOKIN Wendy, b. 1 Nov 1946, New York, New York, USA. Writer. m. James Mnookin, 24 May 1970, 2 sons, 1 daughter. Education: BA, English, Redcliffe College, 1968; MFA, Writing, Vermont College, 1991. Publications: Guenever Speaks, 1991. Contributions to: Bridge; Clockwatch Review; Sow's Ear Poetry Review; Beloit Poetry Journal; Caprice; Cimmaron Review; Eleventh Muse; Harbinger; Kalliope; Kansas Quarterly; Lowell Pearl; Oxford Magazine; Paragraph; Passages North; Poetry Miscellany; Radcliffe Quarterly; Sandscript; Sojourner; Soundings East; Wisconsin Review; Z Miscellaneous. Honours: 2nd Prize for Cities Burning, Harbinger, 1988; 1st Prize for Changing Places, Poetpourri, 1990; 1st Prize for Garden in the Pines, Federal Poets, 1990; 1st Prize for After the Fire at Cocoanut Grove, Poet, 1992; 2nd Prize for Wintering Over, Kansas Quarterly, 1994. Address: 40 Woodchester Drive, Chestnut Hill, MA 02167, USA.

MO Lo-Fu, b. 11 May 1928, Hunan, China. Chief Editor. m. C F Chen, 10 Oct 1961, 1 son, 1 daughter. Education: English Department, Tamkang University, 1968-73; AB, Tamkang University, 1973. Appointments: Commander, Chinese Navy, 1963-73; Lecturer, Soochow University, 1974-77. Publications: Spiritual River; Poems of Beyond; Clamoring of Time; Because of the Wind; Angels Nirvana. Contributions to: United Daily News; China Times; Central Daily News; China News; Epoch Poetry Quarterly; Blue Star Poetry Quarterly;

Modern Poetry; Free China Review; Chinese PEN. Honours: China Times Literary Award; Sun Yat Sen Memorial Literary Award; Wu San-Lien Literary Award; Chinese National Literary and Art Award. Membership: Epoch Poetry Society. Address: 5/F No 10, 197 Alley, Chuang Ching Road, Taipei, Taiwan, China.

MOAT John, b. 1936, India. Writer. m. 1962, 1 son, 1 daughter. Education: Radley; Exeter College, Oxford, English. Publications: 6d per annum, 1967; Thunder of Grass, 1969; The Ballad of the Leat, 1975; Fiesta and the Fox Reviews His Prophecy, 1980; Skeleton Key, 1982; Welcombe Overtures, 1987; Firewater and the Miraculous Mandarin, 1990; Practice, 1994. Contributions to: Temenos; Rialto; Prospice; Scotsman. Address: Crenham Mill, Nr Hartland, North Devon EX39 6HN, England.

MOBBERLEY David Winstone, b. 12 July 1948, Kings Heath, Birmingham, England. Postman. 1 son. Appointments: Pharmaceutical Process Technician, 1964-71; Postman, 1971-. Publications: Equilibrium of Forces, 1992; Beneath the Darkness a Light is Shining, 1993; Sacred Journey, 1995. Contributions to: IOTA; San Fernando Poetry Journal, USA; Envoi; The Plowman - Journal; Envoi Anthology, 1990, 1991; Kaleidoscope Anthology (Poetry Now); Thirteen Plowman Anthologies, 1991-93. Address: 87 Woodthorpe Road, Kings Heath, Birmingham B14 6EG, England.

MOE David J, b. 17 Sept 1938, Morris, Minnesota, USA. Insurance Broker. m. Thordis Hammer, 12 June 1965, 2 daughters. Education: BA, University of Minnesota, 1964; MA, San Francisco State University, 1975. Appointments: Fireman's Fund Insurance Company; Insurance Broker: Fred James and Co, Coroon and Black; Vice President, First Services Corporation; Owner, United Insurance. Publications: Portrait Poems, 1986; Songs of the Soul, 1988; Collected Poems 1980-90, 1991. Contributions to: World Poetry, 1989, 1990; His Precious Love; Love's Greatest Treasures; American Poetry Anthology; Poems from the Last Frontier; Poetic Voice of America. Honour: Honorary Doctorate of Literature, World Academy of Arts and Culture, Bangkok, Thailand, 1988. Membership: World Academy of Arts and Culture. Address: 9011 Tournure, Juneau, AK 99801, USA.

MOFFEIT Tony A, b. 14 Mar 1942, Claremore, Oklahoma, USA. Librarian; Poet. Education: BSc, Psychology, Oklahoma State University, 1964; MLS, University of Oklahoma, 1965. Appointments: Assistant Director, Library, 1980-, Poet-in-Residence, 1986-95, University of Southern Colorado; Director, Pueblo Poetry Project, 1980-. Publications: La Nortenita, 1983; Outlaw Blues, 1983; Shooting Chant, 1984; Coyote Blues, 1985; Hank Williams Blues, 1985; The Spider Who Walked Underground, 1985; Black Cat Bone, 1986; Dancing With the Ghosts of the Dead, 1986; Pueblo Blues, 1986; Boogie Alley, 1989; Luminous Animal, 1989; Poetry is Dangerous, The Poet is an Outlaw, 1995. Contributions to: Journals and magazines. Honours: Jack Kerouac Award, 1986; National Endowment for the Arts Fellowship, 1992. Membership: American Library Association. Address: 1501 East 7th, Pueblo, CO 81001, USA.

MOFFETT Judith, b. 30 Aug 1942, Louisville, Kentucky, USA. Poet; Writer; Teacher. m. Edward B Irving, 1983. Education: BA, Hanover College, Indiana, 1964; MA, Colorado State University, 1966; University of Wisconsin, Madison 1966-67; MA, 1970, PhD, 1971, University of Pennsylvania. Appointments: Fulbright Lecturer, University of Lund, Sweden, 1967-68; Assistant Professor, Behrend College, Pennsylvania State University, 1971-75; Visiting Lecturer, University of Iowa, 1977-78; Visiting Lecturer, 1978-79, Assistant Professor, 1979-86, Adjunct Assistant Professor, 1986-88, Adjunct Associate Professor, 1988-93, Adjunct Professor of English, 1993-94, University of Pennsylvania. Publications: Poetry: Keeping Time, 1976; Whinny Moor Crossing, 1984; Fiction: Pennterra, 1987; The Ragged World, 1991; Time, Like an Ever-Rolling Stream, 1992; Two That Came True, 1992; Other: James Merrill: An Introduction to the Poetry, 1984; Homestead Year: Back to the Land in Suburbia, 1995. Honours: Fulbright Grants, 1967, 1973; American Philosophical Society Grant, 1973; Eunice Tiebens Memorial Prize, 1973; Borestone Mountain Poetry Prize, 1976; Levinson Prize, 1976; Ingram-Merrill Foundation Grants, 1977, 1980, 1989; Columbia University Translation Prize, 1978; Bread Loaf Writers Conferene Tennessee Williams Fellowship, 1978; Swedish Academy Translation Prize, 1982; National Endowment for the Humanities Translation Fellowship, 1983; National Endowment for the Arts Fellowship, 1984; Swedish Academy Translation Grant, 1993. Address: 951 East Laird Avenue, Salt Lake City, UT 84105, USA.

MOHAN RAO Chandramahanti Madan, b. 5 Sept 1936, Talasamudram, India. Educator. Education: BA Hons, 1957; PhD, 1981-82. Appointments: Head, Department of English, MRA College, Vizianagram; Chairman, Board of Studies, English, MRA College; Reader and Principal, MRA College, Vizianagram. Publictions: Manohar Malgonkar and Portrait of Hero in His Novels (criticism), 1993; Occasional Muse (poetry), 1994. Contributions to: Literary Half Yearly; Poet; Indian Express; New India; Levant; Sky Lark; Accent; Byword; Deccan Chronicle; Commonwealth Review; Janata; Samvedana. Memberships: Life Member, Icasel Mysore; Life Member, Indian Society for Commonwealth Studies, New Delhi; Life Friend, PEN India; President, Books and Books, Vizianagram; Arasham; Visakha Rachaitala Sangham. Address: 8-14-70 Maruti, Balajinagar, Vizianagram 3, India.

MOHANTY Niranjan, b. 12 Apr 1953, Calcutta, India. Teacher. m. Jayanti Mohanty, 26 May 1978, 1 son, 1 daughter. Education: BA, 1972; MA, 1974; PhD, 1992. Appointment: Editor, 1975-. Publications: Silencing the Words; Oh, This Bloody Game; Considerations; The Golden Voices; Writing in English; Voices. Contributions to: Critical Quarterly; Toronto South Asian review; Illustrated Weekly of India; Indian PEN; Indian Literature. Memberships: Poetry Time; Poetry; Indian PEN. Address: P G Department of English, Berhampur University, Berhampur 760 007, India.

MOISA Christodoulos Evangeli Georgeau, b. 10 Dec 1948, Lower Hutt, New Zealand. Education: Victoria University; Auckland University; Sir John Cass School of Art, London, England. Appointments: Rare Book Librarian, Archaeological Artist, Education Textbook Editor, Inhouse Magazine Editor, Illustrator, Photographer, Visiting Lecturer at University, Permanent Secondary Teacher, Teacher, Creative Writing to disabled people, pilot project, psychiatric and penal institutions and other creative writing courses; Currently Head of Art, Kapiti College, Raumati, Wellington; 5 one-person exhibitions, paintings and drawings; Founder, Managing Editor, One-Eyed Press Establishment, 1975; Published and Edited various New Zealand poets; Poetry Readings, many venues, New Zealand and overseas. Publications: The Muriwai Motel Sonnets, 1988; Corrigendum, 1980; Elegy, 1987; Thirteen Or So Poems To Inbetween, 1987; Rotlands, 1987. Contributions to: Landfall; Plainwraps; Cornucopia; Takahe; Kangaroo. Honours: Winner, National Poetry Prize, Te Awamutu Rose Festival, 1981; Fellowship to teach Creative Writing to disabled people, Queen Elizabeth II Arts Council, 1983; Winner, Whitereia Poetry Prize, 1991. Memberships: New Zealand PEN, Founding Member, Chairperson, Dunedin Branch, 1982-84, Founding Member, Chairperson, Christchurch Branch, 1985-87, National Executive, 1988. Address: c/o PEN New Zealand, PO Box 34631, Birkenhead, Auckland 10, New Zealand.

MOJIEB-EIMAN Syed Imam Akhlaqi, b. 1 Aug 1934, Patna, Azimabad, India. Professor; Doctor. m. (1) Afsar Jahan, 1 Aug 1952. m. (2) Houda Fadel, 1 Aug 1967. 1 son, 3 daughters. Education: MD, 1st Class, 1959; BA (Hons), 2nd Class, 1961; MA (Hons), Persian, 1963; PhD (Hons), Liberal Arts, 1982; D Litt (Hons), Liberal Arts, 1991. Appointments: General Medical Practitioner, Pakistan, 1959-64; Civil and Public Services, London, England, 1964-80; Retired on medical grounds, 1980; Director of Studies (Honorary, Liberal Arts); Elected Chairman, Academy of Letters, London. Publications: Ashk-e-Shab, 1977; Aah-e-Sahar, 1984; Iram-e-Gham, 1985; Eiman-Aashna, 1991; Gham-Aashna, 1992; Adab-e-Asnaf, 1990; Adab-e-Imbesat, 1990. Contributions to: Queen's Silver Jubilee Poem, to Evening Standard, London; Mah-e-Nau (government publication), Lahore, Pakistan; Aaj-Kal, Delhi; Shama, Delhi, Lahore; Imroz Daily (government newspaper), Lahore, Pakistan; Jang Daily Newspaper, London, Pakistan; Nawa-e-Waqt Daily, Pakistan; Books: In England; Poets of London; Eminent Poets and Their Poetries; Zia-e-Haque; BBC World Service (Urdu); Radio Pakistan World Service; Radio Pakistan, Rawalpindi; Radio Azad Kashmir. Memberships: Writers Guild of Great Britain; Progressive Writers Association, London and Pakistan; Writers Guild of Pakistan; Halqa-e-Arbab-e-Zoque, Pakistan; Academy of Letters, London; Races Amrohuo Academy, Pakistan; Bazm-e-Ghalib, Pakistan; Aligarh Old Boys Association, London and Pakistan; Anjuman Taraqi-e-Urdu, London and Pakistan; Academy of Letters, Islamabad; Iqbal Academy, London. Address: Eiman-Manzil, 13A, Sector Three, Kheyaban-E-Sir Syed, Rawalpindi, Islamabad, Pakistan.

MOKASHI-PUNEKAR Shankar, b. 8 May 1928, Dharwad, India. Educator. m. Girija Gurunath Hadimani, 24 May 1948, 3 sons, 2 daughters. Education: BA Hons, Bombay University, 1948; MA,

Karnatak University, 1953; PhD, Karnatak University, 1965. Appointments: Secondary Schools, 1948-53; Lecturer in English, Lingaraj College, Belgium, 1953-56; Lecturer in English, Kishinchand Chellam College, Churchgate, Bombay, 1956-61; Lecturer and Assistant Professor, Indian Institute of Technology, Bombay, 1961-70; Reader in English, Karnatak University, Dharwad, 1970-80; Professor of English, University of Mysore, 1980-88. Publications: The Captive, 1965; The Cycle of Seasons, 1966; The Pretender, 1968; Epistle to Prof David McCutcheon, satire, 1971; Tent Pole, 1987; Parodims, 1989; Verse translation of Kuvempu's epic Shri Ramayana Darshanam. Contributions to: Sunday Times; Writers Workshop Miscellany. Honours: Karnatak Sahitya Akadami Award, 1977; Kuvempu V V Trust Award, 1977; SUDHA Magazine Prize, 1981; Central Sahitya Akadami Award for Kannada Novel, 1989; Represented India at Struga Poetry Evenings, Yugoslavia. Memberships: Member (for English) General Council, Central Sahitya Akadami, Delhi; Kannada Advisory Board, Bharatiya Jnanapith, New Delhi; Karnatak State Sahitya Akadami, Bangalore. Address: Malmaddi Road 2, Dharwad 580 007, Karnataka, India.

MOLE John Douglas, b. 12 Oct 1941, Tauton, Somerset, England. Teacher; Freelance Writer. m. Mary Norman, 22 Aug 1968, 2 sons. Education: MA, Magdalene College, Cambridge, 1964. Appointments: English Department, Haberdashers' School, Elstree, 1964-73; Exchange to Riverdale School, New York, 1969-70; Head of English Department, Verulam School, 1973-81; Head of English Department, St Albans School, 1981-; Poet-in-Residence, Magdalene College, Cambridge, 1996. Publications: Collections: Feeding The Lake, 1981; In and Out of the Apple, 1984; Homing, 1987; Depending on The Light, 1993; For Young Readers: Boo to a Goose, 1987; The Mad Parrot's Countdown, 1989; Catching the Spider, 1990; The Conjuror's Rabbit, 1992; Criticism: Passing Judgements: Poetry in the Eighties, 1989; Selected Poems, 1995. Contributions to: Sunday Times; Observer; Times Literary Supplement; Spectator; New Statesman; Listener; Poetry Review; PN Review; London Magazine; and others. Honours: Eric Gregory Award, 1970; The Signal Award for Outstanding Contribution to Children's Poetry, 1988; The Cholmondeley Award, 1994. Membership: Vice President, Ver Poets. Address: 11 Hill Street, St Albans, Hertfordshire AL3 4QS, England.

MOLINA LOPEZ Maria Salome, b. 23 Dec 1960, Albacete, Spain. Painter; Writer; Poet. Education: Diploma, International Literature, World Writers Association. Contributions to: World Poetry; Anthology of Contemporary Poetry, Lisbon; World Poetry Society; Sequences Revue Francais de Poesie Contemporaine; Antologia de Poetas Espanoles. Honours: Special Prize for Foreigners, Free Poetry, Free Theme, 1989; 1st Prize, Henry Abattu Medal, Academia des Lettres et des Arts, Perigord, France, 1990. Memberships: Spanish Delegate, Ligue Fraternite Universelle des Poetes et Artistes; International Writers and Artists Association; World Academy of Arts and Culture; Governing Board, World Congress of Poets. Address: c/o Capitam Gomez Descalzo no 16, 02002 Albacete, Spain.

MONACELLI-JOHNSON Linda, b. 31 Mar 1949, Pittsburgh, Pennsylvania, USA. Freelance Writer and Editor. m. Whitman Johnson, 7 May 1983. Education: BA, Saint Mary's College, 1971; MA, Cleveland State University, 1973. Appointments: Printer's Representative, 1975-77; Promotional Writer, 1977-79; Gallery Manager, 1979-81; Freelance Writer, Editor, 1981-. Publications: Weathered; Lacing the Moon; Big Mama; Anthologies: The Spirit That Wants Me, 1991; ¡Saludos! Poemas de Nuevo Mexico, 1994; New Mexico Poetry Renaissance, 1994. Contributions to: Anemone; Fish Drum; Zeta; Crosswinds; Cleveland Anthology; Pembroke; Modern Poetry in Translation; Light Year; La Bella Figura; Christian Science Monitor; Four I's; South Florida Poetry Review; El Palacio; Rio Grande Writers Quarterly. Honours: Poetry in Transit Contest Winner; Cleveland State University Poetry Contest Winner. Memberships: Poets League of Greater Cleveland; Big Mama Poetry Troupe; Last Four Strumpets of the Apocalypse. Address: 308 West Houghton, Santa Fe, NM 87501, USA.

MONAHAN Noel, b. 25 Dec 1949, County Longford, Ireland. Secondary School Teacher. m. Anne O'Leary, 11 Aug 1976, 3 sons. Education: BA, St Patricks College, 1971; H Dip Ed, 1972. Appointments: Humanities Co-ordinator, St Clares College, 1976-89; Senior History Teacher, 1976-; Director, Temenos Theatre, 1990-92; Co-editor, Windows Poetry Broadsheets 1, 2 and 3, 1992-93; Co-editor, Windows Selection, Poetry and Prose, 1993; Co-editor, Windows Authors & Artists, 1994; Compiled and Directed, Half A

Vegetable, Patrick Kavanagh's Poetry for Temenos Theatre, 1994. Publications: Opposite Walls; Snowfire. Contributions to: Sunday Tribune; Honest Ulsterman; Poetry Australia; Poetry Ireland Review; Irish Literary Supplement; Pennine Platform; Green Book; Trinity Poets. Honours: Winner, Hastings Poetry Festival; Winner, Cootehill Arts Festival; The Kilkenny Prize for Poetry, 1992. Memberships: Irish Writers Union; Poetry Ireland; Poetry Society. Address: Auburn Stragella, Cavan, Ireland.

MONEYSMITH Carol Louise Giesbrecht, (Sharleigh Reid, Amber Fielding), b. 28 Nov 1943, Bismarck, North Dakota, USA. Engraver Company Owner; Writer; Poet. m. 17 June 1964, 2 sons, 1 daughter. Education: Cosmetology Licence, Americana Academy of Beauty, 1962; Publishing and Editing Diploma, Institute of Children's Literature, 1982; Computer/Engraving Training, 1990; Private Pilot Certification, Flight School, 1990. Publications: Shirera, anthology of poems, 1961; Lyrical Iowa, 1988; Great Poems of the Western World, 1989. Contributions to: Shenandoah Aviation, 1990. Honours: Golden Poet Award, World of Poetry, 1989; Silver Poet Award, World of Poetry, 1990. Address: PO Box 337, Essex, IA 51638, USA.

MONKS Philip, b. 22 Aug 1960, Leigh, Greater Manchester, England. Freelance TV Floor Manager. m. Jennifer Stephens, 2 Sept 1990, 1 son. Education: BA, St Catherine's College, Cambridge, 1981. Publications: Wake Up; Nursery Verse. Contributions to: Palantir; Argo. Memberships: Canon Poets; Poetry Society. Address: 96 Melton Road, Birmingham B14 7ES, England.

MONROY Lopez Omar Leoncio, b. 30 Mar 1954, Barquito, Chile. State Teacher (Spanish Language); Mining Technician. m. Lividina Sonia Avila George, 9 Dec 1977, 2 sons, 1 daughter. Education: Mine Technician, Universidad Tecnica del Estado, 1972; Diploma, Chilean University, 1977; National Library of Chile, 1978. Appointments: Director, Federico Varela Public Library, Chanaral; President, Rotary Club, Chanaral, 1990-92; President, Erasmo Bernales Gaete Literary Circle, Chanaral. Publications: Seaquake, 1990; Desert Poet, 1991. Contributions to: Newspapers including: Las Ultimas Noticias; La Prensa Austral; Democracia, Argentina; La Prensa, Uruguay; La Discusion; Atacama; Magazines including: Taxa; Plumas Serenenses; Chehueque; Anthologies including: Chanaral and its Poets, 1984; The Lilies and the Sea, 1987; Anthology of Poetry of the American Writers Union in Santiago, 1992. Honours: Gold Medal, 1st Prize, Literary Contest, Carlos Mondaca Literary Circle, La Serena, 1981; 3rd Prize, Regional Poetry Contest, Copiapo, 1983; 1st Prize, Poetry and Story Contest, Chanaral Town Hall, 1987; Diego de Almeida Medal for valuable cultural contributions, Town Hall of Chanaral, 1989; Diploma, International Poetry Meeting, Villa Dolores, Cordoba, Argentina, 1990; Diploma, International Poetry Meeting, La Serena, Chile, 1991; Diploma, Encuentro Poetico Sin Fronteras, Uruguay. Memberships: American Writers Union, Santiago de Chile; Northern Writers Association, Antofagasta; Erasmo Bernales Gaete Literary Circle, Chanaral. Address: Biblioteca Publica Federico Varela, Chanaral, III Region, Chile.

MONTAGUE John (Patrick), b. 1929, Ireland. Author; Educator. Appointments: Worked for State Tourist Board, Dublin, 1956-61; Lecturer in Poetry, University College, Cork. Publications: Forms of Exile, 1958; The Old People, 1960; Poisoned Lands and Other Poems, 1961; The Dolmen Miscellany of Irish Writing (editor), 1962; Death of a Chieftain and Other Stories, 1964; All Legendary Obstacles, 1966; Patriotic Suite, 1966; A Tribute to Austin Clarke on His Seventieth Birthday, 9 May 1966 (edited with Liam Miller), 1966; Home Again, 1967; A Chosen Light, 1967; The Rough Field, 1972; Hymm to the New Imagh Road, 1968; The Bread God: A Lecture, with Illustrations in Verse, 1968; A New Siege, 1969; The Planter and the Gael (with J Hewitt), 1970; Tides, 1970; Small Secrets, 1972; The Rough Field, play, 1972; A Fair House, translation from Irish, 1973; The Cave of Night, 1974; O'Riada's Farewell, 1974; The Faber Book of Irish Verse (editor), 1974; A Slow Dance, 1975; The Great Cloak, 1978; Selected Poems, 1982; The Dead Kingdom, 1984; Mount Eagle, 1989. Address: Department of English, University College, Cork, Republic of Ireland.

MONTE Joanne, b. 21 Nov 1955, Newark, New Jersey, USA. Poet; Writer. m. Kenneth F Potenski. Education: Montclair State College, 1978; Upsala College, 1980. Contributions to: Odessa Poetry Review; Many Voices/Many Lands; American Poetry Anthology; Wide Open Magazine; Contemporary Poets of America and Britain; Mile High Poetry Society; Sparrowgrass Forum; Poet. Honours: Golden Poet Award, 1991; The 11th John David Johnson Memorial Poetry

Award, 1994; The 10th Iva Mary Williams Inspirational Poetry Award, 1995. Memberships: World Poetry Society; Poets and Writers; Poetry Society of America; International Society for the Advancement of Poetry. Address: 1727 Hemlock Farms, Hawley, PA 18428-9070, USA.

MONTEIRO George, b. 23 May 1932, Cumberland, Rhode Island, USA. Teacher. 1 son, 2 daughters. Education: AB, Brown University, 1954; AM, Columbia University, 1956; PhD, Brown University, 1964. Appointment: Instructor to Professor, Brown University, 1961-. Publications: The Coffee Exchange, 1982; Double Weavers Knot, 1990. Contributions to: Denver Quarterly; Centennial Review; NEDGE, New England Journal of Medicine; James River Review. Address: 59 Woodland Drive, Windham, CT 06280, USA.

MOONRAKER Peter. See: **PIERCE Richard Alistair Burnett.**

MOORE Carolyn, b. 17 Oct 1944, New River, North Carolina, USA. Retired University Teacher; Writer; Book Reviewer; Novelist; Poet. m. John T Travis, 27 Dec 1968. Education: BA, Willamette University, Salem, Oregon, Massachusetts, 1966; MA, University of Massachusetts, Amherst, 1968; Postgraduate Studies, San Francisco State University, University of Arizona. Appointment: Lecturer in English, Humboldt State University, 1970-88. Contributions to include: Literature & Belief; Snake Nation Review; The Pen Woman; Poet Pourri; 1989 Roberts Awards, Literary Annual; Cutting Edge Quarterly. Honours: Marion Doyle Memorial Poetry Award, for Best of All Poetry, 1986-88; 1st Prize, Roberts Writing Award for Poetry, 1989; 1st Prize, Literature and Belief Poetry Award, 1988; Finalist for The Pablo Neruda Prize for Poetry, 1988; 1st Prize, Dr Orville Miller Crowder Award for Free Verse, 1988; 1st Prize, Mississippi Valley Poetry Award, 1989. Memberships: National League of American Pen Women; Connecticut Poetry Society; North Coast Writers. Address: 519 Ole Hanson Road, Eureka, CA 95501, USA.

MOORE Diane Marie, (Hermann Solidiane), b. 1 Feb 1964, Jersey, Channel Islands. General Editor. Education: BA, 1st Class Hons, 1986; AKC, 1986; MPhil, 1992; PhD, 1992. Appointments: Part-time Lecturer in French, Central London Polytechnic, 1988-89; Part-time Lecturer in French, Exeter University, 1989; Freelance Photojournalist, 1989-; General Editor, Interactions, poetry and art journal, 1989-96. Publications: Pistachio, 1993; The Lilac Cellar, 1994; Arte Misol, 1995. Contributions to: Interactions; Oltis; Présence; Rencontres; Thinks (journal of C.I. Mensa); Dandelion; Headlock; Krax; Psychopoetica; Purple Patch; Tears in the Fence 1994, Anthology; Poetry Now Anthologies; and others. Honours: CIPAF Honorary Gold Medal, 1990; Grands Concours Internationaux CIPAF, Prix de la Francophonie, 1990; Silver Medal in Free Verse Section, 1991; Amitiés Poétiques de France (Dinan) Silver Medal in Section Jumelage Bretagne, Cote D'Azur, 1991; Highly Commended in Jersey Eisteddfod 1994 Competition; Highly Commended in 1994 Tears in the Fence Competition. Memberships: Cercle International de la Pensée et Des Arts Français (CIPAF), Delegate for Great Britain; Membre Sympathisant, La Légion Violette; Compagnon des Muses, La Poémeraie D'Olt; Société des Amis de Colette; Association des Amis d'André Gide; The Poetry Society; Association Rencontres Artistes Ecrivains Associés; Channel Islands Representative for The Poetry Society, 1995-. Address: St Jacut, Les Six Boules, St Ouen, Jersey JE3 2DA, Channel Islands.

MOORE Gerald Ernest, b. 13 Aug 1926, London, England. Doctor; Dentist. m. (1) Irene Maude Dyer, dec, 10 June 1954. m. (2) Ruth Anne Marie Moore. Education: Eltham College, 1936-40; Italia Conti Drama School, 1940-41; Woolwich Polytechnic, 1943-44; Guys Hospital, 1944-49; Surrey University, 1969-70; LDSRCS (England), 1949; LAH (Dublin), 1954; MSc (Med), 1970; MGDSRCS (England), 1980. Appointments: Dental House Surgeon, Guys Hospital, 1949; Senior Resident Dental Surgeon, The London Hospital, 1950; House Physician, St Olaves Hospital, London, 1956; House Surgeon, St Nicholas Hospital, London, 1957. Publications: Insect On the Leaf, 1952; A Nest of Druids, 1969; Between Silence, 1974; The Singing Dust, co-author, 1976; Collected Poems 1944-91, 1991; Autobiography, Treading in Treacle, 1983; The Cuckoo Who Flew Backwards, a fable, 1977, illustrated by author; Fighting the Developers, Planning Protest, 1991. Contributions to: Aquarius, 1977; More and Matrix, City Literary Institute, 1975-76; North Devon Festival of Art, 1991; Readings, Publications and Broadcasts (BBC). Honour: Prize Winner, Spirit of London, Open Painting Competition, 1981. Membership: Proton Poets. Address: Tordown House, Swimbridge, North Devon EX32 0QY, England.

MOORE Honor, b. 28 Oct 1945, New York, New York, USA. Writer. Education: BA Cum Laude, Radcliffe College; Yale School of Drama, Theatre Administration, 1967-69. Appointments: Visiting Scholar in Poetry and Drama, James Madison University, Harrisonburg, Virginia, 1980; Adjunct Professor, Dramatic Writing Program, New York University, 1980-82; Workshops include: Women's Writing Workshop, Henry Street Settlement House, New York City, 1976; Residency, Women's Writing Workshop, Chatham College, Pittsburgh, 1976, University of Iowa, 1982; Women Writing, Women Telling, 1979-83, 1989; Residency in Poetry, Wells College, Aurora, New York, 1991; Curator/Cataloguer, Works of Margarett Sargent, 1980-; Co-Curator, Retrospective of Margarett Sargent: A Modern Temperament at the Davis Museum and Cultural Center at the Wellesley College, 1996. Publications: The White Blackbird, a life of the Painter, Margarett Sargent by her granddaughter, 1996; Mourning Pictures, in verse, 1974; Memoir, Poems, 1988; Poem in Four Movements by My Sister Marian, 1978; Placemats, 1981. Contributions to: Journals and Magazines: American Review; Village Voice; Nation; New England Review; Paris Review; American Poetry Review; Anthologies include: Writing in a Nuclear Age, 1984; Gay and Lesbian Poetry in Our Time, 1989. Honours: Creative Artists Public Service Grant in Playwrighting, New York State Council on the Arts, 1975; Creative Writing Fellowship in Poetry, National Endowment for the Arts, 1981; Artists Grant, Connecticut Commission on the Arts, 1993. Memberships: PEN American Centre; Poetry Society of America; Poets and Writers. Address: PO Box 305, Kent, CT 06757, USA.

MOORE Lenard Duane, b. 13 Feb 1958, Jacksonville, North Carolina, USA. Poet; Writer; Book Reviewer; Workshop Leader; Contest Judge; Teacher; Public Speaker. m. 15 Oct 1985, 1 daughter. Education: Coastal Carolina Community College, 1976-78; AIT School, 1978; Administrative Specialist Diploma, University of Maryland, 1980-81; North Carolina State University, 1985, 1988-89. Appointments: Poet-in-Residence, Mira Mesa Branch Library, San Diego, 1983; Contributing Editor, The Small Press Book Review, 1987-90; Literary Consultant for Humanities Extension OUTREACH Program, North Carolina State University, 1990-; Writer-in-Residence, United Arts Council of Raleigh and Wake County. Publications: Poems of Love and Understanding, 1982; The Open Eye, 1985; Poems for Performance; Desert Storm: A Brief History. Contributions to: Steppingstones; Pierian Spring; Poetry Canada Review; Frogpond; Pembroke Magazine; St Andrews Review; Painted Bride Quarterly; Haiku Anthology; Kentucky Poetry Review; Writers West. Honours: General Electric Foundation Award for Younger Writers nominee, 1988; Outstanding Young Man of America, 1984, 1988, 1987, 1989; Winner, Third Black Writer's Competition sponsored by the North Carolina Writers' Network, 1991. Memberships: Poetry Society of America; Academy of American Poets; North Carolina Writers Network; Haiku Society of America; National Book Critics Circle; The Raleigh Writing Alliance; National Federation of State Poetry Societies; World Poetry Society; North Carolina Poetry Society. Address: North Carolina Department of Education, 301 North Wilmington Street, Raleigh, NC 27601, USA.

MOORE Miles David, b. 8 Mar 1955, Lancaster, Ohio, USA. Journalist. Education: BSJ summa cum laude, Ohio University, Athens, 1977; Jenny McKean Moore Workshop in Creative Writing, George Washington University, Washington DC, 1990. Appointments: Assistant Editor, Rubber and Plastics News, 1977-80; Washington Correspondent, Rubber and Plastics News and Tire Business, 1980-. Publication: The Bears of Paris, 1995. Contributions to: New York Quarterly; National Review; Poet Lore; Plains Poetry Journal; Bogg; Lip Service; Lyric; Writer's Journal; Black Buzzard Review; Sulphur River Literary Review; Poetry Motel; Impetus; Federal Poet; Pivot; Washington Post Magazine. Honours: Honourable Mention, Orbis/Rhyme Revival Award, World Order of Narrative Poets, 1988; Finalist, Ratner-Ferber Award, Poet Lore, 1989; Winner, Rose LeFcowitz Prize, Poet Lore, 1994. Memberships: National Press Club; Writer's Centre; Federal Poets. Address: 5913 Mayflower Court No 102, Alexandria, VA 22312, USA.

MOORE Val, b. 14 Oct 1943, Linconshire, England. Teacher. m. Peter G Moore, 12 Aug 1972. Education: BA, 1980; PGCE, 1981. Appointments: Clerical Work, 1960-77; Teacher, Adult Education, 1981-91; WEA Tutor, Creative Writing, 1988-91; Teacher of French, 1982-83, 1992; Teacher of English, 1984-85; Supply Teacher, 1981-. Publication: Fledgling Confidence, 1993. Contributions to: Aberystwyth Competition Anthology; Acumen; Bete Noire; Iron; Other Poetry;

Pennine Platform; Poetry Nottingham; Tees Valley Writer; Honest Ulsterman; New Welsh Review; Outposts; Poetry Ireland Review; Proof; Times Literary Supplement; South Coast Poetry Journal, USA. Honours: Merit Award, Yorkshire Competition; Lake Aske Competition; Wea; Lace; Queenie Lee Competition; Tees Valley Writers Competition 2nd Prize; Rosemary Arthur Award, 1993. Address: 16 Magnolia Close, Branston, Lincoln LN4 1PW, England.

MOORE Vincent, (Q.E.D.), b. 29 Feb 1948, Akron, Ohio, USA. Publisher. Education: MFA, Oberlin College, USA, 1963. Appointment: Teacher of English, Japan, 1964-68; Tourist Guide, Berkeley, California, 1968-72; Publisher, True So Press, San Francisco, 1975-. Publications: Uh...No...Maybe, 1962; Bashograms, 1968; No Hassles, 1969; Lids and Caps, 1978; The Duke of Breath, 1982; Rimbaud-Rambo, 1988. Contributions to: Many literary magazines in Japan, Europe and North America. Honour: Silliman Syntax Prize, San Francisco, 1988, for Rimbaud-Rambo. Memberships: Corman Writers Circle, Kyoto, Japan, Treasurer, 1965-68; Poets on the Streets, Oakland, California, 1970-. Address: PO Box 958, Bolinas, CA 94924, USA.

MOORHEAD Andrea D, b. 25 Sept 1947, Buffalo, New York, USA. Teacher. m. Robert Moorhead, 1969. Education: BA, Chatham College, 1969. Appointments: Editor, Publisher, Osiris International Poetry Journal, Deerfield, Massachusetts. Publications: Iris, 1970; Morganstall, 1971; Black Rain, 1975; The Snows of Troy, 1988; Niagara, 1988; Entre nous la neige (with Bonenfant), 1988; Le silence nous entoure, 1992; The Edges of Light, translations of poetry of Helene Dorion, 1993; Winter Light, 1994; La blancheur absolue, 1995. Contributions to: New Directions; Sewanee Review; Oasis; Orbis; Confrontation; Literary Review; Recueil; Estuaire; St Andrews Review; Others. Honours: Phillips Poetry Award, 1986; Pushcart Special Mention, 1990-91; Abraxas Journal Award, 1991. Memberships: American Literary Translators Association; Poets and Writers. Address: PO Box 297, Deerfield, MA 01342, USA.

MOORTHY Krishna Kopparam, (Sudhakar), b. 10 Dec 1929, Sunnapagutta, Karnataka State, India. Teacher; Freelance Writer. m. Vedavalli, 10 June 1969, 1 son, 1 daughter. Education: BA, Madras University, 1952; BEd, Andhra University, 1956; MA (English) 1961, MA (History) 1965, Banaras Hindu University; PhD, (English), Thesis: Bryon as a Humanist, submitted to Madurai-Kamaraj University. Appointments: Teacher; Assistant Professor; Professor; Professor and Head of Department; Retired. Publications: Mother of Melmaruvathur, 1986; Temples of North East India, 1989; Temples of North West India, 1991; Temples of Andhra Pradesh, 1991; Temples of Tramil Nadu, 1991; Temples of Kerala, 1991; Temples of Karnataka, 1991; Temples of Maha Rastra, 1992; Asoka Priyadarsin, 1991; Mighty Atoms for Tiny Tots, 1991; Mantralaya Mahakshetra, 1990; Mata Kanaka Durga, 1992; That Lord Siva To Be Adored, 1995; Telugu-Poorthi Nijamu, 1956; English-Hindu Ethos in Capsules Vol I, 1989; Vishnumayam Jagat, 1996; Temples for Triple Sectts, 1996; Sarum Saktimayam, 1996; English-Hindu Ethos in Capsules Vol II, 1989; One Scene Play, Telugu, 1956. Contributions to: Several periodicals of both Indian and Foreign origin. Memberships: Authors Guild of India, New Delhi. Address: 14-61 Padmavathipwam, Tirupati 517503, India.

MORALES (MILOHNIC) (Juan) Andres, b. 26 May 1962, Santiago, Chile. University Professor. Education: Licenciate in Literature, University de Chile, Santiago, 1984; Doctor of Philosophy and Letters with mention in Hispanic Philology, Universidad Autonoma de Barcelona, Spain, 1988. Appointments: Professor, Classical and Contemporary Spanish Literature, Universidad de Chile, Santiago, 1988-. Publications: Por insulas extranas, 1982; Soliloquio de fuego, 1984; Lazaro siempre llora, 1985; No el azar - Hors du hasard, 1987; Ejercicio del decir, 1988; Verbo, 1991; Vicio de belleza, 1992. Contributions to: Revista Chilena de Literatura; La Gota Pura; Poesia Diaria; Taller de Letras; El Comercio de Lima, Peru; American Joven, Netherlands; Argentina: Ventanal; Corregidor; Mexico: La Brujula en el Bolsillo; Vuelta; USA: Osamayor; Ulula; Spain: Littera. Honours: Manantial Prize, 1980; Vicente Huidobro Prize, Universidad de Chile, 1982; Honourable Mention, Municipal Prize for Literature, Santiago, 1982; Miguel Hernandez International Prize for Poetry, Best Young Latin-American Poet, 1983; Grant for Poetry Writing, Pablo Neruda Foundation, Santiago de Chile, 1988. Memberships: Sociedad de Escritores de Chile; International Writers Association; Sociedad Chilena de Estudios Literarios; Director, Instituto Chileno-Croata de Cultura. Address: Roger de Flor 2900, Depto 122, Las Condes, Santiago de Chile, Chile.

MORAN Daniel Thomas, b. 9 Mar 1957, New York, New York, USA. Dentist. m. Victoria Ann Moran, 28 Mar 1987, 1 son, 2 daughter. Education: BS, Biology, Stony Brook University, 1979; DDS, Howard University, 1983. Appointment: Dentist. Publications: Dancing for Victoria, 1991; Gone to Innisfree, 1993; Sheltered by Islands, 1995. Contributions to: Three Mile Harbor; Long Island Quarterly; Fan; Nassau Review; Inky Blue; Confrontation; Sulfur River Literary Review; New Press Literary Quarterly; Proteus; New York Times; Rain Dog Review; Nomad's Choir; Rocket Literary Quarterly. Honours: Lyceum Award, Suffolk College, 1991; Westhampton Writer's Festival, 1991, 1993. Membership: Host, Poet's Corner on Long Island Public Radio, New York. Address: PO Box 2008, Shelter Island, NY 11964-2008, USA.

MORAND Evelyn Jane, b. 23 June 1934, Waterford, New York, USA. Business and General Manager; Sales and Promotions Director. m. 30 Apr 1955, dec, 1 son, 5 daughters. Education: Pima Community College, Tucson, Arizona, 1979. Appointments: Manager of many hospitality businesses and departments. Publications: Great Poems of the Western World, 1989; World Treasury of Golden Poems, 1990. Honours: Golden Poet Award, 1989; Silver Poet Award, 1990; Outstanding Achievement in Poetry, 1990. Address: 1425 North Dodge Blvd #A, Tucson, AZ 85716-3702, USA.

MOREIGN Rodneigh. (Iconoclastic Only). See: **MOREN Rodney.**

MOREIRA (DA SILVA) Rubenstein, b. 10 Aug 1942, Montevideo, Uruguay. Professor; Editor. m. Norma Suiffet, 22 Dec 1970. 1 son. Education: Teacher of Literature and Spanish Languages, 1970; Teacher of Portuguese, 1980. Appointments: Secondary Teacher, 1970; University Teacher, 1972; Editor and General Co-ordinator, Casa del Poeta Latinoamericano, Uruguay. Publications: Nocturnos de las horas, 1964; Poemas de agosto y un canto por América, 1965; Memoria del Espejo y otros cantos, 1967; Judas o el mar u otras noticias, 1974; Territorios y cantares, 1977; Exequias del tiempo, 1979; Mutilacion, 1981; Los cirios incendiados, 1984; Palabra dada/Primera antologia, 1987; Poesia al hombro/Segunda antologia, 1990. Contributions to: La Urpila; Diario El Dia; Cadernos de Literatura; Ciadernos de Poesia Nueva; Cirreo de la Poesia; Arboleda; Norte; Cultura y Paz; Manxa; Pliego de Murmurios; Puetro Norte y Sur; Ciadernos Reina Amalia de poesia. Honours: Ministryof Education and Culture Prizes, Uruguay, 1986, 1989; Others. Memberships: AUDE; Casa del Poeta Latinoamericano; Centro Cultural Literario e Artistico de Felgueiras, Portugal; Asociacion Prometeo de Poesia, Madrid; Instituto Camoes del Uruguay. Address: Casilla de Correo No 5088 Suc 1, Montevideo, Uruguay.

MORELLI Rolando D H, b. 25 Dec 1953, Denmark. University Professor of Literature. Education: PhD, Spanish, American Literature, Temple University, Philadelphia, 1987. Appointments: Chair, Languages and Literatures Department, Instituto Superior Educational, Cuba, 1979-80; Vice President, Brigada Hnos Saiz of Young Writers and Artists, Vertientes, Camaguey, Cuba, 1978-79; Visiting Professor, Tulane University, 1987. Publications: Leve, para el viento, 1971; Poesia Desolada, 1975; Poetas Cubanos en New York, anthology, 1988. Contributions to: From This Side (Desde este lado), no 1, 1989; El faro, no 17, 1989; El Gato Tuerto Literary Review, 11 and 13, 1989-90; La Nuez, international review of art and literature, nos 8-9, 1991. Memberships: Founder, Poets in Motion, Philadelphia. Address: 2130 Kater Street, Philadelphia, PA 19146, USA.

MOREN Rodney, (Rodneigh Moreign, Nadeena Wada, Jesus Christopher John I), b. 15 Aug 1955, Des Moines, Iowa, USA. Contributions to: Typog, 1972; Chicago Gay Life; Our Western World's Greatest Poems; Golden Treasury of Great Poems; World Treasury of Golden Poems; Telecom USA; Parnassus of World Poets, 1994; Musings, 1994; And Time Stood Still, 1994; Endless Harmony, 1995. Honours: Award of Merit, 1983, 1984, 1988; Golden Poet Award, 1988, 1989; Certificate of Honour, World of Poetry Press, 1990. Membership: Iowa Poetry Association, 1989, 1990. Address: 1111 University Avenue, Des Moines, IA 50314, USA.

MORENO MACHUCA Ernesto, b. 9 Feb 1919. Huauchinango, Puebla, Mexico. Certified Public Accountant. m. Lucila Samaniego Quintero de Moreno. 12 Dec 1960. 2 sons. Education: Public Accounting and Auditing, University of Puebla, 1945. Publications: Sinfonia Cosmica, 1951; Spiritual Landscape of Puebla. 1952; Thesis to Become a Mexican, 2 volumes, 1963. 1972; Light Song for Peace.

1968; Nocturne to My Mother and Other Poems, 1969, 2nd edition, 1992; Let's Talk With Angels, 1975; Poetic Testimony: Homage From The Government of Puebla, 1979; Angels Symphony, 1981. Contributions to: Il Giornale dei Poeti; El Sol de Puebla; World Poetry, 1990; Outstanding Anthology of World Poetry, 1990. Honours: Forjadores de Puebla, Government of the State of Puebla; International Poetry Prize, Siracusa, Rome, 1951; Honorary Major, San Antonio City, Texas, 1972; Pablo Neruda Poetry Award, Santiago de Chile, 1979; 1st Prize in Poetry, Mazatlan, State of Sinaloa, Mexico, 1988; Numerous prizes for poetry in Mexico and from Argentina, Chile, Rome, Naples, New York and Madras, India. Memberships: President, Literary Corporation Bohemia Poblana, Mexico; Mexican Society of Arts and Civic Sciences; Modern Literature Association of Sienna; New York Circle of Iberian Poets and Writers; World Academy of Arts and Culture of San Francisco; Goethe Institute; Vice President, World Poetry Society, Madras, India. Address: Calle 7 Sur No 3105, Col Chula Vista, CP 72420 Puebla, Mexico.

MORGAN Ariel Celeste Heatherley, (Ariel Wingrave, A Celeste Heatherley), b. 30 Sept 1935, Jerusalem, North Carolina, USA. Poet. m. George Tad Morgan, 14 Oct 1967, 3 sons, 1 daughter. Education: Registered Nurse, North Carolina, 1956; BA, English Literature, summa cum laude, University of North Carolina, 1966. Publications: Poems included in I Name Myself Daughter and It is Good, 1981; The Poets Job: To Go Too Far, 1985. Contributions to: George Washington Review; Lapis-Jungian Philosophy; ANIMA; Envoy; Journal of Religious Thought; A Letter Among Friends; Exquisite Corpse; Daughters of Sarah. Honour: Poem, Third Best, Contest by A Letter Among Friends. Membership: Phi Beta Kappa. Address: 4250 North Marine Drive #1802, Chicago, IL 60613, USA.

MORGAN Delane D(urstine), b. 30 Sept 1928, Columbus, Ohio, USA. College Educator. m. (1) Hal M Morgan, 6 Aug 1949, (2) Gordon A Thomas, 9 June 1990, 1 son, 2 daughters. Education: AB, Goucher College, 1949; Masters, Ohio State University, 1951; PhD, Occidental College, 1972. Appointments: Los Angeles Southwest College, 1974; East Los Angeles College, 1975-76; Part-time, Long Beach City College, 1972-83, 1985-96. Publications: Hat With a Plume, 1983; Co-author, Moon Cycle, 1987. Contributions to: Flame; Trace; Palos Verdes Review; Prophetic Voices; CQ; Cycloflame; Archer; Parnassus; Jean's Journal; Voices International; Poetry in the Garden, an anthology, 1996. Honours: 3rd Prize, Chapparral Poets, Any Subject, 1961; 1st Prize, Free Verse, 1962. Memberships: Chaparral Poets; California State Poetry Society; Surfwriters. Address: 512 Esplanade No 302, Redondo Beach, CA 90277, USA.

MORGAN Edwin (George), b. 27 Apr 1920, Glasgow, Scotland. Titular Professor of English Emeritus; Poet; Writer. Education: MA, University of Glasgow, 1947. Appointments: Assistant Lecturer, 1947-50, Lecturer, 1950-65, Senior Lecturer, 1965-71, Reader, 1971-75, Titular Professor of English, 1975-80, Professor Emeritus, 1980-87, University of Glasgow; Visiting Professor, University of Strathclyde, 1987-90; Honorary Professor, University College, Wales, 1991-95. Publications: Poetry includes: Star Gate: Science Fiction Poems, 1979; Poems of Thirty Years, 1982; Grafts/Takes, 1983; Sonnets from Scotland, 1984; Selected Poems, 1985; From the Video Box, 1986; News Poems, 1987; Themes on a Variation, 1988; Tales from Limerick Zoo, 1988; Collected Poems, 1990; Hold Hands Among the Atoms, 1991; Sweeping Out the Dark, 1994; Others include: Nothing Not Giving Messages (interviews), 1990; Crossing the Border: Essays in Scottish Literature, 1990; Language, Poetry, and Language Poetry, 1990; Evening Will Come They Will Sew the Blue Sail, 1991; As Editor includes: Scottish Satirical Verse, 1980; James Thomson: The City of Dreadful Night, 1993; As Translator: Beowulf, 1952; Poems from Eugenio Montale, 1959; Sovpoems, 1961; Vladimir Mayakovsky: Wi the Haill Voice, 1972; Fifty Renaissance Love Poems, 1975; Rites of Passage, 1976; Platen: Selected Poems, 1978; Master Peter Pathelin, 1983; Edmond Rostand: Cyrano de Bergerac: A New Verse Translation, 1992, Collected Translations, 1996. Honours: Cholmondeley Award for Poets, 1968; Scottish Arts Council Book Awards, 1968, 1973, 1975, 1977, 1978, 1983, 1985, 1991, 1992; Hungarian PEN Memorial Medal, 1972; Soros Translation Award, 1985. Address: 19 Whittingehame Court, Glasgow G12 0BG, Scotland.

MORGAN Emma, b. 17 June 1965, Levettown, Pennsylvania, USA. Writer. Education: BA, Writing, Adult Degree Program, Vermont College, 1995. Appointment: Poet-in-the-Schools, First Grade, Crocker Farm Elementary School, Amherst, Massachusetts, 1995. Publications: Gooseflesh, 1993; A Stillness Built of Motion: Living with

Tourette's, 1995. Contributions to: Bay Windows; Lucid Stone; Tourette Perspectives; Daily Hampshire Gazette; Wanting Women: An Anthology of Erotic Lesbian Poetry, 1990; Tuesday Night: Poetry and Fiction by the Valley Lesbian Writers Group, 1992. Membership: The Valley Lesbian Writers' Collective. Address: PO Box 60352, Florence, MA 01060, USA.

MORGAN (George) Frederick, b. 25 Apr 1922, New York, New York, USA. Poet; Writer; Editor. m. (1) Constance Canfield, 1942, div 1957, 6 children, (2) Rose Fillmore, 1957, div 1969, (3) Paula Deitz, 1969. Appointments: Co-Founder, 1947, Editor, 1947-, The Hudson Review; Chair, Advisory Council, Department of Romance Languages and Literatures, Princeton University, 1973-90. Publications: Poetry: A Book of Change, 1972; Poems of the Two Worlds, 1977; Death Mother and Other Poems, 1978; The River, 1980; Northbrook, 1982; Eleven Poems, 1983; Poems, New and Selected, 1987; Poems for Paula, 1995; Other: The Tarot of Cornelius Agrippa, 1978; The Fountain and Other Fables, 1985; Editor: The Hudson Review Anthology, 1961; The Modern Image: Outstanding Stories from "The Hudson Review", 1965. Honour: Chevalier de l'Ordre des Arts et des Lettres, France, 1984. Address: c/o The Hudson Review, 684 Park Avenue, New York, NY 10021, USA.

MORGAN Patrick Malcolm Hulbert, b. 8 Oct 1934, Buenos Aires, Argentina. Business Consultant. m. Margarita Ozcoidi, 4 Oct 1968, 2 sons. Education: Bachelor Degree, St Andrew's Scots School, Buenos Aires, 1952; Licenciado, Literature, University of Buenos Aires, 1994. Appointments: Advertising Manager, Sales Manager, Reckitt & Colman; Marketing Director, Grant Advertising; Area Marketing Manager, Latin America, CPC International; Private Business Consultant; Business News Editor, Buenos Aires Herald. Publications: Landfalls and Departures, 1962; This Life's Eternity, 1962; Selected Poems 1960-1990, 1996. Contributions to: Encounter; Extra Verse; London Welshman; New Measure; Outposts; Poetry Review; A Review of English Literature; Stand; Tribune; Tri-Quarterly; The Perception & Evocation of Literature, USA; The Dublin Magazine; Quest, India. Address: Crámer 381 11 8, 1426 Buenos Aires, Argentina.

MORGAN Robert, b. 3 Oct 1944, Hendersonville, North Carolina, USA. Professor of English; Poet; Writer. m. Nancy K Bullock, 1965, 1 son, 2 daughters. Education: Emory College, Oxford 1961-62; North Carolina State University, Raleigh, 1962-63; BA, University of North Carolina, Chapel Hill, 1965; MFA, University of North Carolina, Greensboro, 1968. Appointments: Instructor, Salem College, Winston-Salem, North Carolina, 1968-69; Lecturer, 1971-73, Assistant Professor, 1973-78, Associate Professor, 1978-84, Professor, 1982-92, Kappa Alpha Professor of English, 1992-, Cornell University. Publications: Poetry: Zirconia Poems, 1969; The Voice in the Crosshairs, 1971; Red Owl, 1972; Land Diving, 1976; Trunk and Thicket, 1978; Groundwork, 1979; Bronze Age, 1981; At the Edge of the Orchard Country, 1987; Sigodlin, 1990; Green River: New and Selected Poems, 1991; Fiction: The Blue Valleys: A Collection of Stories, 1989; The Mountains Won't Remember Us and Other Stories, 1992; The Hinterlands: A Mountain Tale in Three Parts, 1994, The Truest Pleasure, 1995; Non-fiction: Good Measure: Essays, Interviews and Notes on Poetry, 1993. Honours: National Endowment for the Arts Fellowships, 1968, 1974, 1981, 1987; Southern Poetry Review Prize, 1975; Eunice Tietjens Award, 1979; Jacaranda Review Fiction Prize, 1988; Guggenheim Fellowship, 1988-89; Amon Liner Prize, 1989; James G Hanes Poetry Prize, 1991; North Carolina Award in Literature, 1991. Address: c/o Department of English, Goldwin Smith Hall, Cornell University, Ithaca, NY 14853, USA.

MORGAN Robin, b. 29 Jan 1941, Lake Worth, Florida, USA. Writer. 1 son. Education: Non-Matriculating work with poets Louise Bogan, Babette Deutsch and Mark Van Doren, Columbia University, 1959-60; Honorary DHL, University of Connecticut, 1992. Appointments: Freelance: Writer with 15 books of poetry and prose published, Lecturer, Editor, Journalist, Political Activist, 1960-. Publications: Monster, 1971; Lady of the Beasts, 1976; Death Benefits, 1981; Depth Perception, 1982; Upstairs in The Garden: New and Selected Poems, 1990. Contributions to: Yale Review; Antioch Review; The Atlantic; Ms; Sewanee Review; American Poetry Review; Calyx. Honours: National Endowment for the Arts Award, 1980; Yaddo Residency, 1980. Memberships: Advisory Trustee, Women's Institute for Freedom of the Press; Co-Founder, Media Women; Founding Member, National Museum of Women in The Arts; Co-Founder, Women's Ink. Address: c/o Edite Kroll Literary Agency, 12 Grayhurst Park, Portland, ME 04102, USA.

MORGAN Walt, b. 22 Dec 1921, Ledyard, Connecticut, USA. University Professor. Education: BSc, 1946, PhD, 1953, University of Connecticut; MSc, George Washington University, Washington, DC, 1949. Appointments: Research Assistant, National Cancer Institute; Research Associate, Columbia University; Assistant Professor, University of Tennessee; Associate Professor to Professor, South Dakota State University. Publications: Now and Then, 1982; Down Under, 1983; Hitchin' Around, 1985; Here and There, 1990; What's Good About China, 1992. Contributions to: American Scientist; Argus Leader; Bioscience; Bits and Pieces; Register; Music Journal; Pasque Petals; Pequot Trails. Honours: Best Haiku in South Dakota; Honorary Mention in national contest. Memberships: Treasurer, Bardic Round Table; President, Active Board Member, Contest Funder, Judge, South Dakota State Poetry Society; Judge, Contest Sponsor, National Federation of State Poetry Societies. Address: 1610 First Street, Brookings, SD 57006, USA.

MORGAN-JONES Rowena. See: FRENCH Wendy Rowena.

MORLEY David, b. 16 Mar 1964, Lancashire, England. Scientist; Writer. Education: BSc, Bristol, 1985; PhD, London, 1994. Appointments: Frost Fellowship; Vice Chair, Development Officer, NAWE. Publications: Relcasing Stone: A Belfast Kiss; Under the Rainbow; Mandelstram Vocations; The New Poetry. Contributions to: London Magazine; Encounter; Exile; Antigonish Review; Quarry. Honours: Tyrone Guthrie Award; Eric Gregory Award; Northern Poetry Competition; Poetry Business Competition; Hawthornden Fellowship. Address: c/o Bloodaxe Books, PO Box 1SN, Newcastle upon Tyne NE99 1SN, England.

MORRICE (James) Ken(neth Watt), b. 14 July 1924, Aberdeen, Scotland. Psychiatrist. m. Norah Thompson, 5 July 1948, 1 son, 2 daughters. Education: MB ChB, 1946, MD, 1954, Aberdeen University; DPM, London University, 1951; FRCPsych, 1972. Appointments: Consultant Psychiatrist, Dingleton Hospital, Melrose; Consultant, Fort Logan Mental Health Centre, Denver, Colorado; Honorary Lecturer, Edinburgh University; Consultant Psychiatrist, Ross Clinic and Royal Cornhill, Aberdeen; Honorary Fellow, Department of Mental Health, Aberdeen University. Publications: Prototype, 1965; Relations, 1979; Twal Mile Roon, 1985; The Scampering Marmoset, 1990; Selected Poems, 1991. Contributions to: Scotsman; Glasgow Herald; Press and Journal; Lines Review; Chapman; Cencrastus; Akros; Scottish Review; Orbis; Leopard; Aberdeen University Review; Scotia Review; Words; Lallans; Open Space. Honours: McCash Prize for Scottish Poetry, 1979; Scottish Arts Council Book Award, 1982; Scottish International Open Poetry Competition, Diploma for Excellence, 1986. Address: 30 Carnegie Crescent, Aberdeen AB2 4AE, Scotland.

MORRIS Elva A, (Elva Smith), b. 26 July 1917, South Dakota, USA. Service Business; Assistant Librarian. m. John T Morris, 15 Aug 1943, 1 son, 4 stepsons. Education: High School. Appointments: Assistant, Mineral County Library, retired. Publications: Notable American Poets, 1974; Voices of South Dakota, 1977; World Treasury of Poetry, 1980; American Poetry, 1982; World of Poetry Anthology, 1987, 1988, 1989; Nevada Poetry Anthology, 1988. Contributions to: Poet Lore; American Poet; Pasque Petals; Reflections; Idaho Journal; Montana Quarterly; Driftwood; Wings; Kaleidograph; Visions; Arcadian Life; Blue Moon. Honours: Honourable Mention, World of Poetry, 1987, 1988; 5th Honourable Mention, National Poetry Contest, 1988; 2nd Award, 1st Honourable Mention, Nevada Poetry Contest, 1988; 4th Award, World of Poetry, 1989. Memberships: Nevada State Poetry Society; American Society of Authors, Composers and Publishers. Address: Box 1848, Hawthorne, NV 89415, USA.

MORRIS Jennifer (Jenny) Margaret, b. 3 Dec 1940, Ripon, Yorkshire, England. m. (1) Christopher George Hook, 17 Aug 1963, (2) Lawrence Joseph Morris, 16 Apr 1982, 1 son, 1 daughter. Education: University of Southampton, 1961; BA, Open University, 1989. Appointments: Teacher. Publications: Urban Space, 1991; The Sin Eater, 1993. Contributions to: Spectator; Literary Review; Times Educational Supplement; Envoi; Frogmore Papers; Iron; Rialto; Smiths Knoll; Spokes. Honours: Envoi 1st Prize Winner, 1990; Thetford Prize Winner, 1992; Literary Review 1st Prize Winner, twice, 1993; David Thomas Writing Award, Renewal Poetry, 1995. Memberships: Poetry Society; Norwich Poetry Group. Address: 3 Upton Road, Norwich, Norfolk NR4 7PA, England.

MORRIS Stephen, b. 1935, England. Educator; Poet; Writer. Appointments: Assistant Lecturer 1967-69, Lecturer 1969-72, Senior

Lecturer 1972-85, Faculty of Art, Wolverhampton Polytechnic; Full-time Writer, Journalist, TV Scripts Writer, 1985-. Publications: Alien Poets, 1965; Wanted for Writing Poetry (with Peter Finch), 1968; Penny Farthing Madness, 1969; Born Under Leo, 1972; The Revolutionary, 1972; The Kingfisher Catcher, 1974; Death of a Clown, 1976; Widening Circles (anthology with 4 other poets), 1977; The Moment of Truth, 1978; Too Long at the Circus, 1980; The Umbrellas of Mr Parapluie, 1985; Rolling Dice, 1986. Address: Rue Las Cours, Aspiran 34800, France.

MORRIS William Edward, b. 11 Sept 1913. Journalist. m. Patricia Margaret Hamilton, 29 Sept 1990, 1 daughter. Education: Westport Technical College; Part-time at Victoria University. Appointments: Charter President, Lions Club of Te Puke, 1959; Secretary, Te Puke, Maori Education Foundation, 1963; Executive Tauranga Historical Society, 1969; Executive, Tauranga Maori Promotional Committee, 1972. Publications: The Silent Touches of Time, 1971; Alchemy of Time, 1972-73; Children of Zero, 1974; Treadmill of Time, 1975; Good Thinking, poetry and prose, 1976; Please Turn The Page, 1987; Bangkok Collected Poems, 1953-1988, 1988; Crucible, 1980; Please Turn the Page, 1987; Bangkok Collected Poems 1953-88, 1989; Zero's Children, 1989; A Contradiction in Terms, 4 volumes, 1989-93. Contributions to: Poet; Poetry Nippon; Ocarina; Ipse; New Zealand Herald; Various World Poetry anthologies. Honours: International Poet Laureate of New Zealand, 1977; Cultural Doctorate of Literature, 1977; Distinguished Citation, World Poetry Society, 1978; Diploma, Poet Laureate, World Academy of Arts and Culture, 1981; Silver Medal, ABI, 1985; Bronze Medallion, Melbourne Poetry Society, 1990; Silver Medallion, 1995. Memberships: Editor Poet, Oceania Section, 1982-, World Poetry Society International; Life Member, Tagore Institute of Creative Writing; Life Member, World Academy of Arts and Culture; World Literary Academy, 1985; Honorary Vice President, Salamander Oasis Trust. Address: 52A Resolution Road, Welcome Bay, Tauranga, Bay of Plenty, New Zealand.

MORRISON Julia, b. Minneapolis, Minnesota, USA. Writer; Editor. Education: BA, MFA, Writers Workshop, University of Iowa; MA, School of Library and Information Science, University of Minnesota; Graduate Certificate, School of Social Work, Fordham University. Appointments: Assistant Director, St Joseph's College Library, Emmitsburg, Maryland; Assistant Librarian, Downstate Medical Center, State University of New York, Brooklyn; Research Fellow, School of Medicine, University of Minnesota, Minneapolis; Resident Visitor, Acoustics Research, AT&T Bell Labs Inc, Murray Hill, New Jersey; Resident Musician, Columbia-Princeton Electronic Music Studio, New York City; Proofreader, Time-Warner Inc, New York City; Copy Editor, Consumer Electronics, New York City; Freelance writing includes reviews, libretti, drama, business articles, translations. Publication: A Weathervane and Other Poems. Contributions to: New World Writing; Poetry Chicago; Accent; Prism; Confrontation; Minnesota History; Library Journal; Daily Iowan. Honours: Residency, Yaddo; Honourable Mention, Samuel French Drama Competition. Memberships: Poets and Writers; Broadcast Music Inc. Address: 41 West 86th Street 14-D, New York, NY 10024, USA.

MORRISON Robert Hay, b. 11 May 1915, South Yarra, Melbourne, Australia. Poet; Verse Translator. m. Anna Dorothea Booth, 20 Sept 1939, 1 son, 1 daughter. Appointment: Formerly State News Editor for South Australia, Australian Broadcasting Commission. Publications: Lyrics from Pushkin, 1951; Lyric Images, 1954; A Book of South Australian Verse, 1957; Opus 4, 1971; Australia's Russian Poets, 1971; Some Poems of Verlaine, 1972; Australia's Ukrainian Poets, 1973; Leaf-fall, 1974; America's Russian Poets, 1975; Australia's Italian Poets, 1976; In the Ear of Dusk, 1977; The Secret Greenness and Other Poems, 1978; One Hundred Russian Poems, 1979; Ancient Chinese Odes, 1979; Sonnets from the Spanish, 1980; For the Weeks of the Year, 1981; The Cypress Chest (I F Annensky), 1982; Valentina Georgievna Szobovits: A Memoir, 1984; Poems for an Exhibition, 1985; Poems from My Eight Lives, 1989; Poems from Mandelstam, 1990; All I Have Is a Fountain, 1995; The Voice of the Hands, 1996. Contributions to: Canberra Times; Weekend Australian; Sydney Morning Herald; Hemisphere; Southerly; Quadrant; Overland; Australian Book Review; Meanjin; Outrider; Westerly; Temenos; Chapman; Russian Literature Triquarterly; Southern Review; Literary Review; Formalist; Connecticut River Review; Blue Unicorn; Galley Sail Review; Lyric; Hellas; Riverrun; Modern Haiku; Frogpond; Brussels Sprout; Plover; Antigonish Review. Honours: Prize Winner, International Haiku Contest, Ehime, Japan, 1990; Roberts Memorial

Prize, USA, 1994. Address: 6 Bradfield Street, Burnside, South Australia 5066, Australia.

MORTIMER Ian James Forrester, b. 22 Sept 1967, Kent, England. Curatorial Officer. Education: University of Exeter, 1986-89; University College, London, 1992-93. Appointments: Various. Contributions to: Acumen; Outposts; Stand; Honest Ulsterman; Orbis; Lines Review; Poetry Nottingham. Address: c/o The Royal Commission on Historical Manuscripts, Quality House, Quality Court, Chancery Lane, London WC2A 1HP, England.

MORTIMER Peter John Granville, b. 17 Dec 1943, Nottingham, England. Playwright; Poet; Critic; Editor. 1 son. Education: BA, Sheffield University, 1968. Appointments: Editor, Iron Literary Magazine, 1973-; Editor, Poetry of Perestroika, 1991. Publications: The Shape of Bricks; Waiting for History; Utter Nonsense; The Oosquidal; A Rainbow in its Throat. Contributions to: Stand; Acumen; Slow Dancer; Echo Room; Prospice; Poetry Anthologies. Address: 5 Marden Terrace, Cullercoats, North Shields, Northumberland NE30 4PD, England.

MORTON Colin Todd, b. 26 July 1948, Toronto, Ontario, Canada. Writer; Editor. m. Mary Lee Bragg, 30 Aug 1969, 1 son. Education: BA, University of Calgary, 1970; MA, University of Alberta, 1979. Appointments: Creative Writing Instructor, Algonquin College, 1993-94; Writer-in-Residence, Concordia College, 1995-96. Publications: In Transit; Printed Matter; This Wont Last Forever; The Merzbook; Two Decades; How to be Born Again; Primiti Too Taa (poetry film); Oceans Apart (novel), 1995. Contributions to: Anthology of Magazine Verse and Yearbook of American Poetry; Descant; Canadian Literature; Event; Fiddlehead; Praire Fire; Orbis; Prospice; Ariel; Grain; Rampike; Zymergy; Poetry Australia; Waves; Canadian Forum; Poetry Canada Review; Arc; Capital Poets; Nebula; Rune; Quarry; Malahat Review. Honours: Canadian Broadcasting Corporation Award; Archibald Lampman Poetry Award; Best Sound Track; Bronze Apple; Short Grain Prose Poem Award; Jane Jordan Poetry Award. Memberships: League of Canadian Poets; First Draft Society of Artists; Ottawa Independent Writers. Address: 40 Grove Avenue, Ottawa, Ontario K1S 3A6, Canada.

MORTUS Cynthia, b. 19 May 1942, Canada. Writer; Teacher; Desktop Publisher. Education: BA, 1964; MA, 1966. Appointments: Assistant Professor, Radford College; Supervisor, Aetna Life and Casualty; Business Owner, Wordware Inc; Freelancer. Contributions to: Connecticut River Review; Poem; Spoon River Anthology; Earths Daughters; Virginia Country; Cotton Boll; Atlanta Review. Memberships: Modern Language Association; Publication Services Guild. Address: PO Box 870574, Stone Mountain, GA 30087, USA.

MOSDELL Christopher John, b. 9 Nov 1949, Gainsborough, Lincolnshire, England. Lyricist. m. Alice Apel Mosdell, 14 Nov 1978, 2 daughter. Education: MSc Microbiology, Nottingham University, 1972; MSc, Pathology, Exeter University, 1973. Appointments: Lecturer, Department of English, Waseda University, 1976-; Associate Professor of English Literature, Tokyo International University, 1982-. Publications: Equasian, a book and record set featuring VISIC (visual music), 1983; Ink Music: The Lyrics of Chris Mosdell, 1985; LAA... The Dangerous Opera Begins, 1989; The Oracles of Distraction, book and CD set, 1990; Writing The Riot Act in the Illiterate Hour: New and Selected Lyrics, 1991; The Yelp House, 1991. Contributions to: Lyrics and poems to many major publications. Honours: Gold Prize for Lyrics, Tokyo Musical Festival, 1984; Yuki Hayashi-Newkirk Poetry Prize, 1987; Tokyo English Literature Award for Poetry, 1987. Memberships: Poetry Society of America; Tokyo English Literature Society. Address: 3-25-21 Komazawa, Setagaya-ku, Tokyo 154, Japan.

MOSER Norman Calvin, b. 15 Oct 1931, Durham, North Carolina, USA. Writer. m. (1) Hadassah Haskale, 1966, div 1971, (2) Yolanda de Jesus Chitinos, 1978, div 1983, 1 son, (3) Romelia Avila, 15 Mar 1991, div 1993. Appointments: Teacher, Modern Art History, University of Maryland, Ulm, Germany, 1956; Teacher, Contemporary Literature, University of California, Berkeley, 1967-68, University of Arizona, 1969; Contributing Editor, Grande Ronde Review, 1969-72; Managing Editor, The Gar, 1972-74; Staff Writer, North Carolina Anvil, 1974-75. Publications: A Shaman's Songbook, Poems and Tales, 1976; I Live in The South of My Heart, 1980; Open Season, 1980; Shorter Plays and Scenarios, 1981; The Wild Horses and Other Animal Poems, 1983; El Grito del Morte, Stories and Tales, 1984; South by Southwest, poems, 1988; Illuminations Reader, Art and

Writing from Illuminations, Pulse and Gar: Anthology of Literature, Politics and Ecology, 1989. Contributions to: West Coast Review of Books; Film Quarterly; Performing Arts; Southern Poetry Review; Grand Ronde Review; Manas; Oakland Tribune; Berkeley Works; Blue Unicorn; Abraxas; The Sun; Galley Sail Review; Athena Incognito; Cloud Hidden Friends; Shaman's Drum; Minotaur; Xylophone; Mind in Motion; In The Company of Poets; Gypsy; JazziMinds. Honours: National Foundation for The Arts Cash Award, 1966; CCLM Grants to Editors, 1967, 1969, 1974, 1977; Recipient of various other honours and awards. Memberships: Bay Area Poets Coalition; Bay Area Poets Union; Board, 1985-86, Aid for Afghan Refugees. Address: Phoenix Literary Agency, 1731 10th Street, No A, Berkeley, CA 94710, USA.

MOSES Black. See: **THERSON-COFIE Larweh.**

MOSES LaNita Crouch. See: **CROUCH Lynitta.**

MOSONYI Myriam Mason. See: **MASON Myriam (Adelaide).**

MOSS Stanley David, b. 21 June 1925, New York, New York, USA. Editor; Publisher; Private Art Dealer. m. Jane Moss, 2 sons. Education: Trinity College; Yale University. Appointments: Editor, Halycon, Cambridge; Editor, New Directions; Editor, Botteghe Oscure, Rome; Poetry Editor, Book Week, New American Review, and American Review; Editor and Publisher, The Sheep Meadow Press. Publications: The Wrong Angel, 1969; Skull of Adam, 1979; The Intelligence of Clouds, 1989. Contributions to: New Yorker; Times Literary Supplement; Poetry; American Poetry Review; Nation; New Republic; Tikkun; Triquarterly; Vanderbilt Review; Sewanee Review; Encounter, London; Observer; New York Times; Poetry International. Honours: Rockefeller Fellow, 1968; Columbia University Alumni Fellow. Memberships: Trustee, Fine Arts Work Centre, Provincetown; PEN; Poetry Society of America. Address: 5247 Independence Avenue, Riverdale, NY 10471, USA.

MOSSHAM Nat P. See: **THOMPSON Samuel Richard Charles.**

MOTION Andrew, b. 26 Oct 1952, London, England. Writer. m. 9 June 1985, 2 sons, 1 daughter. Education: BA, MLitt, University College, Oxford, 1970-76. Appointments: Lecturer in English, University of Hull, 1976-80; Editor, Poetry Review, 1980-82; Poetry Editor, Chatto and Windus, 1982-89; Professor of Creative Writing, University of East Anglia, 1995-. Publications: Dangerous Play: Selected Poems, 1984; Natural Causes, 1987; Love in a Life, 1991; The Price of Everything, 1994; Philip Larkin: A Writer's Life, 1993. Contributions to: Times Literary Supplement; Observer; Times. Honours: Arvon/Observer Prize, 1982; John Llewelyn Rhys Prize, 1984; Somerset Maugham Prize, 1985; Dylan Thomas Prize, 1987; Whitbread Prize, 1993. Membership: Fellow, Royal Society of Authors. Address: c/o Faber & Faber, 3 Queens Square, London WC1, England.

MOTT Elaine, b. 16 Sept 1946, Brooklyn, New York, USA. Writer. m. Peter H Mott, 5 Jan 1968, 1 son, 1 daughter. Education: BA, City College of New York, 1973; MA, English, Creative Writing, 1990, MA, Applied Linguistics, 1992, Queens College. Contributions to: Croton Review; Pennsylvania Review; Raccoon; Yarrow; Memphis State Review; Cutbank; Madison Review; Cream City Review; Midwest Quarterly; Art and Life; High Plains Literary Review; West Branch; Rhino; Crosscurrents; Green Mountains Review; Brooklyn Review; Nimrod; Primavera; Oxford Magazine. Honours: Honourable Mention, Chester H Jones National Poetry Competition, 1984; 1st Prize, Yarrow Spring Poetry Contest, 1985; Bernard de Voto Scholar, Poetry, Breadloaf Writers Conference, 1986. Address: 8031 210th Street, Hollis Hills, NY 11427, USA.

MOULE Ros, b. 18 Mar 1941, Swansea, Wales. Lecturer. m. Peter Moule, 8 June 1965, div, 1 son, 1 daughter. Education: BA, University College of Swansea, 1962; PGCE, London Institute of Education, 1963. Appointments: Lecturer, American and European Studies, University of London, 1970-75; Lecturer, Kingston College of Further Education, Surrey, 1975-87; Lecturer, Swansea College, 1991-. Contributions to: Poetry Wales; Poetry Digest; Merlin; Westwords; Anglo Welsh Review. Honours: West Wales Writers Umbrella Annual Competition; Swansea Writers Circle Competition. Memberships: West Wales Writers Umbrella; Swansea Writers Circle. Address: 15 Admirals Walk, Sketty, Swansea. West Glamorgan SA2 8LQ. Wales.

MOULIN Monica de Oliveira. See: **BIASE Angela Maria Rocha de.**

MOURE Erin, b. 17 Apr 1955, Calgary, Alberta, Canada. Education: University of Calgary; University of British Columbia. Publications: Sheepish Beauty, Civilian Love; WSW; Furious; Domestic Fuel; Wanted Alive; The Whisky Vigil; Empire, York Street; The Green Word, 1994; Search Procedures, 1996. Contributions to: Descant; Canadian Literature; Quarry; Prism International; Saturday Night; West Coast Line; Writing. Honours: Governor Generals Award; Pat Lowther Memorial Award; National Magazine Award. Memberships: League of Canadian Poets; Writers Union of Canada. Address: c/o Writers Union of Canada, 24 Ryerson Avenue, Toronto, Ontario M5T 2P3, Canada.

MUDGEON Apeman. See: **MITCHELL Adrian.**

MUELLER RosaAnna M, b. 24 Dec 1948, Italy. College Instructor in Foreign Languages and Humanities. m. Robert R Mueller, 27 June 1971, 2 sons. Education: BA, Spanish, Hunter College; MA, Romance Languages, 1977, PhD, Comparative Literature, 1977, City University of New York. Appointments: Morton College, 1982-90; Columbia College, Chicago, Illinois, 1990; Also taught at American University, George Mason College, Illinois Benedictine College and Brooklyn College. Contributions to: Italian Poetry Today; Prairie Light Review; Poetry Now. Honour: Silver Poet Award, 1986. Memberships: Modern Language Association; American Association of Teachers of Spanish and Portuguese. Address: 106 North Madison, LaGrange, IL 60525, USA.

MUIR Mary. See: **TURNER Stella.**

MUKHOPADHYAY Sarat Kumar, (Trishanku), b. 15 Aug 1931, Calcutta, India. Chartered Accountant; Writer. m. Vijaya Dasgupta, 4 July 1967, 1 son. Education: BCom, 1950; Chartered Accountant, 1954; Graduate, British Institute of Management, London, 1961; Postgraduate Certificate, Business Management, Glasgow, 1960. Appointments: Commercial Officer, 1961; Credit Manager, 1962-66; Financial Controller, 1966-76; Secretary, Finance Director, 1976-83; Full-time Literary work, 1983-; Editor, Bengali Poetry Magazine; Columnist; Regular participant, Radio, TV and Stage performances; Counsellor, Creative Writing Programme, Indira Gandhi National Open University Study Centre, Calcutta, 1989; Participated, World Peace Conference, Denmark, and Cultural Observer, Germany, Oct-Nov 1991; Appointed Visiting Professor, Visva Bharati, Santiniketan, 1995. Publications: The Face, in English, 1971; In Bengali: Sonar Harin, 1957; Rimbaud Verlaine Ebang Nijaswa, 1963; Ahata Vrubilash, 1965; Kothai Sei Deergha Chokh, 1969; Na Nishad, 1971; Mourir Bagan O Kichhu Natun Kavita, 1972; Andhakar Lebubon, 1974; Sreshtha Kavita, 1986; Achhi Sangjata Prastoot, 1986; Vasko Popar Kavita, Bengali translation of the Yugoslav poet, 1975; Asroy, (novel); Sonar Pittalmurty Oi (poetry); Abar Europe, (travelogue); 1993; Kavita Samagra (complete poems), 1995. Contributions to: Ananda Bazar Patrika; Desh; Aajkaal; Basumati; Ganashakti; Alinda; Bivab; Several little Bengali Magazines; English translations in many anthologies including Poetry from Bengal, 1989; French translations in Anthologie de la poesie bengalie, 1991. Memberships: PEN, Calcutta; British Council, Calcutta; Prize Selection Panel, Sahitya Akademi, New Delhi. Address: Flat 3C-1, 18-3 Gariahat Road, Calcutta 700 019, India.

MUKHOPADHYAY (MUKHERJEE) Vijaya, b. 11 Mar 1937, Vikrampur, Dhaka, India. Research Fellow in Indology. m. Sarat Kumar Mukhopadhyay, 4 July 1967, 1 son. Education: MA, Sanskrit. Appointments: Lecturer, degree college; Research Fellow, Indology Department, R K Mission Institute of Culture, Gol Park, Calcutta; Edited Bengali literary magazine; Special Correspondent, Desh, 1985; Regular participant, radio, TV and stage performances; Participant, workshops, symposia, other meetings. Publications: Amar Prabhur Janya, 1967; Uranta Namabali, 1970; Jadi Shartaheen, 1971; Bhenge Jay Ananta Badam, 1977; Danrao Tarjani, 1988; Shrestha Kavita, 1990. Contributions to: Desh; Ananda Bazar Patrika; Aajkaal; Basumati; Chaturanga; Many others. Honours: All-Bengal Poetry Award, Prabaha Sahitya Sankalan, 1975; Prize for Creative Work, Pratisruti Parishad, Calcutta, 1979; Bridge-in-the-Making Award for Literary Excellence, 1995. Membership: PEN, India. Address: Flat 3C-1, 18-3 Gariahat Road. Calcutta 700109, India.

MULDOON Paul, b. 1951, Ireland. Radio Producer; Poet. Appointments: Radio Producer, BBC Northern Ireland; Professor,

Princeton University. Publications: Knowing My Place, 1971; New Weather, 1973; Spirit of Dawn, 1975; Mules, 1977; Names and Addresses, 1978; Why Brownlee Left, 1980; Immram, 1980; Quoof, 1983; The Wishbone, 1984; Meeting the British, 1987; Madoc: A Mystery, 1990; Shining Brow, 1993; The Annals of Chile, 1994. Honour: T S Eliot Prize, 1994. Address: c/o Faber & Faber, 3 Queen Square, London WC1N 3AU, England.

MULHERN Maureen, b. 11 May 1957, Birmingham, West Midlands,England. Education: BA, Sarah Lawrence College, 1980; MFA, University of Iowa, 1983. Publication: Parallax, 1986. Honours: Ruth Lake Memorial Award, Poetry Society of America, 1984; Yaddo Fellowship, 1986. Memberships: Poetry Society of America; Academy of American Poets; PEN America; Modern Language Association. Address: Grand Central Station, PO Box 3275, New York, NY 10163, USA.

MULLHOLLAND Theresa. See: **CRAIG Timothy.**

MULLINS Cecil J, b. 8 Feb 1924, West Columbia, Texas, USA. Psychologist. m. Carolyn Elaine, 20 Oct 1948, 2 sons, 2 daughters. Education: BA, University of Houston, 1948; MS, University of Houston, 1950; PhD, University of Houston, 1953. Appointments: Teacher, Psychology and English, Lee College, Baytown, Texas, 1953-57; Part-time Teaching at Our Lady of The Lake; San Antonio College; Palo Alto College; Incarnate Word College; Teaching Psychology, Library Science, Statistics; Psychometrician, US Air Force Research, (a Civilian Scientist position), 1956-85. Publications: Over 120 Papers in Psychology; 4 Book Chapters in Psychology Books; 1 Book of Poetry, 1988; 1 Book of Humor, 1964. Contributions to: Ballstate; Blue Unicorn; Bogg; Candelabrum; Caperock; Chromatones; Experiment; Formalist; GH; Harvest; Hellas; The Lyric; Mobius; National Federation of State Poetry Society; New Earth Review; Plains Poetry Journal; The Poet; Real; Sandcutters National Contest; Voices International. Honours: 1 of 12 Finalists, Formalist Contest, 1995; 1st Prize, Harvest, 1948; Best of Issue, Lyric, 1981; Lyric, Hazek Award, 1985; Best of Issue, Poetry, 1988; 2nd Place, Arkansas Conference; Sandcutters 1st Prize. Address: 100 Dandelion Lane, San Antonio, TX 78213, USA.

MUMFORD Ruth, (Ruth Dallas), b. 29 Sept 1919, Invercargill, New Zealand. Poet; Children's Author. Publications: Country Road and Other Poems, 1953; The Turning Wheel, 1961; Experiment in Form, 1964; Day Book: Poems of a Year, 1966; Shadow Show, 1968; Song for a Guitar, 1976; Walking on the Snow, 1976; Steps of the Sun, 1979; Collected Poems, 1987. Contributions to: Southland Times; New Zealand Listener; Landfall (New Zealand Quarterly); Meanjin (Australian Quarterly); Poetry Australia; Review Magazine of Otago University. Honours: Achievement Award (jointly), New Zealand Literary Fund, 1963; Robert Burns Fellowship, Otago University, 1968; Joint Winner, 1977 Poetry Section of the New Zealand Book Awards; Buckland Literary Award, 1977; Honorary Doctor of Literature, University of Otago, 1978; Commander of the Order of the British Empire, 1989. Membership: PEN New Zealand. Address: 448 Leith Street, Denedin, New Zealand.

MUNDEN Paul Warren Austen, b. 21 Mar 1958, Poole, Dorset, England. Writer; Composer. m. Clare Elizabeth Mallorie, 31 Oct 1981, 2 daughters. Education: BA, University of York, 1980. Appointments: Vice Chair, National Association of Writers in Education, 1991-; Creative Writing Tutor, Hull University, 1991-; Adviser, Yorkshire and Humberside Arts, 1992-; Creative Writing Tutor, Harrogate College, 1992-. Publication: Henderskelfe. Contributions to: Country Life; Encounter; Honest Ulsterman; London Magazine; New Statesman and Society; Poetry Review; Spectator. Honours: Writers Bursary; Eric Gregory Award. Memberships: National Poetry Society; British Film Institute. Address: Three Cottages, Bulmer, York YO6 7BW, England.

MUNDI Dolores. See: **HARR Lorraine Ellis.**

MURA David (Alan), b. 17 June 1952, Great Lakes, Illinois, USA. Poet; Writer; Teacher. m. Susan Sencer, 18 June 1983, 1 daughter. Education: BA, Grinnell College, 1974; Graduate Studies, University of Minnesota, 1974-79; MFA, Vermont College, 1991. Appointments: Instructor, 1979-85, Associate Director, Literature Program, 1982-84, Writers and Artists-in-the-Schools, St Paul, Minnesota; Faculty, The Loft, St Paul, Minnesota, 1984-; Instructor, St Olaf College, 1990-91; Visiting Professor, University of Oregon, 1991; Various poetry readings. Publications: A Male Grief: Notes on

Pornography and Addiction, 1987; After We Lost Our Way (poems), 1989; Turning Japanese, 1991; The Colors of Desire (poems), 1995. Contributions to: Anthologies and magazines. Honours: Fanny Fay Wood Memorial Prize, American Academy of Poets, 1977; US/Japan Creative Artist Fellow, 1984; National Endowment for the Arts Fellowship, 1985; Discovery/Nation Award, 1987; National Poetry Series Contest, 1988; Pushcart Prize, 1990; Minnesota State Arts Board Grant and Fellowship, 1991; New York Times Notable Book of the Year, 1991; Loft McKnight Award of Distinction, 1992. Memberships: Asian-American Renaissance Conference; President, Center for Arts Criticism, 1991-92; Jerome Foundation; Phi Beta Kappa. Address: 1787 Dayton Avenue, St Paul, MN 55104, USA.

MURATORI Fred, b. 30 April 1951, Derby, Connecticut, USA. Reference Librarian. m. Kathleen Caldwell, 16 June 1990. Education: BA, English, Fairfield University, 1973; MA, Creative Writing 1977, MLS, Information Studies 1981, Syracuse University. Appointments: Instructor, Syracuse University, 1977, 1978-79, 1985-88; Reference Librarian, Cornell University. Publications: The Possible, 1988; Despite Repeated Warnings, 1994. Contributions to: Best American Poetry; Spectator; New Directions; Formalist; Denver Quarterly; Northwest Review; Poetry Northwest; New England Review; Literary Review; Talisman; Gargoyle; Mississippi Review; Southern Humanities Review; Others. Honours: Creative Writing Fellowship, Syracuse University, 1973-74; Artist's Fellowship, New York Foundation of the Arts, 1990. Address: 6 Rochester Street, Dryden, NY 13053, USA.

MURAWSKI Elisabeth Anna, b. 27 Sept 1936, Chicago, Illinois, USA. Training Specialist. m. 30 Dec 1961, div 1978, 3 sons. Education: BA, English, DePaul University, 1957; MFA, Creative Writing, George Mason University, 1991. Appointments: Language Arts Editor, Society for Visual Education; Rights and Permissions Editor, Scholastic Magazine; Editor, Catholic University Press; Style Editor, Salesian Studies; Training Specialist, US Census Bureau; Adjunct Professor, University of Virginia, 1993-. Publication: Moon and Mercury, 1990. Contributions to: New Republic; Grand Street; American Poetry Review; Shenandoah; American Voice; Ohio Review; Ohio Journal; Virginia Quarterly Review; Helicon 9; Madison Review; New Mexico Humanities Review; Phoebe; Commonwealth; Christian Century; Carolina Quarterly; Poet and Critic; Mudfish; Crab Creek Review; Literary Review; Poetry Northwest. Honours: 4 grants to Helene Wurlitzer Foundation, Taos, New Mexico, 1988, 1990, 1991, 1993; Washington Writers Publishing House Prize for Moon and Mercury, 1990. Memberships: Associated Writers Program; Writers Center. Address: 6804 Kenyon Drive, Alexandria, VA 22307, USA.

MURPHY Lizz, b. 7 Aug 1950, Belfast, Northern Ireland. Writer. m. Bill Murphy, 21 Sept 1969, 1 son, 1 daughter. Appointments: Editor, Yass Tribune & Yass Post; Public Relations Officer, Canberra School of Art; Managing Editor, Incite, Australian Library and Information Association; Marketing Manager, Aboriginal Studies Press; Selfemployed Writer; Publicity Consultant. Publications: Do Fish Get Seasick, 1994; Pearls and Bullets, 1996; Anthologies: She's a Train and She's Dangerous, 1994; Eat the Ocean, 1996; Wee Girls, 1996. Contributions include: Shrieks; SMH; Earth Against Heaven; Who Do You Think You Are; Canberra Times; Antithesis; Redoubt; Muse; Imago; AWBR; ArS Poetica; Blast; Going Down Swinging; Heartland; Hobo; Pandora; Potpourri; Narcissus; Poetrix; Poetry Australia; Spindrift; Voices; WrN Review; Womanspeak. Honours: ANUtech Poetry Prize, 1994; Project Grants. Memberships: Australian Society of Authors; Poets Union; Island Press Coop; NSW Writers CR; National Book Council; Fellowship of Australian Authors; ACT Writers. Address: PO Binalong, NSW 2584, Australia.

MURPHY Merilene M, b. 20 Mar 1955, New Rochelle, New York, USA. Writer. Education: Journalism, International Affairs, Iowa State University, 1971-75; Zora Neale Hurston Scholar, 1995; Jack Kerouac School of Disembodied Poetics, Boulder. Appointments: Founder, President, Telepoetics. Publication: Under Peace Rising, 1995. Contributions to: Caffeine; Hyena; Trouble; National Poetry Association's National Collage Poem 1995. Honours: Turning Point Magazine's 1995 Living History Maker Arts and Entertainment Award for Telepoetics. Memberships: Poetry Society of America; International Black Writers and Artists; Poets and Writers. Address: 1939 1/4 West Washington Blvd, Los Angeles, CA 90018, USA.

MURPHY Sheila Ellen, b. 5 Apr 1951, Mishawaka, Indiana, USA. Management Consultant; Poet. Education: BA English and Music, Nazareth College; MA English, University of Michigan; PhD

Educational Administration and Supervision, Arizona State University. Appointments: Assistant Professor of English, Bay de Noc Community College, 1974-76; Doctoral Fellow, Arizona State University, 1976-78; Management Development Specialist, Ramada Inc, 1980-85; Director, Ramada Management Institute, 1985-87; Vice President Reservations, 1987-90-; Executive Director, Business and Management Programme, University of Phoenix, 1990-93; President, Shelia Murphy Associate, 1993-. Publications: Lens Rolled in a Heart, co-author; Appropriate Behaviour, 1986; This Stem Much Stronger Than Your Spine, 1989; Memory Transposed Into the Key of C. 1983; Late Summer, 1983; Virtuoso Bird, 1981; Loss Prevention Photograph, Some Pencils and a Memory Elastic, 1988; Sad Isn't the Colour of the Dream, 1991; With House Silence, 1987; TETH, 1991; Tommy and Neil, 1993; Pure Mental Breath, 1994; A Clove of Gender, 1995. Contributions to: Avec; Salt Lick; Paper Air; New York Quarterly; Big Allis; How(ever); Signal; Poetry Australia; Stride; Fennel Stalk; Lost and Found Times; Passages North; Puerto del Sol; Poetry Now; New Mexico Humanities Review; and others. Memberships: Arizona State Poetry Society; Phoenix Poetry Society; Valley Leadership; International Society for Performance Improvement. Address: 3701 East Monterosa No 3, Phoenix, AZ 85018. USA.

MURRAY John. See: **WRIGHT David.**

MURRAY III John E, b. 11 Feb 1973, Jacksonville, Illionis, USA. Writer; Teacher. Education: BA, Psychology, 1995; BA, English Teaching, 1995; Certified in Illionis to teach Psychology and English Grades 6-12. Appointments: Cineplex Odeon Employee, 1995; Assistant Store Manager, Doubleday Bookshop, 1992-96; Walt Disney World Cast Member, Costuming, 1996-. Publications: Rest Best?, 1994; Waiting For What?, 1994; Epitaph of an Angel, 1994; Romance - A Lost Cause, 1994; Most Recent Delight, 1994; Why Life?, 1995; True Friendship, 1995; Let Me Not Begin Anew, 1995; I Await the Day, 1995; Warnings of an Angel, 1995; You Are My Happiness, 1995; Done, 1995. Contributions to: Iliad Press; Arcadia Poetry Press; Quill Books; Amherst Society; Explorer Magazine; Poets Guild; National Library of Poetry; Thumbprints; Creative Arts and Science Enterprises; Sparrowgrass Poetry Forum. Honours: Editors Choice Award, National Library of Poetry, 1994, 1995; Honorable Mention & Presidents Award, Iliad Press, 1994; Accomplishment of Merit, Creative Arts & Science Enterprises, 1995. Memberships: International Society of Poets; National Authors Registry. Address: 2040 Hilltop Road, Hoffman Estates, IL 60195, USA.

MURRAY Les(lie Allan), b. 17 Oct 1938, Australia. Poet; Translator. m. 29 Sept 1962, 3 sons, 2 daughters. Education: BA, Sydney University, 1969; Hon DLitt, University of New England, 1990; Hon DUniv, Stirling, 1992; HonDLitt, ANU, Canberra, 1994. Appointments: Scholarly Translator, Australian National University, 1963-67; Prime Minister's Department, Canberra, 1970; Freelance, 1970-. Publications include: The Ilex Tree (with Geoffrey Lehmann), 1965; The Weatherboard Cathedral, 1969; Poems Against Economics, 1972; Lunch and Counter Lunch, 1974; Selected Poems, The Vernacular Republic, 1976, 2nd Edition, 1982; Ethnic Radio, 1978; The Boys Who Stole the Funeral, 1980; Equanimities, 1982; The People's Otherworld, 1983; Persistence in Folly, 1984; The Australian Year (with Peter Solness, 1986; The Daylight Moon, 1986; Dog Fox Field, 1990; Collected Poems, 1991; The Rabbiter's Bounty, 1992; Translations from the Natural World, 1992; Editor, 1986: Collins Dove Anthology of Australian Religious Verse; New Oxford Book of Australian Verse, 1986. Contributions to: Times Literary Supplement; London Review of Books; PN; Poetry; World International; Poetry Wales; Poetry Ireland Review; Australian; Adelaide Review; Sydney Review; New Republic; Partisan Review; New Yorker; Landfall; Meanjin; New Australia; Trucking Life; Scripsi; Yale Review; Quadrant; Tablet; Paris Reviewer; Planet; Ulitarra; Sport; Canberra Times; Grand Street; Island; Poetry Kanto; Antipodes; Truck and Bus; Others. Honours: Grace Leven Prize, 1965, 1980, 1990; Cook Bi-Centennial Prize, 1970; National Book Awards, 1974, 1984, 1985, 1991, 1993; C J Dennis Memorial Prize, 1976; Gold Medal, Australian Literary Society, 1984; New South Wales Premier's Prize, 1984; Christopher Brennan Medal, Fellowship of Australian Writers, 1985; Canada-Australia Award, 1985; National Poetry Award, 1988; Australian Broadcasting Corporation Bicentennial Prize, 1988; Choice (2), Recommendation (3), Poetry Book Society; Honorary Vice President, Poetry Society of Great Britain; New South Wales and Victoria Premiers Prizes, 1993; The Petrarca Preis, Germany, 1995. Address: Margaret Connolly and Associates, 27 Ormond Street, Paddington, New South Wales 2021, Australia.

MURRAY Patrick. See: **PATTEN Bernard M.**

MURRAY Rona Jean, b. 10 Feb 1924, England. Retired University Lecturer. m. (1) Gerry Haddon, 10 Feb 1944, (2) Walter Dexter, 28 Jan 1972, 2 sons. 1 daughter. Education: Mills College, Oakland, California, 1941-44; BA, 1961, MA, 1968, University of Victoria, British Columbia; PhD, University of Victoria, Kent at Canterbury, 1972. Appointments: Lecturer, University of British Columbia, 1963-66; Selkirk College, British Columbia, 1968-74; Douglas College, British Columbia, 1974-76; University of Victoria, British Columbia, 1977-84; Open University, British Columbia, 1984-. Publications: Blue Ducks Feather and Eagledown, verse play, 1958; The Enchanted Adder, 1965; The Power of the Dog, 1968; Ootischenie, 1974; Selected Poems, 1974; Journey, 1981: Adam and Eve in Middle Age, 1984; Six Poets of British Columbia, 1980; Journey Back to Peshawar, 1993. Contributions to: Canadian Poetry; Commonwealth Poetry; Fiddlehead; Prism International: Canadian Forum; Voices (USA); Alphabet; Alaska Review (USA); Envoy (UK); Poet (India); Blackfish Review; Vanguard; Malahat Review; Event; Bibliographical Archaeologist; Moznaim (Israel); A Canadian Anthology; Contemporary Poets of British Columbia; The New Oxford Book of Canadian Verse, BBC; CBC; Western Listings; Monday Magazine. Honours: Blue Ducks Feather Award, 1958; MacMillan of Canada Creative Writing Award, 1964; Norma Epstein National Award for Creative Writing, 1965; Canadian Council short term grant for book of poems, 1976; Canadian Council B grant for poetry, 1979; Pat Lowther Award for best book of poetry by a woman for that year, 1982. Literary Agent: Carolyn N Swayze, NRPS PO Box 39588, White Rock, British Columbia, V4A 9P3, Canada. Address: 3825 Duke Road, RR4 Victoria, British Columbia, V9B 5T8, Canada.

MURTHY D Srikantha, b. 14 Jan 1952, Mysore, India. Geologist. m. Swarna Murthy, 12 June 1981, 1 son, 1 daughter. Education: BSc; MSc. Appointments: Geologist. Publications: Just Born; Guest for Joy; East West Winds; East West Voices; Life and Love. Contributions to: Samavedana; Poet; Kavita India; Poet International. Honour: International Eminent Poet. Memberships: Chetana Literary Group; International Poets Academy. Address: 251 I Cross 6th Block, Banashankari 3rd Stage, Bangalore 560085, India.

MURTI K V S. See: **KOTIKALAPUDI Venkata Suryanarayana Murti.**

MUSBACH Ruth Ann, b. 20 Mar 1964, Lincoln, Nebraska, USA. Writer. 1 son. Education: Macalester College, 1982-84; Midland Lutheran College, 1985; BA, English and Creative Writing, 1987, University of Minnesota, 1986-87, 1992. Publications: For Love of Michael, volume 1, 1991, Volume 2, 1992. Contributions to: American Knight; Coventry News; Our Journey. Membership: Children's Bookwriter's Society, 1989-90. Address: PO Box 130723, St Paul, MN 55113, USA.

MUSGRAVE Susan, b. 12 Mar 1951, Santa Cruz, California, USA. Poet; Writer; Teacher. m. Stephen Douglas Reid, 1986, 2 daughters. Education: Oak Bay High School. Appointments: Instructor and Writer-in-Residence, University of Waterloo, Ontario, 1983-85; Instructor, Kootenay School of Writing, British Columbia, 1986, Camosun College, Victoria, British Columbia, 1988-90; Writer-in-Residence, University of New Brunswick, Fredericton, 1985, Vancouver Public Library, 1986, Sidney Public Library, British Columbia, 1989, University of Western Ontario, 1992-93, University of Toronto, 1995; Writer-in-Electronic-Residence, York University, 1991-94. Publications include: Poetry: Selected Strawberries and Other Poems, 177; For Charlie Beaulieu..., 1977; Two Poems for the Blue Moon, 1977; Becky Swan's Book, 1978; A Man to Marry, A Man to Bury, 1979; Conversation During the Omelette aux Fines Herbes, 1979; When My Boots Drive Off in a Cadillac, 1980; Taboo Man, 1981; Tarts and Muggers: Poems New and Selected, 1982; The Plane Put Down in Sacramento, 1982; I Do Not Know If Things That Happen Can Be Said To Come To Pass or Only Happen, 1982; Cocktails at the Mausoleum, 1985; Desireless: Tom York, 1947-1988, 1988; Musgrave Landing, 1988; The Embalmer's Art: Poems New and Selected, 1991; In the Small Hours of the Rain, 1991; Forcing the Narcissus, 1994; Fiction: The Dancing Chicken, 1987; Other: Musgrave Landing: Musings on the Writing Life, 1994. Honours: 8 Canada Council Grants, 1969-1991; National Magazine Award, Silver, 1981; Nichol Poetry Chapbook Award, 1991; British Columbia Cultural Fund Grants, 1991, 1994; Reader's Choice Award, Prairie Schooner, 1993. Address:

10301 West Saanich Road, PO Box 2421, Sidney, British Columbia V8L 3Y3, Canada.

MUSICK Martin. See: **GILLILAND Brian Keith.**

MUSSON Cecile Norma. See: **SMITH Cecile Musson.**

MYCUE Edward Delehant, b. 21 Mar 1937, Niagara Falls, New York, USA. Poet. Education: BA, North Texas State University, 1959; Graduate Study at North Texas and Boston University as Lowell Scholar, University of California at Berkeley and University College at Legon, Ghana, 1959-61; International Peoples College, Elsinore, Denmark, 1968-69. Appointments: College and High School Teacher; Editor; US Peace Corps Teacher, Ghana; US Department of Health, Education and Welfare Intergovernmental Relations Specialist to 1968; Freelance Writer and Lecturer; Field Labourer and Dock Worker; Book Shop Employee and Shop Manager; Publisher, Norton Coker Press and Took Magazine. Publications: Damage Within The Community, 1973; Chronicle, 1974; Root, Route and Range, 1977; Root, Route and Range · The Song Returns, 1979; The Singing Man My Father Gave Me, 1980; Edward, 1987; Poems, 1988; No One For Free, 1989; A Grate Country, 1989; Next Year's Words, 1989; Pink Garden/Brown Trees, 1990; Because We Speak the Same Language, 1994; Split: Life As Built From the Inside Out, 1995. Contributions to: European Judaism; Stand; Littack; Meanjin; Crosscurrents; Dalhousie; Caliban; Green's; Gypsy; Amherst; Poetry Ireland Review; On The Bus; Exile; Homocore; Holy Titclamps; Fag Rag; Changing Men; Malcontent; Inside Joke; Peace and Freedom; Score; Minotaur; James White Review; Lynx; Global Tapestry. Honour: MacDowell Colony Fellow, 1974. Memberships: PEN; Local Guilds and Unions. Address: PO Box 640543, San Francisco, CA 94164, USA.

N

NAFTALI Ben. See: OFFEN Yehuda.

NAGAYAMA Mokuo, b. 14 Dec 1929, Kurashiki, Japan. School Teacher. m. Kazuko Hashimoto, 5 May 1960, 1 son, 1 daughter. Education: Doshisha College of Foreign Affairs, 1950. Publications: Snow Bridge, 1976; Mist on the Ridge, 1985; To the Zodiac Animals, 1988. Contributions to: Poetry Nippon; International Poetry; Prophetic Voices; Amber; New Canadian Review; Iron; Poetry Nottingham; Noreal; Poet. Honours: Sangaman Writers International Poetry Contest. USA, 2nd Prize, 1983; Japalish Review Poetry Contest, Japan, 1st Prize, 1985. Memberships: Poetry Society of Japan; British Haiku Society. Address: 1168 Ouchi, Kurashiki, Okayama, Japan.

NAHAR Manak Chand, b. 3 Oct 1944, India. Official Language Instructor. m. Smt Sushila Manak Chand Nahar, 12 Dec 1964, 2 sons, 3 daughters. Education: MA, University of Jabalpur, India. Appointment: Director, Seth Bakhtawar Research Institute. Publications: Sahityakar. Contributions to: Hindi Poet; Rajasthani Poet; Gujrati Poet. Honours: Manak Chand Nahar and His Contributions to the Hindi Literature. MembershipsP: D B Hindi Prachar Sabha. Address: 58 Mylapore Bazaar Road, Mylapore, Madras 600004, India.

NAHRA Nancy Ann, b. 11 May 1947, Bangor, Maine, USA. Poet; Novelist; University Lecturer. m. Willard Sterne Randall, 19 Oct 1985, 1 daughter. Education: BA, Classics, Colby College, Maine, 1968; MA, Classics, Stanford University, 1971; PhD, Romance Languages, Princeton University, 1989. Appointments: Editorial Assistant, Random House, New York City, 1971-72; Editor, Speechwriter, Institute of Signage Research, Palo Alto, California, 1972-77; University Lecturer, Ohio State University, University of Vermont, 1978-93; Poet-in-Residence, John Cabot University, Rome, 1996-. Publication: Personal Reflections on The Lake, 1987; Not From Around Here, 1990; More Charming, 1995. Contributions to: Best New Poets of 1986; American Poetry Anthology; Art of Poetry: A Treasure of Contemporary Verse. Honour: John Masefield Award, Poetry Society of America, 1987. Memberships: Poetry Society of America; Academy of American Poets; Phi Beta Kappa; Founder and Director, Lake Poetry Workshop, Burlington, Vermont; American Society of Eighteenth Century Studies; North American Society for The Study of Jean-Jacques Rousseau; Princeton Club of New York. Address: 200 Summit Street, Burlington, VT 05401, USA.

NAIDU Tulsi, (H Thulasikumari), b. 10 June 1938, Kharagpur, India. Editor; Publisher. m. H M Naidu, 31 Dec 1980. Education: BA, English Literature, 1960; PhD, English Literature, USA, 1994. Appointments: Personnal Secretary to various IAS Officers in Andhra Pradesh Secretariat, Hyderabad, 1960-70; Official Reporter (English), Lok Sabha Secretariat, 1970-81. Publications: Old Wine in New Bottles, 1993; Resurrection - Book I, 1993; Sonnet Century, 1995; Ballads and Ballades, 1995; A Nosegay of New Year Poems, 1996; Lyrics and Limericks, in print. Contributions to: World Poetry; Poet; Poetcrit; Poesie India; Kavita India; Poetry Time; Inner Voice; Prophetic Voices; Skylark; Quest; Writers Forum; United Writers Association Magazine; Lok Patrika; AP Sect Magazine; Samvedana; Canopy; Triveni. Honours: First Prize, AP Sect Magazine; First Prize, Lok Patrika; Honorable Mention, Quest; Citations from Director of Public Libraries; Michael Madhusudan Award, 1996. Memberships: Life Fellow, United Writers Association; Friend of Indian Pen; Writers Forum; Editor-Publisher, Metverse Muse. Address: 21-46/1 Kakani Nagar, NAD Post Office, Visakhapatnam 530009, Andhra Pradesh, India.

NAIK Vihang, b. 2 Sept 1969, Surat. Education: BA, MS, English and Indian Literature, University of Baroda, India, 1993; MA, MS, English and Indian Literature, University of Baroda, 1996. Appointment: Lecturer in English Literature, Pranjii College, near Ahmedabad. Publocations; City Times (a book of poems), 1993. Contributions to: Poems in leading Indian journals includng: The Indian PEN; The Journal of the Poetry Society (India); The Brown Critique; The Journal of Indian Writing in English; Kavya Bharati; Poiesis, a journal of the Poetry Circle, Bombay; The Quest; Poet; Art and Poetry Today; Poetry Time; Anthologies: Poems 96; Poems 97; World Poetry 96; World Poetry 97. Reviews in the Indian Book Chronicle; The Scoria; Poetry Time; Articles in The Times of India; Various readings.

Memberships: The Poetry Society (India); Forum on Contemporary Theory, MSU, Baroda; The Poetry Circle, Bombay; The PEN All-India Center (LF), Bombay; Gujurati Sahitya Parishad, Awmedabad. Address: 3, Kamdurga Society, Sec-2, Opp Ankur bus stop, Naranpura, Ahmedabad 380 013, India.

NAIL Shirley Dianne, b. 14 Jan 1958, Catawba, North Carolina, USA. Editor; Writer. Education: Catawba Valley Technical Institute; Newspaper Institute of American Poetry; BA, Christian Education, Grace Bible College, 1991. Appointments: News Editor, Cut Eye, Catawba Valley Technical Institute; Sports Correspondent, Hickory Daily Record. Contributions to: Anthologies. Honours: Poet of Merit, American Poetry Association, 1989; Honourable Mention, Oxfam Poetry Contest, 1989. Address: Rt 1, Box 442-A, Hickory, NC 28602, USA.

NAIMAN Anatoly G, b. 23 Apr 1936, Leningrad, Russia. Poet; Writer. m. Galina Narinskaia, 1969, 1 son, 1 daughter. Education: Degree, Organic Chemistry, Leningrad Technological Institute, 1958; Diploma, Postgraduate Course in Screenwriting, Moscow, 1964. Appointments: Visiting Professor, Russian Poetry, Bryn Mawr College, USA, 1991; Visiting Fellow, All Souls College, Oxford, England, 1991-92. Publications: The Poems of Anatoly Naiman, in Russian, 1989; Remembering Anna Akhmatova, 1989, 1991-92; The Statue of a Commander and Other Stories, 1992; Translations into Russian: The Poems of Giacomo Leopardi, 1967, 1989; Songs of Troubadours, 1979; Flamenca, 1983, 1984; Floire et Blanceflor, 1985; Le Roman de Renard, 1986; Le Roman de Sept Sages, 1989. Contributions to: Novy Mir; Oktiabr; Continent; Zvezda; Literaturnaia Gazeta; Russkaia Mysl'; L'Espresso; Times Literary Supplement. Honour: Prize for translation of Latvian poetry into Russian, Latvian Union of Writers, 1981. Memberships: Writers Committee, Moscow; PEN Club, French Branch; Formerly: Writers Committee, Leningrad; Leningrad Four Group of Poets. Address: Dmitrovskoye Schosse 29, fl 56, Moscow, Russia.

NAIR Yogesh G, b. 21 Mar 1966, Trichur, Kerala, India. Management Consultant. Education: Graduated in Arts with Psychology, 1987; Master's course in Organisational Psychology, 1989; Postgraduate Diploma in HRD, Mississippi University, 1990; MBA studies with Newport University (USA) through Baroda Productivity Council, Baroda. Appointments: Administrative Assistant, Datapro Information Technology, 1989-90; Executive (Placement), Rightman Placement Services, Baroda; Executive, Baroda Productivity Council, Baroda. Contributions to: Indian Express; Children's World; Home Life; Teenager; Byword; Bharat Protiva; Skylark; Triveni; Poet; Poetry; Poetry Time; Canopy; Eureka; New Literary Horizons; Poésie; City Courier; New Quest; Poetcrit; Rachna India; Samavedna; Kavita India and Commonwealth Quarterly; Around 65 poems published and poems included in 4 anthologies. Memberships: Associate Member, Poetry Society, India; Friend Member, PEN, All India Centre. Address: 14/85 Refinery Township, PO Jawaharnagar, Baroda 391320, Gujarat, India.

NAM Ching Tin. See: WONG Wai Ming (Otis).

NAN Yong Qian, (Yan Yi), b. 3 Mar 1948, Huinan, China. Publisher. m. 27 Jan 1970, 3 sons. Education: Graduated, Liuhe High School, 1967; Graduated, Writers Institute, Jilin, 1987. Appointments: President, Editor-in-Chief, Chang Bai Mountains Publishing House of China; Researcher, Institute for Research in Korean Culture, Beijing University, 1991. Publications: Poems of Longing and Nostalgia, 1987; Poems of Optimism, 1988; Totem Poems, 1990; White Crane Poems, 1992. Contributions to: Poetic Publications, Beijing; National Literature, Beijing; National Writers, Xinjiang; Poets, Changchun; Writers, Changchun; Heaven Pool, Yanji; World Poetry, USA. Honours: Most Effective Writer, 10 times, 1982-92; Chinese Minority Nationalities Literature Prizes, 1985, 1990; Chang Bai Mountains Literature and Art Award, Jilin, 1987; Folk Literature and Art Awards, Chinese Writers Association, 1988, 1992. Memberships: World Academy and Culture Inc; Governing Board, World Congress of Poets; Writers Association; Folk Literature and Art Association of China; Vice Secretary General, Institute of Minority Nationalities of China; Vice President, Korean Culture Exchange Committee of China. Address: 16 Xisidao Street, Nanguan District, Changchun, China.

NANDY Pritish, b. 1947, India. Poet; Translator; Editor. Appointments: Editor, Dialogue Calcutta, later Dialogue India, 1968-. Publications: Of Gods and Olives, 21 poems, 1967; I Hand You in Turn

My Nebbuk Wreath: Early Poems, 1968; On Either Side of Arrogance, 1968; Rites for a Plebian Statue: An Experiment in Verse Drama, 1969; From The Outer Bank of The Brahmaputra, 1969; Ravana's Lament: A Selection From The Abhiseka Swarga of the Meghnad-Badh Kavya of Michael Madhusudhan Data, 1969; Masks to be Interpreted as Messages, 1970; Collected Poems, 1973; Riding the Midnight River: Selected Poems, 1975; Lone Song Street, 1975; Stranger Called I, 1976; In Secret Anarchy, 1976; Nowhere Man, 1978; Anywhere is Another Place, 1979; Tonight This Savage Rite: The Love Poetry of Kamala Das and Pritish Nandy, 1979; The Rainbow Last Night, 1981; Some Friends, 1983; Editor: Getting Rid of Blue Plastic: Poems Old and New, by Margaret Randall, 1968; Some Modern Cuban Poems, 1968; Selected Poems of Subhas Mukhopadhyay, 1969; Selected Poems of Parvez Shadedi, 1969; Selected Poems of G Sankara Kurup, 1969; Selected Poems of Agyeya, 1969; Selected Poems of Amrita Pritam, 1970; Indian Poetry in English Today, 1973; Modern Indian Poetry, 1974; Bengali Poetry Today, 1974; Editor, Translator, The Complete Poems of Samar Sen, 1970. Address: 5 Pearl Road, Calcutta 17, India.

NANGINI Mary Angela, b. 1 Jan 1948, Italy. Teacher. 2 sons, 1 daughter. Education: BA, York University, 1971; BEd, University of Toronto, 1978; BEd. York University, 1985; MA, University of Connecticut-Storrs, 1988; Doctoral Studies, Ontario Institute for Studies in Education, 1995; MTS, St Augustine Seminary of Toronto, 1996-. Appointments: Teacher of the Gifted; Member, Consortium & Educators of the Gifted, Ontario; Artist; Presenter at Gifted Globe, 10th World Congress on Gifted & Talented Education, Toronto, 1993. Publications: Woman in Exile, (book of poetry), 1991; My Ontario Beautiful, (book of poetry), 1995; With a Bang or a Whimper, (play, co-author), 1993. Contributions to: National Library Collections; The Ebbing Tide; Best Poems of the 90s. Honours: Editors Choice Awards, National Library of Poetry, 1995, 1996. Memberships: League of Canadian Poets; International Society of Poets. Address: 42 Brookview Road. Brampton, Ontario L6X 2V9, Canada.

NANNINI Gregg, b. 28 June 1961, Detroit, Michigan, USA. Artist; Poet. Education: BA, English, Western Michigan University, Kalamazoo, 1986. Appointment: Editor and Publisher, Poetry Journal, Kangaroos and Beans, 1990-. Publications: The Lost Generation, 1990; Strange Angels, 1993; Pathways, 1994. Contributions to: Kangaroos and Beans; Cambio Magazine; Fact Sheet Five; New Hope International; Parnassus of World Poets, 1994; White Wall Review; Magic Mountain; Metro Times; Nocturnal Lyric. Honour: Redpath Award for Young Poets, 1990. Membership: Artists Against Censorship. Address: 20484 Kinloch. Redford, MI 48240 1115, USA.

NAOMI French Wallace, b. 17 Aug 1960, USA. Poet; Playwright. Education: BA, Hampshire College. 1982; MFA, University of Iowa, 1986, 1993. Appointments: Teacher of Playwrighting, University of Iowa, 1990-93; Playwright in Residence, Illinois State, 1994. Publications: Slaughter City, (drama); In the Heart of America, (drama); To Dance a Stony Field, (poems). Contributions to: Nation; Massachusetts Review; Antioch Review; Iowa Review; Salmagundi; Three Penny Review; Chicago Review; American Voice; News Letters; Chelsea; London Magazine; Stand; Verse; Bete Noire; American Theatre. Honours: The Nation Discovery Award; Kentucky Arts Council Fellowship; Kentucky Foundation for Women Grant; Mobil Playwrighting Award (UK); Susam Smith Blackburn Playriting Award (UK and USA). Literary Agents: Joyce Ketay Agency, USA, & A P Watt, England. Address: 4575 Hwy 6 SE, Iowa City, IA 52240, USA.

NAPIER (Bernard) Alan, b. 5 June 1945, East Grand Rapids, Michigan, USA. General Manager of screen printing company. m. Shirley M Elsbury. 5 Sept 1970, 1 son, 1 daughter. Education: BA, Comparative Literature, minor Russian Literature, Kent State University, Kent, Ohio, 1973. Contributions to: Four Quarters; American Poetry Review; Chelsea; Juggler's World; Long Islander Newspaper; Nimrod; Hiram Poetry Review; Southern Poetry Review; Negative Capability; Confrontation; Webster Review; MacGuffin; Colorado Review; Key West Review; Mid-American Review; Hibiscus Magazine: Blue Buildings; Green Mountains Review; Spirit That Moves Us; Kentucky Poetry Review; Oxford Magazine. Honours: Finalist, Eve of St Agnes Competition. 1989; Finalist, National Poetry Competition, 1990. Memberships: Academy of American Poets; Poetry Society of America. Address: 3799 Olmsby Drive, Brimfield, OH 44240, USA.

NAPIER Felicity Anne, b. 15 Dec 1943. Croydon, Surrey, England. Creative Writing and Therapy Tutor; Writer of Poetry, Short

Fiction and Drama. m. 10 Jan 1968, 1 daughter. Education: BA, 1st Class Honours, Kingston Polytechnic, 1986. Appointments: Part-time Tutor at various day-centres and hospitals. Contributions to: Honest Ulsterman; Ambit; Spectator; New Statesman; Poetry Review; Literary Review; Outposts; Encounter; Pen; New Welsh Review; Anthologies: Bread and Roses, 1982; No Holds Barred, 1985; Fire The Sun, 1989; Ambit New Poetry, 1990. Honours: Runner-Up, Cheltenham Literary Festival Poetry Competition, 1981; Runner-Up, Stroud Poetry Festival, 1981; Winner, Redcliffe National Poetry Competition, 1983; Winner, Leek Poetry Competition, 1983. Address: 10 Sion Row, Twickenham TW1 3DR, England.

NARASIMHAN Kotur Srinivasan, b. 15 May 1939, Krishnarajsagar, India. Chemical Engineer. Writer. m. Sheela, 7 Mar 1965, 2 daughters. Education: BSc, 1957; DIISc, 1959; PhD, 1964. Appointments: Central Electricity Generating Board, UK, 1964; Council of Scientific and Industrial Research, Government of India, 1965-91; Regional Research Laboratory Bhubaneswar; Consultant in USA, 1991-92; Director, Central Fuel Research Institute, Dhanbad, India, 1992-. Address: Central Fuel Research Institute, Dhanbad, 828108 Bihar, India.

NASH Susan Smith, b. 2 Apr 1958, Ardmore, Oklahoma, USA. Geologist. m. David Nash, 12 Feb 1982, 1 son. Education: BS, 1981. MA, 1989, PhD, 1996, University of Oklahoma. Publications: Pornography, 1992; My Love is Apocalypse and Rhinestone, 1993; Veil in the Sand, 1994; Grammar of the Margin Road, 1993; Liquid Babylon, 1994; A Paleontologists Notebook, 1995; Channel-Surfing the Apocalypse, 1996. Contributions to: Washington Review; World Literature Today; Avec; Talisman; Central Park; Another Chicago Magazine; Paper Air. Honours: Gertrude Stein Award in Innovative Writing; Goldia Cooksey Prize for Creative Accomplishments. Address: 3760 Cedar Ridge Drive, Norman, OK 73072, USA.

NASSAR Eugene Paul, b. 20 Jun 1935. Professor of English. m. Karen Nocian, 30 Dec 1969, 1 son, 2 daughter. Education: BA, Kenyon College, 1957; MA, Worcester College, Oxford University, 1960; PhD, Cornell University, 1962. Appointments: Hamilton College, 1962-64; Utica College of Syracuse University, 1964-. Publications: Selections From a Prose Poem: East Utica, 1971; Wind of The Land: Two Prose Poems, 1979; Other books and articles. Contributions to: College English; Renascence; Essays in Criticism; Paideuma; Mosaic; American Oxonian; Melus; Wallace Stevens Journal; Syracuse Scholar; New York Folklore; Modern Age; Sewanee Review; Bulletin of Research in the Humanities; Dictionary of American Immigration History; Contexts for Criticism. Honours: Grants and Fellowships: Featured in anthology, Grapeleaves: A Century of Arab-American Poetry, 1988. Address: 704 Lansing Street, Utica, NY 13501, USA.

NASSAUER Rudolf, b. 1924. England. Novelist; Writer; Poet. Publications: Poems, 1947; The Holigan, 1959; The Cuckoo, 1962; The Examination, 1973; The Unveiling, 1975; The Agents of Love. 1976; Midlife Feasts, 1977; Reparations, 1981; Kramer's Goats, 1986. Address: 51 St James' Gardens, London W11, England.

NATARASAN Era, b. 8 Dec 1964, Lalgudi, Trichy District, South India. Lecturer in Psychology. Education: Undergraduate, 1982; Graduate, in Physics, 1985; Postgraduation in Psychology, 1988; Diploma in Journalism, 1989. Appointments: Secretary, Bharati Form of Poets, Karur, 1983-85; President, Young Tamil Poets Conference, 1987. Publications: Tamil Poem Collections: Midnight Poems, 1985; Footprints From a Graveyard, 1986; Black War, 1989; Headlines Once Again, 1990; The Started, 1991. Contributions to: Poet, Intercontinental; The Week; Poesy India; Debonire; Manushee; Ananda Vikadan; Junior Vikadan; Kalki; Thai; Kanavu; Nigazh; Thalam; Arangatram; Manin; Vairu; Akalam; Idayam; Kathavu; Kanmadi. Honour: Bharati Medal. 1985. Memberships: Organiser, Voice of Tamil Poets; World Poetry Society, USA; Bangalore Short Journal's Organisation; Faculty, United Writer's Association, Madras; Poets House, Trichy; Puratchi Kavignar Mandram; Faculty, Vizhi (Eye); World University Round Table. Arizona. Address: 23 Renganathan Street, Ganeshnagar, Madras 600032, South India.

NATHAN Leonard Edward, b. 8 Nov 1924, Los Angeles, California, USA. Teacher. m. Carol Gretchen Nash, 27 June 1949, 1 son, 2 daughters. Education: BA (with highest honours), 1950, MA, 1951, PhD, 1961, University of California at Berkeley. Appointments: Instructor, Modesto Junior College, California, 1954-60; Professor, Department of Rhetoric 1961-91, Chairman. Department of Rhetoric

1968-72, Emeritus 1991-, University of California at Berkeley. Publications: Western Reaches, 1958; Glad and Sorry Seasons, 1963; The Matchmakers Lament, 1967; The Day The Perfect Speakers Left, 1969; Flight Plan, 1971; Without Wishing, 1973; Coup and Other Poems, 1975; The Likeness: Poems Out of India, 1975; Returning Your Call, 1975; Teachings of Grandfather Fox, 1976; Lost Distance, 1978; Dear Blood, 1980; Holding Patterns, 1982; Carrying On: New and Selected Poems, 1985; The Tragic Drama of W B Yeats, Figures in a Dance, 1963; The Poet's Work: An Introduction to Czeslaw Milosz, 1991; Diary of a Left-handed Bird Watcher, 1996. Contributions to: Shenandoan; New Yorker; Prairie Schooner; Massachusetts Review; Salmagundi; Quarterly Review of Literature; Antioch Review; Perspective; Antaeus Review; Epoch; Commentary; Nation; New Republic; Georgia Review; Ohio Review; New England Review; Breadloaf Quarterly; and others. Honours: Phalen Award for Narrative Poetry, 1955; Longview Foundation Award for Poetry, 1962; National Institute of Arts and Letters Award for Creative Literature, 1971; Creative Arts Fellowship, University of California, 1963-64, 1973-74; Commonwealth Club Silver Medal for Poetry, 1976, 1980; Guggenheim Fellowship, 1976-77. Memberships: PEN West; Academy of American Poets. Address: 40 Beverly Road, Kensington, CA 94707-1304, USA.

NAVEH David, b. 3 June 1922, Manchester, England. Agronomist. m. 13 Jan 1956, 2 sons. Education: Training Farm, Wiltshire, England, 1941-46; Agronomy, Plant Protection, Orchard Refrigeration-Controlled Atmosphere, Ruppin Agicultural College, Israel. Appointments: Plant Protection Officer, Orchards, Galilee District; Officer for Controlled Atmosphere - Refrigeration, Khar Blum. Publication: A Rhyme in Time, humourous poems, 1992. Contributions to: Jerusalem Post; Link; Kfar Blum; Voices Israel. Honour: 1st Prize for Humour, Reuben Rose International Poetry Competition, 1990. Memberships: Voices Israel; Israel English Poetry Association. Address: Kibbut Kfar Blum, Mobile Post, Upper Galilee 12 150, Israel.

NAZKI Mohammad Farooq, b. 16 Feb 1940, Madar, Bandipore, Kashmir, India. Civil Servant. m. Bilqees, 19 Oct 1963, 1 son, 2 daughters. Education: BA, Philosophy, English Literature, History, Persian; Diploma, Indian Music; MA, Urdu, University of Kashmir; Diploma in TV Programme Production, Sender Fries Berlin, Germany. Appointments: Editor, Daily Mazdoor; Director, Information Division, J & K; Member, Central Committee, Academy of Art, Culture and Languages; Director, All India Radio, Jammu, Srinagar and Leh; Director, Doordarshan Kendra Srinagar. Publications: Kashmiri Dustkariyan (History of Handicrafts of Kashmir), 1970; Akhri Khawab Se Pehley (Anthology of Poetry), 1990; Lafz Lafz Nawah (Poetry in Urdu), 1994; Naar Hatun Kazil Wanus (Poetry in Kashmiri), 1994; Gaye Rutoon Ke Sathi (Poetry in Hindi), 1995; Mahjabeen (Kashmiri Mathnavi), 1996; Rashk-E-Urdu (Poetry), 1996. Contributions to: Aaj Kal; Beeswin Sadi; Qalamkaar; Zehni Jadid; Shiraza. Honours: Sahitya Akadamy Literary Award, for Collection of Poems, 1995; Best Book of Urdu Poetry Award, 1995; Best Book of Kashmiri Poetry Award, 1995. Memberships: Central Committee, J & K Academy of Art, Culture and Languages, Jammu and Kashmir. Address: 1 Shervani Road, Srinagar, 190001 Kashmir, India.

NEAL Herbert. See: **EVERS Jason Harvey**.

NEEF Roger Marie Joseph de, b. 24 June 1941, Wemmel, Belgium. Journalist. m. Anne-Marie Constance Vanden Wijngaert, 17 Sept 1977. Education: University degree in Contemporary History; University degree in Press and Journalism. Appointments: Theatre Critic, BRTN Radio One, 1967-72; Journalist, National Press Agency, Belga, 1972-; Contributor, Literature, Jazz Music and Painting Sections, BRTN, 1977-89. Publications: Winterrunen, 1967; Lichaam mijn landing, 1969; De Grote Wolk, 1972; Gestorven Getal, 1977; Gedichten van Licht en Overspel, 1982; De vertelkunst van de bloemen, 1985; De halsband van de duif, 1993; Empty Bed Blues, 1996. Contributions to: Nieuw Vlaams Tijdschrift; Dietsche Warande en Belfort; Impuls; De Vlaamse Gids; Kentering; Diogenes. Honours: 8 Poetry prizes; De Arkprijs van het Vrije Woord, 1978; Three-yearly State Prize for Poetry, 1982-85. Memberships: PEN Club Flanders; Association of Flemish Authors. Address: Hoeve Winterrunen, Lammeneelstraat nr 11, 2220 Heist-op-den-Berg, Belgium.

NEILL William, (Uilleam Neill), b. 22 Feb 1922, Prestwick, Ayrshire, Scotland. Retired Teacher. m. (1) 2 daughters, (2) Doris Marie Walker Gilmour, 2 April 1970. Education: MA (Hons), University of Edinburgh, 1971; Teacher's Certificate, 1972. Publications:

Scotland's Castle, 1970; Poems, 1970; Four Points of a Saltire (co-author), 1970; Despatches Home, 1972; Galloway Landscape, 1981; Once a Mogail, 1983; Wild Places, 1985; Blossom, Berry, Fall, 1986; Making Tracks, 1991; Straight Lines, 1992; Tales from the Odyssey, 1992; Selected Poems 1969-92, 1994. Contributions to: Chapman; Lines Review; Scotsman; Envoi; Agenda; Cencrastus; Pennine Platform; Orbis; BBC Scotland; BBC Radio 4; STV; Tratti, Italy; Innti, Eire; Pembroke, USA; The Dark Horse. Honours: Bardic Crown, National Gaelic MOD, 1969; Sloan Verse Prize, 1970; Grierson Prize, 1970; Scottish Arts Council Book Award, 1985. Membership: Scottish Branch, PEN International. Address: Burnside, Crossmichael, Castle Douglas, Kirkcudbrightshire DG7 3AP, Scotland.

NELSON Charles Lamar, b. 9 June 1917, Lafayette County, Mississippi, USA. Retired High School Guidance Counsellor. m. Lena Reaves, 1 Oct 1940, 1 son, 1 daughter, dec. Education: BA, 1946, MA, 1947, University of Mississippi; Further study: Auburn University, 1957; Shorter College, 1967. Appointments: Teacher, Principal, Guidance Counsellor in various public schools, 1940-72; Welfare Agent, Adams County Welfare Department, Natchez, Mississippi, 1972-82. Publication: The Marble Urn, 1941; William Faulkner: The Anchorite of Rowan Oak, 1973; A Chain That Breaks a Man, 1975. Contributions to: National Poetry Anthology; Mid-Century Prose and Verse; Mississippi Poetry Journal; Flights of Fancy (A Treasury of Modern Poetry); Poems That Will Live Forever; Our World's Favourite Gold and Silver Poets; Today's Poets. Honours: Golden Poet Awards, 1987, 1989; Silver Poet Award, 1990; Outstanding Achievement in Poetry, World of Poetry. Memberships: Natchez Poetry Society, Co-Founder, 1st President, 1959-60; Mississippi Poetry Society, Treasurer, 1964-65; Columbus Poetry Society, Co-Founder, 1st President, 1980-81; Association of Christian Poets, Co-Founder, Chairman of Publicity, 1984-85; Willian Faulkner Society of International Poets, Founder, 1st President, 1985-86. Address: 712 South 19th Street, Oxford, MS 38655, USA.

NELSON Jo, b. 2 May 1946, Del Norte, Colorado, USA. Bookseller; Real Estate Agent; Writer. Education: BA, German, University of Colorado, Boulder, 1968. Appointments: Secondary Teacher, German, French, Maryland, 1968-70; Secondary Teacher, English, French, German, 1970-72, 1975; Ski Area Office Manager, 1972-75; Restaurant Owner, Chef, 1975-80; Real Estate Agent, 1980-; Antiquarian Bookseller, 1988-. Publication: Seattle Five Plus One poetry anthology. Contributions to: Archer; Chariton Review; Haight Ashbury Literary Review; Portland Review; Poetry Seattle (Seattle Times); San Fernanado Poetry Journal; West Wind Review; Black Buzzard Review; Plainsong; Pacific Coast Journal; Pleides. Memberships: Society Of Children's Book Writers; Society Children's Writers And Illustrators, Washington, Oregon, national chapters. Honour: Washington State Arts Commission Artist In Residence, 1993-95. Address: 1102 Crescent Valley Drive NW, Gig Harbor, WA 98332, USA.

NELSON Marilyn, (Marilyn Waniek), b. 26 Apr 1946, Cleveland, Ohio, USA. University Teacher. m. Roger B Wilkenfeld, 1 son, 1 daughter. Education: BA, 1968; MA, 1970; PhD, 1978. Appointments: Lay Associate, Campus Ministry, Lutheran Church in America; Instructor, Lane Community College; Visiting Assistant Professor, Reed College; Instructor, Norre Nissum Seminarium, Denmark; Assistant Professor, St Olaf College, USA; Instructor, Universitat Hamburg, Germany; Assistant Professor, Associate Professor, Professor, University of Connecticut, Storrs, USA; Visiting Professor, New York University; Instructor, MFA Programme, Vermont College. Publications: For the Body, 1978; Mama's Promises, 1985; The Homeplace, 1990; Partial Truth, 1992; Magnificat, 1994. Contributions to: Ploughshares; Georgia Review; Southern Review; Kenyon Review. Honours: Creative Writing Fellowships, National Endowment for the Arts, 1984, 1990; Pushcart Prize, 1985, 1990; Connecticut Arts Award, 1990; Individual Artist Grant, Connecticut Council for the Arts, 1990; Finalist, National Book Award, 1990; Annisfield Wolf Award, 1991; Fulbright Teaching Fellowship to France, 1995. Memberships: Poetry Society of America; Associated Writing Programs; American Poetry Society; Society for Study of Multi-Ethnic Literature of the USA; Society for Values in Higher Education. Address: 39 Edgewood Lane Ext, Mansfield Center, CT 06250, USA.

NELSON Paul Everett, b. 22 Sept 1961, Chicago, Illinois, USA. Holistic Journalist; Radio Interviewer; Poet. m. Janice Berk, 31 Dec 1985, 1 daughter. Education: BA with Honours, Broadcast Communications, Columbia College, Chicago, Illinois, 1983.

Appointments: Afternoon News Anchor, Music Coordinator and Jazz Host, WCKG, 1981-83; Music Research Intern, Part-Time Air Personality, WMET-FM/Chicago (AOR), 1982-84; Afternoon/Morning On-Air Host, 1988-90, Host and Producer of Sunday Morning Jazz, 1989-90, News and Community Affairs Director, 1990-92, KRWM (NAC); Public Affairs Coordinator, KMTT-FM Seattle (AAA), 1993-96; Founder and President, It Plays in Peoria Productions, non-profit making organisation, 1993-. Publications: We Don't Celebrate Halloween in Cuba: And Other Stories From Auburn, 1996; 99 Lives, 1996. Contributions to: Play Boat Press, 1985; The Source, 1985; Red Sky Anthology; Nobody's Orphan Child, 1996; Seasons, 1996. Memberships: Co-Founder, 19th Drift, Auburn's Literary Arts Group, 1995; Co-Founder, The NW Spoken Word Laboratory, 1996; Co-Director, Telepoetics NW; Board of Directors, Institute for Applied Consciousness Science, Oregon. Address: 520 F Street South East, Auburn, WA 98002-6165, USA.

NELSON-HUMPHRIES Luisa-Teresa (Tessa), b. Yorkshire, England. College Professor of Eighteenth and Nineteenth Century English Literature. m. (1) Kenneth Nelson Brown, 1 June 1957, dec 1962, (2) Cecil Unthank, dec 1979. Education: BA, English; MA, English, University of North Carolina, 1965; PhD, English, University of Liverpool, England, 1974. Appointments: Head of English Department, Richard Thomas Girls School, Walsall, England; Head of English, Elmore Green School, Walsall; Director of English, Windsor College, Buenos Aires, Argentina; Full Professor of English, Cumberland College, Williamsburg, Kentucky, USA, 1964-90; Part-time, English Department, New Mexico State University, Las Cruces, Mew Mexico, 1990-92. Publication: Poem, An Art That's Much Possessed By Death, Envoi Anthology, 1990. Contributions to: Joycean Literary Arts Guild; Blue Unicorn; Z-Miscellaneous; Candles and Lamps; Array; Confrontations; Appalachian Heritage; Society of Women Writers and Journalists Bulletin; Lexicom; McCann's Alaska Journal of Poetry/Philosophy, 1995; Negative Capability, 1995; Bulletin Society Woemn Writers & Journalists, 1995. Honours: 1st Prize, Julia Cairns Silver Trophy for Poetry, England, 1978; 2nd Prize, 1989, 3rd Prize, 1988, Julia Cairns Competition; Numerous Honourable Mentions; Others; Winner, Clemence Dane Trophy for Critical Study on Maria Edgeworth, 1995; Third Prize and Honourable Mention, Julia Cairns Award, 1995. Memberships: Society of Women Writers and Journalists, England; Society of Children's Book Writers, USA; MENSA; American Association of University Women; Vice-President, Mesilla Valley Writers, New Mexico, USA. Address: 3228 Jupiter Rad, 4 Hills, Las Cruces, NM 88012-7742, USA.

NEMM Adolf. See: **FLAMMONDE Paris.**

NES. See: **SAMUELSDOTTIR Norma Elisabet.**

NEVILLE Tam Lin, b. 2 Nov 1944. Poet. m. Herbert J Stern, 30 April 1977, 1 daughter. Education: BA, Religion, Temple University, 1968; MFA, Poetry, Vermont College, 1989. Appointment: Adjunct Instructor, Butler University, Indianapolis, Indiana. Contributions to: American Poetry Review; Ironwood; Massachusetts Review; Indiana Review; Crazyhorse. Honour: Winner, Individual Artist Fellowship, Indiana Arts Commission, 1990-91. Address: 412 Binford Street, Crawfordsville, IN 47933, USA.

NEWCOMB Robert Wayne, b. 27 June 1933, Glendale, California, USA. Electrical Engineer. m. Sarah E Fritz, 22 May 1954, 1 son, 1 daughter. Education: All In Electrical Engineering: BSEE, Purdue University, 1955; MS, Stanford University, 1957; PhD, University of California at Berkeley, 1960. Appointments: Newcomb Electronics, summers, 1951-55; Research Intern, Stanford Research Institute, 1955-57; Teaching and Research Associate, University of California at Berkeley, 1957-60; Assistant and Associate Professor, Stanford University, 1960-70; Professor, University of Maryland at College Park, 1970-; Director of Electrical Engineering Office of Graduate Studies; Director Microsystems Laboratory. Publications: Linear Multiport Synthesis, 1966; Concepts of Linear Systems and Controls, 1968; Active Integrated Circuits Synthesis, 1968; Spanish edition, 1973; Network Theory: The State-Space Approach, 1968; all contain some poetry. Contributions to: Voyages; A Literary Perspective. Honour: Endowed the Academy of American Poets University Prize, University of Maryland. Memberships: Academy of American Poets. Address: Microsystems Laboratory, Electrical Engineering Department, University of Maryland, College Park, MD 20742, USA.

NEWLIN Margaret Elisabeth Rudd, b. 27 Feb 1925, New York, New York, USA. Poet; Writer. m. Nicholas Newlin, 2 April 1956, 4 sons. Education: BA, Bryn Mawr College, 1947; PhD, Reading University, England, 1951. Appointments: Teaching positions at Bryn Mawr College, Harcum Junior College, Washington College; Administration, Bryn Mawr College. Publications: The Fragile Immigrants, 1971; Day of Sirens, 1973; The Snow Falls Upward, Collected Poems, 1976; The Book of Mourning, 1982; Collected Poems 1963-1985, 1986. Contributions to: Southern Review and others; Included in various anthologies. Honours: Gerald and M C Thomas Awards, 1947; Fellow, National Endowment for the Arts, 1977; Honorary DLitt, Washington College, 1980. Membership: Poetry Society of America. Address: Shipley Farm, Secane, PA 19018, USA.

NEWLOVE John (Herbert), b. 13 June 1938, Regina, Saskatchewan, Canada. m. Susan Mary Philips, 1966. Appointments: Writer-in-Residence, various Canadian institutions, 1974-83; English Editor, Office of the Commissioner of Official Languages, Ottawa, 1986-95. Publications include: Grave Sirs, 1962; Elephants, Mothers and Others, 1963; Moving in Alone, 1965; Notebook Pages, 1966; Four Poems, 1967; What They Say, 1967; Black Night Window, 1968; The Cave, 1970; Lies, 1972; The Fat Man: Selected Poems 1962-72, 1977; Dreams Surround Us: Fiction and Poetry (with John Metcalf), 1977; The Green Plain, 1981; Three Poems, 1985; The Night the Dog Smiled, 1986; Apology for Absence: Poems Selected and New, 1993; Editor of volumes of poetry. Honours include: Governor General's Award, 1973, Literary Press Group Award, 1983; Saskatchewan Writers' Guild Founders' Award, 1986; Archibald Lampern Award, 1993. Address: Box 71041, RPO L'Esplanade, Ottawa, Ontario, K2P 2L9 Canada.

NEWMAN Michael Philip, b. 27 Nov 1943, Little Washbourne, England. Teacher; Landscape Gardener; Civil Servant. m. 10 July 1982, 2 sons, 1 daughter. Education: City of Worcester Training College, 1962-65; Hartpury College of Horticulture, 1970-73. Appointments: Teacher, 1960s; Landscape Gardener, 1970s; Civil Servant, 1980s; Various appointments, 1990s. Publications: 28 Poems, 1964; Blow Hot, Blow Cold, 1966; Paperback Writer, 1980; Cotswold Rhapsody, 1986; Poet's World, 1986; Eerie-by-Moonlight, 1986; Moods and Melodies, 1988. Contributions to: Countryman; Cotswold Life; International Cricketer; London Calling; Envoi; Orbis; Outposts; Weyfarers; Doors; Ore; Purple Patch; TOPS; Writer's Rostrum; Third Half; Peotry Nottingham; Pennine Platform; Pennine Ink; Inkshed; Writers' Own Magazine; Tewkesbury Register; Evesham Admay; Frogmore Papers; New Truth; Dada Review; Outrigger. Honours: Cheltenham Poetry Society Open Competition, 1977; 1st Place, 3rd Half National Ghost Poetry Competition, 1987; 1st Place, Writers' Rostrum National Poetry Competition, Poet of the Year, 1989; 1st Place, FAIM Poet of the Year, 1990; 1st Place, Cheltenham Poetry Society Open Competition, 1990. Memberships: Secretary, Cheltenham Poetry Society; International Poetry Society; Poetry Foundation. Address: 18 Courtiers Drive, Bishops Cleeve, Cheltenham, Gloucestershsire GL52 4NU, England.

NEWMAN Paul Nigel, b. 12 Oct 1945, Bristol, England. Writer. Education: Weston-Super-Mare Technical College, 1960-64; St Pauls College, Cheltenham, 1966-69; Certificate Education; Founder and Editor of Abraxas, 1991-. Appointments: Teacher/Lecturer, Orme School, Clevedon/St Austell College. Contributions to: Ore; Krax; Ogmios; Ramraid Extrordinaire; Abraxas; Psychopoetica; Tees Valley Writer; South West Arts; Writers' Viewpoint. Memberships: Stray Dogs (Literary Group run by D M Thomas). Address: 57 Eastbourne Road, St Austell, Cornwall PL25 4SU, England.

NÍ CHUILLEANÁIN Eiléan, b. 28 Nov 1942. Lecturer. m. Macdara Woods, 27 June 1978, 1 son. Education: BA, 1962, MA, 1964, University College Cork; BLitt, Lady Margaret Hall, Oxford, 1969. Appointments: Lecturer in Mediaeval and Renaissance English, Trinity College Dublin, 1966-; Editor, Cyphers Literary Magazine. Publications: Acts and Monuments, 1972; Site Of Ambush, 1975; Cork, 1977; The Second Voyage, 1977, 1986; The Rose-Geranium, 1981; The Magdalene Sermon, 1989; The Brazen Serpent, 1994. Contributions to: Numerous magazines. Honours: Irish Times Poetry Prize, 1966; Patrick Kavanagh Prize, 1972; O'Shaughnessy Poetry Award of Irish-American Cultural Institute, 1992. Memberships: Aosdána; Irish Writers Union. Address: Trinity College, Dublin 2, Ireland.

NI DHOMHNAILL Nuala Maire, b. 16 Feb 1952, St Helens, Lancashire, England. Poet. m. 16 Dec 1973, 1 son, 3 daughter. Education: BA, Honours, English and Irish, 1972, HDipEd, 1973, University College Cork. Appointments: Instructor, METU, Ankara, 1975-80; Writer-in-Residence, University College Cork, 1992-93. Publications: An Dealg Droighinn, 1981; Féar Suaithinseach, 1984; Feis, 1991; Rogla Danta, Selected Poems, 1986, 1988, 1989, 1991; Pharoah's Daughter, 1990; The Astrachan Cloak, 1991. Contributions to: Anthologies: Poets of Munster, 1985; An tonn Gheal - The Bright Wave, 1986, 1988; Pillars of the House, 1987; The Long Embrace, 1987; Contemporary Irish Poetry, 1988; Wildish Things, 1989; Bitter Harvest, 1989; The Penguin Book of Contemporary Irish Poetry, 1990; Magazines include: Anteaus, Comhar, INNTS, Stet, Krino, Irish Times, Diehoren, Eire. Honours: Literary Bursary, Arts Council, 1979, 1981; Oireachtas Poetry Awards, 1982, 1989, 1990; Irish Arts Council Award for Best Collection in Irish Published in 3 Year Period, 1985, 1988; Irish American Foundation O'Shauohnessy Award, 1988; The Ireland Fund Literature Prize, 1991. Memberships: Aosdana; Poetry Ireland; The Irish Writers Union. Address: 2 Little Meadow, Pottery Road, Cabinteely, County Dublin, Ireland.

NICHOLS Larry Sears, b. 13 Feb 1948, Somerset, Kentucky, USA. History and Political Science Professor; Social Worker; Pastor. 1 son, 1 daughter. Education: BS, History, Political Science and Geography, Cumberland College; MA, History and Education, Union College; MDiv, Social Ethics, Asbury Seminary and Lexington Seminary; Dr of Religious Education and US History, International Bible Seminary. Appointments: Social Studies Teacher, Nancy High School, Somerset High School; Executive Program Director, Pulaski YMCA; Part-time Professor, Somerset Community College, Asbury College, Prestonburg Community College and Roane State Community College; Social Worker for Hill Topers Inc, Crossville. Publications: Poems; Methods; I Meant To Do My Work Today; My Teacher; Tennis; Valentines; Christmastime; One Vote; Weekly newspaper column for 6 years; In a Nutshell and Nick Knacks; Books: I'm No Appalachian Shade Tree; Uncle Sam Meets King Jesus. Address: PO Box 1051, Crossville, TN 39557, USA.

NIDITCH B(arry), b. 8 Jan 1943, Boston, Massachusetts, USA. Writer. Education: Graduated, Boston University, 1965. Appointment: Artistic Director, The Original Theatre. Publications: Elements, 1980; Freedom Trail, 1980; A Boston Winter, 1982; A Musical Collection, 1984; Unholy Empire, 1982; Exile, 1986; Ink Dreams, 1986; On the Eve, 1989; Milton: Poems by B Z Niditch, 1992. Contributions to: Encounter; Nottingham Poetry Review; Poetry Review; New Letters; Orbis; Writers Forum; New Hope International; International Poetry Review; Takahe; Denver Quarterly; Webster Review; Fiddlehead; Antigonish Poetry Review; Real Liberales; Miorita; Boston Globe; Midstream; Hawaii Review; Minnesota Review; Ariel; Old Hickory Review; Pittsburgh Quarterly. Honours: 1st Prize, Bitterroot International Poetry Journal; Heershe David-Badonneh Prize. Membership: New England Poetry Club. Address: PO Box 1664, Brookline, MA 02146. USA.

NIELSEN Lone Munksgaard, b. 28 Mar 1968, Ringköbing, Denmark. Writer. Education: High School, 1986. Appointments: Various temporary work. Publications: Poetry: Afvikling, 1993; Frasagn, 1994; Lysvendt/Himmelsöjlen, 1995; Iklædt en andens hud, 1996: Drama: Kapitæler, 1995; Translations: Omvej over himlen (prose and drama of André Breton), 1996. Contributions to: The Danish Periodical, Hvedekorn. Membership: Danish Writers' Union. Address: Lilliendalsvej 26, 2700 Brönshöj, Denmark.

NIELSEN Pia Moeller, b. 5 Dec 1956, Randers, Denmark. Teacher. 1 son. Education: Cand Phil in Esthetic and Culture, University of Aarhus, 1985. Appointments: Teacher at High Schools; Drama Teacher at University. Publications: Hoejsang, 1992. Contributions to: Den Blaa Port; Hvedekorn; Ariel; Atlas; Poetry (in Lithuanian-Vilnius); Broendums Encyclopaedi; Hieroglyf; Banana Split: Et Digit Om Dagen. Membership: The Danish Writers Union. Address: Moellegade 7A, 3.5. 8000 Arhus C. Denmark.

NIEMAN Valerie, b. 6 July 1955, Jamestown, New York, USA. Journalist. Education: West Virginia University, BS, 1978; Jamestown Community College. Appointment: Times-West Virginian, Reporter, Arts Editor, City Editor, 1979-93. Publications: Slipping Out of Old Eve. Contributions to: Bellingham Review; Greenfield Review; Clifton Magazine; Laurel Review; Appalachian Heritage; Wind; Round Table; Poetry; New Letters; West Branch; New Virginia Review. Honours:

National Endowment for the Arts; Chapbook Award; West Virginia Writers. Memberships: Poets and Writers, Science Fiction Writers of America; West Virginia Writers. Address: PO Box 1614, Fairmont, WV 26555, USA.

NIEMINEN Kai Tapani, b. 11 May 1950, Helsinki, Finland. Freelance Poet; Translator of Literature. m. 1 daughter. Education: Studies of Philosophy and Musicology, unfinished, 1970-72; Private studies of Japanese, 1971. Publications: Joki Vie Ajatukseni, 1971; Syntymästa, 1973; Kiireettä, 1977; Tie Jota Oli Kuljettava, 1979; Vain Mies, 1981; Elämän Vuoteessa, 1982; Oudommin Kuin Unessa, 1983; En Minä Tiedä, 1985; Milloin Missäkin Hahmossa, 1987; Keinuva Maa, 1989; Se Vähä Minkä Taivasta Näkee (collected poetry 1969-89), 1990; Fuuga/Fugue (translated into English by Herbert Lomas, 1992; Plus several translations of Japanese poetry and poetical drama. Honours: The National Literature Award, granted by the Ministry of Culture, 1986, 1990. Membership: President, Finnish PEN, 1991-94. Address: Baggböle 99A, 07740 Gammelby, Finland.

NIGHTINGALE Barbra Evans, b. 6 Aug 1949, Chicago, Illinois, USA. Associate Professor of English. m. Preston S Nightingale, 23 Nov 1977, 1 daughter. Education: BS, Health Administration, 1980; MA, English, 1985; EdD, Education, 1991. Appointment: Associate Professor, Broward Community College, 1983-. Publications: Lovers Never Die, 1981; Prelude to a Woman, 1986, 1986; Lunar Equations, 1993; Florida in Poetry, 1995. Contributions to: Kansas Quarterly; The Poet; Cumberlands; Florida Review; Red Light/Blue Light; Visions; Coy Dog Review; Plametto Review; South Florida Poetry Review; Miami Herald; Sun Sentinel; Others. Honour: Grand Prize, National Federation of State Poetry Societies, 1991. Memberships: Poetry Society of America; Poets and Writers; American Academy of Poets; National Federation of State Poetry Societies; Florida State Poets; South Florida Poetry Institute; The Writer's Voice. Address: 2231 North 52nd Avenue, Hollywood, FL 33021, USA.

NIGHTINGALE Gabrielle (Gay), b. London, England. Horticultural Writer. Education: Studied Agriculture and Horticulture, Bicton College, Devon; Read Botany and Zoology, London University; BA, Open University, 1984. Appointments: Teacher; Freelance Writer and Author; Lecturer and Writer. Publications: Editor, Section on Poetry in Growing Cyclamen, 1982, 1987; Other poems unpublished. Memberships: Society of Authors; Garden Writers Guild, Committee Member, Founder Member, 1990-. Address: c/o Batsford Publishers, 4 Fitzhardinge Street, London W1H 0AH, England.

NILSEN Richard Haldor, b. 20 Jan 1948, Gloversville, New York, USA. Director of Mental Health Residence Program. m. Lynda Joy Canary, 23 Sep 1969, 1 son, 2 daughters. Education: BA, English Literature, Houghton College, New York; Master of English Literature, MFA, Creative Writing, University of Arkansas, 1976. Appointments: Caseworker, New York State Department of Social Services, 1985-87; Youth-at-Risk Counsellor, 1987-89; Director, OMH Residence Programme, Upstate New York, 1989-. Contributions to: Antithesis; Ariel II; Arkenstone; Buffalo Spree; Christianity Today; Epoch; Eternity; For the Time Being; Lantern; Milieu; Motif; One Way; Poetry Now; Wellspring. Honours: Poetry Prize, Houghton College, 1969; Poetry Prize, Triton College, 1984. Membership: Poets and Writers. Address: 180 County Highway 142A, Johnstown, NY 12095, USA.

NIMS John Frederick, b. 20 Nov 1913, Muskegan, Michigan, USA. Professor; Editor. m. Bonnie Larkin, 1 son, 2 daughter. Education: AB, 1937, MA, 1939, University of Notre Dame; PhD, University of Chicago, 1945. Appointments: Professor at numerous universities including University of Notre Dame, University of Florence, University of Madrid, University of Illinois, Harvard University and Williams College; Editor, Poetry Chicago, 1978-84. Publications: The Iron Pastoral, 1947; A Fountain in Kentucky, 1950; The Poems of St John of The Cross, translation, 1958, 3rd edition, 1979; Knowledge of The Evening, 1960; Of Flesh and Bone, 1967; Sappho to Valery: Poems in Translation, 1971, 3rd edition, 1990; The Harper Anthology of Poetry, 1980; The Kiss: A Jambalaya, poems, 1982; Selected Poems, 1982; A Local Habitation: Essays on Poetry, 1985; The Six-Cornered Snowflake, 1990; Zany in Denim, 1990. Contributions: Poetry; Hudson Review; Atlantic; Harper's; Times Literary Supplement; Saturday Review. Honours include: National Institute of Arts and Letters Award, 1967; Creative Arts Poetry Award, Brandeis University, 1972; Fellowship, Academy of American Poets, 1982; Guggenheim Fellowship, 1986-87; The Aiken Taylor Award for Modern American

Poetry, 1991; Melville Cane Award, 1992; Hardison Poetry Prize, 1993. Address: 3920 Lake Shore Drive, Chicago, IL 60613, USA.

NINI Taco. See: **SEGUI BENNASSAR Antoni.**

NISHIKAWA Morio, b. 24 May 1943, Kobe, Japan. Teacher of English and Linguistics. m. Sumiko Nishikawa, 3 May 1981. Education: BA, Kobe University of Foreign Studies, 1967; MA, Osaka University, 1969. Appointments: Assistant Teacher, 1969-77, Associate Professor, 1977-88, Professor, 1988-, Kumamoto University. Publications: Han-Getsu (Half Moon), 1980; Gyoka-Soushitsu (Loss of The Songs of Fish), 1983; Kotozute (Message), 1989. Contributions to: Editor, poetry periodical, Genzai; Poetry magazine, Shi to Shisou; Newspaper, Kumamoto Nichi-Nichi Shimbun. Memberships: Poetry Society; Founder, Modern Poetry Forum in Kumamoto, 1987-. Address: Department of English, Kumamoto University, Kyoo-iku-Gakubu, 2-40-1 Kurokami, Kumamoto City 860, Japan.

NITA. See: **RAMAKRISHNAN Nivedita.**

NITCHIE George Wilson, b. 19 May 1921, Chicago, Illinois, USA. Retired Professor of English. m. Laura Margaret Woodard, 19 Jan 1947, 3 daughters. Education: BA, Middlebury College, 1943; MA, 1947, PhD, 1958, Columbia University. Appointments: Instructor in English, 1947, Assistant Professor, 1950, Associate Professor, 1959, Professor, 1966, Chairman, English Department, 1972-79, Professor Emeritus, 1986-, Simmons College. Publications: Human Values in the Poetry of Robert Frost, 1960; Marianne Moore: An Introduction to the Poetry, 1969; Various critical essays on Robert Frost, Robert Lowell, Randall Jarrell, Howard Nemerov, T S Eliot, John Donne, John Milton. Contributions: Poems to various publications. Membership: American Association of University Professors. Address: 50 Pleasantville Avenue, Weymouth, MA 02188, USA.

NITZSCHE Jane Chance. See: **CHANCE Jane.**

NIXON Colin Harry, b. 9 Mar 1939, Putney, London, England. Conciliation Officer with ACAS; Civil Servant. m. Betty Morgan, 2 Sept 1967, 3 daughters. Education: Diploma in Sociology, London University, 1968. Appointments: Civil Servant, 1960-; Disablement Resettlement Officer, 1974-83; ACAS Conciliation Officer, 1983-. Publications: Roads, 1975; Geography of Love, 1977; With all Angels Equal, 1980; The Bright Idea, 1983; included in anthologies: Spongers, 1984; Affirming Flame, 1989; Poetry Street 3, 1991. Contributions to: Outposts; Tribune; Dublin Magazine; Haiku Quarterly; New Cicada, Japan; Poetry Nippon, Japan; Countryman; Cricketer; Tracks; Bogg; New Christian; Christian Century; Symphony; Orbis; Candelabrum; Cricket Quarterly; Ambit; Iron; Third Half; Purple Patch; Ore; Sepia; Periaktos; Poetry Nottingham; X-Calibre; New Hope International; Envoi; Iota; Old Police Station; Vigil; Krax; Doors; Global Tapestry; Moonstone; Magma; Clarity; Editor, various anthologies, Richmond Poetry Society. Honours: George Camp Memorial Prize, 1975, 1983; Emma Civil Service Poetry 1st Prize, 1979; Runner-up, in Voting for Best Small Press Poet, 1986. Address: 72 Barmouth Road, Wandsworth, London SW18 2DS, England.

NOBLESS Dame H E. See: **CRIPPS Dame Joy Beaudette.**

NOCERINO Kathryn, b. 6 Feb 1947, New York, New York, USA. Poet; Reviewer; Editor. Education: BFA, Cooper Union, 1968; MSW, Hunter College, 1972. Appointments: Poetry Reviewer, Home Planet News, WIN; Guest Contributing Editor, Manhattan Poetry Review, 1983-84. Publications: Wax Lips, 1980; Candles in The Daytime, 1986; Death of the Plankton Bar and Grill, 1987. Contributions to: Abraxas; Contact/II; Telephone; Calliope; Home Planet News; Street; Joe Soap's Canoe, UK. Memberships: Poetry Society of America; Poets and Writers. Address: 139 West 19th Street Apt 2B, New York, NY 10011, USA.

NOGUERE Suzanne, b. 1 Dec 1947, Brooklyn, New York, USA. Classified Advertising Manager. m. Henry Grinberg, 5 June 1983. Education: BA magna cum laude, Honours in Philosophy, Barnard College, Columbia University, 1969. Appointments: Classified Advertising Manager, PTN Graphic Arts Network, Melville, New York. Publications: 2 children's natural history books; Whirling Round The Sun, poems, 1996. Contributions to: Nation; Poetry; Jazz; Heresies; Modern Haiku; Parnassus: Poetry in Review; Gradiva; Nathaniel Hawthorne Review; Literary Review; Classical Outlook; Pivot; Poetry Anthology 1912-1977, 1978; A Formal Feeling Comes: Poems in Form

by Contemporary Women, 1994; Sparrow; Lullwater Review; Artist and Influence. Honours: Phi Beta Kappa, 1969; Gertrude B Claytor Memorial Award, Poetry Society of America, 1989; Discovery/The Nation, 1996. Address: 27 West 96th Street, Apt 12B, New York, NY 10025, USA.

NORD Virginia (Gennie) Lana, b. 13 Oct 1946, Tripoli, Wisconsin, USA. Writer; Teacher; Reviewer; Editor. Education: BA, English, 1983, MA, English, 1985, University of Wisconsin; MFA, Creative Writing (Poetry, Fiction), University of Montana, 1988. Appointments: Teaching Assistant, Composition, Creative Writing, University of Wisconsin, University of Montana, 1983-87; Instructor, Fiction, 1987, Instructor, Composition, 1989, Instructor, Literature, 1989-90, University of Montana. Publications: Gathering Place of the Waters: 30 Milwaukee Poets, 1983; Greene's Barn, 1986. Contributions to: North American Review; Bloomsbury Review; Cutbank; Wisconsin Review; Cream City Review; New Voices; Selected Prize-Winning Poets 1984-1988; Academy of American Poets; Ghost Town Quarterly; North Country Review; Ambrosia; Yet Another Small Magazine; Adrift; Periodically Alive; Kinnikinnik; Others. Honours: 1st Prize, Academy of American Poets, 1979, 1983; Wladyslaw Cieszynski Literary Prize, 1983; Richard Hugo Memorial Scholarship in Poetry, University of Montana (first one awarded), 1985-86; Bertha Morton Scholarship, University of Montana, 1986-87; 2nd Prize, Midwest Poetry Contest, 1988. Membership: Hellgate Writers, Missoula. Address: 345112 Blaine, Missoula, MT 59801, USA.

NORDBRANDT Henrik, b. 21 Mar 1945, Copenhagen, Denmark. Writer. Education: Oriental Studies, Chinese, Persian, Turkish and Arabic. Publications: 18 volumes of poetry including: Digte, 1966; Miniaturer, 1967; Sysoverne, 1969; Omgivelser, 1972; Opbrud og ankomstr, 1974; Ode til blaeksprutten, 1976; Guds Hus, 1977; Selected Poems, 1978; Armenia, 1982; Violinbyggernes by, 1985; Glas, 1986; Istid, 1987; Selected Poems, God's House and Armenia available in English. Contributions to: Numerous journals and magazines. Honours: 13 Literary awards including: Major Prize of Danish Academy, Danish Critic's Prize for Best Book of The Year and Life Grant of Honour, Danish State. Address: Plaza Santa Cruz 9, 29700 Velez-Malaga, Spain.

NORRIS Leslie, b. 21 May 1921, Merthyr Tydfil, Wales. Professor. Education: MPhil, 1960; Honorary DLitt, 1994, 1996. Appointments: Principal Lecturer, West Sussex Institute of Education, 1956-74; Professor, Brigham Young University, Utah, USA, 1981-. Publications: Tongue of Beauty, 1941; Poems, 1944; The Lound Winter, 1960; Finding Gold, 1964; Ransoms, 1970; Mountains Polecats Pheasants, 1974; Selected Poems, 1986; Collected Poems, 1996. Contributions to: Atlantic Monthly; New Yorker; New Criterion; Poetry Wales; New Welsh Review; Many others. Honours: British Arts Council Award, 1964; Alice Hunt Bartlett Prize, 1969; Fellow, Royal Society of Literature, 1968; Cholmondeley Poetry Prize, 1979; Fellow, Welsh Academy, 1990. Address: 849 South Carterville Road, Orem, UT 84058, USA.

NORSE Harold George, b. 6 July 1916, New York, New York, USA. Author. Education: BA, Brooklyn College, 1938; MA, New York University, 1951. Appointments: Instructor in English: Cooper Union College, New York, 1949-52; Lion School of English, Rome, Italy, 1956-57; United State Information Service School, Naples, 1958-59; Instructor in Creative Writing, San José State University, California, USA, 1973-75; Currently Freelance Writer; Professor in Creative Writing, New College of California, 1994-95. Publications: The Roman Sonnets of Guiseppe Gioacchino Belli, translations, 1960, 1974; Karma Circuit, London edition, 1967; US edition, 1974; Hotel Nirvana, 1974; Carnivorous Saint, 1977; Mysteries Of Magritte, 1984; Love Poems, 1986; Memoirs of a Bastard Angel, 1989, 90, 91, 92; Seismic Events, 1993. Contributions to: Antaeus; City Lights Review; Kayak; Kenyon Review; Poetry Flash; Advocate; Exquisite Corpse; Semiotexte; Commentary; Transatlantic Review; Christopher Street; Isis, Oxford; Paris Review; Saturday Review; Sewanee Review. Honours: Poetry Fellowship, National Endowment for the Arts, 1974; R H de Young Museum Grant, 1974; Lifetime Achievement Award in Poetry, National Poetry Association, 1991. Membership: PEN. Address: 157 Albion Street, San Francisco, CA 94110, USA.

NORTH Charles Laurence, b. 9 June 1941, New York, New York, USA. Poet; Professor of English. m. 2 June 1963, 1 son, 1 daughter. Education: BA, Tufts University, 1962; MA, Columbia University, 1964. Appointments: Poet-in-Residence, Pace University.

Publications: Lineups, 1972; Elizabethan and Nova Scotian Music, 1974; Six Buildings, 1977; Leap Year, 1978; Gemini, co-author, 1981; The Year Of The Olive Oil, 1989; New and Selected Poems, 1996. Contributions to: Paris Review; Sulfur; Poetry (Chicago); New American Writing; O-blek; Literary Review; Columbia; United Artists; Transfer; Adventures in Poetry; Pequod; Hanging Loose; Best American Poetry, 1995. Honours: Poets Foundation Award, 1972; National Endowment For The Arts Fellowship, 1979; Fund for Poetry Award, 1987, 1989. Membership: PEN. Address: 251 West 92nd Street, No 12E, New York, NY 10025, USA.

NORTH Michael (Mick) Thomas, b. 3 Aug 1958, Lancaster, England. Arts Manager. m. Jani Howker, 15 Oct 1988, 1 son. Education: Lancaster Royal Grammar School, 1971-76; Foundation Course in Art and Design, Wolverhampton Polytechnic, 1977-78; Degree Course in Fine Art (not completed). Appointments: Education and Community Liason Officer, Lancaster Literature Festival, 1983-84; Director, Lancaster Literature Festival, 1984-87; Resources and Development Officer, Ludus Dance Company, 1988-90; Arts Development Officer, Carlisle City Council, 1990-. Publications: Throp's Wife, 1986; The Pheasant Plucker's Son, 1990; Included in Anthologies: The Gregory Poems, 1987; The New Lake Poets, 1991. Contributions to: Spectator; New Statesman; London Magazine; Poetry Review; Stand; Acumen; Argo; Poetry Durham; Iron; Sunk Island Review; Wide Skirt; Resurgence. Honour: Eric Gregory Award, 1986. Memberships: Committee Member, Arvon Foundation at Lumb Bank, 1988-90; Treasurer, Northern Association of Writers in Education, 1987-90; Poetry Society. Address: The Cottage, Cumwhitton, Carlisle, Cumbria CA4 9EX, England.

NORTHNAGEL Ernest W, b. 1 July 1923, Philadelphia, Pennsylvania, USA. Air Traffic Controller (retired). m. Blanca Romain, 21 Sept 1975, 2 daughters. Education: Graduate, South Philadelphia High School, 1942; Numerous college courses. Appointments: Columnist, La Junta (Colorado) Tribune-Democrat, 1954-55; Correspondent, Denver (Colorado) Post, 1956-57; Correspondent, Universal Trade Press Syndicate, 1956-58. Publications: Twenty-Five for Tony, 1969; A Swirl of Tannish Capes, 1971; Images of Vesta, 1979. Contributions to: Caper; Ave Maria; Adam; Alt for Mien, Denmark; Escapade; Reign of Sacred Heart; Travel; Empire Magazine; Desert Magazine; New Mexico Magazine; Popular Science; Newsday; Traveltips; Gent; Modern Man; Frontiers; Others. Honours: Numerous small poetry awards including: Franklin Pierre Davis Contest; Alan Swallow Book Award. Address: PO Box 6155, San Juan, PR 00914, USA.

NORWOOD Victor G(eorge) C(harles), b. 21 Mar 1920, Lincolnshire, England. Poet; Novelist; Playwright. Appointments: Managing Director, Westcliff Literary Agency, 1947-77; Founder, Chairman, North Lines Writers Circle, 1960. Publications: The Know-How of Prospecting, 1976; A Guide to General Prospecting, 1977; Walkabout, 1977; Tressidy's Last Case, 1977; Where the River Ends, 1978; Holocaust, 1978; The Beast of Bulgallon, 1978; Sapphire Seekers, 1979; Venom, 1980; A Lifetime of Cheating Death, 1980; Miracles of Cardiac Surgery, 1980; Across Australia by Volkswagen, 1980; In Canada: Legends of the Forests, 1978; The Carib Hordes, 1978; Diamonds Are Forever, 1979; Numerous publications under pseudonyms in 1950s, 1960s and 1970s. Address: 194 West Common Lane, Westcliff, Scunthorpe DN17 1PD, England.

NOTLEY Alice, b. 8 Nov 1945, Bisbie, Arizona, USA. Poet. m. Douglas Oliver, 10 Feb 1987, 2 sons. Education: BA, Barnard College, 1967; MFA, Writers Workshop, University of Iowa, 1970. Publications: 165 Meeting House Lane, 1971; Phoebe Light, 1973; Incidentals in the Day World, 1973; For Frank O'Hara's Birthday, 1976; Alice Ordered Me To Be Made, 1976; A Diamond Necklace, 1977; When I Was Alive, 1980; Waltzing Matilda, 1981; How Spring Comes, 1981; Margaret and Dusty, 1985; At Night the States, 1988; Parts of a Wedding, 1986; Homer's Art, 1990. Contributions to: Scarlet; Chicago; United Artists. Honours: National Endowment for the Arts Award, 1979; Poetry Centre Award, 1981; General Electric Foundation Award, 1984; Fund for Poetry, 1987, 1990. Address: 101 St Marks Place No 12A, New York City, NY 10009, USA.

NOVAK Lela. See: **NOVAKOVIC Mileva.**

NOVAKOVIC Mileva, (Lela Novak), b. 7 Sept 1938, Zagreb, Yugoslavia. Executive Secretary; Personal Assistant; Business Management Manager. m. Svetozar Novakovic, 21 Feb 1959, 1 son,

1 daughter. Education: Secretarial/Business Management Studies, Pitman's College, Wimbledon, all First Class Passes; Short Story Writer's Course, Premier School of Journalism, Fleet Street, First Class Pass. Appointments: Executive Secretary/Personal Assistant to Chairman of a large Group of Companies; Marketing Director, MAN-VW Truck and Bus Ltd; Technical Director, British Oxygen Ltd; Service/Distribution Director, Rank Radio Ltd; Transport Controller of Rank Organisation; Managing Director, Cubitts International Ltd; Confidential to Joint Managing Directors & Owners of the famous Crockford's Club in Carlton House Terrace, London; Managing Director, London Electrical Manufacturing Company Ltd; Personnel Director, Borax Consolidated Ltd; Currently Self Employed. Business Management-Manager, setting up companies or departments within companies and getting them to run. Publications: Autumn Anthology, 1974; Living Poets, 1976; Spring Poets, 1980; Strand Anthology, 1974; The Grand Anthology of Poetry, 1971; Poetry Panorama, 1971; Poetry, 1971; Poetry, 1970; Poetry published in magazines and papers; Lyricist/Songwriter. Contributions to: Durango Herald; IBA Magazine; Various newspapers in the UK. Honours: Several; Special Mentions. Memberships: British Academy of Songwriters, Composers and Authors; Poetry Society of Great Britain; Fellow, International Biographical Association. Address: 39 The Ridgeway, Gunnersbury Park, London W3 8LW, England.

NOYES Humphrey Farrington, b. 12 May 1918, Portland, Oregon, USA. Psychotherapist. Education: BA, Yale University, 1942; MA, 1950, EdD, 1952, Columbia University. Appointment: Psychologist, private practice, New York. Publications: American Poetry Anthology, 1982; Snowmoon Anthology (USA), 1983; My Rain, My Moon, poems and haiku 1943-1982, 1983; Star Carvings, poems and haiku, 1984; Hawaiian Education Association Contest-Winners Anthologies, 1985, 1986, 1987, 1990; The Blossoming Rudder, Haiku, Senryu and Pithy Sayings, 1987; World Poetry Anthology (Korea), 1987, 1988, 1989, 1990; Anthology of Contemporary Poetry (Lisbon), 1990; Geppo Anthology; 3 Haiku in How to Write and Publish Poetry, 1990; The Moment's Gift, translation of his Haiku into Chinese (China), 1991. Contributions to: Virginia Quarterly Review; American Poetry Magazine; American Weave; Musician; Studia Mystica; Poet (Anthology); Amelia/Cicada; Prophetic Voices; Orphic Lute; Parnassus; Mainichi Daily News; New Cicada (Japan); Ko; Wind Chimes; Modern Haiku; Frogpond; Dragonfly East/West; Brussels Sprout; Woodnotes; Amber (Canada); Red Pagoda; Voices International; Hoosier Challenger; Late Knocking; Piedmont Literary Review; Inkstone (Canada); American Association of Haikuists Newsletter; Winewood Journal. Honours: 1st Prize, Fire Magazine Contest, 1984; 1st Prize, Lucille Sandberg Awards, 1985; 1st Prize, Hawaiian Education Association, 1986; Certificate of Merit, Ko Magazine, 1988; 4th Crown, World Poets Award, Korea, 1990; 1st Prize, North Carolina Haiku Association International Contest, 1991. Memberships: Yukei Tekei Haiku Society; Haiku Society of America; American Association of Haikuists. Address: 7 Kristali Street, Politia, Attikis 145 63, Greece.

NUQUI Efren Banez. See: **FERNANDEZ Querubin D, Jr.**

NUTTALL Jeffrey, b. 8 July 1933, Clitheroe, Lancashire, England. Artist. Div, 5 sons, 1 daughter. Education: Intermediate Examination, Arts and Crafts, Hereford School of Art, 1951; NDD, Painting (Special Level), Bath Academy of Art, Corsham, 1953; ATD, Institute of Education, London University, 1954. Appointment: Sergeant Instructor, Royal Army Education Corps, 1954-56; Art Master, Green lane Secondary School, Leominster, 1956-59; Alder Secondary Modern School, East Finchley, London, 1959-63; Ravenscroft Secondary Modern School, Barnet, Hertfordshire, 1963-67; English Master, Greenacre Secondary Modern School, Great Yarmouth, 1967-68; Lecturer, Foundation Course, Bradford College of Art, 1968-70; Senior Lecturer, Fine Art Department, Leeds Polytechnic, 1970-81; Head, Fine Art Department, Liverpool Polytechnic, 1981-84; Took early retirement, 1984; Occasional broadcasts, London Weekend Television; Granada TV; Yorkshire TV; BBC Radio; Numerous exhibitions, paintings; Actor. Publications: Objects, 1973; Sun Barbs, 1974; Grape Notes-apple Music, 1979; Scenes and Dubs, 1987; Mad With Music, 1987; The Pleasures of Necessity, 1988. Contributions to: Knuckleduster Funnies, 4 issues (edited with Robert Bank), 1986; Poetry criticism to the Guardian, 1979-82; Criticism and comment to numerous journals; Articles for Observer Review; Criticisms for the Independent; Poetry critic, Time Out, 1987-90. Memberships: Chairman, Abergavenny Collective, 1990-. Address: 71 White Hart Lane, Barnes, London SW13 0PP, England.

NYE Robert, b. 15 Mar 1939, London, England. Poet; Novelist; Literary Critic. m. (2) 3 sons, 1 daughter, 1 stepson, 1 stepdaughter. Appointment: Poetry Critic, Times, 1971-. Publications: Juvenilia 1, 1961; Juvenilia 2, 1963; Darker Ends, 1968; Agnus Dei, 1973; Two Prayers, 1974; Five Dreams, 1974; The Seven Deadly Sins: A Mask, 1974; Divisions on a Ground, 1976; A Collection Of Poems, 1955-88, 1989; 14 Poèmes, 1994; Henry James and Other Poems, 1995; Collected Poems, 1995. Honours: Gregory Award, 1963; Scottish Arts Council: Bursary, 1970, 1973; Awards, 1970, 1976; James Hennaway Award, 1970; Guardian Fiction Prize, 1976; Hawthornden Prize, 1977; Society of Authors Travel Scholarship, 1991. Membership: Fellow, Royal Society of Literature. Address: c/o Sheil Land Associates, 43 Doughty Street, London WC1N 2LF, England.

NYSTROM Debra, b. 12 July 1954, Pierre, South Dakota, USA. Writer; College Teacher of Writing and Literature. Education: BA, University of South Dakota, 1976; MFA, Goddard College, 1980; Post-graduate studies, Hoyns Fellowship, University of Virginia. Appointment: Lecturer in Creative Writing and Literature, University of Virginia, 1984-. Publication: A Quarter Turn, 1991. Contributions to: American Poetry Review; Boston Review; Ploughshares; Triquarterly; Virginia Quarterly Review; Denver Quarterly; Threepenny Review; Prairie Schooner; Seattle Review; Missouri Review; Seneca Review; Raccoon; Iris; Five Fingers Review; Poetry East; Antioch Review; Ironwood; Crazy Horse. Honours: Hoyns Fellowship in Poetry, University of Virginia, 1982; Yaddo Fellowship, 1983; Virginia Commission for the Arts Prize, 1987; Balch Prize for Poetry, 1991; Boatwright Prize for Poetry, 1994. Memberships: Associated Writing Programmes; Poetry Society of America. Address: Department of English, 302 Bryan Hall, University of Virginia, Charlottesville, VA 22903, USA.

O

O FIONNAIN See: **FANNING Michael.**

O'BRIEN Angela. See: **MICHAEL Christine.**

O'BRIEN Katharine (Elizabeth), b. Amesbury, Massachusetts, USA. Mathematics Educator. Education: AB, Bates College, 1922; AM, Cornell University, 1924; PhD, Mathematics, Brown University, 1929. Appointments: Instructor to Professor and Chairman, Mathematics Department, College of New Rochelle, 1925-36; Teacher and Head, Mathematics Department, Deering High School, 1940-71; Lecturer, Mathematics, University of Maine, Portland Campus, 1962-73; Lecturer, Mathematics, Brown University, summers 1962-65, 1967. Publication: Excavations and Other Verses, 1967. Contributions to: Saturday Review; Christian Science; Monitor; New York Times; New York Herald Tribune; Boston Herald; American Mathematical Monthly; and about 30 other periodicals and anthologies. Honours: Honorary Degrees: ScDEd 1960, University of Maine; LHD 1965, Bowdoin College; Deborah Morton Award, Westbrook College, 1985. Memberships: Phi Beta Kappa; Poetry Society of America. Address: 130 Hartley Street, Portland, ME 04103, USA.

O'BRIEN   Mark David, b. 31 July 1949. Poet; Journalist. Education: BA English, University of California, 1982. Publication: Breathing, 1990. Contributions to: Margin; Sun; St Andrew's Review. Membership: Academy of American Poets. Literary Agent: Helen McGrath. Address: 2420 Dwight Way No 1, Berkeley, CA 94704, USA.

O'BRIEN Mary Kathryn, b. 13 Nov 1954, Houston, Texas, USA. Editorial Manager. 1 son. Education: BA, University of Arizona, Tucson, 1975. Appointments: Promotion Director, Tucson Newspapers Inc, Tucson, Arizona, 1975-80; Assistant to President, Population Council, 1980-87; Editorial Manager, Sloan Kettering Memorial Cancer Center, New York City, 1989-. Publications: Handbook for Poets, 1977; The Legend of Cherokee Clark, 1989. Contributions to: Art Measure; Black Happiness Journal; Caw's Moss; Everyday Clothes; Fiddlehead; Moon Rock; North Carolina Review; Review La Booche; Waiova Review; Yarns of Silk; Yaphta; The Spirit That Wants Me, anthology, 1991. Membership: Dramatists Guild. Address: 339 East 94th Street 2F, New York, NY 10128, USA.

O'BRIEN Sean Patrick, b. 19 Dec 1952, London, England. Writer. Education: BA, Honours, English, Selwyn College, Cambridge, 1974; MA, Birmingham University, 1977; Hull University, 1976-79; Leeds University, PGCE, 1981. Appointments: Teacher of English, Beacon School, Crowborough, East Sussex, 1981-89; Fellow in Creative Writing, Dundee University, 1989-91; Northern Arts Literary Fellow, 1992-94. Publications: The Indoor Park, 1983; The Frighteners, 1987; Boundary Beach, 1989; HMS Glasshouse, 1991. Contributions to: Times Literary Supplement; Independent; Observer; Sunday Times; Antaeus; Poetry Review; London Magazine; Verse; Bete Noire; PBS Anthology and others; BBC Radio 3, Third Ear, Poetry Now; BBC Radio 4, Time For Verse; Kaleidoscope. Honours: Gregory Award, 1979; Somerset Maughan Award, 1984; Cholmondeley Award, 1988; Arts Council Writer's Bursary, 1992; Fellow in Creative Writing, University of Dundee, 1989-91; Northern Arts Literary Fellow, 1992-94. Address: 15 Connaught Gardens, Forest Hall, Newcastle-upon-Tyne NE12 8AT, England.

O'BRIEN William Patrick, b. 9 Mar 1927, Flushing, New York, USA. Teacher; Writer. m. Dorothea M Neville, 16 Dec 1951, 2 sons, 2 daughters. Education: BS, Fordham University, 1951; MA, Pennsylvania State University, 1965. Publication: Starting From Paumanok, 1971. Contributions to: Anthology of Magazine Verse, 1984, 1986-88; Fiddlehead; Crazy Quilt; Green's Magazine; Kansas Quarterly; Long Pond Review; Newsday; Shenandoah; Southern Humanities Review; Physics Today; West Hills Review. Address: 227 Seville Boulevard, Sayville, NY 11782, USA.

Ó CÉIRÍN Cyril, b. 9 Feb 1934, Ireland. Former Teacher. Education: BA, HDipEd. Publications: Le hAer 's le Fuacht, a collection, 1986; Editor and Contributor to Breith, 1974; Edited: Saltair Muire, 16th Century poem, 1989. Contributions to: Poetry Ireland; Innti; Comhar; New Irish Writing; Irish Press; An Timire; Stony Thursday Book; Anthologies: On The Counterscarp, Nua-Fhili, 3; Rogha an

Fhile. Honours: Poetry Competitions: Feile na Maighe, 1975, An Toireachtas, 1977, 1980, 1982, Listowel Writers Week, 1981; Member of 1979 Bardic Tour of Scotland, Bard to The Inaugural O'Callaghan Clan Gathering, 1988. Address: Teach an Atlantaigh, Lios Duin Bhearna, Co an Chlair, Ireland.

O'CONNELL Richard, b. 25 Oct 1928, New York, New York, USA Poet; Educator. Education: BS, Temple University, 1956; MA, Johns Hopkins University, 1957. Appointment: Professor Emeritus (English), Temple University, 1993-. Publications: Cries Of Flesh And Stone, 1962; Brazilian Happenings, 1966; Terrane, 1967; Epigrams From Martial, 1976; Sappho, 1976; Lorca, 1976; One Hundred Epigrams From The Greek Anthology, 1977; Hudson's Fourth Voyage, 1978; Irish Monastic Poems, 1984; Temple Poems, 1985; Hanging Tough, 1985; Battle Poems, 1987; Lives Of The Poets, 1990; Selected Epigrams, 1990; New Epigrams From Martial, 1991; The Caliban Poems, 1992; Retroworlds, 1993; Simulations, 1993; Voyages, 1995. Contributions to: New Yorker; Paris Review; Atlantic Monthly; National Review; Quarterly Review Of Literature; Littak; Acumen; Texas Quarterly; Others. Honours: Fulbright Lecturer, University of Brazil, 1960; Fulbright Lecturer, University of Navarre, Pamplona, Spain, 1962-63; Contemporary Poetry Prize, 1972; Yaddo Foundation Writing Residency, 1974,75. Memberships: American PEN Club; Modern Language Association; Associated Writing Programmes. Address: 204 Ellesmere D, Deerfield Beach, FL 33442, USA.

O'CONNOR Patrick, b. 26 Aug 1925, Braddock, Pennsylvania, USA. Editor; Critic; Ski Instructor. Education: Catholic University of America, Washington, DC. Appointments: Producer/Director, Rochester Arena Theatre, Rochester, New York; President, O'Connor Productions (TV); Editor-in-Chief: Curtis Books, Popular Library, Pinnacle Books, Washington Square Press; Senior Editor, Warner Books; Dance/Theatre Critic, Jersey Journal, Variety, WNET-TV New York; Cultural Commissar and Commentator, WBAI-FM (Radio), New York; Ski Instructor, Killington, Vermont. Publication: No Poem for Fritz, 1978. Contributions to: Poultry, a magazine of voice; Voices (Israel); Braddock Free Press, Pennsylvania. Memberships: Poetry Society of America; Miss MappSociety, President-for-Life; Nancy Mitford Society, President, 1986-. Address: PO Box 296, Killington, VT 05751, USA.

Ó'CURRAOIN Seán, b. Bearna, Connemara, County Galway, Ireland. Legal Translator to Irish Parliament. Education: BA, Irish and English, 1961; MA, Irish, 1980. Appointments: Linguistic Researcher on the Irish-English Dictionary; Translator and Interpreter, in Dáil. Publications: Soilse ar na Dumhchannaí, 1985; Beairtle, 1985; Tinte Sionnaigh (short stories), 1985. Contributions to: Comhar; Feasta; Innti; Cyphers. Memberships: Irish Translators Association;Folklore of Ireland Society; Irish Writers' Union. Address: 18 Ascaill Verbena, Br. Chill Bharróg, Baile Átha Cliath 13, Ireland.

O'DONNELL Dennis Gerrard, b. 14 Sept 1951, Dechmont, West Lothian, Scotland. Schoolmaster. m. Joan Murphy, 28 Sept 1972, 1 daughter. Education: MA Hons, English Language and Literature, Edinburgh University, 1973; Postgraduate Work on Ezra Pound, (unfinished, no diploma), 1973-76. Appointments: Joiner's Labourer; Nurse in Psychiatric Hospital; Dogsbody in Local Radio; Bus Conductor; Schoolmaster. Contributions to: Acumen; Envoi; Hybrid; Iota; Krax; Lines Magazine; Momentum; New Hope International; Poetry Wales; Psychopoetica; Slow Dancer; Staple; Third Half; Weyfarers; White Rose Magazine; Wire. Address: Almond Lane, The Cross, Blackburn, West Lothian EH47 7QU, Scotland.

O'DONNELL Mary (Elizabeth Eugenie), b. 3 Apr 1954, Monaghan, Ireland. Writer; Poet; Freelance Journalist (theatre and book critic). m. Martin Nugent, 18 June 1977. Education: BA Hons, German and Philosophy, 1977; 1st Class Hons Diploma in Higher Education, Maynooth College, 1983. Appointments: Translator, 1981; Teacher to 1988; Currently Journalist/Theatre Critic; Writer-in-Residence, University College, Dublin; Writer in Residence, County Laois, 1995. Publications: Reading the Sunflowers in September, 1990; Strong Pagans and Other Stories, 1991; The Light-Makers, 1992, 93; Spiderwoman's Third Avenue Rhapsody (poems), 1993. Contributions to: Irish Times; Poetry Review; Oxford Poetry; Orbis; Irish University Review; Honest Ulsterman; Irish Literary Supplement (US); Bloodaxe's New Women Poets, ed Carol Rumens, 1990; Sunday Tribune; North Dakota Quarterly; Midland Review (Oklahoma); Lullwater Review (Georgia); Great Book of Ireland; Seneca Review; Irish Literary Review. Honours: Poetry Award, 1988;

Litowel Writer's Week, 1982; 2nd Prize, Patrick Kavanagh Poetry Award, 1986; 3rd Prize runner-up, Bloodaxe National Poetry Competition, 1987. Memberships: Poetry Ireland (Dublin); Subscriber to Poetry Review (London); The Poetry Society; Irish Council for Civil Liberties. Address: Rook Hollow, Newtown Macabe, Maynooth, Co Kildare, Ireland.

O'DONOGHUE (James) Bernard, b. 14 Dec 1945, Cullen, County Cork, Ireland. University Teacher of English. m. Heather MacKinnon, 23 July 1977, 1 son, 2 daughters. Education: MA, English, 1968; BPhil, Medieval English, 1971; Lincoln College, Oxford. Appointments: Lecturer, Tutor, English, Magdalen College, Oxford, 1971-; Fellow, Wadham College, Oxford, 1995-. Publications: Razorblades and Pencils, 1984; Poaching Rights, 1987; The Absent Signifier, 1990; The Weakness, 1991; Gunpowder, 1995. Contributions to: Times Literary Supplement; Poetry Review; Poetry Ireland Review; Irish Press; Honest Ulsterman; Sunday Tribune; New Statesman; Irish Literary Review. Honour: Southern Arts Literature Prize for The Weakness, 1991; Whitbread Poetry Prize for Gunpowder, 1995. Membership: Poetry Society (London), 1984-. Address: Wadham College, Oxford OX1 3PN, England.

O'DRISCOLL Ciaran, b. 2 Oct 1943, Callan, County Kilkenny, Ireland. Lecturer; Poet; Editor. m. Margaret Farrelly, 3 Sept 1987, 1 son. Education: BA, Hons, English and Philosophy, University College Cork, 1968; MA, Philosophy, Bedford College, University of London, 1978. Appointments: Lecturer, Limerick School of Art and Design; Editor, Limerick Poetry Broad-sheet, 1988-91; Editor, Cyphers, 1992-93. Publications: Gog and Magog, 1987; The Poet and his Shadow, 1990; The Myth of the South, 1992. Contributions to: Ambit; Aquarius; Cyphers; Dedalus Irish Poets (anthology); Die horen (Germany); Fortnight; Hard Lines; Honest Ulsterman; Irish Press; Irish Times; Krino; North Dakota Quarterly; Omens; Orbis; Poetry Ireland Review; Quarry (Canada) Salmon. Honours: Bursary in Literature, Irish Arts Council, 1984; James Joyce Literary Millenium Prize, 1989. Membership: Founder-Member, Chairman, 1986-91, Limerick Poetry Workshop. Address: 5 St Bridget's Avenue, New Street, Limerick, Ireland.

O'FIANNACHTA Padraig, b. 20 Feb 1927, County Kerry, Ireland. Professor. Education: St Brendan's Killarney, 1939-44; St Patrick's College, Maynooth, 1944-48; BA, NUI, 1947; University College Cork, 1949-50; MA, NUI, 1955; MRIA, 1967. Appointments: Lecturer in early Irish and Welsh, 1959, Professor of Early Irish and Lecturer in Welsh, 1960-81, Professor of Modern Irish, 1981-92, St Patrick's College, Maynooth. Publications: Ponc, 1966; Ruin, 1969; Feoirlingi Fileata, 1972; Donn Bo, 1976; Spaisteoireacht, 1982; Deora De, 1987. Contributions to: Comhar; Irisleabhar Mha Nuad; Poetry Ireland; Feasta; An Sagart. Honour: Douglas Hyde Prize for Literature, 1969. Memberships: Cumann na Sagart; Poetry Ireland; President of Oireachtas, 1985; Editor: Maynooth Monographs, Iriseabhar Mha Nuad, Leachtai Cholm Cille, Dan agus Tallann. Address: Ventry, Tralee, Co Kerry, Ireland.

O'GRADY Desmond James Bernard, b. 27 Aug 1935, Limerick, Ireland. Writer. 1 son, 2 daughters. Education: MA, 1964, PhD, 1982, Harvard University. Appointments: Secondary School Teacher, University Professor, 1955-82; Currently Poet, Translator of Poetry; Literary Prose. Publications: Chords and Orchestrations, 1956; Reilly, 1961; Professor Kelleher and the Charles River, 1964; Separazioni, poems with Italian translations, 1965; The Dark Edge of Europe, 1967; The Dying Gaul, 1968; Off Licence, 1968; Hellas, 1971; Separations, 1973; Stations, 1976; Sing Me Creation, 1977; The Gododdin, 1977; A Limerick Rake, 1978; The Headgear of the Tribe, 1979; His Skaldcrane's Nest, 1979; Translator, Grecian Glances, 1981; Alexandria Notebook, 1989; Translator, The Seven Arab Odes, 1990; Tipperary, poems, 1991; Translator, Ten Modern Arab Poets, 1992; My Fields This Springtime, 1993; Alternative Manners, translations, 1993; Trawling Tradition, collected translations 1954-1994; Il Gallo Morente, poems with Italian translations, 1996; The Road Taken, poems, 1956-1996; Works in progress include: Myself Alone, prose memoirs. Contributions to: Many international poetry magazines; Botteghe Oscure; Poetry Ireland Review; Artes; Orbis; Agni Review; Anthologies: Norton Anthology of Modern Poetry; All Anthologies of Modern Irish Poetry. Honours: Founding Member, Ireland's Aosdana of Literature and The Arts; Irish Academy of Arts and Letters; Poet in Residence, American University, Cairo, Egypt. Membership: Aosdana, Ireland. Address: Ardbrack, Kinsdale, County Cork, Ireland.

O'GRADY Irenia Beryle, b. 18 Jan 1931, Magill, South Australia. Journalist; Freelance Poet; Writer; Historian. m. (2) Michael O'Grady, 27 Jan 1978, 1 daughter. Education: Degree in History and English, correspondence courses. Appointments: Journalist, Critic Reviewer to various publications. Publications: The Many Faces of Love; Moods and Fantasies; Of Love, Trust and Other Things; History, Heritage and Humour; Madras, India, 1995. Contributions to: Parnassus of World Poetry, 1994; Richmond Clarion, Victoria; Truth Newspaper; Australian Women's Weekly; Argus Victoria; SA Gazettes; Messenger Press; Advertiser; New Idea; Sunday Mail; People's Friend; My Weekly; Northern Arts Focus; Poem: Positive Thought, in National Stroke Association booklet, USA, 1995. Honours: 4 Awards for radio productions. Memberships include: Tea Tree Gully Library; English Speaking Union, Victoria. Address: Elphin Cottage, Black Hill Road, c/o Houghton Post Office, South Australia 5131, Australia.

O'GRADY Tom, b. 26 Aug 1943. Teacher; Poet; Vintner. Education: BA, University of Baltimore, 1966; MA, Johns Hopkins University, 1967; Advanced Studies, University of Delaware, 1972-74. Appointments: Lecturer, John Hopkins University, 1966-67; Catonsville College, 1969-71; University of Delaware, 1972-74; Hampden Sydney College, 1974-76; Adjunct Professor, Poet in Residence, Hampden Sydney College, 1976. Publications: In the Room of the Just Born, 1989; Carvings of the Moon: A Cycle of Poems, 1992; In The Room Of The Just Born; Shaking The Tree, essays; Carvings Of The Moon; The Gardens of November, a play; Sun, Moon & Stars, poems. Contributions to: Newsletters; Dryad; Enoch; Scene; Pyx; Nimrod; New Laurel Review. Honours include: Leache Prize; Chrysler Museum Arts Poetry Residency; Impact Book Award; Virginia Prize. Address: PO Box 126, Hampden Sydney, VA 23943, USA.

O'HEHIR Diana F, b. 23 May 1922. Writer; College Professor. Div, 2 sons. Education: MA, 1952, PhD, 1970, Johns Hopkins University. Appointments: Lecturer, Assistant Professor, Professor, Mills College, Oakland, 1961-91. Publications: Summoned, 1976; The Power to Change Geography, 1979; Home Free, 1979. Contributions to: Poetry; Paris Review; Iowa Review; Massachusetts Review; Poetry Northwest; Antaeus. Honours: Devins Award for 1st book of poems, 1976; MacDowell Fellowships Fellowships, 1976, 1978, 1980, 1982, 1984; Di Castagnola Award of Poetry Society of America, for work-in-progress, 1980. Memberships: Poets and Writers, Authors Guild; Authors League; Modern Language Association; PEN; Poetry Society. Address: Po Box 510, Bolinas, CA 94924, USA.

O'HIGGINS Michael Cecil Patrick, b. 25 Feb 1935, Dublin, Ireland. Writer; Poet. m. Julie Patricia Bryden, 8 Dec 1962, div 1968. Education: Ruskin College; Magdalen College Oxford. Appointments: American High School Teacher, 1963; Lecturer in Psychology, University of Maryland; In Oxford for the American Armed Forces Education. Publications: A Whisper on the Wind, 1960; Wells and other Poems, 1984; An Adventure of the Mind, 1985; Haiku, illustrated by Dick Boulton, 1985; Schizophrenia, 1988; Much Happy Travelling (poems), 1993. Contributions to: Acumen; Agenda; Contemporary Review; Dublin Magazine; Envoi; Global Tapestry; Iron; Krax; New Epoch; New Irish Writing; Orbis; Ore; Poetry And Audience; Poetry Durham; Poetry Nottingham; Poetry; Sepia; Success; Universities Poetry 6 (anthology); Stay at Homes; Mandeville Press Anthology; Works; and others. Honours: Elmgrant Trust Award, 1963; Mature State Scholarship, Oxford, 1964; South West Arts Literary Award for Poetry, 1984; Winner, Martha Robinson Poetry Competition, 1988; Friends of Mendip Poetry Award, 1988. Membership: Chairman, Wells Poetry Group, 1985-90. Address: 25 Woodbury Avenue, Wells, Somerset BA5 2XW, England.

O'MALLEY Martin J Jr, b. 9 Feb 1924, Passaic, New Jersey, USA. Teacher. Education: BA English 1959, Syracuse University, New York; Teaching Certificate 1958, New Jersey. Appointments: Teacher, 1958-72. Publications: The Lun Yu of Kung Fu, 1960; The Tao of Mao-Tse-Tung, 1961. Contributions to: Class Magazine; AFER, African Ecclesial Review; Baptist Leader; Players; Greater Boston News; Memo Digest. Honours: Golden Poet Award, World of Poetry, Sacramento, 1987-92. Memberships: World of Poetry; National Library; World Poetry, India; International Writers and Artists Association. Address: 222 Paulison Avenue, A-5 Passaic, NJ 07055, USA.

O'NEILL Michael, b. 2 Sept 1953, Aldershot, Hampshire, England. University Lecturer. m. Rosemary McKendrick, 16 July 1977, 1 son, 1 daughter. Education: BA, Class 1, English, 1975, D Phil, 1981,

Oxford University. Appointments: Professor, University of Durham; Editor-Founder, Poetry Durham magazine, 1982. Publication: The Stripped Bed, 1990. Contributions to: Poems: Times Literary Supplement; London Magazine; Spectator; Sunday Times and others; Reviews: Times Literary Supplement; Poetry Review. Honours: Eric Gregory Award, 1983; Cholmondeley Award, 1990. Membership: Editor, founder, Poetry Durham (poetry magazine), 1982-94. Address: School of English, University of Durham, Durham DH1 3JT, England.

O'SULLIVAN Maggie, b. 20 July 1951, Lincoln, England. Poet. Publications: Concerning Spheres: An Incomplete Natural History; A Natural History in 3 Incomplete Parts; Un Assuming Personas; Divisions of Labour; From the Handbook of That and Furriery; States of Emergency; Unofficial Word. Contributions to: City Limits; Reality Studios; Poetry Review; Slow Dancer; Writing Women; Angel Exhaust; Archeus; Palpi; Responses; Critical Quarterly; Inkblot; Writing; Sink; Raddle Moon; Ligne; Avec. Address: Middle Fold Farm, Colden, Hebden Bridge, West Yorkshire HX7 7PG, England.

OAKES Philip, b. 31 Jan 1928, Burslem, Staffordshire, England. m. (1) Stella Fleming, div 1989, (2) Gillian Hodson, 1989. Appointments: Arts Columnist, London Sunday Times, 1965-80; Independent on Sunday, 1990-. Publications include: Unlucky Jonah: Twenty Poems, 1954; In the Affirmative, 1968; Notes by the Provincial Governor, 1972; Married/Singular, 1973; Selected Poems, 1982; Screenplay, The Punch and Judy Man, 1962; Novels and Memoirs. Address: c/o Elaine Greene Ltd, 31 Newington Green, London N16 9PU, England.

OATES Joyce Carol, b. 16 June 1938, Millersport, New York, USA. Author; Dramatist; Poet; Professor; Publisher. m. Raymond Joseph Smith, 23 Jan 1961. Education: BA, Syracuse University, 1960; MA, University of Wisconsin, Madison, 1961. Appointments: Instructor, 1961-65, Assistant Professor, 1965-67, University of Detroit; Faculty, Department of English, University of Windsor, Ontario, Canada, 1967-78; Co-Publisher (with Raymond J Smith), Ontario Review, 1974-; Writer-in-Residence, 1978-81, Professor, 1987-, Princeton University. Publications: Poetry: Women in Love and Other Poems, 1968; Anonymous Sins and Other Poems, 1969; Love and Its Derangements, 1970; Wooded Forms, 1972; Angel Fire, 1973; Dreaming America and Other Poems, 1973; The Fabulous Beasts, 1975; Seasons of Peril, 1977; Women Whose Lives Are Food, Men Whose Lives Are Money, 1978; Celestial Timepiece, 1980; Nightless Nights: Nine Poems, 1981; Invisible Women: New and Selected Poems 1970-1982, 1982; Luxury of Sin, 1984; The Time Traveller: Poems 1983-1989, 1989; Fiction includes: First Love: A Gothic Tale, 1996; Stories include: Haunted Tales of the Grotesque, 1994; Plays include: The Perfectionist and Other Plays, 1995; Other includes: (Woman) Writer: Occasions and Opportunities, 1988; As Editor, includes: Reading the Fights (with Daniel Halpern), 1988. Honours: National Endowment for the Arts Grants, 1966, 1968; Guggenheim Fellowship, 1967; O Henry Awards, 1967, 1973, and Special Awards for Continuing Achievement, 1970, 1986; Rosenthal Award, 1968; National Book Award, 1970; Rea Award, 1990; Heideman Award, 1990; Bobst Lifetime Achievement Award, 1990; Walt Whitman Award, 1995. Membership: American Academy of Arts and Letters. Address: 185 Nassau Street, Princeton, NJ 08540, USA.

OBARSKI Marek b. 2 July 1947, Poznan, Poland. Novelist; Poet; Critic. m. Aleksandra Zaworska, 27 Mar 1982, 2 sons, 1 daughter. Appointments: Director, Flowering Grass, 1974-79; Director, Literary Department, Nurt Literary magazine, 1984-90; Critic, Art For Child magazine, 1989-; Editor, Rebis Publishing House, 1991-93; Europa Cultural Quarterly magazine, 1991. Publications: The Sunken Pipes, 1969; The Countries of Wolves, 1971; The Lightning of Flight, 1978; The Body of Cloud, 1983; The Dancing Stoat, 1987; The Straw Giant, 1987; The Forest Altar, 1989; The Face of Demon. Contributions to: Various magazines and journals. Honours: Medal of Young Art, 1984; Stanislaw Pietak Award, 1985; Nomination, Natalia Gall Prize, 1988. Memberships: Ecologic Association of Creators; Union of Polish Letters, 1979-83; Union des Gens de Lettres Polonais. Address: Osiedle Wl.Lokietka 13 F m 58, 61-616 Poznan, Poland.

ODEGARD Knut, b. 6 Nov 1945, Molde, Norway. Poet. m. Thorgerdur Ingolfsdottir, 2 Aug 1981, 2 daughters. Education: Theology and Philology, Oslo University, 1965. Appointments: Literary Critic, Aftenposten, Norway, 1968-; Director, Noregs Boklag, Oslo, 1975-77; Cultural Director, County of Sor-Trondelag, 1978-84; Managing Director, Scandinavian Centre, Nordens Hus, Reykavik,

1984-89; President, Norwegian Festival of International Literature, 1992-; Consul for Republic of Slovakia, 1995-. Publications: 10 poetry books, debut: The Dreamer, The Wanderer And The Well, 1967; Last poetry books: Ventriloquy, 1994; Selected Poems, 1995; 4 prose books, fiction, 1 study on Iceland. Contributions to; Chief poetry critic, Aftenposten (Norway's leading newspaper), 1968-. Honours: Norwegian State's Stipend for Artists, several times; The Bastian Prize for Best Translation; Knighted by President of Iceland, 1987; Norwegian State Scholar for Life, 1989-; Grand Knight Commander, Order of the Icelandic Falcon, 1993; International Order of Merit, 1993; Knight of The Norwegian Order of Literature (Björnson-orderen), 1995. Memberships: Norwegian Society of Authors; Icelandic Society of Authors; Société Européenne de Culture (Venice); Norwegian Society of Critics, Board, 1971-74; Academy of Norwegian Language; Chairman of The Broadcasting Society, 1975-76; Poetry Society, England, president, 1996; International Literature Festivals in Reyjavik, 1985-87; Norwegian Literary Council, 1991-; Literary Academy of Romania, 1996-. Address: Château, Parkv 42, 6400 Molde, Norway.

OEFFNER Barbara, b. 25 Aug 1944, Southampton, New York, USA. Editor; Publisher. m. Thomas Oeffner, 2 Oct 1991, 1 son, 2 daughters. Education: BSJ, Northwestern University. Appointments: President, Cape Cod Writers Inc; Editor and Publisher, Sandscript Magazine, Cape Cod Writers Inc. Contributions to: Limberlost Review; Poetry/People; WEID American Women Poets Issue; In The West of Ireland; Nantucket Review; Fertile Egg; Sandscript. Honours: CCLM Grant, 1976; Mary Roberts Rinehart Award, 1978; Merit Award, Massachusetts Arts Council, 1980. Memberships: New England Poetry Club; Poets and Writers; CCLM. Address: 1480 Master's Circle No 171, Delray Beach, FL 33445, USA.

OERTLI Cheryl Lyne Gilmore, b. 26 Jan 1951, St Johns, Michigan, USA. Freelance Writer. m. Leroy Louis Oertli, 19 Oct 1972, 2 sons. Education: Graduate, Lansing Community College, 1989. Publication: The Face in the Mirror, poem, 1990. Contributions to: Jesee Poet; American Poetry Association; California State Poetry Society; Allura Magazine; Poets of Now; Peninsula Poets; Watermark Press; World of Poetry; Poetic Pen Pals Newsletter; Nexas News; Poetry Plus; Famous Poets Society. Honours: World of Poetry Golden Poet Awards, 1985-88; Poets of Now Merit Award, 1988; Nominated for inclusion, 5000 Personalities of the World 5th Edition. Memberships: National Federation of State Poetry Societies; Poetry Society of Michigan; Poets of Now; Poetry Study Club; Charter Mbr, Writers Cafe, 1992-. Address: 4523 Sycamore Street, Holt, MI 48842, USA.

OFFEN Yehuda, (Huri Halim, Ben Naftali), b. 4 Apr 1922, Altona, Germany. Writer; Journalist. m. Tova Arbisser, 28 Mar 1946, 1 daughter. Education: BA, London University, 1975; MA, Comparative Literature, Hebrew University, Jerusalem. Appointments: Head of Department, Holland Bank Union, 1950-60; Senior Editor, Al Hamishmar, Daily Guardian, 1960-80. Publications: L'Lo L'An, 1961; Har Vakhol, 1963; Lo Agadat Khoref, 1969; Nofim P'Nima, 1979; N'Vilat Vered, 1983; Shirim Bir'Hov Ayaif, 1984; P'Gishot Me'Ever Laz'man, 1986; Massekhet Av, 1986; Mi Shepa'Am Holid Kochav, 1990; Silly Soil, 1992; Shirim Lir'Fua, Translation of Erich Kaestner's Poems, 1965; Short Stories: In a Closed Circle, 1979; Stoning On The Crossroad, 1988; Poems: Back To Germany, 1994. Contributions to: Moznayim; Iton 77; Apiryon; Al Hamishmar; Yediot Aharonot; Ma'Ariv; Davar; Ha'Aretz; Prosa; Sh'Demot; Gilyonot; Gazith; Also, Bitzaron, USA; Hadoar, USA; Poet, Madras; and others. Honours: ACUM Prize for Literature, 1961, 1979, 1984; Talpir Prize for Literature, 1979; Efrat Prize for Poetry, 1988-89. Memberships: Hebrew Writers' Association in Israel; General Union of Writers in Israel; Societé des Auteurs, Compositeurs et Editeurs en Israel (ACUM); PEN Club, Israel; International Federation of Journalists, Brussels; National Federation of Israeli Journalists; International Academy of Poets, Cambridge. Address: 8 Gazit Street, Tel-Aviv 69417, Israel.

OGDEN Georgine. See: PROKOPOV Georgine Lucile Ogden.

OGDEN Hugh, b. 11 Mar 1937, Erie, Pennsylvania, USA. Teacher. m. Ruth Simpson, 3 Mar 1960, 1 son, 2 daughters. Education: BA, Haverford College, 1959; MA, New York University, 1961; PhD, Michigan University, 1967. Appointments: University of Michigan, Teaching Assistant, 1961-65; Instructor, 1965-67; Assistant Professor, Trinity College, 1967-75; Associate Profesor, 1975-91; Professor, 1992-. Publications: Looking For History, 1991; Two Road and This Spring, 1993; Windfalls, 1996. Contributions to: Poetry

Northwest; Malahat Review; Yankee; Cincinnati Poetry Review; North Dakota Quarterly; Fiddlehead; Blue Line; Passages North; North American Review; Mid-American Review; Negative Capability. Honours: Poetry Project Grant, Connecticut Commission on the Arts, 1990; National Endowment for the Arts, 1993. Memberships: Associated Writing Programs, Poets and Writers; Poetry Society of America. Address: Department of English, Trinity College, Hartford, CT 06106, USA.

OGG Wilson Reid, b. 26 Feb 1928, Alhambra, California, USA. Poet; Graphic Illustrator; Retired Lawyer; Judge. Education: AA, 1947, AB, 1949, JD, 1952, University of California at Berkeley; Ordained as Minister, 1968; Honorary DD, University of Life Church, 1969; DRelig, Humanities, 1970; Credentials as Community College Instructor in Law, Sociology and Real Estate, 1976; Cultural Doctorate in Philosophy of Law, 1983. Appointments: Psychology Instructor, US Armed Forces Institute, Taegu, Korea (during Korean conflict), 1953-54; English Instructor, Taegu English Language Institute, 1954; Private Law Practice, 1955-78; Trustee and Secretary, First Unitarian Church of Berkeley, 1957-58; Research Attorney, Continuing Education of The Bar, University of California, 1958-63; Vice-President, International House Association, 1961-62; President and Board Chairman, California Society for Psychical Study Inc, 1963-65; Arbitrator, American Arbitration Association, 1963-; Curator in Residence, Pinebrook, Berkeley, California, 1964-; Real Estate Broker, 1974-78; Board of Trustees, World University, 1977; Director of Admissions, International Society for Philosophical Enquiry, 1981-85. Contributions to: Numerous anthologies. Memberships: World Academy of Arts and Letters; National Library of Poets; World Literary Academy. Address: Pinebrook at Bret Harte Way, 1104 Keith Avenue, Berkeley, CA 94708-1607, USA.

OHAETO Ezenwa, (Zenwas), b. 31 Mar 1958, Nigeria. Lecturer; Writer. m. 10 Nov 1990. Education: BA, 1979, MA, 1982, University of Nigeria; PhD, University of Benin, 1991. Appointments: Associate Editor, The Muse, 1978-79; Lecturer, 1982-88; Senior Lecturer, 1988-; Editorial Board of Okike. Publications: Songs of Atraueller; I Wan Bi President; Bullets for Buntings; Pieces of Madness. Contributions to: Summer Fires; Fate of Vultures; Kunapipi; Rhythms of Creation; Trinidad and Tobago Review; Okike; Orphic Lute; Proof Rock; Literary Half Yearly; Muse; Ufahamu; Omabe; Nedjma; Kola; Akpata; Bricollages and Collages; Anthill Annual; Guardian; Daily Times. Honours: 1st Prize, Story Competition, University of Nigeria. Memberships: Literary Society of Nigeria; Omabe Poetry Club; Association of Nigerian Authors; Awka Poetry Club; West African Association of Commonwealth. Address: Department of English and Literature, College of Education, PMB 5011, Awka, Anambra State, Nigeria.

OKANZA Okama. See: ADONH Overnak C Antoine.

OKAZAKI Tadao, b. 7 Apr 1943. Physician; Poet. Education: MD, Prefectual Medical School, Japan; State University of New York, USA. Appointments: Editor, New Cicada, Japan, 1984-. Publications: Haiku, Essays on Haiku Ballard Theory. Contributions to: Cicada; Modern Haiku; Frogpond; New Cicada. Honours: Modern Haiku; Cicada Prize; Special Mention Award. Memberships: Haiku Society of America; Haiku Canada; Canadian Poetry. Address: 13 Shimizu Fushiguro, Fukushima 960-05, Japan.

OKON Zbigniew Waldemar, b. 21 July 1945, Chelm, Poland. Teacher. m. Halina Pioro Maciejewska, 6 Oct 1969, 2 sons, 1 daughter. Education: Maria Curie-Sklodowska University, Lublin. Publications: Outlooks and Reflections, 1968; The Soldiers of the Chalk Hills, 1970; Impatience of the Tree, 1979; Intimidation by Twilight, 1986; Calling up the Darkness, 1987; Taste of the Childhood, 1990. Contributions to: Various journals and magazines. Honours: 1st Prize, Poetry Competitions, 1964, 1966, 1968, 1974; Czechowicz Literary Prize, 1987; National Scholarship, Ministry of Culture and Art from the Fund of Literature, 1991. Memberships: Chairman, Pryzmaty, 1983, Stowarzyszenie Ziemi Chelmskiej; Union of Polish Literary Men. Address: ul Kolejowa 86-19, 22-100 Chelm, Poland.

OLABISI Adebayo, b. 25 Sept 1946, Igboho, Nigeria. Teacher. m. Anne Chizoma Ike, 3 Aug 1974, 6 sons. Education: BEd, Honours, Education and Physics, University of Ibadan, Nigeria, 1972; MBA, University of Lagos, Nigeria, 1980. Appointments: Education Officer, Grade I Physics, Federal Government College, Warri, Nigeria, 1972-76; Master Grade I Physics, International School, University of

Ibadan, 1976-77; Marketing Executive, SEMY Limited, Lagos, 1980-81; Assistant General Manager, Macron Services Ltd, Lagos, 1981; Lecturer, Head of Department, Teacher of Education, The Polytechnic, Ibadan, 1982-. Publications: Flakes of Free Verses; Fusion of Reminiscences. Contributions to: The Hard-Time Diviner; Best Poems of the 90's; The Ebbing Tide; Shadows and Light; A Moment in Time; A Walk Through Paradise; Best Poems of 1995; Dance on the Horizon; A Break in the Clouds. Honours: Editors Choice Award, National Library of Poetry, Maryland, USA, 1994; Nomination, Poet of the Year Award, International Society of Poets, 1995, 1996. Memberships: Association of Nigerian Authors; International Society of Poets. Address: PO Box 253, Saki, Oyo State, Nigeria.

OLAFSSON Einar, b. 11 Sept 1949, Reykjavík, Iceland. Writer. m. Gudbjorg Sveinsdottir, 8 Jan 1988, 2 sons, 1 daughter. Education: Studied literature at University of Oslo, 1976-78; BA, History, University of Iceland, 1984. Publications: Litla Stúlkan Og Brúduleikhúsid, 1971; Ljód, 1971; Öll Réttindi Áskilin, 1972; Drepa, Drepa (with Dagur Sigurdason), 1974; Augu Vid Gangstétt, 1983; Sólarbasúnan, 1986; Brynjólfur Bjarnason, Pólitísk Ævisaga, 1989; Mánadúfur, 1995. Membership: Writers Association of Iceland. Address: Tronuhjalli 13, IS-200 Kopavogur, Iceland.

OLAPPAMANNA Subrahmanian Nambudiripad (Olappamanna), b. 10 Jan 1923, Vellinezhi, India. Literary Executive; Agriculturist. m. Sreedevi, 31 Oct 1953, 3 sons, 1 daughter. Education: Government Victoria College, Palakkad under Madras University, 1944-46. Appointments: President, Palakkad District, Rubber Growers Marketing Society, 1966-79; Vice Chairman, 1972-78, Chairman, 1978-84, Kalamandalam Art Centre, Kerala; Director, Nedungadi Bank Ltd, 1982-90. Publications: Veena, 1947; Kalpana, 1948; Kilungunna Kayyamam, 1949; Elathalam, 1949; Asareerikal, 1949; Kulampati, 1950; Rubber Wifum matu kavithakalum, 1951; Theethylam, 1951; Panchali, 1957; Ehisoonari, 1965; Olichupokunna nhan, 1965; Kadha Kavithakal, 1966; Nangemakkutty, 1967; Anamuthu, 1973; Amba, 1973; Subhala, 1974; Dukhamavuka Sukham, 1980; Nizhalana, 1987; Jalakappakshi, 1988. Contributions to: Mangalodayam; Mathrubhumi; Bhashaposhini; Malayala Manorama; Kunkumam; and others. Honours: Award for Best Malayalam Poetical Work of 1950-51 by Madras Government; Kerala Sahithya Akademy Award, 1966; Otakuzhal Award, Guruvayoorappan Trust, 1988; National Award, Central Sahithya Academy, 1989. Memberships: Samastha Kerala Sahithya Parishath, Kerala, 1950-58; Director, Sahithya Pravarthaka Cooperative Society, 1965-74; General Council, Kerala Sahithya Akademy and Executive Committee member, Kerala Sangeetha Nataka Akademy, 1969-72. Address: Hari Sree, Jainmedu, Palakkad, 678 012 Kerala, India.

OLDER Julia D, b. 25 May 1941, Chicago, Illinois, USA. Freelance Writer and Poet. Education: BA, University of Michigan, 1963; MFA, Instituto Allende, Mexico, 1971; Diploma, Conservatorio Arrigo Boito, Parma, Italy, 1966; Iowa Writers' Workshop, one semester, 1962. Appointments: Assistant Children's Book Editor, Putnam Publishing Co, New York, 1969-70; Column Writer and Poetry Editor, New Hampshire Times, 1974-76; Regular Book Reviewer, New Letters Review of Books, Kansas City, 1989-91. Publications: Oonts and Others, 1982; A Little Wild, 1987; Blues For a Black Cat (translations of Boris Vian), 1992; The Island Queen (novel based on poet, Celia Thaxter 1935-94), 1994; Higher Latitudes (poems), 1995. Contributions to: Yankee; International Quarterly; Apalachee Quarterly; Poets and Writers (poetry essay) Salamagundi; New Yorker; Corpse. Honours: Mary Roberts Rinehart Grant for Prose, 1974; GuyAvery Hopwood First Poetry Prize, University of Michigan, 1963; Owen Poetry Award, Southern Review, 1986; Colladay Award, Quarterly Review of Literature, 1989; Judge for Chester Jones National Poetry Competition, (with Diane Wakoski and August Kleinzahler), 1994; Nomination, Pushcart Anthology, 1992. Membership: Academy of American Poets. Literary Agent: Curtis Brown, New York, USA. Address: Box 174, Hancock, NJ 03449, USA.

OLDKNOW Antony, b. 15 Aug 1939, Peterborough, Cambridgeshire, England. Poet; Literary Translator; Professor. Education: BA, Leeds, 1961; PhD, University of North Dakota, 1983. Appointments: Editor, Publisher, Scopcraeft press, 1966-; Editor, The Mainstreeter, 1971-78; Poet in the Schools, North Dakota, 1971-72; Travelling Writer, The Great Plains Book Bus, 1979-81; Writer-in-Residence, Wisconsin Arts Board, 1980-83; Poetry Staff, Cottonwood, 1984-87; Associate Professor, Eastern New Mexico University, 1987-; Chair, ENMU Dept of Languages and Literature,

1991-; Professor (promoted from Associate), 1994. Publications: Lost Allegory; Tomcats and Tigertails; The Rod of the Lord; Consolation for Beggars; Anthem for Rusty Saw and Blue Sky; Clara d'Ellébeuse (translation from Francis Jammes), 1992; The Village (translation from Jammes), 1993; Wanderers (poems), 1995. Contributions to: Numerous journals. Honours: University of North Dakota Poetry Prize; North Dakota State Arts Board Literary Grant; Wisconsin State Arts Board Literary Grant. Address: Department of Languages & Literature, Eastern New Mexico University, Portales, NM 88130, USA.

OLDS Sharon, b. 19 Nov 1942, San Francisco, California, USA. Poet; Associate Professor. Education: BA, Stanford University, 1964; PhD, Columbia University, 1972. Appointments: Lecturer-in-Residence on Poetry, Theodor Herzl Institute, New York, 1976-80; Adjunct Professor, 1983-90, Director, 1988-91, Associate Professor, 1990-, Graduate Program in Creative Writing, New York University; Fanny Hurst Chair in Literature, Brandeis University, 1986-87. Publications: Satan Says, 1980; The Dead and the Living, 1984; The Gold Cell, 1987; The Father, 1992; The Wellspring, 1996. Honours: Creative Arts Public Service Award, 1978; Madeline Sadin Award, 1978; Guggenheim Fellowship, 1981-82; National Endowment for the Arts Fellowship, 1982-83; Lamont Prize, 1984; National Book Critics' Circle Award, 1985; Lila Wallace-Reader's Digest Fellowship, 1993-96. Address: c/o Department of English, New York University, 19 University Place (Room 200) New York, NY 10003, USA.

OLEMA. See: **ONU Johnson Olema.**

OLIVEIRA Joanyr de (Joanir Ferrira de Oliveira), b. 6 Dec 1933, Aimorés, Brazil. Writer; Government Adviser; Journalist; Lawyer. m. 21 Mar 1959, 4 sons. Appointments: Parliament Adviser, now retired, House of Representatives, Brazil; Journalist, 1968-; Lawyer, 1987-; Publisher. Publications: Minha Lira, 1957; Poetas de Brasilia, 1962; Antologia dos Posas de Brasilia, 1971; Cantares, 1977; Antologia da Nova Poesia Evangélica, 1978; O Grito Submerso, 1980; Horas Vagas, short stories, anthology, 1981; Brasilia na Poesia Brasileria, 1982; Casulos do Siléncio, 1988; Soberanas Mitologias e A Cidade do Medo, 1991; Luta A(r)mada, 1992; Numerous unpublished works. Contributions to: SL do Minas Gerais; Caderno Cultural do CB; Dimensao; Literatura; A Seara; International Poetry 12. Honours: Grande Poesia de Brasilia, 1961; Prêmio Secretaria da Educacao e Cultura, Brazil, 1975; I Concurso de Poesia de Florianopolis, São Paolo, Brazil, 1977; Cem Poemas Brasileiros, São Paulo, Brazil, 1979; Veia Poética, São Paulo, 1980; Prêmio Nacional de Poesia Pablo Neruda, Academia Brasiliense de Letras/Embaixada do Chile, Brazil, 1991; Prêmio Nacional de Poesia, Di Instituto de Poesia Internacional, Porto Alegre, 1992; 1st Prize for Poetry, Brazilian Voice Newspaper, Newark, New Jersey, USA, 1992; Prêmio Nacional de Poesia Moacyr Felix, Sindicato des Escritores do Rio de Janeiro, 1992. Address: SQS 105, Block H, Ap 205-70344-080, Brasilia, Brazil.

OLIVER Colin, b. 13 Mar 1946, Tasburgh, Norfolk, England. Primary School Headteacher. m. Carole Oliver, 5 Sept 1968, 1 son, 1 daughter. Education: Education Diploma, University of London Goldsmiths' College. Appointment: Headteacher, Wickambrook Primary School, Suffolk, 1985-. Publications: In the Open, 1974; Seeing, 1980. Contributions to: Guardian; Iron; Lines Review; Middle Way; Oasis; Resurgence; PN Review; Haiku Hundred anthology; Salmon; Smiths Knoll; Staple; Frogmore Papers; Workshop New Poetry; Mountain Path (India). Memberships: Poetry Society, UK; British Haiku Society. Address: 45 Westfield, Clare, Sudbury, Suffolk, England.

OLIVER Mary, b. 10 Sept 1935, Cleveland, Ohio, USA. Poet; Educator. Education: Ohio State University; Vassar College. Appointments: Mather Visiting Professor, Case Western Reserve University, 1980, 1982; Poet-in-Residence, Bucknell University, 1986; Elliston Visiting Professor, University of Cincinnati, 1986; William Blackburn Visiting Professor of Creative Writing, Duke University, 1995; Faculty Bennington College, Bennington, Vermont. Publications: No Voyage, and Other Poems, 1963, augmented edition, 1965; The River Styx, Ohio, and Other Poems, 1972; The Night Traveler, 1978; Twelve Moons, 1978; Sleeping in the Forest, 1979; American Primitive, 1983; Dream Work, 1986; Provincetown, 1987; House of Light, 1990; New and Selected Poems, 1992; A Poetry Handbook, 1994; White Pine: Poems and Prose Poems, 1994; Blue Pastures, 1995. Contributions to: Periodicals in the US and England. Honours: Poetry Society of America 1st Prize, 1962; Devil's Advocate Award, 1968; Shelley Memorial Award, 1972; National Endowment for the Arts

Fellowship, 1972-73; Alice Fay di Castagnola Award, 1973; Guggenheim Fellowship, 1980-81; American Academy and Institute of Arts and Letters Award, 1983; Pulitzer Prize in Poetry, 1984; Christopher Award, 1991; L L Winship Award, 1991; National Book Award for Poetry, 1993. Memberships: PEN; Poetry Society of America. Address: c/o Molly Malone Cook Literary Agency, Box 338, Provincetown, MA 02657, USA.

OLSEN David Leslie, b. 13 Dec 1943, Berkeley, California, USA. Writer; Consultant. m. Barbara Gail Schonborn, 17 Mar 1985, 1 son, 1 daughter. Education: BA, University of California at Berkeley, 1965; MBA, Golden Gate University, 1983; MA, San Francisco State University, 1986. Appointments: Writer, Editor, LSI Logic Co, 1987-89; Consultant, Schonborn Associates, 1989-. Contributions to: Bogg: An Anglo American Journal; Amella; Western Journal of Medicine; Black Bear; Tomcat; Poetry San Francisco; Homeless Not Helpless; Wrestling with the Angel; Alms House Sampler; Vol No; Pegasus Review; Sunrust; Feelings; Cow in the Road; Poetry Connoisseur; Eve's Legacy. Honours: Daly City Arts Commisssion Trophy; Poetry First Prizes: Poetry Olympiad. Memberships: Dramatists Guild; American Academy of Poets; San Francisco Poetry Center. Address: 14 Vine Brook Rd, Westford, MA 01886, USA.

OLSON Toby, (Merle Theodore Olson), b. 17 Aug 1937, Berwyn, Illinois, USA. Poet; Author. m. (1) Ann Yeomans, 1963, div 1965, (2) Miriam Meltzer, 1966. Education: BA, Occidental College, Los Angeles, 1964; MA, Long Island University, New York, 1966. Appointments: Associate Director, Aspen Writers Workshop, Colorado, 1964-67; Assistant Professor, Long Island University, 1966-74; Faculty, New School for Social Research, New York City, 1967-75; Poet-in-Residence, State University of New York, Cortland, 1972, Friends Seminary, New York, 1974-75; Professor of English, Temple University, Philadelphia, 1984. Publications: Poetry includes: The Wrestler and Other Poems, 1974; City, 1974; A Kind of Psychology, 1974; Changing Appearances: Poems 1965-1970, 1975; A Moral Proposition, 1975; Priorities, 1975; Seeds, 1975; Standard-4, 1975; Home, 1976; Three and One, 1976; Doctor Miriam: Five Poems by Her Admiring Husband, 1977; Aesthetics, 1978; The Florence Rooms, 1978; Birdsongs: Eleven New Poems, 1980; Two Standards, 1982; Still/Quiet, 1982; Sitting in Gusevik, 1983; We Are the Fire: A Selection of Poems, 1984; Unfinished Building, 1993; Fiction: The Life of Jesus, 1976; Seaview, 1982; The Woman who Escaped from Shame, 1986; Utah, 1987; Dorit in Lesbos, 1990; At Sea, 1993; Editor: Margins 1976, 1976; Writing Talks: Views on Teaching Writing from Across the Professions (with Muffy E A Siegel), 1983. Honours: Creative Artists Public Service Grant, 1975; PEN Faulkner Award for Fiction, 1983; Pennsylvania Council on the Arts Fellowship, 1983; Guggenheim Fellowship, 1985; Yaddo Colony Fellowship, 1985; National Endowment for the Arts Fellowship, 1985; Rockefeller Foundation Fellowship, 1987. Address: 329 South Juniper Street, Philadelphia, PA 19107, USA.

ONDAATJE (Philip) Michael, b. 12 Sept 1943, Colombo, Ceylon. Poet; Novelist; Dramatist; Teacher; Film Director. Education: St Thomas' College, Columbo; Dulwich College, London; Bishop's University, Lennonxville, Quebec, 1962-64; BA, University of Toronto, 1965; MA, Queen's University, Kingston, Ontario, 1967. Appointments: Teacher, University of Western Ontario 1967-71, Glendon College, York University, Toronto 1971-; Visiting Professor, University of Hawaii 1979, Brown University, Providence, Rhode Island 1990; Film Director. Publications: Poetry: The Dainty Monsters, 1967; The Man with Seven Toes, 1969; The Collected Works of Billy The Kid, 1970; Left Handed Poems, 1970; Rat Jelly, 1973; Elimination Dance, 1978, revised edition, 1980; There's A Trick With A Knife I'm Learning To Do: Poems 1963-1978, 1979; Claude Glass, 1979; Tin Roof, 1982; Secular Love, 1984; All Along the Mazinaw: Two Poems, 1986; Cinnamon Peeler: Selected Poems, 1989. Honours: Ralph Gustafson Award, 1965; Epstein Award, 1966; E J Pratt Medal, 1966; Canadian Governor-General's Awards for Literature, 1971, 1980, 1992; W H Smith/Books in Canada First Novel Award, 1977; Canada-Australia Prize, 1980; City of Toronto Arts Award, 1987; Trillium Book Awards, 1987, 1992; Ritz-Hemingway Prize Nomination, 1987; Booker McConnell Prize, British Book Council, 1992; Canadian Authors Association Author of the Year Award, 1993; Commonwealth Prize (regional), 1993 international nomination; Chianti Ruffino-Antonio Fattore International Literary Prize, 1994; Nelly Sachs Award, 1995; Premio Grinzane Cavour, 1996. Address: c/o Ellen Levine Literary Agency, 15 East 26th Street, Suite 1801, New York, NY 10010, USA.

ONU Johnson Olema, (Olema), b. 30 Jan 1957, Nigeria. Airman. m. Owakoyi Onu, 26 Aug 1978, 2 sons, 4 daughters. Education: Diploma, Personnel Management, Kaduna Polytechnic, Nigeria, 1984; Advanced Diploma, Public Administration, University of Jos, Nigeria, 1994. Appointment: Assistant Chief Clerk, Directorate of Armament, Nigerian Air Force Headquarters, Lagos, Nigeria. Publications: If I Die in the Sturggle, 1992; Travails of Freedom, 1996. Contributions to: Newswatch Magazine; Voice Newspaper; Challenge Magazine. Memberships: Association of Nigerian Authors; Poetry League, Benue State, Nigeria. Address: Headquarters, Nigerian Air Force, Ministry of Defense, Lagos, Nigeria.

ONWY. See: **EVANS Donald.**

ORBAN Otto, b. 20 May 1936, Budapest, Hungary. Poet; Essayist; Translator. m. 23 May 1962, 2 sons. Education: University studies, (unfinished). Appointments: Fulbright Poet in US at Hamline University, Minneapolis, St Paul and University of Minnesota, Minneapolis, 1987. Publications: Aranygyapju, selected verse translations, 1972; Ablak a Foldre, travelogue and essay on India, 1973; Szegenynek lenni, selected poems, 1974; Honnan jon a kolto, selected essays, 1980; Osszegyujott versek, collected poems, 1986; Egyik oldalarol a masikra fordulel, poems, 1992. Contributions to: Senior Editor, Kortars, literary magazine of the Hungarian Writers' Union, 1981-. Honours: Jozsef Attila Prize, 1973, 1985; Robert Graves Prize, 1974; Dery Prize, 1986; Radnoti Prize, 1987; Weores Sandor Prize, 1990; Kossuth Prize, the highest award in Hungary for art and literature, 1992. Memberships: Hungarian Writers' Union; Union of Hungarian Journalists; Vice President, 1989-, Hungarian PEN Club. Address: Becsi ut 88-90, H-1034 Budapest, Hungary.

ORME David John, b. 1 Mar 1948, Stoke-on-Trent, Staffordshire, England. Freelance Writer; Editor; Educational Consultant. m. Helen Bird, 15 Aug 1971, 2 sons. Education: Certificate of Education, Christ Church College, Canterbury; BA, Open University. Appointment: Editor of the educational journal of The Poetry Society, Schools' Poetry Review. Publications: A Fear of Bells, 1982; The Gravedigger's Sandwich, 1992; Heroes and Villains, for children, 1993; Anthologies include: Editor, The Windmill Book of Poetry, 1987; Poetry Show, 1988; Toughie Toffee, 1989; Poetry Street, 1991. Memberships: Director, Schools' Poetry Association, 1982-91; Editor, Schools' Poetry Review; Chairman, Winchester Literature Network. Address: 27 Pennington Close, Colden Common, Near Winchester, Hampshire SO21 1UR, England.

ORME-COLLINS Donna Youngoon, (Morgan Storm), b. 10 Feb 1970, Wimbledon, England. Writer. m. Jonathan R Collins, 23 Dec 1994, 1 daughter. Education: Cleeve House School; Sun Wha Arts School, Korea; High School Diploma, Emerson Preparatory School, Washington DC; Mountvernon College, Washington DC. Appointments: Translator at International Conference; Public Relations; Receptionist, GWBB Studios. Contributions to: South Ash Press, Phoenix, Arizona; Psychopoetica, Hull University, England; Poetry Motel Suburban Wilderpress, Minnesota; Spring Flowers, Arrival Press Poets, England; The Red Candle Press, England; Hyacinth House Publications, USA. Memberships: Arizona Poetry Society. Address: 4925 E Desert Cove, Apt #208, Scottsdale, AZ 85254-7400, USA.

ORMSBY Eric, b. 16 Oct 1941, Atlanta, Georgia, USA. Professor; Writer. m. Irena Murray, 30 Sept 1995, 2 sons. Education: BA, 1971; MA, 1973; MLS, 1978; PhD, 1981. Appointments: Curator, Near East Collections, Princeton University, 1977-83; Director of Libraries, Catholic University, 1983-86; Director of Libraries, 1986-96, Professor, 1996-, McGill University. Publications: Bavarian Shrine, 1990; Coastlines, 1992; For a Modest God: New and Selected Poems, 1997. Contributions include: New Republic; New Yorker; Grand Street; Poetry Wales; Poetry Canada; Paris Review; Southern Review; Gettysburg Review; Chelsea. Honours: Special Commendation, Cheltenham Poetry Competition, 1987; A M Klein Prize for Poetry, 1991; Ingram Merrill Foundation Award, 1992. Address: 2600 Pierre Dupuy, Apt 207, Montreal H3C 3R6, Canada.

ORMSBY Frank, b. 30 Oct 1947, Enniskillen, County Fermanagh, Northern Ireland. Schoolmaster. Education: BA, 1970; MA, 1971. Appointment: Editor, The Honest Ulsterman, 1969-89. Publications: A Store of Candles; A Northern Spring; Poets from the North of Ireland; Northern Windows; The Long Embrace; Thine in Storm and Calm; The Collected Poems of John Hewitt; A Rage for

Order; The Ghost Train. Address: 36 Strathmore Park North, Belfast BT15 5HR, Northern Ireland.

ORR Gregory (Simpson), b. 3 Feb 1947, Albany, New York, USA. Professor of English; Poet; Writer. m. Trisha Winer, 1973, 2 daughters. Education: BA, Antioch College, 1969; MFA, Columbia University, 1972. Appointments: Assistant Professor, 1975-80, Associate Professor, 1980-88, Professor of English, 1988-, University of Virginia; Poetry Consultant, Virginia Quarterly Review, 1976-; Visiting Writer, University of Hawaii, Manoa, 1982. Publications: Poetry: Burning the Empty Nests, 1973; Gathering the Bones Together, 1975; Salt Wings, 1980; The Red House, 1980; We Must Make a Kingdom of It, 1986; New and Selected Poems, 1988; City of Salt, 1995; Non-fiction: Stanley Kunitz: An Introduction to the Poetry, 1985; Richer Entanglements: Essays and Notes on Poetry and Poems, 1993. Honours: Academy of American Poets Prize, 1970; YM-YWHA Discovery Award, 1970; Bread Loaf Writers Conference Transatlantic Review Award, 1976; Guggenheim Fellowship, 1977; National Endowment for the Arts Fellowships, 1978, 1989; Fulbright Grant, 1983. Address: c/o Department of English, University of Virginia, Charlottesville, VA 22903, USA.

ORSZAG-LAND Thomas, b. 12 Jan 1938, Budapest, Hungary. Writer. 2 sons. Publications: Free Women; Berlin Proposal; Bluebeards Castle. Contributions to: Spectator; New York Times; Chapman; Cyphers; New Hope International; Outposts Poetry Quarterly; Envoi; Pen International; Contemporary Review; Acumen; Foolscap. Memberships: International PEN; Society of Authors. Address: PO Box 1213, London N6 5HZ, England.

ORTIZ Simon J(oseph), b. 27 May 1941, Albuquerque, New Mexico, USA. Poet; Writer. m. Marlene Foster, Dec 1981, div Sept 1984, 3 children. Education: Fort Lewis College, 1961-62; University of New Mexico, 1966-68; University of Iowa, 1968-69. Appointments: Instructor, San Diego State University 1974, Institute of American Arts, Santa Fe, New Mexico 1974, Navajo Community College, Tsaile, Arizona 1975-77, College of Marin, Kentfield, California 1976-79, University of New Mexico, Albuquerque 1979-81, Sinte Gleska College, Mission, South Dakota 1985-86, Lewis and Clark College, Portland, Oregon 1990; Consulting Editor, Navajo Community College Press, Tsaile 1982-83, Pueblo of Acoma Press, Acoma, New Mexico 1982-84; Arts Coordinator, Metropolitan Arts Commission, Portland, Oregon, 1990. Publications include: Naked in the Wind, poetry, 1971; Going for the Rain, poetry, 1976; A Good Journey, poetry, 1977; Howbah Indians, short stories, 1978; Song, Poetry, Language, essays, 1978; Fight Back: For The Sake of The People, For the Sake of The Land, poetry and prose, 1980; From Sand Creek: Rising in This Heart Which is Our America, poetry, 1981; After and Before the Lightning, poems, 1994. Editor: Califa: The California Poetry (co-editor), 1978; A Ceremony of Brotherhood (co-editor), 1980; Earth Power Coming, anthology of Native American short fiction, 1983. Contributions to: Various anthologies and textbooks. Honours: National Endowment for the Arts Discovery Award, 1969, and Fellowship, 1981; Honoured Poet, White House Salute to Poetry and American Poets, 1980; New Mexico Humanities Council Humanitarian Award for Literary Achievement. Address: 1270 Calle de Comarcio, No 5, Santa Fe, NM 87501, USA.

ORTT-SAEED Jocelyn Anne, b. 18 Jan 1935, Brisbane, Queensland, Australia. Writer; Educator. m. Mohammed Saeed, 19 Sept 1959, 3 sons, 3 daughters. Education: BA, German and Philosophy, University of Queensland; Teaching Diploma in Language and Literature, Bavarian Ministry of Education, 1961. Appointments: The Friday Times, Lahore; Oxford University Press. Publications: Rainbow of Promise, 1964; Where No Road Goes, 1968; Between Forever and Never, 1971; Selected Poems, with cassette, 1986, 4th edition, 1992; Burning Bush, 1994. Contributions to: Newspapers and poetry magazines in Australia: Bulletin; Poetry Australia; ABC Radio; TV; Pakistani newspapers: Dawn; Frontier Post; The News; Nation; Muslim; Poetry journals and university publications; Regular presentations and readings at home and abroad and readings at PEN; Translations into Urdu, German and Thai. Honours: Cambridge Writers' Workshop, UK, 1990. Memberships: Fellowship, Australian Writers; The Poetry Society; Lahore Arts Forum; Quaid-i-Azam Poets' Reading Group, Lahore. Address: Stillpoint, 72-H Tagore Road, Gulberg III, Lahore, Pakistan.

OSAKI Mark (Stephen), (Matt Ronin), b. 7 Oct 1952, Sacramento, California, USA Writer; Editor. Education: AB,

Journalism, 1972; BA, English, 1976; MFS, 1983; PhD, International Relations, 1985. Appointments: Director of Communications, McGeorge School of Law; Editor-in-Chief, Pacific Citizen, Japanese American Citizens League; Principal Editor, University of California, Berkeley; Analyst, US Foreign Service. Publications: Anthologies: Breaking The Silence; An Anthology of Asian American Poets, 1983; Carrying The Darkness: The Poetry of The Vietnam War, 1985, 1989; Heart Stories, 1992. Contributions to: Georgia Review; South Carolina Review; Fiction Magazine; Cotton Boll/Atlanta Review; Hawaii Review; Crosscurrents; Poetry and The Vietnam Experience; Xanadu; Yellow Silk; Berkeley Poetry Review; Three Rivers Poetry Journal; Boston Monthly; MacGuffin; Strath Poetry Journal, Scotland; LAVA, India; Ergo; Wisconsin Review; New York Quarterly. Honours: Eisner Prize, highest award in the creative arts, University of California at Berkeley; Poets Prize, Academy of American Poets, 1976; National Endowment for The Arts Fellowship, 1981; 1st Prize for Poetry, San Francisco Arts Council, 1987; 1st Prize for Poetry, Seattle Arts Commission, 1989. Memberships: Poetry Society of America; PEN America; Instructor, Poetry in The Schools Programme, National Endowment for The Humanities. Address: 3217 Franklin Boulevard, Sacramento, CA 95818, USA.

OSBORN Howard Andrew Morris, b. 28 Nov 1960, Woking, Surrey, England. Writer. m. Christine Knowles, 22 June 1985. Education: BA, Honours, English Language and Literature, University of Manchester, 1983. Contributions to: Odyssey; Illuminations; Outposts; The Third Half. Address: 2 Asten Buildings, Cowpe, Waterfoot, Rossendale, Lancashire BB4 7DR, England.

OSBORNE Charles Thomas, b. 24 Nov 1927, Brisbane, Queensland, Australia. Author; Critic. Education: Brisbane State High School, 1942-45. Appointments: Assistant Editor, London Magazine, 1958-66; Assistant Literary Director, 1966-71, Director, 1971-86, Arts Council of Great Britain; Chief Theatre Critic, Daily Telegraph, 1986-91; Opera Critic, Jewish Chronicle, 1985-. Publications: The Gentle Planet, 1957; Swansong, 1968; Letter to W H Auden and Other Poems, 1984. Contributions to: Times Literary Supplement; London Magazine; Observer; Sunday Times; Encounter; Anthologies include: Oxford Book of Australian Verse; Australian Writing Today; Australian Poetry; The Queensland Centenary Anthology. Address: c/o Aitken & Stone Ltd, 29 Fernshaw Road, London SW10 0TG, England.

OSERS Ewald, b. 13 May 1917, Prague, Czechoslovakia. Translator. m. Mary Harman, 3 June 1942, 1 son, 1 daughter. Education: Prague University; BA, Honours, University of London; DPhil hc, Olomonuc University, Czechoslovakia; Fellow, Institute of Translating and Interpreting. Appointments: Various posts in BBC; Chairman, Translators Association, 5 years; Vice Chairman, Institute of Linguists; Vice President, International Federation of Translators; Member, International Book Committee. Publications: Wish You Were Here, 1976; Anamneza, Czech translations of his poems, 1986; 31 volumes of poetry translated from Czech, German, Bulgarian and Macedonian. Contributions to: Outposts; Workshop; Christian Science Monitor; Arts Council Anthology; Orbis; Translated poetry: London Magazine; Times Literary Supplement; Observer; Tribune; Jewish Chronicle; Stand; Contemporary Poetry in Translation; Translation, New York, USA; Chicago Review; Dimension; Contemporary Literature in Translation; Partisan Review. Honours: Cyril and Methodius Order, 1st Class, Bulgaria, 1987; European Poetry Translation Prize, 1987; Vitezslaw Nezval Medal, Czechoslovakia, 1987; Golden Pen, Macedonia, 1988; Officer's Cross of Merit, Germany, 1991. Memberships: Fellow, Royal Society of Literature; Society of Authors; Poetry Society; Fellow, English Centre of International PEN. Address: 33 Reades Lane, Sonning Common, Reading, Berkshire RG4 9LL, England.

OSHEROW Jacqueline, b. 15 Aug 1956, Philadelphia, Pennsylvania, USA. Associate Professor of English and Writing, University of Utah. m. Saul Korewa, 16 June 1985, 2 daughters. Education: AB, magna cum laude, History and Literature, Harvard-Radcliffe, 1978; Satisfied Examiners, Trinity College, Cambridge, 1979; PhD, English Literature, Princeton, 1990. Publications: Looking for Angels in New York, 1988; Conversations with Survivors, 1994; With a Moon in Transit, 1996. Contributions to: New Yorker; Times Literary Supplement; Paris Review; Triquarterly; Partisan Review; Shenandoah; Georgia Review; Denver Quarterly; New Republic; Western Humanities Review. Honours: University Chancellor's Medal for English Poem, Cambridge University, 1979; Witter Bynner Prize, American Academy and Institute of Arts and Letters, 1990; John Masefield Memorial Award, 1993; Lucille Medwick Memorial Award, 1995. Membership: Poetry Society of America; PEN; Academy of American Poets. Address: Department of English, 3500 LNCO, University of Utah, Salt Lake City, UT 84112, USA.

OSTERBERG Myra Janet, (Myrna Rose), b. 20 Oct 1931, Salem, South Dakota, USA. Business. m. (1) Dale D Spicer, 26 Mar 1951, 2 daughters, (2) Leland B Osterberg, 7 June 1969, 1 son, 1 daughter. Education: Graduate, Salem St Mary's High School, 1949. Appointments: Legal Secretary, 1955; Accounts Receivable/Billing Department, McCook Electric, 1959; Deputy Clerk of Courts, McCook County, 1975-95; Certified Abstractor, 1980; Proofreader, Tesseract Publications, 1994-; Owner/Manager, The Raven Coffee House, Salem, 1996-. Publications: From My Heart, 1968; Copy Editor: A Sixty-Year Comprehensive Index of Pasque Petals, 1926-1986, 1986. Contributions to: The Sioux Falls Argus Leader; The Salem Special; Pasque Petals; Voices of South Dakota Anthology I, II and III. Memberships: Bardic Round Table, Sioux Falls, 1971; South Dakota State Poetry Society Inc, 1971; Chairman, Annual Poetry Contest, 1992-. Address: P O Box 613, Salem, South Dakota 57058-0613, USA.

OSTRIKER Alicia Suskin, b. 11 Nov 1937, New York, New York, USA. Professor of English. m. 2 Dec 1958, 1 son, 2 daughters. Education: BA, Brandeis University, 1959; MA, 1960, PhD, 1964, University of Wisconsin. Appointment: Assistant to Full Professor, English Department, Rutgers University, 1965-. Publications: Songs, 1969; Once More Out of Darkness and Other Poems, 1974, 76; A Dream of Springtime: Poems, 1970-77, 1978; The Mother-Child Papers, 1980, 86; A Woman Under the Surface, 1983; The Imaginary Lover, 1986; Green Age, 1989; The Nakedness of the Fathers, 1994; The Crack in Everything, 1995; Critical Books: Vision and Verse In William Blake, 1965; Writing Like a Woman, 1982; Stealing the Language, 1986; Feminist Revision and the Bible, 1993. Contributions to: New Yorker; The Nation; American Poetry Review; Iowa Review; Hudson Review; Ontario Review; Poetry; Paris Review; Antaeus; and others. Honours: National Endowment for the Arts Fellowship, 1977; Guggenheim Foundation Fellowship, 1984-85; William Carlos Williams Prize, Poetry Society of America, 1986; Strousse Poetry Prize, Prairie Schooner, 1987; Anna Rosenberg Poetry Award, 1994. Memberships: Poetry Society of America, Board of Governors, 1988-91; PEN; Modern Language Association; Poetry Society of America, 1990-94. Address: 33 Philip Drive, Princeton, NJ 08540, USA.

OURIN Viktor A, b. 3 June 1924. Poet; Publisher; Editor; Sculptor. 1 son. Education: Literary Institute of Maxim Gorky, Moscow, 1945-49; MLit. Appointments: President, The Friends of the Globe Poetry Library, 1971-96; Founder of the Olympoetry Movement Fund; Editor-in-Chief, International Magazine of Poetry; Bridge of Friends, Founder in 1975, Moscow-New York; First Director, Anthology of World Poetry, Korea, 1989; Chairman of Committee, Olympoetry Movement in New York, 1992. Publications: The School Lyrics, 1940; The Spring, 1946; The Road, 1949; Toward, 1952; The Rivers Dream, 1955; South-East, 1956; 179 Days, 1958; Kolyma, Pole of Cold, 1959; Septacolor, 1962; The Iron Stork, 1963; Uzbekistan, 1965; The Big Dipper, 1968; The Mamaev Barrow, 1969; Passport, 1969; The Golden Wedding, 1969; Selected Lyric, 1970; A Ballad of Love, 1970; Outlook, 1971; Carnations Selected Lyric, 1972; The Book of Life, 1974; The Poet's Life in three books, 1979, 1980, 1981; Portraits, 1982; Autokinezis, 1983; The Travelling Tent, 1984; The Bars, 1985; The Squar Babi Yar in New York, 1986; My Beloved Lady, 1986; Selected Lyrics for 50 years 1937-87, collected in 7 volumes, 1988-94; Works of Viktor Ourin in 7 volumes, 1988-94; Author of Complete Olympoetry Anthologies: The First 100, 1980, 1984, 1988, 1992, 1994, 1995, 1996. Contributions to: Novi Mir; Literaturnaia Gazeta; Ogonek; Pravda; Izwestia; Unost; International Anthologies and magazines in various countries. Honours: 1st Prize for International Song, Berlin International Festival, 1968; The Poet Hand on Planet's Pulse Prize, Moscow, 1970; ABI, Medal of Honour, USA, 1984; UPLI Golden Laurel Wreath Laureate Man of Letters, 1986; Korea Golden Crown World Poetry Research Institute; Nominated for Nobel Prize World Poetry, 1988; Winner, 4th World Congress of Cultures and Poetry; 1st Prize, Epos-XX; Best Book by International M Madhusudan Academy, Calcutta, India, 1993; Awarded Alexander of Macedon Medal, Association of Poets of Greece, 1994. Memberships: The New York Forum of Poets; World Congress of Poets; World Academy of Arts and Culture; American Club of Writers. Address: 3395 Neptune Avenue, No 124, Brooklyn, NY 11224, USA.

OVERSEN Ellis, b. 18 July 1923, New Effington, South Dakota, USA. Writer; Artist. m. Thor L Smith, 28 Aug 1949, 2 sons. Education: MA cum laude English, University of Wisconsin, 1948; California Teacher's Credential, 1963; Art minor, San Jose State University. Appointments: Teacher of English, University of Wisconsin, 1946-48; Teacher of English, San Jose State University, 1963-64. Publications: Gloried Grass, 1970; Haloed Paths, 1973; To Those Who Love, 1974; The Last Hour, 1975; Lives Touch, 1976; A Time for Singing (haiku), 1977; A Book of Praises, 1977; Beloved, 1980, 90; Another Man's Mocassins, 1981; The Green Madonna, 1984; The Flowers of God, 1985, 90; The Keeper of the Word, 1985; The Wing Brush, 1986; The Year Of the Snake, 1989; Do Not Go Away, 1990; The Year of the Horse, 1991; Memories Of South Dakota, poetry, 1993. Contributions to: Palo Alto Times; Los Altos Town Crier; Chatelaine; San Diego News; Wee Wisdom; South Dakota Magazine; Plowman; Poetry Quarterly of San Francisco; Wordcraft. Honours: Knighted, Knights of Malta for poetry, art work; Honorary Doctorate, Literature World Academy, Arts and Culture, 1986; Poet of Year, 1990; Silver, Golden Poets Awards, World Of Poetry, 1988, 1989, 1990; American Poetry Association. Memberships: National Writers Club; California Writers Club; Penwoman; Poetry Society of America; California State Poetry Society; Peninisula Poets; World Poetry Society, Madras. Address: Box 482, Los Altos, CA 920023, USA.

OVERY Clara May. See: **BASS Clara May Overy.**

OWEN Eileen, b. 27 Feb 1949, Concord, New Hampshire, USA. Editor; Writer. m. John D Owen, 19 June 1971. Education: BA, University of New Hampshire, 1971; BA, English, 1979; MA, 1981. Publication: Facing The Weather Side. Contributions to: Poetry Northwest; Dark Horse; Tar River Review of Poetry; Passage North; Sojourner; Welter; Seattle Review; Mississippi Mud; Hollow Springs Review; Signpost; Back Door Travel; Arts and Artists. Honours: Artist in Residence; Poems selected, King County Arts Commission; Honourable Mention, Washington Poets Association. Address: 2709 128th Street South East, Everett, WA 98208, USA.

OWEN Jan Jarrold, b. 18 Aug 1940, Adelaide, South Australia. Writer. 2 sons, 1 daughter. Education: BA, University of Adelaide, 1963; ALAA, 1970; MA, University of Adelaide, 1974. Appointments: Librarian, various University andllege Libraries, 1961-84; Writer-in-Residence, Venice Studio of the Literature Board of the Australian Council, 1989; Tasmanian State Institute of Technology, 1990; Brisbane Grammar School, 1993; Tasmanian Writers Union, 1993; B.R. Whiting Library, Rome, 1994. Publications: Boy with a Telescope, 1986; Fingerprints on Light, 1990; Blackberry Season, 1993; Night Rainbows, 1994. Contributions to: Meanjin; Island Magazine; Quadrant; Southerly; Age; Sydney Morning Herald; Bulletin; Voices; Imago; Poetry Wales; New Welsh Review; Verse; Antipodes. Honours: Ian Mudie Prize, 1982; Jessie Litchfield Prize, 1984; Grenfell Henry Lawson Prize, 1985; Harri Jones Memorial Prize, 1986; Anne Elder Award, 1987; Mary Gilmore Prize, 1987; Wesley Michel Wright Poetry Prize, 1992. Memberships: South Australian Writers Centre; National Book Council. Address: 14 Fern Road, Crafers, South Australia 5152, Australia.

OWEN Maureen, b. 6 July 1943, Graceville, Minnesota, USA. Poet. 3 sons. Education: Seattle University, 1961-62; San Francisco State College, 1962-64. Appointments: St Mark's Poetry Project: Administrative Assistant, 1973-76; Co-Director, 1976-78; Coordinator, 1978-80; Catalogue Manager, Inland Book Company, small and independent press distribution, 1982-. Publications: Poetry: Country Rush, 1973; No Travels Journal, 1975; A Brass Choir Approaches the Burial Ground/Big Deal, 1977; Hearts in Space, 1980; Amelia Earhart, 1984; Zombie Notes, 1986; Imaginary Income, 1992; Untapped Maps, 1993. Contributions to: None of The Above, anthology, 1976; Up Late: American Poetry Since 1970; 4 Walls 8 Windows, 1987; Deep Down, anthology, 1988; Talking to the Sun, anthology, 1985; Contemporary American Literature, anthology, Before Columbus, 1978; The Best American Poetry 1994; Educating The Imagination, Vol 2, 1994; Postmodern American Poetry: A Norton Anthology, 1994. Honours: Fellowship in Poetry, National Endowment For The Arts, 1979-80; Amelia Earhart Recipient, Before Columbus American Book Awards, 1985; Recipient, Fund For Poetry Award, 1989, 1990, 1995; Memberships: Vice-Chairperson, Board, Coordinating Council of Literary Magazines; Served on Advisory Board, St Mark's Poetry Project; Before Columbus Foundation. Address: 109 Dunk Rock Road, Guildford, CT 06437, USA.

OWEN Sue Ann, b. 5 Sept 1942, Clarinda, Iowa, USA. Poet. m. 29 Aug 1964. Education: BA, University of Wisconsin, 1964; MFA, Goddard College, 1978. Appointments: Artist in the Schools, 1980-92; Poetry, Instructor, Louisiana State University, 1992-. Publications: Nursery Rhymes for the Dead, 1980; The Book of Winter, 1988. Contributions to: California Quarterly; Epoch; Green House; Greenfield Review; Harvard Review; Harvard Magazine; Iowa Review; Kayak; Massachusetts Review; Nation; New Orleans Review; North American Review; Ploughshares; Poetry; Poetry Northwest; Poetry Now; Southern Review; Virginia Quarterly Review; Bonniers Litterara Magasin-BLM (Sweden); Horisont (Finland); Anthology of Magazine Verse and the Best of Intro (national competitions). Honours: Richard Hugo Fellowship, Port Townsend Writers Conference, 1986; Ohio State University Press, Journal Award in Poetry, 1988. Memberships: Poetry Society of America; Associated Writing Programmes. Address: 2015 General Cleburne Avenue, Baton Rouge, LA 70810, USA.

OWENS Rochelle, b. 2 Apr 1936, Brooklyn, New York, USA. Poet; Dramatist; Critic; Professor; Translator. m. (1) David Owens, 30 Mar 1956, diss 1959, (2) George Economou, 17 June 1962. Education: Theatre Arts, Herbert Berghof Studio, New York City; New School for Social Research, New York City; University of Montreal, Alliance Francaise, Paris, New York City. Appointments: Visiting Lecturer, University of California at San Diego, 1982; Writer-in-Residence, Brown University, Providence, Rhode Island, 1989; Currently, Adjunct Professor in Creative Writing, University of Oklahoma, Norman. Publications: Poetry: Not Be Essence That Cannot Be, 1961; Four Young Lady Poets (with others), 1962; Salt and Core, 1968; I Am the Babe of Joseph Stalin's Daughter: Poems 1961-1971, 1972; Poems from Joe's Garage, 1973; The Joe 82 Creation Poems, 1974; The Joe Chronicles, Part 2, 1979; Shemuel, 1979; French Light, 1984; Constructs, 1985; W C Fields in French Light, 1986; How Much Paint Does the Painting Need, 1988; Black Chalk, 1992; Rubbed Stones and Other Poems, 1994; New and Selected Earlier Poems, 1961-1990, forthcoming. Contributions to: Poems in many anthologies and periodicals; Critical articles and essays in various journals. Honours: Rockefeller Grants, 1965, 1976; Obie Awards, 1965, 1967, 1982; Yale School of Drama Fellowship, 1968; American Broadcasting Corporation Fellowship, 1968; Guggenheim Fellowship, 1971; National Endowment for the Arts Award, 1976; Villager Award, 1982; Franco-Anglais Festival de Poesie, Paris, 1991; Rockefeller Foundation Resident Scholar, Bellagio, Italy, 1993. Memberships: American Society of Composers, Authors and Publishers; Authors League; Dramatists Guild; New York Theatre Strategy; Women's Theatre Council. Address: 1401 Magnolia, Norman, OK 73072, USA.

OXLEY William, b. 29 April 1939, Manchester, England. Poet; Chartered Accountant (part-time). m. Patricia Holmes, 13 April 1963, 2 daughters. Appointments: Chartered accountant; Gardener; Actor; Editor, number of magazines, newsletters, broadsheets; Formerly Assistant Editor, Acumen; Readings, lectures to universities in England and abroad; Visiting Poet and Lecturer, University of Salzburg, three times, 1980s; Readings on radio. Publications: Poetry: The Notebook of Hephaestus and other Poems, 1981; A Map of Time, 1984; The Mansands' Trilogy; Mad Tom On Tower Hill, 1988; Forest Sequence, 1991; The Patient Reconstruction Of Paradise, 1991; The Playboy, 1992; In The Drift of Words, 1992; Cardboard Troy, 1993; Editor: Completing The Picture, anthology of neglected poets, 1995; Translation: Poems of a Black Orpheus (L S Senghor), 1981; Prose includes: The Inner Tapestry, 1985; Of Poets and Poetry (letters Between a Father and Son) ed Patricia Oxley, 1988; Distinguishing Poetry, ed Glyn Pursglove, 1989. Contributions to: New York Times; Formalist (USA); Scotsman; Adam; Poetry Review; Encounter; Spectator; Observer; Others. Poetry to numerous anthologies. Address: 6 The Mount, Higher Furzeham, Brixham, South Devon TQ5 8QY, England.

P

PABISCH Peter Karl, b. 17 Apr 1938, Vienna, Austria. University Professor. m. Patricia Pabisch, 25 Nov 1959, 1 daughter. Education: University of Vienna, 1957-61; MA, 1971, PhD, 1974, University of Illinois, Urbana-Champaign, 1969-74. Appointments: School Teacher and Director, children's homes in Vienna and Italy, 1959-69; Professor of German and Comparative Literature, University of New Mexico, USA, 1972-. Publications include: Arroyo Seco, 1984; Der Morgen leicht wie eine Feder, 1989; Santa Fe, 1990; Sioux, 2nd edition, 1993. Contributions to: Trans-Lit; Literatur und Kritik; Podium; Schatzkammer der Deutschen Sprache; Dimension; Graphie (Greece); Zeitschrift für Kulturaustausch. Honours: Verdienstkreuz, 1st class, der Bundesrepublik Deutschland, 1985; Großes Ehrenzeichen der Republik Österreich, 1986; Pegasus Poet Award, 1992. Memberships: PEN West German Centre; PEN Austrian Center; PEN West US Center, New Mexico; Modern Language Association. Address: c/o Department of Foreign Languages and Literatures, The University of New Mexico, Albuquerque, NM 87131, USA.

PACHE Jean, b. 4 Mar 1933, Lausanne, Switzerland. Teacher. m. (1) Nov 1954, (2) Aug 1967, 2 sons, 1 daughter. Education: Licence es Lettres, University of Lausanne. Appointments: Teacher French Literature, Gymnase de Lausanne; Editor, Literary Series, Editions l'Aire Lausanne, 1970-75; Literary Chronicle. Publications: Les Fenêtres Simultanées, poems, 1955; Poèmes de l'Autre, 1960; Analogies, poems, 1966; Repères, poems, 1969; Rituels, poems, 1971; Anachoniques, récit, 1973; L'Oeil Cérémonial, poems, 1975; Le Corps Morcelé, poems, 1977; La Parodie, fiction, 1980; Lacunaires, poems, 1980; Les Corps Imaginaires, poems, 1983; Baroques, fiction, 1983; Le Fou de Lilith, fiction, 1986; Les Prunelles Ardentes, poems, 1989; Brûlots parmi les dunes, poems, 1989; La Straniera, récit, 1990; Les Soupirs de la Sainte et les Cris de la Fée, poems, 1991; Théodolite, poems, 1993; Le Discours Amoureux D'Un Commis Voyageur, fiction, 1994; Editions H C, 1978-89; Troubles Dans Les Plisements, 1978; Ordonner Les Déserts, 1980;Histoire D'Arbres Et De Roches, 1984; Matière Inscrite, 1984; Anankè, 1988; Dans La Dislocation Des Méridiens, 1989. Contributions to: Les Cahiers Du Sud; La Nouvelle Revue Française; Du; La Revue de Belles-Lettres, Editor-in-Chief, 1959-62; Pays Du Lac, Ed Comm, 1953-55. Honours: Prix de la Fondation, Schiller, 1967, 1978. Memberships: Association des Ecrivains de Langue Francaise; Association Internationale des Critiques Litteraires; Prix Michel Dentan, 1991; Grand Prix de Poésie de la Fondation Vaudoise pour la promotion et la création artistiques, 1993. Address: 14 Route du Signal. CH-1018 Lausanne, Switzerland.

PACK Lola (Catherine) Lee, (L Kathryn Pack), b. 14 Apr 1924, North Carolina, USA. Freelance Writer. m. 6 Mar 1943, 2 sons, 1 daughter. Education: Business College, 2 years. Appointments: Steno-typist; Eligibility Specialist with Department of Social Services. Contributions to: Fayetteville Observer; Pilot; National and International Poetry Journals and Anthologies; State Magazine. Honours: North Carolina Poetry Society Awards, 1972, 1981, 1982, 1983, 1986; Personal Poetry Broadcasts; Poetry featured on Phone-a-Poem Requests, broadcast live coast-to-coast; Song lyrics and words recorded and aired on local radio station. Memberships: North Carolina Poetry Society; National Poetry Society. Address: Route 1, Box 472, Linden, NC 28356, USA.

PACK Robert, b. 29 May 1929, New York, New York, USA. Professor; Poet; Writer. m. (1) Isabelle Miller, 1950, (2) Patricia Powell, 1961, 2 sons, 1 daughter. Education: BA, Dartmouth College, 1951; MA, Columbia University, 1953. Appointments: Teacher, Barnard College, 1957-64; Abernathy Professor, Middlebury College, Vermont, 1970-; Director, Bread Loaf Writers Conferences, 1973-. Publications: Poetry: The Irony of Joy, 1955; A Stranger's Privilege, 1959; Guarded by Women, 1963; Selected Poems, 1964; Home from the Cemetery, 1969; Nothing But Light, 1972; Keeping Watch, 1976; Waking to My Name: New and Selected Poems, 1980; Faces in a Single Tree: A Cycle of Monologues, 1984; Clayfield Rejoices, Clayfield Laments: A Sequence of Poems, 1987; Before It Vanishes: A Packet for Professor Pagels, 1989; Fathering the Map: New and Selected Later Poems, 1993; Other includes: The Long View: Essays on the Discipline of Hope and Poetic Craft, 1991; As Editor, includes: The Bread Loaf Anthology of Contemporary American Short Stories (with Jay Parini), 2 volumes, 1987, 1989; Poems for a Small Planet: An Anthology of

Nature Poetry (with Jay Parini), 1993. Honours: Fulbright Fellowship, 1956; American Academy of Arts and Letters Grant, 1957; Borestone Mountain Poetry Award, 1964; National Endowment for the Arts Grant, 1968. Address: c/o Middlebury College, Middlebury, VT 05742, USA.

PADGETT Ron, b. 17 June 1942, Tulsa, Oklahoma, USA. Writer. Appointments: Director of Publications, Teachers and Writers Collaborative, New York. Publications: Co-author, Bean Spasms, 1967; Great Balls Of Fire, 1969, 1990; Co-author, The Adventures of Mr and Mrs Jim and Ron, 1970; Co-author, Antlers in the Treetops, 1970; Toujours L'Amour, 1976; Tulsa Kid, 1979; Triangles in the Afternoon, 1979; How to be a Woodpecker, 1983; How to be Modern Art, 1984; Among the Blacks, 1988; The Big Something, 1990; Co-author, Supernatural Overtones, 1990; Ted, 1992; New and Selected Poems, 1995; Translations: The Poet Assassinated, 1968; Dialogues with Marcel Duchamp, 1971, 88; Kodak, 1976; The Poems of A O Barnabooth, 1977; The Poet Assassinated and other Stories, 1984; The Complete Poems of Blaise Cendrars, 1992; Anthologies: The Young American Poets, 1968; The World Anthology, 1969; Air Earth Fire & Winter, 1971; Another World, 1971; Contemporary American Poetry, 1972; Bad Moon Rising, 1973; British and American Surrealist Poetry, 1978; Claims for Poetry, 1982; The World Treasury of Children's Literature, 1985; Up Late: American Poetry since 1940, 1987; Postmodern American Poetry, 1994. Contributions to: New Yorker; Poetry; Village Voice; Paris Review; Sulfur; Ms; Artnews; Craft Horizons; Camera Arts; Art and Literature; C; Boulevard; others. Honours: Boar's Head Poetry Award, Columbia University, 1964; Gotham Bookmart Avant-Garde Poetry Prize, 1964; Poets Foundation, 1964, 1969; Fulbright Fellowship, 1965; American Academy of Arts and Letters Awards, 1966, 1971; Columbia University Translation Centre, 1976; National Endowment for the Arts, 1976; New York State Council on the Arts Translation Grant, 1983; Fellowships: 1983, 1986, 1990. Literary Agent: Robert Cornfield Agency. Address: 342 East 13th Street, Apt 6, New York, NY 10003, USA.

PADMANABHAN Neela, b. 26 April 1938, Trivandrum, India. Deputy Chief Engineer, retired. m. 3 July 1963, 1 son, 3 daughters. Education: BSc, 1956; BSc (Eng), 1963, FIE. Appointments: Junior Engineer; Assistant Executive Engineer; Executive Engineer; Deputy Chief Engineer. Publications: Neela Padmanabhan Kavithaikal, 1975 (Tamil); Naa Kaakka, 1984 (Tamil); Surrender and Other Poems, 1982 (English); Peyarilenna, 1993 (Tamil). Contributions to: Ezhutthu; Ilakkiavattam; Deepam; Gnana Ratham; Caravan; Indian Literature; Kunkumam; Mathrubhoomi Weekly; and others. Memberships: Poetry Society of India; Authors Guild of India; PEN. Address: Nilakant 39/1870 Kuriyathi Road, Manacaud PO, Thiruvanantha Puram 695009, Kerala, India.

PAGE Geoff(rey Donald), b. 7 July 1940, Grafton, New South Wales, Australia. Educator. m. Carolyn Mau, 4 Jan 1972, 1 son. Education: BA Hons, Dip Ed, University of New England, Armidale, New South Wales. Appointments: Teacher: New South Wales Department of Education, 1963-72; Australian Capital Territory Schools Authority and Department of Education, 1973-; Head of English Department, Narrabundah College, Canberra, 1974-; Writer-in-Residence, University of Woolongong, New South Wales, 1982. Publications: The Question (in Two Poets), 1971; Smalltown Memorials, 1975; Collecting the Weather, 1978; Cassandra Paddocks, 1980; Clairvoyant in Autumn, 1983; Editor: Shadows from Wire: Poems and Photographs of Australians in the Great War Australian War Memorial, 1983; Benton's Conviction, 1985; Novel: Collected Lives, 1986; Smiling in English, Smoking in French, 1987; Footwork, 1988; Winter Vision, 1989; Novel: Invisible Histories, 1990; Selected Poems, 1991; Gravel Corners, 1992; Human Interest, 1994; Reader's Guide to Contemporary Australian Poetry, 1995; The Great Forgetting, 1996. Contributions to: All major newspapers and magazines in Australia, 1968-; Cambridge Review, UK. Honour: Queensland Premiers Prize, 1990. Memberships: Australian Society of Authors; Australian Teacher's Union; Australian Labour Party. Address: 8 Morehead Street, Curtin, ACT 2605, Australia.

PAGE Jeremy Neil, b. 23 Feb 1958, Folkestone, Kent, England. Trainer of Teachers. Education: BA, Hons, French and Theatre Studies, University of Warwick, 1980; French Drama and Theatre History, University of Bristol, 1983; DipRSA, Teaching English as a Foreign Language; Certificates in Counselling. Appointments: Teacher, International House, Hastings, 1983; Teacher and Trainer, International House, London, 1984-; Director of Studies, International House, London, 1995-; Teacher, Academia Britannica, Arezzo,

Tuscany, Italy, 1987-88; Editor, The Frogmore Papers, 1983-; Founder, Frogmore Poetry Prize, 1987; series Editor, Crabflower Pamphlets, 1990-. Publications: Bliss, 1989; Co-editor, Frogmore Poetry, 1989; Editor, Bush Klaxon Has a Body Like a Trio Sonata, by Bob Mitchell, 1991; Secret Dormitories, 1993. Contributions to: Ego Trip; Frogmore Papers; New Pataphysician; Anthologies; Poetry; Snow Journeys; Envoi Spring Anthology, 1988; Envoi Summer Anthologies, 1989, 1990, 1991; Frogmore Poetry; Acumen; Envoi; Fatchance; Iota; Seam; Tears in the Fence. Honour: 4th Prize, Kent and Sussex Poetry Society Open Competition, 1989; Academy of Paraphysical Science, rank of Grand Transcendent Knight Salamander, 1992. Address: 6 Vernon Road, Hornsey, London N8 0QD, England.

PAGE P(atricia) K(athleen), (Judith Cape, P K Irwin), b. 23 Nov 1916, Swanage, Dorset, England. Writer; Painter. m. W Arthur Irwin, 16 Dec 1950, 1 stepson, 2 stepdaughters. Education: Studied Art with Frank Schaeffer, Brazil, Charles Seliger, New York; Art Students League and Pratt Graphics, New York. Appointments: Sales Clerk, Radio Actress, Saint John, New Brunswick; Filing Clerk, Historical Researcher, Montreal; Co-Editor, Preview; Regional Editor, Northern Review; Scriptwriter, National Film Board, 1946-50; Conducted Workshops, The Writers Workshops, Toronto, 1974-77; Taught, University of Victoria, British Columbia, 1977-78; Member, Advisory Arts Panel, Canada Council, 1976-79; Member, Editorial Board, Malahat Review. Publications: The Sun and the Moon and Other Fictions, 1973; Poems Selected and New, 1974; Editor, To Say the Least (anthology of short poems), 1979; Evening Dance of the Grey Flies (poems and short story), 1981; Text for The Travelling Musicians, 1984; The Glass Air (poetry, essays and drawings), 1985; Brazilian Journal (prose), 1988; I - Sphinx, A Poem for Two Voices; A Flask of Sea Water (fairy story), 1989; The Glass Air - Poems Selected and New, 1991; The Travelling Musicians (childrens book), 1991; Unless the Eye Catch Fire (short story), 1994; The Goat that Flew, 1994; Hologram - A Book of Glosas (poems), 1994; A Children's Hymm for the United Nations, 1995. Contributions to: Ariel; Alphabet; Blackfish; Canadian Forum; Canadian Literature; Journal of Canadian Poetry. Honours: Banff Centre School of Fine Arts National Award, 1989; National Magazines Silver Award for Poetry, 1990; Readers' Choice Award, Prairie Schooner, 1994; Officer of the Order of Canada, 1977; Doctor of Letters, (Honoris Causa), University of Victoria, 1985; Doctor of Laws, (Honoris Causa), Univeristy of Calgary, 1989. Address: 3260 Exeter Road, Victoria, British Columbia, V8R 6A6, Canada.

PAIN Margaret, b. 27 Mar 1922, Woking, Surrey, England. Company Secretary (retired). Education: Private School; Business College; Adult Education: Private Study. Appointments: Company Secretary and Director, R Pain & Sons Ltd (Builders and Engineers), UK, retired. Publications: Walking to Eleusis, 1967; No Dark Legend, 1977; A Fox in the Garden, 1979; Reprinted 1980; Shadow Swordsman, 1988. Contributions to: Country Life; Envoi; Iota; New Poetry; Outposts; Orbis; Printed Matter (Japan); Words Broadsheets; Weyfarers; Poetry Eastwest (USA); Poet's Voice, 1994; In translation, Nea Estia (Athens); Poetry included in anthologies; Poetry South East 1, 1976; International Who's Who In Poetry Anthology, 1972; Ipso Facto (International Poetry Society Anthology), 1975; How Strong The Roots, 1981; Speak To The Hills, 1985; Anthology: Cumbria Poet's England, 1995. Honours: Surrey Poetry Centre Open Competition: 2nd Prize, 1976; 3rd Prize, 1977; 3rd Prize, Eleanor B North Award, 1977; Joint 3rd Prize, Lake Aske Memorial Award. 1977; 1st Prize, New Poetry Competition, 1978; 1st Prize, Surrey Poetry Centre Open Competition, 1981-82; Special Commendation in South East Arts Group Literary Prize, 1985-86. Memberships: Surrey Poetry Society and Wey Poets (previously Deputy Chairman), Chairman, 1987-94. Co-editor, Weyfarers Magazine, 1978-; Administrative Editor, 1984-; Assistant Editor of Envoi (for many years). Address: Hilltop Cottage, 9 White Rose Lane, Woking, Surrey GU22 7JA, England.

PAK T(ae) J(in), b. 9 Sept 1921, Seoul, Korea. Insurance Executive. m. Heiwon Kim, 15 June 1954, 1 daughter. Education: Graduate, University College of St Paul's University, Tokyo, Japan, 1940-45. Appointments: Insurance Executive; English Teacher; London Representative of Shipping Firm, 1957-62. Publications: Transfiguration, 1962; Intimate Talks, 1969; Meaning of day-to-day, 1971; The Daedong River in Retrospection, 1984; Poems as One Narrates, 1987; Where Are They All Gone, 1990. Contributions to: Korean newspapers, periodicals, literary or poetry monthlies; ADAM International Review, 1957. Honour: Korean Literary Critics Society Prize, 1985. Memberships: Korean Writers' Association; Korean PEN;

Soul Poets' Club; Korean Poets' Society. Address: Flat 803 Namsan Mansion, 726-74 Hannam-Dong Yongsan, Seoul, Korea.

PALLANT Cheryl, b. 8 Jan 1960, Bronx, New York, USA. Teacher; Writer; Dancer. Education: BA, MA, Long Island University. Appointments: Editor, Real News, 1978-79; Poetry Editor, Loomings, 1979-80; Poetry Editor, New Southern Literary Messenger, 1985-87; Reviewer, High Performance, 1990-. Publications: Pizza; A Neighbourhood Bar. Contributions to: Oxford Magzine; Ambit; Crescent Review; Assembling; Gyphas; New Rain; High Perfromance; Beanfast; Loomings; Rag Mag; Contact Quarterly. Memberships: Poets & Writers; Virginia Writers Club; Associated Writers Program. Address: 108 South Colonial Aveneue, Richmond, VA 23221, USA.

PALLEY Julian, b. 16 Sept 1925, Atlantic City, New Jersey, USA. Professor of Spanish Literature. m. Shirley Wilson, 17 Sept 1950, 4 sons. Education: BA, Mexico City College, 1950; MA, Spanish, University of Arizone, 1952; PhD, Romance Languages, University of New Mexico, 1958. Appointments: Instructor, Rutgers University, 1956-59; Associate Professor, Arizona State University, 1959-62; Associate Professor, University of Oregon, 1962-66; Professor of Spanish Literature, University of California, 1966-. Publications: Spinoza's Stone, 1976; Bestiary, 1987; Pictures at an Exhibition, 1989; Translations from Spanish: Affirmation, Jorge Guillen, 1968, 1970; Meditation on the Threshold, Rosario Castellanos, 1988; Family Portraits (poetry), 1994. Contributions to: Arizona Quarterly; Beloit Poetry Journal; California Quarterly; Poetry/LA; South Coast Quarterly; Vol No; Galley Sail Review; Translations in: Chicago Quarterly; Northwest Review; Colorado Quarterly; Translation; others. Honours: Arizona Quarterly Poetry Prize, 1956; Jefferson Poetry Prize, 1976. Membership: Chair, Editorial Board, CQ, quarterly of California State Poetry Society. Address: Department of Spanish and Portuguese, University of California, Irvine, CA 92717, USA.

PALM Marion, b. 6 Aug 1940, Brooklyn, New York, USA. Teacher. Div. 2 sons, 1 daughter. Education: Berkeley School of Business; AIS, Normandale Community College, 1976; BA, University of Minnesota, 1978; MS, Bank Street College of Education, 1995. Appointments: Adjunct Professor; Freelance writer, artist, banker. Publications: Nightingale Day Songs; Alice's Forget-Me-Nots; Islands of the Blest; Passages; Riding the West End Express; The Poetry Leaders Guidebook; Editor, Director: Poets Under Glass Workshop Newsletter. Honours: Brooklyn Arts Council, 1995; New York Newsweek, 1995. Memberships: Poets and Writers. Address: 705-41 Street, No 17 Brooklyn, NY 11232, USA.

PALMER Charlene Noel, b. 23 Feb 1930, Los Angeles, California, USA. Poet. m. David Palmer, 16 June 1951, 2 sons, 2 daughters. Education: University of California at Los Angeles, 1948-52. Appointments: Sales Clerk; Night Telegraph Operator; Office Clerk; Library Assistant; Weekend Blood Bank Attendant; Parish Secretary. Publications: Long Stems Colored, 1953; Anthologies: Peace or Perish; Voices for Peace; Anti-War Poem; Exile; 10 Poetry readings, 1979-90. Contributions to: Axios; Chicago Omnibus; Christian Century; Creative Review; December; Descant; Golden Goose; Idiom; Inferno; Living Church; Mainstream; Midland Poetry Review; Odyssey; Olivant Quarterly. Membership: Poets and Writers. Address: 2310 Calumet Street, Flint, MI 48503, USA.

PALMER Leslie Howard, b. 25 Jan 1941, USA. Professor of Literature. m. 27 Aug 1965, 1 son, 1 daughter. Education: PhD, University of Tennessee, 1966. Appointments: Instructor, University of Tennessee, 1966-67; Professor, University of North Texas, 1967-. Publications: A Red Sox Flag, 1984; Ode to a Frozen Dog, 1992; Artemis' Bow, 1993; The Devil Sells Ice Cream, 1994. Contributions to: Laurel Review; New Orleans Review; Samisdat; Smith; Emily Dickinson Reviw; Paideuma; Tennessee Studies in Literature; Travois; Cape Rock; Laughing Bear; Poetry and Audience; Imago (Australia); Bellingham Review. Honours: Beaudoin Gemstone Award, 1962, 1963; Midsouth Poetry Award, 1963; Pushcart Press Nominee, 1984; Cape Rock Poetry Award, 1990. Memberships: Modern Language Association; Modern Humanities Research Association; Coda; PEN. Address: 1905 West Oak, Denton, TX 76201, USA.

PALSSON Sigurdur, b. 30 July 1948, Skinnastadur, Iceland. Writer; Translator; Theatre and TV Director. m. Kristin Johannesdottir, 26 June 1987, 1 son. Education: Baccalaureat, 1967; DUEL Libre 1972, Maitrise libre 1980, DEA 1982, Institut d'Etudes Theatrales Sorbonne, Paris; Diploma in Film Direction 1978, CLCF, Paris.

Appointments: Freelance Writer and Director; Radio Correspondent; Drama Teacher; University Teacher; Critic; Cinema Producer. Publications: Ljod vega salt, 1975; Ljod vega menn, 1980; Ljod vega gerd, 1980; Ljod namu land, 1985; Ljod namu menn, 1988; Ljod namu vold, 1990; Ljudlinudans, 1993; Ljodlinuskip, 1995. Contributions to: Timarit Mals og Menningar; Lesbok Morgun bladsins; Lettre Internationale. Honour: Chevalier de l'Ordre des Arts et des Lettres, 1989, France. Memberships: Writers Union of Iceland, Chairman, 1984-88; Union of Icelandic Theatre Directors, Treasurer, 1983-85; PEN Club of Iceland, Board of Directors, 1983-; Alliance Francaise of Iceland, President, 1976-77. Address: Mavahlid 38, 105 Reykjavik, Iceland.

PANDYA Natavarlal Kuber Bhai, (Ushanas), b. 28 Sept 1920, India. Teacher. m. May 1938, 3 daughters. Education: BA, Hons, 2nd Class with Sanskrit and Gujarate, 1942; MA, 2nd Class with Gujarati, 1946; TD, University of Bombay, 1945; Kovid (Wardha) Rashtrabhasha Hindi, 1st Class, 1948. Appointments: Head of Department of Gujarati, 1957-80; Member of the Senate, SG University, 1964-80. Publications: Prasoon, 1955; Napathye, 1956; Ardra, 1960; Manomudra, 1960; Trin no Qrah, 1964; Spand ane chhand, 1968; Bahrad Saishan, 1974; Ashvattha, 1975; Roop na laya, 1976; Vyakul Vaishnav, 1977; Aroh Avaroh, 1989; Bharat Darshan, 1974. Contributions to: Kumar; Prasthan; Sanskriti; Buddhiprakesh; Khevna; Etadd; Kavita and others. Honours: First Prize, Goverment of Bombay, 1955; 2nd Prize, Gujarat Government, 1960; 1st Prize, Government of Gujarat; Ranji Ram Gold Medal, 1972; Sahitya Akademi Award, 1976; Government of India Award, 1981; Several Gold Medals. Memberships: Central Board, Executive Committee, Gujarati Sahitya Parishad; President, All Gujarati Professors Association, 1980; Vice President, 1989, President, 1991, Gujarati Sahitya Parishad. Address: Laxmi sheri, Madanwad Valsad Pim 396001, Gujarat State, India.

PANIKER Ayyappa, b. 12 Sept 1930, Kavalam, India. Professor of English; Chief Editor. m. Sree Parvathi, 9 Dec 1961, 2 daughters. Education: BA Hons, Travancore University, 1951; MA, Kerala University, 1959; CTE, Ciefl, Hyderabad, 1966; AM, PhD, Indiana University, USA, 1971. Appointments: Lecturer, 1951-73; Reader, 1973-80; Professor and Head, English Department, University of Kerala, 1980-90; Chief Editor, Medieval Indian Literarture, 1990-94; Birla Fellowship, 1994-96. Publications: Ayyappa Panikerude Kritikal I, II, III, 1974, 1982, 1990; Ayyappa Panikerude Lekhanangal, I, 1982; II, 1990; Cuban Kavitakal, 1984; Selected Poems, 1985; Mayakovskiyude Kavitakal, 1987; Ayyappa Panikerude Vivar tadnangal, 1988; Teranjedutta Kavitakal, 1989; Gotrayanam, 1989; Ayyappa Panikerude Avatarikakal 19; Books in English: K M Panikkar; Manjeri Isvaran; Thakazhi Sivasankara Pillai; Editor, Kutiyattam; Indian Renaissance; A Malayalam Anthology; Malayaam Short Stories; Asan, Man and Poet; English and India; The Making of Indian Literature; Dialogues; Modern Indian Poetry in English. Contributions to: Mathrubhoomi; Kalakaumudi; Minnesota Review; Two Plus Two; Indian Literature; Tenor; Frederick Ungar Encyclopedia of 20th Century Literature; Dictionary of National Biography, India. Honours: Awards for Poetry: Kerala Sahitya Akademi, 1975; Kalyani Krishna Menon Prize, 1977; SPCS Award, 1978; Central Sahita Academi, 1984; Bharatiya Bhasha Parishad, 1988; Mahakavi Kuttamath, 1990; Mahakav Ulloor, 1990; Asan Prize, 1991; Kerala Culture Centre, Muscat Award, 1992; Sahitya Parishad Award, 1993. Memberships: AES; ASRC; Rajaram Mohan Roy Library Foundation; National Literary Mission; DLA; Founder-Editor, Keralakavita Quarterly; Chief Editor, Indian Journal of English Studies; National Book Trust; Malayalam Advisory Committee; Sahitya Akademi (General Council and Executive Board); Sangeet Natak Akademi General Council; Malayalam Lexicon Advisory Board. Address: 111 Gandhi Nagar, Trivandrum 65014, India.

PANKEY Eric, b. 25 Feb 1959, Kansas City, Missouri, USA. Director of Writing Programme. m. Jennifer Hale Atkinson, 6 July 1985, 1 daughter. Education: BA, University of Missouri, 1981; MFA, University of Iowa, 1983. Appointments: Director of the Writing Programme, Master of Fine Arts Programme, Washington University. Publications: For the New Year, 1984; Heartwood, 1988; Apocrypha, 1991. Contributions to: Antaeus; Iowa Review; New Republic; New Criterion; New Yorker. Honours: Walt Whitman Award for Poetry, 1984; Ingram Merrill Foundation, 1986; National Endowment for the Arts Fellowship, 1987. Memberships: Associated Writing Programs; Academy of American Poets. Address: 8711 Bridgeport, St Louis, MO 63144, USA.

PAOLUCCI Anne (Attura), b. 1930, Rome, Italy. Poet; Writer; Dramatist; Editor; Professor. m. Henry Paolucci. Education: BA, Barnard College; MA, PhD 1963, Columbia University. Appointments: Assistant Professor of English and Comparative Literature, City College of the City University of New York, 1959-69; Research Professor 1969-, Professor of English 1975-, Chairperson of the English Department 1982-91, Director of the Doctor of Arts Degree Program in English 1982-, St John's University, Jamaica, New York; Visiting Lecturer at various universities in the US and abroad; Founder-Editor, Review of National Literatures 1970-, CNL/Report 1974-; Founder-Executive Director, Council on National Literatures, 1974-. Publications include: Poems Written for Sbek's Mummies, Marie Menken and Other Important Persons, Places and Things, 1977; Riding the Mast Where it Swings, 1980; Tropic of the Gods, 1980; Gorbachev in Concert (and Other Poems), 1991; Queensboro Bridge and Other Poems, 1994. Contributions to: Stories, articles, reviews and poems in numerous journals. Honours: Fulbright Scholarship, 1951-52; Woodbridge Honorary Fellow, Columbia University, 1961-62; Yaddo Colony Residency, 1965; American Council of Learned Societies Grant, 1978; Cavaliere, 1986, Commendatore, Order of Merit 1992, Italy. Memberships include: International Shakespeare Association; PEN American Center; Pirandello Society of America, Vice President 1968-79, President 1979-; World Centre for Shakespeare Studies, Board Director 1972-; National Council on the Humanities, 1986-94; Board Trustees, The City University of New York, 1996-. Address: 166-25 Powells Cove Blvd, Beechurst, NY 11357, USA.

PARADIS Philip M, b. 11 Feb 1951, Connecticut, USA. University Professor. m. Marjorie H Paradis, 27 May 1978. Education: BA, Central Connecticut State College, 1976; MA, University of Utah, 1981; PhD, Oklahoma State University, 1984. Appointments: Oklahoma State University, 1980-85; Iowa State University, 1985-87; Western Carolina University, 1987-90; Iowa State University, 1990-91; Northern Kentucky University, 1992-. Publications: Tornado Alley, 1986, 1987, 1989; From Gobbler's Knob, 1989; Something of Ourselves, 1994; Along the Path, 1996. Contributions to: American Scholar; Chariton Review; Poet and Critic; Tar River Poetry; Kansas Quarterly; College English; Zone 3; Southern Humanities Review. Honours: Academy of American Poets Prize, 1982; Appalachian Writers Association Poetry Award, 1989. Memberships: Associated Writing Programs; Academy of American Poets; National Council of Teachers of English. Address: Department of Literature and Language, Northern Kentucky University, Highland Heights, KY 41099, USA.

PARASKOS Michael, b. 8 Sept 1969, Leeds, Yorkshire, England. Editor. Education: BA, Honours, Fine Art, University of Leeds, 1992. Appointment: Editor, The Tempest Magazine. Contributions to: Poetry and Audience, Leeds; Liberty, Leeds; Understanding, Edinburgh. Honour: Kenneth Hargreaves Prize for Writing, 1992. Memberships: Vice President, 1990-91, English Society, University of Leeds; President, 1990-91, Poetry Society, University of Leeds; Founder and Current Co-Ordinator, New Leeds Art Club. Address: 195 Roundhay Road, Harehills, Leeds, Yorkshire, England.

PARISH Barbara Lu Shirk, b. 28 Nov 1942, Lincoln, Kansas, USA. Writer; Housewife. m. Dr Harlie Albert Parish, Jr, 30 Aug 1964, 1 daughter. Education: AB, English, Fort Hays State University, 1964; MA, English, University of Missouri at Columbia, 1966; MA, Library Science, University of Missouri at Columbia, 1968. Appointments: Cataloguer and Instructor in Library Science, Reference Library, part-time; Tutor, Shelby State Community College, 1995-. Publications: The Kentucky Book, 1979; Maverick Western Verse, 1994. Contributions to: Snapdragon; Prairie Schooner; Kansas Quarterly; Wind; Green's; Plainsongs; Plainswoman; Riverrun; Kentucky Poetry Review; Louisville Review; Small Pond; Shawnee Silhouette; Pegasus; Writer's Journal; Louisville Courier-Journal Magazine; Descant; Cumberlands; Cottonwood Review Anthology; Kansas Women Writers; Cimarron Review; Little Balkans Review; Good Housekeeping; Midwest Quarterly; Sunday Clothes; Writers on the River; Cat's Eye; Forum; Encore; Anthologies: The Kentucky Book; Maverick Western Verse; Journals: Dry Crik Review. Honours: Kentucky State Poetry Society Awards, 1972-94; Appeared on Paul Salyer's Thought for Today, Radio Program, 1980-90. Memberships: Writers Club, Louisville; Kentucky State Poetry Society, Contest Chairman, Chairman of the Board, Board Member, Secretary; Beta Phi Mu, Library Science Honorary Member. Address: 4293 Beechcliff Lane, Memphis, TN 38128, USA.

PARISI Joseph (Anthony), b. 18 Nov 1944, Duluth, Minnesota, USA. Writer; Editor. Education: BA (Hons), College of St Thomas, 1966; MA, University of Chicago, 1967; PhD (with Honours), University of Chicago, 1973. Appointments: Assistant Professor of English, Roosevelt University; Visiting Professor, English, University of Illinois; Associate Editor, Acting Editor, Editor/Writer, Poetry Magazine, Chicago. Publications: The Poetry Anthology 1912-1977, 1978; Viewer's Guide to Voices and Visions, 1987; Marianne Moore: The Art of a Modernist, 1990; Poets in Person, A Listener's Guide, 1992. Contributions to: Yale Review; Georgia Review; Poetry; New Philology; Triquarterly; Shenandoah; Sewanee Review; New Leader; Chicago Tribune; Chicago Sunday Times; Broadcast on National Public Radio, 1991. Address: Poetry, 60 West Walton Street, Chicago, IL 60610, USA.

PARK William, b. 6 May 1962, Hillingdon, West London, England. Tutor in Creative Writing. Appointments: Writer-in-Residence, St Martin's College, Lancaster, 1989; Hawthornden Fellowship, 1991. Publication: The Gregory Anthology, 1987-90, 1990. Contributions to: Oxford Poetry; Poetry Durham; Ambit; Outposts; Poetry Review; Orbis; Iron; Critical Quarterly; Rialto; Acumen; Verse; Bête Noire; Stand. Honour: Major Eric Gregory Award, 1990. Membership: Poetry Society. Address: 25B Dawson Walk, Preston, Lancashire PR1 1NH, England.

PARKER Jean. See: SHARAT CHANDRA Gubbi Shankara Chetty.

PARKS Ian, b. 10 Feb 1959, Yorkshire, England. Poet. Appointments: Writing Fellow, North Riding College, Scarborough, 1986-88; Writer in Education, Humberside, 1990-91. Publications: Gargoyles in Winter, 1985; Sirens, 1994. Contributions to: Poetry Review; Rialto; Other Poetry; Poetry and Audience; Quartz Prospice; New Welsh Review; Orbis; Outposts; Acumen; Bete Noire; Poetry Wales; New Voices in British Poetry. Honours: Yorkshire Arts Association Award, 1984; Hawthornden Fellowship, 1991; Travelling Fellowship to USA, 1993; 3rd Prize, City of Cardiff International Poetry Competition, 1994; 1st Prize, Cascando Travel Writing Competition, 1995. Address: 72 Doncaster Road, Mexborough, South Yorkshire, England.

PARRY Marian, b. 28 Jan 1924, San Francisco, California, USA. Artist. m. Maury David Feld, 4 Apr 1952, 1 son, 1 daughter. Education: BA, University of California, 1946. Appointments: Lecturer, Radcliffe Seminars, 1974-; Lecturer; Assistant Professor. Contributions to: Shenandoah; Atlantic; Antioch Review; Audience Grand Street; Negative Capability; Two Plus Two; Margin; Tendrily Voices; American Weave. Honours: Emily Chamberlain Richardson Cook Poetry Prize; Charles River Festival Poetry Competition. Membership: New England Poetry Society. Address: 60 Martin Street, Cambridge, MA 02138, USA.

PARTRIDGE Dixie Lee, b. 6 July 1943, Wyoming, USA. Homemaker; Writer. m. Jerry A Partridge, 20 Aug 1963, 3 sons, 3 daughters. Education: BA, Brigham Young University, 1965. Publications: Deer in the Haystacks; Watermark. Contributions to: Berkeley Poetry Review; Centennial Review; Christian Science Moniter; Commonwealth; Crosscurrents; Dialogue; Ellipsis; Hollins Critic; Indiana Review; Kaleidescope; Kansas Quarterly; Northern Lights; Passages North; Pittsburgh Quarterly; Quarterly West; Southern Humanities Review; Southern Poetry Review; Cincinnati Poetry Review; Midwest Quarterly; Ploughshares; BYU Studies; Sunstone; A Circle of Women (anthology). Honours: William Stafford Award; Eileen Barnes Award; Literature and Belief Writing Awards; Seattle Arts Commission Writers Award; Bumbershoot Big Book Award. Memberships: Washington Poets Association; Mid Columbia Writers Guild; Rattlesnake Mountain Writers. Address: 1817 Marshall Court, Richland, WA 99352, USA.

PASCHEN Elise Maria, b. 4 Jan 1959, Chicago, Illinois, USA. Arts Administrator. Education: BA, Harvard University, 1982; MPhil, Oxford University, 1984; DPhil, 1988. Appointments: Executive Director, Poetry Society of America. Publications: Houses: Coasts, 1985. Contributions to: Poetry Review; Oxford Magazine; Poetry Ireland Review; Poetry; Harvard Advocate. Honours: Lloyd McKim Garrison Medal for Poetry; Joan Grey Untermeyer Poetry Prize; Richard Selig Prize for Poetry. Memberships: National Arts Club; John Florio Society; Magdalen College. Address: Poetry Society of America, 15 Gramercy Park, New York, NY 10003, USA.

PASTAN Linda, b. 27 May 1932, New York, New York, USA. Poet; m. Ira Pastan, 14 June 1953, 2 sons, 1 daughter. Education: BA, Radcliffe College, 1954; MA, Brandeis University, 1957. Appointment: Poet Laureate of Maryland, 1991-94. Publications: A Perfect Circle of Sun, 1971; Aspects of Eve, 1975; The 5 Stages of Grief, 1978; Waiting for My Life, 1981; PM/AM: New and Selected Poems, 1982; A Fraction of Darkness, 1985; The Imperfect Paradise, 1988; Heros in Disguise, 1991-92; An Early Afterlife, 1995. Contributions to: Atlantic Monthly; New Republic; New Yorker; Poetry; Antaeus; Goergia Review; American Scholar; Grand Street; Gettysburg Review; Nation; Prairie Schooner. Honours: Bess Hoken Prize, 1985; Mauria Erglich Award, 1985; Pushcart Prize; De Castograla Award. Memberships: PEN; Poetry Society of America. Address: 11710 Beall Mt Road, Potomoc, MD 20854, USA.

PASUMPON. See: AYYANARAPPAN Kavikkuil Pon.

PATERSON Alistair Ian, b. 28 Feb 1929, Nelson, New Zealand. Poet; Educationalist. m. Dec 1984, 2 sons, 3 daughters. Education: BA, University of New Zealand, 1961; Diploma in Education, University of Auckland, 1972; Fulbright Fellowship in Education, Police Training, 1977. Appointments: Instructor Lieutenant, RNZN, 1954-62; Instructor Lieutenant Commander, 1962-74; Dean of General Studies, New Zealand Police, 1974-78; Tertiary Inspector, New Zealand Department of Education, 1979-89; Educational Consultant, 1990-. Publications: Short Stories from New Zealand; Garrett on Education; The Toldeo Room; Birds Flying; Climate; Mate; How To Be A Millionaire by Next Wedsnesday, (novel), 1994; Poetry New Zealand (Editor). Contributions to: Landfall; Poetry New Zealand; Poetry Australia; Arena; Buff; Penguin Book of New Zealand Verse; Oxford Anthology of 20th Century New Zealand Verse; New Zealand Listener; New Directions; Blue Mesa Review; Journal of New Zealand Literature; Kite; Literary Olympians, 1992. Honours: University of Auckland, John Cowie Reid Award (Poetry); Katherine Mansfield Award for Fiction, 1993; Creative New Zealand Writing Grant, 1995. Memberships: PEN Auckland Committee Member; Former Member, PEN National Council; Wellington Poetry Society. Address: PO Box 9612, Newmarket, Auckland, New Zealand.

PATERSON Don, b. 30 Oct 1963, Dundee, Scotland. Writer; Musician. Publication: Nil Nil, 1993. Contributions to: Poetry Review; Observer; Verse; New Statesman. Honours: Eric Gregory Award, 1990; Poetry Book Society Choice, summer, 1993. Address: 30 Dyke Road Drive, Brighton BN1 6AJ, England.

PATERSON Stuart A, b. 31 Jan 1966, Truro, Cornwall, England. Writer. Education: James Hamilton Academy, 1977-82; Stirling University, 1988. Publication: Mulaney of Larne and Other Poems, 1991. Contributions to include: Dream State; The New Scottish Poets; The Poets Book of Days; The Forward Book of UK Poetry, 1994; Lines Review; Orbis; Chapman; Northlight; Northwords; Scots Glasnost; Spectrum; Verse; Pennine Platform; Ayrshire; Leader; Squibs; Yonkly. Honour: Eric Gregory Award. Memberships: Founder, Kilmarnock North West Writers Group, 1991; Poetry Prose Review; Artists for Independence; Founder/Editor, Spectrum, poetry/prose review, 1990-; Scottish Poetry Library; Scottish National Party. Address: c/o 2A Leslie Road, New Farm Loch, Kilmarnock, Ayrshire KA3 7RR, Scotland.

PATEY-GRABOWSKA Alicja Wanda. See: GRABOWSKA-STEFFEN Alicja Wanda.

PATNAIK Simanchal, b. 8 Nov 1928, Orissa, India. Advocate. m. Sarala Patnaik, 23 May 1957, 3 sons, 4 daughters. Education: BA, 1951; LLB, 1953. Appointments: Sub Deputy Collector; Munsif; Subordinate Judge; Advocate. Publications: Delightful World of Poems; Sonnets and Other Poems; Bedroom Poems; Poetry in Tranquility; Poetry of Himalayan Wisdom. Contributions to: Poet; Pratibha India; Poetcrit; Poetry; Poetry Time; Statesman; International Poetry; New Hope International Review, England; Prophetic Voices, USA. Honours: Madhusudhan Academy Award; Orissa Sahitya Academy Award; D Litt, World University; International Eminent Poet. Memberships: World Poetry Society; International Poets. Address: Grandhinagar Berhampur 760001, Orissa, India.

PATRICK Joseph. See: SCULLY James.

PATTEN Bernard M, (Patrick Murray), b. 23 Mar 1941, New York, New York, USA. Physician-Neurologist; Poet. m. Ethel Patten, 18 June 1964, 2 sons, 1 daughter. Education: AB summa cum laude,

Columbia College; MD, College of Physicians and Surgeons, Columbia University. Appointments: Attending Neurologist, Methodist Hospital; Associate Professor of Neurology, Baylor College of Medicine. Publications: Numerous. Contributions to: Many reviews, magazines and journals. Honour: Bay Area Writer's League Prize, 1995. Memberships: Modern Poetry Society; World Congress of Poets. Address: 1019 Baronridge, Seabrook, TX 77586, USA.

PATTEN Brian, b. 7 Feb 1946, Liverpool, England. Poet. Appointment: Regents Lecturer, University of California at San Diego, USA. Publications: Poetry: The Mersey Sound: Penguin Modern Poets 10, 1967; Little Johnny's Confession, 1967; The Home Coming, 1969; Notes to The Hurrying Man: Poems, Winter '66 - Summer '68, 1969; The Irrelevant Song, 1970; At Four O'Clock in The Morning, 1971; The Irrelevant Song and Other Poems, 1971; Walking Out: The Early Poems of Brian Patten, 1971; The Eminent Professors and the Nature of Poetry as Enacted Out by Members of the Poetry Seminar One Rainy Evening, 1972; The Unreliable Nightengale, 1973; Vanishing Trick, 1976; Grave Gossip, 1979; Love Poems, 1981; New Volume, 1983; Storm Damage, 1988; Grinning Jack: Selected Poems, 1990; Armada, 1996; Editor: Clare's Countryside: A Book of John Clare, 1981; Children's literature: The Elephant and The Flower: Almost-Fables, 1970; Jumping Mouse, 1972; Manchild, 1973; Mr Moon's Last Case, 1975; The Sly Cormorant and The Fishes: New Adaptations into Poetry of the Aesop Fables, 1977; Gargling with Jelly: A Collection of Poems, 1985; Jimmy Tag-a-long, 1988; Thawing Frozen Frogs, 1990; Grizzelda Frizzle and Other Stories, 1992; The Magic Bicycle, 1993; Impossible Parents, 1994; Frognapped! and Other Stories, 1994; Editor: The House that Jack Built: Poems for Shelter, 1973; Gangsters, Ghosts and Dragonflies: A Book of Story Poems, 1981; The Puffin Book of 20th Century Children's Verse, 1991; Plays: The Pig and the Junk Hill, 1975; Riddle-me-hights; The Tinder Box; The Mouth Trap, 1982; Blind Love, 1983; Gargling with Jelly, 1993. Honour: Special Award, Mystery Writers of America, 1977. Membership: Chelsea Arts Club. Address: c/o Puffin Penguin Books, 27 Wrights Lane, London W8 5TZ, England.

PATTERSON Raymond Richard, b. 14 Dec 1929, USA. University Professor. m. Boydie Alice Cooke, 16 Nov 1957, 1 daughter. Education: BA, Lincoln University, Pennsylvania, 1951; MA, New York University, 1956. Appointments: Instructor in English, Benedict College, Columbia, South Carolina, 1958-59; Teacher, New York City Public Schools, 1959-68; Professor of English, The City College of New York, 1968-92; Professor Emeritus, 1992. Publications: Twenty-Six Ways of Looking at a Black Man and Other Poems, 1969; Elemental Blues, 1983; L'ABC Du Blues, French translation, 1989. Contributions to: Transatlantic Review; Obsidian; Ohio Review; Beloit Poetry Journal; Black Scholar; Race Today Review. Honours: Poetry Awards, Poetry Society of America, 1950; National Endowment for the Arts Award, 1970; Creative Artists Public Service Award, 1977; City College Langston Hughes Award, 1986; National Endowment for the Arts, Collaborative Fellowship, 1989. Memberships: PEN American Centre, Executive Board, 1989-90; The Poetry Society of America, Vice President, 1985-88; Walt Whitman Birthplace Association, Trustee, 1985-. Address: 2 Lee Court, Merrick, NY 11566, USA.

PAUKER Ted. See: **CONQUEST (George) Robert (Acworth)**.

PAULIN Tom, (Thomas Neilson Paulin), b. 25 Jan 1949, Leeds, Yorkshire, England. Poet; Critic; Lecturer in English Literature. m. Munjiet Kaut Khosa, 1973, 2 sons. Education: BA, University of Hull; BLitt, Lincoln College, Oxford. Appointments: Lecturer, 1972-89, Reader in Poetry, 1989-94, University of Nottingham; G M Young Lecturer in English Literature, University of Oxford, 1994-; Fellow, Hertford College, Oxford, 1994-. Publications: Poetry: Theoretical Locations, 1975; A State of Justice, 1977; Personal Column, 1978; The Strange Museum, 1980; The Book of Juniper, 1981; Liberty Tree, 1983; The Argument at Great Tew, 1985; Fivemiletown, 1987; Selected Poems 1972-1990, 1993; Walking a Line, 1994; Other: Thomas Hardy: The Poetry of Perception, 1975; Ireland and the English Crisis, 1984; Editor, The Faber Book of Political Verse, 1986; Co-Editor, Hard Lines 3, 1987; Minotaur: Poetry and the Nation State, 1992. Honours: Eric Gregory Award, 1978; Somerset Maugham Award, 1978; Faber Memorial Prize, 1982; Fulbright Scholarship, 1983-84. Address: c/o Faber and Faber, 3 Queen Square, London, WC1N 3AU, England.

PAZ Octavio, b. 31 Mar 1914, Mexico City, Mexico. Author; Poet; Director. Revista Vuelta. m. Marie Jose Tramini, 1 daughter.

Education: National University of Mexico. Appointments: Founder and Director of Mexican literary reviews: Barandal, 1931, Taller, 1938, El Hijo Prodigo, 1943; Guggenheim Fellowship, USA, 1944; Secretary, Mexican Embassy, Paris, 1946, New Delhi, 1952; Diplomatic Service, 1952-68; Simon Bolivar Professor of Latin-American Studies, Cambridge, 1970; Visiting Professor of Spanish American Literature, University of Texas, Austin and Pittsburgh University, 1968-70; Charles Eliot Norton Professor of Poetry, Harvard University, 1971-72; Editor, Plural, Mexico City, 1971-75. Publications: Semillas para un Himno, 1956; Piedra de Sol, 1957, translated as Sun Stone, 1960; La Estacion Violenta, 1958; Libertad bajo Palabra, poetical works, 1935-1957, 1960; Salamandra, poetical works, 1958-1961, 1962; Viento Entero, 1965; Blanco, 1967; Discos Visuales, 1968; Ladera Este, 1969; La Centena, 1969; Topoemas, 1971; Renga, 1971; New Poetry of Mexico, anthology, 1972; Pasado en Claro, 1975; Vuelta, 1976; Poemas 1935-1975, 1979; Arbol adentro, 1987; In English: Early Poems 1935-37, 1963; Configurations, 1971; A Draft of Shadows and Other Poems, 1979; Airborn/Hijos del Aire, 1981; Selected Poems, 1984; Collected Poems 1957-1987, 1987. Honours: International Poetry Grand Pize, 1963; National Prize for Poetry, Mexico, 1977; Jerusalem Prize, 1977; Golden Eagle, Nice, 1978; Cervantes, Spain, 1982; T S Eliot Prize, Ingersoll Foundation, USA, 1987; Nobel Prize for Literature, 1990. Address: c/o Revista Vuelta, Presidente Canonza 210, Coyoacan, Mexico 4000 DF, Mexico.

PEACOCK Molly, b. 30 June 1947. Poet; Writer. Education: BA, Harpur College, 1969; MA, Johns Hopkins University, 1977. Appointments: Learning Specialist at Friends Seminary, 1981-92; Lecturer, Bucknell University, New York University, Columbia College, Sarah Lawrence College and Hofstra University, 1985-93; Writer in Residence, University of Western Ontario, 1995-96. Publications: And Live Apart, 1980; Raw Heaven, 1984; Take Heart, 1989; Original Love, 1995. Contributions to: New Republic; Nation; New Yorker; Paris Review; many other literary journals. Honours: Ingram Merrill Foundation Award, 1980, 1988; New York Foundation for the Arts Award, 1984, 1989; National Endowment for the Arts Award, 1990; Woodrow Wilson Fellow, 1995. Address: 505 East 14 Street, No 3G, New York, NY 10009, USA.

PEACOCKE M(argaret) R(uth) (Meg), b. 5 Mar 1930, Reading, Berkshire, England. Counsellor; Psychotherapist. Education: Exhibitioner of St Anne's College, Oxford; BA, Oxon, 1951; MA, Oxon, 1954; Diploma in Counselling, Aston University, 1981. Publications: Marginal Land, 1988; Poems included in: The New Lake Poets (anthology), 1991; Northern Poetry Vol 1 (anthology), 1989; Selves, Peterloo Poets, 1995. Contributions to: Poetry Review; London Magazine; Spectator; Pivot (USA). Honours: Commendation, National Poetry Competition, 1985; Commendation, Arvon Poetry Competition, 1987; 1st Prize, Green Book, 1987; 2nd Prize, Bury Metro Arts, 1987; Prizewinner, Peterloo Poets Open Competition, 1986, 1988; Prizewinner, Lancaster Open, 1986, 1988, 1992; Prizewinner, Northern Poetry (Littlewood Press), 1989. Address: Dummah Hill, North Stainmore, Kirkby Stephen, Cumbria, England.

PEARCE Brian Louis, b. 4 June 1933, Acton, London, England. Poet; Author; Lecturer; Occasional Lecturer, National Portrait Gallery, London; Former College Librarian. m. Margaret Wood, 2 Aug 1969, 1 daughter. Education: MA, FLA, FRSA. Appointments: NS, RAF, 1951-53; Examiner in English, Library Association, 1964-70; College Librarian/Senior Lecturer, Richmond upon Thames College, 1977-88; Member, GL Arts Writers in Schools Scheme. Publications: The Vision of Piers Librarian, 1981; Office Hours, 1983; Browne Study, 1984; Palgrave (FT) Selected Poems, edited, 1985; Dutch Comfort: Poetry, Prose, Translations, 1985; Gwen John Talking (poetry), 1985, 2nd Edition, 1996; Victoria Hammersmith (novel), 1987; Shrine Rites (play), 1990; London Clay (stories), 1991; Jack O'Lent (poetry), 1991; Leaving the Corner: Selected Poems 1973-1985, 1992; The Bust of Minerva (fiction), 1992; A Man in his Room (fiction), 1992; The Fashioned Reed: The Poets of Twickenham from 1500, 1992; Coeli et terra (poetry), 1993; Emotional Geology: The Writings of Brian Louis Pearce (symposium), 1993; Thames Listener: Poems 1949-1989, 1993; Battersea Pete (novel), 1994; The Servant of his Country (novel), 1994; City Whiskers (poetry) In The Playing of the Easter Music (with Caws and Caseley), 1995; The Proper Fuss, poetry with essay, 1996; Varieties of Fervour: Portraits of Victorian and Edwardian Poets, 1996. Contributions to: Acumen; Dutch Crossing; The Green Book; Green River Review; New Welsh Review; Ore; Outposts; PEN Broadsheet; Reform; RSA Journal; South Coast Poetry Journal; Swansea Review; Third Way. Honours: Joint 5-6th Place, Poetry

Society 1-Act Verseplay Competition, 1964; 1st Prize, Christian Poetry Competition, 1989. Memberships: The Browning Society; PEN; RSL. Address: The Marish, 72 Heathfield South, Twickenham, Middlesex TW2 7SS, England.

PEASE Peter Pembroke, b. 15 Apr 1941, Columbus, Ohio, USA. Procurement Specialist. m. Julia Feoktistova, 19 July 1996, 2 sons, 1 daughter. Education: BA, MA, Wesleyan University, 1963. Appointments: US Foreign Service, 1965-70; Political Officer, Economic & Commercial Officer, Jordan, Japan; Arabian American Oil Company, 1970-85; Procurement Specialist, Task Manager, World Bank, 1985-. Publication: Rostropovich in Red Square, 1996. Membership: Academy of American Poets. Address: 1050 North Stuart Street, Apt 818, Arlington, VA 22201, USA.

PEASMAIR Arthur. See: **BLACKMAN Roy Alfred Arthur.**

PECK John (Frederick), b. 13 Jan 1941, Pittsburgh, Pennsylvania, USA. Poet. m. Ellen Margaret McKee, 1963, div, 1 daughter. Education: AB, Allegheny College, Meadville, Pennsylvania, 1962; PhD, Stanford University, 1973. Appointments: Instructor, 1968-70, Visiting Lecturer, 1972-75, Princeton University; Assistant Professor, 1977-79, Professor of English, 1980-82, Mount Holyoke College, South Hadley, Massachusetts. Publications: Poetry: Shagbark, 1972; The Broken Blockhouse Wall, 1978; Argura, 1993; Other: The Poems and Translations of Hi-Lo, 1991. Honours: American Academy of Arts and Letters Award, 1975, and Rome Fellowship, 1978; Guggenheim Fellowship, 1981. Address: c/o Englisches Seminar, Plattenstrasse 47, 8032 Zürich, Switzerland.

PECKENPAUGH Angela Johnson, b 21 Mar 1942, Richmond, Virginia, USA. Associate Professor of English; Performing Poet. m. Bill Peckenpaugh, 27 July 1970, 1 daughter. Education: BA, Denison University, Ohio, 1965; MA, Ohio University, 1967; MFA in Writing, University of Massachusetts, 1978. Appointments: Instructor in English, Ohio University; Lecturer in English, University of Wisconsin at Milwaukee; Director of Development, Milwaukee Institute of Art and Design; Director, Writing Programmes for Adults, University of Wisconsin Extension; Professor in English, University of Wisconsin at Whitewater; Editor, Wisconsin Poets Calendar, 1996. Publications: Letters from Lee's Army, 1979; Discovering the Mandala, 1981; A Book of Charms, 1983; Refreshing the Fey, 1986; Remembering Rivers, 1991; A Heathen Herbal, 1993; Always Improving My Appetite, 1994; Inclusion in various anthologies especially: When I am An Old Women I Shall Wear Purple. Contributions to: Women's Review of Books; Calyx; Sing Heavenly Muse; Northwest Review; Virginia Quarterly Review; John O'Hara Journal; Margins; Salthouse; Wisconsin Academy Review; Louisville Review; Wisconsin Poets Calendar; Wind; Buckle; Richmond Broom; Feminist Voices; Milwaukee Journal; Southern Poetry Review; Keltria, 1995. Honours: Honourable Mention, Council of Wisconsin Writers; All University Fellowship, University of Massachusetts; Wisconsin Arts Board Grant. Memberships: Poetry Society of America; Associated Writing Programmes; Wisconsin Fellowship of Poets; Wisconsin Regional Writers. Address: 2513 East Webster Place, Milwaukee, WI 53211, USA.

PEDERSON Cynthia, b. 11 Sept 1956, Oklahoma City, Oklahoma, USA. Teacher. m. Ronald M Pederson, 20 June 1979. Education: BA, Honours magna cum laude, English, Washburn University of Topeka, 1978; MA, Honours, English, University of Kansas, 1983; MFA, Creative Writing, Wichita State University, Kansas, 1988. Appointments: Adjunct Instructor, Washburn University, 1986, Friends University, 1987; Assistant Instructor, Wichita State University, 1988; Instructor, Wilkes Community College, 1988-90; Part-Time Instructor, Danville Community College, 1991-. Publications: Spoken Across a Distance, 1982; Earthcolours, chapbook, 1982; Learning a New Landscape, chapbook, 1987; Fissures, poems, 1993; Poems for children, anthologies: Rhythm Road: Poems to Move To, 1988; Roll Along: Poems on Wheels, 1993; Literary anthologies: Zoo Poems, 1988; Mixed Voices: Contemporary Poems About Music, 1991; Heart of a Flower: Poems for the Sensuous Gardener, 1991; Out of Season, 1993. Contributions to: Metropolitan; Great River Review; Cottonwood; Earth's Daughters; Proof Rock; Visions; Kansas Quarterly; Spoon River Poetry Press; Piedmont Literary Review; River Styx; Connecticut River Review; Plainswoman; Village Idiot; Phoebus; Z Misc; Farmer's Market; Phoenix; Naked Man; Haight Ashbury Literary Journal; Caperock; Crazy Quilt; Midwest Quarterly; KS English; Blue Unicorn; Nebraska; English Journal; Verve. Honours:

Carruth Poetry Contest, University of Kansas, 1983; Great Poets Award, Kansas State Poetry Society, 1989. Address: 1521 College Avenue, Topeka, KS 66604, USA.

PEERADINA Saleem, b. 5 Oct 1944, Bombay, India. Teacher. m. Mumtaz, 11 May 1978, 2 daughters. Education: MA, Bombay University, 1969; MA, Wake Forest University, 1973. Appointments: Director, Open Classroom, Sophia College, Bombay, 1978-84; Copywriter, HTA, Bombay, 1984-87; Visiting Professor to two Michigan Colleges, USA, 1988-89; Assistant Professor of English to Associate Professor of English, Siena Heights College, Michigan, USA, 1989-. Publications: First Offence, 1980; Group Portrait, 1992. Contributions to: Chandrbhaga; Commonwealth Quarterly; Illustrated Weekly; Literary Half-Yearly; Literature East and West; New Quest; Poetry India; Sahitya Akademi Literary Journal; New Letters; Times of India; Voices International; Anthologies: Amerasia; ARC; Oxford Anthology of Modern Indian Poetry; Living in America: Poetry and Fiction by South Asian Writers; Distant Mirrors: America through Foreign Eyes. Honours: Fulbright Travel Grant, 1971; British Council Writer's Grant, 1983. Membership: MLA. Address: 343 Anthony Court, Adrian, MI 49221, USA.

PEGLER Timothy Stuart, b. 26 Sept 1967, Tongala, Victoria, Australia. Journalist. Education: BA, University of Melbourne, 1988. Appointments: Journalist: Suns News Pictorial, 1989-90, Herald-Sun, 1990-91, Weekly Times, 1991-92, Australian Associated Press, 1992, The Age, 1992-. Contributions to: Anthologies: Beneath the Southern Cross; Poetry Day Australia; Magazine: Melbourne University Literary Magazine, Tall Poppies. Honours: Several. Memberships: Melbourne Poetry Society; Victorian Fellowship of Australian Writers. Address: 42 Raphael Street, Abbotsford, Victoria 3067, Australia.

PELC Ryszarda Lidia, b. 20 June 1938, Poland. Writer. m. Karol I Pelc, 24 Sept 1959, 1 son. Education: MA, Literature and Polish Language, University of Wroclaw, 1962. Appointments: Teacher of Polish and European Literature, 1962-85; Librarian, 1962-85; Freelance Writer, 1989-. Publications: Fascinations, Collected Poems, 1989; The Journey, 1989; Somewhere on the Highway, 1990; Watching Seagulls, 1990; The Winter Symphony, 1990; The Vigil, 1991; Lake Biwa, 1996. Contributions to: Lode, Michigan; Peninsula News, Michigan; Panorama, Poland; Przeglad Polski - Weekly Literary Supplement (in Polish); Poems of Great America; American Poetry Annual; American Poetry Anthology. Honours: Certificate of Poetic Achievement, American Poetry Association; Golden Poet Award, 1989, 1990; Certificate of Poetic Achievement, Amherst Society, 1991. Memberships: International Society of Poets, 1991-94; World of Poetry, 1989-91. Address: 390 Lakeview Drive, Hancock, Michigan 49930, USA.

PENDRAGON LE FAY M Malefica Grendelwolf, (Michael L Scarpa), b. 23 Oct 1963. Poet; Playwright; Novelist; Philosopher; Editor; Filmmaker. Appointments: Editor-in-Chief, Excalibur: The Art and Literary Magazine of Jersey City State College, 1988-90; Founder, Current Editor-in-Chief, Publisher, Penny Dreadful: Tales and Poems of Fantastic Terror. Publications: Forthcoming: Much of Madness (novel); Night Magick (play); The Damned (play); Pendragonia (collection of poetry and proverbs); Children of the Night (film screenplay); Blackjack: Twenty-One Pendragonian Grotesques and Arabesques (collection of short stories); Magic Shadow Show: The Metaphysics of Film (college-level textbook); Nocturne: A Symphony of Horror (collection of short stories and poetry), in progress. Contributions to: Poems in: Afterthoughts; Alacrán; The Blue Lady; Delirium; Dragon Dreaming; evernight; Excalibur; Funerary Journal; The Gothic Times; Illya's Honey; The Laureate Letter; Malevolence; The Pannus Index; Penny Dreadful; The Penny Dreadful Review; Pluto's Orchard; Poetry Motel; Portals; Sour Grapes; The Supernatural Magazine; Wyrd; Short stories in: Dragon Dreaming; Excalibur; Grim Commander's Fright Library; Nasty Piece of Work; Penny Dreadful; The Supernatural Magazine. Address: Penny Dreadful, 407 West 50th Street 16, Hell's Kitchen, NY 10019, USA.

PENG Xiang. See: **LI Zhi.**

PENHA James W, b. 1 Feb 1947, New York, New York, USA. Teacher. Education: BA, St John's University, New York, 1967; MA, Pennsylvania State University, 1968; PhD, New York University, 1978. Appointments: Founding Director, The Learning Community, New York, 1969-76; Assistant Dean, St John's University, New York, 1978-85; Assistant Professor of English, St John's University, New

York, 1990-; Director of Planning, University of Detroit, 1985-86; Head, High School English, Hong Kong International School, 1986-89. Publications: Anthologies: Movieworks and American Poetry Confronts the 1990's, both 1990; Back of the Dragon, 1992. Contributions to: Thema; Phoeba; George Mason Review; Hawaii Pacific Review; Bay Windows; Volume Number; Poets On; Lip Service; Slow Dancer; American Land Forum; Impetus; Smackwarm; Taurus; Waterways; San Fernando Poetry Journal; Echoes; Pearl; Milkweed Chronicle; Dark Horse; After Dark; Echoes; Bristlecone; Spectrum; Art Times. Memberships: Poetry Society of America; Poets and Writers; Academy of American Poets; National Writing Project; Teachers and Writers Collaborative; Associated Writing Programmes; Modern Language Association; National Council of Teachers of English. Address: 472 Howard Avenue, 2AA Staten Island, NY 10301, USA.

PENKAL Carolyn Carpenter, b. 22 Nov 1948, Dayton, Ohio, USA. m. Timothy C Penkal, 20 Aug 1982, 1 son, 1 daughter. Appointments: Started writing at High School, in Dayton Daily News, Dayton, Ohio, 1966; Self-publishing own book of poetry, 1996; Attending Writer's Digest School, 1996. Publications: Poetry Press, Celebration of Life, 1996; Quill Books April Anthology, 1996; Amherst Soc, 1996; National Library of Poetry, At Days End, 1994; Sparrowgrass Poetry Forum, Poetic Voices of America, 1996; Poetry Unlimited, Skyline, 1995 & Sweetheart, 1996; JMW Publishing, Rhyme and Reason, 1996. Contributions to: Iliad Press; The Poetry Guild; Creative Arts & Science Ent; Amherst Society; National Library of Poetry; Poets' Guild; Arcadia Poetry Press; Sparrowgrass; International Society of Poet; Poetry Press; Poetry Plus Magazine; Poetry Unlimited; New Castle Courier-Times, New Castle, Indiana. Honours: Special Honour, Poem, Sensitivity, International Society of Poetry Symposium and Convention Marathon Reading, 1994; Creative Arts & Science Poetry, 1994 Editors Choice; Matt Hues 1st Place, 1995; 2nd Place Poetry Unlimited, 1996; Honorable Mention, Iliad Press: Day, poem, 1996, Beyond & Rejoice, poem, 1996. Address: 2910 S CR 850 E, New Castle, IN 47362, USA.

PENWARDEN Andrew John, b. 5 May 1964, London, England. Appointment: Clerk on Government Scheme for Ex-Prisoners over a number of years, restoring ex-offenders to community. Publications: The Girl from Verona, 1995; The Witchfinder General, 1995; The Eye of The Storm, 1996. Contributions to: Ore; The Echo Room; Huddersfield Daily Examiner; Iota; Pennine Platform; The North; The Wide Skirt; Sepia; Poetry Nottingham; Psychopoetica; Inkshed; Krax; Wayfarers; The Third Half; Exiles; The Peoples Poetry; Spook; Symphony; Elim Encounter; Eos; Bifrost. Honours: Mrs Sunderland Annual Poetry Competition, 1995; Runner Up in Pamphlets Competition, 1990. Memberships: Huddersfield Authors Circle. Address: 77 Eldon Road, Marsh, Huddersfield, Yorkshire, England.

PERDIDO Charles. See: **GEROLD Charles.**

PEDRU Charles. See: **GEROLD Charles.**

PEREIRA Teresinka, b. Brazil. Writer; Poet; Professor. m. (1) Heitor Martins, 1968. (2) Pedro Melendez, 1978. (3) Dennis Kann, 1993. 2 sons, 2 daughters. Education: Instituto de Educacao, 1958; BA, Universidade de Minas Gerais, 1960; PhD, University of New Mexico, 1973. Appointments: Instructor of Portuguese, Tulane University, 1962-67; Lecturer of Portuguese, Stanford University, 1968; Visiting Professor, Georgetown University, 1973-74; Assistant Professor of Spanish and Portuguese, University of Colorado, 1975-88, Moorhead State University, 1988-, Bluffton College, 1991-. Publications: Consideracoes Interpretativas de Autores Brasileiros, 1985; Russia: Winter's Poetry, 1985; A Cow on the Sad Plains, 1988; O Absurdo, 1988; A Torre de Mitos, 1972; Trago de Agua Doce, 1987; Back Home, 1995. Contributions to: International Poetry; Revista da Academia Piauiense de Letras; Jornal Ovacion; Brasilia; O Dia; Informe Cultural; Monitor Campista; Arte E Cultura/O Eco do Funchal; el Impulso Literario; Culturales; Jornal de Manha; Confluencia; Poetry; Brasilia; Express Culture. Honours: Poet of the Year, Canadian Society of Poets; Gold Medal for 1st Place Poetry Contest, Brasil; Silver Medal for 2nd Place Poetry Contest, Italy; 1st Place, Poetry Contest, Society of Poets, Portuguese Language, United States; Poet of the Year, Mexico, 1984. Memberships: International Writers and Artists Association; World Poetry Research Institute; Academia Norteamericana de la Lengue Española; Correspondent of Royal Spanish Academy, Committee for Research; Canadian Society of Playwrights. Address: Box 938, Bluffton College, Bluffton, OH 45817, USA.

PEREZ VALIENTE Salvador, b. 24 Jan 1919, Murcia, Spain. m. Viudo. Education: Licentiate, Letters, Philology, Universidad Complutense de Madrid. Appointments: Journalist; Broadcasting Technician; Editor in Chief, Programs for Latin America, and Head of Publications, National Radio of Spain; Professor of Literature. Publications: Gutierre de Cetina, 1942; Cuando ya no hay remedio, 1947; Libro de Elche, 1949; Por tercera vez, 1953; Lo mismo de siempre, 1960; No amanece, 1962; Volcan, 1965; El que busca, 1973; La tarde a perros, 1976; Con odio, con temor, con ira, 1977; La memoria, ese olvido, 1984; Asi en la tierra, 1988; Que trata de un amor, 1992. Contributions to: Numerous journals. Honours: 2nd Prize, Adonais, Madrid, 1952; Polo de Medina, Murcia, 1962; Francisco de Quevedo, Madrid, 1976; Angaro Seville, 1987; Tomas Morales, Las Palmas; The main street of Fortuna, a small town in Murcia, is named after him: Calle del poeta Salvador Perez Valiente; 12 Prizes at meetings of Juegos Florales. Memberships: Sociedad General de Autores; Asociacion de la Prensa de Madrid; Prometeo Poetry Association. Address: Quintana 22, 28008 Madrid, Spain.

PERLMAN John N(iels), b. 13 May 1946, Alexandria, Virginia, USA. Poet; Teacher. m. Janis Hadobas, 26 May 1967, 1 daughter. Education: BA, Ohio State University, 1969; MS, Iona College, 1981. Appointments: Teacher in schools in Minnesota, Georgia, California, New York. Publications: Kachina, 1971; Three Years Rings, 1972; Dinner 650 Warburton Avenue, 1973; Notes Toward a Family, 1975; The Hudson: A Weave, 1976; Nicole, 1976; Self Portrait, 1976; Swath, 1978; Homing, 1981; Powers, 1982; A Wake of, 1983; Longtrail, 1985; Beacons Imaging Within as Promises, 1990; Imperatives of Address, 1992; Anacoustic, 1993. Honours: Academy of American Poets Awards; New York Foundation for the Arts Fellowship; Vanderwater Prize. Address: 29 Lynton Place, White Plains, NY 10606, USA.

PERRIE Walter, b. 5 June 1949, Lanarkshire, Scotland. Author; Poet; Critic; Travel-Writer. Education: MA (Hons), Mental Philosophy, University of Edinburgh, 1975; MPhil, English Studies, University of Stirling, 1989. Appointments: Editor, Chapman, 1970-73; Scottish-Canadian Exchange Fellow, University of British Columbia, 1984-85; Managing Editor, Margin - International Arts Quarterly, 1985-90; Stirling Writing Fellow, University of Stirling, 1991. Publications: Poem on a Winter Night, 1976; A Lamentation for the Children, 1977; By Moon and Sun, 1980; Concerning the Dragon, 1984; Thirteen Lucky Poems, 1991; From Milady's Wood and Other Poems, 1996. Contributions to: Lines Review; New Edinburgh Review; Chapman; Margin; Cencrastus. Honours: Three Scottish Arts Council Writers Bursaries, 1976, 1983, 1994; Eric Gregory Award, 1978; Scottish Arts Council Book Award, 1978; Ingram - Merrill Foundation Award, 1987. Memberships: PEN, Scotland; Society of Authors. Address: 10 Croft Place, Dunning PH2 0SB, Scotland.

PERRIMAN Wendy K(aren), b. 9 July 1958, Stamford, Lincolnshire, England. Teacher; Poet. m. Steven, 8 Aug 1981, 1 son. Education: BA, Honours, Lancaster University, 1979; PGCE, Bristol University, 1980. Appointments: Secondary School Teacher, English and Drama: Dagenham, London, 1980-81, Cornwall School, Dortmund, West Germany, 1981-83, King's School, Gutersloh, West Germany, 1983-85; Head, English and Drama Department, Southampton, Hampshire, England, 1989-94; Poet, USA, 1994-. Publications: Collected Experience, 1996. Contributions to: Poet Magazine; Illyas Honey; Feelings Magazine; In Vein Magazine; Goldfrich. Honours: Honorable Mention, Rhymed Poem, Writer's Digest, 1995; Honorable Mention, John David Johnson Memorial Poetry Award, Poet Magazine, 1995. Memberships: Poetry Society of America; The Academy of American Poets; The International Women's Writing Guild; Women Who Write, New Jersey, Group Co-ordinator and Board Member. Address: P O Box 53, Madison, NJ 07940-0053, USA.

PERRIN Arnold S, b. 26 Nov 1932, Lynn, Massachusetts, USA. Corrections Officer, Maine State Prison. m. Jacquelyn Tucker, 17 Jan 1953, 5 daughters. Education: BE, Plymouth State College of the University of New Hampshire, 1965; Graduate Work: Dartmouth College, 1966, University of Maine at Augusta, 1987. Appointments: Secondary Teacher of English and History; Editor, Publisher, Wings Press; Poetry Editor, New England Sampler. Publications: The Wind's Will, 1979; View From Hill Cabin, 1979; The Essentials of Writing Poetry, 1991; Signs and Seasons, 1991; Noah, 1993; Speaking Inuit, 1994. Contributions to: Maine Life; Christian Science Monitor; Puckerbrush Review; Kennebec; Potato Eyes. Memberships: Maine Writers & Publishers Alliance; Board Member, The Live Poets Society, Rockland, Maine. Address: PO Box 809, Union, ME 04862, USA.

PERRUCCI Christy Lynn, b. 17 July 1973, Abington, Pennsylvania, USA. Poet; Claim Processor; Respite Caregiver. Education: Graduate, William Tennent High School, 1991. Appointments: Claim Processor, Prudential Insurance, 1991-; Caregiver for individuals with developmental disabilities, Indian Creek Foundation, 1996-. Publication: Seasons Of The Heart, Volume 1, 1996. Contributions to: Literary magazines: Poet's Review; The Inspirational Poet; Hayden's Poetry Review; Anthologies: Treasured Poems of America; Anthology of Christian Poetry; The Rainbow's End. Honours: Many honorable mentions; 3rd Prize, Poet's Review, 1995; Outstanding Top Twenty, Cameo Awards, 1996. Address: 274 Henry Avenue, Warminster, PA 18974-4114, USA.

PERRY Colin Ian Henry, b. 4 July 1955, England. State Registered Chiropodist and Podiatrist. m. Agnes Myriam Marcelle, 29 July 1989, 1 son. Education: BSc, Leicester University; Diploma of Podiatric Medicine. Appointments: Independent Practitioner. Publications: Little Things Mean a Lot, 1976; Sliding Magnets, 1982. Contributions to: Another Wing, anthology; Guernsey Press. Membership: Poetry Society. Address: Eastwood, 9 Mount Row, St Peter Port, Guernsey, Channel Islands.

PERRY Marion Judith Helz, b. 2 June 1943, Takoma Park, Maryland, USA. Poet; Professor. m. Franklyn A H Perry, 17 July 1971, 1 son, 1 daughter. Education: BA, 1964; MA, 1966; MFA, 1969; MA, 1979; PhD, 1986. Appointments: Instructor, West Library State College; Instructor, Albright College; Lecturer, State University of New York; Lecturer, Empire State College; Associate Professor, Erie Community College; Professor, Erie Community College. Publications: Icarus, 1980; The Mirror's Image, 1981; Establishing Intimacy, 1982; Dishes, 1989. Contributions to: Footwoork; Esprit; Golden Fleece. Honours: College Arts, 1967; New Gallery, 1980; All Nations Poetry Contests, 1980, 1981. Memberships: Poetry Society of America; Poets and Writers. Address: Erie Community College-South, 4140 Southwestern Boulevard, Orchard Park, NY 14127, USA.

PERRY Ruth, b. 14 Jan 1938, Baltimore, Maryland, USA. Writer. Widow, 1 son. Education: English major, Morgan State College, 1954-57; Honour Student, Cortez Peters Business School, 1960-62. Appointments: Writer; Lyricist. Publications: Poem in Writers' Line, Peace, The Quiet Voice, in Canada. 1985; Poetry Anthologies, 1985, 1986, 1987. Contributions to: Poetry Society of America; Discovery Publishing, children's poetry; Iliad Press, Troy, Michigan; Sewanee Poetry, Florence, Alabama. Honours: 16 Merit Certificates, World of Poetry, Sacramento; 10 Golden Poets Awards, World of Poetry. Memberships: Poetry Society of America; World of Poetry; International Society of Poets. Address: 6713 Ransome Drive, Baltimore, MD 21207, USA.

PERRY HILDEBRAND Mary-Elizabeth, b. 23 Feb 1918, New York, New York, USA. Teacher; Poet; Editor; Publisher. m. (1) John Perry, 25 June 1939, (2) Bert Hildebrand, 6 Nov 1984, 3 sons, 1 daughter. Education: BS, Columbia University, 1967; MA, Teacher's College, Columbia University, 1970. Appointments: Teacher, Drama, English Spanish, 1967-80; Editor, Poetry Magazine, 1986-; Publisher, 1986-; Treasurer for the National League of American Penwomen, 1995-96. Publications: Pegasus, 1986-96; Olé, Olé, 1990; Elizabeth Perry; Gathered Echoes: Book of Poetry, 1992. Contributions to: Archer; Interim; Midwest Poetry Review; Orphic Lute; Parnassus; Pegasus; Penwoman; Reflect; Silver Wings; IRP Review; Las Vegas Sun; Las Vegas Review Journal; One Down, Eight to Go; Cat's Meow, Anthology, 1995. Honours: Distinguished Women of Southern Nevada, 1989, 1990, 1991; Distinguished Women of Southern Nevada, 1995; First Prize, Literary Contest sponsored by National League of American Pen Women, 1995. Memberships: Poetry Society of America; Poets and Writers; Pen Women; Small Press Centre; National League of American Pen Women. Address: 525 Avenue B, Boulder City, NV 89005, USA.

PERSON Stanley Thomas (Tom), b. 7 Oct 1952, Seattle, Washington, USA. Editor. m. Frances Louise Schroeder, 17 Feb 1990. Education: BA, Education and English, Western Washington University, 1974; AA, Music, Shoreline Community College. Appointments: Editor: Laughing Bear Press, 1976-, Laughing Bear Newsletter, 1976-, Laughing Bear, Literary Magazine, 1976-78; Faculty Advisor, Spindrift, Shoreline Community College, 1977-79. Contributions to: Iron; Interstate; Ghost Dance; Nexus; Telephone; Happiness Holding Tank; Rocky Mountain Arsenal of The Arts;

Northwest Review; New York Quarterly. Membership: COSMEP. Address: PO Box 36159, Denver, CO 80236, USA.

PERU Cass. See: **MACLEOD N(orma) J(ean).**

PERUMAL I R, b. 25 July 1952, Injimedu, India. Indian Administrative Service. m. Lalitha Perumal, 13 Sept 1978, 1 son, 1 daughter. Education: MA, 1974; IAS, 1982. Publications: Hasuvina Lokha, 1991; Kannir Kanavu; Pidi Sabam. Contributions to: Poet; Dinasudar; Sanjayvani. Membership: Poet. Address: No 6 Madras Bank Road, Bangalore 560 001, India.

PERVIN Alice. See: **LIST Anneliese. S**

PETERFREUND Stuart Samuel, b. 30 June 1945, Brooklyn, New York, USA. Professor and Chair of English. m. Carol Jean Litzler, 12 Sept 1981, 1 daughter. Education: AB, Cornell University, 1966; MFA, University of California at Irvine, 1968; PhD, University of Washington, Seattle, 1974. Appointments: Assistant Professor of English, University of Arkansas at Little Rock, 1975-78; Northeastern University: Assistant Professor of English, 1978-82, Associate Professor of English, 1982-91, Professor and Chair of English, 1991-. Publications: The Hanged Knife and Other Poems, 1970; Harder Than Rain, 1977; Interstatements, 1986. Contributions to: Worcester Review; Images; Cincinnati Poetry Review; New Orleans Review and others. Honours: First Prize, Writers Digest Contest, Poetry Division, 1970; First Prize, Worcester County Poetry Association Contest, 1989. Memberships: Numerous. Address: Department of English - 406 HO, Northeastern University, 360 Huntington Avenue, Boston, MA 02115, USA.

PETERKIEWICZ Jerzy, b. 29 Sept 1916. Novelist; Poet; Professor of Polish Language and Literature. Education: University of Warsaw; MA, University of St Andrews, 1944; PhD, King's College, London, 1947. Appointments: Freelance Writer to 1950; Lecturer then Reader in Polish Language and Literature, School of Slavonic and East European Studies, 1952-72; Head of Department of East European Languages and Literature, 1972-77; Professor of Polish Language and Literature, University of London, 1972-79. Publications: Prowincja, 1936; Wiersze i poematy, 1938; Pogrzeb Europy, 1946; The Knotted Cord, 1953; Loot and Loyalty, 1955; Polish Prose and Verse, 1956; Antologia liryki angielskiej, 1958; Future to Let, 1958; Isolation, 1959; Co-Author, Five Centuries of Polish Poetry, 1960, enlarged edition, 1970; The Quick and the Dead, 1961; That Angel Burning at My Left Side, 1963; Poematy londynskie, 1965; Inner Circle, 1966; Green Flows the Bile, 1969; The Other Side of Silence, The Poet at the Limits of Language, 1970; The Third Adam, 1975; Editor and Translator, Easter Vigil and Other Poems, by Karol Wojtyla (Pope John Paul II), 1979; Kula magiczna (Poems 1934-52), 1980; Editor and Translator, Collected Poems by Karol Wojtyla (Pope John Paul II), 1982; Poezje Wybrane (Selected Poems), 1986; Literatura polska w perspektywie europejskiej (Polish Literature in its European context; essays translated from English), 1986; Wiersze dobrzynskie (early poems), 1994; The Place Within: The Poetry of Pope John Paul II, 1994, 1995. Contributions to: Various periodicals including: Poetry Quarterly; Botteghe Oscure; Times Literary Supplement; Encounter; Kultura; Tablet; Also Radio Plays for BBC Radio 3. Address: 7 Lyndhurst Terrace, London NW3 5QA, England.

PETERS Lenrie, b. 1 Sept 1932, Bathurst, Gambia. Education: BA, Trinity College, Cambridge, 1955; University College Hospital, London. Appointments: Surgeon, Victoria Hospital, Gambia, 1969-72; Surgeon in private practice, Gambia, 1972-. Publications: Poems, 1964; Satellites, 1967; Katchikali, 1971; Selected Poetry, 1981; Novel: The Second Round, 1965. Contributions to: Many anthologies. Address: Westfield Clinic, PO Box 142, Banjul, Gambia.

PETERS Robert Louis, b. 20 Oct 1924, Wisconsin, USA. Professor of English; Poet. Div, 3 sons, 1 dec, 1 daughter. Education: BA, 1948, MA, 1949, PhD, 1952, University of Wisconsin, Madison. Appointments: Teaching Assistant, University of Wisconsin, 1950-52; Instructor of English, University of Idaho, 1952-53, and Boston University, 1953-55; Assistant Professor of English, Ohio Wesleyan University, 1955-58; Associate Professor of English, Wayne State University, 1958-63; Professor of English, University of California, Riverside, 1963-68, and Irvine, 1968-. Publications: The Drowned Man to the Fish, 1978; Picnic in The Snow: Ludwig of Bavaria, 1982; What Dillinger Meant To Me, 1983; Hawker, 1984; Kane, 1985; Ludwig of Bavaria: Poems and a Play, 1986; The Blood Countess: Poems and a Play, 1987; Haydon, 1988; Brueghel's Pigs, 1989; Poems: Selected and New, 1992; Goodnight Paul: Poems, 1992; Snapshots for a Serial Killer: A Fiction and Play, 1992; Zapped: 2 Novellas, 1993; Nell: A Woman from Eagle River, 1994; Lili Marlene: A Memoir of WWII, 1995. Editions: Victorians in Literature and Art, 1961; Co-author, The Letters of John Addington Symonds, 3 volumes, 1967-69; Gabriel: A Poem by John Addington Symonds, 1974; The Collected Poems of Amnesia Glasscock: John Steinbeck, 1977; Letters to a Tutor: The Tennyson Family Letters to Henry Graham Dakyns, 1988. Honours: Guggenheim Fellowship, 1966-67; Fellowship to Yaddo, MacDowell Colony, and Ossabaw Island Project, 1973-74; National Endowment for the Arts Grant, 1974; Nominee for Senior Fellowship, National Endowment for the Arts, 1989. Memberships: PEN; Writers' Guild; Trustee, American Society for Aesthetics, 1965-68; Contributing Editor, American Book Review, 1976-, Small Press Review, 1973-. Address: 9431 Krepp Drive, Huntington Beach, CA 92646, USA.

PETERSON John. See: **BALON Brett John Steven.**

PETRIE Paul James, b. 1 July 1928, Detroit, Michigan, USA. Retired Professor of English. m. Sylvia Spencer, 21 Aug 1954, 1 son, 2 daughters. Education: BA, Wayne State University, 1950; MA, Wayne State University, 1951; PhD, University of Iowa, 1957. Appointments: Associate Professor, Peru State University, 1958-59; Instructor to Professor, University of Rhode Island, 1959-90. Publications: Confessions of a Non-Conformist, 1963; The Race With Time and the Devil, 1965; From Under the Hill of Night, 1969; The Academy of Goodbye, 1974; Light From the Furnace Rising, 1978; Not Seeing is Believing, 1983; Strange Gravity, 1985; The Runners, 1988. Contributions to: America; American Scholar; Antioch Review; Atlantic; Chicago Review; Colorado Quarterly; Commonweal; Epoch; Esquire; Harvard Magazine; Hudson Review; The Kansas Quarterly; Literary Review; Massachusetts Review; Michigan Quarterly; Nation; New England Review; New Republic; New Yorker; New York Times; Paris Review; Poetry; The Sewanee Review; Southern Review; Stand; Virginia Quarterly Review. Honours: Phi Beta Kappa Poet, Brown University, 1968; Scholarly Achievement Award, University of Rhode Island, 1983; Capricorn Award, Writers Voice, West Side YMCA, 1984; Catholic Press Award, 1985; Wayne State University Arts Achievement Award, 1990. Address: 200 Dendron Road, Peace Dale, RI 02879, USA.

PETRUCCI Mario B, b. 29 Nov 1958, Waterloo, London, England. Research Physicist and Engineer; Teacher. Education: Degree in Physics and Theoretical Physics, 1980; MA, Selwyn College, Cambridge, 1983; Teaching Qualification, London, 1981; PhD, Optoelectronic Materials, Department of Electronics and Electrical Engineering, London University, 1989. Appointments: Teacher, Latymer School, 1981-84; Research Assistant, (Post Doctoral), University of London, 1987-89; Senior Scientist, British Gas Research, 1991-93; Co-Founder, Bound Spiral Magazine. Publications: Anthologies: Conventicle I, Conventicle II, 1987, 1988; Contemporary Christian Poetry, 1990; Envoi Summer Anthology, 1990; Booklets: Mr Bass, 1989; Departures, 1989; Shrapnel and Sheets, 1996. Contributions to: Owl; New Welsh Review; Iron; Coal City Review; Poetry Nottingham; Poetry and Audience; Staple; Foolscap; Sepia; Outposts; Working Titles; Poetry London Newsletter; Acumen; Bete Noire; Smith's Knoll; Envoi; Cobweb. Honours: 3rd Prize, 5th National Convention of Poets and Small Presses, 1989; 2nd Prize, Swanage Arts Festival Poetry Competition, 1990; 1st Prize, Southwest Poetry Competition, 1991; 3rd Prize, First Verse, International Open Poetry Competition, 1992; Winner of London Writers Competition, 1993; Winner, West Sussex Competition, 1993; Winner, Salisbury Competition, 1993; Runner-Up, Sheffield Thursday Competition, 1994; PBS Recommendation, 1996. Memberships: Blue Nose Poets, Organiser, Core Member; Friends of Arvon; Colours Poetry Group, Core Member; Conventicle Poets, Core Member, -1991; Poetry Society, -1991; Co-Founder, The Bound Spiral Magazine. Address: 72 First Avenue, Bush Hill Park, Enfield, Middlesex EN1 1BW, England.

PETTET Simon, b. 6 Nov 1953. Poet. m. Rose Feliu. Education: BA, University of Essex, 1976; MA, University of London, 1977. Appointments: Lecturer at Stevens Institute of Technology, Rutgers University, New School for Social Research, St Marks, Poetry Project and elsewhere, New York, 1977-. Publications: Lyrical Poetry, 1988; Twenty One Love, 1991; Conversations with Rudy Burckhardt, 1988; Talking Pictures, with Rudy Burckhardt, 1994; Selected Poems, 1995. Contributions to: Numerous magazines on both sides of the Atlantic. Memberships: Co-Founder and Administrative Coordinator, Committee

for International Poetry. Address: Apartment 6, 437 East 12th Street, Apt 6, New York, NY 10009, USA.

PETTIT Stephen Lewis Ingham, b. 25 Feb 1921. Company Director; Poet; Anthologist; Historian. 1 daughter. Education: The College, Brighton; RAF College, Cranwell. Appointments: Commission in RAF VR, Pilot; Now Retired; Underwriting Member, Lloyds of London, 1980-. Publications: The Peregrine Instant, 1967; In the Deserts of Time, 1969; For a Moment of Time; Arthur, King of the Britons; Anthology of the Wye Valley, 1972; Today, Upon the Thought-Screen; Omar Khayyam, the Enigma and the Way; Threnody for the Children of the Sun; Land of the Shining Waters; The Elusive Muse; I, Quetzalcoatl; Discovering, At Last, King Arthur - The Reality Behind the Legends, 1995. Contributions to: A/W Review; Poesie Vivante, Geneva; Quill; Breakthru; Platform; Scrip; Expression One; Rainbow; Candelabrum; Viewpoints; Envoi; Manuscript; Several anthologies. Honours: Wilfrid M Appleby Cup; Dr Olive Lamming Memorial Award; Plus, various Certificates of Merit and minor prizes; Sovereign's Commendation for Valuable Service in the air. Memberships: President, Poetry Society of Cheltenham; Founder Fellow, International Poetry Society; Isle of Man Literary Society; Isle of Man Northern Writers Association; Royal Institute of Philosophy, London. Address: The Old Vicarage, May Hill, Ramsey, Isle of Man IM8 2EG, British Isles.

PETTY William Henry, b. 7 Sept 1921, Bradford, Yorkshire, England. Educator; School Governor. m. Margaret Elaine Bastow, 31 May 1948, 1 son, 2 daughters. Education: Bradford Grammar School, 1931-40; Peterhouse, Cambridge, 1940-41;, 1945; MA, Cantab, 1950; BSc, London, 1953; D Litt, Kent, 1983. Appointments: Administrative, Teaching and Lecturing Posts in London, Doncaster, North and West Ridings of Yorkshire, Kent, 1945-73; Chief Education Officer for Kent, 1973-84; Various Voluntary Posts in Education. Publications: No Bold Comfort, 1957; Conquest, 1967; Poems in various anthologies, 1954-96; Springfield: Pieces of the Past, 1994; Genius Loci (with Robert Roberts), 1995. Contributions to: Acumen; Agenda; Ambit; Ariel; English; Envoi; Delta; Foolscap; Frogmore Papers; Iota; New Poems; North; Northern Echo; Orbis; Other Poetry; Outposts; Poetry and Audience; Poetry Review; Poetry South-East; Poetry Business; Poetry Nottingham; Review of English Literature; Rialto; Spectator; Seam; Scrip; Staple; Sunday Times; Tomorrow; Transatlantic Review; Twentieth Century; Yorkshire Life; York Poetry; Yorkshire Post; Zebra; Also the BBC; Castle Poets; Chequer; Community of Poets; Isthmus; South-East Review; Truth. Honours: Commander of the Order of the British Empire, 1981; Prizes: Cheltenham Festival of Literature, 1968; Camden Festival of Music and the Arts, 1969; Greenwood Prize (Poetry Society), 1978; Lake Aske Memorial Award, 1980; Swanage Festival of Literature, 1995; The Ali Competition, 1995; Kent Federation of Writers Prize, 1995. Membership: Poetry Society. Address: Willow Bank, Moat Road, Headcorn, Kent TN27 9NT, England.

PFEIFFER Jeanne, b. 13 Mar 1962, Redwood City, California, USA. Manufacturing Associate. m. Mark D Pfeiffer, 10 Dec 1981, 2 daughters. Education: Youngstown State University; Cleveland State University; Kent State University. Appointments: Technicare, Lead Person; Rockwell Automation, Allen Bradley, Manufacturing Associate. Publications: And Time Stood Still, 1994; A View from the Edge, 1992; Dusting off Dreams, 1995. Contributions to: Twinsburg Connection; Data Highway. Honours: Honorable Mention from Hollywood Famous Poets Soc, 1995; Editor's Choice Award, National Poetry Association, 1993. Membership: National Poetry Assocation. Address: 8227 Clover Lane, Garresttsville, OH 44231, USA.

PHILLIPS H(erbert) I(vor Leason), b. 18 Mar 1913, London, England. Dental Surgeon. m. 28 Sept 1940, 1 son, 1 daughter. Education: Mainly self taught; Regent Street Polytechnic; Chelsea Polytechnic, 1931-34; Diploma Dental Surgery 1940, Dings College Hospital, Dental School, London University. Appointments: School Dentist: East Sussex, 1940-41,Dorset, 1941-47; Fire Leader AFS, Poole, 1941-47; Community Dental Surgeon, LCC, London, 1947-49; Private Practice, Cheam, Surrey, 1949-74; Retired at 61 to write poetry, novels and plays. Contributions to: Daily Mail; Observer; Outposts; Poetry Review; Envoi. Membership: Poetry Society. Address: 15 Sandy Lane, Cheam, Sutton, Surrey SM2 7NU, England.

PHILLIPS Judith Irene, (Judith Irene Tucker), b. 15 Oct 1948, Coose Bay, Oregon, USA. Cattle Rancher; Antique Dealer; Writer; Poet. m. John Valis Tucker, 21 Dec 1982, 1 son. Education: Study of

Psychology, Lane Community College. Appointments: Teacher, Dehydration of Food Products, 7 years; Lecturer, Nutrition; Demonstrator, Therapeutic Exercises. Publications: Award Winning Poetry by Judith I Tucker, 1986; Poems included in: Our World's Best Loved Poems, 1984; Sunshine and Shadows, A Thousand Onward Years, 1985; Our Western World's Most Beautiful Poems, 1985; Visions of Mine, 1986; Lyrical Classics, 1987. Contributions to: Impressions, A Collection of Poetry, 1986; New York Foundation Anthology, 1986; World Poetry Anthology, 1987; Treasured Poems for Young and Old: Cambridge Collection, 1987; Reach for the Stars, A Suwanne Poetry Book, 1987; North American Poetry Review, 1987; Chasing Rainbows, Vol VIII, 1988; National Library of Poetry: Whispers in the Wind, 1993; Tears of Fire, 1993; Outstanding Poets of 1994; After the Storm, 1995. Honours: 23 Awards of Merit Certificates; 6 Golden Poet Awards; 1 Silver Poet Award; 6 Editor's Choice Awards; 2 Women's Inner Circle of Achievement Awards; 1 Woman of the Year Award, 1992; 1 International Cultural Diploma of Honor Award; 2 Gold Medals for Literary Work from the USA. Memberships: World Poetry Society; Poet International. Address: 1387 Romie Howard Road, Yoncalla, OR 97499, USA.

PHILLIPS Michael Joseph, b. 2 Mar 1937, Indianapolis, Indiana, USA. Poet. Education: Purdue University, 1955-56; University of Edinburgh, 1957-58, 1959-60; Alliance Française, 1958; BA, Cum Laude, Wabash College, 1959; MA, Indiana University, 1964; PhD, Indiana University, 1971. Appointments: Lecturer in English, University of Wisconsin 1970, 1971; Instructor in English, Free University of Indianapolis, 1973; Lecturer in English, Indiana University-Purdue University, 1973-78; Instructor, Free University at Indianapolis, 1977-79; Visiting Fellow, Harvard University, 1976-77. Publications include: Libretto for 23 Poems, 1968; Kinetics and Concretes, 1971; The Concrete Book, 1971; 8 Page Poems, 1971; Love, Love, Love, 1975; Visual Sequences, 1975; Abstract Poems, 1978; Underworld Love Poems, 1979; Erotic Concrete Sonnets for Samantha, 1979; Edwin Muir, (criticism), 1979; Selected Love Poems, 1980; Bebop Buets, 1982; Indy Dolls, 1982; Superbeuts, 1983; Selected Concrete Poems, 1986; Dreamgirls, 1989; The Poet of Mythmaker, (criticism), 1990; 11 Poems, 1992; Over 1500 poems. Contributions to: Anthologies and periodicals. Memberships: Modern Language Association of America; American Comparative Literature Association; Society for the Study of Midwestern Literature; Midwest Modern Language Association; Phi Beta Kappa; Mensa. Address: 238 North Smith Road, Springmill, Apt 25, Bloomington, IN 47408, USA.

PHILLIPS Robert Schaeffer, b. 2 Feb 1938, Milford, Milford Delaware, USA. Advertising Executive. m. Judith Anne Bloomingdale, 16 June 1962, 1 son. Education: BA, 1960, MA, 1962, Syracuse University. Appointments: Copywriter, Benton & Bowles, 1963-68; Creative Supervisor, McCann-Erickson, 1968-70; Vice President, Grey Advertising, 1970-78, 1988-, J Walter Thompson, 1980-88; Creative Director, Thompson-Koch, 1978-80. Publications: 8 & 8, 1960; 4 More, 1961; Inner Weather, 1966; The Pregnant Man, 1978; Running on Empty, 1981; Personal Accounts: New and Selected Poems, 1966-1986, 1986; The Wounded Angel, 1987; Public Landing Revisited: Stories, 1992. Contributions to: New Yorker; Hudson Review; Paris Review; Encounter; Partisan Review; Nation; New Republic; Confrontation; Boulevard; Southwest Review; Ontario Review; Poetry; Poets Now; Manhattan Review; Manhattan Poetry Review; New American Review; New Letters; New Mexican Quarterly; Western Humanities Review; South Dakota Review. Honours: Creative Artists' Public Service Award, 1978; Yaddo Fellowships, 1980, 1982; American Academy and Institute of Arts and Letters, 1987; MacDowell Colony Fellowship, 1987; Arents Pioneer Medal, Syracuse University, 1988. Memberships: American PEN Centre; Poets and Writers; Poets' House; The Players National Book Critics' Circle; Authors Guild; American Society of Composers, Authors and Publishers; Wesleyan Writers' Conference Board; Syracuse University Library Associates. Address: Box AF, Katonah, NY 10536, USA.

PHILLIS Yannis A, b. 27 Mar 1950, Greece. Professor. m. Nili Boren, 1 son, 1 daughter. Education: Diploma, National Technical University of Athens, 1973; MS, 1978, Engineering Degree, 1979, PhD, 1980, University of California at Los Angeles. Appointments: Research Assistant, 1977-78, Teaching Associate, 1978-80, University of California at Los Angeles; Assistant Professor, Boston University, 1980-86; Associate Professor, 1986-89, Professor, 1989-, Technical University of Crete. Publications: Starting in Nafplion, 1975; Arctic Zone, 1976; Zarathustra and the Five Vespers, 1985; Beyond the Symplegades, 1991. Contributions to: Harbor Review, USA; Beacon

Review, USA; Stone Country, USA. Honours: Ministry of Culture and Sciences, 1976; Best Book Award, Writers Union, Athens, 1986; Rector, Technical University of Crete, 1993-. Membership: Poets and Writers, USA. Address: Technical University of Crete, Department of Production Engineering and Management, Chania 73100, Greece.

PICKARD Thomas Mariner (Tom), b. 7 Jan 1946, Newcastle-upon-Tyne, England. Freelance Director of Films; Independent Producer. m. 21 July 1978, 2 sons, 1 daughter. Publications: High on The Walls, 1968; Order of Chance, 1972; Guttersnipe, 1971; Dancing Under Fire, 1972; Hero Dust, 1979; Jarrow March, 1982; Custom and Exile, 1987; We Make Ships, 1989. Honours: S D Lewis Fellowship, 1976; Creative Writing Fellowship, Warwick University, 1979-80. Memberships: Co-Founder and Director, Mordern Tower Poetry Readings, Newcastle-upon-Tyne, 1964-75; Organiser, New World Poetry Reading Series, London, 1976-82. Address: c/o Judy Daish Associates Ltd, 2 St Charles Place, London W10 6EG, England.

PICKFORD Stuart, b. 4 Mar 1963, Kent, England. Teacher. Contributions to: Poetry Review; Outposts; Bete Noire; Honest Ulsterman; Foolscap; Staple; The Pen. Honour: Eric Gregory Award. Address: 9 Duchy Grove, Harrogate, North Yorkshire HG2 0ND, England.

PIERCE Richard Alistair Burnett, (Peter Moonraker), b. 14 Apr 1944, Chippenham, Wiltshire, England. Lecturer; Writer; Photographer. m. 14 May 1978. Education: 2nd Class Honours Degree, Sociology with Research, University of Bath, 1986; Postgraduate studies, British Institute, Florence; FAETC; APGCE; MRAI. Appointments: Home Civil Service, EO, MPBW and Land Commission, 1966-69; Insurance Broker, Noble Lowndes/Lowndes Lambert, 1969-80; Mature Student, CTC and University of Bath, 1980-86; Avon CC Lecturer, 1987-90; Access P & W Services, 1991-. Publications: Emergence, 1961; Soundings, 1962; A Radio for You, 1987. Contributions to: Envoi; Countryman; New Statesman; Tribune; Poetry Nottingham; Voice of Youth, Poetry Society; West Coast Review; Venue; Observer; Daily Mail; Wiltshire Gazette and Herald; Off Campus; Sunday Times. Honours: Eisteddfodd, 1960-61; Runner-Up, Bridport, 1980; Prize and Anthology, Bedford Poetry Society, 1988; Runner-Up, Orbis Rhyme Revival, 1990. Memberships: Press Officer, Bath Literary Society, 1987-; Poetry Society; Associate Member, PEN, 1989-; Playwrights' Company; Bath Photographic Society; Bath University Court, 1989-; Friends of Bath Festival; Friends of Arvon. Address: 8 Wedmore Avenue, Chippenham, Wiltshire SN15 1QP, England.

PIERCY Marge, b. 31 Mar 1936, Detroit, Michigan, USA. Poet; Novelist; Essayist. m. 2 June 1982. Education: AB, University of Michigan, 1957; MA, Northwestern University, 1958. Appointments: Poetry Workshop, Cumberland Valley Writers Conference, Vanderbilt University, Tennessee, 1981; Visiting Faculty, Women's Writers Conference, Hartwick College, Oneonta, New York, 1979, 1981, 1984; Master Class in Poetry, Omega Institute, 1990; Advanced Poetry Workshop, Omega Institute, 1991; Poetry Editor, Tikkun Magazine, 1988-; DeRoy Distinguished Visiting Professor, University of Michigan, 1992; University of North Dakota Writers Conference, 1995; Florida Suncoast Writers' Conference, 1996; Many more lectures, readings, given at various workshops in USA and around the world. Publications: To Be of Use, 1973; Living in the Open, 1976; The Twelve-Spoked Wheel Flashing, 1978; The Moon is Always Female, 1980; Circles on the Water: Selected Poems, 1982; Stone, Paper, Knife, 1983; My Mother's Body, 1985; Available Light, 1988; Mars and Her Children, 1992; Editor: The Longings of Women, 1994; Editor: Early Ripening, 1988; Parti-Coloured Block for A Quilt, Poets on Poetry Series, 1982; The Eight Chambers of the Heart: Selected Poems, 1995. Contributions to: An extensive list of newspapers, magazines and journals. Honours: Literature Award, Governor's Commission on the Status of Women, (Massachusetts); Rhode Island School of Design Faculty Association Medal; Carolyn Kizer Poetry Prize, Calapoova College, 1986, 1990; Sheaffer-PEN/New England Award for Literary Excellence; Honorary Doctor of Letters: Lesley College, Bridgewater State College; Golden Rose; May Sarton Award, New England Poetry Club, 1991; Brit ha-Dorot Award, Shalom Centre, 1992; Arthur C Clarke Award, Best Science Fiction, United Kingdon, 1992. Memberships: Authors Guild; Authors League; PEN; Poetry Society of America; National Writers' Union; Israeli Centre for the Arts; American Poetry Centre; New England Poetry Club. Address: Box 1473, Wellfleet, MA 02667, USA.

PIERPOINT Katherine Mary, b. 16 Aug 1961, Northampton, England. Writer. Education: BA, Honours, Modern Languages, University of Exeter, 1984. Appointment: Writer. Publication: Truffle Beds, 1995. Contributions to: New Yorker; Rialto; The Independent; Sunday Times. Honours: Hawthornden International Creative Writing Fellowship, 1993; John Downes/Oppenheim Award, 1994; Somerset Maughan Award, 1996; Sunday Times Young Writers of the Year, 1996. Memberships: Poetry Society; Society of Authors. Address: c/o Left Bank, 17 North Street, Mears Ashby, Northampton NN6 0DW, England.

PILLING Christopher (Robert), b. 20 April 1936, Birmingham, England. Poet; m. Sylvia, 6 Aug 1960, 1 son, 2 daughters. Education: BA Hons, University of Leeds, 1954-57; Diploma, Institut D'Etudes Françaises, Université de Poitiers, 1955; Certificate of Education, Loughborough College, 1958-59. Appointments: Teacher of French and Physical Education, 1959-73; Head of Modern Languages, Knottingley High School, 1973-78; Reviewer, Times Literary Supplement, 1973-74; Tutor, Newcastle University, Department of Adult Education, 1978-80; Head of French, Keswick School, 1980-88. Publications: Snakes and Girls, 1970; In all the Spaces on all the Lines, 1971; Foreign Bodies, 1992; Cross Your Legs and Wish (Bird Poems), 1994; Translations: These Jaundiced Loves (translation of Les Amours Jaunes by Tristan Corbière), 1995; The Oxford Book of Verse in Translation; Peterloo Anthology No 1; Pennine Platform; Modern Poetry in Translation No 8. Contributions to: The Observer; Times Literary Supplement; The New Statesman; London Magazine; Tristan Corbière 150th Anniversary Symposium; Max Jacob 50th Anniversry Symposium; Critical Quarterly; New Welsh Review; Ambit; Encounter; Starwheel Press; Cellar Press; Sceptre Press; Mandeville Press; The Oxford Book of Christmas Poems; Voices of Cumbria; PEN & Arts Council Anthologies; 21 Years of Poetry and Audience; Between Comets; The New Lake Poets; Poems to: Poetry Review; The Independent; The Spectator; Lettres d'Europe; Critical Survey; Poetry Wales. Honours: Arts Council Grant, 1971; Arts Council Translators Grant, 1977; Northern Arts Award, 1985; New Poets Award, 1970; Kate Collingwood Award, 1983; Lauréat Du Concours Européen de Création Littéraire; Tyrone Guthrie Residency, Northern Arts Award, 1993; European Poetry Translation Network Residency, Annaghmakerrig, 1995. Memberships: Cumbrian Poets. Address: 25 High Hill, Keswick, Cumbria CA12 5NY, England.

PINE Ana, b. 13 Nov 1948, Greece. Poet; Editor; Publisher. 1 son, 2 daughters. Education: Purley School of Commerce and Languages. Appointments: Editor, Publisher, Cokefish Literary Magazine, 1989-91; Editor, Publisher, Bouillabaisse Magazine, 1991-. Publications: Broken Silence; New Age Women; Sex on the Interstate; July Moon; Concrete Bologna. Contributions to: Morris County Magazine; Observer; Tribune; Alpha Beat Soup; Global Tapestry Journal; Connections; Chiron Review; Blue Jacket; Moody Street Irregular; New Hope Gazette; Impetus; Free Lunch; XIB; Shock Box. Honour: Alpha Beat Press Poetry Award. Address: PO Box 683, Long Valley, NJ 07853, USA.

PINGEL Martha. See: **TAYLOR Velande Pingel.**

PINKSTON Keli, b. 16 May 1940, Colorado, USA. Writer; Artist. Div, 3 sons, 1 daughter. Education: Emergency Medical Technician Diploma, 1977; BSc, Art, Missouri Valley College, 1987-90. Appointments: Nurse in Obstetrics and Gynaecology, 1971-79; Home Health Nurse, 1982-84; Currently Freelancing. Publications: Window to The World, 1985; American Poetry Annual, 1986; Yesterday's Moments, 1987; New Golden Poems, 1987; American Poetry Showcase, 1987; World Treasury of Great Poems, 1988; Great Poems of Today, 1988; American Poetry Anthology, 1988; Special Poet Series, 1989; Selected Poems of a New Era, 1989; Images, 1989; Laureates, 1990; Another Place Another Time, 1990; Paths Less Travelled, 1990; National Library of Poetry, 1991; Windows of The World, Down Peaceful Paths, 1991; Another Place in Time, 1991; Sunrise Sunset, 1991; Moments of Memory, 1991; Voices on The Wind, 1991. Contributions include: American Poetry Association; Cader Publishing; Marshall Daily Herald; Rolla Daily News; Nimrod. Honours include: Numerous Merit Awards and Golden Poet Awards; Editor's Choice Award, 1989; Special Contribution Award for Poetry, 1989; Certificate of Poetic Achievement, 1990. Memberships: Associate, Academy of American Poets; National Author's Registry. Address: Rt 4, Box 451, Rolla, MO 65401, USA.

PINSKER Sanford, b. 28 Sept 1941, Washington, USA. Professor. m. Ann Getson, 28 June 1968, 1 son, 1 daughter. Education: PhD, University of Washington, 1967. Appointments: Assistant, Associate, Full, Shadek Professor. Publications: Still Life; Memory Breaks Off; Whales at Play; Sketches of Spain; Local News. Contributons to: Harpers; New York Times; Kansas Quarterly; Georgia Review; Response. Address: 700 North Pine Street, Lancaster, PA 17603, USA.

PINSKY Robert, b. 20 Oct 1940, New Jersey, USA. University Teacher. m. 30 Dec 1961, 3 daughters. Education: BA, Rutgers University, 1962; MA, Stanford University, 1966; PhD, Stanford University, 1967. Appointments: Professor of English: Wellesley College, 1968-80, University of California, 1980-88, Boston University, 1988-; Poetry Editor, New Republic, 1978-86; US Poet Laureate, 1997-. Publications: Sadness and Happiness, 1975; An Explanation of America, 1979; History of My Heart, 1984; The Want Bone, 1989; The Inferno of Dante, 1994; New and Collected Poems, 1965-1995. Contributions to: New Yorker; New Republic; Ploughshares; Poetry; Agni Review; Wigwag. Honours: American Academy Prize, 1978; Guggenheim Fellowship, 1978; NEW Award, 1980; William Carlos Williams Award, 1984. Membership: American Academy of Arts and Sciences. Address: c/o Creative Writing, Boston University, 236 Bay State Road, Boston, MA 02215, USA.

PIOMBINO Nicholas (Nick), b. 5 Oct 1942, Manhattan, New York, USA. Psychoanalyst. m. Toni Simon, 25 Nov 1988. Education: BA, City College of New York, 1964; MSW, Fordham, 1971; Certificate in Psychoanalysis and Psychotherapy, 1982. Appointments: School Social Worker, New York, 1976; Private Practice in Psychotherapy, New York, 1976-; Diplomatic Clinical Social Work, 1989-. Publications: Poems, 1988; The Boundary of Blur, essays, 1993; Light Street, poems, 1996. Contributions to: The L A N G U A G E Book; In The American Tree; The Politics of Poetry Form; The Gertrude Stein Awards in Contemporary Poetry. Honours: Postgraduate Center, Literary Award, 1994; New York Foundation for The Arts Fellowship in Poetry, 1992. Memberships: The Academy of American Poets. Address: 680 West End Avenue, #1F, New York City 10025, USA.

PIOTROWSKI   Andrzej   Stanislaw,   (Andrzej Czcibor-Piotrowski), b. 30 Nov 1931, Lwow, Poland. Poet; Translator; Editor. m. Lidia Malgorzata Klimczak, 10 Dec 1977. Education: Master of Slavonic Philology, Warsaw University, 1955. Appointments: Publishing Houses: Pax, 1953-74, KAW, 1975-85. Publications: The Eyes of Snow, 1956; The Horrors, 1959; The Ballads on Two of Us, 1965; We are Creating Worlds, 1963; Susan in the Bath, 1967; Into the Earth, 1969; Testimonies, 1971; Naked in the Candlelight: Selected Poems 1956-1971, 1976; After You, 1980; the Conspiracy of the Dead, 1982; Before the Catastrophe, 1987; Washing the Dead, selected poems, 1991; Prose: Asking for Anne, 1962; Several booklets for children. Contributions to: Various publications. Honours: Poetry and Translation Awards, 1957, 1984; Silver Medal with Ribbon, Czechoslovakia, 1978; P O Hviezdoslav Prize, Slovakia, 1985; V Nezval Prize and Medal, Czechoslovakia, 1986. Memberships: Polish Writers Union; Poets Club; Literrarische Union, Germany. Address: ul Chocimska 35m 21, 00-791 Warsaw, Poland.

PITCHES Douglas Owen, b. 6 Mar 1930, Exning, Suffolk, England. Teacher. m. Barbara Joyce Budgen, 7 Aug 1954. Education: BA, Hons, Open University, 1979. Publications: Poems, 1965; Prayer to the Virgin Mary (Chaucer Translation), 1965; Man in Orbit and Down to Earth, 1981; Art Demands Love Not Homage, 1992. Contributions to: Orbis; Outposts; Envoi; Tribune; Anthologies: Responding; New Voices; Another 5th Poetry Book and others. Address: 14 Linkway, Westham, Pevensey, East Sussex BN24 5JB, England.

PITCHFORD Kenneth S(amuel), b. 24 Jan 1931, Moorhead, Minnesota, USA. Poet; Editor. m. Robin Morgan, 1962, 1 child. Education: BA, University of Minnesota, 1952; MA, New York University, 1959. Appointments: Writer-in-Residence, Yaddo Colony, 1958; Associate Editor, New International Yearbook, 1960-66. Publications: The Blizzard Ape, 1958; A Suite of Angels and Other Poems, 1967; Color Photos of the Atrocities, 1973. Contributions to: Anthologies and Periodicals. Honours: Fulbright Fellowship, 1956-57; Eugene Lee-Hamilton Award for Poetry, 1957; Borestone Mountain Award, 1964. Address: c/o Purchase Press, PO Box 5, Harrison, NY 10528, USA.

PITT-KETHLEY (Helen) Fiona, b. 21 Nov 1954, Edgware, Middlesex, England. Journalist; Travel Writer; Poet; Novelist. Education: BA, Honours, Chelsea School of Art, 1976. Publications: London, 1984; Rome, 1985; The Tower of Glass, 1985; Sky Ray Lolly, 1986; Gesta, 1986; Private Parts, 1987; The Perfect Man, 1989; The Misfortunes of Nigel, 1991; The Literary Companion to Sex, 1992; The Maiden's Progress, 1992; Too Hot To Handle, 1992; Dogs, 1993; The Literary Companion to Low Life (anthology), 1995. Contributions to: Various journals and newspapers, including: Guardian, Independent and Times. Address: 7 Ebenezer Road, Hastings, East Sussex TN34 3BS, England.

PLAICE Stephen James, b. 9 Sept 1951, Watford, Hertfordshire, England. Writer. Education: BA, Hons, German, 1973, MPhil, Comparative Literature, 1979, Sussex University; Attended Universities of Marburg, 1972 and Zürich, 1975. Appointments: Writer-in-Residence, H M Prison, Lewes, 1987-94; Artistic Director, Alarmist Theatre, 1987-. Publications: Rumours of Cousins, 1983; Over the Rollers, 1992. Contributions to: London Magazine; Cumberland Poetry Review; Poetry Durham; Poetry Nottingham; Orbis; Honest Ulsterman; Editor, Printer's Devil, 1990-. Address: 46 Queens Park Road, Brighton, East Sussex BN2 2GL, England.

PLATT Charles, b. 1944, Author; Poet; Freelance Writer. Appointments: Clive Bingley Publishers; Designer, Production Assistant, New Worlds Magazine. Publications: The Garbage World; The City Dwellers; Highway Sandwiches; The Gas; Planet of the Coles; New Worlds; Sweet Evil; Dream Makers; The Uncommon People Who Write Science Fiction. Address: c/o Gollancz, 14 Henrietta Street, London WC2E 8QJ, England.

PLATTHY Jeno, b. 13 Aug 1920, Hungary. Poet; Writer. m. Carol Louise Abell, 25 Sept 1976. Education: Peter Pazmany University, Budapest, 1939-42; Jozsef Ferencz University, 1943-44; Catholic University of America, 1963-65. Appointments: Editor in Chief, Monumenta Classica Perennia, 1967-84; Executive Director, Federation of International Poetry Associations of UNESCO, 1976-; Publisher, New Muses, 1976-. Publications: Sources on the Earliest Greek Libraries with the Testimonia, 1968; Ch'u Yuan, 1975; Collected Poems, 1981; The Mythical Poets of Greece, 1985; Shadows and Numbers, tr, 1985; Bartók: A Critical Biography, 1988; Plato A Critical Biography, 1990; Near-Death Experiences in Antiquity, 1992; Platthy and Antiquity, An Anthology, ed Professor Paul Aström, 1992; 28 volumes of poetry including: Odes Européennes, 1986; Book of Dithyrambs, 1986; Asian Elegies, 1987; Space Eclogues, 1988; Cosmograms, 1988; Nova Comoedia, parts I, II and III, 1988, 1990, 1991; Celebration of Life, 1991; Elegies Asiatiques, 1991; Idylls, 1991; Europaische Oden, 1991; Paeans, 1993; Rhapsodies, 1994; Prosodia, 1994; Visions, 1994; Epodes, 1996; Songs of the Soul, 1996 Sacrifices, 1996. Contributions to: Info; New Muses; Festschriften, among others. Honours: Poet Laureate, 2nd World Congress of Poets, 1973; Confucius, Award, 1974; Poet Laureate, President, 3rd International Congress of Poets, 1976; Jacques Raphael-Leygues Prize of the Société des Poètes Francais; Ordre des Arts et des Lettres (Officer) of the French Republic, 1992. Memberships: International PEN Club; American Society of Composers, Authors and Publishers; International Poetry Society; Die Literarische Union; Academy of American Poets; Association of Literary Critics and Scholars. Address: PO Box 579, Santa Claus, IN 47579, USA.

PLEIJEL Agneta, b. 26 Feb 1940, Stockholm, Sweden. Author. m. Maciej Zaremba, 27 Nov 1982, 1 daughter. Education: MA, 1970. Appointment: Norstedts Publishing Co. Publications: Kollontay; Angels, Drafts; The Hill on the Black Side of the Moon; Eyes of a Dream; He Who Observeth the Wind; Dog Star. Contributions to: Several. Membership: Swedish PEN. Address: Tantogatan 45, 117 42 Stockholm, Sweden.

PLUMLY Stanley (Ross), b. 23 May 1939, Barnesville, Ohio, USA. Poet; Professor. Education: BA, Wilmington College, 1961; MA, Ohio University, 1968. Appointments: Instructor in Creative Writing, Louisiana State University, 1968-70; Professor of English, Ohio University, 1970-74; Editor, Ohio Review 1970-75, Iowa Review 1976-78; Professor of English, University of Houston, 1979-; Visiting Lecturer at several universities. Publications: In the Outer Dark, 1970; How the Plains Indians Got Horses, 1973; Giraffe, 1973; Out-of-the-Body Travel, 1977; Summer Celestial, 1983; Boy on the Step, 1989. Contributions to: Periodicals. Honours: Delmore Schwartz Memorial Award, 1973; Guggenheim Fellowship, 1973; National

Endowment for the Arts Grant, 1977. Address: c/o Department of English & Creative Writing, University of Houston, 4800 Calhoun, Houston, TX 77004, USA.

PO Sar. See: **TU Shiu-tien.**

POBO Kenneth, b. 24 Aug 1954, Elmhurst, Illinois, USA. Associate Professor of English. Education: BA, English, Wheaton College, 1976; MA, English, 1979, PhD, English, 1983, University of Wisconsin, Milwaukee. Appointments: Teacher, University of Wisconsin, Milwaukee, 1977-83; Instructor of English, University of Tennessee, 1983-87; Associate Professor of English, Widener University, Chester, Pennsylvania, 1987-. Publications: Musing From the Porchlit Sea, 1979; Billions of Lit Cigarettes, collection, 1981; Evergreen, 1985; A Pause Inside Disk, 1986; Ferns on Fire, 1991; Yes, Irises, 1992. Contributions to: Over 150 magazines published in USA, UK and Canada, including Orbis, Poetry Durham, Mudfish, University of Windsor Review, Hawaii Review, Poem, Grain, Dalhousie Review, West Branch. Address: Humanities Division, Widener University, Chester, PA 19013, USA.

PODHORODECKI Michael. See: **LEBIODA Dariusz Thomas.**

POETESS LOUISE. See: **WISINSKI Louise Ann Helen.**

POBOG. See: **ZYDANOWICZ Janine Regina.**

POGSON Patricia. See: **HOLLOWAY Patricia.**

POLLARD Roula, (Roula Melitas), b. 2 Feb 1948, Greece. Writer. m. Ian Pollard, 26 July 1982. Education: University of Athens, 1967-72; Leeds University, 1976-77. Appointments: High School Teacher, 1972-75; Part Time Lecturer, Wakefield District College, 1987-90; Priestley Institute of Higher Education, 1989-90. Publications: Presence; Points of Silence; The Birth of Time. Contributions to: Periplous; Zakynthos; Left to Right; Greek Post; Patras Poetry; Anthologies: Symposium Anthology; Proodos; Anthology of Zakynthian Poets; Anthology of Love Poems; Beauty of Spirit, 1994; Zante in Greek and Foreign Poetry, 1995; Zakynthian Poets, 1995. Memberships: Greek Writers Guild; National Association of Writers in Education; Yorkshire Playwrights. Address: The Manor, Main Street, South Hiendley, Barnsley, South Yorkshire S72 9BS, England.

POLLOCK Michael Dean Odin, b. 23 Nov 1953, Marysville, California, USA. 2 sons. Appointments: Musician; Composer; Poet. Publications: Bohemian in Babylon, 1988; The Martial Art of Pagan Diaries, 1994; Poemz, 1983-96. Contributions to: Cafe Review; Kerouac Connection; Howling Mantra; Carnival Serpents Tail; Zig Zag; Thrashing Doves; Tomorrow. Address: Post Box 841, IS-121, Reykjavík, Iceland.

POLOM Stefan, b. 10 Dec 1938, Torun, Poland. Writer; Poet. Education: University of Nicolaus Copernicus, Torin, 1956-60. Publications: De Revolutionbus, 1973; Wlocznie, 1967; Zrodla zapomnienia, 1972; Wiernosc, 1974; W Cieniu sierpnia, 1971; Rok Bez Nieba, 1984; Dzien slonca, 1986; Jezioro Kroleskie, 1988. Contributions to: Kultura; Wspolczesnosc; Nowa Kultura; Poezja; Gazeta Olsztynska; Warmia i Mazury; Komentarze Fromborskie; Wers. Honour: Red Rose, Gdansk, 1986. Membership: Union des Gens de Lettres Polonais. Address: 10-437 Olsztyn, ul Dworcowa 49 m 80, Poland.

POOK John, b. 2 Feb 1942, Neath, Wales. Teacher; Editor. Education: Degree in English, Queen's College, Cambridge, 1964. Publications: That Cornish Facing Door, 1975; Needing the Experience. Contributions to: Poetry Wales; Anglo Welsh Review; Planet; New Hope International; Icon Poetry Quarterly; Pennine Platform; Salmon. Honours: Eric Gregory Award, 1971; Welsh Arts Council Bursary, 1978. Address: c/o Welsh Arts Councils, Museum Place, Cardiff, South Wales.

POOLE Margaret Barbara (Peggy), (Terry Roche, Margaret Thornton), b. 8 Mar 1925, Petham, Kent, England. Freelance Broadcaster/Journalism; Writer. m. Reginald Poole, 10 Aug 1949, 3 daughters. Education: Top Exhibition to Benenden, 1939, Matriculated, 1941. Appointments: Co-organiser of Jabberwocky; Served on literary panel of Merseyside Arts Assocation; Presenter and producer of First Heard, poetry programme on BBC Radio Merseyside, 1976-88; Poetry Consultant, BBC Network Northwest, 1988-96. Publications: Never a

Put-up Job, 1970; Cherry Stones and Other Poems, 1983; No Wilderness in Them, 1984; Midnight Walk, 1986; Hesitations, 1990; Trusting the Rainbow, 1994. Edited: Windfall, 1994; Poet's England, Cumbria, 1995; Marigolds Grow Wild on Platforms, 1996. Contributions to: Countryman; Country Quest; Orbis; Outposts; BBC Radio 4; Poetry included in anthologies: New Christian Poetry, 1990; Poet's England 10: Kent 1990; Stand-up Poetry, 1990; Poet's England 10: Kent, 1990; Stand-up Poetry, 1991; Various SWWJ anthologies and anthologies of prizewinners in England and USA. Honours: Runner-up, Edmund Blunden Memorial Competition, 1979; Twice runner-up, Julia Cairns Trophy; 1st Prize Waltham Forest Competition, 1987; 1st Prize Southport Competition, 1989; Prizewinner, LACE Competition, 1992; Prizewinner in Lancaster Literature Festival, 1987, 1991; Highly Commended or Commended in various other competitions. Memberships: Society of Women Writers and Journalists; Poetry Society; London Writers' Circle. Address: 36 Hilbre Court, West Kirby, Wirral, Merseyside L48 3JU, England.

POOLE Richard Arthur, b. 1 Jan 1945, Yorkshire, England. Tutor in English Literature. m. Sandra Pauline Smart, 18 July 1970, 1 son. Education: BA, University College of North Wales, 1966; MA, University College of North Wales, 1968. Appointments: Tutor in English Literature, Coleg Harlech, 1970-; Editor, Poetry Wales, 1992-96. Publications: Goings and Other Poems, 1978; Words Before Midnight, 1981; Natural Histories, 1989; Autobiographies and Explorations, 1994. Contributions to: Encounter; PN Review; Outposts; Anglo-Welsh Review; Poetry Wales; New Welsh Review; Swansea Review; Planet; NER/BLQ; Chariton Review; Webster Review; Cumberland Poetry Review. Memberships: Yr Academi Gymreig (The Welsh Academy). Address: Glan-y-Werydd, Llandanwg, Harlech, Gwynedd LL46 2SD, Wales.

POPE Deborah, b. Cincinnati, Ohio, USA. Poet; Literary Critic; Teacher. m. Dean A Shangler, 2 sons. Education: BA, Dension University; MA, PhD, University of Wisconsin. Appointments: Professor, Department of English, Duke University, 1979-. Publication: A Separate Vision, 1984; Ties that Bind: Essays on Mothering and Patriarchy, 1990; Fanatic Heart, 1992; Mortal World. Contributions to: Poetry Southern Review; Poetry Northwest; Ohio Review; Prairie Schooner; Three Rivers Poetry Review. Memberships: Phi Beta Kappa; Phi Kappa Phi. Address: Department of English, Duke University, Durham, NC 27706, USA.

POPLE Ian Stewart, b. 25 Oct 1952, Ipswich, Suffolk, England. Teacher of English as a Foreign Language. m. Olivia Michael, 3 Aug 1990. Education: Certificate in Education, Bedford College of Education, 1976; British Council, Athens, Greece, 1986; Diploma TEFL, Royal Society of Arts; MSc, University of Aston, 1990. Appointments: Residential Social Worker, 1977-78; English Teacher, Milton Keynes, 1978-83; English Teacher, El Obeid, Sudan, 1983; English Teacher, Athens, 1984-86; English Instructor, Dhahran Airbase, Saudi Arabia, 1986-90; Freelance English Teacher. Publications: The Same Condemnation, 1989; The Glass Enclosure, 1996; Ways of Reading, 1996. Contributions to: Arvon International Poetry Competition Anthology, 1987; Encounter; Honest Ulsterman; Literary Review; London Review of Books; Oxford Poetry; Poetry Durham; Poetry Review; Times Literary Supplement; Verse; PN Review. Memberships: National Committee, National Association of Writers in Education. Address: 19 Huddersfield Road, Diggle, Saddleworth, Lancashire OL3 5NU, England.

PORTEOUS Katrina, b. 4 Sept 1960, Aberdeen, Scotland. Freelance Writer. Education: Durham High School, 1971-78; BA, Hons, 1st Class, History, 1982, MA, 1986, Trinity Hall, Cambridge; Harkness Fellowship (Creative Writing), University of California at Berkeley and Harvard University, 1982-84. Appointments: Writer-in-Residence, Amble Schools and Library, Northumberland, 1990; Poetry Workshops, Boston Public Schools, USA, 1991; Creative Writing Workshops for Adult Associations, Northumberland, 1991-; Poetry Workshops, Leeds University Adult Extension, 1995; Poet-in-Residence, King's College School, Cambridge, 1995-. Creative works: Morpeth in Flood, musical, co-written with Alistair Anderson and Children of Morpeth Schools, 1996; The Lost Music, 1996. Contributions to: Anthologies: Arvon International Poetry Competition Anthology, 1989; Trees Be Company, 1989; New Women Poets, 1990; Gregory Anthology 1987-1990, 1990; Northern Poetry, Vol 2, 1991; Also contributed poetry to: Texts in the Landscape, National Garden Festival, Gateshead, 1990; The Fisherman, 1994. Honours: Harkness Fellowship for Study and Travel, USA (Creative Writing), 1982-84;

Eisner Prize for Creative Arts (Poetry), University of California, Berkeley, 1983; Arvon International Poetry Competition (Sotheby's Prize), 1987; Placed in Bridport Poetry Competition, 1988; Placed in Newcastle Evening Chronicle Poetry Competition, 1988; Eric Gregory Award, Society of Authors, 1989; Northern Arts Writer's Awards, 1990, 1992; Littlewood Arc, Northern Poetry Competition, 1991; Arts Council Writer's Bursary, 1993. Memberships: Poetry Society; National Association of Writers in Education. Address: Windmillsteads, 58 Harbour Road, Beadnell, Chathill, Northumberland NE67 5BE, England.

PORTER Jan, b. 24 July 1948, Sandwich, Kent, England. Library Assistant. Education: BA, hons, English and American Literature, University of Kent, Canterbury, 1974-77. Appointments: Student Nurse; Novice in Teaching Order; Auxillary Nurse; Filing Clerk; Freelance Marker for Correspondence Course; Part-time Library Assistant, 1996; Part-time Assistant, Boarding Cattery, 1996. Publications: Remember The Time, 1994; Bridging The Gap, 1994; The West In Her Eye, 1995. Contributions to: Envoi; Poetry Nottingham; Psychopoetica; Peace & Freedom; Tandem; Candelabrum; Doors; Never Bury Poets; Dial 174; First Time; Poetry Now; Weyfarers; Krax; Dandelion. Honours: Runner-up, The Mexican Hat Dream, 1993 Competition; First Prize, 1993 Areopagus Poetry Competition; Third Place & Merit Prize, Queenie Lee Memorial Poetry Competition, 1995. Address: Rascals, 1 Barnhill Cottages, Barnhill Road, Wembley, Middlesex HA9 9BU, England.

PORTER Peter Neville Frederick, b. 16 Feb 1929, Brisbane, Queensland, Australia. Freelance Writer. Poet. m. Jannice Henry, 1961, dec 1974, 2 daughters. Appointments: Clerk; Bookseller; Advertising Writer; Poet; Journalist; Reviewer; Broadcaster. Publications: Once Bitten, Twice Bitten; Penguin Modern Poets; Poems Ancient and Modern; A Porter Folio; The Last of England; Preaching to the Converted; After Martial: The Lady and the Unicorn; Living in a Calm Country; The Cost of Seriousness; English Subtitles; Collected Poems; Fast Forward; Narcissus; Possible Worlds. Honour: Duff Cooper Prize. Address: 42 Cleveland Square, London W2, England.

POTTI S K(esavan), b. 30 Aug 1942, Kerala, India. Teacher. m. Saraswathi Potti, 30 Aug 1973, 2 daughters. Education: MA, English Literature, 1969; MPhil, English Literature, 1988. Appointments: Principal and Head of Department of English, Government College, Karkala, 1992-. Publications: Atmagitam, 1960; Love: Ancient and Modern, 1977; Song of Wisdom, 1987. Contributions to: Poet; Mirror; Yuva Bharati; Bhageerath; Youth Karnataka; Deccan Herald; Hindustan Times; Malayalam Literary Survey; Journal of the Poetry Society of India; Journal of Indian Writing in English; Vedanta Kesari; Indian Verse; New Quest. Memberships: Life Member, Poetry Society; World Poetry Society; United Writer's Association; Life Member, Association for Writer's and Ilustrators of Children's Literature. Address: Government College, Karkala 574104, South Kanara, Karnataka, India.

POULSON Joan, (Joan Gregory), b. 25 May 1940, Manchester, England. Writer; Poet. 1 son, 2 daughters. Publication: Celebration, 1992; Girls Are Like Diamonds, 1996. Contributions to: Poetry Nottingham; Slow Dancer; Pennine Platform; PEN International; Smiths Knoll; O Correo Galego; Frogmore Papers; Writing Women. Memberships: International PEN; Society of Authors; Poetry Society. Address: 35 Belmont Road, Sale, Cheshire M33 1HY, England.

POULTNEY Sherman King, b. 18 Mar 1937, USA. Physicist. 1 son. Education: PhD, Physics, Princeton University, 1962. Appointments: Assistant Professor, University of Maryland, 1964-75; Senior Scientist, Hughes Danbury Optical Systems, 1975-. Publications: The Season Transcended, 1, 1990, 11, 1991; The World Transcended, 1993; The World: Not Mine to Keep, 1994; Male and Female: Not Mine to Keep, 1995; A Greek Diptych, 1995. Contributions to: Signal Magazine; Connecticut Writer. Memberships: Connecticut League of Writers; Poetry Society of America; Connecticut Poetry Society, 1990, 1991; Brodine Contest HM, 1994. Address: 24 Spruce Drive, Wilton, CT 06897, USA.

POWELL (John) Craig, b. 16 Nov 1940, New South Wales, Australia. Psychoanalyst. m. Janet Eileen Dawson, 16 Oct 1965, 2 sons, 1 dec, 1 daughter. Education: MBBS, Sydney University, 1965. Appointments: Psychoanalyst in Private Practice, Sydney. Publications: A Different Kind of Breathing, 1966; I Learn by Going,

1968; A Country without Exiles, 1972; Rehearsal for Dancers, 1978; A Face in Your Hands, 1984; The Ocean Remembers it is Visible, 1989; Minga Street: New and Selected Poems, 1993. Contributions to: Poetry Australia; Phoenix Review; Quadrant; Island Magazine; Meajin; Bulletin; Canadian Forum; Poetry Canada Review; Canadian Literature; Quarterly Review of Literature. Honours: Poetry Magazine Award, Sydney, 1964; Henry Lawson Festival Award for Verse, 1969; Mattara Poetry Prize, 1983; Quarterly Review of Literature, International Poetry Competition, 1989. Memberships: League of Canadian Poets, 1974-82; Poets Union, Sydney. Literary Agent: Richard Deutch, 3 Joanne Place, Bilgola Plateau, New South Wales 2107, Australia. Address: 24 Minga Street, Ryde, New South Wales 2112, Australia.

POWELL Joseph E, b. 22 Jan 1952, Ellensburg, Washington, USA. Teacher. Education: BA, University of Washington, 1975; MA, 1978; BA, 1982; MFA, University of Arizona, 1981. Publications: Counting the Change; Winter Insomnia, 1993. Contributions to: Christian Science Monitor; Alaska Quarterly Review; Seattle Review; Southern Poetry Review; Hawaii Review. Honours: Book Award. Memberships: Ellensburg Arts Commission; Alpine Lakes Protection Society. Address: 221 Highway 97, Ellensburg, WA 98926, USA.

POWELL Neil (Ashton), b. 11 Feb 1948, London, England. Writer. Education: BA, English and American Literature, University of Warwick, 1969; MPhil, English Literature, University of Warwick, 1971. Appointments: English Teacher, Kimbolton School, Huntingdon, 1971-74; English Teacher, 1974-78, Head of English, 1978-86, St Christopher School, Letchworth; Bookshop Owner, The Baldock Bookshop, 1986-90; Freelance Writer and Editor, 1990-. Publications: Suffolk Poems, 1975; At the Edge, 1977: Carpenters of Light (criticism), 1979; Out of Time, 1979; A Season of Calm Weather, 1982; Selected Poems of Fulke Greville (editor), 1990; True Colours: New and Selected Poems, 1991; Unreal City (fiction), 1992; The Stones on Thorpeness Beach, 1994; Roy Fuller: Writer and Society (biography), 1995. Contributions to: Bookseller; Critical Quarterly; Encounter; Gay Times; Guardian; Listener; Literary Review; London Magazine; Man Alive; New Statesman; Pacific Quarterly; PN Review; Poetry Review; Poetry Wales; Times Literary Supplement; Also contributor to various anthologies, to The Cambridge Guide to Literature in English, The Oxford Companion to Twentieth-Century Poetry and The Dictionary of Literary Biography. Honours: Gregory Award, Society of Authors, 1969; Authors Foundation Award, Society of Authors, 1992. Memberships: Society of Authors; Poetry Society. Address: c/o A P Watt Ltd, 20 John Street, London WC1N 2DR, England.

PRAISNER Wanda S, b. 15 Dec 1933, Staten Island, New York, USA. Teacher. m. Dr Robert J Praisner, 8 June 1961, 3 sons, 1 dec. Education: BS Early Childhood Education, Magna Cum Laude, Wagner College, 1954; MS Elementary Education, Wagner College, New York, USA, 1957. Appointments: Teacher, Public schools in New York City, California and New Jersey; Educator of the Year, School of St Elizabeth, New Jersey, USA. Publications: Broken Jingles and Moon Shells, 1996; A Fine and Bitter Snow, forthcoming. Contributions to: New York Magazine; The Lullwater Review; The Paterson Literary Review; Journal of New Jersey Poets; Palanquin, USI; Parks and Recreation; Out of Season. Honours: Second Award, Allen Ginsberg Contest, 1992; First Place, The Devil's Millhopper, 1994; Kudzu Contest, 1994; First Place, Maryland Poetry Review's Egan Memorial Poetry Prize, 1995; Poetry Fellowship, New Jersey State Council on the Arts, 1995-96; Read, Geraldine R Dodge International Poetry Festival, Waterloo, New Jersey, 1996. Memberships: Treasurer, South Mountain Poets, New Jersey; USI, Poets, Princeton, New Jersey. Address: 34 Ski Hill Drive, Bedminster, NJ 07921, USA.

PRASAD V S Skanda, b. Sept 1949, Mysore City, India. Bank Executive. m. Suman, May 1980, 1 son. Education: MSc, 1970; DBAIM, 1980. Publications: Explorations and Reflections, 1978; Songs of Cosmos, 1981; East West Winds, 1982; Indo-Australian Flowers, 1984; Sweet Sixteen, 1987; East West Voices, 1988; Glimpses, 1990; Rising Stars and Moving Horizon, 1991; New Global Voice, an International Anthology Poetry, 1994. Contributions to: Samvedana (bulletin); Jaycelite; Kavithaizndia. Honours: International Eminents Poets Award, International Poets Academy, Madras, 1986; DLitt, World Academy of Arts and Culture, 1984; Poetry Prize, Academy of Tarascon, France, 1992; Award of Pegasus of Olympoetry, 1992; Awarded Poetry Editor of the Year, International Writers Association, USA, 1995. Memberships: President, Chetana Literary Group; Editor, House Journal, Mangalore Junior Chambers; Advisory Board, Kavitha

India Literature Journal. Address: Kshema Apartments, Corporation Bank Exec Flat, KMC Men's Hostel Road, Kaprigudda, Mangalore 575001, India.

PRAWER Siegbert Salomon, b. 15 Feb 1925, Cologne, Germany. Author; Artist; Educator. Appointments: Honorary Fellow, Queen's College, Oxford; Professor of German, Emeritus, Oxford University; Lecturer, Birmingham University, 1946-63; Professor of German, London University, 1964-69; Co-Editor, Oxford German Studies, 1971-75; Anglica Germanica, 1973-79. Publications: German Lyric Poetry, 1952; Mörike Und Seine Leser, 1960; Heine's Buch Der Lieder: A Critical Study, 1960; Heine: The Tragic Satirist, 1962; The Penguin Book of Lieder, 1964; Comparative Literary Studies: an Introduction, 1973; Heine's Jewish Comedy: A Study of His Portraits of Jews And Judaism, 1983; The Romantic Period in Germany, 1970; Seventeen Modern German Poets, 1971; A N Stench: Poet Of Whitechapel, 1984; Frankenstein's Island: England and the English in the Writings of Heinrich Heine, 1986; Israel at Vanity Fair: Jews and Judaism in the Writings of W M Thackeray, 1992; Edition of Screenplay of DasKabinett des Doktor Caligari, 1995. Honours: Fellow British Academy; Corresponding Fellow, German Academy of Language and Literature; Honorary Fellow, London University Institute of Germanic Studies (Honorary Director, 1965-68); Honorary Member, Modern Language Association Of America; President, British Comparative Literature Association, 1984-86; Honorary Fellow, British Comparative Literature Association; Goethe Medal; Gold Medal, German Goethe-Gesellschaft; Honorary Doctorates from Universities of Birmingham and Cologne; Isaac Deutscher Prize; Gundolf Prize of the German Academy of Language and Literature. Address: The Queen's College, Oxford, England.

PRESCOTT Richard Chambers, b. 1 April 1952, Houston, Texas, USA. Writer. m. S Elisabeth Grace, 13 Oct 1981. Education: Self taught. Appointments: Writer, 30 years; Newspaper Columnist, 1978-79; Publisher, 1981-96. Publications: The Sage, 1975; Moonstar, 1975; Neuf Songes (Nine Dreams), 1976, second edition, 1991; The Carouse of Soma, 1977; Lions and Kings, 1977; Allah Wake Up, 1978, second edition, 1994; Night Reaper, 1979; Dragon Tales, 1983; Dragon Dreams, 1986, reprinted, 1990; Dragon Prayers, 1988, reprinted, 1990; Dragon Songs, 1988, reprinted, 1990; Dragon Maker, 1989, reprinted, 1990; Dragon Thoughts, 1990; Kings and Sages, 1991; Dragon Sight: A Cremation Poem, 1992; Three Waves, 1992; Disturbing Delights: Waves of the Great Goddess, 1993; Kalee Bhava: The Goddess and Her Moods, 1995; The Skills of Kalee, 1995; Kalee: The Allayer of Sorrows, 1996. Contributions to: The New Times, 1994; The Messenger, 1995. Membership: Houston Poets Guild, 1975-76. Address: 8617 188th St SW, Edmonds, WA 98026, USA.

PRESLEY Frances Elizabeth, b. 30 Aug 1952, Chesterfield, Derbyshire, England. Information Officer. Education: BA Hons, 1st Class, American and English Literature, University of East Anglia, 1975; MA, Comparative Literature, University of Sussex, 1976; MPhil, French Poetry, University of East Anglia, 1986. Appointments: Information Officer, Community Development Foundation, 1982-86; Research Assistant, Free Form Arts Trust, 1986-87; Information Officer, National Council for Voluntary Organisations, 1987-91; Information Officer, King's Fund, Health and Race Project, 1991-; Facilitator, Islington Poetry Workshop, 1993-. Publications: The Sex of Art, 1988; Affirming Flame, anthology, 1990; Hula Hoop, 1993. Contributions to: Critical Quarterly; Oasis; Tenth Decade; Osiris; Vertical Images; Fragmente; Word and Image. Membership: Poetry Society. Address: 19B Marriott Road, London N4 3QN, England.

PRESS Karen Michele, b. 3 Nov 1956, Cape Town, South Africa. Publisher; Author. Education: BA, 1977, Teaching Diploma, 1980, BA Hons, African Studies, 1987, University of Cape Town. Publications: This Winter Coming, 1986; Bird Heart Stoning the Sea, 1990. Contributions to: Magazine: Staffrider, New Coin, Upstream; Anthologies: Siren Songs, Breaking the Silence. Address: PO Box 2580, Cape Town 8000, South Africa.

PRICE Anthony Nigel, b. 15 July 1956, Sutton, Surrey, England. Novelist; Screenwriter. Education: BA Hons, Philosophy and English, St David's University, Wales, 1979. Appointments: Army Officer, Gurkhas, to rank of Major, 1979-91; Sales Director, Asia-Pacific Region. Contributions to: Isthmus; New Christian Poetry; Stand; Poetry Review. Honour: BBC World SVC Competition, runner up and commendation. Memberships: Poetry Society; Poetry Book Society.

Literary Agent: Heather Jeeves Literary Agency. Address: 34 Southway, Carshalton Beeches, Surrey SM5 4HW, England.

PRICE James, b. 6 Feb 1917, Flint, North Wales. Chartered Civil Engineer. m. Mary Eluned Williams, 27 May 1939, 2 sons, 2 daughters. Education: BEng, Hons, 1938, MEng, 1942, Liverpool. Appointments: Swansea Water Department, 1948-56; Nigerian Railways, 1956-57; Chief Resident Engineer, on leading motorways, the historical M1 and Surrey County Council M3, 1957-77. Publications: Price's Progress, 1990; Passages in Paradise, 1994. Contributions to: Anthologies: Echoes of Yesterday, USA National Library of Poetry, 1994; Parnassus of World Poets, India Madras, 1994; Author, Passages in Paradise reviewed by Poetry Now Magazine, 1995. Honours: Editors Choice Award by The National Library of Poetry, USA, 1994. Memberships: Poetry Society, United Kingdom; Welsh Academy; South and Mid-Wales Association of Writers; The Engineering Council; The Institution of Civil Engineers; The Chartered Institution of Water and Environmental Management. Address: Penbre, 13 Liscum Way, Barry, South Glamorgan CF62 8AB, Wales.

PRICE Victor, b. 10 Apr 1930, Newcastle, Northern Ireland. Freelance Journalist. m. Colette Rodot, 20 Oct 1957, 2 sons. Education: Methodist College, Belfast, 1941-47; Queens University, Belfast, 1947-51. Publications: The Death of Achilles; The Other Kingdom; Caliban's Wooing; Two Parts Water. Contributions to: Various articles. Address: 33 Hereford Square, London SW7 4TS, England.

PRIEST Lydia Pallmé, b. 13 Sept 1940, New York, New York, USA. Writer. m. Walter S Priest, 29 Sept 1965, 2 daughters. Education: AB, George Washington University, 1962; AM, George Washington University, 1967; MA, Andover Newton Theological School, 1992. Appointments: English Teacher, 1967-69; Publisher/Reporter for Rockport Eagle. Weekly Newspaper, 1972-84; Pastoral Associate, Salem, Massachusetts, 1985-89; Library Worker, Andover Newton, 1989-92; Reading Teacher and Respite Worker, Association of Retarded Citizens, 1992-95. Publications: Anthologies: At Water's Edge, 1995; Reflections of Light, 1995. Contributions to: Lamp-Post; The Poet's Corner; The Disability Rag and Resource. Honours: Honourable Mentions from: The Gloucester Daily Times Poetry Contest, 1995; International Society of Poets' Magazine; The Poet's Corner, 1996; Newburyport Art Association's Poetry Contest, 1996; Editor's Choice Award, National Library of Poetry, 1995. Memberships: International Society of Poets. Address: 72B Bass Avenue, Gloucester, MA 01930-3119, USA.

PRINCE F(rank) T(empleton), b. 1912, South Africa. Former Professor of English; Author; Poet. Appointments: Professor, University of Southampton, 1957-74; Professor, University of West Indies, Jamaica, 1975-78; Fannie Hurst Professor, Brandeis University, 1978-80; Professor, Washington University, St Louis, 1980-81; Professor, Sana'a University, North Yemen, 1981-83. Publications: Soldiers Bathing and Other Poems; The Italian Element in Milton's Verse; The Stolen Heart; Samson Agonistes by Milton, editor; Paradise Lost I and II, editor; William Shakespeare the Poems, editor; Comus and Other Poems by Milton; Memoirs in Oxford; Penguin Modern Poets; Drypoints of the Hasidim; Afterword on Rupert Brooke; The Yuan Chen Variations; Later on; Walks in Rome; Collected Poems 1935-92, 1993. Contributions to: Keats Country, PN Review, 1995. Address: 32 Brookvale Road, Southampton, Hampshire, England.

PROKOPOV Georgine Lucile Ogden, (Georgine Ogden), b. 3 Nov 1925, Middletown, New York, USA. Writer. m. Theodore S Prokopov, 4 Oct 1968, 1 stepson, 2 stepdaughters. Education: BA, University of Wisconsin, 1947; MIA, Columbia University, 1949; PhD, University of London, 1958. Appointments: Research Writer, US Department of State, 1951-53; Research Assistant, Population Reference Bureau, 1960-64; Research Analyst, Georgetown Research Project, 1965-66; Associate Professor, Upper Iowa University, 1967-73; Administrative Aide, Orange County, New York, Executive's Office, 1975-77; Data Analyst, Hudson Valley HSA, 1975-81, 1984-86; Director of Research and Evaluation, Westchester County Department of Health, 1981-83. Publications: Orange Poems, 1987; Shawangunk and Catskill Chirpings, 1995. Contributions to: Voices of the Majestic Sage; Treasures of the Precious Moments; Dreams and Visions; Anthology Five; Anthology Six; Anthology of Prize Poems, 1988. Honours: Honourable Mention, Beatrice Branch Memorial Award;

Leona Jones Smith Memorial Award. Memberships: National Federation of State Poetry Societies; Florida State Poets Association. Address: PO Box 640578, Beverly Hills, FL 34664, USA.

PROUDFOOT James Mark, b. 21 Feb 1956, Des Moines, Iowa, USA. Visual Artist; Illustrator. Education: Graphic Design, Drake University, 1977. Contributions to: Lyrical Iowa, 1982; Worlds Great Contemporaray Poems, 1981; Family Treasury of Great Poems, 1981. Honours: Iowa State Fair Prize, 1980; Honorable Mentions: Lyrical Iowa Competition, 1982; American Songs Festival, LA, 1981; Music City Song Festival, Nashville, 1981; 1989; 2nd Prize, Music City Song Festival, 1981. Memberships: Iowa Poetry Association. Address: 14 SE Gray St, Des Moines, IA 50315, USA.

PRUTKOV Kozma. See: SNODGRASS W D.

PRYNNE J H, b. 24 June 1936, England. Publications: Kitchen Poems, 1968; The White Stones, 1969; Brass, 1971; Wound Response, 1974; News of Warring Clans, 1977; Poems; The Oval Window, 1983; Bands Around the Throat, 1987; Word Order, 1989; Not-You, 1993; Her Weasels Wild Returning, 1994. Address: Gonville and Caius College, Cambridge CB2 1TA, England.

PUGH Sheenagh, b. 20 Dec 1950, Birmingham, England. m. Michael J H Burns, 1977, 1 son, 1 daughter. Education: BA, Honours, University of Bristol, 1971. Publications include: Crowded by Shadows, 1977; What a Place to Grow Flowers, 1979; Earth Studies and Other Voyages, 1982; Beware Falling Tortoises, 1987; Selected Poems, 1990; Sing for the Taxman, 1993. Honours include: Cardiff International Literature Festival Prize, 1988. Address: 4C Romilly Road, Canton, Cardiff CF5 1FH, Wales.

PUNTER David Godfrey, b. 19 Nov 1949, London, England. Professor of English Studies. m. Caroline Mary Case-Punter, 5 Dec 1988, 1 son, 2 daughters. Education: BA, Hons, 1970, MA, 1974, PhD, 1984, Cambridge University. Appointments: Lecturer, 1973-84, Senior Lecturer, 1984-86, University of East Anglia; Professor, Fudan University, Shanghai, China, 1983, Chinese University of Hong Kong, 1986-88, Stirling University, 1988-. Publications: China and Glass, 1986; Lost in the Supermarket, 1989. Contributions to: PN Review; Encounter; New Poetry; Thames Poetry; Outposts; Plains Review; Orbis; Spectrum; Puckerbrush Review; Peace and Freedom; Other Poetry; Lines Review; Ariel; Kansas Quarterly. Memberships: President, British Association of Romantic Studies; Director, Edinburgh Book Festival. Honours: Michael Johnson Prize, 1981; Bridport Writing Prize, 1985. Address: Department of English Studies, University of Stirling, Stirling FK9 4LA, Scotland.

PURCELL Sally Anne Jane, b. 1 Dec 1944, Worcestershire, England. Writer. Education: BA, Oxford, 1966; MA, 1970. Appointment: Honorary Secretary, Foundation for Islamic Culture, Oxford, 1969-. Publications: The Devil's Dancing Hour; Provençal Poems; The Happy Unicorns: Poetry of Under 25's; The Holly Queen; George Peele; Monarchs And The Muse: Poems By Monarchs And Princes Of England, Scotland and Wales; The Exile Of James Joyce; Charles D'Orléans; Dark Of Day; By The Clear Fountain; Guenever And The Looking Glass; The Early Italian Poets; Gaspara Stampa; Lake And Labyrinth; Amorgós; Heraldic Symbols; Through Lent With Blessed Ramon Lull, 1994; Appearance in William Oxley's anthology, Completing The Picture, 1995. Contributions to: numerous magazines and journals; Acumen; Outposts; Own poetry (and translation of all English into French) Verso 71 (Lyon). Honours: Arts Council Grant. Address: C/o Anvil Press, 69 King George Street, London SE10 8PX, England.

PURDY Al(fred Wellington), b. 30 Dec 1918, Wooler, Ontario, Canada. Poet; Novelist; Editor. m. Eurithe Mary Jane Parkhurst, 1941, 1 son. Education: Albert College, Belleville, Ontario; Trenton Collegiate Institute. Appointments: Royal Canadian Air Force, World War II; Visiting Associate Professor, Simon Fraser University, 1970; Writer-in-Residence, Loyola College, 1973-74; University of Western Ontario, 1977-78; University of Toronto, 1987-88. Publications: Numerous anthologies, Canada, abroad; Editor: The New Romans, 1968; Fifteen Winds, 1969; Storm Warning, 1, 1971; 2, 1976; others; Poems: The Enchanted Echo, 1944; Pressed On Sand, 1956; The Crafte So Longe To Lerne, 1959; Poems for All The Annettes, 1962; The Blur in Between, 1963; The Cariboo Horses, 1965; North of a Summer, 1967; Wild Grape Wine, 1968; Love In a Burning Building, 1970; Hiroshima Poems, 1972; Selected Poems, 1972; On the

Bearpath Sea, 1973; In Search of Owen Roblin, 1974; Sex and Death, 1973; The Poems of Al Purdy, 1976; Sun Dance at Dusk, 1976; At Marsport Drugstore, 1977; No Other Country, 1977; A Handful of Earth, 1977; Being Alive: Poems, 1958-78; No Second Spring, 1978; Moths in the Iron Curtain, 1979; The Stone Bird, 1981; Bursting into Song: An Al Purdy Omnibus, 1982; Birdwatching at the Equator, 1983; Morning and It's Summer: A Memoir, 1984; Bukowski/Purdy Letter, Journal, 1984; Piling Blood, 1984; Collected Poems, 1986; Novel: A Splinter in the Heart, 1990; The Woman on the Shore (poems), 1990; Naked with Summer In Your Mouth (poems), 1994; Margaret Laurence - Al Purdy: A Friendship In Letters, 1993; Starting From Ameliasburgh, Collected Prose, 1995. Honours: Governor General's Awards, 1966; 1987; Order of Canada, 1982; Order of Ontario, 1987; Other awards. Address: RR No 1, Ameliasburgh, Ontario, K0K 1A0, Canada.

PURDY James, b. 14 July 1924, Ohio, USA. Writer; Playwright; Poet. Education: Studied in US, Mexico, Cuba and Spain. Publications: An Oyster is a Wealthy Beast, 1968; The Running Sun, 1971; Sunshine is an Only Child, 1973; Collected Poems, 1990; Collected Stories 1956-1986, 1991; Out With the Stars, 1992. Contributions to: Nvovi Argomenti (Italy). Honours: Oscar Williams and Gene Durwood Poetry Award, 1995; The Morton Dauwen Zabel Award, American Academy of Arts and Letters, Awards, 1993. Memberships: Poetry Society of America; PEN; Author's Guild. Literary Agent: Curtis Brown, 10 Astor Place, NY 10003, USA. Address: 236 Henry Street, Brooklyn, NY 11201, USA.

PURI Rakshat, b. 24 Feb 1924, Lahore, India. m. Meenakshi, 12 Nov 1953, 2 daughters. Education: Graduate in English Literature, Punjab University, Lahore. Appointments: Reporter, 1961-68; Columnist and Editorial Writer, 1969-78, Reporter, 1978-87, The Hindustani Times. Publications: Poems, 1968; 17 Poems, 1975; In the Chronicles, 1978; Love is His Own Power, 1991. Contributions to: Orbis; New Poetry; New Poetry from Oxford; London-Delhi Poetry Quarterly; Resurgence; Journal; Poetry Chronicle; Illustrated Weekly of India. Address: 28 Greville Hall, Greville Place, London NW6 5JS, England.

PYBUS Rodney, b. 5 June 1938, Newcastle upon Tyne, Tyne and Wear, England. Writer. m. Ellen Johnson, 24 June 1961, 2 sons. Education: BA, Hons, Classics, English, MA, 1965, Gonville and Caius College, Cambridge. Appointments: Journalist, TV producer, 1962-76; Lecturer, Macquarie University, Australia, 1976-79; Literature Officer, Cumbria, 1979-81. Publications: In Memoriam Milena, 1973; Bridging Loans, 1976; At the Stone Junction, 1978; The Loveless Letters, 1981; Talitha Cumi, 1985; Cicadas In Their Summers: New and Selected Poems, 1988; Flying Blues, 1994. Contributions to: London Review of Books; New Statesman; London Magazine; Kenyon Review; Ambit; Iowa Review; Sydney Morning Herald; Equivalencias; Poetry Review; Stand; Times Literary Supplement; Critical Survey; Guardian; Independent; Rialto. Honours: Alice Hunt Bartlett Award, Poetry Society, 1974; National Poetry Competition Awards, 1984; 1985; 1988; Peterloo Poetry Competition First Prize, 1989; Arts Council Writer's Fellowships, 1982-84; 1985; Hawthornden Fellowship, 1988. Memberships: Society of Authors; Poetry Society. Address: 21, Plough Lane, Sudbury, Suffolk CO10 6AU, England.

Q

QAZI Moin, b. 4 April 1956, Nagpur, India. Bank Executive; Writer. m. Nahid Qazi, 30 Dec 1994, 2 sons. Education: BA, 1977; LLB, 1980, MA, 1989, Nagpur University; PhD, International University Los Altos, 1992; DLitt, World Academy of Arts and Culture, 1993. Appointment: Bank Manager, State Bank of India, Chandrapur. Publications: A Wakeful Heart, 1989; The Real Face, 1992; Songs of Innocence, 1994. Contributions include: First Time; Poetry International; Symphony; New Hope International; Irish Poetry Review; Resurgence; Northern Perspective; Rocky Hill Lines; Wasteland; New York Times Literary Review; Times of India; Hindu; London Magazine; World Poetry; Art and Poetry. Honours: Commendation Certificates, Poetry Centre, California, USA; International Eminent Poet, 1991; International Poet of the Year, International Poetry Association, WA, USA, 1995; Blue Ribbon Poetry Prize and Commendation Certificates. Membership: Amherst Poetry Society, Baltimore, USA. Address: Ghandhi Chowk, Sadar, Nagpur 440 001, India.

QUARTERMAINE G Gardiner, b. New York, New York, USA. Writer; Poet; Playwright. Education: Oxford University, 1989; BS Communication, American University, Washington, DC, 1981; Lee Strasburg Theatre Institute, New York, 1981. Contributions to: Poet; Dream International Quarterly; Docs; Psychopoetica; Tower Poetry Society; Hot Springs Gazette; Poetalk; Sounds Of Poetry; Ver Poets; Robert Frost Anthology; Poe Sesquicentennial Anthology; Ezra Pound and T S Eliot anthologies. Honours: Mary Carolyn Davies Award, Poetry Society of America, 1987; Outstanding Emerging Artist, Mayor's Arts Awards, 1988. Memberships: Poetry Society of America; Dramatists Guild; Arts Club of Washington; Playwrights Unit (Washington, DC); Academy of American Poets. Address: 1921 Florida Avenue NW, Washignton.**MURRAY III John E,** b. 11 Feb 1973, Jacksonville, Illionis, USA. Writer; Teacher. Education: BA, Psychology, 1995; BA, English Teaching, 1995; Certified in Illionis to teach Psychology & English Grades 6-12. Appointments: Cineplex Odeon Employee, 1995; Assistant Store Manager, Doubleday Bookshop, 1992-96; Walt Disney World Cast Member, Costuming, 1996-. Publications: Rest Best?, 1994; Waiting For What?, 1994; Epitaph of an Angel, 1994; Romance - A Lost Cause, 1994; Most Recent Delight, 1994; Why Life?, 1995; True Friendship, 1995; Let Me Not Begin Anew, 1995; I Await the Day, 1995; Warnings of an Angel, 1995; You Are My Happiness, 1995; Done, 1995. Contributions to: Iliad Press; Arcadia Poetry Press; Quill Books; Amherst Society; Explorer Magazine; Poets Guild; National Library of Poetry; Thumbprints; Creative Arts and Science Enterprises; Sparrowgrass Poetry Forum. Honours: Editors Choice Award, National Library of Poetry, 1994, 1995; Honorable Mention & Presidents Award, Iliad Press, 1994; Accomplishment of Merit, Creative Arts & Science Enterprises, 1995. Memberships: International Society of Poets; National Authors Registry. Address: 2040 Hilltop Road, Hoffman Estates, IL 60195, USA. DC 20009-9328, USA.

QUEFER. See: **FERNANDEZ Querubin D, Jr.**

R

RABORG Frederick Ashton, Jr, (Canyon Kern, Wolf Bronson, Bertha Mayfair, Lee Yay Seok, Gus Fitts), b. 10 Apr 1934, Richmond, Virginia, USA. Writer; Magazine Editor and Publisher. m. Eileen Mary Bradshaw, 19 Oct 1957, 4 sons, 2 daughters. Education: AA, Bakersfield College, 1970; BA, 1973, Secondary credential and graduate studies, 1974-75, California State University, Bakersfield. Appointments: Literary Agent, 1960-62; Journalist, Bakersfield News Bulletin and Bakersfield Californian, 1969-78; Writer 1956-; Editor and Publisher: Amelia Magazine, Cicada Magazine and SPSM&H Magazine, 1983-. Publications: Why Should the Devil Have All the Good Tunes? 1972; Tule, 1988; Hakata, 1991; Posing Nude, 1992. Contributions to: Ladies' Home Journal; Westways; Marriage and Family Living; Chesapeake Bay; Revista/Review Interamericana; Cimarron Review; Epos; Pacific Review; University of Portland Review; Prairie Schooner; Outerbridge; Poetry Australia; Poetry Northwest; Ko; Japanophile; Our Navy; Church Herald; Tendril; Purpose; Junior Discoveries; Grit; Iowa Woman and many more. Honours: Eastside Herald Award, 1974; Bernice Feldman Award, 1974; Louise Louis Award, 1974; Gustaf Davidson Award, 1976; Lillian Steinhauer Award, 1976; Ina Coolbrith Award, 1982; Piedmont Literary Review Award, 1983; Editor's Choice, 1983; Haibun of the Year Award, Dragonfly Magazine, 1983; Ralph Hammond Prize, Alabama State Poetry Society, 1986. Memberships: Poetry Society of America; Authors' League of America; PACT Theatre Guild, Board of Directors 1978-81. Address: PO Box 2385, Bakersfield, CA 93303, USA.

RADAVICH David Allen, b. 30 Oct 1949, Boston, Massachusetts, USA. College Professor. m. Anne Ricketson Zahlan, 2 Jan 1988, 1 stepdaughter. Education: BA, 1971, MA, 1974, PhD, 1979, University of Kansas; Graduate work, Simon Fraser University, Vancouver, British Columbia, 1971-72; University of Aberdeen, Scotland, 1974-75. Appointments: Assistant Instructor, English, Iowa State University, 1982-84; Assistant Professor, Associate Professor, Professor, Eastern Illinois University, 1984-. Publications: Slain Species, 1980; Several chapbooks; Nevertheless...,(drama), 1988. Contributions to: Albany Review; Amaryllis Review; Chapman; Counterpoint; International Poetry Review; Kansas Quarterly; Louisville Review; Lyric; Lyrical Iowa; Orbis; Other Poetry; Plainsongs; Poet and Critic; Poetpourri; Poetry Nottingham; Poetry Now; Success; Times Literary Supplement; Timarit Mals Og Menninger; Trends; Weyfarers; Willow Review; Zebra; Orbis, 1992. Honours: 3rd Prize, Kansas Quarterly, 1976; 1st Prize, Tell-Tale Poetry Competition, 1978; 1st Prize and Special Prize, International Verse Competition, 1983; 3rd Prize, Sucess Competition, 1983; 3rd Prize, Willow Review Competition, 1987; Featured Poet, Rolling Coulter, 1990. Memberships: Poets And Writers; Dramatists Guild. Address: 1832 Ashby Drive, Charleston, IL 61920, USA.

RADULESCU Stella Vinitchi, b. 12 May 1936, Cluj, Romania. Professor. m. Gheorghe Radulescu, 9 May 1959, 1 daughter. Education: PhD, French, University of Bucharest, 1977; MA, French, University of Illinois, Chicago, 1986. Appointments: Assistant Professor, French, University of Bucharest, 1963-83; Lecturer, French, Loyola University, 1986-96; Lecturer, French, Northwestern University, Evanston, Illinois, 1990-. Publications: Versuri, 1969; Dincolo de Alb, 1972; Risipa unei veri, 1978; Singuratatea Cuvintelor, 1981; Blooming Death, 1989; Blood and White Apples, 1993. Contributions to: Luceafarul; Limite; Voices International; Pleiades; Bitterroot. Honour: Honorable Mention, New Voices, 1993. Memberships: Uniunea Scriitorilor, Romania; Academy of American Poets. Address: 5225 North Kenmore 4L, Chicago, IL 60640, USA.

RAE Jacque. See: **SANCHEZ Jacqueline Rae Rawlson.**

RAESCHILD Sheila, b. 4 Nov 1936, Pittsburgh, Pennsylvania, USA. Writer. 3 sons, 3 daughters. Education: BA, Georgia State University, 1967; MA and PhD, Tulane University, 1971. Publications: Lessons in Leaving, 1974. Contributions to: Andover Review; Best College Verse; Centennial Review; Credo; Dekalb Literary Arts Journal; Distaff; Earth's Daughters; East River Review; Hullaballoo; Laureate; New York Quarterly; New Orleans Poets; Painted Bride Quarterly; Rectangles Voices; Shameless Hussey Press Review; Women Together; Zahir. Honours: Several. Memberships: Academy of American Poets; Poetry Society of America; Poets and Writers;

Associated Writers Program; National Writers Union. Address: 1303 Bartlet Court, Santa Fe, NM 87501, USA.

RAGAN James, b. 19 Dec 1944, Pennsylvania, USA. Poet; Playwright; Director; Professor. m. Debora Ann Skovranko, 29 May 1982, 1 son, 2 daughters. Education: BA, Vincent College, 1966; PhD, Ohio University, 1971. Appointments: Director/Professor University of Southern California at Los Angeles Professional Writing Program, 1981-; Poet-in-Residence, Charles University, Prague (summers 1993-); Visiting Professor, CALTECH, 1989-. Publications: In The Talking Hours, 1979; Womb-Weary, 1990; Editor, Yevgeny Yevtushenko, The Collected Poems, 1991; The Hunger Wall, 1995; Lusions, 1996. Contributions to: Nation; Ohio Review; Denver Quarterly; Shenadoah; New Letters; North American Review; Anbtioch Review; Poetry; Yankee; Missouri Review; Southern California Anthology; Expression; Nasi Razgledi; Literaturnaya Gazetta; American Poetry Review; Echo; Gekko; Poetry Magazine; Los Angeles Times; Nimrod; Colorado Review; Trafika; Troubadour; Intro #4; Bomb Magazine. Honours: Humanitarian Award, Swan Foundation, Pittsburgh, 1972; Honorary Doctorate of Humane Letters, St Vincent College, 1990; Medal Of Merit for Poetry, Ohio University, 1990; Co-winner, Gertrude Claytor Award, Poetry Society of America (PSA), 1987. Memberships: Poetry Society of America; Modern Poetry Association; Associated Writing Programs; Modern Language Association; PEN; Writers Guild of America, West; Phi Kappa Phi. Literary Agent: Jennifer Hengen (Sterling Lord Literistic Agency, New York). Address: 1516 Beverwil Drive, Los Angeles, CA 90035, USA.

RAGHUPATHI Kota Varadarajulu, b. 18 Mar 1957, Vellore, Tamil Nadu, India. Teacher. Education: MA, English, 1979, MPhil, 1982, PhD, 1997, Sri Venkateswara University, Tirupati; Diploma in Yoga and Naturopathy, Sri Visweswara Yoga Research Centre, Tirupati, 1995. Publications: Desert Blooms, 1987; Echoes Silent, 1988; The Images of a Growing Dying City, 1989; Voice Eternal, 1991; Symphonies for the Soul, 1997. Widely anthologised and published in various literary journals. Contributions include: Triveni; Literary Half Yearly; Poet; Poetry Times; Canopy; Indian Book Review; Poesie; Rock Pebbles; Brain Wave; Poetry International. Address: 7-96 Second Floor, Shanti Nagar, Tirupati 517 502, India.

RAHBI Saif Al, b. 5 Oct 1956, Oman. Editor. Education: Faculty of Journalism, Cairo University, 1979. Appointments: School Teacher; Editor of Arab newspapers, magazines and periodicals; Correspondent for Arab Press in the Middle East and Europe; Editor in Cultural Affairs. Publications: Madness Albatross; Jabel Al Akhder, 1983; The Bells of Disjunction, 1984; Thoughts of a Voyager, 1986; One Knife is Not Enough to Slaughter a Bird, 1988; The First Step Phase, 1991; Diaspora's Memories, 1992; A Man from the Empty Quarter. Contributions to: Oman; Al Khalij; Al Bayan; Al Awsat; Al Hayyat; Al Nigid Review; Shoun Adabiya Magazine. Address: Koniginnegracht 27, 2514 AB The Hague, Netherlands.

RAHUL. See: **SRIVASTAVA Ram Mohan Lal.**

RAI K B, b. 20 June 1935, Sarai Sidhu, West Pakistan. Administrative Officer, retired. m. Umesh Kanta, 29 May 1970, 2 sons. Education: Matriculation, Punjab University, 1952; BA, Agra University, 1963; MA, English, Delhi University, 1968. Appointments: International Commission on Irrigation and Drainage for 32 years, retiring as Administrative Officer, 1995, Chanakyapuri, New Delhi, India. Publications: Men and Gods and Other Poems, 1985; Miscellany, 1994. Contributions to: Skylark; Poetry; Poetry Time; Poesy; Bridge-in-Making; Canopy; Young India; Poet; Inner Voice; Poetcrit. Address: BB/18C, First Floor, Janakpuri, New Delhi 110058, India.

RAINE Craig Anthony, b. 3 Dec 1944, Shildon, County Durham, England. Writer. m. Ann Pasternak Slater, 27 Apr 1972, 3 sons, 1 daughter. Education: Oxford, 1966; BPhil, 1968. Appointments: Reviews Editor, 1977-79; Editor, Quarto, 1979-80; Poetry Editor, New Statesman, 1981; Faber, 1981-. Publications include: A Martian Sends a Postcard from Home; The Electrification of the Soviet Union; Haydn and the Valve Trumpet. Contributions to: Observer; Sunday Times; Independent on Sunday; New Statesman; Listener; Encounter; London Review of Books; Times Literary Supplement; Literary Review; Grand Street; New Yorker. Honours: Southern Arts Literature Award; Cholmondeley Award. Memberships: PEN; Royal Society of Literature. Address: c/o Faber and Faber, 3 Queen Square, London WC1, England.

RAJA P, b. 7 Oct 1952, India. Lecturer in English. m. Periyanayaki, 6 May 1976, 2 sons, 1 daughter. Education: MA, English Literature and Language, 1975; PhD, 1995. Publications: From Zero To Infinity, 1987; Disturbed Flowers, 1991. Contributions to: Prophetic Voices; Noreal; Spindrift; Writer's Life Line; Now Magazine; Poet; Poesie; Poetry Time; International Poets; Lyric; Skylark; Mirror; Telegraph; Hitavada; Yuva Bharati; Mother India; Indian And Foreign Review; Pratibha India; Canopy; Byword; Language Forum; Kavita India; Sun Times; Creative Forum; Indian Book Chronicle; Samvedana; Muse. Honours: Literary Award, Pondicherry University, 1987; International Eminent Poet Award, Madras, 1988; Michael Madhusudan Award, Calcutta, 1991. Memberships: Poetry Society, New Delhi; Youth Literary Club, Pondicherry. Address: 74 Poincare Street, Olandai Keerapalayam, Pondicherry 605004, India.

RAJAN Tilottama, b. 1 Feb 1951, New York, New York, USA. Professor. Education: BA, Hons, Trinity College, Toronto, 1972; MA, 1973; PhD, 1977, University of Toronto. Appointments: Assistant Professor, Huron College, University of Western Ontario and Queen's University, 1980-83; Associate Professor, 1983-85; Professor, University of Wisconsin at Madison, 1985-90; University of Western Ontario, 1990-; Director, Centre for the Study of Theory and Criticism, University of Western Ontario, 1995-. Publications: Myth In A Metal Mirror, 1967; Dark Interpreter, 1980-; The Supplement of Reading, 1990; Intersections: Nineteenth Century Philosophy and Contemporary Theory, 1995. Contributions to: ELH; Studies In Romanticism; Studies In The Novel; SEL; 19th Century Contexts. Honours: Guggenheim Fellowship, 1987-88; Fellow of the Royal Society of Canada, 1994-. Memberships: Modern Language Association of America; Canadian and American Comparative Literature Associations; International Association of Philosophy and Literature; Society for the Study of Narrative Literature; Keats-Shelley Association; Wordsworth-Coleridge Association; North American Society for the Study of Romanticism. Address: 870 Wellington Street, London, Ontario N6A 5S7, Canada.

RAJANI. See: **ITTYCHERIA Verghese.**

RAJARAM A, (Bramharajan), b. 24 Apr 1953, Salem, Massachusetts. Teacher. m. 9 Nov 1981, 1 daughter. Education: MA; MPhil; PhD. Publications: Known Eternity; Men Sensitive to Pain; Memory Sculpture; Ancient Heart. Contributions to: Poetry Chronicle; Indian Poetry Today; Anuvadha; Indian Express; Book Review; Indian Literature. Memberships: National Poetry Center Bharat Bhavan. Address: Department of English, Government Arts College, Ooty 643 002, India.

RAJU Chethput, b. 28 Jan 1916, Madras, India. m. Eashwari Raju, 14 Nov 1947, 2 sons. Education: BA. Publications: This Modern Age and Other Poems; No Exit. Contributions to: Poetry Review; Poetry Nippon; Purpose; Times of India; Illustrated Weekly; Indian Scholar; Journal of Indian Writing; Skylark. Honour: Prizewinner, All India Poetry Competition. Membership: PEN. Address: 3 Ganga Vihar, 318 Bhalchandra Road, Matunga, C R Bombay 19, India.

RAKOVSZKY Zsuzsa, b. 4 Dec 1950, Sopron, Hungary. Freelance Writer; Translator. Education: Graduate, Faculty of Art, Eotvos University, Budapest, 1975. Appointments: Librarian, 1975-81; Editor, 1981-86; Freelance Writer and Translator, 1986-. Publications: Joslatok es hataridok, 1981; Tovabb egy hazzal, 1987; Feher-fekete, 1991. Contributions to: Kortars; Jelenkor; Alfold; Holmi; 2000; New Hungarian Quarterly. Honours: Graves Prize, 1980; Dery Prize, 1986; Jozsef Attila Prize, 1986. Memberships: Hungarian PEN; Hungarian Writer's Association. Address: Torna u 22, Sopron, Hungary.

RAMAKRISHNAN K V, b. 15 Sept 1935, Kerala, India. m. Santha P, 18 Oct 1967, 2 daughters. Education: MA, English Language and Literature, Malayalam Vidwan. Appointments: Professor of English; Chief Editor, Malayalakavitha (poetry monthly); Assistant Editor, Mathrubhooi Illustrated Weekly. Publications: Sahayaatrikayodu, 1964; Varanda Ganga, 1967; Puthiya Saaradhi, 1975; Chathurangam, 1978; Naazhikavatti, 1980; Ketaavilakku, 1981; Agnisudhi, 1986; Kottum Chiriyum, 1990. Contributions to: Mathrubhoomi Illustrated Weekly; Kumkumam; Kalaakaumudi; Deshabhimani; Malayalanaadu; Thilakam monthly; Bhaashaaposhini; Malayalkavitha; Keralakaviatha. Honours: Mayayalam Poetry Prizes, 1963, 1964; English Poetry Prize, 1963, Kerala University. Memberships: Kerala Sahithya Samithy, Secretary and General Secretary; Edassery Sahithya Samithy; Kerala Sahithya Parashath.

Address: Assistant Editor, Mathrubhoomi Illustrated Weekly, KP Kesava Menon Road, Calicut 873001, India.

RAMAKRISHNAN Nivedita, (Nita), b. 3 Apr 1975, Trivandrum, Kerala, India. Student. Education: BA, English Literature, History and Political Science, Osmania University, Hyderabad, 1995; MA, English Literature and Film (Text and Gender), Keele University, England, 1996. Contributions to: Poetry published in Blitz (weekly), Bombay, and Poet (international monthly), Madras. Address: 2A Atlas Apartments, Road 10, Banjara Hills, Hyderabad 500 034, India.

RAMIREZ-MURZI Marco, b. 3 Dec 1926, San Antonio, Tach, Venezuela. Writer; Lawyer. Education: Doctor of Law and Social Sciences, 1952. Publications: Entre el Cielo y la Tierra, 1948; Antes del Olvido, 1951; Alta Noche, 1955; Otra Soledad, 1956; El Prestidigitador, 1956; Antologia Poetica, 1960; Solo Poemas, 1963; La Rosa y el Verano, 1963; Sin Geografia, 1965; El Bufon de Barba Gris, 1966; De Amar y Andar, 1967; Rito Sagrado, 1967; El Regreso del Agua, 1975; Viento del Oeste, 1978; Contraposiciones, 1981; Los Estigmas, 1987; Todo Poesia, 1990. Contributions to: Revisat Nacional de Cultura; El Tiempo; El Universal; Diario de la Nacion; Diario Catolico. Honours: Numerous. Memberships: Venezuelan Writers Circle, Vice President. Address: Apt 1821, Caracas 1010-A, Venezuela.

RAMKE Bin, b. 19 Feb 1947, Port Neches, Texas, USA. Teacher; Editor; Poet. m. 31 May 1967, 1 son. Education: BA, Louisiana State University, 1970; MA, University of New Orleans, 1971; PhD, Ohio University, 1975. Appointments: Professor, Columbus College, 1976-85 and University of Denver, 1985-; Editor, Contemporary Poetry Series, 1984-; Poetry Editor, The Denver Quarterly, 1985-, Editor, 1994-. Publications: The Language Student; The Difference Between Night and Day; White Monkeys; The Erotic Light of Gardens; Massacre of the Innocents. Contributions to: Poetry; New Yorker; Paris Review. Honours: Yale Younger Poets Award; Texas Institute of Arts and Letters Award; Iowa Poetry Award. Memberships: PEN; Associated Writing Programs; National Book Critics Circle. Address: Department of English, University of Denver, Denver, CO 80208, USA.

RAMNEFALK (Sylvia) Marie Louise, b. 21 Mar 18941, Stockholm, Sweden. Author. Education: FK, 1964, FL, 1968, FD, 1974 (Equivalent to PhD, Literature), Stockholm University. Appointments: Script Supervisor, 1967-68; Tutor, Stockholm and Umea Universities, 1960-70; School for Librarians, Boras, 1970, 1980; Karlstad University, 1986-87; Literary Critic. Publications: Ensskilt Liv Pagar, 1975; Verkligheten Gor Dig Den Aran, 1978; Nagon Har Jag Sett, 1979; Kungsadra, 1981; Sorg, 1982; Levnadskonster, 1983; Adam I Paradiset, 1984; Deb Behovs Nagot Underjordiskt Som Karlek Och Musik, 1987; Julian Såg Gud, 1992; Författaren, världen, språket, 1996. Contributions to: Bonniers Littereara Magasin; Dagens Nyheter; Svenska Dagb; Var Losen; Lyrikvannen; Ord Och Bild. Memberships: Forfattarforbund, Past Executive Board; Statens Kulturrad; Forfattarnas Fotokopieringsfond, Past President; Swedish PEN. Address: Vastra Valhallavagen 25A, S-182 63 Djursholm, Sweden.

RAMSEY Jarold William, b. 1 Sept 1937, Oregon, USA. University Professor. m. Dorothy Ann Quinn, 16 Aug 1959, 1 son, 2 daughters. Education: BA, University of Oregon, 1959; PhD, University of Washington, 1963-65; Assistant Professor, 1965-70, Associate Professor, 1970-80, Professor, 1980-, University of Rochester. Publications: Hand Shadows; Love In An Earthquake; Coyote Was Going There; Reading The Fire; Coyote Goes Upriver (play); The Stories We Tell (with Suzi Jones), 1994. Contributions to: PMLA; Shakespeare Quarterly; Journal of American Folklore; Massachusetts Review; Atlantic; Northwest Review; Iowa Review; American Scholar; Christian Science Monitor. Honours: Phi Beta Kappa; Lilian Fairchild Award; National Endowment for the Arts Writing Award; Ingram Merrill Award; Helen Bullis Prize; Quarterly Review International Poetry Prize, 1989. Membership: Modern Language Association. Address: Department of English, University of Rochester, NY 14627, USA.

RANA Pradeep Shumsher, b. 10 July 1960, Thapathali, Nepal. Education: Matriculation, 1974; IA, 1976; BA, 1978; MA, 1981; MA, 1988; LLB, 1988. Appointments: Supervisor, 1981-1983; Assistant Lecturer, 1984-89; Research Officer, Chief Editor, 1991; Lecturer, JMC Campus, KTM, 1993-1995. Publication: Empty Talk. Contributions to: Himal; Environment; World Poetry; Skylark; Poetry; Atlantic Review; Wascana Review; New Hope International; Broadway Music

Production; International Poets, India. Honours: Golden Poet Award; Special Recording Award; Gold Medal of Honor Award. Memberships: World Of Poetry; International Society of Poets; Creative Writers League Nepal; Nominated Poet Of The Year, International Society of Poets, USA, 1995. Membership: Research Officer, Forum For Developmental Studies, 1991-1995. Address: PO Box 3789, Kathmandu, Nepal.

RANDALL C K. See: **BROCK Randal(l).**

RANDALL Margaret, b. 6 Dec 1936, New York, New York, USA. Writer; Photographer; Teacher; Activist. 1 son, 3 daughters. Appointments: Distinguished Visiting Professor, Women's Studies, University of Delaware, 1991; Managing Editor, Frontiers: A Journal of Women's Studies, University of New Mexico, Albuquerque, 1990-91; Visiting Professor, English Department, Trinity College, Hartford, Connecticut, 1992. Publications: Giant Of Tears, 1959; Ecstasy Is A Number, 1961; Poems Of The Glass, 1964; Small Sounds From The Brass Fiddle, 1964; October, 1965; Twenty-Five Stages Of My Spine, 1967; Getting Rid Of Blue Plastic, 1967; So Many Rooms Has A House But One Roof, 1967; Part Of The Solution, 1972; Day's Coming, 1973; With These Hands, 1973; All My Used Parts, Shackles, Fuel, Tenderness And Stars, 1977; Carlota: Poems And Prose From Havana, 1978; We, 1978; A Poetry Of Resistance, 1983; The Coming Home Poems, 1986; Albuquerque: Coming Back To The USA, 1986; This Is About Incest, 1987; Memory Says Yes, 1988; The Old Cedar Bar, 1992; Dancing With The Doe, 1992; Hunger's Table, The Recipe Poems, 1997; Oral History: Cuban Women Now, 1974; Sandino's Daughters, 1981; Editor: Estos Cantos Habitados/These Living Songs, 1978; Photography: Women Brave In The Face Of Danger, 1985; Nicaragua Libre!, 1985; Editor, Anthologies: Las Mujeres, 1970; Poesia Beat, 1977. Contributions to: Las Mujeres; Poesia Beat; Poetry Chicago; Evergreen Review; Poetry Northwest; Nation; Liberation; Outsider; Ikon; Chelsea Review; Kulcher; Numerous others. Honours include: 1st Prizes, Photography, Nicaraguan Children's Association, 1983; Creating Ourselves National Art Exhibition, 1992. Address: 50 Cedar Hill Road NE, Albuquerque, NM 87122, USA.

RANDELL Elaine, b. 21 Sept 1951, London, England. m. 14 Feb 1982, 3 daughters. Education: CQSW, Mid Kent College. Appointments: Social Worker for London Borough of Bromley, Kent County Council, Guy's Hospital, Children's Society. Publications: Larger Breath of All Things, 1978; This Our Frailty, 1979; Songs for the Sleepless, 1982; Beyond All Other, 1986; Gut Reaction, 1987. Contributions to: Poetry Review; Ambit; New British Poetry; The the Gold of Flesh; Angles of Dine; Writing Women; Slow Dancer; Kite; Not Poetry; North Atlantic Review. Address: The Stable, Snoadhill, Bethersden, nr Ashford, Kent TN26 3DY, England.

RANEY Carolyn, b. 1918, Los Angeles, California, USA. Consultant in Educational Management; Musicologist; University Professor of Creative Writing in English (Germany). m. Saul Schechtman, 2 daughters. Education: BM, University of Rochester, 1938; MM, Cleveland Institute, Case Western University, 1943; PhD, New York University, 1971; IEM, Harvard School of Business, 1980. Appointments: Music Faculties of New York University, City University of New York, AMDA, New York, 1968-73; Co-ordinator of Graduate Studies, Peabody Institute of Johns Hopkins University, 1973-76; Vice President of Academics East Stroudsburg (PA) University, 1976-80; Dean of Graduate School, Schiller International University of Heidelberg, London and Paris. Publications: Inspiration and Apple Pie (Germany); American Poetry Anthology (USA); Carosaul Editions (France); Selected Poems: Realities and Unrealities (UK), 1992. Contributions to: Saturday Evening Post; Christian Science Monitor; Fulbright Funnel (Germany); Paris/Atlantic (France); Cleveland Plain Dealer; Kaleidograph; American Weave; Country Bard; Talaria; Sonnet Sequence; IOTA (UK). Honours: Several. Memberships: Founding President, European Chapter, College Music Society; Life Member, College Music Society; American Society for Composers, Artists and Performers; International Musicological Society; American Association for Higher Education; Sonneck Society; The Authors Guild (USA). Literary Agent: Patricia Allen (USA). Address: 1 Chemin de la Noue, F 57130 Vaux, France.

RANGASWAMI Srinivasa, b. 20 Feb 1924, Madras, India. Retired Parliamentary Official; Freelance Writer. m. Ramapriya C R, 30 June 1944, 1 son. Education: BA (Hons), English Language and Literature, 1944; MA, English Language and Literature, Madras University, 1945. Appointments: Serivce, Parliament of India, 1952-82;

Retired as Joint Director, Library Research and Information Service, Parliament of India, 1982; Officer on Special Duty, Institute of Constitutional & Parliamentary Studies, 1983-91, Head of the Institute, 1987-91. Contributions to: Poet, Madras; Poets International, Bangalore; Journal of the Poetry Society, India; Metverse Muse; Quest; Alive; World Poetry 1996; Poems 1996; Poetry 2000 AD; The Brain Wave, Poets Fantasy, USA. Honours: First Class Honour: Certificate, Second International Youth Exhibition, YMCA, Madras, 1938; The Sir Mark Hunter Memorial Prize at Presidency College, Madras, 1944. Memberships: World Poetry Society Intercontinental, Madras; Poetry Society of India; All India Pen Centre, Bombay; Writers Forum; Fellowship of the United Writers Association, Madras. Address: N/5 Adyar Apartments, Kottur Gardens, Madras 600 085, India.

RANSFORD Tessa, b. 8 July 1938, Bombay, India. Writer; Teacher; Editor. m. (1)Iain Kay Stiven, 29 Aug 1959, div 1986, 1 son, 3 daughters. (2) Callum Macdonald, 7 Dec 1989. Education: MA, University of Edinburgh, 1958; Teacher Training, Craiglockhart College of Education, 1980. Appointments: Previous posts, publishing, adult education, audio-visual aids; Worked in Pakistan (with husband), 1960-68; Director, Scottish Poetry Library, 1984-; Editor, Lines Review, 1988-. Publications: Light Of The Mind, 1980; Fools And Angels, 1984; Shadows From The Greater Hill, 1987; A Dancing Innocence, 1988; Seven Valleys, 1991; Medusa Dozen And Other Poems, 1994. Contributions to: 3 Anthologies; Scotsman; Herald; Lines Review; Chapman; Cencrastus; Stand; Poetry Wales; Poetry Ireland; Fiddlehead (Canada); Review Of The European Association For The Promotion Of Poetry; Ashville Poetry Review, USA; Orbis; Northlight; Northwords; Honours: Scottish Arts Council Book Award, 1980; Howard Sergeant Award for Services to Poetry, 1989. Memberships: RSA; Honorary Member, Saltire Society; Scottish International PEN; Founder and Organiser, The School Of Poets, Edinburgh, 1981-. Address: C/o Scottish Poetry Library, Tweeddale Court, 14 High Street, Edinburgh EH1 1TE, Scotland.

RAO Kanaka Durga, b. 22 Jan 1958, Bombay, India. Educationist. Education: SSC, Bombay Board of Education; PCT, FSBT, Society of Business Teachers, London. Appointments: Former Secretary, Authors Association of India, Bombay; Honorary Director and Member of Editorial Board, International Socio-Literary Foundation, Karnataka State. Publication: Voices of Peace, collection of poems. Contributions to: Indo-Australian Flowers; Skylark; Samvedana; Rising Stars; Greek Anthology; World Poetry, 1995-1996; The Brain Wave; Michael Madhusan Academy; The Quest; International Socio-Literary Foundation. Honours: Internal Eminent Poet and Honorary Fellowship, International Poets Academy, Madras, 1991; Honorary Fellowship, United Writers' Association, Madras, 1991. Membership: Chetana Literary Group. Address: Flat 2, Plot 299, Chandrajyoti Building Ground Floor, Bhimani Street, Matunga, (C/Rly) Mumbai 400 019, India.

RATCH Jerry, b. 9 Aug 1944, Chicago, Illinois, USA. Writer. m. Sherry Karver, 18 Mar 1990. Education: BA, English, 1967; MFA, Creative Writing, 1970. Publications: Puppet X, 1973; Clown Birth, 1975; Osiris, 1977; Chaucer Marginalia, 1979; Hot Weather, 1982; Helen, 1985; Lenin's Paintings, 1987; Light, 1989. Contributions to: Avec; Ironwood; Sonoma Madala; Carolina Quarterly; Washington Review; Contact II; Northeast Journal. Address: 4333 Holden Street, No 54, Emeryville, CA 94608, USA.

RATCLIFFE Eric Hallam, b. 8 Aug 1918, Teddington, Middlesex, England. Retired Physicist; Information Scientist; Assistant Editor. Education: Birbeck College, University of London. Appointments: Assistant Experimental Officer, Experimental Officer, National Physical Laboratory, Teddington; Experimental Officer, Senior Experimental Officer, Water Pollution Research Laboratory, Stevenage; Assistant Editor, Institution of Electrical Engineers, Stevenage, until retirement; Founder, editor, Ore, 1955-95. Publications: The Visitation, 1952; Little Pagan, 1955; The Chronicle Of The Green Man, 1960; Mist On My Eyes, 1961; Gleanings For A Daughter Of Aeolus, 1968; Leo Poems, 1972; Warrior Of The Icenian Queen, 1973; Commius, 1976; A Sun-Red Mantle, 1976; Nightguard Of The Quaternary, 1979; Ballet Class, 1986; Leo Mysticus, 1989; The Runner Of The Seven Valleys, 1990; The Infidelium, 1989; The Ballad Of Polly McPoo, 1991; Hill 60, 1991; Scientary, 1991; Kingdoms, 1992; Ark, 1992; Advent, 1992; Components Of The Nation, 1992; The Golden Heart Man, 1993; The Man In Green Combs, 1993; Fire In The Bush: poems 1955-1992, 1993; William Ernest Henley (1849-1903): An Introduction, 1993; The Caxton Of Her Age: The Career And Family Background Of Emily

Faithfull (1835-95), 1993; Winstanley's Walton, 1649: Events In The Civil War At Walton-On-Thames, 1994; Ratcliffe's Megathersaurus, 1995; Anthropos, 1995. Contributions to: Completing The Picture; Flame; Friday Market; Grub Street; Lynx; Outposts; Fiddlehead (Canada); Quicksilver (USA); Avalon Anthology (USA); PEN New Poems, 1960; Acumen; Rialto; Man; Botteghe Oscure (Italy). Memberships: Scientific and Medical Network; Society for Psychical Research. Address: 7 The Towers, Stevenage, Hertfordshire SG1 1HE, England.

RATCLIFFE Stephen, b. 7 July 1948. Teacher; Publisher; Editor. m. Ashley Perdue Ratcliffe, 17 Nov 1973, div 1994, 1 daughter. Education: BA, 1970, PhD, 1978, University of California atBerkeley. Appointment: Professor of English, Mills College, 1984-. Publications: Criticism Campion: On Song, 1981; Poetry: New York Notes, 1983; Distance, 1986; Mobile/Mobile, 1987; Rustic Diversions, 1988; Spaces in the Light said to be where one/comes from, 1992; Selected Letters, 1992; Private, 1993; Present Tense, 1995. Contributions to: New American Writing; Tuyoni; Caliban; Temblor; Sulfur; Central Park; Talisman: Avec; OiArs; Transfer; Poetry Project Newsletter; Exemplaria; Chain. Honours: Stegner Fellowship in Creative Writing, Stanford University, 1974; Fund for Poetry Awards, 1988, 1991; National Endowment for the Arts Grants, 1991, 1995. Memberships: Associated Writing Programs; Modern Language Association. Address: PO Box 524, Bolinas, CA 94924, USA.

RATH Sashibhusan, b. 30 May 1955, Kalahandi, India. Service; Writer. m. Sanghamitra, 6 Dec 1986, 2 sons. Education: BSc, Hons with Distinction, Social Work, MSc, Physics and Astrophysics, Delhi University; Diploma in Social Work, Indian Institute of Business Management and Social Work, Calcutta University. Appointment: Senior Manager, Personnel and Administration Department, Raw Materials Division, Steel Authority of India Ltd, 1979-. Publications: A Miscellany, in Oriya language, 1992; A book on management, 1995; First anthology, Tributaries, a hundred poems in English, due 1997. Contributions to: Asian Age; Telegraph; Prophetic Voices; Byword; Poetry; Bridge in Making. Honours: Prajatantra, 1970, Dharitree, 1984, for popularisation of science among children. Memberships: Poetry Society, Delhi; Friend of PEN, Bombay. Address: D-3/2 Meghahatuburu, West Singhbhum, Bihar 833223, India.

RATNER Rochelle, b. 2 Dec 1948, Atlantic City, New Jersey, USA. m. Kenneth Thorp, 30 Mar 1990. Appointments: Poetry Columnist, Soho Weekly New, 1976-82; Executive Editor, American Book Review, 1978-; Small Press Columnist, Library Journal, 1982; Poetry Editor, Israel Horizons, 1989-; Board of Directors, National Book Critics Circle, 1995-; Editor, New Literary Online Reading Room, 1995-96. Publications: The Lion's Share; Bobby's Girl; Practicing to be a Woman; Combing the Waves; A Birthday of Waters; False Trees; Someday Songs; Quarry; Trying to Understand What it Means to be a Feminist; Pirate's Song; The Tightrope Walker; Zodiac Arrest. Contributions to: Nation; Antaeus; Minnesota Review; Southern Poetry Review. Memberships: PEN; Authors Guild; National Book Critics Circle; Artists Equity. Address: 609 Columbus Avenue, Apt 16F, New York, NY 10024, USA.

RATTEE Michael Dennis, b. 27 Feb 1953, Holyoke, Massachusetts, USA. Writer. m. Hannelore Quander, 4 Sept 1977, 1 son, 1 daughter, Education: University of Vermont, no degree. Appointments: Editor of Prickly Pear, Tucson (poetry quarterly), 1982-87. Publications: Mentioning Dreams, 1985; Calling Yourself Home, 1986. Contributions to: Blue Unicorn; Contact II; CutBank; Negative Capability; Paragraph; Pivot; Poet Lore; Poery Flash; Signal; Laurel Review; Santa Clara Review. Honour: National Endowment for the Arts Fellowship Grant in Poetry, 1984. Address: 2833 East Kaibab Vista, Tucson, AZ 85713, USA.

RATUSHINSKAYA Irina, b. 4 Mar 1954, Odessa, Russia. Writer. m. Igor Geraschenko, 17 Nov 1979, 2 sons. Education: Diploma, Physics, Odessa University. Appointments: Visiting Scholar, Northwestern University, USA, 1987-88. Publications: No I'm Not Afraid, 1986; A Tale of Three Heads, 1986; Beyond the Limit, 1987; Grey is the Colour of Hope, 1988; Pencil Letter, 1988; In the Beginning, 1990; The Odessans, 1996. Contributions to: Anthologies: Spirits of the Age, 1989; Poetry With an Edge, 1988; Moderne Russiche Poesie seit (Germany), 1990; Poetry Please, 1991; Thin Ice, 1991; Sing Freedom, 1991: Cambridge Contemporary Poets, 1992; Seven Ages, 1992; The Relaxation Letters, 1993; The Calling of the Kindred, 1993; Gather the Fragments, 1993; From the Republic of

Conscience, 1993; Bound to be Free, 1995. Honours: Poetry International Rotterdam Award, 1986; Ross McWhirter Foundation, 1987; Christopher Award (USA), 1988; Individual Templeton UK Award, 1993. Membership: PEN International, London. Address: 15 Crothall Close, London N13 4BN, England.

RAUT-ROY Satchidananda, b. 13 May 1916, Gurujang, Orissa, India. Author; Poet. m. Bhudevi Rautroy, 1945, 2 sons, 2 daughters. Education: Graduated, 1939; Trained in Industrial Relations and Social Welfare, Australia and New Zealand, 1952, ILO, Geneva, Switzerland, 1955. Appointments: Chief Labour Welfare Officer, Executive Officer, Kesoram Cotton Mills Ltd, 1942-62; Founder-President, Diganta Museum and Research Centre, Cuttack; Editor, Diganta (quarterly journal); Founder, Managing Director, Orissa Board Mills, 1962-68; Participated in numerous conferences and seminars worldwide. Publications: Pandulipi, 1932-47; Kavita, 1962; Swagata, 1969; Kavita, 1969; Pallishri; Baji Raut; Abhijan; Chitragriba, novel, 1935; Short stories in 6 volumes; Poems and short stories translated into English and Russian. Contributions to: Journals and international anthologies. Honours: Padma-Shri, 1962; Central Sahitya Akademi Award, National Academy of Letters, 1964; Soviet Land Nehru Award, 1965; President, 1st All-India Poets Conference, Calcutta, 1968; Honorary DLitt, Andhra University, 1977; DLitt, honoris causa, Berhampur University, 1978; Bharat Nayak Award, Sambalpur University, 1983; Jnanpith Award, 1986; Bibhuti Bhusan Bandopadhya Award, Ghatsila, Bihar, 1988; President, Rourkela Session, 1988; Honoured with title of Mahalavi, Rourkela, 1985, Cuttack, 1988; Utkal Ratnamby Utkal Sahitya Samal, 1994; G Rath Award, Cuttack, 1996; Nominated Fellow, Central Sahitya Akademi, New Delhi, 1996. Address: Mission Road, Cuttack 753001, Orissa, India.

RAWNSLEY Irene, b. 20 Jun 1935, Leeds, Yorkshire, England. Poet. Div, 1 son, 1 daughter. Education: Diploma in Education, Leeds University; MA, York University. Appointments: Teacher, Leeds Schools, 22 years. Publications: Poetry for young children: Ask A Silly Question, 1988; Dog's Dinner, 1990, House of A Hundred Cats, 1995; Poetry for young teens: Hiding Out, forthcoming; Poetry for adults: Shall We Gather at The River?, 1990. Contributions to: Encounter; Acumen; Spokes; Wide Skirt; Outposts; BBC Poetry - Poetry Corner (Schools); English Resources (Schools); Pen to Paper, BBC Radio 4; TV, A Bear Behind, children's programme. Honours: Joint First Prize, Rhyme Revival International, 1987; Prizewinner, Northern Poetry Competition (Littlewood), 1989; Prizewinner, The Poetry Business Competition, 1996; 4th Prize, Peterloo Poetry Competition, 1989. Memberships: Poetry Society; Society of Authors, including children's writers' and illustrators' group. Address: 5 Marton Road, Gargrave, Skipton, North Yorkshire BD23 3NL, England.

RAWORTH Thomas (Tom) Moore, b. 19 July 1938, London, England. m. Valerie Murphy, 4 sons, 1 daughter. Education: MA Literature, University of Essex, 1967-70. Appointments: Lecturer, Bowling Green State University, Ohio, 1972-73; Visiting Lecturer, University of Texas, 1974-75; Poet-in-Residence, University of Essex, 1969, Northeastern University, Chicago, 1973-74, Kings College, Cambridge, 1977-78; Visiting Lecturer, University of Cape Town, South Africa, 1991. Publications: Sky Tails, 1978; Nicht Wahr Rosie? 1979; Writing, 1982; Levre de Poche, 1983; Heavy Light, 1984; Tottering State, 1984; Lazy Left Hand, 1986; Visible Shivers, 1987; All Fours, 1991; Catacoustics, 1991; Eternal Sections, 1991; Survival, 1991. Contributions to: New Statesman; Mgur; Zuk; Writing; Verse; Joe Soap's Canoe; Venezia Undertide; L'Implano; Equafinality; Biancaneve; Klinamen; Poesie; Action Poetique; Coyotes Journal. Honours: Alice Hunt Bartlett Prize, 1969; Cholmondley Award, 1972; International Committee on Poetry (NY) Award, 1988. Membership: PEN. Address: 3 St Philip's Road, Cambridge CB1 3AQ, England.

RAY Barnik, b. 21 Jan 1936, Dhaka, India. College Teacher. 2 sons, 1 daughter. Education: MA. Appointments: Teacher in several Government colleges in West Bengal, 37 years. Publications: Poetry: Änander Marmanita Andhakär, 1972; Nil Dupwrer Bhay, 1972; Särírer Udíhijia Chäyäy, 1976; He Amär Mrtyu, 1980; Bälir Ghari, 1984; Sudhu Bëce Achi, 1995; Elomelo Chadä, 1988; Poetry translations from original: Podo Jami (T S Eliot's Waste Land), 1971; Anäbäs (Saint John Perse's Anatase), 1976; Mason William's Poems, 1985. Contributions to: Many newspapers, reviews, magazines, journals and periodicals including: Desh; Statesman; Amrita Bazar Patrika; Pratikshan. Memberships include: Asiatic Society of Bengal; Authors Guild; Sanskrit Society. Address: Puspa Apartment, 4987 Sahid

Hemanta Kumar Basu Sarani, Jawpur, Flat 8, Calcutta 700 074, West Bengal, India.

RAY Bibekananda, b. 24 Mar 1940, West Bengal, India. Official Media Journalist. m. Bandana, 3 Mar 1968, 3 daughters. Education: MA, English Literature, Presidency College, Calcutta, 1963. Appointments: Indian Information Service, 1965; Senior Correspondent, News Editor, All India Radio, Calcutta; Public Relations Officer, Ministry of Defence, Calcutta; Regional Officer, Central Board of Film Censors, Calcutta; Editor-in-Chief, Sainik Samachar, New Delhi, 1983-88; Additional Director General (News), All India Radio, New Delhi, 1991-95; All India Radio Correspondent for Far East, Singapore, 1996-. Publication: Completed Mss on Centenary History of Indian Cinema for Government of India. Contributions to: La Poesie; New Voices, anthology. Honours: Shortlisted, All-India Poetry Contest, 1986. Address: 26 Newton Road, #07-03 Newton View, Singapore 307957.

RAY David Eugene, b. 20 May 1932, Oklahoma, USA. Writer; Professor of English. m. S Judy Ray, 21 Feb 1970. Education: BA, 1952, MA, 1957, University of Chicago. Appointments: Assistant Professor in Humanities, Reed College, Oregon, 1964-66; Visiting Associate Professor, Bowling Green State University, 1970-71; Professor of English, University of Missouri, Kansas City, 1971-95; Visiting Professor: India; New Zealand; Australia. Publications: Poetry Books: X-Rays, 1965; Dragging the Main and Other Poems, 1968; A Hill in Oklahoma, 1972; Gathering Firewood: New Poems and Selected, 1974; Enough of Flying: Poems Inspired by The Ghazals of Ghalib, 1977; The Tramp's Cup, 1978; The Touched Life, 1982; Not Far From The River, 1983; On Wednesday I Cleaned Out My Wallet, 1985; Elysium in The Halls of Hell, 1986; Sam's Book, 1987; The Maharani's New Wall, 1989; Not Far From The River, 1991; Wool Highways, 1993; Kangaroo Paws, 1994. Short Stories: The Mulberries of Mingo, 1978. Contributions include: Atlantic; Harper's; New Yorker; Paris Review; Poetry; Yale Review; Parnassus; Ploughshares; Poetry in Review. Honours: William Carlos Williams Award, Poetry Society of America, 1979, 1994; Bernice Jennings Award for Traditional Poetry, Amelia Magazine, 1987; Emily Dickinson Award, Poetry Society of America, 1988; Maurice English Poetry Award, 1988; Nebraska Review Award, 1989; Passaic Community College National Poetry Award, 1989; 1st Prize, Stanley Hanks Memorial Contest, St Louis Poetry Centre, 1990. Memberships: PEN; Poetry Society of America; Phi Kappa Phi; Friends Association for Higher Education. Address: 2033 E 10th Street, Tucson, AZ 85719, USA.

RAY Suzanne Judy, b. 20 Aug 1939, Sussex, England. m. David E Ray, 21 Feb 1970. Writer; Photographer. Education: BA Hons, University of Southampton, 1960. Appointments: Secretary, Transition Magazine, Kampala, Uganda, 1965-67; Associate Editor, New Letters Magazine, 1971-85; Producer, New Letters on the Air, 1982-86; Executive Director, The Writer's Place, Kansas City, 1992-95. Publications: Pebble Rings, 1980; The Jaipur Sketchbook: Impressions of India, 1991; Pigeons in the Chandeliers, 1993; Contributions to: American Voice; Helicon Nine; Poet and Critic; Poetry Review; West Branch; Cream City Review; Harbor Review; Writers Forum; Anthology of Missouri Women Writers; Getting from Here to There. Memberships: Poetry Society of America. Address: 2033 E 10th St, Tucson, AZ 85719, USA.

RAZ Athar, b. 25 May 1935, India. Teacher. m. Zahra, 27 Jan 1970. Education: BSc (Hons); MA. Appointment: Mathematics Teacher. Publications: The Bud and the Ray; Murgh e Dil; Khanda e Baija; The Yellow Shroud; Life, Like a Candle. Contributions to: Mostly Asian Literary Magazines. Honours: Pakistan Writers Guild and Urdu Tarraqui Board Award. Memberships: 21 Colwood Gardens, Colliers Wood, London SW19 2DS, England.

RE'UBENI Meir. See: **FAERBER Meir Marcell.**

READING Peter, b. 27 July 1946, Liverpool, England. Writer. m. 5 Oct 1968, 1 daughter. Education: BA, Fine Art (Painting), Liverpool College of Art, 1967. Appointments: School Teacher, 1967-68; Lecturer in Art History, Liverpool College of Art, 1968-70-; Worked at Agricultural Feed Mill in Shropshire, 1970-92; Writer-in-Residence, Sunderland Polytechnic, 1980-82. Publications: Water and Waste, 1970; For the Municipality's Elderly, 1974; The Prison Cell and Barrel Mystery, 1976; Nothing for Anyone, 1977; Fiction, 1979; Tom Bedlam's Beauties, 1981; Diplopic, 1983; C, 1984; 5x5x5x5x5, 1983; Ukalele Music, 1985; Stet, 1986; Essential Reading, 1986; Final Demands,

1988; Perduta Gentre, 1989; Shitheads, 1989; Evagatory, 1992; 3 in 1, 1992; Last Poems, 1993. Contributions to: Times Literary Supplement; Sunday Times; Observer; Independent on Sunday. Honours: Chomondeley Award, 1978; Dylan Thomas Award, 1983; Whitbread Award, Poetry Category, 1986; Lannan Foundation, USA, Literary Fellowship, 1990. Memberships: Fellow, Royal Society of Literature, 1988. Address: 1 Ragleth View, Little Stretton, Shropshire, England.

REANEY James Crear, b. 1 Sept 1926, Ontario, Canada. m. 29 Dec 1951, 2 sons, 1 daughter. Education: BA, 1948, MA, 1949, University of Toronto. Appointments: University of Manitoba, Winnipeg, 1948-60; University of Western Ontario, 1960-. Publications: The Red Heart, 1949; Twelve Letters To a Small Town, 1962; Suit of Nettles, 1958; Poems, 1972; Performance Poems, 1990; Lewis Carroll's Alice Through The Looking-Glass, adapted for stage, 1994; The Donnellys, a trilogy: Sticks and Stones, St Nicholas Hotel and Handcuffs, 1994. Contributions to: Under Grad; First Statement Press; Contemporary Verse; Canadian Poetry Magazine; Here and Now; Canadian Forum; Northern Review; Queen's Quarterly; Waterloo Review; Tamarack Review; Poetry Chicago; Some Critics are Music Teachers, in Centre and Labyrinth, Essays in Honour of Northrop Frye, Toronto, 1983. Honours: Governor General Awards, 1949, 1958, 1963; University of Alberta Award for Letters, 1974; Order of Canada, 1975; Chalmers Awards for Drama. Memberships: President, 1959-60, Association of Canadian University Teachers; League of Canadian Poets; Canadian Theatre Co-Op; Guild of Canadian Playwrights. Literary Agent: John Miller Cultural Support Services, 14 Earl Street, Toronto, Canada, M4Y 1M3. Address: 276 Huron Street, London, Ontario N6A 2U9, Canada.

RECTOR Liam, b. 21 Nov 1949, Washington, District of Columbia, USA. Workshop Director; Poetry Editor. m. Tree Swenson, 1 daughter. Education includes: MA, Poetry, Writing Seminars, Johns Hopkins University, 1978; MPA, Administration, Kennedy School of Government, Harvard University, 1992. Appointments: Director of Poetry Programs, Folger Shakespeare Library, 1978-80, 1983; Program Associate, Co-Director, Academy of American Poets, 1980-81; Program Specialist, Literature Program, National Endowment for the Arts, 1983-85; Executive Director, Associated Writing Programs, 1986-91; Founder and Director, Bennington Writing Seminars, Director, Bennington Summer Writing Workshops, Bennington College, 1991-; Poetry Editor, Harvard Magazine, 1994-; Various poetry readings, lectures and panels at colleges, universities and community centres among others, USA. Publications: The Sorrow of Architecture, 1984; American Prodigal, 1994; Editor, The Day I Was Older: On The Poetry of Donald Hall, 1989; Essays, reviews and interviews in various publications including: Oxford Companion to Literature; American Poetry Review. Contributions include: Paris Review; Partisan Review; American Poetry Review; Ploughshares; Boulevard; Agni; Poetry East; Epoch; Kayak; Boston Phoenix. Honours: Fellowship in Poetry, National Endowment for the Arts, 1980; Kenan Grant, Phillips Academy, Andover, Massachusetts, 1982; Postgraduate Fellow, Vermont College, Montpelier, Vermont, 1984; Guggenheim Fellowship in Poetry, New York, 1985-86. Memberships: Board of Directors, Associated Writing Programs, 1995-; Council and Freedom-to-Write Committee, PEN New England, 1994-; Secretary and Executive Committee, Commissioner, Norfolk Commission on The Arts and Humanities, Virginia, 1988-91. Address: 183 Willow Avenue, Somerville, MA 02144, USA.

REDFERN Roger Andrew, b. 9 Nov 1934, Chesterfield, Derbyshire, England. Teacher. Education: Broomfield College of Agriculture; Worcester College of Higher Education. Appointment: Editor, Mountain Craft. Publication: Verses From My Country, 1975. Contributions to: Speak to The Hills, 1985; Poems of The Scottish Hills, 1982; Country Life; The Lady; Mountaineering Press. Membership: International Poetry Society. Address: The Cottage, Old Brampton, Chesterfield, Derbyshire, England.

REDGROVE Peter William, b. 2 Jan 1932. Analytical Psychologist; Poet. m. (1) 2 sons, 1 daughter, (2) Penelope Shuttle, 1 daughter. Education: Queens College, Cambridge. Appointments: Visiting Poet, University of Buffalo, 1961-62; Gregory Fellow in Poetry, Leeds University, 1962-65; O'Connor Professor of Literature, Colgate University, 1974-75; Writer at Large, North Cornwall Arts, 1988. Publications: The Collector, 1960; The Nature of Cold Weather, 1961; At The White Monument, 1963; The Force, 1966; Penguin Modern Poets 11, 1968; Work in Progress, 1969; Dr Faust's Sea-Spiral Spirit, 1972; Three Pieces for Voices, 1972; The Hermaphrodite Album,

1973; Sons of My Skin: Selected Poems, 1975; From Every Chink of The Ark, 1977; Ten Poems, 1977; The Weddings at Nether Powers, 1979; The Apple Broadcast, 1981; The Working of Water, 1984; The Man Names East, 1985; The Mudlark Poems and Grand Buveur, 1986; In The Hall of The Saurians, 1987; The Moon Disposes: Poems 1954-1987, 1987; The First Earthquake, 1989; Dressed as for a Tarot Pack, 1990; Under the Reservoir, 1992; The Laborators, 1993; The Cyclopean Mistress, 1993; My Father's Trapdoors, 1994; Abyssophone, 1995; Assembling a Ghost, 1996; Orchard End, 1997; What the Black Mirror Saw, 1997; The Best of Regrove, 1996. Honours: George Rylands' Verse-Speaking Prize, 1954; Poetry Book Society Choices, 1961, 1966, 1979, 1981; 5 Arts Council Awards, 1969-82; Guardian Fiction Prize, 1973; Prudence Farmer Poetry Award, 1977; Cholmondeley Award, 1985; FRSL, 1982. Address: c/o David Higham Associates, 5-8 Lower John Street, Golden Square, London W1R 4HA, England.

REECE Paul Charles, b. 20 June 1960, Manchester, England. Poet; Trees Secretary. Education: Tameside College, Manchester. Publications: Holy Grail of Love; A Genius Called Love; The Angel Highway; The Candy Floss Tree; Orphans in Renaissance; Birdsong Wine; Love, The Gift of Flight; Maddy Ant Mad; The Butterfly Pauper; A Word with God; Pennines; Peace The Final Frontier; Loves, Wonderful Asylum; The Meditation Sea; A Universal Party; Greekman on Donkey; Tribute to a Street Star; Perception Like Burnt Toast!; Flamingo Sun; A Quench of Dewdrops; Meetings at The Astral Gate; The Last Steam Train; The Essence Ever-Lasting; The Barbed Wire Rainbow, 1994; An Enchantment of Unicorns; Make Love - Not Sex; The Karl Marx Dream; Children's stories: Children of The Unicorn and Angelsneeze. Contributions to: New Hope International; First Time; Peace and Freedom; Global Tapestry; Folio International; Poetry of Love; La Carta de Oliver; International Poetry Yearbook; Poetry Nottingham; Connections; Dandelion Magazine; T.O.P.s; KRAX; Writers Own Magazine; Manchester Evening News; Denton Reporter; North Cheshire Reporter; Tameside Advertiser; Anthologies: Guardian of the State, Voices of Love. Honour: Prize, National Peace Foundation Poetry Competition. Address: 50 Town Lane, Denton, Manchester, M34 1AE, England.

REED Ishmael (Scott), b. 22 Feb 1938, Chattanooga, Tennessee, USA. Writer; Poet; Publisher; Editor; Teacher. m. (1) Priscilla Rose, 1960, div 1970, 1 daughter, (2) Carla Blank-Reed, 1970, 1 daughter. Education: University of Buffalo, 1956-60. Appointments: Lecturer, University of California at Berkeley, 1967-, University of Washington, 1969-70, State University of New York, Buffalo, 1975, 1979, University of Arkansas, 1982, Columbia University, 1983, Harvard University, 1987, University of California, Santa Barbara, 1988; Chairman and President, Yardbird Publishing Company, 1971-; Director, Reed Cannon and Johnson Communications, 1973-; Visiting Professor, 1979, Associate Fellow, 1983-, Calhoun House, Yale University; Visiting Professor, Dartmouth College, 1980; Co-Founder (with Al Young) and Editor, Quilt magazine, 1981-; Associate Fellow, Harvard University Signet Society, 1987-. Publications: Poetry: Catechism of d neoamerican hoodoo church, 1970; Conjure: Selected Poems 1963-1970, 1972; Chattanooga, 1973; A Secretary to the Spirits, 1978; New and Collected Poems, 1988; Fiction includes: Japanese by Spring, 1993; Other includes: Airin' Dirty Laundry, 1993; As Editor, includes: Selections from the American Book Awards, 1980-1990 (with Kathryn Trueblood and Shawn Wong), 1992. Honours: National Endowment for the Arts Grant, 1974; Rosenthal Foundation Award, 1975; Guggenheim Fellowship, 1975; American Academy of Arts and Letters Award, 1975; Michaux Award, 1978. Membership: President, Before Columbus Foundation, 1976-. Address: c/o Ellis J Freeman, 415 Madison Avenue, New York, NY 10017, USA.

REES (Mary) Anne, b. 27 Nov 1952, Norwich, Norfolk, England. Poet; Writer. m. Philip Rees, 4 Jan 1975, 1 son, 2 daughters. Education: BA, English Language and Literature, Lady Margaret Hall, Oxford, 1974. Contributions to: Ambit; Orbis; Rialto; Poetry Wales; Writing Women; Staple; Poetry and Audience; Psychopoetica. Honour: Readers Award for December 1991 issue of Orbis; Runner-up, twice, in Staple First Editions Annual Competitions. Address: 23 Cassiobury Road, London E17 7JD, England.

REEVE F(ranklin) D(olier), b. 18 Sept 1928, Philadelphia, Pennsylvania, USA. Writer; Poet; Teacher. Education: PhD, Columbia University, 1958. Appointments: Professor of Letters, Wesleyan University, 1970-; Editor, Poetry Review, 1982-84; Visiting Professor, Columbia University, 1988. Publications: The Russian Novel, 1966; In

the Silent Stones, 1968; The Red Machines, 1968; Just Over the Border, 1969; The Brother, 1971; The Blue Cat, 1972; White Colors, 1973; Nightway, 1987; The White Monk, 1989; Concrete Music, 1992; Translations, Russian Literature including two-volume Anthology of Russian Plays, 1961-63; An Arrow in the Wall, 1987; The Garden, 1990; The Trouble with Reason, 1993; A Few Rounds of Old Maid and Other Stories, 1995. Contributions to: American Poetry Review; New England Review; Yale Review; Sewanee Review; Manhattan Poetry Review; Confrontation; New Yorker; Kansas Quarterly; North American Review; Kenyon Review; Gettsburg Review; Poetry: A Magazine of Verse; New York Times Book Review. Honours: Literature Award, American Academy and National Institute of Arts and Letters, 1970; PEN, Syndicated Fiction Award, 1985, 1986; New England Poetry Society, Golden Rose, 1994. Memberships: PEN, American Centre; Poetry Society of America, Vice President, 1982-84; Board of Directors, Secretary, Poets House; Advisory Board, Vermont Centre for the Book. Address: RR, Box 206, Wilmington, VT 05363, USA.

REHM Pam, b. 21 October 1967, Camp Hill, Pennsylvania, USA. m. Lew Daly, 27 June 1991, 1 son. Education: BA, English, Shippensburg University, Pennsylvania, 1989; MFA, Creative Writing and Poetry, Brown University, Rhode Island, 1991. Appointment: Inter-Library Loan Technician, 1991-. Publications: Piecework, 1992; Pollux, 1992; The Garment In Which No One Had Slept, 1993; To Give It Up, 1995. Contributions to: Apex Of The M; First Intensity; To; Chicago Review; Notus. Honour: National Poetry Series Winner, 1994. Address: 331 Herkimer Street, Buffalo, NY 14213, USA.

REICH Asher, b. 5 Sept 1937, Jerusalem, Israel. Editor. Education: Literature, University of Jerusalem. Appointments: Consulting Editor, Proza Magazine, 1977-79; Editor, The Literary Magazine, Israel, 1979-90. Publications: The Seventh Year of My Travellings, 1963; Night Shine, 1972; State of Affairs, 1975; A View of the Land, 1978; Women's Rites, 1980; A New Packets, 1983; Selected Poems, 1986; Works on Paper, 1988; Fictional Pacts, 1992; Arbeiten anb Papier, collection of poems, translated in German, 1992; Reminiscence of ag Amnesiac (prose), 1998. Contributions to: Massachusetts Review; Yale Review; Iowa University Review; Poems translated and published in anthologies in France, USA, Holland, Denmark, Hungary, Poland and Russia. Honours: Anna Frank Prize, 1961; Five Writer's Guild Prizes, 1972-85; Chounsky Prize, 1977; Israeli Publishers Organization Poetry Prize, 1987; Tel Aviv's Prize, 1973, 1980, 1988; Prime Minister's Prize, 1989-90; Iowa International Writing Programme Grant, 1985; Deutsche Akademischer Aaustauschdienst Grant, Berlin, 1990. Memberships: Hebrew Writer's Association in Israel; Pen Club, Israel; Writer's Guild. Address: 14 Nechemya Street, Tel Aviv 65604, Israel.

REICHHOLD Jane(t Eileen), b. 18 Jan 1937, Lima, Ohio, USA. Writer; Editor. m. Robert Steiner, 30 Mar 1957, 1 son, 2 daughters. Education: Blueffton College, 1956-58; Ohio University, 1957; Reedley College, 1963-65; Fresno State University, 1966. Appointments: Private Art Teacher; Owner Pottery Studio; Artist; Freelance Journalist; Author; Editor. Publications: Shadows on an Open Window; Thumbtacks on a Calendar; Graffiti; The Land of Seven Realms; Narrow Road to Renga; A Gift of Tanka; Round Renga Round; A Dictionary of Haiku. Contributions to: Mainichi Daily News; Independent Coastal Observer; Modern Haiku; Mirrors; New Hope International; Haiku Quarterly; Poetry Nippon; Haiku Canada. Honour: Merit Book Awards. Memberships: Haiku Society of America; Haiku Poets of Northern California; Haiku Writers of Gualala Arts; Haiku Canada; Poetry Society; Haiku Society of Constanta; German Haiku Society. Address: PO Box 767, Gualala, CA 95445, USA.

REID Alastair, b. 22 Mar 1926, Whithorn, Scotland. Education: MA, Honours, University of St Andrews, 1949. Appointments: Visiting Professor of Latin American Studies at various American and British universities, 1969-79; Staff Writer with the New Yorker, 1959-. Publications include: To Lighten My House, 1953; Oddments Inklings Omens Moments, 1959; Corgi Modern Poets in Focus, with others, 1971; Weathering: Poems and Translations, 1978; Whereabouts: Notes on Being a foreigner, 1987; The Man Who Counted by Malba Tahan, translation with L. Clark, 1993; An Alastair Reid Reader, 1995; Volumes for children; Translations of poetry by Jorge Luis Borges, Pablo Neruda and others. Honours include: Scottish Arts Council Award, 1979. Address: c/o New Yorker, 20 West 43rd Street, New York, NY 10036, USA.

REID Sharleigh. See: **MONEYSMITH Carol Louise Giesbrecht.**

REIFF Andrew Edwin, (Eagin Arthur), b. 25 July 1941, Philadelphia, Pennsylvania, USA. Author; Teacher. m. Patricia Ruth Carlson, 28 Sept 1979, 2 sons, 1 daughter. Education: BS, Drexel University, 1964; MA, University of Iowa, 1966; PhD, University of Texas. Appointments: Instructor of English, Fayetteville University, 1966-68; Associate Professor of English, Bishop College, 1981-86; Editor, Red Rose, Dallas, 1983-85. Publications: A Calendar of Poems, 1975; The Taliessin Poems, 1983; Native Texans, 1984; Planet 3: Help Send This Book Into Space, 1985; A Poetical Reading of The Psalms of David, 1985; The New Earth of Char Beamish, 1994; A Whale Tale of Dolphy, 1994. Contributions to: Several publications. Memberships: Founder, Phoenix Authors of Children's Books, 1992; Co-Chair, Association of Graduate Students of English, University of Texas, Austin, 1971; IMLA Society of Economic Botany. Address: 2645 East Willetta, Phoenix, AZ 85008, USA.

REITER Jennifer Brett (Jendi), b. 13 July 1972, New York, New York, USA. Education: BA, Harvard University; JD, Columbia Law School. Publication: Miller, Reiter and Robbins: Three New Poets, 1991. Contributions to: Poetry; Southern Poetry Review; Lyric; Odessa Poetry Review; Hanging Loose; Pavement Saw; First Things; Best American Poetry, 1990; Roth American Poetry Annual, 1990. Honours: Elias Lieberman Award, Poetry Society of America, 1988; National Endowment for the Humanities Grant, 1989; 1st Prize, College Poetry Contest, 1990; Roger Conant Hatch Poetry Prize, 1991. Memberships: Poetry Society of America; Signet Society of Harvard. Address: 568 Grand Street Apt J 1202, New York, NY 10002, USA.

RENNIE Barbara Muriel, b. 30 June 1930. Writer; Public Speaker. m. Ian Malcolm Rennie, 14 April 1954, 2 sons, 2 daughters. Education: BA, Hons External London degree in English, UCSW, Exeter, 1951. Appointments: Editorial Assistant, 1952, Editor, 1954, Osram-GEC house magazine, Searchlight. Publications: The Sky Wandered By, 1983; As If, 1990; The 50-Minute Hour, 1996. Contributions to: Orbis; Envoi; Weyfarers; Headlock. Honours: Julia Cairns Awards, Society of Women Writers and Journalists; Associate Member, Society of Authors; London Writer Circle; Phoenix Poets, London; Elmbridge Writers' Workshop, Chair, 1982-92. Address: 1 New Road, Stoke Fleming, Dartmouth, Devon TQ6 0NR, England.

REPLANSKY Naomi, b. 23 May 1918, Bronx, New York, USA. Poet. Education: University of California at Los Angeles. Publications: Ring Song, 1952; Twenty-one Poems, Old and New, 1988; The Dangerous World, 1994: New and Selected Poems, 1994. Contributions to: Ploughshares; New York Quarterly; Nation. Honour: Nominated for the National Book Award, 1952. Memberships: PEN American Center; Poetry Society of America. Address: 711 Amsterdam Avenue, No 8E, New York, NY 10025, USA.

REPOSA Carol Jane Coffee, b. 18 Oct 1943, San Diego, California, USA. m. Richare Eugene Reposa, 30 Dec 1967, div 5 Dec 1985, 1 son, 1 daughter. Education: BA 1965, MA 1968, University of Texas at Austin. Appointments: English Instructor, Memorial High School, 1969, San Antonio College, 1969-70, 1982-89 and Trinity University, 1980-82; Assistant Professor of English, San Antonio College, 1989-. Publication: At the Border: Winter Lights, 1989. Contributions to: Texas Observer; River Sedge; Passages North; Inlet; Pax; San Jose Studies; Trinity Review; Concho River Review; Stone Drum; Descant; Imagine; Artists' Alliance Review; Wind; English in Texas. Memberships: Poetry Society of America; National Council of Teachers of English; South Central Modern Language Association; Popular Culture Association; Council of College Teachers of English; Texas Association of Creative Writing Teachers. Address: 263 West Hermine, San Antonio, TX 78212, USA.

RETI Ingrid, b. 16 Sept 1927. Teacher. m. Jerry W Hull, 5 Jan 1991, 1 son, 1 daughter. Education: BA, American Studies, 1971, MA, English, 1975, California State University. Appointments: Instructor, California Polytechnic State University, Extended Education, 1982-. Publications: Ephemera, 1987; Echoes of Silence, 1989. Contributions to: National Forum; Phoenix; Pinehurst Journal; Broomstick; Thirteen; Coffeehouse Poets Quarterly; Perceptions; Iowa Woman; Petroglyph. Memberships: Poets and Writers; Steinbeck Research Center. Address: 1650 Descanso Street, San Luis Obispo, CA 93405, USA.

REYES Carlos, b. 2 June 1935, Missouri, USA. Poet. m. (1) Barbara Anne Hollingsworth, (2) Karen Stoner, 1 son, 3 daughters, (3) Elizabeth Atly. Education: BA, University of Oregon, 1961; MA, University of Arizona, 1965. Publications: The Prisoner; The Windows; The Orange Letters; The Shingle Weavers Journal; At Doolin Quay; Nightmarks; A Suitcase Full of Crows, poems, 1995. Contributions to: Antioch Review; Chelsea; Porch; Minnesota Review; Measure; Poetry Review; Desert Review; Isthmus; Mississippi Mud; Invisible City; Poetry Now; Another Chicago Magazine; Gumbo; Anthologies: A New Geography of Poets, 1992, Men of Our Time: Poetry in The West of Ireland, 1993, Prescott Street Reader, 1995. Honour: Oregon Arts Commission Individual Artists Fellowship; Yaddo Fellow, 1982. Memberships: PEN; Poets and Writers; Co-Chair, PEN Northwest, 1992-93. Address: 3222 North East Schuyler, Portland, OR 97212, USA.

REYNOLDS Craig A, b. 14 Sept 1952, Washington, District of Columbia, USA. Writer; Editor. Education: BA, Howard University, 1970; MA, 1979; PhD, 1989, University of Maryland. Appointment: Writer, Editor, Smithsonian Institution Press, 1988-. Contributions to: Anthologies; Brussels Sprouts; Feelings; Changing Men; Turnstile; Black American Literature Forum; Pegasus; Lip Service; Pegasus Winter; Now Magazine; Durango Herald; World's Word; Country Poet; Deros; Gusto/Driftwood East; Golden Page; Black Light; New Directions Federal Poets. Memberships: Poetry Society of America; Dramatists Guild Inc; Federal Poets, Treasurer, 1981-85, President, 1985-88. Address: 11600 Old Fort Road, Friendly, MD 20744, USA.

REYNOLDS Susan Helen, b. 28 May 1955, Manchester, England. Tutor. m. Michael John Halstead, 22 Aug 1981, diss 1990, 1 son, 1 daughter. Education: Lady Margaret Hall, Oxford, 1972-77; MA, 1979. Appointments: Music Critic, Guardian; Researcher, BBC; Slavonic Secretary, Taylor Institution; Editorial Assistant, Clio Press; Tutor, Oxford Advanced Studies Programme; Oxford Overseas Study Course. Contributions to: Striking Statues; Manchester Poetry 4; Guardians of the State; New Prospects Poetry; Verso; Celtic Dawn. Honours: DuQuesne Award; Kent and Sussex Open Poetry Competition 3rd Prize; National Poetry Competition; Yeats Club International Poetry Competition; Manchester Open Poetry Competition. Memberships: Oxford University Classical Society; Poetry Society; English Goethe Society; Women in German Studies. Address: 12 Marriott Close, Harefields, Oxford OX2 8NT, England.

RHINE David, b. 4 Dec 1950, Lebanon, Pennsylvania, USA. Poet. Education: University of Maryland, 1968-72. Publication: Poems from a Live Nightmare, 1991. Contributions to: Iota Poetry Quarterly; White Rose; Chiron Review; Dan River Anthology; Nihilistic Review; Tucumcari Literary Review; Journal of Sister Moon; Snake River Reflections; Writers Exchange; Brownbag Press; The Matic Poetry Quarterly. Address: Calder Square, PO Box 10445, State College, PA 16805, USA.

RHODAS Virginia, b. Rhodas, Greece. Education: Journalism, Human Public Relations, 1968; East-West Philosophy, 1970-72; Comparative Religions, 1974; Living Languages, 1975; Translation World Literature, 1976. Appointments: Journalist; Freelance poet; Writer; Translation from Spanish into English; From Spanish into Greek; From English into Spanish; From English into Greek and Greek to English; Director, Carta International de Poesia, International Poetry Letter. Publications: Blossoms, 1968; There Will Come A Day... And Other Poems, 1968; Brother Century XX, 1970; Open Letter to Humanity, 1985; Listen to Me Humanity, 1986; Theatre, essays, short stories, plays for children. Contributions to: Publications in Latin America; USA; India; Africa; Germany; England; Italy; Austria; Other European countries; Greece. Memberships: World Poetry Society International and others, India; Latin-American pageant; World Poetry Society Intercontinental; Society of Writers: Greece, India and International Liaison World Day of Prayer, a World Christian Peaceful Movement. Address: Rivadavia 2284-PB J (1034) Buenos Aires, Argentina.

RIACH Alan Scott, b. 1 Aug 1957, Airdrie, Lanarkshire, Scotland. University Lecturer. m. Raewyn Maree Garton, 12 Sept 1992, 1 son. Education: BA, converted to MA, Churchill College, University of Cambridge, 1976-79; PhD, Department of Scottish Literature, University of Glasgow, 1979-84; University of Waikatu, New Zealand. Appointments: Lecturer, Advanced Lecturer, Senior Lecturer, Department of English, University of Waikato, 1990-96. Publications: For What It Is, 1988; This Folding Map, 1990; An Open Return, 1991;

First And Last Songs, 1995. Contributions to: New Writing Scotland; Poetry New Zealand; Landfall; Sport; Verse; Chapman; Gairfish; Westerly; Island; Poetry Australia; Edinburgh Review; Words. Memberships: Secretary, The University of Waikato Scottish Studies Association, 1991-; Association for Scottish Literary Studies. Address: c/o Department of English, University of Waikato, P.B. 3105, Hamilton, New Zealand.

RIBBLE Ron(ald George), b. 7 May 1937, West Reading, Pennsylvania, USA. Psychologist. m. Catalina Tores, 30 Sept 1961, 2 sons, 1 daughter. Education: BSEE, 1968, MS, Electrical Engineering, 1969, MA, Psychology, 1985, PhD, Social Psychology, 1986, University of Missouri, Columbia, USA. Appointments: Advanced through grades to Lieutenant Colonel, United States Air Force, 1956-81; Research Director, Coping Resources Inc, Columbia, Missouri, 1986; Referral Development Coordinator, Laughlin Pavilion Psychiatric Hospital, Kirksville, Missouri, 1987; Psychiatric Program Director, Ellsworth Community Hospital, Iowa Falls, Iowa, 1987-88; Lead Psychotherapist, Gasconade County Counseling Center, Hermann, Missouri, 1988; Associate Clinical Psychologist, Texas Department of Health, San Antonio, Texas, 1989; Lecturer in Psychology, University of Texas at San Antonio, 1989-; President and Co-Owner of Towers and Rushing Ltd, 1989-; Assessment Clinician, Psychiatric Assessment Team, CPC Afton Oaks Hospital, San Antonio, Texas, 1989-91; Psychologist, Olmos Psychological Services, San Antonio, Texas, 1991-93; Columnist for Feelings Magazine and Freelance Writer, 1993-; Lecturer in Psychology, Trinity University, San Antonio, Texas, 1995-96. Publications: Apples, Weeds and Doggie Poo, 1995. Contributions to: The Lyric; Feelings; Midwest Poetry Review; Fauquier Poetry Journal; POET; New Jersey Review of Literature; Words of Wisdom; Timbercreek Review. Honours: Poetry Award, International Platform Association, 1995; The Robert's Memorial Prize in Poetry, 1995. Memberships: Academy of American Poets; Poetry Society of America; National Writers Association. Address: Towers and Rushing Limited, 14023 North Hills Village Drive, San Antonio, Texas 78249-2531, USA.

RICARD Charles, b. 9 Jan 1922, Gap, France. Author. m. J Balmens, 28 July 1951. Education: Professor de Lettres. Publications: Le Puits; La Derniere des Revolutions; Le Mercred des Cendres; A Propos d'Un Piano Casse; Pot a Voudras; Les Ombres du Chemin. Contributions to: Various journals and magazines. Honours: Several Major Prizes; Gold Medals. Memberships: Academy of the French Provinces; Society of French Poets. Address: 20 Rue du Super Gap, 05000 Gap, France.

RICE John, b. 12 Mar 1948, Glasgow, Scotland. Arts Officer. m. Clare Rice, Oct 1970, 2 sons, 1 daughter. Education: St Michaels College. Appointments: Literature Officer, South East Arts; Director, Kent Literature Festival; Director, Metropole Arts Centre; Arts Officer, Kent County Council. Publications: Butterfly Frost; Landscape, Coastscape, Dreamscape; Bears Don't Like Bananas; Dreaming of Dinosaurs; Down at The Dinosaur Fair. Contributions to: Poetry South East; South East Arts Review. Membership: Society of Kent Authors. Address: 47 Hendley Drive, Cranbrook, Kent TN17 3DY, England.

RICH Adrienne, b. 16 May 1929, Baltimore, Maryland, USA. Professor of English and Feminist Studies; Poet; Writer. m. Alfred H Conrad, 1953, dec 1970, 3 sons. Education: AB, Radcliffe College, 1951. Appointments: A D White Professor-at-Large, Cornell University, 1981-85; Clark Lecturer and Distinguished Visiting Professor, Scripps College, Claremont, California, 1983; Visiting Professor, San Jose State University, California, 1985-86; Burgess Lecturer, Pacific Oaks College, Pasadena, California, 1986; Professor of English and Feminist Studies, Stanford University, 1986-. Publications: Poetry includes: A Wild Patience Has Taken Me This Far: Poems 1978-81, 1981; Sources, 1983; The Fact of a Doorframe: Poems Selected and New 1950-1984, 1984; Your Native Land, Your Life, 1986; Time's Power: Poems 1985-1988, 1989; An Atlas of the Difficult World: Poems 1988-1991, 1991; Collected Early Poems 1950-1970, 1993; Dark Fields of the Republic, 1995; Other includes: What is Found There: Notebooks on Poetry and Politics, 1993. Honours: Yale Series of Younger Poets Award, 1951; Guggenheim Fellowships, 1952, 1961; American Academy of Arts and Letters Award, 1961; Bess Hokin Prize, 1963; Eunice Tietjens Memorial Prize, 1968; National Endowment for the Arts Grant, 1970; Shelley Memorial Award, 1971; Ingram Merrill Foundation Grant, 1973; National Book Award, 1974; Fund for Human Dignity Award, 1981; Ruth Lilly Prize, 1986; Brandeis University Creative Arts Award, 1987; Elmer Holmes

Bobst Award, 1989; Commonwealth Award in Literature, 1991; Frost Silver Medal, Poetry Society of America, 1992; Los Angeles Times Book Award, 1992; Lenore Marshall/Nation Award, 1992; William Whitehead Award, 1992; Lambda Book Award, 1992; Harriet Monroe Prize, 1994; John D and Catharine MacArthur Foundation Fellowship, 1994; Honorary doctorates. Address: c/o W W Norton and Company, 500 Fifth Avenue, New York, NY 10110, USA.

RICH Susanna Lippoczy, b. 17 Oct 1951, USA. Professor of English. m. Morton D Rich, 25 May 1980. Education: MA Philosophy, University of North Carolina, Chapel Hill, 1978; PhD Communications, New York University, 1987; MFA, Warren Wilson College. Appointments: Associate Professor of English, Kean College, 1988-; Liberal Arts Coordinator, Sussex County College, 1988. Publication: The Flexible Writer, 1995. Contributions to: Ailanthus; South Coast Poetry Journal; Findings; American Poetry Society of America; South Mountain Poets. Address: 31 Maines Lane, Blairstown, NJ 07825, USA.

RICHARDS Cyndi. See: RICHESON C(ena) G(older).

RICHARDS Melanie, b. 10 Sept 1951, Wisconsin, USA. Writer; Teacher. Education: BA, University of California at Los Angeles, 1976; MFA, Goddard College, 1979. Appointments: Medical Transcriptionist; Senior Lecturer, University of Wisconsin;Community Writer, Artspeople of Wisconsin; Wisconsin Arts Board, Artist-in-Residence. Contributions to: Alembic; Abraxas; Epos; Wisconsin Review; Harvard Review; Yankee; Farmers Market; Milkweed Chronicle; Sing Heavenly Muse; Introll Panache; Journal of Wisconsin; Shenandoah; Negative Capability; North Stone Review; Kinesis. Honours: Gessell Award; AWP Intro Award; Sue Saniel Elkind Poetry Prize; Academy of American Poets Prize; Loft Mentor Award. Address: 16570 22nd Street South, St Marys Point, MN 55043, USA.

RICHARDSON Joanna, b. London, England. Biographer. Education: MA, St Anne's College, Oxford. Publications: Fanny Brawne, 1952; Rachel, 1956; Théophile Gautier: His Life and Times, 1958; Sarah Bernhardt, 1959; Edward FitzGerald, 1960; The Disastrous Marriage: A Study of George IV and Caroline of Brunswick, 1960; The Pre-Eminent Victorian: A Study of Tennyson, 1962; The Everlasting Spell: A Study of Keats and His Friends, 1963; Edward Lear, 1965; George IV: A Portrait, 1966; Creevey and Greville, 1967; Princess Mathilde, 1969; Verlaine, 1971; Enid Starkie, 1973; Translator, Verlaine Poems, 1974, Baudelaire Poems, 1975; Victor Hugo, 1976; Zola, 1978; Keats and His Circle: An Album of Portraits, 1980; Paris Under Siege, 1982; Colette, 1983; The Brownings, 1986; Judith Gautier, 1987; Portrait of a Bonaparte, 1987; Baudelaire, 1994. Contributions to: Times; Times Literary Supplement; Sunday Times; Spectator; New Statesman; New York Times Book Review; Washington Post; French Studies; French Studies Bulletin; Modern Language Review. Honours: Chevalier de l'Ordre des Arts et des Lettres, 1987; Prix Goncourt de la Biographie, 1989. Membership: Fellow, 1959, Council, 1961-86, Royal Society of Literature. Address: c/o Curtis Brown Group, Haymarket House, 28-29 Haymarket, London, SW1Y 4SP, England.

RICHESON C(ena) G(older), (Cyndi Richards, Jessica Jains, Velma Chamberlain), b. 11 April 1941, Oregon, USA. Author; Instructor. m. Jerry Dale Richeson, 3 June 1961, 2 sons. Education: AA, Diablo Valley College, 1962; BA English, California State University, 1972. Appointments: Instructor, Shasta College, California, 1974-76; Columnist, Anderson Press Weekly Newspaper, California, 1976-78; Instructor, Liberty Union High School, Brentwood, California, 1984-85; Frontier Correspondent, The National Tombstone Epitaph, Tucson, Arizona, 1986-; Book Reviewer, Publishers Weekly, New York, 1994-95. Contributions to: Anthologies: The West That Was, 1993, Wild West Show, 1994, The Living West, forthcoming; Hyacinths and Biscuits; Cats; Aim; Green's; Byline; A Galaxy of Verse; Earthwise Poetry Journal; Friend; Shore Anthology; Fault Literature; Creative Urge; New Dawn Poetry; And So It Is Poetry Anthology. Honours: Poet of the Year, 1974; Contra Costa County Fair Awards, 1976; Redwood Acres Fair Award, 1989. Memberships: California Writers Club, President, 1991-92; Society of Children's Book Writers; Zane Grey's West Society, 1986-. Address: PO Box 268, Knightsen, CA 94548, USA.

RICKETTS Mary Jane Gnegy (Marijane G Ricketts), b. 16 July 1925, Maryland, USA. Writer; Editor; Secretary. m. Aubrey Eugene Ricketts, 9 April 1950, 1 son, 1 daughter. Education: BA, West Virginia

Wesleyan College, 1947; Commercial Arts Diploma, Strayer Business College, 1949. Appointments: Secretary, Landon School for Boys, Bethesda, MD, 1960-62, Montgomery County Public Schools, 1962-85, Department of Academic Skills, Montgomery County Public Schools, 1985-88. Publications: Is It The Onion Making Life Pungent?, 1986, 1987; The Poets of Ellicott Street, 1989; A Diamond Anthology of Prose and Poetry, 1992. Contributions to: Shorelines, 1985-87; Poet Magazine, Vols 4 & 5, 1993; Potomac Review, 1995; Earth's Daughter's 41, 1994; Public Voices, 1994, 1995; Dan River Anthology, 1994, 1995, 1996; Metropolitan, 1993, 1994, 1995. Honours: Prize, 1st Honourable Mention, Federation of State Poetry Societies, 1986; Annual Literary Award and Grand Prize for Poetry, Byline Magazine, 1986; Prize, 1987, 1st Prize for Poetry, Arts Project Renaissance Washington, DC, 1992. Memberships: President, 1989-93, Writer's League of Washington; Maryland Poetry and Literary Society; Poetry Society of America, 1987-93; National Federation of State Poetry Societies. Address: 10203 Clearbrook Place, Kensington, MD 20895, USA.

RIEL Steven Joseph, b. 31 Dec 1959, Monson, Massachusetts, USA. Librarian. Education: AB, Georgetown University, 1981; MLS, Simmons College, 1987. Appointments: Cataloguer and Head of Copy Cataloguing, Harvard College Library, Harvard University, 1987-89; Poetry Editor, RFD, published in Liberty, Tennessee, 1987-; Cataloguer, Amherst College, 1990-93; Serials Cataloguer, Harvard University Library, Cambridge, MA, 1993-. Publications: How to Dream, 1992; Anthologies. Contributions to: Christopher Street; Minnesota Review; Antigonish Review; Mouth Of The Dragon; St Andrew's Review; G W Review; Amherst Review; Peregrine; Bay Windows; James White Review; RFD; Fag Rag; Changing Men; Gay Community News; Le FAROG Forum; Amethyst; Evergreen Chronicles. Address: PO Box 679, Natick, MA 01760, USA.

RIELLY Edward James, b. 22 Dec 1943, Darlington, Wisconsin, USA. English Professor. m. Jeanne Smith, 16 Aug 1969, 1 son, 1 daughter. Education: BA, Loras College, 1966; MA, 1968, PhD, 1974, University of Notre Dame. Appointments: English Teacher, 1967-; Professor of English and Dean of Distance Education, St Joseph's College. Publications: Rain Falling Quietly, 1985; Family Portraits, 1987; The Furrow's Edge, 1987; The Breaking of Glass Horses and Other Poems, 1988; My Struggling Soil, 1994. Contributions to: Bitterroot; Wind Chimes; Dragonfly; Webster Review; Cumberland Poetry Review; Soundings East; Farmers Market; Arachne; Rhode Island Review; Frogpond; Plains Poetry Journal; Alchemist; New York Quarterly. Honours: Finalist, Maine Arts Commission Poetry Chapbook Competition, 1983; Merit Book Awards, Haiku Society of America, 1988; Best of Issue Award, Frogpond, 1990. Memberships: Haiku Society of America; Maine Writers and Publishers Alliance. Address: 6 Colony Road, Westbrook, ME 04092, USA.

RIFBJERG Klaus Thorvald, b. 15 Dec 1931, Copenhagen, Denmark. Writer; Publisher. m. Inge Merete, 28 May 1955, 1 son, 2 daughters. Education: Princeton University, 1950-51; University of Copenhagen, 1951-56. Appointments: Theatre Film and Literature Critic for newspaper, Information, 1956-59, Politiken, 1959-70; Editor, literary magazine, Vindrosen, 1959-64. Publications: Under vejr med mig selv, 1956; Efterkrig, 1957; Konfrontation, 1961; Voliere, 1962; Portraet, 1963; Amagerdigte, 1965; Mytologi, 1970; Faedrelandssange, 1967; I Skyttens tegn, 1970; Scener fra det daglige liv, 1973; Desperate Digte, 1974; Stranden, 1976; Selected Poems, 1976; Livsfrisen, 1979; Spansk motiv, 1981; Landet Atlantis, 1980; Udenfor har vinden lagt sig, 1984; Byens tvelys, 1987; Septembersang, 1988; 150 korte og meget korte tekster, 1991; Krigeu, 1992; Kandestedersuiten, 1994; Leksikon, 1996. Contributions to: Lettre Internationale; The Malahat Review; BLM; Literaturug's Gazeta; Horisont; Vinduet. Honours: The Aarestrup Medal, 1963; Danish Academy Major Award, 1968; Holberg Medal, 1985. Memberships: Danish Academy of Arts and Letters; Honorary Professor, Danish Teachers College, Copenhagen; hc phil dr Lund University. Address: Gyldendal Publishers, 3 Klareboderue, DK-1001 Copenhagen, Denmark.

RIGSBEE David Earl, b. 1 Apr 1949. Teacher. Education: BA, University of North Carolina, 1971; MA, Johns Hopkins University, 1972; MALS, Hollins College, 1991; PhD, University of Virginia, 1993. Appointments: Instructor, Hamilton College, 1972-76 and University of North Carolina, 1978-82; Visiting Assistant Professor, Louisiana State University, 1986; Associate Professor, St Andrews College, 1987-88; Instructor, Virginia Tech, 1988-; Presidential Fellow, University of

Virginia, 1991-. Publications: Your Heart Will Fly Away; An Answering Music; The Hopper Light; To Be Here; The Ardis Anthology of New American Poetry; Stamping Ground. Contributions to: New Yorker; Southern Review; Iowa Review; Carolina Quarterly; Literary Review; Quarterly West; Three Rivers Poetry Journal; New Orleans Review; Black Warrior Review. Honours: Academy of American Poets Prize; Djerassi Foundation Resident Artist; Pound Forter Poetry Prize; Writing Fellow, Fine Arts Work Center. Memberships: Academy of American Poets; Poetry Society of America; North Carolina Writers Conference. Address: 418 Lee Street, Blacksburg, VA 24060, USA.

RINALDI Nicholas Michael, b. 2 Apr 1934, Brooklyn, New York, USA. Writer; College Professor. m. Jacqueline Tellier, 29 Aug 1959, 3 sons, 1 daughter. Education: AB, 1957; MA, 1960; PhD, 1963. Appointments: Instructor, Assistant Professor, St Johns University, 1960-65; Lecturer, City University of New York, 1966; Associate Professor, Columbia University, 1966; Assistant Professor, Professor, Fairfield University, 1966-; Professor, University of Connecticut, 1972. Publications: The Resurrection of the Snails; We Have Lost Our Fathers; The Luftwaffe in Chaos; Bridge Fall Down. Contributions to: Yale Review; New American Review; Prairie Schooner; Carolina Quarterly. Honours: Joseph P Slomovich Memorial Award; All Nations Poetry Award; New York Poetry Forum Award; Charles Angoff Literary Award. Memberships: Associated Writing Programs; Poetry Society of America. Address: 190 Brookview Avenue, Fairfield, CT 06432, USA.

RITCHIE Elisavietta Artamonoff, b. 29 June 1932, Missouri, USA. Writer; Poet; Translator; Teacher; Editor. m. (1) Lyell Hale Ritchie Jr, 11 July 1953, div, 2 sons, 1 daughter. (2) Clyde H Farnsworth, 22 June 1991. Education: Sorbonne Degree Superieur, magna cum laude, Cours de Civilisation Francaise; BA, University of California, Berkeley, 1954; MA, French Literature, American University, 1976. Appointments: Various positions held as Writer, Poet, Translator, Teacher and Editor; Readings and workshops at Library of Congress, International Poetry Forum, Folger Library, Harbourfront and abroad. Publications include: Timbot, novella in verse, 1970; Tightening The Circle Over Eel Country, 1974; A Sheath of Dreams and Other Games, 1976; Moving to Larger Quarters, 1977; The Chattanooga Cycles, 1984; The Problem With Eden, 1985; Raking The Snow, 1982; Wild Garlic: The Journal of Maria X, 1995; Elegy For The Other Woman: New and Selected Terribly Female Poems, 1996; The Arc of the Storm, forthcoming; Fiction: Flying Tim: Stories and Half-Stories, 1992, 1996; Editor, The Dolphin's Arc: Poems on Endangered Creatures of The Sea; Founder, Director, The Wineberry Press; Past President of Washington Writers' Publishing House. Contributions to: Poetry; American Scholar; New York Times; Washington Post; New Republic; Christian Science Monitor; New Letters; National Geographic; New York Quarterly; When I'm An Old Woman I Shall Wear Purple; If I Had My Life To Live Over I Would Pick More Daisies; If I Had A Hammer; Grow Old Along With Me The Best Is Yet To Be; Canadian Women's Studies; Confrontation. Honours: Winner 4 times, PEN Syndicated Fiction Project Competition. Memberships: PEN; Poetry Society of America; Poets and Writers. Address: 3207 Macomb Street NW, Washington, DC 20008-2237, USA.

RIVERS Ann, b. 26 Jan 1939, Texas, USA. Poet. Education: BA, 1959. Appointments: Editor-Publisher, SHY, 1974-79; Guest Editor, As-Sharq, 1979; Contributing Editor, Ocarina, 1979-82. Publication: Samos Wine, 1987; A World of Difference, 1995. Contributions to: Ore; Iotà; Orbis; Poetry Nottingham; Pennine Platform. Address: GR 180 40 Hydra, Greece.

RIVES Janet M, b. 10 Feb 1944, Hartford, Connecticut, USA. Professor of Economics. Education: BA, University of Arizona, 1966; Diplome, Cours de Civilisation Francais, Sorbonne, Paris, 1965; MA, 1969, PhD, 1971, Duke University. Appointments: Assistant Professor, Rutgers University, 1970-77; Associate Professor, University of Nebraska, Omaha, 1977-84; Associate Professor, Professor, University of Northern Iowa, 1984-. Contributions to: Lyrikal Iowa; CSS Publications Anthologies; Impressions; American Anthology of Midwestern Poetry; The Whitman Way. Memberships: Iowa Poetry Association; Walt Whitman Guild. Address: 317 Heritage Road, Cedar Falls, IA 50613, USA.

RIZVI I(ftikhar) H(usain), b. 25 June 1936, Bareilly, India. Principal. m. Anis Fatima Rizvi, 24 Oct 1966, 1 son, 4 daughters. Education: MA, English, 1956, MA, History, 1970, Agra University; MA, English, Aligarh University, 1968; BEd, Rajasthan University, 1973.

Appointments: Lecturer in English, 1957, through to Principal, 1988-, Tilak College, Bareilly, Uttar Pradesh, India. Publications: Some poems translated into Spanish, Portuguese, Serbo-Croatian, and Korean among others; Collections of poems in English: Falling Petals, 1975; Unfading Blooms, 1984; Thirsty Pebbles, 1986; Wandering Fragrance, 1988; Wounded Roses Sing, 1993; Snowflakes of Dreams, 1996; Urdu collection: Daman-E-Gul, 1991; Editor, 2 anthologies in English; Editor, Canopy, international journal. Contributions to: Poems included in all the national, international and world anthologies of India in English and in 33 journals of India and world anthologies published in Korea, Portugal, USA and other countries. Honours: DLitt, World University, USA, 1982; 2nd Prize, International Poetry Contest, Brazil, 1987; Honoured by International Poets Academy, USA, 1987, World Poets Congress, Thailand, 1988, Michael Madhusudan Academy, 1989 and by Lions, Jaycees and others. Memberships: Advisor, World Book of Honour, USA, and Michael Madhusudan Academy, Calcutta; International Poets Academy. Address: Rizvi Manzil, Kanghi Tola, Bareilly 243 003, Uttar Pradesh, India.

ROARK Sheila B, b. 17 Dec 1946, New York, New York, USA. Writer. m. V Gail Roark, 10 Feb 1988, 3 daughters. Education: Creative Writing, Profit-Tarrant County Junior College, 1995; Writers Digest School, 1996. Appointment: Writer. Publications: Aids (A Person To Live), 1996; Achieving Excellence - The 1996 Presidents Awards, 1996; Best Poems of the Nineties, 1996; Best New Poems, 1996. Contributions to: Explorer Magazine; Tucumcari Literary Review; House of White Birches; Oatmeal and Poetry; Anterior Poetry Monthly; Lines N Rhymes. Honours: World of Poetry Award of Merit, 1984-87; World of Poetry Golden Poetry Award, 1985-88; First Place Merit Award, 1995; Honorable Mention, Iliad Press, 1995; NLP, Editors Choice, 1995; Creative Arts and Sciences Award of Merit, 1995; NLP, Editors Choice, 1996; Drury's Publishing Achievement Award, 1996. Memberships: National Poets Association; Poets Guild; International Society of Poets. Address: 1881 West Airport Freeway #703, Euless, TX 76040, USA.

ROBBINS Doren Richard, b. 20 Aug 1949, USA. Poet; Critic; Teacher. m. 22 May 1988, 1 daughter. Education: City College of Los Angeles; Portland State University; University of Oregon; University of Iowa; MFA, Iowa Writer's Workshop. Appointments: Creative Writing, University of Iowa, 1991-93; English Instructor, UMPQUA College, 1993-95; Creative Writing, Poetry, UCLA; English Literature, Linfield College, 1994. Publications: Detonated Veils; The Roots and the Towers; Seduction of the Groom; Sympathetic Manifesto; Under the Black Moths Wings; Dignity in Naples and North Hollywood, 1995. Contributions to: Sulfur; Caliban; Kayak; Third Rail; Willow Springs; on the Bus; Sagetreib; North Dakota Quarterly; Hawaii Review; Alembic Willow Springs; Contact II; Lia Weekly; Daily Iowan; American Poetry Review, 1996. Honour: Chester H Jones Commendation Prize, 1994. Memberships: American Poetry Society; Associated Writing Programs. Address: 2735 Olive Street, Eugene, OR 97405, USA.

ROBBINS Jerry Leo, b. 10 Dec 1940, Covington, Tennessee, USA. News Writer. m. Joan L Robbins, 16 Oct 1965, 1 son, 4 daughters. Education: BA, 1964, MA, 1978, Memphis State University. Appointments: Writer, Memphis Press Scimitar, 1969-84, University of Kentucky, 1984-89. Publications: Early Stuff, 1990; The Heat, 1991. Contributions to: Press Scimitar; Pteranodon; Encore; Tennessee Voices; Inside Reporter; Pegasus. Memberships: Vice President, Treasurer, Publicity Director, National Federation of State Poetry Societies; Vice President, Treasurer, Editor of Newsletter, Poetry Society of Tennessee; Board of Directors, Kentucky Poetry Society. Address: 3425 Holwyn Road, Lexington, KY 40503, USA.

ROBBINS Richard Leroy, b. 27 Aug 1953, Los Angeles, California, USA. Poet; College Professor. m. Candace L Black, 8 Sept 1979, 2 sons. Education: AB, San Diego State University, 1975; MFA, University of Montana, 1979. Appointments: Writer in Residence, Montana Arts Council, 1979-81; Instructor, Moorhead State University, 1981-84 and Oregon State University, 1982-84; Assistant, Associate, Professor, Mankato State University, 1984-. Publications: Toward New Weather, 1978; The Invisible Wedding, 1984. Contributions to: Nation; North American Review; Poetry Northwest; Seattle Review. Honours: Robert Winner Award, Poetry Society of America, 1988; National Endowment for the Arts Fellowship, 1992. Memberships: Poetry Society of America; Associated Writing Programs; Western Literature Association. Address: English Department, MSU Box 53, Mankato State University, PO Box 8400, Mankato, MN 56002, USA.

ROBERTS Janet Marie, b. 30 Jan 1947, USA. Lecturer; Writer. m. Thomas Chambers Wayne Roberts II, 18 May 1985, 1 child, sponsored in Thailand. Education: BS, University of Wisconsin; MA, MS, Oxford University, England, 1971. Appointments: Lecturer, University of Pennsylvania, English Seminar; Assistant Professor, Temple University; Lecturer in Poetry and Drama, Fudan University, Shanghai; Dean's Appointed Lecturer, Fordham University; Poet in Schools, Manhattan; Development Director, Akhmatova Memorial Project, Wayne. Publications: Heart's Core; Reaping Song; Elementary Eyelet; Poems Children Love; Toyshop of the Mind. Contributions to: Manhattan Poetry Review; Montage; Shore Poetry Anthology; Strand Poetry Anthology; California Anthology; Aspen Anthology; Ars Textrina, volume 22, 1994; My Lady: Weaving a New Thread of Connection in Ancient Sumer. Honours: Breadloaf Writers Conference Fellowship; Aspen Writers Fellowship; Virginia Centre for the Creative Arts Residency; 1st Place Poetry Award, American Association of University Women; Fellowship, New Jersey State Council of The Arts; Citizen Ambassadorship to Russia, 1994, 1995; National Editor Policy Fellow, Gifted and the Arts, 1981. Memberships: PEN; Poets and Writers; Modern Language Association; Board, English Speaking Union, Chair, Excellence in English Education; Academy of American Poets. Address: 259 West Johnson Street, Apt 4S, Philadelphia, PA 19144, USA.

ROBERTS John Anthony, b. 2 Jan 1935, London, England. Retired Civil Servant. m. Linda Geraldine Cannons, 20 Dec 1969, 3 sons. Education: Honours Degree, Classics and English, Trinity College, Cambridge, 1959; Barrister at Law; Diploma, Librarianship, Ealing College of Higher Education, 1978. Appointments: Clerk, House of Lords, 1960-61; Teacher: Holmleigh Prep School, 1962-63, Bernard Mizeki College, Rhodesia, 1963-64; Legal Assistant, ICL, 1973-76; Clerical Assistant, HM Customs and Excise, 1979-92. Publication: Suburban Reflections, 1990. Contributions to: Success Magazine; Weyfarers; Focus; What's On; Sutton Advertiser. Honour: First Prize, Sutton Library 21st Anniversary Poetry Competition. Memberships: Guildford Poets; Sutton Society of Civil Service Authors; Sutton Writer's Circle. Address: 24 Salisbury Avenue, Cheam, Sutton, Surrey SM1 2DJ, England.

ROBERTS Leonard (Len Roberts), b. 13 Mar 1947, Cohoes, New York, USA. Professor of English. m. 31 Dec 1981, 2 sons, 1 daughter. Education: BA, English, Siena College, Loudonville, NY, 1970; MA, English, University of Dayton, 1972; PhD, English, LeHigh University, 1976. Appointments: Professor of English, Northampton Community College, 1974-82, 1985-88, 1990-; Visiting Professor, Creative Writing, Lafayette College, 1982-85; Fulbright Scholar to Hungary, 1988-89. Publications: Cohoes Theater, 1981; From The Dark, 1984; Sweet Ones, 1988; Black Wings, 1989; Learning About The Heart, chapbook, 1992; Sandor Csoori: Selected Poems, from the Hungarian, 1992; Dangerous Angels, 1993; Counting The Black Angels, 1994. Contributions to: American Poetry Review; Poetry; Paris Review; Partisan Review; Antioch. Honours: Poetry Awards, Pennsylvania Council on The Arts, 1981, 1986, 1987, 1989, 1992; Anthology of Magazine Verse: Yearbook of American Poetry, 1983-; 2 Awards in Poetry, NEA, 1984, 1989; Great Lakes and Prairies Award, 1988; Fulbright Scholar, 1988-89; National Poetry Series, 1989; Translation Awards, Soros Foundation, 1989, 1990, 1992, 1994; Guggenheim Fellowship, 1990-91; Pushcart Prize in Poetry, XVI, 1991; Fulbright Translation Award, to translate Hungarian Poetry, 1991; Witter-Bynner Translation Award, 1991-92; Best American Poetry, 1992; 1st Prize, Wildwood Poetry Contest, 1993; Fulbright Scholar, 1994. Memberships: Modern Language Association; Poet, Literature Advisory Board, Pennsylvania Council on The Arts. Address: 2443 Wassergass Road, Hellertown, PA 18055, USA.

ROBERTS Philippa Mary, b. 7 Aug 1960, Cheltenham, Gloucestershire, England. Writer. 1 son, 1 daughter. Appointments: Fruit Picker; Olive Tree Tender; Waitress; Shop Assistant; Librarian; Writer; Professional Bluestocking. Publications: Poetry Now Anthologies: Pot Pourri, 1991; Guardian of the State, 1992; Tributes in Verse, 1993; A Woman's Place, 1993. Contributions to: Ver Poets, 1983. Honours: Highly Commended, Waterstones Competition, 1990; Highly Commended, Mary & Alfred Wilkins Memorial Competition, 1991; Highly Commended, Writer's Viewpoint Magazine Competition, 1995. Memberships: Cheltenham Shakespeare Society. Address: Cheltenham, Gloucester, England.

ROBERTS Robert (James), b. 11 Jan 1931, Penrith, Cumbria, England. Schoolmaster. m. Patricia Mary Milbourne, 8 Aug 1959, 1 son, dec, 1 daughter. Education: MA, Pembroke College, Cambridge, 1951-55. Appointments: Assistant Master, Fettes, 1955-75; Housemaster, 1970-75; Headmaster, Worksop, 1975-86. Publications: Amphibious Landings, 1990; First Selection, 1994; Genius Loci, 1995; Second Selection, 1995; Worm's Eye View, 1995. Contributions to: Spectator; Countryman; Poetry Review; Acumen; Envoi; Orbis; Outposts; Poetry Nottingham; Staple; Westwords; First Time; Iota; Doors; Otter; Nutshell; Literary Review; Poetry Wales; Seam. Honours: Many awards. Address: Ellon House, Harpford, Sidmouth, Devon EX10 0NH, England.

ROBERTSON Howard W, b. 19 Sept 1947, Eugene, Oregon, USA. Poet. m. Margaret E Collins, 10 Aug 1991, 2 sons, 2 daughters. Education: BA, Russian, 1970, MA, Comparative Literature, 1978, University of Oregon; MSLS, Library Science, University of Southern California, 1975. Appointments: Slavic Catalogue Librarian and Bibliographer, University of Oregon, Eugene, 1975-93; Full-time Poet, 1993-. Publication: To The Fierce Guard in the Assyrian Saloon, 1987. Contributions to: The Ahsahta Anthology; Ergo; Fireweed; Croton Review; Yet Another Little Magazine; Yellow Silk; Negative Capability; Pinchpenny; Assembling; Laughing Unicorn; Laughing Bear; Intown; Pacifica. Honours: Bumbershoot Writers-in-Performance Award, 1993; Pacifica Award, 1995; Honourable Mention, Wildwood Prize, 1995. Membership: Past President, Lane Literary Guild, Lane County, Oregon. Address: 854 Martin Street, Eugene, OR 97405, USA.

ROBERTSON Jennifer Sinclair (Jenny), b. 21 Feb 1942, Datchet, Buckinghamshire, England. Writer; Missionary. m. Stuart Robertson, 19 Feb 1966, 1 son, 1 daughter. Education: MA, Glasgow University, 1963; Diploma in Social Studies, 1966; Postgraduate studies at University of Warsaw, 1965. Appointments: Social Worker; Teacher of Creative Writing; Teacher of English as a Foreign Language; Missionary in St Petersburg. Publications: Touch of Flame, 1988; Beyond the Burden, 1989; Ghetto, 1989. Contributions include: Chapman; Lines Review; Northwords. Honour: Ghetto shortlisted for Winifred Mary Stanford Prize. Address: Chernoretskiy per 4-6, 193167 St Petersburg, Russia.

ROBERTSON William Paul, b. 29 May 1950, Pennsylvania, USA. English Teacher. Education: BS, English, Mansfield University, 1972. Appointments: English Teacher, Otto Eldred High School, 1973-78; Bradford Area School District, 1978-. Publications: Burial Grounds, 1977; Gardez au Froid, 1979; Animal Comforts, 1981; Life After Sex Life, 1983; Waters Boil Bloody, 1990; 1066, 1992; Hearse Verse, 1994; Battle Verse, 1996. Contributions to: Champagne Horror; Cobblestone; Glasgow Magazine; Grue; Lable; Midway Review; Pinehurst Journal; Poetic Knight; Psychopoetica; Slipstream; Stride; Standing Stone; 2AM; Vollmond; Wellspring. Memberships: Poets and Writers; National Writers Association; Genre Writer's Association. Address: PO Box 14532, Savannah, GA 31416, USA.

ROBINSON Mark, b. 20 Oct 1964, Preston, Lancashire, England. Writer; Vegetarian Chef; Literature Development Writer. m. Alison Robinson, 9 July 1988, 1 son, 1 daughter. Education: BA, Honours, English Literature, French, University of Liverpool, 1987. Appointments: Founder, Editor, magazine and press, Scratch, York, 1989-; Literature Development Work, Cleveland, 1993-; Writer-in-Residence, HMP Wealston, 1995. Publications: Rigmarole; The Domesticity Remix, 1992; The Horse Burning Park, 1994; Editor, A Hole Like That: 13 Cleveland Poets, 1994; Magazine and Literary Journals: A Guide, 1994. Contributions to: Rialto; Honest Ulsterman; North; Wide Start; Slow Dancer. Honour: Tyrone Guthrie Award, Northern Arts, 1994. Address: 9 Chestnut Road, Eaglescliffe, Stockton on Tees TS16 0BA, England.

ROBSON Andrew Keith, b. 27 Mar 1949, Leeds, Yorkshire, England. Printer. Education: HNC, Printing, 1971. Appointments: Editor, Krax Magazine, 1971. Contributions to: Boggers All; First Time; Purple Patch; Sandwiches. Membership: Secretary, Treasurer, Yorkshire Federation of Small Presses, 1986-88. Address: 63 Dixon Lane, Leeds, Yorkshire LS12 4RR, England.

ROCHE Terry. See: POOLE Margaret Barbara (Peggy).

RODDEN Bronwyn Anne, b. 26 Nov 1956, Sydney, New South Wales, Australia. Writer. Education: Diploma, Applied Science, Wagga Agriculture College. Appointments: Staff Trainer, New South Wales National Parks and Wildlife Service; Secretary, Women in Prison Task Force Implementation Committee; Technical Officer, Department of

Agriculture, New South Wales; Uniformed Customs Officer, Sydney Water Front. Publications: Wee Girls; The House is Breathing. Contributions to: Hermes; Westerly; Redoubt; Island; Scarp; Four W; Spindrift; Friendly Street Reader; Mattoid. Honours: First New Poets Program Workshop; Selected for New South Wales Bookbinders Anthology. Memberships: Poets Union; Australian Society of Authors; Deakin Literary Society. Address: 14 Bourne Street, Marrickville, NSW 2204, Australia.

RODEFER Stephen (Jean Calais), b. 20 Nov 1940, USA. Writer; Professor. m. Jean Phelps Lowe, 7 July 1985, 3 sons. Education: Amherst College, 1959-63; State University of New York, Buffalo, 1963-67. Appointments: Instructor, State University of New York, 1965-67; Assistant Professor of English, University of New Mexico, 1967-71; Lecturer, San Francisco State University, 1981-85; Curator, Archive for New Poetry, 1985-87, Lecturer, Literature Department, 1985-89, University of California at San Diego; Architecture Department, University of California, Berkeley, 1990-. Publications: The Knife, 1965; Villonny Jean Calais, 1976; One or Two Love Poems From the White World, 1976; The Bell Clerk's Tears Keep Flowing, 1978; Plane Debris, 1981; Four Lectures, 1982; Oriflamme Day, 1984; Safety, 1985; Emergency Measures, 1987. Contributions to: Sulfur; Syzyvva; Oblek; Conjunctions; Sur; Temblor; Jimmy and Lucy's House of K. Honours: Annual Book Award, American Poetry Center, 1983; Grant, Fund for Poetry, 1988. Memberships: Acting Head, Poets Theater; American Literary Translators Association. Address: c/o Rodefer, Overlook Court, Bellaire, OH 43906, USA.

RODGERS Carolyn Marie, b. 14 Dec 1942, Chicago, Illinois, USA. Writer; College Professor. Education: BA, Roosevelt University, 1981; MA, University of Chicago, 1984. Appointments: Columbia College Afro-American Literature Professor, 1969; Albany State College, 1971; Poet-in-Residence, University of Washington, 1970; Malcolm X College, 1971; Poet in Residence, Indiana University, 1974, Roosevelt University, 1983; English Lecturer and Summer Poetry Workshop Co-Ordinator, Columbia College, 1989-91; Founder and Editor, Eden Press, Gale Researcher's Author's Autobiographical Series, 1991. Publications: Paper Soul, 1968; Songs of a Blackbird, 1970; How I Got Ovah, 1976; The Heart as Evergreen, 1978; Translation, 1980; A Little Lower than the Angels, 1984, 1989; Morning Glory, 1989-90; Religious Poetry of Carolyn M Rodgers, Eden and Other Poems, 1993; Daughters of Africa, 1993; We're Only Human, 1994; A Train Called Judah, poetry and prose, 1996. Contributions to: Nation; Ebony; Essence; Black Scholar Magazine; Negro Digest; Black World; Roots and Dreams; Black Dialogue; Caprice; Hands Upon The Heart, vol II, poetry video; Rare Form. Honours: National Endowment of The Arts Award, 1970; First Conrad Kent Rivers Award, 1970; Society of Midland Authors Award, 1970; PEN Grant, 1987; Carnegie Writer's Grant, 1980; Television Gospel Tribute, 1982. Memberships: Founding Member, Organization of Black American Culture, and Gwendolyn Brooks Writing Workshop. Address: PO Box 804271, Chicago, IL 60680, USA.

RODLEY Laura, b. 15 Dec 1955, Wilmington, Delaware, USA. Writer; Certified Nurse's Aide. m. James J Rodley, 10 Apr 1982, 1 son, 2 daughters. Education: Adult Degree Program, Norwich University, Brattleboro. Appointments: Nurse's Aide; Painter; Artist; Quilt-Maker; Horse Painter. Contributions to: Massachusetts Review; Prose Poem; Peregrine; Nurturing; Llama Magazine; Juggler's World. Honour: 2nd Place, Poet's Seat Contest, Greenfield, 1991. Address: 38 South Cemetery Road, Ashfield, MA 01330, USA.

RODNING Charles Bernard, b. 4 Aug 1943, Pipestone, Minnesota, USA. Physician; Surgeon. m. Mary Elizabeth Lipke Rodning, 3 sons. Education: BS, Gustavus Adolphus College, 1965; MD, University of Rochester, 1970; PhD, University of Minnesota, 1979. Appointments: Vice Chairman and Professor, Department of Surgery, Assistant Professor, Department of Structural and Cellular Biology, Director, Surgical Endoscopy Laboratory. Scientist, Cancer Centre, College of Medicine, University of South Alabama, Mobile. Contributions to: Orphic Lute; Piedmont Literary Review; American Poetry Anthology; National Poetry Anthology; Poets at Work; Tightrope; Daring Poetry Quarterly; Parnassus Literary Review; Modern Haiku; Dragonfly; Proof Rock; New Cicada; Old Pond; Wind Chimes; Inkstone; Quill Books; Villager; Poetry Unlimited; American Press; Poetry Nippon; Prophetic Voices; Sumi-e; Image Design; Forum; Amelia; Amherst Review; Modern poetry anthologies include: Yes Press, Sewanee Press, Vantage Press, Word and Image, Haiku Quarterly, Wynham Hall. Memberships: Haiku Society of America;

Sumi-e Society of America; Alabama State Poetry Society; Academy of American Poets; Haiku International Association; Historical Mobile Preservation Society; Southern Poetry Association; Mobile Art Association; Eastern Shore Art Association. Address: 2451 Fillingim Street, Mobile, AL 36617, USA.

RODRIGUES Louis Jerome, b. 20 July 1938, Madras, India. Writer; Translator. m. (1) Malinda Weaving, dec, 1 son, (2) Josefina Bernet Soler, 6 Oct 1984, 1 son. Education: BA Honours, English, 1960, MA, 1962, Intermediate Histories and Logic, Madras, 1955-57; MA, MPhil, Anglo-Saxon, London, 1965-67; MA, Law and English Tripos, 1971-73, 1977; PhD, 1990, Barcelona.Appointments: Assistant Director, Bénédict, Mannheim, 1977; Director of Studies, Inlingua, Barcelona, 1978-82; Director, Phoenix, Barcelona, 1982-87. Publications: A Long Time Waiting, 1979; Anglo-Saxon Riddles, 1990; Seven Anglo-Saxon Elegies, 1991; Chiaroscuro, 1991; The Battles of Maldon and Brunanburh, 1991; Anglo-Saxon Verse Runes, 1992; Translations from Catalan: A Choice of Salvador Espriu's Verse and Salvador Espriu's La Pell de Brau, 1992; Anglo-Saxon Verse Charms, Maxims and Heroic Legends, 1993; Anglo-Saxon Elegiac Verse, 1994; Anglo-Saxon Didactic Verse, 1995; Three Anglo-Saxon Battle Poems, 1995. Contributions to: Ariel; El Correo Catalan; Catalan Review; The Lyric; Orbis; Outposts; Rhyme Revival Anthology; Metamorphoses; In Other Words; Selim. Honour: Poetry Translation Prize, Catholic University of Washington, 1993. Memberships include: Translators Association; Executive Committee, Society of Authors, 1988-91; Royal Society of Literature; International Society of Anglo-Saxonists. Address: 40 Sherlock Close. Cambridge CB3 0HP, England.

RODRIGUEZ Andrés, b. 24 Dec 1955, Kansas City, Missouri, USA. Independent Scholar; Poet. Education: BA, English, 1980; MA, Creative Writing, English, 1984; PhD, Literature, 1990. Appointments: Adjunct Lecturer, Humanities Program, University of Arizona, 1990-91; Instructor, English Department, William Jewell College, spring 1993; Visiting Professor, English Department, Rock-Hurst College, spring 1994. Night Song, 1994; Book of the Heart: The Poetics, Letters, and Life of John Keats, 1993. Contributions to: Bilingual Review, Arizona State University; Sage Trieb, University of Maine, Orono; Lucero, University of California at Berkeley. Memberships: Academy of American Poets; Modern Language Association of America. Address: 3203 Central Street, Kansas City, MO 64111, USA.

RODRIGUEZ Judith (Catherine), b. 13 Feb 1936, Perth, Western Australia. Poet; Dramatist; Librettist; Editor; Lecturer. m. (1) Fabio Rodriguez, 1964, div 1981, 4 children, (2) Thomas Shapcott, 1982. Education: BA, University of Queensland, Brisbane, 1957; MA, Girton College, Cambridge, 1962; Certificate of Education, University of London, 1968. Appointments include: Lecturer in External Studies, University of Queensland, Brisbane, 1959-60; Lecturer in English, Philippa Fawcett College of Education, London 1962-63, University of the West Indies, Kingston, Jamaica 1963-65; Lecturer in English, St Mary's College of Education, Twickenham, 1966-68; Lecturer 1969-75, Senior Lecturer in English 1977-85, La Trobe University, Bundoora, Australia; Senior Lecturer, Deakin University, 1989-; Chair, Committee of Association of Australian Writing Programs, 1996-. Publications: Poetry: Four Poets, 1962; Nu-Plastik Fanfare Red, 1973 and Other Poems, 1973; Water Life, 1976; Shadow on Glass, 1978; Mudcrab at Gambaro's, 1980; Witch Heart, 1982; Floridian Poems, 1986; The House by Water: Selected and New Poems, 1988; The Cold, 1992; Several plays and opera libretti. Contributions to: Numerous publications. Honours: Arts Council of Australia Fellowships, 1974, 1978, 1983; Government of South Australia Biennial Prize for Literature, 1978; International PEN Peter Stuyvesant Prize for Poetry, 1981; Member of the Order of Australia (AM), 1994; Fellowship of Australian Writers Christopher Brennan Award for Poetry, 1994. Memberships: Association for the Study of Australian Literature; Australian Society of Authors; International PEN; South Pacific Association for Commonwealth Language and Literature Studies. Address: PO Box 231, Mont Albert, Victoria 3127, Australia.

RODRIGUEZ Victorino (Victor Roz), b. 24 Jan 1923, Cuba. Lecturer; Instructor; Poet. m. 21 Jan 1966, 1 son, 1 daughter, dec. Education: University of Madrid, 1957-58; Licenciado en Filosofia, Pedagogia, Filologia Romanica. Appointments: Teacher, Markham High School, 1966-67; College Spanish Instructor, East Los Angeles, 1969-92. Publications: Cantos de Cantos; Primera Seleccion, 1969; Segunda Seleccion, 1972; Tercera Seleccion, 1973; Quarta Seleccion, 1974; Quinta Seleccion, 1975; Sexta Seleccion, 1982; Sumas Poeticas, 1990, 1991, 1992. Contributions to: Clarin Gemma;

Americanto; Invitacion a la Poesia; Son de Sometos; Suma de Amor; El Alba de America; VII Antologia de Poesia Contemporanae. Memberships: Liceo Internacional de Cultura; La Cuadratura del Circulo Los Angeles. Address: 8335 Scenic Drive South, San Gabriel, CA 91770, USA.

ROEDER Jill Mary, (Holly Hampden), b. 28 July 1941, Newbury, Berkshire, England. Personnel Manager. Education: St Bernard's Covent, Slough. Appointments: Formerly Associate Editor, Envoi; Text and News Editor, Orbis Magazine. Contributions to: Outposts; Iota; Weyfarers; Spokes; New Prospects; Staple; South; Envoi. Honour: 3rd Prize, Endocrine Research Poetry Competition, 1989. Membership: Chairwoman, Ripley Poetry Association, Bromley, Kent. Address: 6 Green Lane, Chislehurst, Kent BR7 6AG, England.

ROFFMAN DeMaios, b. 6 Jan 1937, New York, New York, USA. Associate Professor of English. m. Bernard Roffman, 31 May 1964, 1 son. Education: BA, Honours, Languages and Literature, CCNY, 1960; MA, English, Asian Studies, University of Hawaii, 1967. Appointments: Writer, TV Guide; Instructor, CCNY; Fulbright Advisor; Instructor, University of Hawaii, Gakushuin University, Aoyama Gakuin, Japan; Writer; Editor; Council on Student Travel and Exchange; Associate Professor, University of Pennsylvania. Publications: Wings of the Rainbow, 1979; Once.. a Miracle, 1981; Living Inland, 1988; First Decade, 1989; A Gathering of Poets, 1992; Co-Editor, Life on the Line: Selections on Healing and Words, 1993; Antologia, 1993; Going to Bed Whole, 1993; Collaborations with composers, D Berlin: No More Masks, 1989, Clippings, 1991, Homage to Theo, 1992, with J Zaimont: Vessels, premiered 1992. Contributions include: Asian Times; Small Press Review; Journal of Popular Literature; College English; Centennial Review; Oxford; Dekalb Literature Arts Review; Sojourner; Laurel Review; Visions; Potato Eyes; Negative Capability; Pittsburgh Poetry Review; Willa; I Have Become the Woman I Wanted, anthology, received American Book Award, 1995. Honours: Best Poem Centennial Award, 1988; Distinguished Faculty Award for Creative Writing, SSHE System, PA; Witter Bynner Foundation Award, 1993, 1994; Best Published Poem for, Small Gratitudes, Pittsburgh Poetry Society, 1995; Nominee for, When You Become All You Detest, Pushcart Poetry Award. Memberships: Poetry Society of America; National Council of Teachers of English; Modern Language Association; World Congress of Poets. Address: 2580 Evergreen Drive, Indiana, PA 15701, USA.

ROGERS Bertha Kay, b. 2 June 1941, Illinois, USA. Product Developer; Doll Designer. m. 27 Aug 1961, div 1987, 2 daughters. Education: Iowa Wesleyan College, 1959-61; University of Iowa, 1962-63; Studio and Forum of Scenic Design, New York City, 1983. Appointments: Consultant, Programme Manager, Metropolitan Museum of Art, New York City; Vice President, Merchandise and Product Development, Collectors Guild Ltd, New York City. Publications: The Reason of Trees, 1987; Clouds, with R Hart, G Saintiny, and T Young, 1988; Sleeper, You Wake, 1991. Contributions include: Bogg; California Quarterly; Sun; Seattle Review; Louisville Review; Salmon Literary Review, Ireland; Yankee; Seems; Slant; Stone Drum; International Poetry Review; Nimrod; Negative Capability; Roanoke Review; Calapooya Collage. Honours: Honourable Mention, Roberts Writing Awards, 1989; Writer's Residency, U Cross Foundation, 1989, MacDowell and Millay Colonies; Finalist, Eve of St Agnes Award, 1992. Memberships: Poetry Society of America; Poets and Writers. Address: Bright Hill Farm, RD 1, Box 545, Delhi, NY 13753, USA.

ROGERS Del Marie, b. 11 Apr 1936, Washington, District of Columbia, USA. Poet; Editor. Div, 1 son, 2 daughters. Education: BA, Baylor University, 1957; MA, English, Philosophy, 1970, PhD study, Vanderbilt University. Appointments: North Carolina State University, 1970-71, Vanderbilt University; Senior Copywriter, catalogue advertising, J C Penney Corporate Headquarters, Dallas, TX. Publications: Breaking Free, 1977; Close to Ground, 1990. Contributions to: Choice; Chicago; Colorado Review; Eighties; Epoch; Ironwood; Kayak; Nation; New Mexico Magazine; Pacific Review; Perspective; Puerto del Sol; Southern Poetry Review; Sun; Texas Observer; Various anthologies. Honours: Monetary Prize, 1970; National Endowment for The Arts Fellowships, 1974-75. Memberships: Poetry Society of America; Academy of American Poets; PEN, USA West. Address: 4017 Bond Street, Rowlett, TX 75088, USA.

ROGERS Linda, b. 10 Oct 1944, Port Alice, British Columbia, Canada. Writer. m. Rick Van Krugel, 3 sons. Education: MA, English

Literature, University of British Columbia. Appointments: Lecturer, University of British Columbia, University of Victoria, Camosum College, Malaspina College. Publications: Some Breath, 1978; Queens of the Next Hot Star, 1981; Witness, 1985; Singing Rib, 1988; Woman at Mile O, 1990; Letters From the Doll Hospital, 1992; The Magic Flute (Mozart for Children), 1992; Hard Candy, 1994; The Half Life of Radium, 1994; Love in The Rainforest, selected poetry, 1996; For children: Worm Sandwich, 1990, Brown Bag Blues, 1991; Frank Zapper and The Disappearing Teacher, 1994; Molly Brown is Not a Clown, 1996. Contributions to: Poetry Canada Review; Orbis International; Canadian Literature; Cross Canada Writers Quarterly; Malahat Review; Border Crossings; Vancouver Sun; Toronto Star. Honours: Canada Council Arts Awards, 1987, 1990; British Columbia Writers Poetry Prize, 1989; Cultural Services Award, 1990; Aya Poetry Prize, 1983; Governor General's Centennial Medal for Poetry and Performance, 1993; Stephen Leacock Award for Poetry, 1994; Dorothy Livesay Award for Poetry, 1995; Peoples Poetry Award, 1996; Stephen Leacock, 1996. Memberships: Board, League of Canadian Poets; President, Federation of British Columbia Writers; Writers Union of Canada; Society of Canadian Composers. Address: 1235 Styles Street, Victoria, BC V9A 3Z6, Canada.

ROGERS Pattiann, b. 23 Mar 1940, Joplin, Missouri, USA. Writer; Poet. m. John R Rogers, 3 Sept 1960, 2 sons. Education: BA, English, University of Missouri, 1961; MA, Creative Writing, University of Houston, 1981. Appointment: Assistant Professor, University of Texas. Publications: The Expectations of Light, 1981; The Tattooed Lady in The Garden, 1986; Legendary Performance, 1987; Splitting and Binding, 1989; Geocentric, 1993. Contributions to: Hudson Review; Poetry; Georgia Review; New England Review; Gettysburg Review; Poetry Northwest; Indiana Review; TriQuarterly; Western Humanities Review; Pushcart Prize Anthology, numbers 10, 11, 14, 17. Honours: Texas Institute of Letters Award, 1982, 1990; Guggenheim Fellowship, 1984; National Endowment for The Arts Grant, 1988; Lannan Fellowship in Poetry, 1991; Strousse Award in Poetry, 1992. Address: 7412 Berkeley Circle, Castle Rock, CO 80104, USA.

ROGGEMAN Willem M, b. 9 July 1935, Brussels, Belgium. m. Jacqueline Nardi, 20 Dec 1975, 1 son, 1 daughter. Education: Economics, University of Ghent. Appointments: Literary and Artistic Critic, Het Laatste Nieuws, Flemish newspaper, 1959-81; Editor, De Vlaamse Gids, 1970-92. Publications: Rhapsody in Blue, 1958; Bij Wijze Van Schrijven, 1960; Baudelaire Verliefd, 1963; Sneeuwblindheid, 1974; Het Zwart Van Goya, 1982; The Revolution Begins in Bruges, 1983; Memoires, 1985; A Vanishing Emptiness, 1988; De Uitvinding Van de Tederheid, 1994. Contributions to: Het Laatste Nieuws; De Vlaamse Gids; Diogenes; Die Zeit; De Tweede Ronde; Poeziekrant; Kunstbeeld. Honours: Dirk Martensprize, 1962; Prize of the City of Brussels, 1975; Prize of St Truiden, 1989. Memberships: Secretary, Flemish PEN Centre, 1968-80; President, L P Boon Society, 1984-91. Address: Luchtlaan 4, 1700 Dilbeek, Belgium.

ROGOFF Jay, b. 21 Feb 1954, New York, New York, USA. College Teacher. Education: BA, English, University of Pennsylvania, 1975; MA, Creative Writing, 1978, Doctor of Arts, English, 1981, Syracuse University. Appointments: Teaching Assistant, Syracuse University, New York, 1975-80; Assistant Professor of English, LeMoyne College, Syracuse, 1980-85; Academic Advisor, Inmate Higher Education Programme, 1985-95, Lecturer in Liberal Studies, 1993-, Skidmore College, Saratoga Springs, New York. Publication: The Cutoff: A Sequence, The Word Works, 1995. Contributions to: Agni; Boundary 2; Chicago Review; Georgia Review; Hudson Review; Kansas Quarterly; Kenyon Review; Mademoiselle; Minnesota Review; MSS; New Republic; New Review; Nimrod; Partisan Review; Poetry Northwest; Poetry Review; Prairie Schooner; Present Tense; Salmagundi; Sewanee Review; Shenandoah; Stand; Yale Review; Zone 3; Manoa; Paris Review; Formalist; Spitball: Literary Baseball Magazine. Honours: Academy of American Poets Award, 1976; Delmore Schwartz Poetry Prize, 1981; John Masefield Memorial Award, Poetry Society of America, 1982; Finalist, Walt Whitman Award, Academy of American Poets, 1986, 1992; Fellow, MacDowell Colony, 1989; Fellow, 1989, Sloan and Solomon Writer in Residence, 1991, Corporation of Yaddo; The Washington Prize for Poetry, 1994. Memberships: Poets and Writers; Associated Writing Programmes; Poetry Society of America; Academy of American Poets. Address: 35 Pinewood Avenue, Saratoga Springs, NY 12866-2622, USA.

ROHEKAR Joel Ezekiel, b. 5 Oct 1942, Nadiad, Gujarat, India. Teacher. m. Sudha, 22 Mar 1974. Education: BA, 1966; Bed, 1971; MA, 1974; IWA honorary, USA. Appointments: Teacher, Mangrule High School, 1971-72; Teacher, Deorukh College, 1974-77; Teacher, New English School, 1976-77; Teacher, T.C. College, 1977; Teacher, S.D.S.M. College, 1977-78; Teacher, English School Junior College, 1979-80; Teacher, P.S. English Medium School and Junior College, 1982-. Publication: Gomatesham Panamami. Contributions to: Hello Student; Shravika; Poet; Poetcrit; Quest; International Poetry; World Poetry, anthology, 1994, 1995, 1996; Poems 96, anthology. Honour: Certificate of Participation with Honour and Excellence, International Writers and Artists Association and Bluffton College, Bluffton, USA, 1995. Memberships: World Poetry Society, Intercontinental; International Writers and Artists Association, USA. Address: 164/65 South Sadar Bazaar, Solapur 413003, Maharashtra State, India.

ROHEN Edward, (Bruton Connors), b. 10 Feb 1931, South Wales. Writer. m. Elizabeth Jarrett, 4 Apr 1961, 1 daughter. Education: ATD, Cardiff College of Art, 1952. Appointments: Art Teacher, Ladysmith High, British Columbia, Canada, 1956-57; Head of Art, St Bonaventures, London, 1958-73; Ilford County High for Boys, Essex, 1973-82. Publications: Nightpriest, 1965; Bruised Concourse, 1973; Old Drunk Eyes Haiku, 1974; Scorpio Broadside 15, 1975; Poems/Poemas, 1976; 109 Haiku and One Seppuku for Maria, 1987; Sonnets for Maria Marriage, 1988; Sonnets: Second Sequence for Maria, 1989. Contributions to: Poetry Wales; Anglo Welsh Review; Irish Press; Mabon; Tribune; Argot; Edge; Little Word Machine; Second Aeon; Planet; Carcanet; Poetry Nippon; Riverside Quarterly; Littack; Wormwood Review; Twentieth Century Magazine. Memberships: Korean War Veterans Writers and Arts Society; Academician, Centro Cultural Literario e Artistico de o Jornal de Felgeiras, Portugal; Welsh Academy. Address: 57 Kinfauns Road, Goodmayes, Ilford, Essex IG3 9QH, England.

RONAN John Joseph, b. 18 June 1944, San Diego, California, USA. University Professor. Education: BA, Loyola University, Chicago; MA, University of Illinois, 1969. Appointments: Assistant Professor, 1973-82, Professor, 1982-, Chairman, Department of Media and Communications, North Shore Community College, Danvers; Director-Producer, The Writer's Block, TV series, WNEC-TV, Gloucester. Contributions to: Ohio Review; New England Quarterly; Greenboro Review; Three Penny Review; Southern Poetry Review; Yankee Magazine; Delaware Literary Review; Louisville Review; New Laurel Review; Epos; Hollins Critic; Andover Review; Lyric; North Essex Review. Honours: Scholarship Winner, Bread Loaf Writers Conference, 1975; Finalist Award, Massachusetts Artists Foundation, 1980; Winner, Willury Farm Competition, 1982; Finalist, Morse Competition, 1988; Capricorn Prize, 1991; National Poetry Series, 1992. Memberships: Poetry Society of America; Academy of American Poets; National Federation of State Poetry Societies. Address: Box 5524, Magnolia, MA 01930, USA.

RONIN Matt. See: OSAKI Mark (Stephen).

ROOT William Pitt, b. 28 Dec 1941, Austin, Texas, USA. Poet; Professor. m. Pamela Uschuk, 6 Nov 1988, 1 daughter. Education: BA, University of Washington, 1964; MFA, University of North Carolina, Greensboro, 1966; Stegman Fellow, Stanford University, 1967-68. Appointments: Assistant Professor, Michigan State University, 1967-68; Visiting Writer-in-Residence, Amherst College, 1971, University of Southwest Louisiana, 1976, Wichita State University, 1976, University of Montana, 1978, 1980, 1982-85, Pacific Lutheran University, 1990; Professor, Hunter College, New York City, 1986-. Publications: The Storm and Other Poems, 1969; Striking The Dark Air For Music, 1973; A Journey South, 1977; Reasons For Going It On Foot, 1981; In The World's Common Grasses, 1981; Invisible Guests, 1984; Faultdancing, 1986; Trace Elements from a Recurring Kingdom, 1994; Selected Odes of Pablo Neruda, 1997. Contributions include: Atlantic; Nation; Harper's; Poetry; New Yorker; APR; Poetry East; Triquarterly; Commonweal. Honours: Academy of American Poetry Prize, 1967; Grants: Rockefeller Foundation, 1969-70, Guggenheim Foundation, 1970-71, National Endowment for The Arts, 1973-74, US-UK Exchange Artist, 1978-79; Best Poems of The Year, Borestone Mountain, 1974; Pushcart Awards, 1977, 1980, 1985; Stanley Kumitz Poetry Award, 1981; Guy Owen Poetry Award, 1984. Address: 2022 East 5th Street, Tucson, AZ 85719, USA.

ROSA ROMERO Jaime Benito, b. 25 July 1949, Bellreguard, Valencia, Spain. Professor. 2 sons. Education: Licentiate in

Philosophy, Universidad de Valencia, 1974; Licentiate and Doctor in Philology, Sorbonne, Paris, 1982. Publications: Poems: Nubes digitales, 1974; Océan Claxon, 1979; La Estación Azul, 1980; Yo Leopardo, 1982; De Rizo Soplo, 1984; Lugar de Polen, 1993. Novels: Arlequin en el laberinto, 1986; Las cuatro caras de la piramide negra, 1990. Contributions to: International Poetry Yearbook, University of Colorado, 1987-88. Honours: Prize for Literary Creativity, Provincial Government of Valencia, 1989; Honorary Doctrate Degree in Literature, World Academy of Arts and Culture. Memberships: World Congress of Poets. Address: C/7 No 134, Urb Parque Montealcedo, 46190-Riba-roja, Valencia, Spain.

ROSDAHL Cecilie, b. 15 Dec 1975, Copenhagen, Denmark. Education: Self-taught Painter. Publications: Lykke Laila, 1993; O (poetry collection), 1996. Address: Viborggade 49 4 MF, DK-2100 Copenhagen 0, Denmark.

ROSE Myrna. See: **OSTERBERG Myra Janet.**

ROSE Susan Ruth, b. 25 July 1959, London, England. Translator. Education: Diplome de Culture Francaise, 1980; BA, Hons, French/English, 1981; Diploma, Bilingual Secretarial Studies, 1985; Diploma in translation, 1990. Appointments: Temporary Seretarial Work, 1986-87; Regional Operations Manager, Rover, 1987-91; Freelance Translator, 1991-. Publications: Inclusion in anthology: Of Eros and of Dust, 1992, A Woman's Place, 1993, As Girls Could Boast, 1994. Contributions to: London Magazine; Orbis; Outposts; Encounter; Writing Women; Skoob Review; Clanjamfrie (Scotland). Honour: Commendation, 1992 National Poetry Competition; Runner Up, Poetry Business Competition, 1992; 8th Prize, Skoob/Index on Censorship Competition, 1989. Memberships: Poetry Society; Society of Authors; AITI. Address: 17 Elmwood Court, Elms Lane, Wembley, Middlesex HA0 2NT, England.

ROSENBAUM Marek. See: **LEBIODA Dariusz Thomas.**

ROSENBLATT Joe, (Joseph Rosenblatt), b. 26 Dec 1933, Toronto, Ontario, Canada. Editor; Poet; Writer. m. Faye Smith, 1970, 1 son. Education: Central Technical School, Toronto; George Brown College, Toronto. Appointments: Editor, Jewish Dialog magazine, 1969-; Writer-in-Residence, University of Western Ontario, London, 1979-80, University of Victoria, British Columbia, 1980-81, Saskatoon Public Library, Saskatchewan, 1985-86; Visiting Lecturer, University of Rome, 1987, University of Bologna, 1987. Publications: Poetry: Voyage of the Mood, 1963; The LSD Leacock, 1966; Winter of the Luna Moth, 1968; The Bumblebee Dithyramb, 1972; Blind Photographer: Poems and Sketches, 1973; Dream Craters, 1974; Virgins and Vampires, 1975; Top Soil, 1976; Loosely Tied Hands: An Experiment in Punk, 1978; Snake Oil, 1978; The Sleeping Lady, 1979; Brides of the Stream, 1983; Poetry Hotel: Selected Poems, 1963-1985, 1985; Gridi nel Buio, 1990; Beds and Consenting Dreamers, 1994; A Tentacled Mother, 1995; Madre Tentacolare, 1995; The Rosenblatt Reader, 1995; The Voluptuous Gardener, 1996; Fiction: Tommy Fry and the Ant Colony, 1979; Other: Doctor Anaconda's Solar Fun Club: A Book of Drawings, 1977; Escape from the Glue Factory: A Memoir of a Paranormal Toronto Childhood in the Late Forties, 1985; The Kissing Goldfish of Siam: A Memoir of Adolescence in the Fifties, 1989. Honours: Canada Council Grants, 1966, 1968, 1973, 1980, 1982; Ontario Arts Council Award, 1970; Governor-General's Award, 1976; BC Book Award, 1986. Address: c/o Olichan Books, Box 10, Lantzville, British Columbia V0R 2H0, Canada.

ROSENSTOCK Gabriel Stefan, b. 29 Sept 1949, County Limerick, Ireland. Editor; Broadcaster; Translator. m. Eithne Ní Chléirigh, 1 son, 3 daughters. Appointment: Former Chairman, Poetry Ireland. Publications: Portrait of The Artist as an Abominable Snowman, 1989; Oráistí, 1991; The Confessions of Henry Hooter the Third, 1992. Contributions to: Poetry Ireland Review; Cyphers; Innti; Comhar; Celtic Dawn; Poetry USA; Irish Times; Ireland Journal; Die Andere; Krino; Poetry, Chicago; Tratti. Honours: Arts Council Bursary, 1988; Irish-American Cultural Foundation Award, 1989; Du Quesne Award, 1990; American Cultural Foundation Award, 1989; Du Quesne Award, 1990; Various Oireachtas prizes. Memberships: Irish Writer's Union; Irish Translators' Association; British Haiku Society. Address: 37 Garrán Arnold, Gleann na gCaorach, County Átha, Cliath, Ireland.

ROSENWALD John, b. 25 June 1943, Oak Park, Illinois, USA. Teacher; Writer. m. Ann Arbor, 7 Aug 1976, 1 daughter. Education: BA, 1964, MA, 1965, University of Illinois; PhD, Duke University, 1969.

Appointments: Assumption College, Worcester, MA, 1969-75; Beloit College, Beloit, Wisconsin, 1976-; Fudan University, Shanghai, China, 1987, 1990, 1996. Publication: Smoking People: Encountering the New Chinese Poetry, 1989. Contributions to: Wisconsin Review; Literary Review; Kansas Quarterly; The South Carolina Review; Kennebec; Northeast; Paintbrush; Wisconsin Poets' Calendar; Manoa; Talus; Descant. Honour: Fulbright Scholarship, 1965-66. Memberships: Modern Language Association; Editorial Board, Beloit Poetry Journal; Robert Bly's Annual Conference on The Great Mother. Address: Granite Rose Farm, Box 389, South Andover, ME 04216, USA.

ROSS Alan, b. 6 May 1922, Calcutta, India. Author; Publisher; Journalist. m. Jennifer Fry, 1949, div 1985, 1 son. Education: St John's College, Oxford. Appointments: Royal Navy, 1942-45; Staff, The Observer, 1950-71, toured as Correspondent with MCC, Australia, 1954-55, 1962-63, South Africa, 1956-57, 1964-65, West Indies, 1960-68; Editor, London Magazine, 1961-; Managing Director, London Magazine Editions (Publishers), 1965-. Publications: The Derelict Day, 1947; Time Was Away, 1948; The Forties, 1950; The Gulf of Pleasure, 1951; The Bandit on the Billiard Table, 1954; Something of the Sea, 1954; Australia 55, 1956, 2nd edition, 1983; Cape Summer and the Australians in England, 1957, 2nd edition, 1986; To Whom it May Concern, 1958; The Onion Man, 1959; Through the Caribbean, 1960; Danger on Grass Island, 1960; African Negatives, 1962; Australia 63, 1963; West Indies at Lord's, 1963, 2nd edition, 1986; North from Sicily, 1965; Poems 1942-1967, 1968; Tropical Ice, 1972; The Taj Express, 1973; Open Sea, 1975; Death Valley and Other Poems, 1980; Colours of War, 1983; Ranji, 1983; Blindfold Games, 1986; The Emissary, 1986; Coastwise Lights, 1988; After Pusan, 1995; Editor: Abroad, 1957, The Cricketer's Companion, 1960, London Magazine Stories, 1-11, 1964-80, Living in London, 1974, Selected Poems of Lawrence Durrell, 1977, The Turf, 1982, Living Out of London, 1984. Honours: Atlantic Award for Literature, Rockefeller Foundation, 1946; FRSL, 1971; Commander of the Order of the British Empire, 1982. Address: 4 Elm Park Lane, London, SW3, England.

ROSS Joe, b. 27 Dec 1960, Pennslyvania, USA. Poet; Writer; Editor. Education: Magna cum laude, Honours Programme, Temple University, 1983. Appointments: Literary Editor, Washington Review, 1990-; Poet in Residence, Pyramid Atlantic, 1991-; Writer and Worker, John F Kennedy Center for the Performing Arts. Publications: Guards of the Heart, 1990; How to Write, or I Used to be in Love With My Jailer, 1992; An American Voyage, 1993; Push, 1994; De-Flections, 1994; Full Silence, 1995. Contributions to: Numerous small press poetry magazines. Membership: Contemporary Arts Educational Project. Address: 1719 South Street North West, No 2, Washington, DC 20009, USA.

ROTHENBERG Jerome (Dennis), b. 11 Dec 1931, New York, New York, USA. Poet. m. Diane Brodatz, 25 Dec 1952, 1 son. Education: BA, City College of New York, 1952; MA, University of Michigan, 1953. Appointments: Professor, English, State University of New York at Binghamton, 1986-88, Visual Arts and Literature, University of California, San Diego, 1989-. Publications: White Sun Black Sun, poetry book, 1960; Poems for The Game of Silence: Selected Poems, 1971; Poland/1931, 1974; A Seneca Journal, 1978; Numbers and Letters, 1980; Vienna Blood, 1980; That Dada Strain, 1983; 15 Flower World Variations, 1984; A Merz Sonata, 1985; New Selected Poems, 1970-85, 1986; Khurbn and Other Poems, 1989; Further Sightings and Conversations, 1989; The Lorca Variations, 1994; Gematria, 1994; Seedings, 1996; Pre-Faces, collected writings on poetics, 1981; An Oracle for Delfi, 1995; Editor: Technicians of The Sacred, 1968; Shaking the Pumpkin, 1972, 1986; America A Prophecy, 1973; A Big Jewish Book, 1977; Symposium of the Whole, 1983; Exiled in The Word, 1989; Revolution of The Word, 1974; Poems for The Millenium, Vol I, 1995; Contributions to: Co-Editor, Alcheringa; Editor, some/thing, New Wilderness Letter; Editor, Poems From the Floating World; Sulfur; Conjunctions; Drama Review; Five Fingers; Ikon; New Directions Annual; Notus; Paris Review; Poetry New York; Poetry USA;Talisman; Talus; Tikkun; Change; Action Poetique; Tumult. Honours: National Endowment for The Arts Fellowship, 1975; Guggenheim Fellowship, 1976; American Book Award, 1982; Josephine Miles Literary Award, PEN Oakland, 1994, 1996; Translation Award, PEN Center, USA West, 1994. Memberships: PEN International; New Wilderness Foundation. Address: Department of Visual Arts 0327, University of California at San Diego, La Jolla, CA 92093, USA.

ROTHSCHILD Anne, b. 16 Mar 1943, New York, New York, USA. Etcher; Painter; Art Professor. 1 son. Education: Graduate School, Columbia University, 1963; Licence es Lettres, Sorbonne, Paris, 1965; Diplome des Beaux-Arts, Geneva, 1973; Certificat d'Aptitude a l'Enseignement, Geneva, 1975. Appointments: Art History and Art Professor, Geneva, 1968-84; Attaché Litteraire à la Promotion des Lettres Belges à Paris, 1988-90. Publications: L'An Prochain a Jerusalem, 1979; L'Errance du Nom, 1982; Sept Branches - Sept Jours, 1983; Sept Figures du Livre, Poems and Aquatints, 1983; Du Desert au Fleuve, Poems and Aquatints, 1986; L'Eau du Marbre, 1987; Le Passeur, 1990; Draperies de l'Oubli, 1990; Le Buisson de Feu, novel, 1992; Les Arbres Voyageurs, 1995. Contributions to: Ecriture; Revue des Belles Lettres; Journal de Geneve; Correspondance; Illustrations for Werner Lambersy, Ireniques and Entrée en Matière; Anthologies include Pardes, Poemonde. Honours: Prix Max-Pol Fouchet, 1983; Grants from Promotion des Lettres Belges, 1983, 1989, 1991, Office Féderal de La Culture, Switzerland, 1984, City of Geneva, 1984, Pro Helvetia, 1985, 1993, CNL, Paris, 1985. Foundation Alain de Rothschild, Paris, 1991. Address: 81 Rue Vieille du Temple, 75003 Paris, France.

ROUPCHEV George, b. 2 Sept 1957, Sofia, Bulgaria. Poet; Translator. m. Valentina Petkova, 1 daughter. Education: Graduated, Bulgarian Philology, Psychology, Sofia University, 1982. Appointment: Freelance Poet and Translator. Publications: Tired of Miracles, 1982; Relief of The Night Guard, 1986; Tibalt's Death, 1989; The Men of The Night, 1991. Contributions to: Magazines. Honours: National Prize for Student Poetry, 1980, 1981, 1982; Sofia University Prize, 1982; Southern Spring Prize, 1983; Union of Bulgarian Translators Prize, 1992, 1994. Memberships: Union of Bulgarian Writers; Union of Bulgarian Translators. Address: Christo Maximov Str 20, 1111 Sofia, Bulgaria.

ROUSSOU Nayia, b. 27 Apr 1935, Larnaca, Cyprus. Senior Lecturer. m. Costas Roussos, 4 June 1967, 1 son, 1 daughter. Education: Graduated, American Academy, Larnaca, 1953; Certificate in Music, National Conservatory of Cyprus, 1966; BA, Mass National Conservatory of Cyprus, 1966; BA, Mass Media, 1972; MA, Mass Media, 1972, Indiana University, Bloomington, USA. Appointments: Teacher of English, History, etc, Terra Santa High School, Larnaca, 1953-56; Cyprus Broadcasting Corporation: Editorial Assistant, 1956-59; Gramophone Librarian, 1959-69, Music Programmes Producer, 1969-70; Study Leave in the United States, 1970-72; CyBC (Contd): Senior Television Programme Producer, 1972-88, Head of Public and International Relations, 1988-95; Senior Lecturer, Inter College, Nicosia, Cyprus, 1995-; Teacher of courses on Mass Media, Public Relations and Advertising at local colleges and at the Government Higher Technological Institute as well as PR Lecturer at Cyprus Police Academy; Representative of Cyprus Broadcasting Corporation, attended Mass Media Seminar of Third World Countries, organized by the American Government, 1979; Represented Cyprus at various international literary congresses; Ran for parliamentary elections for the Democratic Party in Cyprus, 1981. Publications: Weekly column in weekly paper, KYPROS, with articles, literary criticism and journalistic essays, 1964-77; Poetry in Greek, Curtain Hour, 1964; Essays and Poetry: Memories of War, 1975; Channels of Ariadne, 1985; Testimony on the Borderless line - the Attila line, 1988; Short stories in Greek: the Executioner and other stories, 1988; Poetry in English: Transit, 1981; Studies: Reaction of Children to Aggression in TV Cartoons, 1978-(MA Thesis translated in Greek and readjusted); Mass Media: History, Aesthetics, Influence, 1979, used as Textbook in Cyprus and abroad; Visual Dialogues, 1982. Honours include: State prize for Poetry for the poetry collection, Channels of Ariadne, 1985; Honoured for his Poetry in Crete, 1992, Rhodes, 1994. Memberships: Union of Cyprus Writers, 1981-86; Vice President 1984-86; Cyprus Pen Centre, PR Officer in Administrative Council 1986-90, Vice President, 1991-. Hobbies: Reading; Writing; Listening to Music; Swimming. Address: 10C Euripides Street, Aglandja, Nicosia, Cyprus.

ROWBOTHAM Colin Hugh, b. 5 June 1949, Manchester, England. Tutor. m. Maggie Hindley, 1 Sept 1979, 1 son, dec, 2 daughters. Education: BA, Honours, English Literature, York University, 1971; PGCE, Manchester College of Education, 1972; RSA Certificate, TEFL II, 1980. Appointments: Primary School Teacher, Hackney, 1972-77; Part-time ESL/Adult Literacy Tutor, Bow/Mile End, 1973-77; English Teacher, Engelbert-Kaempfer Gymnasium, Germany, 1977-78; Member of Marble Arch EFL Co-Operative, 1979-83; Individual Tutor, Hackney, 1983-. Publications: Total Recall, 1987; Johnny, 1988. Contributions to: Anthologies; Poetry Review;

Orbis; Green Book; Outposts; Other Poetry; Staple; New Spokes; Poetry Nottingham; Rites; New Generation; North. Honours: 1st Prize, Lake Aske Memorial, 1984; 1st Prize, Newbury Festival Competition, 1985; 1st Prize, Old Bull Arts Centre Competition, 1985; 3rd Place, Kent and Sussex Poetry Competition, 1992. Memberships: Highgate Poets, 1984-90; Founder Member, North Seven Poetry Group. Address: 3 Victor Cazalet House, Gaskin Street, London, N1 2RX, England.

ROWSE Alfred Leslie, b. 4 Dec 1903, St Austell, Cornwall, England. Historian; Poet. Education: MA; DLitt; Christchurch, Oxford. Appointments: Fellow, All Souls College, Oxford, 1925-74; Senior Research Associate, Huntington Library, 1963-89. Publications: A Life: Collected Poems, 1981; Transatlantic: Later Poems, 1989; Selected Poems, 1990; Prompting the Age: Poems Early and Late, 1991. Non-Fiction: A Cornish Childhood, 1942; The Elizabethan Age, 4 vols, 1951-72; Prefaces to Shakespeare's Plays, 1984; Shakespeare the Man, 1987; The Sayings of Shakespeare, 1993; Fowl Caroline Portraits, 1993; All Souls in My Time, 1993; Historians I Have Known, 1995. Honours: Benson Medal, Royal Society of Literature, 1982; Hon DLitt; Hon DCL; Hon DL. Memberships: Fellow, Royal Society of Literature; Fellow, British Academy; President, English Association, 1952; President, Shakespeare Club, Stratford upon Avon, 1970-. Address: Trenarren, St Austell, Cornwall PL26 6BH, England.

ROXMAN (Pia) Susanna (Ellinor), b. 29 Aug 1946, Stockholm, Sweden. Writer; Critic. Education: BA (Hons), Comparative Literature, Philosophy, Lund University, 1973; PhD, Comparative Literature, University of Gothenburg, 1984. Appointments: Secretary; Ballet Teacher; Fashion Model; University Lecturer; Freelance Writer, Critic, Guest Lecturer, 1984-; Head of the Centre for Classical Mythology, Lund University, 1996-. Publications: Composed in English: Goodbye to the Berlin Wall, 1991; Broken Angels, 1996; Composed in Swedish: Riva villor, 1978; Nymferna kommer, 1983; Glöm de döda, 1985. Contributions to: Many US university journals including: Oxford Magazine, Roanoke Review, Sanskrit, Ship of Fools, Soundings East, The Spoon River Poetry Review, Webster Review, Westview, and Writers' Forum; others include: New Contrast (South Africa); Poetry Kanto (Japan); Understanding (Scotland); Visions International (USA); Whetstone (Canada). Honours: Grant from the Swedish Authors' Fund, 1979; Arts Grant from Malmöhus Landsting (Malmöhus County Council), Sweden, 1984; The Swedish Balzac Prize, 1990; Editor's Choice Prize, the Marjorie Lees Linn Poetry Award, Elk River Review (USA), 1994, and in 1995; Special Mention in the Open University Poetry Competition (England), 1994. Memberships: Författarcentrum Syd (Authors' Centre South), Sweden; Conservatory of American Letters. Address: Ulrikedal D:201, S-224 58 Lund, Sweden.

ROZ Victor. See: **RODRIGUEZ Victorino.**

RUBIN Diana Kwiatkowski, b. 30 Dec 1958, New York, New York, USA. Poet; Writer; Editor; Critic. m. Paul Rubin, 1 Apr 1986, 1 son. Education: AOS, Wood School, 1983; BA, Marymount Manhattan College, 1988; MA, New York University, 1995. Publications: Panorama, 1979; The Poet Pope, 1980; Spirits in Exile, 1990; Visions of Enchantment, 1991; Poet's Lullaby, 1994. Contributions to: Amelia; Antigonish Review; Fox Cry; Small Press Review; Parnassus; Prophetic Voices. Honours: Lee Shore Quarterly Competition Award, 1989; Iva Mary Williams Inspirational Poetry Competition, 1990. Memberships: Poetry Society of America; Academy of American Poets; Poets and Writers. Address: PO Box 398, Piscataway, NJ 08855, USA.

RUBIN Larry Jerome, b. 14 Feb 1930, New Jersey, USA. Professor of English; Poet. Education: BA, 1951, MA, 1952, PhD, 1956, Emory University, Atlanta. Appointments: Instructor, 1956-58, Assistant Professor, 1958-65, Associate, 1965-73, Professor, 1973-, English, Georgia Tech, Atlanta. Publications: The World's Old Way, 1963; Lanced in Light, 1967; All My Mirrors Lie, 1975. Contributions include: New Yorker; Harper's Magazine; London Magazine; Poetry; Nation; American Scholar; Yale Review; Sewanee Review; Kenyon Review; Virginia Quarterly Review. Honours: Poetry Society of America, 1961, 1973; Sidney Lanier Award, Oglethorpe University, 1964; Poetry Society of New Hampshire, 1965; Georgia Poet of The Year Awards, 1967, 1975; Kansas City Star Award, 1969; Georgia Writers Association, 1973; Georgia Authors Series Award, 1975; All Nations Poetry Award, Triton College, 1980. Memberships: Poetry Societies of America and Georgia. Address: Box 15014, Druid Hills Branch, Atlanta, GA 30333, USA.

RUDMAN Mark, b. 11 Dec 1948, New York, New York, USA. Poet; Critic; Editor; Translator; Adjunct Professor. m. Madelaine Bates, 1 son. Education: BA, New School for Social Research, 1971; MFA, Columbia University, 1974. Appointments: Poetry and Criticism Editor, 1975-, Editor-in-Chief, 1984-, Pequod Journal; Writer-in-Residence, University of Hawaii, 1978, State University of New York, Buffalo, 1979, Wabash College, 1979; Adjunct Lecturer, Queens College, 1980-81; Lecturer, Parsons School of Design, 1983; Poet-in-Residence and Associate Professor, York College, 1984-88; Assistant Director and Adjunct Professor, Graduate Creative Writing Program, New York University, 1986-; Adjunct Professor of Creative Writing, Columbia University, 1988-91; Poet-in-Residence, State University of New York, Purchase, 1991; Adjunct Professor, Columbia University, 1992-. Publications: Book of poems: Rider, 1994 (National Book Critics Circle Award); Books include: Translation with author, Bohdan Boychuk's Selected Poems: Memories of Love; Robert Lowell: An Introduction to the Poetry, 1983; By Contraries: Poems 1970-1984, 1987; The Nowhere Steps, 1990; Diverse Voices: Essays on Poets and Poetry, 1993; Realm of Unknowing: Meditations on Suicide, Art and Other Transformations, 1995; The Millenium Hotel, 1996; Euripides' Daughters of Troy, due 1997; Translations of such poets as Rene Char, Ivan Drach, Horace, and Ovid. Contributions to: Poems in numerous magazines and anthologies; Essays in many anthologies. Honours include: Academy of American Poets Prize; Denver Quarterly Award; Max Hayward Award for Translation, PEN; National Book Critics Circle Award in Poetry, 1995; Guggenheim Fellowship, 1996-97. Memberships: PEN; Board of Governors, Poetry Society of America, 1984-88. Address: 817 West End Avenue, New York, NY 10025, USA.

RUDOLF Anthony, b. 6 Sept 1942, London, England. Publisher; Translator. Div, 1 son, 1 daughter. Education: BA, Trinity College, Cambridge, 1961-64; Diploma, British Institute, Paris, 1961-64. Publications: The Same River Twice, 1976; After the Dream, 1979; Primo Levi's War Against Oblivion, 1990; Mandorla, 1996; Translations of five poetry books. Contributions to: Times Literary Supplement; New Statesman; Stand; Agenda; Transatlantic Review; New Humanist; Nation. Honours: Shortlisted for the New Poets Award, 1969, 1970. Membership: General Council, Poetry Society, 1970-76. Address: 8 The Oaks, Woodside Avenue, London N12 8AR, England.

RUDY Dorothy L, b. 27 June 1924, Ohio, USA. Professor of English and Creative Writing. m. Willis Rudy, 31 Jan 1948, 1 son, 2 daughters. Education: BA, Queens College, 1945; MA, Philosophy, Columbia University, 1948. Appointments: Professor of English and Creative Writing, Montclair State College, 1964-88; Lecturer, Fairleigh Dickinson University, 1988-90. Publications: Quality of Small and Other Poems, 1971; Psyche Afoot and Other Poems, 1978; Grace Notes to the Measure of the Heart, 1979; Voices Through Time and Distant Places, 1993. Contributions to: Passaic Herald News; Letters; Poem; Laurel Review; Just Pulp; Composers; Authors and Artists Quarterly; Scimiter and Song; Bitterroot; Cellar Door; Pet Gazette; Black Buzzard Press. Honour: American Poets Fellowship, 1971. Memberships: Composers, Authors and Artists of America; PEN Women; Bergen Poets; New York Poetry Forum; Browning Society; New England Small Press Association, Women's Board; Scambi International. Address: 161 West Clinton Avenue, Tenafly, NJ 07670, USA.

RUIZ DE TORRES Juan, b. 13 July 1931, Madrid, Spain. Publisher. m. Angela Reyes, 1986, 1 son, 1 daughter. Education: Dr Industrial Engineering, 1962, Lic Hispanic Phil and Computing Science, UAM, University Politecnica de Madrid; Journalism, Esc Oficial de Periodismo, 1955; Currently undertaking PhD. Appointments: President, Ateneo de Cali, Colombia, 1961-65; President, Ateneo de Grecia, 1970-73; President, Asociacion Prometeo de Poesia, Madrid, 1980-94; Counselor, 1985. Publications include: Trece Sonetos, 1977; Trece Sonetos Dedicados, 1978; Poesia Para Sobrevivir, 1980; Trece Nuevos Peomas, 1981; Crisantemos, 1982; Dekatrisfilia, 1983; Las Trece Puertas del Silencio, 1984, 1985; Labio de Hormiga, 1985; Viaje a la Manana, 1987; Calendario Helenico, 1987; Trece por Cinco, 1988; Poesia 1965-79, 1987; Paseos por Nygade, 1989; Arista de Poliedro, 1990; Verano, Verano, 1991; Tres Tiempos del Egeo, 1991; El Cuerpo y sus Lenguajes, 1991; Ti Esti?, 1992; Sic Transit, 1992; El Hombre de Ur, 1995. Contributions to: Founder and current editor/director of the following poetry magazines: Cuadernos de Poesia Nueva; Valor de la Palabra; Carta de la Poesia. Honours include: El Editor Sudamericano, 1988; Iberoamericana de Escritores, 1990; Accademico di Merito, with Gold Palm, Accademia Internazionale di Pontzen, Naples, 1991; Medal of Instituto de Cultura Puertorriquena, 1987. Memberships include: Order de la Encina del Merito Poetico, Founder and Grand Master; Asociacion Cultural El Foro de la Encina, Founder and President; Asociacion Colegial de Escritores. Address: Apartado 007, 28660 Boadilla, Madrid, Spain.

RULEMAN William Arthur, b. 20 Jan 1957, Memphis, Tennessee, USA. College Teacher. m. Elizabeth Howard Sayle, 8 Oct 1983, 1 daughter. Education: BA, University of Virginia, 1979; MA, Memphis State University, 1983. Appointments: Instructor of English, Memphis State University, 1983-84; Graduate Teaching Assistant, University of Arkansas, 1984-87; Instructor, Northwest Missouri State University, 1987-88; Instructor of English, University of Mississippi, 1988-89 and Arkansas State University, 1989-90; Graduate Teaching Assistant, University of Mississippi, 1990-94; Professor of English, Tennessee Wesleyan College, 1994-. Contributions to: Outposts Poetry Quarterly; Poetry and Audience; Psychopoetica; Global Tapestry; Peace and Freedom; Berkeley Poetry Review. Address: 319 North Jackson Street, Athens, TN 37303-3617, USA.

RUMBOLD Lady Pauline Letitia, (Pauline Tennant), b. 6 Feb 1929, London, England. Actress. m. (1) Julian Pitt-Rivers, 1946, (2) Euan Graham, 1954, (3) Sir A Rumbold Bt, 1974, 1 adopted son. Appointments: Stage roles in: Big Top, She Follows Me About, No Medals, The Day After Tomorrow; Films: The Queen of Spades, Great Day. Publications: William Barnes Dorset Poems, translations, 1989; Loaves and Fishes, 1992. Memberships: Vice-Chairman, The William Barnes Society; Poetry Book Society; Prayer Book Society; Friend of Leighton House; Chelsea Arts Club. Address: Hatch Cottage, Cokers Frome, Dorchester, Dorset DT2 7SD, England.

RUMENS Carol Ann, b. 10 Dec 1944, Forest Hill, London, England. Writer. m. David Rumens, 30 July 1965, div, 2 daughters. Education: Studied Philosophy, no degree, London University, 1964-65. Appointments: Writing Fellow, University of Kent, 1983-85; Northern Arts Writing Fellow, 1988-90; Writer-in-Residence, Queens University, Belfast, 1991-. Publications: A Strange Girl in Bright Colours, 1973; Star Whisper, 1983; Unplayed Music, 1983; Direct Dialling, 1985; Selected Poems, 1987; Plato Park, 1988; The Greening of The Snow Beach, 1988; From Berlin to Heaven, 1990. Contributions include: Times Literary Supplement; Observer; Sunday Times; Poetry Review; London Review of Books. Honours: Alice Hunt Bartlett Prize, 1982; Cholmondeley Award, 1984. Membership: Fellow, Royal Society of Literature. Address: 100A Tunis Road, London, W12 7EY, England.

RUSAN Otila Valeria. See: **BLANDIANA Ana.**

RUSS Earlene (Biff), b. 12 Aug 1955, Montague, Massachusetts, USA. Writer. m. James L Ure, 14 Dec 1979. Education: AB, Bryn Mawr College, 1978; MFA, Warren Wilson College, 1983. Publication: Black Method, 1991. Contributions to: Prairie Schooner; Cream City Review; Berkeley Poetry Review; Poetry East; Passages North; Indiana Review; Midwest Quarterly; New Letters Review of Books. Honour: Marianne Moore Poetry Prize for, Black Method, selected by Mona Van Duyn, 1991. Membership: Academy of American Poets. Address: 913 Elmwood Avenue #A1, Evanston, IL 60202, USA.

RUSSELL JONES Selwyn, b. 11 Sept 1909, Aberfan, Glamorgan, Wales. Retired School Master. m. Grethe Whitehead, 2 Sept 1939, 1 son, 1 daughter. Education: South Wales and Monmouth School of Art and Cardiff University College, 1927-32 with Oxford Diploma in Art. Appointments: Senior Arts Master and Housemaster, Kings School, Macclesfield, 1932-73; Served during World War II as Officer in Intelligence Corps, Middle East. Publications: List to Us (co-author), 1982; Directions of the Wind, 1984; Driftwood Odyssey, 1990. Contributions to: Anthologies: Changing Islands; Speak to the Hills; This Climbing Game; Arts Council Anthology; Poetry Magazines: New Poetry; Outposts; Orbis; Envoi; Climber. Honours: Prizes won at various poetry festivals, including Birmingham and Lancaster, and also in poetry magazine competitions. Memberships: Poetry Society; Friend of Arvon Foundation for Poetry. Address: Silvaplana, No 7 Tytherington Park Road, Macclesfield, Cheshire SK10 2EL, England.

RUSSO Albert, b. 26 Feb 1943, Kamina, Zaire. Writer. m. 1 son, 1 daughter. Education: Abschluss Diploma, Heidelberg, Germany; BSc, General Business Administration, New York University, USA. Appointments: Teacher of English, French and Italian in Paris and New

York; Worked in the film department at UNICEF; Member of Jury, Prix de l'Europe, 1982-; One of 12 Jurors for the 1996 Neustadt International Prize for Literature; Stories broadcast by BBC World Service. Publications include: Incandescences, 1970; Eclats de Malachite, 1971; La Pointe du Diable, 1973; Mosaique New Yorkaise, 1975; Your Son Leopold, Princes and Gods and Triality, including excerpts appearing in North American, UK, Indian and African Reviews; Albert Russo I: An Anthology, 1987; Sang Mêlé ou ton Fils Léopold, novel, 1990; Le Cap des Illusions, novel, 1991; Futureyes - Dans La Nuit Bleu-fauve, bilingual poetry collection, 1992; Eclipse sur le Lac Tanganyika, 1994; Venitian Thresholds, 1995; Painting the Tower of Babel, 1996; Zapinette, vidéo novel, 1996; Co-Editor, Paris Transcontinental and Plurilingual Europe. Contributions to: Numerous professional journals including World Literature Today, USA. Honours: Willie Lee Martin Short Story Award, USA, 1987; Silver Medal for, Eclipse sur le Lac Tanganyika, 1995. Memberships: PEN; Authors Guild of America; Writers and Poets; Association of French Speaking Writers. Literary Agents: Béatrix Vernet, Paris, France; Writers House Inc, New York City, USA. Address: BP 640, 75826 Paris Cedex 17, France.

RUTH Sibyl Twilight, b. 12 Sept 1959, Belfast, Northern Ireland. Advice Worker. Education: Cheadle Hulme School, Cheshire, 1967-77; BA, Hons, English Literature, Kings College, Cambridge, 1980. Appointment: Advice Worker. Contributions to: Anthology: Hard Lines 3, 1987; Writing Women; Distaff; People to People; Orbis; Rialto; Smith's Knoll; Envoi; Iron. Address: 8 Surrey House, Crystal Avenue, Stourbridge, West Midlands DY8 4AW, England.

RUTHERFORD Maurice, b. 28 Sept 1922, Hull, East Yorkshire, England. Retired Technical Writer. m. Olive Gray, 12 Apr 1947, 1 son, 1 daughter. Education: Hull College of Commerce, 1936-38. Appointments: Assistant Editor, Envoi, 1979-91; Editor of Proof, 1984-85; Management Advisor for Literature, Lincolnshire and Humberside Arts, 1986-88. Publications: Slipping The Tugs, 1982; This Day Dawning, 1989; Love is a Four-Letter World, 1994; After the Parade, 1996. Contributions to: Critical Survey; Dark Horse; London Magazine; Poetry Review; Rialto; Staple; BBC Radio 3; BBC Radio Humberside; Yorkshire TV. Memberships: Poetry Society; Poetry Book Society; Philip Larkin Society. Address: 58 Wheatley Drive, Bridlington, East Yorkshire YO16 5UF, England.

RUTSALA Vern, b. 5 Feb 1934, McCall, Idaho, USA. Professor of English. m. Joan Colby, 6 Apr 1957, 2 sons, 1 daughter. Education: BA, Reed College, 1956; MFA, University of Iowa, 1960. Appointments: Visiting Professor, University of Minnesota, 1968-69, Bowling Green State University, 1970; Writer-in-Residence, Redlands University, 1979, University of Idaho, 1988. Publications: The Window, 1964; Laments, 1975; The Journey Begins, 1976; Paragraphs, 1978; Walking Home From the Icehouse, 1981; Backtracking, 1985; Ruined Cities, 1987; Selected Poems, 1991; Little-Known Sports, 1994. Contributions to: Atlantic; New Yorker; Nation; New Republic; Poetry; New Statesman; Times Literary Supplement; Stand; Harper's; American Poetry Review; Paris Review. Honours: National Endowment for the Arts Fellowships, 1974, 1979; Northwest Poets Prize, 1975; Guggenheim Fellowship, 1982; Carolyn Kizer Poetry Prize, 1988; Masters Fellowship, Oregon Arts Commission, 1990; Oregon Book Award, Hazel Hall Prize, 1992; Juniper Prize, 1993; Duncan Lawrie Prize, Arvon Foundation, 1994. Memberships: PEN; Poetry Society of America; Associated Writing Programmes; AAUP. Address: 2404 North East 24th Avenue, Portland, OR 97212, USA.

RYAN Patrick. See: **STORER Patrick Antony.**

S

SABA Rathnam, b. 14 Feb 1956, Chettinad, India. Poet. m. Valli Saba, 13 Dec 1985, 1 daughter. Education: BA, English Literature, 1974-77; MA, Philosophy, 1977-79. Publications: The Remembrance of a Dead Red Rose, 1974; Hidden Strength, 1979; Words, Words, Words, 1991; A Bunch of Flowers, anthology, 1977. Contributions to: Poet; Poetry Time; Poetcrit; International Poets. Honour: INTCR National Eminent Poet, International Poets Academy, 1991. Memberships: World Academy of Arts and Culture; International Poets Academy. Address: S Rm CT S House, Chettinad, Tamil Nadu S, India.

SACHIKO Yoshihara, b. 1932, Tokyo, Japan. Poet. Education: Graduated in French Literature, Tokyo University. Appointments: Lead role in Orphée et Euridice, with theatrical group Gekidan Shiki; Poet, 1964-. Publications: Poetry collections: Yônen Rentô, 1964; Natsu no haka, 1964; Hirugao, 1973; Ondine, 1974; Hakkô, 1995; Co-Publisher, poetry periodical Gendai-shi- La Mer (Modern Poetry - La Mer), 1983-93. Honours: Murou Saisei Prize, 1965; Takami Jun Prize, 1973; Hagiwara Sakuturô Prize, 1995. Address: c/o Japan PEN Club, 265 Akasaka Residential Hotel, 9-1-7 Akasaka, Minato-ku, Tokyo 107, Japan.

SACHS Arieh, b. 24 Mar 1932, Tel Aviv, Israel. Poet. m. Rachel Sachs, 1977, 1 son, 2 daughters. Education: BA, MA, Johns Hopkins University, USA, 1952-54; Sorbonne, Paris, France, 1955-56; Fitzwilliam College, Cambridge University, England, 1958-60; PhD, Hebrew University, Israel, 1962. Publications: Passionate Intelligence, 1967; Orange Grove, 1976; The Prankster's Decline, 1978; John Berryman's Dream Songs, 1978; The Pink Book, 1982; Alcohol, 1987; Eros, 1987. Contributions to: Various publications. Honours: Israel Interfaith Prize, 1977; Israel Publishers Association Prize, 1986. Address: 14 Hamefaked Street, Abu Tor, Jerusalem, Israel.

SACKS Peter Michael, b. 15 July 1950, Port Elizabeth, South Africa. Professor of Poetry. m. Barbara Kassel, 8 Jan 1980. Education: BA, Princeton University, USA, 1973; MPhil, Oxford University, England, 1976; PhD, Yale University, USA, 1980. Appointments: Assistant Professor; Associate Professor; Currently Professor. Publications: In These Mountains, 1986; Promised Land, 1990. Contributions to: New Yorker; New Republic; American Poetry Review; Georgia Review; Partisan Review; Tikkun; Boulevard; Seneca Review; Antioch Review; Nation. Address: 35129 Newland Road, Baltimore, MD 21218, USA.

SADIN Marjorie, b. 5 Sept 1954, Englewood, New Jersey, USA. Poet. Education: Oberlin College, 1975; BA, English Literature, George Washington University, 1975-1977; MA, American Literature, George Washington University, 1980-83; Trinity College, 1989-92. Appointments: Professor, 1990-91; Writer with NASA, 1992-96. Publications: The Cliff Edge, 1988; The Black Rose, 1996. Contributions to: The Little Magazine; Dark Horse, Modern Images; Chiron Review; Disability Press; Minotaur Press. Honour: Vivian Nellis Creative Writing Award, 1977. Membership: Writers Center, Bethesda, Maryland. Address: 1330 New Hampshire Ave NW #818, Washington, DC 20036, USA.

SAENZ Gil(bert), b. 17 Oct 1941, Detroit, Michigan, USA. Computer Programmer; Analyst. Education: BA, English Literature, 1969. Accrued 2 years in post-degree studies program, 1980, Wayne State University. Appointment: US Diplomatic Courier Service, Frankfurt, Germany, 1970-71. Publications: Self-published books of poetry: Where Love Is, 1988, Colorful Impressions, 1993; Moments In Time, 1995. Contributions to: North American Poetry Review; Odessa Poetry Review; Several poems published in a local hispanic newspaper, El Central. Honours: Recipient of 4 Editor's Choice Awards; 6th Place in Love Poems contest with, Night Wish, Poetry Press, Pittsburgh, TX, 1992. Membership: Director, 1991-94, Latino Poets Association, Detroit. Address: 6237 Appoline Street, Dearborn, MI 48126-2321, USA.

SAGARIS Lake, b. 29 Sept 1956, Montreal, Quebec, Canada. Writer; Translator; Journalist; Poet. m. Patricio Lanfranco, 1981, 3 sons. Education: BFA, Creative Writing, University of British Columbia, 1981. Appointments: Freelance Journalist; Correspondent, Times of London, Newsweek, Canadian Television (CTV), CBC, BBC Radio. Publications: Exile Home (Exilio en la patria), 1986; Circus Love, 1991; Medusa's Children, 1993; After the First Death: A Journey; Through Chile, Time and Mind, 1996. Contributions include: Anthologies: Cuentos por latinas, 1984, Anthology of Magazine Verse and Yearbook of American Poetry, Words We Come Home To and Frictions; Newspapers and magazines: The Globe and Mail, Saturday Night, Orbis, Palabra de Mujer. Honours: Canada Council Awards for Poetry, 1987, Non-Fiction, 1991 and 1992; MaClean Hunter Fellowship in Arts Journalism, 1989; Banff Writers' Studio, 1989. Memberships: Writers Union of Canada; Sociedad de Escritores de Chile; Periodical Writers Association, Canada; Vice-President, Foreign Press Association, Chile, 1990-91. Address: Casilla 14465, Correo 21, Santiago, Chile.

SAHAY Akhowri Chittaranjan, b. 2 Jan 1925, Muzaffarpur, India. Journal Editor; Former University Educator. m. A Priyamvada Sahay, 17 June 1945. Education: BA, Honours, Distinction, 1945, MA, English, 1947, Patna University; MDEH, National University of EC Homeopathy, Kanpur, 1964; PhD, English, Stanton University, NY, 1985. Appointments: Lecturer, Head, Department of English, Rajendra College, Chapra, 1948-68; Lecturer, University Department of English, L S College, Muzaffarpur, 1968-74; Associate Professor, English, Bihar University, Muzaffarpur, 1974-85; Chief Editor, Kavita India, international quarterly of literature, 1987-. Publications: Hindi poetry: Van Yoothi, 1939; Van Shephali, 1941; Van Geet, 1943; Ajab Desh, 1945; English poetry: Roots and Branches, 1979; Emerald Foliage, 1981; Pink Blossoms, 1983; Golden Pollens, 1985; Vernal Equinox, 1987; Summer Clouds, 1989. Contributions to: Byword; Canopy; Kavita India; Poetry Time; Quest; Skylark; Commonwealth Quarterly; Poets International; Poet; Poesie India; Poetcrit; Rachna; Eureka; Advent; Many anthologies. Honours: Many prizes, medals and certificates of merit. Memberships: Poetry Society, India and UK; PEN All India Centre; International Writers and Artists Association, USA; Writers Club, Madras; World Poetry Society; United Writers Association, Madras; Theosophical Society, Madras. Address: Kavita India House, South-East Chaturbhujasthan, Muzaffarpur 842001, Bihar, India.

SAHU N S, b. 1 Sept 1939, India. Reader in English. m. Shanti Sahu, 17 May 1962, 3 sons. Education: MA, Linguistics, 1970; MA, English Literature, 1973; PhD, Linguistics, 1975; PhD, English, 1978. Appointments: Lecturer in English, Bhilai Steel Plant, Education Department, Bhilainagar, 1971-79; Lecturer, Department of English, University of Gorakhpur, 1979-92, Reader in English, 1992-. Department of English, University of Gorakhpur. Publications: Aspects of Linguistics, 1982, 1990; T S Eliot, The Man as a Poet, Playwright, Prophet and Critic, 1988; A Study of The Works of Matthew Arnold, 1988; Theatre of Protest and Anger, 1988; Toponymy, 1989; Christopher Marlowe and Theatre of Cruelty and Violence, 1990; An Approach to American Literature, 1991; A collection of long and short poems, 1996. Contributions to: Indian Verses by Young Poets; Skylark; Youth Age; New Voices in Indian Poetry; Indian Journal of English Studies; Zephyrs; Priya Darshini; DRSP Nagendra; Eureka; Review Projector; Commonwealth; The Vedic Path; Rajasthan Journal of Educational Studies. Honours: Commemorative Gold Medal of Honour, American Biographical Institute, Raleigh, USA; Attended the First International Conference on the Teaching of Shakespeare, Stratford-upon-Avon, 1992; Recited poems at the Triennial International Conference, EACLALS, University of Graz, Austria, 1993. Memberships: Life: American Studies Research Centre; Linguistic Society of India; International Goodwill Society of India; Journal of Indian Writings in English. Address: 11 New Flat, Hirapuri Colony, University Campus, Gorakhpur 273009, UP, India.

SAIKIA Prayag, b. 7 Oct 1959, Nagaon (Assam), India. Medical Practitioner. m. Dr Rasna Hiloidari, 24 Nov 1990. Education: MBBS, 1985; Fellow, Society for Advanced Studies in Medical Science (FSASMS), 1993. Appointment: Private medical practitioner. Publications: Prithivi Preosy, 1987; Baushit Dukhan Deuka, 1990; Amitabha Phule, 1993. Contributions to: Assamese gariyashi; Prantik; Siralu; Prakash; Nabadut; Ajir Batari; Natun Dainik; Bengali-Jatinga; Ma-Nishad; Durer Kheya; English Poet; World Poetry '96; Poems '96; Sentinal. Memberships: Assam Sahitya Sabha; Kallol Sansritik Gusthi; Advisor of Nagaon Cultural Troup. Address: Dr Prayag Saikia, B Bora Road, Fauzdaripatty, Nagaon - 1, PIN: 782001, Assam, India.

SAIL Lawrence Richard, b. 29 Oct 1942, London, England. Freelance Writer. m. (1) Teresa Luke, 1966, div 1981, 1 son, 1 daughter, (2) Helen Bird, 1994. Education: BA, Honours, Modern

Languages, St John's College, Oxford, 1964. Appointments: Teacher of Modern Languages, Lenana School, Nairobi, Kenya, 1966-71, Millfield School, 1973-74, Blundell's School, Devon, 1975-81, and Exeter School, 1982-91; Visiting Writer, Blundell's School, 1981. Publications: Opposite Views, 1974; The Drowned River, 1978; The Kingdom of Atlas, 1980; Devotions, 1987; Aquamarine, 1988; Out of Land: New and Selected Poems, 1992; Editor: South West Review: A Celebration, 1985; First and Always, 1988; Building into Air, 1995. Contributions to: Encounter; London Magazine; New Statesman; Observer; Oxford Magazine; Poetry Book Society Anthologies; P N Review; Poetry Review; Spectator; Stand; Tribune. Honours: Hawthornden Fellowship, 1992; Arts Council Writer's Bursary, 1993. Memberships: Chairman, Arvon Foundation, 1990-94; Director of 1991 Cheltenham Festival of Literature; Senior Common Room Member, St John's College, Oxford; Committee of Management, Peterloo Poets; Authors' Society; The Poetry Society. Address: Richmond Villa, 7 Wonford Road, Exeter, Devon EX2 4LF, England.

SAINTE-AGATHE Mussy. See: **MARIE Charles P.**

SALAM BRAX Najwa, b. 3 Sept 1948, Aley, Lebanon. Writer; Poet. m. Dr Ghazi Brax, 24 June 1981. Education: BA, 1974, MA, 1983, Faculty of Arts and Human Sciences, Lebanese University. Appointment: Arabic Literature Teacher, 1972-86. Publications: Wings, 1993; Daring Wings, 1996. Contributions to: in over 120 publications, US, Canada, UK, 1990-: Georgia State Poetry Society Newsletter; Hayden's Poetry Review; Poetic Page; Parnassus; Oatmeal & Poetry; Just Write; The Heartlight Journal; Starburst; Illya's Honey; Poetry in Motion; Poetic Eloquence; Poetry Press; Se La Vie; Omnific; Poetry Expressions; Lone Stars; Rhyme Time; Bell's Letters; Moon; Poet's Paradise; Apropos; Poet's Review... (US) Tickled by Thunder; Teak Roundup (Canada); Triumph House; The Arrival Press Perceptions, (UK). Honours: Won more than 120 poetry awards, 1990-: 4 Reader's Choices; 21, 1st's; 20, 2nd's; 19, 3rd's; 4 Editor's Choice Awards; 8 Blue Ribbons; 6 Editor's Preference Awards for Excellence; 2 Golden Poet Awards; 60 HMs, many others. Membership: The Daheshist Publishing Comany, New York City. Address: 163-15 Sanford Avenue, 3rd Floor, Flushing, NY 11358-2640, USA.

SALAMUN Tomaz, b. 4 July 1941, Zagreb. Writer. m. Metka Krasovec, 11 Apr 1979, 1 son, 1 daughter. Education: MA, Art History, Filozofska Fakulteta, University of Ljubljana, Slovenia; Studied Art History in Paris and Rome, 1967; International Writing Program, University of Iowa, Iowa City, 1971-73. Appointments: Assistant Curator, Modern Gallery Ljubljana, 1969-70; Assistant Professor, Academy of Art, Ljubljana, 1970-72; Freelance Writer, 1972-96; Cultural Attaché, Consulate General of Slovenia in New York; Residencies at Yaddo and MacDowell Colonies, USA, 1973, 1974, 1979, 1986, 1987. Publications: Poetry includes: Pesmi (Poems), 1980; Maske (Masks), 1980; Balada za Metko Krasovec (Ballad for Metko Krasovec), 1981; Analogije svetlobe (Anthologies of Light), 1982; Glas (Voice), 1983; Sonet o mleku (Sonnet on Milk), 1984; Soy realidad (I Am Reality), 1985; Ljubljanska pomlad (Ljubljana Spring), 1986; Mera casa, 1987; Ziva rana, zivi sok (Living Wound), 1988; The Selected Poems of Tomaz Salamun, 1988; Otrok in jelen (Boy and Stag), 1990; Ambra (Ambergris), 1994. Contributions to: Paris Review; American Poetry Review; Partisan Review; Nation; Poetry (Chicago); Antaeus; Agni; Chelsea; American Review; Confrontations; Ploughshares; New England Review; Mississippi Review; Poetry (England); Ironwood. Honours: Mladost Prize, 1969; Preseren Foundation Prize, 1973; Zelezara Sisak Prize, 1978; Ljubisa Jocic Prize, 1981; Fulbright Grant, 1986-87; Jenko Prize, 1988; Pushcart Prize, 1994. Memberships: Vice President, Slovenian PEN Centre; Board, Slovenian Writers Association. Address: Dalmatinova 11, 1000 Ljubljana, Slovenia.

SALE James, b. 26 Oct 1952, London, England. Teacher. Education: BA, St Davids University College, 1976. Appointment: Deputy Headteacher, Twynham School, Christchurch, 1990-. Publications: Carnal Spirits, 1983; The Other Side Collection, 1985; The Poetry Show, volumes 1, 2 and 3, 1987-88; Poetry Street, volumes 1, 2 and 3, 1991. Contributions to: Little Word Machine; Ore; South; Doors. Memberships: Deputy Director, Schools' Poetry Association; Director, KQBX Press. Address: 16 Scotter Road, Bournemouth, BH7 6LY, England.

SALEH Ibrahim, b. 15 Oct 1933, Egypt. m. 3 Sept 1981. Education: BA, English, Cairo University, 1957; Teacher's College Diploma, Ain-Shams University, Cairo, 1963. Appointments: School Teacher, 1953-75; Teacher of English, Kuwait, 1971-75; Master and Supervisor of English, Egypt, 1975-80; English Teacher, Bahrain, 1980-84; English Supervisor, School Sub-Principal, Egypt, 1984; Inspector of English, 1987; Director of Public Relations, West Cairo Education Zone, 1988. Publications: Playing on a Deserted String, 1981; I Love You as a Stubborn Dawn, 1990; A Reading In Her Eyes, 1991. Contributions to: Al-Shi'ar, quarterly; Al Thaquafa, monthly; Al Katib, monthly; Al Mawakif, monthly; Akhbar el Khalig, daily; Egyptian Newspapers: Al Ahram, Al Akhbar, Al Masa'a, Al Gomhoria. Honours: Certificates of Appreciation, Al Azhar University, 1977, 1978, Association of Modern Literature, 1981, Public Culture Centres, 1985; Hon DLitt, World Academy of Arts and Culture, 1990. Memberships: World Academy of Arts and Culture; Modern Literature Association, Egypt; Quaseed (Poetry) Club; Teacher's Syndicate; Egyptian Writer's Union; Society of The Poets of Arabism. Address: 24 Musafer Khana Street, Kollaly Azbakia, Cairo, Egypt.

SALEMI Joseph Salvatore, b. 1 Feb 1948, New York, New York, USA. Teacher. Education: BA, Fordham University, 1968; MA, 1970, PhD, 1986, New York University. Appointments: Assistant Professor, English, Hunter College, Fordham University; Associate Professor, Humanities, New York University. Contributions to: Aileron; Amelia; Artful Dodge; Blue Unicorn; Cumberland Poetry Review; Esprit; Formalist; Hollins Critic; Laurel Review; Maledicta; Paintbrush; Plains Poetry Journal; Poem; Translation; University Bookman. Address: 3222 61st Street, Woodside, NY 11377, USA.

SALL Amadou Lamine, b. 26 Mar 1951, Kaolack, Senegal. Education: Lecencie es Lettres; Licencie Sociology; Diploma, Ecole des Hautes Etudes Sociales, Paris; Maitrise, Information and Communication, University of Paris. Appointments: Senegalese Administration, including Ministry of the Interior, 1976-82; Scholarship to Paris, 1983-88; Technical Adviser, Office of Minister of Culture, 1989; Secretary-General, Biennale Internationale des Lettres et des Arts, Dakar, Ministry of Culture and Communication, 1990-. Publications: Mante des Aurores, 1979, 1984; Comme un Iceberg en Flamme, 1982; L'Anthologie des Poetes du Senegal; La Nouvelle Anthologie de la Poesie Negre et Malgache de langue Française; Locataire du Neant, 1989; Kamandalu, 1990; Poems d'Afrique pour les Enfants. Honour: Medaille de Vermeil du Rayonnement de la Langue Française, l'Academie Francaise. Membership: President, l'Association des Ecrivains du Senegal. Address: Ministere de la Culture, Bldg Administratif, Dakar, Senegal.

SALLAH Tijan M, b. 6 Mar 1958, Banjul, The Gambia. Economist, The World Bank. Education: BA, BS, Berea College; MA, PhD, Virginia Technical University. Appointments: Assistant Professor of Economics, University of Pennsylvania, 1987-88; Assistant Professor, North Carolina Agricultural and Technical University, 1988-89; Economist, The World Bank, 1989-. Publications: When Africa Was A Young Woman, 1980; Koraland, 1989; Editor, New Poets of West Africa, anthology, 1992; Dreams of Dusty Roads, 1992. Contributions to: Kentucky Poetry Review; West Africa; Okike; New Africa; Washington Review; Black Scholar; Poet; Wind; Ufahamu; Appalachian Heritage; Mountain Review; Social Science; Linear B. Honour: Honorary Doctorate in Literature, World Poetry Society. Memberships: Continental Regent and Parnassian Jurist, World Poetry Society; African Literature Association. Address: PO Box 124, Banjul, The Gambia.

SALVESEN Christopher Gerald, b. 10 Jan 1935, Edinburgh, Scotland. University Lecturer. m. Charlotte Ann Hunter, 15 Aug 1959, 4 daughters. Education: BA, 1955-58, BLitt, 1959-61, Brasenose College, Oxford. Appointments: Lecturer in English, Trinity College, Dublin, 1962-66; Lecturer in English, 1966-71, Professor of English, 1971-, University of Reading. Publications: Translator, Rilke: Sonnets to Orpheus I: i-x, drawings by William Tucker, 1971; Floodsheaf: From a Parish History, 1974; Among The Goths, 1986. Contributions to: Times Literary Supplement; Listener; New Statesman; Time and Tide; Southern Review; London Review of Books; Quarto; English; Tikkun; New Writing Scotland 5; The Faber Book of Twentieth Century Scottish Poetry. Address: 69 Hamilton Road, Reading, Berkshire, RG1 5RA, England.

SAMARAS Nicholas, b. 1 Aug 1954, Cambridge, England. Education: BA, MA, 1978, Hellenic College; MDiv, MA, 1981, Holy Cross Greek Orthodox Seminary; MFA, Writing, Columbia University, 1985; Doctorate in English and Creative Writing, University of Denver, 1993. Appointments: Teaching Assistant, Lecturer, 1985, Teaching

Fellow, University of Denver, 1989-. Publication: Hands of the Saddlemaker, 1992. Contributions to: New Yorker; Poetry; Ontario Review; Indiana Review; Missouri Review; Aegean Review; Southeastern Review; Intro 13; Aspect; Quarto; Confrontation; Open Places; Green Mountains Review; South Florida Poetry Review; Contemporary Review; Croton Review; Voices International; Albany Review. Honours: Outstanding Literature Award, Quarto Magazine, 1985; New York Foundation for the Arts, 1986-87; Fellowship, University of Denver, 1989; Chamberlain Prize in Poetry, 1989. Memberships: Poetry Society of America; National Arts Club; Associate Editor, Denver Quarterly. Address: 4329 195th Street, Flushing, NY 11358, USA.

SAMBERG Kenneth Franklin, b. 4 May 1945, New York, New York, USA. Poet. Education: BA, English, City University of New York, 1963-67; BA, Anthropology, University of Toronto, 1972-74. Contributions to: Tower; Dalhousie Review; Laomedon Review; Waves; Origins; Antigonish Review; Pierian Spring; UC Review; Poetry WLU; Ariel; Green's Magazine; CBC Anthology; Buffalo Spree; Z Miscellaneous; Pacific Review. Address: 1566 Unionport Road, Bronx, NY 10462, USA.

SAMUELSDOTTIR Norma Elisabet, (NES), b. 7 Sept 1945, Scotland. m. Sigurdur Jon Olafsson, 7 Nov 1971, div, 1 son, 2 daughters. Publications: The Day Before Last of The Year, novel, 1980; The Tree Outside My Window, 1982; Bruises in the Colours of the Rainbow, 1987; The Long Trek, 1990; Over Sensitive, 1991; The Found Key, 1991. Contributions to: Newspapers; Magazines. Membership: Writers Union of Iceland. Address: Miklabraut 16, 105 Reykjavik, Iceland.

SANCHEZ Jacqueline Rae Rawlson, (Jacque Rae), b. 9 Sept 1946, Jackson, Michigan, USA. Publisher. m. Arnulfo H Sanchez, 23 Oct 1965, 1 son, 4 daughters. Education: Graduate, Belleville High School, 1964; Creative Writing, Wayne State University, 1975. Appointments: Publisher, small press, The Sounds of Poetry magazine, 1983-; Founder and Director, Latino Poet's Association, 1983; Poetry readings throughout the State of Michigan including the Jackson Prison; Co-Ordinator with Ken Miller, Annual Coffee House Series; Began the Annual Poetry Outreach Series, 1996-. Contributions to: Harlo's Anthology of Modern-Day Poets and Authors, 1975; Poets and Authors, A Bicentennial Edition, 1976; The Saline Reporter, 1976; Green's Magazine; A Collection of Poems, 1976; Poets of '76; The Shape of American Poetry, 1976; Bountiful A Poetry Digest, 1981; Yearbook of Modern Poetry, 1981; Peninsula Poets, 1981; Detroit La Onda Latina En Poesia, 1985; La Onda Latina En Poesia - Detroit, volume II, 1987; Wayne Literary Review, 1988; Pen and Ink Magazine, 1995; Six limited edition self-published chapbooks of poetry: Gypsy Melody in the Mist of the Sea, 1982; Running Free and More..., 1982; Mine Eyes Have Seen, 1985; Moses and More..., 1985; Wings of Fire, 1992; The Rising Sun, 1996. Memberships: Board Member, Casa de Unidad, 1988-90. Address: The Sounds of Poetry, 2076 Vinewood, Detroit, MI 48216-5506, USA.

SANCHEZ Sonia, b. 9 Sept 1934, Birmingham, Alabama, USA. Professor of English; Poet; Dramatist; Writer. m. Etheridge Knight, div, 2 sons, 1 daughter. Education: BA, Hunter College, 1955; New York University, 1959-60; PhD, Wilberforce University, 1972. Appointments: Instructor, San Francisco State College, 1967-69; Lecturer, University of Pittsburgh, 1969-70, Rutgers University, 1970-71, Manhattan Community College, 1971-73, City University of New York, 1972; Associate Professor, Amherst College, 1972-73, University of Pennsylvania, 1976-77; Associate Professor, 1977-79, Professor of English, 1979-, Temple University. Publications: Poetry: Homecoming, 1969; We a BaddDDD People, 1970; Liberation Poem, 1970; It's a New Day: Poems for Young Brothas and Sistuhs, 1971; Ima Talken Bout the Nation of Islam, 1971; Love Poems, 1973; A Blues Book for Blue Black Magical Women, 1974; I've Been a Woman: New and Selected Poems, 1978, revised edition, 1985; Homegirls and Handgrenades, 1984; Under a Soprano Sky, 1987; Wounded in the House of a Friend, 1995; Plays: The Bronx is Next, 1968; Sister Son/ji, 1969; Dirty Hearts '72, 1973; Uh, Uh: But How Do It Free Us?, 1974; Stories: A Sound Investment, 1980; Other: Crisis in Culture, 1983; Editor: Three Hundred Sixty Degrees of Blackness Comin' at You, 1972; We Be Word Sorcerers: 25 Stories by Black Americans, 1973. Honours: PEN Award, 1969; American Academy of Arts and Letters Award, 1970; National Endowment for the Arts Award, 1978; Smith College Tribute to Black Women Award, 1982; Lucretia Mott Award, 1984; Before Columbus Foundation Award, 1985; PEN Fellow, 1993.

Address: c/o Department of English, Temple University, Philadelphia, PA 19041, USA.

SANDAK-LEWIN Gloria, b. 14 Nov 1940, Cape Town, South Africa. Writer. 1 son. Education: BA, English and Latin, 1960, STD, cum laude, 1962, MA, cum laude, English Literature, 1971, University of Cape Town. Appointments: Tutor, University of Cape Town, 1961; High School Teacher, Cape Town, 1963; Adjudicator, Northern Cape Arts Festival, 1966; Tutor, South African Council for Higher Education, 1971; Lecturer, Centre for Extra Mural Studies, University of Cape Town, 1975; Organizer, Co-Ordinator, Lecturer, Jewish Writers Workshop, 1980-82. Publication: My Father's House, 1985. Contributions to: Jewish Affairs. Honours: Poem included in BBC Award Winning Anthology, The Fate of Vultures: New Poetry of Africa, 1989. Memberships: Poetry Society, London; English Association, Cape Town. Address: 5 Derry Road, Rondebosch, Cape Town, South Africa 7700.

SANDERS (James) Ed(ward), b. 17 Aug 1939, Kansas City, Missouri, USA. Poet; Writer; Singer; Lecturer. m. Miriam Kittell, 5 Oct 1961, 1 child. Education: BA, New York University, 1964. Appointments: Editor-Publisher, Fuck You/A Magazine of the Arts, New York City, 1962-65; Founder-Lead Singer, The Fugs, satiric folk-rock-theatre group, 1964-; Owner, Peace Eye Bookstore, New York City, 1965-70; Visiting Professor of Language and Literature, Bard College, Annandale-on-Hudson, New York, 1979, 1983; Lectures, readings and performances throughout the US and Europe. Publications: A Valorium Edition of the Entire Extent Works of Thales!, 1964; The Fugs' Song Book (with Ken Weaver and Betsy Klein), 1965. Poetry: Poem from Jail, 1963; King Lord/Queen Freak, 1964; The Toe Queen Poems, 1964; Peace Eye, 1965; Egyptian Hieroglyphics, 1973; 20,000 A.D, 1976; The Cutting Prow, 1981; Hymn to Maple Syrup and Other Poems, 1985; Poems for Robin, 1987; Thirsting for Peace in a Raging Century: Selected Poems 1961-1985, 1987; Hymn to the Rebel Cafe: Poems 1987-1991, 1993; Chekhov: A Biography in Verse, 1995. Honours: Frank O'Hara Prize, Modern Poetry Association, 1967; National Endowment for the Arts Awards, 1966, 1970, and Fellowship, 1987-88; Guggenheim Fellowship, 1983-84; American Book Award, 1988. Memberships: New York Foundation for the Arts; PEN. Address: PO Box 729, Woodstock, NY 12498, USA.

SANDY Stephen, b. 2 Aug 1934, Minnesota, USA. Writer. m. Virginia Scoville, 1 son, 1 daughter. Education: BA, Yale University, 1955; MA, 1959, PhD, 1963, Harvard University. Appointments: Lecturer in American Literature, Tokyo University, 1967-68; Visiting Professor, Brown University, 1968-69, Harvard University, 1986-88; McGee Visiting Distinguished Professor of Writing, Davidson College, 1994; Faculty, Bennington College, 1969-; Poetry Workshop Director, Chautauqua Institution, 1975, 1977. Publications: Stresses in the Peaceable Kingdom, 1967; Roofs, 1971; Riding to Greylock, 1983; To a Mantis, 1987; Man in The Open Air, 1988; The Epoch, 1990; Thanksgiving Over The Water, 1992; A Cloak for Hercules, translation of Seneca, Hercules Oetaeus, 1995; Vale of Academe, A Prose Poem for Bernard Malamud, 1996. Contributions to: Atlantic; Agenda; Paris Review; Harvard Magazine; New Yorker; Michigan Quarterly Review; Iowa Review; Harper's; Southwest Review; Salmagundi; Grand Street; American Poetry Review. Honours: Fellowships and Grants, 1961, 1973, 1974, 1985, 1988 (two); Fulbright Visiting Lectureship, Japan, 1967-68; Yaddo Residencies, 1976, 1993; National Endowment for the Arts Poet-in-Residence, Poetry Center, Philadelphia, 1985; MacDowell Colony Fellowships, 1983, 1993; Reader, Academy of American Poets; 50th Anniversary Season, 92 Street, YMHA, Poetry Center, 1989. Address: Box 524, North Bennington, VT 05257, USA.

SANER Reg(inald Anthony), b. 30 Dec 1931, Jacksonville, Illinois, USA. Poet; Writer; Professor. m. Anne Costigan, 16 Aug 1958, 2 sons. Education: BA, St Norbert College, Wisconsin, 1950; MA, 1954, PhD, 1962, University of Illinois at Urbana; Universita per Stranieri, Perugia, 1960-61; Università di Firenze, Florence, 1960-61. Appointments: Assistant Instructor 1956-60, Instructor in English 1961-62, University of Illinois at Urbana; Assistant Professor 1962-67, Associate Professor 1967-72, Professor of English 1972-, University of Colorado at Boulder. Publications: Poetry: Climbing into the Roots, 1976; So This is the Map, 1981; Essay on Air, 1984; Red Letters, 1989. Non-Fiction: The Four-Cornered Falcon: Essays on the Interior West and the Natural Scene, 1993. Contributions to: Poems and essays in numerous anthologies and other publications. Honours: Fulbright Scholar to Florence, Italy, 1960-61; Borestone Mountain Poetry Awards, 1972, 1973; Walt Whitman Award, 1975; National

Endowment for the Arts Creative Writing Fellowship, 1976; Pushcart Prize II, 1977-78; Colorado Governor's Award for Excellence in the Arts, 1983; Quarterly Review of Literature Award, 1989; Rockefeller Foundation Resident Scholar, Bellagio, Italy, 1990; Hazel Barnes Award, University of Colorado, 1993. Memberships: Dante Society; PEN; Renaissance Society; Shakespeare Association. Address: 1925 Vassar, Boulder, CO 80303, USA.

SANFILIP Thomas, b. 28 June 1952, Chicago, Illinois, USA. Writer; Journalist; Teacher. Education: BA, Northern Illinois University, 1975. Publications: By The Hours and The Years, 1974; Myth, 1994. Contributions to: Shore Poetry Anthology; Lyrics of Love; Towers; Ivory Tower; Thalassa; Nit and Wit; Tomorrow; Letter Ex, Walt Whitman Encyclopedia. Address: PO Box 34807, Chicago, IL 60634, USA.

SANFORD Geraldine A Jones, b. 8 Jan 1928, Sioux Falls, South Dakota, USA. Teacher; Editorial Assistant. m. Dayton M Sanford, 28 Aug 1948, 4 sons. Education: BA, English and Psychology, Augustana College, 1971; MA, English, University of South Dakota. Appointments: Instructor and Lecturer in English, University of South Dakota, 1978, 1979; Instructor, University of Minnesota, 1979-82; Editorial Assistant, South Dakota Review, 1973-; Extension Instructor, University of South Dakota, 1991. Publication: Unverified Sightings From Dakota East. Contributions to: Real Dakota; Vermillion Literary Project; Longneck; Mankato Poetry Review; Prairie Winds; South Dakota Magazine; Yearnings; Poets Portfolio; Spirits from Clay; South Dakota Review; North Country; Rocky Mountain Creative Arts Journal; North Country Anvil; Aspect; Sunday Clothes. Honours: Gladys Haase Poetry Prize, 1977; Graduate Student Poetry Award, Unversity of South Dakota, 1976. Address: 306 West 36th Street, Apt 22, Sioux Falls, SD 57105, USA.

SANGUINETI Edoardo, b. 9 Dec 1930, Genoa, Italy. Professor of Italian Literature. m. Luciana Garabello, 30 Sept 1954, 3 sons, 1 daughter. Education: BA, University of Turin, 1956. Appointments: Professor of Italian Literature, University of Salerno, 1968-74, University of Genoa, 1974-. Publications: Laborintus, 1956; Opus Metricum, 1960; Triperuno, 1964; Wirrwarr, 1972; Catamerone, 1974; Postkarten, 1978; Stracciafoglio, 1980; Scartabello, 1981; Segnalibro, 1982; Alfabeto Apocalittico, 1984; Quintine, 1985; Novissimum Testamentum, 1986; Bisbidis, 1987; Omaggio a Catullo, 1991; Senzatitolo, 1992; Libzetto, 1995. Address: via Pergolesi, 20-16159 Genoa, Italy.

SANJUAN Purificacion Martinez de (Pura Sanjuan), b. 2 Apr 1945, Verea, Orente, Spain. Poet. m. Oscar Sanjuan y Lubian, 1 Aug 1974, 2 sons. Education: Pianist, 1965; Teacher, 1966; Computation Engineer, 1977; Master of Educational Management, 1989. Appointments: Teacher of Piano, 1966-77, Teacher of Computation, 1977, Chair, 1978-83, Chief of Computation, 1983-92, Pedagogical University. Publications: Lunita Triguena, 1987; Fantasia y vida, 1988; C'Est le Mont Saint-Michel, 1988; Erase que se era, 1988; Ventisca, 1989; Verano en El Alma, 1989; A corazon abierto, 1989; Ensenar la vida, 1989; Los versos idilicos, 1989; Neblina, nostalgia, llouizno, morrina, 1989; La seleccion, 1990. Memberships: Authors Association; Society of Engineering; Teachers Association. Address: Avda Mediterraneo No 38, 4o B, E Laredo, 28007 Madrid, Spain.

SAPIA Yvonne V, b. New York, New York, USA. Professor of English; Poet. Education: BA, English, Florida Atlantic University, 1970; MA, English, University of Florida, 1976; PhD, English, Florida University, 1990. Appointments: Editor, Newspaper Reporter, The Village Post, Miami, 1971-73; Editorial Assistant, University of Florida, 1974-76; Resident Poet, Professor of English, Lake City Community College, 1976-. Publications: The Fertile Crescent (poems); Valentino's Hair (poems); Valentino's Hair (novel), 1991. Contributions to: South Florida Poetry Review; New Collage; Kalliope; South Coast Journal; Cincinnati Poetry Review; Indiana Review; The Panhandler; The Chattahoochee Review; The Best American Poetry; New Worlds Literature; Hawaii Pacific Review; The MacGuffin; Kansas Quarterly; Innisfree; Forum; Many others. Honours: First Place, Anhinga Press Poetry Chapbook Award, Florida University, 1983; Third Place, Eve of St Agnes Poetry Competition, 1983; First Place, Morse Poetry Prize, Northeastern University Press, 1987; First Place, Tampa-Hillsborough County Arts Council Poetry Competition, 1989; Second Place, Cincinnati Poetry Review Poetry Competition, 1989; Third Place, Apalachee Quarterly Long Poem Contest, 1989; First Place, Nilon Award for Excellence in Minority Fiction, University of Colorado Press

and Fiction, 1991. Address: 702 South Marsh Street, Lake City, FL 32025, USA.

SAPPHIRE. See: **LOFTON Ramona.**

SARGENT Robert Strong, b. 23 May 1912, New Orleans, Louisiana, USA. Electrical Engineer. m. (1) 1 son, 1 daughter, (2) Mary Jane Barnett, 21 July 1985. Education: BS, Electrical Engineering, Mississippi State University, 1993. Appointments: Various electrical engineering posts including US Navy and Department of Defence. Publications: Now is Always the Miraculous Time, 1977; A Woman from Memphis, 1979, 1988; Aspects of a Southern Story, 1983; Fish Galore, 1989; The Cartographer, 1994. Contributions to: Antioch Review; California Quarterly; College English; Georgia Review; Hollins Critic; Kansas Quarterly; Laurel Review; Louisville Review; Mississippi Review; New York Quarterly. Memberships: Poetry Committee for Greater Washington Area, President, 1990; Poetry Society of America; MacDowell Colony Residency; Virginia Center for Creative Arts Fellow. Address: 120 5th Street North East, Washington, DC 20002, USA.

SARMENTO Luis Filipe, b. 12 Oct 1956, Lisbon, Portugal. Writer; Publisher. m. Maria Leonor Boleo Tome, 27 Nov 1980. Appointments: Journalist; Copywriter; Editor. Publications: Trilogia da Noite, 1977; Nuvens, 1978; Orquestras e Coreografias, 1987; Galeria de um sonho intranquilo, 1988; Fim de Paisagem, 1988; Fragmentos de Uma conversa de Quarto, 1989; Ex Posicoes, 1989; Boca Barroca, 1990; Matinas, Laudas, Vesperas e Completas, 1991; Tinturas Alquimicas, 1995; A Intimidade do Sono, 1996. Contributions to: Portugal: Journal de Letras; Coloquio Letras; DL; DPO; Diario de Noticias; Spain: Agalia; El Sol; Diari. Memberships: Associacao Portuguesa de Escritores; Pen Club of Portugal; Association Europeene pour la Promocion de la Poesie; Organization Mondiale des Poetes; World Congress of Poets; World Academy of Arts and Culture. Address: Rua Joao de Deus, 64, 2710 Sintra, Portugal.

SAS Zbigniew, b. 22 April 1954, London, England. Civil Servant. Education: BA, Philosophy, Sussex University, 1977; Postgraduate Diploma in Criminology, Istitute of Criminology, University of Cambridge, 1992; Postgraduate Research, Philosophical Theology, University of Greenwich, 1994-. Publications: Cosmos and Chaos, forthcoming. Contributions to: Interactions; New Hope International; Odyssey; Ore; Outposts; Symphony; Weyfarers. Address: 10 Upper Holly Hill Road, Belvedere, Kent DA17 6HJ, England.

SATYAMURTI Carole, b. 13 Aug 1939, Bromley, Kent, England. Education: BA, Honours, London University, 1960; Diploma in Social Work, University of Birmingham, 1965; MA, University of Illinois, 1967; PhD, University of London, 1979. Appointments: Lecturer, Principal Lecturer, University of East London, 1968-. Publications: Occupational Survival, 1981; Broken Moon (poems), 1987; Changing the Subject (poems), 1990; Striking Distance (poems), 1994. Honours: 1st Prize, National Poetry Competition, 1986; Arts Council of Great Britain Writers Award, 1988. Address: 15 Gladwell Road, London N8 9AA, England.

SAUER Annmarie, (Maria Fischer), b. 30 Apr 1947, Dayton, Ohio, USA. m. Van Leemput Lim, 27 Aug 1968, 1 daughter. Education: University Degree in Translating and Interpreting. Appointments: Professor at an Interpreting School; Interpreter, European Parliament. Publications: Voor Vuinden, 1985; Jardin Public, 1990. Contributions to: Surplus; Symforosa; Chrysales. Memberships: Board, NNVT; National Council of Women; Literaire Tafel.

SAULS Roger Wayne, b. 7 Nov 1944, Lowndes County, Georgia, USA. Marketing Consultant; Publisher. m. 21 Apr 1972, 1 son. Publication: Hard Weather, 1987. Contributions to: Carolina Quarterly; Ironwood; Ploughshares. Address: 1605 The Oaks, Chapel Hill, NC 27514, USA.

SAUNDERS Sally Love, b. 15 Jan 1940, Bryn Mawr, Pennsylvania, USA. Poet; Poetry Therapist; Lecturer; Freelance Writer. Education: BS, George Williams College, Downers Grove, IL, 1965; Poetry Writing Course, The New School, 1968-69; Several other courses. Appointments: Poetry Therapist, Institute of Pennsylvania Hospital, Philadelphia, University of Louisville, Kentucky; Lectures, teaching at schools and other venues; Appearances on TV and radio; Numerous poetry writing workshops; Poetry readings. Publications: Past the Near Meadows, 1961; Pauses, 1978; Fresh Bread, 1982; Random Thoughts, 1992; Patchwork Quilt, 1993. Contributions include:

Times Literary Supplement; New York Times; Mark Twain Journal; Christian Science Monitor; Poetalk; Gate Becomes Bridge; Hoofstrikes; Poetry Magazine; Dan River Anthology, 1986, 1989, 1990; Orchids and Daffodils, 1988; National Poetry Anthology, 1989; Poetic Voices of America, 1990. Honours include: Honourable Mention, New American Poetry Contest, 1988; Silver Poet Award, World of Poetry, 1989; Nutmegger Book Award. Memberships: National Writers Club; Press Club of San Francisco; Poets and Writers Guild; Association for Poetry Therapy; Poetry Society of America; Ina Coolbirth Circle; Pen and Pencil Club, Philadelphia; Academy of American Poets; American Poetry Center. Address: 609 Rose Hill Road, Broomall, PA 19008, USA.

SAVAGE Thomas (Tom), b. 14 July 1948, New York, New York, USA. Poet; Critic. Education: BA, English, Brooklyn College, City University of New York, 1969; Master's Degree, Columbia University School of Library Science, 1980. Appointments: Teaching Assistant, Naropa Institute School of Poetics, 1975; Editor, Roof Magazine, 1976-78; Editor, Gandhabba Magazine, 1981-; Teacher, Words, Music, Words for Poets and Composers, St Mark's Poetry Project, 1983-85. Publications: Personalities, 1978; Filling Spaces, 1980; Slow Waltz on a Glass Harmonica, 1980; Housing Preservation and Development, 1988; Processed Words, 1990; Out of the World, 1991; Political Conditions and Physical States, 1993; Precipice, 1994. Contributions to: Talisman; Oblek; Hanging Loose; Synaesthetic; Downtown; Cover; World; City Magazines; Transfer; Poetry Project Newsletter; Mudfish; Appearances. Honours: PEN Grant, 1978; Grant, Coordinating Council of Literary Magazines, 1981-82. Membership: Coordinating Council of Literary Magazines. Address: 622 East 11th Street, No 14, New York, NY 10009, USA.

SAVVAS Minas, b. 2 Apr 1939, Athens, Greece. Professor of English. m. Angie Savvas, 2 sons. Education: BA, 1963, MA, English, 1965, University of Illinois; PhD, English, University of California, 1970. Appointments: Assistant, 1968-72, Associate, 1972-75, Professor, 1975-, San Diego State University. Publications: Scars and Smiles, 1974; Chronicle of Exile, 1975; The Subterranean Horses, 1977; The House Vacated, 1989. Contributions to: Chicago Review; Poetry Venture; College English; TriQuarterly; Aegean Review; International Poetry Review; Interim; Footwork; Antioch Review; Senecca Review. Honours: Poetry Prize, University of Illinois, 1963, World of Poetry, 1988. Memberships: Poets and Writers; PEN International; Modern Greek Studies Association. Address: Department of English, San Diego State University, San Diego, CA 92182, USA.

SAX Boria, b. New York, New York, USA. Teacher; Author. m. 15 June 1978. Education: BA, Philosophy, University of Chicago, 1973; MA, German, 1978, PhD, German, History, 1983, State University of New York, Buffalo. Appointment: Adjunct Full Professor of German, Pace University, 1985-. Publications: When the Glaciers Melted, 1973; Rheinland Market, 1983; I Am That Snowflake, 1988; The Frog King, 1990; The Parliament of Animals, 1992. Contributions to: Poesie Europe; Kahen; Snowy Egret; Poet and Critic; Foothill Quarterly; Liminar; Archae; Buffalo Evening News. Membership: Poets and Writers. Address: 25 Franklin Avenue, No 2F, White Plains, NY 10601, USA.

SCAMMACCA Nat, b. 20 July 1924, Brooklyn, New York, USA. Editor. m. Nina Scammacca, 1948, 1 son, 2 daughters. Education: BA, Literature and Philosophy, Long Island University; MA, Education, New York University; Graduated in Italian, University of Perugia. Appointments: Pilot, United States Air Force, World War II, serving the India-Burma-China theatre; Social Worker, Italian Board of Guardians; Professor of English, British College, Palermo, now retired; Currently Editor of the "Third Page" of weekly newspaper, Trapani Nuova. Publications: Two Worlds (novel), 1980; Bye Bye America (short stories), 1986; Schammachanat (Italian and English), 1985; Cricepeo (3 volumes in Italian and English), 1990; Sikano L'Amerikano! (short stories), 1991; Co-author, Due Poeti Americani (Italian and English), 1994; The Hump (World War II stories and poems), 1994; Numerous novels and books of short stories. Translations include: New Scots Poetry (poetry anthology into Italian) and The Sicilian Origin of the Odyssey, by Professor L G Pocock. Contributions to: Akros; Phoenix Press; Epoca; Antigruppo; New Voices; Tulipano Rosso(anthology); Antigruppo 73 (anthology); Poetry for Peace; Rosso Fenice; Lettera; Footwork. Honours: Air Medal, Bronze Star, USAF; Taormina City Poetry Prize, 1978; Premio Letterario Sikania Prize, 1988; VII Premio di Poesia Petrosino 91 Prize. Membership: Poets and Writers, New

York City, USA. Address: Villa Schammachanat, Via Argenteria KM4, Trapani, Sicily 91100, Italy.

SCAMMELL William, b. 2 Jan 1939, Hampshire, England. Lecturer. m. Jacqueline Webb, 15 Aug 1964, 2 sons. Education: BA, Honours, English and Philosophy, University of Bristol, 1967. Appointments: Various posts. Publications: Yes and No, 1979; A Second Life, 1982; Jouissance, 1985; Eldorado, 1987; Bleeding Heart Yard, 1992; The Game, 1992; Five Easy Pieces, 1993; Criticism: Keith Douglas: A Study, 1988. Contributions to: Times Literary Supplement; London Magazine; Poetry Review; Observer; New Statesman; Critical Quarterly; Poetry Chicago; Kenyon Review; Encounter; Literary Review; Poetry Durham; Poetry Matters; Verse; PN Review; Honest Ulsterman. Honours: Cholmondeley Award, Society of Authors, 1980; Poetry Book Society Recommendation, 1985; First Prize, National Poetry Competition, Poetry Society, 1989. Memberships: Board, Poetry Book Society; Chairman, Northern Arts Literature Panel. Address: Centre for Continuing Education, The University, Newcastle-upon-Tyne NE1 7RU, England.

SCANNELL Vernon, b. 23 Jan 1922, Spilsby, Lincolnshire, England. Author. m. 4 Oct 1954, 3 sons, 2 daughter. Appointments: Visiting Poet, Shrewsbury School, 1973-75; Writer-in-Residence, Berinsfield, Oxfordshire, 1975-76; Poet-in-Residence, King's School, Canterbury, 1979. Publications: The Fight, 1952; The Wound and the Scar, 1953; The Face of The Enemy, 1960; The Dividing Night, 1962; The Big Time, 1967; New and Collected Poems, 1980; Winterlude, 1983; Funeral Games, 1987; Soldiering On, 1989; A Time for Fires, poems, 1991; Drums of Morning, Growing Up in The 30's, autobiography, 1992; Collected Poems, 1950-1993, 1994. Contributions to: Listener; Observer; Sunday Times; Encounter; London Magazine; Times Literary Supplement; American Scholar; Yale Literary Magazine. Honours: Heinemann Award for Literature, 1960; Cholmondeley Poetry Prize, 1974. Membership: Fellow, Royal Society of Literature, 1961. Address: 51 North Street, Otley, West Yorkshire LS21 1AH, England.

SCARFE Wendy (Elizabeth), b. 1933, Australia. Author; Poet. Publications: Shadow and Flowers, 1964, 1984; The Lotus Throne, novel, 1976; Neither Here Nor There, novel, 1984; Laura My Alter Ego, novel, 1988; The Day They Shot Edward, novel, 1991, 1992; With Allan John Scarfe: A Mouthful of Petals, 1967, 1972; Tiger on a Rein, 1969; People of India, 1972; The Black Australians, 1974; Victims or Bludgers?, 1974, 1981; J P, His Biography, 1975, 1996, (Hindostani Translation, 1978); Labor's Titan, 1983; All That Grief, 1995; In progress: The Sculptor (novel); No Taste for Carnage (biography with Allan Scarfe); Remembering Jayaprakash (biography with Allan Scarfe). Honours: Co-Recipient, Special Purpose Writers Grant, Australia Council Literature Board, 1980, 1988. Membership: Fellowship of Australian Writers. Address: 8 Bostock Street, Warrnambnool, Victoria 3280, Australia.

SCARPA Michael L. See: PENDRAGON LE FAY M Malefica Grendelwolf.

SCATENA Lorraine Borba, b. 18 Feb 1924, San Rafael, California, USA. Ranching; Educator. m. Louis G Scatena, 14 Feb 1960, dec 1995, 1 son, 1 daughter. Education: BA, Dominican College, San Rafael, California, 1945; Elementary Teacher's Credential, State of California, 1946; California School of Fine Arts, San Francisco, 1948; University of California, Berkeley, 1956-57. Appointments: Spanish Teacher, Dominican College, 1946; Teacher of Mentally Handicapped Children, San Anselmo School District, CA, 1946; Fourth Grade Teacher, Fairfax Public Elementary School, CA, 1946-53; Assistant to Mayor, Fairfax City Recreation, 1948-53; Teacher, Librarian, US Dependent Schools, Mainz am Rhine, Germany, 1953-56; Bonding Secretary, America Fore Insurance, San Francisco, 1958-60. Publications: Her unpublished poetry has been written for special occasions and practical reasons. Membership: Nevada Women's History Project. Address: PO Box 247, Yerington, NV 89447-0247, USA.

SCHÄFER Wendel, b. 25 Aug 1940, Bundenbach, Germany. Headmaster. m. Dorothee Schäfer, 22 July 1965, 1 son, 1 daughter. Education: Pedagogical Studies, Universitat Koblenz, Mainz. Appointments: Teacher, 1965-; Teacher Training, 1974-90; Headmaster at school for handicapped children, 1990-. Publications: Teils heiter - teils wolkig, 1979; Eisgirlanden, 1981; Die Musenflunder, 1982; Herbstspuren, 1983; Die Nacht ist nicht nur schwarz, 1983;

Saurer Regen, 1983; Erosionen, 1984; Flügel-schlager, 1985; Guten Morgen Deutschland, 1986; Au den Leib geschrieben, 1988; Bilder kopf und Blumentritt, 1988; Korne im kopf, 1991; Flügel-Spitzen, 1992. Contributions to: 40 anthologies; Numerous periodicals. Honours: Hafiz Satire Prize, 1988, 1990. Memberships: Forderkreis dt Schriftsteller, Rheinland-Pfalz; Regional Advisory Board, Friefrich-Bödecker-Kreis; Veiband olt Schriftsteller (VS). Address: Igelstrasse 2, 56154 Boppard-Buchenau, Germany.

SCHAFFENBURG Carlos A, b. 19 Sept 1919, Mexico City, Mexico. Medical Doctor. m. Lila Marie Williams, 28 June 1952, 2 sons, 1 daughter. Education: MD, Facultad Nacional de Medicina, University of Mexico, 1944. Appointment: Consultant, National Institutes of Health. Publication: Genesis, a poem in eighteen Cantos, 1989; Songs Irreverent and Old, 1995. Contributions to: Excelsior; Linden Lane Magazine; Oktoberfest; La Nuez. Memberships: Writers Centre, Bethesda, Maryland, 1988-89; Poetry Society of America; Academy of American Poets. Address: 5480 Wisconsin Avenue 1014, Chevy Chase, MD 20815, USA.

SCHECHTER Ruth Lisa, b. USA. Poet. Appointments: Founder, Editor, Croton Review; President, Croton Council on The Arts; Consultant Poetry Therapist, Odyssey House, New York City, 1971-78. Publications: Near The Wall of Lion Shadows, 1969, 1970; Movable Parts, 1971; Suddenly Thunder, 1972; Offshore, 1974; Double Exposure, 1978; Clockworks, 1979; Speedway, 1983; Chords and Other Poems, 1986. Address: 9 Van Cortland Place, Croton-on-Hudson, NY 10520, USA.

SCHEDLER Gilbert Walter, b. 11 Mar 1935, British Columbia, Canada. Professor. 1 son, 2 daughters. Education: BA, Concordia College, 1957; BD, Concordia Seminary, 1960; MA, Washington University, 1963; PhD, University of Chicago, 1970. Appointments: Instructor, Washington University, 1962-63; Wittenberg University, 1963-64; Professor, Callison College, 1967-75, University of the Pacific, 1975-. Publications: Waking Before Dawn, 1978; Making Plans, 1980; That Invisible Wall, 1985; Starting Over, 1992. Contributions to: Contemporary Quarterly; California State Poetry Quarterly; Blue Unicorn; Christian Century; California English Journal; Windless Orchard; Gold Dust; Poetry in The Schools; Midwest Chaparral; Minotaur; Western Ohio Journal. Honours: NDEA Fellowship, University of Chicago, 1966; NEH Award, University of California, 1987. Address: 1781 Oxford Way, Stockton, CA 95204, USA.

SCHELLING Andrew, b. 14 Jan 1953, Washington, DC, USA. Poet; Translator. 1 daughter. Education: BA, Religious Studies, UC Santa Cruz, 1975. Appointments: Highway Worker; Baker; Truck Driver; Bookseller; Teacher; Currently, Faculty, The Jack Kerouac School of Disembodied Poetics, The Naropa Institute, Boulder, Colorado. Publications: Dropping the Bow: Poems From Ancient India, 1991; For Love of The Dark One: Songs of Mirabai, 1993; Twilight Speech, 1993; Old Growth: Selected Poems and Notebooks 1986-1994, 1995. Contributions to: Sulfur; Talisman; Colorado Review; Shambhala Sun. Honours: Prize for Translation, Academy of American Poets, 1992; Translation Award, Witter Bynner Foundation for Poetry, 1995. Address: The Naropa Institute, 2130 Arapahoe Avenue, Boulder, CO 80302, USA.

SCHEVILL James (Erwin), b. 10 June 1920, Berkeley, California, USA. Writer; Poet; Dramatist; Professor. m. (1) Helen Shaner, 1942, div. 1966, 2 daughters, (2) Margot Blum, 1966. Education: BS, Harvard University, 1942; MA, Brown University. Appointments: Assistant Professor of Humanities, California College of Arts & Crafts, Oakland, 1951-59; Associate Professor of English, San Francisco State University, 1959-68; Professor of English 1968-88, Professor Emeritus 1988-, Brown University. Publications: Tensions, poems, 1947; The American Fantasies, poems, 1951; Sherwood Anderson: His Life and Work, 1951; High Sinners, Low Angels, musical play, 1953; The Right to Greet, poems, 1956; The Roaring Market and the Silent Tomb, biography of Bern Porter, 1956; The Bloody Tenet, verse play, 1957; Selected Poems 1945-1959, 1959; Private Dooms and Public Destinations: Poems 1945-1962, 1962; Voices of Mass and Capital A, play, 1962; The Stalingrad Elegies, poems, 1964; The Black President and Other Plays, 1965; Violence and Glory: Poems 1962-1967, 1969; Lovecraft's Follies, play, 1971; Breakout! In Search of New Theatrical Environments, 1972; The Buddhist Car and Other Characters, poems, 1973; The Arena of Ants, novel, 1977; The Mayan Poems, 1978; The American Fantasies:

Collected Poems 1945-1982, 1983; Oppenheimer's Chair, play, 1985; Collected Short Plays, 1986; Bern/Porter: A Personal Biography, 1992; 5 Plays 5, 1993; Winter Channels, poems, 1994; The Complete American Fantasies, 1996. Honours: Ford Foundation Grant, 1960-61: Governor's Award in the Arts, Rhode Island, 1975; Guggenheim Fellowship in Poetry, 1981; McKnight Fellowship in Playwriting, 1984; Pawtucket Arts Council Award for Poetry and Theatre, 1987; American Academy & Institute of Arts and Letters Award, 1991. Address: 1309 Oxford Street, Berkeley, CA 94709, USA.

SCHILLER Thelma Shipley (Lucille), b. 14 Oct 1914, Illinois, USA. m. Richard Louis Schiller, 10 July 1943, 2 sons, 2 daughters. Education: AA, Olympic College, 1961; BA, University of Puget Sound, 1964. Publications: Rainbows End, 1988; Where Seabirds Sing, 1988; Fragments, 1990; Sky Goggles, 1992; I Remember Sea Winds, 1995-96. Contributions to: Byline; Grit; Skagit Valley Herald; New Horizons Poetry Club; Poet Magazine; Washington Evergreen State Magazine; Mornings Like This, for The Pegasus Review, 1995; Glimpse of a Parade, for Rhyme Time, 1995-96; Girl Swinging, for The Lyric; Evanescence and Surviving the Storm, for The National League of American Pen Women. Honours: Awards received from Poet Magazine, 1992, and California Federation of Chaparral Poets, 1992; Blue Ribbon Award, Southern Poetry Association, for Locusts and Butterflies in My Garden, 1995; Certificate of Award, for Coming of Summer, 1995; Editor's Choice Award, The National Library of Poetry, 1995; Editor's Choice Award, Rhyme Time, 1995; Rhyme Time Commendations, 1996. Honorable mentions: Poet; Byline; New Horizons Poetry Club; Owl Award, National League of American Pen Women, 1995. Memberships: National Writer's Club; President, 1991-92, Fictioneers Club; New Horizons Poetry Club; Secretary, National League of American Pen Women, 1992-95. Address: 4712 Highway 20, Concrete, WA 98237, USA.

SCHMIDT Carl Anthony, b. 20 Sept 1948, Cleveland, Ohio, USA. Locomotive Engineer. m. Barbara Lee Uselis, 24 April 1971, 1 son, 1 daughter. Appointments: Locomotive Engineer for Conrail; Senior Demolay; Coeur de Lion Chapter, Master Councilor, 1966; Chevilier Degree, 1967; Certified Liscenced Engineer, 1968. Publications: Individual poems published as single contributions to various anthologies; Books include: A Dad for Sale, 1994; America, Our Country, 1995; Adrift, 1995; Back From the Light; Blasted by Love, 1995; Broken Hearted Hummingbirds, 1995; Dusk, 1995; Echo's of Love, 1995; Even for a Minute, 1995; Everyman's Dream, 1995; For No Reason, 1995; A Walk Down the Aisle, 1996. Honours: Award of Merit, 1995. Address: 13029 Fairfield Trail, Chesterland, OH 44026, USA.

SCHMIDT Michael Norton, b. 2 Mar 1947, Mexico City, Mexico. Publisher; Poet. m. Claire Harman, 1979, 1 son, 1 daughter. Education: Harvard University, USA, 1966; BA, Wadham College, Oxford, England, 1969. Appointments: As undergraduate contributed to and helped to edit Carcanet, Oxford undergraduate magazine; Founder, Carcanet Press, publishing small poetry pamphlets, 1969, expanded and moved to Manchester, 1972, Press now considered primary publisher of poetry in Britain; Special Lecturer in Poetry, University of Manchester, 1972; Founder, Editor, PN Review, 1972-. Publications: Black Buildings, 1969; Bedlam and The Oakwood, 1970; Co-Editor, British Poetry Since 1960, 1972; Desert of The Lions, 1972; It Was My Tree, 1972; My Brother Gloucester, 1976; Translated, Flower and Song Poems of The Aztec Peoples, with introduction by Schmidt and Edward Kissam, 1977; A Change of Affairs, 1978; An Introduction to Fifty Modern British Poets, 1979, republished as, A Reader's Guide to Fifty Modern British Poets, 1979; An Introduction to Fifty British Poets 1300-1900, 1979, republished as, A Reader's Guide to Fifty British Poets 1300-1900, 1979; Co-Editor, British Poetry Since 1970, 1980; Tyne Colonist, 1980, republished as, Green Island, 1982; Choosing a Guest: New and Selected Poems, 1983; The Love of Strangers, 1989; Reading Modern Poetry, 1990. Address: c/o Carcanet Press Ltd, 208-212 Corn Exchange Buildings, Manchester M4 3BQ, England.

SCHMIDT-BLEIBTREU Ellen. See: CONRADI-BLEIBTREU Ellen.

SCHMITZ Dennis (Mathew), b. 11 Aug 1937, Dubuque, Iowa, USA. Professor of English; Poet. m. Loretta D'Agostino, 1960, 2 sons, 3 daughters. Education: BA, Loras College, Dubuque, Iowa, 1959; MA, University of Chicago, 1961. Appointments: Instructor, Illinois Institute of Technology, Chicago, 1961-62, University of Wisconsin, Milwaukee,

1962-66; Assistant Professor, 1966-69, Poet-in-Residence, 1966-, Associate Professor, 1969-74, Professor of English, 1974-, California State University, Sacramento. Publications: We Weep for Our Strangeness, 1969; Double Exposures, 1971; Goodwill, Inc, 1976; String, 1980; Singing, 1985; Eden, 1989; About Night: Selected and New Poems, 1993. Honours: New York Poetry Center Discovery Award, 1968; National Endowment for the Arts Fellowships, 1976, 1985, 1992; Guggenheim Fellowship, 1978; di Castagnola Award, 1986; Shelley Memorial Award, 1988. Address: c/o Department of English, California State University at Sacramento, 6000 Jay Street, Sacramento, CA 95819, USA.

SCHNEEMAN Elio, b. 16 Oct 1961, Taranto, Italy. Poet; Librarian. Education: Bard College, 1979-82. Appointments: Librarian, Baker and McKenzie, International Law Firm, USA; Librarian, Teachers College, New York City, 1992-. Publications: In February I Think, 1977; Along the Rails, 1991. Contributions to: Cover Magazine; World; Shiny; Brooklyn Review; Exquisite Corpse; Transfer; Docks; Scarlet; Red Weather; Poetry Project Newsletter; Flatiron News; Talisman; Long News: In The Short Century; GAS; Anthologies: Nice To See You; Homage to Ted Berrigan; Out of This World. Honour: Fund for Poetry, 1990. Memberships: Poets and Writers; St Mark's Church Poetry Project, NY. Address: 29 Saint Marks Place # 3B, New York, NY 10003, USA.

SCHNEIDER Myra Ruth, b. 20 June 1936, London, England. Writer; Teacher. m. Erwin Schneider, 10 Nov 1963, 1 son. Education: English Honours Degree, London University, 1959. Appointments: Publicity Assistant, 1961-63; Teacher, 1964-74; Writing Class Tutor, 1988-. Publications: Fistful of Yellow Hope, 1984; Cat Therapy, 1986, 1989; Cathedral of Birds, 1988; Opening the Ice, 1990; Crossing Point, 1991; Exits, 1994; Anthologies: Chaos of The Night; In Time of War; Blue Nose Poetry Anthology, 1993; Klaonica, Poems for Bosnia, 1994; The Dybbuk of Delight, Five Leaves, 1995. Contributions to: Critical Quarterly; Outposts; Acumen; Poetry Wales; New Spokes; Staple; Green Book; Writing Women; Poetry Nottingham; Orbis; Jewish Quarterly; Pennine Platform; Observer; Independent; New Statesman; Quadrant; The North; Ambit. Honours: Lancaster Poetry Competition, 1990; Merit Prize, Lake Aske Competition, 1990; Commendation, Greenwich, 1991; 2nd Prize, Bournemouth Open Competition, 1993, Aberystwyth Open Competition, 1993; Prizewinner, Lancaster Literature Festival Poetry Competition. Membership: Poetry Library South Bank. Address: 130 Morton Way, Southgate, London N14 7AL, England.

SCHOENFELD Ilan (Ziv Heler, Shlomo Dror, Annand Chatergie, Eshed Esh), b. 22 April 1960, Israel. Literary Editor; PR Manager. Education: BA, Hebrew and English Literature, 1984, MA, Hebrew and English Literature, Tel Aviv University, 1986. Appointments: Literary Editor, Al Hamishmar, Hebrew Daily, 1981-92; Freelance, Magaaim, 1990-94; Editor, The Monthly of the Suzzane Dellal Center of The Arts; Freelance Writer for several papers. Publications/Creative works: The Bewitched Lizard, 1981; The Tongue of Love, 1984; From the Heart of Tel Aviv; Lines to a Friend in Parting, 1987; The Strange Book of Margolis; It Begins With Love, 1989; Shalom, 1992; Arai, 1992; The Dream Stealers, puppet play, 1992; Hey Rimona, cabaret, 1993; Tashlich, poems, 1994; Aray; Tashlir Anthologies: No End to Battles and Massacres, 1983; As You Cross The Border - Poems From The Lebanon War, 1983. Honours: Berenstein Prize, 1983; Kugel Poetry Prize, Tel Aviv Literary Fund, 1988; Dov Sadan Prize for Literary Scholars, Tel Aviv University, 1988; Grant, 1988; Publication Grant, AKUM, 1990; Prime Minister's Prize for Writers, 1991. Memberships: Hebrew Writers Association; AKUM, Israeli Association of Writers and Composers; Israel Public Relations Association. Address: 21 Kfar Saba Street, Neve Tsedek, Tel Aviv 65147, Israel.

SCHOONOVER Amy Jo, b. 25 Apr 1937, Illinois, USA. m. (1) 2 sons, 1 daughter, (2) Samuel J Zook Jr, 15 July 1972. Education: BA, Wittenberg University, 1969; MA, English, 1982, PhD, 1993, West Virginia University. Appointments: Public School Teacher and Tutor, 1961-72; Freelance, 1972-80; Poet in The Schools, 1974-; Graduate Teaching Assistant, 1981-82, 1984-85; Instructor of English, Urbana University, 1986-88, 1992-; Clark State Community College, 1989-91. Publications: Echoes of England, 1975; A Sonnet Sampler, 1979; New and Used Poems, 1988; Threnody, 1994; Editor of revised edition, The Study and Writing of Poetry: American Women Poets Discuss Their Craft, 1995. Contributions include: Christian Science Monitor; Lyric; Descant; Kansas Quarterly; Kentucky Poetry Review; Hiram Poetry

Review; Windless Orchard; Negative Capability; Gryphon; Roanoke Review; Windfall; Canonic Mass, contemporary text for Communion Service, music by Alice Parker, in Hymnal Supplement, 1996. Honour: Poet of the Year, Ohio Poetry Day Association, 1988. Memberships: State President, National League of American Pen Women, Ohio, 1986-90; Contest Chairman, 1974-87, Treasurer, 1988-, Ohio Poetry Day Association; Various offices, Verse Writer's Guild of Ohio; Contest Chairman, 1st Vice President, 1994-96, President, 1996-98, National Federation of State Poetry Societies; Poetry Society of America, 1978-; Illinois State Poetry Society; West Virginia Poetry Society; Society for the Study of Midwestern Literature. Address: 3520 State Route 56, Mechanicsburg, OH 43044, USA.

SCHOTT Erika, b. 28 Dec 1946, Brooklyn, New York, USA. Writer; Artist; Teacher. Education: AA, Packer Collegiate Institute, 1964-66; BA, University of Florida, 1966-68; MA, Arizona State University, 1979-83. Contributions to: Poet; Premier Poet; National Journal of Poetry; View From The Edge; Sounds of Poetry. Honour: Honourable Mention and 1st Prize, Poetry Competition, 1979. Memberships: Arizona Poetry Association; World Poetry Society. Address: 465 Tyende Oui, Flagstaff, AZ 86001, USA.

SCHOULTZ Solveig von, b. 5 Aug 1907, Borga, Finland. Author. m. Erik Bergman, 7 July 1961. Education: Teacher's Qualification. Publications include: Eko av ett rop, 1946; Natet, 1956; Sank ditt ljus, 1963; De fyra flojtspelarna, 1975; Bortom traden hors havet, 1980; En enda minut, 1981; Vattenhjulet, 1987; Alla trad vantar faglar, 1988; Ett satt att rakna tiden, 1989; Längs vattenbrynet, 1992; Samtal med en fjäril, 1994. Honours: The State Literary Prize, 1953, 1957, 1959, 1982; Grand Prize, Svenska Litteratursallskapet, 1959, 1981; Grand Literary Prize, Svenska Akademien, 1972; Honorary Member, Svenska Litteratursallskapet, 1976; Pro Finlandia Medal, 1980; The Church's Literary Prize, 1981; Edith Sodergran Prize, 1984; The Bellman Prize, 1986; PhD Honoris Causa, 1986; Nils Ferlins Prize, 1988. Memberships: PEN Club; Board Member, Finlands forfattareforening. Address: Bergg. 22, C 52, 00100 Helsinki, Finland.

SCHRAMM Werner, b. 28 Apr 1926, Hohenlockstedt, Germany. Author; Painter. Education: Teacher Training Institute; Langemarck Studies. Appointments: Served in the German Army, wounded at age 17 in World War II; Author of numerous published essays on historical, psychological, philosophical and literary-historical themes. Honours include: International Cultural Diploma of Honour, 1987; World Decoration of Excellence, 1989; Lifetime Deputy Governor, 1989; Medal of Honour, 1990; International Order of Merit, 1990; LPIBA, 1990; LFWLA, 1991; HE, 1991; FABI, 1991; Cultural Doctorate in Literature, 1991; Grand Ambassador of Achievement, 1991; Golden Academy Award, 1991; Research Advisor of the Year, 1991; Silver Shield of Valor, 1992; DA, Albert Einstein International Academy Foundation, 1993; AEIAF Commemorative Medallion, 1993; Gold Record of Achievement, 1994; The Order of International Ambassadors, 1995. Memberships include: ABI Research Board of Governors, 1989; IBC Advisory Council, 1990; ABI Research Board of Advisors, 1991. Address: Eckenerweg 8, D-25524 Itzehoe, Germany.

SCHROEDER Andreas Peter, b. 26 Nov 1946, Hoheneggelsen, Germany. Writer; Journalist; Editor; Translator. Education: BA, 1969, MA, Creative Writing, Comparative Literature, 1971, University of British Columbia, Canada. Appointments include: Literary Critic and Columnist, Vancouver Province Newspaper, 1968-73; Founding Editor, Contemporary Literature in Translation Magazine, 1969-80; Teaching Creative Writing; Residence appointments; Translator of screen and radio plays; Maclean-Hunter Chair for Creative Non-Fiction, University of British Columbia, 1993-. Publications: The Ozone, 1969; Universe, 1971; File of Uncertainties, 1970 The Late Man, modern parables, 1972; Shaking it Rough, 1976; Toccata in 'D', 1984; Dust-Ship Glory, 1986; The Mennonites, 1990; The Eleventh Commandment, 1990; Carved From Wood, 1991; Scam, Scandals and Skulduggery, A Selection of the World's Most Ingenious Frauds, 1995; Co-Editor, Contemporary Poetry of British Columbia, volume I, 1970, volume II, 1972; Volvox: Poetry from the Unofficial Languages of Canada, 1971; Editor, Words From Inside, prison anthology, 1976, 1977, 1980. Contributions to: Numerous anthologies and literary magazines; Articles and columns in most major Canadian newspapers, magazines and other publications. Honours: Woodward Memorial Award for Prose, 1969; Finalist, Governor-General's Award for Non-Fiction, 1977, Sealbooks First Novel Award, 1984; Investigative Journalism Award, Canadian Association of Journalists, 1991; Various grants including Canada Council Grants. Memberships include: PEN; Past Chairman,

Writers Union of Canada; League of Canadian Poets; Founding Chairman, Public Lending Right Commission of Canada; Canadian Periodical Publishers Association; ACTRA; Federation of British Columbia Writers. Address: 9564 Erickson Street RR5, Mission, British Columbia V2V 5X4, Canada.

SCHUFF Karen Elizabeth, b. 1 June 1937, Michiganschuler, USA. Poet. m. Henry Clifton Schuff, 7 Sept 1955, 1 son, 1 daughter. Publications: Barefoot Philosopher, 1968; Come, Take My Hand, 1968; Of Rhythm and Cake, 1970; Of June I Sing, 1979; Green as April, 1987. Contributions include: Democrat and Chronicle; Lyric; Amelia; Cyclo-Flame; Parnassus; Perceptions; Poetry Forum; Peninsula Poets; Writer's World; Prophetic Voices; Modern Images Anthology; Alura; Poetry Magic; Piedmont Literary Review; Sunday Independent; Mobius; Byron Poetry Works; Downriver Digest; Ship of Fools; Pen and Ink Magazine; Diarist's Journal; Tucumcari Literary Review; Night Roses; The Oak; Southern Poetry Review; Enlightenments. Honours: 1st Prize for Poetry Manuscript, Poetry Forum, 1990; 3rd Prize, American Sonnet, Parnassus, 1990; 1st Prize for Contemporary Poem, Poetry Society of MI Contest, 1993; 1st Prize, 2nd Prize, 1995, for Poetry, Scottsville, MI Contest; 2nd Prize for Poetry, Monroe County Library System, 1995. Memberships: Society for the Study of Midwestern Literature; Poetry Society of Michigan; Avalon. Address: 15310 Windemere Street, Southgate, MI 48195-3819, USA.

SCHULER Robert Jordan, b. 25 June 1939. California, USA. College Professor. m. Carol Forbis, 7 Sept 1963, 2 sons, 1 daughter. Education: BA, Honours, Political Science, Stanford University, 1961; MA, Comparative Literature, University of California, Berkeley, 1965; PhD, English, University of Minnesota, 1989. Appointments: Instructor in English, Menlo College, 1965-67; Instructor in Humanities, Shimer College, 1967-77; Professor of English, University of Wisconsin, 1978-. Publications: Axle of the Oak, 1978; Seasonings, 1978; Where is Dancers' Hill?, 1979; Morning Raga, 1980; Red Cedar Scroll, 1981; Floating Out of Stone, 1982; Music for Monet, 1984; Grace: A Book of Days, 1995; Journeys Toward the Original Mind, 1995. Contributions include: Caliban; Northeast; Tar River Poetry; Longhouse; Dacotah Territory; Wisconsin Academy Review; Wisconsin Review; North Stone Review; Wisconsin Poetry 1991 Transactions; Hummingbird; Abraxas; Lake Street Review; Inheriting the Earth; Mississippi Valley Review; Coal City Review; Gypsy; Essay, Putting Myself In My Place, in Imagining Home, 1995. Membership: Phi Kappa Phi. Address: 511 Sunset Drive, Menomonie, WI 54751, USA.

SCHULTZ David, b. 20 Nov 1934, Paterson, New Jersey, USA. Teacher; Translator; Poet; Writer. 2 sons. Education: BA, Brandeis University, 1956; MA, Columbia University, 1961. Appointments: High School Teacher, 1958-69; Editor, Translator, 1958-; College Media Center Director, 1969-82; High School and College Teacher, 1986-. Publication: Patches of Paterson, forthcoming. Contributions include: Tin Wreath; The Haven; Footsteps; Horizontes; Transition; Poésie USA; Italian Americana. Membership: Advanced Writers Group, Queens, New York. Address: 162-31 9th Avenue, Whitestone, NY 11357-2010, USA.

SCHULTZ Philip, b. 6 Jan 1945. Writer; Teacher. Education: BA, San Francisco University, 1967; MFA, University of Iowa, 1971. Appointments: Writer-in-Residence, Kalamazoo College, 1971-72, Boston College, 1973-74; Founder, Director, Graduate Programme in Creative Writing, New York University, 1978-88; Founder, Director, The Writers Studio, 1986-. Publications: Like Wings, 1978; Deep Within the Ravine, 1984; My Guardian Angel Stein, 1986. Contributions include: New Yorker; Nation; Poetry; Kenyon Review; North American Review; Georgia Review; American Review; Pequod; Partisan Review; Michigan Quarterly Review; Epoch; New York Quarterly; Anthologies: New American Poets of the 90's; New Anthology, 100 Years of American Poetry by Academy of American Poetry; Articulation; First Light. Honours: Kansas City Star Poetry Award, 1971; Award in Literature, American Academy and Institute of Arts and Letters, 1979; National Endowment for the Arts Fellowship, 1981-82; Fulbright Fellowship, 1983-84; Lamont Poetry Selection, 1984. Memberships: PEN American Centre; Writers Guild; Governing Board, Poetry Society of America, 1984-89. Address: 78 Charles Street, Apt 2R, New York, NY 10014, USA.

SCHUYLER James Marcus, b. 1923, USA. Author; Playwright; Poet. Publications: Alfred and Guinevere, 1958; Salute, 1960; Unpacking The Black Trunk, with Kenward Elmslie, 1965; May 24th Or So, 1966; A Nest of Ninnies, 1969; Freely Espousing: Poems, 1969;

The Crystal Lithium, 1972; Penguin Modern Poets 24, with Kenneth Koch and K Elmslie, 1973; Hymn to Life: Poems, 1974; The Fireproof Floors of Witley Court, 1976; The Home Book: Prose and Poems, 1977; What's For Dinner?, 1978; The Morning of The Poem, 1980; A Few Days, 1985. Address: c/o Maxine Groffsky, 2 Fifth Avenue, New York, NY 10011, USA.

SCHWARTZ Betsy Robin, b. 1 Feb 1956, Newark, New Jersey, USA. Poet. Education: BA, cum laude, English, Speech, Theatre, Kean College of New Jersey, 1977. Appointments: Director, 4 Poetry Reading Series; Host, Producer, Off The Page; TV Show and Reading Series; Featured Reader at more than 100 venues. Publications: I'm not moving across the river. Contributions to: London Observer 1993; Arvon Anthology; 13th Moon; Footwork: The Paterson Literary Review; Longshot; Aquarian Arts Weekly; Up Front Muse International Review; Arbella; Common Journeys; Heartlight Journal; Atelier; Dust Behind the Door. Honours: AVY Award for Directing 1991; 1st Place, Allen Ginsberg Award, 1992; Arvon Foundation Duncan Lawrie Prize, 1993; Proclamations from Woodbridge Township and Metuchen, New Jersey; Poem Nominated for New Jersey State Poem. Membership: American Academy of Poets. Address: 110 Columbia Avenue, Metuchen, NJ 08840, USA.

SCHWARTZ Leonard, b. 7 Oct 1963, Brooklyn, New York, USA. Writer. m. Mingxia Li, 2 Nov 1995. Education: BA, Bard College, 1984; MA, Philosophy, Columbia University, 1986. Appointments: Instructor, The New School for Social Research, 1989-92; Visiting Assistant Professor of English, Bard College, 1992-. Publications: Objects of Thought, Attempts at Speech, 1990; Exiles: Ends, 1990; Gnostic Blessing, 1992. Contributions to: Denver Quarterly; Talisman; First Intensity; Agni Trafika; Alea; The World; Five Fingers Review. Honour: "New Voices" Selection, Academy of American Poets, 1993. Membership: PEN, New York. Address: 561 Hudson Street, Box 44, New York, NY 10014, USA.

SCHWARTZ Lloyd, b. 29 Nov 1941, Brooklyn, New York, USA. Poet; Teacher; Music Critic. Education: BA, Queens College, City University of New York, 1962; MA, 1963, PhD, 1976, Harvard University. Appointments: Classical Music Editor, Boston Phoenix, 1977-; Associate Professor of English, 1982-86; Director of Creative Writing, 1982-, Professor of English, 1986-, University of Massachusetts, Boston; Classical Music Critic, Fresh Air, National Public Radio, 1987-. Publications: These People, 1981; Editor, Elizabeth Bishop and Her Art, 1983; Poems in Best American Poetry, 1991, 1994; Goodnight Gracie, 1992. Contributions: American Review; New York Times; Poetry; New Republic; Pequod; Ploughshares; Shenandoah; Partisan Review; Harvard Magazine; Southwest Review; Poetry Now; Seneca Review. Honours: Deems Taylor Award, ASCAP, 1980, 1987, 1990; Daniel Varoujan Prize, 1984; Pushcart Prize, 1987; Somerville Arts Council Grant, 1987, 1989; National Endowment for the Arts Fellowship, 1990; Runner-up, Gustav Davidson Memorial Award, 1990; Pulitzer Prize in Criticism, 1994. Memberships: Executive Committee, 1983-, PEN New England; Poetry Society of America; New England Poetry Club. Literary Agent: Mark Kelley, New York, USA. Address: 27 Pennsylvania Avenue, Somerville, MA 02145, USA.

SCHWARTZ Rhoda Bette Josephson, b. 28 Dec 1923, New Jersey, USA. Poet; Writer. m. Edward Schwartz, 27 Feb 1944, dec. 1 daughter. Education: Privately tutored. Appointments: Technical Writer, US Veterans Administration; Founding Editor, The American Poetry Review and Pushcart Press. Publications: Anthologies: About Women, 1973; Jewish American Literature, 1974; Speaking for Ourselves, 1975; New World's of Literature, I, 1989, II, 1993; Families, 1990. Contributions to: Nation; Chicago Review; Kansas Quarterly; Carolina Quarterly; Books; Big Moon. Honour: Pushcart Prize, 1976. Membership: Patron, Academy of American Poets. Address: 1901 JFK Boulevard, Apt 2321, Philadelphia, PA 19103, USA.

SCHWEITZER Leah, b. 4 July 1938, Los Angeles, California, USA. Writer; Poet; Teacher; Editor. m. Norm Schweitzer, 3 Feb 1963. Education: BA, English, Immaculate Heart College, Los Angeles, 1980. Publication: Co-Editor, Without a Single Answer: Poems on Contemporary Israel, 1990; Only Morning in Her Shoes, 1990. Contributions: Judaica Book News; Bitterroot; Confrontation; Voices Israel; Jewish Ledger; California State Poetry Quarterly; Apalachee Quarterly; Crosscurrents; Sojourner; Slipstream; Shirim; Heaven Bone; Aim Quarterly. Honour: Alice B Jackson Poetry Award, 1986. Memberships: Board, Women's National Book Association; PEN;

Founding Member, Women Writers West; Creative Jewish Women's Alliance; Poetry Society of America; Academy of American Poets; Authors Guild; National Women's Studies Association. Address: 13322 Maxella Avenue, No 6, Marina del Ray, CA 90292, USA.

SCHWERNER Armand, b. 11 May 1927, Antwerp, Belgium. m. Doloris Holmes, 13 Jan 1961, 2 children. Education: BS, 1950, MA, 1954, Columbia University. Appointments: Professor, Department of English, Speech and World Literature, College of Staten Island, City University of New York. Publications: Tablets XVI, XVII, XVIII and Other Poems, 1975; Bacchae Sonnets, 1977; The Work, The Joy and The Triumph of the Will, 1978; Philoctetes, translation from Sophocles' Greek, 1978; Sounds of the River Naranjana and the Tablets, I-XXIV, 1983; Tablets XXVI, 1989. Contributions: Chelsea; Nation; American Poetry Review; Parnassus; Vort; Performing Arts; Bluefish; Sagetrieb; Dialectical Anthropology; High Performance; Sulfur. Honours: Fellowships and Grants from State University of New York, 1970, 1972, City University of New York, 1971, Creative Artists Public Service Programme, 1973, 1975, NEA, 1973, 1979, 1987, NEH, 1978, 1981, 1985; Creative Incentive Fellowship, CUNY, 1986; Greater New York Development Fund Grant, 1987; Fund for Poetry Grant, 1991; Grant, Rockefeller Foundation Multi-Arts Production Fund for Dragon Bond Rite, a muli-cultural Music-Mask Dance-Theater based on Japanese Noh, 1995; Grant from Mary Flagler Cary Charitable Trust for Dragon Bond Rite libretto, 1995. Address: 20 Bay Street Landing, No B-3C, Staten Island, NY 10301, USA.

SCOTT John A, b. 23 Apr 1948, England. University Lecturer. Education: BA, DipEd, Monash University, Australia, 1970. Appointments: Lecturer, Media Studies, Swinburne Institute, 1975-80; Media Studies, Canberra College of Advanced Education, Australian Capital Territory, 1980-89; Writing, School of Creative Arts, University of Wollongong, 1989-. Publications: The Barbarous Sideshow, 1976; From The Flooded City, 1981; Smoking, 1983; The Quarrel With Ourselves, 1984; Confession, 1984; St Clair, 1986, revised edition, 1990; Blair, 1988; Singles: Shorter Works 1981-1986, 1989; Translation, 1990; What Have I Written, 1993; Translations: Emmanuel Hocquard: Elegies and Other Works, 1989. Contributions to: Age; Antipodes; Meanjin; New American Writing; New Directions; New Poetry; Ninth Decade; Overland; Phoenix Review; Poetry Australia; Scripsi; Shearsman; Southerly; Stand; Voices. Honours: Poetry Society of Australia Award, 1970; Mattara Poetry Prize, 1984; Wesley Michel Wright Awards, 1985, 1988; Victorian Premier's Prize for Poetry, 1986; ANA Award, Fellowship of Australian Writers, 1990. Address: c/o McPhee Gribble Publishers, 56 Claremont Street, South Yarra, Victoria 3141, Australia.

SCOTT Peter Dale, b. 11 Jan 1929, Montreal, Quebec, Canada. Professor. m. Ronna Kabatznick, 14 July 1993, 2 sons, 1 daughter. Education: BA, McGill University, 1979; Studied at Institut d'Etudes Politiques, Paris, 1950; University College, Oxford, 1950-52; PhD, Political Science, McGill University, 1955. Appointments: Lecturer, McGill, 1955-56; Canadian Foreign Service, Ottawa and Poland, 1957-61; Professor of Speech, University of California, Berkeley, 1961-66; of English, University of California, Berkeley, 1966-94. Publications: Poems, 1952; Rumors of No Law, 1981; Coming to Jakarta, 1988; Listening to the Candle, 1992; Crossing Borders, 1994. Contributions: Harvard Review; Times Literary Supplement; Literary Review; Antioch Review; Poetry, Chicago; Tamarack Review; Massachusetts Review; Alphabet; Critical Quarterly; Ironwood; Agni. Honours: Dia Art Foundation, 1989. Address: c/o Department of English, University of California, Berkeley, CA 94720, USA.

SCOTT (Peter) Hardiman, b. 2 Apr 1920, Norfolk, England. Retired. m. (1) 2 sons, (2) 17 June 1966. Appointments: Assistant News Editor, BBC Midland Region; Reporter, BBC Radio and TV, London; Political Correspondent and Political Editor, BBC. Publications: Adam and Eve and Us, 1946; When the Words are Gone, 1972; Part of Silence, 1984; Editor, Selected Poems of Sir Thomas Wyatt, 1996. Contributions to: Poetry Review; Times Literary Supplement; Orbis; Outposts; Rialto; BBC. Honour: Order of the British Empire, 1989. Memberships: Poetry Society; President, Suffolk Poetry Society. Address: The Drey, 4 Butchers Lane, Boxford, Suffolk CO10 5DZ, England.

SCULLY James, (Joseph Patrick), b. 23 Feb 1937, New Haven, Connecticut, USA. Teacher. m. Arlene Marie Steeves, 10 Sept 1960, 2 sons, 1 daughters. Education: BA, 1959, PhD, 1964, University of Connecticut. Publications: Editor, Modern Poetics, 1965; The Marches,

1967; Avenue of The Americas, 1971; Santiago Poems, 1975; Scrap Book, 1977; May Day, 1980; Apollo Helmet, 1983; Line Break: Poetry as Social Practice, 1988; Raging Beauty: Selected Poems, 1994; Translations: Aechylus' Prometheus Bound, with C J Herington, 1975; Quechua Peoples' Poetry, with M A Proser, 1977; Teresa de Jesus' de Repente - All of a Sudden, with Proser and A Scully, 1979. Contributions: Critical Quarterly; Leviathan; Massachusetts Review; Arion; Praxis; New Yorker; Minnesota Review; Literatura Chilena en el Exilio; Harvard Magazine; Poetry Review; Compages; Alcatraz. Honours: Fellowship, Ingram Merrill Foundation, 1962-63; Lamont Poetry Award, 1967; Contributors' Prize, Far Point, 1969; Jenny Taine Memorial Award, Massachusetts Review, 1971; Guggenheim Fellowship, 1973-74; Fellowships, National Endowment for The Arts, 1976-77, 1990-91; Translation Award, Islands and Continents, 1980; Award, Bookcover Design, Bookbuilders of Boston, 1983. Memberships: PEN; Poetry Society of America. Address: 2865 Bryant Street, San Francisco, CA 94110, USA.

SCUPHAM John Peter, b. 24 Feb 1933, Liverpool, England. Teacher; Editor. m. Carola Nance Braunholtz, 6 Aug 1957, 3 sons, 1 daughter. Education: English Honours, Cambridge, 1954-57. Appointment: Ex-Head of English Department, St Christopher School, Letchworth, Hertfordshire. Publications: The Snowing Globe, 1972; Prehistories, 1975; The Hinterland, 1977; Summer Palaces, 1980; Winter Quarters, 1983; Out Late, 1986; The Air Show, 1989; Watching the Perseids', 1990; Selected Poems, 1990; The Ark, 1994. Contributions to: Encounter; Listener; Times Literary Supplement; BBC; Poetry Review; Poetry Nation; Penguin Anthologies. Honour: Fellow, Royal Society of Literature. Address: Old Hall, Norwich Road, South Burlingham, Norfolk NR13 4EY, England.

SEAGER Ralph William, b. 3 Nov 1911, Geneva, New York, USA. Writer. m. Ruth M Lovejoy, 1932, 3 sons. Education: Basic and Advanced Verse, University of California, Berkeley, 1949-51; Studied with Robert Peter Tristam Coffin, University of New Hampshire Writers Conference, 1954, and John Holmes, Harvard, 1956; LittD, Keuka College, 1970. Career: Served United States Navy, South Pacific campaigns, World War II; Assistant Professor of English, Creative Course in Verse Writing, 1960; Professor Emeritus, 1977, Keuka College; Director, Instructor, numerous poetry workshops. Publications: Songs from a Willow Whistle, 1956; Beyond the Green Gate, 1958; Christmas Chimes in Rhyme, 1962; Cup, Flagon and Fountain, 1965; A Choice of Dreams, 1970; Wheatfields and Vineyards, 1975; The Manager Mouse and Other Christmas Poems, 1977; Hiding in Plain Sight, 1982; The Love Tree, 1985; The First Quartet (with 3 other poets), 1988; My Folks and the One-Room Schoolhouse, 1993. Contributions to: Saturday Evening Post; New York Times; Ladies' Home Journal. Memberships: World Parnassian Guild International, 1995. Address: 311 Keuka Street, Penn Yan, NY 14527, USA.

SEAGER Steven A, b. 17 Oct 1958, New York, USA. Accountant; Aspiring Writer. m. Linda A Lee, 11 Oct 1980, 3 daughters. Education: AAS, Accounting Degree, Finger Lakes Community College, New York, 1978; Political Science, Geneseo State College, 1989. Appointment: Board, Phelps Clifton Springs School, 1988-90. Publication: Songs From The Heart, 1988. Contributions to: Lucidity; In-Between Magazine; Six Lakes Arts; Antioch Review; American Review; Quill Books. Honours: Golden Poet Awards, World of Poetry, 1988, 1989, 1990; Poet of Merit Awards, American Poetry Association, 1989, 1990; Editor's Choice Awards, National Library of Poetry, 1988, 1990; Publisher's Choice Award, Watermark Press, 1990. Memberships: Poetry Society of America; Academy of American Poets; National Writers Club. Address: PO Box 69, Phelps, NY 14532, USA.

SEATOR Lynette, b. 23 Mar 1929, Chicago, Illinois, USA. Poet; Freelance Writer. m. Gordon Seator, 8 June 1949, 1 son, 3 daughter. Education: BS, 1963, MA, 1965, PhD, 1972, University of Illinois. Appointments: Instructor, Western Illinois University, 1966-67; Professor of Modern Languages, 1967-89, Pixley Professor of Humanities, 1988, Illinois College; Director of Poetry Workshop, Jacksonville Correctional Center. Publications: After The Light, 1992; Editor of a book of prisoners' writing, funded by Illinois Arts Council Grant, Hear Me Out, forthcoming. Contributions to: Open Places; Mississippi Valley Review; Praxis; Spoon River Quarterly; Pulpsmith; Kalliope; Revista Chicano Riquena; Arts Journal. Honours: Harry J Dunbaugh, Distinguished Professor, 1976; Illinois Arts Council Artist in Residence, 1984, 1985; Lincoln Library, Springfield, Writer of the

Year Award, 1996. Memberships: Board, Illinois Writers, 1983-87, 1993-; Poets and Writers. Address: 1609 Mound Avenue, Jacksonville, IL 62650, USA.

SEGAL Sabra, b. Boston, Massachusetts, USA. Painter; Poet; Ceramic Sculptor; Photographer; Designer and Illustrator; Actress. Education: English major, Elmira College, New York, 1955-57; Painting major, 1957-59, BFA Painting, Sculpture minor, 1961-63, School of Fine and Applied Arts, Boston University, Boston, Massachusetts; MA, Fine Art, 1967-68, MFA, Fine Art, 1968-69, School of Art, Art Education, University of Wisconsin, Madison. Creative works: Museum Exhibits: San Francisco Art Museum, California, 1961, DeCordova Museum, Lincoln, Massachusetts, 1963, Schenectady Museum, New York, 1985, Rice Gallery, Albany Institute of History and Art, New York, 1988-91; Solo exhibits include: Greene County Council of the Arts, New York, 1986, Watermark/Cargo Gallery, Kingston, New York, 1989, FM Artists Coalition, Woodstock, New York, 1991, Froebel Gallery, Albany, New York, 1994; Group exhibitions include: Smithsonian Institution "Good as Gold: Alternative Materials in American Jewelry", Washington DC, 1981-85, Bell Gallery, Rhinebeck and Woodstock, New York, 1988, Donskoj & Co, 1994, and Park West Gallery, 1995, Kingston, New York. Publications: To All Things Alive (poetry book), 1968; The World Turns (poem broadsheets), 1968; The Green Leaf of Time (poem broadsheet), 1968; An Artist's Thoughts (poem drawings), 1996. Contributions to: The New Yorker, San Francisco Literary Magazine, Audience Magazine, Tangent: A Review of Literature and Art, East West Journal, Woodstock Times. Permanent Collections: Library Research Center of The National Museum of Women in the Arts, Washington, DC; University of Wisconsin Memorial Library Rare Books Collection, Madison, Wisconsin; Wexner Collection of Ohio State University. Address: PO Box 821, Woodstock. NY 12498, USA.

SEGERS Gerd, b. 9 Jan 1938, Antwerp, Belgium. Chief Cashier. m. Carol Theijssens, 12 July 1960, 1 daughter. Education: Library School of Antwerp. Publications: Veltro, 1965; Clothilde-Cyclus, 1966; Dagboekje Intiem, 1966; Een Belg in Zwitserland, 1972; Verdwaald ben je er precies pas geweest, 1975; Topografie van een vrouw, 1983; Handschrift van heimwee, 1991. Contributions to: Revolver; Kreatief; HAM; Het Kahier X; Heibel; Yang; Muziek and Woord. Memberships: Review Honest Arts Movements; HC Pernath Foundation; Pen Club, Flanders; Dichters in 't Elzenveld (Poetry International Antwerp), in co-operation with Poetry International Rotterdam. Address: Ludwig Burchardstr 35, B-2050 Antwerp, Belgium.

SEGUI BENNASSAR Antoni, (Taco Nini, A S Bocchoritano), b. 29 Apr 1927, Port de Pollenca, Balears, Spain. Schoolteacher (retired). m. 29 Aug 1953, 2 sons. Education: School Teacher, 1952; National Teacher, 1958; Elementary Teacher in Catalan, 1969; University courses: Catalan, 1978, Spanish Philology, 1979. Appointments: Director, National Unitarian School, 1953-68; Literary Correspondant, Diario de Mallorca, 1959-84; Director, National School, 1968-77; National School Teacher, 1977-89. Publications: Supervivència de Miquel Costa i Liobera, 1973; L'amor en quart creixent, 1977; Un Llorer per a Costa i Liobera, 1982; Bocchoris i els seus forners, 1985; Poesy of Joan Guiraud, 1985; Introductions to: Larry Ashmore's Pollenca Antiga, 1982; J Muntaner's Rost Avall, 1986; My Via-Crucis, 1994. Contributions to: Diario de Mallorca; El Gall; Ponent; Autores-Lectores; Sa Roqueta; Bajari; Lluc; L'Espira; Paris-Baleares; Cala Murta; Tres Branques d'un Mateix Pi; Anuario Poético AHE-81; Programas; Nord; Corona Poètica Felanitx, 1988; Corona Poètica Consolacio, 1989; International Poetry IWA-89. Honours: 1st Prizes: Englantina Felanitx, 1967; Golden Rose, Pau de Castellitx, 1972; Silver Poppy, Sineu, 1980; Xth Spring Poetry Contest, Agrupacion Hispana de Escritores, 1986; 2nd Prizes: Castellitx, 1968, 1979; Coanegra, 1971; Bajari, 1980, 1982, 1983, 1984; Consolacio, 1986, 1988; Gloss Poetry, 1993. Memberships: Agrupacion Hispana de Escritores, Mallorca; International Writers and Artists Association, USA; Obra Cultural Balaer, Mallorca; Centre Cultural, Literario e Artistc, Gazeta del Filgueiras, Portugal; Secretary, Association of Retired Persons 1990-95. Address: C/. Formentor, 2-1er, Apartment 197, 07470 Port de Pollenca, Balears, Spain.

SEIDMAN Hugh, b. 1 Aug 1940, Bronx, New York, USA. Writer; Poet. m. Jayne Holsinger, 2 June 1990. Education: BS, Mathematics, Polytechnic Institute of Brooklyn, 1961; MS, Physics, University of Minnesota, 1964; MFA, Poetry, Columbia University, 1969. Appointments: Faculty, New School for Social Research, 1976-; Assistant Professor, Washington College, 1979; Visiting Lecturer, University of Wisconsin, 1981-, Columbia University, 1985;

Poet-in-Residence, College of William and Mary, 1982; Visiting Poet, Writers Voice, New York City, 1988. Publications: Collecting Evidence, 1970; Blood Lord, 1974; Throne/Falcon/Eye, 1982; People Live, They Have Lives, 1992; Selected Poems, 1965-1995, 1995. Contributions to: New York Times Book Review; Paris Review; Poetry; Atlantic; Pequod; Ironwood; Caterpillar; Ploughshares; Origin; Boulevard. Honours: National Endowment for the Arts Fellowships, 1970, 1972, 1985; Writers Digest Poetry Prize, 1982; Fellowship, New York Foundation for The Arts Fellowships, 1990. Memberships: American PEN; Author's Guild; Author's League; Poetry Society of America. Address: 463 West Street, No H822, New York, NY 10014, USA.

SEIFERLE Rebecca A, b. 14 Dec 1951, Denver, Colorado, USA. Teacher; Poet. m. Phillip Valencia, 11 Aug 1978, 2 daughters, 1 son. Education: BA, English, History, State University of New York, 1982; MFA, Poetry, Warren Wilson College, 1989. Appointments: New Mexico Artists-in-the-Schools, 1986-88; Substitute Teacher, Librarian, Navajo Academy, 1988-89; English Instructor, San Juan College, 1991-. Publications: Trilce, translation from the Spanish poetry of César Vallejo, 1992; The Ripped-Out Seam, poems, 1993; Works in anthologies: New Mexico Poetry Renaissance, 1994, and Saludos: Poemas de Nuevo Mexico, 1995. Contributions to: American Poetry Review; Triquarterly; Calyx; Indiana Review; Taos Review; New Orleans Review; Carolina Quarterly; Nebraska Review; Negative Capability; South Coast Poetry Journal; Blue Mesa Review; Croton Review; American Writer. Honours: Santa Cruz Writers Union Award, 1986; Writers Exchange Award, 1990; George Bogin Memorial Award, 1990. Memberships: Poetry Society of America; Poets and Writers; American Literary Translators Association; Associated Writing Programs. Address: 5602 Tarry Terrace, Farmington, NM 87402, USA.

SELLEN Derek Robert, b. 8 Jan 1948, Kent, England. Teacher. m. Therese Hess, 22 Mar 1975, 2 daughters. Education: BA, English, University of Birmingham, 1969; RSA Diploma in TEFL, 1975; Adult Education Certificate, Open University, 1990. Appointments: Lecturer in English, University of Salamanca; Director of Studies, Stafford House College, Canterbury. Publication: The Dog's-Head Coat, 1996. Contributions to: Agenda; Sunday Telegraph; Poetry Review; Orbis; South East Arts Review; Poetry South East; Ore; Arvon/Sotheby's Competition Anthology; Megaphone; Iron; Alta; Birmingham Post; New Poetry. Honours: Birmingham University Poetry Competition, 1970; Finalist, Cheltenham Festival Competition, 1976; 4th Place National Poetry Competition, 1981; Kent Creative Writing Award, 1986; East Kent Poetry Competition, 1988; Open University Open Competition, 1989; Rhyme International, 1989; Finalist, Canterbury Festival Open Competition, 1994. Membership: Judge, Thanet Poetry Competition, 1990. Address: 5 Lime Kiln Road, Canterbury, Kent CT1 3QH, England.

SELTZER Joanne, b. 21 Nov 1929, Detroit, Michigan, USA. Poet; Writer. m. Stanley Seltzer, 10 Feb 1951, 1 son, 3 daughters. Education: BA, University of Michigan, 1951; MA, College of St Rose, 1978. Appointment: Freelance Writer, 1973-. Publications: Adirondack Lake Poems, 1985; Suburban Landscape, 1988; Inside Invisible Walls, 1989. Contributions to: Village Voice; Painted Bride Quarterly; Blueline; Minnesota Review;MacGuffin; Earth's Daughters; Croton Review; Thirteen; Pegasus Review; Kindred Spirit. Honours: All Nations Poetry Contest, 1978; World Order of Narrative and Formalist Poets Competitions, 1986, 1988, 1990, 1992, 1993, 1994; Tucumcari Literary Review Poetry Contest, 1989. Memberships: Poets and Writers; Associated Writing Programs; American Literary Translators Association; Hudson Valley Writers Guild; Poetry Society of America. Address: 2481 McGovern Drive, Schenectady, NY 12309, USA.

SEOK Lee Yay. See: **RABORG Frederick Ashton, Jr.**

SEQUIERA Desmond, b. 20 Apr 1931, Mangalore, India. Education: Intermediate Degree, Arts and Science, Madras University, 1950; Diploma in Art and Design, Goldsmiths College, London, 1973. Appointments: BEST, Bombay; ARAMCO, Dhahran, Saudi Arabia; Indian High Commission, London; BBC, Broadcasting House, London; Retired, 1991. Publications: Between Times, 1992. Contributions to: Limestone; Litmus; At Waters Edge (Anthology). Honours: Grand Prize, National Library of Poetry, Maryland, USA; Accepted for inclusion in "The Best Poems of 1996" by Library of Congress, USA. Address: 13B Granville Park, London SE13 7DY, England.

SERAZZI AHUMADA Pedro, b. 28 Nov 1944, Chanaral, Chile. Poet; Journalist. Div, 1 son, 1 daughter. Education: Journalist College of Chile, Antofagasta. Appointments: Chief Press, Radio Chanaral, Chanaral City, Radio Diego de Almeida, Diego de Almagro City, Director, Radio Alicanto, El Salvador City, Editor, El Mercurio newspaper, Antofagasta City, Editor, Director, Andino periodicals, El Salvador City, 1966-92. Publications: Al Sur de la Portada, 1976; Diego de Almeida, Pionero del Desierto, 1979; Papito Nunca Mas, 1980; Una Illusion en Caldera, 1982, 1984, 1985, 1990; Tololo Pampa, 1984; Hasta Siempre, Cristian, 1987; Inocencia Perdida, 1991; Mujer Magica, 1992. Contributions to: Magazines: Newspapers. Honours: Medals: Diego de Almagro, Diego de Almagro City, Rafael Torreblanca, Copiano City, Diego de Almeida, Chanaral City; Numerous honours from cities of Ovalle, Santiago de Chile, Copiano, Chanaral, Diego de Almagro. Memberships: Sociedad de Escritores de Chiles, Santiago de Chile; Sociedad de Escritores de Atacama, Copiano; Grupo Literario/turquesa, El Salvador; Circulo Literario Erasmo Bernales Gaete, Chanaral.

SERRAS Dionysis, b. 27 Nov 1947, Greece. Teacher of Greek Literature. Education: Degree in Greek Literature, Athens University, 1971. Publications: Double Voices, 1978; Ode to Dionysius Solomos, 1978; Suns and Nails, 1980; Six Writings for Sepheris, 1987; Antidotes for The Bitter Silence, 1990; Bibliographies of Andrea Kalvo and Ugo Foskolo, 1992; The Poetic March of Lula-Valvi Milona, 1993; Drops in Black White, 1994; Zakynthos in the Greek and Foreign Poetry, anthology, 1994; Editor, literary magazine, Eptanisiaka Filla, 1995. Contributions to: Greek magazines: Lexi; Nea Estia; Sullogi; Epikera; Periplous; Tetramena; Porphyras. Membership: Greek Literary Association. Address: Yfantourgion 39, Zakynthos 29100, Greece.

SETH Vikram, b. 20 June 1952, Calcutta, India. Writer. Education: CCC, BA, Honours, Philosophy, Politics, Economics, 1975, MA, 1978, Oxford, England; MA, Economics, Stanford University, USA, 1977; Diploma, Nanjing University, China, 1982. Appointment: Senior Editor, Stanford University Press, USA, 1984-86. Publications: Mappings, 1980; From Heaven Lake: Travels Through Sinkiang and Tibet, 1983; The Humble Administrator's Garden, 1985; The Golden Gate: A Novel in Verse, 1986; All You Who Sleep Tonight, 1990; Beastly Tales From Here and There (fables in verse), 1992; Three Chinese Poets (translation), 1992; A Suitable Boy (novel), 1993. Contributions to: New Yorker; New Republic; London Magazine; PN Review; Poetry Review; Threepenny Review. Honour: Commonwealth Poetry Prize, 1986. Address: c/o Giles Gordon, Sheil Land Associates, 43 Doughty Street, London WC1N 2LF, England.

SEWERYN Tadeusz. See: **LACZKOWSKI Zdzislaw**.

SEYMOUR-SMITH Martin, b. 24 Apr 1928, London, England. Poet; Writer; Critic; Editor. m. Janet de Glanville, 10 Sept 1952. Education: BA, St Edmund Hall, Oxford, 1951. Appointments: Schoolmaster, 1954-60; Editorial Assistant, The London Magazine, 1955-56; Poetry Editor, Truth Magazine, London, 1955-57, The Scotsman, Edinburgh, 1964-67; Literary Adviser, Hodder and Stoughton, London, 1963-65; General Editor, Gollancz Classic Series, Victor Gollancz Ltd, London, 1967-69. Publications: Poems, with R Taylor and T Hards, 1952; Poems, 1953; Editor, Poetry From Oxford, 1953; All Devils Fading, 1954; Robert Graves, 1956, 1970; Editor, Shakespeare's Sonnets, 1963; Tea With Miss Stockport: 24 Poems, 1963; Bluff Your Way in Literature, 1966, 1972; Editor, Every Man in His Humour, by Ben Jonson, 1966, 1983; Co-Editor, A New Canon of English Poetry, 1967; Fallen Women: A Sceptical Inquiry into The Treatment of Prostitutes, Their Clients and Their Pimps in Literature, 1969; Poets Through Their Letters, 1969; Co-Editor, The Poems of Andrew Marvell, 1969; Editor, Longer Elizabethan Poems, 1970; Inside Poetry, with J Reeves, 1970; Reminiscences of Norma: Poems 1963-1970, 1971; Guide to Modern World Literature, in USA as, Funk and Wagnall's Guide to World Literature, 1973, 3rd edition, 1986; Sex and Society, 1975; Who's Who in Twentieth-Century Literature, 1976; Editor, Selected Poems, by Walt Whitman, 1976; The New Astrologer, 1981; Robert Graves: His Life and Work, 1982; Rudyard Kipling, 1987. Everyman Dictionary of Fictional Characters, 1990; From Bed to Verse: An Anthology of Poems About Lust, 1995. Address: 36 Holliers Hill, Bexhill-on-Sea, Sussex TN40 2DD, England.

SHAFRIR-STILLMAN Moshe D, b. 1935, Tel Aviv, Israel. Poet. m. 3 sons. Education: BSc, Geology and Chemistry, Hebrew University of Jerusalem. Publications include: Hebrew Poems Collections: Belated Rain, 1967; To Ask and to Answer, 1975; The End of the Game, 1983; Presentation, 1989; Belated Loves, 1995; The Promise of Rain, with English translations, 1995. Contributions to: Numerous

periodicals and daily newspapers. Memberships: The Hebrew Writers Association of Israel; PEN Centre Israel. Address: 67 Pinkas Street, Tel Aviv 62157, Israel.

SHAHRYAR Akhlaq Mohd Khan, b. 16 June 1936, Aligarh, India. Teacher. m. 3 Nov 1968, 2 sons, 1 daughter. Education: BA, 1958; MA, 1961; PhD, 1970. Appointments: Literary Assistant; Lecturer; Reader; Professor. Publications: Ism-e-Azam, 1965; Satwa Dar, 1970; Hijr Ke Moasm, 1978; Khuab Ka Darband Hai, 1985; Qafle Yadoon, 1987; The Gateway Dreams Are Closed, 1990. Contributions to: Shabkhoon; Funoon; Adabi Duniya. Honours: UP Urdu Academy and Sahitya Academy Awards, 1975, 1985, 1987. Memberships: General Council and Urdu Board, Sahitya Academy; Sarswati Samman; Iqbal Samman; Editor: Shairo Hikmat Poetry Quarterly and Fikro Nazak Research Quarterly. Address: Department of Urdu, Aligarh Muslim University, Aligarh, UP India.

SHAKESPEARE Eileen Margaret, (Nina Shakespeare, E M Speare), b. 4 July 1929, London, England. Div, 1 son, 1 daughter. Education: Currently studying for Spanish Diploma, Institute of Linguists. Publications: Poetry, 1985; Poems, 1986; Poetry, 1986; Selected Poems, 1986. Contributions to: Outposts; First Time; Pause; Anthologies: Poetry International, American Poetry Association. Memberships: Poetry Society; National Poetry Foundation; Poetry Book Society; Writer's News. Address: 22 Webster Close, Clover Hill Village, Bowthorpe, Norwich NR5 9DF, England.

SHAMBAUGH Frances Joan Dibble, (J D Shambaugh, Joan Dibble Shambaugh, Joan Shambaugh), b. 14 Mar 1928, Michigan, USA. Writer. m. Benjamin Shambaugh, 26 Dec 1950, 2 sons, 1 daughter. Education: AB, Sociology and Education, Duke Women's College, Duke University, 1949; MEd, Lesley College Graduate School. Publications: Poems From Lincoln Hill, 1989; She Who Walks With Trees, 1993. Contributions to: Lincoln Review; Cottage Press; Anthology From Lincoln Hill. Honours: Readings and Presentations at various venues, 1989, 1991. Memberships: Poetry Society of America; New England Poetry Society. Address: PO Box 552, Hardwick, VT 05843, USA.

SHAMLOU Ahmad, (A Bamdad), b. 12 Dec 1925, Tehran, Iran. Poet; Writer; Journalist; Translator. m. Rita Aida Sarkissian, 7 Apr 1964. Appointments: Editor, Ketab-e Hafte, 1962, Khushe, 1967; Lecturer, University of Science and Technology, 1971; Research Associate, Iranian Academy of Languages, 1972-76; Head of Social Research, BuAli University, 1975-76; Editor, Ketab-e Jom-e, 1979-80; Visiting Professor, University of California, Berkeley, 1980. Publications: The Fresh Air, 1957; Mirror Garden, 1959; Moments and Ever, 1963; Aida in the Mirror, 1963; Aida, The Tree, The Dagger and the Memory, 1966; Phoenix in the Rain, 1967; Elegies of the Earth, 1969; Blossoming in the Mist, 1971; Abraham in the Fire, 1972; Dagger in the Dish, 1978; The Small Songs of Exile, 1981; No Appreciated Eulogys, 1991. Contributions to: 40 other volumes including translations; Ketab-e Kutche, An Encyclopaedia of the Persian Folklore; Several magazines, reviews and periodicals. Honour: Human Rights Watch Fund for Free Expression, USA, 1991. Membership: Senior Fellow, Board of Directors, Writers Association of Iran. Address: c/o Entesharate Mazyar, 1430 Enghelab, opposite Tehran University, 1st Floor #4, Tehran 13147, Iran.

SHANGE Ntozake (born Paulette Williams), b. 18 Oct 1948, Trenton, New Jersey, USA. Poet; Dramatist; Writer; Associate Professor of Drama. 1 daughter. Education: BA, Barnard College, 1970; MA, University of Southern California, Los Angeles, 1973. Appointments: Faculty, Sonoma State College, Rohnert Park, California, 1973-75, Mills College, Oakland, California, 1975, City College of the City University of New York, 1975, Douglass College, New Brunswick, New Jersey, 1978; Artist-in-Residence, Equinox Theater, Houston, 1981-; Associate Professor of Drama, University of Houston, 1983-. Publications: Poetry: Melissa and Smith, 1976; Natural Disasters and Other Festive Occasions, 1977; Nappy Edges, 1978; Some Men, 1981; A Daughter's Geography, 1983; From Okra to Greens, 1984; Ridin' the Moon in Texas: Word Paintings, 1988; The Love Space Demands: A Continuing Saga, 1992; Plays: For Colored Girls Who Have Considered Suicide When the Rainbow is Enuf, 1976; A Photograph: Lovers-in-Motion, 1981; Spell #7, 1981; Boogie Woogie Landscapes, 1981; Fiction: Sassafrass: A Novella, 1977; Sassafrass, Cypress, and Indigo, 1982; Betsey Brown, 1985; Liliane: Resurrection of the Daughter, 1995; Non-fiction: See No Evil: Prefaces, Essays, and Accounts 1976-1983, 1984. Honours: New York Drama Critics Circle

Award, 1977; Obie Awards, 1977, 1980; Columbia University Medal of Excellence, 1981; Guggenheim Fellowship, 1981. Address: c/o St Martin's Press, 175 Fifth Avenue, New York, NY 10010, USA.

SHAO Yan Xiang, (Han Yeping), b. 10 June 1933, Beijing, China. Journalist. m. Xie Wenxiu, 27 Jan 1957, 1 son, 1 daughter. Education: L'Universite Franci-Chinoise, 1948-49. Appointments: Managing Editor, 1979-81, Vice Chief Editor, 1981-86, Shi Kan Poetry Magazine. Publications: Singing of the City of Beijing, 1951; Going to the Faraway Place, 1955; To My Comrades, 1956; The Campfire in August, 1956; A Reed Pipe, 1957; Love Song to History, 1980; Making Farewell Smilingly to the Seventies, 1981; At the Faraway Place, 1981; Bearing Witness to Youth, 1982; In Full Blossom Lake Flowers, 1983; Flower Late in Blossom, 1984; Time and Wine, 1985; Collection of Long Lyrics by Shao Yan Xiang, 1985; There's Joy, There's Sorrow, 1988; Selected Poems by Shao Yan Xiang, 1995. Contributions to: People's Literature; Shi kan; Remoin Ribao; Guangming Ribao, 1949-89. Honours: National New Poetry Competition Prize, 1983, 1986. Memberships: PEN Beijing; Presidum, Chinese Writers Association. Address: A15-3-401 Hufang Road, Beijing 100052, China.

SHAPCOTT Jo(anne Amanda), b. 24 Mar 1953, London, England. Poet. Education: Foundation Scholar, 1972-76, 1st Class Honours, English Literature and Language, 1976, Trinity College, Dublin; St Hilda's College, Oxford, 1976-78; Harkness Fellow, Harvard University, 1978-80. Appointments: Lecturer, English, Rolle College, Exmouth, 1980-82; Education Officer, South Bank Centre, London, 1984-91; Judith E Wilson Fellow in Creative Writing, Cambridge University, 1991. Publications: Electroplating the Baby, 1988; Phrase Book, 1992. Contributions to: Times; Sunday Times; New Statesman; Poetry Review; Times Literary Supplement; Verse; Southern Review. Honours: 1st Prize, National Poetry Competition, 1981, 1991; Commonwealth Prize for, Electroplating the Baby, 1988; Autumn Choice for, Phrase Book, Poetry Book Society, 1992. Address: 62a Meadow Road, London SW8 1PP, England.

SHAPCOTT Thomas William, b. 21 Mar 1935, Australia. Writer; Administrator. m. (1) Margaret Hodge, 1960, (2) Judith Rodriguez, 1982, 1 son, 3 daughters. Education: Associate, 1960, Fellow, 1970, Australian Society of Accountants; BA, University of Queensland, 1968; Fellow, Certified Practising Accountant, 1991. Appointments: Public Accountant, 1960-78; Writer, 1978-83, 1990-92; Director, Literature Board, Australia Council, 1983-90; Executive Director, National Book Council, 1992-. Publications include: Sonnets, 1960-1963, 1963; A Taste of Salt Water, 1967; Inwards to the Sunsham, 1969; Fingers at Air, 1969; Begin With Walking, 1973; Shabbytown Calendar, 1975; 7th Avenue Poems, 1976; Selected Poems, 1978; Make The Old Man Sing, 1980; Welcome!, 1983; Travel Dice, 1987; Selected Poems, 1956-1988, 1989; In The Beginning, 1990; The City of Home, 1995; Editor: New Impulses in Australian Poetry, with R Hall, 1967; Australian Poetry Now, 1970; Contemporary American and Australian Poetry, 1975. Contributions to: Australian; Meanjin; Sydney Morning Herald; Australian Poetry; Overland; Sydney Review; New York Times; Poetry Chicago. Honours: Grace Leven Prize, 1961; Sir Thomas White Memorial Prize, 1967; Sidney Myer Charity Trust Awards, 1967, 1969; Churchill Fellowship, 1972; Canada-Australia Literary Prize, 1978; Officer, Order of Australia, 1989; Hon DLitt, Macquarie University, 1989; Gold Wreath, Struga International Poetry Festival, 1989; Christopher Brennan Award for Poetry, 1994. Memberships: Treasurer, Australian Society of Authors; International PEN; Founding Committee, SPACLALS; Chairman, Australia Book Review; ASAL. Literary Agent: Cameron Creswell Agency, Sydney, Australia. Address: PO Box 231, Mont Albert, Victoria 3127, Australia.

SHAPIRO David (Joel), b. 2 Jan 1947, Newark, New Jersey, USA. Violinist; Poet; Art Critic; Teacher. m. Lindsay Stamm, 1970, 1 child. Education: BA, 1968, PhD, 1973, Columbia University; BA, 1970, MA, 1974, Clare College, Cambridge. Appointments: Violinist in various orchestras, 1963-; Instructor and Assistant Professor of English, Columbia University, 1972-80; Visiting Professor, Brooklyn College, City University of New York, 1979, Princeton University, 1982-83; Visiting Professor, Cooper Union, New York City, 1980-; Full Professor, Art History, William Paterson, 1996-. Publications: Poetry: January: A Book of Poems, 1965; Poems from Deal, 1969; A Man Holding an Acoustic Panel, 1971; The Page-Turner, 1973; Lateness, 1978; To an Idea, 1983; House, Blown Apart, 1988; After a Lost Original, 1990; Other: John Ashbery: An Introduction to the Poetry, 1979; Jim Dine: Painting What One Is, 1981; Jasper Johns: Drawings

1954-1984, 1984; Mondrian Flowers, 1990; Alfred Leslie: The Killing Cycle (with Judith Stein), 1991; Editor: An Anthology of New York Poets (with Ron Padgett), 1970. Honours: Bread Loaf Writers Conference Robert Frost Fellowship, 1965; Ingram-Merrill Foundation Fellowship, 1967; Book-of-the-Month Club Fellowship, 1968; Kellett Fellow, Clare College, Cambridge, 1968-70; Creative Artists Public Service Grant, 1974; Morton Dauwen Zabel Award, 1977; National Endowment for the Humanities Fellowships, 1979; National Endowment for the Arts Grants, 1980; Grant for Poetry from the Foundation for Contemporary Performance Art. Address: 3001 Henry Hudson Parkway, Riverdale, NY 10463, USA.

SHAPIRO Harvey, b. 27 Jan 1924, Chicago, Illinois, USA. Poet; Editor. m. 2 July 1953, 2 sons. Education: BA, Yale University, 1947; MA, Columbia, 1948. Appointments: Staff of Commentary, and The New Yorker, 1955-57, New York Times Magazine, 1957-64; Assistant Editor, 1964-75, Editor, 1975-83, New York Times Book Review; Deputy Editor, New York Times Magazine, 1983-. Publications: The Eye, 1953; The Book, 1955; Mountain Fire Thornbush, 1961; Battle Report, 1966; This World, 1971; Lauds, 1975; Lauds and Nightsounds, 1978; The Light Holds, 1984; National Cold Storage Company, New and Selected Poems, 1988; A Day's Portion, 1994. Contributions to: Poetry; Paris Review; Poetry East; Tel Aviv Review; Nation; Quarterly Review of Literature; Mudfish; The Atlantic; Partisan Review; Hanging Loose; New Yorker. Honour: Rockefeller Grant for Poetry, 1967. Address: The New York Times Magazine, 229 West 43rd Street, New York, NY 10036, USA.

SHAPIRO Karl (Jay), b. 10 Nov 1913, Baltimore, Maryland, USA. Professor of English (retired); Poet; Writer. m. Sophie Wilkins, 25 Apr 1985. Education: Johns Hopkins University, 1937-39. Appointments: Consultant in Poetry, Library of Congress, Washington, DC, 1946-47; Associate Professor, Johns Hopkins University, 1947-50; Editor, Poetry, 1950-56, Prairie Schooner, 1956-66; Professor of English, University of Nebraska, 1956-66, University of Illinois, Circle Campus, Chicago, 1966-68, University of California at Davis, 1968-85. Publications: Poetry: Poems, 1935; New and Selected Poems, 1940-46, 1946; Trial of a Poet, 1947; Poems, 1940-53, 1953; Poems of a Jew, 1958; Selected Poems, 1968; White-Haired Lover, 1968; Adult Bookstore, 1976; Collected Poems, 1940-78, 1978; New and Selected Poems, 1940-86, 1987. Novel: Edsel, 1971. Non-Fiction: Beyond Criticism, 1953; In Defense of Ignorance, 1960; Prose Keys to Modern Poetry (with James E Miller Jr and Bernice Slote), 1962; The Bourgeois Poet, 1964; A Prosody Handbook (with Robert Beum), 1964; To Abolish Children, 1968; The Poetry Wreck, 1975; The Younger Son (autobiography), 1988; Reports of My Death (autobiography), 1990; The Old Horsefly, 1993. Honours: Jeanette S Davis Prize, 1942; Levinson Prize, 1943; Contemporary Poetry Prize, 1943; Pulitzer Prize in Poetry, 1945; Shelley Memorial Prize, 1945; Guggenheim Fellowships, 1945-46, 1953-54; Bollingen Prize for Poetry, 1969; Robert Kirsch Award, Los Angeles Times, 1989; Charity Randall Citation, 1990. Memberships: American Academy of Arts and Letters; American Academy of Arts and Sciences; PEN. Address: 211 West 106th Street, No 11C, New York, NY 10025, USA.

SHAPIRO Myra, b. 21 May 1932, New York, USA. Writer. m. Harold M Shapiro, 15 Feb 1953, 2 daughters. Education: BA, University of Tennessee, 1968; MA, Middlebury College, 1973; MFA, Vermont College, 1993. Appointments: Librarian, Chattanooga Public Library, 1965-67; Teacher of English, Notre Dame High School, 1972-77; Instructor in English, Dalton Junior College, 1970's. Publication: Education for Peace: Testimonies From World Religions, 1987. Contributions to: Ploughshares; Ohio Review; Painted Bride Quarterly; Kalliope; Poetry Miscellany; Harvard Review. Honours: McDowell Colony Fellowships, 1984, 1987; Dylan Thomas Poetry Award, The New School, 1981; Selected Reader, Folger Shakespeare Library Midday Muse, 1983. Memberships: Board, Poets House, New York; Poetry Society of America; International Women's Writing Guild. Address: 111 4th Avenue, Apt 12-1, New York, NY 10003, USA.

SHARAT CHANDRA Gubbi Shankara Chetty, (Jean Parker), b. 5 Mar 1938, Nanjangud, India. Professor; Poet. m. Jane Sharat Chandra, 8 Jan 1966, 1 son, 2 daughters. Education: BA, 1956; BL, 1958; MS, 1964; LLM, 1966; MFA, 1968. Appointments: Assistant Professor of English, Washington State University, 1972-80; Fulbright Professor, Malaysia, 1978, Bangladesh, 1989; Assistant Professor, 1983-87, Associate Professor, 1987-92, Professor, 1992-, English, University of Missouri, Kansas City. Publications: April in Nanjangud, 1971; Once or Twice, 1974; The Ghost of Meaning, 1978; Heirloom,

1982; Family of Mirrors, 1993; Immigrants of Loss, 1993. Contributions to: Hippo, UK; The Independent; Encounter; London Magazine; Stand; Outposts Quarterly; Poetry Review; Transatlantic Review; Gallery; Poetry; American Poetry Review; New Criterion; Nation; Paris Review; Iowa Review; Partisan Review. Honours: Artist-in-School Award, National Endowment for Humanities; Award in Poetry, Florida State Arts Council, 1981. Membership: Associated Writing Program, USA. Address: 9916 Juniper, Overland Park, KS 66207, USA.

SHARMA Indra Kumar, b. 1 Jan 1932, Shamli, India. Teaching. m. Sushila Sharma, 1958, 3 sons, 1 daughter. Education: BA, 1953; MA, 1955. Appointments: Lecturer in English, Rajkot, 1955-56; Lecturer, Maharaja's College, Jaipur, 1956-62; Assistant Professor, 1962-83, Associate Professor, 1983-91, retired 1991, University of Rajasthan, Jaipur. Publications: The Shifting Sand-Dunes, 1976; The Native Embers, 1986; Dharamsala and Other Poems, 1993. Contributions to: Thought; Poet; New Quest; Poetry Time; Creative Forum; Poetcrit; Byword; Commonwealth Quarterly; Kavi India; Poetry; Journal of Indian Writing in English; New Letters, USA. Honours: 1st Prize and Gold Medal, Skylark International Poetry Competition, 1977; Honorary DLitt, World University, NY, USA, 1979; Honoured by Rajasthan Sahitya Akademi, 1979. Memberships: World Poetry Society Inter-Continental; Executive Member, Rajasthan Sahitya Akademi; Vice President, Rajasthan Bhasa Prachar Sabha; Associate Editor, Indian Book Chronicle. Address: 1-27 SFS, Mansarovar, Jaipur 302 020, India.

SHARMA Maha Nand, b. 11 July 1924, Bulandshahr, UP India. Teacher. m. Krishna Sharma, 7 Dec 1945, 2 sons, 3 daughters. Education: MA, English Literature, 1950; PhD, 1967. Appointments: Teacher, A.S. Jat High School, 1948-50; Teacher, D.A.V Inter College, 1950-51; Lecturer in Education, Cornation Hindu College, 1951-52; Lecturer in English, S.S.V Degree College, 1952; Lecturer in English, A.S. College, 1952-55; Head, Department of English, A.S. College, 1955-69; Lecturer in English, Meerut University, 1967-82; Reader in English, Meerut University, 1982-85; Retired 1985. Publications: The Pageant of Seasons, 1956; Flowers And Buds, 1984; A Rudraksha Rosary and Other Poems, 1987; A Spiritual Warrior, 1991; Scattered Leaves, 1991; Divine Glimpses, 1996; Gushing Streams, 1996. Contributions to: Kavita India; Metverse Muse. Address: Shiva Kutir D-29, Shastri Nagar, Meerut, UP, India.

SHARP Norman Churchill Craig, b. 6 Nov 1933, Glasgow, Scotland. University Professor. m. (1) 1 son, 1 daughter, (2) Dorothy McNeill, 3 Jan 1976, 1 son. Education: BVMS, MRCVS, Glasgow, 1956; PhD, Glasgow, 1964; FIBiol, 1988; FPEA, FBASES, 1994. Appointments: Lecturer in Veterinary Pathology, 1956-70, Exercise Physiology, 1970-87; Director, Physiological Services, British Olympic Medical Centre, 1987-92; Professor of Sports Science, University of Limerick, 1992-95; Professor of Sports Science, Brunel University, 1995-. Contributions to: Scotsman Newspaper; Chapman Poetry Journal; Radio Clyde as Scottish Poetry Critic. Membership: Scottish Poetry Library Association. Address: 14A Randolph Crescent, Edinburgh EH3 7TT, Scotland.

SHASHOUA-GABBAY Jacqueline, b. 1938, Iraq. Poetess; Writer. m. Salim Shashoua, Oct 1973, 1 daughter. Education: Graduate, Hebrew Literature and Theatrical Arts, Tel Aviv University. Appointments: Teacher, Headmistress for special education school; Stage Director; Managed drama class and literature work groups; Translator in Arabic and Hebrew for Poets and Writers; Interviewer and Conductor of cultural and literary evenings; Presenter of literary programmes and radio programmes. Publications: Another Truth, 1987; In Turbulence of the Individual, 1988, 1989; The Only One, 1991; In the Shade of the Fig Tree, 1997 (in print). Contributions to: A Song of Life, Israeli World Congress of Poets, World Poetry, 1994, 1995, 1996; Anthology of Poetess; Voices Poets in Israel Today; Newspapers and periodicals include: Steps; Mariv; Psifas; Namat; This Week Communication; Mifgash; Mahut; Haouma; Afikim. Honour: Association for Literature and Art Award, 1990. Memberships: Chairwoman, Ramat Gan Israel Branch, International Friends of Literature; Chairwoman, Creative Women's Organisation Namat, Ramat Gan District; Editorial Board, Hebrew Arabic Quarterly, Mifgash. Address: Eked Bar Kochba Street 29, Tel-Aviv, Israel; Tammuz Heh Baieyar Street 12, Tel-Aviv, Israel.

SHATTUCK Roger (Whitney), b. 20 Aug 1923, New York, New York, USA. Writer; Translator; Poet; Editor; Professor. m. Nora Ewing White, 20 Aug 1949, 1 son, 3 daughters. Education: BA, Yale University, 1947. Appointments: Reporter, Chicago Daily News, Paris Office, 1948-49; Assistant Trade Editor, Harcourt, Brace and Co, New York City, 1949-50; Society of Fellows 1950-53, Instructor in French 1953-56, Harvard University; Assistant Professor 1956-59, Associate Professor of Romance Languages 1959-62, Professor of French and English 1962-71, Chairman, Department of French and Italian 1968-71, University of Texas at Austin; Commonwealth Professor of French, University of Virginia, 1974-88; University Professor, Professor of Modern Foreign Languages, Boston University, 1988-; Lecturer at many universities, colleges, art museums and other venues. Publications include: The Forbidden Experiment: The Story of the Wild Boy of Aveyron, 1980; The Innocent Eye: On Literature and the Arts, 1984; Forbidden Knowledge: From Prometheus to Pornography, 1996. Poetry: Half Tame, 1964. Contributions to: Essays, short stories and poems in various publications. Honours: Guggenheim Fellowship, 1958-59; Fulbright Research Fellow, 1958-59; American Council of Learned Societies Research Fellow, 1969-70; National Book Award, 1975; American Academy and Institute of Arts and Letters Award, 1987; Doctorate honoris causa, University of Orleans, France, 1990. Memberships: American Academy of Arts and Sciences, Fellow, 1990; Association of Literary Scholars and Critics, president 1995-96. Address: c/o University Professors Program, Boston University, 745 Commonwealth Avenue, Boston, MA 02215, USA.

SHAW Robert Burns, b. 16 July 1947, Mount Holyoke, Philadelphia, Pennsylvania, USA. Professor of English. m. Hilary Olenchuk, 21 June 1969, 1 son, 1 daughter. Education: AB, Harvard College, 1969; MPhil, 1973, PhD, 1974, Yale University Graduate School. Appointments: Lecturer in English, Harvard University, 1974-76; Assistant Professor, 1976-78, Associate Professor, 1980-83, Yale University; Associate Professor of English, 1983-91, Professor of English, 1991-, Mount Holyoke College. Publications: Curious Questions, 1970; In Witness, 1972; Comforting the Wilderness, 1977; The Wonder of Seeing Double, 1988. Contributions to: Poetry; PN Review; Partisan Review; Yale Review; Paris Review; Shenandoah; Kenyon Review. Honours: George Dillon Prize, 1970; National Endowment for the Arts Fellowship, 1987; Ingram Merrill Fellowship, 1990; James Boatwright Prize for Poetry, 1992. Memberships: PEN American Center; Poetry Society of America. Address: Department of English, Mount Holyoke College, South Hadley, MA 01075, USA.

SHECK Laurie, b. 7 Oct 1953, New York, New York, USA. Professor. m. James Peck, 30 May 1981, 1 daughter. Education: BA, Antioch College, 1975; MFA, University of Iowa, 1978. Appointments: Lecturer, Assistant Professor, 1981-90, Lecturer, Associate, Professor, 1990-, English Department, Rutgers University. Publications: Amarenth, 1981; Lo At Night, 1990. Contributions to: New Yorker; Nation; Paris Review; New York Times Book Review. Address: c/o English Department, Murray Hall CAC, Rutgers University, New Brunswick, NJ 08903, USA.

SHEER Sita, b. 20 July 1920, Turkey. Translator; Writer. m. Isaac Sheer, 6 Aug 1950, 2 daughters. Appointments: Various administrative posts; Sworn Translator, Supreme Court of South Africa. Contributions to: Modern Poetry in Translation; Orbis; Aki Yerushalayim; Jewish Quarterly. Memberships: Institute of Translation and Interpreting; PEN International; PEN South Africa; English PEN; Society of Authors; Translators Association; Society of Women Writers and Journalists. Address: 26 Fairview Court, Linksway, Holders Hill Road, London NW4 1JS, England.

SHEERIN Joe, b. 6 Mar 1941. Teacher. m. 29 Aug 1970, 2 sons. Education: BA, Honours, German, 1969; MA, German, 1970; BA, Honours, English Literature, 1974. Publications: Four, 1976; Poetry Dimensions, 1982; A Crack in The Ice: New Poems. Contributions to: Poetry Review; Poetry Ireland Review; Honest Ulsterman; Paris Review. Address: Colchester College, North Hill, Colchester, Essex, England.

SHEILA. See: **GUJRAL Sheila.**

SHEPARD Neil, b. 29 Jan 1951, Fitchburg, Massachusetts, USA. Professor of Literature and Poetry Writing. m. Kate Riley, 15 Sept 1990. Education: BA, University of Vermont, 1973; MA, Colorado State University, 1976; PhD, Ohio University, 1980. Appointments: Instructor, Louisiana State University, 1980-82; Assistant Professor of Creative Writing and Literature, Rider College, New Jersey, 1983-85; Associate Professor, Creative Writing and Literature, 1985-92, Professor of Literature and Poetry Writing, 1995-, Johnson State

College, VT; Editor, Green Mountains Review Literary Magazine; Writing Co-Ordinator, The Vermont Studio Center Artists Colony. Publication: Scavenging the Country for a Heartbeat, 1993. Contributions to: Yearbook of American Poetry, 1983; Anthology of Magazine Verse, 1986; Antioch Review; Denver Quarterly; Poetry East; Chelsea; Kansas Quarterly; Laurel Review; Nimrod; Poetry Now; Southern Review; AWP Chronicle; Ascent; Another Chicago Magazine; Seneca Review; Southwest Review; Western Humanities Review. Honours: Poetry Fellowships: New Jersey Council on The Arts, 1984; Pennsylvania Council on the Arts, 1985; Vermont Council on The Arts, 1986; 1st Book Prize, Mid-List Press, 1992. Memberships: Associated Writing Programs; Modern Language Association. Address: RD 2, Box 455A, Johnson, VT 05656, USA.

SHEPPERSON Janet Catherine, b. 15 Apr 1954, Edinburgh, Scotland. Writer. m. Nick Acheson, 22 July 1983. Education: MA, Honours, 2:1, English, 1976, Post Graduate Certificate in Primary Education, 1978, Aberdeen University. Appointments: Trainee Journalist, Community Service Volunteer, 1976-77; Primary Teacher, 1978-85; Administrative Assistant, 1987-88; Currently involved in Writers-in-Schools Scheme, Northern Ireland Arts Council, also teaching Creative Writing; Poems read on BBC TV and Schools Radio. Publications: Trio 5, with Martin Mooney and Dennis Greig, 1987; A Ring With a Black Stone, 1989; Madonna of the Spaces, 1994; The Aphrodite Stone, 1995. Contributions to: Southern Review, USA; Poetry Review; Stand; Rialto; Poetry Wales; Poetry Ireland; Honest Ulsterman; Cyphers; Salmon; Belfast Telegraph; Ulster Newsletter; Gown; Fortnight, Northern Ireland; Selection in Canadian anthology, Map-Makers' Colours, 1988. Honours: Calder Prize for Verse, Aberdeen, 1976; Small prize, Bridport Arts Centre Competition, 1989. Memberships: Poetry Society; Poetry Ireland. Address: 30 Ravenhill Park, Belfast 6, Northern Ireland.

SHERIFF Bat-Sheva, b. 28 June 1937, Tel Aviv, Israel. Ministry of Education and Culture Inspector. m. Mordechai Manfred Segal, 1962, 2 sons. Education: Teacher's Diploma, University of Tel Aviv; BA, Philosophy and Literature, Hebrew University, Jerusalem. Appointments: Teacher, Secondary School, 1956-71; Director, Cultural Project for underprivileged Youth in Development Areas, 1971-86; Editor, Monthly Journal for Inspectors; Inspector of Ministry of Education and Culture. Publications: Poems, 1956; Not All The Rivers, 1964; Love Poems, 1972; Persuasive Words, 1974; Festive Poems, 1981; Ashes Instead of Bread, 1982; By Necessity and by Right, 1986; Letters to Bat-Sheva, 1990. Videos: Poems, 1984; Poems, 1985; Home in Jerusalem, 1990; Idenity Card, 1993. Contributions to: Newspapers: Haaretz, Masa, Davar, Maariv; Also to periodicals, radio and television. Memberships: Executive Committee, Hebrew Writers Association; Press Council of Israel; PEN Israel. Address: 10 Emek Refaim, PO Box 7353, Jerusalem 91072, Israel.

SHERIFF Sultan D, b. 6 July 1947, Tiruchi, India. Professor of Biochemistry. m. 23 Sept 1974, 1 son. Education: BSc, MSc, PhD; FACB (USA); FIC (USA); FAZ, Fuwai. Appointments: Lecturer, Assistant, Associate Professor of Biochemistry. Publication: Rising Stars, 1991. Contributions to: Mirror; Medical Journals; Newsletter of Roundtable of India; Some local magazines. Membership: Fellow, United Writers Forum of India. Address: 25 Habib Street, Salem 63001, TN, India.

SHERMAN William David, b. 24 Dec 1940, Philadelphia, Pennsylvania, USA. Poet; Writer. m. Barbara Beaumont, 22 July 1970, div 1978. Education: AB, Temple University, 1962; MA, 1964, PhD, 1968, State University of New York, Buffalo; Dickinson School of Law, 1974-75. Appointments: Teacher, Instructor, and Lecturer in USA and England; Editor; Publisher; Poetry Readings. Publications: The Landscape of Contemporary Cinema (with Leon Lewis), 1967; The Cinema of Orson Welles, 1967; The Springbok (poems), 1973; The Hard Sidewalk (poems), 1974; The Horses of Gwyddno Garanhir (poems), 1976; Mermaids, I, 1977, revised edition, 1985, and II, 1985 (poems); Heart Attack and Spanish Songs in Mandaine Land (poems), 1981; Duchamp's Door (poems), 1983; She Wants to Go to Pago-Pago, 1986; The Tahitian Journals, 1990; A Tale for Tusitala, 1993. Contributions to: Anthologies; Numerous poems, articles and reviews in periodicals. Address: 4805 B Street, Philadelphia, PA 19120, USA.

SHERWOOD Andrea Hilary, b. 27 Sept 1962, Australia. Teacher. m. Brett A M Graham, 15 Aug 1987, div 1996, 1 daughter. Education: BA, Literature; DipEd, Double Method English;

Postgraduate Diploma in Linguistics. Appointments: Emergency Secondary Teacher of English. Publications: Bibliography for Australian Multicultural Writers; One Siren or Another (poetry collection), 1994; Remember the Sound of Footprints (verse narrative), 1996. Contributions to: Meanjin; Bulletin; Southerly; Imago; Otis Rush; Brave New World; Mattoid; Kangaroo 11; Working Titles, UK; New Hope International Writing, UK; Carlton Writers; Overland; Hermes; Linq; Poetry Australia; Fine Line; The Wasteland; Hecate; Going Down Swinging; Prints; New Republica; Westerly; Salt; Verandah. Honours: Grant, Australia Council Literature Board, 1991; Grant, Ministry of The Arts, Victoria, 1991; Anne Elder Award for Best First Collection of Poetry in Australia, 1994; Fellowship B, Australia Council Literature Board, 1996. Memberships: Fellowship of Australian Writers; Victorian Writers Centre; Australian Society of Authors; Poet's Union, Five Bells. Address: 36 Glenlyou Road, Brunswick, Victoria 3056, Australia.

SHIBASAKI Sosuku. See: **CIVASAQUI José.**

SHIBASAWA Naoya. See: **GOTO Takahiko.**

SHIELDS Carol Ann, b. 2 June 1935, Oak Park, Illinois, USA (Canadian citizen, 1974). Professor; Author; Poet. m. Donald Hugh Shields, 20 July 1957, 1 son, 4 daughters. Education: BA, Hanover College, 1957; MA, University of Ottawa, 1975. Appointments: Editorial Assistant, Canadian Slavonic Papers, Ottawa, 1972-74; Lecturer, University of Ottawa, 1976-77, University of British Columbia, 1978-90; Professor, University of Manitoba, 1980-; The Canada Council, 1994-. Publications: Fiction: Small Ceremonies, 1976; The Box Garden, 1977; Happenstance, 1980; A Fairly Conventional Woman, 1982; Various Miracles (short stories), 1985; Swann: A Mystery, 1987; The Orange Fish (short stories), 1989; A Celibate Season (with Blanche Howard), 1991; The Republic of Love, 1992; The Stone Diaries, 1993. Poetry: Others, 1972; Intersect, 1974; Coming to Canada, 1992. Plays: Women Waiting, 1983; Departures and Arrivals, 1984; Thirteen Hands, 1993; Fashion Power Guilt (with Catherine Shields), 1995. Honours: Canada Council Grants, 1973, 1976, 1978, 1986; Canadian Authors Association Fiction Prize, 1976; Canadian Broadcasting Corporation Prizes, 1983, 1984; National Magazine Award, 1985; Arthur Ellis Award, 1987; Governor-General's Award, 1993; National Book Critics Circle Award, 1994, 1995; Pulitzer Prize in Fiction, 1995; Honorary Doctorates, Universities of Ottawa, Winnipeg, Hanover College, British Columbia, 1995; Lire Magazine Book of the Year, France, 1995. Memberships: Jane Austen Society; PEN; Writers Guild of Manitoba; Writers Union of Canada; Canada Council. Address: 701-237 Wellington Crescent, Winnipeg, Manitoba R3M 0A1, Canada.

SHIELDS David Andrew, b. 6 Mar 1964, Folkestone, England. Bookseller. Education: Worcester College, Oxford, 1983-87; MA (Oxon), Classics. Appointments: Organiser, Kent Literary Festival Poetry Competition, 1988; Publicity Officer, Kent Literary Festival, 1990. Publication: Moods and Tenses, 1992. Contributions to: Literary Review; Independent. Address: 14 Herdson Road, Folkestone, Kent CT20 2PB, England.

SHIELDS Michael Joseph, b. 29 Oct 1938. Writer; Translator; Poet. Appointments: Associate Editor, Here Now, 1970-73; Editor, Orbis Magazine, 1980-; Editor, Professional Translator and Interpreter, 1989-93; Consultant Editor, International Who's Who in Poetry, 7th edition, 1993-94. Publications: Helix, 1970; Translations include: Superfine Powders, by Ichinose, 1991; Offshore Structures, vols I & 2, by Clauss, 1991; Submarines of The US Navy, by Terzibaschitsch, 1991; Dubbel, Engineers Handbook, 1992; Fighters of The Luftwaffe, 1992; Bombers of the Luftwaffe, 1993. Contributions to: Outposts; Littack; Writer; New Headland; Poetry Nottingham; Readers Digest; Weekend; Writers News; Publisher. Honours: George Eliot Fellowship Trophy, NFA, 1975, 1977, 1979; John Masefield Award, World Order of Narrative Poets, 1987. Memberships: Society of Authors; Fellow, Institute of Information Scientists; Chairman, Translators Association, 1984-85; Institute of Translating and Interpreting; Royal Over-Seas League. Literary Agent: Peters Fraser and Dunlop. Address: 199 The Long Shoot, Nuneaton, Warwickshire CV11 6JQ, England.

SHIGEMATSU Soiku, b. 13 Oct 1943, Shimizu, Japan. Zen Buddhist Priest; Professor of American Literature. Education: BA, Tokyo University of Foreign Studies, 1967; MA, English, Kyoto University, 1971. Appointments: Lecturer, Shizuoka Women's College, 1972-75, Shizuoka University, 1975-78; Associate Professor, 1978-88, Professor, 1988-, Shizuoka University; Main Priest, Shogenji Zen Temple, 1975-. Publications: A Zen Forest, 1981; A Zen Harvest,

1988; Sun at Midnight, with W S Merwin, 1989; Zen Haiku, 1994. Contributions to: American Poetry Review; Talisman. Honour: Jerome J Shestack Prize, American Poetry Review. Memberships: English Literature Society of Japan; American Literature Society of Japan. Address: Shogenji Zen Temple, Shogenji-cho, Shimizu-shi, Shizuoka-ken 424-02, Japan.

SHIN Chang-Ho, (Alvin C H Shin), b. 18 Sept 1919, Korea. Publishing. m. Jean Park, 10 Mar 1955, 3 sons, 1 daughter. Education: Columbia University of New York, 1948-49. Appointments: President, Founder, Universal Publications Co Ltd, 1958-73; Chairman and Chief Executive Officer, 1973-. Publications: Kamul-kamul Amul-amul, 1988; Long Way to Go Yet, 1989; In the Flux of Time, 1990; White Crane, Black Crow, 1991. Contributions to: Huyndai Munhak and Dongseo Munhak (monthlies); Poems and Poetry. Honour: Pyon-Eun (Cho Byong Hwa) Literary Prize, 1991. Memberships: Co-Chairman, Seoul Poets Club; Korean Literature Writers Association; Korean Poetry Association; International PEN Club. Address: Seoul Poets Club, Jangkyo Building, Suite 2613. 1 Jangkyo Dong, Choong-ku, Seoul 100 760, Korea.

SHIVKUMAR Lalitha, b. 6 Sept 1944, Kumbakonam, India. Writer. m. Wing Commander R Shivkumar, 28 Oct 1966, 2 sons. Education: BSc, 1965; MA, 1973; PhD, 1984; PGCTE, 1984; MA, 1986. Appointments: Teacher, St Joseph's Convent, 1965-66; Research Scholar, Punjab University, 1973-84; Lecturer, BEL College, Lecturer, Mother Theresa Women's University. Publications: Fragrance from Crushed Petals, 1996; Darling Buds of May, forthcoming. Contributions to: Poet; Poet International; Young Poet; Kavita India; Met Verse; Poetry Times; The Quest; World Poetry, 1996; Poet Year Book, 1993-95. Honours: SPCA Annual District Competition, 1961-63; Durga Puja Awd, 1986. Memberships: Writer's Foum; The Poetry Times, Sub Editor. Address: 39 Visweswarayya Street II, Coimbatore 641038, India.

SHOEMAKER Jeannine West, b. 1 July 1960, Texas, USA. m. 26 Feb 1983, 2 daughters. Education: BA, English, Creative Writing, Metropolitan State College of Denver, 1989. Appointments: Freelance Writer; Editor, Voices, 1988-89. Contributions to: Orbis; Metrosphere; Voices; Bayousphere. Honours: Metrofest Prizes for Poetry, 1987, 1989; Orbis Readers Choice, 1987; Bayousphere Prize for Poetry, 1982. Memberships: Sigma Tau Delta, 1989; Rocky Mountain Writers Guild; Southern Poetry Association. Address: 2175 South Saint Paul Street, Denver, CO 80210, USA.

SHOLL Elizabeth Neary, (Betsy Sholl), b. 12 June 1945, Lakewood, Ohio, USA. Poet; Teacher. m. John Douglas Sholl, 17 June 1967, 1 son, 1 daughter. Education: BA, Bucknell University, 1967; MA, University of Rochester, 1969; MFA, Vermont College, 1989. Appointments: Instructor, Lasell Junior College, Massachusetts Institute of Technology, University of Southern Maine. Publications: Changing Faces, 1974; Appalachian Winter, 1978; Rooms Overhead, 1986; Pick a Card, chapbook, 1991; The Red Line, 1992. Contributions to: Field; Ploughshares; Beloit Poetry Journal; Massachusetts Review; Graham House Review; Sojourners; West Branch; Poetry Miscellany. Honours: Maine Chapbook Contest, 1991; Poetry Competition, Associated Writing Programs, 1991; Fellowship to Individual Artist, Maine Arts Commission, 1991. Memberships: Associated Writing Programs; Maine Writers and Publishers Alliance; Literature Panel, Maine Arts Commission; Alice James Publishing Cooperative. Address: 24 Brentwood Street, Portland, ME 04103, USA.

SHORE Herbert, b. 6 June 1924, Philadelphia, Pennsylvania, USA. Writer; Professor. m. Yen Lu Wong, 21 Dec 1974, 1 son, 2 daughters. Education: BA, University of Pennsylvania, 1942; MA, Stanford University, 1953; PhD, International College, 1983. Appointments: Professor, University of Southern California, 1979-; School of Theatre and Master of Professional Writing; Affiliated Scholar, Centre for Multi-Ethnic Transnational Studies; Past Professor, Brandei University, University of Denver, University of Pennsylvania, University of South Florida; Foundation Professor, University of Dar es Salaam, Tanzania; Fellow, The Mayibuye Centre, University of The Western Cape, South Africa. Contributions to: Black Orpheus; Ghala; East African Journal; Chicago Jewish Forum; Wasafiri; Terra Infirma; Southern California Anthology. Honour: Medal of Bagamoyo, Government of Mozambique. Memberships: Pen, USA West; American Poetry Society; National Writers Union; Academy of American Poets. Address: CMTS, University of Southern California, GFS-344 University Park, Los Angeles, CA 90089-1694, USA.

SHRADER Gail, b. 18 Apr 1955, Fort Chaffee, Arkansas, USA. Attending College. m. Kerry Warrior, 30 Oct 1987, 1 son, 1 daughter. Education: Will Graduate Seminole Junior College, 1997, Associate in Applied Science Degree in Office Management. Appointments: Power Machine Operator; Currently in College; Publisher, Editor, Poetic Expressions. Contributions to: Poet's Corner; Greenfeather; Daring Poetry Quarterly; Where Dawn Lingers, anthology published by National Library of Poetry. Honours: Shattered Illusions, read at memorial service, Seminole Junior College in honor of victims of Oklahoma City Bombing. Address: Rt 1, Box 268, Konawa, Oklahoma 74849, USA.

SHUTTLE Penelope Diane, b. 12 May 1947, Middlesex, England. Author. m. Peter Redgrove, 16 Sept 1980, 1 daughter. Publications: The Hermaphrodite Album, 1973; Co-author, The Wise Wound, non-fiction, 1978, 1980, 1986; The Orchard Upstairs, 1980; The Child Stealer, 1983; The Lion from Rio, 1986; Adventures with my Horse, 1988; Taxing the Rain, 1992; Co-author, Alchemy for Women, non-fiction, 1995; Building a City for Jamie, 1996. Contributions to: Times Literary Supplement; Encounter; Outposts; Aylesford Review; Poetry Review; Pequod; Kudos; Prospice; Pink Peace; Gallery; Other Poetry; Bananas; Scotsman; Poetry Australia; Poetry Southwest; Ambit; New Statesman; Harpers and Queen; Tribune; Verse; Poetry Chicago. Honours: 3 Arts Council Awards, 1969, 1972, 1985; Greenwood Poetry Prize, 1972; Radio Times Drama Bursaries Competition Award, 1974; E C Gregory Award for Poetry, 1974. Address: c/o David Higham Associates Ltd, 508 Lower John Street, London W1R 4HA, England.

SIANI Cosma, b. 29 Nov 1945, Foggia, Italy. English Teacher. m. Lina Mazzei, 29 Mar 1979. Education: Degree, Istituto Magistrale, San Giovanni Rotondo, Foggia, 1963; Foreign Languages Degree, Istituto Universtario Orientale, Naples, 1971; Ealing College of Higher Education, London, 1980. Appointments: Teacher, Elementary, 1965-69, Junior High, 1972-76, High School, 1976-. Publications: Ciclo Chiuso, 1972; Lingua E Letteratura, 1992; Microletteratura, 1994; La Percezione Sbagliata, poems, 1996; Translations of British and American Contemporary Poets into Italian, in reviews and anthologies. Contributions to: La Parola del Popolo; Gradiva; La Fusta; Lettera; Piazza Navona; Carte d'Europa; Si Scrive; L'Indice Dei Libri Del Mese; Rivista Di Studi Italiani, Toronto. Membership: President, 1990-92, Editor, 1990-, Tesol-Italy. Address: Via Isole Capo Verde 220, 00121 Lido di Ostia, Rome, Italy.

SIDDIQUI (Mohammed) Naim(uddin), b. 18 Feb 1920, Hyderabad, India. University Teacher. m. Abida, 11 Mar 1956, 1 son, 2 daughters. Education: MA, Osmania University, India, 1942; MA, Oxford, 1963. Appointments: Lecturer, Reader in English, 1942-60, Osmania University, India; Professor of English, University of Liberia, 1969-80. Publication: Paimana-e-Imroze (in Urdu), 1987. Contributions to: Midwest Quarterly; Quest; Kenyon Review; Permafrost; Shahab; Al Moosi; Majilla-e-Osmania; Sabras; Nizam-e-Adab; Siasat. Memberships: Poetry Society of America; Poetry Society of India; Modern Language Association of America; Oxford Society. Address: 1144 Vista Lomas, Corona, CA 91720, USA.

SIDERI Aloi, b. 6 Feb 1929, Lixouri Cefalonia, Greece. Teacher. m. Stratis Sideris, 25 Dec 1953, 1 daughter. Education: Diploma in Greek History and Literature, University of Athens. Appointments: Teacher, Greek Literature, History and Latin Language, High Schools. Publications: Stretcher; Till Death, 1978; Full of Plays (editor), 1980; Dream Visions, 1984; The Dream of the Cat (editor), 1990. Contributions to: Spira; Planodion. Membership: Society of Greek Writers, Board Member, 1995-97.

SIDERIDOU Niki-Stella, (Greczynka), b. 10 May 1915, Smyrni, Greece. General Inspectress. m. Jean Thomopoulos, 15 Feb 1941, 2 daughters. Education: Philosophy and Philology, University of Athens, 1937; Pedagogy, Uppsala University, Sweden, 1950-51; Athens Teachers Training College of Secondary Education, 1958-60. Appointments: Professor in Cyclades Secondary Schools, Syros, Milos, Kea, 1945-52; Teacher, Addis Ababa, Ethiopia, 1953-55, Piraeus, 1958, Athens, 1958-65, Mouzaki, Thessalia, 1965-71, Athens, 1971-81, Syros, 1955-58; Uppsala, 1950-51, Kea, 1951-53; High School Principal, General Inspectress of Secondary Education. Publications: Uncertain Wall, 1964, 2nd edition, 1981; Love in the Stars, 1981; Return, 1981; ...And on the Earth Peace; In the Border of Fantasia. Contributions to: Tharos; Agon; Kenourgia Ephoci; Logotechnico Deltio; Synchoni Sepsi Stathmi Kea Suepsi; Ephorion;

Nea Synora; Enthalpia; Nouvas; Meteora. Honours: Roidi's Premium Prize, Athens Academy, 1956; Giovanni Gronchi Award, Pontedera, 1993; Distinction from the Supreme Council of National Education, 1961; Honorary Ribbon of the Lady of Olympoetry. Memberships: Greek Literature Society; Honorary Chairman, Greek Literature International Society; Distinguished Member, International Movement Committee, Brooklyn, USA; Distinguished Member, International Writers Association, Bluffton, USA. Address: 17 Galaxidiou Street, Athens 104 43, Greece.

SIEGEL Joan I, b. 14 June 1946, New York, USA. English Professor. m. J R Solonche, 12 Jan 1992. Education: BA, Hunter College, 1967; MA, English Literature, New York University, 1972. Contributions to: Commonweal; Literary Review; Yankee; San Jose Studies; Jama; Poet Lore; Hampden-Sydney Poetry Review; Poet and Critic; Wilderness; Interim. Honours: Honourable Mention, Poetry Centre Competition, 1989, Stone Ridge Poetry Society, 1989, 1990; Finalist, Capricorn Poetry Contest, 1992, Anhinga Prize Competition, 1992. Address: PO Box 99, Blooming Grove, NY 10914, USA.

SIEGEL Lee, b. 22 July 1945, Los Angeles, California, USA. Professor of English. 1 son. Education: BA, University of California, Berkeley, 1967; MFA, Columbia University, 1969; DPhil, Oxford University, 1975. Appointments: Instructor, English, Western Washington University, Bellingham, 1969-72; Professor of English, Graduate Programme Chairman, University of Hawaii at Manoa, Honolulu, 1976-; Author, Director, Mask and Mystery, TV series, Media Center, University of Hawaii at Manoa, 1978; Guest Lecturer, Oriental Institute, Oxford University, England, 1985, College de France, 1985. Publications: Vivisection, drawings and poems, 1973; Sacred and Profane Love in Indian Traditions, 1979; Dreams in the Sramanic Traditions, with Jagdish Sharma, 1980; Fires of Love, Waters of Peace: Passion and Renunciation in Indian Culture, 1983; Laughing Matters, Satire and Humour in India, 1987; Sweet Nothings, translation of the Amarusataka, 1988. Contributions to: Encyclopaedia of Religion; Articles and reviews to newspapers and to historical, religious and philosophical journals. Honours: Senior Fellow, American Institute of Indian Studies and Smithsonian Institution, 1979, 1983, 1987; Grants from Center for Asian and Pacific Studies, 1981, American Council of Learned Societies and Social Science Research Council, 1982, 1985, 1987; Presidential Award for Excellence in Teaching, University of Hawaii, 1986. Memberships: International Brotherhood of Magicians; Society of American Magicians; Society of Indian Magicians. Address: Department of Religion, University of Hawaii at Manoa, 2500 Campus Road, Honolulu, HI 96822, USA.

SIEGEL Robert (Harold), b. 18 Aug 1939, Oak Park, Illinois, USA. Poet; Writer; College Professor. m. Roberta Ann Hill, 19 Aug 1961, 3 daughters. Education: BA, Wheaton College, 1961; MA, Johns Hopkins University, 1962; PhD, English, Harvard University, 1968. Appointments: Assistant Professor, 1976-79, Associate Professor, 1979-83, Professor of English, 1983-, University of Wisconsin, Milwaukee, 1983-. Publications: Poetry: The Beasts and the Elders, 1973; In a Pig's Eye, 1980. Fiction: Centauri, 1980; Whalesong, 1981; The Kingdom of Wundle, 1982; The Wyrm of Grog, 1986; The Ice at the End of the World, The Longest Journey, 1994; White Whale: A Novel About Friendship and Courage in the Deep, 1994. Contributions to: Atlantic Monthly; Sewanee Review; Poetry; Poetry Anthology; New York Quarterly; Prairie Schooner; Poetry Northwest; Best Poems of 1976; New England Review; Ploughshares; Cream City Review; Beloit Poetry Journal; Wisconsin Academy Review; Verse. Honours: Grant, University of Wisconsin, 1978, 1984; Ingram Merrill Award, 1979; National Endowment for the Arts Fellowship, 1980; First Prize, Society of Midland Authors, 1981, Council for Wisconsin Writers, 1981; Matson Award, Friends of Literature, 1982; Golden Archer Award, School of Library Science, University of Wisconsin, Oshkosh, 1986; Nomination, Pushcart Prize, 1991, 1995. Address: Department of English, University of Wisconsin, Milwaukee, WI 53201, USA.

SIGURSTEINSSON Gunnar Hersveinn, (Gunnar Hersveinn), b. 28 Mar 1960, Reykjavík, Iceland. Writer; Teacher. m. Margaret Guttormsdottir, 30 Dec 1989, 1 son, 2 daughters. Education: BA, Philosophy, Psychology, University of Iceland, 1986. Appointments: Freelance Journalist, 1986-95; College of Armuli, 1986-87; College of Hamrahlid, 1987-88; College of Breidholt, 1988-91; College of Egilsstadir, 1992-94; Journalist, Morgunbladid, 1995-. Publications: Gaegjugat, 1987; Tre i husi, 1989; The Dual Nature, Philosophy, 1990; Raincity of Silent Houses, 1993. Contributions to: Literary Magazines: Timarit Mals og menningar; Teningur (vettvangur fyrir bokmenntir og

listir); Morgunbladid, newspaper; Nymaeli, selected poems by young poets; Ljoda arbok, poetry yearbook, 1988. Membership: Writers Union of Iceland. Address: Solheimar 46, 104 Reykjavík, Iceland.

SIKÉLIANOS Eléni, b. 31 May 1965, Santa Barbara, California, USA. Poet; Teacher. Education: BFA, 1990, MFA, 1991, Naropa Institute; Diplôme de Langue, l'Institut Catholique, Paris, France. Appointments: Creative Writing Instructor for the Homeless, California Arts Council Residency Grant, 1991-95; Poet-in-the-Schools, 1991-95; Creative Writing Instructor, San Francisco Art Institute, 1995; Freelance Writing Instructor, has taught in prisons, at the Naropa Institute Summer Writing Program, and at many conferences. Publications: To Speak While Dreaming, 1993; Poetics Of The X, 1995; 2 chapbooks forthcoming with Lyric and Press, and Trembling Ladders. Contributions to: The Quarterly; La Main Du Singe, in translation, Paris, France; Aya, Japan; Chain; Zyzzyva; Talisman; The World; Feminist Studies; Black Warrior Review; Exquisite Corpse; also recordings with: Audioliterature; Ruby Throat Productions. Honours: Ted Berrigan Award, 1990; Gertrude Stein Award for Innovative American Writing for, Sun and Moon, 1995; National Endowment for the Arts Creative Writing Fellowship, 1995. Membership: California Poets in the Schools. Address: 3754 12th Avenue, Brooklyn, NY 11218-1921, USA.

SILBERT Layle, b. Chicago, Illinois, USA. Writer; Photographer. m. Abraham Aidenoff, 9 May 1945. Education: BPhil, MA, University of Chicago. Appointment: Freelance Photographer, 1970-. Publications: Making a Baby in Union Park Chicago, 1983; Imaginary People and Other Strangers, 1985; Burkah & Other Stories, 1992. Contributions to: Anthologies: Women on War, 1988; New Poets; Women 1976; Ten Jewish American Poets, 1981; Sarah's Daughters, 1989; Without a Single Answer, 1990. Contributions to: Literary Review; New Letters; Confrontation; Sunbury; West Branch; Jewish Spectator; Lilith; USI Worksheets. Honour: Honorable Mention, Anna Rosenberg Award, 1988. Memberships: Poetry Society of America; PEN American Center. Address: 505 La Guardia Place No 16C, New York, NY 10012, USA.

SILCOCK Ruth Mary, b. 8 Aug 1926, Manchester, England. Retired Social Worker. Education: MA, Cantab, Girton College, Cambridge; Social Science Diploma, Bedford College; Mental Health Certificate, London School of Economics. Appointments: Various posts in the field of social work. Publication: Mrs Carmichael, 1987. Contributions to: Encounter; Spectator; Observer; Poetry Review; among others. Honours: Prizes at Lancaster and Cheltenham Literature Festivals, 1980, 1982 respectively; Duncan Lawrie Prize, Sothebys/Aroon Poetry Competition, 1989. Memberships: Society of Authors; Poetry Society. Address: Fairhaven, South Street, Letcombe Regis near Wantage, Oxon OX12 9JY, England.

SILK Dennis, b. 10 July 1928, London, England. Poet; Playwright. Appointments: Hebrew University of Jerusalem; Freelance Editor. Publications: Retrievements: A Jerusalem Anthology, 1968; Fourteen Israeli Poets: A Selection of Modern Hebrew Poetry, (with Harold Schimmel), 1976; The Punished Land, 1980; Hold Fast, 1984; Catwalk and Overpass, 1990; William the Wonder Kid (plays and theatre writings), forthcoming; 8 Plays produced in Israel. Contributions to: Times Literary Supplement; New York Times; Encounter; Harper's; Midstream; American Poetry Review; Conjunctions; Stand; Literary Review; Tel Aviv Review; Grand Street; Shenandoah; Jerusalem Post; American Voice. Honours: Howard Foundation Fellowship of Brown University, 1966; Peter Schwiefert Prize, Israel, 1976. Memberships: Association of Hebrew Writers in Israel; UNIMA. Address: PO Box 8103, German Colony, Jerusalem, Israel.

SILKIN Jon, b. 2 Dec 1930, London, England. Poet; Editor; Critic. 3 sons (1 dec), 1 daughter. Education: BA, Honours, University of Leeds, 1962. Appointments: Tutor, Writers Workshop, University of Iowa, 1968, 1969, 1991; Visiting Lecturer, University of Sydney, 1974; Tutor, Creative Writing, College of Idaho, 1978; Visiting Poet, Yearly Festival, University of Notre Dame, 1985 and Writers Conference at University of North Alabama, 1987; Distinguished Writer, American University, 1989; Literary Fellow, Dumfries and Galloway Arts Association, 1990; Professor of English and American Literature, University of Tsukuba, Japan, 1991-. Publications: Poems, New and Selected, 1966; Editor, The Penguin Book of First World War Poetry, 1979; Selected Poems, 1980, 1988; Editor, The War Poems of Wilfred Owen, 1985; The Ship's Pasture, 1986; Co-Editor, The Penguin Book of First World War Prose, 1989; The Lens. Contributions to: Times

Literary Supplement; New Statesman; Poetry; Stand; Critical Quarterly; Kenyon Review; London Review of Books; Agenda; Southern Review; Iowa Review; Antioch Review. Honour: Geoffrey Faber Memorial Award, 1966. Memberships: Royal Society of Literature; PEN; Society of Authors. Address: 19 Haldane Terrace, Newcastle upon Tyne NE2 3AN, England.

SILKO Leslie Marmon, b. 1948, Albuquerque, New Mexico, USA. Professor of English; Writer; Poet. 2 sons. Education: BA, English, University of New Mexico, 1969. Appointments: Teacher, University of New Mexico; Professor of English, University of Arizona, Tucson, 1978-. Publications: Fiction: Ceremony, 1977; Almanac of the Dead, 1991; Yellow Woman, 1993; Poetry: Laguna Woman, 1974; Storyteller, 1981; Other: The Delicacy and Strength of Lace: Letters Between Leslie Marmon Silko and James A Wright, 1986; Sacred Water: Narratives and Pictures, 1993. Honours: National Endowment for the Arts Grant, 1974; Chicago Review Award, 1974; Pushcart Prize, 1977; John D and Catharine T MacArthur Foundation Fellowship, 1983. Address: c/o Department of English, University of Arizona at Tucson, Tucson, AZ 85721, USA.

SILLIMAN Ron(ald Glenn), b. 8 May 1946, Pasco, Washington, USA. Editor Poet; m. (1) Rochelle Nameroff, 1965, div 1972, (2) Krishna Evans, 1986, 2 sons. Education: Merritt College, 1965, 1969-72; San Francisco State College, 1966-69; University of California, Berkeley, 1969-71. Appointments: Editor, Tottel's, 1970-81; Director of Research and Education, Committee for Prisoner Humanity and Justice, San Rafael, California, 1972-76; Project Manager, Tenderloin Ethnographic Research Project, San Francisco, 1977-78; Director of Outreach, Central City Hospitality House, San Francisco, 1979-81; Lecturer, San Francisco State University, 1981; Visiting Lecturer, University of California, San Diego, La Jolla, 1982; Writer-in-Residence, New College of California, San Francisco, 1982; Director, Public Relations and Development, 1982-86; Poet-in-Residence, 1983-90, California Institute of Integral Studies, San Francisco; Executive Editor, Socialist Review, 1986-89; Managing Editor, Computer Land, 1989-. Publications: Poetry: Moon in the Seventh House, 1968; Three Syntactic Fictions for Dennis Schmitz, 1969; Crow, 1971; Mohawk, 1973; Nox, 1974; Sitting Up, Standing Up, Taking Steps, 1978; Ketjak, 1978; Tjanting, 1981; Bart, 1982; ABC, 1983; Paradise, 1985; The Age of Huts, 1986; Lit, 1987; What, 1988; Manifest, 1990; Other: A Symposium on Clark Coolidge (Editor), 1978; In the American Tree (Editor), 1986; The New Sentence, 1987. Honours: Hart Crane and Alice Crane Williams Award, 1968; Joan Lee Yang Awards, 1970, 1971; National Endowment for the Arts Fellowship, 1979; California Arts Council Grants, 1979, 1980; Poetry Center Book Award, 1985. Address: 1819 Curtis, Berkeley, CA 94702, USA.

SILLITOE Alan, b. 4 Mar 1928, Nottingham, England. Writer; Poet; Dramatist. m. Ruth Esther Fainlight, 19 Nov 1959, 1 son, 1 daughter (adopted). Education: Principally self-taught. Appointments: Writer, 1948-. Publications: Without Beer or Bread (poems), 1957; Saturday Night and Sunday Morning (novel), 1958, revised edition, 1968; The General (novel), 1960; The Rats and Other Poems, 1960; Key to the Door (novel), 1961; Road to Volgograd (travel), 1964; A Falling Out of Love and Other Poems, 1964; The Death of William Posters (novel), 1965; A Tree on Fire (novel), 1967; A Start in Life (novel), 1967; Shaman and Other Poems, 1968; Love in the Environs of Voronezh and Other Poems, 1968; Travel in Nihilon (novel), 1971; Raw Material (memoir), 1972; The Flame of Life (novel), 1974; Storm and Other Poems, 1974; Barbarians and Other Poems, 1974; Mountains and Caverns: Selected Essays, 1975; The Widower's Son (novel), 1976; The Storyteller (novel), 1979; Snow on the North Side of Lucifer (poems), 1979; Her Victory (novel), 1982; The Lost Flying Boat (novel), 1983; Down from the Hill (novel), 1984; Sun Before Departure (poems), 1984; Life Goes On (novel), 1985; Tides and Stone Walls (poems), 1986; Out of the Whirlpool (novel), 1987; The Open Door (novel), 1989; Lost Loves (novel), 1990; Leonard's War, 1991; Snowstop, 1993; Collected Poems, 1994; Collected Stories, 1995; Leading the Blind (travel), 1995; Life Without Armour (autobiography), 1995. Other: Short stories; Plays. Honours: Author's Club Prize, 1958; Hawthornden Prize, 1960; Honorary Fellow, Manchester Polytechnic, 1977; Honorary Degree: Nottingham Polytechnic, 1990, Nottingham University, 1994; Visiting Professor, De Montfort University, Leicester. Memberships: Royal Geographical Society, fellow; Savage Club; Society of Authors; Writers Action Group. Address: c/o Savage Club, 1 Whitehall Place, London SW1A 2HD, England.

SILLS-DOCHERTY, Jonathan John, (John Docherty), b. 7 Jan 1941, Bowden, Cheshire, England. Humorous Writer; Lyricist; Poet. Education: Fielden Park College, West Didsbury, Manchester, 1977; Poetry Workshop, 1981, Extramural Department, 1986-87, University of Manchester. Appointments: Editor, Guardian Society, 1974; Reporter, Dun and Bradstreet, 1975; Proof Reader, Sub-Editor, Biography Compiler, Odd Fellow Magazine. Publications: A Walk Around the City and Other Groans, 1969, revised, 1973; Words on Paper, 1977; From Bottoms to Tops and Back Again, 1977, limited edition, 1987; Ballads of Fantasy and Reality, 1982; Ballads of Ecstasy and Perspicacity, 1987; Ballads of North West John, with cassette tape, 1987. Contributions to: News-Views; House Journal, Mappin and Webb; Sunday Times; Sunday Telegraph; Manchester Evening News; Stretford and Urmston Journal; Daily Mail; Star; Artful Reporter; What's On In Hulme; Dun and Bradstreet Report Magazine; Radio Manchester. Honours: Poetry Award, North West Arts, 1978; Double Prizewinner, Tribute for St George's Day, Granada TV, 1978; Various other prizes and awards including, Most Prolific Letter Writer to Manchester Evening News. Memberships:Turner Society; Court School of Dancing; Independent Order of Odd Fellows; Friend, North West Arts, Manchester City Art Gallery; Authors North. Address: 43 Cornbrook Park Road, Old Trafford, Manchester M15 4EH, England.

SILVERMAN Sherri, b. 19 Apr 1951, Atlanta, Georgia, USA. Artist; Writer. Education: BA, Emory University, 1971; MA, Brandeis University, 1974; PhD Candidate, The Union Institute, 1996. Appointments: Teaching Fellow, Literature Department, Maharishi International University, Fairfield, Iowa, 1980; Poet, Teacher, California Poets-in-the-Schools, Santa Barbara, 1985-86; Director, Santa Fe Poets-in-the-Schools, New Mwxico, 1989-92; Adjunct Faculty, University of North Florida, 1993; Adjunct Faculty, Florida Community College, 1993; Visiting Faculty, General Honors Program, University of New Mexico, 1996; Visiting Faculty, The Union Institute Graduate School, 1996. Contributions to: Crosswinds, New Mwxico; Sackbut Review; Reconstructionist; Heaven Bone; Wind Chimes; Santa Fe Spirit Magazine; Salome: A Literary Dance Magazine; Seeds of Unfolding; Art of Living Journal. Honours: Grants, Witter Bynner Foundation for Poetry, 1989, 1990. Membership: Poets and Writers: Address: P O Box 66, Santa Fe, NM 87504, USA.

SILVERSTEIN Shel(by), b. 1932, Chicago, Illinois, USA. Cartoonist; Writer; Dramatist; Poet; Composer. Div. 1 daughter. Appointments: Cartoonist, Pacific Stars and Stripes; Writer and Cartoonist, Playboy, 1956-. Publications: Self-Illustrated: Now Here's My Plan: A Book of Futilities, 1960; Uncle Shelby's ABZ Book: A Primer for Tender Young Minds, 1961; Playboy's Teevee Jeebies, 1963; Uncle Shelby's Story of Lafcadio, the Lion Who Shot Back, 1963; The Giving Tree, 1964; Uncle Shelby's Giraffe and a Half, verse, 1964; Uncle Shelby's Zoo: Don't Bump the Glump!, verse, 1964; Who Wants a Cheap Rhinoceros!, 1964; More Playboy's Teevee Jeebies: Do-it-Yourself Dialog for the Late Late Show, 1965; Where the Sidewalk Ends: The Poems and Drawings of Shel Silverstein, 1974; The Missing Piece, 1976; Different Dances, 1979; A Light in the Attic, 1981; The Missing Piece Meets the Big O, 1981; Falling Up, 1996. Plays: The Lady or the Tiger, 1981; Gorilla, 1983; Wild Life, 1983; Remember Crazy Zelda?, 1984; The Crate, 1985; The Happy Hour, 1985; One Tennis Shoe, 1985; Little Feet, 1986; Wash and Dry, 1986; The Devil and Billy Markham, 1989. Screenplay: Things Change (with David Mamet), 1988. Contributions to: The Best American Short Plays 1992-93: The Theatre Annual Since 1937, 1993. Other: Composer and lyricist of many songs. Honours: New York Times Outstanding Book Award, 1974; School Library Journal Best Books Award, 1981; International Reading Association's Children's Choice Award, 1982; Buckeye Awards, 1983, 1985; William Allen White Award, 1984. Address: c/o Grapefruit Productions, 106 Montague Street, Brooklyn, NY 11201, USA.

SIMIC Charles, b. 9 May 1938, Belgrade, Yugoslavia (US citizen, 1971). Associate Professor of English; Poet; Writer. m. Helen Dubin, 1964, 1 son, 1 daughter. Education: University of Chicago, 1956-59; BA, New York University, 1967. Appointments: Faculty, California State College, Hayward, 1970-73; Associate Professor of English, University of New Hampshire, 1973-. Publications: Poetry: What the Grass Says, 1967; Somewhere Among Us a Stone is Taking Notes, 1969; Dismantling the Silence, 1971; White, 1972, revised edition, 1980; Return to a Place Lit by a Glass of Milk, 1974; Biography and a Lament, 1976; Charon's Cosmology, 1977; Brooms: Selected Poems, 1978; School for Dark Thoughts, 1978; Classic Ballroom Dances, 1980; Shaving at Night, 1982; Austerities, 1982; Weather

Forecast for Utopia and Vicinity: Poems 1967-1982, 1983; The Chicken Without a Head, 1983; Selected Poems 1963-1983, 1985, revised edition, 1990; Unending Blues, 1986; The World Doesn't End: Prose Poems, 1989; In the Room We Share, 1990; The Book of Gods and Devils, 1990; Hotel Insomnia, 1992; A Wedding in Hell, 1994; Walking The Black Cat; Others include: Unemployed Fortune Teller, 1994; As Editor, includes: The Essential Campion, 1988; Translator: 12 books, 1970-92. Honours: PEN Awards, 1970, 1980; Guggenheim Fellowship, 1972; National Endowment for the Arts Fellowships, 1974, 1979; Edgar Allan Poe Award, 1975; American Academy of Arts and Letters Award, 1976; Harriet Monroe Poetry Award, 1980; Fulbright Fellowship, 1982; Ingram Merrill Fellowship, 1983; John D and Catharine T MacArthur Foundation Fellowship, 1984; Pulitzer Prize in Poetry, 1990. Address: c/o Department of English, University of New Hampshire, Durham, NH 03824, USA.

SIMMERMAN Jim, b. 5 Mar 1952, Denver, Colorado, USA. Poet; Professor of English. Education: BS, Education, 1973, MA, English, 1976, University of Missouri; MFA, English, University of Iowa, 1980. Appointments: Instructor, 1977-78, Assistant Professor, 1983-86, Associate Professor and Creative Writing Director, 1986-, Department of English, Northern Arizona University. Publications: Home, 1983; Bad Weather, 1988; Once Out of Nature, 1989; Moon Go Away, I Don't Love You No More,1994; Yoyo, 1994. Contributions: Antaeus; Columbia; Crazyhorse; Denver Quarterly; Iowa Review; Missouri Review; New England Review; North American Review; Ploughshares; Poet and Critic; Poetry; Sonora Review; Southern Poetry Review. Honours: Fellowships: Arizona Commission on The Arts, 1983, 1987, National Endowment of the Arts, 1984, Fine Arts Work Center, 1984-85; Best of the Small Presses, Book Fair Selection, 1990; Writer's Choice, 1984 and Pushcart Prize, 1985. Memberships: Associated Writing Programs; Rocky Mountain Modern Language Association. Address: 3601 Mountain Drive, Flagstaff, AZ 86001, USA.

SIMMONS James Stewart Alexander, b. 14 Feb 1933, Londonderry, Northern Ireland. Writer. m. (1) Laura Stinson, (2) Imelda Foley, 1 son, 5 daughters. Education: BA, Honours, Leeds University, England, 1958. Appointments: Lecturer in English, Ahmadu Bello University, Nigeria, 1963-67; Lecturer, Senior Lecturer, English, Chairman, Department of English, University of Ulster, Belfast, Northern Ireland, 1968-83. Publications: Late But in Earnest, 1967; In The Wilderness, 1969; Energy To Burn, 1971; The Long Summer Still to Come, 1973; West Strand Visions, 1976; Judy Garland and The Cold War, 1976; The Selected James Simmons, 1978; Constantly Singing, 1981; Anthologies: Editor, Out on the Edge, New Poems from Ulster, 1971; Ten Irish Poets, 1974; Soundings 3, 1976; From the Irish, 1985; Poems 1956-1986, 1986; Various recordings and settings of poems. Contributions to: Numerous professional journals. Honours: Gregory Award; Cholmondeley Award; Subject of BBC TV program, 1976; Medal for Literature, Irish Book Awards, 1987. Address: 134 My Lady's Road, Belfast BT6 8FE, Northern Ireland.

SIMMS Michael Arlin, (Michael Garcia-Simms), b. 6 Apr 1954, Houston, Texas, USA. College Teacher of Literature and Writing. m. Eva Maria Spork, 29 Sept 1987, 1 son, 1 daughter. Education: Attended School of Irish Studies, 1974; BA, Southern Methodist University, 1976; MFA, University of Iowa, 1978. Appointments: Teaching Assistant, University of Iowa, 1976-78; Instructor of Rhetoric, Southern Methodist University, 1979-87; Instructor of Communication, CCAC, 1988-; Instructor of English, Duquesne University, 1995-. Publications: Notes on Continuing Light, 1980; Migration, 1985; The Fire-Eater, 1988. Contributions to: Southwest Review; Mid-American Review; Blue Buildings; Intro 9; Poets of the West; Telescope; Pittsburgh Poets; Rhetoric Review; Black Warrior Review; West Branch; Pittsburgh Quarterly. Honours: Assistantship, University of Iowa, 1976-78; Yaddo Fellowships, 1979, 1980, 1987; National Endowment for the Humanities Fellowship, 1982; Beyond the Classroom Grants, CCAC, 1988, 1989; International Poetry Forum, 1993. Address: 219 Bigham, Pittsburgh, PA 15211, USA.

SIMON M(argaret) B(allif), (Marge Simon), b. 12 Sept 1942, Washington, District of Columbia, USA. Educator. m. Frank K Simon, 18 June 1981, 1 daughter. Education: BA, 1969, MA, 1970, University of Northern Colorado. Appointments: President, Small Press Writers and Artists Organization, 1988-90. Publications: Editor: Mystic Hoofbeats, 1988; Poets of The Fantastic, 1990; Poetry Editor: Small Press Writers and Artists Organization Showcase, 1990; Recursive Angel, 1990; Eonian Variations, selected works, poetry anthology, 1995. Contributions to: Amazing Stories; Space and Time; Leading Edge; Tales of the Unanticipated; Threshold of Fantasy; Visions; Krax; The Blood Review; Figment; Ellipsis; Buzzworm; Noctulpa; Death Realm; Xenophelia; Eulogy; Glimpses; Moscow, programme book; Barrelhouse; Writer; Ice River. Address: 1412 North East 35th Street, Ocala, FL 34479, USA.

SIMON Maurya, b. 7 Dec 1950, New York, USA. m. Robert Falk, 17 June 1973, 2 daughters. Education: BA, Pitzer College, 1980; MFA, University of California, Irvine, 1984. Appointment: Currently at University of California, Riverside, 1984-. Publications: The Enchanted Room, 1986; Days of Awe, 1989; Speaking in Tongues, 1990; The Golden Labyrinth, 1995. Contributions to: Los Angeles Times; Georgia Review; Grant Street; Hudson Review; Ironwood; Kenyon Review; Literary Review; Michigan Quarterly Review; Missouri Review; Pacific Review; Poetry; Poetry East. Honours: University Award, Academy of American Poets; 1st Prize, National Federation of State Poetry Societies, 1984; 1st Prize, SCCA International Poetry Competition, 1987; Georgia State Poetry Award, 1988; Fulbright, Indo-American Fellowship, 1990. Memberships: Academy of American Poets; Poetry Society of America; Poets and Writers; PEN USA West; Modern Language Association; Associated Writing Programs. Address: 29 Bear Drive, PO Box 203, Mount Baldy, CA 91759, USA.

SIMONSUURI Kirsti Katariina, b. 26 Dec 1945, Helsinki, Finland. Professor; Writer; Poet. Education: BA, 1968, MA, Honours, 1971, University of Helsinki; PhD, University of Cambridge, England, 1977. Appointments: Professor of Literature, University of Oulu, 1978-81; Senior Research Fellow, Academy of Finland, 1981-; Visiting Scholar, Harvard University, USA, 1984-86; Visiting Professor, Columbia University, New York City, 1986-88. Publications: Homer's Original Genius, 1979; Murattikaide, 1980; Tuntematon Tekija, 1982; Europan Ryosto, 1984. Contributions to: World Literature Today; Ploughshares; Horen; Diavaso. Honours: J H Erkko Award for Best First Book, 1980; Wolfson Fellowship Award, British Academy, 1981; Fulbright Postdoctoral Fellowship, 1984. Memberships: PEN International; Finnish Literature Society; Finland's Writers and Authors; Society for The Promotion of Hellenic Studies; International Society for Eighteenth Century Studies; Modern Language Association. Address: 67A Sands Point Road, Port Washington, NY 11050, USA.

SIMPSON Louis Aston Marantz, b. 27 Mar 1923, Jamaica, West Indies. Teacher; Writer. m. Miriam Bachner Butensky, 23 June 1985. Education: BSc, 1944, MA, 1950, PhD, 1959, Columbia University. Appointments: Associate Editor, Bobbs-Merrill Publishing Co, 1950-55; English Instructor, Columbia University, 1955-59; Professor of English, University of California, Berkeley, 1959-67; State University of New York, Stony Brook, 1967-93. Publications: The Arrivistes: Poems 1940-1949, 1949; Good News of Death and Other Poems, 1955; A Dream of Governors, 1959; At The End of The Open Road, 1963; Selected Poems, 1966; Adventures of The Letter I, 1971; Searching for the Ox, 1976; Caviare at the Funeral, 1980; The Best Hour of the Night, 1983; People Live Here: Selected Poems, 1949-1983, 1985; Collected Poems, 1988; In the Room We Share, 1990; There You Are, 1995. Contributions to: Hudson Review; Southern Review; New Criterion; Harvard Review; New York Times. Honours: Fellowships: Hudson Review, 1957, Prix de Rome, 1957, Guggenheim Foundation, 1962, 1970; Pulitzer Prize for Poetry, 1964; Jewish Book Council Award, 1981; Elmer Holmes Bobst Award, 1987. Address: 186 Old Field Road, Setauket, NY 11733, USA.

SIMPSON Matt(hew William), b. 13 May 1936, Lancashire, England. Lecturer in English. m. Monika Ingrid Weydert, 13 Dec 1961, 1 son, 1 daughter. Education: Cert Ed, Liverpool, 1959; MA, Honours, Cantab, 1961. Appointments: Wirral Grammar School for Boys; Studio School of English; Millbank College of Commerce; Liverpool Institute of Higher Education; Poet in Residence, Tasmanian Poetry Festival, 1995. Publications: Letters to Berlin, 1971; A Syke Sequence, 1972; Watercolour From An Approved School, 1975; Uneasy Vespers, 1977; Making Arrangements, 1982; See You on The Christmas Tree, 1984; Dead Baiting, 1989; An Elegy for the Galosherman: New and Selected Poems, 1990; The Pigs Thermal Underwear, 1993; To Tasmania with Mrs Meredith, 1993; Catching Up With History, 1995; Matt, Wes and Pete (for children), 1995; On the Right Side of the Earth, 1995. Contributions to: Critical Quarterly; Iron; Critical Survey; Encounter; English; The Green Book; Honest Ulsterman; Literary Review; London Magazine; London Review of Books; New Review; Outposts. Memberships: Chairman, Trustees of the Windows Project, Merseyside Arts Literature Panel; Vice Chair, Halewood Arts Association. Address: 29 Boundary Drive, Liverpool L25 0QB, England.

SIMPSON Mercer Frederick Hampson, b. 27 Jan 1926, London, England. Schoolmaster; Lecturer; Literary Journalist. m. Betty Cook, 9 Aug 1961, 1 daughter. Education: BA, Honours, English, Magdalene College, Cambridge, 1949; Certificate in Education, University of Bristol, 1950; MA, Cantab, 1970; MA, University College Cardiff, University of Wales, 1975. Appointments: Head of English Department, Monkton House Independent Boys Grammar School, Cardiff, Wales, 1950-66; Lecturer, Liberal Studies, Senior Lecturer, Department of Arts and Languages, University of Glamorgan (formerly Polytechnic of Wales), 1967-81; Editor, BWA Magazine, Welsh Academy, 1986-91; Judge, Welsh Arts Council Literature Awards, 1987; Reader for Publication Grants, Welsh Arts Council, 1987-; Editorial Board, New Welsh Review, 1992-. Publications: East Anglian Wordscapes, 1993; Rain From a Clear Blue Sky, 1994; Anthologies: Hepworth: A Celebration, 1992, Poet's England 15, Suffolk, 1994, and Poet's England 16, Norfolk, 1994. Contributions to: Anglo-Welsh Review; New Welsh Review; Poetry Wales; New Prospects Poetry; Social Care Education; BWA; Old Burian; Powys Review; Cencrastus; Acumen; Bloomsbury Guide to English Literature, Welsh Section. Honour: Elected to Council (Governing Body) of The Welsh Academy, 1993-. Memberships: Various offices, Welsh Academy, 1989-; Cardiff Literature Festival Committee, 1986-; Poetry Society of Great Britain; PEN Wales, 1994-. Address: 1 Dan-y-Graig, Pantmawr, Cardiff CF4 7HJ, Wales.

SIMPSON Nancy. See: **BRANTLEY Nancy Simpson.**

SIMPSON Ronald Albert, b. 1 Feb 1929, Melbourne, Australia. Senior Lecturer; Poet; Editor. m. Pamela Bowles, 27 Aug 1955, 1 son, 1 daughter. Education: Primary Teachers Certificate, 1951; Associate Diploma in Fine Art, Royal Melbourne Institute of Technology, 1966. Appointments: Teacher in junior and secondary schools in Australia and UK, 1951-68; Lecturer, Senior Lecturer, Chisholm Institute of Technology, Melbourne, 1968-87. Publications: The Walk Along the Beach, 1960; This Real Pompeii, 1964; After the Assassination, 1968; Diver, 1972; Poems from Murrumbeena, 1976; The Forbidden City, 1979; Editor: Poems from the Age, 1979; Selected Poems, 1981; Words for a Journey, 1986; Dancing Table, 1992; Poetry Editor, The Age. Honours: Australian Council for Travel, 1977; Category A Fellowship to Write Poetry, 1987; FAW Christopher Brennan Award, 1992. Membership: Australian Society of Authors. Address: 29 Omama Road, Murrumbeena, Melbourne, Victoria 3163, Australia.

SIMS Anthony (Tony) Cyril Martel, b. 22 June 1931, Bath, England. Home Office Official. m. Margaret Patricia Jump, 23 June 1956, 1 daughter. Publication: Poetry in anthology, Sing Freedom, 1991. Contributions to: Agenda; Envoi; Orbis; New Welsh Review; Poetry Nottingham; Spokes; South Coast Poetry Journal, USA. Honour: 1st Prize, Envoi Poetry Competition, 1991. Address: Prospect House, Snowshill, Broadway, Worcestershire WR12 7JU, England.

SINASON Valerie Elaine, b. 17 Dec 1946, London, England. Child Psychotherapist. m. M Sinason, 19 Jan 1969, 1 son, 1 daughter. Education: BA, Honours, English, Language and Literature, 1968, Post-Graduate Teaching Certificate, Drama, English, 1969, London University; MACP, Tavistock Clinic, 1983. Appointment: Principal Child Psychotherapist, Tavistock Clinic, London, 1987-. Publications: Inkstains and Stilettos, 1986. Contributions to: Tribune; Poetry Review; Spare Rib; Ambit; Outposts; Prospice; Arts Council New Poetry; Women's Press; Iron; Omens; PEN; Radio 3 Poetry Now; Thames TV, Angels of Fire; Argo; Wheels; Aquarius; Literary Review; Jewish Chronicle. Memberships: Executive Council, Poetry Society; Past Co-Convenor, Poetry West Hampstead; Founder, Former Member, Prodigal Daughters. Address: Tavistock Clinic, 120 Belsize Lane, London NW3 5BA, England.

SINCLAIR Iain Macgregor, b. 11 June 1943, Cardiff, South Wales. Writer. m. Anna Hadman, 4 Mar 1967, 1 son, 2 daughters. Education: London School of Film Technique; Trinity College, Dublin. Publications: Back Garden Poems, 1970; Muscat's Würm, 1972; Lud Heat, 1975; Suicide Bridge, 1979; Flesh Eggs and Scalp Metal, Selected Poems, 1989; Jack Elam's Other Eye, 1992. Literary Agent: John Parker MBA Literary Agents, London, England. Address: 28 Albion Drive, London E8 4ET, England.

SINCLAIR John, b. 2 Oct 1941, Flint, Michigan, USA. Music Journalist; Poet; Broadcaster; Performer; Lecturer; Educator. m. (1) Magdalene Arndt, 12 June 1965, (2) Patricia (Penny) Brown, 1 Jan 1989, 2 daughters, 2 stepdaughters. Education: Albion College, Albion,

Michigan, 1959-61; BA, English Literature, University of Michigan, Flint, 1964; Graduate studies in American Literature, Wayne State University, Detroit, Michigan, 1964-65. Appointments: Chairman, White Panther Party, 1968-71; President, Strata Associates, 1975-79; Executive Director, Detroit Jazz Center, 1979-81; President, MSA Inc (music management and production company), 1982-88; Editor, City Arts Quarterly, Detroit Council of the Arts, 1988-91; Associate Professor, Music Department, Wayne State University, 1989-91; Radio Show Producer and Host, Blue Sensations, WDET-FM, Detroit, 1989-91, Blues and Roots, WWOZ-FM, New Orleans, Louisiana, 1992-. Creative works: This is Our Music, 1965; Fire Music: A Record, 1966; The Poem For Warner Stringfellow, 1966; Meditations: A Suite for John Coltrane, 1967; We Just Change the Beat, 1988; Fly Right, A Monk Suite, 1992; Fattening Frogs for Snakes: Delta Blues Suite, in progress; Full Moon Night, CD by John Sinclair and His Blues Scholars, 1995; Friday the 13th, LP, John Sinclair with Wayne Kramer; If I Could Be With You, with Ed Moss and the Society Jam Orchestra, 1996; Thelonious: A book of Monk - Volume one, 1996. Contributions to: Jazz Poetry Book; HIP-o-logy; For Malcolm X; Michigan Quarterly Review; Notas; City Arts Quarterly; Detroit Free Press; African-American Scholar, 1995; Mesechabe; Heartland Journal. Honour: Scholarship, Four Young Poets Reading, Berkeley Poetry Conference, 1965. Address: 940 Royal Street #224, New Orleans, LA 70116, USA.

SINGER Davida, b. 31 Oct 1947, Burlington, Vermont, USA. Poet; Writer; Teacher. Education: BA, Writing, Columbia University, 1978; MA, Journalism, New York University, 1991. Appointments: Teacher, Writing Workshops; Co-Director, Poetry Series, Wow Cafe, New York City and Woman Books, New York City. Publications: Shelter Island Poems, 1994; Letters to Women, 1994. Contributions to: Little Magazine; Feminist Studies; Passager; Amaranth Review; Metis; Write-Poems-Women Anthology; Feminist Review; Chelsea Journal; Mouth-of-the-Dragon; Primavera; Caprice; Sinister Wisdom; Peregrine. Membership: Poets and Writers. Address: 162 9th Avenue, No 2C, New York, NY 10011, USA.

SINGER Frieda, b. New York, USA. m. Morris Shapiro, 25 June 1978, 2 step-daughters. Education: BA, English, Hunter College; MA, Columbia University, 1958; MA, Poetry, City College of the City University of New York, 1985. Appointments: Teacher, High School of Fashion, New York and Norman Thomas High School, 1959-79. Publication: Editor, Daughters in High School, 1974. Contributions to: Poetry in Performance; Perception; Infinity Magazine; Negative Capability; Poets Pourri; South Florida Poetry Institute Review; Z Miscellaneous; Blood to Remember: American Poets on The Holocaust. Honours: Poet of The Year, New York Poetry Forum, 1981; Awards from: Shelley Society, 1984; Composers, Authors and Artists of America, 1986, 1990; Florida Freelance Writers, 1986, 1987, 1988, 1990, 1991, 1992; World Order of Narrative Poets, 1986, 1991, 1992; Pen and Brush, 1988, 1989, 1990, 1991, 1992; Poetry Society of America, 1988. Memberships: Poets and Writers; Poetry Society of America; Authors Guild; Pen and Brush; Shelley Society; South Florida Poetry Institute; Florida Freelance Writers Association; Composers, Authors and Artists of America; Poets of Palm Beach. Address: 161-08 Jewel Avenue, No 1C, Flushing, NY 11365, USA.

SINGER Lou. See: **WISINSKI Louise Ann Helen.**

SINGER Sarah Beth, b. 4 July 1915, USA. Poet. m. Leon E Singer, 23 Nov 1938, 1 son, 1 daughter. Education: BA, New York University, 1934. Appointments: Teacher of poetry seminars and workshops, 1968-74, 1981-83. Publications: After the Beginning, 1975; Of Love and Shoes, 1987; The Gathering, book of verse, 1992; Filtered Images, anthology, 1992. Contributions to: Poetry Society of America Bulletin; New York Times; McCall's; New Mexico Quarterly; Commentary; Christian Science Monitor; Yankee; Fiddlehead; Hartford Courant; Poet Lore; Lyric; Anthologies. Honours: Stephen Vincent Benet Narrative Poetry Awards, 1968, 1971; Five Poetry Society of America Awards, 1972-76; National League of American Penwomen Awards, 1976-92; The Lyric, 1981, 1985; Washington Poets Association Award, 1989; Certificate of Merit, Muse Magazine, 1990; Haiku Award, Brussels Sprout, 1992; Metro Bus Award, 1992. Memberships: Vice President, Poetry Society of America, 1974-78; Executive Director, PSA on Long Island, 1979-83; Various positions at branch level, National League of American Penwomen. Address: 2360 43rd Avenue East, Seattle, WA 98112, USA.

SINGH Darshan, b. 14 Sept 1921, India. Spiritual Leader; Poet; Author. m. Harbhajan Kaur, 20 Aug 1943, 2 sons. Education: BA Honours, Government College, Punjab University, Lahore, 1941. Appointments: Spiritual Master, Leader, Sawan Kirpal Ruhani Mission. Publications: Talash-e-Noor, 1965; Mazil-e-Noor, 1969; Cry of the Soul, 1977; Secret of Secrets: Spiritual Discourses, 1978; Spiritual Awakening, 1982; Challenge of Inner Space, 1984; Meaning of Christ, 1985; A Tear and a Star, 1986; Soulergy: Source of All Energy, 1987; Ambassadors of Peacer, 1987. Contributions to: Numerous professional journals and magazines. Honours include: Award Poetry, Urdu Academy, 1969. Memberships: Secretary, Bazame-Adab; Joint Secretary, Halga-e-Arbab-e-Fikr. Address: Kirpal Ashram, 2 Canal Road, Vijay Nagar, Delhi 110009, India.

SINGH Gurcharan, b. 8 Feb 1917, India. Author. m. 12 Feb 1942, 3 sons, 1 daughter. Education: MA, English, 1940; MA, Punjabi, 1953; PhD, 1964. Appointments: Editor, Daily Ranjit, Lahore, 1945, Khalsasewata Amritsar, 1945; Publicity Officer, Pepsu State, 1949; Agricultural Publicity Officer, Nabha, 1950; Editor, Kheti Bare, Nabha, 1951; Lecturer, Mohind64 College, 1954; Reader, Punjabi University, 1966;Chairman, Pre-School Education Board, 1972. Publications: Wan Te Karie, 1946; Wagdi Si Ravi, 1950; Dharti Dan Sandhur, 1977; Sunam Da Surna Shahid, 1977; Behi Sharab, 1987; 20 books of poems. Contributions to: Various journals and magazines. Honours: Pepsu State Awards, 1951, 1952; Punjab State Award, 1963; Government of India Award, 1963; Bal Sahit Academy Award, 1963; Indian Writers Union Award, 1985; Congress Centenary Award, 1985; Many others. Memberships: President, Punjabi Kala Sansar; Shiromany Kav Te Kala-Manoh, Vice President; Punjabi Sahit Academy; Indian Writers Union. Address: 35/9A Chandigarh, India.

SINGH Karnail, b. 28 June 1935, Heir, India. Teaching. m. Shanta, Dec 1963, 1 son, 2 daughters. Education: BA Hons in English, 1954; MA, English, 1956; Graduation in French and Persian, 1957, 1958; PhD, T S Eliot as Critic, 1966; DLitt, The Literary Criticism of F R Leavis w Special Reference to Anglo-American New Criticism. Appointments: Governmentt College for Women Amritsar, 1968-60; Khalsa College Amritsar Professor and Head of P G Department, 1961-93; Professor, Head Postgraduate, Department of English, Sant Singh Sukha Singh College of Commerce for Women, The Mall, Amritsar, India. Publications: The Open Heart, 1993; The Wounded Muse, 1994; And Mysteries of Love, 1996. Contributions to: Art of Living Amritsar; Modern Practical Psychology, 1984-88; Indian Book Chronicle; The Darbar, Khalsa College. Honours: Invited to Taiwan in recognition of the Wounded Muse by Rosemary C Wilkinson Secy General of World Congress of Poets, USA. Memberships: Secretary, Amritsar Literary Society; SSSS Literary Society. Address: 83612, Kot Atma Singh, Amritsar.

SINGH Narenderpal, b. 17 Oct 1924, India. Novelist; Poet; Writer. m. 10 Apr 1948, 2 daughters. Education: BA, Punjab University, 1942; GIANI, Hons in Punjabi Language and Literature, Punjab University. Appointment: Editor of Byword, 1972-. Publications: Malah, 1948; Agammi Wehan, 1948; Ik Rah Ik Para, 1953; Trial Jal, 1957; Khanio Tikhi, 1959; Aryana, 1961; Tapu, 1969; Vikendrit, 1971; Ba Mulhaza Hoshian, 1975; Gaggan Ganga, 1981; The New Moses, 1985; Zero Hour, 1986; Mere to Girdhar Gopal, 1989; Jahanpanah, 1991; Scandal Village, 1991; Crossroads, 1992. Contributions to: Poetry India; New Horizons; Chants Spirituels; Poesi; Poet; Poetry Digest; Echo; Poetry Chronicle of India. Honours: DLitt, United Poets International, Phillipines; Robe of Honour, Government of Punjab; Grande Medaille d'Or de la Ville De Paris, Academy of Arts, Sciences and Letters; Sahitya Akademi Award, India, 1976; Sans National Professor of India, 1983. Memberships: National Commission for UNESCO; Poetry Society of America; PEN International; United Poets International, Philippines. Address: D-203 Defence Colony, New Delhi 110024, India.

SINGH Ram Krishna, b. 31 Dec 1950, Varanasi, India. Teacher; Writer; Poet; Editor. m. Durga, 1 Mar 1978, 1 son, 1 daughter. Education: BA, Harish Chandra College, Varanasi, 1970; MA, English Literature, Banaras Hindu University, 1972; PhD, English, Kashi Vindyapith, 1981. Appointments include: Journalist, Press Trust of India, New Delhi, 1973-74; Lecturer, Royal Bhutan Polytechnic, 1974-76; Assistant Professor, Indian School of Mines, Dhanbad, 1983-93; Professor, Head, Department of Humanities, Indian School of Mines, 1993-. Publications include: Savitri: A Spiritual Epic, 1984; My Silence, 1985; Memories Unmemoried, 1988; Music Must Sound, 1990; Flight of Phoenix, 1990; My Silence and Other Selected Poems

1974-94, 1995. Contributions to: Poet; Skylark; Indian Literature; Journal of Indian Writing in English; Commonwealth Quarterly; Indian and Foreign Review; The Century; Adam and Eve; Rajasthan Journal of English studies; Quill; Poetry Time; Poesie; Indian Book Chronicle; Canopy; Creative Forum; Prophetic Voices; Noreal; Kanora; Indian Literary Panorama. Honours: Honorary DLitt, World Academy of Arts & Culture, Taipei, 1984; Fellowship, International Poets Academy, Madras, 1987; Certificate of Excellence and Mention, Directory of International Writers, 1987; International Man of the Year Award, IBC, 1992/93; Michael Madhusudan Award, Michael Madhusudan Academy, Calcutta, 1994. Memberships include: International Writers and Artists Association; World Poetry Society Intercontinental; International Poets Academy; World Cultural Council; PEN, India. Address: Type VI/4, Teachers Colony, Indian School of Mines, Dhanbad-826004, India.

SINGINGARROW-SMITH. See: CHRYSTOS Christina.

SIRR Peter Anthony, b. 8 June 1960. Director of the Irish Writers' Centre. Education: BA, English and Irish, 1982, MLitt, English, 1984, Trinity College, Dublin. Appointments: Journalist; Teacher; Administrator; Reviewer for the Irish Times. Publications: Marginal Zones, 1984; Talk Talk, 1987; Ways of Falling, 1991. Contributions to: Irish Times; Irish Press; Poetry Ireland Review; Poetry Review London; Oxford Poetry; Ploughshares; Quarry; Anthologies: Penguin Book of Contemporary Irish Poetry; New Younger Irish Poets. Honours: Patrick Kavanagh Award, 1982; Listowel Writers Week Poetry Prize, 1983; Bursaries in Literature by Irish Arts Council, 1985, 1988. Address: Irish Writers Centre, 19 Parnell Square, Dublin 1, Ireland.

SISSON C(harles) H(ubert), b. 22 Apr 1914, Bristol, England. Poet; Writer; Translator; Editor; Retired Civil Servant. m. Nora Gilbertson, 19 Aug 1937, 2 daughters. Education: BA, 1st Class Honours, University of Bristol, 1934; Postgraduate Studies: University of Berlin, University of Freiburg, 1934-35, Sorbonne, University of Paris, 1935-36. Appointments: Assistant Principal, 1936-42, Principal, 1945-53, Assistant Secretary, 1953-62, Undersecretary, 1962-68, Assistant Undersecretary of State, 1962-73, Ministry of Labour, Department of Employment. Publications: Poems, 1959; Twenty-one Poems, 1960; The London Zoo, 1961; Numbers, 1965; The Discarnation: Or, How the Flesh Became Word and Dwelt Among Us, 1967; Metamorphoses, 1968; Roman Poems, 1968; In the Trojan Ditch: Collected Poems and Selected Translations, 1974; The Corridor, 1975; Anchises, 1976; Exactions, 1980; Selected Poems, 1981; Night Thoughts and Other Poems, 1983; Collected Poems 1943-1983, 1984; God Bless Karl Marx!, 1987; Antidotes, 1991; Nine Sonnets, 1991; The Pattern, 1993; What and Who, 1994. Translations: Lucretius: The Poem on Nature, 1976; Dante: The Divine Comedy, 1980; Vingil: The Aeneid, 1986. Contributions to: Agenda; London Magazine; London Review of Books; New Criterion; New York Times Review of Books; Poetry Nation Review; Spectator; Times Literary Supplement. Honours: Senior Simon Research Fellow, University of Manchester; Fellow, Royal Society of London, 1975; Honorary DLitt, University of Bristol, 1980; Companion of Honour, 1993. Address: Moorfield Cottage, The Hill, Langport, Somerset TA10 9PU, England.

SITKA Warren. See: LEVI Steven C.

SITWELL Pauline. Artist; Dancer; Lecturer. Education: Royal Academy Schools Diploma. Publications: Green Song, 1981; Train Journey to Deal and Other Poems, 1982. Contributions to: Numerous publications. Honours: Laureat, Paris Salon for Wood Engraving and Lithography; National Book League Choice for the Frankfurt Book Fair, 1981. Address: 46 Porchester Road, London W2 6ET, England.

SIVAD Niwles. See: DAVIS Selwyn Sylvester.

SJOBERG Leif, b. 15 Dec 1925, Boden, Sweden. m. Inger M Wallervik, 29 Jan 1959, dec 1958. Education: 3 Degrees, Uppsala University. Appointments: Lecturer and Assistant Professor, Columbia University, New York City, 1958-68; Associate Professor, 1968-72, Professor of Scandinavian and Comparative Literature, 1972-91, State, University of New York at Stony Brook. Publications: Gunnar Ekelöf: Selected Poems, 1967, Selected Poems, 1971; Erik Lindergren: The Man Without a Way, 1969; Transtromer: Windows and Stones, 1972; Par Lagerkvist: Evening Land, 1976; Artur Lundkvist: Agadir, 1978, 1980; Gunnar Ekelöf: A Molna Elegy, 1984; Martinson: Wild Bouquet, 1986; Harry Martinson: Aniara, A Review of Man in Time and Space, 1991; Edith Södergran: Violet Twilights, 1993; A Giant Pine: Poems

From Sweden, 1996. Honours: Translation Awards: Swedish Academy, 1967, 1976, 1992, Anglo Swedish Literature Foundation, 1978, Swedish Authors' Fund, 1984, 1994; Nomination, National Book Award, 1972. Memberships: Academy of American Poets; American-Scandinavian Society of New York, 1993; Translation Center; Harry Martinson Society. Address: 50 Morningside Drive Apt 21, New York, NY 10025-1755, USA.

SKAU Michael, b. 6 Jan 1944, Illinois, USA. Professor of English. Education: BA, 1965, MA, 1967, PhD, 1973, University of Illinois. Appointments: Assistant Professor, 1973-78, Associate Professor, 1978-85, Professor, 1985-, University of Nebraska, Omaha. Publication: Me and God Poems, 1990. Contributions include: Midland Review; Cumberland Poetry Review; Nothwest Review; Kentucky Poetry Review; Prophetic Voices; Sequoia; Paintbrush; Galley Sail Review; Carolina Quarterly; Great River Review; Illuminations; Passaic Review; Blue Unicorn; Minotaur. Membership: Modern Language Association. Address: Department of English, University of Nebraska, Omaha, NE 68182, USA.

SKELTON Robin, b. 12 Oct 1925. Easington, East Yorkshire, England. Author; Professor of English. m. Sylvia Mary Jarrett, 1957, 1 son, 2 daughters. Education: BA, 1950, MA, 1951, University of Leeds. Appointments: Served RAF, 1944-47; Assistant Lecturer, English, 1951, Lecturer, 1954, University of Manchester, England; Examiner, NUJMB, 1954-58; Chairman, Examiners, English O Level, 1958-60; Co-Founder, Chairman, Peterloo Group, Manchester, 1857-60; Founding Member, Honorary Secretary, Manchester Institute of Contemporary Arts, 1960-63; Centenary Lecturer, University of Massachusetts, USA, 1962-63; General Editor, Works of J M Synge, 1962-68; Associate Professor, English, 1963-66, Professor, 1966-, Chairman, Creative Writing, 1973-76, University of Victoria, British Columbia, Canada. Publications: Patmos and Other Poems, 1955; Third Day Lucky, 1958; Two Ballads of the Muse, 1960; Begging the Dialect, 1960; The Dark Window, 1962; A Valedictory Poem, 1963; An Irish Gathering, 1964; A Ballad of Billy Barker, 1965; Inscriptions, 1967; Because of This, 1968; The Hold of Our Hands, 1968; Selected Poems, 1944-67, 1968; An Irish Album, 1969; Georges Zuk, selected Verse, 1969; The Hunting Dark, 1971; Two Hundred Poems from the Greek Anthology, 1971; Three for Herself, 1972; Country Songs, 1973; Timelight, 1974; Because of Love, 1977; Landmarks, 1979; Collected Shorter Poems, 1947-77, 1981; Limits, 1981; De Nihilo, 1982; Zuk, 1982; Wordsong, 1983; Distances, 1985; The Edge of Time, 1995. Prose: John Ruskin: The Final Years, 1955; The Poetic Pattern, 1956; Cavalier Poems, 1960; Poetry (Teach Yourself Series), 1963; The Writings of J M Synge, 1971; J M Synge and His World, 1971; The Practice of Poetry, 1971; J M Synge (Irish Writers Series), 1972; Poetic Truth, 1978; Spellcraft, 1978; They Call it the Cariboo, 1980; Talisman Magic, 1985; Numerous edited texts. Contributions to: Anthologies; Others. Address: 1255 Victoria Avenue, British Columbia V8S 4P8, Canada.

SKENE Kathleen Vera, b. 17 Oct 1939, Sault Sainte Marie, Ontario, Canada. Secretary. m. G Leigh Skene, 12 Mar 1960, 1 son, 1 daughter. Education: Lacine High, Matric, 1956; Sir Geo Williams, 1956-57; Diploma, CDN School Commerical Art, 1957-59; Poetry Tutorial, 1988-89; Department for Continuing Education, Oxford, 1993-95. Appointments: Editor, Adventures in Truth, 1986-88; Editor, Victoria Poetry Chapbook #11, 1990; Convener, Canadian Authors Association Workshop, 1991-92. Publications: Pack Rat (Chapbook), 1992; Fire Water, 1994; The Uncertainty Factor/As A Rock (Chapbook), 1995. Contributions to: The Frogmore Papers; Envoi; Psychopoetica; The New Quarterly Ammonite; Ore; The Amethyst Review; Orbis; Grain; Staple; Prism International; Quarry; Carleton Arts Review; Antigonish Review; Canadian Literature; Canadian Author; Dandelion. Honours: Second, Writer of the Year Award, Canadian Authors Association; Honourable Mention, Literary Writes, Federation BC Writers, 1991; Honourable Mention, Writer's Digest, 1992; Third, Hope Writers; Guild, 1992; First Runner Up, Tears in the Fence, East Street Poets, 1994; Honourable Mention, The Amethyst Review, 1994; Second, Orbis, 1994. Memberships: East Street Poets; The Poetry Society; The League of Canadian Poets; Federation of BC Writers; Burnaby Writer's Association. Address: Headbury, Old Malthouse Lane, Langton Matravers, Swanage, Dorset BH19 3JA, England.

SKINNER Jeffrey, b. 8 Dec 1949, Buffalo, New York, USA. Assistant Professor of English and Creative Writing. m. Sarah Gorham, 8 May 1982, 2 daughters. Education: BA, Rollins College,

1971; Graduate Study, University of Bridgeport, 1973-74; MFA, Columbia University, 1978. Appointments: Lecturer, English, University of Bridgeport, Bridgeport, Connecticut, 1978-86; Vice-President, General Manager, Gleason Plant Security Inc, 1978-86; Lecturer, Norwalk Community College, 1982; Creative Writing Teacher to young people: Liberation House, 1982-83, Center for Creative Youth. Wesleyan University, Middletown, Connecticut, 1986-88. Assistant Professor, English, Salisbury State College, Maryland, 1986-88; Advisor, World Prison Poetry Center, 1984-86; Assistant Professor, English, Creative Writing, University of Louisville, Kentucky, 1988-; Poetry readings, colleges and other institutions; Literary Editor, Small Press Book Review. Publications: Late Stars, 1985; A Guide to Forgetting, 1988; Real Toads in Imaginary Gardens, 1991; The Company of Heaven, 1992. Contributions to: Atlantic; Commonwealth; Iowa Review; Nation; New Yorker; Paris Review; Poetry; Anthology of Magazine Verse and Yearbook of American Poetry, 1981, 1984; Anthology of New England Poetry; Other magazines and anthologies. Honours: Fellow: Indiana University Writers Conference, 1973; Colorado Writers Conference, 1975; Provincetown Fine Arts Center, 1981-82; Guest, MacDowell Colony and Yaddo, 1981; Grants: Connecticut Commission on the Arts, 1983; Ingram Merrill Foundation, 1985; Delaware State Arts Council; Fellow, National Endowment for the Arts, 1987; Book Award for A Guide to Forgetting, National Poetry Series, 1987. Address: 1637 Rosewood Avenue, Louisville, KY 40204, USA.

SKINNER Knute Rumsey, b. 25 Apr 1929, St Louis, Missouri, USA. Poet; Professor of English. m. (1) 3 sons, (2) Edna Faye Kiel, 25 Mar 1978. Education: BA, Speech and Drama, University of Northern Colorado, 1951; MA, English, Middlebury College, 1954; PhD, English, University of Iowa, 1958. Appointments: Assistant Professor, 1962-63, Lecturer, 1964-71, Associate Professor, 1971-73, Professor, 1973-, Western Washington University. Publications: Stranger With a Watch, 1965; A Close Sky Over Killaspuglonane, 1968, 1975; In Dinosaur Country, 1969; The Sorcerers - A Loatian Tale, 1972; Hearing of the Hard Times. 1981; The Flame Room, 1983; Selected Poems, 1985; Learning to Spell Zucchini, 1988; The Bears and Other Poems, 1991; What Trudy Knows and Other Poems, 1994. Contributions to: New Republic; Beloit Poetry Journal; Folio; New Orleans Poetry Journal; Chicago Review; Sparrow Magazine; Carolina Quarterly; Prairie Schooner; Colorado Quarterly; Literary Review. Honours: Governor's Invitational Writer's Day Certificate of Recognition, 1968; National Endowment for the Arts Fellowship, 1975; Millay Colony for The Arts Fellowship, 1976; Residency, Tyrone Guthrie Centre, 1985, 1986, 1993. Memberships: Poetry Ireland; Washington Poets Association. Address: Killaspuglonane, Lahinch, County Clare, Ireland.

SKINNER Richard, b. 15 July 1950, London, England. Writer; Counsellor. Education: MA, Natural Science, Cambridge University, 1972; BPhil, CQSW, Social Work, Exeter University, 1982. Appointments: Various posts. Publications: Leaping and Staggering, 1988; In The Stillness, 1990; Is The Clock Slow a Little Up, 1990; The Melting Woman, 1993; Still Staggering..., 1995. Contributions to: Outposts; Orbit; Acumen; Westwords. Address: Little Bystock, Bystock Close, Exeter, Devon EX4 4JJ, England.

SKINNER Susan, b. 22 Feb 1935, Charlton, England. Teacher; Lecturer. m. 28 Jan 1964, 2 sons, 2 daughters. Education: BA Hons, French English, 1955; PGCE, 1956; Certificate in Calligraphy and Bookbinding, 1992. Appointments: Teacher at various schools; Extra Mural Tutor, London University. Publication: Monet's Garden, 1991. Contributions to: Orbis; Outposts; Nursery World; Arvon Anthology. Honours: Julia Cairns Poetry First Prize, 1987, Second Prizes, 1988, 1990; Kent and Sussex Poetry Open Competition, 1991. Memberships: Surrey Poetry Centre, Guest Editor; Southern Writers Conference; Society of Women Writers and Journalists; Dunford Novelists (Founder Member). Address: Bieldside, West Furlong Lane, Hurst Pier Point, Sussex BN6 9RH, England.

SKLAR Morty Edward, b. 28 Nov 1935, Sunnyside, Queens, New York, USA. Editor; Publisher. m. (1) 24 Aug 1981, (2) Marcela Bruno, Oct 1993; 2 sons. Education: Undergraduate work, English, Queens College, New York, 1959-61; Co-Founder, Graduate, Phoenix House Therapeutic Community, Manhattan, 1968; BA, English, University of Iowa, Iowa City, 1972. Appointment: Editor, Publisher, The Spirit That Moves Us Press, Iowa City (now Jackson Heights, Queens, New York), 1975-. Publications: Riverside, 1974; The Night We Stood Up for Our Rights: Poems 1969-75, 1977; Brother Songs: Holy Cowl Press, 1979; A-Z: 200 Contemporary American Poets,

1981; Editor, anthologies: Patchwork of Dreams: Voices From The Heart Of The New America; Editor's Choice: Fiction, Poetry and Art from the US Small Press, 1980, 1987, 1992; Nuke-Rebuke: Writers and Artists Against Nuclear Energy and Weapons, 1984; Men and Women: Together and Alone, 1988. Contributions to: New York Quarterly; New Letters; Abraxas; Open Places; Little Caesar; Poetry Anthology (edited by Robert Creeley); Me Too; Pearl; World Letter; Des Moines Register; Lips; City Scriptum; Beginning; Daily Iowan; Drawing Legion; Pangloss Papers; Postpoetry; Telephone; El Nahuatzen; Yellow Brick Road. Honours: Citation, Excellence in Poetry, University of Iowa, 1972; 1st to publish collection of Jaroslav Seifert's poetry in USA, 1983; Seifert won Novel Prize in 1984; Editor's Grant for vision and excellence, Coordinating Council of Literary Magazines, New York City, 1985. Memberships: Academy of American Poets; Small Press Center; Poets, Essayists and Novelists. Address: The Spirit That Moves Us Press, PO Box 820, Jackson Heights, Queens, NY 11372, USA.

SKOULA-PERIFERAKI Marlena, b. Athens, Greece. Poet; Writer. Education: Lyceum Graduate. Appointments: General Secretary, Greek Author's Association; Greek Society of Civilization, Literature and Arts. Publications: East Nomber One, 1981; At The Twelfth Hour of Love, 1983; Twentieth Century, 1985; New Suns, 1987; In Fancy's Shadow, 1990; Spring Dilemma, 1995. Honours: Gold Medal, 1984, Greek Delegate, Academic Internationale de Lutece, Paris; Silver Medal, Society Francaise d'Encouragement L'Elite, 1989; Hon DLitt, World Academy of Arts and Culture, 1990; Doctor of Literature, World Academy of Arts and Culture, USA, 1990; Diploma, Italian Academy Ferdinandea. Memberships: Academic Internationale de Lutece, France; World Academy of Arts and Culture, USA; Parnassos; Honorary Member, Centro Cultural de Felgueiras, Portugal; Vice President, World Poetry Research Institute, Korea; Greek Astronautical Society. Address: 100 Thiras Street, Athens GR 10446, Greece.

SLADE Quilla. See: LEWIS-SMITH Anne Elizabeth.

SLAPPEY Mary McGowan, b. 22 Nov 1914, North Carolina, USA. Writer; Artist; Publisher; Poet; Novelist. Education: AB, George Washington University, 1947; JD, 1977. Publications: Poetry Power; Immortality Poems; Poems et al; Heartbeats; Swiss Songs, 1995; Pearls From My Memorary Box. Contributions to: Denver Post; Nautilus. Honours: Honorary Cultural Doctorate, World University, 1981; Gold Medals, Winged-Victory Accademia Italia; Laurel Wreath, World Poetry Association, 1978. Memberships: Poetry Society, President, 1976-78; National League of American Pen Women; Writers League; Washington Independent Writers. Address: 4500 Chesapeake Street North West, Washington DC 20016, USA.

SLAVITT David R(ytman), (David Benjamin, Henry Lazarus, Lynn Meyer, Henry Sutton), b. 23 Mar 1935, White Plains, New York, USA. Novelist; Poet; Translator; Lecturer. m. (1) Lynn Nita Meyer, 27 Aug 1956, div. 20 Dec 1977, 2 sons, 1 daughter, (2) Janet Lee Abrahm, 16 Apr 1978. Education: BA, magna cum laude, Yale University, 1956; MA, Columbia University, 1957. Appointments: Instructor in English, Georgia Institute of Technology, Atlanta, 1957-58; Staff, Newsweek Magazine, 1958-63; Assistant Professor, University of Maryland at College Park, 1977; Associate Professor of English, Temple University, Philadelphia, 1978-80; Lecturer in English, Columbia University, 1985-86; Lecturer, Rutgers University, 1987-; Lecturer in English and Classics, University of Pennsylvania, 1991-96; Visiting Professorships; Many university and college poetry readings. Publications: Novels: Rochelle, or Virtue Rewarded, 1966; Feel Free, 1968; Anagrams, 1970; ABCD, 1972; Ringer, 1982; Alice at 80, 1984; The Cliff, 1994. Novels Under the Pseudonym Henry Sutton include: The Sacrifice: A Novel of the Occult, 1978; The Proposal, 1980. Other Pseudonymous Novels: As Lynn Meyer: Paperback Thriller, 1975. As David Benjamin: The Idol, 1979. Other: Editor: Adrien Stoutenburg: Land of Superior Mirages: New and Selected Poems, 1986; Short Stories Are Not Real Life: Short Fiction, 1991. Translator: The Fables of Avianus, 1993; The Metamorphoses of Ovid, 1994. Contributions to: Various other books and periodicals. Honours include: American Academy and Institute of Arts and Letters Award, 1989; Rockefeller Foundation Artist's Residence, 1989. Address: 523 South 41st Street, Philadelphia, PA 19104, USA.

SLESIENSKY Deloris, b. Pennsylvania, USA. Freelance Writer. Education: BA, Political Science, Monmouth College, New Jersey; MA, Human Resources Management, Pepperdine University, California.

Publications: Thoughts in Shadow, 1990; Reflections on a Lopsided World, 1990; Fragments of Yesterday and New, A Long Poem, 1990. Contributions to: Plaza; Psychopoetica; Skylark; Hayden's Poetry Review; Minority Voices; Daily Meditation; Sisters Today; Hob-Nob; Poetry and the Vietnam Experience; Old Hickory Review; Thirteen; Silver Wings; Mill Hunk Herald; Broken Streets; Mobius; Tight; Where Eagles Fly. Honours: Award of Merit, National Federation of State Poetry Societies, 1990; 1st Prize, 1994, 1996 PPS Annual Contest; Nite-Writer's, 1st Annual Award, 1994. Memberships: Wyoming Valley Poetry Society; Pennsylvania Poetry Society; Wyoming Valley Poetry Society; Institute for Senior Learners, Marywood College. Address: 74 Dug Road, Wyoming, PA 18644-9374, USA.

SLIWINSKI Wincenty Piotr, b. 18 Jan 1915, Plock, Poland. Poet; Painter; Constructor of Violins; Physician. Education: University and Engineering College, Warsaw, 1936-39; Academy of Fine Arts, Warsaw, 1936-39, 1948. Appointments: Delegate: International Arts Guild, Monte Carlo, 1969; Haute Academie Internationalede Lutece, Paris, 1969; Comitato Internazionale Centro Studie Scambi Internazionali and Accademia Internazionale Leonardo da Vinci, Roma, Italy, 1970; Hon VP and Inter Execo Commete of Centro Studi e Scambi Internazionali and Accademia Leonardo da Vinci, 1979. Contributions to: Poet: International Monthly, World Poetry Society, Intercontinental, USA, 1974, 1975, 1977; Journals of Poetry International, Madras, India, 1984; International Poets, International Poets Academy, Madras, India, 1986; Rhythm and Rhyme, Auckland, New Zealand, 1986; Others: International Anthology on World Brotherhood and Peace, Manila, Philippines, 1978; World Poetry Europe, Madras, India, 1982; Voices International an Anthology of World Poetry, Madras, India, 1982; Song of Joy and Songs of Sadness, Eminent Poets series, Madras, India, 1985; International Anthology, Taranto, Italy, 1976-93. Honours: Honoris Causa and Gold Medal, Accademia Tomasso Campanella, Rome, 1972; Gold Medal Accademia, Leonardo da Vinci, Rome, 1977; Vermeil Medal, Arts-Sciences-Lettres, Paris, 1979; Gold Medal, Accademia Italia, Parma, 1979; Gold Medal, International Parliament for Safety and Peace, USA, 1982; Gran Premio delle Nazioni and the Statue of Victory, Centro Studi e Ricerche delle Nazioni, Italy, 1983; Albert Einstein Prize and Medal, International Academy Foundation, Delaware, USA, 1984; The Golden Flame, the World Parliament, USA, 1985; Oscar D'Italia, Accademia Italia, Calvatore, Italy, 1985. Memberships: World Poetry Society Interconental, USA; Accademia Leonardo da Vinci, Rome; Accademia Int Tomasso Campanella, Rome; Academia Athenaeum Gentium Pro Pace, Rome; La Haute Academie Internationale du Lutece, Paris; International Academy of Poets, England. Address: 4/78 Tatrzanska St, 00-742 Warsaw, Poland.

SLOAN Mary Margaret (Margy), b. 30 June 1946, Washington, District of Columbia, USA. Poet; Teacher. m. Larry Casalino, 4 July 1984, 1 daughter. Education: BA, Poetics, Humanities, New College of California, 1986. Publications: Infiltration, 1989; The Said Lands, Islands and Premises, 1995. Editor, Moving Borders: Three Decades of Innovative Writing by Women, due 1997. Contributions to: Talisman; Avec; Five Fingers Review; Ironwood; Acts; How(ever); Raddle Moon; Big Allis; Mirage. Address: 45 Stoneman Street, San Francisco, CA 94110, USA.

SMALL Nola Betty, b. 13 Nov 1936, Australia. Freelancer in Art, Drama, Writing and Music. m. John Oliver Small, 30 Mar 1968, 3 sons, 1 daughter. Education: Dip O Therapy, Australia, 1954; OT Reg, Canada, 1959; AMus, 1959; OTR, America, 1960. Appointments: Various Occupational Therapy posts in Australia, England, Canada and USA; Leader of Creative Writing Group - Smalltime. Publications: Off the Top of My Head, 1990; Just Desserts, 1991; Golden Rule Days, 1992; Running Circles, 1992; Going On, 1992; Jeepers Creepers, 1993; Cut Above, 1993; Stair Climbing, 1993; Bright Burning Eyes, 1993; Heavens Above, 1993; Nockasaggabagga, 1994; Pleasant Pastures, 1994; The Jackass Laughs, 1994; Fly High, Dig Deep, 1994; Inside, Looking Out, 1994; Small Heracleia, 1994; Selected Poems, 1994; Scallywag, 1995; Ying Yang Yong, 1995; Black and White, 1995; Yabba Dabba Do, 1995; Words Are Due, 1995; Strolling Words, 1995; Word Camera, 1995; Ruff Stuff, 1995; Blue Stocking Rhymes, 1995; Royal Poets, 1995; Around World, 1995; And There My Love, 1995; First Time; Expression In Verse; First Time Anthology; The Way You Tell 'Em; Triumph House Christian Yearbook; Trouble Shared, 1995; Triumph House Book of Love, 1995; Poems for Mum. Contributions to: Hebridean Magazine; Northam Festival Magazine; Harp Journal; Living Poets Anthology; Collected Verse Anthology; Conquest Magazine; Meriden Magazine; Winter Ensemble; Capital Lines; First Time

Anthology; MAMA Magazine. Honour: Northam Poetry Festival Runner Up, Australia, 1974. Address: 6 Scotts Avenue, Bromley, Kent BR2 0LQ, England.

SMALLSHAW Judith, b. 10 Apr 1935, London, England. Freelance Writer. m. John Smallshaw, 27 Sept 1958, 2 daughters. Education: PNEU, 1939-1951. Appointment: Currently freelance-writer. Publications: Copper Farthings, 1977; By Fell Tarn and Crag, 1978; An Apple in My Pocket, 1984. Contributions to: Lady; Inquirer; Surrey Life; Cumbria; Writers' Review; Exmoor Review; Poems from the Medical World; Woman Journalist; Orbis; Woman's Newspaper, USA; Behaviour and Medicine, USA. Honours: Julia Cairns Silver Salver, 1983, 1984; World Order of Poets, 1987. Memberships: London Writers', 1992; Society of Authors; Society of Women Writers; Poetry Society. Address: 178 Warren Road, Banstead, Surrey SM7 1LB, England.

SMARANDACHE Florentin, b. 10 Dec 1954, Romania. Mathematics Professor. m. Eleonora Niculescu, 28 May 1977, 2 sons. Education: MSc, Mathematics and Computer Science, University of Craiova, 1975-79; Currently pursuing PhD. Appointments: Various posts tutoring mathematics and as software engineer; Founder Paradoxist Literary Movement, 1980's. Publications: Formule Pentru Spirit, 1981; Exercitii Poetice, 1982; Sentimente Fabricate in Laborator, 1982; Legi de Compozitie Interna/Poeme cu Probleme!, 1982; Le Sens du Non-Sens, 1983, 1984; Anti-Chambres et Anti-Poesies ou Bizarreries, 1984, 1989; NonPoems, 1990-91; Inventario del General Malo, 1991; Fugit, 1994; Exist Impotriva Mea, Emigrant La Infinit, NonRoman, Scrieri Defecte, Synapses, 1995. Contributions to: Poetry Nippon; Poetry Time; International Poetry; Meridian; Luceafarul; Orizont; Ramuri; Le Message de la Nation; Le Chalut; Istanbul Accueil. Honours: Premiul Special, Concursul National de Proza Scurta Marin Preda, Alexandria, 1982; Prix Special Etranger, Grand Prix de la Ville de Bergerac, France, 1990; Honourable Mention, Le Concours de L'Academic de Lettres et des Arts du Perigord, France, 1990; Hon DLitt, World Congress of Poets, 1991; Premio della Literatura, Goccia di Luna, Italy, 1995. Memberships: Acting VP, International Writers and Artists Association; World Academy of Arts and Culture; Liga Culturala Oltenia, Romania; Modern Language Association; Academy of Association Poets; Romanian Writers Association. Address: 2456 South Rose Peak Drive, Tucson, AZ 85710, USA.

SMART Harry Watson, b. 6 Mar 1956, Dewsbury, Yorkshire, England. Writer. m. Catriona Stewart Murray, 4 Apr 1979, 1 son. Education: BSc (Hons), Geography, 1978; PhD, Social Theory, 1984, Aberdeen University. Appointments: Travelling Secretary, Universities and Colleges, Christian Fellowship, 1981-85. Publications: Pierrot, 1991; Criticism and Public Rationality, 1991; Shoah, 1993. Contributions to: Lines Review; Chapman; West Coast Magazine; Outposts; Oxford Poetry; Poetry Review; Agenda; Stand Magazine; Times Literary Supplement. Honours: Writer's Bursary, Scottish Arts Council, 1991; Inflatable Dolphin from Ian Duhig, John Hewitt International Summer School, Antrim, 1991. Memberships: Scottish Poetry Library, Edinburgh; Poetry Society, London. Address: c/o Faber and Faber, 3 Queen Square, London WC1N 3AU, England.

SMEV. See: **VOISINE Mary Emma, Sister**.

SMITH Arthur Edwin, b. 17 Apr 1948, Stockton, California, USA. University Professor. Education: BA, 1970, MA, 1971, San Francisco State University; PhD, University of Houston, 1986. Appointments: University of Tennessee. Publications: Elegy on Independence Day, 1985; Orders of Affection, 1996. Contributions to: New Yorker; North American Review; Chicago Review; Poetry; Nation; Georgia Review; New England Review; Crazyhorse. Honours: The Nation - Discovery, 1981; National Endowment for the Arts Fellowship, 1984; Agnes Lynch Starrett Poetry Prize, 1985; Norma Farber First Book Award, 1985. Memberships: International Society of America; Modern Language Association. Address: Department of English, University of Tennessee, Knoxville, TN 37996, USA.

SMITH Cecile Musson (Cécile, Cécile Norma Musson), b. 13 Aug 1914, Bermuda. Educator. m. James A C Smith, 23 Nov 1955. Education: Graduate, Ontario Business College, Canada, 1946; Certificates: American International College, University of Maryland and Queens University, 1955, Cambridge University, 1932, 1956, Bermuda College, 1972. Appointments: Brownie Leader, 1935; News Editor, Recorder, 1941; RCAF, 1946-47; Freelance, Staff,

Parliamentary Reporter, 1947; Founder, Head, Commercial School, 1947; Social Welfare Board, 1965; Arts Council, Juveniles Court, 1969; Now serving Family Court, Updating. Publications: Zephyrs, A Collection of Poetic Thoughts, 1937, reprint in 1942 with donation to RAF War Fund, High Critical Praise from Mid-Ocean News. Contributions to: World's Fair Anthology of Verse, 1940; South and West International, 1942; Poem on BBC, 1961; Rome, Date With The Past, Enjoyment of Poetry, 1965; Poetic Voices of America, 1994. Honours: Honorary Representative, CSSI Leonardo da Vinci, 1963; Honorary Medal, Merit Diploma, 1965; International Great Glory Prize, Rome, 1982; FAME Arts Award, 1983; Government Appreciation, 1989; International Order of Merit, IBC, 1990; Woman of the Year, IBC, 1992-93. Memberships: Founder, 1957, President for 16 years, Bermuda Writers Club; Founding Member, Arts Council, 1969, Board of Governors, ABI; WL Fellow, Academy of Poets; Life Member, IBC Associate Poets Laureate International. Address: Cavendish Apt 2, Block 7, Hibiscus, Devonshire DV 03, Bermuda.

SMITH Charlene Mary-Cath, b. 8 Oct, Manchester, New Hampshire, USA. m. Raymond G Bureau. Contributions to: Hawaii Review; Sulphur River Review Literary Review; White Wall Review, Canada; Fox Cry, Red Brick Review; Aura Literary/Arts Review; Writer's Journal. Honours: Member of Winning Team, 1990s; 15th Annual San Francisco Poetry Film Festival; 1st Place in 1993's New England Regional Holocaust Competition; Ten from Poetalk Award, 1996. Membership: Poetry Society of New Hampshire, 1989-. Address: 283 Lowell Street, Manchester, NH 03104, USA.

SMITH Dave, b. 19 Dec 1942, Portsmouth, Virginia, USA. Professor; Editor. m. Deloras M Weaver, 31 Mar 1966, 1 son, 2 daughters. Education: BA, English, University of Virginia, 1965; MA, English, Southern Illinois University, 1969; PhD, English, Ohio University, 1976. Appointments: Teacher, Poquoson High School, Poquoson, Virginia, 1965-67; Teaching Assistant, Southern Illinois University, 1967-69; Teaching Assistant, Ohio University, 1971-72, 1975-76; Instructor, Western Michigan University, 1973-74; Assistant Professor, Cottey College, Missouri, 1974-75; Assistant Professor/Director, Creative Writing, University of Utah, 1975-77; Associate Professor/Director, Creative Writing, University of Utah, 1977-79; Visiting Professor, SUNY, Binghamton, 1979-80; Associate Professor/Director, Creative Writing, University of Florida, 1980-81; Professor, Virginia Commonwealth University, 1981-90; Professor, LSU, 1990-. Publications: Onliness, 1981; In the House of the Judge, 1983; Southern Delights, 1983; Gray Soldiers, 1984; The Morrow Anthology of Younger American Poets, 1985; The Roundhouse Voices: Selected and New Poems, 1985; Local Assays: On Contemporary American Poetry, 1985; Cuba Night, 1990; The Essential Poem, 1991; Night Pleasures: New and Selected Poems, 1992; Fate's Kite: Poems 1991-95, 1995. Contributions to: American Scholar; Kenyon Review; Georgia Review; Paris Review; Partisan Review; New Yorker; Nation; Poetry. Honours: Lyndhurst Fellowship, 1987-89; Guggenheim Fellowship, 1981; National Endowment for the Arts Fellowship, 1976, 1981; Award from Academy of Arts and Letters, 1979; Reader's Poetry Prize, Prairie Schooner, 1980, 1995; Runner-Up, Pulitzer Prize in Poetry, 1979, 1981. Memberships: Poetry Society of America; Associated Writing Programs; Fellowship of Southern Authors. Address: Editor, The Southern Review, 43 Allen Hall, Louisiana State University, Baton Rouge, LA 70803, USA.

SMITH Deirdre Armes, b. 29 Sept 1922. Teacher. m. 9 Aug 1947, 2 sons, 2 daughters. Education: The College, Saffron Walden, Essex. Appointments: Teacher, St Pauls School, Walkden; Teacher, Autistic Unit, Peel Green; Head, Infant Department, Little Hulton East County Primary School, all in Lancashire, England. Publications: Cycles to The Moon, 1970; Church Bells on a Wet Sunday, 1985; The Real Thing, 1987; Mother of Wales, 1990; With Untold Care, 1991; Winter Tennis Courts, 1987. Contributions to: Lancashire Life; This England; Acumen; Outposts; Poetry Wales; Envoi; Poetry Now; New Hope International; Poetry Nottingham; Writing Women; Writers Own Magazine; Weyfarers; Doors; Write Now; Pause; Spokes. Honours: Invitation to read poetry at Poetry Festival in Maryland, USA, 1992, and Write Now, Radio Merseyside Programme, 1991; Finalist, Bard of the Year Competition, Leicester University, 1993, 1994. Membership: Society of Women Writers and Journalists. Address: Talgarth, 21 Parr Fold Avenue, Worley, Manchester M28 4EJ, England.

SMITH Francis Joseph, b. 22 May 1920, Ohio, USA. Priest; Teacher. Education: Xavier University, Cincinnati, 1943; MA, Loyola University, Chicago, 1949; MA, Oxford University, 1961. Appointments:

Instructor, University of Detroit; Assistant Professor, Associate Professor, Professor, John Carroll University. Publications: First Prelude, 1981; All Is A Prize, 1989. Contributions to: Aethlon; Chicago Poetry Review; New York Quarterly; Samizdat; Snowy Egret; Song; Spoon River Quarterly. Honour: Cuyahoga Writers Workshop First Place. Memberships: Poetry Society of America; Poets and Writers; Modern Language Association. Address: John Carroll University, 20700 North Park Boulevard, Rodman Hall, University Heights, OH 44118, USA.

SMITH Iain Crichton, b. 1 Jan 1928, Isle of Lewis, Scotland. Writer. m. Donalda Gillies Smith, 16 July 1977, 2 stepsons. Education: MA, Honours, English, Aberdeen University, 1945-49. Appointments: Teacher, Clydebank High School, 1952-53; Oban High School, 1955-77. Publications: Thistles and Roses, 1961; The Law and The Grace, 1969; From Bourgeois Land, 1969; Love Poems and Elegies, 1972; The Notebooks of Robinson Crusoe, 1975; A Life, 1980; The Exiles, 1984; Collected Poems, 1992. Contributions to: Times Literary Supplement; Encounter; Stand; Spectator; Listener; New Statesman; Lines Review; Poetry Review. Honours: PEN Poetry Award, 1970; Poetry Society Choice, 1984, Recommendations, 1972, 1975, 1989, 1992; Lines Review Commonwealth Poetry Prize, 1986; Saltire Award, 1992. Memberships: Literature Committee, 1985-91, Main Body, 1985-88, Scottish Arts Council; FRLS. Address: Tigh Na Fuaran, Taynuilt, Argyll, Scotland.

SMITH James Ronald, b. 12 Feb 1949, Savannah, Georgia, USA. Teacher. m. Anita Delores Quinney, 1 Nov 1968, 1 son. Education: BA, English, Philosophy, 1971; MA, English, 1974; MFA, Creative Writing, 1985; MH, 1994. Appointments: Instructor of English; Chairman, Department of English; Robert W Bugg Chair of Distinguished Teaching; Writing-in-Residence. Publication: Running Again in Hollywood Cemetery, 1988. Contributions to: Nation; Kenyon Review; Georgia Review; Kansas Quarterly; New England Review; Virginia Quarterly Review; Southern Poetry Review; Verse; College English; Many others. Honours: Guy Owen Poetry Award, Southern Review, 1986; Theodore Roethke Poetry Prize, Poetry Northwest, 1989. Memberships: Modern Language Association; International James Joyce Foundation; Associated Writing Programs; The Robert Penn Warren Circle; Poetry Society of Virginia; Virginia Writers Club. Address: 616 Maple Ave, Richmond, VA 23226, USA.

SMITH John Charles, (C Busby Smith), b. 5 Apr 1924, High Wycombe, Buckinghamshire, England. Literary Agent. Education: St James Elementary School, Gerrards Cross, Buckinghamshire. Appointments: Joined, 1946, Managing Director, 1958-71, Christy and Moore Ltd; Editor, Poetry Review. Publications: Gates of Beauty and Death, 1948; The Dark Side of Love, 1952; The Birth of Venus, 1954; Excursus in Autumn, 1958; A Letter to Lao Tze, 1973; A Landscape of My Own (selected poems 1948-1982), 1982; Songs for Simpletons, 1984; Poems for Paul Klee, 1990. Contributions to: Windmill; Listener; Saturday Review; New English Review; Poetry Review; Poetry Quarterly; Poetry and Poverty; Modern Reading; New Verse; Northwest Review; Contemporary Review; Tribune; Adam. Honours: Adam International Review Prize, 1952; Poetry Book Society Choice, 1958, 1973; Poetry Book Society Recommendation, 1965; 2nd Borestone Mountain Award, 1971. Memberships: Poetry Society, Member of Executive; PEN Executive; Arts Council, Copywright Panel. Address: 529 Emerald Empire, KNSM Eiland, Amsterdam, Netherlands.

SMITH Jordan, b. 11 Sept 1954, Rochester, New York, USA. Professor. m. Mary Alice Peet, 6 June 1979, 2 sons. Education: Hamilton College, 1972-73; BA, Empire State College, 1973-77; MA, Johns Hopkins University, 1977-78; MFA, University of Iowa, 1979-81. Appointments: Instructor, Johns Hopkins University, 1978-79; Visiting Assistant Professor, 1981-83, Assistant Professor, 1983-88, Associate Professor, 1988-, Union College. Publications: An Apology for Loving The Old Hymns; Lucky Seven; The Household of Continuence. Contributions to: Agni Review; Antaeus; Ironwood; Kenyon Review; New England Review; Breadloaf Quarterly; Paris Review; Poetry; Shenandoah; Yale Review; Quarterly West; Western Humanities Review; Epoch; Transfer. Honours: Fellowships, Guggenheim Foundation, Ingram Merrill Foundation, New York Foundation for The Arts, National Endowment for The Arts. Address: 180 Kingsley Road, Burnt Hills, NY 12027, USA.

SMITH Ken, b. 4 Dec 1938, Rudston, England. Writer. 2 sons, 2 daughters. Education: BA, Leeds, 1963. Appointments: Visiting

Writer, Clark University, Massachusetts, 1972-73; Yorkshire Arts Writer in Residence, Leeds University, 1976-78; Writer in Residence, Kingston Polytechnic, 1979-81; HMP Wormwood Scrubs, 1985-87. Publications: Eleven Poems; Frontwards; Anus Mundi; Tales of the Hunter; Grainy Pictures of the Rain; Inside Time; The Heart, The Border; Berlin: Coming in From the Cold; Tender to the Queen of Spain. Honours: Gregory Award; Co-Editor, Stand; Arts Council of Great Britain Award; Poetry Book Society Recommendation. Address: c/o Bloodaxe Books, PO Box 15N, Newcastle Upon Tyne NE99 1SN, England.

SMITH Margery, b. 21 Mar 1916, Nottingham, England. Teacher; Poet; Editor. Education: Charlotte Mason College, Ambleside, PNEU Teachers Certificate, 1936. Appointments: Editor, L'Umile Pianta, 1972-79; Co-Editor, 5th and 6th Anthologies of Camden Poetry Group. Publications: In Our Time, 1941; Still in My Hand, 1964; In Transit, 1981. Contributions to: Anthologies include: Poems of This War, 1947; Mitre, 1967; Without Adam, 1968; Laudamus Te, 1969; Look Through a Diamond, 1971; Chaos of the Night, 1984; Camden Poetry Society Anthologies; Others: Poetry Review; Anglo-Welsh Review; Yoga Today; The Glass; PNEU Journal; NA Mentor; South and West; Pink Piece; Byron Society Newsletter. Honours: Poetry Review Premium Awards, 1938, 1940; First Prizes for Sonnets, from Lucia Markham, Manifold and Anglo-Welsh Review; Poem included in D Day QEII Concert, 1994. Memberships: Poetry Society, UK, General Council, 1967-69; Poetry Society of America; Nottingham Poetry Society, Co-Founder, Honorary Secretary and Treasurer; Founder-Fellow, International Poetry Society; Camden Poetry Group; Byron Society; Honorary Member, Shelley Society of New York. Address: 12 Springfield Crescent, Horsham, West Sussex RH12 2PP, England.

SMITH R Lester (Bob), b. 14 June 1928, Long Beach, California, USA. US Navy, Retired; Teacher; Pastor. m. Maroline Havens, 1958, 2 sons , 3 daughters. Appointments include: Clam Digger; Wool Presser; Short Order Cook; Bill Collector; Ranch Hand; Helicopter Crewman, Crypto Officer, Mustang Lieutenant, US Navy. Publications: Bread For the Head, 1989; Psalms of Theophilus, 1990; The Spit'N Image, 1993; Ducks in a Row, 1995. Contributions to: Southern Writers Newsletter, Fort Worth, Texas; Omnific; Anterior Poetry Monthly; Ozark Muse; Poet's Voice; Inspirational Poet; Parnassus; Tucumcari Literary Review. Honours: Received Blue Ribbon Awards for Poems, "Time to Rhyme", "Full Circle", "Tree of Degrees", Southern Poetry Association of Pass Christian, Mississippi; Roaring Lamb Award, Amy Foundation of Lansing, Michigan. Address: PO Box 660, Foreman, AR 71836, USA.

SMITH Sam(uel) (David), b. 24 Dec 1946, Blackpool, England. Poet; Editor. m. (1) Judith Bone, 1970, 1 daughter, (2) Stephanie Dart, 2 daughters. Appointments include: Merchant Navy; Plumber; Social Worker; Nurse. Publications: Founding Editor, Journal of Contemporary Anglo-Scandinavian Poetry, 1995-; To Be Like John Clare,collection. Contributions to: Works published in numerous publications worldwide including: Envoi, Cleopatra, Hybrid, New Fiction, New Hope International, Northwords, Orbis, Parnassus of World Poets, Poetry Now, Printed Matter, Purple Patch, Staple, Unicorn, Weyfarers. Memberships: Anglo-Welsh Poetry Society; John Clare Society. Address: 11 Heatherton Park, Bradford-on-Tone, Taunton, Somerset TA4 1EU, England.

SMITH Sheila.See: **HAYWOOD April**.

SMITH Stephen Mark, b. 16 Jan 1964, Worcestershire, England. Writer; Lecturer. Education: BA Honours, English, University College Wales, Aberystwyth; PhD studies. Appointment: Lecturer, Advanced Creative Writing, Sutton College of Liberal Arts. Publications: The Fabulous Relatives, 1993; Included in The Forward Book of Poetry, 1993. Contributions to: Magazines: Bete Noire; Ambit; Honest Ulsterman; Aeirings; Iota; Outposts; London Magazine; Orbis; Wide-Skirt; Envoi; Exile; Scratch; Agenda; Verse; Poetry Nottingham; Cyphers; Foolscap; Echo Room. Honour: Major Gregory Award, 1991. Address: 17 Elgin Court, 12 Bramley Hill, South Croydon CR2 6LT, England.

SMITH Steven James, b. 25 Apr 1972, Wellington, Shropshire, England. Writer; Poet. m. Liesl Smith, 24 Oct 1994. Education: English, History and Philosophy A Levels, Crestwood Sixth Form College, 1990. Appointments: Team Leader of Building Society, 1990-93; Freelance Writer and Poet, 1994-96; Supervisor (Part-time), Kays Postal Department, 1995-96. Publications: My Realm, 1994;

Elysian Dreams, 1996. Contributions to: Tops; Helicon; Poetry Now; Anchor Books; White Tower; National Library of Poetry, USA; Edizioni University, Italy; Reflections; First Time. Honours: Editors Choice Award, National Library of Poetry, USA, 1994, 1995, 1996. Memberships: White Tower Writers Association; The Dreamlands Poetry Group. Address: 106 Windermere Drive, Worcester WR4 9JD, England.

SMITH Thomas R, b. 16 Jan 1948, Chippewa Falls, Wisconsin, USA. Poet; Editor. m. Krista Lynn Spieler, 19 Oct 1985. Education: University of Wisconsin, River Falls,1966-70. Appointments: Director, Artspeople of Wisconsin, 1978-81; Assistant to the President, Natural Resources Corporation, 1982-90; Associate Editor, Ally Press, 1990-. Publications: Keeping the Star, 1988; Horse of Earth, 1994; Editor: Walking Swiftly: Writings and Images on the Occasion of Robert Bly's 65th Birthday, 1992; Editor, What Happened When He Went to the Store for Bread: Poems by Alden Nowlan, 1993; Horse of Earth, 1994. Contributions to: Bloomsbury Review; New Age Journal; Germination; Yellow Silk; Raccoon; Guadalupe Review; Inroads; High Plains Literary Review; Transactions of the Wisconsin Academy of Sciences, Arts and Letters. Honours: Winner, Milkweed Chronicle Poetry Contest, 1982; Winner, Lake Superior Writers Series, 1984, 1991; Poems Selected for Editor's Choice, Sklar and Biggs, The Spirit That Moves Us Press, 1987. Address: 246 Bedford Street, South East 2, Minneapolis, MN 55414, USA.

SMITH Vivian Brian, b. 3 June 1933, Hobart, Tasmania. Reader. m. 15 Feb 1960, 1 son, 2 daughters. Education: MA, 1955; PhD, 1970. Appointments: Lecturer, University of Tasmania, 1955-66; Reader, University of Sydney, 1982-. Publications: The Other Meaning; An Island South; Familiar Places; Tide Country; Selected Poems; New Selected Poems, 1995. Contributions to: Age; Sydney Morning Herald; Bulletin; Australian; Southerly; Quadrant; Times Literary Supplement. Honours: Grace Leven Prize; New South Wales Premier's Prize. Membership: Australian Society of Authors. Address: 19 McLeod Street, Mosman, New South Wales 2088, Australia.

SMITH William Jay, b. 22 Apr 1918, Winnfield, Louisiana, USA. Professor of English Emeritus; Poet; Writer. m. (1) Barbara Howes, 1947, div 1965, 2 sons, (2) Sonja Haussmann, 1966, 1 stepson. Education: BA, 1939, MA, 1941, Washington University, St Louis; Institut de Touraine, Tours, France, 1938; Columbia University, 1946-47; Wadham College, Oxford, 1947-48; University of Florence, 1948-50. Appointments include: Writer-in-Residence, 1965-66, Professor of English, 1967-68, 1970-80, Professor Emeritus, 1980-, Hollins College, Virginia; Consultant in Poetry (Post nour called Poet Laureate), 1968-70, Honorary Consultant, 1970-76, Library of Congress, Washington, DC; Lecturer, Salzburg Seminar in American Studies, 1974; Fulbright Lecturer, Moscow State University, 1981; Poet-in-Residence, Cathedral of St John the Divine, New York City, 1985-88. Publications: Poetry includes: At Delphi: For Allen Tate on His Seventy-Fifth Birthday, 19 November, 1974, 1974; Venice in the Fog, 1975; Verses on the Times (with Richard Wilbur), 1978; Journey to the Dead Sea, 1979; The Tall Poets, 1979; Mr Smith, 1980; The Traveler's Tree: New and Selected Poems, 1980; Oxford Doggerel, 1983; Collected Translations: Italian, French, Spanish, Portuguese, 1985; The Tin Can, 1988; Journey to the Interior, 1988; Plain Talk: Collected Poems 1939-1999, 1990; also 16 books of poetry for children, 1955-90; Epigrams, Epitaphs, Satires, Nonsense, Occasional, Concrete and Quotidian Poems, 1988; Stories include: Army Brat: A Memoir, 1980; As Editor: A Green Place: Modern Poems, 1982. Contributions to: Journals and magazines. Honours: Rhodes Scholar, 1947-48; Ford Foundation Fellowship, 1964; Henry Bellamann Major Award, 1970; National Endowment for the Arts Grant, 1972-95; Loines Award, National Institute Arts and Letters, 1972; National Endowment for the Humanities Grants, 1975, 1989; Gold Medal of Labor, Hungary, 1978, Pro Culture Hungarice Medal, 1993; Ingram Merrill Foundation Grant, 1982. Membership: Vice President for Literature, American Academy of Arts and Letters, 1986-89. Address: 63 Lother Shaw Road, RR 1, Box 151, Cummington, MA 01026, USA.

SMITHER Elizabeth Edwina, b. 15 Sept 1941, New Plymouth, New Zealand. Librarian. m. Michael Duncan Smither, 31 Aug 1963. Education: Victoria and Massey Universities, 1960; New Zealand Library School, 1962. Appointments: Cataloguer; Childrens Librarian; Librarian Information and Advisory. Publications: Here Come the Clouds; You're Very Seductive William Carlos Williams; The Sarah Train; The Legend of Marcello Mastroianni's Wife; Casanova's Ankle;

Shakespeare Virgins; Professor Musgrove's Canary; Gorilla/Guerilla; Animaux; A Pattern of Marching; A Cortège of Daughters, 1993; The Tudor Style, 1993. Contributions to: Times Literary Supplement; PN Review; Bananas; London Magazine; Poetry Review; Samphire; Omens; Encounter; Helix; Poetry Australia; Ariel; Meanjin; Westerly; Listener; Landfall; Island; Poetry Now. Honours: Writing Bursary; Freda Buckland Award; Auckland University Literary Fellowship; Scholarship in Letters; Literary Fund Travelling Bursary; Lilian Ida Smith Award; New Zealand Book Award. Membership: New Zealand Society of Authors (PEN). Address: 19a Mount View Place, New Plymouth, New Zealand.

SMOCK Frederick, b. 23 June 1954. Editor. m. Jacqueline Strange, 3 Sept 1983, 2 sons. Education: BA, Georgetown College, 1976; MA, University of Louisville, 1978. Appointments: Editor, The American Voice; Lecturer, University of Louisville. Publications: The Muhammad Ali Poems, 1989; 12 Poems, 1991; This Meadow of Time: A Provence Journal, 1995. Contributions to: Poetry; Poet and Critic; Iowa Review; La Carta de Oliver; Boulevard; Green Mountains Review; Wind; Plainsong; Thinker Review. Address: 2100 Lavderdale Road, Louisville, KY 40205, USA.

SNEYD Stephen (Steve) Henry, b. 20 Mar 1941, Maidenhead, Berkshire, England. Poet. m. Rita Ann Cockburn, 13 Mar 1964, 1 son, 1 daughter. Education: BSc; DipM; CertEd. Appointments: UK Columnist, Scavenger's Newsletter, USA; Contributing Editor, Poetry, Fantasy Commentator USA, 1992-. Publications: The Legerdemain of Changelings, 1979; Two Humps Not One, 1980; Discourteous Self-Service, 1982; Prug Plac Gamma, 1983; Stone Bones (with Pete Presford), 1983; Fifty-Fifty Infinity, 1989; Bad News from the Stars, 1991; At the Thirteenth Hour, 1991; We Are Not Men, 1991; What Time Has Use For, 1992; A Mile Beyond the Bus, 1992; In Coils of Earthen Hold, 1994. Contributions to: UK: Auguries; Back Brain Recluse; Bogg; Dream; Global Tapestry; Hybrid; Inkshed; Iron; Krax; Ludd's Mill; New Hope International; New Moon; Ore; Pennine Platform; Poetry Nottingham; Psychopoetica; Sanity; Sepia; Star Wine; Stride; Poet's Voice; Trends; Tribune; Wide Skirt; Works; Xenia; Zenos; Others; USA: Aspect; Dark Alley; Dreams and Night-Mares; Fantasy Commentator; Gargoyle; Grasslands Review; Grue; Ice River; International Portland Review; Late Knocking; Magazine of Speculative Poetry; Mernes; Minotaur; New Pathways; New Spokes; New Statesman; Odyssey; Owlflight; Planet Detroit; Red Eft; Space and Time; Star Line; Tenth Muse; Terrible Work; The Third Alternative; Xenophilia. Broadcast: YTV, BBC Radio 4, local stations UK and overseas. Honours: Trend Prize for Peace Poetry, 1967; Northern Star Poetry Prize, 1983; Diploma di Merito, Accademia Italia, 1983; Winner, Best Poet, Small Press and Magazine Awards, 1986; Peterson Prize, 1996. Membership: Science Fiction Poetry Association. Address: 4 Nowell Place, Almondbury, Huddersfield, West Yorkshire HD5 8PB, England.

SNIDER Clifton Mark, b. 3 Mar 1947, Minnesota, USA. College Instructor. Education: BA, California State University, 1969; MA 1971; PhD, University of New Mexico, 1974. Appointments: Lecturer, California State University; Instructor, Long Beach City College. Publications: The Age of the Mother (poems); The Stuff That Dreams Are Made On: A Jungian Interpretation of Literature; Impervious to Piranhas; Blood and Bones; Edwin: A Character in Poems; Jesse and His Son; Bad Smoke Good Body; Jesse Comes Back. Contributions to: Painted Bride Quarterly; Visions; Poetry LA; Rolling Stone; Blue Mesa Review; Blue Light Review; High Rock Review; Pearl; Chiron Review; Bogg. Address: 2719 Eucalyptus Avenue, Long Beach, CA 90806, USA.

SNODGRASS W D, (S S Gardons, Will McConnell, Kozma Prutkov, Dan S Gross), b. 5 Jan 1926, Wilkinsburg, Pennsylvania, USA. Poet; Writer; Dramatist; Professor. m. (1) Lila Jean Hank, 6 June 1946, div Dec 1953, 1 daughter, (2) Janice Marie Ferguson Wilson, 19 Mar 1954, div Aug 1966, 1 stepdaughter, 1 son, (3) Camille Rykowski, 13 Sept 1967, div 1978, (4) Kathleen Ann Brown, 20 June 1985. Education: Geneva College 1943-44, 1946-47; BA, 1949, MA, 1951, MFA, 1953, University of Iowa. Appointments: Instructor in English, Cornell University, 1955-57; Instructor, University of Rochester, New York, 1957-58; Assistant Professor of English, Wayne State University, Detroit, 1959-67; Visiting Professor, Old Dominion University, Norfolk, Virginia, 1978-79; Distinguished Professor 1979-80, Distinguished Professor of Creative Writing and Contemporary Poetry 1980-94, University of Delaware, Newark, 1979-94; Various lectures and poetry readings. Publications: Poetry: Heart's Needle, 1959; After Experience,

1967; As S S Gardons, Remains: A Sequence of Poems, 1970, revised edition 1985; The Fuehrer Bunker: The Complete Cycle, 1977-95; If Birds Build With Your Hair, 1979; D D Byrde Calling Jennie Wrenne, 1984; A Colored Poem, 1986; The House the Poet Built, 1986; A Locked House, 1986; The Kinder Capers, 1986; Selected Poems, 1957-1987, 1987; W D's Midnight Carnival (with DeLoss McGraw), 1988; The Death of Cock Robin, 1989; Each in His Season, 1994; The Fuhrer Bunker: The Complete Cycle, 1995. Contributions to: Many periodicals. Honours: Ingram Merrill Foundation Award, 1958; Government of Romania Centennial Medal, 1977. Memberships: National Institute of Arts & Letters; Poetry Society of America; International PEN. Address: RD 1, Box 51, Erieville, NY 13061, USA.

SNUGGS Olive, (Annie Hughes), b. 26 Nov 1924, Coventry, Warwickshire, England. Poet; Freelance Writer. m. Frederick Eric Snuggs, 29 Jan 1944, 1 son, 4 daughters. Publications: Ollies Overtures; Reflections in Cameo; SAFAW Sunlight & Shadows; Beneath the Southern Cross, Book; One and Two, Anthology of Australian Poetry; Bi Centennial Vintage; New Directions; I Came A Migrant; Salisbury Speaks; Friendly Street ReaderNo 18, 1994; Australian Multicultural Book Review, 1995. Contributions to: Messenger Press; Recreation for Elderly Magazine; Poet International Monthly; Mattoid Deakin University Victoria; Poetry Read Radio; Top Dog Journal, 1995; Scope FAW Queensland, 1992-95. Honours: Celebrating Life Anthology by Writers Over 50 Years; Gawler SA Spring Poetry Competition; The Paddocks House Spring Poetry Competition; MPS 7th Poetry Day Australia, Medallion; MPS 1st Decade Poetry Day. Memberships: Melbourne Poetry Society; Fellowship of Australian Writers, South Australia; Writers Professional Services; South Australian Writers Centre; World Poetry Society; Enfield Writers' Club, South Australia. Address: 6 Jacaranda Drive, Salisbury East, South Australia, Australia.

SNYDER Gary (Sherman), b. 8 May 1930, San Francisco, California, USA. Poet; Writer; Teacher. m. 2 sons, 2 stepdaughters. Education: BA, Reed College, Portland, Oregon, 1951; Graduate Studies in Linguistics, Indiana University, 1951; Graduate School, Department of East Asian Languages, University of California, Berkeley, 1953-56; Studied Zen Buddhism and East Asian Culture in Japan. Appointment: Faculty, University of California, Davis, 1986-. Publications: Poetry: Riprap and Cold Mountain Poems, 1959; Myths and Texts, 1960; A Range of Poems, 1966; Three Worlds, Three Realms, Six Roads, 1966; The Back Country, 1968; The Blue Sky, 1969; Regarding Wave, 1970; Manzanita, 1971; Plute Creek, 1972; The Fudo Trilogy: Spell Against Demons, Smokey the Bear Sutra, The California Water Plan, 1973; Turtle Island, 1974; All in the Family, 1975; Songs for Gaia, 1979; Axe Handles, 1983; Left Out in the Rain: New Poems, 1947-1986, 1986; The Practice of the Wild, 1990; No Nature: New and Selected Poems, 1992; Mountains and Rivers Without End, 1996; Prose: Earth House Hold: Technical Notes and Queries to Fellow Dharma Revolutionaries, 1969; The Old Ways: Six Essays, 1977; He Who Hunted Birds in His Father's Village: The Dimensions of a Haida Myth, 1979; The Real Work: Interviews and Talks, 1964-1979, 1980; Passage Through India, 1984; A Place in Space, 1995. Contributions to: Anthologies. Honours: First Zen Institute of America Scholarship, 1956; American Academy of Arts and Letters Award, 1966; Bollingen Foundation Grant, 1966-67; Frank O'Hara Prize, 1967; Levinson Prize, 1968; Guggenheim Fellowship, 1968-69; Pulitzer Prize in Poetry, 1975; Finalist, National Book Award, 1992. Memberships: American Academy of Arts and Letters; American Academy of Arts and Sciences. Address: 18442 Macnab Cypress Road, Nevada City, CA 95959, USA.

SO Shun. See: **WONG Wai Ming (Otis).**

SOCOLOW Elizabeth Anne, b. 15 June 1940, New York, New York, USA. Teacher. m. Robert Socolow, 10 June 1962, div 1982, 2 sons. Education: BA, Vassar College, 1962; MA, 1963, PhD, 1967, Harvard College. Appointments: Lecturer, Yale University, 1967-70; Rutgers University, 1981-82; High School Teacher, 1986-88, 1990-91, 1992-; Lecturer (Poetry), Bernard and Vassar Colleges, 1988-90; Adjunct Lecturer in English, University of Michigan, Wayne State University, Lawrence Technological Institute, 1992-; Poetry Editor, Delodings. Publication: Laughing at Gravity: Conversations with Issac Newton, 1988. Contributions to: Ploughshares; Poetry East; New England Quarterly; Wayzgoose; The Bridge. Honours: Barnard Women's Poetry Series Winner, 1987; Honorable Mentions, Nimrod, 1987, 1990. Memberships: Modern Language Association; Princeton Research Forum; Society for Literature and Science; US Poets and

Writers Cooperative (Founding Member and Consultant). Address: 29550 Franklin Road, #228, Southfield, MI 48034 1142508, USA.

SOERENSEN Preben Major, b. 14 Apr 1937, Copenhagen, Denmark. Author. Appointment: Co-Editor, Epoke literary magazine, 1983-85. Publications: Ildmesteren, 1965; Vandmandens gilde, 1967; Alfabetets herre, 1970; I vinden begynder samtalerne, 1973; Af en engels erindringer, 1976; Salvatore l'Enigmatico, 1976; Droemmefaengsler, 1978; Genkaldslaer, 1980; Nenia, 1981; Rappaccinis have, 1983; Riget uden graenser, 1984; Vilfarelsen og andre fortaellinger, 1985; Skraemmebilleder, 1986; Ansigter og masker, 1987; Soevnen og skyggerne, 1987; Mishandlinger, 1988; Personlige grunde og afgrunde, 1991; Bevaegelser i Moerket 1993. Contributions to: Argo; Strand; Gyldendals Magasin; Hvedekorn; Ta; Faelleden; Luftskibet; Continent Scandinavia; Politiken; Jyllands Posten; Epoke; Kriterium. Honours: 3 year fellowship for creative work; Holger Drachmann Prize; Sophus Michaelis Mindelegat; Herman Bangs Mindelegat; Beatrice Prize; Henrik Pontoppidans Mindelegat. Membership: Danske skoenlitteraere forfattere. Address: Hovvej 2, 5953 Tranekaer, Denmark.

SOLANKI Mahendra, b. 20 Apr 1956, Nairobi, Kenya. Educator; Poet. m. Hilary Frances Reed, 8 Aug 1986, 2 daughters. Education: BA (Hons), English, Philosophy, Middlesex Polytechnic, England, 1979. Appointments: Freelance Editor; Co-Editor, Other Poetry Magazine, 1982-87; Bookseller; Adult Education Tutor; Associate Director, Leicester Haymarket Theatre; Lecturer, Writer, colleges, schools and universities; Currently Head, Avalon Community Education Project, Leicester. Publications: Shadows of My Making: Poems, 1986; Teaching South Asian Literature in Secondary Schools (co-author), 1986; What You Left Behind, poems, forthcoming. Contributions to: Bazaar; Multicultural Teaching; Other Poetry; Foreword; Leicester Mercury; Others. Honours: Major Writers Bursary for What You Left Behind, 1991-92. Address: 73 Lansdowne Road, Leicester LE2 8AS, England.

SOLEYA Donya. See: **STORHOFF Diana Faye Carmack.**

SOLIDIANE Hermann. See: **MOORE Diane Marie.**

SOLNICKI Jill Louise Newman, b. 27 Mar 1945, Toronto, Ontario, Canada. Writer; Teacher. m. Victor Solnicki, 27 June 1971, 1 son, 1 daughter. Education: BA, University of Toronto, 1966. Publications: This Mortal Coil; The Real Me is Gonna Be a Shock: Year in the Life of a Front-line Teacher, 1992. Contributions to: Atlantis; Grain; Fiddlehead; Toronto Life; Dandelion; Antigonish Review; Room of Ones Own; New Quarterly; Quarry; Anthology of Magazine Verse and Yearbook of American Poetry. Memberships: League of Canadian Poets; Writers' Union of Canada. Address: 53 Hillholm Road, Toronto, Ontario M5P 1M4, Canada.

SOLON Loretta Joseph, (Lady in Black), b. 29 April 1956, Flint, Michigan, USA. Songwriter. m. Robert Joseph Solon, 18 Aug 1992, 4 sons, 2 daughters. Appointments: Former Member Michigan Gospel As, showcased through Stardom and Associates, Gospel Singer, Songwriter, Poet. Publications: East of Sunrise, 1995; Best of the 90s A Red Rose, 1995; The Ebbing Tide a Light Shining Down Early Fall, 1996; The Best of 1996 A Light Shining Late Fall, 1996. Honours: Editors Choice Award, 1995; The International Society of Poets, Poet of Merit Award, 1995. Memberships: The Poets Guild; International Society of Poets. Address: 2258 E Buder, Burton, MI 48529, USA.

SOLWAY David, b. 8 Dec 1941, Montreal, Quebec, Canada. Teacher. m. Karin Semmler, 23 Apr 1980, 2 sons, 2 daughters. Education: BA, 1962, QMA, 1966, McGill University; MA, Concordia University, 1988; MA, Université de Sherbrooke, 1996. Appointments: McGill University, 1966-67; John Abbott College, 1971-76; Brigham Young University, 1993. Publications include: The Road to Arginos, 1976; The Mulberry Men, 1982; Selected Poems, 1982; Stones in Water, 1983; Modern Marriage, 1989; Bedrock, 1993. Contributions to: Atlantic Monthly; Canadian Literature; Partisan Review; Saturday Night; Sewanee Review. Honours: Rutherford Memorial Prize, 1962; York University Poetry Prize, 1977; Qspell Award, 1989, 1990; Bourse du Quebec, 1993. Memberships: PEN International; Union des Écrivains du Québec; President's Club of University of Toronto. Address: 143 Upper McNaughton, Hudson, Quebec J0P 1H0, Canada.

SOLZHENITSYN Aleksandr Isayevich, b. 11 Dec 1918, Kislovodsk, Russia. Writer; Poet. m. (1) Natalya Reshetovskaya, 27

Apr 1940, div, (2) 1956, div 1972, (3) Natalya Svetlova, Apr 1973, 2 sons, 1 stepson. Education: Correspondence course in Philology, Moscow Institute of History, Philosophy and Literature, 1939-41; Degree in Mathematics and Physics, University of Rostock, 1941. Appointments: Commenced writing as a youth; Teacher in secondary school; Commander, Soviet Army, World War II; Exiled as a teacher to Kok-Terek, Kazakhstan, 1953-56; Teacher of Mathematics and Physics in Riazan; Exiled from the Soviet Union, 1974-94. Publications include: One Day in the Life of Ivan Denisovich, novella, 1962; For the Good of the Cause, novella, 1963; A Lenten Letter to Pimen, Patriarch of All Russia, 1972; A World Split Apart, 1979; The Mortal Danger, 1981; Victory Celebrations: A Comedy in Four Acts and Prisoners: A Tragedy, plays, 1983; Rebuilding Russia: Toward Some Formulations, 1991; The Russian Question Toward the End of the Century, 1995. Honours: Priz du Meilleur Livre Etranger, France, 1969; Nobel Prize for Literature, 1970; Freedoms Foundation Award, Stanford University, 1976; Many honorary degrees. Membership: American Academy of Arts & Sciences. Address: c/o Farrar, Straus & Giroux, 19 Union Square West, New York, NY 10003, USA.

SOMARY Wolfgang, b. 30 July 1932, Zürich, Switzerland. Banker. m. Gabriela Hennig, 23 Aug 1958, 2 sons, 2 daughters. Education: BA, MA, Honours in Economics and Political Science, Trinity College, Dublin University, 1951-56. Appointments: Various positions in banking. Publication: Blätter für das Wort, 1978-92. Contributions to: Archipel; Bulletin of Science, Technology and Society; Philosophia Pacis; Midstream; Kink Newsweekly; A Popular Anthology of Earth and Space Poems; Athena Press. Memberships: Co-Founder and President, Intercultural Cooperation Foundation, 1974-; Poetry Society, England. Address: Standthausquai 7, CH-8001 Zurich, Switzerland.

SOMERVILLE Yvonne. See: **MCCLOSKEY Phil(omena Mary)**.

SOMLYO György, b. 28 Nov 1920, Hungary. Div 1988, 1 son. Education: University, 1945-46; Sorbonne, Paris, 1947-48. Appointments: Director, International Poetry Almanach, Arion, 1966-; Literary Director, Associate Editor, French Revue, 1977-. Publications: Numerous. Contributions to: Many Hungarian publications. Honours: Jozsel Attila Prize; Déry Tibor Prize; Prize of the Hungarian Writers Association; Lajos Kassak Prize; Officier de l'Ordre des Arts et des Lettres; Order of the Flag; Medaille, Gabriele Mistral, Chile, 1956. Memberships: Hungarian Academy of Literature and Arts; Hungarian PEN Club; Academie Mallarme, Association of Hungarian Writers; Poetry Biennales of Liège. Address: Irinyi J u 39, H-1111 Budapest, Hungary.

SOMOZA Joseph Manuel, b. 30 Oct 1940, Spain. Poet; Professor. Editor. m. Jill Rosmarie Eggena, 15 June 1963, 2 sons, 1 daughter. Education: BA, English, University of Cincinnati, 1963; MA, English, Roosevelt Univerity, 1966; MFA, Creative Writing, University of Iowa, 1973. Appointments: Instructor, Texas Western College, 1966-68; Colegio Regional de Cayey, Puerto Rico, 1969-71; Instructor, Assistant Professor, and Associate Professor, English, New Mexico State University, 1973-. Publications: Greyhound, 1968; Olive Women, 1976; Backyard Poems, 1986; Out of this World, 1990. Contributions to: Beloit Poetry Review; Bloomsbury Review; Blue Mesa Review; Colorado State Review; Floating Island; Greenfield Review; Hanging Loose; Maryland Poetry Review; Rocky Mountain Review; Sou'Wester; Sumac; Three Rivers Poetry Journal; Z Miscellaneous. Memberships: Poets and Writers, 1983-; Rio Grande Writers Association, 1981-86, Treasurer, 1981-82. Address: 1725 Hamiel Drive, Las Cruces, NM 88001, USA.

SONG Cathy, b. 20 Aug 1955, Honolulu, Hawaii, USA. Poet; Educator. m. Douglas M Davenport, 19 July 1979. Education: BA, Wellesley College, 1977; MA, Boston University, 1981. Publications: Picture Bride, 1983; Frameless Windows, 1988; School Figures, 1994. Contributions to: American Poetry Review; Amerasia; Bamboo Ridge; Black Warrior Review; Columbia; Cream City Review; The Journal; Michigan Quarterly Review; Ploughshares; Poetry; Prairie Schooner; Shenandoah; Zyzzyva; Poetry Ireland; The Southern Review. Honours: Younger Poets Award, Yale University, 1982; Frederick Book Prize for Poetry, 1986; Cades Award for Literature, 88; The Shelley Memorial Award, Poetry Society of America, 1993; The Hawaii Award for Literature, 1993. Address: PO Box 27262, Honolulu, HI 96827, USA.

SONG Lin, b. 20 Jan 1959, China. Teacher. m. Valerie Tehio, 5 June 1991, 1 son. Education: Master of Chinese Language and Literature, East China Normal University, 1983. Publication: Citadins. Contributions to: Today; Poetry Magazine; Shanghai Literature; New Spring; Yellow River; Guandong Literature; Harvest. Honours: Poetry Prizes: Beijing University, 1986; Poetry International, Rotterdam, 1990. Memberships: Societe des Ecrivains Chinois de Shanghai. Address: 55 Rue Greneta, 75002 Paris, France.

SONGLANG. See: **KU Yeonsik**.

SONIAT Katherine, b. 11 Jan 1942, Washington, District of Columbia, USA. Associate Professor of English; Poet. Education: BA, History, 1964; MA, English, 1984. Appointments: Associate Professor, Hollins College, Roanoke, Virginia, 1988-90; Assistant Professor, English, Virginia Polytechnic Institute and State University, Blacksburg, 1990-. Publications: Notes of Departure, 1985; Winter Toys, 1989; Cracking Eggs, 1990; A Shared Life, 1994. Contributions to: Nation; New Republic; Poetry; Kenyon Review; Antioch Review; American Scholar; North American Review; Southern Review; Iowa Review. Honours: Cameden Poetry Prize, Walt Whitman Center for the Arts, 1985; Fellowships to Bread Loaf Writers Conference, Middlebury College, 1987; Virginia Prize for Poetry, 1989; Edwin Ford Piper Award, University of Iowa Press, 1994. Memberships: Academy of American Poets; Associated Writing Programs. Address: Department of English, Virginia Polytechnic Institute and State University, Blacksburg, VA 24061-0112, USA.

SONIAT Katherine, b. Washington, USA. English Educator. Appointments: Instructor, English, VA Polytechnic Institute and State University, Blacksburg, 1985-88; Assistant Professor English, Hollins College, 1989-91; Associate Professor English, VA Polytechnic Institute and State University, Blacksburg, 1991-; Workshop Presenter in Field. Publications: Author: Notes of Departure, poem, 1985; Winter Toys, poem, 1989; Cracking Eggs, poems, 1990; A Shared Life, poem, 1993; Contributor, numerous poems to professional publications. Honours: Recipient, Poetry Society of America; Consuelo Ford Honorable Mention; Ann Stanford Award, University Southern California; Middlebury College Bread Loaf Writers Conference Fellowship & Scholarship in Poetry, 1985, 1989; Camden Poetry Prize Wait Whitman Center for the Arts and Humanities, 1985; VA Prize for Poetry, 1989; Edwin Ford Piper Award University Iowa Press, 1993 Award. Address: Home: 5318 Catawba Creek Road Catawba Creek Road, Catawba, VA 24070-2004; Office: English Department, VA Poly Institute and State University Blacksburg, VA 24061, USA.

SONNENFELD Mark, b. 21 Feb 1956, Newark, New Jersey, USA. Building Clerk. m. Maryann Approvato, 9 April 1983. Education: South Plainfield High School, 1974. Appointment: Writer, 1990-. Publications: Journal V, 1993; Creative Writing, 1994; Miscellany by Mark, 1994; Ten Inch Diagonal, 1994; Dings/Dabbles/Dimensions, 1994; Language Poem Book, 1995; Views Expressed in this Book, 1995; The Poem Thought Equations, 1995; Writing In/Out of Sequence, 1995; Gallery Piece, 1995; Short Fictions, 1996; A Stepping Stone Book, 1996; 17 Chapbooks, 20 Short Stories; Instrumental Music: Classical, Jazz. Contributions to: Joey and the Black Boots; Psychedelic Wasteland; Malcontent; Rip Speed Newsletter; Midnight Toast; Lone Wolf; Transmog; Velocity NYC. Address: 45-08 Old Millstone Drive, East Windsor, New Jersey 08520, USA.

SORESTAD Glen Allan, b. 21 May 1937, Vancouver, British Columbia, Canada. Writer. m. Sonia Diane Talpash, 17 Sept 1960, 3 sons, 1 daughter. Education: BEd, University of Saskatchewan, 1963; Master of Education, 1976. Appointments: Elementary School Teacher, 1957-69; English Teacher, 1969-81; Writer and Publisher, 1981-; President, Thistledown Press, 1975-. Publications: Wind Songs; West Into Night; Prairie Pub Poems; Pear Seeds in My Mouth; Ancestral Dances; Jan Lake Poems; Hold the Rain in Your Hands; Stalking Place; Air Canada Owls. Contributions to: Malahat Review; Poetry Canada Review; Descant; Ariel; Fiddlehead; Prism International; Dalhousie Review; Northward Journal; University of Windsor Review; Grain; Arc; Event; Antigonish Review; Lines Review; Waves; Event; Puerto Del Sol; Wascana Review; Newest Review; Dandelion; Prairie Fire; Sulphur Review; Canadian Forum; Toronto Globe and Mail; English Quarterly; Queens Quarterly. Honours: Hilroy Fellowship; Founders Awards; Canada Council Writing Grant; Saskatchewan Arts Board Writing Grant. Memberships: Saskatchewan Writers Guild; League of Canadian Poets; Writers Union of Canada; International PEN; Assocation of Canadian Publishers; Literary Press

Group. Address: 668 East Place, Saskatoon, Saskatchewan S7J 2Z5, Canada.

SORRENTINO Gilbert, b. 27 April 1929, Brooklyn, New York, USA. Novelist; Poet; Professor. m. (1) Elsene Wiessner, div, (2) Vivian Victoria Ortiz, 3 children. Education: Brooklyn College, 1950-51, 1955-57. Appointments: Editor and Publisher, Neon magazine, New York City, 1956-60; Editor, Grove Press, New York City, 1965-70; Teacher, Columbia University, 1965, Aspen Writers Workshop, 1967, Sarah Lawrence College, 1971-72, and New School for Social Research, New York City, 1976-79; Edwin S Quain Professor of Literature, University of Scranton, 1979; Professor of English, Stanford University, 1982-. Publications: Novels: The Sky Changes, 1966; Steelwork, 1970; Imaginative Qualities of Actual Things, 1971; Splendide-Hotel, 1973; Mulligan Stew, 1979; Aberration of Starlight, 1980; Crystal Vision, 1981; Blue Pastoral, 1983; Odd Number, 1985; Rose Theatre, 1987; Misterioso, 1989; Under the Shadow, 1991; Red the Fiend, 1995; Poetry: The Darkness Surrounds Us, 1960; Black and White, 1964; The Perfect Fiction, 1968; Corrosive Sublimate, 1971; A Dozen Oranges, 1976; White Sail, 1977; The Orangery, 1977; Selected Poems, 1958-80, 1981; Essay: Something Said, 1984; Play: Flawless Play Restored: The Masque of Fungo, 1974; Translator: Sulpiciae Elegidia/Elegiacs of Sulpicia: Gilbert Sorrentino Versions, 1977. Contributions to: Various anthologies and periodicals. Honours: Guggenheim Fellowships, 1973-74, 1987-88; Samuel S Fels Award, 1974; Creative Artists Public Service Grant, 1974-75; Ariadne Foundation Grant, 1975; National Endowment for the Arts Grants, 1975-76, 1978-79, 1983-84; John Dos Passos Prize, 1981; Mildred and Harold Strauss Livings, 1982 (declined); American Academy and Institute of Arts and Letters Award, 1985; Lannan Literary Prize for Fiction, 1992. Membership: PEN American Center. Address: Department of English, Stanford University, Stanford, CA 94305, USA.

SOTO Gary, b. 12 Apr 1952, Fresno, California, USA. Writer; Poet. m. Carolyn Sadako Oda, 24 May 1975, 1 daughter. Education: BA, California State University, Fresno, 1974; MFA, University of California, Irvine, 1976. Appointments: Assistant Professor, 1979-85, Associate Professor of English and Ethnic Studies, 1985-92, Part-time Senior Lecturer in English, 1992-95, University of California, Berkeley; Elliston Professor of Poetry, University of Cincinnati, 1988; Martin Luther King/Cesar Chavez/Rosa Park Visiting Professor of English, Wayne State University, 1990. Publications: Poetry: The Elements of San Joaquin, 1977; The Tale of Sunlight, 1978; Where Sparrows Work Hard, 1981; Black Hair, 1985; Who Will Know Us?, 1990; A Fire in My Hands, 1990; Home Course in Religion, 1992; Neighbourhood Odes, 1992; Canto Familiar/Familiar Song, 1994; New and Selected Poems, 1995; Junior College, 1997; Other includes: The Pool Party, 1993; Crazy Weekend, 1994; Jesse, 1994; Boys at Work, 1995; Chato's Kitchen, 1995; Everyday Seductions (Editor), 1995; Summer on Wheels, 1995; The Old Man and His Door, 1996; Snapshots of the Wedding, 1996; Buried Onions, 1997. Contributions to: Magazines. Honours: Academy of American Poets Prize, 1975; Discovery/The Nation Prize, 1975; United States Award, International Poetry Forum, 1976; Bess Hokin Prize for Poetry, 1978; Guggenheim Fellowship, 1979-80; National Endowment for the Arts Fellowships, 1981, 1991; Levinson Award, Poetry magazine, 1984; American Book Award, Before Columbus Foundation, 1985; California Arts Council Fellowship, 1989; Carnegie Medal, 1993; Tomas Rivera Prize, 1996. Address: 43 The Crescent, Berkeley, CA 94708, USA.

SOUSTER Raymond Holmes, (John Holmes, Raymond Holmes), b. 15 Jan 1921, Toronto, Ontario, Canada. Bank Clerk. m. Rosalia L Geralde, 24 June 1947. Education: University of Toronto Schools, 1932-37; Humberside Collegiate Institute, 1938-39. Appointments: Ground Crew, Royal Canadian Air Force, Eastern Air Command and England, 1941-45; Canadian Imperial Bank of Commerce, retired 1964. Publications: The Eyes of Love; Running Out the Clock; Riding the Long Black Horse; Old Bank Notes; No Sad Songs Wanted Here; Close To Home; 7 Volumes Collected Poems 1955-1988, forthcoming. Contributions to: Montreal Magazine; First Statement; Unit of Five. Honours: Governor General's Award for Poetry in English, 1964; City of Toronto Book Award, 1969; Officer of the Order of Canada, 1995. Membership: Founding Life Member and Chairman 1968-72, League of Canadian Poets. Address: 39 Baby Point Road, Toronto, Ontario M6S 2G2, Canada.

SOUTHGATE Christopher Charles Benedict, b. 26 Sept 1953, Exeter, Devon. Poet; Editor. m. Sandra Joyce Mitchell, 23 June 1981, 1 stepson. Education: BA Hons, Natural Sciences, 1974, MA, PhD,

Biochemistry, 1978, Cambridge; GMC, South-West Ministerial Training course, Exeter, 1991. Appointments: Research Associate, University of North Carolina; Research Officer, Bath Technology; St Lukes Trust Pastoral Assistant, University of Exeter. Publications: Landscape or Land?, 1989; Annotations, 1991; Stonechat - Ten Devon Poets, 1992. Contributions to: Envoi; Nexus; Otter; Pen; Prospice; Westwords; Encounter; Outposts; South Coast Poetry Journal; Crucible; Christian; Company of Poets Anthologies; Collins; New Christian Poetry. Honours: South West Arts Literature Award, 1985; Iolaire Arts Prize, 1987; Sidmouth Arts Festival Prize, 1991; Southwest Open Poetry, Commendation, 1991. Memberships: Poetry Society; Company of Poets; Friends of Arvon Foundation. Address: Parford Cottage, Chagford, Devon TQ13 8JR, England.

SOYINKA Wole (Akinwande Oluwole), b. 13 July 1934, Isara, Nigeria. Poet; Dramatist; Writer; Professor. Education: University of Ibadan; BA, Leeds University, 1959. Appointments: Research Fellow in Drama, 196-61, Chairman, Department of Theatre Arts, 1969-72, University of Ibadan; Lecturer in English, 1962-63, Professor in Dramatic Literature, 1972, Professor of Comparative Literature, 1976-85, University of Ife; Senior Lecturer in English, University of Lagos, 1965-67; Political prisoner, 1967-69; Fellow, Churchill College, Cambridge, 1973-74; Goldwin Smith Professor of Africana Studies and Theatre, Cornell University, 1988-92; Exiled by Nigerian military government, 1995. Publications: Poetry: Idanre and Other Poems, 1967; Poems from Prison, 1969, augmented edition as A Shuttle in the Crypt, 1972; Ogun Abibiman, 1976; Mandela's Earth and Other Poems, 1989; Plays include: The Road, 1965; Kongi's Harvest, 1966; The Trials of Brother Jero, 1967; The Strong Breed, 1967; Madmen and Specialists, 1970; Before the Blackout, 1971; Camwood on the Leaves, 1973; Collected Plays, 2 volumes, 1973, 1974; Death and the King's Horseman, 1975; Opera Wonyosi, 1981; A Play of Giants, 1984; Six Plays, 1984; Requiem for a Futurologist, 1985; From Zia with Love, 1992; A Scourge of Hyacinths, 1992; The Beatification of Area Boy, 1995; Novels: The Interpreters, 1965; Season of Anomy, 1973; Other: The Man Died: Prison Notes of Wole Soyinka, 1972; Myth, Literature and the African World, 1976; Ake: The Years of Childhood, autobiography, 1981; Art, Dialogue and Outrage, 1988; Isara: A Voyage Around "Essay", 1989; The Open Score: A Personal Narrative of the Nigerian Crisis, 1996; Editor: Plays from the Third World: An Anthology, 1971; Poems of Black Africa, 1975. Honours: Rockefeller Foundation Grant, 1960; John Whiting Drama Prize, 1966; Jock Campbell Award, 1968; Nobel Prize for Literature, 1986. Memberships: International Theatre Institute; Union of Writers of the African Peoples; National Liberation Council of Nigeria. Address: c/o Random House Inc, 201 East 50th Street, 22nd Floor, New York, NY 10022, USA.

SPAENS-de VRIEZE Gerde Jozefa Francina, b. 13 July 1946, Etterbeek, Brussels, Belgium. Journalist; Poet. m. Eric Spaens, 12 April 1966, 3 daughters. Publications: Het Kleurrijke wit; Wat De Dag Me Brengt; Het Verschijnsel Man; Van Aap tot Schapen; Rood Licht. Contributions to: G P Averbode; UIT Magazine; 001-Magazine Comet; De Leie Cultuur Magazine. Honours: Prijs Voor Poezie Vlaams, Brussels; Prijs Achste Jong Nederlands Literaire Dagen; St Martens Latem. Memberships: SABAM; BJMH; V.V. Letter kundigen. Address: Henri Storystraat 20, 9030 Gent Mariakerke, Belgium.

SPANGLE Douglas Stewart, b. 8 Feb 1951, Roanoke, Virginia, USA. Marine Reporter. 1 daughter. Education: University of Maryland, Munich Campus, 1968-71; Nicolet Community College, Rhinelander, Wisconsin, 1977-78. Appointments: Associate Editor, Moose Magazine, 1980-82; Associate Editor, Rain City Review, 1992-95; Senior Editor, Rain City Review, 1995-; Organizer and Master of Ceremonies of various events, 1978-; Moderator of Radio Program Talking Earth, 1982-86; Board Member, Portland Poetry Festival, 1986-88. Publications: Initial, chapbook, 1996; 7-page section in the anthology Off the Beaten Track, 1992; Edited the Festschrift Homespun: A Tribute to Mary Barnard, 1994. Contributions to: Fireweed, Eugene, Oregon, 1991-96; Rain City Review, 1993-96; Illya's Honey, 1995; Asia-Pacific American Journal, New York, New York, 1995; Insomnia, Whittier, California, 1995; Mudvein, Portland, Oregon, 1995; Red Brick Review, 1996; Jack Rabbit, Eagle Pass, TX, 1996. Membership: Oregon State Poetry Association. Address: 1304 SE 50th, Portland, OR 97215, USA.

SPAR A J. See: **DAY Kevin K Markwick.**

SPARK Muriel (Sarah), Dame, b. 1 Feb 1918, Edinburgh, Scotland. Author; Poet. m. S O Spark, 1937, diss, 1 son. Education:

Heriot Watt College, Edinburgh. Appointments: Political Intelligence Department, British Foreign Office, 1944-45; General Secretary, Poetry Society, 1947-49; Founder, Forum literary magazine, and Editor, Poetry Review, 1949. Publications: Fiction includes: The Prime of Miss Jean Brodie, 1961; The Hothouse by the East River, 1973; Territorial Rights, 1979; Loitering with Intent, 1981; Bang-Bang You're Dead and Other Stories, 1982; The Only Problem, 1984; The Stories of Muriel Spark, 1985; A Far Cry from Kensington, 1988; Symposium, 1990; The French Window and the Small Telephone, 1993; Omnibus I, 1993; Omnibus II, 1994; Poetry: The Fanfarlo and Other Verse, 1952; Collected Poems I, 1967; Going Up to Sotheby's and Other Poems, 1982; Play: Doctors of Philosophy, 1962; Non-Fiction: Child of Light: A Reassessment of Mary Wollstonecraft Shelley, 1951, revised edition as Mary Shelley, 1987; Emily Brontë: Her Life and Work, 1953; John Masefield, 1953; Curriculum Vitae, autobiography, 1992; The Essence of the Brontës, 1993; Editor: Tribute to Wordsworth, 1950; A Selection of Poems of Emily Brontë, 1952; My Best Mary: The Letters of Mary Shelley, 1953; The Letters of the Brontës: A Selection, 1954; Letters of John Henry Newman, 1957. Contributions to: Various periodicals. Honours: Observer Short Story Prize, 1951; Prix Italia, 1962; Yorkshire Post Book of the Year Award, 1965; James Tait Black Memorial Prize, 1966; Officer of the Order of the British Empire, 1967; 1st Prize, FNAC La Meilleur Recueil des Nouvelles Etrangères, 1987; Scottish Book of the Year Award, 1987; Officier de l'Ordre des Arts et des Lettres, France, 1988; Ingersoll Foundation T S Eliot Award for Creative Writing, 1992; Dame Commander of the Order of the British Empire, 1993. Address: c/o David Higham Associates Ltd, 5-8 Lower John Street, Golden Square, London W1R 4HA, England.

SPARROW. See: **KNELL William H.**

SPARSHOTT Francis (Edward), b. 19 May 1926, Chatham, Kent, England. Philosopher; Writer; Poet; Professor. m. Kathleen Elizabeth Vaughan, 7 Feb 1953, 1 daughter. Education: BA, MA, Corpus Christi College, Oxford, 1950. Appointments: Lecturer 1950-55, Assistant Professor 1955-62, Associate Professor 1962-64, Professor 1964-91, of Philosophy, University of Toronto. Publications: An Enquiry into Goodness and Related Concepts, 1958; The Structure of Aesthetics, 1963; The Concept of Criticism: An Essay, 1967; Looking for Philosophy, 1972; The Theory of the Arts, 1982; Off the Ground: First Steps in the Philosophy of the Art of Dance, 1988; Taking Life Seriously: A Study of the Argument of the Nicomachean Ethic, 1994; A Measured Pace: Toward a Philosophical Understanding of the Art of Dance, 1995. Poetry: A Divided Voice, 1965; A Cardboard Garage, 1969; The Rainy Hills: Verses after a Japanese Fashion, 1979; The Naming of the Beasts, 1979; New Fingers for Old Dikes, 1980; The Cave of Trophonius and Other Poems, 1983; The Hanging Gardens of Etobicoke, 1983; Storms and Screens, 1986; Sculling to Byzantium, 1989; Views from the Zucchini Gazebo, 1994. Contributions to: Various books and periodicals. Honours include: Killam Research Fellowship, 1977-78; First Prize, Poetry, CBC Radio Literary Competition, 1981. Memberships include: Aristotelian Society; League of Canadian Poets, President 1977-78; PEN International, Canadian Centre; Royal Society of Canada, Fellow 1977. Address: 50 Crescentwood Road, Scarborough, Ontario M1N 1E4, Canada.

SPARTA Santino, b. 16 Sept 1943, Randazzo, Sicily. Writer; Journalist; Poet. Education: Dot Litt; Dot Div. Publications: Immutato e il Sorriso tra i Solchi; Vorrei Intervistara il Mistero; I Magi tra storia e Leggenda; Guando Dialoghero Con te. Memberships: Associazione Nazionale dei Critici Italia; Association International des Critique Litteraires. Address: Via Della Transpontina 18, 00193 Rome, Italy.

SPAZIANI Maria Luisa, b. 7 Dec 1924, Torino, Italy. Professor. Education: University of Torino. Appointments: Radio and television, 1960-91; Professor, University of Messina, 1964-66, 1967-91. Publications: Le Acque del Sabato; Utilità della Memoria; L'Occhio del Ciclone; Transito con Catene; Geometria del Disordine; La Stella del Libero Arbitrio; All'America; Giovanna d'Arco; Torri di Vedetta. Contributions to: La Stampa; Botteghe Oscure; Il Tempo; Tempo Presente; Nuovi Argomenti; L'Espresso. Honours: International Byron Award; Premio Carducci; Gran Premio Saint Vincent; Premio Casa Hirta; Premio Viareggio; Premio Il Ceppo; Premio Lerici Pea. Memberships: President, Centro Internazionale Eugenio Montale; SEC; Association Stampa Italiana; Soroptimist Club. Address: Presso Centro Internazionale Eugenio Montale, via Buonarroti 39, 00185 Roma, Italy.

SPEAK Margaret Ann, b. West Yorkshire, England. Teacher. m. 1961, 2 sons. Education: BEd Hons, Leeds; MA, York, 1993. Publication: Giant Steps. Contributions to: Envoi; Staple; Poetry Nottingham; Times Literary Supplement. Honours: Various including most recently: 1st Prize, Lake Aske, 1991. Memberships: Coordinator, York Poetry Workshop; Coordinator, York Open Poetry Competition; Pennine Poets. Address: 32 Spey Bank, Acomb Park, York YO2 2UZ, England.

SPEAKER William. See: **HOLLIDAY David John Gregory.**

SPEARE E M. See: **SHAKESPEARE Eileen Margaret.**

SPEER Laurel, b. 3 Mar 1940, Los Angeles, California, USA. Poet; Essayist; Reviewer. m. Donald P Speer, 27 Jan 1962, div 29 May 1987, 2 sons, 1 daughter. Education: BA English, University of California at Los Angeles, 1962. Publications: Second Thoughts Over Bourget, 1987; Very Frightened Men, 1988; Cold Egg, 1989; Sin, 1990; Grant Drank, 1991; The Destruction of Liars, 1993; Rebecca at the Port Authority, 1994. Contributions to: Editor: 5 & 10+2: Quarterly Essay Review Journal; Contributing Editor, Small Press Review; among others. Honours: Arizona State Commission on Arts Poetry Fellowship, 1991; Barbara Deming Memorial Grant, 1989. Address: PO Box 12220, Tucson, AZ 85732, USA.

SPELIERS Hedwig, b. 11 June 1935, Diksmuide, Belgium. Teacher. m. An Theunynck, 11 July 1961. Publications: Out of Harm's Way in our Cenotaph, 1961; An Abutment of a Bridge, 1963; The Astronaut, 1969; Horrible Dictu, 1972; South of, 1973; Life with Lorenz, 1973; The Man of Paracelsus, 1977; Off from the Cloud, 1980; Dreyfus in the Village, 1981; The Heraldic Creature, 1983; Alpestre, 1986; Villers-la-Ville, 1988; The Mirror of Horta, 1990; Magica Materia, 1990; Beletage, 1992; Photo Sensitive, 1992. Contributions to: Editor, Collaborator: Mep, 1956; Diagram, 1963; Bok, 1964; Daele, 1965; Restant, 1967-80; Poeziekrant, 1980-92; Kunst en'Cultuur, 1992; Columnist: Elseviers Literair Supplement, 1968-72; De Nieuwe, 1964-73; Vrijdag, 1971; Knack, 1971. Honours: Heideland Prize, Zuid en Noord, 1969; 2 Provincial Prizes for Literature, 1972; Dirk Martens Prize, Aalst, 1984. Address: Muscarstraat 12, B-8400 Oostende, Belgium.

SPENCE Noel, b. 25 Dec 1944, Northern Ireland. Film Producer. m. Heather Gardiner, 12 Aug 1971, 1 son, 1 daughter. Education: BA with Honours, English Literature, Queens University, Belfast, 1963-68; Diploma in Education. Appointments: English Department, Orangefield Boys' Secondary School, Belfast, 1968-73; Head of English Department, Victoria College, Belfast, 1973-86; Self Employed Film Producer, 1986-. Publications: Lines and Rhymes, 1995; First Time Out, 1996; A Passage in Time, 1996. Contributions to: Peer International Poetry Magazine. Honour: Runner-Up Award, Peer International Poetry Competition, 1996. Membership: Concordant Poets Society. Address: 22 Drumhirk Road, Comber, County Down, BT23 5LY, Northern Ireland.

SPERANZA Susan, b. 7 June 1951, New York, New York, USA. Writer; Poet; Teacher. m. Alan Knittel, 15 Feb 1978. Education: BA, Queens College of the City University of New York, 1980. Publications: The City of Light; Exile in the Promised Land. Contributions to: Literary Journal of Long Island; Cultural Forum. Honour: Brook House New Poets Award. Memberships: Poetry Society of America; Poetry Project; South Bay Poets Circle. Address: c/o Brook House Press, Mills Pond House, PO Box 52, St James, NY 11780, USA.

SPOONER David Eugene, b. 1 Sept 1941, West Kirby, Wirral, England. Writer; Naturalist. m. Marion O'Neil, 9 Mar 1986, 1 daughter. Education: BA, hons, University of Leeds, 1963; Diploma in Drama, University of Manchester, 1964; PhD, University of Bristol, 1968. Appointments: Lecturer, University of Kent, 1968-73; Visiting Professor, Pennsylvania State University, 1973-74; Lecturer, Manchester Polytechnic, 1974-75; Head of Publishing Borderline Press, 1976-85; Director, Butterfly Conservation, East Scotland. Publications: Unmakings, 1977; The Angelic Fly: The Butterfly in Art, 1992; The Metaphysics of Insect Life, 1995; Creatures of Air, forthcoming 1977. Contributions to: Iron; Interactions; Tandem; Weighbauk; Revue de Littérature Comparée; Bestia (Fable Society of America); Margin; Corbie Press; Butterfly Conservation News; Butterfly News; Field Studies. Memberships: The Welsh Academy Associate; Association of Benjamin Constant. Address: 96 Halbeath Road, Dunfermline, Fife KY12 7LR, Scotland.

SPRIGGS Ruby, b. 25 April 1929, England. m. James William Spriggs, 16 Sept 1950, dec 1988, 1 son, 3 daughters. Appointments: Editor, Haiku Canada Newsletter; Judge; Harold Henderson Haiku Contest, sponsored by The Haiku Society of America, 1993. Publications: Sun Shadow Moon Shadow (book of Haiku); Tanka Splendor; Round Renga Round; The Haiku Hundred; Anthologie de Haiku; How to Write and Publish Poetry. Contributions to: Haiku Canada; Frogpond; Brussels Sprout; Haiku Handbook; New Cicada; Wind Chimes; Ko; Old Pond; Erotic Haiku; Haiku Journal; Iron; Lynx. Honours: Best of Issue; Sanwa Bank Award; 2nd Prize, Tallahassee Writers Association; International Tanka Award; Prize-winner, Japan Airlines International Contests, 1988, 1992; Winner, 2 awards, Canadian Authors Association Contest, 1989. Memberships: Haiku Canada; Haiku Society of America; British Haiku Society. Address: Apt 2609A, 500 Laurier West, Ottawa, Ontario K1R 5E1, Canada.

SQUIRE Shelley. See: **BRENER Rochelle (Diane).**

SREEDHARAN C(herumanalil) K(andothankandy), b. 25 Aug 1921, Cannanore, India. Homoeo Practitioner; Author; Publisher. m. P Karthyayini, 26 Apr 1953. Education: BIET, Bombay; Associated schools, Delhi; Mavelikara, Kerala. Appointments: Clerk, 1940; Clerk, Army Recruiting Office, 1941-42; Clerk, Army Postal Service, 1942-47; Civil Postal Service, 1947-79; Homoeo Practitioner, Author-Publisher, 1978-91. Publications: Uncut Gems; Flowers of Thought; Pearls of Wisdom; Fragrant Flowers. Contributions to: Poet; Kavitha India Muzzaffarpur; Dak Tar P & T Magazine; East West Voices; Rising Stars. Memberships: Authors Guild of India; International Writers and Artists Association, Brazil; United Writers Association, Madras. Address: 107 P & T Colony, Rabindranath Tagore Nagar, Bangalore 560032 Karnataka, South India.

SRINIVAS Krishna (Kesri), b. 26 July 1913, Sriangam, South India. Editor. m. Kothai, 8 July 1933. Education: BA, Madras University, 1932; LittD, Karachi University, Karachi, 1970; DLitt, World University, USA, 1971. Appointments: Bank Accountant, 1936; Script Writer, All India Radio, New Delhi, 1942; Editor, Ajanta 1946; Editor, Indian Industries, 1954; Editor, Poet International Monthly, 1970; Editor, World Poetry, 1990, 1991, 1992, 1993, 1994, 1995, 1996, 1997. Publications: Dance of Dust, 1946; Wheel, 1950; He Walks the Earth, 1954; Magic Pearls, 1956; Niana, 1958; Music of the Soul, 1959; Everest, 1960; Five Elements, 1980; Poetical Works, 1986-89. Contributions to: Laurel Leaves, Manila; Seikyo Shimbu, Toyko; Korea Times, Seoul; Poetry Australia, Sydney; Amrita Bazaar Patricka, Calcutta; Poet, USA. Honours: Poet Laureate, 1973; Hall of Fame, Mala; International Poet Laureate, 1994; S.G.I Award, Tokyo, 1996; Nominated for Nobel Prize in Literature; Michael Madhusuden Award, 1995. Memberships: Now President, World Poetry Society Intercontinental in Six Continents, 1960-; Elected to Korea Academy, Greek Academy, Spanish Academy. Address: 118 Raja Street, Dr Seethapathi Nagar, Velachery, Madras 600 042, India.

SRINIVASAN Indira, (Indu, Indu Sri), b. 30 May 1938, Visakhapatnam, AP, India. Music; Writing; College Professor; Linguist. m. P K Srinivasan, 2 May 1956, 3 sons. Education: Higher Grade in Music, 1953; Sangitha Siromani, Madras University, Kalakshatraj, 1955; Sangitha Vidwan PG course, 1957; PhD with Distinction, California University, USA, 1990; Various other courses. Appointments: Professor, Guest Lecturer, Venkateswala University, Tirupathi College of Music and Dance; Lecturer, Tanjore University, Pondicherry Yoga Seminars, Coins Batore Bharathiar; Volunteer Teacher of Music and Education; Trainer of students for varsity concerts; Tchr of cultural programmes; Gave demonstration lectures on Indian Music in USA and Algeria; Took a group of artists to various countries including Singapore and Thailand. Publications: Published three books; Author of articles, poems, songs; Translator; A collection of her dance dramas, in Tamil; a collection of 88 songs and poems; a collection of her mothers songs and poems, Arumpasi Adakkiya Amudhasurabhi; Indian Cultures and Festivals, in English. Contributions include: Poet (UK), monthly and annual publications; Balamitran (Tamil); Journals and Souvenirs; Indian Express; Flora; Pudhumai and Ilamai; Quest; Brainwave; Madras News. Honours include: Iyatisai Nadaga Mandin, 1995; Fellowship, UWA, 1996, University of Madras, 1996, and Ravi, 1997. Memberships include: Poetry Society of Krishna Srimivas; Life Member, Poet Editor's International Institute of Tamil Studies; Life Member, United Writer's Association; Honorary Patron, World Etamizh Sangam. Address: 22-K South Avenue, Thiruvanmiyur, Madras 600 041, Chennai 41, Tamil Nadu, India.

SRIVASTAVA Ram Mohan Lal, (Dr.Rahul), b. 2 Oct 1952, Khewali, Varanasi, UP, India. m. Madhu Srivastava, 18 Feb 1976, 2 sons, 1 daughter. Education: MA, Banaras Hindu University, Varanasi, UP, 1975; PhD., 1991, DLitt, 1995, Vikramshila Hindi Vidyapeeth, Bhagal Pur, Bihar. Appointment: Food Corporation of India, New Delhi, 1979-. Publications include: Ek Jhalak; Bindi; Yuvasadi; Roti Aur Sansad; Prajatantra; Mittee ki Samvedna; Andhere Se Guzrate Hue; Jangal Hota Shahar; YuGank (epic); Kahin Ant Nahin, Ram Garh Ki Ran Laxmi. Contributions include: Rashtriy Sahara; Swatantra Bharat; Gandeev; Hindustan; Jansatta; Bhasha Setu; India Today; Bat Samyikee. Honours include: Sahitya Shri and Patrakar Shri, 1990-91; Raslok, Sirsa, Haryana, 1991; Dr. Ambedkar Fellowship, 1992; Savita Purskar, 1994; Sadhna Purskar, 1996. Memberships include: Secretary, Bhartiy Lekhak Manch, 1989; President, Akhandta Sangram Nagrik Samiti, 1991-93; President, Bhartiy Sahity Kala Parishad, 1993-95; Editor, Vikas Path; Sub-Editor, Purushottam Jhankar, Lila Abhivyakti; Joint Editor, Sandhan; Executive Editor, Winers Delhi News. Address: Sahitya Kuteer 44, Site 2, Vikas Puri, New Delhi 18, India.

SRIVATSA. See: **CHANDRA SEKHAR, K.**

SRNKOVA Mila. See: **HAUGOVA Mila.**

ST AUBIN DE TERAN Lisa, b. 2 Oct 1953, London, England. Writer. m. (1) Jaime Teran, Oct 1970, div. 1981, 1 daughter, (2) George MacBeth, Mar 1981, div. 1986, 1 son. Appointments: Farmer, sugar cane, avocados, pears, sheep, Venezuela, 1972-78; Writer, 1972-. Publications: The Streak, 1980; The High Place, 1985. Honours: Somerset Maugham Award for novel The Long Way Home, Society of Authors; John Rhys Memorial Prize for novel The Slow Train to Milan, Book Trust, 1983; Eric Gregory Award for Poetry, Society of Authors, 1983. Membership: Fellow, Royal Society of Literature. Address: 7 Canynge Square, Clifton, Bristol, England.

ST AUBYN Edward, b. 14 Jan 1960, London, England. Writer. Education: Oxford University, 1979-82. Publications: Never Mind, 1992; Bad News, 1992; Some Hope, 1994. Honour: Betty Trask Award for Never Mind, 1992. Address: c/o Aitken & Stone, 29 Fernshaw Road, London SW10 0TG, England.

ST CLAIR Patricia Margaret, b. 2 Oct 1937, Hatch End, Middlesex, England. Poet. married, 1 son. Contributions to: BBC; Lady; Spectator; Various other newspapers and magazines. Address: Westwood, 39 Chester Road, Branksome Park, Poole, Dorset BH13 6DE, England.

ST CYR Napoleon, b. 8 May 1924, Franklin, New Hampshire, USA. Editor; Publisher. Education: BA, University of New Hampshire; BS, Certificate of Advanced Study, Fairfield University. Appointments: Editor, The Small Pond Magazine of Literature, 1969-; Literary Advisor, Stratford Cultural Commission, 1975-80; 1 of Final Judges in poetry and history, National Book Awards; Member, Advisory Board of Consultants, Small Press Review of Books, 1985-94; Poetry Editor, Cider Mill Press. Publications: Pebble Ring, 1966; Stones Unturned, 1967. Contributions to: Over 60 journals in form of poetry including: Editor's Line, The Small Pond Magazine of Literature, 1969-. Honour: Sherrard Short Story Prize, Honours Convocation, University of New Hampshire. Memberships: Academy of American Poets; CLMP; Past President, Halsey International Scholarship Programe, University of Bridgeport; French Committee. Address: PO Box 664, Stratford, CT 06497, USA.

ST JOHN Bruce (Carlisle), b. 1923, Barbados. University Lecturer. Appointments: Assistant Master, St Giles' Boys School, 1942-44; Assistant Master, Combermere School, 1944-64; Lecturer, Spanish, 1964-75, Senior Lecturer, Spanish, 1976-, University of the West Indies, Bridgetown; Editor, Ascent Series of Poetry Chap-Books, 1982. Publications: The Foetus Pains, The Foetus Pleasures, 1972; Bruce St John at Kairi House, 1974, 1975; Joyce and Eros and Varia, 1976; The Vests, Aftermath: An Anthology (editor), 1977; Caribanthology (editor), 1981; Bumbatuk I, 1982. Membership: National Council for Arts and Culture, Barbados.

STACHO Jan, b. 1 Jan 1936, Trnava, Czechoslovakia. Physician. 1 daughter. Education: MD, Medical Faculty, Komensky University, Bratislava, 1960. Appointments: Physician, 1960-64; Editor, Slovensky spisovatel publishing house, 1964; Editor-in-Chief, Revue svetovej literatury, 1965-67; Diplomatic Service, 1968-71. Publications:

Svadobne cesta, 1961; Dvojramenne ciste telo, 1964; Zazehy, 1967; Apokryfy, 1969; Z preziteho dna, 1979; Translations of P J de Beranger, J A Rimbaud, A Bertrand, Saint-John Perse, Dylan Thomas. Contributions to: Slovak and Czech magazines, 1960s: Slovenske pohlady; Kulturny zivot; Plamen; Host do domu. Honours: Prize for Poetry, Slovensky spisovatel publishing house, 1961; Jan Holly Prize for translations, 1986. Membership: Spolok slovenskych spisovatelov.

STADIG ALEXANDER, b. 2 Nov 1944, Natick, Massachusetts, USA. m. Alfred G Auel, 19 May 1960, 3 sons, 2 daughters. Education: Writer's Digest School, 1996. Appointments: Freelance Writer; Cin/Data Protection Corp; Volunteer, making tapes and reading to visually impaired, 1994-. Publications: The Seeding of a River, 1989, 1990; Books on tape are: A Light on Crystal Road, 1990; Letters from Roam, 1995, 1996; Limited Edition Greeting Card, In Distant Land, 1995. Contributions to: St Bernard Bugle, Diarist's Journal; Lucidty; My Legacy; Felicity; Rainbows, Vol 4; Memories & Reflections, Vol 4; Awaken to a Dream; Thalia Enquirer; Ohioana Library Association. Honours: Partridge Bicentennial Essay Contest, 1988; University of Cincinnati Reception, Ohioana Library Association Awards, 1989; Writer's Exchange 1st Place, 1988; Lucidty 1st Place, 1989; Golden Poet, 1989, 1990, 1991; International Literary Award, Washington State. Memberships: Hollywood Cable TV; PN Magazine-Poet of the Month, 1994; Radio Reading Service; Friends of Public Library; Friends of University of Cincinnati. Address: 220 Jackson Avenue #3, St Bernard, OH 45217, USA.

STAHL Jayne Lyn, b. 27 Apr 1949, New York, New York, USA. Teacher. Education: BA, State University of New York, 1967; MA, San Francisco State University, 1986. Appointment: Instructor, Valley College, Queens College. Publication: Stiffest of the Corpse, 1989. Contributions to: City Lights Review; Jacaranda; Exquisite Corpse; New York Quarterly; Niagara Review; Pulpsmith; Mouth; Earths; Daughters; Podium; Orange; Echo; Yearbook of Modern Poetry, 1976. Honour: Academy of American Poets Award. Address: 245-84 63 Ave, Douglaston, NY 11362, USA.

STALLWORTHY Jon, b. 18 Jan 1935, London, England. Poet. m. Gillian Waldock, 25 June 1960, 3 children. Education: BA, 1958, BLitt, 1961, Magdalen College, Oxford. Appointments: Served as Lieutenant, Oxfordshire and Buckinghamshire Light Infantry, seconded to Royal West African Frontier Force; Served Nigeria, 15 months, 1954-55; Editor, Oxford University Press, London, England, 1959-71; Visiting Fellow, All Souls College, Oxford, 1971-72; Editor, Clarendon Press, Oxford, 1972-77; Deputy Academic Publisher, Oxford University Press, Oxford, 1974-77; John Wendell Anderson Professor of English Literature, Cornell University, Ithaca, New York, USA, 1977-86; Reader in English Literature, 1986-92, Professor of English Literature, 1992-, Oxford University. Publications: The Earthly Paradise, 1958; The Astronomy of Love, 1961; Between the Lines: Yeats's Poetry in the Making, 1963; Out of Bounds, 1963; The Almond Tree, 1967; A Day in the City, 1967; Vision and Revision in Yeats's Last Poems, 1969; Root and Branch, 1969; Positives, 1969; A Dinner of Herbs, 1970; Hand in Hand, 1974; The Apple Barrel: Selected Poems 1955-63, 1974; Wilfred Owen: A Biography, 1974; Poets of the First World War, 1974; A Familiar Tree, 1978; Boris Pasternak, selected poems (translated with France), 1982; Editor: The Penguin Book of Love Poetry, 1973; The Complete Poems and Fragments of Wilfred Owen, 1983; The Oxford Book of War Poetry, 1984; The Poems of Wilfred Owen, 1985; Henry Reed, Collected Poems, 1991; Louis MacNeice, 1995; The Guest from the Future, 1995. Memberships: Fellow, Royal Society of Literature; Fellow, British Academy. Address: Wolfson College, Oxford, England.

STANDING Sue, b. 14 April 1952, Salt Lake City, Utah, USA. Poet; Teacher. Education: AB, Oberlin College, 1974; MA, Boston University, 1977. Appointments: Lecturer, Wellesley College, 1979; Writer in Residence, Wheaton College, 1979-; Consultant in Writing, J F Kennedy School of Government, 1981-87; Lecturer, MIT, 1993, 1994. Publications: Deception Pass, 1984; Gravida, 1995. Contributions to: Agni; American Poetry Review; American Scholar; Harvard Magazine; Nation; Ohio Review; Partisan Review; Ploughshares; Poetry Northwest; Prairie Schooner; Salmagundi; Southern Review; Southwest Review. Honours: Fellowships; Finalist Award, Massachusetts Artists Foundation; Residency Grants; Bunting Institute Fellowship, 1979; National Endowment for the Arts Fellowship, 1984. Memberships: Poets and Writers; Poetry Society of America; Associated Writing Program. Address: Wheaton College, Norton, MA 02766, USA.

STANNARD Glenys Margaret, (Maggi Stannard), b. 21 June 1942, Wales, England. Teacher. m. Russell Stannard, 25 May 1984, 3 sons. Education: Art Intermediate, 1959; Certificate Education, 1968; BEd Hons, 1984. Contributions to: Speakeasy; Spokes; OU Poets; Poetry Society; Arford Foundation. Honour: Speakeasy 2nd Prize, 1986. Memberships: Poetry Society; OU Poets; Toddington Poets. Address: 21 Alwins Field, Linslade, Beds LU7 7UF, England.

STANNARD Julian Edward, b. 27 May 1962, Kent, England. Lecturer. m. Cristina Angela Ramella, 14 July 1991, 2 sons. Education: BA Hons, English, Medieval Studies, Exeter, 1984; PGCE, English, Department Educational Studies, Oxford, 1986. Appointments: Lecturer, English, University of Genoa, Italy, 1986-93; Lecturer in Literary Studies, Suffolk College, 1994-. Publication: Fleur Adcock in Context: From Movement to Martians, 1996. Contributions to: Nuova Corrente; Quaderno; Orbis; Outposts; Poetry Nottingham; Rialto; Verse; Envoi Summer Anthology; Envoi; London Magazine; Honest Ulsterman; The Poetry Ireland Review; Stand; The North; The Poetry Business Anthology (1993); Acumen; Staple. Honours: Exeter University Literature Prize, 1984; PGCE, English, Oxford University, 1986; MPhil English, University of Exeter. Membership: Postgraduate Association, University of Exeter. Address: Langley House, Blind Lane, Hackney, Matlock, Derbyshire, England.

STANNARD Martin, b. 27 Aug 1952, Reading, England. Poet. m. Diana, 4 Sept 1976, 2 sons. Education: BA, Middlesex Polytechnic, 1981-84; MA, University College, London, 1984-85. Appointment: Editor, Publisher, Joe Soap's Canoe Poetry Magazine. Publications: Half Man Half Hammock Half Marlo Brandon; The Private Life of the Gauze Butterfly; The Lotte Poems; Baffled In Nacton; The Flat of the Land; Something Cold and White; The Gracing of Days; Denying England; From a Recluse to a Roving I Will Go. Contributions to: New Statesman; London Magazine; Ambit; Slow Dancer; Wide Skirt; Hanging Loose; B City; Panoply. Address: 30 Quilter Road, Felixstowe, Suffolk IP11 7JJ, England.

STEAD C(hristian) K(arlson), b. 17 Oct 1932, Auckland, New Zealand. Poet; Writer; Critic; Editor; Professor. m. Kathleen Elizabeth Roberts, 8 Jan 1955, 1 son, 3 daughters. Education: BA, 1954, MA, 1955, University of New Zealand; PhD, University of Bristol, 1961; DLitt, University of Auckland, 1982. Appointments: Lecturer in English, University of New England, Australia, 1956-57; Lecturer 1960-61, Senior Lecturer 1962-64, Associate Professor 1964-67, Professor of English 1967-86, Professor Emeritus 1986-, University of Auckland; Chairman, New Zealand Literary Fund Advisory Committee 1972-75, New Zealand Authors' Fund Committee 1989-91. Publications: Poems: Whether the Will is Free, 1964; Geographies, 1982; Poems of a Decade, 1983; Paris, 1984; Between, 1988; Voices, 1990. Fiction: Smith's Dream, 1971;Five for the Symbol, 1981; All Visitors Ashore, 1984; The Death of the Body, 1986; Sister Hollywood, 1989; The End of the Century at the End of the World, 1992. Criticism: The New Poetic: Yeats to Eliot, 1964, revised edition, 1987; In the Glass Case: Essays on New Zealand Literature, 1981; Pound, Yeats, Eliot and the Modernist Movement, 1986; Answering to the Language: Essays on Modern Writers, 1989. Editor: World's Classics: New Zealand Short Stories, 1966, 3rd edition, 1975; The New Gramophone Room: Poetry and Fiction (with Elizabeth Smither and Kendrick Smithyman), 1985. Contributions to: Poetry, fiction and criticism to various anthologies and periodicals. Honours include: Commander of the Order of the British Empire, 1984; Queen's Medal for Services to New Zealand Literature, 1990. Memberships: New Zealand PEN, chairman, Auckland Branch 1986-89, national vice president 1988-90. Address: 37 Tohunga Crescent, Auckland 1, New Zealand.

STEADMAN John M(arcellus III), b. 25 Nov 1918, USA. College Professor. Education: MA, Emory University, 1941; PhD, Princeton University, 1949. Appointments: Instructor, Georgia Institute of Technology; Assistant Professor, University of North Carolina; Senior Research Associate, Henry E Huntington Library; Professor, University of California. Publications: Ryoanji Temple and Other Poems, 1993; Reconnaissances, 1995. Contributions to: Poet Lore; Verse Craft; Emory University Quarterly; Emory Phoenix. Address: 250 South Oak Knoll Avenue, Apt 109, Pasadena, CA 91101, USA.

STEDHAM Tommy, b. 29 Mar 1967, Anniston, Alabama, USA. College Student. Education: BS, Marketing Major, Sociology Minor, Jacksonville State University, Jacksonville, Alabama, 1989; Currently studying Computer Science Degree, Jacksonville State University. Appointments: Property and Casualty Services Auditor, Alabama

Medicaid Agency (Social Worker), Sears Roebuck & Co, Sales Person. Publications: My Kind of Woman, Echoes from the Silence (anthology), 1995; Baby on the Way (anthology), 1996. Address: 704 West 62nd Street, Anniston, AL 36206, USA.

STEELE Marian, (Clara Marian Szego), b. 23 Mar 1916, Budapest, Hungary. Professor. m. Sidney Roberts, 14 Sept 1943. Education: AB, Hunter College, 1937; MS, University of Minnesota, 1939; PhD, 1942; Biochemistry and Physiology. Appointments: Instructor, University of Minnesota, 1942-43; Cancer Research Fellow, University of Minnesota, 1943-45; Official, Science Research and Development, Washington, DC, 1944-45; Research Instructor, 1945-47; Yale University, 1947-48; Assistant Professor, Professor, University of California, Los Angeles, 1949-. Publications: Submitted: Unquiet River; US: The Lives of a Subcontinent. Approx 160 scientific articles and invited reviews. Contributions to: Archer; Alura; San Ferando Poetry Journal; Plains Poetry Journal; Connecticut River Review; Ellipsis; New Renaissance; Negative Capability; Black Buzzard Review; South Dakota Review; Press. Honour: Guggenheim Fellow in Biochemistry. Memberships: Academy of American Poets; Poetry Society of America; PEN. Address: 1371 Marinette Road, Pacific Palisades, CA 90272, USA.

STEELE Timothy Reid, b. 22 Jan 1948, Vermont, USA. Writer; Teacher. m. Victoria Lee Erpelding, 14 Jan 1979. Education: BA, Stanford University, 1970; PhD, Brandeis University, 1977. Appointments: Jones Lecturer, Stanford University, 1975-77; Lecturer, University of California at Los Angeles, 1977-83; Lecturer, University of California at Santa Barbara, 1986; Professor, California State University, Los Angeles, 1987-. Publications: Uncertainties and Rest; Sapphics Against Anger and Other Poems; Missing Measures; The Color Wheel, 1994; Sapphics and Uncertainties: Poems 1970-86, 1995. Contributions to: Poetry; Threepenny Review; Paris Review; Greensboro Review; Southern Review; Crosscurrents; New Criterion; Numbers; Spectator; Formalist; PN Review. Honours: Stegner Fellowship; Guggenheim Fellowship; Lavan Younger Poets Award; Commonwealth Club of California Medal; Los Angeles Center for PEN Award for Poetry. Memberships: PEN; Academy of American Poets. Address: 1801 Preuss Road, Los Angeles, CA 90035. USA.

STEFANILE Felix Neil, b. 13 Apr 1920, New York, New York, USA. Professor. m. Selma Epstein, 17 Jan 1953. Education: BA, City University of New York, 1944. Appointments: Visiting Poet, Lecturer, 1961-62; Assistant Professor, 1962-64, Associate Professor, 1964-69, Professor, 1969-87, Purdue University, Chairman, Editorial Board, Purdue University Press, 1964-69; Editor, Publisher, Sparrow Press, 1954-89. Publications: If I Were Fire; In That Far Country; The Blue Moustache; Umberto Saba; East River Nocturne; A Fig Tree in America; The Dance at St Gabriel's, 1995. Contributions to: New York Sunday Times Book Review; Sewanne Review; Virginia Quarterly Review; Poetry; Parnassus; TriQuarterly; Hudson Review; New York Times. Honours: Pushcart Press Prize; Standard Oil of Indiana Foundation Award; Virginia Quarterly Review Emily Clark Balch Award; Nathan Haskell Dole Prize; National Endowment for the Arts Prize. Memberships: Poetry Society of America; American Literary Translators Association. Address: 103 Waldron Street, West Lafayette, IN 47906, USA.

STEFFEN Jonathon Neil, b. 5 Oct 1958, London, England. Teacher; Translator. Education: MA English, King's College, Cambridge, 1978-81. Appointment: Teacher, English Department and Department of Translating and Interpreting, Heidelberg University. Publications include: Short Stories: In Seville, 1985; Meeting the Majors, 1987; Carpe Diem, 1991; Cleopatra, 1994; The Story of Icarus, 1994; At Breakfast, 1995; Poems: The Soldier and the Soldier's Son, 1986; German Hunting Party, 1987; The Moving Hand, 1994; The Great Days of the Railway, 1994; Apprentice and Master, 1994; St Francis in the Slaughter, 1995. Contributions to: London Magazine; New Statesman; Spectator; Outposts Poetry Quarterly; Acumen Magazine. Honours: Harper-Wood Travelling Studentship, 1981-82; Hawthornden Creative Writing Fellowship, 1987. Address: Schillerstrasse 16, 69115 Heidelberg, Germany.

STEFFLER John Earl, b. 13 Nov 1947, Toronto, Ontario, Canada. Professor of English Literature. m. Shawn O'Hagan, 30 May 1970. 1 son, 1 daughter. Education: BA, University of Toronto; MA, University of Guelph. Appointments: Professor of English, Memorial University of Newfoundland, 1975-. Publications: An Explanation of Yellow, 1980; The Grey Islands, 1985; The Wreckage of Play, 1988;

The Afterlife of George Cartwright, 1991. Contributions to: Malahat Review; Canadian Literature; Fiddlehead; Queens Quarterly; Event; CV/II; Ariel; Poetry Canada; Orbis; Tickleace. Honours: Norma Epstein Prize for Poetry; Canada Council Awards; Ontario Arts Council Awards; Newfoundland Arts Council Awards; Books in Canada First Novel Award, 1992; Newfoundland Arts Council Artist of The Year Award, 1992; Thomas Raddall Atlantic Fiction Award, 1992; Joseph S Stauffer Prize, 1993. Memberships: Writers Alliance of Newfoundland and Labrador; League of Canadian Poets; PEN International. Literary Agent: Susan Schulman Literary Agency, 454 West 44th St, New York, NY 10036, USA. Address: Department of English, Sir Wilfred Genfell College, Corner Brook, Newfoundland A2H 6P9, Canada.

STEIN Agnes Hippen, b. 14 Aug 1917, Germany. Writer; Translator. m. 26 Aug 1939, 3 daughters. Education: AB, 1939, ABLS, 1940, University of Michigan. Appointment: Lecturer in English, Bloomfield College, 1977-80. Publications: Poetry - Color Composition, 1985; Anthology, Text - The Uses of Poetry, 1975; Translation: Four German Poets, 1979. Contributions to: Purple and Green; Ambit; Orbis; Other Poetry; Rialto; Poetry Nottingham; Poetry Durham; Prospice; Outposts; Osiris; Cumberland Review; River City; Kansas Quarterly; Northstone Review; Translations in anthologies: Making for the Open; Comparative Criticism; Poetry World No 2; Evidence of Fire; Child of Europe. Honour: Poetry Translation Prize, British Comparative Literature Association, 1985. Membership: Poetry Society, London. Address: 1 Carlingford Road, London NW3 1RY, England.

STEIN Hannah, b. 23 Sept 1929, USA. Piano Teacher. m. Sherman Stein, 11 June 1950, 1 son, 2 daughters. Education: BA, Barnard College, 1950. Publication: Schools of Flying Fish, 1990. Contributions to: American Voice; Antioch Review; Poetry Northwest; Prairie Schooner; Yale Review. Honours: National Poetry Competition; Anna Davidson Rosenberg Prize. Memberships: Poets and Writers; Friends of PEN. Address: 1118 Bucknell Drive, Davis, CA 95616, USA.

STEIN Kevin Joseph, b. 1 Jan 1954, Anderson, Indiana, USA. Professor of English. m. Debra Lang, 26 May 1979, 1 son, 1 daughter. Education: BS, summa cum laude, 1976, MA, 1978, Ball State University; MA, Creative Writing, 1982, PhD, 1984, Indiana University. Appointments: Ball State University, 1976-79; Assistant Professor, 1984, Associate Professor, 1988, Professor of English, 1994-, Bradley University. Publications: A Field of Wings, 1986; The Figure Our Bodies Make, 1988; A Circus of Want, 1992; Bruised Paradise, 1996. Contributions to: The American Poetry Review; Poetry; Kenyon Review; Ploughshares; North American Review; Shenandoah; Crazyhorse; Boulevard; The Ohio Review. Honours: Illinois Arts Council Poetry Fellowship, 1986, 1988; Frederick Bock Endowment for the Arts Poetry Fellowship, 1991; Devins Award for Poetry, 1992. Memberships: Society of Midland Authors; Illinois Writers Inc. Address: Department of English, Bradley University, Peoria, IL 61625, USA.

STEINMAN Lisa Malinowski, b. 8 Apr 1950, Willimantic, Connecticut, USA. Professor of English and Humanities. m. James Shugrue, 23 July 1984. Education: BA, 1971, MFA, 1973, PhD, 1976, Cornell University. Appointments: Teaching Assistant, Assistant Professor, Cornell University, 1970-76; Assistant Professor, 1976-82, Associate Professor, 1982-89, Professor, English, Humanities, 1990, Kenan Professor of English Literature and Humanities, 1993, Reed College, Portland, Oregon; Various poetry workshops, New York, Oklahoma, Oregon, Washington, California, 1976-; Director, National Endowment for the Humanities Summer Seminars; 1986, 1988, 1990, 1992; Co-Editor, Hubbub, 1983-. Publications: Lost Poems, 1976; All That Comes to Light, 1989; A Book of Other Days, 1993. Contributions to: Poetry East; Madison Review; Ascent; Birmingham Poetry Review; Pennsylvania English; ZYZZYVA; Threepenny Review; Fine Madness; Boulevard; Albany Review; Colorado Review; Willow Springs; Ironwood; Widner Review; Plain Song; Chicago Review; Another Chicago Magazine; Prism International; Tendril; MSS; Webster review; Penny Dreadful; Epoch; Laurel Review; Small Farm; Concerning Poetry; Hanging Loose; New Poems appearing in New Virginia Review; Michigan Quarterly; Quarterly West; International Quarterly. Honours: Oregon Arts Commission, 1983; National Endowment for the Arts, 1984; Pablo Neruda Award, Nimrod Magazine, 1987; Oregon Book Award, 1993. Memberships: Founding Member, Treasuer, Past Secretary, PEN Northwest; Former Member, Board of Directors, Portland Poetry Festival. Address: Department of English, Reed College, 3203 South East Woodstock Boulevard, Portland, OR 97202, USA.

STEPHEN Ian, b. 29 April 1955. Writer. m. Barbara Ziehm, 2 sons. Education: Nicolson Institute, Stornoway. Appointments: Resigned as Coastguard Officer to become full-time Writer, 1995. Publications: Malin, Hebrides, Minches, 1983; Varying States of Grace, 1989; There Goes the Island - Anthology, 1993; Providence II, 1994. Contributions to: Most Scottish periodicals; Stand; London Magazine; Orbis; Poetry Wales; Waves, Canada; Poetry Canada Review; 11 poems in Best of 84 Poetry Australia. Honours: Scottish Arts Council, Bursaries, 1982, 1995; Inaugural Winner Christian Salvesen/RLS Memorial Award, 1994-95. Membership: Scottish Poetry Library. Literary Agent: Alec Finlay, Morning Star Publications, Edinburgh. Address: Last House, 1 Benside, Newmarket, Isle of Lewis, HS2 0DZ, Scotland.

STEPHENS Meic, b. 23 July 1938, Treforest, Pontypridd, Wales. Editor; Journalist; Consultant; Lecturer. m. Ruth Wynn Meredith, 14 Aug 1965, 1 son, 3 daughters. Education: BA, University College of Wales, Aberystwyth, 1961; University of Rennes, 1960; University College of North Wales, Bangor, 1962. Appointments: French Teacher, 1962-66; Journalist, 1966-67; Literature Director, Welsh Arts Council, 1967-90; Visiting Professor, Brigham Young University, 1991; Lecturer in Journalism, University of Glamorgan, 1994-. Publications: Triad; Poetry Wales; Lilting House; Exiles All; Green Horse; A Book of Wales; Gregynog Poets; Bright Field; A Cardiff Anthology; The Arts in Wales 1950-75; The White Stone; The Curate of Clyro; A Dictionary of Literary Quotations; Oxford Companion to the Literature of Wales; Oxford Illustrated Literary Guide to Great Britain and Ireland; A Most Peculiar People; A Rhondda Anthology; Changing Wales, A Bibliography of Literature in 20th C Wales. Honour: St Davids University College Lampeter. Memberships: Welsh Academy; Gorsedd of Bards. Address: 10 Heol Don, Whitchurch, Cardiff, Wales.

STEPHENS W J. See: **FROEHLICH Joey.**

STERN Gerald, b. 22 Feb 1925, Pittsburgh, Pennsylvania, USA. Poet; Teacher. m. Patricia Miller, 1952, 1 son, 1 daughter. Education: BA, University of Pittsburgh, 1947; MA, Columbia University, 1949. Appointments: Instructor, Temple University, Philadelphia, 1957-63; Professor, Indiana University of Pennsylvania, 1963-67, Somerset County College, New Jersey, 1968-82; Visiting Poet, Sarah Lawrence College, 1977; Visiting Professor, University of Pittsburgh, 1978, Columbia University, 1980, Bucknell University, 1988, New York University, 1989; Faculty, Writers' Workshop, University of Iowa, 1982-94; Distinguished Chair, University of Alabama, 1984; Fanny Hurst Professor, Washington University, St Louis, 1985; Bain Swiggert Chair, Princeton University, 1989; Poet-in-Residence, Bucknell University, 1994. Publications: The Naming of Beasts and Other Poems, 1973; Rejoicings, 1973; Lucky Life, 1977; The Red Coal, 1981; Paradise Poems, 1984; Lovesick, 1987; Leaving Another Kingdom: Selected Poems, 1990; Two Long Poems, 1990; Bread Without Sugar, 1992; Odd Mercy, 1995. Honours: National Endowment for the Arts Grants, 1976, 1981, 1987; Lamont Poetry Selection Award, 1977; Governor's Award, Pennsylvania, 1980; Guggenheim Fellowship, 1980; Bess Hokin Award, 1980; Bernard F Connor Award, 1981; Melville Cane Award, 1982; Jerome J Shestack Prize, 1984; Academy of Poets Fellowship, 1993; Ruth Lilly Poetry Prize, 1996. Address: c/o Department of English, University of Iowa, Iowa City, IA 52242, USA.

STESSEL Harold Edward, b. 24 Apr 1939, Dunkirk, New York, USA. Professor of English. m. Elizabeth Victoria Dewey, 23 Aug 1970, 1 son. Education: BA, English, University of North Carolina, 1959; MA, English, University of Chicago, 1960; MA, American Civilisation, 1972, PhD, American Civilisation, 1980, University of Pennsylvania. Appointments: Assistant Professor, English, Grinnell College, 1974-76; Fulbright Lecturer in American Culture, Gothenburg University, Sweden, 1976-79; Assistant Professor, Humanities, State University of New York, 1981-86; Professor, English, Westfield State College, Massachusetts, 1986-. Publications: American Studies, 1975; Ardis Anthology of New American Poetry, 1977. Contributions to: Ascent; Beloit Poetry Review; Commonwealth Review; Connecticut River Review; Cottonwood Review; Exile; Hiram Poetry Review; Honest Ulsterman, Northern Ireland; Kansas Quarterly; Minnesota Review; Mississippi Review; Moosehead Review, Canada; MSS; Noiseless Spider; Quarry; St Andrews Review; Slow Motion Review; Southern Poetry Review; Windless Orchard; Xanadu. Address: English Department, Westfield State College, Westfield, MA 01086, USA.

STEVEN Kenneth Campbell, b. 25 Nov 1968, Glasgow, Scotland. Writer. Education: Morrisons Academy, 1975-82;

Breadalbane Academy, 1982-86; Student of Scottish, English, Russian and French Literature, Glasgow University. Appointments: Teacher of English, Rognan, Arctic Norway, 1991-92. Publications: The Unborn, 1992; Remembering Peter, 1993; Dan, 1994; The Missing Days, selected poems, 1995. Contributions to: An Anthology of Hope, 1988; Hebridean Connection, 1991; Poetry Now, 1991; New Christian Poetry; Chapman; Lines Review; Orbis; Planet; Poetry Wales; Poetry Australia; Staple; Verse International; Northern Norway Review; Gairm; The Fiddlehead (Canada); Imago (Australia); Northern Perspective (Australia); Outposts Poetry Quarterly; Queen's Quarterly (Canada); Westerly (Australia). Honours: Scottish Poetry Open Poetry Competition Finalist, 1986-91; Michael Bruce Memorial Poetry Competition, Runner Up, 1991; Staple First Editions Award, Runner Up, 1992; Shortlisted, Deo Gloria Award for Fiction, 1992; Nominated - Saltire Book Award, 1994; Hawthornden Fellow, 1995. Address: Boisdale, Old Crieff Road, Aberfeldy PH15 2DH, Scotland.

STEVENS Alex(ander McConnell), b. 17 Dec 1955, New York, USA. Freelance Writer. m. Susan L Helgeson, 1983. Education: BA, University of Louisville, 1976; University of New Hampshire; MA, Writing Seminars, Johns Hopkins University, 1979. Contributions to: New Yorker; Poetry; Shenandoah; New Republic; Georgia Review; Poetry Northwest; Louisville Review; Epoch; Chelsea; Prairie Schooner; Anthology of Magazine Verse and Yearbook of American Poetry, 1981, 1984. Honours: Fellowship, Writing Seminars, Johns Hopkins University; Poetry Fellowship Award, National Endowment for the Arts, 1982-83. Address: 801 Rutland, Houston, TX 77007, USA.

STEVENS Geoffrey, b. 4 June 1942, West Bromwich, England. Industrial Chemist. m. B C Smith, 20 Feb 1965, 1 daughter. Education: Higher National Certificate, Chemistry, 1964. Appointments: Editor, Purple Patch Magazine, 1976-; UK Editor of S-FESt magazines, USA. Publications: From a High Horse, 1977; The 70's, 1986; A Phew Successes, 1986; Not Quite Headlines, 1987; 87 Poems, 1988; Intoxication, 1989; A Guide to the Statues of This Town, 1989; Future Heart Attacks by Appointment Only, 1990; Sits Vacant, 1991; Ecstacy, 1992; A Comparison of Myself with Ivan Blatney, 1992; Field Manual for Poetry Lovers, 1992; Chapbook - Skin Print, with Paul Weinman, 1995. Contribution to: USA: Coal City Review; California State Quarterly; Z Miscellaneous; Manna; Lazer; UK: Workshop New Poetry; Psychopoetica; Periaktos; South; Weyfarers; Pennine Ink; Odyssey; Others; India; Poesie; Quest; Carta del Oliver, Argentina; Greens Magazine, Canada. Membership: Dylan Thomas Society, 1995. Address: 8 Beaconview House, Charlemont Farm, West Bromwich B71 3PL, England.

STEVENS Jean Marian, b. 27 July 1928, Newport Pagnell, Buckinghamshire, England. Former Teacher. m. David Richard Stevens, 14 Aug 1954, 1 son, 2 daughters. Education: Certificate of Education, Hockerill Teacher Training College, Bishops Stortford, Hertfordshire, 1948. Appointments: Assistant Teacher, Primary and Secondary Schools, Bedfordshire and Hertfordshire, 1948-56. Publication: Led by Kingfishers. Contributions to: Outpost Poetry Quarterly; Lady; Woman and Home; Woman Journalist; This England; Ver Poets Voices; Envoi Summer Anthology, 1988; Unsaid Goodnight, 1989; Greetings and Gossip, 1992; Phoenix Poets Anthology, 1994; Anthologies of the Society of Women Writers and Journalists: Valuable Things, 1975; Candles and Lamps, 1979; A Mirror to Our Day, 1984. Honours: Julia Cairns Salver for Poetry, 1974, 1991; Dacorum Poet of the Year, Hemel Hempstead Gazette, 1974. Membership: Vice-President, Past Poetry Adviser, Past Chairman, Past Acting Secretary, Society of Women Writers and Journalists. Address: 3 Nettlecroft, Hemel Hempstead, Herts HP1 1PQ, England.

STEVENS Ron(ald Alfred), b. 17 Mar 1926, New South Wales, Australia. Officer, Royal Australian Navy. m. Clauris Blanche Archer, 9 Dec 1950, 1 son, 3 daughters. Education: BA, Macquarie University, Sydney, 1979. Appointment: Royal Australian Navy. Publications: A Touch of History; A Lighter Touch of History. Contributions to: Overland; Land; Longreach Leader; Ararat Advertiser; Yass Tribune; Northern Perspective; A First Hearing. Honours: Red Earth Poetry Prize; Jessie Litchfield Literary Award; Henry Lawson Society Poetry Prize; Bundaberg Arts Festival Poetry Prize; Geraldton Cultural Trust Literary Award; Botany Bay Bicentennial Poetry Award; Leeton Bicentennial Poetry Award; Melbourne Poetry Society Bicentennial Award; bronze Swagman Poetry Prize. Memberships: Fellowship of Australian Writers; Youngstreet Poets; Henry Lawson Society of New South Wales. Address: 70 Glaston Road, Hornsby, New South Wales 2077, Australia.

STEVENSON Anne Katharine, b. 3 Jan 1933, England. Freelance Writer. m. (1) 2 sons, 1 daughter, (2) Peter David Lucas, 3 Sept 1987. Education: BA, 1954; MA, 1961, University of Michigan. Appointments: School Teacher, 1954-65; Publisher, 1955-56; Part Time Teaching, The Open University, 1970s. Publications: Living in America, 1965; Reversals, 1969; Travelling Behind Glass, 1974; Correspondences, 1974; Enough of Green, 1977; Minute by Glass Minute, 1982; The Fiction Makers, 1985; Winter Time, 1986; Selected Poems, 1987; The Other House, 1990; Four and a Half Dancing Men, 1993; Collected Poems, 1996. Contributions to: TLS; London Review of Books; PN Review; Poetry Review; The New Yorker; Atlantic; Stand; Poetry Wales; Rialto; Poetry Chicago; New England Review. Honours: Major Hopwood Award, 1954; Athena Award, 1990, University of Michigan, 1954; Arts Council Award, 1974; Poetry Book Society Choice, 1985; Five Fellowships. Memberships: Poetry Society GB; FRSL, Arts Council of Great Britian; Society of Authors; University Women's Club, London; Poetry Book Society. Address: 9 Coton Road, Grantchester, Cambridge CB3 9NH, England.

STEVER Edward William, b. 17 Feb 1955, Amityville, New York, USA. Editor. m. Linda Anne Wickers, 25 Sept 1983, 3 daughters. Education: ALA, 1990; Baccalaureate in English Literature, 1993. Appointment: Co-Editor, Prism, literary journal, 1991. Publications: Propulsion, 1992; Transparency, 1990. Contributions to: Long Island Quarterly; Chiron Review; North Atlantic Review; The Portable Wall; Live Poets; The New Press; San Fernando Poetry Journal; Newsday; Kumquat Review; Heaven Bone. Honours: Jean Voege Poetry Awards, 1990, 1991, 1992. Memberships: Academy of American Poets; Long Island Poetry Collective; Live Poet's Society; Walt Whitman Birthplace Association. Address: c/o Writers Edge, Box 284, Ridge, NY 11961, USA.

STEWART Harold Frederick, b. 14 Dec 1916, Sydney, Australia. Poet; Writer; Translator. Education: University of Sydney. Appointments: Broadcaster, Australian Broadcasting Commission; Lecturer, Victorian Council of Adult Education. Publications: Poetry: The Darkening Ecliptic (with James McAuley), 1944; Phoenix Wings: Poems 1940-46, 1948; Orpheus and Other Poems, 1956; The Exiled Immortal: A Song Cycle, 1980; By the Old Walls of Kyoto: A Year's Cycle of Landscape Poems with Prose Commentaries, 1981; Collected Poems (with Ern Malley), 1993. Translator: A Net of Fireflies: Japanese Haiku and Haiku Paintings, 1960; A Chime of Windbells: A Year of Japanese Haiku, 1969; Tannisho: Passages Deploring Deviations of Faith (with Bando Shojun), 1980; The Amida Sutra Mandala (with Inagaki Hisao), 1995. Honours: Sydney Morning Herald Prize for Poetry, 1951; Australia Council Grant, 1978; Senior Emeritus Writers Fellow, Australia Council, 1982; Christopher Brennan Prize for Poetry, 1988. Address: 501 Keifuku Dai-ni Manshon, Yamabana-icho Dacho 7-1, Shugakuin, Sakyo-ku, Kyoto 606, Japan.

STEWART Mary Florence Elinor, b. 17 Sept 1916, Sunderland, England. Writer. m. Frederick Henry Stewart, 24 Sept 1945. Education: BA, 1938, DipEd, 1939, MA, 1941, Durham University. Publications: Madam, Will You Talk?, 1955; Thunder on the Right, 1957; My Brother Michael, 1960; The Moonspinners, 1962; The Merlin Trilogy: The Crystal Cave, 1970; The Hollow Hills, 1973; The Last Enchantment, 1979; The Novel of Mordred: The Wicked Day, 1983; For Children: The Little Broomstick, 1984; Ludo and the Star Horse, 1981; A Walk in Wolf Wood, 1980; Thornyhold, 1988; Forst on the Window and Other Poems, 1990; Stormy Petrel, 1991. Contributions to: Various magazines. Honours: Frederick Niven Prize; Scottish Arts Council Award; Honorary Fellow, Newnham College, Cambridge. Memberships: PEN; New Club. Address: Hodder and Stoughton, 47 Bedford Square, London WC1B 3DP, England.

STEWART Susan Elisabeth, b. 13 June 1953, Lancaster, England. Poet. Education: BA Hons, 2:1, University of Kent, 1979. Appointments: Publishing, London; Full-time Writer and Creative Writing Tutor, schools, adult education, 1982-; Creative Writing Fellowship, Stirling University, 1994-95. Publications: Books of Hours (illustrations by Celia Ward), 1986; Big World, Little World, green anthology of prose and poetry for children (compiler), 1991; Inventing the Fishes, collection 1993; Readings, numerous venues including Poetry Society and South Bank, London. Contributions to: Acumen; Ambit; Blind Serpent; Grand Piano; Illuminations; Independent; London Magazine; Orbis; Other Poetry; Oxford Poetry; Poetry Matters; Poetry Nottingham; Poetry Review; Prospice; Resurgence; South West Review; Strawberry Fare; Times Literary Supplement; Verse; Virtue Without Terror; Women's Review; Anthologies: Delighting the Heart:

A Notebook by Women Writers, 1989; Taking Reality by Notebook by Women Writers, 1989; Taking Reality by Surprise: Writing for Pleasure and Publication, 1991; Compass, 1993. Honours: Book of Hours exhibited at Poetry Society and Mass Gallery, London, and sold to private collector; Finalists, Times Literary Supplement Cheltenham Poetry Competition, 1988; 1st Prize, Formal Section, Rhyme Revival Competition, Orbis, 1988; 5th Prize, Peterloo Poets Open Poetry Competition, 1991; Co-Judge, Southern Arts Literature Prize, 1991; Winner of The Aldeburgh Poetry Festival Prize for Best First Collection for Inventing the Fishes, 1993. Memberships: Council of Management, Arvon Foundation: Poetry Society Poets in Schools Scheme; Steering Committee, Berkshire Literary Festival; Literature Adviser to Southern Arts; Write Connections Scheme, Southern Arts; Reader for Write Reactions, Manuscript Appraisal Service. Address: The Thatched Cottage, Eling, Hermitage, Nr Newbury, Berkshire RG16 9XR, England.

STIMPSON Gerald. See: MITCHELL Adrian.

STOCK Norman, b. 14 July 1940, Brooklyn, New York, USA. Librarian. Education: BA, Brooklyn College, 1962; MLS (Library Services), Rutgers University, 1967; MA, English, Hunter College, 1971. Appointments: Various librarian posts including, most recently at Montclair State University. Publications: Book of Poems: Buying Breakfast for My Kamikaze Pilot, 1994. Contributions to: College English; New York Quarterly; New England Review; Denver Quarterly; Poet Lore; Hanging Loose; Brooklyn Review. Honours: New Voice Award in Poetry, YMCA Writers Voice Program, 1984; National Arts Club Scholar in Poetry, Bread Loaf Writers Conference, 1985; New York to the Heartland Contest, Poets and Writers, 1986; Poetry Prize, Bennington Writing Workshops, 1988; Peregrine Smith Poetry Contest, 1993; Alan Collins Fellow in Poetry, Bread Loaf Writers Conference, 1994; Tennessee Williams Scholar in Poetry, Sewance Writers Conference, 1995. Membership: Poetry Society of America. Address: 77-11 35th Avenue, Apt 2P, Jackson Heights, NY 11372, USA.

STOCKER Stella, b. London, England. Adult Education Lecturer; Reviews Editor; Poet. m. Victor Stocker, 1 son. Education: Queen Mary College, University of London; High Wycombe College of Art and Technology. Appointments: Reviews Editor, Orbis; Creative Writing Tutor; Gives talks on contemporary poetry. Contributions to: Orbis; Envoi; Counterpoint; New Poetry; Outposts; Pennine Platform; Weyfarers; Palantir; Vision On; Keep; Doors; Staple. Honours: Surrey Open Competition: Special Mentions, 1982, 1990, 2nd Prizes, 1987, 1991, 3rd Prize, 1988; 4th Prize Greyfriars Open Competition, 3rd Prize Natural History, Museum Open Competition; Commendations, Ver Poets Open Competitions, 1988, 1991; Commendation, Kent and Sussex Open Competition, 1992; Surrey Open Competition, 1994. Memberships: Poetry Society; Surrey Poetry Centre (Hon General Secretary). Address: Treetops, 18 Hermitage Road, Kenley, Surrey CR8 5EB, England.

STOCKS John Bryan, b. 17 July 1917, Baildon, West Yorkshire, England. Freelance Writer. Education: Leeds University, 1945-50. Publications: Zodiac; Trouble on Helicon; Plays: After You've Gone, comedy in three acts, 1972; Victor's Island, and two other one-act plays, 1990. Contributions to: I Burn for England; Poems From Hospital; More Poems from the Forces; Methuen Book of Theatre Verse; Salamander Oasis Trust; Yorkshire Post; Sunday Times. Memberships: Bradford English Society; Poetry Workshop. Address: Bradda, 11 Halstead Drive, Nr Ilkey, West Yorkshire LS29 6NT, England.

STOKES Daniel Patrick, b. 7 Sept 1945, Dublin, Ireland. Writer. Education: MA, English and Philosophy, Trinity College, Dublin, 1968; HDipEd, National University of Ireland, 1969. Appointments: Teacher, 1969-78; Vice Principal, St Patrick's Cathedral School, 1976-80; Full-time Writer, 1980-. Publications: Keepsake Poems, 1977; Poems for Christmas, 1981; Interest and Other Poems, 1982. Contributions to: New Poetry; Lines Review; Poetry Ireland Review; Sunday Tribune; Journal of Irish Literature; Irish Times; Ariel; Atlantic Review; Dekalb Literary Arts Journal; Studies; Cyphers; Ulster Tatler; Cork Examiner; Connacht Tribune; Prism International. Honours: Yorkshire Poets Award, 1977; New Poetry Competition, 1978; Poetry Athlone Award, 1980; Edinburgh Fringe First for God, Men & God Knows What, a presentation of the works of James Stephens, 1982. Address: 4 New Bridge Drive, Sandymount, Dublin 4, Ireland.

STOLOFF Carolyn, b. 14 Jan 1927, New York, New York, USA. Poet; Painter; Teacher. Education: Dalton School; University of Illinois; BS, Columbia University School of General Studies; Poetry Workshop with Stanley Kunitz. Appointments: Author; Teacher, Manhattanville College, 1957-74; Women's House of Dentention, 1971-72; Baird House, 1973; Stephens College, 1975; Hamilton College, 1985; University of Rochester Summer Writers Workshop, 1985; Poets in Public Service, 1989-90; School Volunteer Program, 1995-. Publications: Stepping Out; Dying to Survive; In the Red Meadow; Lighter-Than-Night Verse; Swiftly Now; A Spool of Blue, New and Selected Poems; You Came to Meet Someone Else, book, 1993. Contributions to: New Yorker Book of Poems; Our Only Hope is Humour; Rising Tides; A Carpet of Sparrows; Alcatraz; New Directions Anthology; A Year in Poetry, anthology, 1995; The Age of Koestler, anthology, 1995. Honours: National Council on the Arts Award for Achievement; Theodore Roethke Award, Poetry Northwest; Silver Anniversary Medal, Audubon Artists; Michael M Engel Memorial Award; Resident Grants: MacDowell Colony, New Hampshire, 1961, 1962, 1970, 1976; Theodore Roethke Award, Poetry Northwest, 1967; First Prize, Poetry from the Miscellany, 1972; Robert Philipp Award 1990; The Bader-Rowney Award for Oil, 1994; The Art Student's League Award for Oil, 1995. Membership: Poetry Society of America. Address: 24 West 8th Street, New York, NY 10011, USA.

STONE Gordon Leonard, b. 27 Feb 1936, Halifax, Nova Scotia. Retired Professor. m. Betty Jean, 10 Aug 1957, 1 daughter. Education: BSc, Forestry, 1960; MSc, Forestry, 1967; MSc, Adult Education, 1975. Appointments: Research Scientist; District Forester; College Professor. Publications: In Search of the Source of Light; Insight into the Mind of a Schizophrenic Friend, 1989; Why I Called?; My Journey of Faith with Telecare, 1996. Address: 145 Princess Crescent, Sault Ste Marie, Ontario P6B 3P4, Canada.

STONE Joan Elizabeth, b. 22 Oct 1930, Port Angeles, Washington, USA. Assistant Professor of English. m. James A Black, 30 July 1990, 4 sons, 1 daughter. Education: BA, magna cum laude, 1970, MA, Creative Writing, 1974, University of Washington. Appointments: Visiting Professor of Poetry, University of Montana, 1974; Director, Creative Writing Workshop, University of Washington, 1975; Assistant Professor of English, Colorado College, 1977-. Publications: The Swimmer and Other Poems, 1975; A Letter to Myself to Water, 1982; Our Lady of the Harbor, 1986. Contributions to: Georgia Review; Poetry Northwest; New York Quarterly; Minnesota Review; Colorado Review; Seattle Review; Indiana Review; Kayak; Green River Review. Honours: Hallmark Honour Prize in Poetry, Academy of American Poets Award, University of Washington, 1969, 1970, 1972; Best Poems of 1973, Borestone Mountain Awards, 1974. Address: c/o Colorado College. 14 East Cache La Poudre, Colorado Springs, CO 80903, USA.

STONE John, b. 7 Feb 1936, Jackson, Mississippi, USA. Physician; Cardiologist; Professor. m. Lu Crymes, 16 Aug 1958, 2 sons. Education: BA, Millsaps College, Jackson, 1958; MD, Washington University, 1962; University of Rochester, Emory University. Appointments: Faculty of Emory University School of Medicine; Assistant Professor to Professor, 1969. Publications: The Smell of Matches; In All This Rain; Renaming the Streets; In the Country of Hearts. Contributions to: New England Review; Shenandoah; Southern Poetry Review; Beloit Poetry Journal; New Orleans Review; Denver Quarterly. Midwest Quarterly; Greenhouse Review; Raven. Honour: Literature Award. Membership: Mississippi Institute of Arts and Letters. Address: c/o Emory University School of Medicine, WHSCAB-1440 Clifton Road North East, Atlanta, GA 30322, USA.

STORER Patrick Antony, (Patrick Ryan), b. 5 Feb 1953, Leicester, England. Senior Teacher. m. Alison Jane Chalmers, 24 Aug 1989. Education: BA, University of Swansea, 1975; MA, 1977; PGCE, Bristol University, 1977. Appointments: Teacher, The Cathedral School, Hereford, 1977-80; Head of Drama, Ross on Wye, 1980-82; Deputy Head of English, South Bromsgrove High School, 1982-85; Head of English, The Castle School, 1985; Senior Teacher, 1992-. Contributions to: Orbis; Envoi; Other Poetry; Westwords; New Prospects; Tandem; Odyssey. Membership: Royal Society of Arts. Address: Brooke Cottage, Blindmoor, Buckland St Mary, Somerset TA20 3RD, England.

STORHOFF Diana Faye Carmack, (Donya Soleya), b. 10 Sept 1946, Anderson, Indiana, USA. Research Scientist. Div, 2 sons.

Education: Bachelor, Chemistry, 1969; MSc, Chemistry, 1973. Appointments: Instructor of Chemistry, Ball State University; Research Scientist, Boehringer Mannheim Corporation. Publications: Live Again; The Promise; A Bridge in Time; My Lovely Valentine; The Locust Serenade; Fire, Fire; Dunkin's Bottom; Its Never Too Late To Start. Contributions to: Musings; Voices; Treasured Poems of America; Mists of Enchantment; A Moment in Time; Nashville Newsletter; Best Poets of 1996. Honours include: Nominated, Poet of the Year, 1995; Editors Choice Certificate, National Library of Poetry; Honorable Mention, Iliad Literary Awards. Memberships: International Society of Poetry; Registered Author, Writers Center of Indianapolis. Address: 2682 DeShong, Pendleton, IN, USA.

STORIE PAHLITZSCH Lori, b. 22 Nov 1948, Tryon, North Carolina, USA. Poet; Writer; Teacher; Editor. m. Robert Pahlitzsch, 30 Dec 1980. Education: Converse College, 1971. Appointments: Writer-in-Residence, Fine Arts Center, Greenville, 1980-84; Creative Writing Faculty, South Carolina Governors School for the Arts, 1981-83; Communications Director, 1981-83; Consultant, 1983-. Publication: Looking for Home: Women Writing About Exile. Contributions to: Poetry Northwest; Poet Lore; Cape Rock; Laurel Review; Arts Journal; Eras Review. Honour: South Carolina Readers Circuit. Membership: Editorial Board, Emrys Journal. Address: 26 Partridge Lane, Greenville, SC 29601, USA.

STORM Morgan. See: ORME-COLLINS Donna Youngoon.

STOUT Frances. See: SUNTREE Susan.

STOUT Robert Joe, b. 3 Feb 1938, Scotts Bluff, Nebraska, USA. Journalist. m. Maureen Ryan, 14 Apr 1988, 2 sons, 3 daughhters. Education: BA, Mexico City College, 1958. Publications: Moving Out, 1973; Trained Bears on Hoops, 1974; The Trick, 1976; Camping Out, 1976; Swallowing Dust, 1978; They Still Play Baseball the Old Way. 1994. Contributions to: Avant-Garde; America; Christian Century; New Orleans Review; New York Times; Invisible City; The Bridge; Southern Poetry Review; South Dakota Review; El Sol; Beloit Poetry Journal; Pivot. Address: PO Box 5074, Chico, CA 95927, USA.

STRAND Mark, b. 11 Apr 1934, Summerside, Prince Edward Island, Canada. Poet; Writer; Professor. m. (1) Antonia Ratensky, 14 Sep 1961, div 1973, 1 daughter, (2) Julia Rumsey Garretson, 15 Mar 1976, 1 son. Education: AB, Antioch College, 1957; BFA, Yale University, 1959; MA, University of Iowa, 1962. Appointments include: Visiting Lecturer, Yale University, 1969-70, and Harvard University, 1980-81; Associate Professor, Brooklyn College, 1971; Bain Swiggett Lecturer, Princeton University, 1972; Fanny Hurst Professor of Poetry, Brandeis University, 1973; Professor, 1981-86, Distinguished Professor, 1986-94, University of Utah; Poet Laureate of USA, 1990-91; Elliott Coleman Professor of Poetry, Johns Hopkins University, 1994-. Publications: Poetry: Sleeping With One Eye Open, 1964; Reasons for Moving, 1968; Darker, 1970; The Sargentville Notebook, 1973; The Story of Our Lives, 1973; The Late Hour, 1978; Selected Poems, 1980; The Continuous Life, 1990; Dark Harbor, 1993; Fiction: Mr and Mrs Baby, short stories; Prose: The Monument, 1978; The Art of the Real, 1983; William Bailey, 1987; Hopper, 1994; Anthologies include: Another Republic (with Charles Simic), 1976; The Best American Poetry 1991 (with David Lehman), 1992; Translations include: Travelling in the Family: The Selected Poems of Carlos Drummond de Andrade, 1986; Children's books: The Planet of Lost Things, 1982; The Night Book, 1985; Rembrandt Takes a Walk, 1986. Contributions to: Poems, book reviews, art reviews, essays on poetry and painting, interviews in numerous periodicals. Honours include: Edgar Allan Poe Prize, 1974; National Institute of Arts and Letters Award, 1975; Writer-in-Residence, American Academy, Rome, 1982; Utah Governor's Award in the Arts, 1992; Bobbitt National Prize for Poetry, 1992; Bollingen Prize for Poetry, 1993. Memberships: American Academy and Institute of Arts and Letters, 1980-; National Academy of Arts and Sciences, 1995-. Address: The Writing Seminars, Johns Hopkins University, 3400 North Charles Street, Baltimore, MD 21218, USA.

STRANDGAARD Charlotte, b. 15 Feb 1943, Brorup, Denmark. Writer. m. (1) Ole Strandgaard, 5 Oct 1962, (2) Jakob Oschlag, 24 June 1978, 1 son, 2 daughters. Education: Graduate, Arhus Katedralskole, 1960. Appointment: Assistant Librarian, Royal Danish Library, 1963-68. Publications: Katalog, 1965; Afstande, 1966; Uafgjort, 1967; Det Var en Lordag Aften, 1968; Naesten Kun Om Kaerlighed, 1977; Braendte Born, 1979; Cellen, 1986. Contributions to:

Several newspapers, magazines, reviews, journals and periodicals. Honour: Scholarship, Danish Fund for the Endowment of the Arts, 1986. Membership: Danish Writers Association. Address: Funkiavej 47, 2300 Copenhagen S, Denmark.

STRAUB Peter Francis, b. 2 Mar 1943, Milwaukee, Wisconsin, USA. Novelist. m. 27 Aug 1966. Education: BA, University of Wisconsin, 1965; MA, Columbia University, 1966. Publications: Ishmael, 1972; Open Air, 1972; Marriage, 1973; Julia, 1975; If You Could See Me Now, 1977; GhostStory, 1979; Shadowland, 1980; Floating Dragon, 1983; Leeson Park and Belsize Park, 1983; The Talisman (with Stephen King), 1984; Koko, 1988; Mystery, 1989; Houses Without Doors, 1990; The Throat, 1992. Contributions to: Times Literary Supplement; New Statesman; Washington Post. Honours: British Fantasy Award, August Derleth Award, for Floating Dragon, 1983; World Fantasy Award; Best Novel for Koko, 1988. Memberships: PEN; Authors League; Authors Guild. Address: 53 W 85th Street, New York, NY 10024, USA.

STROBLAS Laurie, b. Dec 1948, New York, USA. Marketing Manager; Editor; Writer; Teacher; Poet. Education: BA, University of New York, Stony Brook, 1970; MA, University of Massachusetts, 1973. Appointments: Editorial, Promotional Staff, University of Massachusetts; Press Editor, National Academy of Sciences; Book Marketing Manager, Nationala Academy of Sciences; Senior Copywriter, Bureau of National Affairs; Promotion Manager, Urban Institute Press. Contributions to: Science 86; American Speech; Language and Hearing Journal; Washington Review; Poets Laore; Gargoyle; Tendril; Calyx; Outerbridge; Negative Capability; Greenfield Review; New Mexico Humanities Review; Stone Country; Woman Poet; South; Portland Review; Gravida; Window; WPFW.FM Radio Poetry Anthology. Honours: Arts Council Grants for Poetry; National Endowment for the Arts Fellow in Arts Administration; Devoto Scholar Award; Larry Neal Writers Award. Memberships: Folger Shakespeare Library Poetry Committee; Writers Center; Modern Language Association. Address: 2500 Wisconsin Avenue, North West, No 549, Washington, DC 20007, USA.

ŠTROBLOVÁ Jana, b. 1 July 1936, Prague, Czechoslovakia. Poet. m. Otakar Hulec, 21 June 1959, 1 son. Education: Faculty of Arts, Charles University. Appointments: Editor: Publishing House Albatros, 1960-69; Radio, 1990-. Publications: Protěž, 1958; Kdyby nebylo na sůl, 1961; Hostinec u dvou srdcí, 1965; Torza 1969; Úplnek, 1980; Krajina na muří noze, 1984; Čarodeni, 1989; Fatamorgany, 1991; Hra na stvoření světa, 1991. Contributions to: Literarni noviny; Listy; Tvar; Verse; London Anthology; Poetry Review; Sunk Island Review; Borsenblatt; Anthologies: La Poesie tcheque moderne, 1990; Child of Europe, 1990; Equivalencias, 1993; Der Lerchenturm, 1993; Parnassus of World Poets, 1994; Der Herrgott Schuldet Mir Ein Mädchen, 1994; Regenboog aan de Vltava, 1995; La Costa Poetica, 1995. Honour: International Poetry Prize, Florence, 1990. Memberships: Committees of Czech PEN Club and Writers' Union. Address: Detska 176, 100 00, Prague 10, Czechoslovakia.

STROFFOLINO Chris, b. 20 Mar 1963, Reading, Pennsylvania, USA. Teacher. Education: BA, English, Philosophy, Albright College, 1986; MA, English, Temple University, 1988; Currently pursuing PhD, English, State University of New York, Albany. Appointments: Teacher, Temple University, 1986-88, Dreyel University, 1988-89, Peirce Junior College, 1991-92, University of Massachusetts, 1992-93, State University of New York, Albany, 1994-. Publications: Incidents, 1990; Oops, 1991, reprinted 1994; Cusps, 1995. Contributions to: American Poetry Review; Sulfer; New American Writing; O-Blok; Avel; Talisman; Calibah; Sun and Moon; Apex of the M; Tin Fish; Painted Bride Quarterly; Long Shot; The Baffler; New York Quarterly. Memberships: Poets and Writers; Hudson Valley Writers Guild. Address: 365B State Street, Albany, NY 12210, USA.

STRONG Eithne, b. 23 Feb 1923, West Limerick, Ireland. Writer. m. Rupert Strong, 12 Nov 1943, 2 sons, 7 daughters. Education: BA, Trinity College, Dublin. Appointments: Freelance Journalist; Teacher; Writer. Publications: Songs of Living; Sarah in Passing; Flesh the Greatest Sin; Cirt Oibre; Fuil Agus Fallal; My Darling Neighbour; Letlive; Aoife Faoi Ghlas; The Love Riddle; Degrees of Kindred; Patterns; Spatial Nosing. Contributions to: Hiberina; Irish Times; Irish Press; Connaught Tribune; Poetry Ireland Review; Four Quarters; Feathers and Bones; Living Landscape Anthology; Orbis; Living with Monsters; Wildish Things; Poetry Business Anthology; An Cram Fé Bhlath; Irish Poetry New; Thinker Review; Canadian Journal of Irish

Studies. Memberships: Irish Pen; Contadh Na Gaeilge; Irish Writers Union; Poetry Ireland. Address: 17 Eaton Square, Monkstown, Dublin, Ireland.

STROUD Drew McCord, (Ryu Makoto), b. 3 Sept 1944. University Professor. Education: BA, Harvard College, 1966; MA, University of Arizona, 1986. Publications: Lines Drawn Towards, 1980; Poamorio (translation), 1984; The Hospitality of Circumstance, 1992. Contributions to: New Republic; Christopher Street; Expatriate Review; Mediterranean Review; Printed Matter; Noctiluca; Dilettante; Christian Science Monitor. Honours: Witter Bynner Foundation for Poetry Award, 1983; Grand Prize, Tokyo English Literature Society, 1983. Memberships: Poetry Society of America; Tokyo English Literature Society; Asiatic Society of Japan. Address: Temple University, 1-16-7 Kamiochiai, Shinjuku-ku, Tokyo 161, Japan.

STRPKA Ivan, b. 30 June 1944, Hlohovec, Slovak Republic. Geological Researcher. m. 4 May 1968, 2 daughters. Education: Graduated, Spanish Language and Literature, Slovak Language and Literature, Comenius University, Bratislava, 1969. Appointments: Geological Researcher; Journalist; Dramaturgist, Slovak TV; Editor-in-Chief, literary weekly. Publications: Short Childhood of Spearmen, 1968; Tristan bla-bla, 1971; Now and Other Islands, 1981; Before a Change, 1982; News from an Apple, 1985; Everything in a Shell, 1989; Beautiful Naked World, 1990; Rovinsko - SouthWest Death of Mother, 1995; Spasm of Open Fist and Other Essays, 1995; Interplays Headless Marionetts, 1996. Contributions to: Kulturny Zivot, literary weekly; Slovenske Pohlady, literary monthly; Lettres Internationale; Fragment, literary monthly. Honour: Ivan Krasko Prize, 1969. Memberships: Founder, Lonely Runners Literary Group; Community of Slovak Writers; PEN Club, Slovakia. Address: Mlynarovicova 20, 851 03 Bratislava, Slovakia.

STRUTHERS Ann, (Eleanor Mohr Struthers), b. 15 Apr 1930, Terril, USA. Teacher; Writer. m. Melvin Struthers, 27 Dec 1952, 1 son, 3 daughters. Education: BA, Morningside College, 1952; MA, 1979, PhD, 1981, University of Iowa. Appointments: Visiting Associate Professor, Coe College, Cedar Rapids, 1986; Writer-in-Residence, 1991. Publications: From Persia and Other Places; Stoneboat; The Alcott Family Arrives and Other Poems. Contributions to: Poetry; Hudson Review; American Scholar; Southern Humanities Review; Iowa Review; Iowa Women; Seattle Review; Phase and Cycle; Poet and Critic; North American Review; Nebraska Review; Christian Science Monitor; Great River Review; Mid America Review; Minnesota Review; New Letters. Honours: Coolidge Fellowship; Yaddo Writers Colony; Villa Montalro Writers Colony. Memberships: Modern Language Association; Poetry Society of America. Address: 503 Forest Drive, South East, Cedar Rapids, IA 52403, USA.

STUART Dabney, b. 4 Nov 1937, Richmond, Virginia, USA. Professor of English; Editor; Poet; Writer. m. (3) Sandra Westcott, 1983, 2 sons, 1 daughter. Education: AB, Davidson College, North Carolina, 1960; AM, Harvard University, 1962; Appointments: Instructor, College of William and Mary, Williamsburg, Virginia, 1961-65; Instructor, 1965-66, Assistant Professor, 1966-69, Associate Professor, 1969-74, Professor, 1974-91, S Blount Mason Professor of English, 1991-, Washington and Lee University, Lexington, Virginia; Visiting Professor, Middlebury College, 1968-69; Poetry Editor, 1966-76, Editor-in-Chief, 1988-95, Shenandoah; McGuffey Chair in Writing, Ohio University, 1972; Resident Poet, Trinity College, Hartford, Connecticut, 1978; Visiting Poet, University of Virginia, 1981, 1982-83; Poetry Editor, New Virginia Review, 1983. Publications: Poetry: The Diving Bell, 1966; A Particular Place, 1969; Corgi Modern Poets in Focus 3, 1971; The Other Hand, 1974; Friends of Yours, Friends of Mine, 1974; Round and Round: A Triptych, 1977; Rockbridge Poems, 1981; Common Ground, 1982; Don't Look Back, 1987; Narcissus Dreaming, 1990; Light Years: New and Selected Poems, 1994; Second Sight: Poems For Paintings (by Carroll Cloar), 1996; Long Gone, 1996; Fiction: Sweet Lucy Wine: Stories, 1992; Non-fiction: Nabokov: The Dimensions of Parody, 1978. Honours: Dylan Thomas Prize, Poetry Society of America, 1965; Borestone Mountain Awards, 1969, 1974, 1977; National Endowment for the Arts Grant, 1969, and Fellowships, 1974, 1982; Virginia Governor's Award, 1979; Guggenheim Fellowship, 1987-88; Individual Artist's Fellowship, Virginia Commision for the Arts, 1995. Address: c/o Department of English, Washington and Lee University, Lexington, VA 24450, USA.

STUART Derek. See: **FOSTER John Louis.**

STUART (Jessica) Jane, b. 20 Aug 1942, Ashland, Kentucky, USA. Retired. 2 sons. Education: Case Western Reserve University, 1964; AB, Classics (Greek and Latin), Case Western Reserve University, 1964; MA, Classical Languages, Indiana University, 1967; MA, Italian, 1969; PhD, Italian, 1971. Appointment: Teacher, English and Creative Writing. Publications: A Years Harvest, 1956; Eyes of The Mole, 1967; White Barn, 1971; The Wren and Other Poems, 1993; Karnak, 1993; Passage into Time, 1994; White Tock, 1995; Cherokee Lullaby, 1995; Moon Over Miami, 1996. Contributions to: Poetic Eloquence; Byron's Poetry Works; Tampa Review; MOON; Robin's Egg; Hiram Poetry Review; Kansas Magazine; Pegasus; Afterthoughts; White River Quarterly. Honours: Kentucky State Poetry Society Grand Prix, 1992; Different Poetry Prizes including Phoenix Writers Award. Memberships: Kentucky State Poetry Society, Regional Director, Eastern District, 1996; Academy of American Poets. Address: 1000 W-Hollow, Greenup, KY 41144, USA.

STUDEBAKER William V, b. 21 May 1947, Idaho, USA. Assistant Professor; Programme Director. m. 4 children. Education: BA, History, 1970, MA, English, 1972, Idaho State University. Appointments: Assistant Professor, 1975-, Chairman, Department of English, 1980-82, Honors Programme Director, 1990-, College of Southern Idaho. Publications: Everything Goes Without Saying, 1978; Training the Raven, 1983; The Cleaving, 1985; Idaho's Poetry: A Centennial Anthology, 1988; The Rat Lady at the Company Dump, 1990. Contributions to: Ohio Review; Seattle Review; High Country News; Northern Lit Quarterly; Mid-American Review; South Dakota Review; Tar River Poetry; New Mexico Humanities Review; Redneck Review; Expresso Tilt; Greenfield Review; Laurel. Honour: Ethel E Redfield Scholarship, Idaho State University, 1971. Address: Route 4, 2614 East, 4000 North, Twin Falls, ID 83301, USA.

STUDER Constance Elaine Browne, b. 4 Dec 1942, Lodi, Ohio, USA. Professional Writer-Poet; Registered Nurse. Div, 1 son. Education: Nursing Diploma, Toledo Hospital School of Nursing, 1963; BA, Illinois College, 1971; MA, English Literature, Creative Writing, 1978-80, University of Colorado; Artist-in-Residence, Poetry, Rocky Mountain Women's Institute, 1987. Publications: Womanthology, 1977; Hyperion: Black Sun, New Moon, 1980; Wingbone: Poetry from Colorado, 1986; Toward Solomon's Mountain, 1986. Contributions to: Room of Our Own; Eleventh Muse; Kaleidoscope. Honours: Ann Woodbury Hafen Prize, 1977; Finalist, Nimrod Poetry Contest, 1986; 3rd Place, International Kaleidoscope Poetry Contest, 1986; Winners, Embers Poetry Contest, 1986; Winner, Artist-in-Residence Associateship, Poetry, Rocky Mountain Women's Institute, 1987. Address: 1617 Parkside Circle, Lafayette, CO 80026, USA.

SUAREZ Michael Felix, b. New York, New York, USA. Roman Catholic Clergyman; Lecturer. Education: BA, Bucknell University, 1982; MA, Campion Hall, Oxford University, 1987; MDiv, Weston School of Theology, Cambridge, 1993. Appointments: Lecturer, Fordham University, 1987-88; LeMoyne College, 1988-90. Contributions to: Aeolian Harp; America; Berkeley Poetry Review; Great Lakes Review; Month; Sarnidsat; Wallace Stevens Journal. Honours: Sir Roger Newdigat Prize; Chancellor's English Essay Prize; Matthew Arnold Prize; Marshall Scholar; Phi Beta Kappa. Membership: Poetry Society of America. Address: 80 Lexington Avenue, Cambridge, MA 02138, USA.

SUBRAHMANYAM K V V, (Maynam Harbus), b. 11 Oct 1930, Madurai, India. Indian Police. m. Jayalakshmi, 2 Sept 1958, 3 daughters. Education: BS, Madras University. Appointment: Home Secretary to Government, Andhra Pradesh, India. Publication: A Ray of Hope. Contributions to: Triveni; Guntur; New Swatantra Times; Hyderabad; International Congress of Poets. Honour: International Poet by World Congress of Poets. Memberships: Hyderabad Poetry Society; World Congress of Poets. Address: Plot C48 Madhuranagar, Yousufguda, Hyderabad 500 038, India.

SUBRAMANIAM P V, b. 20 Sept 1936, Trichur, Kerala, India. Management. m. Prema, 17 April 1972, 1 son. Education: Degree, Commerce, 1955; Diploma, Administrative Management, 1968. Appointment: Accountant to Chief Accountant, 1963-. Publications: An Executive's Lament, 1993; A Mirror's Verdict, 1995. Contributions to: Times of India Group Publications; The Pioneer; Thought; Indian Verse; Poetcrict. Memberships: The Poetry Society, India; The PEN All India Centre; Poetry Club of India. Address: Officers' Colony, Somaiya Organics (India) Limited, Somaiya Nagar, Barabanki 225123, UP, India.

SUBRAMANIAN (Mary) Belinda, b. 6 Sept 1953, Statesville, North Carolina, USA. Editor. m. S Ramnath, 24 Sept 1977, 2 daughters. Education: MA, California State University, Dominguez Hills, 1990. Appointment: Editor, Gypsy Magazine and Vergin Press, 1983-. Publications: Skin Divers, 1988; The Innocents, 1990; Elephants and Angels, 1991; A New Geography of Poets, 1992. Contributions to: Magazines: Yellow Silk; Arkansas Quarterly; Puerto del Sol; North Coast Review; Amelia; Heaven Bone; Baltimore Sun; Bogg; Chiron Review; Over 300 others; Mondo Barbia, anthology, 1993. Address: PO Box 370322, El Paso, TX 79937, USA.

SUDHAKAR. See: **MOORTHY Krishna Kopparam.**

SULLIVAN Charles, b. 27 May 1933, Massachusetts, USA. Educator. Div. 2 sons, 1 daughter. Education: BA, Swarthmore College, 1955; MA, 1968, PhD, 1973, New York University; MPA, Penn State University, 1978. Appointments: Associate Dean, Georgetown University, 1989; President, American Foundation for the Arts, 1995. Publications: America in Poetry, 1988; Imaginary Gardens, 1989; Ireland in Poetry, 1990; Alphabet Animals, 1991; Children of Promise, 1991; The Lover in Winter, 1991; Numbers at Play, 1992; Circus, 1992; Loving, 1993; Cowboys, 1993; American Beauties, 1994; Fathers and Children, 1995; A Woman of a Certain Age, 1995; Imaginary Animals, 1996. Contributions to: Various. Honours: Various. Memberships: American Poetry Society; Academy of American Poets; Cosmos Club; National Society of Arts and Letters; Folger Poetry Board; Poetry Committee of Greater Washington. Address: 1344 Ballantrae Lane, McLean, VA 22101, USA.

SULLIVAN James (Edward), b. 11 July 1928, Massachusetts, USA. Librarian. m. Frances Elizabeth Lynch, 11 Aug 1963, dec 1976. 1 son, 1 daughter. Education: AB, Greek, Hons, 1948, AM, History, 1950, Boston College. Appointments: Director, Woods Memorial Library, Barre, Massachusetts, 1967-94 (retired). Publications: In Order of Appearance: 400 Poems by James Sullivan, 1988. Contributions to: America; Commonweal; Worcester Review; Barre Gazette. Honour: Worcester County Poetry Association Award, 1972. Membership: Hopkins Society. Address: 590 Sunrise Avenue, Box 451, Barre, MA 01005, USA.

SULLIVAN Sheila, Writer. 3 daughters. Education: MA English Hons, Oxford. Appointments: Oxford University Press; Lycee Francais de Londres. Contributions to: Acumen; Orbis; Countryman; Envoi; Iota; Honest Ulsterman; Lines Review; Oxford Poetry; Rialto. Honours: Celtic Dawn Grand Prize, 1990; Kitley Trust, 1991; Runner up: Ripley Poetry 1990, Poetry Business 1990, Staple 1991. Membership: PEN International; Society of Authors. Address: 69 North End Road, London NW11 7RL, England.

SUNTREE Susan, (Frances Stout), b. 19 May 1946, Los Angeles, California, USA. Writer; Professor. m. 1 son, 1 daughter. Education: BA, University of Arizona, 1968; MA, University of Kent, Canterbury, England, 1970. Appointments: Modesto Community College, 1970-75; North Sierra Regional Co-Ordinator, California Poets in the Schools, 1977-82; Arts Reach Artist in Residence, University of California, Los Angeles, 1983-85; Santa Monica College, 1984-88; East Los Angeles College, 1989-. Publications: Eye of the Womb, 1981; Tulips, 1991 (translations of the poet, Ana Rossetti from Spanish). Contributions to: Not Mixing Up Buddhism - The Kahawai Anthology; Hard Pressed; Anthology of San Francisco Womens Poetry Festival; City of Buds and Flowers - A Berkeley Anthology; Mother Poet Anthology. Honours: California Arts Council Grant, 1978; Eye of the Womb selected for special collections at Yale University Library and University of California Library, Los Angeles, 1981. Memberships: PEN; Poets and Writers. Address: 1223 11th Street, Santa Monica, CA 90401-2002, USA.

SUPRANER Robyn, (Olive Blake, Erica Frost, Elizabeth Warren), b. 14 Sept 1930, Brooklyn, New York, USA. Writer. m. Leon Supraner, 16 Dec 1950, 3 sons, 1 daughter. Education: Pratt Institute and Parsons School of Design, 1944-48; Adelphi University, 1948-51. Appointments: Freelance Song Writer, 1962-72; Writer, 1970; Teacher, Roslyn Creative Arts Workshop, 1973-74. Publications: Draw Me a Cricle; Giggly, Wiggly, Snickety Snick; Magic Tricks You Can Do; The Amazing Mark; No Room for a Sneeze; A Kitten for Rosie; Jonathon's Amazing Adventure. Contributions to: Under Open Sky; Praire Schooner; Ploughshares; Unicorn; Xanadu; Beloit Poetry Journal; Queen Quarterly. Honours: Book of the Year; Poetry Award from Pen and Brush Club. Memberships: Authors Guild; Authors League of

America; Poetry Society of America. Address: 420 Bryant Avenue, Roslyn Harbor, NY 11576, USA.

SURVANT Joseph William, b. 9 Oct 1942, Kentucky, USA. Literature and Writing Professor. m. Jeannie Ashley, 4 Sept 1965, 2 daughters. Education: BA, University of Kentucky, 1964; MA, University of Delaware, 1966; PhD, 1970. Appointments: Instructor, University of Kentucky, 1967-69; Assistant Professor, Professor, Western Kentucky University, 1970-. Publications: Twentieth Anniversary Chapbook, 1993; We Will All Be Changed, 1995; Anne & Alpheus, 1842-1882, 1996. Contributions to: Kentucky Poetry Review; Kentucky Renaissance; Webster Review; Adena; Plainsong; Exploratory Writing; Journal of Evolutionary Psychology; Appalachian Heritage; Zone 3; Rhino; Rilke's Children; Jefferson Review; Stand; Poet and Critic; Chelsea; Hellas; Columbia Poetry Review; Always a River; Chelsea; Stand; The American Voice; Nimrod; Poet & Critic; Zone 3; Hellas; Cincinnati Poetry Review. Honours: Academy of American Poets Prize; Robert Hillyer Award; Frankfort Arts Foundation Poetry Prize; Runner Up Award, Skoob Books, Index on Censorship Poetry Competition, 1989; Poetry Fellowship, Kentucky Arts Council, 1990; Runner Up Award, Robert H Winner Prize, Poetry Society of America, 1994; State Street Press Chapbook Competition, 1994; Arkansas Poetry Prize, 1995. Memberships: Associated Writing Programs; Poetry Society of America. Address: Western Kentucky University, Bowling Green, KY 42101, USA.

SUTHERLAND-SMITH James Alfred, b. 17 June 1948, Aberdeen, Scotland. University Lecturer. m. Viera Schlosserova, 5 Sept 1992, 1 daughter. Education: BA, Leeds University, 1971; Nottingham University, 1974; MA, University of East Anglia, 1988. Appointments: Teacher, 1974-85; Deputy Head of Education, National Guard Signal Corps Training School, 1985-86; Head of English Language Unit Qatar Public Telecom Corp, 1986-88; British Council Lecturer, 1989-. Publications: Four Poetry and Audience Poets; A Poetry Quintet; Trapped Water; A Singer from Sabiya; Naming of the Arrow; Not Waiting for Miracles; Contemporary Slovak Poets. Contributions to: Ambit; Encounter; Poetry Durham; Poetry Review; Rialto; Stand; Times Literary Supplement; Literary Review; Kansas Quarterly; Cumberland Poetry Review; Review; Prairie Schooner; West Branch; BBC Radio 3; Slovak Television. Honours: Eric Gregory Award; National Poetry Competition of Great Britain; Cheltenham Competition; Philips Award; San Jose Studies Poetry Award. Memberships: Poetry Society Reform Movement; Poets Workshop. Address: KAA, UPJS, 17 Novembra c1, 16 Presov, Czechoslovakia.

SUTTON Dorothy Moseley, b. 11 Oct 1938, Todd County, Kentucky, USA. Professor. m. William Sutton, 2 Sept 1961, 2 daughters. Education: BA, Georgetown College, 1960; MA, University of Mississippi, 1963; PhD, University of Kentucky, 1981. Appointments: Professor, Eastern Kentucky, 1971-. Contributions to: Antioch Review; Southern Review; Prairie Schooner; Virginia Quarterly Review; and more than a dozen anthologies. Honours: Artists Award Fellowship; Robert Frost Scholar in Poetry; Twice Winner, Arts Place Competition; Grolier Award; Tyrone Guthrie Award. Memberships: Poetry Society of America; Academy of American Poets; Associated Writing Programs; Poets and Writers. Address: 115 Southland Drive, Richmond, KY 40475, USA.

SUTTON Henry. See: **SLAVITT David R(ytman)**.

SVATEK Kurt Franz, b. 26 Jan 1949, Vienna, Austria. Teacher at a vocational school. m. Herma Kürner, 29 June 1973, 1 daughter. Education: Vienna Academy of Pedagogy; Axel Anderson Academy (Literature, Hamburg, Germany). Appointments: City Government of Vienna, 1968-73; Vocational Teacher (book keeping, correspondence, political science, 1973-; Chairman of works committee, 1990-95; Member of industrial tribunal, Wr Neustadt, 1990-. Publications: Wir alle haben Troja zerstört (short stories), 1988; Bettlerzinken (novel), 1993; Von der Weltunordnung (aphorisms), 1993; Rendezvous mit der Hoffnung (short stories), 1994; Rhapsodie aus leiser Schwermut (poems), 1995; Jahrtausendleben, (haiku-poems), 1995; Auf dem Saumpfad der Zeit (aphorisms), 1995; Wie weit trägt der Wind schon ein Wort (poems), 1997. Contributions to: Over 100 anthologies in English: German Love Poetry, India, 1993; Voices, Israel, 1993; Parnassus of World Poets, India, 1995, 1996, 1997; Parnassus of World Poets, India, 1995, 1996, 1997; The Path Not Taken, USA, 1996; 350 Magazines, over 60 periodicals: Austria, Germany, India, Japan, in English: Poetscrit, India, 1992-; Haiku Suien, Japan; Periodical of the Haiku International Association, Japan. Honours: 9

include: Province of Lower Austria, 1984, 1985; Province of Vienna, 1987; Austrian National Library, 1990; Austrian-Japanese Society, Vienna, 1992; International Haiku Association, Tokyo, 1994; City Government of Neunkirchen, 1994; The National Library of Poetry, Maryland, 1995; Honorary Doctor of Divinity, California, 1995. Memberships: PEN (Austria); International Society of Poets (USA); German Haiku Society (Germany) Der Kreis (Austria). Address: Villa Camena, Schwarzauer Str 42A, A-2624 Breitenau, Austria.

SVEINSSON Audunn Bragi, b. 26 Dec 1923, Selhagi, Hunavatnssysla, Iceland. Primary School Teacher and Principal. m. Guolaug Arnorsdottir, 11 Sept 1949, 4 sons, 1 daughter. Education: Graduated, Icelandic Seminary, 1949; Examination, Reyjavik Gymnasium, 1966; BA, Danish, University of Iceland, 1990. Appointments: Teacher, 36 years, Principal, 24 years, primary schools. Publications: Hunvetningal joo (with others), 1955; Salmar og andleg ljoo, translated from Danish and Norwegian (editor); Smaljoo by Piet Hein, translated from Danish, 1987; Stutt og stuolao, 1989. Contributions to: Various publications. Honour: Represented Writers Union of Iceland at Diktning i Regionarnas Norden Congress, Sweden, 1991. Membership: Writers Union of Iceland. Address: Hjardarhagi 28, 107 Reykjavík, Iceland.

SVOBODA Terese, b. 5 Sept 1950, Ogallala, Nebraska, USA. Poet; Writer; Videomaker. m. Stephen M Bull, 18 July 1981, 3 sons. Education: University of Nebraska, 1968; Montreal Museum of Fine Arts, 1968; Manhattanville, 1968-70; Oxford University, 1969; University of Colorado, 1970; Stanford University, 1971; BFA, University of British Columbia, 1973; MFA, Columbia University, 1978. Appointments: Rare Manuscript Curator, McGill University, 1969; Co-Producer, PBS-TV series Voices and Visions, 1980-82; Distinguished Visiting Professor, University of Hawaii, 1992; Professor, Sarah Lawrence College, 1993. Publications: Poetry: All Aberration, 1985; Cleaned the Crocodile's Teeth, 1985; Laughing Africa, 1990; Mere Mortal, 1995. Fiction: Cannibal, 1995. Honours: Writer's Choice Column Award, New York Times Book Review, 1985; Iowa Prize, 1990; Bobst Prize, 1995. Memberships: PEN; Poets and Writers; Poet's House, founding member and advisory board member 1986-91. Address: 56 Ludlow Street, New York, NY 10002, USA.

SWAIM Alice Mackenzie, b. 5 June 1911, Craigdam, Scotland. Newspaper Correspondent; Poetry Therapy Consultant; Public Relations Director. m. 27 Dec 1932, 2 daughters. Education: Tain Royal Academy, Scotland; Wilson College. Appointments: Columnist, 1st Vice President, American Poetry League; Book Reviewer; Contest and Marketing Editor. Publications: Let the Deep Song Rise; Up to the Stars; Sunshine in a Thimble; Crickets Are Crying Autumn; The Gentle Dragon; Here on the Threshold; Penna Profile; Scented Honeysuckle Days; Beneath a Dancing Star; Beyond my Catnip Garden; And Miles ToGo; Children in Summer; Horizon Makers. Contributions to: Reader's Digest; Christian Science Monitor; Hallmark Cards; New York Times; Poet Scotland; Poet Lore; Lyric Writer's Digest; Dalhousie Review; Anthology of Small Presses and Magazines; Voices International; Bitterroot; South Coast Poetry Journal; Cotton Boll. Honours: 1st Prize, Reader's Digest Contest; American Heritage Award; Poet Laureate of the Sonnet; Knight of the Round Table; Poet Laureate of the Year; Poet of the Year. Memberships: Poetry Society of America; Academy of American Poets; United Poets Laureate International; Studi e Scambi Internazionale. Address: 322 North Second Street, Apt 1606, Harrisburg, PA 17101, USA.

SWANBERG Ingrid, b. 4 Sept 1947, California, USA. Editor; Publisher. m. 27 July 1974, 1 son. Education: BA, English, 1970, MA, English, 1973, California State University, Sacramento; MA, Comparative Literature, 1993, University of Wisconsin; Currently undertaking PhD, Comparative Literature. Appointments: Editor and Publisher, Ghost Pony Press, 1980-, Abraxas Press Inc, 1981-. Publications: Flashlights, 1981; Letter to Persephone and Other Poems, 1984; Editor, Zen Concrete & Etc, 1991. Contributions to: Northeast; Lips; Wisconsin Academy Review; Strange Fruit; Osiris; Le Guépard. Honour: Winner, First Annual Chapbook Award, Rhiannon Press, 1984. Address: 2518 Gregory Street, Madison, WI 53711, USA.

SWANDER Mary Lynch, b. 11 May 1950, Carroll, Iowa, USA. Writer; Professor. Education: BA, University of Iowa, 1973; MFA, 1976. Appointments: Assistant Professor, Lake Forest College, 1976-79; Assistant Professor, 1984-88, Associate Professor, 1988-90 and Visiting Associate Professor, University of Iowa, 1990-91. Publications: Driving the Body Back; Succesion; Needlepoint; Lost Lake; Parsnips in the Snow; Heaven and Earth House. Contributions to: Nation; New Yorker; Poetry; Ploughshares. Honours: National Endowment for the Arts; Carl Sandburg Literary Award; National Discovery Award. Membership: Associated Writing Programs. Address: 203 Ross Hall, English, Iowa State Universty, Ames, IA 50010, USA.

SWANGER David, b. 1 Aug 1940, New Jersey, USA. Professor. m. Lynn Lundstrom, 5 Apr 1969, 1 son, 2 daughters. Education: BA, Swarthmore College, 1963; MAT, 1964, EdD, 1970. Harvard University. Appointments: Assistant Professor, Harvard University, 1970-71; Associate Professor, 1976-85, Professor 1985-, University of California, Santa Cruz. Publications: The Poem as Process, 1971; Lemming Song, 1976; The Shape of Waters, 1978; Inside the Hour, 1981; Essays in Aesthetic Education, 1991; Family, 1994; The Evolution of Education, 1995; This Waking Unafraid, 1995. Contributions to: Georgia Review; Malahat Review; Poetry Northwest; Chariton Review; America Post and Critic; Quarry West; New Letters; Mother Earth News; Negative Capability; Whetstone; Nimrod; Minnesota Review; Cutbank; Tendril; America; Reaper. Honours: Foley Award, 1991; National Endowment for the Arts Poetry Award, 1989. Memberships: Academy of American Poets; Poets and Writers. Address: Porter College, University of California, Santa Cruz, CA 95064, USA.

SWARD Robert (Stuart), b. 23 June 1933, Chicago, Illinois, USA. Poet; Writer; University Lecturer. 2 sons, 3 daughters. Education: BA, University of Illinois, 1956; MA, University of Iowa, 1958; Postgraduate Studies, Middlebury College, Vermont, 1959-60, University of Bristol, 1960-61. Appointments: Poet-in-Residence, Cornell University, 1962-64, University of Victoria, British Columbia, 1969-73, University of California at Santa Cruz, 1987-; Writer-in-Residence, Foothill Writers Conference, summers 1988-; Writer, Writing Programme, Language Arts Department, Cabrillo College, 1989-. Publications: Uncle Dog and Other Poems, 1962; Kissing the Dancer and Other Poems, 1964; Half a Life's History: New and Selected Poems 1957-83, 1983; The Three Roberts (with Robert Zend and Robert Priest), 1985; Four Incarnations: New and Selected Poems 1957-91, 1991; Family (with David Swanger, Tilly Shaw and Charles Atkinson), 1994; Earthquake Collage, 1995; A Much-Married Man (novel), 1996. Contributions to: Anthologies, newspapers and magazines; Contributing Editor, Blue Penny Quarterly and other Internet literary publications. Honours: Fulbright Fellowship, 1960-61; Guggenheim Fellowship, 1965-66; D H Lawrence Fellowship, 1966; Djerassi Foundation Residency, 1990; Way Cool Site Award, editing eSCENE 1996, Internet literary magazine. Memberships: League of Canadian Poets; Modern Poetry Association; National Writers Union, USA; Writers Union of Canada. Address: PO Box 7062, Santa Cruz, CA 95061-7062, USA.

SWEDE George, b. 20 Nov 1940, Latvia. Educator; Writer. m. Anita Krumins, 23 July 1974, 2 sons. Education: BA, University of British Columbia, Vancouver, Canada, 1964; MA, Dalhousie University, 1965. Appointments: Instructor, Vancouver City College, 1966-67; School Psychologist, Scarborough Board of Education, 1967-68; Instructor, 1968-73, Professor, 1973-, Chair, Psychology Department, 1974-75, Ryerson Polytechnic University; Co-Director, Radio Study, CJRT, 1969-70; Director, Developmental Psychology, Open College, 1973-75. Publications: This Morning's Mocking Bird, 1980; Eye to Eye with a Frog, 1981; All of Her Shadows, 1982; Flaking Paint, 1983; Tick Bird, 1983; Frozen Breaths, 1983; Night Tides, 1984; Bifids, 1984; Time is Flies, 1984; High Wire Spider, 1986; I Eat a Rose Petal, 1987; Multiple Personality, 1987; I Throw Stones at the Mountain, 1988; Leaping Lizzard, 1988; Holes in My Cage, 1989; I Want to Lasso Time, 1991; Leaving My Loneliness, 1992. Editor: The Canadian Haiku Anthology, 1979; Cicada Voices, 1983; The Universe is One Poem, 1993; There Will Always Be a Sky, 1993. Contributions to: Daily Yomiuri; ARC; Toronto Life; Canadian Forum; Poetry Canada Review; Tamarack Review; Quarry; Event; Modern Haiku; Antigonish Review; Grain; University of Toronto Review; Literary Cavalcade; Kaldron; Canadian Author and Bookman; Northeast; Greenfield Review; Journal of Humanistic Psychology; Mainichi Daily News; Modern Haiku. Honours: Ontario Arts Council Grants, 1978-82, 1984-86, 1988-89, 1991; Awards: Golden State Bank, 1979; Yuki Teikei Haiku Society, 1980; Museum of Haiku Literature, 1983, 1985, 1992; Co-winner, 5th Annual High-Coo Press Mini-Chapbook Competition, 1982; Our Choice, Canadian Children's Book Centre, 1984, 1985, 1987, 1991, 1992; Author on tour, 10th Annual Children's Book Festival, 1986; Judge, Japan Air Lines World Children's Haiku Contest, 1990. Memberships: Co-Founder, Haiku Canada;

Membership Chair, Writers Union of Canada; PEN; League of Canadian Poets; Canadian Society of Children's Authors, Illustrators and Performers; Haiku Society of America. Address: PO Box 279, Station P, Toronto, Ontario M5S 2S8, Canada.

SWENSON Karen, b. 29 July 1936, New York, New York, USA. Poet; Professor; Journalist. m. Michael Shuter, 27 Nov 1958, 1 son. Education: BA, Barnard College, 1959; MA, New York University, 1971. Appointments: City College, 1968-76; Poet-in-Residence, Clark University, 1976; Skidmore College, 1977-78; University of Idaho, 1979-80; City College of Fordham, 1982-87. Publications: A Sense of Direction, 1989; The Landlady in Bangkok, 1994. Contributions to: New Yorker; Nation; Saturday Review; Prairie Schooner; American Poetry Review; Paris Review; Denver Quarterly; Quarterly Review of Literature; Bennington Review; Texas Quarterly; Virginia Quarterly Review; Poetry. Honours: TransAtlantic Fellowship; Ann Stanford Award; Arvon Award; Pushcart Prize; National Poetry Series. Memberships: Poetry Society of America; Modern Language Association; Academy of American Poets; Poets House; The Century Association. Address: 61 Pierrepont Street, Apt 23, Brooklyn Heights, New York, NY 11201, USA.

SWICKARD David Alexander, b. 5 Dec 1944, Orange, California, USA. Arts Management; Teacher. m. Siv Cedering, 11 Sept 1983. Education: Indiana University, AB, 1967; AM, Harvard University, 1969; PhD, 1975. Appointments: International Analyst Mellow Bank; Research Associate, Twentieth Century Fund; President, American Scandinavian Foundation; Executive Director, East Hampton Historical Society; Local Television. Publications: American Classis; Car Poems. Contributions to: Confrontation; Poet Lore; Nimrod; Panhandler; Bluefish; Pulpsmith; Contact II. Honour: The Scandinavian Review. Memberships: Poetry Society of America; Phi Beta Kappa. Address: PO Box 800, Amagansett, NY 11930, USA.

SWILKY Jody, b. 17 Aug 1951, Brooklyn, New York, USA. College Professor. m. 17 May 1981, 1 son. Education: BA, State University of New York at Genesco, 1973; MFA, University of Iowa, 1975; DA, State University of New York at Albany, 1989. Appointments: Adjunct Lecturer, Hofstra University, 1982-85; Assistant Professor, Drake University, 1989-93. Publication: A City of Fences, 1978. Contributions to: Georgia Review; North American Review; Mid-American Review; Ohio Review; Yale Review; Missouri Review; Chelsea; Poetry Now; New Boston Review. Membership: Poets and Writers. Address: 213 Prospect Avenue, West Des Moines, IA 50265, USA.

SYNEK Jiri (George), (Frantisek Listopad), b. 26 Nov 1921, Prague, Czechoslovakia. University Teacher. Director of Theatre; Television Director, 1 son, 4 daughters. Education: Dr Phil. Publications: Malelasky, 1945; Slava urknuti, 1945; Vzduch, 1946; Prvni veta, 1946; Boj Venezuela, 1947; Jarmark, 1947; Svoboda a jine dvoce, 1960; Tristao ou a Traiçao de um Intelectual, 1960; Cerny bily nevim, 1973; Contos Carcomidos, 1974; Secos & Molhados, 1982; Estreitamento Progressivo, 1983; Primeiro Testamento, 1985; Mar-Seco-Gelado-Quente, 1986; Os Novos Territórios, 1986; Álbum de Família, 1988; Outubro Oriente, 1992; Biografia de Cristal, 1992; Nastroje Pameti, 1992; Final Rondi, 1992; Blizko Daleko, 1993; Meio Conto, 1993; Oprava houslí a Kytar, 1996. Contributions to: Czech, Portuguese, American and French newspapers and reviews. Honours: Academy of Fine Arts, Prague, 1948; Swedish Academy, Lund, 1949; Christian Academy, Rome, 1950; Prize, Radio Free Europe, 1952; Critic's Prizes, Lisbon, 1968, 1970, 1980; Doctor honoris causa, CSFR, 1992. Memberships: PEN Club International; Society of Portuguese Writers. Address: Calcada Conde de Tomar 13, Lisbon 1495, Portugal.

SYOMWANGANGI. See: **KITONGA Ellen Mae.**

SZE Arthur, b. 1 Dec 1950, New York, USA. Poet. 1 son. Education: BA, University of California, Berkeley, 1972. Appointment: Professor, Institute of American Indian Arts, 1984-. Publications: River River; Dazzled; Two Ravens; The Willow Wind; Archipelago, 1995. Contributions to: Paris Review; Chelsea; Harvard Magazine; Mother Jones; New Letters; Manoa; Bloomsbury Review; Seattle Review; River Styx; Tendril; Tyuonyi; The American Poetry Review; The Kenyon Review. Honours: Witter Bynner Foundation for Poetry Grants; New Mexico Arts Division Interdisciplinary Grant; National Endowment for the Arts Creative Writing Fellowships; George A and Eliza Gardener Howard Foundation Fellowship; Eisner Prize; Lannan

Literary Award for Poetry, 1995. Address: PO Box 457, Santa Fe, NM 87504, USA.

SZEGO Clara Marian. See: **STEELE Marian.**

SZIRTES George Gabor Nicholas, b. 29 Nov 1948, Budapest, Hungary. Teacher; Lecturer; Freelance Writer. m. Clarissa Upchurch, 11 July 1970, 1 son, 1 daughter. Education: BA, Fine Art; ATC. Appointments: Part Time Teaching Arts, 1973-75; Head of Art, Hitchin Girls School, 1975-81; Head of Art, St Christophers School, 1982-89; Part Time Teaching, Freelance Writer, Translation. Publications: The Slant Door; November and May; Short Wave; The Photographer in Winter; Metro; Bridge Passages. Contributions to: Observer; Sunday Times; Times Literary Supplement; New Statesman; Spectator; Listener; Encounter; Literary Review; Poetry Review; PN Review; London Magazine. Honours: Faber Memorial Prize; Arts Council Award; Cholmondeley Award; Dery Prize; Gold Medal. Membership: Fellowship: Royal Society of Literature. Address: 20 Old Park Road, Hitchin, Herts SG5 2JR, England.

SZYMBORSKA Wisława, b. 2 July 1923, Bnin, Poland. Poet; Critic; Translator. Education: Jagiellonian University, Kraków, 1945-48. Appointment: Editorial Staff, Zycie Literackie magazine, 1953-81. Publications: Dlatego zyjemy (That's Why We Are Alive), 1952, 2nd edition, 1985; Pytania zadawane sobie (Questioning Oneself), 1954; Wolanie do Yeti (Calling Out to Yeti), 1957; Sól (Salt), 1962; Wiersze wybrane (Selected Verses), 1964; Poezje wybrane (Selected Poems), 1967; Sto pociech (No End of Fun), 1967; Poezje (Poems), 1970; Wszelko wypadek (Could Have), 1972; Wybór wierszy (Selected Verses), 1973; Tarsjusz i inne wiersze (Tarsius and Other Verses), 1976; Wielka liczba (A Large Number), 1977; Poezje wybrane II (Selected Poems II), 1983; Ludzie na moscie (The People on the Bridge), 1986; Wieczór autorski: Wiersze (Author's Evening: Verses), 1992; Koniec i poczatek (The End and the Beginning), 1993; Poetry in English: Sounds, Feelings, Thoughts: Seventy Poems, 1981; People on a Bridge, 1990; View with a Grain of Sand, 1995. Contributions to: Poetry and criticism in various publications. Honours: City of Kraków Prize for Literature, 1954; Polish Ministry of Culture Prize, 1963; Goethe Prize, 1991; Herder Prize, 1995; Honorary doctorates, Adam Mickiewicz University, Poznan, 1995; Nobel Prize for Literature, 1996; Polish PEN Club Prize, 1996. Address: Ul Królewska 82/89, 30-079 Kraków, Poland.

T

T'UNG A. See: **YEH Victor Wei Hsin.**

TABER Roger Noel, b. 21 Dec 1945, Gillingham, Kent, England. Librarian. Education: BA, English and American Literature, University of Kent, 1973; Postgraduate Diploma, Library and Information Science, Ealing School of Librarianship, 1975. Appointments: Freelance Writer/Librarian, 1964-. Publications: August and Genet, 1996; How Can You Write A Poem When You're Dying of Aids, 1993. Contributions to: Nineties Poetry; Helicon; Axiom; Psychopoetica; Broadsword. Honours: Placed in National Competitions. Memberships: The Poetry Society. Address: Flat C, Hammond House, 45A Gaisford Street, London NW5 2EB, England.

TAFARI Levi. See: **KELLY Leonard.**

TAFDRUP Pia, b. 29 May 1952, Copenhagen, Denmark. Poet. m. Bo Hakon Jørgensen, 30 June 1978, 2 sons. Education: BA Copenhagen University, 1977. Publications: When an Angel's Been Grazed, poems, 1981; Nohold, poems, 1982; The Innermost Zone, poems, 1983; Spring Tide, poems 1985 (Eng 1989); White Fever, poems, 1986; The Bridge of Moments, poems, 1988; Death in the Mountains, play, 1988; Walking over the Water, Outline of a Poetics, 1991; The Earth is Blue, play, 1991; The Crystal Forest, poems, 1992. Territorial Song, A Jerusalem Cycle, poems, 1994. Contributions to: More than twenty literary journals in the UK, USA and Canada; Of Thoughts and Words Proceedings of Nobel Symposium, 1992; The Relation Between Language and Mind, 1995. Honours: Three Year Scholarship for Authors from the Danish State Art Foundation, 1984; Holger Drachmann's Grant, 1986; Henri Nathansen's Birthday-Grant, 1987; Otto Rung's Grant, 1987; Tagea Brandt's Grant, 1989; Edith Rode's Grant, 1991; Einer Hansen's Grant, 1991; N Bang's Grant, 1992, Anckerske Grant, 1994, The Literature Prize of Weekend Avisen, 1995, The Grant in Memory of Morten Nielsen, 1995. Memberships: Danish Academy, Danish PEN Centre. Address: Rosenvaengets Sideallé 3.2th, 2100 Copenhagen 0, DK, Denmark.

TAGGART John Paul, b. 5 Oct 1942. University Professor. m. Jennifer A James, 2 daughters. Education: BA, Earlham College, 1965; MA, University of Chicago, 1966; PhD, Syracuse University, 1974. Appointments: English Department, Shippensburg University, 1969-. Publications: Dodeka, 1979; Peace on Earth, 1981; Dehiscence, 1983; Loop, 1991; Prompted, 1991; Aeschylus-Fragments, translation, 1992; Standing Wave, 1993; Remaining in Light, essays, 1993; Songs of Degrees, essays, 1994. Contributions to: Hambone; Conjunctions; Northwest Review; Sulfur; Ironwood; Boundary 2; Epoch; Temblor; Tynonyi. Honours: Writing Fellowships, National Endowment for the Arts, 1976, 1986; Poetry Prize, Chicago Review, 1980; Frank Stanford Poetry Prize, 1982; Writing Fellowship, Pennsylvania Council on the Arts, 1987. Address: 295 East Creek Road, Newburg, PA 17240, USA.

TAGLIABUE John, b. 1 July 1923, Cantu, Italy. Writer; Teacher; Professor Emeritus. m. Grace Ten Eyck, 11 Aug 1946, 2 daughters. Education: BA, CA, Columbia University. Appointments: Teacher, American University of Beirut, 1945; State College of Washington, 1946-47; Alfred University, New York, 1948-50; Fulbright Teacher, University of Pisa, 1950-52; Bates College, Maine, 1953; Tokyo University, 1958-60. Publications: Poems; A Japanese Journal; The Buddha Uproar; The Doorless Door; The Great Day; Collected Poems (1941-95), 1996. Contributions to: Atlantic; Hudson Review; Hobart Review; Harper's; Chicago Review; Kayak; Kenyon Review; Massachusetts Review; New York Quarterly; Poetry; Quarterly Review of Literature; Nation; New Letters. Honours: Fulbright Grants; Rockefeller Bellagio Grant; Fulbright Grant to Indonesia, 1993. Memberships: Academy of American Poets; Poetry Society of America; PEN. Address: 12 Abbott Street, Lewiston, ME 04240, USA.

TAHID. See: **LOCKETT Reginald Franklin.**

TAKACHI Jun'ichiro, b. 7 Mar 1939, Tokushima, Japan. Professor; Poet. Education: BA, Tokushima University, 1964; MA, Hiroshima University, 1964; University of Cambridge, 1979-80; Yale University, 1982-83. Appointments: Lecturer, Hirosaki University, 1965-70; Assistant Professor, 1970-73, Associate Professor, 1973-84, Professor, 1984-, Obirin University. Publications: Spring and Fall in

Cambridge; The Garden of Orpheus; The Summer of Homer; De Construction of Deconstruction; Manna of Love. Contributions to: Shigaku; Gendaishi-Techo; Poetry Tokyo; Japan PoetryReview; Eigo Seinen. Memberships: Japan Contemporary Anglo American Poetry Society; Japan Poets Association; Japan PEN International; International Comparative Literature Association. Address: 4-19-20 Lions City #705, Haramachida, Machida, Japan.

TALAL Marilynn Carole Glick, b. New York, New York, USA. Teacher. m. Norman Talal, 21 June 1959. Education: AB, Sarah Lawrence College, 1959; MA, Columbia University, 1963; PhD, University of Houston, 1993. Appointments: English Instructor, University of Virginia, 1963-65; Marin County Coordinator, California Poets in the Schols, 1978-82; English Instructor, University of Texas at San Antonio, 1982-85. Publication: Being Children, and For Our Dead, in Blood to Remember: American Poets on the Holocaust, 1991. Contributions to: New Republic; Poetry; Present Tense; California Quarterly; Louisville Review; Southern Poetry Review; Bitteroot; Shorelines. Honours: Stella Erhart Memorial Fellowship, University of Houston, 1987; Creative Writing Fellowship, National Endowment for the Arts, 1991. Membership: Academy of American Poets. Address: 106 Village Circle, San Antonio, TX 78232, USA.

TALBOT Norman Clare, b. 14 Sept 1936, Gislingham, Suffolk, England. Poet; Writer; Editor; Literary Consultant; University Professor, retired, 1992. m. 17 Aug 1960, 1 son, 2 daughters. Education: BA, Durham University, Hatfield College, 1959; PhD, Leeds University, 1962. Appointments: Lecturer 1963, Associate Professor 1968, Professor 1973-92, in English, University of Newcastle, NSW, Australia; Visiting Professor, Yale University 1967-68, University of East Anglia 1975-76, University of Aarhus 1976, University of Oregon 1983, University of Leicester 1984, Linacre College, Oxford 1987-88, University of Exeter 1992. Publications: Poetry: Poems for a Female University, 1968; Son of a Female University, 1972; The Fishing Boy, 1975; Find the Lady, 1978; Where Two Rivers Meet, 1981; The Kelly Haiku, 1985; Four Zoas of Australia, 1992; Australian Quaker Christmases, 1993. Criticism: The Major Poems of John Keats, 1967. A Glossary of Poetic Terms, 1980, revised edition, 1982, 1987, 1991; Editor: Another Site to be Mined: The New South Wales Anthology, 1986; Weaving the Heterocosm: An Anthology of British Narrative Poetry, 1989; Roland Robinson: The Nearest the White Man Gets, 1989; Spelling English Revised in Australia, editor, 1990; T H Naisby: The Pink Tongue, 1990. Contributions to: Numerous periodicals. Honours: E C Gregory Memorial Award for Poetry, 1965; American Council of Learned Societies Fellowship, 1967-68. Memberships: William Morris Society; Mythopoeic Literature Association of Australia; Mythopoeic Society (USA); Poetry Book Club of Australia; Poetry at the Pub (Newcastle); Regional Poets' Cooperative of Australia. Address: PO Box 170, New Lambton, NSW 2305, Australia.

TALL Deborah, b. 16 Mar 1951, Washington, District of Columbia, USA. m. David Weiss, 2 daughters. Education: BA, University of Michigan, 1972; MFA, Goddard College, 1979. Appointments: Professor, Hobart and William Smith Colleges; Editor, Seneca Review. Publications: From Where We Stand: Recovering a Sense of Place; Taking Note: From Poet's Notebooks (co-editor); Come Wind, Come Weather; The Island of the White Cow: Memories of an Irish Island; Ninth Life; Eight Colors Wide; The Poet's Notebook, (co-editor) 1995. Honours: Grant from Ingram Merrill Foundation; Fellowships to Yaddo; Hopwood Award for Poetry. Memberships: Poetry Society of America; Academy of American Poets; Associated Writing Programs; Poets and Writers. Address: Department of English, Hobart & William Smith Colleges, Geneva, New York 14456, USA.

TALMOR Avital, b. 17 Aug 1953, Israel. Secretary. Education: BA, Tel Aviv University, 1976; MPhil, University of London, 1981. Contributions to: First Time; Treasures of the Precious Moments (Anthology); Liberal and Fine Arts Review; Rebirth of Artemis; New Letters; Women and Language; Without a Single Answer (Anthology); Voices Israel; Midstream; Pig Iron, anthology; A Moment in Time, anthology. Honour: 4th Prize, International Reuben Rose Memorial Poetry Competition. Address: 4 Bergson Street, Ramat Aviv 69106, Israel.

TALUKDAR Nirodbaran, b. 17 Nov 1903, Rangunia, Chittagong District, Bangladesh. Teaching. Education: MBCHB, Edinburgh University, 1929. Appointments: Medical Practitioner: Rangoon, Burma, 1931, 1932; Pondicherry, India, 1933-38; Personal Attendant and Literary Secretary, Sri Aurobindo, 1938-50; Professor of English and French Literature, Sri Aurobindo International Centre of Education, Pondicherry, 1951-. Publications: Fifty Poems of Nirodbaran with Corrections and Comments by Sri Aurobindo, 1983; Poems by Amal Kiran and Nirodbaran with Sri Aurobindo's Comments, 1987. Address: Sri Aurobindo Ashram, Pondicherry 605002, India.

TAMARACK. See: HARLESS Margaret Michael.

TAMEN Pedro Mario Alles, b. 1 Dec 1934, Lisbon, Portugal. Trustee, Calouste Gulbenkian Foundation. m. Maria Da Graca, 29 Oct 1981, 2 sons, 2 daughters. Education: University of Lisbon, 1957. Appointments: Moraes Publishing House, Director, 1958-75; Flama Magazine, Assistant Editor, 1959-62. Publications: Poema Para Todos Os Dias; O Sangue A Agua E O Vinho; Primeiro Livro De Lapinova; Poemas A Isto; Daniel Na Cova Dos Leoes; Escrito De Memoria; Agora Estar; Poesia, 1956-1978; Horácio e Coriaces; Allegria Del Silenzio; Dentro De Momentos; Delfos, Opus 12 Et Autres Poemes; Tábua das Matérias; Caracois; Depois De Ver. Contributions to: Some of the Most Important in Portugal & Brazil. Honours: D Diniz Prize; Critic Prize, Inapa Prize. Memberships: Portuguese Pen Club, Portuguese Association of Writers. Address: R Luis Pastor De Macedo, Lt 25 50 E, 17150 Lisbon, Portugal.

TANG Shi, b. 28 May 1920, Wenzhou, China. Writer; Poet. m. Chen Aiqiu, July 1946, 2 sons, 2 daughters. Education: AB, National Zhejiang University. Appointments: Editor, Poetic Creation, 1947; Member, Editorial Committee, Contemporary Poetry, 1948; Editor, Drama Monthly, 1954-58; Research Fellow, Wenzhou Art Research Institute, 1986-. Publications: A City in the Tumult, poems, 1947; Heroic Prairie, narrative poem, 1948; Flying Song, poems, 1950; The Collection of Surmiss, reviews of poets-poems, 1950; Hai-lin, the King, 3 historical narrative poems, 1980; The Trip of Charm, sonnets, 1983; The Cataract of Tears, 3 narrative folk-lore poems, 1985; Reverie About Poetry and Beauty, sonnets, 1987; Some Essays About our National Drama, 1987; The Music in the Moonlight, a Collection of Prose, 1988; The New Collection of Surmiss, reviews of poets-poems, 1990; Dreaming of Flute at Glowing Upstair, selected poems, 1993; The Blue Sonnets, selected sonnets, 1993; The Flowery Moonlit Night on the Spring River, 6 historical narrative poems, 1993; The Green Plums, poetry review, 1993; With others: Collection of 9 leaves, selected poems of 9 poets, 1981; Collection of 8 Leaves, selected poems of 8 poets, 1983. Contributions to: Poetry Monthly, Beijing; People's Literature; Hong Kong Literature; Poetry Bi-Monthly, Hong Kong; People's Daily, Beijing; The Star, Chengdu; South River, Hangzhou. Memberships: All-Chinese Art and Literature Association, 1948; Chinese Writers Association; Chinese Dramatists Association. Address: 22-302 Hualiutang New House, Wenzhou, China.

TANZBERG Kris. See: KRANZ Gisbert.

TAPNER Vic(tor David), b. 16 Nov 1950, Watford, Hertfordshire, England. Journalist. m. Rosalind Matthews, 10 Sept 1971, 1 son, 1 daughter. Education: Hitchin College, 1967-69. Appointments: South Wales Guardian, Reporter; Lloyds List, Sub Editor; Telex News Agency, Staff Writer; Contract Journal, Reporter; Building, Assistant Editor; Building Design, Deputy Editor; Financial Times, Night News Editor. Publications: The Icarus Leaf, 1982; Cold Rain: The Icarus, 1982; Cold Rain, 1988. Contributions to: A Package of Poems; Outposts; Envoi; Ore; Smiths Knoll; Poetry Nottingham; Superreal; Cencrastus; Weyfarers; Poetry Now - 1994 Poets; Angel Exhaust; Candelabrum; Interactions. Honours: Lake Aske Memorial Award: Merit 1982; John Clare Poetry Competition: Commendations 1982; International Poetry Competition: Commendation 1983; John Clare Competition: Commendation 1983; Queenie Lee Competition: Commendation, 1984; John Clare Competition: Commendation 1984; All-London Literary Competition: Two Commendations 1987. Membership: Poetry Society. Address: 39 Sun Street, Billericay, Essex CM12 9LW, England.

TAPSCOTT Stephen, b. 5 Nov 1948, Des Moines, Iowa, USA. Poet; Teacher. Education: BA, University of Notre Dame, 1970; PhD, Cornell University, 1975. Appointments: Lecturer in English, University of Kent at Canterbury, England, 1976-77; Teacher, Goddard College, 1976-82; Assistant Professor of English, Massachusetts Institute of Technology, 1977-. Publications: Mesopotamia, poems, 1975; Penobscot: Nine Poems, 1983; American Beauty: William Carlos Williams and the Tradition of the Modernist Whitman, 1984; Pablo Neruda: 100 Love Sonnets, translator from the Spanish, 1985; Another

Body, poems, 1989. Address: 66 Martin Street, No 2, Cambridge, MA 02138, USA.

TARN Nathaniel, b. 30 June 1928, Paris, France. Professor Emeritus; Poet; Writer. m. (1) div, 2 children, (2) Janet Rodney, 1981. Education: BA, 1948, MA, 1952, Cambridge University; MA, 1952, PhD, 1957, University of Chicago. Appointments: Visiting Professor, State University of New York, Buffalo, 1969-70; Princeton University, 1969-70, University of Pennsylvania, 1976, Jilin University, China, 1982; Professor of Comparative Literature, 1970-85, Professor Emeritus, 1985-, Rutgers University. Publications: Poetry: Old Savage/Young City, 1964; Penguin Modern Poets 7 (with Richard Murphy and Jon Silkin), 1966; Where Babylon Ends, 1968; The Beautiful Contradictions, 1969; October: A Sequence of Ten Poems Followed by Requiem Pro Duabus Filiis Israel, 1969; The Silence, 1970; A Nowhere for Vallejo: Choices, October, 1971; Lyrics for the Bride of God: Section: The Artemision, 1973; The Persphones, 1974; Lyrics for the Bride of God, 1975; Narrative of This Fall, 1975; The House of Leaves, 1976; From Alashka: The Ground of Our Great Admiration of Nature, 1977; The Microcosm, 1977; Birdscapes, with Seaside, 1978; The Forest (with Janet Rodney), 1978; Atitlan/Alashka: New and Selected Poems (with Janet Rodney), 1979; The Land Songs, 1981; Weekends in Mexico, 1982; The Desert Mothers, 1984; At the Western Gates, 1985; Palenque: Selected Poems 1972-1984, 1986; Seeing America First, 1989; The Mothers of Matagalpa, 1989; Flying the Body, 1993; Non-fiction: Views from the Weaving Mountain: Selected Essays in Poetics and Anthropology, 1991. Honours: Guinness Prize, 1963; Wenner Gren Fellowships, 1978, 1980; Commonwealth of Pennsylvania Fellowship, 1984; Rockefeller Foundation Fellowship, 1988. Address: PO Box 8187, Santa Fe, NM 87504, USA.

TARTLER (TABARAS) Grete, b. 23 Nov 1948, Bucharest, Romania. Poet; Editor; Musician. m. Stelian Tabaras, 23 Sept 1972, 1 daughter. Education: MA, 1972 and 1976; PhD, 1996. Appointments: Teacher, 1972-88; Editor, 1988, 1990; Diplomate, 1992-. Publications: Apa Vie; Chorale; Hore; Astronomia Ierbii; Substituiri; Achene Zburatoare; Materia Signata; Orient Express. Contributions to: Honest Ulsterman; Poetry Review; Times Literary Supplement; Illuminations; Numbers. Honours: Awards of Writers Union; Poetry Prize; Award of Poetry Society England. Memberships: Writers Union in Romania; PEN. Address: Mihai Bravu ur 1, bld 2 Sc A Apt 7, Sector 2, 73261 Bucharest, Romania.

TATE James (Vincent), b. 8 Dec 1943, Kansas City, Missouri, USA. Poet; Professor. Education: University of Missouri, 1963-64; BA, Kansas State University, 1965; MFA, University of Iowa, 1967. Appointments: Instructor in Creative Writing, University of Iowa, 1966-67; Visiting Lecturer, University of California at Berkeley, 1967-68; Poetry Editor, Dickinson Review, 1967-76; Trustee, Associate Editor, Pym-Randall Press, 1968-80; Assistant Professor of English, Columbia University, 1969-71; Associate Professor, Professor of English, University of Massachusetts at Amherst, 1971-; Poet-in-Residence, Emerson College, 1970-71; Associate Editor, Barn Dream Press. Publications: Poetry: Cages, 1966; The Destination, 1967; The Lost Pilot, 1967; Notes of Woe: Poems, 1968; Camping in the Valley, 1968; The Torches, 1968, revised edition, 1971; Row with Your Hair, 1969; Is There Anything?, 1969; Shepherds of the Mist, 1969; Amnesia People, 1970; Are You Ready Mary Baker Eddy? (with Bill Knott), 1970; Deaf Girl Playing, 1970; The Oblivion Ha-Ha, 1970; Wrong Songs, 1970; Hints to Pilgrims, 1971, 2nd edition, 1982; Absences, 1972; Apology for Eating Geoffrey Movius' Hyacinth, 1972; Hottentot Ossuary, 1974; Viper Jazz, 1976; Riven Doggeries, 1979; Land of Little Sticks, 1981; Constant Defender, 1983; Reckoner, 1986; Distance from Loved Ones, 1990; Selected Poems, 1991; Worshipful Company of Fletchers, 1993. Novel: Lucky Darryl, 1977. Contributions to: Numerous books and periodicals. Honours include: Yale Younger Poets Award, 1966; Pulitzer Prize in Poetry, 1992; National Book Award for Poetry, 1994. Membership: Bollingen Prize Committee, 1974-75. Address: Department of English, University of Massachusetts, Amherst, MA 01003, USA.

TATELBAUM Brenda Loew, b. 1 Apr 1951, Boston, Massachusetts, USA. Publisher. m. Ira Rubin Tatelbaum, 23 Aug 1970, div 1983, 1 son, 1 daughter. Education: BA, Boston University, 1971; MA, Brown University, 1973; Cultural Doctorate, World University, 1992. Appointments: Library Assistant, 1973; Speech Therapist, 1974-77; Chair, Bill Baird Pro Choice Defence League, 1982-; Publisher, 1983-. Publications: Eden Poems; Life Evolves From

Living; Boston Collection of Womens Poetry. Contributions to: Small Magazines, Journals and Periodicals. Honour: Awarded The Lifestyle Award, The Lifestyle Organization. Membership: Former, Poetry Club of New England. Address: c/o EIDOS, PO Box 96, Boston, MA 02137, USA.

TAYLOR Andrew McDonald, b. 19 Mar 1940, Victoria, Australia. m. Beate Josephi, 1 son, 1 daughter. Education: BA, University of Melbourne, 1961; MA, 1970. Appointments: Lockie Fellow, University of Melbourne, 1965-68; Lecturer, University of Adelaide, 1971-74; Senior Lecturer, 1975-92; Professor, Edith Cowan University, 1992-. Publications: The Cool Change; Ice Fishing; The Invention of Fire; Parabolas; The Crystal Absences; Travelling; Selected Poems; Folds in the Map; Miracles of Disbelief; Reading Australian Poetry; Barossa; The Letters of Amalia Dietrich; Sandstone, 1995. Contributions to: Times Literary Supplement; Chelsea; 2 Plus 2; Meanjin; Overland; Quadrant; Westerly; Southern Review; Adelaide Review; Island; Poetry Australia; Age; Sydney Morning Herald; Canberra Times; Australian Broadcasting Corporation. Honours: Pacific Region Winner Commonwealth Poetry Prize; South Australian Festival Awards; Member of Order of Australia. Memberships: Association for the Study of Australian Literature; Australian Society of Authors. Address: c/o English Department, Edith Cowan University, Mount Lawley, Western Australia 6050, Australia.

TAYLOR Anna, b. 14 July 1943, Preston, Lancashire, England. Writer; Teacher; Artistic Collaborator and Translator. m. John E Coombes, 22 Dec 1967, div 1982, 1 son. Education: BA Hons, German, English, Bristol University, 1965; Cert Ed, York University, 1967; MA, Sociology of Literature, Essex University, 1980. Appointments: Various teaching posts, secondary, further and higher education, 1965-, most recently as Lecturer in Post-War British Poetry, Bretton Hall, Wakefield; Invited as writer primarily; Collaborator to French sculptor Serraz, Paris, 1969-89. Publications: Fausta, 1984; Cut Some Cords, 1988. Contributions to: Poetry Anthologies: Purple and Green, 1985; Transformation, 1988; Assemblage, 1989; Pennine Poets, 1986, 1991; Huddersfield Polytechnic Anthology, 1991; Magazines: Green Book, 1990; Folded Sheets; Wide Skirt; Theatre Ireland, 1992. Honours: Short-listed: New Poetry, 1980; York Open Competition, 1985; Wetherby, 1985; Huddersfield Arts Council, 1990; 3rd Prize, Mrs Sunderland, 1991. Memberships: Theatre Writers Union; National Association of Writers in Education, Committee Member, 1991-92; Yorkshire Playwrights, Past Membership: Former Kirklees Poetry Society, Treasurer. Address: 82 Blackhouse Road, Fartown, Huddersfield, West Yorks HD2 1AR, England.

TAYLOR Brian Dormer, b. 17 Sept 1946, Dublin, Ireland. Educator. Education: BSc Econ, 1968, Cert Ed, 1969, LLB, 1974, University of London; MA Urban Processes, Problems and Policies, Council for National Academic Awards, 1984; LLM, Cambridge University, 1985; Associate, London Academy of Music and Dramatic Art, 1967. Appointments: Lecturer, Kingston College of Further Education, 1970-72; Lecturer, 1972-78, Senior Lecturer in Law, School of the Built Environment, Leicester Polytechic (now De Montfort University), 1978-91. Publications: Strong Men Cast Shadows Too, 1982; Anthologies: It's World that Makes the Love Go Round, 1968; Young Winter's Tales 6, 1975; Autumn Anthology, 1977; A Sense of Place, 1986. Contributions to: Breakthru; Expression; First Time; Krax; Morley Magazine; Orbis; Other Poetry; Poetry Review; Riding West; Sepia; Phoenix Broadsheet. Honours: Winner, Open Poetry Competition, Cheltenham Competitive Festival, 1983. Memberships: FRSA, 1977; Poetry Society; Former Member, Council, Leicester Literary and Philosophical Society. Address: Bod Awel, Gors Avenue, Holyhead, Gwynedd LL65 1PB, Wales.

TAYLOR Bruce, b. 19 Feb 1947, Somerville, Massachusetts, USA. Professor of English. m. 4 July 1983, 2 sons. Education: BA, English, Bridgewater State College, Bridgewater, Massachusetts, 1964; MA, MFA, University of Arkansas, 1972. Appointments: Poetry Editor, Transactions: Journal of Wisconsin Academy of Sciences, Arts, Letters; Editor, Publisher, Upriver Press; Professor of English, University of Wisconsin, Eau Claire. Publications: Everywhere the Beauty Gives Itself Away, 1976; Idle Tacde: Early Poems, 1979; The Darling Poems: A Romance, 1982; This Day, 1992; Why That Man Talks That, 1994; Editor: Eating the Menu, 1974; Upriver, 1979; Upriver 2, 1981; Upriver 3, 1984; Upriver 4, 1990; Wisconsin Poetry, 1991. Contributions to: Anglican Theological Review; Kansas Quarterly; Literary Review; Little Magazine; Nation; New Orleans Review; New York Quarterly; Northwest Review; Rocky Mountain

Review; South Coast Poetry Review; Texas Review. Honours: Kenneth Patchen Award for Poetry, 1972; Fellowship, Wisconsin Arts Board, 1981; Writer on the Verge of Significant National Distinction, National Endowment for the Arts and Passages North, 1987; Consulting Humanist and Program Scholar, Voices and Visions: Modern American Poets and Their Poetry, 1988; Faculty Sabbatical, Creative Writing, University of Wisconsin, 1992. Memberships: Associated Writing Programs; Poets, Essayists and Novelists. Address: Department of English, University of Wisconsin, Eau Claire, WI 54702, USA.

TAYLOR C(onciere) M(arlana), b. 30 Oct 1950, New York, New York, USA. Writer; Editor. Education: AA, Queensborough Community College; BFA CW Post College, Long Island University. Appointments: Editor, 1976-80; Editor-in-Chief, 1982; Coordinator of Literary Arts Division, 1976-80. Publication: Cease Fire. Contributions to: New World Anthology; Wings; New York State Waterways Project; Unicorn; Earth's Daughters; Home Planet News; Hearthside; One Page. Memberships: Poets and Writers; Poetry Society of America. Address: 67-08 Parsons Boulevard, No 6B, Flushing, NY 11365, USA.

TAYLOR John (Benjamin), b. 19 Mar 1944, London, England. Teacher. Education: Teachers Certificate, 1977. Appointments: Ocker Hill Juniors, West Bromwich, 1969; Education Certificate, 1972; Poets Workshops, 1972-; Pelham Middle School, Wimbledon, 1978; Pelnam Middle London, 1978-80. Publications: There Were No Lovely Birds, 1974; Three Familiar Birds, 1984; Small Press Items, 1986-; The Manor House (Home), 1988. Contributions to: Southern Arts Magazine, 1975; Chichester Observer; Workshop Poetry; Chichester Chronical; Newsletter; BBC Radio, Television; New Hope International; Positively Poetry, 1995; Mindfull, 1996. Honours: Spring: No Time to Stand and Stare? Hons, 1980. Memberships: Workshop Poetry Agent; Church of England/Methodist; Sussex Writers Club, 1977; Spoken English Member; Pilot Newspaper. Literay Agent, Workshop Press, London, 1974. Address: The Manor House, The Popular Press, 12 Chichester Road, Bognor Regis, West Sussex PO21 2EX, England.

TAYLOR Kent, b. 8 Nov 1940, New Castle, Pennsylvania, USA. Writer; Poet; Widower, 1 son. Education: BA, Ohio Wesleyan University, 1962. Appointment: Medical Research Associate. Publications: Rabbits Have Fled; Late Show at the Starlight Laundry; Driving Like the Sun; Empty Ground; Shit Outside When Eating Berries; Cleveland Dreams; Torn Birds; Late Stations; Fortuitons Mother Fucker; Aleatory Letters; Selected Poems. Contributions to: Quarterly; Swamp Root; Painted Bride Quarterly; Second Aeon; Widener Review; Freelance; Ally; Quixote; Grist; Limberlost Review; The Quarterly; Rain City Review; Atom Mind; Onthebus; Bombay Gin; Grist On-Line, Abraxas, Coracle, Swamp Root, Painted Bride Quarterly, Scree, Vagabond; Second Aeon; many others. Address: 1450 10th Avenue, San Francisco, CA 94122, USA.

TAYLOR Lisa C, b. 16 June 1954, Hartford, Connecticut, USA. Writer; Counselor. m. Russell W Taylor, 8 Aug 1981, 1 son, 1 daughter. Education: BA, English and Comparative Literature, 1979; MA, Counseling, 1981. Appointments: Psychotherapist, Family Therapist for private agencies, 1981-88; Retreats and workshops on creativity and personal growth and writing, 1988-95; Adjunct Faculty, Eastern Connecticut State University, 1988-95; Exploring Yourself Through Writing Group, Middle School and Counseling position, 1988-95. Publications: Falling Open, 1994; Safe Love and Other Political Acts, 1995. Contributions to: Xanadu; Pudding Magazine; Arizona Unconservative; Dream International Quarterly; Poet's Cookbook: Written With A Spoon Anthology, 1995. Honour: First Prize, National Scholastic Writing Award for Poetry, 1972. Memberships: Wolfden Writer's Group; River's Edge Writer's Group; Brick Walk Poets; Cape Cod Writer's Center; Association of Writing Programs. Address: 27 Mulberry Road, Mansfield Center, CT 06250, USA.

TAYLOR Velande Pingel, (Martha Pingel), b. 10 Sept 1923, New York, New York, USA. Writer; Emeritus Professor of Literature and Philosophy. m. Bert Raymond Taylor, Jr, 28 Oct 1961. Education: BA, 1944, MA, 1945, PhD, 1947, Literature and Philosophy; Independent study in art, music, creative writing, poetry and fiction. Appointments: Instructor, Paul Smiths College, New York, 1946-47; Assistant Professor, East Carolina University, North Carolina, 1947-58; Professor and Head, Humanities, Colorado Woman's College, 1958-66; Visiting Professor, St Mary's University, Texas, 1966-69; Professor, Middle Georgia College, 1969-72; Editor, Consultant, Independent Lecturer, 1972-74; Professor, Writer-in-Residence, Hong

Kong Baptist College, 1974-84; Writer; Retreat Facilitator in Poetry and Fiction, WordCraft by Lan, 1984-. Publications: Catalyst, 1951; Mood Montage, 1968; Immortal Dancer, 1968; Mode and Muse in a New Generation, 1979; Variations on the House, 1976; Walking Songs, 1989; Images, 1991; Homilies In The Marketplace: Parables For Our Time?, 1996; Stalking The Shadow, in progress. Contributions to: Pacific Magazine; Rosicrucian Digest; New American Poetry Anthology; HKBC Academic Journal; Radio: KOA, Denver, RTHK, Hong Kong, WWWS-FM, Greenville, North Carolina. Honours: Certificate, International Mark Twain Society, 1947; Miniature Medal, Order of the Danne Brog, 1951; Certificate, Writer's Digest Rhymed Poetry Contest, 1994. Memberships: Secretary, Vice President, International PEN (English), Hong Kong, 1970's; Academy of American Poets. Address: 910 Marion Street #1008, Seattle, WA 98104-1273, USA.

TELLER Gayl, b. 17 June 1946, Bronx, New York, USA. Poet; College English Professor. m. Michael Teller, 14 Aug 1965, 1 son. Education: BA, 1967, MA 1981, Queens College; MA, Columbia University, 1969. Appointments: English Teacher, August Martin High School; Adjunct Assistant Professor, English, Hofstra University; Poetry Teacher, Five Towns Music and Art Foundation. Publication: At the Intersection of Everyting You Have Ever Loved, 1989; Shorehaven, forthcoming. Contributions to: Caesura; South Coast Poetry Journal; Moving Out; Long Island Quarterly; Connecticut Writer; Wyoming - The Hub of the Wheel; Bitteroot; Spring; Half Tones to Jubilee; Small Press Review; Phoebe; Dominion Review. Honours: 1st Place, Peninsula Library Poetry Award, 1984; Poetry Award, National Federation of State Poetry Societies, 1984; Poetry Award, Artemis Magazine, 1985; 1st Place, Poetry Award, Pittenbruach Press, 1989; Poetry Award, National League of American Pen Women, 1992. Memberships: Poetry Society of America; Long Island Poetry Collective; Poetry Center, 92nd Street Y. Address: One Florence Lane, Plainview, NY 11803, USA.

TEMPLETON Fiona, b. 23 Dec 1951, Scotland. Theatre Director. Education: MA, Edinburgh University, 1973; MA, New York University, 1985. Appointments: Co-Founder, Theatre of Mistakes, London, 1974-79; Independent Director. Publications: London, 1984; Elements of Performance Art, 1976; You the City, 1990; Hi Cowboy, 1996; Delirium of Interpretations, 1996. Contributions to: Writing; Conjunctions; Raddle Moon; Poetry Project Letter; Big Allis; Boundary Two; Blatant Artifice; Poetics Journal; Sun and Moon; Appearances; Jaa; Wallpaper. Honour: National Endowment for the Arts Poetry Fellowship, 1995. Memberships: Poets and Writers; New Dramatists. Address: 100 St Marks Place 7, New York, NY 10009, USA.

TENNANT Pauline. See: RUMBOLD Lady Pauline Letitia.

TERENCE Susan, b. 14 Aug 1953, Tucson, Arizona, USA. Writer; Poetry and Arts Teacher; Punch and Judy Puppeteer; Actor. Education: BA, English Education, Spanish, University of Arizona, Tucson, 1975; MA, Inter-Disciplinary Arts, San Francisco State University, California, 1994. Appointments: English Teacher, Tucson, Arizona, 1975-77; Performing Arts Teacher, Tucson, 1981-84; Visiting Artist: Arts in Arizona Towns, 1981-84, Montana Arts Council, 1989-, North Carolina Arts Council, Fulton County, Groegia, Arts Council; California Poets in Schools, 1987-; Residency, Writers' Voice Billings. Contributions to: Negative Capability; Southern Poetry Review; Nebraska Review; Lake Effect; San Francisco Bay Guardian; Halftones to Jubilee; Atlanta Writers' Resource Center; Oktoberfest IV; News From Nowhere; Queen of Hearts Press; California Poets in the Schools Anthologies; National Guardian; Coyote. Honours: 2nd Place, San Francisco Bay Guardian Poetry Contest, 1989; De War's Young Arts Award for Literature, California, 1990. Membership: San Francisco Co-ordinator, California Poets in the Schools. Address: 2153 Hayes, San Francisco, CA 94117, USA.

THABIT JONES Peter, b. 18 May 1951, Swansea, Wales. Writer. m. Hilary, 4 sons, 2 daughters. Education: Diploma in Higher Education, University of Wales; Diploma in Office Studies; Higher National Certificate in Leisure/Conservation Management; Postgraduate Certificate in Education (Further and Higher Education). Appointment: Editor, SWAG Magazine, 1995-. Publications: Tacky Brow, 1974; The Apprenticeship, 1977; Clocks Tick Differently, 1980; Visitors, 1986; The Cold Cold Corner 1995. Contributions to: 2Plus2; Poetry Wales; Poetry Review; Anglo-Welsh Review; Planet; Outposts Poetry Quarterly; Poetry Nottingham; NER/BLQ; Urbane Gorilla; Docks; Cambrensis; Orbis; White Rose; Exile; Iota; Krax; Weyfares; Western Mail; South Wales Evening Post; Momentum; Asp. Honours:

Grants: Royal Literary Fund, 1987, Society of Authors, 1987, Welsh Arts Council, 1990; Commendations from: National Poetry Competition, 1983, 1988; Bridport Arts Festival, 1984; Welsh Arts Council (prose), 1986, (poetry), 1987; Outposts Competition Winner, 1988; Eric Gregory Award for Poetry, 1979, London; Carried out Workshop (with St Thomas School) for Prince Charles, Swansea, April 1995. Memberships: Poetry Society (London); Swansea Writers and Artists Group, Treasurer; Full Member, The Welsh Academy, 1995. Address: Dan y Bryn, 74 Cwm Level Road, Brynhyfryd, Swansea SA5 9DY, Wales.

THAG Bhagwan, b. 24 Jan 1955, Hiwarkhed, Buldana District, India. Government Servant. m. Parvati, 27 June 1977, 3 daughters. Education: BA, Parat II. Appointment: Government Servant, 1974-. Publications: Atmapakshi, 1980; Yuddha, 1985; Anuwad, 1985; Modern Marathi Poetry, (vol I) 1987; (vol II) 1987, (vol III) 1988, (vol IV) 1988, (vol V) 1989, (Vol VI) 1990; Vishw Pratibha, 1988; Japanese Poems, 1986, in Marathi; Anarth, 1991; Dalit Poetry Today, 1991. Contributions to: Poems published in Marathi in numerous periodicals including: Art and Poetry; Poetcrit; Canopi; Skylark; Bhasha; Akata Nagpur Times; Hitwad. Honours include: Dr Ambedkar Award, 1992; Velayudhan Award, 1992; Jagat Jotyi Award, 1992; Bahujan Nayak Award, 1993; Surve Award, 1994; Buldana Gausav Award, 1995. Memberships: Jansahitya Parishad Amaruati; Vidharb Sahitya Sangha Nagpur; Maharashtra Anuwad Parishad; Editor, Tuka Mhane, Yugwani,Anuwad, Vishwavangmay. Address: Editor Tuka Mhane, Rajarshi Shahunagar Chaitnyawadi, Buldana, District Buldana (MS) 443 001, India.

THARP Roland George, b. 6 June 1930, Texas, USA. Professor. 3 sons, 1 daughter. Education: BA, University of Houston, 1957; MA, 1958, PhD, 1961, University of Michigan. Publication: Highland Station. Contributions to: Hawaii Review; Poetry Now; Soney Lonesome; Christianity and Literature; Carolina Quarterly; Volcano Gazette; EPOS; Back Door; Quixote; Port Townsend Journal; Shenandoah; Yankee; Indigo; Hyacinths and Biscuits; Ioon; Bitteroot; Sou'Wester; Prairie Schooner; Small Pond; Kapa; Arizona Quarterly; Voices; Whetstone; Southwest Review; Harvest. Honours: Impact Poetry Book Award Runner Up; Sou'Wester Prize in Poetry; Avery Hopwood Award; Robert Frost Fellowship; Claire Raymer Greenwood Award. Membership: Hawaii Literary Arts Council. Address: Merrill College, University of California, Santa Cruz, CA 95064, USA.

THERSON-COFIE Larweh, (Kwesi Afra, Eddie Cosmos, Black Moses), b. 8 Sept 1943, Ghana. Journalist. m. Rebecca Amobea, 30 Oct 1988, 1 son, 1 daughter. Education: Ghana Institute of Journalism; School of Journalism and Mass Communication, University of Ghana. Appointments: Staff Reporter, 1967; Senior Reporter, 1972; Staff Writer, 1978; Foreign Editor, 1979; Special Correspondent, 1984; Assistant Editor, 1990; Deputy Editor, The Mirror 1992; Director, Afra Golden Age Publications, 1992. Publications: Poets of Our Time; The Lost Eden. Contributions to: World Poetry; Anthology of Contemporary Poetry; Poetry Africa; Rising Stars; Poet; Malahat Review; Literary Review, Fairleigh Dickson University; Mirror. Memberships: World Poetry Society; World Poetry Research Institute; United Poet Laureates League; Pan African Writers Association; Ghana Association of Writers. Address: The Mirror, Editorial Department, Graphic Corporation, PO Box 742, Ghana, West Africa.

THESEN Sharon, b. 1 Oct 1946, Tisdale, Saskatchewan, Canada. Education: BA, Simon Fraser University, British Columbia, 1970. Appointments: Teacher of English, Capilano College, Vancouver. Publications: Artemis Hates Romance, 1980; radio New France Radio, 1982; Holding the Pose, 1983; Confabulations: Poems for Malcolm Lowry, 1984; The Beginning of the Long Dash, 1987; The Pangs of Sunday, 1990; Poetry Editor, Capilano Review, 1978-89.

THOMAS Donald Michael, b. 27 Jan 1935, Redruth, Cornwall, England. Poet; Novelist. 2 sons, 1 daughter. Education: BA 1st Class Honours, English, MA, New College, Oxford. Appointments: Schoolteacher, 1959-63; Lecturer, Hereford College of Education, 1964-78. Publications: Penguin Modern Poets 11, 1968; Two Voices, 1968; Logan Stone, 1971; Love and Other Deaths, 1975; The Honeymoon Voyage, 1978; Dreaming in Bronze, 1981; Selected Poems, 1983; The Puberty Tree: New and Selected Poems, 1992; Translations: Requiem, a Poem Without a Hero, Akhmatova, 1976; Way of All the Earth, Akhmatova, 1979; Bronze Horseman, Pushkin, 1982. Address: The Coach House, Rashleigh Vale, Tregolis Road, Truro, Cornwall TR1 1TJ, England.

THOMAS Henri, b. 7 Dec 1912, Anglemont, Vosges, France; Poet. m. Jacqueline le Beguec, 1957, 1 daughter. Education: Strasbourg University. Appointments: Programme Assistant, BBC French Section, 1947-58; Lecturer, French, Brandeis University, USA, 1955-60; In charge, German Department, Galliards Publishing House, Paris, France, 1960-. Publications: Travaux d'aveugle, 1941; Signe de vie, 1944; Le monde absent, 1947; Nul desordre, 1950; Sous le lien du temps, 1963; Poesies completes, 1970; A quoi tu penses, 1979; Joueur surpris, 1982; Criticism: La chasse aux tresors, 1961; Tristan le Depossede, 1978; Poems: Trézeaux, 1989; Translations: Goethe, Stifter, Jungen, Shakespeare, Pushkin, Melville, Mosley, Kleist, Brentano, Arnim. Honours: Prix Medicis, 1960; Prix Femina, 1961; Prix des Sept; Prix Valery Larbaud, 1970; Chevalier, Legion d'Honneur; Prix de la Ville de Paris, 1985; Grand Prix de la Societe des Gens de Lettres, 1992; Prix Novembre, 1992. Address: Editions Gallimard, 5 rue Sebastien-Bottin, 75007 Paris, France.

THOMAS Norman. See: **HARVEY Marshall L.**

THOMAS R(onald) S(tuart), b. 29 Mar 1913, Cardiff, Wales. Clergyman, retired; Poet. m. Mildred E Eldridge, 1 son. Education: BA, University of Wales, 1935; St Michael's College, Llandaf; Ordained Deacon, 1936, Priest, 1937. Appointments: Curate of Chirk, 1936-40, of Hanmer, 1940-42; Rector, Manafon, 1942-54; Vicar of St Michael's, Eglwysfach, 1954-68, of St Hywyn, Aberdaron, 1968-79; Rector of Rhiw with Llanfaelfhys, 1973-78. Publications: Stones of the Field, 1947; Song at the Year's Turning, 1955; Poetry for Supper, 1958; Tares, 1961; The Bread of Truth, 1963; Pieta, 1966; Not That He Bought Flowers, 1968; H'm, 1972; Selected Poems 1946-68, 1974; Laboratories of the Spirit, 1975; Frequencies, 1978; Between Here and Now, 1981; Later Poems, 1972-82, 1983; Experimenting with an Amen, 1986; Welsh Airs, 1987; Counterpoint, 1990; Mass for Hard Times, 1992; No Truce with the Furies, 1995. Honours: Heinemann Award, Royal Society of Literature, 1956; Sovereign's Gold Medal for Poetry, 1964; Cholmondeley Award, 1978. Address: Cefn du Ganol, Llanfairynghornwy, Holyhead LL65 4LG, Ynys Mon, Wales.

THOMPSON Francis George, b. 29 March 1931, Isle of Lewis, Scotland. Retired Lecturer. m. Margaret Elaine Pullar, 23 April 1960, 1 son, 3 daughters. Education: Fellow, Institution of Electrical Incorporated Engineers. Appointments: Technical Writer; Technical College Lecturer; Senior Lecturer until retirement in 1992. Publications: Void, 1975; First Light, 1977; Touchlines, 1978; Reflections, 1985. Contributions to: Lines Review; Chapman; Prospice; Northwords; Orbis; Words. Honour: Hugh McDiarmid Memorial Cup, Scottish Open Poetry Competition, 1979. Address: 5 Rathad na Muilne, Stornoway, Isle of Lewis, Scotland.

THOMPSON Julius Eric, b. 15 July 1946, Vicksburg, Mississippi, USA. University Teacher. Education: BS, Alcorn State University, Lorman, Mississippi, 1969; MA, History, 1971, PhD, 1973, Princeton University. Appointment: History Department, Jackson State University, Mississippi, 1973-80; Education Division, Lilly Endowment Inc, Indianapolis, Indiana, 1980-81; Social Science Division, Florida Memorial College, 1980-81; State University of New York, Albany, 1983-88; University of Rochester, New York, 1988-89; Associate Professor, History, Black American Studies, Southern Illinois University, Carbondale, 1989-96; Associate Professor, BAS and History, University of Missouri, Columbia, 1996-. Publications: Hopes Tied Up in Promises, 1970; Blues Said: Walk On, 1977; The Anthology of Black Mississippi Poets (editor), 1988; The Black Press in Mississippi, 1865-1985, 1993; Percy Greene and the Jackson Advocate: The Life and Times of a Radical Conservative Black Newspaperman, 1897-1977, 1994. Contributions to: National Poetry Press; Alcorn Herald: Freedomways; Phylon; Black Creation; Hoo Doo; Obsidian I, II; Social Science Speaks, Jackson State University; Negro History Bulletin; Kitabu Cha Jua (Book of the Sun); Callaloo; New Visions; African News; Jackson Advocate; Jackson State University Researcher; Black American Literature Forum. Honours: Danforth Fellow, 1969-73; Doctoral Award, Ford Foundation, 1972-73; National Endowment for the Humanities Summer Seminars for College Teachers, Atlanta University, Georgia, 1979, University of Kansas, 1992; Fulbright Program Award, to Zimbabwe, 1987; National Endowment for the Humanities Fellowship, 1994. Memberships: Southern Black Cultural Alliance; Mississippi Historical Society; Association for the Study of Afro-American Life and History. Address: 2803 Yukon Drive, Columbia, MO 65202, USA

THOMPSON K Lloyd, b. 10 Feb 1945, Jackson, Mississippi, USA. Economist; Physicist. Education: AB, Princeton University, 1966; MSc, London School of Economics, 1967; MA, Stanford University, 1969; PhD, Trinity Hall, Cambridge University, 1979. Publications: Baked Beans, 1994. Contributions to: Agenda; Ambit; Argo; Honest Ulsterman; Literature Review; Orbis; Outposts; Poetry Review; Times Literary Supplement. Honours: Seatonian Prizes, 1987, 1989, 1990, 1991, 1992. Memberships: Judith E Wilson Workshop, Cambridge University; Poetry Society. Address: 4 Napier Street, Cambridge CB1 1HS, England.

THOMPSON Keith, b. 27 Sept 1947. Software Quality Manager. m. Caroline Ann, 18 May 1968, 1 daughter. Education: BA Literature, Open University; Member, Institute of Quality Assurance, 1986; Fellow, Institute of Management Specialist, 1986. Appointments: Royal Air Force, 1963-87; Software Quality Engineer, Manager and Consultant, 1987-95; English Teacher, part-time, Further Education, 1986-87. Publications: Goldmines at Thelnetham, 1991; Jasmine and Honeysuckle Pavilion, 1991; My Affair with Emily, 1991; Pedlar of Dreams, 1993. Contributions to: Open University Poets Workshop Magazine; Open University Poets Anthologies; Suffolk Astrology Journal; Pipesmoker's Guide; Odyssey; Anthologies: Poetry Now: A Deadly Game; Till Death us Do Part; East-Anglia Poetry; Euthanasia, 1996; Timely Poets, 1996; Parnassus of World Poets, 1994, 1995, 1996; Squillet of Wise Fools Gold, 1995; And God Created Woman, 1995. Honours: Scottish Open Poetry Competition Diploma, 1983; 2nd Prize, Newcastle Brown Ale Poetry Competition (poems on the underground), 1992. Memberships: Poetry Society; Open University Poetry Society, Chairman 1988-91; British Computer Society. Address: Bacchus, Hinderclay Road, Thelnetham, Diss, Suffolk IP22 1JZ, England.

THOMPSON Lucille, (E Whitney), b. 23 Aug 1926, Tobago. Teacher. m. 19 June 1954, 3 sons, 1 daughter. Publications: Pocket Book of Verse; Phoenix. Contributions to: Magazine of New Verse; Poetry Press; London Poetry Society. Memberships: London Poetry Society; ICA. Address: 35 Crown Dale, Upper Norwood, London SE19 3PB, England.

THOMPSON Rebecca Patricia, b. 14 Apr 1938, Dover, New Hampshire, USA. Teacher; Writer; Equity Actress. m. Ted van Griethuysen, 26 May 1962. Education: BA, History, English, University of New Hampshire; MA, Theatre Arts, Speech, Pennsylvania State University, 1960; Aesthetic Realism with Eli Siegel, 1961-78. Career: Instructor, Pennsylvania State University, 1959-60; Actress, New York City, 1971-82; Guest Lecturer: Kean College, New Jersey; Queens College, New York, 1970s; Instructor, Baldwin Center, Connecticut, 1984-86; Guest Lecturer, Houstatonic Community College, 1986; Poetry Instructor, Shakespeare Theatre at the Folger, Washington, District of Columbia, 1988-; Instructor, University of South California, 1989; Televised poetry readings, Kean College; 4 poetry recordings, MacMillan and Co, New York City; Lectures on Poetry and Ethics: Stratford Library Association, Connecticut; Libraries and schools throughout Connecticut; Conducts poetry workshops, New York City and Connecticut; Editor, Connecticut River Review national poetry journal. Publications: We Have Been There, essay, 1967; 1st book, 1992; Represented in 10 anthologies including 4 in honour of Poe, Eliot, Frost, Emily Dickinson. Contributions to: New York Quarterly; Midwest Quarterly; Daring Poetry Quarterly; Midwest Review; Notebook; A Little Magazine; Alura; Haven; New Poetry; Mind in Motiion; Pegasus; Slow's Ear; Hightide; Kentucky Poetry Review; Night Roses; Connecticut River Review; Reflect; Pinchpenny; Echoes; Feelings. Memberships: Connecticut Poetry Society, Past Secretary; Poetry Society of America. Address: 116 Sixth Street North East, No 61, Washington, DC 20002, USA.

THOMPSON Samuel Richard Charles, (Nat P. Mossham), b. 9 Feb 1968, London, England. Teacher. Education: BA, English, University of Manchester, 1990; Postgraduate Certificate in Education (Primary), Charlotte Mason College of Education. Appointments: Co-Editor, with the Photographer Simon O'Meara; Muse, literary and creative student based magazine, Manchester, 1989. Publications: Taken by a Wave, 1992; Fresh Fields, 1993; Criticism: A Linguistic Analysis of The Waste Land, 1989; Music in the Poetry of T S Eliot, 1990; These Fragments I Have Shored Against My Ruins - Poetry in the Primary School, 1991. Contributions to: Muse; All usual magazines in The Writers and Artists Yearbook. Honours: Thomas De Quincy Prize, University of Manchester, 1989. Memberships: Former Chair, Manchester University Poetry Society, 1990; Contributor, David

Rosenberg's International Mango Society; Poetry Society. Address: Tree House, 3 Woodsyre, Sydenham Hill, London SE26 6SS, England.

THOMSON Charles Geoffrey, b. 6 Feb 1953, Romford, Essex, England. Poet. m. Andrea Mestanek, 25 Oct 1974, diss 1980, 1 son. Education: Maidstone College of Art, 1975-79; FFIAD, 1979. Appointments: Writer-in-Residence. Borough of Bexley-GLAA, 1985; Resident Poet, Invicta Radio, 1987; Poetry Editor, Kent Companion, 1987-88; Poet-in-Residence, Medway Arts Centre, 1988; Artistic Consultant, National Convention of Poets and Small Presses, 1988; Writer-in-Residence, Stonehouse Hospital, 1989; Poetry Columnist, Kent Life, 1989-90; Poet-in Residence, SCEA Schools, Germany, 1993, 1994, 1995. Publications: The Middle Class, 1982; The Royal Tour, 1983' The End of the Boer War, 1985; The Art of Killing Chickens, 1985; Lunchtime Rhymes, 1988; Something to Sling in Your Shopping Basket, 1991; For Children: The Manic Computer, 1990; The Glurgle Gloop, 1992; I'm Brilliant, 1992. Contributions to: Broadcasts' ITV; TVS; BBC Radio 1; BBC Radio 4. Honours: Southeast Arts Literary Group Award, 1980; 1st Prize, Woman Royal Wedding Party Competition, 1987; The Forward Book of Poetry, 1993. Memberships: Poetry Society; ociety of Authors; National Association of Writers in Education; Betjeman Society; Medway Poets; National Association of Writers in Education, Committee Member. Address: 1 Bank Mansions, Golders Green Road, London NW11 8LG, England.

THOMSON Derick Smith, (Ruaraidh MacThòmais), b. 5 Aug 1921, Stornoway, Isle of Lewis, Scotland. University Teacher. m. Carol Galbraith, 1952, 5 sons, 1 daughter. Education: MA (Aberdeen), 1947; Emmanuel College, Cambridge; BA (Cambridge), 1948; FRSE, 1977; FBA, 1992. Appointments: Assistant in Celtic, University of Edinburgh, 1948-49; Lecturer in Welsh, 1949-56, Professor of Celtic, 1963-91, University of Glasgow; Reader in Celtic, University of Aberdeen, 1956-63. Publications: An Dealbh Briste, 1951; Eadar Samhradh is Foghar, 1967; An Rathad Cian, 1970; The Far Road and Other Poems, 1971; An Introduction to Gaelic Poetry, 1974, 1990; Saorsa agus an Iolaire, 1977; Creachadh na Clarsaich, 1982; The Companion to Gaelic Scotland, 1983, 1994; European Poetry in Gaelic Translation, 1990; Smeur an Dochais, 1992; Editor, Gairm Gaelic Literary Quarterly, 1952-; Gaelic Poetry in the Eighteenth Century, 1993; Meall Garbh/The Rugged Mountain, 1995. Contributions to: Gairm; Lines; Saltire Review; New Saltire; Scottish International; Planet; Stand; Scottish Review; Poetry Australia; Chapman; Courier; New Writing Scotland; Orbis; Poetry Ireland Review; Two Plus Two; Graph; Il Bimestro; Barn; Scotsman; New Dictionary of National Biography. Honours: Publication Award, Scottish Arts Council, 1971; Ossian Prize, FVS Foundation, Hamburg, 1974; Saltire Scottish Book of the Year, 1983; Honorary DLitt, University of Wales, 1987; Publications Award, Scottish Arts Council, 1992; Hon DLitt, University of Aberdeen, 1994. Membership: President, Scottish Gaelic Texts Society; Glasgow Arts Club. Address: 263 Fenwick Road, Giffnock, Glasgow G46 6JX, Scotland.

THOMSON Susan Clark, b. 14 Oct 1966, Scotland. Education: English Literature, Edinburgh University, 1991-95. Contributions to: Frogmore Papers; Third Half; Scratchings; Spokes; Odyssey; First Time; Peace and Freedom; Cokefish (US); Graffiti; Smiths Knoll. Memberships: National Poetry Society; Writers News. Address: 14 Candlemakers Park, Gilmerton, Edinburgh EH17 8TH, Scotland.

THORGEIRSSON Arni Ibsen, (Arni Ibsen), b. 17 May 1948, Stykkisholmur, Iceland. Dramaturg; Writer; Translator. m. Hildur Kristjansdottir, 20 Feb 1971, 3 sons. Education: Teacher's Diploma, Icelandic Teachers Training College, 1971; BA Honours, English, Drama, University of Exeter, England, 1975. Appointment: Teacher of English and Drama, Hafnarfjordur, 1988-, National Theatre of Iceland. Publications: Kom, 1975; Samuel Beckett: Prose, Plays, Poetry (translator, editor), 1987; Vort Skarda Lif, 1990; Plays: Oliver Twist, stage dramatisation, 1981; Skjaldbakan Kemst angad Lika, 1984; Afsakid Hle, 1989; Sky, 1990; Satirical sketches. Contributions to: Timarit Mals og Menningar; Teningur; Samvinnan; Lystraeninginn; Ljodaarbok AB, 1989; Lesbok Morgunbladsins; Transformation, England; Infolio, England; Translations of poetry to magazines; Theatre Companies of the World, 1986; The Cambridge Guide to World Theatre, 1988; Scandinavian Literary History, 1992; World Encyclopedia of Contemporary Theatre, 1993. Honour: Prize for Writing, Icelandic Writers Fund, 1985. Memberships: Icelandic Writers Union; Former Member and Chairman, Executive Committee, Icelandic Writers Fund; Executive Committee, Icelandic Playwrights Union; Former Member, Executive Committee, Reykjavik Arts Festival. Address: Stekkjarkinn 19, 220 Hafnafjordur, Iceland.

THORN Howard Stephen, b. 26 May 1929, London, England. m. 19 Mar 1955. Draughtsman (Electrical and Civil/Structural Engineering). Education: Elementary School, 1936-41; Central School, 1941-45; ONC Mechanical Engineering, Technical College, 1945-50. Publications; The Grand Anthology of Poetry, 1971; An Awakening of the Spirit in Verse, 1973; A Passage in Time, anthology, 1996. Contributions to: Soldiers of the Queen; The Cadmium Blue Literary Journal. Honours: Semi-Finalist, International Society of Poets Competition, 1995. Membership: Authors' Licensing and Collecting Society Limited, London. Address: 37 Crossways, Sittingbourne, Kent ME10 4RJ, England.

THORNE Peter. See: **DANIEL Geoffrey Peter.**

THORNTON Donald Ray, b. 15 Dec 1936, Winnsborro, Louisiana, USA. Educator; Poet; Artist. m. Suzannah Smith. Education: BA, Art Education, Louisiana Tech University, 1960; MA, Design, Louisiana State University, 1967; MA coursework, University of Southwestern Louisiana, 1988. Appointments: Union Arts and Crafts and Gallery Manager, Louisiana State University,1964-67; Instructor, Art, Architecture, University of Southern Louisiana, 1967-73; Artist-in-Residence, College of Mainland, 1973, 1976; Work with gifted children, 1988-92; Illustrator, books, magazines. Publications: Outcry, 1960; Sounding, 1976; A Walk On Water, 1985; Ascending, 1993; Mentor, 1993; Editor: Hypethral; Writeright; Whiffle; Pelican. Contributions to: Poet; Black Creek Review; Still; Southwestern Review; Poetry Texas; Nexus; Pink Chameleon; Poetic Images; Crab Creek Review; Info; Cedar Rock; Published; Slipstream; KRAX; Black Mountain Review; Planets and Plants; ArtBeat; Impetus; RSVP; Implosion; Dark Horse; Museum of Haiku Literature, Tokyo; Bad Haircut; Fireside Poetry Review; Golden Isis; The Pink Chameleon; Skylark; Hoka Hey; Literary Markets; Sidley Center Journal; Piedmont Literary Review; Late Knocking; G W Review; Uncle; Anthologies: Travois, 1976; Ellensburg Anthology, 1985; New Poet's Anthology, 1986; Dan River Anthology, 1987; 9th Annual Anthology, CSS Pub, 1986; Aquarius Anthology, 1986; American Poetry Anthology, 1987; Hearts on Fire, 1987; Suicide Notes, 1987; A New Day, 1987; Poet's 87 Anthology, 1987; Many Voices, Many Lands, 1987; Rainbows and Rhapsodies, 1989. Memberships: Association for Gifted and Talented; Artist Alliance of Lafayette. Address: 1504 Howard Street, New Iberia, LA 70560, USA.

THORNTON Margaret. See: **POOLE Margaret Barbara (Peggy).**

THORODDSEN Dagur Sigurdarson, b. 6 Aug 1937, Reykjavik, Iceland. Poet; Painter. 4 sons, 5 daughters. Education: University study, Literature, Philosophy, 1 year. Appointments: Film Scriptwriter; Opera Librettist; Mountaineer. Publications: Milljónaaevintyri, 1955; Hlutabréf í sólarlaginu, 1958; Nid stong hin meiri, 1965; Nokkur Amerísk ljód, translations of American poems, 1966; Rógmálmur og grásilfur, 1971; Frumskógardrottningin fórnar Tarsan, 1974; Med vitud breikkun á raskati, 1974; Fagurskinna, 1976; Venjuleg husmódir, 1977; Sólskinsfifl, 1980; Drepum Drepum (with Einar Olafsson), 1980; Fyrir Laugavegsgos, 1985; Glimuskjálfti, complete works, 1989. Contributions to: Timarit Máls og menningar; Skirnir; Lystraeninginn; Morgunbladid; Thjódviljinn; Birtingur; Many other papers. Honours: Artists' salary, State of Iceland. Membership: Authors Society of Iceland. Address: Miklubraut 34, 105 Reykjavík, Iceland.

THORPE Dobbin. See: **DISCH Thomas M.**

THRILLING Isobel Marjorie, b. 1935, Hadleigh, Suffolk, England. Teacher; Writer. m. Harold Thrilling, 1961, 1 son, 1 daughter. Education: BA, Hons, Hull University, 1957; PGCE, 1958. Appointments: Various teaching posts; Currently Head of Service ESOL (English for Speakers of Other Languages) for London Borough of Havering. Publications: Ultrasonics of Snow, 1985; Spectrum-Shift, 1991. Contributions to: Torks TV; Encounter; Cornhill Magazine; Arts Council Anthology; Outposts; Country Life; Essex Countryside; Other Poetry; Cosmopolitan; Good Housekeeping; Lady; BBC Radio 3, 4 and 4; Longmans GCSE Anthology, 1992; BBC/Longman Poetry of War, 1991; Viking Anthology, 1992; Poetry Book Society Anthology 2, 1992; Speak to the Hills Anthology; Women's Press Anthology. Honours: Havering Bursary, 1991; 1st Prize, Stroud, 1979; 1st Prize, Bridport (Joint), 1982; 1st Prize, Nottingham; 1st Prize, Full House Competition, 1982; 1st Prize, Kent/Sussex, 1987; 1st Prize, Envoi Competition, 1990; 1st Prize, Essex Challenge Cup; 1st Prize, Suffolk Poetry Competition (Crabbe); Various 2nd and 3rd prizes.

THULASIKUMARI H. See: **NAIDU Tulsi.**

THURIDUR Gudmundsdottir, b. 16 Nov 1939, Iceland. Teacher. Education: Reykjavik City College, 1960; Icelandic Teachers College, 1963. Appointments: Teacher, 1963-82; City Hospital, 1982-89; Currently an Assistant, Association of Invalids in Iceland. Publications: Only One Flower, 1989; Your Cloudy Laughter, 1972; On the Balcony, 1975; And There was Spring, 1980; The Autumn Told Me, 1985; The Words Grow Around Me, 1989; The Night is Listening to Me, 1994. Contributions to: Morgunladid (newspaper); Mal og Menning, Andvari, and 19 Juni, (periodicals); Die Horen (German literary periodical); Innocence of the Zodiac; Ljodspeglar and Ljodspor (collection of poems). Honours: Literature Awards, Writers Union of Iceland, 1973, 1983, 1991. Memberships: Icelandic Authors Association; Writers Union of Iceland. Address: Asvallagata 40, 101 Reykjavík, Iceland.

THWAITE Anthony Simon, b. 23 June 1930, Chester, Cheshire, England. Writer. m. Ann Harrop, 4 Aug 1955, 4 daughters. Education: Kingswood School, Bath, 1944-49; Major Open Scholar, Christ Church, Oxford, BA, 1955, MA, 1959. Appointments: Literary Editor, The Listener, 1962-65; New Statesman, 1968-72; Co-editor, Encounter, 1973-85. Publications: Twentieth Century English Poetry, 1978; Six Centuries of Verse, 1984; Poems 1953-88, 1989; Co-Editor, Penguin Book of Japanese Verse, 1964, latest reprint 1987; Editor: Philip Larkin: Collected Poems, 1988, Selected Letters of Philip Larkin 1940-85, 1992. Contributions to: Numerous publications. Honours: Richard Hillary Memorial Prize, 1968; Cholmondeley Award, 1983; Honorary DLitt, University of Hull, 1989; Officer of the Order of the British Empire, 1990; Honorary Fellow, Westminster College, Oxford, 1990. Memberships: Numerous professional organizations including: Avalon World Arts Association; Modern Poetry Association; American Name Society; National Council of Teachers of English; American Association of University Professors. Address: The Mill House, Low Tharston, Norfolk NR15 2YN, England.

THWAITES (Stephen) Dane, b. 15 June 1950, Inverell, New South Wales, Australia. Bookseller. Separated, 1 son. Education: BA, English Literature, University of Nebraska, Armidale, 1971. Appointments: Delivery Driver; Gardener; Bookseller; Publisher, Black Lightning Press Poetry Series; Manager, Black Lightning Press Poetry Distribution; Formerly, Editor, Compass. Publications: Winter Light, 1983; South China,1994. Contributions to: Compass; Image; New Poetry; Poetry Australia; Lino; Meanjin; Southerly; Overland; ABC. Honour: 1987 Mattara Prize (joint). Address: c/o Butterfly Bookshop, Shop 6, Renae's Arcade, Station Street, Wentworth Falls, New South Wales 2782, Australia.

TICE Arden A, (Arden MacNab, Arden Eckles, Hava Arden), b. 8 Mar 1938, Lawton, Oklahoma, USA. Psychotherapist; Psychologist; Social Worker; Teacher. Education: BA, English/Psychology (minor), University of Texas at Austin, 1951; Master's Degree in Psychology, Saint Matthew University, Columbus, Ohio, 1971; Graduate work: University of New Mexico, Albuquerque, 1968 (12 hours); Mental Health; 1986-87 (6 hours) Creative Writing. Appointments: Director, Alcoholism Treatment, Southwest Mental Health Centre, Las Cruces, New Mexico, 1973-74; Psychology Instructor, El Paso Community College, Texas, 1974-81; Psychotherapist (private practice) El Paso, Texas, 1978-88. Publications: Take It and Fake the Rest, 1974; Wind in My Fist, 1990; The Augmented Moon, 1991; Looking for the Frontier, 1992; A Naming of Women. Contributions to: Wormwood Review; Ferment; Adept; New Mexican; South Dakota Review; Gusher; Texas Observer; University of Houston Forum. Membership: American Association of Artist-Therapists (Registered Poetry and/or Experimental Psychotherapist). Address: PO Box 7403, Albuquerque, NM 87194, USA.

TICE Bradley Scott, b. 6 Oct 1959, Palo Alto, California, USA. Researcher. Education: AA Liberal Arts, De Anza College, 1983; BA History, San Jose State University, 1987; AA, MDL, De Anza College, 1995; PhD Chemistry, Fairfax University, 1996. Appointment: Researcher for Pacific Language Institute Cupertino, California, USA, 1993-. Publication: Suburban White, chapbook, 1996. Contributions to: Anthologies: Crossings, 1995; Inspirations, 1996; A Moment in Time, 1995; Best Poems of 1996, 1996; Walk Through Paradise, 1995; Windows of the Soul, 1995. Honours: Editor's Choice Awd, 1995, 1996; 3rd Prize, North American Open Poetry, 1996; President's Award, 1996; Honorable Mention, 1995; Honorable Mention Summer, 1995;

Citation, 1995. Memberships: International Society of Poets, 1994-95, 1995-96. Address: PO Box 2214, Cupertino, CA 95015-2214, USA.

TICE Richard Ellis, b. 29 Nov 1950, Oakland, California, USA. Editor. m. Kathleen Tripp, 9 Oct 1982, 3 sons, 2 daughters. Education: BA, Comparative Literature, Brigham Young University, 1975. Appointments: English Teacher, Shimamura Foreign Language Institute, Maebashi City, Japan, 1976-80; Student Instructor, Brigham Young University, Utah, USA, 1980-81; Indexer, Proofreader, 1982, Assistant Editor, 1982-86, Associate Editor, 1989-, Deseret Book Company, Salt Lake City, Utah; Editor, Publisher, Dragonfly: East-West Haiku Quarterly, 1985-; Assistant Editor, Ensign Magazine, Salt Lake City, 1986-89. Publication: Station Stop: A Collection of Haiku and Related Forms, 1986. Contributions to: Cicada; Dragonfly; Ensign; Frogpond; Harvest; Inscape; Mainichi Daily News; Mainichi Sande; Poetry Nippon; Poetry Panorama; Sunstone; Yomiuri Shimbun; Anthologies: A Celebration of Christmas; An Anthology of Haiku by People of the United States and Canada; Contemporary Mormon Poems; Utah Sings. Honours: 1st Place, Hart-Larson Poetry Contest, Brigham Young University, 1981; 1st Place, Newcomer's Poetry Category, 1984; 1st Place, Roberts Poetry Category and Published Book Category, 1986; League of Utah Writers Writing Contest. Memberships: Utah State Poetry Society; League of Utah Writers, Past President; Former Member, Poetry Society of Japan. Address: 5737 Middlewood Avenue, Salt Lake City, UT 84118, USA.

TICHY Susan Elizabeth, b. 25 Apr 1952, Washington, District of Columbia, USA. Professor of English. m. Lewis Michael O'Hanlon, 29 Jan 1982. Education: BA, Goddard College, 1976; MA, University of Colorado, 1979; Other coursework at Macalester College, University of California at Berkeley. Appointments: Visiting Associate Professor, Ohio University, 1987; Artist in Residence, Colorado Council on the Arts and Humanities, 1987-88; Assistant Professor, 1988-93, Associate Professor, 1993-, George Mason University, Fairfax, Virginia. Publications: The Hands in Exile, 1983; A Smell of Burning Starts the Day, 1988; Weeping, in manuscript. Contributions to: Antioch Review; American Voice; Beloit Poetry Journal; Five Fingers Review; Indiana Review; High Plains Literary Review; Tonantzin; Northwest Review; Ploughshares; Sing Heavenly Muse; Black Warrior Review; Guadalupe Review. Honours: National Poetry Series, 1983; Eugene Kayden Award, 1985; Pushcart Prize, 1987; National Endowment for the Arts Fellowship, 1988; Nominee for Dewars Performing Arts Award, 1991. Memberships: Poets and Writers; Associated Writing Program; Academy of American Poets. Address: c/o Department of English, George Mason University, Fairfax, VA 22030, USA.

TIERNEY Karl Joseph, b. 15 June 1956, Westfield, Massachusetts, USA. Word Processor; Poet. Education: BA, English, Emory University, Atlanta, Georgia, 1980; MFA, Creative Writing (Poetry), University of Arkansas, 1983. Contributions to: American Poetry Review; Berkeley Poetry Review; James White Review; Crazyquilt Quarterly; Contact II; Exquisite Corpse; Oregonian; San Francisco Sentinel; Equinox. Honours: Finalist, Walt Whitman Award, 1992. Membership: PEN (USA, West division), 1989-. Address: 6-B Sumner Street, San Francisco, CA 94103, USA.

TIERNEY Richard Louis, b. 7 Aug 1936, Spencer, Iowa, USA. Science Fiction and Fantasy Fiction Writer. Education: BS, Entomology, Iowa State University, 1961. Appointments: Canoe Guide, Sommers Canoe Base, Ely, Minnesota, 1956-58; US Forest Laboratory and Field Assistant, Oregon, Alaska, California, New Mexico, Montana, Minnesota, 1958-71; Writer, Editor, Llewellyn Publications, St Paul, Minnesota, 1972-73. Publications: Collected Poems: Nightmares and Visions, 1981; The House of the Toad, 1983. Contributions to: Weird Tales; Twilight Zone. Address: 2419 South Jefferson Mason City, IA 50401, USA.

TIGAR Chad. See: **LEVI Peter.**

TILLINGHAST Richard Williford, b. 25 Nov 1940, Memphis, Tennessee, USA. Professor of English. m. Mary Graves Tillinghast, 22 April 1973, 3 sons, 1 daughter. Education: AB cum laude, English, University of the South, Sewanee, 1962; AM, English, 1963, PhD, English, 1970, Harvard University. Appointments: Editorial Assistant, Sewanee Review, 1961-62; Tutor, Teaching Fellow, 1964-68, Briggs-Copeland Lecturer, 1980-83, Harvard University; Assistant Professor, English, University of California, Berkeley, 1968-73; Instructor, College of Marin, 1976-79; Associate Professor, English,

1983-92, Professor of English, 1992-, University of Michigan. Publications: Sleep Watch, 1969; The Knife and Other Poems, 1980; Sewanee in Ruins, 1981; Our Flag Was Still There, 1984; The Stonecutter's Hand (poems), 1995; Robert Lowell: Damaged Grandeur (critical memoir), 1995. Contributions to: Atlantic Monthly; Nation; New Republic; Poetry; Partisan Review; Sewanee Review; Hudson Review; Southern Review; Antaeus; New Yorker PN Review; New Left Review; Poetry Ireland Review; Ploughshares; Salmon, Ireland; New England Review; Georgia Review; Boston Review; Virginia Quarterly Review; Shenandoah; Michigan Quarterly Review; Harper's; New York Times. Honours: Sinclair-Kennedy Travel Grant, Harvard University, 1966-67; National Endowment for the Humanities Grant, 1981; Mary Roberts Rinehart Foundation Grant, 1982; Michigan Arts Council Grant, 1986; Amy Lowell Travel Fellowship, residence in Ireland, 1990-91; British Council Travel Grant, Northern Ireland, 1993. Memberships: Poetry Society of America; Modern Language Association; Associated Writing Programs. Address: 1317 Granger Avenue, Ann Arbor, MI 48104, USA.

TIMONEY JENKIN Ann, b. 6 July 1933, London, England. Poet. Div. 2 sons, 1 daughter. Education: London University; South Australian Institute of Teachers (Music), 1980. Appointments: Music Teacher, Annesley College, Adelaide, 1980-90; Currently full-time Writer. Publications: Midwinter Light, Collection of Poetry, 1995; Anthologies: The Inner Courtyard, 1990; Poets at Play, 1991; The Sea's White Edge, 1992; Patterson Literary Review, 1992, 1994; Friendly Street Poetry Reader, nos 7-17, 1983-93; Anthologised in Hope & Fear: An Anthology of S A Women's Writing, 1994; Anthologised in: Tuesday Night Live: An Anthology of 15 Years of Friendly Street Poetry, 1994. Contributions to: Bulletin; Quadrant; Poetry Australia; Adelaide Review. Honours: Individual Arts Project Grant, South Australia Department for the Arts and Cultural Heritage. Memberships: Australian Society for Authors; Friendly Street Poets. Address: 10 Margaret Street, Norwood, South Australia 5067, Australia.

TIPTON David John, b. 28 Apr 1934, Birmingham, England. Writer; Publisher; Teacher. m. (1) Ena Hollis, 10 June 1956, (2) Glenys Tipton, Feb 1975, 2 sons, 3 daughters. Education: Certificate of Education, Saltley College, 1959; University of Essex, 1976-77. Appointments: Editor, Rivelin Press, 1974-84, Redbeck Press, 1984-93; Teaching Posts in Buenos Aires, Birmingham, Lima, Sheffield and Bradford. Publications: Millstone Grit, 1972, reprinted 1993; Nomads and Settlers, 1980; Wars of the Roses, 1984; Turning to Alcohol, Horses or Dreams of Travel, 1991; At Night the Cats - translations of the poems of Antonio Cisneros, 1985; Peru, The New Poetry, translations, 1970-76; Green and Purple, 1993; Crossing the Rimac, 1995. Contributions to: Ambit; London Magazine; Poetry Review; Poetry (Chicago); Stand; Beloit Poetry Journal; Evergreen Review; Tribune; Wide Skirt; Echo Room; Outposts; Translation; Tri-Quarterly. Address: 24 Aireville Road, Frizinghall, Bradford BD9 4HH, England.

TOBIAS-TURNER Bessye, b. 10 Oct 1917, Liberty, Mississippi, USA. Poet; Lecturer; Retired Educator. Education: AB, English, Rust College; MA, Literature, MA, Speech, Columbia University; PhD, Literature, World University, 1977. Appointments: Honorary Vice-President, Centro Studi Scambi Internazionale, Italy; Participant, World Congress of Poets, 1976, 1979, 1981, 1988; Director-General, Librae Foundation for the Arts and Culture, 1990-. Publications: La Librae: Anthology of Poetry for Living, 1968; Peace and Love, 1972; Laurel Leaves for Bess, 1977. Contributions to: Anthologies: World Congress of Poets, Seoul, Korea, 1979; International Poetry Conference, Tokyo, 1980; World Congress of Poets, USA, 1981; World of Poetry, Korea, 1983, 1984; Accademia d'Europa, 1984, 1985, 1987, 1990; Poetry Conference, Taipei, Taiwan, 1986; World Congress of Poets, Bangkok, 1989; Masters of Modern Poetry. Honours: Certificate, Award, Clover International Poetry Association, 1976; Crowned Poet Laureate, 1977; Grand Prix Mediterranee, 1983, 1984; Grand Prix Etoiles d'Europa, 1986; Academia d'Europa; Special Guest Poet, Asian Poets Conference, Japan, 1984; Gold Medal, Silver Medal, Centro Studie e Scambi Internazionale; Medal, United Poets Laureate International, 1986, 1987; Gold Medallion, 1986, 1989; Grand Prix Etoiles Mediterranees, 1989. Memberships: World Congress of Poets World Academy of Arts and Poetry, Board Member USA 1981; Associate, Academy of American Poets; Distinguished Member, The International Society of Poets, Associate Membership, 1993. Address: 829 Wall Street. McComb, MS 39648, USA.

TOLMACHYOV Vlad, b. 28 Jan 1962, St Petersburg, Russia. Poet; Computer Consultant. m. Jane Maiskaya, 16 July 1988. Education: BA, New York University, 1985. Appointments: Executive Secretary, Youth Section, Olympoetry-Barcelona 92; Editor, Bridge of Friends. Publications: The Second Beginning, 1990; Poetry of Vlad Tolmachyov, 1991; Under the Dome of a Carrousel, 1992. Contributions to: Bridge of Friends International Poetry Magazine; New Review Magazine; The Russian Daily Newspaper; World Poetry 1990, anthology; Encounters; Almanach-91. Honours: 1st Prize, Poetry Competition, International Pushkin Society, 1990; White Aster for work towards friendship and cooperation of artists of the world, Friends of Globe Poetry, 1991. Memberships: Library of World Poetry; Writers Club, Columbia University Slavic Department. Address: 67 Oxford Street, Glen Ridge, NJ 07028, USA.

TOMALIN Ruth, b. County Kilkenny, Ireland. Writer. m. (2), 1 son. Education: Journalism course, King's College, London, 1939. Appointments: Women's Land Army, 1941-42; Staff Reporter, Evening News, Portsmouth, 1942; Staff Reporter, various newspapers; Press Reporter, London Courts of Law, 1965. Publications: Threnody for Dormice, 1947; Deer's Cry, 1952; Represented in 2 anthologies of poetry from World War II. Contributions to: Observer; Fortnightly Review; Adelphi; Aylesford Review; Others. Address: c/o Faber and Faber, Publishers, 3 Queen Square, London WC1N 3AU, England.

TOMASEVIC Bosko, b. 8 May 1947, Becej, Yugoslavia. Poet; Professor of Literary Theory. m. (1) Rajka Gnjatic, 24 May 1975, div, 2 sons; (2) Vera Kureluk, 12 March, 1995. Education: BA cum laude, Belgrade University, 1972; MA cum laude, University of Belgrade, 1976; PhD, University of Belgrade, 1982. Appointments: Freelance Writer, 1974-90; Visiting Professor of Literary Theory, University of Nancy, 1990-92; Freelance Writer, 1993-96. Publications: Cartesian Passage, 1989; Watchman of the Times, 1990; Celan-Studies, 1991; Repetition and Difference, 1992; Cool Memories, 1994; Live Coals, 1994; Landscape with Wittgenstein and Other Ruins, 1995; Open Space and Presence, 1995; Plan of the Return, 1996. Contributions to: Letopis Matice Srpske; Polja; Oko; Nota Bene; Delo and others. Memberships: European Academy of Sciences, Arts & Literature; New York Academy of Science; Société des Gens des Lettres de France; PEN French Club; International Comparative Literature Association; Martin Heidegger Association. Address: 7/11 rue de St Lambert, Imb 4, Appt 422, F-54000 Nancy, France.

TOMAZOS Criton, b. 13 Apr 1940, Cyprus. Architect; Painter; Writer; Theatre Designer; Dramatist; Journalist; Film and TV Scriptwriter. Education: Diploma, Architecture, Regent St Polytechnic, London, 1964; Scholarship, Theatre Design, Croydon College of Fine Art and Technology, 1977; Scholarship, Advanced Writing, TV, Film, London Academy of TV and Film, 1981. Appointments: Architect, Sir Denys Lasdun, York Rosenburg and Mardall, Sir William Halcrow and Partners, other firms, Greater London Council, London Boroughs of Camden and Haringey, other public authorities; Formerly Actor, Theatre Designer, Writer, at Theatre Technis; Co-Founder, Past Chairman, Resident Playwright, Prometheus Theatre Co. Publications: In English: Lovepoem, 1965; Relationships, 1975; 2 wizuhu cries mice up in nests: Factory Back Yard, 1978; First Explorations, 1990; In Greek: Monologue of the Ancient Hero and Other Poems, 1971; Transparencies (Diaphanies), 1975; Night March, 1979; He Who Left His Fingerprints, 1979; Borders of Memory, 1987-88; The Visit, 1988; To Paramythi tou Nerou, 1990; Poems of 1960-61, in Greek and English, 1981; Represented in 16 Cypriot Poets, 1982; Tora (Now), Poems in Greek, 1994; Environmental Forum: Poetry: Music: Architecture: Graphics (editor), 1970-71. Contributions to: Various magazines and newspapers. Memberships: Theatre Writers Union; Founder, Director, Coordinator, Environmental Forum and Theatre for Mankind; Committee, New Playwrights Trust; Formerly: Arts Together; Poets Conference; Islington Art Circle; Writers Forum; Poetry Society; British Film Institute; International Society of Dramatists; London Screenwriters Workshop; The Centre. Address: c/o Environmental Forum, 12a Ennis Road, London, N4 3HD, England.

TOMBO. See: HARR Lorraine Ellis.

TOMLINSON (Alfred) Charles, b. 8 Jan 1927, Stoke-on-Trent, Staffordshire, England. Professor of English. m. 23 Oct 1948, 2 daughters. Education: Queens' College, Cambridge, 1945-48; BA, MA, Cambridge; MA, London. Appointments: Lecturer, 1956-68, Reader 1968-82, Professor, 1982-92, Emeritus Professor, 1992-, University of Bristol; Visiting Professor, University of New Mexico, USA, 1962-63;

O'Connor Professor, Colgate University, New York, 1967-68, 1989-90; Visiting Fellow of Humanities, Princeton University, 1981; Lamont Professor, Union College, New York, 1987. Publications: Relations and Contraries, 1951; The Necklace, 1955, 1966; Seeing is Believing, 1958; Enlarged Edition, 1960; A Peopled Landscape, 1963; American Scenes, 1966; The Way of a World, 1969; The Poem as Initiation, 1968; Written on Water, 1972; The Way In, 1974; The Shaft, 1978; Selected Poems, 1978; The Flood, 1981; Notes from New York, 1984; Collected Poems, 1985, 1987; The Return, 1987; Poesies Choisies, 1987; Nella pienezza del tempo, 1987; Annunciations, 1989; The Door in the Wall, 1992; Poemas, 1992; Sette Poesie, 1993; Gedichte, 1994; La Insistencia de las cosas, 1994; Jubilation, 1995; In italia, 1995; Zipangu, 1995; Joint collections; Graphics with poems; Poetry translations. Contributions to: Agenda; New Yorker; Antaeus; Cultures, Madrid; Encounter; Essays in Criticism; Northward Journal, Toronto; Exile, Toronto; Hudson Review; Listener; London Magazine; Nation; New Statesman; Parnassus; Paris Review; Times Literary Supplement; Scripsi, Australia; Poetry Chicago; Poetry Review; Poetry Nation Review; Sunday Times; Sagatrieb; Sewanee Review; Spectator; Vuelta, Mexico City; Sunday Observer; Sunday Times; Universities Quarterly. Honours: USA: Bess Hokin Prize, 1956; Oscar Blumenthal Prize, 1960; Union League Arts Foundation Prize, 1961; Inez Boulton Prize, 1964; Frank O'Hara Prize, 1968; Wilbur Award for Poetic Achievement, 1982; Bennett Award for Literature, New York 1992; UK: Cheltenham Poetry Prize, 1976; Cholmondeley Poetry Award, 1979; Italy: Premio Europeo di Cittadella, 1991; Honorary Fellow: Queens' College, Cambridge, 1974; Royal Holloway and Bedford New College, University of London, 1991; Hon Doctorates: Keele University, 1981; Colgate University, 1981; University of New Mexico, 1986. Address: Brook Cottage, Ozleworth Bottom, Wotton-under-Ege, Glos GL12 7QB, England.

TONG Raymond, b. 20 Aug 1922, Winchester, Hampshire, England. British Council Administrator (retired). m. Mariana Apergis, 16 Nov 1946. Education: BSc Honours, Economics, 1948, DipEd, 1949, London University. Appointments: Education Officer, Senior Education Officer, Nigeria, 1949-58 and Uganda, 1958-61; Posts included Principal, Government Teacher Training College, Ibadan; Inspector of Secondary Schools, Western Province, Uganda; British Council, South America, India, Middle East, England, 1961-82; Posts included Director, Baghdad, British Council Representative, Kuwait, Regional Director, Eastern Region, England. Publications: Today The Sun, 1947; Angry Decade, 1950; African Helicon, anthology, 1954, 2nd edition, 1975; Fabled City, 1960; A Matter of History, 1976; Crossing the Border, 1978; Selected Poems, 1994. Contributions to: Adelphi; Review of English Literature; Poetry Review; Ariel; New Poetry; PEN Broadsheet; Contemporary Review; Dublin Magazine; Encounter; Spectator; New Statesman; Outposts Poetry Quarterly; Chapman; Lines Review; New Welsh Review; Iron; Orbis; Samphire; Rialto; Acumen; English; New Humanist; Overseas publications include: Meanjin, Australia; Wormwood Review, USA; Fiddlehead, Canada; Arena, New Zealand; Bim, Barbados. Memberships: Life Member, Poetry Society; West Country Writers Association. Address: 1 Beaufort Road, Clifton, Bristol BS8 2JT, England.

TONOS. See: **MEREDITH Jennifer Margaret (Jenni)**.

TOPAL Carine, b. 5 May 1949, New York, New York, USA. Teacher of Learning Handicapped. m. Victor Gorsky, 12 July 1987, 1 son. Education: BA, Sociology, Anthropology, C W Post College, 1971; MA, Special Education, New York University, 1974. Appointments: Teacher of Profoundly Handicapped, 1975-80; Teacher of Severely Emotionally Disturbed, 1980-88; Teacher of Learning Handicapped, 1988-. Publication: Edging the Nile, chapbook, 1989. Contributions to: Caliban; Pacific Review; Poetry, Los Angeles; Tzunami; California Quarterly; West Word; Interim; Green's Magazine; On the Bus; Vol No; Sculpture Gardens Review; Embers; Blue Building; Pembroke Magazine; Blue Window. Honours: Double 1st Prize, Poetry Contests, Embers, 1988; Finalist, Roberts Writing Award, 1990. Membership: Academy of American Poets. Address: 25061 Via Bajo Cerro, Laguna Niguel, CA 92677, USA.

TORREGIAN Sotère Sheikh Al-Mustapha, b. 25 June 1941. Poet; Scholar; Teacher; Philosopher. Div, 2 daughters. Education: Philosophy, Rutgers University, USA. Appointments: Instructor, Black American Literature, African Literature and Philosophy, Assistant to the Director, Afro-American Studies, 1969-73, Honorary Visiting Scholar, African and Third World Affairs, 1989-90, Stanford University; Visiting Lecturer, African and Third World Ideology, Art and Literature,

University of Santa Clara, Santa Clara, California, 1970-72; Assistant to President, PEDA Corporation, Palo Alto, California, 1990-92. Publications: Song for Woman, 1965; The Golden Palomino Bites the Clock, 1966; The Wounded Mattress, 1968; City of Light, 1971; The Age of Gold, Poems, 1968-70, 1976; The Young Englishwoman, poems and prose manuscript facsimile, 1989; AMTRAK-Trek, poems between Menlo Park, California, en route to New York; The Newark Cantos. Contributions to: Art and Literature, Isère, France; Paris Review; Il Tarocco, Italy; Rutgers Literary Review; Bay Review; Chelsea; Andy Warhol Monster Issue. Honours: Frank O'Hara Award, Modern American Poetry, 1968; Author of the Year, Gotham Book Mart, New York City, 1976. Address: 1010 Tamarack Avenue, San Carlos, CA 94070-3746, USA.

TOTH Eva, b. 30 Jan 1939, Debrecen, Hungary. Writer. m. Gabor Ambrus, 1 son. Education: Hungarian and French Languages and Literatures, 1962, Spanish Language and Literature, 1968, Eotvos Lorand University, Budapest. Appointments: Editor, Hungarian Radio, 1967; Editor in Chief, Corvina weekly, 1984; Fellow, International Writing Program, Iowa, 1982; Merrill Associate, Catherine's College, Oxford, 1989; Foreign Secretary, Hungarian Writers Association, 1990; Council, International Federation of Translators; Co-President, Committee for Translation of Poetry, 1990. Publications: Egyetlen Ertelem, 1977; Hohatá, 1982; Kamfor Benedek, 1986; Wanted, 1992; Limited de las nieves eternas, 1992; Antologia de la poesia hungara, 1981, 1983; Teatro Hungaro, 1984; MA Today Aujourd'hui, Heute, CerogH, 1987. Contributions to: Iowa Review; Feminist Review; Skylark; Insul; Fulbright Visiting Professors, 1992; Vice-President, Hungarian PEN Club, 1994. Memberships: Hungarian Writers Association; Hungarian PEN Club; The American Poetry Review, Promete, Le Spantole. Address: Csalan u 45/B, Fszt 2, 1025, Budapest, Hungary.

TOWNLEY Roderick Carl, b. 7 June 1942, New Jersey, USA. Writer. m. Wyatt Townley, 15 Feb 1986, 1 son, 1 daughter. Education: AB, Bard College, New York; PhD, Rutgers University, New Jersey, 1972. Appointments: Professor of English, Universidad de Concepcion, Chile, South America, 1978-79; National Editorial Writer, TV Guide, magazine, 1980-89; Senior Editor, US, magazine, 1989-90; Freelance Journalist, 1990-95; Executive Director, The Writers Place, Kansas City, Missouri, USA, 1995-96. Publications: Blue Angels, Black Angels, poetry, 1972; The Early Poetry of William Carlos Williams, criticism, 1975; Minor Gods, novel, 1977; Three Musicians, poetry, 1978; Final Approach, poetry, 1986. Contributions include: The Paris Review; The Smith, New York; The Village Voice, Ne York; New Letters; The North American Review; Western Humanities Review. Honours: Co-Winner, 1969, Winner First Prize, 1971, Academy of American Poets University Prize; Finalist, Yale Series of Younger Poets, 1976; Fulbright Professorship, Chile, 1978-79. Address: PO Box 13302, Shawnee Mission, KS 66282, USA.

TOWNLEY Wyatt, b. 20 Sept 1954, Kansas City, Missouri, USA. Writer. m. Roderick Carl Townley, 15 Feb 1986, 1 daughter. Education: BFA, Dance, Purchase College, State University of New York, 1977; North Carolina School of the Arts. Appointments: Co-Artistic Director, Dancers' Portfolio, New York, 1976-80; Dancer, actress and poet, 1980-86; Poet, journalist and teacher, 1986-; Poetry Editor, The Newspaper, Brooklyn, New York, 1988-90; Co-Editor, The Keep, tri-quarterly publication of The Writers' Place, Kansas City, Missouri, USA, 1992-94. Publication: Perfectly Normal, 1990. Contributions include: The Paris Review; New Letters; Western Humanities Review; Pulpsmith; The Midwest Quarterly. Honours: First Recipient, Presidential Award for Outstanding Achievement, Purchase College, State University of New York, 1977; Finalist, The Yale Series of Younger Poets, 1989. Memberships: Academy of American Poets; Society of Children's Book Writers and Illustrators; Board of Governors, The Writers Place. Address: PO Box 13302, Shawnee Mission, KS 66282, USA.

TOWNSEND Ann, b. 5 Dec 1962, Pittsburgh, Pennsylvania, USA. Professor; Poet. m. David Baker, 19 July 1987, 1 daughter. Education: BA, Denison University, 1985; MA, English, 1987, PhD, English, 1991, Ohio State University. Appointment: Assistant Professor, English, Denison University, 1992-. Publication: Modern Love, 1995. Contributions to: The Nation; The Kenyon Review; Tri-Quarterly; The Southern Review; The North America Review. Honours: Breadloaf Scholarship for Poetry, 1991; The Nation Prize for Poetry, 1994; The Pushcart Prize for Poetry, 1995. Memberships:

Associated Writing Programs; Poets and Writers. Address: Department of English, Denison University, Granville, OH 43023, USA.

TOWNSEND Jill, b. 6 Mar 1950, Guildford, Surrey, England. Writer. m. Glyn Davies, 6 Nov 1971. Contributions to: Anthologies: Spoils, The Poetry Business Anthology, 1991; Frogmore Poetry Prize Anthology, 1987-91; Oxford Reading Tree; Poetry Street 2, 1991; Chasing the Sun - the Poetry Society Anthology, 1992; Envoi; Frogmore Papers; Honest Ulsterman; Iota; New Welsh Review; Orbis; Pennine Platform; Periaktos; Prospice; Smoke; Sol; Spokes; Staple; Wide Skirt. Membership: Poetry Society. Address: Merry Meadow, Fullers Road, Wrecclesham, Farnham, Surrey GU10 4LB, England.

TRAKAS Deno, b. 23 Apr 1952, USA. Associate Professor. m. Kathy Jackson, 10 Aug 1974, 1 son, 1 daughter. Education: BA, 1974; MA, 1976; PhD, 1981. Appointments: Associate Professor, Wofford College, 1980-; Instructor, Creative Writing, South California Governors School of the Arts, 1981-; Womens Tennis Coach, Wofford College, 1986-. Publication: The Shuffle of Wings, 1990. Contributions to: Denver Quarterly; Kansas Quarterly; Louisville Review. Honour: Academy of American Poets Prize. Address: Wofford College, 429 North Church Street, Spartanburg, SC 29303, USA.

TRANTER John Ernest, b. 29 Apr 1943, Cooma, New South Wales, Australia. Poet. m. 1968, 1 son, 1 daughter. Education: BA, 1970. Appointments: Senior Editor, Education Division, Angus and Robertson (Publishers), Singapore, 1971-73; Script Editor, Radio Drama and Features Producer, Australian Broadcasting Corporation, 1974-77; Associate Editor, various magazines; Various casual and part-time teaching positions; Publisher, Transit Poetry, 1981-83; Visiting Fellow, Faculty of Arts, Australian National University, 1981; Writer-in-Residence, School of Humanities and Social Sciences, New South Wales Institute of Technology, Sydney, 1983; School of English and Linguistics, Macquarie University, Sydney, 1985; English Department, Australian National University, Canberra, 1987; Rollins College, Winter Park, Florida, 1992; Reading and lecture tours, USA, Europe, 1985, 1986; In charge, Radio Helicon arts programme, ABC Radio National, 1987-88; Poetry Editor, The Bulletin news and arts weekly, Sydney, 1990-93. Publications include: Parallax, 1970; Red Movie, 1972; The Blast Area, 1974; The Alphabet Murders, 1975; 100 Sonnets, 1977; Dazed in the Ladies Lounge, 1970; Selected Poems, 1982; Gloria, 1986; Under Berlin - New Poems, 1988; Anthologies: The New Australian Poetry (compiler, editor), 1979; Norton Anthology of Modern Poetry, 1988; The Tin Wash Dish (compiler), 1989; Penguin Book of Modern Australian Poetry (edited with Philip Mead), 1991. Contributions to: Numerous magazines, Australia, UK, USA; Narrative poem Rain, to Paris Review, 1990. Honours: Kenneth Slessor Prize for Poetry, State Literary Award, for Under Berlin, New South Wales, 1989; Several senior fellowships and grants, Australia Council Literature Board; Australian Artists Creative Fellowship, 1990. Address: PO Box 788, Strawberry Hills, New South Wales 2008, Australia.

TRAYNOR Shaun, b. 19 July 1941, Northern Ireland. Teacher; Poet; Novelist. 2 daughters. Appointments: Southern Arts Writer-in-Residence, Wiltshire Libraries & Museum Service, 1979-81. Publications: The Hardening Ground, 1975; Images in Winter, 1979; Novels for children: Hugo O Hugo The Children's Giant; The Giants' Olympics; A Little Man in England; The Lost City of Belfast. Contributions to: Times Literary Supplement; Times Educational Supplement; Independent on Sunday; London Irish Writer; Fortnight; Irish Aquarius Magazine; ILEA News. Memberships: Society of Authors; United Arts Club, Dublin. Address: 60 Meadow Road, London SW8 1PP, England.

TREBY Ivor C, b. Devonport, Devon, England. Education: MA Hons, School of Biochemistry, Exeter College, Oxford. Publications: Warm Bodies, 1988; Foreign Parts, 1989; Woman with Camellias, 1994. Contributions to: Anthologies: Edge City on Two Different Plans, 1983; Not Love Alone, 1985; Worlds Apart, 1986; Windmill Book of Poetry, 1987; The Faber Book of Fevers and Frets, 1989; Dream Poems (Psychopoetica), 1990; Journals: Acumen; Anglo-Welsh Review; Argo; Pennine Platform; Staple; James White Review; Literary Review; Present Tense; Contemporary Review. Honours: Redcliffe National Poetry Competition Award for verse, which was also performed at the Piccadilly Festival in 1985. Address: Flat 10, 30 Gloucester Terrace, City of Westminster, London W2 3DA, England.

TREMBLAY Gail Elizabeth, b. 15 Dec 1945, Buffalo, New York, USA. College Faculty Member. Education: BA, Drama, University of New Hampshire, 1967; MFA, English, University of Oregon, 1969. Appointments: Part time Instructor, Nathaniel Hawthorne College, Antrim, New Hampshire; Part time Lecturer, University of New Hampshire, Durham; Lecturer, Keene State College, New Hampshire; Assistant Professor, University of Nebraska, Omaha; Faculty, Evergreen State College, Olympia, Washington. Publications: Night Gives Woman the Word, 1979; Talking to the Grandfathers, 1981; Indian Singing in 20th Century America, 1990. Contributions to: Northwest Review; Maize. Address: Evergreen State College, Olympia, WA 98505, USA.

TREMBLAY William (Bill) Andrew, b. 9 June 1940, Massachusetts, USA. Professor. m. Cynthia Ann Crooks, 28 Sept 1962, 3 sons. Education: AB, 1962, MA, 1969, Clark University; MFA, University of Massachusetts, 1972. Appointments: Assistant Professor, Leicester Junior College, 1967-70; Teaching Assistant, University of Massachusetts, 1970-72; Instructor, Springfield College, 1972; Professor, Department of English, Colorado State University, 1973-. Publications: A Time for Breaking; Crying in the Cheap Seats; The Anarchist Heart; Home Front; Second Sun: New and Selected Poems; Duhamel; Ideas of Order in Little Canada; The June Rise. Contributions to: Massachusetts Review; Chicago Review; Minnesota Review; Ohio Review; Indiana Review; Greenfield Review; Green Mountains Review; Cincinnati Poetry Review; Ironwood; Midwest Quarterly; Three Rivers Poetry Journal; Northern Light; Journal; Prism International; Bluefish. Honours: Houyt Poetry Prizes, Clark University, 1960, 1961; Tulsa Poetry Quarterly, 1969; Honourable Mention, Elliston Poetry Prize, University of Cincinnati, 1977; Finalist, National Poetry Contest, 1985; National Endowment for the Arts Fellowship, 1985. Memberships: Associated Writing Programs; High Plains Arts Centre. Address: 3412 Lancaster Drive, Fort Collins, CO 80523, USA.

TRESILLIAN Richard. See: ELLIS Royston.

TRIBE David Harold, b. 17 Dec 1931, Sydney, New South Wales, Australia. Author; Journalist. Education: Open Scholarship, Fellowship, Medicine, University of Queensland,1949-54. Career: Poet, Author, Journalist, Editor, Lecturer, Broadcaster, Artist, Critic, Public Relations Adviser, Publisher, UK, 1954-73; Successively Publicity, Public Relations, Scientific and Policy Officer, New South Wales Public Service, 1973-87; Poet, Author, 1987-. Publications: Why Are We Here?, 1965; Represented in numerous anthologies including: Doves for the Seventies, 1969; A Vein of Mockery: Twentieth-Century Verse Satire, 1973; New Poetry 1, 1975. Contributions to: UK: Sunday Times, New Statesman; Punch; Twentieth Century; New Humanist; Outposts; Weekly satirical-topical poem to Tribune, over 2 years; BBC; Australia: Meanjin; Bulletin; ABC; Several little magazines, UK, Ireland, Canada, USA, Austria, South Africa, Australia. Memberships: Poets Union, Australia: Australian Society of Authors; CAL; UK: Poets Workshop; London Poetry Secretariat; Greater London Arts Association; Poets in Schools Scheme, Arts Council of Great Britain; Society of Authors; Commonwealth Writers Club, Vice President; ALCS. Address: 10 Griffiths Street, Fairlight, New South Wales, 2094, Australia.

TRIPATHY Sailendra Narayan, b. 22 July 1957, Kendrapara, Orissa, India. College Lecturer. m. Ashoka Tripathy, 11 May 1981, 1 son, 1 daughter. Education: BA, English Honours; MA, English, Ravenshaw College, Cuttange, Orissa, 1979; PhD in progress. Appointments: Lecturer, Khallikote Postgraduate College, Lecturer, English, N C College, Jaipur, Orissa; Editor, Poesie, avant-garde poetry quarterly. Publications: I am Phallic God and Other Poems, 1989; The Trapped Word (editor), contemporary poems, 1989; Love Apples, anthology of love poetry, 1992; Juggernaut, poems. Contributions to: Prophetic Voices; New Wave; New Hope International; Poesie; Poetry Time; Canopy; Byword; PoetCrit; Literary Horizons; Samvedana; Avita India; Skylark. Memberships: Life Member, Commonwealth Society; Association of Little Presses, London. Address: Poesie Publications, Shastrinagar, Berhampur 760001, Orissa, India.

TRIPATHY Upendra, b. 5 Oct 1956, Kahakapur, India. Public Servant. m. 2 July 1982, 1 son, 1 daughter. Education: BSc, 1974, BA, Political Science, 1976, Ravanshaw College; MA, Political Science, Jawaharlal Nehru University, New Delhi, 1979. Appointments: Sub-Collector (Puttur), ADM (Development) Chitraduga, DC (Com Tax); Collector (Hassan), Director (Agricultural Marketing), Chief

Secretary, Culbarga, DS (Pinth), New Delhi; Currently Cadre, 1980, batch, All India Service, Indian Administrative Service, Karnataka. Publication: Caged, 1990. Contributions to: Sunday Herald; Poet; My Forest; American Anthology of Poetry. Address: Collector and DM, Hassan, Karnataka, India.

TRISHANKU. See: **MUKHOPADHYAY Sarat Kumar.**

TROUBETZKOY Dorothy Livingston Ulrich, b. Hartford, Connecticut, USA. Writer; Editor. m. Prince Serge Troubetzkoy, 25 Dec 1941, 1 son, 2 daughters. Education: BA, University of Chicago; Columbia University. Appointments: Feature Writer; Columnist; Assistant Editor; Director, Information and Research City of Richmond, 1956-58; Editor, Virginia, 1959-63; The Independent, Virginia, 1971-. Publications include: Outof the Wilderness; Richmond City of Churches; Sagamore Creek; Poems from Korea; Love in the Rain; The Time We Drove All Night. Contributions to: Numerous Magazines, Journals. Honour: Recipient of Numerous Awards inc 11 Poetry Society of America Awards; W H Auden Prize; Mozart Prize. Memberships: Poetry Society of America; New England Poetry Club; Virginia Writers Club; National Federation of Press Women. Address: 2223 Grove Avenue, Richmond, VA 23220, USA.

TROWBRIDGE William L, b. 9 May 1941, Chicago, Illinois, USA. University Teacher. m. 6 July 1963, 2 sons, 1 daughter. Education: AB, 1963, MA, 1965, University of Missouri, Columbia; PhD, Vanderbilt University, 1975. Appointments: University Teacher, 1967-; Currently Distinguished University Professor, English Department, Northwest Missouri State University; Co-Editor, The Laurel Review, 1989-. Publications: The Book of Kong, 1986; Enter Dark Stranger, 1989; O Paradise, 1995. Contributions to: Prairie Schooner; Missouri Review; New Letters; Tar River Poetry; Many others. Honours: Academy of American Poets Prize; Bread Loaf Writers Conference Scholarship. Memberships: Academy of American Poet: Associted Writing Programs; Poetry Society of America; American Association of University Professors. Address: 907 South Dunn, Maryville, MO 64468, USA.

TRUBNIKOV Alexander, b. 5 June 1945, Parnu, Estonia. Sound Engineer. m. Maya Zlot, 12 Jan 1988. 2 sons. Education: Graduated as Computer Programmer, Institute of Technology, USA, 1983. Appointments: Sound Operator, Leningrad Film Company Lenfilm, USSR, 1963-79; Sound Recordist, film and documentary productions, USA. Publication: A Biblical Poetic Retelling, 1991. Contributions to: Ferganskaya Pravda newspaper; Bridge of Friends poetry magazine. Memberships: Friends of the Globe Poetry; Russian Writers Club, Columbia University. Address: 27-30 West 33rd Street, 11 J Brooklyn, NY 11224, USA.

TRUCK Count Robert-Paul, b. 3 May 1917, Calais, France. Poet; Critic; Historian. m. Jeanne Brogniart, 24 July 1942, 1 daughter. Education: Baccalaureat, 1935; French Naval School, 1938. Appointments: Poet, 1938; Naval Officer, 1939; Treasurer, Marine Boulogne-sur-Mer, 1940-43, Art Critic, 1940, Lecturer, 1948; Literary Critic, 1966; Historian, 1975. Publications: Poetry: Heures folles, 1938; Au bord de la Nuit, 1948; Intersignes, 1953; Vertiges (with a study by Roberto Mandel, Prince of Italian Poets: Robert-Paul Truck, Poète du Mysticisme Cosmique), 1989; Bois des Iles, 1992; Marche des Rois, 1993; Cicatrices, 1995; History: Médecins de la Honte (with Betty Truck), 1975; Mengele, l'ange de la mort (with Betty Truck), 1976; 1492-1992 (Foreword of Les Poètes et l'Amérique), 1991. Contributions to include: Quo Vadis; Courrier des Marches; La Voix du Nord; La Métropole; Life; l'Eco del Popolo; Nosta; Historia; Washington Post; Annuaire National des Lettres 1988-89, 1993-94; Anthologies: Les Poètes de la Vie; Les Poètes de la Mer; Poeti Francesi d'Oggi; Les Grandes Anthologies; L'Encyclopédie Poétique (Les Astres); Parnassus of World Poets, 1994, 1995; Séquence 37; Anthologie des Poètes Français d'Aujourd'hui; 50 Ans de Poésie Contemporaine, 1945-95. Honours include: Master of the Intellectual Elite, Italy, 1953; Diploma of Honour, Relations Latines, Milan, 1954; Diploma di Benemerenza, 1983, Targa d'Onore, 1983, Gold Palms, 1984, Leonardo da Vinci International Academy, Rome; Honorary Director for the Western Europe of World Poets, Madras, India, 1995; Medal for Peace with Collar Ribbon, Albert Einstein International Academy, USA, 1989; Cross of Merit with Collar Ribbon, Albert Einstein International Academy, USA, 1992. Memberships: International Academy of Poets; World Literary Academy; Accademia Leonardo da Vinci; Institut Académique de Paris; Société des Poètes Français. Address: Varouna, 49 Rue de Lhomel, 62600 Berck-Plage, France.

TRUE Michael, b. 8 Nov 1933, Oklahoma City, Oklahoma, USA. Teacher; Writer. m. Mary Patricia Delaney, 12 Apr 1958, 3 sons, 3 daughters. Education: BA, 1955; MA, 1957; PhD, Duke University, 1964; Postdoctoral Study, Harvard Divinity School, 1968; Columbia University, 1976-77. Appointments: Founding Editor, Worcester Review, 1973; Professor of English, Assumption College, 1974-; Poetry Editor, English Journal, 1976; Visiting Professor of American Literature, Nanjing University China, 1984-85, 1989; Sheffer Visiting Professor of Religion, Colorado College, USA, 1988, 1990, 1993; Contributing Editor, Spectrum, 1988-; Advisor Peacework; Board, Peace and Change: A Journal of Peace Research, 1996. Publications: Selections in Three Mountains Press Poetry Anthology of 1976; Nonfiction prose: Homemade Social Justice, 1982; Justice-Seekers; Peacemakers: 32 Portraits in Courage, 1985; Ordinary People: Teaching Values in the Family, 1991; Worcester Area Writers, 1680-1980, 1987; To Construct Peace: 30 More Justice-Seekers, Peacemakers, 1992; Daniel Berrigan: Poetry, Drama, Prose (editor), 1988; An Energy Field More Intense Than War: The Nonviolent Tradition and American Literature, 1995. Contributions to: Worcester Review; Peacework; College Composition and Communication; Phoenix; Poetry International (China); Worcester Magazine; Contemporary Poets, 1995. Memberships: Poetry Society of America; Co-Founder, Board Member, Worcester Poetry Association Inc; Convenor, Nonviolence Commission, International Peace Research Association. Address: 4 Westland Street, Worcester, MA 01602, USA.

TU Shiu-tien, (Sar Po), b. 28 July 1944, Taiwan, China. Dentist. Publisher. Tseng Chiu-chu, 22 Nov 1978, 2 sons, 1 daughter. Education: DDS, Dental Department, Kaohsiung Medical College, 1970; Postgraduate courses: Osaka Dental University, Japan, 1972-73; Osaka University, 1973-74; Tokyo University, 1974-77. Appointments: Dentist, Tai Yi Dental Clinic; Publisher, Tai Yi Publishing Company; Director, World Chinese Poets Association, Hong Kong; President, Great Ocean Poetry Magazine, Kaohsiung; Chief Director, Kaohsiung Children's Literature Association. Publications: So, The Streams, 1966; The Running Sound of the Sun, 1983; The Bright Stars, 1986; The Stars Like Children's Poetry, 1987; Sar Po's Essays, 1988; The Spiritual Sea, 1990; Hollow Shells, in English and Chinese, 1990; The Singing River, 1990; Translations into Chinese of T S Eliot, Paul Valery, Japanese Literature. Contributions to: Asian Poets, Korea; Asian Modern Poetry, Japan; Taiwanese Poets, Japan; Contemporary Poetry, Hong Kong; China: Modern Chinese Poetry; Modern Chinese Children's Poetry; Huaxia Poetry; Chinese Poetry; Taiwan: Great Ocean Poetry; Li Poetry; Blue Stars Poetry Quarterly; Modern Literature; Chinese Daily News; Taiwan Times; Taiwan Shin Wen Daily News; Min Chung Daily News. Honour: Kaohsiung Literature Prize. Memberships: World Academy of Arts and Culture, USA; Chinese Poets Association; Chinese Children's Literature Association; Editorial Board, Li Poetry Magazine; Chinese Literature Association. Address: 228 Jen Al First Street, 80027 Kaohsiung, Taiwan, China.

TUCKER Martin, b. 8 Feb 1928, Philadelphia, Pennsylvania, USA. Professor of English; Writer; Poet. Div. Education: BA, 1949, PhD, 1963, New York University; MA, University of Arizona, 1954. Appointments: Associate Editor, Quick Frozen Foods Magazine, 1949-51; Associated Press, Huntington, West Virginia, 1954-56; Long Island University, 1956-. Publications: Homes of Locks and Mystery, 1982; Represented in: Educations, 1985; Food for Thought, 1986; An ABC Bestiary, 1990. Contributions to: Confrontation; Boulevard; New York Times; Monk's Pond; North Atlantic Review; Princeton Journal Spectrum; Union Street Review; Commonwealth; S Anthony's Messenger; Helicon; Loomings; Fire Island Review; West Hills Review; Brooklyn Paper. Honours: Homes of Locks and Mysteries selected for Across the Seas Programme, English-Speaking Union, 1982; Commemorative Reading, Poetry Society of America, 1989; Featured Poet, Union Street Review, 1990. Memberships: Poetry Society of America, Governing Board Member, 1986-90; Executive Board Member, PEN American Center, 1973-; African Literature Association; Modern Language Association; Authors Guild; National Books Critic Association. Address: 90-A Dosoris Lane, Glen Cove, NY 11542, USA.

TULLOS Frances Sue, b. 15 Dec 1945, Orange, Texas, USA. Social Security Representative. Education: BA, English, Sociology, 1969, MA, English, History, 1970, University of Texas, Austin; PhD, Contemporary American Literature, Texas Tech University, 1977. Appointments: College Instructor, 1971-83; Poetry readings: Austin Public Television, 1980; Friends in Art Show Case, 1983, 1985, 1987, 1989; Service Representative, Social Security Administration, 1984-;

Consultant, Cris Cole Rehabilitation Center. Publication: A Pink Disregard for Decorum, 1989. Contributions to: Dialogue; Lifeprints; Women's Brille Press Newsletter; UMC Prophet; OSMT Journal; Log of the Bridge Tender; Davidson Miscellany; Journal of Visual Impairment and Blindness; Arizona Quarterly; Texas Prize Stories and Poems. Honours: Best Poetry Award, Dialogue Magazine, 1976; Jean Kennedy Shriver Award, Excellence in Performing Arts, 1979; 1st Place, 1980, 1981, 2nd Place, 1982, South Plains Writers Association Poetry Contest. Memberships: New Mexico State Poetry Society, Past President, Past 1st Vice President, Past Workshop Presenter; National Federation of Poetry Societies. Address: 506 West Healey, Apt 4, Champaign, IL 61820, USA.

TUNNICLIFFE Stephen, b. 22 May 1925, Wakefield, Yorkshire, England. Teacher and Writer. m. Hilary Katharine Routh, 5 Aug 1949, 3 sons. Education: BA Hons English, 1951, MA English (distinction), 1965, University of London; Certificate of Education, Institute of Education, 1952. Appointments: English Assistant Teacher: Kingston High School, Hull; Head of English, Sowerby Bridge Grammar School, Hull; Head of English, Newton Mill High School, Powys; Music Tutor, Cello and Bass, North Powys. Publications: English in Practice (with Geoffrey Summerfield), 1971; Reading and Discrimination (with Denys Thompson), 1979; Poetry Experience: Teaching and Writing Poetry in Secondary Schools, 1984; Building and Other Poems, 1993; Libretti (for John Joubert): The Martydrom of St Alban; The Raising of Lazarus; The Magus; The Prisoner; The Wayfarers; (for Francis Routh) Circles. Contributions to: Poetry Wales; Anglo-Welsh Review; Use of English. Memberships: Society of Authors. Address: Clairmont, The Square, CLUN, Shropshire SY7 8JA, England.

TURCO Lewis Putnam, (Wesli Court), b. 2 May 1934, Buffalo, New York, USA. Writer. m. Jean Cate Houdlette, 16 June 1956, 1 son, 1 daughter. Education: BA, English, University of Connecticut, 1959; MA, English, University of Iowa, 1962. Appointments: Instructor, Fenn College, 1960-64, Founding Director, Poetry Center, 1961-64, Cleveland State University; Assistant Professor, Hillsdale College, Michigan, 1964-65; Assistant Professor, 1965-68, Associate Professor, 1968-71, Director, Writing Arts, 1969-95, Professor, 1971-, State University of New York College at Oswego; Visiting Professor, State University of New York College at Potsdam, 1968-69; Bingham Poet-in-Residence, University of Louisville, 1982; Writer-in-Residence, Ashland University, Ohio, 1991. Publications: First Poems, 1960; The Book of Forms: A Handbook of Poetics, 1968; Awaken, Bells Falling: Poems 1959-67, 1968; The Inhabitant, 1970; Pocoangelini: A Fantography and Other Poems, 1971; Poetry: An Introduction, 1973; Seasons of the Blood, 1980; The Airs of Wales, 1981; American Still Lifes, 1981; The Compleat Melancholick, 1985; The New Book of Forms, 1986; Visions and Revisions of American Poetry, 1986; A Maze of Monsters, 1986; The Shifting Web: New and Selected Poems, 1989; Dialogue, 1989; A Family Album, 1990; The Public Poet, 1991; Emily Dickinson, Woman of Letters, 1993; Murmurs in the Walls, 1991; Bordello, 1996. Contributions to: New Yorker; Nation; Poetry; Orbis; Carleton Miscellany; Sewanee Review; Tri-Quarterly; Ploughshares; Formalist; Atlantic; Hudson Review; New Republic; Saturday Review; Ontario Review; Kenyon Review; Southern Review; Massachusetts Review. Honours: Resident Fellowships, Yaddo, 1959, 1977; Academy of American Poets Prize, University of Iowa, 1960; Bread Loaf Poetry Fellow, 1961; Chapbook Award, American Weave Press, 1962; Helen Bullis Prize, Poetry Northwest, 1972; 1st Poetry Award, Kansas Quarterly - Kansas Arts Commission, 1984-85; President's Award, State University of New York College, Oswego, 1985; Winner, Chapbook Competition, Silverfish Review, 1989; 1st Place, Chapbook Competition, Cooper House, 1990. Memberships: Maine Antiquesian Booksellers Association. Address: c/o Mathom Press Enterprises, PO Box 362, Oswego, NY 13126, USA.

TURK Eugene M. See: YICTOVE.

TURNBULL Gael Lundin, b. 7 Apr 1928, Edinburgh, Scotland. Former Medical Practitioner; Writer. (1) Jonnie May Draper, 6 June 1952, 3 daughters, (2) Pamela Jill Iles, 28 Dec 1983. Education: BA, Cambridge, 1948; MD, University of Pennsylvania, USA, 1951. Appointments: General Practitioner and Anaethetist, Canada, USA, UK. Publications: A Trampoline: Poems 1952-64, 1968; Scantlings: Poems 1964-1969, 1970; A Gathering of Poems: 1950-1980, 1983; A Winter Journey, 1987; White Breath Persist: New and Selected Poems, 1992; For Whose Delight, 1995. Contributions to: Numerous publications. Honours: Union League Prize, Poetry, Chicago, 1965;

Alice Hunt Bartlet Award, Poetry Society, London, 1969. Address: 12 Strathearn Place, Edinburgh EH9 2AL, Scotland.

TURNER Alberta T, b. 22 Oct 1919, New York, New York, USA. University Teacher (chiefly Creative Writing and Seventeenth Century Poetry). m. William Arthur Turner, 9 Apr 1943, 1 son, 1 daughter. Education: BA, Hunter College, New York, 1940; MA, Wellesley College, Massachusetts, 1941; PhD, Ohio State University, Columbus, 1946. Appointments: Lecturer, Oberlin College, 1946-69; Lecturer, Assistant Professor, Associate Professor, Professor, 1964-90, Director, Poetry Center, 1964-90, Professor Emerita, 1990-, Cleveland State University; Associate Editor: Contemporary Poetry and Poetics, 1970-. Publications: Need, 1971; Learning to Count, 1974; Lid and Spoon, 1977; A Belfry of Knees, 1983; Textbooks: To Make a Poem, 1982; Responses to Poetry, 1990; Editor, anthologies: 50 Contemporary Poets, 1977; Poets Teaching, 1981; 45 Contemporary Poems, 1985; Beginning with And: New and Selected Poems, 1994. Honours: OAC Individual Artists Grant, 1980; Fellowship, MacDowell Colony, 1985; Cleveland Arts Prize for Literature, 1985; Ohio Poetry Award, 1986; Ohio Governor's Award for Arts in Education, 1988. Memberships: Milton Society of America; PEN American Center; Ohio Humanities Council, 1987-92. Address: 482 Caskey Court, Oberlin, OH 44074, USA.

TURNER Brian Lindsay, b. 4 Mar 1944, New Zealand. Publishing Editor; Writer. Div, 1 son. Appointments: Robert Burns Fellow, University of Otago. Publications: Ladders of Rain; Ancestors; Listening to the River; Bones; All That Blue Can Be; Beyond, Timeless Land. Contributions to: New Zealand Listener; Landfall; Metro; Sport; Age Review; Sydney Morning Herald; Quadrant; New Letters. Honours: Commonwealth Poetry Prize; New Zealand Book Award for Poetry, 1993, Scholarship in Letters, 1994. Memberships: New Zealand Society of Authors. Address: 2 Upper Junction Road, Sawyers Bay, Dunedin, New Zealand.

TURNER Frederick, b. 19 Nov 1943, East Haddon, Northamptonshire, England. Professor; Writer. m. Mei Lin Chang, 25 June 1966, 2 sons. Education: BA, 1965, MA, 1967, BLitt, 1967, Oxford University. Appointments: Assistant Professor, University of California, 1967-72; Associate Professor, Kenyon College, 1972-85; Editor, Kenyon Review, 1978-83; Visiting Professor, University of Exeter, 1984-85; Founders Professor, University of Texas, 1985-. Publications: Shakespeare and the Nature of Time; Between Two Lives; A Double Shadow; Counter Terra; The Return; The New World; The Garden; Natural Classicism; Genesis; Rebirth of Value; Tempest, Flute, and Oz; Beauty; April Wind; Translations: Foamy Sky: The major poems of Miklos Radnoti (with Zsuzsanna Ozsvath); The Culture of Hope: A New Birth of the Classical Spirit, 1995. Contributions to: Harper's; Poetry; Wilson Quarterly; National Review; Reason; New Literary History; Southern Review; Poetry Nation Review; New Hungarian Quarterly; Partisan Review. Honours: Djerassi Foundation Grant; Levinson Poetry Prize; Missouri Review Essay Prize; PEN Golden Pen Award; Milan Fust Prize. Memberships: PEN; Modern Language Association; International Society for the Study of Time. Address: 2668 Aster Drize, Richardson, TX 75082, USA.

TURNER Keith Graham, b. 19 Sept 1935, Birmingham, England. Teacher; Lecturer. m. Margaret Eleanor Turner, 21 Mar 1964, 2 sons, 1 daughter. Education: BA Hons English, Birmingham University, 1956; PGCE, London, 1958. Appointments: Assistant Master, Moseley Grammar School, 1958-64; Head of English, Marsh Hill School, Erdington, 1964-66; Lecturer, Senior Lecturer in English, Coventry College of Education, 1966-78. Publication: Allied Powers, 1991. Contributions to: Samphire; Meridian; Isis; Stand; Poetry Review; Poetry Durham; Orbis; New Poetry; Poesie Europe; Other Poetry; Literary Review; Rialto; Iron; People to People. Honours: Duncan Lawrie Award, Arvon/Observer International Poetry Prize, 1989-90. Membership: Poetry Society. Address: 21 Heath Terrace, Leamington Spa, Warwicks, CV32 5NA, England.

TURNER Martin Vernon Lawrence, b. 9 Feb 1948, London, England. Educational Psychologist. m. Farah, 9 Aug 1981, 2 daughters. Education: BA, University of Exeter, 1975; PGCE, St Lukes College, Exeter, 1976; MSc, University of Strathclyde, 1978; MA, University of Kent, 1988. Appointment: Educational Psychologist, Motherwell, Lawarkshire, 1978-79; Educational Psychologist, Newham, 1979-84; Senior Educational Psychologist, Croydon, 1984-91; Head of Psychology, Dyslexia Institute, Staines, 1991-. Publication: Trespass. Contributions to: Ashes; Litmus; Poetry

Durham; Wasafiri; Other Poetry; Poetry Book Society Anthology; Sepia; Poetry World; Comparative Criticism. Honour: Kent Literature Festival National Poetry Competition. Membership: Poetry Society. Address: 120 Gravel Hill, Croydon CR0 5BF, England.

TURNER Stella, (Mary Muir, Harriet Hill), b. 6 Feb 1918, Melbourne, Victoria, Australia. Musician (Cellist); Writer. m. Stanley John Turner, 1 son, dec. Education: Matriculation, 1936. Appointments: Cellist, The Tudor Trio, 1938-41; Taught privately, 1960s, 1970s, 1980s-85; Teaching, Mater Christi Girls School, Belgrave, early 1980s; Started writing seriously, 1985; Poetry readings at public meetings and festivals; Poems read on Radio ABC and 3CR. Publications: From the Dandenongs, 1984; Season of Gold, 1986; Dance Suite, 5 poems set to music, 1988; The Seasons, 5 poems set to music, 1989; Sounds and Music (illustrated by Bob Graham), children's book, 1989; Lost Valley, 4 poems set to music, 1993; 12 single poems set to music. Contributions to: Linq; Northern Perspective; Luna; Studio; Prints; Carringbush Poets; Woorilla; Habitat; Poets for Africa; Up From Below; Small Times; Yarra Valley Writers; Rhythm and Rhyme, New Zealand; Under the Southern Cross; Animal Friends; Arrivals; Herbspin; Flowerspin; Treespin; Skyspin; Birdspin; The Whirling Spindle. Honours: Charles Meeking Prize for Women Poets, 1983; Blue Mountains FAW, 1983; Maryborough Golden Wattle, 1983; Co-recipient, Henry Lawson Award, 1985; Melbourne Poetry Society Competitions, 1986, 1987, 1991; Harold Kesteven Competition, 1986; Northern Territory Literary Awards, 1989; Australia Day Medallion, 1991; Several highly commended poems. Memberships: Society of Women Writers of Australia, Victorian Branch; Script Writing Course, Council of Adult Education, 1992; Poetry Study Group and Workshop with Kathryn Powell; Poetry Workshop, Monash University. Address: Terrigal, 24 Church Street, Emerald, Victoria 3782, Australia.

TURNER William (Bill) Price, b. 14 Aug 1927, York, England. Writer. m. Sylvia Fair. Appointments: Gregory Fellow in Poetry, Leeds University, 1960-62; Creative Writing Fellow, Glasgow University, 1973-75; Writer in Residence, Bedford Central Library, 1979-80; Lincoln Adult Education Center, 1983-84; Cherry Knowle Hospital, 1985-86. Publications: First Offence; The Rudiment of an Eye; The Flying Corset; Fables from Life; Bound to Die; Baldy Bane; Sex Trap; More Fables from Life; Circle of Squares; Another Little Death; The Moral Rocking Horse; Solden's Women; Hot-Foot; Thistles; Fables for Love. Contributions to: Yorkshire Post; Twentieth Century; Poetry Review; Scottish Field; Iron; Samphire; Tribune; Stand; Green Book. Honours: Scottish Arts Council Publication Award; West Midlands Bursary; Prize-winner in five national poetry competitions. Membership: Poetry Society. Address: 38 Arboretum Avenue, Lincoln LN2 5JE, England.

TUROW David, b. 3 Apr 1963, Kiev, Ukraine. Education: BA, New York University; Graduate Certificate in Communications, Pace University. Publications: The Awakening; Poems published in anthologies, Olympoetry-94, Paris and Olympoetry-96, Atlanta, USA; The Torchbearer, Book of Poems, 1996. Contributions to: Periodical Press, USA. Honours: Several Golden Poet Awards from the National Society of Poetry; Awarded with title of Knight of Olympoetry in 1994 and an Order of Pegasus in 1995 from Olympoetry; Consul General of Olympoetry for work with new authors. Address: 138-15 78th Ave, Apta, Flushing, NY 11367, USA.

TURPIN Janet. See: **CRAIG Timothy.**

TUSZYNSKI Felix, b. 19 July 1922, Plock, Poland. Artist. m. Danuta, 3 Aug 1989, 1 son. Education: Studied Oil Painting under Donald Campbell, Melbourne, Australia, 1960-63. Appointments: Exhibitions since 1960; More than 100 Selected Group Exhibitions; 16 One Man Show Exhibitions including Museum, National and Regional Galleries in Australia and Overseas. Publications: Max Germaine Encyclopedia, 1984; The Australian and New Zealand Max Germaine Artists and Galleries, 1990; Art Plock by K Askanas, 1991; A Buyer's Guide to Australian Art by Graham Ryles, 1992; A Palette of Artists by Ken Bendman; Art Business - Polish Art and Antiques, 1994; Melbourne Chronicle, 1995; Antiques and Art in Victoria, 1995; Artists Newsletters and Press. Collections: Holocaust Museum, Sydney; Queensland Art Gallery; Polish National Museum, Mazovia; Mornington Peninsula Art Centre, Shalom Gallery, Warsaw, Poland; Private Collections: USA, Argentina, Poland, France, Israel, Germany, Australia. Honours: First Prize, Chadstone Festival of Art, 1967; First Prize, Victoria Artists Society, 1994; 2 Medals for Contribution to the

Arts; Honorary Art Diploma, City of Plock, Poland; Honorary Award, Victoria Artists Society, S M Melbourne for Contribution and Services in Art. Memberships: Victoria Artists Society; Contemporary Artists Society; Bezalel Artists Society; Five Plus Group. Australia. Address: 1/438 Hawthorn Road, South Caulfield, 3162 Victoria, Australia.

TUWHARE Hone, b. 21 Oct 1922, Kaikohe, New Zealand. Education: Seddon Memorial and Otahuhu Technical Colleges, Auckland, 1939-41. Appointments: Public works in Wellington and Auckland. Publications: No Ordinary Sun, 1964; Come Rain Hail, 1970; Sapwood and Milk, 1972; Something Nothing, 1973; Making a Fist of it, 1978; Selected Poems, 1980; Year of the Dog, 1982; Mihi: Collected Poems, 1987. Honours include: New Zealand Award for Achievement, 1965. Address: c/o John McIndoe Ltd, 51 Crawford Street, PO Box 694, Dunedin, New Zealand.

TYRRELL Richard, b. 19 June 1959, Dublin, Ireland. Arts Manager. Education: BSc, 1981; MA, 1989. Appointments: Festival Director, Worldlinks Readers and Writers Festival, 1988-89; Assistant Director, QMW Launch, 1989-92; Business Development Manager, Brunel University, 1992-. Publications: Happy Hour Conversation, 1991. Contributions to: Irish Press; New Statesman; Poetry Reviewer; London Magazine; Ambit; Outposts; Other Poetry; Independent; Guardian; Times Literary Supplement. Memberships: Society of Authors; Chairman, Poetry Society, 1993-94. Address: 23 Earlsmead Road, London NW10 5QD, England.

U

UHRMAN Celia, b. 14 May 1927, New London, Connecticut, USA. Artist; Poet; Writer; Retired Teacher. Education: BA, Brooklyn College, 1948; MA, Brooklyn College, 1953; Postgraduate Studies: Brooklyn Museum Art School, 1956-57, Teachers College, Columbia University, 1961, City University of New York, 1966; PhD, University of Danzig, 1977; Certificate, Koret Living Library, University of San Francisco, 1982. Appointments: Teacher, New York City School System, 1948-82; Several One-Women Shows; Exhibited, numerous group shows; Partner, Uhrman Studio, Brooklyn, New York, 1973-83. Publications: Poetic Ponderances, 1969; A Pause for Poetry, 1970; Poetic Love Fancies, 1970; A Pause for Poetry for Children, 1973; The Chimps Are Coming, 1975; Love Fancies, 1987. Honours: Personal Poetry Certificate, WEFG Stereo, 1970; Named Poetry Translator Laureate, World Academy of Language Literature, 1972; Poet of Mankind, Academy of Philosophy, 1972; Diploma, Gold Medal, Centro Studi e Scambi Internazionali, 1972; Knight Grand Cross, Order of Ghandi Award of Honor, 1972; Honorary PhD, DLitt, 1973; Certificate of Appreciation, New York City Board of Education, 1982; Several Art Awards. Memberships: Fellow, World Literary Academy; Representative-at-Large, World Poetry Society Intercontinental; Founding Fellow, International Academy of Poets; Honorary Life Member: World Poetry Day Committee: National Poetry Day Committee. Address: 1655 Flatbush Avenue, C106, Brooklyn, NY 11210, USA.

UHRMAN Esther, b. 7 July 1921, New London, Connecticut, USA. Artist; Writer. Education: BA, Traphagen School of Fashion, New York City, 1955; AA, Technical College, 1974; MA, Cornell University, 1976; PhD, Danzig University, 1977. Appointments: Retired Social Worker; Award Winning Artist. Contributions to: Gypsy Logic, Quaderni di Poesia, Italy, 1970; Editor, Inside Detective and Assistant Editor, Detective Group, 1971; Radio broadcast of 2 novels, From Canarsie to Masada, 1978 and Mitras the Second, 1988, and of radio play, 2057, 1984; Contributions to: group magazines, 1980's, to Contemporary Poets of America, 1981-86, to World Poetry and Poets Magazine. Honours: WCBS Award for a Tape Interview Suggestion, 1964; 3rd Place Podiker Essay Award, New York State, 1968; Golden Windmill Radio Drama Contest Award for radio play, 2057, Netherlands, 1971; Diploma di Benemerenza Allavivlta, 1972; Diplome d'Honneur des Beaux Arts, IAG Cultural Exchange Between Nations, 1976; Diploma di Benemerenza Academy Leonardo da Vinci For Poetry, 1980; AFL-C10 Award for News Watch, 1980's; Finalist Dentsu Award, Tokyo, 1985. Memberships: Koret Living Library, University of San Francisco, 1982-; Founding Fellow, International Acadmey of Poets, 1985. Address: 1655 Flatbush Avenue, Apt C 106, Brooklyn, NY 11210, USA.

ULMER James Kenneth, b. 2 Sept 1954, Plainfield, New Jersey, USA. College Professor. m. Robin Kozak, 15 Aug 1985. Education: AB Honours in English, Gettysburg College, 1976; MA, English, University of Washington, 1981; PhD, English, Creative Writing, University of Houston, 1988. Appointments: Instructor, 1986-88, Writer-in-Residence, 1988-, Houston Baptist University, Texas. Contributions to: New Yorker; Antioch Review; Poetry; Black Warrior Review; Crazy-horse; Cincinnati Poetry Review; New Criterion; North American Review; Journal; Intro: Missouri Review; Gulf Coast; Poetry Northwest; Seattle Review; Quarterly West; Three Rivers Poetry Journal; Mississippi Valley Review; Virginia Quarterly Review; Nimrod; Boulevard; Under 35: The New Generation of American Poets. Honours: Academy of American Poets Prize, 1981, 1985; Joan Grayston Poetry Prize, 1981; Henry Hoyns Fellowship in Poetry, University of Virginia, 1981-82; Pablo Neruda Poetry Prize, 1985; National Graduate Fellowship Program Fellow, 1986-87; PEN Southwest Discovery Prize for Poetry, 1987; Artist's Residency, MacDowell Colony, 1988; Creative Artists Program Grant, Cultural Arts Council, Houston, 1989. Memberships: Poetry Society of America; Associated Writing Programs; Modern Language Association. Address: Department of Languages, Houston Baptist University, 7502 Fondren Road, Houston, TX 77074, USA.

UNDERWOOD Juliana Ruth, b. 8 Feb 1938, San Bernardino, California, USA. Counselor. m. Arthur (deceased), 1 son. Education: Ba degree in Music, California State University; PhD, Psychology, University of Humanistic Studies, San Diego, California. Publications:

By the National Library of Poetry, Poems published in Spirit of the Age, 1996; Best Poems of the 90's, 1996; Best Poems of 1997; Poems published by Parnassus of World Poets, 1996, 1997, 1998. Memberships: Treasurer of the Poetry Society of Colorado for 6 years. Address: 618 Soda Creek Drive, Evergreen, CO 80439, USA.

UNGER Barbara, b. 2 Oct 1932, New York, New York, USA. College Professor. m. Theodore Kiichiro Sakano, 31 July 1987, 2 daughters. Education: BA, 1954, MA, 1957, City College of New York. Appointment: Professor, English, Creative Writing, Rockland Community College, State University of New York, 1969-. Publications: Basement: Poems 1959-63, 1975; The Man Who Burned Money, 1980; Inside the Wind, 1986; Learning to Foxtrot, 1989; Blue Depression Glass, 1991. Contributions to: Nation; Massachusetts Review; Midstream; Carolina Quarterly; Southern Humanities Review; Beloit Poetry Journal; Southern Poetry Review; Kansas Quarterly; South Coast Poetry Review; Minnesota Review; Nebraska Review; South Florida Review; Denver Quarterly; Confrontation; Negative Capability; Poet and Critic; Wisconsin Review; Cream City Review; Dalhousie Review; Contact II; South Coast Poetry Journal. Honours: Book Publication Grant, National Endowment for the Arts, 1975; Speaker's Grant, National Endowment for the Humanities, 1975; Breadloaf Scholar, 1978; Fellow, Squaw Valley Committee of Writers, 1980; Creative Writing Fellowship, State University of New York, 1981; Winner, National Poetry Competition, 1982; Chester H Jones Award, 1982; Fellow, Ragdale Foundation, 1985, 1986; HYACA Writer-in-Residence Grant, Rockland Center for the Arts, 1986; Nominee, Pushcart Prize, 1987; Goodman Award in Poetry, 1989; Anna Davidson Rosenberg Award for Poems on the Jewish Experience, 1990; Finalist, New Letters Literary Award, 1990; Literature Residency, Djerassi Foundation, 1991; H G Roberts Writing Award in Poetry, 1991. Membership: Poetry Society of America. Address: 101 Parkside Drive, Suffern, NY 10901, USA.

UPDIKE John (Hoyer), b. 18 Mar 1932, Shillington, Pennsylvania, USA. Writer; Poet; Critic. m. (1) Mary E Pennington, 26 June 1953, div 1977, 2 sons, 2 daughters, (2) Martha R Bernhard, 30 Sep 1977, 3 stepchildren. Education: AB, Harvard University, 1954; Ruskin School of Drawing and Fine Art, Oxford, 1954-55. Publications: Novels include: The Witches of Eastwick, 1984; Roger's Version, 1986; S., 1988; Rabbit at Rest, 1990; Memories of the Ford Administration, 1992; Brazil, 1994; Short stories include: Invasion of the Book Envelopes, 1981; Bech is Back, 1982; The Beloved, 1982; Confessions of a Wild Bore, 1984; More Stately Mansions: A Story, 1987; Trust Me: Short Stories, 1987; The Afterlife and Other Stories, 1994; Poetry: The Carpentered Hen and Other Tame Creatures, 1958; Telephone Poles and Other Poems, 1963; The Angels, 1968; Bath After Sailing, 1968; Midpoint and Other Poems, 1969; Seventy Poems, 1972; Six Poems, 1973; Tossing and Turning, 1977; Sixteen Sonnets, 1979; Five Poems, 1980; Spring Trio, 1982; Jester's Dozen, 1984; Facing Nature: Poems, 1985; Collected Poems, 1953-1993, 1993; Other includes: Assorted Prose, 1965; On Meeting Authors, 1968; A Good Place, 1973; Picked-Up Pieces, 1975; Ego and Art in Walt Whitman, 1980; Emersonianism, 1984; Odd Jobs, 1991; Play: Buchanan Dying, 1974. Contributions to: Many periodicals. Honours: Guggenheim Fellowship, 1959; National Book Award for Fiction, 1966; Prix Medicis Etranger, 1966; O Henry Awards for Fiction, 1966, 1991; MacDowell Medal for Literature, 1981; Pulitzer Prizes in Fiction, 1982, 1991; National Book Critics Circle Awards for Fiction, 1982, 1991, and for Criticism, 1984; PEN/Malamud Memorial Prize, 1988; National Medal of Arts, 1989. Memberships: American Academy of Arts and Letters; American Academy of Arts and Sciences. Address: c/o Alfred A Knopf Inc, 201 East 50th Street, New York, NY 10022, USA.

UPTON Lee, b. 2 June 1953, St Johns, Michigan, USA. Professor of English. m. Eric Jozef Ziolkowski, 31 Mar 1989, 1 daughter. Education: BA, 1977; MFA, 1979; PhD, 1986. Publications: Invention of Kindness, 1984; No Mercy, 1989; Jean Garrigue: A Poetics of Plenitude, criticism, 1991; Approximate Darling, 1996; Obsession and Release: Rereading the Poetry of Louise Bogan, criticism, 1996. Contributions to: Yale Review; American Poetry Review; North American Literary Review; Northwest Review. Honours: National Poetry Series, 1988; Pushcart Prize; Academy of American Poets Prizes. Memberships: Poetry Society of America; Modern Language Association; National Council of Teachers of English. Address: Department of English, Lafayette College, Easton, PA 18042, USA.

URIEL Gila, (Olga Krencel-Stamm) (Tella Vivian), b. 23 Jan 1913, Cracow, Poland. Public and Municipal Administrator; Author; Poet; Translator; Broadcaster. Education: Herzlia College, Tel-Aviv, 1931; High School of Law and Economics, Tel Aviv, 1933; London School of Economics, 1939; UNPA Fellow, England and Wales, 1953. Appointments: Director, Mayor's Parlour, Tel Aviv, 1933-53; Director of Studies and Co-Editor, Public Administration Insitute, Tel Aviv, 1945-60; Director, Organization and Training Department, Tel Aviv Municipality, 1953-73; Advisor, Public Service Improvement, 1973-75. Publications: Gems of World Poetry (translation), 1953; Selected Poems of Heinrich Heine (translation); Murmuring Landscapes (translation), 1972; Yearning - English and Hebrew Poems, 1975; The Poet's World - an Anthology, 1992; The World of The Poetess - an Anthology, 1995. Contributions to: BBC Poetry Broadcasts, London, 1953; Tel-Aviv Poetry Broadcasts, 1953; Poetry Review, London, 1953. Honours: Poetry Review Competition Prize, London, 1953. Memberships: Poetry Society, London; Translators Association, Israel. Address: 9 Prague Street, Tel-Aviv YAFO 63477, Israel.

URSELL Geoffrey Barry, b. 14 May 1943, Canada. Writer; Editor. m. Barbara Davies, 8 July 1967. Education: BA, University of Manitoba, 1965; MA, 1966; PhD, University of London, 1973. Appointments: Writer-in- Residence, Saskatoon Public Library, 1984-85; Winnipeg Public Library, 1989-90; Editor, Grain, 1990-. Publications: Way Out West; The Look Out Tower; Perdue; Trap Lines; Saskatoon Pie; The Running of the Deer. Contributions to: This Magazine; Saturday Night; Canadian Forum; Quarry; Border Crossings; Canadian Fiction Magazine; NeWest Review; Western People in Canada. Honours: Clifford E Lee National Playwriting Award; Special Commendation, Commonwealth Poetry Prize; Books in Canada First Novel Award. Memberships: PEN; Writers Union of Canada; Playwrights Union of Canada; Saskatchewan Writers Guild. Address: c/o Coteau Books, 401-2206 Dewdney Avenue, Regina, Saskatchewan S4R 1H3, Canada.

URSU Liliana. See: **MICU Liliana Maria.**

USHA P (Usha Jayan), b. 23 Oct 1951, Vallicodu, Kottayam, India. Librarian. m. K Jayachandran Nair, 25 Nov 1976, 1 son, 1 daughter. Education: MA, English Language and Literature, 1973; Postgraduate Diploma, Russian, 1981; MLISc, 1984; DCE - Diploma in Creative Writing in English, 1995. Appointment: Assistant Librarian. Contributions to: School Man; Indian Express; Poet; International Poets. Memberships: World Poetry Society Intercontinental, Madras; Writer's Forum, Ranchi. Address: Assistant Librarian, University Library, Cochin University of Science and Technology, Kochi - 22, Kerala, India.

UZEIL-FARCHI Rachel, b. 31 July 1937, Tel Aviv, Israel. Journalist. m. David Farhi, 31 Mar 1957, 1 son. Education: Diploma, Beautician; Diploma, Drama Teacher. Appointments: Computers, 1950-60; Beautician and Drama, 1971-79; Playwright, Radio Israel; Currently Journalist. Publications: A Sheep in the Streets of Jerusalem, 1974; 4 Poets, 1977; A Woman Gave a Man a Bubble, 1986; Flying Balloons between East and West, 1991; Play: Shelter Beneath the Temple, 1981. Contributions to: Davar, 1990, 1991; Voices, Israel, 1982; Dreaming of Winds, 1984; Halykon, 1990; Shelem, 1989; Ha Uma, 1989; 7 Gates, 1985, 1986, 1987; Ariel, 1986; Piut, 1982, 1983; Prosa, 1983, 1985; Apirion, 1986; Lorech Ha Shorot, 1983; Kol Jerushalajm, 1987; Political Poetry Prose, 1987; Maariv, 1985, 1988, 1989; American Anthology, 1990; Without a Single Answer, poems of Contemporary Israel, 1990; Culano. Memberships: Israeli Writers Society; Voices, Israel. Address: Heller St 7/27, Givat Mordechi, Jerusalem 93710, Israel.

V

VACIK Milos, b. 21 June 1922, Kozlany, Czech Republic. Journalist. m. (1) Eva, 27 Mar 1943, (2) Drahomira, 24 Feb 1967, 2 sons, 2 daughters. Education: Studied Literature and Philosophy, Philosophy Faculty, Charles University, Prague, 1947. Appointments: Journalist, President of the Cultural Section of the Union of Liberated Political Prisoners, 1945; Editor-in-Chief, MIR Publishing House, 1947; Journalist, Literary Critic, 1950; Journalist, President of the Weekly New Books (Nové Knihy), 1990. Publications: Kralovstvi (Kingdom), 1943; Mala Kalvarie (Small Calvary), 1946; Sonety z Opusteneho Nadrazi (Sonnets from a Desolate Train Station), 1947; Zeme Jistotna (Land of Certainty), 1949; Zahrada na dva Zamky (Garden Double-Locked), 1983; Nemilostna a Milostna (Unloved and Loved), 1990; Ctyri krahujci (Four Sparrow-hawk), 1991; Kriky Narky Ticha (Cries, Laments, Silences), 1995; Ty jsi ten sad (You are that Orchard), 1996. Contributions to: List Mladych; Blok; Rudé Pravo; Impuls; Nové Knihy; Listy; Tvar; Razgledi; Sodobnost (Slovenija); Nouvel Art de Français (France). Honours: Annual Publishers Award, Melantrich Publishing House, 1990. Memberships: Union of Czechoslovak Writers; Writers Guild; Czech Centre of International PEN. Address: Cukrovarnicka 8, 16200 Prague 6, Czech Republic.

VAGGE Ornello, (Lionello Grifo), b. 10 Aug 1934, Rome, Italy. Poet; Author; Translator; Journalist. Education: Doctor of Political and Social Sciences, Brussels, 1958. Appointments: Stenographer; Reporter for a press agency; Translator and Interpreter for international organisations in Luxembourg, Brussels and Geneva, 1954-58; Founder of a public relations and international credit consultancy company; Retired in 1982 to Spain; Renowned Poet, 1950-. Publications include: Sottovoce, Parole in Cerca di Musica, ETL Torino, 1980; La Mia Poesia, My Poetry. Mi Poesia, 1989; Potgtosem, Warsaw, 1990; Sottovoce Poesia Come Musica and Sempre Sottovoce Poesia Come Vita, 1992; My Poetry, 1993; Hommage To Woman, 1994; Colori, Immagini Emozioni Mediterranee, 1994. Contributions to: Numerous to journals and magazines in Europe and United States; Several conferences on poetry subjects in Italian, Spanish, French and English at European and American universities. Honours: Communaute Europeenne des Journalistes Prize, Malta, 1972; Commenda della Repubblica Italiana, Rome, 1973; Genti e Paesi Prize for Poetry, La Spezia, Regione Liguria and Dante Alighieri Society, 1990; Trofeo Letterario Biellese di Poesia, 1994; Premio Internazionale Lerici PEA, 1995. Memberships: Italian Society of Authors and Publishers, Rome; LF Società Dante Alighieri, Rome; Ordine Nazionale Giornalisti Italiani, Rome; Associazione Stampa Romana; LF World Literary Academy, Cambridge; LF International Society of Poets, Maryland, USA; LF, AME Asociacion Mundial de Escritores, Spain; Research Fellow, ABI; Centro Internazionale Eugenio Montale, Rome; Accademico Ordinario Accademia Euro-Afro-Asiatica del Turismo. Address: c/o Blue Jay Press, Apdo Correos 32, E-30380 La Manga del Mar Menor, Spain.

VAISH Yogi Nandan, b. Aligarh City, India. Writer. Education: BA, 1954; MA, English Literature. 1961. Appointment: English Lecturer, 1974-93. Publication: Dirty Belly, 1991. Contributions to: USA includes: Prophetic Voices; Gusto; Amelia; Cicada; Welter 87; UK: Contemporary Review; London Writer Review; Cork Weekly. Honours: 1st Prize in Poetry, Ireland, 1973; Best Issue Award in Haiku, USA, 1982; Michael Madhusudan Award, India, 1987; Grand Prize Winner in Poetry, USA, ISP, 1995, 1996; Honours of International Biographical Centre. Memberships: Poetry Society; Royal Society of Literature, UK; Fellow, Academy of American Poets; Honorary Life Member, London Writers Circle; Phoenix Poetry Society; Fellow, International Poetry Society, UK; Poetry Society, India; Authors Guild of India; Vice-President, MMA. Address: 9-16 Palamal Street, Aligarh City 202 001, UP, India.

VAJDI Shadab, b. 27 July 1937, Shiraz, Iran. BBC Producer. m. Lotfali Khonji, 25 June 1972, 1 daughter. Education: BA, Persian Literature, 1958, MA, Social Sciences, 1973, Tehran University; PhD, Linguistics, London University, 1976. Appointments: Teacher, Persian Literature, Rezashah High School Tehran; Producer, Persian Section, BBC World Service, England; Chief Examiner for Persian GCSE, London and East Anglia Examination Board. Publications: A Bend in the Alley, 1961; A Song for Little Hands, 1968; To the Memory of the Thirst of Southern Mountain Slopes, 1982; Closed Circuit, 1989; Poetry: Another Day, 1992; Translation from English into Persian:

Inside the Third World by Paul Harrison, 1987; Translation from English into Persian: Return to China, by Ling Heng, 1991. Contributions to: Rialto; Virago Book of Love Poetry; Par, Persian Magazine, USA; Nimeye Digar, Persian Periodical, USA; Barrasiye Ketab, book review, Persian Periodical. Membership: Poetry Society. Address: 31 Sevington Road, London NW4 3RY, England.

VALENTE José Angel, b. 25 Apr 1929, Orense, Spain. Writer. m. Coral Gutierrez-Valente, 24 Nov 1984, 2 daughters. Education: BLitt (Extraordinary Prize), Madrid University, 1953; MA, Oxford University, 1957. Appointments: Lecturer in Spanish Studies, Oxford University, 1955-58; International Civil Servant, Geneva, 1959-80; Chief, Spanish Translation Service, UNESCO, Paris, 1980-84. Publications: A Modo de esperanza, 1955; Pun de la to cero (Poems 1979-89) 1992; Las Palabras de la tribu, 1971; Variaciones sobre el pajaro y la red (essays), 1991; No amanece el cantor, 1992. Contributions to: Insula; Indice; El Pais; ABC; Diario 16. Honours: Premio Adonais, 1954; Premio, Critica, 1960, 1980; Premio, Fundacion Pablo Iglesias, 1984; Premio, Principe de Asturias para las Letras, 1988; Premio nacional de Poesia, 1993. Address: Apartado 195, 04080 Almeria, Spain.

VALENTINE Jean, b. 27 Apr 1934, Chicago, Illinois, USA. Poet; Teacher. m. James Chace, 1957, div 1968, 2 daughters. Education: BA, Radcliffe College, 1956. Appointments: Teacher, Swarthmore College, 1968-70, Barnard College, 1968, 1970, Yale University, 1970, 1973-74, Hunter College of the City University of New York, 1970-75, Sarah Lawrence College, Columbia University, 1974-. Publications: Poetry: Dream Barker and Other Poems, 1965; Pilgrims, 1969; Ordinary Things, 1974; Turn, 1977; The Messenger, 1979; Home, Deep, Blue: New and Selected Poems, 1988; Night Lake, 1992; The River at Wolf, 1992. Honours: Yale Series of Younger Poets Award, 1965; National Endowment for the Arts Grant, 1972; Guggenheim Fellowship, 1976. Address: c/o Department of Writing, Columbia University, New York, NY 10027, USA.

VALERO Roberto, b. 27 May 1955, Matanzas, Cuba. Writer; Assistant Professor. m. Maria Badias, 15 June 1983, 3 daughters. Education: University of Havana, Cuba, 1975-80; PhD with distinction, Latin-American Literature, Georgetown University, Washington DC, 1988. Appointments: Assistant Professor, George Washington University, Washington, District of Columbia, USA, 1988-. Publications: Desde un oscuro anglo, 1982; En fin, la noche, 1984; Dharma, 1985; Venias, 1990. Contributions to: Linden Lane Magazine; Mariel, New York; La Nacion, Costa Rica; El Universal, Venezuela; Poetry reading recordings, Recordings of Hispanic Poets Series, Library of Congress. Honours: Fellowship, Cintas Foundation, New York, 1982-83; Co-winner, 1st Prize for En fin, la noche, Festival de las Artes, Miami; Finalist, Letras de Oro Contest, 1988, 1989; Publication Grant for Venias, University Facilitating Funds, George Washington University. Memberships: World Academy of Arts and Culture; Modern Language Association. Address: 2520 41st Street, North West, No 3, Washington, DC 200007, USA.

VAN DER HOEVEN Jan, b. 3 Nov 1929, Bruges, Belgium. Teacher; Translator. m. Palm Margaret, 16 July 1965, 1 son, 2 daughters. Education: University of Ghent, 1964. Publications: Projekjie Schrjven; Te Woord Staan; Lecina Je Land; Elementair; Hagel En Blank; Anarchipel; Knoop Voor Knoop; Light Verse. Contributions to: Diagram; De Tafelronde; Radar; Diogenes; NVT; De Vlaamse Gids; Yang; Kentering; Kunst Van Nu. Honours: Merendree Poetry Prize; Knokke; Trap; Harelbeke. Memberships: Society of Flemish Writers; Society of West Writers. Address: Brieversweg 89, 8310 Bruges, Belgium.

VAN DUYN Mona (Jane), b. 9 May 1921, Waterloo, Iowa, USA. Poet; Writer; Critic; Editor; Reviewer; Lecturer. m. Jarvis A Thurston, 31 Aug 1943. Education: BA, Iowa State Teachers College, 1942; MA, State University of Iowa, 1943. Appointments: Reviewer, Poetry Magazine, 1944-70; Instructor in English, State University of Iowa 1945, University of Louisville 1946-50; Founder-Editor (with Jarvis A Thurston), Perspective: A Quarterly of Literature, 1947-67; Lecturer in English 1950-67, Adjunct Professor 1983, Visiting Hurst Professor 1987, Washington University, St Louis; Poetry Advisor, College English, 1955-57; Lecturer, Salzburg Seminar in American Studies, 1973; Poet-in-Residence, Breadloaf Writing Conferences, 1974, 1976; Sewanee Writers' Conference, 1990; Poet Laureate of the USA, 1992-93; Numerous poetry readings. Publications: Valentines to the Wide World: Poems, 1959; A Time of Bees, 1964; To See, To Take,

1970; Bedtime Stories, 1972; Merciful Disguises: Poems Published and Unpublished, 1973; Letters from a Father and Other Poems, 1982; If It Be Not I: Collected Poems, 1993; Firefall, 1993. Contributions to: Many anthologies; Poems, criticism, reviews and short stories in various periodicals; Near Changes, 1990. Honours include: Hon DLitt: Washington University, Cornell College, University of Northern Iowa, George Washington University, University of the South, Georgetown University; Harriet Monroe Memorial Prize, 1968; Loines Prize, National Institute of Arts and Letters, 1976; Fellowship, Academy of American Poets, 1981; Sandburg Prize, Cornell College, 1982; Shelley Memorial Award, Poetry Society of America, 1987; Ruth Lilly Prize, 1989; Pulitzer Prize in Poetry, 1991; Bollingen Prize; National Book Award. Memberships: Academy of American Poets, chancellor, 1985; National Academy of Arts and Letters; American Academy of Arts and Science. Address: 7505 Teasdale Avenue, St Louis, MO 63130, USA.

VAN LONDERSELE (Raoul) Roel Richelieu, b. 30 June 1952, Belgium. Teacher. Education: University of Ghent, 1970-74. Appointment: Teacher, Literature, 1974. Publications: Marie Sans Toilette; Appel en Treurigheid; Myn Stilstaand Woord; Mijn Geboomde Vader; Een Nagelaten Liefde; Invoelen; Een Jaar Van September. Contributions to: Numerous. Honours: Vlaamse Poeziedagen Deurle; Vlaamse Club Brussels; Prize City of Ghent; Louis Paul Boonprize. Address: Buffelstraat 2, 9000 Ghent, Belgium.

VAN SOMEREN Gretta June, b. 20 July 1968, Chickishae. Oklahoma, USA. Professional Pianist; Music Teacher; Freelance Poet. m. Jay A Van Someren, 4 Aug 1990, 1 daughter. Education: BM Certificate to teach choral and general music, 1991. Appointments: Music and Choral Teacher, 1990-95: Private Piano Teacher, 1986-95; Professional Pianist, 1986-; Freelance Poet. Publications: National Poets Association Anthology: Miles to Go Before I Sleep, 1997; Why Speak French to An Ilatian, 1996. Contributions to: After Thoughts, The Inner-Fountain; Anterior Poetry Monthly; Apropos; Alpha Beat Press; Poetry in Motion; Poetry Forum; Poets at Work; Family Fun; Joyful Child Journal; Imprint. Memberships: National Poet's Association; UAPAA. Address: 2357 20¼ Street, Rice Lake, WI 54868, USA.

VAN SPANCKEREN Kathryn, b. 14 Dec 1945, Kansas City, Missouri, USA. University Teacher. m. Stephen Breslow, 26 June 1975, 1 son. Education: BA, English, Folklore and Mythology, University of California, Berkeley, 1967; MA, English Literature, Brandeis University, 1968; MA, English Literature, Harvard University, 1969; PhD, English and American Literature, Harvard University, 1976. Appointments: Teaching Fellow, Harvard University, 1970-73; Assistant Professor, Wheaton College, Massachusetts, 1974-79; Program Director, Coordinator, Coordinating Council, Literary Magazines, New York City, 1979-80; Assistant Associate, Full Professor, University of Tampa, Florida, 1982-; Poetry Editor, Tampa Review, 1988-. Publications: Mountains Hidden in Mountains, 1992; Salt and Sweet Water, 1993. Contributions to: Harvard Advocate; American Poetry Review; Boundary 2; Roof; River Styx; Ploughshares; Poets On; En Passant; Thirteenth Moon; Aspect; Carolina Quarterly; Perigraph; Contact 2; Albatross; Assembling; A Carolina Literary Companion; Fine Frenzy, anthology; Our Bodies Ourselves, book. Honours: Honourable Mention, Karen Patricia Barr Dante Memorial Prize, Virginia Commonwealth University, 1978; Honourable Mention, Carolina Quarterly. Memberships: Open Window Literature Association Board of Directors; Modern Language Association, Executive Committee on Popular Culture; American Humor Studies, Past Chair, South Atlantic Region; Founder, Chair, East-West Cultural Relations International Committee; Past President, Margaret Atwood Society; Poetry Society of America; Poets and Writers. Address: 93 Martinique Avenue, Tampa, FL 33606, USA.

VANCE Andrea Elois, b. 20 Mar 1961, Louisville, Kentucky, USA. Poet; Playwright. Education: Psychology Studies, Jefferson Community College, Louisville, 1979-81; BA, Communications, Psychology, University of Louisville, 1983. Appointments: Customer Service Representative, Humana Corp, Louisville, Kentucky; News Clerk, Courier-Journal Newspaper, Louisville; Staff Writer, Louisville Defender Newspaper; Tutor, pre-school and grade school children, YMCA, Louisville; Poetry Reading Interview, Urban Insight, weekly TV programme, Louisville; Participant: Celebration - Voices in the Wind - poetry reading, Black Poet's Day, Kentucky Contemporary Theatre, 1989; Umbhiyozo African American Jazz and Poetry Festival, Kentucky Center for the Arts, 1990. Contributions to: Anthologies and periodicals. Honour: Golden Poet Award; World of Poetry, 1988; Nominated, Outstanding Young Woman in America; Poem "I" recited

at Actor's Theatre, Louisville, 1995. Memberships: Louisville Association of Black Communicators; People for the Ethical Treatment of Animals, Washington DC. Address: 1487 Olive Street, Louisville, KY 40210-1967, USA.

VANICEK Zdenek, b. 24 June 1947, Czechoslovakia. Div. 1 son, 1 daughter. Education: College of Economics, Prague, 1967; LLD, Charles University, Prague, 1980; PhD, Charles University, Prague, 1981; DPhil, Univeristy of Lahore, 1995. Appointments: Czechoslovak Diplomatic Service, 1972-91; Freelance Journalist and Writer, 1991-92; Political and Diplomatic Advisor, 1992-93; Professor of International Relations and Law, 1993-. Publications: Amidst the Ruins of Memories; To the Ends of the Earth, 1992; On the Edge Rain (poetry), 1994; Under The Range of Mountains of Five Fingers (poetry), 1996. Contributions to: Literary Olympians; Orbis; Poetry Review; Scratch; Sunk Island Review; A Happy Christmas 1991; Prairie Schooner. Membership: Poetry Society, London. Literary Agent: Art Van, Prague, Czech Republic. Address: Vladislavova 8, 110 00 Prague 1, Czech Republic.

VANNELLI Maria Antonietta, b. 10 Dec 1946, Livorno, Italy. Journalist. m. Franco Petri, 3 June 1967. Sep, 2 sons. Education: Diploma as French Teacher. Appointments: Journalist, newspapers: La Nazione; Il Tirreno; Il Giorno; Il Sole 24 Ore; Journalist, various cultural periodicals; Currently freelance; Editor-in-charge: Mareggiata; Teleriviera; Journalist: RAI TV; Radio Montecarlo; Promoted numerous socio-cultural events, Versilia. Publications: Un giorno una vita, 1976; Saudade, 1980; La donna di vetro, 1984; Una zattera di liberta, 1991. Contributions to: Controcampo, Turin; Crisi e Letteratura, Rome; Salpare, Calgiari; K Dialogo, Versilia. Honours: 1st Prize, Donne in Poesia, Crespina; Guido Gozzano Special Prize, Turin; La Mole Special Prize, Turin; Jury's Prize, Castiglion de Pepoli; 1st Prize, Citta del Marmo, Carrara; Renato Serra Special Prize Rome; Coreglia Antelminelli Special Prize; Special Prize, Como. Memberships: President, Versilia, Centro Studi e Storia delle Poetiche; Dimensione Donna Club; Azzurro Donna; Gruppo Internazionale di Lettura. Address: Via Piastelli 115, 55043 Lido di Camaiore, Lucca, Italy.

VARJU Livia, b. 17 Sept 1936, Eger, Hungary. International Civil Servant, retired. Education: Numerous courses in many subjects. Appointments: Administrative work, Canadian Broadcasting Corporation, Toronto; Administrative work, translating, editing, World Health Organization; UN High Commission for Refugees. Publications: 1 poem in New Christian Poetry, 1990; Swissericks (co-author), humorous verse and limericks about Switzerland, 1991; Contributions to: WHO Dialogue; UN Special; Guardian of Liberty, Munich; Ex Tempore; Anthology of Eastern European Poetry, Editor-in-Chief. Honour: Gold Medal for translations of Hungarian poetry into English, Arpad Academy, Cleveland, Ohio, USA, 1988. Memberships: Poetry Society, London; Local Writers Group. Address: 4 chem du Repos, 1213 Petit-Lancy, Geneva, Switzerland.

VASSILIEVA Larissa, b. 23 Nov 1935, Kharkov, Russia. Writer; Poet. m. Oleg Vassiliev, 19 Jan 1957, dec 1993, 1 son. Education: Graduated, Department of Philology, Moscow University, 1958. Publications: Linen Moon, 1968; Fire-fly, 1969; The Goose-foot, 1970; Blue Twilight, 1970; Encounter, 1974; A Rainbow of Snow, 1974; Meadows, 1975; Light in the Window, 1978; Russian Names, 1980; Foliage, 1980; Fireflower, 1981; Selected Poetry, 1981; Grove, 1984; Mirror, 1985; Moskvorechie, 1985; Lantern, 1985; Waiting for You in the Sky, 1986; Selected Works, 2 vols, 1989; Strange Quality, 1991; Books of Prose: Books of Essays: Albion and the Secret of Time, 1978; The Cloud of fire, 1988. Contributions to: Literary Gazette; Literary Russia; Pravda; Ogonyok; Novyi Mir; Yunost; Nash Sovremennik; Druzhba Narodov; Krestyanka; Komsomolskaya Pravda. Honours: Moscow Komsomol Prize, 1971; Order of Merit, 1971, 1980; Order of Friendship of People, 1984. Memberships: Union of Writers, USSR, 1968; League of Woman Writers, President. Address: 8 Usievicha Str, Apt 86, Moscow 125319, Russia.

VAUGHAN WILLIAMS Ursula, (Ursula Wood), b. 15 Mar 1911, Malta. Writer. m. (1) Michael Forrester Wood, 24 May 1933, dec 1942. m. (2) Ralph Vaughan Williams OM, 7 Feb 1953, dec 1958. Education: Private. Publications: No Other Choice, 1941; Fall of Leaf, 1944; Need for Speech, 1948; Poems in Pamphlet X, 1952; Silence and Music, 1959; Aspects, 1984; Collected Poems; Staged Opera Libretti: The Sofa; The Brilliant and the Dark; Melita; David and Bathsheba; King of Macedon; Echoes; Canterbury Morning; Words for Songs, Song Cycles, Cantatas (music by various composers): Sons of Light, Four

Last Songs; Break to be Built; Musesd and Grapes; The Icy Mirror; Autumnal; Compassion; Aspects; The Looking Glass; Vision and Echo; King Frost; Jacob and the Angels; The Silver Hound; Lady and Unicorn; Ode to St Cecilia. Address: 66 Gloucester Crescent, London NW1 7EG, England.

VAZQUEZ DIAZ Rene, b. 7 Sept 1952, Caibarien, Cuba. Writer; Translator. Education: Polish Language, Univerity of Lodz; Swedish Language, University of Lund. Appointment: Review Writer, Swedish Journal. Publications: La Era Imaginaria; Querido Traidor; La Isla Del Cundeamor; El últiom Concierto; Difusos Mapas. Contributions to: Sydsvendska Dagladet; Bonniers; El País; El Urogallo; Geo; El Nuevo Herald. Honour: Fellowships. Memberships: Swedish Union of Writers; Swedish Pen Club. Address: Albert Bonniers Forlag, Box 3159, 103-63 Stockholm, Sweden.

VEGA Janine Pommy, b. 5 Feb 1942, Jersey City, New Jersey, USA. Writer; Poet. Education: MFA equivalency: 12 books and chapbooks. Appointments: Poet and Instructor, Poets in the Schools, 1975-88; Director, Incisions/Arts, teaching poetry in prisons and secure centres for youth, 1988-; Alternative Literary Programs in the Schools, 1991-; Teachers and Writers, 1995-. Publications: Poems to Fernando, 1968; Morning Passage, 1976; Here at the Door, 1978; Journal of a Hermit, 1979; The Bard Owl, 1980; Apex of the Earth's Way, 1984; Drunk on a Glacier Talking to Flies, 1988; Island of the Sun, 1991; Threading the Maze, 1992; Red Bracelets, 1994; The Road to Your House is a Mountain Road, 1995; Tracking the Serpent, due 1997. Contributions to: Village Voice; Baltimore Sun; Exquisite Corpse; City Lights Anthology; Mademoiselle Mag; ACM; Out of This World Anthology; El Comercio (Lima, Peru); Tvorba (Prague); IKON; Up Late Anthology. Honours: Operating Grant, New York State Council on the Arts, 1988-96; Heaven Bone Chapbook Competition, 1994. Memberships: Prison Writers Committee, PEN; Poets and Writers. Address: Box 162, Bearsville, NY 12409, USA.

VELARDE Damian John, b. 29 Aug 1938, Liverpool, England. Teacher. m. Eileen Power, 28 July 1964, 1 son, 1 daughter. Education: BSc, Liverpool University, 1960; BA, Open University, 1976; Diploma, Art Education, Birmingham, 1979. Appointments: Teacher of Biology and Art, Liverpool; Head of Biology, Sheffield, 1964-. Contributions to: Poetry and Audience; Poetry Nottingham; Pen to Paper; The New Welsh Review. Honours: Likely Literature Festival; Work included in collection of contemporary Yorkshire Poetry, 1984. Memberships: Poetry Society. Address: 6 Bushey Wood Road, Dore, Sheffield S17 3QB, England.

VELASCO Lola (Garcia), b. 19 Oct 1961, Madrid, Spain. Writer; Literary Critic; Scriptwriter. Education: Study, Litt. Publications: Le Frente de Una Mujer Oblicua, 1986; El Sueno de las Piedras, 1987; La Cometa o las Manos Sobre el Papel, 1992; Included in: Las Diosas Blancas, anthology, 1986; Les Deesses Blanches, 1989; Escritores Espanoles Contemporaneos, 1991; Escritores en Madrid, 1992. Contributions to: Newspapers: ABC, Diario 16, Ya, El Independiente, El Correo Espanol-El Pueblo Vasco; Magazines: Litoral, Barcarola, Revista de Occidente. Honours: Finalist, Hiperion Prize, 1986; Nominee, Icaro Prize, 1990; Participant, 7th International Conference of Contemporary Poetry, Tarascon, France; Summer Courses, El Escorial, Universidad Complutense, Madrid. Address: c/o Costanilla de Santiago 2, 4olzd, 28013 Madrid, Spain.

VENABLES Roger Evelyn Cavendish, b. 4 Mar 1911, Varna, Bulgaria. Poet; Lecturer. Education: Beaumont and Christ Church, Oxford; MA, Oxford University. Publications: Poetry: Combe, 1942; Images of Power, 1960; The Night Comes, 1961; Leaves and Seasons, 1961; Forebodings, 1963, 1975; Memories and Forebodings, 1991; Cornish Themes, including: Farewell to Combe, 1974; The Cornish Hundreds, 1980; War Poetry including: Bari, 1974; Leaflets, 1986; Also: D: Portrait of a Don, biography, 1967; The Hooting Carn, poems 1993. Honour: Bard of Cornish Gorseth, 1984. Memberships: Lancashire Authors Association; Past President, St Just and Pendeen Old Cornwall Society. Address: Atlanta, Pendeen, Penzance, Cornwall, England.

VENEZIANO Patricia Joan Morse, b. 4 Apr 1931, Waterbury, Connecticut, USA. Educator; Librarian; Poet. m. Santo Veneziano, 20 Feb 1965. Education: Fordham University, 1942-54; University of Connecticut, 1956-58; Southeast Connecticut State University, 1959-62. Appointments: Librarian, Silas Bronson Library, Waterbury, 1954-84; Substitute Teacher, Crosby High School, Waterbury, 1985-.

Contributions to: Waterbury Republican-American; Naugatuck Daily News, Connecticut. Memberships: Connecticut Poetry Society; Waterbury Chapter, Connecticut Poetry Society. Address: 170 Hillside Avenue No 3-H, Waterbury, CT 06710, USA.

VERHEGGHE Willie, b. 22 June 1947, Denderleeuw, Belgium. Official. m. Arlet Vanderweeen, 30 May 1970, 2 sons, 1 daughter. Education: Journalism. Appointments: Official Department of Education, 1969-70; Official Department of Culture, 1970-72. Publications: Met Ikaros op Schoot; Van Mensen, Dieren en Dingen; Circus Ricardo & Andere Akrobatieen Tussen Leven; Liefde en Dood; Het Hart Van De Tijger; Miguel Woud Van Wielen; Zilverwerk; Artlantis; Marcinelle. Contributions to: Vooruit; Dimensie; Morgen; Dietsche Warande en Belfort; Avenue; De Vlaamse Gids; Yang; Poeziekrant. Honours: Poetry Prize of Meise; J L De Belder Prize; Vanessa Prize. Memberships: Flemish Pen Club; Literary Foundation Dimensie; Honest Arts Movement. Address: Pollare Dorp 105, B 9401 Ninove, Belgium.

VERRILLI Joseph, b. 2 May 1952, Bridgeport, Connecticut, USA. m. Janet Ochs, 21 Nov 1981. Education: Graduated, Kolbe High School, 1970. Publications: Blessed Events, in The Plowman, 1993; Words From a Little Universe, in JVC Books, 1994; Blues For Angel Face, in JVC Books, 1995; Faces in The Flower Garden, in Caro-Lynn Publication, 1995. Contributions to: Cer-Ber-Us; Zig Zag Zygurat Zyne; Phoenix Rising; Cokefishing in Alpha Beat Soup; Lone Stars; Cokefish; Bouillabaisse; Poetic Page; Poet's Paradise; Window Panes; Khepera. Honours: Editor's Choice Award, National Library of Poetry, 1993, 1994, 1995; 2nd Place, Distinguished Poet Awards, Sparrowgrass Poetry Forum, 1994; 2nd Place and Honorable Mention, Poetic Page, 1995. Membership: Connecticut Poetry Society. Address: 115 Washington Avenue, Apt GH, Bridgeport, CT 06604-3805, USA.

VERTREACE Martha Modena, b. 24 Nov 1945, Washington, District of Columbia, USA. Associate Professor; Writer-in-Residence. Education: BA, English, District of Columbia Teachers College, 1967; MA, English, Roosevelt University, 1972; MPH, Roosevelt University, 1973; MS, Religious Studies, Mundelein College, 1982. Appointments: English Instructor, 1976-85, Assistant Professor, 1986-90, Associate Professor, English, 1991-, Poet-in-Residence, 1986-, Distinguished Professor, 1995-96, Kennedy King College; Assistant Adjunct Professor, English, Rosary College, Illinois, 1982-83; Co-Editor, Rhono; Editor, Class Act. Publications: Second House from the Corner, 1986; Kelly In the Mirror, 1993; Under A Cat's-Eye Moon, 1994; Oracle Bones, 1994; Cinnabar, 1995; Light Caught Bending, 1995. Contributions to: Benchmark: An Anthology of Contemporary Illinois Poetry, 1988; Clockwatch Review; Hawaii Review; Another Chicago Magazine; Chicago Review; Oyez; Poets On; Midwest Quarterly; Willow Review; Monocacy Valley Review; Vincent Brothers Review; Higginson Journal of Poetry; MacGuffin; Crazy Quilt; New College; Phoenix. Honours include: 1st Prize, 4th Annual Salute to the Arts Poetry Contest, Triton College, 1985, 1986, 1987, 1990; Willow Review; Excellence, Professional Writing, Harcourt Brace Jovanovich, 1986; Roberts Writing Awards, 1990; Statewide Reading Series, Illinois, 1992; Fellowship, Hawthornden International Writers Retreat, Scotland, 1992; Poetry Fellow, Writers Centre, Dublin, 1993; Significant Illinois Poet, 1993; National Endowment for the Arts, 1993; Writers Fellowship, Illinois Arts Council, 1993. Memberships: National Federation of State Poetry Societies; Illinois State Poetry Society; Poets Study Club; Society of Writers of Children's Literature; Society of Midland Authors. Address: 1157 East 56th Street, No 3, Chicago, IL 60637-1531, USA.

VETTESE Raymond John, b. 1 Nov 1950, Angus, Scotland. Teacher. m. Maureen Elizabeth, 13 May 1972. Education: Montrose Academy, 1961-67; Dundee College of Education, 1972-75. Appointments: Journalist, 1967-72; Student, 1972-75; Barman, 1975-77; Process Worker, 1977-78; Librarian, 1978-84; Teacher, 1984-. Publications: Four Scottish Poets; The Right Noise and Other Poems; A Keen New Air (poetry), 1995. Contributions to: Akros; Chapman; Cencrastus; Lallans; Lines Review; Orbis; Poetry Ireland; Radical Scotland; Scots Glasnost. Honours: The Saltire Society, The Scotsman Prize, For Best First Book; William Soutar Writers Fellowship. Memberships: Scots Language Society; Scottish Pen; Scots Language Resource Center. Address: 9 Tayock Avenue, Montrose, Angus, Tayside DD10 9AP, Scotland.

VIDAL Francisco Cervantes, b. 7 Apr 1938, Queretoro, Mexico, Journalist and Publisher. Education: High School; Law studies for two years. Publications: Poetry: Los varones senalados/La materia del tributo, 1971; Esta sustancia amarga, 1972; Cantado para nadie, 1982; Heridas que se alternan, 1985; Los huesos peregrinos, 1986; (with Joan Boldo i Climent) El canto del abismo, 1987; Book of short stories: Relatorio sentimental, 1987; Materia de Distintos Lais, 1987; El Libro de Nicole, 1992; Translator of Luso-Brazilian matters. Contributions to: Plural; Vuelta; Revista Unam; UAM; Diora de la Cultura de Excelsior; Revista de Bellas Arteas. Honours: Guggenheim Fellowship, 1977-78; Villaurrotia Prize for Poetry, 1982; Heriberto Frias, Local Government of Queretoro Prize, 1986; Officer, Order of Rio Branco, Brazilian Government for publication of Brazilian matters. Address: Eve Central, Lazaro Cordenas 12, 0600 Mexico DF Hotel Cosmos, Mexico.

VIDALES IBARRA Aura Maria, b. 11 July 1958. Poet; Journalist. m Jose Salvador Guerrero, 11 Dec 1990, 1 son, 1 daughter. Education: Licentiate in Journalism, Escuela Carlos Septien Garcia, 1984. Appointments: Founder, Reporter, Head of Social Section, Cuestion daily newspaper, 1979; Reporter, Channel 11 TV, National Polytechnic Institute, 1980-84; Reporter and Literary Researcher, 1984-90. Publications: Ensueno, 1979; Estalactitas, 1984; Balada para un viento suave, 1987; Ventanas vacias, 1990; Anthologised in Memorias del Sexto Encuentro Nacional de Escritores Jovenes, 1987. Contributions to: Revista de la Universidad de Mexico; Revista Poesia de la UNAM y la Universidad Autonoma Metropolitana; Newspapers: La Journada; El Universal; Novedades; El Nacional; El Sol de Mexico; Excelsior. Honour: Scholarship, National Council for Culture and Arts, 1990. Address: Ingenieros Militaires 94, Colonia Periodista, Mexico DF 11220, Mexico.

VIDOR Vassillil. See: **BARRIERE William J.**

VIERECK Peter (Robert Edwin), b. 5 Aug 1916, New York, New York, USA. Historian; Poet; Professor. m. (1) Anya de Markov, June 1945, div May 1970, 1 son, 1 daughter. (2) Betty Martin Falkenberg, 30 Aug 1972. Education: BS, 1937, MA, 1939, PhD, 1942, Harvard University; Graduate Study as a Henry Fellow, Christ Church, Oxford, 1937-38. Appointments: William R Kenan Chair of History, Mount Holyoke College, 1979-; Director, Poetry Workshop, New York Writers Conferences, 1965-67. Publications: History: Metapolitics: From the Romantics to Hitler, 1941, revised edition as Metapolitics: The Roots of the Nazi Mid, 1961, 2nd revised edition, 1965, updated edition, 1982; Conservatism Revisited: The Revolt Against Revolt 1815-1949, 1949, 2nd edition as Conservatism Revisited and the New Conservatism: What Went Wrong?, 1962, 3rd edition, 1972; Shame and Glory of the Intellectuals: Babbitt, Jr. Versus the Rediscovery of Values, 1953; The Unadjusted Man: A New Hero for Americans: Reflections on the Distinction Between Conserving and Conforming, 1956; Conservatism: From John Adams to Churchill, 1956, revised edition, 1962; Inner Liberty: The Stubborn Grit in the Machine, 1957; Conservatism from Burke and John Adams till 1982: A History and an Anthology, 1982. Poetry: Terror and Decorum: Poems 1940-1948, 1948; Strike Through the Mask: New Lyrical Poems, 1950; The First Morning: New Poems, 1952; Dream and Responsibility: The Tension Between Poetry and Society, 1953; The Persimmon Tree, 1956; The Tree Witch: A Poem and a Play (First of All a Poem), 1961; New and Selected Poems 1932-1967, 1967; Archer in the Marrow: The Applewood Cycles of 1967-1987, 1987; Tide and Continuities: Last and first Poems, 1995-1938, 1995. Contributions to: Monographs, essays, reviews and poems to numerous periodicals. Honours: Pulitzer Prize in Poetry, 1949. Memberships: PEN; Poetry Society of America. Address: 12 Silver Street, South Hadley, MA 01075, USA.

VIERU Grigore Pavel, b. 14 Feb 1935, Moldova. Writer. m. Vieru Raisa Tudor, 8 June 1959, 2 sons. Education: Romanian Language, Chisinau Pedagogic Institute. Appointments: Literary Editor, Children's Publishing House; Reader, Moldovan Writers Union; Freelance Writer. Publications: Alarm, 1957; Variety of books for children and five collections of lyrics for adults. Contributions to: White Flowers; We; Literature and Art; Moldova Youth; Sovereign Moldova; Country Life; Nation's Voice; Journals: Basarabia, Moldova and Columna. Honours: Moldova State Laureate, 1979; Honorary Member, Romanian Academy of Science; Proposed by Romanian Academy of Science as candidate for Nobel Prize, 1992. Memberships: Moldova Writer's Union. Address: Chisinau str Nicolae Iorga 7 ap 10 Moldova, Romania.

VIJAY BHANU A K, (Chaarithra), b. 10 July 1930, Ayyampalayam, Dindigul Q M District, Tamil Nadu, India. Government Servant, Indian Administrative Service (retired); Advocate. m. Gnana

Soundhari, 18 Oct 1956, 2 sons, 1 daughter. Education: BA (Hons), Economics; MA, Economics; Bachelor of Law; DLitt, World University. Appointments: Various government positions. Publications: In English: Silvern Waters, 1987; Revels, 1987; Wood-Nymphs, 1988; Flute, 1988; Ecstasy, 1988; Mystic Rocks, 1988; Goddess, 1989; Honey Comb, 1989; Shadows, 1989. Contributions to: Indian Journals in English. Address: Pearl Castle, S 106, Main Road, Anna Nagar, Madras 40, India.

VILLA Carlo, b. 3 Oct 1931, Rome, Italy. Writer; Poet; Journalist. Education: Graduate. Appointments: Director, Centro Sistema Bibliotecario Cittadino; Secretary-General, Centro Internazionale Eugenio Montale; Book Reviewer, Scriptwriter, RAI TV; Italian Correspondent, Radio Televisione Svizzera Italiana. Publications: Fiera Letteraria, 1959; Il Privilegio di Essere Vivi, 1962; Solo Sperando Nauseati, 1963; Siamo Esseri Antichi, 1964; Gorba, 1972; Le Maesta delle Finte, 1977; Polvere de Miele, 1980; Infanzia del Dettato, 1981; Come la Rosa al Naso, 1984; Corpo a Cuore, 1985; Morte per Lucro, 1988; 100 di Questi Fogli, 1989; Pochades, 1992; L'Apparenza del Nulla, 1992; Simboli Eroici, 1993; L'Ora di Mefistofele, 1993; Several novels, short stories, essays. children, Einaudi, 1975; Il Fortino Sepolto, Literary Textbook, 1980; Essai: V Pratolini: 73, L'Eros Neua Poesia IT Del 900'81; Le Vie Consocari, Roma Su Strada, 1984. Contributions to: Various newspapers and magazines. Honour: Italian nominee, Formentor International Prize, 1964. Membership: International PEN Club, Paso Doble, Rome. Address: Via Virginia Agnelli 24, 00151 Rome, Italy.

VINCENT Elizabeth, (Za), b. 20 Nov 1940, Amersham, Buckingshire, England. Teacher. m. Michael Vincent, 19 Sept 1959, 2 sons. Education: Teachers Certificate in Education, with distinction, 1972; BEd, University of London, 1973. Appointments: Senior Teacher, Primary Education, Sutton, Surrey, 1973-90; Lecturer, Literacy Campaign, Croydon, 1975-78; Lecturer in Communications, Erith, 1977. Publications: Blue Apples, 1958; Green Apples, 1959; The Bride, 1960; Tactical Navigators 1, 1961; Cunt Art Can't, 1962; Mirrors, 1963; Maryelisa, 1969; Beached; Ruiad. Address: Rowans, 20 Byron Close, North Heath Lane, Horsham, West Sussex RH12 5PA, England.

VINCK Catherine de (Baroness), b. Brussels, Belgium. Poet. m. Baron de Vinck, 1 Feb 1945, 4 sons, 2 daughters. Education: Greco-Latin Humanities, 1941. Publications: Time to Gather, 1964, 3rd printing, 1989; Ikon, 1972, 2nd printing, 1974; A Liturgy, 1973, 3rd printing, 1977; A Passion Play, 1975; A Book of Uncommon Prayers, 1976, 2nd printing, 1978; Readings, 1978; A Book of Eve, LP record and text, 1978; A Garland of Straw, 1981; A Book of Peace, 1985; News of the World in Fifteen Stations, 1989; A Peace Cantata, set to music, celebrated at Regis College, Weston, Massachusetts, 1986; Poems of the Hidden Way, 1991; God of a Thousand Names, 1992. Honours: Commencement Speaker, DLitt honoris causa, St Mary's College, Notre Dame, Indiana; Commencement Speaker, DHL honoris causa, St Scholastica College, Duluth, Minnesota, 1986; DLitt honoris causa, Regis College, Weston, Massachusetts, 1986. Address: 672 Franklin Turnpike, Allendale, NJ 07401, USA.

VIRGO Crescent. See: **BALACHANDRAN Kannaiya.**

VISHAL Vijay, b. 17 Oct 1949, Mirzahjaan, District Gurdaspur, India. College Teacher of English. m. Vipan Sharma, 2 Mar 1976, 2 sons, 2 daughters. Education: BA, 1969; MA, English, 1971; University Grants Commission Summer Institute in English Language Teaching for College Teachers, 1973; Refresher Course in English (Phonetics and Spoken English), Central Institute of English and Foreign Languages Regional Centre, Lucknow, 1983. Appointments: Lecturer in English, GGDSD College, Baihnath, 1971; Head, Department of English, GGDSC College, Baijnath. Publications: Speechless Messages: Writers Workshop, 1993; Ehsaas Ke Phool - A Collection of Poems in Hindi, under publication. Contributions to: Skylark; Canopy; The Quest; New Quest; Poetcrit; Kavita India; Rock Pebbles; Rambag; The Young Poet; Indian Book Chronicle; Newspapers: The Tribune; Indian Express; Trigart Times; Palampur Reporter; Radical Thought; Hindi Newspapers: Punjab Kesari; Veer Partaap; Dainik Tribune. Memberships: Poetry Society of India. Address: Mannan House, Preet Nagar, Baijnath 176125, Himachal, Pradesh, India.

VISSER Audrae Eugenie, b. 3 June 1919, Hurley, South Dakota, USA. English Teacher; Poet. 1 son. Education: AA, Black Hills State University, Spearfish, South Dakota, 1942; BS, South Dakota State University, Brookings, 1948; MA, University of Denver, Colorado,

1954. Appointments: Teacher: Country Schools, Moody County, 1939-43; Hot Springs, South Dakota, 1943-45; Elkton High School, 1946-49, 1963-71; DeSmet High School, 1949-50; Pierre Indian School, 1950-51; Pierre High School, 1951-53, 1961-63; Nagoya, Japan, 1954-55; South Dakota State University, 1955-56; Windom, Minnesota, 1956-58; Flandreau High School, South Dakota, 1958-61; Verdi High School, Minnesota, 1974-93. Publications: Rustic Roads, 1961; Poems for Brother Donald, 1974; Meter for Momma, 1974; Poems for Pop, 1976; South Dakota, 1980; Country Cousin, 1986; Pheasant Flights, 1989; Grass Roots Poetry, 1991. Contributions to: Various publications. Honours: Appointed South Dakota State Poet Laureate by Governor Richard F Kneip, 1974; Centennial Poet, South Dakota State Poetry Society, 1989; Woman of Achievement in Fine Arts, General Federation of Women's Clubs, South Dakota, 1990. Memberships include: President, Tau Chapter, Delta Kappa Gamma; United Poets Laureate International; South Dakota State Poetry Society; Black Hills Branch, National League of American Pen Women. Address: 710 Elk Street, Elkton, SD 57026, USA.

VIVIAN Tella. See: **URIEL Gila.**

VOGEL Constance M, b. Wisconsin, USA. Teacher. m. Francis X Vogel, 18 Apr 1959, 2 daughters. Education: BS, Marquette University; MEd, Northeastern Illinois University. Appointments: English Teacher, Nichols Junior High, Evanston, Bay View High, Milwaukee, Alvernia High, Chicago. Contributions to: Orbis; New York Times; Blue Unicorn; Spoon River Quarterly; Oyez Review; Willow Review; Hammers; Eclectic Literary Forum; Pinehurst Journal; Ariel. Honours: Salute to the Arts Contest, Triton College; First Prize, MUSE Contest; Numerous awards in Poets and Patrons contests and National League of American Pen Women contests; 2nd Prize, Ida Mary Williams Inspirational Poetry Contest, Poet Magazine. Memberships: Poets and Patrons (Past President); Poets Club of Chicago; National League of American Pen Women (Poetry Workshop Chairman). Address: 1206 Hutchings, Glenview, IL 60025, USA.

VOGELSANG Arthur, b. 31 Jan 1942, Baltimore, Maryland, USA. Poet. m. Judith Ayers, 14 June 1966. Education: BA, University of Maryland, 1965; MA, Johns Hopkins University, 1966; MFA, University of Iowa, 1970. Appointment: Editor, The American Poetry Review, 1973-. Publications: A Planet, 1983; Twentieth Century Women, 1988; Cities and Towns, 1996. Honours: Fellowships in Poetry Writing, National Endowment for the Arts, 1976, 1985, 1995; California Arts Council, 1994; Juniper Prize, 1995. Address: 1730 North Vista Street, Los Angeles, CA 90046, USA.

VOISINE Sister Mary Emma, (Smev), b.13 June 1914, Bay County, Michigan, USA. Teacher; Librarian. Education: BA, Education, English, College; MA, Library Science, University of Michigan; MTh, Theology, University of Detroit; Various other credentials: Ferris State University, Western Michigan University, University of Notre Dame, Wayne State University, others. Appointments: Elementary Teacher, Grades 1-8, 20 years; Principal, 5 years; High School Teacher in English and Religion, Librarian, Teacher Training, College and University AV-TV Workshops, 20 years; Director, Theology, Religion, Special Education, Elementary and High School Tutor, Adult Instruction, over 20 years; Consultant, Library, AV-TV. Publications: International Platform Association - Poetry Academy Publications; International Anthology of Poetry, 1990, 1991; World Book of Korea, 1991; World Book of Poetry, China, 1992; University of Michigan Class Poetry Publication: Recognition Poems, to be published. Contributions to: Various poems to newspapers. Memberships: International Platform Association; Academy of Poets; Board Member, Secretary, Membership Chair, Michigan Catholic Librarians Association; Michigan State Curriculum Planning Committee, AV Sub-Committee; Michigan State Library Development Committee. Address: McAuley Center, 28750 Eleven Mile Road, Farmington Hills, MI 48336, USA.

VOLDSETH Beverly Ann, b. 23 Oct 1935, Sioux Falls, South Dakota, USA. Teacher; Writer. m. Robert R Allers, 26 June 1958, 3 daughters. Education: BA, English Speech, 1957. Appointments: Teacher, English and Speech; Historical Society Director; Teacher of Writing; Publisher and Editor of Black Hat Press; Freelance Workshops and Readings. Publications: Absorb The Colors, 1984; Tremors Vibrations, 1995; I Am Becoming The Woman I Wanted, 1994. Contributions to: Republican Eagle; Sing Heavenly Muse; Minnesota Review; Poetry Motel; Minnesota Monthly; Fox Cry. Honour: Lake Superior Writers Series Award, 1995. Memberships:

Northfield Women Poets; The Loft; Poets & Writers. Address: Box 12, 508 2nd Avenue, Goodhue, MN 55027, USA.

VOLKOW Veronica, b. 26 Apr 1955, Mexico. Writer; Translator; Art Critic. Education: Licentiate, Spanish Literature, 1978; MA, Comparative Literature, Columbia University, New York, 1981. Publications: La Sibila de Cumas, 1974; Litoral de Tinta, 1979; El Inicio, 1983; Diario de Sudafrica, 1988; Los Caminos, 1989. Contributions to: Vuelta; Sabado; Revista de la UNAM; La Jornada; Poesie 89. Honours: Salvador Novo Fellowship, 1977; International Writers Programme, 1985; Fellowship, Centro Mexicano de Escritores, 1991. Address: Cerro del Vigilante 191, Col Romero de Terreros, CP 04320, Mexico DF, Mexico.

VOLLMAR James Anthony, b. 8 Jan 1952, Wellingborough, Northamptonshire, England. Writer; Poet; Playwright. Education: Queen Mary College, University of London, 1970-72. Appointment: Founder, Editor, Greylag Press, 1977-. Publications: All Stations to Silence; Circles and Spaces; Orkney Poems; Hoy: The Seven Postcards; Warming the Stones; Explorers Log Book. Contributions to: Agenda; Iron; Oasis; Joe Soaps Canoe; Ally; Pacific Quarterly. Memberships: Theatre Writers Union; Association of Little Presses. Address: 2 Grove Street, Higham Ferrers, Northants NN10 8HX, England.

VON WERNICH. See: **KNELL William H.**

W

WACHENJE Vivienne, (Gildersleve), b. 8 Dec 1948, Clapton, London, England. Counsellor. m. Elias Maganga Michael Wachenje, 2 Oct 1971, dec 1984, 2 sons, 1 dec. Education: BA, Honours, Literature, Philosophy, 1984; Postgraduate Diploma, Medical Ethics and Law, King's, London, 1985; RSA Certificate in Counselling and The Development of Learning, 1991, Certificate in Psychodynamic Counselling, Cambridge, 1993. Appointments: Shorthand Typist, 1964-69; State Enrolled Nurse, 1969-72; Childminder, 1974-77; Mature Student, 1977-84; Welfare Assistant, Special Education, 1986-88; Centre Manager and Counsellor, Harlow Well Women Centre, 1988-. Publications: The West in Her Eye, 1995; Poets in Bloom, due 1996; Women's Eye, in progress. Contributions to: Cruse Chronicle, 1988; Catch 99, poem shortlisted, Anglia Literary and Philosophical Society, 1994. Honour: Invited to Birthright charity lunch for poetry reading in the presence of Diana, Princess of Wales, 1988. Memberships: West Essex Literary Society; Associate Member, The Society of Authors; The Poetry Society. Address: 144 The Hornbeams, Harlow, Essex CM20 1PJ, England.

WADA Nadeena. See: **MOREN Rodney.**

WADDINGTON-FEATHER John Joseph, b. 10 July 1933, Keighley, Yorkshire, England. Writer; Priest. m. Sheila Mary Booker, 23 July 1960, 3 daughters. Education: BA, Leeds, 1954; PGCE, Keele, 1974; Ordination Certificate of the Church of England, 1977. Appointments: Various teaching posts including: Wakeman Grammar School, 1969-81; Shrewsbury 6th Form College, 1981-83; Khartoum University, 1984-85; Chaplain, Prestfelde School, 1985-96; Honorary Chaplain, HM Prisons, 1977-; Bronte Society Council Member, 1994-97. Publications: Collection of Verse, 1964; Of Mills, Moors and Men, 1966; Garlic Lane, 1970; Easy Street, 1973; One Man's Road, 1977; Tall Tales from Yukon, 1984; Khartoum Trilogy and other Poems, 1985; Six Christian Monologies, 1990; Six More Christian Poems, 1994; Feather's Foibles, 1995. Contributions to: Poetry Now; Orbis; Symphony; Anglo-Welsh Review; Ore; Pennine Poetry; Borderline. Honours: Bronte Society Prize, 1966; Cyril Hodges Poetry Award, 1974; Carnegie Medal Nomination, 1988. Memberships: FRSA; Life Member, Yorkshire Dialect Society and Bronte Society; Phoenix Poetry Society, USA. Address: Fair View, Old Coppice, Lyth Bank, Shrewsbury SY3 0BW, England.

WAGONER David (Russell), b. 5 June 1926, Massillon, Ohio, USA. Professor of English; Poet; Author. m. (1) Patricia Parrott, 1961, div 1982, (2) Robin H Seyfried, 1982. Education: BA, Pennsylvania State University, 1947; MA, Indiana University, 1949. Appointments: Instructor, DePauw University, 1949-50, Pennsylvania State University, 1950-53; Assistant Professor, 1954-57, Associate Professor, 1958-66, Professor of English, 1966-, University of Washington, Seattle; Editor, Poetry Northwest, 1966-; Elliston Professor of Poetry, University of Cincinnati, 1968. Publications include: Poetry: New and Selected Poems, 1969; Working Against Time, 1970; Riverbed, 1972; Sleeping in the Woods, 1974; A Guide to Dungeness Spit, 1975; Travelling Light, 1976; Collected Poems, 1956-1976, 1976; Who Shall be the Sun?: Poems Based on the Love, Legends, and Myths of Northwest Coast and Plateau Indians, 1978; In Broken Country, 1979; Landfall, 1981; First Light, 1983; Through the Forest: New and Selected Poems, 1977-1987, 1987; Fiction: The Road to Many a Wonder, 1974; Tracker, 1975; Whole Hog, 1976; The Hanging Garden, 1980; Editor: Straw for the Fire: From the Notebooks of Theodore Roethke 1943-1963, 1972. Honours: Guggenheim Fellowship, 1956; Ford Foundation Fellowship, 1964; American Academy of Arts and Letters Grant, 1967; National Endowment for the Arts Grant, 1969; Morton Dauwen Zabel Prize, 1967; Oscar Blumenthal Prize, 1974; Fels Prize, 1975; Eunice Tietjens Memorial Prize, 1977; English-Speaking Union Prize, 1980; Sherwood Anderson Prize, 1980. Membership: Chancellor, Academy of American Poets, 1978. Address: 5416-154th Pl SW, Edmonds, WA 98026, USA.

WAINWRIGHT Jeffrey, b. 19 Feb 1944, Stoke on Trent, Staffordshire, England. Poet; Translator; Lecturer. m. Judith Batt, 22 July 1967, 1 son, 1 daughter. Education: BA, 1965, MA, 1967, University of Leeds. Appointments: Assistant Lecturer, Lecturer, University of Wales, 1967-72; Visiting Instructor, Long Island University, 1970-71; Senior Lecturer, Manchester Polytechnic/Manchester Metropolitan University, 1972-. Publications: Poetry: The Important Men, 1970; Heart's Desire, 1978; Selected Poems, 1985; The Red-Headed Pupil, 1994. Other: Translations of various plays into English. Contributions to: Anthologies; BBC Radio; Many periodicals; Theatre reviews, The Independent. Honour: Judith E Wilson Visiting Fellow, Cambridge University, 1985. Memberships: National Association of Teachers in Further and Higher Education. Address: 11 Hesketh Avenue, Didsbury, Manchester M20 2QN, England.

WAKOSKI Diane, b. 3 Aug 1937, Whittier, California, USA. Poet. m. Robert J Turney, 14 Feb 1982. Education: BA, University of California, Berkeley, 1960. Appointments: Writer in Residence, California Institute of Technology, 1972; University of Virginia, 1972-73; Wilamette University, 1974; University of California at Irvine, 1974; University of Wisconsin, 1976; Whitman College, 1976; University of Washington, 1977; University of Hawaii, 1978; Michigan State University, 1976-. Publications: Coins & Cofins; Discrepancies & Apparitions; The George Washington Poems; Inside the Blood Factory; The Magellanic Clouds; The Motorcycle Betrayal Poems; Smudging; Trilogy; Dancing on the Grave of Son of a Bitch; Virtuoso Literature for Two and Four Hands; Waiting for the King of Spain; The Man Who Shook Hands; Cap of Darkness; The Magicians Feastletter; The Collected Greed; The Rings of Saturn; Why My Mother Likes Liberace; Emerald Ice; Medea The Sorceress, 1991; Jason The Sailor, 1993; The Emerald City of Las Vegas, 1995. Honours: Guggenheim Grant; Fulbright Award for Writers to Yugoslavia; William Carlos Williams Prize. Memberships: PEN; Authors Guild; Poetry Society of America; MLA. Address: 607 Division, East Lansing, MI 48823, USA.

WALCOTT Derek (Alton), b. 23 Jan 1930, Castries, St Lucia, West Indies. Poet; Dramatist; Visiting Professor. m. (1) Fay Moyston, 1954, div 1959, 1 son, (2) Margate Ruth Maillard, 1962, div, 2 daughters, (3) Norline Metivier, 1982. Education: St Mary's College, Castries, 1941-47; BA, University College of the West Indies, Mona, Jamaica, 1953. Appointments: Founder-Director, Little Carib Theatre Workshop, later Trinidad Theatre Workshop, 1959-76; Feature Writer, 1960-62, Drama Critic, 1963-68, Trinidad Guardian, Port-of-Spain; Visiting Professor, Columbia University, 1981, Harvard University, 1982, 1987; Assistant Professor of Creative Writing, 1981, Visiting Professor, 1985-, Brown University. Publications: Poetry includes: Selected Poems, 1964; The Castaway and Other Poems, 1965; The Gulf and Other Poems, 1969; Another Life, 1973; Sea Grapes, 1976; The Star-Apple Kingdom, 1979; Selected Poetry, 1981; The Fortunate Traveller, 1981; The Caribbean Poetry of Derek Walcott and the Art of Romare Bearden, 1983; Midsummer, 1984; Collected Poems 1948-1984, 1986; The Arkansas Testament, 1987; Omeros, 1989; Collected Poems, 1990; Poems 1965-1980, 1992; Derek Walcott: Selected Poems, 1993; Plays include: The Odyssey: A Stage Version, 1993; Non-fiction: The Antilles: Fragments of Epic Memory: The Nobel Lecture, 1993. Honours include: Eugene O'Neill Foundation Fellowship, 1969; Gold Hummingbird Medal, Trinidad, 1969; Obie Award, 1971; Officer of the Order of the British Empire, 1972; Guggenheim Fellowship, 1977; Welsh Arts Council International Writers Prize, 1980; John D and Catharine T MacArthur Foundation Fellowship, 1981; Los Angeles Times Book Prize, 1986; Queen's Gold Medal for Poetry, 1988; Nobel Prize for Literature, 1992. Memberships: Honorary Member, American Academy of Arts and Letters; Fellow, Royal Society of Literature. Address: 165 Duke of Edinburgh Avenue, Diego Martin, Trinidad and Tobago.

WALDMAN Anne, b. 2 Apr 1945, Millville, New Jersey, USA. Poet; Lecturer; Performer. Education: BA, Bennington College, 1966. Appointments: Editor, Angel Hair Magazine, Book, 1965-; Editor, The World, 1966-78; Assistant Director, Poetry Project, St Marks Church In-the Bowery, 1966-68; Director, Poetry Project, New York City, 1968-78; Poetry readings, performance events, throughout the world; Radio and TV Readings; Appeared in documentary, Poetry in Motion and other films; Director, Founder, Jack Kerouac School of Disembodied Poetics, Naropa Institute, Boulder, Colorado. Publications include: Journals and Dreams, 1976; First Baby Poems, 1983; Makeup On Empty Space, 1984; Invention, 1985; Skin Meat Bones, 1985; Blue Mosque, 1987; The Romance Thing, 1987-88; Helping the Dreamer: New and Selected Poems, 1966-1988; Iovis, 1993; Troubairitz, Kill or Cure, 1994; Iovis Book II, 1996; Editor: The World Anthology, 1969; Another World, 1971; Nice to See You: Homage to Ted Berrigan, 1991; In and Out of This World: An Anthology of The St Marks Poetry Project, 1992; Disembodied Poetics: Annuals of the Jack Kerouac School, co-editor with Andrew Shelling,

1991; The Beat Book, 1996; Co-Editor: Talking Poetics From Naropa Institute; Rocky Ledge Cottage Editions; Full Court Press. Contributions to: Paris Review; American Poetry Review; Partisan Review; Poetry, Chicago; Iowa Review; Rolling Stone; Poetry Review, London; Village Voice; Unmuzzled Ox; Honours: Cultural Artists Programme, 1977; National Endowment for the Arts, 1980; Award, Achievement in Poetry, Bennington College Alumni, 1981. Memberships: Committee for International Poetry; PEN; The Shelley Memorial Prize, The Poetry Society of America, 1996. Address: c/o The Naropa Institute, 2130 Arapahoe Avenue, Boulder, CO 80302, USA.

WALDROP Rosmarie, b. 24 Aug 1935, Kitzingen-am-Main, Germany. Poet; Translator. m. Keith Waldrop, 20 Jan 1959. Education: University of Würzburg, 1954-56; University of Aix-Marseille, 1956-57; University of Freiburg, 1957-58; MA, Comparative Literature, 1960, PhD, Comparative Literature, University of Michigan, 1966. Appointments: Assistant Professor, Wesleyan University, USA, 1964-70; Co-Editor, Co-Publisher, Burning Deck Press, 1968-; Visiting Associate Professor, Brown University, 1977-78, 1983, 1990-91; Visiting Lecturer, Tufts University, 1979-81. Publications: The Aggressive Ways of the Casual Stranger, 1972; The Road is Everywhere or Stop This Body, 1978; When They Have Senses, 1980; Nothing Has Changed, 1981; Differences for Four Hands, 1984; Streets Enough to Welcome Snow, 1986; The Reproductions of Profiles, 1987; Peculiar Motions, 1990; Lawn of Excluded Middle, 1992; A Key Into the Language of America, 1994. Contributions to: Acts; Antioch Review; Conjunctions; Credences; Denver Quarterly; Epoch; Ironwood; The Literary Review; Montemora; New American Writing; New Directions; O ARS; O blek; Open Places; Partisan Review; Sulfur; Temblor; Big Allis; Chelsea. Honours include: Major Hopwood Award, 1963; Alexander-von-Humboldt Fellowship, 1970-71, 1975-76; Howard Foundation Fellowship, 1974-75; Translation Center Award, Columbia University, 1978; National Endowment for the Arts Fellowship, 1980; Rhode Island Governor's Arts Award, 1988; Award, Fund for Poetry, 1990; PEN, Book of the Month Club, Citation in Translation, 1991; DAAD Berlin Artist's Program, 1993; National Endowment for the Arts Translation Fellowship, 1994; H M Landon Translation Award, 1994. Memberships: PEN; Wolgamot Society. Address: 71 Elmgrove Aveenue, Providence, RI 02906, USA.

WALKER Alice (Malsenior), b. 9 Feb 1944, Eatonton, Georgia, USA. Author; Poet. m. Melvyn R Leventhal, 17 Mar 1967, div 1976, 1 daughter. Education: BA, Sarah Lawrence College, 1966. Appointments: Writer-in-Residence and Teacher of Black Studies, Jackson State College, 1968-69, Tougaloo College, 1970-71; Lecturer in Literature, Wellesley College, 1972-73, University of Massachusetts, Boston, 1972-73; Distinguished Writer, Afro-American Studies Department, University of California, Berkeley, 1982; Fannie Hurst Professor of Literature, Brandeis University, 1982; Co-Founder and Publisher, Wild Trees Press, Navarro, California, 1984-88. Publications include: The Color Purple, 1982; In Search of Our Mother's Gardens, 1983; Horses Make a Landscape Look More Beautiful, 1984; To Hell With Dying, 1988; Living by the Word: Selected Writings 1973-1987, 1988; The Temple of My Familiar, 1989; Her Blue Body Everything We Know: Earthling Poems 1965-1990, 1991; Finding the Green Stone, 1991; Possessing the Secret of Joy, 1992; Warrior Marks (with Pratibha Parmar), 1993; Double Stitch: Black Women Write About Mothers and Daughters (with others), 1993; Everyday Use, 1994; Editor, I Love Myself When I'm Laughing ... And Then Again When I'm Looking Mean and Impressive, 1979. Honours: Bread Loaf Writer's Conference Scholar, 1966; Ingram Merrill Foundation Fellowship, 1967; McDowell Colony Fellowships, 1967, 1977-78; National Endowment for the Arts Grants, 1969, 1977; Richard and Hinda Rosenthal Pound Award, American Academy and Institute of Arts and Letters, 1974; Guggenheim Fellowship, 1977-78; Pulitzer Prize for Fiction, 1983; American Book Award, 1983; O Henry Award, 1986; Nora Astorga Leadership Award, 1989; Freedom to Write Award, PEN Centre West, 1990; Honorary doctorates. Address: c/o Wendy Weil Agency Inc, 232 Madison Avenue, Suite 1300, New York, NY 10016, USA.

WALKER Edward (Ted) Joseph, b. 28 Nov 1934, Writer; Teacher. m. (1) Lorna Ruth Benfell, 11 Aug 1956, dec 1987, 2 sons, 2 daughters. m. (2) Audrey Joan Hicks, 8 July 1988. Education: St John's College, Cambridge, 1953-56; BA (Hons), Modern and Mediaeval Languages, 1956; MA, 1977. Appointments: Assistant Master, North Paddington School, London, 1956-58; Head, French Department, Southall Technical Grammar School, 1958-63; Head,

Modern Languages Department, Bognor Regis School, 1963-65; Professor of Creative Writing, New England College, 1971-92; Professor Emeritus, 1992. Publications: Fox in a Barn Door, 1965; The Solitaries, 1967; The Night Bathers, 1970; Gloves to the Hangman, 1973; Burning the Ivy, 1978; The Lion's Calvacade, 1980; The High Path, 1982; You've Never Heard Me Sing, 1985; Hands at a Live Fire (Selected Poems), 1987; In Spain, 1987; The Last of England, 1992; Grandad's Seagulls, 1993. Contributions to: New Yorker; New York Times; Sunday Times; Observer; New Statesman; Spectator; Times Literary Supplement; Encounter; Poetry Review; Listener; London Magazine; Stand; Transatlantic Review; Critical Quarterly; Sunday Telegraph. Honours: Eric Gregory Award, 1964; Cholmondeley Award, 1966; Alice Hunt Bartlett Award, 1967; Major Award, Arts Council of Great Britain, 1969; Campion Prize, 1974; Hon DLitt, University of Southampton, 1995. Memberships: Fellow, Royal Society of Literature; Chairman of Judges, Cholmondeley Award for Poetry, 1973-91. Literary Agent: Sheil Land Associates Ltd, 43 Doughty Street, London WC1N 2LF. Address: Argyll House, The Square, Eastergate, Chichester, West Sussex PO20 6UP, England.

WALKER J Brenda, b. 15 Apr 1934, Liverpool, England. Publisher. m. Jolyon William Wilsone Walker, 28 July 1956, dec, Nov 1995, 2 sons, 3 daughters. Education: Teacher's Certificate, Hull, 1964; BA Hons, English Literature, 1977; MA, Educational Psychology, Keele, 1981. Appointments: Senior Lecturer, English Department, Avery Hill College of Education, 1970-76; Head Teacher, London Borough of Waltham Forest, 1976-87; Director of Forest Books, 1988-. Publications: Mind Games, 1989; Poetry Translations and co-translations/tranformations from Romanian, Bulgarian, Urdu, Hindi and Arabic, 1984-96; Night Train (Poems), 1994. Contributions to: Poetry and Literary Magazines as well as national newspapers in Romania, Poland, Hungary, Turkey, Greece, Spain, Syria, Bulgaria, Germany, Switzerland, Portugal, India, Moldavia, Ukraine, Macedonia and Serbia. Honours: New Venture Award, Women in Publishing, 1987; Howard Sergant Award for Services to Poetry, 1990; Romanian Writers Union Award for translating and publishing, 1990. Memberships: Poetry Society; Society of Authors. Address: 20 Forest View, Chingford, London E4 7AY, England.

WALKER Peter Christopher, b. 19 Oct 1973, Lichfield, Birmingham, England. Musician. Contributions to: Publication in a number of media forms. Memberships: Co-founder, The Yellow House, a small group of Artists and Musician/Writers and Poets. Address: 43 Redwood Drive, Burntwood, Staffordshire WS7 8AS, England.

WALKER MURRAY Jeanne, b. 27 May 1944, Parkers Prairie, Minnesota, USA. Professor of English. m. 16 July 1983, 1 son, 1 daughter. Education: BA, English, Wheaton College, Illinois; MA, English, Loyola University, Chicago; PhD, English, University of Pennsylvania, Philadelphia. Appointments: Assistant Professor, English, Haverford College, Pennsylvania; Professor, English, University of Delaware, Newark. Publications: Nailing Up The Home Sweet Home, 1980; Fugitive Angels, 1985; Coming Into History, 1990; Stranger Than Fiction, 1992. Contributions to: American Scholar; Arizona Quarterly; American Poetry Review; Aspen Anthology; Ariel; Poetry Miscellany; Jawbone; Carolina Quarterly; Chicago Tribune; Christian Science Monitor; Cimarron Review; Chariton Review; Critical Quarterly; Georgia Review; Southern Humanities Review; Iowa Review; Kenyon Review; Louisville Review; Lyric; Massachusetts Review; Milkweed Chronicle; Descant; Northwest Review; Christian Century; New England Review; Nantucket Review; Wascona Review; Poet and Critic; 2 Plus 2: Poetry Now; St Andrews Review; Pennsylvania Review; Kansas Quarterly; Seattle Review; Poetry; Shenendoah; Painted Bride Quarterly; Whetstone; Boulevard; Partisan Review. Honours include: 1st Place: Poetry, Fiction, Atlantic Monthly Contest, 1965; Associated Writing Programs Competition, 1980; Cleveland State University Poetry Center Competition, 1980; Fellowship, Delaware Arts Council, 1980; Fellowships, Pennsylvania Council on the Arts, 1984, 1987, 1989, 1991; Strousse Award, Best Sequence of Poems, Prairie Schooner, 1988; Fellow, Center for Advanced Studies, 1993. Memberships: PEN; Poets and Writers; American Poetry Center; Dramatists Guild. Address: University of Delaware, Newark, DE 19711. USA.

WALLACE Ronald William, b. 18 Feb 1945, Cedar Rapids, Iowa, USA. Poet; Professor. m. Margaret Elizabeth McCreight, 3 Aug 1968, 2 daughters. Education: BA, College of Wooster, 1967; MA, 1968; PhD, 1971. Appointments: Director of Creative Writing, University of Wisconsin, 1975-; Series Editor, Brittingham Prize in

Poetry, 1985-; Director, Wisconsin Institute for Creative Writing, 1986-. Publications: Henry James and the Comic Form; Installing the Bees; Cucumbers; The Last Laugh; The Facts of Life; Plums; Stones; Kisses and Hooks; Tunes for Bears to Dance To; God Be With the Clown; The Owl in the Kitchen; People and Dog in the Sun; Vital Signs; The Makings of Happiness; Time's Fancy. Contributions to: New Yorker; Atlantic; Nation; Poetry; Southern Review; Poetry Northwest; Prairie Schooner; Georgia Review; American Scholar. Honours: Hopwood Award; Council for Wisconsin Writers Award; Helen Bullis Prize; Robert E Gard Award; Banta Award; Gerald A Bartell Award in the Arts'. Membership: Poets and Writers. Address: Department of English, 600 North Park Street, University of Wisconsin, Madison, WI 53706, USA.

WALLENSTEIN Barry, b. 13 Feb 1940, New York City, USA. Poet; Professor. m. Lorna Harbus. 19 Mar 1978, 1 son, 1 daughter. Education: PhD, New York University, 1972. Appointments: Professor, City College of New York; Lecturer, The Cooper Union; Writer-in-Residence, Northern Michigan University, Summer 1993. Publications: Short Life of the Five Minute Dancer; Love & Cough; Roller Coaster Kid; Beast Is a Wolf with Brown Fire; In Case You Missed It (recording of my poetry with music), 1995. Contributions to: American Book Review; African American Review; The Nation; American Poetry Review; Ploughshares; Editor, American Book Review. Honours: Residency at MacDowell Colony, 1995. Address: 340 Riverside Drive, New York, NY 10025, USA.

WALTER Colin, b. 23 Sept 1940, Maidstone, Kent, England. Educationalist. m. Cheryl Anne Osborne, 2 Oct 1965, 2 daughters. Education: BEd (Hons), 1972, MA, 1976, University of London. Appointments: Teacher: Essex, Yorkshire, London Borough of Enfield, 1963-72; Teacher, Education, 1972-91, directed MA Language and Literature in Education Courses, Department of Advanced Studies in Education, 1986-91, Goldsmiths College, University of London; Directed experimental undergraduate course to develop theory and practice of teaching poetry in schools, in association with Poetry Society and Tate Gallery; Writer, Educational Consultant, 1991. Publications: Form or Formula? The Practice of Poetry Teaching, in Opening Moves, 1983; Inhabiting Poetry: a formal contribution to the debate upon teaching poetry, 1988; An Early Start to Poetry, 1989; Introduction to BP Teacher: Poetry Resources Files for Primary and Seconday Schools, 1992. Contributions to: Articles include: The Teaching of Poetry in School: formal ways to begin with teacher education, in European Journal of Teacher Education, 1987; Sound in Content: some under-regarded possibilities for the teaching of poetry in school, 1990; A Better Way to Begin Again Together: The value of a comparative approach to teaching poetry in school, 1991; Thinking Through Form: preparing to teach poetry in school, 1993; From Preparation to Progress in Teaching Poetry: young teachers reading, children reading, 1994; All in Education Today; Reviews in The School Librarian. Honours: Fellow, Royal Society of Arts; Fellow, College of Preceptors. Memberships: The Poetry Society. Address: 59 The Highway, Chelsfield, Nr Orpington, Kent BR6 9DQ, England.

WALTER Hugo, b. 3 Dec 1959, Philadelphia, Pennsylvania, USA. College Professor. Education: BA, Princeton University, 1981; PhD in Literature, Yale University, 1985; MA, Old Dominion University, 1989; PhD in Humanities, Drew University, 1986. Career: Instructor, Yale University, 1983-85; Assistant Professor, Rhodes College, 1986-87; Assistant Professor, University of Missouri, 1987-88; Assistant Professor, Washington and Jefferson College, 1989-92; Assistant Professor, Fairleigh Dickinson University, 1992-96; Assistant Professor of Humanities, GMI Engineering and Management Institute, 1996-. Publications: Amber Blossoms and Evening Shadows, 1990; Golden Thorns of Light and Sterling Silhouettes, 1991; Waiting for Babae; Prophecies of Sunflower Dreams, 1992; Along the Maroon, Prismed Threshold of Bronze - Pealing Eternity, 1992; The Light of the Dance is the Music of Eternity, 1993; Dusk - Gloaming Mirrors and Castle- Winding Dreams, 1994; Amaranth-Sage Epiphanies of Dusk-Weaving Paradise, 1995. Memberships: American Association of Poets; International Society of Poets. Address: Department of Humanities, GMI Engineering Institute, 1700 West Third Avenue, Flint, MI 48504, USA.

WANDOR Michelene Dinah, b. 20 Apr 1940, London, England. Writer. 2 sons. Education: BA, Hons, English, Newnham College, Cambridge, 1962; MA, Sociology and Literature, University of Essex, 1976; LTCL, DipTCL, Trinity College of Music, 1993. Appointment: Poetry Editor, Time Out Magazine, 1971-82. Publications: Cutlasses

and Earrings (editor and contributor), 1977; Upbeat, 1981; Touch Papers, 1982; Gardens of Eden, 1984; Gardens of Eden (Selected Poems), 1990. Contributions to: Time Out; Tribune; Kaleidoscope. Address: 71 Belsize Lane, London NW3 5AU, England.

WANG Chi-Lung, (Luti), b. 1 Jan 1942. Publisher; Poet. m. Wang Hung Mei Hung, 12 Mar 1980, 1 son, 4 daughters. Education: Bachelor's Degree, Tam King University, 1954. Appointments: Editor, The Gale Literary Monthly, 1961-68; Publisher, The Nymph, 1972-92; Secretary-General, Chinese Poetry Society, Taipei, 1984-92; Editor, The Long Song Press, Taipei. Publications: Blue Stars, 1962; A Statue in Green, 1963; Castle in the Wind, 1991; Represented in An Anthology of Modern Chinese Poetry, 1964. Contributions to: Gale; Nymph (Chiu Shui Poetry Quarterly). Honours: Honorary Doctor of Literature, World Academy of Arts and Culture, 1987; Poetry Education Award, Minister of Education, China, 1989. Memberships: Secretary-General, Chinese Poetry Society; Deputy Secretary-General, World Academy of Arts and Culture. Address: PO Box 14-57, Taipei, Taiwan.

WANG Chia-Wen, b. 23 Apr 1927, Peng-Lai, Shan-Tung, Taiwan. m. Cho Nai-Fang, June 1974, 1 son, 1 daughter. Education: Pei-Ching National University, Chinese Literature Department, 1940. Appointments: President, Taipei Security Society, 1967-87; President, The Chinese Poetry Art Society, 1995. Publications: Ching Chung, 1961; Shih Kuang Chih Lu, 1993; Chiu Feng Yin, 1994. Contributions to: Taiwan Shin-shen Newspaper. Honours: Poetry Movement Prize of Chinese New Poetry Society, 1995. Memberships: Autumn Water; Grape Garden; World Leaves of Poetry; The Chinese Poetry Art Society. Address: Shintain City, San-Ming Road, No 34-1 57, Taipei Shen, Taiwan.

WANIEK Marilyn. See: NELSON Marilyn.

WANSBROUGH David James, b. 15 Apr 1948, New Zealand. Writer; Painter. m. Roslyn Jones, 5 sons, 2 daughters. Education: DipTeach, Auckland, 1971; LicTheol, 1976, PhL, 1977, Seminary of St Basil, Australia; DTh, St Ephrams, 1994. Appointments: Honorary Resurgent Prisoner, Parramatta Jail, 1975; Director, Australian Institute of Contemporary Studies, 1978-81; The Gavemer Foundation Ltd, 1984; Arunta Investments Pty Ltd, 1988 and Scitec Communications Corporation, 1990; Life Patron, China Education Centre, University of Sydney; Visiting Professor, M V Lomonosov College, Moscow State University, 1993, 1994, 1995, 1996; Visiting Lecturer, The Institute for Pedagogical Innovations of the Russian Academy for Education, 1996. Publications: On the Lip of the Pit, 1981; Seeing Through, 1982; Poetry for a Human Centered Education, 1987; Word Weaving, 1988; A Pillar of Salt?, 1988; At the Edge of Darkness, 1989; A Journey into the Heart, 1993; Dreams, Delights, Fears, Fragments, 1994; Festivals, Seasons and The Southern Sun, 1994; Christianity and the Impulse of East and West, 1995. Honours: Honorary Doctor of Letters (Guiseppe Scicluna), 1987; Medal, Albert Einstein International Academy, 1989; Alfred Nobel Commemmorative Medal, 1991; Winner, New South Wales Writers Centre Poetry Cup, 1992; International Order of Merit, 1992; DTh, St Ephrams, 1994. Memberships: Live Poets Society; Poets Union; Fellow, International Academy of Poets; Life Fellow, World Literary Academy. Literary Agent: Richard King, 42 Old Berrara Road, Sussex Inlet, NSW 2540, Australia. Address: P O Box 424, Street Leonards, NSW 2065, Australia.

WARBURTON Erica Margaret, b. 27 Jan 1939, India. Lecturer. m. John Warburton, 17 Dec 1960, div, 2 sons, 1 daughter. Education: LRAM, 1959; GGSM, 1960; Certificate in Mathematics, 1980. Appointments: School Teacher, 1960-61; Choral Conductor, 1965-70; Sports Coach, 1970-78; Teacher of Mathematics, 1978-. Publication: More Than One Turn. Contributions to: Orbis; Weyfareres; Old Police Station; Hybrid; Bound Spiral; Vigil; Purple Patch; White Rose; Pause; Speakeasy; Word for Word; First Time; Salopoet; Iota. Honours: 1st Prize, Berkshire Moving Poetry, Random Century Writing for Children Competition; 2nd Prize, Stanley Pelter Poetry Competition. Memberships: Poetry Society. Address: 30 Morecambe Avenue, Caversham Heights, Reading, Berkshire RG4 7NL, England.

WARD David John, b. 4 Nov 1949, Northampton, England. Poet. m. Frieda Nyahoe, 26 May 1972, 3 sons, 1 daughter. Education: BA, Hons, English, University of Lancaster. Appointments: Co-ordinator, Windows Poetry Project; Editor, Smoke, poetry magazine. Publications: Jambo, 1993; Candy and Jazzz, 1994; Tracts, 1996.

Contributions to: Poetry Review; Transatlantic Review; Poetry Wales; University of Toronto Review; Die Horen (Germany). Memberships: University of Lancaster Literary Society (Chair); Nemo Poets, Northampton; John Clare Society; Halewood Arts Association (Secretary). Address: 22 Roseheath Drive, Halewood, Merseyside L26 9UH, England.

WARD John Hood, b. 16 Dec 1915, Newcastle-upon-Tyne, England. Former Senior Principal, Civil Service. m. Gladys Hilda Thorogood, 27 July 1940. Education: Newcastle Royal Grammar School, 1925-33; School Certificate (Matriculation), 1931; Higher School Certificate, 1933. Appointments: Senior Principal, Department of Health and Social Security; Retired, 1978. Publications: A Late Harvest, 1982; The Dark Sea, 1983; A Kind of Likeness, 1985; The Wrong Side of Glory, 1986; A Song at Twilight, 1989; Grandfather Best and the Protestant Work Ethic, 1991; The Brilliance of Light, 1994; Winter Song, 1995; Selected Poems, 1968-95, 1996; 4 Pamphlets of Poetry. Contributions to: Anglo-Welsh Review; Contemporary Review; Country Life; Envoi; Pennine Platform; Poetry and Audience; PN Review; Poetry Review; Poetry Durham; Poetry Nottingham; Outposts; Phoenix; New Hope International; Manchester Poetry; Lancaster Festival Anthologies; Iron; Lancashire Life; Cheshire Life. Honours: Imperial Service Order, 1977; Poetry Prize, City of Westminster Arts Council, 1977; Open Poetry Prize, Wharfedale Music Festival, 1978; Prizewinner, Lancaster Festival, 1982, 1987, 1988, 1989, 1994, 1995; 1st Prize, Bury Open Poetry Competition, 1987; 1st Prize, High Peak Open Competition, 1988, 1989; Northern Poetry (Littlewood) Competition, 1989; 1st Prize, Mary & Alfred Wilkins Memorial Competition, 1995; Short Story Prizes. Memberships: Manchester Poets; Society of Civil Service Authors; Poetry Workshop, Society of Civil Service Authors. Address: 42 Seal Road, Bramhall, Stockport, Cheshire SK7 2JS, England.

WARD John Powell, b. 28 Nov 1937, Suffolk, England. University Lecturer. m. Sarah Woodfull Rogers, 16 Jan 1965, 2 sons. Education: BA, Toronto University, 1959; BA, 1961, MA, 1969, Cambridge University; MSc, (Econ), Sociology, University of Wales, 1969. Appointments: Lecturer, Education, 1963-84, Lecturer, English, 1984-86, Senior Lecturer, English 1986-91, Hon Research Fellow, 1991-, University College, Swansea, Wales; Editor, Poetry Wales, 1975-80. Publications: The Other Man, 1970; The Line of Knowledge, 1972; From Alphabet to Logos, 1972; Things, 1980; To Get Clear, 1981; The Clearing, 1984; A Certain Marvellous Thing, 1993. Contributions to: Times Literary Supplement; Listener; Poetry Review; PN Review; Poetry (Chicago); Poetry Australia; Poetry Wales; Poetry Ireland Review; Poetry London Newsletter; Poetry Durham; Poetry Nottingham; Tribune; Time Out; Anglo-Welsh Review; New Welsh Review; New Poetry; Other Poetry; Bananas; Bete Noire; Aquarius; Planet; South-East Review; BBC Radio 3 and 4; Rialto; Orbis; Oasis. Honour: Poetry Prize, Welsh Arts Council, 1985. Address: Court Lodge, Horton Kirby, Dartford, Kent DA4 9BN, England.

WARDMAN Gordon Arthur, b. 16 Feb 1948, England. m. Susan Connor, 25 Nov 1972, 1 son, 1 daughter. Education: BA, Oriel College, Oxford, 1970; CQSW, University of Kent, 1972. Publications: Crispins Spur, 1985; Reparations, 1987; High Country Hank, 1993; The Newfoundland Cantos, 1994; Trolleytown, 1996. Contributions to: Numerous Literary Magazines and Anthologies. Address: 86 Greenhills, Harlow, Essex CM20 3SZ, England.

WARNER Francis (Robert Le Plastrier), b. 21 Oct 1937, Bishopthorpe, Yorkshire, England. Poet; Dramatist. m. (1) Mary Hall, 1958, div 1972, 2 daughters. m. (2) Penelope Anne Davies, 1983, 1 son, 1 daughter. Education: Christ's Hospital, Cambridge, St Catherine's College, MA, BA. Appointments: Fellow and Tutor, St Peter's College, Oxford, 1965-; Vice-Master, St Peter's College, 1987-89; Pro-Proctor, University of Oxford, 1989-90, 1996-97. Publications: Poetry: Perennia, 1962; Early Poems, 1964; Experimental Sonnets, 1965; Madrigals, 1967; The Poetry of Francis Warner, 1970; Lucca Quartet, 1975; Morning Vespers, 1980; Spring Harvest, 1981; Epithalamium, 1983; Collected Poems 1960-1984, 1985; Nightingales, 1996; Plays: Maquettes, 1994; Lying Figures, 1972; Killing Time, 1976; Meeting Ends, 1974; A Conception of Love, 1978; Light Shadows, 1980; Moving Reflections, 1983; Living Creation, 1985; Healing Nature; The Athens of Pericles, 1988; Byzantium, 1990; Vigil and Caesar, 1993; Agora, 1994; King Francis I, 1995. Contributions to: Various Anthologies, Journals. Honour: Messing International Award, 1972; Benemerenti Silver Medal, Kts of St

George, Constantinian Order (Italy), 1990. Address: St Peter's College, Oxford OX1 2DL, England.

WARNER Val, b. 15 Jan 1946, Middlesex, England. Writer. Education: Somerville College, Oxford, 1965-68; BA (Hons), Modern History, 1968. Appointments: Teacher, Inner London Education Authority, 1969-72; Freelance Copy Editor for publishers, 1972-77; Freelance Writer, 1977-. Publications: These Yellow Photos, pamphlet, 1971; Under the Penthouse, 1973; The Centenary Corbière, translation, 1975; Collected Poems and Prose of Charlotte Mew (editor), 1981, 1982; Before Lunch, 1986. Contributions to: Encounter; Tribune; Scotsman; Poetry Review; Lines Review; Critical Quarterly; Ambit; Poetry Wales; PN Review; Antaeus, USA; Cencrastus; Poetry Durham; Other Poetry; Acumen; Bananas; Chapman; Outposts; Honest Ulsterman; Pequod, USA; Green River Review, USA; Cracked Looking Glass; Gairfish; Verse; Blind Serpent; Caret; Folio International; Meridian; Clanjamfrie; New Writing Scotland; Madog; Ostrich; Pick; Vision On; AMF. Honours: Gregory Award for Poetry, 1975; Writer-in-Residence, University College, Swansea, 1977-78; Writer-in-Residence, University of Dundee, 1979-81; 3rd Prize, Lincolnshire Literature Festival Poetry Competition, 1995. Membership: PEN. Address: c/o Carcanet Press Ltd, 402-406 Corn Exchange, Manchester M4 3BY, England.

WARREN Celia Rosemary, b. 17 Jan 1953. Writer. m. Raymond John Albert Kenneth Warren, 20 Sept 1975, 1 son, 1 daughter. Education: Certificate of Education, Loughborough College of Education, 1971-74. Publications: Pathways Series: A Fishy Tale, 1994; Meg's Mad Magnet, 1996; Skittles & Skullbone The Skeletons, 1996. Contributions to: Anthologies: Scrumdiddly, 1992; Dove on the Roof, 1992; Scholastic Collection, 1992; An Armful of Bears, 1993; Them and Us, 1993; 'Ere We Go, 1993; Others: Orbis; Outposts; Staple; Countryman; Haiku Quarterly; Bare Bones; Blithe Spirit; New Prospects; Envoi. Honours: Short-listed for the Lichfield Prize for a novel set recognisably in Lichfield District, 1995. Memberships: National Association of Writers in Education; British Haiku Society; Lichfield & District Writers; Professional Association of Teachers. Address: Meriden, Hopwas Hill, Hopwas, Tamworth, Staffs B78 3AN, England.

WARREN Elizabeth. See: SUPRANER Robyn.

WARREN James E(dward), b. 11 Dec 1908, Atlanta, Georgia, USA. Retired Teacher; Writer. Education: BA, 1930, MAT, 1941, Emory University; Diploma, Yale Summer School, 1960; Other courses: Cambridge University 1930, Georgia University 1940s. Appointments: Teacher 1933-59, Department Head, 2 years, Atlanta School System; Part-time Teacher, Georgia School of Technology night school, 1958-60; Teacher 1959-74, Department Head, 15 years, The Lovett School; Book Reviewer, Atlanta Journal, Atlanta Times, World of Books, Christian Science Monitor. Publications: This Side of Babylon, 1938; Against the Furious Men, 1946; Selected Poems, 1967; Collected Poems, 1980; Poems of Lovett, 1986; 12 poetry chapbooks, 1964-89. Contributions to: Saturday Review; Georgia Review; Poet Lore; Prairie Schooner; Western Humanities Review; Southern Poetry Review; Sewanee Review; Poetry Review; Lyric; La Voix des Poetes; Delphi Quarterly; Blue Unicorn; Paintbrush; International Poetry Review; Lulwater Review; Chattahoochee Review; Educational Review; Emory University Quarterly; New York Times; Atlantic; Southern Humanities Review; New Laurel Review; Independent School Journal; Signature. Honours: Annual Prize, Poetry Society of America, 1937; Barrow Prize, Poetry Society of Georgia, 1945, 1947; Leitch Prize, Poetry Society of Virginia, 1967; Literary Achievement Award, Georgia Writers Association, 1967; Aurelia Austin Writer of the Year Award, Atlanta Writers Club, 1968; Governor's Award, 1980. Memberships: Poetry Society of America; Academy of American Poets; Georgia Writers Association; Cum Laude Society, 1981. Address: St Ann's Terrace, Apt 309, 3100 Northside Parkway North West, Atlanta, GA 30327, USA.

WARSH Lewis, b. 9 Nov 1944, New York, New York, USA. Poet. 1 son, 2 daughters. Education: BA, City College of New York, 1966; MA, 1975. Appointments: Editor, Publisher, United Artists Books; Editor, The World Magazine; Adjunct Associate Professor, Long Island University. Publications: A Free Man; The Corset; Information From the Surface of Venus; Methods of Birth Control; The Maharajahs Son; Blue Heaven; Long Distance; Dreaming As One; Avenue of Escape, 1995. Contributions to: World; The Paris Review; American Poetry Review; Shiny; Transfer; Talisman; Long News; Notus; Broadway;

Cover; United Artists. Honours: New York Foundation of the Arts Award; National Endowment of the Arts Award; Editors Fellowship Award. Address: 701 President Street, Brooklyn, NY 11215, USA.

WASSERMAN Rosanne, b. 29 Nov 1952, Kentucky, USA. Poet; Publisher; Professor; Editor. m. Eugene Daniel Richie, 12 June 1977, 1 son. Education: BA, 1974; MFA, 1976; PhD, 1986. Appointments: Editor, Metropolitan Museum of Art, 1974-91; Poet in Public Schools, 1986-91; Associate Professor, USMMA, 1986-96; Editor, The Groundwater Press, 1976-96. Publications: Apple Perfume, 1989; The Lacemakers, 1992. Contributions to: Best American Poetry; Sulfur; Broadway; Numbers; Talus; Bad Henry Review; Mudfish; Caliban; Joe Soaps Canoe; Private; Gambit; American Letters and Commentary; Poetry New York. Honours: New York Foundation for the Arts Fellowship; Indiana University Writers Conference Award. Address: PO Box 704, Hudson, NY 12534, USA.

WATERMAN Andrew John, b. 28 May 1940, London, England. University Lecturer. Div. 1 son. Education: BA, 1st Class Hons, English, University of Leicester, 1966. Appointments: Lecturer, English, 1968-78, Senior Lecturer, 1978-, University of Ulster, Coleraine, Northern Ireland. Publications: Living Room, 1974; From the Other Country, 1977; Over the Wall, 1980; Out for the Elements, 1981; Selected Poems, 1986; The Poetry of Chess (compiler, editor), 1981; In the Planetarium, 1990; The End of the Pier Show (poetry collection), 1995. Contributions to: All principal UK journals publishing poetry; Some poetry journals, USA, Ireland; Many anthologies. Honours: Poetry Book Society Choice, 1974; Cholmondeley Award for Poetry, 1977; Poetry Book Society Recommendation, 1981; Arvon Poetry Competition Prize, 1981. Address: 15 Hazelbank Road, Coleraine, County Derry, Northern Ireland BT51 3DX.

WATERS Chocolate, b. 21 Jan 1949, Aberdeen, Maryland, USA. Freelance Writer and Designer. Education: BA, Lock Haven State College, Pennsylvania, 1971. Publications: To the Man Reporter from The Denver Post, 1975, 1980; Take Me Like A Photograph, 1977, 1980; Charting New Waters, 1980. Contributions to: Orbis; Westerly; Imago; Mudfish; Downtown; Lips; Sing Heavenly Muse!; Red Start; Caprice; Room of One's Own; Sojourner; Black Maria; Poemail; Z Miscellaneous; Sinister Wisdom; The Leading Edge; Woman Poet-The West; Ordinary Women-Extraordinary Lives; The Hollins Critic; Big Mama Rag; X-It Anthology; PCCCPC Anthology; My Lover Is A Woman; Stand-Up Poetry: The Anthology. Honours: Award, Outstanding Journalistic Achievement, Mt Joy Bulletin, 1967; 2nd Place, Column Writing, 2nd Place Award, Personal Interviewing, Colorado Press Women, Denver, 1975; Honourable Mention, Passaic County Community College Contest, Passaic, New Jersey, 1988; Finalist, Roberts Writing Awards Contest, Pittsburg, Kansas, 1990; 1st Place, Poetry Contest, Poetry Arts Project, 1990, 1991; Grant to complete latest collection, Money for Women, Barbara Deming Memorial Fund Inc, 1990; New York Foundation for the Arts Fellowship in Poetry, 1995. Memberships: Poetry Society of America; Academy of Amerian Poets; National Federation of State Poetry Societies. Address: 415 West 44th Street, No 7, New York, NY 10036, USA.

WATSON John Richard, b. 15 June 1934. Professor of English. m. Pauline Elizabeth Roberts, 21 July 1962, 1 son, 2 daughters. Education: Magdalen College, Oxford; BA, 1958, MA, 1964, Oxford University; PhD, University of Glasgow, 1966. Appointments: Assistant, then Lecturer, University of Glasgow, Scotland, 1962-66; Lecturer, then Senior Lecturer, University of Leicester, England, 1966-78; Professor, English, 1978-, Public Orator, 1989, University of Durham. Publications: A Leicester Calendar, 1976, 2nd Edition, 1978; Everyman's Book of Victorian Verse (editor), 1982; Wordworth's Vital Soul, 1982; English Poetry of the Romantic Period, 1978-1830, 1985, 2nd Edition, 1992. Honours: Prize, Stroud Festival, 1971; Prize, Suffolk Poetry Society, 1975. Memberships: Chairman, Modern Humanities Research Association; Vice President, The Charles Wesley Society; President, International Association of University Professors of English. Address: Stoneyhurst, 27 Western Hill, Durham DH1 4RL, England.

WATSON Scott Harrison (Zenmai), b. 22 Mar 1954, Philadelphia, Pennsylvania, USA. Associate Professor. m. Morie Chiba, 27 Dec 1981, 2 sons. Education: College of William and Mary, 1972-75; BA, Ursinus College, 1979; MA, University of Delaware, 1982. Appointments: English Teacher, Sendai YMCA, Japan, 1980-82; Teacher, Gifted and Talented, Windsor Central High School, USA, 1982-83; Teacher, Hakodate LaSalle High School, 1983-86; Associate

Professor, English Language, American Literature, Tohoku Gakuin University, Japan, 1986-. Publications: First Poems, 1979. Contributions to: Edge, Tokyo; Japan Environment Monitor; Blue Jacket; Poetry Nippon; Collages and Bricolages. Memberships: Sendai Modern Poetry Salon; Poetry Society of Japan; World Congress of Poets; Japan English-American Modern Poetry Society. Address: Tsurugaya Higashi 3-13-16, Sendai-shi, Miyagino-ku, 983 Japan.

WATTS Anthony, b. 3 Feb 1941, Wimbledon, England. Library Assistant. m. Dorothy May Clarke, 18 May 1966, 1 son, 3 daughters. Appointment: Somerset County Library, 1959-. Publication: Strange Gold, 1991. Contributions to: Outposts; PEN; Thames Poetry; Orbis; Envoi; Iron; New Poetry; Poetry Northampton; The Rialto. Honours: Arvon Foundation Prize, 1982; Edmond Blundon Memorial Competition Prize, 1979; Lake Aske Memorial Award, 1978; Michael Johnson Memorial Prize, 1979; Scottish Open Poetry Competition, 1981. Address: Flat 1, Camden Road, Bridgwater, Somerset TA6 3HD, England.

WAUGH Auberon Alexander, b. 17 Nov 1939, Dulverton, Somerset, England. Writer. m. Teresa Onslow, 1961, 2 sons, 2 daughters. Appointments: Editorial Staff, Daily Telegraph, 1960-63; Special Writer, IPC, 1964-67; Chief Fiction Reviewer Spectator, 1970-73; Fortnightly Columnist, 1976-; Policital Correspondent, 1970-76; Columnist, The Times, 1970-71; Sunday Telegraph, 1981-90; Chief Reviewer, Independent, 1986-89; Daily Telegraph, Way to the World Column, 1989-; Editor, Literary Review, 1986-. Publications: The Foxglove Saga; Conside the Lilies; Biafra; Country Topics; Four Crowded Years; In The Lions Den; The Last Word; Auberon Waughs Yearbook; The Diaries of Auberon Waugh; Waugh on Wine; Another Voice; Will This Do?, Autobiography. Honours: British Press Award Commendation; Columnist of the Year. Address: Combe Florey House, Combe Florey, Taunton, Somerset, England.

WAWILOW Danuta, b. 14 Apr 1942, Kozmodemianok, Russia.Writer; Translator. m. Oleg Usenko, 3 Feb 1967, 1 son, 1 daughter. Education: Warsaw University, 1959-63; MA, Russian Literature, Moscow University, 1967. Publications: The Roopaks, 1977; An Awfully Important Thing, 1978; My Secret, 1985; The Wandering, 1986; Rhymes for Naughty Children, 1987; Wild Horses, TV play, 1987; The Little Pipe, 1991; Children in the Wood, 1991; With Oleg Usenko: About a Prince, Kaleidoscopes and an Old Woman, 1980; A Story about 100 King's Fools; An Apple Flies into the Clouds, 1982; A Little Cherry Orchard, Polish Folk Erotic Poems, 1985. Contributions to: Juppi; Jupik; Plomyk; Swierszczryk; Mis Filipinka. Honours: Premio Europeo, Padua, Italy, 1978; Peace Fund Award, USSR, 1987; Polish Prime Minister's Award, 1987. Membership: Polish Writers Association. Address: Anieli Krzywon 2-129, 01-391 Warsaw, Poland.

WAYMAN Tom (Thomas Ethan), b. 13 Aug 1945, Hawkesbury, Ontario, Canada. Poet; Professor. Education: BA, University of British Columbia, 1966; MFA, University of California at Irvine, 1968. Appointments: Instructor, Colorado State University, Fort Collins, 1968-69; Writer-in-Residence, University of Windsor, Ontario, 1975-76; Assistant Professor of English, Wayne State University, Detroit, 1976-77; Writer-in-Residence, University of Alberta, Edmonton, 1978-79; Instructor, David Thompson University Centre, Nelson, British Columbia, 1980-82; Writer-in-Residence, Simon Fraser University, Burnaby, 1983; Instructor, Kootenay School of Writing, Vancouver 1984-87, Kwantlen College, Surrey, British Columbia 1988-89; Professor, Okanagan University College, Kelowna, British Columbia, 1990-91, 1992-95; Instructor, Kootenay School of the Arts, 1991-92, 1995-; Writer-in-Residence, University of Toronto, 1996. Publications include: Mindscapes (with others), 1971; Waiting for Wayman, 1973; For and Against the Moon: Blues, Yells and Chuckles, 1974; Beaton Abbott's Got the Contract: An Anthology of Working Poems (editor), 1974; Money and Rain: Tom Wayman Live!, 1975; Routines, 1976; Transport, 1976; A Government Job at Last: An Anthology of Working Poems, Mainly Canadian (editor), 1976; Kitchener-Chicago/Saskatoon, 1977; Free Time: Industrial Poems, 1977; A Planet Mostly Sea, 1979; Going for Coffee, editor, 1981; Inside Job: Essays on the New Work Writing, 1983; The Face of Jack Munro, 1986; Did I Miss Anything?: Selected Poems 1973-1993, 1993; The Astonishing Weight of the Dead, 1995. Honours: Several prizes and awards. Address: PO Box 163, Winlaw, British Columbia V0G 2J0, Canada.

WEAVER Roger Keys, b. 2 Feb 1935, Portland, Oregon, USA. Professor of English. m. Sharron Beckett, 2 sons. Education: BA,

1957, MFA, 1967, University of Oregon; MA, University of Washington, 1962. Appointments: Assistant Professor, Associate Professor, Full Professor, English, Oregon State University, Corvallis, 1962-. Publications: The Orange and Other Poems, 1978; Twenty-One Waking Dreams, 1985; Traveling on the Great Wheel, 1990; Standing on Earth, Throwing These Sequins at the Stars, 1994. Contributions to: Massachusetts Review; North American Review; Nimrod; Greenfield Review; Dog River Review; Colorado Quarterly; Northwest Review; Fireweed. Honours: Oregon State Poetry Awards Bicentennial, 1976; Tucson Poetry Contest, 1978. Memberships: Academy of American Poets; Willamette Literary Guild. Address: English Department, Oregon State University, Corvallis, OR 97331, USA.

WEBB Bernice Larson, b. Ludell, Kansas, USA. Writer; Consultant; Retired Professor. m. Robert MacHardy Webb, 14 July 1961, 1 son, 1 daughter. Education: AB, University of Kansas, 1956; MA, 1957, PhD, 1961, University of Illinois, University of Aberdeen, 1959-60. Appointments: Assistant Instructor, University of Kansas, 1958-59, 1960-61; Assistant Professor, 1961-67; Associate Professor, 1967-80; Professor, 1980-87; University Consultant, 1987-, University of Southern Louisiana. Book Reviewer: Journal of American Culture, 1980-87; Journal of Popular Culture, 1980-87. Publications: Beware of Ostriches, 1978; Poetry on the Stage, 1979; Spider Web, 1993; The Basketball Man, 1973, 2nd Edition, 1994; Lady Doctor on a Homestead, 1987; Two Peach Baskets, 1991; Born to Be a Loser (co-author), 1993. Contributions to: South Atlantic Quarterly; Kansas City Times; Kansas Quarterly; Twigs; Pawn Review; CEA Critic; Alaska Review; New Orleans Review; Voices International; Louisiana English Journal. Honours: Carruth Memorial Poetry Prize; Morris Rayburn Contest; Freeman Golden Anniversary Award; Heggs Deciquain Contest; Phi Beta Kappa, 1955; Deep South Literary Conference Awards, 1961-79; Nominated Poet Laureate of Louisiana, 1980, 1989. Memberships: President, Louisiana State Poetry Society; Writers Guild of Acadiana; President, Southwest Branch Louisiana State Poetry Society, 1988-; Member of Board, The Deep South Writers Conference, 1978-87; President, South Central College English Association, 1986-87; President, Phi Beta Kappa Association, 1976-77, 1983-84. Literary Agent: K D Writers Service, Beaumont, Texas. Address: 159 Whittington Drive, Lafayette, LA 70503, USA.

WEBB E(ric Christopher), b. 8 July 1969, Pittsburgh, Pennsylvania, USA. Journalist. m. Crystal Allen, 28 May 1995. Education: BS, Lincoln University, 1991; Midwest Newspaper Workshop for Minorities, 1991; Thomson Fellowship, 1992-93; IRE Minority Conference Fellowship, 1995; Paul Miller Washington Reporting Fellowship, Freedom Forum, 1995-96. Literary Appointments: Washington Correspondent, Thomson Newspapers; Reporter, Tribune Chronicle, Warren, Ohio; Executive Director, National Black Authors Tour; Associate Director, NBAT; News Correspondent and Columnist, The Informer, Pittsburgh, Pennsylvania; Campus Representative, Black Excellence Magazine. Publications: Coming of Age: The Waking of Sleeping Giants, 1991; The Recipe for Revolution, 1993; Killing Black Voices, collected writings, early 1996; For Black Coffeehouse Poets Who Believe Their Sh-t Really Matters!?, late 1996. Contributions to: Class Magazine; Grassroots; Da Ghetto Tymz; Poetry Plus. Honours: H Alfred Farrell English Department Award, 1991; H Alfred Farrell Tolson Society Award, 1991; Lincoln University Poet Laureate of the Year, 1991; Distinguished Leadership Award, 1994; Founder's Award, National Black Authors Tour, 1994. Memberships: Executive Director, Associate Director, National Black Authors Tour; Kuntu Writers Workshop; Brothers and Sisters with Books; Endangered Species, performance poetry group. Address: 10425 Campus Way South, Upper Marlboro, MD 20772, USA.

WEBSTER Leonard (Len), b. 6 July 1948, Birmingham, England. Lecturer; Author. m. Emorn Puttalong, 26 Nov 1985. Education: BEd, Warwick University, 1973; MA, Modern English and American Literature, Leicester University, 1976; Poetry Society Adult Verse Speaking Certificate, 1977; Dip RSA TEFLA, 1983; MA, Linguisitics, Birmingham University, 1988. Appointments: Teacher, Oldbury High School, 1976-77; Tarsus American College, Turkey, 1977-78; King Edward VI Grammar School, Handsworth, Birmingham, 1978-84; Lecturer, Ministry of Education, Singapore, 1984-87; 1988-94; Journalist, Birmingham Post and Mail. 1965-68, Coventry Evening Telegraph, 1973-74. Publications: Behind the Painted Veil, 1972; Beneath the Blue Moon, 1992; Hell-Riders, 1994; Flight From the Sibyl, 1994. Contributions to: Journal of Indian Writing in English; Reporter; Singapore Sun; Outposts; Blackcountryman; Sikh Courier; Vedanta for East and West; Holly Leaves; Rainbow; Asiaweek;

Westbere Review. Memberships: Poetry Society; The Society of Authors. Address: c/o 48 Marshall Road, Warley, West Midlands B68 9ED, England.

WEDGE John Francis Newdigate, b. 13 July 1921, London, England. Banker. m. Laura Jacqueline Roberts, 10 Oct 1946, 1 son, 2 daughters. Appointments: Various with Barclays Bank, 1938-81. Contributions to: Anthologies: Poems from the Forces; Poems of the Second World War; The Terrible Rain; Verse of Valour; In Time of War; Poetry Pot Pourri; Echoes of War; Poetry Review. Address: 23 Talbot Road, Carshalton, Surrey SM5 3BP, England.

WEILD Desney. See: JESSENER Stephen.

WEINBERG Robert, b. 28 May 1949, Chicago, Illinois, USA. Respiratory Therapist. Education: BA, Chemistry, University of Illinois, Chicago, 1973; Registered Respiratory Therapist; Workshops with Michael Anania, Paul Hoover and Stanley Rice; Studied with Dr Bernard Brunner, De Paul University. Appointments: Several positions in chemistry until 1978; Respiratory Therapist, 1978-. Contributions to: Lucky Star; Onionhead; European Judaism; Poetry Ireland Review; Poetry Motel. Honours: Dial-A-Poem, 1991, these same poems selected for re-broadcast as part of a 10th Anniversary Dial-A-Poem Program, 1993. Address: 1342 South 50th Avenue #308, Cicero, IL 60650, USA.

WEINFIELD Henry (Michael), b. 3 Jan 1949, Montreal, Quebec, Canada. Associate Professor in Liberal Studies; Poet; Writer. Education: BA, 1970, MA, 1973, PhD, 1985, City College of the City University of New York. Appointments: Lecturer, State University of New York at Binghamton, 1973-74; Adjunct Lecturer, Lehman College 1974-77, Baruch College 1979-81, City College of New York 1982-83; Adjunct Lecturer 1983-84, Special Lecturer 1984-91, New Jersey Institute of Technology; Assistant Professor 1991-96, Associate Professor 1996-, in Liberal Studies, University of Notre Dame. Publications: Poetry: The Carnival Cantata, 1971; In the Sweetness of New Time, 1980; Sonnets Elegiac and Satirical, 1982. Other: The Poet Without a Name: Gray's Elegy and the Problem of History, 1991; The Collected Poems of Stéphane Mallarmé, translated with commentary, 1995. Contributions to: Articles, poems, translations in many publications. Honours: Coordinating Council of Literary Magazines Award, 1975; National Endowment for the Humanities Fellowship, 1989. Memberships: Coordinating Council of Literary Magazines, 1972-76; Modern Language Association, 1985-94; Poetry Society of America, 1988-92. Address: Program of Liberal Studies, University of Notre Dame, Notre Dame, IN 46556, USA.

WEINSTEIN Norman, b. 26 Jan 1948, Pennsylvania, USA. Writer; Educator. m. 14 Mar 1986. Education: BA, Bard College, 1969; MAT, State University of New York. Appointments: Adjunct Faculty, Department of English, Boise State University and State University of New York; Poet-in-Residence, public schools in West Virginia. Publications: Gertrude Stein and The Literature of the Modern Consciousness, 1970; Nigredo, 1982; Albedo, 1984; Suite: Orchid Ska Blues, 1991; A Night in Tunisia: Imaginings of Africa in Jazz, 1992. Contributions to: The Village Voice; IO; Text; Truck; Caterpillar; Tree. Address: 730 East Bannock Street, Boise, ID 83712, USA.

WEISS Theodore Russell, b. 16 Dec 1916, Reading, Pennsylvania, USA. Poet; Professor; Publisher; Editor. m. Renee Karol. Education: BA, 1938; MA, Columbia University, 1940. Appointments: Instructor, University of North Carolina, 1942-44; Yale University, 1941-46; Professor, Band College, 1946-66; Poet-in-Residence, 1966-69; Professor, 1969-85; Monash University, Melbourne, 1982; Editor, Quarterly Review of Literature. Publications: The Catch; Gunsight; The Medium; The Last Day and the First; The World Before Us; Fireweeds; A Slow Fuse; From Princeton One Autumn Afternoon, collected Poems, 1987; A Sum of Destructions; Selected Poems, 1995. Contributions to: Accent; Paris Review; New Yorker; New Criterion; TriQuarterly; Sewannee Review; Hudson Review; Antaeus. Honours: Ford Foundation Fellow; Wallace Stevens Award; Phi Beta Kappa; Ingram Merrill Foundation Fellow; Brandeis Crestive Arts Award; Guggenheim Fellow; Shelly Memorial Award. Memberships: Poetry Society of America. Address: 26 Haslet Avenue, Princeton, NJ 08540, USA.

WELBURN Ron, b 30 Apr 1944. Writer; Professor. m. Cheryl T Donohue, 16 Oct 1988, 2 sons, 1 daughter. Education: BA, Lincoln University, 1968; MA, University of Arizona, 1971; PhD, New York

University, 1983. Appointments: Assistant Professor, Syracuse University, 1970-75; Co-ordinator, Jazz Oral History Project, Institute of Jazz Studies, Rutgers University, Newark, 1980-83; Assistant Professor, 1983; Assistant Professor, Western Connecticut State University; Associate Professor, University of Massachusetts, 1992. Publications: Perpheries; Brownup; The Look in the Night Sky, 1978; Heartland, 1981; Council Decisions, 1991. Contributions to: Greenfield Review; The Eagle; Abraxas; Pig Iron; American Poetry Review; The Phoenix; Gatherings; Archeae; Several Anthologies. Honours: Silver Poetry Award; Certificate of Recognition for Contributing to the Literary Legacy of Langston Hughes. Address: English Department, University of Massachusetts at Amherst, Amherst, MA 01003, USA.

WELCH James, b. 1940, Browning, Montana, USA. Writer; Poet. m. Lois M Welch. Education: Northern Montana College; BA, University of Montana. Publications: Poetry: Riding the Earthboy 40, 1971, revised edition, 1975; Fiction: Winter in the Blood, 1974; The Death of Jim Loney, 1979; Fool's Crow, 1986; The Indian Lawyer, 1990; Non-fiction: Killing Custer: The Battle of the Little Bighorn and the Fate of the Plains Indians (with Paul Stekler), 1994; Editor: Richard Hugo: The Real West Marginal Way: A Poet's Autobiography (with Ripley S Hugg and Lois M Welch), 1986. Contributions to: Periodicals. Honours: National Endowment for the Arts Grant, 1969; Los Angeles Times Book Prize, 1987; Pacific Northwest Booksellers Association Book Award, 1987. Address: 2321 Wylie Street, Missoula, MT 59802, USA.

WELCH Jennifer. See: **BOSVELD Jennifer Miller.**

WELDON Maureen. See: **GARSTON Maureen Beatrice Courtnay.**

WELLMAN Donald, b. 7 July 1944, Nashua, New Hampshire, USA. Poet; Teacher; Editor. m. (1), 1 son, (2) Irene Turner, 2 Jan 1982, 1 daughter. Education: BA, University of New Hampshire, 1967; MA, 1972, DA, 1974, University of Oregon. Appointments: Professor and Chair, Humanities Division, Daniel Webster College, Nashua, New Hampshire; Editor, OARS Inc. Publications: The House in the Fields, 1992; Fields, 1995. Contributions to: Tyuonyi; Puckerbruch Review; Interstate; Zone; Adz; Polis; Boundary-2; Tamarisk; Hyperion; MC; New Maine Writing; Main Review; Generator; Sagetrieb. Address: 21 Rockland Road, Weare, NH 03281, USA.

WELLS Alan Richard, b. 27 Nov 1948. Composer; Music Critic. Education: University of Canterbury, 1970-71; Victoria University of Wellington, 1973-75, 1982-87, 1991-92. Appointments: Secretary for Amnesty International, 1976-77; Assistant Librarian, IHC, 1985-88; Music Critic, New Zealand, 1989-; Judge, New Zealand Poetry Society International Haiku Contest, 1996. Publications: Poems and Haiku in Several Anthologies. Contributions to: Landfall; Argot; Cave; Pacific Moana Quarterly; Plover; Dominion. Honours: New Zealand Poetry Society Competition Runner Up; First Equal New Zealand Poetry Society Haiku Contest; Salient Poetry Contest. Membership: New Zealand Poetry Society. Address: Box 27080, Upper Willis Street, Wellington, New Zealand.

WELLS John David, b. 18 Aug 1964, Newbury, Berkshire, England. Education: BA, History, 1986, MA, 1990, University of Cambridge. Appointments: Research Officer, Location Register of English Literary Manuscripts and Letters, University of Reading, 1987-90; Research Associate, University of Cambridge, 1994-. Publications: Ambion Hill, 1987; Le Pavillon Des Trois Soeurs, 1991; Samuel Taylor Coleridge: Four Letters to Anna and Basil Montagu, editor, 1995. Honours: Eric Gregory Award, 1990; Northern Poets Award, 1991; Hawthornden Fellowship, 1991. Membership: Society of Archivists, 1994-. Address: 6 Porter End, Pyle Hill, Newbury, Berkshire RG14 7JP, England.

WERNER Judith, b. 26 Oct 1941, New York, New York, USA. Writer. m. William Werner, 16 Aug 1975, 1 son, 1 daughter. Education: AB, Barnard College, Columbia University, 1962. Publications: Chapter in books: Elemental I, 1991, Elemental II, 1992; Anthologies: Color Wheel Reader, 1993; Sixteen Voices, 1994. Contributions to: Alea; Bridges; California State Poetry Quarterly; Color Wheel; Eclectic Literary Forum; Four Quarters; The Lyric; River Oak Review; Sequoia; Soujourners; Soundings; South Dakota Review; Visions International; Yankee Magazine; The Christian Century; Miami Beach Times; Spotlight. Honours: Lenore Marshall Poetry Prize, 1962; Academy of American Poets Prize, Columbia University, 1963; Best of Issue Prize.

The Lyric, summer 1992; Ronald J Kemski Prize, 1993. Memberships: Poetry Society of America; Poet's House. Address: 3987 Saxon Avenue, Bronx, NY 10463, USA.

WERNER-KING Janeen Anne, b. 30 Dec 1958, Edmonton, Alberta, Canada. Teacher. m. Robert W King, 11 July 1981. Education: BEd, distinction, University of Alberta; MA, English, University of Calgary. Appointments: English Teacher: Clover Bar School, Alberta, 1981-85, University of Calgary, 1987, Wetaskiwin Composite High School, 1989-91, Our Lady of Peace School, Alberta, 1991-; English Department Head, Bishop Grandin Senior High, 1996. Publications: Bending Light: A Chapbook Anthology, 1993. Contributions to: Orbis; Dandelion; Ariel; Other Voices; Secrets from the Orange Couch; SansCrit; Canadian Broadcasting Corporation Alberta Anthology; Skylines; Eclectic Muse; Alberta Poetry Yearbook; Whetstone; Contemporary Verse 2. Honours: Literary Awards Competition, Edmonton Journal, 1980, 1985; Galbraith Publishing Poetry Contest, 1989. Memberships: Celebration of Women in the Arts, Literary Chair, 1990-92; Member-at-Large, Writers Guild of Alberta; Calgary Writers Association; Calgary Stroll of Poets Coordinator, 1993-95. Address: 7944-71 Avenue North West, Calgary, Alberta, T3B 4J3, Canada.

WEST Colin Edward, b. 21 May 1951, Epping, Essex, England. Author; Illustrator. Education: MA, Royal College of Art, 1972-75. Publications: Not to be Taken Seriously, 1982; A Step in the Wrong Direction, 1984; It's Funny When You Look at It, 1984; What Would You do with a Wobble-Dee-Woo?, 1988; A Moment in Rhyme, 1987; Between the Sun, The Moon and Me, 1990; The Best of West, 1990; I Bought My Love a Tabby Cat, 1988; Long Tales, Short Tales and Tall Tales, 1995. Memberships: Society of Authors; Committee Member, Children's Writers' Group; Society of Authors. Address: 14 High Road, Epping, Essex CM16 4AB, England.

WEST Kathleene, b. 28 Dec 1947, Genoa, Nebraska, USA. Poet; English Professor. Education: BA, University of Nebraska, 1967; MA, University of Washington, 1975; PhD, University of Nebraska, 1986. Appointments: Printer and Book Designer, Copper Canyon Press, 1977-78; Abattoir Editions, 1981-82; Associate Professor of English, New Mexico State University, 1987-; Poetry Editor, Puerto del Sol, 1995-. Publications: Land Bound, 1977; Plainswoman, 1985; Water Witching, 1984; The Farmer's Daughter, 1990. Contributions to: Prairie Schooner; Poetry Northwest; Puerto del Sol; Blue Mesa Review; Calyx; Triquarterly. Honours: Fulbright Scholar, Iceland, 1983-85. Memberships: Associated Writers Program; PEN: Barbara Pym Society. Address: English Department Box 30001, New Mexico State University, Las Cruces, NM 88003, USA.

WESTON Joanna Mary, b. 20 Jan 1938, England. Poet. m. Robert John Weston, 20 May 1967. Education: MA, University of British Columbia, 1969; Education for Ministry Diploma, Victoria, 1988. Appointments: Library Assistant, Kent County Library, Maidstone, 1954-56; McMaster University, Hamilton, 1956-58; Receptionist/Media Managers Assistant, London, 1958-60. Publications: One of These Little Ones; Cuernavaca Diary; Seasons, 1993; All Seasons, 1996. Contributions to: Dandelion; Broken Streets; North Coast Collection; New Hope International; Island Catholic News; Never Bury Poetry; JVC Poetry Newsletter; Envoi; Visions of Flight; Weyfarers. Memberships: Federation of British Columbia Writers; League of Canadian Poets; Cedar Creek Writers; Christian Writers League. Address: 1960 Berger Road, Shawnigan Lake, British Columbia V0R 2W0, Canada.

WEVILL David (Anthony), b. 15 Mar 1935, Yokohama, Japan. Education: BA, Caius College, Cambridge, 1957. Appointment: Teacher, Department of English, University of Texas, Austin. Publications: Penguin Modern Poets 4, 1963; Birth of a Shark, 1964; A Christ of the Ice-Floes, 1966; Firebreak, 1971; Where the Arrow Falls, 1973; Other Names for the Heart; New and Selected Poems, 19164-84, 1985; Figure of Eight, 1987. HOnours include: Eric Gregory Award, 1963; Arts Council Prize and Bursaries. Address: Department of English, University of Texas, Austin, TX 78712, USA.

WHA-PYUNG. See: **JEONG Ki Seok.**

WHALEN Philip (Glenn), b. 20 Oct 1923, Portland, Oregon, USA. Poet; Novelist; Zen Buddhist Priest. Education: BA, Reed College, Portland, Oregon, 1951. Appointments: Writer, 1951-; Ordained Zen Buddhist Priest, 1973; Head Monk, Dharma Sangha, Santa Fe, New Mexico, 1984-87; Abbot, Hartford Street Zen Center,

San Francisco, 1987-96. Publications: Poetry: Three Satires, 1951; Self Portrait from Another Direction, 1959; Memoirs of an Interglacial Age, 1960; Like I Say, 1960; Hymnus ad Patrem, 1963; Three Mornings, 1964; Monday in the Evening, 1964; Goddess, 1964; Every Day, 1965; Highgrade: Doodles, Poems, 1966; T/o, 1967; The Invention of the Letter: A Beastly Morality Being an Illuminated Moral History for the Edification of Younger Readers, 1967; Intransit: The Philip Whalen Issue, 1967; On Bear's Head, 1969; Severance Pay, 1970; Scenes of Life at the Capital, 1971; The Kindness of Strangers: Poems 1969-1974, 1976; Prolegomena to a Study of the Universe, 1976; Decompressions: Selected Poems, 1978; Enough Said: Poems 1974-1979, 1981; Heavy Breathing: Poems 1967-1980, 1983. Novels: You Didn't Even Try, 1967; Imaginary Speeches for a Brazen Head, 1971. Other: Off the Wall: Interviews with Philip Whalen, 1978; The Diamond Noodle, 1980. Contributions to: Anthologies and many periodicals. Honours: Poet Foundation Award, 1962; V K Ratcliff Award, 1964; American Academy of Arts & Letters Grants-in-Aid, 1965, 1991; Committee on Poetry Grants, 1968, 1970, 1971; Morton Dauwen Zabel Award for Poetry, 1986; Fund for Poetry Awards, 1987, 1991. Address: c/o Hartford Street Zen Center, 57 Hartford Street, San Francisco, CA 94114, USA.

WHALLEY Dorothy, (Dorothy Cowlin), b. 16 Aug 1911, Grantham, Lincolnshire, England. Teacher. m. R H Whalley, 12 Apr 1941, 1 daughter. Education: BA, Manchester University, 1929-31. Appointments: Assistant Teacher, St John's, Heaten Mersey, Stockport, and Junior School, Flixton, Lancashire. Publication: The Sound of Rain, self-published, 1991. Contributions include: Envoi; Pennine Platform; Pennine Ink; Airings; Hybrid; Iota; Moonstone; Psychopoetica; New Hope International; Rialto. Honours: Yorkshire TV Competition, 1993. Membership: Scarborough Poetry Workshop. Address: 14 Littledale, Pickering, North Yorkshire, YO18 8PS, England.

WHALLON William, b. 24 Sept 1928. Education: BA, McGill, 1950. Publications: The Oresteia/Apollo & Bacchus; A Book of Time, 1990. Address: 1655 Walnut Heights, East Lansing, MI 48823, USA.

WHEATLEY Jeffery John, b. 31 May 1933, Epsom, Surrey, England. Business Economist. m. 15 Mar 1959, 2 sons, 1 daughter. Education: BSc, Economics, London School of Economics and Political Science, 1956; Honorary Fellow, Telecommunications Engineering Staff College, 1990. Appointments: Independent Consultant, 1990-95; Reviewer for Orbis, 1991-95. Publications: As the Hard Red Sand, 1979; Prince Arthur, 1981. Contributions to: Incept; Linq; Counterpoint; Orbis; Weyfarers; Pennine Platform; Ore; Christian Poetry; Chapman; Iron; Poets Voice; Periaktos, Poets England. Honours: 1st Prize, Maze Poetry Competition, 1992. Memberships: Vice Chair, Surrey Poetry Centre; Panel Editor, Weyfarers; Poetry Society. Address: 9 Copse Edge, Elstead, Godalming, Surrey GU8 6DJ, England.

WHEATLEY Margery Patience, b. 4 Sept 1924, Berkshire, England. Teacher. m. David Irvine Wanklyn, 6 Apr 1948, 1 son, 2 daughters. Education: BA, McGill University, Canada, 1946. Appointments: Teacher of Creative Writing, Thomas More Institute for Adult Education, Montreal. Publications: A Hinge of Spring, 1986; Good-bye to the Sugar Refinery, 1989. Contributions to: Canadian Literary magazines: Antigonish Review; Event; Arc; Canadian Woman Studies; Contemporary Verse II: Descant; The Fiddlehead; Germination; Grain; Poetry Canada Review; Queen's Quarterly; Room of One's Own; Amethyst Review; Pottersfield Portfolio; Wascana Review of Contemporary Poetry and Short Fiction; Anthologies: Anthology of Magazine Verse and Yearbook of American Poetry, California, USA, 1986, 1989; And Other Travels, 1987; Glory to God, 1988; More Garden Varieties, 1989; Bite to Eat Place, 1995; Vintage 95, 1995; Voice of War, 1995. Honour: 1st Prize, Kingston Arts Council Literary Award, 1991. Memberships: Coordinator of the Living Archives Series of the Feminist Caucus, League of Canadian Poets; Chair of Feminist Caucus, 1988-90; Chair, Outreach Committee of Feminist Caucus, 1992; The Poetry Society, London; Writers' Union of Canada. Address: 33 Riverside Drive, Kingston, Ontario K7L 4V1, Canada.

WHEELER Dennis R, b. 1 Jan 1948, North Bend, Oregon, USA. Law Enforcement Officer. m. Dorothy Beyerle, 13 Mar 1971, 2 sons. Education: Associate Arts Degree, San Bernardino Valley College, 1976. Appointments: Vietnam Veteran, 1966-67-68; Lawenforcement Officer, various agencies in South Dakota and California, 1970-; Patrol Sergeant, Rialto Police Department, Rialto, California. Publications: A

Family Affair; A Family Affair II. Contributions to: Mobridge Tribune; Mobridge, South Dakota. Honours: Editors Choice Award, National Library of Poetry, 1996; Certificate, Famous Poet, Famous Poets Society, 1996. Memberships: International Society of Poets; Famous Poets Society. Address: 1148 East Sonora, San Bernardino, CA 92404, USA.

WHEELER Griffith Sylvia, b. 30 May 1930, Kansas, USA. Associate Professor. Div. 2 sons, 1 daughter. Education: University of Kansas, 1968; University of Missouri, 1971. Appointments: Poet in the Schools for Kansas, 1971-88; Associate Editor, BkMk Press, 1971-77; Associate Professor, University of South Dakota, 1977-. Publications: Counting Back; Dancing Alone; This Fool History; This Can't Go On Forever; City Limits; Editor: In the Middle; For Kids/By Kids; Play, The Masters, performed at University of South Dakota, 1995. Contributions to: Prairie Schooner; Chariton Review; Cimarron Review; Minnesota Review; Mississippi Review; New Letters; Paintbrush; Great Rivers Review; Design; Dakotah Territory; Kansas Quarterly. Honours: Award by Witter Bynner Foundation; 3rd Prize Winner, Seaton Award; FMCT Midwestern Playwrights Award; Gwendolyn Brooks Poetry Prize; South Dekota Arts Council Individual Artist Award. Memberships: Poet and Writers; Society for the Study of Midwestern Literature. Address: English Department, University of South Dakota, Vermillion, SD 57069, USA.

WHEELER Susan, b. 16 July 1955, Pittsburgh, Pennsylvania, USA. Education: BA, Bennington College, 1977; University of Chicago, 1979-81. Appointments: Vermont Council on the Arts; Art Institute of Chicago; Poet in Public Service. Publication: Bag o' Diamonds, 1993. Contributions to: Tribune; Boston Review; Massachusetts Review. Honours: Roberts Writing Award; Grolier Poetry Prize; Wurlitzer Foundation Award. Membership: Poetry Society of America. Address: 37 Washington Square West, No 6, New York, NY 10011, USA.

WHINCUP Brenda Rose, b. London, England. Writer. m. Joseph William Whincup, 28 Jan 1961. Appointment: Resident Poet, Master Craftsman Magazine, 1970's. Publication: Triple Echo (a collection). Contributions to: Herb Quarterly; Welter and Radiance; Cat World Annual; Jennings Magazine; Clocks; Bucks and Berks Countryside Magazine; Shropshire Magazine; Anthologies include: Arts Council; Stratford Poets; Phoenix Poets; Penguin Collection of Humour; Poets England Shropshire Book. Honours: Brentwood Writers Competition, 1975, 1978; Contra Costa Fair, USA, 1977, 1980; Ronald Blythe Brentwood Competition, 1980; Gold Medal, Cambridge Festival, 1985; Wrekin Writers Competition, 1990; Theodora Roscoe Cup, 1990; Sutton Writers Competition, 1992; Beryl Lewin Memorial Competition, 1993; Castle Trust Competition, 1994. Memberships: Society of Women Writers and Journalists; London Writers' Society; Anglo-Welsh Poets Society. Address: Mog Cottage, Ruyton Xi Town, Near Shrewsbury, Shropshire SY4 1JB, England.

WHISTLER Laurence, b. 21 Jan 1912, Kent, England. Writer; Glass Engraver. Education: Balliol College, Oxford, 1930-34. Publications: Armed October; Four Walls; The Emperor Heart; In Time of Suspence; Ode to the Sun; Who Live in Unity; The World's Room; Celebrate Her Living; Enter. Honours: Commander of the Order of the British Empire; Honorary DLitt, Oxford; Honorary Fellow of Balliol; Royal Gold Medal for Poetry; Atlantic Award for Literature. Membership: Society of Authors. Address: Scriber's Cottage, Watlington, Oxford OX9 5PY, England.

WHITBY Julie Louise. Writer; Actress. Appointments: Actress, Theatre and TV. Publications: Anthologies. Contributions to: Encounter; Scotsman; Poetry Review; Spare Rib; Country Life; She; Tribune; Countryman; Agenda; Times Literary Supplement; Ambit; Outposts; Core; Contemporary Review; Acumen; New Poetry; Limestone. Memberships: Writers Guild of Great Britain; Poetry Society. Address: c/o Bernard Stone, Turret Bookshop, Lambs Conduit Street, London WC1N 3LH, England.

WHITE Gail (Brockett), b. 1 Apr 1945, Florida, USA. Poet; Editor. m. 27 Mar 1967. Education: BA, Stetson University, 1967. Appointments: Editor, Piedmont Literary Review. Publications: Sibyl & Sphinx; Rockhill Press; All Night in the Churchyard; Irreverent Parables; Fishing for Leviathan; A Formal Feeling Comes. Contributions to: American Scholar; Southern Poetry Review; Lyric; Plains Poetry Journal; South Carolina Review; South Coast Poetry Journal; Christian Century; Outposts; Descant; University of Windsor Review; Room of Ones Own; Kalliope; New Laurel Review; Negative

Capability; Western Humanities Review. Honours: Bernard Meredith Award; Virginia Prize; Seneca Award. Address: 1017 Spanish Moss Lane, Breaux Bridge, LA 70517, USA.

WHITE John Austin The Rev Canon, b. 27 June 1942, England. Canon of St George's Chapel. Education: BA. Appointments: Assistant Curate, Leeds, 1966-69; Chaplain, University of Leeds, 1969-73; Chaplain, Northern Ordination Course, 1973-82; Canon of Windsor, 1982-. Publications: The Poetic Churchman; Anthem for the 40th Anniversary of the Queen's Accession. Membership: Poetry Society. Address: 8 The Cloisters, Windsor Castle, Berkshire SL4 1NJ, England.

WHITE John Roger, b. 2 Jun 1929. Poet. Education: Collegiate Institute, Belleville, Canada. Appointments: Court Reporter, Belleville, 1947-50; Assistant Editor, Canada, 1951-61; Supreme Court of Vancouver, 1961-68; Editor, 1971-83. Publications: Summer Window; Sketches of Abdu Ibaha; Old Songs; New Songs; Different Perspectives; Another Song, Another Season; The Witness of Pebbles; Compendium of the Bahai World; One Bird, One Cage, One Flight; The Shell and the Pearl. Memberships: Guest Editor, Voices; English Langauge Poets of Israel. Address: PO Box 155, 31001 Haifa, Israel.

WHITE Jon (Ewbank) Manchip, b. 22 June 1924, Cardiff, Glamorganshire, Wales. Writer; Poet; Professor of English. m. Valerie Leighton, 2 children. Education: St Catherine's College, Cambridge. 1942-43, 1946-50; Open Exhibitioner in English Literature; MA with Honours, English, Prehistoric Archaeology, and Oriental Languages (Egyptology), and University Diploma in Anthropology. Appointments: Story Editor, BBC TV, London, 1950-51; Senior Executive Officer, British Foreign Service, 1952-56; Independent Author, 1956-67, including a period as screenwriter for Samuel Bronston Productions, Paris and Madrid, 1960-64; Professor of English, University of Texas, El Paso, 1967-77; Lindsay Young Professor of English, University of Tennessee, Knoxville, 1977-. Publications: Novels include: Hour of the Rat, 1962; The Rose in the Brandy Glass, 1965; Nightclimber, 1968; The Game of Troy, 1971; The Garden Game, 1973; Send for Mr Robinson, 1974; The Moscow Papers, 1979; Death by Dreaming, 1981; The Last Grand Master, 1985; Whistling Past the Churchyard, 1992; Poetry: Dragon and Other Poems, 1943; Salamander and Other Poems, 1945; The Rout of San Romano, 1952; The Mountain Lion, 1971; Other includes: Cortés and the Downfall of the Aztec Empire, 1971; A World Elsewhere: One Man's Fascination with the American Southwest, 1975; Everyday Life of the North American Indians, 1979; What To Do When the Russians Come: A Survivor's Handbook (with Robert Conquest), 1984; The Journeying Boy: Scenes from a Welsh Childhood, 1991. Memberships: Honorary, Phi Beta Kappa; Texas Institute of Letters; Welsh Academy. Address: 6817 Northshore Drive, Knoxville, TN 37919, USA.

WHITE June, b. 11 June 1930, Somerset, England. Secretary, Retired. m. Alan White, 8 Mar 1954. Education: Secretarial Training College. Publications: The Living Land; Woodpecker Morning. Contributions to: Northants & Beds Life; Writer Magazine; Writers Own Magazine; Clover International Poetry Anthology; Lilac & English Tea; Salopeot Poetry Anthology; She Magazine. Honours: John McMahon Trophy; Joyce McKay Trophy; Salopian Poetry Society Winner; Writers Review Poetry Competition Winner; Writers Own Magazine Poetry Competition Winner. Membership: Salopian Poetry Society. Address: Sequoia 5 Taylors Ride, Leighton Buzzard, Bedfordshire LU7 7JN, England.

WHITE Kenneth, b. 28 Apr 1936, Glasgow, Scotland. Education: MA, French and German, University of Glasgow, 1959. Appointments: Lecturer in English, Institut Charles V, 1969-83; Professor of 20th Century Poetics, Sorbonne, Paris, 1983-. Publications include: Wild Coal, 1963; En Toute Candeur, 1964; The Cold Wind of Dawn, 1966; The Most Difficult Area, 1968; A Walk Along the Shore, 1977; Le Grand Rivage, 1980; Scienes d'un Monde Flottant, 1983; Terre de diament, 1983; Atlantica: mouvements et mediations, 1986; L'esprit nomade, 1987; The Bird Barth: Collected Longer Poems, 1989; Collected Shorter Poems 1960-1990, 1990; Fiction and essays. Honours include: French Academy Grand Prix de Rayonnement, 1985. Address: Gwenved, Chemin du Goaquer, 22560 Trebeurden, France.

WHITEHEAD Anthony Keith, b. 21 June 1937, Dewsbury, Yorkshire, England. Evangelist. m. Iris Theresa Smith, 26 Dec 1958, 2 sons. Education: City and Guilds Full Technological Certificate in Patternmaking, 1958; BA, Economics, 1971; Postgraduate Certificate in Education, 1972; MPhil, 1978; Certification in Religious Studies, Cambridge University, 1989. Appointments: Patternmaker: Salesman; Retailer; Insurance Agent; Insurance District Manager: Full Time Student; Lecturer; Senior Lecturer; Evangelist. Publication: Another Counsellor, 1995; Prophetic Verse, 1993; People and Employment, 1981. Contributions to: Apostrophe; Areopagus; Broken Streets, USA; Burning Light, USA; Candelabrum; Contemporary Review; Envoi; Good Society Review; Krax; The Month; New Hope International; New Thought Journal, USA; Peace and Freedom; Poetry Nottingham; Psychopoetica; Seam; Studio, Australia; Symphony; Tears in the Fence; The Third Half; Twilight Endings, USA; Working Titles; Yorkshire Journal. Address: Emmaus, 94 Nunn's Lane, Purston, Pontefract, West Yorkshire WF7 5HH, England.

WHITEHEAD John, b. 20 Dec 1924, Esher, Surrey, England. Retired. Education: Winchester College, 1938-43. Publications: Emblems of More; Flash and Outbreak; Murmurs in the Rose. Address: The Coach House, Munslow, Craven Arms, Shropshire SY7 9ET, England.

WHITEHOUSE Anne Cherner, b. 30 Jan 1954, Alabama, USA. Writer. m. Stephen Whitehouse, 24 June 1979, 1 daughter. Education: BA, Harvard University, 1976; MFA, Columbia University, 1979. Publication: The Surveyor's Hand. Contributions to: New England Review; American Voice; Black Warrior Review; Alaska Quarterly Review; Buffalo Spree; Freelance Critic and Feature Writer: New York Times Book Review; Miami Herald; Baltimore Sun; Los Angeles Times; Forward; Atlanta Journal and Constitution. Honour: Academy of American Poets. Memberships: Poetry Society of America; Academy of American Writers, Columbia University Seminar on Latin America. Address: 340 Riverside Drive, New York, NY 10025, USA.

WHITMAN Ruth (Bashein), b. 28 May 1922, New York, USA. Poet; Editor; Translator; Teacher. m. (1) Cedric Whitman, 13 Oct 1941, div 1958, 2 daughters, (2) Firman Houghton, 23 July 1959, div 1964, 1 son, (3) Morton Sacks, 6 Oct 1966. Education: BA, Radcliffe College, 1944; MA, Harvard University, 1947. Appointments: Editorial Assistant 1941-42, Educational Editor 1944-45, Houghton Mifflin Co, Boston; Freelance Editor, Harvard University Press, 1945-60; Poetry Editor, Audience Magazine, 1958-63; Director, Poetry Workshop, Cambridge Center for Adult Education 1964-68, Poetry in the Schools Program, Massachusetts Council on the Arts 1970-73; Scholar-in-Residence, Radcliffe Institute, 1968-70; Instructor in Poetry, Radcliffe College 1970-, Harvard University Writing Program 1979-84; Writer-in-Residence, Visiting Lecturer at various colleges and universities; Many poetry readings. Publications include: Blood and Milk Poems, 1963; Alain Bosquet: Selected Poems, translator with others, 1963; Isaac Bashevis Singer: Short Friday, co-translator, 1966; The Marriage Wig, and Other Poems, 1968; The Selected Poems of Jacob Glatstein, editor and translator, 1972; The Passion of Lizzie Borden: New and Selected Poems, 1973; The Fiddle Rose: Selected Poems of Abraham Sutzkever, translator, 1989; Laughing Gas: Poems New and Selected 1963-1990, 1991; Hatshepsut, Speak to Me, 1992. Contributions to: Anthologies and periodicals. Honours include: John Masefield Award, 1976; Senior Fulbright Fellowship, 1984-85; Urbanarts Award, 1987. Memberships: Authors Guild; Authors League of America; New England Poetry Club; PEN; Phi Beta Kappa; Poetry Society of America. Address: 40 Tuckerman Avenue, Middletown, RI 02840, USA.

WHITNEY E. See: **THOMPSON Lucille.**

WHITT Laurie Anne, b. 3 Aug 1952, San Diego, California, USA. University Professor. Education: BA, College of William and Mary, 1975; MA, Queens University, 1976; PhD, University of Western Ontario, 1985. Appointments: Assistant Professor, Southern Methodist University, 1984-86; Assistant, then Associate Professor of Philosophy, Michigan Technological University, 1986-. Contributions to: Malahat Review; Prism International; Hawaii Review; Wisconsin Review; Ariel; Fiddlehead; Quarry; Poetry Canada Review; Waves; Stone Country; Prairie Journal of Canadian Literature; Cicada; Cross-Canada Writers Quarterly; Anthology: New Voices: A Celebration of Canadian Poetry, 1984; Puerto Del Sol; Cottonwood; The Cream City Review; Northeast; Riverrun. Membership: League of Canadian Poets. Address: PO Box 195, Chassell, MI 49916, USA.

WICHERT Sabine, b. 8 June 1942, Germany. University Teacher. Education: Universities in Frankfurt, Marburg, Berlin,

Mannheim, London and Oxford. Appointments: Lecturer, Queens University, Belfast, 1971-. Publications: Miranda, 1993; Tin Drum Country, 1995. Contributions to: Irish Press; Poetry Ireland Review; Fortnight; Honest Ulsterman; Filmdirections; Raven Introductions; Cyphers; Sunday Tribune; Gown Literary Supplement; Poetry Nottingham; Orbis; Salmon; Big Spoon; Windows Selection; Rustic Rub; Scratch; Envoi; Day by Day; Acumen; Spark; WP Monthly; Writing Women. Honour: Short Listed Hennessy Sunday Tribune Award. Membership: Poetry Society. Address: 63 Vauxhall Park, Stranmillis, Belfast BT9 5HB, Northern Ireland.

WICKER Nina Apple, b. 31 Oct 1927, North Carolina, USA. County Tax Office. m. Julian Talmadge Wicker, 6 July 1951, 3 sons, 1 daughter. Education: Central Carolina Community College; Sandhills Community College. Appointments: Tax Lister, Lee County, North Carolina. Publications: October Rain on My Window, 1984; Winter and Wild Roses, 1989; Where Pelicans Fly, 1991; The Haiku Hundred, 1992; Haiku Moment, 1993. Contributions to: Progressive Farmer; North Carolina Christian Advocate; Carolina Country; Parnassus Literature Journal; Soundings/East; New Earth Review; Pilot; Sandford Herald; Bayleaves; Pegasus; Cairn; Miscellany; Pembroke Magazine; Tower Press; Wind; Piedmont Literature Review. Honours: Mya Pasek Award, 1985; North Carolina Poetry Society Haiku Award, 1990. Memberships: North Carolina Poetry Society, Haiku Society and Writers Network; Haiku Society of America. Address: 4318 Minter School Road, Stanford, NC 27330, USA.

WICKS Susan Jane, b. 24 Oct 1947, Kent, England. Tutor; Writer. m. John Collins, 7 Apr 1973, 2 daughters. Education: BA Hons, French, University of Hull, 1971; DPhil, University of Sussex, 1975. Appointments: University of Dijon, 1974-76; Assistant Lecturer, French, University College, Dublin, 1976-77; Part-time Tutor, University of Kent Centre, Tonbridge, 1983-. Publications: Singing Underwater, 1992; Open Diagnosis, 1994; Driving My Father (prose), 1995. Contributions to: Times Literary Supplement; Observer; LRB; Poetry Review; London Magazine; Ambit; Poetry Durham; Poetry Wales; Poetry East; Women's Review of Books; Orbis; The New Yorker. Honours: Aldeburgh Poetry Festival Prize, 1992; Residency, Hedgebrook, Washington State, 1991; Ragdale Residency, Illinois, 1992; Residency, VCCA, 1994. Memberships: Poetry Society; Kent and Sussex Poetry Society. Literary Agent: Jane Turnbull. Address: c/o University of Kent Centre, Avebury Avenue, Tonbridge, Kent TN9 1TG, England.

WIDDOWS Paul Frederick, b. 5 Aug 1918, London, England. Retired Professor of Classics. m. Huguette Vivers, dec, 5 April 1958. Education: BA, Classics, Oxon, 1948; PhD, Classics, University of Chicago, 1967. Appointments: Teacher, various schools in England and Canada, 1946-60; Professor of Classics, Concordia University, Montreal, 1960-82. Publications: Selected Poems of Emile Nelligan, 1960; Lucan's Civil War, 1988; The Fables of Phaedrus, 1992. Address: 23 Burton Avenue, Westmount, Quebec H3Z 1J6, Canada.

WIEDER Laurance, b. 28 Jun 1946, New York, New York, USA. Writer. m. Andrea Korotky Wieder, 1 daughter. Education: BA, Columbia University, 1968; MA, Cornell University, 1970. Publications: Man's Best Friend, 1982; The Coronet of Tours, 1972; No Harm Done, 1975; Duke: The Poems as told to..., 1990; Full Circle, 1990; The Last Century: Selected Poems, 1992; Chapters into Verse: Poetry in English Inspired by the Bible, 1993; King Solomon's Garden: Poems and Art Inspired by the Old Testament, 1994; The Red Sea Haggadah, 1995; The Poets' Book of Psalms, 1995. Contributions to: Scripsi; Pequod; Boulevard; New Yorker; Pataphysics; Partisan Review; Poetry; Columbia Review; Columbia College Today; Paris Review; Epoch; First Things; Chronicles. Honour: Ingram Merrill Foundation Grant in Poetry, 1974. Address: 114 Oak Street, Patchogue, NY 11772, USA.

WIENERS John (Joseph), b. 6 Jan 1934, Milton, Massachusetts, USA. Poet; Dramatist; Writer. Education: BA, Boston College, 1954; Black Mountain College, North Carolina, 1955-56; State University of New York at Buffalo, 1965-69. Publications: The Hotel Wentley Poems, 1958, revised edition, 1965; Still-Life, play, 1961; Asphodel in Hell's Despite, 1963; Ace Pentacles, 1964; Chinoiserie, 1965; Hart Crane, Harry Crosby, I See You Going Over the Edge, 1966; Anklesox and Five Shoelaces, play, 1966; King Solomon's Magnetic Quiz, 1967; Pressed Water, 1967; Selected Poems, 1968; Unhired, 1968; A Letter to Charles Olson, 1968; Asylum Poems, 1969; Untitled Essay on Frank O'Hara, 1969; A Memory of Black Mountain

College, 1969; Nerves, 1970; Youth, 1970; Selected Poems, 1972; Woman, 1972; The Lanterns Along the Wall, 1972; Playboy, 1972; We Were There!, 1972; Holes, 1974; Behind the State Capitol, or, Cincinnati Pike, 1985; A Superficial Estimation, 1986; Conjugal Contraries and Quart, 1986; Cultural Affairs in Boston: Poetry and Prose, 1956-1985, 1988. Contributions to: Numerous periodicals. Honours: Poet's Foundation Award, 1961; New Hope Foundation Award, 1963; National Endowment for the Arts Grants, 1966, 1968, 1984; Academy Award, 1968; Guggenheim Fellowship, 1985. Address: 44 Joy Street, Apt 10, Boston, MA 02114, USA.

WIER Dara, b. 30 Dec 1949, New Orleans, Louisiana, USA. Poet; Associate Professor. m. (1) Allen Wier, 2 April 1969, div 1983, (2) Michael Pettit, 1 Sept 1983, div 1990, 1 son, 1 daughter. Education: Louisiana State University, 1967-70; BS, Longwood College, 1971; MFA, Bowling Green State University, 1974. Appointments: Instructor in English, University of Pittsburgh, 1974-75; Instructor 1975-76, Assistant Professor of English 1977-80, Hollins College, Virginia; Associate Professor 1980-85, Director of Graduate Studies 1981-82, Director of Writing Program 1983-84, University of Alabama at Tuscaloosa; Associate Professor, 1985-96, Professor, 1996-, University of Massachusetts at Amherst; Visiting poet at various universities; Many poetry readings. Publications: Blood, Hook And Eye, 1977; The 8-Step Grapevine, 1981; All You Have in Common, 1984; The Book of Knowledge, 1988; Blue for the Plough, 1992; Our Master Plan, 1997. Contributions to: Anthologies and many periodicals. Honours: National Endowment for the Arts Fellowship, 1980; Guggenheim Fellowship, 1993-94. Memberships: Associated Writing Programs, President 1981-82; Authors Guild; Authors League of America; PEN; Poetry Society of America. Address: 504 Montague Road, Amherst, MA 01002, USA.

WIGHT Jane (Alison), b. 24 Nov 1935, Wangford, Suffolk, England. Lecturer; Poet. Education: MA, St Andrews, 1959; BA, Reading, 1965. Appointments: Part-time Lecturer in Adult and Further Education including University of Reading Extra-Mural Studies Department, 1977-94. Publications: Author, Brick Building...to 1550, 1972; Author, Mediaeval Floor Tiles, 1975; Poetry: Place and Time, 1978; Thinking in Sentences, 1980; Contour and Cover, 1981; Catching the Sun, 1984; Point the Courses of the Stars, 1986; Linking Islands, 1988; Try Number Seven, 1989; Poetry with illustrations by Helen Stanford: Irregular Measure, 1991; After Image, 1993; Unlatch the Gate, 1996; Edited collection by May Ivimy, The Best Part of the Day, 1992; Co-Editor, Waiting For the Echo, Norwich Poetry Group Anthology, 1994. Contributions to: Ver Poets Voices; Open Competition Anthologies; Odyssey. Memberships: Ver Poets, St Albans; Committee Member, Norwich Poetry Group. Address: 91 Bury Street, Norwich, Norfolk NR2 2DL, England.

WILBER Richard A, b. 4 Sept 1948, St Louis, Missouri, USA. Journalism Professor. m. Robin Smith, 16 Mar 1984, 1 son, 1 daughter. Education: BA, English, Journalism, Southern Illinois University, 1970; MFA English, Southern Illinois University, Edwardsville, 1976; EdD, Southern Illinois University, 1996. Appointments: Associate Editor, The Midwest Motorist, 1970-76; Editor, Fiction Quarterly, 1988-; Journalism Professor, Southern Illinois University, 1988-; Journalism Professor, Florida Southern College, 1980-88; Journalism Professor, University of South Florida, 1988-96. Publications: To Leuchars, 1997. Contributions to: Cencrastus; Poetry Ireland Review; Free Lunch; Asinov's; Spitball; South of Midnight; Whisper of Blood; Dryphon; Fiction Quarterly; Tempa Tribune; Once Upon a Midnight; Starline. Memberships: Textbook Authors Association; Science Fiction Writers of America; Honor Writers of America. Address: 210 Isle Drive, St Pete Beach, FL 33706, USA.

WILBUR Richard (Purdy), b. 1 Mar 1921, New York, New York, USA. Poet; Writer; Translator; Editor; Professor. m. Mary Charlotte Hayes Ward, 20 June 1942, 3 sons, 1 daughter. Education: AB, Amherst College, 1942; AM, Harvard University, 1947. Appointments: Assistant Professor of English, Harvard University, 1950-54; Associate Professor of English, Wellesley College, 1955-57; Professor of English, Wesleyan University, 1957-77; Writer-in-Residence, Smith College, 1977-86; Poet Laureate of the USA, 1987-88; Visiting Lecturer at various colleges and universities. Publications include: Poetry: The Beautiful Changes and Other Poems, 1947; Ceremony and Other Poems, 1950; Things of This World, 1956; Poems 1943-1956, 1957; Advice to a Prophet and Other Poems, 1961; The Poems of Richard Wilbur, 1963; Walking to Sleep: New Poems and Translations, 1969; Digging To China, 1970; Seed Leaves: Homage to R F, 1974; The

Mind-Reader: New Poems, 1976; Seven Poems, 1981; New and Collected Poems, 1988. Honours: Harriet Monroe Memorial Prize, 1948, 1978; Oscar Blumenthal Prize, 1950; Guggenheim Fellowships 1952-53, 1963-64; Prix de Rome Fellowship, American Academy of Arts & Letters, 1954; Edna St Vincent Millay Memorial Award, 1957; Pulitzer Prizes in Poetry, 1957, 1989; National Book Award for Poetry, 1957; Ford Foundation Fellowship, 1960; Bollingen Prizes, 1963, 1971; Brandeis University Creative Arts Award, 1971; Shelley Memorial Award, 1973; Drama Desk Award, 1983; Chevalier, Ordre des Palmes Academiques, 1983; Los Angeles Times Book Prize, 1988; Gold Medal for Poetry, American Academy & Institute of Arts & Letters, 1991; Edward MacDowell Medal, 1991; National Medal of Arts, 1994. Memberships include: Modern Language Association, honorary fellow. Address: 87 Dodwells Road, Cummington, MA 01026, USA.

WILCOX Violet Gaynell, b. 31 Oct 1923, Richmond, Virginia, USA. . m. Richard, 10 Mar 1957, div, 1 son, 3 daughters. Education: Washington School of Art, Port Washington, New York, 1948. Appointments: Worked for Thalhimers Inc, 1946-57; Seamstress, Hub Uniform, 1977-92. Contributions to: Lone Stars; Bell's Letters; Lines N'Rhymes; Silver Wings; Smile, Omnific. Honours: 1st Prize, Aztec Peak, 1986; 1st Prize, Writer's Exchange, 1987; 1st Prize, Poets at Work, 1988, 1989; 3rd Prize, International Contest; 1st for drawing, Psych It; Special Award, Lines N'Rhymes; Joint Winner, Song Contest. Address: 208D Newbridge Circle, Richmond, VA 23223-6265, USA.

WILD Peter, b. 25 Apr 1940, Northampton, Massachusetts, USA. Professor of English; Poet; Writer. m. (1) Sylvia Ortiz, 1966, (2) Rosemary Harrold, 1981. Education: BA, 1962, MA, 1967, University of Arizona; MFA, University of California, Irvine, 1969. Appointments: Assistant Professor, Sul Ross State University, Alpine, Texas, 1969-71; Assistant Professor, 1971-73, Associate Professor, 1973-79, Professor of English, 1979-, University of Arizona; Contributing Editor, High Country News, 1974-; Consulting Editor, Diversions, 1983-. Publications include: Poetry: Cochise, 1973; The Cloning, 1974; Tumacacori, 1974; Health, 1974; Chihuahua, 1976; The Island Hunter, 1976; Pioneers, 1976; The Cavalryman, 1976; House Fires, 1977; Gold Mines, 1978; Barn Fires, 1978; Zuni Butte, 1978; The Lost Tribe, 1979; Jeanne d' Arc: A Collection of New Poems, 1980; Rainbow, 1980; Wilderness, 1980; Heretics, 1981; Bitteroots, 1982; The Peaceable Kingdom, 1983; Getting Ready for a Date, 1984; The Light on Little Mormon Lake, 1984; The Brides of Christ, 1991; Easy Victory, 1994; Other: Pioneer Conservationists of Western America, 2 volumes, 1979, 1983; Enos Mills, 1979; Clarence King, 1981; James Welch, 1983; Barry Lopez, 1984; John Haines, 1985; John Nicholas, 1986; The Saguaro Forest, 1986; John C Van Dyke: The Desert, 1988; Alvar Nunez Cabeza de Vaca, 1991; Ann Zwinger, 1993; Editor: New Poetry of the American West (with Frank Graziano), 1982. Honours: Writer's Digest Prize, 1964; Hart Crane and Alice Crane Williams Memorial Fund Grant, 1969; Ark River Review Prize, 1972; Ohio State University President's Prize, 1982. Address: 1547 East Lester, Tucson, AZ 85719, USA.

WILDHAGEN Dorothy Mabel, (Dorcas), b. 8 July 1942, New York City, New York, USA. Medical Transcriptionist. m. Charles B Wildhagen, 5 Oct 1968, dec, 1975. Education: Theodore Roosevelt High School, 1959; New York Schools of Music, 1955-59; Mandl Medical Assistants School, 1960; City College of New York, 1960-61; Spiritual Development Program, 1986. Appointments: Dictaphone Transcriber; Private Piano Instructor; Religious Candidate, Redemptoristine Nuns; Medical Transcriptionist. Publication: The Eighth of July: Poetry by Dorcas, 1996. Contributions to: National Library of Poetry; Riverdale Press (New York); Poetry Ltd; Poetry Press; Sparrowgrass Forum and Newsletter; Pegasus (Kentucky Poetry Society). Honours: 2 Awards, Editors Choice, National Library of Poetry, 1995. Memberships: Kentucky State Poetry Society; Sparrowgrass Poetry Forum. Address: 3119 Bailey Avenue, Bronx, NY 10463-5732, USA.

WILDWOOD James. See: HANF James Alphonso.

WILEY Valerie, b. 7 April 1954, Philadelphia, Pennsylvania, USA. Poet; Patient Advocate. Education: Temple University; Newspaper Institute. Appointments: Patient Advocate Poet. Publications: Poetry Okayval, 1982; Would You Stand Up, 1996; He's A Prince, 1994. Contributions to: Newspapers; Magazines; Anthologies; Chapbooks; Contests; Radio; TV; Readings. Honours: Danae, 1976. Memberships: PCA; Philadelphia Library; Clover Leaf Poetry Society. Address: 1655 N Allison Street, Philadelphia, PA 19131, USA.

WILKINSON Rosemary Regina Challoner, b. 21 Feb 1924, New Orleans, Louisiana, USA. Poet; Author. m. Henry Bertram Wilkinson, 15 Oct 1949, 3 sons, 1 daughter. Education: San Francisco State University; Livre University, Pakistan. Appointments: Hospital Administration; Literary Career; Teaching, Lecturing, Poetry Reading. Publications: Angels and Poetry, 1992; Cambrian Zepher, 1993. Contributions to: Many. Honours: Bronze Medal, World Poetry Society; Gold/Jade Schilla Dynasty Crown; Centro Cultural Literario e Artistico Award; Universita Delle Arti Award; Leonardo Da Vinci Award; West Bengal Award; American Poets Fellowship; Arti Lettere Scienze Cultura Award. Memberships: American Academy of Poets, New York; Poetry Society of America; Authors League of America; National League of American Pen Women; Poetry Society of London. Addrress: 3146 Buckeye Court, Placerville, CA 95667, USA.

WILL Frederic, b. 4 Dec 1928, New Haven, Connecticut, USA. Professor of Comparative Literature; Poet. Education: AB, Indiana University, 1949; PhD, Yale University, 1954. Appointments: Instructor in Classics, Dartmouth College, 1953-55; Assistant Professor of Classics, Pennsylvania State University 1954-59, University of Texas 1960-64; Associate Professor of English and Comparative Literature 1964-66, Professor of Comparative Literature 1966-71, University of Iowa; Professor of Comparative Literature, University of Massachusetts at Amherst, 1971-; Visiting Lecturer in poetry and criticism at many colleges and universities; Many poetry readings. Publications include: Intelligible Beauty in Aesthetic Thought: From Winckelmann to Victor Cousin, 1958; Mosaic and Other Poems, 1959; A Wedge of Words, poems, 1962; Kostes Palamas: The Twelve Words of the Gypsy, translator, 1964; Hereditas: Seven Essays on the Modern Experience of the Classical, editor, 1964; Metaphrasis: An Anthology from the University of Iowa Translation Workshop, 1964-65, editor, 1965; Flumen historicum: Victor Cousin's Aesthetic and Its Sources, 1965; Literature Inside Out: Ten Speculative Essays, 1966; Planets, poems, 1966; Kostes Palamas: The King's Flute, translator, 1967; Our Thousand Year Old Bodies: Selected Poems 1956-1976, 1980; Entering the Open Hole, 1989; Recoveries, 1993. Contributions to: Many poems and articles in various periodicals. Honours include: Voertman Poetry Awards, Texas Institute of Letters, 1962, 1964; Bollingen Foundation Grant; National Endowment for the Arts Grant. Address: Department of Comparative Literature, University of Massachusetts at Amherst, Amherst, MA 01003, USA.

WILLETTS Ronald Frederick, b. 2 April 1915, Halesowen, West Midlands, England. Scholar; Writer. m. Annie Marion Dann, 10 Feb 1945, 1 daughter. Education: University of Birmingham, 1933-39. Appointments: Schoolmaster, 1939-40; War Service, 1940-46; Lecturer, Greek, 1946-57; Senior Lecturer, 1957-63; Reader, 1963-69; Professor, 1969-75; Chairman of the School of Hellenic and Roman Studies, 1975-81, University of Birmingham. Publications: The Trobriana Islanders; The Baths of Ashrodite; Argo; Pale Moonlight; The Heart of the Matter; Ironies and Hymns; The Plutus of Aristophanes; Rhonian Morning. Contributions to: BBC; Outposts; Greeks Gazette; Birmingham Post; PEN Anthology; Extra Verse. Honour: Mid Century Blues in New Poems. Memberships: PEN; Housman Society; Hellenic Society; Classical Association. Address: 95 Selly Park Road, Selly Park, Birmingham B29 7LH, England.

WILLI RED BEAR. See: KERR Kathryn Ann.

WILLIAMS C(harles) K(enneth), b. 4 Nov 1936, Newark, New Jersey, USA. Poet; Professor. m. Catherine Justine Mauger, April 1975, 1 son, 1 daughter. Education: BA, University of Pennsylvania, 1959. Appointments: Visiting Professor, Franklin and Marshall College, Lancaster, Pennsylvania 1977, University of California at Irvine 1978, Boston University 1979-80; Professor of English, George Mason University, 1982; Visiting Professor, Brooklyn College, 1982-83; Lecturer, Columbia University, 1982-85; Holloway Lecturer, University of California at Berkely, 1986; Professor, Princeton University, 1996-. Publications: A Day for Ann Frank, 1968; Lies, 1969; I Am The Bitter Name, 1972; The Sensuous President, 1972; With Ignorance, 1977; The Women of Trachis, co-translator, 1978; The Lark, The Thrush, The Starling, 1983; Tar, 1983; Flesh and Blood, 1987; Poems 1963-1983, 1988; The Bacchae of Euripedes, translator, 1990; A Dream of Mind, 1992; Selected Poems, 1994. Contributions to: Akzent; Atlantic; Carleton Miscellany; Crazyhorse; Grand Street; Iowa Review; Madison Review; New England Review; New Yorker; Seneca Review; Transpacific Review; TriQuarterly. Honours: Guggenheim Fellowship; National Book Critics Circle Award, 1983; National Endowment for the Arts Fellowship, 1985; Pushcart Press Prizes, 1982, 1983, 1987;

Morton Dauwen Zabel Prize, 1988; Lila Wallace Writers Award, 1993. Membership: PEN. Address: 82 Rue d'Hauteville, 75010 Paris, France.

WILLIAMS Faith, b. 15 Apr 1941, New York, New York, USA. Teacher; Librarian; Poet. m. Stephen Fain Williams, 11 June 1966, 3 sons, 2 daughters. Education: BA, Radcliffe College, 1963; PhD, Columbia University, 1973; Master of Library Science, Catholic University of America, 1992. Contributions to include: Poet Lore; Nimrod; Kansas Quarterly; Bogg; Bridge. Memberships: Poets and Writers, New York; Writer's Center, Bethesda, Maryland. Address: 3768 McKinley Street North West, Washington, DC 20015, USA.

WILLIAMS Hugo, b. 20 Feb 1942, England. Writer. m. Hermine Demoraine, 12 Oct 1966, 1 daughter. Appointments: Assistant Editor, London Magazine, 1961-69; The New Review, 1974; TV Critic, New Statesman, 1982-87; Freelance Columnist Times Literary Supplement, 1988-; Theatre Critic, Sunday Correspondent, 1989-90; Film Critic, Harpers and Queen, 1993-; Freelancing. Publications: Symptoms of Lois; Sugar Daddy; All the Times in the World; Some Sweet Day; Love Life; No Particular Place to Go; Writing Home; Selected Poems; Self Portrait with a Shoe: Dock Leaves. Contributions to: Numerous. Honours: Cholmondely Award; Greyone Award; Faber Prize. Memberships: Royal Society of Literature. Address: 31 Raleigh Street, London N1 8NW, England.

WILLIAMS John Hartley, b. 7 Feb 1942, England. Lecturer. m. Gizella Horvat, 7 Mar 1970, 1 daughter. Education: BA Hons, English, Nottingham University, 1965; MPhil, English and Education, London University, 1974; Certificate in Phonetics, University College, London, 1974. Appointments: Lectureships in English at: Facultes Catholiques, Lille, France; INSA, Toulouse, France; University of Novi Sad, Yugoslavia; Federal University of Cameroon; Free University of Berlin, 1976-. Publications: Cornerless People, 1990; Bright River Yonder, 1987; Hidden Identities, 1982; Double, 1994; Ignoble Sentiments, 1995. Contributions to: Thames Poetry; Rialto; Poetry Review; Observer; Hard Times; Anthologies: The New Poetry; Bloodaxe, 1993; Klaonica - Poems for Bosnia, 1993; Poetry with An Edge, 1993. Honours: Poetry Book Recommendation, 1987; First Prize, Arvon International Poetry Competition, 1983. Membership: Poetry Society. Address: 18 Jenbacherweg, 12209 Berlin, Germany.

WILLIAMS Merryn, b. 9 July 1944, Devon. England. Author. m. John Hemp, 14 April 1973, 1 son, 1 daughter. Education: BA, Cambridge. 1966; PhD, 1970. Appointments: Lecturer, Open University, 1970-71; Editor, The Interpreter's House, 1996-. Publications: The Bloodstream, 1989; Selected Poems of Federico Garcia Lorca, 1992; Wilfred Owen, 1994. Contributions to: Acumen; Aireings; Anglo-Welsh Review; Bedfordshire Times; Bradford Poetry Quarterly; Envoi; Frogmore Papers; Grand Piano; Green Book; Honest Ulsterman; Iron; Lines Review; New Welsh Review; Orbis; Outposts; Oxford Poetry; Poetry Nottingham; Poetry Wales; Prospice; Radical Wales; Smoke; Spokes; Window on Wales; Writing Women. Memberships: Open University; Welsh Academy; Open University Poets. Literary Agent: Meic Stephens, Combrogos Literary Agency, 10 Heol Don, Cardiff, Wales. Address: 10 Farrell Road, Wootton, Bedfordshire MK43 9DU, England.

WILLIAMS Miller, b. 8 Apr 1930, Hoxie, Arkansas, USA. University Press Director. m. Lucille Day, 29 Dec 1951, 1 son, 2 daughters. Education: BS, Arkansas State College, 1950; MS, University of Arkansas, 1952. Appointments: Founder, Editor, New Orleans Review, 1968-70; Advisory Editor, New Orleans Review, 1975-; Contributing Editor, Translation Review, 1976-80. Publications: A Circle of Stone; Recital; Southern Writing in the Sixties; So Long at the Fair; Chile; The Achievement of John Ciardi; The Only World There Is; Emergency Poems; Halfway from Hoxie; A Roman Collection; A Hillside Reader; Living on the Surface; Adjusting to the Light; Points of Department. Contributions to: Letras, (Peru); Oberlin Quarterly; Saturday Review. Honours: Henry Bellaman Poetry Award; Bread Loaf Fellowship; Fulbright Lecturer; Prix de Rome for Literature; Doctor of Humanities, Lander College, 1983; National Poets Prize, 1992; Academy Award for Literature, American Academy of Arts & Letters, 1995; Doctor of Humane Letters, Hendrix College, 1995. Address: University of Arkansas Press, Fayetteville, AR 72701, USA.

WILLIAMS Tyrone, b. 24 Feb 1954, Detroit, Michigan, USA. Associate Professor. Education: BA. 1977; MA, 1983; PhD, 1992. Appointments: Teaching Assistant, Wayne State University, 1979-83; Professor, Xavier University, 1983-. Publication: Convalescence.

Contributions to: Kenyon Review; Obsidian; Colorado Review; World; Transfer. Honours: National Poetry Service, Finalist; Poet Hunt, 2nd Prize; Tompkins Poetry Award, 1st Place. Address: 2217 Victory Parkway, C-1, Cincinnati, OH 45206, USA.

WILLOUGHBY Katrina Agness, b. 8 Mar 1948, New Zealand. Librarian. 1 son, 1 daughter. Education: Central Hawkes Bay College. Appointments: Library Assistant, Army HQ, 1965-66; Schools Library Service, 1966-72; Assistant Information Resource Officer, BP New Zealand, 1984-90; Library Assistant, New Zealand Defence Force, 1992-. Publications: A Green Dreaming; 10 Each. Contributions to: Poetry New Zealand; Takahe; Social Alternatives; Verse; Prism; Plainwraps; West Coast Magazine; Orbis; Amelia; Poetry Magazine. Memberships: PEN; Poetry Society.

WILMER Clive, b. 10 Feb 1945, Harrogate, Yorkshire, England. Freelance Teacher, Lecturer, Writer, Broadcaster. m. Diane Redmond, 12 Sept 1971, div 1986, 1 son, 1 daughter. Education: Kings College, Cambridge, 1964-67, 1968-71; BA, 1st Class Honours, English, 1967; MA, Kings College, Cambridge, 1970. Appointments: Exhibition Committee, Pound's Artists, Tate Gallery, London and Kettle's Yard, Cambridge, 1984-85; Visiting Professor, Creative Writing, University of California, Santa Barbara, 1986; Editor, Numbers, 1986-90; Presenter of BBC Radio 3 Series, Poet of the Month, 1989-90; Mikimoto Memorial Ruskin Lecturer, University of Lancaster, 1996. Publications: Poems: The Dwelling Place, 1977; Devotions, 1982; Of Earthly Paradise, 1992; Selected Poems, 1995; Translated with G Gömöri: Miklós Radnóti, Forced March, 1979; György Petri, Night Song of the Personal Shadow, 1991; George Gömöri, My Manifold City, 1996; Editor of: Thom Gunn; The Occasions of Poetry, 1982; John Ruskin; Unto This Last and other writings, 1985; Dante Gabriel Rossetti: Selected Poems and Translations, 1991; William Morris: News From Nowhere and other writings, 1993; Author of: Poets Talking: The Poet of the Month Interviews from BBC Radio 3, 1994. Contributions to: PN Review; TLS; The Times; The Southern Review; Agenda; Many others. Honours: Writers Grant, Arts Council of Great Britain, 1979; Authors Foundation Grant, 1993. Membership: Companion of the Guild of St George, 1995. Literary Agent: A M Heath. Address: 57 Norwich Street, Cambridge CB2 1ND, England.

WILNER Eleanor, b. 29 July 1937, Ohio, USA. Poet; Teacher. m. Robert Weinberg, 1 daughter. Education: BA, 1959; MA, 1964; PhD, 1971. Appointments: Teacher, Morgan State University, Goucher College, Temple University, Japan; Poet-in-Residence, University of Chicago, University of Iowa, University of Hawaii; Former Editor, American Poetry Review; Associate Editor, Calyx: A Journal of Art and Literature by Women. Publications: Shekhinah, 1984; Sarah's Choice, 1989; Otherwise, 1993. Contributions to: American Poetry Review; Beloit Poetry Journal; Chicago Review; Kenyon Review; New Republic; New Yorker; Southwest Review. Honours: MacArthur Foundation Fellowship; Pennbook Philadelphia Award; Pennsylvania Council on the Arts Fellowship; National Endowment for the Arts Creative Writing Grant. Memberships: PEN; Associated Writing Programs. Address: 324 South 12th Street, Philadelphia, PA 19107, USA.

WILOCH Thomas, b. 3 Feb 1953, Michigan, USA. Writer; Editor. m. Denise R Gottis, 10 Oct 1981. Education: BA, Wayne State University. Appointments: Editor, Gale Research, 1977-; Columnist, Photo Static Magazine, 1988-89; Retrofuturism, 1991-93. Publications: Stigmata Junction; Paper Mask; The Mannikin Cypher; Tales of Lord Shantih, 1990; Night Rain, 1991; Narcotic Signature; Lyrical Brandy; Mr Templeton's Toyshop; Decoded Factories of the Heard, 1995. Contributions to: University of Windsor Review; World Letter; Asylum; Exquisite Corpse; River Styx; Glasgow University Magazine. Honours: Poet Hunt Award; Scantle Magazine Best Chapbook Prize; Pushcart Prize nomination; Rhysling Award Nominations. Memberships: Science Fiction Poetry Association. Address: 43672 Emrick Drive, Canton, MI 48187, USA.

WILSON Allison, b. 14 Mar 1953, York, South Carolina, USA. Professor. m. Rodger E Wilson, 9 Apr 1971. Education: BA, Winthrop College, 1971; MS, Jackson State University, 1972; MAT, Jackson State University, 1973; Ed D, Columbia University Teachers College, 1979. Appointments: Lecturer, 1979-80, Assistant Professor, 1980-86, Associate Professor, 1986-93, Professor, 1993-, Jackson State University. Contributions to: Phi Kappa Phi Journal; Bucks County Panorama; Independent Review; Journal of the Mississippi Poetry Society. Honours: 1st Prize, Independent Review Competition;

Jackson George Regional Library Competition; Mississippi Poetry Society Award; Writers Unlimited Award; Many Honorable Mentions. Memberships: Mississippi Poetry Society; Mississippi Writers Club; Modern Language Association. Address: Department of English and Modern Foreign Languages, Jackson State University, Jackson, MS 39217, USA.

WILSON Donald Douglas, b. 16 July 1930, New York, New York, USA. Professor. m. Carolyn Ann Bliss, 13 July 1968, 1 son, 2 daughters. Education: BA, Wagner College, 1952; MS, 1957; CAS, Wesleyan University, 1971; PhD, St John's University, 1978. Appointments: US Navy, 1952-54; Teacher; Humanities Professor; Fulbright Senior Lecturer, Bulgaria, 1991-92. Publications: Forty Seven Poems From Romania; Milk Like Wine; Lucretilis-Pleasant Hill of Horace; Hush You Nightingales!, versetranslations from Bulgaria; Daydreams and Nightmares (Bulgarian verse translations), 1995; Sean O'Casey's Tragi-comic Vision. Contributions to: Anthology of Magazine Verse and Yearbook of American Poetry; Ararat; Ba Shiru; Dimension; Gryphon; International Poetry Review; Milkweed Chronicle; Modern Poetry in Translation; Ore; Poetry East; Poetry Nippon; Practices of the Wind; Prospice; Pulp; Sepia; Song; St Andrew Review; Associate Editor, Sandhills Review. Honour: Richard Wilbur Prize. Memberships: American Literary Translators Association; Society for Values in Higher Education. Address: Ten Hilltop Drive, Canton, CT 06019, USA.

WILSON Frances Jean, b. 8 July 1937, Wiltshire, England. Teacher. m. Harry Wilson, Apr 1963, 1 son, 1 daughter. Education: BA Hons, English Literature, University College, London, 1958; Diploma of Education, Goldsmiths College, London, 1959. Appointments: Leader of Writing Workshops for local colleges and WEA, 1980-96. Publications: Pamphlet of Poems; Where the Light Gets In, 1992; Too Close To Home, 1993. Contributions to: Times Literary Supplement; Literary Review; Outposts; Staple; Spokes; Writing Women; Iron; The Rialto; Other Poetry; Foolscap; Envoi. Honours: Prizes at: Lace Open Competition, 1987; Orbis Rhyme International Competition, 1987, 1991; Staple Summer Competition, 1987, 1988, 1995; Ver Poets Poemcard Competition, 1988, 1989; Lancaster Competition, 1990, 1992; National Poetry Competiition, 1991; Lake Aske Open, 1995. Memberships: Poetry Society; Joint Founder and Organiser, Ware Poetry Group, 1991-. Address: 52 Watton Road, Ware, Herts SG12 0AT, England.

WILSON Irene K, b. Boston, Massachusetts, USA. Poet; Freelance Writer. m. Edward Osborne Wilson, 30 Oct 1955, 1 daughter. Education: Bay State Community College; University of New York. Appointment: Consultant, Advisor, American Biographical Institute, 1987-. Publications: Wildflowers of the Mind; Poets for Africa Anthology; Only Morning In Her Shoes; Utah State University; In The West of Ireland; Enright House; Ann Eliza Bleeker Anthology, 1993. Contributions to: Rosebud Magazine; Red Book Magazine; Parnassus Literary Journal; Piedmont Literary Review; Dan River Anthology; Haiku Society of America; Mainichi Daily News; Japan; Poetry Nippon; Modern Haiku; The Cathartic; Reflect Magazine; Tucumcari Literary Review; Mobius; Mother Earth; East/West Journal; Pegasus. Honours: Haiku Award; Phi Theta Kappa Award. Memberships: Poetry Society of America; Poets & Writers; Academy of American Poets; Massachusetts State Poetry Society. Address: 9 Foster Road, Lexington, MA 02173, USA.

WILSON James (Jim) C(rawford), b. 16 July 1948, Edinburgh, Scotland. Writer. m. Mik Wilson, 21 Aug 1971. Education: Edinburgh University. Appointments: Lecturer, 1972-81; Writer-in-Residence, 1989-91. Publications: The Loutra Hotel; Six Twentieth Century Poets; Cellos in Hell, 1993. Contributions to: Scotsman; Chapman; Lines Review; Radical Scotland; Times Educational Supplement; Cencrastus; Outposts; Orbis; Acumen; Rialto; Poetry Canada Review; Envoi; 2 Plus 2; Poet's Voice; Iron; Stand; Encounter; Literary Review. Honours: Scottish Arts Council Writer's Bursary, 1987, 1994; 1st Prize, Swanage Arts Festival Literary Competition. Address: 7 Carlton Street, Edinburgh EH4 1NE, Scotland.

WILSON Keith, b. 26 Dec 1927, USA. Poet; Writer. m. Heloise Brigham, 15 Feb 1958, 1 son, 4 daughters. Education: BS, 1950; MA, 1956. Publications: Thantog: Songs of a Jaguar Priest, 1977; The Shaman Deer, 1977; While Dancing Feet Shatter the Earth, 1977; Desert Cenote, 1978; The Streets of San Miguel, 1979; Retables, 1981; Stone Roses: Poems from Transylvania, 1983; Meeting at Jal (with Theodore Ensliu), 1985; Lion's Gate: Selected Poems 1963-1986, 1988; The Wind of Pentcost, 1991; Graves Registry, 1992;

The Way of the Dove, 1994. Contributions to: Evergreen Review; Poetry; Rolling Stone; Coyotes Journal; Prairie Schooner. Honours: National Endowment for the Arts Creative Writing Fellowship; Fulbright-Hays Fellowship; Lawrence Creative Writing Fellowship. Address: 1500 South Locust Street, No C-21, Las Cruces, NM 88001, USA.

WILSON Steve, b. 30 Mar 1960, Fort Sill, Oklahoma, USA. Professor of English. m. Nancy Effinger, 31 July 1982, 2 sons. Education: BA, Letters, University of Oklahoma, 1982; MA, English, Texas Christian University, 1984; MFA, Creative Writing, Wichita State University, 1987. Appointments: Hired by Department of English, 1987, MFA Faculty, 1992-, Southwest Texas State University. Publications: Allegory Dance, 1991; The Singapore Express, 1994; Editor, The Anatomy of Water: A Sampling of Contemporary American Prose Poetry, 1992. Contributions to: New American Writing; Asylum Annual; Midwest Quarterly; The Literary Review; Envoi; Negative Capability; Descant; The Prose Poem: An International Journal. Honour: Fulbright Scholar in Creative Writing, Romania, 1994-95. Address: Department of English, Southwest Texas State University, San Marcos, TX 78666, USA.

WINANS A(llan) D, b. 12 Jan 1936, San Francisco, California, USA. Equal Opportunity Specialist; Retired Civil Rights Investigator. Education: BA, San Francisco State University. Appointments: Editor, Publisher, 1973-89; Editor, Writer, 1975-80; Member, Board of Directors, 1973-75, 1984-85. Publications: In Memoriam; Regan Psalms; Further Adventures of Crazy John; North Beach Poems; ORG Minus One; All the Graffiti on all the Bathroom Walls in the World Can't Hide These Scars of Mine; Straws of Sanity; Crazy John Poems; Carmel Clowns; This Land Isn't My Land. Contributions to: City Lights Journal; Kansas Quarterly; Smith; Beat Scene; New York Quarterly; Confrontation; Chiron Review; Beatitude; Haight Ashbury Quarterly; NIK. Memberships: PEN; Poetry Society of America. Address: PO Box 31249, San Francisco, CA 94131, USA.

WINCH Terence Patrick, b. 1 Nov 1945, New York, New York, USA. Writer; Editor; Musician. m. Susan Francis Campbell, 8 Nov 1981, 1 son. Education: BA, Iona College, 1967; MA, Fordham University, 1968. Appointments: Senior Editor, Acting Chief of Publications, National Museum of American Art, 1986-92; Senior Editor, National Museum of the American Indian, 1992-; Head of Publications, National Museum of the American Indian, Washington, DC. Publications: Luncheonette Jealousy, 1975; Nuns, 1976; The Attachment Sonnets, 1981; Irish Musicians/American Friends, 1986; Contenders, 1989; The Great Indoors (poetry), 1995; Hard New York Days (music recording), 1995. Contributions to: New Republic; Brooklyn Review; Saint Mark's Poetry Project Newsletter; Exquisite Corpse; Washington Review; American Poetry Review; Little Magazine; Shiny; New American Writing; Harvard Magazine; Western Humanities Review. Honours: Yaddo Fellowship, 1975; American Book Award, 1986; National Endowment for the Arts Fellowship, 1992. Memberships: PEN; Associated Writing Programs; American Association of Museums. Address: 10113 Greeley Avenue, Silver Spring, MD 20902, USA.

WINDER Barbara Dietz, b. 14 Oct 1927, New York, New York, USA. Professor. m. Alvin E Winder, 21 June 1949, 2 sons, 2 daughters. Education: BA, University of Chicago, 1950; MFA, University of Massachusetts, 1971; DA, State University of New York at Albany, 1981. Appointments: English Teacher, 1963-67; Instructor, 1970-73; Lecturer, 1973-74; Professor, 1974-90. Publication: Pinochle Under the Stars. Contributions to: Anthology of Magazine Verse; Bear Crossing; Traveling America with Today's Poets; Poetry of Horses; Voices for Peace; Changes of the Day; Mixed Voices; Southern Poetry Review; Yankee; College English; Kansas Quarterly; New Letters; Calyx; Writer; Center Point; Negative Capability; Gravida; Poet & Critic; Northern New England Review; Milkweed. Honours: World of Poetry Golden Award; New Letters Award; City of Harford 350 Anniversary Prize; Hans S Bodenheimer Award; Arts/Wayland Laurel Award; Wildwood Poetry Prize; SCCA International Poetry Contest. Membership: Connecticut Council of Teachers of English. Address: 81 Old Mystic Street, Arlington, MA 02174, USA.

WINDORQUILL Marcus Ivan. See: INDERMILL Marilyn.

WINDSOR Penny Anne, 21 Dec 1946, England. Writer. Education: Teaching Certificate, 1971; BEd, 1972; Diploma in Community Work, 1980. Appointments: Teacher, Rochdale LEA,

1972-73; Teacher, West Glamoragon LEA, 1973-76; Co-Ordinator, Youth Enterprise, Swansea, 1980-87; Writer-in-Residence, Open Learning Centres, West Glamorgan, 1991; Writer-in-Residence, Centre for the Visually Impaired, West Glamorgan, 1995: Lyricist, Performing Right Society; Freelance Writer. Publications: Heroines; Running Wild; Dangerous Women, 1987; Like Oranges, 1989; Love is a Four Letter Word; Crashing The Moon, 1994. Contributions to: New Statesman; Spare Rib; Poetry Wales; New Welsh Review; Other Poetry; Tribune; Ore; New Hope International; Orbis; Tears in The Fence. Honours: Three Year Grant, Royal Literary Society, 1988-91; Grant, Welsh Arts Council, 1993; Grant, Society of Authors, 1992. Memberships: Welsh Academy; Welsh Union of Writers; Writers on Tour (Welsh Arts Council). Address: 7 Taplow Terrace, Pentrechwyth, Swansea SA1 7AD, South Wales.

WIENERS John (Joseph), b. 6 Jan 1934, Milton, Massachusetts, USA. Poet; Dramatist; Writer. Education: BA, Boston College, 1954; Black Mountain College, North Carolina, 1955-56; State University of New York at Buffalo, 1965-69. Publications: The Hotel Wentley Poems, 1958, revised edition, 1965; Still-Life, play, 1961; Asphodel in Hell's Despite, 1963; Ace Pentacles, 1964; Chinoiserie, 1965; Hart Crane, Harry Crosby, I See You Going Over the Edge, 1966; Anklesox and Five Shoelaces, play, 1966; King Solomon's Magnetic Quiz, 1967; Pressed Water, 1967; Selected Poems, 1968; Unhired, 1968; A Letter to Charles Olson, 1968; Asylum Poems, 1969; Untitled Essay on Frank O'Hara, 1969; A Memory of Black Mountain College, 1969; Nerves, 1970; Youth, 1970; Selected Poems, 1972; Woman, 1972; The Lanterns Along the Wall, 1972; Playboy, 1972; We Were There!, 1972; Holes, 1974; Behind the State Capitol, or, Cincinnati Pike, 1985; A Superficial Estimation, 1986; Conjugal Contraries and Quart, 1986; Cultural Affairs in Boston: Poetry and Prose 1956-1985, 1988. Contributions to: Numerous periodicals. Honours: Poet's Foundation Award, 1961; New Hope Foundation Award, 1963; National Endowment for the Arts Grants, 1966, 1968, 1984; Academy Award, 1968; Guggenheim Fellowship, 1985. Address: 44 Joy Street, Apt 10, Boston, MA 02114, USA.

WILMER Clive, b. 10 Feb 1945, Harrogate, West Yorkshire, England. Education: BA, King's College, Cambridge, 1967; MA, 1970. Appointments: Teacher of English, Bell School of Languages, Cambridge, 1973-86; Freelance Writer and Broadcaster, 1986-. Publications include: Shade Mariners, co-author, 1970; The Dwelling Place, 1977; Devotions, 1982; A Catalogue of Flowers, 1986; Amores, 1986; The Infinite Variety, 1989; Of Earthly Paradise, 1992; Poets Talking, 1994; Selected Poems, 1995; Editor and Translator of poetry. Honours include: Artisjus Translation Prize, Hungary, 1980; Authors' Foundation Grant, 1993. Address: 57 Norwich Street, Cambridge CB2 1ND, England.

WINFREE Marie Davis, b. 6 Oct 1939, Johnston, USA. Office Manager; Freelance Writer. m. Ted Harold Winfree, 18 June 1955, 2 sons. Education: Dr, Walters University of North Carolina, 1981; Methodist College, 1984; Community College, North Carolina, 1986. Appointment: Contributing Writer, Carolina Business, 1980-; Feature Writer, 1986, 1988. Publications: New Voices; Southern Images; A Time to Listen, Executive Editor; Rainey Days and Sardine Tins. Contributions to: The State Magazine; Spectra; Wilmington Star News; North Carolina Poetry Society Award Winning Poems; Senior Citizen Review; Sand Paper Magazine; Carolina Magazine; Spring Lake News; World Poetry Anthology. Honours: Fields of Earth Poetry Symp, 1979-80; 3rd, World Poets Award, 1980; Two Arts Service Awards, 1991; Fortner's Honors Award, 1995. Memberships: Writers Ink Guild; North Carolina Poetry Society; Network; Dickens Group. Address: 3109 Phillie Circle, Fayetteville, NC 28306, USA.

WINGRAVE Ariel. See: **MORGAN Ariel Celeste Heatherley.**

WINTERBURN Arthur Dennis, b. 8 Feb 1916, Hull, Yorkshire, England. Retired Schoolmaster. m. Mary Talbot Warwick, 23 May 1942, dec 1987, 1 daughter. Education: BA Hons, 1938, MA, 1941, Emmanuel College, Cambridge; CU Certificate of Education, 1940. Appointments: Head of English Department, Carre's Grammar School, Sleaford, Lincolnshire, 1946-78. Publications: Streaks of the Tulip; Verdure of the Forest; Wolds Poems. Contributions to: Envoi; Orbis; Pennine Platform; Proof; Quaker Monthly. Membership: Secretary, Sleaford Writers Group. Address: 40 Lincoln Road, Ruskington, Sleaford, Lincs NG34 9AP, England.

WISEMAN Christopher Stephen, b. 31 May 1936, Hull, Yorkshire, England. Professor. m. Jean Leytem, 1 Jan 1963, 2 sons. Education: BA, 1959; MA, 1962 (Cantab); PhD, Strathclyde, 1971. Appointment: Assistant, Associate and Professor of English, University of Calgary, Canada, 1969-. Publications: Waiting for the Barbarians, 1971; The Barbarian File, 1974; The Upper Hand, 1981; An Ocean of Whispers, 1982; Postcards Home: Poems New and Selected, 1988; Missing Persons, 1989; Remembering Mr Fox, 1995. Contributions to: Sunday Times; Scotsman; Encounter; Times Literary Supplement; Critical Quarterly; Stand; Ambit; Malahat Review; Transatlantic Review; Glasgow Review; Ontario Review; Descant; Orbis; Canadian Literature; Meridian; Grain; Queen's Quarterly. Honours: Alberta Poetry Awards, 1988, 1989; Writers Guild of Alberta Poetry Award, 1988; Alberta Achievement Award for Excellence in Writing, 1988. Memberships: League of Canadian Poets; Writers Guild of Alberta (President). Address: 8 Varwood Place North West, Calgary, Alberta T3A 0C1, Canada.

WISINSKI Louise Ann Helen, (Lou Singer, Poetess Louise), b. 7 Nov 1947, Milwaukee, Wisconsin, USA. Education: Graduate, Notre Dame High School. Publications: At Day's End, 1994; Today's Great Poems, 1994. Contributions to: Sophomore Jinx, 1994; Allusive Images, 1994. Honours: Editor's Choice Award, National Library of Poetry, 1994; Award of Recognition Famous Poets Society, 1995. Memberships: Poets and Patrons, Chicago, Illinois, USA. Address: 1132 South 57 Street, West Allis, Wisconsin 53214, USA.

WITT Harold Vernon, b. 6 Feb 1923, Santa Ana, California, USA. Writer. m. 8 Sept 1948, 1 son, 2 daughters. Education: BA, 1943; MA, 1947; BLS, 1953. Appointments: Reference Librarian, Washoe County Library, 1953-55; San Jose State University, 1956-59; Co-Editor, California State Poetry Society, 1976; Blue Unicorn, 1977; Consulting Editor, Poet Lore, 1976-91. Publications: Family in the Forest; Superman Unbound; The Death of Venus; Beasts in Clothes; Winesburg by the Sea: A Preview; Pop By, 1940: 40,000; Now, Swim; Surprised By Others at Fort Cronkhite; Winesburg by the Sea; The Snow Prince; Flashbacks and Reruns; The Light at Newport. Contributions to: New Yorker; Poetry; Hudson Review; Kenyon Review; Chicago Tribune; Antioch Review; New Letters; Kansas Quarterly. Honours: Horwood Award; James D Phelan Award; Poetry Society of America Emily Dickinson Award. Address: 39 Claremont Avenue, Orinda, CA 94563, USA.

WITTEN Anne Rubicam, b. 4 Nov 1942, Washington, USA. Poet; Professor. Education: BA, University of Colorado; Boston University. Appointments: Visiting Professor, University of Maine; Lecturer, University of New England. Publications: Stone Stone Water; Touch Touch Touch; O Star. Honours: Colorado Portfolio Poetry Prize; American Institute of Graphic Arts Award; PEN Grant. Memberships: Poets and Writers; Maine Writers and Publishers Alliance; Union of Maine Visual Artists. Address: 15 Adams Street, Peaks Island, ME 04108, USA.

WOERDEHOFF Valorie Anne Breyfogle, (Valorie Anne Broadhurst), b. 5 July 1954, Kansas City, USA. Writer; Public Relations; Marketing and Managing Graphic Design. m. Thomas Alan Woerdehoff, 5 July 1986, 3 sons, 2 daughters. Education: AA, College of Lake County, 1979; BA, Loras College, 1982. Appointments: Community Relations Officer, Clinton Community College, 1984; Director, University Relations, University of Dubuque, 1984-92; Director, Publications, Lonas College, 1994-. Publication: Fourfront. Contributions to: Cottonwood Review; Frog Pond; Spoon River Quarterly; Wind Chimes; Cape Rock; Brussels Sprout; Iowa Woman; Modern Haiku; Woodnotes. Honours: Grant to Artists, Iowa Arts Council; National Endowment for the Arts; 1st Place, 1995 Hawaii Education Association International Haiku Contest, Humorous Division; 1st Place, 1995 Haiku Poets of Northern California Rengay Contest; 1996 Literary Artist of the Year, River Arts Network; Haiku Writing Contest. Memberships: Haiku Society of America; Poets and Writers; Dubuque Writers Guild. Address: 3246 St Anne Drive, Dubuque, IA 52001, USA.

WONG Chung. See: **WONG Wai Ming (Otis).**

WONG Wai Ming (Otis), (Wong Chung, Nam Ching Tin, So Shun), b. 21 Aug 1954, Hong Kong. Civil Servant. m. Lee Shu Hing, 6 Mar 1976, 3 sons. Education: Diploma of English Language and Literature, Shue Yan College, 1981. Appointments: Editor, Poetry, 1976-84; Editor-in-Chief, Modern Poetry - East and West, 1981; Editor,

Shi Bi-Monthly, 1989-94; Editor-in-Chief, Modern Chinese Poetry Anthology, 1995; Editor-in-Chief, Overseas Poetry Series, 1991-. Publications: Modern Poetry - East and West, 1981; Aesculus Chinensis, 1991; Modern Chinese Poetry Anthology, 1995. Contributions to: Poetry; Shi Bi-Monthly; Sing Tao Yat Po; Universal Daily News; Nhat Bao Giai Phong. Honour: Astronimical Project Competition Essay Writing, Open Section, First Prize, 1977. Memberships: Shih Feng Association; Shi Bi-Monthly Association; The Hong Kong Archaeological Society. Address: PO Box 50431, Sai Ying Pun Post Office, Hong Kong.

WOO Kwok Yin, (Ji Hun), b. 20 Oct 1946, Hong Kong. School Principal. m. Li Sook Ling, 11 Nov 1972, 1 son, 2 daughters. Education: BA, 1969, MA, 1972, Diploma in Education, 1974, University of Hong Kong; PhD Candidate, University of Sydney, Australia, 1995. Appointments: Chairman, Drama Sub-committee of North District Arts Advancement Association, 1984-94; Vice Chairman, North District Secondary Schools Headmasters Conference, 1985-94; Chairman, North District Community Youth Club, 1991-94; School Principal, Carlingford Chinese Language School, Sydney, Australia, 1995. Publications: A Vision Revealed, 1964; Blue Beast, 1970; Three Acquaintances, 1976; Broken Spear, 1978; Just Before the Gust Blows, 1987; The Racing Poet, 1980; When the Hill is Still Creeping, 1990; Lest I Fall Asleep Before Dawn, 1991; Unconventional Essays, 1993; One Poem a Week, 1995. Contributions to: Undergrad; Shih Feng Monthly; Shi Bi-Monthly; Hong Kong Literature Monthly; Chinese Students Weekly; One Ninth Poetry Journal; Sing Tao Daily; Blue Stars Poetry Quarterly; Epoch Poetry Quarterly; United Daily News; Chung Hua Daily News; Overseas Digest; Sun Poetry Press; Zhong Yuan Bi-Monthly; Plough Literature; Singapore Literature; Stratosphere; Asian Chinese Writers Magazine; The Independence Daily; The Overseas Chinese Daily. Honours: Merit Award of Chinese Modern Poetry; Adjudicators of Various Literary Awards. Memberships: Shih Feng Association; Singapore Literary Society; Shi Bi-Monthly Association; Australian Chinese Writers Association; Poets Union Inc of Australia. Address: 38 Olive Street, Denistone East, New South Wales 2112, Australia.

WOOD Francis James (Frank), b. 12 Nov 1925, Preston, Lancashire, England. Retired Teacher. m. Margaret Marie-Therese Aspinwall, 7 May 1953, 1 son. Education: Certificate of Education, Dudley College of Education, 1959; Advanced Diploma in English Studies, Leeds University, 1971. Appointments: Teacher, English, Brownedge St Mary's Roman Catholic Secondary School, Lancashire, 1960-67; Lecturer in English, Lancashire Police Cadet School, 1968-73; Head of English, Orwell High School, Felixstowe, 1974-84. Contributions to: Anthologies: Autumn Anthology, 1977; Voices of Today, 1980; Envoi Summer Anthology, 1990; Other: Encounter; Ambit; Outposts; Envoi; New Poetry; Phoenix; Use of English; Joe Soap's Canoe; Samphire; Countryman; Cumbria. Honours: Prizes: Crabbe Memorial Competitions, 1985, 1989; Rhyme Revival International Poetry Competition, 1985; Red Candle Press Poetry Competition, 1986; Red Candle Press Mark Wild Memorial Competition 1986; Kent and Sussex Poetry Society Open Poetry Competition, 1988. Memberships: Poetry Society; Suffolk Poetry Society. Address: 21 Sunningdale Drive, Felixstowe, Suffolk IP11 9LE, England.

WOOD Marguerite Noreen, b. 27 Sept 1923, Ipswich, Suffolk, England. Physiotherapist. m. Douglas James Wood, 12 April 1947, 1 son, 1 daughter. Education: MCSP, Devonshire Royal Hospital, Buxton, 1944; BA Hons, Open University, 1982. Appointments: Justice of the Peace, 1968-93; Physiotherapist, NHS Hospitals, 1968-; Writer in Schools, Eastern Arts Association; WEA Creative Writing Tutor; Assistant Editor, Envoi, 1974-91. Publications: Stone of Vision, 1964; Windows are not Enough, 1971; Crack Me The Shell, 1975; A Line Drawn in Water, 1980; A Wall Cracks, 1993. Contributions to: Poetry Review; Envoi; Orbis; Periacktos; Anthologies: Poems of the Sixties; Writers of East Anglia; Without Adam; Look Through a Diamond; A Touch of Flame; The Secret Christmas; The Poets Gift; Poets England, 1994. Honours: Crabbe Memorial Poetry Competition, 1974; Chelmer Arts Festival, 1979; Norwich Writers Circle, Open Poetry Competition, 1995. Memberships: Poetry Society; Suffolk Poetry Society, Chairman, 1977-78; Magistrates' Assoc. Address: Sandy Hill, Sandy Lane, Woodbridge, Suffolk IP12 4DJ, England.

WOOD Renate, b. 5 Feb 1938, Berlin, Germany. Poet. m. William B Wood, 30 June 1961, 2 sons. Education: PhD, Stanford University, 1970; MFA, Program for Writers, Warren Wilson College,

NC, 1985. Appointments: Lecturer, University of Colorado, Boulder, 1985-91; Faculty, Program for Writers, Warren Wilson College, North Carolina. Publications: Points of Entry, 1981; Raised Underground, 1991. Contributions to: American Poetry Review; Massachusetts Review; The New England Review; Triquarterly; Virginia Review; Seneca Review; Prairie Schooner. Honours: Nominee, Colorado Governor's Award for Excellence in The Arts, 1982; Grant, Colorado Council on the Arts, 1995. Memberships: Associated Writing Programs; Academy of American Poets. Address: 1900 King Avenue, Boulder, CO 80302, USA.

WOOD Ursula. See: VAUGHAN WILLIAMS Ursula.

WOOD Wendy, b. 9 Feb 1957, Ohio, USA. Education: BA, Bennington College, 1983. Contributions to: Bad Henry Review; New Voices; New Observations; Pearl; Thirst; Telephone. Honours: Grant Escandalar; Academy of American Poets College Prize Winner; George Bogin Memorial Award, Poetry Society of America. Memberships: Poets and Writers. Address: PO Box 7333, JAF Station, New York, NY 10011, USA.

WOODBRIDGE Norma (Barnabas), b. 21 Apr 1931, Flushing, New York, USA. Teacher of Piano and English. Education: University of Pennsylvania, 1952; BS, Temple University, 1958. Publications: African Realities, African Dreams; Resting Places; Meditations of a Modern Pilgrim; Dear Child; Joy in the Morning; Conversations with God. Contributions to: New Jersey Poetry Society Anthology; The Princeton Packet. Honours: Fellowship to Yaddo Writing Colony; Honorable Dectorate. Memberships: National League of American Pen Women; New Jersey Poetry Society; ASCAP; Garden State Storytellers League; Christian Writers Fellowship. Address: 2606 Zoysie Lane, North Fort Myers, FL 33917, USA.

WOODBURY Sara Jorgenson (SJW), b. 15 Oct 1944, Wisconsin, USA. Secretary. m. Lon E Woodbury, 23 Aug 1967, div, 1 son, 2 daughters. Education: University of Wisconsin, 1961; University of Idaho, 1962-67; University of Washington, 1971; Eastern Washington University, 1978. Appointments: Secretary, Morgan and Morgan, 1966; US House of Representatives, 1967-70. Publications: Selected Poems; Sketches; Air of Dream; Shadows; Collected Works; Contrasts; Poetry Sampler, All These Years. Contributions to: Nostoc; Archer; Philadelphia Poets; Poetalk; Poetry Peddlar; Hemispheres; Metropolis; Lazer; Tight; Cokefish; Broken Street; Felicity; Wide Open; SOPA Review; Quill Books; Cripes; Red Owl; Ruby; Westbury Anthology; Quest. Honour: Certificate of Excellence. Memberships: Volume II Poets; Spokane Open Poets Association; Pacific Northwest Writers Conference; First Lady Certificate; Lake Hills Jaycees. Address: PO Box 676, Spokane, WA 99210, USA.

WOODCOCK Joan, b. 6 Feb 1908, Bournemouth, Dorset, England. Poet; Artist; Genealogist; Extensive Traveller. m. Alexander Neville Woodcock, 18 Sept 1937, 2 sons, 1 daughter. Publications: The Wandering Years; Borrowing from Time; Stabbed Awake. Contributions to: Envoi; Orbis; Iota; First Time; Outposts and various anthologies. Honours: Prizes: Envoi; Rhyme International; World Order of Narrative and Formalist Poets, New York, USA; Award of Merit from Yeats Club. Memberships: The Poetry Society; Peterloo Poets; Calne Writers Circle; Verse Writers Guild of Ohio, USA; British Haiku Society; National Federation of State Poetry Societies, USA. Address: 6 Hudson Road, Malmesbury, Wiltshire SN16 0BS, England.

WOODFORD Bruce Powers, b. 22 Sept 1919, Astoria, Oregon, USA. Writer; Professor. m. Xanta Grisogono, 19 Nov 1955, 1 daughter. Education: BA, 1948, MA, 1949, PhD, 1958, Denver University. Publications: Twenty-One Poems and a Play, 1958; Love and Other Weathers, 1966; A Suit of Four, 1973; Indiana, Indiana, 1976; The Edges of Distance, 1977. Contributions to: Arizona Quarterly; New Mexico Quarterly Review; Colorado Quarterly; Four Quarters; Uroboros; Wind; Stone; West Ham Review; Quartet. Honours: Phi Beta Kappa, 1948; Foley Best Short Stories List of Distinction, 1948, 1949. Membership: American Poetry Society. Address: 140 Mesa Vista, Santa Fe, NM 87501, USA.

WOODROW Philip James, b. 4 Sept 1957, Surrey, England. Nurse. m. 1 Sept 1984. Education: BA, Literature, Essex, 1979; MA, Victorian Literature, 1980. Appointment: Editor, Eavesdropper, 1989-91. Publications: Matin Songs, 1979; Boudicca, 1982; Post from Armageddon, 1987; A Cloud of Distress, 1989. Contributions to: New Welsh Review; Envoi; New Hope International; Stride; Iota; TOPS;

Memberships: University of Essex Literature Society, Secretary, 1978-79; Founder, 1986, Coordinator, 1986-89, Vertical Images (London); Life: National Poetry Society; Tennyson Association. Address: 30 York Street, Broadstairs, Kent, England.

WOODRUFF Thom (Thom the World Poet), b. 14 June 1949, Brisbane, Queensland, Australia. Poet. m. Wendy A Woodruff, 23 Dec 1993. Education: BA, Queensland, 1967-69; LLB, 1970-72; Dip Ed, Melbourne, 1973. Appointments: Guest performance, Kansas City School of Performing Arts, 1993; Poet-in-Residence, Charles University, 1994; Poet on Tour, Arts Council of Wales, 1994-95; Featured Performer, Cheltenham Literature Festival, 1995-96. Publications: My Father's Son, 1991; Goddess, 1992; Strawberries, 1993; Redemption Poems, 1994; Romance!, 1995; Austin TX, 1995; Moon!, 1995; The Book of Thom, 1996; Persian Limes, 1996; Diamonds, 1996. Contributions to: Chronicle; Coreys; La Mama Poetica; Poesia y Calle. Honours: Poet of the Week, 9 times, Chronicle, 1994-96. Memberships: Programmer, Austin International Poetry Festival; Austin Poets at Large. Address: 5003 Lark Cove, Austin, TX 78745-1830, USA.

WOODS Chris. General Practitioner. Education: MBchB, 1976, MRCGP, 1984, Manchester University. Publication: Recovery, 1993. Contributions to: Acumen; Guardian; Independent; Iron; Kites; Landfall; Lancaster Literature Festival Anthologies; Manchester Poetry; Orbis; Other Poetry; Outposts; Oxford Poetry; GP Writer; Poetry Nottingham; Spectator; Times Literary Supplement; Poetry Review; PN Review. Honours: Prizewinner, Leek Poetry Competition, 1984, Lancaster Literature Festival Competitions, 1985, 1987-94; Peterloo Poets Competition, 1991. Memberships: Manchester Poets; Poetry Society. Address: 103 Holcombe Old Road, Holcombe, Bury, Lancs BL8 4NF, England.

WOODS Gregory Karl Waverling, b. 4 Jan 1953, Egypt. Lecturer. Education: BA, 1974; MA, 1975; PhD, 1983. Appointments: Lector, University of Salerno, 1980-84; Lecturer, Crewe & Alsager College of Higher Education, 1985-90; Nottingham Trent University, 1990-; Reader in Lesbian and Gay Studies, Nottingham Trent University, 1995-. Publications: We Have the Melon; Articulate Flesh: Male Homo-eroticism and Modern Poetry; This Is No Book: A Gay Reader, 1994. Contributions to: James White Review; PN Review; Square Peg; Stand; Gay Times; New Statesman and Society; Times Higher Educational Supplement; Times Literary Supplement. Honour: 3rd Prize, Skoob/Index on Censorship Poetry Competition, 1989. Membership: International Advisory Board, European Gay Review; Editorial Board, PerVersions: The International Journal of Gay and Lesbian Studies. Address: Department of English and Media Studies, Nottingham Trent University, Clifton Lane, Nottingham NG11 8NS, England.

WOODS Simon Andrew, b. 5 Sept 1952, London, England. Education: BA Hons, Law, 1978; Diploma in Publishing, 1982; BA Hons, Fine Art, 1992. Appointments: Articled Clerk; Publishing Assistant; Arts Administrator. Publication: The Leopard, 1981. Contributions to: Poetry Review; Ambit; Stand. Membership: Poetry Society. Address: 69 Ericson Close, Wandsworth, London SW18 1SQ, England.

WOODWARD Gerard Vaughan, b. 4 Dec 1961, London, England. Writer. m. Suzanne Anderson, 16 July 1983. Education: Falmouth School of Art, 1981-83; London School of Economics, 1988-91. Publications: Householder; The Unwriter. Contributions to: Times Literary Supplement; Spectator; Poetry Review; Stand; Ambit; Iron; Orbis; Verse; Critical Quarterly; PN Review; London Magazine. Honours: Eric Gregory Award; Somerset Maugham Award; Mail on Sunday J L Rhys Award. Address: Chatto & Windus, 20 Vauxhall Bridge Road, London SW1V 2SA, England.

WOOLFOLK Miriam R Lamy, b. 14 Feb 1926, Louisville, Kentucky, USA. m. (1) 1944-64, 1 son, 3 daughters. m. (2) Patch G Woolfolk, 8 Aug 1968. 2 stepdaughters. Appointments: President, Lexington Art League, 1975-76; Newsletter Editor, Lexington Art League, 1975-79; Editor, Reaching, Poetry Journal, 1978-88; President, Kentucky State Poetry Society, 1985; Newsletter Editor, Kentucky State Poetry Society, 1985-90; Historian, Lexington Art League; Editor, Pegasus. Publications: Poems by a Kentuckian for Anyone; Seasons; One Plus One; Sunshine and Thunder; For the Birds; Thoughts and Visions. Contributions to: Louisville Courier Journal Newspaper; Ashland Daily Independent; Red Bluff Daily News;

Mainichi Daily News; Kentucky Poetry Review; Wind Literary Journal; Reborn Woman; Hill & Valley; Family Album; Adena; Orbis International Literary Magazine; Poet; Pegasus; Old Hickory Review; Amber; Scripsit (Eastern Kentucky University Journal); The Presbyterian Writer; Parnassus of world Poets (India). Honours: Special Recognition, Alabama Poetry Society National Contest; West Virginia Haiku Poetry Award; Mainichi Daily News Award; Kentucky State Poetry Society President's Award; Award of Special Recognition. Memberships: Kentucky State Poetry Society; National Federation of State Poetry Societies; World Poetry Society Intercontinental; Kentucky Chapter of National Society of Arts and Letters; Life Member, Lexington Art League; Charter Member, Kentucky Watercolor Society. Address: 3289 Hunting Hills Drive, Lexington, KY 40515, USA.

WORLEY Jeff Robert, b. 10 July 1947, Wichita, Kansas, USA. Magazine Editor; Writer. m. Linda Kraus, 10 Jan 1982. Education: BA, 1971, MFA, 1975, Wichita State University. Appointments: Instructor, University of Cincinnati, 1983-84; Assistant Professor, Penn State University, 1984-86; Associate Editor, Odyssey Magazine, 1986-. Publications: Other Heart, 1991; Natural Selections, 1993. Contributions to: Poetry Northwest; College English; Chicago Review; Prairie Schooner; Literary Review; Threepenny Review; Three Rivers Poetry Journal; Malahat Review; New York Quarterly; Anthology of Magazine Verse and Yearbook of American Poetry. Honours: Seaton First Award from Kansas Quarterly; Cincinnati Poetry Review 1st Prize; Al Smith Fellowship; National Endowment for the Arts Fellowship, 1991. Address: 136 Shawnee Place, Lexington, KY 40503, USA.

WRIGHT Amos Jasper III, b. 3 Mar 1952, Gadsden, Alabama, USA. Medical Librarian. m. Margaret Dianne Vargo, 14 June 1980, 1 son, 1 daughter. Education: BA, Auburn University, 1973; MLS, University of Alabama, 1982. Appointments: Clinical Librarian, Department of Anesthesiology Library School of Medicine, 1983-; Cataloger, Tuscaloosa, Alabama, Public Library, 1982-83. Publications: Frozen Fruit; Right Now I Feel Like Robert Johnson. Contributions o: Alabama Poets; A Contemporary Anthology; Aura; Poem; Southern Exposure; Mississippi Review; Negative Capability; Kansas Quarterly; Semiotext; Art/Life. Address: 119 Pintail Drive, Pelham, AL 35124-2121, USA.

WRIGHT Charles, b. 25 Aug 1935, Tennessee, USA. Teacher. m. Holly McIntire, 6 Apr 1969, 1 son. Education: BA, Davidson College, 1957; MFA, University of Iowa, 1963; University of Rome, 1963-64. Appointments: University of California, 1966-83; University of Virginia, 1983-. Publications: The Grave of the Right Hand; Hard Freight; Bloodlines; China Trace; The Southern Cross; Country Music/Selected Early Poems; The Other Side of the River; Zone Journals; Xionia; Halflife, 1988; The World of the Ten Thousand Things; Chickamauga, 1995; Quarternotes, 1995. Contributions to: Poetry Magazine; New Yorker; Southern Review; Antaeus; Field; Yale Review; Paris Review; New Republic; Iowa Review; Gettysburg Review; Verse; Missouri Review. Honours: Edgar Allan Poe Award; Pen Translation Prize; National Book Award; Brandeis University Creative Arts Award; Ruth Lilly Poetry Prize. Memberships: Fellowship of Southern Writers, 1993; American Academy of Arts and Letters, 1995. Address: 940 Locust Avenue, Charlottesville, VA 22901, USA.

WRIGHT David, (John Murray), b. 1920, England. Writer; Poet. Appointments: Staff Member, Sunday Times, 1941-47; Editor, Nimbus, 1955-56, X Magazine, 1959-62; Gregory Fellow in Poetry, University of Leeds, 1965-67. Publications: The Forsaken Garden; Moral Stories; Monologue of a Deaf Man; Seven Victorian Poets; Poems; A Portrait and a Guide; Nerve Ends; A South African Album; A View of the North; The Penguin Book of Everyday Verse; The Canterbury Tales; Deafness. Address: c/o A D Peters Limited, 10 Buckingham Street, Adelphi, London WC2N 6BU, England.

WRIGHT George T(haddeus), b. 17 Dec 1925, New York, New York, USA. Professor; Author; Poet. m. Jerry Honeywell, 28 Apr 1955. Education: BA, Columbia College, 1946; MA, Columbia University, 1947; University of Geneva, 1947-48; PhD, University of California, 1957. Appointments: Teaching Assistant, 1954-55, Lecturer, 1956-57, University of California; Visiting Assistant Professor, New Mexico Highlands University, 1957; Instructor, Assistant Professor, University of Kentucky, 1957-60; Assistant Professor, San Francisco State College, 1960-61; Associate Professor, University of Tennessee, 1961-68; Fulbright Lecturer, University of Aix-Marseilles, 1964-66; University of Thessaloniki, 1977-78; Visiting Lecturer, University of

Nice, 1965; Professor, 1968-89, Chairman, English Department, 1974-77, Regents' Professor, 1989-93, Regents' Professor Emeritus, 1993-, University of Minnesota. Publications: The Poet in the Poem: The Personae of Eliot, Yeats and Pound, 1960; W H Auden, 1969, revised edition, 1981; Shakespeare's Metrical Art, 1988; Editor: Seven American Literary Stylists from Poe to Mailer: An Introduction, 1973. Contributions to: Articles, reviews, poems and translations in many periodicals and books. Honours: Guggenheim Fellowship, 1981-82; National Endowment for the Humanities Fellowship, 1984-85. Memberships: Minnesota Humanities Commission, 1985-88; Modern Language Association; Shakespeare Association of America; Phi Kappa Phi. Address: 2617 West Crown King Drive, Tucson, AZ 85741, USA.

WRIGHT Howard Alan, b. Portadown, County of Armagh, Northern Ireland. Art Teacher. Education: BA, Hons, University of Ulster, 1985; MA, Cardiff, 1986; MPhil, Art History, University of London, 1990. Publication: Yahoo, 1991. Contributions to: Cyphers; Poetry Ireland Review; Salmon; Honest Ulsterman; Belfast Newsletter; Fortnight; Gown; Irish Review; Steeple; Poetry Wales; Verse; New Welsh Review; Irish University Review; Planet; Echo Room; Connacht Tribune; Orbis; Outposts; Oxford Poetry; Fiddlehead; Antigonish Review; Negative Capability; South Coast Poetry Journal. Honour: Runner up, Patrick Kavanagh Award, 1991. Address: Portadown, County Armagh, Northern Ireland.

WRIGHT Judith (Arandell), b. 31 May 1915. Writer. m. J P McKinney, 1 daughter. Education: New South Wales Correspondence School; New England Girls' School. Appointments: Creative Art Fellow, Australia National University, 1974; Australia Council Senior Writers Fellowship, 1977; FAHA, 1970, Dr of Letters (Hon), University of New England, 1963; University of Sydney, 1976; Monash University, 1977; Australia National University, 1981; University of New South Wales, 1985; Griffith University, 1988; University of Melbourne, 1988. Publications: Verse: The Moving Image, 1946; Woman to Man, 1950; The Gateway, 1953; The Oxford Book of Australian Verse, 1954; New Land, New Language (anthology), 1956; The Two Fires, 1955; Birds, 1960; Five Senses, 1963; The Other Half, 1966; Collected Poems, 1971; Alive, 1972; Fourth Quarter, 1976; The Double Tree, 1978; Phantom Dwelling, 1985; A Human Pattern, 1990; Collected Poems, 1942-1985; Prose: The Generations of Men, 1955, new edition, 1995; Preoccupations in Australian Poetry, 1964; The Nature of Love, 1966; Because I Was Invited, 1975; Charles Harpur, 1977; The Coral Battleground, 1977; The Cry for the Dead, 1981; We Call for a Treaty, 1985; Born of the Conquerors, 1991; Going on Talking, 1992; Four Books for Children; Critical Essays and Monographs. Honours: Encyclopaedia Britannica Writer's Award, 1965; Robert Frost Medallion, Fellowship of Australian Writers, 1975; Asan World Prize, Asan Memorial Association, 1984; Queen's Gold Medal for Poetry, 1991. Address: 102 Wallace Street, Braidwood, New South Wales 2622, Australia.

WRIGHT Kit, b. 1944, Kent, England. Education: New College, Oxford. Appointments: Teacher and Lecturer in England and Canada; Brock University, Ontario. Fellow Commoner in Creative Arts, Trinity College, Cambridge, 1977-79. Publications include: Treble Poets, 1974; The Bear Looked Over the Mountain, 1977; Bump-Starting the Hearse, 1983; From the Day Room, 1983; Real Rags and Read, 1988; Poems 1974-1983, 1988; Short Afternoons, 1989; Author and Editor of Poems for Children. Honours include: Geoffrey Faber Memorial Prize, 1978. Address: c/o Century Hutchinson Ltd, Brookmont House, 62-65 Chandos Place, London WC2N 4NW, England.

WRIGHT Michael George Hamilton, b. 16 Oct 1927, Leigh on Sea, Essex, England. Librarian. m. Mary Margaret Hill, 26 Mar 1988. Education: BA, 1952, MA, 1954, St Catharines College, Cambridge; North Western Polytechnic, London, 1955; FLA, 1967. Appointments: Readers Advisor, Ilford Library, 1952-58; Librarian, Army Central Library, 1958-62; Assistant Librarian, Royal Military College of Science, 1962-63; Deputy Librarian, Royal Military Academy, Sandhurst, 1963-87. Publication: Ancestral Voices. Contributions to: Outposts Poetry Quarterly; Orbis; Acumen; Envoi; Iota; Weyfarers; Westwords; Understanding; Candelabrum. Honour: 3rd Place, Farnborough Festival of the Arts. Memberships: RMAS Literary Society; Shirley Society; Friends of Shakespeare's Globe; Jane Austen Society; Basingstoke Poets. Address: Calliope, Parkstone Drive, Camberley, Surrey GU15 2PA, England.

WRIGLEY Robert, b. 27 Feb 1951, East St Louis, Illinois, USA. College Professor. m. Kim Barnes, 1983, 2 sons, 1 daughter. Education: BA, Southern Illinois University, 1974; University of Montana, 1976. Appointments: Poet-in-Residence, Professor, Lewis Clark State College, Idaho, 1977-90; Richard Hugo Poet-in-Residence, University of Montana, 1990; Acting Director, MFA Program. University of Oregon, 1990-91. Publications: Moon In a Mason Jar, 1986; What My Father Believed, 1991; In the Bank of Beautiful Sins, 1995. Contributions to: Poetry; Kenyon Review; Shenandoah; Georgia Review; New England Review; Poetry Northwest; Virginia Quarterly Review. Honours: National Endowment for the Arts Fellowship; Idaho Arts Commission Grant; Celia Wagner Award; Richard Hugo Memorial Award; Frederick Bock Prize; Poet Laureate of Idaho. Memberships: Academy of American Poets; Associated Writing Programs; Poetry Society of America. Address: RRI, Box 96W4, Lenore. ID 83541, USA.

WU Dahan. See: **DU Yunxie.**

WU Jin. See: **DU Yunxie.**

WU Zheng Jimmy, b. 10 Sept 1948, Shanghai, China. Merchant, International Trading; Master, Owner, Music School, m. Lee Mei Mei, 30 May 1978, 2 daughters. Publications: The Budding Seeds; On Wings of Eagles; Hong Kong Viewed Against the Sun; Poetry From a Plain of Love; The Shanghainese; Dee Hunter; Falling in Love; Dreams of Hong Kong; On a Windy Day. Contributions to: Poetry; Li; Stars; Sing Tao Jih Pao; Chinese World; Contemporary People. Memberships: Worlds Association of Chinese Poets; Association of Poets of Hong Kong. Address: P404 Stage 4, Taikoo Shing, Hong Kong.

WURSTER Michael, b. 8 Aug 1940. Illinois, USA. Poet. Education: BA, Dickinson College, 1962. Appointments: Founder, Co-Director, Pittsburgh Poetry Exchange, 1974-; Consultant, Facilitator, Academy of Prison Arts, 1979-83; Coordinator, Carson Street Gallery Poetry Series, 1986-88; Member, Literature Panel, Pennsylvania Council on the Arts, 1990-; Poet-in-Residence, Sweetwater Arts Center, 1990. Publication: The Cruelty of the Desert, 1989. Contributions to: 5 AM; Pittsburgh Quarterly; Poetry; Canada Review; Wind; Interstate; Bassettown Review; Galley Sail Review; Golden Triangle; Flipside; Greenfield Review; Pig Iron; Northern Red Oak; Religious Humanism; Chapter Voice; 4th World Forum; Sunrust. Honours: Pittsburgh Award; Most Valuable Player Award. Memberships: Pittsburgh Poetry Exchange; Academy of American Poets; Poetry Society of America; Canadian Poetry Association. Address: 159 South 16th Street, Pittsburgh, PA 15203, USA.

WYRWA KRZYZANSKI Tadeusz, b. 21 Oct 1947, Poland. Writer. m. Ewa, 27 Feb 1982, 1 daughter. Education: Adam Mickienlnicz University, 1975-76. Appointments: Warsaw Autumn of Poetry, 1983-; International Society of Poetry, 1984-; International Meeting of Writers, 1986. Publications: Dom Ust; Drugi Dom; Fugi x Popiolu; Adoracja Smietnika; Short Stories; Gumtowe Obloki; Kobieta Aniol; Cztery Katy a Pies w Piatym; Puchy Puszki i Poduski; Zloty Cholpiec; Akt Erekcyjiny. Contributions to: Several Professional Journals and Magazines. Honours: Ziemia Nadnotecka; Medal of New Arts; Wilhelma Macha; Stanislawa Pietaka; Red Rose. Membership: Polish Writers Association. Address: Ul Krolowej 11 m 23. 64 920 Pila, Poland.

Y

YADID Andrée. See: **AHARONI Ada.**

YAGUCHI Yorifumi, b. 1 Nov 1932, Japan. University Professor. Education: BA, Tohoku Gakuin University, 1955; MA, International Christian University, 1962; BD, Goshen College Biblical Seminary, 1965. Appointments: Hokusei Gakuen University, 1966-. Publications: A Shadow, 1966; A Myth in Winter, 1967; Ressurection, 1970; A Big Negro Woman, 1972; A Night Forest, 1978; How to Eat Loaches, 1984; Ancestors, 1985; Jesus, 1988. Contributions to: Poetry Nippon; Hokkaido Newspaper; Poetry Australia; London Magazine. Memberships: Poetry Nippon, Editor, 1967-; Japan Pen Club. Address: 12-9 Atsubetsu Minami 7 Chome, Atsubetsuku, Sapporo 004, Japan.

YAN Li, b. 28 Aug 1954, Beijing, China. Poet; Painter; Sculptor; Publisher; Editor. Appointments: Farmer, 1969-70; Factory Machinist, 1970-80; Self Employed Artist, Poet, 1980-. Publications: Selected Poetry of 1990, 1985-89, 1976-85; Drunken Story. Contributions to: 100 Modern Chinese Poems; In Forma di Parole; 5emes Exchanges Internationaux de Poesie Contemporine; Literary Review; Portable Lower East Side; First Line; Today; Village Voice; China Times; Independent Daily; World Journal; Wall Street Journal. Honour: 1st Prize, Poetry, Association of Modern Chinese Literature and Arts of North America. Memberships: Star Art Group; Today Literary Society; First Line Poetry Society. Address: PO Box 418, New York, NY 10013, USA.

YAN Mo. See: **ZHAO Zhenkai.**

YANG Lian, b. 22 Feb 1955, Bern, Switzerland. Poet. m. Liu You Hong, 19 Oct 1989. Appointments: Writer, Central Broadcasting, 1977-88; Visiting Scholar, Auckland University, 1989-90; Sydney University, 1992-93; Writer-in-Residence, Berlin, 1990-91; Fellowship, Amherst College, USA, 1993-94; Poet-in-Residence, Akademie Schloss Solitude. Publications: Li Hun, 1985; Huang Hun, 1986; Pilgerfahrt, 1986; In Symmetry with Death, 1988; Huang, 1989; Ren de Zijue, 1989; Masks and Crocodile, 1990; The Death in Exile, 1990; Yi, 1991; Gedichte, 1992; Gui Hua, 1994; Non-Person Singular, 1994; Geisterreden, 1995; Where the Sea Stands Still, 1995; Hvor Havet Star Stille. Contributions to: Times Literary Supplement; World Apart; Wild Peony; Die Zeit; Die Tageszeitung. Honour: Chinese Poetry Readers Choice, 1986. Memberships: Councillor, Today Literature Research Society; Founder, Survivors Poetry Club; Today Literature Magazine. Address: c/o John Cayley, 1 Grove End House, 150 Highgate Road, London NW5 1PD, England.

YANKEVICH Leo, (Leo Jankiewicz), b. 30 Oct 1961, Pennsylvania, USA. Teacher. m. Danuta Katarzyna Kaminska, 14 Sept 1989, 2 sons. Education: BA, History, Polish Literature, Alliance College, Cambridge Springs, Pennsylvania, 1980-84; Jagiellonian University, Cracow, Poland, 1984-85, 1988, 89. Appointments: Teacher, English, Liceum No 5, Gliwice, Poland, 1989-; Editor and Publisher, Mandrake Poetry Magazine, 1993-. Publications: The Light at the End of the World and Other Poems, 1992; In Polish: Hunger, 1992; Translation into Polish of 14 Dylan Thomas Poems, 1992; The Language of Birds, 1994; The Gnosis of Gnomes, 1995; Grief's Herbs: 18 Poems after the Polish of Stanislaw Grechowiak, 1995. Contributions to: Candelabrum; Riverrun; Nostoc; Blue Unicorn; The MacGuffin; Harp-Strings; Staple; Psychopoetica; New Hope International Writing; Weyfarers. Address: Ul Wielkiej Niedzwiedzicy 35/8, 44-117 Gliwice, Poland.

YAOZ-KEST Itamar, b. 3 Aug 1937, Hungary. Poet; Author. m. Hanna, 1958, 1 son, 1 daughter. Education: BA, University of Tel Aviv. Appointment: Founder, Eked Publishing House. Publications: Nof Beashan; Eyes Heritage; Du Shoresh; Toward Germany; Leshon Hanahar; Leshon Hayan; Tubes of Fire; Poems of the Prayer Siddur; Zimun; Seven Ties. Contributions to: All Israeli Literary Magazines. Honours: Nordau Prize; Talpir Prize; Herzl Prize; Walenrode Prize; Holon Prize; Wertheimer Prize; Lea Goldberg Prize; Prime Minister's Prize. Membership: Association of Hebrew Writers. Address: Meriam HaHashmonait 25, Tel Aviv, Israel.

YATES J(oel) Michael, b. 10 Apr 1938, Fulton, Missouri, USA (Canadian citizen). Education: MA, University of Michigan, 1961.

Appointments: Teacher at universities of Michigan, Ohio, British Columbia, Arkansas and Texas (Dallas, 1976-77); Sales Representative, Mitchell Press, 1978-. Publications: Spital of Mirrors, 1967; Hunt in an Unmapped Interior and Other Poems, 1967; Canticle for Electronic Music, 1967; Parallax, 1968; The Great Bear Lake Meditations, 1970; New and Selected Poems, 1973; Breath of the Snow Leopard, 1974; The Qualicum Physics, 1975; Fugue Brancusi, 1983; The Queen Charlotte Island Meditations, 1983; Selected Shorter Lyrics, 1984; Schedules of Silence: The Collected Longer Poems, 1986; Co-Editor, Contemporary Poetry of British Columbia, 1970-72; Editor, Light Like a Summons: Five Poets, 1989. Honours include: Canada Council Grants and Senior Arts Awards. Address: c/o Sono Nis Press, 1745 Blanshard Street, Victoria, British Columbia V3W 2J8, Canada.

YAU Emily (Yee Ming), (Emily Yau Yee Ming, Chiu Yee Ming), b. 12 Dec 1940, China. Scholar; Poet; Translator; Editor. Education: BA, South China Normal University. Appointments: University Assistant, South China Teachers College, 1962-78; Lecturer, South China Normal University, 1978-88; Senior Lecturer, Hong Kong Shue Yan College, 1989-90; Editor, Consultant, National Poetry Association, 1990-. Publications: Dandelion; Li Qing's Poems; Selected Foreign Poems of 1980's. Contributions to: For Poets Only; Poetalk; Tight; Howl; Poetry USA; Denver Quarterly; World of Poetry. Honours: International First Class Honor; Golden Poet; Award of Merit; Diploma of Distinguished Standing; 1st Prize, English Speech Contest. Memberships: National Poetry Association; World Congress of Poets; International Writers and Artists Association; Chinese Modern Literature and Arts Association; World of Poetry. Address: National Poetry Association, 2nd Floor Building D, Fort Mason Center, San Francisco, CA 94123, USA.

YEH Victor Wei Hsin, (Hai Yien, Ch'ang-Chin, Huang Min-Chi, A T'ung), b. 23 Apr 1935, Hupei, China. General Manager. m. Ellen Pu Yun Wu, 10 Mar 1968, 1 daughter. Education: BA, Tamkang College, 1969; MA, Fu Hsin Kang College, 1972; United States International University, 1981. Appointments: Chinese Army Officer, 1949-83; Teacher, Military Academy, 1981-83; General Manager, Owner, Taico Inc, 1988-91. Publications: A Girl's Will; New Literature; Faith & Pledge. Contributions to: Daily News; I Love My Family; Central Daily News; Poet; Chinese Daily News; Fifth World Congress of Poets. Honour: Central Daily News, The Rhodora. Membership: World Academy of Arts and Culture. Address: 3905 Shawnee Drive, Modesto, California 95356, USA.

YEVTUSHENKO Yevgeny Aleksandrovich, b. 18 July 1933, Stanzia Zima, Siberia, Russia. Poet; Writer. m. (1) Bella Akhmadulina, div, (2) Galina Semyonovna, 1 child. Education: Gorky Literary Institute, 1951-54. Publications in English Translation: Poetry: The Poetry of Yevgeny Yevtushenko 1953-1965, 1965; Bratsk Station, The City of Yes and the City of No, and Other New Poems, 1970; Kazan University and Other New Poems, 1973; From Desire to Desire, 1976; Invisible Threads, 1982; Ardabiola, 1985; Almost at the End, 1987; The Collected Poems, 1952-1990, 1991. Other: A Precocious Autobiography, 1963; Wild Berries, novel, 1984; Divided Twins: Alaska and Siberia, 1988. Honours: Order of the Red Banner of Labour; USSR State Prize, 1984. Memberships: International PEN; Union of Russian Writers. Address: c/o Union of Russian Writers, ul Vorovskogo 52, Moscow, Russia.

YI Yan. See: **NAN Yong Qian.**

YICTOVE (Eugene M Turk), b. 28 Feb 1946, New Orleans, Louisiana, USA. Teacher. 1 daughter. Education: Fine Arts Major, Xavier University, New Orleans, Louisiana, 1967. Appointments: Substitute Teacher, 1980-95; Poet in the Schools, Geraldine Dodge Foundation, 1990-95; Host of poetry series on local cable TV weekly, 1992-95; Host of weekly poetry series at New York Knitting Factory. Publications: No Big Thing, 1967; D J Soliloquy, 1988; Tributes, 1993; Contributions and Other Poems of Love, 1994. Contributions to: Essence Magazine; Rant. Address: 2832 St Bernard Avenue, New Orleans, LA 70128, USA.

YIEN Hai. See: **YEH Victor Wei Hsin.**

YORICK. See: **IVENS Michael William.**

YOSHIMASU Gozo, b. 22 Feb 1939, Tokyo, Japan. Poet; Essayist; Lecturer. m. Marilia, 17 Nov 1973. Education: BA, Keio

University, 1963. Appointments: Chief Editor, Sansai Finer Arts Magazine, 1964-69; Fulbright Visiting Writer, University of Iowa, 1970-71; Poet-in-Residence, Oakland University, Rochester, Michigan, 1979-81; Lecturer, Tama Art University, 1984-; Visiting Lecturer at various institutions; Many poetry readings around the world. Publication in English Translation: A Thousand Steps and More: Selected Poems and Prose, 1964-1984, 1987. Contributions to: Anthologies and periodicals. Honours: Takami Jun Prize, 1971; Rekitei Prize, 1979; Hanatsubaki Modern Poetry Prize, 1984. Memberships: Japan PEN Club; Japan Writers Association. Address: 1-215-5 Kasumi-cho, Hachioji City 192, Japan.

YOUNG Al(bert James), b. 31 May 1939, Ocean Springs, Mississippi, USA. Writer; Poet. m. Arline June Belch, 1963, 1 son. Education: University of Michigan, 1957-61; Stanford University, 1966-67; AB, University of California at Berkeley, 1969. Appointments: Jones Lecturer in Creative Writing, Stanford University, 1969-74; Writer-in-Residence, University of Washington, Seattle, 1981-82; Co-Founder (with Ishmael Reed) and Editor, Quilt magazine, 1981-. Publications: Poetry: Dancing, 1969; The Song Turning Back Into Itself, 1971; Some Recent Fiction, 1974; Geography of the Near Past, 1976; The Blues Don't Change: New and Selected Poems, 1982; Heaven: Collected Poems 1958-1988, 1989; Straight No Chaser, 1994; Fiction: Snakes, 1970; Who is Angelina?, 1975; Sitting Pretty, 1976; Ask Me Now, 1980; Seduction by Light, 1988; Other: Bodies and Soul: Musical Memoirs, 1981; Kinds of Blue: Musical Memoirs, 1984; Things Ain't What They Used to Be: Musical Memoirs, 1987; Mingus/Mingus: Two Memoirs (with Janet Coleman), 1989; Drowning in the Sea of Love: Musical Memoirs, 1995. Honours: National Endowment for the Arts Grants, 1968, 1969, 1974; Joseph Henry Jackson Award, San Francisco Foundation, 1969; Guggenheim Fellowship, 1974; Pushcart Prize, 1980; Before Columbus Foundation Award, 1982. Address: 514 Bryant Street, Palo Alto, CA 94301, USA.

YOUNG Gary, b. 8 Sept 1951, Santa Monica, California, USA. Poet; Artist. m. Margaret Orenstein, 18 Apr 1986, 1 son. Education: BA, University of California at Santa Cruz, 1973; MFA, University of California at Irvine, 1975. Appointments: Instructor, University of California at Santa Cruz, and Gavilan College; Staff Writer, The Sun; Vice President, AE Foundation; Editor, Greenhouse Review Press. Publications: Hands; 6 Prayers; In the Durable World; The Dream of a Moral Life. Contributions to: Periodicals. Honours: Ludwig Vogelstein Foundation Grant; John Ciardi Fellowship; James D Phelan Award; National Endowment for the Humanities Fellowship; National Endowment for the Arts Fellowship. Memberships: Poetry Society of America; Jackalope Society; AE Foundation. Address: 3965 Bonny Doon Road, Santa Cruz, CA 95060, USA.

YOUNG Ian George, b. 5 Jan 1945. Writer; Editor. Appointments: Director, Catalyst, 1969-81. Publications: White Garland; Year of the Quiet Sun; Curieux D'Amour; Double Exposure; Cool Fire; Lions in the Stream; Some Green Moths; Invisible Words; Common Or Garden Gods; Schwule Poesie; Sex Magick; The Male Muse (editor); The Son of the Male Muse (editor). Honours: Several Canada Council and Ontario Arts Council Awards. Address: 2483 Gerrard Street East, Scarborough, Ontario M1N 1W7, Canada.

YOUNG Virginia Brady, b. 2 Dec 1921, New York, New York, USA. Poet. m. Clarence W Young, 28 Feb 1946, 1 son, 1 daughter. Education: Columbia University, 1941-43. Appointments: Secretary, Columbia University Professor, 1929-46; Secretary, Colgate University Professors, 1946-72. Publications: The Clooney Beads; Double Windows; Cold Wind from Aachen; The Way a Live Thing Moves; Chenango Valley; Circle of Thaw; Shedding the River; Waterfall; Warming a Snowflake, 1990. Contributions to: Slant Magazine; Connecticut River Review. Honours: Haiku Prize, Japan Air Lines; Eithime Prefecture; 2nd Prize, Short Story by Croton Review; Winner, Haiku Society of American Annual Merit Book Award; Nominated for the Poet Laurate Connecticut. Memberships: Poetry Society of America; Haiku Society of America; Connecticut Poetry Society; Northern California Poets Society; Connecticut Poetry Society; Academy of American Poets. Address: 44 Currier Place, Cheshire, CT 06410, USA.

YU Kwang-Chung, b. 9 Sept 1928, China. Professor of English. m. Fan Wo-chun, 2 Sept 1956, 4 daughters. Education: BA, National Taiwan University; MFA, State University of Iowa, USA. Appointments: Professor, National Taiwan Normal University, 1966-72, National Chengchi University, 1972-74; Fulbright Visiting Professor, USA,

1964-66, 1969-71; Reader, Chinese University of Hong Kong, 1974-85; Dean of College of Liberal Arts, National Sun Yat-sen University, Kaohsiung, Taiwan, 1985-91. Publications: Poetry: Stalactites, 1960; Halloween, 1960; Associations of the Lotus, 1964; A Youth of T'ang, 1967; The Night City of Heaven, 1968; Music Percussive, 1969; In Time of Cold War, 1969; The White Jade Bitter Gourd, 1974; Sirius, 1976; Tug of War with Eternity, 1979; Kannon Bodhisattva Across the Sea, 1983; The Bauhinia, 1986; Dream and Geography, 1990; The Selected Poetry of Yu Kwang-chung, 1981; Prose includes: Look Homeward, Satyr, 1968; Cremation of the Crane, 1972; Listen to the Cold Rain, 1974; Homesick Border Blues, 1977; Memory Is Where the Railway Reaches, 1987; All by a Map, 1988; Calling for the Ferry-Boat, 1990. Contributions to: United Daily; China Times; China Daily News; Central Daily News; Chung Wai Literary Monthly; Blue Stars Poetry Quarterly; Chinese PEN Quarterly; Poetry Bi-Monthly; Hong Kong Literature Monthly. Honours: The Australian Cultural Award, 1972; Golden Tripod Awards for Lyrics, 1981, 1984; Wu San-lien Award for Prose, 1983; China Times Poetry Award, 1985; National Literary Award for Poetry, 1990; Honorary Fellowship, Hong Kong Translation Society, 1991. Memberships: Taipei Chinese Centre, International PEN, 1990-; Founder of Blue Stars Poetry Society and Publisher of Blue Stars Poetry Quarterly. Address: Institute of Foreign Languages and Literature, National Sun Yat-sen University, Kaohsiung, Taiwan.

YUAN Kejia, b. 18 Sept 1921, Cixi, China. Researcher; Poet; Critic; Translator; Editor. m. Cheng Qi Yun, 20 Jan 1955, 2 daughters. Education: BA, English Literature, Foreign Languages and Literature Department, National South-West Associated University, China, 1946. Appointments: Translator, Department for the English Edition of Mao Ze Dong's Works, Ministry of Propaganda, Chinese Communist Party, 1951-53; Translator, English Department, Foreign Languages Press, Beijing, 1954-56; Assistant Researcher, Department of Western Literature, Research Institute of Foreign Literature, CASS, 1957-78; Associate Researcher, Department of English and American Literature, RIFL, CASS and Associate Professor, Department of Foreign Literature, Postgraduate School, CASS, 1979-82; Professor of English and American Literature, Postgraduate School, CASS, 1983-90; Retired 1991. Publications: A Study of Western Modernist Literature, 1992; On the Modernization of Chinese Poetry, 1988; Editor, An Anthology of Modern Western Poetry, 1992; Editor, Source Materials for the Study of Modernist Literature, 1989; Translator: American Folksongs, 1988; Burns' Poems, 1959, 1981, 1986; Selections of Poems and Essays, 1994. Contributions to: Modern Chinese Poetry; Literary Renaissance; Literary Magazine; Chinese New Poetry; Eight Directions; Ta Kun Pao. Honours: 2nd Class Prize, Foreign Books Award, 1991; 1st Class Prize, Foreign Books Award, 1994. Memberships: Chinese Writers' Union; Editorial Board, Poetic Exploration Review; Council Member, Chinese Translators' Association, Beijing; Advisory Board, All China Society for Literary and Art Theories, 1995. Address: Research Institute of Foreign Literature, 5 Jian Guo Men Nei Da Jie, Beijing 100732, China.

YUASA Nobuyuki, b. 10 Feb 1932, Hiroshima, Japan. Professor; Poet. m. Shigeko, 20 Mar 1967, 2 daughters. Education: BA, English, Hiroshima University, 1954; MA, English, University of California, Berkeley, USA, 1956. Appointments: Lecturer, 1961, Associate Professor, 1965, Professor, 1982, Professor Emeritus, 1995-, Hiroshima University. Publications: The Year of My Life, translation of Issa's Oraga Haru, 1960; The Narrow Road to the Deep North and Other Travel Sketches by Basho, 1966; The Zen Poems by Ryokan, 1981; A Translation of John Donne's Complete Poetry, 1996. Membership: British Haiku Society. Address: 1-1-10 Waseda, Ushita, Higashiku, Hiroshima 732, Japan.

YUDKIN Leon Israel, b. 8 Sept 1939, England. University Lecturer. m. Meirah Goss, 29 Sept 1967. Education: BA, 1960, MA, 1964, University of London. Appointments: Lecturer, Unisa Pretoria, 1965-66; Assistant Lecturer, Lecturer, Manchester, 1966. Publications: Isaac Lamdan, 1971; Escape into Siege, 1974; Jewish Writing & Identity in the 20th Century, 1982; 1948 and After, 1984; Al Shirat Atzag, 1987; Else Lasker Schüler, 1991; Beyond Sequence: Current Israeli Fiction and Its Context, 1992; A Home Within, 1996. Contributions to: Literary Criticism; History of Literature; Reviews in UK, USA, Israel. Honours: Doctor of Literature, University of London, 1995. Memberships: IJA Literary Circle. Address: PO Box 670, London NW3 6HA, England.

YVONNE. See: CHISM-PEACE Yvonne.

Z

ZAHIROVICH Ajsa, b. Sarajevo, Bosnia and Herzegovina. Poet; Researcher. Appointments: Poetess since an early age; Anthologist, 1982-; Researcher of Women's Poetry; Participant at international meetings, conferences and congresses. Publications include: Bridge Has Eyes, Egypt, 1988; Ak Aur Bazghashat (One More Echo), India, 1989; Under the Crown, (Bosnian-English), 1991; Selected Poems (Bosnian-English), 1997; Anthologies: From Verse to Poem, Anthology of Women's Poetry Boznia and Herzegovina from 14th Century to the 1950s, (Sarajevo) 1985; Malaysia - Anthology of Contemporary Poetry, (Sarajevo), 1990; The Poetic Voices of Women from All Meridians, war bibliophilic edition, Sarajevo (English, Bosnian and in original languages), 1992. Contributions to: Numerous magazines and journals in many countries including: Skylark, India; Al-Ahram, Egypt; Al Munteda, Dubai; Puglia, Italy; Dewan Sastera, Malaysia; Migrations Litteraires, France; The Activist, USA; Sesler, Macedonia; Lemon, Japan. Honours: LittD, Thailand, 1988; Gold Crown Kaya, South Korea, 1990; Two Gold Robert Frost Awards, USA, 1990; W B Yeats Award, USA, 1990; International Poets Academy, India, 1991; Silver Crown, Italy, 1991; Michael Madhusudan Award, India, 1991; Australia Day Medal, Australia, 1991; International Prize for Poetry, Greece, 1994; Honorary Member, PEN NZ, 1994; Golden Plate of Humanity, Sarajevo, 1996; Golden Medallion Dove in Peace, Australia, 1996. Memberships: World Academy of Arts and Culture; Council Directors, World Poetry Research Institute, South Korea; International Women's Writing Guild, USA; Co-Editor, Skylark, India; International Poets Academy, India; Editorial Board, World Poetry, India; Writers Association of Boznia and Herzegovina. Address: Str Kranjceviceva 41/3, 71000 Sarajevo, Bosnia and Herzegovina.

ZAHNISER Edward DeFrance, b. 11 Dec 1945, Washington, District of Columbia, USA. Writer; Editor. m. Ruth Christine Hope Duewel, 13 July 1968, 2 sons. Education: AB, Greenville College, Illinois, 1967; Defence Information School, Officer Basic Course, 1971. Appointments: Poetry Editor, The Living Wilderness Magazine, 1972-75; Founding Editor, Some of Us Press, Washington, DC, 1972-75; Arts Editor, Good News Paper, 1981-; Editor, Arts & Kulcher, 1989-91; Poetry Reader, Antietam Review, 1992. Publications: The Way to Heron Mountain (poems), 1974; I Live in a Small Town (with Justin Duewel-Zahniser), 1984; Sheenjek and Denali (poems), 1990; A Calendar of Worship and Other Poems, 1994; Jonathan Edwards (artist book), 1991; Several handbooks on US National Parks and portions of illustrated books on natural history topics in North America; Editor, Where Wilderness Preservation Began: Adirondack Writings by Howard Zahniser, 1992; A Calendar of Worship and Other Poems, 1995. Contributions to: Hollins Critic; Journal of Western American Literature; Carolina Quarterly; Amicus Journal; Wilderness; Antietam Review; Rolling Coulter; Riverrun; December; Backcountry; North of Upstate; Trout; Moneysworth; Mother Earth News; Snowy Egret; Hobo Jungle; Metropolitan; Throw Small Bullets. Honours: Woodrow Wilson Fellow, 1967; First and Second Prizes in Poetry Collection, narrative poetry, in West Virginia Writers Annual Competitions, 1989, 1991, 1992. Address: c/o Atlantis Rising ARC Box G, Shepherdstown, WV 25443, USA.

ZAID Gabriel, b. 24 Jan 1934, Monterrey, Mexico. Business Consultant. m. Basia Batorska, 20 Mar 1973. Education: Monterrey Institute of Technology. Appointments: Junior Trainee-Owner, Business Consulting Firm, 1958-. Publications: Fabula de Narciso y Ariadna; Seguimiento; Campo Nudista; Practica Mortal; Cuestionario; Canciones de Vidyapati; Sonetos y Canciones. Contributions to: La Cultura en Mexico; Plural; Vuelta. Honours: Premio Villaurrutia for Leer Poesia; Premio Magda Donato for La Poesia en la Practica. Memberships: El Colegio Nacional; Academia Mexicana de la Lengua. Address: Gutenberg 224, Mexico 11590, DF, Mexico.

ZAMBARAS Vassilis, b. 1 May 1944, Revmatia, Messenias, Greece. Teacher of English as a Second Language. m. Eleni Nezi, Oct 1980, 1 son, 1 daughter. Education: BA, English, 1970, MA, English, 1972, University of Washington, Seattle. Publications: Sentences, 1976; Aural, 1984; Poetry included in How the Net is Gripped: A Selection of Contemporary American Poetry, 1992. Contributions to: Poetry Northwest; Madrona; West Coast Review; Wisconsin Review; Assay; Edge; Text; Smoot Drive Press; Rialto; Shearsman; Southeastern Review; Southern Poetry Review; Longhouse;

Intermedio; Workshop; Falcon; Klinamen; Apopeira. Honours: Harcourt, Brace and Jovanovich Poetry Fellowship to the University of Colorado, Boulder, 1970; University of Washington Poetry Prizewinner, 1972. Address: 21 K Fotopoulou, Meligalas 24002, Messenias, Greece.

ZANDER William Joseph, b. 28 Apr 1938, USA. Professor. m. Alexandra Halloran, 25 Mar 1978, 2 sons. Education: University of Missouri, 1960; Master of Arts in English, 1961; University of Iowa, 1961-62. Appointments: Undergraduate and Graduate Assistant Teacher; Graduate Assistant, Technical Writing, University of Iowa; Instructor, University of Missouri; Assistant, Associate, Full Professor, Fairleigh Dickinson University; Associate Editor, The Literary Review. Publication: Distances. Contributions to: Beloit Poetry Journal; Yankee; Prairie Schooner; Invisible City; Abraxas; Crazy Horse; Kayak; Poetry Now; New Letters; Blue Unicorn. Honour: State of New Jersey Council of the Arts/Poetry Fellowship. Memberships: Amnesty International; Trout Unlimited; Environmental Defense Fund; League of Conservation Voters. Address: English Department, Fairleigh Dickinson University, 285 Madison Avenue, Madison, NJ 07940, USA.

ZAPATA Miguel-Angel, b. 27 June 1955, Peru. Writer; Professor of Spanish. m. Janice Lynn Kincaid, 4 Feb 1982, 1 son, 2 daughters. Education: BA, Sociology, Universidad Nacionel Mayor de San Marcos, Lima, Peru, 1979; BA, California State University, 1985; MA, University of California at Santa Barbara, 1989. Appointments: Co-Editor, Codice, Journal of Poetry; Co-Editor, Tabla de Poesia Actual. Publications: Partida y ausencia, 1984; Periplos de abandonado, 1986; Imagenes los Juegos, 1987; Poemas para violin y orquesta, 1991. Contributions to: El Comercio, Lima; Delos, Maryland, USA; Inti, USA; Casa de las Americas, Cuba; Hora de Poesia, Spain; Torre de la Palomas, Spain; La Manzana Mordida, Lima; Tabla de Poesia, Princeton, New Jersey; Brujula, New York; La Orquesta, Mexico; Canto, San Francisco, California; Watershead, Chico, California; Melquiades, Irvine, California; Lyra, New Jersey. Honour: 1st Prize, Juegos Red-Tap, Lima, Peru, 1977. Membership: Modern Language Association, USA. Address: 7418 Rupert Avenue, St Louis, MO 63117, USA.

ZAPPALA Simonetta, b. 18 June 1937, Rome, Italy. Poet; Translator. Education: Lower Certificate English Language; Proficiency, English Language and Literature. Publications: Forsele Parole; Il mio Nomednon e Niente Chesospiro; Fiabe; Voce Umanda; Poesied Amore; Elizabeth Jennings Poems Translated; Rime Piccine; Il Marealla Porta. Contributions to: Tempo; Corriere Della Sera; Voce Umana; Fiabe. Honours: Premarosa Poetry Prize; Gold Medal, Centewario of Dante Festival; 1st Prize, Citta Eterna Festival. Memberships: Italian Authors and Editors Guild; Italian Writers Guild; Eugenio Montale Movement; English Poetry Society. Address: Viariccardo Zandonai 75, Rome 00194, Italy.

ZARIN Cynthia Rebecca, b. 9 July 1959, New York, New York, USA. Writer. m. 24 Jan 1988, 1 daughter. Education: AB, Radcliffe College, 1981; MFA, Columbia University, 1984. Appointments: Lecturer, Yale College, Princeton College; Staff Writer, New Yorker Magazine. Publications: The Swordfish Tooth; Fire Lyric, 1993. Contributions to: New Yorker; New Republic; New Criterion; Yale Review; Paris Review; Grand Street. Honours: Ingram Merrill Foundation Award; Fellowship, Corporation of Yaddo; Fellowship, MacDowell Colony. Memberships: Poetry Society of America; Authors Guild. Address: c/o The New Yorker Magazine, 20 West 43rd Street, New York, NY 10036, USA.

ZAVATSKY Bill, b. 1 June 1943, USA. Teacher of English. m. Phyllis Geffen 1968, div 1991. Education: BA, Comparative Literature, Columbia University, 1974; MFA, Writing, Columbia University School of the Arts, 1974. Appointments: Teacher of Poetry Writing Workshops for the Teachers and Writers Collaborative, 1971-86; Instructor in Creative Writing, University of Texas, Austin, 1977-79; Teacher of English, Trinity School, New York City, 1987-; Various other teaching jobs. Publications: Theories of Rain and Other Poems, 1975; For Steve Royal and Other Poems, 1985; The Poems of A O Barnabooth by Valery Larbaud, translator with Ron Padgett, 1977; The Whole World Catalogue 2, editor with Ron Padgett, 1977; Earthlight: Poems of André Breton, translator with Zack Rogow, 1993. Contributions to: Herald; New York Times Book Review; Paris Review; American Poetry Review; Antaeus; SUN; Adventures in Poetry; Marxist Perspectives; Cahiers Renaud-Barrautt (Paris); World. Honours: Creative Artists Public Service Fellowship, 1976; National Endowment for the Arts

Fellowship in Poetry, 1979; Columbia University Translation Centre Award, 1977. Memberships: PEN; Poetry Society of America. Address: 100 West 92 Street, 9D, New York, NY 10025, USA.

ZAWADIWSKY Christina, b. 8 July 1950. Poet; Journalist; Writer; Art Critic; Television Producer. Education: BFA, University of Wisconsin, 1974. Appointments: Contributing Editor to the Pushcart Prize (annual literary anthology), 1977-; Freelance Journalist for Art in Wisconsin, Art Muscle, The Chicago Tribune, The Chicago Reader, Community Connections 14/47, East Side News, RAA World, 1980-; Originator, Interviewer, Producer, TV Series, Where The Waters Meet, 1991-; Riverwest Artists Association Film and Video Exhibition Director and Poetry Director, 1992; Appointed Board Member, Wisconsin Visual Arts, 1993; Judge and Head of Literary Panel, Art Futures Emerging Artists Awards, 1994; Appointed Panel Member, National Alliance for Community Media Task Force, 1995; Judge, National Hometown Video Competition, Professional Documentary Category, 1995. Publications: The World At Large, 1978; Sleeping With The Enemy, 1980; The Hand on the Head of Lazarus, 1986. Contributions to: Pequod; Iowa Review; Ohio Review; Epoch; Memphis State Review; Vanderbilt Review; Georgia Review. Honours include: Best Arts Programming Series in USA and Canada, National Federation of Local Cable Programmers, 1992; Committment to The Mission of Community Television Award from Channels 14/47, 1994; Philo Award for Best in Series - Community Interest from Channels 14/47, 1994; Best Arts Programming Television Series in USA and Canada, National Alliance for Community Media, 1995. Memberships: Poets and Writers, New York, 1971-; National Women's Museum; Riverwest Artists Association; Inner City Arts Council; Milwaukee Press Club, 1991-. Address: 1641 North Humboldt Avenue, Milwaukee, WI 53202, USA.

ZEIGER Lila, b. 6 Dec 1927, USA. Writer; Teacher of Writing; Lecturer. m. David Zeiger, 24 Nov 1949, 1 son, 1 daughter. Education: MA, Cornell University, 1949; MLS, Pratt Institute, 1957. Appointments: Teacher of English, Teacher of Library, Teacher of Writing, Writing Consultant, Lecturer. Publication: The Way to Castle Garden, 1982. Contributions to: Paris Review; Kayak; Georgia Review; New Republic; New Letters; Confrontation; Southern Poetry Review; Madison Review; Yankee; New York Times; Poetry Now; Poets On; Caprice; Dacotah Territory; Some; Oink!; Bogg; West Hills Review; Greenfield Review; Exquisite Corpse; Dominion Review; Sierra Madre Review; Free Lunch. Honours: Witter Bynner Foundation, 1990-91; New York State CAPS Grant, 1983-84; Three awards from the Poetry Society of America: Claytor Award 1978, Hemley Award 1979, Kreymborg Award 1980; Passages North Emerging Writers, 1990; Small Press Tour de Force Award, 1977; CCLM Fels Award in Poetry, 1975; MacDowell Fellowships, 1977, 1979, 1983. Memberships: Executive Board, Governing Board for many years, Poetry Society of America; Long Island Poetry Collective; Poets and Writers. Address: PO Box 4518, Great Neck, NY 11023, USA.

ZENIS Sarah, b. 10 Jan 1925, Lynn, Massachusetts, USA. Freelance Writer. Education: Boston University, 1945; Brandeis University, 1950; Brooklyn College, 1960; The New School, New York, 1970. Publication: Leaders in Poetry for You and Me, 1993. Contributions to: East Coast Writers Anthology; Becoming; Echo; Gotham Memo; Innovators; International Letters. Honours: 3rd Place, National Poetry Contest; Special Honour, North Shore Jewish Historical Society. Memberships: National Writers Club; World Federalist Publicist; New York Poetry Forum; Breadloaf Writers Conference; Katherine Engel Senior Center. Address: 146 West 79th Street, New York, NY 10024, USA.

ZENOFON Fonda, b. 31 Aug 1953, Greece (Australian citizen). Variety Entertainer; Writer. Publications: Three Poetry Books; One Play. Contributions to: Melbourne Observer; Brunswick Sentinel; The Watchamacallit Annual for Children; Australian Womens Weekly; Directory of Australian Poets, 1980; Nation Review; Brunswick Poetry Workshop (founder); Genii Magazine; Max Taylor: Radio Syndication Energy; Earthsong Magazine; Matilda Magazine; The Age Newspaper. Honours: Appointed Poet Laureate of Brunswick City; Awarded Diploma and Fellowship, International Poets Academy. Address: 7 Mountfield Street, Brunswick, Victoria 3056, Australia.

ZENWAS. See: **OHAETO Ezenwa.**

ZEPEDA-HENRIQUEZ Eduardo, b. 6 Mar 1930, Granada, Nicaragua. University Professor. m. Concepcion Aguilar de Ester, 17

Oct 1957, 2 daughters. Education: Studied Law and Literature, Universities of Granda, Nicaragua, Santiago in Chile and Santander, Spain, 1950-55; Studied Spanish Literature and Economic Problems, University of Menendez Pelavo, 1955 and Admon, Pressupuest, 1970. Appointments: Professor, Universidad Centroamericana, Managua; Director, National Library of Nicaragua; Visiting Professor, Seminary of Latin-American Studies, Columbia University; Director General of Nicaraguan Culture; Director de Fondo de Arts, Madrid. Publications: Lirismo, 1948; El Principio del Canto, 1951; Mastiles, 1952; Como llanuras, 1958; A mano alzada, 1964, 1970; En el nombre del mundo, 1980; Horizonte que nunca cicatriza, 1988; Mejores poemas, 1988; Al aire de la vida y otras senales de transito, 1992. Contributions to include: Estanquero, Chile; Correo Literario, Barcelona; Cuadernos Hispanoamericanos, Madrid; Caracola, Malaga; Cuadernos de Agora, Madrid; Blanco y Nagro, Madrid; Punta Europa, Madrid; La Prensa Literaria, Managua; Orto, Managua; La Estafeta Literaria, Madrid; Poesia Hispanica, Madrid; Honours: José Maria Cantilo Prize, Madrid, 1955; Juan Boscan International Prize, Barcelona, 1962; Angaro Prize for Poetry, Seville, 1987; Commander, Order of Ruben Dario, Nicaragua and Order of Isabel la Católica, Spain, 1967, 1968; Knight, Capitulo Hispanoamericano del Corpus Christi en Toledo, 1973; Silver Plaque, Titular Member, Instituto de Cultura Hispanica de Madrid, 1968. Memberships: Academia Nicaragüense de la Lengua; Academia de Geografia e Historia de Nicaragua; Nicaragua Section, Asocicion de Escritores y Artistas Americanos. Address: C/Conde de Aranda, 6-4°d, 28001 Madrid, Spain.

ZEPHANIAH Benjamin Obadiah Iqbal, b. 15 Apr 1958, England. Poet; Writer. m. Amina Iqbal, 17 Mar 1990. Appointments: Writer in Residence, Africa Arts Collective, City of Liverpool, 1 year; Writer in Residence, Hay on Wye Literature Festival; Residency twice at Memphis State University, Tennessee. Publications: Pen Rhythm, 1980; The Dread Affair, 1985; Inna Liverpool, 1988; Rasta Time in Palestine, 1990; City Psalms, 1992; Talking Turkeys, 1994. Contributions to: Guardian; Observer; Poetry Review; Big Issue; New Statesman & Society; Black Parliamentarian. Membership: The Poetry Society. Address: BZ Associates, PO Box 673, East Ham, London E6 3QD, England.

ZHANG Er. See: **LI Mingxia.**

ZHANG Zao, b. 29 Dec 1962, Changsha, Hunan Province, China. Teacher of English Language and Literature. Education: BA, English Language and Literature, Hunan Teachers University, 1982; MA, Anglo-American Literature, Sichuan Institute of Foreign Languages, 1986; Doctoral Candidate in Sinology, University of Trier, Germany. Appointments: English Teacher, Zhuzhou College, Hunan, 1982-83; English Teacher, Sichuan Institute of Foreign Languages, 1983-86; Visiting Scholar and Doctoral Candidate, Department of Sinology, University of Trier, Germany, 1989-. Publications: Selected Poems of April, 1983; Apple Trees, 1984; Who Is It?, 1986. Contributions to: Poems to Major Chinese Literary Magazines, such as Poetry Monthly; Stars; Chinese Writers; Epoch. Memberships: Sichuan Association of Poets; Association of Chinese Writers in Exile; Poetry Editor of Literary Magazine, Jintian (Today). Address: Am Weidengraben 84, D-14550 Trier, Germany

ZHAO Zhenkai, (Bei Dao, Mo Yan), b. 2 Aug 1949, China. Writer. m. Shao Fei, 1 daughter. Appointments: Construction Worker; Editor; Assistant Professor. Publications: The August Sleepwalker; Old Snow. Contributions to: Today. Membership: Today Literature Foundation. Address: Institute of East Asian Studies, University of Aarhus, 800 Aarhus C, Denmark.

ZHENG Min, b. 18 July 1920, Beijing, China. University Professor. m. Professor Shi Bai Tong, 19 Jan 1952, 1 son, 1 daughter. Education: BA, Philosophy, National Southwest Associated University, China, 1943; MA, English Literature, Brown University, Providence, Rhode Island, USA, 1952. Appointments: Editor of Department of Translation, Central News Agency, China, 1945-48; Assistant Research Fellow, Chinese Academy of Social Sciences, 1956-61; Professor of English and American Literature, 1961-; Visiting Professor, Department of Literature, University of California, San Diego, USA, 1985. Publications: Poems 1942-47, 1949; Study of American and English Poetry and Drama, 1983; The Structural and Deconstructive Approach: Poetry, Language, Culture, forthcoming; Editor and Translator: Anthology of Contemporary American Poetry, 1987; Co-writer with seven poets: The Eight Leaves, 1984; Co-Writer with nine poets: The Nine Leaves, 1981; The Quest, 1986; Morning, I

Gather Flowers in the Rain, 1991; Psychic Pictures, 1991. Contributions to: National Poetry Monthly; People's Literature; Stars; Yang-Tze Literature; Xin-Jiang Literature; Milky Way; Poetry Bi-Monthly (Hong Kong); Xing Dao Daily (Hong Kong). Honours: Best Poetry of 1986 Award, Poetry Monthly and The Writer's Association, 1986; Stars Poetry Writing Award, 1982-83; Honorary citizen of San Jose, California, USA, awarded for poetry recital at San Jose, 1986. Memberships: Writer's Association of China; Society of Comparative Literature, China; Shakespearean Society of Shanghai, China. Address: Department of Foreign Languages, Beijing Normal University, Beijing 100875, China.

ZHU Hao, b. 27 May 1969, Shanghai, China. Playwright; Poet. Education: Shi Xi Senior Middle School, 1981-87; Shanghai Drama Institute, 1987-91. Publication: First Frost. Contributions to: Shanghai Literature; Modern Haiku; Frogpond; Windchimes; Mainchi Daily News; Ko Haiku Magazine. Honours: Honorable Mention, Haiku in English Contest; Ko Haiku Magazine Award. Membership: Haiku Societies of America. Address: Lane 906, No 5, Xinzha Road, Shanghai 200041, China.

ZIELINSKI Christopher Thomas, b. 7 Nov 1950, London, England. Publisher. m. Diana Vivien Trimmer, 28 July 1973, 2 sons. Education: BSc, Dundee University, 1971; MSc, Cranfield Institute of Technology, 1977. Appointments: Editor, Translator, Geneva, 1973-75; Editor, UNIDO, Vienna, 1977-78; Editor, FAO, Rome, 1978-82; Chief Reports, WHO, New Delhi, 1982-86; Chief, Editorial Section, FAO, Rome, 1986-90; Director, Health and Biomedical Information, WHO. Publications: Sculled; Artificial Respiration; The Real Canary. Contributions to: Various Small Magazines; New Poetry; Twofold. Honours: 2nd, New Poetry Quarterly Competition; 3rd, Alice Bartlett Hunt Competition. Memberships: Poetry Society; Poetry Book Club; Council of Biology Editors; European Association of Science Editors; International Federation of Scholarly Book Publishers; Middle East Association of Science Editors. Address: MH1 EMRO, c/o WHO, Avenue Appia, CH 1211, Geneva, Switzerland.

ZINNA Lucio, b. 27 Feb 1938, Italy. Poet. m. Giamporcaro Elide, 12 Jan 1970, 2 sons. Education: Laurea in Pedagogia; Abilitazione in Materie Letterarie; Diploma Magistrale. Appointments: Institute Conuitto Nazionale; Di Segretariato Aziendale; Li Colla Boratore Rai TV Sicilia. Publications: Al Chiarore Dell Alba; Il Filo Bus Dei Giorni; Anthimonium 14; Un Rapido Celaire; Sagana; Abbando Nare Trdia; Bonsai; Saganae Dopo; Inoltre, Autbore Di Tre opere Di Narrati. Contributions to: Arenaria; Awisatore; Il Banco Di Lettura; Nuovi Quaderni Del Meridione; Pri Marno; Nouvelle Europe; Equivalencias; Trapani Nvova; Catania Sera; Sicilia Tempo; Sintesi; Revisione. Honours include: Premio Int Le Mediterraneo; Aquila D'Oro; Rhegium Julii; Baldassarre Olimpio Deglo Alessanori; Premio Int Le Citta Di Marineo. Memberships: International Di Poesia Evgenio Montale; Instituto Sicilano Di Cultura; Instituto Di Cultura Romantica. Address: Via Vincenzo Di Marco, 3-90143 Palermo, Italy.

ZINNES Harriet, b. Massachusetts, USA. Poet; Fiction Writer; Literary and Art Critic. m. Irving I Zinnes, 24 Sept 1943, 1 son, 1 daughter. Education: BA, Hunter College, 1939; MA, Brooklyn College, 1944; PhD, New York University, 1953. Appointments: Professor, Queens College, City University of New York, 1962-; Visiting Professor, University of Geneva, 1969; Art and Literature Critic, Weekly Tribune, 1968-70; Art Critic, Pictures on Exhibition, 1971-78. Publications: My Haven't The Flowers Been?; Lover; Blood and Feathers; Book of Twenty; An Eye for An I; Entropisms; I Wanted To See Something Flying; Ezra Pound and the Visual Arts. Contributions to: Hollins Critic; Philadelphia Inquirer; Washington Post Book World; Nation; New York Times; American Scholar; Confrontation; Chelsea; New Directions Annuals; Denver Quarterly; Seattle Review; Women on War; Parnassus; Against Forgetting; I Shudder At Your Touch; Carlton Miscellany; Choice; Poetry Now; New York Quarterly; Prairie Schooner; Mademoisells; For Now; For Chile; New York Times Book of Verse; Out of the War Shadow; A New Folder. Honours: Nominated, Pushcart Prize; Finalist, Small Press Book Award; Finalist, CAPS; Fellow in Residence, MacDowell Colony; Djerassi Foundation; Yaddo Fellowships; Virginia Center for Creative Arts. Memberships: PEN; National Book Critics Circle; Poetry Society of America; Academy of American Poets; International Association of Art Critics. Address: 25 West 54 Street, No 6, New York, NY 10019, USA.

ZITHULELE. See: **MANN Christopher Michael.**

ZOGRAFOU Marina, b. 9 Mar 1937, Komotini, Greece. Poet; Writer; Painter. Education: High School of Economics; Studied Piano, Greek Conservatoire; Certificate, Higher School of Telecommunications for Executives. Appointments: Poetry and prose writer, 1985-. Publications: 10 Books including: Erotiki Tarantella (poems), translated into French (2 prizes, France); Niktes Thyreon (poems), translated into English; Prose: Album of Souvenirs; Requiem; Elegy and Ecstasy; Dispersed Pages of a Diary; Poems: Only the Wind; Apassionata; Other: Studies of 40 Churches in East Thrace. Contributions to: Anthologies: Italian Anthology; Women's Poetry; Anthology of International Poets; World Poetry; New Global Voice; Poeti Greci Contemporani; Contemporani Women Poetry; Poems published in various French Poetical newspapers and reviews including: Santiers Poetiques. Honours include: Hellenic Society of Writers Award, Nominated for Nobel Prize, 1997. Memberships: United Writers of the World; World Poetry Society; World Academy of Arts and Culture; Society of Greek Writers; Society of Greek Arts and Culture. Hobbies: Painting, 3 exhibitions in Athens, Greece; Playing the piano. Address: Hestionos Street 46, Thrakomakedones, 13671 Athens, Greece.

ZOLLER James Alexander, b. 7 Nov 1948, Laramie, Wyoming, USA. College Teacher. m. Donna Dean, 20 June 1970, 3 sons, 1 daughter. Education: BA, History, University of New Hampshire, 1971; MA, English/Creative Writing, San Francisco State University, 1973; DA, State University of New York, Albany, 1984. Contributions to: Poems, stories, articles published in Antaeus; Blueline; Greenfield Review; Kudzu; Other Poetry; Oxford Magazine; HIS; Kentucky Poetry Review; Christianity and Literature; English Record; Zone 3; Spree. Memberships: National Council of Teachers of English; Associated Writing Programs. Address: RD1, Box 3-A, Houghton, NY 14744, USA.

ZOLYNAS Al(girdas Richard Johann), b. 1 June 1945, Dornbirn, Austria. University Professor of English and Literature. m. 24 June 1967. Education: BA, University of Illinois, 1966; MA 1969, PhD 1973, University of Utah. Appointments: Instructor, Assistant Professor, Writer-in-Residence, Southwest State University, Minnesota; Lecturer, Weber State College, Ogden, Utah, San Diego State University, California; Professor, United States International University, San Diego, California. Publications: The New Physics, 1979; 4 Petunia Avenue (chapbook), 1987; Under Ideal Conditions, 1994; Co-editor with Fred Moramarco: Men of Our Time: An Anthology of Male Poetry in Contemporary America, 1992. Contributions to: various anthologies; Kansas City Star; Minneapolis Tribune; Crazy Horse; Poetry Australia; Poetry Now; The Maverick Poets; Stand Up Poetry; A Book of Luminous Things. Honour: San Diego Book Award for Best Poetry, Under Ideal Conditions, 1994. Memberships: Poets and Writers. Address: 2380 Viewridge Place, Escondido, CA 92026, USA.

ZOU Difan, b. 5 May 1917, Hubei, China. Poet; Writer; Literature Editor. m. (1) Shi Zhuen Fong, dec, (2) Gao Si Yong, 29 May 1990, 4 sons, 2 daughters. Education: Graduated, Shi He Middle School, 1935; Graduated, Normal School, 1938; Bachelor's Degree in Economics, Fu Dan University, 1944. Appointments: Chief-Editor, Shi Ken Di Magazine, 1941-43; Translator of US Information Service in Cheng Du and Hankow Branch Office, 1944-48; Executive Editor and Council Member of Editorial Committee, World Literature, 1959-78; Chief-Editor, Shi Kan (Poetry Magazine), 1979-86; Council Member, Editorial Committee, Shi Kan, 1986-. Publications: Carpenter's Shop (long narrative poem); Gambler of Will (poetry collection), 1942; Leap Over (lyrical poem collection), 1949; Lyrical Poems for my Motherland, 1957; Cuckoo and Lilac (poem collection), 1982; Zou Difan Lyrical Poems, 1983; Romantic Songs (poem collection), 1986; Love Struggling with Death (poem collection), 1988; Tremulous Souls (novel), 1988. Contributions to: Harvest; People's Literature; Poetry Magazine; China Writers; Chinese Literature (monthly English edition); People's Daily; Shanghai Encounter Newspaper (Wen Hwei Bao); Hong Kong Encounter newspaper (Hong Kong Wen Hwei Bao). Honour: National Poetry Prize for Zou Difan Lyrical Poems, 1985. Memberships: Council Member, China Writers' Association, 1979; Guest Poet, Bellagio Study and Conference Centre at invitation of Rockefeller Foundation, 1989; Founder-Member, Chinese Writers and Artists Union. Address: Shi-Kan (Poetry Magazine), 10 Non-Zhan Nan Lee, Beijing 100026, China.

ZUCKER Jack S, b. 23 Jan 1935. Teacher of English. m. Helen Zucker, 19 Aug 1959, 2 daughters. Education: BA, City College of New York, 1957; MA, New York University, 1961. Appointments:

Department of Rhetoric, Oakland University, Rochester, Michigan, 1964-. Publications: Beginnings, 1981; From Manhattan, 1985; Editor (with Helen Zucker), The Bridge, literary magazine. Contributions to: Esquire; Poetry Northwest; Literary Review; Southern Poetry Review; Trace; Webster Review; Permaforst. Honour: John Masefield Award, 1977. Address: 14050 Vernon Street, Oak Park, MI 48237, USA.

ZURAKOWSKI Boguslaw, b. 9 Jul 1939, Stanislawow, Poland. Poet; Literary Critic; Academic Lecturer. Education: Dr Humanities and Philology, Wyzsza Szkola Pedagogiczna, 1975. Appointment: Taniec bez ludzi, Poetry, 1962. Publications: Piesno, 1971; Slowa crasu kazdego, 1975; Cialo i swiatlo, 1978; Wybor poezji, 1981; Paradoks poezji, 1982; Koncertciszy, 1984; Grudy ziemi, 1966; Narzecze madziei, 1980; W Swiecie poezi dla dzieci, 1981. Contributions to: Odra; Literatura; Poezja; Opole. Honours: Distinction, International Poetical Competition, PEN Club, London, England, 1965; Pietak Award, Poland, 1979; Award, Periodical Opole, Poland, 1980; Premio Internazionale Pinocchio, 1983. Memberships: PEN; SEC. Address: ul Krupnicza 22/23. 31-123 Cracow, Poland.

ZWICKY Jan, b. 1955, Canada. Appointments: Editor, Brick Books, London, Ontario. Publications: Wittgenstein Elegies, 1986; The New Room, 1989; Lyric Philosophy, 1992; Songs for Relinquishing the Earth, 1996. Contributions to: Many literary periodicals. Address: Box 1149, Mayerthorpe, Alberta T0E 1N0, Canada.

ZWICKY (Julia) Fay, b. 4 July 1933, Melbourne, Victoria, Australia. m. (1) Karl Zwicky, 1957, (2) James Mackie, 1990. Education: BA, University of Melbourne, 1954. Appointments: Senior Lecturer in English, University of Western Australia, 1972-87; Associate Editor, Southerly (Sydney), 1989-. Publications include: Isaac Babel's Fiddle, 1975; Kaddish and Other Poems, 1982; Ask Me, 1990; Editor, Quarry: A Selection of Western Australian Poetry, 1981; Procession: Youngstreet Poets Three, 1987. Honours include: New South Wales Premier's Award, 1982. Address: 30 Goldsmith Road, Claremont, Western Australia 6010. Australia.

ZYCH Adam Alfred, b. 28 July 1945. Czestochowa, Poland. Psychologist; Gerontologist; Poet; Essayist; Translator. m. 24 Dec 1969, 3 sons. Education: MA, Academy of Catholic Theology, Warsaw, 1971; PhD, Institute for Educational Research, Warsaw, 1975; Habilitation, University of Gdansk, 1984. Appointments: Candidate for a Doctor's Degree, Institute for Educational Research, 1971-73; Clerk/Inspector of Vocational Rehabilitation, Center for Health Care, Stettin, 1973-75; Lecturer/Adjunct in Psychology and Pedagogics, University of Pedagogy, Kielce, 1975-86; Visiting Professor, University of Giessen and University of Vienna, 1987-89; Assistant Professor 1987-90. Professor of Pedagogics, University of Pedagogy, Kielce, 1990-; Visiting Scholar, Buehler Center on Aging, Northwestern University, Chicago, 1991-. Publications: Most/The Bridge; Na mojej ziemi byl Oswiecim/Auschwitz Was in My Land, 2 volumes; Psalmy emigracyjne/Emigrant's Psalms; Odlot jest us nas/Departure is in us; Auschwitz-Gedichte. Contributions to: Wspolczesnosc; Kultura; Wiez; Tygodnik Kulturalny; Zycie i Mysl; Nowiny Kurier; Nowy Dziennik; Kurier Zachodni; Zycie; Relax; Bialy Orzel; Moderne polnische Lyrik; Holocaust Poetry; Parnassus of World Poets, 1997. Honours: Medals and awards. Address: ul Sienkiewicza 42 m 6, 25-507 Kielce, Poland.

ZYDANOWICZ Janina Regina, (Pobóg), b. 25 May 1916, Warsaw, Poland. Architect; Painter; Poet. Education: Diploma, Engineer-Architect MSc, Engineering College, Faculty of Architecture, Warsaw; Academy of Fine Arts. Warsaw, 1950-54. Appointments: Design Offices, Warsaw, 1950-76; Superior Designer, General Designer, 1954-76; Art Exhibitons and Competitions, Denmark, France, Italy, Poland, 1973-. Publications: Poesia Religiosa Internazionale, 1979-92; World Poetry Anthology, 1982; Parnassus of World Poets, anthology, 1995-97, 1998; Livre d'Or des 30 Ans de l'Académie Internationale de Lutece, 1997. Contributions to: Rhythm and Rhyme; Poet; Przekró; Quaderni dell ASLA, 1997. Honours: 2nd Prize, 1979-81. 1986, Diploma di Merito, 1982, Medaglia d'argento, 1982-83, 1st Prize Targa Oro, 1987, Diplomi di Segnalazione, 1984-85, 1988, 1990-92, Concorso Internazionale di Poesia, Taranto, Italy; Médaille d'Argent, 1983, Médaille de Vermeil, 1984, Médaille de Bronze, 1987, 1994, Grand Concours International, Académie Internationale de Lutèce, Section Letters, Paris, France; Premio Speciale. 1992. 1993, Menzione d'Onore con Targa, 1995, Segna.azione di Merito, 1996, ASLA Premio Internazionale di Poesia-Sicilia, Palermo, Italy. Memberships: International Arts Guild, Monaco; Comitato Internazionale CSSI, Accademia Internazionale

Leonardo da Vinci, Rome; l'Académie Internationale de Lutéce, Paris; Associazione Siciliana per le Lettere e le Arti, Palermo. Address: Grottgera 11A/3, 00-785 Warsaw, Poland.

APPENDIX A
A SUMMARY OF POETIC FORMS AND RHYME SCHEMES

Rhymes are represented by small letters: thus 'a' represents the first rhyme of poem (eg, red), and is repeated wherever that rhyme appears again (eg, led, bread, said, etc). The second rhyme of the poem is represented by the letter 'b', and so on.

Where a whole line is repeated, a capital letter is used. If a single word or line is used as a refrain throughout the poem, a capital 'R' is used. Where the refrain consists of part of a line, the R is placed in brackets immediately before the rhyming letter of the line in which it appears (eg, (R) a b a b R means that part of the final line of the poem appears again at the end of a four-line stanza as a refrain).

These are very condensed details, and refer only to the rhyme scheme of the poem. For further information, you should consult a dictionary of poetic forms such as *'The Poets' Manual and Rhyming Dictionary'*, by *Frances Stillman* (Thames & Hudson), from which many of these forms are taken.

SONNET
(a) Shakespearian or English:	abab cdcd efef gg
(b) Petrarchan or Italian:	abba abba cde cde (or cdc dcd)
(c) Spenserian:	abab bcbc cdcd ee
(d) Miltonic:	rhyme scheme as Italian but no break

NB: many other sonnet variants exist - see eg Shelley 'Ozymandias' and Mason Sonnet

VILLANELLE A_1bA_2 abA, abA_2 abA, abA_2 abA,A_2
NB: here the first and third lines rhyme and are repeated as marked, hence A, and A_2

BALLADE
(a) eight-line	ababbcbC ababbcbC ababbcbC bcbC
(b) ten-line	ababbccdcD ababbccdcD ababbccdcD ccdcD
(c) seven-line	ababbcC (x4)

NB: there are other ballade variants, such as the double ballade, with 6 stanzas

TERZA RIMA   aba bcb cdc . . . etc xyx yy

OTTAVA RIMA   abababcc . . . (stanza continued ad lib)

RHYME ROYAL   ababbcc . . . (stanza continued ad lib)

RONDEAU, RONDEL, ETC
(a) Rondeau	(R) aabba aabR aabbaR (or (R) abbaabR ababa)
(b) Rondeau of Villon	(R) abba abR abbaR
(c) Rondel	ABbaabABbabaAB (or ABabbaABababAB)
(d) Rondel (13-line)	ABba abAB abbaA
(e) Roundel	abaB bab abaB (or abaR bab abaR)
(f) Chaucerian Roundel	Abb abA abbA
(g) Rondeau Redouble	(R)$A_1B_1A_2B_2$ abbA, abaB, babA, abaB, ababR
(h) Rondelet	AbAabbA

TRIOLET
ABaAabAB

PANTOUM
$A_1B_1A_2B_2$ $B_1C_1B_2C_2$ $C_1D_1C_2D_2$ . . . $X_1A_2X_2A_1$
NB: first and third lines appear <u>reversed</u> in last stanza: poem may be as long as needed.

SESTINA
Basically an unrhymed form, it is neverless included in rhymed poetry because it uses repeated words. The end words of each six-line stanza are repeated in varying pattern as follows:-

123456 615243 364125 532614 451362 246531 plus 3-line envoi using repeated words in the middle and ends of the lines as follows: - 2 - 5 4 - 3 6 - 1

Rhymed sestinas also exist in various forms.

ODE

Many 'odes' of no particular form exist, but Keats used a rhyme scheme ababcdecde

RUBAI OR QUATRAIN

Best know from Fitzgerald's version of Omar Khayyam, stanzas rhyme aaba

ENGLYN

A Welsh syllabic form consisting of 30 syllables arranged in lines as follows:- 10, 6, 7, 7. syllable 6 rhymes with the ends of the last three lines (ie syll's 16, 23 and 30)

LIMERICK

Mainly humorous form rhyming aabba

GLOSA

Spanish 14/15th C form in various rhyme schemes and metres featuring an introductory quatrain followed by four stanzas, each of which ends with one of the lines of the quatrain and comments on (glosses) it.

APPENDIX B
POETS AND OTHER LITERARY FIGURES OF THE PAST

There have been great poets in every century since Homer in the Seventh Century BC and they have come from many nations. The ancient Greeks certainly had their full share and other celebrated poets followed - Roman, Persian, French, English and, more recently, American. All of them, together with poets of other nations, have contributed generously to the world poetry heritage.

It would be difficult indeed (and impractical) to list all of the noted poets and literary figures of the last 27 centuries but here are notes about some 1000 who have been selected for inclusion by our editors.

Abercrombie, Lascelles *(1881-1938),* English poet and critic, best known for his poems in the Georgian manner.

Abū Nuwās *(c.755-c.814),* great Arab poet.

Addison, Joseph *(1672-1719),* distinguished English essayist, poet and politician, author of the poem *The Campaign.*

Aeschylus *(c.515-c.456 BC),* great Greek dramatist, celebrated as the father of Greek tragedy.

Agee, James *(1909-1955),* admired American novelist and poet.

Ai Qing (actually **Jiang Haicheng**) *(1910-1996),* Chinese poet who chronicled the Communist era of his hoemland in popular nationalistic and folk-flavoured works.

Aiken, Conrad (Potter) *(1889-1973),* esteemed American poet and novelist.

Akahito, Yamabe no *(8th Century),* remarkable Japanese poet.

Akhmatova, Anna (actually **Anna Andreyevna Gorenko**) *(1889-1966),*famous Russian poet who masterfully chronicled the horrors of the Stalinst era.

Alcaeus *(c.620-c.580 BC),* famous Greek poet.

Aleixandre, Vicente *(1898-1984),* Spanish poet; won the Nobel Prize for Literature (1977).

Alexander, Cecil Frances (née Humphreys) *(1818-1895),* Irish poet and hymn writer, best remembered for her *All Things Bright and Beautiful, Once in Royal David's City,* and *There is a Green Hill Far Away.*

Alfieri, Count Vittorio *(1749-1803),* Italian poet and dramatist whose output presaged the Risorgimento.

Amis, Sir Kingsley (William) *(1922-1995),* distinguished English novelist and poet, renowned for his novel *Lucky Jim.*

Anacreon *(c.582-c.485 BC),* celebrated Greek poet, renowned for his satires and love poems.

Andersson, Dan(iel) *(1888-1920),* gifted Swedish poet and novelist.

Aneurin *(6th-7th Century),* Welsh poet, known for his *Gododin.*

Antar (acutally **l'Antarah Ibn Shaddād Al-Absi**) *(6th Century),* famous Arab poet and warrior who penned one of the 7 Golden Odes.

Apollonaire, Guillaume (actually **Wilhelm Apollinaris de Kostrowitzki**) *(1880-1918),* Polish-Italian poet of the French avant-garde.

Apollonius Rhodius *(3rd Century BC),* notable Greek poet and grammarian, author of the celebrated epic poem the *Argonautica.*

Arany, János *(1817-1882),* outstanding Hungarian poet.

Archilochus Of Paros *(714-676 BC),* renowned Greek poet, famous for his command of satire.

Aretino, Pietro *(1492-1557),* Italian poet, best known for his *Sonetti Lussuriosi.*

Argensola, Bartolomé Leonardo de *(1562-1631)* and **Lupercio de** *(1559-1613),* Spanish poets who were acclaimed as the "Horaces" of Spain.

Ariosto, Ludovico *(1474-1533),* famous Italian poet, author of the celebrated *Orlando Furioso.*

Aristophanes *(c.448-c.388 BC),* great Greek dramatist, master of comedic writing.

Arndt, Ernst Moritz *(1769-1860),* revered German poet and patriot, known as "Father Arndt".

Arnold, Matthew *(1822-1888),* eminent English poet and critic, admired for such poems as *Dover Beach, The Scholar Gipsy, Sohrab and Rustum,* and *Thyrsis.*

Asturias, Miguel Angel *(1899-1974),* Guatemalan writer and poet; won the Nobel Prize for Literature (1967).

Auden, W(ystan) H(ugh) *(1907-1973),* distinguished English-born American poet and essayist.

Ausonius, Decius Magnus *(c.310-c.395),* fine Latin poet.

Austin, Alfred *(1835-1913),* English poet; became Poet Laureate of the United Kingdom (1896).

Avicebron (actually **Solomon Ben Yehuda Ibn Gabriol**) *(c.1020-c.1070),* renowned Spanish Jewish poet and philosopher.

Babits, Mihály *(1883-1941),* Hungarian poet, novelist and translator.

Baïf, Jean Antoine de *(1532-1589),* notable French poet.

Bailey, Philip James *(1816-1902),* English poet, best remebered for his *Festus.*

Balaguer y Circera, Victor *(1824-1901),* Spanish poet, historian and politician.

Balassa, Bálint *(1555-1591),* Hungarian knight and poet.

Balbuena, Bernardo de *(1568-1627),* Spanish poet and prelate who penned the esteemed epic *El Bernardo o la victoria de Roncesvalles.*

Balmont, Konstantin Dmitrievich *(1867-1943),* Russian poet, essayist, and translator, a leading figure in the Symbolist movement.

Banville, Théodore Faullin de *(1823-1891),* greatly admired French poet and dramatist, acclaimed as the "roi des rimes."

Barbour, John *(c.1325-1395),* famous Scottish poet, scholar and prelate, celebrated as the "father" of Scottish poetry and history, author of the epic *The Brus.*

Barclay, Alexander *(c.1475-1552),* Scottish poet who penned the famous poem *The Shyp of Folys of the Worlde.*

Bardesanes or **Bardaisan** or **Bar Daişān** *(154-c.222),* Syrian Christian Gnostic theologian and poet.

Barham, Richard Harris *(1788-1845),* English poet and churchman, best known for his humorous collection *The Ingoldsby Legends.*

Baring-Gould, Sabine *(1834-1924),* English writer and churchman, author of the hymns *Onward, Christian Soldiers* and *Now the Day is Over.*

Barnes, William *(1800-1886),* English poet and churchman, remembered for his *Poems of Rural Life in the Dorset Dialect.*

Barnfield, Richard *(1574-1627),* English poet in the pastoral tradition.

Bartas, Guillame de Salluste *(1544-1590),* French soldier, diplomat and poet, author of the poem *La Semaine.*

Baudelaire, Charles (Pierre) *(1821-1867),* remarkable French poet of great refinement and originality, renowned for his collection *Les Fleurs du mal.*

Baxter, James Keir *(1926-1972),* New Zealand poet, dramatist and critic.

Beattie, James *(c.1735-1803),* Scottish poet and essayist, author of the poem *The Minstrel.*

Beaumont, Francis *(c.1584-1616),* distinguished English dramatist who collaborated with John Fletcher on a series of outstanding dramas; brother of Sir John Beaumont.

Beaumont, Sir John *(1582-1627),* English poet who introduced the heroic couplet to English verse in his *Bosworth Field*; brother of Francis Beaumont.

Beaumont, Joseph *(1616-1699),* English poet, author of the epic *Psyche.*

Beckett, Samuel *(1906-1989),* renowned Irish dramatist, writer, and poet; won the Nobel Prize for Literature (1969).

Bécquer, Gustavo Adolfo *(1836-1870),* Spanish writer and poet, best remembered for his poems of troubadour love.

Beddoes, Thomas Lovell *(1803-1849),* English poet and physiologist.

Bellay, Joachim du *(1522-1560),* French poet and writer.

Belleau, Rémy *(1528-1577),* French poet, known for his *Avril.*

Belloc, (Joseph-Pierre) Hilaire *(1870-1953),* French-born English writer and poet.

Bely, Andrei (actually **Boris Nikolaievich Bugaiev**) *(1880-1934),* Russian novelist, poet and critic.

Benediktsson, Einar *(1864-1940),* Icelandic poet.

Benét, Stephen Vincent *(1898-1943),* American poet and novelist who penned the well-known poem *John Brown's Body.*

Benn, Gottfried *(1886-1956),* significant German poet.

Bentley, Edmund Clerihew *(1875-1956),* English journalist, writer and versifier who invented the clerihew, a humorous verse form.

Béranger, Pierre-Jean de *(1780-1857),* French poet whose satirical and witty verses brought him great popular acclaim.

Berceo, Gonzalo de *(c.1180-c.1264),* Spanish poet, esteemed for his devotional verses.

Berchet, Giovanni *(1783-1851),* Italian poet, formative figure in the development of Italian Romantic poetry.

Bergman, Bo Hjalmar *(1869-1967),* Swedish poet, novelist and critic.

Bergman, Hjalmar Fredrik Elgérus *(1883-1931),* Swedish poet, novelist and dramatist.

Berryman, John *(1914-1972),* American poet and novelist, best remembered for his collection *77 Dream Songs.*

Berzsenyi, Dániel *(1776-1836),* Hungarian poet who penned the patriotic *Ode to Magyarokhoz.*

Betjeman, Sir John *(1906-1984),* popular English poet; became Poet Laureate of the United Kingdom (1972).

Bhartrhari *(7th Century),* Hindu poet and philosopher.

Bilderdijk, Willem *(1756-1831),* Dutch poet and philologist.

Billinger, Richard *(1893-1965),* Austrian poet and novelist.

Binyon, (Robert) Laurence *(1869-1943),* English poet and art critic, author of the celebrated elegy *For the Fallen.*

Birney, (Alfred) Earle *(1904-1995),* respected Canadian poet, writer, dramatist and critic.

Bishop, Elizabeth *(1911-1979),* distinguished American poet.

Bishop, John Peale *(1892-1944),* American poet, writer and essayist.

Bjørnson, Bjørnstjerne Martinius *(1832-1910),* eminent Norwegian poet, novelist, dramatist and politician, author of Norway's National Anthem *Ja, vi elsker dette landet* (Yes, We Love This Land of Ours); won the Nobel Prize for Literature (1903).

Blair, Robert *(1699-1746),* Scottish poet and preacher who penned the well-remembered *The Grave.*

Blake, William *(1757-1827),* famous English poet, mystic, painter and engraver, renowned for such masterful works as *Songs of Innocence* and *Songs of Experience.*

Blicher, Steen Steensen *(1782-1848),* gifted Danish poet and novelist, author of the notable poetry collection *Traekfuglene* (The Migratory Birds).

Blok, Alexander Alexandrovich *(1880-1921),* Russian poet and dramatist, famed Symbolist.

Bloomfield, Robert *(1766-1823),* English poet who wrote the popular *The Farmer's Boy.*

Blunck, Hans Friedrich *(1888-1961),* German poet and novelist.

Blunden, Edmund Charles *(1896-1974),* English poet and critic.

Blunt, Wilfrid Scawen *(1840-1922),* English poet.

Bocage, Manoel Maria Barbosa du *(1765-1805),* Portuguese poet who displayed a fine gift for both classical and romantic verse.

Boccaccio, Giovanni *(1313-1375),* celebrated Italian poet and writer whose stories in the *Decameron* are renowned the world over.

Boccage, Marie Anne Fiquest du (née Le Page) *(1710-1802),* French poet.

Boiardo, Matteo Maria, Count of Scandiano *(1434-1494),* Italian poet, author of the unfinished *Orlando Innamorato.*

Boileau or **Boileau-Despréaux, Nicolas** *(1636-1711),* important French poet and critic, master of satirical and epistolary writing.

Boito, Arrigo *(1842-1918),* Italian composer and poet who wrote the libretto to his own opera *Mefistofele* as well as to Verdi's operas *Otello* and *Falstaff.*

Boker, George Henry *(1823-1890),* American poet, dramatist and diplomat, remembered for his sonnets and the verse tragedy *Francesca da Rimini.*

Borges, Jorge Luis *(1899-1986),* Argentine poet, essayist and short-story writer.

Bottomley, Gordon *(1874-1948),* English poet and dramatist, author of *Poems of Thirty Years.*

Bouilhet, Louis *(1821-1869),* French poet and dramatist.

Bourget, Paul (-Charles-Joseph) *(1852-1935),* esteemed French poet and novelist.

Bowles, William Lisle *(1762-1850),* English churchman and poet whose works presaged the Romantic era of verse.

Boyd, Martin à Beckett *(1893-1972),* Australian novelist and poet.

Boye, Karin Maria *(1900-1941),* Swedish poet and novelist.

Boyle, Kay *(1902-1992),* American poet, essayist and novelist.

Bradstreet, Anne (née Dudley) *(1612-1672),* English-born American poet, particularly remembered for her collection *The Tenth Muse lately sprung up in America.*

Brady, Nicholas *(1659-1726),* Irish churchman and poet.

Brant, Sebastian *(1458-1521),* German poet, author of the satirical *Narrenschiff* (Ship of Fools).

Brecht, Bertolt (Eugen Friedrich) *(1898-1956),* celebrated German dramatist and poet, master of the modern theatre.

Brennan, Christopher (John) *(1870-1932),* Australian poet and critic.

Brentano, Clemens von *(1778-1842),* important German poet and novelist.

Breton, André *(1896-1966),* French poet, essayist, and critic, known as a proponent of Surrealism.

Breton, Nicholas *(c.1545-c.1626),* English poet and writer, particularly remembered for his poem *The Passionate Shepherd.*

Březina, Otakar *(1868-1929),* Czech poet who excelled in Symbolist imagery.

Bridges, Robert (Seymour) *(1844-1930),* notable English poet, dramatist and critic; became Poet Laureate of the United Kingdom (1913).

Brizieux, Julien Auguste Pélage *(1803-1858),* French poet.

Brod, Max *(1884-1968),* Austrian poet, dramatist, novelist, essayist and biographer.

Brodsky, Joseph Alexandrovich *(1940-1996),* significant Russian-born American poet whose reputation as a master of his craft was secured as an exile in the West; won the Nobel Prize for Literature (1987) and was Poet Laureate of the US (1991-92).

Brontë, Emily Jane *(1818-1848),* remarkable English poet and novelist who wrote under the pseudonym **Ellis Bell** the *Gondal* poems and the novel *Wuthering Heights;* sister of the novelists Anne (1820-1849) and Charlotte (1816-1855) Brontë.

Brooke, (Bernard) Joycelyn *(1908-1966),* English poet and novelist.

Brooke, Rupert (Chawner) *(1887-1915),* admired English poet beloved for such works as *If I Should Die* and *Grantchester;* died in World War I.

Brown, George Mackay *(1921-1996),* Scottish poet and writer.

Brown, Thomas *(1663-1704),* English poet of a satirical bent.

Browne, William *(1591-c.1645),* English poet in the pastoral tradition.

Browning, Elizabeth Barrett *(1806-1861),* eminent English poet of great intellect, famous for such works as *Sonnets from the Portuguese* and *Aurora Leigh;* wife of Robert Browning.

Browning, Robert *(1812-1889),* renowned English poet, and author of the masterful *The Ring and the Book;* husband of Elizabeth Barrett Browning.

Bryant, William Cullen *(1794-1878),* American poet and journalist whose poem *Thanatopsis* became an American classic.

Bryusov, Valeri Yakovlevich *(1873-1924),* Russian poet, critic and translator.

Buchanan, Robert Williams *(1841-1901),* English poet, novelist and dramatist.

Bufalino, Gesualdo *(1920-1996),* Italian writer, poet and translator.

Bukowski, Charles *(1920-1994),* American poet, novelist and screenwriter whose underground career made him a literary cult figure.

Bull, Olav (Jacob Martin Luther) *(1883-1933),* remarkable Norwegian poet in the lyric tradition.

Bunting, Basil *(1900-1985),* English poet.

Bürger, Gottfried August *(1747-1794),* popular German poet whose lyric output secured his reputation in his homeland.

Burns, Robert *(1759-1796),* celebrated Scottish poet, master of the folk tradition of his native land.

Butler, Samuel *(1612-1680),* English poet whose satirical mastery is found in his *Hudibras.*

Byrom, John *(1692-1763),* English poet.

Byron, George Gordon, 6th Baron Byron of Rochdale *(1788-1824),* celebrated English poet, self-created "Byronic hero" of the Romantic age and advocate of political liberty.

Caedmon *(7th Century),* Anglo-Saxon poet, herdsman and monk, earliest Christian poet of England known by name.

Callimachus *(3rd Century BC),* Greek poet, grammarian and critic, author of the elegy *Aitia.*

Calverley, Charles Stuart *(1831-1884),* English poet whose gift of parody is revealed in his *Verses and Translations* and *Fly Leaves.*

Cambridge, Ada *(1844-1926),* English-born Australian novelist and poet.

Camões, Luís (Vaz) de *(c.1524-1580),* significant Portuguese poet who wrote the masterful epic *Os Lusiadas.*

Campbell, (Ignatius) Roy (Dunnachie) *(1901-1957),* South African poet and journalist.

Campbell, Thomas *(1777-1844),* Scottish poet and writer, especially remembered for such poems as *The Battle of the Baltic, Hohenlinden* and *Ye Mariners of England.*

Campbell, William Wilfred *(1861-1918),* Canadian poet and churchman who penned *Lake Lyrics.*

Campion, Thomas *(1567-1620),* English physician, poet and composer, author of both English and Latin poems.

Campoamor y Campoosorio, Ramón de *(1817-1901),* Spanish poet, particularly known for his epigrammatic writing.

Carducci, Giosué *(1835-1907),* prominent Italian poet; won the Nobel Prize for Literature (1906).

Carew, Thomas *(1595-1639),* English poet in the Cavalier tradition, esteemed for his *Rapture.*

Carey, Henry *(c.1690-1743),* English poet and composer, best remembered for his *Sally in Our Alley.*

Carleton, Will(iam McKendree) *(1845-1912),* American poet, best known for his ballads of farm and city life.

Carmen Sylva (actually **Elizabeth, Queen of Romania**) *(1843-1916),* Romanian poet.

Carroll, Lewis (actually **Charles Lutwidge Dodgson**) *(1832-1898),* famous English writer, poet and mathematician, celebrated for his nonsense verse and for his *Alice's Adventures in Wonderland.*

Carter, Elizabeth *(1717-1806),* English poet and translator.

Cartwright, William *(1611-1643),* English poet, dramatist and preacher.

Carver, Raymond *(1939-1988),* American poet and short-story writer.

Castelli, Ignaz Franz *(1781-1862),* Austrian poet.

Casti, Giambattista *(c.1721-1803),* Italian poet.

Castro, Eugénio de *(1869-1944),* Portuguese poet, best remembered for his Symbolist work *Oaristos.*

Cather, Willa Sibert *(1876-1947),* American writer and poet.

Cats, Jacob *(1577-1660),* Dutch statesman and poet, known as "Father" Cats.

Catullus, Gaius Valerius *(c.84-c.54 BC),* celebrated Roman poet, master of lyric verse whose love poems and satirical pieces are exemplary.

Cavafy, Constantine (actually **Konstantínos Pétrou Kaváfis**) *(1863-1933),* esteemed Greek poet.

Cavalcanti, Guido *(c.1255-1300),* Italian poet, admired for his love poems and ballads.

Cendras, Blaise (actually **Frédéric Louis Sauser**) *(1887-1961),* Swiss novelist and poet, especially esteemed for his poems *Le Panama ou Les Aventures de Mes Sept Oncles, Las Paques à New York* and *Transsibérien.*

Cervantes (Saavedra), Miguel de *(1547-1616),* great Spanish novelist and poet, author of the classic novel *Don Quixote* and of the esteemed poem *Viage del Parnaso.*

Chacel, Rosa (Clotilde Cecilia María del Carmen) *(1898-1994),* Spanish novelistand poet.

Chamisso, Adelbert von (actually **Louis-Charles-Adélaïde Chamisso de Boncourt**) *(1781-1838),* French-born German poet, writer and biologist.

Chapelain, Jean *(1595-1674),* French poet and critic.

Chapman, George *(c.1559-1634),* English dramatist and poet, author of the epic poem *Euthymiae and Raptus.*

Chartier, Alain *(c.1385-c.1435),* French poet, writer and courtier, best remembered for his *La belle dame sans merci* and *Livre des quatre dames.*

Chateaubriand, (François-René), Vicomte de *(1768-1848),* prominent French writer and statesman, esteemed for his prose epics and for his remarkable autobiography *Memoires d'outre-tombe.*

Chatterton, Thomas *(1752-1770),* talented English poet who wrote the "Rowley" poems, forgeries he attributed to a mythical 15th Century monk he named Thomas Rowley; committed suicide by arsenic poisoning.

Chaucer, Geoffrey *(c.1343-1400),* great English poet, celebrated for *The Canterbury Tales.*

Chénier, André (-Marie) de *(1762-1794),* French poet, author of *Hermès, L'Invention* and *Suzanne;* guillotined at the close of the Reign of Terror; brother of Marie-Joseph-Blaise de Chénier.

Chénier, Marie-Joseph-Blaise de *(1764-1811),* French poet, dramatist and politician; brother of André de Chénier.

Chesterton, G(ilbert) K(eith) *(1874-1936),* famous English critic, novelist and poet, creator of the detective-priest Father Brown.

Chiabrera, Gabriello *(1552-1638),* Italian poet who introduced the poetical epistle to his homeland in his *Lettere Famigliari.*

Chrétien de Troyes *(12th Century),* celebrated French poet and troubadour.

Christine de Pisan *(1364-c.1430),* gifted French poet, writer and translator.

Cibber, Colley *(1671-1757),* notable English poet, dramatist, and actor; became Poet Laureate of the United Kingdom (1730).

Clare, John *(1793-1864),* English poet, author of *Poems Descriptive of Rural Life.*

Clarke, Austin *(1896-1974),* Irish poet and dramatist.

Claudel, Paul (-Louis-Charles-Marie) *(1868-1955),* eminent French poet, essayist and dramatist, admired for such poetical works as *Cinq Grandes Odes* and *Corona Benignitatis Anni Dei.*

Claudian (actually **Claudius Claudianus**) *(c.370-c.404),* great Roman poet, celebrated for his epic tomes.

Claussen, Sophus (Niels Christen) *(1865-1931),* distinguished Danish poet in the Symbolist manner.

Cleland, William *(c.1661-1689),* Scottish poet; died defending Dunkeld against the Jacobite rebels.

Clemo, Jack (actually **Reginald John Clemo**) *(1916-1994)*, English poet.

Cleveland, John *(1613-1658)*, English poet in the Cavalier tradition.

Clough, Arthur Hugh *(1819-1861)*, English poet, especialy admired for his *Amours de voyage, Dipsychus*, and *The Bothie.*

Cocburn, Alicia or **Alison** *(1713-1794)*, Scottish poet, remembered for her *The Flowers of the Forest.*

Cocteau, Jean *(1889-1963)*, famous French poet, dramatist, novelist and critic.

Coleridge, (David) Hartley *(1796-1849)*, English poet and writer; son of Samuel Taylor Coleridge.

Coleridge, Samuel Taylor *(1772-1834)*, renowned English poet, celebrated for the originality and beauty of his communicative powers in such works as *Christabel, Kubla Khan, Ode to Dejection, Ode to France* and *The Rime of the Ancient Mariner.*

Collier, John *(1708-1786)*, English poet who wrote satirical and humorous verse under the name Tim Bobbin.

Collins, William *(1721-1759)*, English poet, best known for his *Odes.*

Column, Pádraic *(1881-1972)*, Irish poet and dramatist.

Congreve, William *(1670-1729)*, distinguished English dramatist and poet.

Constable, Henry *(1562-1613)*, English poet whose reputation rests upon his sonnets.

Cook, Eliza *(1818-1889)*, English poet.

Coppard, A(lfred) E(dgar) *(1878-1957)*, English short-story writer and poet.

Coppée, François *(1842-1908)*, French poet, active figure in the Parnassien movement.

Corbet, Richard *(1582-1635)*, English poet and churchman.

Corneille, Pierre *(1606-1684)*, celebrated French dramatist, acclaimed as the father of French comedic and tragic writing for the stage; brother of Thomas Corneille.

Corneille, Thomas *(1625-1709)*, French dramatist; brother of Pierre Corneille.

Cory, William Johnson *(1823-1892)*, English poet.

Cotton, Charles *(1630-1687)*, English poet and writer.

Couperus, Louis (Marie Anne) *(1863-1923)*, major Dutch novelist and poet.

Courthope, William John *(1842-1917)*, English poet and critic.

Coward, Sir Noel (Peirce) *(1899-1973)*, famous English actor, dramatist and composer.

Cowley, Abraham *(1618-1667)*, English poet, author of the epic *Davideis.*

Cowper, William *(1731-1800)*, eminent English poet, celebrated for such works as *The Castaway, The Task* and *Yardley Oak.*

Crabbe, George *(1754-1832)*, English poet, admired for his *The Borough, Tales of the Hall, The Parish Register* and *The Village.*

Crane, (Harold) Hart *(1899-1932)*, important American poet, author of *The Bridge* and *White Buildings*; committed suicide by drowning.

Crashaw, Richard *(c.1613-1649)*, English poet of a religious bent.

Cratinus *(c.519-423 BC)*, significant Greek dramatist, master of comedic writing.

Croly, George *(1780-1860)*, Irish poet, writer and churchman.

Csokonai Vitéz, Mihály *(1773-1805)*, Hungarian poet.

Cueva, Juan de la *(c.1550-c.1607)*, Spanish poet and dramatist.

Cullen, Countee *(1903-1946)*, American poet, significant figure in the Harlem Renaissance.

cummings, e e (Edward Estlin) *(1894-1962)*, American poet, writer and painter, renowned for his inventive verse.

Cunningham, Allan *(1784-1842)*, Scottish poet and writer.

Cynewulf *(c.700-c.800)*, Anglo-Saxon poet.

Dahl, Roald *(1916-1990)*, English writer, dramatist and poet, best known for his children's works.

Dahlgren, Karl Fredrik *(1791-1844),* Swedish poet, novelist, dramatist and preacher.

Dahn, Julius Sophus Felix *(1834-1912),* German historian, poet, novelist and dramatist.

Dana, Richard Henry *(1787-1879),* American poet and critic; father of the novelist and lawyer Richard Henry Dana (1815-1882).

Daniel, Arnaut *(12th Century),* important French poet who introduced the sestina in his works.

Daniel, Samuel *(1562-1619),* English poet, dramatist and writer, author of the extensive poetical setting *A History of the Civil Wars between York and Lancaster.*

D'Annunzio, Gabriele *(1863-1938),* Italian poet, novelist, dramatist and political adventurer.

Dantas, Julio *(1876-1962),* Portuguese poet, dramatist and short-story writer.

Dante Alighieri *(1265-1321),* great Italian poet, celebrated for his *Divina Commedia,* one of the supreme achievements in world literature.

Da Ponte, Lorenzo (actually **Emanuele Conegliano**) *(1749-1838),* famous Italian poet who wrote the librettos for Mozart's operas *Cosi fan tutte, Don Giovanni* and *Le Nozze de Figaro.*

Darío, Rubén (actually **Felix Rubén García Sarmiento**) *(1867-1916),* significant Nicaraguan poet, acclaimed for his *Azul* and *Prosas Profanas.*

Darley, George *(1795-1846),* Irish poet, writer, critic and mathematician, remembered for his collection of poems *The Errors of Ecstasie.*

Darwin, Erasmus *(1731-1802),* English physician and poet; father of the naturalist Charles (Robert) Darwin (1809-1882).

Daudet, Alphonse *(1840-1897),* French poet, short-story writer and novelist.

Daurat or **Dorat, Jean** *(c.1510-1588),* important French poet and scholar who excelled in Greek and Latin verse.

D'Avenant, Sir William *(1606-1668),* notable English poet and dramatist; became Poet Laureate of the United Kingdom (1638).

Davidson, John *(1857-1909),* Scottish poet, dramatist and novelist; commited suicide.

Davie, Donald Alfred *(1922-1995),* English poet and critic, a leading figure in the anti-Romantic group known as the Movement.

Davies, Sir John *(1569-1626),* English poet and statesman, author of *Hymns to Astraea, Nosce Te Ipsum* and *Orchestra, or a Poeme of Dancing.*

Davies, William Henry *(1871-1940),* Welsh poet and writer whose early years as a tramp led him to be called the "tramp" poet.

Davis, Idris *(1905-1953),* Welsh poet.

Day-Lewis, C(ecil) *(1904-1972),* admired Irish poet, critic, detective-story writer and translator; became Poet Laureate of the United Kingdom (1968).

Dearmer, Geoffrey *(1893-1996),* English poet, best known for the collection *A Pilgrim's Song,* published in his 100th year.

Defoe, Daniel *(1660-1731),* remarkable English writer and poet, author of such novels as the classic *Robinson Crusoe, Moll Flanders* and *Captain Singleton.*

Dehmel, Richard *(1863-1920),* notable German poet whose works anticipated Expressionism.

Dekker, Thomas *(c.1570-c.1632),* important English dramatist, particularly known for his *The Honest Whore.*

De la Mare, Walter (John) *(1873-1956),* English poet and novelist who won favour with both children and adults.

Delavigne, Jean François Casimir *(1793-1843),* French dramatist.

Delille, Jacques, Abbé *(1738-1813),* French poet and translator.

Delvig, Anton Antonovich, Baron von *(1798-1831),* Russian poet.

Dempster, Thomas *(c.1579-1625),* Scottish poet.

Denham, Sir John *(1615-1669),* Irish poet, known for his *Cooper's Hill.*

Dereme, Tristan (actually **Phillippe Huc**) *(1889-1941),* French poet.

Déroulède, Paul *(1846-1914),* French poet of a strident nationalistic persuasion.

Derozio, Henry Louis Vivian *(1809-1831),* Eurasian poet, remembered for his sonnets.

Derzhavin, Gavril Romanovich *(1743-1816),* admired Russian poet, particularly esteemed for the lyricism of his works.

Deschamps, Eustache *(c.1345-c.1406),* French poet who wrote under the name Morel.

Desmarets, Jean, Sieur de Saint-Sorlen *(1595-1676),* French poet and critic.

De Vere, Aubrey Thomas *(1814-1902),* Irish poet and writer.

Dickey, James (Lafayette) *(1923-1997),* American poet and novelist, admired for his poetry collection *Buckdancer's Choice* and for his novel *Deliverance.*

Dickinson, Emily (Elizabeth) *(1830-1886),* outstanding American poet whose large output revealed a poet of extraordinary gifts.

Dingelstedt, Franz Ferdinand, Freiherr von *(1814-1881),* German poet and dramatist.

Diniz da Cruz e Silva, Antonio *(1731-1799),* Portuguese poet, acclaimed as the "Pindar" of Portugal.

Dixon, Richard Watson *(1833-1900),* English poet and church historian.

Dobell, Sydney Thompson *(1824-1874),* English poet whose works became well known under the name Sydney Yendys.

Dobson, (Henry) Austin *(1840-1921),* English poet, biographer and essayist who penned poems of distinction.

Domett, Alfred *(1811-1887),* English poet and politician; was Prime Minister of New Zealand (1862-63).

Donne, John *(1572-1631),* celebrated English poet, writer and churchman.

Doolittle, Hilda *(1886-1961),* American poet and novelist who wrote under the name H.D.

Dos Passos, John (Roderigo) *(1896-1970),* eminent American novelist, poet and dramatist, author of the sweeping prose trilogy *USA.*

Douglas, Gawin *(c.1474-1522),* Scottish poet, translator and churchman.

Doyle, Sir Francis Hastings Charles, 2nd Baronet *(1810-1888),* English poet, remembered for his ballads.

Drayton, Michael *(1563-1631),* important English poet whose finest achievement is his extensive collection *Polyolbion.*

Drinkwater, John *(1882-1937),* English poet, dramatist and critic.

Droste-Hülshoff, Annette Elisabeth, Baroness von *(1797-1848),* outstanding German poet, renowned for the refined classicism of her works.

Drummond, William, of Hawthornden *(1585-1649),* Scottish poet and writer.

Dryden, John *(1631-1700),* celebrated English poet, dramatist, and translator whose works presaged the neo-Classical movement; was Poet Laureate of the United Kingdom (1668-88).

Du Camp, Maxime *(1822-1894),* French poet, novelist and journalist.

Ducis, Jean-François *(1733-1816),* French poet and dramatist.

Duck, Stephen *(1705-1756),* English poet and churchman; committed suicide by drowning.

Duhamel, Georges *(1884-1966),* eminent French novelist and poet.

Dunbar, Paul Laurence *(1872-1906),* American poet and novelist, some of whose poems in dialect were included in his collection *Lyrics of Lowly Life.*

Dunbar, William *(c.1460-c.1525),* remarkable Scottish poet, renowned for his *Lament for the Makaris* and *The Thrissil and the Rois.*

Dunsany, Edward (John Moreton Drax Plunkett), 18th Baron *(1878-1957),* distinguished Irish poet, novelist and dramatist.

Durrell, Lawrence (George) *(1912-1990),* admired English poet, novelist, dramatist and critic.

Dutt, Michael Madhusudan *(1824-1873),* Indian poet and dramatist who wrote in both English and

Bengali.

Dyer, Sir Edward *(1543-1607)*, English poet and diplomat, particularly remembered for his poem *My Mind to Me a Kingdom*.

Dyer, John *(1699-1757)*, Welsh poet and painter, esteemed for such works as *Grongar Hill*, *The Fleece* and *The Ruin of Rome*.

Ebert, Karl Egon *(1801-1882)*, notable Bohemian poet who penned the national epic *Vlasta*.

Eichendorff, Joseph, Freiherr von *(1788-1857)*, German poet, novelist and critic.

Ekelöf, (Bengt) Gunnar *(1907-1968)*, distinguished Swedish poet.

Ekelund, Vilhelm *(1880-1949)*, Swedish poet and essayist.

Eliot, T(homas) S(tearns) *(1888-1965)*, celebrated American-born English poet, critic and dramatist; won the Nobel Prize for Literature (1948).

Elliott, Ebenezer *(1781-1849)*, English industrialist, poet and political radical, known as the "Corn Law Rhymer" for his attacks upon the corn laws.

Ellis, George *(1753-1815)*, English poet who excelled in satirical verse.

Éluard, Paul (actually **Eugène Grindel**) *(1895-1952)*, French poet, prominent in Surrealist circles.

Emerson, Ralph Waldo *(1803-1882)*, famous American poet and essayist, one of the most important figures in American literary history.

Eminescu (actually **Eminovici**), **Mihail** *(1850-1889)*, distinguished Romanian poet.

Empedocles *(c.490-430 BC)*, Greek philosopher, poet and statesman.

Empson, Sir William *(1906-1984)*, English poet and critic.

Encina or **Enzina, Juan de la** *(c.1468-c.1530)*, Spanish poet and dramatist.

Ennius, Quintus *(c.239-169 BC)*, Roman poet who introduced the hexameter into Latin.

Enríquez Gómez, Antonio (actually **Enríquez de Paz**) *(1602-c.1662)*, Spanish dramatist and poet.

Epicharmus *(c.540-450 BC)*, Greek poet.

Epimenides *(flourished 7th or 6th Century BC)*, Greek poet and priest.

Ercilla y Zuñiga, Alonso de *(1553-c.1595)*, Spanish poet, author of the extensive epic *La Araucana*.

Espronceda (y Delgado), José de *(1808-1842)*, remarkable Spanish poet in the Romantic tradition.

Esquiros, Henri Alphonse *(1814-1876)*, French poet, writer and politician.

Euripides *(c.480-406 BC)*, great Greek dramatist, renowned for his tragedies.

Ewald, Johannes *(1743-1781)*, Danish poet and dramatist, author of the song *King Kristian Stood by the Lofty Mast*, which became the Danish National Anthem.

Ewart, Gavin Buchanan *(1916-1995)*, English poet, best remembered for his verse in a light vein.

Eyvindur (Jónsson) *(10th Century)*, Norwegian poet who was known as Skáldaspillir (The Plagiarist).

Falconer, William *(1732-1769)*, Scottish poet and seaman, author of *The Shipwreck*, who perished in the sinking of the frigate Aurora.

Faria y Sousa, Manual de *(1590-1649)*, Portuguese poet.

Farquhar, George *(1678-1707)*, Irish dramatist, master of comedic invention.

Fawkes, Francis *(1720-1777)*, English poet and translator.

Fay, András *(1786-1864)*, Hungarian poet, dramatist and novelist.

Feith, Rhijnvis *(1753-1824)*, Dutch poet, novelist and critic.

Ferguson, Sir Samuel *(1810-1886)*, Irish poet.

Ferguson, Robert *(1750-1774)*, Scottish poet, best known for his *Auld Reekie*.

Ferreira, António *(1528-1569)*, Portuguese poet in the classical style, known as the "Horace" of his homeland.

Field, Eugene *(1850-1895)*, American poet and writer, author of the popular nursery lullaby *Wynken, Blynken, and Nod*.

Filicaia, Vincenzo da *(1642-1707)*, Italian poet.

Firdausi or **Ferdusi** (actually **Abu-'l Kasim Mansur)** *(c.935-c.1020)*, Persian poet, celebrated for his *Shah Náma* (Book of Kings).

Fitzgerald, Edward *(1809-1883)*, English poet and translator, admired for his translations of quatrains from the *Rubáiyát of Omar Khayyám*.

Flatman, Thomas *(1637-1688)*, English painter and poet.

Flecker, James Elroy (actually **Herman Elroy Fleckner)** *(1884-1915)*, English poet whose gifts were revealed in his *The Bridge of Fire, The Golden Journey to Samarkand* and *Old Ships*.

Flecknoe, Richard *(c.1600-c.1678)*, Irish poet and dramatist.

Fleming, Paul *(1609-1640)*, German poet who introduced the sonnet to his homeland.

Fletcher, Giles *(c.1588-1623)*, English poet, author of *Christ's Victory and Triumph*; brother of Phineas Fletcher and cousin of John Fletcher.

Fletcher, John *(1579-1625)*, notable English dramatist who collaborated with Francis Beaumont on a series of distinguished dramas; cousin of Giles and Phineas Fletcher.

Fletcher, John Gould *(1886-1950)*, American poet and essayist.

Fletcher, Phineas *(1582-1650)*, English poet; brother of Giles Fletcher and cousin of John Fletcher.

Flint, F(rank) S(tewart) *(1885-1960)*, English poet and translator.

Fontane, Theodor *(1819-1898)*, German poet and novelist.

Fontaines, Louis, Marquis de *(1757-1821)*, French poet and politician.

Fontenelle, Bernard Le Bovier, sieur de *(1657-1757)*, French poet and writer.

Ford, Ford Madox (actually **Ford Hermann Hueffer)** *(1873-1939)*, English novelist, editor and poet.

Ford, John *(c.1586-c.1640)*, English dramatist, author of such notable plays as *Perkin Warbeck* and *'Tis Pity She's a Whore*.

Fort, Paul *(1872-1960)*, French poet, dramatist and editor, particularly remembered for his *Ballades françaises*.

Fortiguerra, Niccòlo *(1674-1735)*, Italian poet and prelate who wrote the satirical epic *Il Ricciardetto*.

Frank, Leonhard *(1882-1961)*, German poet and novelist.

Frankl, Ludwig, Ritter von Hochwart *(1810-1893)*, Austrian poet.

Fréchette, Louis-Honoré *(1839-1908)*, Canadian poet, dramatist and writer.

Freeman, John *(1880-1929)*, English poet.

Freiligrath, (Hermann) Ferdinand *(1810-1876)*, German poet, translator and advocate of democracy in his homeland.

Freneau, Philip (Morin) *(1752-1832)*, American poet and sailor whose capture by the British during the American War of Independence inspired him to write *The British Prison Ship*.

Fröding, Gustaf *(1860-1911)*, significant Swedish poet.

Frost, Robert (Lee) *(1874-1963)*, famous American poet.

Fuller, Roy (Broadbent) *(1912-1991)*, English poet and novelist.

Gallus, Gaius Cornelius *(c.70-26 BC)*, Roman poet and creator of the Latin elegy; committed suicide following banishment.

Garborg, Arne Evenson *(1851-1924)*, Norwegian poet and novelist.

García Gutiérrez, Antonio *(1813-1884)*, Spanish poet, dramatist and scientist.

Garcilaso de la Vega *(1503-1536)*, Spanish poet and soldier who introduced the Petrarchian sonnet to Spain; fatally wounded in battle.

Garioch, Robert (actually **Robert Garioch Sutherland)** *(1909-1981)*, Scottish poet, writer and translator.

Garnier, Robert *(c.1545-1590)*, French poet and dramatist, best known for his outstanding tragedies.

Garth, Sir Samuel *(1661-1719)*, English poet and physician, author of the burlesque poem *The*

Dispensary.

Gascoigne, George *(c.1525-1577),* English poet and dramatist.

Gautier, Théophile *(1811-1872),* notable French poet, novelist and critic, champion of Romanticism.

Gay, John *(1685-1732),* famous English poet and dramatist who penned the celebrated *The Beggar's Opera.*

Geibel, (Franz) Emanuel *(1815-1884),* German poet and translator.

Geijer, Erik Gustaf *(1783-1847),* distinguished Swedish poet and historian.

Gellert, Christian Fürchtegott *(1715-1769),* German poet and writer.

Genet, Jean *(1910-1986),* French poet, dramatist and novelist whose writings reflected his experiences as a convict and revolutionary.

George, Stefan *(1868-1933),* German poet and translator.

Gessner, Salomon *(1730-1788),* Swiss poet, painter and engraver.

Gezelle, Guido *(1830-1899),* Flemish poet, writer and churchman.

Gibson, Wilfrid Wilson *(1878-1962),* English poet and dramatist.

Gide, André (Paul Guillaume) *(1869-1951),* eminent French poet, novelist, dramatist and critic; won the Nobel Prize for Literature (1947).

Gil Polo, Gaspar *(c.1535-1591),* Spanish poet who won distinction with his *Diana enamorada.*

Gilbert, Sir W(illiam) S(chwenck) *(1836-1911),* remarkable English poet and librettist, famous for his collaboration as librettist with the composer Sir Arthur Sullivan for a resplendent series of renowned operettas.

Gilmore, Dame Mary Jane *(1865-1962),* Australian poet and writer.

Giraudoux, (Hyppolyte-) Jean *(1882-1944),* French poet and novelist.

Giusti, Giuseppe *(1809-1850),* Italian poet, master of political satire.

Glapthorne, Henry *(1610-c.1644),* English dramatist and poet.

Gleim, Johann Wilhelm Ludwig *(1719-1803),* German poet.

Glen, William *(1789-1826),* Scottish poet, author of the Jacobite lament *Wae's me for Prince Charlie.*

Goethe, Johann Wolfgang von *(1749-1832),* great German poet, dramatist and writer whose *Faust* stands as one of the supreme achievements in world literature.

Goldsmith, Oliver *(1730-1774),* notable Irish dramatist, novelist and poet.

Góngora y Argote, Luis de *(1561-1627),* Spanish poet.

Gonzaga, Tomás António *(1744-1810),* Portuguese poet who penned the greatly admired *Marilia de Dirceu* under the name Dirceu.

Googe, Barnabe *(1540-1594),* English poet.

Gordon, Adam Lindsay *(1833-1870),* Australian poet who won great popularity with his ballads.

Gosse, Sir Edmund William *(1849-1928),* English poet and critic.

Gottfried von Strassburg *(13th Century),* German poet and scholar, author of the German version of *Tristan und Isolde.*

Gourmont, Rémy de *(1858-1915),* French poet, novelist and critic.

Gower, John *(c.1325-1408),* notable English poet, author of *Confessio Amantis, Speculum Meditantis* and *Vox Clamantis.*

Grahame, James *(1765-1811),* Scottish poet.

Grant, Anne (née MacVicar) *(1755-1838),* Scottish poet and essayist.

Graves, Robert (Ranke) *(1895-1985),* distinguished English poet, novelist, essayist and critic.

Gray, David *(1838-1861),* Scottish poet.

Gray, Thomas *(1716-1771),* sublime English poet, celebrated for his *Elegy Written in a Country Churchyard.*

Grenvell, Julian (Henry Francis) *(1888-1915),* English poet, admired for his *Into Battle*; died in World War I.

Greville, Fulke, 1st Baron Brooke *(1554-1628),* English poet and courtier.

Grieg, (Johan) Nordahl Brun *(1902-1943),* Norwegian poet and dramatist; as a member of the Resistance, he was killed when his plane was shot down by the Germans.

Grigson, Geoffrey (Edward Harvey) *(1905-1985),* English poet, editor and critic.

Grillparzer, Franz *(1791-1872),* notable Austrian poet and dramatist.

Grimald, Nicholas *(1519-1562),* English poet, dramatist and translator.

Gringore or **Gringoire, Pierre** *(c.1475-1538),* French poet and dramatist.

Grossi, Tommaso *(1791-1853),* Italian poet, best known for his *I Lombardi alla prima crociata.*

Groth, Klaus *(1819-1899),* German poet and writer, esteemed for his poetry collection *Quickborn.*

Grundtvig, N(ikolai) F(rederik) S(everin) *(1783-1872),* Danish theologian and poet.

Gryphius or **Grief, Andreas** *(1616-1664),* German poet and dramatist.

Guarini, Giovanni Battista *(1538-1612),* Italian poet, author of the celebrated *Il Pastor Fido.*

Guérin, Charles *(1873-1907),* French poet who championed Symbolism.

Guérin, Eugénie de *(1805-1848),* French poet and writer; sister of Georges Maurice de Guérin.

Guérin, Georges Maurice de *(1810-1839),* French poet; brother of Eugénie de Guérin.

Guest, Edgar A(lbert) *(1881-1959),* American poet who wrote the popular *A Heap o' Livin.*

Guimerà, Àngel *(1847-1924),* outstanding Catalan dramatist and poet.

Gumilev, Nikolai Stepanovich *(1886-1921),* Russian poet, champion of the Acmeist movement.

Günther, Johann Christian *(1695-1723),* German poet who was admired for his love poems.

Gustafson, Ralph Barker *(1909-1995),* distinguished Canadian poet who was esteemed for his finely crafted verse.

Habington, William *(1605-1654),* English poet, best known for his *Castara.*

Hāfez (actually **Mohammad Shams Od-Dīn Hāfez**) *(c.1325-c.1390),* famous Persian poet, renowned for his mastery of lyricism.

Hafstein, Hannes (Pétursson) *(1861-1922),* Icelandic politician and poet.

Hagedorn, Friedrich von *(1708-1754),* German poet.

Haidari, Buland al- *(1926-1996),* Iraqi poet of Kurdish descent, an exponent of free verse.

Halevi, Judah ben Samuel (actually **Yehuda Ben Shemuel Ha-Levi**) *(1075-1141),* notable Spanish poet, philosopher and physician, renowned for his famous poem *Zionide* (Ode to Zion).

Halévy (actually **Levi**), **Leon** *(1802-1883),* French poet, novelist, historian and translator.

Haliburton, Hugh (actually **James Logie Robertson**) *(1846-1922),* Scottish poet and essayist.

Halifax, Charles Montagu, 1st Earl of *(1661-1715),* English statesman and poet who collaborated with Matthew Prior on *The Town and Country Mouse,* a parody on Dryden's *The Hind and the Panther.*

Hall, Joseph *(1574-1656),* English churchman, poet and writer, esteemed for his book of political satires *Virgidemairum.*

Hall, (Marguerite) Radclyffe *(1886-1943),* English poet and novelist.

Halleck, Fitz-Greene *(1790-1867),* American poet, best known for his satirical *Fanny.*

Hallgrímsson, Jónas *(1807-1845),* outstanding Icelandic poet.

Hamilton, William *(c.1665-1751),* Scottish poet, author of the *Last Dying Words of Bonny Heck.*

Hamilton, William *(1704-1754),* Scottish poet, best remembered for his ballad *The Braes of Yarrow.*

Hampole, Richard Rolle de *(c.1290-1349),* English poet, known as the "Hermit of Hampole".

Hansson, Ola *(1860-1925),* Swedish poet and novelist.

Hardy, Thomas *(1840-1928),* distinguished English novelist, poet and dramatist.

Harris, Maxwell Henley *(1921-1995)*, Australian poet, editor and publisher.

Harry or **Henry the Minstrel** *(15th Century)*, Scottish poet, author of *Wallace*.

Harte, (Francis) Bret(t) *(1836-1902)*, American poet, editor and short-story writer.

Hartmann von Aue *(c.1170-1215)*, German poet, known for his *Der arme Heinrich*.

Harvey, Gabriel *(c.1545-1630)*, English poet of a satirical turn.

Hasenclever, Walter *(1890-1940)*, German dramatist and poet in the Expressionist manner; a pacifist, he committed suicide while confined in a French internment camp.

Hauptmann, Gerhart *(1862-1946)*, distinguished German dramatist and novelist; won the Nobel Prize for Literature (1912).

Hawes, Stephen *(c.1475-1525)*, English poet, author of *The Passetyme of Pleasure*.

Hawker, Robert Stephen *(1803-1875)*, English poet, remembered for his ballads.

Hayley, William *(1745-1820)*, English poet, dramatist, essayist and biographer.

Heine, Heinrich *(1797-1856)*, famous German poet, essayist and champion of democratic ideals.

Heissenbüttel, Helmut *(1921-1996)*, German novelist and poet of avant-garde persuasion.

Hemans, Felicia Dorothea (née Browne) *(1793-1835)*, English poet, particularly known for her *Casabianca*.

Henley, William Ernest *(1849-1903)*, English poet, dramatist, critic and editor.

Henryson, Robert *(c.1425-c.1508)*, Scottish poet, particularly remembered for his *Testament of Cresseid*.

Herbert, George *(1593-1633)*, English poet and churchman, notable figure in the metaphysical movement.

Herder, Johann Gottfried von *(1744-1803)*, influential German critic and poet.

Heredia, José María *(1803-1839)*, Cuban poet; cousin of José María de Heredia.

Heredia, José María de *(1842-1905)*, Cuban-born French poet, especially admired for his sonnets; cousin of José María Heredia.

Hernández, José *(1834-1886)*, Argentine poet, acclaimed for his epic *El gaucho Martín Fierro*.

Herrera, Fernando de *(c.1534-1597)*, Spanish poet, historian and translator.

Herrick, Robert *(1591-1674)*, admired English poet, esteemed for such poems as *Cherry Ripe* and *Gather ye rosebuds while ye may*.

Hertz, Henrik (actually **Heyman**) *(1797-1870)*, Danish poet and dramatist.

Herwegh, Georg *(1817-1875)*, German poet who championed the revolutionary movements of 1848.

Hesiod *(8th Century BC)*, Greek poet, known for the didactic *Theogony* and *Works and Days*.

Hesse, Hermann *(1877-1962)*, eminent German-born Swiss novelist and poet; won the Nobel Prize for Literature (1946).

Hewlett, Maurice Henry *(1861-1923)*, English poet, novelist and essayist, author of the poem *The Song of the Plow*.

Heywood, Thomas *(c.1574-1641)*, English dramatist, poet and actor.

Hill, Aaron *(1685-1750)*, English poet and dramatist.

Hjartarson, Snorri *(1906-1986)*, Icelandic poet.

Hoccleve or **Occleve, Thomas** *(c.1368-c.1450)*, English poet.

Hodgson, Ralph *(1871-1962)*, English poet.

Hoffmann, August Heinrich *(1798-1874)*, German poet and philologist who wrote under the name Hoffmann von Fallersleben in a patriotic vein; his *Deutschland, Deutschland über Alles* was made the National Anthem of Germany (1922).

Hofmannsthal, Hugo von *(1874-1929)*, notable Austrian poet and dramatist, librettist for several operas by Richard Strauss.

Hogg, James *(1770-1835)*, Scottish poet and writer, known as the "Ettrick Shepherd" after his birthplace.

Hölderlin, (Johann Christian) Friedrich *(1770-1843),* great German poet, famous for his mastery of the ode and the elegy.

Holmes, Oliver Wendell *(1809-1894),* prominent American poet, writer and physician, particularly remembered for *The Autocrat of the Breakfast Table.*

Holtei, Karl von *(1798-1880),* German actor, poet and novelist.

Hölty, Ludwig Heinrich Christoph *(1748-1776),* German poet.

Homer *(8th Century BC),* legendary Greek poet, reputedly the author of the epics the *Iliad* and the *Odyssey,* two of the greatest works in world literature.

Hood, Thomas *(1799-1845),* esteemed English poet and editor, master of humorous verse.

Hope, Laurence (actually **Adela Florence Nicolson née Cory**) *(1865-1904),* English poet.

Hopkins, Gerard Manley *(1844-1889),* exquisite English poet, author of such works as *Pied Beauty, The Windhover* and *The Wreck of the Deutschland.*

Horace (actually **Quintus Horatius Flaccus**) *(65-8 BC),* great Roman poet whose satires, odes and epodes stand as monuments in world literature.

Housman, A(lfred) E(dward) *(1859-1936),* distinguished English poet, admired for his *A Shropshire Lad.*

Hroswitha *(c.932-1002),* German poet and Benedictine nun.

Huerta, Vicente García de *(1730-1787),* Spanish poet and critic.

Hughes, (James Mercer) Langston *(1902-1967),* American poet, dramatist and short-story writer.

Hugo, Victor (Marie) *(1802-1885),* celebrated French poet, novelist and dramatist, author of the classic novels *Les Misérables* and *Notre Dame de Paris.*

Hulme, T(homas) E(rnest) *(1883-1917),* English poet, critic and philosopher; died in battle in France in World War I.

Hunt, (James Henry) Leigh *(1784-1859),* English poet and essayist who wrote the poem *The Story of Rimini* while in prison for libelling the Prince Regent.

Hutten, Ulrich von *(1488-1523),* German religious reformer and poet.

Huxley, Aldous (Leonard) *(1894-1963),* notable English novelist, essayist and poet, author of the classic novel *Brave New World.*

Hyslop, James *(1798-1827),* Scottish poet.

Ibn al-'Arabī *(1165-1240),* Arab poet in the mystic tradition.

Ibsen, Henrik (Johan) *(1828-1906),* great Norwegian dramatist and poet of incalculable importance in the development of the modern drama.

Ibycus *(6th Century BC),* Greek poet.

Ingelow, Jean *(1820-1897),* English poet and novelist, particularly remembered for the poem *High Tide on the Coast of Lincolnshire 1571.*

Ingemann, Bernhard Severin *(1789-1862),* Danish poet and novelist.

Iqbāl, Muhammad *(1876-1938),* Indian poet and philosopher.

Iriarte y Oropesa, Tomas de *(1750-1791),* Spanish poet, writer and translator.

Islam, Kazi Nazrul *(1899-1976),* Bengali poet, acclaimed as the national poet of Bangladesh.

Ivanov, Viacheslav Ivanovich *(1866-1949),* Russian poet and critic.

Jacob, Violet (née **Kennedy-Erskine**) *(1863-1946),* Scottish poet and novelist.

Jalāl ad-Dīn ar-Rūmī *(1207-1273),* famous Persian poet and mystic.

Jāmī *(1414-1492),* Persian poet and writer.

Jammes, Francis *(1868-1938),* French poet and writer.

Jarrell, Randall *(1914-1965),* esteemed American poet and critic; committed suicide.

Jasmin (actually **Jacques Boé**) *(1798-1864),* French poet.

Jensen, Johannes Vilhelm *(1873-1950),* eminent Danish novelist, poet and essayist; won the Nobel Prize for Literature (1944).

Jensen, Wilhelm *(1837-1911),* German poet and novelist.

Jiménez, Juan Ramón *(1881-1958),* admired Spanish poet; won the Nobel Prize for Literature (1956).

Jochumsson, Matthías *(1835-1920),* Icelandic poet, translator and churchman, author of the National Anthem of his homeland.

Jodelle, Étienne *(1532-1573),* French poet and dramatist.

Johannes Secundus, Jan Everts or **Everaerts** *(1511-1536),* Dutch poet, known for his Latin work *Basia.*

John of the Cross, St *(1542-1591),* Spanish mystic and poet, esteemed for such poetical works as the *Cantico espiritual* (Spiritual Cantide) and *Noche oscura del alma* (Dark Night of the Soul).

Johnson, Lionel Pigot *(1867-1902),* English poet, remembered for his *By the Statue of King Charles at Charing Cross.*

Johnson, Samuel *(1709-1784),* famous English writer, critic, lexicographer and poet.

Jones, David Michael *(1895-1974),* English poet and artist.

Jones, Ebenezer *(1820-1860),* English poet, author of *Studies of Sensation and Event.*

Jones, Ernest *(1819-1869),* English poet, leader of the Chartrist movement, who wrote the epic *The Revolt of Hindostan* while in prison.

Jonson, Ben *(1572-1637),* famous English dramatist and poet.

Jónsson, Bólu-Hjálmar *(1796-1875),* Icelandic poet.

Jørgensen, (Jens) Johannes *(1866-1956),* Danish novelist, poet and biographer.

Joyce, James (Augustine Aloysius) *(1882-1941),* greatly significant Irish novelist, short-story writer and poet whose novels *Ulysses* and *Finnegan's Wake* changed the course of modern literature.

Junqueiro, Abílio Manuel Guerra *(1850-1923),* Portuguese poet.

Juvenal (actually **Decimus Junius Juvenalis**) *(c.55-c.140),* Roman lawyer and poet, celebrated for his satirical verse.

Kálidása *(5th Century),* great Indian dramatist, renowned for his *Sakuntala.*

Karlfeldt, Erik Axel *(1864-1931),* Swedish poet; posthumously awarded the Nobel Prize for Literature (1931).

Kästner, Erich *(1899-1974),* German poet and novelist.

Kavanagh, Patrick Joseph *(1905-1967),* Irish poet and novelist.

Kazantzákis, Nikos *(1885-1957),* Greek novelist, dramatist and poet.

Keats, John *(1795-1821),* celebrated English poet, master of Romantic expression.

Keble, John *(1792-1866),* English churchman and poet.

Keller, Gottfried *(1819-1890),* Swiss poet and novelist.

Kellgren, Johan Henrik *(1751-1795),* Swedish poet and journalist.

Kerner, Justinus Andreas Christian *(1786-1862),* German poet.

Key, Francis Scott *(1779-1843),* American lawyer and poet, author of the National Anthem of the US, *The Star-Spangled Banner.*

Keyes, Sydney Arthur Kilworth *(1922-1943),* English poet; died in battle in Libya in World War II.

Kilmer, (Alfred) Joyce *(1886-1918),* American poet who wrote the famous *Trees;* died in battle in France in World War I.

Kingo, Thomas Hansen *(1634-1703),* Danish poet and churchman.

Kingsley, Charles *(1819-1875),* popular English poet, novelist, essayist and churchman.

Kinkel, Gottfried *(1815-1882),* German poet.

Kipling, (Joseph) Rudyard *(1865-1936),* famous English poet, short-story writer and novelist; won the Nobel Prize for Literature (1907).

Kleist, (Bernd) Heinrich (Wilhelm) von *(1777-1811),* German dramatist and poet; committed suicide.

Klopstock, Friedrich Gottlieb *(1724-1803),* eminent German poet of religious expression.

Kollár, Ján *(1793-1852),* Czech poet and scholar.

Körner, (Karl) Theodor *(1791-1813),* German poet; died in battle.

Kraszewski, Jósef Ignacy *(1812-1887),* Polish novelist and poet.

Labé or **Charlieu, Louise (Charly Perrin)** *(c.1520-1566),* French poet.

La Fontaine, Jean de *(1621-1695),* eminent French poet, author of the *Contes et nouvelles en vers* and *Fables choises mises en vers.*

Lagerkvist, Pär (Fabian) *(1891-1974),* distinguished Swedish novelist, poet and dramatist; won the Nobel Prize for Literature (1951).

La Harpe, Jean-François de *(1739-1803),* French poet and critic.

Laidlaw, William *(1780-1845),* Scottish poet.

Lalic, Ivan *(1931-1996),* Serbian poet.

Lamartine, Alphonse (Marie Louis) de *(1790-1869),* prominent French poet, historian and statesman.

Lamb, Charles *(1775-1834),* distinctive English essayist and poet, celebrated especially for his mastery of the essay.

La Motte, Antoine Houdar de *(1672-1731),* French poet and dramatist.

Landor, Walter Savage *(1775-1864),* English poet and writer.

Lang, Andrew *(1844-1912),* esteemed Scottish writer and poet.

Langhorne, John *(1735-1779),* English poet and translator.

Langland or **Langley, William** *(c.1332-c.1400),* English poet, author of the celebrated *Vision of William concerning Piers the Plowman.*

Lanier, Sidney *(1842-1881),* American poet, writer, and composer.

Larkin, Philip (Arthur) *(1922-1985),* admired English poet and essayist.

Larra (y Sánchez de Castro), Mariano José de *(1809-1837),* Spanish poet and writer, noted for his satirical bent.

Lavater, Johann Kasper *(1741-1801),* Swiss physiognomist, theologian and poet.

Lawrence, D(avid) H(erbert) *(1885-1930),* famous English novelist, essayist and poet, known for themes of social and sexual liberation.

Layamon *(13th Century),* English poet and priest, author of *Brut,* the first poem written in Middle English.

Lazarus, Emma *(1849-1887),* American poet whose sonnet *The New Colossus* was inscribed on the Statue of Liberty in New York harbour.

Leconte de Lisle, Charles-Marie-Marie *(1818-1894),* French poet and translator.

Le Gallienne, Richard *(1866-1947),* English writer and poet.

Lehmann, John Frederick *(1907-1989),* English poet, novelist, editor and publisher.

Leino, Eino (actually **Armas Eino Leopold Lónnbohm)** *(1878-1926),* Finnish poet, novelist and translator.

Leiris, Michel (Julien) *(1901-1990),* French anthropologist, writer and poet.

Leland, Charles Godfrey *(1825-1903),* American poet who wrote under the name Hans Breitmann various works in "Pennsylvania Dutch", including the celebrated *Hans Breitmann Ballads.*

Le Maire de Belges, Jean *(c.1473-1525),* Flemish poet.

Lemnius, Simon (actually **Margadant)** *(c.1505-1550),* German poet and scholar.

Lenau, Nikolaus (Niembsch von Strehlenau) *(1802-1850),* German poet.

Leopardi, Giacomo *(1798-1837),* remarkable Italian poet and writer, greatly esteemed for his lyricism in the poetry collection *I Canti.*

Lermontov, Mikhail Yurevich *(1814-1841),* famous Russian poet and novelist; killed in a duel.

Lessing, Gotthold Ephraim *(1729-1781),* celebrated German dramatist, poet and scholar, author of the significant treatise *Laokoon,* the outstanding tragedy *Emilia Galotti* and the notable poem *Nathan der Weise.*

Lewis, Alun *(1915-1944),* Welsh poet, short-story writer and soldier; died in the Burma campaign in World War II.

Lewis, Saunders *(1893-1985),* Welsh dramatist, poet, novelist, essayist and critic.

Leyden, John *(1775-1811),* Scottish poet and orientalist, best known for his ballads.

Lie, Jonas (Lauritz Idemil) *(1833-1908),* Norwegian novelist, poet and dramatist.

Liliencron, (Friedrich Adolf Axel) Detlev, Freiherr von *(1844-1909),* German poet, novelist and dramatist.

Lindsay, (Nicholas) Vachel *(1879-1931),* American poet, remembered for his *General Booth Enters Into Heaven* and *The Congo;* committed suicide.

Li Po *(c.700-762),* great Chinese poet whose works celebrated an unrestrained joy of life and nature.

Lissauer, Ernst *(1882-1937),* German poet and dramatist whose World War I poem *Hassgesang gegen England* won great acclaim in his homeland for its refrain *Gott strafe England.*

Livesay, Dorothy (Kathleen May) *(1909-1996),* Canadian poet whose output reflected her preoccupation with feminist and political issues.

Llull, Ramon *(c.1235-1316),* famous Catalan theologian, mystic and poet, known as the "enlightened doctor".

Lobo, Francisco Rodriques *(c.1580-1622),* admired Portuguese poet and writer; drowned in the Tagus.

Locker-Lampson, Frederick *(1821-1895),* English poet, especially known for his witty verse.

Lodge, Thomas *(c.1558-1625),* English dramatist, writer and poet.

Lofft, Capell *(1751-1824),* English poet, writer and lawyer.

Logan, John *(1748-1788),* Scottish poet, dramatist and churchman.

Lomonosov, Mikhail Vasilievich *(1711-1765),* important Russian scientist, literary scholar and poet.

Longfellow, Henry Wadsworth *(1807-1882),* popular American poet, particularly remembered for *The Courtship of Miles Standish, Evangeline, Hiawatha* and *Paul Revere's Ride.*

Lorca, Federico García *(1899-1936),* notable Spanish poet and dramatist; died in the Spanish Civil War.

Lorris, Guillaume de *(13th Century),* French poet.

Louÿs (actually **Louis), Pierre** *(1870-1925),* outstanding French poet and novelist.

Lovecraft, H(oward) P(hillips) *(1890-1937),* American writer and poet, cult figure among science fiction aficionados.

Lovelace, Richard *(1618-1657),* notable English poet whose *To Althea, from Prison* includes the unforgettable lines "Stone walls do not a prison make/Nor iron bars a cage".

Lowell, Amy *(1874-1925),* remarkable American poet in the imagist manner.

Lowell, James Russell *(1819-1891),* prominent American poet, writer and diplomat.

Lowell, Robert (Traill Spence Jr) *(1917-1977),* notable American poet; great-grand-nephew of James Russell Lowell.

Lucan (actually **Marcus Annaeus Lucanus)** *(39-65),* outstanding Roman poet whose only surviving work is the epic *Pharsalia;* committed suicide after the failure of Piso's conspiracy against Nero.

Lucas, F(rank) L(awrence) *(1894-1967),* English poet and critic.

Lucretius (actually **Titus Lucretius Carus)** *(c.99-55 BC),* notable Roman poet and philosopher, author of the masterful *De Natura Rerum.*

Lydgate, John *(c.1370-c.1451),* English monk and poet.

Lyly, John *(c.1554-1606),* English dramatist, novelist and poet, known as the "Euphuist" after his novel *Euphues.*

Lyndsay or **Lindsay, Sir David of the Mount** *(c.1486-1555)*, Scottish poet, author of the major dramatic work *The Satyre of the Thrie Estaitis*.

Lyte, Henry Francis *(1793-1847)*, Scottish poet and hymn-writer who wrote the famous *Abide with me*.

Lyttelton, George, 1st Baron *(1709-1773)*, English politician, writer and poet.

Lytton, Richard George Earle Bulwer-Lytton, 1st Baron *(1803-1873)*, English novelist, dramatist, essayist, poet and politician.

Lytton, (Edward) Robert Bulwer-Lytton, 1st Earl of *(1831-1891)*, English poet, dramatist and statesman who wrote under the name Owen Meredith.

Macaulay, Thomas Babington, 1st Baron Macaulay *(1800-1859)*, prominent English statesman, writer and poet, celebrated for the poetical *Lays of Ancient Rome*.

MacCaig, Norman Alexander *(1910-1996)*, eminent Scottish poet who was greatly esteemed for the extraordinary craftsmanship of his output.

MacCarthy, Denis Florence *(1817-1882)*, Irish poet and writer.

MacDiarmid, Hugh (actually **Christopher Murray Grieve**) *(1892-1978)*, Scottish poet.

MacDonagh, Thomas *(1878-1916)*, notable Irish poet, critic and nationalist who was executed for his role in the Easter Rising.

Macdonald, George *(1824-1905)*, Scottish poet and novelist.

MacGill, Patrick *(1890-1963)*, Irish novelist and poet.

MacGillivray, James Pittendrigh *(1856-1938)*, Scottish sculptor and poet.

Machado y Ruiz, Antonio *(1875-1939)*, Spanish poet and writer; brother of Manuel Machado y Ruiz.

Machado y Ruiz, Manuel *(1874-1947)*, Spanish poet and writer; brother of Antonio Machado y Ruiz.

Mackay, Robert *(1714-1778)*, Scottish-Gaelic poet who wrote under the name Rob Donn.

Maclean, Sorley (actually **Somhairle MacGill-Eain**) *(1911-1996)*, **outstanding Scottish poet, a master of Gaelic verse.**

MacLeish, Archibald *(1892-1982)*, eminent American poet and dramatist.

MacNeice, Louis *(1907-1963)*, Irish poet and critic.

Macpherson, James *(1736-1796)*, Scottish poet who "translated" the epic verse of the legendary poet and warrior Ossian.

Maerlant, Jacob van *(c.1235-c.1300)*, French poet and translator.

Maeterlinck, Maurice (Polydore-Marie-Bernard) *(1862-1949)*, prominent Belgian dramatist and poet; won the Nobel Prize for Literature (1911).

Maevius *(1st Century BC)*, Roman poet.

Maitland, Sir Richard *(1496-1586)*, Scottish lawyer and statesman.

Malherbe, François de *(1555-1628)*, French poet, critic and translator.

Mallarmé, Stéphane *(1842-1898)*, famous French poet and writer of the Symbolist movement, renowned for his *L'Après-midi d'un faune*.

Mallet (actually **Malloch), David** *(c.1705-1765)*, Scottish poet and dramatist.

Mameli, Goffredo *(1827-1849)*, Italian poet and patriot; died while defending Rome against the French.

Mandelstam, Osip (Yemilievich) *(1891-1938)*, outstanding Russian poet, critic and translator who died a victim of Stalin's tyranny.

Mangan, James Clarence *(1803-1849)*, Irish poet and translator.

Manrique, Jorge *(1440-1479)*, Spanish poet.

Manzoni, Alessandro *(1785-1873)*, outstanding Italian novelist, poet and statesman, author of the notable novel *I Promessi Sposi*.

March, Ausiàs *(1397-1459)*, Catalan poet.

Marie de France *(12th Century)*, French poet who penned the remarkable *Lais*.

Marini, Giambattista *(1569-1625)*, Italian poet.

Marot, Clément *(c.1497-1544)*, remarkable French poet.

Marquis, Don(ald Robert Perry) *(1878-1937)*, American novelist, dramatist and poet.

Marston, John *(1576-1634)*, English dramatist, poet and churchman.

Marston, John Westland *(1819-1890)*, English dramatist and critic; father of Philip Bourke Marston.

Marston, Philip Bourke *(1850-1887)*, English poet and short-story writer; son of John Westland Marston.

Martial (actually **Marcus Valerius Martialis**) *(c.40-c.140)*, celebrated Roman poet, unmatched for his mastery of the epigram.

Martinson, Harry Edmund *(1904-1978)*, Swedish poet and novelist; won the Nobel Prize for Literature (1974).

Marvell, Andrew *(1621-1678)*, notable English poet and writer.

Masefield, John *(1878-1967)*, esteemed English poet and novelist; became Poet Laureate of the United Kingdom (1930).

Mason, William *(1725-1797)*, English poet and churchman.

Massey, Gerald *(1828-1907)*, English poet, writer and mystic.

Massinger, Philip *(1583-1640)*, English dramatist and poet.

Masters, Edgar Lee *(1869-1950)*, celebrated American poet and writer, renowned for his *Spoon River Anthology* and *The New Spoon River*.

Mauriac, François *(1885-1970)*, distinguished French novelist and poet; won the Nobel Prize for Literature (1952).

May, Thomas *(1595-1650)*, English dramatist, poet, historian and translator.

Mayakovsky, Vladimir Vladimirovich *(1893-1930)*, famous Russian poet and dramatist; committed suicide.

McGee, Thomas D'Arcy *(1825-1868)*, Irish-born Canadian poet, writer and politician.

McGonagall, William *(1830-1902)*, Scottish poet and novelist.

McIntyre, Duncan (actually **Donnchad Bàn Macan t-Saoir**) *(1724-1812)*, Scottish-Gaelic poet.

Mei Sheng *(d. 140 BC)*, Chinese poet.

Meinhold, Johann Wilhelm *(1797-1815)*, German pastor, poet and dramatist.

Meleager *(1st Century BC)*, Greek poet, admired for his elegies and epigrams.

Meléndez Valdés, Juan *(1754-1817)*, Spanish poet, esteemed for his fine gift for lyricism.

Melo, Francisco Manuel de *(1608-1666)*, Portuguese soldier, historian, critic and poet.

Menander *(342-292 BC)*, great Greek dramatist, master of comedic writing.

Mendès, Catulle *(1843-1909)*, French poet, dramatist and writer.

Mendoza, Iñigo López de, marqués de Santillana *(15th Century)*, prominent Spanish statesman and poet.

Menéndez y Pelayo, Marcelino *(1856-1912)*, eminent Spanish scholar and poet.

Meredith, George *(1828-1909)*, notable English novelist and poet.

Merezhkovski, Dmitri Sergeievich *(1865-1941)*, Russian novelist, poet and critic.

Merrill, James Ingram *(1926-1995)*, eminent American poet whose output was highly esteemed for its mastery of lyric and epic writing.

Merrill, Stuart Fitzrandolph *(1863-1915)*, American poet who write fine works in the Symbolist manner.

Merriman, Brian *(1747-1805)*, Irish-Gaelic poet, author of the satirical and erotic mock-heroic epic *Cuirt an Mheanin Oidhche* (The Midnight Court).

Metastasio, Pietro (actually **Pietro Antonio Domenico Bonaventura Trapassi**) *(1698-1782)*, famous Italian poet who wrote the librettos for many outstanding operas.

Meun, Jean de *(c.1250-1305)*, French poet and translator, well known for his satirical bent.

Meyer, Conrad Ferdinand *(1825-1898),* Swiss poet and novelist.

Meynell, Alice (Christiana Gertrude née Thompson) *(1847-1922),* English essayist and poet.

Mickiewicz, Adam (Bernard) *(1798-1855),* great Polish poet, acclaimed as the national poet of his homeland.

Mickle, William Julius *(1735-1788),* Scottish poet, best remembered for his *There's nae luck aboot the hoose.*

Millay, Edna St Vincent *(1892-1950),* prominent American poet, admired for her *The Harp Weaver and Other Poems.*

Miller, Joaquin (actually **Cincinnatus Heine**) *(1837-1913),* American poet and writer.

Miller, William *(1810-1872),* Scottish poet, remembered for his *Wee Willie Winkie.*

Milman, Henry Hart *(1791-1868),* English poet and historian.

Milne, A(lan) A(lexander) *(1882-1956),* English writer and poet, celebrated for his verse for children, especially his *Winnie-the-Pooh.*

Milnes, Richard Monckton, 1st Baron Houghton *(1809-1885),* English politician, essayist and poet.

Milton, John *(1608-1674),* great English poet and writer, author of the masterful epic *Paradise Lost.*

Miron, Gaston *(1928-1996),* **French-Canadian poet.**

Mistral, Frédéric *(1830-1914),* esteemed French poet; won the Nobel Prize for Literature (1904).

Mistral, Gabriela (actually **Lucila Godoy de Alcayaga**) *(1889-1957),* Chilean poet; won the Nobel Prize for Literature (1945).

Mitford, John *(1781-1859),* English clergyman, writer and poet.

Moe, Jørgen Engebretsen *(1813-1882),* Norwegian poet and folklorist.

Moir, David Macbeth *(1798-1851),* Scottish physician and poet who wrote under the name Delta.

Molière (actually **Jean-Baptiste Poquelin**) *(1622-1673),* great French dramatist and poet, master of the theatre.

Möller, Poul Martin *(1794-1838),* Danish writer and poet.

Monroe, Harriet *(1860-1936),* American poet and critic.

Montale, Eugenio *(1896-1981),* fine Italian poet; won the Nobel Prize for Literature (1975).

Montemayor, Jorge de *(c.1515-1561),* Spanish novelist and poet.

Montgomerie, Alexander *(c.1545-c.1611),* Scottish poet, best known for his *Cherrie and the Slae* and *To his Mistress.*

Montgomery, James *(1771-1854),* Scottish poet.

Montgomery, Robert *(1807-1855),* English preacher and poet.

Morti, Vincenzo *(1754-1828),* Italian poet.

Moore, Marianne (Craig) *(1887-1972),* distinguished American poet, essayist and editor.

Moore, Thomas *(1779-1852),* renowned Irish poet, author of *Irish Melodies, Lalla Rookh* and *The Loves of the Angels.*

Moore, Thomas Sturge *(1870-1944),* English poet, critic and wood engraver.

Morant, Harry Harbord *(1865-1902),* English-born Australian adventurer and poet; executed by firing squad for murderous actions he committed during the Boer War.

Morata, Olympia *(1526-1555),* Italian poet and scholar.

Moratín, Leandro (Fernández) de *(1760-1828),* Spanish poet and dramatist.

Moréas, Jean (actually **Yannis Papadiamantópoulos**) *(1856-1910),* Greek-born French poet, founder of the Symbolist movement.

Mörike, Eduard Friedrich *(1804-1875),* German poet and novelist.

Morley, Christopher (Darlington) *(1890-1957),* American novelist, essayist and poet.

Morris, George Pope *(1802-1864),* American journalist and poet, best remembered for his poem *Woodman, Spare that Tree.*

Morris, Sir Lewis *(1833-1907),* Welsh poet, dramatist and barrister.

Morris, William *(1834-1896),* English craftsman, socialist, poet and writer.

Mourão-Ferreira, David *(1927-1996),* Portuguese writer and poet.

Muir, Edwin *(1887-1959),* prominent Scottish poet and critic.

Munday, Anthony *(c.1560-1633),* English poet and dramatist.

Mure, Sir William *(1594-1657),* Scottish poet.

Muret, Marc Antoine *(1526-1585),* French poet and scholar.

Murger, (Louis-) Henri *(1822-1861),* French writer and poet.

Murray, Charles *(1864-1941),* Scottish poet.

Murry, John Middleton *(1889-1957),* influential English editor, critic, essayist and poet.

Musaeus *(5th-6th Century),* Greek poet, author of the famous *Hero and Leander.*

Musset, (Louis-Charles-) Alfred de *(1810-1857),* notable French poet and dramatist.

Myers, Ernest James *(1844-1921),* English poet and translator; brother of Frederic William Henry Myers.

Myers, Frederic William Henry *(1843-1901),* English poet and essayist; brother of Ernest James Myers.

Naevius, Gnaeus *(c.270-c.199 BC),* Roman poet and dramatist.

Naidu, Sarojini (née Chattopadhyay) *(1879-1949),* Indian feminist and poet, known as the "nightingale of India".

Nash, (Frederic) Ogden *(1902-1971),* popular American poet, master of wit.

Nashe, Thomas *(1567-1601),* English dramatist, noted for his satire.

Nazor, Vladimir *(1876-1949),* Croatian poet.

Negri, Ada *(1870-1945),* Italian poet and short-story writer.

Nekrasov, Nikolai Alexeievich *(1821-1878),* Russian poet.

Nemerov, Howard *(1920-1991),* admired American poet, writer, and essayist; was Poet Laureate of the US (1988-90).

Neruda, Pablo (Neftali Reyes) *(1904-1973),* prominent Chilean poet; won the Nobel Prize for Literature (1971).

Nerval (actually Labrunie), Gerárd de *(1808-1855),* French writer and poet; dissipation and insanity prompted him to commit suicide.

Newbolt, Sir Henry John *(1862-1939),* English poet and historian, remembered for his sea lyrics.

Noailles, Anna(-Élisabeth), Comtesse de *(1876-1933),* French poet and novelist who was dubbed the "Princesse des lettres".

Nordal, Sigurour (Jóhanneson) *(1886-1974),* Icelandic scholar, poet and short-story writer.

Norton, Caroline Elizabeth Sarah (née Sheridan) *(1808-1877),* Irish poet and novelist.

Novalis (actually **Friedrich Leopold, Freiherr von Hardenberg)** *(1772-1801),* important German poet and novelist, known as the "Prophet of Romanticism".

Noyes, Alfred *(1880-1958),* English poet and dramatist.

Núñez de Arce, Gaspar *(1832-1903),* Spanish poet, dramatist and statesman.

Ó Bruadair, Dáibhidh (David) *(c.1625-1698),* compelling Irish-Gaelic poet.

Oehlenschläger, Adam Gottlob *(1779-1850),* notable Danish poet and dramatist who was acclaimed as the national poet of his homeland.

Ofterdingen, Heinrich von *(12th-13th Century),* celebrated German Minnesinger.

Omar Khayyám *(c.1048-c.1122),* renowned Persian poet, mathematician and astronomer whose *Rubaiyat* are celebrated the world over.

Ormond, John *(1923-1990),* Welsh poet and filmmaker of distinction.

O'Shaughnessy, Arthur (William Edgar), *(1844-1881),* English poet, best known for his *The Music-Makers.*

Ó Súilleabháin, Eoghan Ruadh or **Red Owen O'Sullivan** *(1748-1784),* adventurous Irish-Gaelic poet.

Otway, Thomas *(1652-1685),* notable English dramatist and poet, author of the remarkable drama *Venice Preserved, or a Plot Discovered* and of the fine poem *The Poet's Complaint of his Muse.*

Overbury, Sir Thomas *(1581-1613),* English courtier and poet whose life of intrigue led to his death in the Tower of London.

Øverland, Arnulf *(1889-1968),* Norwegian poet.

Ovid (actually **Publius Ovidius Naso)** *(43 BC-17 AD),* famous Roman poet, celebrated for his *Ars Armatoria* and *Metamorphoses.*

Owen, Wilfrid *(1893-1918),* distinguished English poet who wrote such notable works as *Anthem for doomed Youth* and *Dulce et Decorum Est*; killed in France a week before the Armistice ending World War I.

Palgrave, Francis Turner *(1824-1897),* English poet, critic and editor.

Parini, Giuseppe *(1729-1799),* Italian poet, known for his *Il Giorno.*

Parker, Dorothy (née Rothschild) *(1893-1967),* notable American short-story writer, poet and critic, celebrated for her telling wit.

Parnell, Thomas *(1679-1718),* Irish poet and churchman, author of *The Hermit, Hymn to Contentment* and *The Nightpiece of Death.*

Pascoli, Giovanni *(1855-1912),* Italian poet and writer.

Pasolini, Pier Paolo *(1922-1975),* Italian poet, novelist, critic and film director; was murdered.

Pasternak, Boris Leonidovich *(1890-1960),* renowned Russian poet, novelist and translator whose famous novel *Dr Zhivago* stands as an indictment of the 1917 Bolshevik Revolution; won the Nobel Prize for Literature (1958) but was compelled to refuse it.

Paterson, A(ndrew) B(arton) "Banjo" *(1864-1941),* Australian journalist and poet, author of *Waltzing Matilda,* which was made the national song of Australia.

Patmore, Coventry (Kersey Dighton) *(1823-1896),* English poet, best remembered for his proper Victorian sentiments in the collection *The Angel in the House.*

Pavese, Cesare *(1908-1950),* leading Italian novelist, poet, critic and translator; committed suicide.

Peacock, Thomas Love *(1785-1866),* English novelist and poet.

Peake, Mervyn Laurence *(1911-1968),* English novelist, poet and artist.

Pearse, Patrick or **Padraic Henry** *(1879-1916),* Irish nationalist, poet, short-story writer and dramatist; as commander-in-chief of the insurgent forces in the failed Easter Rising, he was executed.

Peele, George *(c.1558-1598),* English actor, dramatist and poet.

Péguy, Charles Pierre *(1873-1914),* French nationalist, publisher and poet; died in World War I.

Pellico, Silvio *(1789-1854),* Italian patriot, poet and dramatist.

Percival, James Gates *(1795-1856),* American poet and chemist.

Pérez de Ayala, Ramón *(1880-1962),* Spanish novelist, poet and critic.

Persius (actually **Aulus Persius Flaccus**) *(34-62),* Roman poet, known for his satires.

Petersen, Nis *(1897-1943),* Danish poet and novelist.

Petőfi, Sándor *(1823-1849),* important Hungarian poet, founder of the new style of Hungarian verse; died in battle.

Petrarch (actually **Francesco Petrarca**) *(1304-1374),* great Italian poet and scholar, renowned for the extraordinary beauty of his lyricism.

Petronious Arbiter *(1st Century),* famous Roman writer and poet, celebrated for his *Satyricon*; committed suicide.

Pétursson, Hallgrímur *(1614-1674),* significant Icelandic poet whose mastery was revealed in his *Passion Hymns.*

Philips, Ambrose *(c.1674-1749),* English poet.

Philips, John *(1676-1709),* English poet, known for his *Blenheim, Cyder* and *The Spendid Shilling.*

Philips, Katherine (née Fowler) *(1631-1664),* English poet who wrote under the name Orinda.

Phillpotts, Eden *(1862-1960),* English novelist, dramatist and poet.

Picken, Ebenezer *(1769-1816),* Scottish poet.

Pindar (actually **Pindaros**) *(c.522-c.440 BC),* celebrated Greek poet renowned for his odes.

Piozzi or **Thrale, Mrs Hester Lynch (née Salusbury)** *(1741-1821),* Welsh writer and poet.

Piron, Alexis *(1689-1773),* French poet and dramatist, especially admired for his wit.

Plath, Sylvia *(1932-1963),* revealing American poet; committed suicide.

Plautus, Titus Maccius or **Maccus** *(c.250-184 BC),* renowned Roman dramatist, known for his comic works.

Plomer, William (Charles Franklin) *(1903-1973),* English poet and writer.

Po-Chü-I *(772-846),* eminent Chinese poet.

Poe, Edgar Allan *(1809-1849),* imaginative American poet and writer whose poetic genius is equalled in his prose by his mastery of the macabre.

Politian (actually **Angelo Poliziano** or **Ambrogini**) *(1454-1494),* distinguished Italian poet and scholar.

Ponce de Léon, Luis *(1527-1591),* notable Spanish poet, scholar and monk.

Pope, Alexander *(1688-1744),* famous English poet and translator, master of satire.

Porta, Carlo *(1776-1821),* Italian poet.

Pound, Ezra (Loomis) *(1885-1972),* highly significant American poet, critic and translator, author of the challenging *Cantos.*

Prati, Giovanni *(1815-1884),* Italian poet.

Prévert, Jacques *(1900-1977),* French poet and screenwriter.

Pringle, Thomas *(1789-1834),* Scottish writer and poet.

Prior, Matthew *(1664-1721),* prominent English poet and diplomat, best remembered for his witty verse.

Procter, Adelaide Ann *(1825-1864),* English poet who wrote under the name Mary Berwick, winning special recognition for her *Legends and Lyrics* and *The Lost Chord*; daughter of Bryan Walker Procter.

Procter, Bryan Walker *(1787-1874),* English poet who wrote under the name of Barry Cornwall; father of Adelaide Ann Procter.

Propertius, Sextus *(c.48-c.15 BC),* Roman poet, known for his elegiac effusions to his mistress Cynthia.

Prudentius, Aurelius Clemens *(348-c.410),* esteemed Latin poet who excelled in Christian themes.

Prys-Jones, Arthur Glyn *(1888-1987),* eminent Welsh poet.

Pulci, Luigi *(1432-1484),* Italian poet, author of the burlesque epic in Tuscan dialect *Il Morgante Maggiore.*

Pushkin, Alexander Sergeievich *(1799-1837),* great Russian poet, acclaimed as the national poet of his homeland; killed in a duel upholding his wife's honour.

Quarles, Francis *(1592-1644),* English poet and writer.

Quasimodo, Salvatore *(1901-1968),* notable Italian poet; won the Nobel Prize for Literature (1959).

Quental, Antero Tarquínio de *(1842-1891),* Portuguese poet; committed suicide.

Quevedo y Villegas, Francisco Gómez de *(1580-1645),* distinguished Spanish poet and writer.

Quiller-Couch, Sir Arthur Thomas *(1863-1944),* English poet, novelist, essayist and critic.

Quintana, Manuel José *(1772-1857),* eminent Spanish poet; became the national poet of his homeland (1855).

Racine, Jean *(1639-1699),* great French dramatist and poet, master of the tragedy.

Radiguet, Raymond *(1903-1923),* gifted French novelist and poet who was hailed as the "Rimbaud of the novel" and whose early death was lamented.

Rahbek, Knud Lyne *(1760-1830),* Danish poet, dramatist, critic and editor.

Raleigh, Sir Walter *(1554-1618),* famous English courtier, navigator and poet; beheaded.

Ramsay, Allan *(1686-1758),* Scottish poet, best known for his *The Gentle Shepherd, a Pastoral Comedy.*

Randall, James Ryder *(1839-1908),* American poet who extolled the Confederacy.

Randolph, Thomas *(1605-1635),* English poet and dramatist.

Ransom, John Crowe *(1888-1974),* American poet and critic.

Raynouard, François-Juste-Marie *(1761-1836),* French poet and philologist.

Régnier, Henri(-François-Joseph) de *(1864-1936),* French poet, novelist and critc, proponent of Symbolism.

Rhigas, Konstantinos *(1760-1798),* Greek poet and revolutionary; as organizer of the anti-Turkish revolutionary movement in Vienna, he was betrayed and killed.

Rhys, Ernest Percival *(1859-1946),* English editor, writer and poet.

Richards, I(vor) A(rmstrong) *(1893-1979),* English poet and critic.

Richepin, Jean *(1849-1926),* French poet, dramatist and novelist.

Richter, Johann Friedrich *(1763-1825),* famous German novelist, writer and poet, renowned for his *Titan,* who was also known under the name Jean Paul.

Riding, Laura (actually **Laura Reichenthal**) *(1901-1991),* American poet, novelist and critic.

Riley, James Whitcomb *(1849-1916),* American poet, known as the "Hoosier poet", who won success for his homely dialect verses.

Rilke, Rainer Maria *(1875-1926),* outstanding Austrian poet, celebrated for his *Duineser Elegien* and *Die Sonnette an Orpheus.*

Rimbaud, (Jean-Nicolas-) Arthur *(1854-1891),* celebrated French poet, author of the masterful *Les Illuminations.*

Rinuccini, Ottavio *(1562-1621),* Italian poet.

Robinson, Edward Arlington *(1869-1935),* American poet.

Rochester, John Wilmot, 2nd Earl of *(1647-1680),* English courtier and poet.

Roethke, Theodore *(1908-1963),* American poet, best remembered for his *The Waking.*

Rogers, Samuel *(1763-1855),* English poet.

Rolle de Hampole, Richard *(c.1295-1349),* English hermit, mystic and poet.

Ronsard, Pierre de *(1524-1585),* celebrated French poet, master of Gallic verse.

Rosa, Salvator *(1615-1673),* Italian painter and poet.

Rosegger, Peter *(1843-1918),* Austrian poet and novelist.

Rosenberg, Isaac *(1890-1918),* English poet and artist; died in World War I.

Rossetti, Christina Georgina *(1830-1894),* admired English poet, esteemed for her collection *Goblin Market;* daughter of Gabriele Pasquale Rossetti and sister of Dante Gabriel Rossetti.

Rossetti, Dante Gabriel (actually **Gabriel Charles Dante Rossetti**) *(1828-1882),* famous English poet, translator and painter; son of Gabriele Pasquale Rossetti and brother of Christina Georgina Rossetti.

Rossetti, Gabriele Pasquale *(1783-1854),* Italian poet and writer; father of Christina Georgina and Dante Gabriel Rossetti.

Rostand, Edmond *(1868-1918),* French poet and dramatist, particularly known for his drama *Cyrano de Bergerac.*

Rouget de Lisle, Claude-Joseph *(1760-1836),* French poet and writer, author of the words and composer of the music of the French National Anthem, the *Marseillaise.*

Roumanille, Joseph *(1818-1891),* French poet and writer.

Rowe, Nicholas *(1674-1718),* English poet and dramatist; became Poet Laureate of the United Kingdom (1715).

Rozhdestvensky, Robert Ivanovich *(1932-1994),* Russian poet.

Ruccellai, Giovanni *(1475-1525),* Italian poet and dramatist.

Rückert, Friedrich *(1788-1866),* prominent German poet and scholar.

Runeberg, Johan Ludvig *(1804-1877),* eminent Finnish poet and dramatist, author of *Vårt land* (Our Land), which became the Finnish National Anthem.

Russell, George William *(1867-1935),* notable Irish poet, painter, writer and economist who wrote under the name AE.

Sachs, Hans *(1494-1576),* famous German poet, dramatist and writer.

Sachs, Nelly (Leonie) *(1891-1970),* distinguished German-born Swedish poet and dramatist; was co-winner of the Nobel Prize for Literature (1966).

Sackville, Charles, 6th Earl of Dorset *(1638-1706),* English courtier and poet.

Sackville, Thomas, 1st Earl of Dorset *(1536-1608),* English statesman and poet.

Sackville-West, Victoria (Mary) *(1892-1962),* English poet and novelist.

Sa'dī *(c.1213-1292),* celebrated Persian poet and writer, renowned for his *Būstān* (The Orchard) and his *Golestān* (The Rose Garden).

Saint-Amant, Marc-Antoine Girard sieur de *(1594-1661),* French poet.

Sainte-Beuve, Charles Augustin *(1804-1869),* famous French critic, writer, and poet.

Saint-John Perse (actually **Marie René Auguste Alexis Saint-Léger Léger)** *(1887-1975),* French poet and diplomat; won the Nobel Prize for Literature (1960).

Saintine or **Boniface, Joseph Xavier** *(1798-1865),* French dramatist, poet and writer.

Samain, Albert Victor *(1844-1910),* French poet.

Sandburg, Carl *(1878-1967),* popular American poet and biographer of Abraham Lincoln.

Sannazzaro, Jacopo *(1456-1530),* Italian poet.

Santayana, George *(1863-1952),* Spanish philosopher, critic, novelist and poet.

Sappho *(6th Century BC),* celebrated Greek poet, renowned for her love poems.

Sarton, May (actually **Eléanore Marie Sarton)** *(1912-1995),* American poet and writer who became a cult figure in feminist circles.

Sassoon, Siegfried (Lorraine) *(1886-1967),* eminent English poet and novelist.

Savage, Richard *(c.1697-1743),* English poet, remembered for his dissolute life and the poem *The Wanderer.*

Scarron, Paul *(1610-1660),* notable French poet and novelist, creator of the realistic novel.

Scève, Maurice *(1501-1564),* French poet.

Schaukal, Richard *(1874-1942),* Austrian poet of the Symbolist persuasion.

Scheffel, (Joseph) Viktor von *(1826-1886),* German poet and novelist.

Schickele, René *(1883-1940),* Alsatian poet, dramatist and novelist.

Schiller, (Johann Christoph) Friedrich (von) *(1759-1805),* great German dramatist, poet and historian, author of the celebrated dramatic trilogy *Wallenstein.*

Schimper, Carl Friedrich (1803-1867), German naturalist and poet.

Schlegel, August Wilhelm von *(1767-1845),* eminent German critic, translator and editor, a pioneering figure in the Romantic movement; brother of (Karl Wilhelm) Friedrich von Schlegel.

Schlegel, (Karl Wilhelm) Friedrich von *(1772-1829),* distinguished German critic, editor and linguist, a pioneering figure in the Romantic movement; brother of August Wilhelm von Schlegel.

Schubart, Christian Friedrich Daniel *(1739-1791),* German poet.

Schwartz, Delmore *(1913-1966),* esteemed American poet, critic, writer and dramatist.

Scott, Alexander *(c.1525-c.1585),* Scottish poet.

Scott, Sir Walter *(1771-1832),* renowned Scottish novelist and poet.

Scotti, William Bell *(1811-1890),* Scottish painter and poet.

Seaman, Sir Owen *(1861-1936),* English poet and editor.

Sedley, Sir Charles *(1639-1701),* English courtier, poet and dramatist, best remembered for his debauchery and wit at court.

Seferiades, Georgios *(1900-1971),* Greek poet and diplomat who wrote under the name Seferis; won the Nobel Prize for Literature (1963).

Seifert, Jaroslav *(1901-1986),* distinguished Czech poet; won the Nobel Prize for Literature (1984).

Sempill, Robert *(c.1530-1595),* English poet, known for his wit and satire.

Sempill, Robert *(c.1595-c.1665),* Scottish poet.

Seneca, Lucius Annaeus, the Younger *(c.4 BC-65 AD),* celebrated Roman philosopher, statesman and dramatist whose verse tragedies proved influential; committed suicide after the failure of Piso's conspiracy against Nero.

Service, Robert W(illiam) *(1874-1958),* English-born Canadian poet and novelist.

Seward, Anna *(1747-1809),* English poet, known as the "Swan of Lichfield".

Sexton, Anne (née Harvey) *(1928-1974),* American poet; committed suicide.

Shadwell, Thomas *(c.1642-1692),* prominent English dramatist; became Poet Laureate of United Kingdom (1688).

Shakespeare, William *(1564-1616),* immortal English dramatist and poet, celebrated the world over as one of the supremem geniuses of literature.

Shaw, George Bernard *(1856-1950),* famous Irish dramatist, essayist, critic and socialist; won the Nobel Prize for Literature (1925).

Shelley, Mary Wollstonecraft (née Godwin) *(1797-1851),* English novelist, poet and dramatist; wife of Percy Bysshe Shelley.

Shelley, Percy Bysshe *(1792-1822),* celebrated English poet of extraordinary gifts; drowned when his schooner was overturned in a squall in Italy.

Shenstone, William *(1714-1763),* English poet, known for *The Schoolmistress.*

Sheridan, Richard Brinsley (Butler) *(1751-1816),* famous Irish dramatist.

Shevchenko, Taras Grigorievich *(1814-1861),* Ukrainian poet and writer.

Shirely, James *(1596-1666),* outstanding English dramatist, famous for his comedy *The Lady of Pleasure* and for his tragedy *The Traytor*; victim of the Great Fire of London.

Sidney, Sir Philip *(1554-1586),* illustrious English poet, author of *Arcadia, Astrophel and Stella* and *A Defence of Poetry*; died from a wound sustained in an attack on a Spanish convoy.

Sidonius Apollinaris, St (actually **Gaius Sollius)** *(c.430-c.483),* Gallic-Roman poet who was canonized by the Roman Catholic Church.

Sigurjónsson, Jóhann *(1880-1919),* notable Icelandic dramatist and poet.

Silius Italicus (actually **Tiberius Catius Asconius Silius Italicus)** *(25-101),* Roman poet and politician; committed suicide by starving.

Simonides of Ceos *(556-468 BC),* Greek poet.

Sitwell, Dame Edith (Louisa) *(1887-1964),* esteemed English poet and writer whose works included *Elegy for Dead Fashion, Façade* and *Gold Coast Customs*; sister of Sir Osbert and Sacheverell Sitwell.

Sitwell, Sir (Francis) Osbert (Sacheverell) *(1892-1969),* prominent English poet and writer; brother of Dame Edith and Sacheverell Sitwell.

Sitwell, Sir Sacheverell, 6th Baronet *(1897-1988),* notable English writer, art critic, and poet; brother of Dame Edith and Sir Osbert Sitwell.

Skelton, John *(c.1460-1529),* English poet, known for his satirical effusions.

Slessor, Kenneth Adolf *(1901-1971)*, Australian poet and journalist.

Słowacki, Juljusz *(1809-1849)*, remarkable Polish poet and dramatist.

Smart, Christopher *(1722-1771)*, English poet and translator, particularly known for his *A Song to David*.

Smith, Alexander *(1830-1867)*, Scottish poet and essayist.

Smith, Stevie (actually **Florence Margaret Smith**) *(1902-1971)*, English poet and novelist.

Smith, Sydney Goodsir *(1915-1975)*, New Zealand-born Scottish poet.

Södergran, Edith (Irene) *(1892-1923)*, significant Finnish poet, founder of the modernist movement of the Finnish poets writing in Swedish.

Solís y Ribadeneyra, Antonio de *(1610-1686)*, Spanish poet and dramatist.

Solon *(c.640-559 BC)*, renowned Greek lawgiver and poet.

Somerville, William *(1675-1742)*, English poet.

Sophocles *(c.496-406 BC)*, great Greek dramatist, master of the tragedy.

Sorley, Charles Hamilton *(1895-1915)*, Scottish poet; died in World War I.

Soutar, William *(1898-1943)*, Scottish poet and diarist.

Southey, Robert *(1774-1843)*, notable English poet and writer; became Poet Laureate of the United Kingdom (1813).

Southwell, Robert *(c.1561-1595)*, English poet and Jesuit, author of *The Burning Babe*; was martyred.

Spence, (James) Lewis Thomas Chalmers *(1874-1955)*, Scottish poet and anthropologist.

Spender, Sir Stephen (Harold) *(1909-1995)*, eminent English poet and critic, influential figure of the Oxford generation.

Spenser, Edmund *(c.1552-1599)*, great English poet who penned the celebrated *The Faerie Queene*.

Spitteler, Carl Friedrich Georg *(1845-1924)*, Swiss poet and novelist; won the Nobel Prize for Literature (1919).

Spottiswoode, Alicia Ann, Lady John Scott *(1810-1900)*, Scottish poet and songwriter, particularly remembered for her *Annie Laurie* and *Durrisdeer*.

Ssu-ma Hsiang-ju *(179-117 BC)*, important Chinese poet, master of descriptive verse.

Stagnelius, Erik Johan *(1793-1823)*, significant Swedish poet of the Romantic movement.

Statius, Publius Papinius *(c.45-96)*, Roman poet, admired for his *Silvae* and *Thebaïs*.

Stedman, Edmund Clarence *(1833-1908)*, American poet, critic and financier.

Steele, Sir Richard *(1672-1729)*, Irish essayist, dramatist and politician.

Stendahl (actually **Marie-Henri Beyle**) *(1783-1842)*, famous French novelist and writer, celebrated for his novels *La Chartreuse de Parme* and *Le Rouge et le Noir*.

Stephansson, Stephen G (actually **Stefán Guðmundarson**) *(1853-1927)*, Icelandic-born Canadian poet.

Stephens, James *(1882-1950)*, Irish poet.

Sterling, John *(1806-1844)*, Scottish essayist and poet.

Stevens, Wallace *(1879-1955)*, remarkable American poet.

Stevenson, Robert Louis (Balfour) *(1850-1894)*, famous Scottish writer and poet, celebrated for such works as *A Child's Garden of Verses*, *Kidnapped*, *The Strange Case of Dr Jekyll and Mr Hyde* and *Treasure Island.*

Stewart, Douglas Alexander *(1913-1985),* New Zealand-born Australian poet, dramatist, writer and critic.

Stiernhielm, Georg (Olofson) *(1598-1672),* eminent Swedish poet and linguist, known as the "father" of Swedish poetry.

Stirling, William Alexander, 1st Earl of *(c.1576-1640),* Scottish courtier and poet.

Stoddard, Richard Henry *(1825-1903),* American poet and critic.

Stolberg, Christian, Count of *(1748-1821),* German poet and translator; brother of Friedrich Leopold Stolberg.

Stolberg, Friedrich Leopold, Count of *(1750-1819),* German poet, dramatist and translator; brother of Christian Stolberg.

Storm, (Hans) Theodor Woldsen *(1817-1888),* German poet and writer.

Storni, Alfonsina *(1892-1938),* Argentine poet; committed suicide.

Story, William Wetmore *(1891-1895),* American poet and sculptor.

Strindberg, (Johan) August *(1849-1912),* famous Swedish dramatist and novelist who greatly influenced the development of modern drama.

Strode, William *(c.1599-1645),* English churchman and poet.

Strong, Leonard Alfred George *(1896-1958),* English novelist and poet.

Stuckenberg, Viggo *(1863-1905),* Danish poet.

Sturluson, Snorri *(1179-1241),* Icelandic chieftan, historian and poet.

Sully Prudhomme (actually **René-François-Armand Prudhomme**) *(1839-1907),* distinguished French poet and writer; won the first Nobel Prize for Literature (1901).

Supervielle, Jules *(1884-1960),* Uruguayan-born French poet and writer.

Surrey, Henry Howard, Earl of *(c.1517-1547),* English courtier and poet; was executed for high treason.

Su Tung-P'o (actually **Su Shih**) *(1036-1101),* important Chinese painter, calligrapher, poet, philosopher, and statesman.

Sutherland, Efua Theodora *(1924-1996),* Ghanian dramatist, poet and writer.

Swift, Jonathan *(1667-1745),* celebrated Irish poet, writer, and churchman, famous for his mastery of satire, and author of *Gulliver's Travels.*

Swinburne, Algernon Charles *(1837-1909),* outstanding English poet and critic.

Symonds, John Addington *(1840-1893),* English writer, biographer, poet and translator, author of the important study *Renaissance in Italy.*

Symons, Arthur (William) *(1865-1945),* Welsh critic and poet.

Synesius *(c.370-413),* Greek philosopher and poet.

Synge, John Millington *(1871-1909),* influential Irish dramatist, particularly known for his *The Playboy of the Western World.*

Tagore, Rabindranath *(1861-1941),* outstanding Indian poet, novelist and philosopher; won the Nobel Prize for Literature (1913).

Tam'si, Tchicaya U *(1931-1988),* Congolese poet, novelist and dramatist.

T'ang Yin *(1470-1523),* notable Chinese painter and poet.

Tannahill, Robert *(1774-1810),* Scottish poet and songwriter; committed suicide by drowning.

Tasso, Bernardo *(1493-1569),* Italian poet, remembered for his epic *Amadigi di Gaula*; father of Torquato Tasso.

Tasso, Torquato *(1544-1595),* great Italian poet, author of the masterful epic *Gerusalemme Liberata*; son of Bernardo Tasso.

Tate, (John Orley) Allen *(1899-1979),* American poet, biographer and editor.

Tate, Nahum *(1652-1715),* Irish poet and dramatist; became Poet Laureate of the United Kingdom (1692).

Taylor, (James) Bayard *(1825-1878),* American novelist, poet and diplomat.

Taylor, Sir Henry *(1800-1886),* English poet, dramatist and writer.

Taylor, John *(1580-1653),* English poet and writer.

Teasdale, Sara *(1884-1933),* American poet.

Tegnér, Esaias *(1782-1846),* Swedish poet and churchman.

Tennant, William *(1784-1848),* Scottish poet and scholar.

Tennyson, Alfred, Lord *(1809-1892),* eminent English poet, famous for his *Crossing the Bar, In Memoriam, Rizpah, Tiresias* and *To Virgil*; became Poet Laureate of the United Kingdom (1850).

Terence (actually **Publius Terentius Afer**) *(c.185-159 BC),* notable Greek dramatist, known for his comic plays.

Thackeray, William Makepeace *(1811-1863),* prominent English novelist, editor and poet.

Theocritus *(c.310-250 BC),* famous Greek poet, celebrated especially for his idylls.

Theognis *(5th Century BC),* Greek poet, known for his elegies.

Thespis *(6th Century BC),* Greek poet who is considered the founder of Greek tragedy.

Theuriet, André *(1833-1907),* French poet and novelist.

Thomas *(12th Century),* Anglo-Norman poet.

Thomas, Dylan (Marlais) *(1914-1953),* notable Welsh poet, esteemed for his *Under Milk Wood*.

Thomas, (Philip) Edward *(1878-1917),* admired English poet and writer; died in World War I.

Thomas the Rhymer or **Thomas Rymour of Erceldoune** *(c.1220-c.1297),* Scottish seer and poet.

Thompson, Francis *(1859-1907),* esteemed English poet and writer, especially remembered for his poem *Hound of Heaven*.

Thomson, James *(1700-1748),* Scottish poet, author of *Britannia, The Castle of Indolence* and *The Seasons*, who wrote under the name Bysshe Vanolis or B V.

Thomson, James *(1834-1882),* Scottish poet, best known for his *The City of Dreadful Night*.

Thoreau, Henry David *(1817-1862),* famous American essayist and poet, celebrated for the classic prose works *Civil Disobedience* and *Walden, or Life in the Woods*.

Tibullus, (Albius) *(c.54-19 BC),* admired Roman poet, master of the elegy.

Tickell, Thomas *(1686-1740),* English poet and translator.

Tieck, (Johann) Ludwig *(1773-1853),* prominent German critic, editor and poet.

Timon of Phlius *(c.325-c.235 BC),* notable Greek philosopher and poet, proponent of Scepticism.

Todi, Jacopone da *(c.1230-1306),* Italian poet who excelled in religious themes.

Tollens, Hendrik *(1780-1856),* Dutch poet, author of the national hymn of his homeland, *Wien Neerlandsch Bloed*.

Tolstoy, Count Alexei Konstantinovich *(1817-1875),* Russian dramatist, poet and novelist.

Torga, Miguel (actually **Adolfo Correia da Rocha**) *(1907-1995)*, Portuguese poet, dramatist and diarist.

Tourneur, Cyril *(c.1575-1626)*, English dramatist and poet.

Traherne, Thomas *(1637-1674)*, esteemed English writer and poet.

Trench, Frederick Herbert *(1865-1923)*, Irish poet.

Trench, Richard Chenevix *(1807-1886)*, Irish prelate, philologist and poet.

Tripp, John *(1927-1986)*, Welsh poet.

Trumbull, John *(1750-1831)*, American lawyer, judge and poet.

Tulsīdās *(1543-1623)*, famous Indian poet, celebrated for his *Rāmacaritamānas* (The Holy Lake of Rama's Deeds).

Tupper, Martin Farquhar *(1810-1889)*, English writer, poet and novelist, best known for his collection *Proverbial Philosophy*.

Turbervile, George *(c.1540-c.1596)*, English poet and translator, pioneer of blank verse.

Turgenev, Ivan Sergeievich *(1818-1883)*, famous Russian novelist, short-story writer and poet.

Turner (actually **Tennyson**), **Charles** *(1808-1879)*, English poet and churchman; brother of Alfred Tennyson.

Turner, Walter James Redfern *(1889-1946)*, Australian poet, novelist and critic.

Tyard or **Thiard, Pontus de** *(1521-1605)*, French churchman, writer and poet.

Tynan, Katharine *(1861-1931)*, Irish poet and novelist.

Tyrtaeus *(7th Century BC)*, Greek poet.

Tyutchev, Fyodor (Ivanovich) *(1803-1873)*, admired Russian poet of the Romantic school.

Udall, Nicholas *(1504-1556)*, English dramatist, author of the comedy *Ralph Roister Doister*.

Uhland, (Johann) Ludwig *(1787-1862)*, notable German poet and essayist, admired for his lyricism.

Underhill, Evelyn *(1875-1941)*, English mystic, poet and novelist, best remembered for her study *Mysticism*.

Ungaretti, Giuseppe *(1888-1970)*, remarkable Italian poet.

Valéry, Paul (Ambroise) *(1871-1945)*, outstanding French poet, writer and dramatist.

Valle-Inclán, Ramón María del *(1869-1936)*, esteemed Spanish novelist, dramatist, and poet.

Valverde, José María *(1926-1996)*, eminent Spanish poet, literary historian and translator.

Van Doren, Mark (Albert) *(1894-1972)*, eminent American poet and critic.

Varro, Publius Terentius *(c.82-37 BC)*, Roman poet.

Vaughan, Henry *(1622-1695)*, English physician, poet and writer who found inspiration in religious themes.

Vaughan, William *(1577-1641)*, Welsh poet and colonizer.

Vazov, Ivan Minchev *(1850-1921)*, Bulgarian poet.

Vega Carpio, Lope Félix de *(1562-1635)*, notable Spanish dramatist and poet.

Veitch, John *(1829-1894)*, Scottish poet and scholar.

Verdaguer, Mosen Jacinto *(1845-1902)*, Catalan poet.

Vere, Edward de, 17th Earl of Oxford *(1550-1604)*, admired English poet.

Verhaeren, Émile *(1855-1916)*, Belgian poet.

Verlaine, Paul *(1844-1896)*, outstanding French poet, renowned for his *Fêtes galantes* and *Sagesse.*

Very, Jones *(1813-1880)*, American mystic and poet.

Vesaas, Tarjei *(1897-1970)*, Norwegian novelist and poet.

Vian, Boris *(1920-1959)*, French novelist, dramatist and poet.

Viau, Théophile de *(1590-1626)*, French poet.

Vicente, Gil *(c.1470-c.1537)*, significant Portuguese dramatist, called the "father" of Portuguese drama.

Vida, Marco Girolamo *(c.1480-1566)*, Italian poet, known as the "Christian Virgil".

Vielé-Griffin, Francis *(1864-1937)*, American-born French poet in the Symbolist manner.

Vigny, Alfred Victor, Comte de *(1797-1863)*, French poet, dramatist and writer.

Villiers de l'Isle-Adam, Jean-Marie-Mathias-Philippe-Auguste, Comte de *(1838-1889)*, notable French poet, dramatist and novelist, best known for his drama *Axel.*

Villon, François (actually **François de Montcorbier** or **de Logos**) *(1431-c.1463)*, French poet and criminal, author of the *Petit Testament* and the *Grand Testament.*

Virgil (actually **Publius Vergilius Maro**) *(70-19 BC)*, great Roman poet, author of the masterful *Aeneid.*

Vodnik, Valentin *(1758-1819)*, Slovenian poet.

Voiture, Vincent *(1597-1648)*, admired French poet.

Voltaire (actually **François-Marie Arouet**) *(1694-1778)*, great French dramatist, writer and poet.

Vondel, Joost van den *(1587-1679)*, notable Dutch dramatist and poet, esteemed for his dramas *Jephtha* and *Lucifer.*

Vörösmarty, Mihály *(1800-1844)*, important Hungarian poet and dramatist who penned the famous fairy drama *Csongor es Tünde.*

Voss, Johann Heinrich *(1751-1826)*, German poet and translator.

Vrchlický, Jaroslav *(1853-1912)*, Czech poet and translator who wrote under the name Emil Frída.

Wace, Robert *(c.1115-c.1183)*, Anglo-Norman poet.

Wain, John Barrington *(1925-1994)*, English writer, poet, dramatist and critic.

Waller, Edmund *(1606-1687)*, English poet and politician.

Wang Wei *(699-759)*, Chinese poet and painter.

Warner, William *(c.1558-1609)*, English poet.

Warren, Robert Penn *(1905-1989)*, prominent American novelist and poet; was the first Poet Laureate of theUS (1986-87).

Warton, Thomas *(1728-1790)*, English critic and poet; became Poet Laureate of the United Kingdom (1785).

Watkins, Vernon Phillips *(1906-1967)*, distinguished Welsh poet.

Watson, Thomas *(c.1557-1592)*, English poet and translator, admired for his sonnets.

Watts, Alaric Alexander *(1797-1864)*, English journalist and poet.

Watts-Dunton, Walter Theodore *(1832-1914)*, English poet and critic.

Webb, Mary Gladys (née **Meredith**) *(1881-1927)*, English writer and poet.

Webster, John *(c.1580-c.1625),* English dramatist and poet.

Wells, Charles Jeremiah *(c.1800-1879),* English poet.

Wergeland, Henrik Arnold *(1808-1845),* notable Norwegian poet, dramatist and patriot, known as the "Lord Byron" of Norway.

Wheatley, Phillis *(c.1753-1785),* African-born American poet.

White, E(lwyn) B(rooks) *(1899-1985),* esteemed American essayist, writer, and poet.

White, Henry Kirke *(1785-1806),* English poet.

Whitehead, Charles *(1804-1862),* English poet and novelist.

Whitehead, Paul *(1710-1774),* English poet.

Whitehead, William *(1715-1785),* English poet and dramatist; became Poet Laureate of the United Kingdom (1757).

Whitman, Walt(er) *(1819-1892),* famous American poet, celebrated for his liberating collection *Leaves of Grass.*

Whittier, John Greenleaf *(1807-1892),* prominent American poet and abolitionist, remembered for his poem *Barbara Frietchie.*

Wigglesworth, Michael *(1631-1705),* English-born American poet and clergyman, author of the first American epic, *Day of Doom.*

Wilcox, Ella (née Wheeler) *(1850-1919),* American journalist and poet.

Wilde, Lady Jane Francesca *(1826-1896),* Irish poet, known as Speranza.

Wilde, Oscar (Fingal O'Flahertie Wills) *(1854-1900),* celebrated Irish dramatist, novelist, essayist, poet and wit, author of *The Ballad of Reading Gaol,* written during his imprisonment there for homosexuality.

Wildenbruch, Ernst von *(1845-1909),* prominent German dramatist, novelist and poet.

Wildgans, Anton *(1881-1932),* Austrian poet and dramatist.

Williams, Edward *(1747-1826),* Welsh poet, creator of the 14th-century poet Dafydd ap Gwilym and the works he attributed to him.

Williams, Tennessee (actually **Thomas Lanier Williams**) *(1911-1983),* distinguished American dramatist, short-story writer and poet, admired for such dramas as *Cat on a Hot Tin Roof, The Glass Menagerie* and *Summer and Smoke.*

Williams, Waldo *(1904-1971),* Welsh poet.

Williams, William Carlos *(1883-1963),* distinguished American poet, writer and physician.

Wills, William Gorman *(1828-1891),* Irish dramatist and poet, remembered for his ballad *I'll sing thee Songs of Araby.*

Winchilsea, Anne Finch, Countess of (née Kingsmith) *(1661-1720),* English poet.

Winters, (Arthur) Yvor *(1900-1968),* American critic and poet.

Wither, George *(1588-1667),* English writer and poet.

Wodehouse, P(elham) G(renville) *(1881-1975),* prominent English-born American novelist, dramatist and poet.

Wolcot, John *(1738-1819),* English poet and writer who wrote satirical works under the name Peter Pindar.

Wolfe, Charles *(1791-1823),* Irish churchman and poet, known for his *The Burial of Sir John Moore.*

Wolfe, Humbert *(1885-1940),* English poet and critic.

Wolfram von Eschenbach *(13th Century),* famous German poet, renowned as the author of the epic *Parzival.*

Woodcock, George *(1912-1995),* Canadian poet, critic, writer, dramatist and editor.

Woolner, Thomas *(1826-1892),* English poet and sculptor.

Wordsworth, William *(1770-1850),* great English poet, celebrated for his ode *Intimations of Immortality;* became Poet Laureate of the United Kingdom (1843).

Wyat, Sir Thomas, the Elder *(1503-1542),* English courtier and poet.

Wyspiański, Stanisław *(1869-1907),* Polish poet and painter.

Xenophanes *(6th Century BC),* Greek philosopher and poet.

Yeats, William Butler *(1865-1939),* celebrated Irish poet, dramatist and writer; won the Nobel Prize for Literature (1923).

Young, Douglas *(1913-1973),* Scottish poet, dramatist and translator.

Young, Edward *(1683-1765),* esteemed English poet, famous for his *The Complaint, or Night Thoughts on Life, Death and Immortality.*

Young, Marguerite Vivian *(1909-1995),* American novelist and poet.

Yourcenar, Marguerite (actually **Marguerite de Crayencour)** *(1903-1987),* Belgian-born French novelist and poet.

Zangwill, Israel *(1864-1926),* English novelist, poet, dramatist and essayist.

Żeromski, Stefan *(1864-1925),* Polish novelist, dramatist and poet.

Zhukovsky, Vasily Andreievich *(1783-1852),* notable Russian poet.

Zorrilla y Moral, José *(1817-1893),* Spanish poet and dramatist.

Zuckmayer, Carl *(1896-1977),* German dramatist and poet.

Zukofsky, Louis *(1904-1978),* American poet, author of the provocative *First Half of "A".*

Zweig, Stefan *(1881-1942),* Austrian-born English poet, novelist, short-story writer and translator; committed suicide.

APPENDIX C
POETS LAUREATE OF THE UNITED KINGDOM

The Royal Office of Poet Laureate of the United Kingdom commenced with a pension granted to Ben Jonson by James I in 1616. Following Jonson's death in 1637, Sir William D'Avenant was awarded a pension for his services to the crown as poet. Upon D'Avenant's death in 1668, the Royal Office of Poet Laureate was officially established with the appointment of John Dryden.

The Laureateship has become the award for eminence in poetry and is filled automatically when vacant. It is an appointment for life, Dryden being the only Poet Laureate to lose the office when he refused to take the oath of allegiance in the wake of the Revolution of 1688.

This is a list of the Poets Laureate of the United Kingdom with dates of service:

1668-88	John Dryden
1688-92	Thomas Shadwell
1692-1715	Nahum Tate
1715-18	Nicholas Rowe
1718-30	Laurence Eusden
1730-57	Colley Cibber
1757-85	William Whitehead
1785-90	Thomas Warton
1790-1813	Henry James Pye
1813-43	Robert Southey
1843-50	William Wordsworth
1850-96	Alfred (Lord) Tennyson
1896-1913	Alfred Austin
1913-30	Robert Bridges
1930-67	John Masefield
1968-72	C Day-Lewis
1972-84	Sir John Betjeman
1984-	Ted Hughes

APPENDIX D

POETS LAUREATE OF THE UNITED STATES OF AMERICA

The position of Poet Laureate of the United States of America was authorized by the US Senate in 1985 as an adjunct to the Consultant for Poetry of the Library of Congress in Washington, DC. The position is a salaried one but requires no ceremonial verse.

This is a list of the Poets Laureate of the United States of America with dates of service:

1986-87	**Robert Penn Warren**
1987-88	**Richard Wilbur**
1988-90	**Howard Nemerov**
1990-91	**Mark Strand**
1991-92	**Joseph Brodsky**
1992-93	**Mona Van Duyn**
1993-95	**Rita Dove**
1995-97	**Robert Hass**
1997-	**Robert Pinsky**

APPENDIX E
POETS WHO HAVE WON THE NOBEL PRIZE FOR LITERATURE

Alfred B Nobel, the inventor of dynamite, bequeathed US $9 million, the interest from which has been awarded annually since 1901 to those who have made outstanding contributions to mankind in the fields of physics, chemistry, physiology or medicine, literature and peace (economic science was added in 1969). The current value of each prize is US $1,120,000.

Poets who have been awarded the Nobel Prize for Literature since 1901 are:

1901 **Sully Prudhomme** (France)

1903 **Bjørnstjerne Bjørnson** (Norway)

1904 **Frédéric Mistral** (France)

1906 **Giosué Carducci** (Italy)

1907 **Rudyard Kipling** (Great Britain)

1910 **Paul Heyse** (Germany)

1912 **Gerhart Hauptmann** (Germany)

1913 **Rabindranath Tagore** (India)

1916 **Verner von Heidenstam** (Sweden)

1919 **Carl Spitteler** (Switzerland)

1923 **William Butler Yeats** (Ireland)

1931 **Erik Axel Karlfeldt** (Sweden)

1933 **Ivan Bunin** (Russia)

1944 **Johannes V. Jensen** (Denmark)

1945 **Gabriela Mistral** (Chile)

1946 **Hermann Hesse** (Switzerland)

1947 **André Gide** (France)

1948 **T S Eliot** (Great Britain)

1951 **Pär Lagerkvist** (Sweden)

1956 **Juan Ramón Jiménez** (Spain)

1958 **Boris Pasternak** (Russia) (Prize declined)

1959 **Salvatore Quasimodo** (Italy)

1960 **Saint-John Perse** (France)

1963 **Georgios Seferiades** (Greece)

1966 **Nelly Sachs** (Sweden)

1967 **Miguel Angel Asturias** (Guatemala)

1971 **Pablo Neruda** (Chile)

1974 **Harry Martinson** (Sweden)

1975 **Eugenio Montale** (Italy)

1977 **Vicente Aleixandre** (Spain)

1979 **Odysseus Elytis** (Greece)

1980 **Czesław Miłosz** (USA)

1984 **Jaroslav Seifert** (Czechoslovakia)

1986 **Wole Soyinka** (Nigeria)

1987 **Joseph Brodsky** (USA)

1989 **Camilo José Cela** (Spain)

1990 **Octavio Paz** (Mexico)

1992 **Derek Walcott** (West Indies)

1995 **Seamus Heaney** (Ireland)

1996 **Wisława Szymborska** (Poland)

APPENDIX F
THE PULITZER PRIZE FOR AMERICAN POETRY

Joseph Pulitzer *(1847-1911)*, publisher of *The New York World,* endowed the Pulitzer Prizes in a bequest to Columbia University, New York. The prize for American Poetry was established in 1922 and is awarded annually by the President of Columbia University on the recommendation of the Pulitzer Prize Board. Currently, the Poetry Prize is US $3000. The following are the winners from 1922 to the present time:

1922	Edwin Arlington Robinson	*1960*	W D Snodgrass
1923	Edna St Vincent Millay	*1961*	Phyllis McGinley
1924	Robert Frost	*1962*	Alan Dugan
1925	Edwin Arlington Robinson	*1963*	William Carlos Williams
1926	Amy Lowell	*1964*	Louis Simpson
1927	Leonora Speyer	*1965*	John Berryman
1928	Edwin Arlington Robinson	*1966*	Richard Eberhart
1929	Stephen Vincent Benét	*1967*	Anne Sexton
1930	Conrad Aiken	*1968*	Anthony Hecht
1931	Robert Frost	*1969*	George Oppen
1932	George Dillon	*1970*	Richard Howard
1933	Archibald MacLeish	*1971*	William S Merwin
1934	Robert Hillyer	*1972*	James Wright
1935	Audrey Wurdemann	*1973*	Maxine Winokur Kumin
1936	Robert P Tristram Coffin	*1975*	Gary Snyder
1937	Robert Frost	*1976*	John Ashbery
1938	Marya Zaturenska	*1977*	James Merrill
1939	John Gould Fletcher	*1978*	Howard Nemerov
1940	Mark Van Doren	*1979*	Robert Penn Warren
1941	Leonard Bacon	*1980*	Donald Justice
1942	William Rose Benét	*1981*	James Schuyler
1943	Robert Frost	*1982*	Sylvia Plath
1944	Stephen Vincent Benét	*1983*	Galway Kinnell
1945	Karl Shapiro	*1984*	Mary Oliver
1947	Robert Lowell	*1985*	Carolyn Kizer
1948	W H Auden	*1986*	Henry Taylor
1949	Peter Viereck	*1987*	Rita Dove
1950	Gwendolyn Brooks	*1988*	William Meredith
1951	Carl Sandburg	*1989*	Richard Wilbur
1952	Marianne Moore	*1990*	Charles Simic
1953	Archibald MacLeish	*1991*	Mona Van Duyn
1954	Theodore Roethke	*1992*	James Tate
1955	Wallace Stevens	*1993*	Louise Glück
1956	Elizabeth Bishop	*1994*	Yusef Komunyakaa
1957	Richard Wilbur	*1995*	Philip Levine
1958	Robert Penn Warren	*1996*	Jorie Graham
1959	Stanley J Kunitz		

APPENDIX G
KING'S/QUEEN'S GOLD MEDAL FOR POETRY

The King's Gold Medal for Poetry was instituted by King George V in 1933 at the suggestion of the then United Kingdom Poet Laureate, John Masefield. It became the Queen's Gold Medal for Poetry on the accession to the throne of Queen Elizabeth II in 1952.

A small committee, under the chairmanship of the Poet Laureate (currently Ted Hughes), selects the winner. This choice is approved by the Queen and the Medal is presented at Buckingham Palace. It is not awarded every year.

The following is a list of the recipients of the King's/Queen's Gold Medal for Poetry since the inception of the award:

1934	Laurence Whistler
1936	Wystan Hugh Auden
1940	Michael Thwaites
1952	Andrew Young
1953	Arthur Waley
1955	Ruth Pitter*
1956	Edmund Blunder
1957	Siegfried Sassoon
1959	Frances Cornford
1960	John Betjeman
1962	Christopher Fry
1963	William C Plomer
1964	Rev Ronald S Thomas
1965	Philip Larkin
1967	Charles Causley
1968	Robert Graves
1969	Stevie Smith*
1970	Roy Fuller
1971	Stephen Spender
1973	John Heath-Stubbs
1974	Ted Hughes
1977	Norman Nicholson
1981	Dennis J Enright*
1985	Norman MacCaig
1988	Derek Walcott
1989	Allen Curnow*
1990	Sorley Maclean
1991	Judith Wright
1993	Kathleen Raine
1996	Peter Redgrave

* Medal personally presented by Her Majesty.

APPENDIX H
OXFORD UNIVERSITY PROFESSORS OF POETRY

The unique Professorship of Poetry at the University of Oxford, England, was established in 1708 from a bequest by Henry Birkhead, a Fellow of All Souls.

The appointment, which now lasts for five years, is made by the Convocation which consists of all holders of the Master of Arts degree from the University. They are required to vote in person and to hand their ballot papers to the Vice Chancellor or his representative.

The Professor of Poetry must, by Statute, deliver a public lecture each term - a total of 15 lectures.

Only in recent times has the Professor of Poetry been primarily a poet and the list contains many purely academic names.

The following have occupied the Chair of Poetry:

1708-18	Joseph Trapp
1718-28	Thomas Warton
1728-38	Joseph Spence
1738-41	John Whitfield
1741-51	Robert Lowth
1751-56	William Hawkins
1756-66	Thomas Warton
1766-76	Benjamin Wheeler
1776-83	John Randolph
1783-93	Robert Holmes
1793-1802	James Hurdis
1802-12	Edward Copleston
1812-21	John Josias Conybeare
1821-31	Henry Hart Milman
1831-42	John Keble
1842-52	James Garbett
1852-57	Thomas Leigh Claugnton
1857-67	Matthew Arnold
1867-77	Sir Francis Hastings Charles Doyle
1877-85	John Campbell Shairp
1885-95	Francis Turner Palgrave
1895-1900	William John Courthope
1901-06	Andrew Cecil Bradley
1906-11	John William Mackail
1911-16	Sir Thomas Herbert Warren
1920-23	William Paton Ker
1923-28	Heathcote William Garrod
1928-33	Ernest de Selincourt
1933-38	George Gordon
1938-43	Adam Fox

1946-51	Sir Cecil Maurice Bowra
1951-55	Cecil Day-Lewis
1956-61	Wystan Hugh Auden
1961-66	Robert Ranke Graves
1966-68	Edmund Charles Blunden
1968-73	Roy Broadbent Fuller
1973-78	John Barrington Wain
1979-84	Henry John Francis Jones
1984-89	Peter Chad Tigar Levi
1989-94	Seamus Heaney

Vacancies occurred from *1917-19* and from *1944-45*.

APPENDIX I
POETRY PRIZES AND PRIZEWINNERS

The following list covers main poetry prizes and festivals, organziations offering awards and prizes, and, where applicable, recent winners. Conditions and availability of prizes and awards often change with little notice; the most recent situtation can only be ascertained by direct application to the sponsoring organization.

ACADEMY OF AMERICAN POETS FELLOWSHIP
584 Broadway, Suite 1208
New York, NY 10012
USA
Fellows are elected each year by majority vote of the Academy's Board of Chancellors. No applications are accepted. Each Fellow is awarded a stipend of US $20,000.

1937	Edwin Markham
1946	Ridgely Torrence
1948	Percy MacKaye
1950	e e cummings
1952	Padraic Colum
1953	Robert Frost
1954	Louise Townsend Nicholl
	Oliver St John Gogarty
1955	Rolfe Humphries
1956	William Carlos Williams
1957	Conrad Aiken
1958	Robinson Jeffers
1959	Louise Bogan
	Léonie Adams *
1960	Jesse Stuart
1961	Horace Gregory
1962	John Crowe Ransom
1963	Ezra Pound
	Allen Tate
1964	Elizabeth Bishop
1965	Marianne Moore
1966	Archibald MacLeish
	John Berryman
1967	Mark Van Doren
1968	Stanley Kunitz
1969	Richard Eberhart
	Anthony Hecht
1970	Howard Nemerov
1971	James Wright
1972	W D Snodgrass
1973	W S Merwin
1974	Léonie Adams *
1975	Robert Hayden
1976	J V Cunningham
1977	Louise Coxe
1978	Josephine Miles
1979	Mark Strand
	May Swenson
1980	Mona Van Duyn
1981	Richard Hugo
1982	John Ashbery
	John Frederick Nims
1983	Philip Booth
	James Schuyler
1984	Robert Francis
	Richmond Lattimore
1985	Amy Clampitt

	Maxine Kumin
1986	Irving Feldman
	Howard Moss
1987	Alfred Corn
	Josephine Jacobsen
1988	Donald Justice
1989	Richard Howard
1990	William Meredith
1991	J D McClatchy
1992	Adrienne Rich
1993	Gerald Stern
1994	David Ferry
1995	Denise Levertov
1996	Jay Wright

* Only person to receive this honour twice.

ALDEBURGH POETRY FESTIVAL PRIZE
Aldeburgh Poetry Festival
Goldings, Goldings Lane
Leiston, Suffolk IP16 4EB
England
Contact: The Co-ordinator
Awarded annually for the best first full collection of poetry published in Britain and the Republic of Ireland in the preceding twelve months. Submissions are accepted from publishers or individual poets. Winners are announced at the opening event of the festival.
Prize: £500 and invitation to participate at the following year's festival.

1989	Studying Grosz on the Bus by John Lucas
1990	A Sleep of Drowned Fathers by Donald Atkinson
1991	The Hen Ark by Mark Roper
1992	Singing Underwater by Susan Wicks
1993	No prize awarded
1994	Inventing the Fishes by Sue Stewart
1995	Parables and Faxes by Gwyneth Lewis
1996	Could Have Been Funny by Glyn Wright

AMERICAN ACADEMY OF ARTS AND LETTERS
633 West 155th Street
New York, NY 10032
USA

ROSEMARY ARTHUR AWARD
The National Poetry Foundation
27 Mill Road
Fareham, Hants PO16 0TH
England
Annual award founded in 1989 and presented to a poet who has not previuosly has a book of poetry published or self-published.
Prize: Publication of the winner's book, £100 and an engraved brass and carriage clock.
Contact: The Trustees

1990	Robert Roberts
1991	David Lightfoot
1992	Judith Wright
1993	Val Moore
1994	Sheila Simmons
1995	Joan Smith
1996	Patrick Osada

ARVON INTERNATIONAL POETRY COMPETITION
Kilnhurst, Kilnhurst Road
Todmorden, Lancashire OL14 6AX
England
Contact: David Pease, National Director
Biennial awards, including first prize of £5000 for poetry of any length written in English and not previously published or broadcast.

1980	The Letter by Andrew Motion
1982	Ephraim Destiny's Perfectly Utter Darkness by John Hartley Williams
1985	Rorschach Writing by Oliver Reynolds
1987	The Notebook by Selima Hill
1989	Halfway Pond by Sheldon Flory
1991	Thinking Egg by Jacqueline Brown
1993	A Private Bottling by Don Paterson
1995	Laws of Gravity by Paul Farley

ATLANTA REVIEW POETRY COMPETITION
PO Box 8396
Atlanta, GA 30306
USA
Contact: Dan Veach, Editor/Publisher
Annual competition run by Atlanta Review, a leading US literary journal. Approximately
5000 entrants from 30 countries participate. All entries are considered for publication in a special Autumn issue.
Prizes: Gold ($1000), Silver ($500) and Bronze ($250) prizes, plus 50 International Merit awards.

AUSTRALIAN LITERATURE SOCIETY GOLD MEDAL
Association for the Study of Australian Literature Ltd
c/o English Department
University College, ADFA
Campbell, ACT 2600
Australia
Contact: Susan McKernan, Secretary.
Annual award for outstanding Australian literary work or for services to Australian literature.

1983	Fly Away Peter by David Malouf
1984	The People's Other World by Les Murray
1985	Archimedes and the Seagle by David Ireland
1986	Beachmasters by Thea Astley
1987	The Nightmarkets by Alan Wearne
1988	Louisa by Brian Matthews
1989	Forty-Seventeen by Frank Moorhouse
1990	Possible Worlds and Collected Poems by Peter Porter

BOLLINGEN PRIZE IN POETRY
Box 1603A,
Beinecke Library
Yale University,
New Haven, CT 06520
USA
Biennial award of $25,000 for the best book of poetry by an

American poet.
Nominated by jury - no submissions.

1981	Howard Nemerov and May Swenson
1983	Anthony E Hecht and John Hollander
1985	John Ashbury and Fred Chappell
1987	Stanley J Kunitz
1989	Edgar Bowers
1991	Laura (Riding) Jackson and Donald Justice
1993	Mark Strand
1995	Kenneth Koch

BREMEN LITERATURE PRIZE
Bremen City Council, Freie Hansestadt Bremen
Rembertiring 9-11
Senator für Bildung Wisasneschaft und Kunst
D-28195 Bremen
Germany
Annual prize of DM 15,000 awarded to German-speaking writers and poets.

BRIDPORT PRIZE
Bridport Arts Centre, South Street
Bridport, Dorset DT6 3NR
England
Contact: Peggy Chapman-Andrews
Awarded for original poems of not more than 42 lines, and short stories between 1000 and 5000 words. All entries must be written in English and must be previously unpublished or broadcast, nor entered in any other competition.
Prizes: First prize: £2500, Second prize: £1000, Third prize: £500 (in each category), plus discretionary supplementary prizes.

WITTER BYNNER FOUNDATION FOR POETRY
PO Box 10169
Sante Fe, NM 87504
USA
Contact: Executive Director
Annual prize of $25,000 for poetry-related projects.

CANADIAN AUTHORS ASSOCIATION LITERARY AWARDS
c/o CAA, 275 Slater Street, Suite 500
Ottawa, Ontario K1P 5H9
Canada
Contact: Awards Chairman
Annual award of $5000 in each of four categories (fiction, non-fiction, poetry and drama) awarded for book-length works by Canadian writers published during the previous year.
Poetry Award

1980	There's A Trick With A Knife That I'm Learning To Do by Michael Ondaatje
1981	Land of the Peace by Leona Gom
1982	The Acid Test by Gary Geddes
1983	The Presence of Fire by George Amabile
1984	Birding or Desire by Don McKay
1985	Book of Mercy by Leonard Cohen
1986	The Glass Air by P K Page
1987	The Collected Poems, 1956-86 by Purdy
1988	Selected Poems by Pat Lane
1989	Daniel by Bruce Rice
1990	Homeless Heart by Don Bailey
1991	Prelude to the Bacchanal by Richard Lemm

1992	Miner's Pond by Anne Michaels
1993	Inventing the Hawk by Lorna Crozier
1994	Selected Poems by George Bowering

MELVILLE CANE AWARD

Poetry Society of America
15 Gramercy Park
New York, NY 10003, USA
For a published book on poetry (in even-numbered years)
alternating (in odd-numbered years) with a book of poems
published within the award year.
Annual cash award.

1980	Selected Poems by Richard Hugo
1981	The Poet's Calling in the English Ode by Paul Fry
1982	The Red Coal by Gerald Stern
1983	Robert Lowell by Ian Hamilton
1984	New and Collected Poems by Alan Dugan
1985	Kenneth Patchen and American Mysticism by Raymond Nelson
1986	Triumph of Archilles by Louis Gluck
1987	Visions and Revisions of American Poetry by Lewis Turco
1988	Cemetery Nights by Steven Dobyns
	Memories of the Future: The Daybooks of Tina Modotti by Margaret Gibson
1989	Conrad Aiken: Poet of the White Horse Vale by Edward Butscher
1990	Harp Lake by John Hollander
1991	White Paper by J D McClatchy
1992	The 6-Cornered Snowflake by John Frederick Nims
1993	An Essay on French Verse for Readers of English Poetry by Jacques Barzan
1994	Year of the Comet by Nicholas Christopher

GIOSUÉ CARDUCCI PRIZE

Bologna University
Via Zamboni 33
I-40100 Bologna
Italy
Annual prize of 1.5M Lire for poetry, monographs and
essays on poetry and poets.

CHOLMONDELEY AWARD FOR POETS

Society of Authors
84 Drayton Gardens
London SW10 9SB
England
Non-competitive award established in 1966 "for the benefit
and encouragement of poets of any age, sex and
nationality". Awarded for work in general, not for a specific
book. Annual prize of £8,000 (shared).

1980	George Barker
	Terence Tiler
	Roy Fuller
1981	Roy Fisher
	Robert Garioch
	Charles Boyle
1982	Basil Bunting
	Herbert Lomas
	William Scammell
1983	John Fuller
	Craig Raine
	Anthony Thwaite
1984	Michael Baldwin

	Michale Hoffmann
	Carrol Raine
1985	Dannie Abse
	Peter Redgrove
	Brian Taylor
1986	Lawrence Durrell
	James Fenton
	Selima Hill
1987	Wendy Cope
	Matthew Sweeney
	George Szirtes
1988	John Heath-Stubbs
	Sean O'Brien
	John Whitworth
1989	Peter Didsbury
	Douglas Dunn
	E J Scovell
1990	Kinglsey Amis
	Elaine Feinstein
	Michael O'Neill
1991	James Berry
	Sujata Bhatt
	Michael Hulse
	Derek Mahon
1992	Allen Curnow
	Donald Davie
	Carol Ann Duffy
	Roger Woddis
1993	Patricia Beer
	George MacKay Brown
	P J Kavanagh
	Michael Longley
1994	Ruth Fainlight
	Gwen Harwood
	Elizabeth Jennings
	John Mole
1995	U A Fanthorpe
	Christopher Reid
	C H Sisson
	Kit Wright

COUNTY OF CARDIFF INTERNATIONAL POETRY COMPETITION

The Welsh Academy
3rd Floor, Mount Stuart House
Mount Stuart Square,
Cardiff CF1 6DQ
Wales
Annual prize of £5000 for unpublished poems of up to 50
lines written in English.

DANISH ACADEMY PRIZE FOR LITERATURE

Rungstedlund
109 Rungsted Strandvej
DK-2960 Rungsted Kyst
Denmark
Contact: Alan Philip
Prize of DKr 100,000 currently awarded biennially for
outstanding literature.

1980	Henrik Norbrandt
1981	Dorrit Willumsen
1982	Per Højholt
1984	Jess Ornsbo
1986	Henrik Stangerup

1988	Halfdan Rasmussen
1990	Jens Smærup Sørensen

T.S.ELIOT PRIZE

The Poetry Book Society
Book House, 45 East Hill
London SW18 2QZ
England
Contact: Clare Brown
Prize of £5000 awarded annually for books of new poetry, over 32 pages in length, published in the UK and the Republic of Ireland, at least 75% of which must have been previously unpublished in book form.

1993	First Language by Ciaran Carson
1994	The Annals of Chile by Paul Muldoon
1995	My Alexandria by Mark Doty
1996	Subhuman Redneck Peoms by Les Murray

ENGLISH ACADEMY OF SOUTHERN AFRICA

PO Box 124
Witwatersrand 2050
South Africa
Thomas Pringle Awards

1985	Robert Greigg
	Karen Learmont-Batley
	Patrick Cullinan
1986	Gus Silber
	Jan Gorek
	Njabulo Ndebele
1987	David Williams
	Lionel Abrahams
	Mark Swift
1988	John M Coetzee
	Rosie Zwi
1989	Stephen Gray
	Binkie Marwick
	Douglas Livingstone
1990	Dorothy Driver
	Patrick Cullinan
1991	Charlotte Bauer
	Gregory Cunningham
	Tatumkulu Afrika

Olive Schreiner Prize

1985	A State of Fear by Menan du Plessis
1986	Journal of a New Man by Lionel Abrahams
1987	No prize awarded
1988	The Arrowing of the Cane by John Conyngham
1989	Blood of Our Silence by Kelwyn Sole
1990	A Snake in the Garden by Norman Coombe
1991	Missing Persons by Ivan Vladislavic

GEOFFREY FABER MEMORIAL PRIZE

Faber and Faber Ltd
3 Queen Square,
London WC1N 3AU
England
Contact: Sarah Gleadall/Belinda Matthews
Awarded annually (given in alternate years to volumes of prose and fiction), for works published in the UK in the preceding two years. Entrants must be under 40 at the time of publication, and citizens of the UK, Commonwealth, Republic of Ireland or South Africa.
Prize: £1000
Poetry Award

1984	In Memory of War by James Fenton
1986	A Quiet Gathering by David Scott
1988	Agrimony by Michael Hofmann
1990	Shibboleth by Michael Donaghy
1992	Madoc by Paul Muldoon
1994	Myth of the Twin by John Burnside

FORWARD PRIZES FOR POETRY

c/o Coleman Getty PR
126-130 Regent Street
London W1R 5FE
England
Contact: Coleman Getty PR
Three awards for Best Collection of Poetry (£10,000), Best First Collection of Poetry (£5,000) and Best Single Poem (£1000). Poems must be in English, and written by a citizen of the UK or Republic of Ireland.
Best Collection

1992	The Man With Night Sweats by Thom Gunn
1993	Mean Time by Carol Ann Duffy
1994	Harm by Alan Jenkins
1995	Ghost Train by Sean O'Brien
1996	Stones and Fires by John Fuller

Best First Collection

1993	Nil Nil by Don Paterson
1994	Progeny of Air by Kwame Dawes
1995	Breathe Now, Breathe by Jane Duran
1996	Slattern by Kate Clanchy

Best Single Poem

1993	Judith by Vicki Feaver
1994	Autumn by Iain Crichton
1995	In Honour of Love by Jenny Joseph
1996	The Graduates by Kathleen Jamie

FROGMORE POETRY PRIZE

The Frogmore Press
42 Morehall Avenue
Folkestone, Kent CT19 4EF
England
Contact: Jeremy Page
Awarded for unpublished poems of no more than 40 lines written in English. First prize of 100 guineas and a lifetime subscription to The Frogmore Papers; Runners-up prizes of 50 and 25 guineas, and ten shortlisted poems are published in the September issue of the above publication.

1987	David Satherley
1988	Caroline Price
1989	Bill Headon
1990	Caroline Price
1991	John Latham
1992	John Latham
1993	Caroline Price
1994	Diane Brown
1995	Tobias Hill
1996	Mario Petrucci

GOVERNOR-GENERAL'S LITERARY AWARDS

Canada Council
PO Box 1047
350 Albert Street
Ottawa, Ontario K1P 5V8
Canada
Annual awards of $1000 in seven categories including Poetry.

Poetry Award

1980	*McAlmon's Chinese Opera by Stephen Scobie*
1981	*The Collected Poems of FR Scott by FR Scott*
1982	*The Vision Tree: Selected Poems by Phyllis Webb*
1983	*Settlements by David Donnell*
1984	*Celestial Navigation by Paulette Jiles*
1985	*Waiting For Saskatchewan by Fred Wah*
1986	*The Collected Poems of Al Purdy by Al Purdy*
1987	*Afterworlds by Gwendolyn MacEwan*
1988	*Furious by Erin Mouré*
1989	*The Word For Sand by Heather Spears*
1990	*No Time by Margaret Avison*
1991	*Night Field by Don McKay*
1992	*Inventing the Hawk by Lorna Crozier*
1993	*Forests of the Medieval World by Don Coles*

ERIC GREGORY TRUST FUND AWARD
Society of Authors
84 Drayton Gardens
London SW10 9SB
England
Annual award of £27,000 (shared) for poets aged under 30 who are likely to benefit from more time given to writing.

1986	Mick North
	Lachlan Mackinnon
	Oliver Reynolds
	Stephen Romer
1987	Peter McDonald
	Maura Dooley
	Stephen Knight
	Steve Anthony
	Jill Maughan
	Paul Munden
1988	Michael Symmons Robert
	Gwyneth Lewis
	Adrian Blackledge
	Simon Armitage
	Robert Crawford
1989	Gerard Woodward
	David Morley
	Katrina Porteus
	Paul Henry
1990	Nicholas Drake
	Maggie Hannon
	William Park
	Jonathan Davidson
	Lavinia Greenlaw
	Don Paterson
	John Wells
1991	Roddy Lumsden
	Glyn Maxwell
	Stephen Smith
	Wayne Burrows
	Jackie Kay
1992	Jill Dawson
	Hugh Dunkerley
	Christopher Greenhalgh
	Marita Maddah
	Stuart Paterson
	Stuart Pickford
1993	Eleanor Brown
	Joel Lane
	Deryn Rees-Jones
	Sean Boustead

	Tracey Herd
	Angela McSeveney
1994	*Julia Copus*
	Alice Oswald
	Steven Blyth
	Kate Clanchy
	Giles Goodland
1995	*Collette Bryce*
	Sophie Hannah
	Tobias Hill
	Mark Wormald

INGERSOLL PRIZES
Ingersoll Foundation
934 North Main Street
Rockford, IL 61103
USA

INTERNATIONAL PRIZE FOR POETRY
La Maison Internationale de la Poésie
Chaussée de Wavre 150
B-1050 Brussels
Belgium
Biennial prize of 150,000 Belgian Francs awarded by an international jury. No submissions.

IRISH TIMES IRISH LITERATURE PRIZES
Irish Times Ltd
10-16 D'Olier Street
Dublin 2
Ireland
Contact: Gerard Cavanagh, Administrator.
Biennial awards chosen from nominations - no submissions.
Poets must be Irish by birth or be an Irish citizen.

GERALD LAMPERT AWARD
League of Canadian Poets
24 Ryerson Avenue
Toronto, Ontario N5T 2P3
Canada
Contact: Edita Petrauskaite
Annual award of $1000 for a first book of poetry.

1993	*The Night You Called Me A Shadow by Barbara Klar*
1994	*Mad Magellan's Tale by Ilya Tourtidis*

JAMES LAUGHLIN AWARD
(formerly the Lamont Poetry Selcetion)
Academy of American Poets,
584 Broadway, Suite 1208
New York, NY 10012,
USA
Supports the publication of an American poet's second volume of poetry. Only manuscripts already under contract with publisers are considered. Publishers are invited to submit manuscripts by American poets who have already published one volume of poems in a standard edition.
Annual prize of $5000

1954	*The Middle Voice by Constance Carrier*
1955	*Exiles and Marriages by Donald Hall*
1956	*Letter From a Distant Land by Philip Booth*
1957	*Time Without Number by Daniel Berrigan*
1958	*The Night of the Hammer by Ned O'Gorman*
1959	*The Summer Anniversaries by Donald Justice*

1960	The Lovemaker by Donald Justice
1961	Nude Descending a Staircase by X J Kennedy
1962	Stand Up, Friend, With Me by Edward Field
1963	No award given
1964	Heroes, Advise Us by Adrien Stoutenberg
1965	The War of the Secret Agents by Henri Coulette
1966	The Distance Anywhere by Kenneth O Hanson
1967	The Marches by James Scully
1968	The Weather of Six Mornings by Jane Cooper
1969	A Probable Volume of Dreams by Marvin Bell
1970	Treasury Holiday by William Harmon
1971	Concurring Beasts by Stephen Dobyns
1972	Collecting the Animals by Peter Everwine
1973	Presentation Piece by Marilyn Hacker
1974	After Our War by John Balaban
1975	The Private Life by Lisel Mueller
1976	The Afterlife by Larry Lewis
1977	Lucky Life by Gerald Stern
1978	Killing Floor by Ai
1979	Sunrise by Frederick Seidel
1980	More Trouble with the Obvious by Michael Van Walleghen
1981	The Country Between Us by Carolyn Forché
1982	Long Walks in the Afternoon by Margaret Gibson
1983	The Dead and the Living by Sharon Olds
1984	Deep Within the Ravine by Philip Schultz
1985	Victims of the Latest Dance Craze by Cornelius Eady
1986	The Minute Hand by Jane Shore
1987	The River of Heaven by Garrett Kaoru
1988	Unfinished Painting by Mary Jo Salter
1989	Crime Against Nature by Minnie Bruce Pratt
1990	The City in Which I Love You by Li-Young Lee
1991	Campo Santo by Susan Wood
1992	Wildwood Flower by Kathleen Stripling Byer
1993	Stained Glass by Rosanna Warren
1994	Song by Brigit Pegeen Kelly
1995	Neither World by Ralph Angel
1996	Wise Poison by David Rivard

GRACE LEVEN PRIZE FOR POETRY

c/o Perpetual Trustee Company Ltd
39 Hunter Street
Sydney, NSW 2000
Australia
Contact: Charitable Trusts Manager.
Award of $200 in recognition of the best volume of poetry published in the previous year. Poets must be Australian by birth, or naturalised Australians resident in the country for over 10 years.

1980	The Boys Who Stole the Funeral by Leslie Allan Murray
1981	Nero's Poems by Geoffrey Lehmann
1982	Tide Country by Vivian Smith
1983	Collected Poems by Peter Porter
1984	The Three Gates and Other Poems by Rosemary Dobson
1985	Selected Poems by Robert Gray
	The Amorous Cannibal by Chris Wallace Crabbe
1986	Washing the Money by Ryhil McMaster
1987	Occasions of Birds and other Poems by Elizabeth Riddell
1988	Under Berlin by John Tranter
1989	A Tremendous World in Her Head: Selected

	Poems
	by Dorothy Hewett
1990	Dog Fox Field by Les A Murray
1991	The Empire of Grass by Gary Catalano
	Penial by Doctor Kevin Hart

RUTH LILLY POETRY PRIZE

c/o Poetry
Modern Poetry Association
60 West Walton Street
Chicago, IL 60610
USA
Given to a US poet whose accomplishments warrant extraordinary recognition.
Annual prize of $75,000

1986	Adrienne Rich
1987	Philip Levine
1988	Anthony Hecht
1989	Mona Van Duyn
1990	Hayden Carruth
1991	David Wagoner
1992	John Ashbery
1993	Charles Wright
1994	Donald Hall
1995	A R Ammons
1996	Gerald Stern

DOROTHY LIVESAY POETRY PRIZE

West Coast Book Prizes Society
1033 Davie Street #700
Vancouver, BC V6E 1M7
Canada
Contact: Execuitve Director
Regional award of $2000 for poets resident in the area for over 3 years.

LOS ANGELES TIMES BOOK PRIZES

Los Angeles Times
Times Mirror Square
Los Angeles, CA 90053
USA
Contact: PR Supervisor

MAIL ON SUNDAY/JOHN LLEWELLYN RHYS PRIZE

Book Trust
Book House, 45 East Hill
London SW18 2QZ
England
Contact: Sandra Vince
First prize of £5000 for works of fiction, non-fiction, drama or poetry written in English and published in the UK that year. Writers must be under 35 and a citizen of Great Britain or the Commonwealth.

1980	The Diamonds at the Bottom of the Sea by Desmond Hogan
1981	The Laird of Abbotsford by A N Wilson
1982	An Ice-Cream War by William Boyd
1983	The Slow Train to Milan by Lisa St Aubin de Teran
1984	Dangerous Play by Andrew Motion
1985	Out of the Blue by John Milne
1986	Loving Roger by Tim Parks
1987	The Passion by Jeanette Winterson
1988	The March Fence by Matthew Yorke
1989	Sylvia Townsend Warner by Claire Harman

1990	Wittgenstein: The Duty of Genius by Ray Monk
1991	Night Geometry and the Garscadden Trains by A L Kennedy
1992	Sweet Thames by Matthew Kneale
1993	On Foot to the Golden Horn: A Walk to Istanbul by Jason Goodwin
1994	What A Carve Up! by Jonathan Coe

LENORE MARSHALL POETRY PRIZE
Academy of American Poets
584 Broadway, Suite 1208
New York, NY 10012, USA
Recognizes the most outstanding book of poetry published in the US in the previous year. Publishers are invited to submit books.
Annual prize of $10,000

1974	O/I by Cid Corman
1975	The Freeing of the Dust by Denise Levertov
1976	The Names of the Lost by Philip Levine
1977	Collected Poems, 1919-1976 by Allen Tate
1978	Brothers, I Loved You All by Hayden Carruth
1979	The Poems of Stanley Kunitz,1928-1978 by Stanley Kunitz
1980	The Collected Poems of Sterling A Brown by Sterling A Brown
1981	The Bridge of Change: Poems 1974-1980 by John Logan
1982	The Argot Merchant Disaster by George Starbuck
1983	Collected Poems, 1930-83 by Josephine Miles
1984	A Wave by John Ashbery
1985	New Selected Poems by Howard Moss
1986	The Happy Man by Donald Hall
1987	The Sisters: New and Selected Poems by Josephine Jacobsen
1988	Selected Poems, 1938-1988 by Thomas McGrath
1989	God Hunger by Michael Ryan
1990	New Poems, 1980-1988 by John Haines
1991	An Atlas of the Difficult World by Adrienne Rich
1992	The Man with Night Sweats by Thom Gunn
1993	Travels by W S Merwin
1994	Winter Numbers by Marilyn Hacker
1995	Chickamauga by Charles Wright

INGRAM MERRILL FOUNDATION
104 East 40th Street, Suite 302
New York, NY 10016
USA

HAROLD MORTON LANDON TRANSLATION AWARD
Academy of American Poets
584 Broadway, Suite 1208
New York, NY 10012, USA
Awarded to the translator of a published translation of poetry from any language into English. Publishers may submit eligible books.
Annual prize of $1000.

1976	Robert Fitzgerald for the Iliad of Homer
1978	Galway Kinnell for The Poems of François Villon
	Howard Norman for The Wishing Bone Cycle
1980	Saralyn R Daly for The Book of True Love by Juan Ruis
	Edmund Keeley for Ritsos in Parenthesis
1982	Rika Lesser for Guide to the Underworld by Gunnar Ekelöf

1984	Robert Fitzgerlad for The Odyssey of Homer
	Stephen Mitchell for The Selected Poetry of Rainer Maria Rilke
1985	Edward Snow for New Poems (1907) of Rainer Maria Rilke
1986	William Arrowsmith for The Storm and Other Things by Eugenio Montale
1987	Mark Anderson for In the Storm of Roses by Ingeborg Bachmann
1988	Peter Hargitai for Perched on Nothing's Branch by Attila József
1989	Martin Greenberg for Heinrich von Kleist: Five Plays
1990	Stephen Mitchell for Variable Directions by Dan Pagis
1991	Robert Fagles for The Iliad of Homer
1992	John DuVal for The Discovery of America by Cesare Pascarella
	Andrew Schelling for Dropping the Bow: Poems of Ancient India
1993	Charles Simic for The Horse Has Six Legs: An Anthology of Serbian Poetry
1994	Rosmarie Waldrop for The Book of Margins by Edmond Jabès
1995	Robert Pinsky for The Inferno of Dante: A New Verse Translation
1996	Guy Davenport for 7 Greeks

NATIONAL BOOK AWARDS
National Book Awards Foundation
260 Fifth Avenue, 4th Floor
New York, NY 10001
USA
Contact: Executive Director
Award of $10,000 presented annually to living American writers in three categories (fiction, non-fiction and poetry), with $1000 for short-listed works.
Poetry

1991	Philip Levine
1992	Mary Oliver
1993	A R Ammons
1994	James Tate
1995	Stanley J Kunitz

NATIONAL BOOK CRITICS CIRCLE AWARDS
400 North Broad Street
Philadelphia, PA 19103
USA
Contact: The President
Annual award for excellence in biography, criticism, fiction, non-fiction and poetry published for the first time in the previous year by American authors. Nominated by members.
Award: Scroll and citation.

1991	Amy Gerstler
1992	Albert Goldbarth
1993	Hayden Carruth
1994	Mark Doty
1995	Mark Rudman

NATIONAL POETRY COMPETITION
Poetry Society
22 Betterton Street,
London WC2H 9BU
England

Contact: Competition Organizer
Annual award for an unpublished poem of up to 40 lines by anyone over the age of 18.
Prizes: £3000 (1st), £500 (2nd), £250 (3rd), plus lesser prizes.

NEUSTADT INTERNATIONAL PRIZE FOR LITERATURE
World Literature Today
University of Oklahoma
110 Monnet Hall,
Norman, OK 73019
USA
Recognizes outstanding achievement in poetry, fiction or drama written in any language. Awarded only to a living author who has a representative portion of work in English, French and/or Spanish. No applications are accpeted. Biennial prize of $40,000, a replica of an eagle feather cast in silver, and an award certificate.

NOBEL PRIZE FOR LITERATURE
Swedish Academy
Box 5232, Sturegatan 14
S-10245 Stockholm
Sweden
Annual awards with strict eligibilty controls. Prize of US $1,120,000, increasing yearly with inflation.
(See Appendix E for a complete list of poetry winners)

NOVA POETICA OPEN POETRY COMPETITION
14 Pennington Oval
Lymington
Hampshire SO41 8BQ, England
Contact: Adrian Bishop, Editor
First Prize of £300, plus lesser prizes.

OBSERVER NATIONAL CHILDREN'S POETRY COMPETITION
Observer Magazine
Chelsea Bridge House
Queenstown Road
London SW8 4NN
England

OUTPOSTS POETRY COMPETITION
c/o Hippopotamus Press
22 Whitewell Road
Frome, Somerset BA11 4EL
England
Contact: Roland John
Annual prize of £1000 for unpublished works of not more than 40 lines.

PETERLOO POETS OPEN POETRY COMPETITION
2 Kelly Gardens
Calstock, Cornwall PL18 9SA
England
Contact: Lynn Chambers
Annual first prize of £4000, plus lesser prizes, for unpublished poems in English of not more than 40 lines.
1996   *The Magi by John Watts*

POETRY LIFE OPEN POETRY COMPETITION
14 Pennington Oval
Lymington

Hampshire SO41 8BQ
England
Contact: Adrain Bishop, Editor
First prize of £500, plus lesser prizes.

PRIJS DER NEDERLANDSE LETTEREN (Prize for Dutch Letters)
Nederlandse Taalunie
Stadhoudersplantsoen 2
2517 JL The Hague
Netherlands
Contact: The Secretary
A literary prize to celebrate literary writers who write in the Dutch language. Categories for prose, poetry, essays and/or drama.
Prize of f30,000 every three years.

PULITZER PRIZE IN POETRY
Administrator
Columbia University
New York, NY 10027
USA
(See Appendix F for a complete list of poetry winners)

PUSHCART PRIZE: Best of the Small Presses
Pushcart Press
Box 380
Wainscott, NY 11975
USA
Annual award for work published by a small press or literary journal.

QUEEN'S PRESENTATION MEDALS - POETRY
Buckingham Palace
London
England
The Medal is given for a book of verse published in the English Language, but translations of exceptional merit may be considered. It was originally awarded only to British citizens but the scope was widened in 1985 to make Her Majesty's subjects in Commonwealth Monarchies eligible for consideration.
Awarded Gold Medal.
(See Appendix G for a complete list of previous winners)

RAIZISS/DE PALCHI TRANSLATION AWARD
Academy of American Poets
584 Broadway, Suite 1208
New York, NY 10012
USA
Recognizes outstanding translations of modern Italian poetry into English. A $5000 book prize and a $20,000 fellowship is awarded, with the winner of the latter receiving a residency at the American Academy in Rome. No applications are accepted for the book prize. Submissions for the fellowship are accepted in odd-numbered years.
Fellowship
1996   *Anthony Molino for Esercizi di tipologia by Valerio Magrelli*
Book Prize
1996   *W S Di Piero for This Strange Joy: Selected Poems of Sandro Penna*

THEODORE ROETHKE MEMORIAL FOUNDATION
11 West Hannum Boulevard
Saginaw, MI 48602
USA

ROYAL SOCIETY OF LITERATURE AWARD UNDER THE W H HEINEMANN BEQUEST
Royal Society of Literature
1 Hyde Park Gardens
London W2 2LT
England
Annual award of £5000 to works written in English and published in the previous year.

SIGNAL POETRY AWARD
c/o Thimble Press
Lockwood, Station Road,
Woodchester, Stroud,
Glos GL5 5EQ
England
Contact: Nancy Chambers, Editor
Awarded annually since 1979 by Signal, a specialist journal, for excellence in a single-poet collection, poetry anthology or critical work that promote poetry for children. All potery book spublished in Britain are eligible.
Prize: £100 plus award certificate

1979	Moon-Bells and Other Poems by Ted Hughes
1980-81	No award given
1982	You Can't Catch Me! by Mike Rosen and Quentin Blake
1983	The Rattle Bag edited by Seamus Heaney and Ted Hughes
1984	Sky in the Pie by Roger McGough
1985	What is the Truth? by Ted Hughes
1986	Song of the City by Gareth Owen
1987	Early in the Morning by Charles Causely
1988	Boo to a Goose by John Mole
1989	When I Dance by James Berry
1990	Heard It in the Playground by Allan Ahlberg
1991	This Poem Doesn't Rhyme edited by Gerard Benson
1992	Shades of Green edited by Anne Harvey
1993	Two's Company by Jackie Kay
1994	The All-Nite Café by Philip Gross
1995	Secrets by Helen Dunmore
1996	Buns for the Elephants by Mike Harding

W H SMITH LITERARY AWARD
Strand House
7 Holbein Place
London SW1W 8NR
England
Contact: Michale MacKenzie
Annual prize of £10,000 presented for outstanding contributions to English literature in the year under review. Eligible authors must be from Britain, Republic of Ireland or the Commonwealth, and works must be written in English and published in the UK.

STAND INTERNATIONAL POETRY COMPETITION
Stand Magazine
179 Wingrove Road
Newcastle-Upon-Tyne NE4 9DA,
England

Contact: Linda Goldsmith
Awarded for an original poem of no longer than 500 lines written in English. Works must be previously unpublished and unbroadcast.
Prize: £2500 in total prize money, including £1500 first prize.

TANNING PRIZE
Academy of American Poets
584 Broadway, Suite 1208
New York, NY 10012
USA
Recognizes outstanding and proven mastery in the art of poetry. No applicatins are accepted.
Annual prize of $100, 000

1994	W S Merwin
1995	James Tate

WATERSHED FOUNDATION
6925 Willow Street North West, No 201
Washington, DC 20012
USA

WHITBREAD BOOK OF THE YEAR
Booksellers Association
Minster House, 272 Vauxhall Bridge Road
London SW1V 1BA
England
Contact: Corinne Gotch
Prizes awarded annually in five categories, including poetry, to writers resident in the UK or the Republic of Ireland for at least three years. The Whitbread Book of the Year is then chosen from the nominees.
Prizes: £21,000 (Book of the Year), £2000 (all nominees).
Poetry Award

1985	Elegies by Douglas Dunn (and Book of the Year)
1986	Stet by Peter Reading
1987	The Haw Lantern by Seamus Heaney
1988	The Automatic Oracle by Peter Porter
1989	Shibboleth by Michael Donaghy
1990	Daddy, Daddy by Paul Durcan
1991	Gorse Fires by Michael Longley
1992	The Gaze of the Gorgon by Tony Harrison
1993	Mean Time by Carol Ann Duffy
1994	Out of Danger by James Fenton
1995	Gunpowder by Bernard O'Donoghue

WHITING WRITERS AWARD
Mrs Giles Whiting Foundation
1133 Avenue of the Americas
New York, NY 10003
USA
Annual award of $30,000 presented to emergent writers in recognition of their writing achievement as well as promise for producing outstanding future work.
Poetry

1985	Douglas Crase
	Jorie Graham
	Linda Gregg
	James Schuyler
1986	John Ash
	Hayden Carruth
	Frank Stewart
	Ruth Stone
1987	Mark Cox

	Michael Ryan
1988	Michale Burkard
	Sylvia Moss
1989	Russell Edson
	Mary Karr
	C D Wright
1990	Emily Hiestand
	Dennis Nurkse
1991	Thylias Moss
	Franz Wright
1992	Jane Mead
	Roger Fanning
1993	Mark Levine
	Nathaniel Mackey
	Dionisio D Martinez
	Kathleen Pierce
1994	Mark Doty
	Wayne Koestenbaum
	Mary Swander

WALT WHITMAN AWARD

Academy of American Poets
584 Broadway, Suite 1208
New York, NY 10012
USA
Award for a first-book publication by an eminent American poet who has not yet published a book of poetry in a standard edition.
Annual prize of $5000

1975	Climbing into the Roots by Reg Saner
1976	The Hocus-Pocus of the Universe by Laura Gilpin
1977	Guilty Bystander by Lauren Shakely
1978	Wonders by Karen Snow
1979	Shooting Rats at the Bibb County Dump by David Bottoms
1980	Work, for the Night is Coming by Jared Carter
1981	Whispering to Fool the Wind by Alberto Ríos
1982	Jurgis Petraskas by Anthony Petrosky
1983	Across the Mutual Landscape by Christopher Gilbert
1984	For the New Year by Eric Pankey
1985	Bindweed by Christianne Balk
1986	Fragments from the Fire by Chris Llewellyn
1987	The Weight of Numbers by April Bernard
1988	Blackbird Bye Bye by April Bernard
1989	The Game of Statues by Martha Hollander
1990	The Cult of the Right Hand by Elaine Terranova
1991	From the Iron Chair by Greg Glazner
1992	The Fire in All Things by Stephen Yenser
1993	Science and Other Poems by Alison Hawthorne Deming
1994	Because the Brain Can Be Talked into Anything by Jan Richman
1995	Resurrection by Nicole Cooley
1996	Madonna Anno Domini by Joshua Clover

APPENDIX J
ORGANIZATIONS AND EVENTS OF INTEREST TO POETS

The following organizations either offer membership to poets or those interested in poetry, or sponsor events in which poetry plays a major part. For organizations of more general interest to writers, see Appendix B of the **International Authors and Writers Who's Who.**

ACADEMY OF AMERICAN POETS
584 Broadway, Suite 1208
New York, NY 10012
USA

AMERICAN SOCIETY OF COMPOSERS, AUTHORS AND PUBLISHERS
1 Lincoln Plaza
New York, NY 10023
USA

BRITISH HAIKU SOCIETY
Sinodun, Shalford
Braintree, Essex CM7 5HN
England

CANADIAN AUTHORS ASSOCIATION
275 Slater Street, Suite 500
Ottawa, Ontario K1P 5H9
Canada

CANADIAN POETRY ASSOCIATION
PO Box 22571, St George Postal Outlet
Toronto, Ontario M5S 1VO
Canada

CHINA POETRY SOCIETY
17 Beibingmasi Lane
Dongcheng District
Beijing 100009
China

COUNCIL OF LITERARY MAGAZINES AND PRESSES
154 Christopher Street, Suite 3-C
New York, NY 10014
USA

EUROPEAN ASSOCIATION FOR THE PROMOTION OF POETRY
European Poetry House, 'The Seven Sleepers'
J.P. Minckelsstraat 168,
B-3000 Leuven
Belgium

EUROPEAN POETRY LIBRARY
Blidjde Inkommststrasse 9
B-3000 Leuven
Belgium

FEDERATION OF INTERNATIONAL POETRY ASSOCIATIONS
PO Box 579
Santa Claus, IN 47579
USA

HAIKU SOCIETY OF AMERICA
c/o Japan Society Inc
333 East 47th Street
New York, NY 10017
USA

INTERNATIONAL POETRY FORUM
4415 5th Avenue
Pittsburgh, PA 15213
USA

LEAGUE OF CANADIAN POETS
54 Wolseley Street, Suite 204
Toronto, Ontario M5T 1A5
Canada

MAGIC CIRCLE
13455 SW 16 Court #F-405
Pembroke Pines, FL 33027
USA

MODERN POETRY ASSOCIATION
60 West Walton Street
Chicago, IL 60610
USA

NATIONAL FEDERATION OF STATE POETRY SOCIETIES
PO Box 486
Arab, AL 35016
USA

NATIONAL POETRY ASSOCIATION
PO Box 173
Bayport, MN 55003
USA

NATIONAL POETRY FOUNDATION
27 Mill Road
Fareham, Hants PO16 0TH
England

POETRY ASSOCIATION OF SCOTLAND
38 Dovecot Road
Edinburgh EH12 7LE
Scotland

POETRY BOOK SOCIETY
PBS Freepost,
Book House
45 East Hill
London SW18 2BR
England

POETRY IRELAND LTD
Bermingham Tower
Dublin Castle
Dublin 2
Ireland

POETRY LIBRARY
Royal Festival Hall
South Bank Centre
London SE1 8XX
England

POETRY PROJECT
St Mark's Church
131 East 10th Street at 2nd Avenue
New York, NY 10003
USA

POETRY SOCIETY
22 Betterton Street
London WC2H 9BU
England

POETRY SOCIETY OF AMERICA
15 Gramercy Park
New York, NY 10003
USA

POETRY SOCIETY OF INDIA
L-67A Malaviya Nagar
New Delhi 110 017
India

POETS AND WRITERS
72 Spring Street
New York, NY 10012
USA

SCOTTISH POETRY LIBRARY
Tweeddale Court
14 High Street
Edinburgh EH1 1TE
Scotland

SOCIETY OF AUTHORS
84 Drayton Gardens
London SW10 9SB
England

WORLD ACADEMY OF ARTS AND CULTURE
3146 Buckeye Court
Placerville, CA 95667
USA

WORLD POETRY SOCIETY INTERCONTINENTAL
c/o Dr. Seethapthi Nagar
118 Raja Street,
Velacheri
Madras 600 042, Tamil Nadu
India

YUKI TEIKEI HAIKU SOCIETY OF THE UNITED STATES AND CHINA
PO Box 90456
San Jose, CA 95109
USA

APPENDIX K
POETRY BOOK PUBLISHERS

AFRICA

Carrefour Press
PO Box 2629
Cape Town 8000
South Africa

Tree Shrew Press
PO Box 9135
Eldoret
Kenya

Witwatersrand University Press
2050 Johannesburg
South Africa

ASIA

Blue Jacket Press
1-51-54 Sugue-cho
Sanio-shi, Niigata-ken 955
Japan

Chinese Literature Press
24 Baiwanzhuang Road
Beijing 100037
China

New Cicada
40-11 KUBO
Hobara, Fukushima 960-06
Japan

Peacock Books
College Square
Cuttack
Orissa 753003
India

Poetry Nippon Press
11-2, 5-Chome
Nagaike-cho
Showa-ku, Nagoya 466
Japan

Prakalpana Literature
P 40 Nandana Park
Calcutta 700034
West Bengal
India

AUSTRALIA AND NEW ZEALAND

Hecate Press
PO Box 99
St Lucia, QLD 4067
Australia

Islands
4 Sealy Road
Torbay, Auckland 10
New Zealand

Little Esther Books
PO Box 21
North Adelaide, SA 5006
Australia

Night Owl Publishers
PO Box 242
Euroa, VIC 3666
Australia

Pinchgut Press
6 Oaks Avenue
Cremorne
Sydney, NSW 2090
Australia

Visa Books (South Continent Corp Pty Ltd)
PO Box 1024
Richmond North, VIC 3121
Australia

CANADA

Aardvark Enterprises
204 Millbank Drive SW
Calgary
Alberta T2Y 2H9

Beach Holme
4252 Commerce Circle
Victoria
British Columbia V8Z 4M2

Borealis Press Ltd
9 Ashburn Drive
Ottawa,
Onatraio K2E 6N4

Coach House Press
401 (rear) Heron Street
Toronto
Ontario M5S 2GS

Cormorant Books
RR1
Dunvegan
Ontario K0C 1J0

Cosmic Trend
Sheridan Mail Box 47014
Mississauga
Ontario L5K 2R2

DGR Publication
125 Principale North Street, Suite 13,
L'Annonciation
Québec J0T 1T0

Guernica Editions Inc
PO Box 117, Station P
Toronto
Ontario M6C 2W3

Hamilton Haiku Press
237 Prospect Street South
Hamilton
Ontario L8M 2Z6

Insomniac Press
378 Delaware Avenue
Toronto
Ontario M6H 2T8

Marcasite Press
23 Riverside Avenue
Truro
Nova Scotia B2N 4G2

Mekler & Deahl
237 Prospect Street South
Hamilton
Ontario L8M 2Z6

Oolichan Books
PO Box 10
Lantzville
British Columbia V0R 2HL

Prairie Journal Trust
PO Box 61203, Brentwood PO
Calgary
Alberta T2L 2K6

Quarry Press
University of Toronto Press
5201 Dufferin Street
Downsview
Ontario M3H 5T8

Ronsdale Press
3350 West 21st Avenue
Vancouver
British Columbia V6S 1G7

Thistledown Press Ltd
633 Main Street
Saskatoon
Saskatchewan S7J 2Z5

Turnstone Press
607-100 Arthur Street
Winnipeg
Manitoba R3B 1H3

Turnstone Press
University of Toronto Press
5201 Dufferin Street
Downsview
Ontario M3H 5T8

Tyro Publishing
194 Carlbert Street
Sault Ste Marie
Ontario P6A 5E1

Underwhich Editions
PO Box 262
Adelaide Street Station
Toronto
Ontario M5C 2I4

Unfinished Monument Press
237 Prospect Street South

Hamilton
Ontario L8M 2Z6

Véhicule Press
PO Box 125
Place du Parc Station
Montréal
Québec H2W 2M9

West Coast Paradise Publishing
#5 - 9060 Tronson Road
Vernon
British Columbia V1T 6L7

Wolsak and Wynn Publishers Ltd
Box 316
Don Mills Post Office
Ontario M3C 2S7

Women's Press
517 College Street
Suite 233
Toronto
Ontario M6G 4A2

EIRE

Dedalus Poetry Press
24 The Heath
Cypress Down
Dublin 6

Gallery Press
19 Oakdown Road
Dublin 14

Poetry Ireland
Bermingham Tower
Dublin Castle
Dublin 2

Raven Arts
PO Box 1430
Finglas
Dublin 11

Salmon Publishing
The Bridge Mills
Galway

Sunburst Press
25 Newtown Avenue
Blackrock
Co Dublin

Wolfhound Press
68 Mountjoy Square
Dublin 1

EUROPE

Alyscamps Press
35 rue de L'Esperance
75013 Paris
France

Coop Antigruppo Siciliano
Villa Schammachanat
Via Argenteria, KM 4

Trapani-Erice
Sicily, Italy

Expanded Media Editions
PO Box 190136
Prinz Albert Str 65
5300 Bonn 1
Germany

Foreign Languages Press Group
PO Box 33-28
Piata Presei Libere 1
71341 Bucharest
Romania

Handshake Editions
Atelier A2
83 rue de la Tombre-Issoir
75014 Paris
France

Kontexts Publications
Overtoom 444
1954 JW Amsterdam
Netherlands

Maro Verlag
Reidingstr 25/6f
Augsburg
Germany

Model-Peltex Association
3 rue des Couples
67000 Strasbourg
France

Modern Media
PO Box 722
220 07 Lund
Sweden

Modra Musa Publishers
Janovskeho
17000 Prague 7
Czech Republic

My Mother's House
Atini Talo, Villa Remdia
16100 Uusikila
Finland

Nioba, Uitgevers
Maarschalk Geraldstraat 6
2000 Antwerp
Belgium

Vanitas Press
Platslagarevagen 4E1
227 30 Lund
Sweden

LATIN AMERICA AND THE CARIBBEAN

Sandbury Press
PO Box 507
Kingston 10
Jamaica
West Indies

Zagier & Urruty Publicaciones
PO Box 94
Surcusal 19
Buenos Aires 1419
Argentina

UNITED KINGDOM

ENGLAND

Agenda Editions
5 Cranbourne Court
Albert Bridge Road
London SW11 4PE

Anvil Press Poetry Ltd
69 King George Street
London SE10 8PX

Bloodaxe Books Ltd
PO Box 1SN
Newcastle upon Tyne NE99 1SN

Carcanet Press Ltd
208 Corn Exchange Buildings
Manchester M4 3BQ

Dangaroo Books
PO Box 186
Coventry CV4 7HG

Enitharmon Press
36 St George's Avenue
London N7 0HD

Fern Publications
24 Frosty Hollow
East Hunsbury
Northants NN4 0SY

Flambard Press
4 Mitchell Avenue
Jesmond
Newcastle upon Tyne NE2 3LA

Forest Books
20 Forest View
Chingford
London E4 7AY

Frogmore Press
42 Morehall Avenue
Folkestone
Kent CT19 4EF

Greylag Press
2 Grove Street
Higham Ferrers, Rushden
Northants NN10 8HX

Hangman Books
2 May Road
Rochester
Kent ME1 2HY

Headland Publications
38 York Avenue
West Kirby
Wirral
Merseyside

Hippopotamus Press
22 Whitewell Road
Frome
Somerset BA11 4EL

Iron Press
5 Marden Terrace
Cullercoats, North Shields
Northumberland NE30 4PD

Joe Soap's Canoe Publications
30 Quilter Road
Felixstowe
Suffolk IP11 7JJ

KRAX
63 Dixon Lane
Wortly
Leeds LS12 4RR

K T Publications
'Amikeco', 16 Fane Close
Stamford
Lincolnshire PE9 1HG

Lewes Live Literature
All Saints Arts Centre
Friars Walk
Lewes
E Sussex BN7 2LE

Littlewood Arc
The Nanholme Centre
Shaw Wood Road
Todmorden
W Yorks OL14 6DA

Lymes Press
'Greenfields', Agger Hill
Finney Green
Newcastle-under-Lyme
Staffs ST5 6AA

Mammon Press
12 Dartmouth Avenue
Bath
Avon

Mandeville Press
2 Taylor's Hill
Hitchin
Herts

Many Press
15 Norcott Road
London N16 7BJ

Merlin Books Ltd
40 East Street
Braunton
Devon EX33 2EA

Oasis Books
12 Stevenage Road
London SW6 6ES

Peterloo Poets
2 Kelly Gardens
Calstock
Cornwall PH8 9SA

Precious Pearl Publications
71 Harrow Crescent
Romford
Essex RM3 7BJ

Prest Roots Press
34 Alpine Court
Kenilworth CV8 2GP

Redbeck Press
24 Aireville Road
Frizinghall
Bradford BD9 4HH

Rivelin Grapheme Press
Merlin House, Church Street
Hungerford
Berkshire RG17 0JG

Rockingham Press
11 Musley Lane
Ware
Herts SG12 7EN

Shearsman Books
47 Dayton Close
Plymouth
Devon PL6 5DX

Smith/Doorstop
Floor 4, Byram Arcade
Westgate
Huddersfield HD1 1ND

Stride Publications
37 Portland Street
Newtown
Exeter
Devon EX1 2EG

Turret Books
42 Lamb's Conduit Street
London WC1N 3LJ

Vigil Publications
12 Priory Mead
Bruton
Somerset BA10 0DZ

Wide Skirt Press
93 Blackhouse Road
Fartown
Huddersfield HD2 1AP

Writers Forum
89A Petherton Road
London N5 2QT

NORTHERN IRELAND

Blackstaff Press
3 Galway Park
Dundonald
Belfast BT16 0AN

Dissident Editions
71 Ballyculter Road
Loughkeelan
Downpatrick
County Down BT30 7BD

SCOTLAND

Bethany Publications
5 Drynie Place
Muir of Ord
Ross-shire IV6 7RA

Chapman Publishing
4 Broughton Press
Edinburgh EH1 3RX

Gordon Wright Publishing
25 Mayfield Road
Edinburgh EH9 2NQ

Saltire Society
9 Fountain Close
Edinburgh EH1 1TF

WALES

Envoi Poets
2 Pen Ffordd
Newport
Dyfed SA42 0QT

Gomer Press
Llandysul
Ceredigion
Dyfed SA44 4BQ

Honno Ltd
c/o Ailsa Craig
Heol Y Cawl
Dinas Powys
Bro Morgannwg CF64 4AH

Seren Books
1st Floor, 2 Wyndham Street
Bridgend
Mid Glamorgan CF31 1EF

USA

Aldine Press Ltd
304 South Tyson Avenue
Glenside, PA 19038

Allen Publishing
33 W Lancaster Avenue
Ardmore, PA 19003

Alms House Press
PO Box 217
Pearl River, NY 10965

Alpha Beat Press
31 Waterloo Street
New Hope, PA 18938

American Literary Press/Noble House
8019 Belair Road, #10
Baltimore, MD 21236

Anamnesis Press
PO Box 581153
Salt Lake City, UT 84158

Arjuna Library Press
1025 Garner Street, D, Space 18
Colorado Springs, CO 80905

ART Paul Schlosser Inc
214 Dunning Street
Madison, WI 53704

Arte Publico Press
University of Houston
Houston, TX 77204

Artifact Press Ltd
900 Tanglewood Drive
Concord, MA 01742

Atticus Press
PO Box 927428
San Diego, CA 92192

Bennett & Kitchel
PO Box 4422
East Lansing, MI 48826

Black Buzzard Press
1110 Seaton Lane
Falls Church, VA 22046

Black Hat Press
PO Box 12
Goodhue, MN 55027

Black Sparrow Graphic Arts
24 East Tenth Street
Santa Rosa, CA 95401

Bogg Publications
422 North Cleveland Street
Arlington, VA 22201

Bottom Dog Press
c/o Firelands College
Bowling Green State University
Huron, OH 44839

Broken Shadow Publications
472 44th Street
Oakland, CA 94609-2136

Camel Press
General Delivery
Big Cove Tannery, PA 17212

Cerulean Press
18301 Halsted Street
Northridge, CA 91325

City Lights Books
261 Columbus Avenue
San Francisco, CA 94133

Coffee House Press
27 North 4th Street, Suite 400
Minneapolis, MN 55401

Cokefish Press
31 Waterloo Street
New Hope, PA 18938

Conservatory of American Letters
PO Box 298
Thomaston, ME 04861

F Marion Crawford Memorial Society
Saracinesca House
3610 Meadowbrook Avenue

Nashville, TN 37205

Creative with Words Publications
PO Box 223226
Carmel, CA 93922

Curbstone Press
321 Jackson Street
Willimantic, CT 06226

Dark Regions Press
PO Box 6301
Concord, CA 94524

Dragons Teeth Press
7700 Wentworth Springs Road
El Dorado National Forest
Georgetown, GA 95634

Dry Bones Press
PO Box 640345
San Francisco, CA 94164

Ermine Soup
2870 NE 36 Street
Fort Lauderdale, FL 33308

H R Felgenhauer
PO Box 146486
Chicago, IL 60614

Fithian Press
PO Box 1525
Santa Barbara, CA 93102

Fragile Twilight Press
15 W 8th Street
Barnegat Light, NJ 08006

Galileo Press Ltd
15201 Wheeler Lane
Sparks, MD 21152

Gávea-Brown Publications
Department of Portuguese and
  Brazilian Studies
Box 0, Brown University
Providence, RI 02912

Geekspeak Unique Press
PO Box 11443
Indianapolis, IN 46201

George & Mertie's Place: Rooms with a View
PO Box 10335
Spokane, WA 99209

Ghost Pony Press
2518 Gregory Street
Madison, WI 53711

Glass Cherry Press
901 Europe Bay Road
Ellison Bay, WI 54210-9643

GLB Publishers
1028 Howard #503
San Francisco, CA 94103

Golden Isis Press
PO Box 525
Fort Covington, NY 12937

Green Fuse Poetry
3365 Holland Drive
Santa Rosa, CA 95404

Green River Writers Inc
11906 Locust Road
Middletown, KY 40243

Groundwater Press
PO Box 704
Hudson, NY 12534

Harper Square Press
29 East Division Street
Chicago, IL 60610

Heat Press
PO Box 26218
Los Angeles, CA 90026

Heaven Bone Press
PO Box 486
Chester, NY 10918

Highway Poets, MC
PO Box 1400
Brewster, MA 02631

Ion Books
PO Box 111327
Memphis, TN 38111

Inter-Relations
PO Box 11445
Berkeley, CA 94712

Jahbone Press
3787 Maplewood Avenue
Los Angeles, CA 90066

Jungle Man Press
211 W Mulberry Street, 3rd Floor
Baltimore, MD 21201

Karamu Association
Department of English
Eastern Illinois University
Charleston, IL 61920

Kaya Production
8 Harrison Street, Suite 3
New York, NY 10013

Kelsey St Press
2718 Ninth Street
Berkeley, CA 94710

Kenyette Productions
20131 Champ Drive
Euclid, OH 44117-2208

Left Curve Publications
PO Box 472
Oakland, CA 94604

Lotus Press Inc
PO Box 21607
Detroit, MI 48221

Lunar Offensive Press
1910 Foster Avenue
Brooklyn, NY 11230-1902

Luz Bilingual Publishing Inc
PO Box 571062
Tarzana, CA 91357-1062

Manuslave Press
3451 Randolph Street
Jacksonville, FL 32207

Maxrat Press
PO Box 44089
Calabash, NC 28467

MCS Publishing
937 NW 56th
Seattle, WA 98107

Mellen Poetry Press
PO Box 450
Lewiston, NY 14092-0450

Midmarch Arts Press
300 Riverside Drive
New York, NY 10025

Milkweed Editions
430 First Avenue North, Suite 400
Minneapolis, MN 55401

Mind In Motion Publications
PO Box 1118
Apple Valley, CA 92307

M I P Company
PO Box 27484
Minneapolis, MN 55427

Morris Publishing Company
1415 Hemlock Street
Cayce, SC 29033

Mother Road Publications
PO Box 22068
Albuquerque, NM 87154

Mount Olive College Press
624 Henderson Street
Mount Olive, NC 28365

Moving Parts Press
10699 Empire Grade
Santa Cruz, CA 95060

Negative Capability Press
62 Ridgelawn Drive East
Mobile, AL 36608

New Earth Publications
1921 Ashby Avenue
Berkeley, CA 94703

New Native Press
PO Box 661
Cullowhee, NC 28723

nine muses books
3541 Kent Creek Road
Winston, OR 97496

Nite Owl Press
3101 Schieck SE, Suite 100
Pittsburgh, PA 15227

North Star Press of St Cloud Inc

PO Box 451
St Cloud, MN 56302-0451

Office Number One
1708 South Congress Avenue
Austin, TX 78704

Open Hand Publishing Inc
PO Box 22048
Seattle, WA 98112

O!! Zone Press
1266 Fountain View Drive
Houston, TX 77057

Paper Bag Press
PO Box 268805
Chicago, IL 60626

Papyrus Literary Enterprises
102 La Salle Road
PO Box 270797
West Hartford, CT 06127

Paradoxist Movement Association
2456 S Rose Peak Drive
Tucson, AZ 85710

Parallax Press
PO Box 7355
Berkeley, CA 94707

Paris Press Inc
1117 West Road, Ashfield
Williamsburg, MA 01096

Pemmican Press
PO Box 121
Redmond, WA 98073

Pennywhistle Press
PO Box 734
Tesuque, NM 87574

Perivale Press & Agency
13830 Erwin Street
Van Nuys, CA 91401-2914

Pocahontas Press
PO Drawer F
Blacksburg, VA 24063

Poet Band Co
PO Box 4725
Pittsburgh, PA 15206

Poetry Center
Passaic County Community College
1 College Boulevard
Paterson, NJ 07505-1179

Poetry Forum
5713 Larchmont Drive
Erie, PA 16509

Post-Apollo Press
35 Marie Street
Sausalito, CA 94965

Prickly Pear Press
1402 Mimosa Pass
Cedar Park, TX 78613

Protean Press
287-28th Avenue
San Francisco, CA 94121

Pterodactyl Press
PO Box 205
Cumberland, IA 50843

Purple Finch Press
PO Box 758
Dewitt, NY 13214

Pushcart Press
PO Box 380
Wainscott, NY 11975

Rabeth Publishing Company
201 South Cottage Grove/PO Box 171
Kirksville, MO 63501

R C Publications
97 Delaware Avenue
Albany, NY

Red Dragon Press
433 Old Town Court
Alexandria, VA 22314

Red Herring Press
c/o Channing-Murrary Foundation
1209 W Oregon
Urbana, IL 61801

Rising Star Publishers
2105 Amherst Road, Dept G
Hyattsville, MD 20783

Rising Tide Press
PO Box 6136
Santa Fe, NM 87502

Roof Books
303 E 8th Street
New York, NY 10009

Rose Shell Press
15223 Coral Isle Court
Fort Myers, FL 33919

Rowhouse Press
PO Box 23134
Seattle, WA 98102-0434

Runaway Publications
PO Box 1172
Ashland, OR 97520-0040

Salmon Run Publishers
PO Box 231081
Anchorage, AK 99523

Saturday Press Inc.
PO Box 884
Upper Montclair, NJ 07043

Segue Foundation
303 E 8th Street
New York, NY 10009

Serendipity Press
PO Box 16294
St Paul, MN 55116-0294

Shaolin Communications
PO Box 58547
Salt Lake City, UT 84158

Sheep Meadow Press
PO Box 1345
Bronx, NY 10471

Signature Books
564 West 400 North
Salt Lake City, UT 84116

Signpost Press Inc
MS 9053 Western Washington University
Bellingham, WA 98225

Singular Speech Press
Ten Hilltop Drive
Canton, CT 06019

Gibbs Smith
PO Box 667
Layton, UT 84041

Smoke The Soul Press
PO Box 8347
Ann Arbor, MI 48107

Spinning Star Press
1065 E Fairview Boulevard
Inglewood, CA 90302

Spoon River Poetry Press
PO Box 6
Granite Falls, MN 56241

St Andrews College Press
1700 Dogwood Mile
Laurinburg, NC 28352

Wallace Stevens Society Press
Box 5750
Clarkson Univeristy
Potsdam, NY 13699

Sunlight Publishers
PO Box 640545
San Francisco, CA 94109

Sunstone Press
PO Box 2321
Santa Fe, NM 87504

Taffy Productions
33 Dover Road
Durham, NH 03820

Tellstar Productions
PO Box 1264
Huntington, WV 25714

Tesseract Publications
PO Box 505
Hudson, SD 57034

Texture Press
3760 Cedar Ridge Drive
Norman, OK 73072

Three Continents Press Inc
PO Box 38009
Colorado Springs, CO 80937

Tia Chucha Press
c/o Arts Bridge
4753 N Broadway, Suite 918
Chicago, IL 60640

Tilbury House Publishers
132 Water Street
Gardiner, ME 04345

UCA Press
PO Box 5063
Conway, AR 72035

Undulating Bedsheets Productions
PO Box 25760
Los Angeles, CA 90025

Unfinished Monument Press
PO Box 4279
Pittsburgh, PA 15203

Unicorn Press
200 East Bessemer Avenue
Greensboro, NC 27401

University of Missouri Press
2910 Lemane Blvd
Columbia, MO 65201

University of Pittsburgh Press
127 N Bellefield Avenue
Pittsburgh, PA 15260

University of Tampa Press
401 W Kennedy Boulevard
Tampa, FL 33606

VisionWrite
PO Box 588
San Luis Rey, CA 92068

Wampeter Press
PO Box 2626
Key West, FL 33045

Waterworks Publishing
Rte 7, Box 720
Eureka Springs, AR 72632

Wheat Forders Press
PO Box 6317
Washington, DC 20015

Who Who Who Publishing
PO Box 7751
East Rutherford, NJ 07073

Wormwood Books and Magazines
PO Box 4698
Stockton, CA 95204

Ziggurat Press
107 Benevolent Street
Providence, RI 02906

APPENDIX L
POETRY MAGAZINES

ASIA

Blue Jacket
1-51-54 Sugue-cho
Sanjo-shi, Niigata-ken 955
Japan

Chinese Literature
24 Baiwanzhuang Road
Beijing 100037
China

The Indian Writer
C-23 Anna Nagar East
Tamil Nadu
Madras 600 102
India

Lizzengreasy
Dai Ni Kuroda Kopo #203
Funabashi 5-30-6
Setagaya-ku, Tokyo 156
Japan

The Lonsdale
Trash City 3rd Floor
6-18-16 Nishi-Gotanda
Shinigawa-ku, Tokyo 141
Japan

Manushi
C-202 Lajpat Nagar I
New Delhi 110 024
India

New Cicada
40-11 Kubo
Hobara
Fuikushima 960-06
Japan

Parnassus of World Poets
K-13 Todhunter Nagar
Saidapet, Madras 600 015
India

Poetry Kanto
Kanto Gakuin University
Matsuura, Kanazawa-ku
Yokohama 236
Japan

Poetry Nippon
5-11 Nagaike-cho
Showa-ku, Nagoya 466
Japan

Prakalpana Sahitya
P-40 Nandana Park
Calcutta 700 034
West Bengal
India

World Poetry
118 Raja St, Dr. Seethapathi Nagar
Velacheri
Madras 600 042
India

AUSTRALIA AND NEW ZEALAND

Broadsheet
PO Box 56-147
Dominion Road
Auckland
New Zealand

Going Down Swinging
PO Box 64
Coburg, Melbourne, VIC 3058
Australia

Grass Roots
PO Box 242
Euroa, VIC 3666
Australia

Idiom 23
University College of Central Queensland
Rockhampton, QLD 4702
Australia

Islands
4 Sealy Road
Torbay
Auckland 10
New Zealand

Linq
English Department
James Cook Univeristy of North Queensland
Townsville, QLD 4811
Australia

Otis Rush Magazine
PO Box 21
North Adelaide, SA 5006
Australia

Overland
PO Box 14146
Melbourne, VIC 3000
Australia

Poetry Australia
Market Place
Berrima, NSW 2577
Australia

Scarp
PO Box 1144
Wollongon, NSW 2500
Australia

Scripsi
Ormond College, University of Melbourne

Parkville, VIC 3052
Australia

SPIN
7 Megan Avenue
Pakuranga
Auckland 1706
New Zealand

Takahe
PO Box 13-335, 18 Hornsby Street
Bishopdale
Christchurch 8005
New Zealand

Webber's
15 McKillop Street
Melbourne, VIC 3000
Australia

CANADA

Amethyst Review
23 Riverside Avenue
Truro
Nova Scotia B2N 4G2

Antigonish Review
PO Box 5000
St Francis Xavier University
Antigonish
Nova Scotia B2G 2W5

Canadian Literature
2029 West Mall
University of British Columbia
Vancouver
British Columbia V6T 1W5

Dalhousie Review
Dalhousie University Press Ltd
Sir James Dunn Bldg, Suite 314
Halifax
Nova Scotia B3H 3J5

Descant
Box 314, Station P
Toronto
Ontario M5S 2S8

Ellipse
University de Sherbrooke
FLSH Box 10
Sherbrooke
Québec J1K 2R1

Emploi Plus
125 Principale North Street, Suite 13
L'Annonciation
Québec J0T 1T0

Event
Douglas College, PO Box 2503
New Westminster
British Columbia V3L 2B2

Fiddlehead
Box 4400
University of New Brunswick
Fredericton

New Brunswick E3B 5A3

Malahat Review
Box 1700, University of Victoria
Victoria
British Columbia V8W 2YZ

Not A Luxury
517 College Street, Suite 233
Toronto
Ontario M6G 4A2

Para∗Phrase
Sheridan Mall Box 47014
Mississauga
Ontario L5K 2R2

Plowman
Box 414
Whitby
Ontario L1N 5S4

Poemata
237 Prospect Street South
Hamilton
Ontario L8M 2Z6

Poetry Canada
221 King Street East
Kinston
Ontario K7L 4Y5

Poetry Canada Review
307 Coxwell Avenue
Toronto
Ontario M4L 3B5

Poetry Toronto
217 Northwood Drive
Willowdale
Ontario K7L 4Y5

Prairie Journal of Canadian Literature
PO Box 61203
Brentwood PO
Calgary
Alberta T2L 2K6

Teak Roundup
#5 - 9060 Tronson Road
Vernon
British Columbia V1T 6L7

Thalia
Department of English
University of Ottawa
Ottawa
Ontario K1N 6N5

Time for Rhyme
PO Box 1055
Battleford
Sasketchwan S0M 0E0

West Coast Line
2027 East Academic Annex
Simon Fraser University
Burnaby
British Columbia V5A 1S6

EIRE

Irish Review
Cork University Press
University College
Cork

Krino
The Paddocks
Glenrevagh, Corrandulla
Co Galway

Poetry Ireland Review
Bermingham Tower
Dublin Castle
Dublin 2

Salmon Literary Magazine
The Bridge Mills
Galway

EUROPE

Bibliotheque d'Humanisme et Renaissance
Librarie Droz SA, 11r Massot
1211 Geneva 12
Switzerland

Books From Finland
Univeristy of Helsinki
PO Box 15 (Unioninkatu 36)
00014 Helsinki
Finland

Coop. Antigruppo Siciliano
Villa Schammachanat
Via Argenteria Km 4
Trapani-Erice
Sicily, Italy

Frank
104/106 rue Edouard Vaillant
93100 Montreuil Sous Bois
France

Horizon
Stationstraat 232A
1770 Liedekerke
Belgium

Le Journal
22 rue Rene Brut
63110 Beaumont
France

The Lundian
PO Box 722
220 07 Lund
Sweden

Made In USA
PO Box 7024
Limassol
Cyprus

Numero
5 rue des Tulipes
44120 Vertou
France

Romanian Review
Piata Presei Libere 1
Bucharest
Romania

Russian Letter
PO Box 30
St Petersburg 192 282
Russia

Lo Straniero
Via Chiaia 149
Napoli 80121
Italy

Terza Pagina
Villa Schammachanat
Via Argenteria Km 4
Trapani-Erice, Sicily
Italy

Trafika
Veverkova 20
17000 Prague 7
Czech Republic

Transnational Perspectives
CP 161
1211 Geneva 16
Switzerland

2Plus2
Mylabris Press Ltd
Case Postale 35
1000 Lausanne
Switzerland

ISRAEL

Studio Art Magazine
Art Center
Givat Haviva
MP Menashe 37850

Voices Israel
Kibbutz Yizr'el
D N Yizre'el 19350

UNITED KINGDOM

ENGLAND

Acumen
6 The Mount
Furzeham, Brixham
Devon TQ5 8QY

Agenda
5 Cranbourne Court
Albert Bridge Road
London SW11 4PE

Ambit
17 Priory Gardens
Highgate
London N6 5QY

Aquarius
Flat 10

116 Sutherland Avenue
London W9

Argotist
Flat 4
48 Upper Parliament Street
Liverpool L8 7LF

Broadside
c/o The Cannon Poets
Cannon Hill Park
Edgbaston, Birmingham B12 9QH

Cadmium Blue Literary Journal
71 Harrow Crescent
Romford
Essex RM3 7BJ

Dandelion Arts Magazine
24 Frosty Hollow
East Hunsbury
Northants NN4 0SY

Envoi
44 Rudyard Road
Biddulph Moor
Stoke-On-Trent ST8 7JN

Frogmore Papers
42 Morehall Avenue
Folkestone
Kent CT19 4EF

Gallery
3 Honeybourne Road
London NW6 1HH

Global Tapestry
1 Springbank, Longsight Road
Salebury, Blackburn
Lancs BB1 9EU

Green Book
49 Park Street
Bristol BS1 5NT

Hat
1A Church Lane
Croft, Nr Skegness
Lincs

Iota
67 Hady Crescent
Chesterfield
Derbyshire S41 0EB

Iron
5 Marden Terrace
Cullercoats
North Shields
Tyne and Wear NE30 4PD

Issue One
2 Tewkesbury Drive
Grimsby
South Humberside DN34 4TL

Joe Soap's Canoe
30 Quilter Road
Felixstowe
Suffolk IP11 7JJ

KRAX
63 Dixon Lane
Wortly
Leeds LS12 4RR

Many Review
15 Norcott Road
London N16 7BJ

New Hope International
20 Werneth Avenue
Gee Cross, Hyfe
Cheshire SK14 5NL

New Writer
PO Box 60
Cranbrook
Kent TN17 2ZR

North
51 Byram Arcade
Westgate
Huddersfield HD1 1ND

Nova Poetica
14 Pennington Oval
Lymington
Hants SO41 8BQ

Orbis
199 The Long Shoot
Nuneaton
Warks CV11 6JQ

Ore
7 The Towers
Stevenage
Herts SG1 1HE

Ostinato
PO Box 522
London W8 7SX

Outposts
22 Whitewell Road
Frome
Somerset BA11 4EL

Oxford Poetry
Magdalen College
Oxford OX1 4AU

Pennine Platform
Igmanthorpe Hall Farm Cottage
Wetherby
W Yorks LS22 5EQ

Perceptions
73 Eastcombe Avenue
London SE7 7LL

PN Review
208-212 Corn Exchange Buildings
Manchester M4 3BQ

Poetry & Audience
c/o School of English
University of Leeds
Leeds
W Yorks LS2 9JT

Poetry Life
14 Pennington Oval
Lymington
Hants SO41 8BQ

Poetry Nottingham
Summer Cottage
West Street
Shelford
Notts NG12 1EJ

Psychopoetica
Department of Psychology
University of Hull
Hull HU6 7RX

Rialto
32 Grosvenor Road
Norwich
Norfolk NR2 2PZ

Romantic Heir
71 Harrow Crescent
Romford
Essex RM3 7BJ

Slow Dancer
Flat 4
1 Park Valley
Nottingham NG7 1BS

Smoke
40 Canning Street
Liverpool L8 7NP

Spectacular Diseases
83B London Road
Peterborough
Cambridgeshire PE2 9BS

Stand Magazine
179 Wingrove Road
Newcastle-Upon-Tyne NE4 9DA

Staple New Writing
Tor Cottage
81 Cavendish Road
Matlock
Derbyshire DE4 3HX

Sunk Island Review
PO Box 74
Lincoln LN1 1QG

Tears in the Fence
38 Hod View
Stourpaine, nr Blandford Forum
Dorset DT11 8TN

Third Half Magazine
'Amikeco', 16 Fane Close
Stamford
Lincs PE9 1HG

Westwords
15 Trelawney Road
Peverell, Plymouth
Devon PL3 4JS

Weyfarers
Hilltop Cottage

9 Whiterose Lane
Woking
Surrey GU22 7JA

Wide Skirt
93 Blackhouse Road
Fartown
Huddersfield HD2 1AP

Zenos
59B Ilkeston Road
Nottingham NG7 3GR

NORTHERN IRELAND

Celtic Pen
36 Fruithill Park
Belfast BT11 8GE

Haiku Quarterly
71 Ballyculter Road
Loughkeelan
Downpatrick
County Down BT30 7BD

Honest Ulsterman
159 Lower Braniel Road
Belfast BT5 1NN

North Magazine
10 Stranmillis Park
Belfast BT9 5AU

SCOTLAND

Cencrastus
Workshop 1, Abbeymount Techbase,
2 Easter Road
Edinburgh EH8 8EJ

Chapman
4 Broughton Place
Edinburgh EH1 3RX

Edinburgh Review
Edinburgh University Press
22 George Square
Edinburgh EH8 9LF

Gairfish
71 Longlane
Broughty Ferry
Dundee DD5 2AS

Gairm
29 Waterloo Street
Glasgow G2 6BZ

Lallans
8 Strathalmond Road
Edinburgh EH4 8AD

Lines Review
Macdonald Publishing
Edgefield Road, Loanhead
Midlothian EH20 9SY

New Writing Scotland
Department of English
Aberdeen University
Taylor Building, King's College
Aberdeen AB9 2UB

Northwords
68 Strathkinaird
Ullapool
Wester Ross

West Coast Magazine
c/o Em-Dee Productions
Unit F8, Festival Business Centre
150 Brand Street
Glasgow G51 1DH

WALES

New Welsh Review
49 Park Place
Cardiff CF1 3AT

Planet
PO Box 44
Aberystwyth
Dyfed

Poetry Wales
Glan-y-Werydd
Llandanwg
Harlech LL46 2SD

USA

Abraxas
2518 Gregory Street
Madison, WI 53711

ACM (Another Chicago Magazine)
3709 North Kenmore
Chicago, IL 60613

African American Review
English Department
Indiana State University
Terre Haute, IN 47809

Agni
Creative Writers Program
Boston University
236 Bay Street Road
Boston, MA 02215

Aguilar Expression
1329 Gilmore Avenue
Donora, PA 15033

Alabama Literary Review
253 Smith Hall
Troy State University
Troy, AL 36081

Alaska Quarterly Review
College of Arts and Sciences
University of Alaska at Anchorage
3211 Providence Drive
Anchorage, AK 99508

Allegheny Review
Box 232, Allegheny College
Meadville, PA 16335

Alpha Beat Soup
c/o Alpha Beat Press
31 Waterloo Street

New Hope, PA 18938

American Poetry Review
1721 Walnut Street
Philadelphia, PA 19103

American Scholar
1811 Q Street, NW
Washington, DC 20009

Anterior Poetry Monthly
993 Allspice Avenue
Fenton, MO 63026

Antietam Review
7 West Franklin Street
Hagerstown, MD 21740

Antioch Review
PO Box 148
Yellow Springs, OH 45387

Apalachee Quarterly
PO Box 20106
Tallahassee, FL 32316

Arden
PO Box 41008
Philadelphia, PA 19127

Arshile: A Magazine of the Arts
PO Box 3749
Los Angeles, CA 40078

Art and Understanding
25 Monroe Street, Suite 205
Albany, NY 12210-2743

Artful Dodge
English Department
College of Wooster
Wooster, OH 44691

Art: Mag
PO Box 70896
Las Vegas, NV 89170

ART's Garbage Gazzette
214 Dunning Street
Madison, WI 53704

Atlanta Review
PO Box 8396
Atlanta, GA 30306

Atom Mind
PO Box 22068
Albuquerque, NM 87154

Bellingham Review
Signpost Press Inc
MS 9053, Western Washington University
Bellingham, WA 98225

Beloit Poetry Journal
Box 154, RFD 2
Ellsworth, ME 04605

Berkeley Poetry Review
200 MLK Student Union Building
University of California at Berkeley
Berkeley, CA 94720

Berkeley Review of Books
1731 10th Street, Suite A
Berkeley, CA 94710

Black Bear Review
1916 Lincoln Street
Croydon, PA 19021

Black Scholar
PO Box 2869
Oakland, CA 94609

Black Warrior Review
PO Box 2936
Tuscaloosa, AL 35486

Black Willow Poetry Journal
914 Sterling Avenue
Chattanooga, TN 37405

Bloomsbury Review
1028 Bannock Street
Denver, CO 80204

Blue Unicorn
22 Avon Road
Kensington, CA 94707

Bogg
422 North Cleveland Street
Arlington, VA 22201

Borderlands: Texas Poetry Review
PO Box 49818
Austin, TX 78765

Boston Literary Review
PO Box 357
West Somerville, MA 02144

Bottomfish
21250 Stevens Creek Boulevard
Cupertino, CA 95014

Bouillabaisse
c/o Alpha Beat Press
31 Waterloo Street
New Hope, PA 18938

Boulevard
PO Box 30386
Philadelphia, PA 19103

Boundary 2
State University of New York at Binghamton
Binghamton, NY 13901

Bravo: The Poet's Magazine
1081 Trafalgar Street
Teaneck, NJ 07666-1929

Bridge: a journal of fiction and poetry
14050 Vernon Street
Oak Park, MI 48237

Brussels Sprout
PO Box 1551
Mercer Island, WA 98040

Café Review
20 Danforth Street
Portland, ME 04101

Caliban
PO Box 561
Laguna Beach, CA 92652

Callaloo
English Department
Wilson Hall
University of Virginia
Charlottesville, VA 22903

Calliope
Creative Writing Program
Roger Williams University
Bristol, RI 02809

Calyx: A Journal of Art and Literature by Women
PO Box B
Corvallis, OR 97339

Cape Rock
English Department
Southeast Missouri State University
Cape Girardeau, MO 63701

Carolina Quarterly
Greenlaw Hall CB #3520
University of North Carolina at Chapel Hill
Chapel Hill, NC 27599

Cat's Ear
PO Box 946
Kirkville, MO 63501

Catalyst Magazine
236 Forsyth Street, Suite 400
Atlanta, GA 30303

Cathartic
PO Box 1391
Fort Lauderdale, FL 33302

Central Park
PO Box 1446
New York, NY 10023

Chaminade Literary Review
Chaminade University of Honolulu
3140 Waialae Avenue
Honolulu, HI 96816

Chants
R 1, Box 1738
Dexter, ME 04930

Chariton Review
Northeast Missouri State University
Kirksville, MO 63501

Charlotte Poetry Review
PO Box 36701
Charlotte, NC 28236

Chattahoochee Review
DeKalb College
2101 Womanck Road
Dunwoody, GA 30338

Chelsea
Box 773
Cooper Station
New York, NY 10276

Cherotic (r)Evolutionary
PO Box 11445
Berkeley,CA 94712

Chicago Review
5801 South Kenwood
Chicago, IL 60637

Children's Journal
1415 Hemlock Street
Cayce, SC 29033

Chiron Review
522 East South Avenue
St John, KS 67576-2212

Cimarron Review
205 Morrill Hall
Oklahoma State University
Stillwater, OK 74078

Cincinnati Poetry Review
Humanities Department
College of Mount St Joseph
Cincinnati, OH 45233

Circle
125 West Westover Avenue
Colonial Heights, VA 23834

Coffeehouse
PO Box 566
Eastlake, CO 80614

Cokefish
c/o Cokefish Press
31 Waterloo Street
New Hope, PA 18938

Collage & Bricolages
PO Box 86
Clarion, PA 16214

Colorado Review
English Department
Colorado State University
Fort Collins, CO 80523

Columbia: A Magazine of Poetry and Prose
404 Dodge Hall
Columbia University
New York, NY 10027

Compleat Nurse
PO Box 640345
San Francisco, CA 94164

Confrontation
English Department, C W Post College
Greenvale, NY 11548

Conjunctions
Bard College
Annandale-on-Hudson, NY 12504

Connecticut Poetry Review
PO Box 818
Stonington, CT 06378

Connecticut River Review
327 Seabury Drive
Bloomfield, CT 06002

Contact II
PO Box 451
Bowling Green, NY 10004

Context South
Campus Box 4504, Schreiner College
2100 Memorial Boulevard
Kerrville, TX 78028

Cornfield Review
Ohio State University at Marion
1465 Mount Vernon Avenue
Marion, OH 43302

Cottonwood
Box J, 400 Kansas Union
University of Kansas
Lawrence, KS 66045

CPQ
1200 East Ocean Boulevard, No 64
Long Beach, CA 90802

Crab Creek Review
4462 Whitman Avenue North
Seattle, WA 98103

Crazyhorse
English Department
University of Arkansas
2801 South University
Little Rock, AR 72204

Crazyquilt
PO Box 632729
San Diego, CA 92163

Cream City Review
PO Box 413
University of Wisconsin at Milwaukee
Milwaukee, WI 53201

Creeping Bent
433 West Market Street
Bethlehem, PA 18018

Cumberland Poetry Review
PO Box 120128
Acklen Station
Nashville, TN 37212

Cutbank
English Department
University of Montana
Missoula, MT 59812

Dark Regions
PO Box 6301
Concord, CA 94524

December Magazine
PO Box 302
Highland Park, IL 60035

Defined Providence
PO Box 16143
Rumford, RI 02916

Denver Quarterly
University of Denver
Denver, CO 80208

Dimension
PO Box 26673
Austin, TX 78755

Djinni
29 Front Street, No 2
Marblehead, MA 01945

Dog River Review
5976 Billings Road
Parkdale, OR 97041

Dream Whip
PO Box 53832
Lubbock, TX 79453

Driver's Side Airbag
PO Box 25760
Los Angeles, CA 90025

Earth's Daughters: A Feminist Arts Periodical
PO Box 41, Central Park Station
Buffalo, NY 14215

ELF: Eclectic Literary Forum
PO Box 392
Tonawanda, NY 14150

Embers
PO Box 404
Guilford, CT 06437

Emergence
PO Box 1615
Bridgeview, IL 60455

Emrys Journal
PO Box 8813
Greenville, SC 29604

Epoch
251 Goldwin Smith Hall
Cornell University
Ithaca, NY 14853

Ever Dancing Muse
PO Box 7751
East Rutherford, NJ 07073

Evergreen Chronicles
PO Box 8939
Minneapolis, MN 55408

Excursus Literary Arts Journal
PO Box 1056
Knickerbocker Station
New York, NY 10002

Exhibition
261 Madison Avenue South
Bainbridge Island, WA 98110

Expressions Magazine
PO Box 16294
St Paul, MN 55116-0294

Exquisite Corpse
PO Box 25051
Baton Rouge, LA 70894

Eyeball
PO Box 8135
St Louis, MO 63108

Farmer's Market
PO Box 1272
Galesburg, IL 61402

(Feed.)
PO Box 1567
Madison Square Station
New York, NY 10003

Feelings: America's Beautiful Poetry Magazine
PO Box 85
Easton, PA 18044-0085**Fell Swoop**
3000 Ponce De Leon Street
New Orleans, LA 70119

Field
Rice Hall
Oberlin College
Oberlin, OH 44074

Fine Madness
PO Box 31138
Seattle, WA 98103

Five Fingers Review
PO Box 15426
San Francisco, CA 94115

Florida Review
English Department
University of Central Florida
Orlando, FL 32816

Flyway
203 Ross Hall
Iowa State University
Ames, IA 50011

Folio
Literature Department
American University
Washington, DC 20016

Footwork: The Paterson Literary Review
Cultural Affairs Department
Passaic County Community College
1 College Boulevard
Paterson, NJ 07505

Formalist
320 Hunter Drive
Evansville, IN 47711

Four Directions
PO Box 729
Tellico Plains, TN 37385

Four Quartets
LaSalle University
1900 West Olney Avenue
Philadelphia, PA 19141

Fractal
4400 University Drive, MS 206
Fairfax, VA 22030

Free Focus
JAF Station, PO Box 7415
New York, NY 10116

Free Lunch
PO Box 7647
Laguna Niguel, CA 92607-7647

Gaia: A Journal of Literary & Environmental Arts
PO Box 709
Winterville, GA 30683

Galley Sail Review
1630 University Avenue, No 42
Berkeley, CA 94703

Gas: High Octane Poetry
3164 Emerson
Palo Alto, CA 94306

A Gathering of the Tribes
PO Box 20693
Tompkins Square
New York, NY 10009

Gávea-Brown
Dept Portuguese & Brazilian Studies
Box 0, Brown University
Providence, RI 02912

Georgetown Review
400 East College Street
Box 227
Georgetown, KY 40324

Georgia Review
University of Georgia
Athens, GA 30602

Gettysburg Review
Gettysburg College
Gettysburg, PA 17325

Glass Cherry
901 Europe Bay Road
Ellison Bay, WI 54210-9643

Golden Isis
PO Box 525
Fort Covington, NY 12937

Grab-a-Nickel
Alderson-Broaddus College
Philippi, WV 26416

Graham House Review
Box 5000, Colgate University
Hamilton, NY 13346

Grand Street
131 Varick Street, Room 906
New York, NY 10013

Grasslands Review
NT Box 13706
Denton, TX 76203

Great River Review
211 West 7th Street
Winona, MN 55987

Green Fuse Poetry
3365 Holland Drive
Santa Rosa, CA 95404

Green Mountains Review

Johnson State College
Johnson, VT 05656

Greensboro Review
English Department
University of North Carolina at Greensboro
Greensboro, NC 27412

Gulf Coast
English Department
University of Houston
Houston, TX 77204

Gypsy
10708 Gay Brewer Drive
El Paso, TX 79935

Habersham Review
Piedmont College
PO Box 10
Demorest, GA 30535

Hambone
134 Hunolt Street
Santa Cruz, VA 95060

Hammers
1718 Sherman, No 203
Evanston, IL 60201

Hampden-Sydney Poetry Review
PO Box 126
Hampden-Sydney, VA 23943

Hanging Loose
231 Wyckoff Street
Brooklyn, NY 11217

Hanson's Symposium: Of Literary & Social Interest
113 Merryman Court
Annapolis, MD 21401

Happiness Holding Tank
9727 South East Reedway
Portland, OR 97266

Hawaii Review
English Department
University of Hawaii at Manoa
1733 Donaghho Road
Honolulu, HI 96822

Hellas: A Journal of Poetry & the Humanities
304 South Tyson Avenue
Glendside, PA 19038

Heresies: A Feminist Publication on Art and Politics
PO Box 1306
Canal Street Station
New York, NY 10013

High Plains Literary Review
180 Adams Street, Suite 250
Denver, CO 80206

Highway Poet
PO Box 1400
Brewster, MA 02631-7400

Hiram Poetry Review
Box 162
Hiram, OH 44234

Hob-Nob
994 Nissley Road
Lancaster, PA 17601

Hollins Critic
PO Box 9538
Hollins College, VA 24020

Home Planet News
PO Box 415
Stuyvesant Station
New York, NY 10009

Hopewell Review
c/o Arts Indiana Inc
47 South Pennsylvania Street, Suite 701
Indianapolis, IN 46204

Howling Dog
2913 Woodcock Court
Rochester, MI 48306

Hudson Review
684 Park Avenue
New York, NY 10021

Hurricane Alice: A Feminist Quarterly
Lind Hall
207 Church Street South East
Minneapolis, MN 55455

Hyphen
348 South Ahrens
Lombard, IL 60148

Iconoclast
1675 Amazon Road
Mohegan Lake, NY 10547

Ikon
PO Box 1355
Stuyvesant Station
New York, NY 10009

Illinois Review
English Department, Ilinois State University
Normal, IL 61790

Image: A Journal of the Arts and Religion
3100 McCormick Avenue
Wichita, KS 67213

Imagine: International Chicano Poetry Journal
89 Massachusetts Avenue
Boston, MA 02115

In the Company of Poets
PO Box 10786
Oakland, CA 94610

Indiana Review
316 North Jordan Avenue
Indiana University
Bloomington, IN 47405

Interim
English Department
University of Nevada
Las Vegas, NV 89154

International Poetry Review
Romance Language Department

University of North Carolina at Greensboro
Greensboro, NC 27412

International Quarterly
PO Box 10521
Tallahassee, FL 32302

Invisible City
PO Box 2853
San Francisco, CA 94126

Iowa Review
308 EPB
University of Iowa
Iowa City, IA 52242

irresistble impulse
711 Belmont Place East, No 201
Seattle, WA 98102

Jacaranda Review
English Department, 2225 Rolfe Hall
University of California at Los Angeles
Los Angeles, CA 90024

Jack Mackerel Magazine
PO Box 23134
Seattle, WA 98102-0434

James White Review
PO Box 3356
Butler Quarter Station
Minneapolis, MN 55403

Jeopardy Magazine
132 College Hall
Western Washington University
Bellingham, WA 98225

Jordan Creek Anthology
900 North Benton
Springfield, MO 65802

Journal
English Department
Ohio State University
164 West 17th Avenue
Columbus, OH 43210

Journal of Regional Criticism
1025 Garner Street, D, Space 18
Colorado Springs, CO 80905-1774

Kaleidoscope: International Magazine of Literature, Fine Arts, and Disability
326 Locust Street
Akron, OH 44302

Kalliope: A Journal of Women's Art
Florida Community College
3939 Roosevelt Boulevard
Jacksonville, FL 32205

Kansas Quarterly
Kansas State University
Manhattan, KS 66506

Karamu
English Department
Eastern Illinois University
Charleston, IL 61920

Kenyon Review
Kenyon College
Gambier, OH 43022

Kid's World
1300 Kicker Road
Tuscaloosa, AL 35404

Kinesis
PO Box 4007
Whitefish, MT 59937

Kiosk
English Department
302 Clements Hall
State University of New York at Buffalo
Buffalo, NY 14226

Lactuca
159 Jewett Avenue
Jersey City, NJ 07304

Laurel Review
English Department
Northwest Missouri State University
Maryville, MO 64468

Ledge Poetry & Fiction Magazine
64-65 Cooper Avenue
Glendale, NY 11385

Left Curve
PO Box 472
Oakland, CA 94604

Light (Quarterly of Light Verse)
Box 7500
Chicago, IL 60680

Lilliput Review
207 South Millvale Avenue, No 3
Pittsburgh, PA 15224

Lips
PO Box 1345
Montclair, NJ 07042

Literal Latté
61 East 8th Street, Suite 240
New York, NY 10003

Literary Center Quarterly
PO Box 85116
Seattle, WA 98145

Literary Review
Fairleigh Dickinson University
285 Madison Avenue
Madison, NJ 07940

Little Magazine
English Dept, SUNY-Albany
Albany, NY 12222

Long News: In the Short Century
PO Box 150-455
Brooklyn, NY 11215

Long Pond Review
Suffolk Community College
533 College Road
Selden, NY 11784

Long Shot
PO Box 6238
Hoboken, NJ 02030

Lost and Found Times
137 Leland Avenue
Columbus, OH 43214

Louisiana Literature: Literature/Humanities Review
SLU 792
Southeastern Louisiana University
Hammond, LA 70402

Luz en Arte y Literatura
PO Box 571062
Tarzana, CA 91357-1062

Lynx Eye
1880 Hill Drive
Los Angeles, CA 90041

Lyra
PO Box 3188
Guttenburg, NJ 07093

Lyric
307 Dunton Drive South West
Blacksburg, VA 24060

Macguffin
Schoolcraft College
18600 Haggerty Road
Livonia, MI 48152

Magazine of Speculative Poetry
PO Box 564
Beloit, WI 53512

Mail Call: A Journal of the Civil War
PO Box 5031
South Hackensack, NJ 07606

Manhattan Poetry Review
FDR Box 8207
New York, NY 10150

Manhattan Review
440 Riverside Drive, No 45
New York, NY 10027

Manna
2966 West Westcove Drive
West Valley City, UT 84119

Manoa: A Pacific Journal of International Writing
English Department
University of Hawaii
Honolulu, HI 96822

Many Mountains Moving
420 22nd Street
Boulder, CO 80302

Massachusetts Review
Memorial Hall
University of Massachusetts
Amherst, MA 01003

Matrix
c/o Channing-Murray Foundation
1209 W Oregon
Urbana, IL 61801

Men As We Are
PO Box 150615
Brooklyn, NY 11215

Metamorfosis
B523 Padleford Hall, GN-80
University of Washington
Seattle, WA 98195

Metaxy
1630 30th Street, No. 278
Boulder, CO 80301

Metropolitan
6307 North 31st Street
Arlington, VA 22207

Michigan Quarterly Review
3032 Rackham Building
University of Michigan
Ann Arbor, MI 48109

Mid-American Review
English Department
Bowling Green State University
Bowling Green, OH 43403

Midland Review
205 Morrill Hall
Stillwater, OK 74078-4069

Midwest Quarterly
Pittsburg State University
Pittsburg, KS 66762

Mind in Motion
PO Box 1118
Apple Valley, CA 92307

Mindprint Review
PO Box 62
Soulsbyville, CA 95372

Minnesota Review
English Department
East Carolina University
Greenville, NC 27858

Mississippi Mud
150 South Drake Avenue
Austin, TX 78704

Mississippi Review
Southern Stations, Box 5144
Hattiesburg, MS 39406

Mississippi Valley Review
English Department
Western Illinois University
Macomb, IL 61455

Missouri Review
University of Missouri
1507 Hillcrest Hall
Columbia, MO 65211

Mobius
1149 East Mifflin
Madison, WI 53703

Modern Haiku
PO Box 1752

Madison, WI 53701

modern words
350 Bay Street, No 100
Box 325
San Francisco, CA 94133

Moksha Journal of Vajra Printing & Publishing
49 Forrest Place
Amityville, NY 11701

Monocacy Valley Review
English Department
Mount Saint Mary's College
Emmitsburg, MD 21727

Mother Earth International Journal
PO Box 173
Bayport, MN 55003-0173

Mount Olive Review
634 Henderson Street
Mount Olive, NC 28365

Mr Cogito
Humanities
Pacific University
Forest Grove, OR 97116

muae: A Journal of Transcultural Production
8 Harrison Street, Suite 3
New York, NY 10013

Nassau Review
Nassau Community College
State University of New York at Garden City
Garden City, NY 11530

Nebraska Review
212 FA, University of Nebraska at Omaha
Omaha, NE 68182

Negative Capability
62 Ridgelawn Drive East
Mobile, AL 36608

New American Writing
2920 West Pratt
Chicago, IL 60645

New Delta Review
English Department
Louisiana State University
Baton Rouge, LA 70803

New England Review
Middlebury College
Middlebury, VT 05753

New Laurel Review
828 Lesseps Street
New Orleans, LA 70117

New Letters
University of Missouri
Kansas City, MO 64110

New Myths: MSS
State University of New York at Binghamton
Box 530
Binghamton, NY 13901

New Orleans Review
English Department
Loyola University
New Orleans, LA 70118

New Press
53-35 Hollis Court Boulevard
Flushing, NY 11365

new renaissance
9 Heath Road
Arlington, MA 02174

New Virginia Review
1306 East Cary Street, 2A
Richmond, VA 23219

Next Phase
33 Court Street
New Haven, CT 06511

Nimrod
Arts and Humanities Council of Tulsa
2210 South Main
Tulsa, OK 74114

96 Inc
PO Box 15559
Boston, MA 02215

Nit & Wit
PO Box 627
Geneva, IL 60134

Nite-Writer's Literary Arts Journal
3101 Schieck Street, Suite 100
Pittsburgh, PA 15227-4151

No Roses Review
PO Box 14258
Chicago, IL 60614

North American Review
University of Northern Iowa
Cedar Falls, IA 50614

North Atlantic Review
15 Arbutus Lane
Stony Brook, NY 11790

North Dakota Quarterly
University of North Dakota
Box 7209
Grand Forks, ND 58202

Northeast Arts
JFK Station
Boston, MA 02114

Northeast Corridor
Beaver College
450 South Easton Road
Glenside, PA 19038

Northwest Literary Forum
2012 South 314th, Suite 158
Federal Way, WA 98003

Northwest Review
369 PLC, University of Oregon
Eugene, OR 97403

Northwoods Journal
PO Box 298
Thomaston, ME 04861

Oasis, a literary magazine
1833 10th Street South West
Largo, FL 34648

Object Lesson
PO Box 1186
Hampshire College
Amherst, MA 01002

Obsidian II: Black Literature in Review
Box 8105, English Department
North Carolina State University
Raleigh, NC 27695

Odessa Poetry Review
RR 1, Box 39
Odessa, MO 64076

Ogalala Review
PO Box 2699
University of Arkansas
Fayetteville, AR 72701

Ohio Review
209 C Ellis Hall
Ohio University
Athens, OH 45701

Ontario Review
9 Honey Brook Drive
Princeton, NJ 08540

Onthebus
PO Box 481270
Bicentennial Station
Los Angeles, CA 90048

Oracle Poetry & Letters
2105 Amherst Road, Dept G
Hyattsville, MD 20783

Oro Madre
PO Box 143
Getzville, NY 14068

Osiris
Box 297
Deerfield, MA 01342

Ostentatious Mind
JAF Station, Box 7415
New York, NY 10116

Outerbridge
112 East 10th Street
New York, NY 10003

Owen Wister Review
PO Box 4238, University Station
University of Wyoming
Laramie, NY 82071

Oxford American
114 A South Lamar
Oxford, MS 38655

Oyez Review
Roosevelt University

430 South Michigan Avenue
Chicago, IL 60605

O!!Zone
1266 Fountain View Drive
Houston, TX 77057

Pacific Review
English Department
California State University
5500 University Parkway
San Bernardino, CA 92407

Paintbrush: A Journal of Contemporary Multicultural Literature
Division of Language and Literature
Northeast Missouri State University
Kirksville, MO 63501

Painted Bride Quarterly
230 Vine Street
Philadelphia, PA 19106

Panhandler
English Department
University of West Florida
Pensacola, FL 32514

Paper Bag
PO Box 268805
Chicago, IL 60626-8805

Paper Salad Poetry Journal
PO Box 520061
Salt Lake City, UT 84152

Papyrus
102 LaSalle Road, PO Box 270797
West Hartford, CT 06127

The Paradoxist Movement
2456 S Rose Peak Drive
Tucson, AZ 85710

Paris Review
541 East 72nd Street
New York, NY 10021

Parnassus
41 Union Square West, Room 804
New York, NY 10003

Parting Gifts
3413 Wilshire Drive
Greensboro, NC 27408

Partisan Review
236 Bay State Road
Boston, MA 02215

Passages North
Kalamazoo College
1200 Academy
Kalamazoo, MI 49007

Passaic Review
Forstmann Library
195 Gregory Avenue
Passaic, NJ 07055

Pembroke Magazine
Box 60, Pembroke State University

Pembroke, NC 28372

Pemmican
PO Box 121
Redmond, WA 98073

Pennsylvania Review
English Department, 526 CL
University of Pittsburgh
Pittsburgh, PA 15260

Pequod
English Department, 2nd Floor
19 University Place
New York, NY 10003

Peregrine: The Journal of Amherst Writers & Artists
PO Box 1076
Amherst, MA 01004

Permafrost
English Department,
203 Fine Arts Building
University of Alaska
Fairbanks, AK 99775

Piedmont Literary Review
1017 Spanish Moss Lane
Breaux Bridge, LA 70517

Pig Iron
PO Box 237
Youngstown, OH 44501

Pikestaff Forum
PO Box 127
Normal, IL 61761

Pittsburgh Quarterly
36 Haberman Avenue
Pittsburgh, PA 15211

Pivot
250 Riverside Drive, No 23
New York, NY 10025

Plains Poetry Journal
Box 2337
Bismarck, ND 58502

Pleiades
Box 357, 6677 W Colfax
Lakewood, CO 80214

pLopLop
PO Box 11443
Indianapolis, IN 46201-0443

Ploughshares
Emerson College
100 Beacon Street
Boston, MA 02116

Plum Review
PO Box 1347
Philadelphia, PA 19105-1347

Poem
English Department
University of Alabama
Huntsville, AL 35899

Poet Lore
The Writer's Center
Bethesda, MD 20815

Poetic Space Magazine
PO Box 11157
Eugene, OR 97440

Poet's Sanctuary
PO Box 832
Hopkins, MN 55343

Poetpourri
907 Comstock Avenue
Syracuse, NY 13210

Poetry
160 West Walton Street
Chicago, IL 60610

Poetry Connection
13455 SW 16 Court #F-405
Pembroke Pines, FL 33027

Poetry East
English Dept, 802 West Belden
DePaul University
Chicago, IL 60614

Poetry Explosion Newsletter
PO Box 4725
Pittsburgh, PA 15206

Poetry Flash
PO Box 4172
Berkeley, CA 94704

Poetry In Motion
PO Box 173, Dept WW
Bayport, MN 55003

Poetry Miscellany
English Department
University of Tennessee
Chattanooga, TN 37402

Poetry Motel
1619 Jefferson
Duluth, MN 55812

Poetry New York: A Journal of Poetry and Translation
PO Box 3184
Church Street Station
New York, NY 10008

Poetry of the People
PO Box 298
Micanopy, FL 32667

Poetry Project Newsletter
St Mark's Church
131 East 10th Street
New York, NY 10003

Poet's Fantasy
227 Hatten Avenue
Rice Lake, WI 54868

Poets On
29 Loring Avenue
Mill Valley, CA 94941

Poets on the Line
PO Box 020292
Brooklyn, NY 11202-0007

Poets' Roundtable
826 South Center Street
Terre Haute, IN 47807

Portable Wall
c/o Basement Press
215 Burlington
Billings, MT 59101

Portland Review
PO Box 751
Portland, OR 97207

Potato Eyes
PO Box 76
Troy, ME 04987

Potomac Review
PO Box 134
McLean, VA 22101

Potpourri
PO Box 8278
Prairie Village, KS 66208

Prairie Schooner
201 Andrews Hall
University of Nebraska
Lincoln, NE 68588

Primavera
Box 37-7547
Chicago, IL 60637

Prisoners Of The Night
PO Box 688
Yucca Valley
CA 92286-0688

Prolific Writer's Magazine
PO Box 554
Oradell, NJ 07649

Prospect Review
557 10th Street
Brooklyn, NY 11215

Provincetown Arts
650 Commercial Street
Provincetown, MA 02657

Puck: The Unofficial Journal of the Irrepressible
47 Noe Street, No 4
San Francisco, CA 94114

Puckerbrush Review
76 Main Street
Orono, ME 04473

Puerto Del Sol
Box 30001, Department 3E
New Mexico State University
Las Cruces, NM 88003

Quarry West
Porter College
University of California at Santa Cruz
Santa Cruz, CA 95064

Quarterly
650 Madison Avenue, Suite 2600
New York, NY 10021

Quarterly Review of Literature
Contemporary Poetry Series
26 Haslet Avenue
Princeton, NJ 08540

Quarterly West
317 Olpin Union
University of Utah
Salt Lake City, UT 84112

Quartz Hill Journal of Theology
4354 51st Street West
Quartz Hill, CA 93536

Quixote
1812 Marshall
Houston, TX 77098

Raccoon
PO Box 111327
Memphis, TN 38111

Rag Mag
Box 12
Goodhue, MN 55027

Rambunctious Review
1221 West Pratt Boulevard
Chicago, IL 60626

Rant
PO Box 6872
Yorkville Station
New York, NY 10128

Raritan
31 Mine Street
New Brunswick, NJ 08903

Raven Chronicles
PO Box 95918
Seattle, WA 98145

Red Bass
105 West 28th Street
New York, NY 10001

Red Cedar Review
English Department,
17C Morrill Hall
Michigan State University
East Lansing, MI 48824

Red Owl Magazine
35 Hampshire Road
Portsmouth, NH 03801-4815

Renegade
PO Box 314
Bloomfield Hills, MI 48303

Resonance
PO Box 215
Beacon, NY 12508

Reverse
19 West 73rd Street, No 3A
New York, NY 10023

Review
680 Park Avenue
New York, NY 10021

RFD
PO Box 68
Liberty, TN 37095

Rhino
1808 North Larrabee Street
Chicago, IL 60614

River City
English Department
University of Memphis
Memphis, TN 38152

River Oak Review
PO Box 3127
Oak Park, IL 60303

River Styx
3207 Washington
St Louis, MO 63103

Riverside Quarterly
PO Box 12085
San Antonio, TX 78212

Riverwind
Hocking College
Nelsonville, OH 45768

Rocket Literary Quarterly
PO Box 672
Water Mill, NY 11976

Romantist
Saracinesca House
3610 Meadowbrook Avenue
Nashville, TN 37205

Rosebud
Box 459
Cambridge, WI 53523

Saguaro
315 Douglass Building
University of Arizona
Tucson, AZ 85721

SAIL Studies in American Indian Literatures
English Department
California State University
Fullerton, CA 92634

Salmagundi
Skidmore College
Saratoga Springs, NY 12866

Salthouse: A Geopoetics Journal
800 West Main, English Department
University of Wisconsin at Whitewater
Whitewater, WI 53190

San Fernando Poetry Journal
18301 Halsted Street
Northridge, CA 91325

Sandhills Review
Sandhills Community College
2200 Airport Road

Pinehurst, NC 28374

Santa Barbara Review
1309-A State Street
Santa Barbara, CA 93101

Santa Fe Literary Review
PO Box 8018
Santa Fe, NM 87504

Santa Monica Review
1900 Pico Boulevard
Santa Monica, CA 90405

Screens and Tasted Parallels
12714 Barbara Street
Silver Springs, MD 20906

Seattle Review
Padelford Hall, GN-30
University of Washington
Seattle, WA 98195

Seems
Lakeland College
Box 359
Sheboygan, WI 53082

Seneca Review
Hobart and William Smith Colleges
Geneva, NY 14456

Sensations Magazine
2 Radio Avenue, A5
Secaucus, NJ 07094

Sequoia
Storke Publications Building
Stanford, CA 94305

Sewanee Review
735 University Avenue
Sewanee, TN 37383-1000

Shenandoah
Troubadour Theater, 2nd Floor
Washington and Lee University
Lexington, VA 24450

Shooting Star Review
7123 Race Street
Pittsburgh, PA 15208

Sidewalks
Box 321
Champlin, MN 55316

Signal
PO Box 67
Emmett, ID 83617

Silver Wings
PO Box 1000
Pearblossom, CA 93553

Silverfish Review
PO Box 3541
Eugene, OR 97403

Sing Heavenly Muse!
PO Box 13320
Minneapolis, MN 55414

Sinister Wisdom
PO Box 3252
Berkeley, CA 94703

Sistersong: Women Across Cultures
PO Box 7405
Pittsburgh, PA 15213

Situation
10402 Ewell Avenue
Kensington, MD 20895

Slant: A Journal of Poetry
PO Box 5063 (UCA)
Conway, AR 72035

Slate
PO Box 581189
Minneapolis, MN 55458

Slightly West
CAB-320, The Evergreen State College
Olympia, WA 98505

Slipstream
Box 2071
Niagara Falls, NY 14301

Small Pond Magazine
PO Box 664
Stratford, CT 06497

Snail's Pace Review
RR 2, Box 403
Darwin Road
Cambridge, NY 12816

Snake Nation Review
110 No 2 West Force Street
Valdosta, GA 31601

Sonora Review
English Department, University of Arizona
Tucson, AZ 85721

Sophomore Jinx
PO Box 770728
Woodside, NY 11377

South Carolina Review
English Department, Clemson University
Clemson, SC 29634

South Coast Poetry Journal
English Department
California State University at Fullerton
Fullerton, CA 92634

South Dakota Review
University of South Dakota
Vermillion, SD 57069

Southern California Anthology
Master of Professional Writing Program
University of Southern California, WPH 404
Los Angeles, CA 90089

Southern Humanities Review
9088 Haley Center
Auburn University
Auburn, AL 36849

Southern Poetry Review
English Department
University of North Carolina
Charlotte, NC 28223

Southern Review
43 Allen Hall
Louisiana State University
Baton Rouge, LA 70803

Southwest
3490 South Walkup Drive
Flagstaff, AZ 86001

Southwest Review
307 Fondren Library West, Box 374
Southern Methodist University
Dallas, TX 75275

Sou'wester
School of Humanities
Southern Illinois University
Edwardsville, IL 62026

Sow's Ear Poetry Review
19353 Pleasant View Drive
Abingdon, VA 24211

Sparrow Poverty Pamphlets
103 Waldron Street
West Lafayette, IN 47906

Spectrum
Anna Maria College
Paxton, MA 01612

Spoon River Poetry Anthology
English Department
Illinois State University
Normal-Bloomington, IL 61790

Spring: The Journal of the e. e. cummings Society
33-54 164th Street
Flushing, NY 11358

The Steelhead Special
PO Box 219
Bayside, CA 95524

Stet Magazine
PO Box 75
Cambridge, MA 02238

Wallace Stevens Journal
Box 5750 Clarkson University
Potsdam, NY 13699

Stiletto
PO Box 27276
Denver, CO 80227

Sulfur
210 Washtenaw Avenue
Ypsilanti, MI 48197

Sun Dog: The Southeast Review
406 Williams Building
Florida State University
Tallahassee, FL 32306

Sun Magazine
107 North Roberson Street

Chapel Hill, NC 27516

Supernatural Magazine
1415 Hemlock Street
Cayce, SC 29033

Swift Kick
1711 Amherst Street
Buffalo, MY 14214

Sycamore Review
English Department
Purdue University
West Lafayette, IN 47907

Talisman: A Journal of Contemporary Poetry and Poetics
Box 1117
Hoboken, NJ 07030

Tampa Review
University of Tampa
Box 19F, 401 W Kennedy Blvd
Tampa, FL 33606

Taproot/Taproot Literary Review
302 Park Road
Ambridge, PA 15003

Tar River Poetry
English Dept, East Carolina University
Greenville, NC 27834

Texas Review
English Department
Sam Houston State University
Huntsville, TX 77341

Texture
3760 Cedar Ridge Drive
Norman, OK 73072

Thema
Box 74109
Metairie, LA 70033

13th Moon
English Department
 State University of New York at Albany
Albany, NY 12222

This: A Serial Review
6600 Clough Pike
Cincinnati, OH 45244

This is Important
Box 336
Sprague River, OR 97639

Thorny Locust
PO Box 32631
Kansas City, MO 64171

Thoughts For All Seasons
478 NE 56th Street
Miami, FL 33137

360 Degrees: Art and Literary Review
980 Bush Street, Suite 200
San Francisco, CA 94109

Thunder & Honey

PO Box 11386
Atlanta, GA 30310

Tightrope
323 Pelham Road
Amherst, MA 01002

To: A Journal of Poetry, Prose and the Visual Arts
Box 121
Narberth, PA 19072

Tomorrow Magazine
PO Box 148486
Chicago, IL 60614

Took: Modern Poetry in English Series
PO Box 640543
San Francisco, CA 94164

Touchstone: Literary Journal
PO Box 8308
Spring, TX 77387

TriQuarterly
Northwestern University, 2020 Ridge
Evanston, IL 60208

Tucumcari Literary Review
3108 West Bellevue Avenue
Los Angeles, CA 90026

Turnstile
175 Fifth Avenue, Suite 2348
New York, NY 10010

Underground Forest
1701 Bluebell Avenue
Boulder, CO 80302

Unmuzzled Ox
105 Hudson Street
New York, NY 10013

UNo MAS Magazine
PO Box 1832
Silver Spring, MD 20915

Urbanus Magazine
PO Box 192561
San Francisco, CA 94119

Vincent Brothers Review
4566 Northern Circle
Riverside, OH 45424

Vinyl Elephant
700 Cotanche, No 1
Greenville, NC 27858

Virginia Quarterly Review
One West Range
Charlottesville, VA 22903

Visions: International, The World Journal of Illustrated Poetry
1110 Seaton Lane
Falls Church, VA 22046

Vivo
1195 Green Street
San Francisco, CA 94109

Voices International

1115 Gillette Drive
Little Rock, AR 72207

Washington Review
PO Box 50132
Washington, DC 20091

Waterways
393 St Pauls Avenue
Staten Island, NY 10304

Webster Review
English Department
St Louis Community College at Meramec
11333 Big Bend Road
St Louis, MO 63122

West Branch
Bucknell Hall
Bucknell University
Lewisburg, PA 17837

West Hills Review
146 Old Walt Whitman Road
Huntington Station, NY 11746

Western Humanities Review
3500 UNCO
University of Utah
Salt Lake City, UT 84112

Whetstone
PO Box 1266
Barrington, IL 60011

White Clouds Review
PO Box 462
Ketchum, ID 83340

Whole Notes
PO Box 1374
Las Cruces, NM 88004

Whole Terrain
Antioch New England Graduate School
40 Avon Street
Keene, NH 03431

William and Mary Review
PO Box 8795
College of William & Mary
Williamsburg, VA 23187

Willow Review
19351 West Washington Street
Grayslake, IL 60030

Willow Springs
MS-1 526 5th Street
Eastern Washington University
Cheney, WA 99004

Wind
PO Box 24548
Lexington, KY 40524

Windfall
English Department
University of Wisconsin at Whitewater
Whitewater, WI 53190

Windless Orchard
English Department
Indiana University at Fort Wayne
2101 East Coliseum
Fort Wayne, IN 46805

Without Halos
PO Box 1342
Point Pleasant Beach, NJ 08742

Witness
Oakland Community College
27055 Orchard Lake Road
Farmington Hills, MI 48334

Woman Poet
PO Box 60550
Reno, NV 89506

Women's Review of Books
Center for Research on Women
Wellesley College
Wellesley, MA 02181

Women's Words: A Journal of Carolina Writing
128 East Hargett Street, Suite 10
Raleigh, NC 27601

Women's Work
606 Avenue A
Snohomish, WA 98290

Worcester Review
6 Chatham Street
Worcester, MA 01609

World
St Mark's Church
10th Street and 2nd Avenue
New York, NY 10003

World Letter
2726 East Court Street
Iowa City, IA 52245

Wormwood Review
PO Box 4698
Stockton, CA 95204

Writers Forum
University of Colorado at Colorado Springs
Colorado Springs, CO 80933

Writer's Journal
3585 North Lexington Avenue
Arden Hills, MN 55112

Writing For Our Lives
647 N Santa Cruz Avenue, Annex
Los Gatos, CA 95030

Writing Writers Magazine
786 Birch Street
Paradise, CA 95969

Xanadu
Box 773
Huntington, NY 11743

Xavier Review
Box 110C
Xavier University

New Orleans, LA 70125

xib
PO Box 262112
San Diego, CA 92126

X-Ray
PO Box 170011
San Francisco, CA 94117

Yarrow
English Department
Kutztown University
Kutztown, PA 19530

Yellow Silk: A Journal of Erotic Arts
PO Box 6374
Albany, CA 94706

Yet Another Small Magazine
Box 14353
Hartford, CT 06114

Zebra
PO Box 421584
San Francisco, CA 94142

Zukunft
25 East 21st Street
New York, NY 10010

Zuzu's Petals Quarterly
PO Box 4476
Allentown, PA 18105

Zyzzyva
41 Sutter Street, Suite 1400
San Francisco, CA 94104

For Product Safety Concerns and Information please contact our EU representative GPSR@taylorandfrancis.com Taylor & Francis Verlag GmbH, Kaufingerstraße 24, 80331 München, Germany

T - #0007 - 270225 - C0 - 234/156/26 [28] - CB - 9780948875373 - Gloss Lamination